Official Guide to

Bed & Breakfast
guest accommodation

England

There's something different
around every corner

The English Tourism Council

English Tourism Council is the national body for English Tourism. Its mission is to drive forward the quality, competitiveness and wise growth of England's tourism by providing intelligence, setting standards, creating partnerships and ensuring coherence. ETC sets out: to provide leadership and support for the industry – creating the right framework for tourism to flourish and providing a clear focus for tourism policy and promotion; to raise the quality of English tourism – ensuring consumers expectations are met and that tourism contributes to the quality of life; to improve the competitiveness of the industry; to ensure the wise growth of tourism – helping the tourism industry to take better account of the natural and built environment and the communities within which it operates.

Cover Pictures:
  Front Cover: Shrewley Pools Farm, Warwick, Warwickshire
  Front Cover Inset: Promenade Hotel, Minehead, Somerset
  Back Cover: (from top) Stragglethorpe Hall, Stragglethorpe, Lincolnshire
  Tor Cottage, Tavistock, Devon

Photo Credits:
  Cumbria - Cumbria Tourist Board
  Northumbria - Northumbria Tourist Board, Graeme Peacock, Mike Kipling, Colin Cuthbert and Michael Busselle
  North West - North West Tourist Board, Cheshire County Council, Lancashire County Council, Marketing Manchester
  Yorkshire - Yorkshire Tourist Board
  Heart of England - Heart of England Tourist Board
  East of England - East of England Tourist Board Collection
  South West - South West Tourism
  South of England - Southern Tourist Board,
  Peter Titmuss, Chris Cove-Smith and Iris Buckley
  South East England - South East England Tourist Board, Chris Parker and Iris Buckley

  Published by: The English Tourism Council, Thames Tower, Black's Road, Hammersmith, London W6 9EL.
  ISBN 0 86143 252 5

  Publishing Manager: Michael Dewing
  Production Manager: Iris Buckley
  Technical Manager: Marita Sen
  Compilation, Design & Production: www.jacksonlowe.com
  Typesetting: Tradespools Ltd, Somerset and Jackson Lowe Marketing, Lewes
  Maps: © Maps In Minutes™ (1999)
  Printing and Binding: Mozzon Giuntina S.p.A., Florence and Officine Grafiche De Agostini S.p.A., Novara.
  Advertisement Sales: Jackson Lowe Marketing, 173 High Street, Lewes, East Sussex BN7 1YE. (01273) 487487
  © English Tourism Council (except where stated)

Contents

Where to Stay in England 2002

Key to Symbols
A key to symbols can be found on the inside back cover. Keep it open for easy reference.

For short breaks, family holidays, touring holidays or business stop-overs, Where to Stay is all you need. This guide contains details of thousands of places to stay in a wide choice of locations at prices to suit all budgets. Plus places to visit, tourist information centres, maps, events and a whole lot more.

There's no better way to feel refreshed and revitalised than by taking a short break or holiday in England. It offers a rich variety of interest, from dramatic coastal paths, rolling hills and hedgerows to vibrant cities and quality attractions.

Start by looking for a place to stay. The English Tourism Council has assessed all accommodation in this guide for quality, so you can book with confidence that it will meet your expectations.

a warm
welcome

**Welcome to our 27th edition -
it's so easy to use, and packed with information.**

Get away
and do yourself an English
world of good.

How to use the guide

The guide is divided into the 10 English Regional Tourist Board regions (shown on page 14). These regional sections give you all the information you need on the area: accommodation, places to visit, tourist information centres, travel and publications for further information.

Accommodation is listed alphabetically in order of place name. If you would like to know more about the city, town or village in which you wish to stay, you will find brief descriptions at the end of each regional section. Or you can contact the local Tourist Information Centre - the telephone number can be found next to the town name on the accommodation entry pages.

Finding your accommodation

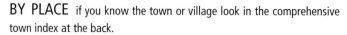

Whether you know exactly where you want to stay or only have an idea of the area you wish to visit, it couldn't be easier to find accommodation:

BY PLACE if you know the town or village look in the comprehensive town index at the back.

BY AREA if you know the area look at the full colour maps starting on page 18. All the places in black offer accommodation featured in this guide.

BY REGION if you know which part of England look in the relevant regional section. These are colour coded at the top of each page. A map showing the regions can be found on page 14.

BY COUNTY if you know which county look at the listing on page 15 to find the region it is in.

Types of accommodation

Guest accommodation is featured in this guide which includes Guesthouses, Small Hotels, Bed and Breakfast, Farmhouses and Inns. Within each entry you will find a brief description of each property and facilities available. (We publish a separate guide for hotel accommodation).

Accommodation entries explained

Each accommodation entry contains detailed information to help you decide if it is right for you. This information has been provided by the proprietors themselves, and our aim has been to ensure that it is as objective and factual as possible. To the left of the establishment name you will find the Diamond rating and quality award, if appropriate.

At-a-glance symbols at the end of each entry give you additional information on services and facilities - a key can be found on the back cover flap. Keep this open to refer to as you read.

A sample entry is shown below.

1. Listing under town or village with map reference
2. ETC Diamond rating (plus Gold and Silver Awards where applicable)
3. Colour picture for enhanced entries
4. Accessible rating where applicable
5. Description - standard entries 25 words; enhanced entries 50 words
6. At-a-glance facility symbols

7. Establishment name, address, telephone and fax numbers, e-mail and web site address
8. Prices for bed and breakfast (B&B) and half board (HB) accommodation
9. Months open
10. Accommodation details including credit cards accepted
11. Special promotions and themed breaks

Exclusive accommodation listings

Where to Stay is the only guide to contain details of ALL guest accommodation in England which has been quality assessed by the English Tourism Council, giving you the widest choice of accommodation.

Accommodation Ratings & Awards

English Tourism Council ratings and awards are an indication of quality which will help you find the most suitable accommodation to meet your needs and expectations. You'll find several in this guide:

DIAMOND RATINGS FOR QUALITY

The English Tourism Council's quality assurance standard awards One to Five Diamonds giving you reliable information about the quality of the accommodation you can expect. (See opposite). You'll find something to suit all budgets and tastes.

SPECIAL AWARDS FOR EXCELLENCE

Gold and Silver Awards - Part of the English Tourism Council scheme, Gold and Silver Awards are given to establishments achieving the highest levels of quality in areas guests have identified as a priority. So if you're looking for somewhere special, turn to page 11 for a list of Gold Award holders which have an entry in the regional sections of this guide. Silver award holders are too numerous to list, but they are clearly indicated in the accommodation entries.

The annual Excellence in England awards are the Oscars of the tourism industry. Winners will be announced in Spring 2002 (see page 13).

NATIONAL ACCESSIBLE SCHEME FOR SPECIAL NEEDS

Establishments which have a National Accessible rating provide access and facilities for wheelchair users and people who have difficulty walking. Turn to page 12 and 13 for further details.

How do Diamond rating? we arrive at a

The English Tourism Council has more than 50 trained assessors throughout England who visit properties annually, generally staying overnight as an anonymous guest. They award ratings based on the overall experience of their stay, and there are strict guidelines to ensure every property is assessed to the same criteria. High standards of housekeeping are a major requirement; heating, lighting, comfort and convenience are also part of the assessment.

THE ASSESSOR'S ROLE - GUEST, ASSESSOR AND ADVISOR

An assessor books their accommodation as a 'normal' guest. He or she will take into account all aspects of the visiting experience, from how the telephone enquiry is dealt with to the quality of the service and facilities on offer.

During their stay the assessor will try to experience as many things as possible including the quality of food, the knowledge of staff and services available. They will even check under the bed!

After paying the bill the assessor reveals who they are and asks to look round the rest of the establishment. The assessor will then advise the proprietor of the Diamond rating they have awarded, discussing the reasons why, as well as suggesting areas for improvement.

So you can see it's a very thorough process to ensure that when you book accommodation with a particular Diamond rating you can be confident it will meet your expectations. After all, meeting customer expectations is what makes happy guests.

Ratings
you can trust

When you're looking for a place to stay, you need a rating system you can trust. The English Tourism Council's ratings give a clear guide to what to expect, in an easy-to-understand form. Properties are visited annually by trained, impartial assessors, so you can have the confidence that your accommodation has been thoroughly checked and rated for quality before you make your booking.

DIAMOND RATINGS

Ratings are awarded from One to Five Diamonds. The more Diamonds, the higher the level of quality and customer care. The brief explanations of the Diamond ratings outlined here show what is included at each rating level (note that each rating also includes what is provided at a lower Diamond rating).

◆ An acceptable overall level of quality and helpful service. Accommodation offering, as a minimum, a full cooked or continental breakfast. Other meals, if provided, will be freshly prepared. Towels are provided and heating and hot water will be available at reasonable times.

◆◆ A good overall level of quality and comfort, with greater emphasis on guest care in all areas.

◆◆◆ A very good overall level of quality in areas such as comfortable bedrooms, well maintained, practical decor, a good choice of quality items at breakfast, customer care and all-round comfort. Where other meals are provided these will be freshly cooked from good quality ingredients.

◆◆◆◆ An excellent level of quality in all areas. Customer care showing very good attention to your needs.

◆◆◆◆◆ An exceptional overall level of quality - for example, ample space with a degree of luxury, a high quality bed and furniture, excellent interior design and customer care which anticipates your needs. Breakfast offering a wide choice of high quality fresh ingredients. Where other meals are provided these will feature fresh, seasonal, and often local ingredients.

Gold and Silver Awards

Look out, too, for the English Tourism Council's Gold and Silver Awards, given to establishments which not only achieve the overall levels of quality within their Diamond rating, but also reach the highest levels of quality in specific areas identified by guests as being really important to them. They reflect the quality of comfort and cleanliness you'll find in bedrooms and bathrooms as well as the quality of service you'll enjoy throughout your stay.

Establishments
Gold Award

Hazel Bank Country House

Establishments featured in the regional sections of this Where to Stay guide, which have achieved a Gold Award for an exceptionally high standard of quality, are listed on this page. Please use the Town Index at the back of the guide to find the page numbers for their full entry.

Silver Awards also represent high standards of quality and there are many establishments within this guide which have achieved this. Gold and Silver Awards are clearly indicated in the accommodation entries.

For further information about Gold and Silver Awards, please see page 9.

- **Blounts Court Farm,** Devizes, Wiltshire
- **Bokiddick Farm,** Bodmin, Cornwall
- **Britannia House,** Lymington, Hampshire
- **Broomshaw Hill Farm,** Haltwhistle, Northumberland
- **Burhill Farm,** Broadway, Worcestershire
- **Burr Bank,** Pickering, North Yorkshire
- **Cannon Croft,** Hathersage, Derbyshire
- **Chalon House,** Richmond, Greater London
- **The Cottage,** Bishop's Stortford, Hertfordshire
- **Cotteswold House,** Bibury, Gloucestershire
- **The Dairy,** Thame, Oxfordshire
- **Efford Cottage,** Lymington, Hampshire
- **Felton House,** Hereford, Herefordshire
- **Field House,** Hindringham, Norfolk
- **Hazel Bank Country House,** Borrowdale, Cumbria
- **Hill House Farm,** Ely, Cambridgeshire
- **Hooke Hall,** Uckfield, East Sussex
- **Jonathan's at The Angel,** Burford, Oxfordshire
- **Knottside Farm,** Pateley Bridge, North Yorkshire
- **Magnolia House,** Canterbury, Kent
- **Manor Farm Oast,** Rye, East Sussex
- **M'Dina Courtyard,** Chipping Campden, Gloucestershire
- **Monkshill,** Bath and North East Somerset
- **Muchelney Ham Farm,** Langport, Somerset
- **Number Twenty Eight,** Ludlow, Shropshire

- **The Old Rectory,** Campsea Ashe, Suffolk
- **The Paddock,** Leominster, Herefordshire
- **Peacock House,** Beetley, Norfolk
- **Ravenscourt Manor,** Ludlow, Shropshire
- **The Ringlestone Inn & Farmhouse,** Maidstone, Kent
- **Tannery House,** Bakewell, Derbyshire
- **The Temple, Longhope,** Gloucestershire
- **Thanington Hotel,** Canterbury, Kent
- **The Three Lions,** Fordingbridge, Hampshire
- **Tor Cottage,** Tavistock, Devon
- **Tregea Hotel,** Padstow, Cornwall

Burr Bank

Britannia House

11

National
Accessible Scheme

The English Tourism Council and National and Regional Tourist Boards throughout Britain assess all types of places to stay, on holiday or business, that provide accessible accommodation for wheelchair users and others who may have difficulty walking.

Accommodation establishments taking part in the National Accessible Scheme, and which appear in the regional sections of this guide are listed opposite. Use the Town Index at the back to find the page numbers for their full entries.

The Tourist Boards recognise three categories of accessibility:

CATEGORY 1	Accessible to all wheelchair users including those travelling independently.
CATEGORY 2	Accessible to a wheelchair user with assistance.
CATEGORY 3	Accessible to a wheelchair user able to walk short distances and up at least three steps.

If you have additional needs or special requirements of any kind, we strongly recommend that you make sure these can be met by your chosen establishment before you confirm your booking.

The criteria the English Tourism Council and National and Regional Tourist Boards have adopted do not necessarily conform to British Standards or to Building Regulations. They reflect what the Boards understand to be acceptable to meet the practical needs of wheelchair users.

The National Accessible Scheme is currently in the process of being updated. Consultation has been conducted throughout 2001 with introduction during 2002.

The National Accessible Scheme forms part of the Tourism for All Campaign that is being promoted by the English Tourism Council and National and Regional Tourist Boards. Additional help and guidance on finding suitable holiday accommodation for those with special needs can be obtained from:

Holiday Care,
2nd Floor, Imperial Buildings,
Victoria Road,
Horley, Surrey RH6 7PZ

Tel: (01293) 774535
Fax: (01293) 784647
Email: holiday.care@virgin.net
Internet: www.holidaycare.org.uk
Minicom: (01293) 776943

HOLIDAY CARE

CATEGORY 1

- **Bath, Bath and North East Somerset** - Carfax Hotel
- **Minehead, Somerset** - Promenade Hotel
- **Selsey, West Sussex** - St Andrews Lodge
- **Wilmslow, Cheshire** - Dean Bank Hotel

 CATEGORY 2

- **Southport, Merseyside** - Sandy Brook Farm

 CATEGORY 3

- **Arundel, West Sussex** - Mill Lane House
- **Bakewell, Derbyshire** - Tannery House
- **Boscastle, Cornwall** - The Old Coach House
- **Bridgnorth, Shropshire** - Bulls Head Inn
- **Carlisle, Cumbria**
  - Bessiestown Farm Country Guesthouse
- **Colyton, Devon** - Smallicombe Farm
- **Durham, County Durham** - St Aidan's College

- **Earls Colne, Essex** - Riverside Lodge
- **Exeter, Devon** - St Andrews Hotel
- **Heathfield, East Sussex** - Spicers Bed & Breakfast
- **Henley-on-Thames, Oxfordshire** - Holmwood
- **Lenham, Kent** - The Dog & Bear Hotel
- **Leominster, Herefordshire** - The Paddock
- **Lower Whitley, Cheshire** - Tall Trees Lodge
- **Moreton-in-Marsh, Gloucestershire** - Treetops
- **Norwich, Norfolk** - Elm Farm Country House
- **Okehampton, Devon** - Week Farm Country Holidays
- **Otterburn, Northumberland** - Redesdale Arms Hotel
- **Salisbury, Wiltshire** - Byways House
- **Sarre, Kent** - Crown Inn
  (The Famous Cherry Brandy House)
- **Skegness, Lincolnshire** - Saxby Hotel
- **Skipton, North Yorkshire** - Craven Heifer Inn
- **Stratford-upon-Avon, Warwickshire** - Church Farm
- **Warwick, Warwickshire** - Woodside
- **Weston-super-Mare, North Somerset**
  - Moorlands Country Guesthouse
- **Whitley Bay, Tyne and Wear** - Marlborough Hotel
- **Winchester, Hampshire** - Shawlands

(The information contained on these pages was correct at the time of going to press.)

The Excellence in England
AWARDS 2002

The Safeway Excellence in England Awards are all about blowing English tourism's trumpet and telling the world what a fantastic place England is to visit, whether it's for a two week holiday, a weekend break or a day trip.

Formerly called England for Excellence, the Awards are now in their 13th year and are run by the English Tourism Council in association with England's ten regional tourist boards. There are 13 categories including B&B of the Year, Hotel of the Year and Visitor Attraction of the Year. New for 2002 are Short Break Destination of the Year and Most Improved Seaside Resort.

Winners of the 2002 awards will receive their trophies at a fun and festive event to be held on St George's Day (23 April) at the Royal Opera House in London. The day will not only celebrate excellence in tourism but also Englishness in all its diversity.

For a truly exceptional experience, look out for accommodation and attractions displaying a Safeway Excellence in England Award from April 2002 onwards.

Safeway, one of the UK's leading food retailers, is delighted to be sponsoring these awards as a part of a range of initiatives to help farming communities and the tourism industry.

For more information on Safeway Stores please visit: www.safeway.co.uk
For more information about the Excellence in England Awards visit: www.englishtourism.org.uk

Regional
Tourist Board
Areas

This Where to Stay guide is divided into 10 regional sections as shown on the map below. To identify each regional section and its page number, please refer to the key below. The county index overleaf indicates in which regional section you will find a particular county.

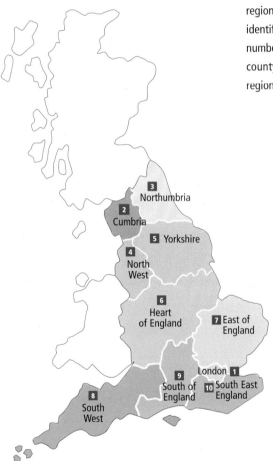

Each of the ten English regions shown here has a Regional Tourist Board which can give you information about things to see or do locally. Contact details are given both at the beginning and end of each regional section.

LOCATION MAPS

Colour location maps showing all the cities, towns and villages with accommodation in the regional sections of this guide can be found on pages 18-30. Turn to the Town Index at the back of this guide for the page number on which you can find the relevant accommodation.

In which **region** is the **county** I wish to **visit**?

COUNTY/UNITARY AUTHORITY	REGION
Bath & North East Somerset	South West
Bedfordshire	East of England
Berkshire	South of England
Bristol	South West
Buckinghamshire	South of England
Cambridgeshire	East of England
Cheshire	North West
Cornwall	South West
Cumbria	Cumbria
Derbyshire	Heart of England
Devon	South West
Dorset (Eastern)	South of England
Dorset (Western)	South West
Durham	Northumbria
East Riding of Yorkshire	Yorkshire
East Sussex	South East England
Essex	East of England
Gloucestershire	Heart of England
Greater London	London
Greater Manchester	North West
Hampshire	South of England
Herefordshire	Heart of England
Hertfordshire	East of England
Isle of Wight	South of England
Isles of Scilly	South West
Kent	South East England
Lancashire	North West
Leicestershire	Heart of England
Lincolnshire	Heart of England
Merseyside	North West
Norfolk	East of England
North East Lincolnshire	Yorkshire
North Lincolnshire	Yorkshire
North Somerset	South West
North Yorkshire	Yorkshire
Northamptonshire	Heart of England
Northumberland	Northumbria
Nottinghamshire	Heart of England
Oxfordshire	South of England
Rutland	Heart of England
Shropshire	Heart of England
Somerset	South West
South Gloucestershire	South West
South Yorkshire	Yorkshire
Staffordshire	Heart of England
Suffolk	East of England
Surrey	South East England
Tees Valley	Northumbria
Tyne & Wear	Northumbria
Warwickshire	Heart of England
West Midlands	Heart of England
West Sussex	South East England
West Yorkshire	Yorkshire
Wiltshire	South West
Worcestershire	Heart of England
York	Yorkshire

UNITARY AUTHORITIES

Please note that many new unitary authorities have been formed - for example Brighton & Hove and Bristol - and are officially separate from the county in which they were previously located. To aid the reader we have only included the major unitary authorities in the list above and on the colour maps.

Making a Booking

Please remember that changes may occur after the guide is printed. When you have found a suitable place to stay we advise you to contact the establishment to check availability, and to confirm prices and any specific facilities which may be important to you. Further advice on how to make a booking can be found at the back of this guide, together with information about deposits and cancellations. If you have time, it is always advisable to confirm your booking in writing.

Welcome Host

Welcome Host is a nationally recognised customer care initiative, sponsored in England by the English Tourism Council. When visiting accommodation in this guide you may find this sign on display. It demonstrates commitment to courtesy and service and an aim to provide high standards of service and a warm welcome for all visitors.

www.travelengland.org.uk

Log on to travelengland.org.uk and discover something different around every corner. Meander through pages for ideas of places to visit and things to do. Spend time in each region and discover the diversity - from busy vibrant cities to rural village greens; rugged peaks to gentle rolling hills; dramatic coastline to idyllic sandy beaches. England might be a small country but it is brimming with choice and opportunity. Visit www.travelengland.org.uk and see for yourself.

England

Tourist
information
Centres

When it comes to your next England break, the first stage of your journey could be closer than you think. You've probably got a Tourist Information centre nearby which is there to serve the local community- as well as visitors. knowledgeable staff will be happy to help you, wherever you're heading.

Many Tourist information Centres can provide you with maps and guides, and sometimes it's even possible to book your accommodation, too.

Across the country, there are more than 550 Tourist Information Centres. You'll find the address of your nearest Tourist Information Centre in your local Phone Book.

MAP 1

A   B

Location
Maps

Every place name featured in the regional accommodation sections of this Where to Stay guide has a map reference to help you locate it on the maps which follow. For example, to find Colchester, Essex, which has 'Map ref 3B2', turn to Map 3 and refer to grid square B2.

All place names appearing in the regional sections are shown in black type on the maps. This enables you to find other places in your chosen area which may have suitable accommodation - the Town Index (at the back of this guide) gives page numbers.

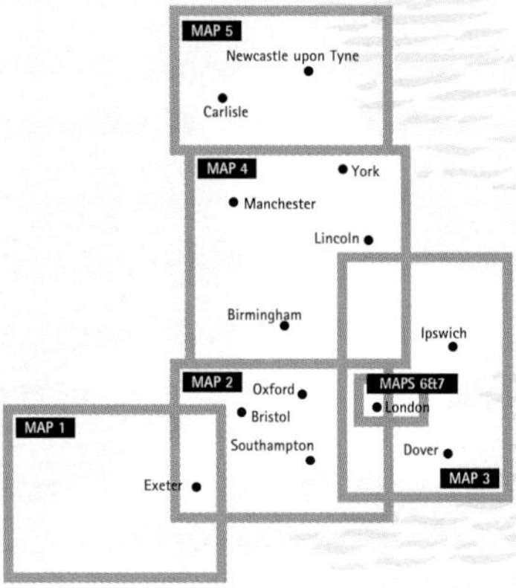

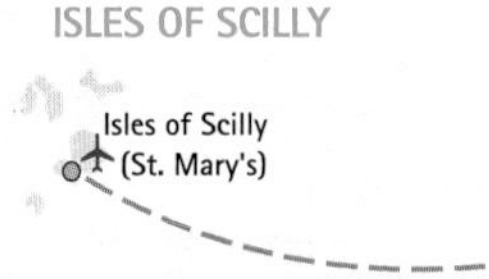

MAP 5
Newcastle upon Tyne
Carlisle
MAP 4   York
Manchester
Lincoln
Birmingham
Ipswich
MAP 2 Oxford   MAPS 6&7
Bristol   London
MAP 1   Southampton   Dover
Exeter   MAP 3

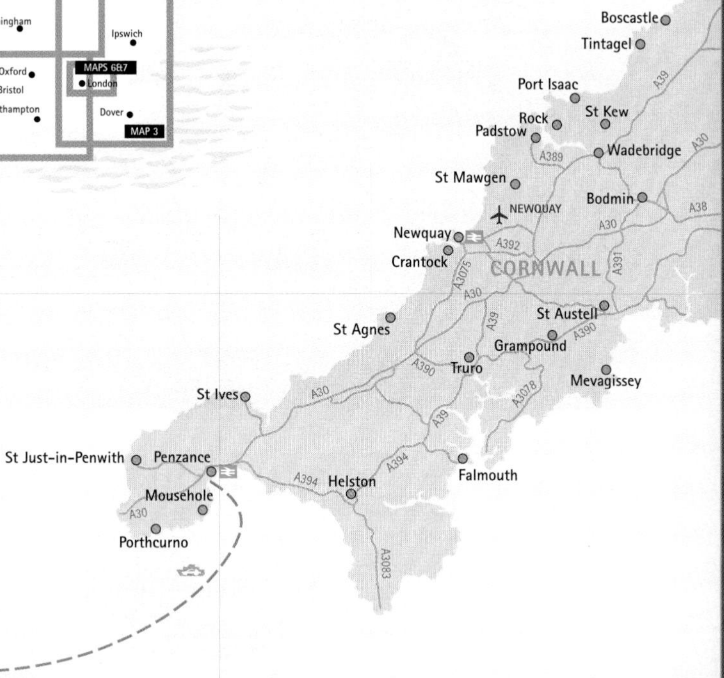

Boscastle
Tintagel
Port Isaac   A39
Rock   St Kew
Padstow   Wadebridge
A389   A30
St Mawgen
Bodmin   A38
NEWQUAY   A30   A391
Newquay   A392
Crantock   CORNWALL
A30
St Agnes   St Austell   A390
Grampound
A390   Truro   Mevagissey
St Ives   A30   A3078
A39
St Just-in-Penwith   Penzance   A394   Helston   A394   Falmouth
Mousehole   A30
Porthcurno   A3083

ISLES OF SCILLY

Isles of Scilly
(St. Mary's)

Key to regions: South West

MAP 1

All place names in black offer accommodation in this guide.

MAP 2

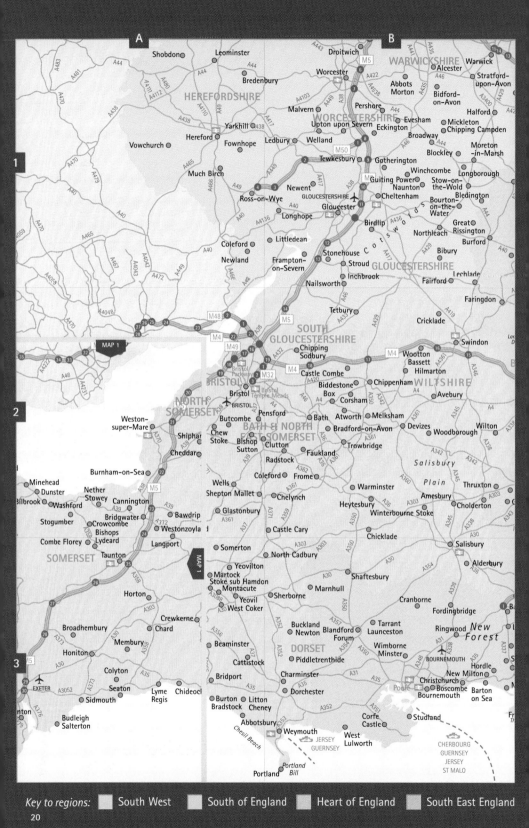

MAP 2

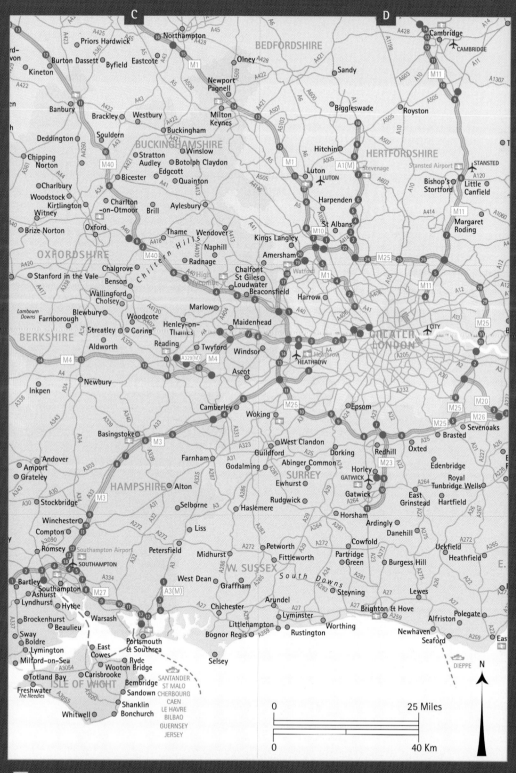

East of England

All place names in black offer accommodation in this guide.

MAP 3

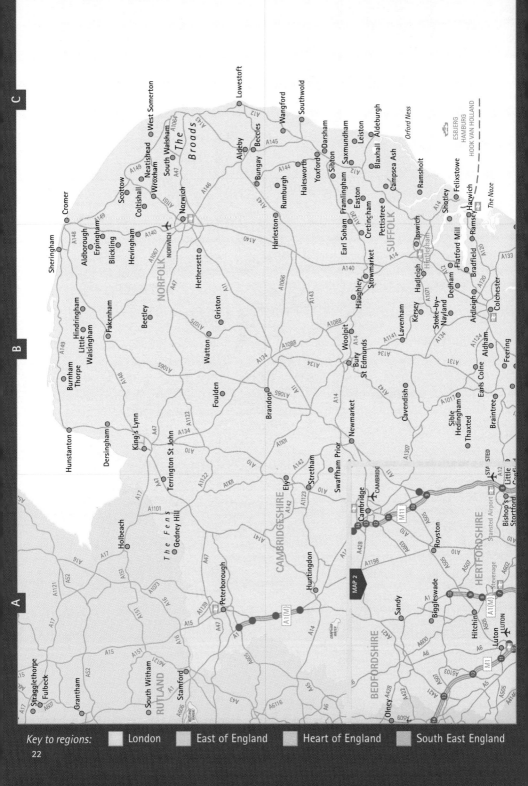

Key to regions: London   East of England   Heart of England   South East England

MAP 3

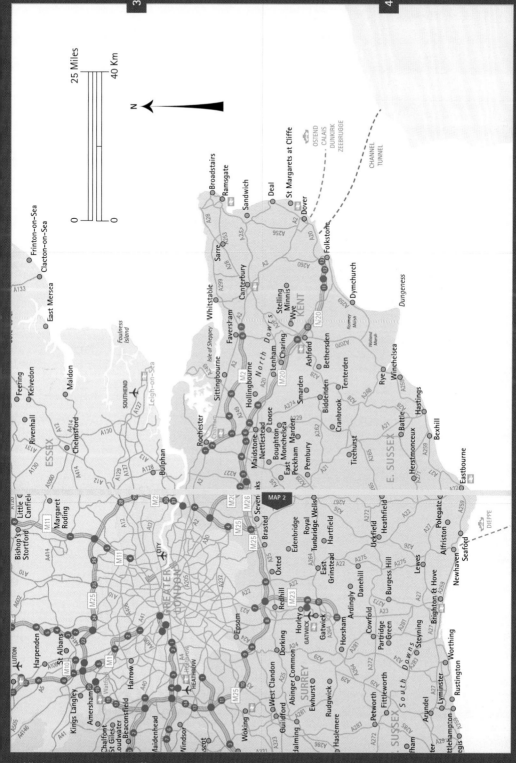

All place names in black offer accommodation in this guide.

MAP 4

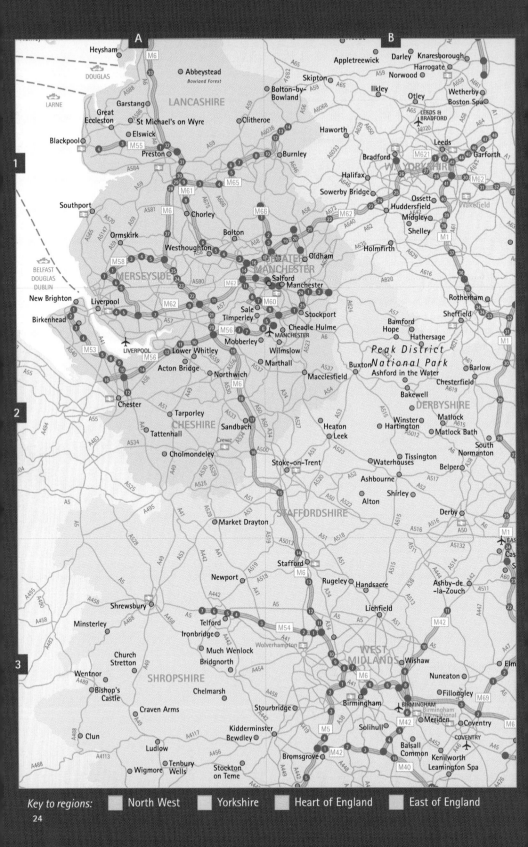

MAP 4

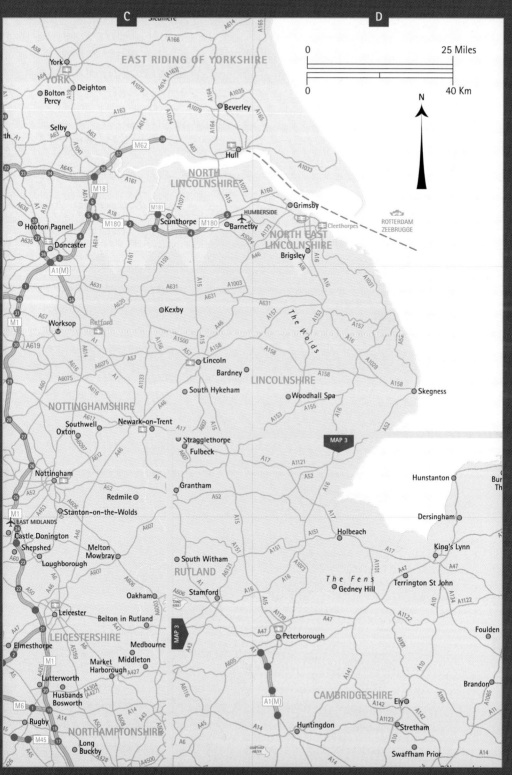

MAP 4

0 — 25 Miles
0 — 40 Km
N

EAST RIDING OF YORKSHIRE

York
Deighton
Bolton Percy
Selby
YORK

Beverley

Hull

NORTH LINCOLNSHIRE

Scunthorpe
Barnetby
HUMBERSIDE
Grimsby
Cleethorpes

ROTTERDAM ZEEBRUGGE

NORTH EAST LINCOLNSHIRE

Brigsley

Hooton Pagnell
Doncaster
Worksop
Retford

Kexby

The Wolds

Skegness

Lincoln
Bardney
South Hykeham

LINCOLNSHIRE

Woodhall Spa

NOTTINGHAMSHIRE

Southwell
Oxton
Newark-on-Trent

Stragglethorpe
Fulbeck

MAP 3

Hunstanton

Bur
Th

Dersingham

Nottingham

Grantham

Redmile
Stanton-on-the-Wolds

EAST MIDLANDS
Castle Donington
Shepshed
Loughborough

Melton Mowbray

South Witham

Holbeach

King's Lynn

RUTLAND

Oakham
Stamford

The Fens
Gedney Hill

Terrington St John

Foulden

LEICESTERSHIRE
Elmesthorpe
Leicester

Belton in Rutland

Medbourne
Market Harborough
Middleton

Lutterworth
Husbands Bosworth

Peterborough

MAP 3

Brandon

CAMBRIDGESHIRE
Ely
Stretham

Rugby

NORTHAMPTONSHIRE
Long Buckby

Huntingdon

Swaffham Prior

All place names in black offer accommodation in this guide.

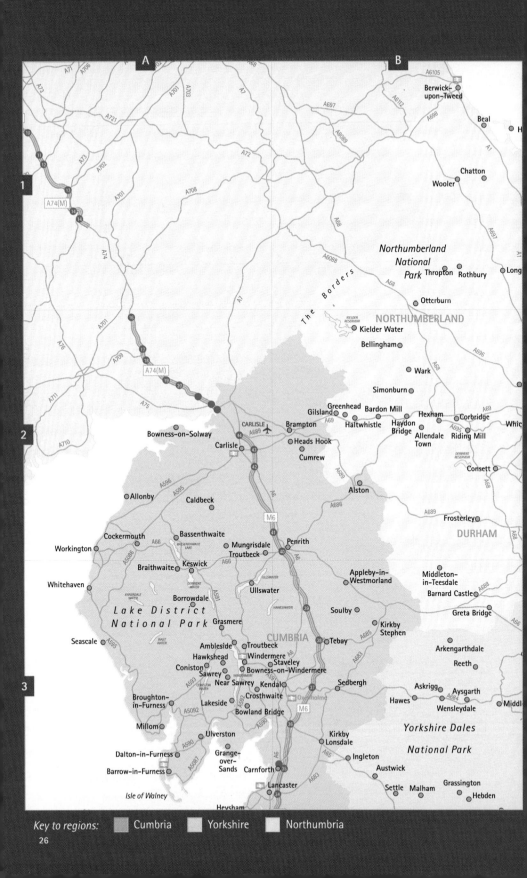

A **B**

A71 A706 A701 A703 A7 A68 A6105
Berwick-upon-Tweed

A73 A73 A721 A697 A6698 Beal

10 A74(M) A702 A701 A708 A72 A8089 Chatton

1 11 12 A73 A701 Wooler Long

13 A74(M) A708 A1 A68

14 A74 A697

16 A709 A74(M) A75 *Northumberland*
National Thropton Rothbury
Park Otterburn

17 18 19 20 A711 A710 **The Borders** KIELDER RESERVOIR **NORTHUMBERLAND**
Kielder Water
Bellingham A696

A6088 A68 Wark A68

Bowness-on-Solway Simonburn A69

CARLISLE Gilsland Greenhead Bardon Mill Hexham Corbridge
Brampton A69 Haltwhistle Haydon Allendale Riding Mill Whic
2 Carlisle Heads Hook Bridge Town A695

Cumrew DERWENT RESERVOIR Consett

A596 Alston **DURHAM**
A595 A686 A689 Frosterley

Allonby Caldbeck M6 A689

Cockermouth A66 Appleby-in- Middleton-
Workington A595 Bassenthwaite BASSENTHWAITE LAKE Penrith Westmorland in-Teesdale A698
Mungrisdale Barnard Castle
Braithwaite Keswick Troutbeck A66 Greta Bridge
Whitehaven DERWENT WATER A591 ULLSWATER Soulby A66

ENNERDALE WATER Borrowdale Ullswater Arkengarthdale
Seascale A595 *Lake District* HAWESWATER Reeth
National Park Grasmere **CUMBRIA** Kirkby
WAST WATER Stephen Askrigg Aysgarth
Ambleside Troutbeck Tebay A684 Middl
Hawkshead Windermere A685 Hawes Wensleydale
Coniston Staveley A683
Sawrey Bowness-on-Windermere Sedbergh Yorkshire Dales
3 Near Sawrey Kendal
CONISTON WATER Crosthwaite Oxenholme *National Park*
Broughton- A593 A592 M6
in-Furness Lakeside Bowland Bridge A65
A5092 Kirkby
Millom Bowness- Lonsdale Grassington
Ulverston A590 A65 Ingleton Austwick Hebden
Dalton-in-Furness Grange- Austwick
A5087 over- Carnforth Settle Malham
Barrow-in-Furness Sands A683
Isle of Walney Lancaster
Heysham

MAP 5

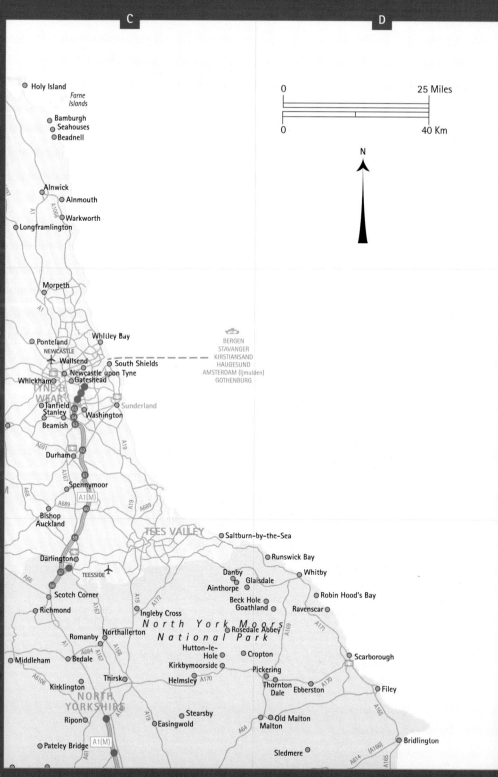

All place names in black offer accommodation in this guide.

MAP 6

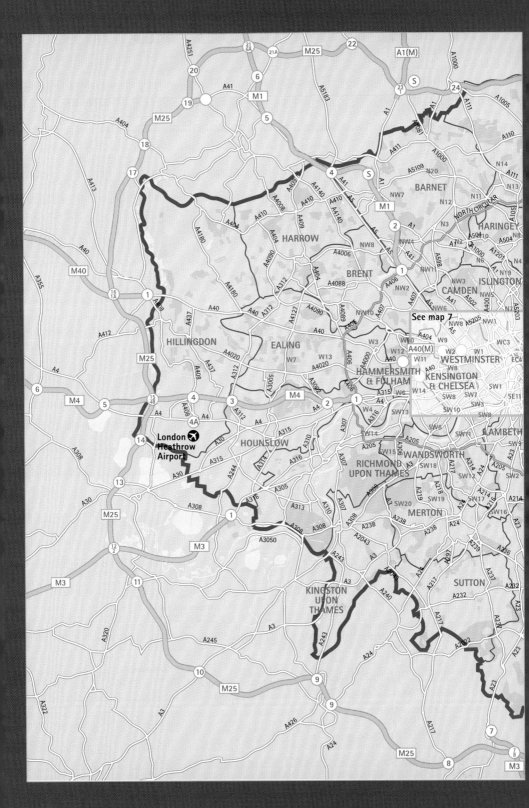

MAP 6

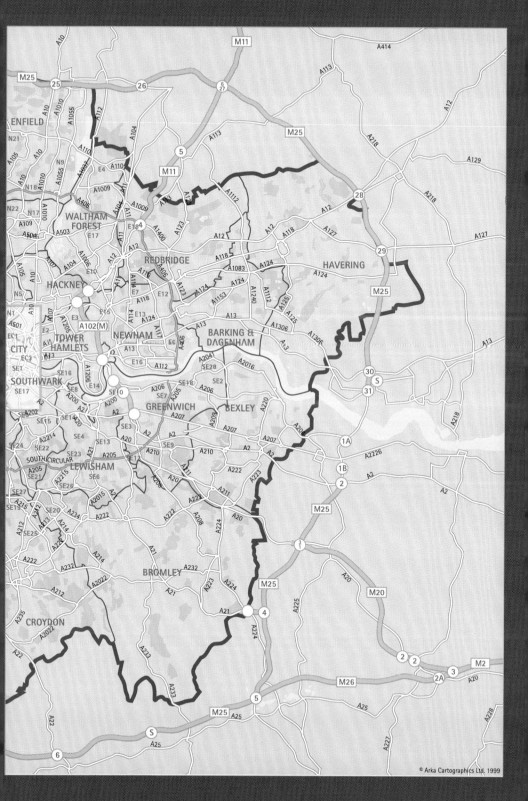

© Arka Cartographics Ltd. 1999

MAP 7

Central London

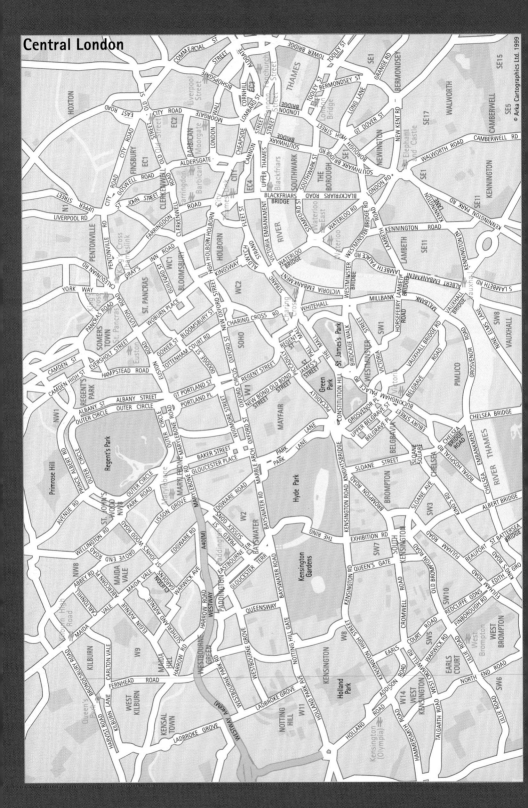

LONDON

A dynamic mix of history and heritage, cool and contemporary. Great museums, stunning art collections, royal palaces, hip nightlife and stylish shopping, from ritzy Bond Street to cutting-edge Hoxton.

classic sights

St Paul's Cathedral – Wren's famous church
Tower of London – 900 years of British history
London Eye – spectacular views from the world's highest 'big wheel'

arts for all

National Gallery – Botticelli, Rembrandt, Turner and more
Tate Modern – 20th century art in a former power station
Victoria & Albert Museum – decorative arts

city lights

Theatre: musicals – West End; drama – Royal Court and National Theatre;
Music: classical – Wigmore Hall and Royal Festival Hall;
jazz – Ronnie Scott's; ballet & opera – Royal Opera House

insider london

Dennis Severs's House, E1 – candlelit tours of this authentically 18th century house

Greater London, comprising the 32 London Boroughs

FOR MORE INFORMATION CONTACT:
**London Tourist Board
6th Floor, Glen House, Stag Place,
London SW1E 5LT
Telephone enquiries - see London Line on page 36
Internet: www.LondonTouristBoard.com**

The Pictures:
1 Tower Bridge
2 Hampton Court
3 Piccadilly Circus

Places to Visit - see pages 32-36
Where to Stay - see pages 39-62

31

PLACES to visit

You will find hundreds of interesting places to visit during your stay, just some of which are listed in these pages. Contact any Tourist Information Centre in and around London for more ideas on days out.

Bank of England Museum

Bartholomew Lane, London, EC2R 8AH
Tel: (020) 7601 5545 www.bankofengland.co.uk
The museum is housed within the Bank of England. It traces the history of the Bank from its foundation by Royal Charter in 1694 to its role today as the nation's central bank.

British Airways London Eye

Jubilee Gardens, South Bank, London, SE1
Tel: (0870) 5000 600 www.ba-londoneye.com
At 443 ft (135 m) high, this is the world's highest observation wheel. It provides a 30-minute slow-moving flight over London

British Library

96 Euston Road, London, NW1 2DB
Tel: (020) 7412 7332 www.bl.uk
Exhibition galleries, bookshop, piazza displaying Magna Carta, Gutenberg Bible, Shakespeare's First Folio and illuminated manuscripts, temporary exhibitions.

British Museum

Great Russell Street, London, WC1B 3DG
Tel: (020) 7323 8000 www.thebritishmuseum.ac.uk
One of the great museums of the world, showing the works of man from prehistoric to modern times with collections drawn from the whole world.

Cabinet War Rooms

Clive Steps, King Charles Street, London, SW1A 2AQ
Tel: (020) 7930 6961 www.iwm.org.uk
The underground headquarters used by Winston Churchill and the British Government during World War II. Includes Cabinet Room, Transatlantic Telephone Room and Map Room.

Chessington World of Adventures

Leatherhead Road, Chessington, KT9 2NE
Tel: (01372) 729560 www.chessington.com
Visitors will be in for a big adventure as they explore the theme park's amazing new attractions.

Design Museum

28 Shad Thames, London, SE1 2YD
Tel: (020) 7403 6933 www.designmuseum.org
The Design Museum is one of London's most inspiring attractions, concerned solely with the products, technologies and buildings of the 20thC and 21stC.

Hampton Court Palace

Hampton Court, East Molesey, KT8 9AU
Tel: (020) 8781 9500 www.hrp.org.uk
The oldest Tudor palace in England with many attractions including the Tudor kitchens, tennis courts, maze, State Apartments and King's Apartments.

HMS Belfast

Morgan's Lane, Tooley Street, London, SE1 2JH
Tel: (020) 7940 6300 www.iwm.org.uk
World War II cruiser weighing 11,500 tonnes, now a floating naval museum, with 9 decks to explore.

Imperial War Museum

Lambeth Road, London, SE1 6HZ
Tel: (020) 7416 5320 www.iwm.org.uk
Museum tells the story of 20thC war from Flanders to
Bosnia. Special features include the Blitz Experience,
the Trench Experience and the World of Espionage.

Kensington Palace State Apartments

Kensington Gardens, London, W8 4PX
Tel: (020) 7937 7079 www.hrp.org.uk
Furniture and ceiling paintings from Stuart-Hanoverian
periods, rooms from Victorian era and works of art from
the Royal Collection. Also Royal Ceremonial Dress
Collection.

Kew Gardens (Royal Botanic Gardens)

Kew Richmond TW9 3AB
Tel: (020) 8940 1171 Rec.
300 acres (121 ha) containing living collections of over
40,000 varieties of plants. Seven spectacular glasshouses,
2 art galleries, Japanese and rock garden.

London Dungeon

28-34 Tooley Street, London, SE1 2SZ
Tel: (020) 7403 7221 www.thedungeons.com
The world's first medieval fully interactive horror
attraction. Relive the 'Great Fire of London', unmask
'Jack the Ripper' and take the 'Judgement Day' ride.

London Planetarium

Marylebone Road, London, NW1 5LR
Tel: (0870) 400 3000 www.london-planetarium.com
Visitors can experience a virtual reality trip through space
and wander through the interactive Space Zones before
the show.

London Transport Museum

Covent Garden Piazza, London, WC2E 7BB
Tel: (020) 7379 6344 www.ltmuseum.co.uk
The history of transport for everyone, from spectacular
vehicles, special exhibitions, actors and guided tours to
film shows, gallery talks and children's craft workshops.

London Zoo

Regent's Park, London, NW1 4RY
Tel: (020) 7722 3333 www.londonzoo.co.uk
One of the world's most famous zoos and home to over
600 species. Including the new 'Web of Life' exhibition,
as well as a full daily events programme.

Madame Tussaud's

Marylebone Road, London, NW1 5LR
Tel: (0870) 400 3000 www.madame-tussauds.com
World-famous collection of wax figures in themed
settings which include The Garden Party, 200 Years,
Superstars, The Grand Hall, The Chamber of Horrors and
The Spirit of London.

National Army Museum

Royal Hospital Road, Chelsea, London, SW3 4HT
Tel: (020) 7730 0717
www.national-armymuseum.ac.uk
The story of the British soldier in peace and war, through
five centuries. Exhibits range from paintings to uniforms
and from the English Civil War to Kosovo.

National History Museum

Cromwell Road, London, SW7 5BD
Tel: (020) 7942 5000 www.nhm.ac.uk
Home of the wonders of the natural world, one of the
most popular museums in the world and one of London's
finest landmarks.

The Pictures:
1 London by night, Piccadilly Circus
2 Big Ben
3 Buckingham Palace
4 Albert Hall
5 Harrods
6 Horseguards Parade

National Portrait Gallery

St Martin's Place, London, WC2H 0HE
Tel: (020) 7306 0055 www.npg.org.uk
Permanent collection of portraits of famous men and women from the Middle Ages to the present day. Free, but charge for some exhibitions.

Royal Air Force Museum

Grahame Park Way, Hendon, London, NW9 5LL
Tel: (020) 8205 2266 www.rafmuseum.com
Britain's National Museum of Aviation features over 70 full-sized aircraft, Flight Simulator, 'Touch and Try' Jet Provost Trainer and Eurofighter 2000 Theatre.

Royal Mews

Buckingham Palace, London, SW1A 1AA
Tel: (020) 7839 1377 www.royal.gov.uk
Her Majesty The Queen's carriage horses, carriages and harness used on State occasions (Coronation Coach built 1761).

Royal Observatory Greenwich

Greenwich Park, London, SE10 9NF
Tel: (020) 8858 4422 www.nmm.ac.uk
Museum of time and space and site of the Greenwich Meridian. Working telescopes and planetarium, timeball, Wren's Octagon Room and intricate clocks and computer simulations.

Science Museum

Exhibition Road, London, SW7 2DD
Tel: (0870) 870 4868 www.sciencemuseum.org.uk
See, touch and experience the major scientific advances of the last 300 years. With over 40 galleries, and over 2,000 hands-on exhibits to captivate and inspire all.

Shakespeare's Globe Exhibition and Tour

New Globe Walk, Bankside, London, SE1 9DT
Tel: (020) 7902 1500 www.shakespeares-globe.org
Against the historical background of Elizabethan Bankside, the City of London's playground in Shakespeare's time, the exhibition focuses on actors, architecture and audiences.

St Paul's Cathedral

St Paul's Churchyard, London, EC4M 8AD
Tel: (020) 7236 4128 www.stpauls.co.uk
Wren's famous cathedral church of the diocese of London incorporating the Crypt, Ambulatory and Whispering Gallery.

Tate Britain

Millbank, London, SW1P 4RG
Tel: (020) 7887 8000 www.tate.org.uk
Tate Britain presents the world's greatest collection of British art in a dynamic series of new displays and exhibitions.

Theatre Museum

Russell Street, London, WC2E 7PA
Tel: (020) 7943 4700 www.theatremuseum.org
Five galleries illustrating the history of performance in the United Kingdom. The collection includes displays on theatre, ballet, dance, musical stage, rock and pop music.

Tower of London

Tower Hill, London, EC3N 4AB
Tel: (020) 7709 0765 www.hrp.org.uk
Home of the `Beefeaters' and ravens, the building spans 900 years of British history. On display are the nation's Crown Jewels, regalia and armoury robes.

Victoria and Albert Museum

Cromwell Road, London, SW7 2RL
Tel: (020) 7942 2000 www.vam.ac.uk
The V&A holds one of the world's largest and most diverse collections of the decorative arts, dating from 3000BC to the present day.

Vinopolis, City of Wine

1 Bank End, London, SE1 9BU
Tel: (0870) 241 4040 www.vinopolis.co.uk
Vinopolis offers all the pleasures of wine under one roof. The Wine Odyssey tour includes free tastings from over 200 wines; also 2 restaurants on site.

Westminster Abbey

Parliament Square, London, SW1P 3PA
Tel: (020) 7222 5152 www.westminster-abbey.org
One of Britain's finest Gothic buildings. Scene of the coronation, marriage and burial of British monarchs. Nave and cloisters, Royal Chapels and Undercroft Museum.

Find out more about
London

Millennium Wheel

LONDON TOURIST BOARD

London Tourist Board and Convention Bureau
6th Floor, Glen House, Stag Place, London SW1E 5LT
www.LondonTouristBoard.com

TOURIST INFORMATION CENTRES

POINT OF ARRIVAL

- **Heathrow Terminals 1, 2, 3** Underground Station Concourse, Heathrow Airport, TW6 2JA.
  Open: Daily 0800-1800; 1 Jun-30 Sep, Mon-Sat 0800-1900, Sun 0800-1800.

- **Liverpool Street Underground Station**, EC2M 7PN.
  Open: Daily 0800-1800; 1 Jun-30 Sep, Mon-Sat 0800-1900, Sun 0800-1800.

- **Victoria Station Forecourt**, SW1V 1JU
  Open: 1 Jun-30 Sep, Mon-Sat 0800-2100, Sun 0800-1800; 1 Oct-Easter, daily 0800-1800; Easter-31 May, Mon-Sat 0800-2000, Sun 0800-1800.

- **Waterloo International Terminal**
  Arrivals Hall, London SE1 7LT. Open: Daily 0830-2230.

INNER LONDON

- **Britain Visitor Centre**, 1 Regent Street, Piccadilly Circus, SW1Y 4XT.
  Open: Mon 0930-1830, Tue-Fri 0900-1830, Sat & Sun 1000-1600; Jun-Oct, Sat 0900-1700.

- **Greenwich TIC**, Pepys House, 2 Cutty Sark Gardens, Greenwich SE10 9LW.
  Tel: 0870 608 2000; Fax: 020 8853 4607.
  Open: Daily 1000-1700; 1 Jul-31 Aug, daily 1000-2000.

- **Lewisham TIC**, Lewisham Library, 199-201 Lewisham High Street, SE13 6LG.
  Tel: 020 8297 8317; Fax: 020 8297 9241.
  Open: Mon 1000-1700, Tue-Fri 0900-1700, Sat 1000-1600, Sun closed.

- **Liverpool Street Underground Station**, EC2M 7PN.
  Open: Mon-Fri 0800-1800, Sat 0800-1730, Sun 0900-1730.

- **Southwark Information Centre**,
  London Bridge, 6 Tooley Street, SE1 2SY.
  Tel: 020 7403 8299; Fax: 020 7357 6321.
  Open: Easter-31 Oct, Mon-Sat 1000-1800, Sun 1030-1730; 1 Nov-Easter, Mon-Sat 1000-1600, Sun 1100-1600.

- **Tower Hamlets TIC**, 18 Lamb Street, E1 6EA.
  Fax: 020 7375 2539.
  Open: Mon, Tue, Thu & Fri 0930-1330 & 1430-1630, Wed 0930-1300, Sat closed, Sun 1130-1430.

- **Victoria Station Forecourt**, SW1V 1JU.
  Open: Jan-Feb, Mon-Sat 0800-1900; Mar-May, Mon-Sat 0800-2000; Jun-Sep, Mon-Sat 0800-2100; Oct-Dec, Mon-Sat 0800-2000, Sun 0800-1815.

- **London Visitor Centre, Arrivals Hall,**
  Waterloo International Terminal, London SE1 7LT.
  Open: Daily 0830-2230.

OUTER LONDON

- **Bexley Hall Place TIC,** Bourne Road, Bexley, Kent, DA5 1PQ.
  Tel: 01322 558676; Fax 01322 522921.
  Open: Mon-Sat 1000-1630, Sun 1400-1730.

- **Croydon TIC, Katharine Street,** Croydon, CR9 1ET.
  Tel: 020 8253 1009; Fax: 020 8253 1008.
  Open: Mon, Tues, Wed & Fri 0900-1800, Thu 0930-1800, Sat 0900-1700, Sun 1400-1700.

- **Harrow TIC, Civic Centre,** Station Road, Harrow, HA1 2XF.
  Tel: 020 8424 1103; Fax: 020 8424 1134.
  Open: Mon-Fri 0900-1700, Sat & Sun closed.

- **Heathrow Terminals 1,2,3 Underground Station**
  Concourse, Heathrow Airport, TW6 2JA.
  Open: Daily 0800-1800.

- **Hillingdon TIC,** Central Library, 4-15 High Street, Uxbridge, UB8 1HD.
  Tel: 01895 250706; Fax: 01895 239794.
  Open: Mon, Tue & Thu 0930-2000, Wed 0930-1730, Fri 1000-1730, Sat 0930-1600, Sun closed.

- **Hounslow TIC,** The Treaty Centre, High Street, Hounslow, TW3 1ES.
  Tel: 020 8583 2929; Fax: 020 8583 4714.
  Open: Mon, Wed, Fri & Sat 0930-1730, Tue & Thu 0930-2000, Sun closed.

- **Kingston TIC,** Market House, Market Place, Kingston upon Thames, KT1 1JS.
  Tel: 020 8547 5592; Fax: 020 8547 5594.
  Open: Mon-Fri 1000-1700, Sat 0900-1600, Sun closed.

- **Richmond TIC,** Old Town Hall, Whittaker Avenue; Richmond, TW9 1TP.
  Tel: 020 8940 9125 Fax: 020 8940 6899.
  Open: Mon-Sat 1000-1700; Easter Sunday-end Sep, Sun 1030-1330.

- **Swanley TIC,** London Road, BR8 7AE.
  Tel: 01322 614660; Fax: 01322 666154.
  Open: Mon-Thur 0930-1730, Fri 0930-1800, Sat 0900-1600, Sun closed.

- **Twickenham TIC,** The Atrium, Civic Centre, York Street, Twickenham, Middlesex, TW1 3BZ.
  Tel: 020 8891 7272; Fax: 020 8891 7738.
  Open: Mon-Thu 0900-1715, Fri 0900-1700, Sat & Sun closed.

LONDON LINE

London Tourist Board's recorded telephone information service provides information on museums, galleries, attractions, river trips, sight seeing tours, accommodation, theatre, what's on, changing of the Guard, children's London, shopping, eating out and gay and lesbian London.

Available 24 hours a day. Calls cost 60p per minute as at July 2001. Call 09068 663344.

ARTSLINE

London's information and advice service for disabled people on arts and entertainment. Call (020) 7388 2227.

HOTEL ACCOMMODATION SERVICE

Accommodation reservations can be made throughout London. Call the London Tourist Board's Telephone Accommodation Service on (020) 7932 2020 with your requirements and Mastercard/Visa/Switch details or email your request on book@londontouristboard.co.uk

Reservations on arrival are handled at the Tourist Information Centres at Victoria Station, Heathrow Underground, Liverpool Street Station and Waterloo International. Go to any of them on the day when you need accommodation. A communication charge and a refundable deposit are payable when making a reservation.

WHICH PART OF LONDON?

The majority of tourist accommodation is situated in the central parts of London and is therefore very convenient for most of the city's attractions and night life.

However, there are many hotels in outer London which provide other advantages, such as easier parking. In the 'Where to Stay' pages which follow, you will find accommodation listed under INNER LONDON (covering the E1 to W14 London Postal Area) and OUTER LONDON (covering the remainder of Greater London). Colour maps 6 and 7 at the front of the guide show place names and London Postal Area codes and will help you to locate accommodation in your chosen area of London.

Getting to
London

BY ROAD: Major trunk roads into London include: A1, M1, A5, A10, A11, M11, A13, A2, M2, A23, A3, M3, A4, M4, A40, M40, A41, M25 (London orbital). London Transport is responsible for running London's bus services and the underground rail network. (020) 7222 1234 (24 hour telephone service; calls answered in rotation).

BY RAIL: Main rail termini:
Victoria/Waterloo/Charing Cross - serving the South/South East;
King's Cross - serving the North East; Euston - serving the North West/Midlands;
Liverpool Street - serving the East; Paddington - serving the Thames Valley/West.

The Pictures:
1 China Town
2 Houses of Parliament

Finding
accommodation
is as easy as 1 2 3

Where to Stay makes it quick and easy to find a place to stay.
There are several ways to use this guide.

1

Town Index

The town index, starting on page 812, lists all the places with accommodation featured in the regional sections. The index gives a page number where you can find full accommodation and contact details.

2

Colour Maps

All the place names in black on the colour maps at the front have an entry in the regional sections. Refer to the town index for the page number where you will find one or more establishments offering accommodation in your chosen town or village.

3

Accommodation listing

Contact details for **all** English Tourism Council assessed accommodation throughout England, together with their national Star rating are given in the listing section of this guide. Establishments with a full entry in the regional sections are shown in blue. Look in the town index for the page number on which their full entry appears.

LONDON INDEX

Where to stay in London

Accommodation entries in this region are listed under Inner London (covering the postcode areas E1 to W14) and Outer London (covering the remainder of Greater London) - please refer to the colour location maps 6 and 7 at the front of this guide.

At-a-glance symbols at the end of each accommodation entry give useful information about services and facilities. A key to symbols can be found inside the back cover flap. Keep this open for easy reference.

A complete listing of all the English Tourism Council assessed accommodation covered by this guide appears at the back of the guide.

INNER LONDON
LONDON E4

◆◆◆◆
Silver
Award

AUCKLANDS
25 Eglington Road,
North Chingford, London E4 7AN
T: (020) 8529 1140
F: (020) 8529 9288

Bedrooms: 2 double/
twin

Lunch available
Evening meal available

B&B per night:
S Min £35.00
D Min £70.00

OPEN All year round

Comfortable Edwardian period family home with exclusive facilities in quiet suburb, easy access to City. Solar-heated swimming pool in landscaped garden.

 12

LONDON E7

◆

FOREST VIEW HOTEL
227 Romford Road, Forest Gate,
London E7 9HL
T: (020) 8534 4844
F: (020) 8534 8959

Bedrooms: 8 single,
7 double/twin, 5 triple/
multiple
Bathrooms: 4 en suite,
3 private

Evening meal available
CC: Delta, Mastercard,
Switch, Visa

B&B per night:
S £36.00–£42.00
D £58.00–£70.00

HB per person:
DY £50.00–£65.00

OPEN All year round

Catering for business and tourist clientele. En suite rooms with tea/coffee making, direct-dial telephone and TV. Full English breakfast. Warm and friendly atmosphere.

 P

IMPORTANT NOTE Information on accommodation listed in this guide has been supplied by the proprietors. As changes may occur you are advised to check details at the time of booking.

LONDON E7 continued

◆ GRANGEWOOD LODGE HOTEL

104 Clova Road, Forest Gate,
London E7 9AF
T: (020) 8534 0637 & 8503 0941
F: (020) 8503 0941
E: grangewoodlodgehotel@talk21.
com
I: www.grangewoodlodgehotel.co.
uk

Bedrooms: 9 single,
5 double/twin, 3 triple/
multiple
Bathrooms: 2 en suite

CC: Mastercard, Switch,
Visa

B&B per night:
S £22.00–£25.00
D £34.00–£44.00

OPEN All year round

Comfortable budget accommodation in a quiet road. Pleasant garden. Easy access to central London, Docklands and M11. Twelve minutes to Liverpool Street station.

LONDON N1

◆◆◆ KANDARA GUEST HOUSE

68 Ockendon Road, London
N1 3NW
T: (020) 7226 5721 & 7226 3379
F: (020) 7226 3379
E: admin@kandara.co.uk
I: www.kandara.co.uk

Bedrooms: 4 single,
3 double/twin, 4 triple/
multiple

CC: Delta, Mastercard,
Visa

B&B per night:
S £41.00–£47.00
D £51.00–£59.00

OPEN All year round

Small family-run guesthouse near the Angel, Islington. Free street parking and good public transport to West End and City.

LONDON N4

◆◆ COSTELLO PALACE HOTEL

374 Seven Sisters Road,
Finsbury Park, London N4 2PG
T: (020) 8802 6551
F: (020) 8802 9461
E: costellopalacehotel@uk2net.co
I: www.costellopalacehotel.co.uk

Bedrooms: 3 single,
37 double/twin, 4 triple/
multiple
Bathrooms: 44 en suite

CC: Delta, Mastercard,
Switch, Visa

B&B per night:
S £45.00–£50.00
D £68.00–£70.00

OPEN All year round

Ideally situated for all amenities, exhibition centres, bus and underground. Bedrooms are attractively decorated with en suite facilities, direct-dial telephone, Sky TV, tea and coffee facilities. Free parking.

LONDON N6

Rating
Applied For

THE RAJ HIDEAWAY BED & BREAKFAST

67 Highgate High Street, Highgate Village,
London N6 5JX
T: (0208) 3488760 & 3483972

B&B per night:
S £25.00–£40.00
D £40.00–£60.00

HB per person:
DY £35.00–£50.00

OPEN All year round

Though tucked away on top of the 'Whittington Hill' of Highgate, N6, easy to get to from: the North by the circular road by car, Gatwick via Victoria and Finsbury Park, then 210 bus. Heathrow via Finsbury Park and 210 bus. Stanstead via Liverpool Street and 214 bus. Highgate is 20 minutes from Theatreland.

Bedrooms: 2 single,
2 double/twin
Bathrooms: 4 en suite

Lunch available
Evening meal available

25% discount for 2nd night, 33% for 3rd and subsequent nights.

LONDON N7

◆◆◆ EUROPA HOTEL

60-62 Anson Road, London N7 0AA
T: (020) 7607 5935
F: (020) 7607 5909

Bedrooms: 7 single,
12 double/twin, 9 triple/
multiple
Bathrooms: 28 en suite

CC: Delta, Mastercard,
Switch, Visa

B&B per night:
S £30.00–£35.00
D £45.00–£55.00

OPEN All year round

Two Georgian properties, all rooms en suite. Free zone parking. Nearest station Tufnell Park. Convenient for West End, London Zoo, Highgate. Two miles from Kings Cross.

LONDON N7 continued

FIVE KINGS GUEST HOUSE

◆◆

59 Anson Road, Tufnell Park,
London N7 0AR
T: (020) 7607 3996 & 7607 6466
F: (020) 7609 5554
I: www.hotelregister.co.uk/hotel/
fivekings.asp

Bedrooms: 6 single,
6 double/twin, 4 triple/
multiple
Bathrooms: 11 en suite

CC: Mastercard, Visa

B&B per night:
S £25.00–£30.00
D £38.00–£46.00

OPEN All year round

Privately-run guesthouse in a quiet residential area. 15 minutes to central London and convenient for London Zoo and most tourist attractions. Unrestricted parking in road.

LONDON N8

WHITE LODGE HOTEL

◆◆◆

1 Church Lane, Hornsey, London
N8 7BU
T: (020) 8348 9765
F: (020) 8340 7851

Bedrooms: 7 single,
6 double/twin, 3 triple/
multiple
Bathrooms: 8 en suite

Evening meal available
CC: Mastercard, Visa

B&B per night:
S £30.00–£32.00
D £40.00–£48.00

OPEN All year round

Small, friendly, family hotel offering personal service. Easy access to all transport, for sightseeing and business trips.

LONDON N22

PANE RESIDENCE

◆◆

154 Boundary Road, Wood Green,
London N22 6AE
T: (020) 8889 3735

Bedrooms: 1 single,
2 double/twin

B&B per night:
S £22.00–£24.00
D £32.00–£36.00

OPEN All year round

In a pleasant location 6 minutes' walk from Turnpike Lane underground station and near Alexandra Palace. Kitchen facilities available.

LONDON NW3

DILLONS HOTEL

◆

21 Belsize Park, Hampstead, London
NW3 4DU
T: (020) 7794 3360
F: (020) 7431 7900
E: desk@dillonshotel.com
I: www.dillonshotel.com

Bedrooms: 1 single,
8 double/twin, 4 triple/
multiple
Bathrooms: 8 en suite

CC: Delta, Mastercard,
Switch, Visa

B&B per night:
S £32.00–£42.00
D £48.00–£58.00

OPEN All year round

Victorian stucco-fronted house, convenient for central London and just 6 minutes from either Swiss Cottage or Belsize Park tube stations. Most rooms have private shower/wc.

LONDON NW6

CAVENDISH GUEST HOUSE

◆◆◆◆

24 Cavendish Road, London
NW6 7XP
T: (020) 8451 3249
F: (020) 8451 3249

Bedrooms: 2 single,
2 double/twin, 2 triple/
multiple
Bathrooms: 3 en suite

B&B per night:
S £33.00–£45.00
D £52.00–£59.00

OPEN All year round

In a quiet residential street, 5 minutes' walk from Kilburn underground station, 15 minutes' travelling time to the West End. Easy access to Wembley Stadium, Heathrow, Gatwick.

AT-A-GLANCE SYMBOLS

Symbols at the end of each accommodation entry give useful information about services and facilities. A key to symbols can be found inside the back cover flap. Keep this open for easy reference.

LONDON NW10

◆◆◆

J AND T GUEST HOUSE

98 Park Avenue North, Willesden Green,
London NW10 1JY
T: (020) 8452 4085
F: (020) 8450 2503
E: jandthome@aol.com
I: www.jandtguesthouses.com

B&B per night:
S £42.00–£49.00
D £52.00–£62.00

OPEN All year round

J and T Guest House, situated in a quiet residential area of Willesden Green, is only a few minutes' walk from the underground station and buses. In 10-15 minutes you are in the heart of the West End with shops, restaurants, theatres, and close to all major tourist attractions. Free parking.

Bedrooms: 1 single, 4 double/twin, 1 triple/ multiple
Bathrooms: 6 en suite

CC: Amex, Delta, Mastercard, Switch, Visa

LONDON SE3

◆◆◆

49 FOXES DALE
Blackheath, London SE3 9BH
T: (020) 8852 1076 &
07770 583487
F: (020) 8852 1076

Bedrooms: 3 double/ twin

Evening meal available

B&B per night:
S £40.00–£45.00
D £55.00–£60.00

HB per person:
DY £40.00

Comfortable family home on a private estate close to bustling Blackheath Village, historic Greenwich and the river Thames, 15 minutes from central London.

◆◆

59 LEE TERRACE
Blackheath, London SE3 9TA
T: (020) 8852 6334
E: susan.bedbreakfast@virgin.net

Bedrooms: 1 single, 1 double/twin, 1 triple/ multiple
Bathrooms: 1 en suite

B&B per night:
S £24.00–£25.00
D £48.00–£50.00

OPEN All year round

A Grade II Listed Georgian building with most of its original features. Situated near the centre of Blackheath village and Greenwich Park. Train station to central London 100 metres.

LONDON SE6

Rating Applied For

THE HEATHERS
71 Verdant Lane, Catford, London SE6 1JD
T: (020) 8698 8340
F: (020) 8461 3980
E: berylheath@yahoo.co.uk
I: theheathersbb.com

Bedrooms: 2 double/ twin

B&B per night:
S £30.00–£35.00
D £45.00–£50.00

A comfortable family run, 'home from home'. Beryl and Ron will do their best to ensure you really enjoy your visit.

◆◆◆

THORNSBEACH
122 Bargery Road, Catford, London SE6 2LR
T: (020) 8695 6544 & 8244 5554
F: (020) 8695 9577
E: helen@thornsbeach.co.uk
I: www.thornsbeach.co.uk

Bedrooms: 1 single, 1 double/twin
Bathrooms: 1 en suite

CC: Delta, Mastercard, Switch, Visa

B&B per night:
S £28.00–£30.00
D £56.00–£68.00

OPEN All year round

Spacious, comfortable Edwardian house within conservation area. Substantial organic breakfasts. Ample parking. Five minutes' walk to cinema and shops. Convenient for City, West End, Lewisham and Kent.

CONFIRM YOUR BOOKING
You are advised to confirm your booking in writing.

LONDON SE6 continued

◆◆◆ TULIP TREE HOUSE

41 Minard Road, Catford, London
SE6 1NP
T: (020) 8697 2596
F: (020) 8698 2020

Bedrooms: 1 single,
2 double/twin

Evening meal available

B&B per night:
S £25.00
D £46.00

OPEN All year round

English home in quiet residential area off A205 South Circular Road. 10 minutes' walk to Hither Green station for 20-minute journey to central London.

LONDON SE8

◆◆ M B GUEST HOUSE

7 Bolden Street, Deptford, London
SE8 4JF
T: (020) 8692 7030
F: (020) 8691 6241

Bedrooms: 1 double/
twin, 1 triple/multiple

B&B per night:
S £25.00–£35.00
D £55.00–£60.00

HB per person:
DY £33.00–£43.00

OPEN All year round

Listed building in a cul-de-sac. All rooms are bright with central heating, colour TV, own sink and tea/coffee-making facilities. Full English breakfast. Two minutes' walk from station.

LONDON SE9

◆ WESTON HOUSE

8 Eltham Green, Eltham, London
SE9 5LB
T: (020) 8850 5191
F: (020) 8850 0030
E: reservation@westonhousehotel.
co.uk
I: www.westonhousehotel.co.uk

Bedrooms: 3 single,
5 double/twin, 2 triple/
multiple
Bathrooms: 8 en suite

CC: Delta, Mastercard,
Switch, Visa

B&B per night:
S £35.00–£40.00
D £45.00–£50.00

OPEN All year round

Victorian hotel set in quiet conservation area. Close to Maritime Greenwich, City Airport, Canary Wharf. Easy access to central London (20 minutes by train) and A2, M2, A20, M20, M25.

LONDON SE10

◆◆ GREENWICH PARKHOUSE HOTEL

1-2 Nevada Street, Greenwich,
London SE10 9JL
T: (020) 8305 1478
E: B&B@
greenwich-parkhouse-hotel.co.uk
I: www.
greenwich-parkhouse-hotel.co.uk

Bedrooms: 1 single,
5 double/twin, 2 triple/
multiple
Bathrooms: 2 en suite,
1 private

B&B per night:
S £33.00–£50.00
D £40.00–£50.00

OPEN All year round

Small hotel. Beautifully situated in the centre of the World Heritage Site, by the gates of Greenwich Royal Park.

LONDON SE20

◆◆◆◆ MELROSE HOUSE

89 Lennard Road, London SE20 7LY
T: (020) 8776 8884 &
07956 357714
F: (020) 8776 8480
E: melrose.hotel@virgin.net
I: www.uk-bedandbreakfast.com

Bedrooms: 4 double/
twin; suites available
Bathrooms: 3 en suite

CC: Delta, Mastercard,
Switch, Visa

B&B per night:
S £35.00–£45.00
D £45.00–£65.00

OPEN All year round

Pleasant, friendly accommodation with spacious en suite bedrooms. Good wholesome food and easy access to West End. Quiet, respectable and welcoming.

www.travelengland.org.uk
Log on for information and inspiration. The latest information on places to visit, events and quality assessed accommodation.

LONDON SE22

◆◆◆◆

DRAGON HOUSE

39 Marmora Road, London SE22 0RX
T: (020) 8693 4355 & 07956 645894
F: (020) 8693 7954
E: dulwichdragon@hotmail.com
I: www.thedragonhouse.co.uk

B&B per night:
S £45.00–£55.00
D £60.00–£70.00

OPEN All year round

A wonderful welcome is assured at this beautiful Victorian home. Spacious bedrooms and bright and luxuriously furnished, with fruit, flowers and books. Meals are served in the Aga-warmed kitchen or garden. Dinner on request. Sitting room with log fire, library and piano. French windows open on to a mature garden leading to parkland. Pets welcomed.

Bedrooms: 4 double/ twin
Bathrooms: 1 ensuite

Evening meal available

Luxury travel in classic car with guide by hour, day or week for sightseeing or wedding hire.

LONDON SW1

◆◆

AIRWAYS HOTEL NATIONLODGE LTD
29-31 St George's Drive, Victoria, London SW1V 4DG
T: (020) 7834 0205 & 7834 3567
F: (020) 7932 0007
E: sales@airways-hotel.com
I: www.airways-hotel.com

Bedrooms: 9 single, 20 double/twin, 10 triple/multiple
Bathrooms: 39 en suite

CC: Amex, Delta, Diners, Mastercard, Switch, Visa

B&B per night:
S £45.00–£60.00
D £50.00–£80.00

OPEN All year round

Within walking distance of Buckingham Palace and Westminster Abbey. Convenient for Harrods and theatreland. Friendly personal service. Full English breakfast.

◆◆

BLAIR VICTORIA HOTEL
78-84 Warwick Way, London SW1V 1RZ
T: (020) 7828 8603
F: (020) 7976 6536
E: sales@blairvictoria.com
I: www.blairvictoria.com

Bedrooms: 4 single, 37 double/twin, 7 triple/ multiple
Bathrooms: 48 en suite

CC: Amex, Delta, Diners, Mastercard, Switch, Visa

B&B per night:
S £40.00–£60.00
D £50.00–£80.00

OPEN All year round

Situated close to Victoria station. Behind a period facade, the Blair Victoria offers comfort and service in the heart of London.

◆◆

CARLTON HOTEL
90 Belgrave Road, Victoria, London SW1V 2BJ
T: (020) 7976 6634 & 7932 0913
F: (020) 7821 8020
E: info@cityhotelcarlton.co.uk
I: www.cityhotelcarlton.co.uk

Bedrooms: 4 single, 6 double/twin, 7 triple/ multiple
Bathrooms: 13 en suite

CC: Amex, Delta, Diners, Mastercard, Switch, Visa

B&B per night:
S £49.00–£59.00
D £59.00–£69.00

OPEN All year round

Small, friendly B&B near Victoria station and within walking distance of famous landmarks such as Buckingham Palace, Trafalgar Square, Piccadilly Circus. A lot to offer at a moderate all-inclusive rate.

◆◆

DOVER HOTEL
44 Belgrave Road, London SW1V 1RG
T: (020) 7821 9085
F: (020) 7834 6425
E: reception@dover-hotel.co.uk
I: www.dover-hotel.co.uk

Bedrooms: 4 single, 20 double/twin, 9 triple/ multiple
Bathrooms: 29 en suite

CC: Amex, Delta, Diners, Mastercard, Switch, Visa

B&B per night:
S £55.00–£65.00
D £65.00–£75.00

OPEN All year round

Friendly bed and breakfast hotel within minutes of Victoria station and Gatwick Express. Most rooms with satellite TV, shower/WC, telephone, hairdryer. Very competitive prices.

◆ **HUTTONS HOTEL**
55 Belgrave Road, London SW1V 2BB
T: (020) 7834 3726
F: (020) 7834 3389
E: reservations@huttons-hotel.co.uk

Bedrooms: 8 single, 33 double/twin, 13 triple/multiple
Bathrooms: 54 en suite

CC: Amex, Delta, Diners, Mastercard, Switch, Visa

B&B per night:
S £60.00–£65.00
D £70.00–£80.00

OPEN All year round

5 minutes' walk from Victoria and Pimlico, easy access to central London.

◆◆◆◆ **KNIGHTSBRIDGE GREEN HOTEL**
159 Knightsbridge, London SW1X 7PD
T: (020) 7584 6274
F: (020) 7225 1635
E: thekghotel@aol.com
I: www.thekghotel.co.uk

Bedrooms: 7 single, 9 double/twin, 12 triple/multiple; suites available
Bathrooms: 28 en suite

CC: Amex, Diners, Mastercard, Visa

B&B per night:
S £120.50
D £166.00–£191.00

OPEN All year round

Small family-owned hotel close to Harrods, offering spacious accommodation at competitive rates. Finalist in 1997 and 1998 London Tourism Awards.

◆◆

LUNA–SIMONE HOTEL
47 Belgrave Road, London SW1V 2BB
T: (020) 7834 5897
F: (020) 7828 2474
E: lunasimone@talk21.com
I: www.lunasimone.com

B&B per night:
S £35.00–£40.00
D £50.00–£80.00

OPEN All year round

Our family-run hotel in the heart of London offers a range of comfortable rooms with full English breakfast. All rooms have colour TV, tea/coffee facilities, safety deposit boxes and most have en suite facilities.

Bedrooms: 2 single, 21 double/twin, 10 triple/multiple
Bathrooms: 19 en suite

CC: Mastercard, Visa

◆◆◆ **MELITA HOUSE HOTEL**
35 Charlwood Street, Victoria, London SW1V 2DU
T: (020) 7828 0471 & 7834 1387
F: (020) 7932 0988
E: reserve@melitahotel.com
I: www.melitahotel.com

Bedrooms: 4 single, 10 double/twin, 8 triple/multiple
Bathrooms: 22 en suite

CC: Amex, Delta, Diners, Mastercard, Switch, Visa

B&B per night:
S £60.00–£65.00
D £85.00–£90.00

OPEN All year round

Elegant, family-run hotel in excellent location close to Victoria station. Rooms have extensive modern facilities. Warm, friendly welcome, full English breakfast included.

◆◆

STANLEY HOUSE HOTEL
19-21 Belgrave Road, London SW1V 1RB
T: (020) 7834 5042 & 7834 7292
F: (020) 7834 8439
E: cmahotel@aol.com
I: www.affordablehotelsonline.com

B&B per night:
S £40.00–£50.00
D £50.00–£60.00

OPEN All year round

In elegant Belgravia, only a few minutes' walk from Victoria station and with easy access to West End. All rooms en suite, with colour TV, direct-dial telephone, hairdryer. Friendly, relaxing atmosphere at affordable rates.

Bedrooms: 4 single, 30 double/twin, 10 triple/multiple
Bathrooms: 44 en suite

CC: Amex, Delta, Diners, Mastercard, Switch, Visa

◆◆◆◆
Silver
Award

WINDERMERE HOTEL

142-144 Warwick Way, Victoria, London
SW1V 4JE
T: (020) 7834 5163 & 7834 5480
F: (020) 7630 8831
E: windermere@compuserve.com
I: www.windermere-hotel.co.uk

B&B per night:
S £69.00–£96.00
D £89.00–£139.00

HB per person:
DY £59.35–£72.35

OPEN All year round

BTA Trophy winner. An intimate boutique hotel renowned for its friendly and personalised service. Well-equipped and individually designed bedrooms. English breakfast and dinner are served in the elegant licensed restaurant. Parking available. Situated within minutes walk from Victoria station, Buckingham Palace and Westminster.

Bedrooms: 4 single,
15 double/twin, 3 triple/
multiple
Bathrooms: 20 en suite

Evening meal available
CC: Amex, Delta,
Mastercard, Switch, Visa

LONDON SW5

◆◆
HOTEL EARLS COURT
28 Warwick Road, Earls Court,
London SW5 9UD
T: (020) 7373 7079 & 7373 0302
F: (020) 7912 0582
E: res@hotelearlscourt.com
I: www.hotelearlscourt.com

Bedrooms: 6 single,
6 double/twin, 5 triple/
multiple
Bathrooms: 6 private

CC: Amex, Diners,
Mastercard, Visa

B&B per night:
S £30.00–£49.00
D £49.00–£60.00

OPEN All year round

A friendly, clean and comfortable, centrally located bed and breakfast, opposite Earl's Court Exhibition Hall and 50 yards from Earl's Court underground station (Warwick Road exit)

◆◆◆
KENSINGTON INTERNATIONAL HOTEL
4 Templeton Place, London
SW5 9LZ
T: (020) 7370 4333
F: (020) 7244 7873
E: hotel@
kensingtoninternationalhotel.com
I: www.
kensingtoninternationalhotel.com

Bedrooms: 15 single,
40 double/twin, 3 triple/
multiple
Bathrooms: 58 en suite

CC: Amex, Delta, Diners,
Mastercard, Switch, Visa

B&B per night:
S £75.00–£100.00
D £85.00–£100.00

OPEN All year round

A boutique hotel with individually designed rooms. Located just two minutes from underground station and within easy reach of all sights of London.

◆◆

LORD JIM HOTEL

23-25 Penywern Road, London SW5 9TT
T: (020) 7370 6071 & 07957 167081
F: (020) 7373 8919
E: lordjimhotel@cs.com
I: www.igh-hotels.com

B&B per night:
S £30.00–£60.00
D £40.00–£70.00

OPEN All year round

A good quality hotel for both business travellers and tourists. Bedrooms are modern and mostly en suite, with colour TVs, telephone and hairdryers. Two minutes' walk from Earls Court station which is directly linked to Heathrow and Gatwick Airports (via Victoria). Earls Court and Olympia exhibition halls within walking distance.

Bedrooms: 9 single,
12 double/twin,
14 triple/multiple
Bathrooms: 21 en suite

CC: Amex, Delta, Diners,
Mastercard, Switch, Visa

Special discounts available in low seasons.

MERLYN COURT HOTEL

2 Barkston Gardens, London SW5 0EN
T: (020) 7370 1640
F: (020) 7370 4986
E: london@merlyncourt.demon.co.uk
I: www.smoothhound.co.uk/hotels/merlyn.html

B&B per night:
S £30.00–£50.00
D £50.00–£80.00

OPEN All year round

Well-established, family-run, good value hotel in quiet Edwardian square, close to Earl's Court and Olympia. Direct underground link to Heathrow, the West End and rail stations. Easy access to motorways and airports. Car park nearby.

Bedrooms: 4 single, 8 double/twin, 5 triple/multiple
Bathrooms: 11 en suite

CC: Delta, Mastercard, Switch, Visa

Nov-Mar: 2-3 night stays at reduced rates on application.

MOWBRAY COURT HOTEL

28-32 Penywern Road, Earl's Court, London SW5 9SU
T: (020) 7370 2316 & 7370 3690
F: (020) 7370 5693
E: mowbraycrthot@hotmail.com
I: www.m-c-hotel.mcmail.com

Bedrooms: 30 single, 30 double/twin, 28 triple/multiple
Bathrooms: 72 en suite

CC: Amex, Delta, Diners, Mastercard, Switch, Visa

B&B per night:
S £46.00–£55.00
D £57.00–£65.00

OPEN All year round

Close to Earl's Court underground and West Brompton Station with links to Heathrow and Gatwick airports. Good shopping available in the locality of Kensington and Knightsbridge.

CREDIT CARD BOOKINGS If you book by telephone and are asked for your credit card number it is advisable to check the proprietor's policy should you cancel your reservation.

USE YOUR *i*s

There are more than 550 Tourist Information Centres throughout England offering friendly help with accommodation and holiday ideas as well as suggestions of places to visit and things to do. You'll find TIC addresses in the local Phone Book.

◆◆ **OLIVER PLAZA HOTEL**

33 Trebovir Road, Earl's Court, London SW5 9NF
T: (020) 7373 7183
F: (020) 7244 6021
E: oliverplaza@capricornhotels.co.uk
I: www.capricornhotels.co.uk

Bedrooms: 3 single, 27 double/twin, 8 triple/multiple
Bathrooms: 38 en suite

CC: Amex, Delta, Diners, Mastercard, Switch, Visa

B&B per night:
S £40.00–£55.00
D £50.00–£85.00

OPEN All year round

Friendly hotel with emphasis on efficiency of service and comfort for guests. Fully refurbished in 1999. Good access to public transport and shopping facilities.

◆◆◆

HOTEL PLAZA CONTINENTAL

9 Knaresborough Place, Earls Court, London SW5 0TP
T: (020) 7370 3246
F: (020) 7373 9571
E: hpc@lgh-hotels.com
I: www.lgh-hotels.com

B&B per night:
S £35.00–£72.00
D £45.00–£85.00

OPEN All year round

Good quality hotel, recently refurbished, for the needs of both business travellers and tourists. Only 2 minutes' walk from Earls Court station and within walking distance of Earls Court and Olympia exhibition halls. Favourably positioned within easy reach of London's West End and Theatreland, Hyde Park and museums.

Bedrooms: 6 single, 12 double/twin, 3 triple/multiple
Bathrooms: 21 en suite

CC: Amex, Delta, Diners, Mastercard, Switch, Visa

◆◆

Ad p10

RAMSEES HOTEL

32-36 Hogarth Road, Earl's Court, London SW5 0PU
T: (020) 7370 1445
F: (020) 7244 6835
E: ramsees@rasool.demon.co.uk
I: www.ramseeshotel.com

B&B per night:
S £35.00–£44.00
D £50.00–£57.00

OPEN All year round

Our friendly staff are here to make your stay comfortable. Ideally located in fashionable Kensington, close to the heart of the city. One minutes' walk Earl's Court station, making major shopping areas of Knightsbridge, Oxford Street and tourist attractions of Buckingham Palace, Tower of London and museums within easy reach.

Bedrooms: 15 single, 39 double/twin, 13 triple/multiple
Bathrooms: 56 en suite

CC: Amex, Delta, Diners, Mastercard, Switch, Visa

QUALITY ASSURANCE SCHEME

For an explanation of the quality and facilities represented by the Diamonds please refer to the front of this guide. A more detailed explanation can be found in the information pages at the back.

◆◆
Ad p10

RASOOL COURT HOTEL

19-21 Penywern Road, Earl's Court,
London SW5 9TT
T: (020) 7373 8900
F: (020) 7244 6835
E: rasool@rasool.demon.co.uk
I: www.rasoolcourthotel.com

B&B per night:
S £35.00-£44.00
D £50.00-£57.00

OPEN All year round

Family-run hotel ideally located in fashionable Kensington, within 1 minutes' walk of Earl's Court station, which makes the shopping areas of Knightsbridge, Oxford Street and tourist attractions of Buckingham Palace, the Tower of London and museums within easy reach. The immediate area has a variety of restaurants and shops for your convenience.

Bedrooms: 25 single, 24 double/twin, 8 triple/ multiple
Bathrooms: 35 en suite

CC: Amex, Delta, Diners, Mastercard, Switch, Visa

◆◆◆

SWISS HOUSE HOTEL

171 Old Brompton Road, London SW5 0AN
T: (020) 7373 2769 & 7373 9383
F: (020) 7373 4983
E: recep@swiss-hh.demon.co.uk
I: www.swiss-hh.demon.co.uk

B&B per night:
S £50.00-£72.00
D £89.00-£105.00

OPEN All year round

The Swiss House Hotel is located in the heart of South Kensington, one of London's smartest and most fashionable districts, and is close to most of London's main attractions. Whether your visit is for business or pleasure, the Swiss House extends a warm welcome and ensures a comfortable stay.

Bedrooms: 5 single, 7 double/twin, 4 triple/ multiple
Bathrooms: 15 en suite

CC: Amex, Delta, Diners, Mastercard, Switch, Visa

◆

Ad p47

WINDSOR HOUSE

12 Penywern Road, London SW5 9ST
T: (020) 7373 9087
F: (020) 7385 2417
E: bookings@windsor-house-hotel.com
I: www.windsor_house.com

B&B per night:
S £24.00-£46.00
D £19.00-£36.00

OPEN All year round

Central London. Friendly, family-run bed and breakfast. Beautiful Victorian building. Excellent budget standard. Spacious, comfortable rooms. Ideal for double/family rooms (3,4,5). Children – the more the merrier! Use of new hotel kitchen for preparing own teas/meals. Super garden. NCP parking.

Bedrooms: 1 single, 8 double/twin, 9 triple/ multiple
Bathrooms: 12 en suite

Super special savers for stays of 3 nights or more. Discounts for children. 3/4/5 bedroom family rooms from £12-£26pp.

ACCESSIBILITY

Look for the symbols which indicate accessibility for wheelchair users. A list of establishments is at the front of this guide.

LONDON SW5 continued

YORK HOUSE HOTEL

◆◆

27-28 Philbeach Gardens, London SW5 9EA
T: (020) 7373 7519 & 7373 7579
F: (020) 7370 4641
E: yorkhh@aol.com
I: www.smoothhound.co.uk/hotels/yorkhousehotel.html

Bedrooms: 16 single, 6 double/twin, 5 triple/multiple
Bathrooms: 3 en suite

CC: Amex, Delta, Diners, Mastercard, Switch, Visa

B&B per night:
S £35.00–£49.00
D £56.00–£75.00

OPEN All year round

Conveniently located in Kensington close to Earl's Court and Olympia exhibition centres and the West End. Underground direct to Heathrow Airport.

LONDON SW7

ASTER HOUSE

◆◆◆◆◆

Silver Award

3 Sumner Place, London SW7 3EE
T: (020) 7581 5888
F: (020) 7584 4925
E: AsterHouse@btinternet.com
I: www.AsterHouse.com

Bedrooms: 3 single, 11 double/twin
Bathrooms: 14 en suite

CC: Delta, Mastercard, Switch, Visa

B&B per night:
S £75.00–£99.00
D £135.00–£180.00

OPEN All year round

Aster House aims to provide their guests with a clean and comfortable accommodation together with a healthy breakfast. Value for money and entirely no smoking.

◆◆◆◆

Awarded 'best small hotel'. In South Kensington, one of the most stylish and sought-after locations in London, the hotel brings the charm and elegance of a former age to the 20thC. Ideally placed for visiting the sights. This family-owned and run hotel offers excellent service and personal attention.

FIVE SUMNER PLACE HOTEL

5 Sumner Place, South Kensington, London SW7 3EE
T: (020) 7584 7586
F: (020) 7823 9962
E: reservations@sumnerplace.com
I: www.sumnerplace.com

Bedrooms: 3 single, 10 double/twin
Bathrooms: 13 en suite

CC: Amex, Mastercard, Switch, Visa

B&B per night:
S £85.00–£130.00
D £140.00–£152.00

OPEN All year round

LONDON SW14

THE PLOUGH INN

◆◆◆

42 Christchurch Road, East Sheen, London SW14 7AF
T: (020) 8876 7833 & 8876 4533
F: (020) 8392 8801
E: ploughthe@hotmail.com

Bedrooms: 1 single, 6 double/twin, 1 triple/multiple
Bathrooms: 8 en suite

Lunch available
Evening meal available
CC: Amex, Delta, Mastercard, Switch, Visa

B&B per night:
S £65.00–£70.00
D £85.00–£90.00

HB per person:
DY £75.00–£80.00

OPEN All year round

Delightful old pub, part 16thC, next to Richmond Park. En suite accommodation, traditional ales, home-cooked food.

LONDON SW18

THE BREWERS INN

◆◆◆

147 East Hill, Wandsworth, London SW18 2QB
T: (020) 8874 4128
F: (020) 8877 1953
E: brewersinn@youngs.co.uk
I: www.youngs.co.uk

Bedrooms: 4 single, 12 double/twin
Bathrooms: 16 en suite

Lunch available
Evening meal available
CC: Amex, Delta, Mastercard, Switch, Visa

B&B per night:
S £62.00–£82.00
D £72.00–£92.00

OPEN All year round

Sixteen en suite bedrooms, all with air conditioning. Large bar and bistro, a la carte restaurant. Patio garden and car park. Excellent full English breakfast included.

RATING All accommodation in this guide has been rated, or is awaiting a rating, by a trained English Tourism Council assessor.

LONDON W1

◆◆◆ **BLANDFORD HOTEL**
80 Chiltern Street, London
W1U 5AF
T: (020) 7486 3103
F: (020) 7487 2786
E: blandfordhotel@dial.pipex.com
I: www.capricornhotels.co.uk

Bedrooms: 8 single,
14 double/twin,
11 triple/multiple
Bathrooms: 33 en suite

CC: Amex, Delta,
Mastercard, Switch, Visa

B&B per night:
S £45.00–£70.00
D £65.00–£90.00

OPEN All year round

Centrally located hotel, close to Baker Street underground station and Madame Tussauds. Oxford Street and other attractions in the West End are within walking distance.

◆◆

LINCOLN HOUSE HOTEL-CENTRAL LONDON

33 Gloucester Place, London W1U 8HY
T: (020) 7486 7630
F: (020) 7935 7089
E: reservations@lincoln-house-hotel.co.uk
I: www.lincoln-house-hotel.co.uk

B&B per night:
S £59.00–£79.00
D £79.00–£89.00

OPEN All year round

Built in the days of King George III, this hotel offers Georgian charms and character. En suite rooms with modern comforts. Competitively priced. Located in the heart of London's West End, next to Oxford Street and most famous shopping attractions, close to theatreland. Ideal for business and leisure.

Bedrooms: 8 single,
10 double/twin, 4 triple/
multiple
Bathrooms: 22 en suite

CC: Amex, Delta, Diners,
Mastercard, Switch, Visa

Long-stay discounts on request; most Sun discounted. For other special offers visit our website.

◆◆ **MARBLE ARCH INN**
49-50 Upper Berkeley Street,
Marble Arch, London W1H 7PN
T: (020) 7723 7888
F: (020) 7723 6060
E: sales@marblearch-inn.co.uk
I: www.marblearch-inn.co.uk

Bedrooms: 2 single,
18 double/twin, 9 triple/
multiple
Bathrooms: 23 en suite,
2 private

CC: Amex, Delta, Diners,
Mastercard, Switch, Visa

B&B per night:
S £45.00–£75.00
D £65.00–£75.00

OPEN All year round

Friendly bed and breakfast hotel within minutes of Hyde Park, Oxford Street, Heathrow Express. Most rooms with satellite TV, shower/WC, telephone, hairdryer. Very competitive prices.

LONDON W2

◆◆

ALLANDALE HOTEL

3 Devonshire Terrace, Lancaster Gate,
London W2 3DN
T: (020) 7723 8311 & 7723 7807
F: (020) 7723 8311
E: info@allandalehotel.co.uk
I: www.allandalehotel.co.uk

B&B per night:
S £50.00–£55.00
D £65.00–£70.00

HB per person:
DY £50.00–£55.00

OPEN All year round

Quietly situated, family-run hotel. All bedrooms have private shower, toilet and TV. Full English breakfast. Close to 2 Underground stations, Lancaster Gate and Paddington. Stroll in Hyde Park or take a bus to Oxford Street, West End theatres, museums and art galleries. Saturday Portobello antiques, Sunday Bayswater Road open air art.

Bedrooms: 4 single,
10 double/twin, 6 triple/
multiple
Bathrooms: 18 en suite

CC: Amex, Delta, Diners,
Mastercard, Visa

£3 discount per night on 2-night stays. £5 discount per night on 3-night stays.

WHERE TO STAY
Please mention this guide when making your booking.

◆◆

BARRY HOUSE HOTEL
12 Sussex Place, London W2 2TP
T: (020) 7723 7340
F: (020) 7723 9775
E: hotel@barryhouse.co.uk
I: www.barryhouse.co.uk

B&B per night:
S £40.00–£45.00
D £80.00–£85.00

OPEN All year round

We believe in family-like care. Comfortable en suite rooms with TV, telephone and hospitality tray. Located close to Hyde Park, the West End, Paddington Station and many tourist attractions. We offer tourist information, sightseeing and tours arranged, theatre tickets and taxis booked.

Bedrooms: 4 single, 11 double/twin, 3 triple/ multiple
Bathrooms: 15 en suite

CC: Amex, Delta, Diners, Mastercard, Switch, Visa

◆◆

CLASSIC HOTEL
92 Sussex Gardens, Hyde Park, London W2 1UH
T: (020) 7706 7776
F: (020) 7706 8136
E: bookings@classic-hotel.com
I: www.classic-hotel.com

Bedrooms: 2 single, 7 double/twin, 4 triple/ multiple
Bathrooms: 13 en suite

CC: Amex, Delta, Diners, Mastercard, Switch, Visa

B&B per night:
S £45.00–£52.00
D £60.00–£76.00

OPEN All year round

Rooms with private shower and toilet, colour TV, fridge. Parking facility. Ideal for business, shopping, leisure. Close to Paddington mainline and underground station. Buses nearby.

◆◆

DYLAN HOTEL
14 Devonshire Terrace, Lancaster Gate, London W2 3DW
T: (020) 7723 3280
F: (020) 7402 2443
E: booking@dylan-hotel.com
I: www.dylan-hotel.com

Bedrooms: 4 single, 11 double/twin, 3 triple/ multiple
Bathrooms: 7 en suite

CC: Amex, Delta, Diners, Mastercard, Switch, Visa

B&B per night:
S £35.00–£50.00
D £52.00–£72.00

OPEN All year round

Small hotel in central location, 4 minutes from Paddington and Lancaster Gate underground stations. Marble Arch, Hyde Park and Oxford Street close by. Not just a hotel, a home from home.

◆

HYDE PARK ROOMS HOTEL
137 Sussex Gardens, Hyde Park, London W2 2RX
T: (020) 7723 0225 & 7723 0965

Bedrooms: 5 single, 8 double/twin, 3 triple/ multiple
Bathrooms: 6 en suite

CC: Amex, Diners, Mastercard, Visa

B&B per night:
S £30.00–£40.00
D £45.00–£60.00

OPEN All year round

Small centrally located private hotel with personal service. Clean, comfortable and friendly. Within walking distance of Hyde Park and Kensington Gardens. Car parking available.

USE YOUR *i*s

There are more than 550 Tourist Information Centres throughout England offering friendly help with accommodation and holiday ideas as well as suggestions of places to visit and things to do. You'll find TIC addresses in the local Phone Book.

LONDON W2 continued

♦♦♦

KINGSWAY PARK HOTEL HYDE PARK

139 Sussex Gardens, Hyde Park, London W2 2RX
T: (020) 7723 5677 & 7724 9346
F: (020) 7402 4352
E: kingswaypark@hotel.com
I: www.kingsway-hotel.com

B&B per night:
S £47.00–£65.00
D £64.00–£85.00

HB per person:
DY £55.00–£73.00

OPEN All year round

The hotel is situated in the heart of London 3 minutes from Paddington station and Hyde Park and 10 minutes walk to Marble Arch and Oxford Street. Completely refurbished to a high standard, all rooms have en suite facilities, direct dial phone, tea/coffee-making facilities, hairdryer, Sky TV and ironing facilities. 24 hour reception.

Bedrooms: 4 single, 7 double/twin, 11 triple/multiple
Bathrooms: 22 en suite

Evening meal available
CC: Amex, Delta, Diners, Mastercard, Switch, Visa

10% discount on weekly bookings.

♦♦♦

LONDON GUARDS HOTEL
36-37 Lancaster Gate, London W2 3NA
T: (020) 7402 1101
F: (020) 7262 2551
E: info@londonguardshotel.co.uk
I: www.londonguardshotel.co.uk

Bedrooms: 2 single, 25 double/twin, 13 triple/multiple
Bathrooms: 40 en suite

Evening meal available
CC: Amex, Delta, Diners, Mastercard, Switch, Visa

B&B per night:
S £95.00–£120.00
D £105.00–£128.00

OPEN All year round

Close to Hyde Park, 6 minutes' walk to Heathrow Express, in a quiet residential area of Lancaster Gate. Bar and speciality restaurant.

♦

MANOR COURT HOTEL
7 Clanricarde Gardens, London W2 4JJ
T: (020) 7727 5407 & 7792 3361
F: (020) 7229 2875

Bedrooms: 5 single, 9 double/twin, 6 triple/multiple
Bathrooms: 6 en suite, 3 private

CC: Amex, Delta, Diners, Mastercard, Switch, Visa

B&B per night:
S £30.00–£50.00
D £50.00–£65.00

OPEN All year round

Family-run bed and breakfast hotel within walking distance of Hyde Park and Kensington Gardens. Near Notting Hill Gate underground and Airbus stop. All rooms have colour TV and telephone.

♦♦

OLYMPIC HOUSE HOTEL
138-140 Sussex Gardens, London W2 1UB
T: (020) 7723 5935
F: (020) 7224 8144
E: olympichousehotel@btinternet.com
I: www.olympichousehotel.co.uk

Bedrooms: 9 single, 12 double/twin, 15 triple/multiple
Bathrooms: 30 en suite

CC: Amex, Mastercard, Switch, Visa

B&B per night:
S £40.00–£55.00
D £60.00–£74.00

OPEN All year round

Small, centrally-located, privately-run hotel. Offers both comfort and personal service in warm and friendly atmosphere. All rooms have shower, WC, hairdryer, telephone, radio, colour TV and satellite.

♦♦

OXFORD HOTEL
13-14 Craven Terrace, Paddington, London W2 3QD
T: (020) 7402 6860 & 0800 318798
F: (020) 7262 7574
E: info@oxfordhotellondon.co.uk
I: www.oxfordhotellondon.co.uk

Bedrooms: 8 double/twin, 9 triple/multiple
Bathrooms: 17 en suite

CC: Amex, Delta, Mastercard, Switch, Visa

B&B per night:
S £50.00–£60.00
D £60.00–£66.00

OPEN All year round

Located in a quiet one-way street, close to underground and bus routes to Oxford Street. 5 minutes' walk from Hyde Park.

 HALF BOARD PRICES Half board prices are given per person, but in some cases these may be based on double/twin occupancy.

LONDON W2 continued

♦♦

SPRINGFIELD HOTEL
154 Sussex Gardens, London W2 1UD
T: (020) 7723 9898
F: (020) 7723 0874
E: info@springfieldhotellondon.co.uk
I: www.springfieldhotellondon.co.uk

B&B per night:
S £35.00–£45.00
D £65.00–£70.00

OPEN All year round

Small family-run bed and breakfast hotel close to Hyde Park, Marble Arch, Paddington and Oxford Street. All the comforts you require: all rooms are en suite, colour satellite TV, direct dial telephone, tea/coffee facilities, full central heating. Generous full English breakfast.

Bedrooms: 2 single, 12 double/twin, 6 triple/ multiple
Bathrooms: 20 en suite

CC: Amex, Delta, Mastercard, Switch, Visa

Ⓜ 🐾 ♿ & ☎ 🖥 ▯ ✆ 🛆 Ⓢ 🎱 ◑ 🖵 🕹 ✎ P

LONDON W4

♦♦♦

CHISWICK LODGE
104 Turnham Green Terrace, London W4 1QN
T: (020) 8994 9926 & 8994 1712
F: (020) 8742 8238
E: chishot@clara.net
I: www.chiswick-hotel.co.uk

Bedrooms: 9 double/ twin
Bathrooms: 9 en suite

CC: Amex, Delta, Mastercard, Switch, Visa

B&B per night:
S £55.00–£57.00
D £75.00–£77.00

OPEN All year round

New high quality accommodation, furnished to a high standard. All rooms are en suite.

♿ ☎ ▯ ✆ Ⓢ ◑ 🖵 🛆 🐕 🚗 P

♦♦

FOUBERT'S HOTEL
162-166 Chiswick High Road, London W4 1PR
T: (020) 8994 5202 & 8995 6743

Bedrooms: 15 single, 13 double/twin, 3 triple/ multiple
Bathrooms: 31 en suite

Lunch available
Evening meal available
CC: Mastercard, Visa

B&B per night:
S £50.00–£55.00
D £70.00–£75.00

OPEN All year round

Family-run hotel, close to central London and Heathrow Airport. Fully licensed cafe/ restaurant open daily 8am to 11pm.

Ⓜ 🐾 ▯ 🏆 Ⓢ ✂ 🕹 🖵 🛆 ⛾ ❄ ✎

♦♦

IVY GATE HOUSE
6 Temple Road, Chiswick, London W4 5NW
T: (020) 8994 8618
E: thejones@ivygatehouse.co.uk
I: www.ivygatehouse.co.uk

Bedrooms: 2 double/ twin

B&B per night:
S £45.00–£55.00
D £55.00–£75.00

OPEN All year round

Family terraced house in west London close to the tube station, Chiswick House, Kew Gardens and Heathrow Airport.

🐾 ▯ ✆ Ⓢ ✂ 🖵 🚗

LONDON W5

♦♦

ABBEY LODGE HOTEL
51 Grange Park, Ealing, London W5 3PR
T: (020) 8567 7914
F: (020) 8579 5350
E: enquiries@londonlodgehotels. com
I: www.londonlodgehotels.com

Bedrooms: 10 single, 3 double/twin, 3 triple/ multiple
Bathrooms: 16 en suite

CC: Delta, Diners, Mastercard, Switch, Visa

B&B per night:
S Min £47.00
D Min £59.00

OPEN All year round

All rooms en suite, with colour TV, tea/coffee-making facilities and radio alarm clocks. Very close to 3 underground lines. Midway central London and Heathrow.

🐾 ♿ & ☎ ▯ ✆ Ⓢ ✂ 🕹 🖵 🛆 ❄ ⛾

QUALITY ASSURANCE SCHEME
Diamond ratings and awards were correct at the time of going to press but are subject to change. Please check at the time of booking.

LONDON W5 continued

GRANGE LODGE HOTEL

48-50 Grange Road, London
W5 5BX
T: (020) 8567 1049
F: (020) 8579 5350
E: enquiries@londonlodgehotels.
com
I: www.londonlodgehotels.com

Bedrooms: 8 single,
3 double/twin, 3 triple/
multiple
Bathrooms: 9 en suite

CC: Delta, Diners,
Mastercard, Switch, Visa

B&B per night:
S £35.00–£47.00
D £48.00–£59.00

OPEN All year round

Quiet, comfortable hotel, close to 3 underground stations. Midway central London and Heathrow. Colour TV, tea/coffee-making facilities, radio/alarm, most rooms en suite.

LONDON W6

HOTEL ORLANDO

83 Shepherds Bush Road, Hammersmith,
London W6 7LR
T: (020) 7603 4890
F: (020) 7603 4890
E: hotelorlando@btconnect.com
I: www.hotelorlando.co.uk

B&B per night:
S £35.00–£40.00
D £48.00–£56.00

OPEN All year round

Family-run business for the last 22 years. Situated near Hammersmith tube station, ideal for easy connection to central London. Newly decorated and all rooms have en suite facilities and colour TV. Homely welcome from Italian proprietor.

Bedrooms: 4 single,
6 double/twin, 4 triple/
multiple
Bathrooms: 14 en suite

CC: Amex, Delta,
Mastercard, Switch, Visa

ST PETERS HOTEL

407-411 Goldhawk Road, London
W6 0SA
T: (020) 8741 4239
F: (020) 8748 3845

Bedrooms: 5 single,
13 double/twin
Bathrooms: 12 en suite

Evening meal available
CC: Amex, Delta,
Mastercard, Switch, Visa

B&B per night:
S £45.00–£58.00
D £58.00–£75.00

OPEN All year round

A small, well-appointed establishment where customer care is a priority. Within easy reach of Heathrow and central London. Good value for money.

LONDON W8

HOTEL ATLAS-APOLLO

18-30 Lexham Gardens, London W8 5JE
T: (020) 7835 1155 & 7835 1133
F: (020) 7370 4853
E: reservations@atlas-apollo.com
I: www.atlas-apollo.com

B&B per night:
S £75.00
D £90.00–£100.00

OPEN All year round

Friendly, long established hotel, situated close to Earl's Court and Olympia exhibition centres and the shopping areas of Knightsbridge and Kensington High Street. Spacious, well-furnished bedrooms all with colour TV, direct-dial telephone and en suite bathroom.

Bedrooms: 28 single,
51 double/twin,
14 triple/multiple
Bathrooms: 93 en suite

CC: Amex, Delta,
Mastercard, Switch, Visa

CLEARLAKE HOTEL

18-19 Prince of Wales Terrace,
Kensington, London W8 5PQ
T: (020) 7937 3274
F: (020) 7376 0604
E: clearlake@talk21.com

Bedrooms: 2 single,
6 double/twin, 6 triple/
multiple
Bathrooms: 14 en suite

CC: Amex, Diners,
Mastercard, Visa

B&B per night:
S £40.00–£50.00
D £53.00–£70.00

OPEN All year round

Comfortable rooms in a hotel in a quiet cul-de-sac, with view of Hyde Park. Self-catering apartments also available. Close to shops and transport.

♦♦♦

CRESCENT HOTEL

49-50 Cartwright Gardens, Bloomsbury,
London WC1H 9EL
T: (020) 7387 1515
F: (020) 7383 2054
E: General.Enquiries@
CrescentHotelofLondon.com
I: www.CrescentHotelofLondon.com

B&B per night:
S £44.00–£71.00
D £82.00–£85.00

OPEN All year round

Comfortable, elegant, family-run hotel in quiet Georgian crescent, with private garden square and tennis courts. All rooms have colour TV, tea/coffee tray and direct-dial telephone, most en suite. The individually prepared English breakfast will sustain you for the best part of the day.

Bedrooms: 12 single, 5 double/twin, 10 triple/ multiple
Bathrooms: 18 en suite

CC: Delta, Mastercard, Switch, Visa

'3 night special' 10% discount on stays of 3 nights, to include Sun and Mon (excl Christmas and New Year).

♦♦♦

EURO HOTEL

53 Cartwright Gardens, London WC1H 9EL
T: (020) 7387 4321
F: (020) 7383 5044
E: Reception@eurohotel.co.uk
I: www.eurohotel.co.uk

Bedrooms: 8 single, 16 double/twin, 10 triple/multiple
Bathrooms: 10 en suite

CC: Amex, Delta, Mastercard, Switch, Visa

B&B per night:
S £49.00–£70.00
D £69.00–£89.00

OPEN All year round

Centrally located hotel close to the West End and British Museum. Bright, spacious rooms with TV, radio, direct-dial telephone, tea/coffee facilities, video films, satellite channel.

♦

GOWER HOUSE HOTEL

57 Gower Street, London WC1E 6HJ
T: (020) 7636 4685
F: (020) 7636 4685

Bedrooms: 4 single, 8 double/twin, 4 triple/ multiple
Bathrooms: 3 en suite

CC: Mastercard, Switch, Visa

B&B per night:
S £40.00–£45.00
D £50.00–£75.00

OPEN All year round

Friendly bed and breakfast hotel within easy walking distance of the British Museum, shops, theatres and restaurants. Near Goodge Street underground station.

♦♦

GUILFORD HOUSE HOTEL

6 Guilford Street, London WC1N 1DR
T: (020) 7430 2504
F: (020) 7430 0697
E: guilford-hotel@lineone.net
I: www.guilfordhotel.co.uk

Bedrooms: 3 single, 3 double/twin, 6 triple/ multiple

CC: Amex, Delta, Diners, Mastercard, Switch, Visa

B&B per night:
S £35.00–£39.00
D £54.00–£59.00

OPEN All year round

Centrally located bed and breakfast, walking distance to British Museum, Trafalgar Square, Piccadilly Circus, Oxford Street, Theatreland and West End. Easy access to public transport.

♦

ST ATHANS HOTEL

20 Tavistock Place, Russell Square, London WC1H 9RE
T: (020) 7837 9140 & 7837 9627
F: (020) 7833 8352

Bedrooms: 14 single, 28 double/twin, 6 triple/ multiple
Bathrooms: 8 en suite

CC: Amex, Diners, Mastercard, Visa

B&B per night:
S £30.00–£40.00
D £40.00–£50.00

OPEN All year round

Simple, small but clean family-run hotel offering bed and breakfast.

NB **IMPORTANT NOTE** Information on accommodation listed in this guide has been supplied by the proprietors. As changes may occur you are advised to check details at the time of booking.

LONDON WC1 continued

◆◆◆◆

STAUNTON HOTEL

13-15 Gower Street, Bloomsbury, London WC1E 6HE
T: (020) 7580 2740
F: (020) 7580 3554
E: enquiries@stauntonhotel.com
I: www.stauntonhotel.com

B&B per night:
S £60.00–£70.00
D £90.00–£140.00

OPEN All year round

A beautiful Grade II Listed Georgian town house. The Staunton Hotel boasts of its luxurious décor and warm atmosphere. Situated in the heart of central London, the hotel is only a few minutes walk from the British Museum, Oxford Street, Theatreland, Covent Garden and much more. All rooms are en suite.

Bedrooms: 1 single, 16 double/twin; suites available
Bathrooms: 17 en suite

CC: Amex, Delta, Diners, Mastercard, Switch, Visa

Special weekend rate starting on Fridays. 3 nights for the price of 2 nights.

LONDON WC2

◆◆

ROYAL ADELPHI HOTEL

21 Villiers Street, London WC2N 6ND
T: (020) 7930 8764
F: (020) 7930 8735
E: info@royaladelphi.co.uk
I: www.royaladelphi.co.uk

Bedrooms: 20 single, 25 double/twin, 2 triple/ multiple
Bathrooms: 34 en suite

Lunch available
Evening meal available
CC: Amex, Delta, Diners, Mastercard, Switch, Visa

B&B per night:
S £54.00–£72.00
D £76.00–£98.00

OPEN All year round

Centrally located and ideal for theatreland, near Embankment and Charing Cross underground. All rooms with colour TV, hairdryer, tea/coffee facilities. Most rooms have private bathrooms.

OUTER LONDON BEXLEYHEATH

◆◆◆◆

VIVENDA HOUSE

1 Ferndale Close, Bexleyheath DA7 4ES
T: (020) 8304 5486 & 07956 848050
E: francisvivenda@aol.com
I: www.vivendahouse.co.uk

B&B per night:
S £25.00–£35.00
D £56.00–£65.00

HB per person:
DY £38.00–£48.00

OPEN All year round

A haven of peace, yet only 45 minutes to London. Elegant house with quality furnishings throughout to provide highest standard of accommodation. A warm welcome awaits you with home cooking a speciality. We are an ideal base for touring and business. Garden features – sunken barbecue, koi pool, games room.

Bedrooms: 3 double/ twin
Bathrooms: 1 en suite, 1 private

Lunch available
Evening meal available
CC: Mastercard, Switch, Visa

CROYDON *Tourist Information Centre Tel: (020) 8253 1009*

◆◆◆

CROYDON HOTEL

112 Lower Addiscombe Road, Croydon CR0 6AD
T: (020) 8656 7233
F: (020) 8655 0211

Bedrooms: 1 single, 5 double/twin, 2 triple/ multiple
Bathrooms: 6 en suite

CC: Delta, Mastercard, Visa

B&B per night:
S £35.00–£55.00
D £55.00–£70.00

OPEN All year round

Close to central Croydon (route A222) and 10 minutes' walk from East Croydon station. Opposite shops and restaurants. Frequent direct trains to Victoria and Gatwick Airport.

IDEAS For ideas on places to visit refer to the introduction at the beginning of this section.

CROYDON continued

Rating Applied For

CROYDON FRIENDLY GUESTHOUSE

16 St Peter's Road, Croydon
CR0 1HD
T: (020) 8680 4428 & 07989 924 988
F: (020) 8658 5385
E: bilal@bhasan.fsnet.co.uk

Bedrooms: 7 single,
1 double/twin
Bathrooms: 2 en suite

B&B per night:
S £25.00–£45.00
D £40.00–£50.00

OPEN All year round

Detached house with comfortable, well-appointed rooms, all with private facilities. Friendly, family atmosphere with ample off-road parking. Perfect base for London or Croydon.

HAMPTON

♦♦♦

FRIARS COTTAGE

2B Priory Road, Hampton
TW12 2WR
T: (020) 8287 4699

Bedrooms: 3 single

B&B per night:
S £23.00–£26.00

OPEN All year round

Detached house in a very quiet cul-de-sac. Good parking facilities. Near buses, 5 minutes from trains to Waterloo and Hampton Court.

HARROW

♦♦♦

HINDES HOTEL

8 Hindes Road, Harrow HA1 1SJ
T: (020) 8427 7468 & 8427 7272
F: (020) 8424 0673
E: reception@hindeshotel.com
I: www.hindeshotel.com

Bedrooms: 4 single,
10 double/twin
Bathrooms: 7 en suite

Evening meal available
CC: Amex, Delta, Diners, Mastercard, Switch, Visa

B&B per night:
S £39.00–£49.00
D £49.00–£59.00

OPEN All year round

Situated near the M4 and M1. West End 15 minutes by Underground. Convenient for Wembley Stadium and Heathrow airport (25 minutes). Tube and train 5 minutes walk.

HEATHROW AIRPORT

See under Hounslow

HOUNSLOW *Tourist Information Centre Tel: (020) 8572 8279*

♦♦♦♦

ASHDOWNE HOUSE

9 Pownall Gardens, Hounslow TW3 1YW
T: (020) 8572 0008
F: (020) 8570 1939
E: mail@ashdownehouse.com
I: www.ashdownehouse.com

B&B per night:
S Min £65.00
D Min £79.00

OPEN All year round

Very comfortable Victorian house with elegant rooms, all en suite and non-smoking. Walking distance of the high street and Hounslow Central underground station (for access to central London and Heathrow Airport). Hampton Court Palace, Kew Gardens, Twickenham rugby ground and Syon Park are easily reached by car or bus.

Bedrooms: 2 single,
5 double/twin
Bathrooms: 7 en suite

CC: Delta, Mastercard, Switch, Visa

♦♦♦

LAMPTON PARK GUESTHOUSE

4 Lampton Park Road, Hounslow
TW3 4HS
T: (020) 8572 8622
E: michael.duff1@virgin.net

Bedrooms: 2 single,
2 double/twin
Bathrooms: 2 en suite

B&B per night:
S £35.00
D £55.00–£60.00

OPEN All year round

Large converted family house in quiet cul-de-sac, close to shops, amenities and only 35 minutes to London's West End by tube.

SYMBOLS The symbols in each entry give information about services and facilities. A key to these symbols appears at the back of this guide.

HOUNSLOW continued

◆◆ **SKYLARK BED & BREAKFAST**
297 Bath Road, Hounslow TW3 3DB
T: (020) 8577 8455
F: (020) 8577 8741
E: skylarkgh@ukonline.co.uk
I: web.ukonline.co.uk/skylarkgh

Bedrooms: 8 single,
8 double/twin, 2 triple/
multiple
Bathrooms: 18 en suite

CC: Amex, Delta,
Mastercard, Visa

B&B per night:
S £45.00–£50.00
D £60.00–£65.00

HB per person:
DY £40.00–£50.00

OPEN All year round

Skylark Bed & Breakfast is 100 yards from Hounslow West Underground station and 3 miles from Heathrow Airport. All rooms are en suite.

🛏️ 🖃 📠 ☎ 🖥️ □ ↓ 🍷 S ↙ ◑ 🏭 💻 ☼ 🐾 ⌂ P

KEW

◆◆◆◆ **11 LEYBORNE PARK**
Kew, Richmond TW9 3HB
T: (020) 8948 1615 &
07778 123736
F: (020) 8255 1141
E: garriganx2@hotmail.com

Bedrooms: 1 single,
2 double/twin
Bathrooms: 1 en suite,
1 private

B&B per night:
S £27.00–£40.00
D £55.00–£75.00

OPEN All year round

Comfortable, newly refurbished house in quiet street close to Kew Gardens and Public Record Office. Easy access to central London, 3 minutes' walk from tube.

🛏️ 🖃 □ ↓ 🍷 S ↙ 🏭 💻 ⌂ P

◆◆◆ **WEST LODGE**
179 Mortlake Road, Kew, Richmond
TW9 4AW
T: (020) 8876 0584 & 8876 5375
F: (020) 8876 0584
E: westlodge@thakria.demon.co.uk

Bedrooms: 1 double/
twin
Bathrooms: 1 en suite

B&B per night:
S £35.00–£45.00
D £50.00–£60.00

OPEN All year round

Accommodation in a Grade II Listed Georgian house. Close to Public Records Office and Underground.

🛏️ □ ↓ 🍷 S 🏭 💻 ☼ 🐎 ⌂ P

MORDEN

◆◆ **28 MONKLEIGH ROAD**
Morden SM4 4EW
T: (020) 8542 5595 & 8287 7494

Bedrooms: 1 single,
1 double/twin

B&B per night:
S Min £18.00
D Min £36.00

OPEN All year round

Clean and comfortable family-run bed and breakfast. With easy access to main London attractions and Wimbledon tennis. Approximately 45 minutes to Heathrow or Gatwick.

🛏️5 🖃 🍷 S ↙ 🏭 💻 ☼ ⌂ P

PURLEY

◆◆◆ **FOXLEY MOUNT**
44 Foxley Lane, Purley CR8 3EE
T: (020) 8660 9751
F: (020) 8645 9368

Bedrooms: 1 single,
1 double/twin, 1 triple/
multiple

B&B per night:
S £25.00–£35.00
D £45.00

OPEN All year round

Large Edwardian house, family-run bed and breakfast. Walking distance to Purley station. Twenty minutes to Gatwick or central London by train.

🛏️5 □ ↓ 🍷 S ↙ 🏭 💻 ⌂ P

RICHMOND *Tourist Information Centre Tel: (020) 8940 9125*

◆◆◆◆◆
**Gold
Award**

CHALON HOUSE
8 Spring Terrace, Paradise Road, Richmond
TW9 1LW
T: (020) 8332 1121
F: (020) 8332 1131
E: virgilioz@aol.com

B&B per night:
S £70.00
D £75.00–£80.00

Listed Georgian townhouse. Quality en suite bedrooms with big comfortable beds and breakfast tailored to your taste. 5-minute walk to Richmond station and 7 miles to central London. Picnic in Kew Gardens or relax at one of the many traditional pubs along the Thames.

Bedrooms: 3 double/
twin
Bathrooms: 3 en suite

🖃 □ ↓ 🍷 S ↙ 🍴 🏭 💻 ☼ ⌂ P

RICHMOND continued

◆◆◆

HOBART HALL HOTEL

43-47 Petersham Road, Richmond
TW10 6UL
T: (020) 8940 0435 & 8940 1702
F: (020) 8332 2996
E: hobarthall@aol.com
I: www.smoothhound.co.uk/hotels/
hobarthall.html

Built c1690. Past tenants inlcude the Earl of Buckinghamshire and the Duke of Clarence (King William IV). Situated on the banks of the River Thames, but also in the historic town of Richmond, guests have the best of both worlds. Richmond has tubes and trains and is 15 minutes from Heathrow.

Bedrooms: 7 single,
8 double/twin, 4 triple/
multiple
Bathrooms: 15 en suite,
3 private

CC: Amex, Diners,
Mastercard, Switch, Visa

Subject to availability, weekend special deals recommended at great prices. Play golf, watch rugby, watch history unfold before your eyes.

B&B per night:
S £45.00–£70.00
D £65.00–£90.00

OPEN All year round

◆◆◆

PRO KEW GARDENS B & B

15 Pensford Avenue, Kew Gardens,
Richmond TW9 4HR
T: (020) 8876 3354
E: info@prokewbandb.demon.co.uk

Quiet, detached period Edwardian house, close to Kew Gardens, Public Records Office and underground station. Unrestricted parking on street. The rooms on the first floor are for exclusive use of guests and are non-smoking. Hospitable welcome, continental breakfast. Minimum stay 2 nights.

Bedrooms: 2 single,
2 double/twin
Bathrooms: 1 en suite

B&B per night:
S £30.00
D £55.00–£65.00

OPEN All year round

◆◆◆

QUINNS HOTEL

48 Sheen Road, Richmond
TW9 1AW
T: (020) 8940 5444
F: (020) 8940 1828
I: www.quinnshotel.com

Bedrooms: 6 single,
31 double/twin, 1 triple/
multiple
Bathrooms: 23 en suite

CC: Amex, Delta, Diners,
Mastercard, Switch, Visa

B&B per night:
S £40.00–£70.00
D £60.00–£90.00

OPEN All year round

Ideally located for business or pleasure, within easy reach of central London, airports and local places of interest.

◆◆◆

RIVERSIDE HOTEL

23 Petersham Road, Richmond
TW10 6UH
T: (020) 8940 1339
F: (020) 8948 0967
E: riversidehotel@yahoo.com
I: www.smoothhound.co.uk/hotels/
riversid.html

Bedrooms: 6 single,
12 double/twin, 2 triple/
multiple
Bathrooms: 20 en suite

CC: Amex, Delta, Diners,
Mastercard, Switch, Visa

B&B per night:
S £65.00–£75.00
D £85.00–£90.00

OPEN All year round

Elegant Victorian townhouse overlooking the Thames in Richmond town centre. The rooms are en suite and offer satellite TV and tea/coffee facilities.

---

www.travelengland.org.uk

Log on for information and inspiration. The latest information on places to visit, events and quality assessed accommodation.

RICHMOND continued

◆◆◆ **WEST PARK GARDENS**
105 Mortlake Road, Kew, Richmond
TW9 4AA
T: (020) 88766842
F: (020) 88766842
E: edwardsnjdr@aol.com

Bedrooms: 1 double/
twin
Bathrooms: 1 en suite

B&B per night:
S £35.00–£40.00
D £50.00–£55.00

OPEN All year round

Three-room suite including small conservatory. Victorian house. Breakfast in main conservatory. Near Kew Gardens, PRO, London Underground (5 mins), M3, M4. Off-street parking.

SIDCUP

◆◆◆ **HILBERT HOUSE**
Halfway Street, Sidcup DA15 8DE
T: (020) 8300 0549 &
07719 721521

Bedrooms: 1 triple/
multiple
Bathrooms: 1 en suite

Evening meal available

B&B per night:
S £25.00
D £50.00

HB per person:
DY Min £35.00

OPEN All year round

Comfortable home offering one family en suite room for bed and breakfast. 15 minutes walk from station, 25 minutes to central London.

TWICKENHAM *Tourist Information Centre Tel: (020) 8891 7272*

◆◆◆ **3 WALDEGRAVE GARDENS**
Strawberry Hill, Twickenham
TW1 4PQ
T: (020) 8892 3523

Bedrooms: 3 double/
twin

B&B per night:
S Min £25.00
D Min £50.00

OPEN All year round

Large house with garden, close to Strawberry Hill station and 30 minutes by train to Waterloo.

UPMINSTER

◆◆◆ **CORNER FARM**
Corner Farm, Fen Lane,
North Ockendon, Upminster
RM14 3RB
T: (01708) 851310
F: (01708) 852025
E: corner.farm@virgin.net

Bedrooms: 1 single,
2 double/twin, 1 triple/
multiple
Bathrooms: 1 en suite

CC: Mastercard, Visa

B&B per night:
S £25.00–£35.00
D £35.00–£37.50

OPEN All year round

Attractive detached bungalow in rural setting. Breakfast served in farmhouse conservatory (30 metres). No public transport. Friendly atmosphere. Parking. No smoking, children under 10 or pets.

WEMBLEY

◆

AARON (WEMBLEY PARK) HOTEL LTD

8 Forty Lane, Wembley HA9 9EB
T: (020) 8904 6329 & 8908 5711
F: (020) 8385 0472
E: info@aaronhotel.com
I: www.aaronhotel.com

B&B per night:
S £29.00–£59.00
D £55.00–£69.00

OPEN All year round

We are a small, family-run hotel which has just been refurbished. Within easy reach of Wembley Park station and Wembley Stadium, Arena and Conference Centre. Easily accessible from A406 (North Circular Road), M1 and A1. West End of London is approximately 20 minutes away.

Bedrooms: 3 single,
1 double/twin, 6 triple/
multiple
Bathrooms: 9 en suite,
1 private

Lunch available
Evening meal available
CC: Amex, Delta, Diners,
Mastercard, Switch, Visa

10% discount for bookings over 5 days.

PRICES
Please check prices and other details at the time of booking.

WEMBLEY continued

◆◆◆ ADELPHI HOTEL

4 Forty Lane, Wembley HA9 9EB
T: (020) 8904 5629 & 89085629
F: (020) 8908 5314
E: adel@dial.pipex.com
I: www.hoteladelphi.co.uk

Bedrooms: 4 single,
7 double/twin, 2 triple/
multiple
Bathrooms: 9 en suite

CC: Amex, Delta, Diners,
Mastercard, Switch, Visa

B&B per night:
S £35.00–£42.00
D £45.00–£55.00

OPEN All year round

Close to Wembley Stadium and Wembley Park underground, 15 minutes from West End. Attractive decor. TV lounge, tea/coffee in rooms.

◆◆◆ ARENA HOTEL

6 Forty Lane, Wembley HA9 9EB
T: (020) 8908 0670 & 8904 0019
F: (020) 8908 2007
E: enquiry@arenahotel.fsnet.co.uk
I: www.arena-hotel.co.uk

Bedrooms: 2 single,
5 double/twin, 6 triple/
multiple
Bathrooms: 13 en suite

CC: Amex, Delta, Diners,
Mastercard, Switch, Visa

B&B per night:
S £45.00–£49.00
D £55.00–£59.00

OPEN All year round

All rooms en suite, with satellite TV, tea/coffee-making facilities and direct-dial telephone. Ideally situated, with Wembley Stadium complex only 1 mile away.

◆◆◆ ELM HOTEL

1-7 Elm Road, Wembley HA9 7JA
T: (020) 8902 1764
F: (020) 8903 8365
E: elm.hotel@virgin.net
I: www.elmhotel.co.uk

Bedrooms: 6 single,
18 double/twin, 9 triple/
multiple
Bathrooms: 30 en suite

CC: Amex, Delta,
Mastercard, Switch, Visa

B&B per night:
S Max £48.00
D Max £65.00

OPEN All year round

Ten minutes' walk (1200 yards) from Wembley Stadium, Conference Centre, and Arena, 150 yards from Wembley Central station, underground and mainline station.

WORCESTER PARK

◆◆◆ THE GRAYE HOUSE

24 The Glebe, Worcester Park
KT4 7PF
T: (020) 8330 1277 &
07733 150621
F: (020) 8255 7850
E: graye.house@virgin.net
I: www.smoothhound.co.uk

Bedrooms: 4 double/
twin, 2 triple/multiple
Bathrooms: 4 en suite

B&B per night:
S £30.00–£40.00
D £50.00–£55.00

OPEN All year round

A modern, comfortable townhouse, which serves as a family home. Rooms are en suite. Close to stations and amenities. Annexe with 4 larger rooms also available.

AT-A-GLANCE SYMBOLS

Symbols at the end of each accommodation entry give useful information about services and facilities. A key to symbols can be found inside the back cover flap. Keep this open for easy reference.

CUMBRIA

Cumbria's dramatic and breathtaking landscapes, from the famous Lakes to the rugged mountains and fells, have inspired poets and artists for hundreds of years.

classic sights
Hadrian's Wall – a reminder of Roman occupation
Lake Windermere – largest lake in England

coast & country
Scafell Pike – England's highest mountain
Whitehaven – historic port

literary links
William Wordsworth – The poet's homes: Wordsworth House, Dove Cottage and Rydal Mount
Beatrix Potter – Her home, Hill Top; her watercolours at the Beatrix Potter Gallery and the tales at The World of Beatrix Potter

distinctively different
The Gondola – sail Coniston Water aboard the opulent 1859 steam yacht Gondola
Cars of the Stars Museum – cars from TV and film, including Chitty Chitty Bang Bang and the Batmobile

The county of Cumbria

FOR MORE INFORMATION CONTACT:
Cumbria Tourist Board
Ashleigh, Holly Road, Windermere,
Cumbria LA23 2AQ
Tel: (015394) 44444 Fax: (015394) 44041
Email: mail@cumbria-tourist-board.co.uk
Internet: www.golakes.co.uk

The Pictures:
1 Lake Windermere
2 Muncaster Castle
3 Walking at Wasdale

Places to Visit - see pages 64-67
Where to Stay - see pages 68-108

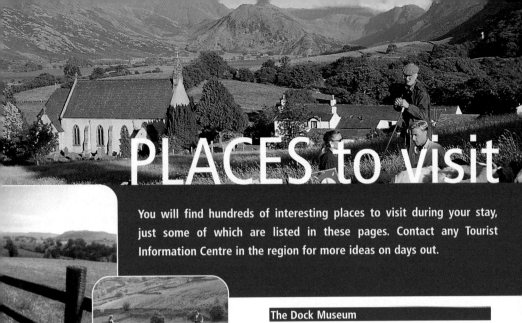

PLACES to visit

You will find hundreds of interesting places to visit during your stay, just some of which are listed in these pages. Contact any Tourist Information Centre in the region for more ideas on days out.

The Beacon

West Strand, Whitehaven, Cumbria CA28 7LY
Tel: (01946) 592302 www.copelandbc.gov.uk
Discover the industrial, maritime and social history of Whitehaven and surrounding area. Includes Meteorology Office weather gallery with satellite-linked equipment.

Birdoswald Roman Fort

Gilsland, Carlisle, Cumbria CA8 7DD
Tel: (016977) 47602
Remains of Roman fort on one of the best parts of Hadrian's Wall with excellent views of the Irthing Gorge. Exhibition, shop, tearooms and excavations.

Brantwood, Home of John Ruskin

Coniston, Cumbria LA21 8AD
Tel: (015394) 41396 www.brantwood.org.uk
Superb lake and mountain views. Works by Ruskin and contemporaries, memorabilia, Ruskin watercolours, craft and picture gallery, gardens.

Cars of the Stars Motor Museum

Standish Street, Keswick, Cumbria CA12 5LS
Tel: (017687) 73757 www.carsofthestars.com
Features TV and film vehicles including the Batmobile, Chitty Chitty Bang Bang, the James Bond collection, Herbie, FAB 1, plus many other famous cars and motorcycles.

The Dock Museum

North Road, Barrow-in-Furness, Cumbria LA14 2PW
Tel: (01229) 894444 www.barrowtourism.co.uk
The museum presents the story of steel shipbuilding, for which Barrow is famous, and straddles a Victorian graving dock. Interactive displays, nautical adventure playground.

Dove Cottage and Wandsworth Museum

Town End, Grasmere, Ambleside, Cumbria LA22 9SH
Tel: (015394) 35544 www.wordsworth.org.uk
Wordsworth's home 1799-1808. Poet's possessions. Museum with manuscripts, farmhouse reconstruction, paintings and drawings. Special events throughout the year.

Eden Ostrich World

Langwathby Hall Farm, Langwathby Hall, Langwathby, Penrith, Cumbria CA10 1LW
Tel: (01768) 881771 www.ostrich-world.com
Working farm with ostriches and other rare breed animals. Play areas, riverside walk, tearooms and gift shop. An enjoyable day out for the whole family.

Furness Abbey

Barrow-in-Furness, Cumbria LA13 0TJ
Tel: (01229) 823420
Ruins of 12thC Cistercian abbey, the 2nd wealthiest in England. Extensive remains include transepts, choir and west tower of church, canopied seats, arches, church.

Gleaston Water Mill

Gleaston, Ulverston, Cumbria LA12 0QH
Tel: (01229) 869244 www.watermill.co.uk
Water-driven corn mill in working order. Impressive wooden machinery and water-wheel. Farm equipment and tools display. Craft workshop, craft videos and rare breeds.

Heron Glass

The Lakes Glass Centre, Oubas Hill, Ulverston, Cumbria LA12 7LY
Tel: (01229) 581121
Heron Glass is a combined visitor centre and workshop where you will find traditional glass-making demonstrations daily with a chance of purchasing glassware at the factory shop.

Hill Top

Near Sawrey, Ambleside, Cumbria LA22 0LF
Tel: (015394) 36269 www.nationaltrust.org.uk
Beatrix Potter wrote many of her popular Peter Rabbit stories and other books in this charming little house which still contains her own china and furniture.

Jennings Brothers, The Castle Brewery

Cockermouth, Cumbria CA13 9NE
Tel: (01900) 821011 www.jenningsbrewery.co.uk
Guided tours of Jennings traditional brewery. The brewery uses the finest well water, malt, hops, sugar and yeast to brew distinctive local beers.

K Village Outlet Centre

Lound Road, Netherfield, Kendal, Cumbria LA9 7DA
Tel: (01539) 732363 www.kvillage.co.uk
Famous named brands such as K-shoes, Van Heusen, Denby, National Trust Shop, Tog24 and Ponden Mill, all at discounts. Open 7 days per week with full disabled access.

The Lake District Coast Aquarium

Maryport South Quay, Maryport, Cumbria CA15 8AB
Tel: (01900) 817760
www.lakedistrict-coastaquarium.co.uk
Purpose-built independent aquarium with over 35 displays. Largest collection of native marine species in Cumbria. Cafe and gift shop.

The Lake District Visitor Centre

Brockhole, Windermere, Cumbria LA23 1LJ
Tel: (015394) 46601 www.lake-district.gov.uk
Interactive exhibitions, audio-visual show, shop, gardens, grounds, adventure playground, dry-stone walling area, trails, events and croquet. Cafe with home-cooked food.

Lakeland Motor Museum

Holker Hall, Cark in Cartmel, Grange-over-Sands, Cumbria LA11 7PL
Tel: (015395) 58509 www.holker-hall.co.uk
Over 10,000 exhibits including rare motoring automobilia. A 1930s garage re-creation and the Campbell Legend Bluebird Exhibition.

Lakeland Sheep and Wool Centre

Egremont Road, Cockermouth, Cumbria CA13 0QX
Tel: (01900) 822673 www.shepherdshotel.co.uk
An all-weather attraction with live sheep shows including working-dog demonstrations. Also large screen and other tourism exhibitions on the area, a gift shop and cafe.

Lakeland Wildlife Oasis

Hale Milnthorpe, Cumbria LA7 7BW
Tel: (015395) 63027 www.wildlifeoasis.co.uk
A wildlife exhibition where both living animals and inanimate hands-on displays are used to illustrate evolution in the animal kingdom. Includes gift shop and cafe.

The Pictures:
1 Kirkstile Inn
2 Watendlath Bridge
3 Loughrigg
4 Shoreline, Derwentwater

Lowther Parklands

Hackthorpe, Penrith, Cumbria CA10 2HG
Tel: (01931) 712523
Attractions include exotic birds and animals, rides, miniature railway, boating lake, play areas, adventure fort, Tarzan trail, international circus and a puppet theatre.

Muncaster Castle, Gardens, Owl Centre and Meadow Vole Maze

Ravenglass, Cumbria CA18 1RQ
Tel: (01229) 717614 www.muncastercastle.co.uk
Muncaster Castle has the most beautifully situated Owl Centre in the world. See the birds fly, picnic in the gardens, and visit the Pennington family home.

Ravenglass and Eskdale Railway

Ravenglass, Cumbria CA18 1SW
Tel: (01229) 717171 www.ravenglass-railway.co.uk
England's oldest narrow-gauge railway runs for 7 miles through glorious scenery to the foot of England's highest hills. Most trains are steam hauled.

Rheged - The Village in the Hill

Redhills, Penrith, Cumbria CA11 0DQ
Tel: (01768) 868000 www.rheged.com
Cumbria's new visitor attraction with Europe's largest grass-covered building. Discover speciality shops, restaurants, artist exhibitions, pottery demonstrations, children's play area and The National Mountaineering Exhibition.

The Rum Story

27 Lowther Street, Whitehaven, Cumbria CA28 7DN
Tel: (01946) 592933 www.rumstory.co.uk
'The Rum Story' - an authentic, heritage-based experience, depicting the unique story of the UK rum trade in the original Jefferson's wine merchant premises.

Sizergh Castle

Kendal, Cumbria LA8 8AE
Tel: (015395) 60070 www.nationaltrust.org.uk
Strickland family home for 750 years, now National Trust owned. With 14thC pele tower, 15thC great hall, 16thC wings. Stuart connections. Rock garden, rose garden, daffodils.

South Lakes Wild Animal Park Ltd

Crossgates, Dalton-in-Furness, Cumbria LA15 8JR
Tel: (01229) 466086 www.wildanimalpark.co.uk
Wild zoo park in over 17 acres (7 ha) of grounds. Large waterfowl ponds, cafe, toilets, car/coach park, miniature railway. Over 120 species of animals from all around the world.

South Tynedale Railway

Railway Station, Alston, Cumbria CA9 3JB
Tel: (01434) 381696 www.strps.org.uk
Narrow-gauge railway operating along 2.25 mile line from Alston to Kirkhaugh through the scenic South Tyne Valley. Steam- and diesel-hauled passenger trains.

Steam Yacht Gondola

Pier Cottage, Coniston, Cumbria LA21 8AJ
Tel: (015394) 41962
Victorian steam-powered vessel now National Trust owned and completely renovated with an opulently upholstered saloon. Superb way to appreciate the beauty of Coniston Water.

Theatre by the Lake

Lakeside, Keswick, Cumbria CA12 5DJ
Tel: (017687) 74411 www.theatrebythelake.com
Main auditorium of 400 seats, studio of 80. Exhibitions all year round. Cafe and bar.

Tullie House Museum and Art Gallery

Castle Street, Carlisle, Cumbria CA3 8TP
Tel: (01228) 534781 www.historic-carlisle.org.uk
Major tourist complex housing museum, art gallery, education facility, lecture theatre, shops, herb garden, restaurant and terrace bars.

Windermere Lake Cruises

Lakeside Pier, Newby Bridge, Ulverston, Cumbria LA12 8AS
Tel: (015395) 31188
www.windermere-lakecruises.co.uk
Steamers and launches sail between Ambleside, Bowness and Lakeside with connections for the Steam Railway, Brockhole, Ferry House, Fell Foot and the Aquarium of the Lakes.

Windermere Steamboat Museum

Rayrigg Road, Bowness-on-Windermere, Windermere, Cumbria LA23 1BN
Tel: (015394) 45565 www.steamboat.co.uk
A wealth of interest and information about life on bygone Windermere. Regular steam launch trips, vintage vessels and classic motorboats. Model boat pond, lakeside picnic area.

The World Famous Old Blacksmith's Shop Centre

Gretna Green, Gretna DG16 5EA
Tel: (01461) 338441 www.gretnagreen.com
The original Blacksmith's Shop museum and a shopping centre selling cashmere and woollen knitwear, crystal and china. Taste local produce in the Old Smithy Restaurant.

Find out more about
Cumbria

Further information about holidays and attractions in Cumbria is available from:

CUMBRIA TOURIST BOARD

Ashleigh, Holly Road, Windermere, Cumbria LA23 2AQ.

Tel: (015394) 44444 Fax: (015394) 44041

Email: mail@cumbria-tourist-board.co.uk

Internet: www.golakes.co.uk

The following publications are available from Cumbria Tourist Board:

Cumbria Tourist Board Holiday Guide (free) Tel: 08705 133059

Events Listings (free)

Cumbria The Lake District Touring Map
including tourist information and touring caravan and camping parks - £3.95

Laminated Poster - £4.50

Getting to
Cumbria

BY ROAD: The M1/M6/M25/M40 provide a link with London and the South East and the M5/M6 provide access from the South West. The M62/M6 link Hull and Manchester with the region. Approximate journey time from London is 5 hours, from Manchester 2 hours.

BY RAIL: From London (Euston) to Oxenholme (Kendal) takes approximately 3 hours 30 minutes. From Oxenholme (connecting station for all main line trains) to Windermere takes approximately 20 minutes. From Carlisle to Barrow-in-Furness via the coastal route, with stops at many of the towns in between, takes approximately 2 hours. Trains from Edinburgh to Carlisle take 1 hour 45 minutes. The historic Settle-Carlisle line also runs through the county bringing passengers from Yorkshire via the Eden Valley.

The Pictures:

1 Ullswater
2 Buttermere
3 Lake Windermere

www.travelcumbria.co.uk

Where to stay in Cumbria

Accommodation entries in this region are listed in alphabetical order of place name, and then in alphabetical order of establishment.

Map references refer to the colour location maps at the front of this guide. The first number indicates the map to use; the letter and number which follow refer to the grid reference on the map.

At-a-glance symbols at the end of each accommodation entry give useful information about services and facilities. A key to symbols can be found inside the back cover flap. Keep this open for easy reference.

A brief description of the towns and villages offering accommodation in the entries which follow, can be found at the end of this section.

A complete listing of all the English Tourism Council assessed accommodation covered by this guide appears at the back of the guide.

ALLONBY, Cumbria Map ref 5A2

SHIP HOTEL
Main Street, Allonby, Maryport
CA15 6PD
T: (01900) 881017 & 881115
F: (01900) 881017

Bedrooms: 1 single,
3 double/twin, 4 triple/
multiple; suites available
Bathrooms: 4 en suite

Lunch available
Evening meal available
CC: Mastercard, Visa

B&B per night:
S £23.50–£30.00
D £58.75–£82.25

OPEN All year round

A 17thC Grade II Listed coaching inn where Charles Dickens and Wilkie Collins stayed in 1857. Situated on the Solway coastline, close to Lake District.

ALSTON, Cumbria Map ref 5B2

BROWNSIDE HOUSE
Leadgate, Alston CA9 3EL
T: (01434) 382169 & 382100
E: brownside_hse@hotmail.com
I: www.cumbria1st.com/
brown_side/index.htm

Bedrooms: 3 double/
twin

Evening meal available
CC: Mastercard, Visa

B&B per night:
S £18.00
D £36.00

HB per person:
DY £24.50

OPEN All year round

Brownside House (dated 1849) is set in the countryside just outside Alston, with superb views of the South Tyne Valley. Easy reach Lake District/Hadrian's Wall.

CREDIT CARD BOOKINGS If you book by telephone and are asked for your credit card number it is advisable to check the proprietor's policy should you cancel your reservation.

AMBLESIDE, Cumbria Map ref 5A3 *Tourist Information Centre Tel: (015394) 32582*

◆◆◆ BROADVIEW

Low Fold, Lake Road, Ambleside
LA22 0DN
T: (01539) 432431
E: enquiries@
broadview-guesthouse.co.uk
I: www.broadview-guesthouse.co.uk

Bedrooms: 4 double/
twin, 2 triple/multiple
Bathrooms: 3 en suite,
1 private

CC: Amex, Delta,
Mastercard, Switch, Visa

B&B per night:
S £18.00–£25.00
D £36.00–£50.00

OPEN All year round

Spacious, comfortable Victorian guesthouse near lake and village. Some rooms en suite with lovely views. Great breakfasts and a warm welcome. Non-smoking establishment.

◆◆◆◆ THE DOWER HOUSE

Wray Castle, Ambleside LA22 0JA
T: (01539) 433211

Bedrooms: 3 double/
twin
Bathrooms: 3 en suite

Evening meal available

B&B per night:
S £26.00–£27.00
D £26.00

HB per person:
DY £39.00

OPEN All year round

The house overlooks Lake Windermere, 3 miles from Ambleside. Through the main gates of Wray Castle and up the drive.

◆◆◆◆ ELDER GROVE

Lake Road, Ambleside LA22 0DB
T: (015394) 32504
F: (015394) 32504
E: info@eldergrove.co.uk
I: www.eldergrove.co.uk

Bedrooms: 2 single,
7 double/twin, 1 triple/
multiple
Bathrooms: 10 en suite

CC: Delta, Mastercard,
Switch, Visa

B&B per night:
S £25.00–£32.00
D £50.00–£68.00

OPEN All year round

Enjoy quality accommodation and service in our Victorian house. Pretty bedrooms with private bathrooms, relaxing bar and lounge, hearty Cumbrian breakfast, car park. Non-smoking.

◆◆◆ FERN COTTAGE

6 Waterhead Terrace, Ambleside
LA22 0HA
T: (01539) 433007

Bedrooms: 3 double/
twin

B&B per night:
S £18.00–£20.00
D £30.00–£34.00

OPEN All year round

Homely Lakeland-stone cottage on edge of village. Two minutes to head of Lake Windermere and steamer pier. Friendly atmosphere, hearty breakfast. Non-smoking.

◆◆◆ FERNDALE HOTEL

Lake Road, Ambleside LA22 0DB
T: (01539) 432207

Bedrooms: 1 single,
8 double/twin, 1 triple/
multiple
Bathrooms: 10 en suite

CC: Delta, Mastercard,
Switch, Visa

B&B per night:
S £22.00–£25.00
D £40.00–£50.00

OPEN All year round

Small family-run hotel in the heart of The Lakes, offering comfortable accommodation and traditional English fare. En suite bedrooms, some with views of the surrounding mountains and fells.

◆◆◆

GHYLL HEAD HOTEL
Waterhead, Ambleside LA22 0HD
T: (01539) 432360
F: (01539) 434062
E: ghyllhead@hotel.fsnet.co.uk
I: www.hotelcumbria.com

B&B per night:
S £40.00–£50.00
D £70.00–£120.00

OPEN All year round

Splendidly situated Lakeland hotel in its own grounds overlooking Lake Windermere and the rolling fells and mountains beyond, just a short stroll from Ambleside town. All spacious bedrooms have en suite facilities and colour TVs. Private parking available.

Bedrooms: 8 double/
twin, 4 triple/multiple;
suites available
Bathrooms: 12 en suite

Evening meal available
CC: Mastercard, Switch,
Visa

◆◆◆◆

GLENSIDE
Old Lake Road, Ambleside LA22 0DP
T: (01539) 432635
E: david-janice@glenside22fsnet.
co.uk

18thC farmhouse with old world charm, offering high standard of accommodation. Ideally situated between village and lake. Private parking, non-smoking, walks from the door.

Bedrooms: 1 single,
3 double/twin

B&B per night:
D £32.00–£38.00

◆◆◆◆◆

Silver
Award

A warm welcome awaits visitors to Pamela and David Veen's country house. This delightful former vicarage enjoys magnificent views of the Brathay River and fells. The house is tastefully furnished with antiques and bric-a-brac. Most en suite bedrooms have antique or 4-poster beds. Good traditional cooking is enjoyed by all.

GREY FRIAR LODGE COUNTRY HOUSE HOTEL
Clappersgate, Ambleside LA22 9NE
T: (01539) 433158
F: (01539) 433158
E: greyfriar@veen.freeserve.co.uk
I: www.cumbria-hotels.co.uk

Bedrooms: 8 double/
twin
Bathrooms: 7 en suite,
1 private

3 and 7-day break rates.

Evening meal available
CC: Delta, Mastercard,
Switch, Visa

B&B per night:
S £36.00–£80.00
D £52.00–£88.00

HB per person:
DY £19.50–£22.50

◆◆◆◆

HOLMESHEAD FARM
Skelwith Fold, Ambleside LA22 0HU
T: (01539) 433048
I: www.amblesideonline.co.uk

Bedrooms: 2 double/
twin, 1 triple/multiple
Bathrooms: 3 en suite

Evening meal available

300-acre livestock farm. Comfortable farmhouse nestling between Ambleside/Hawkshead in the hamlet of Skelwith Fold at the foot of the famous Langdale Valley.

B&B per night:
S £30.00–£34.00
D £20.00–£25.00

HB per person:
DY £34.00–£39.00

OPEN All year round

◆◆◆

Substantial detached Victorian house once visited by children's author Beatrix Potter. Spacious en suite bedrooms, some with 4-poster beds and jacuzzi, decorated in William Morris style, with fell views. Within easy walking distance of Lake Windermere and 1 minute's walk from Ambleside village. Accessible private car park.

LAUREL VILLA
Lake Road, Ambleside LA22 0DB
T: (01539) 433240
E: laurelvilla_hotel@hotmail.com
I: www.hotel-ambleside.co.uk

Bedrooms: 7 double/
twin, 2 triple/multiple
Bathrooms: 9 en suite

B&B per night:
S £30.00–£50.00
D £50.00–£70.00

OPEN All year round

ACCESSIBILITY

Look for the 🔣🔣🔣 symbols which indicate accessibility for wheelchair users. A list of establishments is at the front of this guide.

◆◆◆

LYNDALE

Low Fold, Lake Road, Ambleside LA22 0DN
T: (01539) 434244
E: wendy@lyndale-guesthouse.co.uk
I: www.lyndale-guesthouse.co.uk

B&B per night:
S £17.00–£21.00
D £19.00–£25.00

OPEN All year round

A Victorian house surrounded by the most beautiful scenery in the country. Take full advantage of Lyndale's central location midway between Lake Windermere and Ambleside. Feel comfortable in our spacious accommodation and, after a hearty breakfast, enjoy one of the many walks starting from our door. Great value for money!

Bedrooms: 2 single,
2 double/twin, 2 triple/
multiple
Bathrooms: 2 en suite

CC: Amex, Delta,
Mastercard, Switch, Visa

3 nights for the price of 2, Oct–Mar (excl Christmas and New Year).

◆◆◆

LYNDHURST HOTEL
Wansfell Road, Ambleside LA22 0EG
T: (01539) 432421
F: (01539) 432421
E: lyndhurst@amblesidehotels.co.uk
I: www.amblesidehotels.co.uk

Bedrooms: 6 double/
twin
Bathrooms: 6 en suite

Evening meal available

B&B per night:
S £25.00–£40.00
D £40.00–£58.00

HB per person:
DY £36.00–£45.00

OPEN All year round

Small, attractive Lakeland-stone hotel with private car park. Quietly situated for town and lake. Pretty rooms, delicious food – a delightful experience.

◆◆◆◆

RIVERSIDE HOTEL

Under Loughrigg, Rothay Bridge,
Ambleside LA22 9LJ
T: (01539) 432395
F: (01539) 432440
E: info@riverside-at-ambleside.co.uk
I: www.riverside-at-ambleside.co.uk

B&B per night:
S £26.00–£40.00
D £52.00–£80.00

OPEN All year round

Riverside is a beautiful and stylish Victorian country house and gardens, situated on the River Rothay, on a quiet lane within 10 minutes' walk of the village. Riverside provides high quality bed and breakfast and is ideally situated for easy access to all Lake District attractions.

Bedrooms: 4 double/
twin, 1 triple/multiple
Bathrooms: 5 en suite

CC: Delta, Mastercard,
Visa

Up to 15% discount for stays of 3 nights or more. Special rates for anniversary and special occasions.

QUALITY ASSURANCE SCHEME

For an explanation of the quality and facilities represented by the Diamonds please refer to the front of this guide. A more detailed explanation can be found in the information pages at the back.

◆◆◆◆◆
Silver
Award

ROWANFIELD COUNTRY GUESTHOUSE

Kirkstone Road, Ambleside LA22 9ET
T: (01539) 433686
F: (01539) 431569
E: email@rowanfield.com
I: www.rowanfield.com

Idyllic, quiet countryside setting, central Lakeland. Rowanfield enjoys breathtaking lake and mountain views. A beautiful period house with Laura Ashley style decor. All bedrooms en suite with powerful showers, some have baths, queen and king beds. Fabulous food created by chef patron. Dinner available certain weeks of the year. Superior breakfasts.

Bedrooms: 7 double/ twin, 1 triple/multiple
Bathrooms: 8 en suite

Evening meal available
CC: Delta, Mastercard, Switch, Visa

Reduced rates for longer stays. Special DB&B breaks, May and Oct. Superb Christmas and New Year all inclusive packages.

B&B per night:
S £55.00–£67.00
D £65.00–£100.00

HB per person:
DY £57.50–£74.00

OPEN Mar–Nov &
Christmas

M ⛺ 8 🖭 ❑ ⅊ ⅃ Ⓢ ⅂ 🛏 🖳 🖨 ☼ 🚲 ⋈ 🏠 P

◆◆◆

THE RYSDALE HOTEL

Rothay Road, Ambleside LA22 0EE
T: (01539) 432140 & 433999
F: (01539) 433999
I: www.rysdalehotel.co.uk

Bedrooms: 4 single,
3 double/twin, 2 triple/ multiple
Bathrooms: 7 en suite,
2 private

Family-run hotel with magnificent views over park and fells. Good food, licensed bar. Friendly, personal service. Ideal walking base. No smoking.

B&B per night:
S £23.00–£30.00
D £44.00–£62.00

M ⛺ 8 🖭 ❑ ⅊ 🍷 Ⓢ ⅂ 🛏 🖳 🖨 🐕 🚲 ⋈ P

◆◆◆◆

STEPPING STONES COUNTRY HOUSE

Under Loughrigg, Ambleside LA22 9LN
T: (01539) 433552
F: (01539) 433552
E: info@steppingstonesambleside.com
I: www.steppingstonesambleside.com

Lakeland-stone Victorian house set in outstanding location with spectacular views over river and famous stepping stones and fells beyond. Beautifully appointed, spacious, en suite bedrooms with period furnishings.

Bedrooms: 3 double/ twin
Bathrooms: 3 en suite

B&B per night:
D £50.00–£70.00

OPEN All year round

⛺ 🏠 🖭 ❑ ⅊ 🍷 Ⓢ ⅂ 🖳 🖨 ☼ 🚲 P

◆◆◆

TOCK HOW FARM

High Wray, Ambleside LA22 0JF
T: (01539) 436106 & 436294
F: (01539) 436294
I: www.tock-how-farm.com

Bedrooms: 1 double/ twin, 1 triple/multiple
Bathrooms: 2 en suite

Family-run farm with spectacular views overlooking Blelham Tarn and towards Ambleside. Comfortable accommodation with traditional farmhouse breakfast. All rooms en suite. Log fires.

B&B per night:
S £22.00–£25.00
D £40.00–£46.00

OPEN All year round

M ⛺ ❑ ⅊ 🍷 Ⓢ ⅂ 🛏 🖳 🖨 ☼ 🐕 🚲 🏠 P

◆◆◆◆

WANSLEA GUEST HOUSE

Lake Road, Ambleside LA22 0DN
T: (01539) 433884
F: (01539) 433884
E: wanslea.guesthouse@virgin.net

Bedrooms: 1 single,
2 double/twin, 4 triple/ multiple
Bathrooms: 4 en suite

Evening meal available
CC: Delta, Mastercard, Switch, Visa

Spacious, comfortable, family-run Victorian house offering good food, wines and fine views. Easy walk to lake and village. Families welcome and pets by arrangement.

B&B per night:
S £20.00–£30.00
D £18.50–£27.50

OPEN Feb–Dec

M ⛺ ❑ ⅊ Ⓢ ⅂ 🛏 🖳 🖨 ☼ 🐕 🚲

APPLEBY–IN–WESTMORLAND, Cumbria Map ref 5B3 *Tourist Information Centre Tel: (017683) 51177*

BROOM HOUSE
◆◆◆

Long Marton, Appleby-in-Westmorland CA16 6JP
T: (01768) 361318
F: (01768) 361318
E: sandra@bland01.freeserve.co.uk

Bedrooms: 1 double/twin, 1 triple/multiple

B&B per night:
S £25.00
D £40.00–£44.00

HB per person:
DY £32.50–£35.00

Former farmhouse with large garden, lovely views of the Pennines and countryside. Appleby is 2.5 miles, easy access to A66 and M6.

BARROW–IN–FURNESS, Cumbria Map ref 5A3 *Tourist Information Centre Tel: (01229) 894784*

ARLINGTON HOUSE HOTEL AND RESTAURANT
◆◆◆◆

200-202 Abbey Road, Barrow-in-Furness LA14 5LD
T: (01229) 831976
F: (01229) 870990
E: arlington@tinyworld.co.uk

Bedrooms: 8 double/twin
Bathrooms: 8 en suite

Evening meal available
CC: Amex, Mastercard, Visa

B&B per night:
S Min £60.00
D Min £80.00

OPEN All year round

Relaxed hotel with an elegant restaurant. In the town, yet not far away from the Lakes and sea.

BASSENTHWAITE LAKE, Cumbria Map ref 5A2

◆◆◆◆
Ad p17

LAKESIDE
Dubwath, Bassenthwaite Lake, Cockermouth CA13 9YD
T: (01768) 776358
F: (01768) 776163

B&B per night:
S Min £23.00
D Max £27.00

OPEN All year round

Elegant Edwardian double-fronted house with oak floors and panelled entrance hall, standing in its own garden overlooking Bassenthwaite Lake. All rooms en suite with tea-making facilities and TV. Private car park and parking in grounds.

Bedrooms: 7 double/twin, 1 triple/multiple
Bathrooms: 7 en suite, 1 private

Any 3 nights B&B £70pp.

◆◆◆◆

LINK HOUSE
Bassenthwaite Lake, Cockermouth CA13 9YD
T: (01768) 776291
F: (01768) 776670
E: linkhouse@lineone.net
I: www.link-house.co.uk

B&B per night:
S £23.00–£29.00
D £55.00–£58.00

HB per person:
DY £38.00–£44.00

OPEN All year round

A warm, friendly, family-run, late-Victorian country house set in the quieter part of the Lake District National Park mid way between Keswick and Cockermouth with stunning views of the surrounding forests and fells. All the attractive bedrooms have en suite facilities, colour TV and tea/coffee-making facilities.

Bedrooms: 3 single, 5 double/twin, 1 triple/multiple
Bathrooms: 8 en suite, 1 private

Evening meal available
CC: Amex, Delta, Mastercard, Switch, Visa

Winter breaks-3 nights B&B, £70pp (excl Christmas, New Year and Public Hols), from 1 Nov-1 Mar only.

QUALITY ASSURANCE SCHEME
Diamond ratings and awards were correct at the time of going to press but are subject to change. Please check at the time of booking.

BORROWDALE, Cumbria Map ref 5A3

◆◆◆◆
Silver
Award

GREENBANK COUNTRY HOUSE HOTEL

Borrowdale, Keswick CA12 5UY
T: (01768) 777215
F: (01768) 777215
E: jeanwwood@lineone.net

B&B per night:
S £30.00–£35.00
D £60.00–£70.00

HB per person:
DY £45.00–£50.00

A refurbished Victorian country house, Greenbank is the friendliest hotel in the Lake District. It stands in an acre of garden high up on the wooded slopes in the heart of Borrowdale. Superb walking and touring area. En suite bedrooms, log fires, restaurant licence. Excellent home-cooked food from local produce.

Bedrooms: 1 single,
7 double/twin, 1 triple/
multiple
Bathrooms: 9 en suite

Evening meal available
CC: Delta, Mastercard,
Switch, Visa

3 nights for the price of 2 for B&B Nov-Feb incl.

◆◆◆◆◆
Gold
Award

HAZEL BANK COUNTRY HOUSE

Rosthwaite, Borrowdale, Keswick CA12 5XB
T: (01768) 777248
F: (01767) 877373
E: enquiries@hazelbankhotel.co.uk
I: www.hazelbankhotel.co.uk

HB per person:
DY £47.50–£64.50

OPEN All year round

Exquisite Victorian country house set in 4-acre grounds. Peaceful, idyllic location, superb views of central Lakeland Fells. Bedrooms all en suite. Award-winning cuisine using local produce. Puddings and sauces a speciality, vegetarians welcome. Ideal base for walking. Non-smokers only. No pets. Self catering cottage for 2 in grounds.

Bedrooms: 8 double/
twin; suites available
Bathrooms: 8 en suite

Evening meal available
CC: Delta, Mastercard,
Switch, Visa

Discounts available when bookings are made more than 3 months in advance of arrival.

BOWLAND BRIDGE, Cumbria Map ref 5A3

◆◆◆

HARE AND HOUNDS COUNTRY INN

Bowland Bridge, Grange-over-
Sands LA11 6NN
T: (01539) 568333 & 568777
F: (01539) 568993
E: innthelakes@supanet.com
I: www.bowlandbridge.co.uk

Bedrooms: 12 double/
twin, 2 triple/multiple
Bathrooms: 12 en suite

Lunch available
Evening meal available
CC: Amex, Delta,
Mastercard, Switch, Visa

B&B per night:
S £30.00–£44.50
D £40.00–£69.00

OPEN All year round

Surrounded by the Cartmel Fells in the Winster Valley. A former coaching inn dating back to the 17thC. Complimentary leisure club nearby.

USE YOUR *i*s

There are more than 550 Tourist Information Centres throughout England offering friendly help with accommodation and holiday ideas as well as suggestions of places to visit and things to do. You'll find TIC addresses in the local Phone Book.

◆◆◆◆

WALLSEND

The Old Rectory, Church Lane, Bowness-on-Solway, Carlisle CA7 5AF
T: (016973) 51055
E: wallsend@btinternet.com
I: www.wallsend.net

B&B per night:
S £22.00–£25.00
D £40.00

OPEN All year round

Peaceful old rectory located in own wooded grounds at end of Hadrian's Wall in Solway AONB. All rooms en suite. Picturesque village on Solway Firth with local pub/restaurant 150 yards away. Easy access to/from historic city of Carlisle, North Lakes and Scotland. Ideal for walkers, cyclists and just 'getting away'. Warm welcome and relaxing atmosphere.

Bedrooms: 1 single, 2 double/twin, 1 triple/ multiple
Bathrooms: 4 en suite

Evening meal available

1) 3 night special-10% Off 2) Bird holiday specials-Nov–Feb expert guide tours-2 night and 4 night specials.

See also Windermere

◆◆◆

BISKEY HOWE VILLA HOTEL

Craig Walk, Bowness-on-Windermere, Windermere LA23 3AX
T: (01539) 443988
F: (01539) 488379
E: biskey-howe@lakes-pages.com
I: www.biskey-howe-hotel.co.uk

B&B per night:
S £35.00–£38.00
D £60.00–£70.00

OPEN Mar–Oct

In a peaceful spot above Lake Windermere commanding beautiful views of the lake and surrounding mountains. Close to Bowness Bay, and only a few minutes' walk from centre of Bowness village. All bedrooms en suite, with telephone, TV, clock/radio, hairdryer, tea and coffee. Private parking, terraced gardens and patios.

Bedrooms: 1 single, 6 double/twin, 3 triple/ multiple
Bathrooms: 10 en suite

Lunch available
CC: Amex, Delta, Mastercard, Switch, Visa

Reduced rates for 3 nights and longer.

◆◆◆◆

LAUREL COTTAGE

St Martin's Square, Kendal Road, Bowness-on-Windermere, Windermere LA23 3EF
T: (01539) 445594
F: (01539) 445594
E: enquiries@laurelcottage-bnb.co.uk
I: www.laurelcottage-bnb.co.uk

B&B per night:
S £19.00–£26.00
D £40.00–£68.00

OPEN All year round

Charming early 17thC cottage (1613), originally the village grammar school, located one minute's stroll from the lake at Bowness Bay. Ideally situated for all local attractions and amenities. Whilst the cottage retains many original features we continue to give all our guests the comforts of the present. Free membership of local leisure club.

Bedrooms: 2 single, 9 double/twin, 2 triple/ multiple
Bathrooms: 11 en suite

CC: Delta, Mastercard, Switch, Visa

BRAITHWAITE, Cumbria Map ref 5A3

◆◆◆ COLEDALE INN

Braithwaite, Keswick CA12 5TN
T: (01768) 778272

Bedrooms: 1 single,
7 double/twin, 4 triple/
multiple
Bathrooms: 12 en suite

Lunch available
Evening meal available
CC: Delta, Mastercard,
Switch, Visa

B&B per night:
S £21.00–£25.00
D £52.00–£60.00

OPEN All year round

Victorian country house hotel and Georgian inn, in a peaceful hillside position away from traffic, with superb mountain views. Families and pets welcome.

◆◆◆◆

MAPLE BANK

Braithwaite, Keswick CA12 5RY
T: (01768) 778229
F: (01768) 778000
E: maplebank@aol.com
I: www.maplebank.co.uk

B&B per night:
S £25.00–£35.00
D £48.00–£52.00

HB per person:
DY £36.50–£45.50

OPEN All year round

A friendly and relaxing, family-run, Edwardian country establishment with superb views of Skiddaw across the Derwent Valley. Situated at the foot of Whinlatter Pass and with ample secluded parking and bike storage. We offer delicious home-cooking to test your will power, some ingredients being home-grown! Open 4 seasons.

Bedrooms: 5 double/
twin, 2 triple/multiple
Bathrooms: 7 en suite

Evening meal available
CC: Delta, Mastercard,
Visa

1 Nov-31 Mar: 4 nights B&B for price of 3 (excl Bank Hols). 3 Jan-1 Mar: 3 nights for 2 B&B. See website for competitions.

BRAMPTON, Cumbria Map ref 5B2

◆◆◆ BLACKSMITHS ARMS HOTEL

Talkin Village, Brampton CA8 1LE
T: (01697) 73452
F: (01697) 73396

Bedrooms: 5 double/
twin
Bathrooms: 5 en suite

Lunch available
Evening meal available
CC: Amex, Delta,
Mastercard, Switch, Visa

B&B per night:
S £30.00
D £45.00

OPEN All year round

Country inn in scenic countryside half a mile from Talkin Tarn. Walking, golf, pony trekking, sailing, windsurfing, fishing, Hadrian's Wall and Lake District within easy reach.

◆◆◆ OAKWOOD PARK HOTEL

Longtown Road, Brampton
CA8 2AP
T: (01697) 72436 & 42679
F: (01697) 72436
E: donal.collier@amserve.net

Bedrooms: 3 double/
twin, 1 triple/multiple
Bathrooms: 4 en suite

Evening meal available
CC: Delta, Mastercard,
Visa

B&B per night:
S Max £30.00
D Max £50.00

OPEN All year round

Victorian hotel, 8 miles east of Carlisle. Situated half a mile from Brampton on the A6071, 200 yards off the road.

◆◆◆ SOUTH VIEW

Banks, Brampton CA8 2JH
T: (016977) 2309
E: sandrahodgson@
southviewbanks.f9.co.uk
I: www.southviewbanks.f9.co.uk

Bedrooms: 1 double/
twin, 1 triple/multiple
Bathrooms: 2 en suite

B&B per night:
S £20.00–£22.00
D £40.00–£44.00

OPEN Feb–Dec

Situated in the village of Banks between Lanercost Priory and Birdoswald Roman Fort offering well-appointed bed and breakfast accommodation.

CHECK THE MAPS

The colour maps at the front of this guide show all the cities, towns and villages for which you will find accommodation entries.
Refer to the town index to find the page on which they are listed.

◆◆◆◆

VALLUM BARN

Irthington, Carlisle CA6 4NN
T: (01697) 742478

B&B per night:
S £21.00–£26.00
D £38.00–£42.00

OPEN All year round

Relax and unwind in our spacious converted barn 5 minutes' walk from Hadrian's Wall footpath and country pub serving evening meals. Comfortable lounge with wood floor and open fire, ground floor bedroom suitable for disabled guests. Ideal base for touring Hadrian's Wall, Lake District and Scottish Borders, lovely walks in the area.

Bedrooms: 2 triple/ multiple
Bathrooms: 2 en suite

Evening meal available

3 nights for price of 2 Oct-Mar. Reduced summer rate for 3 nights or more.

◆◆◆

WALTON HIGH RIGG

Walton, Brampton CA8 2AZ
T: (01697) 72117

B&B per night:
S £18.00–£21.00
D £34.00–£40.00

202-acre mixed farm. 18thC Listed farmhouse on roadside, 1 mile from Walton and Roman wall, 3.5 miles from Brampton. Family run with pedigree cattle and sheep, farm trail to waterfall. Friendly atmosphere, delicious food. Good stop over or holiday base. Ideal centre for walking, fishing, golf and horse-riding.

Bedrooms: 1 triple/ multiple
Bathrooms: 1 private

Evening meal available

Discounts for 3 days or more. Children half price.

◆◆◆◆

BROOM HILL

New Street, Broughton-in-Furness LA20 6JD
T: (01229) 716358 & 0797 4135971
F: (01229) 716358

Bedrooms: 3 double/ twin
Bathrooms: 2 en suite, 1 private

B&B per night:
S £24.00
D £48.00

Beautiful Georgian country mansion with secluded grounds and magnificent views, yet within walking distance of the centre of this unspoilt village.

◆◆◆◆

THE WORKSHOP STUDIOS

Church Street, Broughton-in-Furness LA20 6HJ
T: (01229) 716159
F: (01229) 716159
E: workshop.accom@virgin.net

Bedrooms: 4 double/ twin
Bathrooms: 4 en suite

CC: Mastercard, Switch, Visa

B&B per night:
S £22.00–£24.00
D £40.00–£46.00

OPEN All year round

18thC building, used for the past 110 years for a family painting and decorating business. Recently refurbished to form stylish studios. Tranquil location in heart of village.

◆◆◆

THE BRIARS

Friar Row, Caldbeck, Wigton CA7 8DS
T: (01697) 478633

Bedrooms: 1 single, 2 double/twin
Bathrooms: 1 en suite

B&B per night:
S £20.00–£21.00
D £40.00–£42.00

OPEN All year round

140-acre mixed farm. In lovely village of Caldbeck overlooking Caldbeck Fells. Ideal for touring Lakes and Scottish Borders. Right on Cumbria Way route.

◆◆◆◆

SWALEDALE WATCH

Whelpo, Caldbeck, Wigton CA7 8HQ
T: (01697) 478409
F: (01697) 478409
E: nan.savage@talk21.com

B&B per night:
S £20.00–£24.00
D £36.00–£42.00

HB per person:
DY £30.00–£37.00

OPEN All year round

A working farm outside picturesque Caldbeck. Enjoy great comfort, excellent food and a warm welcome amidst peaceful unspoilt countryside. Central for touring, walking or discovering the rolling northern fells. A memorable walk into Caldbeck is through 'The Howk', a limestone gorge. Relax 'at home' with open fires – your happiness is our priority.

Bedrooms: 2 double/ twin, 2 triple/multiple
Bathrooms: 4 en suite

Evening meal available

CARLISLE, Cumbria Map ref 5A2 *Tourist Information Centre Tel: (01228) 625600*

◆◆◆◆◆

Silver Award

BESSIESTOWN FARM COUNTRY GUESTHOUSE

Catlowdy, Longtown, Carlisle CA6 5QP
T: (01228) 577219 & 577019
F: (01228) 577019
E: bestbb2000@cs.com
I: www.smoothhound.co.uk/hotels/bessies

B&B per night:
S £33.00–£35.00
D £50.00–£60.00

HB per person:
DY £38.50–£45.00

OPEN All year round

As featured on TV. Multi award-winning Best Guesthouse offering warm, lighthearted welcome, peace and quiet, delightful public rooms, beautiful en suite bedrooms, luxury honeymoon suite, delicious real food. Open all year. Indoor heated swimming pool is open end May to September. Easy access M6, M74, A7. Carlisle 14 miles.

Bedrooms: 5 double/ twin, 1 triple/multiple; suites available
Bathrooms: 6 en suite

Evening meal available
CC: Mastercard, Visa

Specialist country craft courses. Telephone for more details.

◆◆◆

BROOKLYN HOUSE
42 Victoria Place, Carlisle CA1 1EX
T: (01228) 590002

Bedrooms: 1 single, 2 double/twin, 2 triple/ multiple

B&B per night:
S £18.00–£25.00
D £34.00–£38.00

OPEN All year round

Comfortable, friendly, family-run guesthouse. Recently refurbished. All rooms have welcome trays and colour TV. Lounge with Sky TV. Close to all amenities.

◆◆◆

CHATSWORTH GUESTHOUSE
22 Chatsworth Square, Carlisle CA1 1HF
T: (01228) 524023
F: (01228) 524023
E: chatsworth22@aol.com
I: www.visitcarlise.com

Bedrooms: 1 single, 3 double/twin, 1 triple/ multiple
Bathrooms: 4 en suite, 1 private

B&B per night:
S £25.00
D £38.00–£44.00

OPEN All year round

Ornate city centre listed Victorian townhouse in quiet conservation area overlooking Chatsworth Gardens. 5 minutes from bus and rail stations, convenient for Sands Centre (sports and leisure). Street parking.

SPECIAL BREAKS

Many establishments offer special promotions and themed breaks. These are highlighted in red. (All such offers are subject to availability.)

♦♦♦♦

CORNERWAYS GUEST HOUSE
107 Warwick Road, Carlisle
CA1 1EA
T: (01228) 521733

Bedrooms: 4 single,
4 double/twin, 2 triple/
multiple
Bathrooms: 3 en suite

B&B per night:
S £16.00–£20.00
D £30.00–£36.00

OPEN All year round

Five minutes to rail and bus stations and city centre. M6 exit 43. Colour TV, central heating in all bedrooms. Tea and coffee facilities. Lounge, payphone.

♦♦♦

CROFT END
Hurst, Ivegill, Carlisle CA4 0NL
T: (01768) 484362 & 07762 346349

Bedrooms: 2 double/
twin

B&B per night:
S £17.00
D £34.00

OPEN All year round

Rural bungalow situated midway between junctions 41 and 42 of M6, 4 miles west of Southwaite service area. Ideal stopover for northbound or southbound travellers.

♦♦♦

HAZELDENE GUEST HOUSE
Orton Grange, Wigton Road,
Carlisle CA5 6LA
T: (01228) 711953

Bedrooms: 2 single,
2 double/twin
Bathrooms: 2 en suite

Lunch available
Evening meal available

B&B per night:
S Min £19.00
D £36.00–£38.00

HB per person:
DY Min £27.00

OPEN All year round

Friendly and comfortable accommodation in detached house with extensive gardens, 3 miles west of Carlisle. During your stay enjoy a massage, reflexology or Reiki treatment.

♦♦♦♦
Silver Award

MARCHMAIN HOUSE
151 Warwick Road, Carlisle CA1 1LU
T: (01228) 529551
F: (01228) 529551

B&B per night:
S £18.00–£22.00
D £38.00–£40.00

HB per person:
DY £30.00–£40.00

OPEN All year round

An elegantly refurbished, family-run Georgian townhouse. Central location. Close to bus and rail station. Easy access from M6 (jct 43). All rooms offer welcome tray, colour TV and many hidden extras. Residents' lounge with satellite TV, overlooking exquisite floral display. Cordon Bleu evening meals and packed lunches by request.

Bedrooms: 1 single,
2 double/twin, 1 triple/
multiple
Bathrooms: 2 en suite,
2 private

Lunch available
Evening meal available

Discount breaks for long weekends off-peak. Baby/pet sitting service.

♦♦♦♦

NEW PALLYARDS
Hethersgill, Carlisle CA6 6HZ
T: (01228) 577308
F: (01228) 577308
E: info@newpallyards.freeserve.co.uk
I: www.newpallyards.freeserve.co.uk

B&B per night:
S £23.90–£29.00
D £42.00–£47.80

HB per person:
DY £34.00–£36.90

OPEN All year round

National Gold Award for best breakfast in Britain. Friendly hospitality, warmth and comfort await you in our country farmhouse. Ideal stop-over, or better still take a longer stay to explore our wonderful countryside. Hadrian's wall, Scottish borders, northern Wales, Kielder Water and forest are all under 1 hour's drive.

Bedrooms: 1 single,
2 double/twin, 1 triple/
multiple; suites available
Bathrooms: 3 en suite,
1 private

Evening meal available
CC: Delta, Mastercard,
Visa

Book 7 nights' B&B and get a free meal every night. 4 nights' B&B £72pp (excl Bank Hols and Aug. Subject to availability).

◆◆◆◆

THE MELBREAK HOTEL

Winscales Road, Little Clifton,
Nr Cockermouth CA14 1XS
T: (01900) 61443
F: (01900) 606589

B&B per night:
S £45.00–£55.00
D £55.00–£65.00

HB per person:
DY £70.00–£80.00

OPEN All year round

Family-run motel-style country house. All rooms are tastefully decorated with en suite and beverage-making facilities, television and telephones. Private car park, large relaxing bar area with cosy fireside seating and a very popular restaurant. We are situated close to the Lake District and Workington town centre.

Bedrooms: 32 double/
twin, 3 triple/multiple
Bathrooms: 35 en suite

Lunch available
Evening meal available
CC: Amex, Mastercard,
Switch

Special 2 nigh break DB&B, £70 per couple per night, 4 course table d'hote menu.

◆◆◆

ROSE COTTAGE

Lorton Road, Cockermouth CA13 9DX
T: (01900) 822189
F: (01900) 822189
I: www.rosecottageguest.co.uk

B&B per night:
S £27.00–£35.00
D £42.00–£50.00

HB per person:
DY £36.00–£40.00

OPEN All year round

In a pleasant position and only a 10-minute walk from the town, this family-run guesthouse is within easy reach of the Lakes and the coast. Home cooking. Large private car park. An ideal base for walking or touring.

Bedrooms: 1 single,
5 double/twin, 2 triple/
multiple
Bathrooms: 8 en suite

Evening meal available
CC: Amex, Delta,
Mastercard, Switch, Visa

Mid-week or weekend breaks available all year (min 2 nights). Family group packages also available all year (min 12 people).

◆◆◆◆

BANK GROUND

East of Lake, Coniston LA21 8AA
T: (01539) 441264
F: (01539) 441900
E: info@bankground.co.uk
I: www.bankground.co.uk

B&B per night:
S £25.00–£40.00
D £40.00–£70.00

OPEN All year round

'Storybook' location, with Arthur Ransome's 'Swallows and Amazons' being both written and filmed here. A mere 150 yards from the property's own half-mile stretch of Coniston shoreline, there are uninterrupted views over the lake to Coniston village and its magnificent backdrop of Lakeland fells. Ideal for all outdoor activities.

Bedrooms: 4 double/
twin, 3 triple/multiple
Bathrooms: 5 en suite

Evening meal available
CC: Delta, Mastercard,
Switch, Visa

MAP REFERENCES The map references refer to the colour maps at the front of this guide. The first figure is the map number; the letter and figure which follow indicate the grid reference on the map.

CONISTON continued

◆◆◆◆

CROWN HOTEL
Coniston LA21 8EA
T: (01539) 441243
F: (01539) 441804
E: enntiidus@crown-hotel-coniston.com
I: www.crown-hotel-coniston.com

B&B per night:
S £35.00–£45.00
D £60.00–£75.00

HB per person:
DY £45.00–£65.00

OPEN All year round

The Crown Hotel has been completely refurbished to a very high standard to ensure the comfort of all our guests. Enjoy the delights of Coniston and the lake where Donald Campbell attempted to break the world water speed record.

Bedrooms: 11 double/twin, 1 triple/multiple
Bathrooms: 12 en suite

Lunch available
Evening meal available
CC: Amex, Delta, Diners, Mastercard, Switch, Visa

2 day break for only £160 for 2 people, all meals included.

◆◆◆

OAKLANDS
Yewdale Road, Coniston LA21 8DX
T: (01539) 441245
F: (01539) 441245

Bedrooms: 1 single, 3 double/twin
Bathrooms: 1 en suite

B&B per night:
S £20.00
D £20.00–£25.00

OPEN All year round

Spacious 100-year-old Lakeland house, village location, mountain views. Quality breakfast, special diets, owner's personal attention. Parking. Non-smoking.

◆◆◆◆

OLD RECTORY HOTEL
Torver, Coniston LA21 8AX
T: (015394) 41353
F: (015394) 41156
E: enquiries@theoldrectoryhotel.com

B&B per night:
D £40.00–£70.00

HB per person:
DY £35.00–£53.00

OPEN All year round

The house, built 1868, is in 3 acres of gardens and woodland, and has majestic views of Coniston Old Man. We offer a peaceful setting, an opportunity to unwind, and an ideal base from which to explore. And in the evening enjoy a candlelit dinner in our conservatory dining room.

Bedrooms: 7 double/twin, 1 triple/multiple
Bathrooms: 8 en suite

Evening meal available
CC: Delta, Mastercard, Switch, Visa

3 nights for the price of 2, Nov-Mar (excl Christmas and New Year).

◆◆◆

WILSON ARMS
Torver, Coniston LA21 8BB
T: (01539) 441237
F: (01539) 441590

B&B per night:
S £27.00–£30.00
D £50.00–£60.00

OPEN All year round

In the small village of Torver, 2.5 miles from Coniston. Ideal walking area. Well stocked bar, log fire on cooler days. Good central location for touring the Lakes. Meals prepared with local fresh produce. Surrounded by beautiful fells.

Bedrooms: 1 single, 5 double/twin, 2 triple/multiple
Bathrooms: 7 en suite, 1 private

Lunch available
Evening meal available
CC: Delta, Diners, Mastercard, Switch, Visa

IMPORTANT NOTE Information on accommodation listed in this guide has been supplied by the proprietors. As changes may occur you are advised to check details at the time of booking.

CROSTHWAITE, Cumbria Map ref 5A3

◆◆◆◆ CROSTHWAITE HOUSE

Crosthwaite, Kendal LA8 8BP
T: (01539) 568264
F: (01539) 568264
E: bookings@crosthwaitehouse.co.uk
I: www.crosthwaitehouse.co.uk

Bedrooms: 1 single,
5 double/twin
Bathrooms: 6 en suite

Evening meal available

B&B per night:
S £22.00–£25.00
D £44.00–£50.00

HB per person:
DY £37.00–£40.00

Mid-18thC building with unspoilt views of the Lyth and Winster valleys, 5 miles from Bowness and Kendal. Family atmosphere and home cooking. Self-catering cottages also available.

◆◆◆◆ THE PUNCH BOWL INN

Crosthwaite, Kendal LA8 8HR
T: (01539) 568237
F: (01539) 568875
E: enquiries@punchbowl.fsnet.co.uk
I: www.punchbowl.fsnet.co.uk

Bedrooms: 3 double/twin
Bathrooms: 3 en suite

Lunch available
Evening meal available
CC: Delta, Mastercard, Switch, Visa

B&B per night:
S £40.00–£45.00
D £60.00–£65.00

HB per person:
DY £60.00–£65.00

Coaching inn with 3 double bedrooms, all with private facilities. Adjacent to Crosthwaite Church in the Lyth Valley, 5 miles from Windermere and Kendal.

CUMREW, Cumbria Map ref 5B2

◆◆◆◆

CUMREW HOUSE

Cumrew, Heads Nook, Carlisle CA8 9DD
T: (01768) 896115
E: rabduff@aol.com
I: www.countrysport-lodge.com

B&B per night:
S £40.00
D £60.00

OPEN All year round

Cumrew House dates from 1753 and is situated in a conservation area on the edge of Cumrew village overlooking a sheltered, mature garden. It includes stabling, traditional dog kennels, tennis court and working walled garden. A large, comfortable drawing room is always available and a delicious breakfast awaits you in the dining room.

Bedrooms: 3 double/twin
Bathrooms: 3 en suite

Evening meal available

Three nights or more-10% discount. View website www.countrysport-lodge.com.

DALTON-IN-FURNESS, Cumbria Map ref 5A3

◆◆ BLACK DOG INN

Holmes Green, Broughton Road,
Dalton-in-Furness LA15 8JP
T: (01229) 462561 & 07931 751282
F: (01229) 468036
E: jack@blackdoginn.freeserve.co.uk

Bedrooms: 2 double/twin
Bathrooms: 2 en suite

Lunch available
Evening meal available
CC: Mastercard, Switch, Visa

B&B per night:
S £15.00–£25.00
D £35.00–£40.00

HB per person:
DY £20.00–£30.00

OPEN All year round

Old coaching inn, situated in rural surroundings, with log fires, cask ales and home-cooked food. Local Camra Pub of the Year 1998 and 1999.

TOWN INDEX

This can be found at the back of the guide. If you know where you want to stay, the index will give you the page number listing accommodation in your chosen town, city or village.

◆◆◆◆

BUSH NOOK

Upper Denton, Gilsland, Carlisle CA8 7AF
T: (016977) 47194
F: (016977) 47790
E: paulaibarton@bushnook.freeserve.co.uk
I: www.hadriansway.co.uk

B&B per night:
S £18.00
D £45.00–£50.00

HB per person:
DY £28.00–£40.00

OPEN All year round

18thC former farmhouse set in open countryside overlooking Birdoswall Fort on Hadrian's Wall. Spectacular views on all sides, peaceful, charming and restful accommodation easily accessed from the M6 or A1. Award-winning home cooking is our speciality. Ideal base for exploring Roman Wall country and the North Pennines.

Bedrooms: 1 single, 3 double/twin; suites available
Bathrooms: 2 en suite, 1 private

Evening meal available

Any 3 nights for price of 1, Oct-Mar (excl Christmas and New Year). 3 nights or more discount all year.

◆◆◆◆

BIRCHLEIGH GUEST HOUSE

Kents Bank Road, Grange-over-Sands LA11 7EY
T: (01539) 532592
F: (01539) 532592

B&B per night:
S £24.00
D £40.00–£44.00

HB per person:
DY £30.00–£32.00

OPEN All year round

There's a warm welcome at this comfortable Victorian guesthouse, ideally placed for exploring the Lake District. All rooms tastefully decorated, with colour TV and tea/coffee tray. Excellent breakfasts. Lunch available on request. Non-smoking. Pets welcome. Private parking.

Bedrooms: 2 double/twin, 2 triple/multiple
Bathrooms: 4 en suite

Evening meal available

Weekly terms for 1 person £135. 2 people sharing a double room for 1 night £22ppn, for 3 nights £20ppn.

◆◆◆

CORNER BEECH

Kents Bank Road, Grange-over-Sands LA11 7DP
T: (01539) 533088
F: (01539) 535288
E: david@cornerbeech.ndirect.co.uk
I: www.cornerbeech.ndirect.co.uk

Bedrooms: 3 double/twin, 2 triple/multiple
Bathrooms: 5 en suite

Evening meal available
CC: Delta, Mastercard, Switch, Visa

B&B per night:
S £25.00–£30.00
D £47.00–£60.00

HB per person:
DY £35.00–£41.50

Elegant Edwardian house overlooking Morecambe Bay close to the promenade. Spacious, centrally heated en suite rooms. Restaurant/bar and separate lounge. Home cooking.

CHECK THE MAPS

The colour maps at the front of this guide show all the cities, towns and villages for which you will find accommodation entries. Refer to the town index to find the page on which they are listed.

◆◆◆◆

ELTON HOTEL

Windermere Road, Grange-over-Sands
LA11 6EQ
T: (01539) 532838
F: (01539) 532838
E: chris.crane@btclick.com

B&B per night:
S £26.00–£30.00
D £42.00–£50.00

HB per person:
DY £32.00–£36.00

Our superior rooms have all the little extras to make them 'home from home', with the emphasis on clean and comfortable. Good home cooking a speciality. Two minutes on level to all amenities. Ground floor rooms. Ideal location for touring Lakes. Come and enjoy a warm welcome from Ian and Christine.

Bedrooms: 6 double/ twin, 1 triple/multiple
Bathrooms: 5 en suite

Evening meal available

◆◆◆◆

MAYFIELDS
3 Mayfield Terrace,
Kents Bank Road, Grange-over-Sands LA11 7DW
T: (01539) 534730
I: www.accommodata.co.uk/ 010699.htm

Bedrooms: 1 single, 2 double/twin
Bathrooms: 2 en suite

Lunch available
Evening meal available

B&B per night:
S £25.00
D £50.00

HB per person:
DY £37.00

OPEN All year round

Victorian terraced townhouse, tastefully furnished and equipped to a high standard. In a pleasant position on fringe of town close to promenade and open countryside.

◆◆◆◆

METHVEN HOTEL

Kents Bank Road, Grange-over-Sands
LA11 7DU
T: (01539) 532031

B&B per night:
S £32.00–£37.00
D £52.00–£62.00

HB per person:
DY £38.00–£48.00

A delightful family-run hotel set in own grounds offers a warm and relaxing atmosphere with uninterrupted views of Morecambe Bay and surrounding fells. All rooms are well-appointed and have en suite facilities and high quality furnishings. All meals are prepared by the proprietor, a qualified chef.

Bedrooms: 8 double/ twin, 2 triple/multiple
Bathrooms: 10 en suite

Lunch available
Evening meal available

◆◆◆

SOMERSET HOUSE
Kents Bank Road, Grange-over-Sands LA11 7EY
T: (01539) 532631

Bedrooms: 3 single, 2 double/twin, 3 triple/ multiple

Lunch available
Evening meal available

B&B per night:
S £19.00–£22.00
D £34.00–£44.00

HB per person:
DY £24.00–£31.00

OPEN All year round

Enjoy our small privately-run hotel and relax. Excellent home-cooked meals. Close to shops, lakes and beautiful homes and estates. Ideal area for walkers and relaxing.

◆◆◆◆

ASH COTTAGE GUEST HOUSE
Red Lion Square, Grasmere, Ambleside LA22 9SP
T: (01539) 435224

Bedrooms: 1 single, 6 double/twin, 1 triple/ multiple
Bathrooms: 8 en suite

Evening meal available

B&B per night:
S £25.00–£30.00
D £46.00–£60.00

HB per person:
DY £36.00–£42.00

OPEN All year round

Detached guesthouse with comfortable en suite bedrooms, personal attention and fine home cooking. Licensed. Pleasant award-winning garden. Private parking.

GRASMERE continued

◆◆◆◆ DUNMAIL HOUSE

Keswick Road, Grasmere, Ambleside LA22 9RE T: (01539) 435256 E: enquiries@dunmailhouse. freeserve.co.uk I: www.dunmailhouse.com	Bedrooms: 1 single, 2 double/twin, 1 triple/ multiple Bathrooms: 3 en suite, 1 private	B&B per night: S £20.00–£27.00 D £44.00–£54.00 OPEN All year round

Traditional stone house in lovely grounds, with friendly family atmosphere and beautiful views from all rooms.

⋔☎6⬜♿🍴Ⓢ✂🅿️🏧💻🖥️☀️🚗♦P

◆◆◆ THE HARWOOD

Red Lion Square, Grasmere, Ambleside LA22 9SP T: (01539) 435248 F: (01539) 435545 E: harwoodlan@aol.com I: members.aol.com/harwoodian	Bedrooms: 2 single, 6 double/twin Bathrooms: 4 en suite, 4 private	Lunch available CC: Delta, Mastercard, Switch, Visa	B&B per night: S £18.50–£32.50 D £37.00–£65.00 OPEN All year round

Traditional Lakeland stone-built Victorian hotel in the heart of Grasmere. Comfortable rooms all with private facilities and TV. Friendly and welcoming, speciality Cumbrian breakfasts.

⋔☎🏇⬜♿Ⓢ✂💻🖥️🚗♦P

◆◆◆ HOW FOOT LODGE

Town End, Grasmere, Ambleside LA22 9SQ T: (01539) 435366	Bedrooms: 6 double/ twin Bathrooms: 6 en suite	CC: Delta, Mastercard, Switch, Visa	B&B per night: S £33.00–£35.00 D £44.00–£52.00

Beautiful Victorian house in peaceful surroundings. Spacious rooms with lovely views. Ideal base for walking and exploring the Lake District.

⋔☎2🛋️⬜♿Ⓢ✂🅿️💻🖥️☀️🐴🚗♦🏠P

◆◆◆◆ LAKE VIEW COUNTRY HOUSE

Lake View Drive, Grasmere LA22 9TD T: (015394) 35384 E: info@lakeview-grasmere.com I: www.lakeview-grasmere.com	Bedrooms: 1 single, 4 double/twin Bathrooms: 3 en suite	Evening meal available CC: Delta, Mastercard, Switch, Visa	B&B per night: D £40.00–£71.00 HB per person: DY £33.50–£49.00 OPEN All year round

Beautifully situated, family-run house in tranquil setting close to village centre. Lake views, private lakeshore access, substantial gardens.

⋔🏛️⬜♿🍴Ⓢ✂🅿️🖥️🚗🎵▶️☀️🐴🚗♦P

◆◆◆ RAISE VIEW GUEST HOUSE

Traditional Lakeland-stone house situated at the northern edge of Grasmere, with uninterrupted views of Easedale and easy access to many fine walks. Comfortably furnished, en suite rooms. Cosy lounge with roaring log fires in the late and early seasons. A warm and friendly welcome awaits you.

White Bridge, Grasmere, Ambleside LA22 9RQ
T: (01539) 435215
F: (01539) 435126
E: john@raisevw.demon.co.uk
I: www.raisevw.demon.co.uk

Bedrooms: 6 double/
twin
Bathrooms: 6 en suite

Discount of £3 per room, per night, for bookings of 3 nights or more.

B&B per night:
D £48.00–£56.00

⋔☎5⬜♿Ⓢ✂🅿️🌙💻🖥️🚗☀️🚗P

◆◆◆◆

REDMAYNE COTTAGE

Grasmere, Ambleside LA22 9QY

T: (01539) 435635 & 07977 596133

B&B per night:
D £44.00–£54.00

OPEN Feb–Nov

From its superb elevated private situation in Grasmere, Redmayne Cottage enjoys breathtaking panoramic views of the lake and mountains. Spacious luxury en suite double bedrooms have colour TV, hospitality tray and many thoughtful extras. Choice of delicious breakfasts. Exclusively for non-smokers. Regret no children or pets. Private enclosed parking.

Bedrooms: 3 double/twin
Bathrooms: 3 en suite

 P

◆◆◆◆

SILVER LEA GUEST HOUSE

Easedale Road, Grasmere,
Ambleside LA22 9QE
T: (015394) 35657
F: (015394) 35657

Bedrooms: 1 single,
4 double/twin
Bathrooms: 2 en suite,
3 private

Evening meal available

B&B per night:
S £28.00–£31.00
D £56.00–£64.00

HB per person:
DY £36.00–£43.00

OPEN Feb–Nov

Cosy, comfortable Lakeland-stone house close to village centre. Home cooking and a warm welcoming atmosphere. Special breaks February-May.

11 P

◆◆◆◆

TITTERINGDALES GUEST HOUSE

Pye Lane, Grasmere LA22 9RQ

T: (015394) 35439

E: titteringdales@grasmere.net

I: www.grasmere.net

B&B per night:
S £20.00–£25.00
D £37.00–£50.00

OPEN Feb–Nov

Titteringdales is a small, family-owned and run guesthouse quietly situated in the village of Grasmere. We can offer you clean and comfortable accommodation, with an excellent breakfast and very good off-road parking. So why not base yourselves with us to explore the rest of the Lake District?

Bedrooms: 7 double/twin
Bathrooms: 6 en suite

CC: Delta, Mastercard, Switch, Visa

2, 3 and 7 night rates available on request.

12 P

◆◆◆◆

WOODLAND CRAG GUEST HOUSE

How Head Lane, Grasmere, Ambleside LA22 9SG

T: (01539) 435351

F: (01539) 435351

E: woodlandcrag@aol.com

I: www.woodlandcrag.com

B&B per night:
S £20.00–£28.00
D £42.00–£70.00

OPEN All year round

Traditional Lakeland-stone Victorian country house in secluded location, a short walk from village centre. Dove Cottage (William Wordsworth) 200 metres. Lovely lake and fell views. One acre woodland garden. Tastefully decorated rooms. Drying room. Enclosed parking. Vegetarians catered for. Ideal for touring. Many walks radiate from here.

Bedrooms: 2 single,
3 double/twin
Bathrooms: 3 en suite

CC: Amex, Delta,
Mastercard, Switch, Visa

10% discount for 3 nights or more. 3 nights for the price of 2, 1 Nov-28 Feb.

12 P

◆◆◆◆
Silver
Award

BORWICK LODGE

Hawkshead, Ambleside LA22 0PU
T: (01539) 436332
F: (01539) 436332
E: borwicklodge@talk21.com
I: www.borwicklodge.com

B&B per night:
S £35.00–£45.00
D £50.00–£72.00

OPEN All year round

A leafy driveway entices you to a rather special 17thC country house with panoramic lake and mountain views, quietly secluded in the heart of the Lakes. Beautiful en suite bedrooms include special occasions and romantic breaks with king-size 4-poster beds. Rosemary and Colin Haskell welcome you to this most beautiful corner of England. Totally non-smoking.

Bedrooms: 5 double/twin, 1 triple/multiple
Bathrooms: 6 en suite

◆◆◆◆
Silver
Award

GRIZEDALE LODGE HOTEL
Grizedale, Ambleside LA22 0QL
T: (01539) 436532
F: (01539) 436572
E: enquiries@grizedale-lodge.com
I: www.grizedale-lodge.com

Bedrooms: 8 double/twin
Bathrooms: 8 en suite

Lunch available
CC: Amex, Mastercard, Switch, Visa

B&B per night:
S £35.00–£42.50
D £70.00–£90.00

OPEN All year round

Luxurious, licensed, former shooting lodge; elegant 4 poster suites, patio, sun terrace. Near Hawkshead. Romantic setting, lovely forest views and close to famous sculpture walks.

◆◆◆◆

YEWFIELD VEGETARIAN GUEST HOUSE

Yewfield, Hawkshead, Ambleside LA22 0PR
T: (01539) 436765
F: (01539) 436096
E: derek.yewfield@btinternet.com
I: www.yewfield.co.uk

B&B per night:
S £27.00–£32.00
D £44.00–£75.00

A peaceful and quiet retreat in the heart of the Lakes, perfect for lovely walking holidays, an impressive Gothic vegetarian guesthouse set in its own 30-acre organic gardens and grounds. All rooms individually appointed to a very high standard with en suite bath and shower. Completely non-smoking.

Bedrooms: 3 double/twin
Bathrooms: 3 en suite

CC: Delta, Mastercard, Switch, Visa

Classical concerts throughout the year. See website for dates.

COUNTRY CODE Always follow the Country Code ✿ Enjoy the countryside and respect its life and work ✿ Guard against all risk of fire ✿ Fasten all gates ✿ Keep your dogs under close control ✿ Keep to public paths across farmland ✿ Use gates and stiles to cross fences, hedges and walls ✿ Leave livestock, crops and machinery alone ✿ Take your litter home ✿ Help to keep all water clean ✿ Protect wildlife, plants and trees ✿ Take special care on country roads ✿ Make no unnecessary noise

◆◆◆◆◆
**Silver
Award**

BLAVEN HOMESTAY

Blaven, Middleshaw, Old Hutton, Kendal
LA8 0LZ
T: (01539) 734894 & 740490
F: (01539) 727447
E: hospitality@greenarrow.demon.co.uk
I: www.blavenhomestay.co.uk

B&B per night:
S £35.00–£38.50
D £55.00–£64.00

HB per person:
DY £47.00–£62.00

OPEN Jun–Dec

Peacefully located beside a pretty Lakeland trout stream, this beautifully appointed, sympathetically converted barn is convenient for the M6 and touring the Lake District and Yorkshire Dales. Amiable, welcoming hosts Janet and Barry offer gourmet meals, fine wine and every comfort to guests. Local walks, wood fires, lovely garden, safe parking.

Bedrooms: 1 double/
twin, 1 triple/multiple
Bathrooms: 2 en suite

Evening meal available
CC: Mastercard, Visa

Business courses-'Running a Bed and Breakfast' and cookery demonstrations-'Innovative Breakfast and Brunch Cookery' twice monthly.

◆◆◆
FAIRWAYS GUEST HOUSE
102 Windermere Road, Kendal
LA9 5EZ
T: (01539) 725564
E: mp@fairways1.fsnet.co.uk

Bedrooms: 3 double/
twin
Bathrooms: 3 en suite

B&B per night:
S £25.00–£30.00
D £38.00–£42.00

OPEN All year round

On the main Kendal-Windermere road. Victorian guesthouse with en-suite facilities. TV, tea and coffee in all rooms. Four-poster bedrooms. Private parking.

◆◆◆
HILLSIDE GUEST HOUSE
4 Beast Banks, Kendal LA9 4JW
T: (01539) 722836

Bedrooms: 2 single,
4 double/twin
Bathrooms: 4 en suite

B&B per night:
S £18.00–£21.00
D £36.00–£42.00

OPEN Apr–Oct

Small elegant Victorian guesthouse near shops and town facilities, convenient for the Lakes, Yorkshire Dales and Morecambe Bay. En suite and appointed to a very high standard.

◆◆◆◆
ABACOURT HOUSE
26 Stanger Street, Keswick
CA12 5JU
T: (01768) 772967
E: abacourt@btinternet.com
I: www.abacourt.co.uk

Bedrooms: 5 double/
twin
Bathrooms: 5 en suite

B&B per night:
D £22.00

OPEN All year round

Victorian townhouse, lovingly restored to a high standard in 1992. Beautifully furnished, fully double glazed. Superior en-suites in all bedrooms. Central, quiet, cosy and friendly. Brochure available.

◆◆◆◆
**Silver
Award**

ACORN HOUSE HOTEL
Ambleside Road, Keswick CA12 4DL
T: (01768) 772553
F: (01768) 775332
E: info@acornhousehotel.co.uk
I: www.acornhousehotel.co.uk

Bedrooms: 8 double/
twin, 2 triple/multiple
Bathrooms: 9 en suite,
1 private

CC: Delta, Mastercard,
Switch, Visa

B&B per night:
S £28.00–£35.00
D £50.00–£62.00

OPEN Feb–Nov

Elegant Georgian house set in colourful garden. All bedrooms tastefully furnished, some 4-poster beds. Cleanliness guaranteed. Close to town centre. Good off-street parking. Strictly no smoking.

CREDIT CARD BOOKINGS If you book by telephone and are asked for your credit card number it is advisable to check the proprietor's policy should you cancel your reservation.

KESWICK continued

♦♦♦

THE ANCHORAGE
14 Ambleside Road, Keswick
CA12 4DL
T: (01768) 772813

Bedrooms: 1 single, 3 double/twin, 2 triple/multiple
Bathrooms: 6 en suite

Evening meal available

Comfortable house, serving good home cooking, with owners who make every effort to please.

5 P

B&B per night:
S £20.00–£23.00
D £40.00–£46.00

HB per person:
DY £32.00–£34.00

OPEN All year round

♦♦♦♦

ANWORTH HOUSE

27 Eskin Street, Keswick CA12 4DQ
T: (01768) 772923
I: www.anworthhouse.co.uk

Ideally situated for the town centre, theatre, lake and fells. Each of the five en suite bedrooms is individually co-ordinated and tastefully furnished to the highest standards. A relaxed atmosphere and excellent home cooking. Special diets catered for. For the comfort of guests, Anworth House is a no smoking establishment.

Bedrooms: 5 double/twin
Bathrooms: 5 en suite

CC: Mastercard, Switch, Visa

Special winter breaks: 3 nights for the price of 2, 1 Nov 2001-21 Mar 2002 (excl Christmas and New Year).

6

B&B per night:
S £25.00
D £46.00–£54.00

OPEN All year round

♦♦♦♦

AVONDALE GUEST HOUSE
20 Southey Street, Keswick
CA12 4EF
T: (01768) 772735
F: (01768) 775431
E: enquiries@avondaleguesthouse.com
I: www.avondaleguesthouse.com

Bedrooms: 1 single, 5 double/twin
Bathrooms: 6 en suite

CC: Amex, Delta, Mastercard, Switch, Visa

High quality, comfortable guesthouse with well-appointed en suite rooms. Close to town centre, theatre, lake and parks. Non-smokers only, please.

12

B&B per night:
S £22.00–£23.50
D £44.00–£47.00

OPEN All year round

♦♦♦

BECKSTONES FARM GUEST HOUSE

Thornthwaite, Keswick CA12 5SQ
T: (01768) 778510
E: beckstones@lineone.net
I: website.lineone.net/~beckstones

Friendly, quality, en suite B&B in converted Georgian farmhouse. Peacefully situated beneath the forest and overlooking green fields to the magnificent mountain scenery of Skiddaw and the Helvellyn Range. Lounge. Keswick 10 minutes' drive, Bassenthwaite Lake 10 minutes' walk. Bar meals 3 minutes walk. Ample parking. Cycle lock-up. Dogs by arrangement. Brochure.

Bedrooms: 1 single, 5 double/twin, 1 triple/multiple
Bathrooms: 6 en suite

Weekly rates: £150pp double room; £165pp single room.

8 P

B&B per night:
S £23.50–£27.00
D £43.00–£50.00

OPEN All year round

MAP REFERENCES

Map references apply to the colour maps at the front of this guide.

KESWICK continued

BONSHAW GUEST HOUSE

◆◆◆

20 Eskin Street, Keswick CA12 4DG
T: (01768) 773084
E: sylviasanderson@compuserve.com

Bedrooms: 3 single, 4 double/twin
Bathrooms: 4 en suite

Evening meal available
CC: Delta, Mastercard, Switch, Visa

B&B per night:
S £17.00–£20.00
D £38.00–£44.00

HB per person:
DY £28.50–£34.00

OPEN All year round

Small, friendly, comfortable guesthouse, providing good home cooking. Convenient for town centre and all amenities. En suite rooms available. Private car park. Non-smoking.

CHERRY TREES

◆◆◆◆

16 Eskin Street, Keswick CA12 4DQ
T: (017687) 71048
E: cherry.trees@virgin.net

B&B per night:
S £19.00–£22.00
D £38.00–£48.00

HB per person:
DY £28.00–£36.00

OPEN All year round

Distinguished Victorian townhouse, quietly situated yet only a 5-minute walk to town centre. Spacious, en suite rooms with tea/coffee-making facilities, colour TV, hairdryer, clock/radio. King-sized comfortable beds. A warm welcome and good home cooking are guaranteed.

Bedrooms: 1 single, 3 double/twin, 1 triple/multiple
Bathrooms: 4 en suite, 1 private

Evening meal available
CC: Delta, Mastercard, Switch, Visa

3 nights for the price of 2, Nov–Mar.

EDWARDENE HOTEL

◆◆◆◆

26 Southey Street, Keswick CA12 4EF
T: (01768) 773586
F: (01768) 773824
E: enquiries@edwardenehotel.com
I: www.edwardenehotel.com

Bedrooms: 2 single, 8 double/twin, 1 triple/multiple
Bathrooms: 11 en suite

Evening meal available
CC: Amex, Delta, Mastercard, Switch, Visa

B&B per night:
S £28.00–£31.00
D £52.00–£58.00

HB per person:
DY £39.00–£44.00

OPEN All year round

Centrally located, the Edwardene provides stylish accommodation. Beautifully furnished bedrooms varying in size. There is a cosy residents' lounge and a delightfully decorated dining room.

GLENDALE GUEST HOUSE

◆◆◆

7 Eskin Street, Keswick CA12 4DH
T: (01768) 773562
E: glendale.guesthouse@talk21.com
I: www.glendale-keswick.freeserve.co.uk

Bedrooms: 1 single, 2 double/twin, 3 triple/multiple
Bathrooms: 3 en suite

Evening meal available

B&B per night:
S £18.00–£26.00
D £40.00–£44.00

OPEN All year round

Victorian townhouse only minutes from town, lake and hills. Ideal base for exploring the Lake District. Excellent breakfast with various options.

AT-A-GLANCE SYMBOLS

Symbols at the end of each accommodation entry give useful information about services and facilities. A key to symbols can be found inside the back cover flap. Keep this open for easy reference.

◆◆◆◆◆
Silver
Award

THE GRANGE COUNTRY HOUSE HOTEL

Manor Brow, Ambleside Road, Keswick
CA12 4BA
T: (01768) 772500
F: (01768) 772500
E: duncan.miller@btconnect.com

B&B per night:
S £28.00–£37.50
D £56.00–£75.00

OPEN Feb–Nov

The Grange is an immaculate Lakeland property which overlooks Keswick and the surrounding fells. Located in its own grounds of 1 acre, a 10 minute stroll to this popular and bustling market town. Walking advice, ample parking, spacious lounges, lovely bedrooms and an exceptional breakfast will make your stay unforgettable.

Bedrooms: 10 double/twin
Bathrooms: 10 en suite

Evening meal available
CC: Delta, Mastercard, Visa

Reduced tariff for 3 day stay or longer. Theatre by the Lake ticket included with any 6 day stay.

◆◆◆◆

GREYSTONES HOTEL

Ambleside Road, Keswick CA12 4DP
T: (01768) 773108
E: greystones@keslakes.freeserve.co.uk

B&B per night:
S £23.00–£26.00
D £46.00–£52.00

OPEN All year round

Greystones enjoys an enviable, tranquil location, with splendid mountain views. Yet, the hotel is only a short walk from Lake Derwentwater and the historic Market Square with its restaurants, traditional pubs and craft shops. The accommodation is stylish and comfortable. Private car park.

Bedrooms: 1 single, 7 double/twin
Bathrooms: 7 en suite, 1 private

CC: Mastercard, Visa

Mid-week special rates available.

◆◆◆

HEDGEHOG HILL GUESTHOUSE

18 Blencathra Street, Keswick
CA12 4HP
T: (01768) 774386
F: (01768) 780622
E: hedhil@fsbdial.co.uk

Bedrooms: 2 single, 4 double/twin
Bathrooms: 4 en suite

CC: Delta, Mastercard, Switch, Visa

B&B per night:
S £17.50–£18.50
D £42.00–£46.00

OPEN All year round

Friendly Victorian guest house near town centre and lake. Lovely views, comfortable en suite rooms, freshly cooked breakfast with choice, vegetarian options.

◆◆◆

LINNETT HILL

4 Penrith Road, Keswick CA12 4HF
T: (01768) 773109
E: Pete@linnetthill.co.uk
I: www.linnetthill.co.uk

B&B per night:
S £26.00
D £48.00–£50.00

OPEN All year round

Georgian house built in 1812. Overlooks Fitz Park and the River Greta. View of Skiddaw and Latrigg. Close to Keswick's market square and short level walk to the shores of Derwentwater. All rooms en suite with colour TV, hairdryer and tea/coffee-making facilities. Large car park and secure cycle storage.

Bedrooms: 1 single, 9 double/twin
Bathrooms: 10 en suite

CC: Amex, Delta, Diners, Mastercard, Switch, Visa

Reduced winter rates available.

♦♦♦ **LITTLETOWN FARM**
Newlands, Keswick CA12 5TU
T: (01768) 778353
F: (01768) 778437

Bedrooms: 1 single,
6 double/twin, 2 triple/
multiple
Bathrooms: 6 en suite

Evening meal available
CC: Mastercard, Visa

B&B per night:
S £30.00–£34.00
D £60.00–£68.00

HB per person:
DY £40.00–£44.00

150-acre mixed farm. In the beautiful, unspoilt Newlands Valley. Comfortable residents' lounge, dining room and cosy bar. Traditional 4-course dinner 6 nights a week.

♦♦♦♦

LYNWOOD HOUSE

35 Helvellyn Street, Keswick CA12 4EP
T: (01768) 772398
F: (01768) 774090
E: lynwoodho@aol.com

B&B per night:
S £18.50–£19.00
D £17.00–£21.00

OPEN All year round

Situated in a quiet, residential area, our family-run Victorian guesthouse is a 5-minute stroll from Keswick town centre. Each room has TV and tea/coffee facilities, while a comfortable lounge with extensive collection of books is available for your relaxation. Breakfast menu options include traditional, vegetarian and organic dishes.

Bedrooms: 1 single,
2 double/twin, 1 triple/
multiple
Bathrooms: 1 en suite

♦♦♦♦
Silver
Award

PARKFIELD GUESTHOUSE

The Heads, Keswick CA12 5ES
T: (01768) 772328
E: parkfield@kencomp.net
I: www.kencomp.net/parkfield

B&B per night:
S Min £32.00
D Min £54.00

OPEN All year round

Quiet but central, Parkfield offers high quality accommodation exclusively for non-smokers. Only 2 minutes' walk from Lake, bus station and Theatre by the Lake. Private parking at the rear. There is a large guests' lounge with superb views overlooking the golf course and mountains beyond. All en suite rooms.

Bedrooms: 8 double/
twin
Bathrooms: 8 en suite

CC: Amex, Delta,
Mastercard, Switch, Visa

♦♦♦♦
Silver
Award

RAVENSWORTH HOTEL

29 Station Street, Keswick CA12 5HH
T: (01768) 772476
F: (01768) 775287
E: info@ravensworth-hotel.co.uk
I: www.ravensworth-hotel.co.uk

B&B per night:
S £25.00–£35.50
D £45.00–£57.00

OPEN All year round

This elegant Victorian townhouse offers quality accommodation, a fantastic breakfast and a very warm welcome. Close to the lake, the theatre and the lower fells, the Ravensworth is the perfect base for an exploration of the town and lakes and for those interested in walking, fishing, golf and horse-riding.

Bedrooms: 8 double/
twin
Bathrooms: 7 en suite,
1 private

CC: Amex, Delta,
Mastercard, Switch, Visa

◆◆◆◆

RICKERBY GRANGE
Portinscale, Keswick CA12 5RH
T: (01768) 772344
F: (01768) 775588
E: val@ricor.demon.co.uk
I: www.ricor.demon.co.uk

B&B per night:
S £30.00–£32.00
D £60.00–£64.00

HB per person:
DY £43.00–£45.00

OPEN All year round

Detached country hotel in its own gardens, quietly situated in the pretty village of Portinscale, 0.75 miles from Keswick. Easy access to all parts of the Lakes. Comfort and good service, a cosy bar, elegant restaurant, imaginative cooking, comfortable lounge all there for your enjoyment. Ground floor rooms available.

Bedrooms: 2 single, 8 double/twin, 3 triple/ multiple
Bathrooms: 11 en suite

Evening meal available
CC: Delta, Mastercard, Switch, Visa

Winter breaks available. Victorian weekend. Christmas and New Year party nights. Group bookings taken.

 🅰️ ⛺ 5 ♨ 🖥️ 🔌 🕯️ ♀ 🍷 Ⓢ ✂ 🅿️ 🖥️ 🍴 ❋ 🐎 🚲 🐾 P

◆◆◆

SANDON GUESTHOUSE
13 Southey Street, Keswick CA12 4EG
T: (01768) 773648
I: www.sandoncleworth.supanet. com

Bedrooms: 2 single, 3 double/twin, 1 triple/ multiple
Bathrooms: 4 en suite

Evening meal available

B&B per night:
S £17.00–£18.00
D £40.00–£42.00

OPEN All year round

Charming Lakeland-stone Victorian guesthouse, conveniently situated for town, theatre or lake. Friendly, comfortable accommodation. Ideal base for walking or cycling holidays. Superb English breakfast.

⛺ 4 🖥️ 🔌 ♀ 🕯️ Ⓢ ✂ 🖥️ 🍴 ❋ 🚲 🐾

◆◆◆◆

SUNNYSIDE GUEST HOUSE
25 Southey Street, Keswick CA12 4EF
T: (01768) 772446
F: (01768) 774447
E: raynewton@survey.u-net.com
I: www.survey.u-net.com

B&B per night:
S £25.00
D £40.00–£50.00

OPEN All year round

We offer a friendly and flexible welcome to our comfortable Victorian house that has been extensively modernised to provide well equipped and tastefully furnished rooms, 5 being en suite and the other 2 having adjacent private facilities. Relaxing guest lounge. Central location. Parking for 8 cars. Non-smoking throughout.

Bedrooms: 1 single, 5 double/twin, 1 triple/ multiple
Bathrooms: 5 en suite, 2 private

🅰️ ⛺ 🖥️ 🔌 ♀ 🕯️ Ⓢ ✂ 🖥️ 🐎 🚲 P

◆◆◆

SWINSIDE INN
Newlands, Keswick CA12 5UE
T: (01768) 778253 & 778285
F: (01768) 778253
E: theswinsideinn@btinternet.com
I: www.kesnet.co.uk

Bedrooms: 5 double/ twin, 1 triple/multiple
Bathrooms: 4 en suite

Lunch available
Evening meal available
CC: Delta, Mastercard, Switch, Visa

B&B per night:
D £44.00–£54.00

OPEN All year round

Situated amidst stunning views and great walks. 500 year-old inn, log fires, spacious en suite and standard rooms, excellent food and ales. Drying room and parking.

🅰️ ⛺ 1 🖥️ ♀ 🍷 Ⓢ ✂ 🖥️ 🍴 🍸 ♣ ❋ 🐎 🚲 🎣 P

ACCESSIBILITY
Look for the ♿ ♿ 🚶 symbols which indicate accessibility for wheelchair users. A list of establishments is at the front of this guide.

KESWICK continued

♦♦♦ **WATENDLATH GUEST HOUSE**
15 Acorn Street, Keswick CA12 4EA
T: (01768) 774165
F: (01768) 74165
E: linda@wakendlathguesthouse.
co.uk
I: www.wakendlathguesthouse.co.
uk

Bedrooms: 2 double/
twin, 2 triple/multiple
Bathrooms: 4 en suite

B&B per night:
D £36.00–£42.00

Within easy walking distance of the lake, hills and town centre. We offer a warm and friendly welcome and traditional English breakfast.

KIRKBY LONSDALE, Cumbria Map ref 5B3 *Tourist Information Centre Tel: (015242) 71437*

♦♦ **THE COPPER KETTLE**
3-5 Market Street, Kirkby Lonsdale,
Carnforth LA6 2AU
T: (01524) 271714
F: (01524) 271714

Bedrooms: 3 double/
twin, 1 triple/multiple
Bathrooms: 3 en suite

Lunch available
Evening meal available
CC: Amex, Delta, Diners,
Mastercard, Switch, Visa

B&B per night:
S £23.00
D £17.50–£20.50

HB per person:
DY £23.00–£28.00

OPEN All year round

Part of an old manor house, built in 1610, on the border between the Yorkshire Dales and the Lakes.

KIRKBY STEPHEN, Cumbria Map ref 5B3 *Tourist Information Centre Tel: (017683) 71199*

Rating
Applied For

WEST VIEW
Ravenstonedale, Kirkby Stephen
CA17 4NG
T: (01539) 623415

Bedrooms: 3 double/
twin
Bathrooms: 2 en suite,
1 private

Evening meal available

B&B per night:
S £22.00–£25.00
D £40.00–£44.00

HB per person:
DY £30.00–£32.00

OPEN All year round

Westview is a lovely old farmhouse overlooking the village green, in a picturesque, quiet village with churches, pubs, small golf course and lovely walking area.

LAKESIDE, Cumbria Map ref 5A3

♦♦♦♦

The Knoll is a traditional Victorian country house set in its own grounds surrounded by wooded countryside at the southern tip of Lake Windermere. The house is beautifully appointed with large, recently refurbished en suite bedrooms. A relaxing rural retreat with open fires offering a warm welcome, excellent cuisine and wines.

THE KNOLL COUNRTY HOUSE

Lakeside, Nr Newby Bridge, Ulverston
LA12 8AU
T: (01539) 531347
F: (01539) 530850
E: info@theknoll-lakeside.co.uk
I: www.theknoll-lakeside.co.uk

Bedrooms: 6 double/
twin, 2 triple/multiple
Bathrooms: 8 en suite

Evening meal available
CC: Delta, Mastercard,
Switch, Visa

B&B per night:
S £35.00–£45.00
D £55.00–£70.00

HB per person:
DY £45.00–£55.00

OPEN All year round

MILLOM, Cumbria Map ref 5A3

♦♦♦♦ **THE DUDDON PILOT HOTEL**
Devonshire Road, Millom LA18 4JT
T: (01229) 774116
F: (01229) 774116

Bedrooms: 1 single,
4 double/twin, 1 triple/
multiple
Bathrooms: 6 en suite

Lunch available
Evening meal available

B&B per night:
S £25.00
D £50.00

OPEN All year round

The hotel is built on the site of old ironworks. Decorated in a nautical theme which is real to the area.

QUALITY ASSURANCE SCHEME
Diamond ratings and awards are explained at the back of this guide.

MUNGRISDALE, Cumbria Map ref 5A2

◆◆◆ **MOSEDALE END FARM**

Mungrisdale, Penrith CA11 0XQ
T: (017687) 79605
E: armstrong@awmcmanus.
screaming.net
I: www.smoothhound.co.uk/hotels/
mosedale.html

Bedrooms: 1 double/
twin, 1 triple/multiple
Bathrooms: 2 en suite

B&B per night:
S £20.00–£22.00
D £40.00–£44.00

OPEN All year round

A 17thC farmhouse in a peaceful location surrounded by mountains, rivers and green fields in the Central Lakes.

NEAR SAWREY, Cumbria Map ref 5A3

◆◆◆ **TOWER BANK ARMS**

Near Sawrey, Ambleside LA22 0LF
T: (01539) 436334
F: (01539) 436334

Bedrooms: 3 double/
twin
Bathrooms: 3 en suite

Lunch available
Evening meal available
CC: Amex, Delta,
Mastercard, Switch, Visa

B&B per night:
S Min £37.00
D Min £52.00

OPEN All year round

Next door to Hill Top, the former home of Beatrix Potter. It features in the tale of Jemima Puddleduck.

PENRITH, Cumbria Map ref 5B2 *Tourist Information Centre Tel: (01768) 867466*

◆◆◆ **ALBANY HOUSE**

5 Portland Place, Penrith CA11 7QN
T: (01768) 863072
F: (01768) 863072
I: www.albanyhouse.com.uk

Bedrooms: 1 double/
twin, 4 triple/multiple
Bathrooms: 2 en suite

B&B per night:
D £37.00–£50.00

OPEN All year round

Large Victorian terraced house run by proprietress and providing good facilities. Ideal for Lake District and stopover to or from Scotland. Children welcome, special diets on request.

◆◆◆◆

BEACON BANK HOTEL

Beacon Edge, Penrith CA11 7BD
T: (01768) 862633
F: (01768) 899055
E: beaconbank.hotel@virgin.net
I: www.smoothhound.com

B&B per night:
S Min £35.00
D £50.00–£60.00

HB per person:
DY £40.00–£50.00

OPEN All year round

A beautiful Victorian house of character, set in peaceful, secluded landscaped gardens on the outskirts of Penrith. M6 5 minutes. Spacious, comfortable accommodation of a high standard with many interesting features. Ample off-street parking. Ideally placed for touring the Lakes, the Eden Valley and Southern Scotland. A no smoking hotel.

Bedrooms: 6 double/
twin, 2 triple/multiple
Bathrooms: 8 en suite

Evening meal available
CC: Delta, Mastercard,
Switch, Visa

◆◆◆ **BLUE SWALLOW GUESTHOUSE**

11 Victoria Road, Penrith CA11 8HR
T: (01768) 866335
E: blueswallows@lineone.net
I: www.blueswallow.co.uk

Bedrooms: 2 double/
twin, 3 triple/multiple
Bathrooms: 3 en suite

B&B per night:
S £22.00–£30.00
D £18.00–£20.00

OPEN All year round

Family-run, mid-Victorian townhouse, comfortable and well-appointed throughout. Situated in Eden Valley, 5 minutes from Lakeland. Hearty breakfast and cleanliness assured.

◆◆◆◆

HORNBY HALL
COUNTRY GUEST HOUSE

Hornby Hall, Brougham, Penrith CA10 2AR
T: (01768) 891114
F: (01768) 891114

B&B per night:
S £30.00–£33.00
D £50.00–£75.00

HB per person:
DY £48.00–£56.00

OPEN All year round

You will receive a warm welcome to this 16thC farmhouse. It is situated in open farmland yet only 4 miles from the M6. Fresh flowers, log fires in winter and full of antiques. Home-cooked local produce, generous breakfast. Easy reach of Lakes and Yorkshire. Private fishing available on River Eamont.

Bedrooms: 1 single, 6 double/twin
Bathrooms: 3 en suite, 2 private

Evening meal available
CC: Delta, Mastercard, Switch, Visa

◆◆◆◆
Silver
Award

ROUNDTHORN
COUNTRY HOUSE

Beacon Edge, Penrith CA11 8SJ
T: (01768) 863952
F: (01768) 864100
E: enquiries@roundthorn.co.uk
I: www.roundthorn.co.uk

B&B per night:
S £44.55–£49.50
D £61.20–£68.00

OPEN All year round

Grade II Listed Georgian mansion, set in landscaped grounds, from which there are panoramic views of the Eden Valley, Pennines and Lakeland fells. All rooms are en suite and have TV and tea/coffee-making facilities. The house is fully licensed and rates include a hearty Cumbrian breakfast.

Bedrooms: 8 double/twin, 2 triple/multiple
Bathrooms: 10 en suite

Evening meal available
CC: Amex, Delta, Diners, Mastercard, Switch, Visa

◆◆◆◆

BUCKLE YEAT GUEST HOUSE
Sawrey, Ambleside LA22 0LF
T: (01539) 436446 & 436538
F: (01539) 436446
E: info@buckle-yeat.co.uk
I: www.buckle-yeat.co.uk

Bedrooms: 1 single, 6 double/twin
Bathrooms: 6 en suite, 1 private

CC: Amex, Delta, Mastercard, Switch, Visa

B&B per night:
S £27.50–£30.00
D £55.00–£60.00

OPEN All year round

17thC oak-beamed cottage, famous for its connections with Beatrix Potter, provides a warm, friendly and centrally located base, and excellent value for money.

◆◆◆◆

LAKEFIELD

Near Sawrey, Ambleside LA22 0JZ
T: (01539) 436635
F: (01539) 436635

B&B per night:
D £50.00–£58.00

OPEN All year round

A warm welcome awaits at our modern bungalow overlooking Esthwaite Water, offering a high standard of comfort in en suite bedrooms with colour TV, tea/coffee-making facilities. Central heating, delicious hearty breakfasts. Ample parking, secure cycle store. An ideal location for fell and valley walks. Exclusively non-smoking.

Bedrooms: 2 double/twin
Bathrooms: 2 en suite

3 nights for the price of 2, Nov-Feb (excl Christmas and New Year) Sun-Thur.

An elegant Victorian stone-built house, renovated to a high standard and complemented by fine antique furnishings and prints found throughout the house. This coupled with superb fell views from all its spacious en suite bedrooms makes West Vale an ideal base to relax or explore the Lake District.

WEST VALE COUNTRY HOUSE

Far Sawrey, Hawkshead, Ambleside
LA22 0LQ
T: (01539) 442817
F: (01539) 45302
E: westvalehouse@yahoo.co.uk

Bedrooms: 3 double/ twin, 3 triple/multiple; suites available
Bathrooms: 6 en suite

Evening meal available
CC: Amex, Delta, Mastercard, Switch, Visa

Take advantage of our free fishing weekend. Hire a small country house for the weekend. Winter warmer weekends.

B&B per night:
D £56.00–£66.00

HB per person:
DY £44.00–£49.00

OPEN All year round

SEASCALE, Cumbria Map ref 5A3

Victorian building where Swiss chef/ patron specialises in English and continental cooking – Swiss fondue nights a speciality. Lovely bedrooms, all en suite, some with sea views. Beautiful west coast, close to the highest mountain and deepest lake in England. Tennis courts and 18-hole golf course nearby.

VICTORIA VILLA HOTEL AND EGLOFF'S EATING HOUSE

58 Gosforth Road, Seascale CA20 1JG
T: (01946) 727309
F: (01946) 727158
I: www.egloffeatinghouse.co.uk

Bedrooms: 6 double/ twin
Bathrooms: 6 en suite

Lunch available
Evening meal available
CC: Delta, Mastercard, Switch, Visa

Fondue nights and 3 for 2 night offers weekends only.

B&B per night:
S £28.00–£45.00
D £56.00–£65.00

HB per person:
DY £38.00–£55.00

OPEN All year round

SEDBERGH, Cumbria Map ref 5B3

ASH HINING FARM
Howgill, Sedbergh LA10 5HU
T: (01539) 620957
F: (01539) 620957

Bedrooms: 2 double/ twin

Evening meal available

B&B per night:
S £20.00
D £18.00–£20.00

Beef breeding farm situated in the Howgill Fells and with panoramic views. Five miles M6, 20 miles Windermere. Ideal for walking or touring. Excellent home cooking.

HB per person:
DY £30.00–£32.00

All rooms refurbished July 2001 with solid hand-made beds, wardrobes and vanity units in a very traditional theme. To complement the bedrooms, a huge menu in our restaurant, with many dishes cooked on an open chargrill – curry, sausage, fish and vegetarian sections – children catered for. Cheap lunchtime menu also.

DALESMAN COUNTRY INN

Main Street, Sedbergh LA10 5BN
T: (01539) 621183
F: (01539) 621311
I: www.thedalesman.co.uk

Bedrooms: 1 single, 1 double/twin, 5 triple/ multiple
Bathrooms: 7 en suite

Lunch available
Evening meal available
CC: Delta, Diners, Mastercard, Switch, Visa

B&B per night:
S £25.00–£30.00
D £50.00–£60.00

OPEN All year round

◆◆◆

THE LODGE
10 Loftus Manor, Sedbergh LA10 5SQ
T: (01539) 621855
E: anne.thelodge@talk21.com
I: www.thedalesway.co.uk/thelodge

B&B per night:
S £20.00–£22.50
D £40.00–£45.00

HB per person:
DY £32.50–£35.00

OPEN All year round

Lovely lodge, just 50m from the Dales Way. We offer spacious, comfortable accommodation, hearty breakfasts and delicious home-cooked evening meals using fresh local produce. Packed lunches are also available. Ideal for exploring both the Yorkshire Dales and the Lake District, offering opportunities for walking, cycling, horse-riding and bird-watching.

Bedrooms: 2 double/twin

Evening meal available

One night's free B&B on bookings over 3 nights. Complimentary wine with evening meals.

ⓜ🐎12🛏️🍳👍🍷Ⓢ🔭🖥️🛋️🚶↑🏵️🐕🚌🅿

◆◆◆◆

RIDDLESAY FARM
Soulby, Kirkby Stephen CA17 4PX
T: (01768) 371474 & 0772 0811611
E: mrarmstrong@btinternet.com

Bedrooms: 2 double/twin
Bathrooms: 2 en suite

Evening meal available

B&B per night:
S £18.00–£24.00

OPEN All year round

Warm and friendly 18thC farmhouse in the Eden Valley. Good food and accommodation. One mile north of Kirkby Stephen on A66. Dog-friendly kennels available.

ⓜ🐎🖥️🛏️👍🍷Ⓢ🔭🖥️🐕🚌🅿

◆

EAGLE AND CHILD HOTEL
Kendal Road, Staveley, Kendal LA8 9LP
T: (01539) 821320
E: eaglechildinn@btinternet.com
I: www.eaglechildinn.co.uk

B&B per night:
D £30.00–£49.90

HB per person:
DY £25.00–£35.00

OPEN All year round

Traditional country inn situated in the quiet village of Staveley. Ten minutes from Kendal or Windermere, ideal touring location. Excellent walking, cycling, fishing and golf nearby. All rooms tastefully refurbished 2001. Fresh local produce, 4 real ales, Good Beer guide, riverside beer garden and new terrace. Children welcome.

Bedrooms: 4 double/twin, 1 triple/multiple
Bathrooms: 4 en suite

Lunch available
Evening meal available
CC: Delta, Mastercard, Switch, Visa

Autumn 4 winter breaks-3 nights for price of 2. Guided walking and cycling holidays, organised golf breaks. Call for details.

ⓜ🐎🛏️👍🍷Ⓢ🔭🖥️🛋️🚶🎣🎵↑🏵️🅿

◆◆◆◆

PRIMROSE COTTAGE
Orton Road, Tebay, Penrith
CA10 3TL
T: (01539) 624791 & 07778 520930
E: primrosecottebay@aol.com

Bedrooms: 3 double/twin
Bathrooms: 1 en suite, 2 private

Evening meal available

B&B per night:
S £25.00–£30.00
D £40.00–£45.00

HB per person:
DY £31.00–£41.00

OPEN All year round

Close to M6, junction 38. Overnight stops/short breaks. North Lakes and Yorkshire Dales nearby. Excellent facilities include 4-poster bed, jacuzzi bath. Also self-catering flat and bungalow.

ⓜ🐎🛏️🖥️🛏️👍🍷Ⓢ🖥️🛋️🚶🏵️🐕🚌🅿

COLOUR MAPS Colour maps at the front of this guide pinpoint all places under which you will find accommodation listed.

GILL HEAD FARM

Troutbeck, Penrith CA11 0ST
T: (01768) 779652
F: (01768) 779130
E: gillhead@talk21.com
I: www.gillheadfarm.co.uk

B&B per night:
S £20.00
D £40.00

HB per person:
DY £28.00

OPEN All year round

Stay in our lovely 17thC farmhouse set against the dramatic backdrop of the northern fells, where a warm welcome and traditional hospitality is assured. Relax in the comfort of our attractive en suite rooms, log fires in our cosy oak-beamed sitting room and of course lots of delicious home cooking!

Bedrooms: 5 double/twin
Bathrooms: 5 en suite

Evening meal available

Discounts for group bookings.

HIGH FOLD FARM
Troutbeck, Windermere LA23 1PG
T: (015394) 32200
F: (015394) 34970

Bedrooms: 2 double/twin, 3 triple/multiple
Bathrooms: 3 en suite

B&B per night:
S £26.00–£34.00
D £42.00–£54.00

OPEN All year round

Unbeatable views over the Troutbeck Valley. Well furnished, comfortable accommodation of the highest standard. Excellent breakfasts. An ideal centre for walkers and for touring Lakeland.

HIGH GREEN LODGE
High Green, Troutbeck, Windermere LA23 1PN
T: (01539) 433005

Bedrooms: 3 double/twin
Bathrooms: 3 en suite

CC: Mastercard, Switch, Visa

B&B per night:
S £25.00–£45.00
D £50.00–£90.00

OPEN All year round

Here all mornings are magical – sun, swans, Swallows and Amazons. 2002 4-posters/jacuzzis, en suite/king-size rooms in peaceful lodge with fantastic views down valley/Lake Garbon Pass.

BANK HOUSE FARM

Matterdale End, Penrith CA11 0LF
T: (01768) 482040

B&B per night:
S £30.00
D £60.00

OPEN All year round

Set above the small Lakeland hamlet of Matterdale End with magnificent views of the Ullswater Fells. This delightful farmhouse offers a peaceful, tranquil base from which to explore the National Park. Comfortable surroundings, Aga-cooked breakfast and 7 acres to relax in, make this the perfect holiday location.

Bedrooms: 3 double/twin
Bathrooms: 3 en suite

Short breaks of 3 or more nights available at special rates.

CREDIT CARD BOOKINGS If you book by telephone and are asked for your credit card number it is advisable to check the proprietor's policy should you cancel your reservation.

Silver Award ◆◆◆◆

ELM HOUSE

Pooley Bridge, Penrith CA10 2NH
T: (01768) 486334
F: (01768) 486851
E: b&b@elmhouse.demon.co.uk
I: www.elmhouse.demon.co.uk

B&B per night:
S £25.00–£28.00
D £38.00–£45.00

OPEN All year round

Splendid Victorian family-run bed and breakfast on fringe of Pooley Bridge, a short stroll away from Lake Ullswater. Warm, friendly welcome assured in comfortable, relaxed surroundings. Our renowned breakfasts use only good quality, fresh, local produce. Ideal base for exploring lakes/fells. Easy reach of M6.

Bedrooms: 5 double/twin
Bathrooms: 4 en suite, 1 private

CC: Delta, Mastercard, Switch, Visa

Discount for 3 nights or more-10% per room for 3rd and any further consecutive night (not Bank Hols).

◆◆◆

KNOTTS MILL COUNTRY LODGE

Watermillock, Penrith CA11 0JN
T: (01768) 486699
E: knottsmill@cwcom.net
I: www.knottsmill.cwc.net

B&B per night:
S £25.00–£37.50
D £47.00–£55.00

HB per person:
DY £35.50–£42.45

OPEN All year round

A country lodge offering quality serviced accommodation and delicious home-cooked food. In private grounds set in magnificent scenery around Ullswater with stunning views of the surrounding hills. Ideal for walking, touring, bird-watching and sailing. Relaxed welcoming atmosphere in a peaceful setting, yet only 10 minutes from the M6.

Bedrooms: 6 double/twin, 3 triple/multiple
Bathrooms: 9 en suite

Evening meal available
CC: Delta, Mastercard, Switch, Visa

Off-peak discounts, e.g. 7 for 6. 'Special Occasion Breaks'. Ullswater Steamers and Rheged discount vouchers. All inclusive, guided walking holidays.

◆◆◆

LAND ENDS

Watermillock, Ullswater, Penrith CA11 0NB
T: (01768) 486438
F: (01768) 486959
E: infolandends@btinternet.com
I: www.landends.btinternet.co.uk

B&B per night:
S £30.00
D £52.00–£56.00

OPEN All year round

A haven of peace and quiet, set in 25 acres with two pretty lakes, ducks, red squirrels and wonderful birdlife, our traditional farmhouse has been tastefully restored providing en suite bedrooms, one with 4-poster. Light snacks available evenings. Cosy lounge and bar. Close to lake Ullswater and high fells.

Bedrooms: 3 single, 6 double/twin
Bathrooms: 9 en suite

Evening meal available

SPECIAL BREAKS

Many establishments offer special promotions and themed breaks. These are highlighted in red. (All such offers are subject to availability.)

ULLSWATER continued

◆◆◆

MOSS CRAG
Eagle Road, Glenridding, Penrith CA11 0PA
T: (01768) 482500 & 0789 9777419
F: (01768) 482500
E: info@mosscrag.co.uk
I: www.mosscrag.co.uk

B&B per night:
S £30.00–£35.00
D £41.00–£57.00

HB per person:
DY £36.00–£43.00

OPEN Jan–Nov

Small, friendly family-run guesthouse overlooking Glenridding Beck, and close to Ullswater shore. Individually tastefully decorated rooms await your arrival. All rooms have TV, hospitality tray, etc. A good wholesome breakfast will start your day, whether walking, climbing, fishing, sailing or just touring the area.

Bedrooms: 6 double/twin
Bathrooms: 4 en suite

3 day and weekly break packages.

Lunch available
Evening meal available
CC: Delta, Mastercard, Switch, Visa

ᗯ੭5🛏🖪⌨⬇♨🍸Ⓢ⅋♿🖩🛋♨️🚲🅿

ULVERSTON, Cumbria Map ref 5A3 *Tourist Information Centre Tel: (01229) 587120*

◆◆◆◆

VIRGINIA HOUSE HOTEL
24 Queen Street, Ulverston
LA12 7AF
T: (01229) 584844
F: (01229) 588565
E: virginia@ulverstonhotels.co.uk
I: www.ulverstonhotels.com

Bedrooms: 3 single,
4 double/twin
Bathrooms: 7 en suite

CC: Amex, Delta, Diners, Mastercard, Switch, Visa

B&B per night:
S £25.00–£40.00
D £50.00–£65.00

OPEN All year round

Elegant Georgian townhouse situated in the town centre, Grade II Listed building

📞🖪⌨⬇♨🍸Ⓢ⅋♿🖩🛋☼🚲🏠

WHITEHAVEN, Cumbria Map ref 5A3 *Tourist Information Centre Tel: (01946) 852939*

◆◆◆◆

CORKICKLE GUEST HOUSE
1 Corkickle, Whitehaven CA28 8AA
T: (01946) 692073
F: (01946) 692073
E: corkickle@tinyworld.co.uk

Bedrooms: 2 single,
4 double/twin
Bathrooms: 4 en suite,
2 private

Evening meal available

B&B per night:
S £22.50–£35.00
D £45.00–£50.00

OPEN All year round

Elegant Georgian townhouse close to town centre, offering high standards of comfort. Ideal base for business or leisure visitors.

ᗯ੭🖪⌨⬇♨Ⓢ⅋♿🖩🛋☼🐕🚲🏠🅿

WINDERMERE, Cumbria Map ref 5A3 *Tourist Information Centre Tel: (015394) 46499*

See also Bowness-on-Windermere

◆◆◆

APPLEGARTH HOTEL
College Road, Windermere LA23 1BU
T: (015394) 43206
F: (015394) 46636
I: www.smoothhound.co.uk/hotels/apple.html

B&B per night:
S £25.00–£50.00
D £40.00–£76.00

OPEN All year round

Detached, elegant Victorian mansion house in quiet area of central Windermere. Large, comfortable bar, sun lounge, car park, fell views. Four-poster rooms. Warm welcome and excellent service. Free leisure facilities nearby.

Bedrooms: 4 single,
11 double/twin, 3 triple/multiple
Bathrooms: 18 en suite

CC: Delta, Mastercard, Switch, Visa

3 nights mid-week from £66pp, weekend from £75pp.

ᗯ੭10🛏📞🖪⌨⬇♨🍸Ⓢ⅋♿🖩🛋☼🐕🚲🏠🅿

MAP REFERENCES The map references refer to the colour maps at the front of this guide. The first figure is the map number; the letter and figure which follow indicate the grid reference on the map.

◆◆◆

APPLETHWAITE HOUSE

1 Upper Oak Street, Windermere LA23 2LB
T: (015394) 44689
E: applethwaitehouse@btinternet.com
I: www.btinternet.com/
~applethwaitehouse

B&B per night:
S £16.00–£40.00
D £32.00–£52.00

OPEN All year round

We offer you a warm welcome and a hearty breakfast in our family-run guesthouse. Clean, comfortable rooms with colour TV and complimentary hot drinks. Situated in a quiet cul-del-sac just minutes from the village centre. Garage for cycle storage. Families, vegetarians and pets all most welcome.

Bedrooms: 1 double/
twin, 3 triple/multiple
Bathrooms: 3 en suite,
1 private

CC: Delta, Diners,
Mastercard, Switch, Visa

◆◆◆◆

THE ARCHWAY

13 College Road, Windermere LA23 1BU
T: (01539) 445613 & 445328
F: (01539) 445328
E: archway@btinternet.com
I: www.communiken.com/archway

B&B per night:
S £25.00–£40.00
D £40.00–£60.00

HB per person:
DY £40.00–£45.00

OPEN All year round

The Archway is a comfortable Victorian guesthouse, entirely non-smoking, tastefully furnished with superb mountain views and a breakfast well worth getting up for. Quietly situated yet close to the centre of Windermere or the railway station. Easy access to the Lakes and an ideal base for touring.

Bedrooms: 4 double/
twin, 1 triple/multiple
Bathrooms: 5 en suite

Lunch available
Evening meal available

◆◆◆

AUTUMN LEAVES GUEST HOUSE

29 Broad Street, Windermere
LA23 2AB
T: (01539) 448410

Bedrooms: 1 single,
4 double/twin, 1 triple/
multiple
Bathrooms: 3 en suite

CC: Delta, Mastercard,
Switch, Visa

B&B per night:
D £30.00–£50.00

OPEN All year round

A comfortable Victorian guesthouse located in the heart of Windermere, providing an excellent quality of service and friendly atmosphere.

◆◆◆◆◆

**Silver
Award**

THE BEAUMONT

Holly Road, Windermere LA23 2AF
T: (01539) 447075
F: (01539) 447075
E: thebeaumonthotel@btinternnet.com
I: www.lakesbeaumont.co.uk

B&B per night:
S £32.00–£40.00
D £56.00–£98.00

OPEN Feb–Nov

The Beaumont is an elegant Victorian villa occupying an enviable position for all amenities of Windermere/Bowness and is an ideal base from which to explore Lakeland. The highest standards prevail and the lovely en suite bedrooms are immaculate. We provide all modern comforts, superb breakfasts, genuine hospitality, excellent value. Private car park.

Bedrooms: 1 single,
8 double/twin, 1 triple/
multiple
Bathrooms: 10 en suite

CC: Delta, Mastercard,
Switch, Visa

Please ring or e-mail for details of current special offers. Free leisure facilities at nearby country club.

WINDERMERE continued

◆◆ BOWFELL COTTAGE

Middle Entrance Drive, Storrs Park, Bowness-on-Windermere, Windermere LA23 3JY
T: (01539) 444835

Bedrooms: 2 double/ twin, 1 triple/multiple
Bathrooms: 1 en suite

Evening meal available

B&B per night:
S £20.00–£25.00
D £40.00–£45.00

HB per person:
DY £31.50–£34.00

OPEN All year round

Cottage in a delightful setting, about 1 mile south of Bowness just off the A5074, offering traditional Lakeland hospitality. Secluded parking in own grounds.

◆◆◆ BROOK HOUSE

30 Ellerthwaite Road, Windermere LA23 2AH
T: (01539) 444932

Bedrooms: 1 single, 5 double/twin
Bathrooms: 3 en suite

B&B per night:
S £17.00–£20.00
D £35.00–£50.00

OPEN All year round

This immaculately kept guesthouse, in a quiet part of Windermere, offers en suite facilities, tea/coffee making, private car park, good food, warm personal welcome.

◆◆◆ BROOKLANDS

Ferry View, Bowness-on-Windermere, Windermere LA23 3JB
T: (01539) 442344
E: brooklandsferryview@btinternet.com
I: www.smoothhound.co.uk/hotels/brooklands

Bedrooms: 1 single, 3 double/twin, 2 triple/multiple
Bathrooms: 5 en suite, 1 private

Evening meal available
CC: Delta, Mastercard, Switch, Visa

B&B per night:
S £20.00–£25.00
D £36.00–£50.00

HB per person:
DY £28.00–£35.00

OPEN All year round

Comfortable guesthouse in rural setting on the outskirts of Bowness, with fine views of the lake and Cumbrian fells. Close to Lake Windermere marina and shops. Golf nearby. Car parking.

◆◆◆ CLIFTON HOUSE

28 Ellerthwaite Road, Windermere LA23 2AH
T: (01539) 444968
E: info@cliftonhse.co.uk
I: www.cliftonhse.co.uk

Bedrooms: 1 single, 3 double/twin, 1 triple/multiple
Bathrooms: 5 en suite

B&B per night:
S £15.00–£44.00
D £30.00–£50.00

OPEN All year round

Small, family-run guesthouse, situated in a very quiet part of the village. Excellent English breakfast. Friendly service.

◆◆◆ COLLEGE HOUSE

15 College Road, Windermere LA23 1BU
T: (01539) 445767 & 0798 0000992
E: clghse@aol.com
I: www.college-house.com

Bedrooms: 3 double/twin
Bathrooms: 3 en suite

B&B per night:
S £25.00–£30.00
D £36.00–£56.00

OPEN All year round

Warm, comfortable, Victorian family house. En suite rooms with gorgeous mountain views. Nice garden. Quiet location. Close to village centre. Private parking. Non-smoking.

◆◆◆ DUNVEGAN GUEST HOUSE

Broad Street, Windermere LA23 2AB
T: (01539) 443502
F: (01539) 447721
E: bryan.twaddle@btinternet.com
I: www.smoothhound.co.uk/hotels/dunvegan

Bedrooms: 1 single, 2 double/twin, 1 triple/multiple
Bathrooms: 3 en suite, 1 private

B&B per night:
S £19.00–£23.00
D £34.00–£46.00

Dunvegan is a friendly, family-run guesthouse, quietly situated away from the main road in Windermere village. A traditional Lakeland-stone house.

CONFIRM YOUR BOOKING
You are advised to confirm your booking in writing.

◆◆◆◆

THE FAIRFIELD

Brantfell Road, Bowness-on-Windermere,
Windermere LA23 3AE
T: (01539) 446565
F: (01539) 446565
E: ray&barb@the-fairfield.co.uk
I: www.the-fairfield.co.uk

B&B per night:
S £26.00–£33.00
D £52.00–£66.00

OPEN Feb–Nov

*Small, friendly, family-run, 200-
year-old Lakeland guesthouse for
non-smokers. Set in a peaceful
garden environment, close to
Bowness village and lake shore.
Well-appointed and tastefully
furnished bedrooms all with TV,
hairdryers, welcome tray,etc.
Breakfasts are a speciality. Leisure
club facilities nearby. Genuine
hospitality and a warm welcome.*

Bedrooms: 1 single,
6 double/twin, 2 triple/
multiple
Bathrooms: 8 en suite,
1 private

CC: Delta, Mastercard,
Switch, Visa

Reduced prices of 2, 3 or more nights.

◆◆◆◆

FIR TREES

Lake Road, Windermere LA23 2EQ
T: (01539) 442272
F: (01539) 442512
E: firtreeshotel@email.msn.com
I: www.fir-trees.com

B&B per night:
S £30.00–£45.00
D £44.00–£60.00

OPEN All year round

*Built in 1888 as a Victorian
gentleman's residence and offering
elegant accommodation. Situated
between Windermere village and the
lake. Lovely bedrooms, scrumptious
breakfasts and warm hospitality at
exceptional value for money. Guests
staying 2 nights or more have free
use of Parklands Country Club leisure
facilities.*

Bedrooms: 6 double/
twin, 2 triple/multiple
Bathrooms: 8 en suite

CC: Amex, Delta,
Mastercard, Switch, Visa

Mid-week special offers Nov-Mar (excl Christmas
and New Year).

◆◆◆

FIRGARTH

Ambleside Road, Windermere
LA23 1EU
T: (01539) 446974
F: (01539) 442384
E: thefirgarth@netscapeonline.co.
uk

Bedrooms: 1 single,
3 double/twin, 4 triple/
multiple
Bathrooms: 8 en suite

CC: Amex, Delta, Diners,
Mastercard, Switch, Visa

B&B per night:
S £17.50–£25.00
D £35.00–£45.00

OPEN All year round

*Elegant Victorian country house offering good breakfast, friendly atmosphere, private
parking, close to lake viewpoint. Ideally situated for touring all areas of Lakeland. Tours
arranged.*

◆◆◆

GREENRIGGS GUEST HOUSE

8 Upper Oak Street, Windermere
LA23 2LB
T: (01539) 442265
F: (01539) 442265
E: greenriggs@talk21.com

Bedrooms: 2 single,
4 double/twin, 1 triple/
multiple
Bathrooms: 4 en suite

B&B per night:
S £15.00–£25.00
D £30.00–£50.00

OPEN All year round

*Comfortable, friendly guesthouse. Central but quiet, convenient for shops, buses and
trains. Single, double and family/twin rooms, parking. Seven minutes' walk from station.
Tours arranged.*

RATING All accommodation in this guide has been rated, or is awaiting
a rating, by a trained English Tourism Council assessor.

WINDERMERE continued

◆◆◆◆

HAZELBANK

Hazel Street, Windermere LA23 1EL
T: (01539) 445486
F: (01539) 445486

B&B per night:
S £30.00–£35.00
D £45.00–£60.00

OPEN All year round

Elegant detached Victorian house with matured walled garden and own private car park; situated in a quiet cul-de-sac close to the centre of Windermere village. En suite bedrooms (including four-poster) are spacious and individually decorated. Non-smoking.

Bedrooms: 3 double/ twin
Bathrooms: 3 en suite

Please enquire about spring, autumn, pre-Christmas and New Year breaks and offers.

 P

◆◆◆◆

Silver Award

HIGH VIEW

Sun Hill Lane, Troutbeck Bridge, Windermere LA23 1HJ
T: (01539) 444618 & 442731
F: (01539) 444618
E: info@accommodationlakedistrict.com
I: www.accommodationlakedistrict.com

Bedrooms: 1 double/ twin, 1 triple/multiple
Bathrooms: 2 en suite

B&B per night:
S £19.50–£24.00
D £39.00–£48.00

OPEN All year round

A delightful bungalow in an elevated position overlooking Lake Windermere. Within walking distance of Troutbeck, Windermere and Bowness. Breakfast a real speciality.

P

◆◆◆

HOLLY LODGE

6 College Road, Windermere LA23 1BX
T: (01539) 443873
F: (01539) 443873
E: doyle@hollylodge20.fsnet.co.uk

B&B per night:
S £19.00–£27.00
D £38.00–£54.00

OPEN All year round

Traditional Lakeland family-run guesthouse in a quiet location close to shops, restaurants, buses and trains. Friendly atmosphere. Good English breakfast with varied menu. Each bedroom individually furbished, with refreshment tray. Separate lounge with open fire. Advice is readily available to make your stay with us memorable.

Bedrooms: 1 single, 7 double/twin, 3 triple/ multiple
Bathrooms: 6 en suite

CC: Delta, Mastercard, Switch, Visa

P

◆◆◆◆

HOLLY PARK HOUSE

1 Park Road, Windermere LA23 2AW
T: (01539) 442107
F: (01539) 448997
I: www.s-h-systems.co.uk/hotels/hollypk.html

Bedrooms: 3 double/ twin, 3 triple/multiple
Bathrooms: 6 en suite

CC: Amex, Delta, Diners, Mastercard, Switch, Visa

B&B per night:
S £30.00–£40.00
D £42.00–£62.00

OPEN All year round

Handsome stone-built Victorian guesthouse with spacious en suite rooms. Quiet area, but convenient for village shops, coach and rail services.

P

IMPORTANT NOTE Information on accommodation listed in this guide has been supplied by the proprietors. As changes may occur you are advised to check details at the time of booking.

WINDERMERE continued

◆◆◆ **HOLMLEA**

Kendal Road, Bowness-on-Windermere, Windermere
LA23 3EW
T: (01539) 442597

Bedrooms: 2 single, 4 double/twin
Bathrooms: 4 en suite

B&B per night:
S £20.00–£28.00
D £40.00–£56.00

OPEN All year round

Friendly, comfortable guesthouse in quiet location 3 minutes' walk from lake and amenities. Car park, generous breakfast, warm welcome assured.

◆◆◆ **KAYS COTTAGE**

7 Broad Street, Windermere
LA23 2AB
T: (01539) 444146
F: (01539) 444146
E: kayscottage@freenetname.co.uk
I: www.kayscottage.co.uk

Bedrooms: 1 single, 2 double/twin, 2 triple/multiple
Bathrooms: 5 en suite

CC: Delta, Mastercard, Switch, Visa

B&B per night:
S £20.00–£30.00
D £40.00–£52.00

OPEN All year round

Friendly, comfortable cottage, ideally situated, with large en suite bedrooms, colour TVs and generous breakfasts. Prices shown do not apply to Easter.

◆◆◆◆◆
Silver
Award

LAKESHORE HOUSE

Ecclerigg, Windermere LA23 1LJ
T: (01539) 433202
F: (01539) 433213
E: lakeshore@lakedistrict.uk.com
I: www.lakedistrict.uk.com

B&B per night:
S £85.00–£112.50
D £130.00–£170.00

OPEN All year round

Fine lodgings in a haven of peace and tranquillity for the discerning on the shores of Lake Windermere. Unsurpassed comfort in glorious surroundings – with simply the best view in England. Highest standard bed/breakfast with own private access. Breakfast is served in Lakeshore's 45ft long, carpeted conservatory/pool.

Bedrooms: 3 double/twin; suites available
Bathrooms: 3 en suite

CC: Mastercard, Switch, Visa

3 nights, 10% discount. 5 nights, 15% discount.

◆◆◆ **LINDISFARNE**

Sunny Bank Road, Windermere
LA23 2EN
T: (01539) 446295 & 0775 9925528
F: (01539) 46295
E: lindisfarne@zoom.co.uk

Bedrooms: 3 double/twin, 1 triple/multiple
Bathrooms: 2 en suite, 2 private

Evening meal available

B&B per night:
S £20.00–£25.00
D £37.00–£45.00

HB per person:
DY £30.00–£33.00

OPEN All year round

Traditional detached Lakeland stone house, ideally situated in quiet area, close to lake, shops and scenic walks. Varied breakfasts, friendly and flexible hours.

◆◆◆◆

LINGWOOD

Birkett Hill, Bowness-on-Windermere, Windermere LA23 3EZ
T: (01539) 444680
F: (01539) 448154
E: enquiries@lingwood-guesthouse.co.uk
I: www.lingwood-guesthouse.co.uk

B&B per night:
S £19.00–£30.00
D £38.00–£60.00

OPEN All year round

Small, friendly, family-run guesthouse set in own gardens but within 400 yards of lake shore, shops and restaurants. Hearty breakfast provided. With ample private car parking and safe storage for bicycles, Lingwood is ideally placed for exploring both the Lake District and surrounding areas.

Bedrooms: 3 double/twin, 3 triple/multiple
Bathrooms: 4 en suite, 2 private

CC: Delta, Mastercard, Switch, Visa

3 nights for the price of 2 Nov–Mar (excl Bank Hols).

◆◆◆◆

RAYRIGG VILLA GUEST HOUSE

Ellerthwaite Square, Windermere LA23 1DP
T: (01539) 488342
E: rayriggvilla@nascr.net
I: www.rayriggvilla.co.uk

B&B per night:
S £25.00–£35.00
D £40.00–£60.00

OPEN All year round

Lakeland-stone detached guesthouse built in 1873 as the home for a prosperous corn merchant. Ideally situated on edge of Windermere village, facing Library Gardens. All bedrooms have en suite or private facilities. Extensive full English breakfast with alternatives. Private parking. Convenient for buses and trains. A warm welcome assured.

Bedrooms: 6 double/ twin, 1 triple/multiple
Bathrooms: 5 en suite, 2 private

CC: Delta, Mastercard, Switch, Visa

Reductions available for breaks of 3 nights or more (excl Bank Holiday periods).

 🐎 ♨ ▢ ♦ ⑤ ⊀ 🏄 🎞 🍴 🚗 P

◆◆◆

ST JOHN'S LODGE

Lake Road, Windermere LA23 2EQ
T: (01539) 443078
F: (01539) 488054
E: mail@st-johns-lodge.co.uk
I: www.st-johns-lodge.co.uk

B&B per night:
S £20.00–£30.00
D £38.00–£60.00

OPEN All year round

Attractive Lakeland guesthouse ideally situated between Windermere village and the lake and Bowness and close to all amenities. Well known for excellent quality and choice of breakfasts and comfortable, spotlessly clean en suite bedrooms. We offer a relaxed atmosphere, good service, a little bit of humour and excellent value for money.

Bedrooms: 2 single, 9 double/twin, 3 triple/ multiple
Bathrooms: 12 en suite, 2 private

Evening meal available
CC: Delta, Mastercard, Switch, Visa

🏨 🐎 4 ♨ ▢ ♦ ⑤ ⊀ 🎞 🍴 🐴 🚗 🖐 P

◆◆◆

SANDOWN

Lake Road, Bowness-on-Windermere, Windermere LA23 2JF
T: (01539) 445275
F: (01539) 445275

Bedrooms: 7 double/ twin
Bathrooms: 7 en suite

B&B per night:
S £25.00–£38.00
D £44.00–£60.00

OPEN All year round

Large modern detached house, set in landscaped area with trees and shrubs, 10 minutes' walk from Lake Windermere. Golf, riding, sailing nearby. Safe parking in grounds. SAE or telephone for details.

🏨 ♨ ▢ ♦ ⑤ 🏄 🎞 🍴 ♿ ∪ � 🐴 🚗 🖐 P

◆◆

UPPER OAKMERE

3 Upper Oak Street, Windermere LA23 2LB
T: (01539) 445649 & 07798 806732
E: upperoakmere@hotmail.com
I: www.upperoakmere.co.uk

Bedrooms: 4 double/ twin, 1 triple/multiple
Bathrooms: 3 en suite

B&B per night:
S £16.00–£22.00
D £32.00–£44.00

OPEN All year round

Ideal location, 100 yards from main High Street. Friendly atmosphere, home cooking. Single people/party bookings. Pets welcome. Fifteen minutes' walk to Lake Windermere.

🏨 🐎 ▢ ♦ ⑤ ⊀ 🏄 🎞 🍴 ∪ ↄ 🐴 🚗 🏡 P

♦♦♦♦

VILLA LODGE GUEST HOUSE

25 Cross Street, Windermere LA23 1AE
T: (01539) 443318
F: (01539) 443318
E: rooneym@btconnect.com
I: www.villa-lodge.co.uk

Traditional Lakeland guesthouse in an elevated setting in Windermere. All bedrooms en suite, 4-poster bed for that special occasion. Excellent home cooking, evening meal optional extra. Residential licence. Two minutes from rail and bus station. Private car park. Pets welcome by arrangement.

Bedrooms: 2 single, 6 double/twin
Bathrooms: 8 en suite

Evening meal available
CC: Delta, Mastercard, Switch, Visa

B&B per night:
S £24.00–£35.00
D £48.00–£70.00

HB per person:
DY £39.00–£50.00

OPEN All year round

♦♦♦

WESTLAKE HOTEL

Lake Road, Windermere LA23 2EQ
T: (01539) 443020
F: (01539) 443020
E: westlake@clara.net

Bedrooms: 5 double/twin, 2 triple/multiple
Bathrooms: 7 en suite

Evening meal available

Small, friendly hotel near lake, restaurants. All rooms en suite with colour TV, tea/coffee, hairdryer. Four-poster, de luxe doubles, lounge, car parking. English/continental breakfast.

B&B per night:
S £20.00–£25.00
D £38.00–£52.00

HB per person:
DY Min £34.50

OPEN All year round

♦♦♦

MORVEN GUEST HOUSE

Siddick Road, Siddick, Workington CA14 1LE
T: (01900) 602118
F: (01900) 602118
E: cnelsonmorven@aol.com

Bedrooms: 2 single, 4 double/twin
Bathrooms: 6 en suite

Lunch available
Evening meal available

Detached house north-west of town. Ideal base for western Lakes and coast. Start of C2C cycleway. Car park, cycle storage.

B&B per night:
S £24.00–£28.00
D £44.00–£48.00

OPEN All year round

QUALITY ASSURANCE SCHEME

For an explanation of the quality and facilities represented by the Diamonds please refer to the front of this guide. A more detailed explanation can be found in the information pages at the back.

A brief guide to the main Towns and Villages offering accommodation in Cumbria

A ALLONBY, CUMBRIA - Small village on Solway Firth with good sandy beaches, once famous for its herring fishing and as a fashionable resort of Victorian gentry. Good views across the Firth to Criffel and the Galloway mountains.

• **ALSTON, CUMBRIA** - Alston is the highest market town in England, set amongst the highest fells of the Pennines and close to the Pennine Way in an Area of Outstanding Natural Beauty. Mainly 17th C buildings and steep, cobbled streets.

• **AMBLESIDE, CUMBRIA** - Market town situated at the head of Lake Windermere and surrounded by fells. The historic town centre is now a conservation area and the country around Ambleside is rich in historic and literary associations. Good centre for touring, walking and climbing.

• **APPLEBY-IN-WESTMORLAND, CUMBRIA** - Former county town of Westmorland, at the foot of the Pennines in the Eden Valley. The castle was rebuilt in the 17th C, except for its Norman keep, ditches and ramparts. It now houses a Rare Breeds Survival Trust Centre. Good centre for exploring the Eden Valley.

B BARROW-IN-FURNESS, CUMBRIA - On the Furness Peninsula in Morecambe Bay, an industrial and commercial centre with sandy beaches and nature reserves on Walney Island. Ruins of 12th C Cistercian Furness Abbey. The Dock Museum tells the story of the area and Forum 28 houses a modern theatre and arts centre.

• **BASSENTHWAITE LAKE, CUMBRIA** - The northernmost and only true 'lake' in the Lake District. Visited annually by many species of migratory birds.

• **BORROWDALE, CUMBRIA** - Stretching south of Derwentwater to Seathwaite in the heart of the Lake District, the valley is walled by high fellsides. It can justly claim to be the most scenically impressive valley in the Lake District. Excellent centre for walking and climbing.

• **BOWLAND BRIDGE, CUMBRIA** - Pretty hamlet in the Lyth Valley. Ideal starting point for rambling woodland and country walks.

• **BOWNESS-ON-SOLWAY, CUMBRIA** - Coastal village near the site of the Roman fort Maia at the western end of Hadrian's Wall.

• **BOWNESS-ON-WINDERMERE, CUMBRIA** - Bowness is the older of the two towns of Bowness and Windermere and dates from the 11th C. It is a busy tourist resort set on the shores of Lake Windermere, England's largest lake. Good location for touring, walking, boating and fishing.

• **BRAITHWAITE, CUMBRIA** - Braithwaite nestles at the foot of the Whinlatter Pass and has a magnificent backdrop of the mountains forming the Coledale Horseshoe.

• **BRAMPTON, CUMBRIA** - Excellent centre for exploring Hadrian's Wall. Wednesday is market day around the Moot Hall in this delightful sandstone-built town. Wall plaque marks the site of Bonnie Prince Charlie and his Jacobite army headquarters whilst they laid siege to Carlisle Castle in 1745.

• **BROUGHTON-IN-FURNESS, CUMBRIA** - Old market village whose historic charter to hold fairs is still proclaimed every year on the first day of August in the market square. Good centre for touring the pretty Duddon Valley.

C CALDBECK, CUMBRIA - Quaint limestone village lying on the northern fringe of the Lake District National Park. John Peel, the famous huntsman who is immortalised in song, is buried in the churchyard. The fells surrounding Caldbeck were once heavily mined, being rich in lead, copper and barytes.

• **CARLISLE, CUMBRIA** - Cumbria's only city is rich in history. Attractions include the small red sandstone cathedral and 900-year-old castle with magnificent view from the keep. Award-winning Tullie House Museum and Art Gallery brings 2,000 years of Border history dramatically to life. Excellent centre for shopping.

• **COCKERMOUTH, CUMBRIA** - Ancient market town at confluence of Rivers Cocker and Derwent. Birthplace of William Wordsworth in 1770. The house where he was born is at the end of the town's broad, tree-lined main street and is now owned by the National Trust. Good touring base for the Lakes.

• **CONISTON, CUMBRIA** - The 803m fell Coniston Old Man dominates the skyline to the east of this village at the northern end of Coniston Water. Arthur Ransome set his 'Swallows and Amazons' stories here. Coniston's most famous resident was John Ruskin, whose home, Brantwood, is open to the public. Good centre for walking.

• **CROSTHWAITE, CUMBRIA** - Small village in the picturesque Lyth Valley off the A5074.

D DALTON-IN-FURNESS, CUMBRIA - Conveniently located between Ulverston and Barrow. There exists the remains of a 14th C tower in the main street of the village.

G GRANGE-OVER-SANDS, CUMBRIA - Set on the beautiful Cartmel Peninsula, this tranquil resort, known as Lakeland's Riviera, overlooks Morecambe Bay. Pleasant seafront walks and beautiful gardens. The bay attracts many species of wading birds.

• **GRASMERE, CUMBRIA** - Described by William Wordsworth as 'the loveliest spot that man hath ever found', this village, famous for its gingerbread, is in a beautiful setting overlooked by Helm Grag. Wordsworth lived at Dove Cottage. The cottage and museum are open to the public.

H HAWKSHEAD, CUMBRIA - Lying near Esthwaite Water, this village has great charm and character. Its small squares are linked by flagged or cobbled alleys and the main square is dominated by the market house, or Shambles, where the butchers had their stalls in days gone by.

K KENDAL, CUMBRIA - The 'Auld Grey Town' lies in the valley of the River Kent with a backcloth of limestone fells. Situated just outside the Lake District National Park, it is a good centre for touring the Lakes and surrounding country. Ruined castle, reputed birthplace of Catherine Parr.

• **KESWICK, CUMBRIA** - Beautifully positioned town beside Derwentwater and below the mountains of Skiddaw and Blencathra. Excellent base for walking, climbing, watersports and touring. Motor-launches operate on Derwentwater and motor boats, rowing boats and canoes can be hired.

• **KIRKBY LONSDALE, CUMBRIA** - Charming old town of narrow streets and Georgian buildings, set in the superb scenery of the Lune Valley. The Devil's Bridge over the River Lune is probably 13th C.

- **KIRKBY STEPHEN, CUMBRIA** - Old market town close to the River Eden, with many fine Georgian buildings and an attractive market square. St Stephen's Church is known as the 'Cathedral of the Dales'. Good base for exploring the Eden Valley and the Dales.

L LAKESIDE, CUMBRIA - Lakeside lies at the foot of Lake Windermere and is linking point between the Lakeside and Haverthwaite Railway and the Windermere steamers, both of which run during the summer months.

M MILLOM, CUMBRIA - Town on the west side of the Duddon Estuary and once a busy centre for iron ore. Birthplace of poet Norman Nicholson, who is celebrated in the town's Folk Museum.

- **MUNGRISDALE, CUMBRIA** - Set in an unspoilt valley, this hamlet has a simple, white church with a 3-decker pulpit and box pews.

N NEAR SAWREY, CUMBRIA - Lies near Esthwaite water. Famous for Hill Top Farm, home of Beatrix Potter, now owned by the National Trust and open to the public.

P PENRITH, CUMBRIA - Ancient and historic market town, the northern gateway to the Lake District. Penrith Castle was built as a defence against the Scots. Its ruins, open to the public, stand in the public park. High above the town is the Penrith Beacon, made famous by William Wordsworth.

S SAWREY, CUMBRIA - Far Sawrey and Near Sawrey lie near Esthwaite Water. Both villages are small but Near Sawrey is famous for Hill Top Farm, home of Beatrix Potter, now owned by the National Trust and open to the public.

- **SEASCALE, CUMBRIA** - Attractive small seaside town with an uncrowded sand and shingle beach.

- **SEDBERGH, CUMBRIA** - This busy market town set below the Howgill Fells is an excellent centre for walkers and touring the Dales and Howgills. The noted boys' school was founded in 1525.

- **STAVELEY, CUMBRIA** - Large village built in slate, set between Kendal and Windermere at the entrance to the lovely Kentmere Valley.

T TEBAY, CUMBRIA - Village lying amongst high fells at the north end of the Lune Gorge.

- **TROUTBECK, CUMBRIA** - Most of the houses in this picturesque village are 17th C, some retain their spinning galleries and oak-mullioned windows. At the south end of the village is Townend, owned by the National Trust and open to the public, an excellently preserved example of a yeoman farmer's or statesman's house.

- **TROUTBECK, CUMBRIA** - On the Penrith to Keswick road, Troutbeck was the site of a series of Roman camps. The village now hosts a busy weekly sheep market.

U ULLSWATER, CUMBRIA - This beautiful lake, which is over 7 miles long, runs from Glenridding to Pooley Bridge. Lofty peaks ranging around the lake make an impressive background. A steamer service operates along the lake between Pooley Bridge, Howtown and Glenridding in the summer.

- **ULVERSTON, CUMBRIA** - Market town lying between green fells and the sea. There is a replica of the Eddystone lighthouse on the Hoad which is a monument to Sir John Barrow, founder of the Royal Geographical Society. Birthplace of Stan Laurel, of Laurel and Hardy.

W WHITEHAVEN, CUMBRIA - Historic Georgian port on the west coast. The town was developed in the 17th C and many fine buildings have been preserved. The Beacon Heritage Centre includes a Meteorological Office Weather Gallery. Start or finishing point of Coast to Coast, Whitehaven to Sunderland, cycleway.

- **WINDERMERE, CUMBRIA** - Once a tiny hamlet before the introduction of the railway in 1847, now adjoins Bowness which is on the lakeside. Centre for sailing and boating. A good way to see the lake is a trip on a passenger steamer. Steamboat Museum has a fine collection of old boats.

- **WORKINGTON, CUMBRIA** - A deep-water port on the west Cumbrian coast. There are the ruins of the 14th C Workington Hall, where Mary Queen of Scots stayed in 1568.

NORTHUMBRIA

Romans, sailors and industrial pioneers have all left their mark here. Northumbria's exciting cities, castle – studded countryside and white-sanded coastline make it an undiscovered gem.

classic sights

Lindisfarne Castle – on Holy Island
Housesteads Roman Fort – the most impressive Roman fort on Hadrian's Wall

coast & country

Kielder Water and Forest Park – perfect for walking, cycling and watersports
Saltburn – beach of broad sands
Seahouses – picturesque fishing village

maritime history

HMS Trincomalee – magnificent 1817 British warship
Captain Cook – birthplace museum and replica of his ship, Endeavour
Grace Darling – museum commemorating her rescue of shipwreck survivors in 1838

arts for all

Angel of the North – awe-inspiring sculpture by Antony Gormley

distinctively different

St Mary's lighthouse – great views from the top

The counties of County Durham, Northumberland, Tees Valley and Tyne & Wear

FOR MORE INFORMATION CONTACT:
Northumbria Tourist Board
Aykley Heads, Durham DH1 5UX
Tel: (0191) 375 3009 Fax: (0191) 386 0899
Internet: www.visitnorthumbria.com

The Pictures:
1 Lindisfarne Castle, Holy Island
2 Bamburgh, Northumberland
3 Washington Old Hall,
   Tyne & Wear

Places to Visit - see pages 112-115
Where to Stay - see pages 116-135

PLACES to visit

You will find hundreds of interesting places to visit during your stay, just some of which are listed in these pages. Contact any Tourist Information Centre in the region for more ideas on days out.

Alnwick Castle

The Estate Office, Alnwick, Northumberland NE66 1NQ
Tel: (01665) 510777 www.alnwickcastle.com
Largest inhabited castle in England, after Windsor Castle, and home of the Percys, Dukes of Northumberland since 1309.

ARC

Dovecot Street, Stockton-on-Tees, Stockton TS18 1LL
Tel: (01642) 666600 www.arconline.co.uk
Arts venue which aims to provide the region with an extensive and innovative programme. Two theatres, a dance studio, recording studio and rehearsal rooms.

Bamburgh Castle

Bamburgh, Northumberland NE69 7DF
Tel: (01668) 214515 www.bamburghcastle.com
Magnificent coastal castle completely restored in 1900. Collections of china, porcelain, furniture, paintings, arms and armour.

Bede's World

Church Bank, Jarrow, Tyne & Wear NE32 3DY
Tel: (0191) 489 2106 www.bedesworld.co.uk
Discover the exciting world of the Venerable Bede, early medieval Europe's greatest scholar. Church, monastic site, museum with exhibitions and recreated Anglo-Saxon farm.

Bowes Museum

Barnard Castle, Durham DL12 8NP
Tel: (01833) 690606 www.bowesmuseum.org.uk
French-style chateau housing art collections of national importance and archaeology of south west Durham.

Captain Cook Birthplace Museum

Stewart Park, Marton, Middlesbrough, Cleveland TS7 6AS
Tel: (01642) 311211
Early life and voyages of Captain Cook and the countries he visited. Temporary exhibitions. One person free with every group of 10 visiting.

Chesters Roman Fort (Cilurnum)

Chollerford, Hadrian's Wall, Humshaugh, Hexham, Northumberland NE46 4EP
Tel: (01434) 681379
Fort built for 500 cavalrymen. Remains include 5 gateways, barrack blocks, commandant's house and headquarters. Finest military bath house in Britain.

Cragside House, Gardens and Estate

Cragside, Rothbury, Morpeth, Northumberland NE65 7PX
Tel: (01669) 620333 www.nationaltrust.org.uk
House built 1864-84 for the first Lord Armstrong, a Tyneside industrialist. Cragside was the first house to be lit by electricity generated by water power.

Discovery Museum

Blandford House, Blandford Square, Newcastle upon Tyne, Tyne & Wear NE1 4JA
Tel: (0191) 232 6789
The Museum is currently undergoing a £10.7 million redevelopment. Visit the Science Maze, Fashion Works, Live Wires, Maritime Gallery, A Soldier's Life Gallery and The Newcastle Story (the new John George Jolcey Museum).

Durham Castle

Palace Green, Durham DH1 3RW
Tel: (0191) 374 3863 www.durhamcastle.com
Castle founded in 1072, Norman chapel dating from 1080, kitchens and great hall dated 1499 and 1284 respectively. Fine example of motte-and-bailey castle.

Durham Cathedral

The Chapter Office, The College, Durham DH1 3EH
Tel: (0191) 386 4266 www.durhamcathedral.co.uk
Durham Cathedral is thought by many to be the finest example of Norman church architecture in England. Visit the tombs of St Cuthbert and The Venerable Bede.

Gisborough Priory

Church Street, Guisborough, Redcar & Cleveland TS14 6HG
Tel: (01287) 633801
Remains of a priory founded by Robert de Brus in AD1119. A priory for Augustinian canons in the grounds of Guisborough Hall. Main arch and window of east wall virtually intact.

Hall Hill Farm

Lanchester, Durham DH7 0TA
Tel: (01388) 730300 www.hallhillfarm.co.uk
Family fun set in attractive countryside with an opportunity to see and touch the animals at close quarters. Farm trailer ride, riverside walk, teashop and play area.

Hartlepool Historic Quay

Maritime Avenue, Hartlepool, Cleveland TS24 0XZ
Tel: (01429) 860006 www.thisishartlepool.com
Hartlepool Historic Quay is an exciting reconstruction of a seaport of the 1800s with buildings and lively quayside, authentically reconstructed.

Housesteads Roman Fort (Vercovicum)

Hadrian's Wall, Haydon Bridge, Hexham, Northumberland NE47 6NN
Tel: (01434) 344363
Best preserved and most impressive of the Roman forts. Vercovicium was a 5-acre fort for an extensive 800 civil settlement. Only example of a Roman hospital.

Killhope, The North of England Lead Mining Museum

Cowshill, Weardale, St John's Chapel, Bishop Auckland, County Durham DL13 1AR
Tel: (01388) 537505 www.durham.gov.uk/killhope
Most complete lead mining site in Great Britain. Mine tours available, 10m (34ft) diameter water-wheel, reconstruction of Victorian machinery, miners lodging and woodland walks.

Kirkleatham Old Hall Museum

Kirkleatham, Redcar, Redcar & Cleveland TS10 5NW
Tel: (01642) 479500
Displays depicting local life, industry, commerce, local history, sea rescue, artists, social and natural history and the story of Kirkleatham.

Laing Art Gallery

New Bridge Street, Newcastle upon Tyne, Tyne & Wear NE1 8AJ
Tel: (0191) 232 7734
Paintings, including watercolours by Northumbrian-born artist John Martin. Award-winning interactive displays 'Art on Tyneside' and 'Children's Gallery'. Cafe and shop.

Life Interactive World

Times Square, Scotswood Road, Newcastle upon Tyne, Tyne & Wear NE1 4EP
Tel: (0191) 243 8210 www.lifeinteractiveworld.co.uk
Life Interactive World is an amazing action-packed journey. Experience the longest motion ride in the world, magical 3D, theatre shows, virtual games and Interactives.

National Glass Centre

Liberty Way, Sunderland, Tyne & Wear SR6 0GL
Tel: (0191) 515 5555 www.nationalglasscentre.com
A large gallery presenting the best in contemporary and historical glass. Master craftspeople will demonstrate glass-making techniques. Classes and workshops available.

Nature's World at the Botanic Centre

Nature's World at the Botanic Centre
Ladgate Lane, Acklam, Middlesbrough,
Tees Valley TS5 7YN
Tel: (01642) 594895 www.naturesworld.org.uk
Demonstration gardens, wildlife pond, white garden, environmental exhibition hall, shop, tearooms and River Tees model now open. Hydroponicum and visitor exhibition centre.

Newcastle Cathedral Church of St Nicholas

St Nicholas Street, Newcastle upon Tyne,
Tyne & Wear NE1 1PF
Tel: (0191) 232 1939
www.newcastle-ang-cathedral-stnicholas.org.uk
13thC and 14thC church, added to in 18thC-20thC. Famous lantern tower, pre-reformation font and font cover, 15thC stained glass roundel in the side chapel.

The North of England Open Air Museum

Beamish, County Durham DH9 0RG
Tel: (0191) 370 4000 www.beamish.org.uk
Visit the town, colliery village, working farm, Pockerley Manor and 1825 railway, recreating life in the North East in the early 1800s and 1900s.

Ormesby Hall

Church Lane, Ormesby, Middlesbrough TS7 9AS
Tel: (01642) 324188 www.nationaltrust.org.uk
Georgian, 18thC mansion. Impressive contemporary plasterwork. Magnificent stable block attributed to Carr of York. Model railway exhibition and layout.

Raby Castle

PO Box 50, Staindrop, Darlington, County Durham DL2 3AH
Tel: (01833) 660202 www.rabycastle.com
The medieval castle, home of Lord Barnard's family since 1626, includes a 200-acre deer park, walled gardens, carriage collection, adventure playground, shop and tearooms.

Sea Life Aquarium

Grand Parade, Tynemouth, Tyne & Wear NE30 4JF
Tel: (0191) 257 6100
More than 30 hi-tech displays provide encounters with dozens of sea creatures. Journey beneath the North Sea and discover thousands of amazing creatures.

South Shields Museum and Art Gallery

Ocean Road, South Shields, Tyne & Wear NE33 2JA
Tel: (0191) 456 8740
Discover how the area's development has been influenced by its natural and industrial past through lively hands-on displays. Exciting programme of temporary exhibitions.

Thomas Bewick Birthplace Museum

Cherryburn, Station Bank, Mickley, Stocksfield,
Northumberland NE43 7DB
Tel: (01661) 843276
Birthplace cottage (1700) and farmyard. Printing house using original printing blocks. Introductory exhibition of the life, work and countryside.

Vindolanda (Chesterholm)

Chesterholm Museum, Hadrian's Wall, Bardon Mill,
Hexham, Northumberland NE47 7JN
Tel: (01434) 344277 www.vindolanda.com
Visitors may inspect the remains of the Roman fort and settlement, and see its extraordinary finds in the superb museum. Full-scale replicas of Roman buildings.

Washington Old Hall

The Avenue, District 4, Washington, Tyne & Wear NE38 7LE
Tel: (0191) 416 6879
From 1183 to 1399 the home of George Washington's direct ancestors, remaining in the family until 1613. The manor, from which the family took its name, was restored in 1936.

Wet 'N Wild

Rotary Way, Royal Quays, North Shields,
Tyne & Wear NE29 6DA
Tel: (0191) 296 1333 www.wetnwild.co.uk
Tropical indoor water park. A fun water playground providing the wildest and wettest indoor rapid experience. Whirlpools, slides and meandering lazy river.

Wildfowl and Wetlands Trust

Washington, District 15, Washington, Tyne & Wear NE38 8LE
Tel: (0191) 416 5454 www.wwt.org.uk
Collection of 1,000 wildfowl of 85 varieties. Viewing gallery, picnic areas, hides and winter wild bird-feeding station, flamingos and wild grey heron. Food available.

Find out more about Northumbria

Dunstanburgh Castle

Further information about holidays and attractions in Northumbria is available from:

NORTHUMBRIA TOURIST BOARD
Aykley Heads, Durham DH1 5UX.
Tel: (0191) 375 3009 Fax: (0191) 386 0899
Internet: www.visitnorthumbria.com

The following publications are available from Northumbria Tourist Board unless otherwise stated:

Northumbria 2002
information on the region, including hotels, bed and breakfast and self-catering accommodation, caravan and camping parks, attractions, shopping, eating and drinking

Going Places
information on where to go, what to see and what to do. Combined with the award-winning Powerpass promotion which offers 2-for-1 entry into many of the region's top attractions

Group Travel Directory
guide designed specifically for group organisers, detailing group accommodation providers, places to visit, suggested itineraries, coaching information and events

Educational Visits
information to help plan educational visits within the region. Uncover a wide variety of places to visit with unique learning opportunities

Discover Northumbria on two wheels
information on cycling in the region including an order form allowing the reader to order maps/leaflets from a central ordering point

Freedom
caravan and camping guide to the North of England. Available from Freedom Holidays, tel: 01202 252179

Getting to Northumbria

BY ROAD: The north/south routes on the A1 and A19 thread the region as does the A68. East/west routes like the A66 and A69 easily link with the western side of the country. Within Northumbria you will find fast, modern interconnecting roads between all the main centres, a vast network of scenic, traffic-free country roads to make motoring a pleasure and frequent local bus services operating to all towns and villages.

BY RAIL: London to Edinburgh InterCity service stops at Darlington, Durham, Newcastle and Berwick upon Tweed. 26 trains daily make the journey between London and Newcastle in just under 3 hours. The London to Middlesbrough journey takes 3 hours. Birmingham to Darlington 3 hours 15 minutes. Bristol to Durham 5 hours and Sheffield to Newcastle just over 2 hours. Direct services operate to Newcastle from Liverpool, Manchester, Glasgow, Stranraer and Carlisle. Regional services to areas of scenic beauty operate frequently, allowing the traveller easy access. The Tyne & Wear Metro makes it possible to travel to many destinations within the Tyneside area, such as Gateshead, South Shields, Whitley Bay and Newcastle International Airport, in minutes.

Where to stay in Northumbria

Accommodation entries in this region are listed in alphabetical order of place name, and then in alphabetical order of establishment.

Map references refer to the colour location maps at front of this guide. The first number indicates the map to use; the letter and number which follow refer to the grid reference on the map.

At a glance symbols at the end of each accommodation entry give useful information about services and facilities. A key to symbols can be found inside the back cover flap. Keep this open for easy reference.

A brief description of the towns and villages offering accommodation in the entries which follow, can be found at the end of this section.

A complete listing of all the English Tourism Council assessed accommodation covered by this guide appears at the back of the guide.

ALLENDALE TOWN, Northumberland Map ref 5B2

◆◆◆

MANOR HOUSE FARM
Ninebanks, Hexham NE47 8DA
T: (01434) 345068
F: (01434) 345068
E: manorhouse@ukonline.co.uk
I: www.manorhouse.ntb.org.uk

B&B per night:
S £20.00–£25.00
D £40.00–£50.00

HB per person:
DY £32.00–£35.00

OPEN All year round

Situated on the A686 Penrith to Corbirdge 'recognised beautiful drive'. Manor House Farm is a working 333-acre hill farm. The Georgian farmhouse is complete with 0.5 acre landscaped garden and children's play area. The farm is ideal for visiting Hadrian's Wall, the Lakes and Metrocentre.

Bedrooms: 2 triple/ multiple

Evening meal available

CREDIT CARD BOOKINGS If you book by telephone and are asked for your credit card number it is advisable to check the proprietor's policy should you cancel your reservation.

ALNMOUTH, Northumberland Map ref 5C1

BEECH LODGE

8 Alnwood, Alnmouth, Alnwick NE66 3NN
T: (01665) 830709 & 07713 011526

B&B per night:
D £45.00–£50.00

A warm welcome awaits guests at our modern, detached bungalow in quiet woodland setting in heart of unique coastal village. One comfortable, spacious, ground floor, double en suite room is furnished and decorated to a high standard and has all facilities. Alnmouth has all amenities, an ideal base for visiting beautiful Northumberland.

Bedrooms: 1 double/twin
Bathrooms: 1 en suite

ALNWICK, Northumberland Map ref 5C1 *Tourist Information Centre Tel: (01665) 510665*

AYDON HOUSE
South Road, Alnwick NE66 2NT
T: (01665) 602218

Bedrooms: 2 single, 4 double/twin, 2 triple/multiple
Bathrooms: 8 en suite

B&B per night:
S £20.00–£24.00
D £36.00–£44.00

OPEN Mar–Oct

Old established licensed guesthouse offering 8 comfortable and clean en suite bedrooms at sensible prices. Large private car park. Residents' lounge, friendly welcome.

BONDGATE HOUSE HOTEL
20 Bondgate Without, Alnwick NE66 1PN
T: (01665) 602025
F: (01665) 602025
E: kenforbes@lineone.net
I: www.bondgatehotel.ntb.org.uk

Bedrooms: 1 single, 4 double/twin, 3 triple/multiple
Bathrooms: 5 en suite

Evening meal available
CC: Delta, Mastercard, Switch, Visa

B&B per night:
S £25.00–£30.00
D £45.00–£47.00

HB per person:
DY £35.50–£37.00

OPEN All year round

Small family-run hotel near the medieval town gateway and interesting local shops. Well-placed for touring. Most rooms are en suite.

CHARLTON HOUSE
2 Aydon Gardens, Alnwick NE66 2NT
T: (01665) 605185
I: www.s-h-systems.co.uk/hotels/charlt2.html

Bedrooms: 1 single, 4 double/twin
Bathrooms: 5 en suite

B&B per night:
S £20.00–£22.00
D £40.00–£48.00

Victorian townhouse on the edge of historic Alnwick, where a warm welcome awaits. Beautiful en suite bedrooms, TV, hospitality tray. Breakfasts to suit all tastes.

THE GEORGIAN GUEST HOUSE
3 Hotspur Street, Alnwick NE66 1QE
T: (01665) 602 398
F: (01665) 602 398
E: georgianguesthouse@eggconnect.net

Bedrooms: 3 double/twin, 1 triple/multiple
Bathrooms: 4 en suite

B&B per night:
S Min £25.00
D £18.00–£20.00

OPEN All year round

Georgian house very close to town centre, near famous Hotspur Tower. All rooms on ground floor. Very handy for Alnwick gardens. Private parking.

ACCESSIBILITY
Look for the symbols which indicate accessibility for wheelchair users. A list of establishments is at the front of this guide.

BAMBURGH, Northumberland Map ref 5C1

Silver Award

◆◆◆◆

GLENANDER GUEST HOUSE
27 Lucker Road, Bamburgh
NE69 7BS
T: (01668) 214336
F: (01668) 214100

Bedrooms: 3 double/twin
Bathrooms: 3 en suite

B&B per night:
D £50.00–£70.00

Built early last century and recently carefully and tastefully modernised, providing quality accommodation. All rooms en suite with hospitality tray, hairdryer, colour TV. All day access.

◆◆◆◆

SQUIRREL COTTAGE
1 Friars Court, Bamburgh NE69 7AE
T: (01668) 214494 & 214572
E: theturnbulls2k@btinternet.com
I: www.geocities.com/thetropics/bay/3021

Bedrooms: 3 double/twin
Bathrooms: 2 en suite, 1 private

B&B per night:
D £50.00–£55.00

OPEN Feb–Nov

Quality, detached house, minutes from the magnificent castle and beaches. En suite rooms with sea or castle views. Local produce served.

BARDON MILL, Northumberland Map ref 5B2

◆◆◆

STRAND COTTAGE BED AND BREAKFAST
Main Road (A69), Bardon Mill, Hexham
NE47 7BH
T: (01434) 344643 & 07833 968655
E: strandcottage@aol.com
I: www.strand-cottage.co.uk

B&B per night:
S £20.00–£25.00
D £34.00–£44.00

OPEN All year round

Welcoming family home in the heart of picturesque Northumberland. The accommodation provides an excellent base from which to visit Hadrian's Wall, Kielder Forest, Lake District, Scottish Borders and Haltwhistle, the centre of Britain. Comfortable en suite rooms. Children and dogs welcome in our large detached family room which sleeps 6.

Bedrooms: 2 double/twin, 1 triple/multiple
Bathrooms: 3 en suite

Discounts for group bookings or stays 3 nights or over. Mid-week rates Mon-Thurs available on request.

BARNARD CASTLE, Durham Map ref 5B3 *Tourist Information Centre Tel: (01833) 690909*

◆◆◆

MONTALBO HOTEL
Montalbo Road, Barnard Castle
DL12 8BP
T: (01833) 637342
F: (01833) 637342
E: suzannethomas@montalbohotel.co.uk
I: www.montalbohotel.co.uk

Bedrooms: 5 double/twin, 1 triple/multiple
Bathrooms: 6 en suite

Lunch available
Evening meal available
CC: Delta, Mastercard, Switch, Visa

B&B per night:
S £30.00–£35.00
D £50.00–£60.00

OPEN All year round

Small family-run hotel offering attractive and comfortable bedrooms with en suite facilities. Excellent choice of food served every evening.

USE YOUR *i*s

There are more than 550 Tourist Information Centres throughout England offering friendly help with accommodation and holiday ideas as well as suggestions of places to visit and things to do. You'll find TIC addresses in the local Phone Book.

◆◆◆

MOORCOCK INN

Hill Top, Gordon Bank, Eggleston,
Barnard Castle DL12 0AU
T: (01833) 650395
F: (01833) 650052
E: zach1@talk21.com
I: www.moorcock-Inn.co.uk

Country inn with scenic views over Teesdale. Ideal walking country. Cosy en suite bedrooms, open log fire in lounge bar. Over 50 malt whiskies and a selection of real ales. Excellent home-cooked food using local produce. Our speciality is Teesdale lamb and locally produced beef and pork. Also, extensive fish menu.

Bedrooms: 2 single,
5 double/twin
Bathrooms: 4 en suite

Lunch available
Evening meal available
CC: Delta, Mastercard,
Switch, Visa

B&B per night:
S £20.00–£25.00
D £32.00–£37.00

OPEN All year round

◆◆◆

SPRING LODGE
Newgate, Barnard Castle DL12 8NW
T: (01833) 638110
F: (01833) 638110
E: ormston@telinco.co.uk
I: www.springlodgebandb.co.uk

Bedrooms: 3 double/
twin
Bathrooms: 2 en suite,
1 private

B&B per night:
S £27.50–£32.50
D £45.00–£55.00

OPEN All year round

Regency Villa built in 1825 standing in its own grounds and gardens on the outskirts of this historical town.

◆◆◆

STRATHMORE LAWN EAST

81 Galgate, Barnard Castle DL12 8ES
T: (01833) 637061
E: strathmoreebb@talk21.co.uk

B&B per night:
S Max £24.00
D Max £23.00

OPEN All year round

Elegant Victorian stone-built house, within 5 minutes walk of town centre. Whether fishing, walking or relaxing in this beautiful rural area, this is the place to stay. Personally supervised food, varied to your taste. Guaranteed to please. Hair salon on ground floor.

Bedrooms: 1 single,
1 double/twin, 1 triple/
multiple
Bathrooms: 1 en suite

Stay for 4 nights and pay for 3, Mon-Fri.

◆◆◆

THE NEW BEADNELL TOWERS HOTEL

Beadnell, Chathill NE67 5AU
T: (01665) 721211
F: (01665) 720424
E: beadnell@towers.fsnet.co.uk

Bedrooms: 9 double/
twin, 3 triple/multiple
Bathrooms: 11 en suite

Lunch available
Evening meal available
CC: Delta, Mastercard,
Switch, Visa

B&B per night:
S £60.00–£70.00
D £90.00–£110.00

HB per person:
DY £65.00–£80.00

OPEN All year round

After an extensive period of refurbishment, The New Beadnell Towers re-opened in June 2001, offering well-appointed en suite bedrooms. A choice of 2 bars provide a wide range of ales and bar food, whilst our 70-seat restaurant serves freshly produced innovative cuisine.

Stay Fri and Sat on our DB&B rate and stay free for Sun B&B.

BEAL, Northumberland Map ref 5B1

◆◆◆ **BROCK MILL FARMHOUSE**

Brock Mill, Beal, Berwick-upon-
Tweed TD15 2PB
T: (01289) 381283 & 07889 099517
F: (01289) 381283

Bedrooms: 1 single,
2 double/twin, 1 triple/
multiple
Bathrooms: 1 en suite

B&B per night:
S £20.00–£25.00
D £40.00–£46.00

220-acre mixed farm. Peaceful farmhouse, ideal for touring and golf, situated just off Holy Island road. Spacious, comfortable rooms. Private lounge/dining room. Walled garden.

BEAMISH, Durham Map ref 5C2

◆◆◆◆ **THE COACH HOUSE**

High Urpeth, Beamish, Stanley
DH9 0SE
T: (0191) 370 0309
F: (0191) 370 0046
E: coachhouse@foreman25.
freeserve.co.uk
I: www.coachhousebeamish.ntb.
org.uk

Bedrooms: 3 double/
twin
Bathrooms: 1 en suite,
2 private

Lunch available
Evening meal available
CC: Mastercard, Visa

B&B per night:
S £25.00–£30.00
D £40.00–£45.00

HB per person:
DY £38.50–£43.50

OPEN All year round

Converted coach house in rural situation. Eight miles from Durham/Newcastle. Excellent touring base for Northumbria and northern dales. Five minutes from the A1(M).

BELLINGHAM, Northumberland Map ref 5B2 *Tourist Information Centre Tel: (01434) 220616*

Rating Applied For

WESTFIELD HOUSE

Bellingham, Hexham NE48 2DP
T: (01434) 220340
F: (01434) 220354
I: www.westfield-house.net

Bedrooms: 1 double/
twin, 2 triple/multiple
Bathrooms: 2 en suite

Evening meal available
CC: Delta, Mastercard,
Visa

B&B per night:
S £28.00–£30.00
D £56.00–£60.00

HB per person:
DY £44.00–£46.00

OPEN All year round

The guesthouse you always wished to find. Excellent, freshly cooked food, good touring spot for Kielder and Hadrian's Wall. Let us spoil you.

BERWICK-UPON-TWEED, Northumberland Map ref 5B1 *Tourist Information Centre Tel: (01289) 330733*

◆◆◆ **THE CAT INN**

Great North Road, Cheswick,
Berwick-upon-Tweed TD15 2RL
T: (01289) 387251
F: (01289) 387251

Bedrooms: 5 double/
twin, 2 triple/multiple
Bathrooms: 4 en suite

Lunch available
Evening meal available

B&B per night:
S £18.00–£25.00
D £36.00–£40.00

OPEN All year round

Seven-bedroom inn situated 5 miles south of Berwick. Providing accommodation, good food and range of ales and lagers. Excellent location for local attractions.

◆◆◆◆ **DERVAIG GUEST HOUSE**

1 North Road, Berwick-upon-Tweed
TD15 1PW
T: (01289) 307378
F: (01289) 307378
E: dervaig@talk21.com

Bedrooms: 2 double/
twin, 3 triple/multiple
Bathrooms: 5 en suite

B&B per night:
S £20.00–£40.00
D £45.00–£50.00

OPEN All year round

Beautiful Victorian house, tastefully furnished, with spacious garden. 2 minute from train station, 5 minutes from centre of town. Private car park. Rooms en suite.

◆◆◆ **LADYTHORNE HOUSE**

Cheswick, Berwick-upon-Tweed
TD15 2RW
T: (01289) 387382
F: (01289) 387073
E: valparker@ladythorneguesthouse.
freeserve.co.uk
I: www.ladythorneguesthouse.
freeserve.co.uk

Bedrooms: 1 single,
3 double/twin, 2 triple/
multiple

B&B per night:
S £15.00–£17.00
D £30.00–£34.00

OPEN All year round

Grade II Listed Georgian house dated 1721. Magnificent views of the countryside, close to unspoilt beaches. Large garden, families welcome. Meals available within 5 minutes' drive.

BERWICK-UPON-TWEED continued

ROB ROY

Dock Road, Tweedmouth, Berwick-upon-Tweed TD15 2BQ
T: (01289) 306428
E: therobroy@btinternet.com
I: www.therobroy.co.uk

B&B per night:
S Min £33.00
D Min £52.00

OPEN All year round

Stone-built pub with cosy bar and log fire. One mile to Berwick centre from our riverside location. Our restaurant and bar menus offer choice local seafood, lobster, oysters, scallops. Visit Northumbria's beautiful coastline and castles, walk the Cheviots or the beautiful Tweed Valley. Or just enjoy Rob Roy hospitality.

Bedrooms: 2 double/twin
Bathrooms: 2 en suite

Lunch available
Evening meal available
CC: Amex, Delta, Diners, Mastercard, Switch, Visa

Reduced out of season offers. Nov-May deals on website.

BISHOP AUCKLAND, Durham Map ref 5C2 *Tourist Information Centre Tel: (01388) 604922*

FIVE GABLES GUEST HOUSE

Binchester, Bishop Auckland DL14 8AT
T: (01388) 608204
F: (01388) 663092
E: book.in@fivegables.co.uk
I: www.fivegables.co.uk

Bedrooms: 1 single, 1 double/twin, 1 triple/multiple
Bathrooms: 3 en suite

Evening meal available
CC: Delta, Mastercard, Switch, Visa

B&B per night:
S Max £28.50
D £46.00–£48.00

OPEN All year round

Three miles from Bishop Auckland, 15 minutes from Durham. Victorian house in country. Recommended by Which? Good B&B Guide. Self catering cottage available, sleeping 5.

CHATTON, Northumberland Map ref 5B1

SOUTH HAZELRIGG FARMHOUSE

South Hazelrigg, Chatton, Alnwick NE66 5RZ
T: (01668) 215216 & 07710 346076
E: sdodds@farmhousebandb.co.uk
I: www.farmhousebandb.co.uk

Bedrooms: 1 single, 2 double/twin

B&B per night:
S £20.00–£25.00
D £45.00–£50.00

OPEN Mar–Oct

Spacious farmhouse, magnificent views over lovely countryside. Elegant dining-room, large drawing room with access to extensive grounds. Full central heating, tea/coffee-making, TV, private parking.

CONSETT, Durham Map ref 5B2

BEE COTTAGE FARM

Castleside, Consett DH8 9HW
T: (01207) 508224

Bedrooms: 1 single, 7 double/twin, 4 triple/multiple; suites available
Bathrooms: 5 en suite

Lunch available

B&B per night:
S £28.00–£35.00
D £44.00–£80.00

OPEN Mar–Oct

Quiet, pleasant walks, unspoilt views in peaceful surroundings. Ideal base for Beamish Museum, Durham Cathedral, Hadrian's Wall. Some ground floor rooms. You will be very welcome.

CORBRIDGE, Northumberland Map ref 5B2

DILSTON MILL

Corbridge NE45 5QZ
T: (01434) 633493
F: (01434) 633513
E: susan@distonmill.com
I: www.dilstonmill.com

Bedrooms: 2 double/twin, 1 triple/multiple
Bathrooms: 2 private

B&B per night:
S £30.00–£35.00
D £50.00

OPEN All year round

Somewhere special. Historic former watermill in beautiful riverside position. Warm welcome, excellent breakfasts, homemade jams. Peaceful, secluded location yet convenient for all amenities.

CORBRIDGE continued

◆◆◆◆ FELLCROFT

Station Road, Corbridge NE45 5AY
T: (01434) 632384
F: (01434) 633918
E: tove.brown@ukonline.co.uk

Bedrooms: 1 double/
twin, 1 triple/multiple
Bathrooms: 1 en suite,
1 private

Evening meal available

B&B per night:
S £21.00–£23.00
D £35.00–£38.00

HB per person:
DY £27.50–£33.00

OPEN All year round

Well-appointed stone-built Edwardian house with full private facilities. Quiet road in country setting, half a mile south of market square. Non-smokers only, please.

◆◆◆◆

LOW FOTHERLEY FARMHOUSE BED AND BREAKFAST

Riding Mill NE44 6BB
T: (01434) 682277
F: (01434) 682277
E: hugh@lowfotherley.fsnet.co.uk
I: www.westfarm.freeserve.co.uk

Bedrooms: 2 double/
twin
Bathrooms: 1 en suite,
1 private

Special breaks Nov–Mar £17.50pppn.

B&B per night:
S £25.00
D £40.00–£50.00

OPEN All year round

Imposing Victorian farmhouse on a working farm in the Northumberland countryside. On the A68, close to the market towns of Hexham, Corbridge and to Hadrian's Wall. Recently refurbished and decorated to a high standard. We offer warm, spacious and comfortable bedrooms. Families are very welcome.

DARLINGTON, Durham Map ref 5C3 *Tourist Information Centre Tel: (01325) 388666*

◆ ABERLADY GUEST HOUSE

51 Corporation Road, Darlington
DL3 6AD
T: (01325) 461449 & 07970 379939

Bedrooms: 2 single,
3 double/twin, 2 triple/
multiple

B&B per night:
S £15.00–£18.00
D £30.00

OPEN All year round

Large Victorian house near town centre. Short walking distance to Railway Museum. Within easy reach of 4 golf courses and leisure centre.

◆◆◆ BOOT & SHOE

Church Row, Darlington DL1 5QD
T: (01325) 287501 & 362121
F: (01325) 287501

Bedrooms: 9 double/
twin
Bathrooms: 7 en suite,
2 private

CC: Mastercard, Switch,
Visa

B&B per night:
S £25.00–£35.00
D £50.00–£70.00

OPEN All year round

A Grade II Listed building situated on Darlington's busy market-place, fully refurbished in 2000. Only minutes away from train and bus station and A1.

◆◆◆ HAREWOOD LODGE

40 Grange Road, Darlington
DL1 5NP
T: (01325) 358152
E: Harewood.Lodge@NTLWorld.
com

Bedrooms: 2 single,
2 double/twin
Bathrooms: 3 en suite,
1 private

B&B per night:
S £25.00–£35.00
D Min £45.00

OPEN All year round

Victorian townhouse on outskirts of town. Short walk to town centre and golf course. Rooms en suite or private facilities.

DURHAM, Durham Map ref 5C2 *Tourist Information Centre Tel: (0191) 384 3720*

◆◆◆◆ 60 ALBERT STREET

Western Hill, Durham DH1 4RJ
T: (0191) 386 0608 &
07855 086266
F: (0191) 370 9739
E: laura@sixtyalbertstreet.co.uk
I: www.sixtyalbertstreet.co.uk

Bedrooms: 1 single,
2 double/twin, 1 triple/
multiple
Bathrooms: 2 en suite

CC: Delta, Mastercard,
Switch, Visa

B&B per night:
S £25.00–£27.00
D £47.00–£56.00

OPEN All year round

Elegantly restored Victorian townhouse situated in quiet conservation area near railway station. Five minutes' walk to central market square, cathedral, shops and restaurants. Private parking.

DURHAM continued

◆◆◆

BAY HORSE INN
Brandon Village, Durham DH7 8ST
T: (0191) 378 0498

B&B per night:
S £35.00–£40.00
D £45.00–£50.00

OPEN All year round

Ten stone-built chalets 3 miles from Durham city centre. All have shower, toilet, TV, tea and coffee facilities and telephone. Ample car parking. Lunch and evening meals available at extra cost. Bar meals from £1.80, Al a carte from £4.00. Close location to tourist sights.

Bedrooms: 9 double/ twin, 1 triple/multiple
Bathrooms: 10 en suite

Lunch available
Evening meal available
CC: Amex, Delta, Mastercard, Switch, Visa

◆◆◆◆

CASTLE VIEW GUEST HOUSE
4 Crossgate, Durham DH1 4PS
T: (0191) 386 8852
F: (0191) 386 8852
E: castle_view@hotmail.com

Bedrooms: 1 single, 5 double/twin
Bathrooms: 6 en suite

CC: Delta, Mastercard, Switch, Visa

B&B per night:
S £40.00–£45.00
D £55.00–£58.00

OPEN All year round

250-year-old, Listed building in the heart of the old city, with woodland and riverside walks and a magnificent view of the cathedral and castle.

◆◆◆

CASTLEDENE
37 Nevilledale Terrace, Durham DH1 4QG
T: (0191) 384 8386 &
07710 425921
F: (0191) 384 8386
E: lornabyrne@tinyworld.co.uk

Bedrooms: 2 double/ twin

B&B per night:
S £20.00–£25.00
D Max £42.00

OPEN All year round

Edwardian end-of-terrace house half a mile west of the market place. Within walking distance of the riverside, cathedral and castle.

◆

COLLEGE OF SAINT HILD AND SAINT BEDE (GUEST ROOMS & GABLES)
St Hild's Lane, Durham DH1 1SZ
T: (0191) 374 3069 & 374 3064
F: (0191) 374 4740
E: l.c.hugill@durham.ac.uk
I: www.dur.ac.uk/HildBede

Bedrooms: 2 single, 3 double/twin

Lunch available
Evening meal available

B&B per night:
S £20.00–£27.00

University accommodation set in spectacular grounds, close proximity to historic city centre and cathedral.

◆◆◆

THE GILESGATE MOOR HOTEL
Teasdale Terrace, Gilesgate, Durham DH1 2RN
T: (0191) 386 6453
F: (0191) 386 6453

B&B per night:
S £20.00–£28.00
D £38.00–£45.00

OPEN All year round

Comfortable family-run inn on the outskirts of Durham City. The accommodation throughout is finished to the highest standard and offers an ideal base for exploring Durham City and the surrounding area. We guarantee a warm, friendly welcome and high standards of service throughout your stay.

Bedrooms: 1 single, 6 double/twin, 1 triple/ multiple
Bathrooms: 4 en suite

CC: Mastercard, Visa

◆◆◆ GREEN GROVE

99 Gilesgate, Durham DH1 1JA
T: (0191) 384 4361
E: bill-dockery@guesthouse.fsnet.co.uk
I: www.smoothhound.co.uk/hotels/greengro.html

Bedrooms: 2 single, 5 double/twin, 1 triple/multiple
Bathrooms: 3 en suite

B&B per night:
S £20.00–£30.00
D £40.00–£50.00

OPEN All year round

Victorian guesthouse, public rooms with high ceilings and period fireplaces. Easy access from the motorway.

◆◆◆ THE LOVES

17 Front Street, Broompark, Durham DH7 7QT
T: (0191) 384 9283
E: karen.paul@tinyonline.co.uk

Bedrooms: 1 double/twin, 1 triple/multiple
Bathrooms: 1 en suite, 1 private

B&B per night:
S £25.00–£30.00
D £50.00–£60.00

OPEN All year round

Village pub approximately 120 years old. Near Deerness Valley, lovely walks on disused railway line. Approximately 5 minutes from historic city centre of Durham.

◆◆◆ ST AIDAN'S COLLEGE

University of Durham, Windmill Hill, Durham DH1 3LJ
T: (0191) 374 3269
F: (0191) 374 4749
E: aidans.conf@durham.ac.uk
I: www.st-aidans.org.uk

Bedrooms: 72 single, 24 double/twin
Bathrooms: 96 en suite

Lunch available
Evening meal available
CC: Delta, Mastercard, Switch, Visa

B&B per night:
S £20.00–£30.00
D £36.00–£54.00

HB per person:
DY £32.50–£42.50

OPEN Mar–Apr, Jul–Sep, Dec

Set in landscaped gardens, overlooking one of the most visually attractive cities in Britain, Durham. Ideal base to visit Northumbria. Adjacent golf course, free tennis.

Rating Applied For — SAINT JOHNS COLLEGE (CRUDDAS)

3 South Bailey, Durham DH1 3RJ
T: (0191) 374 3579
F: (0191) 374 3573
E: s.l.hobson@durham.ac.uk
I: www.stjohnscollege-durham.com

Bedrooms: 26 single, 7 double/twin

Evening meal available
CC: Delta, Diners, Mastercard, Switch, Visa

B&B per night:
S £20.00–£24.00
D £40.00–£48.00

College buildings are skilfully adapted, 18thC townhouses. Situated in the heart of the city alongside Durham Cathedral and Durham Castle.

◆◆ TREVELYAN COLLEGE (MACAULAY WING)

Elvet Hill Road, Durham DH1 3LN
T: (0191) 374 3765 & 374 3768
F: (0191) 374 3789
E: trev.coll@durham.ac.uk
I: www.dur.ac.uk/~dtr0www/conference.html

Bedrooms: 253 single, 27 double/twin
Bathrooms: 50 en suite

Lunch available
Evening meal available
CC: Delta, Mastercard, Switch, Visa

B&B per night:
S £20.00–£30.00
D £36.00–£54.00

HB per person:
DY Min £29.25

OPEN Jan, Mar–Apr, Jul–Oct, Dec

Set in parkland within easy walking distance of Durham City. Air-conditioned Cloister Bar, TV lounges, tennis court, ample parking. Standard and en suite rooms available.

TOWN INDEX

This can be found at the back of the guide. If you know where you want to stay, the index will give you the page number listing accommodation in your chosen town, city or village.

FROSTERLEY, Durham Map ref 5B2

HIGH LAITHE
10A Hill End, Frosterley, Bishop Auckland
DL13 2SX
T: (01388) 526421

B&B per night:
S £19.00
D £38.00

HB per person:
DY £29.00

OPEN All year round

Peacefully situated, overlooking the village of Frosterley. A real 'home from home' offering privacy in a relaxed atmosphere. Rooms have splendid views across the dale. Attractive garden. Excellent for walking, cycling, touring the Land of the Prince Bishops, designated an Area of Outstanding Natural Beauty. Own horses welcome.

Bedrooms: 1 single,
1 double/twin
Bathrooms: 2 private

Evening meal available

GATESHEAD, Tyne and Wear Map ref 5C2 *Tourist Information Centre Tel: (0191) 477 3478*

SHAFTESBURY GUEST HOUSE
245 Prince Consort Road,
Gateshead NE8 4DT
T: (0191) 478 2544
F: (0191) 478 2544

Bedrooms: 2 single,
6 double/twin, 2 triple/
multiple
Bathrooms: 2 en suite

B&B per night:
S £24.00–£34.00
D £36.00–£46.00

OPEN All year round

Charming, family-run guesthouse. Ideal for MetroCentre, Newcastle City/Arena, Gateshead Stadium. Opposite Gateshead leisure centre. A1 north, A167 Gateshead (south). A1 south, A181 Gateshead.

GREENHEAD, Northumberland Map ref 5B2

FOUR WYNDS
Longbyre, Greenhead, Brampton
CA8 7HN
T: (01697) 747330
F: (01697) 747330
E: rozbonnarhadrianswall@talk21.
com

Bedrooms: 3 double/
twin
Bathrooms: 3 en suite

B&B per night:
S £25.00–£30.00
D £40.00

OPEN All year round

Stone-built house overlooking Pennine Way/Coast to Coast Walk/Hadrian's Wall. Easy reach Thirlwall Castle, Birdoswald, and Vindolanda. Golf club and friendly pubs nearby.

GRETA BRIDGE, Durham Map ref 5B3

Silver
Award

THE COACH HOUSE
Greta Bridge, Barnard Castle
DL12 9SD
T: (01833) 627201
E: info@coachhousegreta.co.uk
I: www.coachhousegreta.co.uk

Bedrooms: 2 double/
twin, 1 triple/multiple
Bathrooms: 2 en suite,
1 private

CC: Delta, Mastercard,
Switch, Visa

B&B per night:
S £45.00
D £64.00

HB per person:
DY £52.00–£65.00

OPEN All year round

Former coaching inn on the River Greta, ideally situated for the dales and lakes. Extremely comfortably furnished, charming garden and lovely walks.

CHECK THE MAPS
The colour maps at the front of this guide show all the cities, towns and villages for which you will find accommodation entries. Refer to the town index to find the page on which they are listed.

HALTWHISTLE, Northumberland Map ref 5B2 *Tourist Information Centre Tel: (01434) 322002*

♦♦♦♦♦
Gold
Award

BROOMSHAW HILL FARM

Willia Road, Haltwhistle NE49 9NP
T: (01434) 320866 & 0771 483 5828
F: (01434) 320866
E: broomshaw@msn.com
I: www.broomshaw.co.uk

Original 18thC farmhouse, enlarged and modernised to high standards, whilst retaining its original features. The house stands on the side of a valley on the conjunction of a bridleway and footpath, both leading to Hadrian's Wall. Close to all major Roman sites. Town amenities less than three quarters of a mile.

Bedrooms: 3 double/twin
Bathrooms: 2 en suite, 1 private

B&B per night:
S £25.00–£30.00
D £46.00–£48.00

♦♦♦

THE GREY BULL HOTEL
Main Street, Haltwhistle NE49 0DL
T: (01434) 321991
F: (01434) 320770
E: PamGreyB@aol.com

An 18thC coaching inn.

Bedrooms: 1 single, 4 double/twin, 2 triple/multiple

Lunch available
Evening meal available
CC: Mastercard, Visa

B&B per night:
S £17.50
D £35.00

♦♦♦

OAKY KNOWE FARM

Haltwhistle NE49 0NB
T: (01434) 320648
F: (01434) 320648

B&B per night:
S £20.00–£25.00
D £36.00–£40.00

HB per person:
DY £28.00–£35.00

OPEN All year round

18-acre equestrian and sheep farm, overlooking the scenic Tyne Valley, within walking distance of Haltwhistle and the Roman wall. Stabling for your horse should you wish to bring it along. The farmhouse offers a friendly and relaxing atmosphere.

Bedrooms: 1 double/twin, 1 triple/multiple
Bathrooms: 1 private

Evening meal available

HAMSTERLEY FOREST

See under Barnard Castle, Bishop Auckland, Frosterley

HAYDON BRIDGE, Northumberland Map ref 5B2

♦♦♦

HADRIAN LODGE
Hindshield Moss,
North Road, Nr Hadrians Wall,
Haydon Bridge, Hexham NE47 6NF
T: (01434) 688688
F: (01434) 684867
E: hadrianlodge@hadrianswall.co.uk
I: www.hadrianswall.co.uk

Bedrooms: 1 single, 5 double/twin, 4 triple/multiple
Bathrooms: 6 en suite

Evening meal available
CC: Amex, Mastercard, Switch, Visa

B&B per night:
S £20.00–£29.50
D £40.00–£49.50

HB per person:
DY £28.00–£37.50

Idyllic rural location, overlooking lakes (fishing available), near Housesteads Roman Fort and Hadrian's Wall. Cosy residents' bar, delicious home-cooked meals. Warm welcome. Write/ring for brochure.

WHERE TO STAY
Please mention this guide when making your booking.

HEXHAM, Northumberland Map ref 5B2

◆◆◆◆ HETHERINGTON
Wark-on-Tyne, Hexham NE48 3DR
T: (01434) 230260
F: (01434) 230260
E: a_nichol@hotmail.com

Bedrooms: 3 double/twin
Bathrooms: 2 en suite, 1 private

B&B per night:
S Min £20.00
D £40.00–£52.00

Northumbrian farmhouse on 400-acre mixed farm on a public road. Stabling available. Excellent facilities. Ideal walking and touring area – the Pennine Way runs through the farm.

 10 🛏 🖤 ⑤ 🎯 Ⅲ ♪ ♦ ❄ 🐴 ⛽ P

◆◆◆ ROSE AND CROWN INN
Main Street, Slaley, Hexham
NE47 0AA
T: (01434) 673263
F: (01434) 673305
E: rosecrowninn@supanet.com
I: www.smoothhound.co.uk/hotels/rosecrowninn.html

Bedrooms: 1 single, 2 double/twin
Bathrooms: 3 en suite

Lunch available
Evening meal available
CC: Amex, Delta, Mastercard, Switch, Visa

B&B per night:
S £27.50–£35.00
D £45.00–£50.00

OPEN All year round

Warm, friendly, family-run business with good wholesome home cooking and a la carte restaurant. All bedrooms en suite in this 200-year-old Listed village freehouse in Slaley.

 7 🖼 🖵 🖤 ☕ ⑤ ✂ 🎯 Ⅲ 🚲 ♪ ♦ ❄ ⛽ 🛁 🎪 P

HOLY ISLAND, Northumberland Map ref 5C1

◆◆◆ BRITANNIA
Britannia House, Holy Island,
Berwick-upon-Tweed TD15 2RX
T: (01289) 389218

Bedrooms: 2 double/twin, 1 triple/multiple
Bathrooms: 1 en suite

B&B per night:
S £20.00–£35.00
D £40.00–£44.00

Comfortable, friendly bed and breakfast in centre of Holy Island. Tea-making facilities in all rooms. TV lounge. En suite available.

 🖤 ⑤ 🎯 Ⅲ 🚲 ♦ ⛽ P

◆◆◆◆ THE BUNGALOW
Holy Island, Berwick-upon-Tweed
TD15 2SE
T: (01289) 389308
E: bungalow@celtic121.demon.co.uk
I: www.lindisfarne.org.uk/bungalow

Bedrooms: 3 double/twin
Bathrooms: 3 en suite

B&B per night:
S £35.00–£45.00
D £50.00–£55.00

OPEN All year round

Magnificent views of the sea, Lindisfarne Castle and countryside. Private car park. Open all year. Secluded garden.

 🖼 🖵 🖤 ⑤ ✂ Ⅲ ❄ ⛽ P

◆◆◆ THE SHIP
Marygate, Holy Island, Berwick-upon-Tweed TD15 2SJ
T: (01289) 389311
F: (01289) 389316
E: theship@holyisland7.freeserve.co.uk
I: www.lindisfarneaccommodate.com

Bedrooms: 1 double/twin, 2 triple/multiple
Bathrooms: 3 en suite

Lunch available
Evening meal available
CC: Delta, Mastercard, Switch, Visa

B&B per night:
S £40.00
D £58.00

Historical building, totally refurbished but retaining its character and charm. A tearoom and quality gift and craft shop is attached.

 🖼 🖵 🖤 ☕ ☕ ⑤ ✂ Ⅲ 🚲 ♦ ❄ 🎪 P

KIELDER FOREST

See under Bellingham, Wark. See also Keilder Water

QUALITY ASSURANCE SCHEME
Diamond ratings and awards were correct at the time of going to press but are subject to change. Please check at the time of booking.

KIELDER WATER, Northumberland Map ref 5B2

◆◆◆◆

THE PHEASANT INN (BY KIELDER WATER)

Stannersburn, Falstone, Hexham NE48 1DD
T: (01434) 240382
F: (01434) 240382
E: thepheasantinn@kielderwater.demon.co.uk

B&B per night:
S £30.00–£40.00
D £50.00–£65.00

HB per person:
DY £45.00–£50.00

OPEN All year round

Charming 16thC inn, retaining its character while providing comfortable, modern en suite accommodation. Features include stone walls and low-beamed ceilings in the bars, antique artefacts and open fires. Emphasis on traditional home cooking, using fresh vegetables, served in bar or dining room. Sunday roasts are renowned for their quality.

Bedrooms: 7 double/ twin, 1 triple/multiple	Lunch available
Bathrooms: 8 en suite	Evening meal available
	CC: Delta, Mastercard, Switch, Visa

Reduced rates Oct-May, DB&B £45pppn.

LONGFRAMLINGTON, Northumberland Map ref 5C1

◆◆◆◆

THE ANGLER'S ARMS

Weldon Bridge, Longframlington,
Morpeth NE65 8AX
T: (01665) 570655 & 570271
F: (01665) 570041
I: www.anglersarms.com

Bedrooms: 4 double/ twin, 1 triple/multiple	Lunch available
Bathrooms: 5 en suite	Evening meal available
	CC: Delta, Diners, Mastercard, Switch, Visa

B&B per night:
S £35.00
D £50.00

OPEN All year round

Grade II Listed Georgian country inn, by river Coquet amid Northumberland countryside. With character bar and Pullman restaurant.

MIDDLETON-IN-TEESDALE, Durham Map ref 5B3

◆◆◆

BELVEDERE HOUSE

54 Market Place, Middleton-in-Teesdale, Barnard Castle DL12 0QH
T: (01833) 640884
F: (01833) 640884
E: belvedere@thecoachhouse.net
I: www.thecoachhouse.net/belvedere

| Bedrooms: 3 double/ twin | |
| Bathrooms: 3 en suite | |

B&B per night:
S £18.00
D £34.00

OPEN All year round

18thC house, centrally situated in dales village. Enjoy a warm welcome and great breakfast. Explore Teesdale's beautiful countryside and places of historic interest. Magnificent waterfalls.

◆◆◆

BLUEBELL HOUSE

Market Place, Middleton-in-Teesdale, Barnard Castle DL12 0QG
T: (01833) 640584
I: www.bluebellhouse-teesdale.co.uk

| Bedrooms: 4 double/ twin | |
| Bathrooms: 3 en suite, 1 private | |

B&B per night:
S £21.00–£25.00
D £32.00–£34.00

OPEN All year round

Former coaching inn, offering en suite/private facilities. Some ground floor rooms. Tea, coffee, TV in rooms. Guests' lounge. Ideal for walking. Cycle hire avaliable.

COUNTRY CODE Always follow the Country Code ✤ Enjoy the countryside and respect its life and work ✤ Guard against all risk of fire ✤ Fasten all gates ✤ Keep your dogs under close control ✤ Keep to public paths across farmland ✤ Use gates and stiles to cross fences, hedges and walls ✤ Leave livestock, crops and machinery alone ✤ Take your litter home ✤ Help to keep all water clean ✤ Protect wildlife, plants and trees ✤ Take special care on country roads ✤ Make no unnecessary noise

COTTAGE VIEW GUEST HOUSE

6 Staithes Lane, Morpeth NE61 1TD
T: (01670) 518550
F: (01670) 510840
E: cottageview.morpeth@virgin.net
I: www.cottageview.co.uk

B&B per night:
S £30.00–£35.40
D £42.00–£47.40

OPEN All year round

Centrally situated, licensed, family-run, guesthouse with all facilities to make your stay at Morpeth more enjoyable. Facilities include private car parking, laundry service, reception bar, 2 lounges (1 private), email/fax facilities and a night porter for your convenience. And now we can accommodate up to 60 people.

Bedrooms: 20 double/twin, 5 triple/multiple
Bathrooms: 19 en suite

CC: Amex, Delta, Diners, Mastercard, Switch, Visa

Child discounts available.

JESMOND PARK HOTEL

74-76 Queens Road, Jesmond,
Newcastle upon Tyne NE2 2PR
T: (0191) 281 2821 & 281 1913
F: (0191) 281 0515
E: vh@jespark.fsnet.co.uk
I: www.jesmondpark.com

Bedrooms: 6 single, 7 double/twin, 5 triple/multiple
Bathrooms: 12 en suite

Evening meal available
CC: Amex, Delta, Mastercard, Switch, Visa

B&B per night:
S £24.00–£35.00
D £42.00–£48.00

OPEN All year round

Clean and friendly hotel offering good English breakfast. Residents' bar, free parking, close to city centre and handy for MetroCentre and Hadrian's Wall.

THE KEELMAN'S LODGE

Grange Road, Newburn,
Newcastle upon Tyne NE15 8NL
T: (0191) 267 1689 & 267 0772
F: (0191) 499 0041
E: admin@petersen-stainless.co.uk
I: www.petersen-stainless.co.uk

B&B per night:
S £16.00–£39.00
D Max £55.00

OPEN All year round

Purpose-built stone lodge in riverside country park. Close to A1, A69, railway stations and airport. Ideal base for exploring Hadrian's Wall, Holy Island and Tyne Valley. Local pursuits include cycling, walking, fishing, golf. Big Lamp Brewery and pub adjacent with children's playground. Quality accommodation highly rated by previous customers.

Bedrooms: 6 triple/multiple
Bathrooms: 6 en suite

Lunch available
Evening meal available
CC: Amex, Delta, Mastercard, Switch, Visa

Free child places. Weekend special: 2nd and 3rd nights half-price.

AT-A-GLANCE SYMBOLS

Symbols at the end of each accommodation entry give useful information about services and facilities. A key to symbols can be found inside the back cover flap. Keep this open for easy reference.

OTTERBURN, Northumberland Map ref 5B1 *Tourist Information Centre Tel: (01830) 520093*

◆◆◆◆

BUTTERCHURN GUEST HOUSE

Main Street, Otterburn,
Newcastle upon Tyne NE19 1NP
T: (01830) 520585
F: (01830) 520874
E: keith@butterchurn.freeserve.co.uk
I: www.butterchurn.freeserve.co.uk

Excellent family-run guesthouse in quiet village location renowned for its welcome, quality of service and ambiance. Situated in Northumberland National Park, on the scenic route to Scotland. Central for Hadrian's Wall, Kielder Water, coast and castles. Everyone welcome in the county known as the 'Land of Far Horizons'.

Bedrooms: 4 double/twin, 3 triple/multiple
Bathrooms: 7 en suite

CC: Delta, Mastercard, Visa

B&B per night:
S £25.00
D £40.00

OPEN All year round

◆◆◆◆

REDESDALE ARMS HOTEL

Rochester, Newcastle upon Tyne NE19 1TA
T: (01830) 520668
F: (01830) 520063
E: redesdalehotel@hotmail.com
I: www.redesdale-hotel.co.uk

Bedrooms: 8 double/twin, 2 triple/multiple
Bathrooms: 10 en suite

Lunch available
Evening meal available
CC: Amex, Delta, Mastercard, Switch, Visa

B&B per night:
S £38.00-£43.00
D £60.00-£70.00

OPEN All year round

Family-run old coaching inn with log fires and fine food. Central for Hadrian's Wall and the Kielder Forest. Beautiful en suite country bedrooms.

PONTELAND, Northumberland Map ref 5C2

◆◆◆◆

HAZEL COTTAGE

Eachwick, Dalton, Newcastle upon Tyne NE18 0BE
T: (01661) 852415
F: (01661) 854797
E: hazelcottage@eachwick.fsbusiness.co.uk

A warm welcome awaits you in our comfortable, traditional Northumbrian farmhouse, set in a lovely, tranquil rural area. Delightful en suite bedrooms with TV, tea-making facilities and everything for your comfort. Freshly prepared evening meals and splendid breakfasts. Newcastle, Hexham, Hadrian's wall, Metrocentre within easy reach. Non-smoking.

Bedrooms: 4 double/twin
Bathrooms: 4 en suite

Evening meal available
CC: Mastercard, Visa

B&B per night:
S £25.00-£28.00
D £40.00-£44.00

HB per person:
DY £33.00-£41.00

OPEN All year round

◆◆◆

STONEHAVEN LODGE

Prestwick Road End, Ponteland,
Newcastle upon Tyne NE20 9BX
T: (01661) 872363
E: brenanderson@ncletw.freeserve.co.uk

Bedrooms: 1 single, 2 double/twin
Bathrooms: 1 en suite

B&B per night:
S £25.00
D £40.00

OPEN All year round

Stone semi facing the Cheviots on the Prestwick roundabout, on the A696 to Jedburgh. Two hundred yards past Newcastle Airport.

HALF BOARD PRICES Half board prices are given per person, but in some cases these may be based on double/twin occupancy.

RIDING MILL, Northumberland Map ref 5B2

◆◆◆

BROOMLEY FELL FARM
Riding Mill NE44 6AY
T: (01434) 682682 & 07802 676143
F: (01434) 682728
E: enquiries@broomleyfell.co.uk
I: www.broomleyfell.co.uk

B&B per night:
S £20.00–£25.00
D £40.00–£50.00

HB per person:
DY Min £27.50

OPEN All year round

Warm welcome in cosy separate annexe in farmhouse. Open beams and log fire. Very relaxing. Evening meals available. Lovely surrounding area.

Bedrooms: 1 single, 1 triple/multiple
Bathrooms: 1 en suite, 1 private

Evening meal available
CC: Delta, Mastercard, Switch, Visa

ROTHBURY, Northumberland Map ref 5B1

◆◆◆◆

THE CHIRNELLS
Thropton, Morpeth NE65 7JE
T: (01669) 621507 & 07866 081747

Bedrooms: 2 double/twin
Bathrooms: 1 en suite, 1 private

Evening meal available

B&B per night:
D Min £45.00

HB per person:
DY Min £63.00

OPEN All year round

Georgian farmhouse, built late 1700s, stands in own grounds 2.5 miles from market town of Rothbury. Spectacular views overlooking the Coquet Valley and Cheviot Hills.

◆◆◆◆

KATERINA'S GUEST HOUSE
Sun Buildings, High Street,
Rothbury, Morpeth NE65 7TQ
T: (01669) 620691 & 07977 555692
E: cath@katerinasguesthouse.co.uk
I: www.katerinasguesthouse.co.uk

Bedrooms: 3 double/twin
Bathrooms: 3 en suite

Evening meal available

B&B per night:
S £30.00
D £44.00–£46.00

OPEN All year round

Situated in beautiful country village. All rooms en suite, 4-poster beds, TV. Ideal centre for exploring Northumberland hills, beaches, Scottish Borders. Evening meals by arrangement.

SALTBURN-BY-THE-SEA, Cleveland Map ref 5C3 *Tourist Information Centre Tel: (01287) 622422*

◆◆◆◆

THE ROSE GARDEN
20 Hilda Place, Saltburn-by-the-Sea
TS12 1BP
T: (01287) 622947
F: (01287) 622947
E: enquiries@therosegarden.co.uk
I: www.therosegarden.co.uk

Bedrooms: 3 double/twin
Bathrooms: 2 en suite, 1 private

B&B per night:
S £20.00–£30.00
D Max £50.00

OPEN Feb–Dec

Large Victorian terraced house with small front garden. Well situated for all amenities in a charming seaside town. Homemade preserves a speciality.

SEAHOUSES, Northumberland Map ref 5C1

◆◆◆

BRAIDSTONE LODGE
1 Braidstone Square, Seahouses
NE68 7RP
T: (01665) 720055

Bedrooms: 2 double/twin
Bathrooms: 1 en suite

B&B per night:
S £22.50–£25.00
D £37.00–£50.00

OPEN Jan–Nov

Stone-built bungalow in private courtyard, around the corner from the harbour. Offering friendly and comfortable en suite and standard accommodation.

◆◆◆

LEEHOLME
93 Main Street, Seahouses
NE68 7TS
T: (01665) 720230
& 0780 838 1590

Bedrooms: 3 double/twin
Bathrooms: 1 en suite

Lunch available

B&B per night:
S £20.00–£25.00
D £36.00–£50.00

A warm welcome awaits you at this small homely bed and breakfast. 5 minutes' walk to Seahouses harbour and shops. Hearty breakfast assured.

SEAHOUSES continued

THE LODGE
◆◆

146 Main Street, Seahouses
NE68 7UA
T: (01665) 720158

Bedrooms: 3 double/
twin, 2 triple/multiple;
suites available
Bathrooms: 5 en suite

Evening meal available
CC: Delta, Mastercard,
Switch, Visa

B&B per night:
S £22.00–£24.00
D £22.00–£24.00

OPEN All year round

Fully licensed hotel with motel-style rooms in quiet walled garden. A cosy pine bar with indoor aquarium. Private parking. Families and pets welcome.

WYNDGROVE HOUSE
◆◆◆

156 Main Street, North Sunderland,
Seahouses NE68 7UA
T: (01665) 720658

Bedrooms: 3 double/
twin, 4 triple/multiple
Bathrooms: 2 en suite

CC: Delta, Mastercard,
Switch, Visa

B&B per night:
S £20.00–£25.00
D £38.00–£48.00

OPEN All year round

Family-run guesthouse offering comfort and friendliness. Ideal accommodation for friends, couples, families or group bookings and as a base for coastline, castles and countryside.

SIMONBURN, Northumberland Map ref 5B2

SIMONBURN GUEST HOUSE
◆◆◆

1 The Mains, Simonburn, Hexham
NE48 3AW
T: (01434) 681321 & 07801 229866

Bedrooms: 3 triple/
multiple

B&B per night:
S £22.00–£25.00
D £37.00–£40.00

OPEN All year round

Two-hundred-year-old guesthouse set in beautiful little quiet village famed for the filming of Catherine Cookson's books. Located in Hadrian's Wall country.

SOUTH SHIELDS, Tyne and Wear Map ref 5C2 *Tourist Information Centre Tel: (0191) 454 6612*

AINSLEY GUEST HOUSE
◆◆◆

59 Ocean Road, South Shields
NE33 2JJ
T: (0191) 454 3399 &
07879 461492
F: (0191) 454 3399
E: ainsleyguesthouse@hotmail.
com

Bedrooms: 1 single,
2 double/twin, 3 triple/
multiple

B&B per night:
S £20.00–£25.00
D £35.00

OPEN All year round

Victorian 3-storey terraced townhouse retaining many original features. Comfortable, attractive bedrooms. Close to town centre, seafront, parks and beaches. Relaxed and friendly atmosphere assured.

THE KINGSMERE
◆◆◆

9 Urfa Terrace, South Shields
NE33 2ES
T: (0191) 456 0234
F: (0191) 425 5026

Bedrooms: 3 single,
3 double/twin, 1 triple/
multiple

Lunch available
Evening meal available

B&B per night:
S £17.00–£21.00
D £32.00–£35.00

HB per person:
DY £22.00

OPEN All year round

Friendly hospitality offered in a Victorian house close to parks, town centre, Roman Fort and seafront amenities. Cable TV or video facilities in all rooms.

SPENNYMOOR, Durham Map ref 5C2

IDSLEY HOUSE
◆◆◆◆

4 Green Lane, Spennymoor
DL16 6HD
T: (01388) 814237

Bedrooms: 1 single,
3 double/twin, 1 triple/
multiple
Bathrooms: 4 en suite,
1 private

CC: Amex, Delta,
Mastercard, Switch, Visa

B&B per night:
S £32.00–£35.00
D £48.00

OPEN All year round

Detached Victorian residence in quiet area at junction of A167/A688, opposite council offices. Just 8 minutes south of Durham City. Tastefully furnished, spacious bedrooms, safe parking on premises.

IDEAS For ideas on places to visit refer to the introduction at the beginning of this section.

STANLEY, Durham Map ref 5C2

◆◆◆

BUSHBLADES FARM
Harperley, Stanley DH9 9UA
T: (01207) 232722

B&B per night:
S £25.00–£30.00
D £37.00–£42.00

OPEN All year round

60-acre livestock farm. Georgian house with large garden in rural setting. All rooms are spacious with colour TV, tea/coffee facilities and comfortable chairs. Ideal base or stopover. A1M 10 minutes. Easy reach of Durham City, Beamish Museum, Hadrian's Wall and the Northumberland Coast. Ample parking.

Bedrooms: 3 double/twin
Bathrooms: 1 en suite

🛋12 ♿ ⬚ ↟ 🍵 S ⛿ 🎹 ∰ ✿ 🚗 P

◆◆◆

HARPERLEY HOTEL
Harperley, Stanley DH9 9TY
T: (01207) 234011
F: (01207) 232325
E: harperley-hotel@supernet.com

Bedrooms: 2 single, 3 double/twin
Bathrooms: 5 en suite

Lunch available
Evening meal available
CC: Amex, Delta, Mastercard, Switch, Visa

B&B per night:
S £35.00–£40.00
D £45.00–£50.00

OPEN All year round

Converted granary on the outskirts of Stanley, in the country park area close to the old watermill. Recently refurbished to a high standard.

🛋🖼📞⬚↟🍴🏆 S ∠ ∰ 🖴 🍴 ↟ 🐴 🚗 🔌 🏛 P

TANFIELD, Durham Map ref 5C2

◆◆◆

TANFIELD GARDEN LODGE
Tanfield Lane, Tanfield, Stanley DH9 9QF
T: (01207) 282821
& 0797 039 8890
F: (01207) 282821

Bedrooms: 2 double/twin, 2 triple/multiple
Bathrooms: 2 en suite

B&B per night:
S £28.00–£32.00
D £38.00–£45.00

OPEN All year round

Guesthouse in private grounds offering first-class accommodation. Close to Beamish Museum and MetroCentre. Also within easy reach of Durham and Newcastle. Private parking.

📶🛋🖼⬚↟🍵 S ∠🎹∰🖴✿P

THROPTON, Northumberland Map ref 5B1

◆◆◆

DEMESNE FARMHOUSE
Thropton, Morpeth NE65 7LT
T: (01669) 620196

Bedrooms: 3 double/twin
Bathrooms: 2 en suite, 1 private

Evening meal available

B&B per night:
S Min £28.00
D Max £46.00

OPEN All year round

Traditional stone-built farmhouse with panoramic views across the Coquetdale Valley. On the edge of Northumbria National Park.

📶⬚↟🍵 S ∠🎹∰🖴✿🚗🔌P

QUALITY ASSURANCE SCHEME

For an explanation of the quality and facilities represented by the Diamonds please refer to the front of this guide. A more detailed explanation can be found in the information pages at the back.

◆◆◆

IMPERIAL GUEST HOUSE

194 Station Road, Wallsend NE28 8RD
T: (0191) 236 9808
F: (0191) 236 9808
E: enquiries@imperialguesthouse.co.uk
I: www.imperialguesthouse.co.uk

B&B per night:
S £20.00–£29.00
D £40.00–£50.00

Behind the plain and unassuming terraced frontage lies a guesthouse with a difference. At the Imperial we are committed to providing the highest standards of service. This Victorian house has been superbly restored to create an elegant and supremely comfortable interior. Ideally situated for the city centre, coast and Northumbria.

Bedrooms: 2 double/ twin; suites available
Bathrooms: 1 en suite

Evening meal available

Candlelit dinners and 'VIP welcome'. Please enquire for details.

◆◆◆

BATTLESTEADS HOTEL

Wark, Hexham NE48 3LS
T: (01434) 230209
F: (01434) 230730
E: info@battlesteads-hotel.co.uk
I: www.Battlesteads-Hotel.co.uk

B&B per night:
S £30.00–£35.00
D £60.00

HB per person:
DY £47.95–£72.95

OPEN All year round

18thC inn, formerly a farmhouse, in the heart of rural Northumberland, close to the Roman Wall and Kielder Water. An ideal centre for exploring Border country and for relaxing, walking, cycling or horse-riding. Collection and delivery service operated for walkers and cyclists.

Bedrooms: 1 single, 7 double/twin, 2 triple/ multiple
Bathrooms: 10 en suite

Lunch available
Evening meal available
CC: Amex, Delta, Mastercard, Switch, Visa

Please see web page.

◆◆◆◆

NORTH COTTAGE
Birling, Warkworth, Morpeth
NE65 0XS
T: (01665) 711263
E: edithandjohn@another.com
I: www.accta.co.uk/north

Bedrooms: 1 single, 3 double/twin
Bathrooms: 3 en suite

B&B per night:
S £20.00–£22.00
D £40.00–£44.00

OPEN All year round

Attractive cottage, with ground floor, en suite non-smoking rooms. Extensive gardens, with patio where visitors are welcome to relax. Off-street parking.

◆◆◆◆

WILLOW LODGE
12 The Willows, Washington
NE38 8JE
T: (0191) 419 4363
F: (0191) 419 4363
E: glover@nobrad.demon.co.uk

Bedrooms: 1 double/ twin, 1 triple/multiple

B&B per night:
S £25.00
D £40.00

OPEN All year round

Two double bedrooms with tea making facilities and colour TV. Full English breakfast. Secure parking. Close to Newcastle, Gateshead and Durham.

CHECK THE MAPS
The colour maps at the front of this guide show all the cities, towns and villages for which you will find accommodation entries.
Refer to the town index to find the page on which they are listed.

WHICKHAM, Tyne and Wear Map ref 5C2

Silver Award

EAST BYERMOOR GUEST HOUSE

Fellside Road, Whickham,
Newcastle upon Tyne NE16 5BD
T: (01207) 272687
F: (01207) 272145
E: eastbyermoor-gh.arbon@virgin.net

Bedrooms: 6 double/twin	Evening meal available	B&B per night:
Bathrooms: 5 en suite, 1 private	CC: Delta, Mastercard, Switch, Visa	S £23.00–£25.00
		D £46.00–£50.00
		OPEN All year round

Former farmhouse (approximately 200 years old) in open countryside. Near Gateshead MetroCentre, Newcastle, Durham and Sunderland. Rural but convenient.

WHITLEY BAY, Tyne and Wear Map ref 5C2 *Tourist Information Centre Tel: (0191) 200 8535*

MARLBOROUGH HOTEL

20-21 East Parade, The Promenade,
Whitley Bay NE26 1AP
T: (0191) 251 3628
F: (0191) 252 5033
E: reception@marlborough-hotel.com
I: www.marlborough-hotel.com

Bedrooms: 6 single, 7 double/twin, 3 triple/multiple	Evening meal available	B&B per night:
Bathrooms: 13 en suite	CC: Amex, Delta, Mastercard, Switch, Visa	S £22.00–£38.00
		D £45.00–£65.00
		HB per person:
		DY £34.00–£50.00
		OPEN All year round

Seaside hotel with fine sea views. Comfortable, modern accommodation with friendly service. Close to MetroCentre and ferry terminal.

WOOLER, Northumberland Map ref 5B1

LORETO GUEST HOUSE

1 Ryecroft Way, Wooler NE71 6BW
T: (01668) 281 350

Bedrooms: 1 single, 4 double/twin, 1 triple/multiple	Evening meal available	B&B per night:
Bathrooms: 6 en suite		S £18.00–£21.00
		D £18.00–£21.00
		HB per person:
		DY £25.00–£27.50
		OPEN All year round

Family-run early Georgian house in spacious grounds, in lovely Cheviot village. Central for touring and walking and close to coastline. All rooms en suite.

USE YOUR *i*s

There are more than 550 Tourist Information Centres throughout England offering friendly help with accommodation and holiday ideas as well as suggestions of places to visit and things to do. You'll find TIC addresses in the local Phone Book.

A brief guide to the main Towns and Villages offering accommodation in

Northumbria

ALNMOUTH, NORTHUMBERLAND - Quiet village with pleasant old buildings, at the mouth of the River Aln where extensive dunes and sands stretch along Alnmouth Bay. 18th C granaries, some converted to dwellings, still stand.

ALNWICK, NORTHUMBERLAND - Ancient and historic market town, entered through the Hotspur Tower, an original gate in the town walls. The medieval castle, the second biggest in England and still the seat of the Dukes of Northumberland, was restored from ruin in the 18th C.

BAMBURGH, NORTHUMBERLAND - Village with a spectacular red sandstone castle standing 150 ft above the sea. On the village green the magnificent Norman church stands opposite a museum containing mementoes of the heroine Grace Darling.

BARDON MILL, NORTHUMBERLAND - Small hamlet midway between Haydon Bridge and Haltwhistle, within walking distance of Vindolanda, an excavated Roman settlement, and near the best stretches of Hadrian's Wall.

BARNARD CASTLE, DURHAM - High over the Tees, a thriving market town with a busy market square. Bernard Baliol's 12th C castle (now ruins) stands nearby. The Bowes Museum, housed in a grand 19th C French chateau, holds fine paintings and furniture. Nearby are some magnificent buildings.

BEADNELL, NORTHUMBERLAND - Charming fishing village on Beadnell Bay. Seashore lime kilns (National Trust), dating from the 18th C, recall busier days as a coal and lime port and a pub is built on to a medieval pele tower which survives from days of the border wars.

BEAL, NORTHUMBERLAND - Tiny hamlet with an inn at the junction of the A1 which leads on to the causeway to Holy Island. Some farmhouses and buildings are dated 1674.

BEAMISH, DURHAM - Village made famous by the award-winning Beamish, North of England Open Air Museum, which covers every aspect of the life, buildings and artefacts of the North East of 1913. Also in the area are Causey Arch and Tanfield Railway.

BELLINGHAM, NORTHUMBERLAND - Set in the beautiful valley of the North Tyne close to the Kielder Forest, Kielder Water and lonely moorland below the Cheviots. The church has an ancient stone wagon roof fortified in the 18th C with buttresses.

BERWICK-UPON-TWEED, NORTHUMBERLAND - Guarding the mouth of the Tweed, England's northernmost town with the best 16th C city walls in Europe. The handsome Guildhall and barracks date from the 18th C. Three bridges cross to Tweedmouth, the oldest built in 1634.

BISHOP AUCKLAND, DURHAM - Busy market town on the bank of the River Wear. The Bishop's Palace, a castellated Norman manor house altered in the 18th C, stands in beautiful gardens. Entered from the market square by a handsome 18th C gatehouse, the park is a peaceful retreat of trees and streams.

CHATTON, NORTHUMBERLAND - Lovely village in the foothills of the Cheviot Hills, peaceful now but much troubled in the past. Nearby are Chillingham Castle and the famous herd of Chillingham Wild White cattle.

CONSETT, DURHAM - Former steel town on the edge of rolling moors. Modern development includes the shopping centre and a handsome Roman Catholic church, designed by a local architect. To the west, the Derwent Reservoir provides water sports and pleasant walks.

CORBRIDGE, NORTHUMBERLAND - Small town on the River Tyne. Close by are extensive remains of the Roman military town Corstopitum, with a museum housing important discoveries from excavations. The town itself is attractive with shady trees, a 17th C bridge and interesting old buildings, notably a 14th C vicarage.

DARLINGTON, DURHAM - Largest town in County Durham, standing on the River Skerne and home of the earliest passenger railway which first ran to Stockton in 1825. Now the home of a railway museum. Originally a prosperous market town occupying the site of an Anglo-Saxon settlement, it still holds an open market.

DURHAM, DURHAM - Ancient city with its Norman castle and cathedral, now a World Heritage site, set on a bluff high over the Wear. A market and university town and regional centre, spreading beyond the market-place on both banks of the river.

FROSTERLEY, DURHAM - Old quarrying village on the limestone slopes of Weardale. The rich Frosterley marble, black when polished, graces the fonts and columns of many local churches, including Durham Cathedral.

GATESHEAD, TYNE AND WEAR - Facing Newcastle across the Tyne, a busy industrial centre which grew rapidly early in the 20th century. Now it is a town of glass, steel and concrete buildings. Home of Europe's largest indoor shopping and leisure complex, the Metro Centre.

GREENHEAD, NORTHUMBERLAND - Small hamlet, overlooked by the ruins of Thirlwall Castle, at the junction of the A69 and the B6318 which runs alongside Hadrian's Wall. Some of the finest sections of the wall and the Carvoran Roman Military Museum are nearby.

HALTWHISTLE, NORTHUMBERLAND - Small market town with interesting 12th C church, old inns and blacksmith's smithy. North of the town are several important sites and interpretation centres of Hadrian's Wall. Ideal centre for archaeology, outdoor activity or touring holidays.

HAYDON BRIDGE, NORTHUMBERLAND - Small town on the banks of the South Tyne with an ancient church, built of stone from sites along the Roman Wall just north. Ideally situated for exploring Hadrian's Wall and the Border country.

HEXHAM, NORTHUMBERLAND
- Old coaching and market town near Hadrian's Wall. Since pre-Norman times a weekly market has been held in the centre with its market-place and abbey park, and the richly-furnished 12th C abbey church has a superb Anglo-Saxon crypt.

HOLY ISLAND, NORTHUMBERLAND
- Still an idyllic retreat, tiny island and fishing village and cradle of northern Christianity. It is approached from the mainland at low water by a causeway. The clifftop castle (National Trust) was restored by Sir Edwin Lutyens.

KIELDER WATER, NORTHUMBERLAND - A magnificent man-made lake, the largest in Northern Europe, with over 27 miles of shoreline. On the edge of the Northumberland National Park and near the Scottish border, Kielder can be explored by car, on foot or by ferry.

LONGFRAMLINGTON, NORTHUMBERLAND - Pleasant village with an interesting church of the Transitional style. On Hall Hill are the remains of a camp with triple entrenchment. Brinkburn Priory is nearby.

MIDDLETON-IN-TEESDALE, DURHAM - Small stone town of hillside terraces overlooking the river, developed by the London Lead Company in the 18th C. Five miles up-river is the spectacular 70-ft waterfall, High Force.

MORPETH, NORTHUMBERLAND
- Market town on the River Wansbeck. There are charming gardens and parks, among them Carlisle Park which lies close to the ancient remains of Morpeth Castle. The chantry building houses the Northumbrian Craft Centre and the bagpipe museum.

NEWCASTLE UPON TYNE, TYNE AND WEAR - Commercial and cultural centre of the North East, with a large indoor shopping centre, Quayside market, museums and theatres which offer an annual 6 week season by the Royal Shakespeare Company. Norman castle keep, medieval alleys, old Guildhall.

OTTERBURN, NORTHUMBERLAND
- Small village set at the meeting of the River Rede with Otter Burn, the site of the Battle of Otterburn in 1388. A peaceful tradition continues in the sale of Otterburn tweeds in this beautiful region, which is ideal for exploring the Border country and the Cheviots.

PONTELAND, NORTHUMBERLAND
- A place of great antiquity, now a dormitory town for Newcastle. The fine Norman church, fortified rectory, Vicar's Pele and old inn, formerly a 17th C manor house, make this town particularly interesting.

RIDING MILL, NORTHUMBERLAND
- Small village on the south bank of the River Tyne, near historic Corbridge and the Thomas Bewick Museum.

ROTHBURY, NORTHUMBERLAND
- Old market town on the River Coquet near the Simonside Hills. It makes an ideal centre for walking and fishing or for exploring this beautiful area from the coast to the Cheviots. Cragside House and Gardens (National Trust) are open to the public.

SALTBURN-BY-THE-SEA, CLEVELAND
- Set on fine cliffs just north of the Cleveland Hills, a gracious Victorian resort with later developments and wide, firm sands. A handsome Jacobean mansion at Marske can be reached along the sands.

SEAHOUSES, NORTHUMBERLAND
- Small modern resort developed around a 19th C herring port. Just offshore, and reached by boat from here, are the rocky Farne Islands (National Trust) where there is an important bird reserve. The bird observatory occupies a medieval pele tower.

SOUTH SHIELDS, TYNE AND WEAR
- At the mouth of the Tyne, shipbuilding and industrial centre developed around a 19th C coalport and occupying the site of an important Roman fort and granary port. The town's museum has mementoes of the earliest self-righting lifeboat, built here in 1789.

SPENNYMOOR, DURHAM - Booming coal and iron town from the 18th C until early in the 20th century when traditional industry gave way to lighter manufacturing and trading estates were built. On the moors south of the town there are fine views of the Wear Valley.

STANLEY, DURHAM - Small town on the site of a Roman cattle camp. At the Beamish North of England Open Air Museum numerous set-pieces and displays recreate industrial and social conditions prevalent during the area's past.

THROPTON, NORTHUMBERLAND
- Pretty village in Coquetdale with an ancient but well-preserved castle house at the west end of the village. Cragside (National Trust) is 2 miles to the east.

WARK, NORTHUMBERLAND - Set in the beautiful North Tyne Valley amid the Northumbrian fells, old village just above the meeting of Warks Burn with the North Tyne. Grey stone houses surround the green with its shady chestnut trees and an iron bridge spans the stream. The mound of a Norman castle occupies the riverbank.

WARKWORTH, NORTHUMBERLAND
- A pretty village overlooked by its medieval castle. A 14th C fortified bridge across the wooded Coquet gives a superb view of 18th C terraces climbing to the castle. Upstream is a curious 14th C Hermitage and in the market square is the Norman church of St Lawrence.

WASHINGTON, TYNE AND WEAR
- New Town based on an old coal-mining village. The original pit-head buildings and mining apparatus now serve as a museum. The Old Hall (National Trust), seat of George Washington's ancestors, was rescued from its dilapidated state in the 1930s, restored and furnished.

WHITLEY BAY, TYNE AND WEAR
- Traditional seaside resort with long beaches of sand and rock and many pools to explore. St Mary's lighthouse is open to the public.

WOOLER, NORTHUMBERLAND
- Old grey-stone town, market-place for foresters and hill farmers, set at the edge of the north-east Cheviots. This makes a good base for excursions to Northumberland's loveliest coastline, or for angling and walking in the Borderlands.

Where to Stay

2002

The official and best selling guides,
offering the reassurance of quality assured accommodation

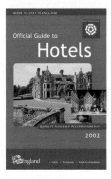

Hotels, Townhouses and
Travel Accommodation
in England 2002
£10.99

Guesthouses, Bed &
Breakfast, Farmhouses
and Inns in England 2002
£11.99

Self Catering
Holiday Homes
in England 2002
£9.99

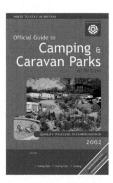

Camping & Caravan Parks
in Britain 2002
£5.99

Somewhere Special
in England 2002
£7.99

Look out also for:
**SOMEWHERE SPECIAL
IN ENGLAND 2002**

Accommodation
achieving the highest
standards in facilities
and quality of service -

the perfect guide for the
discerning traveller.

**NOW ALSO FEATURING
SELF CATERING
ACCOMMODATION**

The guides include

• Accommodation entries packed with information • Full colour maps
• Places to visit • Tourist Information Centres

INFORMATIVE • EASY TO USE • GREAT VALUE FOR MONEY

From all good bookshops or by mail order from the ETC Fulfilment Centre,
PO Box 22489, London W6 9FR
Tel: 0870 606 7204 Fax: 020 8563 3048
Email: fulfilment@englishtourism.org.uk Web: www.englishtourism.org.uk

NORTH WEST

Home of pop stars, world famous football teams, Blackpool Tower and Coronation Street, the great North West has vibrant cities, idyllic countryside and world class art collections too.

classic sights

Blackpool Tower & Pleasure Beach – unashamed razzamatazz
Football – museums and tours at Manchester United and Liverpool football clubs
The Beatles – The Beatles Story, Magical Mystery Tour Bus and Macca's former home

coast & country

The Ribble Valley – unchanged rolling landscapes
Formby – a glorious beach of sand dunes and pine woods
Wildfowl & Wetlands Trust, near Ormskirk – 120 types of birds including flamingoes

arts for all

The Tate Liverpool – modern art
The Lowry – the world's largest collection of LS Lowry paintings

distinctively different

Granada Studios – tour the home of many TV classics

The counties of Cheshire, Greater Manchester, Lancashire, Merseyside and the High Peak District of Derbyshire

FOR MORE INFORMATION CONTACT:

**North West Tourist Board
Swan House, Swan Meadow Road,
Wigan Pier, Wigan WN3 5BB
Tel: (01942) 821222 Fax: (01942) 820002
Internet: www.visitnorthwest.com**

The Pictures:
1 Manchester United
    Football Club
2 Healey Dell, Rochdale
3 Blackpool Beach

Places to Visit - see pages 140-143
Where to Stay - see pages 144-159

PLACES to visit

You will find hundreds of interesting places to visit during your stay, just some of which are listed in these pages. Contact any Tourist Information Centre in the region for more ideas on days out.

The Albert Dock Company Limited

Suite 22, Edward Pavilion, Albert Dock, Liverpool, Merseyside L3 4AF
Tel: (0151) 708 7334 www.albertdock.com
Britain's largest Grade I Listed historic building. Restored four-sided dock including shops, bars, restaurants, entertainment, marina and the Maritime Museum.

The Beatles Story

Britannia Vaults, Albert Dock, Liverpool, Merseyside L3 4AA
Tel: (0151) 709 1963
Liverpool's award-winning visitor attraction with a replica of the original Cavern Club. Available for private parties.

Beeston Castle

Beeston, Tarporley, Cheshire CW6 9TX
Tel: (01829) 260464
A ruined 13thC castle situated on top of the Peckforton Hills, with views of the surrounding countryside. Exhibitions are also held featuring the castle's history.

Blackpool Pleasure Beach

525 Ocean Boulevard, South Shore, Blackpool, Lancashire FY4 1EZ
(0870) 444 5577
www.blackpoolpleasurebeach.co.uk
Europe's greatest show and amusement park. Blackpool Pleasure Beach offers over 145 rides and attractions, plus spectacular shows.

Blackpool Sea Life Centre

The Promenade, Blackpool, Lancashire FY1 5AA
Tel: (01253) 622445
Tropical sharks up to 8 ft (2.5 m) housed in a 100,000-gallon (454,609-litre) water display with an underwater walkway. The new 'Lost City of Atlantis' is back with the feature exhibition.

Blackpool Tower

The Promenade, Blackpool, Lancashire FY1 4BJ
Tel: (01253) 622242 www.blackpoollive.com
Inside Blackpool Tower you will find the Tower Ballroom, a circus, entertainment for the children, the Tower Top Ride and Undersea World.

Boat Museum

South Pier Road, Ellesmere Port, Cheshire CH5 4FW
Tel: (0151) 355 5017
Over 50 historic crafts, largest floating collection in the world with restored buildings, traditional cottages, workshops, steam engines, boat trips, shop and cafe.

Bridgemere Garden World

Bridgemere, Nantwich, Cheshire CW5 7QB
Tel: (01270) 520381
Bridgemere Garden World, 25 fascinating acres (10 ha) of plants, gardens, greenhouses and shop. Coffee shop, restaurant and over 20 different display gardens in the Garden Kingdom.

Camelot Theme Park

Park Hall Road, Charnock Richard, Chorley, Lancashire PR7 5LP
Tel: (01257) 453044 www.camelotthemepark.co.uk
The magical kingdom of Camelot is a world of thrilling rides, fantastic entertainment and family fun, with over 100 rides and attractions to enjoy.

CATALYST: The Museum of Chemical Industry

Gossage Building, Mersey Road, Widnes, Cheshire WA8 0DF
Tel: (0151) 420 1121
Catalyst is the award-winning family day out where science and technology come alive.

Chester Zoo

Upton-by-Chester, Chester, Cheshire CH2 1LH
Tel: (01244) 380280 www.demon.co.uk/chesterzoo
Chester Zoo is one of Europe's leading conservation zoos, with over 5,000 animals in spacious and natural enclosures. Now featuring the new 'Twilight Zone'.

Dunham Massey Hall Park and Garden

Altrincham, Cheshire WA14 4SJ
Tel: (0161) 941 1025 www.thenationaltrust.org.uk
An 18thC mansion in a 250-acre (100ha) wooded deer park with furniture, paintings and silver. A 25-acre (10ha) informal garden with mature trees and waterside plantings.

East Lancashire Railway

Bolton Street Station, Bury, Greater Manchester BL9 0EY
Tel: (0161) 764 7790 www.east-lancs-rly.co.uk
Eight miles of preserved railway, operated principally by steam. Traction Transport Museum close by.

Gawsworth Hall

Gawsworth, Macclesfield, Cheshire SK11 9RN
Tel: (01260) 223456 www.gawsworthhall.com
Gawsworth Hall is a Tudor half-timbered manor-house with tilting ground. Featuring pictures, sculpture and furniture and an open-air theatre.

Jodrell Bank Science Centre, Planetarium and Arboretum

Lower Withington, Macclesfield, Cheshire SK11 9DL
Tel: (01477) 571339 www.jb.man.ac.uk/scicen
Exhibition and interactive exhibits on astronomy, space, energy and the environment. Planetarium and the world-famous Lovell telescope, plus a 35-acre (14-ha) arboretum.

Knowsley Safari Park

Prescot, Merseyside L34 4AN
Tel: (0151) 430 9009 www.knowsley.com
A 5-mile safari through 500 acres (202 ha) of rolling countryside, and the world's wildest animals roaming free – that's the wonderful world of freedom you'll find at the park.

Lady Lever Art Gallery

Port Sunlight Village, Higher Bebington, Wirral, Merseyside CH62 5EQ
Tel: (0151) 478 4136 www.nmgm.org.uk
The 1st Lord Leverhulme's magnificent collection of British paintings dated 1750-1900, British furniture, Wedgwood pottery and oriental porcelain.

The Pictures:
1 The River Ribble and Pendle Hill, Lancashire
2 Japanese Garden, Tatton Park
3 Lytham, Lancashire
4 Pavilion Gardens, Buxton
5 Blackpool Pleasure Beach

Lancaster Castle

Shire Hall, Castle Parade, Lancaster, Lancashire LA1 1YJ
Tel: (01524) 64998
www.lancashire.gov.uk/resources/ps/castle/index.htm
Shire Hall has a collection of coats of arms, a crown court, a grand jury room, a 'drop room' and dungeons. Also external tour of castle.

Lyme Park

Disley, Stockport, Greater Manchester SK12 2NX
Tel: (01663) 762023 www.nationaltrust.org.uk
Lyme Park is a National Trust country estate set in 1,377 acres (541 ha) of moorland, woodland and park.This magnificent house has 17 acres (7 ha) of historic gardens.

The Museum of Science & Industry, in Manchester

Liverpool Road, Castlefield, Manchester M3 4FP
Tel: (0161) 832 1830 www.msim.org.uk
The Museum of Science and Industry in Manchester is based in the world's oldest passenger railway station with galleries that amaze, amuse and entertain.

National Football Museum

Deepdale Stadium, Preston, Lancashire PR1 6RU
Tel: (01772) 908442
www.nationalfootballmuseum.com
The Football Museum exists to explain how and why football has become the people's game.

Norton Priory Museum and Gardens

Tudor Road, Runcorn, Cheshire WA7 1SX
Tel: (01928) 569895 www.nortonpriory.org
Medieval priory remains, purpose-built museum, St Christopher's statue, sculpture trail and award-winning walled garden, all set in 39 acres (16 ha) of beautiful gardens.

Quarry Bank Mill

Styal, Wilmslow, Cheshire SK9 4LA
Tel: (01625) 527468
www.rmplc.co.uk/orgs/quarrybankmill
A Georgian water-powered cotton-spinning mill, with four floors of displays and demonstrations and 300 acres (121 ha) of parkland surroundings.

Rufford Old Hall

Rufford, Ormskirk, Lancashire L40 1SG
Tel: (01704) 821254 www.nationaltrust.org.uk
One of the finest 16thC buildings in Lancashire with a magnificent hall, particularly noted for its immense moveable screen.

Sandcastle

South Promenade, Blackpool, Merseyside FY4 1BB
Tel: (01253) 343602
Wave pool, leisure pools, giant water flumes, white-knuckle water slides, kiddies' safe harbour, play area, catering, bar, shops and amusements.

Smithills Hall & Park Trust

Smithills Hall, Smithills Dean Road, Bolton, Greater Manchester BL1 7NP
Tel: (01204) 332377
Smithills Hall is a fascinating example of the growth of a great house which mirrors the changes in fashion and living conditions from the late 14thC.

Southport Zoo and Conservation Trust

Princes Park, Southport, Merseyside PR8 1RX
Tel: (01704) 538102
Zoological gardens and conservation trust. Southport Zoo has been run by the Petrie family since 1964. Talks on natural history are held in the schoolroom.

Stapley Water Gardens & Palms Tropical Oasis

London Road, Stapeley, Nantwich, Cheshire CW5 7LH
Tel: (01270) 623868
www.stapeleywatergardens.com
Large water garden centre filled with display lakes, pools and fountains. Trees and shrubs, pot plants, gifts, garden sundries and pets. Thousand of items on display.

Tate Liverpool

Albert Dock, Liverpool, Merseyside L3 4BB
Tel: (0151) 702 7445 www.tate.org.uk
The Tate at Liverpool exhibits the National Collection of Modern Art.

Tatton Park

Knutsford, Cheshire WA16 6QN
Tel: (01625) 534400 www.tattonpark.org.uk
Historic mansion with a 50-acre (20-ha) garden, traditional working farm, Tudor manor-house, 2,000-acre (809-ha) deer park and children's adventure playground.

Wigan Pier

Trencherfield Mill, Wigan, Lancashire WN3 4EF
Tel: (01942) 323666 www.wiganmbc.gov.uk
Wigan Pier combines interaction with displays and reconstructions and the Wigan Pier Theatre Company. Facilities include shops and a cafe.

Find out more about the
North West

Further information about holidays and attractions in the North West is available from:

NORTH WEST TOURIST BOARD
Swan House, Swan Meadow Road, Wigan Pier, Wigan WN3 5BB.
Tel: (01942) 821222 Fax: (01942) 820002
Internet: www.visitnorthwest.com

The following publications are available from North West Tourist Board:

Best of the North West
a guide to information on the region including hotels, self-catering establishments, caravan and camping parks. Also includes attractions, major events, shops and restaurants

Discovery Map
a non-accommodation guide, A1 folded to A4 map including list of visitor attractions, what to see and where to go

Bed and Breakfast Map
forming part of a family of maps for England, this guide provides information on bed and breakfast establishments in the North West region

Freedom
forming part of a family of publications about caravan and camping parks in the north of England

Stay on a Farm
a guide to farm accommodation in the north of England

Group Travel Planner
a guide to choosing the right accommodation, attraction or venue for group organisers

Venues
a 6-monthly newsletter about conference venues in the North West region

Schools Out
a 6-monthly newsletter aimed at schools providing information about where to go and what to see

The Pictures:
Derbyshire
Barca Cafe Bar, Manchester

Getting to the
North West

BY ROAD:
Motorways intersect within the region which has the best road network in the country. Travelling north or south use the M6 and east or west the M62.

BY RAIL:
Most North West coastal resorts are connected to InterCity routes with trains from many parts of the country and there are through trains to major cities and towns.

Where to stay in the North West

Accommodation entries in this region are listed in alphabetical order of place name, and then in alphabetical order of establishment.

Map references refer to the colour location maps at front of this guide. The first number indicates the map to use; the letter and number which follow refer to the grid reference on the map.

At-a-glance symbols at the end of each accommodation entry give useful information about services and facilities. A key to symbols can be found inside the back cover flap. Keep this open for easy reference.

A brief description of the towns and villages offering accommodation in the entries which follow, can be found at the end of this section.

A complete listing of all the English Tourism Council assessed accommodation covered by this guide appears at the back of the guide.

ABBEYSTEAD, Lancashire Map ref 4A1

◆◆◆

GREENBANK FARMHOUSE

Abbeystead, Lancaster LA2 9BA
T: (01524) 792063 & 792063
E: tait@greenbankfarmhouse.freeserve.co.uk.
I: www.greenbankfarmhouse.co.uk

Stone-built farmhouse set in peaceful countryside with glorious views of the Bowland Fells, yet only 4.5 miles from junction 33 of M6 and 5 miles from Lancaster University. Set in extensive gardens on the edge of the Forest of Bowland, ideal base for Lakes, dales and historic Lancaster.

Bedrooms: 3 double/twin
Bathrooms: 2 en suite

B&B per night:
S £20.00–£25.00
D £34.00–£38.00

OPEN All year round

12 P

SPECIAL BREAKS

Many establishments offer special promotions and themed breaks. These are highlighted in red. (All such offers are subject to availability.)

ACTON BRIDGE, Cheshire Map ref 4A2

◆◆◆◆

MANOR FARM

Cliff Road, Acton Bridge, Northwich
CW8 3QP
T: (01606) 853181
F: (01606) 853181
E: terri.mac.manorfarm@care4free.net

B&B per night:
S £22.00–£25.00
D £44.00–£50.00

OPEN All year round

Peaceful, elegantly furnished country house. Open views from all rooms. Situated down long private drive, above wooded banks of the River Weaver. Large garden provides access to private path through woodland into the picturesque valley. In central Cheshire, ideal location for business or pleasure, convenient for Chester, Merseyside and motorways.

Bedrooms: 1 single,
2 double/twin
Bathrooms: 1 en suite,
2 private

BAY HORSE, Lancashire Map ref 4A1

◆◆◆

STANLEY LODGE FARMHOUSE

Cockerham Road, Bay Horse,
Lancaster LA2 0HE
T: (01524) 791863
F: (01524) 793115

Bedrooms: 1 single,
1 double/twin, 1 triple/
multiple
Bathrooms: 1 en suite

B&B per night:
S £18.00–£20.00
D £36.00–£40.00

OPEN All year round

Family-run bed and breakfast. Leave M6 junction 33 on to A6 Garstang for 1 mile. Turn right signed Glasson, on to Cockerham Road, further mile to house

BIRKENHEAD, Merseyside Map ref 4A2 *Tourist Information Centre Tel: (0151) 647 6780*

◆◆◆

SHREWSBURY LODGE HOTEL AND RESTAURANT

31 Shrewsbury Road, Oxton,
Birkenhead CH43 2JB
T: (0151) 652 4029
F: (0151) 653 4079
E: info@shrewsbury-hotel.com
I: www.shrewsbury-hotel.com

Bedrooms: 7 single,
5 double/twin, 4 triple/
multiple
Bathrooms: 9 en suite

Evening meal available
CC: Delta, Mastercard,
Switch, Visa

B&B per night:
S £26.50–£36.50
D £48.00

HB per person:
DY £32.50–£48.00

OPEN All year round

Friendly hotel with relaxed atmosphere. Restaurant, licensed bar and function room. Private car park. Satellite TV. Close to the M53.

BLACKPOOL, Lancashire Map ref 4A1 *Tourist Information Centre Tel: (01253) 478 222*

◆◆◆

ARNCLIFFE HOTEL

24 Osborne Road, Blackpool FY4 1HJ
T: (01253) 345209 & 07802 438907
F: (01253) 345209
E: arncliffehotel@talk21.com
I: www.blackpool-internet.co.uk/
HOMEarncliffe.html

B&B per night:
S £15.00–£20.00
D £36.00–£50.00

HB per person:
DY £27.00–£34.00

Hotel of the Year 2000, Blackpool Tourism Award 2000. Small family-run hotel, convenient for all road, rail and air links. Situated in the South Shore, one minute from the Promenade, Pleasure Beach and Sandcastle leisure complex. Catering for couples and families only. Cleanliness and good home cooking assured. Credit cards accepted.

Bedrooms: 2 single,
5 double/twin, 1 triple/
multiple
Bathrooms: 5 en suite

Evening meal available
CC: Delta, Mastercard,
Visa

Mon-Fri breaks at reduced prices incl free night at cabaret show; discounted tickets for Pleasure Beach, Tower and zoo.

SYMBOLS The symbols in each entry give information about services and facilities. A key to these symbols appears at the back of this guide.

BLACKPOOL continued

◆◆◆ ASHCROFT HOTEL

42 King Edward Avenue,
North Shore, Blackpool FY2 9TA
T: (01253) 351538 & 07765 542306

Bedrooms: 3 single,
5 double/twin, 2 triple/
multiple
Bathrooms: 7 en suite

Evening meal available
CC: Delta, Mastercard,
Switch, Visa

B&B per night:
S £18.00–£23.00
D £36.00–£46.00

HB per person:
DY £23.00–£29.00

OPEN All year round

Small, friendly hotel off Queens Promenade, 2 minutes from sea and Gynn Gardens. Offering personal service. Cleanliness assured.

◆◆◆ BEVERLEY HOTEL

25 Dean Street, Blackpool FY4 1AU
T: (01253) 344426
E: beverley.hotel@virgin.net
I: www.beverleyhotel-blackpool.co.uk

Bedrooms: 1 single,
6 double/twin, 4 triple/
multiple
Bathrooms: 11 en suite

Evening meal available
CC: Delta, Diners,
Mastercard, Switch, Visa

B&B per night:
S £21.00–£24.00
D £36.00–£40.00

HB per person:
DY £27.00–£30.00

OPEN All year round

Licensed family-run hotel, with good home-cooked food. All rooms en suite. Adjacent promenade, Pleasure Beach and swimming complex, with local shopping facilities nearby.

◆◆◆ BONA VISTA HOTEL

104-106 Queens Promenade,
Blackpool FY2 9NX
T: (01253) 351396
F: (01253) 594985
E: bona.vista@talk21.com
I: www.bonavista@freeservers.com

Bedrooms: 2 single,
10 double/twin, 4 triple/
multiple
Bathrooms: 15 en suite

Evening meal available
CC: Amex, Delta, Diners,
Mastercard, Switch, Visa

B&B per night:
S £22.00
D £44.00

HB per person:
DY £30.50

OPEN All year round

Detached seafront hotel on North Shore overlooking sea and cliff walks. Furnished to high standard with large car park. Choice of dinner menu. Full English breakfast.

◆◆◆◆ COLLINGWOOD HOTEL

8-10 Holmfield Road, North Shore,
Blackpool FY2 9SL
T: (01253) 352929
F: (01253) 352929
E: enquiries@collingwoodhotel.co.uk
I: www.collingwoodhotel.co.uk

B&B per night:
S £20.00–£27.00
D £40.00–£54.00

HB per person:
DY £25.00–£32.00

OPEN All year round

Family supervised hotel, established for 25 years, in a select area just off Queens Promenade, near Gynn Gardens. Decorated and furnished to the highest standard with all the comforts of a modern hotel. Fine restaurant with plenty of choice. A warm and friendly welcome assured. Excellence is our standard. Private car park.

Bedrooms: 2 single,
11 double/twin, 4 triple/
multiple
Bathrooms: 17 en suite

Evening meal available
CC: Amex, Delta, Diners,
Mastercard, Switch, Visa

Tinsel and Turkey weekends, Theatre weekends, over 55s offers, early season special, Christmas and New Year house party.

◆◆◆◆ CROYDON HOTEL

12 Empress Drive, Blackpool FY2 9SE
T: (01253) 352497

B&B per night:
S £18.00–£26.00
D £36.00–£52.00

HB per person:
DY £22.00–£30.00

The Croydon is a small, warm and friendly family-run hotel. All rooms equipped with private shower and toilet, colour TV and tea-making facilities. Private car park. Resident owners Keith and Mary Staniland winners of award for best steak and kidney pies in the UK.

Bedrooms: 2 single,
6 double/twin, 2 triple/
multiple
Bathrooms: 10 en suite

Evening meal available

BLACKPOOL continued

◆◆◆

THE FERN ROYD HOTEL

35 Holmfield Road, North Shore, Blackpool
FY2 9TE
T: (01253) 351066
E: info@fernroydhotel.co.uk
I: www.fernroydhotel.co.uk

B&B per night:
S £18.00–£25.00
D £36.00–£50.00

HB per person:
DY £24.50–£31.50

OPEN All year round

Quiet, family-run hotel adjacent Queens Promenade, close to Gynn Gardens and a few minutes from sea. Spacious, comfortably furnished en suite bedrooms with TV and tea/coffee-making facilities professionally prepared meals. Offering a choice of menu. Separate smoking and non-smoking lounges.

Bedrooms: 2 single, 6 double/twin, 2 triple/ multiple
Bathrooms: 10 en suite

Evening meal available
CC: Delta, Mastercard, Switch, Visa

Special offers Mon-Fri all year including Illuminations.

◆◆◆

FYLDE HOTEL

93 Palatine Road, Blackpool
FY1 4BX
T: (01253) 623735
F: (01253) 622801
E: fyldehotel@talk21.com

Bedrooms: 5 single, 9 double/twin
Bathrooms: 11 en suite

Evening meal available
CC: Delta, Diners, Mastercard, Switch, Visa

B&B per night:
S £17.00–£24.00
D £34.00–£48.00

HB per person:
DY £23.50–£30.50

OPEN All year round

The hotel whose theme is old Blackpool was a turn-of-the-century town-centre vicarage. Situated between the seafront and Stanley Park. Bicycle loan scheme.

◆◆◆

RAFFLES HOTEL

73-75 Hornby Road, Blackpool
FY1 4QJ
T: (01253) 294713
F: (01253) 294240
I: www.raffleshotelblackpool.co.uk

Bedrooms: 1 single, 15 double/twin, 2 triple/ multiple
Bathrooms: 18 en suite

Evening meal available
CC: Amex, Delta, Mastercard, Switch, Visa

B&B per night:
S £20.00–£27.00
D £40.00–£54.00

HB per person:
DY Min £29.50

OPEN All year round

Excellent location for theatres, promenade, shops, restaurants, tourist spots and conference venues. Family-run private hotel with character. The proprietor is also the chef.

◆◆◆

SUNNYSIDE HOTEL

36 King Edward Avenue, North Shore,
Blackpool FY2 9TA
T: (01253) 352031
F: (01253) 354255
E: stuart@sunnysidehotel.com
I: www.sunnysidehotel.com

B&B per night:
S £18.50–£25.00
D £32.00–£45.00

HB per person:
DY £22.00–£29.00

OPEN All year round

Small hotel, BIG welcome, situated adjacent to promenade in a select, quiet area of North Shore yet near the town centre attractions. South-facing sun lounge, bar lounge, spacious dining area with varied menu to suit your needs. All bedrooms are en suite. Unrestricted street parking, and parking for 4 on site.

Bedrooms: 1 single, 3 double/twin, 4 triple/ multiple
Bathrooms: 8 en suite

Evening meal available

Early season savers except Bank Hols, Feb-Jun. Illuminations short breaks Fri-Mon, Mon-Fri Sep and Oct.

◆◆◆

WINDSOR PARK HOTEL

96 Queens Promenade, Blackpool
FY2 9NS
T: (01253) 357025

Bedrooms: 1 single, 9 double/twin, 1 triple/ multiple
Bathrooms: 11 en suite

Evening meal available
CC: Delta, Mastercard, Visa

B&B per night:
S £17.50–£26.00
D £35.00–£56.00

HB per person:
DY £23.00–£26.00

OPEN Jan–Oct &
Christmas

Hotel overlooking the Irish Sea. All bedrooms have en suite facilities. Full central heating, licensed bar, car park.

BOLTON, Greater Manchester Map ref 4A1 *Tourist Information Centre Tel: (01204) 334400*

◆◆◆ **FOURWAYS HOTEL**

13-15 Bolton Road, Moses Gate,
Farnworth, Bolton BL4 7JN
T: (01204) 573661
F: (01204) 862488
E: fourwayshotel@pureapshalt.co.uk

Bedrooms: 4 single,
5 double/twin, 1 triple/
multiple
Bathrooms: 7 en suite

Evening meal available
CC: Delta, Mastercard,
Switch, Visa

B&B per night:
S £34.00–£45.00
D £49.00–£59.00

HB per person:
DY £41.00–£53.00

OPEN All year round

New, quality hotel offering a high standard of service and facilities rarely found in small hotels. Noted English/Chinese restaurant. Two minutes from motorway network, 15 minutes from Manchester, 5 minutes from Bolton.

BOLTON-BY-BOWLAND, Lancashire Map ref 4B1

◆◆◆◆ **COPY NOOK HOTEL**

Bolton-by-Bowland, Clitheroe
BB7 4NL
T: (01200) 447205
F: (01200) 447004
E: copynookhotel@btinternet.com
I: www.copynookhotel.com

Bedrooms: 1 single,
4 double/twin, 1 triple/
multiple
Bathrooms: 6 en suite

Lunch available
Evening meal available
CC: Amex, Delta,
Mastercard, Switch, Visa

B&B per night:
S Max £40.00
D Max £60.00

OPEN All year round

Traditional country inn, set in rural countryside. All the charm and atmosphere of yesteryear combined with the modern comforts of today. Only 3 minutes from A59.

BURNLEY, Lancashire Map ref 4B1 *Tourist Information Centre Tel: (01282) 664421*

◆◆◆ **ORMEROD HOTEL**

121-123 Ormerod Road, Burnley
BB11 3QW
T: (01282) 423255

Bedrooms: 4 single,
4 double/twin, 2 triple/
multiple
Bathrooms: 10 en suite

B&B per night:
S £25.00–£28.00
D £40.00–£42.00

OPEN All year round

Small bed and breakfast hotel in quiet, pleasant surroundings facing local parks. Recently refurbished, all en suite facilities. 5 minutes from town centre.

CARNFORTH, Lancashire Map ref 5B3

◆◆◆◆ **GRISEDALE FARM**

Leighton, Carnforth LA5 9ST
T: (01524) 734360

Bedrooms: 2 double/
twin

B&B per night:
D £40.00

OPEN All year round

Working family farm set in an Area of Outstanding Natural Beauty. Leighton Moss RSPB 300yds. Convenient for lakes and dales. Ten minutes from M6.

CHEADLE HULME, Greater Manchester Map ref 4B2

◆◆◆ **SPRING COTTAGE GUEST HOUSE**

60 Hulme Hall Road,
Cheadle Hulme, Cheadle SK8 6JZ
T: (0161) 485 1037

Bedrooms: 1 single,
5 double/twin
Bathrooms: 3 en suite

CC: Delta, Mastercard,
Switch, Visa

B&B per night:
S £23.00–£30.00
D £39.00–£42.00

OPEN All year round

Beautifully-furnished Victorian house, in historic part of Cheadle Hulme. Convenient for airport, rail station and variety of local restaurants.

TOWN INDEX

This can be found at the back of the guide. If you know where you want to stay, the index will give you the page number listing accommodation in your chosen town, city or village.

CHESTER, Cheshire Map ref 4A2 *Tourist Information Centre Tel: (01244) 402111*

◆◆◆

ALTON LODGE HOTEL
78 Hoole Road, Chester CH2 3NT
T: (01244) 310213
F: (01244) 319206
E: enquiries@altonlodge.co.uk
I: www.altonlodge.co.uk

B&B per night:
S £45.00–£50.00
D £50.00–£70.00

OPEN All year round

Family-run, motel-style in attractive setting. Newly refurbished with 17 well-equipped en suite bedrooms. Emphasis on high standard and good value. City centre and railway station less than a mile. Easy access exit M53 at junction 12 into Chester.

Bedrooms: 1 single, 12 double/twin, 4 triple/ multiple
Bathrooms: 17 en suite

Evening meal available
CC: Delta, Mastercard, Switch, Visa

Short breaks available throughout the year. Early bird breaks available Jan-Mar.

◆◆◆

CHEYNEY LODGE HOTEL
77-79 Cheyney Road, Chester CH1 4BS
T: (01244) 381925

Bedrooms: 1 single, 6 double/twin, 1 triple/ multiple
Bathrooms: 8 en suite

Lunch available
Evening meal available
CC: Delta, Mastercard, Switch, Visa

B&B per night:
S £24.00–£30.00
D £39.90–£48.00

HB per person:
DY £30.90–£35.95

OPEN All year round

Small, friendly hotel of unusual design, featuring indoor garden and fish pond. 10 minutes' walk from city centre and on main bus route. Personally supervised, emphasis on good food.

◆◆◆◆

CHIPPINGS
10 Cranford Court, Chester CH4 7LN
T: (01244) 679728
F: (01244) 659470

Bedrooms: 1 double/ twin
Bathrooms: 1 en suite

B&B per night:
S £22.00–£25.00
D £38.00–£44.00

A modern property with a newly refurbished double room en suite. Convenient for motorway, good parking. Unlimited access. Call Elaine.

◆◆◆

GROSVENOR PLACE GUEST HOUSE
2-4 Grosvenor Place, Chester CH1 2DE
T: (01244) 324455 & 10244 400225
F: (01244) 400225

Bedrooms: 3 single, 4 double/twin, 3 triple/ multiple
Bathrooms: 6 en suite

CC: Delta, Mastercard, Switch, Visa

B&B per night:
S £25.00
D £36.00–£45.00

OPEN All year round

City centre guesthouse within the walls, two minutes from famous Rows, surrounded by restaurants, in quiet cul-de-sac. Most rooms en suite.

◆◆◆◆

GROVE HOUSE
Holme Street, Tarvin, Chester CH3 8EQ
T: (01829) 740893
F: (01829) 741769
E: helen_s@btinternet.com

B&B per night:
S £30.00–£40.00
D £40.00–£70.00

OPEN All year round except Christmas and New Year

Warm welcome in relaxing environment. Spacious, comfortable rooms, attractive garden. Ample parking. Within easy reach of Chester (4 miles) and major North West and North Wales tourist attractions. NWTB Place to Stay Award 1996 and 1997. Closed Christmas and New Year.

Bedrooms: 1 single, 2 double/twin
Bathrooms: 2 en suite, 1 private

PRICES
Please check prices and other details at the time of booking.

◆◆◆◆

THE GUESTHOUSE AT OLD HALL COUNTRY CLUB
Aldford Road, Chester CH3 6EA
T: (01244) 311593 & 317273
F: (01244) 313785
E: info@oldhallcountryclub.com
I: www.oldhallcountryclub.com

Six beautifully decorated en suite rooms in lovely landscaped rural setting only 5 minutes from historic city centre and station. Indoor/outdoor pools, saunas, steam, superb gym, tennis, yoga, aerobics, Aveda and Matis beauty spa, lounge bar serving excellent food. Awarded 'Club of the Year 2000'.

Bedrooms: 1 single, 5 double/twin
Bathrooms: 6 en suite

Lunch available
Evening meal available
CC: Delta, Mastercard, Switch, Visa

Luxury spa packages incl B&B from £150. Hen weekends from £130 (incl treatments and gourmet dinner).

B&B per night:
S £60.00–£75.00
D £95.00–£120.00

HB per person:
DY Min £85.00

OPEN All year round

◆◆◆

LABURNUM HOUSE
2 St Anne Street, Chester CH1 3HS
T: (01244) 380313
F: (01244) 380313

Bedrooms: 1 single, 1 double/twin, 1 triple/multiple
Bathrooms: 3 en suite

B&B per night:
S £22.00
D £44.00

OPEN All year round

A fine townhouse situated 4 minutes' walk from cathedral and city centre. Warm, comfortable en suite rooms complete with TV and hospitality tray. Private parking.

◆

LLOYD'S GUEST HOUSE
108 Brook Street, Chester CH1 3DU
T: (01244) 325838
F: (01244) 317491

Bedrooms: 4 single, 9 triple/multiple
Bathrooms: 7 en suite

B&B per night:
S £15.00–£20.00
D £30.00–£35.00

OPEN All year round

Family-run guesthouse, 5 minutes from train station and city centre.

◆◆◆◆

Silver
Award

MITCHELLS OF CHESTER GUEST HOUSE
28 Hough Green, Chester CH4 8JQ
T: (01244) 679004
F: (01244) 659567
E: mitoches@dialstart.net
I: www.mitchellsofchester.com

Bedrooms: 1 single, 4 double/twin, 1 triple/multiple
Bathrooms: 6 en suite

CC: Mastercard, Switch, Visa

B&B per night:
S £30.00–£38.00
D £48.00–£60.00

OPEN All year round

Tastefully restored, elegant Victorian residence, with steeply pitched slated roofs, sweeping staircase, antique furniture in tall rooms with moulded cornices. Compact landscaped gardens. Close city centre.

◆◆◆

RECORDER HOTEL
19 City Walls, Chester CH1 1SB
T: (01244) 326580
F: (01244) 401674
E: reservations@recorderhotel.co.uk
I: www.recorderhotel.co.uk

Bedrooms: 7 double/twin, 5 triple/multiple
Bathrooms: 12 en suite

Evening meal available
CC: Amex, Delta, Mastercard, Switch, Visa

B&B per night:
S £45.00–£50.00
D £55.00–£80.00

HB per person:
DY £38.00–£50.00

OPEN All year round

Centrally-situated Grade II Listed building on the walls of Chester overlooking the river. En suite rooms with TV and coffee-making facilities.

MAP REFERENCES The map references refer to the colour maps at the front of this guide. The first figure is the map number; the letter and figure which follow indicate the grid reference on the map.

CHOLMONDELEY, Cheshire Map ref 4A2

◆◆◆◆

MANOR FARM
Egerton, Cholmondeley, nr Malpas
SY14 8AW
T: (01829) 720261

B&B per night:
S £20.00–£30.00
D £19.00–£25.00

HB per person:
DY £25.00–£30.00

OPEN All year round

Charming farmhouse set in lovely grounds close to the Bickerton Hills. Peaceful location down private drive, but convenient for Chester and North Wales. Three miles from Carden Park and 1 mile from Cholmondeley Castle. All rooms en suite including 1 ground floor bedroom. Guests' comfort top priority.

Bedrooms: 1 single, 3 double/twin; suites available
Bathrooms: 2 en suite, 1 private

Lunch available
Evening meal available

Low season breaks £19pp 2 nights or more.

CHORLEY, Lancashire Map ref 4A1

◆◆◆◆

PARR HALL FARM
Parr Lane, Eccleston, Chorley PR7 5SL
T: (01257) 451917
F: (01257) 453749
E: parrhall@talk21.com

B&B per night:
S £30.00–£35.00
D £50.00–£60.00

OPEN All year round

Georgian farmhouse built in 1721 and tastefully restored. Quiet rural location within easy walking distance of good public houses and restaurants and village amenities. Conveniently situated for Lancashire coast and countryside, Lake District and Yorkshire Dales. Manchester Airport 45 minutes, junction 27 (M6) 5 miles north on B5250.

Bedrooms: 1 single, 3 double/twin
Bathrooms: 4 en suite

CC: Delta, Mastercard, Switch, Visa

CLITHEROE, Lancashire Map ref 4A1 *Tourist Information Centre Tel: (01200) 425566*

◆◆◆◆

RAKEFOOT FARM
Chaigley, Clitheroe BB7 3LY
T: (01995) 61332 & 07889 279063

Bedrooms: 5 double/twin, 3 triple/multiple
Bathrooms: 6 en suite, 2 private

B&B per night:
S £17.00–£25.00
D £37.00–£42.00

HB per person:
DY £29.00–£37.00

OPEN All year round

Working family farm. 17thC farmhouse and traditional stone barn conversion, between Clitheroe and Chipping. Panoramic views in Forest of Bowland. Home cooking. Also self-catering cottages.

ELSWICK, Lancashire Map ref 4A1

◆◆◆◆

THORNTON HOUSE
High Street, Elswick, Preston
PR4 3ZB
T: (01995) 671863
F: (01995) 671863
E: john_tizard@lineone.net

Bedrooms: 3 double/twin
Bathrooms: 3 en suite

B&B per night:
S Min £22.00
D Min £36.00

OPEN All year round

Comfortable friendly home, spacious rooms, kingsize beds. Situated in the Fylde countryside. Ideal base for exploring west coast resorts and many Fylde golf courses.

GARSTANG, Lancashire Map ref 4A1 *Tourist Information Centre Tel: (01995) 602125*

◆◆◆

Friendly, family-run thatched canalside hamlet, with restaurant, flagged floored Tavern Pizzeria, en suite lodgings, craft shops, cricket ground and thatched pavilion (all-weather wicket), crown green bowling (special events, corporate days), conference centre. Blackpool, Lake District, Yorkshire Dales within easy reach. Off junction 32 of M6, then 3 miles north on A6 to Garstang.

GUY'S THATCHED HAMLET

Canalside, St Michael's Road, Bilsborrow, Garstang, Preston PR3 0RS
T: (01995) 640010 & 640020
F: (01995) 640141
E: guyshamlet@aol.com
I: www.guysthatchedhamlet.co.uk

Bedrooms: 48 double/
twin, 5 triple/multiple
Bathrooms: 53 en suite

Lunch available
Evening meal available
CC: Amex, Delta, Diners,
Mastercard, Switch, Visa

Champagne weekends. Oyster Festival 31 Aug-4 Sept.

B&B per night:
S £48.50–£58.25
D £54.25–£64.00

HB per person:
DY £39.13–£45.50

OPEN All year round

🏔🐎⛵🌳🕴🍷Ⓢ✂🅗🕙🏢🍴♨✗⚕☕☾♪ꜛ❄🐴🖐🈁P

◆◆◆ **WOODACRE HALL FARM**
Scorton, Preston PR3 1BN
T: (01995) 602253
F: (01995) 602253

Bedrooms: 3 double/
twin
Bathrooms: 2 en suite,
1 private

B&B per night:
S £20.00–£22.00
D £36.00–£38.00

HB per person:
DY £28.00–£32.00

150-acre dairy and livestock farm. Built in the late 1600s, the former home of the 4th Duke of Hamilton, written about in A Hewitson's book 'Northward', chapter XIII.

🏢🌳☕Ⓢ✗⚕☕♪❄🐴🖐🈁P

◆◆◆ **CARTFORD HOTEL**
Cartford Lane, Little Eccleston,
Preston PR3 0YP
T: (01995) 670166
F: (01995) 671785

Bedrooms: 1 single,
5 double/twin
Bathrooms: 6 en suite

Lunch available
Evening meal available
CC: Delta, Mastercard,
Switch, Visa

B&B per night:
S £36.00–£40.00
D £48.00–£60.00

OPEN All year round

Country riverside pub and coaching inn, CAMRA Pub of the Year winner. Hosts on site Hart Brewery. Easy access to Blackpool and the Lake District.

🏔🐎🌳☕Ⓢ✗🏢♨⚕♪🐴🖐P

◆◆◆ **IT'L DO**
15 Oxcliffe Road, Heysham LA3 1PR
T: (01524) 850763

Bedrooms: 2 double/
twin

B&B per night:
S £15.00
D £28.00

OPEN All year round

Comfortable, welcoming atmosphere. Conveniently situated for Port of Heysham and delightful Heysham village. Ideal for touring, good links to M6 and Lancaster.

🐎🌳☕Ⓢ✗🏢🖐P

◆◆◆ **LOW HOUSE FARM**
Claughton, Lancaster LA2 9LA
T: (01524) 221260
E: shirley@lunevalley.freeserve.co.uk

Bedrooms: 1 single,
1 double/twin, 1 triple/
multiple
Bathrooms: 1 en suite,
1 private

B&B per night:
S £20.00–£25.00
D £40.00

OPEN All year round

130-acre mixed farm. Working mixed dairy farm in beautiful Lune Valley with large garden and within walking distance of country pub.

🏔🐎🖼🌳☕Ⓢ✗🏢♨⚕❄🐴🖐🈁P

IMPORTANT NOTE Information on accommodation listed in this guide has been supplied by the proprietors. As changes may occur you are advised to check details at the time of booking.

152

LIVERPOOL, Merseyside Map ref 4A2

◆◆◆ DOLBY HOTEL LIVERPOOL LTD

36-42 Chaloner Street,
Queen's Dock, Liverpool L3 4DE
T: (0151) 708 7272
F: (0151) 708 7266
E: liverpool@dolbyhotels.co.uk
I: www.dolbyhotels.co.uk

Bedrooms: 65 triple/
multiple
Bathrooms: 65 en suite

Evening meal available
CC: Amex, Delta,
Mastercard, Switch, Visa

B&B per night:
D £39.90–£46.90

OPEN All year round

On the famous Liverpool waterfront, 10 minutes from city centre. Free parking. All rooms are en suite and sleep up to 3 people.

◆◆ THE FEATHERS INN

1 Paul Street, Vauxhall Road,
Liverpool L3 6DX
T: (0151) 236 1203
F: (0151) 236 0081

Bedrooms: 2 single,
5 double/twin, 1 triple/
multiple
Bathrooms: 3 en suite

CC: Amex, Delta, Diners,
Mastercard, Switch, Visa

B&B per night:
S £25.00–£30.00
D £40.00–£50.00

OPEN All year round

Family-run, elegant stone house, 10 minutes' walk to city centre, ferry terminal. Large, attractive bedrooms with colour TV, tea/coffee facilities, hairdryer. Parking.

◆◆ HOLME LEIGH GUEST HOUSE

93 Woodcroft Road, Wavertree,
Liverpool L15 2HG
T: (0151) 734 2216 & 726 9980
F: (0151) 728 9521
E: bridges01@cableinet.co.uk

Bedrooms: 4 single,
6 double/twin
Bathrooms: 6 en suite

CC: Amex, Mastercard,
Switch, Visa

B&B per night:
S £15.00–£20.00
D £30.00–£35.00

OPEN All year round

Victorian red brick 3-storey corner dwelling and fashion shop, facing on to Lawrence Road. Just 2.5 miles from city centre, 2 miles from M62.

LOWER WHITLEY, Cheshire Map ref 4A2

◆◆◆ TALL TREES LODGE

Tarporley Road, Lower Whitley,
Warrington WA4 4EZ
T: (01928) 790824 & 715117
F: (01928) 791330
E: booking@talltreeslodge.co.uk
I: www.talltreeslodge.co.uk

Bedrooms: 14 double/
twin, 6 triple/multiple
Bathrooms: 20 en suite

CC: Amex, Delta,
Mastercard, Switch, Visa

B&B per night:
S £39.95–£45.00
D £39.95–£45.00

OPEN All year round

2.5 miles south of junction 10 of the M56. Take A49 towards Whitchurch. Little Chef and BP garage on site. A warm welcome awaits you.

MACCLESFIELD, Cheshire Map ref 4B2 *Tourist Information Centre Tel: (01625) 504114*

◆◆◆ MOORHAYES HOUSE HOTEL

27 Manchester Road, Tytherington,
Macclesfield SK10 2JJ
T: (01625) 433228
F: (01625) 429878
E: helen@moorhayes.co.uk
I: www.smoothhound.co.uk/hotels/
moorhaye

Bedrooms: 1 single,
6 double/twin, 1 triple/
multiple
Bathrooms: 8 en suite

CC: Delta, Mastercard,
Switch, Visa

B&B per night:
S £35.00–£40.00
D £52.00–£55.00

OPEN All year round

Warm welcome, comfortable house with gardens and parking. Half a mile from town centre. Hearty breakfasts. Rooms en suite with tea/coffee, TV and telephone.

CHECK THE MAPS

The colour maps at the front of this guide show all the cities, towns and villages for which you will find accommodation entries. Refer to the town index to find the page on which they are listed.

◆◆◆

DOLBY HOTEL MANCHESTER WEST LTD

55 Blackfriars Road, Manchester M3 7DB
T: (0161) 907 2277
F: (0161) 907 2266
E: manchester@dolbyhotels.co.uk
I: www.dolbyhotels.co.uk

Modern purpose-built hotel offering excellent value for money. Free car parking, city-centre location, close to railway station. Five minutes' walk from the MEN Arena, residents' bar open open until 1 am. Breakfast from £1.95 to £5.95 for a full English.

Bedrooms: 37 double/twin, 28 triple/multiple
Bathrooms: 65 en suite

Evening meal available
CC: Amex, Delta, Mastercard, Switch, Visa

B&B per night:
D £43.40–£50.40

OPEN All year round

MANCHESTER AIRPORT

See under Cheadle Hulme, Manchester, Mobberley, Sale, Salford, Stockport, Wilmslow

MARTHALL, Cheshire Map ref 4A2

◆◆◆

MOAT HALL MOTEL
Chelford Road, Marthall, Knutsford WA16 8SU
T: (01625) 860367 & 861214
F: (01625) 861136
E: val@moathall.fsnet.co.uk
I: www.moathallmotel.co.uk

Bedrooms: 3 single, 3 double/twin
Bathrooms: 6 en suite

B&B per night:
S £25.00–£35.00
D £40.00–£45.00

OPEN All year round

Modern accommodation on Cheshire farm, 6 miles from Manchester Airport. Knutsford 3 miles (M6 junction 19). All rooms en suite overlooking courtyard. Suitable for business and touring guests.

MOBBERLEY, Cheshire Map ref 4A2

◆◆◆◆
Silver Award

THE HINTON

Town Lane, Mobberley, Knutsford WA16 7HH
T: (01565) 873484
F: (01565) 873484

Award-winning bed and breakfast for both business and private guests. Within easy reach of M6, M56, Manchester Airport and InterCity rail network. Ideal touring base, on the B5085 between Knutsford and Wilmslow. Beautifully appointed rooms with many extras. All good home cooking.

Bedrooms: 2 single, 2 double/twin, 1 triple/multiple
Bathrooms: 5 en suite

Evening meal available
CC: Amex, Diners, Mastercard, Visa

B&B per night:
S £38.00–£44.00
D £50.00–£58.00

HB per person:
DY £49.15–£55.15

OPEN All year round

NEW BRIGHTON, Merseyside Map ref 4A2

◆◆◆

SHERWOOD GUEST HOUSE
55 Wellington Road, New Brighton, Wirral CH45 2ND
T: (0151) 639 5198
E: frankbreo@btinternet.com

Bedrooms: 1 single, 3 double/twin, 2 triple/multiple
Bathrooms: 3 en suite

Evening meal available

B&B per night:
S £16.00–£19.00
D £30.00–£35.00

HB per person:
DY £24.00–£27.00

OPEN All year round

Family guesthouse facing promenade and Irish Sea. Close to station and M53. Ideal centre for Chester, North Wales, Lakes and Liverpool (15 minutes).

MAP REFERENCES

Map references apply to the colour maps at the front of this guide.

◆◆◆ **WELLINGTON HOUSE HOTEL**

65 Wellington Road, New Brighton, Wirral CH45 2NE T: (0151) 639 6594 F: (0151) 639 6594 I: www.wellington-house-hotel.freeserve.co.uk	Bedrooms: 2 single, 5 double/twin, 4 triple/ multiple Bathrooms: 8 en suite	Evening meal available CC: Delta, Mastercard, Switch, Visa	B&B per night: **S £20.00–£25.00** **D £36.00–£45.00** OPEN All year round

Family-run hotel. Convenient for bus, train and boat, Mersey Tunnel and motorways. Evening meals/bar snacks available. Licensed bar. Enclosed car park. 24-hour CCTV.

NORTHWICH, Cheshire Map ref 4A2 *Tourist Information Centre Tel: (01606) 353534*

◆◆◆ **PARK DALE GUEST HOUSE**

140 Middlewich Road, Rudheath, Northwich CW9 7DS T: (01606) 45228 F: (01606) 331770	Bedrooms: 3 single, 2 double/twin, 1 triple/ multiple Bathrooms: 3 en suite	Lunch available Evening meal available CC: Delta, Mastercard, Switch, Visa	B&B per night: **S £21.00–£27.00** **D £42.00–£48.00** HB per person: **DY £27.00–£33.00** OPEN All year round

Warm and friendly accommodation within easy reach of town centre and the tourist attractions of the North West. Convenient for motorway links and Manchester Airport.

OLDHAM, Greater Manchester Map ref 4B1 *Tourist Information Centre Tel: (0161) 627 1024*

◆◆◆◆

TEMPLE BAR FARM
Wallhill Road, Dobcross, Oldham OL3 5BH
T: (01457) 870099 & 872003
F: (01457) 872003
E: info@templebarfarm.co.uk
I: www.templebarfarm.co.uk

B&B per night:
S £28.00–£35.00
D £42.00–£49.00

OPEN All year round except Christmas

A picturesque 18thC farmhouse, tastefully restored and surrounded by large gardens. Spectacular Pennine views. Beautifully appointed en suite bedrooms. Famed for our hospitality and home cooking. Ample parking. Manchester and motorways within easy reach. Central location makes us an ideal base for exploring the North of England.

Bedrooms: 3 double/twin
Bathrooms: 2 en suite, 1 private

Reductions available for longer stays. Painting weekends (with tuition) during the summer months.

ORMSKIRK, Lancashire Map ref 4A1

◆◆◆◆

THE MEADOWS
New Sutch Farm, Sutch Lane, Ormskirk L40 4BU
T: (01704) 894048

B&B per night:
S Min £22.00
D Min £38.00

OPEN All year round

Lovely 17thC farmhouse situated down a private country lane. Relaxed and friendly atmosphere. Three pretty en suite ground floor bedrooms with all home comforts. Both lounge and dining room overlook beautiful gardens. Enjoy a hearty breakfast whilst listening to the birdsong. Welcome pot of tea. M6, 15 minutes, A59, 5 minutes.

Bedrooms: 1 single, 2 double/twin
Bathrooms: 2 en suite, 1 private

QUALITY ASSURANCE SCHEME

Diamond ratings and awards are explained at the back of this guide.

◆◆◆◆

TULKETH HOTEL

209 Tulketh Road, Ashton, Preston PR2 1ES
T: (01772) 728096 & 726250
F: (01772) 723743
I: www.smoothhound.co.uk/hotels/tulketh.html

B&B per night:
S £37.50–£40.00
D £49.50–£60.00

OPEN All year round

Many original features have been retained in this fine Edwardian hotel, situated in a quiet residential area and fronted by mature gardens and large landscaped car park. There is a bar/lounge and a dining room off a most impressive period hallway. All bedrooms have modern facilities and are tastefully decorated.

Bedrooms: 5 single,
8 double/twin
Bathrooms: 13 en suite

Evening meal available
CC: Amex, Delta,
Mastercard, Switch, Visa

See under Clitheroe

◆◆◆◆

COMPTON HOUSE
Garstang Road,
St Michael's on Wyre, Preston
PR3 0TE
T: (01995) 679378
F: (01995) 679378
E: dave@compton-hs.co.uk
I: www.compton-hs.co.uk

Bedrooms: 3 double/
twin
Bathrooms: 3 en suite

B&B per night:
S £25.00–£30.00
D £40.00

OPEN All year round

Well-furnished country house in own grounds in a picturesque village, near M6 and 40 minutes from Lake District. Fishing in the Wyre. 'Best-Kept Guesthouse' award 1995 and 1996.

◆◆◆◆

CORNERSTONES

230 Washway Road, Sale M33 4RA
T: (0161) 283 6909
F: (0161) 283 6909
E: cornerstones.hotel@aol.com
I: www.cornerstoneshotel.com

B&B per night:
S £27.00–£35.00
D £54.00

HB per person:
DY £35.00–£50.00

OPEN All year round

Elegantly refurbished, offering every comfort and service. Ideally situated on the A56 only minutes from city and airport. 5 minutes' walk to Metro station and 10 minutes' drive to Trafford Centre, Manchester United football ground and LCCC.

Bedrooms: 3 single,
6 double/twin
Bathrooms: 7 en suite

Lunch available
Evening meal available
CC: Delta, Mastercard,
Visa

For 2-night weekend stays we will arrange a night at any theatre with a visit to a top Manchester restaurant.

◆

WHITE LODGE PRIVATE HOTEL
87-89 Great Cheetham Street West,
Salford M7 2JA
T: (0161) 792 3047

Bedrooms: 3 single,
6 double/twin

B&B per night:
S Min £20.00
D Min £34.00

OPEN All year round

Small, family-run hotel, close to city centre amenities and sporting facilities.

COLOUR MAPS Colour maps at the front of this guide pinpoint all places under which you will find accommodation listed.

SANDBACH, Cheshire Map ref 4A2

♦♦♦♦ **MOSS COTTAGE FARM**

Hassall Road, Winterley, Sandbach
CW11 4RU
T: (01270) 583018

Bedrooms: 1 single,
2 double/twin
Bathrooms: 1 en suite

Evening meal available

B&B per night:
S £22.00–£25.00
D £40.00–£45.00

OPEN All year round

Beamed farmhouse in quiet location just off A534, close junction 17 of M6. 1 double en suite. All rooms have TV, tea-making. Evening meals available.

SOUTHPORT, Merseyside Map ref 4A1 *Tourist Information Centre Tel: (01704) 533333*

♦♦♦♦ **AMBASSADOR PRIVATE HOTEL**

13 Bath Street, Southport PR9 0DP
T: (01704) 543998
F: (01704) 536269
E: ambassador.walton@virgin.net
I: www.ambassadorprivatehotel.co.uk

Bedrooms: 6 double/
twin, 2 triple/multiple
Bathrooms: 8 en suite

Lunch available
Evening meal available
CC: Amex, Delta,
Mastercard, Switch, Visa

B&B per night:
S £25.00–£36.00
D £50.00

HB per person:
DY £35.00–£46.00

OPEN All year round

Delightful small quality hotel with residential licence, 200 yards from promenade, conference facilities, Lord Street and gardens. All bedrooms en suite.

♦♦♦ **SANDY BROOK FARM**

52 Wyke Cop Road, Scarisbrick,
Southport PR8 5LR
T: (01704) 880337
F: (01704) 880337

Bedrooms: 1 single,
3 double/twin, 2 triple/
multiple
Bathrooms: 6 en suite

B&B per night:
S £21.00
D £36.00

OPEN All year round

27-acre arable farm. Comfortable accommodation in converted farm buildings in rural area of Scarisbrick, 3.5 miles from Southport. Special facilities for disabled guests.

STOCKPORT, Greater Manchester Map ref 4B2 *Tourist Information Centre Tel: (0161) 474 4444*

♦♦♦

HALLFIELD GUEST HOUSE

50 Hall Street, Stockport SK1 4DA
T: (0161) 429 8977 & 429 6153
F: (0161) 429 9017
E: hallfieldhouse@btconnect.com
I: www.hallfieldguesthouse.co.uk

B&B per night:
S £25.00–£30.00
D £40.00–£50.00

OPEN All year round

Spacious and comfortably refurbished Victorian house, ideally located for easy access to Manchester city centre and the Peak District. Stockport town centre is within walking distance where there is a main bus and railway station. There is a wide variety of restaurants in the area.

Bedrooms: 1 single,
4 double/twin
Bathrooms: 5 en suite

CC: Delta, Mastercard,
Switch, Visa

Rating Applied For

NEEDHAMS FARM

Uplands Road, Werneth Low,
Gee Cross, Hyde SK14 3AG
T: (0161) 368 4610
F: (0161) 367 9106
E: charlotte@needhamsfarm.demon.co.uk
I: www.needhamsfarm.co.uk

Bedrooms: 2 single,
4 double/twin, 1 triple/
multiple
Bathrooms: 6 en suite,
1 private

Evening meal available
CC: Mastercard, Visa

B&B per night:
S £20.00–£22.00
D £34.00–£36.00

HB per person:
DY Min £24.00

OPEN All year round

30-acre non-working farm. 500-year-old farmhouse with exposed beams and open fire in bar/dining room. Excellent views. Well placed for Manchester city and airport.

www.travelengland.org.uk
Log on for information and inspiration. The latest information on places to visit, events and quality assessed accommodation.

TARPORLEY, Cheshire Map ref 4A2

◆◆◆ **FORESTERS ARMS**
92 High Street, Tarporley CW6 0AX
T: (01829) 733151
F: (01829) 730020

Bedrooms: 4 double/
twin
Bathrooms: 1 en suite

Lunch available
Evening meal available
CC: Amex, Delta,
Mastercard, Switch, Visa

B&B per night:
S £24.50–£30.00
D £36.00–£45.00

HB per person:
DY £30.00–£38.00

OPEN All year round

Country public house, on the edge of the village of Tarporley, offering a homely and friendly service. Weekly rates negotiable.

TATTENHALL, Cheshire Map ref 4A2

◆◆◆ **BROAD OAK FARM**
Birds Lane, Tattenhall, Chester
CH3 9NL
T: (01829) 770325
F: (01829) 771546

Bedrooms: 3 double/
twin

B&B per night:
S £20.00–£22.00
D £36.00–£38.00

OPEN All year round

An 18thC country farmhouse with excellent views of Beeston Castle. Ideal, quite rural location.

TIMPERLEY, Greater Manchester Map ref 4A2

◆◆◆ **ACORN OF OAKMERE**
Oakmere, 6 Wingate Drive,
Timperley, Altrincham WA15 7PX
T: (0161) 980 8391
F: (0161) 980 8391
E: oakmere6@cwctv.net

Bedrooms: 1 single,
1 double/twin

B&B per night:
S £25.00–£50.00
D £50.00–£100.00

OPEN All year round

Comfortable quiet accommodation. With sunken spa bath, and separate dining room. Private walled garden. Two minutes' walk from golf course. Close to the airport and motorways.

WESTHOUGHTON, Greater Manchester Map ref 4A1

◆◆◆ **DAISY HILL HOTEL**
3 Lower Leigh Road, Daisy Hill,
Westhoughton, Bolton BL5 2JP
T: (01942) 812096 & 797180
F: (01942) 797180
E: daisy.hill@cwcom.net
I: www.daisyhillhotel.co.uk

Bedrooms: 2 single,
2 double/twin
Bathrooms: 4 en suite

CC: Delta, Diners,
Mastercard, Switch, Visa

B&B per night:
S £25.00–£30.00
D £35.00–£45.00

OPEN All year round

En suite rooms with TV, tea/coffee, fridge, safe, hairdryer, microwave. Private parking. Ideal for Reebok stadium, Harwich, Bolton, Leigh, Atherton, Wigan, all within 7 mile radius.

WILMSLOW, Cheshire Map ref 4B2

◆◆◆ **DEAN BANK HOTEL**
Adlington Road, Wilmslow SK9 2BT
T: (01625) 524268
F: (01625) 549715

Bedrooms: 11 double/
twin, 5 triple/multiple
Bathrooms: 16 en suite

Evening meal available
CC: Amex, Mastercard,
Visa

B&B per night:
S £36.00–£42.00
D £47.50–£55.00

HB per person:
DY £28.75–£32.50

OPEN All year round

Family-run, countryside hotel in a peaceful setting, ideal for leisure breaks, long or short stay business accommodation and Manchester Airport.

◆◆◆◆ **HOLLOW BRIDGE GUEST HOUSE**
90 Manchester Road, Wilmslow
SK9 2JY
T: (01625) 537303
F: (01625) 528718
E: lynandjack@hollowbridge.com
I: www.hollowbridge.com

Bedrooms: 2 single,
2 double/twin
Bathrooms: 4 en suite

CC: Delta, Mastercard,
Visa

B&B per night:
S £35.00–£40.00
D £48.00–£50.00

OPEN All year round

Recently refurbished house, en suite bedrooms, garden room dining, reading room. Off-road parking. Manchester Airport and motorway 10 minutes, Wilmslow centre 5 minutes.

CONFIRM YOUR BOOKING
You are advised to confirm your booking in writing.

◆◆◆◆ **MARIGOLD HOUSE**
132 Knutsford Road, Wilmslow
SK9 6JH
T: (01625) 584414 & 0793 9514609

Bedrooms: 3 double/
twin
Bathrooms: 3 en suite

B&B per night:
S £35.00
D £45.00

OPEN All year round

18thC period house with oak beams, flagged floors and antique furnishings. Log fires in winter. Private sitting room and dining room. Courtesy car to airport.

WIRRAL

See under Birkenhead, New Brighton

COUNTRY CODE

Always follow the Country Code ♧
Enjoy the countryside and respect
its life and work ♧ Guard against
all risk of fire ♧ Fasten all gates
♧ Keep your dogs under close control
♧ Keep to public paths across
farmland ♧ Use gates and stiles to
cross fences, hedges and walls ♧
Leave livestock, crops and machinery
alone ♧ Take your litter home ♧
Help to keep all water clean ♧
Protect wildlife, plants and trees ♧
Take special care on country roads ♧
Make no unnecessary noise ♧

A brief guide to the main Towns and Villages offering accommodation in the North West

A ACTON BRIDGE, CHESHIRE - Village with old farmsteads and cottages on a picturesque section of the River Weaver. Riverside walks pass the great Dutton Viaduct on the former Grand Junction Railway and shipping locks on the Weaver Navigation Canal.

B BIRKENHEAD, MERSEYSIDE - Founded in the 12th C by monks who operated the first Mersey ferry service, Birkenhead has some fine Victorian architecture and one of the best markets in the north west. Attractions include the famous Mersey Ferry and Birkenhead Park, opened in 1847, the first public park in the country.

• **BLACKPOOL, LANCASHIRE** - Britain's largest fun resort, with Blackpool Pleasure Beach, 3 piers and the famous Tower. Host to the spectacular autumn illuminations.

• **BOLTON, GREATER MANCHESTER** - On the edge of the West Pennine Moors and renowned for its outstanding town centre architecture and fine shopping facilities. The Octagon Theatre has national recognition for its theatre in the round. Samuel Crompton, inventor of the spinning mule, is buried here.

• **BOLTON-BY-BOWLAND, LANCASHIRE** - Village near the Ribble Valley with 2 greens, one with stump of 13th C market cross and stocks. Whitewashed and greystone cottages.

• **BURNLEY, LANCASHIRE** - A town amidst the Pennines. Towneley Hall has fine period rooms and is home to Burnley's art gallery and museum. The Kay-Shuttleworth collection of lace and embroidery can be seen at Gawthorpe Hall (National Trust). Burnley Mechanics Arts Centre is a well-known jazz and blues venue.

C CARNFORTH, LANCASHIRE - Carnforth station was the setting for the film 'Brief Encounter'. Nearby are Borwick Hall, an Elizabethan manor house, and Leighton Hall which has good paintings and Gillow furniture and is open to the public.

• **CHEADLE HULME, GREATER MANCHESTER** - Residential area near Manchester with some older buildings dating from 19th C once occupied by merchants and industrialists from surrounding towns. Several fine timber-framed houses, shopping centre and easy access to Manchester Airport.

• **CHESTER, CHESHIRE** - Roman and medieval walled city rich in treasures. Black and white buildings are a hallmark, including 'The Rows' - two-tier shopping galleries. 900-year-old cathedral and the famous Chester Zoo.

• **CHORLEY, LANCASHIRE** - Set between the Pennine moors and the Lancashire Plain, Chorley has been an important town since medieval times, with its covered markets. The rich heritage includes Astley Hall and Park, Hoghton Tower, Rivington Country Park and the Leeds-Liverpool Canal.

• **CLITHEROE, LANCASHIRE** - Ancient market town with a 800-year-old castle keep and a wide range of award-winning shops. Good base for touring Ribble Valley, Trough of Bowland and Pennine moorland. Country market on Tuesdays and Saturdays.

G GARSTANG, LANCASHIRE - Market town. The gateway to the fells, it stands on the Lancaster Canal and is a popular cruising centre. Close by are the remains of Greenhalgh Castle (no public access) and the Bleasdale Circle. Discovery Centre shows history of Over Wyre and Bowland fringe areas.

L LANCASTER, LANCASHIRE - Interesting old county town on the River Lune with history dating back to Roman times. Norman castle, St Mary's Church, Customs House, City and Maritime Museums, Ashton Memorial and Butterfly House are among places of note. Good centre for touring the Lake District.

• **LIVERPOOL, MERSEYSIDE** - Vibrant city which became prominent in the 18th C as a result of its sugar, spice and tobacco trade with the Americas. Today the historic waterfront is a major attraction. Home to the Beatles, the Grand National, two 20th C cathedrals and many museums and galleries.

M MACCLESFIELD, CHESHIRE - Cobbled streets and quaint old buildings stand side by side with modern shops and three markets. Centuries of association with the silk industry; museums feature working exhibits and social history. Stunning views of the Peak District National Park.

• **MANCHESTER, GREATER MANCHESTER** - The Gateway to the North, offering one of Britain's largest selections of arts venues and theatre productions, a wide range of chain stores and specialist shops, a legendary, lively nightlife, spectacular architecture and a plethora of eating and drinking places.

N NEW BRIGHTON, MERSEYSIDE - This resort on the Mersey Estuary has 7 miles of coastline, with fishing off the sea wall and pleasant walks along the promenade. Attractions include New Palace Amusements, Floral Pavilion Theatre, ten pin bowling and good sports facilities.

• **NORTHWICH, CHESHIRE** - An important salt-producing town since Roman times, Northwich has been replanned with a modern shopping centre and a number of black and white buildings. Unique Anderton boat-lift on northern outskirts of town.

CHECK THE MAPS

The colour maps at the front of this guide show all the cities, towns and villages for which you will find accommodation entries.
Refer to the town index to find the page on which they are listed.

O OLDHAM, GREATER MANCHESTER - The magnificent mill buildings which made Oldham one of the world's leading cotton-spinning towns still dominate the landscape. Ideally situated on the edge of the Peak District, it is now a centre of culture, sport and shopping. Good art gallery.

• **ORMSKIRK, LANCASHIRE** - Market town with interesting parish church of St Peter and St Paul containing bells brought from nearby Burscough Priory after its dissolution; half-timbered medieval manor houses, museum of Lancashire folk life and Martin Mere Wildfowl and Wetlands Centre

P PRESTON, LANCASHIRE - Scene of decisive Royalist defeat by Cromwell in the Civil War and later of riots in the Industrial Revolution. Local history exhibited in Harris museum. Famous for its Guild and the celebration that takes place every 20 years.

S SALE, GREATER MANCHESTER - Located between Manchester and Altrincham, Sale owes its name to the 12th C landowner Thomas de Sale. It is now home to Trafford Water Sports Centre and Park which offers the best in aquatic leisure and countryside activities.

• **SALFORD, GREATER MANCHESTER** - Industrial city close to Manchester with Roman Catholic cathedral and university. Lowry often painted Salford's industrial architecture and much of his work is in the local art gallery. Salford Quays provide a backdrop to pubs, walkways and a large cinema complex.

• **SANDBACH, CHESHIRE** - Small Cheshire town, originally important for salt production. Contains narrow, winding streets, timbered houses and a cobbled market-place. Town square has 2 Anglo-Saxon crosses to commemorate the conversion to Christianity of the King of Mercia's son.

• **SOUTHPORT, MERSEYSIDE** - Delightful Victorian resort noted for gardens, sandy beaches and 6 golf-courses, particularly Royal Birkdale. Attractions include the Atkinson Art Gallery, Southport Railway Centre, Pleasureland and the annual Southport Flower Show. Excellent shopping, particularly in Lord Street's elegant boulevard.

• **ST MICHAEL'S ON WYRE, LANCASHIRE** - Lancashire Village near Blackpool with interesting 13th C church of St Michael containing medieval stained glass window depicting sheep shearing, and clock tower bell made in 1548.

• **STOCKPORT, GREATER MANCHESTER** - Once an important cotton-spinning and manufacturing centre, Stockport has an impressive railway viaduct, a shopping precinct built over the River Mersey and a new leisure complex. Lyme Hall and Vernon Park Museum nearby.

T TARPORLEY, CHESHIRE - Old town with gabled houses and medieval church of St Helen containing monuments to the Done family, a historic name in this area. Spectacular ruins of 13th C Beeston Castle nearby.

• **TIMPERLEY, GREATER MANCHESTER** - Located between the towns of Sale and Altrincham, Timperley retains its village atmosphere with spacious tree-lined roads, excellent shopping facilities, restaurants and hostelries offering traditional ales, hearty meals and local speciality dishes.

W WILMSLOW, CHESHIRE - Nestling in the valleys of the Rivers Bollin and Dane, Wilmslow retains an intimate village atmosphere. Easy-to-reach attractions include Quarry Bank Mill at Styal. Lindow Man was discovered on a nearby common.

Our Countryside Matters!

Country Code

- Always follow the Country code
- Guard against all risk of fire
- Keep your dogs under close control
- Use gates and stiles to cross fences, hedges and walls
- Take your litter home
- Protect wildlife, plants and trees
- Make no unnecessary noise
- Enjoy the countryside and respect its life and work
- Fasten all gates
- Keep to public paths across farmland
- Leave livestock, crops and machinery alone
- Help to keep all water clean
- Take special care on country roads

We hope the countryside will fully open in 2002. However, given the serious nature of Foot and Mouth Disease please be ready to follow this additional advice and respect any further precautions given in local authority notices:

- Don't go onto farmland if you have handled farm animals in the last 7 days
- Avoid contact with farm animals and keep dogs on a lead where they are present
- If you step in dung, remove it before you leave the field • Don't go on paths with a local authority 'closed' notice.

For more information contact Tourist information Centres or Countryside Agency web site www.countryside.gov.uk which links to other local authority web sites providing details about rights of way and access opportunities across England.

Ratings
you can trust

English Tourism Council

◆ ◆ ◆

**GUEST
ACCOMMODATION**

When you're looking for a place to stay, you need a rating system you can trust. The **English Tourism Council's** ratings are your clear guide to what to expect, in an easy-to-understand form. Properties are visited annually by our trained, impartial assessors, so you can have confidence that your accommodation has been thoroughly checked and rated for quality before you make a booking.

Using a simple One to five Diamond rating, the system puts great emphasis on quality and is based on research which shows exactly what consumers are looking for when when choosing accommodation.

"Guest Accommodation" covers a wide variety of serviced accommodation for which England is renowned, including guesthouses, bed and breakfasts, ,inns and farmhouses. Establishments are rated from One to Five Diamonds. Progressively higher levels of quality and customer care must be provided for each of the One to Five Diamond ratings. The rating reflects the unique character of Quest Accommodation, and covers areas such as cleanliness, service and hospitality, bedrooms, bathrooms and food quality.

Look out, too for the english Tourism Council's Gold and Silver Awards, which are awarded to those establishments which not only achieve the overall quality required for their Diamond rating, but also reach the highest levels of quality in those specific areas which guests identify as being really important for them. They will reflect the quality of comfort and cleanliness you'll find in the bedrooms and bathrooms and the quality of service you'll enjoy throughout your stay.

The ratings are you sign of quality assurance, giving you the confidence to book the accommodation that meets your expectations.

YORKSHIRE

Yorkshire combines wild and brooding moors with historic cities, elegant spa towns and a varied coastline of traditional resorts and working fishing ports.

classic sights
Fountains Abbey & Studley Royal – 12th century Cistercian abbey and Georgian water garden
Nostell Prior – 18th century house with outstanding art collection
York Minster – largest medieval Gothic cathedral north of the Alps

coast & country
The Pennines – dramatic moors and rocks
Whitby – unspoilt fishing port, famous for jet (black stone)

literary links
Brontë parsonage, Haworth – home of the Brontë sisters; inspiration for 'Wuthering Heights' and 'Jane Eyre'

arts for all
National Museum of Photography, Film and Television – hi-tech and hands-on

distinctively different
The Original Ghost Walk of York – spooky tours every night

The counties of North, South, East and West Yorkshire, and Northern Lincolnshire

FOR MORE INFORMATION CONTACT:
Yorkshire Tourist Board
312 Tadcaster Road, York YO24 1GS
Tel: (01904) 707070 (24-hr brochure line) Fax: (01904) 701414
Email: info@ytb.org.uk Internet: www.yorkshirevisitor.com

The Pictures:
1 Roseberry Topping
2 Skidby Windmill
3 The Beach at Bridlington

Places to Visit - see pages 164-167
Where to Stay - see pages 168-214

PLACES to visit

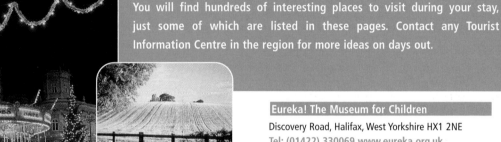

You will find hundreds of interesting places to visit during your stay, just some of which are listed in these pages. Contact any Tourist Information Centre in the region for more ideas on days out.

Eureka! The Museum for Children

Discovery Road, Halifax, West Yorkshire HX1 2NE
Tel: (01422) 330069 www.eureka.org.uk
Eureka! is the first museum of its kind designed especially for children up to the age of 12 with over 400 hands-on exhibits.

Beningbrough Hall & Gardens

Beningbrough, York, North Yorkshire YO30 1DD
Tel: (01904) 470666
Handsome Baroque house, built in 1716, with 100 pictures from the National Portrait Gallery, Victorian laundry, potting shed and restored walled garden.

Camp Modern History Theme Museum

Malton, North Yorkshire YO17 6RT
Tel: (01653) 697777 www.edencamp.co.uk
Modern history theme museum depicting civilian way of life during World War II. Millennium features.

Cusworth Hall Museum of South Yorkshire Life

Cusworth Hall, Cusworth Lane, Doncaster,
South Yorkshire DN5 7TU
Tel: (01302) 782342
www.museum@doncaster.gov.uk
Georgian mansion in landscaped park containing Museum of South Yorkshire Life. Special educational facilities.

The Deep

79 Ferensway, Hull, Kingston upon Hull HU2 8LE
Tel: (01482) 615789 www.hull.ac.uk
The Deep consists of 4 elements: a visitor attraction, learning centre, research facility and a business centre.

Flamingo Land Theme Park, Zoo and Holiday Village

Kirby Misperton, Malton, North Yorkshire YO17 6UX
Tel: (01653) 668287 www.flamingoland.co.uk
One-price family funpark with over 100 attractions, 7 shows and Europe's largest privately owned zoo. Europe's only triple-looping coaster, Magnum Force.

Fountains Abbey and Studley Royal

Studley Park, Ripon, North Yorkshire HG4 3DY
Tel: (01765) 608888 www.fountainsabbey.org.uk
Largest monastic ruin in Britain, founded by Cistercian monks in 1132. Landscaped garden laid between 1720-40 with lake, formal water garden, temples and deer park.

Hornsea Freeport

Rolston Road, Hornsea,
East Riding of Yorkshire HU18 1UT
Tel: (01964) 534211
Set in 25 acres (10 ha) of landscaped gardens with over 40 quality high-street names all selling stock with discounts of up to 50%, licensed restaurant. Leisure attractions.

Last of the Summer Wine Exhibition (Compo's House)

30 Huddersfield Road, Holmfirth, Huddersfield,
West Yorkshire HD6 1JS
Tel: (01484) 681408
Collection of photographs and memorabilia connected
with the television series 'Last of the Summer Wine'.

Leeds City Art Gallery

The Headrow, Leeds, West Yorkshire LS1 3AA
Tel: (0113) 247 8248
www.leeds.gov.uk/tourinfo/attract/museums/artgall.html
Art gallery containing British paintings, sculptures, prints
and drawings of the 19thC and 20thC. Henry Moore
gallery with permanent collection of 20thC sculpture.

Lightwater Valley Theme Park

North Stainley, Ripon, North Yorkshire HG4 3HT
Tel: (01765) 635321 www.lightwatervalley.net
Set in 175 acres (71 ha) of parkland, Lightwater Valley
features a number of white-knuckle rides and children's
rides along with shopping malls, a restaurant and picnic
areas.

Magna

Sheffield Road, Templeborough, Rotherham,
South Yorkshire S60 1DX
Tel: (01709) 720002 www.magnatrust.org.uk
Magna is the UK's first science adventure centre set in
the vast Templeborough steelworks in Rotherham. Fun is
unavoidable here with giant interactives.

Midland Railway Centre

Butterley Station, Ripley, North Yorkshire DE5 3QZ
Tel: (01773) 747674
Over 50 locomotives and over 100 items of historic
rolling stock of Midland and LMS origin with a steam-
hauled passenger service, a museum site, country and
farm park.

Mother Shipton's Cave & the Petrifying Well

Prophesy House, High Bridge, Knaresborough,
North Yorkshire HG5 8DD
Tel: (01423) 864600 www.mothershipton.co.uk
Mother Shipton's Cave and Petrifying Well are the oldest
tourist attractions in Britain, opened in 1630. Cave, well,
museum, playground and 12 acres (5 ha) of riverside
grounds.

National Museum of Photography, Film & Television

Bradford, West Yorkshire BD1 1NQ
Tel: (01274) 202030 www.nmpft.org.uk
This fascinating and innovative museum houses the three
types of media that have transformed the 20thC.
Millennium grant awarded.

National Railway Museum

Leeman Road, York, North Yorkshire YO26 4XJ
Tel: (01904) 621261 www.nrm.org.uk
For a fun-packed family day out come along to the
National Railway Museum and experience the incredible
story of the train.

North Yorkshire Moors Railway

Pickering Station, Park Street, Pickering,
North Yorkshire YO18 7AJ
Tel: (01751) 472508 www.nymr.demon.co.uk
Evening and Sunday lunchtime dining service trains offer
a unique and nostalgic experience with a wonderful
selection of menus to suit all tastes.

The Pictures:
1 Boats in harbour, Whitby, North Yorkshire
2 Hull Fair
3 Countryside near Grimsby
4 The Humber Bridge
5 Flamborough Head
6 Felixkirk, North York Moors

YORKSHIRE

Piece Hall

Halifax, West Yorkshire HX1 1RE
Tel: (01422) 358087 www.calderdale.gov.uk
Built in 1779 and restored in 1976, this Grade I Listed building forms a unique and striking monument to the wealth and importance of the wool trade.

Pleasure Island Family Theme Park

Kings Road, Cleethorpes, North East Lincolnshire DN35 0PL
Tel: (01472) 211511 www.pleasure-island.co.uk
The East Coast's biggest fun day out, with over 50 rides and attractions. Whatever the weather, fun is guaranteed with lots of undercover attractions. Shows from around the world.

Ripley Castle

Ripley, Harrogate, North Yorkshire HG3 3AY
Tel: (01423) 770152 www.ripleycastle.co.uk
Ripley Castle, home to the Ingilby family for over 26 generations, is set in the heart of a delightful estate with Victorian walled gardens, deer park and pleasure grounds.

Royal Armouries Museum

Armouries Drive, Leeds, West Yorkshire LS10 1LT
Tel: (0870) 510 6666 www.armouries.org.uk
Experience more than 3,000 years of history covered by over 8,000 spectacular exhibits and stunning surroundings. Arms and armour.

Sheffield Botanical Gardens

Clarkehouse Road, Sheffield, South Yorkshire S10 2LN
Tel: (0114) 250 0500 www.sbg.org.uk
Extensive gardens with over 5,500 species of plants, Grade II Listed garden pavilion (now closed).

Skipton Castle

Skipton, North Yorkshire BD23 1AQ
Tel: (01756) 792442 www.skiptoncastle.co.uk
Fully-roofed Skipton Castle is in excellent condition. One of the most complete and well-preserved medieval castles in England.

Temple Newsam House

Leeds, West Yorkshire LS15 0AE
Tel: (0113) 264 7321 www.leeds.gov.uk
Tudor/Jacobean house, birthplace of Lord Darnley. Paintings, furniture by Chippendale and others. Gold and silver c1600 onwards. Ceramics, especially Leeds pottery.

Thirsk Museum

14-16 Kirkgate, Thirsk, North Yorkshire YO7 1PQ
Tel: (01845) 527707
Exhibits of local life and industry and cricket memorabilia. The building was the home of Thomas Lord, founder of Lords cricket ground in London.

The Viking City of Jorvick

Coppergate, York, North Yorkshire YO1 9WT
Tel: (01904) 643211 www.jorvik-viking-centre.co.uk
Technology of the 21stC transforms real archaeological evidence into a dynamic vision of the City of York in the10thC.

Wensleydale Cheese Visitor Centre

Wensleydale Creamery, Gayle Lane, Hawes, North Yorkshire DL8 3RN
Tel: (01969) 667664
Museum, video and interpretation area, viewing gallery. Handmade Wensleydale cheese, licensed restaurant, specialist cheese shop, farm animals in natural environment.

Wigfield Farm

Haverlands Lane, Worsbrough Bridge, Barnsley, South Yorkshire S70 5NQ
Tel: (01226) 733702
Open working farm with rare and commercial breeds of farm animals including pigs, cattle, sheep, goats, donkeys, ponies, small animals, snakes and other reptiles.

York Castle Museum

The Eye of York, York, North Yorkshire YO1 9RY
Tel: (01904) 653611 www.york.gov.uk
England's most popular museum of everyday life including reconstructed streets and period rooms.

York Dungeon

12 Clifford Street, York, North Yorkshire YO1 9RD
Tel: (01904) 632599 www.thedungeons.com
Set in dark, musty, atmospheric cellars and featuring life-size tableaux of Dark Age deaths, medieval punishments and persecution/torture of heretics.

York Minster

Deangate, York, North Yorkshire YO1 7HH
Tel: (01904) 557200 www.yorkminster.org
York Minster is the largest medieval Gothic cathedral north of the Alps. Museum of Roman/Norman remains. Chapter house.

Find out more about Yorkshire

Further information about holidays and attractions in Yorkshire is available from:

YORKSHIRE TOURIST BOARD
312 Tadcaster Road, York YO24 1GS.
Tel: (01904) 707070 (24-hour brochure line)
Fax: (01904) 701414
Email: info@ytb.org.uk
Internet: www.yorkshirevisitor.com

The following publications are available from Yorkshire Tourist Board:

Yorkshire Visitor Guide 2002
information on the region, including hotels, self-catering, caravan and camping parks.
Also attractions, shops, restaurants and major events

Yorkshire - A Great Day Out
non-accommodation A5 guide listing where to go, what to see and where to eat,
the list goes on! Including map

Bed & Breakfast Touring Map
forming part of a 'family' of maps covering England, this guide provides information on
bed and breakfast establishments in Yorkshire

Group Operators' Guide 2002
a guide to choosing the right venue for travel trade and group organisers including hotels,
attractions and unusual venues

Conference and Venue Guide 2002
a full-colour, comprehensive guide to conference facilities in the region

The Pictures:
1 Walker in the Yorkshire Dales
2 York Minster

Getting to Yorkshire

BY ROAD: Motorways: M1, M62, M606, M621, M18, M180, M181, A1(M). Trunk roads: A1, A19, A57, A58, A59, A61, A62, A63, A64, A65, A66.

BY RAIL: InterCity services to Bradford, Doncaster, Harrogate, Kingston upon Hull, Leeds, Sheffield, Wakefield and York. Frequent regional railway services city centre to city centre including Manchester Airport service to Scarborough, York and Leeds.

Where to stay in
Yorkshire

Accommodation entries in this region are listed in alphabetical order of place name, and then in alphabetical order of establishment.

Map references refer to the colour location maps at front of this guide. The first number indicates the map to use; the letter and number which follow refer to the grid reference on the map.

At-a-glance symbols at the end of each accommodation entry give useful information about services and facilities. A key to symbols can be found inside the back cover flap. Keep this open for easy reference.

A brief description of the towns and villages offering accommodation in the entries which follow, can be found at the end of this section.

A complete listing of all the English Tourism Council assessed accommodation covered by this guide appears at the back of the guide.

AINTHORPE, North Yorkshire Map ref 5C3

◆◆◆◆ **THE FOX & HOUNDS INN**
45 Brook Lane, Ainthorpe, Whitby
YO21 2LD
T: (01287) 660218
F: (01287) 660030
E: ajbfox@globalnet.co.uk
I: www.foxandhounds.org

Bedrooms: 7 double/ twin
Bathrooms: 7 en suite

Lunch available
Evening meal available
CC: Amex, Delta, Diners, Mastercard, Switch, Visa

B&B per night:
S £33.00–£35.00
D £56.00–£60.00

OPEN All year round

16thC former coaching inn, now a high quality residential country inn and restaurant. Set amidst the beautiful North York Moors National Park.

APPLETREEWICK, North Yorkshire Map ref 4B1

◆◆◆◆ **KNOWLES LODGE**
Appletreewick, Skipton BD23 6DQ
T: (01756) 720228
F: (01756) 720381
E: chris.knowlesfitton@totalise.co.uk
I: www.knowleslodge.com

Bedrooms: 3 double/ twin
Bathrooms: 3 en suite

Evening meal available

B&B per night:
S Max £33.00
D Max £56.00

HB per person:
DY Max £45.00

OPEN All year round

In a spectacular setting of garden, meadow and woodland, Knowles Lodge overlooks River Wharfe. Accommodation comprises three stylishly appointed bedrooms, each with en suite bathrooms.

CREDIT CARD BOOKINGS If you book by telephone and are asked for your credit card number it is advisable to check the proprietor's policy should you cancel your reservation.

ARKENGARTHDALE, North Yorkshire Map ref 5B3

♦♦♦♦

THE CHARLES BATHURST INN

Arkengarthdale, Richmond DL11 6EN
T: (01748) 884567 & 884058
F: (01748) 884599
E: info@cbinn.co.uk
I: www.cbinn.co.uk

An 18thC inn steeped in local history offering outstanding fresh food in a warm and friendly atmosphere. Open fires and antique pine now furnish the bar and restaurant. Each of the en suite rooms has been individually designed and decorated and commands marvellous views of the Stang and Arkengarthdale.

Bedrooms: 18 double/
twin
Bathrooms: 18 en suite

Lunch available
Evening meal available
CC: Delta, Mastercard,
Switch, Visa

Special offers posted on our website throughout the year.

B&B per night:
S £40.00–£65.00
D £55.00–£75.00

HB per person:
DY £42.50–£50.00

OPEN All year round

ASKRIGG, North Yorkshire Map ref 5B3

♦♦♦

HOME FARM

Stalling Busk, Askrigg, Leyburn DL8 3DH
T: (01969) 650360

Situated amidst breathtaking scenery overlooking Semerwater Lake in Wensleydale. The 17thC beamed farmhouse with log fires is beautifully furnished with antiques, brass beds, patchwork quilts, etc. Bed and breakfast with optional evening meal. Traditional cooking and home-made bread are the order of the day. Licensed.

Bedrooms: 3 double/
twin

Evening meal available

B&B per night:
D £38.00

HB per person:
DY £30.00

OPEN All year round

AUSTWICK, North Yorkshire Map ref 5B3

♦♦♦♦

WOODVIEW GUEST HOUSE

The Green, Austwick, Lancaster
LA2 8BB
T: (01524) 251268

Bedrooms: 4 double/
twin, 2 triple/multiple
Bathrooms: 6 en suite

Evening meal available
CC: Delta, Mastercard,
Switch, Visa

One of the oldest (c1700) farmhouses in Austwick, an elegant Grade II Listed building on The Green. All rooms en suite. Packed lunch available. Welcome drink on arrival.

B&B per night:
S Min £36.00
D £55.00–£66.00

HB per person:
DY £43.50–£49.00

OPEN All year round

AYSGARTH, North Yorkshire Map ref 5B3

♦♦♦

CORNLEE

Aysgarth, Leyburn DL8 3AE
T: (01969) 663779 & 663053
F: (01969) 663779
E: cornlee@tesco.net
I: www.cornlee.co.uk

Bedrooms: 3 double/
twin
Bathrooms: 2 en suite,
1 private

Overlooking the village green in Aysgarth opposite The George and Dragon Inn. A short walk from Aysgarth waterfalls.

B&B per night:
S £25.00
D £40.00–£45.00

OPEN Feb–Dec

ACCESSIBILITY

Look for the symbols which indicate accessibility for wheelchair users. A list of establishments is at the front of this guide.

BARNETBY, South Humberside Map ref 4C1

REGINALD HOUSF
27 Queens Road, Barnetby
DN38 6JH
T: (01652) 688566
F: (01652) 688510

Bedrooms: 1 single,
2 double/twin
Bathrooms: 3 en suite

Evening meal available

B&B per night:
S £20.00–£25.00
D £35.00–£40.00

OPEN All year round

Quiet, family-run guesthouse in Barnetby village. Five minutes from M180 and railway station, 3 miles from Humberside Airport. Near to Grimsby, Scunthorpe and Hull.

BECK HOLE, North Yorkshire Map ref 5D3

Silver Award

BROOKWOOD FARM
Beck Hole, Whitby YO22 5LE
T: (01947) 896402
I: www.brookwoodfarm.co.uk

B&B per night:
S £35.00–£37.50
D £50.00–£55.00

OPEN All year round

Grade II Listed farmhouse with rooms enhanced in a romantic country style. We feel we have captured the timeless tranquillity of the countryside without sacrificing 21stC luxuries. Breakfast served in the sunny conservatory overlooking courtyard. Set in 18 acres of ancient meadows, ideally situated for woodland and moorland walks.

Bedrooms: 3 double/twin
Bathrooms: 3 en suite

Discounted winter breaks. Oriental food weekends as available Nov-Feb.

BEDALE, North Yorkshire Map ref 5C3

THE CASTLE ARMS INN
Snape, Bedale DL8 2TB
T: (01677) 470270
F: (01677) 470837
E: castlearms@aol.com

B&B per night:
S £45.00
D £59.00

HB per person:
DY Min £51.50

OPEN All year round

A family-run 14thC inn which has been completely refurbished. Nine en suite twin/double bedrooms have been added, all furnished to an exceptional standard and including TV and tea/coffee-making facilities. A warm welcome awaits you, with open fires, traditional ales and real home cooking.

Bedrooms: 9 double/twin
Bathrooms: 9 en suite

Lunch available
Evening meal available
CC: Delta, Mastercard, Switch, Visa

ELMFIELD COUNTRY HOUSE
Arrathorne, Bedale DL8 1NE
T: (01677) 450558
F: (01677) 450557
E: stay@elmfieldhouse.freeserve.co.uk
I: www.countryhouse.co.uk

Bedrooms: 7 double/twin, 2 triple/multiple
Bathrooms: 9 en suite

Evening meal available
CC: Delta, Mastercard, Switch, Visa

B&B per night:
S Max £37.00
D £50.00–£60.00

HB per person:
DY £37.00–£49.00

OPEN All year round

Country house in own grounds with special emphasis on standards and home cooking. All rooms en suite. Bar, games room, solarium. Ample secure parking.

QUALITY ASSURANCE SCHEME
Diamond ratings and awards were correct at the time of going to press but are subject to change. Please check at the time of booking.

BEVERLEY, North Humberside Map ref 4C1 *Tourist Information Centre Tel: (01482) 867430*

◆◆◆◆ BECK VIEW GUEST HOUSE

Beck View House, 1a Blucher Lane,
Beverley HU17 0PT
T: (01482) 882332
E: BeckViewHouse@aol.com

Bedrooms: 1 single,
4 double/twin
Bathrooms: 2 en suite,
3 private

B&B per night:
S Min £23.00
D £35.00–£38.00

OPEN All year round

Beck View House is a large modern bungalow with ample parking. Offering high-quality accommodation in a warm and friendly atmosphere.

◆◆◆ EASTGATE GUEST HOUSE

7 Eastgate, Beverley HU17 0DR
T: (01482) 868464
F: (01482) 871899

Bedrooms: 5 single,
8 double/twin, 3 triple/
multiple
Bathrooms: 7 en suite

B&B per night:
S £22.00–£38.00
D £35.00–£49.00

OPEN All year round

Family-run Victorian guesthouse, established and run by the same proprietor for 31 years. Close to town centre, Beverley Minster, Museum of Army Transport and railway station.

BOLTON PERCY, North Yorkshire Map ref 4C1

◆◆◆◆ GLEBE FARM

Bolton Percy, York YO23 7AL
T: (01904) 744228

Bedrooms: 1 double/
twin
Bathrooms: 1 en suite

B&B per night:
S £22.00–£24.00
D £44.00–£48.00

225-acre mixed farm. Excellent accommodation in self-contained en suite annexe on family-run farm. Conservatory, garden, ample parking.

BOSTON SPA, West Yorkshire Map ref 4B1

◆◆◆ CROWN HOTEL

128 High Street, Boston Spa,
Wetherby LS23 6BW
T: (01937) 842608
F: (01937) 541373

Bedrooms: 6 double/
twin, 1 triple/multiple
Bathrooms: 7 en suite

Lunch available
Evening meal available
CC: Delta, Mastercard,
Switch, Visa

B&B per night:
S £33.00
D £50.00

OPEN All year round

Small private hotel one mile from A1 and within easy reach of Yorkshire Dales, Harrogate, York and Leeds. An ideal base for a sightseeing and shopping break. Live jazz every Saturday.

BRADFORD, West Yorkshire Map ref 4B1 *Tourist Information Centre Tel: (01274) 753678*

◆◆ IVY GUEST HOUSE

3 Melbourne Place, Bradford
BD5 0HZ
T: (01274) 727060
F: (01274) 306347
E: 101524.3725@compuserve.com

Bedrooms: 2 single,
8 double/twin

CC: Amex, Delta, Diners,
Mastercard, Switch, Visa

B&B per night:
S £20.00
D £34.00

OPEN All year round

Large, detached, listed Yorkshire stone house. Close to city centre, National Museum of Photography, Film and Television, Alhambra Theatre and the University of Bradford.

AT-A-GLANCE SYMBOLS

Symbols at the end of each accommodation entry give useful information about services and facilities. A key to symbols can be found inside the back cover flap. Keep this open for easy reference.

BRIDLINGTON, East Riding of Yorkshire Map ref 5D3 *Tourist Information Centre Tel: (01262) 673474*

◆◆◆

BOSVILLE ARMS COUNTRY HOTEL

High Street, Rudston, Driffield YO25 4UB
T: (01262) 420259
F: (01262) 420259
E: hogan@bosville.freeserve.co.uk
I: www.bosville.freeserve.co.uk

B&B per night:
S £29.95
D £49.40–£57.40

OPEN All year round

Family-run country motel with village pub and quality restaurant. All rooms en suite. Located in beautiful historic Wolds village, only minutes from coast and golf courses. Art breaks with resident artist available. Quality accommodation, good food and fine ale, in a friendly country environment.

Bedrooms: 3 double/
twin, 3 triple/multiple
Bathrooms: 6 en suite

Lunch available
Evening meal available
CC: Delta, Mastercard, Switch, Visa

Residential art breaks with Yorkshire artist Tony Hogan. Small groups. All media and abilities catered for. All year round.

◆◆◆

THE GRANTLEA GUEST HOUSE

2 South Street, Bridlington
YO15 3BY
T: (01262) 400190

Bedrooms: 2 single,
4 double/twin
Bathrooms: 3 en suite

Evening meal available

B&B per night:
S £15.00–£17.00
D £30.00–£34.00

OPEN All year round

Situated on the south side, 1 minute from the beach, spa, theatre and harbour. Within easy walking distance of the town centre and coach/rail stations.

◆◆◆

THE WHITE ROSE

123 Cardigan Road, Bridlington
YO15 3LP
T: (01262) 673245 & 07860 159208

Bedrooms: 4 double/
twin, 1 triple/multiple
Bathrooms: 4 en suite

Lunch available
Evening meal available
CC: Mastercard, Visa

B&B per night:
S £20.00–£22.00
D £40.00–£44.00

HB per person:
DY £27.00–£29.00

OPEN All year round

Personal attention with warm, friendly hospitality and emphasis on food. No hidden extras. Near the South Beach, spa and harbour. Special pensioners' weeks at discount prices.

BRIGSLEY, South Humberside Map ref 4D1

◆◆◆◆

PROSPECT FARM

Waltham Road, Brigsley, Grimsby
DN37 0RQ
T: (01472) 826491
E: prospectfarm@btchick.com
I: www.nelincs.gov.uk

B&B per night:
S £22.50–£25.00
D £45.00–£50.00

OPEN All year round

Prospect Farm is situated down a long leafy lane. The house offers tranquil views of horses and sheep grazing. The bedrooms are attractively furnished with either en suite or private bathroom (with jacuzzi bath). Aga cooked breakfasts, and the snug with its open fire for your relaxation.

Bedrooms: 1 single,
2 double/twin
Bathrooms: 1 en suite

CHECK THE MAPS

The colour maps at the front of this guide show all the cities, towns and villages for which you will find accommodation entries.
Refer to the town index to find the page on which they are listed.

CROPTON, North Yorkshire Map ref 5C3

Silver Award

HIGH FARM

Cropton, Pickering YO18 8HL
T: (01751) 417461
F: (01751) 417807
E: highfarmcropton@aol.com

B&B per night:
S £24.99
D £44.00

OPEN All year round

Relax in the friendly atmosphere of this elegant Victorian farmhouse surrounded by beautiful gardens, on the edge of quiet, unspoilt village and overlooking North York Moors National Park. Peaceful base for walkers, nature/garden lovers. Steam railway and Castle Howard nearby. Village inn has own brewery. A warm welcome awaits.

Bedrooms: 3 double/twin
Bathrooms: 3 en suite

CC: Delta, Mastercard, Switch, Visa

DANBY, North Yorkshire Map ref 5C3

DUKE OF WELLINGTON INN

Danby, Whitby YO21 2LY
T: (01287) 660351
E: landlord@dukeofwellington.freeserve.co.uk
I: www.danby-dukeofwellington.co.uk

B&B per night:
S £30.00–£35.00
D £60.00

HB per person:
DY £39.95

OPEN All year round

An ivy-clad traditional 18thC inn located in the tranquil village of Danby at the heart of the North Moors. Enjoy our home cooked meals, real ales, interesting wines and malt whiskies whilst seated by the open fire. An ideal base for exploring the Moors, Whitby and coast.

Bedrooms: 1 single, 5 double/twin, 1 triple/multiple
Bathrooms: 7 en suite

Lunch available
Evening meal available
CC: Delta, Mastercard, Switch, Visa

ROWANTREE FARM
Ainthorpe, Whitby YO21 2LE
T: (01287) 660396
E: krbsatindall@aol.com

Bedrooms: 1 double/twin, 1 triple/multiple

Evening meal available

B&B per night:
S £17.00–£18.00
D £34.00–£36.00

HB per person:
DY £26.00–£27.00

OPEN All year round

120-acre mixed farm on the outskirts of Danby village. Panoramic moorland views and ample car parking facilities. Home cooking. Ideal walking country. Friendly atmosphere.

SYCAMORE HOUSE
Danby Dale, Danby, Whitby YO21 2NW
T: (01287) 660125 & 07703 714676
F: (01287) 669122
E: sycamore.danby@btinternet.com
I: www.smoothhound.co.uk/hotels/sycamore1.html

Bedrooms: 2 double/twin, 1 triple/multiple
Bathrooms: 1 en suite

Evening meal available

B&B per night:
S £20.00
D £40.00

HB per person:
DY £32.00

OPEN All year round

A comfortable 17thC stone-built home offering modern facilities and conveniences. Stunning views reinforce the welcome that awaits you. Please contact us for a brochure.

RATING All accommodation in this guide has been rated, or is awaiting a rating, by a trained English Tourism Council assessor.

DARLEY, North Yorkshire Map ref 4B1

◆◆◆◆ **ELSINGLEA GUEST HOUSE**
Sheepcote Lane, Darley, Harrogate
HG3 2RW
T: (01423) 781069 & 0777 391 4642
I: www.elsingleaguesthouse.homestead.com/homepage.html

Bedrooms: 1 single, 2 double/twin
Bathrooms: 3 en suite

B&B per night:
S £30.00–£35.00
D £45.00–£48.00

OPEN All year round

Property was once an old barn which we have carefully converted, but still retaining its unique character. Over-looking the beautiful Nielderdale valley. Independent access.

DEIGHTON, North Yorkshire Map ref 4C1

◆◆◆ **GRIMSTON HOUSE**
Deighton, York YO19 6HB
T: (01904) 728328
F: (01904) 720093
E: grimstonhouse@talk21.com
I: www.grimstonhouse.com

Bedrooms: 1 double/twin, 6 triple/multiple
Bathrooms: 5 en suite

B&B per night:
S £31.00–£38.00
D £45.00–£50.00

OPEN All year round

Country house in well-established gardens, 5 miles from York and close to good pub food.

DONCASTER, South Yorkshire Map ref 4C1 *Tourist Information Centre Tel: (01302) 734309*

◆◆◆◆ **LOW FARM**
The Green, Clayton, Doncaster
DN5 7DB
T: (01977) 648433 & 640472
F: (01977) 640472
E: bar@lowfarm.freeserve.co.uk
I: www.lowfarm.freeserve.co.uk

Bedrooms: 1 single, 5 double/twin, 1 triple/multiple
Bathrooms: 4 en suite

B&B per night:
S £22.00–£30.00
D £40.00–£56.00

OPEN All year round

Restored 17thC farmhouse and restored barns in rural village with 10 other working farms. In conservation village in South Yorkshire, within easy reach of Doncaster.

EASINGWOLD, North Yorkshire Map ref 5C3

◆◆◆ **YEOMAN'S COURSE HOUSE**
Thornton Hill, Easingwold, York
YO61 3PY
T: (01347) 868126
F: (01347) 868129
E: chris@yeomanscourse.fsnet.co.uk

Bedrooms: 3 double/twin

B&B per night:
S £18.50–£20.50
D £37.00–£39.00

Built c1800 as part of Newburgh Priory Estate. Set in the Howardian Hills overlooking the Vale of York and beyond.

EBBERSTON, North Yorkshire Map ref 5D3

◆◆◆ **GIVENDALE HEAD FARM**
Ebberston, Scarborough YO13 9PU
T: (01723) 859383
F: (01723) 859383
E: sue.gwilliam@talk21.com
I: www.visityorkshire.com

Bedrooms: 3 double/twin
Bathrooms: 3 en suite

Evening meal available

B&B per night:
S £20.00–£22.00
D £36.00–£40.00

OPEN All year round

A warm welcome and good food awaits on family-run farm. Quiet location, lovely views. Dalby Forest on our doorstep. A good base for touring, walking and mountain biking.

FILEY, North Yorkshire Map ref 5D3

◆◆ **PEBBLES GUEST HOUSE**
5-6 Brooklands, Filey YO14 9BA
T: (01723) 513366 & 07944 917238

Bedrooms: 3 single, 4 double/twin, 1 triple/multiple

B&B per night:
S Min £15.00
D Min £30.00

Family-run guesthouse with good sized rooms, lounge and a passenger lift to all floors. Close to shops, gardens and beach. Disabled access and facilities.

WHERE TO STAY
Please mention this guide when making your booking.

GARFORTH, West Yorkshire Map ref 4B1

◆◆◆ **MYRTLE HOUSE**
31 Wakefield Road, Garforth, Leeds
LS25 1AN
T: (0113) 286 6445

Bedrooms: 1 single,
2 double/twin, 3 triple/
multiple

B&B per night:
S £18.50–£21.00
D £38.00–£42.00

Spacious Victorian terraced house between M62 and A1 (M1, junction 47). All rooms have tea and coffee making facilities, TV, vanity basins and central heating.

OPEN All year round

GLAISDALE, North Yorkshire Map ref 5C3

◆◆◆ **HOLLINS FARM**
Glaisdale, Whitby YO21 2PZ
T: (01947) 897516

Bedrooms: 1 double/
twin, 1 triple/multiple

B&B per night:
S £16.00–£17.00
D £32.00–£34.00

Comfortable farmhouse bed and breakfast and good camping facilities. Near moors, short drive Whitby, steam railway, many pretty villages and good places to eat.

OPEN All year round

◆◆◆ **LONDON HOUSE FARM**
Dale Head, Glaisdale, Whitby
YO21 2PZ
T: (01530) 836122
F: (01947) 897166
E: marydanaher@hotmail.com

Bedrooms: 2 double/
twin, 1 triple/multiple
Bathrooms: 3 en suite

Evening meal available
CC: Mastercard, Visa

B&B per night:
S £25.00–£35.00
D £44.00–£58.00

HB per person:
DY £32.00–£44.00

Tasty home cooking using fresh local produce at our traditional farmhouse situated in a beautiful, quiet dale in the heart of the North York moors.

GOATHLAND, North Yorkshire Map ref 5D3

◆◆◆ **FAIRHAVEN COUNTRY HOTEL**
The Common, Goathland, Whitby
YO22 5AN
T: (01947) 896361
E: royellis@thefairhavenhotel.co.uk
I: www.thefairhavenhotel.co.uk

Bedrooms: 2 single,
4 double/twin, 3 triple/
multiple
Bathrooms: 5 en suite

Evening meal available
CC: Delta, Mastercard,
Switch, Visa

B&B per night:
S £22.00–£35.00
D £46.00–£54.00

HB per person:
DY £36.00–£49.00

Edwardian country house with superb moorland views in the centre of Goathland village. Warm hospitality and fine food in a relaxed atmosphere. Dogs welcome.

OPEN All year round

◆◆◆

HEATHERDENE HOTEL
The Common, Goathland, Whitby
YO22 5AN
T: (01947) 896334
F: (01947) 896334
E: info@heatherdenehotel.co.uk
I: www.heatherdenehotel.co.uk

B&B per night:
S £35.00
D £50.00–£70.00

HB per person:
DY £37.00–£50.00

OPEN All year round

Heatherdene is a licensed hotel situated in Goathland. Formerly a vicarage, the accommodation is spacious and comfortable with magnificent views. Home cooking and a warm welcome are Heatherdene specialities. An ideal base for exploring the national park. The North Yorkshire Moors Railway is only a short walk from the hotel.

Bedrooms: 1 single,
3 double/twin, 2 triple/
multiple
Bathrooms: 6 en suite

Evening meal available
CC: Delta, Mastercard,
Switch, Visa

SPECIAL BREAKS

Many establishments offer special promotions and themed breaks. These are highlighted in red. (All such offers are subject to availability.)

GOATHLAND continued

◆◆◆◆

PRUDOM GUEST HOUSE

Goathland, Whitby YO22 5AN
T: (01947) 896368
F: (01947) 896030
E: info@prudomhouse.co.uk
I: www.prudomhouse.co.uk

B&B per night:
S £25.00–£28.00
D £25.00–£30.00

A warm welcome awaits you at our cosy family-owned 18thC farmhouse in the village of Goathland. Situated opposite the church and surrounded by magnificent moorland views. Perfect for walking and touring. Quality accommodation, log fires, pretty cottage gardens and excellent food using local produce.

Bedrooms: 1 single, 5 double/twin
Bathrooms: 6 en suite

GRASSINGTON, North Yorkshire Map ref 5B3 *Tourist Information Centre Tel: (01756) 752774*

◆◆◆

CLARENDON HOTEL

Hebden, Grassington, Skipton
BD23 5DE
T: (01756) 752446
E: clarhotel@aol.com
I: www.theclarendonhotel.co.uk

Bedrooms: 3 double/twin
Bathrooms: 3 en suite

Lunch available
Evening meal available
CC: Delta, Mastercard, Switch, Visa

B&B per night:
D £46.00–£50.00

OPEN All year round

Yorkshire Dales village inn serving good food and ales. Personal supervision at all times. Steaks and fish dishes are specialities. Seven nights for the price of six.

◆◆◆

FORESTERS ARMS HOTEL

20 Main Street, Grassington,
Skipton BD23 5AA
T: (01756) 752349
F: (01756) 753633
E: theforesters@totalise.co.uk

Bedrooms: 5 double/twin, 2 triple/multiple
Bathrooms: 7 en suite

Lunch available
Evening meal available
CC: Delta, Mastercard, Switch, Visa

B&B per night:
S £25.00–£35.00
D £50.00

OPEN All year round

Formerly an old coaching inn, situated in picturesque village, serving lunch and evening meals. Hand-pulled ales and en suite accommodation.

◆◆◆

NEW LAITHE HOUSE

Wood Lane, Grassington, Skipton
BD23 5LU
T: (01756) 752764
E: enquiries@newlaithehouse.co.uk
I: www.newlaithehouse.co.uk

Bedrooms: 5 double/twin, 1 triple/multiple
Bathrooms: 4 en suite, 1 private

B&B per night:
D £46.00–£54.00

OPEN All year round

Situated in a quiet location. An ideal base for walking or fishing and for visiting the many historic towns in North and West Yorkshire.

GRIMSBY, North East Lincolnshire Map ref 4D1

◆◆◆◆

SUNNYVIEW GUESTHOUSE

Carr Lane, Healing, Grimsby
DN41 7QR
T: (01472) 885015
F: (01472) 885015
E: starian@btinternet.com

Bedrooms: 1 double/twin, 1 triple/multiple

B&B per night:
S Max £35.00
D Max £50.00

OPEN All year round

Luxury, non-smoking establishment in a quiet rural setting 1.5 miles from A180(T). Fishing pond, 9 holes pitch-and-putt in grounds. Supervised pets welcome.

MAP REFERENCES The map references refer to the colour maps at the front of this guide. The first figure is the map number; the letter and figure which follow indicate the grid reference on the map.

HALIFAX, West Yorkshire Map ref 4B1 *Tourist Information Centre Tel: (01422) 368725*

◆◆◆ THE ELMS

Keighley Road, Illingworth, Halifax HX2 8HT T: (01422) 244430 E: sylvia@theelms.f9.co.uk	Bedrooms: 2 single, 1 double/twin, 1 triple/ multiple Bathrooms: 3 en suite, 1 private	Evening meal available

Victorian residence with gardens and original ornate ceilings, within 3 miles of Halifax. Traditional Yorkshire family welcome. Sorry, no late night keys after 1am.

B&B per night:
S £21.00–£23.00
D £40.00–£42.00

HB per person:
DY £30.00–£32.00

OPEN All year round

◆◆◆ MOZART HOUSE

34 Prescott Street, Halifax HX1 2QW T: (01422) 340319 & 256419 F: (01422) 340319	Bedrooms: 1 single, 5 double/twin Bathrooms: 5 en suite, 1 private	CC: Amex, Delta, Diners, Mastercard, Switch, Visa

En-suite B&B, rooms with TV, tea/coffee facilities, microwave, fridge. Close to town centre, theatre, cinema and swimming baths. Easy access to motorways.

B&B per night:
S Max £25.00
D Max £36.00

OPEN All year round

HARROGATE, North Yorkshire Map ref 4B1 *Tourist Information Centre Tel: (01423) 537300*

◆◆◆◆ ALAMAH

88 Kings Road, Harrogate HG1 5JX T: (01423) 502187 F: (01423) 566175	Bedrooms: 2 single, 4 double/twin, 1 triple/ multiple Bathrooms: 6 en suite	CC: Delta, Mastercard, Visa

Comfortable rooms, personal attention, friendly atmosphere and full English breakfast. 300 metres from town centre, 150 metres from Exhibition Centre. Garages/parking.

B&B per night:
S £28.00–£33.00
D £52.00–£54.00

OPEN All year round

◆◆◆◆ ASHBROOKE HOUSE HOTEL

140 Valley Drive, Harrogate HG2 0JS T: (01423) 564478 F: (01423) 564458 E: ashbrooke@harrogate.com I: www.harrogate.com/ashbrooke	Bedrooms: 2 single, 2 double/twin, 2 triple/ multiple Bathrooms: 4 en suite	CC: Mastercard, Visa

An elegant Victorian townhouse offering high standards of accommodation. Well situated for the many conferences and exhibitions which take place each year in Harrogate.

B&B per night:
S £27.00–£35.00
D £50.00–£55.00

OPEN All year round

◆◆◆◆

ASHLEY HOUSE HOTEL

36-40 Franklin Road, Harrogate HG1 5EE
T: (01423) 507474
F: (01423) 560858
E: ron@ashleyhousehotel.com
I: www.ashleyhousehotel.com

B&B per night:
S £39.50–£70.00
D £59.50–£80.00

OPEN All year round

Close to the town centre, Ashley House is a friendly hotel aiming to give you a memorable stay and value for money. Delightful bar with extensive collection of whiskies. Excellent restaurants within walking distance. Tour the Yorkshire Dales and Moors from our convenient location in this lovely spa town.	Bedrooms: 5 single, 13 double/twin Bathrooms: 18 en suite Bargain breaks available out of conference/ exhibition periods. Bed and breakfast from £29.75 pppn, minimum 3 nights.	CC: Amex, Delta, Diners, Mastercard, Switch, Visa

◆◆◆◆ CAVENDISH HOTEL

3 Valley Drive, Harrogate HG2 0JJ T: (01423) 509637 F: (01423) 504434	Bedrooms: 3 single, 6 double/twin Bathrooms: 9 en suite	CC: Delta, Mastercard, Visa

Overlooking the beautiful Valley Gardens in a quiet location yet close to conference centre and extensive shopping area. Ideal for business or pleasure.

B&B per night:
S £35.00–£50.00
D £55.00–£80.00

OPEN All year round

HARROGATE continued

◆◆◆◆

GARDEN HOUSE HOTEL
14 Harlow Moor Drive, Harrogate
HG2 0JX
T: (01423) 503059
F: (01423) 503059
E: gardenhouse@hotels.harrogate.
com
I: www.harrogate.com/
gardenhouse

Bedrooms: 3 single,
4 double/twin
Bathrooms: 5 en suite

Evening meal available
CC: Mastercard, Visa

B&B per night:
S Min £24.00
D Min £52.00

OPEN All year round

Small, family-run, Victorian hotel overlooking Valley Gardens, in a quiet location with unrestricted parking. Non-smokers only please.

◆◆◆

HOLLINS HOUSE
17 Hollins Road, Harrogate HG1 2JF
T: (01423) 503646
F: (01423) 503646
I: www.hollinshouse.co.uk

Bedrooms: 1 single,
5 double/twin
Bathrooms: 4 en suite

CC: Delta, Mastercard,
Switch, Visa

B&B per night:
S £26.00–£30.00
D £42.00–£48.00

OPEN All year round

Non-smoking establishment offering quiet, clean accommodation in warm, friendly, family-run Victorian house. Excellent food. Close to shops, leisure facilities and restaurants.

◆◆◆◆◆

Silver
Award

RUSKIN HOTEL
1 Swan Road, Harrogate HG1 2SS
T: (01423) 502045
F: (01423) 506131
E: ruskin.hotel@virgin.net
I: www.ruskinhotel.co.uk

Bedrooms: 2 single,
4 double/twin, 1 triple/
multiple
Bathrooms: 7 en suite

Lunch available
Evening meal available
CC: Amex, Delta,
Mastercard, Switch, Visa

B&B per night:
S £60.00–£75.00
D £85.00–£135.00

HB per person:
DY £67.00–£99.50

OPEN All year round

Award-winning 7-bedroomed Victorian town house hotel, lovely gardens, offers luxury accommodation in town centre. Individually-designed bedrooms. Lots of antiques. Elegant drawing room. Private car park.

◆◆◆

SCOTIA HOUSE HOTEL
66-68 Kings Road, Harrogate
HG1 5JR
T: (01423) 504361
F: (01423) 526578
E: info@scotiahotel.harrogate.net
I: www.scotiahotel.harrogate.net

Bedrooms: 6 single,
8 double/twin, 1 triple/
multiple
Bathrooms: 12 en suite

Evening meal available
CC: Amex, Delta,
Mastercard, Switch, Visa

B&B per night:
S £27.00–£34.00
D £54.00–£64.00

OPEN All year round

Award-winning, warm, friendly hotel opposite conference centre and close to town and amenities. Individually styled bedrooms offering colour TV, telephone, beverage tray, modem point etc.

HAWES, North Yorkshire Map ref 5B3 *Tourist Information Centre Tel: (01969) 667450*

◆◆

BEECH HOUSE
Burtersett Road, Hawes DL8 3NP
T: (01969) 667486

Bedrooms: 2 double/
twin

B&B per night:
D £32.00–£34.00

Semi-detached stone house with drive and garage, facing on to a main road. Central heating and double glazing, off-road parking.

◆◆◆◆

COCKETTS HOTEL AND RESTAURANT
Market Place, Hawes DL8 3RD
T: (01969) 667312
F: (01969) 667162
E: enquiries@cocketts.co.uk
I: www.cocketts.co.uk

Bedrooms: 7 double/
twin, 1 triple/multiple
Bathrooms: 8 en suite

Lunch available
Evening meal available
CC: Delta, Mastercard,
Switch, Visa

B&B per night:
D £44.00–£59.00

HB per person:
DY £37.95–£45.45

OPEN All year round

17thC stone-built hotel in the market place. Ideally situated for touring the dales. English and French cuisine.

HALF BOARD PRICES Half board prices are given per person, but in some cases these may be based on double/twin occupancy.

HAWES continued

◆◆◆ **EBOR GUEST HOUSE**
Burtersett Road, Hawes DL8 3NT
T: (01969) 667337
F: (01969) 667337
E: gwen@eborhouse.freeserve.co.
uk

Bedrooms: 3 double/
twin
Bathrooms: 2 en suite

B&B per night:
D £36.00–£40.00

OPEN All year round

Small, family-run guesthouse, double-glazed and centrally-heated throughout. Walkers are particularly welcome. Centrally located for touring the dales.

◆◆◆

LABURNUM HOUSE
The Holme, Hawes DL8 3QR
T: (01969) 667717
F: (01969) 667 041
E: janetbatty@hotmail.com

B&B per night:
D Min £21.00

OPEN All year round

18thC dales house in Hawes, central for walking and touring. Warm welcome, hearty breakfast.

Bedrooms: 2 double/
twin, 1 triple/multiple
Bathrooms: 3 en suite

3 night break Nov-20 Mar £50pp (excl Christmas and New Year).

◆◆◆ **WHITE HART INN**
Main Street, Hawes DL8 3QL
T: (01969) 667259
F: (01969) 667259
E: whitehart@wensleydale.org
I: www.wensleydale.org

Bedrooms: 1 single,
6 double/twin

Lunch available
Evening meal available
CC: Delta, Diners,
Mastercard, Switch, Visa

B&B per night:
S £23.00–£25.00
D £42.00–£45.00

OPEN All year round

17thC coaching inn with a friendly welcome, offering traditional fare. Open fires, Yorkshire ales. Central for exploring the dales.

HAWORTH, West Yorkshire Map ref 4B1 *Tourist Information Centre Tel: (01535) 642329*

◆◆◆ **THE APOTHECARY GUEST HOUSE**
86 Main Street, Haworth, Keighley
BD22 8DA
T: (01535) 643642
F: (01535) 643642
E: apot@sisley86.freeserve.co.uk
I: www.sisley86.freeserve.co.uk

Bedrooms: 1 single,
5 double/twin, 1 triple/
multiple
Bathrooms: 6 en suite,
1 private

CC: Mastercard, Visa

B&B per night:
S £20.00–£25.00
D £40.00–£45.00

OPEN All year round

At the top of Haworth Main Street opposite the famous Bronte church, 1 minute from the Parsonage and moors. Ten minutes' walk from steam railway.

◆◆◆ **EBOR HOUSE**
Lees Lane, Haworth, Keighley
BD22 8RA
T: (01535) 645869
E: derekbelle@aol.com

Bedrooms: 3 double/
twin
Bathrooms: 1 en suite

B&B per night:
S £18.00–£19.00
D £34.00–£36.00

OPEN All year round

Yorkshire stone-built house of character, conveniently placed for the main tourist attractions of Haworth, including the Worth Valley Railway and Bronte Parsonage and Museum.

NB IMPORTANT NOTE Information on accommodation listed in this guide has been supplied by the proprietors. As changes may occur you are advised to check details at the time of booking.

◆◆◆

THE OLD REGISTRY

2-4 Main Street, Haworth, Keighley
BD22 8DA
T: (01535) 646503
F: (01535) 646503
E: oldregistry.haworth@virgin.net
I: www.old-registry.co.uk

B&B per night:
S £25.00–£40.00
D £40.00–£50.00

OPEN All year round

Situated in prime position, on the main cobbled street overlooking the park, this beautiful guesthouse offers the very best in bed and breakfast, with its themed rooms, all decorated to a high standard. Most rooms have 4-poster beds, all have private bathrooms or are en suite. Whether it's business or pleasure, you'll be glad it was us you chose.

Bedrooms: 1 single,
3 double/twin, 1 triple/
multiple
Bathrooms: 4 en suite,
1 private

CC: Delta, Mastercard,
Switch, Visa

Book our very special winter package: 2 nights, 2 people, 4-poster bed £80.

◆◆◆

THE OLD SILENT INN

Hob Lane, Stanbury, Keighley
BD22 0HW
T: (01535) 647437
F: (01535) 646449

Bedrooms: 2 single,
5 double/twin, 2 triple/
multiple
Bathrooms: 9 en suite

Lunch available
Evening meal available
CC: Amex, Delta,
Mastercard, Switch, Visa

B&B per night:
S £48.00
D £56.00

OPEN All year round

The Old Silent Inn offers true hospitality and comfort with open log fires, real home-made food, complemented by traditional ales and fine wines.

◆◆◆

COURT CROFT

Church Lane, Hebden, Skipton
BD23 5DX
T: (01756) 753406

Bedrooms: 2 double/
twin

B&B per night:
S £20.00–£25.00

OPEN All year round

500-acre livestock farm. Newly-built farmhouse in village location. Close to the Dalesway.

◆◆◆

THE HAWNBY HOTEL

Hawnby, York YO62 5QS
T: (01439) 798202
F: (01439) 798344
E: info@hawnbyhotel.co.uk
I: www.hawnbyhotel.co.uk

B&B per night:
S £45.00–£49.00
D £60.00–£69.00

OPEN All year round

Situated in an unspoilt village in the heart of the North Yorkshire Moors National Park, offering spectacular views from its hilltop location. Six exceptional en suite bedrooms. 25-seat 'Mexborough' restaurant offering home-made English fare. Cosy country pub soaking up the village atmosphere, both past and present. A peaceful relaxing break at any time of year.

Bedrooms: 6 double/
twin
Bathrooms: 6 en suite

Lunch available
Evening meal available
CC: Delta, Mastercard,
Switch, Visa

3 night stay £60 per room per night at any time.

HELMSLEY continued

◆◆◆◆

LASKILL FARM
Hawnby, York YO62 5NB
T: (01439) 798268
F: (01439) 798498
E: suesmith@laskillfarm.fsnet.co.uk
I: www.laskillfarm.co.uk

B&B per night:
S £27.00–£30.00
D £25.00–£30.00

HB per person:
DY £38.50–£43.50

OPEN All year round

700-acre mixed farm, peaceful setting within North York Moors National Park. Ideal for stately homes and walking. Natural spring water. Peace and tranquillity, idyllic surroundings, every comfort. York 45 minutes. Laskill Farm has earned its reputation from attention to detail, friendly, personal service and, most of all, value for money. Recommended on 'Holiday' programme.

Bedrooms: 1 single,
5 double/twin
Bathrooms: 5 en suite,
1 private

Lunch available
Evening meal available
CC: Mastercard, Switch,
Visa

HOLMFIRTH, West Yorkshire Map ref 4B1 *Tourist Information Centre Tel: (01484) 222444*

◆◆◆

RED LION INN
Sheffield Road, Jackson Bridge,
Holmfirth, Huddersfield HD7 7HS
T: (01484) 683499

Bedrooms: 1 single,
5 double/twin
Bathrooms: 4 en suite

Lunch available
Evening meal available
CC: Mastercard, Switch,
Visa

B&B per night:
S £24.00–£28.00
D £37.00–£44.00

OPEN All year round

Well-appointed, family-run inn in attractive 'Summer Wine' country, close to the Peak District and Yorkshire Dales.

HOOTON PAGNELL, South Yorkshire Map ref 4C1

◆◆◆

ROCK FARM
Hooton Pagnell, Doncaster DN5 7BT
T: (01977) 642200 & 07785 916186

Bedrooms: 1 single,
1 triple/multiple
Bathrooms: 1 en suite

B&B per night:
S Max £20.00
D Max £40.00

OPEN All year round

200-acre mixed farm. Traditional farmhouse in an unspoilt, picturesque stone village on the B6422, 6 miles north-west of Doncaster and 1.5 miles west of the A1.

HUDDERSFIELD, West Yorkshire Map ref 4B1 *Tourist Information Centre Tel: (01484) 223200*

◆◆◆

THE MALLOWS GUEST HOUSE
55 Spring Street, Springwood,
Huddersfield HD1 4AZ
T: (01484) 544684

Bedrooms: 1 single,
5 double/twin
Bathrooms: 3 en suite

B&B per night:
S £19.50–£29.50
D £35.00–£40.00

OPEN All year round

An elegant, impeccably maintained Listed building with tastefully furnished, spacious bedrooms. Close to town centre, 1.5 miles from M62.

HULL, East Riding of Yorkshire Map ref 4C1 *Tourist Information Centre Tel: (01482) 223559 (Paragon Street)*

◆◆◆◆

CONWAY-ROSEBERRY HOTEL
86 Marlborough Avenue, Hull
HU5 3JT
T: (01482) 445256 & 07909 517328
F: (01482) 343215
I: www.smoothhound.co.uk/hotels/
conwayhtml

Bedrooms: 1 single,
1 double/twin, 2 triple/
multiple
Bathrooms: 4 en suite

CC: Mastercard, Visa

B&B per night:
S £19.00–£30.00
D £34.00–£42.00

OPEN All year round

Comfortable guesthouse in quiet conservation area. Emphasis on good food, cleanliness and service, in a friendly atmosphere.

YORKSHIRE

HUTTON-LE-HOLE, North Yorkshire Map ref 5C3

◆◆◆ **BARN HOTEL AND TEA ROOM**
Hutton-le-Hole, York YO62 6UA
T: (01751) 417311
E: fairhurst@lineone.net

Bedrooms: 1 single,
6 double/twin
Bathrooms: 5 en suite

Lunch available
Evening meal available
CC: Delta, Mastercard,
Visa

B&B per night:
S £25.00–£30.00
D £50.00–£60.00

HB per person:
DY £35.00–£43.00

OPEN All year round

Stone walls, log fires and homemade food in the peaceful family-run hotel, situated in the moorland village of Hutton-le-Hole.

ILKLEY, West Yorkshire Map ref 4B1

◆◆◆◆

GROVE HOTEL
66 The Grove, Ilkley LS29 9PA
T: (01943) 600298
F: 0870 706 5587
E: info@grovehotel.org
I: www.grovehotel.org

B&B per night:
S £47.00–£54.00
D £64.00–£69.00

OPEN All year round

This very well cared for, friendly hotel offers thoughtfully equipped bedrooms together with a cosy lounge and small bar. Breakfast is served in the bright dining room. The hotel is convenient for several local restaurants and shops. Complementary use for hotel guests of the private health club adjacent to the hotel.

Bedrooms: 4 double/
twin, 2 triple/multiple
Bathrooms: 6 en suite

CC: Amex, Delta, Diners,
Mastercard, Switch, Visa

◆◆◆◆ **ONE TIVOLI PLACE**
Ilkley LS29 8SU
T: (01943) 600328 & 07860 293193
F: (01943) 600320
E: tivolipl@aol.com

Bedrooms: 3 double/
twin, 1 triple/multiple
Bathrooms: 3 en suite,
1 private

Evening meal available
CC: Mastercard, Switch,
Visa

B&B per night:
S £35.00
D £50.00–£60.00

HB per person:
DY Min £45.00

OPEN All year round

Warm, friendly guesthouse with en suite facilities offering a high standard of accommodation and excellent home cooking.

◆◆◆ **SUMMERHILL GUEST HOUSE**
24 Crossbeck Road, Ilkley LS29 9JN
T: (01943) 607067

Bedrooms: 2 single,
3 double/twin
Bathrooms: 1 en suite

B&B per night:
S £19.00–£25.00
D £38.00–£44.00

OPEN All year round

Elegant Victorian villa with beautiful garden opening on to Ilkley Moor. Quiet position, lovely views, private parking. Easy walking distance to town.

INGLEBY CROSS, North Yorkshire Map ref 5C3

◆ **BLUE BELL INN**
Ingleby Cross, Northallerton
DL6 3NF
T: (01609) 882272
E: david.kinsella@tesco.net

Bedrooms: 5 double/
twin
Bathrooms: 5 en suite

Lunch available
Evening meal available

B&B per night:
S £22.00
D Max £40.00

HB per person:
DY Max £30.00

OPEN All year round

On the edge of the North York Moors. Ideal base for walking the Cleveland Way, Coast to Coast or the Lyke Wake Walk. Close to Teesside.

ACCESSIBILITY
Look for the symbols which indicate accessibility for wheelchair users. A list of establishments is at the front of this guide.

◆◆◆◆

FERNCLIFFE COUNTRY GUEST HOUSE

55 Main Street, Ingleton, via Carnforth
LA6 3HJ
T: (01524) 242405
E: ferncliffe@hotmail.com

B&B per night:
S £29.00–£30.00
D £46.00–£48.00

Ferncliffe is a Victorian, dales-style, detached house on the edge of Ingleton. A warm welcome is assured from your hosts Susan and Peter Ring. An ideal base to explore the Yorkshire Dales and South Lakes area. The comfortable rooms are en suite, with beverage tray and colour TV.

Bedrooms: 5 double/ twin
Bathrooms: 5 en suite

Evening meal available
CC: Mastercard, Visa

◆◆◆◆

INGLEBOROUGH VIEW GUEST HOUSE

Main Street, Ingleton, Carnforth
LA6 3HH
T: (01524) 241523
E: anne@ingleboroughview.co.uk
I: www.ingleboroughview.co.uk

Bedrooms: 3 double/ twin, 1 triple/multiple
Bathrooms: 2 en suite, 2 private

B&B per night:
S £25.00–£30.00
D £38.00–£42.00

OPEN All year round

Attractive Victorian house with picturesque riverside location. All rooms have superb views. Highly recommended for food, comfort and hospitality. Ideally situated for local walks/touring dales.

◆◆◆

INGLENOOK GUEST HOUSE

20 Main Street, Ingleton, Carnforth
LA6 3HJ
T: (01524) 241270
E: phillsmith@
inglenookguesthouse.fsbusiness.co.uk
I: www.nebsweb.co.uk/inglenook

Bedrooms: 4 double/ twin, 1 triple/multiple
Bathrooms: 4 en suite, 1 private

Evening meal available
CC: Delta, Mastercard, Visa

B&B per night:
D £40.00–£42.00

HB per person:
DY £27.00–£31.00

OPEN All year round

Victorian guesthouse with riverside location. Our recently refurbished, tastefully co-ordinated en suite bedrooms have superb views. Reputation for good food and friendly service. Ground floor bedroom.

◆◆◆◆

PINES COUNTRY HOUSE

Ingleton, Carnforth LA6 3HN
T: (01524) 241252
F: (01524) 241252
E: pineshotel@aol.com
I: www.yorkshirenet.co.uk/stayat/
thepines

Bedrooms: 7 double/ twin, 1 triple/multiple
Bathrooms: 8 en suite

Lunch available
Evening meal available
CC: Mastercard, Visa

B&B per night:
S £27.00–£32.00
D £48.00–£54.00

HB per person:
DY £37.00–£40.00

Splendid Victorian country house, excellent rooms, food and view. Licensed, sauna, car park. Beautiful conservatory dining room. Quality assured. Brochure sent with pleasure.

QUALITY ASSURANCE SCHEME

For an explanation of the quality and facilities represented by the Diamonds please refer to the front of this guide. A more detailed explanation can be found in the information pages at the back.

INGLETON continued

◆◆◆

Detached Victorian villa, large garden with patio down to River Greta. Home grown vegetables in season, home cooking. Private fishing. Pets welcome.

SPRINGFIELD COUNTRY HOUSE HOTEL

Main Street, Ingleton, Carnforth LA6 3HJ
T: (01524) 241280
F: (01524) 241280
I: www.destination-england.co.uk. springfield

Bedrooms: 4 double/ twin, 1 triple/multiple
Bathrooms: 5 en suite

Evening meal available
CC: Amex, Delta, Diners, Mastercard, Visa

Special terms for 2 or more days. Weekly terms.

B&B per night:
S £21.00–£23.00
D £42.00–£46.00

HB per person:
DY £32.00–£34.00

OPEN All year round

KIRKBYMOORSIDE, North Yorkshire Map ref 5C3

◆◆◆◆

Walk or drive round 5 valleys from our door. Spacious rooms with king-size beds and TV/video. Spacious lounge/diner with picture windows overlooking Rosedale. Historic Lion Inn is opposite. Local attractions include castle, museums and the coast. Garage kennel for pets. Parking. Peace, comfort and a warm welcome await you.

HIGH BLAKEY HOUSE

Blakey Ridge, Kirkbymoorside,
North Yorkshire YO62 7LQ
T: (01751) 417186
E: highblakey.house@virginnet.co.uk
I: freespace.virginnet.co.uk/highblakey. house/

Bedrooms: 1 single,
1 double/twin, 2 triple/ multiple
Bathrooms: 1 en suite

Weekly rate for 2 or more £99pp. Discount for 2nd nights or bookings of 3 or more.

B&B per night:
S £25.00–£30.00
D £46.00–£54.00

OPEN All year round

KIRKLINGTON, North Yorkshire Map ref 5C3

◆◆◆◆

Elegant house on moated site in beautiful open countryside. The land was once owned by Katherine Parr. Ideally placed for moors and dales, historic buildings and stately homes. En suite rooms. Drawing room with log fire. Delicious breakfasts cooked on the Aga.

UPSLAND FARM

Kirklington, Bedale DL8 2PA
T: (01845) 567709
F: (01845) 567709
E: upsand@btinternet.com
I: www.btinternet.com/upsand

Bedrooms: 3 double/ twin
Bathrooms: 3 en suite

Evening meal available

Weekly rate £175.

B&B per night:
D £55.00

HB per person:
DY £43.50

OPEN All year round

KNARESBOROUGH, North Yorkshire Map ref 4B1

◆◆◆

EBOR MOUNT

18 York Place, Knaresborough
HG5 0AA
T: (01423) 863315
F: (01423) 863315

Bedrooms: 1 single,
5 double/twin, 2 triple/ multiple
Bathrooms: 8 en suite

CC: Delta, Mastercard, Switch, Visa

B&B per night:
S £22.00–£38.00
D £44.00

Charming 18thC townhouse with private car park, providing bed and breakfast accommodation in recently refurbished rooms. Ideal touring centre.

KNARESBOROUGH continued

◆◆◆◆ HOLLY CORNER

3 Coverdale Drive, High Bond End,
Knaresborough HG5 9BW
T: (01423) 864204 & 07713 135713
F: (01423) 864204
E: hollycorner@ukhotelguide.net
I: www.knaresborough.co.uk/
guest-accom/

Bedrooms: 1 single,
2 double/twin; suites
available
Bathrooms: 2 private

B&B per night:
S £28.00–£35.00
D £48.00–£54.00

OPEN All year round

Tudor-style house in quiet, private drive on town outskirts. Friendly B&B. Personal service guaranteed. Easy access town, Dales, A1(M). No smoking. Parking. Plants/preserves for sale.

◆◆◆◆ NEWTON HOUSE HOTEL

5-7 York Place, Knaresborough
HG5 0AD
T: (01423) 863539
F: (01423) 869748
E: newtonhouse@btinternet.com
I: www.newtonhousehotel.com

Bedrooms: 1 single,
11 double/twin
Bathrooms: 11 en suite,
1 private

Evening meal available
CC: Delta, Mastercard,
Switch, Visa

B&B per night:
S £35.00–£65.00
D £55.00–£65.00

HB per person:
DY Min £42.50

OPEN Jan, Mar–Dec

Charming, family-run, 17thC former coaching inn, 2 minutes' walk from the market square, castle and river. Spacious and comfortable accommodation. Ideal Harrogate, York, Dales.

◆◆◆

WATERGATE LODGE

Watergate Haven, Ripley Road,
Knaresborough HG5 9BU
T: (01423) 864627
F: (01423) 861087
E: watergate.haven@virgin.net
I: business.virgin.net/watergate.haven

B&B per night:
S £29.50–£37.50
D £49.50–£54.50

OPEN All year round

Comfortable en suite bedrooms, ideal for business or holidays. Tastefully appointed with many personal touches. Spectacular setting with woodland walks to River Nidd, Knaresborough and the beautiful Nidd Gorge. Good travel links to all areas. Conference facilities. Many nearby attractions. Convenient for Harrogate, York and the Yorkshire Dales. Also self-catering apartments.

Bedrooms: 3 double/
twin, 1 triple/multiple
Bathrooms: 4 en suite

Weekend breaks-Sun night free (min 2 persons, 3 nights). 10% discount for stays of more than 4 nights.

LEEDS, West Yorkshire Map ref 4B1 *Tourist Information Centre Tel: (0113) 242 5242*

◆◆ AINTREE HOTEL

38 Cardigan Road, Headingley,
Leeds LS6 3AG
T: (0113) 275 8290 & 275 7053
F: (0113) 275 8290

Bedrooms: 5 single,
6 double/twin
Bathrooms: 6 en suite

Evening meal available
CC: Delta, Mastercard,
Switch, Visa

B&B per night:
S £27.00–£37.00
D £39.00–£47.00

HB per person:
DY £34.00–£44.00

OPEN All year round

Small, comfortable, licensed family hotel overlooking Headingley Cricket Ground. Close to amenites, public transport, Headingley shopping centre, 1.5 miles from city centre.

◆◆◆ BROOMHURST HOTEL

12 Chapel Lane, Off Cardigan Road,
Headingley, Leeds LS6 3BW
T: (0113) 278 6836 & 278 5764
F: (0113) 230 7099

Bedrooms: 9 single,
6 double/twin, 4 triple/
multiple
Bathrooms: 13 en suite

Evening meal available
CC: Delta, Mastercard,
Switch, Visa

B&B per night:
S £27.00–£37.00
D £39.00–£47.00

HB per person:
DY £34.00–£44.00

OPEN All year round

Small, comfortable hotel in a quiet, pleasantly wooded conservation area, 1.5 miles from the city centre. Convenient for Yorkshire County Cricket Ground and university. Warm welcome.

LEEDS continued

◆◆

CITY CENTRE HOTEL
51A New Briggate, Leeds LS2 8JD
T: (0113) 242 9019
F: (0113) 242 9019

Bedrooms: 3 single,
6 double/twin, 4 triple/
multiple
Bathrooms: 9 en suite

CC: Mastercard, Switch,
Visa

B&B per night:
S Min £27.00
D £40.00–£50.00

OPEN All year round

Family-run hotel in the heart of the city opposite Grand Theatre and close to all major shops and restaurants.

◆◆◆

GLENGARTH HOTEL
162 Woodsley Road, Leeds LS2 9LZ
T: (0113) 245 7940
F: (0113) 216 8033

B&B per night:
S £26.00–£40.00
D £38.00–£50.00

HB per person:
DY £26.00–£45.00

OPEN All year round

Attractive, clean family-run hotel close to city centre, university and city hospital. 20 minutes from Leeds City Airport. Easy access to M1 and M62. Most of the rooms have en suite facilities and colour TVs.

Bedrooms: 8 single,
2 double/twin, 4 triple/
multiple
Bathrooms: 10 en suite

Lunch available
Evening meal available
CC: Mastercard, Switch,
Visa

Special discount for group bookings.

◆◆◆

PREMIER LODGE
City West Office Park,
Gelderd Road, Leeds LS12 6SN
T: 0870 700 1414
F: 0870 700 1415

Bedrooms: 90 double/
twin, 36 triple/multiple
Bathrooms: 126 en suite

Evening meal available
CC: Amex, Delta, Diners,
Mastercard, Switch, Visa

B&B per night:
S £52.00–£56.00
D £58.00–£62.00

OPEN All year round

Budget hotel offering excellent accommodation. Conference facilities available. Excellent location next to M621 opposite side of Elland Road.

◆◆

MANXDENE PRIVATE HOTEL
154 Woodsley Road, Leeds LS2 9LZ
T: (0113) 243 2586

Bedrooms: 6 single,
3 double/twin, 3 triple/
multiple

Evening meal available

B&B per night:
S Min £27.00
D Min £40.00

HB per person:
DY £33.00–£45.00

OPEN All year round

A family-run hotel. Convenient for city centre, adjacent to universities and hospitals. Comfortable and friendly atmosphere.

◆◆◆◆

PINEWOOD HOTEL
78 Potternewton Lane, Leeds LS7 3LW
T: (0113) 262 2561 & 0800 096 7463

B&B per night:
S Max £39.00
D Max £49.00

HB per person:
DY Max £52.00

OPEN All year round
except Christmas

An attractively decorated and well-furnished hotel, with many extras. A warm welcome in a small hotel of distinction. Convenient for shopping, theatre, visiting the famous Yorkshire Dales and moors. Special weekend rates. Closed Christmas and New Year. At first roundabout leaving Leeds centre, turn right and hotel is 600 yards on left.

Bedrooms: 5 single,
5 double/twin
Bathrooms: 10 en suite

Evening meal available
CC: Amex, Delta,
Mastercard, Visa

Weekend breaks, minimum 2 nights. Single £22.50 per night. Double £40 per night. Incl full English breakfast.

IDEAS For ideas on places to visit refer to the introduction at the beginning of this section.

LEEDS continued

♦♦♦ **ST MICHAEL'S TOWER HOTEL**

5 St Michael's Villas, Cardigan Road, Headingley, Leeds LS6 3AF T: (0113) 275 5557 & 275 6039 F: (0113) 230 7491	Bedrooms: 7 single, 14 double/twin, 2 triple/ multiple Bathrooms: 12 en suite	Evening meal available CC: Delta, Mastercard, Switch, Visa

B&B per night:
S £25.00–£33.00
D £39.00–£44.00

HB per person:
DY £32.00–£40.00

OPEN All year round

Comfortable, licensed hotel, 1.5 miles from city centre and close to Headingley Cricket Ground and university. Easy access to Yorkshire countryside. Warm welcome from friendly staff.

LEEDS/BRADFORD AIRPORT

See under Bradford, Leeds, Otley

MALHAM, North Yorkshire Map ref 5B3

♦♦♦ **BECK HALL GUEST HOUSE**

Malham, Skipton BD23 4DJ T: (01729) 830332	Bedrooms: 1 single, 11 double/twin, 2 triple/ multiple Bathrooms: 10 en suite, 1 private	Lunch available Evening meal available CC: Delta, Mastercard, Switch, Visa

B&B per night:
S £20.00–£35.00
D £36.00–£50.00

HB per person:
DY £25.00–£32.00

OPEN All year round

Family-run guesthouse set in a spacious riverside garden. Homely atmosphere, 4-poster beds, log fires, large car park.

MALTON, North Yorkshire Map ref 5D3 *Tourist Information Centre Tel: (01653) 600048*

♦♦♦♦ **THE OLD RECTORY**

West Heslerton, Malton YO17 8RE T: (01944) 728285 & 07778 064580 F: (01944) 720430 E: bhillas@supanet.com I: www.oldrectoryny.fsnet.co.uk/	Bedrooms: 3 double/ twin Bathrooms: 3 en suite	CC: Mastercard, Visa

B&B per night:
S £21.00
D £42.00

OPEN All year round

The Old Rectory is a fine Georgian house built in 1818. Ideally situated for moors and coast, no smoking. Pets welcome.

MIDDLEHAM, North Yorkshire Map ref 5C3

♦♦♦ **THE PRIORY**

West End, Middleham, Leyburn DL8 4QG T: (01969) 623279	Bedrooms: 2 single, 4 double/twin, 2 triple/ multiple Bathrooms: 4 en suite, 1 private

B&B per night:
S £26.00–£30.00
D £46.00–£52.00

Friendly, family-run Georgian property opposite Richard III castle. Local amenities and ideal centre for walking, golfing and touring in surrounding beautiful dales countryside. Brochure.

♦♦♦ **RICHARD III HOTEL**

Market Place, Middleham, Leyburn DL8 4NP T: (01969) 623240	Bedrooms: 6 double/ twin Bathrooms: 6 en suite	Lunch available Evening meal available CC: Delta, Mastercard, Switch, Visa

B&B per night:
S Max £30.00
D Max £50.00

OPEN All year round

A 17thC historic hotel in the heart of Wensleydale. We stand in front of historic Middleham Castle, home of Richard III, in the Yorkshire Dales.

MIDGLEY, West Yorkshire Map ref 4B1

♦♦♦ **MIDGLEY LODGE MOTEL**

Bar Lane, Midgley, Wakefield WF4 4JJ T: (01924) 830069 F: (01924) 830087 I: www.scoot.co.uk/ midgley-lodge-motel	Bedrooms: 15 double/ twin, 10 triple/multiple Bathrooms: 25 en suite	CC: Amex, Delta, Diners, Mastercard, Switch, Visa

B&B per night:
S £42.75–£43.50
D £54.50–£56.00

OPEN All year round

New purpose-built family owned motel providing above average luxury accommodation. Every room has panoramic view of open countryside.

NORTHALLERTON, North Yorkshire Map ref 5C3 *Tourist Information Centre Tel: (01609) 776864*

♦♦♦

ALVERTON GUEST HOUSE
26 South Parade, Northallerton
DL7 8SG
T: (01609) 776207
F: (01609) 776207

Bedrooms: 2 single,
2 double/twin, 1 triple/
multiple
Bathrooms: 3 en suite

Evening meal available

B&B per night:
S £21.50–£26.00
D £40.00–£43.00

OPEN All year round

Family-run guesthouse convenient for county town facilities and ideal for touring the dales, moors and coastal areas.

♦♦♦♦

ELMSCOTT
10 Hatfield Road, Northallerton
DL7 8QX
T: (01609) 760575
E: elmscott@freenet.co.uk
I: www.elmscottbedandbreakfast.
co.uk

Bedrooms: 2 double/
twin
Bathrooms: 2 en suite

B&B per night:
S £30.00
D £25.00

OPEN All year round

Elmscott is a charming cottage-style property set in a delightful landscaped garden close to the centre of this thriving market town.

♦♦♦

HEYROSE FARM
Lovesome Hill, Northallerton
DL6 2PS
T: (01609) 881554
F: (01609) 881554
E: heyrosefarm@hotmail.com

Bedrooms: 2 double/
twin
Bathrooms: 1 en suite

Evening meal available

B&B per night:
S £18.00–£25.00
D £36.00–£50.00

OPEN All year round

Rural setting, eggs and home produce in season. See our Gloucester Old Spot and Tamworth pigs, Wiltshire Horn sheep, ducks and chickens. Warm welcome.

NORWOOD, North Yorkshire Map ref 4B1

♦♦♦♦

THE OLD PRIMARY
Bland Hill, Norwood, Harrogate
HG3 1TB
T: (01943) 880472

Bedrooms: 1 double/
twin
Bathrooms: 1 private

B&B per night:
D £45.00

OPEN All year round

Converted school built 1875. Situated in the beautiful Washburn Valley. Warm welcome and comfortable atmosphere. Excellent home-cooked local food. Cosy log fire in winter.

OLD MALTON, North Yorkshire Map ref 5D3

Rating
Applied For

THE WENTWORTH ARMS

111 Town Street, Old Malton, Malton
YO17 7HD
T: (01653) 692618
F: (01653) 600061
E: wentwortharms@btinternet.com

B&B per night:
S £25.00–£30.00
D £52.00–£60.00

OPEN All year round

Former coaching inn built in the early 1700s, offering a friendly welcome for guests looking for a central base to explore York, the East Coast and the North Yorkshire Moors. Well furnished en suite bedrooms. Excellent home-cooked food available in our restaurant or bar.

Bedrooms: 5 double/
twin
Bathrooms: 4 en suite,
1 private

Lunch available
Evening meal available
CC: Delta, Mastercard,
Switch, Visa

QUALITY ASSURANCE SCHEME

Diamond ratings and awards were correct at the time of going to press but are subject to change. Please check at the time of booking.

OSSETT, West Yorkshire Map ref 4B1

♦♦♦

HEATH HOUSE

Chancery Road, Ossett WF5 9RZ
T: (01924) 260654 & 273098
F: (01924) 260654
E: jo.holland@amserve.net
I: www.heath-house.co.uk

B&B per night:
S £25.00–£35.00
D £42.00–£48.00

OPEN All year round

Set in spacious gardens, a warm welcome awaits you at Heath House. Our family home for over half a century, we take great pleasure in sharing it with our guests. Ideally situated 1.5 miles west of junction 40 M1 on the A638. Leeds, Bradford, Wakefield and Dewsbury easily accessible.

Bedrooms: 3 double/ twin
Bathrooms: 3 en suite

CC: Amex, Delta, Mastercard, Visa

♦♦♦♦

MEWS HOTEL

Dale Street, Ossett WF5 9HN
T: (01924) 273982 & 07973 137547
F: (01924) 279389
E: enquiries@mews-hotel.co.uk
I: www.mews-hotel.co.uk

Bedrooms: 5 single, 8 double/twin, 1 triple/ multiple
Bathrooms: 14 en suite

Lunch available
Evening meal available
CC: Amex, Delta, Diners, Mastercard, Switch, Visa

B&B per night:
S £42.00–£46.00
D £55.00–£60.00

HB per person:
DY £42.50–£66.00

OPEN All year round

Family-run hotel, public bar. Excellent dining facilities. Set in attractive mews courtyard. Just off M1 at junction 40, 10 minutes from Leeds.

OTLEY, West Yorkshire Map ref 4B1 *Tourist Information Centre Tel: (0113) 247 7707*

♦♦♦

PADDOCK HILL

Norwood, Otley LS21 2QU
T: (01943) 465977
E: chenbeaumont@connectfree.co.uk

Bedrooms: 2 single, 2 double/twin

B&B per night:
S £16.00–£17.00
D £32.00–£36.00

OPEN All year round

Converted farmhouse on B6451. Open fires, lovely views; quiet, rural setting. Convenient for 'Emmerdale' and 'Heartbeat' country and for the Dales. Leeds 16 miles, York 28 miles.

PATELEY BRIDGE, North Yorkshire Map ref 5C3

Gold Award

KNOTTSIDE FARM

The Knott, Pateley Bridge, Harrogate HG3 5DQ
T: (01423) 712927
F: (01423) 712927

B&B per night:
D £60.00–£64.00

HB per person:
DY £48.00–£50.00

OPEN All year round

This elegant, beautifully furnished, comfortable 17thC country house has superb views overlooking Nidderdale and is within easy reach of York, Harrogate, dales and moors. Nigel is Cordon Bleu trained – cooking is the love of his life and he responds to all dietary needs. A perfect spot for a relaxing break.

Bedrooms: 2 double/ twin
Bathrooms: 1 en suite, 1 private

Evening meal available

CHECK THE MAPS

The colour maps at the front of this guide show all the cities, towns and villages for which you will find accommodation entries.
Refer to the town index to find the page on which they are listed.

PICKERING, North Yorkshire Map ref 5D3 *Tourist Information Centre Tel: (01751) 473791*

♦♦♦♦♦ Gold Award

BURR BANK

Cropton, Pickering YO18 8HL
T: (01751) 417777 & 0776 884 2233
F: (01751) 417789
E: bandb@burrbank.com
I: www.burrbank.com

Winner 'Guest Accommodation of the Year'. Comfortable, quiet, spacious with home cooking and personal attention. Two acre garden, 80 acres grounds. Wonderful views of moors and forest. Close to York, moors, dales, coast. Excursions and route plans. Local golf, fishing and riding.

Bedrooms: 3 double/twin
Bathrooms: 3 en suite

Evening meal available

12 [S] P

B&B per night:
S £27.00
D £54.00

HB per person:
DY £43.00

OPEN All year round

♦♦♦

CLENT HOUSE
15 Burgate, Pickering YO18 7AU
T: (01751) 477928 & 07960 243446
E: bb1315@swiftlink.pnc-uk.net
I: www.swiftlink.pnc-uk.net/bb/1315.htm

Bedrooms: 3 double/twin
Bathrooms: 3 en suite

Enjoy your stay in this recently restored late 18thC Grade II Listed house, close to town centre and local attractions including Moors railway and castle. Brochure available.

[S] P

B&B per night:
S £20.00–£25.00
D £40.00–£44.00

OPEN All year round

♦♦♦♦

COTTAGE LEAS COUNTRY HOTEL

Nova Lane, Middleton, Pickering YO18 8PN
T: (01751) 472129
F: (01751) 474930
E: cottageleas@aol.com

Charming 18thC country hotel in an idyllic setting, with 2 acres of gardens and surrounded by open countryside. Excellent base for touring the moors, the coast or York. Comfortable lounge with log fire. Restaurant with views of the Vale of Pickering. Table d'hote and seasonal a la carte menus nightly.

Bedrooms: 8 double/twin, 4 triple/multiple; suites available
Bathrooms: 12 en suite

Lunch available
Evening meal available
CC: Delta, Mastercard, Switch, Visa

Christmas and New Year holidays, seasonal breaks for 3 days or more. Ideal country location for civil marriages.

[S] P

B&B per night:
S £42.50–£48.50
D £75.00–£87.00

HB per person:
DY £44.00–£65.50

OPEN All year round

♦♦♦♦

FOX AND HOUNDS COUNTRY INN

Sinnington, York YO62 6SQ
T: (01751) 431577
F: (01751) 432791
E: foxhoundsinn@easynet.co.uk

Family-run inn with relaxed friendly atmosphere. Our priority is good food, fine wine and excellent service. Comfort and exceptional cuisine in one of Yorkshire's prettiest villages.

Bedrooms: 1 single, 8 double/twin, 1 triple/multiple
Bathrooms: 10 en suite

Lunch available
Evening meal available
CC: Amex, Mastercard, Switch, Visa

2 night breaks often available throughout the year. Telephone for last minute offers.

[S] P

B&B per night:
S £35.00–£50.00
D £50.00–£80.00

OPEN All year round

PICKERING continued

◆◆◆◆ **THE OLD MANSE GUEST HOUSE**

Middleton Road, Pickering
YO18 8AL
T: (01751) 476484
F: (01751) 477124
E: valerie-a-gardner@talk21.com

Bedrooms: 1 single,
7 double/twin, 2 triple/
multiple
Bathrooms: 10 en suite

B&B per night:
S £23.00–£28.00
D £44.00–£54.00

HB per person:
DY £34.00–£40.00

OPEN All year round

Fine Edwardian house in 1 acre of garden/orchard. A short walk to steam railway and town centre. All rooms en suite, car parking on site.

RAVENSCAR, North Yorkshire Map ref 5D3

◆◆◆ **BIDE-A-WHILE**

3 Loring Road, Ravenscar,
Scarborough YO13 0LY
T: (01723) 870643
F: (01723) 871577

Bedrooms: 2 double/
twin, 1 triple/multiple
Bathrooms: 2 en suite

Lunch available
Evening meal available

B&B per night:
S Max £25.00
D £37.00–£43.00

HB per person:
DY £23.00–£33.50

OPEN All year round

Small guesthouse offering clean, comfortable accommodation in a homely atmosphere. Home cooking with fresh produce. Sea views from all rooms. Edge of North York Moors.

◆◆◆

SMUGGLERS ROCK COUNTRY HOUSE

Staintondale Road, Ravenscar,
Scarborough YO13 0ER
T: (01723) 870044
E: info@smugglersrock.co.uk
I: www.smugglersrock.co.uk

B&B per night:
S £26.00–£31.00
D £46.00–£52.00

OPEN All year round

Georgian country house, reputedly a former smugglers' haunt, with panoramic views over national park and sea. In open countryside with wonderful walks. Ideal country holiday area – located at southern end of Robin Hood's Bay. Whitby, Scarborough and 'Heartbeat' Country within easy reach. Two self-catering cottages also available.

Bedrooms: 1 single,
4 double/twin, 3 triple/
multiple
Bathrooms: 8 en suite

Evening meal available
CC: Delta, Mastercard,
Visa

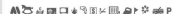

REETH, North Yorkshire Map ref 5B3

◆◆◆ **ELDER PEAK**

Arkengarthdale Road, Reeth,
Richmond DL11 6QX
T: (01748) 884770

Bedrooms: 2 double/
twin

B&B per night:
S £17.00–£20.00
D Min £34.00

OPEN Apr–Oct

Quiet, comfortable family home, within easy walking distance of village centre. Panoramic views across the valley.

RICHMOND, North Yorkshire Map ref 5C3 *Tourist Information Centre Tel: (01748) 850252*

◆◆◆ **EMMANUEL GUEST HOUSE**

41 Maison Dieu, Richmond
DL10 7AU
T: (01748) 823584 & 0585 272
2361
F: (01748) 821554

Bedrooms: 2 single,
3 double/twin
Bathrooms: 1 en suite

B&B per night:
S £17.00–£18.00
D £19.00–£20.00

OPEN All year round

Small stone-built family-run guesthouse offering a warm welcome. Tea or coffee on arrival.

SPECIAL BREAKS

Many establishments offer special promotions and themed breaks. These are highlighted in red. (All such offers are subject to availability.)

◆◆◆ **THE RESTAURANT ON THE GREEN**
5-7 Bridge Street, Richmond
DL10 4RW
T: (01748) 826229
F: (01748) 826229
E: accom.bennett@talk21.com
I: www.coast2coast.co.uk/
restaurantonthegreen

Bedrooms: 2 double/ twin	Evening meal available	B&B per night:
Bathrooms: 2 en suite	CC: Delta, Mastercard, Switch, Visa	S Min £25.00 D Min £40.00
		OPEN All year round

Handsome Grade II Listed William and Mary house with Georgian sundials and inglenook. Near town centre, river and countryside. Chef/family run. Excellent food and wines.

◆◆◆ **BISHOPTON GROVE HOUSE**
Bishopton, Ripon HG4 2QL
T: (01765) 600888
E: wimpress@bronco.co.uk

Bedrooms: 3 double/ twin	Evening meal available	B&B per night: S £20.00–£25.00 D £36.00–£40.00
Bathrooms: 2 en suite, 1 private		HB per person: DY £30.50–£32.50
		OPEN All year round

Restored Georgian (pink) house in a lovely rural corner of Ripon, near the River Laver and Fountains Abbey. Ten minutes' walk to town centre.

◆◆◆ **THE COOPERS**
36 College Road, Ripon HG4 2HA
T: (01765) 603708
E: joe_cooper74@hotmail.com

Bedrooms: 1 single, 1 double/twin, 1 triple/ multiple	B&B per night: S £20.00 D £36.00–£40.00
Bathrooms: 1 en suite	OPEN All year round

Spacious, comfortable Victorian house in quiet area. En suite facilities available. Special rates for children. Cyclists welcome (storage for bicycles). Take-away meals acceptable in rooms.

◆◆◆◆ **MOOR END FARM**
Knaresborough Road, Littlethorpe,
Ripon HG4 3LU
T: (01765) 677419
E: pspensley@ukonline.co.uk
I: www.yorkshirebandb.co.uk

Bedrooms: 3 double/ twin	B&B per night: D £39.00–£47.00
Bathrooms: 2 en suite, 1 private	OPEN All year round

Relax in the friendly, peaceful atmosphere of this Victorian farmhouse. Well furnished and decorated. Delicious breakfast. Pleasant garden. Safe parking. Excellent meals found locally. Non-smoking.

◆◆◆◆  **SHAROW CROSS HOUSE**
Dishforth Road, Sharow, Ripon HG4 5BQ
T: (01765) 609866 & 0786 683 0741
E: sharowcrosshouse@btinternet.com
I: www.sharowcrosshouse.com

B&B per night:
S £30.00–£35.00
D £50.00–£60.00

HB per person:
DY £36.50–£45.00

OPEN All year round

This elegant country house has 3 double en suite rooms, recently refurbished, offering a very high standard of comfortable accommodation. High quality home cooking a speciality. A peaceful setting, within 1 mile of Ripon, an ideal base for exploring the beautiful North Yorkshire countryside, including Fountains Abbey, Newby Hall, York.

Bedrooms: 3 double/ twin	Evening meal available
Bathrooms: 3 en suite	

Price reduction for 2nd night stay.

 SYMBOLS The symbols in each entry give information about services and facilities. A key to these symbols appears at the back of this guide.

ROBIN HOOD'S BAY, North Yorkshire Map ref 5D3

◆◆◆◆

FLASK INN

Robin Hood's Bay, Whitby
YO22 4QH
T: (01947) 880305
F: (01947) 880592
E: flaskinn@aol.com
I: www.flaskinn.com

Bedrooms: 4 double/
twin, 2 triple/multiple
Bathrooms: 6 en suite

Lunch available
Evening meal available
CC: Delta, Diners,
Mastercard, Switch, Visa

B&B per night:
S £30.00
D £50.00

OPEN All year round

Originally a 16thC monks' hostel, situated on the Whitby to Scarborough road (A171) in the glorious North York Moors National Park.

◆◆◆◆

FLASK INN TRAVEL LODGE

Robin Hoods Bay, Fylingdales, Whitby
YO22 4QH
T: (01947) 880692 & 880592
F: (01947) 880592
E: flaskinn@aol.com
I: www.flaskinn.com

Small country lodge adjoining the Flask Inn. Ideally situated between Scarborough and Whitby on the A171, within easy reach of all major tourist attractions. All rooms are ground floor, centrally heated, en suite and include colour TV and tea/coffee facilities.

Bedrooms: 1 single,
4 double/twin, 1 triple/
multiple
Bathrooms: 6 en suite

Lunch available
Evening meal available
CC: Delta, Mastercard,
Switch, Visa

B&B per night:
S £30.00
D £50.00

OPEN All year round

ROMANBY, North Yorkshire Map ref 5C3

◆◆

BRIDGE END

159 Chantry Road, Romanby,
Northallerton DL7 8JJ
T: (01609) 772655 & 07831 388
112
F: (01609) 772655

Bedrooms: 1 single,
2 double/twin

B&B per night:
S Min £17.00
D Min £34.00

OPEN All year round

Pleasant family house. Close to all amenities, railway station, golf course, leisure centre and town centre. Spacious yet cosy rooms. Nice local walks and childrens' play areas.

ROSEDALE ABBEY, North Yorkshire Map ref 5C3

◆◆◆

THE ORANGE TREE

Rosedale East, Rosedale Abbey,
Nr Pickering YO18 8RH
T: (01751) 417219
F: (01751) 417219
E: relax@theorangetree.com
I: www.theorangetree.com

Bedrooms: 4 double/
twin, 1 triple/multiple
Bathrooms: 5 en suite

Lunch available
Evening meal available

B&B per night:
S £26.00–£29.00
D £40.00–£50.00

OPEN All year round

Fine Victorian building amid beautiful scenery in National Park. Completely refurbished, good food and wine, peace and tranquility. Ideal for walking. Sauna, massage, relaxation studio.

ROTHERHAM, South Yorkshire Map ref 4B2

◆◆◆

FITZWILLIAM ARMS HOTEL

Taylors Lane, Parkgate, Rotherham
S62 6EE
T: (01709) 522744
F: (01709) 710110

Bedrooms: 1 single,
17 double/twin; suites
available
Bathrooms: 18 en suite

Lunch available
Evening meal available
CC: Delta, Mastercard,
Switch, Visa

B&B per night:
S £29.37–£33.32
D £35.25–£43.15

HB per person:
DY £40.27

OPEN All year round

Public house, hotel with 18 en suite bedrooms. Children's area with video games and pool tables. Function room available. Extensive car parking facilities.

PRICES

Please check prices and other details at the time of booking.

RUNSWICK BAY, North Yorkshire Map ref 5D3

THE FIRS

26 Hinderwell Lane, Runswick Bay,
Nr Whitby TS13 5HR
T: (01947) 840433
F: (01947) 841616
E: mandy.shackleton@talk21.com
I: www.the-firs.co.uk

Bedrooms: 1 single,
6 double/twin, 4 triple/
multiple
Bathrooms: 11 en suite

Evening meal available

B&B per night:
S £30.00
D £50.00

HB per person:
DY £37.50–£42.50

In a coastal village, 8 miles north of Whitby. All rooms en suite, with colour TV, tea/coffee facilities. Private parking. Children and dogs welcome.

SCARBOROUGH, North Yorkshire Map ref 5D3 *Tourist Information Centre Tel: (01723) 373333*

AIREDALE GUEST HOUSE

23 Trafalgar Square, Scarborough
YO12 7PZ
T: (01723) 366809
E: shaunatairedale@aol.com

B&B per night:
D £32.00–£40.00

OPEN All year round

A small friendly establishment noted for good food and cleanliness. Quietly situated in a tree-lined square and convenient for town, beach and Northside attractions. Tastefully decorated en suite rooms offer central heating, TVs, complimentary beverage tray. Rooms to the rear have views over the County Cricket Ground and countryside beyond.

Bedrooms: 4 double/
twin, 2 triple/multiple
Bathrooms: 6 en suite

Early and late season reductions on short stays. Please ring for latest offers.

Evening meal available

HOTEL ALMAR

116 Columbus Ravine, Scarborough
YO12 7QZ
T: (01723) 372887
F: (01723) 372887

B&B per night:
S £18.00–£20.00
D £36.00–£40.00

HB per person:
DY £24.50–£26.50

OPEN All year round

Beautifully positioned licensed small hotel, peaceful yet near to all North Bay attractions. Comfortable interior, all bedrooms en suite with colour TV and tea/coffee-making facilities, hairdryer and alarm clock radios. Home cooking with tureen service. Ideal base for exploring the beautiful north east coast and York.

Bedrooms: 2 single,
4 double/twin, 3 triple/
multiple; suites available
Bathrooms: 7 en suite,
2 private

Low season per week £161, high season per week £175. Special rates for senior citizens. 50% reduction for children sharing.

Evening meal available

USE YOUR *i*s

There are more than 550 Tourist Information Centres throughout England offering friendly help with accommodation and holiday ideas as well as suggestions of places to visit and things to do. You'll find TIC addresses in the local Phone Book.

SCARBOROUGH continued

◆◆

THE ANCHOR GUEST ACCOMMODATION

61 Northstead Manor Drive, Scarborough
YO12 6AF
T: (01723) 364518
F: (01723) 364518
E: theanchor@hotmail.com

In rural setting overlooking Peasholm Park, yet close to the beach, swimming pools and Bowls Centre. Short walk to town centre. The ideal touring base for this area of outstanding beauty. YTB inspector's quote 'the owners show very high levels of hospitality and have the guests' welfare very much at heart'.

Bedrooms: 3 single, 5 double/twin, 2 triple/multiple
Bathrooms: 10 en suite

Lunch available
Evening meal available
CC: Delta, Mastercard, Switch, Visa

3 nights B&B, £45pp, 4 nights B&B £59pp (excl July, August and Bank Hols).

B&B per night:
S £16.00–£29.00
D £32.00–£48.00

HB per person:
DY £20.00–£37.00

OPEN All year round

◆◆◆

BRINCLIFFE EDGE HOTEL
105 Queens Parade, Scarborough
YO12 7HY
T: (01723) 364834
E: brincliffeedgehotel@hotmail.com
I: www.brincliffeedgehotel.co.uk

Bedrooms: 2 single, 5 double/twin, 3 triple/multiple
Bathrooms: 7 en suite

Evening meal available

Welcoming hotel overlooking North Bay. Car park, sea views, en suites available. Home cooking, separate tables. Cleanliness assured. Comfortable walking distance from most attractions and shops.

B&B per night:
S £19.00–£25.00
D £44.00–£49.00

◆◆◆

HARCOURT HOTEL
45 Esplanade, Scarborough
YO11 2AY
T: (01723) 373930
E: harcourthotel@netscapeonline.co.uk

Bedrooms: 2 single, 10 double/twin, 3 triple/multiple
Bathrooms: 14 en suite

Evening meal available
CC: Mastercard, Visa

Comfortable, licensed hotel, overlooking the South Bay. The town, beach and cliff lift to the Spa Complex is just a short walk from the hotel.

B&B per night:
S £25.00–£28.00
D £50.00–£62.00

HB per person:
DY £31.00–£37.00

◆◆◆◆

HILLCREST PRIVATE HOTEL
2 Peasholm Avenue, Scarborough
YO12 7NE
T: (01723) 361981
E: peacock@hillcresthotel.fsnet.co.uk
I: www.hillcresthotel.fsnet.co.uk

Bedrooms: 2 single, 4 double/twin, 1 triple/multiple
Bathrooms: 7 en suite

Evening meal available

Small, detached non-smoking hotel with emphasis on food, friendliness, comfort and service. Close to Peasholm Park and all other attractions.

B&B per night:
S £23.00
D £46.00

HB per person:
DY £32.00–£34.00

OPEN All year round

◆◆◆◆

KILLERBY COTTAGE FARM
Killerby Lane, Cayton, Scarborough
YO11 3TP
T: (01723) 581236
F: (01723) 585465
E: val@green-glass.demon.co.uk
I: www.yorkshire.co.uk/valgreen

Bedrooms: 2 double/twin, 1 triple/multiple
Bathrooms: 3 en suite

CC: Delta, Mastercard, Switch, Visa

400-acre arable farm. Character farmhouse, adjacent to stained glass craft centre. 1.5 miles from Cayton Bay, between Scarborough and Filey.

B&B per night:
S £25.00–£35.00
D £50.00–£65.00

OPEN Jan–Nov

REGIONAL TOURIST BOARD The symbol in an establishment entry indicates that it is a Regional Tourist Board member.

SCARBOROUGH continued

◆◆◆ PARMELIA HOTEL

17 West Street, Southcliff,
Scarborough YO11 2QN
T: (01723) 361914
E: parmeliahotel@btinternet.com
I: www.parmeliahotel.co.uk

Bedrooms: 2 single,
8 double/twin, 4 triple/
multiple
Bathrooms: 11 en suite,
1 private

Evening meal available

B&B per night:
S £19.50–£25.50
D £39.00–£46.00

HB per person:
DY £29.50–£35.50

OPEN Mar–Nov

Spacious, licensed hotel with emphasis on comfort, quality and home cooking. On the South Cliff near the Esplanade Gardens, the cliff lift to the Spa and the beach.

◆◆ REX HOTEL

9 Crown Crescent, South Cliff,
Scarborough YO11 2BJ
T: (01723) 373297 & 07771 697023
F: (01723) 373297
E: ibstewart@talk21.com

Bedrooms: 1 single,
3 double/twin, 5 triple/
multiple
Bathrooms: 9 en suite

Evening meal available
CC: Mastercard, Visa

B&B per night:
S £20.00–£22.00
D £40.00–£44.00

HB per person:
DY £27.00–£29.00

A friendly family hotel in South Cliff, within easy walking distance of South Bay, Spa Complex and the town centre.

◆◆◆◆ WHARNCLIFFE HOTEL

26 Blenheim Terrace, Scarborough
YO12 7HD
T: (01723) 374635
F: (01723) 374635
E: wharncliffe.hotel@virgin.net
I: freespace.virgin.net/wharncliffe.
hotel

Bedrooms: 8 double/
twin, 4 triple/multiple
Bathrooms: 12 en suite

B&B per night:
5 £26.00–£29.00
D £42.00–£50.00

OPEN Mar–Oct

Directly overlooking the North Bay and castle. Close to town with amenities. Friendly service with emphasis on cleanliness. All rooms en suite. Bar with unusual puzzles.

SCOTCH CORNER, North Yorkshire Map ref 5C3

◆◆◆ VINTAGE HOTEL

Scotch Corner, Richmond DL10 6NP
T: (01748) 824424 & 822961
F: (01748) 826272

Bedrooms: 3 single,
5 double/twin
Bathrooms: 5 en suite

Lunch available
Evening meal available
CC: Amex, Delta, Diners,
Mastercard, Switch, Visa

B&B per night:
S £27.00–£42.50
D £36.50–£53.50

HB per person:
DY £35.50–£50.00

OPEN All year round

Family-run roadside inn with friendly atmosphere, conveniently situated on A66 (Penrith road) only 200 metres from A1 Scotch Corner junction. (Richmond 3 miles).

SCUNTHORPE, South Humberside Map ref 4C1

◆◆◆ BEVERLEY HOTEL

55 Old Brumby Street, Scunthorpe
DN16 2AJ
T: (01724) 282212
F: (01724) 270422

Bedrooms: 5 single,
8 double/twin, 2 triple/
multiple
Bathrooms: 15 en suite

Lunch available
Evening meal available
CC: Delta, Mastercard,
Switch, Visa

B&B per night:
S £38.50–£45.00
D £48.50–£55.00

OPEN All year round

In the pleasant, quiet residential district of Old Brumby off the A18, close to Scunthorpe town centre and M180 motorway.

◆◆ KIRKS KORNER

12 Scotter Road, Scunthorpe
DN15 8DR
T: (01724) 855344 & 281637
E: paul.kirk1@ntlworld.com

Bedrooms: 1 single,
4 double/twin, 2 triple/
multiple
Bathrooms: 4 en suite

CC: Delta, Mastercard,
Switch, Visa

B&B per night:
S £19.95–£24.95
D £29.95

OPEN All year round

Friendly, family-run motel, furnished to a high standard. Situated 1 mile from M181, opposite Warren Lodge Big Steak Pub.

MAP REFERENCES The map references refer to the colour maps at the front of this guide. The first figure is the map number; the letter and figure which follow indicate the grid reference on the map.

SELBY, North Yorkshire Map ref 4C1 *Tourist Information Centre Tel: (01757) 703263*

◆◆ **HAZELDENE GUEST HOUSE**

34 Brook Street, Doncaster Road,
Selby YO8 4AR
T: (01757) 704809
F: (01757) 709300
E: selbystay@breathe.com
I: www.hazeldene-selby.co.uk

Bedrooms: 2 single,
6 double/twin
Bathrooms: 5 en suite

CC: Mastercard, Visa

B&B per night:
S £30.00–£32.00
D £42.00–£46.00

OPEN All year round

Victorian townhouse in a pleasant market town location, 12 miles south of York. On the A19 with easy access to the A1 and M62 motorways.

🅰🛏12🔥🖵🚿⑤✂🖳🖬🚗♿P

SETTLE, North Yorkshire Map ref 5B3 *Tourist Information Centre Tel: (01729) 825192*

◆◆◆◆ **ARBUTUS GUEST HOUSE**

Riverside, Clapham LA2 8DS
T: (01524) 251240
F: (01524) 251197
E: info@arbutus.co.uk
I: www.arbutus.co.uk

Bedrooms: 1 single,
3 double/twin, 2 triple/
multiple
Bathrooms: 5 en suite

Evening meal available

B&B per night:
S £20.00–£21.50
D £49.00–£52.00

HB per person:
DY £40.00–£41.50

OPEN All year round

Situated in the heart of the beautiful village of Clapham. Country guesthouse offering traditional home cooking and a friendly atmosphere. Ideal for touring, walking and relaxing.

🅰🛏🔥🖵♿🍷⑤✂🖳🖳🖬🚗♫⌖♪🐕☀🏇🚗🐾P

◆◆◆◆

MAINSFIELD

Stackhouse Lane, Giggleswick, Settle
BD24 0DL
T: (01729) 823549 & 07790 379247

B&B per night:
S £20.00–£25.00
D £46.00–£50.00

OPEN All year round

A fine Edwardian residence, spacious accommodation with 4-poster rooms. Oak panelling. It is also written that Edward Elgar played his violin in the music room at Mainsfield (now dinning room), also snooker or pool table. Well decorated rooms with fine views over countryside. Some rooms 4-posters and 1 half tester.

Bedrooms: 3 double/
twin
Bathrooms: 2 en suite,
1 private

4-poster honeymoon suite, champagne and chocolates.

🖼🖵♿🍷⑤✂🖳🖬🚗☀🚗🏠P

◆◆◆ **MAYPOLE INN**

Maypole Green, Main Street,
Long Preston, Skipton BD23 4PH
T: (01729) 840219
E: landlord@maypole.co.uk
I: www.maypole.co.uk

Bedrooms: 1 single,
3 double/twin, 2 triple/
multiple
Bathrooms: 6 en suite

Lunch available
Evening meal available
CC: Delta, Mastercard,
Switch, Visa

B&B per night:
S £29.00
D £47.00

OPEN All year round

17thC inn, with open fires, on village green. Many attractive walks in surrounding dales. Four miles from Settle. Winter breaks.

🅰🛏📞🖳🖵♿🍷⑤✂🖳🖬🚗🍴♦♫☀🏇P

◆◆◆◆ **PENMAR COURT**

Duke Street, Settle BD24 9AS
T: (01729) 823258
F: (01729) 823258
E: stay@penmarcourt.freeserve.co.
uk

Bedrooms: 3 double/
twin
Bathrooms: 3 en suite

CC: Delta, Mastercard,
Switch, Visa

B&B per night:
S £27.00–£30.00
D £45.00–£50.00

OPEN All year round

Large, late Victorian townhouse well situated in Settle for wining and dining, walking and touring, railway and scenery. Guest lounge with panoramic views. Car park.

🅰🛏🖼🖳🖵♿⑤✂🖳🖬🚗☀🚗P

SYMBOLS The symbols in each entry give information about services and facilities. A key to these symbols appears at the back of this guide.

◆◆◆

STATION HOUSE

Settle BD24 9AA
T: (01729) 822533
E: stationhouse@btinternet.com
I: www.stationhouse.btinternet.com

B&B per night:
S £30.00–£35.00
D £40.00–£50.00

The original stationmaster's house built in 1875 retains much of the charm and character of those old railway days. The house stands in an elevated position with spectacular views of open countryside. Settle's market square is only a stroll away and yet our garden is a haven of tranquility.

Bedrooms: 2 double/twin

Evening meal available

10% reduction given for more than 3 nights.

◆◆◆

WHITEFRIARS COUNTRY GUEST HOUSE

Church Street, Settle BD24 9JD
I: (01729) 823753
I: www.whitefriars-settle.co.uk

Bedrooms: 1 single, 6 double/twin, 2 triple/multiple
Bathrooms: 5 en suite, 1 private

Evening meal available

B&B per night:
S £19.00–£24.00
D £38.00–£48.00

HB per person:
DY £31.95–£37.50

OPEN All year round

17thC family home, set in spacious gardens, town centre location. This delightful guesthouse offers traditional, pleasantly furnished accommodation and fully no smoking. Private parking.

SHEFFIELD, South Yorkshire Map ref 4B2 *Tourist Information Centre Tel: (0114) 221 1900*

◆◆◆

LINDRICK HOTEL

226-230 Chippinghouse Road, Sheffield S7 1DR
T: (0114) 258 5041
F: (0114) 255 4758
E: reception@thelindrick.co.uk
I: www.thelindrick.co.uk

Bedrooms: 16 single, 5 double/twin, 2 triple/multiple
Bathrooms: 15 en suite

Evening meal available
CC: Amex, Delta, Mastercard, Switch, Visa

B&B per night:
S £28.00–£39.00
D £50.00

OPEN All year round

Family-run hotel with parking at the front and rear, only minutes from the city centre.

SHELLEY, West Yorkshire Map ref 4B1

◆◆

THREE ACRES INN AND RESTAURANT

Roydhouse, Shelley, Huddersfield HD8 8LR
T: (01484) 602606
F: (01484) 608411
E: 3acres@globalnet.co.uk

Bedrooms: 6 single, 14 double/twin
Bathrooms: 20 en suite

Lunch available
Evening meal available
CC: Amex, Delta, Mastercard, Switch, Visa

B&B per night:
S £50.00–£60.00
D £75.00–£80.00

OPEN All year round

An attractive country inn conveniently situated for all of Yorkshire's major conurbations and motorway networks. Restaurant. Traditional beers.

TOWN INDEX

This can be found at the back of the guide. If you know where you want to stay, the index will give you the page number listing accommodation in your chosen town, city or village.

CRAVEN HEIFER INN

Grassington Road, Skipton BD23 3LA
T: (01756) 792521 & 07767 476077
F: (01756) 794442
E: philandlynn@cravenheifer.co.uk
I: www.cravenheifer.co.uk

B&B per night:
S £44.95
D £44.95

OPEN All year round

Traditional country inn, serving cask ale and excellent home-cooked food, all day every day. Bar food or enjoy a meal in our restaurant overlooking the Yorkshire Dales. Excellent car parking. Most rooms ground floor. Non-smoking restaurant. Non-smoking rooms available. Prices shown are per room (max 2 people) including buffet breakfast.

Bedrooms: 1 single,
15 double/twin, 4 triple/
multiple
Bathrooms: 17 en suite

Lunch available
Evening meal available
CC: Delta, Mastercard,
Switch, Visa

THE TRITON INN

Sledmere, Driffield YO25 3XQ
T: (01377) 236644
E: thetritoninn@sledmere.
fsbusiness.co.uk

Bedrooms: 1 single,
3 double/twin, 1 triple/
multiple
Bathrooms: 2 en suite

Lunch available
Evening meal available
CC: Delta, Mastercard,
Switch, Visa

B&B per night:
S £24.00–£29.00
D £44.00–£52.00

OPEN All year round

18thC coaching inn, in heart of Yorkshire Wolds adjacent to Sledmere House. Ideal touring and walking base, twixt York and East Coast.

PARK VILLA GUEST HOUSE

Bolton Brow, Sowerby Bridge
HX6 2BE
T: (01422) 832179

Bedrooms: 3 double/
twin

Lunch available
Evening meal available

B&B per night:
S Min £17.50
D Min £35.00

OPEN All year round

This Victorian house was originally a presbytery to the adjacent St Patricks Church, and now offers comfortable good value accommodation.

THE GRANARY

Stearsby, York YO61 4SA
T: (01347) 888652
F: (01347) 888652
E: robertturl@thegranary.org.uk

B&B per night:
S £28.00–£30.00
D £46.00–£50.00

OPEN All year round

18thC converted granary set in beautiful 1-acre garden. Surrounded by woodland, yet only 12 miles from York. Ideally located for York, Yorkshire Dales, North Yorkshire Moors and Herriot country. En suite rooms with own sitting rooms in Barn Annexe, en suite double in main house. Breakfast in south-facing conservatory, overlooking the pool.

Bedrooms: 3 double/
twin; suites available
Bathrooms: 3 en suite

THIRSK, North Yorkshire Map ref 5C3 *Tourist Information Centre Tel: (01845) 522755*

◆◆ FOURWAYS GUEST HOUSE

Town End, Thirsk YO7 1PY
T: (01845) 522601
F: (01845) 522131
E: fourways@nyorks.fsbusiness.co.uk

Bedrooms: 3 single, 4 double/twin, 1 triple/multiple	Lunch available
Bathrooms: 7 en suite	Evening meal available
	CC: Delta, Mastercard, Visa

B&B per night:
S £19.00–£21.00
D £38.00–£40.00

HB per person:
DY £27.00–£28.00

OPEN All year round

Guesthouse close to town centre, 2 minutes' walk from the surgery of famous vet and author James Herriot. Centrally located for touring North Yorkshire Moors and Yorkshire Dales.

◆◆◆ LAVENDER HOUSE

27 Kirkgate, Thirsk YO7 1PL
T: (01845) 522224
E: susie.dodds@btinternet.com
I: www.lavenderhouse.org

Bedrooms: 1 single,
2 triple/multiple

B&B per night:
S Max £19.00
D Max £38.00

OPEN All year round

Let us offer you a warm welcome to Lavender House. We are next to the World of James Herriot and close to the market square.

◆◆◆ TOWN PASTURE FARM

Boltby, Thirsk YO7 2DY
T: (01845) 537298

Bedrooms: 1 double/twin, 1 triple/multiple
Bathrooms: 2 en suite

Evening meal available

B&B per night:
S Min £20.00
D Min £20.00

HB per person:
DY Min £31.50

OPEN All year round

180-acre mixed farm. Farmhouse with views of the Hambleton Hills, in picturesque Boltby village within the boundary of the North York Moors National Park.

THORNTON DALE, North Yorkshire Map ref 5D3

◆◆◆ THE BUCK HOTEL

Chestnut Avenue, Thornton Dale, Pickering YO18 7RW
T: (01751) 474212
F: (01751) 474212

Bedrooms: 3 double/twin, 1 triple/multiple
Bathrooms: 4 en suite

Lunch available
Evening meal available

B&B per night:
S £27.50
D £45.00

OPEN All year round

In the beautiful village of Thornton Dale, a comfortable family-run hotel with excellent en suite accommodation. Village inn atmosphere. Quality food. Open all year.

WENSLEYDALE, North Yorkshire Map ref 5B3

◆◆◆ IVY DENE COUNTRY GUESTHOUSE

West Witton, Leyburn DL8 4LP
T: (01969) 622785
F: (01969) 622785

Bedrooms: 4 double/twin, 1 triple/multiple
Bathrooms: 4 en suite, 1 private

Evening meal available

B&B per night:
S £30.00–£35.00
D £40.00–£46.00

HB per person:
DY £34.50–£49.50

OPEN All year round

17thC old world licensed guesthouse in Dales National Park. Warm welcome, good food and fine accommodation. Excellent for walking, touring and golf.

WETHERBY, West Yorkshire Map ref 4B1 *Tourist Information Centre Tel: (0113) 247 7251*

◆◆ PROSPECT HOUSE

8 Caxton Street, Wetherby
LS22 6RU
T: (01937) 582428

Bedrooms: 1 single,
5 double/twin
Bathrooms: 4 en suite

B&B per night:
S £22.50–£25.00
D £45.00–£50.00

OPEN All year round

Established 40 years. En suite rooms available. Near York, Harrogate, Dales, Herriot country. Midway London/Edinburgh. Restaurants nearby. Pets welcome.

www.travelengland.org.uk
Log on for information and inspiration. The latest information on places to visit, events and quality assessed accommodation.

WHITBY, North Yorkshire Map ref 5D3 *Tourist Information Centre Tel: (01947) 602674*

♦♦♦

ARCHES GUESTHOUSE

8 Havelock Place, Hudson Street, Whitby
YO21 3ER
T: (01947) 601880
F: (01947) 601880
E: archeswhitby@freeola.com
I: www.whitbyguesthouses.co.uk

B&B per night:
S £22.00–£25.00
D £38.00–£44.00

OPEN All year round

Friendly, family-run guesthouse, where a warm welcome and large breakfast is always assured. The ideal base for experiencing the old world charms of this historic seaside town, exploring the beautiful North Yorkshire moors, or just relaxing. Ground floor rooms available. Pets welcome. This non-smoking establishment is open all year.

Bedrooms: 1 single,
7 double/twin, 3 triple/
multiple
Bathrooms: 8 en suite,
1 private

Lunch available
Evening meal available
CC: Delta, Mastercard,
Switch, Visa

Book for 7 nights and pay for only 6.

♦♦♦♦

CRESCENT LODGE

27 Crescent Avenue, Whitby YO21 3EW
T: (01947) 820073

B&B per night:
D £40.00–£45.00

OPEN All year round

Crescent Lodge has a friendly caring atmosphere. All rooms are comfortable, attractive with en suite or private facilities and there is a high standard of cleanliness. Breakfasts are varied and generous and vegetarians are welcome. We are conveniently located, and close to the North York Moors. Strictly non-smoking.

Bedrooms: 5 double/
twin, 2 triple/multiple
Bathrooms: 6 en suite,
1 private

Short breaks available Dec-Mar (excl Christmas and
New Year).

♦♦♦♦

MORNINGSIDE HOTEL

10 North Promenade, West Cliff, Whitby
YO21 3JX
T: (01947) 602643 & 604030

B&B per night:
S £30.00–£32.00
D £50.00–£58.00

HB per person:
DY £40.00–£44.00

Within easy distance of sports ground, indoor swimming pool, Spa Theatre and Pavilion, and 0.5 miles to the 18-hole golf course. Set in quiet location overlooking the sea. All rooms en suite, TV and welcome tray. Table d'hote menu using fresh local produce. Senior citizens reductions. Hospitable staff guarantee a warm welcome.

Bedrooms: 1 single,
14 double/twin, 1 triple/
multiple
Bathrooms: 16 en suite

Evening meal available
CC: Mastercard, Visa

3 or 4 night mid-week breaks from £69pp for 3
nights, from £92pp for 4 nights, excl Aug and Bank
Hols.

CREDIT CARD BOOKINGS If you book by telephone and are asked for your credit card number it is advisable to check the proprietor's policy should you cancel your reservation.

◆◆◆◆

NETHERBY HOUSE

90 Coach Road, Sleights, Whitby YO22 5EQ
T: (01947) 810211
F: (01947) 810211
E: netherby-house@hotmail.com

B&B per night:
S £23.50–£28.50
D £47.00–£57.00

HB per person:
DY £37.50–£42.50

Elegant Victorian villa set in 1.5 acres of garden with superb views over the Esk Valley. Very attractive en suite bedrooms with some available on the ground floor. Good food served in attractive dining room. Licensed, private car park. Ideal base for the coast, moors and North Yorkshire.

Bedrooms: 1 single,
9 double/twin, 1 triple/
multiple
Bathrooms: 11 en suite

Evening meal available
CC: Delta, Mastercard,
Switch, Visa

Special bargain breaks available outside high season and bank hols.

◆◆◆◆

NUMBER SEVEN GUEST HOUSE

7 East Crescent, Whitby YO21 3HD
T: (01947) 606019
F: (01947) 606019
E: numberseven@whitbytown.freeserve.co.uk
I: www.1up.co.uk/whitby

B&B per night:
S £20.00
D £42.00–£46.00

Centrally-located period property offering modern facilities with access to town centre, beach, abbey and other tourist attractions. All rooms have colour TV and tea/coffee-making facilities. The rooms at the front have extensive views over the sea, Whitby and the Abbey. Limited private parking available.

Bedrooms: 2 single,
5 double/twin, 1 triple/
multiple
Bathrooms: 5 en suite

◆◆◆

PARTRIDGE NEST FARM
Eskdaleside, Sleights, Whitby
YO22 5ES
T: (01947) 810450 & 811412
F: (01947) 811413
E: pnfarm@aol.com
I: www.tmis.uk.com/partridge-nest/

Bedrooms: 2 triple/
multiple

B&B per night:
S Min £20.00
D Min £36.00

OPEN All year round

Farmhouse B&B with 2 double rooms with unbeatable views and informal, friendly, relaxed atmosphere. Farm is also a working equestrian centre.

◆◆◆◆

WHEELDALE HOTEL

11 North Promenade, Whitby YO21 3JX
T: (01947) 602365 & 07710 994277
E: wheeldale-hotel@lineone.net
I: www.wheeldale_hotel.co.uk

B&B per night:
D £50.00–£60.00

HB per person:
DY £40.00–£45.00

OPEN Feb–Nov

Premier non-smoking, seafront hotel in quiet peaceful location. Tastefully decorated and furnished. All bedrooms en suite with courtesy trays and colour TV. Central heating. Beautiful sea view lounge/bar and dining room. Vegetarians catered for. Private car park. Personally run by proprietors Liz and Ian. Autumn and spring specials.

Bedrooms: 9 double/
twin
Bathrooms: 9 en suite

Evening meal available
CC: Delta, Mastercard,
Visa

Mid-week special, 3 nights for the price of 2, up to 16 May and from 7 Oct, excl bank holidays.

YORK, North Yorkshire Map ref 4C1 *Tourist Information Centre Tel: (01904) 621756*

♦♦♦

ABBEY GUEST HOUSE

14 Earlsborough Terrace, Marygate, York
YO30 7BQ
T: (01904) 627782
F: (01904) 671743
E: abbey@rsummers.cix.co.uk
I: www.cix.co.uk/~munin/sworld/abbey.
htm

*Peacefully situated on banks of River
Ouse, just 5 minutes' stroll away
from city centre and railway station.
All rooms have colour TV, hairdryer,
tea/coffee-making facilities, washbasins. Double en suites with
4-poster beds, twin en suites on
ground floor. TV lounge, private car
park. Non-smoking.*

Bedrooms: 2 single,
4 double/twin, 1 triple/
multiple
Bathrooms: 5 en suite

CC: Delta, Mastercard,
Switch, Visa

B&B per night:
S £25.00–£32.00
D £45.00–£58.00

OPEN All year round

♦♦♦♦ P

♦♦♦♦
Silver
Award

THE ACER HOTEL

52 Scarcroft Hill, York YO24 1DE
T: (01904) 653839 & 677017
F: (01904) 677017
E: info@acerhotel.co.uk
I: www.acerhotel.co.uk

*Elegant, award-winning hotel,
tastefully restored to a high
standard. Superior en suite
accommodation is provided in a
relaxed and pleasant atmosphere.
Beautiful 4-poster room. Special
occasion requests for champagne,
flowers and chocolates catered for. A
substantial 4-course breakfast is
offered. Ten minutes' walk to
attractions and railway station.*

Bedrooms: 2 double/
twin, 1 triple/multiple
Bathrooms: 3 en suite

CC: Amex, Delta,
Mastercard, Switch, Visa

Special mid-week breaks-4 nights for the price of 3
during Jan and Feb, subject to availability.

B&B per night:
S £35.00
D £52.00–£76.00

OPEN All year round

♦♦

ALDWARK GUEST HOUSE

30 St Saviourgate, Aldwark, York
YO1 8NN
T: (01904) 627781 & 07771 530160
E: aldwark@hotmail.com

Bedrooms: 2 double/
twin, 2 triple/multiple
Bathrooms: 3 en suite

CC: Amex, Delta, Diners,
Mastercard, Switch, Visa

B&B per night:
S £20.00–£35.00
D £30.00–£40.00

OPEN All year round

*City-centre guesthouse, close to the Minster and all amenities, offering en suite rooms
and a warm, friendly atmosphere. Listed building 1702.*

CHECK THE MAPS

The colour maps at the front of this guide show
all the cities, towns and villages for which you will
find accommodation entries. Refer to the town
index to find the page on which they are listed.

◆◆◆◆

ASCOT HOUSE
80 East Parade, York YO31 7YH
T: (01904) 426826
F: (01904) 431077
E: j&tk@ascot-house-york.demon.co.uk
I: www.smoothhound.co.uk/hotels/ascothou.html

B&B per night:
S £20.00–£46.00
D £44.00–£60.00

OPEN All year round

A family-run, 15-bedroomed Victorian villa, built in 1869, with en suite rooms of character and many 4-poster or canopy beds. Delicious traditional English breakfasts. Fifteen minutes' walk to city centre, Jorvik Viking Museum or York Minster. Residential licence and residents' lounge, sauna, private enclosed car park.

Bedrooms: 1 single, 11 double/twin, 3 triple/multiple
Bathrooms: 12 en suite, 1 private

CC: Delta, Diners, Mastercard, Switch, Visa

◆◆◆◆

ASHBOURNE HOUSE
139 Fulford Road, York YO10 4HG
T: (01904) 639912
F: (01904) 631332
E: ashbourneh@aol.com

Bedrooms: 5 double/twin, 2 triple/multiple
Bathrooms: 6 en suite, 1 private

CC: Amex, Delta, Diners, Mastercard, Switch, Visa

B&B per night:
S £35.00–£40.00
D £40.00–£60.00

OPEN All year round

Charming, comfortable, family-owned and run licensed private house. On main route into York from the South and within walking distance of city centre.

◆◆◆

ASTLEY HOUSE
123 Clifton, York YO30 6BL
T: (01904) 634745 & 621327
F: (01904) 621327
E: astley123@aol.com
I: www.astley123.co.uk

B&B per night:
S £25.00–£50.00
D £50.00–£66.00

OPEN All year round

Superb accommodation, centrally situated. 10 minutes' walk from York Minster. All en suite, TV's etc, 4-poster beds, hearty English breakfasts. Car parking. Special 3 night midweek breaks.

Bedrooms: 9 double/twin, 3 triple/multiple
Bathrooms: 12 en suite

CC: Delta, Mastercard, Switch, Visa

◆◆◆

BARRINGTON HOUSE
15 Nunthorpe Avenue, Scarcroft Road, York YO23 1PF
T: (01904) 634539

B&B per night:
S £19.00–£25.00
D £38.00–£50.00

OPEN Feb–Nov

Beautiful Edwardian guesthouse in quiet cul-de-sac. Ten minutes' walk from city centre and all York's attractions. Near station, racecourse and theatres. All en suite and hearty breakfasts. Parking on street. From A64 take York west A1036. Approximately 2 miles, turn right into Scarcroft Road, 2nd right into Nunthorpe Avenue.

Bedrooms: 1 single, 4 double/twin, 2 triple/multiple
Bathrooms: 7 en suite

CC: Delta, Mastercard, Switch, Visa

♦♦♦

BEDFORD HOTEL

108-110 Bootham, York YO30 7DG
T: (01904) 624412
F: (01904) 632851
E: info@bedford-hotel.fsnet.co.uk
I: www.bedford-hotel.fsnet.co.uk

B&B per night:
S £35.00–£45.00
D £50.00–£68.00

HB per person:
DY £36.00–£45.00

OPEN All year round

Enjoy a relaxing stay in this tastefully converted Victorian house where the resident family owners assure you of a warm welcome and a comfortable stay. York Minster and city centre are just a short walk away. Private car park to rear of hotel. Traditional home cooked evening meals available.

Bedrooms: 2 single, 10 double/twin, 5 triple/ multiple
Bathrooms: 17 en suite

Evening meal available
CC: Amex, Delta, Diners, Mastercard, Switch, Visa

♦♦♦

BEECH HOUSE

6-7 Longfield Terrace, Bootham, York YO30 7DJ
T: (01904) 634581 & 630951

B&B per night:
S £28.00–£32.00
D £50.00–£56.00

Beech House is centrally situated in a quiet tree-lined street about 5 minutes' walk from York Minster and the city centre. You can stroll through the museum gardens or along the riverside. All rooms have en suite, shower, toilet, colour TV, clock/radio, hairdryer, tea-making facilities and direct-dial telephone.

Bedrooms: 1 single, 9 double/twin
Bathrooms: 10 en suite

CC: Mastercard, Visa

♦♦♦

BLAKENEY HOTEL

180 Stockton Lane, York YO31 1ES
T: (01904) 422786
F: (01904) 422786
E: reception@blakeneyhotel-york. co.uk
I: www.blakeneyhotel-york.co.uk

Bedrooms: 2 single, 5 double/twin, 10 triple/ multiple
Bathrooms: 9 en suite, 1 private

Lunch available
Evening meal available
CC: Amex, Delta, Mastercard, Visa

B&B per night:
S £31.00–£36.50
D £50.00–£60.00

HB per person:
DY £36.00–£48.50

OPEN All year round

Comfortable, family-run, licensed hotel. Located within easy reach of the city centre and attractions. Ground floor en suite rooms. Evening meals available. Car park. Brochure available.

♦♦♦

BLUE BRIDGE HOTEL

Fishergate, York YO10 4AP
T: (01904) 621193
F: (01904) 671571
E: info@bluebridgehotel.co.uk
I: www.bluebridgehotel.co.uk

B&B per night:
S £39.00–£45.00
D £55.00–£69.00

HB per person:
DY £39.00–£46.00

OPEN All year round

Located a short stroll from the town centre along the banks of York's beautiful River Ouse. With free parking, the hotel offers an ideal location to enjoy this historic city. Rooms are traditionally furnished with the usual trimmings. Craig's restaurant, offering incredible choice and value, public cellar bar and residents' lounge bar.

Bedrooms: 2 single, 12 double/twin, 4 triple/ multiple
Bathrooms: 16 en suite

Evening meal available
CC: Delta, Mastercard, Switch, Visa

◆◆◆◆

BOOTHAM PARK

9 Grosvenor Terrace, Bootham, York
YO30 7AG
T: (01904) 644262
F: (01904) 645647
E: boothampark@aol.com

B&B per night:
S £28.00–£32.00
D £56.00–£70.00

OPEN All year round

Sandy and Philip personally welcome you to their elegant Victorian townhouse. Only five minutes' pleasant stroll from city centre. Individually styled en suite bedrooms with all facilities. Delicious choice of freshly prepared breakfasts, catering for all tastes. Fully non-smoking, car parking available. Hospitality and a relaxing atmosphere always assured.

Bedrooms: 1 single, 4 double/twin, 2 triple/ multiple
Bathrooms: 6 en suite

Winter breaks: late Nov-Feb, 4 nights price of 3.

CC: Mastercard, Visa

 7 🛈 🖭 ⌨ ↯ 🗡 S ✂ 📖 ☎ ✿ ⌂ P

◆◆◆

BRIAR LEA GUEST HOUSE

8 Longfield Terrace, Bootham, York
YO30 7DJ
T: (01904) 635061 & 07703 344302
F: (01904) 330356
E: briargh8l@aol.com

Bedrooms: 4 double/ twin, 2 triple/multiple
Bathrooms: 6 en suite

Evening meal available
CC: Delta, Mastercard, Switch, Visa

B&B per night:
S £25.00–£35.00
D £40.00–£50.00

OPEN All year round

Victorian house with all rooms en-suite, 6 minutes' walk from the city centre and railway station.

♦ 🎠 🖭 ↯ 🍷 S 📺 🖭 🖭 ↤ 🦮 ⛽ P

◆◆◆

CAVALIER HOTEL

39 Monkgate, York YO31 7PB
T: (01904) 636615
F: (01904) 636615
E: julia@cavalierhotel.co.uk
I: www.cavalierhotel.co.uk

B&B per night:
S £35.00–£55.00
D £45.00–£69.00

OPEN All year round

Georgian family-run hotel close to the city centre, only yards from the ancient Bar Walls, Minster and many of York's famous historic landmarks.

Bedrooms: 2 single, 6 double/twin, 2 triple/ multiple
Bathrooms: 7 en suite

CC: Delta, Mastercard, Switch, Visa

♦ 🎠 🖭 🖭 ↯ 🍷 S ✂ 📺 🖭 🖭 🖭 ⛽ ⌂ P

◆◆◆◆
Silver Award

CITY GUEST HOUSE

68 Monkgate, York YO31 7PF
T: (01904) 622483
E: info@cityguesthouse.co.uk
I: www.cityguesthouse.co.uk

Bedrooms: 1 single, 6 double/twin
Bathrooms: 6 en suite, 1 private

CC: Delta, Mastercard, Visa

B&B per night:
S £30.00–£35.00
D £50.00–£58.00

OPEN All year round

Small, friendly, family-run guesthouse in attractive Victorian townhouse. Five minutes' walk to York Minster, close to attractions. Private parking. Cosy en suite rooms. Restaurants nearby. Non-smoking.

♦ 🎠 12 ♿ 🖭 🖭 ↯ 🍷 S ✂ 📺 🖭 🖭 ⛽ P

COUNTRY CODE Always follow the Country Code ❧ Enjoy the countryside and respect its life and work ❧ Guard against all risk of fire ❧ Fasten all gates ❧ Keep your dogs under close control ❧ Keep to public paths across farmland ❧ Use gates and stiles to cross fences, hedges and walls ❧ Leave livestock, crops and machinery alone ❧ Take your litter home ❧ Help to keep all water clean ❧ Protect wildlife, plants and trees ❧ Take special care on country roads ❧ Make no unnecessary noise

◆◆◆

Just 10 minutes' walk to the historic and beautiful city of York. This 18-bedroom hotel offers all en suite rooms, licensed bar, restaurant, telephones in all rooms, large car park with adjacent bowling green and children's park.

CLARENCE GARDENS HOTEL

Haxby Road, York YO31 8JS
T: (01904) 624252
F: (01904) 671293
E: clarencehotel@hotmail.com
I: www.clarencegardenhotel.com

Bedrooms: 1 single, 12 double/twin, 6 triple/ multiple
Bathrooms: 19 en suite

Evening meal available
CC: Amex, Delta, Mastercard, Switch, Visa

Our luxurious new dorm is now available for group bookings-hen/stag parties, shopping trips, sports groups etc.

B&B per night:
S £30.00–£45.00
D £50.00–£65.00

HB per person:
DY £36.00–£43.00

OPEN All year round

ⓜ🕿♨✆🖥⌨📺▽ⓢ🅷🄾🛏🛋🍽✎P

◆◆◆

COOK'S GUEST HOUSE

120 Bishopthorpe Road, York YO23 1JX
T: (01904) 652519 & 07946 577247
F: (01904) 652519
E: cooks@talk21.com

Bedrooms: 1 double/ twin, 1 triple/multiple
Bathrooms: 2 en suite

CC: Visa

B&B per night:
D £40.00–£50.00

OPEN All year round

Featured on TV's 'This Morning', small, friendly and comfortable guesthouse with unique decor. 10 minutes' walk to city, railway station and racecourse.

ⓜ🕿7⌨▽🗝ⓢ🔥🄷🛏🛋✿🚗🛶

◆◆◆

CORNMILL LODGE VEGETARIAN GUEST HOUSE

120 Haxby Road, York YO31 8JP
T: (01904) 620566
F: (01904) 620566
E: cornmillyork@aol.com
I: www.cornmillyork.co.uk

Bedrooms: 1 single, 3 double/twin, 1 triple/ multiple
Bathrooms: 4 en suite, 1 private

CC: Delta, Mastercard, Visa

B&B per night:
S £22.00–£28.00
D £44.00–£56.00

OPEN All year round

Well-appointed guesthouse only 12 minutes' walk from York Minster. Most rooms en suite. No smoking. Car park. Launderette nearby. Friendly welcome. Vegetarian/vegan/organic where possible.

ⓜ🕿🖥⌨▽ⓢ🔥🛏🛋✿🚗P

◆◆◆◆

CROOK LODGE

26 St Mary's, Bootham, York YO30 7DD
T: (01904) 655614
F: (01904) 655614
E: crooklodge@hotmail.com
I: www.crooklodge.co.uk

Bedrooms: 7 double/ twin
Bathrooms: 7 en suite

B&B per night:
S £30.00–£60.00
D £50.00–£60.00

Early Victorian residence 450 yards from city centre. Bedrooms all en suite with colour TV, radio. Private car park. Special breaks. No smoking, no children.

ⓜ♨🖥⌨▽🗝ⓢ🔥🄷🛏🛋▶🚗P

◆◆◆

CUMBRIA HOUSE

2 Vyner Street, Haxby Road, York YO31 8HS
T: (01904) 636817
E: clark@cumbriahouse.freeserve.co.uk
I: www.cumbriahouse.com

Bedrooms: 1 single, 3 double/twin, 2 triple/ multiple
Bathrooms: 2 en suite

CC: Delta, Mastercard, Switch, Visa

B&B per night:
S £22.00–£30.00
D £40.00–£50.00

OPEN All year round

Family-run guesthouse, 12 minutes' walk from York Minster. En suites available. Easily located from ring road. Private car park. Brochure.

ⓜ🕿3🖥⌨▽ⓢ🔥🛏🛋🚗P

◆◆◆◆

CURZON LODGE AND STABLE COTTAGES

23 Tadcaster Road, Dringhouses, York
YO24 1QG
T: (01904) 703157
F: (01904) 703157
I: www.smoothhound.co.uk/hotels/curzon.html

Charming 17thC Listed house and former stables in a conservation area overlooking York racecourse. Ten comfortable en suite rooms, some with 4-poster or brass beds. Country antiques, books, prints, fresh flowers and complimentary sherry lend traditional ambience. Delicious breakfasts. Warm relaxed atmosphere with restaurants a minute's walk. Entirely non-smoking. Parking in grounds.

Bedrooms: 1 single, 7 double/twin, 2 triple/multiple
Bathrooms: 10 en suite

CC: Delta, Mastercard, Switch, Visa

B&B per night:
S £39.00–£49.00
D £49.00–£70.00

OPEN All year round

♦♦♦

FAIRTHORNE
356 Strensall Road, Earswick, York
YO32 9SW
T: (01904) 768609
F: (01904) 768609

Bedrooms: 1 double/twin, 1 triple/multiple
Bathrooms: 2 en suite

B&B per night:
S £20.00
D £16.00

OPEN All year round

Detached dormer bungalow with spacious gardens, 4 miles from York city centre. Family-run guesthouse with private car parking and en suite.

◆◆◆

FARTHINGS HOTEL

5 Nunthorpe Avenue, York YO23 1PF
T: (01904) 653545
F: (01904) 628355
E: farthings@york181.fsbusiness.co.uk

Bill and Barbara Dixon extend a warm welcome to their guests. Ideally situated in a quiet cul-de-sac 10 minutes' stroll to city centre. The Farthings is a charming Victorian residence. Selection of quality rooms including en suite, all fully equipped. Breakfast freshly cooked including vegetarian. Unrestricted street parking. Non-smoking throughout.

Bedrooms: 1 single, 6 double/twin, 2 triple/multiple
Bathrooms: 5 en suite

CC: Delta, Mastercard, Switch, Visa

Winter breaks and mid-week packages available- prices on request. (Excl Bank Hols, Christmas and New Year).

B&B per night:
S £25.00–£35.00
D £40.00–£50.00

OPEN All year round

◆◆◆

FOSS BANK GUEST HOUSE

16 Huntington Road, York YO31 8RB
T: (01904) 635548

Overlooking the River Foss, this Victorian town house provides comfortable accommodation in individually furnished rooms. Our private car park allows you to leave your car and take a 10 minute stroll into the city via Monkgate Bar, one of the original stone gateways through the city walls.

Bedrooms: 2 single, 3 double/twin, 1 triple/multiple
Bathrooms: 2 en suite

B&B per night:
S £23.00–£25.00
D £42.00–£52.00

OPEN All year round

◆◆◆

FOURPOSTER LODGE HOTEL

68-70 Heslington Road, Barbican Road,
York YO10 5AU
T: (01904) 651170
F: (01904) 651170
E: fourposter.lodge@virgin.net
I: www.smoothhound.co.uk/hotels/
fourposter.html

Your hosts Shirley and Gary welcome you to their Victorian villa. Enjoy the comfort and luxury of our 4-poster beds. Start the day with the house speciality 'a hearty English breakfast'. Ten minutes' walk to the city centre, close to The Barbican Centre, Fulford Golf Course, and York University. Licensed. Car park.

Bedrooms: 1 single,
7 double/twin, 2 triple/
multiple
Bathrooms: 9 en suite,
1 private

Evening meal available
CC: Mastercard, Visa

Reduction for 3 nights or more, all year round.

B&B per night:
S £40.00–£55.00
D £52.00–£65.00

HB per person:
DY £41.00–£80.00

OPEN All year round

🛇🛏🖨📠💻♨🍷Ⓢ🗝🎖🏧🖥🐕🐾🐈P

◆◆◆

FRIARS REST GUEST HOUSE

81 Fulford Road, York YO10 4BD
T: (01904) 629823 & 07802 798427
F: (01904) 629823
E: friarsrest@btinternet.com
I: www.smoothhound.co.uk/hotels/
friars.html

Bedrooms: 4 double/
twin, 3 triple/multiple
Bathrooms: 7 en suite

CC: Amex, Mastercard,
Visa

B&B per night:
S £19.00–£29.00
D £38.00–£64.00

OPEN All year round

Small, family run guesthouse, with a friendly atmosphere. Leave your car in our car park and enjoy a 10-minute riverside walk to York centre.

Ⓜ🛇🛏🖨💻♨Ⓢ🗝🖥🐾🐾🐕P

◆◆◆◆

Silver
Award

THE HAZELWOOD

24-25 Portland Street, York YO31 7EH
T: (01904) 626548
F: (01904) 628032
E: Reservations@thehazelwoodyork.com
I: www.thehazelwoodyork.com

Situated in the very heart of York in an extremely quiet residential area only 400 yards from York Minster. Elegant Victorian townhouse with private car park providing high-quality accommodation in individually-designed en suite bedrooms. Wide choice of delicious breakfasts catering for all tastes including vegetarian. Completely non-smoking.

Bedrooms: 1 single,
11 double/twin, 2 triple/
multiple
Bathrooms: 14 en suite

CC: Delta, Mastercard,
Switch, Visa

B&B per night:
S £35.00–£85.00
D £70.00–£100.00

OPEN All year round

Ⓜ🛇8🛏🖨📠💻♨🍷Ⓢ🗝🎖🖥🐾🐾🏧P

AT-A-GLANCE SYMBOLS

Symbols at the end of each accommodation entry give useful information about services and facilities. A key to symbols can be found inside the back cover flap. Keep this open for easy reference.

◆◆◆

HILLCREST GUEST HOUSE

110 Bishopthorpe Road, York YO23 1JX
T: (01904) 653160
F: (01904) 656168
E: hillcrest@accommodation.gbr.fm
I: www.accommodation.gbr.fm

B&B per night:
S £19.00–£28.00
D £34.00–£54.00

OPEN All year round

Spaciously, elegant Victorian townhouse 10 minutes' walk from city centre and racecourse. Next to Rowantree Park. Private car park. Highly complimented, generous breakfast selection. Special diets catered for. En suite ground floor room available. Enjoy comfort, cleanliness and personal attention in a relaxed and homely atmosphere. Bargain breaks, November – March. Non-smoking.

Bedrooms: 3 single, 7 double/twin, 3 triple/ multiple
Bathrooms: 7 en suite

Evening meal available
CC: Delta, Mastercard, Visa

◆◆◆◆

HOLLY LODGE

206 Fulford Road, York YO10 4DD
T: (01904) 646005
I: www.thehollylodge.co.uk

B&B per night:
S £48.00–£68.00
D £58.00–£68.00

OPEN All year round

Beautifully appointed Georgian Grade II building where you are assured of a warm welcome. 10 minutes' riverside stroll to centre, conveniently located for all York's attractions including Barbican and university. All rooms individually furnished, each overlooking garden or terrace. On-site parking, easy to find. Booking recommended.

Bedrooms: 4 double/ twin, 1 triple/multiple
Bathrooms: 5 en suite

CC: Delta, Mastercard, Visa

◆◆◆◆

HOLMWOOD HOUSE HOTEL

114 Holgate Road, York YO24 4BB
T: (01904) 626183
F: (01904) 670899
E: holmwood.house@dial.pipex.com
I: www.holmwoodhousehotel.co.uk

B&B per night:
S £50.00–£85.00
D £65.00–£110.00

OPEN All year round

Elegant Victorian house with a secure car park. Carefully restored and furnished with antiques. Five minutes' walk from the city walls, 10 minutes' walk from the station. Two family suites available.

Bedrooms: 13 double/ twin, 1 triple/multiple
Bathrooms: 14 en suite

CC: Amex, Delta, Mastercard, Switch, Visa

Gourmet breaks with York's top restaurants from £110pp for 2 nights. 3 nights for price of 2 offers, mid-week, off-peak.

QUALITY ASSURANCE SCHEME

Diamond ratings and awards were correct at the time of going to press but are subject to change. Please check at the time of booking.

♦♦♦

MIDWAY HOUSE HOTEL
145 Fulford Road, York YO10 4HG
T: (01904) 659272
E: midway.house@virgin.net
I: www.s-h-systems.co.uk/hotels/midway.html

B&B per night:
D £40.00–£64.00

OPEN All year round

Welcome to our elegant 1897 Victorian villa, totally non-smoking. Four-poster and ground floor en suite rooms available. We are close to York via Riverside walk, centre and university and have a spacious on-site car park for all rooms. Freshly cooked English breakfast served in a friendly and informal atmosphere.

Bedrooms: 1 single, 9 double/twin, 2 triple/multiple
Bathrooms: 10 en suite

CC: Delta, Mastercard, Switch, Visa

7 night and 3 night mid-week en suite breaks (excl New Year and Valentine's Day).

♦♦♦

MONKGATE GUEST HOUSE
65 Monkgate, York YO31 7PA
T: (01904) 655947
E: jmb@monkgate.swinternet.co.uk

B&B per night:
S £27.00–£35.00
D £50.00–£56.00

OPEN All year round

Georgian cottages, tastefully renovated to retain original character, cosy and rambling. Very easy walk to York Minster and city attractions. Private parking. Non-smoking. Families welcome.

Bedrooms: 2 single, 5 double/twin, 2 triple/multiple
Bathrooms: 2 en suite, 1 private

♦♦♦

MONT CLARE GUEST HOUSE
32 Claremont Terrace, Gillygate, York YO31 7EJ
T: (01904) 627054 & 651011
F: (01904) 627054
E: montclarey@aol.com
I: www.mont-clare.co.uk

B&B per night:
S £40.00–£50.00
D £60.00–£80.00

OPEN All year round

Take advantage and enjoy the convenience of city centre accommodation with car parking in a quiet location, close to the magnificent cathedral. A warm and friendly welcome awaits you at Mont Clare, a small bed and breakfast offering you every comfort in the tastefully equipped, centrally-heated rooms. All rooms en suite, with some 4-posters.

Bedrooms: 1 single, 6 double/twin, 2 triple/multiple
Bathrooms: 9 en suite

CC: Delta, Mastercard, Switch, Visa

♦♦♦♦
Silver Award

NUNMILL HOUSE
85 Bishopthorpe Road, York YO23 1NX
T: (01904) 634047
F: (01904) 655879
E: info@nunmill.co.uk
I: www.nunmill.co.uk

Bedrooms: 7 double/twin, 1 triple/multiple
Bathrooms: 7 en suite, 1 private

B&B per night:
S £45.00–£50.00
D £47.50–£65.00

OPEN Feb–Dec

Splendid Victorian house with well-appointed rooms, 4-poster beds. Just outside the medieval walls, convenient for the racecourse and railway station. Walking distance to all attractions.

YORK continued

♦♦♦ OAKLANDS GUEST HOUSE

351 Strensall Road, Earswick, York
YO32 9SW
T: (01904) 768443
E: mavmo@oaklands5.fsnet.co.uk
I: www.holidayguides.com

Bedrooms: 2 double/
twin, 1 triple/multiple
Bathrooms: 2 en suite

B&B per night:
S £19.00–£26.00
D £36.00–£42.00

OPEN All year round

*A very warm welcome awaits you at our attractive and comfortable home set in open
countryside, yet only 3 minutes north of the City of York.*

ⓜ ☎ 🖼 ⌨ ♿ ⏻ ⓢ ✂ 📺 ▥ 🖨 ✿ 🚲 P

♦♦ OLGA'S LICENSED GUEST HOUSE

12 Wenlock Terrace, Fulford Road,
York YO10 4DU
T: (01904) 641456 & 07850 225682
F: (01904) 641456
I: olgasguesthouseyork@
talk21.com
I: www.
olgas-guesthouse-york-
england-uk.com

Bedrooms: 4 single,
4 double/twin, 2 triple/
multiple
Bathrooms: 6 en suite

CC: Delta, Mastercard,
Visa

B&B per night:
S £18.00–£25.50
D £40.00–£50.00

OPEN Feb–Oct

*Built for cavalry officers in 1800s. Quiescent locale, congenial company, copacetic cuisine,
superlative service. Close proximity to all major attractions and city centre.*

ⓜ ☎ ⌨ ♿ ⏻ ⓢ ✂ 📺 ▥ 🖨 🍴 🏵 P

♦♦♦ PARK VIEW GUEST HOUSE

34 Grosvenor Terrace, Bootham,
York YO30 7AG
T: (01904) 620437
F: (01904) 620437
E: park_view@talk21.com

Bedrooms: 1 single,
2 double/twin, 3 triple/
multiple
Bathrooms: 5 en suite,
1 private

B&B per night:
S £25.00–£35.00
D £45.00–£50.00

OPEN All year round

*Family-run Victorian house with views of York Minster, close to city centre off the A19.
Reductions for children sharing.*

ⓜ ☎ ♿ 🖼 ⌨ ♿ ⏻ ✂ ▥ 🖨 🍴 🚲

♦♦♦

PRIORY HOTEL & GARTH RESTAURANT

126-128 Fulford Road, York YO10 4BE
T: (01904) 625280
F: (01904) 637330
E: reservations@priory-hotelyork.co.uk
I: www.priory-hotelyork.co.uk

B&B per night:
S £42.00–£60.00
D £60.00–£90.00

HB per person:
DY £35.00–£70.00

OPEN All year round

*A Victorian-style family-run hotel,
only a few minutes' walk to city
centre. The university, and
racecourse are only 1.5 miles, the
McArthurGlen Centre and Golf
course 2 miles. Pam's Bar and Garth
Restaurant. Ample parking. Please
send for brochure.*

Bedrooms: 1 single,
8 double/twin, 7 triple/
multiple
Bathrooms: 16 en suite

Evening meal available
CC: Amex, Delta, Diners,
Mastercard, Switch, Visa

Enquire about our Special Breaks in York, 3 nights,
DB&B.

ⓜ ☎ ⓒ ⌨ ♿ ⏻ 🍴 ⓢ 📺 ▥ 🖨 🍴 ✿ 🐕 🏵 P

♦♦♦

RIVERSIDE WALK GUEST HOUSE

9 Earlsborough Terrace, Marygate, York
YO30 7BQ
T: (01904) 620769 & 646249
F: (01904) 627782
E: riverside@rsummers.cix.co.uk
I: www.riversidewalkbb.demon.co.uk

B&B per night:
S £34.00–£36.00
D £50.00–£58.00

OPEN All year round

*Charming B&B, 450-yard riverside
walk to city and 5 minutes' walk to
York Minster, rail/bus stations and all
main attractions. Quiet location,
private car park. Bargain breaks in
low season. All rooms en suite, no
smoking.*

Bedrooms: 2 single,
10 double/twin
Bathrooms: 10 en suite,
2 private

CC: Delta, Mastercard,
Switch, Visa

ⓜ ☎ ♿ 🖼 🖼 ⌨ ♿ ⏻ ⓢ ✂ 📺 ▥ 🖨 ✿ 🚲 P

◆◆◆

ROMLEY GUEST HOUSE

2 Millfield Road, Scarcroft Road, York
YO23 1NQ
T: (01904) 652822
E: info@romleyhouse.co.uk
I: www.romleyhouse.co.uk

B&B per night:
S £18.00–£21.00
D £36.00–£52.00

OPEN All year round

Family-run guesthouse, few minutes' walk from city centre and all attractions, offers happy atmosphere, hearty breakfast, home comforts. All rooms are well appointed (en suite available) with colour TV, clock radio alarms, tea/ coffee-making facilities. Comfortable residents' lounge with licensed bar.

Bedrooms: 1 single, 3 double/twin, 2 triple/ multiple
Bathrooms: 2 en suite

CC: Delta, Mastercard, Visa

◆◆◆

ST DENY'S HOTEL

51 St Denys Road, York YO1 9QD
T: (01904) 622207 & 646776
F: (01904) 624800
E: info@stdenyshotel.co.uk
I: www.stdenyshotel.co.uk

B&B per night:
S £35.00–£50.00
D £45.00–£80.00

OPEN All year round

A warm welcome awaits you at St Deny's. City centre location within the walls of historic York, with on-site parking. Newly refurbished licensed bar. Corporate accounts and group bookings welcome. With the Jorvik Viking Centre 2 minutes' walk away, we offer the ideal base from which to explore this beautiful city.

Bedrooms: 2 single, 8 double/twin, 3 triple/ multiple
Bathrooms: 13 en suite

CC: Mastercard, Switch, Visa

◆◆◆

ST PAUL'S HOTEL
120 Holgate Road, York YO24 4BB
T: (01904) 611514
F: (01904) 623188
E: normfran@supernet.com

Bedrooms: 1 single, 1 double/twin, 4 triple/ multiple
Bathrooms: 6 en suite

Evening meal available

B&B per night:
S £30.00–£40.00
D £50.00–£80.00

OPEN All year round

Close to York's many attractions, this small, family-run hotel has a warm atmosphere and serves a hearty breakfast. Come as a guest and leave as a friend.

◆◆◆

SKELTON GRANGE FARMHOUSE

Orchard View, Skelton, York YO30 1XQ
T: (01904) 470780
F: (01904) 470229
E: info@skelton-farm.co.uk
I: www.skelton-farm.co.uk

B&B per night:
S £25.00–£45.00
D £49.00–£55.00

OPEN All year round

Welcoming 18thC farmhouse. Five charming motel-style rooms to rear of this former dairy farm. All rooms tastefully decorated en suite and at ground floor level. Half a mile from York Park and Ride. Courtesy tray, colour TV, hairdryers and other simple finishing touches. Delightful breakfast menu. Private parking. Traditional pubs, restaurants and golf nearby.

Bedrooms: 1 single, 3 double/twin, 1 triple/ multiple
Bathrooms: 5 en suite

CC: Mastercard, Switch, Visa

3 night breaks for parties of 8-10 guests, with optional celebration candlelit private dinner party 1 evening.

◆ ◆ ◆

TYBURN HOUSE

11 Albemarle Road, The Mount,
York YO2 1EN
T: (01904) 655069
F: (01904) 655069
E: york@tyburnhotel.freeserve.co.
uk

Bedrooms: 2 single,
6 double/twin, 5 triple/
multiple
Bathrooms: 12 en suite,
1 private

B&B per night:
S £30.00–£40.00
D £58.00–£80.00

Family-owned and run guesthouse overlooking the racecourse. In a quiet and beautiful area, close to the city centre and railway station.

◆ ◆ ◆

WARRENS GUEST HOUSE

30 Scarcroft Road, York YO23 1NF
T: (01904) 643139
F: (01904) 658297
I: www.warrens.ndo.co.uk

B&B per night:
S £35.00–£50.00
D £50.00–£60.00

OPEN Feb–Nov

Friendly and family-run Victorian townhouse (1880). Attractive bedrooms all en suite with colour TV and beverage tray, some ground floor rooms and 4-poster beds, lovely lounge in which to relax after a day's sightseeing. Colourful garden area in which to sit. Secure car park with CCTV.

Bedrooms: 3 double/
twin, 3 triple/multiple
Bathrooms: 6 en suite

Reductions for 3 or more days Sun-Thurs inclusive (excl Bank Hols and race days).

P

A brief guide to the main Towns and Villages offering accommodation in Yorkshire

A AINTHORPE, NORTH YORKSHIRE - Eskdale village on the banks of the River Esk, in the picturesque North York Moors National Park.

APPLETREEWICK, NORTH YORKSHIRE - Wharfedale village below the craggy summit of Simon's Seat. Halfway through the village is Monks Hall, stands High Hall, former home of the Craven family.

ARKENGARTHDALE, NORTH YORKSHIRE - Picturesque Yorkshire dale, in the valley of Arkle Beck, once an important and prosperous lead-mining valley developed by Charles Bathurst in the 18th C.

ASKRIGG, NORTH YORKSHIRE - The name of this dales village means 'ash tree ridge'. It is centred on a steep main street of high, narrow 3-storey houses and thrived on cotton and later wool in 18th C. Once famous for its clock making.

AUSTWICK, NORTH YORKSHIRE - Picturesque, peaceful dales village with pleasant cottages, a green, an old cross and an Elizabethan Hall.

AYSGARTH, NORTH YORKSHIRE - Famous for its beautiful Falls - a series of 3 cascades extending for half a mile on the River Ure in Wensleydale. There is a coach and carriage museum at Yore Mill and a National Park Centre. A single-arched Elizabethan bridge spans the River Ure.

B BECK HOLE, NORTH YORKSHIRE - Tiny, picturesque village on the moors with a handful of cottages, an inn and a green where quoits are played.

BEDALE, NORTH YORKSHIRE - Ancient church of St Gregory and Georgian Bedale Hall occupy commanding positions over this market town situated in good hunting country. The hall, which contains interesting architectural features including great ballroom and flying-type staircase, now houses a library and museum.

BEVERLEY, NORTH HUMBERSIDE - Beverley's most famous landmark is its beautiful medieval Minster dating from 1220, with Percy family tomb. Many attractive squares and streets, notably Wednesday and Saturday Market and North Bar Gateway. Famous racecourse. Market cross dates from 1714.

BOLTON PERCY, NORTH YORKSHIRE - Secluded village of limestone with red-brick buildings. Exceptional 15th C parish church contains medieval stained glass and monument to Fairfaxes. 15th C half-timbered gatehouses with carved timber-work.

BOSTON SPA, WEST YORKSHIRE - Largest of a cluster of villages on the lower Wharfe built of limestone from Tadcaster quarries. Saline waters were discovered in 1774 and the town developed as a spa with fine Georgian houses until superseded by Harrogate.

BRADFORD, WEST YORKSHIRE - City founded on wool, with fine Victorian and modern buildings. Attractions include the cathedral, city hall, Cartwright Hall, Lister Park, Moorside Mills Industrial Museum and National Museum of Photography, Film and Television.

BRIDLINGTON, EAST RIDING OF YORKSHIRE - Lively seaside resort with long sandy beaches, Leisure World and busy harbour with fishing trips in cobles. Priory church of St Mary whose Bayle Gate is now a museum. Mementoes of flying pioneer, Amy Johnson, in Sewerby Hall. Harbour Museum and Aquarium.

C CROPTON, NORTH YORKSHIRE - Moorland village at the top of a high ridge with stone houses, some of cruck construction, a Victorian church and the remains of a 12th C moated castle. Cropton Forest and Cropton Brewery nearby.

D DANBY, NORTH YORKSHIRE - Eskdale village 12 miles west of Whitby. Visit the Moors Centre at Danby Lodge, a former shooting lodge in 13 acres of grounds including woodland and riverside meadow. Remains of medieval Danby Castle.

DARLEY, NORTH YORKSHIRE - Picturesque village 4 miles south-east of Pateley Bridge.

DONCASTER, SOUTH YORKSHIRE - Ancient Roman town famous for its heavy industries, butterscotch and racecourse (St Leger), also centre of agricultural area. Attractions include 18th C Mansion House, Cusworth Hall Museum, Doncaster Museum, St George's Church, The Dome and Doncaster Leisure Park.

E EASINGWOLD, NORTH YORKSHIRE - Market town of charm and character with a cobbled square and many fine Georgian buildings.

EBBERSTON, NORTH YORKSHIRE - Picturesque village with a Norman church and hall, overlooking the Vale of Pickering.

F FILEY, NORTH YORKSHIRE - Resort with elegant Regency buildings along the front and 6 miles of sandy beaches bounded by natural breakwater, Filey Brigg. Starting point of the Cleveland Way. St Oswald's church, overlooking a ravine, belonged to Augustinian canons until the Dissolution.

G GARFORTH, WEST YORKSHIRE - Town 7 miles east of Leeds, between Temple Newsam Estate and Lotherton Hall. Old coal mining district of Leeds.

GLAISDALE, NORTH YORKSHIRE - Set in a wooded valley with the 350-year-old shingle stone arch Beggars Bridge spanning the River Esk. Often described as the Queen of the Dales, central for the North York Moors National Park and close to Whitby. Numerous lovely walks and bridle paths.

GOATHLAND, NORTH YORKSHIRE - Spacious village with several large greens grazed by sheep, an ideal centre for walking the North York Moors. Nearby are several waterfalls, among them Mallyan Spout. Plough Monday celebrations held in January. Location for filming of TV 'Heartbeat' series.

GRASSINGTON, NORTH YORKSHIRE - Tourists visit this former lead-mining village to see its 'smiddy', antique and craft shops and Upper Wharfedale Museum of country trades. Popular with fishermen and walkers. Cobbled market square, numerous prehistoric sites. Grassington Feast in October. National Park Centre.

GRIMSBY, NORTH EAST LINCOLNSHIRE - Founded 1000 years ago by a Danish fisherman named Grim, Grimsby is today a major fishing port and docks. It has modern shopping precincts and National Fishing Heritage Centre, voted England's top tourist attraction in 1992.

H HALIFAX, WEST YORKSHIRE - Founded on the cloth trade, and famous for its building society, textiles, carpets and toffee. Most notable landmark is Piece Hall where wool merchants traded, now restored to house shops, museums and art gallery. Home also to Eureka! The Museum for Children.

- **HARROGATE, NORTH YORKSHIRE** - Major conference, exhibition and shopping centre, renowned for its spa heritage and award-winning floral displays, spacious parks and gardens. Famous for antiques, toffee, fine shopping and excellent tea shops, also its Royal Pump Rooms and Baths. Annual Great Yorkshire Show in July.

- **HAWES, NORTH YORKSHIRE** - The capital of Upper Wensleydale on the famous Pennine Way, Yorkshire's highest market town and renowned for great cheeses. Popular with walkers. Dales National Park Information Centre and Folk Museum. Nearby is spectacular Hardraw Force waterfall.

- **HAWORTH, WEST YORKSHIRE** - Famous since 1820 as home of the Bronte family. The Parsonage is now a Bronte Museum where furniture and possessions of the family are displayed. Moors and Bronte waterfalls nearby and steam trains on the Keighley and Worth Valley Railway pass through.

- **HEBDEN, NORTH YORKSHIRE** - Situated between Grassington and Pateley Bridge. The present bridge across the ravine was built in 1827, but the old stone bridge can still be seen. Close by is Scala Force. Abundant remains of lead-mining activity.

- **HELMSLEY, NORTH YORKSHIRE** - Delightful small market town with red roofs, warm stone buildings and cobbled market square, on the River Rye at the entrance to Ryedale and the North York Moors. Remains of 12th C castle, several inns and All Saints' Church.

- **HOLMFIRTH, WEST YORKSHIRE** - Village on the edge of the Peak District National Park, famous as the location for the filming of the TV series 'Last of the Summer Wine'.

- **HUDDERSFIELD, WEST YORKSHIRE** - Founded on wool and cloth, has a famous choral society. Town centre redeveloped, but several good Victorian buildings remain, including railway station, St Peter's Church, Tolson Memorial Museum, art gallery and nearby Colne Valley Museum.

- **HULL, EAST RIDING OF YORKSHIRE** - Busy seaport with a modern city centre and excellent shopping facilities. Maritime traditions in the town, docks museum, and the home of William Wilberforce, the slavery abolitionist, whose house is now a museum. The Humber Bridge is 5 miles west.

- **HUTTON-LE-HOLE, NORTH YORKSHIRE** - Listed in the Domesday Book, this pretty village of red-tiled stone cottages situated around Hutton Beck became a refuge for persecuted Quakers in the 17th C. Ryedale Folk Museum.

I ILKLEY, WEST YORKSHIRE - Former spa with an elegant shopping centre and famous for its ballad. The 16th C manor house, now a museum, displays local prehistoric and Roman relics. Popular walk leads up Heber's Ghyll to Ilkley Moor, with the mysterious Swastika Stone and White Wells, 18th C plunge baths.

- **INGLEBY CROSS, NORTH YORKSHIRE** - Located north-east of Northallerton at crossroads adjoining Ingleby Arncliffe to the south east.

- **INGLETON, NORTH YORKSHIRE** - Thriving tourist centre for fell-walkers, climbers and pot-holers. Popular walks up beautiful Twiss Valley to Ingleborough Summit, Whernside, White Scar Caves and waterfalls.

K KIRKBYMOORSIDE, NORTH YORKSHIRE - Attractive market town with remains of Norman castle. Good centre for exploring moors. Nearby are wild daffodils of Farndale. Kirklington, North Yorkshire, Attractive village situated between Masham and Thirsk. Much altered church dates from the 16th C.

- **KNARESBOROUGH, NORTH YORKSHIRE** - Picturesque market town on the River Nidd. The 14th C keep is the best-preserved part of John of Gaunt's castle, and the manor house with its chequerboard walls was presented by James I to his son Charles as a fishing lodge. Prophetess Mother Shipton's cave. Boating on river.

L LEEDS, WEST YORKSHIRE - Large city with excellent modern shopping centre and splendid Victorian architecture. Museums and galleries including Temple Newsam House (the Hampton Court of the North), Tetley's Brewery Wharf and the Royal Armouries Museum; also home of Opera North.

M MALHAM, NORTH YORKSHIRE - Hamlet of stone cottages amid magnificent rugged limestone scenery in the Yorkshire Dales National Park. Malham Cove is a curving, sheer white cliff 240 ft high. Malham Tarn, one of Yorkshire's few natural lakes, belongs to the National Trust. National Park Centre.

- **MALTON, NORTH YORKSHIRE** - Thriving farming town on the River Derwent with large livestock market. Famous for racehorse training. The local museum has Roman remains and the Eden Camp Modern History Theme Museum transports visitors back to wartime Britain. Castle Howard within easy reach.

- **MIDDLEHAM, NORTH YORKSHIRE** - Town famous for racehorse training, with cobbled squares and houses of local stone. Norman castle, once principal residence of Warwick the Kingmaker and later Richard III. Ancient stronghold of the Neville family was taken over by the Crown after the Battle of Barnet in 1471.

N NORTHALLERTON, NORTH YORKSHIRE - Formerly a staging post on coaching route to the North and later a railway town. Today a lively market town and administrative capital of North Yorkshire. Parish church of All Saints dates from 1200. Dickens stayed at The Fleece.

O OSSETT, WEST YORKSHIRE - Small town lying just off the M1 west of Dewsbury. Noted for its textiles, engineering and coal mining. World coal-carrying championship takes place every Easter Monday.

- **OTLEY, WEST YORKSHIRE** - Charming market and small manufacturing town in Lower Wharfedale, the birthplace of Thomas Chippendale, painted by Turner. Old inns, medieval 5-arched bridge, local history museum, maypole, historic All Saints' Church. Beautiful countryside. Annual carnival.

P PATELEY BRIDGE, NORTH YORKSHIRE - Market town at centre of Upper Nidderdale. Flax and linen industries once flourished in this remote and beautiful setting. Remains of Bronze Age settlements and disused lead mines.

- **PICKERING, NORTH YORKSHIRE** - Market town and tourist centre on edge of North York Moors. Parish church has complete set of 15th C wall paintings depicting lives of saints. Part of 12th C castle still stands. Beck Isle Museum. The North York Moors Railway begins here.

R RAVENSCAR, NORTH YORKSHIRE - Splendidly positioned small coastal resort with magnificent views over Robin Hood's Bay. Its Old Peak is the end of the famous Lyke Wake Walk or 'corpse way'.

- **REETH, NORTH YORKSHIRE** - Once a market town and lead-mining centre, Reeth today serves holiday-makers in Swaledale with its folk museum and 18th C shops and inns lining the green at High Row.

- **RICHMOND, NORTH YORKSHIRE** - Market town on edge of Swaledale with 11th C castle, Georgian and Victorian buildings surrounding cobbled market-place. Green Howards' Museum is in the former Holy Trinity Church. Attractions include the Georgian Theatre, restored Theatre Royal, Richmondshire Museum, Easby Abbey.

RIPON, NORTH YORKSHIRE - Ancient city with impressive cathedral containing Saxon crypt which houses church treasures from all over Yorkshire. Charter granted in 886 by Alfred the Great. 'Setting the Watch' tradition kept nightly by horn-blower in Market Square. Fountains Abbey nearby.

ROBIN HOOD'S BAY, NORTH YORKSHIRE - Picturesque village of red-roofed cottages with main street running from cliff top down ravine to seashore, a magnet for artists. Scene of much smuggling and shipwrecks in 18th C. Robin Hood reputed to have escaped to continent by boat from here.

ROSEDALE ABBEY, NORTH YORKSHIRE - Sturdy hamlet built around Cistercian nunnery in the reign of Henry II, in the middle of Rosedale, largest of the moorland valleys. Remains of 12th C priory. Disused lead mines on the surrounding moors.

ROTHERHAM, SOUTH YORKSHIRE - In the Don Valley, Rotherham became an important industrial town in the 19th C with discovery of coal and development of iron and steel industry by Joshua Walker who built Clifton House, now the town's museum. Magnificent 15th C All Saints Church is town's showpiece.

RUNSWICK BAY, NORTH YORKSHIRE - Holiday and fishing village on the west side of Runswick Bay.

S SCARBOROUGH, NORTH YORKSHIRE - Large, popular East Coast seaside resort, formerly a spa town. Beautiful gardens and two splendid sandy beaches. Castle ruins date from 1100; fine Georgian and Victorian houses. Scarborough Millennium depicts 1,000 years of town's history. Sea Life Centre.

SCOTCH CORNER, NORTH YORKSHIRE - Famous milestone at the junction of the A1 and A66 near Richmond.

SCUNTHORPE, SOUTH HUMBERSIDE - Consisted of 5 small villages until 1860 when extensive ironstone beds were discovered. Today an industrial 'garden town' with some interesting modern buildings. Nearby Normanby Hall contains fine examples of Regency furniture.

SELBY, NORTH YORKSHIRE - Small market town on the River Ouse, believed to have been birthplace of Henry I, with a magnificent abbey containing much fine Norman and Early English architecture.

SETTLE, NORTH YORKSHIRE - Town of narrow streets and Georgian houses in an area of great limestone hills and crags. Panoramic view from Castleberg Crag which stands 300 ft above town.

SHEFFIELD, SOUTH YORKSHIRE - Local iron ore and coal gave Sheffield its prosperous steel and cutlery industries. The modern city centre has many interesting buildings - cathedral, Cutlers' Hall, Crucible Theatre, Graves and Mappin Art Galleries. Meadowhall Shopping Centre nearby.

SHELLEY, WEST YORKSHIRE - West Yorkshire village south of Huddersfield and close to Kirklees Light Railway.

SKIPTON, NORTH YORKSHIRE - Pleasant market town at gateway to dales, with farming community atmosphere, a Palladian Town Hall, parish church and fully roofed castle at the top of the High Street. The Clifford family motto, 'Desoramis' is sculpted in huge letters on the parapet over the castle gateway.

SOWERBY BRIDGE, WEST YORKSHIRE - Busy little town in the Calder Valley near the Calder Hebble Canal. Birthplace of essayist John Foster.

T THIRSK, NORTH YORKSHIRE - Thriving market town with cobbled square surrounded by old shops and inns. St Mary's Church is probably the best example of Perpendicular work in Yorkshire. House of Thomas Lord - founder of Lord's Cricket Ground - is now a folk museum.

THORNTON DALE, NORTH YORKSHIRE - Picturesque village with Thorntondale Beck, traversed by tiny stone footbridges at the edge of pretty cottage gardens.

W WETHERBY, WEST YORKSHIRE - Prosperous market town on the River Wharfe, noted for horse-racing.

WHITBY, NORTH YORKSHIRE - Holiday town with narrow streets and steep alleys at the mouth of the River Esk. Captain James Cook, the famous navigator, lived in Grape Lane. 199 steps lead to St Mary's Church and St Hilda's Abbey overlooking harbour. Dracula connections. Gothic weekend every April.

Y YORK, NORTH YORKSHIRE - Ancient walled city nearly 2,000 years old, containing many well-preserved medieval buildings. Its Minster has over 100 stained glass windows and is the largest Gothic cathedral in England. Attractions include Castle Museum, National Railway Museum, Jorvik Viking Centre and York Dungeon.

Finding
accommodation
is as easy as 1 2 3

Where to Stay makes it quick and easy to find a place to stay.
There are several ways to use this guide.

1 Town Index

The town index, starting on page 812, lists all the places with accommodation featured in the regional sections. The index gives a page number where you can find full accommodation and contact details.

2 Colour Maps

All the place names in black on the colour maps at the front have an entry in the regional sections. Refer to the town index for the page number where you will find one or more establishments offering accommodation in your chosen town or village.

3 Accommodation listing

Contact details for **all** English Tourism Council assessed accommodation throughout England, together with their national Star rating are given in the listing section of this guide. Establishments with a full entry in the regional sections are shown in blue. Look in the town index for the page number on which their full entry appears.

HEART of England

The home of Shakespeare, fine china and the grandest palaces in Britain, the region is full of surprises, from the thriving multicultural cities of Birmingham and Nottingham to countryside both dramatic and picturesque.

classic sights

Hardwick Hall – probably Britain's greatest Elizabethan house

Pottery & porcelain – factory tours of Royal Crown Derby, Wedgewood, Spode and more

Ironbridge Gorge – the world's first cast-iron bridge

country

The Cotswolds – picturebook England

The Peak District – moorland, limestone gorges and ancient woodlands

literary links

Stratford-upon-Avon – Royal Shakespeare Company; the homes of Shakespeare and his family

Nottingham – DH Lawrence Birthplace Museum

arts for all

Walsall – The New Art Gallery

Wightwick Manor – arts & crafts masterpiece

Arts Festivals – Bromsgrove, Malvern and Cheltenham

distinctively different

Cadbury World – Chocaholic heaven

The counties of Derbyshire, Gloucestershire, Herefordshire, icestershire, Lincolnshire, Northamptonshire, Nottinghamshire, Rutland, opshire, Staffordshire, Warwickshire, Worcestershire and West Midlands

FOR MORE INFORMATION CONTACT:

Heart of England Tourist Board
Larkhill Road, Worcester WR5 2EZ
Tel: (01905) 761100 Fax: (01905) 763450
Internet: www.visitheartofengland.com

The Pictures:
1 South Shropshire Hills
2 Brindley Place, Birmingham
3 Stratford-upon-Avon

Places to Visit - see pages 220-224
Where to Stay - see pages 225-301

219

PLACES to visit

You will find hundreds of interesting places to visit during your stay, just some of which are listed in these pages. Contact any Tourist Information Centre in the region for more ideas on days out.

Acton Scott Historic Working Farm

Wenlock Lodge, Acton Scott, Church Stretton, Shropshire SY6 6QN
Tel: (01694) 781306 www.actonscotmuseum.co.uk
Acton Scott Historic Working Farm demonstrates farming and rural life in south Shropshire at the close of the 19thC.

Alton Towers Theme Park

Alton, Stoke-on-Trent, Staffordshire ST10 4DB
Tel: (0870) 520 4060 www.alton-towers.co.uk
Theme Park with over 125 rides and attractions including Oblivion, Nemesis, Haunted House, Runaway Mine Train, Congo River Rapids, Log Flume and many children's rides.

The American Adventure

Ilkeston, Derbyshire DE7 5SX
Tel: (01773) 531521 www.americanadventure.co.uk
The American Adventure has action and entertainment for all ages including the Missile white-knuckle rollercoaster, Europe's tallest skycoaster and the world's wettest log flume.

Belton House, Park and Gardens

Belton, Grantham, Lincolnshire NG32 2LS
Tel: (01476) 566116
The crowning achievement of restoration country house architecture, built in 1685-88 for Sir John Brownlow with alterations by James Wyatt in 1777.

Belvoir Castle Estate Office

Belvoir, Grantham, Lincolnshire NG32 1PD
Tel: (01476) 870262 www.belvoircastle.com
The present castle is the fourth to be built on this site and dates from 1816. Art treasures include works by Poussin, Rubens, Holbein and Reynolds. Queen's Royal Lancers display.

Birmingham Botanical Gardens and Glasshouses

Westbourne Road, Edgbaston, Birmingham, West Midlands B15 3TR
Tel: (0121) 454 1860
www.bham-bot-gdns.demon.co.uk
15 acres (6 ha) of ornamental gardens and glasshouses. Widest range of plants in the Midlands from tropical rainforest to arid desert. Aviaries with exotic birds, children's play area.

Black Country Living Museum

Tipton Road, Dudley, West Midlands DY1 4SQ
Tel: (0121) 557 9643 www.bclm.co.uk
A warm welcome awaits you at Britain's friendliest open-air museum. Wander around original shops and houses, or ride on fair attractions and take a look down the mine.

Blenheim Palace

Woodstock, Oxford, Oxfordshire OX7 1PX
Tel: (01993) 811325
Home of the 11th Duke of Marlborough, birthplace of Sir Winston Churchill. Designed by Vanbrugh in the English Baroque style. Park landscaped by 'Capability' Brown.

Butlins Family Entertainment Resort

Roman Bank, Skegness, Lincolnshire PE25 1NJ
Tel: (01754) 762311
Butlins Family Entertainment Resort has a skyline pavilion, toyland, sub-tropical waterworld, tenpin bowling and entertainments' centre with live shows.

Cadbury World

Linden Road, Bournville, Birmingham, West Midlands B30 2LD
Tel: (0121) 451 4180 www.cadburyworld.co.uk
Story of Cabdury's chocolate includes chocolate-making demonstration and attractions for all ages.

Chatsworth House and Garden

Bakewell, Derbyshire DE45 1PP
Tel: (01246) 582204 www.chatsworth-house.co.uk
Built in 1687-1707 with a collection of fine pictures, books, drawings and furniture. Garden laid out by 'Capability' Brown with fountains, cascades, a farmyard and playground.

Cotswold Farm Park

Guiting Power, Cheltenham, Gloucestershire GL54 5UG
Tel: (01451) 850307
Collection of rare breeds of British farm animals. Pets' corner, adventure playground, Tractor School, picnic area, gift shop, cafe and seasonal farming displays.

Drayton Manor Family Theme Park

Tamworth, Staffordshire B78 3TW
Tel: (01827) 287979 www.draytonmanor.co.uk
A major theme park with over 100 rides and attractions, plus children's rides, Zoo, farm, museums and the new, live 'Popeye Show'.

The Elgar Birthplace Museum

Crown East Lane, Lower Broadheath, Worcester, Worcestershire WR2 6RH
Tel: (01905) 333224 www.elgar.org
Country cottage birthplace displaying Elgar's desk and family possessions, complemented by new Elgar Centre. Memorabilia, sounds and special events illustrate his life.

The Galleries of Justice

Shire Hall, High Pavement, Lace Market, Nottingham, Nottinghamshire NG1 1HN
Tel: (0115) 952 0555 www.galleriesofjustice.org.uk
A museum of law located in and around a 19thC courthouse and county gaol, brought to life by costumed interpreters.

The Heights of Abraham Cable Cars, Caverns and Country Park

Matlock Bath, Matlock, Derbyshire DE4 3PD
Tel: (01629) 582365 www.heights-of-abraham.co.uk
A spectacular cable car ride takes you to the summit where, within the grounds, there is a wide variety of attractions for young and old alike. Gift shop and coffee shop.

Ikon Gallery

1 Oozells Square, Brindleyplace, Birmingham, West Midlands B1 2HS
Tel: (0121) 248 0708 www.ikongallery.co.uk
Ikon Gallery is one of Europe's foremost galleries for presenting the work of living artists within an innovative educational framework.

The Pictures:
1 Cottage Gardens, River Arrow, Herefordshire
2 Darwin Statue, Shrewsbury
3 Packwood House, Warwickshire
4 Rutland Water
5 Rockingham Castle, Northamptonshire

Ironbridge Gorge Museum

Ironbridge, Telford, Shropshire TF8 7AW
Tel: (01952) 433522 www.ironbridge.org.uk
World's first cast-iron bridge, Museum of the Gorge
Visitor Centre, Tar Tunnel, Jackfield Tile Museum, Coalport
China Museum, Rosehill House, Blists Hill Museum and
Museum of Iron.

Lincoln Castle

Castle Hill, Lincoln, Lincolnshire LN1 3AA
Tel: (01522) 511068
A medieval castle, including towers and ramparts, with a
Magna Carta exhibition, a prison chapel experience,
reconstructed Westgate and popular events throughout
the summer.

Museum of British Road Transport

Hales Street, Coventry, West Midlands CV1 1PN
Tel: (024) 7683 2425 www.mbrt.co.uk
200 cars and commercial vehicles from 1896 to date, 200
cycles from 1818 to date, 90 motorcycles from 1920 to
date and the 'Thrust 2' land speed story.

National Sea Life Centre

The Water's Edge, Brindleyplace, Birmingham,
West Midlands B1 2HL
Tel: (0121) 633 4700 www.sealife.co.uk
Over 55 fascinating displays. The opportunity to come
face-to-face with literally hundreds of fascinating sea
creatures, from sharks to shrimps.

The National Tramway Museum

Crich, Matlock, Derbyshire DE4 5DP
Tel: (01773) 852565 www.tramway.co.uk
A collection of over 70 trams from Britain and overseas
from 1873-1969 with tram rides on a 1-mile route, a
period street scene, depots, a power station, workshops
and exhibitions.

Nottingham Industrial Museum

Courtyard Buildings, Wollaton Park, Nottingham,
Nottinghamshire NG8 2AE
Tel: (0115) 915 3910 www.nottinghamcity.gov.uk
An 18thC stables presenting the history of Nottingham's
industries: printing, pharmacy, hosiery and lace. There is
also a Victorian beam engine, a horse gin and transport.

Peak District Mining Museum

The Pavilion, Matlock Bath, Matlock, Derbyshire DE4 3NR
Tel: (01629) 583834 www.peakmines.co.uk
A large exhibition on 3,500 years of lead mining with
displays on geology, mines and miners, tools and
engines. The climbing shafts make it suitable for children
as well.

Rockingham Castle

Rockingham, Market Harborough, Leicestershire LE16 8TH
Tel: (01536) 770240 www.rockinghamcastle.com
An Elizabethan house within the walls of a Norman
castle with fine pictures, extensive views, gardens with
roses and an ancient yew hedge.

Rugby School Museum

10 Little Church Street, Rugby, Warwickshire CV21 3AW
Tel: (01788) 556109
Rugby School Museum tells the story of the school, scene
of 'Tom Brown's Schooldays', and contains the earlier
memorabilia of the game invented on the school close.

Severn Valley Railway

The Railway Station, Bewdley, Worcestershire DY12 1BG
Tel: (01299) 403816 www.svr.co.uk
Preserved standard gauge steam railway running 16
miles between Kidderminster, Bewdley and Bridgnorth.
Collection of locomotives and passenger coaches.

Shakespeare's Birthplace

Henley Street, Stratford-upon-Avon, Warwickshire CV37 6QW
Tel: (01789) 204016 www.shakespeare.org.uk
The world-famous house where William Shakespeare was
born in 1564 and where he grew up. See the highly
acclaimed Shakespeare Exhibition.

The Shrewsbury Quest

193 Abbey Foregate, Shrewsbury, Shropshire SY2 6AH
Tel: (01743) 243324 www.shrewsburyquest.com
12thC medieval visitor attraction. Solve mysteries, create
illuminated manuscripts, play medieval games and relax
in unique herb gardens. Gift shop and cafe.

Shugborough Estate

Shugborough, Milford, Stafford, Staffordshire ST17 0XB
Tel: (01889) 881388 www.staffordshire.gov.uk
18thC mansion house with fine collection of furniture.
Gardens and park contain beautiful neo-classical
monuments.

Skegness Natureland Seal Sanctuary

North Parade, The Promenade, Skegness,
Lincolnshire PE25 1DB
Tel: (01754) 764345 www.skegnessnatureland.co.uk
Collection of performing seals, baby seals, penguins,
aquarium, crocodiles, snakes, terrapins, scorpions, tropical
birds, butterflies (April-October) and pets.

Snibston Discovery Park

Ashby Road, Coalville, Leicester, Leicestershire LE67 3LN
Tel: (01530) 278444 www.leics.gov.uk/museums
An all-weather and award-winning science and
industrial heritage museum.

Spode Visitor Centre

Spode, Church Street, Stoke-on-Trent,
Staffordshire ST4 1BX
Tel: (01782) 744011 www.spode.co.uk
Visitors are shown the various processes in the making of
bone china. Samples can be bought at the Spode Shop.

The Tales of Robin Hood

30-38 Maid Marian Way, Nottingham,
Nottinghamshire NG1 6GF
Tel: (0115) 948 3284
Join the world's greatest medieval adventure. Ride
through the magical green wood and play the Silver
Arrow game, in the search for Robin Hood.

Twycross Zoo

Twycross, Atherstone, Warwickshire CV9 3PX
Tel: (01827) 880250 www.twycrosszoo.com
A zoo with gorillas, orang-utans, chimpanzees, a modern
gibbon complex, elephants, lions, giraffes, a reptile
house, pets' corner and rides.

Walsall Arboretum

Lichfield Street, Walsall, West Midlands WS1 1TJ
Tel: (01922) 653148 www.walsallarboretum.co.uk
Picturesque Victorian park with over 79 acres (32 ha) of
gardens, lakes and parkland.

Warwick Castle

Warwick, Warwickshire CV34 4QU
Tel: (01926) 406600 www.warwick-castle.co.uk
Set in 60 acres (24 ha) of grounds with state rooms,
armoury, dungeon, torture chamber, clock tower, A Royal
Weekend Party 1898, Kingmaker – a preparation for
battle attractions.

The Wedgwood Story Visitor Centre

Barlaston, Stoke-on-Trent, Staffordshire ST12 9ES
Tel: (01782) 204218 www.thewedgwoodstory.com
New £4.5 million visitor centre. It exhibits centuries of
craftsmanship on a plate. Audio guided tour includes
exhibition and demonstration areas. Shop and
restaurants.

The Wildfowl and Wetlands Trust

The Wildfowl and Wetlands Trust
Slimbridge, Gloucester, Gloucestershire GL2 7BT
Tel: (01453) 890333 www.wwt.org.uk
Tropical house, hides, heated observatory, exhibits, shop,
restaurant, children's playground, pond zone.

Worcester Cathedral

10A College Green, Worcester,
Worcestershire WR1 2LH
Tel: (01905) 611002
Norman crypt and chapter house, King John's Tomb,
Prince Arthur's Chantry, medieval cloisters and buildings.
Touch and hearing control visually impaired facilities
available.

The Pictures:
1 Alford Craft Market, Lincolnshire
2 Chatsworth House, Derbyshire

Find out more about
HEART of England

Further information about holidays and attractions in Heart of England is available from:

HEART OF ENGLAND TOURIST BOARD
Larkhill Road, Worcester WR5 2EZ.
Tel: (01905) 761100 Fax: (01905) 763450
Internet: www.visitheartofengland.com

The following publications are available free from the Heart of England Tourist Board:

Heart of England - The Official Guide 2002
Bed & Breakfast Touring Map including Caravan and Camping

Getting to the
HEART of England

BY ROAD: Britain's main motorways (M1/M6/M5) meet in the Heart of England; the M40 links with the M42 south of Birmingham while the M4 provides fast access from London to the south of the region. These road links ensure that the Heart of England is more accessible by road than any other region in the UK.

BY RAIL: The Heart of England lies at the centre of the country's rail network. There are direct trains from London and other major cities to many towns and cities within the region.

The Pictures:
1 River Avon, Evesham
2 Black Country Museum, Dudley

Where to stay in the Heart of England

Accommodation entries in this region are listed in alphabetical order of place name, and then in alphabetical order of establishment. As West Oxfordshire and Cherwell are promoted in both Heart of England and South of England, places in these areas with accommodation are listed in this section. See South of England for full West Oxfordshire and Cherwell entries.

Map references refer to the colour location maps at front of this guide. The first number indicates the map to use; the letter and number which follow refer to the grid reference on the map.

At-a-glance symbols at the end of each accommodation entry give useful information about services and facilities. A key to symbols can be found inside the back cover flap. Keep this open for easy reference.

A brief description of the towns and villages offering accommodation in the entries which follow, can be found at the end of this section.

A complete listing of all the English Tourism Council assessed accommodation covered by this guide appears at the back of the guide.

ABBOTS MORTON, Worcestershire Map ref 2B1

◆◆◆◆

THE COTTAGE APARTMENT
The Cottage,
Gooms Hill, Abbots Morton Manor,
Abbots Morton, Worcester WR7 4LT
T: (01386) 792783
F: (01386) 792783
E: cottage@bedbrek.fsnet.co.uk
I: www.bedbrek.co.uk

Bedrooms: 1 double/twin
Bathrooms: 1 en suite

B&B per night:
S £25.00–£30.00
D £40.00–£50.00

OPEN All year round

Beautiful apartment in grounds of timber-framed cottage c1455. Malvern views. Set in peaceful countryside with fabulous walks, pubs and history. Central for all tourist sites.

P

USE YOUR *i*s

There are more than 550 Tourist Information Centres throughout England offering friendly help with accommodation and holiday ideas as well as suggestions of places to visit and things to do. You'll find TIC addresses in the local Phone Book.

ALCESTER, Warwickshire Map ref 2B1

♦♦♦♦

THE GLOBE HOTEL

54 Birmingham Road, Alcester B49 5EG
T: (01789) 763287 & 07956 442767
F: (01789) 763287
E: info@theglobehotel.com
I: www.theglobehotel.com

B&B per night:
S £49.50–£55.00
D £55.00–£65.00

OPEN All year round

Family-run hotel on the edge of historic market town (7 miles Stratford-upon-Avon). Stylish, comfortable and spacious en suite rooms, pine furniture and fitted desk-top working areas, colour TV and hospitality trays. Elegant dining room and separate conservatory lounge-bar. Ground floor room, disabled toilet. Ample private parking.

Bedrooms: 1 single, 7 double/twin, 1 triple/ multiple
Bathrooms: 8 en suite, 1 private

Lunch available
Evening meal available
CC: Delta, Mastercard, Switch, Visa

Seasonal weekend breaks £99 per room for 2 nights based on 2 sharing a double or twin room B&B.

ALTON, Staffordshire Map ref 4B2

♦♦♦♦

FIELDS FARM

Chapel Lane, Threapwood, Alton,
Stoke-on-Trent ST10 4QZ
T: (01538) 752721 & 07850 310381
F: (01538) 757404
E: pat.massey@ukonline.co.uk

B&B per night:
S Min £23.00
D £34.00–£41.00

HB per person:
DY £24.00–£32.00

OPEN All year round

Traditional farmhouse hospitality and comfort in picturesque Churnet Valley, 10 minutes from Alton Towers. Near Peak Park and within easy reach of Potteries and many stately homes. Stabling available. Ideal for walking, cycling, riding and fishing. Dogs by arrangement. Proprietor Pat Massey.

Bedrooms: 3 double/ twin
Bathrooms: 2 en suite, 1 private

Evening meal available

♦♦♦

HILLSIDE FARM

Alton Road, Denstone, Uttoxeter ST14 5HG
T: (01889) 590760
I: www.smoothhound.co.uk/hotels/ hillside.html

Bedrooms: 1 double/ twin, 3 triple/multiple
Bathrooms: 1 en suite, 1 private

B&B per night:
S £20.00–£25.00
D £32.00–£38.00

Victorian farmhouse with extensive views to the Weaver Hills and Churnet Valley. Situated 2 miles south of Alton Towers on B5032.

TOWN INDEX

This can be found at the back of the guide. If you know where you want to stay, the index will give you the page number listing accommodation in your chosen town, city or village.

ASHBOURNE, Derbyshire Map ref 4B2 *Tourist Information Centre Tel: (01335) 343666*

◆◆◆

THE BLACK HORSE INN

Main Road, Hulland Ward, Ashbourne
DE6 3EE
T: (01335) 370206
F: (01335) 370206

B&B per night:
S £40.00–£45.00
D £60.00–£70.00

OPEN All year round

Dating from the 1690s and personally run by owners. Four-poster en suite accommodation. Home-cooked food, vegetarian options, traditional Sunday carvery. Guest beers, bar games, beer garden. Set in Derbyshire Dales on edge of Peak District National Park, 4 miles Ashbourne. Ideal for Carsington Water, Alton Towers, Chatsworth and Dovedale.

Bedrooms: 4 double/ twin
Bathrooms: 4 en suite

Lunch available
Evening meal available
CC: Delta, Mastercard, Switch, Visa

◆◆◆◆

CROSS FARM

Main Road, Ellastone, Ashbourne
DE6 2GZ
T: (01335) 324668
F: (01335) 324039
E: janecliffe@hotmail.com

Bedrooms: 2 double/ twin, 1 triple/multiple
Bathrooms: 3 en suite

B&B per night:
S £20.00–£25.00
D £36.00–£38.00

OPEN All year round

19thC farmhouse near Alton Towers, Potteries, National Trust properties. Good accommodation and traditional Aga cooking in village location. Pub within walking distance.

◆◆◆

MONA VILLAS BED AND BREAKFAST

1 Mona Villas, Church Lane,
Mayfield, Ashbourne DE6 2JS
T: (01335) 343773
F: (01335) 343773

Bedrooms: 3 double/ twin
Bathrooms: 3 en suite

B&B per night:
S £20.00–£26.00
D £40.00–£50.00

OPEN All year round

A warm, friendly welcome to our Edwardian home with new purpose-built en suite accommodation. Beautiful views over open countryside. Near Alton Towers, Dovedale etc.

◆◆◆◆

STANSHOPE HALL

Stanshope, Ashbourne DE6 2AD
T: (01335) 310278
F: (01335) 310470
E: naomi@stanshope.demon.co.uk
I: www.stanshope.demon.co.uk

Bedrooms: 3 double/ twin
Bathrooms: 3 en suite

Evening meal available
CC: Delta, Mastercard, Switch, Visa

B&B per night:
S £25.00–£40.00
D £50.00–£80.00

HB per person:
DY £46.00–£61.00

OPEN All year round

Historic hall providing imaginatively decorated en suite bed and breakfast accommodation, with home cooking using garden and local produce, in Peak Park near Dovedale.

ASHBY-DE-LA-ZOUCH, Leicestershire Map ref 4B3 *Tourist Information Centre Tel: (01530) 411767*

◆◆◆◆

MEASHAM HOUSE FARM

Gallows Lane, Measham,
Swadlincote DE12 7HD
T: (01530) 270465 & 273128
F: (01530) 270465
E: jjlovett@meashamhouse.
freeserve.co.uk

Bedrooms: 2 double/ twin, 1 triple/multiple
Bathrooms: 3 en suite

B&B per night:
S Max £24.00
D Max £48.00

OPEN All year round

500-acre mixed farm. 200-year-old Grade II Listed Georgian farmhouse. 2 miles from A42 junction 12, 8 miles from M1 junction 22.

QUALITY ASSURANCE SCHEME

Diamond ratings and awards are explained at the back of this guide.

ASHFORD IN THE WATER, Derbyshire Map ref 4B2

♦♦♦♦
Silver
Award

GRITSTONE HOUSE
Greaves Lane, Ashford in the Water,
Bakewell DE45 1QH
T: (01629) 813563
F: (01629) 813563

Bedrooms: 3 double/
twin
Bathrooms: 1 en suite

B&B per night:
D £45.00–£50.00

OPEN All year round

Charming 18thC Georgian house offering friendly service and accommodation designed with comfort and style in mind. Ideal centre for exploring the Peak District's scenery.

BAKEWELL, Derbyshire Map ref 4B2 *Tourist Information Centre Tel: (01629) 813227*

♦♦♦

CASTLE CLIFFE
Monsal Head, Bakewell DE45 1NL
T: (01629) 640258
F: (01629) 640258
E: relax@castle-cliffe.co.uk
I: www.castle-cliffe.com

B&B per night:
S £30.00–£32.50
D £45.00–£55.00

OPEN All year round

Stunning position overlooking the beautiful Monsal Dale. Noted for its friendly atmosphere, hearty breakfasts and exceptional views. Drinks in the garden or around open log fire in winter. Centrally situated for Chatsworth, Haddon Hall and other attractions. Choice of dinner venues within an easy stroll. Walks in all directions.

Bedrooms: 4 double/
twin, 2 triple/multiple
Bathrooms: 6 en suite

3 nights for the price of 2 Nov–Mar incl.

CC: Delta, Mastercard,
Switch, Visa

♦♦♦♦♦
Gold
Award

TANNERY HOUSE
Matlock Street, Bakewell DE45 1EE
T: (01629) 815011 & 815327
F: (01629) 815327
I: www.tanneryhouse.co.uk

Bedrooms: 3 double/
twin
Bathrooms: 3 en suite

B&B per night:
S £32.50–£35.00
D £50.00–£55.00

OPEN All year round

Central Bakewell: Grade II Listed building, with guest wing, set in secluded gardens. Bedrooms en suite, opening onto garden. Private dining room overlooks swimming pool.

BALSALL COMMON, West Midlands Map ref 4B3

♦♦

AVONLEA
135 Kenilworth Road,
Balsall Common, Coventry CV7 7EU
T: (01676) 533003
F: (01676) 533003

Bedrooms: 1 single,
3 double/twin

B&B per night:
S £22.00–£27.00
D £44.00–£50.00

OPEN All year round

19thC cottage extended to provide spacious and comfortable accommodation, set back from main A425 road. Ample off-road parking. Near NEC, NAC and motorways.

♦♦♦

BLYTHE PADDOCKS
Barston Lane, Balsall Common,
Coventry CV7 7BT
T: (01676) 533050
F: (01676) 533050

Bedrooms: 2 single,
2 double/twin
Bathrooms: 1 en suite

B&B per night:
S £18.00–£20.00
D £40.00–£44.00

OPEN All year round

Family home standing in 5 acres. Ten minutes from Birmingham Airport and National Exhibition Centre. NAC Stoneleigh 8 miles. Countryside location. Find us in Birmingham A-Z page 168 square 1D.

CHECK THE MAPS

The colour maps at the front of this guide show all the cities, towns and villages for which you will find accommodation entries. Refer to the town index to find the page on which they are listed.

BALSALL COMMON continued

◆◆◆ **CAMP FARM**
Hob Lane, Balsall Common,
Coventry CV7 7GX
T: (01676) 533804
F: (01676) 533804

Bedrooms: 3 double/
twin

B&B per night:
S £26.00–£27.00
D £40.00–£41.00

OPEN All year round

200-year-old farmhouse used as a campsite by Cromwell for the siege of Kenilworth. 'Home from home' accommodation.

🐎 Ⓢ ♨ 🖾 ☎ ☼ 🐴 🚲 🎮 P

BAMFORD, Derbyshire Map ref 4B2

◆◆◆◆

PIONEER HOUSE
Station Road, Bamford, Hope Valley,
S33 0BN
T: (01433) 650638
E: pioneerhouse@yahoo.co.uk
I: www.pioneerhouse.co.uk

B&B per night:
S £30
D £40.00–£44.00

OPEN All year round

Pioneer House is a comfortable Edwardian home with spacious en suite bedrooms, beautifully decorated in turn-of-the-century style but with all modern conveniences. Nestling in the Hope Valley, we are ideally placed for visiting the Peak District and the Derbyshire Dales. Hearty breakfasts in a warm and friendly atmosphere.

Bedrooms: 2 double,
1 twin
Bathrooms: 2 en suite,
1 private

Parking for 6

3 nights for the price of 2 during low season.

🅰 🐎 12 🖾 ☐ ↓ 🔍 🖳 Ⓢ 🗡 🖾 ☎ ☼

BANBURY

See South of England region for entries

BARDNEY, Lincolnshire Map ref 4C2

◆◆◆

THE BLACK HORSE
16 Wragby Road, Bardney, Lincoln LN3 5XL
T: (01526) 398900
F: (01526) 399281
E: black-horse@lineone.net

B&B per night:
S £30.00
D £50.00

HB per person:
DY £30.00–£40.00

OPEN All year round

A warm welcome awaits you at this traditional 16thC former public house, fully refurbished as a guesthouse and tearoom. Set in a peaceful village location on the Viking Way and Sustrans Cycle Route. An ideal base for exploring the City of Lincoln and the Wolds. Homemade cakes a speciality.

Bedrooms: 3 double/
twin, 1 triple/multiple
Bathrooms: 4 en suite

Lunch available
Evening meal available

Short break-B&B £47.50 per couple per night.
Minimum stay 3 nights to incl Sat.

🅰 🐎 1 ☐ ↓ 🍷 Ⓢ 🗡 ♨ 🖾 ☾ ☼ 🚲 🎮 P

BARLOW, Derbyshire Map ref 4B2

◆◆◆◆
Silver
Award

MILLBROOK

Furnace Lane, Monkwood, Barlow,
Dronfield S18 7SY
T: (0114) 2890253 & 07831 398373
F: (0114) 2891365

B&B per night:
S £30.00
D £50.00–£54.00

OPEN All year round

Situated down a quiet country lane surrounded by lovely countryside with many walks around. On the edge of the Peak District, with Chatsworth House and Haddon Hall nearby, yet within easy reach of Sheffield and Chesterfield. Millbrook is spacious and comfortably furnished with attention to detail to make your stay as enjoyable as possible.

Bedrooms: 2 double/
twin
Bathrooms: 2 en suite

BELPER, Derbyshire Map ref 4B2

◆◆◆

THE OLD SHOP

10 Bakers Hill, Heage, Belper
DE56 2BL
T: (01773) 856796

Bedrooms: 1 single,
1 double/twin

B&B per night:
S Min £17.00
D Min £32.00

HB per person:
DY Min £23.00

OPEN All year round

Old house in a small village. Two bedrooms, stairlift access available for able-bodied and disabled guests. Transport and outings arranged to tourist attractions, evening events.

BELTON IN RUTLAND, Rutland Map ref 4C3

◆◆

THE OLD RECTORY

4 New Road, Belton in Rutland, Oakham
LE15 9LE
T: (01572) 717279
F: (01572) 717343
E: bb@stablemate.demon.co.uk
I: www.rutnet.co.uk/orb

B&B per night:
S £19.00–£32.00
D £40.00–£72.00

OPEN All year round

Victorian country house and guest annexe on 14-acre smallholding. Conservation village overlooking the Eye Brook Valley and rolling Rutland countryside. Cottage-style en suite rooms, quiet, friendly atmosphere. Families welcome. Continental or full farmhouse cooked breakfast. Excellent local pubs and restaurants for your evening meal.

Bedrooms: 1 single,
6 double/twin, 2 triple/
multiple
Bathrooms: 5 en suite

CC: Delta, Mastercard,
Visa

Mid-week breaks: 4 nights for price of 3.

COUNTRY CODE Always follow the Country Code ✿ Enjoy the countryside and respect its life and work ✿ Guard against all risk of fire ✿ Fasten all gates ✿ Keep your dogs under close control ✿ Keep to public paths across farmland ✿ Use gates and stiles to cross fences, hedges and walls ✿ Leave livestock, crops and machinery alone ✿ Take your litter home ✿ Help to keep all water clean ✿ Protect wildlife, plants and trees ✿ Take special care on country roads ✿ Make no unnecessary noise

BEWDLEY, Worcestershire Map ref 4A3 *Tourist Information Centre Tel: (01299) 404740*

◆◆◆

WINBROOK COTTAGE

Cleobury Road, Bewdley DY12 2BA
T: (01299) 405686 & 07967 700758

B&B per night:
S £21.00–£25.00
D £40.00–£45.00

OPEN All year round

Detached cottage circa 1782, five minutes' walk into Bewdley town centre. Ample off-road parking. Double bedroom has its own private balcony overlooking gardens. Home cooking a speciality. Friendly welcoming atmosphere. Children/ dogs welcome. Ideal for Severn Valley Railway, fishing (safe storage for tackle), West Midland Safari Park, Wyre Forest.

Bedrooms: 1 single,
1 double/twin

☎ 🖵 ⚓ Ⓢ ⚲ 🖩 ✳ ⚞ 🐴 P

BIBURY, Gloucestershire Map ref 2B1

◆◆◆◆
Gold
Award

COTTESWOLD HOUSE

Arlington, Bibury, Cirencester GL7 5ND
T: (01285) 740609
F: (01285) 740609
E: cotteswold.house@btclick.com
I: www.home.btclick.com/cotteswold.house

B&B per night:
S Max £35.00
D Max £48.00

Situated in this picturesque village, Cotteswold House offers high quality accommodation in a relaxed, friendly atmosphere. Three tastefully furnished bedrooms with en suite facilities, colour TV and tea/coffee. Spacious guest lounge/dining room. Cotteswold House is an ideal centre for touring Cotswolds and surrounding area. No smoking/pets. Private parking.

Bedrooms: 3 double/ twin
Bathrooms: 3 en suite

CC: Mastercard, Visa

☎ 🖥 🖵 ⚓ 🦪 Ⓢ ⚲ 🖩 ✳ ⚞ P

BICESTER

See South of England region for entries

BIDFORD-ON-AVON, Warwickshire Map ref 2B1

◆◆◆◆

AVONVIEW HOUSE

Stratford Road, Bidford-on-Avon, Alcester
B50 4LU
T: (01789) 778667
F: (01789) 778667
E: avonview@talk21.com

B&B per night:
S £28.00–£31.00
D £46.00–£52.00

HB per person:
DY Max £40.00

OPEN All year round

Convenience meets country life at Avonview House. A base for exploring Shakespeare Country and the warm heart of England, or just passing through, you will be made welcome in our 200-year-old converted stone barn with beamed bedrooms, set in ancient orchard and paddocks. Opposite a pay-as-you-play golf course.

Bedrooms: 2 double/ twin
Bathrooms: 2 private

Evening meal available

♈ ☎ 10 🖵 ⚓ 🦪 Ⓢ ⚲ 🖩 ♿ 🐾 ✳ 🐴 ⚞ P

BIDFORD-ON-AVON continued

◆◆◆

BROOM HALL INN
Bidford Road, Broom, Alcester B50 4HE
T: (01789) 773757

B&B per night:
S £25.00–£37.50
D £40.00–£60.00

HB per person:
DY Min £34.50

OPEN All year round

Family-owned country inn with carvery restaurant and extensive range of bar meals. Close to Stratford-upon-Avon and Cotswolds. Roaring log fires in the winter and a large garden with rare trees to relax in the summer months.

Bedrooms: 4 single,
8 double/twin
Bathrooms: 9 en suite,
3 private

Lunch available
Evening meal available
CC: Mastercard, Visa

BIRDLIP, Gloucestershire Map ref 2B1

◆◆◆

BEECHMOUNT
Birdlip, Gloucester GL4 8JH
T: (01452) 862262
F: (01452) 862262
E: thebeechmount@breathemail.net

Bedrooms: 3 double/twin, 3 triple/multiple
Bathrooms: 2 en suite

Evening meal available
CC: Delta, Mastercard, Switch, Visa

B&B per night:
S £17.00–£31.00
D £36.00–£44.00

OPEN All year round

Warm hospitality in family-run guesthouse, ideal centre for the Cotswolds. All rooms individually decorated. Choice of menu for breakfast. Evening meal by arrangement. Unrestricted access.

BIRMINGHAM, West Midlands Map ref 4B3 *Tourist Information Centre Tel: (0121) 643 2514 (City Arcade)*

◆◆◆

ASHLEY HOUSE
18 Alcott Lane, Marston Green,
Birmingham B37 7AT
T: (0121) 779 5368
F: (0121) 779 5368

Bedrooms: 2 double/twin
Bathrooms: 2 en suite

B&B per night:
S £25.00–£30.00
D £40.00–£45.00

OPEN All year round

Comfortable friendly accommodation near Marston Green station, convenient for the National Exhibition Centre, airport and Birmingham International station.

◆◆◆

ATHOLL LODGE
16 Elmdon Road, Acocks Green,
Birmingham B27 6LH
T: (0121) 707 4417
F: (0121) 707 4417

Bedrooms: 5 single,
4 double/twin, 1 triple/multiple
Bathrooms: 2 en suite

Lunch available
Evening meal available

B&B per night:
S £23.00–£30.00
D £45.00–£55.00

OPEN All year round

Friendly guesthouse in a quiet location on the south side of Birmingham. The National Exhibition Centre, airport and town centre are all within easy reach.

◆◆◆

CENTRAL GUEST HOUSE
1637 Coventry Road, South Yardley,
Birmingham B26 1DD
T: (0121) 706 7757
F: (0121) 706 7757
E: mmou826384@aol.com
I: www.centralguesthouse.com

Bedrooms: 1 single,
3 double/twin, 1 triple/multiple
Bathrooms: 4 en suite,
1 private

CC: Mastercard, Switch, Visa

B&B per night:
S £18.50–£22.50
D £40.00–£45.00

OPEN All year round

Aside Birmingham A45 road into city, close to local amenities, airport, NEC, railway station. All rooms en suite. Full English breakfast. 'Home from home'.

◆◆◆

ELMDON GUEST HOUSE
2369 Coventry Road, Sheldon,
Birmingham B26 3PN
T: (0121) 742 1626 & 688 1720
F: (0121) 7421626

Bedrooms: 2 single,
4 double/twin, 1 triple/multiple
Bathrooms: 7 en suite

Lunch available
Evening meal available
CC: Delta, Mastercard, Switch, Visa

B&B per night:
S £32.00–£38.00
D £45.00–£55.00

HB per person:
DY £32.00–£37.00

OPEN All year round

Family-run guesthouse with en suite facilities. TV in all rooms, including Sky. On main A45 close to the National Exhibition Centre, airport, railway and city centre.

BIRMINGHAM continued

◆◆◆ GABLES NEST

1639 Coventry Road, South Yardley,
Birmingham B26 1DD
T: (0121) 708 2712
F: (0121) 707 3396
E: malatgables@aol.com
I: www.guesthousebirmingham.co.uk

Bedrooms: 1 single,
2 double/twin, 2 triple/
multiple
Bathrooms: 4 en suite,
1 private

Lunch available
Evening meal available
CC: Amex, Delta, Diners,
Mastercard, Switch, Visa

B&B per night:
S £20.00–£25.00
D £40.00–£45.00

OPEN All year round

Family-run guesthouse, close to the National Exhibition Centre, Birmingham Airport, international railway station, Birmingham city centre and Solihull. All major credit cards taken.

◆◆◆ HOMELEA

2399 Coventry Road, Sheldon,
Birmingham B26 3PN
T: (0121) 742 0017
F: (0121) 688 1879

Bedrooms: 1 single,
2 double/twin, 1 triple/
multiple
Bathrooms: 2 en suite,
1 private

CC: Delta, Mastercard,
Switch, Visa

B&B per night:
S £22.00–£30.00
D £40.00–£45.00

OPEN All year round

A friendly bed and breakfast close to National Exhibition Centre and airport. Comfortable rooms all with TV. Full English breakfast included. Pubs and restaurants within walking distance.

◆◆◆ LYNDHURST HOTEL

135 Kingsbury Road, Erdington,
Birmingham B24 8QT
T: (0121) 373 5695
F: (0121) 373 5697
E: info@lyndhurst-hotel.co.uk
I. www.lyndhurst-hotel.co.uk

Bedrooms: 10 single,
4 double/twin
Bathrooms: 13 en suite,
1 private

Evening meal available
CC: Amex, Delta,
Mastercard, Visa

B&B per night:
S £30.00–£44.00
D £42.00–£56.00

HB per person:
DY £42.00–£54.00

OPEN All year round

Within half a mile of M6 (junction 6) and within easy reach of city and National Exhibition Centre. Comfortable bedrooms, spacious restaurant. Personal service in a quiet, friendly atmosphere.

◆◆ ROLLASON WOOD HOTEL

130 Wood End Road, Erdington,
Birmingham B24 8BJ
T: (0121) 373 1230
F: (0121) 382 2578
E: rollwood@globalnet.co.uk

Bedrooms: 19 single,
11 double/twin, 5 triple/
multiple
Bathrooms: 11 en suite

Evening meal available
CC: Amex, Delta, Diners,
Mastercard, Switch, Visa

B&B per night:
S £18.00–£38.00
D £32.00–£49.50

OPEN All year round

Friendly, family-run hotel, 1 mile from M6, exit 6. Convenient for city centre, NEC and convention centre. A la carte restaurant and bar.

◆◆ WENTWORTH HOTEL

103 Wentworth Road, Harborne,
Birmingham B17 9SU
T: (0121) 427 2839 & 427 6818
F: (0121) 427 2839
E: wentworthhotel@freeuk.com
I: www.hotelbirminghamuk.com

Bedrooms: 6 single,
7 double/twin, 1 triple/
multiple
Bathrooms: 14 en suite

Evening meal available
CC: Amex, Delta, Diners,
Mastercard, Switch, Visa

B&B per night:
S £32.00–£35.00
D £45.00–£55.00

OPEN All year round

Family-run hotel, 16 bedrooms en suite with TV, tea/coffee in all rooms. Victorian building with bar. Quiet location, yet close to all amenities.

◆ WOODVILLE HOUSE

39 Portland Road, Edgbaston,
Birmingham B16 9HN
T: (0121) 454 0274
F: (0121) 454 5965

Bedrooms: 4 single,
5 double/twin, 1 triple/
multiple
Bathrooms: 4 en suite

B&B per night:
S £18.00–£25.00
D £30.00–£35.00

OPEN All year round

High standard accommodation, 1 mile from city centre. Full English breakfast. All rooms have colour TV and tea/coffee-making facilities. En suite bedrooms available.

BIRMINGHAM AIRPORT

See under Balsall Common, Birmingham, Coventry, Meriden, Solihull

♦♦♦

THE CASTLE HOTEL
The Square, Bishop's Castle SY9 5BN
T: (01588) 638403
F: (01588) 638403
I: www.bishops-castle.co.uk/castlehotel

B&B per night:
S £38.00
D £65.00

OPEN All year round

Five very comfortable en suite bedrooms, oak-panelled no-smoking dining room, 3 bars, open fires, Good Beer Guide since 1990. Wonderful walking country (Shropshire Way, Offa's Dyke, Wild Edric's Way). Special breaks.

Bedrooms: 1 single, 4 double/twin
Bathrooms: 5 en suite

Lunch available
Evening meal available
CC: Delta, Mastercard, Switch, Visa

2 nights' DB&B £80pp, 4 nights for the price of 3 Sun to Thurs only.

♦♦♦♦

THE SUN AT NORBURY
Norbury, Bishop's Castle SY9 5DX
T: (01588) 650680
E: sun@norbury99.fsbusiness.co.uk
I: www.thesunatnorbury.co.uk

B&B per night:
S £35.00–£45.00
D £60.00–£75.00

OPEN All year round

In a secret corner of Shropshire where time has stood still for centuries, this ancient inn full of antiques and atmosphere has an excellent restaurant and comfortable en-suite rooms in the Old Coach House. Beautiful walking/cycling routes from the village and a wealth of wildlife and local history.

Bedrooms: 3 double/twin
Bathrooms: 3 en suite

Lunch available
Evening meal available
CC: Delta, Mastercard, Switch, Visa

'Antiques Buying Breaks' courier service for dealers/collectors. Auction, sales, Shopshire/North Wales. (Transport/collection incl). Minimum 2 nights.

♦♦♦♦

KINGS HEAD INN AND RESTAURANT
The Green, Bledington, Oxford OX7 6XQ
T: (01608) 658365
F: (01608) 658902
E: kingshead@orr-ewing.com
I: www.kingsheadinn.net

B&B per night:
S £45.00–£75.00
D £60.00–£90.00

OPEN All year round

A hot buttered experience can be expected at this quintessential 15thC inn on village green with brook and ducks. Much of medieval character remains, exposed stone walls, inglenook fireplace, trestles and pews. Delightful accommodation complemented by full facilities and thoughtful extras. Award-winning restaurant. Ideally situated for main tourist attractions.

Bedrooms: 12 double/twin
Bathrooms: 12 en suite

Lunch available
Evening meal available
CC: Amex, Delta, Mastercard, Switch, Visa

SPECIAL BREAKS
Many establishments offer special promotions and themed breaks. These are highlighted in red. (All such offers are subject to availability.)

BLOCKLEY, Gloucestershire Map ref 2B1

♦♦♦ **THE MALINS**
21 Station Road, Blockley,
Moreton-in-Marsh GL56 9ED
T: (01386) 700402
F: (01386) 700402
E: johnmalin@talk21.com
I: members.home.com/panthers-3/
TheMalinsBnB.html

Bedrooms: 3 double/
twin
Bathrooms: 3 en suite

B&B per night:
S £26.00–£30.00
D £40.00–£42.00

OPEN All year round

Beautifully presented Cotswold-stone house on edge of delightful village. Ideal base for touring Cotswolds and Shakespeare Country. Tastefully decorated, comfortable, non-smoking accommodation. A warm welcome awaits.

BOURTON-ON-THE-WATER, Gloucestershire Map ref 2B1 *Tourist Information Centre Tel: (01451) 820211*

♦♦♦♦
Silver
Award

COOMBE HOUSE
Rissington Road, Bourton-on-the-Water,
Cheltenham GL54 2DT
T: (01451) 821966 & 822367
F: (01451) 810477
E: coombe.house@virgin.net
I: www.coombehousecotswolds.co.uk

B&B per night:
S £35.00–£50.00
D £45.00–£60.00

OPEN Mar–Dec

A charming peaceful house in lovely gardens with sun terrace. Five minutes' riverside walk from the centre of the village and restaurants. Pretty en suite bedrooms thoughtfully equipped. Guests' lounge and attractive dining room where traditional breakfast is served. Parking. Licensed. The perfect place from which to explore the Cotswolds.

Bedrooms: 6 double/
twin
Bathrooms: 6 en suite

CC: Delta, Mastercard,
Switch, Visa

Discounts available for off-season breaks.
Telephone for further details.

♦♦♦ **THE COTSWOLD HOUSE**
Lansdowne, Bourton-on-the-
Water, Cheltenham GL54 2AR
T: (01451) 822373

Bedrooms: 2 double/
twin, 2 triple/multiple
Bathrooms: 2 en suite,
2 private

B&B per night:
S £25.00–£35.00
D £40.00–£50.00

OPEN All year round

Lovely detached Cotswold-stone house. Elegant hall, curved stairs to galleried landing, spacious en suite rooms overlooking pretty garden. Homely atmosphere.

♦♦♦♦

LANSDOWNE HOUSE
Lansdowne, Bourton-on-the-Water,
Cheltenham GL54 2AT
T: (01451) 820812
F: (01451) 822484
E: heart@lansdownehouse.co.uk
I: www.lansdownehouse.co.uk

B&B per night:
D £40.00–£45.00

OPEN All year round

Large period stone family house. Tastefully furnished en suite accommodation with a combination of old and antique furniture. All rooms have tea/coffee trays and colour TV. There is parking and a garden for guests' use and a good selection of guide books to help you explore the area.

Bedrooms: 2 double/
twin, 1 triple/multiple
Bathrooms: 3 en suite

MAP REFERENCES The map references refer to the colour maps at the front of this guide. The first figure is the map number; the letter and figure which follow indicate the grid reference on the map.

BOURTON-ON-THE-WATER continued

◆◆◆ MOUSETRAP INN

Lansdowne, Bourton-on-the-
Water, Cheltenham GL54 2AR
T: (01451) 820579
F: (01451) 822393
E: mtinn@waverider.co.uk
I: www.mousetrap-inn.co.uk

Bedrooms: 9 double/
twin
Bathrooms: 9 en suite

Lunch available
Evening meal available
CC: Delta, Mastercard,
Switch, Visa

B&B per night:
D £45.00–£62.00

HB per person:
DY £32.50–£41.00

OPEN All year round

Small homely inn. All rooms en suite with TV and tea/coffee facilities. Excellent food served in relaxed surroundings. Open fire in the winter.

◆◆◆◆ THE RIDGE
Silver Award

Whiteshoots Hill, Bourton-on-the-
Water, Cheltenham GL54 2LE
T: (01451) 820660
F: (01451) 822448

Bedrooms: 3 double/
twin, 1 triple/multiple
Bathrooms: 3 en suite,
1 private

B&B per night:
S £30.00–£35.00
D £48.00–£50.00

OPEN All year round

Large country house surrounded by beautiful grounds. Central for visiting many places of interest and close to all amenities. Ground floor en suite bedrooms available.

Rating Applied For

STATION VILLA

2 Station Villa, Station Road, Bourton-on-
the-Water, Cheltenham GL54 2ER
T: (01451) 810406
F: (01451) 821359
E: rooms@stationvilla.com
I: www.stationvilla.com

Liz and Nigel welcome you to their home. Station Villa bed and breakfast is conveniently situated in Bourton-on-the-Water, 5 minutes' walk to the centre of the village where you will find the River Windrush, Motor Museum, Model Railway, Birdland plus the Perfumery and some of the best tearooms in the area.

Bedrooms: 3 double/
twin
Bathrooms: 3 en suite

B&B per night:
S £25.00–£30.00
D £40.00–£45.00

OPEN All year round

BRACKLEY, Northamptonshire Map ref 2C1 *Tourist Information Centre Tel: (01280) 700111*

◆◆◆ THE THATCHES

Whitfield, Brackley NN13 5TQ
T: (01280) 850358

Bedrooms: 3 double/
twin

B&B per night:
S £20.00–£30.00
D £35.00–£60.00

200-year-old house, facing south, with lovely views, in a quiet village location. Close to Stowe gardens (NT), Silverstone, Oxford and other interesting places.

BREDENBURY, Herefordshire Map ref 2A1

◆◆ REDHILL FARM

Bredenbury, Bromyard HR7 4SY
T: (01885) 483255 & 483535
F: (01885) 483535

Bedrooms: 2 double/
twin

B&B per night:
S £18.00–£20.00
D £34.00–£36.00

OPEN All year round

17thC farmhouse in 86 acres of peaceful countryside with panoramic views. Central for Malvern, Hereford, Worcester, Ledbury, Ludlow. Children and pets welcome. Horses, and 0.5 mile gallop.

IMPORTANT NOTE Information on accommodation listed in this guide has been supplied by the proprietors. As changes may occur you are advised to check details at the time of booking.

BRIDGNORTH, Shropshire Map ref 4A3 *Tourist Information Centre Tel: (01746) 763257*

♦♦♦

BASSA VILLA BAR AND GRILL

48 Cartway, Bridgnorth WV16 4BG
T: (01746) 763977 &
(01952) 691184
F: (01952) 691604
E: sugarloaf@globalnet.co.uk
I: www.bassavilla.com

Bedrooms: 1 double/
twin, 1 triple/multiple
Bathrooms: 2 en suite

Lunch available
Evening meal available
CC: Delta, Mastercard,
Switch, Visa

B&B per night:
S £40.00–£45.00
D £50.00–£60.00

OPEN All year round

Comfortable en suite accommmodation provided in a delightful 16thC riverside inn. Award-winning restaurant, cosy bar offers fine wines, several draught ales. Friendly staff guarantee warm welcome.

♦♦♦♦

BULLS HEAD INN

Chelmarsh, Bridgnorth WV16 6BA
T: (01746) 861469
F: (01746) 862646
E: dave@bullshead.fsnet.co.uk
I: www.virtual-shropshire.co.uk/
bulls-head-inn

B&B per night:
S £32.00–£35.00
D £46.00–£52.00

OPEN All year round

17thC country inn offering excellent accommodation and country fare, approximately 4 miles from Bridgnorth. All bedrooms are en suite with tea/coffee-making facilities. Three ground floor bedrooms for people with disabilities. Choice of cottages/apartments for self-catering or bed and breakfast. Fishing parties welcome – lock-up store for tackle and bait.

Bedrooms: 1 single,
5 double/twin, 3 triple/
multiple
Bathrooms: 9 en suite

Lunch available
Evening meal available
CC: Delta, Mastercard,
Switch, Visa

BRIZE NORTON

See South of England region for entries

BROADWAY, Worcestershire Map ref 2B1

♦♦♦♦♦
Gold
Award

BURHILL FARM

Buckland, Broadway WR12 7LY
T: (01386) 858171
F: (01386) 858171

B&B per night:
D £45.00–£55.00

OPEN All year round

A warm welcome awaits guests at our mainly grass farm lying in the folds of the Cotswolds, just 2 miles south of Broadway. Both guest rooms are en suite and have TV and tea/coffee facilities. The Cotswold Way runs through the middle of the farm providing many lovely walks.

Bedrooms: 2 double/
twin
Bathrooms: 2 en suite

AT-A-GLANCE SYMBOLS

Symbols at the end of each accommodation entry give useful information about services and facilities. A key to symbols can be found inside the back cover flap. Keep this open for easy reference.

◆◆◆

CROWN AND TRUMPET INN

Church Street, Broadway WR12 7AE
T: (01386) 853202
F: (01386) 834650
E: ascott@cotswoldholidays.co.uk
I: www.cotswoldholidays.co.uk

B&B per night:
D £50.00–£70.00

OPEN All year round

17thC Cotswold-stone inn in picturesque Broadway, gateway to the Cotswolds and an ideal touring base. Extensive menu of seasonal and local dishes, many home-made, and fine selection of traditional beers and seasonal drinks. Oak beams, log fires in winter. Special offers for off-season and extended stays – telephone for details.

Bedrooms: 5 double/twin
Bathrooms: 5 en suite

Lunch available
Evening meal available
CC: Delta, Mastercard, Switch, Visa

3 night stays available Oct-May (excl Christmas, New Year, Easter).

◆◆◆◆
Silver Award

LEASOW HOUSE
Laverton Meadow, Broadway
WR12 7NA
T: (01386) 584526
F: (01386) 584596
E: leasow@clara.net
I: www.leasow.co.uk

Bedrooms: 5 double/twin, 2 triple/multiple
Bathrooms: 7 en suite

CC: Amex, Mastercard, Visa

B&B per night:
S £40.00–£55.00
D £55.00–£70.00

OPEN All year round

Set in tranquil countryside close to Broadway. Leasow House is a 16thC farmhouse, ideally based for touring the Cotswolds and Shakespeare Country.

◆◆◆◆

LOWERFIELD FARM

Willersey, Broadway WR11 5HF
T: (01386) 858273 & 07703 343996
F: (01386) 854608
E: info@lowerfield-farm.co.uk
I: www.lowerfield-farm.co.uk

B&B per night:
S £35.00–£45.00
D £45.00–£75.00

HB per person:
DY £37.50–£52.50

OPEN All year round

2000-acre mixed farm. Genuine farmhouse comfort and hospitality, in a late 17thC Cotswold-stone farmhouse. Delightful accommodation, all en suite, with panoramic views over hills. Peaceful location provides an ideal base from which to explore the Cotswolds, Shakespeare Country and Hidcote Gardens. Evening meals by arrangement, colour brochure available.

Bedrooms: 2 double/twin, 1 triple/multiple
Bathrooms: 3 en suite

Evening meal available
CC: Delta, Mastercard, Switch, Visa

3 nights for the price of 2 from 30 Oct-30 Mar (excl Christmas/New Year).

QUALITY ASSURANCE SCHEME

For an explanation of the quality and facilities represented by the Diamonds please refer to the front of this guide. A more detailed explanation can be found in the information pages at the back.

◆◆◆◆

MILESTONE HOUSE

Upper High Street, Broadway WR12 7AJ
T: (01386) 853432
E: milestone.house@talk21.com

B&B per night:
S Min £45.00
D £55.00–£65.00

OPEN All year round

A 17thC Listed property situated in the upper High Street of Broadway. There is a wealth of period charm in the 4 comfortably appointed double bedrooms. Guests can relax in either of the 2 sitting rooms and breakfast is served in the conservatory overlooking the courtyard garden.

Bedrooms: 4 double/twin
Bathrooms: 4 en suite

CC: Mastercard, Switch, Visa

 ♘ ☐ ♨ ⁇ ⑤ ⌦ 🕮 🖳 🖴 ► ⁑ ⁂ 🏠 P

◆◆◆◆

SHENBERROW HILL
Stanton, Broadway WR12 7NE
T: (01386) 584468
F: (01386) 584468
E: michael.neilan@talk21.com
I: www.cotswold-way.co.uk

Bedrooms: 1 double/twin, 2 triple/multiple
Bathrooms: 3 en suite

B&B per night:
S £30.00
D £50.00–£55.00

OPEN All year round

Attractive country house, quietly situated in beautiful unspoilt Cotswold village. Heated swimming pool. Friendly, helpful service. Inn nearby. Ideal base touring, walking, riding.

♘3 🖴 ☐ ♨ ⁇ ⑤ 🕮 🖳 ⌦ 🐾 U ⁑ 🐕 🐑 🏠 P

◆◆◆◆

SOUTHWOLD GUEST HOUSE

Station Road, Broadway WR12 7DE
T: (01386) 853681
F: (01386) 854610
E: sueandnick.southwold@talk21.com

B&B per night:
S £27.00–£30.00
D £48.00–£55.00

OPEN All year round

Sue and Nick Smiles invite you to their spacious and tastefully decorated Edwardian house situated in one of the Cotswolds' most picturesque villages. We are 3 minutes' walk from pubs, restaurants and the Cotswolds Way. Well appointed rooms available with en suites (single with private facilities), hospitality tray, colour TV. Hairdryer. Guest lounge.

Bedrooms: 1 single, 6 double/twin, 1 triple/multiple
Bathrooms: 7 en suite, 1 private

CC: Mastercard, Switch, Visa

 ♘ ☐ ♨ ⁇ ⑤ ⌦ 🕮 🖳 🖴 🐑 🏠 P

◆◆◆◆
Silver
Award

WHITEACRES

Station Road, Broadway WR12 7DE
T: (01386) 852320
E: whiteacres@btinternet.com
I: www.broadway-cotswolds.co.uk/whiteacres.html

B&B per night:
D £50.00–£55.00

OPEN All year round

This beautiful Edwardian property offers 5 en suite bedrooms, 2 with 4-poster beds, all with colour TV, tea/coffee-making facilities, hairdryer and many thoughtful extras. There is a guests' lounge and ample car parking space. The house is decorated to a high standard and our aim is to provide a comfortable, happy base for a perfect holiday.

Bedrooms: 5 double/twin
Bathrooms: 5 en suite

 ♘ 🖭 📷 ☐ ♨ ⁇ ⑤ ⌦ 🕮 🖳 🖴 🏠 P

BROADWAY continued

◆◆◆◆ Silver Award

WINDRUSH HOUSE

Station Road, Broadway WR12 7DE
T: (01386) 853577 & 853790
F: (01386) 853790
E: richard@broadway-windrush.co.uk
I: www.broadway-windrush.co.uk

Bedrooms: 5 double/twin, 1 triple/multiple
Bathrooms: 6 en suite

CC: Delta, Mastercard, Switch, Visa

B&B per night:
S £30.00–£45.00
D £50.00–£65.00

HB per person:
DY £62.00–£80.00

OPEN All year round

Windrush House is an outstanding example of Edwardian elegance, located a few minutes' walk from the centre of Broadway – the 'jewel' of the Cotswolds. The house provides spacious, relaxed and sophisticated surroundings combined with a homely and welcoming atmosphere to make your stay one of those unforgettable memories.

BROMSGROVE, Worcestershire Map ref 4B3 *Tourist Information Centre Tel: (01527) 831809*

◆◆◆◆

BROMSGROVE COUNTRY HOTEL

249 Worcester Road, Stoke Heath, Bromsgrove B61 7JA
T: (01527) 835522
F: (01527) 871257
E: bchotel@talk21.com

Bedrooms: 6 double/twin, 3 triple/multiple
Bathrooms: 8 en suite, 1 private

Evening meal available
CC: Delta, Mastercard, Switch, Visa

B&B per night:
S £49.00
D £55.00

HB per person:
DY £69.00–£75.00

OPEN All year round

Quiet, elegant, Victorian residence with modern amenities. Close to M6/M42/M5 and historic countryside. A pleasant stay ensured under personal supervision of the proprietors.

◆◆

12 MOORFIELD DRIVE

Bromsgrove B61 8EJ
T: (01527) 835056 & 0796 8087966

Bedrooms: 1 single, 1 double/twin

B&B per night:
S £18.00–£22.00
D £36.00–£44.00

OPEN All year round

Quiet, comfortable accommodation in detached family home. Close to town centre and a few minutes to M42 motorway. No smoking.

◆◆◆◆

OVERWOOD BED AND BREAKFAST

Woodcote Lane, Woodcote, Bromsgrove B61 9EE
T: (01562) 777193
F: (01562) 777689
E: info@overwood.net
I: www.overwood.net

Bedrooms: 3 double/twin
Bathrooms: 2 en suite, 1 private

Lunch available
Evening meal available

B&B per night:
S Min £29.00
D Min £48.00

OPEN All year round

Pretty cottage in rural surroundings, but convenient for M5/M42. Very comfortable rooms and high quality breakfasts with eggs from our own free-range hens.

BURFORD

See South of England region for entries

BURTON DASSETT, Warwickshire Map ref 2C1

◆◆◆◆

THE WHITE HOUSE BED AND BREAKFAST

Burton Dassett, Southam CV47 2AB
T: (01295) 770143 & 0476 458314
E: lisa@whitehouse10.freeserve.co.uk

B&B per night:
S £35.00–£45.00
D £45.00–£50.00

HB per person:
DY £37.50–£40.00

OPEN All year round

Large country house situated at the top of the Burton Dassett Hills, enjoying superb views over the Warwickshire and Oxfordshire countryside. Evening meal and packed lunch on request. A high standard of accommodation, both homely and welcoming. Convenient for Warwick, Stratford-upon-Avon, Cotswolds, Birmingham and NEC. Please phone for a brochure.

Bedrooms: 3 double/twin
Bathrooms: 3 en suite

BUXTON, Derbyshire Map ref 4B2 *Tourist Information Centre Tel: (01298) 25106*

◆◆◆◆

ALL SEASONS GUEST HOUSE

4 Wye Grove, Buxton SK17 9AJ
T: (01298) 74628 & 07970 186715
E: chrisandruss@allseasonsguesthouse.fsnet.co.uk
I: www.allseasonsguesthouse.fsnet.co.uk

Bedrooms: 3 double/twin
Bathrooms: 3 en suite

Evening meal available

A warm and friendly Victorian house in a quiet area yet within 5 minutes' walk to all amenities and attractions. All rooms to a high standard.

🐴 📺 ☐ ☕ ⚲ [S] 🚭 ▥ 🧺 ✿ 🚗 ⊘ P

B&B per night:
S £25.00–£30.00
D £40.00–£45.00

HB per person:
DY £30.00–£40.00

OPEN All year round

◆◆◆◆

BUXTON VIEW

74 Corbar Road, Buxton SK17 6RJ
T: (01298) 79222 & 07710 516846
F: (01298) 79222
E: rogerbuxtonview@aol.com

Lovely stone house in a 'classy' residential area. Comfortable en suite bedrooms, residents' lounge. Easy walking distance to Buxton's gracious town centre. Pretty gardens, with woodland and moorland walks leading from the front door. Your hosts are Val and Roger Broad, whose hospitality is renowned.

Bedrooms: 1 single, 3 double/twin, 1 triple/multiple
Bathrooms: 4 en suite, 1 private

Evening meal available
CC: Delta, Mastercard, Switch, Visa

Any 2 nights or more 10% discount (excl Christmas).

[M] 🐴 📺 ☐ ☕ ⚲ [S] 🚭 [RL] ▥ 🧺 ✿ 🚗 P

B&B per night:
S £21.00–£26.00
D £42.00–£47.00

HB per person:
DY £33.00–£35.50

OPEN All year round

◆◆◆◆◆
Silver Award

BUXTON'S VICTORIAN GUESTHOUSE

3A Broad Walk, Buxton SK17 6JE
T: (01298) 78759 & 07801 861227
F: (01296) 74732
E: buxvic@x-stream.co.uk
I: www.smoothhound.co.uk

Bedrooms: 6 double/twin, 2 triple/multiple
Bathrooms: 8 en suite

Built in 1860 by Duke of Devonshire. Now fully refurbished in classical Victorian style. On a quiet freeze-lined promenade, overlooking Pavilion Gardens and Opera House.

[M] 🐴 5 ♿ 📠 📺 ☐ ☕ [S] 🚭 [RL] ▥ 🧺 ⚑ 🚗 ⊘ 🏠 P

B&B per night:
S £35.00–£45.00
D £50.00–£65.00

OPEN All year round

◆◆◆

DEVONSHIRE ARMS

Peak Forest, Buxton SK17 8EJ
T: (01298) 23875 & 07831 707325
I: www.devarms.com

Bedrooms: 2 double/twin, 1 triple/multiple
Bathrooms: 3 en suite

Lunch available
Evening meal available
CC: Amex, Delta, Mastercard, Switch, Visa

Traditional Peak District inn. Rooms refurbished to high standard, en suite, TV and coffee facilities. Excellent food and traditional ales. Good walking country. Dogs and children free.

[M] 🐴 ☐ ☕ ⚲ 🍷 [S] 🚭 ▥ 🧺 U ✿ 🐕 🚗 P

B&B per night:
S Min £28.50
D Min £46.00

OPEN All year round

◆◆

FAIRHAVEN

1 Dale Terrace, Buxton SK17 6LU
T: (01298) 24481
F: (01298) 24481
E: paulandcatherine@fairhavenguesthouse.freeserve.co.uk

Bedrooms: 1 single, 3 double/twin, 3 triple/multiple

Evening meal available
CC: Amex, Delta, Mastercard, Switch, Visa

Within easy reach of the Opera House, Pavilion Gardens, 2 golf courses and the many and varied attractions of Derbyshire's Peak District.

[M] 🐴 📺 ☐ ☕ [S] 🚭 ▥ 🚗

B&B per night:
S £17.50–£25.00
D £31.00–£40.00

OPEN All year round

WEB

www.travelengland.org.uk
Log on for information and inspiration. The latest information on places to visit, events and quality assessed accommodation.

BUXTON continued

◆◆◆◆ **GROSVENOR HOUSE**
1 Broad Walk, Buxton SK17 6JE
T: (01298) 72439
F: (01298) 72439
I: www.SmoothHound.co.uk/hotels/
grosvenr.html

Bedrooms: 6 double/
twin, 2 triple/multiple
Bathrooms: 8 en suite

B&B per night:
S £45.00–£50.00
D £50.00–£75.00

OPEN All year round

Privately-run, Victorian residence enjoying splendid views of Pavilion Gardens/theatre. Homely and peaceful atmosphere. Bedrooms non-smoking. Home-cooked traditional English food. Comfort and hospitality assured.

◆◆◆◆
Silver
Award

▼ **HAREFIELD**
15 Marlborough Road, Buxton SK17 6RD
T: (01298) 24029
F: (01298) 24029
E: hardie@harefield1.freeserve.co.uk
I: www.harefield1.freeserve.co.uk

B&B per night:
S £23.00–£25.00
D £46.00–£50.00

HB per person:
DY £35.50–£37.50

OPEN All year round

Elegant Victorian property set in its own grounds overlooking Buxton. Quiet location just a few minutes' walk from the historic town centre and an ideal base for exploring the beautiful Peak District. Spacious and comfortable accommodation with all bedrooms en suite. Friendly atmosphere, delicious food and lovely gardens to enjoy.

Bedrooms: 1 single,
4 double/twin, 1 triple/
multiple
Bathrooms: 5 en suite,
1 private

Lunch available
Evening meal available

◆◆◆◆
Silver
Award

KINGSCROFT
10 Green Lane, Buxton SK17 9DP
T: (01298) 22757 & 07889 977971
F: (01298) 27858

B&B per night:
S £25.00–£30.00
D £50.00–£60.00

OPEN All year round

Welcome to our Victorian luxury guesthouse. Central yet quiet location. Take a relaxing break in comfortable surroundings with period furnishings. Enjoy our hearty, delicious full English or vegetarian breakfasts. Fully licensed bar. All 8 rooms are en suite with TV/video and well-stocked hospitality tray. Private car park.

Bedrooms: 2 single,
6 double/twin
Bathrooms: 8 en suite

Evening meal available

10% discount on stays of 4 nights or more.

◆◆◆◆ **LAKENHAM GUESTHOUSE**
11 Burlington Road, Buxton
SK17 9AL
T: (01298) 79209

Bedrooms: 4 double/
twin, 2 triple/multiple
Bathrooms: 5 en suite,
1 private

B&B per night:
D Min £60.00

OPEN All year round

Elegant Victorian house in own grounds overlooking Pavilion Gardens. Furnished in Victorian manner and offering personal service in a friendly, relaxed atmosphere.

CREDIT CARD BOOKINGS If you book by telephone and are asked for your credit card number it is advisable to check the proprietor's policy should you cancel your reservation.

BUXTON continued

◆◆◆ STADEN GRANGE COUNTRY HOUSE

Staden Lane, Staden, Buxton
SK17 9RZ
T: (01298) 24965
F: (01298) 72067
E: staden@grange100.fsbusiness.
co.uk

Bedrooms: 11 double/
twin
Bathrooms: 10 en suite

CC: Amex, Delta,
Mastercard, Switch, Visa

B&B per night:
S £40.00–£42.50
D £50.00–£55.00

OPEN All year round

250-acre beef farm. Spacious residence 1.5 miles from Buxton, in a magnificent scenic area. Carefully extended, uninterrupted views over open farmland. Ground floor rooms available.

◆◆ TEMPLETON GUESTHOUSE

Compton Road, Buxton SK17 9DN
T: (01298) 25275 & 07831 606601
F: (01298) 25275
E: tembux@lineone.net

Bedrooms: 3 double/
twin
Bathrooms: 3 en suite

Evening meal available

B&B per night:
S £21.50–£23.50
D £37.00–£39.00

HB per person:
DY Min £28.50

OPEN All year round

Spacious Victorian residence in quiet but central residential area. En suite rooms. Licensed. Private off-street parking. Ideal base for discovering the Peak District.

BYFIELD, Northamptonshire Map ref 2C1

◆◆◆ GLEBE FARM BED AND BREAKFAST

Glebe Farm, 61 Church Street,
Byfield, Daventry NN11 6XN
T: (01327) 260512 & 07773 398550
F: (01327) 260512
E: sagem12924@talk21.com

Bedrooms: 2 double/
twin

Evening meal available

B&B per night:
S £25.00–£30.00
D £40.00–£60.00

HB per person:
DY £20.00–£33.00

OPEN All year round

Breakfast with the family in this modern farm bungalow, while enjoying panoramic views over the rolling Northamptonshire countryside. Althorp, Silverstone, Warwick and Stratford easily accessible.

CASTLE DONINGTON, Leicestershire Map ref 4C3

◆◆◆◆ CASTLETOWN HOUSE

4 High Street, Castle Donington,
Derby DE74 2PP
T: (01332) 812018 & 814550
F: (01332) 814550
E: enquiry@castletownhouse.co.uk
I: www.castletownhouse.com

Bedrooms: 5 double/
twin
Bathrooms: 5 en suite

CC: Delta, Mastercard,
Switch, Visa

B&B per night:
S Min £35.00
D Min £50.00

OPEN All year round

17thC Tudor wood-framed farmhouse in village centre, with wood beams in most rooms. Ample parking. New barn development. All rooms very spacious.

CHALBURY

See South of England region for entries

CHARLTON-ON-OTMOOR

See South of England region for entries

CHELMARSH, Shropshire Map ref 4A3

◆◆ UNICORN INN

Hampton Loade, Chelmarsh,
Bridgnorth WV16 6BN
T: (01746) 861515
F: (01746) 861515
E: unicorninn.bridgnorth@
virginnet.co.uk
I: freespace.virginnet.co.uk/
unicorninn.bridgnorth

Bedrooms: 2 single,
6 double/twin, 1 triple/
multiple
Bathrooms: 9 en suite

Lunch available
Evening meal available
CC: Delta, Mastercard,
Switch, Visa

B&B per night:
S Min £20.00
D Min £38.00

HB per person:
DY £23.50–£26.95

OPEN All year round

Situated in the heart of the Severn Valley. Easy walking distance for railway and river. Ideal for fishing and country walkers.

COLOUR MAPS Colour maps at the front of this guide pinpoint all places under which you will find accommodation listed.

CHELTENHAM, Gloucestershire Map ref 2B1 *Tourist Information Centre Tel: (01242) 522878*

◆◆◆ HOPE ORCHARD

Gloucester Road, Staverton,
Cheltenham GL51 0TF
T: (01452) 855556
F: (01452) 530037
E: info@hopeorchard.com
I: www.hopeorchard.com

Bedrooms: 5 double/
twin, 3 triple/multiple
Bathrooms: 8 en suite

CC: Delta, Mastercard,
Switch, Visa

B&B per night:
S Max £32.00
D Max £47.00

OPEN All year round

Attractive guesthouse in its own grounds. Chalet-style bedrooms. Excellent breakfast. Ideally located for the Cotswolds and Forest of Dean. Two minutes from the M5.

◆◆◆ IVYDENE GUEST HOUSE

145 Hewlett Road, Cheltenham
GL52 6TS
T: (01242) 521726 & 525694
F: (01242) 525694
E: jvhopwood@ivydenehouse.
freeserve.co.uk
I: www.ivydenehouse.freeserve.co.
uk

Bedrooms: 3 single,
4 double/twin, 2 triple/
multiple
Bathrooms: 5 en suite,
2 private

CC: Delta, Mastercard,
Switch, Visa

B&B per night:
S £27.50–£35.00
D £55.00–£60.00

OPEN All year round

A stylish, yet good value, Victorian house close to city centre. 'Themed' en suite rooms (e.g, Tuscan, Greek, Oriental). Hearty English breakfasts.

◆◆◆◆

PIKE HOUSE

Fossebridge, Cheltenham GL54 3JR
T: (01285) 720223 & 07765 482068
F: (01285) 720223

B&B per night:
S Min £50.00
D £50.00–£64.00

HB per person:
DY Min £45.50

OPEN All year round

A Cotswold-stone period cottage, 270-years old, with many original features including flagstone floor, inglenook fireplace and window seat. Spacious accommodation with en suite bathrooms. All rooms have colour TV, hot beverage facilities and hairdryer. In an area of Outstanding Natural Beauty. Ample car parking space. No smoking.

Bedrooms: 3 double/
twin; suites available
Bathrooms: 3 en suite

Evening meal available
CC: Mastercard, Switch,
Visa

◆◆◆◆ THE WYNYARDS

Butts Lane, Woodmancote,
Cheltenham GL52 4QH
T: (01242) 673876
E: graham@wynyards1.freeserve.
co.uk
I: www.smoothhound.co.uk/hotels/
wynyards.html

Bedrooms: 3 double/
twin
Bathrooms: 1 en suite,
1 private

B&B per night:
S £25.00
D £38.00

OPEN All year round

Secluded old Cotswold-stone house in elevated position with panoramic views. Set in open countryside on outskirts of small village, 4 miles from Cheltenham.

CHESTERFIELD, Derbyshire Map ref 4B2 *Tourist Information Centre Tel: (01246) 345777*

◆◆◆ ABIGAILS

62 Brockwell Lane, Chesterfield
S40 4EE
T: (01246) 279391 & 07970 777909
F: (01246) 854468
E: gail@abigails.fsnet.co.uk
I: www.abigailsguesthouse.co.uk

Bedrooms: 2 single,
5 double/twin
Bathrooms: 7 en suite

B&B per night:
S £28.00
D £42.00

OPEN All year round

Relax taking breakfast in the conservatory overlooking Chesterfield and surrounding moorlands. Garden with pond and waterfall, private car park. Best B&B winners 2000.

CHESTERFIELD continued

♦♦♦♦ Silver Award

BROOK HOUSE

45 Westbrook Drive, Brookside,
Chesterfield S40 3PQ
T: (01246) 568535

Bedrooms: 1 double/
twin, 1 triple/multiple
Bathrooms: 1 en suite,
1 private

B&B per night:
S £30.00
D £45.00

OPEN All year round

Welcoming, delightful luxury accommodation in lovely rural setting adjacent fields and footpaths edging Peak National Park. Chatsworth is 10 minutes away. Good home cooking/baking.

♦♦♦

CLARENDON GUESTHOUSE

32 Clarence Road, West Bars,
Chesterfield S40 1LN
T: (01246) 235004

Bedrooms: 2 single,
3 double/twin
Bathrooms: 4 en suite

Evening meal available

B&B per night:
S £15.50–£20.00
D £30.00–£36.00

HB per person:
DY £21.00–£25.50

OPEN All year round

Victorian town residence, near town centre, cricket ground, leisure facilities and Peak District National Park. Special diets catered for. Overnight laundry service.

♦♦♦

SHAKESPEARE VILLA

3 Saint Margarets Drive, Saltergate,
Chesterfield S40 4SY
T: (01246) 200704

Bedrooms: 2 single,
3 triple/multiple
Bathrooms: 3 en suite

B&B per night:
S £15.00–£22.00
D £30.00–£38.00

HB per person:
DY £21.00–£28.00

OPEN All year round

Only 2 minutes from the town centre, our detached house has large, sunny rooms and leaded glass feature windows.

CHIPPING CAMPDEN, Gloucestershire Map ref 2B1

♦♦♦♦ Silver Award

A prime timber-framed residence, opposite the historic Market Hall on the most perfect of high streets. Open daily as tea rooms serving excellent home-made fayre. Bedrooms are of good size with en suite facilites. Plentiful breakfasts served at individual tables in breakfast room. Smoking not permitted in the house.

BADGERS HALL TEAROOMS

High Street, Chipping Campden GL55 6HB
T: (01386) 840839
E: badgershall@talk21.com
I: www.stratford.upon.avon.co.uk/
badgershall.htm

Bedrooms: 1 double/
twin
Bathrooms: 1 en suite

Three day breaks based on 2 persons sharing: any two nights £55 per night–third night £40 inclusive of VAT and excellent breakfast.

B&B per night:
D £50.00–£60.00

OPEN All year round

USE YOUR *i*s

There are more than 550 Tourist Information Centres throughout England offering friendly help with accommodation and holiday ideas as well as suggestions of places to visit and things to do. You'll find TIC addresses in the local Phone Book.

CHIPPING CAMPDEN continued

◆◆◆

THE EIGHT BELLS
Church Street, Chipping Campden GL55 6JG
T: (01386) 840371
F: (01386) 841669
I: www.eightbellsinn.co.uk

B&B per night:
S £40.00–£45.00
D £60.00–£70.00

OPEN All year round

An unspoilt 14thC Cotswold inn featuring open fires in winter and candlelit tables all year round. In addition there is a sun-drenched courtyard and terraced beer garden which overlooks the church. All accommodation is en suite, food is of the very highest standard and a friendly but informal welcome awaits you.

Bedrooms: 2 single, 3 double/twin, 1 triple/ multiple
Bathrooms: 6 en suite

Lunch available
Evening meal available
CC: Delta, Mastercard, Switch, Visa

◆◆◆◆
Gold Award

M'DINA COURTYARD
Park Road, Chipping Campden GL55 6EA
T: (01386) 841752
F: (01386) 840942
E: chilver@globalnet.co.uk
I: www.mdina-bandb.co.uk

B&B per night:
S £45.00–£50.00
D £55.00–£65.00

OPEN All year round

Character Cotswold-stone house, apartment and 250-year-old cottage, in idyllic courtyard setting. Located at the quieter end of Chipping Campden's historic High Street. Extensive breakfast menu using local produce wherever possible. All rooms en suite with colour TV, hairdryer, tea/coffee facilities and much more. Off-road parking.

Bedrooms: 2 double/ twin, 1 triple/multiple; suites available
Bathrooms: 3 en suite

◆◆◆◆

MANOR FARM
Weston Subedge, Chipping Campden GL55 6QH
T: (01386) 840390 & 07889 108812
F: 08701 640 638
E: lucy@manorfarmbnb.demon.co.uk
I: www.manorfarmbnb.demon.co.uk

B&B per night:
S £35.00–£45.00
D £45.00–£50.00

OPEN All year round

A warm, friendly welcome and a hearty, full English breakfast are assured for all guests at Manor Farm, a traditional 17thC Cotswold-stone, oak-beamed farmhouse. Excellent base for exploring the Cotswolds and Shakespeare Country from our 800 acre working farm. Superb choice of eating houses. 1.5 miles from Chipping Campden.

Bedrooms: 3 double/ twin
Bathrooms: 3 en suite

Reductions for stays of 4 nights or more.

ACCESSIBILITY
Look for the 🚿 symbols which indicate accessibility for wheelchair users. A list of establishments is at the front of this guide.

◆◆◆◆

NINEVEH FARM

Campden Road, Mickleton,
Chipping Campden GL55 6PS
T: (01386) 438923 & 07880 737649
E: stay@ninevehfarm.co.uk
I: www.ninevehfarm.co.uk

B&B per night:
D £50.00–£55.00

OPEN All year round

18thC farmhouse with oak beams, flagstone floors and a warm welcome. Gardens of 1.5 acres in open countryside just a quarter mile from village pubs. Ideal for exploring Cotswolds, Stratford-upon-Avon and Warwick. Cream teas and free loan of cycles.

Bedrooms: 4 double/ twin, 1 triple/multiple
Bathrooms: 5 en suite

CC: Amex, Delta, Mastercard, Switch, Visa

Details of short breaks on request.

CHIPPING NORTON

See South of England region for entries

CHURCH STRETTON, Shropshire Map ref 4A3

◆◆◆◆

BELVEDERE GUEST HOUSE

Burway Road, Church Stretton
SY6 6DP
T: (01694) 722232
F: (01694) 722232
E: belv@bigfoot.com
I: www.smoothhound.co.uk/hotels/
belvedere.html

Bedrooms: 3 single, 5 double/twin, 4 triple/ multiple
Bathrooms: 6 en suite

CC: Delta, Mastercard, Switch, Visa

B&B per night:
S £25.00–£31.00
D £50.00–£56.00

OPEN All year round

Quiet detached house set in its own grounds, convenient for Church Stretton town centre and Longmynd Hills. Adequate parking.

◆◆◆◆

SAYANG HOUSE

Hope Bowdler, Church Stretton SY6 7DD
T: (01694) 723981
E: madegan@aol.com
I: www.sayanghouse.com

B&B per night:
S £27.50–£30.00
D £50.00–£55.00

HB per person:
DY £40.00–£45.00

OPEN All year round

Our house is 1 mile from Church Stretton set in an acre of landscaped gardens, commanding views of the surrounding countryside. All bedrooms are en suite and furnished to the highest standard. Delicious home-prepared meals on request, served in our homely oak-beamed sitting room. We have a full residents' licence.

Bedrooms: 1 double/ twin, 2 triple/multiple
Bathrooms: 3 en suite

Evening meal available

Out-of-season special offers. Reductions for 3 day stays.

CLUN, Shropshire Map ref 4A3

◆◆◆

THE OLD FARMHOUSE

Woodside, Clun, Craven Arms
SY7 0JB
T: (01588) 640695
F: (01588) 640501
E: helen@vuan1.freeserve.co.uk
I: www.tuckedup.com/
theoldfarmhouse.html

Bedrooms: 1 double/ twin, 1 triple/multiple

Evening meal available

B&B per night:
S £16.00–£22.50
D £32.00–£45.00

HB per person:
DY £21.00–£34.50

250-year-old farmhouse, 1 mile and 300 feet above Clun, overlooking the picturesque Clun Valley. Ordnance Survey ref. S0310802.

COLEFORD, Gloucestershire Map ref 2A1 *Tourist Information Centre Tel: (01594) 812388*

♦♦♦ **GRAYGILL**
Duke of York Road, Staunton,
Coleford GL16 8PD
T: (01600) 712536

Bedrooms: 2 double/
twin
Bathrooms: 2 en suite

B&B per night:
S Min £18.50
D Min £37.00

OPEN All year round

Secluded family house set in 11 acres of pasture adjoining forestry, offering en suite bed and breakfast accommodation. Ideal for walking, cycling and touring.

ＡＤ 🐴 🖥 💻 ♨ 🔔 ⓢ 🏠 ▥ 📻 🐾 🦃 ⟲ P

COTSWOLDS

See under Bibury, Birdlip, Bledington, Blockley, Bourton-on-the-Water, Broadway, Cheltenham, Chipping Campden, Fairford, Gloucester, Great Rissington, Guiting Power, Lechlade, Mickleton, Moreton-in-Marsh, Nailsworth, Naunton, Northleach, Stonehouse, Stow-on-the-Wold, Stroud, Tetbury, Tewkesbury, Winchcombe

See also Cotswolds in South of England region

COVENTRY, West Midlands Map ref 4B3 *Tourist Information Centre Tel: (024) 7622 7264*

♦♦♦ **ABIGAIL GUESTHOUSE**
39 St. Patrick's Road, Coventry
CV1 2LP
T: (024) 7622 1378
E: ag002a@netgates.co.uk
I: www.abigailuk.com

Bedrooms: 3 single,
2 double/twin, 1 triple/
multiple

B&B per night:
S £20.00–£25.00
D £38.00–£40.00

OPEN All year round

Family-run establishment in centre of city, very clean and friendly. Convenient for station, cathedral and city centre shopping, also NEC and NAC.

🐴 🖥 ♨ ⓢ ▥ 🦃 ⟲

♦♦♦♦ **ABURLEY**
23 St Patricks Road, Cheylesmore,
Coventry CV1 2LP
T: (024) 76251348 & 07957 925596
F: (024) 76223243

Bedrooms: 1 single,
1 double/twin, 1 triple/
multiple
Bathrooms: 3 en suite

CC: Delta, Mastercard,
Switch, Visa

B&B per night:
S £26.00–£35.00
D £50.00–£60.00

OPEN All year round

A semi-detached Victorian house situated in the city centre. Close to railway station, easy access to National Exhibition Centre and motorway network. Small and friendly.

ＡＤ 🐴 🖥 💻 ♨ 🔔 ⓢ ⚷ ▥ 📻 🐾 🦃 ⟲ 🏠

♦♦♦

ASHDOWNS GUEST HOUSE
12 Regent Street, Earlsdon, Coventry
CV1 3EP
T: (024) 7622 9280

B&B per night:
S £25.00–£40.00
D £45.00–£50.00

OPEN All year round

Family-run guesthouse offering quality accommodation. Convenient for city centre, rail and bus services, NEC, NAC, university and Birmingham International Airport. A warm welcome awaits you in this relaxed, non-smoking family home. Private car park at rear.

Bedrooms: 2 single,
5 double/twin, 1 triple/
multiple
Bathrooms: 7 en suite

Long stay and short break offers, weddings and parties.

🐴5 ⚶ 📞 🖥 💻 ♨ 🔔 ⓢ ⚷ ▥ 📻 🦃 P

♦♦♦ **ASHLEIGH HOUSE**
17 Park Road, Coventry CV1 2LH
T: (024) 7622 3804
F: (024) 76223804

Bedrooms: 3 single,
5 double/twin, 2 triple/
multiple
Bathrooms: 8 en suite

B&B per night:
S £23.50–£27.50
D £40.00–£44.00

HB per person:
DY Min £32.00

OPEN All year round

Recently renovated guesthouse only 100 yards from the railway station. All city amenities within 5 minutes' walk. Licensed, evening meals.

🐴 💻 ♨ ⓢ ▥ 📻 🦃 P

CONFIRM YOUR BOOKING
You are advised to confirm your booking in writing.

COVENTRY continued

◆◆◆◆ BROOKFIELDS

134 Butt Lane, Allesley, Coventry CV5 9FE T: (024) 7640 4866 F: (024) 7640 2022 E: brookfieldscoventry@easicom. com	Bedrooms: 2 single, 2 double/twin Bathrooms: 4 en suite	B&B per night: S £28.00–£35.00 D £48.00–£55.00 OPEN All year round

Small, friendly guesthouse offering quality accommodation and service. Convenient city centre, National Exhibition Centre, Birmingham International Airport, Jaguar Cars/ museum, NAC Stoneleigh. Ample parking.

♬☆5 ⌂ ▤ ♨ ℚ ⓈⱮ ▥ ⌂ ⇔ P

◆◆ HIGHCROFT GUEST HOUSE

65 Barras Lane, Coundon, Coventry CV1 4AQ T: (024) 7622 8157 F: (024) 7663 1609	Bedrooms: 2 single, 3 double/twin, 2 triple/ multiple Bathrooms: 3 en suite	B&B per night: S £18.00–£20.00 D £32.00–£40.00 OPEN All year round

Large detached guesthouse close to the city centre. A family-run business that endeavours to make guests feel at home. Discounts available.

☆▤⌂♨ℚⓈⱮ▥⌂⋇⟟⁂ 🏇 ⚲ P

◆◆◆ WESTWOOD COTTAGE

79 Westwood Heath Road, Westwood Heath, Coventry CV4 8GN T: (024) 7647 1084 F: (024) 7647 1084	Bedrooms: 3 single, 2 double/twin Bathrooms: 5 en suite	B&B per night: S £23.00 D £42.00 OPEN All year round

One of 4 sandstone farm cottages, circa 1834, in rural surroundings. Recently converted but with character maintained and offering comfortable accommodation for a small number of guests.

☆⌂⌂♨ℚⓈⱮ▥⌂⁂🏠P

CRAVEN ARMS, Shropshire Map ref 4A3

◆◆◆◆ EARNSTREY HILL HOUSE

Abdon, Craven Arms SY7 9HU T: (01746) 712579 F: (01746) 712631 E: hugh.scurfield@smwh.org.uk	Bedrooms: 3 double/ twin Bathrooms: 1 en suite, 1 private	B&B per night: S £20.00–£25.00 D £40.00 HB per person: DY £35.50–£40.50 OPEN All year round

Comfortable light stone and brick house built 12 years ago. On site of farm cottage, 1200 ft up Brown Clee Hill. Superb views.

☆⌂ⓈⱮ▥⌂⁂🏇⚲P

DEDDINGTON

See South of England region for entries

DERBY, Derbyshire Map ref 4B2 *Tourist Information Centre Tel: (01332) 255802*

◆◆◆ BONEHILL FARM

Etwall Road, Mickleover, Derby DE3 5DN T: (01332) 513553 E: bonehillfarm@hotmail.com	Bedrooms: 2 double/ twin, 1 triple/multiple Bathrooms: 2 en suite	B&B per night: S £20.00–£25.00 D £40.00–£44.00 OPEN All year round

A 120-acre mixed farm. Georgian farmhouse in rural setting, 3 miles from Derby. Alton Towers, Peak District, historic houses and the Potteries within easy reach.

☆▤⌂♨Ⓢ Ɱ▥⌂⁂🏇⚲🏠P

DROITWICH, Worcestershire Map ref 2B1 *Tourist Information Centre Tel: (01905) 774312*

◆◆ RICHMOND GUEST HOUSE

3 Ombersley St. West, Droitwich WR9 8HZ T: (01905) 775722 F: (01905) 794642 I: www.infotel.co.uk/hotels/36340. htm	Bedrooms: 6 single, 3 double/twin, 2 triple/ multiple	B&B per night: S £20.00–£22.00 D £34.00–£36.00 OPEN All year round

Victorian-built guesthouse in the town centre, 5 minutes from railway station and bus route. English breakfast. 30 minutes from National Exhibition Centre via M5/M42.

☆⌂⌂♨Ⓢ Ɱ▥⌂🏇P

Silver Award

WEST FARM
Gayton Road, Eastcote, Towcester
NN12 8NS
T: (01327) 830310
F: (01327) 830310
E: west.farm@eastcote97.fsnet.co.uk

B&B per night:
S £25.00–£30.00
D £50.00–£60.00

OPEN All year round

Recently built stone farmhouse situated half a mile off the public highway, which gives a real sense of tranquillity. The garden is spacious with a small lake. Enjoy a walk on the farm or visit some of the local attractions which include Althorp, Silverstone and Sulgrave Manor. Easy access to M1.

Bedrooms: 3 double/ twin
Bathrooms: 2 en suite

THE ANCHOR INN AND RESTAURANT
Cotheridge Lane, Eckington,
Pershore WR10 3BA
T: (01386) 750356
F: (01386) 750356
E: anchoreck@aol.com
I: www.anchoreckington.co.uk

Bedrooms: 5 double/ twin
Bathrooms: 5 en suite

Lunch available
Evening meal available
CC: Mastercard, Visa

B&B per night:
S £30.00–£40.00
D £45.00–£80.00

HB per person:
DY £30.00–£40.00

OPEN All year round

Traditional village inn off the main road, comfortable lounge, separate restaurant. Chef-prepared cuisine. Central for Worcester, Evesham, Cheltenham and Tewkesbury.

BADGERS MOUNT
6 Station Road, Elmesthorpe, Leicester
LE9 7SG
T: (01455) 848161
F: (01455) 848161
E: info@badgersmount.com
I: www.badgersmount.com

B&B per night:
S £35.00–£42.00
D £45.00–£60.00

OPEN All year round

Set in countryside surroundings between M1 and M69 for easy travel to Leicester, Coventry, Birmingham and many Midlands tourist attractions. The atmosphere is relaxed and informal. Residential licence, bar room overlooking large patio and spacious gardens and outdoor heated swimming pool for summer use.

Bedrooms: 10 double/ twin, 2 triple/multiple
Bathrooms: 12 en suite

Lunch available
Evening meal available
CC: Amex, Delta, Mastercard, Switch, Visa

PARK VIEW HOTEL
Waterside, Evesham WR11 6BS
T: (01386) 442639
E: mike.spires@btinternet.com
I: www.superstay.co.uk

Bedrooms: 10 single, 13 double/twin, 1 triple/ multiple

Evening meal available
CC: Amex, Delta, Mastercard, Switch, Visa

B&B per night:
S £23.00–£27.00
D £40.00–£47.00

OPEN All year round

Family-run hotel offering comfortable accommodation in a friendly atmosphere. Riverside situation, close to town centre. Ideal base for touring the Cotswolds and Shakespeare Country.

RATING   All accommodation in this guide has been rated, or is awaiting a rating, by a trained English Tourism Council assessor.

FAIRFORD, Gloucestershire Map ref 2B1

♦♦♦ **MILTON FARM**

Fairford GL7 4HZ	Bedrooms: 3 double/	B&B per night:
T: (01285) 712205	twin	S £25.00–£30.00
F: (01285) 711349	Bathrooms: 2 en suite,	D £38.00–£50.00
E: milton@farmersweekly.net	1 private	
I: www.miltonfarm.co.uk		OPEN All year round

Impressive Georgian farmhouse with large en suite bedrooms and high-ceiling public rooms. Central heating, quiet pleasant outlook on edge of most attractive small Cotswold town.

♦♦ **WAITEN HILL FARM**

Fairford GL7 4JG	Bedrooms: 3 double/	B&B per night:
T: (01285) 712652	twin	S £20.00–£25.00
F: (01285) 712652	Bathrooms: 2 en suite	D £35.00–£40.00

350-acre mixed farm. Imposing 19thC farmhouse, overlooking River Coln, old mill and famous church. Short walk to shops, pubs, restaurants. Ideal for touring Cotswolds and water parks.

OPEN All year round

FILLONGLEY, Warwickshire Map ref 4B3

♦♦♦♦ **MANOR HOUSE FARM**

Silver Award

Green End Road, Fillongley,	Bedrooms: 1 double/	B&B per night:
Coventry CV7 8DS	twin	S £20.00–£25.00
T: (01676) 540256	Bathrooms: 1 en suite	D Min £40.00

The groom's cottage at Manor House Farm was built in 1874 and offers a double room with en suite facilities.

OPEN All year round

FOREST OF DEAN

See under Coleford, Littledean, Newent, Newland

FOWNHOPE, Herefordshire Map ref 2A1

♦♦♦ **THE TAN HOUSE**

Fownhope, Hereford HR1 4NJ	Bedrooms: 3 double/	B&B per night:
T: (01432) 860549	twin	D £18.00–£22.00
F: (01432) 860466	Bathrooms: 1 en suite	
E: vera@ukbu.co.uk		OPEN All year round

16thC Grade II Listed house with working cider mill and cellar including display of antique agricultural implements and tools.

FRAMPTON-ON-SEVERN, Gloucestershire Map ref 2B1

♦♦♦♦ **ARCHWAY HOUSE**

The Green, Frampton-on-Severn,	Bedrooms: 5 double/	Evening meal available	B&B per night:
Gloucester GL2 7DY	twin		S £25.00–£35.00
T: (01452) 740752	Bathrooms: 1 private		D £40.00–£50.00
F: (01452) 741629			
E: mike.brown@archwayhouse.			HB per person:
fsnet.co.uk			DY £35.00–£50.00

200-year-old Georgian house in a Gloucestershire village, fronting on to 'Rosamunds Green'. Set in good walking country near the River Severn. Non-smoking establishment.

OPEN All year round

FULBECK, Lincolnshire Map ref 3A1

♦♦♦ **THE HARE AND HOUNDS COUNTRY INN**

The Green, Fulbeck, Grantham	Bedrooms: 6 double/	Lunch available	B&B per night:
NG32 3JJ	twin, 2 triple/multiple	Evening meal available	S £25.00–£39.50
T: (01400) 272090	Bathrooms: 8 en suite	CC: Delta, Mastercard,	D £45.00–£50.00
F: (01400) 273663		Switch, Visa	

Privately owned and family run 17thC freehouse, log fires, real ales, bar menu and a la carte, patio garden. Only 10 minutes A1, 20 minutes Lincoln.

HB per person:
DY Min £30.00

OPEN All year round

WHERE TO STAY
Please mention this guide when making your booking.

251

◆◆◆

SYCAMORE FARMHOUSE

6 Station Road, Gedney Hill, Spalding
PE12 ONP
T: (01406) 330445 & 07889 147001
F: (01406) 330445
E: sycamore.farm@virgin.net
I: www.farmhousebedandbreakfast.
freeserve.co.uk

A warm and comfortable welcome awaits you at this 150-year-old home in small Lincolnshire village on the B1166. Dining room and lounge with TV. Shops and pubs nearby. Close to Fenland Airfield, Wisbech and Spalding. Flying, gliding, golf, fishing and clay pigeon shooting available locally.

Bedrooms: 1 double/ twin, 1 triple/multiple
Bathrooms: 2 private

Evening meal available

B&B per night:
S Min £25.00
D Min £50.00

OPEN All year round

◆◆◆

BROOKTHORPE LODGE

Stroud Road, Brookthorpe, Gloucester
GL4 0UQ
T: (01452) 812645
F: (01452) 812645
E: enq@brookthorpelodge.demon.co.uk
I: www.brookthorpelodge.demon.co.uk

Licensed, family-run, spacious and comfortable Georgian detached house on the outskirts of Gloucester (3.5 miles). Set in lovely countryside at the foot of the Cotswold escarpment. Close to ski-slope and golfing facilities. Excellent walking country. Ideal base for visiting the Cotswolds, Cheltenham, Bath and nearby WWT reserve at Slimbridge.

Bedrooms: 3 single, 5 double/twin, 2 triple/ multiple
Bathrooms: 6 en suite

Evening meal available
CC: Delta, Mastercard, Switch, Visa

Special discounts on 3 day weekend and 5 day mid-week breaks.

B&B per night:
S £22.50–£23.50
D £45.00–£50.00

HB per person:
DY £30.00–£35.00

OPEN All year round

◆◆◆◆

CYDER PRESS FARM

The Leigh, Gloucester GL19 4AG
T: (01242) 680661
F: (01242) 680023
E: archers@cyderpressfarm.freeserve.co.uk

Beautifully restored 15thC half-timbered farmhouse set in 4 acres. A tranquil country retreat ideally situated for Cheltenham, Gloucester, Cotswolds and Forest of Dean. You will be assured of a warm welcome and we are happy to accommodate children and pets. We use local and homegrown produce. Quality assured!

Bedrooms: 2 double/ twin
Bathrooms: 2 en suite

B&B per night:
S £30.00–£40.00
D £60.00–£80.00

OPEN All year round

◆

GEORGIAN GUEST HOUSE
85 Bristol Road, Gloucester
GL1 5SN
T: (01452) 413286
F: (01452) 413286

Bedrooms: 2 single, 3 double/twin, 4 triple/ multiple
Bathrooms: 5 en suite

On the main Bristol Road, 15 minutes' walk from Gloucester city centre.

B&B per night:
S £15.00
D £33.00

OPEN All year round

◆◆◆

KILMORIE SMALL HOLDING
Gloucester Road, Corse, Snigs End,
Staunton, Gloucester GL19 3RQ
T: (01452) 840224
F: (01452) 840224
E: sheila-barnfield@supanet.com
I: www.SmoothHound.co.uk/hotels/
kilmorie.html

All ground floor quality rural accommodation, within a conservation area. Colour TV, tea tray, radio all bedrooms. Most are en suite, Grade II Listed Chartist smallholding (c.1848) keeping free-range hens which provide excellent eggs for breakfast. Ample parking. Ideally situated for walking countryside or touring Cotswolds, Forest of Dean, Malvern Hills.

Bedrooms: 1 single,
3 double/twin, 1 triple/
multiple
Bathrooms: 3 en suite,
2 private

Lunch available
Evening meal available

Reduced rates on full week stays. Reduced rates for children 5-12 years.

B&B per night:
S £18.00–£22.00
D £36.00–£40.00

HB per person:
DY Min £26.00

OPEN Mar–Oct

◆◆ **NICKI'S HOTEL & TAVERNA**
105-107 Westgate Street,
Gloucester GL1 2PG
T: (01452) 301359

Bedrooms: 15 single,
7 double/twin, 3 triple/
multiple; suites available
Bathrooms: 12 en suite

Lunch available
Evening meal available
CC: Mastercard, Visa

B&B per night:
S £28.00–£33.00
D £40.00–£50.00

HB per person:
DY £38.00–£43.00

OPEN All year round

Restaurant with lounge bar and full a la carte menu. English and Greek food. Near city centre, Cathedral and Docks.

GOTHERINGTON, Gloucestershire Map ref 2B1

◆◆◆ **PARDON HILL FARM**
Prescott, Gotherington,
Cheltenham GL52 9RD
T: (01242) 672468 & 07802 708814
F: (01242) 672468
E: janet@pardonhillfarm.freeserve.
co.uk
I: www.glosfarmhols.co.uk

Bedrooms: 1 single,
2 double/twin
Bathrooms: 3 en suite

B&B per night:
S Min £30.00
D Min £50.00

OPEN All year round

300-acre mixed, family-run farm. Outstanding views from all rooms. Ideal centre for walking and touring.

GRANTHAM, Lincolnshire Map ref 3A1 *Tourist Information Centre Tel: (01476) 406166*

◆◆◆

THE RED HOUSE
74 North Parade, Grantham NG31 8AN
T: (01476) 579869
F: (01476) 401597
E: redhousebb@aol.com
I: www.smoothhound.co.uk/hotels/
theredhouse1.html

An elegant Grade II Listed Georgian townhouse situated conveniently close to the town centre. A short walk from local bars and restaurants, 2 miles from major golf clubs. All rooms are en suite and non-smoking. Evening meals by prior arrangement, special diets catered for. Ample parking and rear garden.

Bedrooms: 1 double/
twin, 2 triple/multiple
Bathrooms: 3 en suite

Evening meal available
CC: Delta, Mastercard,
Switch, Visa

3-course evening meals £6.95 include coffee or tea (must be booked in advance).

B&B per night:
S £21.00–£28.00
D £34.00–£38.00

HB per person:
DY £23.95–£34.95

OPEN All year round

HALF BOARD PRICES Half board prices are given per person, but in some cases these may be based on double/twin occupancy.

253

GREAT RISSINGTON, Gloucestershire Map ref 2B1

◆◆◆

LOWER FARMHOUSE

Great Rissington, Cheltenham
GL54 2LH
T: (01451) 810163 & 810187
F: (01451) 810187
E: B&B@lowerfarmhouse.co.uk

Bedrooms: 1 single, 1 double/twin

B&B per night:
S £18.00–£22.00
D £36.00–£44.00

OPEN All year round

Grade II Listed Georgian home with separate guest rooms in Cotswold barn conversion. On north-west edge of peaceful village, yet close to attractions.

P

◆◆◆

STEPPING STONE

Rectory Lane, Great Rissington,
Cheltenham GL54 2LL
T: (01451) 821385
E: stepping-stone-b-b@excite.com

B&B per night:
S £27.50–£37.00
D £55.00–£65.00

OPEN All year round

Set in large garden at the edge of a picturesque village, providing quiet and comfortable accommodation for B&B and longer stays (two self-contained doubles). Located 3 miles from Bourton-on-the-Water and just 200 metres from The Lamb restaurant and bar. Open all year.

Bedrooms: 1 single, 4 double/twin; suites available
Bathrooms: 3 en suite, 2 private

CC: Delta, Mastercard, Visa

Special offers: 10% off for stays of 3 nights or more mid-week. Winter specials Nov-1 Mar: 3 nights for the price of 2.

P

GUITING POWER, Gloucestershire Map ref 2B1

◆◆◆

THE HOLLOW BOTTOM

Winchcombe Road, Guiting Power,
Cheltenham GL54 5UX
T: (01451) 850392
F: (01451) 850945

B&B per night:
S £30.00
D £50.00

OPEN All year round

17thC Cotswold inn, with a horse racing theme, set in the pretty village of Guiting Power, a designated Area of Outstanding Natural Beauty. En suite accommodation, real ales, log fire, warm and welcoming. Ideal for walking and or touring in the North Cotswolds. Golf, fishing, riding nearby. HB price varies according to meal choice.

Bedrooms: 2 double/twin, 1 triple/multiple
Bathrooms: 2 en suite, 1 private

Lunch available
Evening meal available
CC: Delta, Mastercard, Switch, Visa

3 P

HANDSACRE, Staffordshire Map ref 4B3

◆◆◆

THE OLDE PECULIAR

The Green, Handsacre, Rugeley
WS15 4DP
T: (01543) 491891
F: (01543) 493733

Bedrooms: 2 double/twin
Bathrooms: 2 en suite

Lunch available
Evening meal available
CC: Mastercard, Switch, Visa

B&B per night:
S £29.50–£32.00
D £42.00–£45.00

OPEN All year round

A traditional village pub serving real ales and homemade food. Situated 4 miles from Lichfield city centre on the A513.

P

QUALITY ASSURANCE SCHEME

Diamond ratings and awards were correct at the time of going to press but are subject to change. Please check at the time of booking.

◆◆◆

WOLFSCOTE GRANGE

Hartington, Buxton SK17 0AX
T: (01298) 84342
E: wolfscote@btinternet.com

B&B per night:
S Min £25.00
D Min £50.00

OPEN All year round

Listen to the silence, take in the stunning views of the walkable hills and dales from our uniquely positioned farmhouse on the edge of the Dove Valley. Wind along the ancient corridors steeped in history (dating from the Domesday Book) enjoy its old world touches, pretty en suite rooms, cosy log fires, flower garden and leisurely breakfast with local produce and specialities.

Bedrooms: 3 double/ twin
Bathrooms: 2 en suite, 1 private

Private farm trail. Badger viewing. Weekend short breaks available.

◆◆◆◆
Gold
Award

CANNON CROFT

Cannonfields, Hathersage, Hope Valley
S32 1AG
T: (01433) 650005 & 0771 3352327
F: (01433) 650005
E: soates@cannoncroft.fsbusiness.co.uk
I: www.cannoncroft.fsbusiness.co.uk

B&B per night:
S £28.00–£32.00
D £42.00–£45.00

OPEN All year round

Enjoy stunning, panoramic views from the conservatory and our extensive breakfast menu – try our sundancer eggs! Private parking. Visit Chatsworth/Hardwick Halls. Cycling, walking, climbing all abilities. Pubs/restaurants in walking distance. First class accommodation with many extras in individually designed rooms. We look forward to welcoming you to our home.

Bedrooms: 3 double/ twin
Bathrooms: 3 en suite

◆◆◆◆

THE PLOUGH INN

Leadmill Bridge, Hathersage, Hope Valley
S32 1BA
T: (01433) 650319 & 650180
F: (01433) 651049

B&B per night:
S £49.50–£60.00
D £60.00–£89.50

OPEN All year round

17thC stone-built inn, formerly a farmhouse, standing in 9 acres of land bounded by the River Derwent. Situated in the Peak National Park an ideal base for visiting the stately homes of Chatsworth House and Haddon Hall. The inn is noted for its excellent food and warm atmosphere.

Bedrooms: 6 double/ twin; suites available
Bathrooms: 6 en suite

Lunch available
Evening meal available
CC: Delta, Mastercard, Switch, Visa

3 nights for the price of 2, Oct-Mar (excl Christmas and New Year).

CHECK THE MAPS

The colour maps at the front of this guide show all the cities, towns and villages for which you will find accommodation entries.
Refer to the town index to find the page on which they are listed.

♦♦♦

GUN END BED AND BREAKFAST

The Barn, Swythamley SK11 0SJ
T: (01260) 227391

Bedrooms: 1 double/ twin
Bathrooms: 1 en suite

B&B per night:
D £40.00

OPEN All year round

En suite room with private rear yard. Beautiful, peaceful area. Eight miles Macclesfield, 10 miles Stoke. Leek 6 miles, market town and antiques. Walking and fishing.

♦♦♦♦

THE BOWENS COUNTRY HOUSE

Fownhope, Hereford HRI 4PS

T: (01432) 860430
F: (01432) 860430

B&B per night:
S Min £32.50
D Min £65.00

HB per person:
DY Min £47.50

OPEN All year round

Delightful Georgian house set in peaceful Wye Valley village, midway Hereford and Ross-on-Wye (B4224). Well appointed en suite rooms (including ground floor, single and family rooms). All home-cooked meals using local produce. Vegetarians welcome. Fully licensed bar, good wine list. Large garden, putting green and grass tennis court (summer only).

Bedrooms: 2 single, 6 double/twin, 2 triple/ multiple
Bathrooms: 10 en suite

Lunch available
Evening meal available
CC: Delta, Mastercard, Switch, Visa

DB&B short breaks available all year.

♦♦♦

CEDAR GUEST HOUSE

123 Whitecross Road, Whitecross, Hereford HR4 0LS

T: (01432) 267235
F: (01432) 267235
E: info@cedarguesthouse.com
I: www.cedarguesthouse.com

B&B per night:
S Min £25.00
D £39.00–£46.00

OPEN All year round

Former Victorian gentleman's residence, retaining many of the original features. Family-run offering spacious accommodation, within easy walking distance of Hereford's historic city centre. Situated on major tourist route, also close to the excellent coarse angling on River Wye.

Bedrooms: 3 double/ twin, 3 triple/multiple
Bathrooms: 2 en suite

Evening meal available
CC: Delta, Mastercard, Switch, Visa

TOWN INDEX

This can be found at the back of the guide. If you know where you want to stay, the index will give you the page number listing accommodation in your chosen town, city or village.

HEREFORD continued

♦♦♦♦ Gold Award

FELTON HOUSE

Felton, Hereford HR1 3PH
T: (01432) 820366
F: (01432) 820366
E: bandb@ereal.net
I: www.bandbherefordshire.co.uk

B&B per night:
S £25.00
D £50.00

OPEN All year round

On arrival relax with complimentary refreshments in a country house of character set in beautiful, tranquil gardens. Taste excellent evening meals in 3 local inns. Sleep soundly in a 4-poster or brass bed; awake refreshed to enjoy a healthy large breakfast selected from a wide choice of Herefordshire and vegetarian dishes.

Bedrooms: 1 single, 3 double/twin
Bathrooms: 2 en suite, 2 private

🚶 🐴 🛏 ☕ 💨 [S] 🚭 📖 📺 🔥 ✿ 🐕 🚗 🏠 P

♦♦♦♦

HEDLEY LODGE

Belmont Abbey, Abergavenny Road, Hereford HR2 9RZ
T: (01432) 277475
F: (01432) 277318
E: hedleylodge@aol.com
I: www.hedleylodge.com

B&B per night:
S £31.50–£33.50
D £53.00–£56.00

HB per person:
DY £38.00–£43.00

OPEN All year round

Set in lovely grounds of Belmont Abbey (above), this friendly, modern guesthouse offers 17 bedrooms comfortably appointed with en suite facilities, TV and telephone. Our licensed restaurant offers a wide selection of snacks or main meals. Located 2.5 miles from Hereford off A465, an ideal venue for visiting the Wye Valley.

Bedrooms: 16 double/twin, 1 triple/multiple
Bathrooms: 17 en suite

Lunch available
Evening meal available
CC: Delta, Mastercard, Switch, Visa

🚶 🐴 ☎ 📺 ☕ 🍷 [S] 🚭 📺 🔥 🍸 ✿ 🚭 🏠 P

♦♦♦

HERON HOUSE BED & BREAKFAST

Heron House,
Canon Pyon Road, Portway,
Burghill, Hereford HR4 8NG
T: (01432) 761111
F: (01432) 760603
E: bb.hereford@tesco.net
I: www.homepages.tesco.net/~bb.hereford/heron.html

Bedrooms: 2 double/twin
Bathrooms: 1 en suite

B&B per night:
S £18.00
D £42.00

OPEN All year round

Country location with panoramic view, 4 miles north of Hereford city. Off-road parking. Excellent centre for country pursuits and places of historic interest. No smoking.

🐴10 📺 ☕ [S] 🚭 📺 🚗 🚭 P

♦♦♦♦

MONTGOMERY HOUSE

12 St Owen Street, Hereford HR1 2PL
T: (01432) 351454 & 07971 649787
F: (01432) 344463
E: lizforbes@lineone.net

Bedrooms: 2 double/twin
Bathrooms: 2 en suite

B&B per night:
S £35.00–£40.00
D £50.00–£55.00

OPEN All year round

Elegant bed and breakfast accommodation in Georgian Grade II Listed townhouse in centre of Hereford. Spacious en suite facilities, kingsize beds and luxury linen. Hearty breakfasts include award-winning local produce.

📺 ☕ 💨 [S] 🚭 📺 🔥 🚗 🏠 P

IDEAS For ideas on places to visit refer to the introduction at the beginning of this section.

HOLBEACH, Lincolnshire Map ref 3A1

◆◆

THE BULL INN
Old Main Road,
Fleet Hargate, Holbeach, Spalding
PE12 8LH
T: (01406) 426866

Bedrooms: 3 double/
twin

Lunch available
Evening meal available
CC: Mastercard, Switch,
Visa

B&B per night:
S Min £18.00
D Min £30.00

OPEN All year round

Ancient coaching inn on the road round The Wash. Grade II Listed building, site of archaeological interest. Bar, restaurant, rooms, car park and beer garden.

◆◆◆◆
Silver
Award

CACKLE HILL HOUSE
Cackle Hill Lane, Holbeach, Spalding
PE12 8BS
T: (01406) 426721 & 07930 228755
F: (01406) 424659
E: cacklehill2@netscapeonline.co.
uk

Bedrooms: 3 double/
twin
Bathrooms: 2 en suite,
1 private

B&B per night:
S £25.00
D £40.00–£44.00

OPEN All year round

We welcome you to our farm situated in a rural position just off the A17. Spacious accommodation, tea/coffee facilities, excellent traditional breakfasts.

HOPE, Derbyshire Map ref 4B2

◆◆◆◆◆
Silver
Award

UNDERLEIGH HOUSE
Off Edale Road, Hope, Hope Valley S33 6RF
T: (01433) 621372 & 621324
F: (01433) 621324
E: underleigh.house@btinternet.com
I: www.underleighhouse.co.uk

B&B per night:
S £33.00–£46.00
D £60.00–£66.00

OPEN All year round

Secluded cottage and barn conversion near the village of Hope with magnificent countryside views. Ideal for walking and exploring the Peak District. Delicious breakfasts featuring local and home-made specialities, served in flagstoned dining hall. Welcoming and relaxing atmosphere with a log fire on chilly evenings in the charming, beamed lounge.

Bedrooms: 6 double/
twin; suites available
Bathrooms: 6 en suite

CC: Delta, Mastercard,
Switch, Visa

Low season 3 night breaks: £50 B&B per room per night.

HUSBANDS BOSWORTH, Leicestershire Map ref 4C3

◆◆

MRS ARMITAGE'S
31-33 High Street,
Husbands Bosworth, Lutterworth
LE17 6LJ
T: (01858) 880066

Bedrooms: 1 single,
1 double/twin, 1 triple/
multiple

B&B per night:
S £17.00–£18.00
D £34.00–£36.00

OPEN All year round

Village centre home of character on A4304/A427, with wholesome cooking and warm welcome. Good choice of reasonably-priced evening meals at local inns.

INCHBROOK, Gloucestershire Map ref 2B1

◆◆◆

THE CROWN INN
Bath Road, Inchbrook, Stroud
GL5 5HA
T: (01453) 832914 & 07977 096224
F: (01453) 832914
E: inchbrook@cwcom.net
I: www.inchbrook.cwc.net

Bedrooms: 4 double/
twin
Bathrooms: 4 en suite

Lunch available
Evening meal available
CC: Mastercard, Switch,
Visa

B&B per night:
S £25.00–£30.00
D £45.00

OPEN All year round

A quiet family-run inn in the hamlet of Inchbrook on the A46 between Stroud and Nailsworth. Disabled-friendly ground floor rooms available.

SYMBOLS The symbols in each entry give information about services and facilities. A key to these symbols appears at the back of this guide.

♦♦♦

BIRD IN HAND INN

Waterloo Street, Ironbridge, Telford
TF8 7HG
T: (01952) 432226

B&B per night:
S £25.00–£45.00
D £35.00–£55.00

HB per person:
DY £38.00–£50.00

OPEN All year round

The inn, built in 1774, has been run by the Poultons for 15 years, during which time they have built up an excellent reputation for its comfortable 3 Diamond en suite accommodation with superb food and real ales. Situated in the centre of the Ironbridge Gorge with spectacular views over the River Severn.

Bedrooms: 3 single,
2 double/twin, 1 triple/
multiple
Bathrooms: 3 en suite

Lunch available
Evening meal available
CC: Delta, Mastercard,
Switch, Visa

Book 3 nights DB&B and receive your 3rd night accommodation free. From £165 per couple incl from Nov-Mar.

♦♦♦♦♦

**Silver
Award**

BRIDGE HOUSE

Buildwas, Telford TF8 7BN
T: (01952) 432105
F: (01952) 432105
E: janethedges@talk21.com
I: www.smoothhound.co.uk/

B&B per night:
S £40.00–£45.00
D £55.00–£60.00

OPEN All year round

Charming 17thC country house situated by the River Severn and close to the famous Ironbridge. A house full of character and charm. Beautiful rooms all individually decorated and en suite, with a breakfast to be remembered. In all, the place to stay when visiting the famous Ironbridge Gorge.

Bedrooms: 3 double/
twin, 1 triple/multiple;
suites available
Bathrooms: 4 en suite

♦♦

LORD HILL GUEST HOUSE
Duke Street, Broseley TF12 5LU
T: (01952) 884270 & 580792

Bedrooms: 2 single,
5 double/twin
Bathrooms: 3 en suite,
1 private

B&B per night:
S £18.00–£22.00
D £38.00–£44.00

OPEN All year round

Former public house. Friendly atmosphere, full English breakfast, parking. Easy access to Ironbridge, Bridgnorth, Shrewsbury and Telford.

♦♦♦♦

ENDERLEY GUEST HOUSE
20 Queens Road, Kenilworth
CV8 1JQ
T: (01926) 855388
F: (01926) 850450
E: enderleyguesthouse@supanet.
com

Bedrooms: 1 single,
4 double/twin, 1 triple/
multiple
Bathrooms: 6 en suite

B&B per night:
S £27.00
D £45.00–£50.00

OPEN All year round

Family-run guesthouse, quietly situated near town centre and convenient for Warwick, Stratford-upon-Avon, Stoneleigh, Warwick University and National Exhibition Centre.

♦♦♦♦

FERNDALE GUEST HOUSE
45 Priory Road, Kenilworth CV8 1LL
T: (01926) 853214
F: (01926) 858336
E: derekwilson1@canpuserve.com

Bedrooms: 1 single,
4 double/twin, 2 triple/
multiple
Bathrooms: 7 en suite

B&B per night:
S £26.00–£30.00
D £40.00

OPEN All year round

Delightfully modernised Victorian house. Attractive en suite bedrooms with colour TV, tea/coffee facilities. Ideal for NEC, NAC and Warwick University. Private parking.

KENILWORTH continued

◆◆◆◆ VICTORIA LODGE HOTEL

180 Warwick Road, Kenilworth
CV8 1HU
T: (01926) 512020
F: (01926) 858703
E: info@victorialodgehotel.co.uk
I: www.victorialodgehotel.co.uk

Bedrooms: 1 single,
8 double/twin
Bathrooms: 9 en suite

Lunch available
CC: Amex, Delta,
Mastercard, Switch, Visa

B&B per night:
S Min £40.00
D Min £59.00

OPEN All year round

Prestigious small hotel with a warming ambience. Luxurious bedrooms, with individual appeal and character, complemented by traditional hospitality. Non-smoking.

 🕐12 ♿ 🏠 ☎ ▤ 🖵 ♨ 🍷 🅂 🗡 🏵 🎞 🖂 🛏 ✱ 🚲 P

KEXBY, Lincolnshire Map ref 4C2

◆◆◆ THE GRANGE

Kexby, Gainsborough DN21 5PJ
T: (01427) 788265

Bedrooms: 1 single,
1 double/twin
Bathrooms: 1 private

Lunch available
Evening meal available

B&B per night:
S Min £17.00
D Min £34.00

HB per person:
DY Min £29.00

OPEN All year round

650-acre mixed farm. Victorian farmhouse offering warm welcome. 4 miles from Gainsborough. Convenient for Lincoln, Hemswell Antique Centre and Wolds. Double room has private bathroom.

 ▤ 🖵 ♨ 🅂 🏵 🎞 ♪ ✱ 🚲 P

KIDDERMINSTER, Worcestershire Map ref 4B3

◆◆◆ VICTORIA HOTEL

15 Comberton Road, Kidderminster
DY10 1UA
T: (01562) 67240
F: (01562) 67240

Bedrooms: 3 single,
2 double/twin, 2 triple/
multiple
Bathrooms: 5 en suite

CC: Delta, Mastercard,
Switch, Visa

B&B per night:
S £25.00–£28.00
D £45.00

OPEN All year round

Select family-run hotel offering traditional bed and breakfast accommodation, complete with service and hospitality.

 🅰🕐2 ▤ 🖵 ♨ 🅂 🎞 🖂 🚲 P

KINETON, Warwickshire Map ref 2C1

◆◆◆ THE CASTLE

Edgehill, Kineton, Warwick
OX15 6DJ
T: (01295) 670255
F: (01295) 670521
E: castleedgehill@msn.com.
I: www.our-web-site.com/
the-castle-inn

Bedrooms: 1 double/
twin, 2 triple/multiple
Bathrooms: 3 en suite

Lunch available
Evening meal available
CC: Amex, Delta, Diners,
Mastercard, Switch, Visa

B&B per night:
S £35.00–£45.00
D £55.00–£65.00

OPEN All year round

'Folly' built by Sanderson-Miller. Copy of Guy's Tower at Warwick Castle. Erected to commemorate 100th aniversary of Battle of Edgehill (1642) traditionally where King Charles I stood.

🅰♿🏠☎▤🖵♨🍷🅂🗡🎞🖂🔍✱🐎🚲🏠P

KIRTLINGTON

See South of England region for entries

LEAMINGTON SPA, Warwickshire Map ref 4B3 *Tourist Information Centre Tel: (01926) 742762*

◆◆◆◆
Silver
Award

8 CLARENDON CRESCENT

Leamington Spa CV32 5NR
T: (01926) 429840
F: (01926) 424641
E: lawson@lawson71.fsnet.co.uk
I: www.shakespeare-country.co.uk

B&B per night:
S £35.00–£40.00
D £55.00–£60.00

OPEN All year round

Grade II Listed Regency house overlooking private dell, in quiet backwater of Leamington Spa with its many shops and restaurants. Elegantly furnished with antiques. Individually designed en suite bedrooms. Five minutes' walk town centre, convenient for Warwick, Stratford, Royal Agricultural Centre and NEC.

Bedrooms: 2 single,
2 double/twin
Bathrooms: 3 en suite,
1 private

 🕐4 🖵 ♨ 🅂 🏵 🎞 🖂 ✱ 🐎 🚲 🏠 P

LEAMINGTON SPA continued

◆◆◆◆ THE COACH HOUSE

Snowford Hall Farm, Hunningham, Leamington Spa CV33 9ES T: (01926) 632297 F: (01926) 633599 E: the_coach_house@lineone.net I: lineone.net/~the_coach_house	Bedrooms: 3 double/ twin Bathrooms: 2 en suite, 1 private	B&B per night: S £30.00–£32.00 D £40.00–£44.00 OPEN All year round

200-acre arable farm. Converted barn farmhouse off the Fosse Way, on the edge of Hunningham village. On elevated ground overlooking quiet surrounding countryside.

ⵏⴽ ⵣ ⵛ ⵉ ⵇ ⵛ [S] ⵁ ⵙ ▥ ⵔ ⵜ P

◆◆◆◆ HILL FARM

Lewis Road, Radford Semele, Leamington Spa CV31 1UX T: (01926) 337571	Bedrooms: 5 double/ twin Bathrooms: 3 en suite	B&B per night: D £40.00–£50.00 OPEN All year round

350-acre mixed farm. Farmhouse set in large attractive garden, 2 miles from Leamington town centre and close to Warwick Castle and Stratford-upon-Avon.

ⵏⴽ ⵣ ⵛ ⵡ ⵇ [S] ⵁ ⵙ ▥ ⵔ ⵜ P

◆◆◆◆ LANSDOWNE HOTEL

87 Clarendon Street, Leamington Spa CV32 4PF T: (01926) 450505 F: (01926) 421313 E: thelansdowne@cwcom.net I: www.thelansdowne.cwc.net	Bedrooms: 4 single, 10 double/twin Bathrooms: 14 en suite	Evening meal available CC: Amex, Delta, Mastercard, Switch, Visa	B&B per night: S £40.00–£54.95 D £50.00–£68.00 HB per person: DY £58.95–£73.90

Central Regency townhouse recently re-decorated throughout, dinner available if requested. All rooms en suite with TV, tea/coffee facilities, central heating and double glazing.

OPEN All year round

ⵏⴽ ⵣ 5 ⵣ ⵛ ⵣ ⵡ ⵇ ⵟ [S] ⵁ ⵙ ▥ ⵔ ⵜ ⵎ P

◆◆◆ 4 LILLINGTON ROAD

Leamington Spa CV32 5YR T: (01926) 429244 E: pauline.burton@btinternet.com	Bedrooms: 3 double/ twin	B&B per night: S £20.00 D £40.00

Attractive Victorian house within 5 minutes' walk of the town centre. Within easy reach of the NAC, NEC, Stratford-upon-Avon, Warwick and the Cotswolds.

OPEN All year round

ⵏⴽ ⵣ ⵡ [S] ⵁ ⵙ ▥ ⵔ ⵜ

◆◆◆◆ VICTORIA PARK HOTEL

12 Adelaide Road, Leamington Spa CV31 3PW T: (01926) 424195 F: (01926) 421521 I: www. victoriaparkhotelleamingtonspa.co. uk	Bedrooms: 6 single, 7 double/twin, 7 triple/ multiple Bathrooms: 20 en suite	Lunch available Evening meal available CC: Amex, Delta, Mastercard, Switch, Visa	B&B per night: S £36.00–£45.00 D £55.00–£75.00 OPEN All year round

Victorian house close to bus and railway stations and town centre. Park, Pump Room, gardens, bowls, tennis and river all 3 minutes' walk away.

ⵏⴽ ⵣ ⵛ ⵣ ⵡ ⵇ ⵟ [S] ⵁ ⵙ ▥ ⵔ ⵜ ⵎ P

◆◆◆◆ WYMONDLEY LODGE
Silver Award

8 Adelaide Road, Leamington Spa CV31 3PW T: (01926) 882669 F: (01926) 882669	Bedrooms: 2 double/ twin Bathrooms: 2 en suite	B&B per night: S £35.00 D £50.00

Elegant Victorian townhouse, few minutes walk from town centre, shops, restaurants and railway station. Convenient for historic Warwick, Kenilworth, Stratford and the NAC.

ⵏⴽ ⵣ 5 ⵣ ⵡ [S] ⵁ ⵙ ▥ ⵔ ⵜ ⵎ P

LECHLADE, Gloucestershire Map ref 2B1

◆◆◆◆ CAMBRAI LODGE

Oak Street, Lechlade GL7 3AY T: (01367) 253173 & 07860 150467	Bedrooms: 2 single, 5 double/twin; suites available Bathrooms: 2 en suite	B&B per night: S £29.00–£39.00 D £47.00–£59.00 OPEN All year round

Friendly, family-run guesthouse, recently modernised, close to River Thames. Ideal base for touring the Cotswolds. Four-poster bedroom, garden and ample parking.

ⵏⴽ ⵣ ⵣ ⵛ ⵣ ⵡ ⵇ [S] ⵁ ▥ ⵔ ⵜ ⵎ P

LECHLADE continued

NEW INN HOTEL
♦♦♦

Market Square, Lechlade-on-
Thames, Lechlade GL7 3AB
T: (01367) 252296
F: (01367) 252315
E: info@newinnhotel.com
I: www.newinnhotel.com

Bedrooms: 2 single,
17 double/twin
Bathrooms: 19 en suite

Lunch available
Evening meal available
CC: Amex, Delta, Diners,
Mastercard, Switch, Visa

B&B per night:
S £42.50–£60.00
D £50.00–£69.00

HB per person:
DY £35.00–£42.50

OPEN All year round

Situated in a tranquil riverside setting, offering a comfortable blend of traditional hospitality and all modern advantages. Private parking. Restaurant and freehouse with en suite bedrooms.

LEDBURY, Herefordshire Map ref 2B1 *Tourist Information Centre Tel: (01531) 636147*

BROOK HOUSE
♦♦♦♦

Birtsmorton, Malvern WR13 6AF
T: (01531) 650664
F: (01531) 650664
E: maryd@lineone.net
I: website.lineone.net/~maryd

Bedrooms: 3 double/
twin
Bathrooms: 2 en suite,
1 private

B&B per night:
S £18.00
D £36.00–£40.00

A beautiful 17thC timber-framed property set in the countryside close to the Malvern Hills and 3 Counties showground. Convenient for Eastnor, Ledbury and Tewkesbury.

LEEK, Staffordshire Map ref 4B2 *Tourist Information Centre Tel: (01538) 483741*

PROSPECT HOUSE
♦♦♦♦

334 Cheadle Road, Cheddleton,
Leek ST13 7BW
T: (01782) 550639 & 07973 179478
E: prospect@talk21.com
I: www.touristnetuk.com/wm/
prospect/index.htm

Bedrooms: 1 single,
2 double/twin, 2 triple/
multiple
Bathrooms: 5 en suite

Evening meal available
CC: Delta, Mastercard,
Switch, Visa

B&B per night:
S £21.00–£22.50
D £42.00–£45.00

HB per person:
DY £34.00–£35.50

OPEN All year round

A 19thC converted coach house in a tranquil courtyard setting, offering superior accommodation and a personal service tailored to your individual needs.

LEICESTER, Leicestershire Map ref 4C3 *Tourist Information Centre Tel: (0116) 299 8888*

BURLINGTON HOTEL
♦♦♦

Elmfield Avenue, Stoneygate,
Leicester LE2 1RB
T: (0116) 270 5112
F: (0116) 270 4207
E: welcome@burlingtonhotel.co.uk
I: www.burlingtonhotel.co.uk

Bedrooms: 9 single,
6 double/twin, 1 triple/
multiple
Bathrooms: 11 en suite

Evening meal available
CC: Amex, Delta,
Mastercard, Visa

B&B per night:
S £32.00–£45.00
D £48.00–£60.00

OPEN All year round

A friendly welcome awaits you at this family-run hotel. Situated in a quiet residential area close to the city centre.

♦♦♦

SPINDLE LODGE HOTEL
2 West Walk, Leicester LE1 7NA
T: (0116) 233 8801
F: (0116) 233 8804
E: spindlelodgeleicester@orange.net
I: www.smoothhound.co.uk/hotels/spindle.html

B&B per night:
S £27.50–£50.00
D £46.00–£65.00

OPEN All year round

Located in a tree-lined conservation area and built in 1876, charming Spindle Lodge is in a quiet location, yet centrally positioned. A family-run Victorian house with a friendly atmosphere, within easy walking distance of city centre, railway station, universities, civic and entertainment centres.

Bedrooms: 6 single,
5 double/twin, 2 triple/
multiple
Bathrooms: 8 en suite

Evening meal available
CC: Delta, Mastercard,
Switch, Visa

◆◆◆◆
Gold
Award

THE PADDOCK
Shobdon, Leominster HR6 9NQ
T: (01568) 708176
F: (01568) 708829
E: thepaddock@talk21.com

B&B per night:
S £32.00–£35.00
D £42.00–£47.00

HB per person:
DY £35.00–£49.00

Delightful ground floor accommodation set in beautiful countryside bordering Wales. All rooms en suite. Large garden and patio, ample off-road parking. Guests' lounge and dining room. We offer delicious home-cooked food and a very warm welcome. For brochure telephone 01568 708176.

Bedrooms: 5 double/ twin
Bathrooms: 5 en suite

Evening meal available

◆◆◆
TYN-Y-COED
Shobdon, Leominster HR6 9NY
T: (01568) 708277
F: (01568) 708277
E: jandrews@shobdondesign.kc3. co.uk

Bedrooms: 2 double/ twin
Bathrooms: 1 en suite, 1 private

B&B per night:
S Max £20.00
D £40.00

OPEN Apr–Oct

Country house in large garden on Mortimer Trail, close to Croft Castle and Berrington Hall (NT). Convenient for Leominster, Ludlow and Presteigne.

◆◆◆
ALTAIR HOUSE
21 Shakespeare Avenue, Lichfield WS14 9BE
T: (01543) 252900 & 07968 265843

Bedrooms: 1 single, 2 double/twin

B&B per night:
S £20.00
D £36.00–£40.00

OPEN All year round

House situated in quiet cul-de-sac south side of Lichfield, walking distance rail and bus stations. Three miles Whittington Barracks, 15 miles NEC. Motorway link M6, A38.

◆◆◆◆

8 THE CLOSE
Lichfield WS13 7LD
T: (01543) 418483
F: (01543) 418483
E: gilljones@talk21.com
I: www.ldb.co.uk/accommodation.htm

B&B per night:
S Max £28.00
D £48.00–£52.00

OPEN All year round

Grade II Listed building in historic Close overlooking Lichfield Cathedral, within easy walking distance of the city centre and numerous restaurants. Just 15 minutes from junction 9, M42 and convenient for Drayton Manor, The Belfry, Birmingham and East Midlands Airports and NEC.

Bedrooms: 3 double/ twin
Bathrooms: 1 en suite

SPECIAL BREAKS
Many establishments offer special promotions and themed breaks. These are highlighted in red. (All such offers are subject to availability.)

LICHFIELD continued

◆◆◆

Detached guesthouse of character and charm in its own grounds. Conservatory dining room, large walled garden with patio, guests' own lounge, residential licence. All bedrooms non-smoking. Off-road parking. Easy access to M6, M42 and M1, Lichfield, Walsall and Birmingham. 16 miles to NEC, 6 miles Whittington Barracks. Motorcyle friendly.

COPPERS END GUEST HOUSE

Walsall Road, Muckley Corner, Lichfield
WS14 0BG
T: (01543) 372910
F: (01543) 360423
I: www.coppersendguesthouse.co.uk

Bedrooms: 6 double/twin	CC: Amex, Delta, Diners, Mastercard, Visa
Bathrooms: 4 en suite	

B&B per night:
S £26.00–£34.00
D £41.00–£50.00

OPEN All year round

◆◆◆◆
Silver Award

THE FARMHOUSE

Lysway Lane, Longdon Green
WS15 4PZ
T: (0121) 378 4552 &
(01543) 490416
F: (0121) 311 2915
E: jaynetdrury@aol.com
I: www.chez.com/thefarmhouse

Bedrooms: 1 single,
2 double/twin
Bathrooms: 2 en suite,
1 private

Country residence with elegant bedrooms, cosy lounge. Within easy reach of the NEC, Belfry sporting club, Shugborough Hall. Lichfield 2.5 miles. Evening meals by arrangement.

B&B per night:
S £25.00–£30.00
D £55.00–£60.00

OPEN All year round

◆◆

THE WHITE HOUSE

Market Lane, Wall, Lichfield
WS14 0AS
T: (01543) 480384

Bedrooms: 2 double/twin

CC: Visa

House built on site of Roman Baths. Some old beams in the house. Very peaceful, good garden. Near to Motorway, NEC etc.

B&B per night:
S Min £18.00
D Min £36.00

OPEN All year round

LINCOLN, Lincolnshire Map ref 4C2 *Tourist Information Centre Tel: (01522) 873213 & 873256*

◆◆◆

NEWPORT GUEST HOUSE

26-28 Newport, Lincoln LN1 3DF
T: (01522) 528590
F: (01522) 542868
E: info@newportguesthouse.co.uk
I: www.newportguesthouse.co.uk

Bedrooms: 1 single,
5 double/twin, 2 triple/multiple
Bathrooms: 7 en suite

CC: Amex, Delta, Diners, Mastercard, Switch, Visa

A Victorian double-fronted property, walking distance from historic centre of Lincoln. Own off-street parking for guests.

B&B per night:
S £16.00–£28.00
D £32.00–£45.00

OPEN All year round

◆◆◆

WELBECK COTTAGE

Meadow Lane, South Hykeham,
Lincoln LN6 9PF
T: (01522) 692669 & 07799 741000
F: (01522) 692669
E: mad@wellbeck1.demon.co.uk

Bedrooms: 2 double/twin
Bathrooms: 2 en suite

Lunch available
Evening meal available

120-year-old semi-detached cottage in village location. Well decorated, real fire in winter. Near City of Lincoln.

B&B per night:
S £20.00
D £38.00

HB per person:
DY £25.00–£28.00

OPEN All year round

MAP REFERENCES The map references refer to the colour maps at the front of this guide. The first figure is the map number; the letter and figure which follow indicate the grid reference on the map.

LITTLEDEAN, Gloucestershire Map ref 2B1

Rating
Applied For

THE COTTAGE
Green Bottom, Cinderford
GL14 3LH
T: (01594) 823665 & 07909 717966
E: pmccoy45@aol.com

Bedrooms: 2 double/
twin

B&B per night:
S Min £25.00
D Min £40.00

HB per person:
DY Min £30.00

Large attractive cottage set in pretty gardens in small tranquil hamlet. Adjacent to beautiful Forest of Dean. Riding, golf 5 miles. Ideal for nature lovers.

LONG BUCKBY, Northamptonshire Map ref 4C3

♦♦♦

MURCOTT MILL
Murcott, Long Buckby,
Northampton NN6 7QR
T: (01327) 842236
F: (01327) 844524
E: bhart6@compuserve.com

Bedrooms: 3 double/
twin
Bathrooms: 3 en suite

Evening meal available

B&B per night:
S £25.00
D £42.00

HB per person:
DY £35.00

OPEN All year round

A hundred-acre livestock farm. Imposing Georgian mill house overlooking open countryside. Recently renovated to a high standard, with open fires and en suite bedrooms. Ideal stopover for M1 travellers.

LONGBOROUGH, Gloucestershire Map ref 2B1

♦♦♦

LUCKLEY FARM BED AND BREAKFAST
Luckley Farm, Longborough,
Moreton-in-Marsh GL56 0RD
T: (01451) 870885
F: (01451) 831481
E: luckleyholidays@talk21.com
I: www.luckley-holidays.co.uk

Bedrooms: 3 double/
twin
Bathrooms: 3 private

B&B per night:
S £30.00–£40.00
D £50.00–£70.00

OPEN All year round

Luckley is set in the very heart of the north Cotswolds in open countryside. The rooms are sympathetically renovated farm buildings.

LONGHOPE, Gloucestershire Map ref 2B1

♦♦♦♦

THE OLD FARM
Barrel Lane, Longhope GL17 0LR
T: (01452) 830252 & 0789 9831998
F: (01452) 830252
E: lucyr@avnet.co.uk
I: www.avnet.co.uk/theoldfarm

B&B per night:
S £29.00
D £40.00–£52.00

OPEN All year round

Charming 16thC farmhouse with a wealth of character. A peaceful haven in idyllic rural location, yet convenient for Gloucester, the Wye Valley and the Royal Forest of Dean. Comfortable, well-equipped, en suite rooms including a 4-poster. Relax in front of the fire or in the sunny garden. Wonderful walks. Dogs welcome.

Bedrooms: 3 double/
twin
Bathrooms: 3 en suite

3 nights for the price of 2, Nov-Mar (excl Bank Hols).

QUALITY ASSURANCE SCHEME

For an explanation of the quality and facilities represented by the Diamonds please refer to the front of this guide. A more detailed explanation can be found in the information pages at the back.

LONGHOPE continued

◆◆◆◆◆ Gold Award

THE TEMPLE

Old Monmouth Road, Longhope GL17 0NZ
T: (01452) 831011
F: (01452) 831776
E: tricia.ferguson@virgin.net

B&B per night:
S £35.00–£40.00
D £60.00–£70.00

OPEN All year round

Run by Tricia and Keith Ferguson formerly from Cullin House, Broadway. The Temple is a fine Georgian house in over an acre of formal gardens. It is beautifully furnished and ideally situated for Cheltenham, Gloucester and the Forest of Dean. Delicious home made meals with barbeques on a summer's evening.

Bedrooms: 2 double/twin
Bathrooms: 1 en suite, 1 private

Evening meal available

P

LOUGHBOROUGH, Leicestershire Map ref 4C3 *Tourist Information Centre Tel: (01509) 218113*

◆◆◆

CHARNWOOD LODGE

136 Leicester Road, Loughborough LE11 2AQ
T: (01509) 211120
F: (01509) 211121
E: charnwoodlodge@charwat.freeserve.co.uk
I: www.charnwoodlodge.com

B&B per night:
S £30.00–£45.00
D £40.00–£45.00

HB per person:
DY £37.50–£55.00

OPEN All year round

Elegant Victorian licensed guesthouse in pretty gardens with private parking. Peaceful, yet close to town centre, steam railway, university and Charnwood Forest. Spacious, comfortable interior with very attractive en suite rooms including a 4-poster suite. Ideal base for Leicester, Nottingham, Derby, East Midlands Airport and Donington Racecourse. Warm, friendly service assured.

Bedrooms: 1 single, 5 double/twin, 2 triple/multiple
Bathrooms: 7 en suite

Lunch available
Evening meal available
CC: Delta, Diners, Mastercard, Switch, Visa

P

◆◆◆

FOREST RISE HOTEL LTD

55-57 Forest Road, Loughborough LE11 3NW
T: (01509) 215928
F: (01509) 210506

B&B per night:
S £25.00–£50.00
D £45.00–£70.00

OPEN All year round

Family-run establishment, friendly personal service, excellent standards throughout. Short walking distance to the town centre, university. Easy access to M1, M42, airport, Donington Park, Prestwold and Beaumanour Halls. Ample secure car parking, large garden and patio to the rear. 23 en suite bedrooms including executive, bridal, family, 4-poster rooms. All prices include full English breakfast.

Bedrooms: 8 single, 11 double/twin, 4 triple/multiple
Bathrooms: 19 en suite

Evening meal available
CC: Delta, Diners, Mastercard, Switch, Visa

P

PRICES
Please check prices and other details at the time of booking.

◆◆◆ **GARENDON PARK HOTEL**

92 Leicester Road, Loughborough	Bedrooms: 3 single,	Evening meal available	B&B per night:
LE11 2AQ	5 double/twin, 1 triple/	CC: Delta, Diners,	**S £25.00–£35.00**
T: (01509) 236557	multiple	Mastercard, Switch, Visa	**D £38.00–£48.00**
F: (01509) 265559	Bathrooms: 7 en suite		
E: info@garendonparkhotel.co.uk			OPEN All year round
I: www.garendonparkhotel.co.uk			

Warm, friendly welcome and high standards in bright, comfortable surroundings. Five minutes from town centre. Local attractions include Great Central Railway, bell foundry, surrounding countryside.

♦♫▦♌↯▨⑂▤Ⅲ▱❈⛃

◆◆◆ **THE MOUNTSORREL HOTEL**

217 Loughborough Road,	Bedrooms: 4 single,	Lunch available	B&B per night:
Mountsorrel, Loughborough	9 double/twin, 1 triple/	Evening meal available	**S £25.00–£45.00**
LE12 7AR	multiple	CC: Amex, Delta,	**D £45.00–£65.00**
T: (01509) 412627 & 416105	Bathrooms: 11 en suite	Mastercard, Switch, Visa	
F: (01509) 416105			HB per person:
E: mountsorrelhotel@route56.co.			**DY £31.50–£78.00**
uk			
I: www.uktourism.com/			OPEN All year round
le-mountsorrel			

A small, friendly, family-run hotel in secluded grounds off the old A6, midway between Leicester and Loughborough. Bradgate Park and Charnwood Forest Steam Railway are nearby.

♦♫⚓▦♌↯▨⑂▤Ⅲ▱♪▸❈⛃⚲P

◆◆◆ **NEW LIFE GUESTHOUSE**

121 Ashby Road, Loughborough	Bedrooms: 4 single,		B&B per night:
LE11 3AB	2 double/twin, 1 triple/		**S £16.00 £26.50**
T: (01509) 216699	multiple		**D £40.00–£46.00**
F: (01509) 210020	Bathrooms: 2 en suite		
E: jean_of_newlife@assureweb.			OPEN All year round
com			

Family-run, luxurious Victorian villa. Five minutes' Loughborough centre, university, M1. Finalist Best Bed and Breakfast Leicestershire 2000. Attractions: steam railway, National Space Centre, Taylors Bell Foundry, national forest.

♦♫▦♌↯▨⑂✂▤Ⅲ▱❈⚷P

◆◆ **PEACHNOOK**

154 Ashby Road, Loughborough	Bedrooms: 2 single,		B&B per night:
LE11 3AG	2 double/twin, 2 triple/		**S £15.00–£30.00**
T: (01509) 264390 & 217525	multiple; suites available		**D £38.00–£45.00**
I: www.smoothhound.co.uk/hotels/	Bathrooms: 1 en suite		
peachnohtml			OPEN All year round

Small, friendly guesthouse built around 1890. Near all amenities. TV and tea-making facilities in all rooms. Ironing facilities.

♦♫5⚓♌↯▨▱❈⚷⛉🅿P

◆◆◆ **BULL HOTEL**

14 The Bull Ring, Ludlow SY8 1AD	Bedrooms: 3 double/	Lunch available	B&B per night:
T: (01584) 873611	twin, 1 triple/multiple	CC: Amex, Delta,	**S £30.00–£45.00**
F: (01584) 873666	Bathrooms: 4 en suite	Mastercard, Visa	**D £45.00**
E: bull.ludlow@btinternet.com			
I: www.ludlow.org.uk/bullhotel			OPEN All year round

Situated in town centre. Oldest pub in Ludlow, earliest mention c1343. Was known as Peter of Proctors House and probably dates back to c1199.

⚓♌↯▨⑂▤Ⅲ▱♟∪▸❈⚲🅿P

◆◆◆ **CECIL GUEST HOUSE**

Sheet Road, Ludlow SY8 1LR	Bedrooms: 2 single,	Evening meal available	B&B per night:
T: (01584) 872442	5 double/twin, 2 triple/	CC: Delta, Mastercard,	**S £20.00–£35.00**
F: (01584) 872442	multiple	Visa	**D £42.00–£56.00**
	Bathrooms: 4 en suite		
			OPEN All year round

Attractive guesthouse 15 minutes' walk from town centre and station. Freshly cooked food from local produce. Residents' bar and lounge. Off-street parking.

♦♫⚓♌↯▨⑂✂▤Ⅲ▱❈⛃P

♦♦♦♦♦
Gold Award

NUMBER TWENTY EIGHT

28 Lower Broad Street, Ludlow SY8 1PQ
T: (01584) 876996 & 0800 0815000
F: (01584) 876860
E: ross@no28.co.uk
I: www.no28.co.uk

B&B per night:
D £80.00–£100.00

OPEN All year round

Six period town houses of great charm and character, in old Ludlow town. Each room individually furnished providing superb en suite accommodation (suites available). More Michelins within walking distance than anywhere. Come to Ludlow to eat like Lords; to No. 28 to stay like them! The place where guests come first.

Bedrooms: 9 double/ twin; suites available
Bathrooms: 9 en suite

CC: Delta, Mastercard, Switch, Visa

3 for the price of 2, except Bank Hols, Fri and Sat, Nov-Mar.

♦♦♦♦
Gold Award

RAVENSCOURT MANOR

Woofferton, Ludlow SY8 4AL
T: (01584) 711905
F: (01584) 711905
I: www.virtual-shropshire.co.uk/ ravenscourt-manor

B&B per night:
S £35.00–£40.00
D £55.00–£65.00

Historic beamed manor-house, 3 miles from Ludlow with its famous restaurants, castle and festival. Excellent en suite accommodation, tastefully decorated and furnished with antiques. Central heating, TV, tea/coffee-making facilities. Beautiful area for walking and touring. Warm welcome assured.

Bedrooms: 3 double/ twin
Bathrooms: 3 en suite

♦♦♦♦

THE WHEATSHEAF INN
Lower Broad Street, Ludlow
SY8 1PQ
T: (01584) 872980
F: (01584) 877990
E: karen.wheatsheaf@tinyworld.co.uk

Bedrooms: 5 double/ twin
Bathrooms: 5 en suite

Lunch available
Evening meal available
CC: Delta, Mastercard, Switch, Visa

B&B per night:
S £30.00–£50.00
D £45.00–£50.00

OPEN All year round

Family-run mid-17thC beamed inn, 100 yards from the town centre, nestling under Ludlow's historic 13thC Broad Gate, the last remaining of 7 town gates.

COUNTRY CODE Always follow the Country Code ☙ Enjoy the countryside and respect its life and work ☙ Guard against all risk of fire ☙ Fasten all gates ☙ Keep your dogs under close control ☙ Keep to public paths across farmland ☙ Use gates and stiles to cross fences, hedges and walls ☙ Leave livestock, crops and machinery alone ☙ Take your litter home ☙ Help to keep all water clean ☙ Protect wildlife, plants and trees ☙ Take special care on country roads ☙ Make no unnecessary noise

LUTTERWORTH, Leicestershire Map ref 4C3

◆◆◆◆

ORCHARD HOUSE
Church Drive, Gilmorton, Lutterworth
LE17 5LR
T: (01455) 559487
F: (01455) 553047
E: diholman@hotmail.com

B&B per night:
S £23.00–£25.00
D £38.00–£40.00

OPEN All year round

Orchard House provides comfortable accommodation in a quiet village setting. Home-cooked breakfast and a warm and relaxing atmosphere awaits you. One en suite double room and 1 twin room with adjacent bathroom available. Stanford Hall, Rugby, Leicester M1/M6 motorways within easy reach.

Bedrooms: 2 double/twin
Bathrooms: 1 en suite

 P

MALVERN, Worcestershire Map ref 2B1 *Tourist Information Centre Tel: (01684) 892289*

◆◆◆◆

BEREWE COURT
Whiting Lane, Berrow, Malvern
WR13 6AY
T: (01531) 650250 & 07702 303810
E: susanmaryprice@hotmail.com
I: www.ourworcester.net/
berewecourt

Bedrooms: 2 double/twin, 1 triple/multiple
Bathrooms: 3 en suite

B&B per night:
S £30.00–£36.00
D £52.00–£54.00

OPEN All year round

Converted barn in very peaceful rural setting close to Malvern Hills. Also within easy access of Tewkesbury, Malvern and Ledbury towns.

P

◆◆◆

HARCOURT COTTAGE
252 West Malvern Road,
West Malvern, Malvern WR14 4DQ
T: (01684) 574561
F: (01684) 574561
E: harcourtcottage@lineone.net

Bedrooms: 3 double/twin
Bathrooms: 3 en suite

Evening meal available

B&B per night:
S Min £30.00
D Min £40.00

HB per person:
DY £32.50–£42.50

OPEN All year round

Nestling on the west side of the Malvern Hills, well placed for walking holidays or as a base for touring. English and French cuisine.

P

MARKET DRAYTON, Shropshire Map ref 4A2 *Tourist Information Centre Tel: (01630) 652139*

◆◆

HEATH FARM BED AND BREAKFAST
Heath Farm, Wellington Road,
Hodnet, Market Drayton TF9 3JJ
T: (01630) 685570
F: (01630) 685570
E: adrysdale@telco4u.net

Bedrooms: 3 double/twin

B&B per night:
S £19.00–£21.00
D £38.00–£42.00

OPEN All year round

60-acre mixed farm. Traditional farmhouse welcome. Situated 1.5 miles south of Hodnet off A442, approached by private drive. Hodnet Hall, Hawkstone, Potteries, Ironbridge, Shrewsbury.

5 P

MARKET HARBOROUGH, Leicestershire Map ref 4C3 *Tourist Information Centre Tel: (01858) 821270*

◆◆◆◆

THE GEORGE AT GREAT OXENDON
Great Oxendon, Market Harborough
LE16 8NA
I: (01858) 465205
F: (01858) 465205

Bedrooms: 3 double/twin
Bathrooms: 3 en suite

Lunch available
Evening meal available
CC: Amex, Delta,
Mastercard, Switch, Visa

B&B per night:
S Min £52.50
D Min £59.50

HB per person:
DY £75.00–£95.00

OPEN All year round

Bedroom accommodation and restaurant with bars and conservatory, all with views of the garden. Ex-QE2 chef/proprietor. Established 1986.

P

MATLOCK, Derbyshire Map ref 4B2 *Tourist Information Centre Tel: (01629) 583388*

◆◆◆ **HOME FARM**
Ible, Grange Mill, Matlock DE4 4HS
T: (01629) 650349

Bedrooms: 1 double/ twin, 1 triple/multiple
Bathrooms: 2 en suite

Evening meal available

B&B per night:
D £32.00–£36.00

HB per person:
DY £23.00–£25.00

OPEN All year round

A retired farm, but still a few animals. Plenty of walks and places to visit, and a warm welcome to all.

◆◆◆◆ **THE WHITE LION INN**
195 Starkholmes Road, Matlock
DE4 5JA
T: (01629) 582511
F: (01629) 582511
E: whitelion@ntlworld.com
I: www.rightfast.com/whitelion/

Bedrooms: 3 double/ twin
Bathrooms: 2 private

Lunch available
Evening meal available
CC: Amex, Mastercard, Switch, Visa

B&B per night:
D £48.00

OPEN All year round

Converted stone cottages with a panoramic view over Matlock Bath. Bedrooms in old pine furniture with shower rooms.

MATLOCK BATH, Derbyshire Map ref 4B2

◆◆ **ASHDALE**
92 North Parade, Matlock Bath,
Matlock DE4 3NS
T: (01629) 57826 & 07714 106402
E: ashdale@matlockbath.fsnet.co.uk
I: www.ashdaleguesthouse.co.uk

Bedrooms: 2 double/ twin, 2 triple/multiple; suites available
Bathrooms: 4 en suite

CC: Amex, Delta, Diners, Mastercard, Switch, Visa

B&B per night:
S £25.00–£30.00
D £40.00–£50.00

OPEN All year round

A Grade II Listed Georgian villa situated in the centre of Matlock Bath. Large comfortable rooms, level walking to local amenities and station.

◆◆◆◆

HODGKINSONS HOTEL
150 South Parade, Matlock Bath, Matlock
DE4 3NR
T: (01629) 582170
F: (01629) 584891
E: enquiries@hodgkinsons-hotel.co.uk
I: www.hodgkinsons-hotel.co.uk

B&B per night:
S £38.00–£50.00
D £68.00–£95.00

HB per person:
DY £55.00–£77.00

OPEN All year round

Grade II Listed Georgian hotel dating from 1770, overlooking River Derwent in former spa town. Beautifully restored with original features and open fires. All rooms individually decorated and furnished, all with en suite facilities. Imaginative dinners prepared with best of local produce. Car parking available.

Bedrooms: 1 single, 6 double/twin
Bathrooms: 7 en suite

Evening meal available
CC: Amex, Delta, Mastercard, Switch, Visa

Bargain breaks–DB&B £54.50pp minimum 2 night stay.

AT-A-GLANCE SYMBOLS
Symbols at the end of each accommodation entry give useful information about services and facilities. A key to symbols can be found inside the back cover flap. Keep this open for easy reference.

MEDBOURNE, Leicestershire Map ref 4C3

◆◆◆◆

HOMESTEAD HOUSE
5 Ashley Road, Medbourne,
Market Harborough LE16 8DL
T: (01858) 565724
F: (01858) 565324

B&B per night:
S Min £25.00
D Min £42.00

OPEN All year round

In an elevated position overlooking the Welland Valley on the outskirts of Medbourne, a picturesque village dating back to Roman times. Surrounded by open countryside and within easy reach of many places of interest. Three tastefully decorated bedrooms with rural views. A warm welcome awaits you.

Bedrooms: 3 double/twin
Bathrooms: 3 en suite

Evening meal available
CC: Mastercard, Switch, Visa

MELTON MOWBRAY, Leicestershire Map ref 4C3 *Tourist Information Centre Tel: (01664) 480992*

◆◆◆◆

TOLE COTTAGE
10 Main Street, Kirby Bellars,
Melton Mowbray LE14 2EA
T: (01664) 812932
E: michael@handjean.freeserve.co.uk

B&B per night:
S £25.00
D £42.00–£45.00

HB per person:
DY £35.00

OPEN All year round

Situated in the heart of the picturesque Wreake Valley, a warm welcome awaits you at Tole Cottage. This charming, early 19thC traditional home has a colourful garden and inspirational interior. Ideal for touring or weekend breaks, guests can enjoy the relaxed atmosphere and home-cooked food in quiet, comfortable surroundings. Three miles south Melton Mowbray.

Bedrooms: 1 single, 1 double/twin, 1 triple/multiple; suites available
Bathrooms: 1 en suite

Evening meal available

Combine a relaxing break with a decorative folk painting weekend. Jean Payne, author of 'Decorative Folk Painting' caters for all abilities.

MERIDEN, West Midlands Map ref 4B3

◆◆

BONNIFINGLAS GUEST HOUSE
3 Berkswell Road, Meriden,
Coventry CV7 7LB
T: (01676) 523193 & 07900 20116
F: (01676) 523193

Bedrooms: 2 single, 5 double/twin, 1 triple/multiple
Bathrooms: 8 en suite

B&B per night:
S Max £25.00
D Max £40.00

OPEN All year round

Country house, all rooms en suite with TV. Several pubs and restaurants within walking distance.

MICKLETON, Gloucestershire Map ref 2B1

◆◆◆◆

MYRTLE HOUSE
High Street, Mickleton,
Chipping Campden GL55 6SA
T: (01386) 430032 & 07971 938085
F: (01386) 438965
E: kate@myrtlehouse.co.uk
I: www.myrtlehouse.co.uk

Bedrooms: 4 double/twin, 1 triple/multiple
Bathrooms: 5 en suite

Evening meal available
CC: Delta, Mastercard, Switch, Visa

B&B per night:
S £35.00–£50.00
D £55.00–£70.00

OPEN All year round

A Georgian house situated between Stratford and the Cotswolds, with full en suite facilities, TV tea and coffee. Open fire, non-smoking property with a safe walled garden.

MAP REFERENCES
Map references apply to the colour maps at the front of this guide.

MIDDLETON, Northamptonshire Map ref 4C3

◆◆◆ VALLEY VIEW

3 Camsdale Walk, Middleton,
Market Harborough LE16 8YR
T: (01536) 770874

Bedrooms: 2 double/
twin

B&B per night:
S £18.00–£20.00
D £36.00–£40.00

Elevated, stone-built house with panoramic views of the Welland Valley. Within easy distance of Market Harborough, Corby and Rockingham raceway.

OPEN All year round

MINSTERLEY, Shropshire Map ref 4A3

◆◆◆◆ CRICKLEWOOD COTTAGE

Plox Green, Minsterley, Shrewsbury
SY5 0HT
T: (01743) 791229
E: paul.crickcott@bushinternet.
com
I: www.SmoothHound.co.uk/hotels/
crickle

Bedrooms: 3 double/
twin
Bathrooms: 3 en suite

Lunch available

B&B per night:
D £47.00–£52.00

OPEN All year round

Delightful 18thC cottage in unspoilt Shropshire countryside. Charming en suite bedrooms. Breakfast in the Sun Room overlooking a beautiful cottage garden and trout stream. Brochure available.

MORETON–IN–MARSH, Gloucestershire Map ref 2B1

◆◆ ACACIA

2 New Road, Moreton-in-Marsh
GL56 0AS
T: (01608) 650130

Bedrooms: 1 single,
2 double/twin, 1 triple/
multiple
Bathrooms: 1 en suite

B&B per night:
S £20.00–£22.00
D £34.00–£36.00

OPEN All year round

Old Cotswold stone-built house, leaded-light windows. Just off centre of High Street.

◆◆◆ BLUE CEDAR HOUSE

Stow Road, Moreton-in-Marsh
GL56 0DW
T: (01608) 650299
E: gandsib@dialstart.net

Bedrooms: 1 single,
2 double/twin, 1 triple/
multiple
Bathrooms: 2 en suite

Evening meal available

B&B per night:
S Min £22.00
D Min £44.00

HB per person:
DY Min £31.50

OPEN Jan–Dec

Attractive detached residence set in half-acre garden in the Cotswolds, with pleasantly decorated, well-equipped accommodation and garden room. Complimentary tea/coffee. Close to village centre.

◆◆◆ DITCHFORD FARMHOUSE

Stretton on Fosse, Moreton-in-
Marsh GL56 9RD
T: (01608) 663307 & 07812 415357
E: randb@ditchford-farmhouse.co.
uk
I: www.ditchford-farmhouse.co.uk

Bedrooms: 4 double/
twin, 2 triple/multiple
Bathrooms: 3 en suite,
3 private

B&B per night:
S £27.00–£32.00
D £46.00–£52.00

OPEN All year round

1000-acre arable farm. Secluded Georgian farmhouse in lovely north Cotswold countryside. Large garden with children's corner. Home-grown produce and country cooking. Winter breaks with log fires.

◆◆◆◆ FOSSEWAY FARM B&B

Stow Road, Moreton-in-Marsh
GL56 0DS
T: (01608) 650503

Bedrooms: 3 double/
twin, 1 triple/multiple
Bathrooms: 4 en suite

CC: Mastercard, Visa

B&B per night:
S £25.00–£35.00
D £45.00–£50.00

OPEN All year round

Fosseway Farm is just a 5 minute walk into Morton-in-Marsh town. All rooms have en suite, TV, hairdryer and refreshments. Camping facilities.

◆◆◆

NEW FARM
Dorn, Moreton-in-Marsh GL56 9NS
T: (01608) 650782
F: (01608) 652704
E: cath.righton@amserve.net
I: www.smoothhound.co.uk

B&B per night:
S £20.00–£25.00
D £40.00–£45.00

OPEN All year round

Guests can enjoy first class accommodation at very competitive terms in this old farmhouse. Beautiful double 4-poster bed and very pretty twin room. All rooms spacious, colour TV, coffee/tea and private facilities and furnished with antiques. Dining room has large impressive fireplace. Breakfast served with hot crispy bread. Menu.

Bedrooms: 3 double/twin
Bathrooms: 2 en suite, 1 private

◆◆◆

OLD FARM
Dorn, Moreton-in-Marsh GL56 9NS
T: (01608) 650394
F: (01608) 650394
E: simon@righton.freeserve.co.uk

B&B per night:
S Min £25.00
D Min £40.00

Enjoy the delights of a 15thC farmhouse on a 250-acre mixed farm surrounded by beautiful Cotswold countryside. Spacious en suite double bedrooms including 4-poster, twin room available. Croquet on lawn. Children welcome. Peaceful setting for relaxing break, ideal base for visiting Cotswolds/Stratford and only 1 mile from Moreton.

Bedrooms: 3 double/twin
Bathrooms: 2 en suite

◆◆◆◆

TREETOPS
London Road, Moreton-in-Marsh
GL56 0HE
T: (01608) 651036
F: (01608) 651036
E: treetops1@talk21.com

Bedrooms: 5 double/twin, 1 triple/multiple
Bathrooms: 6 en suite

CC: Delta, Mastercard, Switch, Visa

B&B per night:
S Min £35.00
D £45.00–£50.00

OPEN All year round

Family guesthouse on the A44, set in half an acre of secluded gardens. 5 minutes' walk from the village centre.

MUCH BIRCH, Herefordshire Map ref 2A1

◆◆◆

THE OLD SCHOOL
Much Birch, Hereford HR2 8HJ
T: (01981) 541317

Bedrooms: 2 single, 2 double/twin
Bathrooms: 2 en suite

B&B per night:
S £18.00–£20.00
D £40.00–£45.00

OPEN All year round

Interesting Victorian school on A49 Hereford to Ross road. A warm welcome and varied food are 2 of our specialities.

MUCH WENLOCK, Shropshire Map ref 4A3

◆◆◆

THE LONGVILLE ARMS
Longville in the Dale,
Much Wenlock TF13 6DT
T: (01694) 771206
F: (01694) 771742

Bedrooms: 2 double/twin, 2 triple/multiple
Bathrooms: 4 en suite

Lunch available
Evening meal available
CC: Amex, Delta, Mastercard, Switch, Visa

B&B per night:
S £30.00–£34.00
D £46.00–£48.00

OPEN All year round

The main building dates back to 1726 and inside are all original exposed beams. The bedrooms are converted from an old stable.

MUCH WENLOCK continued

◆◆◆ **TALBOT INN**

Much Wenlock TF13 6AA
T: (01952) 727077
F: (01952) 728436

Bedrooms: 1 single,
5 double/twin
Bathrooms: 6 en suite

Lunch available
Evening meal available
CC: Amex, Delta,
Mastercard, Switch, Visa

B&B per night:
S £35.00–£45.00
D £60.00–£70.00

The Talbot has been tending to the needs of visitors for 600 years. The Malt House, with its quiet rooms, is situated in the medieval courtyard.

HB per person:
DY £45.00–£49.95

OPEN All year round

NAILSWORTH, Gloucestershire Map ref 2B1

◆◆◆◆ **AARON FARM**

Nympsfield Road, Nailsworth,
Stroud GL6 0ET
T: (01453) 833598
F: (01453) 833626
E: aaronfarm@aol.com
I: www.
aaronfarm-bedandbreakfast.co.uk

Bedrooms: 3 double/
twin
Bathrooms: 3 en suite

Evening meal available

B&B per night:
S £30.00–£32.00
D £42.00–£44.00

HB per person:
DY £35.00–£36.00

OPEN All year round

Former farmhouse, with large en suite bedrooms and panoramic views of the Cotswolds. Ideal touring centre. Many walks and attractions. Home cooking. Brochure on request.

NAUNTON, Gloucestershire Map ref 2B1

◆◆◆ **FOX HILL**

Old Stow Road, Naunton,
Cheltenham GL54 5RL
T: (01451) 850496 & 07798 822477
F: (01451) 850602

Bedrooms: 2 double/
twin, 1 triple/multiple
Bathrooms: 3 en suite

B&B per night:
S £25.00–£30.00
D £40.00–£50.00

OPEN All year round

This rural idyll in the high Cotswolds offers bed and breakfast in a sympathetically converted 17thC pub. All facilities, pets welcome.

◆◆◆

NAUNTON VIEW GUESTHOUSE

Naunton, Cheltenham GL54 3AS
T: (01451) 850482
F: (01451) 850482

B&B per night:
S £30.00–£35.00
D £45.00–£50.00

OPEN All year round

Recently opened family-run guesthouse in picturesque village near Bourton-on-the-Water. Good base for touring the Cotswolds and within easy reach of Bath and Stratford as well as having excellent walks in the area. All rooms en suite with TV and tea-making facilities. Good views over the village and plenty of safe off-road parking.

Bedrooms: 3 double/
twin
Bathrooms: 3 en suite

CC: Delta, Mastercard,
Switch, Visa

QUALITY ASSURANCE SCHEME

For an explanation of the quality and facilities represented by the Diamonds please refer to the front of this guide. A more detailed explanation can be found in the information pages at the back.

◆◆◆◆

THE BOOT AND SHOE INN

Main Street, Flintham, Newark NG23 5LA
T: (01636) 525246

B&B per night:
S Max £32.00
D Max £48.00

OPEN All year round

A 17thC village pub recently renovated to a high standard. All rooms en suite. Situated in an unspoilt conservation area at the edge of the Vale of Belvoir, 6 miles from Newark. Easy access off A46 to Nottingham, Leicester and Lincoln.

Bedrooms: 1 single, 1 double/twin, 3 triple/ multiple
Bathrooms: 5 en suite

Lunch available
Evening meal available
CC: Delta, Mastercard, Switch, Visa

◆◆◆

NEWENT GOLF AND LODGES

Newent Golf Course, Coldharbour Lane, Newent GL18 1DJ
T: (01531) 820478
F: (01531) 820478
E: tomnewentgolf@aol.com
I: www.short-golf-break.com

B&B per night:
S £30.00
D £50.00–£60.00

OPEN All year round

Set in lovely countryside with views to the Forest of Dean and Malvern Hills. Each lodge has its own entrance on to landscaped courtyard with trellised seating areas. Licensed clubhouse.

Bedrooms: 1 single, 5 double/twin, 2 triple/ multiple; suites available
Bathrooms: 8 en suite

Lunch available
CC: Delta, Mastercard, Switch, Visa

Golf packages available: 2 nights B&B free golf, £60 per person, based on 2 sharing.

◆◆◆◆◆

THREE CHOIRS VINEYARDS
Newent GL18 1LS
T: (01531) 890223
F: (01531) 890877
E: info@threechoirs.com
I: www.threechoirs.com

Bedrooms: 6 double/ twin, 2 triple/multiple
Bathrooms: 8 en suite

Lunch available
Evening meal available
CC: Delta, Mastercard, Switch, Visa

B&B per night:
S £65.00–£85.00
D Min £85.00

HB per person:
DY £57.50–£95.00

OPEN All year round

Relax and enjoy the beauty of England's leading vineyard. Each room is spacious and very well-appointed. All rooms have en suite bathrooms and views over vineyards.

◆◆◆

TAN HOUSE FARM
Newland, Coleford GL16 8NP
T: (01594) 832222
F: (01594) 833501

Bedrooms: 2 double/ twin, 1 triple/multiple
Bathrooms: 2 en suite, 1 private

B&B per night:
S £23.00–£26.00
D £46.00–£52.00

OPEN All year round

14-acre livestock farm. Post Restoration. Queen Anne house dating from 1670, situated in one of the most beautiful villages in the Forest of Dean. Walking distance of 16thC pub.

◆◆◆◆

Silver Award

LANE END FARM
Chetwynd, Newport TF10 8BN
T: (01952) 550337 & 0777 1632255
F: (01952) 550337
E: lane1.endfarm@ondigital.com
I: www.virtual-shropshire.co.uk/lef

Bedrooms: 3 double/ twin
Bathrooms: 2 en suite, 1 private

Evening meal available

B&B per night:
S £25.00–£30.00
D £40.00

HB per person:
DY £31.00–£41.00

OPEN All year round

Delightful period farmhouse in lovely countryside, on A41 near Newport. Ideal for business/leisure, with good local walks. Reductions for 3 nights or more.

◆◆◆

NORWOOD HOUSE HOTEL AND RESTAURANT

Pave Lane, Newport TF10 9LQ
T: (01952) 825896
F: (01952) 825896

Bedrooms: 1 single,
3 double/twin, 1 triple/
multiple
Bathrooms: 5 en suite

Lunch available
Evening meal available
CC: Delta, Mastercard,
Switch, Visa

B&B per night:
S £35.00–£37.50
D £45.00–£47.50

Family-run hotel of character, just off the A41 Wolverhampton to Whitchurch road. Close to Lilleshall National Sports Centre, RAF Cosford and Ironbridge Gorge.

HB per person:
DY Max £47.95

OPEN All year round

◆◆

AARANDALE REGENT HOTEL AND GUESTHOUSE

6-8 Royal Terrace,
Barrack Road (A508), Northampton
NN1 3RF
T: (01604) 631096
F: (01604) 621035
E: info@aarandale.co.uk
I: www.aarandale.co.uk

Bedrooms: 3 single,
12 double/twin, 4 triple/
multiple
Bathrooms: 3 en suite

Evening meal available
CC: Delta, Mastercard,
Switch, Visa

B&B per night:
S £26.00–£38.00
D £40.00–£54.00

OPEN All year round

Small and cosy, family-run hotel/guesthouse within easy walking distance of town centre, bus and train stations.

◆◆◆◆
Silver
Award

NORTHFIELD BED AND BREAKFAST

Cirencester Road (A429),
Northleach, Cheltenham GL54 3JL
T: (01451) 860427
F: (01451) 860820
E: nrthfield0@aol.com

Bedrooms: 2 double/
twin, 1 triple/multiple
Bathrooms: 3 en suite

Evening meal available
CC: Delta, Mastercard,
Switch, Visa

B&B per night:
D £48.00–£54.00

HB per person:
DY £35.00–£40.00

Detached family house with large gardens and home-grown produce. Evening meals available. Excellent centre for visiting the Cotswolds. A warm welcome awaits you.

OPEN All year round

◆◆◆◆

CALERIN HOUSE
21 Redcliffe Road, Mapperley Park,
Nottingham NG3 5BW
T: (0115) 960 5366
F: (0115) 985 8423

B&B per night:
S £30.00–£45.00
D £50.00–£65.00

Delightful Victorian gentleman's residence c1875, 0.75 miles from the centre of Nottingham in a quiet residential area. Superior accommodation. Hospitality tray, trouser press, colour TV, hairdryer. Car parking and lovely gardens. Nearby are places of interest, including Newstead Abbey, Chatsworth House, Belvoir Castle, Nottingham Castle Museum and Sherwood Forest.

Bedrooms: 1 single,
2 double/twin, 1 triple/
multiple
Bathrooms: 4 en suite

◆◆◆◆

ORCHARD COTTAGE

The Old Workhouse, Trowell,
Nottingham NG9 3PQ
T: (0115) 9280933 & 07790 817597
F: (0115) 9280933
E: orchardcottage.bandb@virgin.
net
I: www.orchardcottages.com

Bedrooms: 3 double/
twin
Bathrooms: 3 en suite

CC: Delta, Mastercard,
Switch, Visa

B&B per night:
S £45.00–£55.00
D £55.00–£70.00

OPEN All year round

Opened in 1795, Trowell Workhouse was rebuilt in 1817. In tranquil open farmland. Used as a school from 1835, Napolianic war heros Shaw and Waplington believed to attend.

NOTTINGHAM continued

♦♦ **PARK HOTEL CITY CENTRE**

7 Waverley Street, Nottingham
NG7 4HF
T: (0115) 978 6299 & 942 0010
F: (0115) 942 4358
E: enquiries@parkhotelcitycentre.
co.uk
I: www.parkhotelcitycentre.co.uk

Bedrooms: 9 single,
13 double/twin, 5 triple/
multiple; suites available
Bathrooms: 11 en suite,
16 private

Lunch available
Evening meal available
CC: Delta, Mastercard,
Switch, Visa

B&B per night:
S £48.00–£68.00
D £68.00–£90.00

HB per person:
DY £58.00–£68.00

OPEN All year round

Victorian building with garden setting facing the park. Specialising in stag nights and hen nights. Group bookings taken.

NUNEATON, Warwickshire Map ref 4B3 *Tourist Information Centre Tel: (024) 7638 4027*

♦♦ **LA TAVOLA CALDA**

70 Midland Road, Abbey Green,
Nuneaton CV11 5DY
T: (024) 7638 3195 &
07747 010702
F: (024) 7638 1816

Bedrooms: 1 single,
5 double/twin, 2 triple/
multiple
Bathrooms: 8 en suite

Evening meal available
CC: Amex, Delta, Diners,
Mastercard, Switch, Visa

B&B per night:
S £20.00–£25.00
D £35.00

HB per person:
DY £35.00–£48.00

OPEN All year round

Family-run Italian restaurant and hotel.

OAKHAM, Leicestershire Map ref 4C3 *Tourist Information Centre Tel: (01572) 724329*

♦♦♦

HALL FARM

Cottesmore Road, Exton, Oakham
LE15 8AN
T: (01572) 812271 & 07711 979628
F: (01572) 812271

B&B per night:
S £20.00–£24.50
D £35.00–£44.00

OPEN All year round

25-acre arable and horses farm. Early 19thC Grade II Listed stone farmhouse in open countryside. Approximately 2 miles from Rutland Water north shore and 1 mile from Geoff Hamilton's TV gardens. TV, hairdryer and hot drinks in all rooms. Many of our guests are now making frequent return visits. Reduced prices for children

Bedrooms: 2 double/
twin, 1 triple/multiple
Bathrooms: 1 en suite

♦♦♦

THE TITHE BARN

Clatterpot Lane, Cottesmore, Oakham
LE15 7DW
T: (01572) 813591
F: (01572) 812719
E: jpryke@thetithebarn.co.uk
I: www.tithebarn-rutland.co.uk

B&B per night:
S £20.00–£35.00
D £39.00–£50.00

OPEN All year round

17thC converted tithe barn. Outstanding original dovecote. Spacious and comfortable en suite rooms with a wealth of original features. Panelled dining room and attractive garden. In the heart of unspoilt Rutland, 5 minutes from Rutland Water, Geoff Hamilton's Barnsdale Gardens, Stamford, Oakham and A1. Children and dogs welcome.

Bedrooms: 3 double/
twin, 1 triple/multiple
Bathrooms: 3 en suite,
1 private

CC: Delta, Mastercard,
Switch, Visa

QUALITY ASSURANCE SCHEME

Diamond ratings and awards are explained at the back of this guide.

OXTON, Nottinghamshire Map ref 4C2

♦♦♦

FAR BAULKER FARM
Oxton, Southwell NG25 0RQ
T: (01623) 882375 & 0797 1087605
F: (01623) 882375
E: j.esam@virgin.net

B&B per night:
S Min £22.00
D £40.00–£50.00

OPEN All year round

300-acre mixed farm. An attractive farmhouse with pleasant gardens, in very good decorative order and situated in a peaceful, rural environment. A family-run business in the heart of Sherwood, yet within easy reach of Nottingham, Newark and Mansfield. A warm welcome awaits you.

Bedrooms: 3 double/ twin
Bathrooms: 2 en suite

PEAK DISTRICT

See under Ashbourne, Ashford in the Water, Bakewell, Barlow, Buxton, Calver, Hartington, Hathersage, Hope, Winster

PERSHORE, Worcestershire Map ref 2B1 *Tourist Information Centre Tel: (01386) 554262*

♦♦♦♦
Silver
Award

ALDBURY HOUSE
George Lane, Wyre Piddle, Pershore
WR10 2HX
T: (01386) 553754
F: (01386) 553754
E: aldbury@onetel.net.uk

Bedrooms: 3 double/ twin
Bathrooms: 3 en suite

B&B per night:
S £30.00–£35.00
D £44.00–£50.00

OPEN All year round

Quietly situated, all rooms en suite, guests' lounge and safe parking. Friendly welcome assured. Catering pub nearby. Ideally situated for visits to Worcester, Stratford, The Malverns.

♦♦♦♦
Silver
Award

ARBOUR HOUSE
Main Road, Wyre Piddle, Pershore
WR10 2HU
T: (01386) 555833
F: (01386) 555833
E: arbourhouse@faxvia.net

B&B per night:
S £26.00–£36.00
D £46.00–£52.00

OPEN All year round

A fine Grade II Listed home with oak beams and log fires, overlooking Bredon Hill and close to the River Avon. Comfortable accommodation and good food in a relaxed, friendly atmosphere. Excellent riverside pub opposite. An ideal base for visiting the Cotswolds, Stratford, Worcester and Malvern.

Bedrooms: 3 double/ twin
Bathrooms: 3 en suite

PRIORS HARDWICK, Warwickshire Map ref 2C1

♦♦♦

HILL FARM
Priors Hardwick, Southam
CV47 7SP
T: (01327) 260338 & 07740 853085
E: simon.darbishire@farming.co.uk
I: www.farming_holidays.co.uk

Bedrooms: 2 double/ twin

B&B per night:
S Min £25.00
D Min £40.00

OPEN All year round

We offer an ideal rural retreat! Relax, and take in outstanding westerly views, beautiful sunsets, over peaceful countryside. Excellent location for M40(J12), Stratford, Warwick, Banbury.

REDMILE, Leicestershire Map ref 4C2

♦♦♦ **PEACOCK FARM GUESTHOUSE AND THE FEATHERS RESTAURANT**

Redmile, Nottingham NG13 0GQ	Bedrooms: 3 double/	Lunch available	B&B per night:
T: (01949) 842475	twin, 5 triple/multiple	Evening meal available	S £38.00–£42.00
F: (01949) 843127	Bathrooms: 8 en suite	CC: Amex, Delta, Diners,	D £52.00–£56.00
E: peacockfarm@primeuk.net		Mastercard, Switch, Visa	
I: www.peacock-farm.co.uk			HB per person:

*Nicky Need welcomes you to an 18thC Belvoir Vale farmhouse where professional service
is combined with old-fashioned hospitality. Art gallery and giftshop.*

DY £38.50–£54.50

OPEN All year round

㊉🐎♿🖨️🖥️🖐️🎣🍽️$✂️📺🖥️💺🍵☕🥃⏱️↻🎿🏇☼🐴🐾P

ROSS-ON-WYE, Herefordshire Map ref 2A1 *Tourist Information Centre Tel: (01989) 562768*

♦♦♦ **THE ARCHES**

Walford Road, Ross-on-Wye	Bedrooms: 5 double/	Evening meal available	B&B per night:
HR9 5PT	twin, 1 triple/multiple	CC: Amex, Switch, Visa	S £25.00
T: (01989) 563348	Bathrooms: 6 en suite		D £50.00
F: (01989) 563348			
E: the.arches@which.net			OPEN All year round

*Small, family-run hotel, 10 minutes' walk from town centre. Warm, friendly atmosphere.
All rooms with views of the garden. Victorian-style conservatory, half-acre of lawned
garden to enjoy in summer.*

🐎🖥️🖐️🎣$✂️🖥️💺🏇🐴🐾P

♦♦♦

BROOKFIELD HOUSE

Over Ross, Ross-on-Wye HR9 7AT

T: (01989) 562188

Γ: (01989) 504053

E: reception@brookfieldhouse.co.uk

I: www.brookfieldhouse.co.uk

B&B per night:
S £17.50–£25.00
D £37.00–£50.00

OPEN All year round

*Queen Anne and Georgian Grade II
Listed house close to town centre.
Large private car park. All rooms
have colour TV and tea and coffee-
making facilities, some en suite.
Central heating. Come and go as you
please. Pets with well-behaved
owners welcome. You are offered a
warm and friendly welcome.*

Bedrooms: 2 single,	CC: Amex, Mastercard,
6 double/twin	Visa
Bathrooms: 3 en suite	

🐎🖥️🖐️$🖥️💺🏇☼🐴🐾🎰P

♦♦♦ **THE FALCON GUEST HOUSE**

How Caple, Hereford HR1 4TF	Bedrooms: 3 double/	Evening meal available
T: (01989) 740223	twin, 1 triple/multiple	
F: (01989) 740223	Bathrooms: 4 en suite	
E: falconguesthouse@tinyworld.co.		
uk		

B&B per night:
S Max £25.00
D Max £39.00

HB per person:
DY Min £26.50

*Delightful Georgian house set in Wye Valley between Hereford and Ross-on-Wye.
Excellent base for walking, bird-watching and historic attractions. Close to M50.*

OPEN All year round

㊉🐎♿🖥️🖐️$✂️🖥️💺🏇🐴🎰P

USE YOUR *i*s

There are more than 550 Tourist Information
Centres throughout England offering friendly help
with accommodation and holiday ideas as well as
suggestions of places to visit and things to do.
You'll find TIC addresses in the local Phone Book.

♦♦♦

THE HILL HOUSE
Howle Hill, Ross-on-Wye HR9 5ST
T: (01989) 562033
E: welcome@thehillhouse.dabsol.co.uk
I: www.thehillhouse.dabsol.co.uk/index.html

B&B per night:
S £20.00–£30.00
D £30.00–£50.00

HB per person:
DY £20.00–£35.00

OPEN All year round

Something different: secluded private woodland setting, on Wye Valley Walk. Spectacular views, close to Ross, local organic produce, slow food, friendly ghosts, sauna and massage. Amazing rooms including 'The Dryad Suite' with 7ft 4-poster bed, sheepskin rugs in front of woodburning stove, perfect for honeymoons or naughty weekends. Brochure available.

Bedrooms: 1 double/twin, 1 triple/multiple
Bathrooms: 2 en suite

Evening meal available

Special weekends, local festivals, send for details including: books, poetry, music, food, ghost-hunting, cider, relaxation, paganism, ballooning, rambling, story-telling, poker.

♦♦♦

THE MILL HOUSE
Walford, Ross-on-Wye HR9 5QS
T: (01989) 764339 & 07780 812507
F: (01989) 763231

B&B per night:
S £35.00
D £40.00–£50.00

OPEN All year round

The Mill House is a 300-year-old country house nestled in the Wye Valley on the fringes of Ross-on-Wye. The house benefits from far-reaching views over the river, Kerne Bridge and Goodrich Castle. We offer comfortable, traditional accommodation in a friendly family atmosphere. Dogs welcome.

Bedrooms: 2 double/twin
Bathrooms: 1 en suite, 1 private

♦♦♦♦

THE OLD RECTORY
Hope Mansell, Ross-on-Wye HR9 5TL
T: (01989) 750382
F: (01989) 750382
E: rectory@mansell.wyenet.co.uk

Bedrooms: 3 double/twin
Bathrooms: 1 private

B&B per night:
D £49.00

OPEN All year round

Georgian house in beautiful rural surroundings near Ross-on-Wye. Friendly atmosphere, comfortable rooms with period furniture. Lovely mature gardens, tennis court, children's play facilities.

♦♦♦

THATCH CLOSE
Llangrove, Ross-on-Wye HR9 6EL
T: (01989) 770300
E: thatch.close@virgin.net

B&B per night:
D £38.00–£42.00

HB per person:
DY £31.50–£33.50

OPEN All year round

13-acre mixed farm. Secluded, peaceful and homely Georgian country farmhouse midway between Ross-on-Wye and Monmouth. Home-produced vegetables and meat. Ideal for country lovers of any age. Guests welcome to help with animals. Map sent on request. Ordnance Survey: 51535196.

Bedrooms: 3 double/twin
Bathrooms: 2 en suite, 1 private

Lunch available
Evening meal available

RUGBY, Warwickshire Map ref 4C3 *Tourist Information Centre Tel: (01788) 534970*

♦♦♦♦
Silver
Award

VILLAGE GREEN HOTEL
The Green, Dunchurch, Rugby CV22 6NX
T: (01788) 813434 & 07710 576867
F: (01788) 814714
E: villagegreenhotel.rugby@btinternet.
com
I: www.villagegreenhotelrugby.com

B&B per night:
S £39.00–£54.00
D £49.00–£69.00

OPEN All year round

Located in the historic and
picturesque coaching village of
Dunchurch in Warwickshire, this
award-winning hotel provides
excellent accommodation, facilities
and service for business visitors and
tourists. Ten bedrooms, all en suite,
some with 4-poster beds, all with Sky
TV. Small conference room available.
Full English or buffet breakfast
included.

Bedrooms: 4 single,
6 double/twin
Bathrooms: 10 en suite

CC: Amex, Delta,
Mastercard, Switch, Visa

Special weekend rates: single from £39 night B&B.
Double from £49 night B&B. Romantic nights from
£119. Pampering weekend breaks.

♦♦♦
WHITE LION INN
Coventry Road, Pailton, Rugby
CV23 0QD
T: (01788) 832359
F: (01788) 832359

Bedrooms: 9 double/
twin
Bathrooms: 5 en suite

Lunch available
Evening meal available
CC: Delta, Mastercard,
Switch, Visa

B&B per night:
S £22.00–£32.00
D £39.00–£49.00

OPEN All year round

*17thC coaching inn, recently refurbished but retaining all old world features. Close to
Rugby, Coventry and Stratford. Within 2 miles of motorways. Home-cooked food served
daily.*

RUGELEY, Staffordshire Map ref 4B3

♦♦♦
PARK FARM
Hawkesyard, Armitage Lane,
Rugeley WS15 1ED
T: (01889) 583477
F: (01889) 583477

Bedrooms: 2 triple/
multiple; suites available
Bathrooms: 2 en suite

B&B per night:
S £19.00–£21.00
D £40.00–£42.00

OPEN All year round

*40-acre livestock farm. While convenient for towns and attractions in the area, Park Farm
is quietly tucked away in scenic hills.*

RUTLAND WATER

See under Belton in Rutland, Oakham

SHEPSHED, Leicestershire Map ref 4C3

♦♦♦
CROFT GUESTHOUSE
21 Hall Croft, Shepshed,
Loughborough LE12 9AN
T: (01509) 505657
F: 0870 0522266
E: ray@croftguesthouse.demon.co.
uk
I: www.croftguesthouse.demon.co.
uk

Bedrooms: 5 double/
twin, 2 triple/multiple
Bathrooms: 7 en suite

CC: Delta, Mastercard,
Switch, Visa

B&B per night:
S Min £20.00
D Min £38.00

OPEN All year round

*The property is a Victorian terrace with attractive green and gold frontage, a family run
traditional bed and breakfast with a warm and friendly welcome.*

♦♦♦♦
THE GRANGE COURTYARD
The Grange, Forest Street,
Shepshed, Loughborough LE12 9DA
T: (01509) 600189
E: lindalawrence@
thegrangecourtyard.co.uk
I: www.thegrangecourtyard.co.uk

Bedrooms: 12 double/
twin; suites available
Bathrooms: 12 en suite

Evening meal available
CC: Delta, Mastercard,
Switch, Visa

B&B per night:
S £35.00–£55.00
D £70.00–£75.00

OPEN All year round

*11thC former farmhouse with additions in Tudor and Georgian periods. Beautifully
refurbished with original beams. Close to East Midlands Airport, Donington Park and M1
junction 23.*

SHERWOOD FOREST

See under Newark, Oxton, Southwell, Worksop

SHIRLEY, Derbyshire Map ref 4B2

 ◆◆◆◆

THE OLD BYRE GUESTHOUSE
Hollington Lane, Shirley, Ashbourne
DE6 3AS
T: (01335) 360054
F: (01335) 360054
E: alan@theoldbyre.fsbusiness.co.uk
I: www.theoldbyre.fsbusiness.co.uk

Bedrooms: 2 single,
2 double/twin

Lunch available

B&B per night:
S £22.50
D £45.00

HB per person:
DY £22.50

OPEN All year round

18thC converted barn in quiet village, in the heart of the Derbyshire countryside. Four-poster room, inglenook fireplace, beams and log fires. Traditional English breakfast. Convenient for Alton Towers and Peak District.

SHOBDON, Herefordshire Map ref 2A1

 ◆◆◆

FOUR OAKS
Uphampton, Shobdon, Leominster
HR6 9PA
T: (01568) 708039
F: (01568) 708039
E: fouroaksBandB@hotmail.com

Bedrooms: 2 double/twin
Bathrooms: 1 en suite,
1 private

B&B per night:
S £35.00
D £50.00

OPEN All year round

Comfortable AD2000 house within 1860s walls. Splendid countryside views and easy access to the Mortimer Trail, delightful villages and ancient towns.

SHREWSBURY, Shropshire Map ref 4A3 *Tourist Information Centre Tel: (01743) 281200*

◆◆◆◆
Silver
Award

ASHTON LEES
Dorrington, Shrewsbury SY5 7JW
T: (01743) 718378

B&B per night:
S £21.00–£24.00
D £42.00–£48.00

OPEN Feb–Dec

For many years we have welcomed guests to our family home. On winter evenings, roaring fires entice you to curl up and read a book, with a drink purchased from our small licensed bar. In summer we serve teas in the tree-shaded garden. A place of relaxation and tranquility.

Bedrooms: 3 double/twin
Bathrooms: 2 en suite

◆◆

AVONLEA
33 Coton Crescent, Coton Hill,
Shrewsbury SY1 2NZ
T: (01743) 359398

Bedrooms: 1 single,
2 double/twin

B&B per night:
S £18.00–£20.00
D £34.00–£40.00

OPEN All year round

A comfortable Edwardian house with spacious rooms in a crescent of similar houses. Close to historic town centre, all public transport, records and research library.

◆◆◆

CHATFORD HOUSE
Bayston Hill, Shrewsbury SY3 0AY
T: (01743) 718301

Bedrooms: 3 double/twin

B&B per night:
S Min £17.00
D Min £34.00

Comfortable farmhouse built in 1776, 5.5 miles south of Shrewsbury off A49. Through Bayston Hill, take third right (Stapleton) then right to Chatford.

www.travelengland.org.uk
Log on for information and inspiration. The latest information on places to visit, events and quality assessed accommodation.

◆◆◆◆

NORTH FARM
Eaton Mascot, Shrewsbury SY5 6HF
T: (01743) 761031
F: (01743) 761854
E: northfarm@talk21.com
I: www.northfarm.co.uk

B&B per night:
S £30.00
D £50.00

OPEN All year round

Victorian farmhouse on a mixed arable farm, set within beautiful, countryside yet only 5 miles from Shrewsbury. Three large bedrooms decorated in styles to suit a Victorian house. A friendly, informal atmosphere is our aim, a relaxed, stress-free at-home feeling. Shrewsbury, Ironbridge, Church Stretton and Much Wenlock are within easy reach.

Bedrooms: 3 double/twin
Bathrooms: 2 en suite, 1 private

10% discount on 2-3 night stays.

◆◆◆

SANDFORD HOUSE HOTEL
St Julian's Friars, Shrewsbury
SY1 1XL
T: (01743) 343829
F: (01743) 343829
E: sandfordhouse@lineone.net
I: www.sandfordhouse.co.uk

Bedrooms: 1 single, 5 double/twin, 4 triple/multiple; suites available
Bathrooms: 8 en suite, 2 private

CC: Amex, Delta, Mastercard, Switch, Visa

B&B per night:
S £40.00–£55.00
D £55.00–£65.00

OPEN All year round

Family-run Grade II Listed townhouse, close to the river, with pleasant walks and access to good fishing. Easy parking and within a few minutes of the town centre.

◆◆◆

THE STIPERSTONES GUEST HOUSE
18 Coton Crescent, Coton Hill, Shrewsbury
SY1 2NZ
T: (01743) 246720 & 350303
F: (01743) 350303
E: stiperston@aol.com
I: www.stiperstones.net

B&B per night:
S £22.50–£25.00
D £38.00–£42.00

OPEN All year round

Always a warm welcome. Very comfortable, tastefully furnished, quality accommodation. High standard of cleanliness. Extensive facilities include off-road parking, direct-dial phones, teletext TVs, hospitality trays, comfortable guest lounge. Business facilities. Close to town centre, railway station, river walks. Vegetarian breakfasts available. Directions available. Ideal for a relaxing break.

Bedrooms: 1 single, 4 double/twin, 1 triple/multiple

◆◆◆

EASTLEIGH
60 Scarbrough Avenue, Skegness
PE25 2TB
T: (01754) 764605 & 07719 626232
F: (01754) 764605
I: www.eastleigh-skegness.co.uk

Bedrooms: 1 single, 4 double/twin, 3 triple/multiple
Bathrooms: 8 en suite

B&B per night:
S £21.00–£24.00
D £42.00–£46.00

HB per person:
DY £30.00–£35.00

On a tree-lined avenue adjacent to pier, 2 minutes' walk to the Embassy Theatre, shopping centre and seafront amenities. Bowling greens and golf clubs nearby.

COLOUR MAPS Colour maps at the front of this guide pinpoint all places under which you will find accommodation listed.

SKEGNESS continued

◆◆◆ SAXBY HOTEL

12 Saxby Avenue, Skegness	Bedrooms: 1 single,	Lunch available	B&B per night:
PE25 3LG	9 double/twin, 3 triple/	Evening meal available	S £25.00
T: (01754) 763905	multiple	CC: Delta, Mastercard,	D £50.00
F: (01754) 763905	Bathrooms: 13 en suite	Switch, Visa	

HB per person:
DY £32.00

A family-run hotel, on a corner in a quiet residential area of Skegness, 300 yards from the seafront.

SOLIHULL, West Midlands Map ref 4B3 *Tourist Information Centre Tel: (0121) 704 6130*

◆◆◆◆ ACORN GUEST HOUSE

29 Links Drive, Solihull B91 2DJ	Bedrooms: 2 single,	B&B per night:
T: (0121) 7055241	3 double/twin	S £22.00–£30.00
E: acorn.wood@btinternet.com	Bathrooms: 1 en suite	D £44.00–£50.00

Comfortable, quiet family home with ample private facilities, overlooking golf course. Parking and easy access to NEC, airport, M42 and Solihull centre.

OPEN All year round

◆◆◆ CHALE GUEST HOUSE

967 Stratford Road, Shirley, Solihull	Bedrooms: 3 single,	B&B per night:
B90 4BG	2 double/twin, 1 triple/	S £24.00–£32.00
T: (0121) 744 2846 &	multiple	D £48.00–£55.00
07974 323018	Bathrooms: 5 en suite,	
F: (0121) 6240044	1 private	OPEN All year round
E: chale.guesthouse@iname.com		
I: www.smoothhound.co.uk/hotels/		
chalegue.htm		

A family-run Edwardian guesthouse within easy access to the NEC. Warm friendly atmosphere, comfortable accommodation.

◆◆◆◆ CHELSEA LODGE

48 Meriden Road,	Bedrooms: 3 double/	B&B per night:
Hampton in Arden, Solihull B92 0BT	twin	S Min £25.00
T: (01675) 442408	Bathrooms: 2 en suite,	D £45.00–£55.00
F: (01675) 442408	1 private	
E: chelsealodgebnb@aol.com		OPEN All year round
I: www.chelsealodgebnb.co.uk ALSO		
www.tempera.co.uk/pchapman		

Comfortable, detached property with delightful gardens. Walking distance to Hampton in Arden station (direct NEC/Birmingham Airport) and village pubs. Village location, 3 miles NEC/Solihull.

◆◆◆ THE GATE HOUSE

Barston Lane, Barston, Solihull	Bedrooms: 1 single,	B&B per night:
B92 0JN	2 double/twin	S £25.00–£35.00
T: (01675) 443274	Bathrooms: 2 en suite	D £48.00–£60.00
F: (01675) 443274		
E: gatehouse@jjemmett.fsnet.co.uk		OPEN All year round

Early Victorian mansion house set in beautiful countryside. Close to National Exhibition Centre, International Convention Centre, airport and motorway.

SOULDERN

See South of England region for entries

CREDIT CARD BOOKINGS If you book by telephone and are asked for your credit card number it is advisable to check the proprietor's policy should you cancel your reservation.

SOUTH NORMANTON, Derbyshire Map ref 4B2

◆◆◆◆
Silver
Award

THE BOUNDARY LODGE
Lea Vale, Broadmeadows,
South Normanton, Alfreton DE55 3NA
T: (01773) 819066
E: manager@boundarylodgefs.net.co.uk
I: theboundary.co.uk

B&B per night:
D £53.85–£96.85

OPEN All year round

Just 5 minutes' drive from junction 28 of the M1 and close to many local attractions and superb shopping. Our spacious rooms are all en suite and extremely well appointed. On-site facilities include family pub/restaurant with children's indoor and outdoor play areas and weekend entertainment.

Bedrooms: 11 double/ twin, 2 triple/multiple
Bathrooms: 13 en suite

Lunch available
Evening meal available
CC: Delta, Mastercard, Switch, Visa

Weekend breaks: Fri/Sat or Sat/Sun. Free continental breakfast (max. 2 per room). Reserve 14 days in advance only.

ᗰᕵᗶᏓᖴᏃᕫᗴᖲᏕᐢᎆᐅᛘᕫᏆᕄᏗᖽᙁP

SOUTH WITHAM, Lincolnshire Map ref 3A1

◆◆◆◆
BARN OWL HOUSE
20 High Street, South Witham,
Grantham NG33 5QB
T: (01572) 767688 & 07932 000870
F: (01572) 767688
E: margaret@mcclambert.fsnet.co.uk
I: www.rutnet.co.uk/barnowl

Bedrooms: 3 double/ twin
Bathrooms: 3 en suite

CC: Delta, Mastercard, Switch, Visa

B&B per night:
S £30.00–£35.00
D £45.00

OPEN All year round

An 18thC stone-built house, all rooms en suite, private parking, fishing, watersports and bird-watching nearby. Packed lunches and freezer facilities available.

ᕵᖴᏃᕫᗴᖽᏕᐢᎆᐅᛘP

◆◆◆
THE BLUE COW INN AND BREWERY
29 High Street, South Witham,
Grantham NG33 5QB
T: (01572) 768432
F: (01572) 768432
E: richard@thirlwell.fslife.co.uk
I: www.thebluecowinn.co.uk

Bedrooms: 4 double/ twin, 2 triple/multiple
Bathrooms: 6 en suite

Lunch available
Evening meal available
CC: Delta, Mastercard, Switch, Visa

B&B per night:
S £40.00–£45.00
D £45.00–£55.00

OPEN All year round

13thC beamed freehouse with log fires, real ales and home-cooked meals. Convenient for A1, Grantham, Oakham, Stamford and Melton Mowbray. Brewery on premises, brewing own beers.

ᗰᕵᏓᖴᏃᕫᗴᖲᏕᐅᎆᐢᏆᕄᏗᖽᙁᛘP

SOUTHWELL, Nottinghamshire Map ref 4C2

◆◆◆◆
CHURCH STREET BED AND BREAKFAST
56 Church Street, Southwell
NG25 0HG
T: (01636) 812004 & 0798 995 1665
E: ian.wright5@btinternet.com

Bedrooms: 3 double/ twin
Bathrooms: 1 en suite

B&B per night:
S £20.00–£35.00
D £40.00–£50.00

OPEN All year round

Breakfast is our speciality! Beautifully restored Georgian Grade II townhouse offering a friendly, relaxed atmosphere. Town centre 5 minutes. Southwell Minster, pubs and restaurants.

ᗰᕵᗶᖴᏃᕫᗴᖲᏕᐢᎆᐢᛘP

ACCESSIBILITY
Look for the 🖮 🖮 🖮 symbols which indicate accessibility for wheelchair users. A list of establishments is at the front of this guide.

STAFFORD, Staffordshire Map ref 4B3 *Tourist Information Centre Tel: (01785) 619619*

◆◆◆◆

LITTYWOOD HOUSE
Bradley, Stafford ST18 9DW
T: (01785) 780234 & 780770
F: (01785) 780770

B&B per night:
S £25.00–£35.00
D £40.00–£45.00

OPEN All year round

Littywood is a beautiful double moated 14thC manor house, set in its own grounds, surrounded by open countryside. Tastefully furnished with antiques and tapestries throughout. We are easily accessible from the M6 motorway. Ideally situated for Alton Towers, Shugborough Hall, Weston Park and The Potteries. Centrally heated.

Bedrooms: 2 double/
twin
Bathrooms: 1 en suite,
1 private

STAMFORD, Lincolnshire Map ref 3A1 *Tourist Information Centre Tel: (01780) 755611*

◆◆

DOLPHIN GUESTHOUSE
12 East Street, Stamford PE9 1QD
T: (01780) 757515 & 481567
F: (01780) 757515
E: mikdolphin@mikdolphin.demon.co.uk

Bedrooms: 7 double/
twin, 1 triple/multiple;
suites available
Bathrooms: 6 en suite

CC: Delta, Mastercard,
Visa

B&B per night:
S £20.00–£35.00
D £40.00–£50.00

OPEN All year round

En suite hotel-style accommodation next to the Dolphin Inn, renowned for its cask ales, friendliness and food. Off-road secure car parking and only 100 yards from the town centre.

STANTON-ON-THE-WOLDS, Nottinghamshire Map ref 4C2

◆◆◆

LAUREL FARM
Browns Lane, Stanton-on-the-Wolds, Keyworth, Nottingham
NG12 5BL
T: (0115) 937 3488
F: (0115) 9376490
E: laurelfarm@yahoo.com
I: www.s-h-systems.co.uk/laurelfa.html

Bedrooms: 3 double/
twin
Bathrooms: 2 en suite,
1 private

Evening meal available
CC: Delta, Mastercard,
Switch, Visa

B&B per night:
S £35.00–£37.50
D £45.00–£47.50

OPEN All year round

Old farmhouse with NGS garden. Lovely en suite/private rooms with many extras. Only fresh local produce used for breakfast. Strictly no smoking. Nearest roads M1, A46, A606.

STOCKTON ON TEME, Worcestershire Map ref 4A3

◆◆◆

WHARF FARM
Pensax Lane, Stockton on Teme,
Worcester WR6 6XF
T: (01584) 881341
E: wharf.farm@cwcom.net

Bedrooms: 1 double/
twin
Bathrooms: 1 en suite

B&B per night:
S £20.00
D £40.00

OPEN Apr–Oct

An 1840s modernised farmhouse in beautiful Teme Valley. Horses and sheep to see. Easily accessible for Worcester, Hereford and Ludlow. Warm welcome.

STOKE-ON-TRENT, Staffordshire Map ref 4B2 *Tourist Information Centre Tel: (01782) 236000*

◆

FLOWER POT HOTEL
44-46 Snow Hill, Shelton,
Stoke-on-Trent ST1 4LY
T: (01782) 207204

Bedrooms: 5 single,
4 double/twin, 3 triple/
multiple
Bathrooms: 2 en suite

CC: Mastercard, Visa

B&B per night:
S £15.00–£20.00
D £30.00–£35.00

OPEN All year round

A small hotel, central for Alton Towers and the Potteries attractions, about 5 miles from the motorway and 0.5 miles from the main bus/rail stations.

STOKE-ON-TRENT continued

◆◆◆ STAR HOTEL

92 Marsh Street North, Hanley,
Stoke-on-Trent ST1 5HH
T: (01782) 207507 & 289989
F: (01782) 289989

Bedrooms: 2 single,
6 double/twin, 1 triple/
multiple
Bathrooms: 7 en suite

CC: Delta, Mastercard,
Visa

B&B per night:
S £25.00–£26.00
D £40.00–£42.00

OPEN All year round

A small hotel in the city centre, offering spacious en suite accommodation with a friendly service. An ideal base for visiting Alton Towers and the Potteries.

◆◆◆ VERDON GUEST HOUSE

44 Charles Street, Hanley,
Stoke-on-Trent ST1 3JY
T: (01782) 264244 & 07711 514682
F: (01782) 264244
E: debbie@howlett18.freeserve.co.uk
I: business.thisisstaffordshire.co.uk/verdon

Bedrooms: 1 single,
6 double/twin, 6 triple/
multiple
Bathrooms: 4 en suite

CC: Mastercard, Visa

B&B per night:
S £22.00
D £38.00–£42.00

OPEN All year round

Large, friendly guesthouse in town centre close to bus station. Convenient for pottery visits, museum. Alton Towers 20 minutes, M6 10 minutes. All rooms cable TV, some 4-poster beds.

STONEHOUSE, Gloucestershire Map ref 2B1

◆◆ MERTON LODGE

8 Ebley Road, Stonehouse GL10 2LQ
T: (01453) 822018

Bedrooms: 3 double/
twin
Bathrooms: 1 en suite

B&B per night:
S £19.00–£21.00
D £38.00–£42.00

OPEN All year round

Former gentleman's residence offering a warm welcome. Non-smoking. Three miles from M5 junction 13, over 4 roundabouts. Along Ebley old road, under footbridge.

STOURBRIDGE, West Midlands Map ref 4B3

◆◆◆◆

ST. ELIZABETH'S COTTAGE

Woodman Lane, Clent, Stourbridge
DY9 9PX
T: (01562) 883883
F: (01562) 885034
E: st_elizabeth_cot@btconnect.com

Bedrooms: 3 double/
twin
Bathrooms: 3 en suite

B&B per night:
S £30.00–£32.00
D £55.00–£60.00

OPEN All year round

Beautiful country cottage with lovely garden and swimming pool. Interior professionally decorated throughout. Close to all motorway links. Destinations within easy reach – Symphony Hall, Convention Centre in Birmingham, Black Country Museum, Stourbridge crystal factories, Severn Valley railway. 25 minutes from NEC and Birmingham Airport.

STOW-ON-THE-WOLD, Gloucestershire Map ref 2B1 *Tourist Information Centre Tel: (01451) 831082*

◆◆◆ CORSHAM FIELD FARMHOUSE

Bledington Road, Stow-on-the-
Wold, Cheltenham GL54 1JH
T: (01451) 831750

Bedrooms: 4 double/
twin, 4 triple/multiple
Bathrooms: 6 en suite

B&B per night:
S £25.00–£30.00
D £35.00–£45.00

OPEN All year round

100-acre mixed farm. Homely farmhouse with breathtaking views, ideal for exploring Cotswolds. En suite and standard rooms. TVs, guest lounge, tea/coffee facilities. Good pub food 5 minutes' walk.

CONFIRM YOUR BOOKING

You are advised to confirm your booking in writing.

◆◆◆

MAUGERSBURY MANOR

Stow-on-the-Wold, Cheltenham GL54 1HP
T: (01451) 830581
F: (01451) 870902
E: karen@manorholidays.co.uk
I: www.manorholidays.co.uk

B&B per night:
S £30.00–£45.00
D £45.00

A warm, friendly welcome awaits you at this Jacobean manor house, in the heart of the beautiful Cotswold countryside. Situated near Stow, this is an ideal place to visit picturesque villages and historic towns. Oxford, Cheltenham, Stratford all within easy reach. Quiet, comfortable accommodation. Ample parking and lovely views.

Bedrooms: 3 double/twin; suites available
Bathrooms: 2 en suite

◆◆◆

SOUTH HILL FARMHOUSE

Fosseway, Stow-on-the-Wold, Cheltenham GL54 1JU
T: (01451) 831888
F: (01451) 832255
E: info@southhill.co.uk
I: www.southhill.co.uk

B&B per night:
S £32.00–£35.00
D £45.00–£48.00

OPEN All year round

A friendly family-run B&B in a listed Cotswold-stone farmhouse on the outskirts of Stow-on-the-Wold. Ideally situated for touring, walking or cycling in the Cotswolds. The town square is only 10 minutes' walk away and we have ample parking for guests.

Bedrooms: 1 single, 4 double/twin, 1 triple/multiple
Bathrooms: 5 en suite, 1 private

CC: Delta, Mastercard, Switch, Visa

◆◆◆◆

WOODLANDS

Upper Swell, Stow-on-the-Wold, Cheltenham GL54 1EW
T: (01451) 832346

Bedrooms: 1 single, 4 double/twin
Bathrooms: 5 en suite

CC: Mastercard, Visa

B&B per night:
S Min £30.00
D Min £52.00

OPEN All year round

Small guesthouse in quaint Cotswold village, 1 mile from Stow-on-the-Wold. Set in half-acre gardens with breathtaking views of the Cotswolds. Guest lounge where light snacks can be served.

◆◆◆◆◆

WYCK HILL LODGE

Burford Road, Stow-on-the-Wold, Cheltenham GL54 1HT
T: (01451) 830141
E: gkhwyck@compuserve.com

Bedrooms: 3 double/twin
Bathrooms: 3 en suite

B&B per night:
D £46.00–£50.00

Tastefully furnished Victorian lodge in peaceful rural surroundings. Renowned for comfort, fine breakfasts and hospitality. Extensive views. 1 mile from Stow-on-the-Wold. Ample parking. Non-smokers only, please.

QUALITY ASSURANCE SCHEME

Diamond ratings and awards were correct at the time of going to press but are subject to change. Please check at the time of booking.

◆◆◆◆
Silver
Award

STRAGGLETHORPE HALL

Stragglethorpe, Lincoln LN5 0QZ
T: (01400) 272308
F: (01400) 273816
E: stragglethorpe@compuserve.com
I: www.stragglethorpe.com

B&B per night:
S £25.00–£40.00
D £60.00–£90.00

OPEN All year round

Situated just south of Lincoln, Stragglethorpe is a Grade II Tudor manor set in formal gardens and furnished with antiques. Individually furnished en suites, including two 4-poster rooms, have all modern amenities. Ideal for touring the country or simply stopping over between York and Cambridge off the A1.

Bedrooms: 3 double/twin
Bathrooms: 3 en suite

Meals provided for parties of 5 or more.

Evening meal available

◆◆◆

AMELIA LINHILL GUESTHOUSE
35 Evesham Place, Stratford-upon-Avon CV37 6HT
T: (01789) 292879
F: (01789) 299691
E: Linhill@bigwig.net
I: Linhillguesthouse.co.uk

Bedrooms: 1 single, 2 double/twin, 3 triple/multiple
Bathrooms: 3 en suite

Lunch available
Evening meal available
CC: Amex, Delta, Mastercard, Switch, Visa

B&B per night:
S £20.00–£30.00
D £40.00–£65.00

HB per person:
DY £25.00–£35.00

Comfortable Victorian guesthouse offering warm welcome and good food. 5 minutes' walk from town centre and theatres and convenient for Cotswolds. Baby sitting service.

OPEN All year round

◆◆◆◆

AVONLEA

47 Shipston Road, Stratford-upon-Avon CV37 7LN
T: (01789) 205940
F: (01789) 209115
E: avonlea-stratford@lineone.net
I: www.avonlea-stratford.co.uk

B&B per night:
S £30.00–£45.00
D £44.00–£72.00

OPEN All year round

Stylish Victorian townhouse situated only 5 minutes' walk from the theatre and town centre. All rooms are en suite and furnished to the highest quality. Our guests are assured of a warm welcome and friendly atmosphere.

Bedrooms: 2 single, 4 double/twin, 1 triple/multiple
Bathrooms: 6 en suite, 1 private

CC: Mastercard, Switch, Visa

3 nights for the price of 2 from Oct-Mar.

◆◆◆

THE BLUE BOAR INN

Temple Grafton, Alcester B49 6NR
T: (01789) 750010
F: (01789) 750635
E: blueboar@covlink.co.uk
I: www.stratford.upon.avon.co.uk/blueboar

B&B per night:
S £45.00–£50.00
D £65.00–£75.00

HB per person:
DY £30.00–£45.00

OPEN All year round

This family-owned 16thC country inn is ideally located in the heart of rural Warwickshire, within easy reach of the Cotswolds, Birmingham NEC, NAC, Warwick Castle and Shakespeare's Stratford-upon-Avon. It has beautiful gardens, warm fires and is renowned for its good food, real ales and fine wines.

Bedrooms: 11 double/twin, 4 triple/multiple
Bathrooms: 15 en suite

Lunch available
Evening meal available
CC: Amex, Delta, Diners, Mastercard, Switch, Visa

3 nights for the price of 2 (doubles only) from 1 Oct-28 Feb.

STRATFORD-UPON-AVON continued

◆◆◆ BRETT HOUSE
8 Broad Walk, Stratford-upon-Avon CV37 6HS
T: (01789) 266374
F: (01789) 414027
I: www.bretthouse.co.uk

Bedrooms: 1 single, 2 double/twin, 1 triple/multiple
Bathrooms: 3 en suite, 1 private

B&B per night:
S £21.00–£22.00
D £44.00–£46.00

OPEN All year round

In walking distance of the theatre and town centre. Ample parking. Hospitality trays. English, continental and vegetarian breakfasts.

◆◆◆ BROADLANDS GUEST HOUSE
23 Evesham Place, Stratford-upon-Avon CV37 6HT
T: (01789) 299181
F: (01789) 551382
E: broadlands.com@virgin.net

Bedrooms: 1 single, 4 double/twin
Bathrooms: 5 en suite

B&B per night:
S £22.00–£35.00
D £44.00–£60.00

OPEN All year round

Victorian house in Old Town conservation area. Friendly atmosphere. Private parking. Complimentary tea/coffee facilities all rooms. 5-10 minutes' walk town centre/theatres/station.

◆◆◆◆ BURTON FARM

Bishopton, Stratford-upon-Avon CV37 0RW
T: (01789) 293338
F: (01789) 262877
E: tony.crook@ukonline.co.uk

B&B per night:
S £35.00–£38.00
D £50.00–£55.00

OPEN All year round

150-acre mixed farm with Elizabethan farmhouse. It has large gardens which include a collection of interesting plants, designed to encourage wildlife, such as birds and frogs. Situated in rural surroundings, 1.5 miles from Stratford-upon-Avon.

Bedrooms: 1 single, 3 double/twin, 1 triple/multiple
Bathrooms: 4 en suite, 1 private

◆◆◆ CHURCH FARM

Dorsington, Stratford-upon-Avon CV37 8AX
T: (01789) 720471 & 07831 504194
F: (01789) 720830
E: chfarmdorsington@aol.com
I: www.churchfarmstratford.co.uk

Bedrooms: 5 double/twin, 2 triple/multiple
Bathrooms: 6 en suite, 1 private

B&B per night:
S £24.00–£26.00
D £40.00–£43.00

OPEN All year round

127-acre mixed farm. Situated on Heart of England Way, in pretty village. Most rooms en suite, TV, tea and coffee facilities. Close Stratford-upon-Avon, Warwick, Cotswolds, Evesham.

◆◆◆ CURTAIN CALL
142 Alcester Road, Stratford-upon-Avon CV37 9DR
T: (01789) 267734
F: (01789) 267734
E: curtaincall@btinternet.com
I: www.curtaincallguesthouse.co.uk

Bedrooms: 2 single, 3 double/twin, 1 triple/multiple
Bathrooms: 4 en suite

Evening meal available
CC: Delta, Mastercard, Switch, Visa

B&B per night:
S £20.00–£30.00
D £45.00–£60.00

HB per person:
DY £37.00–£45.00

OPEN All year round

Ten minutes' walk from town centre. We offer professional service with exacting standards. Friendly, relaxed atmosphere, en suite themed rooms, 4-poster beds, all offering value for money.

RATING All accommodation in this guide has been rated, or is awaiting a rating, by a trained English Tourism Council assessor.

◆◆◆

HIGHCROFT

Banbury Road, Stratford-upon-Avon
CV37 7NF

T: (01789) 296293
F: (01789) 415236
E: suedavies_highcroft@hotmail.com
I: www.Smoothhound.co.uk

B&B per night:
S £25.00–£28.00
D £40.00–£50.00

OPEN All year round

*Lovely country house and converted
barns in 2 acres of landscaped
gardens in the heart of rural
Warwickshire but only 2 miles from
Stratford-upon-Avon and close to
Cotswolds and Warwick. We
welcome you with tea and home-
made cakes and then ask you to
relax and enjoy our home. Rooms
both en suite, sitting room with open
fire.*

Bedrooms: 1 double/
twin, 1 triple/multiple
Bathrooms: 2 en suite

◆◆◆◆◆

HOWARD ARMS

Lower Green, Ilmington, Shipston-
on-Stour CV36 4LT
T: (01608) 682226
F: (01608) 682226
E: howard.arms@virgin.net
I: www.howardarms.com

Bedrooms: 3 double/
twin
Bathrooms: 3 en suite

Lunch available
Evening meal available
CC: Delta, Mastercard,
Switch, Visa

B&B per night:
S Max £50.00
D £80.00–£90.00

HB per person:
DY £58.50–£63.50

*16thC inn set beside village green widely known for good food and our 3 lovely bedrooms.
Delightful garden. Ideal for Stratford-upon-Avon and the Cotswolds.*

OPEN All year round

◆◆◆◆

MELITA PRIVATE HOTEL

37 Shipston Road, Stratford-upon-Avon
CV37 7LN

T: (01789) 292432
F: (01789) 204867
E: Melita37@email.msn.com
I: www.melitahotel.co.uk

B&B per night:
S £37.00–£59.00
D £52.00–£82.00

OPEN All year round

*Once a Victorian home, the Melita is
now a warm and friendly hotel
managed by caring proprietors.
Accommodation and service are of a
high standard, and breakfasts are
individually prepared to suit guests'
requirements. The Melita is only 400
metres from the theatres and town
centre and has free private on-site
car parking.*

Bedrooms: 3 single,
7 double/twin, 2 triple/
multiple
Bathrooms: 10 en suite,
2 private

CC: Amex, Delta,
Mastercard, Switch, Visa

Discounts available Nov-Mar 2002, excl Sat and
locally important dates.

◆◆◆

MOONLIGHT BED & BREAKFAST

144 Alcester Road, Stratford-upon-
Avon CV37 9DR
T: (01789) 298213

Bedrooms: 1 single,
2 double/twin, 1 triple/
multiple
Bathrooms: 2 en suite

B&B per night:
S £16.00–£18.00
D £34.00–£36.00

OPEN All year round

*Small family guesthouse near town centre and station, offering comfortable
accommodation at reasonable prices. Tea/coffee-making facilities, colour TV. En suite
rooms available.*

CHECK THE MAPS

The colour maps at the front of this guide show all the cities, towns
and villages for which you will find accommodation entries.
Refer to the town index to find the page on which they are listed.

◆◆◆◆ **MOSS COTTAGE**

61 Evesham Road, Stratford-upon-Avon CV37 9BA
T: (01789) 294770
F: (01789) 294770
E: pauline_rush@onetel.net.uk

Bedrooms: 2 double/twin
Bathrooms: 2 en suite

B&B per night:
S £35.00
D £42.00–£44.00

OPEN All year round

Pauline and Jim Rush welcome you to their charming detached cottage. Walking distance theatre/town. Spacious en suite accommodation. Hospitality tray, TV. Parking.

◆◆◆◆ **THE MYRTLES BED AND BREAKFAST**

6 Rother Street, Stratford-upon-Avon CV37 6LU
T: (01789) 295511

Bedrooms: 3 double/twin
Bathrooms: 3 en suite

CC: Mastercard, Visa

B&B per night:
S £35.00–£40.00
D £55.00–£57.50

OPEN All year round

Victorian house opposite market square. En suite bedrooms are immaculate, bright and prettily furnished and have a range of quality toiletries. Cosy breakfast room with attractive patio.

◆◆◆

OXSTALLS FARM

Warwick Road, Stratford-upon-Avon
CV37 0NS
T: (01789) 205277 & 730224
F: (01789) 205277

B&B per night:
S £28.00–£38.00
D £44.00–£64.00

OPEN All year round

Thoroughbred stud farm overlooking the beautiful Welcombe Hills and golf course. Situated 1 mile from Stratford-upon-Avon and easy access to NEC, M40 etc. Delightful en suite rooms, many with 4-poster beds in The Barn or Cowshed complex. Ideal location for touring the Cotswolds or exploring Warwick Castle and Stratford-upon-Avon.

Bedrooms: 1 single, 15 double/twin, 7 triple/multiple
Bathrooms: 16 en suite

◆◆◆ **PARKFIELD**

3 Broad Walk, Stratford-upon-Avon CV37 6HS
T: (01789) 293313
F: (01789) 293313
E: parkfield@btinternet.com
I: www.parkfieldbandb.co.uk

Bedrooms: 1 single, 5 double/twin, 1 triple/multiple
Bathrooms: 6 en suite, 1 private

CC: Diners, Mastercard, Visa

B&B per night:
S £25.00–£26.00
D £45.00–£48.00

OPEN All year round

Delightful Victorian house. Quiet location, 5 minutes' walk from theatre and town. Most rooms en suite. Colour TV, tea and coffee facilities and parking. Choice of breakfast, including vegetarian. A non-smoking house.

◆◆◆ **QUILT AND CROISSANTS**

33 Evesham Place, Stratford-upon-Avon CV37 6HT
T: (01789) 267629
F: (01789) 551651
E: rooms@quilt-croissants.demon.co.uk
I: www.smoothhound.co.uk/hotels/quilt.html

Bedrooms: 3 single, 3 double/twin, 2 triple/multiple
Bathrooms: 6 en suite

Evening meal available

B&B per night:
S £16.00–£30.00
D £40.00–£50.00

OPEN All year round

Young, family-run business in Victorian premises in the heart of Stratford-upon-Avon. Comfortable, tastefully decorated and only five minutes from the centre of town.

WHERE TO STAY
Please mention this guide when making your booking.

♦♦♦

RAVENHURST
2 Broad Walk, Stratford-upon-Avon
CV37 6HS
T: (01789) 292515
E: ravaccom@waverider.co.uk
I: www.ravenhurstguesthouse.co.uk

B&B per night:
D £44.00–£50.00

OPEN All year round

Victorian townhouse built in 1865, quiet location, a few minutes' walk from town centre, historical buildings and Royal Shakespeare Theatre. Comfortable home. Breakfasts a speciality. Off-street parking available. All bedrooms en suite, non-smoking. Richard Workman and family offer you a warm welcome and a vast amount of local knowledge.

Bedrooms: 5 double/
twin
Bathrooms: 5 en suite

CC: Amex, Mastercard,
Visa

♦♦♦ **SALAMANDER GUEST HOUSE**

40 Grove Road, Stratford-upon-
Avon CV37 6PB
T: (01789) 205728 & 297843
F: (01789) 205728
E: sejget@nova88.freeserve.co.uk

Bedrooms: 1 single,
2 double/twin, 4 triple/
multiple
Bathrooms: 4 en suite,
1 private

CC: Delta, Mastercard,
Switch, Visa

B&B per night:
S £20.00–£28.00
D £40.00–£56.00

OPEN All year round

5 minutes' walk from the town centre, the Royal Shakespeare Theatre and many historic houses. Close to railway and bus stations.

See South of England region for entries

♦♦♦

DOWNFIELD HOTEL
134 Cainscross Road, Stroud GL5 4HN
T: (01453) 764496
F: (01453) 753150
E: messenger@downfieldotel.demon.co.uk
I: www.downfieldotel.demon.co.uk

B&B per night:
S £28.00–£43.00
D £40.00–£55.00

HB per person:
DY £40.00–£50.00

OPEN All year round

Set in the heart of the beautiful south Cotswolds, this is a favourite for thousands of guests. Whether you are staying for a few days, exploring the surrounding hills and valleys and the numerous attractions or breaking a long journey, you can enjoy warm hospitality, home-cooked food, spacious lounges and cosy bar.

Bedrooms: 4 single,
16 double/twin, 1 triple/
multiple
Bathrooms: 11 en suite

Evening meal available
CC: Amex, Delta,
Mastercard, Switch, Visa

♦♦♦♦ **PRETORIA VILLA**

Wells Road, Eastcombe, Stroud
GL6 7EE
T: (01452) 770435
F: (01452) 770435
E: Glynis@G.salomon.freeserve.co.
uk

Bedrooms: 1 single,
2 double/twin
Bathrooms: 1 en suite,
2 private

Evening meal available

B&B per night:
S £22.00
D £44.00

HB per person:
DY £35.00

OPEN All year round

Cotswold-stone double-fronted detached house, built c1900, with private gardens. In quiet village lane with beautiful views.

◆◆◆ **FALCON HOTEL**

Holyhead Road, Wellington, Telford TF1 2DD T: (01952) 255011 E: falconhotel@hotmail.com	Bedrooms: 2 single, 8 double/twin, 1 triple/ multiple Bathrooms: 8 en suite	Lunch available Evening meal available CC: Delta, Mastercard, Visa

Small, family-run 18thC coaching hotel, 10 miles from Shrewsbury, 4 miles from Ironbridge, 18 miles from M6 at the end of M54 (exit 7).

B&B per night:
S £31.00–£42.00
D £39.00–£51.00

OPEN All year round

 🐴 ☐ ⅃ ♈ 🅂 🄿 ▥ 🍴 ⚑ 🐎 🏠 P

◆◆◆ **GROVE HOUSE GUESTHOUSE**

Stafford Street, St Georges, Telford TF2 9JW T: (01952) 616140 F: (01952) 616140	Bedrooms: 3 single, 5 double/twin Bathrooms: 7 en suite, 1 private

Originally built as a hunting lodge. Close to Telford town centre/Exhibition centre/ Ironbridge. Accessed from junction 4, M54. Centrally situated for Shropshire attractions.

B&B per night:
S £22.00–£28.00
D £38.00

OPEN All year round

🐴 ⛵ ▤ ☐ ♈ 🄿 ▥ ⚑ 🐎 P

◆◆◆◆ **THE MILL HOUSE**

Shrewsbury Road, High Ercall, Telford TF6 6BE T: (01952) 770304 F: (01952) 770394 E: mill-house@talk21.com I: www.virtual-shropshire.co.uk/ millhouse	Bedrooms: 1 double/ twin, 1 triple/multiple

A Grade II Listed watermill (no machinery) incorporating a working smallholding and family home, beside River Roden. Convenient for Ironbridge, Shrewsbury and mid Wales.

B&B per night:
S £30.00–£35.00
D £40.00–£45.00

OPEN All year round

🐴 ▤ ♈ 🅂 ▥ 🍴 ⚑ ⚓ 🐎 🏠 P

◆◆◆◆ **THE OLD VICARAGE COUNTRY HOUSE**

Church Street, St George's, Telford TF2 9LZ
T: (01952) 616437
F: (01952) 616952
E: skristian@aol.com
I: www.oldvicarage.uk.com

Charming 1860 period vicarage set in extensive picturesque gardens and countryside location. Enjoy a warm welcome and a comfortable, relaxing stay with a breakfast never to be forgotten. Just minutes from Telford town centre and the M54. Within easy reach of Ironbridge, Weston Park and many other tourist attractions.

Bedrooms: 1 single, 5 double/twin, 1 triple/ multiple; suites available Bathrooms: 5 en suite, 1 private	CC: Delta, Mastercard, Switch, Visa

B&B per night:
S £30.00–£35.00
D £45.00–£50.00

OPEN All year round

🐴 ⛵ ▤ ☐ ♈ 🅂 🄿 ▥ 🍴 🐎 🏠 P

◆◆◆◆ **ELLIOTT HOUSE FARM**

Vine Lane, Kyre, Tenbury Wells WR15 8RL T: (01885) 410302 & 07836 533049 F: (01885) 410240	Bedrooms: 2 double/ twin Bathrooms: 2 en suite	Lunch available Evening meal available

Beautiful modern farmhouse offering luxurious accommodation, with spacious lounge and conservatory, it boasts spectacular views. We offer real farmhouse cooking using home produced products.

B&B per night:
S Min £25.00
D Min £38.00

HB per person:
DY Min £31.50

OPEN All year round

🐴 ☐ ♈ 🅂 🄿 ▥ 🍴 ⚑ 🐎 P

SPECIAL BREAKS

Many establishments offer special promotions and themed breaks. These are highlighted in red. (All such offers are subject to availability.)

TETBURY, Gloucestershire Map ref 2B2 *Tourist Information Centre Tel: (01666) 503552*

FOLLY FARM COTTAGES

Long Newnton, Tetbury GL8 8XA	Bedrooms: 1 single,	CC: Mastercard, Switch,
T: (01666) 502475	3 double/twin	Visa
F: (01666) 502358	Bathrooms: 4 en suite	
E: info@gtb.co.uk		
I: www.gtb.co.uk		

B&B per night:
S £35.00–£45.00
D £45.00

OPEN All year round

220-acre dairy farm.Queen Anne farmhouse, just 3 minutes' walk into Royal Tetbury and close to M4 and M5 motorways. Resident host.

TEWKESBURY, Gloucestershire Map ref 2B1 *Tourist Information Centre Tel: (01684) 295027*

ABBOTS COURT FARM
Church End, Twyning, Tewkesbury
GL20 6DA
T: (01684) 292515
F: (01684) 292515
E: bernieabbotscourt.fsbusiness.co.uk

B&B per night:
S £21.00–£23.00
D £36.00–£40.00

OPEN All year round

450-acre arable and dairy farm. Large, comfortable farmhouse in excellent touring area. Most rooms en suite. Three games rooms, grass tennis court, fishing lakes.

Bedrooms: 1 single,
3 double/twin, 4 triple/
multiple
Bathrooms: 6 en suite

Rating Applied For

TOWN STREET FARM
Tirley, Gloucester GL19 4HG
T: (01452) 780442
F: (01452) 780890
E: townstreetfarm@hotmail.com

B&B per night:
S £25.00–£26.00
D £44.00–£45.00

OPEN All year round

A friendly welcome awaits you at our 18thC farmhouse close to the River Severn. Unspoilt views of our 500 acres of grassland on which we farm mostly cattle with a few horses and sheep. The comfortable en suite bedrooms and full English breakfasts will complement your stay.

Bedrooms: 2 double/
twin, 1 triple/multiple
Bathrooms: 2 en suite,
1 private

TISSINGTON, Derbyshire Map ref 4B2

BASSETT WOOD FARMHOUSE BED AND BREAKFAST

Bassett Wood Farm, Tissington,	Bedrooms: 2 double/	Lunch available
Ashbourne DE6 1RD	twin, 1 triple/multiple	
T: (01335) 350254	Bathrooms: 2 en suite,	
E: janet@bassettwood.freeserve.co.uk	1 private	
I: www.peakdistrictfarmhols.co.uk		

B&B per night:
S £30.00–£55.00
D £50.00–£60.00

OPEN All year round

160-acre dairy and livestock farm. A working farm, twice a day milking. Pets paddock. Light snacks available. Warm friendly farming family welcome you.

MAP REFERENCES The map references refer to the colour maps at the front of this guide. The first figure is the map number; the letter and figure which follow indicate the grid reference on the map.

◆◆◆◆

TILTRIDGE FARM AND VINEYARD

Upper Hook Road, Upton-upon-Severn, Worcester WR8 0SA
T: (01684) 592906
F: (01684) 594142
E: elgarwine@aol.com

B&B per night:
S £28.00–£30.00
D £44.00–£48.00

OPEN All year round

Sympathetically restored Georgian farmhouse between Malvern Hills and the attractive riverside town of Upton-on-Severn. Set in vineyards. One double, one twin and one family room, all en suite with TV. Bumper breakfast with our own eggs, homemade preserves and locally sourced produce. Free wine tasting. Three counties showground four minutes away.

Bedrooms: 2 double/ twin, 1 triple/multiple
Bathrooms: 3 en suite

Third night at a cheaper rate. Free wine tasting.

◆◆◆◆
Silver Award

UPPER GILVACH FARM

St. Margarets, Vowchurch, Hereford HR2 0QY
T: (01981) 510618
F: (01981) 510618
E: ruth@uppergilvach.freeserve.co.uk
I: www.golden-valley.co.uk/gilvach

B&B per night:
S Min £30.00
D £50.00–£60.00

HB per person:
DY £39.00–£45.00

OPEN All year round

A warm welcome awaits you on this family farm between the Golden Valley and Black Mountains. The 300-year-old farmhouse offers 3 spacious, attractively furnished bedrooms, all en suite with colour TV and hospitality tray. Delicious evening meals and hearty farmhouse breakfasts using local wines and produce. Plenty of parking. Licensed.

Bedrooms: 1 single, 1 double/twin, 1 triple/ multiple
Bathrooms: 2 en suite, 1 private

Evening meal available
CC: Mastercard, Switch, Visa

◆◆◆
AUSTIN HOUSE
96 Emscote Road, Warwick CV34 5QJ
T: (01926) 493583
F: (01926) 493679
E: mike@austinhouse96.freeserve.co.uk

Bedrooms: 1 single, 4 double/twin, 2 triple/ multiple; suites available
Bathrooms: 5 en suite

CC: Delta, Mastercard, Visa

B&B per night:
S £19.00–£23.00
D £38.00–£46.00

OPEN All year round

Black and white Victorian house 1 mile from Warwick town and Castle. Three miles from Royal Leamington Spa, 8 miles from Stratford-upon-Avon.

◆◆◆◆
Silver Award

THE COACH HOUSE
Old Budbrooke Road, Budbrooke, Warwick CV35 7DU
T: (01926) 410893
F: (01926) 490453
E: johnmannion@hotmail.com

Bedrooms: 3 double/ twin
Bathrooms: 1 en suite, 1 private

B&B per night:
S £33.00–£40.00
D £46.00–£58.00

Elegant c1820 coach house conversion in rural setting, 1 mile from Warwick town centre, 8 miles from Stratford-upon-Avon. Convenient for NEC/NAC. Friendly atmosphere. French and German spoken.

HALF BOARD PRICES Half board prices are given per person, but in some cases these may be based on double/twin occupancy.

◆◆◆◆

THE CROFT GUESTHOUSE
Haseley Knob, Warwick CV35 7NL
T: (01926) 484447
F: (01926) 484447
E: david@croftguesthouse.co.uk
I: www.croftguesthouse.co.uk

B&B per night:
S Min £34.00
D Min £46.00

OPEN All year round

A non-smoking, friendly family guesthouse providing high quality clean and comfortable en suite accommodation at reasonable prices. Centrally located (off A4177) for exploring Warwick, Stratford, Coventry and Kenilworth, or for visiting NEC (15 minutes), National Agricultural Centre (15 minutes). Sky TV, fax and e-mail facilities. More details on our website.

Bedrooms: 2 single, 3 double/twin, 2 triple/ multiple
Bathrooms: 6 en suite, 1 private

CC: Amex, Delta, Mastercard, Switch, Visa

 🐴 🚗 📧 🖥 💧 🍷 Ⓢ ✂ 🖨 💻 🛏 ⌲ ✳ 🐴 🐎 P

◆◆◆◆

Silver Award

FORTH HOUSE
44 High Street, Warwick CV34 4AX
T: (01926) 401512
F: (01926) 490809
E: info@forthhouseuk.co.uk
I: www.forthhouseuk.co.uk

Bedrooms: 1 double/ twin, 1 triple/multiple; suites available
Bathrooms: 2 en suite

CC: Delta, Mastercard, Switch, Visa

B&B per night:
S £40.00–£48.00
D £60.00–£70.00

OPEN All year round

Ground floor and first floor guest suites with private sitting rooms and bathrooms. At the back of the house, overlooking peaceful garden, in town centre.

🐴 🚗 📧 🖥 💧 🍷 Ⓢ ✂ 🖨 💻 🛏 ⌲ U ⌲ ✳ 🐎 🏠 P

◆◆◆◆

HIGH HOUSE
Old Warwick Road, Rowington, Warwick CV35 7AA
T: (01926) 843270 & 0774 8592656
F: (01926) 843689

B&B per night:
S Max £40.00
D Max £60.00

OPEN All year round

Beautiful country house built 1690. Beamed rooms, open fireplaces and gorgeous 4-poster beds. Magnificent secluded rural postition with outstanding views and excellent walks. Super breakfasts. Convenient for NEC, Birmingham, NAC, Kenilworth, Warwick Castle, Stratford, National Trust Houses and Warwick University.

Bedrooms: 3 double/ twin
Bathrooms: 3 en suite

🏠 📧 🖥 💧 🍷 Ⓢ ✂ 🖨 💻 🛏 ⌲ U ✳ 🐎 🏠 P

TOWN INDEX
This can be found at the back of the guide. If you know where you want to stay, the index will give you the page number listing accommodation in your chosen town, city or village.

WARWICK continued

◆◆◆◆
Silver
Award

LOWER ROWLEY
Wasperton, Warwick CV35 8EB
T: (01926) 624937
F: (01926) 620053
E: cliffordveasey@lower-rowley.freeserve.
co.uk

B&B per night:
S £25.00–£35.00
D £45.00–£48.00

OPEN All year round

Peace and quiet in luxurious non-smoking accommodation, 4 miles from Warwick and 6 miles from Stratford-upon-Avon. Beautiful rural surroundings, with River Avon at bottom of the garden. En suite accommodation with colour TV, hostess tray, hairdryer and many more extras to make your stay enjoyable.

Bedrooms: 2 double/twin
Bathrooms: 1 en suite, 1 private

Reduction for 3 nights or more.

◆◆◆◆
Silver
Award

NORTHLEIGH HOUSE
Five Ways Road, Hatton, Warwick
CV35 7HZ
T: (01926) 484203 & 07774 101894
F: (01926) 484006
I: www.northleigh.co.uk

B&B per night:
S £36.00–£43.00
D £52.00–£62.00

Comfortable, peaceful country house where the freshly decorated rooms are individually designed, each having an en suite bathroom, TV, fridge and kettle and many thoughtful extras. A full English breakfast is specially cooked to suit each guest. Handy for Warwick, Stratford-upon-Avon and the Exhibition Centres.

Bedrooms: 1 single, 6 double/twin
Bathrooms: 7 en suite

CC: Mastercard, Visa

◆◆◆◆
Silver
Award

SHREWLEY POOLS FARM
Haseley, Warwick CV35 7HB
T: (01926) 484315
E: cathydodd@hotmail.com
I: www.s-h-systems.co.uk/hotels/shrewley.html

B&B per night:
S £30.00–£45.00
D £45.00–£55.00

HB per person:
DY £40.00–£60.00

OPEN All year round

Glorious 17thC traditional family farmhouse with log fires, oak floors, beams, etc, set in an acre of outstanding garden featuring herbaceous borders and unusual trees and shrubs. Two spacious en suite bedrooms and own sitting room with books and games. Perfectly situated for numerous attractions. Surrounded by picturesque farmland.

Bedrooms: 1 double/twin, 1 triple/multiple
Bathrooms: 2 en suite

Evening meal available

Stay 3 nights, 2 people sharing and get fishing half price.

◆◆◆◆

THE TILTED WIG
11 Market Place, Warwick CV34 4SA
T: (01926) 410466 & 411740
F: (01926) 495740

Bedrooms: 4 double/twin
Bathrooms: 4 en suite

Lunch available
Evening meal available
CC: Amex, Delta, Diners, Mastercard, Switch, Visa

B&B per night:
S £55.00
D £55.00

OPEN All year round

Grade II Listed building situated comfortably in the market place, blending in with the town's historic architecture. A cafe bar, brasserie, wine bar atmosphere.

WARWICK continued

♦♦♦

WOODSIDE
Langley Road, Claverdon, Warwick
CV35 8PJ
T: (01926) 842446
F: (01926) 843697
E: ab021@dial.pipex.com

Bedrooms: 4 double/
twin, 1 triple/multiple
Bathrooms: 1 en suite

Evening meal available

B&B per night:
S £27.00–£30.00
D £50.00–£60.00

HB per person:
DY £40.00–£43.00

OPEN All year round

Charming country house with acres of garden and woodland nature reserve. Full central heating, open fires, good home cooking. Very central for Stratford-upon-Avon and Warwick.

WATERHOUSES, Staffordshire Map ref 4B2

♦♦♦♦
Silver
Award

LEE HOUSE FARM
Leek Road, Waterhouses, Stoke-on-
Trent ST10 3HW
T: (01538) 308439

Bedrooms: 3 double/
twin
Bathrooms: 3 en suite

B&B per night:
S £30.00
D £40.00–£50.00

OPEN All year round

Charming 18thC house in centre of a Staffordshire Moorlands village in Peak National Park. Ideal for Derbyshire Dales, Potteries and Alton Towers.

WELLAND, Worcestershire Map ref 2B1

♦♦♦♦

THE LOVELLS
Welland, Malvern WR13 6NF
T: (01684) 310795

Bedrooms: 1 double/
twin
Bathrooms: 1 private

B&B per night:
S Min £27.50
D Min £55.00

A renovated farmhouse featured in 25 Beautiful Homes magazine. Wonderful views to Bredon/Malvern Hills, 2 miles to Three Counties showground.

WENTNOR, Shropshire Map ref 4A3

♦♦♦♦

CROWN INN
Wentnor, Bishop's Castle SY9 5EE
T: (01588) 650613
F: (01588) 650436
E: crowninn@wentnor.com
I: www.wentnor.com

B&B per night:
S £27.50–£31.00
D £52.00–£54.00

HB per person:
DY £42.50–£60.00

OPEN All year round

Traditional 16thC country inn with log fires, beams and horse brasses. Set in the rolling hills of South Shropshire with easy access to Midland Gliding Club, several golf clubs, trout fishing, horse riding and hill walking. Guaranteed warm welcome in this family-run establishment.

Bedrooms: 3 double/
twin
Bathrooms: 2 en suite,
1 private

Lunch available
Evening meal available
CC: Delta, Mastercard,
Switch, Visa

WIGMORE, Herefordshire Map ref 4A3

♦♦♦♦

PEAR TREE FARM
Wigmore, Leominster HR6 9UR
T: (01568) 770140 & 770141
F: (01568) 770140
E: steveandjill@peartreefarmco.
freeserve.co.uk
I: www.peartreefarmco.freeserve.
co.uk

Bedrooms: 3 double/
twin
Bathrooms: 2 en suite,
1 private

Lunch available
Evening meal available

B&B per night:
S £30.00–£45.00
D £50.00–£70.00

HB per person:
DY £60.00–£70.00

OPEN All year round

17thC Listed farmhouse 7 miles from historic Ludlow. Flavours of Herefordshire Guesthouse of the Year 2000. Superior en suite accommodation and 4-course dinner. Licensed.

IDEAS For ideas on places to visit refer to the introduction at the beginning of this section.

◆◆◆

THE WHITE HART INN AND RESTAURANT

High Street, Winchcombe, Cheltenham
GL54 5LJ
T: (01242) 602359 & 609220
F: (01242) 602703
E: enquiries@the-white-hart-inn.com
I: www.the-white-hart-inn.co.uk

B&B per night:
S £40.00–£70.00
D £55.00–£95.00

HB per person:
DY £50.00–£70.00

OPEN All year round

Charming 16thC family-run coaching inn. Centrally located in historic Winchcombe. Ideal for touring the Cotswolds, within easy reach of Cheltenham, Broadway and Stratford. Brasserie-style restaurant serving continental and Scandinavian cuisine using fresh, local produce. Extensive bar snack menu also available. Eight individually decorated en suite rooms.

Bedrooms: 6 double/ twin, 2 triple/multiple
Bathrooms: 8 en suite

Lunch available
Evening meal available
CC: Delta, Mastercard, Switch, Visa

Two-night break. Accommodation, breakfast, 1 night's dinner, entrance to Sudeley Castle and Gardens. Third night discount.

🐕🏠📞🖥️♿🍷S✕🏛️🛏️🍴🍷🖊️☼🐴🚗🖧🏦P

◆◆◆◆

BRAE COTTAGE
East Bank, Winster, Matlock
DE4 2DT
T: (01629) 650375

Bedrooms: 2 double/ twin
Bathrooms: 2 en suite

B&B per night:
D £40.00–£60.00

OPEN All year round

18thC cottage in tranquil surroundings. Picturesque village in Peak District National Park. En suite accommodation, separate from cottage, furnished to high standard. Private courtyard parking.

♫🐕♿🖥️📞♿🍷S✕🛏️☼🐴🚗🏦P

◆◆◆

ASH HOUSE
The Gravel, Wishaw,
Sutton Coldfield B76 9QB
T: (01675) 475782 & 07850 414000
E: kate@rectory80.freeserve.co.uk

Bedrooms: 3 single, 2 double/twin, 1 triple/ multiple
Bathrooms: 4 en suite, 1 private

CC: Delta, Mastercard, Visa

B&B per night:
S £30.00–£35.00
D £50.00–£60.00

OPEN All year round

Former rectory with lovely views. Few minutes' walk from Belfry Golf and Leisure Hotel. Half a mile M42, 10 minutes' drive from Birmingham Airport/NEC.

🐕5🖥️♿🍷S✕🏛️🛏️◡🖊️🚗🏦P

See South of England region for entries

◆◆

CLAREMONT GUESTHOUSE
9-11 Witham Road, Woodhall Spa
LN10 6RW
T: (01526) 352000

Bedrooms: 2 single, 3 double/twin, 5 triple/ multiple
Bathrooms: 3 en suite

Evening meal available

B&B per night:
S £15.00–£20.00
D £30.00–£40.00

OPEN All year round

Homely B&B in unspoilt Victorian guesthouse within easy reach of the town's sporting and leisure facilities. Off-street car parking. Good choice of food nearby.

🐕♿🖥️♿S🍴🍷☼🐴🚗P

See South of England region for entries

◆◆◆

FORESTERS GUEST HOUSE
2 Chestnut Walk, Worcester
WR1 1PP
T: (01905) 20348
F: (01905) 20348

Bedrooms: 1 single, 8 double/twin
Bathrooms: 7 en suite

Evening meal available

B&B per night:
S £20.00–£30.00
D £40.00–£50.00

OPEN All year round

Close to city centre and bus and rail stations, away from main road. Cricket ground, racecourse, sports complex all within easy walking distance.

🐕3♿🖥️📞♿🍷S✕🏛️🍴☼🐴🚗P

WORKSOP, Nottinghamshire Map ref 4C2 *Tourist Information Centre Tel: (01909) 501148*

♦♦♦ **SHERWOOD GUESTHOUSE**

57 Carlton Road, Worksop S80 1PP
T: (01909) 474209
F: (01909) 476470
E: CHERWOULD@aol.com

Bedrooms: 1 single,
4 double/twin, 1 triple/
multiple
Bathrooms: 2 en suite

B&B per night:
S £21.00–£26.00
D £42.00–£47.00

OPEN All year round

In Robin Hood Country, near M1 and A1. Close to station and town centre. Comfortable rooms with TV and tea/coffee facilities. Accent on 'service'.

WYE VALLEY

See under Fownhope, Hereford, Much Birch, Ross-on-Wye

YARKHILL, Herefordshire Map ref 2A1

♦♦♦ **GARFORD FARM**

Yarkhill, Hereford HR1 3ST
T: (01432) 890226
F: (01432) 890707
E: garfordfarm@lineone.net

Bedrooms: 1 double/
twin, 1 triple/multiple
Bathrooms: 1 en suite,
1 private

B&B per night:
S £25.00
D £45.00

OPEN All year round

Picturesque black and white farmhouse with comfortable en suite bedrooms. Very quiet but with easy access to the A4103 Hereford/Worcester road. Dogs/horses taken by arrangement.

COUNTRY CODE

Always follow the Country Code ⚘
Enjoy the countryside and respect
its life and work ⚘ Guard against
all risk of fire ⚘ Fasten all gates
⚘ Keep your dogs under close control
⚘ Keep to public paths across
farmland ⚘ Use gates and stiles to
cross fences, hedges and walls ⚘
Leave livestock, crops and machinery
alone ⚘ Take your litter home ⚘
Help to keep all water clean ⚘
Protect wildlife, plants and trees ⚘
Take special care on country roads ⚘
Make no unnecessary noise ⚘

A brief guide to the main Towns and Villages offering accommodation in the

Heart of England

A ALCESTER, WARWICKSHIRE - Town has Roman origins and many old buildings around the High Street. It is close to Ragley Hall, the 18th C Palladian mansion with its magnificent baroque Great Hall.

ALTON, STAFFORDSHIRE - Alton Castle, an impressive 19th C building, dominates the village which is set in spectacular scenery. Nearby is Alton Towers, a romantic 19th C ruin with innumerable tourist attractions within one of England's largest theme parks in its 800 acres of magnificent gardens.

ASHBOURNE, DERBYSHIRE - Market town on the edge of the Peak District National Park and an excellent centre for walking. Its impressive church with 212-ft spire stands in an unspoilt old street. Ashbourne is well-known for gingerbread and its Shrovetide football match.

ASHBY-DE-LA-ZOUCH, LEICESTERSHIRE - Lovely market town with late 15th C church, impressive ruined 15th C castle, an interesting small museum and a wide, sloping main street with Georgian buildings. Twycross Zoo is nearby.

ASHFORD IN THE WATER, DERBYSHIRE - Limestone village in attractive surroundings of the Peak District approached by 3 bridges over the River Wye. There is an annual well-dressing ceremony and the village was well-known in the 18th C for its black marble quarries.

B BAKEWELL, DERBYSHIRE - Pleasant market town, famous for its pudding. It is set in beautiful countryside on the River Wye and is an excellent centre for exploring the Derbyshire Dales, the Peak District National Park, Chatsworth and Haddon Hall.

BALSALL COMMON, WEST MIDLANDS - Close to Birmingham NEC and Kenilworth and within easy reach of Coventry.

BARLOW, DERBYSHIRE - Lying 4 miles north-west of Chesterfield, its recorded history dates back to William the Conqueror. The major event is annual well-dressing week.

BELPER, DERBYSHIRE - Pleasant old market town in the valley of the River Derwent. Attractive scenery and a wealth of industrial history.

BELTON IN RUTLAND, RUTLAND - Conservation village with the oldest church in Rutland. Close to Rutland Water and 'Barnsdale' TV gardens.

BEWDLEY, WORCESTERSHIRE - Attractive town on the River Severn, approached by a bridge designed by Telford. The town has many elegant buildings and an interesting craft and folk museum. On the Severn Valley Steam Railway.

BIBURY, GLOUCESTERSHIRE - Village on the River Coln with stone houses and the famous 17th C Arlington Row, former weavers' cottages. Arlington Mill is now a folk museum. Trout farm and Barnsley House Gardens nearby are open to the public.

BIDFORD-ON-AVON, WARWICKSHIRE - Attractive village with an ancient 8-arched bridge. Riverside picnic area and a main street with some interesting 15th C houses.

BIRDLIP, GLOUCESTERSHIRE - Hamlet at the top of a very steep descent down to the Gloucester Vale with excellent viewpoint over Crickley Hill Country Park.

BIRMINGHAM, WEST MIDLANDS - Britain's second city, whose attractions include Centenary Square and the ICC with Symphony Hall, the NEC, the City Art Gallery, Barber Institute of Fine Arts, 17th C Aston Hall, science and railway museums, Jewellery Quarter, Cadbury World, 2 cathedrals and Botanical Gardens.

BISHOP'S CASTLE, SHROPSHIRE - A 12th C Planned Town with a castle site at the top of the hill and a church at the bottom of the main street. Many interesting buildings with original timber frames hidden behind present day houses. On the Welsh border close to the Clun Forest in quiet, unspoilt countryside.

BLEDINGTON, GLOUCESTERSHIRE - Village close to the Oxfordshire border, with a pleasant green and a beautiful church.

BLOCKLEY, GLOUCESTERSHIRE - This village's prosperity was founded in silk mills and other factories but now it is a quiet, unspoilt place. An excellent centre for exploring pretty Cotswold villages, especially Chipping Campden and Broadway.

BOURTON-ON-THE-WATER, GLOUCESTERSHIRE - The River Windrush flows through this famous Cotswold village which has a green, and cottages and houses of Cotswold stone. Its many attractions include a model village, Birdland, a Motor Museum and the Cotswold Perfumery.

BRACKLEY, NORTHAMPTONSHIRE - Historic market town of mellow stone, with many fine buildings lining the wide High Street and Market Place. Sulgrave Manor (George Washington's ancestral home) and Silverstone Circuit are nearby.

BRIDGNORTH, SHROPSHIRE - Red sandstone riverside town in 2 parts - High and Low - linked by a cliff railway. Much of interest including a ruined Norman keep, half-timbered 16th C houses, Midland Motor Museum and Severn Valley Railway.

BROADWAY, WORCESTERSHIRE - Beautiful Cotswold village called the 'Show village of England', with 16th C stone houses and cottages. Near the village is Broadway Tower with magnificent views over 12 counties and a country park with nature trails and adventure playground.

BROMSGROVE, WORCESTERSHIRE - This market town near the Lickey Hills has an interesting museum and craft centre and 14th C church with fine tombs and a Carillon tower. The Avoncroft Museum of Buildings is nearby where many old buildings have been re-assembled, having been saved from destruction.

BURTON DASSETT, WARWICKSHIRE - The church tower looks out over the site of the Battle of Edgehill and it is said that Cromwell himself climbed the tower to watch the fighting. Nearby is a 16th C beacon tower from which news of the battle was sent.

CREDIT CARD BOOKINGS If you book by telephone and are asked for your credit card number it is advisable to check the proprietor's policy should you cancel your reservation.

BUXTON, DERBYSHIRE - The highest market town in England and one of the oldest spas, with an elegant Crescent, Poole's Cavern, Opera House and attractive Pavilion Gardens. An excellent centre for exploring the Peak District.

☐ CASTLE DONINGTON, LEICESTERSHIRE - A Norman castle once stood here. The world's largest collection of single-seater racing cars is displayed at Donington Park alongside the racing circuit, and an Aeropark Visitor Centre can be seen at nearby East Midlands International Airport.

CHELMARSH, SHROPSHIRE - An unspoilt village near the River Severn, with old timbered cottages and an imposing 14th C church.

CHELTENHAM, GLOUCESTERSHIRE - Cheltenham was developed as a spa town in the 18th C and has some beautiful Regency architecture, in particular the Pittville Pump Room. It holds international music and literature festivals and is also famous for its race meetings and cricket.

CHESTERFIELD, DERBYSHIRE - Famous for the twisted spire of its parish church, Chesterfield has some fine modern buildings and excellent shopping facilities, including a large, traditional open-air market. Hardwick Hall and Bolsover Castle are nearby.

CHIPPING CAMPDEN, GLOUCESTERSHIRE - Outstanding Cotswold wool town with many old stone gabled houses, a splendid church and 17th C almshouses. Nearby are Kiftsgate Court Gardens and Hidcote Manor Gardens (National Trust).

CHURCH STRETTON, SHROPSHIRE - Church Stretton lies under the eastern slope of the Longmynd surrounded by hills. It is ideal for walkers, with marvellous views, golf and gliding. Wenlock Edge is not far away.

CLUN, SHROPSHIRE - Small, ancient town on the Welsh border with flint and stone tools in its museum and Iron Age forts nearby. The impressive ruins of a Norman castle lie beside the River Clun and there are some interesting 17th C houses.

COLEFORD, GLOUCESTERSHIRE - Small town in the Forest of Dean with the ancient iron mines at Clearwell Caves nearby, where mining equipment and geological samples are displayed. There are several forest trails in the area.

COVENTRY, WEST MIDLANDS - Modern city with a long history. It has many places of interest including the post-war and ruined medieval cathedrals, art gallery and museums, some 16th C almshouses, St Mary's Guildhall, Lunt Roman fort and the Belgrade Theatre.

CRAVEN ARMS, SHROPSHIRE - Busy village on A49 renowned for its sheep markets. Close to Wenlock Edge and the Longmynd and an ideal centre for walking with many fine views. Nearby Stokesay Castle, a 13th C fortified manor house, the ruins of Hopton Castle and Ludlow.

☐ DERBY, DERBYSHIRE - Modern industrial city but with ancient origins. There is a wide range of attractions including several museums (notably Royal Crown Derby), a theatre, a concert hall, and the cathedral with fine ironwork and Bess of Hardwick's tomb.

DROITWICH, WORCESTERSHIRE - Old town with natural brine springs, now incorporated into the Brine Baths Health Centre, developed as a spa at the beginning of the 19th C. Of particular interest is the Church of the Sacred Heart with splendid mosaics. Fine parks and a Heritage Centre.

☐ ECKINGTON, WORCESTERSHIRE - Large and expanding village in a fruit growing and market gardening area beside the Avon, which is crossed here by a 15th C bridge. Half-timbered houses are much in evidence.

ELMESTHORPE, LEICESTERSHIRE - Silhouetted against the horizon, the picturesque church of St Mary has a 17th C tower and 12th or 13th C font and is set in a beautiful churchyard with lovely views.

EVESHAM, WORCESTERSHIRE - Market town in the centre of a fruit-growing area. There are pleasant walks along the River Avon and many old houses and inns. A fine 16th C bell tower stands between 2 churches near the medieval Almonry Museum.

☐ FAIRFORD, GLOUCESTERSHIRE - Small town with a 15th C wool church famous for its complete 15th C stained glass windows, interesting carvings and original wall paintings. It is an excellent touring centre and the Cotswolds Wildlife Park is nearby.

FILLONGLEY, WARWICKSHIRE - Small and tranquil farming village in leafy north Warwickshire, retaining its old character and with many old buildings and thatched cottages.

FOWNHOPE, HEREFORDSHIRE - Attractive village close to the River Wye with black and white cottages and other interesting houses. It has a large church with a Norman tower and a 14th C spire.

FRAMPTON-ON-SEVERN, GLOUCESTERSHIRE - Near the River Severn in the Berkeley Vale, the village has a remarkably large green with an interesting range of buildings, the most notable being Frampton Court built around 1733. Beside the Sharpness Canal, close by is Berkeley Castle and Slimbridge Wildfowl Trust.

☐ GLOUCESTER, GLOUCESTERSHIRE - A Roman city and inland port, its cathedral is one of the most beautiful in Britain. Gloucester's many attractions include museums and the restored warehouses in the Victorian docks containing the National Waterways Museum, Robert Opie Packaging Collection and other attractions.

GOTHERINGTON, GLOUCESTERSHIRE - A small village 5 miles north of Cheltenham, at the edge of the Cotswolds, looking towards Langley Hill and Prescott Hill. Famous for the special classic car climbs, close to Tewkesbury and Sudeley Castle.

GRANTHAM, LINCOLNSHIRE - On the old Great North Road (A1), Grantham's splendid parish church has a fine spire and chained library. Sir Isaac Newton was educated here and his statue stands in front of the museum which includes displays on Newton and other famous local people.

GREAT RISSINGTON, GLOUCESTERSHIRE - One of two villages overlooking the River Windrush near Bourton-on-the-Water.

GUITING POWER, GLOUCESTERSHIRE - Unspoilt village with stone cottages and a green. The Cotswold Farm Park, with a collection of rare breeds, an adventure playground and farm trail, is nearby.

☐ HARTINGTON, DERBYSHIRE - Village with a large market-place set in fine surroundings near the River Dove, well-known for its fishing and Izaak Walton, author of 'The Compleat Angler'.

HATHERSAGE, DERBYSHIRE - Hillside village in the Peak District, dominated by the church with many good brasses and monuments to the Eyre family which provide a link with Charlotte Bronte. Little John, friend of Robin Hood, is said to be buried here.

HEREFORD, HEREFORDSHIRE - Agricultural county town, its cathedral containing much Norman work, a large chained library and the world-famous Mappa Mundi exhibition. Among the city's varied attractions are several museums including the Cider Museum and the Old House.

HOLBEACH, LINCOLNSHIRE - Small town, mentioned in the Domesday Book, has splendid 14th C church with a fine tower and spire. The surrounding villages also have interesting churches, and the area is well-known for its bulbfields.

HOPE, DERBYSHIRE - Village in the Hope Valley which is an excellent base for walking in the Peak District and for fishing and shooting. There is a well-dressing ceremony each June and its August sheep dog trials are well-known. Castleton Caves are nearby.

- **HUSBANDS BOSWORTH, LEICESTERSHIRE** - This village is situated at the crossroads between Lutterworth and Market Harborough and the A50, Northampton/Leicester. Stanford Hall is within easy reach.

- ◪ **IRONBRIDGE, SHROPSHIRE** - Small town on the Severn where the Industrial Revolution began. It has the world's first iron bridge built in 1779. The Ironbridge Gorge Museum, of exceptional interest, comprises a rebuilt turn-of-the-century town and sites spread over 6 square miles.

- ◪ **KENILWORTH, WARWICKSHIRE** - The main feature of the town is the ruined 12th C castle. It has many royal associations but was damaged by Cromwell. A good base for visiting Coventry, Leamington Spa and Warwick.

- **KIDDERMINSTER, WORCESTERSHIRE** - The town is the centre for carpet manufacturing. It has a medieval church with good monuments and a statue of Sir Rowland Hill, a native of the town and founder of the penny post. West Midlands Safari Park is nearby. Severn Valley Railway station.

- **KINETON, WARWICKSHIRE** - Attractive old village in rolling countryside. 1 mile from site of famous battle of Edgehill. Medieval church of St Peter.

- ◪ **LEAMINGTON SPA, WARWICKSHIRE** - 18th C spa town with many fine Georgian and Regency houses. The refurbished 19th C Pump Rooms with Heritage Centre. The attractive Jephson Gardens are laid out alongside the river.

- **LECHLADE, GLOUCESTERSHIRE** - Attractive village on the River Thames and a popular spot for boating. It has a number of fine Georgian houses and a 15th C church. Nearby is Kelmscott Manor, with its William Morris furnishings, and 18th C Buscot House (National Trust).

- **LEDBURY, HEREFORDSHIRE** - Town with cobbled streets and many black and white timbered houses, including the 17th C market house and old inns. In attractive countryside nearby is Eastnor Castle, a venue for many events, with an interesting collection of tapestries and armour.

- **LEEK, STAFFORDSHIRE** - Old silk and textile town, with some interesting buildings and a number of inns dating from the 17th C. Its art gallery has displays of embroidery. Brindley Mill, designed by James Brindley, has been restored as a museum.

- **LEICESTER, LEICESTERSHIRE** - Modern industrial city with a wide variety of attractions including Roman remains, ancient churches, Georgian houses and a Victorian clock tower. Excellent shopping precincts, arcades and market, museums, theatres, concert hall and sports and leisure centres.

- **LEOMINSTER, HEREFORDSHIRE** - The town owed its prosperity to wool and has many interesting buildings, notably the timber-framed Grange Court, a former town hall. The impressive Norman priory church has 3 naves and a ducking stool. Berrington Hall (National Trust) is nearby.

- **LICHFIELD, STAFFORDSHIRE** - Lichfield is Dr Samuel Johnson's birthplace and commemorates him with a museum and statue. The 13th C cathedral has 3 spires and the west front is full of statues. Among the attractive town buildings is the Heritage Centre. The Regimental Museum is in Whittington Barracks.

- **LINCOLN, LINCOLNSHIRE** - Ancient city dominated by the magnificent 11th C cathedral with its triple towers. A Roman gateway is still used and there are medieval houses lining narrow, cobbled streets. Other attractions include the Norman castle, several museums and the Usher Gallery.

- **LITTLEDEAN, GLOUCESTERSHIRE** - Village in the Forest of Dean close to the River Severn with magnificent views of the Severn Valley. Traces of a Roman paved road leading to the mines can be seen near the village.

- **LONG BUCKBY, NORTHAMPTONSHIRE** - Stretching for one and a half miles, this is a village with individuality and character.

- **LONGBOROUGH, GLOUCESTERSHIRE** - Cotswold village close to the 18th C Sezincote House built in Indian style, whose gardens are open to the public. The Jacobean Chastleton House with its 17th C topiary garden is also nearby.

- **LONGHOPE, GLOUCESTERSHIRE** - Set in beautiful hilly countryside on the edge of the Forest of Dean, this ancient village is mentioned in the Domesday Book. The church is 12th C and other buildings of historic interest include the medieval Harts Barn.

- **LOUGHBOROUGH, LEICESTERSHIRE** - Industrial town famous for its bell foundry and 47-bell Carillon Tower. The Great Central Railway operates steam railway rides of over 8 miles through the attractive scenery of Charnwood Forest.

- **LUDLOW, SHROPSHIRE** - Outstandingly interesting border town with a magnificent castle high above the River Teme, 2 half-timbered old inns and an impressive 15th C church. The Reader's House, with its 3-storey Jacobean porch, should also be seen.

- ◪ **MALVERN, WORCESTERSHIRE** - Spa town in Victorian times, its water is today bottled and sold worldwide. 6 resorts, set on the slopes of the Hills, form part of Malvern. Great Malvern Priory has splendid 15th C windows. It is an excellent walking centre.

- **MARKET DRAYTON, SHROPSHIRE** - Old market town with black and white buildings and 17th C houses, also acclaimed for its gingerbread. Hodnet Hall is in the vicinity with its beautiful landscaped gardens covering 60 acres.

- **MARKET HARBOROUGH, LEICESTERSHIRE** - There have been markets here since the early 13th C, and the town was also an important coaching centre, with several ancient hostelries. The early 17th C grammar school was once the butter market.

- **MATLOCK, DERBYSHIRE** - The town lies beside the narrow valley of the River Derwent surrounded by steep wooded hills. Good centre for exploring Derbyshire's best scenery.

- **MATLOCK BATH, DERBYSHIRE** - 19th C spa town with many attractions including several caverns to visit, a lead mining museum and a family fun park. There are marvellous views over the surrounding countryside from the Heights of Abraham, to which a cable car gives easy access.

- **MEDBOURNE, LEICESTERSHIRE** - Picturesque village with medieval bridge.

- **MELTON MOWBRAY, LEICESTERSHIRE** - Close to the attractive Vale of Belvoir and famous for its pork pies and Stilton cheese which are the subjects of special displays in the museum. It has a beautiful church with a tower 100 ft high.

- **MERIDEN, WEST MIDLANDS** - Village halfway between Coventry and Birmingham. Said to be the centre of England, marked by a cross on the green.

- **MICKLETON, GLOUCESTERSHIRE** - Mickleton lies in the Vale of Evesham and is close to Hidcote Manor Gardens (National Trust) and to the beautiful Cotswold town of Chipping Campden.

- **MINSTERLEY, SHROPSHIRE** - Village with a curious little church of 1692 and a fine old black and white hall. The lofty ridge known as the Stiperstones is 4 miles to the south.

- **MORETON-IN-MARSH, GLOUCESTERSHIRE** - Attractive town of Cotswold stone with 17th C houses, an ideal base for touring the Cotswolds. Some of the local attractions include Batsford Park Arboretum, the Jacobean Chastleton House and Sezincote Garden.

- **MUCH BIRCH, HEREFORDSHIRE** - Village on the road between Ross-on-Wye and Hereford, with splendid views towards the Black Mountains.

• **MUCH WENLOCK, SHROPSHIRE** - Small town close to Wenlock Edge in beautiful scenery and full of interest. In particular there are the remains of an 11th C priory with fine carving and the black and white 16th C Guildhall.

N NAILSWORTH, GLOUCESTERSHIRE - Ancient wool town with several elegant Jacobean and Georgian houses, surrounded by wooded hillsides with fine views.

• **NAUNTON, GLOUCESTERSHIRE** - A high place on the Windrush, renowned for its wild flowers and with an attractive dovecote.

• **NEWARK, NOTTINGHAMSHIRE** - The town has many fine old houses and ancient inns near the large, cobbled market-place. Substantial ruins of the 12th C castle, where King John died, dominate the riverside walk and there are several interesting museums. Sherwood Forest is nearby.

• **NEWENT, GLOUCESTERSHIRE** - Small town with the largest collection of birds of prey in Europe at the Falconry Centre. Flying demonstrations daily. Glass workshop where visitors can watch glass being blown. There is a seconds shop. North of the village are the Three Choirs Vineyards.

• **NEWLAND, GLOUCESTERSHIRE** - Probably the most attractive of the villages of the Forest of Dean. The church is often referred to as 'the Cathedral of the Forest'; it contains a number of interesting monuments and the Forest Miner's Brass. Almshouses nearby were endowed by William Jones, founder of Monmouth School.

• **NEWPORT, SHROPSHIRE** - Small market town on the Shropshire Union Canal has a wide High Street and a church with some interesting monuments. Newport is close to Aqualate Mere which is the largest lake in Staffordshire.

• **NORTHAMPTON, NORTHAMPTONSHIRE** - A bustling town and a shoe manufacturing centre, with excellent shopping facilities, several museums and parks, a theatre and a concert hall. Several old churches include 1 of only 4 round churches in Britain.

• **NORTHLEACH, GLOUCESTERSHIRE** - Village famous for its beautiful 15th C wool church with its lovely porch and interesting interior. There are also some fine houses including a 17th C wool merchant's house containing Keith Harding's World of Mechanical Music. The Cotswold Countryside Collection is in the former prison.

• **NOTTINGHAM, NOTTINGHAMSHIRE** - Attractive modern city with a rich history. Outside its castle, now a museum, is Robin Hood's statue. Attractions include 'The Tales of Robin Hood'; the Lace Hall; Wollaton Hall; museums and excellent facilities for shopping, sports and entertainment.

• **NUNEATON, WARWICKSHIRE** - Busy town with an art gallery and museum which has a permanent exhibition of the work of George Eliot. The library also has an interesting collection of material. Arbury Hall, a fine example of Gothic architecture, is nearby.

O OAKHAM, LEICESTERSHIRE - Pleasant former county town of Rutland. Fine 12th C Great Hall, part of its castle, with a historic collection of horseshoes. An octagonal Butter Cross stands in the market-place and Rutland County Museum, Rutland Farm Park and Rutland Water are of interest.

P PERSHORE, WORCESTERSHIRE - Attractive Georgian town on the River Avon close to the Vale of Evesham, with fine houses and old inns. The remains of the beautiful Pershore Abbey form the parish church.

• **PRIORS HARDWICK, WARWICKSHIRE** - This tiny village is in peaceful Warwickshire countryside beside the Oxford Union Canal and route of the Walk, situated 5 miles SE of Southam is within easy reach of the many attractions of Stratford, Leamington Spa and Banbury.

R REDMILE, LEICESTERSHIRE - Vale of Belvoir village, overlooked by the hilltop castle.

• **ROSS-ON-WYE, HEREFORDSHIRE** - Attractive market town with a 17th C market hall, set above the River Wye. There are lovely views over the surrounding countryside from the Prospect and the town is close to Goodrich Castle and the Welsh border.

• **RUGBY, WARWICKSHIRE** - Town famous for its public school which gave its name to Rugby Union football and which featured in Tom Brown's Schooldays.

• **RUGELEY, STAFFORDSHIRE** - Town close to Cannock Chase which has over 2,000 acres of heath and woodlands with forest trails and picnic sites. Nearby is Shugborough Hall (National Trust) with a fine collection of 18th C furniture and interesting monuments in the grounds.

S SHIRLEY, DERBYSHIRE - Village in a pretty setting among little hills, with a tiny 14th C church.

• **SHREWSBURY, SHROPSHIRE** - Beautiful historic town on the River Severn retaining many fine old timber-framed houses. Its attractions include Rowley's Museum with Roman finds, remains of a castle, Clive House Museum, St Chad's 18th C round church, rowing on the river and the Shrewsbury Flower Show in August.

• **SKEGNESS, LINCOLNSHIRE** - Famous seaside resort with 6 miles of sandy beaches and bracing air. Attractions include swimming pools, bowling greens, gardens, Natureland Marine Zoo, golf-courses and a wide range of entertainment at the Embassy Centre. Nearby is Gibraltar Point Nature Reserve.

• **SOLIHULL, WEST MIDLANDS** - On the outskirts of Birmingham. Some Tudor houses and a 13th C church remain amongst the new public buildings and shopping centre. The 16th C Malvern Hall is now a school and the 15th C Chester House at Knowle is now a library.

• **SOUTH NORMANTON, DERBYSHIRE** - Village near the Nottinghamshire border and close to Hardwick Hall, Newstead Abbey and the National Tramway Museum at Crich.

• **SOUTH WITHAM, LINCOLNSHIRE** - Well placed for the A1 and easy access to the historic towns of Stamford and Grantham.

• **SOUTHWELL, NOTTINGHAMSHIRE** - Town dominated by the Norman minster which has some beautiful 13th C stone carvings in the Chapter House. Charles I spent his last night of freedom in one of the inns. The original Bramley apple tree can still be seen.

• **STAFFORD, STAFFORDSHIRE** - The town has a long history and some half-timbered buildings still remain, notably the 16th C High House. There are several museums in the town and Shugborough Hall and the famous angler Izaak Walton's cottage, now a museum, are nearby.

• **STAMFORD, LINCOLNSHIRE** - Exceptionally beautiful and historic town with many houses of architectural interest, several notable churches and other public buildings all in the local stone. Burghley House, built by William Cecil, is a magnificent Tudor mansion on the edge of the town.

• **STANTON-ON-THE-WOLDS, NOTTINGHAMSHIRE** - Quiet village with golf course, just off the main route between Nottingham and Melton Mowbray, giving easy access to nearby attractions.

• **STOKE-ON-TRENT, STAFFORDSHIRE** - Famous for its pottery. Factories of several famous makers, including Josiah Wedgwood, can be visited. The City Museum has one of the finest pottery and porcelain collections in the world.

• **STONEHOUSE, GLOUCESTERSHIRE** - Village in the Stroud Valley with an Elizabethan Court, later restored and altered by Lutyens.

• **STOURBRIDGE, WEST MIDLANDS** - Town on the River Stour, famous for its glassworks. Several of the factories can be visited and glassware purchased at the factory shops.

- **STOW-ON-THE-WOLD, GLOUCESTERSHIRE** - Attractive Cotswold wool town with a large market-place and some fine houses, especially the old grammar school. There is an interesting church dating from Norman times. Stow-on-the-Wold is surrounded by lovely countryside and Cotswold villages.

- **STRATFORD-UPON-AVON, WARWICKSHIRE** - Famous as Shakespeare's home town, Stratford's many attractions include his birthplace, New Place where he died, the Royal Shakespeare Theatre and Gallery and Hall's Croft (his daughter's house).

- **STROUD, GLOUCESTERSHIRE** - This old town, surrounded by attractive hilly country, has been producing broadcloth for centuries and the local museum has an interesting display on the subject. Many of the mills have been converted into craft centres.

- **TELFORD, SHROPSHIRE** - New Town named after Thomas Telford, the famous engineer who designed many of the country's canals, bridges and viaducts. It is close to Ironbridge with its monuments and museums to the Industrial Revolution, including restored 18th C buildings.

- **TENBURY WELLS, WORCESTERSHIRE** - Small market town on the Teme possessing many fine black and white buildings. In 1839 mineral springs were found here and there were hopes of a spa centre developing. The waters never became fashionable and today only the old Pump Room remains.

- **TETBURY, GLOUCESTERSHIRE** - Small market town with 18th C houses and an attractive 17th C Town Hall. It is a good touring centre with many places of interest nearby including Badminton House and Westonbirt Arboretum.

- **TEWKESBURY, GLOUCESTERSHIRE** - Tewkesbury's outstanding possession is its magnificent church, built as an abbey, with a great Norman tower and beautiful 14th C interior. The town stands at the confluence of the Severn and Avon and has many medieval houses, inns and several museums.

- **UPTON-UPON-SEVERN, WORCESTERSHIRE** - Attractive country town on the banks of the Severn and a good river cruising centre. It has many pleasant old houses and inns, and the pepperpot landmark is now the Heritage Centre.

- **VOWCHURCH, HEREFORDSHIRE** - Close to the Welsh border, its church has 15 dedications which were all confirmed in one day in 1348.

- **WARWICK, WARWICKSHIRE** - Castle rising above the River Avon, 15th C Beauchamp Chapel attached to St Mary's Church, medieval Lord Leycester's Hospital almshouses and several museums. Nearby is Ashorne Hall Nickelodeon and the National Heritage museum at Gaydon.

- **WATERHOUSES, STAFFORDSHIRE** - Village in the valley of the River Hamps, once the terminus of the Leek and Manifold Light Railway, 8 miles of which is now a macadamised walkers' path.

- **WENTNOR, SHROPSHIRE** - Village near the lovely countryside of the Long Mynd and close to the Welsh border and Offa's Dyke.

- **WIGMORE, HEREFORDSHIRE** - Village with a Norman church and some attractive half-timbered houses. There are the remains of Wigmore Castle and Wigmore Abbey. Croft Castle (National Trust) is nearby.

- **WINCHCOMBE, GLOUCESTERSHIRE** - Ancient town with a folk museum and railway museum. To the south lies Sudeley Castle with its fine collection of paintings and toys and an Elizabethan garden.

- **WINSTER, DERBYSHIRE** - Village with some interesting old gritstone houses and cottages, including the 17th C stone market hall now owned by the National Trust. It is a former lead mining centre.

- **WISHAW, WARWICKSHIRE** - A village with interesting features in the small church, and is now well known as the location of the National Golf Centre within easy reach of jct. 9 of the M42, close to Sutton Coldfield.

- **WOODHALL SPA, LINCOLNSHIRE** - Attractive town which was formerly a spa. It has excellent sporting facilities with a championship golf-course and is surrounded by pine woods.

- **WORCESTER, WORCESTERSHIRE** - Lovely riverside city dominated by its Norman and Early English cathedral, King John's burial place. Many old buildings including the 15th C Commandery and the 18th C Guildhall. There are several museums and the Royal Worcester porcelain factory.

- **WORKSOP, NOTTINGHAMSHIRE** - Market town close to the Dukeries, where a number of Ducal families had their estates, some of which, like Clumber Park, may be visited. The upper room of the 14th C gatehouse of the priory housed the country's first elementary school in 1628.

- **YARKHILL, HEREFORDSHIRE** - Thatched cottages, oasthouses and a medieval church among the old hopfields and orchards.

EAST of England

A region of remote and wild beauty, with vast expanses of open country, unspoilt coastline, sweeping views and big skies. It's renowned for its charming half-timbered towns and villages, ancient sites, historic country houses and nature reserves.

classic sights
Blickling Hall – one of England's great Jacobean houses
Sutton Hoo – important Anglo-Saxon burial site

coast & country
Blakeney Point – good for seal and bird watching
Hatfield Forest – medieval royal hunting forest
Norfolk Broads – miles of waterways through glorious countryside

arts for all
Aldeburgh Festival – classical music in a picturesque setting
Dedham Vale – the landscapes of John Constable; his home and early studio are at East Bergholt. Also the home of Sir Alfred Munnings, famous for his paintings of horses
Sudbury – Gainsborough's house, with fine collection of paintings

delightfully different
Whipsnade Tree Cathedral – unique, 26 acres (10.5ha) cathedral made of trees

The counties of Bedfordshire, Cambridgeshire, Essex, Hertfordshire, Norfolk and Suffolk

FOR MORE INFORMATION CONTACT:
**East of England Tourist Board
Toppesfield Hall, Hadleigh, Suffolk IP7 5DN
Tel: (01473) 822922 Fax: (01473) 823063
Email: eastofenglandtouristboard@compuserve.com
Internet: www.eastofenglandtouristboard.com**

The Pictures:
1 Horsey Mere, Norfolk
2 King's College, Cambridge
3 Norwich

Places to Visit - see pages 308-312
Where to Stay - see pages 313-351

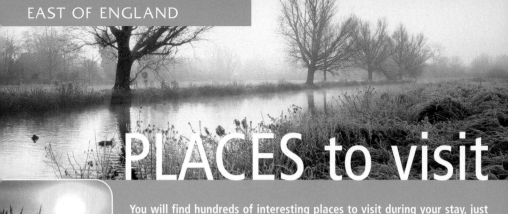

PLACES to visit

You will find hundreds of interesting places to visit during your stay, just some of which are listed in these pages. Contact any Tourist Information Centre in the region for more ideas on days out.

Blickling Hall

Blickling, Norwich, Norfolk NR11 6NF
Tel: (01263) 738030 www.nationaltrust.org.uk
A Jacobean redbrick mansion with garden, orangery, parkland and lake. There is also a display of fine tapestries and furniture.

Audley End House and Park

Audley End, Saffron Walden, Essex CB11 4JF
Tel: (01799) 522399
A palatial Jacobean house remodelled in the 18thC-19thC with a magnificent Great Hall with 17thC plaster ceilings. Rooms and furniture by Robert Adam and park by 'Capability' Brown.

Bressingham Steam Experience and Gardens

Bressingham, Diss, Norfolk IP22 2AB
Tel: (01379) 687386 www.bressingham.co.uk
Steam rides through five miles of woodland. Six acres (2 ha) of the Island Beds plant centre. Mainline locomotives, the Victorian Gallopers and over 50 steam engines.

Banham Zoo

The Grove, Banham, Norwich, Norfolk NR16 2HE
Tel: (01953) 887771 www.banhamzoo.co.uk
Wildlife spectacular which will take you on a journey to experience tigers, leopards and zebra and some of the world's most exotic, rare and endangered animals.

Bure Valley Railway

Aylsham Station, Norwich Road, Aylsham, Norwich, Norfolk NR11 6BW
Tel: (01263) 733858 www.bvrw.co.uk
A 15-inch narrow-gauge steam railway covering nine miles of track from Wroxham, in the heart of the Norfolk Broads, to Aylsham, a bustling market town.

Barleylands Farm

Barleylands Road, Billericay, Essex CM11 2UD
Tel: (01268) 290229
Visitor centre with a rural museum, animal centre, craft studios, blacksmith's shop, glass-blowing studio with a viewing gallery, miniature steam railway and a restaurant.

Colchester Castle

Colchester, Essex CO1 1TJ
Tel: (01206) 282931
www.colchestermuseums.org.uk
A Norman keep on the foundations of a Roman temple. The archaeological material includes much on Roman Colchester (Camulodunum).

Colchester Zoo

Maldon Road, Stanway, Colchester, Essex CO3 5SL
Tel: (01206) 331292 www.colchester-zoo.co.uk
Zoo with 200 species and some of the best cat and primate collections in the UK, 60 acres (27 ha) of gardens and lakes, award-winning animal enclosures and picnic areas.

Ely Cathedral

Chapter House, The College, Ely, Cambridgeshire CB7 4DL
Tel: (01353) 667735
One of England's finest cathedrals with guided tours and tours of the Octagon and West Tower, monastic precincts and also a brass-rubbing centre and Stained Glass Museum.

Fritton Lake Country World

Fritton, Great Yarmouth, Norfolk NR31 9HA
Tel: (01493) 488208
A 250-acre (101-ha) centre with a children's assault course, putting, an adventure playground, golf, fishing, boating, wildfowl, heavy horses, cart rides, falconry and flying displays.

The Gardens of the Rose

The Royal National Rose Society, Chiswell Green, St Albans, Hertfordshire AL2 3NR
Tel: (01727) 850461 www.roses.co.uk
The Royal National Rose Society's Garden with 27 acres (11 ha) of garden and trial grounds for new varieties of rose. Roses of all types displayed with 1,700 different varieties.

Hatfield House, Park and Gardens

Hatfield, Hertfordshire AL9 5NQ
Tel: (01707) 287010 www.hatfield-house.co.uk
Magnificent Jacobean house, home of the Marquess of Salisbury. Exquisite gardens, model soldiers and park trails. Childhood home of Queen Elizabeth I.

Hedingham Castle

Castle Hedingham, Halstead, Essex CO9 3DJ
Tel: (01787) 460261
www.hedinghamcastle@aspects.net
The finest Norman keep in England, built in 1140 by the deVeres, Earls of Oxford. Visited by Kings Henry VII and VIII and Queen Elizabeth I and besieged by King John.

Holkham Hall

Wells-next-the-Sea, Norfolk NR23 1AB
Tel: (01328) 710227 www.holkham.co.uk
A classic 18thC Palladian-style mansion. Part of a great agricultural estate and a living treasure house of artistic and architectural history along with a bygones collection.

Ickworth House, Park and Gardens

The Rotunda, Horringer, Bury St Edmunds, Suffolk IP29 5QE
Tel: (01284) 735270 www.nationaltrust.org.uk
An extraordinary oval house with flanking wings, begun in 1795. Fine paintings, a beautiful collection of Georgian silver, an Italian garden and stunning parkland.

Imperial War Museum

Duxford, Cambridge, Cambridgeshire CB2 4QR
Tel: (01223) 835000 www.iwm.org.uk
Over 180 aircraft on display with tanks, vehicles and guns, an adventure playground, shops and a restaurant.

The Pictures:
1 River Wensum, Norfolk
2 Punting on the River Cam, Cambridge
3 Globe Inn, Linslade, Bedfordshire
4 Thorpeness, Suffolk
5 Tulip fields

Kentwell Hall

Long Melford, Sudbury, Suffolk CO10 9BA
Tel: (01787) 310207 www.kentwell.co.uk
A mellow redbrick Tudor manor surrounded by a moat, this family home has been interestingly restored with Tudor costume displays, a 16thC house and mosaic Tudor rose maze.

Knebworth House, Gardens and Park

Knebworth, Stevenage, Hertfordshire SG3 6PY
Tel: (01438) 812661 www.knebworthhouse.com
Tudor manor house, re-fashioned in the 19thC, housing a collection of manuscripts, portraits and Jacobean banquet hall. Formal gardens and adventure playground.

Leighton Buzzard Railway

Page's Park Station, Billington Road, Leighton Buzzard, Bedfordshire LU/ 4IN
Tel: (01525) 373888 www.buzzrail.co.uk
An authentic narrow-gauge light railway, built in 1919, offering a 65-minute return journey into the Bedfordshire countryside.

Marsh Farm Country Park

Marsh Farm Road, South Woodham Ferrers, Chelmsford, Essex CM3 5WP
Tel: (01245) 321552
www.marshfarmcountrypark.co.uk
A farm centre with sheep, a pig unit, free-range chickens, milking demonstrations, indoor and outdoor adventure play areas, nature reserve, walks, picnic area and pets' corner.

Melford Hall

Long Melford, Sudbury, Suffolk CO10 9AA
Tel: (01787) 880286
www.nationaltrust.org.uk/eastanglia
Turreted brick Tudor mansion with 18thC and Regency interiors. Collection of Chinese porcelain, gardens and a walk in the grounds. Dogs on leads, where permitted.

Minsmere Nature Reserve

Westleton, Saxmundham, Suffolk IP17 3BY
Tel: (01728) 648281 www.rspb.org.uk
RSPB reserve on the Suffolk coast with bird-watching hides and trails, year-round events, guided walk and visitor centre with large shop and welcoming tearooms.

National Horseracing Museum and Tours

99 High Street, Newmarket, Suffolk CB8 8JL
Tel: (01638) 667333 www.nhrm.co.uk
Award-winning display of the people and horses involved in racing's amazing history. Minibus tours to gallops, stables and equine pool. Hands-on gallery with horse simulator.

National Stud

Newmarket, Suffolk CB8 0XE
Tel: (01638) 663464 www.nationalstud.co.uk
A visit to the National Stud consists of a conducted tour which will include top thoroughbred stallions, mares and foals.

Norfolk Lavender Limited

Caley Mill, Heacham, King's Lynn, Norfolk PE31 7JE
Tel: (01485) 570384 www.norfolk-lavender.co.uk
Lavender is distilled from the flowers and the oil made into a wide range of gifts. There is a slide show when the distillery is not working.

Norwich Cathedral

The Close, Norwich, Norfolk NR1 4EH
Tel: (01603) 218321 www.cathedral.org.uk
A Norman cathedral from 1096 with 14thC roof bosses depicting bible scenes from Adam and Eve to the Day of Judgement. Cloisters, cathedral close, shop and restaurant.

Oliver Cromwell's House

29 St Marys Street, Ely, Cambridgeshire CB7 4HF
Tel: (01353) 662062 www.elyeastcambs.co.uk
The family home of Oliver Cromwell with a 17thC kitchen, parlour, a haunted bedroom, a Tourist Information Centre, souvenirs and craft shop.

Peter Beales Roses

London Road, Attleborough, Norfolk NR17 1AY
Tel: (01953) 454707 www.classicroses.co.uk
Two and a half acres (1 ha) of display rose garden set in rural surroundings.

Pleasure Beach

South Beach Parade, Great Yarmouth, Norfolk NR30 3EH
Tel: (01493) 844585
Rollercoaster, Terminator, log flume, Twister, monorail, galloping horses, caterpillar, ghost train and fun house. Height restrictions are in force on some rides.

Pleasurewood Hills Theme Park

Leisure Way, Corton, Lowestoft, Suffolk NR32 5DZ
Tel: (01502) 586000 pleasurewoodhills.co.uk
Crazy coaster, tidal wave watercoaster, log flume, chairlift, two railways, pirate ship, Aladdin's cave, parrot and sea-lion shows, the cannonball express and rattlesnake rides.

Sainsbury Centre for Visual Arts

University of East Anglia, Norwich, Norfolk NR4 7TJ
Tel: (01603) 456060 www.uea.ac.uk/scva
Housing the Sainsbury collection of works by Picasso, Bacon and Henry Moore alongside many objects of pottery and art. Also a cafe and an art bookshop with activities monthly.

Sandringham

Sandringham, King's Lynn, Norfolk PE35 6EN
Tel: (01553) 772675 www.sandringhamestate.co.uk
The country retreat of HM The Queen. A delightful house and 60 acres (24 ha) of grounds and lakes. There is also a museum of royal vehicles and royal memorabilia.

Shuttleworth Collection

Old Warden Aerodrome, Biggleswade, Bedfordshire SG18 9EP
Tel: (01767) 627288 www.shuttleworth.org
A unique historical collection of aircraft, from a 1909 Bleriot to a 1942 Spitfire (in flying condition), and cars, dating from an 1898 Panhard (in running order).

Somerleyton Hall and Gardens

Somerleyton, Lowestoft, Suffolk NR32 5QQ
Tel: (01502) 730224 www.somerleyton.co.uk
Anglo Italian-style mansion with state rooms, a maze, 12-acre (5-ha) gardens with azaleas and rhododendrons, miniature railway, shop and tearooms.

Stondon Museum

Station Road, Lower Stondon, Henlow Camp, Henlow, Bedfordshire SG16 6JN
Tel: (01462) 850339 www.transportmuseum.co.uk
A museum with transport exhibits from the early 1900s to the 1980s. The largest private collection in England of bygone vehicles from the beginning of the century.

Thursford Collection

Thursford Green, Thursford, Fakenham, Norfolk NR21 0AS
Tel: (01328) 878477
Musical evenings some Tuesdays from mid-July to the end of September. A live musical show with nine mechanical organs and a Wurlitzer show starring Robert Wolfe (daily 29 March-mid October).

Whipsnade Wild Animal Park

Dunstable, Bedfordshire LU6 2LF
Tel: (01582) 872171 www.whipsnade.co.uk
Whipsnade Wild Animal Park has over 2,500 animals and is set in 600 acres (243 ha) of beautiful parkland. The Great Whipsnade Railway and free animal demonstrations.

Wimpole Hall and Home Farm

Arrington, Royston, Hertfordshire SG8 0BW
Tel: (01223) 207257 www.wimpole.org
An 18thC house in a landscaped park with a folly, Chinese bridge. Plunge bath and yellow drawing room in the house, the work of John Soane. Home Farm has a rare breeds centre.

Woburn Abbey

Woburn, Milton Keynes, Bedfordshire MK17 9WA
Tel: (01525) 290666 www.woburnabbey.co.uk
An 18thC Palladian mansion, altered by Henry Holland, the Prince Regent's architect, containing a collection of English silver, French and English furniture and art.

Woburn Safari Park

Woburn, Milton Keynes, Bedfordshire MK17 9QN
Tel: (01525) 290407 www.woburnsafari.co.uk
Drive through the safari park with 30 species of animals in natural groups just a windscreen's width away, plus the action-packed Wild World Leisure Area with shows for all.

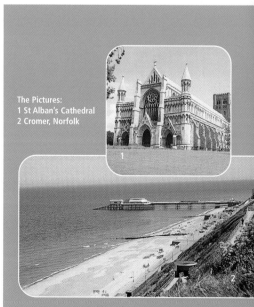

The Pictures:
1 St Alban's Cathedral
2 Cromer, Norfolk

Find out more about the
East of England

Further information about holidays and attractions in the East of England is available from:

EAST OF ENGLAND TOURIST BOARD
Toppesfield Hall, Hadleigh, Suffolk IP7 5DN
Tel: (01473) 822922 Fax: (01473) 823063
Email: eastofenglandtouristboard@compuserve.com
Internet: www.eastofenglandtouristboard.com

The following publications are available from The East of England Tourist Board:

East of England - The Official Guide 2002
an information packed A5 guide featuring all you need to know about places to visit and things to see
and do in the East of England. From historic houses to garden centres, from animal collections to craft
centres - the Guide has it all, including film and TV locations, city, town and village information, events,
shopping, car tours plus lots more! Price £3.99 (excl. p&p)

England's Cycling Country
the East of England offers perfect cycling country - from quiet country lanes to ancient trackways. This
free publication promotes the many Cycling Discovery Maps that are available to buy (£1.50 excl. p&p),
as well as providing useful information for anyone planning a cycling tour of the region

Getting to the
East of England

BY ROAD: The region is easily accessible. From London and the south via the A1, M11,
M25, A10, M1, A46 and A12. From the north via the A17, A1, A15, A5, M1 and A6.
From the west via the A14, A47, A421, A428, A418, A41 and A427.

BY RAIL: Regular fast trains run to all major cities and towns in the region. London
stations which serve the region are Liverpool Street, Kings Cross, Fenchurch Street,
Moorgate, St Pancras, London Marylebone and London Euston. Bedford, Luton and
St Albans are on the Thameslink line which runs to Kings Cross and onto London Gatwick
Airport. There is also a direct link between London Stansted Airport and Liverpool Street.
Through the Channel Tunnel, there are trains direct from Paris and Brussels to Waterloo
Station, London. A short journey on the Underground will bring passengers to those
stations operating services into the East of England. Further information on rail journeys
in the East of England can be obtained on (0845) 748 4950.

Where to stay in the East of England

Accommodation entries in this region are listed in alphabetical order of place name, and then in alphabetical order of establishment.

Map references refer to the colour location maps at front of this guide. The first number indicates the map to use; the letter and number which follow refer to the grid reference on the map.

At-a-glance symbols at the end of each accommodation entry give useful information about services and facilities. A key to symbols can be found inside the back cover flap. Keep this open for easy reference.

A brief description of the towns and villages offering accommodation in the entries which follow, can be found at the end of this section.

A complete listing of all the English Tourism Council assessed accommodation covered by this guide appears at the back of the guide.

ALDBOROUGH, Norfolk Map ref 3B1

◆◆◆ **BUTTERFLY COTTAGE**
The Green, Aldborough, Norwich
NR11 7AA
T: (01263) 768198
F: (01263) 768198

Bedrooms: 1 single,
2 triple/multiple
Bathrooms: 3 en suite

B&B per night:
S £20.00–£22.00
D £40.00

HB per person:
DY £36.00–£38.00

OPEN All year round

On the Weavers Way. Comfortable cottage-style, well-equipped, friendly atmosphere. Rooms overlook large garden or village green. Each has own entrance. Car parking.

🐎 👍 🖵 👌 🐚 S 🏛 🖃 ※ 🏇 🕸 P

ALDEBURGH, Suffolk Map ref 3C2 *Tourist Information Centre Tel: (01728) 453637*

◆◆◆ **LIME TREE HOUSE B&B**
Benhall Green, Saxmundham
IP17 1HU
T: (01728) 602149

Bedrooms: 2 double/
twin

B&B per night:
S £18.00–£25.00
D £40.00–£50.00

HB per person:
DY £25.00–£30.00

OPEN All year round

Old village house behind ivy-covered walls. Large, airy rooms overlooking beautiful gardens in which to wander. Private parking. Good breakfasts. A warm welcome.

🐎 👌 🐚 S ✂ 🍴 🖃 ※ 🏇 🕸 🏨 P

IMPORTANT NOTE Information on accommodation listed in this guide has been supplied by the proprietors. As changes may occur you are advised to check details at the time of booking.

ALDEBY, Norfolk Map ref 3C1

THE OLD VICARAGE

Rectory Road, Aldeby, Beccles
NR34 0BJ
T: (01502) 678229
E: butler@beccles33.freeserve.co.
uk

Bedrooms: 2 double/
twin, 1 triple/multiple
Bathrooms: 1 en suite,
2 private

B&B per night:
S £18.00–£22.00
D £36.00–£40.00

OPEN All year round

Spacious old vicarage, quiet rural location. Convenient for Norfolk Broads, boating, wildlife and bird-watching. Non-smoking, no dogs. Ample parking for cars, bicycles and canoes.

ALDHAM, Essex Map ref 3B2

OLD HOUSE

Ford Street, Aldham, Colchester
CO6 3PH
T: (01206) 240456
F: (01206) 240456

Bedrooms: 1 single,
1 double/twin, 1 triple/
multiple
Bathrooms: 1 en suite,
2 private

CC: Delta, Mastercard,
Visa

B&B per night:
S £27.50–£32.50
D £45.00–£55.00

OPEN All year round

Historic 14thC 'old hall' house. Family home with friendly atmosphere, oak beams, log fires, large garden, ample parking. On A1124 5 miles west of Colchester.

ARDLEIGH, Essex Map ref 3B2

MALTING FARM

Malting Farm Lane, Ardleigh,
Colchester CO7 7QG
T: (01206) 230207

Bedrooms: 1 double/
twin, 1 triple/multiple
Bathrooms: 2 en suite

B&B per night:
S Min £24.00
D Min £40.00

OPEN All year round

Medieval farmhouse quietly located in countryside with easy access to Colchester, Dedham Vale, A12 and port of Harwich. Set in 6 acres.

BECCLES, Suffolk Map ref 3C1

CATHERINE HOUSE

2 Ringsfield Road, Beccles
NR34 9PQ
T: (01502) 716428
F: (01502) 716428

Bedrooms: 3 double/
twin
Bathrooms: 2 en suite,
1 private

B&B per night:
S £20.00–£30.00
D £40.00–£42.50

OPEN All year round

Family home, tastefully decorated to high standard, in quiet position overlooking Waveney Valley. Five minutes' walk to town centre.

COLVILLE ARMS MOTEL

Lowestoft Road, Worlingham,
Beccles NR34 7EF
T: (01502) 712571
F: (01502) 712571
E: pat@thecolvillearms.freeserve.
co.uk

Bedrooms: 2 single,
8 double/twin
Bathrooms: 10 en suite

Lunch available
Evening meal available
CC: Amex, Delta,
Mastercard, Switch, Visa

B&B per night:
S £30.00–£35.00
D £45.00–£55.00

HB per person:
DY Min £37.50

OPEN All year round

Village setting half an hour Lowestoft, Norwich and Yarmouth, 5 minutes to Broads. Excellent fishing, golf, country walks. All rooms en suite, TV, tea-making. Ample parking.

COUNTRY CODE Always follow the Country Code. Enjoy the countryside and respect its life and work. Guard against all risk of fire. Fasten all gates. Keep your dogs under close control. Keep to public paths across farmland. Use gates and stiles to cross fences, hedges and walls. Leave livestock, crops and machinery alone. Take your litter home. Help to keep all water clean. Protect wildlife, plants and trees. Take special care on country roads. Make no unnecessary noise

◆◆◆

THE KINGS HEAD
New Market, Beccles NR34 9HA
T: (01502) 712147
F: (01502) 715386
E: enquiries@kingsheadhotel-uk.co.uk
I: www.kingsheadhotel-uk.co.uk

B&B per night:
S £47.50–£55.00
D £57.50–£65.00

HB per person:
DY £45.00–£55.00

OPEN All year round

Grade II Listed coaching inn dating back to 1700, set in a small and bustling town centre, in the heart of the Norfolk Broads. Enjoy quality food in our Tylers' Restaurant. Relax in our friendly bar offering a choice of quality hand-pulled local beers and good value bar meals.

Bedrooms: 2 single, 8 double/twin, 2 triple/ multiple
Bathrooms: 8 en suite, 4 private

Lunch available
Evening meal available
CC: Amex, Delta, Diners, Mastercard, Switch, Visa

Ⓜ🐴📞📠🖥🛆🍷Ⓢ🔑🏠🛆🍴※🐾♿🅿

BEETLEY, Norfolk Map ref 3B1

◆◆◆◆
Gold
Award

PEACOCK HOUSE
Peacock Lane, Beetley, East Dereham NR20 4DG
T: (01362) 860371 & 0797 9013258
E: PeackH@aol.com
I: www.smoothhound.co.uk/hotels/ peacockh.html/

B&B per night:
S £21.00–£27.00
D £42.00–£45.00

OPEN All year round

Beautiful old farmhouse, peacefully situated in lovely garden and grounds. Offering excellent accommodation with all facilities, guests' lounge, open fires, beamed dining room, home cooking and a warm welcome. Centrally situated with Norwich, Sandringham, NT houses and the coast all within easy reach, and golf, fishing and swimming all close by.

Bedrooms: 3 double/ twin
Bathrooms: 3 en suite

Evening meal available

Ⓜ🐴📠🖥🛆Ⓢ🔑🎿🖥🛆♻🔱🚶🐴🐎♿🅿

◆◆◆

SHILLING STONE
Church Road, Beetley, East Dereham NR20 4AB
T: (01362) 861099 & 07721 306190
F: (01362) 869153
E: jeannepartridge@ukgateway.net
I: www.norfolkshillingstone.co.uk

B&B per night:
S £22.00–£24.00
D £40.00–£42.00

OPEN All year round

A large country house on the edge of Beetley. Excellent accommodation with large double and twin rooms, all en suite with colour TV. Full English breakfast. Ideal base for touring Norfolk coast, Broads, Norwich, Sandringham and Gressenhall Rural Life Museum. A warm welcome awaits you. Children and pets welcome. Golf and fishing nearby.

Bedrooms: 3 double/ twin
Bathrooms: 3 en suite

Evening meal available
CC: Amex, Delta, Mastercard, Switch, Visa

Ⓜ🐴📠🖥🛆Ⓢ🔑🎿🖥🛆🍴🎱🏹♻🔱🚶🐴🐎♿🅿

BIGGLESWADE, Bedfordshire Map ref 2D1

◆◆◆

OLD WARDEN GUESTHOUSE
Shop and Post Office, Old Warden, Biggleswade SG18 9HQ
T: (01767) 627201

Bedrooms: 3 double/ twin
Bathrooms: 3 en suite

B&B per night:
S £27.00
D £42.00

OPEN All year round

Listed, 19th C building, adjacent to shop and post office. Between Biggleswade and Bedford. One mile from Shuttleworth Collection. All rooms en suite.

🐴📠🖥🛆Ⓢ🖥🛆※🚲🏠🅿

BISHOP'S STORTFORD, Hertfordshire Map ref 2D1 *Tourist Information Centre Tel: (01279) 655831*

♦♦♦♦
Gold
Award

THE COTTAGE
71 Birchanger Lane, Birchanger,
Bishop's Stortford CM23 5QA
T: (01279) 812349
F: (01279) 815045

B&B per night:
S £38.00–£52.00
D £68.00–£70.00

OPEN All year round

The Cottage is a 17thC Listed house with panelled rooms and wood-burning stove. Conservatory-style breakfast room overlooks large mature garden. Quiet and peaceful village setting yet near M11 jct 8, Stansted Airport and Bishop's Stortford. Guest rooms are furnished in a traditional cottage style, all with colour TV and tea/coffee facilities.

Bedrooms: 3 single,
12 double/twin
Bathrooms: 12 en suite,
1 private

CC: Delta, Mastercard,
Switch, Visa

BLAXHALL, Suffolk Map ref 3C2

♦♦
THE SHIP INN
Blaxhall, Woodbridge IP12 2DY
T: (01728) 688316
F: (01728) 688316

Bedrooms: 4 double/
twin
Bathrooms: 4 en suite

Lunch available
Evening meal available
CC: Delta, Mastercard,
Switch, Visa

B&B per night:
S £32.00–£36.00
D £40.00–£50.00

OPEN All year round

The Ship Inn is a traditional 17thC village inn. We offer real ales from local breweries and a variety of home-cooked food.

BLICKLING, Norfolk Map ref 3B1

♦♦♦
THE BUCKINGHAMSHIRE ARMS
Blickling, Norwich NR11 6NF
T: (01263) 732133

Bedrooms: 3 double/
twin
Bathrooms: 1 en suite

Lunch available
Evening meal available
CC: Amex, Delta, Diners,
Mastercard, Switch, Visa

B&B per night:
S £25.00–£30.00
D £50.00–£60.00

OPEN All year round

Historic 17thC inn next to Blickling Hall. Four-posters and delicious food. Real English inn.

BRADFIELD, Essex Map ref 3B2

♦♦♦
EMSWORTH HOUSE
Ship Hill, Bradfield, Manningtree
CO11 2UP
T: (01255) 870860 & 07767 477771
E: emsworthhouse@hotmail.com
I: www.emsworthhouse.co.uk

Bedrooms: 3 double/
twin
Bathrooms: 1 en suite

Lunch available
Evening meal available

B&B per night:
S £28.00–£45.00
D £38.00–£56.00

HB per person:
DY £50.00–£76.00

OPEN All year round

Formerly the vicarage. Spacious rooms with stunning views of the countryside and River Stour. Near Colchester and Harwich. On holiday, business or en route to the continent, it's perfect!

BRAINTREE, Essex Map ref 3B2 *Tourist Information Centre Tel: (01376) 550066*

♦♦♦
BROOK FARM
Wethersfield, Braintree CM7 4BX
T: (01371) 850284 & 07770 881966
F: (01371) 850284

Bedrooms: 2 double/
twin, 1 triple/multiple
Bathrooms: 1 en suite,
1 private

B&B per night:
S £25.00
D £40.00–£50.00

OPEN All year round

Beautiful Listed farmhouse, parts dating back to 13thC. On edge of picturesque village. Spacious, comfortable rooms, guest lounge. Thirty minutes from Stansted. Camping available.

www.travelengland.org.uk
Log on for information and inspiration. The latest information on places to visit, events and quality assessed accommodation.

BRAINTREE continued

70 HIGH GARRETT

Braintree CM7 5NT	Bedrooms: 1 single,	B&B per night:
T: (01376) 345330	1 double/twin, 1 triple/	S £20.00
	multiple	D £40.00

Three-bedroom bed and breakfast situated on main road between Braintree and Halstead. Convenient for Colchester, Chelmsford, Constable Country. Half hour to London. Non-smokers only.

OPEN All year round

⑤ ⊬ 𝄞 ▥. ▶ ✽ 🚗 P

BRANDON, Suffolk Map ref 3B2

THE LAURELS

162 London Road, Brandon	Bedrooms: 2 double/	B&B per night:
IP27 0LP	twin	S £16.50–£20.00
T: (01842) 812005	Bathrooms: 1 en suite,	D £33.00–£37.00
	1 private	

A cosy welcome awaits you in our comfortable bungalow with tea or coffee on arrival. Close to forest, market town and other places of interest.

OPEN All year round

⛨ ♿ 🖻 ▢ ♨ ⛉ ⑤ ⊬ ▥. ▱ ✽ 🐴 🚗 P

BULPHAN, Essex Map ref 3B3

BONNY DOWNS FARM

Doesgate Lane, Bulphan, Upminster	Bedrooms: 2 double/	B&B per night:
RM14 3TB	twin, 1 triple/multiple	S £17.50
T: (01268) 542129		D £35.00

60-acre mixed farm. Large comfortable farmhouse offering home-cooked food. Conveniently placed for road links: M25, A13 and A127 to London and south-east England.

OPEN All year round

⛨ ♿ 🖻 ▢ ♨ ⛉ ⑤ ⊬ 𝄞 ▥. ▱ ▶ ✽ 🚗 P

BUNGAY, Suffolk Map ref 3C1

CLEVELAND HOUSE

2 Broad Street, Bungay NR35 1EE	Bedrooms: 2 double/	B&B per night:
T: (01986) 896589	twin	S Min £40.00
F: (01986) 892311	Bathrooms: 2 en suite	D Min £56.00

Small bed and breakfast, with its own charming icecream parlour, in historic market town. Suffolk coast within easy reach. Golf, walking and cycling paths nearby.

OPEN All year round

🖻 ▢ ♨ ⑤ ⊬ ▥. ▱ ✽ 🚗

BURNHAM THORPE, Norfolk Map ref 3B1

WHITEHALL FARM

Burnham Thorpe, King's Lynn	Bedrooms: 2 triple/	B&B per night:
PE31 8HN	multiple	S £27.00–£44.00
T: (01328) 738416 & 07831 794029	Bathrooms: 2 private	D £44.00
F: (01328) 730937		
E: barry.southerland@amserve.net		

Barry and Valerie welcome you for a quiet relaxed stay in north Norfolk, 2 miles from coast. Family rooms with full facilities in 16thC farmhouse.

OPEN All year round

⛨ 🖻 ▢ ♨ ⛉ ⑤ 𝄞 ▥. ▱ ✽ 🐴 🚗 ▨ 🏠 P

AT-A-GLANCE SYMBOLS

Symbols at the end of each accommodation entry give useful information about services and facilities. A key to symbols can be found inside the back cover flap. Keep this open for easy reference.

BURY ST EDMUNDS, Suffolk Map ref 3B2 *Tourist Information Centre Tel: (01284) 764667*

◆◆◆◆

BRIGHTHOUSE FARM
Melford Road, Lawshall, Bury St Edmunds
IP29 4PX
T: (01284) 830385 & 07711 829546
F: (01284) 830385
E: brighthousefarm@supanet.com
I: www.brighthousefarm.fsnet.co.uk

B&B per night:
S £25.00–£40.00
D £40.00–£60.00

OPEN All year round

A warm welcome awaits you at this 200-year-old Georgian farmhouse. Tastefully presented en suite rooms, outstanding breakfasts served in spacious conservatory. 3 acres of glorious gardens and farm trail to explore. Close to a wealth of interesting places to visit, good pubs and restaurants nearby. Send SAE for brochure.

Bedrooms: 5 double/ twin
Bathrooms: 5 en suite

◆◆◆

DUNSTON GUESTHOUSE/HOTEL
8 Springfield Road,
Bury St Edmunds IP33 3AN
T: (01284) 767981

Bedrooms: 7 single,
7 double/twin, 3 triple/
multiple
Bathrooms: 8 en suite,
3 private

B&B per night:
S £25.00–£35.00
D £60.00

OPEN All year round

Victorian guesthouse/hotel in a tree-lined road 5-10 minutes' walk from town centre. Comfortable residents' lounge, peaceful sun lounge, gardens, car park. Small groups by arrangement.

◆◆◆◆

SOUTH HILL HOUSE
43 Southgate Street,
Bury St Edmunds IP33 2AZ
T: (01284) 755650
F: (01284) 752718
E: southill@cwcom.net
I: www.southill.cwc.net

Bedrooms: 3 double/
twin
Bathrooms: 3 en suite

CC: Delta, Mastercard,
Switch, Visa

B&B per night:
S £30.00–£39.00
D £45.00–£54.00

OPEN All year round

Grade II* Listed townhouse, reputed to be the school mentioned in Charles Dickens' 'Pickwick Papers'. 10 minutes' walk town centre, 2 minutes' drive A14. Less 10% for 2+ nights.

◆◆◆

SYCAMORE HOUSE
23 Northgate Street,
Bury St Edmunds IP33 1HP
T: (01284) 755828
E: m.chalkley@ntlworld.com
I: www.sycamorehouse.net

Bedrooms: 2 double/
twin
Bathrooms: 1 en suite,
1 private

B&B per night:
S £35.00–£40.00
D £50.00–£55.00

OPEN All year round

A comfortable Victorian home offering a warm and friendly atmosphere. The premises is centrally situated and features an attractive two-tiered garden. Non-smokers only.

CAMBRIDGE, Cambridgeshire Map ref 2D1 *Tourist Information Centre Tel: (01223) 322640*

◆◆◆

ARBURY LODGE GUESTHOUSE
82 Arbury Road, Cambridge
CB4 2JE
T: (01223) 364319 & 566988
F: (01223) 566988
E: arburylodge@ntlworld.com
I: www.guesthousecambridge.com

Bedrooms: 1 single,
5 double/twin, 1 triple/
multiple
Bathrooms: 4 en suite

CC: Amex, Delta,
Mastercard, Switch, Visa

B&B per night:
S £27.00–£50.00
D £45.00–£62.00

OPEN All year round

Comfortable family-run guesthouse, 1.5 miles north of city centre and colleges. Easy access from A14/M11. Large car park and garden.

SYMBOLS The symbols in each entry give information about services and facilities. A key to these symbols appears at the back of this guide.

◆◆◆ **ASHLEY HOTEL**

74 Chesterton Road, Cambridge	Bedrooms: 2 single,	CC: Mastercard, Visa
CB4 1ER	6 double/twin, 2 triple/	
T: (01223) 350059	multiple	
F: (01223) 350900	Bathrooms: 8 en suite	
E: info@arundelhousehotels.co.uk		
I: www.arundelhousehotels.co.uk		

B&B per night:
S £49.50–£59.50
D £59.50–£69.50

OPEN All year round

Well-appointed recently refurbished small hotel with modern facilities close to city centre. Nearby Arundel House Hotel's facilities available to Ashley residents (under same ownership).

♈☎♿☎❒▢♒☜⑤☵◐▥.☎✲♦P

◆◆◆ **ASHTREES GUESTHOUSE**

128 Perne Road, Cambridge	Bedrooms: 2 single,	Lunch available
CB1 3RR	4 double/twin, 1 triple/	Evening meal available
T: (01223) 411233	multiple	CC: Mastercard, Visa
F: (01223) 411233	Bathrooms: 3 en suite	
E: mandy@mhill22.fsnet.co.uk		
I: www.smoothhound.co.uk/hotels/		
ashtrees.html		

B&B per night:
S £23.00–£38.00
D £39.00–£45.00

HB per person:
DY £33.00–£48.00

OPEN Feb–Dec

Comfort and an enjoyable stay are the priorities. Individually decorated rooms to a high standard. Home cooking. Garden and car park.

☎♿▢♒☜⑤✂▥.☎✲♦P

◆◆◆

ASSISI GUESTHOUSE

193 Cherry Hinton Road, Cambridge
CB1 7BX

T: (01223) 246648 & 211466
F: (01223) 412900

B&B per night:
S Min £35.00
D Min £50.00

OPEN All year round

Warm, welcoming, family-run guesthouse, ideally situated for the city, colleges and Addenbrookes Hospital. All modern facilities. Large car park.

Bedrooms: 4 single,	CC: Amex, Delta, Diners,
12 double/twin, 1 triple/	Mastercard, Switch, Visa
multiple	
Bathrooms: 16 en suite,	
1 private	

♈☎♿☎❒▢♒☜⑤✂☵▥.☎✲❒P

◆◆◆◆

AYLESBRAY LODGE GUESTHOUSE

5 Mowbray Road, Cambridge CB1 7SR

T: (01223) 240089
F: (01223) 528678
E: aylesbray.lodge@ntlworld.com
I: www.smoothhound.co.uk/hotels/
aylesbray.html

B&B per night:
S £35.00–£45.00
D £50.00–£70.00

OPEN All year round

All rooms are en suite, tastefully decorated and have complimentary extras. Four-poster rooms, satellite TV. Direct-dial telephones, radio alarm and hairdryer, free car parking. Close to Addenbrookes Hospital and within easy reach of rail station, Colleges and historic city centre. Easy access to M11, A14, A10. Convenient for local businesses.

Bedrooms: 1 single,	CC: Amex, Delta,
2 double/twin, 2 triple/	Mastercard, Switch, Visa
multiple	
Bathrooms: 5 en suite	

☎♿▦☎❒▢♒☜⑤✂☵▥.☎✲❒P

◆◆◆ **CAM GUESTHOUSE**

17 Elizabeth Way, Cambridge	Bedrooms: 3 single,
CB4 1DD	3 double/twin, 3 triple/
T: (01223) 354512	multiple
F: (01223) 353164	Bathrooms: 4 en suite
E: camguesthouse@btinternet.com	
I: www.camguesthouse.co.uk	

B&B per night:
S £32.00–£35.00
D Min £50.00

OPEN All year round

Guesthouse close to the River Cam, within 15 minutes' walking distance of the city centre and 5 minutes from Grafton shopping centre. En suite jacuzzi bath. Parking.

☎▢♒☜⑤✂▥.☎✲✖♈P

◆◆◆

CAROLINA BED & BREAKFAST

148 Perne Road, Cambridge CB1 3NX
T: (01223) 247015 & 07716 83424
F: (01223) 247015
E: carolina.amabile@tesco.net
I: www.smoothhound.co.uk/hotels/carol.html

Comfortable home offering a warm and friendly service. Easy access from and to M11 and A14. Close to city centre, railway station, bus station, Addenbrookes Hospital and colleges. Excellent breakfast, parking, discount for long-term booking. Credit cards accepted, children welcome, non-smokers. We can cater for all your needs.

Bedrooms: 2 double/twin
Bathrooms: 2 en suite

CC: Delta, Mastercard, Switch, Visa

B&B per night:
S £25.00–£45.00
D £38.00–£60.00

HB per person:
DY £35.00–£55.00

OPEN All year round

♦♦♦ A ⅍ ♿ 📺 ❏ ♦ ◌ § ⅄ 🛏 🍴 ☎ 🐾 P

◆◆◆

CRISTINAS

47 St Andrews Road, Cambridge
CB4 1DH
T: (01223) 365855 & 327700
F: (01223) 365855
E: cristinas.guesthouse@ntlworld.com
I: www.smoothhound.co.uk/hotels/cristina.html

Bedrooms: 8 double/twin, 1 triple/multiple
Bathrooms: 7 en suite

B&B per night:
S £38.00–£49.00
D £48.00–£56.00

OPEN All year round

Established in 1986, Cristinas Guest House provides a very warm welcome and a comfortable and contented stay for guests. Walking distance of city centre.

♦♦♦ A ⅍ 📺 ❏ ♦ ◌ § ⅄ 🍴 ☎ P

◆◆◆

DRESDEN VILLA GUESTHOUSE

34 Cherry Hinton Road, Cambridge
CB1 7AA
T: (01223) 247539
F: (01223) 410640

Bedrooms: 6 single, 5 double/twin, 2 triple/multiple
Bathrooms: 13 en suite

Evening meal available

B&B per night:
S £34.00–£36.00
D £50.00–£52.00

HB per person:
DY £46.00–£48.00

OPEN All year round

Family-run guesthouse offering friendly service. All rooms en suite, tea/coffee. Situated approximately 1 mile from city centre and Addenbrookes Hospital.

♦♦♦ A ⅍ ♿ ❏ ♦ ◌ § ⅄ 🍴 ☎ 🐎 🐾 P

◆◆◆

DYKELANDS GUESTHOUSE

157 Mowbray Road, Cambridge CB1 7SP
T: (01223) 244300
F: (01223) 566746
E: dykelands@fsbdial.co.uk
I: www.dykelands.com

Highly recommended guesthouse in south of city, only 1.75 miles from historic city centre. Ideally located for city and for touring. We offer modern, spacious accommodation, most en suite. Two bedrooms on ground floor. A non-smoking establishment. Traditional English breakfast or vegetarian alternatives. Car parking on site.

Bedrooms: 1 single, 4 double/twin, 3 triple/multiple
Bathrooms: 6 en suite

CC: Delta, Mastercard, Switch, Visa

B&B per night:
S £30.00–£47.00
D £38.00–£47.00

OPEN All year round

♦♦♦ A ⅍ ♿ 📺 ❏ ♦ § ⅄ 🍴 ☎ ✳ 🐎 🚲 P

PRICES

Please check prices and other details at the time of booking.

◆◆◆◆ **FINCHES**

144 Thornton Road, Girton,
Cambridge CB3 0ND
T: (01223) 276653 & 07710 179214
F: (01223) 276653
E: liz.green.b-b@talk21.com
I: www.smoothhound.co.uk/hotels/
finches

Bedrooms: 3 double/
twin
Bathrooms: 3 en suite

B&B per night:
S £45.00–£60.00
D £50.00–£60.00

OPEN All year round

A 3 bedroom bed and breakfast establishment situated on the corner of Huntingdon Road, Cambridge. All en suite.

🐴 🕭 🖼 �占 ♨ 🖐 🕄 🖵 ✂ 🔲 ⌂ ❋ 🐴 🐾 P

◆◆◆

HAMILTON HOTEL

156 Chesterton Road, Cambridge CB4 1DA
T: (01223) 365664
F: (01223) 314866

B&B per night:
S £22.00–£45.00
D £45.00–£65.00

HB per person:
DY Min £32.00

OPEN All year round

Recently refurbished hotel less than 1 mile from centre of city. Easy access from A14 and M11. Most rooms have en suite shower and toilet. All rooms have colour TV, direct-dial telephone and hospitality tray.

Bedrooms: 5 single,
16 double/twin, 4 triple/
multiple
Bathrooms: 20 en suite

Evening meal available
CC: Amex, Delta, Diners,
Mastercard, Switch, Visa

🐴 ♨ ♿ 🖵 ♨ 🕄 🍷 🕄 🐴 ⬤ 🔲 ⌂ P

◆◆◆◆ **HILLS GUESTHOUSE**

157 Hills Road, Cambridge CB2 2RJ
T: (01223) 214216
F: (01223) 214216

Bedrooms: 1 single,
3 double/twin
Bathrooms: 4 en suite

CC: Amex, Delta,
Mastercard, Switch, Visa

B&B per night:
S £33.00–£40.00
D Max £50.00

OPEN All year round

We are a friendly family-run guesthouse. Bedrooms are cosy and spacious. Situated in between Addenbrookes Hospital, railway station and city centre.

⚠🐴 🖵 ♨ 🕄 🖵 ✂ 🐴 🔲 ⌂ ❋ 🐾 P

◆◆◆◆ **KING'S TITHE**

13a Comberton Road, Barton,
Cambridge CB3 7BA
T: (01223) 263610
F: (01223) 263610
E: thornebarton@lineone.net

Bedrooms: 2 double/
twin

B&B per night:
S £34.00–£36.00
D £50.00–£60.00

OPEN All year round

Guests return often to this up-market quiet home. Both rooms with countryside views. Excellent breakfasts. Good village pub. Near M11 junction 12 (west A603 to B1046).

🐴8 🖼 🖵 ♨ 🕄 🔲 ⌂ ❋ 🐾 P

◆◆◆◆ **LENSFIELD HOTEL**

53 Lensfield Road, Cambridge
CB2 1EN
T: (01223) 355017
F: (01223) 312022
E: reservations@lensfield.co.uk
I: www.lensfieldhotel.co.uk

Bedrooms: 6 single,
21 double/twin, 2 triple/
multiple
Bathrooms: 29 en suite

Evening meal available
CC: Amex, Delta, Diners,
Mastercard, Switch, Visa

B&B per night:
S £45.00–£78.00
D £85.00–£89.00

HB per person:
DY £55.00–£88.00

OPEN All year round

Family-run hotel in central location for all parts of the city's splendour – the 'Bridges and Backs', Botanical Gardens, colleges, entertainment and shopping.

🐴 ♨ ♿ 🖵 ♨ 🕄 🍷 🕄 ✂ 🐴 ⬤ 🔲 ⌂ ❋ 🏠 P

◆◆◆ **SEGOVIA LODGE**

2 Barton Road, Newnham,
Cambridge CB3 9JZ
T: (01223) 354105
F: (01223) 323011

Bedrooms: 1 single,
3 double/twin
Bathrooms: 1 en suite,
1 private

B&B per night:
D £55.00–£58.00

OPEN All year round

Within walking distance city centre and colleges. Next to cricket and tennis fields. Warm welcome, personal service, both rooms with private facilities. Non-smokers only, please.

🐴10 🖼 🖵 ♨ 🕄 🖵 ✂ 🔲 ⌂ ❋ 🐾 P

CAMBRIDGE continued

♦♦♦ SOUTHAMPTON GUEST HOUSE

7 Elizabeth Way, Cambridge
CB4 1DE
T: (01223) 357780
F: (01223) 314297
E: southamptonhouse@telco4u.net
I: www.smoothhound.co.uk/hotels/
sout.htlm

Bedrooms: 1 single,
1 double/twin, 3 triple/
multiple
Bathrooms: 5 en suite

B&B per night:
S £35.00–£45.00
D £40.00–£55.00

OPEN All year round

Victorian property with friendly atmosphere, only 15 minutes' walk along riverside to city centre, colleges and new shopping mall.

ⓢ ♿ ⌂ ☎ ⬇ Ⓢ ✂ 🛏 🖨 🚭 🅿

♦♦♦♦ SYCAMORE HOUSE

56 High Street, Great Wilbraham,
Cambridge CB1 5JD
T: (01223) 880751 & 07711 845300
F: (01223) 880751
E: barry@thesycamorehouse.co.uk
I: www.thesycamorehouse.co.uk

Bedrooms: 1 single,
2 double/twin

B&B per night:
S £22.50–£25.00
D £45.00–£50.00

Pleasantly situated detached house in small village with shop and pub. Five miles to Cambridge and Newmarket. Excellent for racing, cycling and touring.

ⓢ ☎ ⬇ Ⓢ 🚭 🅿

♦♦♦♦ VICTORIA

57 Arbury Road, Cambridge
CB4 2JB
T: (01223) 350086
F: (01223) 350086
E: vicmaria@globalnet.co.uk
I: www.victoriaguesthouse.co.uk

Bedrooms: 2 double/
twin, 2 triple/multiple;
suites available
Bathrooms: 4 en suite

CC: Delta, Mastercard,
Switch, Visa

B&B per night:
S £22.00–£49.00
D £38.00–£65.00

OPEN All year round

Situated close to the city centre. Excellent decor. Extremely clean. Excellent breakfasts. En suite rooms. TV and complimentary tea and coffee. Self-catering also available.

Ⓜ ⓢ ♿ 🖥 ☎ ⬇ ♉ Ⓢ ✂ 🛏 🖨 ✳ 🚭 🏠 🅿

CAMPSEA ASHE, Suffolk Map ref 3C2

♦♦♦♦♦ THE OLD RECTORY
Gold Award

Campsea Ashe, Woodbridge
IP13 0PU
T: (01728) 746524
F: (01728) 746524

Bedrooms: 1 single,
6 double/twin
Bathrooms: 7 en suite

Evening meal available
CC: Amex, Diners,
Mastercard, Visa

B&B per night:
S £45.00
D £65.00–£75.00

HB per person:
DY £48.50–£68.00

OPEN All year round

Large, family country house in mature grounds offering comfortable accommodation with food and wine under the owner's supervision.

ⓢ 🖥 ⬇ 🍽 Ⓢ ✂ 🛏 🖨 ♉ ☺ ✳ 🐎 🚭 🏠 🅿

CAVENDISH, Suffolk Map ref 3B2

♦♦♦♦ Silver Award

EMBLETON HOUSE BED & BREAKFAST

Melford Road, Cavendish, Sudbury
CO10 8AA
T: (01787) 280447
F: (01787) 282396
E: silverned@aol.com
I: www.smoothhound.co.uk/hotels/
embleton

B&B per night:
S £35.00–£45.00
D £55.00–£75.00

OPEN All year round

A large 1930s house, set well back from the road, within its own secluded mature gardens at the eastern edge of Cavendish village. Five spacious recently appointed en suite bedrooms. Stour Valley views. Suffolk breakfast. Good pub within 8 minutes' walk. An ideal base for exploring Long Melford, Clare, Lavenham and beyond.

Bedrooms: 5 double/
twin
Bathrooms: 5 en suite

Evening meal available

Special rates for stays of 3 nights or more. 'Stress Busting'-holistic therapies, heated pool (May-Sept) and tennis court.

ⓢ 8 ♿ 🖥 ☎ ⬇ ♉ Ⓢ ✂ 🛏 🖨 ♌ ☺ ✳ 🐎 🚭 🏠 🅿

CHELMSFORD, Essex Map ref 3B3 *Tourist Information Centre Tel: (01245) 283400*

♦♦♦ BEECHCROFT PRIVATE HOTEL
211 New London Road, Chelmsford CM2 0AJ
T: (01245) 352462 & 250861
F: (01245) 347833
E: beechcroft.hotel@btinternet.com
I: www.beechcrofthotel.com

Bedrooms: 11 single, 6 double/twin, 2 triple/multiple
Bathrooms: 13 en suite

CC: Delta, Diners, Mastercard, Switch, Visa

B&B per night:
S £44.00–£46.00
D £59.00–£60.00

OPEN All year round

Central hotel offering clean and comfortable accommodation with friendly service. Under family ownership and management. Within walking distance of town centre.

♦♦♦♦ BOSWELL HOUSE HOTEL
118 Springfield Road, Chelmsford CM2 6LF
T: (01245) 287587
F: (01245) 287587

Bedrooms: 5 single, 6 double/twin, 2 triple/multiple
Bathrooms: 13 en suite

Lunch available
Evening meal available
CC: Amex, Delta, Diners, Mastercard, Switch, Visa

B&B per night:
S £48.00–£50.00
D £65.00

HB per person:
DY £60.00–£62.00

OPEN All year round

Victorian townhouse in central location, offering high-standard accommodation in friendly and informal surroundings. Family atmosphere and home cooking, lounge bar.

♦♦ NEPTUNE CAFE MOTEL
Burnham Road, Latchingdon, Chelmsford CM3 6EX
T: (01621) 740770

Bedrooms: 6 double/twin, 4 triple/multiple
Bathrooms: 10 en suite

Lunch available
Evening meal available

B&B per night:
S £25.00
D £35.00

OPEN All year round

Cafe with adjoining chalet block, which includes 2 units suitable for physically disabled. Village location between Maldon and Burnham-on-Crouch.

♦♦♦♦ OLD BAKERY
Waltham Road, Terling, Chelmsford CM3 2QR
T: (01245) 233363

Bedrooms: 2 double/twin
Bathrooms: 2 en suite

B&B per night:
S £22.50–£24.00
D £45.00–£48.00

OPEN All year round

Converted bakery in small village, 4 miles from A12 overlooking open farmland and on the Essex Way.

♦♦♦ TANUNDA HOTEL
217-219 New London Road, Chelmsford CM2 0AJ
T: (01245) 354295 & 258799
F: (01245) 345503

Bedrooms: 8 single, 12 double/twin
Bathrooms: 11 en suite

CC: Amex, Delta, Diners, Mastercard, Switch, Visa

B&B per night:
S £36.00–£55.00
D £52.00–£60.00

OPEN All year round

We are on the main road to London and Harwich and 5 minutes from the town centre.

♦♦ WARDS FARM
Loves Green, Highwood Road, Highwood, Chelmsford CM1 3QJ
T: (01245) 248812
F: (01245) 248812
E: alsnbrtn@aol.com

Bedrooms: 3 double/twin

Evening meal available

B&B per night:
S £25.00–£28.00
D £50.00–£55.00

HB per person:
DY £32.00–£40.00

Farm with horses. Traditional oak-beamed 16thC farmhouse set in moated grounds. Log fires and a warm welcome.

CLACTON-ON-SEA, Essex Map ref 3B3 *Tourist Information Centre Tel: (01255) 423400*

♦♦♦ SANDROCK HOTEL
1 Penfold Road, Marine Parade West, Clacton-on-Sea CO15 1JN
T: (01255) 428215
F: (01255) 428215

Bedrooms: 7 double/twin, 1 triple/multiple
Bathrooms: 8 en suite

Lunch available
Evening meal available
CC: Amex, Delta, Diners, Mastercard, Switch, Visa

B&B per night:
S £35.00–£37.00
D £52.00–£54.00

HB per person:
DY £38.00–£50.00

OPEN All year round

Private hotel in central position, just off seafront and close to town. Comfortable bedrooms with co-ordinated soft furnishings. Excellent, freshly cooked food. Licensed. Car park.

COLCHESTER, Essex Map ref 3B2 *Tourist Information Centre Tel: (01206) 282920*

◆◆◆ **APPLE BLOSSOM HOUSE**

8 Guildford Road, Colchester
CO1 2YL
T: (01206) 512303
F: (01206) 870260

Bedrooms: 2 single,
1 double/twin
Bathrooms: 1 en suite

B&B per night.
S £20.00–£24.00
D £35.00–£40.00

OPEN All year round

Detached house near town centre, bus station, sports centre. Bright rooms, private facilities, shower robes, TV, clock radio. Driveway parking. Healthy breakfasts. Company rates.

◆◆◆◆ **FRIDAYWOOD FARM**

Bounstead Road, Colchester
CO2 0DF
T: (01206) 573595 & 07970 836285
F: (01206) 547011

Bedrooms: 2 double/
twin
Bathrooms: 1 en suite,
1 private

B&B per night:
S £30.00–£35.00
D £40.00–£45.00

OPEN All year round

Working farm. Period farmhouse in woodland, convenient for bird-watching, Beth Chatto Gardens, countryside and coast.

◆◆◆◆ **OLD COURTHOUSE INN**

Harwich Road, Great Bromley,
Colchester CO7 7JG
T: (01206) 250322 & 251906
F: (01206) 251346
E: oldcourthoseinn@21.com

Bedrooms: 1 single,
3 double/twin, 1 triple/
multiple
Bathrooms: 5 en suite

Lunch available
Evening meal available
CC: Amex, Delta,
Mastercard, Switch, Visa

B&B per night:
S £30.00–£35.00
D £50.00–£60.00

HB per person:
DY £38.00–£48.00

OPEN All year round

17thC inn, all en suite rooms, bar and restaurant. Just off A120, ideally situated for Harwich, Colchester, coastal resorts. Beth Chatto garden 2 miles.

◆◆ **PEVERIL HOTEL**

51 North Hill, Colchester CO1 1PY
T: (01206) 574001
F: (01206) 574001

Bedrooms: 4 single,
12 double/twin, 1 triple/
multiple
Bathrooms: 7 en suite

Lunch available
Evening meal available
CC: Amex, Delta, Diners,
Mastercard, Switch, Visa

B&B per night:
S £28.00–£45.00
D £40.00–£55.00

HB per person:
DY £35.00–£80.00

OPEN All year round

Friendly, family-run hotel with fine restaurant and bar. All rooms have colour TV and all facilities. Some en suite available.

◆◆ **SCHEREGATE HOTEL**

36 Osborne Street,
via St John's Street, Colchester
CO2 7DB
T: (01206) 573034
F: (01206) 541561

Bedrooms: 11 single,
14 double/twin, 2 triple/
multiple
Bathrooms: 10 en suite

CC: Delta, Mastercard,
Switch, Visa

B&B per night:
S £24.00–£35.00
D £40.00–£50.00

OPEN All year round

Interesting 15thC building, centrally situated, providing accommodation at moderate prices.

THE HEDGES GUESTHOUSE

Tunstead Road, Coltishall, Norwich
NR12 7AL
T: (01603) 738361
F: (01603) 738983
E: thehedges@msn.com
I: www.hedgesbandb.co.uk

Hear evening owlsong and the dawn chorus at this friendly family-run guesthouse. Set in large, peaceful gardens surrounded by open countryside, yet convenient for local amenities. Ideal base for exploring the Norfolk Broads, Norwich and Norfolk coast. Families welcome, spacious lounge with log fire, licensed, plenty of parking.

Bedrooms: 3 double/ twin, 2 triple/multiple
Bathrooms: 5 en suite

Evening meal available
CC: Delta, Mastercard, Switch, Visa

B&B per night:
S £22.00–£30.00
D £44.00–£47.00

OPEN All year round

TERRA NOVA LODGE
14 Westbourne Road, Coltishall,
Norwich NR12 7HT
T: (01603) 736264

Bedrooms: 2 double/ twin
Bathrooms: 2 en suite

B&B per night:
S £36.00–£38.00
D £40.00–£46.00

Accommodation within a large detached bungalow in this Broadland village, close to Norwich. Spacious rooms, both en suite, central heating, colour TV, pleasing decor and secluded gardens.

OPEN All year round

Silver Award

THE CRETINGHAM BELL

The Street, Cretingham, Woodbridge
IP13 7BJ
T: (01728) 685419

B&B per night:
S £39.95
D £58.75

OPEN All year round

In the quiet village of Cretingham. Its Tudor beams, log fires, luxury accommodation, old world charm, traditional home-cooked food, locally brewed ales and a warm welcome make The Bell the ideal stop for travellers seeking peace and tranquillity.

Bedrooms: 2 double/ twin; suites available
Bathrooms: 2 en suite

Lunch available
Evening meal available
CC: Delta, Mastercard, Switch, Visa

Silver Award

SHRUBBERY FARMHOUSE

Chapel Hill, Cretingham, Woodbridge
IP13 7DN
T: (01473) 737494 & 07860 352317
F: (01473) 737312
E: sm@marmar.co.uk
I: www.shrubberyfarmhouse.co.uk

Charming part 16thC listed Suffolk farmhouse set in some of the most quiet and beautiful countryside in East Anglia. Winter log fires. Al fresco summer breakfasts with fresh eggs from the farmhouse hens make this the ideal base for exploring Suffolk's Heritage Coast. Comfortable bedrooms, gymnasium and tennis court.

Bedrooms: 1 single, 2 double/twin
Bathrooms: 1 en suite, 2 private

Lunch available
Evening meal available

B&B per night:
S £29.00–£35.00
D £58.00

HB per person:
DY £44.00–£49.00

OPEN All year round

CROMER, Norfolk Map ref 3C1 *Tourist Information Centre Tel: (01263) 512497*

◆◆◆ **BIRCH HOUSE**

34 Cabbell Road, Cromer NR27 9HX
T: (01263) 512521

Bedrooms: 1 single,
7 double/twin
Bathrooms: 3 en suite,
3 private

CC: Delta, Mastercard,
Switch, Visa

B&B per night:
S £19.00–£21.00
D £38.00–£44.00

A family-run guesthouse in a quiet position but close to the seafront and all amenities. A non-smoking establishment with some en suite rooms.

OPEN All year round

DARSHAM, Suffolk Map ref 3C2

◆◆◆ **WHITE HOUSE FARM**

Main Road, Darsham, Saxmundham
IP17 3PP
T: (01728) 668632

Bedrooms: 3 double/
twin
Bathrooms: 1 en suite

B&B per night:
S £25.00–£35.00
D £40.00–£55.00

Small, family-run, modernised farmhouse with pleasant gardens, on edge of village. Easy access to Aldeburgh, Southwold, Dunwich, Minsmere. Large gardens. Hearty farmhouse breakfasts.

OPEN All year round

DEDHAM, Essex Map ref 3B2

◆◆◆◆ **MAY'S BARN FARM**

May's Lane, Off Long Road West,
Dedham, Colchester CO7 6EW
T: (01206) 323191
E: maysbarn@talk21.com
I: www.mays.barn.btinternet.co.uk

Bedrooms: 2 double/
twin
Bathrooms: 1 en suite,
1 private

B&B per night:
S £25.00–£28.00
D £40.00–£45.00

350-acre arable farm. Tranquil old farmhouse with outstanding views over Dedham Vale in Constable Country. Quarter mile down private lane. Comfortable, spacious rooms, with private facilities.

OPEN All year round

DERSINGHAM, Norfolk Map ref 3B1

◆◆◆ **ASHDENE HOUSE**

Dersingham, King's Lynn PE31 6HQ
T: (01485) 540395
I: www.mistral.co.uk/ashdene

Bedrooms: 5 double/
twin
Bathrooms: 5 en suite

Lunch available
Evening meal available
CC: Delta, Mastercard,
Switch, Visa

B&B per night:
S £20.00–£24.00
D £40.00–£48.00

HB per person:
DY £29.00–£31.50

An elegant Victorian house in village centre, convenient for country walks and seaside activities. Pleasant garden and adequate car park.

OPEN All year round

EARL SOHAM, Suffolk Map ref 3C2

◆◆◆◆
Silver
Award

BRIDGE HOUSE

Earl Soham, Woodbridge IP13 7RT
T: (01728) 685473 & 685289
F: (01728) 685289
E: bridgehouse46@hotmail.com
I: www.jenniferbaker.co.uk

Bedrooms: 3 double/
twin
Bathrooms: 3 en suite

Lunch available
Evening meal available

B&B per night:
S Min £27.50
D Min £45.00

HB per person:
DY Min £34.50

Bridge House is an attractive, 16thC property near Heritage Coast. A warm welcome and excellent food add charm to well-appointed, comfortable accommodation.

OPEN All year round

EARLS COLNE, Essex Map ref 3B2

◆◆◆

RIVERSIDE LODGE

40 Lower Holt Street, Earls Colne,
Colchester CO6 2PH
T: (01787) 223487
F: (01787) 223487

Bedrooms: 5 double/
twin
Bathrooms: 5 en suite

Lunch available
Evening meal available
CC: Mastercard, Visa

B&B per night:
S £38.50–£40.50
D £47.00–£51.00

OPEN All year round

On the A1124 Colchester-Halstead road, single storey en suite chalets on the banks of the River Colne. Restaurants, pubs and village amenities within walking distance.

REGIONAL TOURIST BOARD The **M** symbol in an establishment entry indicates that it is a Regional Tourist Board member.

EAST MERSEA, Essex Map ref 3B3

◆◆◆◆ **MERSEA ISLAND VINEYARD**
Rewsalls Lane, East Mersea,
Colchester CO5 8SX
T: (01206) 385900
F: (01206) 383600
E: jacqui.barber@merseawine.com
I: www.merseawine.com

Bedrooms: 3 double/
twin
Bathrooms: 3 en suite

B&B per night:
S £35.00
D £50.00

Newly constructed house and winery overlooking established vineyard and Colne and Blackwater estuaries. Walking distance to sea wall and beach. Colchester 9 miles.

EASTON, Suffolk Map ref 3C2

◆◆◆◆ **ATLANTIS STUD FARM**
Framlingham Road, Easton,
Woodbridge IP13 0EW
T: (01728) 621553
F: (01728) 621553
E: atlantisbandb@yahoo.co.uk

Bedrooms: 3 double/
twin
Bathrooms: 3 en suite

B&B per night:
D £48.00–£58.00

OPEN All year round

Newly rebuilt barn, set in an acre of Suffolk countryside, with ultra modern facilities. Local produce, all rooms en suite, use of lounge and garden.

ELY, Cambridgeshire Map ref 3A2 *Tourist Information Centre Tel: (01353) 662062*

◆◆◆◆
Gold
Award

HILL HOUSE FARM
9 Main Street, Coveney, Ely CB6 2DJ
T: (01353) 778369

B&B per night:
D £48.00–£50.00

OPEN All year round

Fine Victorian farmhouse on arable working farm 3 miles west of Ely. First class breakfast served in traditional dining room. Open views of surrounding countryside. No smoking, no pets, children over 12 welcome. Access from A142 or A10. Situated in the centre of quiet village. Convenient for Ely, Cambridge, Newmarket.

Bedrooms: 3 double/
twin
Bathrooms: 3 en suite

CC: Delta, Mastercard,
Switch, Visa

◆◆◆◆

SPINNEY ABBEY
Stretham Road, Wicken, Ely CB7 5XQ
T: (01353) 720971
E: spinney.abbey@tesco.net
I: www.spinneyabbey.co.uk

B&B per night:
D £45.00–£48.00

OPEN All year round

This attractive Georgian Grade II Listed farmhouse, surrounded by pasture fields, stands next to our dairy farm which borders the NT Nature Reserve 'Wicken Fen', on the southern edge of the Fens. Guests are welcome to full use of spacious garden and all-weather tennis court. All rooms have private facilities.

Bedrooms: 2 double/
twin, 1 triple/multiple
Bathrooms: 2 en suite,
1 private

Nov-Feb-10% discount for three night bookings.

CREDIT CARD BOOKINGS If you book by telephone and are asked for your credit card number it is advisable to check the proprietor's policy should you cancel your reservation.

SARACENS HEAD INN

Wolterton, Erpingham, Norwich
NR11 7LX
T: (01263) 768909
F: (01263) 768993
I: www.broadland.com/
saracenshead

Bedrooms: 4 double/
twin
Bathrooms: 4 en suite

Lunch available
Evening meal available
CC: Amex, Delta, Diners,
Mastercard, Switch, Visa

B&B per night:
S £30.00–£40.00
D £50.00–£60.00

OPEN All year round

Unusual country inn with comfortable en suite rooms, delightful garden and log fires in winter. Renowned for cuisine.

ABBOTT FARM

Walsingham Road, Binham, Fakenham
NR21 0AW
T: (01328) 830519 & 0780 884 7582
F: (01328) 830519
E: abbot.farm@btinternet.com

B&B per night:
S £20.00–£25.00
D £40.00–£50.00

HB per person:
DY £30.00–£35.00

OPEN All year round

126-acre arable farm. A modern, brick-built farm bungalow with a loft conversion, an airy conservatory and rural views of north Norfolk including the historic Binham Priory. Liz and Alan offer a warm welcome to their guesthouse and are there to make you feel at home.

Bedrooms: 2 double/
twin
Bathrooms: 2 en suite

HOLLY LODGE

The Street, Thursford Green, Fakenham
NR21 0AS
T: (01328) 878465
F: (01328) 878465
E: hollyguestlodge@talk21.com
I: www.hollylodgeguesthouse.co.uk

B&B per night:
S £35.00–£45.00
D £50.00–£70.00

OPEN Feb–mid Dec

Warm and welcoming friendly atmosphere at our 18thC house and guest cottages. Picturesque setting, recently renovated, period charm. Stylish luxurious rooms, all en suite, centrally heated, TV/video, tea/coffee facilities, beams, 4-poster, antique furniture. Home-cooked breakfast, car parking. Ideally situated for places of interest, Norfolk Coast and countryside.

Bedrooms: 3 double/
twin
Bathrooms: 3 en suite

7 nights for the price of 6.

SOUTHVIEW

Lynn Road, Sculthorpe, Fakenham
NR21 9QE
T: (01328) 851300

Bedrooms: 1 double/
twin
Bathrooms: 1 en suite

B&B per night:
D £45.00

OPEN All year round

Private house, 1 twin bedded letting room and dining room for guests.

THE OLD ANCHOR

132 Feering Hill, Feering, Colchester
CO5 9PY
T: (01376) 572855
F: (01376) 572855

Bedrooms: 1 single,
5 double/twin
Bathrooms: 6 en suite

Lunch available
Evening meal available
CC: Delta, Mastercard,
Switch, Visa

B&B per night:
S £50.00–£55.00
D £60.00–£65.00

HB per person:
DY £37.00–£40.00

OPEN All year round

Traditional wood-beamed inn, offering fine food, real ales and accommodation that blends the old with the requirements of today's traveller.

◆◆◆

OLD WILLS FARM

Feering, Colchester CO5 9RP
T: (01376) 570259
F: (01376) 570259
E: janecrayston@barclays.net

B&B per night:
S Min £22.50
D Min £45.00

OPEN All year round

Attractive and comfortable Essex farmhouse on a working arable farm with a large garden. Offering homely surroundings and atmosphere. Ideal relaxing base from which to sample the many and varied visitor attractions in the area, including historic sites, coastal regions and good restaurants.

Bedrooms: 1 single,
1 double/twin, 1 triple/
multiple
Bathrooms: 1 en suite,
1 private

 P

FELIXSTOWE, Suffolk Map ref 3C2 *Tourist Information Centre Tel: (01394) 276770*

◆◆

DOLPHIN HOTEL
41 Beach Station Road, Felixstowe
IP11 2EY
T: (01394) 282261
F: (01394) 278319

Bedrooms: 3 single,
5 double/twin, 1 triple/
multiple
Bathrooms: 2 en suite

Lunch available
Evening meal available
CC: Amex, Delta,
Mastercard, Switch, Visa

B&B per night:
S £20.00–£30.00
D £34.00–£46.00

OPEN All year round

Private hotel, 5 minutes from beach and 10 minutes from town centre. Fully licensed bar, traditional bar menu. Family room.

P

FLATFORD MILL, Suffolk Map ref 3B2

Rating
Applied For

THE GRANARY

Granary Museum,
Flatford Mill, East Bergholt, Colchester
CO7 6UL
T: (01206) 298111 & 299100
E: flatfordmill@fsdial.co.uk

B&B per night:
D £40.00

OPEN All year round

Delightful, beamed accommodation set in the very heart of Constable Country at Flatford Mill, with lawned garden, adjoining river and surrounded by wonderful countryside. Once owned by Constable family, Flatford Mill is halfway between Ipswich and Colchester. From A12 take B1070 to East Bergholt, follow signs to Flatford.

Bedrooms: 2 triple/
multiple
Bathrooms: 2 en suite

P

FOULDEN, Norfolk Map ref 3B1

◆◆◆

THE WHITE HART INN
White Hart Street, Foulden,
Thetford IP26 5AW
T: (01366) 328638
E: sylvia.chisholm@virgin.net

Bedrooms: 1 single,
2 double/twin
Bathrooms: 3 en suite

Lunch available
Evening meal available
CC: Delta, Mastercard,
Switch, Visa

B&B per night:
S £27.25–£35.00
D £35.00–£45.00

OPEN All year round

Traditional country inn with beer garden, conservatory and car park. Home-cooked food and real ale. Accommodation in former barn.

P

ACCESSIBILITY
Look for the symbols which indicate accessibility for wheelchair users. A list of establishments is at the front of this guide.

FRAMLINGHAM, Suffolk Map ref 3C2

♦♦♦ **SHIMMENS PIGHTLE**
Dennington Road, Framlingham,
Woodbridge IP13 9JT
T: (01728) 724036

Bedrooms: 3 double/
twin

B&B per night:
D £44.00–£49.00

OPEN Mar–Oct

*Comfortable home in an acre of landscaped garden, overlooking fields on outskirts of
Framlingham. Ground floor accommodation. Home-made marmalade and locally cured
bacon.*

 ⏰8 ♨ 🖥 ♦ ⌖ Ⓢ ✂ 🕮 Ⅲ ☎ ✲ 🖙 P

FRINTON-ON-SEA, Essex Map ref 3C2

♦♦♦ **UPLANDS GUESTHOUSE**
41 Hadleigh Road, Frinton-on-Sea
CO13 9HQ
T: (01255) 674889 &
(01255) 679232
E: info@uplandsguesthouse.
freeserve.co.uk

Bedrooms: 1 single,
3 double/twin
Bathrooms: 4 en suite

B&B per night:
S £20.00–£28.00
D £46.00–£56.00

OPEN All year round

*A quiet and comfortable house just 3 minutes from beautiful beach and excellent shops.
Ample parking. Golf and tennis clubs nearby. A no smoking house.*

 ⏰ ♦ Ⓢ ✂ 🕮 Ⅲ ☎ 🖙 P

GRISTON, Norfolk Map ref 3B1

♦♦♦♦ **PARK FARM BED & BREAKFAST**
Park Farm, Caston Road, Griston,
Thetford IP25 6QD
T: (01953) 483020 & 07974 772485
F: (01953) 483056
E: parkfarm@eidosnet.co.uk
I: www.parkfarmbreckland.co.uk

Bedrooms: 2 double/
twin
Bathrooms: 2 en suite

B&B per night:
S £25.00–£30.00
D £40.00–£50.00

*Working arable farm with en suite accommodation in converted outbuildings. Rural
location, peaceful surroundsings. Large lounge/dining for residents only. Vist our web site.*

🅰 ⏰ ♨ 🖥 ▢ ♦ ⌖ Ⓢ ✂ 🕮 Ⅲ ☎ ✲ 🖙 P

HADLEIGH, Suffolk Map ref 3B2

♦♦♦ **THE WHITE HART**
46 Bridge Street, Hadleigh, Ipswich
IP7 6DB
T: (01473) 822206
F: (01473) 822206
E: enquiries@whiteharthadleight.
co.uk
I: www.whiteharthadleigh.co.uk

Bedrooms: 4 double/
twin
Bathrooms: 4 en suite

Lunch available
Evening meal available
CC: Mastercard, Switch,
Visa

B&B per night:
S £30.00
D £55.00

HB per person:
DY £40.00

OPEN All year round

*A picturesque 16thC beamed country pub and restaurant located on the outskirts of
Hadleigh overlooking the local cricket ground.*

🅰 ⏰ ♨ 🖥 ▢ ♦ ⌖ 🍷 Ⓢ ✂ ◐ Ⅲ ✲ 🐎 🖙 ⚟ 🏤 P

HALESWORTH, Suffolk Map ref 3C2

♦♦♦

THE ANGEL HOTEL
Thoroughfare, Halesworth IP19 8AH
T: (01986) 873365
F: (01986) 874891
E: angel@halesworth.ws
I: www.halesworth.ws/angel/

B&B per night:
S £35.00–£39.00
D £50.00–£55.00

OPEN All year round

*A characterful 16thC coaching inn
situated at the centre of the thriving
market town of Halesworth. Apart
from the 7 very individual en suite
bedrooms the inn has 3 bars, a
central glass-roofed courtyard and a
60-seat Italian restaurant.
Traditional bar food also served. Car
parking. Bicycle store.*

Bedrooms: 7 double/
twin
Bathrooms: 7 en suite

20% discount on stays over 5 nights.

Lunch available
Evening meal available
CC: Amex, Delta, Diners,
Mastercard, Switch, Visa

⏰ 📞 🖥 ▢ ♦ ⌖ 🍷 Ⓢ ✂ Ⅲ ☎ ▶ ✲ 🐎 🏤 P

HALESWORTH continued

◆◆◆ FEN WAY GUEST HOUSE

Fen Way, School Lane, Halesworth
IP19 8BW
T: (01986) 873574

Bedrooms: 3 double/twin
Bathrooms: 1 en suite

B&B per night:
S £20.00–£25.00
D £36.00–£46.00

Spacious bungalow in 7 acres of peaceful medowland, pets include sheep and lambs. Five minutes' walk from town centre. Convenient for many places including Southwold 9 miles.

OPEN All year round

🏠5 🛁 🖭 🖵 🗣 🖎 ⑤ ⌦ 🖾 🛏 🗗 ∪ ⊦ ☼ 🚲 P

◆◆◆ THE HUNTSMAN AND HOUNDS

Stone Street, Spexhall, Halesworth
IP19 0RN
T: (01986) 781341
E: huntmanspexhall@aol.com

Bedrooms: 3 double/twin
Bathrooms: 3 en suite

Lunch available
Evening meal available
CC: Delta, Diners, Mastercard, Switch, Visa

B&B per night:
S £30.00
D £44.00

HB per person:
DY £33.00

A 15thC inn with original beams, beautiful garden and pond. A family-run business specialising in good food, real ale and a warm welcome.

OPEN All year round

🏠 🐎 🖵 🗣 🍷 ⑤ ⌦ 🖾 ☼ 🐕 🚲 🏬 P

HARLESTON, Suffolk Map ref 3C2

◆◆◆

WESTON HOUSE FARM

Mendham, Harleston IP20 0PB
T: (01986) 782206 & 07803 099203
F: (01986) 782414
E: holden@farmline.com

B&B per night:
S £24.00–£29.00
D £40.00–£50.00

HB per person:
DY £32.00–£41.00

This peacefully located 17thC Grade II Listed farmhouse set in a one-acre garden offers comfortable, spacious accommodation on a 300-acre mixed farm on the Norfolk/Suffolk border. It is within easy reach of Suffolk Heritage Coast, Minsmere Nature Reserve, Norfolk Broads, the historic city of Norwich and nearby otter sanctuary.

Bedrooms: 3 double/twin
Bathrooms: 3 en suite

Evening meal available
CC: Amex

🏠 🐎 🖭 🖵 🗣 ⑤ ⌦ 🖾 🛏 🛏 ∪ ☼ 🐕 🚲 🏬 P

HARPENDEN, Hertfordshire Map ref 2D1

◆◆◆ MILTON HOTEL

25 Milton Road, Harpenden
AL5 5LA
T: (01582) 762914

Bedrooms: 2 single, 8 double/twin
Bathrooms: 8 en suite

CC: Mastercard, Visa

B&B per night:
S £30.00–£45.00
D £55.00

Family-run, comfortable hotel in residential area close to mainline station, junctions 9/10 of M1 and convenient for M25. Car park.

OPEN All year round

🅰️ 🏠 🖭 🖵 🗣 🖎 ⑤ 🖾 🛏 🖾 🍷 ☼ P

HARWICH, Essex Map ref 3C2 *Tourist Information Centre Tel: (01255) 506139*

◆◆◆ NEW FARM HOUSE

Spinnels Lane, Wix, Manningtree
CO11 2UJ
T: (01255) 870365
F: (01255) 870837
E: newfarmhouse@which.net
I: www.newfarmhouse.com

Bedrooms: 2 single, 4 double/twin, 5 triple/multiple
Bathrooms: 9 en suite

Evening meal available
CC: Delta, Mastercard, Switch, Visa

B&B per night:
S £29.00–£39.00
D £44.00–£58.00

OPEN All year round

Large, non-working farmhouse in 4 acres of grounds, 10 minutes' drive from Harwich, convenient for Colchester and Constable Country. Spacious public rooms. Home cooking, licensed.

🅰️ 🏠 🐎 🖭 🖵 🗣 🍷 ⑤ ⌦ 🖾 🛏 ☼ 🚲 P

QUALITY ASSURANCE SCHEME

Diamond ratings and awards were correct at the time of going to press but are subject to change. Please check at the time of booking.

HARWICH continued

◆◆◆ **PASTON LODGE**
1 Una Road, Parkeston, Harwich
CO12 4PP
T: (01255) 551390 & 07867 888498
F: (01255) 551390
E: dwright@globalnet.co.uk

Bedrooms: 1 single,
1 double/twin, 1 triple/
multiple
Bathrooms: 3 en suite

B&B per night:
S £21.00–£26.00
D £42.00–£48.00

OPEN All year round

Edwardian house offering comfortable en suite bed and breakfast facilities, situated within walking distance of Harwich International port.

HAUGHLEY, Suffolk Map ref 3B2

◆◆◆◆ **RED HOUSE FARM**
Station Road, Haughley,
Stowmarket IP14 3QP
T: (01449) 673323
F: (01449) 675413
E: mary@noy1.fsnet.co.uk
I: www.farmstayanglia.co.uk

Bedrooms: 2 single,
2 double/twin
Bathrooms: 4 en suite

B&B per night:
S £28.00
D £45.00

Attractive farmhouse in rural location on small grassland farm. First class breakfast. Central heating and large garden.

HETHERSETT, Norfolk Map ref 3B1

◆◆◆ **MAGNOLIA HOUSE**
Cromwell Close, Hethersett,
Norwich NR9 3HD
T: (01603) 810749
F: (01603) 810749

Bedrooms: 2 single,
3 double/twin

B&B per night:
S £22.00–£26.00
D £44.00–£48.00

OPEN All year round

Family-run B&B. All rooms centrally heated, colour TV, hot water, tea/coffee making facilities. Laundry, public telephone and fax available. Weekend break discounts. Private car park.

HEVINGHAM, Norfolk Map ref 3B1

◆◆◆◆ **MARSHAM ARMS INN**
Holt Road, Hevingham, Norwich
NR10 5NP
T: (01603) 754268
F: (01603) 754839
E: nigelbradley@marshamarms.co.uk
I: www.marshamarms.co.uk

Bedrooms: 8 double/
twin
Bathrooms: 8 en suite

Lunch available
Evening meal available
CC: Amex, Delta,
Mastercard, Switch, Visa

B&B per night:
S £42.50–£45.00
D £60.00–£70.00

OPEN All year round

Set in peaceful Norfolk countryside within reach of Norwich, the Broads and the coast. Comfortable and spacious accommodation, good food and a fine selection of ales.

HINDRINGHAM, Norfolk Map ref 3B1

◆◆◆◆◆
Gold
Award

FIELD HOUSE
Moorgate Road, Hindringham, Fakenham
NR21 0PT
T: (01328) 878726
T: (01328) 878955
E: wendyfieldhouse@lineone.net
I: www.northnorfolk.co.uk/fieldhouse

B&B per night:
D £50.00–£70.00

HB per person:
DY £45.00–£55.00

OPEN All year round

Field House stands in lovely gardens on the edge of the peaceful village, close to the north Norfolk Coast, and enjoys fine views of the Norfolk countryside. Luxury bedrooms with many thoughtful extras. The lounge and dining room are superbly furnished. Quality cooking with dinner being a highlight.

Bedrooms: 2 double/
twin
Bathrooms: 2 en suite

Evening meal available

HITCHIN, Hertfordshire Map ref 2D1

◆◆◆

THE LORD LISTER HOTEL
1 Park Street, Hitchin SG4 9AH
T: (01462) 432712 & 459451
F: (01462) 438506

B&B per night:
S £45.00–£65.00
D £55.00–£75.00

OPEN All year round

18thC country-style hotel on the edge of Hitchin town centre. Warm atmosphere with friendly and helpful staff. Individually furnished rooms, all en suite, some non-smoking. Lounge, cosy bar, free car park. Good choice of menu offered for breakfast. Special weekend rates.

Bedrooms: 4 single, 13 double/twin, 3 triple/ multiple
Bathrooms: 20 en suite

CC: Amex, Delta, Diners, Mastercard, Switch, Visa

HUNSTANTON, Norfolk Map ref 3B1 *Tourist Information Centre Tel: (01485) 532610*

◆◆◆

ECCLES COTTAGE
Heacham Road, Sedgeford,
Hunstanton PE36 5LU
T: (01485) 572688
E: mike99.barker@virgin.net

Bedrooms: 1 double/ twin
Bathrooms: 1 en suite

Evening meal available

B&B per night:
S £22.50
D £45.00

HB per person:
DY £28.50

OPEN All year round

Traditional-style Norfolk cottage in rural location with uninterrupted views of countryside. Ample secure parking, 3 miles to sea. Village on Pedars Way.

◆◆◆◆

THE GABLES
28 Austin Street, Hunstanton PE36 6AW
T: (01485) 532514
E: bbatthegables@aol.com

B&B per night:
S Min £25.00
D £38.00–£50.00

HB per person:
DY £31.99–£37.99

OPEN All year round

A warm welcome awaits at our lovely refurbished Edwardian house, built of local Norfolk carrstone, with retains many original features combined with modern en suite facilities with many luxuries. Glorious sea views, superb breakfasts, delicious evening meals. Ideal location for beach, sailing, golfing, windsurfing, kitesurfing, birdwatching, rambling or just relaxing.

Bedrooms: 2 double/ twin, 3 triple/multiple
Bathrooms: 5 en suite

Lunch available
Evening meal available

Small groups welcome and special group discount on 2 night stays available at certain times of the year.

HUNTINGDON, Cambridgeshire Map ref 3A2 *Tourist Information Centre Tel: (01480) 388588*

◆◆◆

GRANGE HOTEL
115 High Street, Brampton,
Huntingdon PE28 4RA
T: (01480) 459516
F: (01480) 459391
E: enquiries@
grangehotelbrampton.com
I: www.grangehotelbrampton.
com .co.uk

Bedrooms: 4 single, 3 double/twin, 1 triple/ multiple
Bathrooms: 7 en suite

Lunch available
Evening meal available
CC: Amex, Delta, Mastercard, Switch, Visa

B&B per night:
S £50.00–£65.00
D £65.00–£85.00

HB per person:
DY £65.00–£75.00

OPEN All year round

Period house converted to small hotel. A la carte restaurant, bar meals and extensive wine list. Quiet, convenient location close to A1/A14 and Huntingdon.

MAP REFERENCES
Map references apply to the colour maps at the front of this guide.

HUNTINGDON continued

 PRINCE OF WALES

Potton Road, Hilton, Huntingdon	Bedrooms: 2 single,	Lunch available
PE28 9NG	2 double/twin	Evening meal available
T: (01480) 830257	Bathrooms: 4 en suite	CC: Amex, Delta,
F: (01480) 830257		Mastercard, Switch, Visa
E: princeof wales.hilton@talk21.		
com		

B&B per night:
S £45.00–£50.00
D £65.00

OPEN All year round

Friendly traditional village inn only a short drive from Huntingdon, St Ives, Cambridge and Peterborough. CAMRA Good Beer Guide listed, real ale and good value, hearty meals.

人 ꗃ 5 ᐸ 🕭 ❑ ⬇ ⚲ 🍽 🆂 📖 🖥 🔍 ∪ ✲ 🐴 🚲 P

IPSWICH, Suffolk Map ref 3B2 *Tourist Information Centre Tel: (01473) 258070*

◆◆◆◆
Silver
Award

MOCKBEGGARS HALL

Paper Mill Lane, Claydon, Ipswich IP6 0AH
T: (01473) 830239 & 0770 2627770
F: (01473) 832989
E: pru@mockbeggars.co.uk
I: www.mockbeggars.co.uk

B&B per night:
S £32.00–£42.00
D £45.00–£55.00

OPEN All year round

Jacobean manor house, Grade II	Bedrooms: 2 double/	Evening meal available
Listed, with spacious, comfortable	twin, 4 triple/multiple	CC: Delta, Mastercard,
accommodation in rural setting, but	Bathrooms: 6 en suite	Switch, Visa
close to Ipswich. A warm welcome is		
extended to our guests in a relaxed	Winter breaks (minimum 2 nights). Sailing days or	
atmosphere. Ideally placed for	short breaks, also tuition. 35' yacht. Enjoy our	
sightseeing around Suffolk and	complementary therapies, appointment necessary.	
North Essex or for business in the		
town. Bed and breakfast and self		
catering offered. Brochures available.		

人 ꗃ 🕭 ❑ ⬇ ⚲ 🆂 ⅃ 📖 🖥 🍴 ✲ 🐴 🚲 🎠

KELVEDON, Essex Map ref 3B3

◆◆◆ **HIGHFIELDS FARM**

Kelvedon, Colchester CO5 9BJ	Bedrooms: 3 double/
T: (01376) 570334	twin
F: (01376) 570334	Bathrooms: 3 en suite
E: HighfieldsFarm@farmersweekly.	
net	

B&B per night:
S Min £24.00
D £44.00–£46.00

OPEN All year round

700-acre arable and horse farm. Timber-framed farmhouse in quiet location in open countryside. Easy access to A12. Heating in all rooms.

ꗃ 🖊 ❑ ⬇ ⚲ 🆂 ⅃ 📖 🖥 ∪ ✲ 🐴 🚲 🎠 P

KERSEY, Suffolk Map ref 3B2

◆◆◆ **RED HOUSE FARM**

Wickerstreet Green, Kersey, Ipswich	Bedrooms: 1 single,	Evening meal available
IP7 6EY	2 double/twin	
T: (01787) 210245	Bathrooms: 2 en suite	

B&B per night:
S £25.00–£28.00
D £40.00–£44.00

HB per person:
DY £29.00–£38.00

OPEN All year round

Comfortable, Listed farmhouse between Kersey and Boxford, central for Constable Country. Rooms have TV and tea-making facilities. Swimming pool.

🖊 🕭 ❑ ⬇ ⚲ 🆂 📖 🖥 ⇆ ↱ ✲ 🐴 🚲 🎠 P

KING'S LYNN, Norfolk Map ref 3B1 *Tourist Information Centre Tel: (01553) 763044*

◆◆◆◆ **FAIRLIGHT LODGE**

79 Goodwins Road, King's Lynn	Bedrooms: 2 single,
PE30 5PE	5 double/twin
T: (01553) 762234	Bathrooms: 4 en suite
F: (01553) 770280	
E: joella@nash42.freeserve.co.uk	
I: www.fairlightlodge.co.uk	

B&B per night:
S £20.00–£25.00
D £36.00–£42.00

OPEN All year round
except Christmas

Lovely owner-run Victorian house with friendly atmosphere and well appointed rooms. Ground floor en suite rooms available. Private parking. Closed Christmas.

人 ꗃ 🖊 ❑ ⬇ ⚲ 🆂 ⅃ 📖 🖥 🖊 ✲ 🐴 🚲 🎠 P

◆◆◆ **MARANATHA GUESTHOUSE**

115-117 Gaywood Road,	Bedrooms: 2 single,	CC: Amex, Mastercard,	B&B per night:
King's Lynn PE30 2PU	6 double/twin, 3 triple/	Switch, Visa	S £20.00–£25.00
T: (01553) 774596 & 772331	multiple		D £36.00–£45.00
F: (01553) 763747	Bathrooms: 5 en suite		

OPEN All year round

Large family-run guesthouse, 10 minutes' walk town centre, Lynnsport and Queen Elizabeth Hospital. Direct road to Sandringham and coast. Special rates for group bookings.

🐎 ⬜ 🛏 Ⓢ ✂ ⌕ 🖥 🖨 ✳ 🐾 P

KINGS LANGLEY, Hertfordshire Map ref 2D1

◆◆◆◆ **WOODCOTE HOUSE**

7 The Grove, Whippendell,	Bedrooms: 2 single,	Evening meal available	B&B per night:
Chipperfield, Kings Langley	2 double/twin		S £24.00–£30.00
WD4 9JF	Bathrooms: 4 en suite		D £42.00–£48.00
T: (01923) 262077			
F: (01923) 266198			OPEN All year round
E: leveridge@btinternet.com			

Timber-framed house, sitting in 1 acre of landscaped gardens with quiet rural aspect. Convenient for M1 and M25 and close to Watford and Hemel Hempstead.

🐎 🖥 Ⓢ ✂ ⌕ 🖥 🖨 ∪ ✳ 🐾 P

LAVENHAM, Suffolk Map ref 3B2

◆◆◆◆ **BRETT FARM**

The Common, Lavenham, Sudbury	Bedrooms: 3 double/		B&B per night:
CO10 9PG	twin		S Min £30.00
T: (01787) 248533	Bathrooms: 2 en suite,		D £45.00–£50.00
	1 private		

OPEN All year round

Riverside bungalow set in rural surroundings within walking distance of Lavenham High Street. Three comfortable bedrooms, 2 en suite, 1 private bath. Stabling available.

🐎 🖥 ⬜ 🛏 🔒 Ⓢ ✂ ⌕ 🖥 🖨 ✳ 🐾 P

◆◆◆◆
Silver
Award

LAVENHAM GREAT HOUSE HOTEL

Market Place, Lavenham, Sudbury
CO10 9QZ
T: (01787) 247431
F: (01787) 248007
E: info@greathouse.co.uk
I: www.greathouse.co.uk

B&B per night:
S £65.00–£90.00
D £75.00–£150.00

HB per person:
DY £63.95–£90.00

OPEN Feb–Dec

Delightful 16thC house with award-winning restaurant, on magnificent Lavenham square. Beautifully decorated, individual bedooms, all furnished with antiques. Most have sitting areas and provide every comfort to modern travellers. Daily changing lunch and dinner (not Saturday) set menus offer excellent value. (One 4-poster bedroom).

Bedrooms: 4 double/	Lunch available
twin, 1 triple/multiple;	Evening meal available
suites available	CC: Amex, Delta,
Bathrooms: 5 en suite	Mastercard, Switch, Visa

2-3 night stay from £62.95pppn incl DB&B and full English breakfast. Available Tues-Thurs incl.

🏰 🐎 🖥 ☎ ⬜ 🛏 🔒 Ⓨ Ⓢ ✂ ⌕ 🖥 🖨 ✳ 🐾 🏮 P

◆◆◆◆

THE OLD CONVENT

The Street, Kettlebaston, Ipswich IP7 7QA
T: (01449) 741557
E: holidays@kettlebaston.fsnet.co.uk
I: www.kettlebaston.fsnet.co.uk

B&B per night:
S £27.50–£30.00
D £45.00–£60.00

OPEN All year round

A warm welcome awaits you in our comfortable 17thC Grade II Listed thatched house. Attractive bedrooms with en suite facilities. Exposed beams; seasonal log fires. Ample off-street parking. Guests' TV lounge. Centrally located for touring. Colour brochure available.

| Bedrooms: 3 double/ |
| twin |
| Bathrooms: 3 en suite |

🏰 🖥 🛏 🔒 Ⓢ ✂ ⌕ 🖥 🖨 ∪ ✳ 🐾 🏮 P

LEISTON, Suffolk Map ref 3C2

◆◆◆◆
Silver
Award

FIELD END
1 Kings Road, Leiston IP16 4DA
T: (01728) 833527
F: (01728) 833527
E: pwright@field-end.freeserve.co.uk
I: www.field-end.freeserve.co.uk

Bedrooms: 2 single,
2 double/twin, 1 triple/
multiple; suites available
Bathrooms: 1 en suite,
4 private

Evening meal available

B&B per night:
S £28.00–£35.00
D £48.00–£52.00

OPEN All year round

A comfortable, newly refurbished Edwardian house with many original features; in ideal central position for touring the Suffolk Heritage Coast.

🏍🐎🖭⬜♨🍴⑂Ⓢ⤢🎝🖳🖩🛋🚲P

LITTLE CANFIELD, Essex Map ref 2D1

◆◆◆◆◆
Silver
Award

CANFIELD MOAT
High Cross Lane West, Little Canfield,
Dunmow CM6 1TD
T: (01371) 872565 & 07881 165 049
F: (01371) 876264
E: falk@canfieldmoat.co.uk
I: www.canfieldmoat.co.uk

B&B per night:
D £55.00–£68.00

OPEN All year round

A Georgian rectory set in 8 acres including lawns, paddocks, woodland and a small lake. All rooms are spacious and beautifully furnished. Antique furniture and log fires feature in the public rooms. Breakfast includes eggs from our own chickens. Afternoon tea with homemade cakes often available at no extra cost.

Bedrooms: 2 double/
twin
Bathrooms: 2 en suite

🐎10🖭⬜♨🍴Ⓢ⤢🖳🖩🛋⚲🔍⏻🌣🚲🅿P

LITTLE WALSINGHAM, Norfolk Map ref 3B1

◆◆

ST DAVID'S HOUSE
Friday Market, Little Walsingham,
Walsingham NR22 6BY
T: (01328) 820633 & 07710 044452
E: stdavidshouse@amserve.net
I: www.stilwell.co.uk

Bedrooms: 3 double/
twin, 2 triple/multiple
Bathrooms: 2 en suite

Lunch available
Evening meal available

B&B per night:
S £22.00–£25.00
D £44.00–£50.00

HB per person:
DY £34.00–£37.00

OPEN All year round

16thC brick house in a delightful medieval village. The village is fully signposted from Fakenham (A148). Four miles from the coast.

🐎🖭♨🍴Ⓢ⤢🖳🖩🛋⚲🐾🐕🚲🏺

LOWESTOFT, Suffolk Map ref 3C1

◆◆◆◆

ALBANY HOTEL
400 London Road South, Lowestoft
NR33 0BQ
T: (01502) 574394
F: (01502) 581198
E: geoffrey.ward@btclick.com
I: www.albanyhotel-lowestoft.co.uk

Bedrooms: 3 single,
2 double/twin, 3 triple/
multiple
Bathrooms: 6 en suite

Evening meal available
CC: Delta, Mastercard,
Switch, Visa

B&B per night:
S £20.00–£30.00
D £42.00–£55.00

HB per person:
DY £26.95–£42.50

OPEN All year round

'The small hotel with the BIG welcome' offers standard and luxury accommodation within easy reach of town centre and three minutes from award-winning beach.

🏍🐎🖭⬜♨🍷Ⓢ🖳🖩🛋🐕🚲🔊P

USE YOUR *i*s

There are more than 550 Tourist Information Centres throughout England offering friendly help with accommodation and holiday ideas as well as suggestions of places to visit and things to do. You'll find TIC addresses in the local Phone Book.

♦♦♦♦♦

CHURCH FARM

Corton, Lowestoft NR32 5HX
T: (01502) 730359
F: (01502) 733426
E: medw149227@aol.com

B&B per night:
S Max £30.00
D £40.00–£45.00

OPEN Mar–Oct

Britain's most easterly farm near rural beach and cliff walks. Victorian farmhouse, attractive, high standard en suite double-bedded rooms. Generous traditional English breakfast. Non-smoking. German spoken. On A12 from Lowestoft to Great Yarmouth into Stirrups Lane, Church Farm opposite Corton Parish Church.

Bedrooms: 3 double/twin
Bathrooms: 3 en suite

♦♦♦

THE SANDCASTLE
35 Marine Parade, Lowestoft
NR33 0QN
T: (01502) 511799
F: (01502) 511799
E: rocketfuel@lineone.net

Bedrooms: 1 double/twin, 2 triple/multiple; suites available
Bathrooms: 2 en suite

CC: Mastercard, Visa

B&B per night:
S £20.00–£25.00
D £40.00–£45.00

OPEN All year round

A world of comfort, care and Aga cuisine await you and your family at this beautifully appointed Victorian seafront house.

♦♦♦

ADARA LODGE
539 Hitchin Road, Luton LU2 7UL
T: (01582) 731361

Bedrooms: 1 double/twin
Bathrooms: 1 private

Evening meal available

B&B per night:
S Min £25.00
D Min £50.00

HB per person:
DY Min £37.50

OPEN All year round

Very comfortable, peaceful home with beautiful garden and off-road parking. Home cooking. Convenient M1, airport, station, town and sports centre.

♦♦

44 SKELTON CLOSE
Barton Hills, Luton LU3 4HF
T: (01582) 495205

Bedrooms: 1 single, 1 double/twin
Bathrooms: 2 private

B&B per night:
S £20.00–£24.00
D £32.00–£36.00

OPEN All year round

Quiet, detached house 4 miles from Luton Airport (good taxi service). Easy reach of M1, A6 and trains to London.

♦♦♦

LITTLE OWLS
Post Office Road,
Woodham Mortimer, Maldon
CM9 6ST
T: (01245) 224355 & 07889 964584
F: (01245) 224355
E: the.bushes@virgin.net

Bedrooms: 3 double/twin
Bathrooms: 1 en suite, 1 private

B&B per night:
S £20.00–£30.00
D £40.00–£50.00

OPEN All year round

Friendly, family-run establishment, set in rural Essex. Bedrooms are light and spacious with panoramic views over surrounding countryside. Large garden with heated indoor swimming pool.

CHECK THE MAPS

The colour maps at the front of this guide show all the cities, towns and villages for which you will find accommodation entries. Refer to the town index to find the page on which they are listed.

◆◆◆◆

GARNISH HALL
Margaret Roding, Dunmow CM6 1QL
T: (01245) 231209 & 231224
F: (01245) 231224

B&B per night:
S £30.00–£33.00
D £55.00

HB per person:
DY £42.50–£48.00

OPEN All year round

A 16thC manor house, once moated. Graceful curved staircase. Bedrooms with lovely views of the island. On A1060 Chelmsford road, adjacent to a Norman church which boasts perhaps the most attractive doorway in Essex. Black swans, carp. Tennis court, walled garden. Walking distance of Reid Rooms, popular for the Punchbowl.

Bedrooms: 3 double/ twin; suites available
Bathrooms: 2 en suite, 1 private

Lunch available
Evening meal available

Mid-week breaks-3 nights for the price of 2 (Mon-Thurs).

🛇🐴☐➡🖤🏐🏆Ⓢ✂🛏🖩🛋🍴🔍☽⚘ 🚜 🐾 🏛 P

◆◆◆

GREYS
Ongar Road, Margaret Roding, Dunmow CM6 1QR
T: (01245) 231509

Bedrooms: 3 double/ twin

B&B per night:
S £24.00–£25.00
D Min £45.00

OPEN All year round

B&B in old beamed cottage on family arable/sheep farm. A no smoking house. Turn off A1060 in village at sign to Berners Roding, half a mile along.

🏐Ⓢ✂🛏🖩⚘ 🚜 🏛 P

◆◆◆◆

REGENCY GUESTHOUSE
The Street, Neatishead, Norwich NR12 8AD
T: (01692) 630233
F: (01692) 630233
E: wrigleyregency@talk21.com
I: www.norfolkbroads.com/regency

Bedrooms: 5 double/ twin
Bathrooms: 3 en suite

Evening meal available
CC: Diners

B&B per night:
D £44.00–£48.00

OPEN All year round

Peaceful Broads village. Ideal nature rambles, wildlife, bird-watching. Six miles coast/10 miles Norwich. Personal service. Renowned for generous English breakfasts. Laura Ashley rooms. Eating places nearby.

🛇☐➡🖤🏐Ⓢ✂🛏🛋⚘🐓⚘ 🚜 🐾 🏛 P

◆◆◆◆

THE MEADOW HOUSE
2A High Street, Burwell, Cambridge
CB5 0HB
T: (01638) 741926 & 741354
F: (01638) 743424
E: hilary@themeadowhouse.co.uk
I: www.themeadowhouse.co.uk

B&B per night:
S £25.00–£30.00
D £42.00–£45.00

OPEN All year round

Large well equipped modern house set in grounds of 2 acres, close to Newmarket Racecourse, Cambridge and Ely. King size double beds. Large car park. Generous breakfasts.

Bedrooms: 3 double/ twin, 3 triple/multiple
Bathrooms: 3 en suite

🛇1🅿☐➡🖤🏐Ⓢ✂🖩🛋⚘🐓⚘ 🚜 P

See under Beccles, Bungay, Coltishall, Hevingham, Lowestoft, Neatishead, Norwich, South Walsham, Wroxham

SPECIAL BREAKS
Many establishments offer special promotions and themed breaks. These are highlighted in red. (All such offers are subject to availability.)

◆◆◆ **BECKLANDS**

105 Holt Road, Horsford, Norwich NR10 3AB	Bedrooms: 4 single, 5 double/twin	CC: Diners, Mastercard, Visa	B&B per night: S £25.00–£30.00 D £40.00–£45.00
T: (01603) 898582 F: (01603) 754223	Bathrooms: 7 en suite, 1 private		

Quietly located modern house overlooking open countryside. 5 miles north of Norwich. Central for the Broads and coastal areas.

🛋 ♿ 📺 ☎ 🖐 Ⓢ 🕯 🏠 ☕ ✳ 🚲 P

◆◆◆◆

THE BLUE BOAR INN
259 Wroxham Road, Sprowston, Norwich
NR7 8RL
T: (01603) 426802
F: (01603) 487749
E: turnbull101@hotmail.com
I: www.norwich2nite.co.uk/pubs/blue boar/

B&B per night:
S £40.00–£50.00
D £45.00–£70.00

HB per person:
DY £55.00–£60.00

OPEN All year round

Well-situated 10 minutes' drive from blueboar.htm
the city centre, yet a few minutes from lovely countryside. Broads 15 minutes, coast 25 minutes. Five superb en suite bedrooms, executive standard. Two bars, an all non-smoking restaurant, delicious home-cooked food. Beautiful gardens and great kids' play area.

Bedrooms: 5 double/ twin	Lunch available Evening meal available
Bathrooms: 4 en suite, 1 private	CC: Amex, Delta, Mastercard, Switch, Visa

🛋 ☎ 📺 🖐 🌙 ♟ 🍷 Ⓢ 🕯 🏠 ☕ ➤ ✳ 🚲 P

◆◆◆ **CAVELL HOUSE**

Swardeston, Norwich NR14 8DZ T: (01508) 578195	Bedrooms: 1 single, 2 double/twin	Lunch available Evening meal available	B&B per night: S £18.00–£20.00 D £30.00–£40.00

Birthplace of nurse Edith Cavell. Rural Georgian farmhouse on edge of Swardeston village. Off B1113 south of Norwich, 5 miles from centre. Near university, new hospital.

OPEN All year round

🛋 📺 ☎ 🖐 🌙 Ⓢ 🕯 🏠 ☕ 🔍 ✳ 🐴 🚲 🏠 P

◆◆◆ **CHURCH FARM GUESTHOUSE**

Church Street, Horsford, Norwich NR10 3DB	Bedrooms: 4 double/ twin, 2 triple/multiple	CC: Delta, Diners, Mastercard, Visa	B&B per night: S £30.00–£35.00 D £45.00–£50.00
T: (01603) 898020 F: (01603) 891649 E: churchfarm.guesthouse@ btinternet.com I: www.btinternet.com/ ~churchfarm.guesthouse	Bathrooms: 6 en suite		OPEN All year round

Quiet, modernised 17thC farmhouse. Separate entrance, lounge and dining room for guests. Approximately 4 miles north of Norwich. All rooms en suite.

🛋 ♿ 📺 ☎ 🖐 🌙 Ⓢ 🕯 🏠 ☕ ✳ 🚲 P

◆◆◆◆ **EARLHAM GUESTHOUSE**

147 Earlham Road, Norwich NR2 3RG	Bedrooms: 3 single, 3 double/twin, 1 triple/ multiple	CC: Amex, Delta, Mastercard, Switch, Visa	B&B per night: S £24.00–£42.00 D £42.00–£48.00
T: (01603) 454169 F: (01603) 454169 E: earlhamgh@hotmail.com	Bathrooms: 2 en suite		OPEN All year round

Smart, non-smoking family guesthouse convenient for city and university. Vegetarian choices. Personal keys, hospitality tray, colour TV. Amex, Mastercard, Visa welcome.

📶 🛋 10 ☎ 🖐 Ⓢ 🕯 🏠 ☕ ✳ 🚲

MAP REFERENCES The map references refer to the colour maps at the front of this guide. The first figure is the map number; the letter and figure which follow indicate the grid reference on the map.

◆◆◆

EDMAR LODGE
64 Earlham Road, Norwich NR2 3DF
T: (01603) 615599
F: (01603) 495599
E: edmar@btconnect.com
I: www.edmarlodge.co.uk

B&B per night:
S £28.00–£32.00
D £40.00–£44.00

OPEN All year round

Edmar Lodge is a family-run guesthouse where you will receive a warm welcome from Ray and Sue. We are situated only 10 minutes' walk from the city centre. All rooms have en suite facilities and cable TV. We are well-known for our excellent breakfasts that set you up for the day.

Bedrooms: 4 double/ twin, 1 triple/multiple
Bathrooms: 5 en suite

CC: Amex, Delta, Diners, Mastercard, Switch, Visa

Weekend breaks Oct-Mar-special rates including discount on evening meals at local restaurant.

◆◆◆◆

ELM FARM COUNTRY HOUSE
55 Norwich Road, St Faiths
NR10 3HH
T: (01603) 898366
F: (01603) 897129
E: pmpbelmfarm@aol.com

Bedrooms: 3 single, 9 double/twin, 2 triple/ multiple
Bathrooms: 14 en suite

Lunch available
CC: Amex, Delta, Mastercard, Switch, Visa

B&B per night:
S £33.00–£38.00
D £54.00–£60.00

OPEN All year round

Situated in quiet, pretty village 4 miles north of Norwich. Ideal base for touring Norfolk and Suffolk. En suite chalet bedrooms. Breakfast served in farmhouse dining room. Licensed.

◆◆◆◆

THE GABLES GUESTHOUSE
527 Earlham Road, Norwich NR4 7HN
T: (01603) 456666
F: (01603) 250320

B&B per night:
S £40.00
D £58.00–£63.00

Friendly, family-run, non-smoking guesthouse with very high quality en suite accommodation, residents' lounge and full-size snooker table. Illuminated private car park at rear within secluded gardens. Situated within easy walking distance of university and close to Research Park and city centre.

Bedrooms: 10 double/ twin, 1 triple/multiple
Bathrooms: 11 en suite

CC: Delta, Mastercard, Switch, Visa

◆◆◆◆

KINGSLEY LODGE
3 Kingsley Road, Norwich NR1 3RB
T: (01603) 615819
F: (01603) 615819
E: kingsley@paston.co.uk

B&B per night:
S £30.00–£36.00
D £40.00–£46.00

Quiet, friendly, non-smoking Edwardian house in central Norwich. Close to the bus station and less than 10 minutes' walk to the Market Place, castle, shops and restaurants. All rooms have en suite bathroom, colour TV and tea/coffee making facilities. Full English breakfast, using mostly organic food, cooked to order. Parking permits provided.

Bedrooms: 1 single, 2 double/twin
Bathrooms: 3 en suite

◆◆◆◆

MANOR BARN HOUSE
Back Lane, Rackheath, Norwich NR13 6NN
T: (01603) 783543

B&B per night:
S £22.00–£25.00
D £44.00–£50.00

OPEN All year round

Traditional Norfolk barn conversion with exposed beams in quiet setting with pleasant gardens. Just off A1151, 2 miles from the heart of the Broads, 5 miles Norwich. Ideally situated for golf (2 minutes away), fishing, horse-riding. All rooms are en suite with colour TV, tea/coffee-making facilities. Guest lounge.

Bedrooms: 5 double/twin
Bathrooms: 4 en suite, 1 private

◆◆◆

MARLBOROUGH HOUSE HOTEL
22 Stracey Road, Norwich NR1 1EZ
T: (01603) 628005
F: (01603) 628005

Bedrooms: 9 single, 9 double/twin, 2 triple/multiple
Bathrooms: 12 en suite

Evening meal available

B&B per night:
S £26.00–£35.00
D £48.00–£54.00

HB per person:
DY £38.00–£47.00

OPEN All year round

Long established family hotel, close city centre, new Riverside development, Castle Mall, museum, cathedral. All double, twin and family rooms are en suite. Licensed bar, car park.

◆◆◆◆
Silver
Award

THE OLD RECTORY
Hall Road, Framingham Earl,
Norwich NR14 7SB
T: (01508) 493590
F: (01508) 495110
E: brucewellings@drivedevice.freeserve.co.uk

Bedrooms: 2 double/twin

B&B per night:
S £26.00–£30.00
D £46.00–£52.00

OPEN All year round

Beautifully renovated and extended 17thC family house set in 2 acres of country garden. Wealth of beams in lounge and dining room. Village 4.5 miles south-east of Norwich.

◆◆

ROSEDALE
145 Earlham Road, Norwich
NR2 3RG
T: (01603) 453743 & 07949 296542
F: (01603) 259887
E: drcbac@aol.com
I: www.members.aol.com/drcbac

Bedrooms: 2 single, 2 double/twin, 2 triple/multiple

CC: Delta, Mastercard, Switch, Visa

B&B per night:
S £22.00–£28.00
D £40.00–£48.00

OPEN All year round

Friendly, family-run, non-smoking Victorian guesthouse, on B1108, 1 mile from city centre. Restaurants, shops and university nearby, convenient for coast and Broads. Cards taken.

TOWN INDEX
This can be found at the back of the guide. If you know where you want to stay, the index will give you the page number listing accommodation in your chosen town, city or village.

♦♦♦

WEDGEWOOD HOUSE

42 St Stephens Road, Norwich NR1 3RE
T: (01603) 625730
F: (01603) 615035
E: stay@wedgewoodhouse.co.uk
I: www.wedgewoodhouse.co.uk

B&B per night:
S £28.00–£49.00
D £48.00–£55.00

OPEN All year round

Comfortable city centre Victorian home. Easy to find. Very close to Norwich's main sights, shops and bus station. Individually decorated rooms, most with en suite bath or shower. Dining room and most guest rooms are non-smoking. Freshly prepared breakfast. Children welcome under supervision of their parents. Parking.

Bedrooms: 2 single,
7 double/twin, 3 triple/
multiple
Bathrooms: 8 en suite,
2 private

CC: Delta, Mastercard,
Switch, Visa

Courtesy breaks Nov-Mar (excl public hol). 2 nights £23pppn. Single supplement. Must include a Sat.

ᛚᚱᚴᏚ☐☝◖Ⓢ✂⊯▥,☐☕P

♦♦♦

THE ANCHOR LODGE

28 Percival Street, Peterborough PE3 6AU
T: (01733) 312724 & 07767 611911

B&B per night:
S Min £20.00
D Min £40.00

OPEN All year round

Friendly establishment, 7 minutes' walk from shopping centre and railway. Ten minutes' drive to East of England Showground and A1.

Bedrooms: 4 double/
twin
Bathrooms: 3 en suite,
1 private

ᚱᏚ☐☝◖Ⓢ✂⊯▥,☐☕✳☘⊯P

♦♦♦

PARK ROAD GUESTHOUSE
67 Park Road, Peterborough
PE1 2TN
T: (01733) 562220
F: (01733) 344279

Bedrooms: 2 single,
2 double/twin, 1 triple/
multiple
Bathrooms: 4 en suite,
1 private

B&B per night:
S £28.00–£30.00
D £40.00–£45.00

OPEN All year round

Comfortable, family-run, 5 mins from city centre, close to coach and railway station. Good English breakfast, central heated. All rooms en suite, tea/coffee, colour TV and hairdryers.

ᚱ5᚛☐☝◖Ⓢ▥,☐☘⊯P

♦♦♦

THE THREE TUNS COACHING INN

Main Road, Pettistree, Woodbridge
IP13 0HW
T: (01728) 747979 & 746244
F: (01728) 746244
E: jon@threetuns-coachinginn.co.uk
I: www.threetuns-coachinginn.co.uk

B&B per night:
S £45.00–£55.00
D £65.00–£75.00

HB per person:
DY £45.00–£67.50

OPEN All year round

John and Brenda invite you to visit their enchanting coaching inn, ideally situated for visiting the Suffolk Heritage Coast. All rooms are en suite and fully equipped. After experiencing local ales at the bar and fine food in the restaurant, just relax in the comfortable lounge with its open log fires.

Bedrooms: 1 single,
10 double/twin
Bathrooms: 11 en suite

Lunch available
Evening meal available
CC: Amex, Delta,
Mastercard, Switch, Visa

ᛚᚱᚴᏚᛚᛒ☐☝◖Ⓨ☐Ⓢ✂⊯▥,☐✦▸✳☘⊞P

RAMSEY, Essex Map ref 3B2

◆◆◆◆ **WOODVIEW COTTAGE**

Wrabness Road, Ramsey, Harwich
CO12 5ND
T: (01255) 886413 & 07714 600134
E: pcohen@cix.co.uk
I: www.woodview-cottage.co.uk

Bedrooms: 1 double/ twin
Bathrooms: 1 private

B&B per night:
S £25.00–£30.00
D £42.00–£45.00

OPEN All year round

Spacious homely accommodation in pretty country cottage adjacent to nature reserve and the beautiful Stour estuary. Four miles from Harwich International.

RAMSHOLT, Suffolk Map ref 3C2

◆◆◆

THE RAMSHOLT ARMS

Dock Road, Ramsholt, Woodbridge
IP12 3AB
T: (01394) 411229
F: (01394) 411818

B&B per night:
S £37.50–£47.50
D £75.00–£95.00

OPEN All year round

A glorious tidal estuary setting, with a large terrace overlooking the River Deben, a sandy beach and a grassy area between. Surely the most beautiful pub lcoation in Suffolk. Voted the ninth best pub in the country (The Independent). Friendly staff, lovely atmosphere. Excellent food, good local walks, country accommodation.

Bedrooms: 4 double/ twin

Lunch available
Evening meal available
CC: Delta, Mastercard, Switch, Visa

Free hire of the marquee in summer.

RIVENHALL, Essex Map ref 3B3

◆◆◆◆

NORTH FORD FARM

Church Road, Rivenhall, Witham CM8 3PG
T: (01376) 583321 & 07957 862112
F: (01376) 583321

B&B per night:
S Min £30.00
D Min £50.00

Attractive and comfortable country property within short distance of mainline railway and trunk road, 30 minutes Stansted airport, M11, Harwich, 10 minutes Colchester. Non-smoking, twin en suite room. TV, tea and coffee-making facilities.

Bedrooms: 1 double/ twin, 1 triple/multiple
Bathrooms: 2 en suite

ROYSTON, Hertfordshire Map ref 2D1

◆◆◆◆ **HALL FARM**

Great Chishill, Royston SG8 8SH
T: (01763) 838263
F: (01763) 838263
E: wisehall@farming.co.uk
I: www.hallfarmbb.co.uk

Bedrooms: 2 double/ twin, 1 triple/multiple
Bathrooms: 1 en suite

B&B per night:
S £30.00–£35.00
D £40.00–£55.00

OPEN All year round

805-acre arable farm. Beautiful farmhouse accommodation on working farm, in secluded gardens on the highest point in Cambridgeshire. Royston 5 miles, Duxford Museum 4 miles, Cambridge 12 miles.

IMPORTANT NOTE Information on accommodation listed in this guide has been supplied by the proprietors. As changes may occur you are advised to check details at the time of booking.

343

RUMBURGH, Suffolk Map ref 3C2

♦♦♦♦ **RUMBURGH FARM**
Rumburgh, Halesworth IP19 0RU
T: (01986) 781351
F: (01986) 781351
E: binder@rumburghfarm.
freeserve.co.uk
I: www.rumburghfarm.freeserve.co.
uk

Bedrooms: 2 double/
twin
Bathrooms: 2 en suite

B&B per night:
S £25.00–£27.00
D £38.00–£45.00

OPEN All year round

20-acre mixed farm. A friendly welcome in an attractive 17thC Suffolk farmhouse peacefully situated on a working farm.

ST ALBANS, Hertfordshire Map ref 2D1 *Tourist Information Centre Tel: (01727) 864511*

♦♦♦♦

FERN COTTAGE
116 Old London Road, St Albans AL1 1PU
T: (01727) 834200 & 07957 484349
E: dorotheabristow@ntlworld.com
I: www.ferncottage.uk.net

B&B per night:
S £35.00–£45.00
D £50.00–£55.00

OPEN All year round

A warm welcome awaits you at this charming 19thC locally Listed character cottage. All tastefully decorated bedrooms are en suite with tea/coffee facilities. Off-street parking available. Situated within walking distance of the historic town centre, cathedral and Thameslink station. Kings Cross, London is only 20 minutes' journey by train.

Bedrooms: 3 double/
twin
Bathrooms: 3 en suite

♦♦♦♦
Silver
Award

RIVERSIDE
24 Minister Court, St Albans
AL2 2NF
T: (01727) 758780 & 0771 5824936
F: (01727) 758760
E: Ellispatriciam@aol.com

Bedrooms: 1 single,
1 triple/multiple; suites
available
Bathrooms: 1 en suite,
1 private

B&B per night:
S £30.00–£35.00
D £55.00–£60.00

HB per person:
DY £65.00–£70.00

OPEN All year round

Spacious Edwardian villa-type residence, offering high standard accommodation, in a rural river and lakeside setting. Close access to all motorway and railway links.

♦♦♦♦

TRESCO
76 Clarence Road, St Albans
AL1 4NG
T: (01727) 864880
F: (01727) 864880
E: pat.leggatt@talk21.com
I: www.twistedsilicon.co.uk/76/
index.htm

Bedrooms: 1 single,
1 double/twin

B&B per night:
S £30.00–£35.00
D £50.00–£55.00

OPEN All year round

Spacious Edwardian house with quiet, comfortable rooms and pleasant conservatory. Park nearby. Easy walk to station for fast trains to London (20 minutes).

CHECK THE MAPS
The colour maps at the front of this guide show all the cities, towns and villages for which you will find accommodation entries. Refer to the town index to find the page on which they are listed.

◆◆◆◆◆
Silver
Award

HIGHFIELD FARM
Great North Road, Sandy SG19 2AQ
T: (01767) 682332
F: (01767) 692503
E: stay@highfield-farm.co.uk

B&B per night:
S £30.00–£50.00
D £50.00–£60.00

OPEN All year round

Beautifully peaceful, welcoming farmhouse in own grounds on attractive arable farm. Wonderful location well back from A1. Bedford, Cambridge, Biggleswade, St Neots Hitchin and Stevenage all within easy reach. London just 50 minutes by train. Delightful sitting room for guests' use. Hospitality tray in each bedroom. Safe parking. Most guests return.

Bedrooms: 6 double/ twin, 2 triple/multiple
Bathrooms: 6 en suite, 1 private

CC: Delta, Mastercard, Switch, Visa

◆◆◆◆
MOAT HOUSE FARM
Rendham Road, Carlton,
Saxmundham IP17 2QN
T: (01728) 602228
F: (01728) 602228
E: sally@goodacres.com
I: www.goodacres.com

Bedrooms: 2 double/ twin
Bathrooms: 2 en suite

B&B per night:
S £25.00–£28.00
D £40.00–£50.00

OPEN All year round

Detached property set in grounds of 3.5 acres with traditional Suffolk barns. We are surrounded by open farmland. Easy access to the A12 trunk road.

◆◆◆◆◆
Silver
Award

NORTH LODGE GUEST HOUSE
6 North Entrance, Saxmundham IP17 1AY
T: (01728) 603337
E: northlodgetoto@aol.com

B&B per night:
S £37.50–£45.00
D £55.00–£75.00

OPEN All year round

Explore Suffolk and its Heritage Coast from our beautifully renovated Grade II Listed guesthouse. Relax in our library. Unwind with a drink in our residents' lounge with its grand piano and open fire. Amble in our walled garden. Enjoy the delights of good home cooking from our kitchen.

Bedrooms: 5 double/ twin, 1 triple/multiple
Bathrooms: 6 en suite

Lunch available
Evening meal available
CC: Delta, Mastercard, Switch, Visa

◆◆◆◆
HOLMWOOD HOUSE
Tunstead Road, Scottow, Norwich
NR10 5DA
T: (01692) 538386
F: (01692) 538386
E: holmwoodhouse@lineone.net
I: www.norfolkbroads.com/
holmwood

Bedrooms: 3 double/ twin
Bathrooms: 2 en suite, 1 private

B&B per night:
S £25.00–£27.00
D £36.00–£42.00

OPEN All year round

Situated edge of village, rural views, secluded garden, ample parking, ensuite/private bathroom. Tea/coffee. Television/Hairdryer in all bedrooms. Guests lounge, full English breakfast .

◆◆◆

THE BURLINGTON LODGE

5 St Nicholas Place, Sheringham NR26 8LF
T: (01263) 820931 & 822053
F: (01263) 820964
E: r.mcdermott@hemscott.net

B&B per night:
S £22.50–£27.50
D £45.00–£55.00

HB per person:
DY £32.50–£37.50

OPEN All year round

Edwardian villa set in extensive gardens and only 100 yards to the Blue Flag beach, and 2 minutes' walk to the town centre. All bedrooms are en suite, with sea or garden views from most rooms. The spacious family rooms also have the use of a kitchen facility including fridge and microwave.

Bedrooms: 7 double/ twin, 4 triple/multiple
Bathrooms: 11 en suite

Evening meal available

🏠🛏🖥📺♿🕯🄎🍴🅿 P

◆◆◆

CAMBERLEY GUESTHOUSE

62 Cliff Road, Sheringham NR26 8BJ
T: (01263) 823101
F: (01263) 821433
E: graham@camberleyguesthouse.co.uk
I: www.camberleyguesthouse.co.uk

B&B per night:
S £25.00–£32.00
D £40.00–£54.00

OPEN All year round

Friendly, relaxing comfortable and spacious. By the sea in a quiet part of Sheringham, views overlooking sea, town and countryside. Slipway to beach opposite. All bedrooms en suite, soap, towels, hairdryers and colour TV. Comfortably furnished lounge. Attractive setting for breakfast. Access to rooms at all times. Car parking in grounds.

Bedrooms: 4 double/ twin
Bathrooms: 4 en suite

🄰🏠📺♿🕯🄎🍴U⚓☼🚗 P

◆◆◆◆

WILLOW LODGE

6 Vicarage Road, Sheringham NR26 8NH
T: (01263) 822204
F: (01263) 822204

Bedrooms: 5 double/ twin, 2 triple/multiple
Bathrooms: 5 en suite

CC: Delta, Mastercard, Switch, Visa

B&B per night:
S £35.00
D £50.00–£56.00

OPEN All year round

In a quiet residential area, approximately 10 minutes' walk to town centre and sea. All beds en suite with central heating, TV, hairdryer, tea/coffee-making.

🏠5📺♿🕯🄎🍴☼🚗 P

Rating Applied For

HILL HOUSE FARM

Wades Lane, Shotley, Ipswich IP9 1EW
T: (01473) 787318 & 787111
F: (01473) 787111
E: richard@rjwrinch.fsnet.co.uk

Bedrooms: 1 double/ twin
Bathrooms: 1 private

B&B per night:
S Max £25.00
D Max £45.00

OPEN Mar–Oct

Georgian farmhouse, tastefully furnished, on 600-acre mixed farm. Unrivalled breathtaking views of Orwell Estuary. Five minutes' walk to riverbank. 10 minutes' from A14.

🏠12📺♿🄎🍴☼🐎🚗♨ P

SIBLE HEDINGHAM, Essex Map ref 3B2

◆◆◆◆

TOCAT HOUSE
9 Potter Street, Sible Hedingham,
Halstead CO9 3RG
T: (01787) 461942

Bedrooms: 3 double/
twin

Lunch available
Evening meal available

B&B per night:
S Min £30.00
D Min £50.00

HB per person:
DY £45.00

Victorian Grade II Listed building. Comfortable, elegant family home with 3 tastefully furnished bedrooms. Mature, spacious garden with stunning views.

OPEN All year round

SIBTON, Suffolk Map ref 3C2

◆◆◆◆◆
Silver
Award

CHURCH FARM
Yoxford Road, Sibton, Saxmundham
IP17 2LX
T: (01728) 660101
F: (01728) 660102
E: dixons@church-farmhouse.demon.co.uk
I: www.church-farmhouse.demon.co.uk

B&B per night:
S £25.00–£35.00
D £46.00–£60.00

OPEN All year round

A warm welcome is assured at our period country house set in grounds of 3.5 acres amidst beautiful Suffolk countryside. A convenient location for the Heritage Coast. Relax in your elegant, light and exceptionally well-appointed bedroom and unwind in the deep sofas of the spacious and comfortable lounge.

Bedrooms: 3 double/
twin
Bathrooms: 2 en suite,
1 private

Special rates for stays of 5 nights or more.

SOUTH WALSHAM, Norfolk Map ref 3C1

◆◆◆◆

OLD HALL FARM
Newport Road, South Walsham,
Norwich NR13 6DS
T: (01603) 270271 & 270017
F: (01603) 270017
E: rdewing@freenet.co.uk
I: www.oldhallfarm.co.uk

Bedrooms: 3 double/
twin
Bathrooms: 3 en suite

B&B per night:
S £22.00–£25.00
D £44.00–£50.00

OPEN All year round

Recently restored 17thC thatched farmhouse. Comfortable rooms, all en suite. Wide range of cooked breakfasts. Ideal centre for Norwich coast and Norfolk Broads. Non-smoking.

SOUTHWOLD, Suffolk Map ref 3C2

◆◆◆

'NO 21' NORTH PARADE
Southwold IP18 6LT
T: (01502) 722573
F: (01502) 724326
E: richard.comrie@cwcom.net

B&B per night:
S Min £35.00
D £55.00–£70.00

OPEN All year round

Panoramic sea views overlooking a Blue Flag beach and promenade, ideally situated for exploring the Heritage Coast. Close to all amenities.

Bedrooms: 3 double/
twin
Bathrooms: 2 en suite,
1 private

3 nights for the price of 2, mid-week. 1 Nov-31 Mar
(excl Christmas and New Year).

CREDIT CARD BOOKINGS If you book by telephone and are asked for your credit card number it is advisable to check the proprietor's policy should you cancel your reservation.

◆◆◆◆ **NORTHCLIFFE GUESTHOUSE**

20 North Parade, Southwold
IP18 6LT
T: (01502) 724074 & 07702 588554
F: (01502) 724074
I: www.s-h-systems.co.uk/hotels/
northcli.html

Bedrooms: 1 single,
6 double/twin
Bathrooms: 5 en suite,
2 private

B&B per night:
S £35.00–£60.00
D £55.00–£70.00

OPEN All year round

Select en suite accommodation. Individually designed rooms of a high standard. Panoramic sea views. In quiet location next to beach, close to town centre. Lounge with log fire. Licensed.

◆◆◆◆

THE OLD VICARAGE
Wenhaston, Halesworth IP19 9EG
T: (01502) 478339
F: (01502) 478068
E: theycock@aol.com
I: www.southend.blythweb.co.uk/
oldvicarage

B&B per night:
S £25.00–£35.00
D £50.00–£60.00

OPEN All year round

Our period house in large grounds offers a peaceful stay. Close to Southwold, Minsmere Bird Reserve and Heritage Coast. You will receive a warm welcome and be able to stay in comfortable surroundings, with a full English breakfast in the morning to look forward to.

Bedrooms: 3 double/
twin
Bathrooms: 3 private

◆◆◆◆ **PROSPECT PLACE**

33 Station Road, Southwold
IP18 6AX
T: (01502) 722757
E: sally@prospect-place.demon.co.
uk
I: www.prospect-place.demon.co.uk

Bedrooms: 4 double/
twin, 1 triple/multiple
Bathrooms: 5 en suite

B&B per night:
S £25.00–£35.00
D £40.00–£50.00

OPEN All year round

Compact 15 bedroom hotel, all en suite. Attractive a la carte and table d hote restaurant, and bar lounge. Private meetings/wedding receptions can be booked in Wightman room.

◆◆◆◆
Silver
Award

THE ANGEL INN

Polstead Street, Stoke-by-Nayland,
Colchester CO6 4SA
T: (01206) 263245
F: (01206) 263373
I: www.angelhotel.com

Bedrooms: 6 double/
twin
Bathrooms: 6 en suite

Lunch available
Evening meal available
CC: Delta, Mastercard,
Switch, Visa

B&B per night:
S £52.00
D £67.00

OPEN All year round

Beautifully restored freehouse and restaurant in the historic village of Stoke-by-Nayland, in the heart of Constable Country.

◆◆◆◆ **THE STEP HOUSE**

Hockey Hill, Wetheringsett,
Stowmarket IP14 5PL
T: (01449) 766476
F: (01449) 766476
E: stephouse@talk21.com

Bedrooms: 2 double/
twin; suites available
Bathrooms: 2 en suite

B&B per night:
S £28.00
D £50.00

OPEN All year round

Built in the early 15thC. Orginally a hall house. Recently restored. Heavily beamed. Private garden. Inglenook fireplaces. Ideal for touring and the Heritage Coast.

QUALITY ASSURANCE SCHEME
Diamond ratings and awards are explained at the back of this guide.

STRETHAM, Cambridgeshire Map ref 3A2

◆◆◆

THE RED LION

High Street, Stretham, Ely CB6 3JQ
T: (01353) 648132
F: (01353) 648327
E: frank.hayes@gateway.net
I: www.redlion.org

B&B per night:
S Max £39.75
D Max £45.75

OPEN All year round

A village inn, completely refurbished, with 12 en suite bedrooms, ideally situated for visiting the Fens and other tourist attactions. Four miles from Ely on A10. Cambridge 12 miles, Newmarket 14 miles away. Pets welcome, car park. Non-smoking conservatory restaurant.

Bedrooms: 2 single, 7 double/twin, 3 triple/ multiple
Bathrooms: 12 en suite

Lunch available
Evening meal available
CC: Amex, Delta, Mastercard, Switch, Visa

SWAFFHAM PRIOR, Cambridgeshire Map ref 3B2

◆◆◆

STERLING FARM

Heath Road, Swaffham Prior, Cambridge CB5 0LA
T: (01638) 741431

Bedrooms: 2 double/ twin

B&B per night:
S £25.00
D £40.00–£50.00

OPEN All year round

Modernised farmhouse in 3-acre grounds, peaceful location with views over open countryside, ample parking space. Conveniently situated for Newmarket, Cambridge and Ely.

TERRINGTON ST JOHN, Norfolk Map ref 4D3

◆◆◆◆

SOMERVILLE HOUSE

Church Road, Terrington St John, Wisbech PE14 7RY
T: (01945) 880952
F: (01945) 880952
E: somervillemc@hotmail.com
I: www.somervillehouse.co.uk

Bedrooms: 1 single, 2 double/twin
Bathrooms: 2 en suite

Lunch available
Evening meal available
CC: Delta, Mastercard, Switch, Visa

B&B per night:
S £30.00–£35.00
D £50.00–£55.00

HB per person:
DY £38.50–£49.50

OPEN All year round

Period country house in large mature gardens. Comfortable, spacious accommodation with licensed fine dining restaurant. Small, friendly, family-run business.

THAXTED, Essex Map ref 3B2

◆◆◆◆
Silver
Award

CROSSWAYS GUESTHOUSE

32 Town Street, Thaxted, Dunmow CM6 2LA
T: (01371) 830348

Bedrooms: 2 double/ twin
Bathrooms: 2 en suite

B&B per night:
S £35.00–£38.00
D £53.00–£56.00

OPEN All year round

Elegant 16thC house with Georgian additions, situated on B184 in centre of Thaxted opposite the 600-year-old Guildhall.

◆◆◆

THE FARMHOUSE INN

Monk Street, Thaxted, Dunmow CM6 2NR
T: (01371) 830864
F: (01371) 831196

B&B per night:
S £38.50
D £50.00

OPEN All year round

A character rural inn with excellent cuisine, set in a tranquil backwater yet, only 8 miles from Stanstead Airport.

Bedrooms: 10 double/ twin
Bathrooms: 10 en suite

Lunch available
Evening meal available
CC: Amex, Delta, Mastercard, Switch, Visa

COLOUR MAPS Colour maps at the front of this guide pinpoint all places under which you will find accommodation listed.

WANGFORD, Suffolk Map ref 3C2

◆◆◆◆

POPLAR HALL
Frostenden Corner, Frostenden,
Wangford, Beccles NR34 7JA
T: (01502) 578549
I: www.southwold.co.uk/
poplar-hall/

Bedrooms: 1 single,
2 double/twin
Bathrooms: 1 en suite

B&B per night:
S £25.00
D £48.00–£56.00

OPEN All year round

An early 16thC house, in 1.5 acres of garden, surrounded by countryside only 2.5 miles from the sea and 3.5 miles from the charming town of Southwold. Luxury accommodation en suite, double or single.

WATTON, Norfolk Map ref 3B1

◆◆◆◆

THE WILLOW HOUSE
2 High Street, Watton, Thetford IP25 6AE
T: (01953) 881181 & (01760) 440760
F: (01953) 885885
E: willowhousewatton@barbox.net
I: www.willowhouse.net

B&B per night:
S £39.00–£45.00
D £45.00–£60.00

HB per person:
DY £50.00–£60.00

OPEN All year round

16thC thatched building with large open fireplaces and low-beamed bedrooms. Seven en suite bedrooms. Quality restaurant with a la carte and table d'hote menus. All food cooked to order using locally sourced produce whenever possible. Family-run with quality service.

Bedrooms: 6 double/
twin, 1 triple/multiple
Bathrooms: 7 en suite

Lunch available
Evening meal available
CC: Amex, Delta,
Mastercard, Switch, Visa

3 nights for price of 2, Oct-Mar (excl Christmas and New Year). Gourmet food weekends.

WEST SOMERTON, Norfolk Map ref 3C1

◆◆◆◆

THE WHITE HOUSE FARM
The Street, West Somerton,
Great Yarmouth NR29 4EA
T: (01493) 393991
E: prued@hotmail.com

B&B per night:
S Max £25.00
D Max £40.00

OPEN All year round

A 17thC farmhouse, providing a special location in all season – sunny conservatory, sheltered garden, log fires, books and videos, good and varied breakfasts, private/en suite bath/shower rooms, comfortable bedrooms and attractive guest sitting room. Near lovely beach and Broads waterways. Rowing dinghy available.

Bedrooms: 3 double/
twin
Bathrooms: 1 en suite,
2 private

Evening meal available

WOOLPIT, Suffolk Map ref 3B2

◆◆◆

THE BULL INN & RESTAURANT
The Street, Woolpit,
Bury St Edmunds IP30 9SA
T: (01359) 240393
E: trevor@howling.fsbusiness.co.uk

Bedrooms: 1 single,
2 double/twin, 1 triple/
multiple
Bathrooms: 4 en suite

Lunch available
Evening meal available
CC: Amex, Delta,
Mastercard, Switch, Visa

B&B per night:
S £25.00–£27.00
D £45.00–£50.00

HB per person:
DY £30.00–£40.00

OPEN All year round

Public house and restaurant offering good accommodation in centre of pretty village. Large garden, ample parking. Ideal base for touring Suffolk.

ACCESSIBILITY
Look for the 🛇 symbols which indicate accessibility for wheelchair users. A list of establishments is at the front of this guide.

WROXHAM PARK LODGE

142 Norwich Road, Wroxham,
Norwich NR12 8SA
T: (01603) 782991
E: prklodge@nascr.net
I: www.smoothhound.co.uk/hotels/
wroxhamp.html

Bedrooms: 3 double/
twin
Bathrooms: 3 en suite

B&B per night:
S £22.00–£27.00
D £40.00–£48.00

OPEN All year round

Warm welcome in comfortable Victorian house. All rooms en suite. In Broads capital of Wroxham, central for touring all Broads and North Norfolk. Garden. Private parking.

THE OLD METHODIST CHAPEL

High Street, Yoxford, Saxmundham
IP17 3EU
T: (01728) 668333 & 07931 668681
F: (01728) 668333
E: browns@chapelsuffolk.co.uk
I: www.chapelsuffolk.co.uk

Bedrooms: 2 double/
twin
Bathrooms: 1 en suite,
1 private

B&B per night:
S £33.00–£40.00
D £55.00–£65.00

OPEN Feb–Nov

Stay somewhere special: a beautifully converted Grade II Listed Victorian chapel set in a pretty Suffolk village. Both bedrooms are finely appointed and overlook the secluded courtyard garden. Ideally situated for exploring the Heritage Coast and the Suffolk countryside, Yoxford has an interesting selection of pubs and shops.

COUNTRY CODE Always follow the Country Code ✿
Enjoy the countryside and respect its life and work ✿ Guard
against all risk of fire ✿ Fasten all gates ✿ Keep your dogs
under close control ✿ Keep to public paths across farmland
✿ Use gates and stiles to cross fences, hedges and walls ✿
Leave livestock, crops and machinery alone ✿ Take your litter
home ✿ Help to keep all water clean ✿ Protect wildlife,
plants and trees ✿ Take special care on country roads ✿
Make no unnecessary noise

A brief guide to the main Towns and Villages offering
accommodation in the

East of England

A ALDBOROUGH, NORFOLK
- Aldborough is a picturesque village with a large green and winner of Best Kept Village 1999. Situated on the Weaver's Way. The location is ideal for visiting local National Trust properties, Norfolk Broads and the North Norfolk coastal area.

• **ALDEBURGH, SUFFOLK**
- A prosperous port in the 16th C, now famous for the Aldeburgh Music Festival held annually in June. The 16th C Moot Hall, now a museum, is a timber-framed building once used as an open market.

• **ALDHAM, ESSEX** - Small village in the Colne Valley convenient for Colchester.

• **ARDLEIGH, ESSEX** - 2.5 miles north-east of Colchester on the A137. Ardleigh Reservoir has a large bird-watching area.

B BECCLES, SUFFOLK - Fire destroyed the town in the 16th C and it was rebuilt in Georgian red brick. The River Waveney, on which the town stands, is popular with boating enthusiasts and has an annual regatta. Home of Beccles and District Museum.

• **BEETLEY, NORFOLK** - Rural village close to Dereham with its picturesque pargeted cottages.

• **BIGGLESWADE, BEDFORDSHIRE** -
Busy centre for market gardening set on the River Ivel spanned by a 14th C bridge. Some interesting old buildings in the market-place. Nearby are the Shuttleworth collection of historic aeroplanes and Jordan's Mill.

• **BISHOP'S STORTFORD, HERTFORDSHIRE** - Fine old town on the River Stort with many interesting buildings, particularly Victorian, and an imposing parish church. The vicarage where Cecil Rhodes was born is now a museum.

• **BLAXHALL, SUFFOLK** - Unspoilt village featured in the writings on country lore of George Ewart Evans. Sheep used to graze on the former common lands beside the River Alde and smuggling was popular.

• **BRAINTREE, ESSEX** - The Heritage Centre in the Town Hall describes Braintree's former international importance in wool, silk and engineering. St Michael's parish church includes some Roman bricks. Braintree market was first chartered in 1199.

• **BRANDON, SUFFOLK** - Set on the edge of Thetford Forest in an area known as Breckland. Old stone 5-arched bridge links Suffolk with Norfolk. 3 miles north-east is Grime's Graves, the largest prehistoric flint mine in Europe.

• **BULPHAN, ESSEX** - Small village, convenient for Brentwood, Basildon and Thurrock.

• **BUNGAY, SUFFOLK** - Market town and yachting centre on the River Waveney with the remains of a great 12th C castle. In the market-place stands the Butter Cross, rebuilt in 1689 after being largely destroyed by fire. Nearby at Earsham is the Otter Trust.

• **BURY ST EDMUNDS, SUFFOLK**
- Ancient market and cathedral town which takes its name from the martyred Saxon King, St Edmund. Bury St Edmunds has many fine buildings including the Athenaeum and Moyses Hall, reputed to be the oldest Norman house in the county.

C CAMBRIDGE, CAMBRIDGESHIRE
- A most important and beautiful city on the River Cam with 31 colleges forming one of the oldest universities in the world. Numerous museums, good shopping centre, restaurants, theatres, cinema and fine bookshops.

• **CAVENDISH, SUFFOLK** - One of the most picturesque villages in East Anglia, with a number of pretty thatched timber-framed and colour-washed cottages grouped around a large green. Sue Ryder Foundation Museum and coffee room are in the High Street.

• **CHELMSFORD, ESSEX** - The county town of Essex, originally a Roman settlement, Caesaromagus, thought to have been destroyed by Boudicca. Growth of the town's industry can be traced in the excellent museum in Oaklands Park. 15th C parish church has been Chelmsford Cathedral since 1914.

• **CLACTON-ON-SEA, ESSEX**
- Developed in the 1870s into a popular holiday resort with pier, pavilion, funfair, theatres and traditional amusements. The Martello Towers on the seafront were built like many others in the early 19th C to defend Britain against Napoleon.

• **COLCHESTER, ESSEX** - Britain's oldest recorded town standing on the River Colne and famous for its oysters. Numerous historic buildings, ancient remains and museums. Plenty of parks and gardens, extensive shopping centre, theatre and zoo.

• **COLTISHALL, NORFOLK** - On the River Bure, with an RAF station nearby. The village is attractive with many pleasant 18th C brick houses and a thatched church.

• **CROMER, NORFOLK** - Once a small fishing village and now famous for its fishing boats that still work off the beach and offer freshly caught crabs. Excellent bathing on sandy beaches fringed by cliffs. The town boasts a fine pier, theatre, museum and a lifeboat station.

D DARSHAM, SUFFOLK - Well placed for touring North Suffolk and the coast. The nearby Otter Trust is fascinating to visit.

• **DEDHAM, ESSEX** - A former wool town. Dedham Vale is an Area of Outstanding Natural Beauty and there is a countryside centre in the village. This is John Constable country and Sir Alfred Munnings lived at Castle House which is open to the public.

• **DERSINGHAM, NORFOLK** - Large parish church, mostly of Perpendicular period, with 14th C font and Elizabethan barn dated 1672.

E EARL SOHAM, SUFFOLK - A good base for visiting Bury St Edmunds, Ipswich and the east of Suffolk. The church of St Mary is notable for its hammerbeam nave roof decorated with angels and its 17th C pulpit with hour-glasses.

• **EARLS COLNE, ESSEX** - In the Colne Valley. Large village with a fine 14th C church and some old houses with interesting pargeting.

- **EASTON, SUFFOLK** - Picturesque little village with a delightful crinkle-crankle wall, the longest in England, and some decorative round cottages, Regency in date. All Saints is a small decorated Perpendicular church. Home of Easton Farm Park, Victorian setting for many species of farm animals.

- **ELY, CAMBRIDGESHIRE** - Until the 17th C, when the Fens were drained, Ely was an island. The cathedral, completed in 1189, dominates the surrounding area. One particular feature is the central octagonal tower with a fan-vaulted timber roof and wooden lantern.

- **F FAKENHAM, NORFOLK** - Attractive, small market town dates from Saxon times and was a Royal Manor until the 17th C. Its market place has 2 old coaching inns, both showing traces of earlier work behind Georgian facades, and the parish church has a commanding 15th C tower.

- **FELIXSTOWE, SUFFOLK** - Seaside resort that developed at the end of the 19th C. Lying in a gently curving bay with a 2-mile-long beach and backed by a wide promenade of lawns and floral gardens.

- **FRAMLINGHAM, SUFFOLK** - Pleasant old market town with an interesting church, impressive castle and some attractive houses round Market Hill. The town's history can be traced at the Lanman Museum.

- **FRINTON-ON-SEA, ESSEX** - Sedate town that developed as a resort at the end of the 19th C and still retains an air of Victorian gentility. Fine sandy beaches, good fishing and golf.

- **H HADLEIGH, SUFFOLK** - Former wool town, lying on a tributary of the River Stour. The church of St Mary stands among a remarkable cluster of medieval buildings.

- **HALESWORTH, SUFFOLK** - Small market town which grew firstly with navigation on the Blyth in the 18th C and then with the coming of the railways in the 19th C. Opposite the church in a beautiful 14th C building is the Halesworth Gallery.

- **HARLESTON, SUFFOLK** - Attractive small town on the River Waveney with 2 market-places and a museum. Candler's House is an outstanding example of an early Georgian town house. At Starston, 1 mile away, is a restored wind-pump.

- **HARPENDEN, HERTFORDSHIRE** - Delightful country town with many scenic walks through surrounding woods and fields. Harpenden train station provides a fast service into London.

- **HARWICH, ESSEX** - Port where the Rivers Orwell and Stour converge and enter the North Sea. The old town still has a medieval atmosphere with its narrow streets. To the south is the seaside resort of Dovercourt with long sandy beaches.

- **HAUGHLEY, SUFFOLK** - In the heart of Suffolk, very well placed for touring.

- **HETHERSETT, NORFOLK** - Conveniently located for Norwich.

- **HEVINGHAM, NORFOLK** - Located with easy access to Norwich, North Norfolk Coast, Broads and Blickling Hall.

- **HITCHIN, HERTFORDSHIRE** - Once a flourishing wool town. Full of interest, with many old buildings around the market square. These include the 17th C almshouses, old inns and the Victorian Corn Exchange.

- **HUNSTANTON, NORFOLK** - Seaside resort which faces the Wash. The shingle and sand beach is backed by striped cliffs and many unusual fossils can be found here. The town is predominantly Victorian. The Oasis family leisure centre has indoor and outdoor pools.

- **HUNTINGDON, CAMBRIDGESHIRE** - Attractive, interesting town which abounds in associations with the Cromwell family. The town is connected to Godmanchester by a beautiful 14th C bridge over the River Great Ouse.

- **I IPSWICH, SUFFOLK** - Interesting county town and major port on the River Orwell. Birthplace of Cardinal Wolsey. Christchurch Mansion, set in a fine park, contains a good collection of furniture and pictures, with works by Gainsborough, Constable and Munnings.

- **K KELVEDON, ESSEX** - Village on the old Roman road from Colchester to London. Many of the buildings are 18th C but there is much of earlier date. The famous preacher Charles Spurgeon was born here in 1834.

- **KERSEY, SUFFOLK** - A most picturesque village, which was famous for cloth-making, set in a valley with a water-splash. The church of St Mary is an impressive building at the top of the hill.

- **KINGS LANGLEY, HERTFORDSHIRE** - Between Hemel Hempstead and Watford. The Church of All Saints has parts which date from the 13th C.

- **KING'S LYNN, NORFOLK** - A busy town with many outstanding buildings. The Guildhall and Town Hall are both built of flint in a striking chequer design. Behind the Guildhall in the Old Gaol House the sounds and smells of prison life 2 centuries ago are recreated.

- **L LAVENHAM, SUFFOLK** - A former prosperous wool town of timber-framed buildings with the cathedral-like church and its tall tower. The market-place is 13th C and the Guildhall now houses a museum.

- **LEISTON, SUFFOLK** - Centrally placed for visiting the Suffolk Heritage Coast, Leiston is a bustling, working town in a rural setting famous for Leiston Abbey and the award winning Long Shop Museum.

- **LITTLE WALSINGHAM, NORFOLK** - Little Walsingham is larger than its neighbour Great Walsingham and more important because of its long history as a religious shrine to which many pilgrimages were made. The village has many picturesque buildings of the 16th C and later.

- **LOWESTOFT, SUFFOLK** - Seaside town with wide sandy beaches. Important fishing port with picturesque fishing quarter. Home of the famous Lowestoft porcelain and birthplace of Benjamin Britten. East Point Pavilion's exhibition describes the Lowestoft story.

- **LUTON, BEDFORDSHIRE** - Bedfordshire's largest town with its own airport, several industries and an excellent shopping centre. The town's history is depicted in the museum and art gallery in Wardown Park. Luton Hoo has a magnificent collection of treasures.

- **M MALDON, ESSEX** - The Blackwater Estuary has made Maldon a natural base for yachtsmen. Boat-building is also an important industry. Numerous buildings of interest. The 13th C church of All Saints has the only triangular church tower in Britain. Also a museum and maritime centre.

- **MARGARET RODING, ESSEX** - One of the six Rodings, a group of old villages clustered in the rural Roding Valley. The church features some fine Norman work.

- **N NEWMARKET, SUFFOLK** - Centre of the English horse-racing world and the headquarters of the Jockey Club and National Stud. Racecourse and horse sales. The National Horse Racing Museum traces the history and development of the Sport of Kings.

NORWICH, NORFOLK - Beautiful cathedral city and county town on the River Wensum with many fine museums and medieval churches. Norman castle, Guildhall and interesting medieval streets. Good shopping centre and market.

PETERBOROUGH, CAMBRIDGESHIRE - Prosperous and rapidly expanding cathedral city on the edge of the Fens on the River Nene. Catherine of Aragon is buried in the cathedral. City Museum and Art Gallery. Ferry Meadows Country Park has numerous leisure facilities.

ROYSTON, HERTFORDSHIRE - Old town lying at the crossing of the Roman road Ermine Street and the Icknield Way. It has many interesting old houses and inns.

SANDY, BEDFORDSHIRE - Small town on the River Ivel on the site of a Roman settlement. Sandy is mentioned in Domesday.

SAXMUNDHAM, SUFFOLK - The church of St John the Baptist has a hammer-beam roof and contains a number of good monuments.

SHERINGHAM, NORFOLK - Holiday resort with Victorian and Edwardian hotels and a sand and shingle beach where the fishing boats are hauled up. The North Norfolk Railway operates from Sheringham station during the summer. Other attractions include museums, theatre and Splash Fun Pool.

SOUTH WALSHAM, NORFOLK - Village famous for having 2 churches in adjoining churchyards. South Walsham Broad consists of an inner and outer section, the former being private. Alongside, the Fairhaven Garden Trust has woodland and water-gardens open to the public.

SOUTHWOLD, SUFFOLK - Pleasant and attractive seaside town with a triangular market square and spacious greens around which stand flint, brick and colour-washed cottages. The parish church of St Edmund is one of the greatest churches in Suffolk.

ST ALBANS, HERTFORDSHIRE - As Verulamium this was one of the largest towns in Roman Britain and its remains can be seen in the museum. The Norman cathedral was built from Roman materials to commemorate Alban, the first British Christian martyr.

STOKE-BY-NAYLAND, SUFFOLK - Picturesque village with a fine group of half-timbered cottages near the church of St Mary, the tower of which was one of Constable's favourite subjects. In School Street are the Guildhall and the Maltings, both 16th C timber-framed buildings.

STOWMARKET, SUFFOLK - Small market town where routes converge. There is an open-air museum of rural life at the Museum of East Anglian Life.

STRETHAM, CAMBRIDGESHIRE - On the edge of the Fens, Stretham is noted for its 20 ft high village cross from around 1400.

THAXTED, ESSEX - Small town rich in outstanding buildings and dominated by its hilltop medieval church. The magnificent Guildhall was built by the Cutlers' Guild in the late 14th C. A windmill built in 1804 has been restored and houses a rural museum.

WOOLPIT, SUFFOLK - Village with a number of attractive timber-framed Tudor and Georgian houses. St Mary's Church is one of the most beautiful churches in Suffolk and has a fine porch. The brass eagle lectern is said to have been donated by Elizabeth I.

WROXHAM, NORFOLK - Yachting centre on the River Bure which houses the headquarters of the Norfolk Broads Yacht Club. The church of St Mary has a famous doorway and the manor house nearby dates back to 1623.

YOXFORD, SUFFOLK - Village given a unique character by the timbered, bow-windowed and balconied houses along the main street. In the surrounding area are Grove Park, Rookery Park and Cockfield Hall, built in 1540, where Katherine Grey, sister of Lady Jane Grey, lived out her last months.

SOUTH WEST

A land of myths and legends – and beautiful beaches. The region has cathedral cities, Georgian Bath and maritime Bristol, mysterious castles, evocative country houses and sub-tropical gardens to discover too.

classic sights
Newquay – surfers' paradise
English Riviera – family-friendly beaches
Dartmoor – wild open moorland and rocky tors

coast & country
Runnymede – riverside meadows and woodland
Pegwell Bay & Goodwin Sands – a haven for birds and seals

glorious gardens
Stourhead – 18th century landscape garden
Lost Gardens of Heligan – 19th century gardens

art for all
Tate Gallery St Ives – modern art and the St Ives School
Arnolfini Gallery, Bristol – contemporary arts

distinctively different
Daphne du Maurier – Cornwall inspired many of her novels
Agatha Christie – follow the trail in Torquay

The counties of Bath, Bristol, Cornwall, Devon, Dorset (Western),Isles of Scilly, Somerset, South Gloucestershire and Wiltshire

FOR MORE INFORMATION CONTACT:
South West Tourism
Admail 3186, Exeter EX2 7WH
Tel: (0870) 442 0880 Fax: (0870) 442 0881
Email: info@westcountryholidays.com
Internet: www.westcountryholidays.com

The Pictures:
1 Weston-super-Mare
2 Bath

Places to Visit - see pages 356-360
Where to Stay - see pages 361-439

PLACES to visit

You will find hundreds of interesting places to visit during your stay, just some of which are listed in these pages. Contact any Tourist Information Centre in the region for more ideas on days out.

At Bristol Harbourside
Bristol, Avon BS1 5DB
Tel: (0117) 915 5000 www.at-bristol.org.uk
A £97 million Millennium Landmark project on Bristol's revitalised harbourside. It consists of 3 world-class visitor attractions.

Atwell-Wilson Motor Museum Trust
Downside, Stockley Lane, Calne, Wiltshire SN11 0NF
Tel: (01249) 813119 www.atwell-wilson.org
Motor museum with vintage, post-vintage and classic cars, including American models. Classic motorbikes. A 17thC water meadow walk. Car clubs welcome for rallies. Play area.

Avebury Manor and Garden
Avebury, Marlborough, Wiltshire SN8 1RF
Tel: (01672) 539250
Manor house, regularly altered and of monastic origins. Present buildings date from the early 16thC with Queen Anne alterations and Edwardian renovations. Gardens.

Babbacombe Model Village
Hampton Avenue, Babbacombe, Torquay, Devon TQ1 3LA
Tel: (01803) 315315
www.babbacombemodelvillage.co.uk
Over 400 models, many with sound and animation, with four acres (1.6 ha) of award-winning gardens. See modern towns, villages and rural areas. Stunning illuminations.

Bristol City Museum & Art Gallery
Queen's Road, Bristol, Avon BS8 1RL
Tel: (0117) 922 3571
www.bristol-city.gov.uk/museums
Collection representing applied, oriental and fine art, archaeology, geology, natural history, ethnography and Egyptology.

Bristol Zoo Gardens
Clifton, Bristol, Avon BS8 3HA
Tel: (0117) 973 8951 www.bristolzoo.org.uk
Enjoy an exciting, real life experience and see over 300 species of wildlife in beautiful gardens.

Buckland Abbey
Yelverton, Devon PL20 6EY
Tel: (01822) 853607
Originally a Cistercian monastery, then home of Sir Francis Drake. Ancient buildings, exhibitions, herb garden, craft workshops and estate walks.

Cheddar Caves and Gorge

Cheddar, Somerset BS27 3QF
Tel: (01934) 742343 www.cheddarcaves.co.uk
Beautiful caves located in Cheddar Gorge. Gough's Cave with its cathedral-like caverns, and Cox's Cave with stalagmites and stalactites. Also 'The Crystal Quest' fantasy adventure.

The Combe Martin Motor Cycle Collection

Cross Street, Combe Martin, Ilfracombe, Devon EX34 0DH
Tel: (01271) 882346
www.motorcycle-collection.co.uk
Collection of motorcycles, scooters and invalid carriages, displayed against a background of old petrol pumps, signs and garage equipment. Motoring nostalgia.

Combe Martin Wildlife and Dinosaur Park

Jurassic Hotel, Combe Martin, Ilfracombe, Devon EX34 0NG
Tel: (01271) 882486
Wildlife park and life-size models of dinosaurs.

Crealy Park

Sidmouth Road, Clyst St Mary, Exeter, Devon EX5 1DR
Tel: (01395) 233200 www.crealy.co.uk
One of Devon's largest animal farms. Milk a cow, feed a lamb and pick up a piglet. Adventure playgrounds. Dragonfly Lake and farm trails.

Dairyland Farm World

Newquay, Cornwall TR8 5AA
Tel: (01872) 510246 www.dairylandfarmworld.com
One hundred and seventy cows milked in rotary parlour. Heritage centre. Farm nature trail. Farm park with animals, pets and wildfowl. Daily events. Also conservation area.

Eden Project

Watering Lane Nursery, Pentewan, St Austell, Cornwall PL26 6EN
Tel: (01726) 222900
A 37-acre (15-ha) china clay pit has been dramatically transformed to accommodate the planthouses, visitor centre and temperate parkland.

Exmoor Falconry & Animal Farm

West Lynch Farm, Allerford, Minehead, Somerset TA24 8HJ
Tel: (01643) 862816 www.exmoorfalconry.co.uk
Farm animals, rare breeds, pets' corner, birds of prey and owls. Flying displays daily. Historic farm buildings.

Flambards Village

Culdrose Manor, Helston, Cornwall TR13 0QA
Tel: (01326) 573404 www.flambards.co.uk
Life-size Victorian village with fully stocked shops, plus carriages and fashions. 'Britain in the Blitz' life-size wartime street, historic aircraft, exploratorium.

Heale Garden & Plant Centre

Middle Woodford, Salisbury, Wiltshire SP4 6NT
Tel: (01722) 782504
Mature, traditional-type garden with shrubs, musk and other roses, and kitchen garden. Authentic Japanese teahouse in water garden. Magnolias. Snowdrops and aconites in winter.

International Animal Rescue Animal Tracks

Ash Mill, South Molton, Devon EX36 4QW
Tel: (01769) 550277 www.iar.org.uk
A 60-acre (24-ha) animal sanctuary with a wide range of rescued animals, from monkeys to chinchillas and shire horses to other horses and ponies. Also rare plant nursery.

The Pictures:
1 Lands End, Cornwall
2 Clifton Suspension Bridge, Bristol
3 Stonehenge
4 Interior of Salisbury Cathedral
5 Shaftesbury Hill, Dorset

Jamaica Inn Museums (Potters Museum of Curiosity)

Jamaica Inn Courtyard, Bolventor, Launceston,
Cornwall PL15 7TS
Tel: (01566) 86838
Museums contain lifetime work of Walter Potter, a
Victorian taxidermist. Exhibits include Kittens' Wedding,
Death of Cock Robin and The Story of Smuggling.

Longleat

The Estate Office, Warminster, Wiltshire BA12 7NW
Tel: (01985) 844400 www.longleat.co.uk
Elizabethan stately home, safari park, plus a wonderland
of family attractions. 'World's Longest Hedge Maze',
Safari Boats, Pets' Corner, Longleat railway.

The Lost Gardens of Heligan

Heligan, Pentewan, St Austell, Cornwall PL26 6EN
Tel: (01726) 845100 www.heligan.com
Heligan Gardens is the scene of the largest garden
restoration project undertaken since the war. Public
access to parts of 'Home Farm'.

Lyme Regis Philpot Museum

Bridge Street, Lyme Regis, Dorset DT7 3QA
Tel: (01297) 443370 www.lymeregismuseum.co.uk
Fossils, geology, local history and lace exhibitions.
Museum shop.

National Marine Aquarium

Rope Walk, Coxside, Plymouth, Devon PL4 0LF
Tel: (01752) 600301 www.national-aquarium.co.uk
The United Kingdom's only world-class aquarium, located
in the heart of Plymouth. Visitor experiences will include
a mountain stream and Caribbean reef complete with
sharks.

Newquay Zoo

Trenance Park, Newquay, Cornwall TR7 2LZ
Tel: (01637) 873342 www.newquayzoo.co.uk
A modern, award-winning zoo where you can have fun
and learn at the same time. A varied collection of
animals, from Acouchi to Zebra.

Paignton Zoo Environmental Park

Totnes Road, Paignton, Devon TQ4 7EU
Tel: (01803) 557479 www.paigntonzoo.org.uk
One of England's largest zoos with over 1,200 animals in
the beautiful setting of 75 acres (30 ha) of botanical
gardens. The zoo is one of Devon's most popular family
days out.

Plant World

St Marychurch Road, Newton Abbot, Devon TQ12 4SE
Tel: (01803) 872939
Four acres (1.6 ha) of gardens including the unique 'map
of the world' gardens. Cottage garden. Panoramic views.
Comprehensive nursery of rare and more unusual plants.

Powderham Castle

The Estate Office, Kenton, Exeter, Devon EX6 8JQ
Tel: (01626) 890243 www.powderham.co.uk
Built c1390, restored in the 18thC. Georgian interiors,
china, furnishings and paintings. Family home of the
Courtenays for over 600 years. Fine views across deer
park and River Exe.

Plymouth Dome

The Hoe, Plymouth, Devon PL1 2NZ
Tel: (01752) 603300
Purpose-built visitor interpretation centre showing the
history of Plymouth and its people from Stone Age
beginnings to satellite technology. Situated on
Plymouth Hoe.

Railway Village Museum

34 Faringdon Road, Swindon, Wiltshire SN1 5BJ
Tel: (01793) 466553 www.swindon.gov.uk
Foreman's house in original Great Western Railway
village. Furnished to re-create a Victorian
working-class home.

Roman Baths

Pump Room, Abbey Church Yard, Bath BA1 1LZ
Tel: (01225) 477785 www.romanbaths.co.uk
Roman baths and temple precinct, hot springs and
Roman temple. Jewellery, coins, curses and votive
offerings from the sacred spring.

St Michael's Mount

Marazion, Cornwall TR17 0HT
Tel: (01736) 710507
Originally the site of a Benedictine chapel, the castle on
its rock dates from the14thC. Fine views towards Land's
End and the Lizard. Reached by foot, or ferry at high tide
in summer.

Steam – Museum of the Great Western Railway

Kemble Drive, Churchward, Swindon, Wiltshire SN2 2TA
Tel: (01793) 466646 www.steam-museum.org.uk
Historic Great Western Railway locomotives, wide range
of nameplates, models, illustrations, posters and tickets.

Stonehenge

Amesbury, Salisbury, Wiltshire SP4 7DE
Tel: (01980) 623108
www.stonehengemasterplan.org
World-famous prehistoric monument built as a
ceremonial centre. Started 5,000 years ago and
remodelled several times in next 1,500 years.

Stourhead House and Garden

The Estate Office, Stourton, Warminster, Wiltshire BA12 6QD
Tel: (01747) 841152 www.nationaltrust.org.uk
Landscaped garden, laid out c1741-80, with lakes,
temples, rare trees and plants. House, begun in c1721 by
Colen Campbell, contains fine paintings and Chippendale
furniture.

Tate Gallery St Ives

Porthmeor Beach, St Ives, Cornwall TR26 1TG
Tel: (01736) 796226 www.tate.org.uk
Opened in 1993 and offering a unique introduction to
modern art. Changing displays focus on the modern
movement St Ives is famous for. Also an extensive
education programme.

Teignmouth Museum

29 French Street, Teignmouth, Devon TQ14 8ST
Tel: (01626) 777041
Exhibits include a16thC cannon and artefacts from the
Armada wreck, local history, c1920s pier machines and
c1877 cannon.

Tintagel Castle

Tintagel, Cornwall PL34 0HE
Tel: (01840) 770328 www.english-heritage.org.uk
Medieval ruined castle on wild, wind-swept coast.
Famous for associations with Arthurian legend. Built
largely in the 13thC by Richard, Earl of Cornwall.
Used as a prison in the 14thC.

Tithe Barn Children's Farm

New Barn Road, Abbotsbury, Weymouth, Dorset DT3 4JF
Tel: (01305) 871817
Extensive children's farm for children under 11 years.
Activities include hand-feeding (with bottles) milk to
lambs and kids. Replicas of Terracotta Warriors on display
in barn.

Totnes Costume Museum – Devonshire Collection of Period Costume

Bogan House, 43 High Street, Totnes, Devon TQ9 5NP
Tel: (01803) 863821
New exhibition of costumes and accessories each season,
displayed in one of the historic merchant's houses of
Totnes. Bogan House recently restored by Mitchell Trust.

Woodlands Leisure Park

Blackawton, Totnes, Devon TQ9 7DQ
Tel: (01803) 712598
www.woodlands-leisure-park.co.uk
All-weather fun guaranteed with unique combination of
indoor and outdoor attractions: 3 watercoasters,
toboggan run, massive indoor adventure centre with
rides. Falconry and animals.

Wookey Hole Caves and Papermill

Wookey Hole, Wells, Somerset BA5 1BB
Tel: (01749) 672243 www.wookey.co.uk
Spectacular caves and legendary home of the Witch of
Wookey. Working Victorian papermill including Old Penny
Arcade, Magical Mirror Maze and Cave Diving Museum.

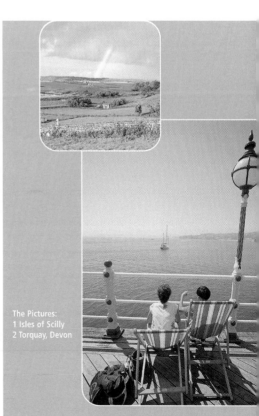

The Pictures:
1 Isles of Scilly
2 Torquay, Devon

Find out more about the
SOUTH WEST

Further information about holidays and attractions in the South West is available from:

SOUTH WEST TOURISM
Admail 3186, Exeter EX2 7WH.
Tel: (0870) 442 0880
Fax: (0870) 442 0881
Email: info@westcountryholidays.com
Internet: www.westcountryholidays.com

The following publications are available free from South West Tourism:
Bed & Breakfast Touring Map
West Country Holiday Homes & Apartments
West Country Hotels and Guesthouses
Glorious Gardens of the West Country
Camping and Caravan Touring Map
Tourist Attractions Touring Map
Trencherman's West Country, Restaurant Guide

Getting to the
SOUTH WEST

BY ROAD: Somerset, Devon and Cornwall are well served from the North and Midlands by the M6/M5 which extends just beyond Exeter, where it links in with the dual carriageways of the A38 to Plymouth, A380 to Torbay and the A30 into Cornwall. The North Devon Link Road A361 joins Junction 37 with the coast of north Devon and A39, which then becomes the Atlantic Highway into Cornwall.

BY RAIL: The main towns in the South West are served throughout the year by fast, direct and frequent rail services from all over the country. InterCity 125 trains operate from London (Paddington) to Chippenham, Swindon, Bath, Bristol, Weston-super-Mare, Taunton, Exeter, Plymouth and Penzance, and also from Scotland, the North East and the Midlands to the South West. A service runs from London (Waterloo) to Exeter, via Salisbury, Yeovil and Crewkerne. Sleeper services operate between Devon and Cornwall and London as well as between Bristol and Glasgow and Edinburgh. Motorail services operate from strategic points to key South West locations.

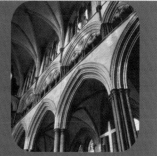

Where to stay in the South West

Accommodation entries in this region are listed in alphabetical order of place name, and then in alphabetical order of establishment.

Map references refer to the colour location maps at front of this guide. The first number indicates the map to use; the letter and number which follow refer to the grid reference on the map.

At-a-glance symbols at the end of each accommodation entry give useful information about services and facilities. A key to symbols can be found inside the back cover flap. Keep this open for easy reference.

A brief description of the towns and villages offering accommodation in the entries which follow, can be found at the end of this section.

A complete listing of all the English Tourism Council assessed accommodation covered by this guide appears at the back of the guide.

ABBOTSBURY, Dorset Map ref 2A3

♦♦♦ **SWAN LODGE**

Rodden Row, Abbotsbury, Weymouth DT3 4JL	Bedrooms: 5 double/ twin	Lunch available	B&B per night:
T: (01305) 871249	Bathrooms: 2 en suite	Evening meal available	S £33.00–£43.00
F: (01305) 871249		CC: Mastercard, Visa	D £46.00–£58.00

Situated on the B3157 coastal road between Weymouth and Bridport. Swan Inn public house opposite, where food is served all day in season, is under the same ownership.

OPEN All year round

ALDERBURY, Wiltshire Map ref 2B3

♦♦♦ **WISTERIA COTTAGE**

Silver Street, Alderbury, Salisbury SP5 3AN	Bedrooms: 2 single, 1 double/twin	B&B per night:
T: (01722) 710274	Bathrooms: 2 en suite	S £30.00–£35.00
		D £45.00–£47.00

Situated in village of Alderbury, 3 minutes from Salisbury. Quiet gravel lane with beautiful views, unusual bed and breakfast.

HB per person:
DY £35.00

OPEN All year round

QUALITY ASSURANCE SCHEME

Diamond ratings and awards were correct at the time of going to press but are subject to change. Please check at the time of booking.

ALLERFORD, Somerset Map ref 1D1

◆◆◆◆

FERN COTTAGE
Allerford, Minehead TA24 8HN
T: (01643) 862215
F: (01643) 862215
E: ferncottage@bushinternet.com
I: www.smoothhound.co.uk/hotels/ferncott

B&B per night:
S £39.00
D £58.00

HB per person:
DY £42.75

OPEN All year round

Comfortable, large, traditional Exmoor cottage, circa 16thC, set in a tiny National Trust village in a wood-fringed vale. Exhilarating walks in dramatic hill and coastal scenery start on doorstep. Noted for fine classic/bistro cooking and comprehensive cellar. A non-smoking house.

Bedrooms: 3 triple/ multiple
Bathrooms: 3 en suite

Evening meal available
CC: Amex, Delta, Mastercard, Switch, Visa

The Exmoor break...3 nights DB&B £122pp (based on 2 people sharing). Single Exmoor break £154.50.

Ⓜ️🐎11 ▤☕🍷Ⓢ✄🅿️🎗️.🛍️Ʊ↾🐾🚲🐾P

AMESBURY, Wiltshire Map ref 2B2 *Tourist Information Centre Tel: (01980) 622833*

◆◆◆

THE OLD BAKERY
Netton, Salisbury SP4 6AW
T: (01722) 782351
E: valahen@aol.com
I: members.aol.com/valahen

Bedrooms: 3 double/ twin
Bathrooms: 2 en suite, 1 private

B&B per night:
S £25.00–£30.00
D £36.00–£44.00

OPEN All year round

Pleasantly modernised former bakery in small, quiet, picturesque village. Views over fields and water meadows. Ideal base for Stonehenge/Salisbury. Short walk to local inns.

🐎5 ▤☕🍷Ⓢ🎗️.🛍️♪↾☀️🚲P

◆◆◆

SOLSTICE FARMHOUSE
39 Holders Road, Amesbury, Salisbury SP4 7PH
T: (01980) 625052 & 07944 709869
E: williams@btinternet.com

Bedrooms: 2 double/ twin

B&B per night:
S £25.00–£28.00
D £42.00–£45.00

OPEN All year round

Grade II Listed farmhouse boasts a woodburning stove and large, attractive garden with pond and water feature. Comfortable rooms with private en suite showers.

Ⓜ️🐎12 ▤☕☕🍷Ⓢ🛍️☀️🚲🏠P

◆◆◆

VALE HOUSE
Figheldean, Salisbury SP4 8JJ
T: (01980) 670713

Bedrooms: 1 single, 2 double/twin
Bathrooms: 1 en suite

B&B per night:
S £18.00–£20.00
D £36.00–£40.00

OPEN All year round

Secluded house in centre of picturesque village, 4 miles north of Amesbury on A345, 2 miles from Stonehenge.

🐎▤☕☕🍷Ⓢ✄🅿️🎗️.🛍️☀️🚲P

ASHBURTON, Devon Map ref 1C2

◆◆◆◆
Silver Award

GAGES MILL
Buckfastleigh Road, Ashburton, Newton Abbot TQ13 7JW
T: (01364) 652391
F: (01364) 652391
E: moore@gagesmill.co.uk
I: www.gagesmill.co.uk

B&B per night:
S £23.00–£30.00
D £46.00–£60.00

HB per person:
DY £37.00–£44.00

14thC former wool mill in over an acre of gardens. A friendly welcome and comfortable accommodation. High standard of cooking. Licensed. One mile from the ancient Stannary town of Ashburton. An ideal base for exploring South Devon, with its many National Trust properties, pretty villages and, of course, Dartmoor.

Bedrooms: 1 single, 7 double/twin
Bathrooms: 7 en suite

Evening meal available

Ⓜ️🐎12 ▤☕☕🍷🏆Ⓢ✄🅿️🎗️.🛍️☀️🚲🏠P

◆◆◆◆

THE RISING SUN
Woodland, Ashburton, Newton Abbot
TQ13 7JT
T: (01364) 652544
F: (01364) 654202
E: mail@risingsunwoodland.co.uk
I: www.risingsunwoodland.co.uk

B&B per night:
S £28.00–£36.00
D £53.00–£58.00

OPEN All year round

*Recommended inn and restaurant
with super food, specialising in fresh
local produce, real ales and fine
wines. Splendidly situated in
beautiful countryside on the edge of
Dartmoor but also convenient for
Torbay. Just 1.5 miles from the A38,
ideal for a stopover to Cornwall or
for the Plymouth ferry.*

Bedrooms: 2 double/
twin
Bathrooms: 2 en suite

Lunch available
Evening meal available
CC: Amex, Delta,
Mastercard, Switch, Visa

◆◆◆◆
Silver
Award

SLADESDOWN FARM
Landscove, Ashburton, Newton Abbot
TQ13 7ND
T: (01364) 653973
F: (01364) 653973
E: sue@sladesdownfarm.co.uk
I: www.sladesdownfarm.co.uk

B&B per night:
S £22.50–£25.00
D £45.00–£50.00

*A warm welcome awaits you at
Sladesdown Farm. Set in the heart of
the country, with peaceful, scenic
walks. Close to the moors and coast,
2 miles off the A38. Two spacious,
attractive bedrooms, en suite, with
sitting area, plus family room with
private bathroom, TV and hot drinks
facilities.*

Bedrooms: 3 double/
twin, 1 triple/multiple
Bathrooms: 2 en suite,
2 private

◆◆◆

CHURCH FARM
Atworth, Melksham SN12 8JA
T: (01225) 702215 & 07974 786387
F: (01225) 702215
E: chrchfarm@tinyonline.co.uk
I: www.churchfarm-atworth.
freeserve.co.uk

Bedrooms: 2 double/
twin
Bathrooms: 1 en suite,
1 private

B&B per night:
S £20.00–£30.00
D £35.00–£50.00

OPEN Mar–Nov

*Working dairy farm. Grade II Listed farmhouse. Large garden with patio area. Within
walking distance of local pub. Easy access Bath, Lacock and Bradford-on-Avon.*

◆◆◆◆

MANOR FARM
Avebury, Marlborough SN8 1RF
T: (01672) 539294
F: (01672) 539294

Bedrooms: 2 double/
twin
Bathrooms: 2 private

B&B per night:
S £40.00–£45.00
D £57.00–£65.00

OPEN All year round

*Listed 18thC farmhouse in Avebury stone circle. Large, comfortable rooms, guests enjoy
sleeping within the famous ring. Pub 100 yards.*

CHECK THE MAPS
The colour maps at the front of this guide show all the cities, towns
and villages for which you will find accommodation entries.
Refer to the town index to find the page on which they are listed.

BARNSTAPLE, Devon Map ref 1C1 *Tourist Information Centre Tel: 0845 4582003*

♦♦♦♦ **BRADIFORD COTTAGE**
Bradiford, Barnstaple EX31 4DP
T: (01271) 345039
F: (01271) 345039
E: tony@humesfarm.co.uk
I: www.humesfarm.co.uk

Bedrooms: 1 single,
3 double/twin

B&B per night:
S £17.00–£20.00
D £34.00–£40.00

OPEN All year round

Family-run 17thC cottage set in countryside just 1 mile from Barnstaple. Ideal for exploring the Atlantic coast and Exmoor. Lovely, comfortable rooms, attractive garden and use of pool.

ⓜ ⛊ 8 🕮 ▢ ⬇ ⚲ ⑤ ⤢ ⋈ ▥ 🖻 ✿ 🐎 P

♦♦♦♦
Silver
Award

THE SPINNEY
Shirwell, Barnstaple EX31 4JR
T: (01271) 850282
E: thespinny@shirwell.fsnet.co.uk
I: www.northdevon.com

B&B per night:
S £18.00–£22.00
D £36.00–£44.00

HB per person:
DY £28.00–£32.00

OPEN All year round

Set in over an acre of grounds with views towards Exmoor, a former rectory. Spacious accommodation, en suite available. Centrally heated. Delicious meals cooked by chef/ proprietor, served during summer months in our restored Victorian conservatory under the ancient vine. Residential licence. The Spinney is non-smoking.

Bedrooms: 1 single,
2 double/twin, 2 triple/
multiple
Bathrooms: 3 en suite

Evening meal available

ⓜ ⛊ 🕮 ▢ ⬇ ⑤ ⤢ ▥ 🖻 🝔 ✿ 🐎 🐕 🏠 P

BATH, Bath and North East Somerset Map ref 2B2 *Tourist Information Centre Tel: (01225) 477101*

♦♦♦♦ **ASHLEY VILLA HOTEL**
26 Newbridge Road, Bath BA1 3JZ
T: (01225) 421683 & 428887
F: (01225) 313604
E: ashleyvilla@clearface.co.uk
I: www.ashleyvilla.co.uk

Bedrooms: 1 single,
12 double/twin, 5 triple/
multiple
Bathrooms: 16 en suite,
2 private

Lunch available
Evening meal available
CC: Amex, Delta,
Mastercard, Switch, Visa

B&B per night:
S £49.00–£69.00
D £69.00–£130.00

HB per person:
DY £64.00–£85.00

OPEN All year round

Friendly, family run hotel with relaxing, informal atmosphere. Close to city centre. Car park, bar, restaurant, garden and outdoor pool. Premier rooms inlcuding 4 poster.

ⓜ ⛊ 🛏 🏠 📞 ▢ ⬇ ⚲ 🍽 ⑤ ⤢ ▥ 🖻 🝔 🍴 ⚲ ✿ P

♦♦♦ **ASTOR HOUSE**
14 Oldfield Road, Bath BA2 3ND
T: (01225) 429134
F: (01225) 429134
E: astorhouse.visitus@virgin.net

Bedrooms: 6 double/
twin, 2 triple/multiple;
suites available
Bathrooms: 7 en suite,
1 private

CC: Delta, Mastercard,
Switch, Visa

B&B per night:
D £45.00–£55.00

OPEN All year round

Comfortable, spacious Victorian home with lovely views of the city and countryside yet only a short walk to the centre. Friendly welcome, varied delicious breakfasts.

ⓜ ⛊ 2 🏠 🕮 ▢ ⬇ ⑤ ⤢ ▥ 🖻 🝔 🍴 ✿ P

AT-A-GLANCE SYMBOLS
Symbols at the end of each accommodation entry give useful information about services and facilities. A key to symbols can be found inside the back cover flap. Keep this open for easy reference.

◆◆◆◆◆
Silver
Award

ATHOLE GUEST HOUSE

33 Upper Oldfield Park, Bath BA2 3JX
T: (01225) 334307
F: (01225) 320000
E: info@atholehouse.co.uk
I: www.atholehouse.co.uk

B&B per night:
S £45.00–£55.00
D £65.00–£75.00

OPEN All year round

Large Victorian home restored to give bright, inviting, quiet bedrooms, sleek furniture, sparkling bathrooms, hotel facilities (mini-bar, laptop connection, satellite TV, safe). Hospitality is old-style, award-winning breakfasts. Relax in our gardens, or let us help you explore the area. Secure parking behind remote-control gates or in garage.

Bedrooms: 2 double/
twin, 1 triple/multiple
Bathrooms: 3 en suite

CC: Amex, Delta,
Mastercard, Switch, Visa

4 nights incl 1 night free, all year. 3 nights (incl 1 night free) or 5 nights (incl 2 nights free), Nov-Feb incl.

Ⓜ 🐎 📞 🖥 💻 🍺 🍷 Ⓢ ✂ 🏖 🖳 ❄ 🚲 P

◆◆◆◆◆

AYRLINGTON HOTEL

24/25 Pulteney Road, Bath BA2 4EZ
T: (01225) 425495
F: (01225) 469029
E: mail@ayrlington.com
I: www.ayrlington.com

B&B per night:
S £75.00–£145.00
D £90.00–£145.00

OPEN All year round

Located within an easy 5-minute level walk of Bath city centre, The Ayrlington is a small, tranquil, non-smoking luxury hotel. Its 12 elegantly appointed rooms boast every modern amenity, and some feature 4-poster beds and spa baths. Private parking and access to a nearby golf course are among its many facilities.

Bedrooms: 12 double/
twin
Bathrooms: 12 en suite

CC: Amex, Delta,
Mastercard, Switch, Visa

3 nights for the price of 2. Mon/Thur, Dec-Feb.

Ⓜ 🐎 ⛳ 📞 🖥 💻 🍺 🍷 Ⓢ ✂ 🏖 ◐ 🖳 ⚓ 🚲 🍴 ⭐ ❄ 🚲 🏨 P

◆◆◆

BAILBROOK LODGE HOTEL

35/37 London Road West, Bath BA1 7HZ
T: (01225) 859090
F: (01225) 852299
E: hotel@bailbrooklodge.demon.co.uk
I: www.bailbrooklodge.demon.co.uk

B&B per night:
S £40.00–£60.00
D £60.00–£80.00

HB per person:
DY £42.00–£45.00

OPEN All year round

Welcome to a fine Georgian house offering 12 bedrooms, all en suite (some 4-posters) with antiques and many original features. The lounge bar and dining room overlook the patio and lawns. Excellently located 1 mile from Bath's centre and close to junctions for M4 and beautiful surrounding countryside. Ample car parking.

Bedrooms: 8 double/
twin, 4 triple/multiple
Bathrooms: 12 en suite

Evening meal available
CC: Amex, Delta, Diners,
Mastercard, Switch, Visa

3rd night half price (excl Sat); 2 nights for the price of 1, Nov-Feb (excl Sat).

Ⓜ 🐎 ⛳ 🖥 📞 🍺 🍷 Ⓢ ✂ 🏖 🖳 ⚓ 🍴 ⭐ ❄ 🏨 P

◆◆◆◆

BROMPTON HOUSE

St John's Road, Bath BA2 6PT
T: (01225) 420972
F: (01225) 420505
E: bromptonhouse@btinternet.com
I: www.bromptonhouse.co.uk

Bedrooms: 1 single,
14 double/twin, 1 triple/
multiple
Bathrooms: 16 en suite

CC: Amex, Delta,
Mastercard, Switch, Visa

B&B per night:
S £32.00–£65.00
D £60.00–£95.00

OPEN All year round

Charming Georgian rectory in beautiful secluded gardens. 5-6 minutes' level walk to city centre. Free private car park. No smoking, please.

Ⓜ 🐎 📞 🖥 💻 🍺 🍷 Ⓢ ✂ 🏖 🖳 ⚓ ❄ 🚲 🏨 P

◆◆◆◆

CARFAX HOTEL

Great Pulteney Street, Bath
BA2 4BS
T: (01225) 462089
F: (01225) 443257
E: reservations@carfaxhotel.co.uk
I: www.carfaxhotel.co.uk

Bedrooms: 12 single,
21 double/twin, 3 triple/
multiple
Bathrooms: 35 en suite,
1 private

Evening meal available
CC: Amex, Delta,
Mastercard, Switch, Visa

B&B per night:
S £52.00–£65.00
D £78.00–£99.50

HB per person:
DY £48.50–£59.25

A trio of Georgian houses, overlooking Henrietta Park and surrounded by Bath's beautiful hills. A short stroll from Pump Rooms and Roman Baths.

OPEN All year round

◆◆◆

CHESTERFIELD HOUSE

11 Great Pulteney Street, Bath
BA2 4BR
T: (01225) 460953
F: (01225) 448770
E: info@chesterfieldhouse.com
I: www.chesterfieldhouse.com

Bedrooms: 4 single,
15 double/twin, 1 triple/
multiple
Bathrooms: 20 en suite

CC: Amex, Delta, Diners,
Mastercard, Switch, Visa

B&B per night:
S £45.00–£60.00
D £60.00–£100.00

OPEN All year round

Townhouse in Bath's prestigious and central Great Pulteney Street with the peaceful gardens of Henrietta Park to the rear.

◆◆◆

CHURCH FARM

Monkton Farleigh, Bradford-on-
Avon BA15 2QJ
T: (01225) 858583 & 07889 596929
F: (01225) 852474
E: rebecca@tuckerb.fsnet.co.uk
I: www.tuckerb.fsnet.co.uk

Bedrooms: 2 double/
twin, 1 triple/multiple
Bathrooms: 3 en suite

B&B per night:
D £45.00

OPEN All year round

Converted farmhouse barn with exceptional views in peaceful, idyllic setting. Ten minutes from Bath, ideal base for touring/walking South West England. Families/dogs welcome.

◆◆◆

EDGAR HOTEL

64 Great Pulteney Street, Bath
BA2 4DN
T: (01225) 420619
F: (01225) 466916

Bedrooms: 2 single,
13 double/twin, 1 triple/
multiple
Bathrooms: 16 en suite

CC: Delta, Mastercard,
Switch, Visa

B&B per night:
S £40.00–£50.00
D £45.00–£85.00

OPEN All year round

Georgian townhouse hotel, close to city centre and Roman Baths. Privately run. All rooms with en suite facilities. Four-poster bed available.

◆◆◆

FLAXLEY VILLA

9 Newbridge Hill, Bath BA1 3PW
T: (01225) 313237 & 480574

Bedrooms: 3 double/
twin
Bathrooms: 2 en suite

B&B per night:
S £20.00–£36.00
D £36.00–£55.00

OPEN All year round

Comfortable Victorian house, just a few minutes by car to city centre and within easy reach of Royal Crescent and main attractions.

QUALITY ASSURANCE SCHEME

For an explanation of the quality and facilities represented by the Diamonds please refer to the front of this guide. A more detailed explanation can be found in the information pages at the back.

◆◆◆◆

THE GAINSBOROUGH
Weston Lane, Bath BA1 4AB
T: (01225) 311380
F: (01225) 447411
E: gainsborough_hotel@compuserve.com
I: www.gainsboroughhotel.co.uk

B&B per night:
S £42.00–£62.00
D £60.00–£95.00

OPEN All year round

Spacious and comfortable country-house style bed and breakfast hotel. Situated in own grounds near the Botanical Gardens and within easy walking distance of the city. Large guests' lounge with books, magazines, also a small friendly bar. High ground, nice views, sun terraces, car park. Five-course breakfast, friendly staff. Warm welcome.

Bedrooms: 1 single,
10 double/twin, 6 triple/
multiple
Bathrooms: 17 en suite

CC: Amex, Delta,
Mastercard, Switch, Visa

◆◆◆◆

HAUTE COMBE HOTEL
174/176 Newbridge Road, Bath BA1 3LE
T: (01225) 420061 & 339064
F: (01225) 446077
E: enquiries@hautecombe.com
I: www.hautecombe.com

B&B per night:
S £49.00–£59.00
D £59.00–£89.00

OPEN All year round

Conveniently situated hotel with period charm. Attractive, no-smoking bedrooms, patio and garden with all the extras of a modern hotel. Satellite TV. Bar and smoking/no-smoking lounges. A la carte menu. Large monitored car park. Frequent shuttle or level walk to abbey. Free unlimited golf locally.

Bedrooms: 2 single,
6 double/twin, 5 triple/
multiple
Bathrooms: 11 en suite,
2 private

Evening meal available
CC: Amex, Delta, Diners,
Mastercard, Switch, Visa

◆◆◆

HENRIETTA HOTEL
32 Henrietta Street, Bath BA2 6LR
T: (01225) 447779
F: (01225) 444150

Bedrooms: 9 double/
twin, 1 triple/multiple
Bathrooms: 10 en suite

CC: Delta, Mastercard,
Switch, Visa

B&B per night:
S £40.00–£50.00
D £45.00–£85.00

Privately-run Georgian townhouse hotel, close to city centre and Roman Baths. All rooms with en suite facilities. Four-poster bed available.

OPEN All year round

◆◆◆

HERMITAGE
Bath Road, Box, Corsham SN13 8DT
T: (01225) 744187
F: (01225) 743447
E: hermitage@telecall.co.uk

Bedrooms: 4 double/
twin, 1 triple/multiple
Bathrooms: 5 en suite

B&B per night:
S £35.00–£40.00
D £45.00–£55.00

Six miles from Bath on A4 to Chippenham, 1st drive on left by 30 mph sign. 16thC house with heated pool in summer. Dining room with vaulted ceiling.

OPEN All year round

◆◆◆◆◆
Silver
Award

HOLLY LODGE
8 Upper Oldfield Park, Bath BA2 3JZ
T: (01225) 424042 &
(01255) 339187
F: (01225) 481138
E: stay@hollylodge.co.uk
I: www.hollylodge.co.uk

Bedrooms: 1 single,
6 double/twin
Bathrooms: 7 en suite

CC: Amex, Delta, Diners,
Mastercard, Switch, Visa

B&B per night:
S £48.00–£55.00
D £79.00–£97.00

OPEN All year round

Elegant Victorian house set in its own grounds, enjoying magnificent views of the city. Visit my web site for further information.

367

BATH continued

◆◆◆ LAMP POST VILLA

3 Crescent Gardens,
Upper Bristol Road, Bath BA1 2NA
T: (01225) 331221
F: (01225) 426783

Bedrooms: 3 double/
twin, 1 triple/multiple
Bathrooms: 4 en suite

CC: Delta, Mastercard,
Switch, Visa

B&B per night:
S £35.00–£45.00
D £55.00–£60.00

OPEN All year round

Semi-detached bay windowed property of Edwardian period, still maintaining many original features.

◆◆◆◆ LAURA PLACE HOTEL

3 Laura Place,
Great Pulteney Street, Bath
BA2 4BH
T: (01225) 463815
F: (01225) 310222

Bedrooms: 7 double/
twin, 1 triple/multiple
Bathrooms: 7 en suite

CC: Amex, Mastercard,
Visa

B&B per night:
S Min £60.00
D £72.00–£93.00

18thC townhouse, centrally located in Georgian square. 2 minutes from Roman Baths, Pump Rooms and abbey.

◆◆◆◆ LINDISFARNE GUEST HOUSE

41a Warminster Road, Bathampton,
Bath BA2 6XJ
T: (01225) 466342 & 07740 741541
F: (01225) 444062
E: lindisfarne-bath@talk21.com
I: www.bath.org/hotel/lindisfarne.htm

Bedrooms: 3 double/
twin, 1 triple/multiple
Bathrooms: 4 en suite

CC: Mastercard, Visa

B&B per night:
S £35.00–£40.00
D £48.00–£60.00

OPEN All year round

Spacious house with friendly proprietors. Within walking distance of good eating places, about 1.5 miles from Bath city centre. Large car park.

◆◆◆◆ MARLBOROUGH HOUSE

1 Marlborough Lane, Bath BA1 2NQ
T: (01225) 318175
F: (01225) 466127
E: mars@manque.dircon.co.uk
I: www.marlborough-house.net

B&B per night:
S £45.00–£75.00
D £65.00–£95.00

HB per person:
DY £47.50–£95.00

OPEN All year round

An enchanting and unusual vegetarian townhouse in the centre of Bath. Exquisitely furnished with antiques, but run in a relaxed and friendly style, we specialise in organic, vegetarian world cuisine. Breakfast choices include San Francisco pancakes with organic maple syrup and delicate omelettes with breakfast potatoes. Unique and elegant accommodation.

Bedrooms: 2 single,
4 double/twin, 1 triple/
multiple
Bathrooms: 7 en suite

Lunch available
Evening meal available
CC: Amex, Delta, Diners,
Mastercard, Switch, Visa

Vegetarian Christmas-3 days of exotic dining, all meals included. Vegetarian New Years-3 days of exotic dining all meals included.

◆◆◆◆ MIDWAY COTTAGE

10 Farleigh Wick, Bradford-on-
Avon BA15 2PU
T: (01225) 863932
F: (01225) 866836
E: midway_cottage@hotmail.com

Bedrooms: 3 double/
twin
Bathrooms: 3 en suite

B&B per night:
S £25.00–£29.00
D £40.00–£45.00

OPEN All year round

Friendly cottage run by 'Landlady of the Year 2000' finalist. On A363 midway between Bathford and Bradford-on-Avon, next door to a country inn serving excellent food.

SPECIAL BREAKS

Many establishments offer special promotions and themed breaks. These are highlighted in red. (All such offers are subject to availability.)

◆◆◆◆◆
Gold
Award

MONKSHILL

Shaft Road, Monkton Combe, Bath
BA2 7HL
T: (01225) 833028
F: (01225) 833028
E: monks.hill@virgin.net

B&B per night:
S £50.00–£65.00
D £65.00–£80.00

OPEN All year round

You are assured of a warm welcome in this secluded and very comfortable country residence surrounded by its own extensive gardens. The emphasis is on luxurious comfort. The individually-styled bedrooms are graciously appointed and command excellent views over the garden, with its croquet lawn, the woodland and valley below.

Bedrooms: 3 double/
twin
Bathrooms: 2 en suite,
1 private

CC: Amex, Delta,
Mastercard, Switch, Visa

◆◆◆◆

NUMBER 30 CRESCENT GARDENS

Bath BA1 2NB
T: (01225) 337393
F: (01225) 337393
E: david.greenwood12@btinternet.
com
I: www.stay@numberthirty.co.uk

Bedrooms: 1 single,
5 double/twin
Bathrooms: 5 en suite,
1 private

CC: Mastercard, Switch,
Visa

B&B per night:
S £55.00–£70.00
D £65.00–£85.00

OPEN All year round

A small privately owned Victorian house in the centre of Bath. 'Outstanding' housekeeping. Private car parking. Easy walking to shops and to Roman Baths.

◆◆◆◆

ROMAN CITY GUEST HOUSE

18 Raby Place, Bathwick Hill, Bath BA2 4EH
T: (01225) 463668 & 07899 777953
E: romancityguesthse@amserve.net
I: www.romancityguesthouse.co.uk

B&B per night:
S £35.00–£50.00
D £50.00–£75.00

OPEN All year round

Enjoy any and every occasion in this beautifully restored and tastefully decorated house. Built in 1810, full of character and charm. Relaxing rooms, 4-poster beds, superb views. Easy car parking. Short walk to Bath Abbey. Warm welcome, friendly service. Truly a perfect setting for a perfect memory.

Bedrooms: 3 double/
twin, 1 triple/multiple

Special offers all year-please ring for update.
Special occasions caringly catered for. Mid-week reductions.

CC: Mastercard, Visa

◆◆

SAMPFORD

11 Oldfield Road, Bath BA2 3ND
T: (01225) 310053
E: robert.dolby@btinternet.com

Bedrooms: 2 double/
twin, 1 triple/multiple
Bathrooms: 3 private

B&B per night:
D £44.00

OPEN All year round

In a quiet residential area half a mile south of city centre off the A367 Exeter/Radstock/ Shepton Mallet road. No commerical sign is displayed.

MAP REFERENCES The map references refer to the colour maps at the front of this guide. The first figure is the map number; the letter and figure which follow indicate the grid reference on the map.

◆◆◆◆

SOMERSET HOUSE HOTEL

35 Bathwick Hill, Bath BA2 6LD
T: (01225) 466451 & 463471
F: (01225) 317188
E: somersethouse@compuserve.com
I: www.somersethouse.co.uk

An elegant Georgian house (1827), owned and run by the Seymour family. Large garden. Good views of city. Non-smoking house. 12 minutes' walk from Roman Baths and Abbey. Car park. Innovative buffet, continental and English breakfasts served each morning in the old Georgian kitchen. Restaurant available for family celebrations.

Bedrooms: 1 single, 4 double/twin, 5 triple/multiple
Bathrooms: 10 en suite

CC: Amex, Delta, Diners, Mastercard, Switch, Visa

B&B per night:
S £29.00–£54.00
D £58.00–£73.50

OPEN All year round

🏍🐎6♨☎🖥🖵👤🍷🖺⛱🚺🛋🍺🍴🚬🐎🚲🐕🏛P

BAWDRIP, Somerset Map ref 1D1

◆◆◆

KINGS FARM
10 Eastside Lane, Bawdrip,
Bridgwater TA7 8QB
T: (01278) 683233 & 07801 079138

Bedrooms: 2 single,
1 double/twin
Bathrooms: 2 en suite

B&B per night:
S Max £18.00
D Max £18.00

OPEN All year round

Accommodation in fine 17thC farmhouse. Dining in grand dining and sitting room with open fireplaces. Wonderful views and wildlife including deer, buzzards and badgers.

🏍🐎🖵👤🍷🖺⛱🚺🛋🍴🚬🐎🚲🏛

BEAMINSTER, Dorset Map ref 2A3

◆◆◆◆

SLAPE HILL BARN

Waytown, Bridport DT6 5LQ
T: (01308) 488429

B&B per night:
D Min £53.00

HB per person:
DY Min £39.00

OPEN All year round

Deep in the quiet, unspoilt countryside of south-west Dorset, beautiful scenery, lovely hamstone villages, the coast nearby. Excellent home cooking, lovely views, comfortable drawing room with television, wood-burning stove, 4 acres of garden to enjoy, village pub. We offer hospitality, comfort and a warm welcome – let us look after you.

Bedrooms: 2 double/twin
Bathrooms: 1 en suite, 1 private

Lunch available
Evening meal available

🚺🍷⛱🚺🛋🚬🐕🚲P

◆◆◆◆
Silver
Award

THE WALNUTS
2 Prout Bridge, Beaminster DT8 3AY
T: (01308) 862211

Bedrooms: 3 double/twin
Bathrooms: 2 en suite

B&B per night:
D £56.00–£60.00

OPEN All year round

Tastefully refurbished building with very attractive bedrooms. Friendly, family-run establishment. Very well situated within short walk of local inns and tasteful small shops.

🐎8🖵♨⛱🚺🛋🚲P

IMPORTANT NOTE Information on accommodation listed in this guide has been supplied by the proprietors. As changes may occur you are advised to check details at the time of booking.

BEAMINSTER continued

◆◆◆◆
Silver
Award

WATER MEADOW HOUSE
Bridge Farm, Hooke, Beaminster
DT8 3PD
T: (01308) 862619
F: (01308) 862619
E: enquiries@watermeadowhouse.
co.uk
I: www.watermeadowhouse.co.uk

Bedrooms: 1 double/
twin, 1 triple/multiple
Bathrooms: 1 en suite,
1 private

CC: Delta, Mastercard,
Switch, Visa

B&B per night:
S £26.00–£30.00
D £44.00–£48.00

OPEN Mar–Oct

280-acre dairy and livestock farm. New Georgian-style farmhouse in quiet village of Hooke, by the river. Good walking country, lovely countryside.

Ⓜ 🐎 🖥 🖵 ♨ 🔍 ⓢ ⊁ 🖾 🛏 🚶 🌸 ⛟ P

BIDDESTONE, Wiltshire Map ref 2B2

◆◆◆◆

HOME FARM
Harts Lane, Biddestone,
Chippenham SN14 7DQ
T: (01249) 714475 & 07966 549759
F: (01249) 701488
E: audrey.smith@homefarmbandb.
co.uk
I: www.homefarmbandb.co.uk

Bedrooms: 1 single,
1 double/twin, 2 triple/
multiple
Bathrooms: 3 en suite,
1 private

B&B per night:
S £27.00–£32.00
D £45.00–£50.00

OPEN All year round

200-acre mixed farm. 17thC farmhouse in a beautiful Cotswold village. Stroll across the village green to the local pub. Close to Bath, Castle Combe and Lacock.

Ⓜ 🐎 🖩 🖥 🖵 ♨ 🔍 ⓢ ⊁ 🖾 🛏 🌸 ⛟ 🏠 P

BIDEFORD, Devon Map ref 1C1 *Tourist Information Centre Tel: (01237) 477676*

◆◆◆◆

THE MOUNT
Northdown Road, Bideford EX39 3LP
T: (01237) 473748
F: (01271) 342268
E: andrew@themountbideford.fsnet.co.uk
I: www.themount1.cjb.net

B&B per night:
S £26.00–£28.00
D £50.00–£54.00

OPEN All year round

Elegant Georgian licensed guesthouse, comfortably furnished. All rooms en suite. Peaceful garden for guests' use. Short walk to town centre. Convenient for trips to Lundy, Clovelly, Exmoor, Dartmoor and North Devon coast. No smoking.

Bedrooms: 3 single,
4 double/twin, 1 triple/
multiple
Bathrooms: 8 en suite

CC: Delta, Mastercard,
Switch, Visa

Ⓜ 🐎 🖩 🖵 ♨ 🔍 ⓢ ⊁ 🖾 🛏 🚶 🌸 ⛟ 🏠 P

◆◆◆

SUNSET HOTEL
Landcross, Bideford EX39 5JA
T: (01237) 472962
F: (01237) 422520
E: hazellamb@hotmail.com

B&B per night:
S £36.00–£50.00
D £55.00–£62.00

HB per person:
DY £40.00–£44.00

Small, elegant country hotel set in beautiful gardens in a quiet, peaceful location, overlooking spectacular scenery. 1.5 miles from town. Beautifully decorated and spotlessly clean. Highly recommended quality accommodation. All en suites with colour TV and beverages. Superb cooking, everything home-made. Special needs catered for. Licensed, private parking. Non-smoking establishment.

Bedrooms: 2 double/
twin, 2 triple/multiple
Bathrooms: 4 en suite

Evening meal available
CC: Mastercard, Visa

Reduced rates for 3 and 5 day breaks.

Ⓜ 🐎 🖵 ♨ 🍽 ⓢ ⊁ 🖾 🖩 🛏 🌸 ⛟ P

CONFIRM YOUR BOOKING
You are advised to confirm your booking in writing.

◆◆◆◆

STEPS FARMHOUSE
Bilbrook, Minehead TA24 6HE
T: (01984) 640974
E: info@stepsfarmhouse.co.uk
I: www.stepsfarmhouse.co.uk

B&B per night:
S £22.00–£25.00
D £40.00–£46.00

OPEN Feb–Nov

Traditional 16thC former farmhouse situated close to Dunster and Minehead, offering a selection of individual en suite bed and breakfast accommodation in barn conversions, located in beautiful secluded gardens with views towards Exmoor. Breakfasts are served in our cosy dining room, with oak beams and inglenook fireplace.

Bedrooms: 2 double/ twin, 1 triple/multiple
Bathrooms: 3 en suite

CC: Amex, Delta, Diners, Mastercard, Switch, Visa

BISHOP SUTTON, Bath and North East Somerset Map ref 2A2

◆◆◆

WITHYMEDE
The Street, Bishop Sutton, Bristol BS39 5UU
T: (01275) 332069

Bedrooms: 2 double/ twin
Bathrooms: 2 en suite

B&B per night:
S £23.00–£25.00
D £37.00–£40.00

Detached house, ample parking. Chew Valley Lake half a mile. Bath/Wells/Bristol all approximately 20 minutes' drive. Bristol Airport/Farrington Golf Course 15 minutes' drive.

BISHOP'S LYDEARD, Somerset Map ref 1D1

◆◆◆◆

WEST VIEW
Minehead Road, Bishop's Lydeard, Taunton TA4 3BS
T: (01823) 432223
F: (01823) 432223
E: westview@pattemore.freeserve.co.uk

Bedrooms: 3 double/ twin
Bathrooms: 2 en suite, 1 private

B&B per night:
S £20.00–£30.00
D £44.00–£50.00

OPEN All year round

Attractive Victorian house in the village close to the privately-owned West Somerset Steam Railway. Within easy reach of Taunton and the M5.

BODMIN, Cornwall Map ref 1B2 *Tourist Information Centre Tel: (01208) 76616*

◆◆◆

BEDKNOBS
Polgwyn, Castle Street, Bodmin PL31 2DX
T: (01208) 77553
F: (01208) 77885
E: gill@bedknobs.co.uk
I: www.bedknobs.co.uk

Bedrooms: 1 double/ twin, 1 triple/multiple
Bathrooms: 1 en suite, 1 private

CC: Delta, Mastercard, Switch, Visa

B&B per night:
S £25.00–£35.00
D £40.00–£50.00

OPEN All year round

A rambling Victorian villa offering spacious accommodation, a warm welcome and real home comforts. A perfect base for exploring Cornwall. The Eden Project within easy reach.

USE YOUR *i*s

There are more than 550 Tourist Information Centres throughout England offering friendly help with accommodation and holiday ideas as well as suggestions of places to visit and things to do. You'll find TIC addresses in the local Phone Book.

Gold
Award

BOKIDDICK FARM
Lanivet, Bodmin PL30 5HP
T: (01208) 831481
F: (01208) 831481
E: gillhugo@bokiddickfarm.co.uk
I: www.bokiddickfarm.co.uk

B&B per night:
S £28.00–£32.00
D £46.00–£50.00

OPEN All year round

Welcome to our lovely Georgian farmhouse in central Cornwall. A peaceful location with magnificent views, yet only 2 miles from A30. Close to exciting Eden Project and magnificent NT Lanhydrock House and Gardens. Oak beams, wood panelling, pretty en suite bedrooms, delicious Aga cooked breakfasts. The perfect place for that special break.

Bedrooms: 2 double/
twin, 1 triple/multiple
Bathrooms: 3 en suite

BOSCASTLE, Cornwall Map ref 1B2

◆◆◆◆

THE OLD COACH HOUSE
Tintagel Road, Boscastle PL35 0AS
T: (01840) 250398
F: (01840) 250346
E: parsons@old-coach.co.uk
I: www.old-coach.co.uk

Bedrooms: 5 double/
twin, 3 triple/multiple
Bathrooms: 8 en suite

CC: Delta, Mastercard,
Switch, Visa

B&B per night:
S £18.00–£44.00
D £36.00–£44.00

OPEN All year round

Relax in beautiful 300-year-old former coach house. All rooms en suite with colour TV, teamaker, hairdryer, etc. Friendly and helpful owners. Good parking.

BOVEY TRACEY, Devon Map ref 1D2

◆◆◆◆
Silver
Award

BROOKFIELD HOUSE
Challabrook Lane, Bovey Tracey,
Newton Abbot TQ13 9DF
T: (01626) 836181
F: (01626) 836182
E: brookfieldh@tinyworld.co.uk
I: www.hotellink.co.uk/bovey/brookfield/
index.htm

B&B per night:
D £50.00–£64.00

OPEN Feb–Nov

Spacious early Edwardian residence situated on the edge of Bovey Tracey and Dartmoor. Set in 2 acres with panoramic moor views and bounded by the gently flowing Pottery Leat. Secluded tranquillity yet within easy walking distance of town, local attractions and moorland. Individually decorated bedrooms, all with comfortable seating areas.

Bedrooms: 3 double/
twin
Bathrooms: 2 en suite,
1 private

Evening meal available
CC: Amex, Mastercard,
Switch, Visa

BOX, Wiltshire Map ref 2B2

◆◆◆◆

LORNE HOUSE
London Road, Box, Corsham
SN13 8NA
T: (01225) 742597
E: lornehousebandb@aol.com

Bedrooms: 3 double/
twin, 1 triple/multiple
Bathrooms: 4 en suite

CC: Delta, Mastercard,
Switch, Visa

B&B per night:
S £30.00–£35.00
D £45.00–£50.00

OPEN All year round

Listed in guide books in Germany, Canada and America, this Victorian property boasts excellent service and accommodation to discerning travellers. Situated 6 miles from Bath.

RATING All accommodation in this guide has been rated, or is awaiting a rating, by a trained English Tourism Council assessor.

373

♦♦♦

SPRINGFIELDS
182a Great Ashley, Bradford-on-Avon
BA15 2PP
T: (01225) 866125
E: christine.rawlings@farmersweekly.net
I: www.bed-and-breakfast.org

B&B per night:
S £30.00–£35.00
D £40.00–£45.00

OPEN All year round

Delightful, quiet country setting in 0.5 acres of cottage gardens between Bradford-on-Avon and Bath. En suite double ground floor accommodation, with adjoining private lounge/dining room. Delicious breakfast, all tastes catered for, home preserves, eggs from our own chickens.

Bedrooms: 1 double/ twin; suites available
Bathrooms: 1 en suite

10% reduction on 3 nights or more.

Evening meal available

 ♦♦♦♦

WOODPECKERS
Holt Road, Bradford-on-Avon
BA15 1TR
T: (01225) 865616
F: (01225) 865615
E: b+b@wood-peckers.co.uk
I: www.wood-peckers.co.uk

Bedrooms: 3 double/ twin, 2 triple/multiple
Bathrooms: 4 en suite

CC: Delta, Mastercard, Switch, Visa

B&B per night:
S £30.00–£35.00
D £50.00–£60.00

OPEN Feb–Nov

Woodpeckers offer bright, spacious rooms, all en suite. A lift, ample parking and a large open garden with a patio.

♦♦♦♦

COKERHURST FARM
87 Wembdon Hill, Bridgwater
TA6 7QA
T: (01278) 422330 & 07850 692065
F: (01278) 422330
E: cokerhurst@clara.net
I: www.cokerhurst.clara.net

Bedrooms: 2 double/ twin, 1 triple/multiple
Bathrooms: 3 en suite

B&B per night:
S £26.00
D £52.00

OPEN All year round

16thC Somerset longhouse with 3 pretty en suite bedrooms, all with comfortable beds. Picturesque location overlooking the garden and lake beyond. Four miles from M5.

♦♦♦♦

MODEL FARM
Perry Green, Wembdon, Bridgwater
TA5 2BA
T: (01278) 433999
E: rmodelfarm@aol.com
I: www.modelfarm.com

B&B per night:
S £35.00–£40.00
D £50.00–£60.00

HB per person:
DY £37.00–£58.00

OPEN All year round

Peacefully situated in a rural setting, Model Farm is a licensed country house retreat, offering spacious en suite accommodation. A set evening meal is available by prior arrangement, guests being joined by their hosts. A warm welcome and friendly atmosphere awaits all who visit whether business or leisure.

Bedrooms: 1 single, 2 double/twin
Bathrooms: 3 en suite

Evening meal available
CC: Amex, Delta, Mastercard, Switch, Visa

BRIDGWATER continued

◆◆◆ QUANTOCK VIEW GUEST HOUSE

Bridgwater Road, North Petherton,
Bridgwater TA6 6PR
T: (01278) 663309
E: irene@quantockview.freeserve.
co.uk

Bedrooms: 2 double/
twin, 2 triple/multiple
Bathrooms: 3 en suite,
1 private

Evening meal available
CC: Amex, Delta,
Mastercard, Switch, Visa

B&B per night:
S £23.00–£25.00
D £38.00–£40.00

HB per person:
DY £24.00–£33.00

OPEN All year round

Comfortable, family-run guesthouse in central Somerset. En suite facilities available. Close to hills and coast, yet only minutes from M5, junction 24.

BRIDPORT, Dorset Map ref 2A3 *Tourist Information Centre Tel: (01308) 424901*

◆◆◆ BRIDPORT ARMS HOTEL

West Bay, Bridport DT6 4EN
T: (01308) 422994
F: (01308) 425141

Bedrooms: 3 single,
7 double/twin, 3 triple/
multiple
Bathrooms: 6 en suite

Lunch available
Evening meal available
CC: Delta, Mastercard,
Switch, Visa

B&B per night:
S £25.00–£35.00
D £50.00–£70.00

HB per person:
DY £40.00–£45.00

OPEN All year round

16thC thatched hotel on beach. Restaurant specialising in local sea food. 2 bars, real local ales and bar meals.

◆◆◆◆ BRITMEAD HOUSE

West Bay Road, Bridport DT6 4EG
T: (01308) 422941
F: (01308) 422516
E: britmead@talk21.com
I: www.britmeadhouse.co.uk

Bedrooms: 5 double/
twin, 2 triple/multiple
Bathrooms: 7 en suite

Evening meal available
CC: Delta, Mastercard,
Switch, Visa

B&B per night:
S £26.00–£40.00
D £44.00–£64.00

OPEN All year round

Elegant, spacious, tastefully decorated house. Lounge and dining room overlooking garden. West Bay Harbour/Coastal Path, 10 minutes' walk away. Renowned for hospitality and comfort.

◆◆◆◆ CANDIDA HOUSE

Whitchurch Canonicorum DT6 6RQ
T: (01297) 489629
F: (01297) 489629
E: candida@globalnet.co.uk
I: www.holidayaccom.com/
candida-house.htm

Bedrooms: 3 double/
twin
Bathrooms: 3 en suite

Lunch available

B&B per night:
S Min £25.00
D £40.00–£60.00

OPEN All year round

Comfortable en suite rooms in elegant spacious Georgian rectory. Peaceful village 2 miles from the sea. Special breakfasts. Warm hospitality and restful ambience.

◆◆◆◆ POLLY'S

22 West Allington, Bridport
DT6 5BG
T: (01308) 458095 & 07957 856112
F: (01308) 421834
E: mail@hime.org.uk

Bedrooms: 2 double/
twin
Bathrooms: 1 en suite,
1 private

B&B per night:
S £25.00–£35.00
D £44.00–£50.00

OPEN All year round

Welcome to our home. Delightful bedsitting rooms with TV and private bathroom, in a Georgian Grade II Listed house.

BRISTOL Map ref 2A2 *Tourist Information Centre Tel: (0117) 926 0767*

◆◆◆◆◆ THE HUNTERS REST
Silver
Award

King Lane, Clutton Hill, Bristol
BS39 5QL
T: (01761) 452303
F: (01761) 453308
E: paul@huntersrest.co.uk
I: www.huntersrest.co.uk

Bedrooms: 3 double/
twin, 1 triple/multiple;
suites available
Bathrooms: 4 en suite

Lunch available
Evening meal available
CC: Delta, Mastercard,
Switch, Visa

B&B per night:
S £40.00–£65.00
D £70.00–£100.00

HB per person:
DY £40.00–£70.00

OPEN All year round

Close to Bath and Bristol. This country inn is renowned for home-cooked food, warm welcome and luxury accommodation with stunning views.

WHERE TO STAY
Please mention this guide when making your booking.

BRISTOL continued

◆◆◆ **NASEBY HOUSE HOTEL**
105 Pembroke Road, Clifton, Bristol
BS8 3EF
T: (0117) 9737859 & 9080011
F: (0117) 9737859
I: www.nasebyhousehotel.co.uk

Bedrooms: 2 single,
12 double/twin
Bathrooms: 13 en suite

CC: Delta, Mastercard,
Switch, Visa

B&B per night:
S £48.00
D £63.00–£72.00

OPEN All year round

Small family-run hotel near Clifton Village. Approximately 1 mile from city centre. Near zoo, downs and suspension bridge. Quiet garden.

◆◆◆ **ROWAN LODGE HOTEL**
41 Gloucester Road North,
Filton Park, Bristol BS7 0SN
T: (0117) 931 2170
F: (0117) 975 3601

Bedrooms: 1 single,
3 double/twin, 2 triple/
multiple
Bathrooms: 3 en suite

CC: Mastercard, Visa

B&B per night:
S £26.00–£34.00
D £40.00

OPEN All year round

Small family-run hotel. On A38 access to motorways M4, M5, M32 and city. Residential area. Ample parking.

◆◆◆ **TRICOMO HOUSE B & B**
183 Cheltenham Road, Cotham,
Bristol BS6 5RH
T: (0117) 9248082
F: (0117) 9248082
E: tricomohouse1@activemail.
co.uk

Bedrooms: 1 single,
2 double/twin, 2 triple/
multiple

B&B per night:
S £25.00–£35.00
D £42.00–£50.00

OPEN All year round

Small family-run bed and breakfas on A38, half a mile from Bristol centre. Five minutes' drive from Bristol University, BBC. Close to rail and coach stations.

BRIXHAM, Devon Map ref 1D2 Tourist Information Centre Tel: 0906 680 1268 (Premium rate number)

◆◆◆

ANCHORAGE GUEST HOUSE
170 New Road, Brixham TQ5 8DA
T: (01803) 852960
F: (01803) 852960

B&B per night:
S £16.00–£21.50
D £32.00–£43.00

HB per person:
DY £25.50–£31.00

OPEN All year round

The chalet style bungalow, set in award-winning gardens, offers very comfortable, mostly en suite, accommodation. With good home cooking, a friendly atmosphere and ample parking. The Anchorage is a good base for exploring Dartmoor and the South Devon Coast. 'Brixham's best kept secret' – Daily Telegraph, June 1999.

Bedrooms: 2 single,
4 double/twin, 1 triple/
multiple
Bathrooms: 4 en suite,
1 private

Evening meal available
CC: Amex, Delta,
Mastercard, Switch, Visa

TOWN INDEX
This can be found at the back of the guide. If you know where you want to stay, the index will give you the page number listing accommodation in your chosen town, city or village.

◆◆◆◆

You will be warmly welcomed at our unique and picturesque turn-of-the-19thC residence, with ample parking, overlooking Brixham's outer harbour, marina and the panoramic beauty of Torbay. Home-cooked meals are prepared from local produce and served in our elegant dining room which overlooks the garden.

RANSCOMBE HOUSE HOTEL

Ranscombe Road, Brixham TQ5 9UP
T: (01803) 882337
F: (01803) 882337
E: ranscombe@lineone.net
I: www.RanscombeHouseHotel.co.uk

Bedrooms: 2 single, 4 double/twin, 3 triple/ multiple
Bathrooms: 9 en suite

Evening meal available
CC: Amex, Delta, Mastercard, Switch, Visa

3-day break DB&B £108-£114. 7-day break DB&B £245-£259.

B&B per night:
S £27.00–£30.00
D £54.00–£60.00

Ᵽ🐎☕🛏♨♿🍷Ⓢ🚭🕍🖥🛋❄🏰 P

◆◆◆ **RICHMOND HOUSE HOTEL**

Higher Manor Road, Brixham TQ5 8HA
T: (01803) 882391
F: (01803) 882391
E: juliegiblett@richmondhse.hoteloneman.fsnet.co.uk

Bedrooms: 4 double/ twin, 2 triple/multiple
Bathrooms: 5 en suite, 1 private

CC: Delta, Mastercard, Switch, Visa

B&B per night:
D £36.00–£44.00

OPEN All year round

Detached Victorian house with well-appointed accommodation, sun-trap garden and adjacent car park. Convenient for shops and harbour, yet quiet location. First left after Golden Lion.

Ᵽ🐎♿☕🛏♨Ⓢ🚭🕍🖥🛋▶❄🐎🚬🏰 P

◆◆◆ **SAMPFORD HOUSE**

57-59 King Street, Brixham TQ5 9TH
T: (01803) 857761
F: (01803) 857761
E: carole.boulton@btinternet.com

Bedrooms: 6 double/ twin; suites available
Bathrooms: 5 en suite, 1 private

B&B per night:
S £25.00–£40.00
D £34.00–£50.00

OPEN All year round

An 18thC family-run house overlooking fishing harbour and Torbay. Individual breakfasts catered for.

Ᵽ🐎🛏♨Ⓢ🕍🖥🛋❄🐎🚬🏰

◆◆◆◆◆ **STAFFORD BARTON FARM**

Broadhembury, Honiton EX14 3LU
T: (01404) 841403
E: djwalters@uk.packardbell.org

Bedrooms: 2 double/ twin
Bathrooms: 2 en suite

B&B per night:
S £22.50–£25.00
D £45.00–£50.00

OPEN All year round

55-acre mixed farm. Delightful modern Scandinavian-style house, on genuine working farm, close to thatched village. Beautiful gardens and views.

🐎♿♨Ⓢ🚭🛋❄🐎🚬

CHECK THE MAPS

The colour maps at the front of this guide show all the cities, towns and villages for which you will find accommodation entries. Refer to the town index to find the page on which they are listed.

BUCKLAND NEWTON, Dorset Map ref 2B3

◆◆◆◆
Silver
Award

A warm welcome awaits you at this hamstone and flint farmhouse. Situated at the head of the Blackmore Vale the character rooms enjoy panoramic views over unspoilt countryside. Ideal for walks along the Wessex Way and Hardy Trail and within 30 minutes of the sea.

WHITEWAYS FARMHOUSE ACCOMMODATION

Bookham, Buckland Newton, Dorchester
DT2 7RP
T: (01300) 345511
F: (01300) 345511
E: bookhamfarm@netscapeonline.co.uk

Bedrooms: 1 double/
twin, 1 triple/multiple
Bathrooms: 2 en suite

B&B per night:
S £22.00–£25.00
D £44.00–£50.00

OPEN All year round

BUDE, Cornwall Map ref 1C2 *Tourist Information Centre Tel: (01288) 354240*

◆◆◆◆

ATLANTIC CALM

30 Downs View, Bude EX23 8RG
T: (01288) 359165
E: atlanticcalm@btinternet.com
I: www.atlanticcalm.co.uk

B&B per night:
S £17.00–£25.00
D £32.00–£49.00

HB per person:
DY £26.00–£34.50

OPEN All year round

Delightful guesthouse offering the very best in comfortable accommodation and personal service. Attractively decorated rooms – view them all on our website. Quality home cooking using local produce. Guests' lounge with log burner for those cooler months. Ideally situated for town, beaches and an excellent base to explore Cornwall and Devon.

Bedrooms: 1 single,
6 double/twin, 1 triple/
multiple
Bathrooms: 7 en suite,
1 private

Evening meal available
CC: Amex, Delta, Diners,
Mastercard, Switch, Visa

3 night B&B and 4 course evening meal £79pp.
Available 1 Feb to 24 May (excl Bank Hols) and 21
Sept to 31 Oct.

◆◆◆◆

CLIFF HOTEL
Crooklets Beach, Bude EX23 8NG
T: (01288) 353110
F: (01288) 353110
I: www.cliffhotel.co.uk

Bedrooms: 1 double/
twin, 14 triple/multiple
Bathrooms: 15 en suite

Lunch available
Evening meal available
CC: Delta, Mastercard,
Switch, Visa

B&B per night:
S £35.40–£40.20
D £59.00–£39.50

HB per person:
DY £39.50–£45.00

OPEN Mar–Oct

Indoor pool, mini-gym, putting, tennis court, bowling green, 5 acres next to National Trust cliffs, 200 yards from the beach. Chef/proprietor. Open Mar to Oct.

◆◆◆◆

LINK'S SIDE
7 Burn View, Bude EX23 8BY
T: (01288) 352410
E: linksidebude@north-cornwall.
co.uk
I: www.north-cornwall.co.uk/bude/
client/linkside

Bedrooms: 5 double/
twin, 1 triple/multiple
Bathrooms: 5 en suite

B&B per night:
S Min £18.00
D Min £34.00

OPEN All year round

Town centre location overlooking golf course and within walking distance of beaches and coastal paths.

CREDIT CARD BOOKINGS If you book by telephone and are asked for your credit card number it is advisable to check the proprietor's policy should you cancel your reservation.

Silver Award

LUFFLANDS
Yettington, Budleigh Salterton EX9 7BP
T: (01395) 568422
F: (01395) 568810
E: Lufflands@compuserve.com
I: www.lufflands.co.uk

B&B per night:
S £22.00
D £44.00

OPEN All year round

A warm welcome can be found at Lufflands, a 17thC former farmhouse. All rooms equipped to a high standard and your breakfast is freshly cooked to order in the guest dining room/lounge with inglenook and bread ovens. Large garden, ample off-street parking. Close to beaches. Excellent walking.

Bedrooms: 1 single, 1 double/twin, 1 triple/ multiple
Bathrooms: 2 en suite, 1 private

CC: Delta, Mastercard, Switch, Visa

Short breaks-minimum 3 nights. Apr-Oct £20pppn, Nov-Mar £18.50pppn.

ALSTONE COURT FARM
Alstone Lane, Highbridge TA9 3DS
T: (01278) 789417
F: (01278) 784582

Bedrooms: 2 double/ twin, 1 triple/multiple

B&B per night:
S Min £16.00
D Min £32.00

250-acre mixed farm. 17thC farmhouse with a warm and friendly atmosphere. Horse riding on farm, qualified instructors available. River walks.

OPEN Mar-Nov

KNIGHTS REST
9 Dunstan Road, Burnham-on-Sea
TA8 1ER
T: (01278) 782318

Bedrooms: 1 single, 2 double/twin

Evening meal available

B&B per night:
S £17.00-£18.50
D £34.00-£37.00

Edwardian residence. 4 minutes' easy walk to town and beach. Off-road parking. A quiet family home, where a friendly welcome awaits.

OPEN All year round

PROSPECT FARM GUEST HOUSE
Strowlands, East Brent, Highbridge TA9 4JH
T: (01278) 760507

B&B per night:
S £19.00-£25.00
D £38.00-£50.00

OPEN All year round

17thC Somerset farmhouse with inglenook fireplaces, bread ovens, beamed ceilings and a colourful history. Surrounded by the natural West Country beauty of the Somerset Levels, near legendary Brent Knoll, with remains of Iron Age and Roman settlements. 2 miles junction 22 M5, 3 miles Burnham-on-Sea. Variety of small farm animals and pets. Children welcome.

Bedrooms: 1 double/ twin, 2 triple/multiple
Bathrooms: 1 en suite

Stay longer and save. 2-6 nights less 5%. 7-13 nights less 10%. 14 nights less 15%.

ACCESSIBILITY
Look for the symbols which indicate accessibility for wheelchair users. A list of establishments is at the front of this guide.

◆◆◆

SOMEWHERE HOUSE

68 Berrow Road, Burnham-on-Sea TA8 2EZ
T: (01278) 795236
E: di@somewherehouse.com
I: www.somewherehouse.com

B&B per night:
S £26.00
D £40.00

OPEN All year round

A large Victorian residence near Burnham's extensive sandy beach and other local amenities including Burnham and Berrow championship golf course. All rooms have the usual facilities including colour TV and hairdryer and we have a comfortable lounge with widescreen digital TV. No smoking throughout.

Bedrooms: 2 double/ twin, 3 triple/multiple
Bathrooms: 5 en suite

CC: Delta, Mastercard, Switch, Visa

◆◆◆◆

PEBBLE BEACH LODGE
Coast Road, Burton Bradstock,
Bridport DT6 4RJ
T: (01308) 897428
F: (01308) 897428
E: pebblebeachlodge@supanet.com
I: www.burtonbradstock.org.uk/pebblebeachlodge

Bedrooms: 1 single, 6 double/twin, 3 triple/multiple; suites available
Bathrooms: 10 en suite

B&B per night:
S £25.00–£30.00
D £50.00–£55.00

Located on B3157 coast road, affording panoramic views of heritage coastline. Direct access to beach. Spacious and attractive accommodation, large conservatory.

◆◆◆◆

BUTCOMBE FARM

Aldwick Lane, Butcombe, Bristol BS40 7UW
T: (01761) 462380
F: (01761) 462300
E: info@butcombe-farm.demon.co.uk
I: www.butcombe-farm.demon.co.uk

B&B per night:
S £30.00–£39.00
D £40.00–£54.00

OPEN All year round

Originally a 14thC medieval hall house, Butcombe Farm is now a beautiful manor house with en suite bed and breakfast and individual self-catering accommodation. Set in several acres amid peaceful countryside. Close to Bristol, Bath, Cheddar, Wells, Mendips and Exmoor. For more information, please contact Barry and Josephine Harvey.

Bedrooms: 3 double/ twin, 2 triple/multiple
Bathrooms: 5 en suite

CC: Delta, Mastercard, Switch, Visa

Out of season short breaks to include clay pigeon shoots, archery, paint ball, horse-riding, aromatherapy massage, wine tasting and more.

◆◆◆

DOZMARY
Tors View Close, Tavistock Road,
Callington PL17 7DY
T: (01579) 383677
E: dozmarybb@aol.com

Bedrooms: 2 double/ twin, 1 triple/multiple
Bathrooms: 2 en suite, 1 private

B&B per night:
S £20.00–£21.00
D £34.00–£36.00

OPEN All year round

Deceptively spacious dormer bungalow providing comfortable accommodation with good facilities, just a few minutes from Callington town centre.

HALF BOARD PRICES Half board prices are given per person, but in some cases these may be based on double/twin occupancy.

CALLINGTON continued

GREEN PASTURES

Longhill, Callington PL17 8AU
T: (01579) 382566
E: greenpast@aol.com

Bedrooms: 2 double/
twin, 1 triple/multiple
Bathrooms: 2 en suite,
1 private

B&B per night:
S £20.00–£22.00
D £35.00–£37.00

OPEN All year round

Spacious detached bungalow set within 5 acres of pastural land. Large car park. Extensive views towards Dartmoor, Tamar Valley. Cotehele, Morwellam Quay within easy reach.

CANNINGTON, Somerset Map ref 1D1

THE FRIENDLY SPIRIT

Brook Street, Cannington, Bridgwater
TA5 2HP
T: (01278) 652215
F: (01278) 653636

B&B per night:
S £25.00–£30.00
D £40.00–£50.00

OPEN All year round

A long established country inn (with resident ghost) lying within an attractive conservation area by the village green and brook. Ideal base for exploring the Quantocks and North Somerset coast. Cycle hire, golf and other attractions nearby. As featured on Carlton Television and winner of 'Perfect Pint' award 1999-2000.

Bedrooms: 7 double/
twin, 1 triple/multiple
Bathrooms: 8 en suite

Lunch available
Evening meal available
CC: Delta, Mastercard,
Switch, Visa

CASTLE CARY, Somerset Map ref 2B2

THE HORSE POND INN AND MOTEL

The Triangle, Castle Cary BA7 7BD
T: (01963) 350318 & 351762
F: (01963) 351764
E: horsepondinn@aol.com

B&B per night:
S £40.00–£50.00
D £55.00–£60.00

HB per person:
DY £45.00–£60.00

OPEN All year round

The inn and motel nestles at the foot of Castle Cary. Centrally located, making it an ideal base for travelling around Somerset, West Devon, Dorset and Wiltshire either for business or pleasure. A small country town, where streets and shops retain the character of bygone days.

Bedrooms: 2 double/
twin, 2 triple/multiple;
suites available
Bathrooms: 4 en suite

Lunch available
Evening meal available
CC: Diners, Mastercard,
Switch, Visa

Stay for 4 nights (4th night 50% reduction); stay for 7 nights (7th night free).

CASTLE COMBE, Wiltshire Map ref 2B2

FOSSE FARMHOUSE

Nettleton Shrub, Nettleton,
Chippenham SN14 7NJ
T: (01249) 782286 & 07780 694935
F: (01249) 783066
E: caroncooper@compuserve.com
I: www.fossefarmhouse.8m.com

Bedrooms: 2 double/
twin, 1 triple/multiple
Bathrooms: 3 en suite

Lunch available
Evening meal available
CC: Amex, Mastercard,
Switch, Visa

B&B per night:
S £55.00–£65.00
D £85.00–£125.00

HB per person:
DY £67.50–£90.00

OPEN All year round

Nestling beside the Roman Fosse Way in an Area of Outstanding Natural Beauty. Take the A420 from Chippenham to Bristol, turn right at the 'Shoe' pub, 1.5 miles along the Fosse Way on the left hand side.

QUALITY ASSURANCE SCHEME

Diamond ratings and awards were correct at the time of going to press but are subject to change. Please check at the time of booking.

CASTLE COMBE continued

♦♦♦ **THORNGROVE COTTAGE**

Summer Lane, Castle Combe, Chippenham SN14 7LG
T: (01249) 782607 & 0780 1304676
E: chrisdalene@compuserve.com

Bedrooms: 1 double/twin
Bathrooms: 1 en suite

B&B per night:
S £22.00–£25.00
D £44.00–£50.00

OPEN All year round

We are situated in a quiet location, close to Bath and Bristol. With 7 good pubs within 2 miles.

CATTISTOCK, Dorset Map ref 2A3

♦♦♦ **GREYSTONES**

Cattistock, Dorchester DT2 OJB
T: (01300) 320477
E: j_f.fletcher@virgin.net

Bedrooms: 2 double/twin

B&B per night:
S £20.00–£22.00
D £40.00–£44.00

OPEN All year round

Spacious, comfortable family home with adjoining annexe situated in beautiful quiet village in the heart of West Dorset.

CHAGFORD, Devon Map ref 1C2

♦♦♦♦ **GLENDARAH HOUSE**

Silver
Award

Lower Street, Chagford, Newton Abbot TQ13 0BZ
T: (01647) 433270
F: (01647) 433483
E: enquiries@glendarah-house.co.uk
I: www.glendarah-house.co.uk

Bedrooms: 1 single, 6 double/twin
Bathrooms: 7 en suite

CC: Delta, Mastercard, Switch, Visa

B&B per night:
S £25.00–£29.00
D £50.00–£58.00

OPEN All year round

Non-smoking Victorian house with beautiful views in peaceful location, a short walk from village centre. Friendly service, en suite rooms with all facilities.

CHARD, Somerset Map ref 1D2 *Tourist Information Centre Tel: (01460) 67463*

♦♦♦♦♦ **BELLPLOT HOUSE HOTEL**

High Street, Chard TA20 1QB
T: (01460) 62600
F: (01460) 62600
E: bellplothousehotel@talk21.com

Bedrooms: 1 single, 5 double/twin, 1 triple/multiple
Bathrooms: 7 en suite

Evening meal available
CC: Delta, Mastercard, Switch, Visa

B&B per night:
S £52.50–£62.50
D £70.00–£80.00

OPEN All year round

Grade II Listed Georgian house with 7 luxury en suite bedrooms, where you will be assured of a warm welcome. Award-winning food cooked by Dennis.

♦♦♦♦

HORNSBURY MILL

Eleighwater, Chard TA20 3AQ
T: (01460) 63317
F: (01460) 63317
E: horsburymill@btclick.com
I: www.hornsburymill.co.uk

B&B per night:
S £50.00–£55.00
D £70.00–£75.00

HB per person:
DY £45.00–£50.00

OPEN All year round

Lying in lush Somerset countryside. Close to Devon and Dorset boarders. Ideal for touring, close to many attractions. This 200-year-old working watermill is surrounded by 4 acres of landscaped water gardens. Renowned restaurant, cream teas, relaxing atmosphere. All rooms en suite and furnished to high standard.

Bedrooms: 5 double/twin
Bathrooms: 5 en suite

Lunch available
Evening meal available
CC: Amex, Delta, Diners, Mastercard, Switch, Visa

3 nights for the price of 2, Oct–Mar (excl Christmas and New Year). Themed breaks.

CHECK THE MAPS

The colour maps at the front of this guide show all the cities, towns and villages for which you will find accommodation entries.
Refer to the town index to find the page on which they are listed.

◆◆◆

WAMBROOK FARM
Wambrook, Chard TA20 3DF
T: (01460) 62371
F: (01460) 68827

B&B per night:
S £25.00
D £40.00

A listed farmhouse and buildings in the beautiful countryside of the Blackdown Hills, 2 miles from Chard in peaceful, rural village. An ideal base for visiting Devon, Dorset and Somerset, Forde Abbey and gardens, Lyme Regis, Honiton antiques and NT properties. Excellent pub food in village.

Bedrooms: 1 double/ twin, 1 triple/multiple
Bathrooms: 2 en suite

CHARMINSTER, Dorset Map ref 2B3

◆◆◆

THREE COMPASSES INN
Charminster, Dorchester DT2 9QT
T: (01305) 263618

Bedrooms: 1 single, 2 double/twin, 1 triple/ multiple
Bathrooms: 2 en suite

Lunch available
Evening meal available

B&B per night:
S £20.00–£25.00
D £40.00–£45.00

OPEN All year round

Traditional village public house/inn with skittle alley, set in village square.

CHEDDAR, Somerset Map ref 1D1

◆◆◆

MARKET CROSS HOTEL
The Cross, Church Street, Cheddar
BS27 3RA
T: (01934) 742264
F: (01934) 741411
E: annfieldhouse@aol.com
I: www.marketcrosshotel.co.uk

Bedrooms: 2 single, 2 double/twin, 2 triple/ multiple
Bathrooms: 3 en suite

Lunch available
Evening meal available
CC: Delta, Mastercard, Switch, Visa

B&B per night:
S £21.50–£30.00
D £43.00–£56.00

HB per person:
DY £35.00–£45.00

OPEN All year round

Delightful Regency hotel. Good walking area, 5 minutes' walk from Cheddar Gorge, caves and Mendip Hills. Wells, Glastonbury, Bristol, Bath, Weston-super-Mare within easy reach.

◆◆◆◆

TOR FARM
Nyland, Cheddar BS27 3UD
T: (01934) 743710
F: (01934) 743710
E: bcjbkj@aol.com

Bedrooms: 1 single, 5 double/twin, 1 triple/ multiple
Bathrooms: 5 en suite

CC: Delta, Mastercard, Switch, Visa

B&B per night:
S £25.00–£30.00
D £35.00–£48.00

OPEN All year round

33-acre mixed farm. On A371 between Cheddar and Draycott. On Somerset Levels. Ideally situated for visiting Cheddar, Bath, Wookey Hole, Glastonbury, Wells and coast.

CHELSTON, Devon Map ref 1D2

◆◆◆◆

ELMDENE HOTEL
Rathmore Road, Chelston, Torquay
TQ2 6NZ
T: (01803) 294940
F: (01803) 294940
E: elmdenehoteltorqy@amserve. nett
I: www.s-h-systems.co.uk/hotels/ elmdene.html

Bedrooms: 2 single, 5 double/twin, 4 triple/ multiple
Bathrooms: 7 en suite

Evening meal available
CC: Amex, Mastercard, Visa

B&B per night:
S £20.00–£27.00
D £40.00–£55.00

HB per person:
DY £29.00–£37.00

OPEN All year round

A lovely Victorian hotel in rural setting, on the level and close to seafront, Torre Abbey and amenities. Own car park and licensed bar.

IDEAS For ideas on places to visit refer to the introduction at the beginning of this section.

CHELYNCH, Somerset Map ref 2B2

◆◆◆◆ **THE OLD STABLES**
Hurlingpot Farm, Chelynch,
Shepton Mallet BA4 4PY
T: (01749) 880098 & 07798 600752
E: maureen.keevil@amserve.net
I: www.the-oldstables.co.uk

Bedrooms: 1 double/
twin, 1 triple/multiple
Bathrooms: 1 en suite,
1 private

B&B per night:
S £30.00–£35.00
D £40.00–£45.00

*Carefully restored Grade II Listed barn offering a high standard of accommodation, set in
300 acres of Somerset countryside. Open April 2001.*

CHEW STOKE, Bath and North East Somerset Map ref 2A2

◆◆◆ **ORCHARD HOUSE**
Bristol Road, Chew Stoke, Bristol
BS40 8UB
T: (01275) 333143
F: (01275) 333754
E: orchardhse@ukgateway.net
I: www.orchardhse.ukgateway.net

Bedrooms: 1 single,
5 double/twin, 1 triple/
multiple
Bathrooms: 6 en suite,
1 private

Evening meal available
CC: Delta, Mastercard,
Switch, Visa

B&B per night:
S £20.00–£27.00
D £40.00–£50.00

HB per person:
DY £32.00–£39.00

OPEN All year round

*Comfortable accommodation in a carefully modernised Georgian house and coach house
annexe. Home cooking using local produce.*

CHICKLADE, Wiltshire Map ref 2B2

◆◆◆◆ **THE OLD RECTORY**
Chicklade, Hindon, Salisbury
SP3 5SU
T: (01747) 820226
F: (01747) 820783
E: vbronson@old-rectory.co.uk
I: www.old-rectory.co.uk

Bedrooms: 3 double/
twin

Evening meal available

B&B per night:
S Min £28.00
D Min £50.00

HB per person:
DY £28.50–£41.50

OPEN All year round

*A 17thC rectory guesthouse ideally placed between Bath and Salisbury as a Wessex
touring centre set in beautiful natural gardens.*

CHIDEOCK, Dorset Map ref 1D2

◆◆◆◆ **BETCHWORTH HOUSE**
Chideock, Bridport DT6 6JW
T: (01297) 489478
F: (01297) 489932
E: jffldg@aol.com
I: www.lymeregis.co.uk

Bedrooms: 4 double/
twin, 1 triple/multiple
Bathrooms: 3 en suite,
2 private

CC: Amex, Delta,
Mastercard, Switch, Visa

B&B per night:
S £30.00–£35.00
D £50.00–£60.00

OPEN All year round

*Charming 17thC guesthouse offering a high standard of accommodation. Dorset cream
teas served in attractive dining-room or pretty cottage garden.*

CHIPPENHAM, Wiltshire Map ref 2B2 *Tourist Information Centre Tel: (01249) 706333*

◆◆◆◆

CHURCH FARM
Hartham Park, Corsham SN13 0PU
T: (01249) 715180 & 07977 910775
F: (01249) 715572
E: kmjbandb@aol.com
I: www.churchfarm.cjb.net

B&B per night:
S £22.00–£25.00
D £44.00–£50.00

OPEN All year round

*Cotswold farmhouse on working
dairy and mixed farm, offering
superb views over open countryside.
Glorious walks nearby with plenty of
wildlife. Garden available for guests'
use. Local produce used wherever
possible. Warm family welcome.
Secure off-road parking. Good road/
rail links, easy access Bath, Castle
Combe and Lacock.*

Bedrooms: 1 single,
1 double/twin, 1 triple/
multiple
Bathrooms: 2 en suite,
1 private

Reductions for more than 2 nights.

CHIPPENHAM continued

♦♦ **75 ROWDEN HILL**
Chippenham SN15 2AL
T: (01249) 652981

Bedrooms: 3 double/ twin

Near National Trust village of Lacock and attractive Castle Combe. Corsham Court also nearby. Friendly welcome assured.

B&B per night:
S Max £20.00
D Max £30.00

OPEN All year round

CHIPPING SODBURY, South Gloucestershire Map ref 2B2

♦♦♦♦ **THE SODBURY HOUSE HOTEL**
Badminton Road, Old Sodbury,
Bristol BS37 6LU
T: (01454) 312847
F: (01454) 273105
E: sodhousehotel@tesco.net

Bedrooms: 6 single,
9 double/twin, 2 triple/ multiple
Bathrooms: 17 en suite

CC: Amex, Diners,
Mastercard, Switch, Visa

B&B per night:
S £45.00–£54.00
D £65.00–£90.00

OPEN All year round

A warm welcome awaits you at this former farmhouse offering well-appointed en suite accommodation in attractive rural setting, within easy reach M4/M5, Bath, Bristol and Cotswolds.

CLOVELLY, Devon Map ref 1C1

♦♦♦ **FUCHSIA COTTAGE**
Burscott, Clovelly, Bideford
EX39 5RR
T: (01237) 431398
E: tomsuecurtis.fuchsiacot@ currantbun.com
I: www.clovelly-holidays.co.uk

Bedrooms: 1 single,
1 double/twin, 1 triple/ multiple
Bathrooms: 2 en suite

Evening meal available

B&B per night:
S Max £16.00
D Max £38.00

OPEN All year round

Fuchsia Cottage has comfortable ground and first floor en suite accommodation. Surrounded by beautiful views of sea and country. Good walking area. Ample parking.

CLUTTON, Bath and North East Somerset Map ref 2A2

♦♦♦

CHOLWELL HALL
Clutton, Bristol BS39 5TE
T: (01761) 452380
I: www.cholwellhall.co.uk

B&B per night:
D £40.00–£90.00

OPEN All year round

Elegant stone-built house with extensive grounds in a pastoral, Mendip setting. Bath, Bristol and Wells are each just 11 miles away. Family-run, very large, comfortable rooms with views, easy to find and ample parking. Groups welcome. Residents' lounge with log fire. Walking/riding/golf locally in outstanding scenery.

Bedrooms: 1 single,
5 double/twin
Bathrooms: 3 en suite,
1 private

Fancy dress costumes available for hire for themed parties, murder mystery etc. Discounts for stays of 3 nights, please enquire.

Lunch available

COLEFORD, Somerset Map ref 2B2

♦♦ **BROOK COTTAGE**
Highbury Street, Coleford, Bath
BA3 5NW
T: (01373) 812633
F: (01373) 812633

Bedrooms: 1 single,
2 double/twin; suites available
Bathrooms: 1 en suite

Evening meal available

B&B per night:
S Max £16.00
D £32.00–£36.00

HB per person:
DY £24.00–£52.00

OPEN All year round

Homely accommodation with stairlift, good food, friendly cottage, overlooking lovely countryside. Half hour drive to Bath, Wells, Longleat and Cheddar.

SYMBOLS The symbols in each entry give information about services and facilities. A key to these symbols appears at the back of this guide.

◆◆◆◆

SMALLICOMBE FARM

Northleigh, Colyton EX24 6BU
T: (01404) 831310
F: (01404) 831431
E: maggie_todd@yahoo.com
I: www.smallicombe.com

B&B per night:
S £25.00–£30.00
D £44.00–£50.00

HB per person:
DY £34.50–£37.50

OPEN All year round

Idyllic setting with only the sights and sounds of the countryside yet close to the coast. Meet friendly farm animals including Berkshire pigs. Explore picturesque villages and historic houses and gardens. Return to enjoy a scrumptious farmhouse meal in our licensed restaurant.

Bedrooms: 1 single,
1 double/twin, 1 triple/
multiple; suites available
Bathrooms: 3 en suite

Evening meal available

'Piggy Weekend': 2 nights en suite B&B plus evening meal on one night and a day with the pigs including lunch £65pp.

◆◆◆◆

REDLANDS

Trebles Holford, Combe Florey, Taunton
TA4 3HA
T: (01823) 433159
E: redlandshouse@hotmail.com
I: www.escapetothecountry.co.uk

B&B per night:
S £28.00
D £48.00–£53.00

OPEN All year round

Escape to the country to our peacefully located barn conversion set beside a stream adjacent to the Quantock Hills. Enjoy the outdoors or let off steam on the West Somerset Railway. Within easy reach are gardens, National Trust properties, the coast and Exmoor. Ground floor room suitable for disabled guests.

Bedrooms: 2 double/
twin
Bathrooms: 2 en suite

◆◆◆◆

HEATHERLY COTTAGE

Ladbrook Lane, Gastard, Corsham
SN13 9PE
T: (01249) 701402
F: (01249) 701412
E: ladbrook1@aol.com
I: www.smoothhound.co.uk/hotels/
heather3.html

B&B per night:
S £27.00
D £46.00–£50.00

OPEN All year round

Delightful 17thC cottage set in 1.5 acres with views over open coutryside. Guests' accommodation is a separate wing of the house with its own front door and staircase. Our attractively furnished rooms are all en suite and have TV and hospitality trays. Many pubs serving food nearby. Bath 9 miles. Ample parking.

Bedrooms: 3 double/
twin
Bathrooms: 3 en suite

SPECIAL BREAKS

Many establishments offer special promotions and themed breaks. These are highlighted in red. (All such offers are subject to availability.)

CRANTOCK, Cornwall Map ref 1B2

◆◆◆

HIGHFIELD LODGE HOTEL

Halwyn Road, Crantock, Newquay TR8 5TR
T: (01637) 830744
E: highfieldlodge@tinyworld.co.uk

B&B per night:
S £18.00–£23.00
D £36.00–£46.00

OPEN All year round

Highfield Lodge is a small, friendly, non-smoking hotel in the picturesque coastal village of Crantock. An ideal centre for touring Cornwall with nearby facilities for coarse and sea fishing, riding, surfing and golf. Crantock beach a mere stroll away. Bar meals available in our cosy licensed bar.

Bedrooms: 2 single, 8 double/twin, 1 triple/ multiple
Bathrooms: 8 en suite

CC: Delta, Mastercard, Switch, Visa

 P

CREDITON, Devon Map ref 1D2 *Tourist Information Centre Tel: (01363) 772006*

◆◆

GREAT PARK FARM

Crediton EX17 3PR
T: (01363) 772050

B&B per night:
S £17.00–£21.00
D £32.00–£40.00

OPEN Mar–Dec

Listed farmhouse on working dairy farm. Attractive, comfortable rooms, all with wonderful views TVs and beverage facilities. Tranquil, picturesque location yet within easy walking distance of town. Golf, fishing, swimming. Inns and shops close by. Enjoy the peace of Great Park whilst exploring Devon.

Bedrooms: 2 double/ twin, 1 triple/multiple
Bathrooms: 1 en suite

P

CREWKERNE, Somerset Map ref 1D2

◆◆◆

THE GEORGE HOTEL & COURTYARD RESTAURANT
Market Square, Crewkerne TA18 7LP
T: (01460) 73650
F: (01460) 72974
E: eddie@thegeorgehotel.sagehost.co.uk
I: www.thegeorgehotel.saganet.co.uk

Bedrooms: 3 single, 8 double/twin, 2 triple/ multiple
Bathrooms: 7 en suite, 2 private

Lunch available
Evening meal available
CC: Amex, Delta, Diners, Mastercard, Switch, Visa

B&B per night:
S £25.00–£50.00
D £50.00–£80.00

OPEN All year round

Recently refurbished 17thC Grade II Listed coaching inn in the market square. Ideally located for touring. Fine food, real ales, warm welcome!

P

CRICKLADE, Wiltshire Map ref 2B2

◆◆

THE WHITE LION
50 High Street, Cricklade, Swindon SN6 6DA
T: (01793) 750443
E: info@whitelion-inn.com
I: www.whitelion-inn.com

Bedrooms: 4 double/ twin, 1 triple/multiple
Bathrooms: 5 en suite

Lunch available
Evening meal available
CC: Amex, Delta, Diners, Mastercard, Switch, Visa

B&B per night:
S £37.50–£85.00
D £50.00–£85.00

OPEN All year round

The White Lion is an old Coaching Inn dating back to the late 1600's. Built in the 9thC Saxon town of Cricklade.

P

 PRICES
Please check prices and other details at the time of booking.

HOOKS HOUSE

Crowcombe, Taunton TA4 4AE

T: (01984) 618691

B&B per night:
S £22.50–£35.00
D £45.00

OPEN All year round

Delightful country house situated on the southern slopes of the Quantock Hills, in the historic village of Crowcombe. Short walk from pub. Footpaths into hills close by. Super views. Relaxed family atmosphere. Ideal for touring, walking and the West Somerset Railway.

Bedrooms: 3 double/twin

DARTMOOR

See under Ashburton, Bovey Tracey, Chagford, Dunsford, Hexworthy, Moretonhampstead, Okehampton, Tavistock, Widecombe-in-the-Moor, Yelverton

Silver Award

WOODSIDE COTTAGE BED & BREAKFAST

Blackawton, Totnes TQ9 7BL

T: (01803) 712375

F: (01803) 712375

E: woodside-cottage@lineone.net

I: www.woodside-cottage-devon.co.uk

B&B per night:
D £27.00–£35.00

OPEN Feb–Dec & New Year

Comfortably refurbished 18thC gamekeeper's lodge in tranquil setting with stunning views over unspoilt valley, 4 miles from Dartmouth and short walk from historic village with two inns. All bedrooms are en suite, having carefully co-ordinated furnishings and lovely views. Charming reception rooms with alcoves. Conservatory and large sheltered outside terrace.

Bedrooms: 3 double/twin
Bathrooms: 3 en suite

Gold Award

BLOUNTS COURT FARM

Coxhill Lane, Potterne, Devizes SN10 5PH

T: (01380) 727180

E: blountscourtfarm@tinyworld.co.uk

B&B per night:
S £32.00–£37.00
D £50.00–£55.00

OPEN All year round

Situated in a peaceful countryside setting of 150 acres with woodland backdrop. Traditional stone-built farmhouse with ground floor guest accommodation in recently converted stables adjoining house. Beautifully furnished rooms including 4-poster bed. Guests' own sitting room. Warm and homely atmosphere. Ideal base to explore this exciting part of Wiltshire.

Bedrooms: 2 double/twin
Bathrooms: 2 en suite

DODDISCOMBSLEIGH, Devon Map ref 1D2

WHITEMOOR FARM

Doddiscombsleigh, Exeter EX6 7PU
T: (01647) 252423
E: blaceystaffyrescue@easicom.com

B&B per night:
S £18.50–£19.50
D £35.00–£36.00

OPEN All year round

16thC thatched farmhouse surrounded by gardens and farmland in the picturesque Teign Valley, ideal for those appreciating peace and quiet. The house has oak beams, log fires in winter, central heating throughout. Home produce a speciality. Swimming pool available. Within easy reach of Exeter, forest walks, the sea and Dartmoor.

Bedrooms: 2 single,
2 double/twin

Evening meal available

DORCHESTER, Dorset Map ref 2B3 *Tourist Information Centre Tel: (01305) 267992*

CHURCHVIEW GUEST HOUSE

Winterbourne Abbas, Dorchester DT2 9LS
T: (01305) 889296
F: (01305) 889296
E: stay@churchview.co.uk
I: www.churchview.co.uk

B&B per night:
S £27.00–£34.00
D £48.00–£60.00

HB per person:
DY £38.00–£45.00

OPEN All year round

Beautiful 17thC guesthouse set in a small village near Dorchester, offers a warm welcome and delicious home-cooked meals. Character bedrooms with hospitality trays, TV and radio. Two comfortable lounges and licensed bar. Your hosts will give every assistance with information to ensure a memorable stay.

Bedrooms: 1 single,
7 double/twin, 1 triple/
multiple
Bathrooms: 8 en suite,
1 private

Evening meal available
CC: Delta, Mastercard,
Switch, Visa

Prices reduced by £2 pp daily, for stays of 2 nights or more with evening meals.

JOAN'S BED AND BREAKFAST
119 Bridport Road, Dorchester
DT1 2NH
T: (01305) 267145 & 0774 8947610
F: (01305) 267145
E: b_and_b@joancox.freeserve.
co.uk

Bedrooms: 1 single,
2 double/twin

B&B per night:
S £20.00–£22.00
D £40.00–£44.00

OPEN All year round

Detached house. Comfortable relaxed atmosphere, close to all amenities. Excellent breakfast. Light airy bedrooms, bathroom and shower room. Guest lounge. Lovely garden.

COUNTRY CODE Always follow the Country Code 🌳 Enjoy the countryside and respect its life and work 🌳 Guard against all risk of fire 🌳 Fasten all gates 🌳 Keep your dogs under close control 🌳 Keep to public paths across farmland 🌳 Use gates and stiles to cross fences, hedges and walls 🌳 Leave livestock, crops and machinery alone 🌳 Take your litter home 🌳 Help to keep all water clean 🌳 Protect wildlife, plants and trees 🌳 Take special care on country roads 🌳 Make no unnecessary noise

◆◆◆◆

THE OLD RECTORY

Winterbourne Steepleton, Dorchester
DT2 9LG
T: (01305) 889468
F: (01305) 889737
E: trees@eurobell.co.uk
I: www.trees.eurobell.co.uk

B&B per night:
S £55.00
D £45.00–£100.00

OPEN All year round

Built 1850 on one acre of private ground in a quiet hamlet, surrounded by spectacular walks, 6 miles from historic Dorchester, 8 miles from Weymouth's sandy beach. We offer a peaceful stay with a memorable breakfast including many home-made organic products. Excellent local pubs and restaurants. French spoken.

Bedrooms: 4 double/ twin
Bathrooms: 4 en suite

Evening meal available

◆◆◆◆◆

YALBURY COTTAGE HOTEL AND RESTAURANT

Lower Bockhampton, Dorchester DT2 8PZ
T: (01305) 262382
F: (01305) 266412
E: yalburycottage@aol.com
I: www.smoothhound.co.uk/hotels/yalbury.html

B&B per night:
S £55.00
D £86.00

HB per person:
DY £71.95–£83.95

OPEN Feb–Dec

Nestling amidst winding rivers and peaceful fields, Yalbury Cottage is the ideal place to relax and unwind. This friendly, 17thC thatched hotel is at the heart of Thomas Hardy's Wessex. Its pretty restaurant offers head chef Russell Brown's excellent award-winning food, in an atmosphere enhanced by oak beams and inglenooks.

Bedrooms: 7 double/ twin, 1 triple/multiple
Bathrooms: 8 en suite

Evening meal available
CC: Delta, Mastercard, Switch, Visa

Short breaks available for DB&B throughout the year. Christmas package.

◆◆◆◆
Silver
Award

TOWN MILLS

High Street, Dulverton TA22 9HB
T: (01398) 323124
E: townmills@onetel.net.uk

B&B per night:
D £40.00–£52.00

OPEN All year round

Escape for a while to enjoy comfort and peace in our secluded 19thC mill house situated in the centre of Dulverton. We serve full English breakfast in our attractive and spacious bedrooms, some having their own log fire. We are an ideal centre for exploring Exmoor.

Bedrooms: 5 double/ twin; suites available
Bathrooms: 3 en suite

MAP REFERENCES The map references refer to the colour maps at the front of this guide. The first figure is the map number; the letter and figure which follow indicate the grid reference on the map.

Silver
Award

OAK LODGE
The Court, Dunsford, Exeter EX6 7DD
T: (01647) 252829 & 0771 404 0648
E: shirley.hodge@virgin.net
I: www.oaklodge-devon.co.uk

B&B per night:
S Min £25.00
D £40.00–£48.00

OPEN All year round

Attractive detached house peacefully situated in a picturesque village within the Dartmoor National Park. Seven miles from Exeter. Ideally situated for touring, walking and relaxing. 200yds from local pub/ restaurant. Spacious and comfortable rooms with colour TVs and video in all rooms. Award-winning breakfast using local produce.

Bedrooms: 1 single,
2 double/twin
Bathrooms: 1 en suite,
2 private

Bargain breaks for 3 nights or more. Negotiable rates for longer stays and families. Reduced-rate winter promotions.

SPEARS CROSS HOTEL
1 West Street, Dunster, Minehead
TA24 6SN
T: (01643) 821439
E: mjcapel@aol.com
I: www.smoothhound.co.uk/hotels/
spearsx.html

Bedrooms: 2 double/
twin, 1 triple/multiple
Bathrooms: 3 en suite

Lunch available
Evening meal available
CC: Delta, Mastercard,
Switch, Visa

B&B per night:
S £27.00–£32.00
D £46.00–£55.00

OPEN Feb–Dec

Pretty 15thC small hotel with old world charm but up-to-date facilities. Situated in picturesque village in the Exmoor National Park. No smoking. Private car parking.

THE GRANGE
Stoke Hill, Exeter EX4 7JH
T: (01392) 259723
E: dudleythegrange@aol.com

Bedrooms: 4 double/
twin
Bathrooms: 4 en suite

B&B per night:
S £26.00–£28.00
D £36.00–£42.00

Country house set in 3 acres of woodlands, 1.5 miles from the city centre. Ideal for holidays and off-season breaks. En suite rooms.

OPEN All year round

HAYNE BARTON
Whitestone, Exeter EX4 2JN
T: (01392) 811268

B&B per night:
S £26.00–£30.00
D £44.00–£50.00

OPEN All year round

Listed Grade II farmhouse (Domesday Book, 1086) with Saxon cellar, in 16 acres of gardens, fields, streams and woods. Views to Dartmoor and Exe Estuary, 3 miles west of Exeter. Both bedrooms en suite with colour TV. Ample parking. Dogs welcome. Stabling available. Bedding plant sales. Brochure available. 90 minutes from Eden project.

Bedrooms: 2 double/
twin
Bathrooms: 2 en suite

REGIONAL TOURIST BOARD The **A** symbol in an establishment entry indicates that it is a Regional Tourist Board member.

◆◆◆◆

ST ANDREWS HOTEL
28 Alphington Road, Exeter EX2 8HN
T: (01392) 276784
F: (01392) 250249

B&B per night:
S £40.00–£49.00
D £55.00–£65.00

OPEN All year round

A warm welcome awaits you at this long established family-run hotel, retaining the features of a large Victorian house but with all the facilities of a modern hotel. Offering a very high standard of comfort and service in a friendly, relaxing atmosphere. Weekend breaks. Brochure on request.

Bedrooms: 4 single, 11 double/twin, 2 triple/ multiple
Bathrooms: 17 en suite

Lunch available
Evening meal available
CC: Amex, Delta, Diners, Mastercard, Switch, Visa

Weekend breaks all year, must include Sat night. Ideally situated for Christmas shopping or summer touring breaks.

EXMOOR

See under Allerford, Bilbrook, Dulverton, Dunster, Lynton, Minehead, Porlock, Winsford, Parracombe

FALMOUTH, Cornwall Map ref 1B3 *Tourist Information Centre Tel: (01326) 312300*

◆◆◆◆

APPLE TREE COTTAGE
Laity Moor, Ponsanooth, Truro TR3 7HR
T: (01872) 865047
E: appletreecottage@talk21.com
I: www.cornwall-online.co.uk

B&B per night:
S £25.00
D £46.00–£50.00

OPEN All year round

Set amid countryside between Falmouth and Truro with a river meandering through the gardens. Rooms are furnished in a country style and guests are offered traditional farmhouse fare cooked on the Aga. Close to superb Cornish gardens and beaches. No smoking. Member Falmouth Hotel Association. For brochure contact Mrs A Tremayne.

Bedrooms: 2 double/ twin

◆◆◆◆

IVANHOE GUEST HOUSE
7 Melvill Road, Falmouth TR11 4AS
T: (01326) 319083
F: (01326) 319083
E: ivanhoe@enterprise.net
I: www.smoothhound.co.uk/hotels/ivanhoe

Bedrooms: 2 single, 3 double/twin, 1 triple/ multiple
Bathrooms: 4 en suite

B&B per night:
S £18.00–£22.00
D £44.00–£50.00

OPEN All year round

A warm and comfortable guesthouse with particularly well equipped en suite rooms. Minutes from the beaches, harbour and town. Off-road parking.

WICKHAM GUEST HOUSE

21 Gyllyngvase Terrace, Falmouth
TR11 4DL
T: (01326) 311140 & 07977 573575
E: enquiries@wickhamhotel.freeserve.co.uk

B&B per night:
S £19.00
D £38.00–£42.00

HB per person:
DY £28.00–£30.00

OPEN All year round

Small, friendly, no-smoking guesthouse. Situated between harbour and beach with views over Falmouth Bay, Wickham is the ideal base for exploring Falmouth and South Cornwall's gardens, castles, harbours, coastal footpath and much more. All rooms have TV and tea/coffee facilities, some have sea views.

Bedrooms: 2 single, 2 double/twin, 2 triple/ multiple
Bathrooms: 3 en suite

Evening meal available
CC: Mastercard, Visa

4 nights' HB for the price of 3, Mar and Oct.

AT-A-GLANCE SYMBOLS

Symbols at the end of each accommodation entry give useful information about services and facilities. A key to symbols can be found inside the back cover flap. Keep this open for easy reference.

DOLVEAN HOTEL

50 Melvill Road, Falmouth TR11 4DQ

Welcome to our Victorian gentleman's residence, dating from 1870, in historic Falmouth. With it's beautiful natural harbour and splendid Tudor castle, the area is one of Cornwall's finest locations for exploring the South-West of England.
Step inside, and experience the elegance and comfort of our Victorian home. We have carefully chosen interesting antiques, fine china, and fascinating books to create an ambience where you can relax and feel at home.
Each of our bedrooms has it's own individual character. Pretty pictures, china, Victorian photographs and of course lots of ribbon and lace create an atmosphere that makes you feel special. All our bedrooms enjoy full en suite facilities, with fluffy white towels, and a range of luxury toiletries. Thoughtful extra's include cookies, mineral water, and chocolates by your bedside.
Superb Bed and Breakfast in a non-smoking environment, from £30.00 - £40.00 per person.

Tel: 01326 313658 Fax: 01326 313995
Email: reservations@dolvean.freeserve.co.uk
www.dolvean.co.uk

FAULKLAND, Somerset Map ref 2B2

♦♦♦♦

LIME KILN FARM
Faulkland, Bath BA3 5XE
T: (01373) 834305
E: limekiln@btinternet.com

B&B per night:
S £48.00–£65.00
D £60.00–£70.00

OPEN All year round

Enjoy the hospitality of our family home or cottage from converted barn. Set in open countryside. Best of both worlds in the tranquility of the countryside and yet only 15 minutes south of Bath. Easy access all major tourist attractions.

Bedrooms: 5 double/twin
Bathrooms: 5 en suite

FROME, Somerset Map ref 2B2 *Tourist Information Centre Tel: (01373) 467271*

♦♦♦♦

Silver
Award

KOZY-GLEN
Rooks Lane, Berkley Marsh, Frome BA11 5JD
I: (01373) 464767

Bedrooms: 3 double/twin
Bathrooms: 1 en suite

Evening meal available

B&B per night:
D £36.00–£40.00

OPEN All year round

Charming bungalow situated in a quiet hamlet, 2 miles from Frome with easy access to Bath and all West Country attractions.

♦♦♦

WADBURY HOUSE
Mells, Frome BA11 3PA
T: (01373) 812359
E: sbrinkmann@btinternet.com

B&B per night:
S £32.00–£38.00
D £60.00–£72.00

HB per person:
DY £42.00–£50.00

OPEN All year round

Wadbury is an historic country house with galleried hall, surrounded by gardens and parkland affording complete peace and quiet. Magnificent views, elegant comfortable rooms, heated outdoor pool for summer, log fires in winter, home produce and a warm welcome. Opportunities for walking, riding and golf. Many places of interest nearby.

Bedrooms: 3 double/twin, 1 triple/multiple
Bathrooms: 3 en suite, 1 private

Lunch available
Evening meal available

GLASTONBURY, Somerset Map ref 2A2 *Tourist Information Centre Tel: (01458) 832954*

♦♦♦

LITTLE ORCHARD
Ashwell Lane, Glastonbury BA6 8BG
T: (01458) 831620
E: the.littleorchard@lineone.net
I: www.smoothhound.co.uk/hotels/orchard.html

Bedrooms: 2 single, 1 double/twin, 2 triple/multiple

B&B per night:
S £18.00–£21.00
D £36.00–£42.00

OPEN All year round

On the A361 Glastonbury to Shepton Mallet road. Good central position for touring the West Country. At the foot of historic Glastonbury Tor, with views over the Vale of Avalon.

www.travelengland.org.uk
Log on for information and inspiration. The latest information on places to visit, events and quality assessed accommodation.

◆◆◆

MEADOW BARN

Middlewick Farm, Wick Lane, Glastonbury
BA6 8JW
T: (01458) 832351
F: (01458) 832351
I: www.smoothhound.co.uk/hotels/
middlewi.html

B&B per night:
S £27.00–£28.00
D £44.00–£48.00

HB per person:
DY £35.00–£37.00

OPEN All year round

Meadow Barn is ground floor en suite accommodation, in an old converted barn. It has country-style decor and old world charm, set in beautiful grounds, cottage gardens, meadows and apple orchards. Lovely walks and beautiful views of the Somerset Levels and the Mendip Hills beyond. Indoor heated swimming pool.

Bedrooms: 3 double/
twin
Bathrooms: 3 en suite

Evening meal available

◆◆◆◆

MEARE MANOR

60 St Marys Road, Meare, Glastonbury
BA6 9SR
T: (01458) 860449
F: (01458) 860449
E: info@mearemanor.co.uk
I: www.mearemanor.co.uk

B&B per night:
S £25.00–£30.00
D £50.00–£70.00

OPEN All year round

A 200-year-old manor built by the Abbots of Glastonbury. Imposing, friendly, restaurant, licensed, tea rooms, parking, gardens, local walks. All rooms en suite, TV, tea trays, lift, disabled facilities, dogs welcome. Near Wells and Cheddar, 12 minutes M5. Apartments, suites and rooms.

Bedrooms: 1 single,
4 double/twin, 2 triple/
multiple; suites available
Bathrooms: 7 en suite

Evening meal available
CC: Delta, Mastercard,
Switch, Visa

Book 7 nights for the price of 6, plus a bottle of
wine on your arrival.

◆◆◆

THE WHO'D A THOUGHT IT INN
17 Northload Street, Glastonbury
BA6 9JJ
T: (01458) 834460
F: (01458) 831039
E: reservations@
whodathoughtit.co.uk
I: www.reservations.
whodathoughtit.co.uk

Bedrooms: 5 double/
twin
Bathrooms: 5 en suite

Lunch available
Evening meal available
CC: Delta, Mastercard,
Switch, Visa

B&B per night:
S Min £40.00
D Min £58.00

OPEN All year round

18thC Grade II Listed traditional inn. Full of reclaimed interesting artefacts and memorabilia. Real ales. Quality food always available.

◆◆◆

PERRAN HOUSE
Fore Street, Grampound, Truro
TR2 4RS
T: (01726) 882066
F: (01726) 882936

Bedrooms: 2 single,
4 double/twin
Bathrooms: 3 en suite

CC: Delta, Mastercard,
Visa

B&B per night:
S £16.00–£18.00
D £32.00–£40.00

OPEN All year round

Delightful 17thC cottage in the pretty village of Grampound, between St Austell and Truro. Central for touring and visiting the many local gardens and Eden Project.

CREDIT CARD BOOKINGS If you book by telephone and are asked for your credit card number it is advisable to check the proprietor's policy should you cancel your reservation.

♦♦♦ **THE GEORGE**

Market Street, Hatherleigh,	Bedrooms: 2 single,	Lunch available	B&B per night:
Okehampton EX20 3JN	7 double/twin	Evening meal available	S £40.00–£48.00
T: (01837) 810454	Bathrooms: 9 en suite	CC: Delta, Mastercard,	D £69.50–£79.50
F: (01837) 810901		Switch, Visa	
E: jfpozzetto@yahoo.co.uk			OPEN All year round

15thC coaching inn with cobbled courtyard, thatched roof, cob walls, blackened beams and blazing log fires. A la carte restaurant, 2 character bars. Traditional 4-poster beds.

⋔☆🏢🛏️🚪⛳🍷🆂✂️🎪🍽️♨️🍴🎿♨️∪♪⛵⛄🐴🐎P

♦♦♦

LONGSTONE FARM
Coverack Bridges, Trenear, Helston
TR13 0HG
T: (01326) 572483
F: (01326) 572483
E: longstonehse@lineone.net
I: www.longstonehse.co.uk

B&B per night:
S Min £22.00
D Min £40.00

HB per person:
DY Min £30.00

Enjoy the warm and friendly atmosphere of our home, off the beaten track overlooking rolling fields and peaceful countryside. Central for sandy beaches and many attractions, particularly Flambards. Delicious meals using local produce attractively presented in our dining room overlooking the spacious garden. Relax and unwind in our TV lounge and sun-lounge.

Bedrooms: 2 double/ twin, 3 triple/multiple
Bathrooms: 3 en suite, 2 private

Evening meal available

⋔☆🛁🏢🛏️🆂🎪🍽️♨️🍴⛄🐴🐎P

♦♦♦♦

THE FOREST INN
Hexworthy, Yelverton PL20 6SD
T: (01364) 631211
F: (01364) 631515
E: forestinn@hotmail.com

B&B per night:
S £22.00–£35.00
D £44.00–£59.00

OPEN Feb–Dec

A haven for walkers, riders, fishermen or anyone just looking for an opportunity to enjoy the natural beauty of Dartmoor. The restaurant specialises in homemade food using local produce wherever possible. As an alternative, there is an extensive range of meals that can be enjoyed in the more informal setting if the Huccaby room. Dogs and muddy boots welcome.

Bedrooms: 2 single, 8 double/twin
Bathrooms: 7 en suite, 3 private

Lunch available
Evening meal available
CC: Delta, Mastercard, Switch, Visa

Stay any 2 nights (Sun-Wed) and get your 3rd night free.

⋔☆🏢🚪🍷🆂✂️🍽️♨️🍴∪♪♨️🐴🐎🐕🐎P

♦♦ **RED LION HOTEL**

42a High Street, Heytesbury,	Bedrooms: 3 triple/	Lunch available	B&B per night:
Warminster BA12 0EA	multiple	Evening meal available	S £26.50–£28.00
T: (01985) 840315	Bathrooms: 3 en suite	CC: Mastercard, Visa	D £45.00–£47.00

Unpretentious village inn, in beautiful countryside. Offering home-cooked food complemented by fine ales, in comfortable and friendly surroundings. Be assured of a warm welcome.

HB per person:
DY £28.00–£38.00

OPEN All year round

⋔☆🚪🍷🆂🍽️♨️🍴♨️∪♪♨️🐴🐎P

MAP REFERENCES
Map references apply to the colour maps at the front of this guide.

HILMARTON, Wiltshire Map ref 2B2

◆◆◆◆

BURFOOTS
The Close, Hilmarton, Calne
SN11 8TH
T: (01249) 760492
F: (01249) 760609
E: anncooke@burfoots.co.uk
I: www.burfoots.co.uk

Bedrooms: 2 double/
twin, 1 triple/multiple
Bathrooms: 3 en suite

B&B per night:
S £25.00–£27.00
D £42.00–£50.00

OPEN All year round

Large private house on edge of lovely village, 6 miles from M4. Ideally situated for Avebury, Lacock, Bowood, Lyneham, Castle Combe and Bath.

Ⓜ🏠10 🖭 🖵 🌢 🖳 Ⓢ ↙ 🅜 🎞 🗐 🟡🏷 🎇 📶 P

HOLBETON, Devon Map ref 1C3

◆◆◆◆
Silver
Award

BUGLE ROCKS
The Old School, Battisborough, Holbeton,
Plymouth PL8 1JX
T: (01752) 830422
F: (01752) 830558
E: buglerocks@hotmail.com

B&B per night:
S £25.00
D £50.00

OPEN All year round

Located in an Area of Outstanding Natural Beauty, converted coach house and stable block. Formerly part of a gentleman's country residence, in a secluded valley overlooking the sea. Close to the spectacular coastal footpath, 5 minutes from the famous Mothecombe beach.

Bedrooms: 2 double/
twin
Bathrooms: 1 en suite,
1 private

Ⓜ🖐🖵🌢Ⓢ🅜🎞🎇🐎📶P

HOLSWORTHY, Devon Map ref 1C2

◆◆◆◆
Silver
Award

LEWORTHY FARMHOUSE BED & BREAKFAST
Leworthy Farmhouse, Lower Leworthy,
Pyworthy, Holsworthy EX22 6SJ
T: (01409) 259469

B&B per night:
S £25.00–£35.00
D £40.00–£44.00

HB per person:
DY £35.00–£50.00

OPEN All year round

Beautiful Georgian farmhouse nestling in unspoilt backwater, relaxing gardens, orchard, fishing lake. Charming en suites. Fresh flowers, milk, pretty china, chintzy curtains, glossy mags, books. Peaceful lounge. Chiming old clocks, sparkling china, comfy old sofas, Victoriana. Delightful breakfast choice – traditional or yogurt prunes, fruit salad. Warm, friendly and discreet hosts.

Bedrooms: 3 double/
twin, 1 triple/multiple
Bathrooms: 3 en suite,
1 private

Evening meal available

Ⓜ🏠🖭🖵🌢🖳Ⓢ↙🅜🗐🍴🎇📶🏠P

QUALITY ASSURANCE SCHEME

For an explanation of the quality and facilities represented by the Diamonds please refer to the front of this guide. A more detailed explanation can be found in the information pages at the back.

◆◆◆◆

FAIRMILE INN
Fairmile, Ottery St Mary EX11 1LP
T: (01404) 812827
F: (01404) 815806

B&B per night:
S £32.50
D £45.00

HB per person:
DY £30.00–£45.00

OPEN All year round

Lovely Grade II East Devon inn, parts of which are 400 years old, privately owned/managed, comfortable en suite accommodation, good pub guide 2000, a la carte restaurant open 7 days a week, good English food, real ales. Half a mile off new A30, free collection Exeter Airport, nearest bus and rail station.

Bedrooms: 3 double/twin
Bathrooms: 2 en suite

Lunch available
Evening meal available
CC: Delta, Mastercard, Switch, Visa

Stay 3 nights pay for 2 (subject to availability). Weekend breaks, Fri night to Mon morning, full board £75pp (excl Bank Hols).

🏰🖼️📺♨️🍳🏆Ⓢↈ🎱🛏️🪑🍺∪♪✤�GP

◆◆◆◆

THE OLD VICARAGE
Yarcombe, Honiton EX14 9BD
T: (01404) 861594
F: (01404) 861594
E: jonannstockwell@aol.com
I: members.aol.com/Jonannstockwell/

B&B per night:
S £24.00–£30.00
D £39.00–£50.00

HB per person:
DY £39.00–£45.00

OPEN All year round

Relaxed and gracious living at its best. The house and hosts are a delight! Surrounded by spectacular countryside, this imposing period house provides an excellent holiday base and spacious accommodation. Guest louge, TV lounge, games room and elegant dining room. Large garden. Ample parking. Meals or DIY barbecue by arrangement.

Bedrooms: 3 double/twin

Evening meal available

Sundays we can arrange informative pleasure flights over historic sites. £140 for 2-3 persons. Weather permitting. No fly-no pay!

🏰🐴5♨️Ⓢ🍳🛏️🪑🍺▶✤🚚🏠P

◆◆◆◆
Silver
Award

WESSINGTON FARM
Awliscombe, Honiton EX14 3NU
T: (01404) 42280
F: (01404) 45271
E: b&b@eastdevon.com
I: www.eastdevon.com/bedandbreakfast

B&B per night:
S Min £21.00
D £42.00–£50.00

OPEN All year round

140-acre dairy farm. Elegant Victorian stone farmhouse, situated in an Area of Outstanding Natural Beauty, with wonderful panoramic views over open countryside. On A373, 2 miles from Honiton, picturesque East Devon coastline 20 minutes, historic Exeter 16 miles. High standard rooms, warm, friendly atmosphere, traditional Aga-cooked breakfast.

Bedrooms: 3 double/twin
Bathrooms: 2 en suite, 1 private

4x4 off-road driving centre on site.

🐴🖼️📺♨️♨️Ⓢ🍳🛏️🪑✤🚚P

ACCESSIBILITY
Look for the 🚻🦽🚶 symbols which indicate accessibility for wheelchair users. A list of establishments is at the front of this guide.

HORTON, Somerset Map ref 1D2

◆◆◆ **LYMPOOL HOUSE**

Forest Mill Lane, Horton, Ilminster
TA19 9QU
T: (01460) 57924

Bedrooms: 2 single,
1 double/twin

B&B per night:
S £24.00
D £40.00

Quality, tranquil accommodation in elegant stone-built house set in 1.5 acres of beautiful gardens. Next to nature reserve. Ample parking. Easy access coast/moors.

OPEN Mar–Sep

ILFRACOMBE, Devon Map ref 1C1 *Tourist Information Centre Tel: 0845 4583630*

◆◆◆ **CAPSTONE HOTEL AND RESTAURANT**

St James Place, Ilfracombe
EX34 9BJ
T: (01271) 863540
F: (01271) 862277
E: steve@capstone.freeserve.co.uk
I: www.ilfracombe2000.freeserve.
co.uk

Bedrooms: 2 single,
7 double/twin, 3 triple/
multiple
Bathrooms: 12 en suite

Lunch available
Evening meal available
CC: Amex, Delta,
Mastercard, Switch, Visa

B&B per night:
S £19.50–£21.50
D £37.00–£42.00

HB per person:
DY £25.00–£29.50

OPEN Apr–Oct

Family-run hotel, with restaurant on ground floor. Close to harbour and all amenities. Local seafood a speciality.

◆◆◆◆

GLEN TOR HOTEL

Torrs Park, Ilfracombe EX34 8AZ
T: (01271) 862403
F: (01271) 862403
E: info@glentorhotel.co.uk
I: www.glentorhotel.co.uk

B&B per night:
S Min £22.00
D £48.00–£64.00

HB per person:
DY £37.00–£44.00

OPEN All year round

A beautiful, small, family-run, licensed hotel nestled in the quiet conservation area of Torrs Park and enjoying panoramic views of the surrounding hills, across the town, and to the sea. A gentle stroll to the town, theatre, pubs and restaurants, the main beaches, promenade, and dramatic cliff-top walks.

Bedrooms: 1 single,
5 double/twin, 1 triple/
multiple
Bathrooms: 5 en suite,
2 private

Open Christmas and New Year. Autumn mid-week breaks. 4 nights for the price of 3. Alternative therapy weekend courses.

Evening meal available
CC: Delta, Mastercard,
Switch, Visa

◆◆◆◆ **LYNCOTT HOUSE**

56 St Brannock's Road, Ilfracombe
EX34 8EQ
T: (01271) 862425
F: (01271) 862425
E: david@ukhotels.com
I: www.s-h-systems.co.uk/hotels/
lyncott.html and www./
yncottdevon.com

Bedrooms: 1 single,
3 double/twin, 2 triple/
multiple
Bathrooms: 6 en suite

Evening meal available

B&B per night:
S £19.00–£22.00
D £38.00–£48.00

HB per person:
DY £31.00–£34.00

OPEN All year round

Relax, smoke-free, at elegant, lovingly restored, Victorian Lyncott House. Spacious, individually designed en suite bedrooms. Delicious home-made fare. Near lovely Bicclescombe Park. Private parking.

◆◆◆◆
Silver
Award

STRATHMORE HOTEL

57 St Brannocks Road, Ilfracombe
EX34 8EQ
T: (01271) 862248 & 862243
F: (01271) 862243
E: strathmore@ukhotels.com
I: www.strathmore.ukhotels.com

Bedrooms: 2 single,
3 double/twin, 4 triple/
multiple; suites available
Bathrooms: 9 en suite

Lunch available
Evening meal available
CC: Mastercard, Switch,
Visa

B&B per night:
S £25.00–£35.00
D £40.00–£60.00

HB per person:
DY £39.95–£49.95

OPEN All year round

Quality hotel recommended for its superbly prepared home-cooked food, comfort and service. Licensed bar and parking. Close to beautiful beaches and Exmoor. Pets, children welcome.

ILFRACOMBE continued

◆◆◆ **THE TOWERS HOTEL**

Chambercombe Park Road, Ilfracombe EX34 9QN T: (01271) 862809 F: (01271) 879442 E: info@thetowers.co.uk I: www.thetowers.co.uk	Bedrooms: 1 single, 7 double/twin Bathrooms: 4 en suite, 1 private	Evening meal available CC: Delta, Mastercard, Switch, Visa	B&B per night: S £21.00–£24.00 D £42.00–£48.00 HB per person: DY £30.00–£66.00

Quiet location, sea views, private parking, family run. Special diets by arrangement. Pets welcome.

ISLES OF SCILLY Map ref 1A3 *Tourist Information Centre Tel: (01720) 422536*

◆◆◆ **NUNDEEPS**

Rams Valley, St Mary's TR21 0JX T: (01720) 422517	Bedrooms: 3 double/twin Bathrooms: 1 en suite	B&B per night: D £48.00–£58.00 OPEN All year round

Situated in a quiet cul-de-sac within easy reach of the town centre and quay, for any boating excursions to the off islands.

◆◆◆

POLREATH GUEST HOUSE

Higher Town, St Martin's TR25 0QL
T: (01720) 422046
F: (01720) 422046

B&B per night:
S £35.00–£38.00
D £70.00–£90.00

HB per person:
DY £50.00–£60.00

OPEN Mar–Oct

Friendly, family-run licensed guesthouse situated on St Martins. Attractive bedrooms, all with sea views. Conservatory, lounge, glasshouse and private gardens available for guests' use. Evening meals available on selected nights. Good home cooking is our speciality. Tea room open daily for light lunches and homemade cakes.

Bedrooms: 1 single, 4 double/twin
Bathrooms: 2 en suite

Lunch available
Evening meal available
CC: Delta, Mastercard, Switch, Visa

10% discount for stays of 5 nights or more during low season only. Offer excludes evening meals and drinks.

IVYBRIDGE, Devon Map ref 1C2 *Tourist Information Centre Tel: (01752) 897035*

◆◆◆◆

HILLHEAD FARM

Ugborough, Ivybridge PL21 0HQ
T: (01752) 892674 & 07785 915612
F: (01752) 690111

B&B per night:
S £20.00–£22.00
D £40.00–£44.00

HB per person:
DY £32.50–£34.50

OPEN All year round

Antique furniture and light, sunny rooms combine to create a welcoming atmosphere in this peaceful, friendly farmhouse with lovely views over rolling Devon countryside. Turn off A38 at Wrangation, turn left, take 3rd right, continue over next crossroads, after three quarters of a mile, turn left at Hillhead, entrance 75 yards on left.

Bedrooms: 3 double/twin
Bathrooms: 2 en suite, 1 private

Evening meal available

QUALITY ASSURANCE SCHEME

Diamond ratings and awards were correct at the time of going to press but are subject to change. Please check at the time of booking.

KENTON, Devon Map ref 1D2

♦♦♦ **DEVON ARMS**

Fore Street, Kenton, Exeter EX6 8LD	Bedrooms: 2 double/	Lunch available	B&B per night:
T: (01626) 890213	twin, 4 triple/multiple	Evening meal available	S £30.00–£35.00
F: (01626) 891678	Bathrooms: 6 en suite	CC: Mastercard, Switch,	D £45.00–£55.00
E: devon.arms@ukgateway.net		Visa	

Family-run inn on A379 between Exeter and Dawlish. Adjacent to Powderham Castle. Good base to explore Devon countryside: close to beach. All rooms en suite.

OPEN All year round

Ⓜ️🐎❑♨🍷ⓈⅢ🖼️🍴🕭☾❊🚢🏮P

KINGSAND, Cornwall Map ref 1C3

♦♦♦ **HALFWAY HOUSE INN**

Fore Street, Kingsand, Torpoint	Bedrooms: 2 single,	Lunch available	B&B per night:
PL10 1NA	3 double/twin, 1 triple/	Evening meal available	S £28.00–£38.00
T: (01752) 822279	multiple	CC: Amex, Delta,	D £56.00–£66.00
F: (01752) 823146	Bathrooms: 6 en suite	Mastercard, Switch, Visa	
E: halfway@eggconnect.net			OPEN All year round
I: www.crappot.co.uk			

Comfortable family-run inn. Ideal for coastal and valley walks, water sports or just relaxing. Good food. On Cawsand Bay, in Cornwall's forgotten corner.

Ⓜ️🐎🖼️❑♨🍷Ⓢ✂🖼️Ⅲ🖼️🍴🚢✎🏮

KINGSBRIDGE, Devon Map ref 1C3 *Tourist Information Centre Tel: (01548) 853195*

♦♦♦ **ASHLEIGH HOUSE**

Ashleigh Road, Kingsbridge	Bedrooms: 6 double/	Evening meal available	B&B per night:
TQ7 1HB	twin, 2 triple/multiple	CC: Delta, Mastercard,	S £26.00–£30.00
T: (01548) 852893 & 07967 737875	Bathrooms: 8 en suite	Switch, Visa	D £42.00–£50.00
E: reception@ashleigh-house.co.uk			
I: www.ashleigh-house.co.uk			HB per person:
			DY £30.00–£42.00

Comfortable, informal licensed Victorian guesthouse. Edge of town, easy walk. All rooms en suite, colour TV and beverage tray. Sun lounge, bar. Off-road parking.

OPEN All year round

Ⓜ️🐎❑♨🍷Ⓢ✂🖼️❊🍴🏮P

♦♦♦

SHUTE FARM

South Milton, Kingsbridge TQ7 3JL
T: (01548) 560680

B&B per night:
S £20.00–£21.00
D £40.00–£42.00

OPEN All year round

Working mixed farm of 140 acres, situated in a quiet position on the edge of a small, partly thatched village, 1.5 miles from Thurlestone Sands and only a short drive from Salcombe. The 16thC farmhouse has plenty of character and a wealth of oak beams.

Bedrooms: 2 double/
twin, 1 triple/multiple
Bathrooms: 2 en suite,
1 private

Ⓜ️🐎♨Ⓢ🖼️Ⅲ🖼️❊🍴🏮P

♦♦♦ **SLOOP INN**

Bantham, Kingsbridge TQ7 3AJ	Bedrooms: 3 double/	Lunch available	B&B per night:
T: (01548) 560489 & 560215	twin, 2 triple/multiple	Evening meal available	S £31.00–£39.00
F: (01548) 561940	Bathrooms: 5 en suite	CC: Delta, Switch	D £62.00–£68.00

Part 16thC inn in old world fishing village west of Kingsbridge. Some rooms overlook sea and estuary. Menu majors on local seafood. Featured in all major pub guides.

OPEN All year round

Ⓜ️🐎🖼️❑♨🍷ⓈⅢ🖼️🍴🏮P

CHECK THE MAPS

The colour maps at the front of this guide show all the cities, towns and villages for which you will find accommodation entries. Refer to the town index to find the page on which they are listed.

◆◆◆◆
Silver
Award

SOUTH ALLINGTON HOUSE

Chivelstone, Kingsbridge TQ7 2NB
T: (01548) 511272
F: (01548) 511421
E: barbara@sthallingtonbnb.demon.co.uk
I: www.sthallingtonbnb.demon.co.uk

B&B per night:
S £24.00–£47.00
D £47.00–£67.00

OPEN All year round

Georgian country house in 4 acres of beautiful grounds, also 140 acres of mixed farm. Abundance of birds, wonderful coastline. Ideal for walking the coastal path. Between Start Point and Prawle Point. If you want peace and quiet, this is just the place for you. Croquet, coarse fishing and tennis court.

Bedrooms: 1 single,
7 double/twin, 1 triple/
multiple
Bathrooms: 7 en suite,
2 private

10% reduction for 3 nights mid-week bookings May and Jun (excl Bank Hols).

Ⓜ 🅰 4 🏠 🖳 ⬚ ⬚ 📺 Ⓢ ⬚ 🅼 🏛, ⬚ ⬚ ⬚ ⬚ 🚲 🏮 P

LANGPORT, Somerset Map ref 1D1

◆◆◆◆◆
Gold
Award

MUCHELNEY HAM FARM
Muchelney, Langport TA10 0DJ
T: (01458) 250737
F: (01458) 250737
I: www.muchelneyhamfarm.co.uk

Bedrooms: 2 double/
twin, 1 triple/multiple
Bathrooms: 3 en suite

B&B per night:
S £25.00–£36.00
D £50.00–£65.00

OPEN All year round

103-acre mixed farm. Beautiful, traditional, Somerset farmhouse, mainly mid 17thC, tastefully furnished with period furniture. Beams and inglenook fireplace. Three sitting rooms with colour TVs for guest use only.

🅰 ⬚ 🖳 ⬚ ⬚ 📺 Ⓢ ⬚ 🅼 🏛, ⬚ ⬚ 🚲 ⬚ 🏮 P

◆◆◆

THE OLD POUND INN

Aller, Langport TA10 0RA
T: (01458) 250469
F: (01458) 250469

B&B per night:
S £35.00
D £55.00

OPEN All year round

Built in 1571 and upgraded to modern standards, with en suite bedrooms, 50-seat dining room and function room for 200. Log fires. Bar meals from £1.95. Ideal for country lovers, walking, fishing, bird watching. Winner of JPC national award of 'Best Pub of the Year 1999'.

Bedrooms: 1 single,
4 double/twin, 1 triple/
multiple
Bathrooms: 6 en suite

Lunch available
Evening meal available
CC: Amex, Delta,
Mastercard, Switch, Visa

🅰 🏠 🖳 ⬚ 🍷 Ⓢ ⬚ 🅼 🏛, ⬚ 🍴 🔑 ⬚ 🚲 P

LEWDOWN, Devon Map ref 1C2

◆◆

STOWFORD GRANGE FARM
Lewdown, Okehampton EX20 4BZ
T: (01566) 783298

Bedrooms: 2 double/
twin, 1 triple/multiple

Lunch available
Evening meal available

B&B per night:
S £16.50–£17.00
D £32.00–£34.00

HB per person:
DY £23.00–£25.00

220-acre mixed farm. Listed building in quiet village. Home-cooked food, fresh vegetables, poultry. Ten miles from Okehampton, 7 miles Launceston. Half a mile from old A30, turn right at Royal Exchange.

Ⓜ 🅰 ⬚ ⬚ Ⓢ ⬚ 🅼 🏛, ⬚ ⬚ 🚲 🏮 P

LISKEARD, Cornwall Map ref 1C2

◆◆◆◆

TREGONDALE FARM
Menheniot, Liskeard PL14 3RG
T: (01579) 342407
F: (01579) 342407
E: tregondale@connectfree.co.uk
I: www.tregondalefarm.co.uk

Bedrooms: 3 double/
twin
Bathrooms: 2 en suite,
1 private

Evening meal available
CC: Amex, Delta, Diners,
Mastercard, Switch, Visa

B&B per night:
S £25.00–£30.00
D £45.00–£50.00

HB per person:
DY £35.00–£43.50

OPEN All year round

200-acre mixed farm. Character farmhouse in beautiful countryside. Home-produced food our speciality. Log fires, tennis court. North east of Menheniot, between A38/A390.

Ⓜ 🅰 ⬚ 🖳 ⬚ ⬚ 📺 Ⓢ ⬚ 🅼 🏛, ⬚ ⬚ 🔦 ⬚ 🚲 P

CHARITY FARM

Litton Cheney, Dorchester DT2 9AP
T: (01308) 482574
E: charityfarm@eurolink.ltd.net

B&B per night:
S £23.00–£25.00
D £46.00–£50.00

Charity Farm is a working dairy farm set in the beautiful Bride Valley, in 122 acres of fertile pasture and water meadows. Relax in our spacious farmhouse and explore the glorious unspoilt surroundings of Litton Cheney. We are 3 miles from the sea.

Bedrooms: 3 double/ twin

Evening meal available

Silver
Award

BUCKLAWREN FARM

St Martin-by-Looe, Looe PL13 1NZ
T: (01503) 240738
F: (01503) 240481
E: bucklawren@compuserve.com
I: www.cornwallexplore.co.uk/bucklawren

B&B per night:
S £23.00–£30.00
D £46.00–£50.00

HB per person:
DY £36.50–£38.50

OPEN Mar–Nov

Delightful farmhouse set in glorious countryside with spectacular sea views. Quiet location, situated 1 mile from the beach and 3 miles from the fishing village of Looe. An award-winning farm with all bedrooms en suite. Enjoy dinner in our candlelit restaurant.

Bedrooms: 4 double/ twin, 2 triple/multiple
Bathrooms: 6 en suite

Lunch available
Evening meal available
CC: Mastercard, Visa

COOMBE FARM
COUNTRY HOUSE HOTEL

Widegates, Looe PL13 1QN
T: (01503) 240223 & 240329
F: (01503) 240895
E: coombe_farm@hotmail.com
I: www.coombefarmhotel.co.uk

B&B per night:
D £68.00–£78.00

HB per person:
DY £52.00–£56.00

Lovely, award-winning country house in a wonderful setting with superb views down a wooded valley to the sea. Delicious food, candlelit dining, log fires, heated outdoor pool, warm friendly hospitality. Nearby golf, fishing, riding, moorland walks, the Cornish Coastal Path, sandy beaches, coves, National Trust houses, glorious gardens and Eden project.

Bedrooms: 1 double/ twin, 9 triple/multiple
Bathrooms: 10 en suite

Evening meal available
CC: Amex, Mastercard, Switch, Visa

Bargain break discounts for 2 nights HB or more.

SPECIAL BREAKS
Many establishments offer special promotions and themed breaks. These are highlighted in red. (All such offers are subject to availability.)

◆◆◆◆

LITTLE LARNICK FARM
Pelynt, Looe PL13 2NB
T: (01503) 262837
F: (01503) 262837
E: littlelarnick@btclick.com

B&B per night:
D £42.00–£48.00

OPEN All year round

200-acre dairy farm situated in the beautiful West Looe River valley. The farmhouse and newly converted barn offer peaceful and relaxing character en suite accommodation, including a barn suite and ground floor bedroom. Wonderful walks from the door. Drying room available. Special 'Winter Warmer' breaks.

Bedrooms: 5 double/ twin, 1 triple/multiple
Bathrooms: 6 en suite

CC: Amex, Delta, Diners, Mastercard, Switch, Visa

'Winter Warmer' breaks Nov-Mar.

◆◆◆◆

THE PANORAMA HOTEL
Hannafore Road, Looe PL13 2DE
T: (01503) 262123
F: (01503) 265654
E: stay@looe.co.uk
I: www.looe.co.uk

Bedrooms: 2 single,
3 double/twin, 4 triple/ multiple
Bathrooms: 9 en suite

Evening meal available
CC: Delta, Mastercard, Switch, Visa

B&B per night:
S £24.50–£37.00
D £46.00–£74.00

HB per person:
DY £38.00–£52.00

OPEN All year round

Family-run hotel, good food, friendly atmosphere. Magnificent setting overlooking harbour, beach and miles of beautiful coastline.

◆◆

STONEROCK COTTAGE
Portuan Road, Hannafore,
West Looe, Looe PL13 2DN
T: (01503) 263651
F: (01503) 263414

Bedrooms: 1 single,
2 double/twin, 1 triple/ multiple
Bathrooms: 2 en suite, 1 private

B&B per night:
S £17.00–£18.00
D £38.00–£44.00

Modernised old world cottage facing south to the Channel and overlooking Looe Island in quiet residential area. Close to beach and amenities. Ample private parking.

◆◆◆◆

CHARNWOOD GUEST HOUSE
21 Woodmead Road, Lyme Regis DT7 3AD
T: (01297) 445281
E: charnwood@lymeregis62.freeserve.co.uk
I: www.lymeregisaccommodation.com

B&B per night:
S £21.00–£25.00
D £42.00–£50.00

OPEN All year round

Quaint Edwardian guesthouse in quiet area, 5 to 10 minutes' walk from main shops/restaurants and the sea. Off road car parking. Sea views from 3 rooms. We serve an English, vegetarian, or fruit and yoghurt breakfast and can cater for most special requirements. Visit fossil walk, beach, enjoy!

Bedrooms: 1 single,
6 double/twin, 1 triple/ multiple
Bathrooms: 7 en suite, 1 private

CC: Delta, Mastercard, Switch, Visa

Sun to Thurs, 5% discount on 3/4 nights, 10% discount on 5 night stays. 10% on 7 nights or more.

MAP REFERENCES The map references refer to the colour maps at the front of this guide. The first figure is the map number; the letter and figure which follow indicate the grid reference on the map.

◆◆◆◆◆
Silver
Award

CLAPPENTAIL HOUSE
Uplyme Road, Lyme Regis DT7 3LP
T: (01297) 445739
F: (01297) 444794
E: pountain@clappentail.freeserve.co.uk

B&B per night:
S £21.00–£30.00
D £42.00–£60.00

OPEN All year round

Grade II Listed house, Lyme's first 5 Diamond B&B, offering comfort, good food and a warm welcome. Kingsize beds, power showers, all modern facilities. Superb breakfasts including house specialities. Cosy visitors' lounge, secluded courtyard, garden with seating overlooking Lyme Valley. Few minutes' walk to shops, restaurants and seafront.

Bedrooms: 3 double/ twin; suites available
Bathrooms: 3 en suite

Special breaks out of season on HB basis.

Evening meal available
CC: Delta, Mastercard, Switch, Visa

🐎10 🖳📞♿Ⓢ✂🛏🖥🛋☼ 🐾❄🐾P

◆◆◆
LUCERNE
View Road, Lyme Regis DT7 3AA
T: (01297) 443752
E: lucerne@lineone.net

Bedrooms: 1 single, 4 double/twin
Bathrooms: 4 en suite, 1 private

B&B per night:
S £23.00–£25.00
D £38.00–£46.00

OPEN All year round

Private house in quiet residential area. Excellent sea and coastal views. Comfortably furnished, non-smoking. All rooms en suite or private with colour TV, tea/coffee.

🐎📞♿Ⓢ✂🛏🖥🛋🐴🐾P

◆◆◆◆

ORCHARD COUNTRY HOTEL
Rousdon, Lyme Regis DT7 3XW
T: (01297) 442972
F: (01297) 443670
E: the.orchard@btinternet.com

B&B per night:
S £25.00–£42.00
D £50.00–£78.00

HB per person:
DY £38.00–£53.00

OPEN All year round

Superb food (including vegetarian), quality en suite accommodation (ground floor available) and a friendly atmosphere. Totally non-smoking. Bar, sun terrace, gardens and ample parking. Good location for visiting National Trust properties and gardens, walking, fossil hunting, bird-watching, golf – and relaxing. Short breaks. Groups welcome. Brochure available.

Bedrooms: 2 single, 10 double/twin
Bathrooms: 9 en suite, 3 private

Short breaks available.

Evening meal available
CC: Delta, Switch

Not Sunday.

🐎8🛋🖳📞♿🍷Ⓢ✂🛏🖥🛋♂♪☼🐾P

◆◆◆

SPRINGFIELD
Woodmead Road, Lyme Regis DT7 3LJ
T: (01297) 443409
F: (01297) 443685
E: springfield@lymeregis.com
I: www.lymeregis.com/springfield

B&B per night:
D £40.00–£48.00

Elegant Georgian house in partly walled garden with conservatory. Well proportioned rooms, all with far-reaching views over the sea and Dorset coastline. A short walk to the shops and seafront. Close to major footpaths. Concession at local golf course.

Bedrooms: 3 double/ twin, 2 triple/multiple
Bathrooms: 4 en suite, 1 private

🐎📞♿Ⓢ✂🛏🖥🛋♂☼🐴🐾P

◆◆◆◆ **WHITE HOUSE**
47 Silver Street, Lyme Regis
DT7 3HR
T: (01297) 443420

Bedrooms: 1 single,
6 double/twin
Bathrooms: 7 en suite

B&B per night:
D £38.00–£50.00

Fine views of Dorset coastline from rear of this 18thC guesthouse. A short walk from beach, gardens and shops.

LYNTON, Devon Map ref 1C1 *Tourist Information Centre Tel: 0845 458 3775*

◆◆◆

THE DENES GUEST HOUSE
15 Longmead, Lynton EX35 6DQ
T: (01598) 753573
F: (01598) 753573
E: j.e.mcgowan@btinternet.com
I: www.thedenes.com

B&B per night:
S £16.00–£22.50
D £32.00–£45.00

HB per person:
DY £26.00–£35.00

OPEN All year round

Homely, friendly guesthouse with spacious rooms, some having en suite facilities. Optional home-cooked evening meals and licensed for diners. The Denes has ample parking and offers baby sitting by arrangement. Situated at the entrance to the Valley of Rocks, it makes an ideal spot for walking, birdwatching and exploring Exmoor.

Bedrooms: 2 double/
twin, 3 triple/multiple
Bathrooms: 3 en suite

Lunch available
Evening meal available
CC: Delta, Mastercard,
Switch, Visa

Beaujolais Nouveau weekend. Christmas and New Year specials. Gift vouchers.

◆◆◆

LEE HOUSE
27 Lee Road, Lynton EX35 6BP
T: (01598) 752364
F: (01598) 752364
E: leehouse@freeuk.com
I: www.smoothhound.co.uk/hotels/lee.html

B&B per night:
D £36.00–£50.00

OPEN All year round

Delightful Victorian house enjoying sunny position. Walk from the door to the Valley of the Rocks or the famous Cliff Railway. Enjoy traditional home cooking using fresh local and organic produce whenever possible. All rooms en suite. Comfortable lounge. Small residents' bar. Private parking. A warm welcome awaits.

Bedrooms: 6 double/
twin, 2 triple/multiple
Bathrooms: 8 en suite

Evening meal available
CC: Delta, Mastercard,
Switch, Visa

◆◆◆

MILLSLADE COUNTRY HOUSE HOTEL
Brendon, Lynton EX35 6PS
T: (01598) 741322
F: (01598) 741355
E: bobcramp@millslade.freeserve.co.uk
I: www.brendonvalley.co.uk/millslade.htm

B&B per night:
S £35.00–£50.00
D £50.00–£80.00

HB per person:
DY £42.00–£55.50

OPEN All year round

Small, family-run hotel nestling alongside the East Lyn River in a secluded valley on Exmoor. We have a restaurant featuring the best of locally sourced specialities, and are ideally poised for walking, riding and exploring the beauty and wildlife of Exmoor, Lorna Doone Country and the North Devon coast.

Bedrooms: 6 double/
twin
Bathrooms: 3 en suite,
3 private

Lunch available
Evening meal available
CC: Amex, Mastercard,
Visa

3 day break: DB&B from £120–£150pp (excl Bank Hols).

◆◆◆◆

ROCKVALE HOTEL

Lee Road, Lynton EX35 6HW

T: (01598) 752279 & 753343

E: JudithWoodland@rockvale.fsbusiness.co.uk

I: www.rockvalehotel.co.uk

B&B per night:
S £24.00–£26.00
D £52.00–£56.00

HB per person:
DY £43.00–£45.00

OPEN Mar–Oct

Delightful Victorian property situated in its own grounds on the sunny south facing slopes of Hollerday Hill. Glorious panoramic views across the town towards Countisbury and Watersmeet Valley. Award-winning home cooking and hospitality. Peaceful and relaxing. Pretty bedrooms with many thoughtful extras. Large level car park. Totally non-smoking.

Bedrooms: 1 single, 5 double/twin, 2 triple/multiple
Bathrooms: 7 en suite, 1 private

Evening meal available
CC: Delta, Mastercard, Switch, Visa

⌕4🛏📞🖂📺♿🍷⑤✂🅿💻🚗🚲P

◆◆◆

SINAI HOUSE

Lynway, Lynton EX35 6AY
T: (01598) 753227
F: (01598) 752633
E: enquires@sinaihouse.co.uk
I: www.sinaihouse.co.uk

Bedrooms: 1 single, 8 double/twin
Bathrooms: 7 en suite, 2 private

Evening meal available
CC: Mastercard, Visa

B&B per night:
S £30.00–£35.00
D £50.00–£55.00

OPEN All year round

Elegant Victorian house set in terraced gardens, renowned for its spectacular views over Lynmouth Bay and within easy walking dstance of Lynton and its facilities.

🅰️🖾📺♿⑤✂🅿🖥💻🚗∪☆🐕🚲🏮P

◆◆◆

VICTORIA FERNERY

Lydiate Lane, Lynton EX35 6AJ

T: (01598) 752440

F: (01598) 752396

E: enquiries@theferney.co.uk

I: www.theferney.co.uk

B&B per night:
S £20.00–£22.00
D £38.00–£42.00

OPEN All year round

Set in the old village, this unique house is steeped in history. Beautiful decor, spacious and comfortable. Delightful walled garden, complete with fernery. Delicious food, friendly and informal atmosphere. Refresh youself with spectacular scenery and miles of unspoilt coastal, moor and tumbling river walks. A very warm welcome awaits you.

Bedrooms: 3 double/twin
Bathrooms: 1 en suite, 2 private

Evening meal available

Special breaks are available (except Christmas and New Year). Please contact us for details.

🅰️🛏12📺♿🍷⑤✂💻🚗☆🚲🏮

MARTOCK, Somerset Map ref 2A3

◆◆◆◆

WYCHWOOD

7 Bearley Road, Wychwood, Martock TA12 6PG
T: (01935) 825601
F: (01935) 825601
E: wychwoodmartock@yahoo.co.uk
I: www.theaa.co.uk/region8/76883.html

Bedrooms: 3 double/twin
Bathrooms: 2 en suite, 1 private

CC: Delta, Mastercard, Switch, Visa

B&B per night:
S £34.00–£36.00
D £46.00–£50.00

OPEN Mar–Nov

ETC England for Excellence Silver Award for Outstanding Customer Service. Top 20 finalist for Landlady of the Year Award. Small, comfortable bed and breakfast ideally situated for visiting the 10 Classic Gardens of South Somerset. Close to A303.

🅰️🖾📺♿🍷⑤✂💻🚗▶☆🚲P

QUALITY ASSURANCE SCHEME

Diamond ratings and awards are explained at the back of this guide.

MELKSHAM, Wiltshire Map ref 2B2 *Tourist Information Centre Tel: (01225) 707424*

◆◆◆

LONGHOPE GUEST HOUSE

9 Beanacre Road, Melksham
SN12 8AG
T: (01225) 706737
F: (01225) 706737

Bedrooms: 1 single, 3 double/twin, 2 triple/multiple
Bathrooms: 6 en suite

B&B per night:
S £25.00–£28.00
D Max £45.00

OPEN All year round

Situated in its own grounds on the A350 Melksham-Chippenham road. Half a mile from Melksham town centre, 10 miles from M4 junction 17.

P

MEMBURY, Devon Map ref 1D2

◆◆◆◆

GOODMANS HOUSE

Furley, Membury, Axminster EX13 7TU
T: (01404) 881690
F: (01404) 881690

B&B per night:
S £27.00–£32.00
D £56.00–£60.00

HB per person:
DY £47.00–£50.00

OPEN All year round

Cleverly converted stone cottages/suites close to 16thC Georgian restored country house set in 9 acres botanist-landscaped grounds. Specimen trees, carp lake, orchards, wonderful Devon valley views all units. Peace and tranquility. Ideal location 3 counties, coast, gardens. Uniquely flexible tariff offers superb fresh produce, imaginative menus (lots organic), candlelit dining.

Bedrooms: 1 single, 6 double/twin; suites available
Bathrooms: 7 en suite

Evening meal available

Special inclusive offers, spring, autumn, early summer. Christmas and New Year. Fine food, flexible breaks. Valentine romantic weekend.

P

MEVAGISSEY, Cornwall Map ref 1B3

◆◆◆

SEAPOINT HOUSE HOTEL

Battery Terrace, Mevagissey,
St Austell PL26 6QS
T: (01726) 842684 & 844627
F: (01726) 842266
E: mevatele@compuserve.com
I: ourworld.compuserve.com/homepages/mevatele

Bedrooms: 8 double/twin, 2 triple/multiple
Bathrooms: 10 en suite

Lunch available
Evening meal available
CC: Amex, Mastercard, Visa

B&B per night:
S £28.00–£42.00
D £56.00–£76.00

HB per person:
DY £40.00–£56.00

OPEN All year round

The only hotel in Mevagissey overlooking both the harbour and bay. Quiet cul-de-sac location. Direct access to Coastal Path. 3 minute walk to village. Close to Heligan Gardens and Eden Project.

P

MINEHEAD, Somerset Map ref 1D1 *Tourist Information Centre Tel: (01643) 702624*

◆◆◆

FIELD HOUSE

The Parks, Minehead TA24 8BU
T: (01643) 706958
F: (01643) 704335

Bedrooms: 1 single, 2 double/twin
Bathrooms: 2 en suite, 1 private

B&B per night:
S £19.00
D £38.00

OPEN All year round

Field House has fine views over the hills from the Quantocks to Exmoor, accessible to North Hill but yet a stroll into town.

3 P

USE YOUR *i*s

There are more than 550 Tourist Information Centres throughout England offering friendly help with accommodation and holiday ideas as well as suggestions of places to visit and things to do. You'll find TIC addresses in the local Phone Book.

PROMENADE HOTEL
The Esplanade, Minehead TA24 5QS
T: (01643) 702572
F: (01643) 702572
E: jgph@globalnet.co.uk
I: www.johngroons.org.uk

B&B per night:
S £26.00–£32.00
D £52.00–£64.00

HB per person:
DY £36.00–£45.00

A 12-bedroomed hotel on the seafront with 8 of the 12 bedrooms adapted for disabled people. With parking, garden and conservatory.

Bedrooms: 1 single, 7 double/twin, 3 triple/ multiple
Bathrooms: 11 en suite

Lunch available
Evening meal available
CC: Mastercard, Switch, Visa

£25pp H/B, minimum stay 3 nights (1 Nov 2001-1 March 2002).

MONTACUTE, Somerset Map ref 2A3

MAD HATTERS TEAROOMS
1 South Street, Montacute
TA15 6XD
T: (01935) 823024
E: montacutemuseum@aol.com
I: www.montacotemuseum.com

Bedrooms: 1 double/ twin
Bathrooms: 1 en suite

Lunch available
Evening meal available

B&B per night:
S £24.00–£28.00
D £38.00–£42.00

OPEN All year round

Listed Georgian property in the centre of picturesque conservation village. Pubs and restaurants close by. On the Leland trail and South Somerset cycle route.

MORETONHAMPSTEAD, Devon Map ref 1C2

Silver Award

GREAT SLONCOMBE FARM
Moretonhampstead, Newton Abbot
TQ13 8QF
T: (01647) 440595
F: (01647) 440595
E: hmerchant@sloncombe.
freeserve.co.uk
I: www.greatsloncombefarm.co.uk

Bedrooms: 3 double/ twin
Bathrooms: 3 en suite

Evening meal available

B&B per night:
S £23.00–£25.00
D £46.00–£50.00

HB per person:
DY Min £36.00

OPEN All year round

13thC farmhouse in a magical Dartmoor valley. Meadows, woodland, wildflowers, animals. Farmhouse breakfast with new baked bread. Everything provided for an enjoyable break.

GREAT WOOSTON FARM BED & BREAKFAST
Moretonhampstead, Newton Abbot
TQ13 8QA
T: (01647) 440367 & 07798 670590
F: (01647) 440367

Bedrooms: 3 double/ twin
Bathrooms: 2 en suite, 1 private

CC: Mastercard, Switch, Visa

B&B per night:
S £22.00–£25.00
D £40.00–£46.00

OPEN All year round

Great Wooston is a peaceful haven with views across the moor and walks nearby.Two rooms en suite, one with 4-poster. Quality accommodation. Brochure available.

TOWN INDEX
This can be found at the back of the guide. If you know where you want to stay, the index will give you the page number listing accommodation in your chosen town, city or village.

MOUSEHOLE, Cornwall Map ref 1A3

♦♦♦♦

KERRIS FARMHOUSE
Kerris, Paul, Penzance TR19 6UY
T: (01736) 731309
E: susangiles@btconnect.com
I: www.cornwall-online.co.uk/kerris-farm

B&B per night:
S £20.00–£25.00
D £40.00–£42.00

HB per person:
DY £32.00–£35.00

OPEN Mar–Dec

Stay with a Cornish farming family. Granite farmhouse in peaceful location with splendid rural views. Clean surroundings, ample parking. En suite with TV and refreshment trays, full central heating, log burning stove. Evening meals. Ideal for visiting anywhere between Land's End, Minack Theatre and St Ives. Close to Mousehole, Penzance, Lamorna.

Bedrooms: 1 double/ twin, 1 triple/multiple
Bathrooms: 1 en suite

Special 2-night breaks from 16 Dec to see the famous Mousehole Christmas lights.

Evening meal available

NETHER STOWEY, Somerset Map ref 1D1

♦♦♦♦

Silver Award

CASTLE OF COMFORT COUNTRY HOUSE
Dodington, Nether Stowey, Bridgwater TA5 1LE
T: (01278) 741264 & 07050 642002
F: (01278) 741144
E: reception@castle-of-comfort.co.uk
I: www.castle-of-comfort.co.uk

Bedrooms: 1 single, 4 double/twin, 1 triple/ multiple
Bathrooms: 6 en suite

Lunch available
Evening meal available
CC: Delta, Mastercard, Switch, Visa

B&B per night:
S £39.00–£61.00
D £74.00–£101.00

OPEN All year round

16thC country house hotel nestling in the Quantock Hills with 4 acres of grounds. Luxuriously re-furbished accommodation of the highest standard.

NEWQUAY, Cornwall Map ref 1B2 *Tourist Information Centre Tel: (01637) 854020*

♦♦♦

ALOHA
122 Henver Road, Newquay TR7 3EQ
T: (01637) 878366
E: Alohanewqu@aol.com
I: www.mjiggins.freeserve.co.uk/ aloha/index.html

Bedrooms: 1 single, 4 double/twin, 2 triple/ multiple
Bathrooms: 6 en suite

Evening meal available
CC: Amex, Delta, Diners, Mastercard, Switch, Visa

B&B per night:
S £13.00–£23.00
D £26.00–£46.00

OPEN All year round

Friendly and cosy with en suite rooms and home comforts. Well situated for beaches and touring Cornwall. Garden overlooking Trencreek Valley. Ample parking. Close to centre.

♦

CHICHESTER
14 Bay View Terrace, Newquay TR7 2LR
T: (01637) 874216
F: (01637) 874216
E: sheila.harper@virgin.net
I: www.freespace.virgin.net/sheila. harper

Bedrooms: 2 single, 4 double/twin, 1 triple/ multiple

Evening meal available

B&B per night:
S £16.50
D £33.00

HB per person:
DY £22.00

OPEN All year round

Comfortable, licensed establishment convenient for shops, beaches and gardens. Showers in most bedrooms, many extras. Walking, mineral collecting, archaeology and Cornish heritage holidays in spring and autumn.

NORTH CADBURY, Somerset Map ref 2B3

♦♦

THE CATASH INN
North Cadbury, Yeovil BA22 7DH
T: (01963) 440248
F: (01963) 440248
E: clive&sandra@catash.com
I: www.catash.com

Bedrooms: 2 double/ twin, 1 triple/multiple
Bathrooms: 2 en suite

Lunch available
Evening meal available
CC: Delta, Mastercard, Switch, Visa

B&B per night:
S £30.00–£35.00
D Min £45.00

OPEN All year round

17th C inn with restaurant and large car park, in centre of North Cadbury a mile from A303. Close to Sparkford Motor Museum and Yeovilton Air Base.

◆◆◆◆

HIGHER CADHAM FARM

Jacobstowe, Okehampton EX20 3RB
T: (01837) 851647
F: (01837) 851410
I: www.highercadham.co.uk

B&B per night:
S £20.00–£25.00
D £40.00–£50.00

HB per person:
DY £32.50–£37.50

OPEN All year round

139-acre mixed farm. For a real Devonshire welcome come to our farm in the secluded Okement Valley near Dartmoor. Famous for our excellent farmhouse food. Plenty of interesting things to amuse the family including farm trail. Well worth the drive out.

Bedrooms: 1 single,
5 double/twin, 3 triple/
multiple
Bathrooms: 5 en suite

Lunch available
Evening meal available
CC: Delta, Mastercard,
Switch, Visa

◆◆◆◆

WEEK FARM COUNTRY HOLIDAYS

Bridestowe, Okehampton EX20 4HZ
T: (01837) 861221
F: (01837) 861221
E: accom@weekfarmonline.com
I: www.weekfarmonline.com

B&B per night:
S £24.00–£25.00
D £48.00–£50.00

OPEN All year round

200-acre sheep farm. A warm welcome awaits at this homely 17thC farmhouse, in Devonshire countryside and 6 miles Okehampton. Three new coarse fishing lakes. Good home cooking assured and every comfort. Ideal touring base Dartmoor and coasts, walking, cycling, pony trekking, fishing. Outdoor heated swimming pool. Come and spoil yourselves.

Bedrooms: 2 double/
twin, 2 triple/multiple
Bathrooms: 4 en suite

Evening meal available

Fishing weekend breaks. 3 well stocked coarse fishing lakes, something for the whole family.

Rating
Applied For

THE OLD MILL HOUSE

Little Petherick, Wadebridge PL27 7QT
T: (01841) 540388
F: 0870 056 9360
E: dwalker@oldmillbandb.demon.co.uk

B&B per night:
S £45.00–£48.00
D £60.00–£64.00

OPEN Apr–Oct

Grade II Listed 16thC corn mill with water wheel in an Area of Outstanding Natural Beauty. Guest bedrooms overlook the garden and stream. Delicious breakfasts served to your individual table in the Mill Room. Licensed. Ideal location for exploring the whole of Cornwall. Two miles from Padstow.

Bedrooms: 4 double/
twin
Bathrooms: 4 en suite

CC: Delta, Mastercard,
Switch, Visa

IMPORTANT NOTE Information on accommodation listed in this guide has been supplied by the proprietors. As changes may occur you are advised to check details at the time of booking.

PADSTOW continued

◆◆◆◆◆
Gold
Award

TREGEA HOTEL
16-18 High Street, Padstow PL28 8BB
T: (01841) 532455
F: (01841) 533542
E: reservations@tregea.co.uk
I: www.tregea.co.uk

B&B per night:
S £45.00–£68.00
D £64.00–£92.00

OPEN All year round

Beautiful 17thC house in quiet old part of Padstow, close to harbour, beaches and coastal walks. A small family-run hotel with personal, friendly service and comfortable accommodation of a very high standard. Off street parking.

Bedrooms: 8 double/ twin
Bathrooms: 8 en suite

Special out-of-season offers. Summer offers for stays of more than 3 nights.

CC: Delta, Mastercard, Switch, Visa

◆◆◆◆
TREVONE BAY HOTEL
Trevone Bay, Padstow PL28 8QS
T: (01841) 520243
F: (01841) 521195
E: hamilton@trevonebay.demon. co.uk

Bedrooms: 3 single, 7 double/twin, 2 triple/ multiple
Bathrooms: 12 en suite

Lunch available
Evening meal available
CC: Delta, Mastercard, Switch, Visa

B&B per night:
S £30.00–£36.00
D £52.00–£72.00

HB per person:
DY £36.00–£46.00

OPEN Mar–Oct

Take a real break! Friendly, spotless, non-smoking hotel in beautiful, peaceful village location. Excellent cooking and personal service. Overlooking beautiful sandy beach and rugged coastline.

◆◆◆
TREVORRICK FARM
St Issey, Wadebridge PL27 7QH
T: (01841) 540574
F: (01841) 540574
E: info@trevorrick.co.uk
I: www.trevorrick.co.uk

Bedrooms: 2 double/ twin, 1 triple/multiple
Bathrooms: 3 en suite

Lunch available
Evening meal available

B&B per night:
S £31.00–£35.00
D £42.00–£50.00

OPEN All year round

Beautiful, peaceful location. Farmhouse by footpath to Camel Trail offers en suite rooms and welcomes families. Indoor heated swimming pool. Near sandy beaches.

PAIGNTON, Devon Map ref 1D2 *Tourist Information Centre Tel: 0906 680 1268 (Premium rate number)*

◆◆◆
COLIN HOUSE
2 Colin Road, Paignton TQ3 2NR
T: (01803) 550609
F: (01803) 550609
E: colin-house@talk21.com
I: www.paigntondevon.co.uk/ colinhouse.htm

Bedrooms: 1 single, 3 double/twin, 2 triple/ multiple
Bathrooms: 6 en suite

CC: Mastercard, Visa

B&B per night:
S £16.00–£19.00
D £32.00–£38.00

Beautifully maintained select en suite bed and breakfast accommodation. Personally managed by dedicated professional ex hoteliers. Ample parking facilities. Only 50 yards from seafront.

◆◆◆
DEVON HOUSE HOTEL
20 Garfield Road, Paignton TQ4 6AX
T: (01803) 559371
F: (01803) 550054
E: devon.house.hotel@lineone.net
I: www.lineone.net/~devon.house. hotel/

Bedrooms: 3 single, 4 double/twin, 3 triple/ multiple
Bathrooms: 4 en suite

Evening meal available
CC: Amex, Delta, Mastercard, Switch, Visa

B&B per night:
D £28.00–£36.00

OPEN All year round

Quiet, family-run, non-smoking, licensed hotel. Home-cooked food, open all year round, situated off seafront, near town centre. Credit cards taken. En suite rooms.

---

www.travelengland.org.uk
Log on for information and inspiration. The latest information on places to visit, events and quality assessed accommodation.

PAIGNTON continued

◆◆◆◆ THE LINTON HOTEL
7 Elmsleigh Road, Paignton
TQ4 5AX
T: (01803) 558745
F: (01803) 527345

Bedrooms: 2 single,
6 double/twin, 2 triple/
multiple
Bathrooms: 10 en suite

Evening meal available

B&B per night:
S £17.00–£21.00
D £34.00–£38.00

HB per person:
DY £23.00–£25.00

Semi-detached Victorian building, built approximately c1882 with local sandstone blocks, faced with plaster. Lawned front garden with flower beds. Car park.

OPEN Mar–Oct &
Christmas

🏠1 ♨ ⌷ ♿ ⚲ ⑤ ♩ Ⅲ ☕ ✻ ⛽ ⚲ P

PENSFORD, Bath and North East Somerset Map ref 2A2

◆◆◆ GREEN ACRES
Stanton Wick, Pensford BS39 4BX
T: (01761) 490397
F: (01761) 490397

Bedrooms: 2 single,
3 double/twin
Bathrooms: 1 en suite

B&B per night:
S £20.00–£25.00
D £40.00–£50.00

A friendly welcome awaits you in peaceful setting, off A37/A368. Relax and enjoy panoramic views across Chew Valley to Dundry Hills.

OPEN All year round

🏠 ♨ ⌷ ♿ ⚲ ⑤ ⚿ ♩ Ⅲ ☕ ⚶ ✕ ✦ ✻ ⛺ ⛽ P

PENZANCE, Cornwall Map ref 1A3 *Tourist Information Centre Tel: (01736) 362207*

◆◆◆

MENWIDDEN FARM
Ludgvan, Penzance TR20 8BN

T: (01736) 740415

B&B per night:
S £18.00
D £36.00–£44.00

HB per person:
DY Min £25.00

Small mixed farm, centrally situated in West Cornwall. Warm, family atmosphere with comfortable beds and good home cooking. Within easy reach of both coasts and Lands End. A warm welcome awaits you. Turn right at Crowlas crossroads on the A30 from Hayle, signpost Vellanoweth on right turn. Last farm on left.

Bedrooms: 1 single,
4 double/twin
Bathrooms: 1 en suite

Evening meal available

Ⓜ ♿ ⑤ ⚿ ♩ ♨ ✻ ✦ ⛽ P

◆◆◆ PENMORVAH HOTEL
Alexandra Road, Penzance TR18 4LZ
T: (01736) 363711
F: (01736) 363711

Bedrooms: 2 single,
2 double/twin, 4 triple/
multiple
Bathrooms: 8 en suite

Evening meal available
CC: Amex, Delta,
Mastercard, Switch, Visa

B&B per night:
S £18.00–£25.00
D £36.00–£50.00

HB per person:
DY £32.00–£40.00

350 yards from promenade in tree-lined avenue. Easy reach of town centre and an ideal location for touring.

OPEN All year round

Ⓜ 🏠 ♨ ▨ ⌷ ♿ ⚲ Ⓨ ⑤ ♩ Ⅲ ☕ ✦

◆◆◆

This elegant Victorian house is situated at the foot of a tree-lined avenue, 200 metres from the sea. Constructed of Cornish granite, it has a restful, spacious atmosphere. Art galleries, antique shops, excellent restaurants nearby. The romantic Lamorna Cove must be visited on one's way to Lands End.

TREVENTON GUEST HOUSE
Alexandra Place, Penzance TR18 4NE

T: (01736) 363521
F: (01736) 361873
I: www.ukholidayaccommodation.com/
treventonguesthouse

Bedrooms: 1 single,
5 double/twin, 1 triple/
multiple
Bathrooms: 4 en suite

B&B per night:
S £16.00–£23.00
D £32.00–£40.00

OPEN All year round

🏠5 ⌷ ♿ ⑤ ♩ Ⅲ ⛽

◆◆◆◆

THE POACHERS INN

Piddletrenthide, Dorchester DT2 7QX
T: (01300) 348358
F: (01300) 348153
E: thepoachersinn@piddletrenthide.
fsbusiness.co.uk
I: www.thepoachersinn.co.uk

B&B per night:
S £35.00
D £60.00

HB per person:
DY £42.00

OPEN All year round

Country inn, with riverside garden and swimming pool, within easy reach of all Dorset's attractions. All rooms en suite, restaurant where half board guests choose from our a la carte menu at no extra cost.

Bedrooms: 17 double/ twin, 1 triple/multiple
Bathrooms: 18 en suite

Lunch available
Evening meal available
CC: Delta, Mastercard, Switch, Visa

Short breaks: stay 2 nights DB&B £84pp 3rd night DB&B free 1 Oct 2001-30 Apr 2002 (excl Bank Hols).

Ⓜ🛉⚓🏠🛏🖥🔌🐕🍷Ⓢ🛁🖥🚲🍽🧺❄🐎🚙 P

◆◆◆

THE WEARY FRIAR INN
Pillaton, Saltash PL12 6QS
T: (01579) 350238
F: (01579) 350238

Bedrooms: 2 single, 8 double/twin, 1 triple/ multiple
Bathrooms: 11 en suite

Lunch available
Evening meal available
CC: Delta, Mastercard, Switch, Visa

B&B per night:
S £40.00–£45.00
D £50.00–£60.00

OPEN All year round

Charming country inn noted for its quality food and interesting combination of modern comforts with 12thC character. Ideally placed for exploring inland and coastal areas.

Ⓜ🐎10🖥🔌🍷Ⓢ🛁🖥🚲🍽🐕🐎 P

◆◆◆◆

BERKELEYS OF ST JAMES
4 St James Place East, The Hoe,
Plymouth PL1 3AS
T: (01752) 221654
F: (01752) 221654
I: www.smoothhound.co.uk/hotels/ berkely2html.

Bedrooms: 1 single, 3 double/twin, 1 triple/ multiple
Bathrooms: 4 en suite, 1 private

CC: Delta, Mastercard, Switch, Visa

B&B per night:
S £28.00–£35.00
D £40.00–£60.00

OPEN All year round

Non-smoking Victorian townhouse ideally situated for seafront, Barbican, theatre, ferry port and city centre. Flexible accommodation between double/twin/triple. Excellent breakfast menu.

Ⓜ🐎⚓🏠🖥🔌🐕🍷Ⓢ🖥🧺🚙 P

◆◆◆◆◆
Silver
Award

BOWLING GREEN HOTEL

9-10 Osborne Place, Lockyer Street,
Plymouth PL1 2PU
T: (01752) 209090 & 667485
F: (01752) 209092
E: dave@bowlinggreenhotel.freeserve.
co.uk
I: www.smoothhound.co.uk/hotels/
bowling.html

B&B per night:
S Min £38.00
D £52.00–£54.00

OPEN All year round

Opposite Drake's bowling green, this elegant Victorian hotel has superbly appointed bedrooms offering all modern facilities. Our friendly and efficient staff will make your stay a memorable one. Centrally situated for the Barbican, Theatre Royal, leisure/conference centre, ferry port, National Marine Aquarium, with Dartmoor only a few minutes away.

Bedrooms: 1 single, 10 double/twin, 1 triple/ multiple
Bathrooms: 12 en suite

CC: Amex, Delta, Diners, Mastercard, Switch, Visa

Special weekend breaks Nov-Mar inclusive. Prices on application.

Ⓜ🐎⚓🖥🔌🐕🍷Ⓢ🛁🖥🍴◐🖥🚲🐕 P

CREDIT CARD BOOKINGS If you book by telephone and are asked for your credit card number it is advisable to check the proprietor's policy should you cancel your reservation.

414

♦♦♦ **GABBER FARM**

Down Thomas, Plymouth PL9 0AW
T: (01752) 862269
F: (01752) 862269

Bedrooms: 1 single,
2 double/twin, 2 triple/
multiple
Bathrooms: 2 en suite

Evening meal available

B&B per night:
S £18.00–£20.00
D £36.00–£40.00

HB per person:
DY £28.00–£30.00

OPEN All year round

Courteous welcome at this farm, near coast and Bovisand diving centre. Lovely walks. Special weekly rates, especially for senior citizens and children. Directions provided.

♦♦♦ **LAMPLIGHTER HOTEL**

103 Citadel Road, The Hoe,
Plymouth PL1 2RN
T: (01752) 663855
F: (01752) 228139
E: lampligherhotel@ukonline.co.uk

Bedrooms: 7 double/
twin, 2 triple/multiple
Bathrooms: 7 en suite,
2 private

CC: Amex, Delta,
Mastercard, Visa

B&B per night:
S £25.00–£35.00
D £35.00–£42.00

OPEN All year round

Small friendly hotel on Plymouth Hoe, 5 minutes' walk from the city centre and seafront.

♦♦♦ **MOUNTBATTEN HOTEL**

52 Exmouth Road, Stoke, Plymouth
PL1 4QH
T: (01752) 563843
F: (01752) 606014

Bedrooms: 4 single,
4 double/twin, 2 triple/
multiple
Bathrooms: 8 en suite

Evening meal available
CC: Delta, Mastercard,
Switch, Visa

B&B per night:
S £20.00–£25.00
D £46.00–£50.00

HB per person:
DY £28.50–£34.95

OPEN All year round

Family-owned hotel overlooking parkland in quiet cul-de-sac. Easy reach city centre and ferry port, particularly good access to Cornwall. Secure parking.

♦♦♦♦

ROSALAND HOTEL

32 Houndiscombe Road, Plymouth
PL4 6HQ
T: (01752) 664749
F: (01752) 256984
E: manager@rosalandhotel.com
I: www.rosalandhotel.com

B&B per night:
S £18.00–£30.00
D £34.00–£42.00

HB per person:
DY £30.00–£42.00

OPEN All year round

Victorian private hotel in quiet residential area, close to city centre, university and railway station. Plymouth Hoe and Barbican only 15 minutes' walk away. Well-appointed rooms. Licensed bar. Comfortable lounge with surround-sound TV. Evening dinners available. Warm welcome assured.

Bedrooms: 4 single,
3 double/twin, 2 triple/
multiple
Bathrooms: 4 en suite

Evening meal available
CC: Amex, Delta,
Mastercard, Switch, Visa

♦♦♦♦ **SMEATONS TOWER HOTEL**

40-42 Grand Parade, The Hoe,
Plymouth PL1 3DJ
T: (01752) 221007
F: (01752) 221664
E: info@smeatonstowerhotel.co.uk
I: www.smeatonstowerhotel.co.uk

Bedrooms: 2 single,
4 double/twin, 4 triple/
multiple
Bathrooms: 10 en suite

Lunch available
CC: Delta, Mastercard,
Switch, Visa

B&B per night:
S £30.00–£35.00
D £45.00–£55.00

OPEN All year round

Family-run, friendly hotel adjacent to Plymouth Hoe and ferry services. Town centre 3 minutes by car. Plymouth Pavilions nearby. Easy routes to moors and Cornwall.

ACCESSIBILITY

Look for the 🦽🦽🚶 symbols which indicate accessibility for wheelchair users. A list of establishments is at the front of this guide.

PORLOCK, Somerset Map ref 1D1

◆◆◆ **MYRTLE COTTAGE**

High Street, Porlock, Minehead
TA24 8PU
T: (01643) 862978
F: (01243) 862978
E: bob.steer@talk21.com
I: www.smoothhound.co.uk

Bedrooms: 3 double/
twin, 2 triple/multiple
Bathrooms: 5 en suite

CC: Delta, Mastercard,
Switch, Visa

B&B per night:
S £25.00–£30.00
D £45.00–£50.00

OPEN All year round

Charming 16thC thatched cottage situated in the centre of this picturesque village. Ideal base for walking and exploring Exmoor.

PORT ISAAC, Cornwall Map ref 1B2

◆◆◆ **THE SLIPWAY HOTEL & RESTAURANT**

Harbour Front, Port Isaac PL29 3RH
T: (01208) 880264
F: (01208) 880408
E: slipwayhotel@portisaac.com
I: www.portisaac.com

Bedrooms: 9 double/
twin, 3 triple/multiple;
suites available
Bathrooms: 10 en suite

Lunch available
Evening meal available
CC: Amex, Delta,
Mastercard, Switch, Visa

B&B per night:
S £42.00–£75.00
D £56.00–£100.00

HB per person:
DY £48.00–£95.00

OPEN Feb–Dec

A 16thC small friendly hotel in heart of beautiful historic fishing village of Port Isaac overlooking the harbour.

PORTHCURNO, Cornwall Map ref 1A3

◆◆◆◆ **THE PORTHCURNO HOTEL**

The Valley, Porthcurno, St Levan,
Penzance TR19 6JX
T: (01736) 810119
F: (01736) 810711
E: porthcurnohotel@
netscapeonline.co.uk
I: www.porthcurnohotel.co.uk

Bedrooms: 11 double/
twin, 1 triple/multiple
Bathrooms: 8 en suite

Lunch available
Evening meal available
CC: Delta, Mastercard,
Switch, Visa

B&B per night:
S £25.00–£55.00
D £44.00–£65.00

HB per person:
DY £36.00–£46.00

OPEN All year round

Hotel set in large gardens 600 yards from beach, offering quality accommodation and restaurant. Minack Theatre and Museum of Submarine Telegraphy within 6 minutes' walking distance.

PORTLAND, Dorset Map ref 2B3

◆◆◆ **ALESSANDRIA HOTEL**

71 Wakeham Easton, Portland
DT5 1HW
T: (01305) 822270 & 820108
F: (01305) 820561
I: www.s-h-systems.co.uk/hotels/
alessand.html

Bedrooms: 6 single,
6 double/twin, 3 triple/
multiple; suites available
Bathrooms: 10 en suite,
1 private

Evening meal available
CC: Amex, Delta,
Mastercard, Visa

B&B per night:
S £28.00–£48.00
D £48.00–£65.00

OPEN All year round

18thC Portland-stone building in quiet location. Comfortable rooms with facilities, 2 on ground floor. Free parking. Excellent fresh food and warm, friendly hospitality from Giovanni Bisogno..

RADSTOCK, Bath and North East Somerset Map ref 2B2

◆◆◆◆

THE ROOKERY

Wells Road, Radstock, Bath BA3 3RS
T: (01761) 432626
F: (01761) 432626
E: rookery@iname.com
I: www.therookeryguesthouse.co.uk

B&B per night:
S £38.50–£40.00
D £55.00–£62.00

HB per person:
DY Min £47.50

OPEN All year round

A 200-year-old family run property centrally situated for Bath, Wells and the Mendips. We have a relaxing lounge, residents' bar and restaurant and offer the best in service coupled with an easy-going atmosphere. En suite rooms with hot beverage facilities, TV, telephone and hairdryer. Large car park.

Bedrooms: 1 single,
8 double/twin, 3 triple/
multiple
Bathrooms: 12 en suite

Evening meal available
CC: Delta, Mastercard,
Switch, Visa

For £35pppn, get away and relax in a warm and friendly atmosphere: Afternoon tea, dinner, B&B, newspaper and welcome drink.

ROCK, Cornwall Map ref 1B2

◆◆◆ **SILVERMEAD**

Rock, Wadebridge PL27 6LB
T: (01208) 862425
F: (01208) 862919
E: barbara@silvermead.freeserve.co.uk
I: www.silvermeadguesthouse.co.uk

Bedrooms: 2 single, 5 double/twin, 2 triple/multiple
Bathrooms: 6 en suite

Evening meal available

B&B per night:
S £20.00
D £40.00–£52.00

HB per person:
DY £30.00–£36.00

OPEN All year round

Family-run licensed guesthouse over looking the Camel estuary on the North Cornwall coast. Spacious accommodation, most en suite with colour television. Watersports centre nearby.

ST AGNES, Cornwall Map ref 1B3

◆◆

PENKERRIS
Penwinnick Road, Penkerris, St Agnes
TR5 0PA
T: (01872) 552262
F: (01872) 552262
E: info@penkerris.co.uk
I: www.penkerris.co.uk

B&B per night:
S £17.50–£30.00
D £30.00–£50.00

HB per person:
DY £25.00–£35.00

OPEN All year round

Creeper-clad Edwardian residence with garden in unspoilt Cornish village. Log fires in winter, real home cooking. Children welcome, dogs accepted. Rooms with colour TV, H&C, kettles, some en suite. Two bathrooms, large shower room. Liquor licence – drinks served in lounge or garden. Dramatic cliff walks and beaches are nearby.

Bedrooms: 2 single, 4 double/twin, 2 triple/multiple
Bathrooms: 3 en suite

Evening meal available
CC: Amex, Mastercard, Visa

ST AUSTELL, Cornwall Map ref 1B3

◆◆◆◆

POLGREEN FARM
London Apprentice, St Austell PL26 7AP
T: (01726) 75151
F: (01726) 75151
E: polgreen.farm@btclick.com

B&B per night:
S £20.00–£25.00
D £38.00–£46.00

OPEN All year round

Situated in an Area of Outstanding Natural Beauty, 1 mile from the coast and 4 miles from the picturesque fishing village of Mevagissey. Centrally placed for touring Cornwall. Cornish Way leisure trail adjoining. Within a few miles' drive of the spectacular Eden Project and Heligan Gardens. All rooms with private facilities, colour TV, tea/coffee.

Bedrooms: 4 double/twin, 1 triple/multiple
Bathrooms: 3 en suite

ST IVES, Cornwall Map ref 1B3 *Tourist Information Centre Tel: (01736) 796297*

◆◆◆◆ **THE ANCHORAGE GUEST HOUSE**

5 Bunkers Hill, St Ives TR26 1LJ
T: (01736) 797135
F: (01736) 797135
E: james@theanchoragebb.fsnet.co.uk
I: www.theanchoragebb.fsnet.co.uk

Bedrooms: 1 single, 4 double/twin, 1 triple/multiple
Bathrooms: 5 en suite

CC: Amex, Mastercard, Visa

B&B per night:
S £20.00–£25.00
D £40.00–£50.00

OPEN All year round

18thC fisherman's cottage, 30 yards from harbour front and beaches, full of old world charm. Two minutes from Tate Gallery. Open all year.

◆◆◆◆

BLUE HAYES HOTEL

Trelyon Avenue, St Ives TR26 2AD

T: (01736) 797129

F: (01736) 797129

E: malcolm@bluehayes.fsbusiness.co.uk

I: www.bluehayes.co.uk

B&B per night:
S £49.00–£75.00
D £78.00–£120.00

OPEN Feb–Nov

A country house by the sea at St Ives, with ample parking, situated in its own grounds on Porthminster Point, overlooking St Ives bay and harbour, above one of the finest sandy beaches in the country – just a few minutes' walk along the coastal path, from the bottom of the garden. Recently completely refurbished to a high standard.

Bedrooms: 1 single, 6 double/twin; suites available

Bathrooms: 7 en suite

Evening meal available

CC: Mastercard, Switch, Visa

◆◆◆

BOSAVERN HOUSE

St Just-in-Penwith TR19 7RD

T: (01736) 788301

F: (01736) 788301

E: marcol@bosavern.u-net.com

I: www.bosavern.u-net.com

B&B per night:
S £21.00–£28.00
D £42.00–£56.00

OPEN All year round

A charming 17thC country house offering the very best in good taste and comfort at an affordable price. All rooms offer en suite facilities, TV, hairdryer and refreshment tray. Relax in our extensive gardens, walk the coastal footpath to an isolated sandy cove or explore West Cornwall. The choice is yours.

Bedrooms: 1 single, 4 double/twin, 3 triple/ multiple

Bathrooms: 7 en suite, 1 private

CC: Amex, Delta, Mastercard, Switch, Visa

QUALITY ASSURANCE SCHEME

Diamond ratings and awards were correct at the time of going to press but are subject to change. Please check at the time of booking.

◆◆◆◆

TREGELLIST FARM
Tregellist, St Kew, Bodmin PL30 3HG
T: (01208) 880537
F: (01208) 881017
E: jillcleave@tregellist.fsbusiness.co.uk

B&B per night:
S £26.00–£30.00
D Min £44.00

HB per person:
DY £36.00–£40.00

OPEN All year round

Delightful farmhouse set in pleasant countryside 130-acre sheep farm. Delicious home cooking. All bedrooms are en suite with colour TVs and tea/coffee facilities. Some ground floor bedrooms are disabled-friendly. Close to north Cornwall beaches and moors. Camel trail. Within easy reach of Eden Project and Lost Gardens of Heligan.

Bedrooms: 4 double/ twin, 1 triple/multiple
Bathrooms: 5 en suite

Evening meal available

◆◆◆◆

THE FALCON INN
St Mawgan, Newquay TR8 4EP
T: (01637) 860225
F: (01637) 860884
E: abanks@cwcom.net
I: www.falcon-inn.net

B&B per night:
S £20.00
D £48.00–£60.00

OPEN All year round

16thC wisteria-covered inn with beautiful gardens in the Vale of Lanherne. Unspoilt peaceful situation, offering quality accommodation and excellent food. Only 20 minutes from Eden Project and the closest Inn to Newquay Airport. Log fires, malt whisky and a good wine list enhance the experience.

Bedrooms: 1 single, 3 double/twin
Bathrooms: 2 en suite

Lunch available
Evening meal available
CC: Delta, Diners, Mastercard, Switch, Visa

10% off stays of more than two nights

◆◆◆◆

TORRE VIEW HOTEL
Devon Road, Salcombe TQ8 8HJ
T: (01548) 842633
F: (01548) 842633
E: bouttle@torreview.eurobell.
co.uk
I: www.smoothhound.co.uk/hotels/
torreview.html

Bedrooms: 7 double/ twin, 1 triple/multiple
Bathrooms: 5 en suite, 3 private

Evening meal available
CC: Delta, Mastercard, Visa

B&B per night:
S £30.00–£35.00
D £55.00–£60.00

HB per person:
DY £40.00–£45.00

OPEN Mar–Oct

Detached Victorian residence with every modern comfort, commanding extensive views of the estuary and surrounding countryside yet within reach of the town. No smoking, please.

◆◆◆◆

THE BARFORD INN
Barford St Martin, Salisbury
SP3 4AB
T: (01722) 742242
F: (01722) 743606
E: ido@barfordinn.co.uk
I: www.barfordinn.co.uk

Bedrooms: 4 double/ twin
Bathrooms: 4 en suite

Lunch available
Evening meal available
CC: Delta, Mastercard, Switch, Visa

B&B per night:
S £40.00–£55.00
D £40.00–£65.00

HB per person:
DY £40.00–£45.00

OPEN All year round

A 16thC coaching inn, beautifully furnished throughout, comprising 50-seater open-plan restaurant, cosy bar complete with log fires and 4 luxurious en suite letting rooms.

◆◆◆

BYWAYS HOUSE

31 Fowlers Road, City Centre, Salisbury
SP1 2QP
T: (01722) 328364
F: (01722) 322146
E: byways@bed-breakfast-salisbury.co.uk
I: www.bed-breakfast-salisbury.co.uk

B&B per night:
S Min £30.00
D Min £50.00

OPEN All year round

Attractive family-run Victorian house close to cathedral in quiet area of city centre. Large car park. Bedrooms with private bathrooms and colour satellite TV, 4-poster beds. Traditional English and vegetarian breakfasts. From Byways you can walk all around Salisbury. Ideal for Stonehenge and Wilton House.

Bedrooms: 4 single,
10 double/twin, 9 triple/
multiple
Bathrooms: 19 en suite

CC: Delta, Mastercard,
Switch, Visa

◆◆◆

CASTLEWOOD

45 Castle Road, Salisbury SP1 3RH
I: (01722) 324809 & 07733 331599
F: (01722) 421494

Bedrooms: 2 single,
1 double/twin, 3 triple/
multiple
Bathrooms: 3 en suite

Evening meal available

B&B per night:
S £25.00–£27.00
D £45.00–£48.00

HB per person:
DY £31.00–£40.00

OPEN All year round

Large Edwardian house, tastefully restored throughout. Pleasant 10 minutes' riverside walk to city centre and cathedral.

◆ ◆

LEENA'S GUEST HOUSE

50 Castle Road, Salisbury SP1 3RL
T: (01722) 335419
F: (01722) 335419

Bedrooms: 1 single,
4 double/twin, 1 triple/
multiple
Bathrooms: 5 en suite

B&B per night:
S £24.00–£41.00
D £39.00–£50.00

OPEN All year round

Friendly, family-run guesthouse with pretty bedrooms and delightful public areas. Close to riverside walk to city centre and cathedral.

◆◆◆◆

MANOR FARM

Burcombe, Salisbury SP2 0EJ
T: (01722) 742177
F: (01722) 744600
E: SACombes@talk.com

B&B per night:
D £44.00–£46.00

Comfortable farmhouse, warm and attractively furnished, on 960-acre mixed farm in a quiet, pretty village quarter of a mile off A30 west of Salisbury. Ideal base for touring this lovely area. Nearby attractions include Wilton House, Salisbury and Stonehenge. Wonderful walks, good riding. Pub with good food nearby. No smoking.

Bedrooms: 2 double/
twin
Bathrooms: 2 en suite

CC: Amex, Delta, Diners,
Mastercard, Switch, Visa

Reduction for stays of 3 nights or more.

CHECK THE MAPS

The colour maps at the front of this guide show all the cities, towns and villages for which you will find accommodation entries.
Refer to the town index to find the page on which they are listed.

♦♦♦♦♦
Silver
Award

NEWTON FARM HOUSE
Southampton Road, Whiteparish, Salisbury
SP5 2QL
T: (01794) 884416
F: (01794) 884416
E: enquiries@newtonfarmhouse.co.uk
I: www.newtonfarmhouse.co.uk

B&B per night:
S £25.00–£35.00
D £38.00–£60.00

HB per person:
DY £41.00–£51.00

OPEN All year round

Historic 16thC farmhouse, once part of the Trafalgar Estate. Delightfully decorated en suite bedrooms, 5 with genuine 4-posters (see our website). Beamed dining room with flagstones, bread oven and Nelson memorabilia. Superb breakfasts include fresh fruits, home-made bread, preserves and free-range eggs. Extensive grounds with swimming pool.

Bedrooms: 5 double/
twin, 3 triple/multiple
Bathrooms: 8 en suite

Evening meal available

♦♦♦♦
THE OLD RECTORY BED & BREAKFAST
75 Belle Vue Road, Salisbury
SP1 3YE
T: (01722) 502702
F: (01722) 501135
E: stay@theoldrectory-bb.co.uk
I: www.theoldrectory-bb.co.uk

Bedrooms: 3 double/
twin
Bathrooms: 2 en suite,
1 private

B&B per night:
S £28.00 .00
D £40.00 .00

OPEN All year round

Victorian rectory in quiet street, a short walk from the heart of Salisbury and convenient for all attractions. Warm, welcoming atmosphere. Visit our web site.

♦♦♦♦

THE ROKEBY GUEST HOUSE
3 Wain-a-Long Road, Salisbury SP1 1LJ
T: (01722) 329800
F: (01722) 329800
I: www.smoothhound.co.uk/hotels/rokeby.html

B&B per night:
S £38.00–£40.00
D £50.00–£55.00

HB per person:
DY £40.00–£55.00

OPEN All year round

Beautiful, nostalgic, Victorian guesthouse, quietly situated, 10 minutes' stroll city centre/cathedral. Large landscaped gardens, summerhouse, elegant 2-storey conservatory, satellite TV, licensed restaurant, gymnasium. Brochure available.

Bedrooms: 4 double/
twin, 3 triple/multiple;
suites available
Bathrooms: 5 en suite,
2 private

Evening meal available

Organised tandem parachute descents with qualified British Parachute Associate instructors-ideal for sponsored charity fund-raising.

♦♦♦
VICTORIA LODGE GUEST HOUSE
61 Castle Road, Salisbury SP1 3RH
T: (01722) 320586
F: (01722) 414507
E: mail@viclodge.co.uk
I: www.viclodge.co.uk

Bedrooms: 4 single,
10 double/twin, 2 triple/
multiple
Bathrooms: 16 en suite

Lunch available
Evening meal available
CC: Delta, Mastercard,
Switch, Visa

B&B per night:
S Min £40.00
D Min £55.00

HB per person:
DY Min £37.50

OPEN All year round

Victorian lodge, a short riverside walk to city centre and cathedral. Home-cooked evening meals, good parking. Licensed bar. Stonehenge 15 minutes, Bath and Winchester 45 minutes.

See under Alderbury, Amesbury, Chicklade, Hindon, Salisbury, Warminster, Winterbourne Stoke

◆◆◆◆

BEAUMONT
Castle Hill, Seaton EX12 2QW
T: (01297) 20832
F: 0870 0554708
E: tony@lymebay.demon.co.uk
I: www.smoothound.co.uk/hotels/
beaumont.html

B&B per night:
D £46.00–£54.00

HB per person:
DY £38.00–£42.00

OPEN All year round

Attractive and spacious guesthouse in select seafront position, offering en-suite comfort, personal attention and freedom to relax in beautiful surroundings. Unrivalled views over Lyme Bay and the cliffs of Beer Head. Half-mile esplanade opposite. Golf, bowling, tennis etc nearby.

Bedrooms: 2 double/
twin, 3 triple/multiple
Bathrooms: 5 en suite

Evening meal available

◆◆◆◆◆

KNAPPS FARM
Doulting, Shepton Mallet BA4 4LA
T: (01749) 880471

Bedrooms: 2 double/
twin
Bathrooms: 2 en suite

B&B per night:
S £30.00–£35.00
D £45.00–£50.00

HB per person:
DY £40.00–£60.00

OPEN All year round

Secluded 1825 farmhouse, extensive views and gardens, log fires, evening meals by arrangement, non-smoking in bedrooms.

◆◆◆◆
Silver
Award

THE ALDERS
Sandford Orcas, Sherborne DT9 4SB
T: (01963) 220666
F: (01963) 220106
E: jonsue@thealdersbb.com
I: www.thealdersbb.com

B&B per night:
D £45.00–£50.00

OPEN All year round

Secluded stone house set in old walled garden, in picturesque conservation village near Sherborne. House is tastefully furnished, with original watercolour paintings and hand-made pottery. There is a woodburning fire in lounge inglenook fireplace. Good breakfasts served around large farmhouse table. Excellent food available in traditional friendly village pub.

Bedrooms: 3 double/
twin
Bathrooms: 3 en suite

◆◆◆◆
Silver
Award

CROMWELL HOUSE
Long Street, Sherborne DT9 3BS
T: (01935) 813352
I: www.smoothound.co.uk/
a53281.html

Bedrooms: 3 double/
twin
Bathrooms: 2 en suite,
1 private

CC: Mastercard, Visa

B&B per night:
S £30.00–£35.00
D £50.00

OPEN All year round

A charming old manse c1740. Quietly situated in the heart of Sherborne in the conservation area.

SPECIAL BREAKS
Many establishments offer special promotions and themed breaks.
These are highlighted in red. (All such offers are subject to availability.)

◆◆◆ **CROWN INN**
Green Hill, Sherborne DT9 4EP
T: (01935) 812930
F: (01935) 812930

Bedrooms: 3 double/
twin, 1 triple/multiple
Bathrooms: 2 en suite

Lunch available
Evening meal available
CC: Delta, Mastercard,
Switch, Visa

B&B per night:
S £28.00–£38.00
D £40.00–£49.00

Friendly and comfortable freehouse. Excellent English and French cuisine. Quality wines and real ales. In the heart of Sherborne on the A30.

HB per person:
DY Min £30.00

OPEN All year round

🛎🗋💧🍷ⓢ�▥🍴↻▶🚲P

◆◆◆◆◆
Silver
Award

HEARTSEASE COTTAGE
North Street, Bradford Abbas, Sherborne
DT9 6SA
T: (01935) 475480 & 07929 717019
F: (01935) 475480
E: heartsease@talk21.com

B&B per night:
S £22.00–£30.00
D £44.00–£60.00

HB per person:
DY £37.00–£48.00

OPEN All year round

'Heartsease' describes our cottage better than any brochure. Delightful old honey-coloured stone cottage, huge conservatory looking on to idyllic garden, beautiful Dorset village lane. Themed bedrooms, guests' sitting room. Large choice of breakfasts and dinners, that you would love to have at home – but don't have time. Discounts over 1 night.

Bedrooms: 2 double/
twin
Bathrooms: 1 en suite,
1 private

Lunch available
Evening meal available

♠🐎8🖼💧🎣ⓢ🅟▥🖥✳🚲🐾P

◆◆◆◆◆

THE OLD VICARAGE HOTEL
Sherborne Road, Milborne Port, Sherborne
DT9 5AT
T: (01963) 251117
F: (01963) 251515
E: theoldvicarage@milborneport.freeserve.
co.uk
I: www.milborneport.freeserve.co.uk

B&B per night:
S £31.00–£36.00
D £57.00–£101.00

HB per person:
DY £45.00–£71.50

OPEN Feb–Dec

Listed Victorian Gothic building, elegantly furnished with antiques, set in 3.5 acres of beautiful grounds. The spacious lounge and the dining room afford magnificent views of open country. On Fridays and Saturdays one of the partners, a highly acclaimed chef, prepares dinner. On other nights food can be provided by a pub restaurant 200 yards away.

Bedrooms: 1 single,
5 double/twin, 1 triple/
multiple
Bathrooms: 7 en suite

Evening meal available
CC: Amex, Delta,
Mastercard, Switch, Visa

DB&B for 2 Fri and Sat from £180 (2 nights).

♠🐎5🍴📞🗋💧🎣🍷ⓢ🅟▥🖥↻✳🐴🚲P

◆◆◆ **VILLAGE VACATIONS**
Brookmead, Rimpton, Yeovil
BA22 8AQ
T: (01935) 850241
F: (01935) 850241
E: villagevac@aol.com
I: www.villagevacations.co.uk

Bedrooms: 2 double/
twin
Bathrooms: 1 en suite,
1 private

CC: Delta, Mastercard,
Switch, Visa

B&B per night:
S £20.00–£22.00
D £40.00–£44.00

OPEN All year round

Comfortable detached house in quiet village location. Friendly welcome, large garden. Touring, walking. Three miles from A303. Near Sherborne/Yeovil. Also all inclusive customised tours.

♠🐎10🗋💧🎣ⓢ🅟▥🖥▶✳🐴🚲P

COLOUR MAPS Colour maps at the front of this guide pinpoint all places under which you will find accommodation listed.

SHIPHAM, Somerset Map ref 1D1

◆◆◆ **PENSCOT FARMHOUSE HOTEL**

The Square, Shipham, Winscombe
BS25 1TW
T: (01934) 842659
F: (01934) 842576
I: www.minotel.com

Bedrooms: 5 single,
10 double/twin
Bathrooms: 12 en suite

Lunch available
Evening meal available
CC: Delta, Mastercard,
Switch, Visa

B&B per night:
S £30.00–£35.00
D £60.00–£65.00

HB per person:
DY £45.00–£60.00

OPEN All year round

Cosy old world atmosphere with log fires in winter, oak beams and English-style food. Situated in Mendip foothills with lovely views and walks.

SIDMOUTH, Devon Map ref 1D2 *Tourist Information Centre Tel: (01395) 516441*

◆◆◆ **CANTERBURY GUEST HOUSE**

Salcombe Road, Sidmouth
EX10 8PR
T: (01395) 513373
& 0800 328 1775
E: cgh@eclipse.co.uk

Bedrooms: 5 double/
twin, 3 triple/multiple
Bathrooms: 8 en suite

Evening meal available
CC: Amex, Mastercard,
Switch, Visa

B&B per night:
S £18.00–£21.50
D £36.00–£43.00

HB per person:
DY £27.50–£30.00

OPEN All year round

Old house of charm and character adjacent to River Sid. Close to shops, seafront and National Trust parkland. Non-smoking policy.

SOMERTON, Somerset Map ref 2A3

◆◆◆◆◆

MILL HOUSE

Barton St. David, Somerton TA11 6DF
T: (01458) 851215
F: (01458) 851372
E: knightsmillhouse@aol.com
I: www.smoothhound.co.uk/hotels/
millhouse3.html

B&B per night:
S £26.00–£28.00
D £48.00–£52.00

OPEN All year round

Beautifully restored Listed Georgian mill house in a peaceful garden with the mill stream still running through one end of the house. Set in lovely countryside but conveniently accessible from the A303. Spacious bedrooms all en suite. Close to Glastonbury and Wells. A warm welcome awaits you.

Bedrooms: 1 single,
2 double/twin; suites
available
Bathrooms: 3 en suite

Evening meal available
CC: Delta, Mastercard,
Switch, Visa

SPREYTON, Devon Map ref 1C2

◆◆◆

THE TOM COBLEY TAVERN

Spreyton, Crediton EX17 5AL
T: (01647) 231314
F: (01647) 231506
E: fjwfilor@tomcobley.fsnet.co.uk

B&B per night:
S £22.50
D £45.00

OPEN All year round

A small village inn serving its isolated community and offering a warm welcome to all guests. Real ales are on draught and food is home cooked on the premises. Rooms are comfortable, quiet and well equipped, service is cheerful and friendly. Dartmoor is 2 miles to the south.

Bedrooms: 2 single,
2 double/twin

Lunch available
Evening meal available

MAP REFERENCES The map references refer to the colour maps at the front of this guide. The first figure is the map number; the letter and figure which follow indicate the grid reference on the map.

STOGUMBER, Somerset Map ref 1D1

♦♦♦ **HALL FARM**

Stogumber, Taunton TA4 3TQ
T: (01984) 656321

Bedrooms: 1 single,
4 double/twin, 1 triple/
multiple
Bathrooms: 3 en suite,
2 private

Lunch available
Evening meal available

B&B per night:
S £18.50–£20.00
D £37.00–£40.00

HB per person:
DY £28.50–£30.00

Hall Farm is situated in the centre of picturesque Stogumber, between the Brendon and Quantock Hills. Close to sea and quaint villages of Dunster and Porlock.

OPEN All year round

STOKE SUB HAMDON, Somerset Map ref 2A3

♦♦♦♦ **CASTLE FARM**

Stoke sub Hamdon TA14 6QS
T: (01935) 822231
F: (01935) 822057

Bedrooms: 2 double/
twin, 1 triple/multiple
Bathrooms: 3 en suite

B&B per night:
S £25.00–£30.00
D £40.00–£45.00

Castle Farm is an 18thC farmhouse, part of the Duchy of Cornwall estate, next to the A303 and close to Montacute House.

OPEN All year round

SWINDON, Wiltshire Map ref 2B2 *Tourist Information Centre Tel: (01793) 530328*

♦♦♦♦ **COURTLEIGH HOUSE**

40 Draycott Road, Chiseldon,
Swindon SN4 0LS
T: (01793) 740246

Bedrooms: 2 double/
twin
Bathrooms: 1 en suite,
1 private

B&B per night:
S £22.00–£27.00
D £40.00–£45.00

Large detached village house with downland views, ample parking, tennis court and gardens. Comfortable, relaxing rooms. Easy access to Marlborough, Swindon, M4 and Cotswolds.

OPEN All year round

TAUNTON, Somerset Map ref 1D1 *Tourist Information Centre Tel: (01823) 336344*

♦♦♦ **NORTH DOWN FARM BED & BREAKFAST**

Pyncombe Lane, Wiveliscombe,
Taunton TA4 2BL
T: (01984) 623730 &
077 9 0 858450
F: (01984) 623730

Bedrooms: 1 single,
1 double/twin, 1 triple/
multiple
Bathrooms: 2 en suite,
1 private

Evening meal available

B&B per night:
S Min £20.00
D Min £40.00

HB per person:
DY Min £32.00

Family-run livestock farm on edge Exmoor, 10 miles Taunton, 1 mile Wiveliscombe. Magnificent views. Relaxed friendly atmosphere. Home-produced meat and vegetables. Delicious farmhouse meals.

OPEN All year round

TAVISTOCK, Devon Map ref 1C2 *Tourist Information Centre Tel: (01822) 612938*

♦♦♦♦ **ACORN COTTAGE**

Heathfield, Tavistock PL19 0LQ
T: (01822) 810038
E: viv@acorncot.fsnet.co.uk
I: www.visitbritain.com

Bedrooms: 3 double/
twin
Bathrooms: 3 en suite

Evening meal available

B&B per night:
S £25.00–£30.00
D £30.00–£40.00

OPEN All year round

17thC Grade II Listed. Many original features, lovely views, peaceful location. Lydford Gorge 3.5 miles and near Brentor medieval church. Central to many activities – bordering Dartmoor. Send for brochure.

QUALITY ASSURANCE SCHEME

For an explanation of the quality and facilities represented by the Diamonds please refer to the front of this guide. A more detailed explanation can be found in the information pages at the back.

Rating
Applied For

HARRABEER COUNTRY HOUSE HOTEL

Harrowbeer Lane, Yelverton PL20 6EA
T: (01822) 853302 & 855811
F: (01822) 853302
E: reception@harrabeer.co.uk
I: www.harrabeer.co.uk

B&B per night:
S £27.00–£39.00
D £55.00–£62.00

HB per person:
DY £42.50–£54.50

OPEN All year round

Delightful country house hotel in beautiful rural surroundings. Specialising in food, comfort and service. Not open at Christmas or New Year. Small conferences by arrangement.

Bedrooms: 6 double/
twin; suites available
Bathrooms: 4 en suite,
2 private

Evening meal available
CC: Amex, Mastercard,
Switch, Visa

Special offers for weekly and out of season breaks.
Visit our website for up-to-date information.

◆◆◆◆

OLD RECTORY FARM
Mary Tavy, Tavistock PL19 9PP
T: (01822) 810102

Bedrooms: 2 double/
twin
Bathrooms: 2 en suite

Lunch available

B&B per night:
D £36.00–£40.00

OPEN All year round

Modern traditional-style house on western edge of Dartmoor, with en suite rooms. Friendly welcome, local produce. Excellent for moorland walking and riding. Stabling available.

◆◆◆◆◆
Gold
Award

TOR COTTAGE

Chillaton, Tavistock PL16 OJE
T: (01822) 860248
F: (01822) 860126
E: info@torcottage.co.uk
I: www.torcottage.co.uk

B&B per night:
S £89.00
D £115.00

OPEN Feb–Nov

National winner of English Tourist Board England for Excellence Gold Award. Tor Cottage has a warm, relaxed atmosphere and nestles in a private valley. Lovely streamside gardens, wildlife hillsides, heated swimming pool. Luxurious en suite bedsitting rooms, each with log fire, private garden or conservatory. Renowned vegetarian and traditional cuisine.

Bedrooms: 4 double/
twin; suites available
Bathrooms: 4 en suite

CC: Delta, Mastercard,
Switch, Visa

Autumn/winter/spring breaks: 3 nights for price of 2. Valentine breaks include special dinners.

COUNTRY CODE Always follow the Country Code 🌳 Enjoy the countryside and respect its life and work 🌳 Guard against all risk of fire 🌳 Fasten all gates 🌳 Keep your dogs under close control 🌳 Keep to public paths across farmland 🌳 Use gates and stiles to cross fences, hedges and walls 🌳 Leave livestock, crops and machinery alone 🌳 Take your litter home 🌳 Help to keep all water clean 🌳 Protect wildlife, plants and trees 🌳 Take special care on country roads 🌳 Make no unnecessary noise

THORNBURY, Devon Map ref 1C2

◆◆◆

FORDA FARM
Thornbury, Holsworthy EX22 7BS
T: (01409) 261369

B&B per night:
S Min £20.00
D £40.00–£44.00

HB per person:
DY £32.00–£34.00

OPEN All year round

Relax and unwind at Forda with its 300-year-old farmhouse and cosy welcoming bedrooms, beamed ceilings and an inglenook fireplace for cooler evenings. Enjoy a complimentary cream tea on arrival and discover unspoilt Devon and Cornwall, a wildlife paradise with picturesque villages, dramatic coastline and market towns. Many activities close by. Open all year.

Bedrooms: 1 single,
2 double/twin
Bathrooms: 1 en suite

Evening meal available

3 nights B&B plus 1 evening meal, complimentary bottle of wine £62pp (2 sharing) excl Bank Hols, available Mar-Jun, Sept-Nov.

⋔ 🐎 Ⓢ ⊬ 🏛 💻 ☎ ∪ ✳ 🐎 ⚲ P

TINTAGEL, Cornwall Map ref 1B2

◆◆◆◆

PORT WILLIAM INN
Trebarwith Strand, Tintagel PL34 0HB
T: (01840) 770230
F: (01840) 770936
E: william@eurobell.co.uk

B&B per night:
S £52.00–£59.00
D £69.00–£83.00

OPEN All year round

Probably the best-located inn in Cornwall, overlooking sea and beach. All rooms en suite with TV and telephone. Extensive menu, including local seafood. Open all day, all year.

Bedrooms: 3 double/
twin, 3 triple/multiple
Bathrooms: 6 en suite

Lunch available
Evening meal available
CC: Amex, Delta,
Mastercard, Switch, Visa

⋔ 🐎 ☎ 🖥 ⊡ ♦ 🍷 ▼ Ⓢ ⊬ 🏛 ◖ ∪ ⊦ ✳ 🐎 ⚲ 🏨 P

TORQUAY, Devon Map ref 1D2 *Tourist Information Centre Tel: 0906 680 1268 (Premium rate number)*

◆◆◆

AVENUE PARK GUEST HOUSE
3 Avenue Road, Torquay TQ2 5LA
T: (01803) 293902
F: (01803) 293902
E: avenuepark@bushinternet.com
I: www.torbay.gov.uk/tourism/
t-hotels/avepark.htm

Bedrooms: 1 single,
3 double/twin, 4 triple/
multiple
Bathrooms: 8 en suite

B&B per night:
S £16.00–£20.00
D £32.00–£40.00

OPEN All year round

Friendly family-run guesthouse overlooking parkland. Seafront 350 yards, close to town, Riviera Centre, Abbey Gardens. Railway station nearby. Cleanliness and comfort assured.

⋔ 🐎 ♨ ⊡ ♦ Ⓢ ⊬ 🏛 💻 ✳ 🐎 P

◆◆◆◆

CEDAR COURT HOTEL
3 St Matthew's Road, Chelston,
Torquay TQ2 6JA
T: (01803) 607851

Bedrooms: 3 single,
5 double/twin, 2 triple/
multiple
Bathrooms: 10 en suite

Evening meal available

B&B per night:
S £20.00–£30.00
D £40.00–£60.00

HB per person:
DY £30.00–£50.00

OPEN All year round

Situated in peaceful surroundings within easy walking distance of seafront, town centre and railway station. All rooms en suite. Quality accommodation and meals. Craft courses.

⋔ 🐎 2 ♨ 🖥 ⊡ ♦ 🍷 Ⓢ ⊬ 🏛 💻 ✳ 🐎 P

IMPORTANT NOTE Information on accommodation listed in this guide has been supplied by the proprietors. As changes may occur you are advised to check details at the time of booking.

◆◆◆

CHESTER COURT HOTEL
30 Cleveland Road, Torquay TQ2 5BE
T: (01803) 294565
F: (01803) 294565
E: kevin@kpmorris.freeserve.co.uk
I: www.kpmorris.freeserve.co.uk/cch.html

B&B per night:
S £17.50–£22.00
D £35.00–£44.00

OPEN All year round

Small, family-run unlicensed hotel. Ample parking. All rooms en suite with colour TV, tea-making and full central heating for your comfort out of season. No-smoking rooms available. Varied menu, home cooking, English breakfast in spacious dining room. Level walk to Riviera Centre and seafront.

Bedrooms: 1 single, 4 double/twin, 5 triple/ multiple
Bathrooms: 9 en suite

Evening meal available
CC: Delta, Mastercard, Visa

10% discount for pensioners, Sep-Jun inclusive. Reductions for children sharing with 2 adults.

◆◆◆

CLOVELLY GUEST HOUSE
91 Avenue Road, Chelston, Torquay TQ2 5LH
I: (01803) 292286
F: (01803) 242286
E: clovellyguesthouse@ntlworld.com
I: homepage.ntlworld.com/clovelly.guesthouse

Bedrooms: 2 single, 3 double/twin, 1 triple/ multiple
Bathrooms: 2 en suite

Lunch available
Evening meal available

B&B per night:
S £12.00–£18.00
D £28.00–£36.00

OPEN All year round

Excellent accommodation with friendly atmosphere. Excellent food with choice of menu, special rates for families. Level walk to beach.

◆◆◆◆◆
Silver
Award

CRANBORNE HOTEL
58 Belgrave Road, Torquay TQ2 5HY
T: (01803) 298046
F: (01803) 215477

Bedrooms: 3 single, 6 double/twin, 1 triple/ multiple
Bathrooms: 10 en suite

Evening meal available
CC: Delta, Mastercard, Switch, Visa

B&B per night:
S £25.00
D £50.00

HB per person:
DY £40.00–£45.00

OPEN All year round

Victorian terraced hotel in excellent situation, being close to seafront, town centre and Riviera Centre. Torquay's only 5 Diamond Silver award hotel.

◆◆◆◆

THE CRANMORE
89 Avenue Road, Torquay TQ2 5LH
T: (01803) 298488
F: (01803) 298488
E: dave@thecranmore.fsnet.co.uk

Bedrooms: 7 double/ twin, 1 triple/multiple
Bathrooms: 8 en suite

Evening meal available
CC: Amex, Mastercard, Visa

B&B per night:
S £16.00–£19.00
D £32.00–£38.00

OPEN All year round

Friendly, family-run hotel. All rooms are en suite, clean, well decorated, warm and comfortable, with all usual facilities. Centrally placed close to all amenities.

◆◆◆

GAINSBORO HOTEL
22 Rathmore Road, Torquay TQ2 6NY
T: (01803) 292032
F: (01803) 292032
E: gainsboro@freeuk.com

Bedrooms: 1 single, 6 double/twin
Bathrooms: 4 en suite

Evening meal available
CC: Delta, Mastercard, Switch, Visa

B&B per night:
S £18.00–£22.00
D £36.00–£44.00

HB per person:
DY £29.50–£33.50

OPEN All year round

Victorian house of character. Idyllic setting, level walk to seafront (400 yards), and all amenities. En suite facilities, evening meal optional. Open all year.

---

www.travelengland.org.uk
Log on for information and inspiration. The latest information on places to visit, events and quality assessed accommodation.

TORQUAY continued

◆◆◆

THE GREEN PARK HOTEL
25 Morgan Avenue, Torquay TQ2 5RR
T: (01803) 293618
E: greenpark@eclipse.co.uk
I: www.greenpark.eclipse.co.uk

Bedrooms: 2 single, 6 double/twin, 3 triple/multiple
Bathrooms: 8 en suite, 1 private

Evening meal available
CC: Mastercard, Switch, Visa

B&B per night:
S £16.00–£24.00
D £32.00–£48.00

OPEN All year round

Small family hotel with resident proprietors. Close to town centre and only a short walk to shops, harbour and seafront. Residential licence. En suite rooms.

🚶 🐴 📺 ☕ 🍷 [S] 🛏 📻 🚿 ✿ 🚗 🚭 P

◆◆◆

MAPLE LODGE
36 Ash Hill Road, Torquay TQ1 3JD
T: (01803) 297391

Bedrooms: 1 single, 4 double/twin, 2 triple/multiple
Bathrooms: 6 en suite, 1 private

CC: Amex, Delta, Mastercard, Switch, Visa

B&B per night:
S £17.00–£23.00
D £34.00–£46.00

OPEN All year round

Detached guesthouse with beautiful views. Relaxed atmosphere, home cooking, en suite rooms. Centrally situated for town and beaches.

🚶 🐴 📺 ☕ [S] 🛏 📻 🚿 ✿ 🚗 P

◆◆

THE HOTEL NEWBURGH
14 Scarborough Road, Torquay TQ2 5UJ
T: (01803) 293270
E: the-newburgh-torquay@hotels.activebooking.com

Bedrooms: 4 double/twin, 2 triple/multiple
Bathrooms: 6 en suite

Evening meal available
CC: Mastercard, Visa

B&B per night:
S £21.00–£30.00
D £32.00–£44.00

HB per person:
DY £24.00–£30.00

OPEN All year round

A family-run hotel where the accent is on comfort. Just 10 minutes' walk to the beach or town, yet set in a quiet location.

🚶 🐴 📺 ☕ [S] 🛏 📻 🚿 ✿ 🚗 🚭 P

◆◆◆◆

ROBIN HILL INTERNATIONAL HOTEL

74 Braddons Hill Road East, Torquay TQ1 1HF
T: (01803) 214518
F: (01803) 291410
E: jo@robinhillhotel.co.uk
I: www.robinhillhotel.co.uk

'Our priorities are simple, they're yours'. David and Joanna's 35 years' experience in hotels ensures first class service at this award-winning hotel. Four years recipient of the prestigious 'Commitment to Quality Award'. Upgraded yearly. Imposingly situated in pretty south-facing terraced gardens. Only 450 metres from harbour, shop and restaurants.

Bedrooms: 4 single, 12 double/twin, 2 triple/multiple
Bathrooms: 17 en suite, 1 private

Evening meal available
CC: Delta, Mastercard, Switch, Visa

B&B per night:
S £26.00–£35.00
D £52.00–£70.00

🚶 🐴 ☎ 📺 ☕ 🍷 [S] 🛏 📻 🚿 ✿ 🐕 🚗 P

◆◆◆

SANDPIPER HOTEL

Rowdens Road, Torquay TQ2 5AZ
T: (01803) 292779

Modern, detatched, family-run licensed hotel. Close to Abbey Gardens, beach, Riviera Centre and entertainment. Relax in a friendly atmosphere, where good food and cleanliness are of first importance. En suite bedrooms with colour TV and beverage facilities, sun terrace and gardens. Ample parking in own grounds.

Bedrooms: 1 single, 9 double/twin, 1 triple/multiple
Bathrooms: 8 en suite, 1 private

Evening meal available
CC: Delta, Mastercard, Switch, Visa

3 nights for the price of 2 Oct–Feb (excl Christmas and New Year).

B&B per night:
S £16.00–£22.00
D £32.00–£44.00

HB per person:
DY £25.00–£30.00

OPEN All year round

🚶 🐴 📺 ☕ 🍷 [S] 🛏 📻 🚿 ✿ 🚭 P

TOTNES, Devon Map ref 1D2 *Tourist Information Centre Tel: (01803) 863168*

◆◆◆◆ **THE HUNGRY HORSE RESTAURANT**

Old Road, Harbertonford, Totnes TQ9 7TA	Bedrooms: 3 double/ twin	Evening meal available CC: Amex, Delta,	B&B per night: D £42.00–£54.00
T: (01803) 732441	Bathrooms: 3 en suite	Mastercard, Switch, Visa	
F: (01803) 732780			OPEN Feb–Dec

Denise and Brian invite you to stay in this delightful old building and sample some of the finest food in the South West. Fine dining at affordable prices!

🏇🐎🖵🛆🍷⌧✂🛍⊙🖩🖴✿🐎 P

◆◆◆◆◆
Silver
Award

OLD FOLLATON

Plymouth Road, Totnes TQ9 5NA

T: (01803) 865441
F: (01803) 863597
E: bandb@oldfollaton.co.uk
I: www.oldfollaton.co.uk

B&B per night:
S £40.00–£45.00
D £50.00–£60.00

HB per person:
DY £43.00–£57.00

OPEN All year round

Delightful Georgian country house set in peaceful surroundings and offering accommodation of the highest standard in a friendly and informal atmosphere. It is the ideal location surrounded by a wealth of places to visit, superb coastal and countryside walks and the splendour of Dartmoor.

Bedrooms: 3 double/ twin; suites available
Bathrooms: 3 en suite

Evening meal available

🏇5🖳🖵🛆🍷⌧✂🛍🖩🖴✿🐎 P

TROWBRIDGE, Wiltshire Map ref 2B2 *Tourist Information Centre Tel: (01225) 777054*

◆◆◆ **62B PAXCROFT COTTAGES**

Devizes Road, Hilperton, Trowbridge BA14 6JB	Bedrooms: 3 double/ twin	Evening meal available	B&B per night: S £22.00–£25.00 D £44.00–£50.00
T: (01225) 765838	Bathrooms: 2 en suite, 1 private		
E: paxcroftcottages@hotmail.com			HB per person: DY £29.00–£32.00

Comfortable house with lovely views, in rural situation, 1.5 miles from town. Lovely gardens and good food. Central for Wiltshire's attractions and only 10 miles from Bath.

OPEN All year round

🏇🖳🖵🛆🍷⌧✂🛍🖩🖴✿🐎🏠 P

TRURO, Cornwall Map ref 1B3 *Tourist Information Centre Tel: (01872) 274555*

◆◆◆◆
Silver
Award

BISSICK OLD MILL

Ladock, Truro TR2 4PG

T: (01726) 882557
F: (01726) 884057

B&B per night:
S £39.95
D £54.00–£69.00

OPEN All year round

17thC water mill sympathetically converted to provide well-appointed accommodation with exceptional standards throughout and a relaxing, friendly atmosphere. All bedrooms en suite and well equipped. Candlelit dinners prepared with fresh, quality ingredients and served in a beamed dining room. Ideal base for exploring all areas of Cornwall.

Bedrooms: 1 single, 4 double/twin
Bathrooms: 5 en suite

Evening meal available
CC: Delta, Mastercard, Switch, Visa

🏇10⛄🕭🖳🖵🛆🍷⌧✂🛍🖩🖴✿🐎🏠 P

◆◆◆◆

MARCORRIE HOTEL
20 Falmouth Road, Truro TR1 2HX
T: (01872) 277374
F: (01872) 241666
E: marcorrie@aol.com
I: www.hotelstruro.com

B&B per night:
S £39.50–£45.00
D £42.00–£46.00

OPEN All year round

Victorian townhouse with en suite bedrooms, only 5 minutes' walk to city centre and cathedral. Centrally situated for visiting all of Cornwall by car or bus. Many country houses and gardens, coastal and river walks nearby. Ample parking. Traditional English cuisine served in period dining room.

Bedrooms: 3 single, 5 double/twin, 4 triple/ multiple
Bathrooms: 12 en suite

CC: Amex, Delta, Mastercard, Switch, Visa

◆◆◆◆

ROCK COTTAGE
Blackwater, Truro TR4 8EU
T: (01872) 560252 & 07971 941399
F: (01872) 560252
E: rockcottage@yahoo.com

B&B per night:
S £26.00–£28.00
D £44.00–£48.00

OPEN All year round

18thC, beamed cob cottage, formerly the village schoolmaster's home. A haven for non-smokers. Centrally heated throughout, all bedrooms en suite. Guest sitting room with colour TV. Cosy dining room with antique Cornish range. Private parking. Gardens. Village location, 3 miles ocean and 6 miles Truro. No pets or children.

Bedrooms: 3 double/ twin
Bathrooms: 3 en suite

CC: Delta, Mastercard, Switch, Visa

◆◆◆◆ **TREVISPIAN-VEAN FARM GUEST HOUSE**
St Erme, Truro TR4 9AT
T: (01872) 279514
F: (01872) 263730
I: www.guesthousestruro.com

Bedrooms: 4 double/ twin, 6 triple/multiple
Bathrooms: 10 en suite

Evening meal available

B&B per night:
S £21.00–£24.00
D £42.00

HB per person:
DY £31.00–£34.00

300-acre arable & livestock farm. Beautifully situated 7 miles from coast in heart of the countryside, the farmhouse combines modern comforts with all the charm of a 300-year-old farm.

AT-A-GLANCE SYMBOLS
Symbols at the end of each accommodation entry give useful information about services and facilities. A key to symbols can be found inside the back cover flap. Keep this open for easy reference.

WADEBRIDGE, Cornwall Map ref 1B2 *Tourist Information Centre Tel: (01208) 813725*

◆◆◆◆

KIVELLS

Chapel Amble, Wadebridge PL27 6EP
T: (01208) 841755
E: kivells@cwcom.net
I: www.kivellsbandb.co.uk

B&B per night:
S £25.00
D £40.00–£48.00

HB per person:
DY £28.00–£33.00

OPEN Mar–Oct

Kivells lies in lovely countryside close to the market town of Wadebridge, the stunning North Cornwall coast and other attractions including the Eden Project. All bedrooms and the guests' sitting room face south, overlooking the gardens and swimming pool. Quite simply, the perfect place for the holiday you deserve!

Bedrooms: 3 double/twin
Bathrooms: 1 en suite

◆◆◆

TREGOLLS FARM

St Wenn, Bodmin PL30 5PG
T: (01208) 812154
F: (01208) 812154
E: tregollsfarm@btclick.com
I: www.tregollsfarm.co.uk

B&B per night:
S £18.00–£21.00
D £36.00–£42.00

HB per person:
DY £28.00–£31.00

OPEN All year round

Grade II Listed farmhouse set in a picturesque valley overlooking fields of cows and sheep. Ideal for walkers. Farm trail links up with Saints Way Footpath. Camel Trail close by. Children's games room. Pets' corner. Padstow, Eden Project and Lost Gardens of Heligan all within 25 minutes.

Bedrooms: 2 single, 2 double/twin

Evening meal available
CC: Amex, Delta, Diners, Mastercard, Switch, Visa

3-night break available at a special price.

WARMINSTER, Wiltshire Map ref 2B2 *Tourist Information Centre Tel: (01985) 218548*

◆◆◆◆◆
Silver Award

BUGLEY BARTON

Victoria Road, Warminster
BA12 7RB
T: (01985) 213389
F: (01985) 300450
E: bugleybarton@aol.com

Bedrooms: 3 double/twin
Bathrooms: 2 en suite, 1 private

B&B per night:
S £40.00
D £60.00–£65.00

OPEN All year round

A hospitable stay is assured in this elegant and spacious Georgian farmhouse. Mature formal gardens. Close to Longleat, Bath and Sailsbury. Good food locally. Easy parking.

WASHFORD, Somerset Map ref 1D1

◆◆◆

GREEN BAY

Washford, Watchet TA23 0NN
T: (01984) 640303
E: greenbay@tinyonline.co.uk

Bedrooms: 3 double/twin
Bathrooms: 2 en suite, 1 private

Evening meal available

B&B per night:
S £17.50–£20.00
D £35.00–£38.00

HB per person:
DY £24.50–£26.00

OPEN All year round

Charming period cottage. Ideal location near coast, Exmoor, Dunster, Watchet harbour, Cleeve Abbey and steam railway. Friendly hosts, comfortable rooms and good home cooking.

ACCESSIBILITY

Look for the symbols which indicate accessibility for wheelchair users. A list of establishments is at the front of this guide.

◆◆◆

BURCOTT MILL HISTORIC WATERMILL & GUESTHOUSE

Wookey Road, Wookey, Wells BA5 1NJ
T: (01749) 673118
F: (01749) 677376
E: theburts@burcottmill.com
I: www.burcottmill.com

Authentically restored Victorian watermill dating from Domesday, still stonegrinding flour daily. Enjoy a personal tour with the miller. Families especially welcome: playground, ponies, birds, small animals.Tearoom, craftshops. Opposite country pub for evening meals. Ideal for Cheddar, Wells, Glastonbury. Flexible accommodation. Wheelchair friendly suite. Wells 1 mile. You won't be disappointed.

Bedrooms: 1 single,
1 double, 4 triple/
multiple
Bathrooms: 5 en suite,
1 private

CC: Mastercard, Switch,
Visa

Somerset's Cream Tees golfing minibreaks. Ambling, rambling and birdwatching breaks. Birthday, wedding and school parties catered for.

B&B per night:
S £24.00
D £42.00–£64.00

OPEN All year round

◆◆◆

FRANKLYNS FARM

Chewton Mendip, Bath BA3 4NB
T: (01761) 241372

Bedrooms: 3 double/
twin; suites available
Bathrooms: 2 en suite,
1 private

Cosy farmhouse in heart of Mendip. Superb views, peaceful setting. Large garden with tennis court. Offering genuine hospitality and delicious breakfast. Ideal touring Bath, Wells, Cheddar.

B&B per night:
S Min £25.00
D Min £40.00

OPEN All year round

◆◆◆◆

LITTLEWELL FARM GUEST HOUSE "NON WORKING FARM"

Coxley, Wells BA5 1QP
T: (01749) 677914

Delightful 18thC farmhouse on non-working farm, set in pretty garden and enjoying extensive views over beautiful countryside. Charming en suite bedrooms with antique furniture offer comfort and high standards coupled with personal and thoughtful touches. Our candlelit dinner is skilfully prepared and beautifully presented, using only the best of local produce. One mile south-west of Wells.

Bedrooms: 1 single,
4 double/twin
Bathrooms: 4 en suite,
1 private

Evening meal available

B&B per night:
S £24.00–£28.00
D £39.00–£50.00

HB per person:
DY £40.00–£46.00

OPEN All year round

◆◆◆◆

THE OLD STORES

Westbury-sub-Mendip, Wells
BA5 1HA
T: (01749) 870817 & 07721 514306
F: (01749) 870980
E: moglin980@aol.com

Bedrooms: 3 double/
twin; suites available
Bathrooms: 2 en suite,
1 private

Midway between Wells and Cheddar this 300-year-old cottage is ideal for walking and exploring Somerset's history. Local and homemade produce. Opposite village inn.

B&B per night:
S £21.00–£22.00
D £22.00–£24.00

OPEN All year round

CONFIRM YOUR BOOKING

You are advised to confirm your booking in writing.

◆◆◆

THE POUND INN

Burcott Lane, Coxley, Wells BA5 1QZ
T: (01749) 672785
E: poundinnwells@aol.com

B&B per night:
D £40.00

OPEN All year round

Expect a warm welcome at our traditional 17thC village inn. 1.5 miles from Wells on A39 to Glastonbury. Varied menu making good use of fresh local produce with a range of wines and beers to complement and a high standard of service to match. Convenient base for local tourist attractions.	Bedrooms: 1 double/ twin, 1 triple/multiple Bathrooms: 2 en suite	Lunch available Evening meal available CC: Delta, Mastercard, Switch, Visa

🐾🖥️❑♨️🍽️§✂️🛏️🖨️🔌🚶U☼🚗🖼️P

◆◆◆◆

WORTH HOUSE HOTEL

Worth, Wookey, Wells BA5 1LW
T: (01749) 672041
F: (01749) 672041
E: mblomeley2001@yahoo.co.uk

Bedrooms: 1 single, 5 double/twin, 1 triple/ multiple
Bathrooms: 7 en suite

Lunch available
Evening meal available
CC: Delta, Mastercard, Switch, Visa

B&B per night:
S £25.00–£28.00
D £40.00–£46.00

HB per person:
DY £32.00–£36.00

OPEN All year round

Small country hotel, dating from the 16th C, 2 miles from Wells on the B3139. Exposed beams and log fires.

🔼🐾🖥️❑♨️🍽️§✂️🖨️🔌☼🚗🖼️P

◆◆◆◆

MILLBROOK HOUSE

92 High Street, West Coker, Yeovil BA22 9AU
T: (01935) 862840
F: (01935) 863846

Bedrooms: 3 double/ twin
Bathrooms: 2 en suite, 1 private

Evening meal available

B&B per night:
S £28.00–£35.00
D £45.00–£60.00

OPEN All year round

Charming 18thC hamstone house set on edge of attractive village. Parking on premises. En suite accommodation. Cosy wood fires. Evening meals.

🖥️❑♨️🍲§✂️🖨️🔌☼🚗P

◆◆◆◆

BRAESIDE HOTEL

2 Victoria Park, Weston-super-Mare BS23 2HZ
T: (01934) 626642
F: (01934) 626642
E: braeside@tesco.net
I: www.braesidehotel.co.uk

B&B per night:
S £25.00
D £50.00

OPEN All year round

Fabulous views over Weston Bay; 2 minutes' walk from sandy beach. Quiet location with unrestricted on-street parking. Single rooms always available. Directions: with sea on left, take first right after Winter Gardens, then first left into Lower Church Road. Victoria Park is on the right after the left-hand bend.	Bedrooms: 2 single, 5 double/twin, 2 triple/ multiple Bathrooms: 9 en suite Stay 2 nights and have a 3rd night free, 1 Nov-end Apr (excl Easter).	

🔼🐾🖥️❑♨️§✂️🖨️🔌🐕🚗

QUALITY ASSURANCE SCHEME

Diamond ratings and awards were correct at the time of going to press but are subject to change. Please check at the time of booking.

◆◆◆

MOORLANDS COUNTRY GUESTHOUSE

Hutton, Weston-super-Mare BS24 9QH
T: (01934) 812283
F: (01934) 812283
E: margaret_holt@email.comm
I: www.guestaccom.co.uk/35.htm

B&B per night:
S £20.00–£30.00
D £40.00–£50.00

OPEN All year round

Family-run 18thC house in mature landscaped grounds. The Holts have been at Moorlands for the past 35 years. Hutton is a pretty village with a pub serving meals. Close to hill and country walks, many places of interest easily reached by car. Riding can be arranged for children.

Bedrooms: 3 double/ twin, 3 triple/multiple
Bathrooms: 5 en suite

CC: Amex, Diners, Mastercard, Visa

◆◆◆◆

Silver
Award

STADDLESTONES GUEST HOUSE

3 Standards Road, Westonzoyland, Bridgwater TA7 0EL
T: (01278) 691179
F: (01278) 691333
E: staddlestones@euphony.net
I: www.staddlestonesguesthouse. co.uk

Bedrooms: 3 double/ twin
Bathrooms: 2 en suite, 1 private

CC: Delta, Mastercard, Switch, Visa

B&B per night:
S £30.00–£35.00
D £50.00–£56.00

OPEN All year round

Elegant, Georgian, converted 17thC farmhouse in centre of village. Comfortable rooms with private facilities. Guest lounge, large garden, parking.

◆◆◆

THE PUFFINS INN

123 Bay View Road, Westward Ho!, Bideford EX39 1BJ
T: (01237) 473970
F: (01237) 422815
E: thepuffins@breathemail.net

Bedrooms: 2 double/ twin, 3 triple/multiple
Bathrooms: 5 en suite

Lunch available
Evening meal available
CC: Delta, Mastercard, Switch, Visa

B&B per night:
S £22.50–£25.00
D £45.00–£50.00

HB per person:
DY £31.00–£33.50

OPEN All year round

Former gentleman's residence overlooking Northam Burrows Country Park. Car park and garden.

◆◆◆

BRUNSWICK GUEST HOUSE

9 Brunswick Terrace, Weymouth DT4 7RW
T: (01305) 785408 & 07776 485600

B&B per night:
S £16.00–£20.00
D £36.00–£48.00

OPEN All year round

Enjoy our seafront cul-de-sac position in a picturesque Georgian terrace, with panoramic views of the bay. You are assured of a warm welcome and hearty breakfasts. Walk along the esplanade to the many amenities and attractions. Rail, bus, coach approximately 5 minutes' walk. Full central heating, ideal for out of season breaks.

Bedrooms: 1 single, 4 double/twin, 2 triple/ multiple
Bathrooms: 6 en suite

CC: Delta, Mastercard, Switch, Visa

RATING All accommodation in this guide has been rated, or is awaiting a rating, by a trained English Tourism Council assessor.

WEYMOUTH continued

◆◆◆ **WEYSIDE GUEST HOUSE**

1a Abbotsbury Road, Weymouth
DT4 0AD
T: (01305) 772685
E: weysideguesthouse@btinternet.
com
I: www.weysideguesthouse.
btinternet.co.uk

Bedrooms: 2 double/
twin, 2 triple/multiple
Bathrooms: 4 en suite

B&B per night:
S £22.50
D £45.00

OPEN All year round

A well-established guesthouse within walking distance to all attractions. All rooms en suite with television. Catering for families and couples. Own car park.

WIDECOMBE-IN-THE-MOOR, Devon Map ref 1C2

◆◆◆ **HIGHER VENTON FARM**

Widecombe-in-the-Moor,
Newton Abbot TQ13 7TF
T: (01364) 621235
F: (01364) 621382

Bedrooms: 3 double/
twin
Bathrooms: 2 en suite

Evening meal available

B&B per night:
S £20.00–£25.00
D £22.00–£48.00

HB per person:
DY £30.00–£37.00

OPEN All year round

40-acre farm. 17thC thatched farmhouse with a homely atmosphere and farmhouse cooking. Ideal for touring Dartmoor. 16 miles from the coast.

WILTON, Wiltshire Map ref 2B2

◆◆◆◆ **THE PEMBROKE ARMS HOTEL**

Minster Street, Wilton,
Marlborough SP2 0BH
T: (01722) 743328
F: (01722) 744886
E: reservations@pembrokearms.
co.uk

Bedrooms: 1 single,
5 double/twin, 2 triple/
multiple
Bathrooms: 8 en suite

Lunch available
Evening meal available
CC: Delta, Mastercard,
Switch, Visa

B&B per night:
S £55.00–£65.00
D £75.00–£90.00

HB per person:
DY Min £60.00

OPEN All year round

This elegant hotel has an emphasis on excellence, with superb cuisine, attractive rooms and friendly atmosphere. Situated in 2 acres of grounds, opposite Wilton House.

WINKLEIGH, Devon Map ref 1C2

◆◆◆

THE OLD PARSONAGE

Court Walk, Winkleigh EX19 8JA
T: (01837) 83772
F: (01837) 680074

B&B per night:
S £25.00
D £40.00–£47.00

HB per person:
DY £37.00

OPEN All year round

Typical Devon thatched and cob-walled house, once the residence of the local squire. Park-like gardens have many magnificent trees, rhododendrons and azaleas. Comfortable en suite bedrooms with lots of old world charm. Garden gate leads to village square and the Kings Arms where excellent food is served.

Bedrooms: 3 double/
twin; suites available
Bathrooms: 3 en suite

Evening meal available

WINSFORD, Somerset Map ref 1D1

◆◆◆ **KEMPS FARM**

Winsford, Minehead TA24 7HT
T: (01643) 851312

Bedrooms: 3 double/
twin
Bathrooms: 2 en suite,
1 private

Evening meal available

B&B per night:
S £18.00–£18.50
D £36.00–£37.00

HB per person:
DY £25.00–£25.50

OPEN All year round

Spacious farmhouse with stunning views over Exe Valley. Superb walking, delicious home cooking with local produce. Guests' comfort is paramount. Hostess trays in all rooms.

WHERE TO STAY

Please mention this guide when making your booking.

WINSFORD continued

◆◆◆◆

LARCOMBE FOOT

Winsford, Minehead TA24 7HS
T: (01643) 851306

B&B per night:
S Min £23.00
D Min £46.00

HB per person:
DY Min £35.50

Attractive period house in beautiful, tranquil Exe Valley. Guests' comfort within a warm, happy atmosphere is paramount. Footpath access to the moor and surrounding wildlife make Larcombe Foot an idyllic rural retreat. Dogs welcome.

Bedrooms: 1 single, 2 double/twin
Bathrooms: 1 en suite, 1 private

Evening meal available

🐴6 📺 ☕ 💨 [S] 🛏 ▦ 🧺 🎣 ✿ 🐕 🚗 P

WINTERBOURNE STOKE, Wiltshire Map ref 2B2

◆◆◆◆

SCOTLAND LODGE FARM

Winterbourne Stoke, Salisbury SP3 4TF
T: (01980) 621199
F: (01980) 621188
E: william.lockwood@bigwig.net
I: www.smoothhound.co.uk/hotels/scotlandl.html

B&B per night:
S £28.00–£30.00
D £46.00–£48.00

OPEN All year round

Warm welcome at family-run competition yard set in 46 acres of grassland. Lovely views and walks, Stonehenge/Salisbury nearby. Dogs, children and horses welcomed – stabling available on shavings. Conservatory for guests' use. French, German, Italian spoken. Easy access off A303 with entry through automatic gate. Excellent local pubs.

Bedrooms: 3 double/twin
Bathrooms: 2 private

CC: Delta, Mastercard, Switch, Visa

🅰 🐴 🛋 📺 ☕ 💨 [S] 🚭 🛏 ▦ 🧺 ✿ 🐕 🚗 P

WOODBOROUGH, Wiltshire Map ref 2B2

◆◆◆◆

PANTAWICK
Woodborough, Pewsey SN9 5PG
T: (01672) 851662
F: (01672) 851662
E: pantawick@aol.com

Bedrooms: 2 double/twin
Bathrooms: 2 en suite

B&B per night:
S £25.00–£30.00
D £40.00–£45.00

OPEN All year round

Modern fully centrally-heated house. One double room en suite and 1 twin en suite. Tea/coffee trays. Colour TV. Ample parking. No smoking, please.

📺 📺 ☕ 💨 [S] 🚭 ▦ 🧺 🚗 P

QUALITY ASSURANCE SCHEME

For an explanation of the quality and facilities represented by the Diamonds please refer to the front of this guide. A more detailed explanation can be found in the information pages at the back.

◆◆◆◆

GULL ROCK HOTEL
Mortehoe, Woolacombe EX34 7EA
T: (01271) 870534
F: (01271) 870534
E: info@thegullrockhotel.co.uk
I: www.thegullrockhotel.co.uk

B&B per night:
S £22.00–£30.00
D £44.00–£60.00

HB per person:
DY £32.00–£40.00

OPEN Mar–Oct

Delightful detached Edwardian house hotel with spectacular views, close to scenic walks, sandy beaches and secluded coves. It has a friendly relaxed atmosphere with a high standard of comfort, food and service and overlooks Combesgate and Woolacombe beaches. All its en suite rooms, south-facing terrace, spacious TV lounge, separate bar/ games room, have superb sea views.

Bedrooms: 1 double/
twin, 4 triple/multiple
Bathrooms: 4 en suite,
1 private

Evening meal available

Special low season 3,5 & 7 day breaks from £88
including B&B and 5-course evening meals.

⌂4♨▤⬛♿♨▓⬛◗🐾P

◆◆◆

THE HOLLIES
Greenhill, Hook, Wootton Bassett,
Swindon SN4 8EH
T: (01793) 770795
F: (01793) 770795

Bedrooms: 2 single,
2 double/twin
Bathrooms: 1 en suite

B&B per night:
S £20.00–£23.00
D £38.00–£45.00

OPEN All year round

In beautiful countryside looking across the valley to the Cotswolds. Large garden, ample parking, non-smoking. One room en suite. 4 miles west of Swindon, 8 miles Cotswold Water Park.

♠⌂3♨▤⬛♿▓⬛🐾P

◆◆◆◆

TORRFIELDS
Sheepstor, Yelverton PL20 6PF
T: (01822) 852161
E: torrfields@beeb.net

Bedrooms: 2 double/
twin
Bathrooms: 2 en suite

Evening meal available

B&B per night:
S £20.00
D £40.00

HB per person:
DY £30.00–£35.00

OPEN All year round

Detached property in own grounds, with good views and direct access on to moorland. Super setting in Dartmoor National Park – ideal for walkers.

♠⌂♨▤⬛♿▓⬛◗∪▎🐾P

◆◆◆◆

JESSOPS
Vagg Lane, Chilthorne Domer, Yeovil
BA22 8RY
T: (01935) 841097
F: (01935) 841097

B&B per night:
S £20.00–£25.00
D £45.00–£50.00

OPEN All year round

New bungalow with 2 double bedrooms (1 en suite, 4-poster), 1 twin bedroom. TV, tea/coffee in all rooms. Full English breakfast, excellent accommodation, panoramic views. Good pub food, 5 minutes' walk. Yeovil town and A303 ten minutes' drive. Riding stables 2 miles. Lovely walks at Ham Hill and Stoke Subhampton.

Bedrooms: 3 double/
twin
Bathrooms: 1 en suite

♠⌂♨▤⬛♿⬛🐾P

HALF BOARD PRICES Half board prices are given per person, but in some cases these may be based on double/twin occupancy.

♦♦♦

COURTRY FARM

Bridgehampton, Yeovil BA22 8HF

T: (01935) 840327

F: (01935) 840964

I: www.courtryfarm@hotmail.com

B&B per night:
S £22.00–£25.00
D Min £40.00

600-acre mixed working farm. Warm welcome at farmhouse and annexed accommodation. Ground floor rooms, en suite, TV, tea-making facilities. Tennis court and garden. Just off A303 – three quarters of a mile. Fleet Air Arm Museum half a mile. Local attractions include Stourhead, Tintinhull and Montacute gardens. Longleat 40 minutes. Leland Trail for walkers and cycle trails.

Bedrooms: 1 double/
twin, 1 triple/multiple
Bathrooms: 2 en suite

USE YOUR *i*s

There are more than 550 Tourist Information Centres throughout England offering friendly help with accommodation and holiday ideas as well as suggestions of places to visit and things to do. There may well be a centre in your home town which can help you before you set out. You'll find addresses in the local Phone Book.

A brief guide to the main Towns and Villages offering accommodation in the South West

A **ABBOTSBURY, DORSET** - Beautiful village near Chesil Beach, with a long main street of mellow stone and thatched cottages and the ruins of a Benedictine monastery. High above the village on a hill is a prominent 15th C chapel. Abbotsbury's famous swannery and sub-tropical gardens lie just outside the village.

ALLERFORD, SOMERSET - Village with picturesque stone and thatch cottages and a packhorse bridge, set in the beautiful Vale of Porlock.

AMESBURY, WILTSHIRE - Standing on the banks of the River Avon, this is the nearest town to Stonehenge on Salisbury Plain. The area is rich in prehistoric sites.

ASHBURTON, DEVON - Formerly a thriving wool centre and important as one of Dartmoor's four stannary towns. Today's busy market town has many period buildings. Ancient tradition is maintained in the annual ale-tasting and bread-weighing ceremony. Good centre for exploring Dartmoor or the south Devon coast.

AVEBURY, WILTSHIRE - Set in a landscape of earthworks and megalithic standing stones, Avebury has a fine church and an Elizabethan manor. Remains from excavations may be seen in the museum. The area abounds in important prehistoric sites, among them Silbury Hill. Stonehenge stands about 20 miles due south.

B **BARNSTAPLE, DEVON** - At the head of the Taw Estuary, once a ship-building and textile town, now an agricultural centre with attractive period buildings, a modern civic centre and leisure centre. Attractions include Queen Anne's Walk, a charming colonnaded arcade and Pannier Market.

BATH, BATH AND NORTH EAST SOMERSET - Georgian spa city beside the River Avon. Important Roman site with impressive reconstructed baths, uncovered in 19th C. Bath Abbey built on site of monastery where first king of England was crowned (AD 973). Fine architecture in mellow local stone. Pump Room and museums.

BEAMINSTER, DORSET - Old country town of mellow local stone set amid hills and rural vales. Mainly Georgian buildings; attractive almshouses date from 1603. The 17th C church with its ornate, pinnacled tower was restored inside by the Victorians. Parnham, a Tudor manor house, lies 1 mile south.

BIDEFORD, DEVON - The home port of Sir Richard Grenville, the town with its 17th C merchants' houses flourished as a shipbuilding and cloth town. The bridge of 24 arches was built about 1460. Charles Kingsley stayed here while writing Westward Ho!

BISHOP SUTTON, BATH AND NORTH EAST SOMERSET - Village at edge of Chew Valley Lake.

BISHOP'S LYDEARD, SOMERSET - Village 5 miles north-west of Taunton, the county town. Terminus for the West Somerset steam railway.

BODMIN, CORNWALL - County town south-west of Bodmin Moor with a ruined priory and church dedicated to St Petroc. Nearby are Lanhydrock House and Pencarrow House.

BOSCASTLE, CORNWALL - Small, unspoilt village in Valency Valley. Active as a port until onset of railway era, its natural harbour affords rare shelter on this wild coast. Attractions include spectacular blow-hole, Celtic field strips, part-Norman church. Nearby St Juliot Church was restored by Thomas Hardy.

BOVEY TRACEY, DEVON - Standing by the river just east of Dartmoor National Park, this old town has good moorland views. Its church, with a 14th C tower, holds one of Devon's finest medieval rood screens.

BOX, WILTSHIRE - Village in an Area of Outstanding Natural Beauty, 7 miles south-west of Chippenham. It is famed for Box ground stone, used for centuries on buildings of national importance.

BRADFORD-ON-AVON, WILTSHIRE - Huddled beside the river, the buildings of this former cloth-weaving town reflect continuing prosperity from the Middle Ages. There is a tiny Anglo-Saxon church, part of a monastery. The part-14th C bridge carries a medieval chapel, later used as a gaol.

BRIDGWATER, SOMERSET - Former medieval port on the River Parrett, now small industrial town with mostly 19th C or modern architecture. Georgian Castle Street leads to West Quay and site of 13th C castle razed to the ground by Cromwell. Birthplace of Cromwellian Admiral Robert Blake is now museum. Arts centre.

BRIDPORT, DORSET - Market town and chief producer of nets and ropes just inland of dramatic Dorset coast. Old, broad streets built for drying and twisting and long gardens for rope-walks. Grand arcaded Town Hall and Georgian buildings. Local history museum has Roman relics.

BRISTOL - Famous for maritime links, historic harbour, Georgian terraces and Brunel's Clifton suspension bridge. Many attractions including SS Great Britain, Bristol Zoo, museums and art galleries and top name entertainments. Events include Balloon Fiesta and Regatta.

BRIXHAM, DEVON - Famous for its trawling fleet in the 19th C, a steeply-built fishing port overlooking the harbour and fish market. A statue of William of Orange recalls his landing here before deposing James II. There is an aquarium and museum. Good cliff views and walks.

BROADHEMBURY, DEVON - Thatch-and-cob village with 14th/15th C church built largely of local Beer stone. South-east of the village, 884ft above sea level, is the Iron Age Hembury Fort.

BUCKLAND NEWTON, DORSET - Village in an Area of Outstanding Natural Beauty, on the edge of the Dorset Downs midway between Dorchester and Sherborne.

BUDE, CORNWALL - Resort on dramatic Atlantic coast. High cliffs give spectacular sea and inland views. Golf-course, cricket pitch, folly, surfing, coarse-fishing and boating. Mother-town Stratton was base of Royalist Sir Bevil Grenville.

BUDLEIGH SALTERTON, DEVON - Small resort with pebble beach on coast of red cliffs, setting for famous Victorian painting 'The Boyhood of Raleigh'. Sir Walter Raleigh was born at Hayes Barton. A salt-panning village in medieval times, today's resort has some Georgian houses.

BURNHAM-ON-SEA, SOMERSET - Small Victorian resort famous for sunsets and sandy beaches, a few minutes from junction 22 of the M5. Ideal base for touring Somerset, Cheddar and Bath. Good sporting facilities, championship golf-course.

BURTON BRADSTOCK, DORSET - Lying amid fields beside the River Bride, a village of old stone houses, a 14th C church and a village green. The beautiful coast road from Abbotsbury to Bridport passes by and Iron Age forts top the surrounding hills. The sheltered river valley makes a staging post for migrating birds.

CALLINGTON, CORNWALL - A quiet market town standing on high ground above the River Lynher. The 15th C church of St Mary's has an alabaster monument to Lord Willoughby de Broke, Henry VII's marshal. A 15th C chapel, 1 mile east, houses Dupath Well, one of the Cornish Holy Wells.

CANNINGTON, SOMERSET - Quantock Hills village with Brymore House, birthplace of John Pym, a leading statesman in the reign of Charles I, lying to the west. Three fine old 16th C houses are close by.

CASTLE CARY, SOMERSET - One of south Somerset's most attractive market towns, with a picturesque winding high street of golden stone and thatch, market-house and famous round 18th C lock-up.

CASTLE COMBE, WILTSHIRE - One of England's prettiest villages, in a steep woodland valley by a brook. The Perpendicular church recalls the village's prosperous times as a cloth-weaving centre. No trace remains of the castle, but the 13th C effigy of its founder Walter de Dunstanville lies in the church.

CATTISTOCK, DORSET - 9 miles north-west of Dorchester, amidst fine downland scenery near the River Frome.

CHAGFORD, DEVON - Handsome stone houses, some from the Middle Ages, grace this former stannary town on northern Dartmoor. Popular centre for walking in beautiful scenery and ideal base for exploring the West Country. There is a splendid 15th C granite church, said to be haunted by the poet Godolphin.

CHARD, SOMERSET - Market town in hilly countryside. The wide main street has some handsome buildings, among them the Guildhall, court house and almshouses. Modern light industry and dairy produce have replaced 19th C lace making which came at decline of cloth trade.

CHARMINSTER, DORSET - Village just north of the county town of Dorchester, with its museums and Maiden Castle Iron Age hillfort. Within easy reach of Thomas Hardy's Cottage and the Cerne Giant hillside figure.

CHEDDAR, SOMERSET - Large village at foot of Mendips just south of the spectacular Cheddar Gorge. Close by are Roman and Saxon sites and famous show caves. Traditional Cheddar cheese is still made here.

CHEW STOKE, BATH AND NORTH EAST SOMERSET - Attractive village in the Mendip Hills with an interesting Tudor rectory and the remains of a Roman villa. To the south is the Chew Valley reservoir with its extensive leisure facilities.

CHIDEOCK, DORSET - Village of sandstone thatched cottages in a valley near the dramatic Dorset coast. The church holds an interesting processional cross in mother-of-pearl and the manor house close by is associated with the Victorian Roman Catholic church. Seatown has a pebble beach and limestone cliffs.

CHIPPENHAM, WILTSHIRE - Ancient market town with modern industry. Notable early buildings include the medieval Town Hall and the gabled 15th C Yelde Hall, now a local history museum. On the outskirts Hardenhuish has a charming hilltop church by the Georgian architect John Wood of Bath.

CHIPPING SODBURY, SOUTH GLOUCESTERSHIRE - Old market town, its buildings a mixture of Cotswold stone and mellowed brickwork. The 15th C church and the market cross are of interest. Horton Court (National Trust) stands 4 miles north-east and preserves a very rare Norman hall.

CLOVELLY, DEVON - Clinging to wooded cliffs, fishing village with steep cobbled street zigzagging, or cut in steps, to harbour. Carrying sledges stand beside whitewashed flower-decked cottages. Charles Kingsley's father was rector of the church set high up near the Hamlyn family's Clovelly Court.

COLYTON, DEVON - Surrounded by fertile farmland, this small riverside town was an early Saxon settlement. Medieval prosperity from the wool trade built the grand church tower with its octagonal lantern and the church's fine west window.

CORSHAM, WILTSHIRE - Growing town with old centre showing Flemish influence, legacy of former prosperity from weaving. The church, restored last century, retains Norman features. The Elizabethan Corsham Court, with additions by Capability Brown, has fine furniture.

CRANTOCK, CORNWALL - Pretty village of thatched cottages and seaside bungalows. Village stocks, once used against smugglers, are in the churchyard and the pub has a smugglers' hideout.

CREDITON, DEVON - Ancient town in fertile valley, once prosperous from wool, now active in cider-making. Said to be the birthplace of St Boniface. The 13th C Chapter House, the church governors' meeting place, holds a collection of armour from the Civil War.

CREWKERNE, SOMERSET - This charming little market town on the Dorset border nestles in undulating farmland and orchards in a conservation area. Built of local sandstone with Roman and Saxon origins. The magnificent St Bartholomew's Church dates from 15th C; St Bartholomew's Fair is held in September.

CRICKLADE, WILTSHIRE - Standing on the upper Thames, an old town and former Anglo-Saxon settlement. The Roman road from Cirencester passes through and canals pass to north and south. The church, its lofty Tudor tower dominating the town, has work of varying periods from the 12th C to 1930.

CROWCOMBE, SOMERSET - Village at the foot of the Quantock Hills, with an early medieval market cross. The church is adorned with rich 16th C bench-ends and the fine church house is of about the same period. A large Georgian house, Crowcombe Court, stands next to the church.

DARTMOUTH, DEVON - Ancient port at mouth of Dart. Has fine period buildings, notably town houses near Quay and Butterwalk of 1635. Harbour castle ruin. In 12th C Crusader fleets assembled here. Royal Naval College dominates from Hill. Carnival, June; Regatta, August.

DEVIZES, WILTSHIRE - Old market town standing on the Kennet and Avon Canal. Rebuilt Norman castle, good 18th C buildings. St John's church has 12th C work and Norman tower. Museum of Wiltshire's archaeology and natural history reflects wealth of prehistoric sites in the county.

DODDISCOMBSLEIGH, DEVON - Riverside village amid hilly countryside just east of Dartmoor. Former manor house stands beside granite church. Spared from the Roundheads by its remoteness, the church's chief interest lies in glowing 15th C windows said to contain Devon's finest collection of medieval glass.

DORCHESTER, DORSET - Busy medieval county town destroyed by fires in 17th and 18th C. Cromwellian stronghold and scene of Judge Jeffreys' Bloody Assize after Monmouth Rebellion of 1685. Tolpuddle Martyrs were tried in Shire Hall. Museum has Roman and earlier exhibits and Hardy relics.

DULVERTON, SOMERSET - Set among woods and hills of south-west Exmoor, a busy riverside town with a 13th C church. The Rivers Barle and Exe are rich in salmon and trout. The information centre at the Exmoor National Park Headquarters at Dulverton is open throughout the year.

DUNSFORD, DEVON - Picturesque village of thatched white walled cottages 4 miles north-east of Moretonhampstead and on the edge of the Dartmoor National Park.

DUNSTER, SOMERSET - Ancient town with views of Exmoor. The hilltop castle has been continuously occupied since 1070. Medieval prosperity from cloth built 16th C octagonal Yarn Market and the church. A riverside mill, packhorse bridge and 18th C hilltop folly occupy other interesting corners in the town.

E EXETER, DEVON - University city rebuilt after the 1940s around its cathedral. Attractions include 13th C cathedral with fine west front; notable waterfront buildings; Guildhall; Royal Albert Memorial Museum; underground passages; Northcott Theatre.

F FALMOUTH, CORNWALL - Busy port and fishing harbour, popular resort on the balmy Cornish Riviera. Henry VIII's Pendennis Castle faces St Mawes Castle across the broad natural harbour and yacht basin Carrick Roads, which receives 7 rivers.

FROME, SOMERSET - Old market town with modern light industry, its medieval centre watered by the River Frome. Above Cheap Street with its flagstones and watercourse is the church showing work of varying periods. Interesting buildings include 18th C wool merchants' houses.

G GLASTONBURY, SOMERSET - Market town associated with Joseph of Arimathea and the birth of English Christianity. Built around its 7th C abbey said to be the site of King Arthur's burial. Glastonbury Tor with its ancient tower gives panoramic views over flat country and the Mendip Hills.

GRAMPOUND, CORNWALL - Village on the River Fal, 6 miles south-west of St Austell. Probus Gardens 3 miles south-west.

H HATHERLEIGH, DEVON - Set in pastoral countryside, small town with thatched cottages and a cattle market. There are trout and salmon streams close by.

HELSTON, CORNWALL - Handsome town with steep, main street and narrow alleys. In medieval times it was a major port and stannary town. Most buildings date from Regency and Victorian periods. The famous May dance, the Furry, is thought to have pre-Christian origins. A museum occupies the old Butter Market.

HILMARTON, WILTSHIRE - Village 3 miles north of Calne. Traces of prehistoric burial mounds and a medieval village in the area.

HOLSWORTHY, DEVON - Busy rural town and centre of a large farming community. Market day attracts many visitors.

HONITON, DEVON - Old coaching town in undulating farmland. Formerly famous for lace-making, it is now an antiques trade centre and market town. Small museum.

ILFRACOMBE, DEVON - Resort of Victorian grandeur set on hillside between cliffs with sandy coves. At the mouth of the harbour stands an 18th C lighthouse, built over a medieval chapel. There are fine formal gardens and a museum. Chambercombe Manor, an interesting old house, is nearby.

ISLES OF SCILLY - Picturesque group of islands and granitic rocks south-west of Lands End. Peaceful and unspoilt, they are noted for natural beauty, romantic maritime history, silver sands, early flowers and sub-tropical gardens on Tresco. Main island is St. Mary's.

IVYBRIDGE, DEVON - Town set in delightful woodlands on the River Erme. Brunel designed the local railway viaduct. South Dartmoor Leisure Centre.

K KENTON, DEVON - Village between Exeter and Dawlish, separated from the Exe estuary by the large estate of Powderham Castle. Fine 14th C church of red sandstone with a massive medieval rood screen and loft.

KINGSAND, CORNWALL - On Cawsand Bay, on the Cornish side of Plymouth Sound.

KINGSBRIDGE, DEVON - Formerly important as a port, now a market town overlooking head of beautiful, wooded estuary winding deep into rural countryside. Summer art exhibitions; Cookworthy Museum.

L LANGPORT, SOMERSET - Small market town with Anglo-Saxon origins, sloping to River Parrett. Well-known for glove making and, formerly, for eels. Interesting old buildings include some fine local churches.

LEWDOWN, DEVON - Small village on the very edge of Dartmoor. Lydford Castle is 4 miles to the east.

LISKEARD, CORNWALL - Former stannary town with a livestock market and light industry, at the head of a valley running to the coast. Handsome Georgian and Victorian residences and a Victorian Guildhall reflect the prosperity of the mining boom. The large church has an early 20th C tower and a Norman font.

LITTON CHENEY, DORSET - Village 6 miles east of Bridport with stream running past its yellow stone cottages. St Mary's Church dates from the 15th C and contains many brasses and monuments.

LOOE, CORNWALL - Small resort developed around former fishing and smuggling ports occupying the deep estuary of the East and West Looe Rivers. Narrow winding streets, with old inns; museum and art gallery are housed in interesting old buildings. Shark fishing centre, boat trips; busy harbour.

LYME REGIS, DORSET - Pretty, historic fishing town and resort set against the fossil-rich cliffs of Lyme Bay. In medieval times it was an important port and cloth centre. The Cobb, a massive stone breakwater, shelters the ancient harbour which is still lively with boats.

LYNTON, DEVON - Hilltop resort on Exmoor coast linked to its seaside twin, Lynmouth, by a water-operated cliff railway which descends from the town hall. Spectacular surroundings of moorland cliffs with steep chasms of conifer and rocks through which rivers cascade.

M MARTOCK, SOMERSET - Large village with many handsome buildings of hamstone and a beautiful old church with tie-beam roof. Medieval treasurer's house where a 10' x 6' medieval mural has recently been discovered during National Trust restoration work. Georgian market house, 17th C manor.

MELKSHAM, WILTSHIRE - Small industrial town standing on the banks of the River Avon. Old weavers' cottages and Regency houses are grouped around the attractive church which has traces of Norman work. The 18th C Round House, once used for dyeing fleeces, is now a craft centre.

MEVAGISSEY, CORNWALL - Small fishing town, a favourite with holidaymakers. Earlier prosperity came from pilchard fisheries, boat-building and smuggling. By the harbour are fish cellars, some converted, and a local history museum is housed in an old boat-building shed. Handsome Methodist chapel; shark fishing, sailing.

MINEHEAD, SOMERSET - Victorian resort with spreading sands developed around old fishing port on the coast below Exmoor. Former fishermen's cottages stand beside the 17th C harbour; cobbled streets climb the hill in steps to the church. Boat trips, steam railway. Hobby Horse festival 1 May.

MONTACUTE, SOMERSET - Picturesque village named after its steep hill and noted for its splendid hamstone Elizabethan mansion. By the church stands the gatehouse of a Cluniac priory, built with stone from the hilltop castle. An 18th C folly now crowns the hill, where the Holy Cross of Waltham Abbey was found.

MORETONHAMPSTEAD, DEVON - Small market town with a row of 17th C almshouses standing on the Exeter road. Surrounding moorland is scattered with ancient farmhouses, prehistoric sites.

MOUSEHOLE, CORNWALL - Old fishing port completely rebuilt after destruction in the 16th C by Spanish raiders. Twisting lanes and granite cottages with luxuriant gardens rise steeply from the harbour; just south is a private bird sanctuary.

NETHER STOWEY, SOMERSET - Winding village below east slopes of Quantocks with attractive old cottages of varying periods. A Victorian clock tower stands at its centre, where a village road climbs the hill beside a small stream. Cottage owned by Coleridge is open to the public.

NEWQUAY, CORNWALL - Popular resort spread over dramatic cliffs around its old fishing port. Many beaches with abundant sands, caves and rock pools; excellent surf. Pilots' gigs are still raced from the harbour and on the headland stands the stone Huer's House from the pilchard-fishing days.

OKEHAMPTON, DEVON - Busy market town near the high tors of northern Dartmoor. The Victorian church, with William Morris windows and a 15th C tower, stands on the site of a Saxon church. A Norman castle ruin overlooks the river to the west of the town. Museum of Dartmoor Life in a restored mill.

PADSTOW, CORNWALL - Old town encircling its harbour on the Camel Estuary. The 15th C church has notable bench-ends. There are fine houses on North Quay and Raleigh's Court House on South Quay. Tall cliffs and golden sands along the coast and ferry to Rock. Famous 'Obby 'Oss Festival on 1 May.

PAIGNTON, DEVON - Lively seaside resort with a pretty harbour on Torbay. Bronze Age and Saxon sites are occupied by the 15th C church, which has a Norman door and font. The beautiful Chantry Chapel was built by local landowners, the Kirkhams.

PENSFORD, BATH AND NORTH EAST SOMERSET - Village 6 miles south of Bristol and within easy reach of the City of Bath. Chew Valley and Blagdon Lakes close by.

PENZANCE, CORNWALL - Resort and fishing port on Mount's Bay with mainly Victorian promenade and some fine Regency terraces. Former prosperity came from tin trade and pilchard fishing. Grand Georgian style church by harbour. Georgian Egyptian building at head of Chapel Street and Morrab Gardens.

PIDDLETRENTHIDE, DORSET - Situated on the River Piddle, north of Puddletown and Dorchester. Norman church with 15th C towers.

PILLATON, CORNWALL - Peaceful village on the slopes of the River Lynher in steeply-wooded country near the Devon border. Within easy reach of the coast and rugged walking country on Bodmin Moor.

PLYMOUTH, DEVON - Devon's largest city, major port and naval base. Old houses on the Barbican and ambitious architecture in modern centre, with new National Marine Aquarium, museum and art gallery, the Dome - a heritage centre on the Hoe. Superb coastal views over Plymouth Sound from the Hoe.

PORLOCK, SOMERSET - Village set between steep Exmoor hills and the sea at the head of beautiful Porlock Vale. The narrow street shows a medley of building styles. South westward is Porlock Weir with its old houses and tiny harbour and further along the shore at Culbone is England's smallest church.

PORT ISAAC, CORNWALL - Old fishing port of whitewashed cottages, twisting stairways and narrow alleys. A stream splashes down through the centre to the harbour. Nearby stands a 19th C folly, Doyden Castle, with a magnificent view of the coast.

PORTHCURNO, CORNWALL - Beautifully-sited village near a beach with white sand and turquoise sea enclosed in granite cliffs. The Minack open air theatre of concrete and granite slabs, perched 200 ft above the sea, has a good view of Treryn Dinas to the east.

PORTLAND, DORSET - Joined by a narrow isthmus to the coast, a stony promontory sloping from the lofty landward side to a lighthouse on Portland Bill at its southern tip. Villages are built of the white limestone for which the 'isle' is famous.

RADSTOCK, BATH AND NORTH SOMERSET - Thriving small town ideally situated for touring the Mendip Hills.

ROCK, CORNWALL - Small resort and boating centre beside the abundant sands of the Camel Estuary. A fine golf-course stretches northward along the shore to Brea Hill, thought to be the site of a Roman settlement. Passenger ferry service from Padstow.

SALCOMBE, DEVON - Sheltered yachting resort of whitewashed houses and narrow streets in a balmy setting on the Salcombe Estuary. Palm, myrtle and other Mediterranean plants flourish. There are sandy bays and creeks for boating.

SALISBURY, WILTSHIRE - Beautiful city and ancient regional capital set amid water meadows. Buildings of all periods are dominated by the cathedral whose spire is the tallest in England. Built between 1220 and 1258, it is one of the purest examples of Early English architecture.

SEATON, DEVON - Small resort lying near the mouth of the River Axe. A mile-long beach extends to the dramatic cliffs of Beer Head. Annual art exhibition in July.

SHEPTON MALLET, SOMERSET - Historic town in the Mendip foothills, important in Roman times and site of many significant archaeological finds. Cloth industry reached its peak in the 17th C, and many fine examples of cloth merchants' houses remain. Beautiful parish church, market cross, local history museum, Collett Park.

SHERBORNE, DORSET - Dorset's 'Cathedral City' of medieval streets, golden hamstone buildings and great abbey church, resting place of Saxon kings. Formidable 12th C castle ruins and Sir Walter Raleigh's splendid Tudor mansion and deer park. Street markets, leisure centre, many cultural activities.

SHIPHAM, SOMERSET - Peaceful village on the slopes of the Mendip Hills.

SIDMOUTH, DEVON - Charming resort set amid lofty red cliffs where the River Sid meets the sea. The wealth of ornate Regency and Victorian villas recalls the time when this was one of the south coast's most exclusive resorts. Museum; August International Festival of Folk Arts.

SOMERTON, SOMERSET - Old market town, important in Saxon times, situated at a gap in the hills south-east of Sedgemoor. Attractive red-roofed stone houses surround the 17th C octagonal market cross and among other handsome buildings are the Town Hall and almshouses of about the same period.

SPREYTON, DEVON - Village situated 6 miles east of Okehampton, just north of the Dartmoor National Park. In 1802, Tom Cobley and his friends travelled from the village to Widecombe Fair.

ST AGNES, CORNWALL - Small town in a once-rich mining area on the north coast. Terraced cottages and granite houses slope to the church. Some old mine workings remain, but the attraction must be the magnificent coastal scenery and superb walks. St Agnes Beacon offers one of Cornwall's most extensive views.

ST AUSTELL, CORNWALL - Leading market town, the meeting point of old and new Cornwall. One mile from St Austell Bay with its sandy beaches, old fishing villages and attractive countryside. Ancient narrow streets, pedestrian shopping precincts. Fine church of Pentewan stone and Italianate Town Hall.

ST IVES, CORNWALL - Old fishing port, artists' colony and holiday town with good surfing beach. Fishermen's cottages, granite fish cellars, a sandy harbour and magnificent headlands typify a charm that has survived since the 19th C pilchard boom. Tate Gallery opened in 1993.

ST JUST-IN-PENWITH, CORNWALL - Coastal parish of craggy moorland scattered with engine houses and chimney stacks of disused mines. The old mining town of St Just has handsome 19th C granite buildings. North of the town are the dramatic ruined tin mines at Botallack.

ST KEW, CORNWALL - Old village sheltered by trees standing beside a stream. The church is noted for its medieval glass showing the Passion and the remains of a scene of the Tree of Jesse.

ST MAWGAN, CORNWALL - Pretty village of great historic interest, on wooded slopes in the Vale of Lanherne. At its centre, an old stone bridge over the River Menahyl is overlooked by the church with its lofty buttressed tower. Among ancient stone crosses in the churchyard is a 15th C lantern cross with carved figures.

SWINDON, WILTSHIRE - Wiltshire's industrial and commercial centre, an important railway town in the 19th C, situated just north of the Marlborough Downs. The railway village created in the mid-19th C has been preserved. Railway museum, art gallery, theatre and leisure centre. Designer shopping village.

TAUNTON, SOMERSET - County town, well-known for its public schools, sheltered by gentle hill-ranges on the River Tone. Medieval prosperity from wool has continued in marketing and manufacturing and the town retains many fine period buildings. Museum.

TAVISTOCK, DEVON - Old market town beside the River Tavy on the western edge of Dartmoor. Developed around its 10th C abbey, of which some fragments remain, it became a stannary town in 1305 when tin-streaming thrived on the moors. Tavistock Goose Fair, October.

TINTAGEL, CORNWALL - Coastal village near the legendary home of King Arthur. There is a lofty headland with the ruin of a Norman castle and traces of a Celtic monastery are still visible in the turf.

TORQUAY, DEVON - Devon's grandest resort, developed from a fishing village. Smart apartments and terraces rise from the seafront and Marine Drive along the headland gives views of beaches and colourful cliffs.

TOTNES, DEVON - Old market town steeply built near the head of the Dart Estuary. Remains of motte and bailey castle, medieval gateways, a noble church, 16th C Guildhall and medley of period houses recall former wealth from cloth and shipping, continued in rural and water industries.

TROWBRIDGE, WILTSHIRE - Wiltshire's administrative centre, a handsome market and manufacturing town with a wealth of merchants' houses and other Georgian buildings.

TRURO, CORNWALL - Cornwall's administrative centre and cathedral city, set at the head of Truro River on the Fal Estuary. A medieval stannary town, it handled mineral ore from west Cornwall; fine Georgian buildings recall its heyday as a society haunt in the second mining boom.

WADEBRIDGE, CORNWALL - Old market town with Cornwall's finest medieval bridge, spanning the Camel at its highest navigable point. Twice widened, the bridge is said to have been built on woolpacks sunk in the unstable sands of the river bed.

WARMINSTER, WILTSHIRE - Attractive stone-built town high up to the west of Salisbury Plain. A market town, it originally thrived on cloth and wheat. Many prehistoric camps and barrows nearby, along with Longleat House and Safari Park.

WASHFORD, SOMERSET - Village 2 miles west of Williton and a good centre for many interesting walks. On the edge of the village is Cleeve Abbey, founded in the 13th C by the Cistercians, and with remarkably complete dormitory and refectory.

WELLS, SOMERSET - Small city set beneath the southern slopes of the Mendips. Built between 1180 and 1424, the magnificent cathedral is preserved in much of its original glory and with its ancient precincts forms one of our loveliest and most unified groups of medieval buildings.

WESTON-SUPER-MARE, NORTH SOMERSET - Large, friendly resort developed in the 19th C. Traditional seaside attractions include theatres and a dance hall. The museum has a Victorian seaside gallery and Iron Age finds from a hill fort on Worlebury Hill in Weston Woods.

WESTWARD HO!, DEVON - Small resort, whose name comes from the title of Charles Kingsley's famous novel, on Barnstaple Bay, close to the Taw and Torridge Estuary. There are good sands and a notable golf-course - one of the oldest in Britain.

WEYMOUTH, DORSET - Ancient port and one of the south's earliest resorts. Curving beside a long, sandy beach, the elegant Georgian esplanade is graced with a statue of George III and a cheerful Victorian Jubilee clock tower. Museum, Sea-Life Centre.

WIDECOMBE-IN-THE-MOOR, DEVON - Old village in pastoral country under the high tors of East Dartmoor. The 'Cathedral of the Moor' stands near a tiny square, once used for archery practice, which has a 16th C Church House among other old buildings.

WILTON, WILTSHIRE - In ancient times a county town, now an important sheep trading centre and famous for its carpets and 16th C Wilton House. Fragments of medieval churches and hospitals remain and the flamboyant 19th C Italianate church stands near a series of ruined arches.

WINSFORD, SOMERSET - Small village in Exmoor National Park, on the River Exe in splendid walking country under Winsford Hill. On the other side of the hill is a Celtic standing stone, the Caratacus Stone, and nearby across the River Barle stretches an ancient packhorse bridge, Tarr Steps.

WOOLACOMBE, DEVON - Between Morte Point and Baggy Point, Woolacombe and Mortehoe offer 3 miles of the finest sand and surf on this outstanding coastline. Much of the area is owned by the National Trust.

WOOTTON BASSETT, WILTSHIRE - Small hillside town with attractive old buildings and a 13th C church. The church and the half-timbered town hall were both restored in the 19th C and the stocks and ducking pool are preserved.

YELVERTON, DEVON - Village on the edge of Dartmoor, where ponies wander over the flat common. Buckland Abbey is 2 miles south-west, while Burrator Reservoir is 2 miles to the east.

YEOVIL, SOMERSET - Lively market town, famous for glove making, set in dairying country beside the River Yeo. Interesting parish church. Museum of South Somerset at Hendford Manor.

YEOVILTON, SOMERSET - Village just south of A303. Royal Naval Air Station and Fleet Air Arm Museum situated close by.

SOUTH of England

A seafaring region with 800 years of nautical heritage to enjoy in its busy harbours and family resorts. For landlubbers there's gentle countryside, Georgian towns, modern cities and outstanding historic houses too.

classic sights

Blenheim Palace – a gilded Italian palace in an English park
Oxford – University town with ancient colleges
Claydon House – unusual interiors in the Rococo, Gothick and Chinoiserie styles

coast & country

Chiltern Hills – tranquil country walks
New Forest – historic wood and heathland
Studland Bay – glorious sweeping beach

glorious gardens

Cliveden – a series of distinctive and delightful gardens
Mottisfont Abbey – the perfect English rose garden

maritime history

Portsmouth Historic Dockyard – Henry VIII's Mary Rose, HMS Victory and HMS Warrior

distinctively different

Sandham Memorial Chapel – houses Stanley Spencer's WW1 murals

The counties of Berkshire, Buckinghamshire, Dorset (Eastern), Hampshire, Isle of Wight and Oxfordshire

FOR MORE INFORMATION CONTACT:
Southern Tourist Board
40 Chamberlayne Road, Eastleigh,
Hampshire SO50 5JH
Tel: (023) 8062 5505 Fax: (023) 8062 0010
Email: info@southerntb.co.uk
Internet: www.visitbritain.com

The Pictures:
1 Freshwater Bay, Isle of Wight
2 Radcliffe Camera, Oxford
3 Lulworth Cove, Dorset

Places to Visit - see pages 446-449
Where to Stay - see pages 450-498

PLACES to visit

You will find hundreds of interesting places to visit during your stay, just some of which are listed in these pages. Contact any Tourist Information Centre in the region for more ideas on days out.

Beaulieu National Motor Museum

Beaulieu, Brockenhurst, Hampshire SO42 7ZN
Tel: (01590) 612345 www.beaulieu.co.uk
Motor museum with over 250 exhibits showing the history of motoring from 1896. Also Palace House, Wheels Experience, Beaulieu Abbey ruins and a display of monastic life.

Bekonscot Model Village

Warwick Road, Beaconsfield, Buckinghamshire HP9 2PL
Tel: (01494) 672919 www.bekonscot.org.uk
The oldest model village in the world, Bekonscot depicts rural England in the 1930s, where time has stood still for 70 years.

Blenheim Palace

Woodstock, Oxfordshire OX20 1PX
Tel: (01993) 811325 www.blenheimpalace.com
Home of the 11th Duke of Marlborough. Birthplace of Sir Winston Churchill. Designed by Vanbrugh in the English baroque style. Landscaped by `Capability' Brown.

Breamore House

Breamore, Fordingbridge, Hampshire SP6 2DF
Tel: (01725) 512233
Elizabethan manor house of 1583, with fine collection of works of art. Furniture, tapestries, needlework, paintings mainly 17thC and 18thC Dutch School.

Broughton Castle

Banbury, Oxfordshire OX15 5EB
Tel: (01295) 276070
Medieval moated house built in 1300 and enlarged between 1550 and 1600. The home of Lord and Lady Saye and Sele and family home for 600 years. Has Civil War connections.

Buckinghamshire County Museum

Church Street, Aylesbury, Buckinghamshire HP20 2QP
Tel: (01296) 331441
www.buckscc.gov.uk/tourism/museum
Lively hands-on, innovative museum complex consisting of county heritage displays, regional art gallery and Roald Dahl Children's Gallery in lovely garden setting.

Carisbrooke Castle

Newport, Isle of Wight PO30 1XY
Tel: (01983) 522107 www.english-heritage.org.uk
A splendid Norman castle where Charles I was imprisoned. The governor's lodge houses the county museum. Wheelhouse with wheel operated by donkeys.

Compton Acres

Canford Cliffs Road, Canford Cliffs,
Poole, Dorset BH13 7ES
Tel: (01202) 700778 www.comptonacres.co.uk
Ten separate and distinct gardens of the world. The gardens include Italian, Japanese, Indian glen and Spanish water garden. Country crafts and 'Off the Beaten Track Trail'.

Cotswold Wildlife Park

Bradwell Grove, Burford, Oxford, Oxfordshire OX18 4JW
Tel: (01993) 823006
Wildlife park in 200 acres (81 ha) of gardens and woodland with a variety of animals from all over the world.

The D Day Museum and Overlord Embroidery

Clarence Esplanade, Portsmouth, Hampshire PO5 3NT
Tel: (023) 9282 7261
www.portsmouthmuseums.co.uk
The magnificent 272 ft- (83 m-) long 'Overlord Embroidery' depicts the allied invasion of Normandy on 6 June 1944. Sound guides available in 4 languages.

Dicot Railway Centre

Great Western Society, Didcot, Oxfordshire OX11 7NJ
Tel: (01235) 817200
www.didcotrailwaycentre.org.uk
Living museum recreating the golden age of the Great Western Railway. Steam locomotives and trains, engine shed and small relics museum.

Exbury Gardens

Exbury Estate Office, Exbury, Southampton, Hampshire SO45 1AZ
Tel: (023) 8089 1203 www.exbury.co.uk.
Over 200 acres (81 ha) of woodland garden, including the Rothschild collection of rhododendrons, azaleas, camellias and magnolias.

Flagship Portsmouth

Porter's Lodge, 1/7 College Road, HM Naval Base, Portsmouth, Hampshire PO1 3LJ
Tel: (023) 9286 1533 www.flagship.org.uk
The world's greatest historic ships: Mary Rose, HMS Victory, HMS Warrior 1860. Royal Naval Museum, 'Warships by Water' tours, Dockyard Apprentice exhibition.

Gilbert White's House and Garden and The Oats Museum

The Wakes, High Street, Selborne, Alton, Hampshire GU34 3JH
Tel: (01420) 511275
Historic house and garden, home of Gilbert White, author of 'The Natural History of Selborne'. Exhibition on Frank Oates, explorer, and Captain Lawrence Oates of Antarctica fame.

The Hawk Conservancy and Country Park

Andover, Hampshire SP11 8DY
Tel: (01264) 772252 www.hawk-conservancy.org
Unique to Great Britain – 'Valley of the Eagles' held here daily at 1400.

Jane Austen's House

Chawton, Alton, Hampshire GU34 1SD
Tel: (01420) 83262
A 17thC house where Jane Austen lived from 1809-1817 and wrote or revised her six great novels. Letters, pictures, memorabilia, garden with old-fashioned flowers.

Kingston Lacy

Wimborne Minster, Dorset BH21 4EA
Tel: (01202) 883402 www.nationaltrust.org.uk
A 17thC house designed for Sir Ralph Bankes by Sir Roger Pratt, altered by Sir Charles Barry in the19thC. Collection of paintings, 250-acre (101-ha) wooded park, herd of Devon cattle.

Legoland Windsor

Winkfield Road, Windsor, Berkshire SL4 4AY
Tel: (0870) 504 0404 www.legoland.co.uk
A family park with hands-on activities, rides, themed playscapes and more Lego bricks than you ever dreamed possible!

The Pictures:
1 Blenheim Palace, Oxfordshire
2 HMS Victory, Portsmouth
3 Deer at Bolderwood, New Forest
4 Poole, Dorset
5 Oxford
6 Swan Green, New Forest

The Living Rainforest

Hampstead Norreys, Newbury, Berkshire RG18 0TN
Tel: (01635) 202444 www.livingrainforest.org
Two tropical rainforests, all under cover, approximately 20,000 sq ft (1,858 sq m). Collection of rare and exotic tropical plants together with small representation of wildlife in rainforest.

Manor Farm (Farm and Museum)

Manor Farm Country Park, Pylands Lane, Bursledon, Southampton, Hampshire SO30 2ER
Tel: (01489) 787055
www.hants.gov.uk/countryside/manorfarm
Traditional Hampshire farmstead with range of buildings, farm animals, machinery and equipment, pre-1950s farmhouse and 13thC church set for 1900.
Living history site.

Marwell Zoological Park

Colden Common, Winchester, Hampshire SO21 1JH
Tel: (01962) 777407
Set in 100 acres (40.5 ha) of parkland surrounding Marwell Hall. Venue suitable for all age groups including disabled.

Oceanarium

Pier Approach, West Beach, Bournemouth, Dorset BH2 5AA
Tel: (01202) 311993 www.oceanarium.co.uk
Situated in the heart of Bournemouth next to the pier, the Oceanarium will take you on a fascinating voyage of the undersea world with creatures such as elegant seahorses and sinister sharks.

Osborne House

Yorke Avenue, East Cowes, Isle of Wight PO32 6JY
Tel: (01983) 200022 www.english-heritage.com
Queen Victoria and Prince Albert's seaside holiday home. Swiss Cottage where royal children learnt cooking and gardening. Victorian carriage service to Swiss Cottage.

The Oxford Story

6 Broad Street, Oxford, Oxfordshire OX1 3AJ
Tel: (01865) 728822 www.heritageattractions.co.uk
An excellent introduction to Oxford – experience 900 years of University history in one hour. From scientists to poets, astronomers to comedians.

Paultons Park

Ower, Romsey, Hampshire SO51 6AL
Tel: (023) 8081 4442
A full day out for all the family with over 40 attractions. Rides, play areas, entertainments, museums, birds and animals, beautiful gardens and lots more.

River and Rowing Museum

Mill Meadows, Henley-on-Thames, Oxfordshire RG9 1BF
Tel: (01491) 415600 www.rrm.co.uk
A unique, award-winning museum with galleries dedicated to rowing, the River Thames and the town of Henley. Special exhibitions run throughout the year.

Royal Navy Submarine Museum and HMS Alliance

Haslar Jetty Road, Gosport, Hampshire PO12 2AS
Tel: (023) 9252 9217 www.rnsubmus.co.uk
HM Submarine Alliance, HM Submarine No 1 (Holland 1), midget submarines and models of every type of submarine from earliest days to present nuclear age.

Swanage Railway

Station House, Swanage, Dorset BH19 1HB
Tel: (01929) 425800 www.swanrail.demon.co.uk
Enjoy a nostalgic steam train ride on the Purbeck line. Steam trains run every weekend throughout the year with daily running from April to October.

The Vyne

Sherborne St John, Basingstoke, Hampshire RG24 9HL
Tel: (01256) 881337 www.nationaltrust.org.uk
Original house dating back to Henry VIII's time. Extensively altered in the mid 17thC. Tudor chapel, beautiful gardens and lake.

Waterperry Gardens

Waterperry, Oxford, Oxfordshire OX33 1JZ
Tel: (01844) 339254 www.waterperrygardens.co.uk
Ornamental gardens covering six acres (2 ha) of the 83-acre (33.5-ha) 18thC Waterperry House estate. Saxon village church, garden shop, teashop and art and craft gallery.

Whitchurch Silk Mill

28 Winchester Street, Whitchurch, Hampshire RG28 7AL
Tel: (01256) 892065
Unique Georgian silk-weaving watermill, now a working museum producing fine silk fabrics on Victorian machinery. Riverside garden, tearooms for light meals, silk gift shop.

Windsor Castle

Windsor, Berkshire SL4 1NJ
Tel: (01753) 869898 www.royal.gov.uk
Official residence of HM The Queen and royal residence for 9 centuries. State apartments, Queen Mary's Doll's House.

Find out more about the
SOUTH of England

Further information about holidays and attractions in the South of England is available from:

SOUTHERN TOURIST BOARD
40 Chamberlayne Road, Eastleigh, Hampshire SO50 5JH.
Tel: (023) 8062 5505 Fax: (023) 8062 0010
Email: info@southerntb.co.uk
Internet: www.visitbritain.com

Getting to the
SOUTH of England

BY ROAD: A good road network links London and the rest of the UK with major Southern destinations. The M27 provides a near continuous motorway route along the south coast and the M25/M3/A33 provides a direct route from London to Winchester and Southampton. The scenic A31 stretches from London, through Hampshire and to mid Dorset, whilst the M40/A34 have considerably cut travelling times from the West Midlands to the South. The M25 has speeded up access to Berkshire on the M4, Buckinghamshire and Oxfordshire on the M40.

BY RAIL: From London's Waterloo, trains travel to Portsmouth, Southampton and Bournemouth approximately three times an hour. From these stations, frequent trains go to Poole, Salisbury and Winchester. Further information on rail journeys in the South of England can be obtained from 08457 484950.

he Pictures:
River Isis, Oxford
Alum Bay, Isle of Wight

Where to stay in the South of England

Accommodation entries in this region are listed in alphabetical order of place name, and then in alphabetical order of establishment.

Map references refer to the colour location maps at front of this guide. The first number indicates the map to use; the letter and number which follow refer to the grid reference on the map.

At-a-glance symbols at the end of each accommodation entry give useful information about services and facilities. A key to symbols can be found inside the back cover flap. Keep this open for easy reference.

A brief description of the towns and villages offering accommodation in the entries which follow, can be found at the end of this section.

A complete listing of all the English Tourism Council assessed accommodation covered by this guide appears at the back of the guide.

ALDWORTH, West Berkshire Map ref 2C2

◆◆◆◆

FIELDVIEW COTTAGE
Bell Lane, Aldworth, Reading RG8 9SB
T: (01635) 578964
E: chunt@fieldview.freeserve.co.uk

B&B per night:
S £25.00–£30.00
D £50.00–£60.00

OPEN All year round

Fieldview is a pretty cottage in the centre of Aldworth, situated high on the Downs and adjoining the Ridgeway, an ideal base for walking, cycling and horse riding. M4/A34 J12/13, Oxford, Bath, Windsor and Heathrow within easy reach. Only 2.5 miles from main railway line – Paddington 45 minutes.

Bedrooms: 2 double/twin
Bathrooms: 2 private

⋒ 🐎 ⌂ 🖿 ♿ 🕯 🖩 ⑤ ✂ 🎞 🖪 🚜 P

CHECK THE MAPS
The colour maps at the front of this guide show all the cities, towns and villages for which you will find accommodation entries. Refer to the town index to find the page on which they are listed.

◆◆◆◆
Silver
Award

Situated on the edge of the Meon Valley and on the boundary of the village of Lower Farringdon. Guests are assured of a warm welcome with comfortable accommodation in a relaxed atmosphere. Lovely garden; excellent breakfast. Ideal touring/ walking base. Many places of interest and good pubs/restaurants nearby. Parking.

BOUNDARY HOUSE
B & B
Gosport Road, Lower Farringdon, Alton
GU34 3DH
T: (01420) 587076
F: (01420) 587047
E: BoundaryS@messages.co.uk

Bedrooms: 1 single,
2 double/twin
Bathrooms: 1 en suite,
2 private

CC: Delta, Mastercard,
Switch, Visa

B&B per night:
S £25.00
D £50.00

♪ ⌘ ▤ ⛶ ⛭ ⌧ ⦿ ▥ ⌕ ⎙ ⚑ ⚘ ⛟ P

◆◆◆

THE VICARAGE
East Worldham, Alton GU34 3AS
T: (01420) 82392 & 07778 800804
F: (01420) 82367
E: wenrose@bigfoot.com
I: www.altonbedandbreakfast.co.uk

Bedrooms: 1 single,
1 double/twin, 1 triple/
multiple

B&B per night:
S £18.00–£20.00
D £34.00–£36.00

OPEN All year round

Warm, friendly, peaceful country vicarage near Selbourne and Chawton. Half an hour from Portsmouth and Winchester. Chaucer's wife buried in church opposite. Good food in nearby pub.

♪ ⌘5 ▤ ⛶ ⛭ ⌧ ⦿ ⌕ ⎙ ⚑ ⚘ 🐎 ⛟ P

◆◆◆◆

39 QUARRENDON ROAD
Amersham HP7 9EF
T: (01494) 727959

Bedrooms: 1 single,
1 double/twin

B&B per night:
S £25.00–£30.00
D £48.00–£52.00

Detached house, comfortable, with friendly atmosphere. Residents' lounge, private parking, pleasant garden. One mile to London Underground station, easy reach of M25, M40 and A40.

⌘12 ▤ ⛶ ⛭ ⌧ ⦿ ▨ ⎙ ⚘ ⛟ P

◆◆◆◆

Listed thatched cottage in delightful secluded garden, providing relaxed and cosy atmosphere in peaceful village setting. Large bedrooms with en suite facilities. Sitting room with open log fire in winter. Excellent stopover for West Country and airport travellers (A303 half a mile). Stonehenge only 15 minutes' drive, Salisbury and Winchester 30 minutes.

BROADWATER
Amport, Andover SP11 8AY
T: (01264) 772240
F: (01264) 772240
E: carolyn@dmac.co.uk
I: www.dmac.co.uk/carolyn

Bedrooms: 2 double/
twin
Bathrooms: 2 en suite

CC: Delta, Mastercard,
Switch, Visa

B&B per night:
S £30.00–£35.00
D £50.00–£60.00

OPEN All year round

♪ ⌘ ▤ ⛭ ⌧ ⦿ ▨ ⎙ ⚑ ⚘ ⛟ ⌂ P

SPECIAL BREAKS
Many establishments offer special promotions and themed breaks.
These are highlighted in red. (All such offers are subject to availability.)

ANDOVER, Hampshire Map ref 2C2 *Tourist Information Centre Tel: (01264) 324320*

 ♦♦♦

AMBERLEY HOTEL
70 Weyhill Road, Andover
SP10 3NP
T: (01264) 352224 & 364676
F: (01264) 392555
E: amberleyand@fsbdial.co.uk.

Compact 15 bedroom hotel, all en suite. Attractive a la carte and table d'hote restaurant and bar lounge. Private meetings, wedding receptions can be booked in Wightman room.

Bedrooms: 3 single,
9 double/twin, 3 triple/
multiple
Bathrooms: 15 en suite

Lunch available
Evening meal available
CC: Amex, Diners,
Mastercard, Switch, Visa

B&B per night:
S £45.00–£60.00
D Min £60.00

HB per person:
DY Min £40.00

OPEN All year round

ASCOT, Berkshire Map ref 2C2

♦♦♦♦
Silver
Award

ASCOT CORNER
Wells Lane, Ascot SL5 7DY
T: (01344) 627722
F: (01344) 873965
E: susan.powell@easynet.co.uk

Georgian-style family home in lovely gardens. Ample enclosed parking. Walking distance Ascot racecourse/Windsor Great Park. Welcoming caring atmosphere of casual luxury and elegance.

Bedrooms: 5 double/
twin
Bathrooms: 5 en suite

Evening meal available
CC: Amex, Delta,
Mastercard, Switch, Visa

B&B per night:
D £75.00–£90.00

OPEN Jan–Dec

♦♦♦

TANGLEWOOD
Birch Lane, off Longhill Road,
Chavey Down, Ascot SL5 8RF
T: (01344) 882528

Spacious, modern bungalow. Quiet, secluded location, large wooded garden, safe parking. Convenient Wentworth, Sunningdale, Ascot, Bracknell, Thames Valley and London. Telephone for directions/map. Non-smoking.

Bedrooms: 2 single,
2 double/twin
Bathrooms: 4 en suite

B&B per night:
S £40.00–£60.00
D £60.00–£100.00

OPEN All year round

ASHURST, Hampshire Map ref 2C3

♦♦♦

FOREST GATE LODGE
161 Lyndhurst Road, Ashurst,
Southampton SO40 7AW
T: (023) 8029 3026

B&B per night:
S Min £23.00
D Min £46.00

OPEN All year round

Large Victorian house with direct access to New Forest and its attractions – walks, riding, cycling. Pubs and restaurants nearby, Lyndhurst – 'capital of the New Forest' – 5 minutes' drive. Full English breakfast or vegetarian by prior arrangement. Special rates October–March: 3 nights for the price of 2.

Bedrooms: 1 single,
3 double/twin, 2 triple/
multiple
Bathrooms: 5 en suite

Special rates: 3 nights for price of 2, weekdays 1 Oct–1 Apr.

AYLESBURY, Buckinghamshire Map ref 2C1 *Tourist Information Centre Tel: (01296) 330559*

♦♦♦

THE OLD FORGE BARN
Ridings Way, Cublington,
Leighton Buzzard LU7 0LW
T: (01296) 681194
F: (01296) 681194
E: waples@ukonline.co.uk

Converted barn in village location, close to Aylesbury, Leighton Buzzard, Milton Keynes. Restaurants and pubs nearby. Friendly welcome.

Bedrooms: 1 double/
twin

B&B per night:
S £25.00
D £40.00

OPEN All year round

MAP REFERENCES The map references refer to the colour maps at the front of this guide. The first figure is the map number; the letter and figure which follow indicate the grid reference on the map.

◆◆◆◆ **THE LODGE**

Main Road, Middleton Cheney,
Banbury OX17 2PP
T: (01295) 710355

Bedrooms: 2 double/
twin
Bathrooms: 2 en suite

B&B per night:
D £54.00–£56.00

OPEN All year round

200-year-old lodge in lovely countryside, on outskirts of historic village, 2 miles east of Banbury on A422 and 1 mile from M40.

🐎3 🔧 ⑤ 👗 ◐ ⬛ ☐ ❋ 🚲 🏫 P

◆◆◆

PROSPECT HOUSE
GUEST HOUSE

70 Oxford Road, Banbury OX16 9AN
T: (01295) 268749 & 07798 772578
F: (01295) 268749

B&B per night:
S £34.00–£38.00
D £42.00–£48.00

OPEN All year round

Detached house standing in lovely gardens, situated on the A4260 only a few minutes' walk from Banbury Cross and Oxfordshire's newest regional shopping centre (Castle Quay). Modern en suite rooms, TV, tea and coffee, on-site parking. Conveniently situated for Blenheim Palace, Warwick Castle and Stratford-upon-Avon.

Bedrooms: 1 single,
5 double/twin, 4 triple/
multiple
Bathrooms: 10 en suite

CC: Amex, Mastercard,
Visa

Special weekend rates Jan–May.

⚔🐎 🔧 📧 ☐ ✦ ⑤ ✂ 👗 ⬛ ☐ ❋ 🚲 P

◆◆◆ **ST MARTINS HOUSE**

Warkworth, Banbury OX17 2AG
T: (01295) 712684
F: (01295) 712838

Bedrooms: 2 double/
twin
Bathrooms: 1 en suite,
1 private

Lunch available
Evening meal available

B&B per night:
S £25.00–£27.50
D £50.00–£55.00

HB per person:
DY £43.00–£45.50

OPEN All year round

600-year-old Listed converted barn with galleried dining room. Comfortable en suite rooms with TV. Safe parking, evening meals, French and English country cooking.

⚔🐎2 ☐ 🍷 ⑤ ✂ ⬛ ☐ ❋ 🐐 🚲 🏫 P

◆◆◆◆ **BARTLEY FARMHOUSE**

Ringwood Road, Bartley,
Southampton SO40 7LD
T: (023) 8081 4194
F: (023) 8081 4117

Bedrooms: 3 double/
twin
Bathrooms: 3 private

B&B per night:
S £40.00
D £50.00–£60.00

OPEN All year round

Whether bringing your horse to ride in the forest, needing a mountain bike or simply a chair in the garden, a truly delightful place to stay.

⚔🍷 ⑤ ✂ 👗 ⬛ ☐ ∪ ❋ 🐐 🚲 P

TOWN INDEX

This can be found at the back of the guide. If you know where you want to stay, the index will give you the page number listing accommodation in your chosen town, city or village.

♦♦♦♦

EVERGLADES

81 Sea Road, Barton on Sea, New Milton
BH25 7ND
T: (01425) 617350 & 0773 017 7625

B&B per night:
S £23.00–£35.00
D £46.00–£56.00

OPEN All year round

Charming cottage, beautifully appointed en suite bedrooms, one ground floor, will delight any discerning guest, yards from level cliff-top walks, with panoramic views across the Solent and Isle of Wight. Beaches, golf, glorious New Forest all nearby. Christchurch, Bournemouth, Lymington, Southampton short drive. Excellent restaurants close by. Spoilt for choice.

Bedrooms: 2 double/twin
Bathrooms: 2 en suite

⬚⬚⬚⬚⬚⬚⬚⬚⬚⬚⬚⬚⬚⬚⬚ P

♦♦♦

WESTBURY HOUSE

12 Greenacre, Barton on Sea, New Milton
BH25 7BS
T: (01425) 620935 & 07976 871756
E: les@westbury-house.freeserve.co.uk
I: www.westbury-house.freeserve.co.uk

B&B per night:
S £25.00–£35.00
D £50.00

OPEN All year round

Come and experience our welcome. Awaken to the morning bird song in our quiet cul-de-sac. Breakfast in our flower filled conservatory overlooking our lovely garden and water features. Walk to superb local restaurants, a theatre, the sea and golf course. Drive to the New Forest, Bournemouth, Poole, Southampton, Lymington.

Bedrooms: 3 double/twin
Bathrooms: 3 en suite

CC: Amex, Delta, Mastercard, Switch, Visa

⬚⬚12⬚⬚⬚⬚⬚⬚⬚⬚⬚⬚⬚⬚⬚⬚ P

♦♦♦

CEDAR COURT
Reading Road, Hook RG27 9DB
T: (01256) 762178
F: (01256) 762178

Bedrooms: 2 single, 4 double/twin
Bathrooms: 5 en suite

CC: Delta, Mastercard, Switch, Visa

B&B per night:
S £30.00–£45.00
D £45.00–£50.00

OPEN All year round

Comfortable ground floor accommodation with delightful gardens. On B3349 between the M3 and M4, 6 miles east of Basingstoke, 1 hour from London and the coast.

⬚⬚⬚⬚⬚⬚⬚⬚⬚⬚⬚⬚ P

♦♦♦♦
Silver
Award

FERNBANK HOTEL
4 Fairfields Road, Basingstoke
RG21 3DR
T: (01256) 321191
F: (01256) 321191
E: availability@fernbankhotel.co.uk
I: www.fernbankhotel.co.uk

Bedrooms: 8 single, 8 double/twin
Bathrooms: 16 en suite

CC: Amex, Delta, Mastercard, Switch, Visa

B&B per night:
S £62.00–£80.00
D £70.00–£90.00

OPEN All year round

Extremely well-appointed family-run hotel, full of character. In residential area within a short walk of town's facilities. Charming conservatory/lounge. First class breakfast.

⬚⬚⬚⬚⬚⬚⬚⬚⬚⬚⬚⬚⬚⬚⬚ P

IMPORTANT NOTE
Information on accommodation listed in this guide has been supplied by the proprietors. As changes may occur you are advised to check details at the time of booking.

BEACONSFIELD, Buckinghamshire Map ref 2C2

◆◆◆◆ **HIGHCLERE FARM**

Newbarn Lane, Seer Green,	Bedrooms: 1 single,	CC: Amex, Delta, Diners,
Beaconsfield HP9 2QZ	6 double/twin, 2 triple/	Mastercard, Switch, Visa
T: (01494) 875665 & 874505	multiple	
F: (01494) 875238	Bathrooms: 9 en suite	

B&B per night:
S £45.00
D £60.00

OPEN Jan, Mar–Dec

Comfortable, family-run annexed farm accommodation with all rooms en suite. Two family rooms available. Quiet location, yet within easy reach of Windsor (12 miles) and London.

BEAULIEU, Hampshire Map ref 2C3

◆◆◆

DALE FARM HOUSE
Manor Road, Applemore Hill, Dibden,
Southampton SO45 5TJ
T: (023) 8084 9632
F: (023) 8084 0285
E: chris@dalefarmhouse.fsnet.co.uk

B&B per night:
S £25.00–£30.00
D £40.00–£48.00

OPEN All year round

Beautiful 18thC converted farmhouse in secluded wooded setting with direct access for walks or cycling. Peaceful garden in which to unwind and a bird-watcher's paradise. Excellent food to satisfy your appetite. Barbecues on request. Spoil yourself at this BBC holiday programme featured bed and breakfast.

Bedrooms: 1 single,
4 double/twin, 1 triple/
multiple
Bathrooms: 4 en suite

10% discount for Christmas breaks on a room-only basis. Ideal for family visitors.

◆◆◆ **LEYGREEN FARM HOUSE**

Lyndhurst Road, Beaulieu,	Bedrooms: 3 double/
Brockenhurst SO42 7YP	twin
T: (01590) 612355	Bathrooms: 3 en suite
F: (01590) 612355	
I: www.newforest.demon.co.uk/	
leygreen.htm	

B&B per night:
S £26.00–£28.00
D £44.00–£50.00

OPEN All year round

Comfortable Victorian farmhouse with large garden. Convenient for Beaulieu, Bucklers Hard museums and Exbury Gardens. Reductions for 3 days or more.

BEMBRIDGE, Isle of Wight Map ref 2C3 *Tourist Information Centre Tel: (01983) 813818*

◆◆◆◆ **SEA CHANGE**

22 Beachfield Road, Bembridge	Bedrooms: 3 double/
PO35 5TN	twin
T: (01983) 875558 & 875557	Bathrooms: 3 en suite
F: (01983) 875667	
E: curzon@compuserve.com	

B&B per night:
S Min £25.00
D £40.00–£48.00

OPEN Mar–Oct

Modern detached home in quiet location on coastal path 100 metres from sea. Three en suite rooms with TV and fridge. Beach cafe, pub restaurant nearby.

BENSON, Oxfordshire Map ref 2C2

◆◆◆◆
Silver
Award

FYFIELD MANOR

Benson, Wallingford OX10 6HA	Bedrooms: 2 double/
T: (01491) 835184	twin
F: (01491) 825635	Bathrooms: 2 en suite
E: ffbrown@fifield-software.	
demon.co.uk	

B&B per night:
S £35.00–£40.00
D £55.00

OPEN All year round

A 12thC manor house, situated between Benson and Ewelme, 20 minutes from Oxford and 15 minutes from Henley. Luxury en suite rooms.

IDEAS For ideas on places to visit refer to the introduction at the beginning of this section.

BENSON continued

Rating Applied For

RAINBOW COTTAGE
19 Littleworth Road, Benson,
Wallingford OX10 6LY
T: (01491) 837488

Bedrooms: 1 single,
1 double/twin
Bathrooms: 2 private

B&B per night:
S £20.00–£24.00
D £50.00–£55.00

OPEN All year round

This little 18thC farmworker's cottage offers a warm welcome, and lovely views across fields. Close to Thames Path and Oxfordshire Cycleway. Vegetarians catered for.

BICESTER, Oxfordshire Map ref 2C1 *Tourist Information Centre Tel: (01869) 369055*

♦♦♦

PRIORY HOUSE
86 Chapel Street, Bicester
OX26 6BD
T: (01869) 325687
E: anderson@prioryhouse.fsnet.co.uk

Bedrooms: 2 double/
twin, 1 triple/multiple
Bathrooms: 2 en suite

B&B per night:
S £25.00–£45.00
D £50.00–£70.00

OPEN All year round

Friendly family run guesthouse, 2 minutes walk from town centre yet in quiet location. Convenient for M40, Oxford, Cotswolds. En suite bedrooms available. Off-road parking.

BLANDFORD FORUM, Dorset Map ref 2B3 *Tourist Information Centre Tel: (01258) 454770*

♦♦♦

FARNHAM FARM HOUSE
Farnham, Blandford Forum
DT11 8DG
T: (01725) 516254
F: (01725) 516306
E: patricia.bed.and.breakfast@farmersweekly.net

Bedrooms: 3 double/
twin
Bathrooms: 3 en suite

B&B per night:
S £35.00
D £43.00–£50.00

OPEN All year round

350-acre arable farm. 19thC farmhouse in the Cranborne Chase with extensive views to the south. Within easy reach of the coast.

♦♦♦♦
Silver Award

MEADOW HOUSE
Tarrant Hinton, Blandford Forum
DT11 8JG
T: (01258) 830498
F: (01258) 830498

Bedrooms: 1 single,
1 double/twin, 1 triple/
multiple

B&B per night:
S £19.50–£25.00
D £39.00–£50.00

OPEN All year round

Farmhouse set in 4.5 acres. Warm welcome in peaceful, clean and comfortable family home. Noted for delicious home-produced English breakfast. Excellent base for touring.

BLEWBURY, Oxfordshire Map ref 2C2

♦♦♦

THE BARLEY MOW
London Road, Blewbury, Didcot
OX11 9NU
T: (01235) 850296
F: (01235) 850296

Bedrooms: 1 single,
4 double/twin
Bathrooms: 3 en suite

B&B per night:
S Max £45.00
D Max £60.00

HB per person:
DY Max £55.00

Traditional village inn offering good food, picturesque surroundings and friendly atmosphere, only minutes from A34.

CHECK THE MAPS
The colour maps at the front of this guide show all the cities, towns and villages for which you will find accommodation entries. Refer to the town index to find the page on which they are listed.

BOLDRE, Hampshire Map ref 2C3

◆◆

PINECROFT
Coxhill, Boldre, Lymington SO41 8PS
T: (01590) 624260 & 07980 309384
F: (01590) 624025
E: enquiries@pinecroftbandb.co.uk
I: www.pinecroftbandb.co.uk

B&B per night:
S £25.00–£35.00
D £45.00–£60.00

OPEN All year round

Standing in approximately 2 acres, only the garden gate separates this charming and pretty Victorian cottage from the heart of the New Forest. An ideal base for exploring the forest and surrounding area. Within walking distance of the award-winning Hobler Inn. We even supply torches for your journey home.

Bedrooms: 1 double/ twin, 1 triple/multiple
Bathrooms: 2 en suite

BONCHURCH, Isle of Wight Map ref 2C3 *Tourist Information Centre Tel: (01983) 813818*

◆◆◆◆

THE LAKE HOTEL
Shore Road, Bonchurch, Ventnor PO38 1RF
T: (01983) 852613
F: (01983) 852613
E: enquiries@lakehotel.co.uk
I: www.lakehotel.co.uk

B&B per night:
S £26.00–£32.00
D £52.00–£64.00

HB per person:
DY £35.00–£40.00

OPEN Mar–Oct

Charming country house hotel in 2 acres of beautiful gardens. Located on the seaward side of Bonchurch pond in the old world village of Bonchurch. Run by the same family for over 35 years. We are confident of offering you the best value accommodation and food on our beautiful island.

Bedrooms: 1 single, 12 double/twin, 7 triple/ multiple
Bathrooms: 20 en suite

Evening meal available

BOSCOMBE, Dorset Map ref 2B3

◆◆◆

AUDMORE HOTEL
3 Cecil Road, Boscombe, Bournemouth BH5 1DU
T: (01202) 395166
I: www.audmorehotel.co.uk

Bedrooms: 2 single, 3 double/twin, 5 triple/ multiple
Bathrooms: 6 en suite

Evening meal available

B&B per night:
S £18.00–£22.00
D £34.00–£44.00

HB per person:
DY £28.00–£32.00

Friendly, family-run licensed hotel only a few minutes from beach, shops and theatres.

BOTOLPH CLAYDON, Buckinghamshire Map ref 2C1

◆◆◆◆

HICKWELL HOUSE
40 Botyl Road, Botolph Claydon, Buckingham MK18 2LR
T: (01296) 712217 & 07703 115972
F: (01296) 712217

Bedrooms: 2 double/ twin, 1 triple/multiple

Evening meal available

B&B per night:
S £27.00
D £50.00

HB per person:
DY £37.00

OPEN All year round

Thatched 17thC country house with homely atmosphere. Situated in beautiful village with open aspect over lovely Buckinghamshire countryside.

www.travelengland.org.uk
Log on for information and inspiration. The latest information on places to visit, events and quality assessed accommodation.

457

◆◆◆◆

ALEXANDER LODGE HOTEL

21 Southern Road, Southbourne,
Bournemouth BH6 3SR
T: (01202) 421662
F: (01202) 421662
E: alexanderlodge@yahoo.com
I: www.smoothhound.co.uk/a28852.html

B&B per night:
D £39.00–£52.00

HB per person:
DY £30.00–£46.00

OPEN All year round

Delightful small hotel offering a friendly welcome, in quiet Bournemouth suburb. 200 yards from Blue Flag sandy beach, cliff top and lift. Excellent home-cooked meals, comfortable en suite rooms, licensed bar, parking. Low season specials! Ideal for holidays, short breaks and stopovers. Perfect for visiting Christchurch, New Forest, Bournemouth and Dorset.

Bedrooms: 4 double/ twin, 2 triple/multiple
Bathrooms: 5 en suite

Evening meal available
CC: Delta, Mastercard, Switch, Visa

3 night specials available from Sept-Jun. Prices from £59pp B&B, £85pp DB&B.

◆◆◆◆

FAIRMOUNT HOTEL

15 Priory Road, West Cliff, Bournemouth
BH2 5DF
T: (01202) 551105
F: (01202) 551105
E: reservations@fairmount-hotel.co.uk
I: www.fairmount-hotels.co.uk

B&B per night:
S £25.00–£35.00
D £49.00–£70.00

HB per person:
DY £34.00–£44.00

Clean, comfortable family-run hotel within 3 minutes of beach, pier, conference centre, main shopping centre and leisure facilities. All rooms with private facilities. Large, secure car/boat park. Renowned cuisine.

Bedrooms: 3 single, 11 double/twin, 5 triple/ multiple
Bathrooms: 18 en suite, 1 private

Evening meal available
CC: Delta, Mastercard, Switch, Visa

Discounts available at many local tourist attractions. 3 nights for the price of 2, Oct-Mar (excl Christmas and New Year).

◆◆◆

GERVIS COURT HOTEL

38 Gervis Road, Bournemouth BH1 3DH
T: (01202) 556871
F: (01202) 556871
E: enquiries@gerviscourthotel.co.uk
I: www.gerviscourthotel.co.uk

B&B per night:
S £20.00–£30.00
D £40.00–£60.00

OPEN All year round

Gervis Court is a detached Victorian villa set in its own grounds with ample parking. Located in a lovely tree-lined road yet only a few minutes' walk to the town centre, beach, BIC, restaurants and other amenities. All rooms are en suite and no smoking is permitted inside the hotel.

Bedrooms: 1 single, 10 double/twin, 2 triple/ multiple
Bathrooms: 13 en suite

CC: Mastercard, Visa

Special promotions can be found on our website.

MAYFIELD GUEST HOUSE

46 Frances Road,
Knyveton Gardens, Bournemouth
BH1 3SA
T: (01202) 551839
F: (01202) 551839
E: accom@may-field.co.uk
I: www.may-field.co.uk

Bedrooms: 1 single,
6 double/twin, 1 triple/
multiple
Bathrooms: 7 en suite,
1 private

Evening meal available

B&B per night:
S £20.00–£22.00
D £40.00–£44.00

HB per person:
DY £26.50–£28.50

OPEN Jan–Nov

Ideally situated for all amenities, opposite Knyveton Gardens with bowling greens, sensory garden, tennis courts. Handy for rail/ coach stations, sea, shops and BIC.

 ROSEDENE COTTAGE HOTEL

St Peter's Road, Bournemouth
BH1 2LA
T: (01202) 554102
F: (01202) 246995
E: enquiries@
rosedenecottagehotel.co.uk
I: www.rosedenecottagehotel.co.uk

Bedrooms: 2 single,
6 double/twin, 1 triple/
multiple
Bathrooms: 8 en suite,
1 private

CC: Amex, Delta, Diners,
Mastercard, Switch, Visa

B&B per night:
S £26.00–£40.00
D £48.00–£70.00

Town centre location. Old world cottage hotel, quiet. A short stroll to pier, shops, gardens, Bournemouth International Centre, theatres and beaches. 20 minutes from airport.

Silver Award

ST WINIFRIDES HOTEL

1 Studland Road, Alum Chine,
Bournemouth BH4 8HZ
T: (01202) 761829

B&B per night:
S £25.00–£45.00
D £50.00–£90.00

HB per person:
DY £30.00–£50.00

Awarded Four Diamonds with Silver merit. Our 'home from home' family-run hotel, 40 metres from the sandy beach, offers refurbished en suite rooms with full facilities, some with views of the sea. High standards of food, cleanliness and hospitality. Motto 'arrive as a guest, leave as a friend'.

Bedrooms: 1 single,
14 double/twin, 5 triple/
multiple
Bathrooms: 20 en suite

Evening meal available

Special Valentine's Weekend. Family parties catered for.

 SHORELINE HOTEL

7 Pinecliffe Avenue, Southbourne,
Bournemouth BH6 3PY
T: (01202) 429654
F: (01202) 429654
E: timjonshorelinebb@amserve.net

Bedrooms: 2 single,
6 double/twin, 2 triple/
multiple
Bathrooms: 5 en suite

B&B per night:
S £13.00–£22.00
D £26.00–£42.00

OPEN All year round

Small hotel providing comfortable accommodation and home cooking. Close to beach and local shops, in quiet area of Southbourne.

Silver Award

THE TWIN TOPS

33 Wheelers Lane, Bournemouth
BH11 9QQ
T: (01202) 570080 & 07890 332742
F: (01202) 570080
E: twintops@btinternet.com
I: www.thetwintops.com

Bedrooms: 1 single,
1 double/twin, 1 triple/
multiple
Bathrooms: 1 en suite

Evening meal available

B&B per night:
S Min £25.00
D £40.00–£70.00

HB per person:
DY £40.00–£50.00

OPEN All year round

Tranquil, semi-rural setting between Bournemouth and Poole. Several golf courses within a short distance. Antique furniture in all rooms. First-rate Italian cuisine.

 SYMBOLS The symbols in each entry give information about services and facilities. A key to these symbols appears at the back of this guide.

BOURNEMOUTH continued

◆◆◆ THE VINE HOTEL

22 Southern Road, Southbourne,
Bournemouth BH6 3SR
T: (01202) 428309
F: (01202) 428309
E: thevinehotel@faxvia.net

Bedrooms: 8 double/twin
Bathrooms: 8 en suite

Evening meal available
CC: Delta, Mastercard, Switch, Visa

B&B per night:
S £20.00–£24.00
D £40.00–£48.00

OPEN All year round

Small family hotel close to local amenities. Superb location twixt Bournemouth and Christchurch. Beaches and Hengistbury Head nearby. Residential licence. Parking. Dogs welcome. No smoking.

ⓜ☜2▭⬥♨️🍽️🅢✄💺▦🖥️🅓🐴🚐♒P

◆◆◆ WRENWOOD HOTEL

11 Florence Road, Boscombe,
Bournemouth BH5 1HH
T: (01202) 395086 & 250793
F: (01202) 396511
E: bookings@wrenwood.co.uk
I: www.wrenwood.co.uk

Bedrooms: 4 double/twin, 6 triple/multiple
Bathrooms: 10 en suite

Evening meal available
CC: Delta, Mastercard, Switch, Visa

B&B per night:
S £22.00–£34.00
D £36.00–£50.00

HB per person:
DY £27.00–£35.00

OPEN All year round

Licensed, family hotel, 5 minutes' walk to pier, shopping centre and entertainments. Convenient for tennis, bowling, golf and New Forest area. Close to buses/coaches.

ⓜ☜🖃▭⬥🍷🍽️🅢✄💺▦🖥️🅓❉🐴♒P

◆◆◆◆

WYCHCOTE HOTEL

2 Somerville Road, West Cliff,
Bournemouth BH2 5LH
T: (01202) 557898
E: info@wychcote.co.uk
I: www.wychcote.co.uk

B&B per night:
S £30.00–£40.00
D £55.00–£84.00

OPEN Feb–Nov &
Christmas

Small, well-appointed Victorian house hotel peacefully situated in own tree lined grounds. Short walk to town centre, beach and entertainment. Two lounges overlooking the garden. Standard, deluxe and superior rooms available including 4-poster, all en suite. All have colour TV, hospitality tray and radio alarm. No smoking.

Bedrooms: 2 single, 10 double/twin
Bathrooms: 11 en suite, 1 private

Evening meal available
CC: Delta, Mastercard, Visa

ⓜ☜5🖃🖃▭⬥🅢✄💺▦🖥️🅓❉🚐♒P

BRILL, Buckinghamshire Map ref 2C1

◆◆◆◆ LAPLANDS FARM

Ludgershall Road, Brill, Aylesbury
HP18 9TZ
T: (01844) 237888
F: (01844) 238870
E: enquiries@intents-
marquees.co.uk
I: www.intents-marquees.co.uk

Bedrooms: 3 double/twin
Bathrooms: 3 en suite

B&B per night:
S £30.00–£35.00
D £50.00–£55.00

OPEN All year round

17thC Listed, timbered farmhouse. Quiet woodland location. Attractive grounds with rare breed animal collection. Luxury accommodation, guests' lounge, dining room. Indoor pool and games room available in summer.

☜5🖃🖃⬥🅢💺▦🖥️●🔍❉🚐

COUNTRY CODE Always follow the Country Code 🌳 Enjoy the countryside and respect its life and work 🌳 Guard against all risk of fire 🌳 Fasten all gates 🌳 Keep your dogs under close control 🌳 Keep to public paths across farmland 🌳 Use gates and stiles to cross fences, hedges and walls 🌳 Leave livestock, crops and machinery alone 🌳 Take your litter home 🌳 Help to keep all water clean 🌳 Protect wildlife, plants and trees 🌳 Take special care on country roads 🌳 Make no unnecessary noise

BRIZE NORTON, Oxfordshire Map ref 2C1

Rating
Applied For

THE PRIORY MANOR FARM

Manor Road, Brize Norton, Carterton
OX18 3NA
T: (01993) 843062 & 0771 838 6264

B&B per night:
S £30.00–£40.00
D £45.00–£65.00

HB per person:
DY £40.00–£50.00

OPEN All year round

Beautiful character house in natural stone. Set in 0.75 acres of beautiful gardens with ample parking. Comfortable rooms with tea/coffee-making facilities and colour TV. Close to many Cotswold attractions, Burford, Blenheim Palace. Oxford and golf. Ground floor accommodation available.

Bedrooms: 1 double/
twin, 1 triple/multiple
Bathrooms: 1 en suite,
1 private

Evening meal by arrangement. Prices for longer stay
B&B negotiable.

BROCKENHURST, Hampshire Map ref 2C3

◆◆

GOLDENHAYES
9 Chestnut Road, Brockenhurst
SO42 7RF
T: (01590) 623743

Bedrooms: 1 double/
twin

B&B per night:
S £15.00–£20.00
D £30.00–£35.00

OPEN All year round

Single owner occupied home, single storey, in central but quiet situation. Close to village, station and open forest. Large garden.

◆◆◆

HILDEN BED & BREAKFAST
Southampton Road, Boldre,
Brockenhurst SO41 8PT
T: (01590) 623682 & 07802 668658
F: (01590) 624444
I: www.newforestbandb-hilden.co.
uk

Bedrooms: 1 double/
twin, 2 triple/multiple
Bathrooms: 3 en suite

CC: Delta, Mastercard,
Switch, Visa

B&B per night:
S £20.00–£40.00
D £40.00–£55.00

OPEN All year round

Attractive Edwardian house set in own grounds, 25 yards from open forest, 175 yards excellent pub. Two miles from Brockenhurst and Lymington. Families and pets welcome.

BUCKINGHAM, Buckinghamshire Map ref 2C1 *Tourist Information Centre Tel: (01280) 823020*

Rating
Applied For

HUNTSMILL HOUSE B & B
Huntsmill Farm, Shalstone,
Buckingham MK18 5ND
T: (01280) 704852
F: (01280) 704852

Bedrooms: 3 double/
twin
Bathrooms: 3 en suite

B&B per night:
S Min £30.00
D £45.00–£70.00

HB per person:
DY Min £35.00

OPEN All year round

Quality bed and breakfast in lovely converted stone barns in peaceful countryside location, yet M40 only 10 minutes away. Local walks through open countryside. Home cooking.

◆◆◆◆

RADCLIVE DAIRY FARM
Radclive Road, Gawcott,
Buckingham MK18 4AA
T: (01280) 813433
F: (01280) 813433

Bedrooms: 2 double/
twin
Bathrooms: 2 en suite

B&B per night:
S Max £25.00
D Max £50.00

OPEN All year round

Elegant farmhouse offers quality accommodation in this unspoilt countryside. All rooms have facilities en suite. Spacious rooms and very quiet.

ACCESSIBILITY
Look for the 🚹🚹🚹 symbols which indicate accessibility for wheelchair users. A list of establishments is at the front of this guide.

◆◆◆

THE HIGHWAY

117 High Street, Burford, Oxford OX18 4RG
T: (01993) 822136
F: (01993) 824740
E: rbx20@dial.pipex.com
I: www.oxlink.co.uk/burford

B&B per night:
S £30.00–£50.00
D £50.00–£65.00

OPEN All year round

Built circa 1520, The Highway was old when Elizabeth I was on the throne. Today this beamed medieval Cotswold guesthouse offers 9 en suite bedrooms with TV, telephones, hairdryers etc. Perfect base for touring the Cotswolds. Also incorporating the highly acclaimed needlecraft centre.

Bedrooms: 9 double/
twin, 2 triple/multiple
Bathrooms: 9 en suite

CC: Amex, Delta, Diners,
Mastercard, Switch, Visa

◆◆◆◆◆
Gold
Award

JONATHAN'S AT THE ANGEL

14 Witney Street, Burford, Oxford
OX18 4SN
T: (01993) 822714
F: (01993) 822069
E: jo@theangel-uk.com

B&B per night:
S £65.00–£75.00
D £80.00–£95.00

OPEN All year round
except mid Jan–early
Feb

Jonathan's at the Angel is a 16thC former coaching inn serving brasserie-style food. With 3 en suite themed letting rooms, Madras (Indian), Camargue (French) and Simione (Italian), the accent is firmly on comfort and quality. Situated off Burford's historic High Street, The Angel has a south-facing courtyard and walled garden.

Bedrooms: 3 double/
twin
Bathrooms: 3 en suite

Lunch available
Evening meal available
CC: Delta, Mastercard,
Switch, Visa

◆◆◆

ST WINNOW
160 The Hill, Burford, Oxford
OX18 4QY
T: (01993) 823843
I: www.stwinnow.com

Bedrooms: 1 single,
2 double/twin

B&B per night:
S £30.00–£40.00
D £45.00–£55.00

OPEN All year round

Comfortable 16thC Cotswold house above the historic high street. Close to restaurants and shops. Garden, garage and parking at rear. Organic and special diets provided.

◆◆◆

TUDOR COTTAGE
40 Witney Street, Burford, Oxford
OX18 4SN
T: (01993) 823251
F: (01993) 823251

Bedrooms: 2 double/
twin
Bathrooms: 2 private

B&B per night:
D £50.00–£55.00

OPEN All year round

Elegant and very beautiful old Cotswold cottage in central Burford. Lovely garden and extremely comfortable en suite rooms. Quiet and peaceful. Ideally situated for all amenities.

◆◆◆

ALVINGTON MANOR FARM
Carisbrooke, Newport PO30 5SP
T: (01983) 523463
F: (01983) 523463

Bedrooms: 3 triple/
multiple
Bathrooms: 3 en suite

B&B per night:
S £25.00
D £40.00–£45.00

OPEN All year round

17thC farmhouse, gardens and parking, 3 en suite double/twin rooms. Ideal base in centre of island for walking, cycling etc.

CHALFONT ST GILES, Buckinghamshire Map ref 2D2

◆◆◆◆ **THE WHITE HART INN**

Three Households, Chalfont St Giles
HP8 4LP
T: (01494) 872441

Bedrooms: 2 single,
9 double/twin
Bathrooms: 11 en suite

Lunch available
Evening meal available
CC: Delta, Mastercard,
Switch, Visa

B&B per night:
S Min £67.50
D Min £87.50

OPEN All year round

One-hundred-year-old village pub with non-smoking restaurant, large gardens and parking. Detached stable conversion accommodation. Plus new 7 bedroomed lodge.

CHALGROVE, Oxfordshire Map ref 2C2

◆◆◆ **CORNERSTONES**

1 Cromwell Close, Chalgrove,
Oxford OX44 7SE
T: (01865) 890298
F: (01865) 890298

Bedrooms: 2 double/
twin

B&B per night:
S £25.00
D £40.00

OPEN All year round

Bungalow in pretty village with thatched cottages. The Red Lion (half a mile away) serves good and reasonably priced food.

CHARLBURY, Oxfordshire Map ref 2C1

◆◆◆◆ **BANBURY HILL FARM**

Enstone Road, Charlbury, Oxford
OX7 3JH
T: (01608) 810314
F: (01608) 811891
E: angelawiddows@gfwiddows.f9.
co.uk
I: www.charlburyoxfordaccom.co.uk

Bedrooms: 1 single,
5 double/twin, 7 triple/
multiple
Bathrooms: 11 en suite

CC: Mastercard, Switch,
Visa

B&B per night:
S £22.00–£35.00
D £36.00–£50.00

OPEN Mar–Oct

54-acre mixed farm. Cotswold-stone farmhouse with extensive views across Evenlode Valley. Ideal touring centre for Blenheim Palace, Oxford and the Cotswolds. Scrumptious breakfasts.

CHARLTON-ON-OTMOOR, Oxfordshire Map ref 2C1

◆◆ **HOME FARM**

Mansmoor Lane, Charlton-on-
Otmoor, Kidlington OX5 2US
T: (01865) 331267 & 07774 710305
F: (01865) 331267

Bedrooms: 1 single,
1 double/twin

B&B per night:
S £20.00–£25.00
D £40.00–£50.00

Modern farmhouse on sheep and arable farm. In quiet location 0.5 mile from village. Pets welcome. Stabling available. Central for Bicester, Woodstock, Oxford and Thame.

CHIPPING NORTON, Oxfordshire Map ref 2C1 *Tourist Information Centre Tel: (01608) 644379*

◆◆◆◆
Silver
Award

LOWER PARK FARM

Great Tew, Oxford OX7 4DE
T: (01608) 683170
F: (01608) 683859
E: lowerparkfarm@talk21.com
I: members.tripod.co.uk/lowerparkfarm

B&B per night:
S £45.00
D £60.00

OPEN All year round

This Grade II Listed building, set in the picturesque parkland landscape designed by Loudon, has recently been refurbished to a very high standard and retains many of its original features. Whether you are on business, enjoy walking, bird-watching or wish to explore the Cotswolds, we are the ideal destination.

Bedrooms: 3 double/
twin
Bathrooms: 3 en suite

CC: Delta, Mastercard,
Switch, Visa

PRICES

Please check prices and other details at the time of booking.

CHIPPING NORTON continued

♦♦♦

SOUTHCOMBE LODGE GUEST HOUSE

Southcombe, Chipping Norton
OX7 5QH
T: (01608) 643068
F: (01608) 642948
E: georgefinlysouthcombelodge@tinyworld.co.uk

Bedrooms: 5 double/twin, 1 triple/multiple
Bathrooms: 4 en suite

Lunch available
Evening meal available

B&B per night:
S £30.00–£36.00
D £48.00–£56.00

OPEN All year round

Well-decorated pebbledash guesthouse set in 3.5 acres, at the junction of the A44/A3400, close to Chipping Norton.

🐴 🪑 📺 ☕ [S] 🚭 🍴 ♨ 👕 ⛳ ✿ 🐕 🚗 🚫 P

CHOLDERTON, Hampshire Map ref 2B2

♦♦♦♦

PARKHOUSE MOTEL

Cholderton, Salisbury SP4 0EG
T: (01980) 629256
F: (01980) 629256

Bedrooms: 6 single, 24 double/twin, 3 triple/multiple; suites available
Bathrooms: 23 en suite, 10 private

Evening meal available
CC: Delta, Mastercard, Switch, Visa

B&B per night:
S £32.00–£46.00
D £52.00–£58.00

HB per person:
DY £38.95–£52.95

OPEN All year round

Attractive family-run 17thC former coaching inn, 5 miles east of Stonehenge, 10 miles north of Salisbury and 7 miles west of Andover.

[M] 🐴 🪑 📺 ☕ 🍷 [S] 🍴 ♨ 👕 🍸 ✿ 🐕 🚫 🏠 P

CHOLSEY, Oxfordshire Map ref 2C2

♦♦♦

THE WELL COTTAGE

Caps Lane, Cholsey, Wallingford
OX10 9HQ
T: (01491) 651959 & 07887 958920
F: (01491) 651675
E: thewellcottage@talk21.com
I: www.thewellcottage.co.uk

Bedrooms: 3 double/twin
Bathrooms: 2 en suite, 1 private

B&B per night:
S £20.00–£30.00
D £30.00–£50.00

OPEN All year round

A delightful cottage with en suite bedrooms in secluded garden flat. Close to River Thames and historic town of Wallingford.

🐴 🪑 ☎ 📺 ☕ 💇 [S] ♨ 👕 ⛳ ✿ 🐕 🚗 P

CHRISTCHURCH, Dorset Map ref 2B3 *Tourist Information Centre Tel: (01202) 471780*

♦♦♦♦

BEVERLY GLEN GUEST HOUSE

1 Stuart Road, Highcliffe,
Christchurch BH23 5JS
T: (01425) 273811

Bedrooms: 1 single, 5 double/twin
Bathrooms: 6 en suite

CC: Mastercard, Visa

B&B per night:
S £24.00–£30.00
D £42.00–£56.00

OPEN All year round

On A337, ample parking. 6 minutes' walk beaches, Highcliffe shops, restaurants, 10 minutes' drive to New Forest. All rooms en-suite, TV, tea-making, toiletries etc.

🐴6 ☎ 📺 ☕ 💇 [S] 🍴 ♨ 👕 🐕 🚗 P

♦♦♦♦

THE WHITE HOUSE

428 Lymington Road, Highcliffe BH23 5HF
T: (01425) 271279
F: (01425) 276900
E: thewhitehouse@themail.co.uk
I: www.thewhite-house.co.uk

B&B per night:
S £26.00–£30.00
D £48.00–£52.00

OPEN All year round

Eileen and Fred welcome you to their beautiful Victorian house, furnished and decorated to high standards. Award-winning Highcliffe beach, shops and restaurants are just a short walk away. The New Forest, local golf course are also nearby. Rooms are equipped with hairdryer, clock/radio, colour TV and tea/coffee-making facilities. Private car park.

Bedrooms: 1 single, 5 double/twin
Bathrooms: 5 en suite

CC: Delta, Mastercard, Switch, Visa

Oct-Mar: special rates for 3 nights or more. Ask for Fred or Eileen.

[M] 🐴 ☎ 📺 ☕ 💇 [S] 🚭 ♨ 👕 🚗 P

REGIONAL TOURIST BOARD The [M] symbol in an establishment entry indicates that it is a Regional Tourist Board member.

COMPTON, Hampshire Map ref 2C3

◆◆

MANOR HOUSE

Place Lane, Compton, Winchester
SO21 2BA
T: (01962) 712162

Bedrooms: 1 double/
twin

B&B per night:
S £16.00
D £32.00

Comfortable country house in a large garden, 8 minutes from Shawford railway station and 2 miles from city of Winchester. Non-smokers preferred.

OPEN All year round

CORFE CASTLE, Dorset Map ref 2B3

◆◆◆◆
Silver
Award

Relax and unwind in our period farmhouse in the heart of Purbeck on 550-acre farm. Spacious, attractively furnished rooms with superb views. We guarantee a breakfast to set you up for the day using home-made produce. A warm, friendly atmosphere is assured, come and sample what we have to offer. Local pub 1 mile.

BRADLE FARMHOUSE

Bradle Farm, Church Knowle, Wareham
BH20 5NU
T: (01929) 480712
F: (01929) 481144
E: hole.bradle@farmersweekly.net
I: www.smoothhound.co.uk/hotels/bradle.html

Bedrooms: 3 double/
twin
Bathrooms: 2 en suite,
1 private

B&B per night:
S £25.00–£40.00
D £45.00–£50.00

OPEN All year round

COTSWOLDS

See under Brize Norton, Burford, Chalbury, Chipping Norton, Witney, Woodstock

See also Cotswolds in Heart of England region

CRANBORNE, Dorset Map ref 2B3

◆◆◆◆

THE FLEUR DE LYS

5 Wimborne Street, Cranborne,
Wimborne Minster BH21 5PP
T: (01725) 517282 & 517765
F: (01725) 517631
E: fleurdelys@btinternet.com
I: www.btinternet.com/fleurdelys/

Bedrooms: 1 single,
7 double/twin
Bathrooms: 7 en suite

Lunch available
Evening meal available
CC: Amex, Delta,
Mastercard, Switch, Visa

B&B per night:
S £30.00–£35.00
D £45.00–£65.00

HB per person:
DY £40.00–£45.00

Charming old-world coaching inn, close to the New Forest. Cosy atmosphere, friendly hospitality. Restaurant, bar, en suite accommodation.

OPEN All year round

DEDDINGTON, Oxfordshire Map ref 2C1

◆◆

HILL BARN

Milton Gated Road, Deddington,
Banbury OX15 0TS
T: (01869) 338631
F: (01869) 338631
E: hillbarn-bb@supanet.com

Bedrooms: 3 double/
twin

B&B per night:
S £25.00–£30.00
D £45.00–£55.00

OPEN All year round

Converted barn set in open countryside. Banbury-Oxford road, half a mile before Deddington, turn right to Milton Gated Road. Hill Barn is 100 yards on right.

◆◆

STONECROP GUEST HOUSE

Hempton Road, Deddington,
Banbury OX15 0QH
T: (01869) 338335 & 338496
F: (01869) 338505

Bedrooms: 1 single,
2 double/twin, 1 triple/
multiple

B&B per night:
S £18.00–£20.00
D £36.00–£40.00

OPEN All year round

Modern, detached accommodation, close to major roads, shops and places of interest.

MAP REFERENCES

Map references apply to the colour maps at the front of this guide.

SOUTH OF ENGLAND

EAST COWES, Hampshire Map ref 2C3 *Tourist Information Centre Tel: (01983) 813818*

◆◆◆◆ **THE DOGHOUSE**

Crossways Road, East Cowes
PO32 6LJ
T: (01983) 293677
E: timindoghouse@beeb.net

Bedrooms: 2 double/ twin
Bathrooms: 2 en suite

B&B per night:
S £25.00–£35.00
D £46.00–£60.00

OPEN All year round

The house everyone knows. Well-favoured, en suite, 4 Diamond bed and breakfast on coastal path, between Osborne House and Whippingham. Southampton ferries and East Cowes Marina nearby.

EDGCOTT, Buckinghamshire Map ref 2C1

◆◆ **PERRY MANOR FARM**

Buckingham Road, Edgcott,
Aylesbury HP18 0TR
T: (01296) 770257

Bedrooms: 1 single,
2 double/twin

B&B per night:
S £20.00
D £36.00

OPEN All year round

200-acre working sheep farm, offering peaceful and comfortable accommodation, with en suite toilet and basin. Extensive views over Aylesbury Vale. Walkers welcome. Non-smokers only, please.

FARINGDON, Oxfordshire Map ref 2B2 *Tourist Information Centre Tel: (01367) 242191*

◆◆◆ **PORTWELL HOUSE HOTEL**

Market Place, Faringdon SN7 7HU
T: (01367) 240197 & 242413
F: (01367) 244330
E: portwellh@aol.com

Bedrooms: 1 single,
5 double/twin, 2 triple/ multiple
Bathrooms: 8 en suite

Evening meal available
CC: Delta, Mastercard, Switch, Visa

B&B per night:
S £40.00–£50.00
D £50.00–£70.00

HB per person:
DY £37.50–£57.50

OPEN All year round

Small, family-run hotel within easy reach of Oxford, Thames, Ridgeway and Cotswolds. A warm welcome awaits you. Freshly cooked evening meals on request.

FARNBOROUGH, Hampshire Map ref 2C2

◆◆ **COLEBROOK GUEST HOUSE**

56 Netley Street, Farnborough
GU14 6AT
T: (01252) 542269
F: (01252) 542269
E: derek.clark@ukonline.co.uk

Bedrooms: 3 single,
4 double/twin, 1 triple/ multiple
Bathrooms: 4 en suite, 2 private

CC: Amex, Delta,
Mastercard, Switch, Visa

B&B per night:
S £20.00–£30.00
D £45.00–£60.00

OPEN All year round

Late Victorian detached, double fronted house on 3 floors, in quiet residential area.

FORDINGBRIDGE, Hampshire Map ref 2B3

◆◆◆◆ **BROOMY**

Ogdens, Fordingbridge SP6 2PY
T: (01425) 653264

Bedrooms: 3 double/ twin
Bathrooms: 3 en suite

B&B per night:
S £25.00–£35.00
D £45.00–£55.00

OPEN All year round

Originally built in 1930s. Secluded, peaceful location with direct access on to forest. Ideally situated for walks, riding and touring. Good base for the south.

◆◆◆ **THE CROWN INN**

62 High Street, Fordingbridge
SP6 1AX
T: (01425) 652552
F: (01425) 655752
E: CandM.Bell@ukgateway.net

Bedrooms: 3 double/ twin
Bathrooms: 3 en suite

CC: Delta, Mastercard,
Switch, Visa

B&B per night:
S £30.00
D £39.00

Old coaching inn situated on edge of New Forest. Real ales, home-cooked food and friendly atmosphere.

◆◆◆◆◆ **THE THREE LIONS**
Gold Award

Stuckton, Fordingbridge SP6 2HF
T: (01425) 652489
F: (01425) 656144
E: the3lions@btinternet.com

Bedrooms: 3 double/ twin
Bathrooms: 3 en suite

Lunch available
Evening meal available
CC: Amex, Delta,
Mastercard, Switch, Visa

B&B per night:
S £59.00–£75.00
D £65.00–£85.00

OPEN All year round except mid Jan–early Feb

Quiet, rural restaurant with rooms, all individually decorated. Ground floor room. Wheelchair access. Whirlpool jacuzzi. English/French cuisine. Rosettes awarded for food.

FRESHWATER, Isle of Wight Map ref 2C3 *Tourist Information Centre Tel: (01983) 813818*

◆◆◆◆

SEAHORSES
Victoria Road, Freshwater PO40 9PP
T: (01983) 752574
F: (01983) 752574
E: lanterncom@aol.com

Bedrooms: 2 double/
twin, 2 triple/multiple
Bathrooms: 4 en suite

B&B per night:
S £23.00–£28.00
D £46.00–£56.00

Peaceful restored 18thC country house, standing in secluded gardens, retaining its original charm and character. Near beaches, nature reserve and the Tennyson Downs.

 P

FRESHWATER BAY, Isle of Wight Map ref 2C3 *Tourist Information Centre Tel: (01983) 813818*

◆◆◆◆

WIGHTHAVEN
Afton Road, Freshwater Bay PO40 9TT
T: (01983) 753184 & 755957
E: wighthaven@btinternet.com

B&B per night:
S £33.00
D £50.00

OPEN All year round

Victorian detached house built 1895. Set in the heart of an Area of Outstanding Natural Beauty, facing Afton marshes. Wighthaven is the perfect base for beach and walking holidays, surrounded by National Trust downland, 400 yards from the beach. Beautiful walks to The Needles and Alum Bay via Tennyson Down.

Bedrooms: 3 double/
twin
Bathrooms: 3 en suite

7 nights for the price of 6. Off-season 3 nights for the price of 2 (excl Easter, Christmas and New Year).

 P

GORING, Oxfordshire Map ref 2C2

◆◆◆

MILLER OF MANSFIELD
High Street, Goring, Reading
RG8 9AW
T: (01491) 872829
F: (01491) 874200
I: www.millerofmansfield.co.uk

Bedrooms: 2 single,
8 double/twin
Bathrooms: 10 en suite

Lunch available
Evening meal available
CC: Delta, Mastercard,
Switch, Visa

B&B per night:
S £57.50–£59.50
D £75.00–£80.00

OPEN All year round

Ivy-covered inn with Tudor-style exterior. Interior has original beams, open fires and comfortable bedrooms. Excellent bar and restaurant serving quality food, wines and beers.

P

GRATELEY, Hampshire Map ref 2C2

◆◆◆◆
Silver
Award

GUNVILLE HOUSE
Grateley, Andover SP11 8JQ
T: (01264) 889206
F: (01264) 889060
E: pct@onetel.net.uk

Bedrooms: 1 single,
1 triple/multiple
Bathrooms: 2 en suite

Lunch available
Evening meal available
CC: Mastercard, Switch,
Visa

B&B per night:
S £30.00
D £50.00

HB per person:
DY £40.00–£45.00

OPEN All year round

Charming, thatched, beamed family house in secluded, rural position. Within easy reach of Salisbury, Stonehenge, Worcester, Marlborough, Bath and Oxford. Five minutes from A303.

P

HENLEY-ON-THAMES, Oxfordshire Map ref 2C2 *Tourist Information Centre Tel: (01491) 578034*

◆◆◆◆

ALFTRUDIS
8 Norman Avenue, Henley-on-
Thames RG9 1SG
T: (01491) 573099 & 07802 408643
F: (01491) 411747
E: b&b@alftrudis.fsnet.co.uk
I: www.alftrudis.co.uk

Bedrooms: 3 double/
twin
Bathrooms: 2 en suite,
1 private

B&B per night:
S £45.00–£55.00
D £55.00–£65.00

OPEN All year round

Friendly, detached Victorian home in quiet, tree-lined cul-de-sac a minute's walk from the town centre, station and river.

P

QUALITY ASSURANCE SCHEME
Diamond ratings and awards are explained at the back of this guide.

HENLEY-ON-THAMES continued

◆◆ **BANK FARM**

The Old Road, Pishill, Henley-on-Thames RG9 6HS
T: (01491) 638601 & 07799 752 933
F: (01491) 638601
E: bankfarm@btinternet.com

Bedrooms: 1 double/twin, 1 triple/multiple
Bathrooms: 1 en suite

B&B per night:
S £20.00–£24.00
D £40.00–£48.00

OPEN All year round

Peaceful, listed farmhouse in AONB. Good walking, birdwatching (red kites), reading (secondhand bookshop). Ideal for visiting London, Oxford and the Thames from Windsor to Abingdon.

◆◆◆◆ **COLDHARBOUR HOUSE**

3 Coldharbour Close, Henley-on-Thames RG9 1QF
T: (01491) 575229
F: (01491) 575229
E: coldharbourhouse@cs.com

Bedrooms: 1 single, 2 double/twin
Bathrooms: 1 en suite

B&B per night:
S £30.00–£45.00
D £55.00–£65.00

OPEN All year round

Old farmhouse-style home with walled garden, in a quiet close, 15 minutes' walk from town centre and river. Off-street parking.

◆◆◆ **HENLEY HOUSE**

School Lane, Medmenham, Marlow SL7 2HJ
T: (01491) 576100
F: (01491) 571764
E: dres@crownandanchor.co.uk
I: www.crownandanchor.co.uk

Bedrooms: 3 double/twin
Bathrooms: 3 en suite

B&B per night:
S £50.00–£55.00
D £50.00–£55.00

OPEN All year round

Elegant, spacious property, set in a Victorian walled garden in an AONB. All modern home comforts, relaxed, friendly atmosphere. Convenient for M4 and access to London, Oxford, Windsor.

◆◆◆◆

HOLMWOOD

Shiplake Row, Binfield Heath, Henley-on-Thames RG9 4DP
T: (0118) 947 8747
F: (0118) 947 8637

B&B per night:
S £40.00
D £60.00

OPEN All year round

Large, elegant, peaceful Georgian country house with very beautiful gardens and views over the Thames Valley. All bedrooms are large and en suite and furnished with period and antique furnishings. Holmwood is in Binfield Heath, which is signposted off the A4155, equidistant from Henley-on-Thames and Reading.

Bedrooms: 1 single, 4 double/twin
Bathrooms: 5 en suite

CC: Delta, Mastercard, Switch, Visa

AT-A-GLANCE SYMBOLS

Symbols at the end of each accommodation entry give useful information about services and facilities. A key to symbols can be found inside the back cover flap. Keep this open for easy reference.

◆◆◆◆

THE KNOLL
Crowsley Road, Shiplake,
Henley-on-Thames RG9 3JT
T: (01189) 402705 & 406538
F: (01189) 402705
E: theknollhenley@aol.com
I: www.theknollhenley.com

B&B per night:
S £45.00
D £55.00–£58.00

OPEN All year round

Beautifully restored home with every modern convenience, riverside walks and landscaped garden. Good base for Cotswolds, Oxford, Windsor, London and Heathrow. Free internet access. 'We had the best time ever staying in your beautiful home.' 'We had such an unforgettable time in your wonderful home.'

Bedrooms: 2 double/
twin, 1 triple/multiple;
suites available
Bathrooms: 1 en suite

◆◆◆◆◆

LENWADE
3 Western Road, Henley-on-Thames
RG9 1JL
T: (01491) 573468 & 07774 941629
F: (01491) 573468
E: lenwadeuk@compuserve.com
I: www.w3b-ink.com/lenwade

B&B per night:
S £45.00–£50.00
D £55.00–£65.00

OPEN All year round

Lenwade has been awarded an ETC 5 diamond rating which ensures you the highest standard of service and comfort. This beautiful Victorian home is in a quiet residential road within walking distance of town, river and station. Ample parking. Superb individually cooked breakfasts. Convenient base for Oxford, Heathrow, Windsor.

Bedrooms: 3 double/
twin
Bathrooms: 2 en suite,
1 private

◆◆

PARK VIEW FARM
Lower Assendon,
Henley-on-Thames RG9 6AN
T: (01491) 414232 & 0786 766
0814
F: (01491) 577515
E: thomasmartin@globalnet.co.uk
I: www.thomasmartin.co.uk

Bedrooms: 2 double/
twin

B&B per night:
S £20.00
D £20.00

OPEN All year round

An equestrian property with stunning Chiltern views. On bridle/footpath yet only 1 mile outside Henley. X39 bus stop nearby. Horses welcome.

◆◆◆◆

SOMEWHERE TO STAY
c/o Loddon Acres, Bath Road,
Twyford, Reading RG10 9RU
T: (0118) 934 5880 &
07798 801088
F: (0118) 934 5880

Bedrooms: 1 single,
2 double/twin, 1 triple/
multiple
Bathrooms: 3 en suite,
1 private

B&B per night:
S £35.00–£49.00
D £45.00–£59.00

OPEN All year round

Quality bed and breakfast in separate cottage next to owners house in beautiful river – fronted 2-acre garden. Rooms en suite, TV, tea/coffee. Near Windsor, Henley, Reading.

QUALITY ASSURANCE SCHEME
Diamond ratings and awards were correct at the time of going to press but are subject to change. Please check at the time of booking.

◆◆◆◆◆
Silver
Award

THAMESMEAD HOUSE HOTEL

Remenham Lane, Remenham,
Henley-on-Thames RG9 2LR
T: (01491) 574745
F: (01491) 579944
E: thamesmead@supanet.com
I: www.thamesmeadhousehotel.co.uk

Small, family-owned and managed hotel in a quiet location close to the town and river with the famous regatta course. The rooms are bright, stylish and contemporary. The art and decor is interesting, the ambiance chic, and the atmosphere...totally relaxed.

Bedrooms: 1 single,
5 double/twin
Bathrooms: 6 en suite

Lunch available
Evening meal available
CC: Amex, Delta,
Mastercard, Switch, Visa

Autumn and winter weekend breaks, stay Sat night
and get Sun night half-price.

B&B per night:
S £105.00–£115.00
D £125.00–£135.00

OPEN All year round

♙🐎⌖🛏️🖥️📠🛜⚡🍷ⓈⒺ🖨️💻🍴🐇🐕🐾P

HORDLE, Hampshire Map ref 2B3

◆◆◆
LONG ACRE FARM
Vaggs Lane, Hordle, Lymington
SO41 0FP
T: (01425) 610443 & 07946 577530
F: (01425) 613026
E: long.acre@amserve.net

Bedrooms: 1 single,
2 double/twin
Bathrooms: 1 en suite,
1 private

B&B per night:
S £20.00–£30.00
D £40.00–£50.00

HB per person:
DY £25.00–£35.00

OPEN All year round

Stylish old farmhouse set within 18 acres. Extremely comfortable ground floor (4-poster) en suite double room and charming twin room and holiday horse livery available.

🐎⌖🛜⚡ⓈⒺ🖨️💻🚲🐾P

HYTHE, Hampshire Map ref 2C3

◆◆◆◆

CHANGRI-LA

12 Ashleigh Close, Hythe, Southampton
SO45 3QP
T: (023) 8084 6664

B&B per night:
S Min £19.50
D Min £39.00

OPEN All year round

Comfortable home in unique position on edge of New Forest, a few minutes' drive from Beaulieu National Motor Museum, Bucklers Hard, Exbury Gardens, Calshot Activities Centre, for sailing, windsurfing etc, and many other places of interest.

Bedrooms: 2 double/
twin
Bathrooms: 2 private

⌖🖥️⚡Ⓢ🕘◐💻🖨️🚲P

INKPEN, Berkshire Map ref 2C2

◆◆◆◆

THE CROWN & GARTER

Great Common, Inkpen, Hungerford
RG17 9QR
T: (01488) 668325
F: (01488) 669072
I: www.crownandgarter.com

A 16thC inn, newly built en suite bedrooms arranged around a private garden. Interesting and reasonably priced food and real ales in beautiful surroundings. Terrific walking and cycling on the doorstep, Bath, Bristol, Oxford and Windsor are nearby. Warm, friendly and relaxing.

Bedrooms: 8 double/
twin
Bathrooms: 8 en suite

Lunch available
Evening meal available
CC: Delta, Diners,
Mastercard, Switch, Visa

Fri and Sat: Relaxing breaks with special prices for
DB&B.

B&B per night:
S £45.00
D £65.00

OPEN All year round

🐎⌖🛏️🍷🖥️⚡Ⓢ🖨️💻🌐🚲🍴🔍♨️🎵⌖🐇🐕🐾P

◆◆◆◆

THE SWAN INN
Inkpen, Hungerford RG17 9DX
T: (01488) 668326
F: (01488) 668306
E: enquiries@theswaninn-organics.co.uk
I: www.theswaninn-organics.co.uk

B&B per night:
S £40.00–£65.00
D £75.00–£90.00

HB per person:
DY £45.00–£70.00

OPEN All year round

17thC inn located in an Area of Outstanding Natural Beauty, one mile from Coombe Gibbet, the highest point in Southern England (965ft). En suite bedrooms. Owned by local organic beef farmers, the bar food and restaurant use the best, fresh organic ingredients. West Berkshire Camra 'Pub of the Year' 2000.

Bedrooms: 1 single,
9 double/twin
Bathrooms: 10 en suite

Lunch available
Evening meal available
CC: Delta, Mastercard,
Switch, Visa

ISLE OF WIGHT

See under Bembridge, Bonchurch, Carisbrooke, East Cowes, Freshwater, Freshwater Bay, Ryde, Sandown, Shanklin, Totland Bay, Whitwell, Wootton Bridge

---

KIRTLINGTON, Oxfordshire Map ref 2C1

◆◆◆◆

VICARAGE FARM
Kirtlington, Oxford OX5 3JY
T: (01869) 350254
F: (01869) 350254
E: jahunter@freenet.co.uk
I: www.country-accom.co.uk/
vicaragefarm

Bedrooms: 3 double/
twin
Bathrooms: 1 private

B&B per night:
S £25.00–£30.00
D £45.00–£50.00

OPEN Feb–Nov

On A4095 just outside Kirtlington. Close to Woodstock, Blenheim Palace, Bicester village and many places of interest. Modern farmhouse. Oxford, Stratford and Warwick Castle easily accessible.

LISS, Hampshire Map ref 2C3

◆◆◆

GREYWALLS HOUSE
London Road, Hillbrow, Liss GU33 7QR
T: (01730) 894246 & 895596
F: (01730) 894865
E: hillbrow.la@lineone.net
I: www.bidbury.co.uk

B&B per night:
S £35.00–£40.00
D £50.00–£70.00

HB per person:
DY £45.00–£80.00

Stone-built Victorian country house set in extensive beautiful woodland gardens. Very peaceful yet within 5 minutes of Petersfield and downland. Good golf, walking and riding nearby. 30 minutes from Winchester, Chichester, Portsmouth and Guildford. Spacious and comfortable lounge with log fire. All bedrooms have private facilities. French spoken.

Bedrooms: 1 single,
2 double/twin
Bathrooms: 2 en suite,
1 private

Evening meal available

LOUDWATER, Buckinghamshire Map ref 2C2

Rating
Applied For

TREVONA
7 Derehams Lane, Loudwater,
High Wycombe HP10 9RH
T: (01494) 526715

Bedrooms: 2 double/
twin

B&B per night:
S £25.00–£30.00
D £45.00–£50.00

OPEN All year round

Small quiet country location, 3 minutes M40. Midway between London and Oxford. Within easy reach of Henley, Marlow, Windsor. Indoor heated pool. Parking.

◆◆◆◆◆
Gold
Award

BRITANNIA HOUSE

Mill Lane, Lymington SO41 9AY
T: (01590) 672091
F: (01590) 672091
E: enquiries@britannia-house.com
I: www.britannia-house.com

B&B per night:
S £50.00–£70.00
D £60.00–£85.00

OPEN All year round

Luxurious 1870 character guesthouse providing every comfort, yet only 2 minutes' walk from picturesque Lymington Quay, shops, restaurants and marinas. Very comfortable double bedrooms with en suite facilities, luxury breakfast in a cosy farmhouse kitchen, attractive courtyard garden, on-site parking, residential supper and liquor license.

Bedrooms: 3 double/
twin; suites available
Bathrooms: 2 en suite,
1 private

In-house beauty treatments available. Private yacht hire, horse riding, picnic hampers and many more outside activities can be arranged.

Evening meal available
CC: Delta, Mastercard,
Switch, Visa

◆◆◆◆◆
Gold
Award

EFFORD COTTAGE

Everton, Lymington SO41 0JD
T: (01590) 642315
F: (01590) 641030
E: effcottage@aol.com
I: www.smoothhound.co.uk/hotels/
effordco.html

B&B per night:
D £50.00–£60.00

OPEN All year round

Friendly, spacious Georgian cottage in an acre of garden. Award-winning guesthouse. Elegant bedrooms, luxury facilities. Delicious, 4-course breakfast from a wide and varied menu. Home-made bread/preserves. Patricia, a qualified chef, uses home-grown produce for traditional country cooking. Special midweek winter breaks. 'Your comfort is our concern'.

Bedrooms: 2 double/
twin, 1 triple/multiple;
suites available
Bathrooms: 3 en suite

Easter, Valentine specials, winter breaks, course and training weekends available on application.

Lunch available
Evening meal available

◆◆◆◆

BURWOOD LODGE

27 Romsey Road, Lyndhurst SO43 7AA
T: (023) 8028 2445
F: (023) 8028 4104

B&B per night:
S £25.00–£30.00
D £44.00–£50.00

OPEN All year round

Lovely Edwardian house in half-acre grounds, located just 3 minutes' walk to village high street, 5 minutes from open forest. Guest lounge and separate dining room overlook the gardens, enhancing a relaxing environment. Bedrooms tastefully decorated: family, twin, single and a 4-poster room for those special, romantic occasions.

Bedrooms: 1 single,
4 double/twin, 1 triple/
multiple
Bathrooms: 6 en suite

CHECK THE MAPS

The colour maps at the front of this guide show all the cities, towns and villages for which you will find accommodation entries.
Refer to the town index to find the page on which they are listed.

◆◆◆◆
Silver
Award

CLAYHILL HOUSE

Clayhill, Lyndhurst SO43 7DE
T: (023) 8028 2304 & 07989 536837
F: (023) 8028 2093
E: clayhillhouse@tinyworld.co.uk
I: www.newforest.demon.co.uk/clayhill.htm

B&B per night:
S £25.00–£35.00
D £45.00–£50.00

OPEN All year round

Warm and friendly, Georgian house, built in 1830. Beautifully decorated, all en suites, spacious rooms ideal for couples, families and honeymooners. Long or short stays. Close to forest walks and cycling paths. Good pub food nearby.

Bedrooms: 3 double/ twin
Bathrooms: 3 en suite

CC: Delta, Mastercard, Switch, Visa

3 nights for price 2, Oct–Mar (excl Christmas and New Year).

♠ ⛺ 10 🍴 ⬜ ♨ 🔍 S 🔍 🕮 🖥 🍷 🐾 🐕 P

◆◆◆◆
Silver
Award

FOREST COTTAGE

High Street, Lyndhurst SO43 7BH
T: (023) 8028 3461
I: www.forestcottage.i12.com

B&B per night:
S £22.00–£24.00
D £44.00–£48.00

OPEN All year round

Charming 300-year-old cottage, in the village yet close to the forest. Guest lounge with TV, library of natural history books, maps and local literature. Tea/coffee always available. Warm, pretty bedrooms. The garden contains an interesting collection of plants. Private parking. Riding and bicycle hire available locally.

Bedrooms: 1 single, 2 double/twin

⛺ 14 S 🔍 🕮 🖥 🖥 🐾 🐕 P

◆◆◆◆

THE PENNY FARTHING HOTEL

Romsey Road, Lyndhurst SO43 7AA
T: (023) 8028 4422
F: (023) 8028 4488
E: stay@pennyfarthinghotel.co.uk
I: www.pennyfarthinghotel.co.uk

B&B per night:
S £35.00–£45.00
D £59.00–£90.00

OPEN All year round

Welcome to our cheerful hotel, conveniently situated a moment's walk from the village centre. Our cosy centrally heated bedrooms have multiple en suite shower or bath and WC, colour TV, clock, radio and tea/coffee-making facilities. We also provide a residents' bar/lounge, lock-up bicycle store and large private car park.

Bedrooms: 4 single, 9 double/twin, 2 triple/ multiple
Bathrooms: 15 en suite

CC: Amex, Delta, Diners, Mastercard, Switch, Visa

♠ ⛺ 🏠 ⬜ 🍷 S 🔍 🕮 🖥 ∪ 🐾 🐕 P

◆◆◆

ROSEDALE BED & BREAKFAST

24 Shaggs Meadow, Lyndhurst SO43 7BN
T: (023) 8028 3793
E: jenny@theangels.freeserve.co.uk

Bedrooms: 1 double/ twin, 1 triple/multiple
Bathrooms: 1 en suite

Evening meal available

B&B per night:
S £18.00–£24.75
D £36.00–£49.50

HB per person:
DY £24.00–£30.75

OPEN All year round

Family-run bed and breakfast in the centre of Lyndhurst. We cater for families. Colour TV, tea/coffee facilities. Breakfast served at your convenience. Evening meals by arrangement.

♠ ⛺ ⬜ ♨ 🔍 S 🔍 🖥 🐾 🐕 P

◆◆◆ **SOUTHVIEW**
Gosport Lane, Lyndhurst SO43 7BL
T: (023) 8028 2224
E: gburbidge@virgin.net

Bedrooms: 1 single,
5 double/twin
Bathrooms: 4 en suite

B&B per night:
S £25.00–£35.00
D £45.00–£50.00

OPEN Jan–Nov

*Comfortable rooms, close to town centre and in the middle of the New Forest. En suite
have baths and showers. Lock up garages if required.*

◆◆◆◆

TEMPLE LODGE GUEST HOUSE
Queens Road, Lyndhurst SO43 7BR
T: (023) 8028 2392
F: (023) 8028 4590
E: templelodge@lineone.net

B&B per night:
S £22.50–£30.00
D £50.00

OPEN All year round

*Robyn and Eddie Richey invite guests
to come and enjoy a break in our
gracious Victorian home situated in
the heart of the New Forest. We offer
en suite accommodation. TV in all
rooms, hairdryer and hospitality tray.
Choice of breakfasts. Spacious public
guest rooms and off-road parking.*

Bedrooms: 5 double/
twin, 1 triple/multiple
Bathrooms: 6 en suite

CC: Delta, Mastercard,
Switch, Visa

◆ **CARTLANDS COTTAGE**
Kings Lane,
Cookham Dean, Cookham,
Maidenhead SL6 9AY
T: (01628) 482196

Bedrooms: 1 triple/
multiple
Bathrooms: 1 en suite

B&B per night:
S £25.00–£30.00
D £45.00–£55.00

OPEN All year round

*Family room in self-contained garden studio. Meals in delightful timbered character
cottage with exposed beams. Traditional cottage garden. National Trust common land.
Very quiet.*

◆◆◆

ACORN LODGE
79 Marlow Bottom Road, Marlow Bottom,
Marlow SL7 3NA
T: (01628) 472197 & 0771 8757601
F: (01628) 472197

B&B per night:
S £40.00–£55.00
D £55.00–£65.00

OPEN All year round

*Backing on to woodland. Outdoor
swimming pool. En suite rooms,
comfortable beds, Victorian brass
4-poster or twin beds, ceiling fans,
remote TV. Suite has a sitting room,
whirlpool bath. Warm welcome,
super breakfast, 2 happy dogs. Easy
reach Heathrow, Windsor, Legoland,
1.5 miles Marlow centre. We own a
natural therapy centre 50 yards
away.*

Bedrooms: 3 double/
twin; suites available
Bathrooms: 3 en suite

CC: Amex, Delta,
Mastercard, Switch, Visa

Weekend workshops availble in pain management
and divorce, separated and bereavment recovery
and bio-spiritual focusing. Prices on application.

◆◆ **16 CLAREMONT ROAD**
Marlow SL7 1BW
T: (01628) 471334 & 07774 107445
E: sue@gladeend.com
I: www.gladeend.com

Bedrooms: 1 single,
1 double/twin

B&B per night:
S £30.00–£35.00
D £55.00–£60.00

OPEN All year round

*Warm welcome in a family home a few minutes' walk from the town centre, business area,
railway station and river. Easy access to M4 and M40.*

MARLOW continued

◆◆◆◆ **THE INN ON THE GREEN LIMITED**

The Old Cricket Common, Cookham Dean, Cookham, Maidenhead SL6 9NZ	Bedrooms: 1 single, 7 double/twin	Lunch available Evening meal available	B&B per night: S £80.00–£120.00 D £90.00–£140.00
T: (01628) 482638	Bathrooms: 8 en suite	CC: Amex, Delta, Mastercard, Switch, Visa	

T: (01628) 482638
F: (01628) 487474
E: enquiries@theinnonthegreen.com
I: www.theinnonthegreen.com

Beautiful country house hotel in heart of the countryside. Freshly prepared modern French/British menu. Stunning al fresco courtyard. Close to Marlow, Windsor, Henley and Cookham.

HB per person:
DY £65.00–£80.00

OPEN All year round

ⓜ🐎♿🏠📞🖥️🖵↻🍽️Ⓢ🖩◼️🍷↻☼🐴🚲🍃♿P

◆◆◆ **RED BARN FARM**

Marlow Road, Marlow SL7 3DQ
T: (01494) 882820
F: (01494) 883545

Bedrooms: 1 single, 1 double/twin, 1 triple/multiple
Bathrooms: 1 en suite

B&B per night:
S Max £25.00
D Max £55.00

OPEN All year round

Detached farmhouse 10 acres grazed by horses and ponies. Oxford, Henley, London within easy reach. Theatres. Heated outdoor pool in pleasant garden.

ⓜ🐎🖥️↻Ⓢ🖩◼️🍃☼🚲🍃P

◆◆◆◆

ROSEMARY COTTAGE BED & BREAKFAST

99 Heath End Road, Flackwell Heath, High Wycombe HP10 9ES

T: (01628) 520635
F: (01628) 520635
E: mike.1@virgin.net
I: www.reservation.co.uk

Bedrooms: 3 double/twin
Bathrooms: 1 en suite

B&B per night:
S £45.00–£50.00
D £50.00–£65.00

OPEN All year round

A charming character cottage with stunning panoramic views across the Thames Valley towards Marlow and Maidenhead. Convenient for London, Windsor, Oxford, access to M40, M25 and M4 motorways. Flackwell Heath is situated in a beautiful part of the Chilterns and a perfect base for exploring the surrounding area.

ⓜ🐎🖥️🖵↻Ⓢ🖩◼️🍃🚲P

MARNHULL, Dorset Map ref 2B3

◆◆◆ **THE OLD BANK**

Burton Street, Marnhull, Sturminster Newton DT10 1PH
T: (01258) 821019
F: (01258) 821019

Bedrooms: 2 double/twin, 1 triple/multiple

B&B per night:
S £20.00
D £40.00

OPEN All year round

Stone-built (1730) house in quiet Dorset country village. Attractive courtyard bordered by barns, leading to pretty garden. Pub approximately 100 yards away. Friendly, family-run home.

🐎🖵↻Ⓢ🖩◼️🍃☼🚲🍃P

MILFORD-ON-SEA, Hampshire Map ref 2C3

◆◆◆◆ **ALMA MATER**

4 Knowland Drive, Milford-on-Sea, Lymington SO41 0RH	Bedrooms: 3 double/twin	Evening meal available	B&B per night: S £30.00–£35.00 D £45.00–£50.00

T: (01590) 642811
F: (01590) 642811
E: bandbalmamater@aol.com
I: www.almamater.org.uk

Bathrooms: 3 en suite

HB per person:
DY £37.50–£40.00

OPEN All year round

Detached, quiet, spacious, non-smoking chalet bunglow with en suite bedrooms overlooking lovely garden. Close to village, beaches, New Forest and IoW. Evening meals by request.

ⓜ🐎♿🏠🖵↻Ⓢ🖩◼️🍃☼🚲🍃P

MILFORD-ON-SEA continued

◆◆◆◆◆ THE BAY TREES

Silver Award

8 High Street, Milford-on-Sea,
Lymington SO41 0QD
T: (01590) 642186
F: (01590) 645461
E: thebaytrees@netscapeonline.co.uk
I: www.newforestbandb.com

Bedrooms: 2 double/twin
Bathrooms: 2 en suite

B&B per night:
S £30.00–£40.00
D £60.00–£70.00

OPEN All year round

The Bay Tree is a luxurious 17thC home situated in the heart of picturesque Milford-on-Sea, on the edge of the New Forest and only a few minutes' walk from the sea.

◆◆◆ COMPTON HOTEL

59 Keyhaven Road, Milford-on-Sea,
Lymington SO41 0QX
T: (01590) 643117
F: (01590) 643117
E: dbembo@talk21.com

Bedrooms: 2 single,
3 double/twin, 1 triple/
multiple
Bathrooms: 4 en suite

Evening meal available

B&B per night:
S £32.00–£35.00
D £45.00–£47.00

HB per person:
DY £32.00–£35.00

OPEN All year round

Compton is a small, private hotel, with the facilities of a larger hotel, run by the same proprietors and family for 20 years.

MILTON KEYNES, Buckinghamshire Map ref 2C1

◆◆◆ CHANTRY FARM

Pindon End, Hanslope,
Milton Keynes MK19 7HL
T: (01908) 510269 & 07850 166122
F: (01908) 510269

Bedrooms: 3 double/twin
Bathrooms: 1 en suite

B&B per night:
S £20.00–£30.00
D £40.00–£60.00

OPEN All year round

500-acre farm. Stone farmhouse, 1650, with inglenook. Surrounded by beautiful countryside. Swimming pool, trout lake, table tennis, croquet, clay pigeon shooting. 15 minutes' from centre.

◆◆◆ MILL FARM

Gayhurst, Newport Pagnell
MK16 8LT
T: (01908) 611489 & 07714 719640
F: (01908) 611489
E: adamsmillfarm@aol.com

Bedrooms: 3 double/
twin, 1 triple/multiple
Bathrooms: 2 en suite,
1 private

B&B per night:
S £20.00–£25.00
D £40.00–£50.00

OPEN All year round

500-acre mixed farm. 17thC farmhouse with hard tennis court, fishing on River Ouse, which flows through farm. Good touring centre. Easy reach of Oxford, Cambridge, Woburn Abbey and Whipsnade.

◆◆◆ VIGNOBLE

2 Medland, Woughton Park,
Milton Keynes MK6 3BH
T: (01908) 666804
F: (01908) 666626
E: vignoblegh@aol.com

Bedrooms: 1 single,
2 double/twin

B&B per night:
S £28.00–£37.00
D £48.00–£50.00

OPEN All year round

In a quiet cul-de-sac within walking distance of the Open University and 2.5 miles from the city centre. A warm welcome home from home in 3 languages.

QUALITY ASSURANCE SCHEME

For an explanation of the quality and facilities represented by the Diamonds please refer to the front of this guide. A more detailed explanation can be found in the information pages at the back.

◆◆◆

WOODPECKERS
244 Main Road, Naphill, High Wycombe
HP14 4RX
T: (01494) 563728 & 07775 694015
E: angela.brand@virgin.net

B&B per night:
S £20.00–£25.00
D £40.00–£45.00

Situated in Chiltern Hills. Accommodation in modernised annexe with garden which can also be rented as a separate holiday cottage. Rooms en suite. Easily accessible for London, Oxford, Windsor, Henley, Heathrow Airport. Beautiful walks, pub food and places of interest minutes away. Warm welcome guaranteed.

Bedrooms: 1 single,
2 double/twin
Bathrooms: 2 en suite,
1 private

🐎 Ⓢ 🄿 🕮 🍴 ❄ 🐕 ⛟ 🅿

NEW FOREST

See under Ashurst, Bartley, Barton on Sea, Beaulieu, Boldre, Brockenhurst, Fordingbridge, Hordle, Hythe, Lymington, Lyndhurst, Milford-on-Sea, New Milton, Ringwood, Sway

---

◆◆◆◆

JOBZ-A-GUDN
169 Stem Lane, New Milton
BH25 5ND
T: (01425) 615435 & 07866 881426
F: (01425) 615435

Bedrooms: 1 double/
twin
Bathrooms: 1 en suite

B&B per night:
S £20.00–£25.00
D £40.00–£45.00

OPEN All year round

Lovely family bungalow overlooking farmland. Accommodation of 1 double room with beautiful new en suite. Excellent 4-course breakfast.

🛏 🍴 🖥 Ⓢ 🄿 🕮 ❄ 🐕 ⛟ 🅿

◆◆◆

WILLY'S WELL
Bashley Common Road, Wootton,
New Milton BH25 5SF
T: (01425) 616834
E: myoramac2@hotmail.com

B&B per night:
S £25.00–£30.00
D £45.00–£50.00

OPEN All year round

A warm welcome awaits you at our mid-1700s Listed thatched cottage standing in 1 acre of mature gardens also available for your enjoyment. We have direct forest access through 6 acres of pasture and are 3 miles from the sea. Ideal for walking, cycling, horse-riding.

Bedrooms: 2 double/
twin
Bathrooms: 1 en suite,
1 private

🛏 🍴 🖥 Ⓢ 🕮 🐾 ⛟ ♪ ► ❄ 🐕 ⛟ 🅿

USE YOUR *i*s
There are more than 550 Tourist Information Centres throughout England offering friendly help with accommodation and holiday ideas as well as suggestions of places to visit and things to do. You'll find TIC addresses in the local Phone Book.

◆◆◆◆

THE OLD FARMHOUSE
Downend Lane, Chieveley, Newbury
RG20 8TN
T: (01635) 248361 & 07970 583373
F: (01635) 528195
E: palletts@aol.com
I: www.smoothhound.co.uk/hotels/
oldfarmhouse

B&B per night:
S £35.00–£37.00
D £52.00–£55.00

OPEN All year round

Period farmhouse on edge of village within 2 miles of M4/A34 (junction 13), 5 miles north of Newbury. Accommodation in ground-floor annexe comprising hall, kitchenette, sitting room (with bed-settee), double bedroom, bathroom. Large gardens overlooking countryside. Oxford, Bath, Windsor and Heathrow Airport within easy reach. London approximately one hour.

Bedrooms: 1 triple/
multiple
Bathrooms: 1 en suite

◆◆◆

WHITE COTTAGE
Newtown, Hungerford RG20 9AP
T: (01635) 43097 & 07721 613224
F: (01635) 43097
E: ellie@p-p-i.fsnet.co.uk

Bedrooms: 1 single,
2 double/twin

B&B per night:
S £27.00
D £45.00

OPEN All year round

Delightful cottage in semi-rural position, just 2 miles south of Newbury. Comfortable, quiet accommodation. Children and dogs welcome.

◆◆◆◆

THE WHITE HART INN
Kintbury Road, Hamstead Marshall,
Newbury RG20 0HW
T: (01488) 658201
F: (01488) 657192

B&B per night:
S £60.00–£70.00
D £80.00–£90.00

OPEN All year round

Traditional, elegant country inn and restaurant with lovely walled garden and views of open countryside. We offer a relaxed atmosphere and are renowned for our Italian cooking. The stylish bedrooms are peacefully situated in adjacent barn conversion.

Bedrooms: 2 single,
2 double/twin, 2 triple/
multiple
Bathrooms: 6 en suite

Lunch available
Evening meal available
CC: Mastercard, Visa

◆◆◆◆◆

Silver
Award

THE LIMES
North Square, Newport Pagnell MK16 8EP
T: (01908) 617041 & 07860 908925
F: (01908) 217292
E: royandruth@8thelimes.freeserve.co.uk

B&B per night:
S £45.00–£60.00
D £65.00–£80.00

HB per person:
DY £65.00–£80.00

OPEN All year round

Georgian townhouse with river frontage, off-road parking, private fishing and established gardens. Comfortable and beautifully furnished with antiques. All bedrooms have en suite facilities and one has a 4-poster bed. Good home cooking. Meeting/conference room available. Three miles from M1 junction 14.

Bedrooms: 3 double/
twin
Bathrooms: 3 en suite

Evening meal available
CC: Amex, Delta,
Mastercard, Switch, Visa

NEWPORT PAGNELL continued

♦♦♦ RECTORY FARM

North Crawley, Newport Pagnell
MK16 9HH
T: (01234) 391213

Bedrooms: 2 double/
twin

B&B per night:
S £17.50–£20.00
D £35.00–£40.00

350-acre arable & livestock farm. A family-run farm situated 1 mile from North Crawley and 2 miles from Newport Pagnell. A non-smoking establishment.

OPEN All year round

⚫🐎7 Ⓢ ⤢ ⬛ ❄ 🚗 P

OLNEY, Buckinghamshire Map ref 2C1

♦♦♦♦ COLCHESTER HOUSE

26 High Street, Olney MK46 4BB
T: (01234) 712602
F: (01234) 240564
I: www.olneybucks.co.uk

Bedrooms: 4 double/
twin; suites available
Bathrooms: 2 en suite

B&B per night:
S £27.50–£40.00
D £50.00–£60.00

Listed townhouse within short walk of pubs and restaurants. Two annexe en suite doubles in garden, double and twin with shared bathroom in house. Warm welcome.

OPEN All year round

🐎🏃💷🖥🖵💧❓Ⓢ⤢🏠⬛❄🚗🏨P

OXFORD, Oxfordshire Map ref 2C1 *Tourist Information Centre Tel: (01865) 726871*

♦♦ BEAUMONT GUEST HOUSE

234 Abingdon Road, Oxford
OX1 4SP
T: (01865) 241767
F: (01865) 241767
E: info@beaumont.sagehost.co.uk
I: www.beaumont.sagehost.co.uk

Bedrooms: 1 single,
3 double/twin, 1 triple/
multiple
Bathrooms: 1 en suite

CC: Delta, Mastercard,
Switch, Visa

B&B per night:
S £28.00–£45.00
D £46.00–£62.00

OPEN All year round

Small, friendly guesthouse situated near the river. Oxford city centre is 10 minutes' walk away.

⚫🐎🖵💧Ⓢ⤢⬛🚙🚗

♦♦♦ THE BUNGALOW

Cherwell Farm, Mill Lane,
Old Marston, Oxford OX3 0QF
T: (01865) 557171 & 07703 162125

Bedrooms: 3 double/
twin
Bathrooms: 1 en suite

B&B per night:
S £30.00–£45.00
D £46.00–£52.00

Modern bungalow set in 5 acres, in quiet location with views over open countryside, 3 miles from city centre. No smoking. No bus route – car essential.

⚫🐎6🖥🖵💧❓Ⓢ⤢⬛🚙❄🚗P

♦♦♦♦♦
Silver
Award

CHESTNUTS GUEST HOUSE

45 Davenant Road, Off Woodstock Road,
Oxford OX2 8BU
T: (01865) 553375
F: (01865) 553375
E: stay@chestnutsguesthouse.co.uk

B&B per night:
S £50.00–£55.00
D £70.00–£72.00

OPEN All year round

Elegant house set in beautiful garden. Peaceful, yet near to the city centre. Spacious, comfortable interior with very attractive bedrooms, all en suite. Home cooking is our speciality. Ideal base for exploring this beautiful college city and surrounding countryside. Hospitable staff guarantee a warm welcome.

Bedrooms: 1 single,
4 double/twin, 1 triple/
multiple
Bathrooms: 6 en suite

CC: Amex, Delta, Diners,
Mastercard, Switch, Visa

🐎12🖥🖵💧❓Ⓢ⤢🏠⬛❄🚗🚫P

♦♦♦ DIAL HOUSE

25 London Road, Headington,
Oxford OX3 7RE
T: (01865) 769944
F: (01865) 769944
E: dialhouse@aol.com
I: www.oxfordcity.co.uk/accom/
dialhouse

Bedrooms: 7 double/
twin, 1 triple/multiple
Bathrooms: 7 en suite,
1 private

CC: Amex, Delta,
Mastercard, Switch, Visa

B&B per night:
S £45.00–£60.00
D £60.00–£80.00

OPEN All year round

Small family-run guesthouse built in a Tudor style. Close to city centre, on main bus route to London.

⚫🐎🖵💧❓Ⓢ⤢⬛🚗🐴P

◆◆◆◆ **HIGH HEDGES**
8 Cumnor Hill, Oxford OX2 9HA
T: (01865) 863395
F: (01865) 437351
E: tompkins@btinternet.com
I: www.smoothhound.co.uk/hotels/
highhedges

Bedrooms: 1 single,
2 double/twin, 1 triple/
multiple
Bathrooms: 2 en suite

CC: Delta, Mastercard,
Switch, Visa

B&B per night:
S £26.00–£30.00
D £48.00–£56.00

OPEN All year round

Close to city centre. High standard of accommodation, including en suite rooms with TV/Sky and tea/coffee facilities, making your stay a comfortable one.

◆◆◆ **HIGHFIELD WEST**
188 Cumnor Hill, Oxford OX2 9PJ
T: (01865) 863007
E: highfieldwest@email.msn.com

Bedrooms: 2 single,
2 double/twin, 1 triple/
multiple
Bathrooms: 3 en suite

B&B per night:
S £27.50–£31.00
D £47.50–£60.00

OPEN All year round

Non-smoking. Comfortable accommodation with good access to city centre and ring road. Large outdoor, heated swimming pool (summer season only). Vegetarians welcome.

◆◆ **ISIS GUEST HOUSE**
45-53 Iffley Road, Oxford OX4 1ED
T: (01865) 248894 & 242466
F: (01865) 243492
E: isis@herald.ox.ac.uk

Bedrooms: 12 single,
23 double/twin, 2 triple/
multiple
Bathrooms: 14 en suite

CC: Mastercard, Switch,
Visa

B&B per night:
S £26.00–£32.00
D £52.00–£56.00

OPEN Jul–Sep

Modernised, Victorian, city centre guesthouse within walking distance of colleges and shops. Easy access to ring road.

◆◆◆◆ **MARLBOROUGH HOUSE HOTEL**
321 Woodstock Road, Oxford OX2 7NY
T: (01865) 311321
F: (01865) 515329
E: enquiries@marlbhouse.win-uk.net
I: www.oxfordcity.co.uk/hotels/
marlborough

B&B per night:
S £73.00
D £84.00

OPEN All year round

Immaculate, spacious, privately owned hotel located in attractive leafy area of Victorian houses, 1.5 miles city centre. Bedrooms equipped with a kitchenette containing fridge, microwave, tea and coffee making facilities, telephone and TV, comfortable chairs, dining table and desk. Restaurants and shops are located within 10 minutes' walk.

Bedrooms: 2 single,
12 double/twin, 2 triple/
multiple
Bathrooms: 16 en suite

CC: Amex, Delta, Diners,
Mastercard, Switch, Visa

◆◆◆ **MILKA'S GUEST HOUSE**
379 Iffley Road, Oxford OX4 4DP
T: (01865) 778458
F: (01865) 776477
E: reservations@milkas.co.uk
I: www.milkas.co.uk

Bedrooms: 3 double/
twin
Bathrooms: 1 en suite

CC: Amex, Delta,
Mastercard, Switch, Visa

B&B per night:
S £35.00–£40.00
D £55.00–£60.00

OPEN All year round

Pleasant semi-detached house on main road, 1 mile from city centre.

◆◆◆ **MULBERRY GUEST HOUSE**
265 London Road, Headington,
Oxford OX3 9EH
T: (01865) 767114
F: (01865) 767114
E: mulberryguesthouse@hotmail.
com

Bedrooms: 5 double/
twin
Bathrooms: 4 en suite,
1 private

CC: Mastercard, Visa

B&B per night:
D £60.00–£70.00

OPEN All year round

Detached house close to BMW factory (M40 exit 8), Brookes University and local hospitals. Parking. Bus stops outside for Oxford colleges, Heathrow and Gatwick. Good touring base.

◆◆◆

NEWTON HOUSE

82-84 Abingdon Road, Oxford OX1 4PL
T: (01865) 240561
F: (01865) 244647
E: newton.house@btinternet.com
I: www.oxfordcity.co.uk/accom/newton

B&B per night:
S £34.00–£52.00
D £42.00–£65.00

OPEN All year round

Centrally situated. Two handsome Victorian townhouses linked to form a sizable guesthouse, retaining many original features and period furniture. Conveniently located close to the city's restaurants, pubs and shops, university and River Thames (with punting).

Bedrooms: 6 double/ twin, 7 triple/multiple
Bathrooms: 10 en suite

CC: Amex, Delta, Mastercard, Switch, Visa

◆◆◆

THE OLD BLACK HORSE HOTEL

102 St Clements, Oxford OX4 1AR
T: (01865) 244691
F: (01865) 242771

B&B per night:
S £50.00
D £85.00–£95.00

OPEN All year round

Former coaching inn, c1650, privately owned. Large, secure car park. Close to the historic High Magdalen Bridge, colleges, riverside walks and the city centre. The area has a wide variety of restaurants. Easy access M40 north and south. London and airport coaches stop close by.

Bedrooms: 1 single, 7 double/twin, 2 triple/ multiple
Bathrooms: 10 en suite

Lunch available
Evening meal available
CC: Amex, Delta, Mastercard, Switch, Visa

◆◆◆◆

PICKWICKS GUEST HOUSE

15-17 London Road, Headington, Oxford OX3 7SP
T: (01865) 750487
F: (01865) 742208
E: pickwicks@x-stream.co.uk
I: www.oxfordcity.co.uk/accom/pickwicks/

B&B per night:
S £30.00–£45.00
D £65.00–£70.00

OPEN All year round

Comfortable, friendly, family-run guesthouse within five minutes' drive of Oxford ring road and M40 motorway. Nearby coach stop for 24-hour service to central London, Heathrow and Gatwick airports. Close to Oxford Brookes University, John Radcliffe, Nuffield and Churchill hospitals. Translation service available.

Bedrooms: 4 single, 7 double/twin, 4 triple/ multiple
Bathrooms: 14 en suite

CC: Amex, Delta, Diners, Mastercard, Switch, Visa

SPECIAL BREAKS

Many establishments offer special promotions and themed breaks. These are highlighted in red. (All such offers are subject to availability.)

♦♦♦♦

PINE CASTLE HOTEL
290 Iffley Road, Oxford OX4 4AE
T: (01865) 241497 & 728887
F: (01865) 727230
E: stay@pinecastle.co.uk
I: www.oxfordcity.co.uk/hotels/pinecastle

B&B per night:
S £55.00–£60.00
D £69.00–£74.00

OPEN All year round

Beautiful hotel built at the turn of the country. Situated 1 mile from the city centre. Excellent bus service. Spacious bedrooms, all en suite and non-smoking. Breakfasts tailored to suit all tastes. Cosy lounge where guests are welcome to smoke. Open all year. Car park.

Bedrooms: 7 double/ twin, 1 triple/multiple
Bathrooms: 8 en suite

CC: Amex, Delta, Mastercard, Switch, Visa

♦♦♦

RIVER HOTEL
17 Botley Road, Oxford OX2 0AA
T: (01865) 243475
F: (01865) 724306
E: info@southerntb.co.uk
I: www.riverhotel.co.uk

Bedrooms: 4 single, 10 double/twin, 6 triple/ multiple
Bathrooms: 18 en suite, 2 private

CC: Mastercard, Visa

B&B per night:
S £60.00–£70.00
D £70.00–£01.00

OPEN All year round

Excellent location on River Thames walk. Residents' bar, car park on site. Walking distance to city colleges, bus/rail stations. 'Large enough to be comfortable, small enough to be friendly.'

♦♦♦♦

THE TOWER HOUSE
15 Ship Street, Oxford OX1 3DA
T: (01865) 246828
F: (01865) 246828

Bedrooms: 7 double/ twin
Bathrooms: 4 en suite

CC: Delta, Mastercard, Switch, Visa

B&B per night:
S £45.00–£55.00
D £80.00–£95.00

OPEN All year round

17thC guesthouse in universtiy city centre. Renowned for its warm hospitality and good hearty breakfast. Recently awarded 4 diamonds. Establisment is also of historical interest.

♦♦♦

WEST FARM
Eaton, Appleton, Abingdon OX13 5PR
T: (01865) 862908
F: (01865) 865512

B&B per night:
S £25.00–£30.00
D £50.00–£55.00

1100-acre arable and livestock farm. Comfortable, centrally heated farmhouse on working farm, 6 miles west of Oxford, 3 miles from A34, 1 mile from A420 (Oxford – Swindon road). Children welcome (equipment, toys, etc). Excellent centre for touring, also frequent cheap coaches from Oxford to London and airports. Good local pubs.

Bedrooms: 1 single, 1 double/twin, 1 triple/ multiple
Bathrooms: 1 private

♦♦♦

ROSE COTTAGE
1 The Mead, Liss GU33 7DU
T: (01730) 892378

Bedrooms: 1 single, 2 double/twin

B&B per night:
S £17.50–£20.00
D £34.00–£40.00

Semi-detached, 4-bedroom house with lounge and dining area. Three minutes' walk to station.

OPEN All year round

PETERSFIELD continued

◆◆◆ 1 THE SPAIN

Sheep Street, Petersfield GU32 3JZ	Bedrooms: 3 double/	B&B per night:
T: (01730) 263261 & 261678	twin	**S £20.00–£28.00**
F: (01730) 261084	Bathrooms: 1 en suite	**D £40.00–£45.00**
E: allantarver@cwcom.net		
		OPEN All year round

18thC house with charming walled garden, in conservation area of Petersfield. Good eating places nearby, lovely walks, plenty to see and do.

PORTSMOUTH & SOUTHSEA, Hampshire Map ref 2C3

◆◆◆ BEMBELL COURT HOTEL

69 Festing Road, Southsea,	Bedrooms: 2 single,	Evening meal available	B&B per night:
Portsmouth PO4 0NQ	7 double/twin, 3 triple/	CC: Amex, Delta, Diners,	**S £39.50–£45.00**
T: (023) 9273 5915 & 9275 0497	multiple	Mastercard, Visa	**D £52.00–£60.00**
F: (023) 9275 6497	Bathrooms: 10 en suite		
E: keith@bembell.freeserve.co.uk			OPEN All year round
I: www.bembell.com			

Friendly, family-run hotel ideally situated in Portsmouth's prime holiday area. A short stroll from shops, restaurants, pubs, boating lake, Rose Gardens. Close to ferries.

◆◆◆ THE ELMS GUEST HOUSE

48 Victoria Road South, Southsea	Bedrooms: 1 double/	CC: Delta, Mastercard,	B&B per night:
PO5 2BT	twin, 4 triple/multiple	Switch, Visa	**S £35.00–£48.00**
T: (023) 9282 3924	Bathrooms: 5 en suite		**D £42.00–£48.00**
F: (023) 9282 3924			
E: theelmsgh@aol.com			OPEN All year round
I: www.resort-guide/portsmouth/			
elms			

Warm, friendly, totally no-smoking guesthouse within 8 minutes' walk of the seafront and restaurants. Close to the maritime attractions and ferry ports.

◆◆◆◆ HAMILTON HOUSE

95 Victoria Road North, Southsea	Bedrooms: 1 single,	CC: Delta, Mastercard,	B&B per night:
PO5 1PS	5 double/twin, 3 triple/	Switch, Visa	**S £21.00–£40.00**
T: (023) 9282 3502	multiple		**D £42.00–£50.00**
F: (023) 9282 3502	Bathrooms: 5 en suite		
E: sandra@hamiltonhouse.co.uk			OPEN All year round
I: www.resort-guide.co.uk/			
portsmouth/hamilton			

Delightful Victorian townhouse. Five minutes – Continental/I.O.W. Ferry ports, centres, stations, university, historic ships/museums, Gunwarf Quays. Ideal touring base. Breakfast served from 6.15am.

◆◆◆◆ THE ROWANS

43 Festing Grove, Southsea	Bedrooms: 3 double/	B&B per night:
PO4 9QB	twin	**S £23.00–£30.00**
T: (023) 9273 6614	Bathrooms: 2 en suite	**D £23.00–£26.00**
F: (023) 9282 3711		
		OPEN All year round

Elegant Victorian guesthouse in quiet residential area. Close to seafront and all amenities. Convenient for ferry ports. Early breakfasts available. Off and on street parking.

QUAINTON, Buckinghamshire Map ref 2C1

◆◆◆ WOODLANDS FARMHOUSE

Doddershall, Quainton, Aylesbury	Bedrooms: 3 double/	B&B per night:
HP22 4DE	twin, 1 triple/multiple	**S Min £25.00**
T: (01296) 770225	Bathrooms: 4 en suite	**D Min £50.00**
		OPEN All year round

18thC farmhouse offering peaceful accommodation in 11 acres of grounds. Large en suite rooms with individual entrances in barn conversion.

COLOUR MAPS Colour maps at the front of this guide pinpoint all places under which you will find accommodation listed.

RADNAGE, Buckinghamshire Map ref 2C1

♦♦♦♦ HIGHLANDS

26 Green Lane, Radnage, High Wycombe HP14 4DN T: (01494) 484835 F: (01494) 482633 E: janekhighlands@aol.com I: www.country-accom.co.uk	Bedrooms: 2 double/ twin; suites available Bathrooms: 2 en suite	B&B per night: S Min £35.00 D Min £50.00 OPEN All year round

Chalet bungalow in the hamlet of Radnage where red kites fly. Close to Oxford, Windsor, 2.5 miles from M40 junctions. Ideal for walking, relaxing and business.

READING, Berkshire Map ref 2C2 *Tourist Information Centre Tel: (0118) 956 6226*

♦♦♦ BATH HOTEL

54 Bath Road, Reading RG1 6PG T: (0118) 957 2019 F: (0118) 950 3203	Bedrooms: 7 single, 11 double/twin, 3 triple/ multiple Bathrooms: 21 en suite	Lunch available Evening meal available CC: Amex, Delta, Mastercard, Switch, Visa	B&B per night: S £39.00–£70.00 D £55.00–£90.00 HB per person: DY £53.00–£84.00 OPEN All year round

Victorian-built hotel, ideally situated for town centre, M4 and Reading Station.

♦♦♦ CRESCENT HOTEL

35 Coley Avenue, Reading RG1 6LL T: (01189) 507980 F: (01189) 574299	Bedrooms: 4 single, 10 double/twin, 4 triple/ multiple Bathrooms: 15 en suite	Evening meal available CC: Amex, Mastercard, Visa	B&B per night: S £40.00–£50.00 D £60.00–£70.00 HB per person: DY £40.00–£50.00 OPEN All year round

Family-run licensed hotel, in the centre of Reading and close to all amenities. Trouser press and hair dryer in most rooms. Free car park. Close to town centre and railway station.

♦♦♦ DITTISHAM GUEST HOUSE

63 Tilehurst Road, Reading RG30 2JL T: (0118) 956 9483 & 07889 605193 E: dittishamgh@aol.com	Bedrooms: 4 single, 1 double/twin Bathrooms: 3 en suite	CC: Delta, Mastercard, Switch, Visa	B&B per night: S £29.50–£37.50 D £39.00–£60.00 OPEN All year round

Renovated Edwardian property with garden, in a quiet but central location. Good value and quality. On bus routes for centre of town. Car park.

♦♦♦ THE OLD FORGE

109 Grovelands Road, Reading RG30 2PB T: (0118) 958 2928 F: (0118) 958 2408 E: rees.family@virgin.net	Bedrooms: 4 single, 8 double/twin Bathrooms: 9 en suite	CC: Delta, Mastercard, Switch, Visa	B&B per night: S £32.00–£38.00 D £47.50–£55.00 OPEN All year round

Family-run guesthouse, approximately 1.5 miles west of Reading town centre. Detached premises, large car park. Comfortable rooms all with tea/coffee and TV.

RINGWOOD, Hampshire Map ref 2B3

♦♦♦ THE AULD KENNELS

215 Christchurch Road, Moortown, Ringwood BH24 3AN T: (01425) 475170 F: (01425) 461577	Bedrooms: 2 double/ twin Bathrooms: 2 en suite	Evening meal available	B&B per night: S £18.00–£24.00 D £36.00–£40.00 HB per person: DY £27.50–£33.50 OPEN All year round

Comfortable thatched family cottage on edge of New Forest. Home from home surroundings. Hearty breakfast, centrally situated for all amenities.

CONFIRM YOUR BOOKING
You are advised to confirm your booking in writing.

ROMSEY, Hampshire Map ref 2C3 *Tourist Information Centre Tel: (01794) 512987*

◆◆◆ **RANVILLES FARM HOUSE**
Ower, Romsey SO51 6AA
T: (023) 8081 4481
F: (023) 8081 4481

Bedrooms: 1 single,
2 double/twin, 1 triple/
multiple
Bathrooms: 4 en suite

B&B per night:
S £35.00
D £50.00–£55.00

OPEN All year round

An historic farmhouse near Winchester, Salisbury, the New Forest and 1 mile from Romsey. Peaceful situation, set in 5 acres of gardens and paddocks. Extra large beds.

◆◆◆◆ **ROSELEA**
Hamdown Crescent, East Wellow,
Romsey SO51 6BJ
T: (01794) 323262
F: (01794) 323262
E: pennyc@tcp.co.uk

Bedrooms: 2 double/
twin
Bathrooms: 2 en suite

B&B per night:
S £20.00–£25.00
D £35.00–£40.00

OPEN All year round

Quiet ground floor accommodation on the edge of the New Forest. Honey from our own bees, together with homemade honey marmalade served at breakfast.

RYDE, Isle of Wight Map ref 2C3 *Tourist Information Centre Tel: (01983) 813818*

◆◆◆ **SEAWARD GUEST HOUSE**
14-16 George Street, Ryde
PO33 2EW
T: (01983) 563168 &
0800 915 2966
F: (01983) 563168
E: seaward@fsbdial.co.uk

Bedrooms: 1 single,
4 double/twin, 2 triple/
multiple
Bathrooms: 2 en suite

Evening meal available

B&B per night:
S £19.00–£21.00
D £32.00–£46.00

OPEN All year round

Family-run guesthouse close to beach, pier and all amenities. English, continental or vegetarian breakfast available. An ideal base for touring the island.

◆◆◆◆ **SILLWOOD ACRE**
Church Road, Binstead, Ryde
PO33 3TB
T: (01983) 563553
E: sillwood.acre@virgin.net

Bedrooms: 2 double/
twin, 1 triple/multiple
Bathrooms: 3 en suite

B&B per night:
S £20.00
D £40.00

OPEN All year round

Large Victorian house near Ryde, convenient for the ferry and hovercraft terminals. Three spacious en suite rooms. Non-smoking. Relaxed, friendly, quiet atmosphere.

◆◆◆ **THE VINE GUEST HOUSE**
16 Castle Street, Ryde PO33 2EG
T: (01983) 566633
F: (01983) 566633
E: vine@guesthouse49.freeserve.
co.uk

Bedrooms: 5 double/
twin
Bathrooms: 2 en suite

Evening meal available
CC: Diners, Mastercard,
Switch, Visa

B&B per night:
S £23.00–£29.00
D £36.00–£48.00

HB per person:
DY £26.00–£37.00

Comfortable, 5 double/twin-bedded guesthouse, close to all amenities. Most rooms have sea views, some en suite. Family rooms available from 2002.

TOWN INDEX

This can be found at the back of the guide. If you know where you want to stay, the index will give you the page number listing accommodation in your chosen town, city or village.

◆◆◆◆

ST MICHAELS HOTEL
33 Leed Street, Sandown PO36 8JE
T: (01983) 403636

B&B per night:
S £21.00–£26.00
D £42.00–£52.00

HB per person:
DY £25.00–£31.00

OPEN Mar–Oct

Friendly, family-run hotel with own parking. Excellent home-cooked food, licensed bar and TV lounge. All rooms are en suite and have colour TV and tea-making facilities. Ground floor rooms available. Set in a quiet side street 4 minutes from the beach and 3 minutes from Sandown High Street.

Bedrooms: 2 single, 5 double/twin, 5 triple/ multiple
Bathrooms: 12 en suite

Evening meal available
CC: Delta, Mastercard, Visa

Senior citizens' discounts early and late season. Any day bookings available.

◆◆◆◆

8 GOSLINGS CROFT
Selborne, Alton GU34 3HZ
T: (01420) 511285
F: (01420) 587451

Bedrooms: 1 double/ twin
Bathrooms: 1 en suite

B&B per night:
S £20.00
D £40.00

OPEN All year round

Family home, set on edge of historic village, adjacent to National Trust land. Ideal base for walking and touring. Non-smokers only, please.

◆◆◆◆

IVANHOE
Oakhanger, Selborne, Alton
GU35 9JG
T: (01420) 473464

Bedrooms: 2 double/ twin
Bathrooms: 1 private

B&B per night:
S Min £25.00
D Min £40.00

OPEN All year round

Comfortable, homely accommodation in a small hamlet, with views to open countryside. Central base for tourists and business people. Good pub nearby.

◆◆◆◆

THE GROVE ARMS INN
Ludwell, Shaftesbury SP7 9ND
T: (01747) 828328
F: (01747) 828960
I: www.wiltshireacommodation.com

B&B per night:
S Min £40.00
D Min £50.00

Grade II Listed 17thC inn and hotel. Very attractive en suite bedrooms. Good position for walking in beautiful countryside. We pride ourselves on the quality of our food and service.

Bedrooms: 2 single, 4 double/twin
Bathrooms: 6 en suite

Lunch available
Evening meal available
CC: Delta, Mastercard, Switch, Visa

◆◆◆◆

THE KINGS ARMS INN
East Stour Common, East Stour, Gillingham SP8 5NB
T: (01747) 838325
E: jenny@kings-arms.fsnet.co.uk

Bedrooms: 3 double/ twin
Bathrooms: 3 en suite

Lunch available
Evening meal available
CC: Delta, Mastercard, Switch, Visa

B&B per night:
S Min £25.50
D Min £45.00

OPEN All year round

Attractive inn in beautiful rural Dorset. Restaurant, good food, real ales. En suite accommodation, garden and car park.

RATING All accommodation in this guide has been rated, or is awaiting a rating, by a trained English Tourism Council assessor.

SHAFTESBURY continued

◆◆◆◆
Silver
Award

THE KNOLL
Bleke Street, Shaftesbury SP7 8AH
T: (01747) 855243
E: pickshaftesbury@compuserve.com
I: www.pick-art.org.uk

B&B per night:
S £35.00–£52.00
D £52.00–£54.00

OPEN All year round

Conveniently situated in the town centre, our guest rooms all have wonderful countryside and garden views. Lots of restaurants, pubs and famous 'Hovis' Gold Hill within 5 minutes' walk. Superb centre for Stonehenge, Salisbury, Bath and South Coast. Welcome to the home of a quilter and a watercolourist. Non-smoking.

Bedrooms: 2 double/ twin
Bathrooms: 2 en suite

Discount for 3 or more nights.

◆◆◆◆
THE RETREAT
47 Bell Street, Shaftesbury SP7 8AE
T: (01747) 850372
F: (01747) 850372
E: at.retreat@virgin.net
I: www.the-retreat.org.uk

Bedrooms: 1 single, 4 double/twin, 5 triple/ multiple
Bathrooms: 10 en suite

CC: Mastercard, Switch, Visa

B&B per night:
S £25.00–£35.00
D £50.00–£60.00

OPEN All year round

Family-run Georgian town house in a quiet part of this beautiful Saxon hilltop town. A warm and friendly welcome awaits you. Just along from the Tourist Information Centre.

SHANKLIN, Isle of Wight Map ref 2C3 *Tourist Information Centre Tel: (01983) 813818*

◆◆◆◆

CULHAM LODGE HOTEL
31 Landguard Manor Road, Shanklin
PO37 7HZ
T: (01983) 862880
F: (01983) 862880
E: metcalf@culham99.freeserve.co.uk
I: www.isleofwight-hotel.co.uk

B&B per night:
S £24.00–£25.00
D £48.00–£50.00

HB per person:
DY £33.00–£35.00

Charming hotel in beautiful tree-lined road. Heated swimming pool in secluded garden, conservatory, home cooking and personal service. All rooms have TV with satellite channels, tea-maker and hairdryer. Culham Lodge is well placed for country walks and cycle trails. We can book your ferry crossing and save you money!

Bedrooms: 1 single, 9 double/twin
Bathrooms: 10 en suite

Evening meal available
CC: Delta, Mastercard, Switch, Visa

◆◆◆
HAZELWOOD HOTEL
14 Clarence Road, Shanklin
PO37 7BH
T: (01983) 862824
F: (01983) 862824
E: barbara.tubbs@thehazelwood.
free-online.co.uk
I: www.thehazelwood.free-online.
co.uk

Bedrooms: 1 single, 5 double/twin, 2 triple/ multiple; suites available
Bathrooms: 8 en suite

Evening meal available
CC: Amex, Diners, Mastercard, Visa

B&B per night:
S £19.00–£21.00
D £38.00–£42.00

HB per person:
DY £26.00–£28.00

OPEN All year round

Detached, friendly, comfortable hotel in a quiet tree-lined road, close to all amenities. Daily bookings taken. Parking available. All rooms en suite, family suites available.

WHERE TO STAY

◆◆◆ **HOLLY LODGE B & B**
29 Queens Road, Shanklin
PO37 6DQ
T: (01983) 863604

Bedrooms: 4 double/ twin
Bathrooms: 2 en suite

B&B per night:
D £44.00–£48.00

Victorian house close to beautiful beaches, station and town centre, offering a wide selection of shops and eating venues.

🐕10 ▤ ▢ ♦ Ⓢ ⊁ ▥ 🖫 ✿ 🐎 P

◆◆◆ **RYEDALE PRIVATE HOTEL**
3 Atherley Road, Shanklin PO37 7AT
T: (01983) 862375 & 07831 413233
F: (01983) 862375
E: ryedale@dottydots.co.uk
I: www.smoothhound.co.uk/hotels/ryedalep.html

Bedrooms: 1 single, 2 double/twin, 4 triple/ multiple
Bathrooms: 4 en suite, 1 private

CC: Amex, Delta, Mastercard, Switch, Visa

B&B per night:
S £18.00–£23.00
D £40.00–£46.00

Small and friendly, close to all amenities. Child stays free until late July and from early September. Discounts in selected local restaurants. Free parking available.

🎠🐕 🛴 ▤ ▢ ♦ Ⓢ 🖫 ✿ 🐎 🐕

◆◆◆

ST BRELADES HOTEL
15 Hope Road, Shanklin PO37 6EA
T: (01983) 862967
E: julie@st-brelades-hotel.co.uk
I: www.st-brelades-hotel.co.uk

B&B per night:
S £22.00–£25.00
D £44.00–£50.00

HB per person:
DY £31.00–£36.00

OPEN Jan–Dec

Enjoy a traditional seaside family holiday or short break close to clean, safe, sandy beaches and coastal cliff top walks and local attractions. Choose from our seasonal market menu with local specialities complemented by our range of wines and bar drinks. Ferry discounts. Secluded rear patio garden.

Bedrooms: 1 single, 9 double/twin, 6 triple/ multiple
Bathrooms: 13 en suite

Lunch available
Evening meal available
CC: Delta, Mastercard, Switch, Visa

Peaceful and relaxing 'Wight Christmas' 3-night break 24-27 Dec £260 full board, choice menus, children's discounts.

🎠🐕 🛴 ▤ ▢ ♦ ⚘ 🍷 Ⓢ ⊁ 🖫 ✿ 🐎 P

◆◆

THE TRITON HOTEL
23 Atherley Road, Shanklin PO37 7AU
T: (01983) 862494

B&B per night:
S £17.00–£19.00
D £34.00–£44.00

HB per person:
DY £23.50–£26.50

OPEN All year round

Family-run small hotel. Ideal base close to railway, shops, beach and Shanklin old village. Tastefully furnished with attractive and comfortable bedrooms. Home cooking is our speciality. All diets catered for. A very warm welcome awaits from staff and proprietor.

Bedrooms: 4 single, 10 double/twin, 3 triple/ multiple
Bathrooms: 9 en suite

Evening meal available
CC: Delta, Mastercard, Switch, Visa

🐕 🛴 ▤ ▢ ♦ ⚘ 🍷 Ⓢ 🖫 ✿ 🐎 🐕 P

◆◆ **THE FOX INN**
Fox Lane, Souldern, Bicester
OX27 7JW
T: (01869) 345284
F: (01869) 345667

Bedrooms: 4 double/ twin
Bathrooms: 2 en suite

Lunch available
Evening meal available
CC: Amex, Delta, Mastercard, Switch, Visa

B&B per night:
S £34.00–£40.00
D £45.00–£55.00

OPEN All year round

Traditional country inn, in the centre of a beautiful Cotswold stone village. Real ales and food served in bar/dining room. Convenient for Oxford, Banbury, Silverstone, Stratford and the Cotswolds.

🐕 ▢ ♦ 🍷 Ⓢ ▥ ✿ 🐎 🐕 P

SOULDERN continued

◆◆◆ **TOWER FIELDS**

Tusmore Road, Souldern, Bicester OX27 7HY T: (01869) 346554 F: (01869) 345157 E: hgould@strayduck.com	Bedrooms: 1 single, 1 double/twin, 1 triple/ multiple Bathrooms: 3 en suite	B&B per night: **S £30.00** **D £50.00–£52.00** OPEN All year round

Converted 18thC cottages and 14-acre smallholding with rare breeds of poultry, sheep and cattle. Small collection of vintage cars.

SOUTHAMPTON, Hampshire Map ref 2C3

◆◆◆ **ASHELEE LODGE**

36 Atherley Road, Shirley, Southampton SO15 5DQ T: (023) 8022 2095 F: (023) 8022 2095	Bedrooms: 1 single, 2 double/twin, 1 triple/ multiple	Evening meal available CC: Mastercard, Visa	B&B per night: **S £20.00** **D £38.00–£44.00** OPEN All year round

Homely guesthouse, garden with pool. Half a mile from city centre, near station, M27 and Red Funnel Docks ferryport. Good touring base for New Forest, Salisbury and Winchester. Near university.

◆◆ **BANISTER HOUSE HOTEL**

Banister Road, Southampton SO15 2JJ T: (023) 8022 1279 & 8022 5753 F: (023) 8022 6551 E: banisterhouse@lineone.net	Bedrooms: 12 single, 8 double/twin, 2 triple/ multiple Bathrooms: 12 en suite	Evening meal available CC: Delta, Mastercard, Switch, Visa	B&B per night: **S £26.00–£30.00** **D £42.00–£48.00** HB per person: **DY £25.00–£30.00** OPEN All year round

Friendly, warm welcome in this family-run hotel which is central and in a residential area. Off A33 (The Avenue) into Southampton.

◆◆◆ **EATON COURT HOTEL**

32 Hill Lane, Southampton SO15 5AY T: (023) 8022 3081 F: (023) 8032 2006 E: ecourthot@aol.com I: www.eatoncourtsouthampton.co. uk	Bedrooms: 8 single, 6 double/twin Bathrooms: 7 en suite	Evening meal available CC: Amex, Delta, Diners, Mastercard, Switch, Visa	B&B per night: **S £28.00–£36.00** **D £42.00–£46.00** OPEN All year round

Comfortable, small, owner-run hotel for business or leisure stays. Bedrooms have all amenities and a generous traditional breakfast is served.

SOUTHSEA

See under Portsmouth & Southsea

STANFORD IN THE VALE, Oxfordshire Map ref 2C2

◆◆◆ **STANFORD PARK HOUSE**

Park Lane, Stanford in the Vale, Faringdon SN7 8PF T: (01367) 710702 & 07831 242694 F: (01367) 710329 E: gjd34@dial.pipex.com I: www.stanfordpark.co.uk	Bedrooms: 2 double/ twin	B&B per night: **S £30.00–£35.00** **D £50.00–£55.00**

Large country house, in the heart of the countryside. Near Oxford, Cotswolds, Windsor, Blenheim Palace and many other interesting places to visit.

MAP REFERENCES The map references refer to the colour maps at the front of this guide. The first figure is the map number; the letter and figure which follow indicate the grid reference on the map.

◆◆◆

CARBERY GUEST HOUSE
Salisbury Hill, Stockbridge SO20 6EZ
T: (01264) 810771
F: (01264) 811022

B&B per night:
S £29.00–£36.00
D £51.00–£55.00

HB per person:
DY £43.50–£50.50

OPEN All year round

Fine old Georgian house in an acre of landscaped gardens and lawns, overlooking the River Test. Games and swimming facilities, riding and fishing can be arranged. Ideal for touring the South Coast and the New Forest.

Bedrooms: 4 single, 6 double/twin, 1 triple/ multiple
Bathrooms: 8 en suite

Evening meal available
CC: Delta, Mastercard, Switch, Visa

◆◆◆

THE OLD SCHOOL
Mill Road, Stratton Audley, Bicester OX6 9BJ
T: (01869) 277371
E: sawertheimer@euphony.net
I: www.old-school.co.uk

Bedrooms: 1 single, 3 double/twin

B&B per night:
S £30.00–£35.00
D £60.00–£70.00

OPEN All year round

400-year-old house in tranquil village, 7 minutes from Bicester. Tea/coffee and homemade cakes on arrival. From Bicester take Buckingham road, turn right at sign to Stratton Audley.

◆◆◆◆

PENNYFIELD
The Coombe, Streatley, Reading RG8 9QT
T: (01491) 872048 & 07774 946182
F: (01491) 872048
E: mandrvanstone@hotmail.com
I: web.onetel.net.uk/
~mandrvanstone

Bedrooms: 3 double/ twin
Bathrooms: 3 en suite

B&B per night:
S £45.00–£50.00
D £45.00–£50.00

OPEN All year round

Charming house in beautiful Thames-side village, situated on Thames path, Ridgeway Walk routes. Featuring 4-poster bed and heated spa pool. One mile to rail station.

◆◆◆

THE BANKES ARMS HOTEL
Manor Road, Studland, Swanage BH19 3AU
T: (01929) 450225 & 450310
F: (01929) 450307

B&B per night:
S £27.00–£36.00
D £54.00–£72.00

OPEN All year round

Award-winning lovely old inn with large gardens, overlooking the sea. Eight real ales, log fires, extensive home-cooked menu (open all day for food during the season). Fresh fish a speciality. Sandy beaches, water sports, golf, riding and coastal walks.

Bedrooms: 1 single, 4 double/twin, 3 triple/ multiple
Bathrooms: 6 en suite

Lunch available
Evening meal available
CC: Delta, Diners, Mastercard, Switch, Visa

SWAY, Hampshire Map ref 2C3

◆◆◆ **MANOR FARM**
Coombe Lane, Sway, Lymington
SO41 6BP
T: (01590) 683542

Bedrooms: 1 double/
twin, 1 triple/multiple
Bathrooms: 2 en suite

B&B per night:
S £20.00–£22.00
D £40.00–£44.00

Small working farm. 18thC, Grade II Listed farmhouse, surrounded by open fields and forest. Off B3055 Sway-Brockenhurst road.

OPEN All year round

◆◆◆ **TIVERTON**
9 Cruse Close, Sway, Lymington
SO41 6AY
T: (01590) 683092
F: (01590) 683092
E: ronrowe@talk21.com

Bedrooms: 2 triple/
multiple; suites available
Bathrooms: 2 en suite

B&B per night:
S £30.00–£35.00
D £40.00–£45.00

OPEN All year round

Quiet friendly accommodation in the village centre. Your suite of rooms includes own private sitting room, with TV, video and fridge. Delicious breakfast. Very relaxing.

TARRANT LAUNCESTON, Dorset Map ref 2B3

◆◆◆◆ **RAMBLERS COTTAGE**
Tarrant Launceston,
Blandford Forum DT11 8BY
T: (01258) 830528
E: sworrall@ramblerscottage.fsnet.co.uk
I: www.ramblerscottage.fsnet.co.uk

Bedrooms: 2 double/
twin
Bathrooms: 2 en suite

B&B per night:
S £28.00
D £50.00

OPEN All year round

Traditional country cottage set in a quiet village. Very friendly, peaceful location.

THAME, Oxfordshire Map ref 2C1 *Tourist Information Centre Tel: (01844) 212834*

◆◆◆◆◆ Gold Award **THE DAIRY**
Moreton, Thame OX9 2HX
T: (01844) 214075
F: (01844) 214075
E: thedairy@freeuk.com
I: www.thedairy.freeuk.com

Bedrooms: 3 double/
twin
Bathrooms: 3 en suite

CC: Amex, Mastercard, Visa

B&B per night:
S Min £62.00
D Min £86.00

OPEN All year round

Former milking parlour, set in 4.5 acres of lawns and native trees, enjoying a quiet village location with views of the Chilterns.

THRUXTON, Hampshire Map ref 2B2

◆◆◆◆ Silver Award

MAY COTTAGE
Thruxton, Andover SP11 8LZ
T: (01264) 771241 & 07768 242166
F: (01264) 771770

B&B per night:
S £35.00–£45.00
D £50.00–£65.00

OPEN All year round

May Cottage dates back to 1740 and is situated in the heart of this picturesque tranquil village. All rooms have en suite/private bathrooms, TV, radio and beverage trays. Guests' own sitting room/ dining room. Pretty, secluded garden with stream. Many National Trust and stately homes/gardens within easy reach. Ample private parking. A non-smoking establishment.

Bedrooms: 3 double/
twin
Bathrooms: 2 en suite,
1 private

www.travelengland.org.uk
Log on for information and inspiration. The latest information on places to visit, events and quality assessed accommodation.

TOTLAND BAY, Isle of Wight Map ref 2C3 *Tourist Information Centre Tel: (01983) 813818*

◆◆◆ **NORTON LODGE**

Granville Road, Totland Bay
PO39 0AZ
T: (01983) 752772 & 07971 815460
E: jacquie.simmons@talk21.com

Bedrooms: 1 double/
twin, 1 triple/multiple
Bathrooms: 1 en suite

B&B per night:
S £15.00–£25.00
D £30.00–£40.00

OPEN All year round

Large family home with friendly and relaxed atmosphere.Three lovely rooms available. Children welcome. Close to beaches, downs and the famous Needles.

TWYFORD, Berkshire Map ref 2C2

◆◆◆ **CHESHAM HOUSE**

79 Wargrave Road, Twyford,
Reading RG40 9PE
T: (0118) 932 0428
E: maria.ferguson@virgin.net

Bedrooms: 2 double/
twin
Bathrooms: 2 en suite

B&B per night:
S £35.00–£40.00
D £60.00–£65.00

OPEN All year round

In triangle formed by Reading, Maidenhead and Henley-on-Thames. Each room has en suite bathroom, colour TV, refrigerator, tea and coffee facilities. Parking in grounds.

WALLINGFORD, Oxfordshire Map ref 2C2 *Tourist Information Centre Tel: (01491) 826972*

◆◆◆ **LITTLE GABLES**

166 Crowmarsh Hill,
Crowmarsh Gifford, Wallingford
OX10 8BG
T: (01491) 837834 & 07860 148882
F: (01491) 834426
E: jill@stayingaway.com
I: www.stayingaway.com

Bedrooms: 1 single,
2 triple/multiple
Bathrooms: 1 en suite,
2 private

B&B per night:
S £35.00–£40.00
D £55.00–£60.00

OPEN All year round

Detached house, close to Ridgeway and Wallingford. Includes single and family room (cot), or twin, double or triple en suite. Tea/coffee making, colour TV, fridge.

WARSASH, Hampshire Map ref 2C3

◆◆◆◆

A tranquil Victorian house set in an attractive garden, featuring 12 en suite bedrooms one of which is a superior queen bedded room. All with tea and coffee making facilities, direct dial telephones, hair dryers and remote control televisions. Close to River Hamble, Southampton, Portsmouth and local business parks.

DORMY HOUSE HOTEL

21 Barnes Lane, Sarisbury Green,
Southampton SO31 7DA
T: (01489) 572626
F: (01489) 573370
E: dormyhousehotel@warsash.globalnet.co.uk
I: www.silverblue.co.uk/dormy

Bedrooms: 3 single,
7 double/twin, 2 triple/
multiple
Bathrooms: 12 en suite

Evening meal available
CC: Mastercard, Switch,
Visa

B&B per night:
S £44.00–£49.00
D £54.00–£68.00

OPEN All year round

WENDOVER, Buckinghamshire Map ref 2C1 *Tourist Information Centre Tel: (01296) 696759*

◆ **BELTON HOUSE**

26 Chiltern Road, Wendover,
Aylesbury HP22 6DB
T: (01296) 622351

Bedrooms: 1 single,
1 triple/multiple

B&B per night:
S £15.00
D £30.00

OPEN All year round

Tall, Victorian semi-detached house. Kitchen upstairs for guests' use. Breakfast, food, tea and coffee provided.

CREDIT CARD BOOKINGS If you book by telephone and are asked for your credit card number it is advisable to check the proprietor's policy should you cancel your reservation.

WEST LULWORTH, Dorset Map ref 2B3

LULWORTH COVE HOTEL
Main Road, West Lulworth,
Wareham BH20 5RQ
T: (01929) 400333
F: (01929) 400534
E: hotel@lulworth-cove.com
I: www.lulworth-cove.com

Bedrooms: 1 single,
14 double/twin, 2 triple/
multiple
Bathrooms: 13 en suite,
1 private

Lunch available
Evening meal available
CC: Amex, Delta,
Mastercard, Switch, Visa

B&B per night:
S £25.00–£40.00
D £48.00–£72.50

HB per person:
DY £33.00–£47.00

OPEN All year round

One hundred metres from the cove on the Dorset Coastal Path. Some sea-view balcony rooms. Wide variety of restaurant and bar meals.

WESTBURY, Buckinghamshire Map ref 2C1

MILL FARM HOUSE
Westbury, Brackley NN13 5JS
T: (01280) 704843
F: (01280) 704843

Bedrooms: 1 single,
1 double/twin, 1 triple/
multiple
Bathrooms: 1 en suite

B&B per night:
S £25.00–£30.00
D £45.00–£50.00

OPEN All year round

1000-acre mixed farm. Grade II Listed farmhouse, overlooking a colourful garden including a covered heated swimming pool. Situated in the centre of Westbury village.

WHITWELL, Isle of Wight Map ref 2C3 *Tourist Information Centre Tel: (01983) 813818*

Silver Award

THE OLD RECTORY
Ashknowle Lane, Whitwell, Ventnor
PO38 2PP
T: (01983) 731242
F: (01983) 731288
E: rectory@ukonline.co.uk
I: www.wightonline.co.uk/oldrectory

B&B per night:
S £30.00–£35.00
D £50.00–£60.00

OPEN All year round

Enjoy the comfort of spacious, traditionally furnished en suite bedrooms at our Victorian rectory in this historic village. All rooms with colour TV, fridge, hairdryer. Guests' sitting room. Secluded garden. Car park. Church, Post Office, stores and pub nearby. Good centre for walking, cycling and touring. Ventnor 3 miles.

Bedrooms: 2 double/twin
Bathrooms: 2 en suite

WIMBORNE MINSTER, Dorset Map ref 2B3 *Tourist Information Centre Tel: (01202) 886116*

Silver Award

ASHTON LODGE
10 Oakley Hill, Wimborne Minster
BH21 1QH
T: (01202) 883423
F: (01202) 886180
E: ashtonlodge@ukgateway.net
I: www.ashtonlodge.ukgateway.net

B&B per night:
S Min £24.00
D £48.00–£50.00

OPEN All year round

Spacious, detached family house with ample off-street parking. Relaxed friendly atmosphere with all the comforts of home on offer, including a full English breakfast served in the dining room overlooking the attractively laid garden. All bedrooms are centrally heated, tastefully decorated and furnished to a high standard.

Bedrooms: 1 single,
1 double/twin, 2 triple/
multiple
Bathrooms: 2 en suite,
2 private

Spring/autumn/winter savers 10% discount for couples staying 3 nights or more Oct-Apr.

ACCESSIBILITY
Look for the symbols which indicate accessibility for wheelchair users. A list of establishments is at the front of this guide.

♦♦♦♦

HEMSWORTH MANOR FARM
Witchampton, Wimborne Minster
BH21 5BN
T: (01258) 840216
F: (01258) 841278

B&B per night:
S £27.50–£30.00
D £55.00–£60.00

OPEN All year round
except Christmas

Lovely old manor house and garden in outstanding peaceful location. 800 acres, mainly arable, with cattle, sheep, pigs and horses. Four spacious rooms (3 en suite), colour TV, fully equipped. Guests' sitting room. Half an hour Bournemouth, Poole, Salisbury, Dorchester, New Forest. Excellent local pubs. Open all year except Christmas. Brochure available.

Bedrooms: 3 double/
twin, 1 triple/multiple
Bathrooms: 4 en suite

♦♦♦

HOMESTAY
22 West Borough, Wimborne Minster
BH21 1NF
T: (01202) 849015
F: (01202) 849015

B&B per night:
S £25.00–£30.00
D £45.00–£55.00

OPEN All year round

A warm welcome to our Grade II Listed Georgian townhouse, just one minutes' walk from the town centre, with its many restaurants and pubs, and the Tivoli Theatre. Bedrooms are individually furnished to a high standard of comfort with tea/coffee facilities. All are en suite or have private facilities.

Bedrooms: 3 double/
twin
Bathrooms: 2 en suite,
1 private

♦♦♦

TWYNHAM
67 Poole Road, Wimborne Minster
BH21 1QB
T: (01202) 887310

Bedrooms: 3 double/
twin

B&B per night:
S £18.00–£20.00
D £30.00–£34.00

OPEN All year round

Friendly family home, recently refurbished, with vanity unit, TV and beverages in rooms. Within walking distance of town centre.

♦♦

12 CHRISTCHURCH ROAD
Winchester SO23 9SR
T: (01962) 854272

Bedrooms: 2 double/
twin

B&B per night:
S £25.00–£30.00
D £35.00–£40.00

OPEN All year round

Family house, with much old furniture, conservatory and garden. In tree-lined residential area, 10 minutes' walk from the cathedral and city centre.

QUALITY ASSURANCE SCHEME
Diamond ratings and awards were correct at the time of going to press but are subject to change. Please check at the time of booking.

◆◆◆◆

SHAWLANDS
46 Kilham Lane, Winchester SO22 5QD
T: (01962) 861166
F: (01962) 861166
E: kathy@pollshaw.u-net.com

B&B per night:
S £30.00–£32.00
D £40.00–£50.00

OPEN All year round

Attractive modern house in a quiet, elevated position overlooking open countryside, 1.5 miles from city centre. Bedrooms are spotlessly clean, bright and attractively decorated. Extra comforts include colour TV, hairdryer and welcome tray with tea and coffee. The inviting breakfast includes home-made bread and preserves with fruit from the garden.

Bedrooms: 4 double/ twin, 1 triple/multiple
Bathrooms: 1 en suite

CC: Delta, Mastercard, Visa

WINDSOR, Berkshire Map ref 2D2 *Tourist Information Centre Tel: (01753) 743900*

◆◆◆◆ **BEAUMONT LODGE**
1 Beaumont Road, Windsor
SL4 1HY
T: (01753) 863436 & 07774 841273
F: (01753) 863436
E: bhamshere@beaumontlodge.
demon.co.uk
I: www.smoothound.co.uk/hotels/
beaulos.html

Bedrooms: 3 double/ twin
Bathrooms: 3 en suite

CC: Delta, Mastercard, Switch, Visa

B&B per night:
D £65.00–£75.00

OPEN All year round

All rooms have colour TV, video, clock/radio alarm, tea/coffee facilities and trouser press. Double has spa bath.

◆◆ **CLARENCE HOTEL**
9 Clarence Road, Windsor SL4 5AE
T: (01753) 864436
F: (01753) 857060

Bedrooms: 4 single, 10 double/twin, 6 triple/ multiple
Bathrooms: 20 en suite

CC: Amex, Delta, Diners, Mastercard, Switch, Visa

B&B per night:
S £45.00–£56.00
D £55.00–£67.00

OPEN All year round

Comfortable hotel with licensed bar and steam room, near town centre, castle and Eton. All rooms en suite, TV, hairdryer, radio and tea-maker. Convenient for Heathrow Airport and Legoland.

◆◆ **JEANS**
1 Stovell Road, Windsor SL4 5JB
T: (01753) 852055
F: (01753) 842932

Bedrooms: 2 double/ twin
Bathrooms: 2 private

B&B per night:
D £50.00

OPEN All year round

Self-contained garden flat with its own lounge. Only 100 yards to river and leisure centre and 7 minutes' walk to town centre.

◆◆◆ **OSCAR HOTEL**
65 Vansittart Road, Windsor
SL4 5DB
T: (01753) 830613
F: (01753) 833744
E: info@oscarhotel.com
I: www.oscarhotel.com

Bedrooms: 4 single, 5 double/twin, 4 triple/ multiple
Bathrooms: 13 en suite

Evening meal available
CC: Amex, Delta, Diners, Mastercard, Switch, Visa

B&B per night:
S £58.00–£65.00
D £75.00–£80.00

OPEN All year round

Fully licensed bar. All rooms en suite with direct-dial telephone, colour TV, tea/coffee facilities. Own car park. Minutes' drive to Legoland and Heathrow.

HALF BOARD PRICES Half board prices are given per person, but in some cases these may be based on double/twin occupancy.

WINSLOW, Buckinghamshire Map ref 2C1

◆◆

'WITSEND'

9 Buckingham Road, Winslow, Buckingham MK18 3DT
T: (01296) 712503 & 715499
E: sheila.spatcher@tesco.net

Bedrooms: 2 double/twin
Bathrooms: 2 en suite

Homely semi-detached chalet bungalow with en suite bedrooms. Close to town centre, colour TV, tea/coffee facilities. A warm welcome assured. Great breakfast!

[S] P

B&B per night:
S Min £25.00
D Min £50.00

OPEN All year round

WITNEY, Oxfordshire Map ref 2C1 *Tourist Information Centre Tel: (01993) 775802*

◆◆◆

THE COURT INN

43 Bridge Street, Witney OX8 6DA
T: (01993) 703228
F: (01993) 700980
E: info@thecourt.co.uk

Bedrooms: 2 single, 9 double/twin
Bathrooms: 8 en suite

Lunch available
Evening meal available
CC: Delta, Mastercard, Switch, Visa

Historic inn with dining room and 2 bars. TV and telephone in all bedrooms. Car park. Friendly service.

☎ [S] P

B&B per night:
S £30.00–£45.00
D £50.00–£60.00

OPEN All year round

◆◆

THE WITNEY HOTEL

7 Church Green, Witney OX28 4AZ
T: (01993) 702137
F: (01993) 705337
E: bookings@thewitneyhotel.co.uk

Bedrooms: 1 single, 7 double/twin, 2 triple/multiple
Bathrooms: 10 en suite

CC: Delta, Mastercard, Switch, Visa

Small, family-run bed and breakfast situated in a Listed building overlooking historic Church Green. Centrally located. Clean and comfortable accommodation at reasonable prices.

[S]

B&B per night:
S £30.00–£36.00
D Min £52.00

OPEN All year round

WOODCOTE, Oxfordshire Map ref 2C2

◆◆◆

HEDGES

South Stoke Road, Woodcote, Reading RG8 0PL
T: (01491) 680461

Bedrooms: 2 single, 2 double/twin
Bathrooms: 1 private

Peaceful, rural situation on edge of village. Historic Area of Outstanding Natural Beauty. Good access Henley, Oxford, Reading (Heathrow link), M4, M40.

[S] P

B&B per night:
S £17.00–£19.00
D £34.00–£38.00

OPEN All year round

WOODSTOCK, Oxfordshire Map ref 2C1 *Tourist Information Centre Tel: (01993) 813276*

◆◆◆

BURLEIGH FARM

Bladon Road, Cassington, Oxford OX29 4EA
T: (01865) 881352
E: j.cook@farmline.com

Bedrooms: 1 double/twin, 1 triple/multiple
Bathrooms: 2 en suite

360-acre farm on Blenheim Estate (home of Duke of Marlborough) at Woodstock. 6 miles north-west of Oxford, halfway between Cassington (A40) and Bladon (A4095), south of Woodstock.

[S] P

B&B per night:
S £25.00–£35.00
D £45.00–£55.00

OPEN All year round

CHECK THE MAPS

The colour maps at the front of this guide show all the cities, towns and villages for which you will find accommodation entries. Refer to the town index to find the page on which they are listed.

◆◆◆◆

GORSELANDS HALL

Boddington Lane, North Leigh, Witney
OX29 6PU
T: (01993) 882292 & 881895
F: (01993) 883629
E: hamilton@gorselandshall.com
I: www.gorselandshall.com

B&B per night:
S £35.00
D £45.00–£50.00

OPEN All year round

Old Cotswold-stone country house with oak beams and flagstone floors. All rooms en suite with colour TV. Large secluded garden. Croquet lawn. Tennis court. Snooker. Quiet rural location. Convenient for Oxford, Blenheim Palace and Cotswolds. Stratford 32 miles, Heathrow 1.25 hours by car and London (Paddington) 1.25 hours by train.

Bedrooms: 5 double/ twin, 1 triple/multiple
Bathrooms: 6 en suite

10% reduction for stays of 4 nights or more. Winter discounts available.

CC: Amex, Delta, Diners, Mastercard, Switch, Visa

◆◆◆◆
Silver Award

THE LAURELS

Hensington Road, Woodstock,
Oxford OX20 1JL
T: (01993) 812583
F: (01993) 812583
I: www.smoothhound.co.uk/hotels/thelaur.html

Bedrooms: 3 double/ twin
Bathrooms: 2 en suite, 1 private

CC: Delta, Mastercard, Switch, Visa

B&B per night:
S £40.00–£48.00
D £48.00–£58.00

OPEN All year round

Fine Victorian house, charmingly furnished with an emphasis on comfort and quality. Just off town centre and a short walk from Blenheim Palace.

◆◆

THE LAWNS

2 Flemings Road, Woodstock, Oxford
OX20 1NA
T: (01993) 812599
F: (01993) 812599
E: thelawns@amserve.net
I: www.smoothhound.co.uk/hotels/thelawns2

B&B per night:
S £28.00–£30.00
D £38.00–£45.00

OPEN All year round

Attractive, well maintained property. Homely, comfortable and welcoming. Free local taxi service. Also chauffeured service (air conditioned car) and free car washing. Free laundry. Ironing services. Save £s – free collection from Oxford rail or bus stations. Flag of country upon reception table. Quiet. Five minutes' walk to town centre and Blenheim Palace gates.

Bedrooms: 1 single, 2 double/twin

CC: Visa

10% discount 2 days or more.

COUNTRY CODE Always follow the Country Code ✤ Enjoy the countryside and respect its life and work ✤ Guard against all risk of fire ✤ Fasten all gates ✤ Keep your dogs under close control ✤ Keep to public paths across farmland ✤ Use gates and stiles to cross fences, hedges and walls ✤ Leave livestock, crops and machinery alone ✤ Take your litter home ✤ Help to keep all water clean ✤ Protect wildlife, plants and trees ✤ Take special care on country roads ✤ Make no unnecessary noise

◆◆◆

THE PUNCHBOWL INN
12 Oxford Street, Woodstock, Oxford
OX20 1TR
T: (01993) 811218
F: (01993) 811393
E: info@punchbowl-woodstock.co.uk
I: www.punchbowl-woodstock.co.uk

B&B per night:
S £50.00–£55.00
D £60.00–£65.00

OPEN All year round

18thC Grade II Listed inn situated in the centre of Woodstock. A traditional inn serving bar meals, afternoon teas/coffee. Ten guest en suite bedrooms are available, and a residents' car park. Ideal base for visiting Blenheim Palace, Oxford, Stratford-upon-Avon and the Cotswolds.

Bedrooms: 1 single, 9 double/twin	Lunch available
	Evening meal available
Bathrooms: 9 en suite, 1 private	CC: Delta, Mastercard, Switch, Visa

---

◆◆◆

SHEPHERDS HALL INN
Witney Road, Freeland, Oxford
OX29 8HQ
T: (01993) 881256
F: (01993) 883455

Bedrooms: 1 single, 3 double/twin, 1 triple/ multiple
Bathrooms: 5 en suite

Lunch available
Evening meal available
CC: Delta, Mastercard, Switch, Visa

B&B per night:
S £25.00–£35.00
D £45.00–£55.00

OPEN All year round

Well-appointed inn offering good accommodation. All rooms en suite. Ideally situated for Oxford, Woodstock and the Cotswolds, on the A4095 Woodstock to Witney road.

◆◆◆◆

THE TOWNHOUSE
15 High Street, Woodstock, Oxford
OX20 1TE
T: (01993) 810843 & 0780 359 9001
F: (01993) 810843
E: info@woodstock-townhouse. com
I: www.woodstock-townhouse.com

Bedrooms: 5 double/ twin
Bathrooms: 5 en suite

CC: Amex, Mastercard, Visa

B&B per night:
S £40.00–£50.00
D £60.00–£75.00

OPEN Mar–Dec

Character, 18thC stone-built house in centre of historic Woodstock. All rooms en suite. Recently refurbished to high standard. Dining room overlooks charming walled garden.

◆◆

ISLAND CHARTERS SEA URCHIN
26 Barge Lane, Wootton Creek, Wootton Bridge, Ryde PO33 4LB
T: (01983) 882315 & 07889 038877
F: (01983) 882315

Bedrooms: 13 double/ twin, 1 triple/multiple
Bathrooms: 1 en suite

B&B per night:
S Max £20.00
D Max £40.00

98ft heated static based Floatel, 10 double or single cabins. Also 65ft luxury cruiser. All modern facilites, brochure available.

AT-A-GLANCE SYMBOLS
Symbols at the end of each accommodation entry give useful information about services and facilities. A key to symbols can be found inside the back cover flap. Keep this open for easy reference.

A brief guide to the main Towns and Villages offering accommodation in the South of England

A **ALTON, HAMPSHIRE** - Pleasant old market town standing on the Pilgrim's Way, with some attractive Georgian buildings. The parish church still bears the scars of bullet marks, evidence of a bitter struggle between the Roundheads and the Royalists.

- **AMERSHAM, BUCKINGHAMSHIRE** - Old town with many fine buildings, particularly in the High Street. There are several interesting old inns.

- **ANDOVER, HAMPSHIRE** - Town that achieved importance from the wool trade and now has much modern development. A good centre for visiting places of interest.

- **ASCOT, BERKSHIRE** - Small country town famous for its racecourse which was founded by Queen Anne. The race meeting each June is attended by the Royal Family.

- **ASHURST, HAMPSHIRE** - Small village on the A35, on the edge of the New Forest and three miles north-east of Lyndhurst. Easy access to beautiful forest lawns.

- **AYLESBURY, BUCKINGHAMSHIRE** - Historic county town in the Vale of Aylesbury. The cobbled market square has a Victorian clock tower and the 15th C King's Head Inn (National Trust). Interesting county museum and 13th C parish church.

B **BANBURY, OXFORDSHIRE** - Famous for its cattle market, cakes, nursery rhyme and Cross. Founded in Saxon times, it has some fine houses and interesting old inns. A good centre for touring Warwickshire and the Cotswolds.

- **BARTLEY, HAMPSHIRE** - Small village on the north-east edge of the New Forest.

- **BARTON ON SEA, HAMPSHIRE** - Seaside village with views of the Isle of Wight. Within easy driving distance of the New Forest.

- **BASINGSTOKE, HAMPSHIRE** - Rapidly developing commercial and industrial centre. The town is surrounded by charming villages and places to visit.

- **BEACONSFIELD, BUCKINGHAMSHIRE** - Former coaching town with several inns still surviving. The old town has many fine houses and an interesting church. Beautiful countryside and beech woods nearby.

- **BEAULIEU, HAMPSHIRE** - Beautifully situated among woods and hills on the Beaulieu river, the village is both charming and unspoilt. The 13th C ruined Cistercian abbey and 14th C Palace House stand close to the National Motor Museum. There is a maritime museum at Bucklers Hard.

- **BEMBRIDGE, ISLE OF WIGHT** - Village with harbour and bay below Bembridge Down - the most easterly village on the island. Bembridge Sailing Club is one of the most important in southern England.

- **BENSON, OXFORDSHIRE** - On a river plain by the Thames, this village is notable for its 13th C church and 17th C coaching inn. Nearby is a large airfield, famous for housing the Queen's Flight.

- **BICESTER, OXFORDSHIRE** - Market town with a large army depot and well-known hunting centre with hunt established in the late 18th C. The ancient parish church displays work of many periods. Nearby is the Jacobean mansion of Rousham House with gardens landscaped by William Kent.

- **BLANDFORD FORUM, DORSET** - Almost completely destroyed by fire in 1731, the town was rebuilt in a handsome Georgian style. The church is large and grand and the town is the hub of a rich farming area.

- **BOLDRE, HAMPSHIRE** - An attractive village with pretty views of the village from the bridge. The white plastered church sits on top of a hill.

- **BONCHURCH, ISLE OF WIGHT** - Sheltered suburb at the foot of St Boniface Down.

- **BOURNEMOUTH, DORSET** - Seaside town set among the pines with a mild climate, sandy beaches and fine coastal views. The town has wide streets with excellent shops, a pier, a pavilion, museums and conference centre.

- **BRIZE NORTON, OXFORDSHIRE** - Village closely associated with the American Air Force. The medieval church is the only church in England dedicated to St Brice, from whom the village takes its name.

- **BROCKENHURST, HAMPSHIRE** - Attractive village with thatched cottages and a ford in its main street. Well placed for visiting the New Forest.

- **BUCKINGHAM, BUCKINGHAMSHIRE** - Interesting old market town surrounded by rich farmland. It has many Georgian buildings, including the Town Hall and Old Jail and many old almshouses and inns. Stowe School nearby has magnificent 18th C landscaped gardens.

- **BURFORD, OXFORDSHIRE** - One of the most beautiful Cotswold wool towns with Georgian and Tudor houses, many antique shops and a picturesque High Street sloping to the River Windrush.

C **CARISBROOKE, ISLE OF WIGHT** - Situated at the heart of the Isle of Wight and an ideal base for touring. Boasts a Norman church, formerly a monastic church, and a castle built on the site of a Roman fortress.

- **CHALFONT ST GILES, BUCKINGHAMSHIRE** - Pretty, old village in wooded Chiltern Hills yet only 20 miles from London and a good base for visiting the city. Excellent base for Windsor, Henley, the Thames Valley, Oxford and the Cotswolds.

- **CHARLBURY, OXFORDSHIRE** - Large Cotswold village with beautiful views of the Evenlode Valley just outside the village and close to the ancient Forest of Wychwood.

- **CHIPPING NORTON, OXFORDSHIRE** - Old market town set high in the Cotswolds and an ideal touring centre. The wide market-place contains many 16th C and 17th C stone houses and the Town Hall and Tudor Guildhall.

- **CHRISTCHURCH, DORSET** - Tranquil town lying between the Avon and Stour just before they converge and flow into Christchurch Harbour. A fine 11th C church and the remains of a Norman castle and house can be seen.

- **CORFE CASTLE, DORSET** - One of the most spectacular ruined castles in Britain. Norman in origin, the castle was a Royalist stronghold during the Civil War and held out until 1645. The village had a considerable marble-carving industry in the Middle Ages.

- **CRANBORNE, DORSET** - Village with an interesting Jacobean manor house. Lies south-east of Cranborne Chase, formerly a forest and hunting preserve.

D **DEDDINGTON, OXFORDSHIRE** - On the edge of the Cotswolds and settled since the Stone Age, this is the only village in England to have been granted a full Coat of Arms, displayed on the 16th C Town Hall in the picturesque market square. Many places of interest include the Church of St Peter and St Paul.

E EDGCOTT, BUCKINGHAMSHIRE - Small village within easy reach of Aylesbury, Milton Keynes and Bicester.

F FARINGDON, OXFORDSHIRE - Ancient stone-built market town in the Vale of the White Horse. The 17th C market hall stands on pillars and the 13th C church has some fine monuments. A great monastic tithe barn is nearby at Great Coxwell.

• **FARNBOROUGH, HAMPSHIRE** - Home of the Royal Aircraft Establishment and the site of the biennial International Air Show. St Michael's Abbey was built by the Empress Eugenie, wife of Napoleon III of France, and together they and their son are buried in the crypt.

• **FORDINGBRIDGE, HAMPSHIRE** - On the north-west edge of the New Forest. A medieval bridge crosses the Avon at this point and gave the town its name. A good centre for walking, exploring and fishing.

• **FRESHWATER, ISLE OF WIGHT** - This part of the island is associated with Tennyson, who lived in the village for 30 years. A monument on Tennyson's Down commemorates the poet.

G GORING, OXFORDSHIRE - Riverside town on the Oxfordshire/Berkshire border, linked by an attractive bridge to Streatley with views to the Goring Gap.

H HENLEY-ON-THAMES, OXFORDSHIRE - The famous Thames Regatta is held in this prosperous and attractive town at the beginning of July each year. The town has many Georgian buildings and old coaching inns and the parish church has some fine monuments.

• **HORDLE, HAMPSHIRE** - A mixture of suburban and rural dwellings 4 miles west of Lymington.

• **HYTHE, HAMPSHIRE** - Waterside village with spectacular views over Southampton Water. Marina with distinctive 'fishing village' style development, 117-year-old pier, wide range of interesting shops.

L LISS, HAMPSHIRE - Village including East and West Liss on the Hampshire/Sussex border.

• **LYMINGTON, HAMPSHIRE** - Small, pleasant town with bright cottages and attractive Georgian houses, lying on the edge of the New Forest with a ferry service to the Isle of Wight. A sheltered harbour makes it a busy yachting centre.

• **LYNDHURST, HAMPSHIRE** - The 'capital' of the New Forest, surrounded by attractive woodland scenery and delightful villages. The town is dominated by the Victorian Gothic-style church where the original Alice in Wonderland is buried.

M MAIDENHEAD, BERKSHIRE - Attractive town on the River Thames which is crossed by an elegant 18th C bridge and by Brunel's well-known railway bridge. It is a popular place for boating with delightful riverside walks. The Courage Shire Horse Centre is nearby.

• **MARLOW, BUCKINGHAMSHIRE** - Attractive Georgian town on the River Thames, famous for its 19th C suspension bridge. The High Street contains many old houses and there are connections with writers including Shelley and T S Eliot.

• **MARNHULL, DORSET** - Has a fine church and numerous attractive houses.

• **MILFORD-ON-SEA, HAMPSHIRE** - Victorian seaside resort with shingle beach and good bathing, set in pleasant countryside and looking out over the Isle of Wight. Nearby is Hurst Castle, built by Henry VIII. The school chapel, former abbey church, can be visited.

• **MILTON KEYNES, BUCKINGHAMSHIRE** - Designated a New Town in 1967, Milton Keynes offers a wide range of housing and is abundantly planted with trees. It has excellent shopping facilities and 3 centres for leisure and sporting activities. The Open University is based here.

N NEW MILTON, HAMPSHIRE - New Forest residential town on the mainline railway.

• **NEWBURY, BERKSHIRE** - Ancient town surrounded by the Downs and on the Kennet and Avon Canal. It has many buildings of interest, including the 17th C Cloth Hall, which is now a museum. The famous racecourse is nearby.

• **NEWPORT PAGNELL, BUCKINGHAMSHIRE** - Busy town situated on 2 rivers with some Georgian as well as modern buildings.

O OXFORD, OXFORDSHIRE - Beautiful university town with many ancient colleges, some dating from the 13th C, and numerous buildings of historic and architectural interest. The Ashmolean Museum has outstanding collections. Lovely gardens and meadows with punting on the Cherwell.

P PETERSFIELD, HAMPSHIRE - Grew prosperous from the wool trade and was famous as a coaching centre. Its attractive market square is dominated by a statue of William III. Close by are Petersfield Heath with numerous ancient barrows and Butser Hill with magnificent views

• **PORTSMOUTH & SOUTHSEA, HAMPSHIRE** - There have been connections with the Navy since early times and the first dock was built in 1194. HMS Victory, Nelson's flagship, is here and Charles Dickens' former home is open to the public. Neighbouring Southsea has a promenade with magnificent views of Spithead.

Q QUAINTON, BUCKINGHAMSHIRE - Rural village with many 17th and 18th C monuments, including a large monument which is unsigned. Some Georgian buildings.

R READING, BERKSHIRE - Busy, modern county town with large shopping centre and many leisure and recreation facilities. There are several interesting museums and the Duke of Wellington's Stratfield Saye is nearby.

• **RINGWOOD, HAMPSHIRE** - Market town by the River Avon comprising old cottages, many of them thatched. Although just outside the New Forest, there is heath and woodland nearby and it is a good centre for horse-riding and walking.

• **ROMSEY, HAMPSHIRE** - Town grew up around the important abbey and lies on the banks of the River Test, famous for trout and salmon. Broadlands House, home of the late Lord Mountbatten, is open to the public.

• **RYDE, ISLE OF WIGHT** - The island's chief entry port, connected to Portsmouth by ferries and hovercraft. 7 miles of sandy beaches with a half-mile pier, esplanade and gardens.

S SANDOWN, ISLE OF WIGHT - The 6-mile sweep of Sandown Bay is one of the island's finest stretches, with excellent sands. The pier has a pavilion and sun terrace; the esplanade has amusements, bars, eating-places and gardens.

• **SELBORNE, HAMPSHIRE** - Village made famous by Gilbert White, who was a curate here and is remembered for his classic book 'The Natural History of Selborne', published in 1788. His house is now a museum.

• **SHAFTESBURY, DORSET** - Hilltop town with a long history. The ancient and cobbled Gold Hill is one of the most attractive in Dorset. There is an excellent small museum containing a collection of buttons for which the town is famous.

HALF BOARD PRICES Half board prices are given per person, but in some cases these may be based on double/twin occupancy.

• **SHANKLIN, ISLE OF WIGHT** - Set on a cliff with gentle slopes leading down to the beach, esplanade and marine gardens. The picturesque, old thatched village nestles at the end of the wooded chine.

• **SOUTHAMPTON, HAMPSHIRE** - One of Britain's leading seaports with a long history, now a major container port. In the 18th C it became a fashionable resort with the assembly rooms and theatre. The old Guildhall and the Wool House are now museums. Sections of the medieval wall can still be seen.

• **STOCKBRIDGE, HAMPSHIRE** - Set in the Test Valley which has some of the best fishing in England. The wide main street has houses of all styles, mainly Tudor and Georgian.

• **STREATLEY, BERKSHIRE** - Pretty village on the River Thames, linked to Goring by an attractive bridge. It has Georgian houses and cottages and beautiful views over the countryside and the Goring Gap.

• **STUDLAND, DORSET** - On a beautiful stretch of coast and good for walking, with a National Nature Reserve to the north. The Norman church is the finest in the country, with superb rounded arches and vaulting. Brownsea Island, where the first scout camp was held, lies In Poole Harbour.

• **SWAY, HAMPSHIRE** - Small village on the south-western edge of the New Forest. It is noted for its 220-ft tower, Peterson's Folly, built in the 1870s by a retired Indian judge to demonstrate the value of concrete as a building material.

■**THAME, OXFORDSHIRE** - Historic market town on the River Thames. The wide, unspoilt High Street has many styles of architecture with medieval timber-framed cottages, Georgian houses and some famous inns.

• **TOTLAND BAY, ISLE OF WIGHT** - On the Freshwater Peninsula. It is possible to walk from here around to Alum Bay.

• **TWYFORD, BERKSHIRE** - Stands on the edge of the Loddon water meadows. There is a pleasant group of almshouses built by Sir Richard Harrison in 1640. The 19th C church is notable for the coloured marble on the floor of the baptistry.

■**WALLINGFORD, OXFORDSHIRE** - Site of an ancient ford over the River Thames, now crossed by a 900-ft-long bridge. The town has many timber-framed and Georgian buildings, Gainsborough portraits in the 17th C Town Hall and a few remains of a Norman Castle.

• **WARSASH, HAMPSHIRE** - On the edge of Southampton Water. Warships were built here in Napoleonic times.

• **WENDOVER, BUCKINGHAMSHIRE** - Historic town on the Icknield Way set amid beautiful scenery and spectacular views of the Chilterns. There are many old timbered cottages and inns, one visited by Oliver Cromwell. The church has some interesting carving.

• **WESTBURY, BUCKINGHAMSHIRE** - Village close to Buckingham and within easy reach of Milton Keynes and Banbury.

• **WEST LULWORTH, DORSET** - Well-known for Lulworth Cove, the almost landlocked circular bay of chalk and limestone cliffs.

• **WHITWELL, ISLE OF WIGHT** - West of Ventnor, with interesting church, thatched inn and youth hostel. Good walking area.

• **WIMBORNE MINSTER, DORSET** - Market town centred on the twin-towered Minster Church of St Cuthberga which gave the town the second part of its name. Good touring base for the surrounding countryside, depicted in the writings of Thomas Hardy.

• **WINCHESTER, HAMPSHIRE** - King Alfred the Great made Winchester the capital of Saxon England. A magnificent Norman cathedral, with one of the longest naves in Europe, dominates the city. Home of Winchester College founded in 1382.

• **WINDSOR, BERKSHIRE** - Town dominated by the spectacular castle, home of the Royal Family for over 900 years. Parts are open to the public. There are many attractions including the Great Park, Eton and trips on the river.

• **WINSLOW, BUCKINGHAMSHIRE** - Small town with Georgian houses, a little market square and a fine church with 15th C wall-paintings. Winslow Hall, built to the design of Sir Christopher Wren in 1700, is open to the public.

• **WITNEY, OXFORDSHIRE** - Town famous for its blanket-making and mentioned in the Domesday Book. The market-place contains the Butter Cross, a medieval meeting place, and there is a green with merchants' houses.

• **WOODCOTE, OXFORDSHIRE** - Town in the Chilterns close to Goring and Henley-on-Thames.

• **WOODSTOCK, OXFORDSHIRE** - Small country town clustered around the park gates of Blenheim Palace, the superb 18th C home of the Duke of Marlborough. The town has well-known inns and an interesting museum. Sir Winston Churchill was born and buried nearby.

Ratings
you can trust

English Tourism Council

◆ ◆ ◆

**GUEST
ACCOMMODATION**

When you're looking for a place to stay, you need a rating system you can trust. The **English Tourism Council's** ratings are your clear guide to what to expect, in an easy-to-understand form. Properties are visited annually by our trained, impartial assessors, so you can have confidence that your accommodation has been thoroughly checked and rated for quality before you make a booking.

Using a simple One to five Diamond rating, the system puts great emphasis on quality and is based on research which shows exactly what consumers are looking for when when choosing accommodation.

"Guest Accommodation" covers a wide variety of serviced accommodation for which England is renowned, including guesthouses, bed and breakfasts, ,inns and farmhouses. Establishments are rated from One to Five Diamonds. Progressively higher levels of quality and customer care must be provided for each of the One to Five Diamond ratings. The rating reflects the unique character of Quest Accommodation, and covers areas such as cleanliness, service and hospitality, bedrooms, bathrooms and food quality.

Look out, too for the english Tourism Council's Gold and Silver Awards, which are awarded to those establishments which not only achieve the overall quality required for their Diamond rating, but also reach the highest levels of quality in those specific areas which guests identify as being really important for them. They will reflect the quality of comfort and cleanliness you'll find in the bedrooms and bathrooms and the quality of service you'll enjoy throughout your stay.

The ratings are you sign of quality assurance, giving you the confidence to book the accommodation that meets your expectations.

SOUTH EAST England

The White cliffs of Dover, beach huts and piers, yachts at Chichester – this distinctive coast combines with famous gardens and the apples and hops of Kent to make a quintessentially English region.

classic sights
Battle of Hastings – audio tour brings the battle to life
Hever Castle – romantic moated castle, home of Anne Boleyn

coast & country
Runnymede – riverside meadows and woodland
Pegwell Bay & Goodwin Sands – a haven for birds and seals

gorgeous gardens
Sissinghurst – celebrated garden of Vita Sackville-West
Leonardslee – rhododendrons and azaleas ablaze with colour in May

literary links
Charles Dickens – Rochester; his home Gad's Hill Place
Rudyard Kipling – Bateman's, his momento filled home
Chaucer – The Canterbury Tales

arts for all
Brighton Festival – international performers, artists and writers every May

distinctively different
Royal Pavilion – exotic palace of King George IV

The counties of East Sussex, Kent, Surrey and West Sussex

FOR MORE INFORMATION CONTACT:
South East England Tourist Board
The Old Brew House, Warwick Park,
Tunbridge Wells, Kent TN2 5TU
Tel: (01892) 540766 Fax: (01892) 511008
Email: enquiries@seetb.org.uk
Internet: www.SouthEastEngland.uk.com

The Pictures:
1 Bodiam Castle, East Sussex
2 Southover Grange Gardens,
   Lewes, East Sussex

Places to Visit - see pages 504-507
Where to Stay - see pages 508-553

PLACES to visit

You will find hundreds of interesting places to visit during your stay, just some of which are listed in these pages. Contact any Tourist Information Centre in the region for more ideas on days out.

Alfriston Clergy House

The Tye, Alfriston, Polegate, East Sussex BN26 5TL
Tel: (01323) 870001 www.nationaltrust.org.uk
A thatched, half-timbered 14thC building with exhibition on Wealden house-building. It was the first building acquired by The National Trust in 1896. Cottage garden.

Amberley Museum

Houghton Bridge, Amberley, Arundel, West Sussex BN18 9LT
Tel: (01798) 831370 www.amberleymuseum.co.uk
Open-air industrial history centre in chalk quarry. Working craftsmen, narrow-gauge railway, early buses, working machines and other exhibits. Nature trail/visitor centre.

Anne of Cleves House Museum

52 Southover High Street, Lewes, East Sussex BN7 1JA
Tel: (01273) 474610 www.sussexpast.co.uk
A 16thC timber-framed Wealden hall-house which contains collections of Sussex interest. Displays feature Lewes from the 16thC to the present day.

Arundel Castle

Arundel, West Sussex BN18 9AB
Tel: (01903) 883136 www.arundelcastle.org
An impressive Norman stronghold in extensive grounds, much restored in the 18thC and 19thC. 11thC keep, 13thC barbican, barons' hall, armoury, chapel. Van Dyck and Gainsborough paintings.

Basingstoke Canal Visitor Centre

Mytchett Place Road, Mytchett, Camberley, Hampshire GU16 6DD
Tel: (01252) 370073 www.basingstoke-canal.co.uk
A canal interpretation centre with an exhibition displaying the history of canals over the past 200 years. Boat trips and boat hire available. Adventure playground.

Battle Abbey and Battlefield

High Street, Battle, East Sussex TN33 0AD
Tel: (01424) 773792 www.english-heritage.org.uk
An abbey founded by William the Conqueror on the site of the Battle of Hastings. The church altar is on the spot where King Harold was killed. Battlefield views and exhibition.

Beaver Zoological Gardens

Waylands Farm, Approach Road, Tatsfield, Westerham, Kent TN16 2JT
Tel: (01959) 577747 www.beaverwaterworld.com
Visitors to Beaver Zoological Gardens can see reptiles, tropical and cold water fish, Canadian beavers, aviary birds, rabbits and chipmunks. Play area, sandpit and cafe.

Borde Hill Garden

Balcombe Road, Haywards Heath, West Sussex RH16 1XP
Tel: (01444) 450326 www.bordehill.co.uk
Winner of two prestigious awards. A garden of contrasts where botanical interest and garden design play equally important roles. Extended colour throughout the year.

Brooklands Museum

Brooklands Road, Weybridge, Surrey KT13 0QN
Tel: (01932) 857381 www.motor-software.co.uk
Original 1907 motor racing circuit. Features the most
historic and steepest section of the old banked track and
1-in-4 test hill. Motoring village and Grand Prix
exhibition.

The Canterbury Tales Visitor Attraction

St Margaret's Street, Canterbury, Kent CT1 2TG
Tel: (01227) 479227 www.canterburytales.org.uk
An audiovisual recreation of life in medieval England.
Visitors join Chaucer's pilgrims on their journey from
London's Tabard Inn to Thomas Becket's shrine at
Canterbury.

Charleston

Firle, Lewes, East Sussex BN8 6LL
Tel: (01323) 811265 www.charleston.org.uk
A 17thC-18thC farmhouse, home of Vanessa Bell and
Duncan Grant of the Bloomsbury Set. House and contents
decorated by the artists. Traditional walled garden.

Chartwell

Westerham, Kent TN16 1PS
Tel: (01732) 866368 www.nationaltrust.org.uk
The home of Sir Winston Churchill with study, studio,
museum rooms with gifts, uniforms and photos. Garden,
Golden Rose Walk, lakes. 'Years at Chartwell' exhibition.

Chatley Heath Semaphore Tower

Pointers Road, Cobham, Surrey KT11 1PQ
Tel: (01483) 517595
A restored historic semaphore tower, set in woodland,
displaying the history of overland naval communications
in the early 19thC. Working semaphore mast and models.

Drusillas Park

Alfriston, East Sussex BN26 5QS
Tel: (01323) 874100 www.drusillas.co.uk
South East England Tourist Board Visitor Attraction of the
Year. Jungle Adventure Golf, adventure playground,
toddlers' play village, zoolympics and small-gauge
railway.

Eagle Heights

Hulberry Farm, Lullingstone Lane, Eynsford,
Dartford, Kent DA4 0JB
Tel: (01322) 866466 www.eagleheights.co.uk
Bird of prey centre housed undercover where visitors can
see eagles, hawks, falcons, owls and vultures from all
over the world. Reptile centre, play area and sandpit.

English Wine Centre

Alfriston Roundabout, Alfriston, East Sussex BN26 5QS
Tel: (01323) 870164 www.weddingwine.co.uk
The English Wine Centre was established in 1972 and
stocks a large range of English wines, fruit wines and
ciders within the attractive wine shop. Tours and tastings
available.

Goodwood House

Goodwood, Chichester, West Sussex PO18 0PX
Tel: (01243) 755040 www.goodwood.co.uk
A magnificent Regency house, home to the Earl of
March, extensively refurbished in 1997 and set in a large
area of open parkland. Fine furnishings, tapestries and
porcelain.

Kent & East Sussex Railway

Tenterden Town Station, Tenterden, Kent TN30 6HE
Tel: (01580) 765155 www.kesr.org.uk
Full-size steam railway with restored Edwardian stations
at Tenterden and Northiam. 14 steam engines, Victorian
coaches and Pullman carriages. Museum and children's
play area.

Leeds Castle and Gardens

Maidstone, Kent ME17 1PL
Tel: (01622) 765400 www.leeds-castle.co.uk
A castle built on two islands in a lake, dating from the
9thC. Furniture, tapestries, art treasures, dog collar
museum, gardens, duckery, aviaries, maze, grotto,
vineyard and greenhouses.

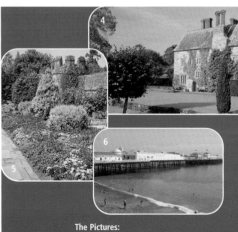

The Pictures:
1 River Wey, Nr. Guildford
2 Chiddingfold Village, Surrey
3 Leeds Castle, Kent
4 Bateman's, East Sussex
5 Chichester Cathedral Gardens, West Sussex
6 Brighton Pier

Port Lympne Wild Animal Park, Mansion and Gardens

Port Lympne, Hythe, Kent CT21 4PD
Tel: (01303) 264647 www.howletts.net
A 300-acre (121-ha) wild animal park specialising in rare breeds including gorillas, deer, rhino, tigers, elephants etc. Mansion with art gallery exhibitions, murals and gardens. Trailer rides.

Rural Life Centre

Old Kiln Museum, Reeds Road, Tilford,
Farnham, Surrey GU10 2DL
Tel: (01252) 792300
www.surreyweb.org.uk/rural-life
A museum with a comprehensive collection of farm machines, implements, wagons, displays on past village life, small arboretum and a woodland walk.

The Savill Garden

Windsor Great Park, Wick Lane, Englefield Green,
Egham, Surrey TW20 0UU
Tel: (01753) 847518 www.savillgarden.co.uk
Woodland garden with formal gardens and herbaceous borders offering much of great interest and beauty in all seasons. Landscaped Queen Elizabeth Temperate House.

Scotney Castle Garden

Lamberhurst, Royal Tunbridge Wells, Kent TN3 8JN
Tel: (01892) 891081 www.nationaltrust.org.uk
Romantic gardens created around the ruins of a 14thC moated castle containing exhibitions. Gardens created by the Hussey family with shrubs, winding paths and good views.

Sculpture at Goodwood

Hat Hill Copse, Goodwood, Chichester, West Sussex PO18 0QP
Tel: (01243) 538449 www.sculpture.org.uk
A changing collection of contemporary British sculpture set in 20 acres (8 ha) of beautiful grounds on the South Downs overlooking Chichester.

St Mary's House and Gardens

Bramber, Steyning, West Sussex BN44 3WE
Tel: (01903) 816205
A medieval, timber-framed Grade I Listed house with rare 16thC wall-leather, fine panelled rooms and a unique painted room. Topiary gardens.

South of England Rare Breeds Centre

Highlands Farm, Woodchurch, Ashford, Kent TN26 3RJ
Tel: (01233) 861493 www.rarebreeds.org.uk
Large collection of rare farm breeds on a working farm with children's play activities. Georgian farmstead under reconstruction. Home to the 'Tamworth Two'. Woodland walks.

Titsey Place and Gardens

Oxted, Surrey RH8 0SD
Tel: (01273) 407056 www.titsey.com
A guided tour of Titsey Place includes the library, old servants' hall, dining room and drawing room. The gardens comprise 10 acres (4 ha) of formal gardens and a walled garden.

Weald and Downland Open Air Museum

Singleton, Chichester, West Sussex PO18 0EU
Tel: (01243) 811348 www.wealddown.co.uk
Over 40 rescued historic buildings from South East England, reconstructed on a downland country park site. Homes and workplaces of the past include a medieval farmstead.

West Dean Gardens

West Dean Estate, West Dean, Chichester,
West Sussex PO18 0QZ
Tel: (01243) 818210 www.westdean.org.uk
Extensive downland garden with specimen trees, 300 ft (91 m) pergola, rustic summerhouses and restored walled kitchen garden. Walk in parkland and 45-acre (18-ha) arboretum.

Wilderness Wood

Hadlow Down, Uckfield, East Sussex TN22 4HJ
Tel: (01825) 830509 www.wildernesswood.co.uk
A family-run working woodland of 60 acres (24 ha), beautiful in all seasons. There are trails, a bluebell walk, a play area, workshop and a timber barn with exhibitions.

The Wildfowl and Wetlands Trust

Mill Road, Arundel, West Sussex BN18 9PB
Tel: (01903) 883355 www.wwt.org.uk
A wildlife paradise and a haven of peace and tranquility for swans, ducks and geese from around the world. Visitor centre and viewing gallery.

Winkworth Arboretum

Hascombe Road, Hascombe, Godalming, Surrey GU8 4AD
Tel: (01483) 208477 www.cornuswwweb.co.uk
One hundred acres (40 ha) of hillside planted with rare trees and shrubs. Good views, lakes, newly restored boathouse, azaleas, bluebells, wild spring flowers and autumn colours.

Find out more about
SOUTH EAST England

Further information about holidays and attractions in South East England is available from:

SOUTH EAST ENGLAND TOURIST BOARD
The Old Brew House, Warwick Park, Tunbridge Wells, Kent TN2 5TU.
Tel: (01892) 540766 Fax: (01892) 511008
Email: enquiries@seetb.org.uk
Internet: www.SouthEastEngland.uk.com

The following publications are available from the South East England Tourist Board:

South East Holiday and Short Breaks Guide
a detailed guide to the region including places to visit and inspected accommodation

Bed and Breakfast Touring map 2002 - including Camping and Caravan Parks in the South East
a useful touring map detailing inspected guest accommodation in the South East and London regions. Also contains camping and caravan parks

Eating and Drinking at Traditional Inns
in partnership with Whitbread Pubs, a guide to some of the fine inns to be found in the South and South East of England

Churches and Cathedrals of the South of England
a guide detailing some of the region's finest churches and cathedrals, their fascinating history and architecture

Spoilt for Choice - 100s of Places to Visit in South East England
the definitive guide to over 300 places to visit in South East England. Also contains a Web site directory, map and information on the network of Tourist Information Centres

Leisure Map and Gazetteer - South East England
produced in conjunction with Estate Publications Ltd, a colourful tourist map of the South East showing roads, railways, hundreds of places to visit and the topography of the region

pictures:
Guildford Castle

Getting to
SOUTH EAST England

BY ROAD: From the north of England - M1/M25; the west and Wales - M4/M25; the east of England - M25; the south of England M3/M25; London - M20 or M2.

BY RAIL: Regular services from London's Charing Cross, Victoria and Waterloo East stations to all parts of South East England.

Where to stay in
South East
England

Accommodation entries in this region are listed in alphabetical order of place name, and then in alphabetical order of establishment.

Map references refer to the colour location maps at front of this guide. The first number indicates the map to use; the letter and number which follow refer to the grid reference on the map.

At-a-glance symbols at the end of each accommodation entry give useful information about services and facilities. A key to symbols can be found inside the back cover flap. Keep this open for easy reference.

A brief description of the towns and villages offering accommodation in the entries which follow, can be found at the end of this section.

A complete listing of all the English Tourism Council assessed accommodation covered by this guide appears at the back of the guide.

ABINGER COMMON, Surrey Map ref 2D2

◆◆◆◆

LEYLANDS FARM
Leylands Lane, Abinger Common, Dorking
RH5 6JU
T: (01306) 730115 & 0781 8422881
F: (01306) 731675

B&B per night:
S £40.00
D £55.00

OPEN All year round

Attractively furnished, self-contained annexe of period farmhouse. Double bedroom, en suite bathroom, lounge, own television and tea-making facilities. Central heating. Log fire. Set in lovely 7-acre gardens amidst woodland. Easy access to airports and motorways.

Bedrooms: 1 triple/
multiple; suites available

 P

ALFRISTON, East Sussex Map ref 2D3

◆◆◆◆

RIVERDALE HOUSE
Seaford Road, Alfriston, Polegate
BN26 5TR
T: (01323) 871038
I: www.cuckmere-valley.co.uk/
riverdale/

Bedrooms: 5 double/
twin, 1 triple/multiple
Bathrooms: 4 en suite,
2 private

CC: Mastercard, Visa

B&B per night:
D £50.00–£60.00

OPEN All year round

Lovely Victorian home, peacefully located on the edge of famous village. Wonderful views of the South Downs. Minimum stay of two nights on summer weekends.

 P

ARDINGLY, West Sussex Map ref 2D3

◆◆◆

STONELANDS WEST LODGE
Ardingly Road, West Hoathly,
East Grinstead RH19 4RA
T: (01342) 715372

B&B per night:
S £20.00–£25.00
D £45.00–£50.00

OPEN All year round

Victorian lodge on B2028 between Ardingly and Turners Hill. Convenient for Gatwick, Brighton, Ardingly Showground, Bluebell Railway and several National Trust gardens, with Wakehurst Place 1 mile away. Ground floor annexe with en suite. Full English breakfast. Warm welcome. White Hart Inn next door offers excellent food. Strictly non-smoking.

Bedrooms: 1 single,
2 double/twin
Bathrooms: 1 en suite

🐴🛋🖵👌🗑Ⓢ🏦▥ ☎☀🐴🚲P

ARUNDEL, West Sussex Map ref 2D3 *Tourist Information Centre Tel: (01903) 882268*

◆◆◆

MEDLAR COTTAGE
Poling Street, Poling, Arundel
BN18 9PT
T: (01903) 883106
F: (01903) 883106

Bedrooms: 1 single,
3 double/twin
Bathrooms: 2 en suite

B&B per night:
S £25.00–£35.00
D £45.00–£50.00

OPEN All year round

Relax and enjoy warm comfortable accommodation in picturesque setting close to historic Arundel. Lovely views, extensive breakfast menu. Excellent pub food nearby

Ⅲ🐴🛋🖳🖵👌🗑Ⓢ🏦▥ ☎🍴☀🚲P

◆◆◆

MILL LANE HOUSE
Slindon, Arundel BN18 0RP
T: (01243) 814440
F: (01243) 814436

Bedrooms: 4 double/
twin, 1 triple/multiple;
suites available
Bathrooms: 5 en suite

Evening meal available

B&B per night:
S £29.50
D £47.00

OPEN All year round

17thC house in beautiful National Trust village. Magnificent views to coast. Pubs within easy walking distance. One mile from A29/A27 junction.

Ⅲ🐴🛋🖵Ⓢ▥🏠☎☀🐴🚲🏦P

ASHFORD, Kent Map ref 3B4 *Tourist Information Centre Tel: (01233) 629165*

◆◆◆

DEAN COURT FARM
Challock Lane, Westwell, Ashford
TN25 4NH
T: (01233) 712924

Bedrooms: 3 double/
twin
Bathrooms: 1 en suite,
1 private

Evening meal available

B&B per night:
S £25.00
D £45.00

HB per person:
DY Min £67.00

OPEN All year round

Period farmhouse on working farm with modern amenities. Magnificent views in quiet valley. Comfortable accommodation with separate sitting room for guests.

🐴🖳👌Ⓢ🏠▥ ☎☀🚲🏦P

◆◆◆

MAYFLOWER HOUSE
61 Magazine Road, Ashford
TN24 8NR
T: (01233) 621959
F: (01233) 621959

Bedrooms: 2 single,
1 double/twin

Evening meal available

B&B per night:
S £20.00–£22.00
D £35.00–£37.00

HB per person:
DY £32.00–£35.00

OPEN All year round

Family-run establishment, all rooms with colour TV and tea/coffee making facilities. Friendly atmosphere. Close to M20 and Ashford International station.

Ⅲ🐴📞🖳🖵👌🗑Ⓢ🏠▥ ☎☀🐴🚲

CHECK THE MAPS
The colour maps at the front of this guide show all the cities, towns and villages for which you will find accommodation entries.
Refer to the town index to find the page on which they are listed.

◆◆◆

17thC former coaching inn with oak beams. Extensive bar, restaurant menu and 10 en suite bedrooms. Ideal for short breaks, touring and walking the Kent countryside and coast, and as a countryside stop-over for the Shuttle, Eurostar and ferries. Wye village is not far from the A2 and the M20.

NEW FLYING HORSE INN

Upper Bridge Street, Wye, Ashford
TN25 5AN
T: (01233) 812297
F: (01233) 813487
E: newflyhorse@shepherd-neame.co.uk
I: www.shepherd-neame.co.uk

Bedrooms: 4 single, 5 double/twin, 1 triple/ multiple	Lunch available Evening meal available CC: Amex, Delta, Mastercard, Switch, Visa
Bathrooms: 10 en suite	

HB daily price is based on a minimum 2-night stay for 2 people.

B&B per night:
S Min £50.00
D Min £65.00

HB per person:
DY Min £55.00

OPEN All year round

🏇🐴⚕🖼📞🖥🖵♿☕🍷Ⓢ🏧,🛋☼🐴🐎🦮📮P

◆◆◆

QUANTOCK HOUSE
Quantock Drive, Ashford TN24 8QH
T: (01233) 638921
E: tucker100@madasafish.com

Bedrooms: 1 single, 1 double/twin, 1 triple/ multiple	
Bathrooms: 3 en suite	

Small, family-run establishment within easy walking distance from town centre with all its facilities, but within a quiet residential area.

B&B per night:
S £22.00–£25.00
D £40.00–£45.00

OPEN All year round

🏇🐴7⚕🖵☕🍷Ⓢ✂🖵,🛋🦮P

◆◆◆

WARREN COTTAGE HOTEL AND RESTAURANT
136 The Street, Willesborough,
Ashford TN24 0NB
T: (01233) 621905 & 632929
F: (01233) 623400
E: general@warrencottage.co.uk
I: www.warrencottage.co.uk

Bedrooms: 1 single, 4 double/twin, 1 triple/ multiple	Lunch available CC: Delta, Mastercard, Switch, Visa
Bathrooms: 6 en suite	

17thC hotel set in 2.5 acres. All rooms en suite. Large car park, M20 Junc 10 and minutes to Ashford International Station and Channel Tunnel.

B&B per night:
S £39.90–£45.00
D £59.90–£69.90

HB per person:
DY £52.00–£63.00

OPEN All year round

🏇🐴🖼🖵☕🍷Ⓢ✂🖵,🛋🍽♿☼🐴🦮📮P

◆◆◆

MOONS HILL FARM
The Green, Ninfield, Battle
TN33 9LH
T: (01424) 892645
F: (01424) 892645

Bedrooms: 3 double/ twin	
Bathrooms: 3 en suite	

10-acre mixed farm. Modernised farmhouse in Ninfield village centre, in the heart of '1066' Country. A warm welcome and Sussex home cooking. Pub opposite. Large car park.

B&B per night:
S £20.00–£25.00
D £40.00–£50.00

OPEN Mar–Nov

🏇🐴⚕🖼🖵☕🍷Ⓢ🖵,🛋Ↄ▷☼🐴🦮P

QUALITY ASSURANCE SCHEME

For an explanation of the quality and facilities represented by the Diamonds please refer to the front of this guide. A more detailed explanation can be found in the information pages at the back.

BETHERSDEN, Kent Map ref 3B4

◆◆◆

THE COACH HOUSE
Oakmead Farm, Bethersden, Ashford
TN26 3DU
T: (01233) 820583
F: (01233) 820583

B&B per night:
S £25.00
D £40.00

Comfortable family home, set well back from road, in 5 acres of garden and paddocks. Breakfast of your choice served in the dining room or conservatory, also used as a sitting room for guests. One mile from village – central for ferries, Channel Tunnel, Eurostar, Canterbury, Leeds Castle, Sissinghurst and many tourist attractions. Dutch spoken.

Bedrooms: 5 double/twin
Bathrooms: 2 en suite, 1 private

BEXHILL, East Sussex Map ref 3B4 *Tourist Information Centre Tel: (01424) 732208*

◆◆◆◆
Silver Award

THE AROSA HOTEL
6 Albert Road, Bexhill TN40 1DG
T: (01424) 212574 & 08000 748041
F: (01424) 212574

Bedrooms: 1 single, 5 double/twin, 3 triple/multiple
Bathrooms: 6 en suite

Lunch available
Evening meal available
CC: Delta, Mastercard, Switch, Visa

B&B per night:
S £25.00–£30.00
D £40.00–£50.00

HB per person:
DY £29.00–£39.00

OPEN All year round

Family-run hotel offering wide range of accommodation to suit all budgets. Good home cooking with quality service and accommodation. Half-board breaks available.

◆◆◆

PARK LODGE HOTEL
16 Egerton Road, Bexhill TN39 3HH
T: (01424) 216547 & 215041
F: (01424) 217460

Bedrooms: 8 double/twin, 2 triple/multiple
Bathrooms: 8 en suite

Evening meal available
CC: Amex, Diners, Mastercard, Visa

B&B per night:
S £23.00–£26.00
D £43.00–£48.00

HB per person:
DY £32.00–£35.00

OPEN All year round

Informal family-run hotel with home-from-home feel, renowned for high standards and fresh home cooking. Seafront shops and theatre 50 yards.

BIDDENDEN, Kent Map ref 3B4

◆◆◆◆

HERON COTTAGE
Biddenden, Ashford TN27 8HH
T: (01580) 291358

Bedrooms: 3 double/twin
Bathrooms: 3 en suite

Evening meal available

B&B per night:
S £25.00–£35.00
D £35.00–£50.00

HB per person:
DY £30.00–£47.50

Peacefully set in unspoilt countryside. Walled garden with pond for fishing and animals to visit. Situated between the historic village of Biddenden and Sissinghurst Castle.

BOGNOR REGIS, West Sussex Map ref 2C3 *Tourist Information Centre Tel: (01243) 823140*

◆◆◆

JUBILEE GUEST HOUSE
5 Gloucester Road, Bognor Regis
PO21 1NU
T: (01243) 863016 & 07702 275967
F: (01243) 868017
E: jubileeguesthouse@breathemail.net
I: www.jubileeguesthouse.com

Bedrooms: 2 single, 1 double/twin, 3 triple/multiple
Bathrooms: 2 en suite

CC: Delta, Mastercard, Switch, Visa

B&B per night:
S £20.00–£35.00
D £40.00–£70.00

OPEN All year round

Family-run business, 75 yards from seafront and beach. Ideal for visiting 'Butlin's family entertainment resort', Chichester, Goodwood, Fontwell, Arundel, Portsmouth and IOW.

IDEAS For ideas on places to visit refer to the introduction at the beginning of this section.

BOGNOR REGIS continued

◆◆◆ **REGIS LODGE**

3 Gloucester Road, Bognor Regis
PO21 1NU
T: (01243) 827110 & 07768 117770
F: (01243) 827110
E: frank@regislodge.fsbusiness.co.
uk
I: www.regislodge.tripod.com

Bedrooms: 2 single,
2 double/twin, 8 triple/
multiple
Bathrooms: 12 en suite

B&B per night:
S £25.00–£30.00
D £40.00–£50.00

OPEN Apr–Oct

Family-run guesthouse, friendly atmosphere, comfortable rooms. 40 yards from beach, opposite South Coast World. Close to town centre, shops, restaurants, park, leisure centre, Goodwood and Fontwell.

BOUGHTON MONCHELSEA, Kent Map ref 3B4

◆◆◆ **WIERTON HALL FARM**

East Hall Hill,
Boughton Monchelsea, Maidstone
ME17 4JU
T: (01622) 743535
F: (01622) 743535

Bedrooms: 3 double/
twin
Bathrooms: 1 en suite

Evening meal available

B&B per night:
S £19.00–£21.50
D £38.00–£43.00

HB per person:
DY £29.00–£31.50

OPEN All year round

20-acre fruit farm. 200-year-old converted stable barn. Beautiful views, 3 miles Leeds Castle. Friendly and warm welcome. Good base for visiting many historic places of interest

BRASTED, Kent Map ref 2D2

◆◆◆ **THE MOUNT HOUSE**

Brasted, Westerham TN16 1JB
T: (01959) 563617
F: (01959) 561296
E: jpaulco@webspeed.net

Bedrooms: 1 single,
2 double/twin
Bathrooms: 1 en suite

B&B per night:
S £25.00
D £50.00–£60.00

OPEN All year round

Large early Georgian family residence in centre of village. Listed Grade II.

BRIGHTON & HOVE, East Sussex Map ref 2D3

◆◆◆◆ **AINSLEY HOUSE HOTEL**

28 New Steine, Brighton BN2 1PD
T: (01273) 605310
F: (01273) 688604
E: ahhotel@fastnet.co.uk
I: www.ainsleyhotel.com

Bedrooms: 3 single,
7 double/twin
Bathrooms: 8 en suite

Evening meal available
CC: Amex, Delta, Diners,
Mastercard, Switch, Visa

B&B per night:
S £26.00–£33.00
D £45.00–£79.00

OPEN All year round

Regency townhouse on garden square, overlooking the sea. All rooms comfortably furnished, some non-smoking. Close to all amenities. Extensive breakfast menu, warm welcome guaranteed.

◆◆◆◆

AMBASSADOR HOTEL

22 New Steine, Marine Parade, Brighton
BN2 1PD
T: (01273) 676869
F: (01273) 689988
E: ambassadorhoteluk@hotmail.com
I: www.ambassadorhotelbrighton.com

B&B per night:
S £30.00–£38.00
D £60.00–£75.00

OPEN All year round

Family-run, licensed hotel in a seafront garden square, overlooking the sea and Palace Pier. Close to Royal Pavilion, shops, conference halls and entertainments. All rooms en suite with colour TV, direct-dial telephone, radio, hospitality tray. Ground floor and no-smoking rooms available.

Bedrooms: 7 single,
7 double/twin, 9 triple/
multiple
Bathrooms: 23 en suite

CC: Amex, Delta, Diners,
Mastercard, Switch, Visa

SYMBOLS The symbols in each entry give information about services and facilities. A key to these symbols appears at the back of this guide.

◆◆◆◆
Silver
Award

ARLANDA HOTEL

20 New Steine, Brighton BN2 1PD
T: (01273) 699300
F: (01273) 600930
E: arlanda@brighton.co.uk
I: www.arlandahotel.co.uk

B&B per night:
S £30.00–£48.00
D £60.00–£120.00

OPEN All year round

Charming Grade II Regency townhouse, situated in a garden square adjacent to the seafront. The hotel provides a peaceful and relaxing base for exploring historic Brighton, the countryside and outstanding coastline. Whether your journey is for business or pleasure you are assured a warm welcome and a clean and comfortable stay.

Bedrooms: 4 single, 9 double/twin, 1 triple/ multiple
Bathrooms: 14 en suite

CC: Amex, Delta, Diners, Mastercard, Switch, Visa

◆◆

DIANA HOUSE
25 St Georges Terrace, Brighton BN2 1JJ
T: (01273) 605797
F: (01273) 600533
E: diana@enterprise.net
I: www.dianahouse.co.uk

Bedrooms: 9 double/ twin, 1 triple/multiple
Bathrooms: 6 en suite

CC: Mastercard, Visa

B&B per night:
S £22.00–£25.00
D £44.00–£50.00

OPEN All year round

Large, friendly guesthouse close to sea, town and conference centre. All rooms have TV, hospitality tray, clock/radio, shaver point. Some rooms en suite. 24-hour access.

◆◆◆◆

FYFIELD HOUSE

26 New Steine, Brighton BN2 1PD
T: (01273) 602770
F: (01273) 602770
E: fyfield@aol.com
I: www.brighton.co.uk/hotels/fyfield

B&B per night:
S £25.00–£45.00
D £50.00–£90.00

OPEN All year round

Excellent, clean, home-from-home private hotel, where Anna and Peter have welcomed their guests for the last 30 years. Central to all attractions in and out of town. All rooms are tastefully decorated and most have en suite facilities. Superb breakfast menu, from the traditional to the home-made vegetarian sausage.

Bedrooms: 4 single, 5 double/twin
Bathrooms: 6 en suite

Evening meal available
CC: Amex, Delta, Diners, Mastercard, Switch, Visa

Low season Sun-Thurs reduced rates available.

◆◆◆

RUSSELL GUEST HOUSE
19 Russell Square, Brighton BN1 2EE
T: (01273) 327969
F: (01273) 821535
E: russell.brighton@btinternet.com

Bedrooms: 4 double/ twin, 4 triple/multiple
Bathrooms: 8 en suite

CC: Amex, Delta, Mastercard, Switch, Visa

B&B per night:
D £46.00–£72.00

OPEN All year round

Five-storey townhouse in pleasant garden square. Close Brighton centre, seafront, main shopping area. Unrestricted access. Theatres, cinemas, nightclubs all within easy walking distance.

SPECIAL BREAKS
Many establishments offer special promotions and themed breaks. These are highlighted in red. (All such offers are subject to availability.)

◆◆

SANDPIPER GUEST HOUSE

11 Russell Square, Brighton
BN1 2EE
T: (01273) 328202
F: (01273) 329974
E: sandpiper@brighton.co.uk

Bedrooms: 3 single,
2 double/twin, 1 triple/
multiple

Evening meal available
CC: Amex, Delta,
Mastercard, Switch, Visa

B&B per night:
S £15.00–£28.00
D £30.00–£56.00

OPEN All year round

Newly refurbished guesthouse, 2 minutes from conference centre, shopping area, leisure centres and seafront. All rooms have central heating, colour TV, tea/coffee. Unrestricted access.

◆◆◆

HOTEL SEAFIELD

23 Seafield Road, Hove, Brighton
BN3 2TP
T: (01273) 735912
F: (01273) 323525
I: www.brighton.co.uk/hotels/seafield/

Bedrooms: 2 single,
7 double/twin, 5 triple/
multiple
Bathrooms: 12 en suite

Lunch available
Evening meal available
CC: Delta, Mastercard,
Switch, Visa

B&B per night:
S £35.00–£60.00
D £70.00–£100.00

OPEN All year round

Family-run hotel with home-cooked food, close to seafront and main shopping centre. Free street and private parking. Most rooms en suite with shower/toilet.

◆◆◆

BAY TREE HOTEL

12 Eastern Esplanade, Broadstairs
CT10 1DR
T: (01843) 862502
F: (01843) 860589

B&B per night:
S £28.00–£32.00
D £56.00–£64.00

HB per person:
DY £42.00–£46.00

OPEN All year round

Situated on the lovely Eastern Esplanade overlooking Stone Bay, the hotel enjoys panoramic sea views across the English Channel. Minutes from the town centre and sandy beaches. A warm welcome awaits you at this family-run hotel.

Bedrooms: 1 single,
10 double/twin
Bathrooms: 11 en suite

Evening meal available
CC: Delta, Mastercard,
Switch, Visa

◆◆◆◆

THE VICTORIA

23 Victoria Parade, Broadstairs
CT10 1QL
T: (01843) 871010
F: (01843) 860888
E: mullin@thevictoriabroadstairs.
co.uk
I: www.thevictoriabroadstairs.co.uk

Bedrooms: 6 double/
twin
Bathrooms: 6 en suite

CC: Mastercard, Visa

B&B per night:
S £30.00–£60.00
D £50.00–£100.00

OPEN All year round

Spacious, elegant, well appointed rooms. Some with panoramic views over Viking Bay and Broadstairs Harbour.

USE YOUR *i*s

There are more than 550 Tourist Information Centres throughout England offering friendly help with accommodation and holiday ideas as well as suggestions of places to visit and things to do. You'll find TIC addresses in the local Phone Book.

BURGESS HILL, West Sussex Map ref 2D3 *Tourist Information Centre Tel: (01444) 247726*

◆◆◆◆

THE HOMESTEAD

Homestead Lane, Valebridge Road, Burgess Hill RH15 0RQ
T: (01444) 246899 & 0800 064 0015
F: (01444) 246899
E: homestead@burgess-hill.co.uk
I: www.burgess-hill.co.uk

Quiet, comfortable, friendly home in peaceful setting of 7.5 acres at end of private lane. All rooms en suite with refreshment facilities and TV. Two ground-floor bedrooms have wheelchair access. Glyndebourne, numerous gardens, National Trust locations and Bluebell steam railway nearby. Wivelsfield railway station 1 km – Brighton/Gatwick/Lewes 15 minutes, London 50 minutes. Parking. Strictly no smoking.

Bedrooms: 3 double/twin
Bathrooms: 3 en suite

CC: Delta, Mastercard, Visa

B&B per night:
S £25.00–£30.00
D £50.00–£60.00

OPEN All year round

CAMBERLEY, Surrey Map ref 2C2

◆◆◆

ABACUS
7 Woodside, Blackwater, Camberley GU17 9JJ
T: (01276) 38339

Bedrooms: 2 single

Attractive cottage in quiet lane yet convenient for shops, superstores and M3. Off-road parking. Rooms tastefully refurbished, with TV, tea/coffee.

B&B per night:
S £16.00–£20.00
D £30.00–£36.00

OPEN All year round

CANTERBURY, Kent Map ref 3B3 *Tourist Information Centre Tel: (01227) 766567*

◆◆

ASHLEY GUEST HOUSE
9 London Road, Canterbury CT2 8LR
T: (01227) 455863

Bedrooms: 2 double/twin

A cosy and friendly atmosphere at this 16thC guesthouse. Close to city centre. Private parking. Tea/coffee-making facilities.

B&B per night:
S £15.00–£20.00
D £32.00–£40.00

OPEN All year round

◆◆◆

CATHEDRAL GATE HOTEL

36 Burgate, Canterbury CT1 2HA
T: (01227) 464381
F: (01227) 462800
E: cgate@cgate.demon.co.uk
I: www.smoothhound.co.uk/cathedra.html

Pilgrims slept here! This 1438 building with massive beams, sloping floors and low doorways, offers modern comfort, centrally situated at the main cathedral gateway. Our rooms have telephone, TV, welcome tray. Quiet lounge, bar and home-cooked meals in our bow-window dining room. Continental breakfast included, cooked breakfast extra.

Bedrooms: 6 single, 16 double/twin, 5 triple/multiple
Bathrooms: 12 en suite

Evening meal available
CC: Amex, Delta, Diners, Mastercard, Switch, Visa

Special breaks (DB&B and full English breakfast) available-2 nights' stay minimum.

B&B per night:
S £23.50–£55.50
D £45.00–£83.50

OPEN All year round

MAP REFERENCES The map references refer to the colour maps at the front of this guide. The first figure is the map number; the letter and figure which follow indicate the grid reference on the map.

CANTERBURY continued

♦♦♦♦

CHAUCER LODGE

62 New Dover Road, Canterbury CT1 3DT
T: (01227) 459141
F: (01227) 459141
E: wchaucerldg@aol.com
I: www.thechaucerlodge.co.uk

B&B per night:
S £24.00–£35.00
D £44.00–£52.00

HB per person:
DY £35.00–£50.00

OPEN All year round

Alistair and Maria Wilson extend a very warm welcome to their family-run guesthouse. The highest standards of cleanliness and service are provided in a friendly and relaxed atmosphere. Large, well appointed quiet en suite bedrooms, elegantly decorated. Ideally situated close to city centre, cathedral, bus, coach and railway station.

Bedrooms: 1 single, 3 double/twin, 2 triple/ multiple
Bathrooms: 6 en suite

Evening meal available
CC: Delta, Mastercard, Visa

20% discount for 3 nights Nov–Mar (excl Christmas and New Year).

♦♦♦♦
Silver
Award

CLARE-ELLEN GUEST HOUSE

9 Victoria Road, Wincheap, Canterbury CT1 3SG
T: (01227) 760205
F: (01227) 784482
E: loraine.williams@clareellenguesthouse.co.uk
I: www.clareellenguesthouse.co.uk

B&B per night:
S £27.00–£30.00
D £49.00–£54.00

OPEN All year round

A warm welcome and bed and breakfast in style. Large, quiet, elegant en suite rooms all with colour TV, clock/radio, hairdryer and tea/coffee-making facilities. Full English breakfast. Vegetarian and special diets on request. Six minutes' walk to city centre, 5 minutes' to Canterbury East train station. Car park/garage available.

Bedrooms: 1 single, 2 double/twin, 2 triple/ multiple
Bathrooms: 5 en suite

CC: Delta, Mastercard, Switch, Visa

Discounts for 2/3 night stay Nov–Mar (excl Christmas and New Year).

♦

THE COACH HOUSE
34 Watling Street, Canterbury CT1 2UD
T: (01227) 784324

Bedrooms: 3 double/ twin, 3 triple/multiple

B&B per night:
S £25.00–£30.00
D £40.00–£50.00

OPEN All year round

An elegant Georgian townhouse in the city centre. All travel routes accessible. Park and ride facilities adjacent.

♦♦♦

THE DICKENS INN AT HOUSE OF AGNES HOTEL

71 St Dunstan's Street, Canterbury CT2 8BN
T: (01227) 472185
F: (01227) 464527
E: enq@dickens-inn.co.uk
I: www.dickens-inn.co.uk

B&B per night:
S £39.50–£59.50
D £54.00–£74.00

HB per person:
DY £39.50–£49.50

OPEN All year round

Home of Agnes Wickfield from Charles Dickens' novel 'David Copperfield', this friendly hotel combines the atmosphere of bygone days with modern comforts.

Bedrooms: 2 single, 5 double/twin, 2 triple/ multiple
Bathrooms: 9 en suite

Lunch available
Evening meal available
CC: Delta, Diners, Mastercard, Switch, Visa

◆◆◆ **THE GREEN HOUSE**
86 Wincheap, Canterbury CT1 3RS
T: (01227) 453338
F: (01227) 452185
E: chrismac@greenhouse48.fsnet. co.uk
I: www.bednbreakfastkent.co.uk

Bedrooms: 2 single, 2 double/twin, 1 triple/ multiple	CC: Delta, Mastercard, Switch, Visa	B&B per night: S £25.00–£30.00 D £45.00–£50.00
Bathrooms: 5 en suite		OPEN All year round

An all en suite Victorian house. Clean, comfortable, very good value. Close to city centre and very child friendly. Excellent breakfast variety offered.

♘ 🐴 ⚑ 🖭 ☐ ↓ ¶ Ⓢ ⚹ 🎬 🖉 ✿ ⛽ P

◆◆◆◆◆
Gold
Award

MAGNOLIA HOUSE
36 St Dunstans Terrace, Canterbury
CT2 8AX
T: (01227) 765121 & 07885 595970
F: (01227) 765121
E: magnolia_house_canterbury@yahoo. com
I: freespace.virgin.net/magnolia.canterbury

B&B per night:
S £48.00–£65.00
D £78.00–£125.00

OPEN All year round

Charming late Georgian house in quiet residential street, a 10-minute stroll from the city centre. Bedrooms, individually co-ordinated, have every facility for an enjoyable stay. Varied breakfasts are served overlooking the attractive walled garden, where you are welcome to relax after a busy day's sightseeing.

Bedrooms: 1 single, 6 double/twin	Evening meal available
Bathrooms: 7 en suite	CC: Amex, Delta, Diners, Mastercard, Switch, Visa

♘ 🐴 | 2 ⚑ 🏠 🖭 ⊔ ↓ ¶ Ⓢ ⚹ 🎬 🖉 ✿ ⛽ ⌂ P

◆◆◆◆
Silver
Award

ORIEL LODGE
3 Queens Avenue, Canterbury CT2 8AY
T: (01227) 462845
F: (01227) 462845
E: info@oriel-lodge.co.uk
I: www.oriel-lodge.co.uk

B&B per night:
S £27.00–£34.00
D £45.00–£67.00

OPEN All year round

In a tree-lined residential avenue, very near the city centre and restaurants, an attractive Edwardian house with 6 well-furnished bedrooms and clean, up-to-date facilities. Afternoon tea served in the garden or lounge with log fire. Restricted smoking. Private parking.

Bedrooms: 1 single, 4 double/twin, 1 triple/ multiple	CC: Delta, Diners, Mastercard, Switch, Visa
Bathrooms: 2 en suite	

Short break and weekly terms available.

♘ 🐴 6 🖭 ☐ ↓ ¶ Ⓢ 🎬 🖉 ✿ ⛽ ⌂ P

◆◆◆

RENVILLE OAST
Bridge, Canterbury CT4 5AD
T: (01227) 830215
F: (01227) 830215
E: renville.oast@virgin.net
I: freespace.virgin.net/joan.hill/index.html

B&B per night:
S £25.00–£36.00
D £45.00–£55.00

OPEN All year round

The 150-year-old Oast was once used for drying hops for the brewery trade. Enjoy a stay in beautiful Kentish countryside as well as experiencing the history of a magnificent cathedral city. Many interesting castles, historic houses and gardens within easy reach. All rooms comfortably furnished. Warm welcome awaits you.

Bedrooms: 2 double/ twin, 1 triple/multiple	
Bathrooms: 2 en suite, 1 private	

🐴 🖭 ↓ ¶ Ⓢ ⚹ 🎬 🖉 ✦ ✿ ⛽ ⌂ P

CANTERBURY continued

◆◆◆◆◆
Gold Award

THANINGTON HOTEL
140 Wincheap, Canterbury CT1 3RY
T: (01227) 453227
F: (01227) 453225
E: thanington@lineone.net
I: www.thanington-hotel.co.uk

Bedrooms: 13 double/ twin, 2 triple/multiple
Bathrooms: 15 en suite

CC: Amex, Delta, Diners, Mastercard, Switch, Visa

B&B per night:
S £50.00–£55.00
D £68.00–£90.00

OPEN All year round

Special Georgian bed and breakfast hotel, only minutes' walk from city centre and Cathedral. Spacious en suite accommodation. Secure car park. Indoor heated swimming pool.

◆◆◆◆
Silver Award

TWIN MAYS
Plumpudding Lane, Dargate, Faversham ME13 9EX
T: (01227) 751346
E: janetm@harper128.freeserve.co.uk

Bedrooms: 1 triple/ multiple
Bathrooms: 1 en suite

B&B per night:
S £30.00–£35.00
D £55.00–£58.00

HB per person:
DY £45.00–£50.00

OPEN Feb–Dec

Ideallity situated for Canterbury, Whitstable and Faversham. Charming country property, 1 spacious double with sitting area, 1 twin, luxury bathroom. Homemade bread and preserves.

◆◆◆◆

WHITE HORSE INN
Boughton, Faversham ME13 9AX
T: (01227) 751700 & 751343
F: (01227) 751090
E: whitehorse@shepherd-neame.co.uk
I: www.shepherd-neame.co.uk

B&B per night:
S Min £60.00
D Min £80.00

HB per person:
DY £60.00–£80.00

OPEN All year round

15thC coaching inn with lime-washed beams and inglenook fireplaces. Newly refurbished with 12 en suite bedrooms. The menu features many regional specialities and ever changing specials all of which are freshly prepared. Situated in the picturesque village of Boughton just off the A2, close to Canterbury and Faversham.

Bedrooms: 11 double/ twin, 2 triple/multiple
Bathrooms: 13 en suite

HB daily price is based on a minimum 2-night stay for 2 people.

Lunch available
Evening meal available
CC: Amex, Delta, Mastercard, Switch, Visa

◆◆◆◆

THE WHITE HOUSE
6 St Peters Lane, Canterbury CT1 2BP
T: (01227) 761836
E: whwelcome@aol.com

B&B per night:
S £30.00–£35.00
D £50.00–£55.00

OPEN All year round

Regency house situated in quiet location within city walls by the Marlowe Theatre. Superior family-run accommodation, all rooms en suite. Two minutes' walk to a charming mix of shops, restaurants, pretty parks and rivers. Cathedral and other major attractions also close by. Excellent English or vegetarian breakfast.

Bedrooms: 1 single, 6 double/twin, 2 triple/ multiple
Bathrooms: 9 en suite

IMPORTANT NOTE Information on accommodation listed in this guide has been supplied by the proprietors. As changes may occur you are advised to check details at the time of booking.

◆◆◆

WOODLANDS FARM

The Street, Adisham, Canterbury CT3 3LA
T: (01304) 840401 & 07720 861765
F: (01304) 841985
E: woodlands.farm@btinternet.com

B&B per night:
S £35.00–£40.00
D £45.00–£50.00

HB per person:
DY £34.50–£45.00

OPEN All year round

Charming 15thC farmhouse, peacefully located yet within easy reach of Canterbury and Channel ports. Beautiful gardens, private woodlands, inglenooks, beams, log fire and panelled dining-room; elegant surroundings which provide a tranquil, relaxing setting in which to be pampered. Speciality first class cuisine featuring fresh, organic and home-grown produce.

Bedrooms: 2 double/twin; suites available
Bathrooms: 1 en suite

Lunch available
Evening meal available
CC: Amex, Delta, Diners, Mastercard, Switch, Visa

◆◆◆

THE WOOLPACK INN

High Street, Chilham, Canterbury CT4 8DL
T: (01227) 730208 & 730351
F: (01227) 731053
E: woolpack@shepherd-neame.co.uk
I: www.shepherd-neame.co.uk

B&B per night:
S £45.00–£60.00
D £80.00–£120.00

HB per person:
DY £60.00–£85.00

OPEN All year round

This ancient inn, c1422, with inglenook fireplaces and oak-beamed restaurant, has 14 newly refurbished en suite bedrooms. Locally renowned restaurant with extensive menu serving local produce. Situated in the picturesque village of Chilham, it is an ideal location for touring the Kent countryside and is quite close to Canterbury and Ashford.

Bedrooms: 1 single, 10 double/twin, 3 triple/multiple; suites available
Bathrooms: 14 en suite

Lunch available
Evening meal available
CC: Amex, Delta, Mastercard, Switch, Visa

HB daily price is based on a minimum 2-night stay for 2 people.

◆◆◆

ROYAL OAK INN

5 High Street, Charing, Ashford TN27 0HU
T: (01233) 712612
F: (01233) 713355
E: theroyal-oak.charingtn27@barbox.net

Bedrooms: 4 single, 5 double/twin, 1 triple/multiple
Bathrooms: 10 en suite

Lunch available
Evening meal available
CC: Amex, Mastercard, Switch, Visa

B&B per night:
S £43.50–£50.00
D £53.50–£65.00

OPEN All year round

A village pub in the medieval village of Charing serving a cross section of customers, farmers, horse people, business and tourists.

TOWN INDEX

This can be found at the back of the guide. If you know where you want to stay, the index will give you the page number listing accommodation in your chosen town, city or village.

◆◆◆◆

THE COACH HOUSE
Binderton, Chichester PO18 0JS
T: (01243) 539624 & 07710 536085
F: (01243) 539624
E: spightling@aol.com

B&B per night:
S £20.00–£25.00
D £40.00–£50.00

OPEN All year round

Converted flint and brick coach house of 17thC origin, peacefully set in 2 acres of walled gardens overlooking the unspoilt Lavant Valley on the slopes of the South Downs. Ten minutes' drive Chichester, Goodwood, West Dean Gardens. Convenient for country walks, local pub. Recently updated, spacious accommodation, delicious English breakfast.

Bedrooms: 1 double/
twin, 1 triple/multiple
Bathrooms: 1 private

◆◆◆◆

THE OLD STORE GUEST HOUSE
Stane Street, Halnaker, Chichester
PO18 0QL
T: (01243) 531977
F: (01243) 531977
E: alandavis@theoldstore.fsnet.co.uk
I: www.smoothhound.co.uk/hotels/store.html

Bedrooms: 1 single,
5 double/twin, 1 triple/
multiple
Bathrooms: 7 en suite

CC: Delta, Mastercard,
Switch, Visa

B&B per night:
S £25.00–£28.00
D £50.00–£55.00

OPEN All year round

Lovely 18thC Grade II Listed home. Seven comfortable rooms all ensuite. Adjoins Goodwood Estate. Close to Chichester, convenient for Petworth, Arundel and the coast.

◆◆◆

COACH HOUSE
Horsham Road, Cowfold, Horsham
RH13 8BT
T: (01403) 864247
F: (01403) 865329
E: coachhousecowfold@talk21.com

Bedrooms: 1 single,
13 double/twin, 1 triple/
multiple
Bathrooms: 15 en suite

Lunch available
Evening meal available
CC: Delta, Mastercard,
Switch, Visa

B&B per night:
S £28.00–£35.50
D £46.00–£56.00

OPEN All year round

Roadside Inn. Fifteen en suite bedrooms, including 1 room designed for disabled guests. Village bar with open fires. Bar and restaurant. Only 7 miles to Horsham.

◆◆◆

SWATTENDEN RIDGE
Swattenden Lane, Cranbrook
TN17 3PR
T: (01580) 712327

Bedrooms: 2 double/
twin
Bathrooms: 1 en suite,
1 private

Lunch available
Evening meal available
CC: Mastercard, Visa

B&B per night:
S Min £34.00
D Min £44.00

HB per person:
DY £30.50–£35.50

OPEN Mar–Nov

Modern quiet farmhouse with wonderful views and ancient woodlands. 15 miles from Hastings, Maidstone and Tunbridge Wells. Outdoor pool for summer use.

www.travelengland.org.uk
Log on for information and inspiration. The latest information on places to visit, events and quality assessed accommodation.

◆◆◆◆

NEW GLENMORE
Sliders Lane, Furners Green, Uckfield
TN22 3RU
T: (01825) 790783
E: alan.robinson@bigfoot.com

B&B per night:
S £35.00–£45.00
D £35.00–£45.00

OPEN All year round

New Glenmore is a spacious bungalow set in 6 acres of grounds in a rural location close to the Bluebell Steam Railway and Sheffield Park National Trust property. We have a large family en suite room, a double and a twin room. Breakfast comes with our own eggs and honey.

Bedrooms: 1 double/ twin, 1 triple/multiple
Bathrooms: 2 private

◆◆◆◆

HARDICOT GUEST HOUSE
Kingsdown Road, Walmer, Deal CT14 8AW
T: (01304) 373867 & 389234
F: (01304) 389234
E: guestbuss@talk21.com
I: smoothhound.co.uk/hotels/hardicot.html

B&B per night:
S £22.00–£25.00
D £44.00–£50.00

OPEN All year round

Large, quiet, detached Victorian house with Channel views and secluded garden, situated 100 yards from the beach. Guests have unrestricted access to rooms. Close to 3 championship golf courses, ferries, and the Channel Tunnel. Ideal centre for cliff walks and exploring Canterbury and the castles and gardens of East Kent.

Bedrooms: 3 double/ twin
Bathrooms: 1 en suite, 2 private

◆◆◆

FAIRDENE GUEST HOUSE
Moores Road, Dorking RH4 2BG
T: (01306) 888337
E: zoe@fairdene5.freeserve.co.uk

Bedrooms: 6 double/ twin, 1 triple/multiple

B&B per night:
S £27.50–£30.00
D £45.00–£50.00

OPEN All year round

Late-Victorian house in convenient location, close to town centre, Gatwick Airport and North Downs Way. Friendly and homely atmosphere. Off-street parking.

CHECK THE MAPS
The colour maps at the front of this guide show all the cities, towns and villages for which you will find accommodation entries. Refer to the town index to find the page on which they are listed.

DOVER, Kent Map ref 3C4 *Tourist Information Centre Tel: (01304) 205108*

◆◆◆

BLAKES OF DOVER

52 Castle Street, Dover CT16 1PJ
T: (01304) 202194 & 211263
F: (01304) 202194
E: blakes-of-dover@hotels.activebooking.com

Situated in the shadow of Dover Castle, close to town centre, yet a few minutes from the ferry and cruise terminals. Offering 5 beautifully furnished and decorated en suite rooms, an internationally renowned restaurant serving local caught fish, steaks and vegetarian dishes. Unquestionably the perfect location for business or pleasure.

Bedrooms: 2 double/twin, 3 triple/multiple
Bathrooms: 5 en suite

Lunch available
Evening meal available
CC: Delta, Mastercard, Switch, Visa

Early Bird evening menu, 6-7.30pm daily May-Oct. 2 courses and wine £10.80pp.

B&B per night:
D £45.00–£55.00

OPEN All year round

◆◆◆◆

COLRET HOUSE

The Green, Coldred, Dover CT15 5AP
T: (01304) 830388
F: (01304) 830388
E: jackie.colret@evnet.co.uk

An early Edwardian property with modern, purpose-built, en suite garden rooms, standing in extensive well maintained grounds. Situated beside the village green in a conservation area on downs above Dover. Ideally situated for overnight stays when travelling by ferries or shuttle. Close to Canterbury and Sandwich. Ample secure parking.

Bedrooms: 2 double/twin
Bathrooms: 2 en suite

Evening meal available

B&B per night:
S £25.00–£30.00
D £50.00–£60.00

OPEN All year round

◆◆◆◆

LODDINGTON HOUSE HOTEL
14 East Cliff,
(Seafront - Marine Parade), Dover
CT16 1LX
T: (01304) 201947
F: (01304) 201947

Bedrooms: 1 single, 5 double/twin
Bathrooms: 4 en suite, 2 private

Evening meal available
CC: Amex, Mastercard, Visa

Well-positioned small hotel in Georgian terrace overlooking harbour. Quality food and wine – prices on request. Yards from east ferry terminal.

B&B per night:
S £45.00–£50.00
D £54.00–£60.00

OPEN All year round

◆◆◆

LONGFIELD GUEST HOUSE

203 Folkestone Road, Dover CT17 9SL
T: (01304) 204716

A clean and highly recommended guesthouse, 2 minutes from Dover Priory station, Hoverport and town centre, 10 minutes from Channel Tunnel. Single, double, twin and family rooms, some en suite, with colour TV, tea/coffee facilities, washbasins and central heating. Large car park and lock-up garage.

Bedrooms: 4 single, 2 double/twin, 1 triple/multiple
Bathrooms: 1 en suite, 1 private

Evening meal available
CC: Delta, Mastercard, Switch, Visa

B&B per night:
S £15.00–£22.00
D £28.00–£40.00

HB per person:
DY £22.00–£30.00

OPEN All year round

♦♦♦♦
**Silver
Award**

OWLER LODGE
Alkham Valley Road, Alkham, Dover
CT15 7DF
T: (01304) 826375
F: (01304) 826375
E: owlerlodge@aol.com
I: www.smoothhound.co.uk/hotels/
owlerlodge.html

*Small guesthouse situated in the
beautiful Alkham Valley between
Dover and Folkestone, 3 miles from
Channel Tunnel, 4 miles from Dover
Docks. Ideal base for touring East
Kent. All rooms have en suite shower,
toilet, colour TV, clock/radio,
hairdryer and tea-making facilities.
Beautiful garden with our Koi ponds.
Off-street parking. A non-smoking
residence.*

Bedrooms: 2 double/	Lunch available
twin, 1 triple/multiple	Evening meal available
Bathrooms: 3 en suite	

B&B per night:
S £36.00–£39.00
D £46.00–£50.00

OPEN All year round

♦♦♦♦

THE PARK INN
1-2 Park Place, Ladywell, Dover CT16 1DQ
T: (01304) 203300
F: (01304) 203324
E: theparkinn@cs.com
I: www.theparkinnatdover.co.uk

*The feel of Victorian England
immediately embraces guests on
arrival at the Park Inn. An extremely
high standard of finish in decor,
furnishings and fittings prevails in
our en suite rooms which
complement our successful inn and
restaurant. All our rooms are cosy
and comfortable and contain many
facilities.*

Bedrooms: 1 single,	Lunch available
3 double/twin, 1 triple/	Evening meal available
multiple	CC: Amex, Delta, Diners,
Bathrooms: 5 en suite	Mastercard, Switch, Visa

Special accommodation offers for our monthly
music by candlelight evenings, superb quaterly
theme nights and bank hol Sunday night
entertainment.

B&B per night:
S £35.00–£45.00
D £54.00–£74.00

OPEN All year round

♦♦♦♦

TALAVERA HOUSE
275 Folkestone Road, Dover
CT17 9LL
T: (01304) 206794
F: (01304) 207067
E: john-jan@talavera-house.
freeserve.co.uk
I: www.smoothhound.co.uk/hotels

*Comfortable family home, offering high standards of accommodation and service.
Convenient for ferries and Channel Tunnel.*

Bedrooms: 2 double/	Evening meal available
twin, 1 triple/multiple	CC: Delta, Mastercard,
Bathrooms: 1 en suite	Switch, Visa

B&B per night:
S £21.00–£26.00
D £36.00–£46.00

HB per person:
DY £29.50–£34.50

OPEN All year round

COUNTRY CODE Always follow the Country Code 🌳
Enjoy the countryside and respect its life and work 🌳 Guard
against all risk of fire 🌳 Fasten all gates 🌳 Keep your dogs
under close control 🌳 Keep to public paths across farmland
🌳 Use gates and stiles to cross fences, hedges and walls 🌳
Leave livestock, crops and machinery alone 🌳 Take your litter
home 🌳 Help to keep all water clean 🌳 Protect wildlife,
plants and trees 🌳 Take special care on country roads 🌳
Make no unnecessary noise

◆◆◆◆

Cottage-style house offering comfortable rooms and attractive gardens, ideally situated for Channel crossings and touring historic Romney Marsh countryside by foot or transport. Experience the RH&D railway, visit Port Lympne Wild Animal Park or stroll along nearby sandy beaches, finally enjoying a drink or meal from our varied menu.

WATERSIDE GUEST HOUSE

15 Hythe Road, Dymchurch, Romney Marsh TN29 0LN
T: (01303) 872253
F: (01303) 872253
E: info@watersideguesthouse.co.uk
I: www.watersideguesthouse.co.uk

Bedrooms: 4 double/ twin, 1 triple/multiple
Bathrooms: 5 en suite

Lunch available
Evening meal available
CC: Delta, Mastercard, Switch, Visa

Two, 3 or 4 day short breaks (DB&B). Also Christmas specials-contact for details.

B&B per night:
S £25.00–£30.00
D £40.00–£45.00

HB per person:
DY £27.00–£32.00

OPEN All year round

◆◆◆

CRANSTON HOUSE
Cranston Road, East Grinstead RH19 3HW
T: (01342) 323609
F: (01342) 323609
E: accommodation@cranstonhouse.screaming.net
I: www.cranstonhouse.co.uk

Bedrooms: 3 double/ twin
Bathrooms: 2 en suite, 1 private

B&B per night:
S £28.00–£34.00
D £40.00–£45.00

OPEN All year round

Attractive detached house in quiet location near town centre and station, 15 minutes' drive from Gatwick. Spacious high quality en suite accommodation. Ample parking off-road.

◆◆◆

The inn is set in the oldest part of this Surrey village, close to 15thC parish church of St Peter and Paul. Here you can experience all the pleasures of a traditional English inn: a warm friendliness, real comfort, excellent food, ales, wines and a room for the night.

THE STAR INN

Church Road, Lingfield RH7 6AH
T: (01342) 832364
F: (01342) 832364
E: thestarinn@breathemail.net
I: www.starinnlingfield.co.uk

Bedrooms: 6 double/ twin, 1 triple/multiple
Bathrooms: 7 en suite

Lunch available
Evening meal available
CC: Amex, Delta, Mastercard, Switch, Visa

Weekend special deals. Free parking when using us as an airport stop-over.

B&B per night:
S £40.00
D £55.00

HB per person:
DY £50.00–£70.00

OPEN All year round

◆◆

TOWN HOUSE
6 De La Warr Road, East Grinstead RH19 3BN
T: (01342) 300310
F: (01342) 315122

Bedrooms: 3 double/ twin

B&B per night:
S £25.00–£30.00
D £40.00–£50.00

OPEN All year round

Cosy, friendly, quiet, very clean, en suite rooms. Five minutes from train, town centre, 2 minutes from shops, restaurants, 15 minutes from Gatwick.

CREDIT CARD BOOKINGS If you book by telephone and are asked for your credit card number it is advisable to check the proprietor's policy should you cancel your reservation.

EAST PECKHAM, Kent Map ref 2D2

◆◆◆ **ROYDON HALL**

Seven Mile Lane, East Peckham,	Bedrooms: 5 single,	Lunch available	B&B per night:
Tonbridge TN12 5NH	12 double/twin, 2 triple/	Evening meal available	S £30.00–£50.00
T: (01622) 812121	multiple	CC: Delta, Mastercard,	D £40.00–£65.00
F: (01622) 813959	Bathrooms: 7 en suite	Switch, Visa	
E: roydonhall@btinternet.com			HB per person:

16thC Tudor manor set in 10 acres of gardens, terraces and woodlands. Commanding a fine view of Weald of Kent.

DY £38.00–£58.00

OPEN All year round

EASTBOURNE, East Sussex Map ref 3B4 *Tourist Information Centre Tel: (01323) 411400*

◆◆◆

BIRLING GAP HOTEL

Birling Gap, Seven Sisters Cliffs, East Dean, Eastbourne BN20 0AB

T: (01323) 423197
F: (01323) 423030
E: info@birlinggaphotel.co.uk
I: birlinggaphotel.co.uk

B&B per night:
S £20.00–£50.00
D £30.00–£65.00

OPEN All year round

Magnificent Seven Sisters clifftop position, with views of country, sea, beach. Superb downland and beach walks. Old world 'Thatched Bar' and 'Oak Room Restaurant'. Coffee shop and games room, function and conference suite. Off A259 coast road at East Dean, 1.5 miles west of Beachy Head.

Bedrooms: 1 single,
5 double/twin, 3 triple/
multiple
Bathrooms: 9 en suite

Lunch available
Evening meal available
CC: Amex, Delta, Diners,
Mastercard, Switch, Visa

3 nights for the price of 2, Oct–Mar (except Christmas and New Year). Pre-booked only.

◆◆◆◆
Silver
Award

BRAYSCROFT HOTEL

13 South Cliff Avenue, Eastbourne
BN20 7AH

T: (01323) 647005
F: (01323) 720705
E: brayscroft@hotmail.com
I: www.brayscrofthotel.co.uk

B&B per night:
S £27.00–£29.50
D £54.00–£59.00

HB per person:
DY £39.00–£41.50

OPEN All year round

Elegant award-winning small hotel, one of only a handful in Eastbourne with coveted ETC 4 Diamonds – Silver Award for 'outstanding accommodation and hospitality'. Superb position less than a minute from seafront in fashionable Meads district and ideally situated for South Downs, theatres, restaurants and town centre. Totally non-smoking.

Bedrooms: 1 single,
5 double/twin
Bathrooms: 6 en suite

Evening meal available
CC: Delta, Mastercard,
Switch, Visa

Upgrade from single room to double/twin at no extra cost except at peak holiday times. 4 night and weekly breaks.

AT-A-GLANCE SYMBOLS

Symbols at the end of each accommodation entry give useful information about services and facilities. A key to symbols can be found inside the back cover flap. Keep this open for easy reference.

EASTBOURNE continued

◆◆◆◆
Silver
Award

CHERRY TREE HOTEL

15 Silverdale Road, Eastbourne BN20 7AJ
T: (01323) 722406
F: (01323) 648838
E: anncherrytree@aol.com
I: www.eastbourne.org/cherrytree-hotel

B&B per night:
S £28.00–£36.00
D £56.00–£72.00

HB per person:
DY £40.50–£48.50

OPEN All year round

Tastefully converted Edwardian residence, this award-winning family-run licensed hotel retains its original charm, elegance and character yet offers all the comfort and convenience expected by today's discerning guest. Quiet location close to seafront, downlands and theatres, the hotel is noted for its excellent traditional English cuisine. Non-smoking.

Bedrooms: 3 single, 6 double/twin, 1 triple/ multiple
Bathrooms: 10 en suite

Evening meal available
CC: Amex, Delta, Diners, Mastercard, Switch, Visa

Special 2 and 3 day breaks available during low and mid season. Full details, prices on request.

◆◆◆◆

LITTLE FOXES

24 Wannock Road, Eastbourne BN22 7JU
T: (01323) 640670
F: (01323) 640670
E: chris@foxholes55.freeserve.co. uk

Bedrooms: 1 single, 1 double/twin; suites available
Bathrooms: 2 en suite

B&B per night:
S £20.00–£26.00
D £40.00–£52.00

OPEN All year round

Personally run B&B. Close to beach and 1 kilometre town centre. En suite facilities. Guests' lounge with Sky TV. All ages welcome. No smoking.

◆◆◆◆

SEA BEACH HOUSE HOTEL

39-40 Marine Parade, Eastbourne BN22 7AY
T: (01323) 410458 & 410459
E: enquiries@seabeachhousehotel.com
I: www.seabeachhousehotel.com

B&B per night:
S £26.00–£29.50
D £59.00–£65.00

HB per person:
DY £39.50–£78.50

OPEN All year round

Charming, characterful, listed Georgian hotel where Tennyson once lodged. Furnished in keeping with a hotel of its age and with many original features. From your en suite bedroom see the sun rise over the sea or the flowers in our tea garden. For old-fashioned warmth, friendliness and hospitality visit us soon.

Bedrooms: 2 single, 8 double/twin, 1 triple/ multiple
Bathrooms: 10 en suite, 1 private

Evening meal available
CC: Amex, Mastercard, Visa

Winter breaks Nov-May (excl Easter): 3 nights for price of 2. Summer weekly rates: 7 nights for price of 6 (Quote SEEB).

◆◆

STRATFORD HOTEL & RESTAURANT

59 Cavendish Place, Eastbourne BN21 3RL
T: (01323) 724051 & 726391
F: (01323) 726391

Bedrooms: 2 single, 9 double/twin, 2 triple/ multiple
Bathrooms: 11 en suite

Lunch available
Evening meal available
CC: Delta, Mastercard, Visa

B&B per night:
S £22.00–£24.00
D £40.00–£44.00

HB per person:
DY £25.00–£28.00

OPEN All year round

Ideally situated near promenade, coaches and shopping centre. Licensed, centrally heated throughout. Ground floor and family rooms available. Most rooms with modern en suite.

ACCESSIBILITY

Look for the 🚹 symbols which indicate accessibility for wheelchair users. A list of establishments is at the front of this guide.

EASTBOURNE continued

◆◆◆◆
Silver
Award

TREVINHURST LODGE

10 Baslow Road, Meads, Eastbourne
BN20 7UJ
T: (01323) 410023
F: (01323) 643238
E: enquiries@trevinhurstlodge.com
I: www.trevinhurstlodge.com

B&B per night:
S £40.00–£50.00
D £60.00–£72.00

HB per person:
DY £60.00–£70.00

OPEN All year round

A warm welcome awaits those looking for a discerning break in a non-smoking, relaxed, informal atmosphere. With just 3 attractive, spacious bedrooms we can guarantee the individual attention you would expect. Fine food offered in our elegant dining room completes the picture.Speciality watercolour courses are also available.

Bedrooms: 3 double/ twin
Bathrooms: 2 en suite, 1 private

Proprietor Brian Smith, a professional artist, offers weekend or mid-week residential watercolour courses for small groups.

Evening meal available

🅰🐎8 🖼️📠❄️🍷Ⓢ🗝️Ⓜ️🖥️ ✲ ♿ P

EDENBRIDGE, Kent Map ref 2D2 *Tourist Information Centre Tel: (01732) 868110*

◆◆◆◆

YE OLD CROWN INN

74-76 The High Street, Edenbridge
TN8 5AR
T: (01732) 867896
F: (01732) 868316
I: www.lionheartinns.co.uk

B&B per night:
S £59.00
D £74.00

OPEN All year round

Once the haunt of the infamous Ramsey Gang, this 14thC inn carries a distinctive landmark to Edenbridge – the pub's original 'Crown Post' dating back to circa 1325. Superior en suite bedrooms, air-conditioned restaurant and a good range of local ales. Ideal base for Hever Castle and visits to National Trust properties and gardens.

Bedrooms: 1 single, 5 double/twin
Bathrooms: 6 en suite

Lunch available
Evening meal available
CC: Amex, Delta, Mastercard, Switch, Visa

🅰🐎📞🖼️📠❄️🍷🍽️Ⓢ🖥️🛗📠🎠 ✲ ♿ P

◆◆◆◆

SHOSCOMBE

Mill Hill, Edenbridge TN8 5DA
T: (01732) 866781
F: (01732) 867807

B&B per night:
S £22.50–£25.00
D Min £45.00

OPEN Jan–Nov

Georgian-style house situated on the south of Edenbridge. Shoscombe offers a double and single bedroom with their own bathroom. Both bedrooms have tea/coffee-making facilities. Guests have use of their own TV sitting room. From the garden there is access by foot paths to the River Eden.

Bedrooms: 1 single, 1 double/twin
Bathrooms: 2 private

🐎❄️🍷Ⓢ🗝️Ⓜ️🖥️🛗🎠 ✲ ♿ P

QUALITY ASSURANCE SCHEME

Diamond ratings and awards were correct at the time of going to press but are subject to change. Please check at the time of booking.

♦♦♦♦

WHITE HOUSE HOTEL
Downs Hill Road, Epsom KT18 5HW
T: (01372) 722472
F: (01372) 744447
E: hopkins.epsom@virgin.net

B&B per night:
S £49.50–£79.50
D £61.50–£85.50

OPEN All year round

Charming, spacious, traditional mansion converted into a modern hotel. Epsom town and station are only minutes away, with regular train services to London. Convenient for Gatwick and Heathrow airports and London via A23 and M25.

Bedrooms: 7 single, 5 double/twin, 1 triple/ multiple
Bathrooms: 7 en suite

Lunch available
Evening meal available
CC: Amex, Delta, Diners, Mastercard, Switch, Visa

♦♦♦

YARD FARM
Ewhurst, Cranleigh GU6 7SN
T: (01483) 276649
F: (01483) 276649

Bedrooms: 1 single, 3 double/twin
Bathrooms: 2 en suite

Evening meal available

B&B per night:
S £25.00–£30.00
D £50.00

OPEN All year round

350-acre mixed farm. A 16thC farmhouse surrounded by countryside. Working farm, mainly grass with sheep and horses.

♦♦♦♦♦

Silver Award

SOUTH LODGE
Gravel Hill Road, Holt Pound, Farnham GU10 4LG
T: (01420) 520960
F: (01420) 520961
E: southlodge1@aol.com
I: www.southlodge.org.uk

B&B per night:
S £29.50
D £59.00

OPEN All year round

A detached, Spanish-style bungalow offering delightful accommodation with private parking. Ground floor en suite bedrooms overlooking our south-facing gardens, providing a relaxing and tranquil setting. Backing onto 'Birdworld', Britain's largest bird park, and adjacent to Alice Holt Woodland Park. Located 3 miles south of Farnham off the A325.

Bedrooms: 2 double/ twin
Bathrooms: 2 en suite

Evening meal available

♦♦♦

BARNSFIELD
Fostall, Hernhill, Faversham ME13 9JH
T: (01227) 750973 & 07889 836259
F: (01227) 273098
E: barnsfield@yahoo.com
I: www.barnsfield.co.uk

Bedrooms: 3 double/ twin
Bathrooms: 1 en suite

Evening meal available

B&B per night:
S £14.00–£24.00
D £28.00–£48.00

OPEN All year round

Listed Grade II country cottage accommodation, just off A299, set in 3 acres of orchards. 6 miles from Canterbury. Convenient for ports and touring.

CHECK THE MAPS
The colour maps at the front of this guide show all the cities, towns and villages for which you will find accommodation entries. Refer to the town index to find the page on which they are listed.

◆◆◆

OWENS COURT FARM
Selling, Faversham ME13 9QN
T: (01227) 752247
F: (01227) 752247

B&B per night:
S £25.00
D £40.00

OPEN All year round

A gracious Grade II Listed farmhouse with large comfortable rooms overlooking the farm. Situated in a quiet lane 3 miles from Faversham, 9 from Canterbury, its situation is ideal for holidaying in Kent or travelling to the continent. A lovely garden and a warm welcome await you.

Bedrooms: 1 single, 1 double/twin, 1 triple/ multiple

◆◆◆◆

Silver Award

PRESTON LEA
Canterbury Road, Faversham ME13 8XA
T: (01795) 535266
F: (01795) 533388
E: preston.lea@which.net
I: homepages.which.net/~alan.turner10

B&B per night:
S £35.00–£40.00
D £50.00–£60.00

OPEN All year round

A unique and elegant Victorian Gothic house with turrets, set in large secluded gardens. Spacious, sunny bedrooms with garden views and antique furniture. Beautiful guest drawing room, panelled dining room and delicious breakfasts. Only 15 minutes from Canterbury, 35 minutes from ports, Eurotunnel, 70 minutes train to London.

Bedrooms: 3 double/ twin
Bathrooms: 2 en suite, 1 private

CC: Delta, Mastercard, Switch, Visa

◆◆◆◆

THE OLD POST OFFICE
Lower Street, Fittleworth, Pulborough RH20 1JE
T: (01798) 865315
F: (01798) 865315
E: sue.moseley@ukgateway.net

Bedrooms: 2 double/ twin

B&B per night:
S £30.00–£35.00
D £40.00–£50.00

OPEN All year round

Warm welcome extended to the first post office in this village. Convenient for Arundel, Petworth and Goodwood. Children welcome.

◆◆◆◆

SWAN INN
Lower Street, Fittleworth, Pulborough RH20 1EN
T: (01798) 865429
F: (01798) 865721
E: hotel@swaninn.com
I: www.swaninn.com

B&B per night:
S £30.00–£40.00
D £60.00–£75.00

HB per person:
DY £42.95–£53.25

OPEN All year round

Listed 14thC building in centre of village, well placed for visiting many of the historic houses and places of interest in the area. Public bar and cosy oak-beamed restaurant provide a comfortable environment renowned for food. Awarded Food Pub of the Year 2000.

Bedrooms: 3 single, 12 double/twin
Bathrooms: 15 en suite

Lunch available
Evening meal available
CC: Amex, Delta, Mastercard, Switch, Visa

FOLKESTONE, Kent Map ref 3B4 *Tourist Information Centre Tel: (01303) 258594*

◆◆◆ **BEACHBOROUGH PARK**

Newington, Folkestone CT18 8BW	Bedrooms: 6 double/	Lunch available	B&B per night.
T: (01303) 275432	twin, 2 triple/multiple	Evening meal available	S £25.00–£27.50
F: (01843) 845131	Bathrooms: 8 en suite	CC: Mastercard, Switch,	D £41.00–£50.00
I: www.kentaccess.org.uk		Visa	
			OPEN All year round

Beautiful setting, ideal for sightseeing and very convenient for tunnel and ferries. Very comfortable for both active people and those just seeking peace and quiet.

GATWICK, West Sussex Map ref 3A4

◆◆◆ **COLLENDEAN BARN**

Collendean Lane, Norwood Hill,	Bedrooms: 1 double/	B&B per night:
Horley RH6 0HP	twin, 1 triple/multiple	S £30.00–£40.00
T: (01293) 862433	Bathrooms: 2 en suite	D £50.00–£60.00
F: (01293) 863102		
E: collendean.barn@amserve.net		OPEN All year round

Bed and breakfast in a self-contained, converted barn with en suite, on a 16thC farm in lovely countryside, 3 miles from Gatwick and trains.

◆◆◆ **GAINSBOROUGH LODGE**

39 Massetts Road, Horley RH6 7DT	Bedrooms: 7 single,	CC: Diners, Mastercard,	B&B per night:
T: (01293) 783982 & 430830	15 double/twin, 4 triple/	Switch, Visa	S £33.00–£40.00
F: (01293) 785365	multiple		D Max £54.00
E: gainsbor@eurobell.co.uk	Bathrooms: 24 en suite		
I: www.gainsboroughlodge.co.uk			OPEN All year round

Extended Edwardian house set in attractive garden. Five minutes' walk from Horley station and town centre. Five minutes' drive from Gatwick Airport.

GATWICK AIRPORT

See under East Grinstead, Gatwick, Horley, Horsham, Redhill

GODALMING, Surrey Map ref 2D2

◆◆◆ **HEATH HALL FARM**

Bowlhead Green, Godalming	Bedrooms: 1 single,	B&B per night:
GU8 6NW	2 double/twin	S £25.00–£30.00
T: (01428) 682808	Bathrooms: 2 en suite,	D Min £50.00
F: (01428) 684025	1 private	
E: heathhallfarm@btinternet.com		OPEN All year round

Farmhouse on the edge of hamlet. Converted stable courtyard. Free-range fowl, sheep and horse. Tennis court. Farmhouse atmosphere. Pets welcome if under control.

GRAFFHAM, West Sussex Map ref 2C3

◆◆◆◆◆ **BROOK BARN**
Silver
Award

Selham Road, Graffham, Petworth	Bedrooms: 1 double/	B&B per night:
GU28 0PU	twin	S £30.00–£40.00
T: (01798) 867356	Bathrooms: 1 en suite	D £50.00–£60.00
E: jollands@lineone.net		
		OPEN All year round

Large double bedroom with en suite bathroom and its own conservatory, which leads to beautiful secluded 2 acre garden. From the garden is direct access to woodland walks.

GUILDFORD, Surrey Map ref 2D2 *Tourist Information Centre Tel: (01483) 444333*

◆◆◆ **BEEVERS FARM**

Chinthurst Lane, Bramley, Guildford	Bedrooms: 3 double/	B&B per night:
GU5 0DR	twin	D £36.00–£50.00
T: (01483) 898764	Bathrooms: 1 en suite	
F: (01483) 898764		
E: beevers@onetel.net.uk		

In peaceful surroundings 2 miles from Guildford, near villages with pubs and restaurants. Own preserves, honey, eggs. Friendly atmosphere. Non-smokers. Convenient for Heathrow/ Gatwick Airports.

GUILDFORD continued

♦♦♦ CHALKLANDS

Beech Avenue, Effingham,
Leatherhead KT24 5PJ
T: (01372) 454936
F: (01372) 459569
E: rreilly@onetel.net.uk

Detached house backing on to Effingham golf course. 30 minutes from Heathrow/Gatwick Airports, 35 minutes from London Waterloo station. Excellent pub food nearby.

Bedrooms: 3 double/
twin
Bathrooms: 2 en suite,
1 private

Evening meal available

B&B per night:
S £30.00–£40.00
D £45.00–£48.00

HB per person:
DY £35.00–£45.00

OPEN All year round

♦♦♦ HIGH EDSER

Shere Road, Ewhurst, Cranleigh
GU6 7PQ
T: (01483) 278214 & 0777 5865125
F: (01483) 278200
E: franklinadams@highedser.
demon.co.uk

Early 16thC family home in Area of Outstanding Natural Beauty. 6 miles from Guildford and Dorking, easy reach airports and many tourist attractions. Non-smokers only, please.

Bedrooms: 3 double/
twin

B&B per night:
S £25.00–£35.00
D £50.00–£55.00

OPEN All year round

♦♦♦ LITTLEFIELD MANOR

Littlefield Common, Guildford
GU3 3HJ
T: (01483) 233068 & 07860 947439
F: (01483) 233686

120-acre mixed farm. 17thC Listed manor house with Tudor origins. Enjoy the walled rose garden in summer or the blazing log fire in winter.

Bedrooms: 3 double/
twin
Bathrooms: 3 en suite

Evening meal available
CC: Amex, Delta,
Mastercard, Switch, Visa

B&B per night:
S £45.00
D £60.00

OPEN All year round

♦♦♦♦ PLAEGAN HOUSE

96 Wodeland Avenue, Guildford
GU2 4LD
T: (01483) 822181 & 07961 919430
E: roxanne@plaegan.fsnet.co.uk

Large room in friendly accommodating house with lovely views directly on to the North Downs. Tastefully refurbished property in walking distance of town centre and university.

Bedrooms: 1 double/
twin
Bathrooms: 1 en suite

B&B per night:
D £52.00–£56.00

OPEN All year round

HARTFIELD, East Sussex Map ref 2D2

♦♦♦

BOLEBROKE CASTLE LTD

Edenbridge Road, Hartfield TN7 4JJ
T: (01892) 770061
F: (01892) 771041
E: bolebroke@btclick.com
I: www.bolebrokecastle.co.uk

B&B per night:
D £50.00–£78.00

OPEN All year round

Henry VIII's hunting lodge set in a stunningly beautiful location on 30-acre estate away from main roads and noise. Two lakes, woodlands, views to Ashdown Forest, original beamed ceilings, 2nd largest fireplace in England, 4-poster suite, TV, tea/coffee. Tunbridge Wells 5 minutes, Brighton 30 minutes.

Bedrooms: 6 double/
twin
Bathrooms: 5 en suite,
1 private

Regular medieval banquets.

CC: Delta, Mastercard,
Switch, Visa

SPECIAL BREAKS

Many establishments offer special promotions and themed breaks. These are highlighted in red. (All such offers are subject to availability.)

HASLEMERE, Surrey Map ref 2C2

◆◆◆

CHAWTON
17 Marley Combe Road, Haslemere
GU27 3SN
T: (01428) 658023
E: hannah@hlnewman.freeserve.co.uk

B&B per night:
D £40.00–£44.00

OPEN All year round

1930s brick-built house set in attractive garden surrounded by National Trust woodland – ideal for walking. Comfortable accommodation in a peaceful location, within easy reach of A3 and Haslemere railway station giving access to Guildford and London or the south coast. Relaxed, happy and friendly atmosphere.

Bedrooms: 2 double/ twin

◆◆◆

SHEPS HOLLOW
Henley Common, Haslemere
GU27 3HB
T: (01428) 653120

Bedrooms: 2 single,
2 double/twin
Bathrooms: 2 en suite,
1 private

Lunch available
Evening meal available

B&B per night:
S £30.00–£35.00
D £60.00–£70.00

HB per person:
DY £40.00–£45.00

OPEN All year round

Charming 500-year-old cottage in a rural setting. Newly renovated. Sky TV in rooms. Self-catering annexe for two.

HASTINGS, East Sussex Map ref 3B4 *Tourist Information Centre Tel: (01424) 781111*

◆◆◆◆

EAGLE HOUSE HOTEL
12 Pevensey Road, St Leonards-on-Sea,
Hastings TN38 0JZ
T: (01424) 430535 & 441273
F: (01424) 437771
E: info@eaglehousehotel.com
I: www.eaglehousehotel.com

B&B per night:
S £30.00–£33.00
D £48.00–£52.00

HB per person:
DY £45.40–£49.40

OPEN All year round

You are assured of a warm welcome at the Eagle House Hotel. The charm and style of a bygone age is reflected in the spacious Victorian reception rooms. Our competitive rates include full English breakfast and free parking. Few minutes' walk from Warrior Square railway station.

Bedrooms: 16 double/
twin, 2 triple/multiple
Bathrooms: 18 en suite

Lunch available
Evening meal available
CC: Amex, Delta, Diners,
Mastercard, Switch, Visa

◆◆◆

SEA SPRAY GUEST HOUSE
54 Eversfield Place, St Leonards on Sea,
Hastings TN37 6DB
T: (01424) 436583
F: (01424) 436583
E: seaspraybb@faxvia.net
I: www.seaspraybb.co.uk

B&B per night:
S Max £18.00
D £40.00–£50.00

OPEN All year round

Newly refurbished family-run seafront bed and breakfast, 100m west of pier, 5 minutes level walk to town centre, station and local amenities. All rooms central heating/ double glazing, tea/coffee facilities, ceiling fans, TV, radio alarm. Extensive breakfast, all tastes catered for. No smoking policy, payphone, children welcome.

Bedrooms: 2 single,
5 double/twin
Bathrooms: 5 en suite

◆◆◆◆

SUMMERFIELDS HOUSE
Bohemia Road, Hastings TN34 1EX
T: (01424) 718142
F: (01424) 420135

B&B per night:
S £22.00–£30.00
D £40.00–£50.00

OPEN All year round

Welcome to Summerfields House, set in beautiful parkland but within minutes' walking distance of Hastings town centre, Horntye Cricket Ground, leisure/sports centres, pier and seafront. Luxury rooms, mostly en suite with TV, hospitality tray, bath robe and hairdryer. Full English breakfast served with many healthy options. Private secure parking. Stunning gardens.

Bedrooms: 3 double/
twin
Bathrooms: 2 en suite,
1 private

Special rates for children in family rooms.

HEATHFIELD, East Sussex Map ref 2D3

◆◆◆◆

SPICERS BED & BREAKFAST
21 Spicers Cottages, Cade Street,
Heathfield TN21 9BS
T: (01435) 866363 & 07973 188138
F: (01435) 866363
E: beds@spicersbb.co.uk
I: www.spicersbb.co.uk

Bedrooms: 1 single,
2 double/twin
Bathrooms: 1 en suite,
2 private

CC: Delta, Mastercard,
Switch, Visa

B&B per night:
S £20.00–£25.00
D £40.00–£45.00

HB per person:
DY £32.00–£37.00

OPEN All year round

Beamed cottage in hamlet of Cade Street near Heathfield on the High Weald, between Eastbourne and Tunbridge Wells. Convenient for many places of interest.

HERSTMONCEUX, East Sussex Map ref 3B4

◆◆◆◆

SANDHURST
Church Road, Herstmonceux,
Hailsham BN27 1RG
T: (01323) 833088
F: (01323) 833088
E: junerussell@compuserve.com

Bedrooms: 2 double/
twin, 2 triple/multiple
Bathrooms: 3 en suite,
1 private

B&B per night:
S £35.00–£45.00
D £50.00–£60.00

OPEN All year round

Large bungalow with plenty of off road parking. Within walking distance of Herstmonceux village. Twenty minutes' drive to sea. Close to Herstmonceux Castle.

◆◆◆

THE STUD FARM
Bodle Street Green, Herstmonceux,
Hailsham BN27 4RJ
T: (01323) 833201
F: (01323) 833201
E: philippa@miroted.freeserve.co.
uk

Bedrooms: 3 double/
twin
Bathrooms: 1 en suite

Evening meal available

B&B per night:
S £23.00–£26.00
D £42.00–£44.00

OPEN All year round

70-acre mixed farm. Upstairs, 2 bedrooms and bathroom let as one unit to party of 2, 3 or 4. Downstairs, twin-bedded en suite room. Guests' sitting room and sunroom.

HOLLINGBOURNE, Kent Map ref 3B3

◆◆◆◆

WOODHOUSES
49 Eyhorne Street, Hollingbourne,
Maidstone ME17 1TR
T: (01622) 880594
F: (01622) 880594

Bedrooms: 3 double/
twin
Bathrooms: 3 en suite

Lunch available

B&B per night:
S £22.00–£25.00
D £40.00

OPEN All year round

Interconnected listed cottages dating from 17thC, with inglenook fireplace, exposed wooden beams and cottage garden. Short walk to Leeds Castle, close to village pubs.

HORLEY, Surrey Map ref 2D2

THE LAWN GUEST HOUSE

♦♦♦♦ Silver Award

30 Massetts Road, Gatwick
RH6 7DE
T: (01293) 775751 & 784370
F: (01293) 821803
E: info@lawnguesthouse.co.uk
I: www.lawnguesthouse.co.uk

Bedrooms: 6 double/
twin, 6 triple/multiple
Bathrooms: 12 en suite

CC: Amex, Delta,
Mastercard, Switch, Visa

B&B per night:
D £50.00–£52.50

OPEN All year round

Classic Victorian house with mature garden, 2 minutes from Horley centre, restaurants, pubs and main rail station to London/Brighton. 5 minutes' drive to Gatwick, long-term parking. Non-smoking.

ROSEMEAD GUEST HOUSE

♦♦♦♦

19 Church Road, Horley RH6 7EY
T: (01293) 784965
F: (01293) 430547
E: rosemead@globalnet.co.uk
I: www.rosemeadguesthouse.co.uk

B&B per night:
S £34.00–£38.00
D £50.00

OPEN All year round

Edwardian guesthouse 5 minutes from Gatwick; close to shops, restaurants and pubs. Non-smoking. All rooms individually decorated with all the extras to make your stay comfortable and pleasant including full central heating, colour TV, beverage trays and tin of biscuits. Full English breakfast served in our newly refurbished dining room.

Bedrooms: 2 single,
2 double/twin, 2 triple/
multiple
Bathrooms: 5 en suite,
1 private

CC: Delta, Mastercard,
Switch, Visa

SPRINGWOOD GUEST HOUSE

♦♦♦

58 Massetts Road, Horley RH6 7DS
T: (01293) 775998
F: (01293) 823103
E: ernest@springwood58.u-net.com
I: www.networkclub.co.uk/springwood

B&B per night:
S Min £37.00
D £49.00–£52.00

OPEN All year round

Springwood is an elegant Victorian house with an attractive garden, situated close to Gatwick airport. Long-term parking and courtesy transport provided. It is within walking distance of Horley town centre with shops, restaurants and pubs. You can catch a main-line train to London, Brighton or the South Coast.

Bedrooms: 3 single,
5 double/twin, 3 triple/
multiple
Bathrooms: 10 en suite,
1 private

CC: Amex, Delta,
Mastercard, Switch, Visa

HORSHAM, West Sussex Map ref 2D2 *Tourist Information Centre Tel: (01403) 211661*

THE LARCHES

♦♦♦

28 Rusper Road, Horsham
RH12 4BD
T: (01403) 263392
F: (01403) 249980

Bedrooms: 1 single,
1 double/twin, 1 triple/
multiple
Bathrooms: 1 en suite

Evening meal available

B&B per night:
S £20.00–£30.00
D £38.00–£45.00

HB per person:
DY £25.00–£35.00

Friendly family house, close to town and stations. All rooms TV, fridge, hot drinks. Some rooms en suite. Full English breakfast. Evening meal available. Separate guest entrance.

HOVE

See under Brighton & Hove

PRICES

Please check prices and other details at the time of booking.

◆◆◆

THE DOG & BEAR HOTEL

The Square, Lenham, Maidstone ME17 2PG
T: (01622) 858219
F: (01622) 859415
E: dogbear@shepherd-neame.co.uk
I: www.shepherd-neame.co.uk

B&B per night:
S Min £50.00
D Min £65.00

HB per person:
DY £55.00–£65.00

OPEN All year round

15thC coaching inn with 24 en suite bedrooms, extensive bar and restaurant menu, Kent ale, lagers and fine wines. Close to Leeds Castle, ideal for touring the Kent countryside and close to historic Maidstone. Just a few minutes from the M20 makes it easy to reach the Channel ports and London.

Bedrooms: 3 single, 18 double/twin, 3 triple/multiple
Bathrooms: 24 en suite

Lunch available
Evening meal available
CC: Amex, Delta, Mastercard, Switch, Visa

HB daily price is based on a minimum 2-night stay for 2 people.

◆◆◆◆
Silver
Award

EAST LENHAM FARM

Lenham, Maidstone ME17 2DP
T: (01622) 858686
F: (01622) 859474
E: eastlenham@farmline.com
I: www.members.farmline.com/abarr

B&B per night:
D £60.00–£65.00

OPEN Jan, Mar–Dec

Spacious old farmhouse set at the end of avenue of 100-year-old trees. Ground floor en suite bedroom and adjacent sitting room face west over ha-ha across fields and lake. Ideal base for exploring Kent. Leeds Castle 5 miles, Channel Tunnel 20 miles. Good choice of pubs and restaurants within easy reach.

Bedrooms: 1 double/twin
Bathrooms: 1 en suite

Oct–Jan 3 nights £150 (excl Christmas and New Year).

◆◆

THE CROWN INN

High Street, Lewes BN7 2NA
T: (01273) 480670
F: (01273) 480679
E: sales@crowninn-lewes.co.uk
I: www.crowninn-lewes.co.uk

Bedrooms: 7 double/twin, 1 triple/multiple
Bathrooms: 6 en suite

Lunch available
CC: Delta, Mastercard, Switch, Visa

B&B per night:
S £37.50–£50.00
D £49.00–£65.00

OPEN All year round

Family-run inn at the centre of historic town offering traditional food. Licensed bar open all day. Most rooms en suite. Meeting room available.

◆◆◆

DOWNSVIEW

15 Montacute Road, Lewes BN7 1EW
T: (01273) 472719

Bedrooms: 1 single, 3 double/twin, 1 triple/multiple
Bathrooms: 4 en suite

B&B per night:
S £25.00–£30.00
D £45.00–£50.00

OPEN All year round

Downsview is situated in a residential area with easy access to the main A27. Ample parking available.

MAP REFERENCES The map references refer to the colour maps at the front of this guide. The first figure is the map number; the letter and figure which follow indicate the grid reference on the map.

◆◆◆◆

ECKINGTON HOUSE

Ripe Lane, Ripe, Lewes BN8 6AR
T: (01323) 811274
F: (01323) 811140
E: sue@eckingtonhouse.co.uk
I: www.eckingtonhouse.co.uk

B&B per night:
S £25.00–£35.00
D £45.00–£60.00

OPEN All year round

Historic 16thC Listed property with oak beams and inglenook fireplaces. Set in mature, peaceful gardens. Clients can enjoy total relaxation, yet still be close to the interesting and ancient town of Lewes, the South Downs, Glyndebourne Opera House and Charleston farmhouse. With the nearby coastal resorts of Eastbourne and Brighton.

Bedrooms: 1 single,
3 double/twin, 1 triple/
multiple
Bathrooms: 3 en suite

ঠ8 ⌗ ⌂ ♦ ⏹ Ⓢ ⊁ ⥮ ⊞ ⛾ ∪ ☼ ⋘ ⬚ ⊞ P

◆◆◆

HALE FARM HOUSE

Chiddingly, Lewes BN8 6HQ
T: (01825) 872619 & 07702 340631
F: (01825) 872619
E: s.burrough@virgin.net
I: www.cuckmere-valley.co.uk/hale

B&B per night:
S £20.00–£25.00
D £40.00–£50.00

HB per person:
DY £25.00–£30.00

OPEN All year round

14thC framed farmhouse in 65 acres on Weald Way, overlooking South Downs 12 miles from Eastbourne. Riding horses/ponies, cross-country course, schooling area. Bed and breakfast, family holidays, English language activity holidays with horse riding, cycling, walking, canoeing, golf, swimming and trips.

Bedrooms: 3 double/
twin
Bathrooms: 1 en suite

Evening meal available

4 nights for the price of 3 (excl Sat and Sun night).

Ⱥ ঠ ⊞ ⌂ ♦ Ⓢ ⊁ ⊞ ◲ ∪ ⊦ ☼ ⛾ ⋘ ⊞ P

◆◆◆

13 HILL ROAD

Lewes BN7 1DB
T: (01273) 477723 & 07881 911929
F: (01273) 486032
E: kmyles@btclick.com

Bedrooms: 1 double/
twin
Bathrooms: 1 en suite

B&B per night:
S Min £30.00
D Min £50.00

OPEN All year round

House with self-contained flat which is the only part to be let. Property positioned on a hill with far reaching views.

ঠ ⊞ ⌂ ♦ ⏹ Ⓢ ⊁ ⊞ ◲ ⋋ ☼ ⋘ ⬚ P

◆◆◆◆

RACECOURSE HOUSE

Old Lewes Racecourse, Lewes
BN7 1UR
T: (01273) 480804
F: (01273) 486478
E: a.heyes@btinternet.com

Bedrooms: 2 double/
twin
Bathrooms: 2 en suite

B&B per night:
S £35.00–£65.00
D £60.00–£80.00

Area of Outstanding Natural Beauty. Historic racecourse now racehorse training centre. Convenient for Glyndebourne, Brighton and Gatwick (25 minutes). Tasteful en suite rooms with TV.

ঠ10 ⊞ ⌂ ♦ Ⓢ ⥮ ⊞ ◲ ∪ ⊦ ☼ SP ⊞ P

IMPORTANT NOTE Information on accommodation listed
in this guide has been supplied by the proprietors. As changes may occur
you are advised to check details at the time of booking.

◆◆◆◆

SETTLANDS
Wellgreen Lane, Kingston, Lewes BN7 3NP
T: (01273) 472295
F: (01273) 472295
E: diana-a@solutions-inc.co.uk

B&B per night:
S £25.00–£35.00
D £45.00–£55.00

OPEN All year round

Picturesque Swedish chalet bungalow located in the attractive village of Kingston overlooking the South Downs. Ideal for walking holidays, yet only a few minutes from Brighton, Glyndebourne, universities and ferries. Pub lunches, evening meals can be enjoyed at village pub hearby. A warm welcome awaits all our guests.

Bedrooms: 2 double/ twin

Lunch available

LITTLEHAMPTON, West Sussex Map ref 2D3

◆◆◆

ARUN SANDS
84 South Terrace, Seafront,
Littlehampton BN17 5LJ
T: (01903) 732489
F: (01903) 732489
E: info@arun-sands.co.uk
I: www.arun-sands.co.uk

Bedrooms: 1 single,
1 double/twin, 5 triple/
multiple
Bathrooms: 7 en suite

CC: Mastercard, Visa

B&B per night:
S Min £25.00
D Min £45.00

OPEN All year round

Friendly seafront guesthouse. All rooms en suite with colour TV, tea/coffee facilities, hairdryer, clock radio/alarm, bedtime story book and teddy bear.

Rating
Applied For

RACING GREENS
70 South Terrace, Littlehampton BN17 5LQ
T: (01903) 732972 & 719389
F: (01903) 732932
E: urban.surfer@easynet.co.uk

B&B per night:
S £20.00–£35.00
D £20.00–£27.50

OPEN All year round

You can smell the surf from the seafront dining room whilst enjoying a hearty breakfast prior to indulging in the sporting or scenic attractions of Arundel, Goodwood, Fontwell Park and Brighton, or simply stroll across the green for the relaxing pleasures of our beach and leisure facilities.

Bedrooms: 2 double/ twin

CC: Delta, Mastercard,
Switch, Visa

We can accommodate up to 8 persons for special occasions, using our self-catering apartment.

◆◆◆

TUDOR LODGE GUEST HOUSE
2 Horsham Road, Littlehampton
BN17 6BU
T: (01903) 716203 & 07803 821440
F: (01903) 716203

Bedrooms: 2 single,
1 double/twin, 3 triple/
multiple
Bathrooms: 2 en suite

CC: Delta, Mastercard,
Switch, Visa

B&B per night:
S £16.00–£25.00
D £16.00–£25.00

OPEN All year round

Friendly, family-run guesthouse. Our comfortable rooms are equipped with colour TV and tea/coffee-making facilities. En-suite available. Within easy reach of all local amenities. Sandy beaches, sports centre, sea fishing, river trips, golf. Ideal base for visiting Arundel, Bognor, Chichester, Worthing.

---

www.travelengland.org.uk
Log on for information and inspiration. The latest information on places to visit, events and quality assessed accommodation.

LOOSE, Kent Map ref 3B4

◆◆◆ **VALE HOUSE**
Old Loose Hill, Loose, Maidstone
ME15 0BH
T: (01622) 743339 & 743400
F: (01622) 743103
E: vansegethin@hotmail.com

Bedrooms: 3 double/
twin
Bathrooms: 1 private

B&B per night:
S £30.00–£40.00
D £45.00–£55.00

OPEN All year round

Listed Georgian house in 3-acre garden in the centre of historic village. Three miles south of Maidstone and five miles from Leeds Castle and M20 motorway.

ᛗᏫ♦⚲⑤⊬⊞.◢℀⇔🏠P

LYMINSTER, West Sussex Map ref 2D3

◆◆◆◆ **SANDFIELD HOUSE**
Lyminster, Littlehampton BN17 7PG
T: (01903) 724129
F: (01903) 715041
E: thefbs@aol.com

Bedrooms: 2 double/
twin

B&B per night:
D £38.00–£42.00

OPEN All year round

Spacious country-style family house in 2 acres. Between Arundel and sea, near Area of Outstanding Natural Beauty. Tourist Board Blue Badge Guide available.

ᛗ⛐🖳☐♦⑤⊬ꝑ⊞.◢✲⇔P

MAIDSTONE, Kent Map ref 3B3 *Tourist Information Centre Tel: (01622) 602169*

◆◆◆ **51 BOWER MOUNT ROAD**
Maidstone ME16 8AX
T: (01622) 762948
F: (01622) 202753
E: sylviabnb@compuserve.com

Bedrooms: 2 double/
twin

B&B per night:
S £22.00–£25.00
D £34.00–£38.00

OPEN All year round

Comfortable Edwardian semi-detached house. TV and tea and coffee making facilities in all rooms. Within walking distance of the town and easy access to the M20.

ᗷ9🖳☐♦⑤⊬⊞.◢✲

◆◆◆◆◆
Gold
Award

THE RINGLESTONE INN & FARMHOUSE HOTEL
Ringlestone Hamlet, Harrietsham,
Maidstone ME17 1NX
T: (01622) 859900 & 07973 612261
F: (01622) 859966
E: bookings@ringlestone.com
I: www.ringlestone.com

B&B per night:
S £97.00–£107.00
D £119.00–£126.00

OPEN All year round

On the tranquil North Downs, just 10 minutes from Leeds Castle, this character Kentish farmhouse is luxuriously furnished in rustic oak throughout, including a canopied 4-poster bed. Opposite, the famous 16thC Ringlestone Inn is recommended for interesting Kentish fare incorporating English fruit wines in the traditional recipes.

Bedrooms: 2 double/
twin, 1 triple/multiple;
suites available
Bathrooms: 3 en suite

Lunch available
Evening meal available
CC: Amex, Delta, Diners,
Mastercard, Switch, Visa

ᛗ⛐🖾ℓ🖳☐♦⚲🍷⑤⊬ꝑ⊞.◢🍴✲🏠P

MARDEN, Kent Map ref 3B4

◆◆◆◆ **TANNER HOUSE**
Tanner Farm, Goudhurst Road,
Marden, Tonbridge TN12 9ND
T: (01622) 831214
F: (01622) 832472
E: tannerhouse@cs.com
I: www.tannerfarmpark.co.uk

Bedrooms: 3 double/
twin
Bathrooms: 3 en suite

Evening meal available
CC: Delta, Mastercard,
Switch, Visa

B&B per night:
S Min £30.00
D £45.00–£50.00

HB per person:
DY £37.50–£45.00

OPEN All year round

150-acre arable farm. Tudor farmhouse in centre of attractive family farm. Inglenook dining room. Off B2079. Car essential. Shire horses bred on farm.

ᛗ⛐12🖾🖳☐♦⚲⑤⊬ꝑ⊞.◢♒✲⇔🏠P

MIDHURST, West Sussex Map ref 2C3 *Tourist Information Centre Tel: (01730) 817322*

◆◆◆◆

10 ASHFIELD CLOSE
Midhurst GU29 9RP
T: (01730) 814858

Bedrooms: 2 double/
twin
Bathrooms: 2 private

B&B per night:
S £25.00–£30.00
D £45.00–£50.00

OPEN All year round

Located in the heart of Midhurst, quiet cul-de-sac. Choice of twin or double bedroom with private bathroom including power shower. Warm, friendly welcome.

◆◆◆

THE ELSTED INN
Elsted Marsh, Midhurst GU29 0JT
T: (01730) 813662
F: (01730) 813662

Bedrooms: 4 double/
twin
Bathrooms: 4 en suite

Lunch available
Evening meal available
CC: Delta, Mastercard,
Switch, Visa

B&B per night:
S Min £40.00
D Min £60.00

OPEN All year round

Pretty, en suite bedrooms in old brewhouse. Set in country garden of the Elsted Inn, known for its good food and good ales.

NETTLESTEAD, Kent Map ref 3B4

◆◆◆◆
Silver
Award

Friendly but professional family-run bed and breakfast. Newly converted 1810 granary set in rural Heart of Kent, on a working farm, with easy access to M20, M25 and south coast. Ideal for exploring Kent. Beautifully furnished bedrooms with en suite or sole use facilities. High standards and quality accommodation is our aim.

THE GRANARY BED & BREAKFAST

Rock Farm, Gibbs Hill, Nettlestead,
Maidstone ME18 5HT
T: (01622) 814547
F: (01622) 813905
E: robcorfe@thegranary-bnb.co.uk
I: www.thegranary-bnb.co.uk

Bedrooms: 1 single,
1 double/twin, 1 triple/
multiple; suites available
Bathrooms: 2 en suite

Evening meal available

B&B per night:
S £30.00–£40.00
D £50.00–£60.00

OPEN All year round

◆◆◆◆

ROCK FARM HOUSE
Gibbs Hill, Nettlestead, Maidstone
ME18 5HT
T: (01622) 812244
F: (01622) 812244

Bedrooms: 3 double/
twin
Bathrooms: 2 en suite,
1 private

B&B per night:
S £30.00–£35.00
D £50.00

OPEN All year round

This delightful 18thC Kentish farmhouse situated in a quiet and idyllic position on a farm in an Area of Outsanding Natural Beauty with extensive views.

NEWHAVEN, East Sussex Map ref 2D3

◆

A comfortable, bright, family-run establishment located close the Newhaven/Dieppe ferry terminal. Newhaven Lodge also caters for visitors to nearby Brighton and Lewes who wish to take advantage of the South Downs. The establishment motto is 'Arrive as a guest and leave as a friend.'

NEWHAVEN LODGE GUEST HOUSE

12 Brighton Road, Newhaven BN9 9NB
T: (01273) 513736 & 07776 293398
F: (01273) 734619
E: newhavenlodge@aol.com

Bedrooms: 1 double/
twin, 4 triple/multiple
Bathrooms: 1 en suite

CC: Mastercard, Switch,
Visa

Discounts given to groups of 10 or more who are willing to share family rooms.

B&B per night:
S £17.50–£25.00
D £45.00–£50.00

OPEN All year round

OXTED, Surrey Map ref 2D2

◆◆◆ ARAWA

58 Granville Road, Limpsfield, Oxted RH8 0BZ
T: (01883) 714104 & 0800 298 5732
F: (01883) 714104
E: david@davidgibbs.co.uk

Bedrooms: 2 double/ twin, 1 triple/multiple
Bathrooms: 2 en suite

B&B per night:
S £25.00–£50.00
D £50.00–£70.00

OPEN All year round

Family home near North Downs Way, Chartwell and Hever. Near rail service to London and 30 minutes to Gatwick by car. Friendly and comfortable. Enjoy your stay!

◆◆◆ THE NEW BUNGALOW

Old Hall Farm, Tandridge Lane, Oxted RH8 9NS
T: (01342) 892508
F: (01342) 892508
E: donnunn@compuserve.com

Bedrooms: 3 double/ twin
Bathrooms: 1 en suite

B&B per night:
S £24.00–£30.00
D £38.00–£42.00

OPEN All year round

Spacious, modern bungalow set in green fields and reached by a private drive. 5 minutes' drive from M25. London easily accessible by train.

PARTRIDGE GREEN, West Sussex Map ref 2D3

◆◆◆ POUND COTTAGE BED & BREAKFAST

Mill Lane, Littleworth, Partridge Green, Horsham RH13 8JU
T: (01403) 710218 & 711285
F: (01403) 711337
E: poundcottagebb@amserve.net
I: www.horsham.co.uk/ poundcottage.html

Bedrooms: 1 single, 2 double/twin

B&B per night:
S £20.00–£22.00
D £40.00–£44.00

OPEN All year round

Pleasant country house in quiet surroundings. 8 miles from Horsham, 25 minutes from Gatwick. Just off the B2135 West Grinstead to Steyning road.

PEMBURY, Kent Map ref 3B4

◆◆◆ GATES HOUSE

5 Lower Green Road, Pembury, Royal Tunbridge Wells TN2 4DZ
T: (01892) 822866
F: (01892) 824626
E: simon@s.galway.freeserve.co.uk

Bedrooms: 1 single, 2 double/twin

B&B per night:
S £22.00
D £44.00

OPEN All year round

Lovely old house and gardens. Excellent location for sightseeing in the heart of Kent all year round. Close airports, rail, Euroterminals, London and coast.

PETWORTH, West Sussex Map ref 2D3

◆◆◆◆ EEDES COTTAGE

Bignor Park Road, Bury Gate, Pulborough RH20 1EZ
T: (01798) 831438
F: (01798) 831942

Bedrooms: 3 double/ twin
Bathrooms: 1 en suite

B&B per night:
S £25.00–£30.00
D £45.00–£50.00

OPEN All year round

Quiet country house surrounded by farmland. Convenient main roads to Arundel, Chichester and Brighton. Dogs, horses accommodated. TV in all rooms.

POLEGATE, East Sussex Map ref 2D3

◆◆◆◆ THE COTTAGE

Dittons Road, Polegate BN26 6HS
T: (01323) 482011
F: (01323) 482011

Bedrooms: 3 double/ twin

B&B per night:
S £25.00–£30.00
D £40.00

The Cottage is situated on the rural outskirts of Polegate. Ample well lit parking available and easy access to the A27.

MAP REFERENCES

Map references apply to the colour maps at the front of this guide.

RAMSGATE, Kent Map ref 3C3 *Tourist Information Centre Tel: (01843) 583333*

◆◆◆ GLENDEVON GUEST HOUSE

8 Truro Road, Ramsgate CT1 8DB
T: (01843) 570909 & 0800 0352110
F: (01843) 570909
E: glendevon@currantbun.com
I: www.glendevon-guesthouse.
co.uk

Bedrooms: 4 double/
twin, 2 triple/multiple
Bathrooms: 6 en suite

Lunch available
CC: Mastercard, Switch,
Visa

B&B per night:
S £20.00–£24.00
D Max £40.00

OPEN All year round

Delightful converted Victorian house near beach, harbour and town. Very comfortable rooms, all en suite and each containing attractive feature of modern kitchen/dining area.

◆◆◆ THE ROYALE GUEST HOUSE

7 Royal Road, Ramsgate CT11 9LE
T: (01843) 594712
F: (01843) 594712
E: theroyaleguesthouse@talk21.
com

Bedrooms: 4 single,
4 double/twin, 1 triple/
multiple
Bathrooms: 2 en suite

B&B per night:
S £17.00–£20.00
D £34.00–£42.00

OPEN All year round

Our homely, comfortable, friendly guesthouse welcomes you to bed and full English breakfast. Very close to port, harbour and all amenities.

REDHILL, Surrey Map ref 2D2

◆◆◆◆ ASHLEIGH HOUSE HOTEL

39 Redstone Hill, Redhill RH1 4BG
T: (01737) 764763
F: (01737) 780308

Bedrooms: 1 single,
5 double/twin, 2 triple/
multiple
Bathrooms: 6 en suite

CC: Mastercard, Visa

B&B per night:
S £40.00–£54.00
D £56.00–£60.00

OPEN All year round

Friendly, family-run early Edwardian house with most rooms en suite. 500 yards from railway station, London 30 minutes, Gatwick Airport 15 minutes.

ROCHESTER, Kent Map ref 3B3 *Tourist Information Centre Tel: (01634) 843666*

◆◆◆ KING CHARLES HOTEL

Brompton Road, Gillingham
ME7 5QT
T: (01634) 830303
F: (01634) 829430
E: enquiries@kingcharleshotel.
co.uk
I: www.kingcharleshotel.co.uk

Bedrooms: 1 single,
54 double/twin,
31 triple/multiple
Bathrooms: 86 en suite

Lunch available
Evening meal available
CC: Amex, Delta, Diners,
Mastercard, Switch, Visa

B&B per night:
S £34.00
D £40.00

HB per person:
DY £25.00–£44.00

OPEN All year round

Friendly, modern hotel run by family, catering for all requirements at very reasonable rates in comfortable accommodation. Ideal for groups.

◆◆◆ ST MARTIN

104 Borstal Road, Rochester
ME1 3BD
T: (01634) 848192
E: icolvin@stmartin.freeserve.co.uk

Bedrooms: 3 double/
twin

Evening meal available

B&B per night:
S £18.00
D £34.00

Victorian family home overlooking the River Medway, close to city centre. Ideal for North Downs Way.

ROYAL TUNBRIDGE WELLS, Kent Map ref 2D2 *Tourist Information Centre Tel: (01892) 515675*

◆◆◆◆ BLUNDESTON

Eden Road, Royal Tunbridge Wells
TN1 1TS
T: (01892) 513030
F: (01892) 540255
E: daysblundeston@excite.co.uk

Bedrooms: 2 double/
twin
Bathrooms: 2 en suite

B&B per night:
S £35.00–£45.00
D £45.00–£52.00

OPEN All year round

Beautiful period home, tranquil private location, centre of old Tunbridge Wells within minutes of Pantiles, common land and main line station.

QUALITY ASSURANCE SCHEME
Diamond ratings and awards are explained at the back of this guide.

◆◆◆ **HADLEIGH**
69 Sandown Park,
Royal Tunbridge Wells TN2 4RT
T: (01892) 822760
F: (01892) 823170

Bedrooms: 2 double/
twin
Bathrooms: 2 private

B&B per night:
S £22.00–£25.00
D £44.00–£46.00

OPEN All year round

Quiet comfortable house within easy reach of Royal Tunbridge Wells, the Kent countryside, Gatwick Airport and M25. Off-street parking.

◆◆◆

MANOR COURT FARM
Ashurst, Royal Tunbridge Wells TN3 9TB
T: (01892) 740279
F: (01892) 740919
E: jsoyke@jsoyke.freeserve.co.uk
I: www.manorcourtfarm.co.uk

B&B per night:
S £22.00–£28.00
D £44.00–£48.00

OPEN All year round

Georgian farmhouse with friendly atmosphere, spacious rooms and lovely views of Medway Valley. 350-acre mixed farm, good base for walking. Many animals. Penshurst Place, Hever Castle, Chartwell, Sissinghurst, etc, all within easy reach by car. London 50 minutes by train from Tonbridge. Guest lounge. Excellent camping facilities. On A264 half a mile east of Ashurst village.

Bedrooms: 3 double/
twin

Reductions for longer stays.

◆◆◆

NUMBER TEN
Modest Corner, Southborough,
Royal Tunbridge Wells TN4 0LS
T: (01892) 522450
F: (01892) 522450
E: modestanneke@lineone.net

B&B per night:
D £45.00–£50.00

OPEN All year round

Number Ten is situated in a lovely tranquil hamlet on the edge of Tunbridge Wells, with easy access to M25 and a host of historic places. A warm welcome is assured in this attractive home, where the owner's artistic touches can be seen throughout.

Bedrooms: 3 double/
twin
Bathrooms: 3 private

Evening meal available

◆◆ **80 RAVENSWOOD AVENUE**
Royal Tunbridge Wells TN2 3SJ
T: (01892) 523069

Bedrooms: 1 single,
1 double/twin

B&B per night:
S £20.00
D £40.00

Quietly located house one mile from town centre, off street parking, comfortable lounge, TV, tea/coffee served. Home made preserves. Overseas visitors and UK guests welcome. Cyclists catered for.

◆◆◆ **VALE ROYAL HOTEL**
54-57 London Road,
Royal Tunbridge Wells TN1 1DS
T: (01892) 525580 & 525968
F: (01892) 526022
E: reservations@valeroyalhotel.
co.uk
I: www.valeroyalhotel.co.uk

Bedrooms: 12 single,
24 double/twin, 3 triple/
multiple
Bathrooms: 26 en suite

Lunch available
Evening meal available
CC: Delta, Diners,
Mastercard, Switch, Visa

B&B per night:
S £48.00–£55.00
D £68.00–£75.00

HB per person:
DY £60.00–£65.00

OPEN All year round

Family hotel, overlooking the common, set in beautiful secluded shrub garden. All rooms have telephone, TV, tea and coffee-making facilities. Victorian conservatory leading on to the patio.

RUDGWICK, West Sussex Map ref 2D2

◆◆◆ **THE MUCKY DUCK INN**
Loxwood Road, Tismans Common,
Rudgwick, Horsham RH12 3BW
T: (01403) 822300
F: (01403) 822300
E: mucky_duck_pub@msn.com
I: www.mucky-duck-inn.co.uk

Bedrooms: 6 double/
twin
Bathrooms: 6 en suite

Lunch available
Evening meal available
CC: Delta, Mastercard,
Switch, Visa

B&B per night:
S £50.00–£55.00
D £75.00–£80.00

OPEN All year round

*Family pub in the heart of the countryside. Home-made food, real ales. Open all day.
Secure family garden and play area. Large en suite luxury rooms.*

RUSTINGTON, West Sussex Map ref 2D3

◆◆◆◆
Silver
Award

KENMORE
Claigmar Road, Rustington, Littlehampton
BN16 2NL
T: (01903) 784634
F: (01903) 784634
E: kenmoreguesthouse@amserve.net
I: www.kenmoreguesthouse.co.uk

B&B per night:
S £23.50–£30.00
D £47.00–£60.00

OPEN All year round

*Secluded Edwardian house in a
garden setting in the heart of the
village and close to sea. Attractive en
suite rooms, individually decorated
and comfortably furnished. Private
parking. Ideal for touring historic
towns, castles, cathedrals and stately
homes. Sylvia and Ray Dobbs offer a
warm and friendly welcome.*

Bedrooms: 1 single,
2 double/twin, 4 triple/
multiple
Bathrooms: 7 en suite

CC: Amex, Mastercard,
Visa

RYE, East Sussex Map ref 3B4 *Tourist Information Centre Tel: (01797) 226696*

◆◆◆◆
Silver
Award

DURRANT HOUSE HOTEL
2 Market Street, Rye TN31 7LA
T: (01797) 223182
F: (01797) 226940
E: kingslands@compuserve.com
I: www.durranthouse.com

B&B per night:
S £45.00–£72.00
D £60.00–£80.00

HB per person:
DY £35.00–£80.00

*A charming Listed building located in
the centre of ancient Rye. It has 6
comfortable and individually
decorated bedrooms, including
4-poster and triple rooms, all
equipped to a high standard. The
hotel offers an informal and friendly
atmosphere, wholesome food and is
the perfect location for a relaxing
break.*

Bedrooms: 5 double/
twin, 2 triple/multiple
Bathrooms: 6 en suite,
1 private

Evening meal available
CC: Delta, Mastercard,
Switch, Visa

Nov-Easter: Sun-Fri mini-breaks; 2 nights or more
10% discount based on 2 people sharing a room.

QUALITY ASSURANCE SCHEME
For an explanation of the quality and facilities
represented by the Diamonds please refer to the
front of this guide. A more detailed explanation
can be found in the information pages at the back.

RYE continued

◆◆◆◆◆
Silver
Award

JEAKE'S HOUSE
Mermaid Street, Rye TN31 7ET
T: (01797) 222828
F: (01797) 222623
E: jeakeshouse@btinternet.com
I: www.jeakeshouse.com

B&B per night:
S £33.00–£67.00
D £65.00–£103.00

OPEN All year round

Ideally located historic house, on winding cobbled street in the heart of ancient medieval town. Individually restored rooms provide traditional luxury combined with all modern facilities. A book-lined bar and cosy parlours. Extensive breakfast menu to suit all tastes. Easy walking distance to restaurants and shops. Private car park.

Bedrooms: 1 single, 8 double/twin, 3 triple/ multiple; suites available
Bathrooms: 9 en suite, 1 private

Reductions for a stay of 4 or more nights. Mid-week winter breaks.

CC: Delta, Mastercard, Switch, Visa

◆◆◆◆◆
Silver
Award

LITTLE ORCHARD HOUSE
West Street, Rye TN31 7ES
T: (01797) 223831
F: (01797) 223831
I: www.littleorchardhouse.com

Bedrooms: 2 double/ twin
Bathrooms: 2 en suite

CC: Delta, Mastercard, Switch, Visa

B&B per night:
S £45.00–£65.00
D £64.00–£90.00

OPEN All year round

Georgian townhouse in centre of Rye. Antique furnishings and large walled garden give country-house atmosphere. 4-poster beds, generous free-range/organic breakfast. Parking available.

◆◆◆◆◆
Gold
Award

MANOR FARM OAST
Workhouse Lane, Icklesham, Winchelsea TN36 4AJ
T: (01424) 813787
F: (01424) 813787
E: manor.farm.oast@lineone.net

B&B per night:
S £35.00–£45.00
D £55.00–£64.00

HB per person:
DY £47.50–£52.00

OPEN All year round

Three-roundel oast house in the heart of 1066 country. Quiet and secluded in orchards, close to Rye, Battle and Hastings. Beautiful walled garden for romantic breaks, wedding receptions and honeymoons. All rooms are tastefully furnished, the original round room particularly restful. Home-cooked dinners exceptionally good using local produce.

Bedrooms: 3 double/ twin
Bathrooms: 2 en suite, 1 private

Murder mystery dinners for groups. Honeymoon breaks. Specialist romantic dinners for two.

Evening meal available
CC: Delta, Mastercard, Switch, Visa

◆◆◆
THE OLD VICARAGE
Rye Harbour, Rye TN31 7TT
T: (01797) 222088
F: (01797) 229620
E: jonathan@
oldvicarageryeharbour.fsnet.co.uk

Bedrooms: 2 double/ twin

B&B per night:
S £20.00–£45.00
D £37.00–£52.00

OPEN All year round

Imposing Victorian former vicarage, quietly situated close to sea and nature reserve. Antique furniture and open fires. Magnificent English breakfast. Classic excellence and old fashioned hospitality.

CREDIT CARD BOOKINGS If you book by telephone and are asked for your credit card number it is advisable to check the proprietor's policy should you cancel your reservation.

RYE continued

◆◆◆◆◆
Silver Award

PLAYDEN COTTAGE GUESTHOUSE

Military Road, Rye TN31 7NY
T: (01797) 222234
I: www.rye.org.uk.playdencottage

B&B per night:
D £58.00–£68.00

HB per person:
DY £41.00–£50.00

Large character cottage, said to be 'Grebe' from E.F. Benson's Mapp and Lucia novels. Personal service in a comfortable family home. Pretty gardens, rural aspect, peaceful – and a very warm welcome. Every third night free during winter period.

Bedrooms: 3 double/twin
Bathrooms: 3 en suite

Evening meal available
CC: Mastercard, Visa

12 [S] P

◆◆◆◆

THE STRAND HOUSE

Tanyard's Lane, Winchelsea, Rye TN36 4JT
T: (01797) 226276
F: (01797) 224806
E: strandhouse@winchelsea98.fsnet.co.uk
I: www.s-h-systems.co.uk/hotels/strand.html

B&B per night:
S £30.00–£35.00
D £48.00–£70.00

OPEN All year round

A warm welcome awaits in the 15thC old world charm of Winchelsea's old workhouse. Now a Grade II Listed building with oak beams and inglenooks. Overlooking National Trust pastureland. Four-poster bedroom. Residents' bar. Traditional breakfasts utilising local produce served in the heavily beamed dining room. Log fires in season. Pretty gardens.

Bedrooms: 9 double/twin, 1 triple/multiple
Bathrooms: 9 en suite, 1 private

Evening meal available
CC: Delta, Mastercard, Switch, Visa

Winter weekend breaks (2 nights min). Special rates off-season mid-week (3 nights min).

5 [S] P

◆◆◆

THE WINDMILL GUEST HOUSE

Mill Lane, (off Ferry Road), Rye TN31 7DW
T: (01797) 224027
F: (01797) 227211
I: www.rye-tourism.co.uk/windmill

Bedrooms: 8 double/twin
Bathrooms: 8 en suite

B&B per night:
S £35.00–£45.00
D £60.00–£70.00

OPEN All year round

An old windmill with a modern extension to house the letting rooms. Situated on the banks of the River Tillingham. Very peaceful.

[S] P

ST-MARGARETS-AT-CLIFFE, Kent Map ref 3C4

◆◆◆◆

HOLM OAKS

Dover Road, St-Margarets-at-Cliffe, Dover CT15 6EP
T: (01304) 852990 & 853473
F: (01304) 853433
E: holmoaks852@icqmail.com

B&B per night:
S £25.00–£40.00
D £50.00–£60.00

OPEN All year round

Holm Oaks is situated in the beautiful village of St Margarets. We offer a friendly atmosphere along with private parking. Our bedrooms are spacious and well equipped with tea tray, TV, hairdryer and plenty of good reading material. En suite bathrooms have a full range of accessories.

Bedrooms: 2 double/twin
Bathrooms: 2 en suite

[S] P

SANDWICH, Kent Map ref 3C3

◆◆◆

DURLOCK LODGE

Durlock, Minster-in-Thanet, Ramsgate
CT12 4HD
T: (01843) 821219 & 07880 725150
E: david@durlocklodge.co.uk
I: www.durlocklodge.co.uk

B&B per night:
S £44.00–£73.00
D £47.00–£76.00

OPEN All year round

Welcoming 18thC lodge in quiet historical village between Ramsgate and Sandwich. Charming inns and restaurants within 5 minutes walk. This tranquil bed and breakfast is an ideal location for exploring South East Kent with fine beaches, coastal walks and golf courses all within 5 miles. Self catering also available.

Bedrooms: 3 double/ twin
Bathrooms: 3 en suite

CC: Amex, Delta, Mastercard, Switch, Visa

Book 2 nights in 4-poster room and receive a bottle of champagne and chocolate on arrival. £152 all inclusive.

🐄🏠🖳🏳💧🔌⑤🖳🛋🏀🐴�🏮P

◆◆◆

FLEUR DE LIS HOTEL INN & RESTAURANT
6-8 Delf Street, Sandwich CT13 9BZ
T: (01304) 611131
F: (01304) 611199
E: thefleur@verinitaverns.co.uk
I: www.verinitaverns.co.uk

Bedrooms: 8 double/ twin, 2 triple/multiple
Bathrooms: 10 en suite

Lunch available
Evening meal available
CC: Amex, Diners, Mastercard, Visa

B&B per night:
S £50.00–£55.00
D £60.00–£65.00

OPEN All year round

A 17thC coaching house situated in the heart of historical Sandwich, with 10 highly presentable en suite letting rooms.

♒🐄🏠🖳💧🍷⑤🔪🖳🛋🍴🐾🐴�🏮

SARRE, Kent Map ref 3C3

◆◆◆◆

CROWN INN (THE FAMOUS CHERRY BRANDY HOUSE)

Ramsgate Road, Sarre, Birchington CT7 OLF
T: (01843) 847808
F: (01843) 847914
E: crown@shepherd-neame.co.uk
I: www.shepherd-neame.co.uk

B&B per night:
S Min £60.00
D Min £80.00

HB per person:
DY £55.00–£75.00

OPEN All year round

Ancient traditional inn, with inglenook fireplaces and oak-beamed restaurant. 12 newly refurbished en suite bedrooms. Friendly hospitality, extensive bar and restaurant menu serving local produce. Ideal for a country break, close to Canterbury and the coastal towns of Margate, Broadstairs and Ramsgate, as well as the ferry ports and Eurotunnel.

Bedrooms: 10 double/ twin, 2 triple/multiple
Bathrooms: 12 en suite

Lunch available
Evening meal available
CC: Amex, Delta, Mastercard, Switch, Visa

HB daily price is based on a minimum 2-night stay for 2 people.

♒🐄🏖🥂🔔🖳🏳💧⑤🔪🕐🖳🛋🍴🐴�🏮P

SEAFORD, East Sussex Map ref 2D3 *Tourist Information Centre Tel: (01323) 897426*

◆◆

THE OASIS CLEARVIEW HOTEL
36-38 Claremont Road, Seaford
BN25 2BD
T: (01323) 890138
F: (01323) 896534

Bedrooms: 2 single, 4 double/twin, 5 triple/ multiple
Bathrooms: 11 en suite

Lunch available
Evening meal available
CC: Delta, Diners, Mastercard, Switch, Visa

B&B per night:
S £30.00–£40.00
D £50.00–£70.00

HB per person:
DY £40.00–£50.00

OPEN All year round

Hotel with all rooms en suite, bar and restaurant. Family-run, close to beautiful countryside and sea view.

♒🐄🔔🖳🏳💧⑤🔪🏵🖳🛋🐾�🐾P

ACCESSIBILITY

Look for the 🔲🔲🚶 symbols which indicate accessibility for wheelchair users. A list of establishments is at the front of this guide.

SEAFORD continued

◆◆◆◆

THE SILVERDALE

21 Sutton Park Road, Seaford BN25 1RH
T: (01323) 491849
F: (01323) 891131
E: silverdale@mistral.co.uk
I: www.mistral.co.uk/silverdale/silver.htm

B&B per night:
S £25.00–£45.00
D £35.00–£60.00

HB per person:
DY £18.50–£55.00

OPEN All year round

Small, expertly run house-hotel in the centre of peaceful Edwardian seaside town. Beautifully prepared food and a host of English wines. Over 120 single malt whiskies. Only a few minutes' walk from the seaside, the antique shops and the friendly local pubs. We'd love to meet you.

Bedrooms: 1 single, 5 double/twin, 2 triple/ multiple
Bathrooms: 6 en suite

Lunch available
Evening meal available
CC: Amex, Delta, Diners, Mastercard, Switch, Visa

Special 2 night theatre breaks and many others. Contact us for a more detailed list.

◆◆◆◆

TUDOR MANOR HOTEL

Eastbourne Road, Seaford BN25 4DB
T: (01323) 896006
F: (01323) 896006

B&B per night:
S £40.00
D £70.00–£80.00

HB per person:
DY Min £60.00

OPEN All year round

Outstandingly beautiful manor house set in delightful landscaped gardens. Luxurious bedrooms. Excellent choice of breakfast served in the dining room which is furnished as a banqueting room, with arms and armour. Guests' lounge with a cosy inglenook fireplace and beamed ceiling. A 4-poster suite is available for that special night.

Bedrooms: 1 single, 3 double/twin, 1 triple/ multiple
Bathrooms: 4 en suite, 1 private

Evening meal available
CC: Delta, Mastercard, Switch, Visa

SELSEY, West Sussex Map ref 2C3

◆◆◆

NORTON LEA

Upper Norton, Selsey, Chichester PO20 9EA
T: (01243) 605454
F: (01243) 605456
E: 100013.3142@compuserve.com

Bedrooms: 2 double/ twin, 1 triple/multiple

B&B per night:
S Min £25.00
D £40.00–£50.00

OPEN All year round

Comfortable country house ideally situated for visiting Pagham Harbour Nature Reserve, local countryside including Goodwood and the coast. Guests' TV lounge. Ample off-road car parking.

◆◆◆◆

ST ANDREWS LODGE

Chichester Road, Selsey, Chichester PO20 0LX
T: (01243) 606899
F: (01243) 607826
E: info@standrewslodge.co.uk
I: www.standrewslodge.co.uk

Bedrooms: 1 single, 5 double/twin, 4 triple/ multiple; suites available
Bathrooms: 10 en suite

Evening meal available
CC: Amex, Delta, Diners, Mastercard, Switch, Visa

B&B per night:
S £27.50–£50.00
D £58.00–£85.00

OPEN All year round

Family-run, friendly relaxed atmosphere, licensed. En suite bedrooms, cosy lounge, log fire, peaceful suntrap garden. Close to natural beaches and countryside, south of Chichester.

QUALITY ASSURANCE SCHEME

Diamond ratings and awards were correct at the time of going to press but are subject to change. Please check at the time of booking.

♦♦♦♦

HORNSHAW HOUSE
47 Mount Harry Road, Sevenoaks TN13 3JN
T: (01732) 465262
E: embates@hornshaw47.freeserve.co.uk
I: www.hornshaw-house.co.uk

B&B per night:
S £30.00–£35.00
D £45.00–£50.00

OPEN All year round

Attractive family house in quiet garden setting. Warm bedrooms with comfortable beds and en suite baths and showers. Off road parking. Visit Kent's castles and gardens, or go sight-seeing in London, only 30 minutes by train from here; Hornshaw House is a 5 minute walk from Sevenoaks station.

Bedrooms: 2 double/ twin
Bathrooms: 2 en suite

Lunch available
Evening meal available

♦♦♦

THE MOORINGS HOTEL
97 Hitchen Hatch Lane, Sevenoaks
TN13 3BE
T: (01732) 452589 & 742323
F: (01732) 456462
E: theryans@mooringshotel.co.uk
I: www.mooringshotel.co.uk

Bedrooms: 5 single, 16 double/twin, 2 triple/ multiple
Bathrooms: 23 en suite

Lunch available
Evening meal available
CC: Amex, Delta, Diners, Mastercard, Switch, Visa

B&B per night:
S £43.00–£53.00
D £65.00–£75.00

OPEN All year round

Friendly family hotel offering high standard accommodation for tourists and business travellers. 30 minutes from London. Close to BR station.

♦♦♦♦♦

HEMPSTEAD HOUSE
London Road, Bapchild, Sittingbourne
ME9 9PP
T: (01795) 428020
F: (01795) 436362
E: info@hempsteadhouse.co.uk
I: www.hempsteadhouse.co.uk

B&B per night:
S £70.00
D £80.00

HB per person:
DY £62.50–£95.00

OPEN All year round

Exclusive privately-owned Victorian country house hotel and restaurant situated in rural location, but on the main A2 between Canterbury and Sittingbourne. Set in 3 acres of beautifully landscaped gardens, we offer beautifully appointed accommodation, fine cuisine, prepared solely from fresh, local produce, elegant reception rooms and friendly hospitality.

Bedrooms: 12 double/ twin, 2 triple/multiple
Bathrooms: 14 en suite

Lunch available
Evening meal available
CC: Amex, Delta, Diners, Mastercard, Switch, Visa

USE YOUR *i*s
There are more than 550 Tourist Information Centres throughout England offering friendly help with accommodation and holiday ideas as well as suggestions of places to visit and things to do. You'll find TIC addresses in the local Phone Book.

SMARDEN, Kent Map ref 3B4

◆◆◆◆

CHEQUERS INN

The Street, Smarden, Ashford TN27 8QA
T: (01233) 770217
F: (01233) 770623

B&B per night:
S £40.00–£45.00
D £60.00–£75.00

OPEN All year round

Listed 14thC inn, in heart of the Weald. Wealth of oak beams, beautifully landscaped gardens with duck pond. All rooms individually decorated. Ideal for touring and visiting many places of historic interest, including Leeds Castle and Sissinghurst Gardens. Many interesting walks, 5 golf courses nearby. Good food always available.

Bedrooms: 3 double/
twin, 1 triple/multiple
Bathrooms: 4 en suite

Lunch available
Evening meal available
CC: Delta, Mastercard,
Switch, Visa

STELLING MINNIS, Kent Map ref 3B4

◆◆◆◆

Silver
Award

GREAT FIELD FARM
Misling Lane, Stelling Minnis,
Canterbury CT4 6DE
T: (01227) 709223
F: (01227) 709223
E: Greatfieldfarm@aol.com

Bedrooms: 3 double/
twin; suites available
Bathrooms: 3 en suite

CC: Delta, Mastercard,
Switch, Visa

B&B per night:
S £30.00–£40.00
D £40.00–£50.00

OPEN All year round

Delightful farmhouse amidst beautiful countryside, gardens and paddocks. Enjoy peace and privacy in our suites, B&B or self catering. 10 minutes Canterbury/Channel Tunnel.

STEYNING, West Sussex Map ref 2D3

◆◆◆

CHEQUER INN

41 High Street, Steyning BN44 3RE
T: (01903) 814437
F: (01903) 879707
E: chequerinn@btinternet.com

B&B per night:
S Min £35.00
D Min £45.00

OPEN All year round

A fine historic hostelry in the heart of picturesque Steyning. The Chequer Inn is over 500 years old with open fires and many original features. En suite rooms are comfortably appointed and the inn offers fine food and an excellent cellar. A perfect base to explore the beauty of Sussex.

Bedrooms: 3 double/
twin
Bathrooms: 3 en suite

Lunch available
Evening meal available
CC: Amex, Delta,
Mastercard, Switch, Visa

TENTERDEN, Kent Map ref 3B4

◆◆◆

OLD BURREN
25 Ashford Road, Tenterden
TN30 6LL
T: (01580) 764442 & 764254
E: poo@burren.fsbusiness.co.uk
I: www.oldburren.co.uk

Bedrooms: 2 double/
twin
Bathrooms: 1 en suite,
1 private

B&B per night:
D £45.00–£55.00

OPEN All year round

Old Burren is a 17thC home where a warm friendly welcome awaits you. The 2 bedrooms are tastefully furnished to a high standard. Perfect.

CHECK THE MAPS

The colour maps at the front of this guide show all the cities, towns and villages for which you will find accommodation entries. Refer to the town index to find the page on which they are listed.

TENTERDEN continued

WHITE LION HOTEL
High Street, Tenterden TN30 6BD
T: (01580) 765077
F: (01580) 764157

B&B per night:
S £59.00
D £74.00

OPEN All year round

◆◆◆◆

This traditional coaching inn, set in the lovely market town of Tenterden, has been welcoming visitors since before 1623. High standard en suite rooms – some with 4-poster – hearty breakfasts, imaginative lunch and dinner menus coupled with a well-stocked cellar and hospitable service makes the White Lion a 'must visit'.

Bedrooms: 13 double/ twin, 2 triple/multiple
Bathrooms: 15 en suite

Lunch available
Evening meal available
CC: Amex, Delta, Diners, Mastercard, Switch, Visa

TICEHURST, East Sussex Map ref 3B4

◆◆◆

CHERRY TREE INN
Dale Hill, Ticehurst, Wadhurst TN5 7DG
T: (01580) 201229
F: (01580) 201325
E: leondiane@aol.com

B&B per night:
S £40.00–£45.00
D £45.00–£55.00

OPEN All year round

Delightful country pub on the edge of the village of Ticehurst. Bewl Water is within walking distance as is Dalehill Golf Course. All rooms are en suite. The beamed bar offers a wide range of meals lunchtime and evenings, together with wines and cask beers. Charming patio and gardens.

Bedrooms: 3 double/ twin
Bathrooms: 3 en suite

Lunch available
Evening meal available
CC: Delta, Mastercard, Switch, Visa

TUNBRIDGE WELLS

See under Royal Tunbridge Wells

UCKFIELD, East Sussex Map ref 2D3

◆◆◆◆◆◆
Gold
Award

HOOKE HALL
250 High Street, Uckfield TN22 1EN
T: (01825) 761578
F: (01825) 768025
E: a.percy@virgin.net

Bedrooms: 10 double/ twin
Bathrooms: 10 en suite

CC: Mastercard, Visa

B&B per night:
S £55.00–£85.00
D £80.00–£135.00

OPEN All year round

Elegant Queen Anne townhouse, recently completely refurbished, with individual comfortably designed rooms equipped to a high standard. Friendly and informal atmosphere.

◆◆◆◆
Silver
Award

OLD MILL FARM
High Hurstwood, Uckfield
TN22 4AD
T: (01825) 732279
F: (01825) 732279

Bedrooms: 1 single, 1 double/twin, 1 triple/ multiple
Bathrooms: 2 en suite, 1 private

B&B per night:
S £24.00–£30.00
D £48.00–£60.00

OPEN All year round

Sussex barn and buildings converted to a comfortable home, situated in the quiet village of High Hurstwood, off A26. Ashdown Forest nearby.

COLOUR MAPS Colour maps at the front of this guide pinpoint all places under which you will find accommodation listed.

WEST CLANDON, Surrey Map ref 2D2

◆◆◆◆ **WAYS COTTAGE**
Lime Grove, West Clandon,
Guildford GU4 7UT
T: (01483) 222454

Bedrooms: 2 double/
twin
Bathrooms: 1 en suite

Evening meal available

B&B per night:
S £25.00–£27.00
D £36.00–£40.00

Rural detached house in quiet location, 5 miles from Guildford. Easy reach of A3 and M25. Close to station on Waterloo/Guildford line.

HB per person:
DY £37.50–£39.50

OPEN All year round

🗲🗆⊛🖑⑤⊬🅜🎟🖳🖉✳☻P

WEST DEAN, West Sussex Map ref 2C3

◆◆◆ **LODGE HILL FARM**
West Dean, Chichester PO18 0RT
T: (01243) 535245

Bedrooms: 2 double/
twin
Bathrooms: 1 private

B&B per night:
S £20.00–£25.00
D £40.00–£50.00

Flint farmhouse built in 1813 on the South Downs, superb views, near Goodwood, 15 minutes to Chichester, ideal for walkers.

🗲5🕻🗆⊛🖑⑤⊬🅜🎟🖳☻P

WHITSTABLE, Kent Map ref 3B3 *Tourist Information Centre Tel: (01227) 275482*

◆◆◆ **HOTEL CONTINENTAL**
29 Beach Walk, Whitstable CT5 2BP
T: (01227) 280280
F: (01227) 280257
E: dec2@ukc.ac.uk
I: www.oysterfishery.co.uk

Bedrooms: 1 single,
21 double/twin
Bathrooms: 22 en suite

Lunch available
Evening meal available
CC: Amex, Delta, Diners,
Mastercard, Switch, Visa

B&B per night:
S £49.50–£65.00
D £55.00–£125.00

OPEN All year round

Refurbished hotel, located directly on seafront. With 1930s decor, the hotel provides good food and quality accommodation.

🗲🖦🗆🍷⑤⊬🅜◐🖳☻🍸☻P

◆◆◆

MARINE
Marine Parade, Tankerton, Whitstable
CT5 2BE
T: (01227) 272672
F: (01227) 264721
E: marine@shepherd-neame.co.uk
I: www.shepherd-neame.co.uk

B&B per night:
S £48.50–£55.00
D £68.50–£75.00

HB per person:
DY £40.00–£50.00

OPEN All year round

The Marine is situated on top of the Tankerton Cliffs overlooking the sea, offering exceptional comfort with 25 en suite bedrooms. Lovingly restored and refurbished, retaining much original character. Extensive bar and restaurant menu. Ideally located for touring Kent's coast. Next to delighful Whitstable, famous for its oysters, and close to Canterbury.

Bedrooms: 2 single,
21 double/twin, 2 triple/
multiple
Bathrooms: 25 en suite

Lunch available
Evening meal available
CC: Amex, Delta,
Mastercard, Switch, Visa

♪🗲🖪🕻🖃🗆⊛🖑🍷⑤⊬🅜🖳☻🍸🔍✳🐎🐾🎠P

◆◆◆◆

WINDYRIDGE GUEST HOUSE
Wraik Hill, Whitstable CT5 3BY
T: (01227) 263506
F: (01227) 771191

B&B per night:
S £30.00
D £50.00

HB per person:
DY £45.00

Impressive country house set in 3 acres, 1 mile Whitstable and sea. Outstanding views over countryside and sea, famous for beautiful sunsets. Five miles Canterbury, ideal base to visit a host of quaint villages and seaside resorts. Regular train service to London. Lovely lounge, pretty dining room.

Bedrooms: 2 single,
5 double/twin, 3 triple/
multiple
Bathrooms: 10 en suite

Evening meal available
CC: Delta, Mastercard,
Switch, Visa

🗲🖦🖪🕻🖃🗆⊛🖑🍷⑤⊬🅜🎟🖳☻▶✳🐎🎠P

◆◆◆

THE NEW INN

German Street, Winchelsea TN36 4EN
T: (01797) 226252
E: newinnwsea@aol.com

B&B per night:
S £30.00–£50.00
D £50.00–£70.00

OPEN All year round

Lovely 18thC inn in the centre of ancient and historic town of Winchelsea. Very attractive bedrooms all en suite, including one 4-poster room. Fresh local fish our speciality, excellent homemade dishes, succulent steaks and much more. Real log fire in winter. Beautiful, peaceful Winchelsea is a must for visitors.

Bedrooms: 5 double/ twin, 1 triple/multiple
Bathrooms: 6 en suite

Lunch available
Evening meal available
CC: Delta, Mastercard, Switch, Visa

3 nights for the price of 2, Nov–Mar (excl Christmas and New Year).

🐕 🏠 📺 🛆 🍷 S ✂ 🖥 🛋 🔍 ❄ 📻 🚭 🐴 P

◆◆◆

GRANTCHESTER

Boughton Hall Avenue, Send, Woking GU23 7DF
T: (01483) 225383
F: (01483) 596490
E: gary@hotpotmail.com

B&B per night:
S £25.00
D £48.00

OPEN All year round

Attractive family house with large superbly kept garden. Situated 4 minutes from Guildford and Woking town centres. Close to M25 and A3 motorways. Parking available. Long stays welcome. Close to Heathrow and Gatwick Airports, Wisley Gardens and Clandon Park.

Bedrooms: 3 double/ twin

🏔 ♨ 📺 ♨ S ✂ 🖥 🛋 ❄ 🚭 P

◆◆◆◆

ANGEL LODGE

19 Malvern Close, Worthing BN11 2HE
T: (01903) 233002 & 0777 921 7734
F: (01903) 233002
E: angellodge19@aol.com
I: www.angellodge.co.uk

B&B per night:
D £40.00–£50.00

OPEN All year round

Ideal base for touring beautiful Sussex! Very friendly atmosphere. Fifteen years of B&B experience. Attractive detached house. One minute from seafront in a very quiet road. Access at all times. Beautiful bedroom, TV, tea/coffee/choc facilities, with exclusive use of private bathroom (with jacuzzi). Lovely landscape gardens to relax in.

Bedrooms: 1 double/ twin
Bathrooms: 1 en suite

📺 📺 ♨ S 🖥 ❄ 🐴 🚭 P

SPECIAL BREAKS

Many establishments offer special promotions and themed breaks. These are highlighted in red. (All such offers are subject to availability.)

WORTHING continued

◆◆◆ **WOODLANDS GUEST HOUSE**

20-22 Warwick Gardens, Worthing BN11 1PF T: (01903) 233557 & 231957 F: (01903) 536925 E: woodlandsghse@cwcom.net I: www.woodlands20-22.freeserve.co.uk	Bedrooms: 3 single, 8 double/twin, 3 triple/ multiple Bathrooms: 11 en suite, 1 private	Evening meal available CC: Delta, Mastercard, Switch, Visa	B&B per night: S £25.00–£32.00 D £46.00–£56.00 HB per person: DY £33.00–£40.00 OPEN All year round

Edwardian guesthouse providing excellent food and comfortable accommodation. Quiet area close to town and seafront. Honeymoon suite. Ideal touring base for Sussex. Free parking.

WYE, Kent Map ref 3B4

◆◆◆ **MISTRAL**

3 Oxenturn Road, Wye, Ashford TN25 5BH T: (01233) 813011 F: (01233) 813011 E: geoff@chapman.invictanet.co.uk I: www.wye.org	Bedrooms: 1 single, 1 double/twin	B&B per night: S £25.00 D £50.00 OPEN All year round

Small bed and breakfast offering high quality food and facilities in a central but secluded part of Wye village. Parking is available by arrangement.

COUNTRY CODE

Always follow the Country Code ⚘
Enjoy the countryside and respect
its life and work ⚘ Guard against
all risk of fire ⚘ Fasten all gates
⚘ Keep your dogs under close control
⚘ Keep to public paths across
farmland ⚘ Use gates and stiles to
cross fences, hedges and walls ⚘
Leave livestock, crops and machinery
alone ⚘ Take your litter home ⚘
Help to keep all water clean ⚘
Protect wildlife, plants and trees ⚘
Take special care on country roads ⚘
Make no unnecessary noise ⚘

A brief guide to the main Towns and Villages offering accommodation in South East England

A ABINGER COMMON, SURREY - Small hamlet 4 miles south-west of Dorking.

- **ALFRISTON, EAST SUSSEX** - Old village in the Cuckmere Valley and a former smugglers' haunt. The 14th C Clergy House was the first building to be bought by the National Trust. Spacious 14th C St Andrew's church is known as the 'Cathedral of the South Downs' and the 13th C Star Inn is one of the oldest in England.

- **ARDINGLY, WEST SUSSEX** - Home of the South of England Agricultural Showground with its famous antique fairs and the public school. Nearby is Wakehurst Place (National Trust), the gardens of which are administered by the Royal Botanic Gardens, Kew.

- **ARUNDEL, WEST SUSSEX** - Picturesque, historic town on the River Arun, dominated by Arundel Castle, home of the Dukes of Norfolk. There are many 18th C houses, the Wildfowl and Wetlands Centre and Museum and Heritage Centre.

- **ASHFORD, KENT** - Once a market centre for the farmers of the Weald of Kent and Romney Marsh. The town centre has a number of Tudor and Georgian houses and a museum. Eurostar trains stop at Ashford International station.

B BATTLE, EAST SUSSEX - The Abbey at Battle was built on the site of the Battle of Hastings, when William defeated Harold II and so became the Conqueror in 1066. The museum has a fine collection relating to the Sussex iron industry and there is a social history museum - Buckleys Yesterday's World.

- **BETHERSDEN, KENT** - Typical Wealden village with plenty of weatherboarded houses. Famous in the Middle Ages for its marble, used in Canterbury and Rochester Cathedrals.

- **BEXHILL, EAST SUSSEX** - Popular resort with beach of shingle and firm sand at low tide. The impressive 1930s designed De la Warr Pavilion has good entertainment facilities. Costume Museum in Manor Gardens.

- **BIDDENDEN, KENT** - Perfect village with black and white houses, a tithe barn and a pond. Part of the village is grouped around a green with a village sign depicting the famous Biddenden Maids. It was an important centre of the Flemish weaving industry, hence the beautiful Old Cloth Hall. Vineyard nearby.

- **BOGNOR REGIS, WEST SUSSEX** - Five miles of firm, flat sand has made the town a popular family resort. Well supplied with gardens.

- **BOUGHTON MONCHELSEA, KENT** - Pleasant village mainly built of ragstone, a material that has been quarried nearby for over 7 centuries and was used in the building of Westminster Abbey. Leeds Castle nearby.

- **BRASTED, KENT** - Standing in a park adjoining the village is 18th C Brasted Place (not open to visitors). The work of Robert Adam, this fine house was once the home of Napoleon III.

- **BRIGHTON & HOVE, EAST SUSSEX** - Brighton's attractions include the Royal Pavilion, Volks Electric Railway, Sea Life Centre and Marina Village, Conference Centre, 'The Lanes' and several theatres.

- **BROADSTAIRS, KENT** - Popular seaside resort with numerous sandy bays. Charles Dickens spent his summers at Bleak House where he wrote parts of 'David Copperfield'. The Dickens Festival is held in June, when many people wear Dickensian costume.

C CAMBERLEY, SURREY - Well-known for the Royal Staff College and the nearby Royal Military Academy, Sandhurst.

- **CANTERBURY, KENT** - Place of pilgrimage since the martyrdom of Becket in 1170 and the site of Canterbury Cathedral. Visit St Augustine's Abbey, St Martin's (the oldest church in England), Royal Museum and Art Gallery and the Canterbury Tales. Nearby is Howletts Wild Animal Park. Good shopping centre.

- **CHARING, KENT** - Delightful village with many 15th C houses. The parish church has a fine timbered roof with painted beams and a medieval pulpit.

- **CHICHESTER, WEST SUSSEX** - The county town of West Sussex with a beautiful Norman cathedral. Noted for its Georgian architecture but also has modern buildings like the Festival Theatre. Surrounded by places of interest, including Fishbourne Roman Palace, Weald and Downland Open-Air Museum and West Dean Gardens.

- **CRANBROOK, KENT** - Old town, a centre for the weaving industry in the 15th C. The 72-ft high Union Mill is a 3-storey windmill, still in working order. Sissinghurst Gardens (National Trust) nearby.

D DEAL, KENT - Coastal town and popular holiday resort. Deal Castle was built by Henry VIII as a fort and the museum is devoted to finds excavated in the area. Also the Time-Ball Tower museum. Angling available from both beach and pier.

- **DORKING, SURREY** - Ancient market town and a good centre for walking, delightfully set between Box Hill and the Downs. Denbies Wine Estate - England's largest vineyard - is situated here.

- **DOVER, KENT** - A Cinque Port and busiest passenger port in the world. Still a historic town and seaside resort beside the famous White Cliffs. The White Cliffs Experience attraction traces the town's history through the Roman, Saxon, Norman and Victorian periods.

- **DYMCHURCH, KENT** - For centuries the headquarters of the Lords of the Level, the local government of this area. Probably best known today because of the fame of its fictional parson, the notorious Dr Syn, who has inspired a regular festival.

E EAST GRINSTEAD, WEST SUSSEX - A number of fine old houses stand in the High Street, one of which is Sackville College, founded in 1609.

- **EASTBOURNE, EAST SUSSEX** - One of the finest, most elegant resorts on the south-east coast situated beside Beachy Head. Long promenade, well known Carpet Gardens on the seafront, Devonshire Park tennis and indoor leisure complex, theatres, Towner Art Gallery, 'How We Lived Then' Museum of Shops and Social History.

- **EDENBRIDGE, KENT** - Small Wealden town with timbered houses. Nearby are Hever Castle, a romantic, moated castle, once the home of Anne Boleyn, and Haxted Watermill and Museum.

- **EPSOM, SURREY** - Horse races have been held on the slopes of Epsom Downs for centuries. The racecourse is the home of the world-famous Derby. Many famous old homes are here, among them the 17th C Waterloo House.

- **EWHURST, SURREY** - Once a prosperous centre of the woollen trade. Nearby is Elstead Moat, a national nature reserve.

F FARNHAM, SURREY - Town noted for its Georgian houses. Willmer House (now a museum) has a facade of cut and moulded brick with fine carving and panelling in the interior. The 12th C castle has been occupied by Bishops of both Winchester and Guildford.

- **FAVERSHAM, KENT** - Historic town, once a port, dating back to prehistoric times. Abbey Street has more than 50 listed buildings. Roman and Anglo-Saxon finds and other exhibits can be seen in a museum in the Maison Dieu at Ospringe. Fleur de Lys Heritage Centre.

- **FITTLEWORTH, WEST SUSSEX** - Quiet village that attracts artists and anglers. Groups of cottages can be found beside the narrow lanes and paths in the woodlands near the River Rother.

- **FOLKESTONE, KENT** - Popular resort. The town has a fine promenade, the Leas, from where orchestral Horse-racing at Westenhanger Racecourse nearby.

G GODALMING, SURREY -Several old coaching inns are reminders that the town was once a staging point. The old Town Hall is now the local history museum. Charterhouse School moved here in 1872 and is dominated by the 150-ft Founder's Tower.

- **GUILDFORD, SURREY** - Bustling town with Lewis Carroll connections and many historic monuments, one of which is the Guildford clock jutting out over the old High Street. The modern cathedral occupies a commanding position on Stag Hill.

H HARTFIELD, EAST SUSSEX - Pleasant village in Ashdown Forest, the setting for A A Milne's Winnie the Pooh stories.

- **HASLEMERE, SURREY** - Town set in hilly, wooded countryside, much of it in the care of the National Trust. Its attractions include the educational museum and the annual music festival.

- **HASTINGS, EAST SUSSEX** - Ancient town which became famous as the base from which William the Conqueror set out to fight the Battle of Hastings. Later became one of the Cinque Ports, now a leading resort. Castle, Hastings Embroidery inspired by the Bayeux Tapestry and Sea Life Centre.

- **HEATHFIELD, EAST SUSSEX** - Old Heathfield is a pretty village which was one of the major centres of the Sussex iron industry.

- **HERSTMONCEUX, EAST SUSSEX** - Pleasant village noted for its woodcrafts and the beautiful 15th C moated Herstmonceux Castle with its Science Centre and gardens open to the public. The only village where traditional Sussex trug baskets are still made.

- **HOLLINGBOURNE, KENT** - Pleasant village near romantic Leeds Castle in the heart of orchard country at the foot of the North Downs. Some fine half-timbered houses and a flint and ragstone church.

- **HORLEY, SURREY** - Town on the London to Brighton road, just north of Gatwick Airport, with an ancient parish church and 15th C inn.

- **HORSHAM, WEST SUSSEX** - Busy town with much modern development but still retaining its old character. The museum in Causeway House is devoted chiefly to local history and the agricultural life of the county.

L LENHAM, KENT - Shops, inns and houses, many displaying timber-work of the late Middle Ages, surround a square which is the centre of the village. The 14th C parish church has one of the best examples of a Kentish tower.

- **LEWES, EAST SUSSEX** - Historic county town with Norman castle. The steep High Street has mainly Georgian buildings. There is a folk museum at Anne of Cleves House and the archaeological museum is in Barbican House.

- **LITTLEHAMPTON, WEST SUSSEX** - Ancient port at the mouth of the River Arun, now a popular holiday resort, offering flat, sandy beaches, sailing, fishing and boat trips. The Sussex Downs are a short walk inland.

- **LYMINSTER, WEST SUSSEX** - Links up with Littlehampton looking inland, and across the watermeadows to the churches and towers of Arundel. There is a vineyard here.

M MAIDSTONE, KENT - Busy county town of Kent on the River Medway has many interesting features and is an excellent centre for excursions. Museum of Carriages, Museum and Art Gallery, Mote Park.

- **MARDEN, KENT** - The village is believed to date back to Saxon times, though today more modern homes surround the 13th C church.

- **MIDHURST, WEST SUSSEX** - Historic, picturesque town just north of the South Downs, with the ruins of Cowdray House, medieval castle and 15th C parish church. Polo at Cowdray Park. Excellent base for Chichester, Petworth, Glorious Goodwood and the South Downs Way.

N NEWHAVEN, EAST SUSSEX - Town has the terminal of a car-ferry service to Dieppe in France. Paradise Park family attraction and indoor ski-slope.

O OXTED, SURREY - Pleasant town on the edge of National Trust woodland and at the foot of the North Downs. Chartwell (National Trust), the former home of Sir Winston Churchill, is close by.

P PARTRIDGE GREEN, WEST SUSSEX - Small village between Henfield and Billingshurst.

- **PEMBURY, KENT** - Large residential village with 14th C church on the outskirts of Tunbridge Wells. Orchards to the north and east.

- **PETWORTH, WEST SUSSEX** - Town known as an antique centre and dominated by Petworth House (National Trust), the great 17th C mansion, set in 2000 acres of parkland laid out by Capability Brown. The house contains wood-carvings by Grinling Gibbons.

- **POLEGATE, EAST SUSSEX** - Polegate used to be an important junction for the London, Brighton and South Coast Railway. Polegate Windmill and Milling Museum can be visited.

R RAMSGATE, KENT - Popular holiday resort with good sandy beaches. At Pegwell Bay is a replica of a Viking longship.

- **REDHILL, SURREY** - Part of the borough of Reigate and now the commercial centre with good shopping facilities. Gatwick Airport is 3 miles to the south.

- **ROCHESTER, KENT** - Ancient cathedral city on the River Medway. Has many places of interest connected with Charles Dickens (who lived nearby) including the fascinating Dickens Centre. Also massive castle overlooking the river and Guildhall Museum.

- **ROYAL TUNBRIDGE WELLS, KENT** - This 'Royal' town became famous as a spa in the 17th C and much of its charm is retained, as in the Pantiles, a shaded walk lined with elegant shops. Heritage attraction 'A Day at the Wells'. Excellent shopping centre.

- **RUSTINGTON, WEST SUSSEX** - Village with thatched cottages and a medieval church.

- **RYE, EAST SUSSEX** - Cobbled, hilly streets and fine old buildings make Rye, once a Cinque Port, a most picturesque town. Noted for its church with ancient clock, potteries and antique shops. Town Model Sound and Light Show gives a good introduction to the town.

S SANDWICH, KENT - Delightful old market town, once a Cinque Port, now 2 miles from the sea. Many interesting old buildings including the 16th C Barbican and the Guildhall which contains the town's treasures. Several excellent golf-courses.

- **SARRE, KENT** - Attractive Dutch-gabled houses can be seen in this Thanet village. Names of many famous people are inscribed on the walls of the 16th C Crown Inn, noted for the manufacture of cherry brandy.

- **SEAFORD, EAST SUSSEX** - The town was a bustling port until 1579 when the course of the River Ouse was diverted. The downlands around the town make good walking country, with fine views of the Seven Sisters cliffs.

- **SELSEY, WEST SUSSEX** - Almost surrounded by water, with the English Channel on two sides and an inland lake, once Pagham Harbour, and the Brook on the other two. Ideal for yachting, swimming, fishing and wildlife.

- **SEVENOAKS, KENT** - Set in pleasant wooded country, with a distinctive character and charm. Nearby is Knole (National Trust), home of the Sackville family and one of the largest houses in England, set in a vast deer park.

- **SITTINGBOURNE, KENT** - Set in pleasant wooded country, with a distinctive character and charm. Nearby is Knole (National Trust), home of the Sackville family and one of the largest houses in England, set in a vast deer park.

- **SMARDEN, KENT** - Pretty village with a number of old, well-presented buildings. The 14th C St Michael's Church is sometimes known as the 'Barn of Kent' because of its 36-ft roof span.

- **STELLING MINNIS, KENT** - Off the Roman Stone Street, this quiet, picturesque village lies deep in the Lyminge Forest, south of Canterbury.

- **STEYNING, WEST SUSSEX** - An important market town and thriving port before the Norman Conquest, lying at the foot of the South Downs. Retains a picturesque charm with fascinating timber-framed and stone buildings.

- **ST-MARGARETS-AT-CLIFFE, KENT** - Small resort 4 miles north-east of Dover on St Margarets Bay.

T **TENTERDEN, KENT** - Most attractive market town with a broad main street full of 16th C houses and shops. The tower of the 15th C parish church is the finest in Kent. Fine antiques centre.

U **UCKFIELD, EAST SUSSEX** - Once a medieval market town and centre of the iron industry, Uckfield is now a busy country town on the edge of the Ashdown forest.

W **WEST CLANDON, SURREY** - Home of the Clandon Park (National Trust), the Palladian mansion built in the early 1730s and home of the Queen's Royal Surrey Regiment Museum.

- **WHITSTABLE, KENT** - Seaside resort and yachting centre on Kent's north shore. The beach is shingle and there are the usual seaside amenities and entertainments and a museum.

- **WINCHELSEA, EAST SUSSEX** - Edward I laid out the present town on its hilltop site in the 13th C to replace the ancient Cinque Port which was eventually engulfed by the sea.

- **WOKING, SURREY** - One of the largest towns in Surrey, which developed with the coming of the railway in the 1830s. Old Woking was a market town in the 17th C and still retains several interesting buildings. Large arts and entertainment centre.

- **WORTHING, WEST SUSSEX** - Town in the West Sussex countryside and by the South Coast, with excellent shopping and many pavement cafes and restaurants. Attractions include the award-winning Museum and Art Gallery, beautiful gardens, pier, elegant town houses, Cissbury Ring hill fort and the South Downs.

- **WYE, KENT** - Well known for its agricultural and horticultural college. The Olantigh Tower, with its imposing front portico, is used as a setting for part of the Stour Music Festival held annually in June.

Welcome Host

Welcome Host is a nationally recognised customer care initiative, sponsored in England by the English Tourism Council. When visiting accommodation in this guide you may find this sign on display. It demonstrates commitment to courtesy and service and an aim to provide high standards of service and a warm welcome for all visitors.

English Tourism Council
assessed

Accommodation

On the following pages you will find an exclusive listing of all guest accommodation in England that has been assessed for quality by the English Tourism Council.

The information includes brief contact details for each place to stay, together with its Diamond rating, and quality award if appropriate. The listing also shows if an establishment has a National Accessible rating (see the front of the guide for further information).

More detailed information on all the places shown in blue can be found in the regional sections (where establishments have paid to have their details included). To find these entries please refer to the appropriate regional section, or look in the town index at the back of this guide.

The list which follows was compiled slightly later than the regional sections. For this reason you may find that, in a few instances, a Diamond rating and quality award may differ between the two sections. This list contains the most up-to-date information and was correct at the time of going to press.

INNER LONDON
E4

Aucklands ◆◆◆◆
25 Eglington Road, North
Chingford, London E4 7AN
T: (020) 8529 1140
F: (020) 8529 9288

Ridgeway Hotel Limited ◆◆◆
115-117 The Ridgeway LTD,
North Chingford, London
E4 6QU
T: (020) 8529 1964
F: (020) 8542 9130

E7

Forest View Hotel ◆
227 Romford Road, Forest Gate,
London E7 9HL
T: (020) 8534 4844
F: (020) 8534 8959

Grangewood Lodge Hotel ◆
104 Clova Road, Forest Gate,
London E7 9AF
T: (020) 8534 0637 & 8503 0941
F: (020) 8503 0941
E: grangewoodlodgehotel@
talk21.com
I: www.grangewoodlodgehotel.
co.uk

E15

Park Hotel ◆◆
81 Portway, Stratford, London
E15 3QJ
T: (0208) 2579034
F: (0208) 2798094

N1

Kandara Guest House ◆◆◆
68 Ockendon Road, London
N1 3NW
T: (020) 7226 5721 & 7226 3379
F: (020) 7226 3379
E: admin@kandara.co.uk
I: www.kandara.co.uk

N4

Costello Palace Hotel ◆◆
374 Seven Sisters Road, Finsbury
Park, London N4 2PG
T: (020) 8802 6551
F: (020) 8802 9461
E: costellopalacehotel@uk2net.
co
I: www.costellopalacehotel.co.uk

N6

**The Raj Hideaway Bed &
Breakfast**
Rating Applied For
67 Highgate High Street,
Highgate Village, London N6 5JX
T: (0208) 3488760 & 3483972

N7

Europa Hotel ◆◆◆
60-62 Anson Road, London
N7 0AA
T: (020) 7607 5935
F: (020) 7607 5909

Five Kings Guest House ◆◆
59 Anson Road, Tufnell Park,
London N7 0AR
T: (020) 7607 3996 & 7607 6466
F: (020) 7609 5554
I: www.hotelregister.
co.uk/hotel/fivekings.asp

Queens Hotel ◆◆
33 Anson Road, Tufnell Park,
London N7 0RB
T: (020) 7607 4725
F: (020) 7697 9725
E: queens@stavrouhotels.co.uk

N8

White Lodge Hotel ◆◆◆
1 Church Lane, Hornsey, London
N8 7BU
T: (020) 8348 9765
F: (020) 8340 7851

N10

The Muswell Hill Hotel ◆◆◆
73 Muswell Hill Road, London
N10 3HT
T: (020) 8883 6447
F: (020) 8883 5158
E: demos@fhlon.freeserve.co.uk

N16

Rose Hotel ◆◆
69-71 Stoke Newington Road,
London N16 8AD
T: (020) 7254 5990 & 7923 0483
F: (020) 7923 0483
E: rosehotel6971@aol.com
I: smoothhound.co.uk/rosehotel.
html

N20

The Corner Lodge ◆◆◆◆
9 Athenaeum Road, Whetstone,
London N20 9AA
T: (020) 8446 3720
F: (020) 8446 3720

N22

Pane Residence ◆◆
154 Boundary Road, Wood
Green, London N22 6AE
T: (020) 8889 3735

NW1

Americana Hotel ◆◆◆
172 Gloucester Place, Regent's
Park, London NW1 6DS
T: (020) 7723 1452
F: (020) 7723 4641
E: manager@americanahotel.
demon.co.uk

Four Seasons Hotel ◆◆◆◆
173 Gloucester Place, London
NW1 6DX
T: (020) 7724 3461 & 7723 9471
F: (020) 7402 5594
E: fourseasons@dial.pipex.com
I: www.4seasonshotel.co.uk

NW3

Dillons Hotel ◆
21 Belsize Park, Hampstead,
London NW3 4DU
T: (020) 7794 3360
F: (020) 7431 7900
E: desk@dillonshotel.com
I: www.dillonshotel.com

NW6

Cavendish Guest House
◆◆◆◆
24 Cavendish Road, London
NW6 7XP
T: (020) 8451 3249
F: (020) 8451 3249

Dawson House Hotel ◆◆◆◆
72 Canfield Gardens, London
NW6 3ED
T: (020) 7624 0079 & 7624 6525
F: (020) 7644 6321
E: dawsonhtl@aol.com
I: www.dawsonhouse.com

NW10

Aran Guest House ◆◆
21 Holland Road, Kensal Green,
London NW10 5AH
T: (020) 8968 6402 & 8968 2153

J and T Guest House ◆◆◆
98 Park Avenue North, Willesden
Green, London NW10 1JY
T: (020) 8452 4085
F: (020) 8450 2503
E: jandthome@aol.com
I: www.jandtguesthouses.com

NW11

Anchor-Nova Hotel ◆◆◆
10 West Heath Drive, Golders
Green, London NW11 7QH
T: (020) 8458 8764 & 8458 4311
F: (020) 8455 3204
E: reserv@anchor-hotel.co.uk
I: www.anchor-hotel.co.uk

SE3

64 Beaconsfield Road ◆◆
Blackheath, London SE3 7LG
T: (020) 8858 1685

49 Foxes Dale ◆◆◆
Blackheath, London SE3 9BH
T: (020) 8852 1076 &
07770 583487
F: (020) 8852 1076

The Grovers ◆◆◆
96 Merriman Road, London
SE3 8RZ
T: (020) 8488 7719 & 07730 877
656
F: (020) 8488 7719

Hill Crest Guesthouse ◆◆
2 Hardy Road, Blackheath,
London SE3 7NR
T: (020) 8305 0120 & 8305 2203
E: hillcrest@dial.pipex.com
I: ds.dial.pipex.
com/town/drive/xsd11/

59a Lee Road ◆◆
Blackheath, London SE3 9EN
T: (020) 8318 7244
F: (020) 8318 7244

59 Lee Terrace ◆◆
Blackheath, London SE3 9TA
T: (020) 8852 6334
E: susan.bedbreakfast@virgin.
net

Mrs Dove's ◆◆
68 Wricklemarsh Road,
Blackheath, London SE3 8DS
T: (020) 8856 1331
F: (020) 8480 6653
E: mrsdove@cwcom.net
I: www.mrsdove.co.uk

**Number Nine Blackheath
Limited** ◆◆◆◆
9 Charlton Road, Blackheath,
London SE3 7EU
T: (020) 8858 4175 &
07957 361997
F: (020) 8858 4175
E: derek@
numbernineblackheath.com
I: www.numbernineblackheath.
com

3 Tilbrook Road ◆◆
3 Tilbrook Road, Kidbrooke,
London SE3 9QD
T: (020) 8319 8843

SE4

Crofton Park Holdenby ◆◆
28 Holdenby Road, Crofton Park,
London SE4 2DA
T: (020) 8694 0011
E: savitri.gaines@totalise.co.uk

66 Geoffrey Road ◆◆
London SE4 1NT
T: (020) 8691 3887 &
07790 467061
F: (020) 8691 3887
E: andrea.dechamps@btclick.
com

SE6

The Heathers
Rating Applied For
71 Verdant Lane, Catford,
London SE6 1JD
T: (020) 8698 8340
F: (020) 8461 3980
E: berylheath@yahoo.co.uk
I: theheathersbb.com

Thornsbeach ◆◆◆
122 Bargery Road, Catford,
London SE6 2LK
T: (020) 8695 6544 & 8244 5554
F: (020) 8695 9577
E: helen@thornsbeach.co.uk
I: www.thornsbeach.co.uk

Tulip Tree House ◆◆◆
41 Minard Road, Catford,
London SE6 1NP
T: (020) 8697 2596
F: (020) 8698 2020

SE7

Old Rectory Guest House ◆◆◆
80 Maryon Road, London
SE7 8DL
T: (020) 8317 9694

SE8

M B Guest House ◆◆
7 Bolden Street, Deptford,
London SE8 4JF
T: (020) 8692 7030
F: (020) 8691 6241

SE9

Abigail House ◆◆◆
68 Dunvegan Road, Eltham,
London SE9 1SB
T: (020) 8859 3924

Benvenuti ◆◆◆◆
217 Court Road, Eltham, London
SE9 4TG
T: (020) 8857 4855
F: (020) 8265 5635
E: val.smith.benvenuti@cwcom.
net
I: www.benvenuti.cwc.net

Boru House ◆◆
70 Dunevegan Road, Eltham,
London SE9 1SB
T: (020) 8850 0584

Century House ◆◆◆
100 Dumbreck Road, London
SE9 1XD
T: (020) 8859 1927

33 Glenshiel Road ◆◆◆
33 Glenshiel Road, Eltham,
London SE9 1AQ
T: (020) 8850 4958 &
07940 544123
E: astone@astone.new.labour.
org.uk

80 Rennets Wood Road ◆◆◆
Eltham, London SE9 2NH
T: (020) 8850 1829 &
07866 650514

Weston House ◆
8 Eltham Green, Eltham, London
SE9 5LB
T: (020) 8850 5191
F: (020) 8850 0030
E: reservation@
westonhousehotel.co.uk
I: www.westonhousehotel.co.uk

SE10

69 Ashburnham Place ◆◆
Greenwich, London SE10 8UG
T: (020) 8692 9065

Greenwich Parkhouse Hotel
◆◆
1-2 Nevada Street, Greenwich,
London SE10 9JL
T: (020) 8305 1478
E: B&B@
greenwich-parkhouse-hotel.
co.uk
I: www.
greenwich-parkhouse-hotel.
co.uk

81 Greenwich South Street
◆◆◆◆
London SE10 8NT
T: (020) 8293 3121
E: bandbwade.greenwich@
talk21.com

Mitre Inn ◆◆◆
291 Greenwich High Road,
London SE10 8NA
T: (020) 8355 6760 & 8293 0037
F: (020) 8355 6761

SE12

The Corner House ◆◆◆
81 Micheldever Road, London
SE12 8LU
T: (020) 8852 2604 &
0786 7887888
E: joannacourtney@aol.com

SE13

Blue Danube Guest House
◆◆◆
54 Albacore Crescent, Lewisham,
London SE13 7HP
T: (020) 8244 3019 &
07941 286183
F: (020) 8690 4147
E: maz.anita@lc24.net

Manna House ◆◆◆
320 Hither Green Lane,
Lewisham, London SE13 6TS
T: (020) 8461 5984 & 8695 5316
F: (020) 8695 5316
E: mannahouse@aol.com
I: members.aol.
com/mannahouse

13 Wellmeadow Road ◆
Hither Green, London SE13 6SY
T: (020) 8697 1398
F: (020) 8697 1398

8 Yeats Close ◆◆
Eliot Park, London SE13 7ET
T: (020) 8318 3421 & 8694 3495
F: (020) 8318 3421
E: pathu@tesco.net

SE17

Hampton Court Palace Hotel
◆◆◆◆
Hampton Street, London
SE17 3AN
T: (020) 7703 0011
F: (020) 7703 6464
E: hcpal@aol.co.uk
I: www.hampton-hotel.com/

SE18

Home from Home ◆◆
29 Tellson Avenue, Shooters Hill
Road, London SE18 4PD
T: (020) 8856 9213 &
07712 494836
F: (020) 8856 9213
E: 106440,2211@compuserve.
com
I: www.ourworld.compuserve.
com/homepages/
PTNdedicatedservices

268 Shooters Hill Road ◆
Blackheath, London SE18 4LX
T: (020) 8319 2699 &
07713 422912

SE20

Happy Home Bed & Breakfast
◆◆◆
186 Anerley Road, London
SE20 8BL
T: (020) 8289 2252 & 8289 2252
F: (020) 82892252

Melrose House ◆◆◆◆
89 Lennard Road, London
SE20 7LY
T: (020) 8776 8884 &
07956 357714
F: (020) 8776 8480
E: melrose.hotel@virgin.net
I: www.
guesthouseaccommodation.
co.uk

SE22

Dragon House ◆◆◆◆
39 Marmora Road, London
SE22 0RX
T: (020) 8693 4355 &
07956 645894
F: (020) 8693 7954
E: dulwichdragon@hotmail.com
I: www.thedragonhouse.co.uk

SW1

Airways Hotel Nationlodge Ltd
◆◆
29-31 St George's Drive,
Victoria, London SW1V 4DG
T: (020) 7834 0205 & 7834 3567
F: (020) 7932 0007
E: sales@airways-hotel.com
I: www.airways-hotel.com

Blair Victoria Hotel ◆◆
78-84 Warwick Way, London
SW1V 1RZ
T: (020) 7828 8603
F: (020) 7976 6536
E: sales@blairvictoria.com
I: www.blairvictoria.com

Carlton Hotel ◆◆
90 Belgrave Road, Victoria,
London SW1V 2BJ
T: (020) 7976 6634 & 7932 0913
F: (020) 7821 8020
E: info@cityhotelcarlton.co.uk
I: www.cityhotelcarlton.co.uk

Caswell Hotel ◆◆
25 Gloucester Street, London
SW1V 2DB
T: (020) 7834 6345
E: manager@hotellondon.co.uk
I: www.hotellondon.co.uk

Central House Hotel
Rating Applied For
39 Belgrave Road, London
SW1V 2BB
T: (020) 7834 8036 & 7828 0644
F: (020) 7834 1854
I: www.splendidhotels.com

Colliers Hotel ◆
97 Warwick Way, London
SW1V 1QL
T: (020) 7834 6931 & 7828 0210
F: (020) 7834 8439
E: cmahotel@aol.com
I: www.affordablehotel.com

Collin House ◆◆◆
104 Ebury Street, London
SW1W 9QD
T: (020) 7730 8031
F: (020) 7730 8031
E: collin.house@faxvia.net

Dover Hotel ◆◆
44 Belgrave Road, London
SW1V 1RG
T: (020) 7821 9085
F: (020) 7834 6425
E: reception@dover-hotel.co.uk
I: www.dover-hotel.co.uk

Elizabeth Hotel ◆◆
37 Eccleston Square, Victoria,
London SW1V 1PB
T: (020) 7828 6812
F: (020) 7828 6814
E: info@elizabethhotel.com
I: www.elizabethhotel.com

Georgian House Hotel ◆◆
35-39 St George's Drive, London
SW1V 4DG
T: (020) 7834 1438
F: (020) 7976 6085
E: georgian@wildnet.co.uk
I: www.georgianhousehotel.
co.uk

Hanover Hotel ◆◆◆
30-32 St George's Drive, London
SW1V 4BN
T: (020) 7834 0367 & 7834 7617
F: (020) 7976 5587
E: reservations@hanoverhotel.
co.uk
I: www.hanoverhotel.co.uk

Huttons Hotel ◆
55 Belgrave Road, London
SW1V 2BB
T: (020) 7834 3726
F: (020) 7834 3389
E: reservations@huttons-hotel.
co.uk

Knightsbridge Green Hotel
◆◆◆◆
159 Knightsbridge, London
SW1X 7PD
T: (020) 7584 6274
F: (020) 7225 1635
E: thekghotel@aol.com
I: www.thekghotel.co.uk

Luna-Simone Hotel ◆◆
47 Belgrave Road, London
SW1V 2BB
T: (020) 7834 5897
F: (020) 7828 2474
E: lunasimone@talk21.com
I: www.lunasimone.com

Melita House Hotel ◆◆◆
35 Charlwood Street, Victoria,
London SW1V 2DU
T: (020) 7828 0471 & 7834 1387
F: (020) 7932 0988
E: reserve@melitahotel.com
I: www.melitahotel.com

Oxford House Hotel ◆
92 Cambridge Street, Victoria,
London SW1V 4QG
T: (020) 7834 6467
F: (020) 7834 0225
E: oxfordhousehotel@hotmail.
com

Stanley House Hotel ◆◆
19-21 Belgrave Road, London
SW1V 1RB
T: (020) 7834 5042 & 7834 7292
F: (020) 7834 8439
E: cmahotel@aol.com
I: www.affordablehotelsonline.
com

Vandon House Hotel ◆◆◆
1 Vandon Street, London
SW1H 0AH
T: (020) 7799 6780
F: (020) 7799 1464
E: info@vandonhouse.com
I: www.vandonhouse.com

Victor Hotel ◆◆◆
51 Belgrave Road, London
SW1V 2BB
T: (020) 7592 9853
F: (020) 7592 9854

The Victoria Inn ◆◆◆
65-67 Belgrave Road, London
SW1V 2BG
T: (020) 7834 6721 & 7834 0182
F: (020) 7931 0201
E: info@victoriainn.co.uk
I: www.victoriainn.co.uk

Windermere Hotel ◆◆◆◆
142-144 Warwick Way, Victoria,
London SW1V 4JE
T: (020) 7834 5163 & 7834 5480
F: (020) 7630 8831
E: windermere@compuserve.
com
I: www.windermere-hotel.co.uk

SW5

The Albany Hotel ◆◆◆
4-12 Barkston Gardens, London
SW5 0EN
T: (020) 7370 6116
F: (020) 7244 8024
E: albany@realco.co.uk
I: www.realco.co.uk

The Ambassadors Hotel X
◆◆◆
16 Collingham Road, London
SW5 0LX
T: (020) 7373 1075
F: (020) 7244 8375

Beaver Hotel ◆◆◆
57-59 Philbeach Gardens,
London SW5 9ED
T: (020) 7373 4553
F: (020) 7373 4555
E: hotelbeaver@hotmail.com
I: www.beaverhotel.co.uk

Buosi Hotel ◆◆
50 Nevern Square, London
SW5 9PF
T: (020) 7370 3325
F: (020) 7370 3103
E: 6088@mjbart.demon.co.uk
I: www.hotelbuosi.com

Comfort Inn Earl's Court ◆◆
11-13 Penywern Road, Earl's Court, London SW5 9TT
T: (020) 7373 6514
F: (020) 7370 3639
E: cihotel@compuserve.com

Hotel Earls Court ◆◆
28 Warwick Road, Earls Court, London SW5 9UD
T: (020) 7373 7079 & 7373 0302
F: (020) 7912 0582
E: res@hotelearlscourt.com
I: www.hotelearlscourt.com

Henley House Hotel ◆◆◆
30 Barkston Gardens, Earl's Court, London SW5 0EN
T: (020) 7370 4111
F: (020) 7370 0026
E: henleyhse@aol.com
I: www.henleyhousehotel.co.uk

Kensington Court Hotel ◆◆◆
33 Nevern Place, London SW5 9NP
T: (020) 7370 5151 & 7370 3499
F: (020) 7370 3499
E: kensington_court_hotel@visit.uk.com
I: www.visit.uk.com

Kensington International Hotel ◆◆◆
4 Templeton Place, London SW5 9LZ
T: (020) 7370 4333
F: (020) 7244 7873
E: hotel@kensingtoninternationalhotel.com
I: www.kensingtoninternationalhotel.com

London Town Hotel ◆◆◆
15 Penywern Road, Earl's Court, London SW5 9TT
T: (020) 7370 4356
F: (020) 7370 7923
E: townhotel@compuserve.com
I: www.londontownhotel.com

Lord Jim Hotel ◆◆
23-25 Penywern Road, London SW5 9TT
T: (020) 7370 6071 & 07957 167081
F: (020) 7373 8919
E: lordjimhotel@cs.com
I: www.igh-hotels.com

Maranton House Hotel ◆◆◆
14 Barkston Gardens, Earls Court, London SW5 0EN
T: (020) 7373 5782
F: (020) 7244 9543
E: marantonhotel@hotmail.com

Mayflower Hotel ◆◆
26-28 Trebovir Road, Earls Court, London SW5 9NJ
T: (020) 7370 0991
F: (020) 7370 0994
E: mayfhotel@aol.com
I: members.aol.com/mayfhotel/private/may.htm

Merlyn Court Hotel ◆◆
2 Barkston Gardens, London SW5 0EN
T: (020) 7370 1640
F: (020) 7370 4986
E: london@merlyncourt.demon.co.uk
I: www.smoothhound.co.uk/hotels/merlyn.html

Mowbray Court Hotel ◆◆
28-32 Penywern Road, Earl's Court, London SW5 9SU
T: (020) 7370 2316 & 7370 3690
F: (020) 7370 5693
E: mowbraycrthot@hotmail.com
I: www.m-c-hotel.mcmail.com

Hotel Oliver ◆◆
198 Cromwell Road, London SW5 0SN
T: (020) 7370 6881
F: (020) 7370 6556
E: reservations@hoteloliver.freeserve.co.uk
I: www.hoteloliver.co.uk

Oliver Plaza Hotel ◆◆
33 Trebovir Road, Earl's Court, London SW5 9NF
T: (020) 7373 7183
F: (020) 7244 6021
E: oliverplaza@capricornhotels.co.uk
I: www.capricornhotels.co.uk

Hotel Plaza Continental ◆◆◆
9 Knaresborough Place, Earls Court, London SW5 0TP
T: (020) 7370 3246
F: (020) 7373 9571
E: hpc@lgh-hotels.com
I: www.lgh-hotels.com

Ramsees Hotel ◆◆
32-36 Hogarth Road, Earl's Court, London SW5 0PU
T: (020) 7370 1445
F: (020) 7244 6835
E: ramsees@rasool.demon.co.uk
I: www.ramseeshotel.com

Rasool Court Hotel ◆◆
19-21 Penywern Road, Earl's Court, London SW5 9TT
T: (020) 7373 8900
F: (020) 7244 6835
E: rasool@rasool.demon.co.uk
I: www.rasoolcourthotel.com

Swiss House Hotel ◆◆◆
171 Old Brompton Road, London SW5 0AN
T: (020) 7373 2769 & 7373 9383
F: (020) 7373 4983
E: recep@swiss-hh.demon.co.uk
I: www.swiss-hh.demon.co.uk

Windsor House ◆
12 Penywern Road, London SW5 9ST
T: (020) 7373 9087
F: (020) 7385 2417
E: bookings@windsor-house-hotel.com
I: www.windsor_house.com

York House Hotel ◆◆
27-28 Philbeach Gardens, London SW5 9EA
T: (020) 7373 7519 & 7373 7579
F: (020) 7370 4641
E: yorkhh@aol.com
I: www.smoothhound.co.uk/hotels/yorkhousehotel.html

SW7

Aster House ◆◆◆◆◆
3 Sumner Place, London SW7 3EE
T: (020) 7581 5888
F: (020) 7584 4925
E: AsterHouse@btinternet.com
I: www.AsterHouse.com

Eden Plaza Hotel ◆
68-69 Queensgate, London SW7 5JT
T: (020) 7370 6111
F: (020) 7370 0932
E: eden_plaza_hotel@visit.uk.com
I: www.visit.uk.com

Five Sumner Place Hotel ◆◆◆◆
5 Sumner Place, South Kensington, London SW7 3EE
T: (020) 7584 7586
F: (020) 7823 9962
E: reservations@sumnerplace.com
I: www.sumnerplace.com

Hotel Number Sixteen ◆◆◆◆◆
16 Sumner Place, London SW7 3EG
T: (020) 7589 5232
F: (020) 7584 8615
E: reservations@numbersixteenhotel.co.uk
I: www.numbersixteenhotel.co.uk

Stuart Hotel ◆
110-112 Cromwell Road, London SW7 4ES
T: (020) 7373 1004
F: (020) 7370 2548
E: the-stuart-hotel@visit.uk.com
I: www.visit.uk.com/the-stuart-hotel

SW11

Lavender Guest House ◆◆◆
18 Lavender Sweep, London SW11 1HA
T: (020) 7585 2767 & 7223 1973
F: (020) 7924 6274

SW14

106 East Sheen Avenue ◆◆◆
London SW14 8AU
T: (020) 8255 1900
F: (020) 8876 8084
E: rpratt@easynet.co.uk

The Plough Inn ◆◆◆
42 Christchurch Road, East Sheen, London SW14 7AF
T: (020) 8876 7833 & 8876 4533
F: (020) 8392 8801
E: ploughthe@hotmail.com

SW16

The Konyots ◆
95 Pollards Hill South, London SW16 4LS
T: (020) 8764 0075

SW18

The Brewers Inn ◆◆◆
147 East Hill, Wandsworth, London SW18 2QB
T: (020) 8874 4128
F: (020) 8877 1953
E: brewersin@youngs.co.uk
I: www.youngs.co.uk

Grosvenor Arms ◆◆◆
204 Garratt Lane, Wandsworth, London SW18 4ED
T: (020) 8874 2709
F: (020) 8874 0813

2 Melrose Road ◆◆◆
London SW18 1NE
T: (020) 8871 3259

SW19

Trochee Hotel ◆◆
21 Malcolm Road, Wimbledon, London SW19 4AS
T: (020) 8946 3924
F: (020) 8946 1579
E: rosina@dhala.com
I: www.trocheehotel.co.uk

Trochee Hotel Annexe ◆◆
52 Ridgway Place, Wimbledon, London SW19 4SW
T: (020) 8946 9425 & 8946 9400
F: (020) 8785 4058

W1

Bentinck House Hotel ◆◆
20 Bentinck Street, London W1M 5RL
T: (020) 7935 9141
F: (020) 7224 5903
E: b.hh@virgin.net

Berkeley Court Hotel ◆◆
22 Upper Berkeley Street, London W1H 7PF
T: (020) 7262 3091
F: (020) 7258 0290
E: berkeleycourthotel@yahoo.co.uk
I: www.smoothhound.co.uk/hotels/berkeleycourt.html

Blandford Hotel ◆◆◆
80 Chiltern Street, London W1U 5AF
T: (020) 7486 3103
F: (020) 7487 2786
E: blandfordhotel@dial.pipex.com
I: www.capricornhotels.co.uk

The Edward Lear Hotel ◆◆
30 Seymour Street, Marble Arch, London W1H 5WD
T: (020) 7402 5401
F: (020) 7706 3766
E: edwardlear@aol.com
I: www.edlear.com

Hallam Hotel ◆◆◆
12 Hallam Street, Portland Place, London W1W 6JF
T: (020) 7580 1166
F: (020) 7323 4527

Kenwood House Hotel ◆
114 Gloucester Place, London W1H 3DB
T: (020) 7935 3473 & 7935 9455
F: (020) 7224 0582
E: kenwoodhouse@yahoo.co.uk
I: www.kenwoodhousehotel.com

Lincoln House Hotel – Central London ◆◆
33 Gloucester Place, London W1U 8HY
T: (020) 7486 7630
F: (020) 7935 7089
E: reservations@lincoln-house-hotel.co.uk
I: www.lincoln-house-hotel.co.uk

Marble Arch Inn ◆◆
49-50 Upper Berkeley Street, Marble Arch, London W1H 7PN
T: (020) 7723 7888
F: (020) 7723 6060
E: sales@marblearch-inn.co.uk
I: www.marblearch-inn.co.uk

Hotel La Place ◆◆◆
17 Nottingham Place, London
W1V 5LG
T: (020) 7486 2323
F: (020) 7486 4335
E: reservations@hotellaplace.
com
I: www.hotellaplace.com

Saint George Hotel ◆◆◆◆
49 Gloucester Place, London
W1H 3PE
T: (020) 7486 8586
F: (020) 7486 6567
E: reservations@stgeorge-hotel.
net
I: www.stgeorge-hotel.net

Ten Manchester Street ◆◆◆◆
10 Manchester Street, London
W1V 4DG
T: (020) 7486 6669
F: (020) 7224 0348
E: stay@10manchesterstreet.
fsnet.co.uk
I: www.10manchesterstreet.com

Wigmore Court Hotel ◆◆◆
23 Gloucester Place, Portman
Square, London W1H 3PB
T: (020) 7935 0928
F: (020) 7487 4254
E: info@wigmore-court-hotel.
co.uk
I: www.wigmore-court-hotel.
co.uk

Wyndham Hotel ◆◆◆
30 Wyndham Street, London
W1H 1EB
T: (020) 7723 7204 & 7723 9400
F: (020) 7724 2893
E: wyndhamhotel@talk21.com

W2

**Abbey Court & Westpoint
Hotel ◆◆**
170-174 Sussex Gardens,
London W2 1TP
T: (020) 7402 0281 & 7402 5060
F: (020) 7224 9114
E: info@abbeycourt.com
I: www.abbeycourt.com

Admiral Hotel ◆◆
143 Sussex Gardens, Hyde Park,
London W2 2RY
T: (020) 7723 7309
F: (020) 7723 8731
E: frank@admiral143.demon.
co.uk
I: www.admiral-hotel.com

Allandale Hotel ◆◆
3 Devonshire Terrace, Lancaster
Gate, London W2 3DN
T: (020) 7723 8311 & 7723 7807
F: (020) 7723 8311
E: info@allandalehotel.co.uk
I: www.allandalehotel.co.uk

Apollo Hotel ◆◆◆
64 Queensborough Terrace,
London W2 3SH
T: (020) 7727 3066
F: (020) 7727 2800
E: apollohotel@btinternet.com
I: www.hotelapollo.com

Ashley Hotel ◆◆
15 Norfolk Square, London
W2 1RU
T: (020) 7723 3375 & 7723 9966
F: (020) 7723 0173
E: ashhot@btinternet.com
I: www.ashleyhotels.com

Athena Hotel ◆◆◆
110-114 Sussex Gardens,
London W2 1UA
T: (020) 7706 3866
F: (020) 7262 6143
E: athena@stavrouhotels.co.uk
I: www.stavrouhotels.co.uk

Barry House Hotel ◆◆
12 Sussex Place, London W2 2TP
T: (020) 7723 7340
F: (020) 7723 9775
E: hotel@barryhouse.co.uk
I: www.barryhouse.co.uk

The Brunel Hotel ◆◆◆
78-81 Gloucester Terrace,
Bayswater, London W2 3HB
T: (0207) 2624481
F: (0207) 7063611
E: brunel.hotel@visit.uk.com
I: www.visit.uk.com

Caring Hotel ◆
24 Craven Hill Gardens, London
W2 3EA
T: (020) 7262 8708
F: (020) 7262 8590
E: caring@lineone.net
I: www.caringhotel.co.uk

Classic Hotel ◆
92 Sussex Gardens, Hyde Park,
London W2 1UH
T: (020) 7706 7776
F: (020) 7706 8136
E: bookings@classic-hotel.com
I: www.classic-hotel.com

Duke of Leinster ◆◆
34 Queen's Gardens, London
W2 3AA
T: (020) 7258 0079 & 7258 1839
F: (020) 7262 0741
E: dukeshotel@aol.com
I: WWW.SCOOT.CO.
UK/DUKE-OF-LEINST

Dylan Hotel ◆◆
14 Devonshire Terrace, Lancaster
Gate, London W2 3DW
T: (020) 7723 3280
F: (020) 7402 2443
E: booking@dylan-hotel.com
I: www.dylan-hotel.com

Hotel Edward ◆◆
1A Spring Street, Hyde Park,
London W2 3RA
T: (0207) 2622671
F: (0207) 7062962
E: hotel_edward@visit.uk.com
I: www.visit.uk.com

Europa House Hotel ◆◆
151 Sussex Gardens, London
W2 2RY
T: (020) 7723 7343 & 7402 1923
F: (020) 7224 9331
E: europahouse@enterprise.net
I: www.europahousehotel.com

Gower Hotel ◆◆
129 Sussex Gardens, Hyde Park,
London W2 2RX
T: (020) 7262 2262
F: (020) 7262 2006
E: gower@stavrouhotels.co.uk
I: www.stavrouhotels.co.uk

Hyde Park House ◆
48 St Petersburgh Place,
Queensway, London W2 4LD
T: (020) 7229 9652 & 7229 1687

**Hyde Park Radnor Hotel
◆◆◆◆**
7-9 Sussex Place, Paddington,
London W2 2SX
T: (020) 7723 5969
F: (020) 7262 8955
I: www.hydeparkradnor.com

Hyde Park Rooms Hotel ◆
137 Sussex Gardens, Hyde Park,
London W2 2RX
T: (020) 7723 0225 & 7723 0965

**Kensington Gardens Hotel
◆◆◆**
9 Kensington Gardens Square,
London W2 4BH
T: (020) 7221 7790
F: (020) 7792 8612
E: kensingtongardenshotel@
phoenixhotel.co.uk
I: www.kensingtongardenshotel.
co.uk

Kings Arms Hotel ◆◆
254 Edgware Road, Paddington,
London W2 1DS
T: (020) 7262 8441
F: (020) 7258 0556
E: kingsarmshotel@
compuserve.com

Kingsway Hotel ◆◆
27 Norfolk Square, Hyde Park,
London W2 1RX
T: (020) 7723 5569 & 7723 7784
F: (020) 7723 7317
E: kingswyh@aol.com
I: www.kingswayhotel.net

**Kingsway Park Hotel Hyde Park
◆◆◆**
139 Sussex Gardens, Hyde Park,
London W2 2RX
T: (020) 7723 5677 & 7724 9346
F: (020) 7402 4352
E: kingswaypark@hotmail.com
I: www.kingsway-hotel.com

Lancaster Court Hotel ◆◆
202-204 Sussex Gardens, Hyde
Park, London W2 3UA
T: (020) 7402 8438 & 7402 6369
F: (020) 7706 3794
E: lancohot@cs.com
I: www.lancaster-court-hotel.
co.uk/

Linden House Hotel ◆◆
4-6 Sussex Place, London
W2 2TP
T: (020) 7723 9853 & 7262 0804
F: (020) 7724 1454
E: lindenhse@
sussexplacelondon.freeserve.
co.uk
I: www.smoothhound.
co.uk/hotels/lindenho.html

London Guards Hotel ◆◆◆
36-37 Lancaster Gate, London
W2 3NA
T: (020) 7402 1101
F: (020) 7262 2551
E: info@londonguardshotel.
co.uk
I: www.londonguardshotel.co.uk

Manor Court Hotel ◆
7 Clanricarde Gardens, London
W2 4JJ
T: (020) 7727 5407 & 7792 3361
F: (020) 7229 2875

Olympic House Hotel ◆◆
138-140 Sussex Gardens,
London W2 1UB
T: (020) 7723 5935
F: (020) 7224 8144
E: olympichousehotel@
btinternet.com
I: www.olympichousehotel.co.uk

Oxford Hotel ◆◆
13-14 Craven Terrace,
Paddington, London W2 3QD
T: (020) 7402 6860 &
0800 318798
F: (020) 7262 7574
E: info@oxfordhotellondon.
co.uk
I: www.oxfordhotellondon.co.uk

Park Lodge Hotel ◆◆◆
73 Queensborough Terrace,
Bayswater, London W2 3SU
T: (020) 7229 6424
F: (020) 7221 4772
E: smegroup.kfc@cwcom.net
I: www.angelfive.
com/sol/parklodgehotel

Parkwood Hotel ◆◆
4 Stanhope Place, London
W2 2HB
T: (020) 7402 2241
F: (020) 7402 1574
E: pkwdhotel@aol.com
I: www.parkwoodhotel.com

Pembridge Palace Hotel ◆◆
52-57 Prince's Square, London
W2 4PX
T: (020) 7229 6262
F: (020) 7792 3868
E: pembridge_palace_hotel@
visit.uk.com
I: www.visit.uk.
com/pembridge_palace_hotel

Reem Hotel ◆◆◆
50-51 Princes Square,
Bayswater, London W2 4PX
T: (0207) 2438516
F: (0207) 2296821
E: reem_hotel@visit.uk.com
I: www.visit.uk.com

Rhodes House Hotel ◆◆◆
195 Sussex Gardens, London
W2 2RJ
T: (020) 7262 5617 & 7262 0537
F: (020) 7723 4054
E: chris@rhodeshotel.com
I: www.rhodeshotel.com

Rose Court Hotel ◆◆◆
1-3 Talbot Square, London
W2 1TR
T: (020) 7723 5128 & 7723 8671
F: (020) 7723 1855
E: rosehotel@aol.com
I: www.rosecourthotel.com

Sass Hotel ◆◆
10-11 Craven Terrace, London
W2 3QD
T: (020) 7262 2325
F: (020) 7262 0889
E: info@sasshotel.com
I: www.sasshotel.com

Springfield Hotel ◆◆
154 Sussex Gardens, London
W2 1UD
T: (020) 7723 9898
F: (020) 7723 0874
E: info@springfieldhotellondon.
co.uk
I: www.springfieldhotellondon.
co.uk

W3

Acton Park Hotel ♦♦
116 The Vale, Acton, London
W3 7JT
T: (020) 8743 9417
F: (020) 8743 9417

W4

Chiswick Lodge ♦♦♦
104 Turnham Green Terrace,
London W4 1QN
T: (020) 8994 9926 & 8994 1712
F: (020) 8742 8238
E: chishot@clara.net
I: www.chiswick-hotel.co.uk

Foubert's Hotel ♦♦
162-166 Chiswick High Road,
London W4 1PR
T: (020) 8994 5202 & 8995 6743

Ivy Gate House ♦♦
6 Temple Road, Chiswick,
London W4 5NW
T: (020) 8994 8618
E: thejones@ivygatehouse.co.uk
I: www.ivygatehouse.co.uk

W5

Abbey Lodge Hotel ♦♦
51 Grange Park, Ealing, London
W5 3PR
T: (020) 8567 7914
F: (020) 8579 5350
E: enquiries@
londonlodgehotels.com
I: www.londonlodgehotels.com

Creffield Lodge ♦♦
2-4 Creffield Road, Ealing,
London W5 3HN
T: (020) 8993 2284
F: (020) 8992 7082
E: jiealing.rs@jarvis.co.uk

Grange Lodge Hotel ♦♦♦
48-50 Grange Road, London
W5 5BX
T: (020) 8567 1049
F: (020) 8579 5350
E: enquiries@
londonlodgehotels.com
I: www.londonlodgehotels.com

W6

Brook Green Hotel ♦♦♦♦
170 Shepherds Bush Road,
Hammersmith, London W6 7PB
T: (020) 7603 2516
F: (020) 7603 6827
E: brookgreen@youngs.co.uk

Hotel Orlando ♦♦
83 Shepherds Bush Road,
Hammersmith, London W6 7LR
T: (020) 7603 4890
F: (020) 7603 4890
E: hotelorlando@btconnect.com
I: www.hotelorlando.co.uk

St Peters Hotel ♦♦♦
407-411 Goldhawk Road,
London W6 0SA
T: (020) 8741 4239
F: (020) 8748 3845

W7

Boston Manor Hotel ♦♦♦
146-152 Boston Road, Hanwell,
London W7 2HJ
T: (020) 8566 1534
F: (020) 8567 9510
E: bmh@bostonmanor.com
I: www.bostonmanor.com

W8

Hotel Atlas-Apollo ♦♦♦
18-30 Lexham Gardens, London
W8 5JE
T: (020) 7835 1155 & 7835 1133
F: (020) 7370 4853
E: reservations@atlas-apollo.
com
I: www.atlas-apollo.com

Clearlake Hotel ♦♦
18-19 Prince of Wales Terrace,
Kensington, London W8 5PQ
T: (020) 7937 3274
F: (020) 7376 0604
E: clearlake@talk21.com

Vicarage Private Hotel ♦
10 Vicarage Gate, Kensington,
London W8 4AG
T: (020) 7229 4030
F: (020) 7792 5989
E: reception@
londonvicaragehotel.com
I: londonvicaragehotel.com/

W11

Kensington Guest House ♦♦
72 Holland Park Avenue,
Kensington, London W11 3QZ
T: (020) 7229 9233 & 7460 7080
F: (020) 7221 1077
E: HoteLondon@aol.com
I: www.HoteLondon.co.uk

W14

Avonmore Hotel ♦♦♦♦
66 Avonmore Road, Kensington,
London W14 8RS
T: (020) 7603 3121 & 7603 4296
F: (020) 7603 4035
E: avonmore.hotel@dial.pipex.
com
I: www.avonmore.hotel.dial.
pipex.com

Holland Court Hotel ♦♦♦
31-33 Holland Road,
Kensington, London W14 8HJ
T: (020) 7371 1133
F: (020) 7602 9114
E: reservations@
hollandcourthotel.com
I: www.hollandcourthotel.com

WC1

Arran House Hotel ♦♦
77 Gower Street, London
WC1E 6HJ
T: (020) 7636 2186 & 7637 1140
F: (020) 7436 5328
E: arran@dircon.co.uk
I: www.london-hotel.co.uk

Crescent Hotel ♦♦♦
49-50 Cartwright Gardens,
Bloomsbury, London WC1H 9EL
T: (020) 7387 1515
F: (020) 7383 2054
E: General.Enquiries@
CrescentHotelofLondon.com
I: www.CrescentHotelofLondon.
com

Euro Hotel ♦♦♦
53 Cartwright Gardens, London
WC1H 9EL
T: (020) 7387 4321
F: (020) 7383 5044
E: Reception@eurohotel.co.uk
I: www.eurohotel.co.uk

Garth Hotel ♦
69 Gower Street, London
WC1E 6HJ
T: (020) 7636 5761
F: (020) 7637 4854
E: garth.hotel@virgin.net
I: www.garthhotel-london.com

George Hotel ♦♦♦
58-60 Cartwright Gardens,
London WC1H 9EL
T: (020) 7387 8777
F: (020) 7387 8666
E: ghotel@aol.com
I: www.georgehotel.com

Gower House Hotel ♦
57 Gower Street, London
WC1E 6HJ
T: (020) 7636 4685
F: (020) 7636 4685

Guilford House Hotel ♦♦
6 Guilford Street, London
WC1N 1DR
T: (020) 7430 2504
F: (020) 7430 0697
E: guilford-hotel@lineone.net
I: www.guilfordhotel.co.uk

St Athans Hotel ♦
20 Tavistock Place, Russell
Square, London WC1H 9RE
T: (020) 7837 9140 & 7837 9627
F: (020) 7833 8352

Staunton Hotel ♦♦♦♦
13-15 Gower Street,
Bloomsbury, London WC1E 6HE
T: (020) 7580 2740
F: (020) 7580 3554
E: enquiries@stauntonhotel.
com
I: www.stauntonhotel.com

WC2

Royal Adelphi Hotel ♦♦
21 Villiers Street, London
WC2N 6ND
T: (020) 7930 8764
F: (020) 7930 8735
E: info@royaladelphi.co.uk
I: www.royaladelphi.co.uk

OUTER LONDON
BECKENHAM

Amberlea ♦♦
1 Lodge Gardens, Eden Park,
Beckenham, Kent BR3 3DP
T: (020) 8663 3638
F: (020) 8663 3638

BEXLEY

66 Arcadian Avenue ♦♦♦
Bexley, Kent DA5 1JW
T: (020) 8303 5732

**Buxted Lodge Bed and
Breakfast ♦♦**
40 Parkhurst Road, Bexley, Kent
DA5 1AS
T: (01322) 554010 &
07904 299601
E: buxted.lodge@cwcom.net

BEXLEYHEATH

Vivenda House ♦♦♦♦
1 Ferndale Close, Bexleyheath,
Kent DA7 4ES
T: (020) 8304 5486 &
07956 848050
E: francisvivenda@aol.com
I: www.vivendahouse.co.uk

BRENTFORD

Kings Arms ♦♦♦
19 Boston Manor Road,
Brentford, Middlesex TW8 8EA
T: (020) 8560 5860
F: (020) 8847 4416

BROMLEY

Avondale House ♦♦♦♦
56 Avondale Road, Bromley,
BR1 4EP
T: (020) 8402 0844
E: fortis@ukonline.co.uk

Glendevon House Hotel ♦♦
80 Southborough Road, Bickley,
Bromley, BR1 2EN
T: (020) 8467 2183
F: (020) 8295 0701

Westfields ♦♦♦
78 Hayes Lane, Bromley BR2 9EE
T: (020) 8462 5591

CROYDON

63 Addington Road ♦♦♦
Sanderstead, South Croydon,
Surrey CR2 8RD
T: (020) 8657 8776
F: (020) 8657 8776

Alpha Guest House ♦♦
99 Brigstock Road, Thornton
Heath, Surrey CR7 7JL
T: (020) 8684 4011 & 8665 0032
F: (020) 8405 0302

Bramley ♦♦♦
7 Green Court Avenue, Shirley
Park, Croydon, CR0 7LD
T: (020) 8654 6776 &
07909 510061
F: (020) 8654 6776

15A Birdhurst Road ♦♦♦
Croydon, CR2 7EF
T: (0208) 6499116 &
07850 235481
E: mikeaf@lineone.net

**Croydon Friendly Guesthouse
Rating Applied For**
16 St Peter's Road, Croydon,
CR0 1HD
T: (020) 8680 4428 & 07989 924
988
F: (020) 8658 5385
E: bilal@bhasan.fsnet.co.uk

Croydon Hotel ♦♦♦
112 Lower Addiscombe Road,
Croydon, CR0 6AD
T: (020) 8656 7233
F: (020) 8655 0211

Ginetta Guest House ♦♦
32 Rylandes Road, Selsdon,
South Croydon, Surrey CR2 8EA
T: (020) 8657 3132 &
07720 935299

Stocks ♦♦♦
51 Selcroft Road, Purley, Surrey
CR8 1AJ
T: (020) 8660 3054
F: (020) 8660 3054
E: joycestock@ukonline.co.uk

ENFIELD

1 Chinnery Close ♦♦♦
Enfield, Middlesex EN1 4AX
T: (020) 8363 3887
F: (020) 8366 5496

HAMPTON

Friars Cottage ◆◆◆
2B Priory Road, Hampton,
Middlesex TW12 2WR
T: (020) 8287 4699

14 Nightingale Road ◆◆◆◆
Hampton, Middlesex TW12 3HX
T: (020) 8979 8074

Riverine ◆◆◆
Taggs Island, Hampton Court
Road, Hampton, Middlesex
TW12 2HA
T: (020) 89792266
F: (020) 82554001
E: malcolm@cootpoint.
freeserve.co.uk
I: www.feedtheducks.com

HARROW

Central Hotel ◆◆
6 Hindes Road, Harrow,
Middlesex HA1 1SJ
T: (020) 8427 0893
F: (020) 84248797
E: central@hindeshotel.com

Cresent Hotel ◆◆◆
58-62 Welldon Crescent,
Harrow, Middlesex HA1 1QR
T: (020) 8863 5491
F: (020) 8427 5965
E: jivraj@crsnthtl.demon.co.uk
I: www.crsnthtl.demon.co.uk

Hindes Hotel ◆◆◆
8 Hindes Road, Harrow,
Middlesex HA1 1SJ
I: (020) 8427 7468 & 8427 7272
F: (020) 8424 0673
E: reception@hindeshotel.com
I: www.hindeshotel.com

HAYES

Shepiston Lodge ◆◆◆
31 Shepiston Lane, Hayes,
Middlesex UB3 1LJ
T: (020) 8573 0266 & 8569 2536
F: (020) 8569 2536
E: shepistonlodge@aol.com
I: www.shepistonlodge.co.uk

HOUNSLOW

Ashdowne House ◆◆◆◆
9 Pownall Gardens, Hounslow,
Middlesex TW3 1YW
T: (020) 8572 0008
F: (020) 8570 1939
E: mail@ashdownehouse.com
I: www.ashdownehouse.com

Civic Guest House ◆◆
87-89 Lampton Road,
Hounslow, Middlesex TW3 4DP
T: (020) 8572 5107 & 8570 1851
F: (020) 8814 0203
E: enquiries@civicguesthouse.
freeserve.co.uk
I: www.civicguesthouse.
freeserve.co.uk

Lampton Park Guesthouse
◆◆◆
4 Lampton Park Road,
Hounslow, Middlesex TW3 4HS
T: (020) 8572 8622
E: michael.duff1@virgin.net

Shalimar Hotel ◆◆
215-221 Staines Road,
Hounslow, Middlesex TW3 3JJ
T: (020) 8577 7070 &
0500 238239
F: (020) 8569 6789
I: www.s-h-systems.
co.uk/hotels/shalimar.htm

Skylark Bed & Breakfast ◆◆
297 Bath Road, Hounslow,
Middlesex TW3 3DB
T: (020) 8577 8455
F: (020) 8577 8741
E: skylarkgh@ukonline.co.uk
I: web.ukonline.co.uk/skylarkgh

ILFORD

Cranbrook Hotel ◆◆
24 Coventry Road, Ilford, Essex
IG1 4QR
T: (020) 8554 6544 & 8554 4765
F: (020) 8518 1463

Park Hotel ◆◆◆
327 Cranbrook Road, Ilford,
Essex IG1 4UE
T: (020) 8554 9616 & 8554 7187
F: (020) 8518 2700
E: parkhotelilford@
netscapeonline.co.uk
I: www.the-park-hotel.co.uk

ISLEWORTH

80 Bassett Gardens ◆◆
Osterley, Isleworth, Middlesex
TW7 4QY
T: (020) 8570 8362

KENLEY

Appledore ◆◆◆
6 Betula Close, Kenley, Surrey
CR8 5ET
T: (020) 8668 4631
F: (020) 8668 4631

KEW

35 Beechwood Avenue ◆◆◆◆
Kew, Richmond, Surrey
TW9 4DD
T: (020) 8878 0049 &
07990 613821
F: (020) 8878 0049

1 Chelwood Gardens ◆◆◆
Kew, Richmond, Surrey TW9 4JG
T: (020) 8876 8733 &
07860 811998
F: (020) 8255 0171
E: MrsLJGray@aol.com

11 Leyborne Park ◆◆◆◆
Kew, Richmond, Surrey
TW9 3HB
T: (020) 8948 1615 &
07778 123736
F: (020) 8255 1141
E: garriganx2@hotmail.com

40 Marksbury Avenue ◆◆◆
Kew, Richmond, Surrey TW9 4JF
T: (020) 8878 9572 &
07890 696040

West Lodge ◆◆◆
179 Mortlake Road, Kew,
Richmond, Surrey TW9 4AW
T: (020) 8876 0584 & 8876 5375
F: (020) 8876 0584
E: westlodge@thakria.demon.
co.uk

29 West Park Road ◆◆◆
Kew, Richmond, Surrey
TW9 4DA
T: (020) 8878 0505
E: alanbrooklands@aol.uk

MORDEN

28 Monkleigh Road ◆◆
Morden, Surrey SM4 4EW
T: (020) 8542 5595 & 8287 7494

NORTHOLT

**Brenda & Bertie Woosters
Guesthouse** ◆◆◆
5 Doncaster Drive, Northolt,
Middlesex UB5 4AS
T: (020) 8423 5072

PINNER

Delcon ◆◆
468 Pinner Road, Pinner,
Middlesex HA5 5RR
T: (020) 8863 1054
F: (020) 8863 1054

PURLEY

Arcadia ◆◆
212 Brighton Road, Purley,
Surrey CR8 4HB
T: (020) 8668 2486

Conifers ◆◆◆
214 Brighton Road, Purley,
Surrey CR8 4HB
T: (020) 8668 6580 &
(0208) 66686580

Foxley Mount ◆◆◆
44 Foxley Lane, Purley, Surrey
CR8 3EE
T: (020) 8660 9751
F: (020) 8645 9368

Guest House ◆◆
The Nook Guest House, 12
Grasmere Road, Purley, Surrey
CR8 1DU
T: (020) 8660 1742
E: agmandrews@callnet.uk.com

The Maple House ◆◆◆
174 Foxley Lane, Purley, Surrey
CR8 3NF
T: (020) 8407 5123

Purley Cross Guest House
◆◆◆
50 Brighton Road, Purley, Surrey
CR8 2LG
T: (020) 8668 4964
F: (020) 8407 2133
E: purleycross@hotmail.com

Woodlands ◆◆
2 Green Lane, Purley, Surrey
CR8 3PG
T: (020) 8660 3103

RICHMOND

Anna Guest House ◆
37 Church Road, Richmond,
Surrey TW9 1UA
T: (020) 8940 5237

8 Cardigan Mansions ◆◆
19 Richmond Hill, Richmond,
Surrey TW10 6RD
T: (020) 8940 1654 &
07885 405420

Chalon House ◆◆◆◆◆
8 Spring Terrace, Paradise Road,
Richmond, Surrey TW9 1LW
T: (020) 8332 1121
F: (020) 8332 1131
E: virgilioz@aol.com

Doughty Cottage ◆◆◆◆◆
142a Richmond Hill, Richmond,
Surrey TW10 6RN
T: (020) 8332 9434
F: (020) 8332 9434
E: deniseoneill425@
netscapeonline.co.uk
I: www.smoothhound.
co.uk/hotels/doughtycott

Dukes Head Inn ◆◆◆
42 The Vineyards, Richmond,
Surrey TW10 6AW
T: (020) 8948 4557
F: (020) 8948 4557
E: thedukeshead@yahoo.com
I: www.dukeshead.com

Fox House ◆◆◆
Ham Common, Ham, Richmond,
Surrey TW10 5LA
T: (020) 8940 9086 &
07881 588243

Hobart Hall Hotel ◆◆◆
43-47 Petersham Road,
Richmond, Surrey TW10 6UL
T: (020) 8940 0435 & 8940 1702
F: (020) 8332 2996
E: hobarthall@aol.com
I: www.smoothhound.
co.uk/hotels/hobarthall.html

Ivy Cottage ◆◆
Upper Ham Road, Ham
Common, Richmond, Surrey
TW10 5LA
T: (020) 8940 8601
F: (020) 8940 3865
E: taylor@dbta.freeserve.co.uk
I: www.dbta.freeserve.co.uk

Pro Kew Gardens B & B ◆◆◆
15 Pensford Avenue, Kew
Gardens, Richmond, Surrey
TW9 4HR
T: (020) 8876 3354
E: info@prokewbandb.demon.
co.uk

Quinns Hotel ◆◆◆
48 Sheen Road, Richmond,
Surrey TW9 1AW
T: (020) 8940 5444
F: (020) 8940 1828
I: www.quinnshotel.com

Reston Lodge ◆◆◆◆
Petersham Road, Petersham,
Richmond, Surrey TW10 7AD
T: (020) 8332 9350

Richmond Inn Hotel ◆◆◆◆
50-56 Sheen Road, Richmond,
Surrey TW9 1UG
T: (020) 8940 0171
F: (020) 8332 2596

Richmond Park Hotel ◆◆◆
3 Petersham Road, Richmond,
Surrey TW10 6UH
T: (020) 8948 4666
F: (020) 8940 7376
E: richmdpk@globalnet.co.uk

Riverside Hotel ◆◆◆
23 Petersham Road, Richmond,
Surrey TW10 6UH
T: (020) 8940 1339
F: (020) 8948 0967
E: riversidehotel@yahoo.com
I: www.smoothhound.
co.uk/hotels/riversid.html

31 Rothesay Avenue ◆◆◆
Richmond, Surrey TW10 5EB
T: (020) 8876 2331

248 Sandycombe Road ◆◆◆
Kew, Richmond, Surrey TW9 3NP
T: (020) 8940 5970

9 Selwyn Court ◆◆
Church Road, Richmond, Surrey
TW10 6LR
T: (020) 8940 3309

**454 Upper Richmond Road
West** ◆◆◆
Richmond, Surrey TW10 5DY
T: (020) 8876 0327

West Park Gardens ◆◆◆
105 Mortlake Road, Kew,
Richmond, Surrey TW9 4AA
T: (020) 88766842
F: (020) 88766842
E: edwardsnjdr@aol.com

ROMFORD

The Orchard Guest House ◆◆◆
81 Eastern Road, Romford,
RM1 3PB
T: (01708) 744099
F: (01708) 768881
E: johnrt@globalnet.co.uk

SIDCUP

The Chimneys ◆◆◆
6 Clarence Road, Sidcup, Kent
DA14 4DL
T: (020) 8309 1460
F: (020) 83065177

Hilbert House ◆◆◆
Halfway Street, Sidcup, Kent
DA15 8DE
T: (020) 8300 0549 &
07719 721521

SOUTH CROYDON

Dereen ◆◆
14 St Augustine's Avenue, South
Croydon, Surrey CR2 6BS
T: (020) 8686 2075

Owlets ◆◆◆
112 Arundel Avenue, South
Croydon, Surrey CR2 8BH
T: (020) 8657 5213
F: (020) 8657 5213

Waldenbury ◆◆◆
33 Crossways, Selsdon, South
Croydon, Surrey CR2 8JQ
T: (020) 8657 7791
F: (020) 8657 7791

SOUTH HARROW

4 Shaftesbury Avenue ◆◆
South Harrow, Harrow,
Middlesex HA2 0PH
T: (020) 8357 2548 &
07939 017983
E: mckeefourguests@
bushinternet.com

TEDDINGTON

93 Clarence Road ◆◆◆◆
Teddington, Middlesex
TW11 0BN
T: (020) 8977 3459
F: (020) 8943 1560

Glenhurst ◆◆◆
93 Langham Road, Teddington,
Middlesex TW11 9HG
T: (020) 8977 6962 &
07836 782132
F: (020) 8977 6962
E: stayinteddington@aol.com

6 Grove Gardens ◆◆◆
Teddington, Middlesex
TW11 8AP
T: (020) 8977 6066

Hazeldene ◆◆◆◆
58 Hampton Road, Teddington,
Middlesex TW11 0JX
T: (020) 8286 8500
E: glasslisa58@hotmail.com

King Edwards Grove ◆◆◆
Teddington, Middlesex
TW11 9LY
T: (020) 8977 7251

126 Kingston Road ◆◆◆
Teddington, Middlesex
TW11 9JA
T: (020) 8943 9302

187 Kingston Road ◆◆◆
Teddington, Middlesex
TW11 9JN
T: (020) 8977 3392 &
07951 173139
F: 0870 1352140
E: teddingtonaccom@aol.com
I: www.members.aol.
com/teddingtonaccom

**Polly's Bed and Breakfast
◆◆◆**
166 High Street, Teddington,
Middlesex TW11 8HU
T: (020) 8287 1188 &
07767 402231
E: polly31@fsnet.co.uk

THORNTON HEATH

The Lloyd's House ◆◆
41 Moffatt Road, Thornton
Heath, Surrey CR7 8PY
T: (020) 8768 1827

TWICKENHAM

Avalon Cottage ◆◆◆
50 Moor Mead Road, St
Margarets, Twickenham,
TW1 1JS
T: (020) 8744 2178
F: (020) 8891 2444
E: avalon@mead99.freeserve.
co.uk

59 Court Way ◆◆
Twickenham, TW2 7SA
T: (020) 8892 4254 & 8744 0959
F: (020) 87440959

136 London Road ◆◆◆
Twickenham, TW1 1HD
T: (020) 8892 3158 &
07956 499819
E: jenniferjfinnerty@hotmail.
com

St Margarets Guest House ◆◆
53-55 Crown Road, St
Margarets, Twickenham,
TW1 3EJ
T: (020) 8744 2990 &
07836 763872
F: (020) 8744 2953

Mrs Durnham's B&B ◆◆
18 Heathcote Road, St
Margarets, Twickenham,
TW1 1RX
T: (020) 8892 4745 & 077 7916
0298
F: (020) 8892 4745

11 Spencer Road ◆◆◆
11 Spencer Road, Strawberry
Hill, Twickenham, TW2 5TH
T: (020) 8894 5271
F: (020) 8994 4751
E: bruceduff@hotmail.com

Susi Lever ◆◆
27 The Avenue, St Margaret's,
Twickenham, TW1 1QP
T: (020) 8892 7679 &
07703 355793
F: (020) 8892 5596

3 Waldegrave Gardens ◆◆◆
Strawberry Hill, Twickenham,
TW1 4PQ
T: (020) 8892 3523

UPMINSTER

Corner Farm ◆◆◆
Corner Farm, Fen Lane, North
Ockendon, Upminster, Essex
RM14 3RB
T: (01708) 851310
F: (01708) 852025
E: corner.farm@virgin.net

WELLING

De + Dees B & B ◆◆◆◆
91 Welling Way, Welling, Kent
DA16 2RW
T: (020) 8319 1592
F: (020) 8319 1592

WEMBLEY

**Aaron (Wembley Park) Hotel
Ltd ◆**
8 Forty Lane, Wembley,
Middlesex HA9 9EB
T: (020) 8904 6329 & 8908 5711
F: (020) 8385 0472
E: info@aaronhotel.com
I: www.aaronhotel.com

Adelphi Hotel ◆◆◆
4 Forty Lane, Wembley,
Middlesex HA9 9EB
T: (020) 8904 5629 & 89085629
F: (020) 8908 5314
E: adel@dial.pipex.com
I: www.hoteladelphi.co.uk

Arena Hotel ◆◆◆
6 Forty Lane, Wembley,
Middlesex HA9 9EB
T: (020) 8908 0670 & 8904 0019
F: (020) 8908 2007
E: enquiry@arenahotel.fsnet.
co.uk
I: www.arena-hotel.co.uk

Elm Hotel ◆◆◆
1-7 Elm Road, Wembley,
Middlesex HA9 7JA
T: (020) 8902 1764
F: (020) 8903 8365
E: elm.hotel@virgin.net
I: www.elmhotel.co.uk

WORCESTER PARK

The Graye House ◆◆◆
24 The Glebe, Worcester Park,
Surrey KT4 7PF
T: (020) 8330 1277 &
07733 150621
F: (020) 8255 7850
E: graye.house@virgin.net
I: www.smoothhound.co.uk

CUMBRIA

AINSTABLE
Cumbria

Bell House ◆◆◆◆
Ainstable, Carlisle, Cumbria
CA4 9RE
T: (01768) 896255 &
07767 888636
F: (01768) 896255
E: mrobinson@bellhouse.
fsbusiness.co.uk

ALLONBY
Cumbria

Ship Hotel ◆◆◆
Main Street, Allonby, Maryport,
Cumbria CA15 6PD
T: (01900) 881017 & 881115
F: (01900) 881017

ALSTON
Cumbria

Brownside House ◆◆◆
Leadgate, Alston, Cumbria
CA9 3EL
T: (01434) 382169 & 382100
E: brownside_hse@hotmail.com
I: www.cumbria1st.
com/brown_side/index.htm

Greycroft ◆◆◆◆
Middle Park, The Raise, Alston,
Cumbria CA9 3AR
T: (01434) 381383
E: enquiry@greycroft.co.uk
I: www.greycroft.co.uk

AMBLESIDE
Cumbria

Ambleside Lodge ◆◆◆◆
Rothay Road, Ambleside,
Cumbria LA22 0EJ
T: (01539) 431681
F: (01539) 434547
E: cherryho@globalnet.co.uk
I: www.ambleside-lodge.com

Amboseli Lodge ◆◆◆◆
Rothay Road, Ambleside,
Cumbria LA22 0EE
T: (01539) 431110
F: (01539) 488441
E: royfry@assureweb.com
I: www.fryamboseli@aol.com

The Anchorage ◆◆◆
Rydal Road, Ambleside, Cumbria
LA22 9AY
T: (015394) 32046
E: robanj@yahoo.com

**Barnes Fell Guest House
◆◆◆◆**
Low Gale, Ambleside, Cumbria
LA22 0BB
T: (01539) 433311
F: (01539) 43493

Borrans Park Hotel ◆◆◆◆
Borrans Road, Ambleside,
Cumbria LA22 0EN
T: (01539) 433454
F: (01539) 433003
E: mail@borranspark.co.uk
I: www.borranspark.co.uk

Brantfell House ◆◆◆◆
Rothay Road, Ambleside,
Cumbria LA22 0EE
T: (01539) 432239 & 434124
F: (01539) 432239
E: brantfell@kencomp.net

Broadview ◆◆◆
Low Fold, Lake Road, Ambleside,
Cumbria LA22 0DN
T: (01539) 432431
E: enquiries@
broadview-guesthouse.co.uk
I: www.broadview-guesthouse.
co.uk

3 Cambridge Villas ◆◆◆
Church Street, Ambleside,
Cumbria LA22 9DL
T: (01539) 432307

Claremont House ◆◆◆
Compston Road, Ambleside,
Cumbria LA22 9DJ
T: (01539) 433448
F: (01539) 433448
E: olwenm@supanet.com

Compston House ◆◆◆◆
Compston Road, Ambleside,
Cumbria LA22 9DJ
T: (01539) 432305
E: compston@globalnet.co.uk
I: www.compstonhouse.co.uk

The Dower House ◆◆◆◆
Wray Castle, Ambleside, Cumbria
LA22 0JA
T: (01539) 433211

Easedale Guest House ◆◆◆◆
Compston Road, Ambleside,
Cumbria LA22 9DJ
T: (01539) 432112
F: (01539) 432112
E: soar@easedaleambleside.
co.uk
I: www.easedaleambleside.co.uk

Elder Grove ◆◆◆◆
Lake Road, Ambleside, Cumbria
LA22 0DB
T: (015394) 32504
F: (015394) 32504
E: info@eldergrove.co.uk
I: www.eldergrove.co.uk

Fern Cottage ◆◆◆
6 Waterhead Terrace, Ambleside,
Cumbria LA22 0HA
T: (01539) 433007

Ferndale Hotel ◆◆◆
Lake Road, Ambleside, Cumbria
LA22 0DB
T: (01539) 432207

Fisherbeck Garden ◆◆◆
Old Lake Road, Ambleside,
Cumbria LA22 0DH
T: (015394) 33088
E: janice@fisherbeck.net1.co.uk

Foxghyll ◆◆◆◆
Under Loughrigg, Ambleside,
Cumbria LA22 9LL
T: (015394) 33292
E: foxghyll@hotmail.com
I: www.smoothhound.
co.uk/hotels/foxghyll.html

Freshfields ◆◆◆◆
Wansfell Road, Ambleside,
Cumbria LA22 0EG
T: (01539) 434469
F: (01539) 434469
E: info@freshfieldsguesthouse.
co.uk
I: www.freshfieldsguesthouse.
co.uk

The Gables ◆◆◆
Church Walk, Ambleside,
Cumbria LA22 9DJ
T: (01539) 433272
F: (01539) 434734
E: the.old.vicarage@kencomp.
net
I: www.oldvicarageambleside.
co.uk

Ghyll Head Hotel ◆◆◆
Waterhead, Ambleside, Cumbria
LA22 0HD
T: (01539) 432360
F: (01539) 434062
E: ghyllhead@hotel.fsnet.co.uk
I: www.hotelcumbria.com

Glenside ◆◆◆◆
Old Lake Road, Ambleside,
Cumbria LA22 0DP
T: (01539) 432635
E: david-janice@
glenside22fsnet.co.uk

Greenbank ◆◆◆◆
Skelwith Bridge, Ambleside,
Cumbria LA22 9NW
T: (01539) 433236
E: greenbank@bigwig.net
I: www.visitgreenbank.co.uk

**Grey Friar Lodge Country
House Hotel** ◆◆◆◆◆
Clappersgate, Ambleside,
Cumbria LA22 9NE
T: (01539) 433158
F: (01539) 433158
E: greyfriar@veen.freeserve.
co.uk
I: www.cumbria-hotels.co.uk

High Wray Farm ◆◆◆◆
High Wray, Ambleside, Cumbria
LA22 0JE
T: (01539) 432280
E: sheila@highwrayfarm.co.uk
I: www.highwrayfarm.co.uk

Highfield
Rating Applied For
Lake Road, Ambleside, Cumbria
LA22 0DB
T: (015394) 32671
E: t.m.wright@talk21.com

Hillsdale ◆◆◆
Church Street, Ambleside,
Cumbria LA22 0BT
T: (01539) 433174
F: (01539) 431226
E: gstaley@hillsdale.freeserve.
co.uk
I: www.hillsdale.freeserve.co.uk

Holmeshead Farm ◆◆◆◆
Skelwith Fold, Ambleside,
Cumbria LA22 0HU
T: (01539) 433048
I: www.amblesideonline.co.uk

Howe Farm ◆◆◆◆
Hawkshead, Ambleside, Cumbria
LA22 0QB
T: (015394) 36345
E: howefarm@nascr.net

Kent House ◆◆◆◆
Lake Road, Ambleside, Cumbria
LA22 0AD
T: (015394) 33279
F: (015394) 33279
E: info@kent-house.com
I: www.kent-house.com

Lattendales Guest House ◆◆◆
Compston Road, Ambleside,
Cumbria LA22 9DJ
T: (01539) 432368
E: admin@latts.freeserve.co.uk
I: www.latts.freeserve.co.uk

Laurel Villa ◆◆◆
Lake Road, Ambleside, Cumbria
LA22 0DB
T: (01539) 433240
E: laurelvilla_hotel@hotmail.
com
I: www.hotel-ambleside.co.uk

Lyndale ◆◆◆
Low Fold, Lake Road, Ambleside,
Cumbria LA22 0DN
T: (01539) 434244
E: wendy@lyndale-guesthouse.
co.uk
I: www.lyndale-guesthouse.
co.uk

Lyndhurst Hotel ◆◆◆
Wansfell Road, Ambleside,
Cumbria LA22 0EG
T: (01539) 432421
F: (01539) 432421
E: lyndhurst@amblesidehotels.
co.uk
I: www.amblesidehotels.co.uk

Meadowbank ◆◆◆
Rydal Road, Ambleside, Cumbria
LA22 9BA
T: (01539) 432710 &
07989 623450
F: (01539) 432710
E: catherine@meadowbank10.
freeserve.co.uk

Melrose ◆◆◆
Church Street, Ambleside,
Cumbria LA22 0BT
T: (01539) 432500

Norwood House
Rating Applied For
Church Street, Ambleside,
Cumbria LA22 0BT
T: (01539) 433349
F: (01539) 434938
E: mail@norwoodhouse.net
I: www.norwoodhouse.net

The Old Vicarage ◆◆◆◆
Vicarage Road, Ambleside,
Cumbria LA22 9DH
T: (01539) 433364
F: (01539) 434734
E: theoldvicarage@kencomp.net
I: www.oldvicarageambleside.
co.uk

Red Bank Guest House ◆◆◆◆
Wansfell Road, Ambleside,
Cumbria LA22 0EG
T: (01539) 434637
F: (01539) 434637
E: info@red-bank.co.uk
I: www.red-bank.co.uk

Riverside Hotel ◆◆◆◆
Under Loughrigg, Rothay Bridge,
Ambleside, Cumbria LA22 9LJ
T: (01539) 432395
F: (01539) 432440
E: info@riverside-at-ambleside.
co.uk
I: www.riverside-at-ambleside.
co.uk

**Rowanfield Country
Guesthouse** ◆◆◆◆◆
Kirkstone Road, Ambleside,
Cumbria LA22 9ET
T: (01539) 433686
F: (01539) 431569
E: email@rowanfield.com
I: www.rowanfield.com

The Rysdale Hotel ◆◆◆
Rothay Road, Ambleside,
Cumbria LA22 0EE
I: (01539) 432140 & 433999
F: (01539) 433999
I: www.rysdalehotel.co.uk

**Stepping Stones Country
House** ◆◆◆◆
Under Loughrigg, Ambleside,
Cumbria LA22 9LN
T: (01539) 433552
F: (01539) 433552
E: info@
steppingstonesambleside.com
I: www.
steppingstonesambleside.com

Thorneyfield Guest House
◆◆◆◆
Compston Road, Ambleside,
Cumbria LA22 9DJ
T: (015394) 32464
F: (015394) 32464
E: info@thorneyfield.co.uk
I: www.thorneyfield.co.uk

Tock How Farm ◆◆◆
High Wray, Ambleside, Cumbria
LA22 0JF
T: (01539) 436106 & 436294
F: (01539) 436294
I: www.tock-how-farm.com

Walmar Hotel ◆◆◆
Lake Road, Ambleside, Cumbria
LA22 0DB
T: (01539) 432454

Wanslea Guest House ◆◆◆◆
Lake Road, Ambleside, Cumbria
LA22 0DN
T: (01539) 433884
F: (01539) 433884
E: wanslea.guesthouse@virgin.
net

APPLEBY-IN-WESTMORLAND
Cumbria

Bridge End Farm ◆◆◆◆◆
Kirkby Thore, Penrith, Cumbria
CA10 1UZ
T: (01768) 361362

Broom House ◆◆◆
Long Marton, Appleby-in-
Westmorland, Cumbria
CA16 6JP
T: (01768) 361318
F: (01768) 361318
E: sandra@bland01.freeserve.
co.uk

**Sycamore House Bed &
Breakfast**
Rating Applied For
Dufton, Appleby-in-
Westmorland, Cumbria
CA16 6DB
T: (01768) 351296
E: o_halloran@hotmail.com

ARNSIDE
Cumbria

Willowfield Hotel ◆◆◆◆
The Promenade, Arnside,
Cumbria LA5 0AD
T: (01524) 761354
E: info@willowfield.net1.co.uk
I: www.willowfield.uk.com

BARROW-IN-FURNESS
Cumbria

Arlington House Hotel and Restaurant ◆◆◆◆
200-202 Abbey Road, Barrow-in-Furness, Cumbria LA14 5LD
T: (01229) 831976
F: (01229) 870990
E: arlington@tinyworld.co.uk

BASSENTHWAITE LAKE
Cumbria

Herdwick Croft Guest House ◆◆◆
Bassenthwaite, Keswick, Cumbria CA12 4RD
T: (01768) 776241
E: stayinthelakes@BTconnect.com
I: www.stayinthelakes.co.uk

Kiln Hill Barn ◆◆◆
Bassenthwaite, Keswick, Cumbria CA12 4RG
T: (01768) 776454
F: (01768) 776454
E: ken@kilnhillbarn.freeserve.co.uk
I: www.kilnhillbarn.co.uk

Lakeside ◆◆◆◆
Dubwath, Bassenthwaite Lake, Cockermouth, Cumbria CA13 9YD
T: (01768) 776358
F: (01768) 776163

Link House ◆◆◆◆
Bassenthwaite Lake, Cockermouth, Cumbria CA13 9YD
T: (01768) 776291
F: (01768) 776670
E: linkhouse@lineone.net
I: www.link-house.co.uk

Ravenstone Lodge ◆◆◆◆
Bassenthwaite, Keswick, Cumbria CA12 4QG
T: (017687) 76629 & 76638
F: (017687) 76629
E: ravenstone.lodge@talk21.com
I: www.ravenstonelodge.co.uk

Robin Hood House ◆◆◆◆
Bassenthwaite, Keswick, Cumbria CA12 4RJ
T: (01768) 776296

BEETHAM
Cumbria

Barn Close/North West Birds ◆◆◆
Beetham, Milnthorpe, Cumbria LA7 7AL
T: (01539) 563191 & 07752 620658
F: (01539) 563191
E: mike@nwbirds.co.uk
I: www.nwbirds.co.uk

BIRKBY
Cumbria

The Retreat Hotel and Restaurant ◆◆◆◆
Birkby, Maryport, Cumbria CA15 6RG
T: (01900) 814056

BOLTON
Cumbria

Eden Grove Farm House ◆◆◆◆
Bolton, Appleby-in-Westmorland, Cumbria CA16 6AX
T: (01768) 362321
E: edengrovecumbria@aol.com
I: www.ukworld.net/edengrove

Tarka House ◆◆◆
Bolton, Appleby-in-Westmorland, Cumbria CA16 6AW
T: (01768) 361422 & 0771 966 1514

BOOT
Cumbria

The Burnmoor Inn ◆◆◆
Boot, Holmrook, Cumbria CA19 1TG
T: (01946) 723224
F: (01946) 723337
E: stay@burnmoor.co.uk
I: www.burnmoor.co.uk

BORROWDALE
Cumbria

Greenbank Country House Hotel ◆◆◆◆
Borrowdale, Keswick, Cumbria CA12 5UY
T: (01768) 777215
F: (01768) 777215
E: jeanwwood@lineone.net

Hazel Bank Country House ◆◆◆◆◆
Rosthwaite, Borrowdale, Keswick, Cumbria CA12 5XB
T: (01768) 777248
F: (01767) 877373
E: enquiries@hazelbankhotel.co.uk
I: www.hazelbankhotel.co.uk

BOWLAND BRIDGE
Cumbria

Hare and Hounds Country Inn ◆◆◆
Bowland Bridge, Grange-over-Sands, Cumbria LA11 6NN
T: (01539) 568333 & 568777
F: (01539) 568993
E: innthelakes@supanet.com
I: www.bowlandbridge.com

BOWNESS-ON-SOLWAY
Cumbria

Maia Lodge ◆◆◆
Bowness-on-Solway, Carlisle CA7 5BH
T: (01697) 351955

Wallsend ◆◆◆◆
The Old Rectory, Church Lane, Bowness-on-Solway, Carlisle CA7 5AF
T: 016973 51055
E: wallsend@btinternet.com
I: www.wallsend.net

BOWNESS-ON-WINDERMERE
Cumbria

Aphrodites Themed Accommodation ◆◆◆◆
Longtail Hill, Bowness-on-Windermere, Windermere, Cumbria LA23 2EQ
T: (01539) 446702
E: enquires@dalegarthe.demon.co.uk
I: www.dalegarthe.demon./bordriggshtm.co.uk

Beechwood Private Hotel ◆◆◆◆
South Craig, Beresford Road, Bowness-on-Windermere, Windermere, Cumbria LA23 2JG
T: (015394) 43403
F: (015394) 43403

Belsfield House ◆◆◆◆
4 Belsfield Terrace, Kendal Road, Bowness-on-Windermere, Windermere, Cumbria LA23 3EQ
T: (01539) 445823

Biskey Howe Villa Hotel ◆◆◆
Craig Walk, Bowness-on-Windermere, Windermere, Cumbria LA23 3AX
T: (01539) 443988
F: (01539) 488379
E: biskey-howe@lakes-pages.com
I: www.biskey-howe-hotel.co.uk

Craig Wood Guest House ◆◆◆
119 Craig Walk, Bowness-on-Windermere, Windermere, Cumbria LA23 3AX
T: (015394) 44914

Elim Lodge ◆◆◆
Biskey Howe Road, Bowness-on-Windermere, Windermere, Cumbria LA23 2JP
T: (01539) 447299
F: (01539) 447299
E: enquiries@elimlodge.co.uk
I: www.elimlodge.co.uk

Latimer House ◆◆◆
Lake Road, Bowness-on-Windermere, Windermere, Cumbria LA23 2JJ
T: (01539) 446888
F: (01539) 446888
E: latimerhouse@hotmail.com
I: www.latimerhouse.co.uk

Laurel Cottage ◆◆◆◆
St Martin's Square, Kendal Road, Bowness-on-Windermere, Windermere, Cumbria LA23 3EF
T: (01539) 445594
F: (01539) 445594
E: enquiries@laurelcottage-bnb.co.uk
I: www.laurelcottage-bnb.co.uk

Little Longtail ◆◆◆
Ferry view, Bowness-on-Windermere, Windermere, Cumbria LA23 3JB
T: (01539) 443884

The Lonsdale ◆◆◆
Lake Road, Bowness-on-Windermere, Windermere, Cumbria LA23 2JJ
T: (015394) 43348
F: (015394) 43348
E: lonsdale@fsbdial.co.uk

Lowfell ◆◆◆◆
Ferney Green, Bowness-on-Windermere, Windermere, Cumbria LA23 3ES
T: (015394) 45612 & 48411
F: (015394) 48411
E: lowfell@talk21.com
I: www.low-fell.co.uk

White Foss ◆◆◆◆
Longtail Hill, Bowness-on-Windermere, Windermere, Cumbria LA23 3JD
T: (015394) 46593
E: nicholson@whitefoss.freeserve.co.uk

BRAITHWAITE
Cumbria

Coledale Inn ◆◆◆
Braithwaite, Keswick, Cumbria CA12 5TN
T: (01768) 778272

Maple Bank ◆◆◆◆
Braithwaite, Keswick, Cumbria CA12 5RY
T: (01768) 778229
F: (01768) 778000
E: maplebank@aol.com
I: www.maplebank.co.uk

BRAMPTON
Cumbria

Blacksmiths Arms Hotel ◆◆◆
Talkin Village, Brampton, Cumbria CA8 1LE
T: (01697) 73452
F: (01697) 73396

Howard House Farm ◆◆◆◆
Gilsland, Carlisle CA8 7AJ
T: (01697) 747285

Langthwaite ◆◆◆
Lanercost Road, Brampton, Cumbria CA8 1EN
T: (01697) 72883
E: anneharding@nicetoseeyou.co.uk

Low Rigg Farm ◆◆◆
Walton, Brampton, Cumbria CA8 2DX
T: (01697) 73233
E: lowrigg@lineone.net
I: www.smoothhound.co.uk/hotels/lowrigg.html

New Mills House ◆◆◆
Brampton, Cumbria CA8 2QS
T: (01697) 73376
F: (01697) 73457
E: newmills@btinternet.com
I: www.info@newmillshouse.co.uk

Oakwood Park Hotel ◆◆◆
Longtown Road, Brampton, Cumbria CA8 2AP
T: (01697) 72436 & 42679
F: (01697) 72436
E: donal.collier@amserve.net

South View ◆◆◆
Banks, Brampton, Cumbria CA8 2JH
T: (016977) 2309
E: sandrahodgson@southviewbanks.f9.co.uk
I: www.southviewbanks.f9.co.uk

Vallum Barn ◆◆◆◆
Irthington, Carlisle CA6 4NN
T: (01697) 742478

Walton High Rigg ◆◆◆
Walton, Brampton, Cumbria CA8 2AZ
T: (01697) 72117

BRIGSTEER
Cumbria

Low Plain ◆◆◆◆
Brigsteer, Kendal, Cumbria LA8 8AX
T: (01539) 568464
F: (01539) 568916
E: farmhouse@lowplain.co.uk
I: www.lowplain.co.uk

BROUGH
Cumbria

River View ◆◆◆
Brough, Kirkby Stephen,
Cumbria CA17 4BZ
T: (017683) 41894
F: (017683) 41894
E: riverviewbb@talk21.com

BROUGHAM
Cumbria

Keepers Cottage ◆◆◆
Brougham, Penrith, Cumbria
CA10 2DE
T: (01768) 865280 &
07790 660427
F: (01768) 865280
E: stay@keeperscottage.co.uk
I: www.keeperscottage.co.uk

BROUGHTON-IN-FURNESS
Cumbria

Broom Hill ◆◆◆◆
New Street, Broughton-in-
Furness, Cumbria LA20 6JD
T: (01229) 716358 &
0797 4135971
F: (01229) 716358

The Dower House ◆◆◆
High Duddon, Broughton-in-
Furness, Cumbria LA20 6ET
T: (01229) 716279
F: (01229) 716279

Manor Arms ◆◆◆
The Square, Broughton-in-
Furness, Cumbria LA20 6HY
T: (01229) 716286
F: (01229) 716729

Middlesyke ◆◆◆◆
Church Street, Broughton-in-
Furness, Cumbria LA20 6ER
T: (01229) 716549

Oak Bank ◆◆
Ulpha, Broughton-in-Furness,
Cumbria LA20 6DZ
T: (01229) 716393

The Workshop Studios ◆◆◆◆
Church Street, Broughton-in-
Furness, Cumbria LA20 6HJ
T: (01229) 716159
F: (01229) 716159
E: workshop.accom@virgin.net

CALDBECK
Cumbria

The Briars ◆◆◆
Friar Row, Caldbeck, Wigton,
Cumbria CA7 8DS
T: (01697) 478633

Gate House ◆◆◆
Caldbeck, Wigton, Cumbria
CA7 8EL
T: (01697) 478092
E: ray@caldbeckgatehouse.
co.uk
I: www.caldbeckgatehouse.co.uk

Swaledale Watch ◆◆◆◆
Whelpo, Caldbeck, Wigton,
Cumbria CA7 8HQ
T: (01697) 478409
F: (01697) 478409
E: nan.savage@talk21.com

CARLETON
Cumbria

River Forge Bed and Breakfast
◆◆◆◆
River Forge, Carleton, Carlisle
CA4 0AA
T: (01228) 523569

Terracotta Restaurant ◆◆◆◆
London Road, Carleton, Carlisle
CA1 3DP
T: (01228) 524433 &
07879 846630
F: (01228) 524433
I: www.terracotta-restaurant.
co.uk

CARLISLE
Cumbria

Abbey Court ◆◆◆◆
24 London Road, Carlisle,
CA1 2EL
T: (01228) 528696
F: (01228) 528696

Ashleigh House ◆◆◆◆
46 Victoria Place, Carlisle,
CA1 1EX
T: (01228) 521631

Avondale ◆◆◆◆
3 St Aidan's Road, Carlisle,
CA1 1LT
T: (01228) 523012
F: (01228) 523012
E: www.beeanbee@hotmail.
com
I: www.beeanbee.co.uk

Bessiestown ◆◆◆◆◆
Catlowdy, Longtown, Carlisle
CA6 5QP
T: (01228) 577219 & 577019
F: (01228) 577019
E: bestbb2000@cs.com
I: bessiestown.co.uk

Brooklyn House ◆◆◆
42 Victoria Place, Carlisle,
CA1 1EX
T: (01228) 590002

Caldew View ◆◆◆
Metcalfe Street, Denton Holme,
Carlisle, CA2 5EU
T: (01228) 595837

Calreena Guest House ◆◆
123 Warwick Road, Carlisle,
CA1 1JZ
T: (01228) 525020 & 598260

Chatsworth Guesthouse ◆◆◆
22 Chatsworth Square, Carlisle,
CA1 1HF
T: (01228) 524023
F: (01228) 524023
E: chatsworth22@aol.com
I: www.visitcarlise.com

Claremont Guest House ◆◆◆
30 London Road, Carlisle,
CA1 2EL
T: (01228) 524691
F: (01228) 524691

Corner House Hotel and Bar
◆◆◆
4 Grey Street, Off London Road,
Carlisle, Cumbria CA1 2JP
T: (01228) 533239
F: (01228) 546628

Cornerways Guest House
◆◆◆◆
107 Warwick Road, Carlisle,
CA1 1EA
T: (01228) 521733

Courtfield House ◆◆◆◆
169 Warwick Road, Carlisle,
CA1 1LP
T: (01228) 522767
E: mdawes@courtfieldhouse.
fsnet.co.uk

Croft End ◆◆◆
Hurst, Ivegill, Carlisle CA4 0NL
T: (01768) 484362 &
07762 346349

Dalroc ◆◆◆
411 Warwick Road, Carlisle,
CA1 2RZ
T: (01228) 542805
E: www.dalroc.co.uk

East View Guest House ◆◆◆
110 Warwick Road, Carlisle,
CA1 1JU
T: (01228) 522112
F: (01228) 522112
I: www.guesthousecarlisle.co.uk

1 Etterby Street ◆◆◆
Stanwix, Carlisle, Cumbria
CA3 9JB
T: (01228) 547285 & 0789 994
8711

Fern Lee Guest House ◆◆◆◆
9 St Aidans Road, Carlisle,
CA1 1LT
T: (01228) 511930
F: (01228) 511930

Hazeldene Guest House ◆◆◆
Orton Grange, Wigton Road,
Carlisle, CA5 6LA
T: (01228) 711953

Howard Lodge Guesthouse
◆◆◆◆
90 Warwick Road, Carlisle,
CA1 1JU
T: (01228) 529842

Kates Guest House ◆◆◆
6 Lazonby Terrace, London Road,
Harraby Green, Carlisle, CA1 2PZ
T: (01228) 539577 & 0776 980
6321
E: katesguesthouse@hotmail.
com

Langleigh House ◆◆◆◆
6 Howard Place, Carlisle,
CA1 1HR
T: (01228) 530440
F: (01228) 530440
E: james@langleigh.f9.co.uk
I: www.langleigh.f9.co.uk

Lynebank House ◆◆◆◆
Westlinton, Carlisle CA6 6AA
T: (01228) 792820
F: (01228) 792820
E: jan@lynebank.co.uk
I: www.lynebank.co.uk

Marchmain House ◆◆◆◆
151 Warwick Road, Carlisle,
CA1 1LU
T: (01228) 529551
F: (01228) 529551

Naworth Guest House ◆◆◆◆
33 Victoria Place, Carlisle,
CA1 1HP
T: (01228) 521645
E: stay@naworth.com
I: www.naworth.com

New Pallyards ◆◆◆◆
Hethersgill, Carlisle CA6 6HZ
T: (01228) 577308
F: (01228) 577308
E: info@newpallyards.freeserve.
co.uk
I: www.newpallyards.freeserve.
co.uk

Newfield Grange Hotel ◆◆◆
Newfield Drive, Kingstown,
Carlisle CA3 0AF
T: (01228) 819926
F: (01228) 546323
E: bb@newfield53.freeserve.
co.uk
I: www.newfield53.freeserve.
co.uk
(木)

Number Thirty One ◆◆◆◆◆
31 Howard Place, Carlisle,
CA1 1HR
T: (01228) 597080
F: (01228) 597080
E: bestpep@aol.com
I: number31.freeservers.com

Stratheden ◆◆◆◆
93 Warwick Road, Carlisle,
CA1 1EB
T: (01228) 520192

Vallum House Garden Hotel
◆◆◆
Burgh Road, Carlisle, CA2 7NB
T: (01228) 521860

Warren Guesthouse ◆◆◆
368 Warwick Road, Carlisle,
CA1 2RU
T: (01228) 533663 & 512916
F: (01228) 533663

Warwick Lodge ◆◆◆◆
112 Warwick Road, Carlisle,
CA1 1LF
T: (01228) 523796
F: (01228) 546789
E: warwick112@aol.com

White Lea Guest House ◆◆◆
191 Warwick Road, Carlisle,
CA1 1LP
T: (01228) 533139
F: (01228) 533139

CARTMEL
Cumbria

Bank Court Cottage ◆◆◆
The Square, Cartmel, Grange-
over-Sands, Cumbria LA11 6QB
T: (01539) 536593 &
07798 790710
F: (01539) 536593

Prior's Yeat
Rating Applied For
Aynsome Road, Cartmel,
Grange-over-Sands, Cumbria
LA11 6PR
T: (01539) 535178
F: (01539) 535178
E: priorsyeat@hotmail.com

CARTMEL FELL
Cumbria

Lightwood Farmhouse Country
Guesthouse◆◆◆◆
Cartmel Fell, Grange-over-
Sands, Cumbria LA11 6NP
T: (01539) 531454
T: (01595) 31454
E: enquiries@
lightwoodguesthouse.co.uk
I: www.lightwoodguesthouse.
co.uk

COCKERMOUTH
Cumbria

The Melbreak Hotel ◆◆◆◆
Winscales Road, Little Clifton,
Workington, Cumbria CA14 1XS
T: (01900) 61443
F: (01900) 606589

Rose Cottage ♦♦♦
Lorton Road, Cockermouth,
Cumbria CA13 9DX
T: (01900) 822189
F: (01900) 822189
I: www.rosecottageguest.co.uk

Arrowfield Country Guest House ♦♦♦♦
Little Arrow, Coniston, Cumbria
LA21 8AU
T: (01539) 441741

Bank Ground ♦♦♦♦
East of Lake, Coniston, Cumbria
LA21 8AA
T: (01539) 441264
F: (01539) 441900
E: info@bankground.co.uk
I: www.bankground.co.uk

Beech Tree Guest House ♦♦♦♦
Yewdale Road, Coniston,
Cumbria LA21 8DX
T: (01539) 441717

Brigg House ♦♦♦♦
Torver, Coniston, Cumbria
LA21 8AY
T: (01539) 441592
F: (01539) 441092
E: brigg.house@virgin.net
I: www.brigghouse.co.uk

Coniston Lodge ♦♦♦♦♦
Station Road, Coniston, Cumbria
LA21 8HH
T: (015394) 41201
F: (015394) 41201
E: info@coniston-lodge.com
I: www.coniston-lodge.com

Crown Hotel ♦♦♦♦
Coniston, Cumbria LA21 8EA
T: (01539) 441243
F: (01539) 441804
E: enntiidus@
crown-hotel-coniston.com
I: www.crown-hotel-coniston.
com

Cruachan ♦♦♦♦
Collingwood Close, Coniston,
Cumbria LA21 8DZ
T: (01539) 441628
F: (01539) 441628
E: cruachan21@lineone.net

How Head Cottage ♦♦♦
East of Lake, Coniston, Cumbria
LA21 8AA
T: (01539) 441594
E: howhead@lineone.net
I: www.howheadcottages.co.uk

Lakeland House ♦♦♦
Tilberthwaite Avenue, Coniston,
Cumbria LA21 8ED
T: (01539) 441303
E: lakelandhouse_coniston@
hotmail.com

Oaklands ♦♦♦
Yewdale Road, Coniston,
Cumbria LA21 8DX
T: (01539) 441245
F: (01539) 441245

Old Rectory Hotel ♦♦♦♦
Torver, Coniston, Cumbria
LA21 8AX
T: (015394) 41353
F: (015394) 41156
E: enquiries@
theoldrectoryhotel.com

Orchard Cottage ♦♦♦♦
18 Yewdale Road, Coniston,
Cumbria LA21 8DU
T: (01539) 441373

Shepherds Villa ♦♦♦
Tilberthwaite Avenue, Coniston,
Cumbria LA21 8ED
T: (01539) 441337
F: (01539) 441337

Sunny Brae Cottage ♦♦♦
Haws Bank, Coniston, Cumbria
LA21 8AR
T: (01539) 441654 & 441532
F: (01539) 441532
E: sunnybraecottage@aol.com

Thwaite Cottage ♦♦♦♦
Waterhead, Coniston, Cumbria
LA21 8AJ
T: (01539) 441367
E: m@thwaitcot.freeserve.co.uk
I: www.thwaitcot.freeserve.co.uk

Townson Ground ♦♦♦♦
East of Lake Road, Coniston,
Cumbria LA21 8AA
T: (015394) 41272
F: (015394) 41110
E: info@townsonground.co.uk
I: www.townsonground.co.uk

Wheelgate Country Guesthouse ♦♦♦♦♦
Little Arrow, Coniston, Cumbria
LA21 8AU
T: (01539) 441418
F: (01539) 441114
E: wheelgate@
conistoncottages.co.uk
I: www.wheelgate.co.uk

Wilson Arms ♦♦♦
Torver, Coniston, Cumbria
LA21 8BB
T: (01539) 441237
F: (01539) 441590

Hillfarm House ♦♦♦♦
Cowgill, Sedbergh, Cumbria
LA10 5RF
T: (01539) 625144
F: (01539) 625144
I: homepage.ntworld.com/r.
metcalfe2

Mitchelland House ♦♦♦♦
Steeles Lane, Crook, Kendal,
Cumbria LA8 8LL
T: (01539) 448589
E: marie.mitchelland@talk21.
com

Crosby House ♦♦♦♦
Crosby-on-Eden, Carlisle
CA6 4QZ
T: (01228) 573239
F: (01228) 573338
E: enquiries@norbyways.
demon.co.uk
I: www.northumbria-byways.
com/crosby

Wickerslack Farm ♦♦♦
Crosby Ravensworth, Penrith,
Cumbria CA10 3LN
T: (01931) 715236

Crosthwaite House ♦♦♦♦
Crosthwaite, Kendal, Cumbria
LA8 8BP
T: (01539) 568264
F: (01539) 568264
E: bookings@crosthwaitehouse.
co.uk
I: www.crosthwaitehouse.co.uk

The Punch Bowl Inn ♦♦♦♦
Crosthwaite, Kendal, Cumbria
LA8 8HR
T: (01539) 568237
F: (01539) 568875
E: enquiries@punchbowl.fsnet.
co.uk
I: www.punchbowl.fsnet.co.uk

The Black Swan Inn ♦♦♦♦
Culgaith, Penrith, Cumbria
CA10 1QW
T: (01768) 88223
F: (01768) 88223

Cumrew House ♦♦♦♦
Cumrew, Heads Nook, Carlisle
CA8 9DD
T: (01768) 896115
E: rabduff@aol.com
I: www.countrysport-lodge.com

Park House Farm ♦♦♦
Dalemain, Penrith, Cumbria
CA11 0HB
T: (01768) 486212
F: (01768) 486212
E: park.house@faxvia.net
I: www.eden-in-cumbria.
co.uk/parkhouse

Black Dog Inn ♦♦
Holmes Green, Broughton Road,
Dalton-in-Furness, Cumbria
LA15 8JP
T: (01229) 462561 &
07931 751282
F: (01229) 468036
E: jack@blackdoginn.freeserve.
co.uk

George and Dragon Hotel
♦♦♦
Main Street, Dent, Sedbergh,
Cumbria LA10 5QL
T: (01539) 625256

Smithy Fold ♦♦♦
Whernside, Dent, Sedbergh,
Cumbria LA10 5RE
T: (01539) 625368

Stone Close Tea Shop ♦♦♦
Main Street, Dent, Sedbergh,
Cumbria LA10 5QL
T: (01539) 625231
F: (01539) 726567
E: accommodation@stoneclose.
co.uk
I: www.stoneclose.co.uk

Sun Inn ♦♦♦
Main Street, Dent, Sedbergh,
Cumbria LA10 5QL
T: (01539) 625208 & 625256
I: www.dentbrewery.co.uk/

Old Vicarage Guest House
♦♦♦
Oaklands, Egremont, Cumbria
CA22 2NX
T: (01946) 841577

Elterwater Park ♦♦♦♦
Skelwith Bridge, Ambleside,
Cumbria LA22 9NP
T: (01539) 432227
F: (01539) 431768
E: enquiries@elterwater.com
I: www.elterwater.com

High Side Farm ♦♦♦♦
Embleton, Cockermouth,
Cumbria CA13 9TN
T: (017687) 76893
E: marshall@highsidehols.co.
freeserve.co.uk

Forest How ♦♦♦
Eskdale, Holmrook, Cumbria
CA19 1TR
T: (019467) 23201
F: (019467) 23190
E: fcarter@easynet.co.uk
I: www.
foresthow-eskdale-cumbria.
co.uk/

The Gatehouse Outward Bound
♦♦♦
Eskdale, Holmrook, Cumbria
CA19 1TE
T: (019467) 23281
F: (019467) 23393
E: professional@
outwardbound-uk.org
I: www.outwardbound-uk.org

Woolpack Inn ♦♦♦
Boot, Eskdale, Holmrook,
Cumbria CA19 1TH
T: (01946) 723230
F: (01946) 723230
E: woolpack@eskdale.dial.
lakesnet.co.uk
I: www.insites.
co.uk/guide//cumbria/accom/
woolpack

High Windy Hall Hotel and Restaurant♦♦♦♦
Middleton-in-Teesdale Road,
Garrigill, Alston, Cumbria
CA9 3EZ
T: (01434) 381547
F: (01434) 382477
E: sales@hwh.u-net.com
I: www.hwh.u-net.com

Bush Nook ♦♦♦♦
Upper Denton, Gilsland, Carlisle
CA8 7AF
T: (01697) 747194
F: (01697) 747790
E: paulaibarton@bushnook.
freeserve.co.uk
I: www.hadriansway.co.uk

The Hill on the Wall ♦♦♦♦
Gilsland, Carlisle CA6 7DA
T: (01697) 747214
F: (01697) 747214
E: thehill@hadrians-wall.
demon.co.uk
I: www.
hadrians-wallbedandbreakfast.
com

Slack House Farm ♦♦♦
Gilsland, Carlisle, Cumbria
CA6 7DB
T: (016977) 47351

GRANGE-OVER-SANDS
Cumbria
Birchleigh Guest House
♦♦♦♦
Kents Bank Road, Grange-over-
Sands, Cumbria LA11 7EY
T: (01539) 532592
F: (01539) 532592

Corner Beech ♦♦♦
Kents Bank Road, Grange-over-
Sands, Cumbria LA11 7DP
T: (01539) 533088
F: (01539) 535288
E: david@cornerbeech.ndirect.
co.uk
I: www.cornerbeech.ndirect.
co.uk

Elton Hotel ♦♦♦♦
Windermere Road, Grange-over-
Sands, Cumbria LA11 6EQ
T: (01539) 532838
F: (01539) 532838
E: chris.crone@btclick.com

The Laurels Bed and Breakfast
♦♦♦♦
Berriedale Terrace, Lindale Road,
Grange-over-Sands, Cumbria
LA11 6ER
T: (015395) 35919
F: (015395) 35919
E: gml@thelaurels71.freeserve.
co.uk

Mayfields ♦♦♦♦
3 Mayfield Terrace, Kents Bank
Road, Grange-over-Sands,
Cumbria LA11 7DW
T: (01539) 534730
I: www.accommodata.
co.uk/010699.htm

Methven Hotel ♦♦♦♦
Kents Bank Road, Grange-over-
Sands, Cumbria LA11 7DU
T: (01539) 532031

Somerset House ♦♦♦
Kents Bank Road, Grange-over-
Sands, Cumbria LA11 7EY
T: (01539) 532631

GRASMERE
Cumbria
Ash Cottage Guest House
♦♦♦♦
Red Lion Square, Grasmere,
Ambleside, Cumbria LA22 9SP
T: (01539) 435224

Beck Allans ♦♦♦♦
College Street, Grasmere,
Cumbria LA22 9SZ
T: (015394) 35563
F: (015394) 35563
E: mail@beckallans.com
I: www.beckallans.com

Chestnut Villa ♦♦♦
Keswick Road, Grasmere,
Ambleside, Cumbria LA22 9RE
T: (015394) 35218

Dunmail House ♦♦♦♦
Keswick Road, Grasmere,
Ambleside, Cumbria LA22 9RE
T: (01539) 435256
E: enquiries@dunmailhouse.
freeserve.co.uk
I: www.dunmailhouse.com

Forest Side Hotel ♦♦♦
Grasmere, Ambleside, Cumbria
LA22 9RN
T: (015394) 35250
F: (015394) 35947
E: hotel@forestsidehotel.com
I: www.forestsidehotel.com

The Harwood ♦♦♦
Red Lion Square, Grasmere,
Ambleside, Cumbria LA22 9SP
T: (01539) 435248
F: (01539) 435545
E: harwoodlan@aol.com
I: members.aol.com/harwoodlan

How Foot Lodge ♦♦♦
Town End, Grasmere, Ambleside,
Cumbria LA22 9SQ
T: (01539) 435366

Lake View Country House
♦♦♦♦
Lake View Drive, Grasmere,
Ambleside, Cumbria LA22 9TD
T: (015394) 35384
E: info@lakeview-grasmere.com
I: www.lakeview-grasmere.com

Raise View Guest House ♦♦♦
White Bridge, Grasmere,
Ambleside, Cumbria LA22 9RQ
I: (01539) 435215
F: (01539) 435126
E: john@raisevw.demon.co.uk
I: www.raisevw.demon.co.uk

Redmayne Cottage ♦♦♦♦
Grasmere, Ambleside, Cumbria
LA22 9QY
T: (01539) 435635 &
07977 596133

Silver Lea Guest House ♦♦♦♦
Easedale Road, Grasmere,
Ambleside, Cumbria LA22 9QE
T: (015394) 35657
F: (015394) 35657

Titteringdales Guest House
♦♦♦♦
Pye Lane, Grasmere, Cumbria
LA22 9RQ
T: (015394) 35539
E: titteringdales@grasmere.net
I: www.grasmere.net

Travellers Rest ♦♦♦
Grasmere, Ambleside, Cumbria
LA22 9RR
T: (015394) 35604 & 0870 011
2152
I: www.lakelandsheart.com

Woodland Crag Guest House
♦♦♦♦
How Head Lane, Grasmere,
Ambleside, Cumbria LA22 9SG
T: (01539) 435351
F: (01539) 435351
E: woodlandcrag@aol.com
I: www.woodlandcrag.com

GRAYRIGG
Cumbria
Grayrigg Hall Farm ♦♦
Grayrigg, Kendal, Cumbria
LA8 9BU
T: (01539) 824689

Punchbowl House ♦♦♦♦
Grayrigg, Kendal, Cumbria
LA8 9BU
T: (01539) 824345
F: (01539) 824345
E: enquiries@punchbowlhouse.
co.uk
I: www.punchbowlhouse.co.uk

GREAT CLIFTON
Cumbria
The Clifton Hotel ♦♦♦♦
2 Moor Road, Great Clifton,
Workington, Cumbria CA14 1TS
T: (01900) 64616
F: (01900) 873384
E: slaes@cliftonhotel.com
I: www.cliftonhotel.com

HAWKSHEAD
Cumbria
Betty Fold Country House
♦♦♦♦
Hawkshead Hill, Ambleside,
Cumbria LA22 0PS
T: (01539) 436611
E: holidays@bettyfold.freeserve.
co.uk
I: www.bettyfold.freeserve.co.uk

Borwick Lodge ♦♦♦♦
Hawkshead, Ambleside, Cumbria
LA22 0PU
T: (01539) 436332
F: (01539) 436332
E: borwicklodge@talk21.com
I: www.borwicklodge.com

The Drunken Duck Inn ♦♦♦♦
Barngates, Ambleside, Cumbria
LA22 0NG
T: (015394) 36347
F: (015394) 36781
E: info@drunkenduckinn.co.uk
I: www.drunkenduckinn.co.uk

Grizedale Lodge Hotel ♦♦♦♦
Grizedale, Ambleside, Cumbria
LA22 0QL
T: (01539) 436532
F: (01539) 436572
E: enquiries@grizedale-lodge.
com
I: www.grizedale-lodge.com

High Grassings ♦♦♦♦
Sunny Brow, Outgate,
Ambleside, Cumbria LA22 0PU
T: (01539) 436484
F: (01539) 436140
E: info@highgrassings.com
I: www.highgrassings.com

Ivy House Hotel ♦♦♦♦
Main Street, Hawkshead,
Ambleside, Cumbria LA22 0NS
T: (015394) 36204 & 0800 056
3533
F: (015394) 36171
E: david@ivyhousehotel.com
I: www.ivyhousehotel.com

The Sun Inn ♦♦♦♦
Main Street, Hawkshead,
Ambleside, Cumbria LA22 0NT
T: (015394) 36236 & 36353
F: (015394) 36155
E: thesuninn@hawkshead98.
freeserve.co.uk
I: www.suninn.co.uk

**Yewfield Vegetarian Guest
House** ♦♦♦♦
Yewfield, Hawkshead,
Ambleside, Cumbria LA22 0PR
T: (01539) 436765
F: (01539) 436096
E: derek.yewfield@btinternet.
com
I: www.yewfield.co.uk

HIGH LORTON
Cumbria
Swinside End Farm ♦♦♦
Scales, High Lorton,
Cockermouth, Cumbria
CA13 9UA
T: (01900) 85134
F: (01900) 85134

Terrace Farm ♦♦♦
Lorton, Cockermouth, Cumbria
CA13 9TX
T: (01900) 85278

HOLME
Cumbria
Marwin House ♦♦
Duke Street, Holme, Carnforth,
Lancashire LA6 1PY
T: (01524) 781144 & 0774 782
0435
F: (01524) 781144

HOUGHTON
Cumbria
The Steadings ♦♦♦
Townhead Farm, Houghton,
Carlisle CA6 4JB
T: (01228) 523019
F: (01228) 590178

IREBY
Cumbria
Daleside Farm ♦♦♦♦
Ireby, Carlisle CA5 1EW
T: (016973) 71268

Woodlands Country House
♦♦♦♦
Ireby, Cumbria CA7 1EX
T: (016973) 71791
F: (016973) 71482
E: hj@woodlnd.u-net.com
I: www.woodlnd.u-net.com

KENDAL
Cumbria
Blaven Homestay ♦♦♦♦♦
Blaven, Middleshaw, Old Hutton,
Kendal, Cumbria LA8 0LZ
T: (01539) 734894 & 740490
F: (01539) 727447
E: hospitality@greenarrow.
demon.co.uk
I: www.blavenhomestay.co.uk

Burrow Hall ♦♦♦♦
Plantation Bridge, Kendal,
Cumbria LA8 9JR
T: (01539) 821711
E: burrowhall@supanet.com

Cragg Farm ♦♦♦
New Hutton, Kendal, Cumbria
LA8 0BA
T: (01539) 721760
E: knowles.cragg@ukgateway.
net
I: www.cragg-farm.sagenet.
co.uk

Fairways Guest House ♦♦♦
102 Windermere Road, Kendal,
Cumbria LA9 5EZ
T: (01539) 725564
E: mp@fairways1.fsnet.co.uk

Fell View ◆◆◆
100 Windermere Road, Kendal,
Cumbria LA9 5EZ
T: (01539) 728431

Gateside Farm ◆◆◆
Windermere Road, Kendal,
Cumbria LA9 5SE
T: (01539) 722036
E: gatesidefarm@aol.com

The Glen ◆◆◆
Oxenholme, Kendal, Cumbria
LA9 7RF
T: (01539) 726386
E: greenintheglen@btinternet.
com
I: www.smoothhound.
co.uk/hotels/glen2.html

Hillside Guest House ◆◆◆
4 Beast Banks, Kendal, Cumbria
LA9 4JW
T: (01539) 722836

Hollin Root Farm ◆◆◆
Garth Row, Kendal, Cumbria
LA8 9AW
T: (01539) 823638
E: b-and-b@hollin-root-farm.
freeserve.co.uk
I: www.hollinrootfarm.co.uk

Kendal Arms and Hotel ◆◆
72 Milnthorpe Road, Kendal,
Cumbria LA9 5HG
T: (01539) 720956
F: (01539) 724851

**Lakeland Natural Vegetarian
Guesthouse** ◆◆◆
Low Slack, Queens Road, Kendal,
Cumbria LA9 4PH
T: (01539) 733011
F: (01539) 733011
E: relax@lakelandnatural.co.uk
I: www.lakelandnatural.co.uk

Newalls Country House
◆◆◆◆
Skelsmergh, Kendal, Cumbria
LA9 6NU
T: (01539) 723202

Riversleigh ◆◆◆
49 Milnthorpe Road, Kendal,
Cumbria LA9 5QG
T: (01539) 726392

Sonata ◆◆◆
19 Burneside Road, Kendal,
Cumbria LA9 4RL
T: (01539) 732290
F: (01539) 732290
E: chris@sonataguesthouse.
freeserve.co.uk.
I: www.sonataguesthouse.co.uk

7 Thorny Hills ◆◆◆◆
Kendal, Cumbria LA9 7AL
T: (01539) 720207
E: martyn.jowett@btinternet.
com

Union Tavern ◆◆◆
159 Stricklandgate, Kendal,
Cumbria LA9 4RF
T: (01539) 724004
E: uniontavern@edirectory.
co.uk
I: www.edirectory.
co.uk/uniontavern

KENTMERE
Cumbria

Maggs Howe ◆◆◆
Kentmere, Kendal, Cumbria
LA8 9JP
T: (01539) 821689
I: www.smoothhound.
co.uk/hotels/maggs.html

KESWICK
Cumbria

Abacourt House ◆◆◆◆
26 Stanger Street, Keswick,
Cumbria CA12 5JU
T: (01768) 772967
E: abacourt@btinternet.com
I: www.abacourt.co.uk

Acorn House Hotel ◆◆◆◆
Ambleside Road, Keswick,
Cumbria CA12 4DL
T: (01768) 772553
F: (01768) 775332
E: info@acornhousehotel.co.uk
I: www.acornhousehotel.co.uk

Amble House Guest House
◆◆◆◆
23 Eskin Street, Keswick,
Cumbria CA12 4DQ
I: (01768) 773288
F: (01768) 780220
E: foye_house@keswick98.
freeserve.co.uk

The Anchorage ◆◆◆
14 Ambleside Road, Keswick,
Cumbria CA12 4DL
T: (01768) 772813

Anworth House ◆◆◆◆
27 Eskin Street, Keswick,
Cumbria CA12 4DQ
T: (01768) 772923
I: www.anworthhouse.co.uk

Avondale Guest House ◆◆◆◆
20 Southey Street, Keswick,
Cumbria CA12 4EF
T: (01768) 772735
F: (01768) 775431
E: enquiries@
avondaleguesthouse.com
I: www.avondaleguesthouse.
com

Badgers Wood ◆◆◆◆
30 Stanger Street, Keswick,
Cumbria CA12 5JU
T: (01768) 772621
F: (01768) 772621
E: enquiries@badgers-wood.
co.uk
I: www.badgers-wood.co.uk

Beckside Guest House
Rating Applied For
5 Wordsworth Street, Keswick,
Cumbria CA12 4HU
T: (01768) 773093
F: (01768) 780977
E: info@5beckside.fsnet.co.uk
I: www.smoothhound.co.uk

Beckstones Farm Guest House
◆◆◆
Thornthwaite, Keswick, Cumbria
CA12 5SQ
T: (01768) 778510
E: beckstones@lineone.net
I: website.lineone.
net/~beckstones

Berkeley Guest House ◆◆◆◆
The Heads, Keswick, Cumbria
CA12 5ER
T: (017687) 74222
E: berkeley@tesco.net
I: www.berkeley-keswick.
homepage.com

Birkrigg Farm ◆◆◆
Newlands, Keswick, Cumbria
CA12 5TS
T: (01768) 778278

Bonshaw Guest House ◆◆◆
20 Eskin Street, Keswick,
Cumbria CA12 4DG
T: (01768) 773084
E: sylviasanderson@
compuserve.com

Bowfell House ◆◆◆
Chestnut Hill, Keswick, Cumbria
CA12 4LR
T: (01768) 774859
E: bowfell.keswick@easicom.
com
I: www.stayinkeswick.co.uk

Braemar ◆◆◆◆
21 Eskin Street, Keswick,
Cumbria CA12 4DQ
T. (01768) 773743
E: enquires@
braemar-guesthouse.co.uk
I: www.braemar-guesthouse.
co.uk

Brierholme Guest House ◆◆◆
21 Bank Street, Keswick,
Cumbria CA12 5JZ
T: (01768) 772938
E: enquiries@brierholme.co.uk
I: www.brierholme.co.uk

The Cartwheel ◆◆◆
5 Blencathra Street, Keswick,
Cumbria CA12 4HW
T: (017687) 73182
E: info@thecartwheel.co.uk
I: www.thecartwheel.co.uk

Charnwood Guest House
◆◆◆◆
6 Eskin Street, Keswick, Cumbria
CA12 4DH
T: (01768) 774111 &
07711 773925

Charnwood Lodge ◆◆◆
Thrushwood, Keswick, Cumbria
CA12 4PG
T: (01768) 771318

Cherry Trees ◆◆◆◆
16 Eskin Street, Keswick,
Cumbria CA12 4DQ
T: (017687) 71048
E: cherry.trees@virgin.net

Clarence House ◆◆◆◆
14 Eskin Street, Keswick,
Cumbria CA12 4DQ
T: (01768) 773186
F: (01768) 772317
E: clarenceho@aol.com
I: users.aol.
com/clarenceho/index.html

Cottage in the Wood ◆◆◆◆
Whinlatter Pass, Keswick,
Cumbria CA12 5TW
T: (01768) 778409
F: (01768) 778064
E: cottage@lake-district.net
I: www.lake-district.net/cottage

Cumbria House ◆◆◆◆
1 Derwentwater Place,
Ambleside Road, Keswick,
Cumbria CA12 4DR
T: (01768) 773171
F: (01768) 773171
E: bta@cumbriahouse.co.uk
I: www.cumbriahouse.co.uk

**Dalegarth House Country
Hotel** ◆◆◆◆
Portinscale, Keswick, Cumbria
CA12 5RQ
T: (01768) 772817
F: (01768) 772817
E: john@dalegarthhousehotel.
freeserve.co.uk
I: www.dalegarth-house.co.uk

Derwentdale Guesthouse ◆◆◆
8 Blencathra Street, Keswick,
Cumbria CA12 4HP
T: (01768) 774187

Dolly Waggon ◆◆◆
17 Helvellyn Street, Keswick,
Cumbria CA12 4EN
T: (01768) 773593
E: gjosborn@aol.com

Dunsford Guest House ◆◆◆◆
16 Stanger Street, Keswick,
Cumbria CA12 5JU
T: (01768) 775059
E: enquiries@dunsford.net
I: www.dunsford.net

The Easedale Hotel ◆◆◆
Southey Street, Keswick,
Cumbria CA12 4EG
T: (01768) 772710 & 771127
F: (01768) 771127
E: easedaleh@aol.com
I: www.milford.
co.uk/go/easedale.html

Edwardene Hotel ◆◆◆◆
26 Southey Street, Keswick,
Cumbria CA12 4EF
T: (01768) 773586
F: (01768) 773824
E: enquiries@edwardenehotel.
com
I: www.edwardenehotel.com

Ellergill Guest House ◆◆◆◆
22 Stanger Street, Keswick,
Cumbria CA12 5JU
T: (01768) 773347 &
07762 021390
E: stay@ellergill.uk.com
I: www.ellergill.uk.com

Fell House ◆◆◆◆
28 Stanger Street, Keswick,
Cumbria CA12 5JU
T: (01768) 772669
F: (01768) 772669
E: info@fellhouse.co.uk
I: www.fellhouse.co.uk

Glencoe Guest House ◆◆◆◆
21 Helvellyn Street, Keswick,
Cumbria CA12 4EN
T: (01768) 771016 &
07711 376407
F: 07803 605385
E: enquiries@
glencoeguesthouse.co.uk
I: www.glencoeguesthouse.co.uk

Glendale Guest House ◆◆◆
7 Eskin Street, Keswick, Cumbria
CA12 4DH
T: (01768) 773562
E: glendale.guesthouse@talk21.
com
I: www.glendale-keswick.
freeserve.co.uk

The Grange Country House Hotel ◆◆◆◆◆
Manor Brow, Ambleside Road, Keswick, Cumbria CA12 4BA
T: (01768) 772500
F: (01768) 772500
E: duncan.miller@btconnect.com

Grassmoor Guest House
Rating Applied For
10 Blencathra Street, Keswick, Cumbria CA12 4HP
T: (017687) 74008

Greystones Hotel ◆◆◆◆
Ambleside Road, Keswick, Cumbria CA12 4DP
T: (01768) 773108
E: greystones@keslakes.freeserve.co.uk

Hedgehog Hill Guesthouse ◆◆◆
18 Blencathra Street, Keswick, Cumbria CA12 4HP
T: (01768) 774386
F: (01768) 780622
E: hedhil@fsbdial.co.uk

Howe Keld Lakeland Hotel ◆◆◆◆
5-7 The Heads, Keswick, Cumbria CA12 5ES
T: (017687) 72417
F: (017687) 72417
E: david@howekeld.co.uk
I: www.howekeld.co.uk

Hunters Way Guest House ◆◆◆◆
4 Eskin Street, Hunters Way, Keswick, Cumbria CA12 4DH
T: (01768) 772324

Kalgurli Guest House ◆◆◆
33 Helvellyn Street, Keswick, Cumbria CA12 4EP
T: (01768) 772935

Keskadale Farm ◆◆◆◆
Newlands Valley, Keswick, Cumbria CA12 5TS
T: (01768) 778544 & 778150
E: keskadale.b.b@kencomp.net

Latrigg House ◆◆◆◆
St Herbert Street, Keswick, Cumbria CA12 4DF
T: (01768) 773068
F: (01768) 772801
E: latrigghse@aol.com
I: members.aol.com/latrigghse/index.html

Lindisfarne ◆◆◆
21 Church Street, Keswick, Cumbria CA12 4DX
T: (01768) 773218 & 773261

Linnett Hill ◆◆◆
4 Penrith Road, Keswick, Cumbria CA12 4HF
T: (01768) 773109
E: Pete@linnetthill.co.uk
I: www.linnetthill.co.uk

Littlebeck ◆◆◆◆
Chestnut Hill, Keswick, Cumbria CA12 4LT
T: (01768) 772972
E: littlebeck@btinternet.com

Littletown Farm ◆◆◆
Newlands, Keswick, Cumbria CA12 5TU
T: (01768) 778353
F: (01768) 778437

Lynwood ◆◆◆◆
12 Ambleside Road, Keswick, Cumbria CA12 4DL
T: (01768) 772081
E: lynwood.keswick@virgin.net
I: www.thelynwoodguesthouse.co.uk

Lynwood House ◆◆◆◆
35 Helvellyn Street, Keswick, Cumbria CA12 4EP
T: (01768) 772398
F: (01768) 774090
E: lynwoodho@aol.com

Melbreak House ◆◆◆
29 Church Street, Keswick, Cumbria CA12 4DX
T: (017687) 73398
F: (017687) 73398
E: melbreakhouse@btinternet.com
I: www.melbreakhouse.co.uk

The Paddock ◆◆◆◆
Wordsworth Street, Keswick, Cumbria CA12 4HU
T: (01768) 772510
E: val@keswickonderwentwater.fsnet.co.uk
I: www.keswickguesthouse.com

Parkfield Guesthouse ◆◆◆◆
The Heads, Keswick, Cumbria CA12 5ES
T: (01768) 772328
E: parkfield@kencomp.net
I: www.kencomp.net/parkfield

Ravensworth Hotel ◆◆◆◆
29 Station Street, Keswick, Cumbria CA12 5HH
T: (01768) 772476
F: (01768) 775287
E: info@ravensworth-hotel.co.uk
I: www.ravensworth-hotel.co.uk

Richmond House ◆◆◆
37-39 Eskin Street, Keswick, Cumbria CA12 4DG
T: (01768) 773965
E: richmondhouse@tesco.net

Rickerby Grange ◆◆◆◆
Portinscale, Keswick, Cumbria CA12 5RH
T: (01768) 772344
F: (01768) 775588
E: val@ricor.demon.co.uk
I: www.ricor.demon.co.uk

Sandon Guesthouse ◆◆◆
13 Southey Street, Keswick, Cumbria CA12 4EG
T: (01768) 773648
I: www.sandoncleworth.supanet.com

Seymour House ◆◆◆
36 Lake Road, Keswick, Cumbria CA12 5DQ
T: (017687) 72764 & 0800 0566 401
F: (017687) 71289
E: andy042195@aol.com
I: www.seymour-house.com

Shemara Guest House ◆◆◆◆
27 Bank Street, Keswick, Cumbria CA12 5JZ
T: (01768) 773936
E: shemaraguesthouse@yahoo.co.uk

Skiddaw Grove Country Guest House ◆◆◆◆
Vicarage Hill, Keswick, Cumbria CA12 5QB
T: (01768) 773324
F: (01768) 773324

Stonegarth ◆◆◆◆
2 Eskin Street, Keswick, Cumbria CA12 4DH
T: (01768) 772436
E: info@stonegarth.com
I: www.stonegarth.com

Strathmore Guest House ◆◆◆◆
8 St John's Terrace, Ambleside Road, Keswick, Cumbria CA12 4DP
T: (01768) 772584
F: (01768) 772584
E: pbrown@strathmore-lakes.demon.co.uk
I: www.keswick.net/strathmore.htm

Sunnyside Guest House ◆◆◆◆
25 Southey Street, Keswick, Cumbria CA12 4EF
T: (01768) 772446
F: (01768) 774447
E: raynewton@survey.u-net.com
I: www.survey.u-net.com

Swinside Inn ◆◆◆
Newlands, Keswick, Cumbria CA12 5UE
T: (01768) 778253 & 778285
F: (01768) 778253
E: theswinsideinn@btinternet.com
I: www.kesnet.co.uk

Tarn Hows ◆◆◆◆
3-5 Eskin Street, Keswick, Cumbria CA12 4DH
T: (01768) 773217
F: (01768) 773217
E: david@tarnhows40.freeserve.co.uk
I: www.smoothhound.co.uk/hotels/tarnhows.html

Watendlath Guest House ◆◆◆
15 Acorn Street, Keswick, Cumbria CA12 4EA
T: (01768) 774165
F: (01768) 74165
E: linda@wakendlathguesthouse.co.uk
I: www.wakendlathguesthouse.co.uk

West View Guest House ◆◆◆◆
The Heads, Keswick, Cumbria CA12 5ES
T: (01768) 773638

Whitehouse Guest House ◆◆◆◆
15 Ambleside Road, Keswick, Cumbria CA12 4DL
T: (01768) 773176
F: (01768) 773176
E: jj_taylor1@hotmail.com

KIRKBY-IN-FURNESS
Cumbria

Commercial Inn ◆◆◆
Askew Gate Brow, Kirkby-in-Furness, Cumbria LA17 7TE
T: (01229) 889039

KIRKBY LONSDALE
Cumbria

Capernwray House ◆◆◆◆
Borrans Lane, Capernwray, Carnforth, Lancashire LA6 1AE
T: (01524) 732363
F: (01524) 732363
E: thesmiths@capernwrayhouse.com
I: www.capernwrayhouse.com

The Copper Kettle ◆◆
3-5 Market Street, Kirkby Lonsdale, Carnforth, Lancashire LA6 2AU
T: (01524) 271714
F: (01524) 271714

KIRKBY STEPHEN
Cumbria

Ing Hill Lodge ◆◆◆◆
Mallerstang Dale, Kirkby Stephen, Cumbria CA17 4JT
T: (01768) 371153
E: inghill@fsbdial.co.uk

Jolly Farmers Guest House ◆◆◆◆
63 High Street, Kirkby Stephen, Cumbria CA17 4SH
T: (017683) 71063
F: (017683) 71063
E: jollyf@cumbria.com
I: www.cumbria.com/jollyf/

The Old Court House ◆◆◆◆
High Street, Kirkby Stephen, Cumbria CA17 4SH
T: (017683) 71061
F: (017003) 71001
E: hilary.claxton@virgin.net

West View
Rating Applied For
Ravenstonedale, Kirkby Stephen, Cumbria CA17 4NG
T: (01539) 623415

KIRKLINTON
Cumbria

Clift House Farm ◆◆◆
Kirklinton, Carlisle CA6 6DE
T: (01228) 675237 & 07790 758272
F: (01228) 675237

Fergushill ◆◆◆
Kirklinton, Carlisle CA6 6DA
T: (01228) 675785
F: (01228) 675785
E: info@fergushill.co.uk
I: www.fergushill.co.uk

LAKESIDE
Cumbria

The Knoll Country House ◆◆◆◆
Lakeside, Newby Bridge, Ulverston, Cumbria LA12 8AU
T: (01539) 531347
F: (01539) 530850
E: info@theknoll-lakeside.co.uk
I: www.theknoll-lakeside.co.uk

LANGWATHBY
Cumbria

Langstanes ◆◆◆◆
Culgaith Road, Langwathby, Penrith, Cumbria CA10 1NA
T: (01768) 881004
F: (01768) 881004

LAZONBY
Cumbria

Banktop House ♦♦♦
Lazonby, Penrith, Cumbria
CA10 1AQ
T: (01768) 898268
F: (01768) 898851
E: hartsop@globalnet.co.uk

Harlea ♦♦♦♦
Lazonby, Penrith, Cumbria
CA10 1BX
T: (01768) 897055
E: harlea.eden@ukgateway.net

LINDALE
Cumbria

Greenacres Country Guesthouse ♦♦♦♦
Lindale, Grange-over-Sands,
Cumbria LA11 6LP
T: (01539) 534578
F: (01539) 534578
I: www.smoothhound.
co.uk/hotels/greenacres.html

LONGTOWN
Cumbria

Briar Lea House ♦♦♦♦
Brampton Road, Longtown,
Carlisle CA6 5TN
T: (01228) 791538
F: (01228) 791538
E: briarlea@cltministries.co.uk
I: www.cltministries.co.uk

Craigburn ♦♦♦
Catlowdy, Longtown, Carlisle
CA6 5QP
T: (01228) 577214
F: (01228) 577014
E: louiselawson@hotmail.com
I: www.craigburnfarmhouse.
co.uk

Orchard House ♦♦♦♦
Blackbank, Longtown, Carlisle
CA6 5LQ
T: (01461) 338596
E: orchard.gretna@virgin.net
I: www.gretnaweddings.
com/orchardhouse.html

LOWESWATER
Cumbria

Askhill Farm ♦♦♦
Loweswater, Cockermouth,
Cumbria CA13 0SU
T: (01946) 861640

LOWICK
Cumbria

Everard Lodge ♦♦♦
Lowick, Ulverston, Cumbria
LA12 8ER
T: (01229) 885245
F: (01229) 885245

Garth Row ♦♦♦
Lowick Green, Ulverston,
Cumbria LA12 8EB
T: (01229) 885633
E: b&b@garthrow.freeserve.
co.uk

MAULDS MEABURN
Cumbria

Trainlands Bed & Breakfast ♦♦♦
Maulds Meaburn, Penrith,
Cumbria CA10 3HX
T: (017683) 51249
F: (017683) 53983
E: bousfield@trainlands.u-net.
com

MIDDLETON
Cumbria

Swan Inn ♦♦♦
Middleton, Sedbergh, Cumbria
LA6 2NB
T: (01524) 276223 &
07811 352913
E: ghl@swaninn.freeserve.co.uk
I: www.theswaninn.com

MILBURN
Cumbria

Slakes Farm ♦♦♦
Milburn, Penrith, Cumbria
CA16 6DP
T: (01768) 361385

MILLOM
Cumbria

The Duddon Pilot Hotel ♦♦♦♦
Devonshire Road, Millom,
Cumbria LA18 4JT
T: (01229) 774116
F: (01229) 774116

The Pavilion Hotel ♦♦♦♦
36 Duke Street, Millom, Cumbria
LA18 5BB
T: (01229) 770700
F: (01229) 770700

MOSEDALE
Cumbria

Mosedale House ♦♦♦♦
Mosedale, Penrith, Cumbria
CA11 0XQ
T: (01768) 779371
E: colin.smith2@ukonline.co.uk
I: www.northlakes.
co.uk/mosedalehouse
♿

MUNGRISDALE
Cumbria

Mosedale End Farm ♦♦♦
Mungrisdale, Penrith, Cumbria
CA11 0XQ
T: (017687) 79605
E: armstrong@awmcmanus.
screaming.net
I: www.smoothhound.
co.uk/hotels/mosedale.html

Near Howe Hotel ♦♦♦
Mungrisdale, Penrith, Cumbria
CA11 0SH
T: (01768) 779678
F: (01768) 779678

NEAR SAWREY
Cumbria

Beechmount Country House ♦♦♦
Near Sawrey, Ambleside,
Cumbria LA22 0JZ
T: (01539) 436356
I: www.
beechmountcountryhouse.co.uk

High Green Gate Guest House ♦♦♦
Near Sawrey, Ambleside,
Cumbria LA22 0LF
T: (01539) 436296
E: highgreengate@amserve.net

Tower Bank Arms ♦♦♦
Near Sawrey, Ambleside,
Cumbria LA22 0LF
T: (01539) 436334
F: (01539) 436334

NEWBIGGIN-ON-LUNE
Cumbria

Tranna Hill ♦♦♦
Newbiggin-on-Lune, Kirkby
Stephen, Cumbria CA17 4NY
T: (015396) 23227 &
07989 892368
E: trannahill@hotmail.com

NEWBY BRIDGE
Cumbria

Low Graythwaite Hall ♦♦♦♦
Graythwaite, Newby Bridge,
Ulverston, Cumbria LA12 8AZ
T: (01539) 531676
F: (01539) 531948

Old Barn Farm
Rating Applied For
Fiddler Hall, Newby Bridge,
Cumbria LA12 8NQ
T: (015395) 31842
F: (015395) 31842
E: barch@btinternet.com

NEWLANDS
Cumbria

Uzzicar Farm ♦♦♦
Newlands, Keswick, Cumbria
CA12 5TS
T: (017687) 78367

OUTGATE
Cumbria

Bracken Fell ♦♦♦
Outgate, Ambleside, Cumbria
LA22 0NH
T: (01539) 436289
F: (01539) 436142
E: hart.brackenfell@virgin.net
I: www.brackenfell.com

OXENHOLME
Cumbria

Station Inn ♦♦♦
Oxenholme, Kendal, Cumbria
LA9 7RF
T: (01539) 724094

PARDSHAW
Cumbria

Sunny Corner ♦♦♦♦
Pardshaw, Cockermouth,
Cumbria CA13 0SP
T: (01900) 826380
F: (01900) 826380

PATTERDALE
Cumbria

Deepdale Hall ♦♦♦♦
Patterdale, Penrith, Cumbria
CA11 0NR
T: (01768) 482369 & 482608
E: brown@deepdalehall.
freeserve.co.uk
I: www.deepdalehall.co.uk

Ullswater View Bed and Breakfast ♦♦♦♦
Ullswater View, Patterdale,
Penrith, Cumbria CA11 0NW
T: (017684) 82175
F: (017684) 82181
E: ext@btinternet.com
I: www.ullswater-view.co.uk

PENRITH
Cumbria

Albany House ♦♦♦
5 Portland Place, Penrith,
Cumbria CA11 7QN
T: (01768) 863072
F: (01768) 863072
I: www.albanyhouse.com.uk

Beacon Bank Hotel ♦♦♦♦
Beacon Edge, Penrith, Cumbria
CA11 7BD
T: (01768) 862633
F: (01768) 899055
E: beaconbank.hotel@virgin.net
I: www.smoothhound.com

Blue Swallow Guesthouse ♦♦♦
11 Victoria Road, Penrith,
Cumbria CA11 8HR
T: (01768) 866335
E: blueswallows@lineone.net
I: www.blueswallow.co.uk

Brandelhow Guest House ♦♦♦
1 Portland Place, Penrith,
Cumbria CA11 7QN
T: (01768) 864470

The Friarage ♦♦♦♦
Friargate, Penrith, Cumbria
CA11 7XR
T: (01768) 863635
F: (01768) 863635

Glendale ♦♦♦
4 Portland Place, Penrith,
Cumbria CA11 7QN
T: (01768) 862579
F: (01768) 867934
E: glendale@lineone.net
I: www.smoothhound.
co.uk/hotels/glendgh.html

Greenfields ♦♦♦♦
Ellonby, Penrith, Cumbria
CA11 9SJ
T: (01768) 484671
F: (01768) 484671
E: greenfields@gofornet.co.uk
I: www.smoothhound.
co.uk/hotels/grenfields.html

Hornby Hall Country Guest House ♦♦♦♦
Hornby Hall, Brougham, Penrith,
Cumbria CA10 2AR
T: (01768) 891114
F: (01768) 891114

Limes Country Hotel ♦♦♦
Redhills, Penrith, Cumbria
CA11 0DT
T: (01768) 863343
F: (01768) 867190
E: jdhanton@aol.com
I: www.members.aol.
com/jdhanton/index.htm

Little Blencowe Farm ♦♦♦
Blencowe, Penrith, Cumbria
CA11 0DG
T: (017684) 83338
F: (017684) 83054
E: bart.fawcett@ukgateway.net

Queen's Head Inn ♦♦
Tirril, Penrith, Cumbria CA10 2JF
T: (01768) 863219
F: (01768) 863243
E: bookings@queensheadinn.
co.uk
I: www.queensheadinn.co.uk

Roundthorn Country House ♦♦♦♦
Beacon Edge, Penrith, Cumbria
CA11 8SJ
T: (01768) 863952
F: (01768) 864100
E: enquiries@roundthorn.co.uk
I: www.roundthorn.co.uk

The White House ♦♦♦♦
Clifton, Penrith, Cumbria
CA10 2EL
T: (01768) 865115

Woodland House Hotel ◆◆◆
Wordsworth Street, Penrith,
Cumbria CA11 7QY
T: (01768) 864177
F: (01768) 890152
E: ivordavies@woodlandhouse.
co.uk
I: www.woodlandhouse.co.uk

POOLEY BRIDGE
Cumbria

Sun Inn ◆◆◆
Pooley Bridge, Penrith, Cumbria
CA10 2NN
T: (01768) 486205
F: (01768) 486913

PORTINSCALE
Cumbria

Derwent Cottage ◆◆◆◆◆
Portinscale, Keswick, Cumbria
CA12 5RF
T: (01768) 774838
E: enquires@dercott.demon.
co.uk
I: www.dercott.demon.co.uk

Thirnbeck Guest House ◆◆◆
Portinscale, Keswick, Cumbria
CA12 5RD
T: (01768) 772869
E: mls@thirnbeck.fsnet.co.uk

RYDAL
Cumbria

Nab Cottage Guest House
◆◆◆
Nab Cottage, Rydal, Ambleside,
Cumbria LA22 9SD
T: (01539) 435311
F: (01539) 435493
E: ell@nab.dial.lakesnet.co.uk
I: www.lakesnet.
net/homepages/ell/nab

Rydal Lodge Hotel ◆◆◆
Rydal, Ambleside, Cumbria
LA22 9LR
T: (015394) 33208

ST BEES
Cumbria

Stonehouse Farm ◆◆◆
Main Street, St Bees, Cumbria
CA27 0DE
T: (01946) 822224
E: csmith.stonehouse@virgin.
net

SANDSIDE
Cumbria

**Kingfisher House and
Restaurant** ◆◆◆
Sandside, Milnthorpe, Cumbria
LA7 7HW
T: (015395) 63909
F: (015395) 64022
E: kingfisherest@tinyworld.
co.uk

Plantation Cottage ◆◆◆◆
Arnside Road, Sandside,
Milnthorpe, Cumbria LA7 7JU
T: (01524) 762069 &
07768 353202

SATTERTHWAITE
Cumbria

Town End ◆◆◆◆
Satterthwaite, Ulverston,
Cumbria LA12 8LN
T: (01229) 860936 &
07967 879452

SAWREY
Cumbria

Buckle Yeat Guest House
◆◆◆◆
Sawrey, Ambleside, Cumbria
LA22 0LF
T: (01539) 436446 & 436538
F: (01539) 436446
E: info@buckle-yeat.co.uk
I: www.buckle-yeat.co.uk

Lakefield ◆◆◆◆
Near Sawrey, Ambleside,
Cumbria LA22 0JZ
T: (01539) 436635
F: (01539) 436635

Sawrey House Country Hotel
◆◆◆◆◆
Near Sawrey, Ambleside,
Cumbria LA22 0LF
T: (015394) 36387
F: (015394) 36010
E: enquiries@sawrey-house.
com
I: www.sawrey-house.com

West Vale Country House
◆◆◆◆
Far Sawrey, Hawkshead,
Ambleside, Cumbria LA22 0LQ
T: (01539) 442817
F: (01539) 45302
E: westvalehouse@yahoo.co.uk

SCOTBY
Cumbria

Windsover ◆◆◆◆
Lambley Bank, Scotby, Carlisle
CA4 8BX
T: (01228) 513550
E: jimcallaghan@tinyworld.
co.uk
I: www.windsover.co.uk

SEASCALE
Cumbria

**Victoria Villa Hotel and
Egloff's Eating House** ◆◆◆◆
58 Gosforth Road, Seascale,
Cumbria CA20 1JG
T: (01946) 727309
F: (01946) 727158
I: www.egloffeatinghouse.co.uk

SEBERGHAM
Cumbria

Stockwell Hall ◆◆◆◆
Sebergham, Carlisle, Cumbria
CA5 7DY
T: (016974) 76364
F: (01694) 76364

SEDBERGH
Cumbria

Ash Hining Farm ◆◆◆
Howgill, Sedbergh, Cumbria
LA10 5HU
T: (01539) 620957
F: (01539) 620957

Bridge House ◆◆◆◆
Brigflatts, Sedbergh, Cumbria
LA10 5HN
T: (01539) 621820
F: (01539) 621820

Bull Hotel ◆◆◆◆
Main Street, Sedbergh, Cumbria
LA10 5BL
T: (01539) 620264
F: (01539) 620212
E: bullhotel@btinternet.com
I: www.bullatsedbergh.co.uk

Dalesman Country Inn ◆◆◆◆
Main Street, Sedbergh, Cumbria
LA10 5BN
T: (01539) 621183
F: (01539) 621311
I: www.thedalesman.co.uk

The Lodge ◆◆◆
10 Loftus Manor, Sedbergh,
Cumbria LA10 5SQ
T: (01539) 621855
E: anne.thelodge@talk21.com
I: www.thedalesway.
co.uk/thelodge

St Mark's ◆◆◆◆
Cautley, Sedbergh, Cumbria
LA10 5LZ
T: (015396) 20287 & 21585
F: (015396) 21585
E: 100540.1376@compuserve.
com

SELSIDE
Cumbria

Hollowgate Farm ◆◆◆
Hollowgate, Selside, Kendal,
Cumbria LA8 9LG
T: (01539) 823258
E: hollowgate@talk21.com

SOULBY
Cumbria

Riddlesay Farm ◆◆◆◆
Soulby, Kirkby Stephen, Cumbria
CA17 4PX
T: (01768) 371474 &
0772 0811611
E: mrarmstrong@btinternet.
com

STAVELEY
Cumbria

Eagle and Child Hotel ◆
Kendal Road, Staveley, Kendal,
Cumbria LA8 9LP
T: (01539) 821320
E: eaglechildinn@btinternet.
com
I: www.eaglechildinn.co.uk

Tarn House ◆◆◆◆
18 Danes Road, Staveley, Kendal,
Cumbria LA8 9PW
T: (01539) 821656 &
07771 516156

Watermill Inn ◆◆◆
Ings, Staveley, Kendal, Cumbria
LA8 9PY
T: (01539) 821309
F: (01539) 822309
E: all@watermill-inn.demon.
co.uk
I: www.watermill-inn.demon.
co.uk

TALKIN
Cumbria

Hullerbank ◆◆◆
Talkin, Brampton, Cumbria
CA8 1LB
T: (016977) 46668
F: (016977) 46668
E: info@hullerbank.freeserve.
co.uk
I: www.smoothhound.
co.uk/hotels/huller.html

TEBAY
Cumbria

Primrose Cottage ◆◆◆◆
Orton Road, Tebay, Penrith,
Cumbria CA10 3TL
T: (01539) 624791 &
07778 520930
E: primrosecottebay@aol.com

THORNTHWAITE
Cumbria

Jenkin Hill Cottage ◆◆◆◆
Thornthwaite, Keswick, Cumbria
CA12 5SG
T: (017687) 78443 & 0777 594
2861
F: (017687) 78445
E: quality@jenkinhill.co.uk
I: www.jenkinhill.co.uk

Thornthwaite Hall ◆◆◆◆
Thornthwaite, Keswick, Cumbria
CA12 5SA
T: (017687) 78424
F: (017687) 78122
E: thornthwaite@msn.com

THRELKELD
Cumbria

**Scales Farm Country
Guesthouse** ◆◆◆◆
Scales, Threlkeld, Keswick,
Cumbria CA12 4SY
T: (01768) 779660
F: (01768) 779660
E: scales@scalesfarm.com.
I: www.scalesfarm.com

TROUTBECK
Cumbria

Gill Head Farm ◆◆◆
Troutbeck, Penrith, Cumbria
CA11 0ST
T: (01768) 779652
F: (01768) 779130
E: gillhead@talk21.com
I: www.gillheadfarm.co.uk

High Fold Farm ◆◆◆◆
Troutbeck, Windermere, Cumbria
LA23 1PG
T: (015394) 32200
F: (015394) 34970

High Green Lodge ◆◆◆◆
High Green, Troutbeck,
Windermere, Cumbria LA23 1PN
T: (01539) 433005

Lane Head Farm Guest House
◆◆◆◆
Troutbeck, Penrith, Cumbria
CA11 0SY
T: (01768) 779220
F: (01768) 779220
E: info@laneheadfarm.
freeserve.co.uk
I: www.laneheadfarm.co.uk

Troutbeck Inn ◆◆◆◆
Troutbeck, Penrith, Cumbria
CA11 0SJ
T: (01768) 483635
F: (01768) 483928
E: enquiries@troutbeck_inn.
com
I: www.troutbeck_inn.com

ULLSWATER
Cumbria

Bank House Farm ◆◆◆
Matterdale End, Penrith,
Cumbria CA11 0LF
T: (01768) 482040

Elm House ◆◆◆◆
Pooley Bridge, Penrith, Cumbria
CA10 2NH
T: (01768) 486334
F: (01768) 486851
E: b&tb@elmhouse.demon.co.uk
I: www.elmhouse.demon.co.uk

Knotts Mill Country Lodge ♦♦♦
Watermillock, Penrith, Cumbria
CA11 0JN
T: (01768) 486699
E: knottsmill@cwcom.net
I: www.knottsmill.cwc.net

Land Ends ♦♦♦
Watermillock, Ullswater, Penrith,
Cumbria CA11 0NB
T: (01768) 486438
F: (01768) 486959
E: infolandends@btinternet.
com
I: www.landends.btinternet.
co.uk

Moss Crag ♦♦♦
Eagle Road, Glenridding, Penrith,
Cumbria CA11 0PA
T: (01768) 482500 &
0789 9777419
F: (01768) 482500
E: info@mosscrag.co.uk
I: www.mosscrag.co.uk

Netherdene Guest House ♦♦♦
Troutbeck, Penrith, Cumbria
CA11 0SJ
T: (01768) 483475 & 483475
F: (01768) 483475

Tymparon Hall ♦♦♦
Newbiggin, Stainton, Penrith,
Cumbria CA11 0HS
T: (01768) 483236
F: (01768) 483236
E: margaret@peeearson.
freeserve.co.uk
I: www.peeearson.freeserve.
co.uk

Ullswater House ♦♦♦
Pooley Bridge, Penrith, Cumbria
CA10 2NN
T: (01768) 486259

Whitbarrow Farm ♦♦♦
Berrier, Penrith, Cumbria
CA11 0XB
T: (01768) 483366 &
07720 9838304
E: gmharris@farmersweekly.net

ULVERSTON
Cumbria
Trinity House Hotel ♦♦♦♦
Prince's Street, Ulverston,
Cumbria LA12 7NB
T: (01229) 587639 &
07802 226273
F: (01229) 588552
E: hotel@trinityhouse.furness.
co.uk

Virginia House Hotel ♦♦♦♦
24 Queen Street, Ulverston,
Cumbria LA12 7AF
T: (01229) 584844
F: (01229) 588565
E: virginia@ulverstonhotels.
co.uk
I: www.ulverstonhotels.com

UNDERBARROW
Cumbria
High Gregg Hall Farm ♦♦♦
Underbarrow, Kendal, Cumbria
LA8 8BL
T: (01539) 568318

Tranthwaite Hall ♦♦♦♦
Underbarrow, Kendal, Cumbria
LA8 8HG
T: (01539) 568285
E: tranthwaitehall@hotmail.
com

Tullythwaite House ♦♦♦♦
Underbarrow, Kendal, Cumbria
LA8 8BB
T: (01539) 568397

WALTON
Cumbria
Town Head Farm ♦♦♦
Walton, Brampton, Cumbria
CA8 2DJ
T: (01697) 72730

WARWICK BRIDGE
Cumbria
**Brookside Bed and Breakfast
♦♦♦♦**
Warwick Bridge, Carlisle
CA4 8RE
T: (01228) 560250
E: brookside@contactme.co.uk
I: www.
brooksidebedandbreakfast.
homestead.com

WATERHEAD
Cumbria
**Waterhead Country Guest
House ♦♦♦**
Waterhead, Ambleside, Cumbria
LA21 8AJ
T: (01539) 441442
F: (01539) 441476
E: steve-waterhead@lineone.
co.uk

WHITEHAVEN
Cumbria
Corkickle Guest House ♦♦♦♦
1 Corkickle, Whitehaven,
Cumbria CA28 8AA
T: (01946) 692073
F: (01946) 692073
E: corkickle@tinyworld.co.uk

**The Cottage Bed and Breakfast
♦♦**
The Cottage, Mirehouse Road,
Whitehaven, Cumbria CA28 9UD
T: (01946) 695820

**Glenfield
Rating Applied For**
Corkicle, Whitehaven, Cumbria
CA28 7TS
T: (01946) 691911
E: glenfield_hotel@talk21.com

WINDERMERE
Cumbria
Acton House ♦♦♦
41 Craig Walk, Windermere,
Cumbria LA23 2HB
T: (01539) 445340

Almaria House ♦♦♦
17 Broad Street, Windermere,
Cumbria LA23 2AB
T: (015394) 43026

Applegarth Hotel ♦♦♦
College Road, Windermere,
Cumbria LA23 1BU
T: (015394) 43206
F: (015394) 46636
E: applegarthhotel@zoom.co.uk
I: www.smoothhound.
co.uk/hotels/apple.html

Applethwaite House ♦♦♦
1 Upper Oak Street, Windermere,
Cumbria LA23 2LB
T: (01539) 444689
E: applethwaitehouse@
btinternet.com
I: www.btinternet.
com/~applethwaitehouse

The Archway ♦♦♦♦
13 College Road, Windermere,
Cumbria LA23 1BU
T: (01539) 445613 & 445328
F: (01539) 445328
E: archway@btinternet.com
I: www.communiken.
com/archway

Ashleigh Guest House ♦♦♦♦
11 College Road, Windermere,
Cumbria LA23 1BU
T: (01539) 442292 &
07940 598634
F: (01539) 442292

Aspen Cottage ♦♦
6 Havelock Road, Windermere,
Cumbria LA23 1EH
T: (01539) 443946 &
07930 959110

**Autumn Leaves Guest House
♦♦♦**
29 Broad Street, Windermere,
Cumbria LA23 2AB
T: (01539) 448410
I: www.autumnleaves.gbr.cc

The Beaumont ♦♦♦♦♦
Holly Road, Windermere,
Cumbria LA23 2AF
T: (01539) 447075
F: (01539) 447075
E: thebeaumonthotel@
btinternet.com
I: www.lakesbeaumont.co.uk

Beaumont ♦♦♦♦
Thornbarrow Road, Windermere,
Cumbria LA23 2DG
T: (01539) 445521
F: (01539) 446267
E: etc@beaumont-holidays.
co.uk
I: www.beaumont-holidays.
co.uk
🏠

Beckmead House ♦♦♦
5 Park Avenue, Windermere,
Cumbria LA23 2AR
T: (015394) 42757
F: (015394) 42757

Beckside Cottage ♦♦♦
4 Park Road, Windermere,
Cumbria LA23 2AW
T: (01539) 442069 & 488105

Boston House ♦♦♦♦
4 The Terrace, Windermere,
Cumbria LA23 1AJ
T: (01539) 443654
E: info@bostonhouse.co.uk
I: www.bostonhouse.co.uk

Bowfell Cottage ♦♦
Middle Entrance Drive, Storrs
Park, Bowness-on-Windermere,
Windermere, Cumbria LA23 3JY
T: (01539) 444835

Braemount House ♦♦♦♦
Sunny Bank Road, Windermere,
Cumbria LA23 2EN
T: (01539) 445967 & 447737
F: (01539) 445967
E: braemount.house@virgin.net
I: freespace.virgin.
net/braemount.house

Brook House ♦♦♦
30 Ellerthwaite Road,
Windermere, Cumbria LA23 2AH
T: (01539) 444932

Brooklands ♦♦♦
Ferry View, Bowness-on-
Windermere, Windermere,
Cumbria LA23 3JB
T: (01539) 442344
E: brooklandsferryview@
btinternet.com
I: www.smoothhound.
co.uk/hotels/brooklands

Cambridge House ♦♦♦
9 Oak Street, Windermere,
Cumbria LA23 1EN
T: (015394) 43846
F: (015394) 46662
E: reservations@
cambridge-house.fsbusiness.
co.uk
I: www.cambridge-house.
fsbusiness.co.uk

Clifton House ♦♦♦
28 Ellerthwaite Road,
Windermere, Cumbria LA23 2AH
T: (01539) 444968
E: info@cliftonhse.co.uk
I: www.cliftonhse.co.uk

College House ♦♦♦
15 College Road, Windermere,
Cumbria LA23 1BU
T: (01539) 445767 &
0798 0000992
E: clghse@aol.com
I: www.college-house.com

The Common Farm ♦♦♦
Windermere, Cumbria LA23 1JQ
T: (01539) 443433

The Cottage ♦♦♦
Elleray Road, Windermere,
Cumbria LA23 1AG
T: (01539) 444796
F: (01539) 444796
E: janetfox@
thecottageguesthouse.com
I: www.thecottageguesthouse.
com

**Denehurst Guest House
♦♦♦♦**
40 Queens Drive, Windermere,
Cumbria LA23 2EL
T: (015394) 44710 & 0771 297
5987
F: (015394) 44710
E: denehurst@btconnect.com
I: www.smoothhound.
co.uk/hotels/dene.html

Dunvegan Guest House ♦♦♦
Broad Street, Windermere,
Cumbria LA23 2AB
T: (01539) 443502
F: (01539) 447721
E: bryan.twaddle@btinternet.
com
I: www.smoothhound.
co.uk/hotels/dunvegan

Eastbourne ♦♦♦♦
Biskey Howe Road, Bowness-
on-Windermere, Windermere,
Cumbria LA23 2JR
T: (01539) 443525
F: (01539) 443525
E: eastbourne@lakes-pages.
co.uk
I: www.lakes-pages.co.uk

The Fairfield ♦♦♦♦
Brantfell Road, Bowness-on-
Windermere, Windermere,
Cumbria LA23 3AE
T: (01539) 446565
F: (01539) 446565
E: ray&barb@the-fairfield.co.uk
I: www.the-fairfield.co.uk

Fir Trees ◆◆◆◆
Lake Road, Windermere,
Cumbria LA23 2EQ
T: (01539) 442272
F: (01539) 442512
E: firtreeshotel@email.msn.com
I: www.fir-trees.com

Firgarth ◆◆◆
Ambleside Road, Windermere,
Cumbria LA23 1EU
T: (01539) 446974
F: (01539) 442384
E: thefirgarth@netscapeonline.
co.uk

Glenville Hotel ◆◆◆◆
Lake Road, Windermere,
Cumbria LA23 2EQ
T: (01539) 443371
F: (01539) 443371
E: glenville1@btinternet.com
I: www.glenville1.btinternet.com

Greenriggs Guest House ◆◆◆
8 Upper Oak Street, Windermere,
Cumbria LA23 2LB
T: (01539) 442265
F: (01539) 442265
E: greenriggs@talk21.com

Haisthorpe Guest House
◆◆◆◆
Holly Road, Windermere,
Cumbria LA23 2AF
T: (015394) 43445
F: (015394) 48875
E: haisthorpe@clara.net
I: www.haisthorpe-house.co.uk

Hawksmoor ◆◆◆◆
Lake Road, Windermere,
Cumbria LA23 2EQ
T: (01539) 442110
F: (01539) 442110
E: enquiries@hawksmoor.com
I: www.hawksmoor.com

HazelBank ◆◆◆◆
Hazel Street, Windermere,
Cumbria LA23 1EL
T: (01539) 445486
F: (01539) 445486

Heatherbank Guest House
◆◆◆
13 Birch Street, Windermere,
Cumbria LA23 1EG
T: (01539) 446503 &
07970 634050
F: (01539) 446503
E: heatherbank@btinternet.com

High View ◆◆◆◆
Silver Award
Sun Hill Lane, Troutbeck Bridge,
Windermere, Cumbria LA23 1HJ
T: (01539) 444618 & 442731
F: (01539) 444618
E: info@
accommodationlakedistrict.com
I: www.
accommodationlakedistrict.com

Hilton House ◆◆◆◆
New Road, Windermere,
Cumbria LA23 2EE
T: (01539) 443934
F: (01539) 443934

Holly Lodge ◆◆◆
6 College Road, Windermere,
Cumbria LA23 1BX
T: (01539) 443873
F: (01539) 443873
E: doyle@hollylodge20.fsnet.
co.uk
I: www.hollylodge20.fsnet.co.uk

Holly Park House ◆◆◆◆
1 Park Road, Windermere,
Cumbria LA23 2AW
T: (01539) 442107
F: (01539) 448997
I: www.s-h-systems.
co.uk/hotels/hollypk.html

Holly-Wood ◆◆◆◆
Holly Road, Windermere,
Cumbria LA23 2AF
T: (01539) 442219

Holmlea ◆◆◆
Kendal Road, Bowness-on-
Windermere, Windermere,
Cumbria LA23 3EW
T: (01539) 442597

Ivy Bank ◆◆◆◆
Holly Road, Windermere,
Cumbria LA23 2AF
T: (015394) 42601 &
07808 516245
E: ivybank@clara.co.uk
I: www.ivybank.clara.co.uk

Kays Cottage ◆◆◆◆
7 Broad Street, Windermere,
Cumbria LA23 2AB
T: (01539) 444146
F: (01539) 444146
E: kayscottage@freenetname.
co.uk
I: www.kayscottage.co.uk

Kirkwood Guest House ◆◆◆◆
Prince's Road, Windermere,
Cumbria LA23 2DD
T: (01539) 443907
F: (01539) 443907
E: neil.cox@kirkwood51.
freeserve.co.uk
I: www.kirkwood51.freeserve.
co.uk/

Lakes Hotel ◆◆◆
1 High Street, Windermere,
Cumbria LA23 1AF
T: (015394) 42751
F: (015394) 46026
E: admin@lakes-hotel.com
I: www.lakes-hotel.com

Lakeshore House ◆◆◆◆◆
Ecclerigg, Windermere, Cumbria
LA23 1LJ
T: (01539) 433202
F: (01539) 433213
E: lakeshore@lakedistrict.uk.
com
I: www.lakedistrict.uk.com

Langdale View Guest House
◆◆◆
114 Craig Walk, Off Helm Road,
Bowness-on-Windermere,
Windermere, Cumbria LA23 3AX
T: (01539) 444076

Laurel Cottage ◆◆◆◆
8 Park Road, Windermere,
Cumbria LA23 2BJ
T: (01539) 443053
E: wendy@laurelcottage8.
freeserve.co.uk
I: www.guesthouseswindermere.
co.uk

Lindisfarne ◆◆◆
Sunny Bank Road, Windermere,
Cumbria LA23 2EN
T: (01539) 446295 &
0775 9925528
F: (01539) 46295
E: lindisfarne@zoom.co.uk

Lingwood ◆◆◆◆
Birkett Hill, Bowness-on-
Windermere, Windermere,
Cumbria LA23 3EZ
T: (01539) 444680
F: (01539) 448154
E: enquiries@
lingwood-guesthouse.co.uk
I: www.lingwood-guesthouse.
co.uk

Lynwood Guest House ◆◆◆
Broad Street, Windermere,
Cumbria LA23 2AB
T: (01539) 442550
F: (01539) 442550

Meadfoot Guest House ◆◆◆◆
New Road, Windermere,
Cumbria LA23 2LA
T: (01539) 442610
F: (01539) 445280
E: enquiries@
meadfoot-guesthouse.co.uk
I: www.meadfoot-guesthouse.
co.uk

Melbourne Guest House ◆◆◆
2-3 Biskey Howe Road,
Bowness-on-Windermere,
Windermere, Cumbria LA23 2JP
T: (01539) 443475
F: (01539) 442475

Mount View Guest House
◆◆◆
New Road, Windermere,
Cumbria LA23 2LA
T: (01539) 445548

Mylne Bridge House ◆◆◆
Brookside, Lake Road,
Windermere, Cumbria LA23 2BX
T: (01539) 443314
F: (01539) 448052
E: mylnebridgehouse@talk21.
com
I: www.s-h-systems.
co.uk/hotels/mylne.html

Oakbank House ◆◆◆◆◆
Helm Road, Bowness-on-
Windermere, Cumbria LA23 3BU
T: (015394) 43386
F: (015394) 47965
E: enquiries@
oakbarnkhousehotel.co.uk
I: www.oakbankhousehotel.
co.uk

Oldfield House ◆◆◆◆
Oldfield Road, Windermere,
Cumbria LA23 2BY
T: (015394) 88445
F: (015394) 43250
E: pat.reeves@virgin.net

Orrest Cottage ◆◆◆
17 Church Street, Windermere,
Cumbria LA23 1AQ
T: (01539) 488722

Park Beck ◆◆◆
3 Park Road, Windermere,
Cumbria LA23 2AW
T: (015394) 44025

Rayrigg Villa Guest House
◆◆◆◆
Ellerthwaite Square,
Windermere, Cumbria LA23 1DP
T: (01539) 488342
E: rayriggvilla@nascr.net
I: www.rayriggvilla.co.uk

Rocklea ◆◆◆
Brookside, Lake Road,
Windermere, Cumbria LA23 2BX
T: (01539) 445326
F: (01539) 445326
E: rocklea.co.uk@virginnet
I: www.rocklea.co.uk

St John's Lodge ◆◆◆
Lake Road, Windermere,
Cumbria LA23 2EQ
T: (01539) 443078
F: (01539) 488054
E: mail@st-johns-lodge.co.uk
I: www.st-johns-lodge.co.uk

Sandown ◆◆◆
Lake Road, Bowness-on-
Windermere, Windermere,
Cumbria LA23 2JF
T: (01539) 445275
F: (01539) 445275

Storrs Gate House ◆◆◆◆
Longtail Hill, Bowness-on-
Windermere, Windermere,
Cumbria LA23 3JD
T: (01539) 443272
E: enquiries@storrsgatehouse.
co.uk
I: www.storrsgatehouse.co.uk

Tarn Rigg ◆◆◆◆
Thornbarrow Road, Windermere,
Cumbria LA23 2DG
T: (01539) 488777
E: stay@tarn-rigg.co.uk
I: www.tarn-rigg.co.uk

Thornbank House ◆◆◆
4 Thornbarrow Road,
Windermere, Cumbria LA23 2EW
T: (01539) 443724
F: (01539) 443724

Thornleigh Guest House ◆◆◆
Thornbarrow Road, Windermere,
Cumbria LA23 2EW
T: (01539) 444203
F: (01539) 444203

Upper Oakmere ◆◆
3 Upper Oak Street, Windermere,
Cumbria LA23 2LB
T: (01539) 445649 &
07798 806732
E: upperoakmere@hotmail.com
I: www.upperoakmere.co.uk

Villa Lodge Guest House
◆◆◆◆
25 Cross Street, Windermere,
Cumbria LA23 1AE
T: (01539) 443318
F: (01539) 443318
E: rooneym@btconnect.com
I: www.villa-lodge.co.uk

Virginia Cottage ◆◆◆
1 and 2 Crown Villas, Kendal
Road, Bowness-on-Windermere,
Windermere, Cumbria LA23 3EJ
T: (01539) 444891 & 444855
F: (01539) 444891
E: enquiries@virginia-cottage.
co.uk
I: www.virginia-cottage.co.uk

Waverley Hotel ◆◆◆
College Road, Windermere,
Cumbria LA23 1BX
T: (01539) 445026 & 444528
F: (01539) 445549
E: info@waverley.com
I: www.waverleyhotel.com

Westbourne Hotel ◆◆◆◆
Biskey Howe Road, Bowness-
on-Windermere, Cumbria
LA23 2JR
T: (015394) 43625 &
07702 025305
F: (015394) 43625
E: westbourne@btinternet.com
I: www.milford.co.uk

Westbury House ◆◆◆
27 Broad Street, Windermere,
Cumbria LA23 2AB
T: (01539) 446839
F: (01539) 442784
E: tonybaker@aol.com

Westlake Hotel ◆◆◆
Lake Road, Windermere,
Cumbria LA23 2EQ
T: (01539) 443020
F: (01539) 443020
E: westlake@clara.net

White Lodge Hotel ◆◆◆◆
Lake Road, Windermere,
Cumbria LA23 2JJ
T: (015394) 43624
F: (015394) 44749
E: enquiries@whitelodgehotel.
com
I: www.whitelodgehotel.com

White Rose ◆◆◆
Broad Street, Windermere,
Cumbria LA23 2AB
T: (01539) 445180
F: (01539) 445180
E: whiteroselakes@lineone.net
I: www.smoothhound.
co.uk/hotels/whiteroselakes

The Windermere Hotel ◆◆◆
Kendal Road, Windermere,
Cumbria LA23 1AL
T: (015394) 42251

Woodlands ◆◆◆◆
New Road, Windermere,
Cumbria LA23 2EE
T: (01539) 443915
F: (01539) 443915

WORKINGTON
Cumbria

Morven Guest House ◆◆◆
Siddick Road, Siddick,
Workington, Cumbria CA14 1LE
T: (01900) 602118
F: (01900) 602118
E: cnelsonmorven@aol.com

NORTHUMBRIA

ACOMB
Northumberland

The Sun Inn ◆◆◆◆
Main Street, Acomb, Hexham,
Northumberland NE46 4PW
T: (01434) 602934
F: (01434) 606635
E: sun_inn@hotmail.com

ALLENDALE
Northumberland

Kings Head Hotel ◆◆
Market Place, Allendale,
Hexham, Northumberland
NE47 9BD
T: (01434) 683681

Oakey Dene ◆◆◆◆
Allendale, Hexham,
Northumberland NE47 9EL
T: (01434) 683572

Struthers Farm ◆◆◆
Catton, Allendale, Hexham,
Northumberland NE47 9LP
T: (01434) 683580

Thornley House ◆◆◆◆
Allendale, Hexham,
Northumberland NE47 9NH
T: (01434) 683255
E: e.finn@ukonline.co.uk
I: web.ukonline.co.uk/e.finn

ALLENDALE TOWN
Northumberland

Manor House Farm ◆◆◆
Ninebanks, Hexham,
Northumberland NE47 8DA
T: (01434) 345068
F: (01434) 345068
E: manorhouse@ukonline.co.uk
I: www.manorhouse.ntb.org.uk

ALNMOUTH
Northumberland

Beech Lodge ◆◆◆◆
8 Alnwood, Alnmouth, Alnwick,
Northumberland NE66 3NN
T: (01665) 830709 &
07713 011526

Bilton Barns Farmhouse
◆◆◆◆
Alnmouth, Alnwick,
Northumberland NE66 2TB
T: (01665) 830427
F: (01665) 830063
E: dorothy@biltonbarns.co.uk
I: www.biltonbarns.co.uk

The Grange ◆◆◆◆
Northumberland Street,
Alnmouth, Alnwick,
Northumberland NE66 2RJ
T: (01665) 830401
F: (01665) 830401
E: thegrange.alnmouth@virgin.
net

High Buston Hall ◆◆◆◆◆
High Buston, Alnmouth,
Alnwick, Northumberland
NE66 3QH
T: (01665) 830606
F: (01665) 830707
E: highbuston@aol.com
I: www.highbuston.com

Hipsburn Farm ◆◆◆◆
Alnmouth, Alnwick,
Northumberland NE66 3PY
T: 07710 896430 & 896430
F: (01665) 830206

Hope and Anchor Hotel ◆◆◆
44 Northumberland Street,
Alnmouth, Alnwick,
Northumberland NE66 2RA
T: (01665) 830363

**Marine House Private Hotel
(Alnmouth) Ltd**◆◆◆◆
1 Marine Road, Alnmouth,
Alnwick, Northumberland
NE66 2RW
T: (01665) 830349
F: (01665) 830349
E: tanney@marinehouse.
freeserve.
co.uk
I: www.northumberland-hotel.
co.uk

Sefton House ◆◆◆
15 Argyle Street, Alnmouth,
Alnwick, Northumberland
NE66 2SB
T: (01665) 830002
E: Victoriana@supanet.com

ALNWICK
Northumberland

Aln House ◆◆◆◆
South Road, Alnwick,
Northumberland NE66 2NZ
T: (01665) 602265
E: bill@alnhousealnwick.
worldonline.co.uk

Aydon House ◆◆◆
South Road, Alnwick,
Northumberland NE66 2NT
T: (01665) 602218

Bondgate House Hotel ◆◆◆
20 Bondgate Without, Alnwick,
Northumberland NE66 1PN
T: (01665) 602025
F: (01665) 602025
E: kenforbes@lineone.net
I: www.bondgatehotel.ntb.org.
uk

21 Boulmer Village ◆◆◆◆
Alnwick, Northumberland
NE66 3BS
T: (01665) 577262

Charlton House ◆◆◆◆
2 Aydon Gardens, Alnwick,
Northumberland NE66 2NT
T: (01665) 605185
I: www.s-h-systems.
co.uk/hotels/charlt2.html

Crosshills House ◆◆◆◆
40 Blakelaw Road, Alnwick,
Northumberland NE66 1BA
T: (01665) 602518

East Cawledge Park Farm
◆◆◆
Alnwick, Northumberland
NE66 2HB
T: (01665) 605705
F: (01665) 605963

The Georgian Guest House ◆◆
3 Hotspur Street, Alnwick,
Northumberland NE66 1QE
T: (01665) 602 398
F: (01665) 602 398
E: georgianguesthouse@
eggconnect.net

Hawkhill Farmhouse ◆◆◆◆
Lesbury, Alnwick,
Northumberland NE66 3PG
T: (01665) 830380
F: (01665) 830093

Ingleside ◆◆◆◆
23 Stott Street, Alnwick,
Northumberland NE66 1QA
T: (01665) 602229

Lilburn Grange ◆◆◆
West Lilburn, Alnwick,
Northumberland NE66 4PP
T: (01668) 217274

Limetree Cottage ◆◆◆◆
38 Eglingham Village, Alnwick,
Northumberland NE66 2TX
T: (01665) 578322

Masons Arms ◆◆◆◆
Stamford, Rennington, Alnwick,
Northumberland NE66 3RX
T: (01665) 577275
F: (01665) 577894
E: masonsarms@lineone.net
I: www.masonsarms.net

Norfolk ◆◆◆◆
41 Blakelaw Road, Alnwick,
Northumberland NE66 1BA
T: (01665) 602892
I: www.norfolk.ntb.org.uk

Reighamsyde ◆◆◆◆
The Moor, Alnwick,
Northumberland NE66 2AJ
T: (01665) 602535

Rock Midstead Farm House
◆◆◆
Rock Midstead, Rock, Alnwick,
Northumberland NE66 2TH
T: (01665) 579225 & 579326
E: ian@rockmidstead.freeserve.
co.uk

Rooftops ◆◆◆◆
14 Blakelaw Road, Alnwick,
Northumberland NE66 1AZ
T: (01665) 604201
E: rooftops.alnwick@talk21.com
I: www.rooftops.ntb.org.uk

Roseworth ◆◆◆◆
Alnmouth Road, Alnwick,
Northumberland NE66 2PR
T: (01665) 603911
E: bowden@roseworthann.
freeserve.co.uk

Tower Guest Rooms ◆◆◆◆
10 Bondgate Within, Alnwick,
Northumberland NE66 1TD
T: (01665) 603888 & 0797 102
3692
F: (01665) 603222
E: hotspurtower@aol.com
I: www.hotspur-tower.com

AMBLE-BY-THE-SEA
Northumberland

Bisley Place ◆◆◆
37 Bisley Road, Amble-by-the-
Sea, Morpeth, Northumberland
NE65 0NP
T: (01665) 710473 &
07773 162545

Coquetside ◆◆◆◆
16 Broomhill Street, Amble-by-
the-Sea, Morpeth,
Northumberland NE65 0AN
T: (01665) 710352 &
07719 708829
I: coquetside.future.easyspace.
com

The Hollies ◆◆◆
3 Riverside Park, Amble-by-the-
Sea, Morpeth, Northumberland
NE65 0YR
T: (01665) 712323 & 712708
E: terrihollies@clara.co.uk
I: www.baldeagle50.demon.
co.uk/Holliesmain.htm

Togston Hall Farmhouse ◆◆◆
North Togston, Morpeth,
Northumberland NE65 0HR
T: (01665) 712699 &
07971 541365
F: (01665) 712699

BAMBURGH
Northumberland

Broome ◆◆◆◆
22 Ingram Road, Bamburgh,
Northumberland NE69 7BT
T: (01668) 214287 &
07971 248230
E: mdixon4394@aol.com
I: www.member.xoom.
com/bamburgh

Burton Hall ◆◆◆
Bamburgh, Northumberland
NE69 7AR
T: (01668) 214213 & 214458
F: (01668) 214538
E: evehumphreys@aol.com
I: www.burtonhall.co.uk

Glenander Guest House
◆◆◆◆
27 Lucker Road, Bamburgh,
Northumberland NE69 7BS
T: (01668) 211330
F: (01668) 214100

Green Gates ◆◆◆
34 Front Street, Bamburgh,
Northumberland NE69 7BJ
T: (01668) 214535
E: bamburgh.sunset@talk21.
com

Squirrel Cottage ◆◆◆◆
1 Friars Court, Bamburgh,
Northumberland NE69 7AE
T: (01668) 214494 & 214572
E: theturnbulls2k@btinternet.
com
I: www.geocities.
com/thetropics/bay/3021

BARDON MILL
Northumberland

Carrsgate East ◆◆◆◆
Bardon Mill, Hexham,
Northumberland NE47 7EX
T: (01434) 344376 &
07710 981533
F: (01434) 344011
E: lesley@armstrongrl.freeserve.
co.uk
I: carrsgate-east.com

Crindledykes Farm ◆◆◆◆
Nr Housesteads, Bardon Mill,
Hexham, Northumberland
NE47 7AF
T: (01434) 344316
F: (01434) 344316

Gibbs Hill Farm
Rating Applied For
Once Brewed, Bardon Hill,
Hexham, Once Brewed,
NE47 7AP
T: (01434) 344030
F: (01434) 344030
E: val@gibbshillfarm.co.uk
I: www.gibbshillfarm.co.uk

The Old Stables, Montcoffer
◆◆◆◆
Bardon Mill, Hexham,
Northumberland NE47 7HZ
T: (01434) 344138 &
07715 911024
F: (01434) 344730
E: john-dehlia@talk21.com
I: www.montcoffer.co.uk
🅿

**Strand Cottage Bed and
Breakfast** ◆◆◆
Main Road (A69), Bardon Mill,
Hexham, Northumberland
NE47 7BH
T: 1434 344643 & 7833 968655
E: strandcottage@aol.com
I: www.strand-cottage.co.uk

Vallum Lodge Hotel ◆◆◆◆
Military Road, Twice Brewed,
Bardon Mill, Hexham,
Northumberland NE47 7AN
T: (01434) 344248
F: (01434) 344488
E: vallum.lodge@ukonline.co.uk
I: www.vallumlodge.ntb.org.uk

BARNARD CASTLE
Durham

Bowes Moor Hotel ◆◆◆
Bowes Moor, Barnard Castle,
County Durham DL12 9RH
T: (01833) 628331
F: (01833) 628331
E: bowesmoorhotel@
barnard-castle.co.uk
I: www.barnard-castle.co.uk

Bowfield Farm ◆◆
Scargill, Barnard Castle, County
Durham DL12 9SU
T: (01833) 638636

Cloud High ◆◆◆◆
Eggleston, Barnard Castle,
County Durham DL12 0AU
T: (01833) 650644
F: (01833) 650644
E: cloudhigh@btinternet.com
I: www.cloudhigh-teesdale.co.uk

Demesnes Mill ◆◆◆◆◆
Barnard Castle, County Durham
DL12 8PE
T: (01833) 637929
F: (01833) 637974
E: millbb2@ic24.net
I: www.webproze.com/millbb

East Mellwaters Farm ◆◆◆
Bowes, Barnard Castle, County
Durham DL12 9RH
T: (01833) 628269 & 628022
F: (01833) 628269
E: trishmilner@ic24.net

George & Dragon Inn ◆◆◆
Boldron, Barnard Castle, County
Durham DL12 9RF
T: (01833) 638215

Greta House ◆◆◆◆
89 Galgate, Barnard Castle,
County Durham DL12 8ES
T: (01833) 631193
F: (01833) 631193
I: gretahousebc@btclock.com

The Homelands ◆◆◆◆
85 Galgate, Barnard Castle,
County Durham DL12 8ES
T: (01833) 638757
E: homelands@barnard-castle.
fsnet.co.uk

Marwood House ◆◆◆◆
98 Galgate, Barnard Castle,
County Durham DL12 8BJ
T: (01833) 637493
F: (01833) 637493
E: john&sheila@kilgarriff.
demon.co.uk
I: www.kilgarriff.demon.co.uk

Montalbo Hotel ◆◆◆
Montalbo Road, Barnard Castle,
County Durham DL12 8BP
T: (01833) 637342
F: (01833) 637342
E: suzannethomas@
montalbohotel.co.uk
I: www.montalbohotel.co.uk

Moorcock Inn ◆◆◆
Hill Top, Gordon Bank,
Eggleston, Barnard Castle,
County Durham DL12 0AU
T: (01833) 650395
F: (01833) 650052
E: zach1@talk21.com
I: www.moorcock-Inn.co.uk

33 Newgate ◆◆◆
Barnard Castle, County Durham
DL12 8NJ
T: (01833) 690208
E: peter.whittaker@tinyworld.
co.uk
I: www.barnard-castle.
co.uk/accommodation/
whittaker.html

Old Well Inn ◆◆◆
21 The Bank, Barnard Castle,
County Durham DL12 8PH
T: (01833) 690130
F: (01833) 690140
E: reservations@oldwellinn.
co.uk
I: www.oldwellinn.co.uk

Raygill Farm ◆◆◆
Lartington, Barnard Castle,
County Durham DL12 9DG
T: (01833) 690118
F: (01833) 690118

Spring Lodge ◆◆◆
Newgate, Barnard Castle,
County Durham DL12 8NW
T: (01833) 638110
F: (01833) 638110
E: ormston@telinco.co.uk
I: www.springlodgebandb.co.uk

Strathmore Lawn East ◆◆◆
81 Galgate, Barnard Castle,
County Durham DL12 8ES
T: (01833) 637061
E: strathmoreebb@talk21.co.uk

Wilson House ◆◆◆◆
Barningham, Richmond, North
Yorkshire DL11 7EB
T: (01833) 621110
F: (01833) 621110

BARRASFORD
Northumberland

Barrasford Arms ◆◆◆
Barrasford, Hexham,
Northumberland NE48 4AA
T: (01434) 681237
F: (01434) 681237

BEADNELL
Northumberland

Beach Court ◆◆◆◆◆
Harbour Road, Beadnell,
Chathill, Northumberland
NE67 5BJ
T: (01665) 720225 &
07703 555125
F: (01665) 721499
E: info@beachcourt.com
I: www.beachcourt.com

Beadnell House Hotel ◆◆◆
Beadnell, Chathill,
Northumberland NE67 5AT
T: (01665) 721380
F: (01665) 720217
E: enquiries@beadnellhouse.
co.uk
I: www.beadnellhouse.co.uk

7 Benthall ◆◆◆◆
Beadnell, Chathill,
Northumberland NE67 5BQ
T: (01665) 720900
F: (01665) 720900
E: stay@7benthall.co.uk
I: www.7benthall.co.uk

Low Dover Beadnell Bay
◆◆◆◆
Harbour Road, Beadnell,
Chathill, Northumberland
NE67 5BJ
T: (01665) 720291 &
07971 444070
F: (01665) 720291
E: kathandbob@lowdover.co.uk
I: www.lowdover.co.uk

**The New Beadnell Towers
Hotel** ◆◆◆
Beadnell, Chathill,
Northumberland NE67 5AU
T: (01665) 721211
F: (01665) 720424
E: beadnell@towers.fsnet.co.uk

Shepherds Cottage ◆◆◆◆
Beadnell, Chathill,
Northumberland NE67 5AD
T: (01665) 720497 &
07703 455131
F: (01665) 720497
I: www.shepherdscottage.ntb.
org.uk

BEAL
Northumberland

Brock Mill Farmhouse ◆◆◆
Brock Mill, Beal, Berwick-upon-
Tweed TD15 2PB
T: (01289) 381283 &
07889 099517
F: (01289) 381283

West Mains House ◆◆◆
Beal, Berwick-upon-Tweed
TD15 2PD
T: (01289) 381227

BEAMISH
Durham

The Beamish Mary Inn ◆◆◆
No Place, Beamish, Stanley,
County Durham DH9 0QH
T: (0191) 370 0237
F: (0191) 370 0091

The Coach House ◆◆◆◆
High Urpeth, Beamish, Stanley,
County Durham DH9 0SE
T: (0191) 370 0309
F: (0191) 370 0046
E: coachhouse@foreman25.
freeserve.co.uk
I: www.coachhousebeamish.ntb.
org.uk

Malling House ◆◆◆
1 Oakdale Terrace, Newfield,
Chester-le-Street, County
Durham DH2 2SU
T: (0191) 370 2571 & 0750 856
5967
F: (0191) 370 1391
E: heather@mallingguesthouse.
co.uk
I: www.mallinghouse.com

No Place House Bed &
Breakfast ◆◆
Beamish, Stanley, County
Durham DH9 0QH
T: (0191) 370 0891
E: margaret@
noplaceguesthouse.freeserve.
co.uk

BELFORD
Northumberland

Easington Farm ◆◆◆◆
Belford, Northumberland
NE70 7EG
T: (01668) 213298

The Farmhouse Guest House
◆◆◆
24 West Street, Belford,
Northumberland NE70 7QE
T: (01668) 213083

Fenham-le-Moor ◆◆◆◆
Belford, Northumberland
NE70 7PN
T: (01668) 213247
F: (01668) 213247

Oakwood House ◆◆◆◆
3 Cragside Avenue, Belford,
Northumberland NE70 7NA
T: (01668) 213303
E: maureenatoakwood@talk21.
com

Rosebank ◆◆◆
5 Cragside Avenue, Belford,
Northumberland NE70 7NA
T: (01668) 213762
F: (01668) 213762

11 West Street ◆◆◆
Belford, Northumberland
NE70 7QA
T: (01668) 213480

BELLINGHAM
Northumberland

Bridgeford Farm
Rating Applied For
Bridgeford, Bellingham,
Hexham, Northumberland
NE48 2HU
T: (01434) 220940

The Cheviot Hotel ◆◆◆
Bellingham, Hexham,
Northumberland NE48 2AU
T: (01434) 220696
F: (01434) 220696

Ivy Cottage ◆◆◆
Lanehead, Tarset, Hexham,
Northumberland NE48 1NT
T: (01434) 240337
F: (01434) 240073

Lyndale Guest House ◆◆◆◆
Off The Square, Bellingham,
Hexham, Northumberland
NE48 2AW
T: (01434) 220361 &
03778 925479
F: (01434) 220361
E: ken&joy@lyndalegh.fsnet.
co.uk
I: www.SmoothHound.
co.uk/hotels/lyndale.html

Westfield House
Rating Applied For
Bellingham, Hexham,
Northumberland NE48 2DP
T: (01434) 220340
F: (01434) 220354
I: www.westfield-house.net

BELMONT
Durham

Moor End House Bed and
Breakfast ◆◆◆
7-8 Moor End Terrace, Belmont,
Durham DH1 1BJ
T: (0191) 384 2796
F: (0191) 3842796

BERWICK-UPON-TWEED
Northumberland

Alannah House ◆◆◆◆
84 Church Street, Berwick-
upon-Tweed, TD15 1DU
T: (01289) 307252
I: www.alannahhouse.co.uk

Bridge View ◆◆◆◆
14 Tweed Street, Berwick-upon-
Tweed, TD15 1NG
T: (01289) 308098

The Castle ◆◆◆
103 Castlegate, Berwick-upon-
Tweed, TD15 1LF
T: (01289) 307900 & 306471
F: (01289) 307900

The Cat Inn ◆◆◆◆
Great North Road, Cheswick,
Berwick-upon-Tweed, TD15 2RL
T: (01289) 387251
F: (01289) 387251

Cear Urfa ◆◆◆◆
15 Springfield Park, East Ord,
Berwick-upon-Tweed, TD15 2FD
T: (01289) 303528

Clovelly House ◆◆◆◆
58 West Street, Berwick-upon-
Tweed, TD15 1AS
T: (01289) 302337
F: (01289) 302052
E: vivroc@clovelly53.freeserve.
co.uk
I: www.clovelly53.freeserve.
co.uk

Cobbled Yard Hotel ◆◆◆
40 Walkergate, Berwick-upon-
Tweed, TD15 1DJ
T: (01289) 308407
F: (01289) 330623
E: cobbledyardhotel@
berwick35.fsnet.co.uk
I: www.cobbledyardhotel.com

Dervaig Guest House ◆◆◆◆
1 North Road, Berwick-upon-
Tweed, TD15 1PW
T: (01289) 307378
F: (01289) 307378
E: dervaig@talk21.com

Drousha Guest House ◆◆◆
11 Sandgate, Berwick-upon-
Tweed, TD15 1EP
T: (01289) 306659

Fairholm ◆◆◆◆
East Ord, Berwick-upon-Tweed,
TD15 2NS
T: (01289) 305370

The Friendly Hound ◆◆◆◆
Ford Common, Berwick-upon-
Tweed, TD15 2QD
T: (01289) 388554
E: friendlyhound.b.b@talk21.
com

Heron's Lee ◆◆◆◆
Thornton, Berwick-upon-Tweed,
TD15 2LP
T: (01289) 382000
F: (01289) 382000
E: john_burton@btconnect.com
I: www.northumbandb.co.uk

High Letham Farmhouse
◆◆◆◆◆
High Letham, Berwick-upon-
Tweed, TD15 1UX
T: (01289) 306585
F: (01289) 304194
E: hlf-b@fantasyprints.co.uk
I: www.wolsey-lodges.co.uk

Ladythorne House ◆◆◆
Cheswick, Berwick-upon-Tweed,
TD15 2RW
T: (01289) 387382
F: (01289) 387073
E: valparker@
ladythorneguesthouse.freeserve.
co.uk
I: www.ladythorneguesthouse.
freeserve.co.uk

Meadow Hill Guest House
◆◆◆◆
Duns Road, Berwick-upon-
Tweed, TD15 1UB
T: (01289) 306325
F: (01289) 306325
E: barryandhazel@meadow-hill.
co.uk
I: www.meadow-hill.co.uk

Middle Ord Manor House
◆◆◆◆◆
Middle Ord Farm, Berwick-
upon-Tweed, TD15 2XQ
T: (01289) 306323
F: (01289) 308423
E: joan@middleordmanor.co.uk
I: www.middleordmanor.com

No 1 Sallyport ◆◆◆◆
Bridge Street, Berwick-upon-
Tweed, TD15 1EZ
T: (01289) 308827 &
07703 116796
F: (01289) 308827
E: info@
1sallyport-bedandbreakfast.com
I: www.
1sallyport-bedandbreakfast.com

4 North Road ◆◆◆◆
Berwick-upon-Tweed,
Northumberland TD15 1PL
T: (01289) 306146 & 0771 242
6145
F: (01289) 306146
E: sandra@thorntonfour.
freeserve.co.uk

6 North Road ◆◆◆◆
Berwick-upon-Tweed, TD15 1PL
T: (01289) 308949

The Old Vicarage Guest House
◆◆◆◆
24 Church Road, Tweedmouth,
Berwick-upon-Tweed TD15 2AN
T: (01289) 306909
F: (01289) 309052
E: stay@oldvicarageberwick.
co.uk
I: www.oldvicarageberwick.co.uk

Orkney House ◆◆
37 Woolmarket, Berwick-upon-
Tweed, TD15 1DH
T: (01289) 331710

6 Parade ◆◆◆
Berwick-upon-Tweed, TD15 1DF
T: (01289) 308454

40 Ravensdowne ◆◆◆◆
Berwick-upon-Tweed, TD15 1DQ
T: (01289) 306992
F: (01289) 301606
E: petedot'dmuckle.freeserve.
co.uk
I: www.secretkingdom.
com/40/ravensdowne.htm

Rob Roy ◆◆◆◆
Dock Road, Tweedmouth,
Berwick-upon-Tweed TD15 2BQ
T: (01289) 306428
E: therobroy@btinternet.com
I: www.therobroy.co.uk

Whyteside House ◆◆◆◆
46 Castlegate, Berwick-upon-
Tweed, Northumberland
TD15 1JT
T: (01289) 331019
F: (01289) 331419
E: albert@whyteside100.
freeserve.co.uk
I: www.secretkingdom.
com/whyte/side.htm

BISHOP AUCKLAND
Durham

Albion Cottage Guest House
◆◆◆
Albion Terrace, Bishop Auckland,
County Durham DL14 6EL
T: (01388) 602217
F: (01388) 602217
E: bookings@albioncottage.
co.uk

Five Gables Guest House ◆◆◆
Binchester, Bishop Auckland,
County Durham DL14 8AT
T: (01388) 608204
F: (01388) 663092
E: book.in@fivegables.co.uk
I: www.fivegables.co.uk

The Old Farmhouse ◆◆◆
Grange Hill, Bishop Auckland,
County Durham DL14 8EG
T: (01388) 602123
F: (01388) 602123

BOWBURN
Durham

Prince Bishop Guest House
◆◆◆
1 Oxford Terrace, Bowburn,
Durham DH6 5AX
T: (0191) 377 8703 & 3736914

BRIGNALL
Durham

Lily Hill Farm ◆◆◆
Brignall, Barnard Castle, County
Durham DL12 9SF
T: (01833) 627254

CAMBO
Northumberland

Shieldhall ◆◆◆◆
Wallington, Cambo, Morpeth,
Northumberland NE61 4AQ
T: (01830) 540387
F: (01830) 540490
E: robinson.gay@btinternet.com

CASTLESIDE
Durham

Castleneuk Guest House ◆◆
18-20 Front Street, Castleside,
Consett, County Durham
DH8 9AR
T: (01207) 506634
E: jan@castleneuk.co.uk
I: www.castleneuk.co.uk

Deneview ◆◆◆
15 Front Street, Castleside,
Consett, County Durham
DH8 9AR
T: (01207) 502925 &
07957 948498
E: cyndyglancy@lineone.net

CHATHILL
Northumberland

North Charlton Farm ◆◆◆◆◆
Chathill, Northumberland
NE67 5HP
T: (01665) 579443 &
07812 579407
F: (01665) 579407
E: ncharlton1@agricplusnet

West Link Hall Farmhouse
◆◆◆◆
Alnwick, Northumberland
NE67 5HU
T: (01665) 579306 &
(01655) 577262

CHATTON
Northumberland

South Hazelrigg Farmhouse
◆◆◆◆
South Hazelrigg, Chatton,
Alnwick, Northumberland
NE66 5RZ
T: (01668) 215216 &
07710 346076
E: sdodds@farmhousebandb.
co.uk
I: www.farmhousebandb.co.uk

CHESTER-LE-STREET
Durham

Hollycroft ◆◆◆◆
11 The Parade, Chester-le-
Street, County Durham DH3 3LR
T: (0191) 388 7088 &
07932 675069
E: cutter@hollycroft11.
freeserve.co.uk

Low Urpeth Farm House
◆◆◆◆
Ouston, Chester-le-Street,
County Durham DH2 1BD
T: (0191) 410 2901
F: (0191) 410 0088
E: lowurpeth@hotmail.com
I: www.lowurpeth.co.uk

Waldridge Fell House ◆◆◆◆
Waldridge Lane, Waldridge,
Chester-le-Street, County
Durham DH2 3RY
T: (0191) 389 1908
E: BBchesterlestreet@
btinternet.com

CONSETT
Durham

Bee Cottage Farm ◆◆◆
Castleside, Consett, County
Durham DH8 9HW
T: (01207) 508224

CORBRIDGE
Northumberland

Clive House ◆◆◆◆
Appletree Lane, Corbridge,
Northumberland NE45 5DN
T: (01434) 632617

Dilston Mill ◆◆◆◆
Corbridge, Northumberland
NE45 5QZ
T: (01434) 633493
F: (01434) 633513
E: susan@distonmill.com
I: www.dilstonmill.com

Fellcroft ◆◆◆◆
Station Road, Corbridge,
Northumberland NE45 5AY
T: (01434) 632384
F: (01434) 633918
E: tove.brown@ukonline.co.uk

The Hayes ◆◆◆
Newcastle Road, Corbridge,
Northumberland NE45 5LP
T: (01434) 632010
F: (01434) 632010
E: mjct@matthews.fsbusiness.
co.uk
I: www.hayes-corbridge.co.uk

Holmlea ◆◆◆
Station Road, Corbridge,
Northumberland NE45 5AY
T: (01434) 632486

**Low Fotherley Farmhouse Bed
and Breakfast** ◆◆◆◆
Riding Mill, Northumberland
NE44 6BB
T: (01434) 682277
F: (01434) 682277
E: hugh@lowfotherley.fsnet.
co.uk
I: www.westfarm.freeserve.co.uk

Priorfield ◆◆◆◆
Hippingstones Lane, Corbridge,
Northumberland NE45 5JA
T: (01434) 633179 &
07860 962448
F: (01434) 633179
E: nsteenberg@lineone.net

Riverside Guest House ◆◆◆◆
Main Street, Corbridge,
Northumberland NE45 5LE
T: (01434) 632942
F: (01434) 633883
E: riverside@ukonline.co.uk
I: web.ukonline.co.uk/riverside/

Town Barns ◆◆◆◆
Off Trinity Terrace, Corbridge,
Northumberland NE45 5HP
T: (01434) 633345

COTHERSTONE
Durham

Fox and Hounds ◆◆◆
Cotherstone, Barnard Castle,
County Durham DL12 9PF
T: (01833) 650241 &
07710 351822
F: (01833) 650241
E: mcarlisle@foxcothe.
freenetname.com
I: foxcotherstone.co.uk

Glendale ◆◆◆
Cotherstone, Barnard Castle,
County Durham DL12 9UH
T: (01833) 650384
I: www.barnard-castle.co.uk

COXHOE
Durham

The Black Horse ◆◆
Station Road East, Coxhoe,
Durham DH6 4AT
T: (0191) 377 9574
F: (0191) 377 9555
E: ian@blackhorse11.co.uk

CRAGHEAD
Durham

The Punch Bowl ◆◆
Craghead, Stanley, County
Durham DH9 6EF
T: (01207) 232917

CRASTER
Northumberland

Cottage Inn ◆◆◆
Dunstan Village, Craster,
Alnwick, Northumberland
NE66 3SZ
T: (01665) 576658
F: (01665) 576788

Howick Scar Farmhouse ◆◆◆
Craster, Alnwick,
Northumberland NE66 3SU
T: (01665) 576665
F: (01665) 576665
E: howickscar@lineone.net

Stonecroft ◆◆◆◆
Dunstan, Craster, Alnwick,
Northumberland NE66 3SZ
T: (01665) 576433
F: (01665) 576311
E: sally@stonestaff.freeserve.
co.uk
I: www.stonecroft.ntb.org.uk

CRESSWELL
Northumberland

Cresswell House ◆◆◆◆
Cresswell, Morpeth,
Northumberland NE61 5LA
T: (01670) 861302

CROOK
Durham

Watergate Lane Farm ◆◆◆
Rumby Hill, Crook, County
Durham DL15 8EN
T: (01388) 766913
F: (01388) 764727

CROOKHAM
Northumberland

The Coach House at Crookham
◆◆◆◆
Cornhill-on-Tweed,
Northumberland TD12 4TD
T: (01890) 820293
F: (01890) 820284
E: thecoachouse@englandmail.
com
I: www.coachhousecrookham.
com
♿

CROXDALE
Durham

Croxdale Inn ◆◆◆
Front Street, Croxdale, Durham
DH6 5HX
T: (01388) 815727 & 420294
F: (01388) 815368
E: croxdale@talk21.com

DARLINGTON
Durham

Aberlady Guest House ◆
51 Corporation Road,
Darlington, County Durham
DL3 6AD
T: (01325) 461449 &
07970 379939

Boot & Shoe ◆◆◆
Church Row, Darlington, County
Durham DL1 5QD
T: (01325) 287501 & 362121
F: (01325) 287501

The Chequers Inn ◆◆◆
Darlington, County Durham
DL2 2NT
T: (01325) 721213 & 722307
F: (01325) 722357

Clow–Beck House ◆◆◆◆◆
Monk End Farm, Croft,
Darlington, County Durham
DL2 2SW
T: (01325) 721075 & 0779 908
4526
F: (01325) 720419
E: david@clowbeckhouse.co.uk
I: www.clowbeckhouse.co.uk

The Cricketers Hotel
Rating Applied For
55 Parkgate, Darlington, County
Durham DL1 1RR
T: (01325) 384444

The Dalesman Hotel ◆◆
96–100 Victoria Road,
Darlington, County Durham
DL1 5JW
T: (01325) 466695 & 357654
F: (01325) 467855

Greenbank Guest House ◆◆◆
90 Greenbank Road, Darlington,
County Durham DL3 6EL
T: (01325) 462624
F: (01325) 250233

Harewood Lodge ◆◆◆
40 Grange Road, Darlington,
County Durham DL1 5NP
T: (01325) 358152
E: Harewood.Lodge@NTLWorld.
com

DURHAM
Durham

60 Albert Street ◆◆◆◆
Western Hill, Durham, DH1 4RJ
T: (0191) 386 0608 &
07855 086266
F: (0191) 370 9739
E: laura@sixtyalbertstreet.co.uk
I: www.sixtyalbertstreet.co.uk

The Anchorage ◆◆◆
25 Langley Road, Newton Hall,
Durham, DH1 5LR
T: (0191) 386 2323
F: (0191) 3862323
E: anchorageb@aol.com

**The Autumn Leaves Guest
House** ◆◆◆
Dragonville, Durham, DH1 2DX
T: (0191) 386 3394

12 The Avenue ◆◆◆
Durham, DH1 4ED
T: (0191) 384 1020
E: janhanim@aol.com

The Avenue Inn ◆
Avenue Street, High Shincliffe,
Durham DH1 2PT
T: (0191) 386 5954
E: wenmah@aol.com

Bay Horse Inn ◆◆◆
Brandon Village, Durham,
DH7 8ST
T: (0191) 378 0498

Belle Vue Guest House ◆◆◆
4 Belle Vue Terrace, Gilesgate
Moor, Durham, DH1 2HR
T: (0191) 386 4800

Broom Farm Guest House
◆◆◆◆
Broom Farm, Broom Park Village,
Durham, DH7 7QX
T: (0191) 386 4755

Castle View Guest House
◆◆◆◆
4 Crossgate, Durham, DH1 4PS
T: (0191) 386 8852
F: (0191) 386 8852
E: castle_view@hotmail.com

Castledene ◆◆◆
37 Nevilledale Terrace, Durham,
DH1 4QG
T: (0191) 384 8386 &
07710 425921
F: (0191) 384 8386
E: lornabyrne@tinyworld.co.uk

Cathedral View Guest House
◆◆◆◆
212 Gilesgate, Durham, Co
Durham DH1 1QN
T: (0191) 386 9566
E: cathedralview@hotmail.com

College of Saint Hild and Saint
Bede (Guest Rooms & Gables)
◆
St Hild's Lane, Durham, DH1 1SZ
T: (0191) 374 3069 & 374 3064
F: (0191) 374 4740
E: l.c.hugill@durham.ac.uk
I: www.dur.ac.uk/HildBede

Collingwood College Cumbrian
Wing ◆◆◆
South Road, Durham, DH1 3LT
T: (0191) 374 4568
F: (0191) 374 4595
E: collingwood_college.
conference@durham.ac.uk

Farnley Tower ◆◆◆◆
The Avenue, Durham, DH1 4DX
T: (0191) 375 0011
F: (0191) 383 9694
E: enquiries@farnley-tower.
co.uk
I: www.farnley-tower.co.uk

The Georgian Town House
◆◆◆◆
10 Crossgate, Durham, DH1 4PS
T: (0191) 386 8070
F: (0191) 386 8070
E: enquiries@
georgian-townhouse.fsnet.com

10 Gilesgate ◆◆
Durham, DH1 1QW
T: (0191) 386 2026 &
07711 956476
F: (0191) 386 2026

14 Gilesgate ◆◆
Top of Claypath, Durham,
County Durham DH1 1QW
T: (0191) 384 6485
F: (0191) 386 5173
E: bb@nimmins.co.uk
I: www.nimmins.co.uk

The Gilesgate Moor Hotel
◆◆◆
Teasdale Terrace, Gilesgate,
Durham DH1 2RN
T: (0191) 386 6453
F: (0191) 386 6453

Green Grove ◆◆◆
99 Gilesgate, Durham, DH1 1JA
T: (0191) 384 4361
E: bill-dockery@guesthouse.
fsnet.co.uk
I: www.smoothhound.
co.uk/hotels/greengro.html

Grey College (Holgate) ◆◆
South Road, Durham, DH1 3LG
T: (0191) 374 2965 & 374 2965
F: (0191) 374 2968
E: joyce.dover@durham.ac.uk
I: www.dur.ac.uk/GreyCollege

Hatfield College, Jevons ◆◆
North Bailey, Durham, DH1 3RQ
T: (0191) 374 3165
F: (0191) 374 7472
E: a.m.ankers@durham.ac.uk
I: www.dur.ac.
uk/Hatfield/college/confrnce.
html

Hill Rise Guest House
Rating Applied For
13 Durham Road West,
Bowburn, Durham DH6 5AU
T: (0191) 377 0302
F: (0191) 377 0898
E: hillrise.guesthouse@
btinternet.com
I: www.hill-rise.com

Knights Rest ◆◆◆
1 Anchorage Terrace, Durham,
DH1 3DL
T: (0191) 386 6229 & 0780 170
0896
F: (0191) 386 6229

The Loves ◆◆◆
17 Front Street, Broompark,
Durham DH7 7QT
T: (0191) 384 9283
E: karen.paul@tinyonline.co.uk

The Newton Grange Hotel
◆◆◆
Finchal Road, Brasside, Durham
DH1 5SA
T: (0191) 386 0872
F: (0191) 386 0872

O'Neills Inn ◆◆
91a Claypath, Durham, DH1 1RG
T: (0191) 383 6951

Pelaw Rise ◆◆◆◆
Leazes Road, Durham, DH1 1TS
T: (0191) 386 5778 &
07802 697965
F: (0191) 386 5778
E: hospitality@pelawrise.
freeserve.co.uk

St Aidan's College ◆◆◆
University of Durham, Windmill
Hill, Durham, DH1 3LJ
T: (0191) 374 3269
F: (0191) 374 4749
E: aidans.conf@durham.ac.uk
I: www.st-aidans.org.uk
♿

St Chad's College ◆◆
18 North Bailey, Durham,
DH1 3RH
T: (0191) 374 3364
F: (0191) 374 3309
E: St-Chads.www@durham.ac.
uk
I: www.dur.ac.uk/StChads/

Saint Cuthberts Society ◆◆
12 South Bailey, Durham,
DH1 3EE
T: (0191) 374 3464 & 374 3400
F: (0191) 374 4753
E: i.d.barton@durham.ac.uk
I: www.dur.ac.
uk/~dcb0www/conf.htm

Saint Johns College (Curddas)
Rating Applied For
3 South Bailey, Durham DH1 3RJ
T: (0191) 374 3579
F: (0191) 374 3573
E: s.i.hobson@durham.ac.uk
I: www.
stjohnscollege-durham.com

Seven Stars Inn ◆◆◆
Shincliffe Village, Durham,
DH1 2NU
T: (0191) 384 8454
F: (0191) 386 0640

Three Horse Shoes Inn ◆◆◆
Running Waters, Sherburn
House, Durham DH1 2SR
T: (0191) 372 0286 & 372 3386
F: (0191) 372 3386
E: m.s.parkinson@
threehorseshoes.fsbosiness.
co.uk
I: www.smoothhounds.co.uk/

Trevelyan College (Macaulay
Wing) ◆◆◆
Elvet Hill Road, Durham,
DH1 3LN
T: (0191) 374 3765 & 374 3768
F: (0191) 374 3789
E: trev.coll@durham.ac.uk
I: www.dur.ac.
uk/~dtr0www/conference.html

Triermayne ◆◆◆◆
Nevilles Cross Bank, Durham,
DH1 4JP
T: (0191) 384 6036

Van Mildert College (Tunstall
Stairs) ◆◆◆
Mill Hill Lane, Durham, DH1 3LH
T: (0191) 374 3900
F: (0191) 374 3974
E: van-mildert.college@durham.
ac.uk
I: www.dur.ac.
uk/VanMildert/Conferences/
together.htm

Victoria Inn ◆◆◆
86 Hallgarth Street, Durham,
DH1 3AS
T: (0191) 386 5269 & 386 0465
F: (0191) 386 0465

Waterside ◆◆◆◆
Elvet Waterside, Durham,
DH1 3BW
T: (0191) 384 6660 & 384 6996
F: (0191) 384 6996
♿

EASINGTON
Tees Valley
The Grapes ◆◆◆
Scaling Dam, Easington,
Saltburn-by-the-Sea, Cleveland
TS13 4TP
T: (01287) 640461
E: mark79@kenny7997.
freeserve.co.uk
I: www.touristnetuk.
com/ne/grapes/

EAST ORD
Northumberland
Inverleacainn ◆◆◆◆
4 Springfield Park, East Ord,
Berwick-upon-Tweed TD15 2FD
T: (01289) 304627

Tweed View House ◆◆◆
East Ord, Berwick-upon-Tweed
TD15 2NS
T: (01289) 332378
F: (01289) 332378
E: khdobson@aol.com

EASTGATE-IN-WEARDALE
Durham
Rose Hill Farm Bed and
Breakfast ◆◆◆◆
Rose Hill Farm, Eastgate-in-
Weardale, Bishop Auckland,
County Durham DL13 2LB
T: (01388) 517209 &
07808 402425
E: june@rosehillfarm.fsnet.co.uk
I: www.rosehillfarmholidays.
co.uk

EGLINGHAM
Northumberland
Ash Tree House ◆◆◆◆
The Terrace, Eglingham, Alnwick,
Northumberland NE66 2UA
T: (01665) 578533
I: www.ashtreehouse.com

ELLINGHAM
Northumberland
Pack Horse Inn ◆◆◆
Ellingham, Chathill,
Northumberland NE67 5HA
T: (01665) 589292 &
07050 189333
F: (01665) 589063
E: graham.simpson@farmline.
com
I: www.thepackhorseinn.co.uk

EMBLETON
Northumberland
Blue Bell Inn ◆◆◆
Embleton, Alnwick,
Northumberland NE66 3UP
T: (01665) 576573 & 576639

Rock Farmhouse ◆◆◆
Rock Village, Alnwick,
Northumberland NE66 3SE
T: (01665) 579235
F: (01665) 579215
E: rockfarmbb@cs.com
I: www.rockfarmhouse.
freeserve.co.uk

The Sportsman ◆◆◆
Sea Lane, Embleton, Alnwick,
Northumberland NE66 3XF
T: (01665) 576588
F: (01665) 576524

ESCOMB
Durham
The Gables ◆◆◆
3 Lane Ends, Escomb, Bishop
Auckland, County Durham
DL14 7SR
T: (01388) 604745

FALSTONE
Northumberland
The Blackcock Inn ◆◆◆
Falstone, Hexham,
Northumberland NE48 1AA
T: (01434) 240200
F: (01434) 240200
E: blackcock@falstone.
fsbusiness.co.uk
I: www.smoothhound.
co.uk/hotels/black.html

High Yarrow Farm ◆◆◆
Falstone, Hexham,
Northumberland NE48 1BG
T: (01434) 240264

Woodside ◆◆◆◆
Yarrow, Falstone, Hexham,
Northumberland NE48 1BG
T: (01434) 240443

FELTON
Northumberland
Cook and Barker Inn ◆◆◆◆
Newton-on-the-Moor, Felton, Morpeth, Northumberland NE65 9JY
T: (01665) 575234
F: (01665) 575234

FENHAM
Tyne and Wear
The Brighton ◆◆
47-49 Brighton Grove, Fenham, Newcastle upon Tyne NE4 5NS
T: (0191) 273 3600
F: (0191) 226 0563

FIR TREE
Durham
Duke of York Inn ◆◆◆◆
Fir Tree, Crook, County Durham DL15 8DG
T: (01388) 762848

FORD
Northumberland
The Estate House ◆◆◆◆
Ford, Berwick-upon-Tweed, Northumberland TD15 2PX
T: (01890) 820668 &
07715 313989
F: (01890) 820672
E: theestatehouse@supanet.com

Hay Farm Farmhouse ◆◆◆◆
Ford, Berwick-upon-Tweed TD12 4TR
T: (01890) 820617 & 820650
F: (01890) 820659

The Old Post Office ◆◆◆
2 Old Post Office Cottages, Ford, Berwick-upon-Tweed TD15 2QA
T: (01890) 820286 &
07803 819452
E: jwait309139627@aol.com
I: www.secretkingdom.com

FOREST-IN-TEESDALE
Durham
High Force Hotel ◆◆◆
Forest-in-Teesdale, Barnard Castle, County Durham DL12 0XH
T: (01833) 622222

FOURSTONES
Northumberland
8 St Aidans Park ◆◆◆◆
Fourstones, Hexham, Northumberland NE47 5EB
T: (01434) 674073
F: (01434) 674073
E: janet@hadrians-wall.co.uk
I: www.hadrians-wall.co.uk

FOXTON
Northumberland
Out of Bounds ◆◆◆
Foxton, Alnwick, Northumberland NE66 3BE
T: (01665) 830150
F: (01665) 830150

FROSTERLEY
Durham
High Laithe ◆◆◆
10A Hill End, Frosterley, Bishop Auckland, County Durham DL13 2SX
T: (01388) 526421

GAINFORD
Durham
Queens Head Hotel ◆◆◆
11 Main Road, Gainford, Darlington, County Durham DL2 3DZ
T: (01325) 730958

GATESHEAD
Tyne and Wear
The Bewick Hotel ◆◆◆
145 Prince Consort Road, Gateshead, Tyne and Wear NE8 4DS
T: (0191) 477 1809 & 477 3401
F: (0191) 477 6146
E: bewickenquiries@145bewick.fsnet.co.uk
I: www.bewickhotel.co.uk

Shaftesbury Guest House ◆◆◆
245 Prince Consort Road, Gateshead, Tyne and Wear NE8 4DT
T: (0191) 478 2544
F: (0191) 478 2544

GREAT TOSSON
Northumberland
Tosson Tower Farm ◆◆◆◆
Great Tosson, Morpeth, Northumberland NE65 7NW
T: (01669) 620228
F: (01669) 620228
E: ann@tossontowerfarm.com
I: www.tossontowerfarm.com

GREENHAUGH
Northumberland
Hollybush Inn ◆◆◆
Greenhaugh, Hexham, Northumberland NE48 1PW
T: (01434) 240391 & 240228

GREENHEAD
Northumberland
Four Wynds ◆◆◆
Longbyre, Greenhead, Brampton, Cumbria CA8 7HN
T: (01697) 747330
F: (01697) 747330
E: rozbonnarhadrianswall@talk21.com

Greenhead Hotel ◆◆◆
Greenhead, Brampton, Cumbria CA8 7HB
T: (01697) 747411

Holmhead Guest House ◆◆◆◆
Thirlwall Castle Farm, Hadrian's Wall, Greenhead, Brampton, Cumbria CA8 7HY
T: (01697) 47402
F: (01697) 47402
E: Holmhead@hadrianswall.freeserve.co.uk
I: www.bandbhadrianswall.com

GRETA BRIDGE
Durham
The Coach House ◆◆◆◆◆
Greta Bridge, Barnard Castle, County Durham DL12 9SD
T: (01833) 627201
E: info@coachhousegreta.co.uk
I: www.coachhousegreta.co.uk

HALTWHISTLE
Northumberland
Ashcroft ◆◆◆◆
Lantys Lonnen, Haltwhistle, Northumberland NE49 0DA
T: (01434) 320213
F: (01434) 320213
E: enquiries@ashcroftguesthouse.freeserve.co.uk
I: www.ashcroftguesthouse.co.uk

Brookside House Vegetarian Bed and Breakfast ◆◆◆◆
Brookside House, Town Foot, Haltwhistle, Northumberland NE49 0ER
T: (01434) 322481
E: brooksideveg-b-and-b@lineone.net
I: website.lineone.net/~billstapleton

Broomshaw Hill Farm ◆◆◆◆◆
Willia Road, Haltwhistle, Northumberland NE49 9NP
T: (01434) 320866 & 0771 483 5828
F: (01434) 320866
E: broomshaw@msn.com
I: www.broomshaw.co.uk

Doors Cottage Bed and Breakfast ◆◆◆
Shield Hill, Haltwhistle, Northumberland NE49 9NW
T: (01434) 322556 &
07867 668574
E: doors-cottage@supanet.com

The Grey Bull Hotel ◆◆◆
Main Street, Haltwhistle, Northumberland NE49 0DL
T: (01434) 321991
F: (01434) 320770
E: PamGreyB@aol.com

Hall Meadows ◆◆◆
Main Street, Haltwhistle, Northumberland NE49 0AZ
T: (01434) 321021

Kirkholmedale ◆◆◆
Lantys Lonnen, Haltwhistle, Northumberland NE49 0HQ
T: (01434) 322948

Oaky Knowe Farm ◆◆◆
Haltwhistle, Northumberland NE49 0NB
T: (01434) 320648
F: (01434) 320648

The Old School House ◆◆◆◆
Fair Hill, Haltwhistle, Northumberland NE49 9EE
T: (01434) 322595
F: (01434) 322595
E: vera@oshouse.freeserve.co.uk
I: www.oshouse.freeserve.co.uk

Saughy Rigg Farm ◆◆◆
Twice Brewed, Haltwhistle, Northumberland NE49 9PT
T: (01434) 344120
E: kathandbrad@aol.com
I: www.saughyrigg.co.uk

Spring House ◆◆◆◆
Comb Hill, Haltwhistle, Northumberland NE49 9NS
T: (01434) 320334

HAMSTERLEY
Durham
Dryderdale Hall ◆◆◆◆
Hamsterley, Bishop Auckland, County Durham DL13 3NR
T: (01388) 488494 & 0780 328 3222
F: (01388) 488195

HARBOTTLE
Northumberland
The Byre Vegetarian B&B ◆◆◆◆
Harbottle, Morpeth, Northumberland NE65 7DG
T: (01669) 650476
E: rosemary@the-byre.co.uk
I: www.the-byre.co.uk
🏃

HARTFORD BRIDGE
Northumberland
Woodside ◆◆◆◆
Hartford Bridge Farm, Hartford Bridge, Bedlington, Northumberland NE22 6AL
T: (01670) 822035

HARTLEPOOL
Tees Valley
Brafferton Guest House ◆◆
161 Stockton Road, Hartlepool, Cleveland TS25 1SL
T: (01429) 273875
E: jwilson.brafferton@virgin.net

Hillcarter Hotel ◆◆◆◆
31-32 Church Street, Hartlepool, Cleveland TS24 7DJI
T: (01429) 855800 & 855826
F: (01429) 855829
E: hillcarter@btinternet.com
I: www.hillcarterhotel.co.uk

The Oakroyd Hotel ◆◆◆
133 Park Road, Hartlepool, Cleveland TS26 9HT
T: (01429) 864361
F: (01429) 890535

The York Hotel ◆◆◆
185 York Road, Hartlepool, Cleveland TS26 9EE
T: (01429) 867373
F: (01429) 867220
E: info@theyorkhotel.co.uk
I: www.theyorkhotel.co.uk

HAYDON BRIDGE
Northumberland
Anchor Hotel ◆◆◆
John Martin Street, Haydon Bridge, Hexham, Northumberland NE47 6AB
T: (01434) 684227
F: (01434) 684586
E: anchor.hotel@virgin.net
I: www.freespace.virgin.net/alan.mcjannet4/index.html

Hadrian Lodge ◆◆◆
Hindshield Moss, North Road, Haydon Bridge, Hexham, Northumberland NE47 6NF
T: (01434) 688688
F: (01434) 684867
E: hadrianlodge@hadrianswall.co.uk
I: www.hadrianswall.co.uk

Railway Hotel ◆◆◆
Church Street, Haydon Bridge, Hexham, Northumberland NE47 6JG
T: (01434) 684254

West Mill Hills ♦♦♦
Haydon Bridge, Hexham,
Northumberland NE47 6JR
T: (01434) 684387

HEXHAM
Northumberland

10 Alexandra Terrace ♦♦
Hexham, Northumberland
NE46 3JQ
T: (01434) 601954
E: davesue@onetel.net.uk
I: www.hexham.lookscool.com

Anick Grange ♦♦♦
Hexham, Northumberland
NE46 4LP
T: (01434) 603807

The Coach and Horses ♦♦♦
Priestpopple, Hexham,
Northumberland NE46 1PQ
T: (01434) 601004 & 600492

Corio House ♦♦♦
3 Woodlands, Corbridge Road,
Hexham, Northumberland
NE46 1HT
T: (01434) 603370 &
07790 397161

**The County Hotel
Rating Applied For**
Priestpopple, Hexham,
Northumberland NE46 1PS
T: (01434) 603601
F: (01434) 603616
E: the-county-hotel-hexham@
supanet.com

Dene House ♦♦♦♦
Juniper, Hexham,
Northumberland NE46 1SJ
T: (01434) 673413
F: (01434) 673413
E: margaret@
denehouse-hexham.co.uk
I: www.denehouse-hexham.
co.uk

Dukesfield Hall Farm ♦♦♦
Steel, Hexham, Northumberland
NE46 1SH
T: (01434) 673634
E: cath@dukesfield.supanet.
com

The Fairway ♦♦♦♦
4 Shaws Park, Hexham,
Northumberland NE46 3BJ
T: (01434) 604846
E: gailcowley@aol.com

Hetherington ♦♦♦
Wark-on-Tyne, Hexham,
Northumberland NE48 3DR
T: (01434) 230260
F: (01434) 230260
E: a_nichol@hotmail.com

High Reins ♦♦♦♦
Leazes Lane, Hexham,
Northumberland NE46 3AT
T: (01434) 603590
E: walton45@hotmail.com
I: www.highreins.co.uk

Kitty Frisk House ♦♦♦♦
Corbridge Road, Hexham,
Northumberland NE46 1UN
T: (01434) 601533
F: (01434) 601533
E: alan@kittyfriskhouse.co.uk
I: www.kittyfriskhouse.co.uk

Laburnum House ♦♦♦♦
23 Leazes Crescent, Hexham,
Northumberland NE46 3JZ
T: (01434) 601828
E: laburnum.house@virginnet.
co.uk

**Number 18 Hextol Terrace
♦♦♦**
Hexham, Northumberland
NE46 2DF
T: (01434) 602265

Old Redhouse Farm ♦♦♦♦
Dipton Mill, Hexham,
Northumberland NE46 1XY
T: (01434) 604463
E: susanbradley@ukonline.co.uk

Peth Head Cottage ♦♦♦♦
Juniper, Juniper, Hexham,
Northumberland NE47 0LA
T: (01434) 673286
F: (01434) 673038
E: tedliddle@compuserve.com
I: www.pethheadcottage.ntb.
org.uk

Queensgate House ♦♦♦
Cockshaw, Hexham,
Northumberland NE46 3QU
I: (01434) 605592
F: (01434) 608940
E: njareed@aol.com

Rose and Crown Inn ♦♦♦
Main Street, Slaley, Hexham,
Northumberland NE47 0AA
T: (01434) 673263
F: (01434) 673305
E: rosecrowninn@supanet.com
I: www.smoothhound.
co.uk/hotels/rosecrowninn.html

Rye Hill Farm ♦♦♦♦
Slaley, Hexham,
Northumberland NE47 0AH
T: (01434) 673259
F: (01434) 673259
E: enquiries@consult-courage.
co.uk
I: www.ryehillfarm.co.uk

Thistlerigg Farm ♦♦♦
High Warden, Hexham,
Northumberland NE46 4SR
T: (01434) 602041 &
07790 384675
F: (01434) 602041

Topsy Turvy ♦♦♦♦
9 Leazes Lane, Hexham,
Northumberland NE46 3BA
T: (01434) 603152
E: topsy.turvy@ukonline.co.uk

Ventnor House ♦♦♦
23 Elvaston Road, Hexham,
Northumberland NE46 2HA
T: (01434) 607814 &
07866 826437

West Close House ♦♦♦♦
Hextol Terrace, Hexham,
Northumberland NE46 2AD
T: (01434) 603307 &
07971 529949

West Wharmley ♦♦♦♦
Hexham, Northumberland
NE46 2PL
T: (01434) 674227 &
07788 711112

Westbrooke Hotel ♦♦♦
Allendale Road, Hexham,
Northumberland NE46 2DE
T: (01434) 603818

Woodley Field ♦♦♦
Allendale Road, Hexham,
Northumberland NE46 2NB
T: (01434) 601600

HIGH SHINCLIFFE
Durham

Shincliffe Station House ♦♦♦
High Shincliffe, Durham
DH1 2TE
T: (0191) 384 6906
E: joan@shincliffe.demon.co.uk
I: www.shincliffe.demon.co.uk

HOLY ISLAND
Northumberland

Britannia ♦♦♦
Britannia House, Holy Island,
Berwick-upon-Tweed TD15 2RX
T: (01289) 389218

The Bungalow ♦♦♦♦
Holy Island, Berwick-upon-
Tweed TD15 2SE
T: (01289) 389308
E: bungalow@celtic121.demon.
co.uk
I: www.lindisfarne.org.
uk/bungalow

Crown & Anchor Hotel ♦♦♦
Market Place, Holy Island,
Berwick-upon-Tweed TD15 2RX
T: (01289) 389215
F: (01289) 389215

Open Gate ♦♦♦♦
Marygate, Holy Island, Berwick-
upon-Tweed TD15 2SD
T: (01289) 389222
E: info@theopengate.org.uk
I: www.lindisfarne.org.
uk-accommodation

The Ship ♦♦♦
Marygate, Holy Island, Berwick-
upon-Tweed TD15 2SJ
T: (01289) 389311
F: (01289) 389316
E: theship@holyisland7.
freeserve.co.uk
I: www.
lindisfarneaccommodate.com

HOLYSTONE
Northumberland

**The Kennels
Rating Applied For**
Holystone, Morpeth,
Northumberland NE65 7AJ
T: (01669) 650429
F: (01669) 650429
E: stay@thekennelsholystone.
co.uk
I: www.thekennelsholystone.
co.uk

HORSLEY
Northumberland

Belvedere ♦♦♦♦
Harlow Hill, Horsley, Newcastle
upon Tyne NE15 0QD
T: (01661) 853689
E: pat.carr@btinternet.com
I: www.belvederehouse.co.uk

HOUSESTEADS
Northumberland

Moss Kennels Farm ♦♦♦♦
Housesteads, NE47 9NL
T: (01434) 344016 &
07889 111885
F: (01434) 344016
E: tim.mosskennels@virgin.net

HUMSHAUGH
Northumberland

Greencarts Farm ♦♦♦
Humshaugh, Hexham,
Northumberland NE46 4BW
T: (01434) 681320

**Haughton Strother Bed and
Breakfast ♦♦♦♦**
Haughton Strother House,
Humshaugh, Hexham,
Northumberland NE46 4BX
T: (01434) 681438
F: (01434) 681438
E: joycehhunt@hotmail.com

HUTTON MAGNA
Durham

Rokeby Close Farm ♦♦♦♦
Hutton Magna, Richmond,
North Yorkshire DL11 7HN
T: (01833) 627171 &
07710 745961
F: (01833) 627662
E: don.wilkinson@farmline.com

KIELDER
Northumberland

Deadwater Farm ♦♦♦♦
Kielder, Hexham,
Northumberland NE48 1EW
T: (01434) 250216

Gowanburn ♦♦♦
Kielder, Hexham,
Northumberland NE48 1HL
T: (01434) 250254

KIELDER WATER
Northumberland

**The Pheasant Inn (by Kielder
Water) ♦♦♦♦**
Stannersburn, Falstone, Hexham,
Northumberland NE48 1DD
T: (01434) 240382
F: (01434) 240382
E: thepheasantinn@
kielderwater.demon.co.uk

Ridge End Farm ♦♦♦♦
Falstone, Hexham,
Northumberland NE48 1DE
T: (01434) 240395
E: ridge_end_farm@talk21.com

KIRKWHELPINGTON
Northumberland

Cornhills Farmhouse ♦♦♦♦
Cornhills, Kirkwhelpington,
Newcastle upon Tyne NE19 2RE
T: (01830) 540232
F: (01830) 540388
E: cornhills@farming.co.uk
I: www.
northumberlandfarmhouse.
co.uk

LANCHESTER
Durham

**Maiden Hall Farmhouse Bed
and Breakfast♦♦♦**
Maiden Law, Lanchester,
Durham DH7 0QX
T: (01207) 520796 &
07932 973686

LITTLETOWN
Durham

Littletown Lodge ♦♦♦
Front Street, Littletown, Durham
DH6 1PZ
T: 0771 3322667 &
(0191) 3723712
F: (0191) 3723712

Establishments printed in blue have a detailed entry in this guide

LONGFRAMLINGTON
Northumberland
The Angler's Arms ◆◆◆◆
Weldon Bridge,
Longframlington, Morpeth,
Northumberland NE65 8AX
T: (01665) 570655 & 570271
F: (01665) 570041
I: www.anglersarms.com

Lee Farm ◆◆◆◆
Longframlington, Morpeth,
Northumberland NE65 8JQ
T: (01665) 570257
F: (01665) 507257
E: enqs@leefarm.co.uk
I: www.leefarm.co.uk

LONGHORSLEY
Northumberland
The Baronial ◆◆◆
Cross Cottage, Longhorsley,
Morpeth, Northumberland
NE65 8TD
T: (01670) 788378
F: (01670) 788378

Kington ◆◆◆
East Linden, Longhorsley,
Morpeth, Northumberland
NE65 8TH
T: (01670) 788554
F: (01670) 788747
E: clive@taylor-services.
freeserve.co.uk

Thistleyhaugh Farm ◆◆◆◆◆
Longhorsley, Morpeth,
Northumberland NE65 8RG
T: (01665) 570629
F: (01665) 570629

LOWICK
Northumberland
Black Bull Inn ◆◆◆◆
Main Street, Lowick, Berwick-
upon-Tweed TD15 2UA
T: (01289) 388228
F: (01289) 388395
E: tom@blackbullowick.
freeserve.co.uk

The Old Manse ◆◆◆◆
5 Cheviot View, Lowick, Berwick-
upon-Tweed TD15 2TY
T: (01289) 388264
E: glenc99@aol.com

Southwood ◆◆◆◆
75 Main Street, Lowick, Berwick-
upon-Tweed, Northumberland
TD15 2UD
T: (01289) 388619
F: (01289) 388619
E: anne.waite@virgin.net
I: freespace.virgin.net/anne.
waite

MARLEY HILL
Tyne and Wear
Hedley Hall ◆◆◆◆
Hedley Lane, Marley Hill,
Newcastle upon Tyne NE16 5EH
T: (01207) 231835
E: sfr1008452@aol.com

MATFEN
Northumberland
Matfen High House ◆◆◆◆
Matfen, Newcastle upon Tyne
NE20 0RG
T: (01661) 886592
F: (01661) 886592
E: struan@struan.
enterprise-plc.com

MICKLETON
Durham
Pine Grove ◆◆◆
Lowside, Mickleton, Barnard
Castle, County Durham
DL12 0JR
T: (01833) 640886
E: chris@cgillings.freeserve.
co.uk
I: www.barnardcastleindex.i12.
com

MIDDLETON
Northumberland
East Shaftoe Hall ◆◆◆◆
Middleton, Morpeth,
Northumberland NE61 4EA
T: (01830) 530249
F: (01830) 530249
E: charlotterobson@shaftoe.
fsbusiness.co.uk
I: www.s-h-systems.
co.uk/hotels/eastshaf.html

MIDDLETON-IN-TEESDALE
Durham
Belvedere House ◆◆◆
54 Market Place, Middleton-in-
Teesdale, Barnard Castle, County
Durham DL12 0QH
T: (01833) 640884
F: (01833) 640884
E: belvedere@thecoachhouse.
net
I: www.thecoachhouse.
net/belvedere

Bluebell House ◆◆◆
Market Place, Middleton-in-
Teesdale, Barnard Castle, County
Durham DL12 0QG
T: (01833) 640584

Brunswick House ◆◆◆◆
55 Market Place, Middleton-in-
Teesdale, Barnard Castle, County
Durham DL12 0QH
T: (01833) 640393
F: (01833) 640393
E: enquiries@brunswickhouse.
net
I: www.brunswickhouse.net

Grove Lodge ◆◆◆◆
Hude, Middleton-in-Teesdale,
Barnard Castle, County Durham
DL12 0QW
T: (01833) 640798

Ivy House ◆◆◆
Stanhope Road, Middleton-in-
Teesdale, Barnard Castle, County
Durham DL12 0RT
T: (01833) 640603

Lonton South Farm ◆◆◆
Middleton-in-Teesdale, Barnard
Castle, County Durham
DL12 0PL
T: (01833) 640409

**Marketplace Guest House
◆◆◆**
16 Market Place, Middleton-in-
Teesdale, Barnard Castle, County
Durham DL12 0QG
T: (01833) 640300

Snaisgill Farm ◆◆◆
Middleton-in-Teesdale, Barnard
Castle, County Durham
DL12 0RP
T: (01833) 640343

Wemmergill Hall Farm ◆◆◆
Lunedale, Middleton-in-
Teesdale, Barnard Castle, County
Durham DL12 0PA
T: (01833) 640379
F: (01833) 640379
E: wemmergill@freenet.co.uk
I: www.wemmergill-farm.co.uk

MORPETH
Northumberland
**Cottage View Guest House
◆◆◆**
6 Staithes Lane, Morpeth,
Northumberland NE61 1TD
T: (01670) 518550
F: (01670) 510840
E: cottageview.morpeth@virgin.
net
I: www.cottageview.co.uk

Elder Cottage ◆◆◆◆
High Church, Morpeth,
Northumberland NE61 2QT
T: (01670) 517664
F: (01670) 517644
E: cook@eldercot.freeserve.
co.uk
I: www.eldercottage.co.uk

**Riverside Bed and Breakfast
◆◆◆**
77 Newgate Street, Morpeth,
Northumberland NE61 1BX
T: (01670) 515026
F: (01670) 514647
E: elaine.riverside@virgin.net
I: www.riverside-guesthouse.
co.uk

NEW BRANCEPETH
Durham
**Alum Waters Guest House
◆◆◆◆**
Unthank Farmhouse, Alum
Waters, New Brancepeth,
Durham DH7 7JJ
T: (0191) 373 0628
F: (0191) 373 0628
E: tony@alumwaters.freeserve.
co.uk

NEWBIGGIN-BY-THE-SEA
Northumberland
Seaton House ◆◆◆
20 Seaton Avenue, Newbiggin-
by-the-Sea, Northumberland
NE64 6UX
T: (01670) 816057

NEWBROUGH
Northumberland
**Allerwash Farmhouse
◆◆◆◆◆**
Newbrough, Hexham,
Northumberland NE47 5AB
T: (01434) 674574
F: (01434) 674574

Newbrough Park ◆◆◆◆◆
Newbrough, Hexham,
Northumberland NE47 5AR
T: (01434) 674545
F: (01434) 674544

NEWCASTLE UPON TYNE
Tyne and Wear
Avenue Hotel ◆◆◆
2 Manor House Road, Jesmond,
Newcastle upon Tyne NE2 2LU
T: (0191) 281 1396
F: (0191) 281 6588

Chirton House Hotel ◆◆◆
46 Clifton Road, Off Grainger
Park Road, Newcastle upon
Tyne, NE4 6XH
T: (0191) 273 0407 & 273 3454
F: (0191) 273 0407

Eldon Hotel ◆◆
24 Akenside Terrace, Jesmond,
Newcastle upon Tyne NE2 1TN
T: (0191) 281 2562
F: (0191) 213 0546

Elm Cottage ◆◆
37 Sunniside Road, Sunnise,
Newcastle upon Tyne, NE16 5NA
T: (0191) 496 0156 & 07759 326
2298

Jesmond Park Hotel ◆◆◆
74-76 Queens Road, Jesmond,
Newcastle upon Tyne NE2 2PR
T: (0191) 281 2821 & 281 1913
F: (0191) 281 0515
E: vh@jespark.fsnet.co.uk
I: www.jesmondpark.com

The Keelman's Lodge ◆◆◆◆
Grange Road, Newburn,
Newcastle upon Tyne NE15 8NL
T: (0191) 267 1689 & 267 0772
F: (0191) 499 0041
E: admin@petersen-stainless.
co.uk
I: www.petersen-stainless.co.uk

The Lynnwood ◆◆◆
1 Lynwood Terrace, Newcastle
upon Tyne, NE4 6UL
T: (0191) 273 3497
F: (0191) 273 3497

**University of Northumbria
Claude Gibb Hall's of
Residence◆◆**
Room 107, Ellison Terrce, Ellison
Place, Newcastle upon Tyne,
NE1 8ST
T: (0191) 227 4024 & 227 4403
F: (0191) 227 3197
E: carmel.wright@unn.ac.uk
I: www.unn.ac.uk/~amu6

Westland Hotel ◆◆◆
27 Osborne Avenue, Jesmond,
Newcastle upon Tyne NE2 1JR
T: (0191) 281 0412
F: (0191) 281 5005

NEWFIELD
Durham
The Newfield Inn ◆◆◆
New Field Road, Chester-le-Street, County
Durham DH2 2SP
T: (0191) 370 0565 & 370 3988

NEWTON
Northumberland
Crookhill Farm ◆◆◆
Newton, Stocksfield,
Northumberland NE43 7UX
T: (01661) 843117
F: (01661) 844702

NORHAM
Northumberland
Dromore House ◆◆◆
12 Pedwell Way, Norham,
Berwick-upon-Tweed,
Northumberland TD15 2LD
T: (01289) 382313

**Rosemary Cottage
Rating Applied For**
14 West Street, Norham,
Berwick-upon-Tweed,
Northumberland TD15 2LB
T: (01289) 382247

Threeways ♦♦♦
Norham, Berwick-upon-Tweed
TD15 2JZ
T: (01289) 382795

NORTH HYLTON
Tyne and Wear
The Shipwrights Hotel ♦♦♦
Ferry Boat Lane, North Hylton,
Sunderland SR5 3HW
T: (0191) 549 5139
F: (0191) 549 7464
E: tony@theshipwrights.
freeserve.co.uk

NORTH SUNDERLAND
Northumberland
132 Main Street ♦♦♦♦
North Sunderland, Seahouses,
Northumberland NE68 7TZ
T: (01665) 720729
F: (01665) 720729

NORTON
Tees Valley
Grange Guest House ♦♦♦
33 Grange Road, Norton,
Stockton-on-Tees, Cleveland
TS20 2NS
T: (01642) 552541
I: www.shlwell.co.uk

OTTERBURN
Northumberland
**Butterchurn Guest House
♦♦♦♦**
Main Street, Otterburn,
Newcastle upon Tyne NE19 1NP
T: (01830) 520585
F: (01830) 520874
E: keith@butterchurn.freeserve.
co.uk
I: www.butterchurn.freeserve.
co.uk

**Dunns Houses Farmhouse Bed
and Breakfast♦♦♦♦**
Dunns Houses, Otterburn,
Newcastle upon Tyne NE19 1LB
T: (01830) 520677 & 0780 859
2701
F: (01830) 520677
E: dunnshouses@hotmail.com
I: www.dunnshouses.freeserve.
co.uk

Low Byrness ♦♦♦♦
Rochester, Newcastle upon Tyne
NE19 1TF
T: (01830) 520648
F: (01830) 520733
E: pdq@globalnet.co.uk
I: www.lowbyrness.co.uk

Redesdale Arms Hotel ♦♦♦♦
Rochester, Newcastle upon Tyne
NE19 1TA
T: (01830) 520668
F: (01830) 520063
E: redesdalehotel@hotmail.com
I: www.redesdale-hotel.co.uk
🛉

OVINGTON
Northumberland
Southcroft ♦♦♦♦
Ovington, Prudhoe,
Northumberland NE42 6EE
T: (01661) 830651 & 832515
F: (01661) 834312

PIERCEBRIDGE
Durham
The Bridge House ♦♦♦
Piercebridge, Darlington, County
Durham DL2 3SG
T: (01325) 374727
E: ceformstone@
netscapeonline.co.uk

Holme House ♦♦♦
Piercebridge, Darlington, County
Durham DL2 3SY
T: (01325) 374280
F: (01325) 374280
E: graham@holmehouse22.
freeserve.co.uk
I: www.destinationengland.
co.uk/holmehouse.html

PITY ME
Durham
**The Lambton Hounds Inn
♦♦♦**
Front Street, Pity Me, Durham
DH1 5DE
T: (0191) 386 4742
F: (0191) 375 0805
E: lambtonhounds@aol.com

PLAWSWORTH
Durham
Lilac Cottage ♦♦
Wheatley Well Lane,
Plawsworth, Chester-le-Street,
County Durham DH2 3LD
T: (0191) 371 2969

PONTELAND
Northumberland
Hazel Cottage ♦♦♦♦
Eachwick, Dalton, Newcastle
upon Tyne NE18 0BE
T: (01661) 852415
F: (01661) 854797
E: hazelcottage@eachwick.
fsbusiness.co.uk

Stone Cottage ♦♦♦
Prestwick Road End, Ponteland,
Newcastle upon Tyne NE20 9BX
T: (01661) 823957 & 823947
E: klee@euphony.net
I: www.stonecottageguesthouse.
com

Stonehaven Lodge ♦♦♦
Prestwick Road End, Ponteland,
Newcastle upon Tyne NE20 9BX
T: (01661) 872363
E: brenanderson@ncletw.
freeserve.co.uk

QUEBEC
Durham
Hamsteels Hall ♦♦♦
Hamsteels Lane, Quebec,
Durham DH7 9RS
T: (01207) 520388
F: 07754 751795
E: June@hamsteelshall.co.uk
I: www.hamsteelshall.co.uk

Hamsteels Inn ♦♦
Front Street, Quebec, Durham,
County Durham DH7 9DF
T: (0191) 373 7604
F: (0191) 373 7604

RAMSHAW
Northumberland
**The Bridge Inn
Rating Applied For**
1 Gordon Lane, Ramshaw,
Bishop Auckland, County
Durham DL14 0NS
T: (01388) 832509
F: (01388) 832509
E: bridgeinnramshaw@barbox.
com

REDCAR
Tees Valley
Claxton Hotel ♦♦♦
196 High Street, Redcar,
Cleveland TS10 3AW
T: (01642) 486745
F: (01642) 486522
E: enquiries@claxtonhotel.co.uk
I: www.claxtonhotel.co.uk

Falcon Hotel ♦♦♦
13 Station Road, Redcar,
Cleveland TS10 1AH
T: (01642) 484300
🛉

RIDING MILL
Northumberland
Broomley Fell Farm ♦♦♦
Riding Mill, Northumberland
NE44 6AY
T: (01434) 682682 &
07802 676143
F: (01434) 682728
E: enquiries@broomleyfell.co.uk
I: www.broomleyfell.co.uk

Woodside House ♦♦♦
Sandy Bank, Riding Mill,
Northumberland NE44 6HS
T: (01434) 682306

ROMALDKIRK
Durham
Mill Riggs Cottage ♦♦♦
Romaldkirk, Barnard Castle,
County Durham DL12 9EW
T: (01833) 650392

ROOKHOPE
Durham
High Brandon ♦♦♦♦
Rookhope, Bishop Auckland,
County Durham DL13 2AF
T: (01388) 517673
E: highbrandonbb@aol.com
I: members.aol.
com/highbrandonbb

ROTHBURY
Northumberland
Alexandra House ♦♦♦♦
High Street, Rothbury, Morpeth,
Northumberland NE65 7TE
T: (01669) 621463
E: lucy@alexandrahouse.fsnet.
co.uk
I: www.alex-house.co.uk

The Chirnells ♦♦♦♦
Thropton, Morpeth,
Northumberland NE65 7JE
T: (01669) 621507 &
07866 081747

Farm Cottage ♦♦♦♦
Thropton, Morpeth,
Northumberland NE65 7NA
T: (01669) 620831 & 0798 041
9774
F: (01669) 620831
E: joan@
farmcottageguesthouse.co.uk
I: www.farmcottageguesthouse.
com

The Haven ♦♦♦
Backcroft, Rothbury, Morpeth,
Northumberland NE65 7YA
T: (01669) 620577 &
07885 431814
F: (01669) 620577
E: dogmikec@aol.com

**Katerina's Guest House
♦♦♦♦**
Sun Buildings, High Street,
Rothbury, Morpeth,
Northumberland NE65 7TQ
T: (01669) 620691 &
07977 555692
E: cath@katerinasguesthouse.
co.uk
I: www.katerinasguesthouse.
co.uk

Lorbottle West Steads ♦♦♦
Thropton, Morpeth,
Northumberland NE65 7JT
T: (01665) 574672 &
07833 392966
F: (01665) 574672
E: helen.farr@farming.co.uk
I: www.cottageguide.
co.uk/lorbottle.html

Newcastle Hotel ♦♦♦
Rothbury, Morpeth,
Northumberland NE65 7UT
T: (01669) 620334
F: (01669) 620334

Orchard Guest House ♦♦♦♦
High Street, Rothbury, Morpeth,
Northumberland NE65 7TL
T: (01669) 620684
E: jpickard@orchardguesthouse.
co.uk
I: www.orchardguesthouse.co.uk

Silverton House ♦♦♦♦
Silverton Lane, Rothbury,
Morpeth, Northumberland
NE65 7RJ
T: (01669) 621395
E: maggie.wallacel@virgin.net
I: www.silvertonhouse.ntb.org.
uk

Silverton Lodge ♦♦♦♦
Silverton Lane, Rothbury,
Morpeth, Northumberland
NE65 7RJ
T: (01669) 620144
F: (01669) 621920
E: silverton.lodge@btinternet.
com
I: www.silvertonlodge.co.uk

Wagtail Farm ♦♦♦
Rothbury, Morpeth,
Northumberland NE65 7PL
T: (01669) 620367
E: wagtail@tinyworld.co.uk

**Whitton Farmhouse Hotel
♦♦♦♦**
Whitton, Rothbury, Morpeth,
Northumberland NE65 7RL
T: (01669) 620811
F: (01669) 620811
I: www.smoothound.
co.uk/hotels
🛉

RUSHYFORD
Durham
Garden House ♦♦♦♦
Windlestone Park, Windlestone,
Rushyford, Ferryhill, County
Durham DL17 0LZ
T: (01388) 720217 & 0797 929
7374

RYTON
Tyne and Wear
Hedgefield House ◆◆◆
Stella Road, Ryton, Tyne and
Wear NE21 4LR
T: (0191) 413 7373 &
07958 304942
F: (0191) 413 7373

ST JOHN'S CHAPEL
Durham
Low Chesters Guesthouse
Rating Applied For
St John's Chapel, Bishop
Auckland, County Durham
DL13 1QP
T: (01388) 537406

SALTBURN-BY-THE-SEA
Tees Valley
The Rose Garden ◆◆◆◆
20 Hilda Place, Saltburn-by-the-
Sea, Cleveland TS12 1BP
T: (01287) 622947
F: (01287) 622947
E: enquiries@therosegarden.
co.uk
I: www.therosegarden.co.uk

SEAHAM
Durham
**Seaham Hall Hotel and
Oriental Spa**
Rating Applied For
Lord Byron's Walk, Seaham,
County Durham SR7 7AG
T: (0191) 516 1400
F: (0191) 516 1410
E: simon@tonscompanies.com
I: www.seaham-hall.com

SEAHOUSES
Northumberland
Braidstone Lodge ◆◆◆
1 Braidstone Square, Seahouses,
Northumberland NE68 7RP
T: (01665) 720055

Kingsway ◆◆◆◆
19 Kings Street, Seahouses,
Northumberland NE68 7XW
T: (01665) 720449
F: (01665) 720449

Leeholme ◆◆◆
93 Main Street, Seahouses,
Northumberland NE68 7TS
T: (01665) 720230 & 0780 838
1590

The Links Hotel
Rating Applied For
8 King Street, Seahouses,
Northumberland NE68 7XP
T: (01665) 720062
F: (01665) 720988
E: linkshotel@hotmail.com
I: www.smoothhound.
co.uk/hotels/inks4.html

The Lodge ◆◆
146 Main Street, Seahouses,
Northumberland NE68 7UA
T: (01665) 720158

Railston House ◆◆◆◆
133 Main Street, North
Sunderland, Seahouses,
Northumberland NE68 7TS
T: (01665) 720912

Rowena ◆◆◆
99 Main Street, Seahouses,
Northumberland NE68 7TS
T: (01665) 721309

St Aidan Hotel ◆◆◆
1 St Aidans, Seafield Road,
Seahouses, Northumberland
NE68 7SR
T: (01665) 720355
F: (01665) 721989
E: staidan@globalnet.co.uk
I: www.users.globalnet.
co.uk/~staidan/

Slate Hall Riding Centre
◆◆◆◆
174 Main Street, Seahouses,
Northumberland NE68 7UA
T: (01665) 720320
F: (01665) 720199
E: ian@slatehall.freeserve.co.uk
I: www.slatehallridingcentre.
com

Stoneridge ◆◆◆
15 Quarry Field, Seahouses,
Northumberland NE68 7TB
T: (01665) 720835

Union Cottage Guest House
◆◆◆◆
11 Union Street, Seahouses,
Northumberland NE68 7RT
T: (01665) 720521
F: (01665) 720521
E: carruthers@unioncottage.
freeserve.co,uk
I: www.unioncottage.freeserve.
co.uk

Wyndgrove House ◆◆◆
156 Main Street, North
Sunderland, Seahouses,
Northumberland NE68 7UA
T: (01665) 720658

SEATON CAREW
Tees Valley
Altonlea Lodge Guest House
◆◆◆
19 The Green, Seaton Carew,
Hartlepool, Cleveland TS25 1AT
T: (01429) 271289
E: enquiries@altonlea.co.uk
I: www.altonlea.co.uk

Norton Hotel ◆
The Green, Seaton Carew,
Hartlepool, Cleveland TS25 1AR
T: (01429) 268317
F: (01429) 268317
E: steve@leeholme.1.freeserve.
co.uk

SEDGEFIELD
Durham
Forge Cottage ◆◆◆
2 West End, Sedgefield,
Stockton-on-Tees, Cleveland
TS21 2BS
T: (01740) 622831 & 620031
F: (01740) 622831
E: forgecottage@line.net

Glower-Oer-Him Farm ◆◆
Sedgefield, Stockton-on-Tees,
Cleveland TS21 3HO
T: (01740) 622737

Todds House Farm ◆◆◆
Sedgefield, Stockton-on-Tees,
Cleveland TS21 3EL
T: (01740) 620244
F: (01740) 620244
E: edgoosej@aol.com
I: www.toddshousefarm.co.uk

SHINCLIFFE
Durham
The Bracken Hotel ◆◆◆◆
Bank Foot, Shincliffe, Durham
DH1 2PD
T: (0191) 386 2966
F: (0191) 384 5423

SHOTLEY BRIDGE
Durham
The Manor House Inn ◆◆◆◆
Carterway Heads, Shotley
Bridge, Consett, County Durham
DH8 9LX
T: (01207) 255268 & 255332
F: (01207) 255268
I: www.scoot.co.uk/manor.
house/

SIMONBURN
Northumberland
Simonburn Guest House ◆◆◆
1 The Mains, Simonburn,
Hexham, Northumberland
NE48 3AW
T: (01434) 681321 &
07801 229866

SKELTON
Tees Valley
The Wharton Arms ◆◆
133 High Street, Skelton,
Saltburn-by-the-Sea, Cleveland
TS12 2DY
T: (01287) 650618

SLALEY
Northumberland
Flothers Farm ◆◆◆
Slaley, Hexham,
Northumberland NE47 0BJ
T: (01434) 673240 & 673587
F: (01434) 673240
E: dart@flothers.fsnet.co.uk
I: www.flothers.co.uk

The Strothers ◆◆◆◆
Slaley, Hexham,
Northumberland NE47 0AA
T: (01434) 673417 &
007803 280379
F: (01434) 673417
E: edna.hardy@the-strothers.
co.uk
I: www.the-strothers.co.uk

Travellers Rest ◆◆◆◆
Slaley, Hexham,
Northumberland NE47 1TT
T: (01434) 673231
F: (01434) 673906
E: enq@travellersrest.sagehost.
co.uk
I: www.travellersrest.sagesite.
co.uk

SOUTH SHIELDS
Tyne and Wear
Ainsley Guest House ◆◆◆
59 Ocean Road, South Shields,
Tyne and Wear NE33 2JJ
T: (0191) 454 3399 &
07879 461492
F: (0191) 454 3399
E: ainsleyguesthouse@hotmail.
com

Algarve Guest House ◆◆
77 Ocean Road, South Shields,
Tyne and Wear NE33 2JJ
T: (0191) 455 3783

Beaches Guest House ◆◆◆
81 Ocean Road, South Shields,
Tyne and Wear NE33 2JJ
T: (0191) 456 3262
F: (0191) 422 2021
E: beaches@cableinet.co.uk

Dunlin Guest House ◆◆◆
11 Urfa Terrace, South Shields,
Tyne and Wear NE33 2ES
T: (0191) 456 7442
F: (0191) 456 7442

Forest Guest House ◆◆◆◆
117 Ocean Road, South Shields,
Tyne and Wear NE33 2JL
T: (0191) 454 8160
F: (0191) 454 8160
E: abne02579@cableinet.co.uk
I: www.forest-house.pwp.
blueyonder.co.uk

The Kingsmere ◆◆◆
9 Urfa Terrace, South Shields,
Tyne and Wear NE33 2ES
T: (0191) 456 0234
F: (0191) 425 5026

Marina Guest House ◆◆◆
32 Seaview Terrace, South
Shields, Tyne and Wear
NE33 2NW
T: (0191) 456 1998
F: (0191) 456 1998

North View ◆◆◆
12 Urfa Terrace, South Shields,
Tyne and Wear NE33 2ES
T: (0191) 454 4950
F: (0191) 454 4950

Ravensbourne Guest House
◆◆
106 Beach Road, South Shields,
Tyne and Wear NE33 2NE
T: (0191) 456 5849

River's End Guest House ◆◆◆
41 Lawe Road, South Shields,
Tyne and Wear NE33 2EU
T: (0191) 456 4229
F: (0191) 456 4229
E: Brian@riversend.fsnet.co.uk
I: www.riversend.fsnet.co.uk

Royale Guest House ◆◆◆
13 Urfa Terrace, South Shields,
Tyne and Wear NE33 2ES
T: (0191) 4559 085

Saraville Guest House ◆◆◆
103 Ocean Road, South Shields,
Tyne and Wear NE33 2JL
T: (0191) 454 1169 &
07961 907435
F: (0191) 454 1169
E: Emma@saraville.freeserve.
co.uk
I: www.geocities.
com/saravillehouse

Sir William Fox Hotel
Rating Applied For
5 Westoe Village, South Shields,
Tyne and Wear NE33 3D2
T: (0191) 456 4554
F: (0191) 427 6312
I: www.sirwilliamfox.co.uk

South Shore ◆◆◆
115 Ocean Road, South Shields,
Tyne and Wear NE33 2JL
T: (0191) 454 4049 &
07711 567053
F: (0191) 454 4049

SPENNYMOOR
Durham

The Gables ♦♦♦
10 South View, Middlestone
Moor, Spennymoor, County
Durham DL16 7DF
T: (01388) 817544
F: (01388) 812533
E: thegablesghouse@aol.com

Highview Country House ♦♦♦
Kirkmerrington, Spennymoor,
County Durham DL16 7JT
T: (01388) 811006

Idsley House ♦♦♦♦
4 Green Lane, Spennymoor,
County Durham DL16 6HD
T: (01388) 814237

SPITTAL
Northumberland

All Seasons ♦♦♦
46 Main Street, Spittal, Berwick-
upon-Tweed TD15 1QY
T: (01289) 308452 &
07833 567983

The Roxburgh ♦♦
117 Main Street, Spittal,
Berwick-upon-Tweed TD15 1RP
T: (01289) 306266

STAINTON
Tees Valley

Stainton House
Rating Applied For
2 Hemlington Road, Stainton,
Middlesbrough, Cleveland
TS8 9AJ
T: (01642) 594221

STAMFORDHAM
Northumberland

**The Stamfordham Bay Horse
Inn** ♦♦♦♦
Southside, Stamfordham,
Newcastle upon Tyne NE18 0PB
T: (01661) 886244
E: stay@stamfordham-bay.
co.uk

STANHOPE
Durham

Horsley Hall ♦♦♦♦♦
Eastgate, Stanhope, Bishop
Auckland, County Durham
DL13 2LJ
T: (01388) 517239 &
07850 425615
F: (01388) 517608
E: hotel@horsleyhall.co.uk
I: www.horsleyhall.co.uk

STANLEY
Durham

Bushblades Farm ♦♦♦
Harperley, Stanley, County
Durham DH9 9UA
T: (01207) 232722

Harperley Hotel ♦♦♦
Harperley, Stanley, County
Durham DH9 9TY
T: (01207) 234011
F: (01207) 232325
E: harperley-hotel@supernet.
com

STANNERSBURN
Northumberland

Spring Cottage ♦♦♦♦
Stannersburn, Hexham,
Northumberland NE48 1DD
T: (01434) 240388
E: springcottage2000@yahoo.
co.uk

STANNINGTON
Northumberland

**Cheviot View Farmhouse Bed
& Breakfast** ♦♦♦♦
North Shotton Farm,
Stannington, Morpeth,
Northumberland NE61 6EU
T: (01670) 789231

STOCKSFIELD
Northumberland

Old Ridley Hall ♦♦♦
Stocksfield, Northumberland
NE43 7RU
T: (01661) 842816
E: oldridleyhall@talk21.com

Wheelbirks Farm ♦♦♦♦
Stocksfield, Northumberland
NE43 7HY
T: (01661) 843378
F: (01661) 842613
I: www.wheelbirks.ndo.co.uk

SUNDERLAND
Tyne and Wear

**Abingdon and Belmont Guest
House** ♦♦♦
5 St George's Terrace, Roker,
Sunderland, SR6 9LX
T: (0191) 567 2438 &
07973 318210
E: belmontguesthouse@
hotmail.com
I: www.belmontguesthouse.com

Acorn Guest House ♦♦
10 Mowbray Road, Hendon,
Sunderland SR2 8EN
T: (0191) 514 2170
E: theacornguesthouse@
hotmail.com

Anchor Lodge Guest House
♦♦♦
16 Roker Terrace, Roker
Seafront, Sunderland, SR6 9NB
T: (0191) 567 4154

April Guest House ♦♦♦♦
12 Saint Georges Terrace, Roker,
Sunderland, SR6 9LX
T: (0191) 565 9550
F: (0191) 565 9550
E: ghunter@aprilguesthouse.
freeserve.co.uk and gary@
aprilguesth
I: www.aprilguesthouse.com

Areldee Guest House ♦♦♦
18 Roker Terrace, Sunderland,
SR6 9NB
T: (0191) 514 1971 &
07775 856335
F: (0191) 514 0678
E: peter@areldeeguesthouse.
freeserve.co.uk

The Ashborne ♦♦♦
7 St George's Terrace, Roker,
Sunderland, Tyne and Wear
SR6 9LX
T: (0191) 565 3997
F: (0191) 565 3997

Beach View ♦♦♦
15 Roker Terrace, Sunderland,
Tyne and Wear SR6 9NB
T: (0191) 567 0719

Braeside Holiday Guest House
♦♦
26 Western Hill, (Beside
University), Sunderland,
SR2 7PH
T: (0191) 565 4801 & 0771 282
8723
F: (0191) 552 4198
E: george@the20thhole.co.uk
I: www.the20thhole.co.uk

Brendon House ♦♦♦
49 Roker Park Road, Roker,
Sunderland, SR6 9PL
T: (0191) 548 9303 & 529 2365
E: BrendonHouse@talk21.com

Brookside Bed and Breakfast
♦♦♦
6 Brookside Terrace, Tunstall
Road, Sunderland, SR2 7RN
T: (0191) 565 6739

The Chaise Guest House ♦♦
5 Roker Terrace, Roker Seafront,
Sunderland, SR6 9NB
T: (0191) 565 9218
F: (0191) 565 9218
E: thechaise@aol.com

Felicitations ♦♦♦
94 Ewesley Road, High Barnes,
Sunderland, SR4 7RJ
T: (0191) 522 0960
F: (0191) 551 8915
E: felicitations_uk@talk21.com

Lemonfield Hotel ♦♦♦
Sea Lane, Seaburn, Sunderland,
Tyne & Wear SR6 8EE
T: (0191) 529 3018 & 529 5735
F: (0191) 529 5952
E: ian@lemonfield.fsnet.co.uk

Mayfield Hotel ♦♦♦
Sea Lane, Seaburn, Sunderland,
SR6 8EE
T: (0191) 529 3345
F: (0191) 529 3345

SWALWELL
Tyne and Wear

The Angel Guest House ♦♦♦
6 Front Street, Swalwell,
Newcastle upon Tyne NE16 3DW
T: (0191) 496 0186
F: (0191) 496 0186
E: angel@swalwell6.freeserve.
com

SWARLAND
Northumberland

Swarland Old Hall ♦♦♦♦
Swarland, Morpeth,
Northumberland NE65 9HU
T: (01670) 787642 &
07801 688153
E: proctor@swarlandoldhall.
fsnet.co.uk

TANFIELD
Durham

Tanfield Garden Lodge ♦♦♦
Tanfield Lane, Tanfield, Stanley,
County Durham DH9 9QF
T: (01207) 282821 & 0797 039
8890
F: (01207) 282821

Tanfield Lane Farm ♦♦♦
Tanfield, Stanley, County
Durham DH9 9QE
T: (01207) 232739

TANTOBIE
Durham

Oak Tree Inn ♦♦
Tantobie, Stanley, County
Durham DH9 9RF
T: (01207) 235445
F: (01207) 230438
🐾

THROPTON
Northumberland

Demesne Farmhouse ♦♦♦
Thropton, Morpeth,
Northumberland NE65 7LT
T: (01669) 620196

TOW LAW
Durham

Bracken Hill Weardale ♦♦♦♦
Thornley, Tow Law, Bishop
Auckland, County Durham
DL13 4PQ
T: (01388) 731329
E: enquiriesfarrow@
bracken-hill.com
I: www.bracken-hill.com

TYNEMOUTH
Tyne and Wear

Martineau Guest House
♦♦♦♦
57 Front Street, Tynemouth,
North Shields, Tyne and Wear
NE30 4BX
T: (0191) 296 0746
E: martineau.house@
ukgateway.net
I: www.martineau-house.co.uk

WALL
Northumberland

St Oswalds Farm ♦♦
Wall, Hexham, Northumberland
NE46 4HB
T: (01434) 681307
E: ereay@fish.co.uk

WALLSEND
Tyne and Wear

Imperial Guest House ♦♦♦
194 Station Road, Wallsend,
Tyne and Wear NE28 8RD
T: (0191) 236 9808
F: (0191) 236 9808
E: enquiries@
imperialguesthouse.co.uk
I: www.imperialguesthouse.
co.uk

WARK
Northumberland

Battlesteads Hotel ♦♦♦
Wark, Hexham, Northumberland
NE48 3LS
T: (01434) 230209
F: (01434) 230730
E: info@battlesteads-hotel.
co.uk
I: www.Battlesteads-Hotel.co.uk

Black Bull Hotel ♦♦♦♦
Main Street, Wark, Hexham,
Northumberland NE48 3LG
T: (01434) 230239
F: (01434) 230239

WARKWORTH
Northumberland

Beck 'N' Call ♦♦♦♦
Birling West Cottage,
Warkworth, Morpeth,
Northumberland NE65 0XS
T: (01665) 711653
E: beck-n-call@lineone.net
I: www.beck-n-call.co.uk

Bide A While ◆◆◆
4 Beal Croft, Warkworth,
Morpeth, Northumberland
NE65 0XL
T: (01665) 711753
F: (01665) 510267

North Cottage ◆◆◆◆
Birling, Warkworth, Morpeth,
Northumberland NE65 0XS
T: (01665) 711263
E: edithandjohn@another.com
I: www.accta.co.uk/north

The Old Manse ◆◆◆◆
20 The Butts, Warkworth,
Morpeth, Northumberland
NE65 0SS
T: (01665) 710850

WASHINGTON
Tyne and Wear

Willow Lodge ◆◆◆◆
12 The Willows, Washington,
Tyne and Wear NE38 8JE
T: (0191) 419 4363
F: (0191) 419 4363
E: glover@nobrad.demon.co.uk

Ye Olde Cop Shop ◆◆◆◆
6 The Green, Washington
Village, Washington, Tyne and
Wear NE38 7AB
T: (0191) 416 5333
E: yeoldecopshop@btinternet.
com

WATERHOUSES
Durham

Ivesley ◆◆◆◆
Waterhouses, Durham DH7 9HB
T: (0191) 373 4324
F: (0191) 373 4757
E: ivesley@msn.com
I: www.ridingholidays-ivesley.
co.uk

WEST AUCKLAND
Durham

Wheatside Hotel ◆
Bildershaw Bank, West
Auckland, Bishop Auckland,
County Durham DL14 9PL
T: (01388) 832725
F: (01388) 832485

WEST WOODBURN
Northumberland

Bay Horse Inn ◆◆◆◆
West Woodburn, Hexham,
Northumberland NE48 2RX
T: (01434) 270218
F: (01434) 270118

Plevna House ◆◆◆◆
West Woodburn, Hexham,
Northumberland NE48 2RA
T: (01434) 270369 &
07703 778323
F: (01434) 270179
E: plevnaho@aol.com
I: www.plevnahouse.ntb.org.uk

Yellow House Farm ◆◆◆◆
Yellow House, West Woodburn,
Hexham, Northumberland
NE48 2RA
T: (01434) 270070
F: (01434) 270070
E: avril-yellowhous@faxvia.net

WESTGATE-IN-WEARDALE
Durham

Lands Farm ◆◆◆◆
Westgate-in-Weardale, Bishop
Auckland, County Durham
DL13 1SN
T: (01388) 517210
F: (01388) 517210

WHICKHAM
Tyne and Wear

**East Byermoor Guest House
◆◆◆◆**
Fellside Road, Whickham,
Newcastle upon Tyne NE16 5BD
T: (01207) 272687
F: (01207) 272145
E: eastbyermoor-gh.arbon@
virgin.net

WHITLEY BAY
Tyne and Wear

**Caprice Hotel
Rating Applied For**
14-16 South Parade, Whitley
Bay, Tyne and Wear NE26 2RG
T: (0191) 253 0141
F: (0191) 253 0141
E: stay@caprice-hotel.co.uk
I: www.caprice-hotel.co.uk

The Cara ◆◆◆◆
9 The Links, Whitley Bay, Tyne
and Wear NE26 1PS
T: (0191) 253 0172
I: www.thecara.co.uk

Chedburgh Hotel ◆◆◆
12 The Esplanade, Whitley Bay,
Tyne and Wear NE26 1AH
T: (0191) 253 0415 & 0780 128
6606
F: (0191) 253 0415
E: scottcarlucci@freenetname.
co.uk
I: www.SmoothHound.co.uk

**The Glen Esk Guest House
◆◆◆**
8 South Parade, Whitley Bay,
Tyne and Wear NE26 2RG
T: 07970 710 364 & (0191) 291
0128
F: (0191) 2530 103
E: the.glenesk@talk21.com

Marlborough Hotel ◆◆◆◆
20-21 East Parade, The
Promenade, Whitley Bay, Tyne
and Wear NE26 1AP
T: (0191) 251 3628
F: (0191) 252 5033
E: reception@
marlborough-hotel.com
I: www.marlborough-hotel.com
🏠

Shan-Gri-La ◆
29 Esplanade, Whitley Bay, Tyne
and Wear NE26 2AL
T: (0191) 253 0230

The Waterford Arms ◆◆◆◆
Collywell Bay Road, Whitley Bay,
Tyne and Wear NE26 4QZ
T: (0191) 237 0450
F: (0191) 298 0990

York House Hotel ◆◆◆◆
30 Park Parade, Whitley Bay,
Tyne and Wear NE26 1DX
T: (0191) 252 8313
F: (0191) 251 3953
E: reservations@
yorkhousehotel.com
I: www.yorkhousehotel.com
🏠

WHITTINGHAM
Northumberland

**Callaly Cottage Bed and
Breakfast ◆◆◆◆**
Callaly, Alnwick,
Northumberland NE66 4TA
T: (01665) 574684 &
07712 502284
E: callaly@alnwick.org.uk
I: www.callaly.alnwick.org.uk

WITTON GILBERT
Durham

The Coach House ◆◆◆◆
Stobbilee House, Witton Gilbert,
Durham DH7 6TW
T: (0191) 373 6132 &
07802 320439
F: (0191) 373 6711
E: suzanne.cronin@genie.co.uk
I: www.stobbilee.com

Prospect House ◆◆
5 Dene Terrace, Front Street,
Witton Gilbert, Durham DH7 6SS
T: (0191) 371 0760 &
07932 959238

WOLSINGHAM
Durham

Bay Horse Hotel ◆◆
59 Uppertown, Wolsingham,
Bishop Auckland, County
Durham DL13 3EX
T: (01388) 527220 & 528739
F: (01388) 528721

Holywell Farm ◆◆◆
Wolsingham, Bishop Auckland,
County Durham DL13 3HB
T: (01388) 527249

The Mill Race Hotel ◆◆
West End, Wolsingham, Bishop
Auckland, County Durham
DL13 3AP
T: (01388) 526551
F: (01388) 526551

WOOLER
Northumberland

Loreto Guest House ◆◆
1 Ryecroft Way, Wooler,
Northumberland NE71 6BW
T: (01668) 281 350

The Old Manse ◆◆◆◆◆
New Road, Chatton, Alnwick,
Northumberland NE66 5PU
T: (01668) 215343
E: chattonbb@aol.com
I: www.oldmansechatton.ntb.
org.uk

Ryecroft Hotel ◆◆◆
28 Ryecroft Way, Wooler,
Northumberland NE71 6AB
T: (01668) 281459 & 281233
F: (01668) 282214
E: ryecrofthotel@lineone.net

Saint Hilliers ◆◆◆
6 Church Street, Wooler,
Northumberland NE71 6DA
T: (01668) 281340

Sheileen ◆◆◆◆
17 Victoria Road, Wooler,
Northumberland NE71 6DX
T: (01668) 281924
F: (01668) 281026
E: billyates@wjyates.freeserve.
co.uk

Tilldale House ◆◆◆◆
34-40 High Street, Wooler,
Northumberland NE71 6BG
T: (01668) 281450
F: (01668) 281450
E: tilldalehouse@freezone.co.uk

**West Weetwood Farmhouse
◆◆◆◆**
West Weetwood, Wooler,
Northumberland NE71 6AQ
T: (01668) 281497
F: (01668) 281497

Winton House ◆◆◆
39 Glendale Road, Wooler,
Northumberland NE71 6DL
T: (01668) 281362
F: (01668) 281362
E: winton.house@virgin.net
I: www.wintonhouse.ntb.org.uk

WYLAM
Northumberland

Wormald House ◆◆◆◆
Main Street, Wylam,
Northumberland NE41 8DN
T: (01661) 852529 & 852552
F: (01661) 852529
E: john.craven3@btinternet.com

YARM
Tees Valley

**Hotel Tall Trees
Rating Applied For**
Green Lane, Yarm, Cleveland
TS15 9PE
T: (01642) 781050
F: (01642) 788250
E: hotel@talltrees.co.uk
I: www.talltrees.co.uk

NORTH WEST

ABBEYSTEAD
Lancashire
Greenbank Farmhouse ◆◆◆
Abbeystead, Lancaster LA2 9BA
T: (01524) 792063 & 792063
E: tait@greenbankfarmhouse.
freeserve.co.uk
I: www.greenbankfarmhouse.
co.uk

ACCRINGTON
Lancashire
Horizons Hotel and Restaurant Traders Brasserie◆◆◆
The Globe Centre, St James Square, Accrington, Lancashire BB5 0RE
T: (01254) 602020 & 602022
F: (01254) 602021
E: horizonshotel@hotmail.com

ACTON BRIDGE
Cheshire
Manor Farm ◆◆◆◆
Cliff Road, Acton Bridge, Northwich, Cheshire CW8 3QP
T: (01606) 853181
F: (01606) 853181
E: terri.mac.manorfarm@
care4free.net

AINTREE
Merseyside
Church View Guest House ◆◆
7 Church Avenue, Aintree, Liverpool L9 4SG
T: (0151) 525 8166

ALPRAHAM
Cheshire
Tollemache Arms ◆◆◆
Chester Road, Alpraham, Tarporley, Cheshire CW6 9JE
T: (01829) 260030
F: (01829) 260030

ALSAGER
Cheshire
Sappho Cottage ◆◆◆◆
118 Crewe Road, Alsager, Stoke-on-Trent ST7 2JA
T: (01270) 882033
F: (01270) 883556
E: reception@sappho-cottage.
demon.co.uk
I: www.sappho-cottage.demon.
co.uk

ALTRINCHAM
Greater Manchester
Belvedere Guest House
Rating Applied For
58 Barrington Road, Altrincham, Cheshire WA14 1HY
T: (0161) 941 5996 &
07885 692419
E: paddykel@aol.com

Cornbrooke Guest House ◆◆
15 Manchester Road, Altrincham, Cheshire WA14 4RG
T: (0161) 941 2789
E: cornbrooke@callnetuk.com
I: www.cornbrooke.hypermart.
net

APPLETON
Cheshire
Birchdale Hotel ◆◆◆
Birchdale Road, Appleton, Warrington WA4 5AW
T: (01925) 263662
F: (01925) 860607
E: rfw@birchdalehotel.co.uk
I: www.birchdalehotel.co.uk

ARKHOLME
Lancashire
Redwell Inn ◆◆◆
Kirkby Lonsdale Road, Arkholme, Carnforth, Lancashire LA6 1BQ
T: (01524) 221240
F: (01524) 221107
E: julie@redwellinn.co.uk
I: www.redwellinn.co.uk

The Tithe Barn ◆◆◆◆
Arkholme, Carnforth, Lancashire LA6 1AU
T: (015242) 22236
F: (015242) 22207
E: enquiries@tithe-barn.com
I: www.mallerassoc.co.uk

ASHLEY
Greater Manchester
Birtles Farm ◆◆◆◆
Ashley, Altrincham, Cheshire WA14 3QH
T: (0161) 928 0458

ASHTON–UNDER–LYNE
Greater Manchester
Lynwood Hotel ◆◆◆
3 Richmond Street, Ashton-under-Lyne, Lancashire OL6 7TX
T: (0161) 330 5358
F: (0161) 330 5358

BACUP
Lancashire
Irwell Inn ◆◆
71 Burnley Road, Bacup, Lancashire OL13 8DB
T: (01706) 873346
E: kevin@irwellinn.com
I: www.irwellinn.com

Pasture Bottom Farm ◆◆◆
Bacup, Lancashire OL13 9UZ
T: (01706) 873790
F: (01706) 873790
E: ha.isherwood@zen.co.uk
I: www.smoothhound.
co.uk/hotels/pasture.html

BARLEY
Lancashire
The Pendle Inn ◆◆◆
Barley, Burnley, Lancashire BB12 9JX
T: (01282) 614808
F: (01282) 614808
E: john@pendleinn.freeserve.
co.uk
I: www.pendleinn.freeserve.
co.uk

BASHALL EAVES
Lancashire
Hodder House B&B ◆◆◆
Hodder House Farm, Mitton Road, Bashall Eaves, Clitheroe, Lancashire BB7 3LZ
T: (01254) 826328
F: (01254) 826328
E: heather@hodderhousebb.
freeserve.co.uk
I: www.hodderhousebb.
freeserve.co.uk

BAY HORSE
Lancashire
Stanley Lodge Farmhouse ◆◆◆
Cockerham Road, Bay Horse, Lancaster LA2 0HE
T: (01524) 791863
F: (01524) 793115

BILLINGTON
Lancashire
Rosebury ◆◆◆
51 Pasturelands Drive, Billington, Clitheroe, Lancashire BB7 9LW
T: (01254) 822658 & 780 927 4910
E: enquiries@
rosebury-guest-house.freeserve.
co.uk
I: www.rosebury-guest-house.
co.uk

BIRKDALE
Merseyside
Belgravia Hotel ◆◆◆
11 Trafalgar Road, Birkdale, Southport, Merseyside PR8 2EA
T: (01704) 565298
F: (01704) 562728
E: belgravias@aol.com
I: www.hotelsouthport.com

BIRKENHEAD
Merseyside
Shrewsbury Lodge Hotel and Restaurant◆◆◆
31 Shrewsbury Road, Oxton, Birkenhead, Merseyside CH43 2JB
T: (0151) 652 4029
F: (0151) 653 4079
E: info@shrewsbury-hotel.com
I: www.shrewsbury-hotel.com

Victoria House ◆◆
12 Shrewsbury Road, Oxton, Birkenhead, Merseyside CH43 1UX
T: (0151) 652 8379 &
07771 618778
F: (0151) 342 3037
E: maryjohnatherton@aol.com

Villa Venezia ◆◆◆
14-16 Prenton Road West, Birkenhead, Merseyside CH42 9PN
T: (0151) 608 9212
F: (0151) 608 6671

BISPHAM
Lancashire
Cliff Head Hotel ◆◆
174 Queens Promenade, Bispham, Blackpool, Blackpool, Lancashire FY2 9JN
T: (01253) 591086 &
04111 047100
F: (01253) 590952

Cliff Head Hotel ◆◆
174 Queens Promenade, Bispham, Blackpool, Blackpool, Lancashire FY2 9JN
T: (01253) 591086 &
04111 047100
F: (01253) 590952

BLACKBURN
Lancashire
The Fernhurst & Star Lodge
Rating Applied For
466 Bolton Road, Blackburn, BB2 4JP
T: (01254) 693541
F: (01254) 695221

Shalom ◆◆◆◆
531b Livesey Branch Road, Blackburn, Lancashire BB2 5DF
T: (01254) 209032
F: (01254) 209032
E: paul@shalomblackburn.co.uk
🅐

BLACKPOOL
Lancashire
Adelaide House Hotel ◆◆◆
66-68 Adelaide Street, Blackpool, FY1 4LA
T: (01253) 625172
F: (01253) 625172

Alderley Hotel ◆◆◆
581 South Promenade, Blackpool, FY4 1NG
T: (01253) 342173

Arncliffe Hotel ◆◆◆
24 Osborne Road, Blackpool, FY4 1HJ
T: (01253) 345209 &
07802 438907
F: (01253) 345209
E: arncliffehotel@talk21.com
I: www.blackpool-internet.
co.uk/HOMEarncliffe.html

Ashcroft Hotel ◆◆◆
42 King Edward Avenue, North Shore, Blackpool, FY2 9TA
T: (01253) 351538 &
07765 542306

Astoria Guest house ◆◆
50 Park Road, Blackpool, FY1 4HT
T: (01253) 622377
F: (01253) 291321
E: astoria@IC24.net
I: www.astoria.IC24.net

Baricia ◆◆◆
40-42 Egerton Road, Blackpool, FY1 2NW
T: (01253) 623130
E: TKBariciahotel@aol.com

Baron Hotel
Rating Applied For
296 North Promenade, Blackpool, FY1 2EY
T: (01253) 622729
F: (01253) 297165
E: baronhotel@btinternet.com

Beachcomber Hotel ◆◆◆
78 Reads Avenue, Blackpool, FY1 4DE
T: (01253) 621622
F: (01253) 299254
E: beachcomber@euphony.net

Beauchief Hotel ◆◆◆
48 King Edward Avenue, Blackpool, FY2 9TA
T: (01253) 353314
F: (01253) 353314
E: beauchiefhotel@blackpool.
net
I: www.fyldecoast.
co.uk/beauchief

The Beaucliffe Hotel ◆◆◆
20-22 Holmfield Road,
Blackpool, FY2 9TB
T: (01253) 351663
E: don.siddall@talk21.com
I: members.netscapeonline.
co.uk/beaucliffe

Berwick Hotel ◆◆◆
23 King Edward Avenue, North
Shore, Blackpool, FY2 9TA
T: (01253) 351496
F: (01253) 351496
E: chris@berwickhotel.fsnet.
co.uk
I: www.berwickhotel.freeserve.
co.uk

Berwyn Hotel ◆◆◆◆
1 Finchley Road, Gynn Square,
Blackpool, FY1 2LP
T: (01253) 352896
F: (01253) 594391
I: www.blackpool-holidays.com

Beverley Hotel ◆◆◆
25 Dean Street, Blackpool,
FY4 1AU
T: (01253) 344426
E: beverley.hotel@virgin.net
I: www.beverleyhotel-blackpool.
co.uk

Boltonia Hotel ◆◆◆
124-126 Albert Road, Blackpool,
FY1 4PN
T: (01253) 620248
F: (01253) 299064
E: info@boltoniahotel.co.uk
I: www.boltoniahotel.co.uk

Bona Vista Hotel ◆◆◆
104-106 Queens Promenade,
Blackpool, FY2 9NX
T: (01253) 351396
F: (01253) 594985
E: bona.vista@talk21.com
I: www.bonavista@freeservers.
com

Braeside Hotel ◆◆◆
6 Willshaw Road, Gynn Square,
Blackpool, FY2 9SH
T: (01253) 351363
I: www.
blackpoolholidays-braeside.
co.uk

The Brayton ◆◆◆
7-8 Finchley Road, Gynn Square,
Blackpool, FY1 2LP
T: (01253) 351645
F: (01253) 595500
E: brayton@btinternet.com
I: www.brayton.btinternet.co.uk

Briny View ◆◆
2 Woodfield Road, Blackpool,
FY1 6AX
T: (01253) 346584

Hotel Camelot ◆◆◆
487 Promenade, Blackpool,
FY4 1AZ
T: (01253) 404597 & 341948
F: (01253) 341948

Canasta Hotel ◆◆◆
288 North Promenade,
Blackpool, FY1 2EY
T: (01253) 290501 & 752518
F: (01253) 290501
E: canasta@blackpool.net
I: www.blackpool.
net/canastahotel/

Cardoh Lodge ◆◆◆
21 Hull Road, Blackpool,
FY1 4QB
T: (01253) 627755
F: (01253) 292624
E: cardoh.lodge@btinternet.
com
I: www.blackpoolhotels.og.
uk/cardohlodge.html

The Cheslyn ◆◆◆
21 Moore Street, Blackpool,
FY4 1DA
T: (01253) 349672

Cliftonville Hotel ◆◆◆
14 Empress Drive, Blackpool,
Lancashire FY2 9SE
T: (01253) 351052
F: (01253) 590052
I: www.cliftonville-blackpool.
co.uk

Collingwood Hotel ◆◆◆◆
8-10 Holmfield Road, North
Shore, Blackpool, FY2 9SL
T: (01253) 352929
F: (01253) 352929
E: enquiries@collingwoodhotel.
co.uk
I: www.collingwoodhotel.co.uk

Colris Hotel ◆◆◆
209 Central Promenade,
Blackpool, FY1 5DL
T: (01253) 625461

Courtneys of Gynn Square
◆◆◆◆
1 Warbreck Hill Road, Blackpool,
FY2 9SP
T: (01253) 352179 &
07802 786117
F: (01253) 352179

The Cresta ◆◆◆
85 Withnell Road, Blackpool,
FY4 1HE
T: (01253) 343866
E: john@snelly.co.uk
I: www.snelly.co.uk

Croydon Hotel ◆◆◆◆
12 Empress Drive, Blackpool,
FY2 9SE
T: (01253) 352497

Denely Private Hotel ◆◆
15 King Edward Avenue,
Blackpool, FY2 9TA
T: (01253) 352757

Derwent Private Hotel ◆◆◆
42 Palatine Road, Blackpool,
FY1 4BY
T: (01253) 620004
F: (01253) 620004

Elgin Hotel ◆◆◆
36 - 42 Queens Promenade,
Blackpool, FY2 9RW
T: (01253) 351433
F: (01253) 353535
E: info@elginhotel.com
I: www.elginhotel.com

Fairway Hotel ◆◆◆
34-36 Hull Road, Blackpool,
FY1 4QB
T: (01253) 623777
F: (01253) 753455
E: bookings@fairway.gb.com
I: www.fairway.gb.com

The Fern Royd Hotel ◆◆◆
35 Holmfield Road, North Shore,
Blackpool, FY2 9TE
T: (01253) 351066
E: info@fernroydhotel.co.uk
I: www.fernroydhotel.co.uk

Fylde Hotel ◆◆◆
93 Palatine Road, Blackpool,
FY1 4BX
T: (01253) 623735
F: (01253) 622801
E: fyldehotel@talk21.com

The Grand Hotel ◆◆◆
Station Road, Blackpool,
FY4 1EU
T: (01253) 343741
F: (01253) 408228
E: max@grandholidayflats.co.uk
I: www.grandholidayflats.co.uk

Granville Hotel ◆◆◆
12 Station Road, Blackpool,
FY4 1BE
T: (01253) 343012
F: (01253) 408594
E: wilft@thegranvillehotelfsnet.
co.uk
I: www.thegranvillehotel.co.uk

Happy Return Hotel ◆◆◆
17-19 Hull Road, Blackpool,
FY1 4QB
T: (01253) 622596
F: (01253) 290024

Hartshead Private Hotel ◆◆◆
17 King Edward Avenue,
Blackpool, FY2 9TA
T: (01253) 353133 & 357111

Hertford Hotel ◆◆◆
18 Lord Street, North Shore,
Blackpool, FY1 2BD
T: (01253) 622793
F: (01253) 622793
E: ceges@dircon.co.uk
I: www.ceges.dircon.co.uk

Holmsdale Hotel ◆◆◆
6-8 Pleasant Street, North
Shore, Blackpool, FY1 2JA
T: (01253) 621008
F: 0870 133 1487
E: holmsdale@talk21.com
I: www.blackpool-hotels.
co.uk/holmsdale.html

Homecliffe Hotel ◆◆◆
5-6 Wilton Parade, North
Promenade, Blackpool, FY1 2HE
T: (01253) 625147
F: (01253) 292667
E: douglas@homecliffe56.
freeserve.co.uk

Hornby Villa ◆◆◆
130 Hornby Road, Blackpool,
FY1 4QS
T: (01253) 624959
E: hornby.villa@virgin.net

Hurstmere Hotel ◆◆◆
5 Alexandra Road, Blackpool,
FY1 6BU
T: (01253) 345843
F: (01253) 347188

Inglewood Hotel ◆◆◆
18 Holmfield Road, Blackpool,
FY2 9TB
T: (01253) 351668
F: (01253) 351668
E: elaine_hodgin@talk21.com
I: www.blackpool-hotels.
co.uk/inglewood.html

Jay-Mar Guesthouse ◆◆◆
36 Egerton Road, North Shore,
Blackpool, FY1 2NW
T: (01253) 297626

Jeanne Hotel ◆◆
45 Station Road, Blackpool,
FY4 1EU
T: (01253) 343430

The Kimberley ◆◆◆
25 Gynn Avenue, Blackpool,
FY1 2LD
T: (01253) 352264

Lynmoore Guest House ◆◆◆
25 Moore Street, Blackpool,
FY4 1DA
T: (01253) 349888

Manor Grove Hotel ◆◆
24 Leopold Grove, Blackpool,
FY1 4LD
T: (01253) 625577
F: (01253) 625577
E: lyndon@evans2ooo.
freeserve.co.uk
I: www.manorgrovehotel.com

Manor Private Hotel ◆◆◆
32 Queens Promenade,
Blackpool, FY2 9RN
T: (01253) 351446
F: (01253) 355449
E: holidays@manorblackpool.
co.uk
I: manorblackpool.co.uk

Marlow Lodge Hotel ◆◆◆
76 Station Road, Blackpool,
FY4 1EU
T: (01253) 341580
F: (01253) 408330
E: hotelreception@yahoo.co.uk
I: www.blackpoolmarlowhotel.
co.uk

May-Dene Licensed Hotel
◆◆◆
10 Dean Street, Blackpool,
FY4 1AU
T: (01253) 343464
F: (01253) 401424
E: may_dene_hotel@hotmail.
com

Hotel Montclair ◆◆◆
95 Albert Road, Blackpool,
FY1 4PW
T: (01253) 625860

The Moores Hotel ◆◆◆
42 Banks Street, Blackpool,
FY1 2BE
T: (01253) 623638
F: (01253) 623638

Motel Mimosa ◆◆
24A Lonsdale Road, Blackpool,
FY1 6EE
T: (01253) 341906

New Bond Hotel ◆◆◆
72 Lord Street, Blackpool,
FY1 2DG
T: (01253) 628123 & 0771 298
1328

Newholme Private Hotel ◆◆◆
2 Wilton Parade, Blackpool,
FY1 2HE
T: (01253) 624010
I: www.fyldecoast.
co.uk/newholme.

North Crest Hotel ◆◆◆
22 King Edward Avenue,
Blackpool, FY2 9TD
T: (01253) 355937

Northlands Hotel ◆◆◆
31-33 Hornby Road, Blackpool,
FY1 4QG
T: (01253) 625795
F: (01253) 625795
E: northlands.hotel@virgin.net
I: www.northlandshotel.co.uk

The Old Coach House ◆◆◆◆◆
50 Dean Street, Blackpool,
FY4 1BP
T: (01253) 349195
F: (01253) 344330
E: blackpool@
theoldcoachhouse.freeserve.
co.uk
I: www.theoldcoachhouse.
freeserve.co.uk

Pembroke Private Hotel ◆◆◆◆
11 King Edward Avenue,
Blackpool, FY2 9TD
T: (01253) 351306
F: (01253) 351306
E: stay@pembrokehotel.com
I: www.pembrokehotel.com

Penrhyn Hotel ◆◆◆
38 King Edward Avenue,
Blackpool, FY2 9TA
T: (01253) 352762
E: ericpenrhyn@talk21.com

Pickwick Hotel ◆◆◆
93 Albert Road, Blackpool,
FY1 4PW
T: (01253) 624229
F: (01253) 624229

Raffles Hotel ◆◆◆
73-75 Hornby Road, Blackpool,
FY1 4QJ
T: (01253) 294713
F: (01253) 294240
I: www.raffleshotelblackpool.
co.uk

Regent Hotel
Rating Applied For
18 Springfield Road, Blackpool,
FY1 1QL
T: (01253) 620299 & 473825
F: (01253) 620299

The Robin Hood Hotel ◆◆◆
100 Queens Promenade,
Blackpool, FY2 9NS
T: (01253) 351599

Rosedale Private Hotel ◆◆◆
9 Chatsworth Avenue, Bispham,
Blackpool, FY2 9AN
T: (01253) 352661
F: (01253) 352661
E: mail@rosedaleprivatehotel.
co.uk
I: www.rosedaleprivatehotel.
co.uk

The Royal Seabank Hotel ◆◆◆
219-221 Central Promenade,
Blackpool, FY1 5DL
T: (01253) 622717 & 622173
F: (01253) 295148
E: royalseabank@hotmail.com
I: www.blackpool.
net/wwwroyalseabank

Rutlands Hotel ◆◆◆
13 Hornby Road, Blackpool,
FY1 4QG
T: (01253) 623067

Sands Hotel ◆◆◆
485 South Promenade,
Blackpool, FY4 1AZ
T: (01253) 349262 & 407081
F: (01253) 407081

Seabreeze ◆◆◆
1 Gynn Avenue, Blackpool,
FY1 2LD
T: (01253) 351427
F: (01253) 310713
E: info@vbreezey.co.uk
I: www.vbreezey.co.uk

Seaforth Hotel ◆◆◆
18 Lonsdale Road, Blackpool,
FY1 6EE
T: (01253) 345820 & 405079
F: (01253) 345820
E: enquiries@seaforthhotel.
co.uk
I: www.seaforthhotel.co.uk

Sheron House ◆◆◆
21 Gynn Avenue, Blackpool
North Shore, Blackpool, FY1 2LD
T: (01253) 354614
E: sheronhouse@amserve.net
I: www.hotels.f9.co.uk/sheron

Hotel Skye ◆◆
571-573 New South Promenade,
Blackpool, FY4 1NG
T: (01253) 343220 & 345446
F: (01253) 401244
E: office@blackpool-hotel.co.uk
I: www.blackpool-hotel.co.uk

Somerville Hotel ◆◆◆
72 Station Road, Blackpool,
FY4 1EU
T: (01253) 341219
F: (01253) 341219
E: michacl.haigh@btclick.com
I: www.somervillehotel.co.uk/

South Lea Hotel ◆◆◆
4 Willshaw Road, Blackpool,
FY2 9SH
T: (01253) 351940 & 595758
F: (01253) 595758
E: southlea@hotmail.com
I: www.blackpool-holidays.
com/southlea.htm.

Stuart Hotel ◆◆
27-29 Clifton Drive, Blackpool,
FY4 1NT
T: (01253) 345485
F: (01253) 406239

Sunnymede Hotel
Rating Applied For
50 King Edward Avenue,
Blackpool, FY2 9TA
T: (01253) 352877
E: enquiries@sunnymedehotel.
co.uk
I: www.sunnymedehotel.co.uk

Sunnyside Hotel ◆◆◆
36 King Edward Avenue, North
Shore, Blackpool, FY2 9TA
T: (01253) 352031
F: (01253) 354255
E: stuart@sunnysidehotel.com
I: www.sunnysidehotel.com

Tudor Rose Original ◆◆◆◆
5 Withnell Road, Blackpool,
FY4 1HF
T: (01253) 343485
E: tudororiginal@aol.com

Victoria House ◆◆◆
14 Regent Road, Blackpool,
FY1 4LY
T: (01253) 626967
F: (01253) 626967

Vidella Hotel ◆◆◆
80-82 Dickson Road, Blackpool,
FY1 2BU
T: (01253) 621201
F: (01253) 620319

Waverley Hotel ◆◆◆
95 Reads Avenue, Blackpool,
FY1 4DG
T: (01253) 621633
F: (01253) 753581
E: wavehotel@aol.com
I: www.thewaverleyhotel.com

Westdean Hotel ◆◆◆
59 Dean Street, Blackpool,
FY4 1BP
T: (01253) 342904
F: (01253) 342926
E: mikeball@westdeanhotel.
freeserve.co.uk
I: www.westdeanhotel.com

Wilmar ◆◆◆
42 Osborne Road, Blackpool,
FY4 1HQ
T: (01253) 346229

Wilton Hotel ◆◆◆
108-112 Dickson Road,
Blackpool, FY1 2HF
T: (01253) 627763
F: (01253) 295379

The Windsor Hotel ◆◆◆◆
21 King Edward Avenue, North
Shore, Blackpool, FY2 9TA
T: (01253) 353735

Windsor Park Hotel ◆◆◆
96 Queens Promenade,
Blackpool, FY2 9NS
T: (01253) 357025

Ycalm Guest House ◆◆
32 Reads Avenue, Blackpool,
FY1 4BP
T: (01253) 625398 & 0800 074
3453

Blundellsands Bed & Breakfast ◆◆◆◆
9 Elton Avenue, Blundellsands,
Liverpool L23 8UN
T: (0151) 924 6947
F: (0151) 287 4113
E: liz@bsbb.freeserve.co.uk
I: visitbritain.visitnorthwest.com

Cheetham Arms ◆◆◆
987 Blackburn Road, Sharples,
Bolton, BL1 7LG
T: (01204) 301372
F: (01204) 598209
E: mike@cheethamarms.
freeserve.co.uk

Fourways Hotel ◆◆◆
13-15 Bolton Road, Moses Gate,
Farnworth, Bolton BL4 7JN
T: (01204) 573661
F: (01204) 862488
E: fourwayshotel@pureapshalt.
co.uk

The Grosvenor Guest House ◆◆◆
46 Bradford Street, Bolton,
BL2 1JJ
T: (01204) 391616

The Highgrove Guest House ◆◆◆
63 Manchester Road, Bolton,
BL2 1ES
T: (01204) 384928
F: (01204) 384928

Morden Grange Guest House
Rating Applied For
15 Chadwick Street, The Haulgh,
Bolton, BL2 1JN
T: (01204) 522000
I: www.mordengrange.co.uk

Pelton Fold Farm ◆◆◆◆
Bury Road, Turton, Bolton,
BL7 0BS
T: (01204) 852207

The Woods ◆◆◆
6 Oakenclough Drivc, Bolton,
BL1 5QY
T: (01204) 492100 &
07719 976657
F: (01204) 492100
E: neilmags@cwcom.net
I: www.boltonbandb.co.uk

Copy Nook Hotel ◆◆◆◆
Bolton-by-Bowland, Clitheroe,
Lancashire BB7 4NL
T: (01200) 447205
F: (01200) 447004
E: copynookhotel@btinternet.
com
I: www.copynookhotel.com

Middle Flass Lodge ◆◆◆◆
Forest Becks Brow, Settle Road,
Bolton-by-Bowland, Clitheroe,
Lancashire BB7 4NY
T: (01200) 447259
F: (01200) 447300
I: www.mflodge.freeservers.
com/

Regent Maritime Hotel ◆◆◆
58-62 Regent Road, Liverpool,
L20 8DB
T: (0151) 922 4090
F: (0151) 922 6308
E: regent_maritime_hotel@
hotmail.com
I: www.regentmaritimehotel.
co.uk

Dibbinsdale Inn ◆◆
Dibbinsdale Road,
Bromborough, Wirral,
Merseyside CH63 0HJ
T: (0151) 334 5171
F: (0151) 334 0097

Woodlands Guest House ◆◆◆
66 Woodyear Road,
Bromborough, Wirral,
Merseyside CH62 6AZ
T: (0151) 327 3735
F: (0151) 328 1572

The Poplars ◆◆◆◆
58 Horseshoe Lane, Bromley
Cross, Bolton BL7 0RR
T: (01204) 308001 &
07980 140635
F: (01204) 308001
E: patricia@v-b-elec.u-net.com
I: www.v-b-elec.u-net.com

Ormerod Hotel ◆◆◆
121-123 Ormerod Road,
Burnley, Lancashire BB11 3QW
T: (01282) 423255

Thorneyholme Farm Cottage
Rating Applied For
Barley New Road, Roughlee,
Burnley, Lancashire BB12 9LH
T: (01282) 612452

**Brandreth Barn Brandreth
Farm◆◆◆**
Tarlscough Lane, Burscough,
Ormskirk, Lancashire L40 0RJ
T: (01704) 893510

Martin Inn ◆◆◆
Martin Lane, Burscough,
Ormskirk, Lancashire L40 0RT
T: (01704) 892302 &
07768 352216
F: (01704) 895735

BURY
Greater Manchester
The Bolholt Country Park Hotel
Rating Applied For
Walshaw Road, Bury, Lancashire
BL8 1PU
T: (0161) 764 5239 &
0800 174141
F: (0161) 763 1789
E: enquiries@bolholt.co.uk
I: www.bolholt.co.uk

CALDY
Merseyside
Cheriton ◆◆◆◆
151 Caldy Road, Caldy, Wirral,
Merseyside CH48 1LP
T: (0151) 625 5271
F: (0151) 625 5271
E: cheriton151@hotmail.com

CAPERNWRAY
Lancashire
New Capernwray Farm
◆◆◆◆◆
Capernwray, Carnforth,
Lancashire LA6 1AD
T: (01524) 734284
F: (01524) 734284
E: info@newcapfarm.co.uk
I: www.newcapfarm.co.uk

CARNFORTH
Lancashire
Dale Grove ◆◆◆
162 Lancaster Road, Carnforth,
Lancashire LA5 9EF
T: (01524) 733382 &
07974 125426
E: cal.craig@ntlworld.com
I: www.dalegrove.co.uk

Galley Hall Farm ◆◆◆◆
Shore Road, Carnforth,
Lancashire LA5 9HZ
T: (01524) 732544

The George Washington ◆◆◆
Main Street, Warton, Carnforth,
Lancashire LA5 9PJ
T: (01524) 732865

Grisedale Farm ◆◆◆◆
Leighton, Carnforth, Lancashire
LA5 9ST
T: (01524) 734360

High Bank ◆◆◆◆
Hawk Street, Carnforth,
Lancashire LA5 9LA
T: (01524) 733827

Longlands Hotel ◆◆◆
Tewitfield, Carnforth, Lancashire
LA6 1JH
T: (01524) 781256
F: (01524) 781004
E: info@thelonglandshotel.
co.uk

The Manse Bed and Breakfast
◆◆
74 Kellet Road, Carnforth,
Lancashire LA5 9LP
T: (01524) 732623 & 07979 571
412
F: (01524) 732623
E: yvonne.hetherington@
lineone.net

CATON
Lancashire
Ellerdene ◆◆◆◆
85 Horby Road, Caton,
Lancaster, Lancashire LA2 9QR
T: (01524) 770625

Kilcredan ◆
14 Brookhouse Road, Caton,
Lancaster LA2 9QT
T: (01524) 770271

CHEADLE
Greater Manchester
Curzon House ◆◆◆
3 Curzon Road, Heald Green,
Cheadle, Cheshire SK8 3LN
T: (0161) 436 2804 & 493 9990
E: curzonhouse@aol.com

CHEADLE HULME
Greater Manchester
The Governor's House ◆◆◆
43 Ravenoak Road, Cheadle
Hulme, Cheadle, Cheshire
SK8 7EQ
T: (0161) 488 4222
F: (0161) 486 1850

Spring Cottage Guest House
◆◆◆
60 Hulme Hall Road, Cheadle
Hulme, Cheadle, Cheshire
SK8 6JZ
T: (0161) 485 1037

CHELFORD
Cheshire
Astle Farm East ◆◆
Chelford, Macclesfield, Cheshire
SK10 4TA
T: (01625) 861270

CHESTER
Cheshire
Abbotsford Court Hotel ◆◆
17 Victoria Road, Chester,
CH2 2AX
T: (01244) 390898
F: (01244) 390898
E: abbotsford_court_hotel@
hotmail.com

Alton Lodge Hotel ◆◆◆
78 Hoole Road, Chester,
CH2 3NT
T: (01244) 310213
F: (01244) 319206
E: enquiries@altonlodge.co.uk
I: www.altonlodge.co.uk

Bawn Park Hotel ◆◆◆
10 Hoole Road, Chester,
CH2 3NH
T: (01244) 324971
F: (01244) 310951
E: robert.bawn@tesco.net

Bowman Lodge ◆◆◆
52 Hoole Road, Chester,
CH2 3NL
T: (01244) 342208
E: cig.davies@virgin.net
I: freespace.virgin.net/cig.
davies/bowman.htm

Carmeletta Guest House ◆◆◆
18 Hough Green, Chester,
CH4 8JG
T: (01244) 677876
F: (01244) 677876
E: john@carmeletta.fsbusiness.
co.uk
I: www.carmetlettafsbusiness.
co.uk

Castle House ◆◆◆
23 Castle Street, Chester,
CH1 2DS
T: (01244) 350354
F: (01244) 350354

Chester Town House ◆◆◆
23 King Street, Chester,
CH1 2AH
T: (01244) 350021
F: (01244) 350021
E: davidbellis@
chestertownhouse.co.uk
I: www.chestertownhouse.co.uk

Cheyney Lodge Hotel ◆◆◆
77-79 Cheyney Road, Chester,
CH1 4BS
T: (01244) 381925

Chippings ◆◆◆◆
10 Cranford Court, Chester,
CH4 7LN
T: (01244) 679728
F: (01244) 659470

Comfort Inn Chester ◆◆◆◆
74 Hoole Road, Chester,
CH2 3NL
T: (01244) 327542
F: (01244) 344889
E: comfortinn@chestergb.u-net.
com
🛈

The Commercial Hotel ◆◆
St Peters Churchyard, Chester,
Cheshire CH1 2HG
T: (01244) 320749
F: (01244) 348318
I: www.stayhereuk.com

Dee Hills Lodge ◆◆◆◆
7 Dee Hills Park, Boughton,
Chester, CH3 5AR
T: (01244) 325719

Derry Raghan Lodge ◆◆◆
54 Hoole Road, Chester,
CH2 3NL
T: (01244) 318740
I: www.derryraghanlodge.co.uk

Donegal House ◆◆◆
73 Whitchurch Road, Boughton,
Chester, CH3 5QB
T: (01244) 311342 &
07968 436045
E: donegalhouse@aol.com

Eastern Guest House ◆◆◆
1 Eastern Pathway, Queens Park,
Handbridge, Chester, CH3 7AQ
T: (01244) 680104

Eaton House ◆◆◆
36 Eaton Road, Handbridge,
Chester, CH4 7EN
T: (01244) 680349 & 659021
F: (01244) 659021
E: grahamd@aol.com

Edwards House Hotel ◆◆◆
61-63 Hoole Road, Chester,
CH2 3NJ
T: (01244) 318055
F: (01244) 310948
E: steanerob@sypanet.com
I: www.smoothhound.
co.uk/hotels/edwardhou.html

Elliots ◆◆◆◆
2 Abbey Green, Northgate
Street, Chester, CH1 2JH
T: (01244) 329932
F: (01244) 314659

Gables Guest House ◆◆◆
5 Vicarage Road, Off Hoole
Road, Chester, CH2 3HZ
T: (01244) 323969
F: (01244) 401060

Golborne Manor ◆◆◆◆
Platts Lane, Hatton Heath,
Chester CH3 9AN
T: (01829) 770310 &
07774 695268
F: (01829) 770370
E: ann.ikin@golbornemanor.
co.uk

Grosvenor Place Guest House
◆◆◆
2-4 Grosvenor Place, Chester,
CH1 2DE
T: (01244) 324455 &
10244 400225
F: (01244) 400225

Grove House ◆◆◆◆
Holme Street, Tarvin, Chester
CH3 8EQ
T: (01829) 740893
F: (01829) 741769
E: helen_s@btinternet.com

Grove Villa ◆◆◆
18 The Groves, Chester, CH1 1SD
T: (01244) 349713
E: GroveVilla@tesco.net

**The Guesthouse at Old Hall
Country Club**◆◆◆◆
Aldford Road, Chester, CH3 6EA
T: (01244) 311593 & 317273
F: (01244) 313785
E: info@oldhallcountryclub.com
I: www.oldhallcountryclub.com

Halcyon House ◆◆◆
18 Eaton Road, Handbridge,
Chester, CH4 7EN
T: (01244) 676159
F: (01244) 676159

Hameldaeus ◆◆◆
9 Lorne Street, Chester, Cheshire
CH1 4AE
T: (01244) 374913
E: joyce33@brunton81.
freeserve.co.uk

Holly House ◆◆◆
41 Liverpool Road, Chester,
CH2 1AB
T: (01244) 383484
E: fjb5@tutor.open.ac.uk

Homeleigh Guest House ◆◆◆
14 Hough Green, Chester,
CH4 8JG
T: (01244) 676761
F: (01244) 679977
I: www.scoot.
co.uk/homeleigh_guest_house/

Kent House ◆◆
147 Boughton, Chester,
CH3 5BH
T: (01244) 324171
F: (01244) 319758
I: kent-house@turner10101.
freeserve.co.uk

Kilmorey Lodge ◆◆◆
50 Hoole Road, Chester,
Cheshire CH2 3NL
T: (01244) 324306

The Kings Hotel
Rating Applied For
14 Eaton Road, Handbridge,
Chester, CH4 7EN
T: (01244) 671249

Laburnum House ◆◆◆
2 St Anne Street, Chester,
CH1 3HS
T: (01244) 380313
F: (01244) 380313

Latymer Swiss Hotel ◆◆◆
82 Hough Green, Chester,
CH4 8JW
T: (01244) 675074
F: (01244) 683413
E: markus@latymerhotel.fsnet.
co.uk
I: www.latymerhotel.com

Laurels ◆◆◆◆
14 Selkirk Road, Curzon Park,
Chester, Cheshire CH4 8AH
T: (01244) 697682
E: howell@ellisroberts.freeserve.
co.uk

The Laurels Guest House
Rating Applied For
61 Tarvin Road, Boughton,
Chester, CH3 5DY
T: (01244) 346292 & 403943
E: carlton40@btinternet.com

The Limes Hotel ◆◆◆◆
12 Hoole Road, Hoole, Chester
CH2 3NJ
T: (01244) 328239
F: 07968 404105
E: rhowardbraydon@btinternet.
com

Lloyd's Guest House ◆
108 Brook Street, Chester,
CH1 3DU
T: (01244) 325838
F: (01244) 317491

**Mitchells of Chester Guest
House** ◆◆◆◆
28 Hough Green, Chester,
CH4 8JQ
T: (01244) 679004
F: (01244) 659567
E: mitoches@dialstart.net
I: www.mitchellsofchester.com

Newton Hall ◆◆◆◆
Tattenhall, Chester CH3 9NE
T: (01829) 770153
F: (01829) 770655
E: newton.hall@farming.co.uk

Recorder Hotel ◆◆◆
19 City Walls, Chester, CH1 1SB
T: (01244) 326580
F: (01244) 401674
E: reservations@recorderhotel.
co.uk
I: www.recorderhotel.co.uk

Rowland House ◆◆◆
No 2 Chichester Street, Chester,
CH1 4AD
T: (01244) 390967
F: (01244) 390967
E: rowlandhousechester@
hotmail.com

Strathearn Guest House ◆◆◆
38 Hoole Road, Chester,
CH2 3NL
T: (01244) 321522
F: (01244) 321522
E: strathearn@breathemail.net

Ten The Groves ◆◆◆
10 The Groves, Chester, Cheshire
CH1 1SD
T: (01244) 317907
E: ten-the-groves@freeuk.com

Tentry Heys ◆◆
Queens Park Road, Chester,
CH4 7AD
T: (01244) 677857
F: (01244) 659439
E: njarthur@btconnect.com

Tower House ◆◆◆◆
14 Dee Hills Park, Chester,
CH3 5AR
T: (01244) 341936
E: sue.heather@talk21.com

Walpole House ◆◆◆◆
26 Walpole Street, Chester,
CH1 4HG
T: (01244) 373373
F: (01244) 373373
E: walphse@aol.com

CHILDWALL
Merseyside

Childwall Abbey Hotel
Rating Applied For
Score Lane, Childwall, Liverpool
L16 5EY
T: (0151) 722 5293
F: (0151) 722 0438

The Real McCoy ◆◆◆
126 Childwall Park Avenue,
Childwall, Liverpool L16 0JH
T: (0151) 722 7116 &
07971 161542
F: (0151) 722 7116

CHOLMONDELEY
Cheshire

Manor Farm ◆◆◆◆
Egerton, Malpas, Cheshire
SY14 8AW
T: (01829) 720261

CHORLEY
Lancashire

Parr Hall Farm ◆◆◆◆
Parr Lane, Eccleston, Chorley,
Lancashire PR7 5SL
T: (01257) 451917
F: (01257) 453749
E: parrhall@talk21.com

CHRISTLETON
Cheshire

The Cheshire Cat ◆◆◆
Whitchurch Road, Christleton,
Chester CH3 6AE
T: (01244) 332200 &
07885 952810
F: (01244) 336415
I: www.thecheshirecat.co.uk

CLAUGHTON
Lancashire

The Old Rectory ◆◆◆◆
Claughton, Lancaster LA2 9LA
T: (015242) 21150
F: (015242) 21098
E: info@rectorylancs.co.uk
I: www.rectorylancs.co.uk

CLAYTON-LE-MOORS
Lancashire

Maple Lodge Hotel ◆◆◆
70 Blackburn Road, Clayton-le-
Moors, Accrington, Lancashire
BB5 5JH
T: (01254) 301284
F: (01254) 388152
E: maplelod@aol.com
I: www.maplelodgehotel.co.uk

CLEVELEYS
Lancashire

Briardene Hotel ◆◆◆◆
56 Kelso Avenue, Cleveleys,
Blackpool FY5 3JG
T: (01253) 852312 & 852379
F: (01253) 851190

CLITHEROE
Lancashire

Brooklands ◆◆◆
9 Pendle Road, Clitheroe,
Lancashire BB7 1JQ
T: (01200) 422797 & 422797
F: (01200) 422797
E: kenandjean@tesco.net
I: www.ribblevalley.gov.
uk/hotel/brooklan/index.htm

Don Dino ◆◆◆◆
78-82 Whalley Road, Clitheroe,
Lancashire BB7 1EE
T: (01200) 424450

The Old Post House Hotel
Rating Applied For
48 King Street, Clitheroe,
Lancashire BB7 2EU
T: (01200) 422025
F: (01200) 423059
E: rooms@posthousehotel.co.uk
I: www.posthousehotel.co.uk

Rakefoot Farm ◆◆◆◆
Chaigley, Clitheroe, Lancashire
BB7 3LY
T: (01995) 61332 &
07009 279063

Selborne Guest House ◆◆◆
Back Commons, Kirkmoor Road,
Clitheroe, Lancashire BB7 2DX
T: (01200) 423571 & 422236
F: (01200) 423571
E: selbornehouse@lineone.net
I: selbornehouse@lineone.net

The Swan & Royal ◆◆◆
Castle Street, Clitheroe,
Lancashire BB7 2BX
T: (01200) 423130
F: (01200) 444351
E: skilshaw@jenningsbrewery.
co.uk
I: www.jenningsbrewery.co.uk

Timothy Cottage ◆◆◆
Whalley Road, Hurst Green,
Clitheroe, Lancashire BB7 9QJ
T: (01254) 826337 &
07889 194507
F: (01254) 826737
E: jgordon@dial.pipex.com

COLNE
Lancashire

Blakey Hall Farm ◆◆◆
Red Lane, Colne, Lancashire
BB8 9TD
T: (01282) 863121

Higher Wanless Farm ◆◆◆◆
Red Lane, Barrowford, Nelson,
Lancashire BB9 7JP
T: (01282) 865301
F: (01282) 865823
E: wanlessfarm@bun.com
I: www.stayinlancs.co.uk

Middle Beardshaw Head Farm
◆◆◆
Burnley Road, Trawden, Colne,
Lancashire BB8 8PP
T: (01282) 865257

Reedymoor Farm ◆◆◆◆
Reedymoor Lane, Foulridge,
Colne, Lancashire BB8 7LJ
T: (01282) 865074

Wickets ◆◆◆◆
148 Keighley Road, Colne,
Lancashire BB8 0PJ
T: (01282) 862002
F: (01282) 859675
E: wickets@colne148.fsnet.
co.uk

CONDER GREEN
Lancashire

Stork Hotel ◆◆◆
Conder Green, Lancaster
LA2 0AN
T: (01524) 751234
F: (01524) 752660

CONGLETON
Cheshire

The Plough at Eaton
Rating Applied For
Macclesfield Road, Eaton,
Congleton, Cheshire CW12 2NR
T: (01260) 280207
F: (01260) 298377
E: trev@plough76.fsnet.co.uk

Sandhole Farm ◆◆◆◆
Hulme Walfield, Congleton,
Cheshire CW12 2JH
T: (01260) 224419
F: (01260) 224766
E: veronica@sandholefarm.
co.uk
I: www.sandholefarm.co.uk
🏃

The Woodlands ◆◆◆◆
Quarry Wood Farm, Wood
Street, Mow-Cop, Congleton,
Cheshire ST7 3PF
T: (01782) 518877
F: (01782) 518877

Yew Tree Farm ◆◆◆◆
North Rode, Congleton, Cheshire
CW12 2PF
T: (01260) 223569
E: kiddyewtreefarm@
netscapeonline.co.uk

COPSTER GREEN
Lancashire

**The Brown Leaves Country
Hotel**
Rating Applied For
Longsight Road, Copster Green,
Blackburn BB1 9EU
T: (01254) 249523
F: (01254) 245240
I: www.brownleavescountry.
hotel.co.uk

CREWE
Cheshire

Balterley Green Farm ◆◆◆◆
Deans Lane, Balterley Green,
Crewe, Cheshire CW2 5QJ
T: (01270) 820214
E: greenfarm@balterley.fsnet.
co.uk
I: www.greenfarm.freeserve.
co.uk

Coole Hall Farm ◆◆◆◆
Hankelow, Crewe, CW3 0JD
T: (01270) 811232
E: goodwin280@hotmail.com

CULCHETH
Cheshire

99 Hob Hey Lane ◆◆◆◆
Culcheth, Warrington WA3 4NS
T: (01925) 763448
F: (01925) 763448

DENTON
Greater Manchester

Manchester Shelton Hotel
Rating Applied For
121 - 123 Twon Lane, Denton,
Manchester M34 2DJ
T: (0161) 320 7606
F: (0161) 336 1600
E: sheltonmanchester@hotmail.
com
I: www.sheltonhotelmanchester.
co.uk

DISLEY
Cheshire

The Grey Cottage ◆◆◆◆
20 Jacksons Edge Road, Disley,
Stockport, Cheshire SK12 2JE
T: (01663) 763286
E: carol.greycottage@talk21.
com

DUKINFIELD
Greater Manchester

Barton Villa Guest House
◆◆◆
Crescent Road, Dukinfield,
Cheshire SK16 4EY
T: (0161) 330 3952
F: (0161) 285 8488
E: bartonvillas.fsnet.co.uk
I: www.bartonvilla.co.uk

DUNSOP BRIDGE
Lancashire

Wood End Farm ◆◆◆◆
Dunsop Bridge, Clitheroe,
Lancashire BB7 3BE
I: (01200) 448223
E: spencers@beatrix-freeserve.
co.uk
I: www.members.tripod.
co.uk/Woodend

EATON
Cheshire

**The Cottage at The Waggon
and Horses**◆◆◆◆
Manchester Road, Eaton,
Congleton, Cheshire CW12 2JD
T: (01260) 224229
F: (01260) 224238
I: www.waggonandhorses.com

ELSWICK
Lancashire

Thornton House ◆◆◆◆
High Street, Elswick, Preston
PR4 3ZB
T: (01995) 671863
F: (01995) 671863
E: john_tizard@lineone.net
I: website.lineone.
net/~john_tizard

FARNWORTH
Greater Manchester

Fernbank Guest House ◆◆◆◆
61 Rawson Street, Farnworth,
Bolton BL4 7RJ
T: (01204) 708832

FOULRIDGE
Lancashire

Bankfield Guest House ◆◆◆
Skipton Road, Foulridge, Colne,
Lancashire BB8 7PY
T: (01282) 863870 &
07702 033637
F: (01282) 863870

Hare And Hounds Inn ◆◆◆
Old Skipton Road, Foulridge,
Colne, Lancashire BB8 7PD
T: (01282) 864235
F: (01282) 865966
E: hareandhounds1@hotmail.
com
I: www.hareandhoundsinn.com

FULWOOD
Lancashire

Kiwi House ◆◆◆◆
6 Sharoe Green Park, Fulwood,
Preston PR2 8HW
T: (01772) 719873
F: (01772) 719873

GARSTANG
Lancashire

Ashdene ◆◆◆
Parkside Lane, Nateby, Preston
PR3 0JA
T: (01995) 602676 &
07957 745624
E: ashdene@supanet.com

Guy's Thatched Hamlet ◆◆◆
Canalside, St Michael's Road,
Bilsborrow, Garstang, Preston
PR3 0RS
T: (01995) 640010 & 640020
F: (01995) 640141
E: guyshamlet@aol.com
I: www.guysthatchedhamlet.
co.uk

Tudor Farm ◆◆◆
Sowerby Road, St Michaels,
Garstang, Preston PR3 0TT
T: (01995) 679717

Woodacre Hall Farm ◆◆◆
Scorton, Preston PR3 1BN
T: (01995) 602253
F: (01995) 602253

GARSTON
Merseyside

Aplin House Hotel ◆◆
35 Clarendon Road, Garston,
Liverpool L19 6PJ
T: (0151) 427 5047

GAWSWORTH
Cheshire

Rough Hey Farm ◆◆◆◆
Leek Road, Gawsworth,
Macclesfield, Cheshire SK11 0JQ
T: (01260) 252296
E: roughheyfarm@bushinternet.
com

GOODSHAW
Lancashire

The Old White Horse ◆◆◆◆
211 Goodshaw Lane, Goodshaw,
Rossendale, Lancashire BB4 8DD
T: (01706) 215474 &
07703 763448
E: johnandmaggie54@hotmail.
com
I: www.211oldwhitehorse.
freeserve.co.uk

GOOSNARGH
Lancashire

Isles Field Barn ◆◆◆
Syke, Goosnargh, Preston
PR3 2EN
T: (01995) 640398

GREAT ECCLESTON
Lancashire

Cartford Hotel ◆◆◆
Cartford Lane, Little Eccleston,
Preston PR3 0YP
T: (01995) 670166
F: (01995) 671785

GREAT HARWOOD
Lancashire

Royal Hotel ◆◆◆
Station Road, Great Harwood,
Blackburn BB6 7BA
T: (01254) 883541

HALE
Greater Manchester

Clovelly Court ◆◆◆◆
224 Ashley Road, Hale,
Altrincham, Cheshire WA15 9SR
T: (0161) 927 7027 &
07947 437211

HARTFORD
Cheshire

The Coachman ◆◆◆
Chester Road, Hartford,
Northwich, Cheshire CW8 1QU
T: (01606) 871359 & 77199
F: (01606) 871359

HESKIN
Lancashire

Farmers Arms ◆◆◆
85 Wood Lane, Heskin, Chorley,
Lancashire PR7 5NP
T: (01257) 451276 & 453562
E: andy@farmersarms.co.uk
I: www.farmersarms.co.uk

HESWALL
Merseyside

The Hotel Victoria ◆◆◆
45 Gayton Road, Heswall, Wirral,
Merseyside CH60 8QE
T: (0151) 342 6021 & 342 3191
F: (0151) 342 6564
E: mail@hotelvictoria.co.uk
I: www.hotelvictoria.co.uk

HEYSHAM
Lancashire

It'l Do ◆◆◆
15 Oxcliffe Road, Heysham,
LA3 1PR
T: (01524) 850763

HEYWOOD
Greater Manchester

Albany Hotel ◆◆◆
87-89 Rochdale Road East,
Heywood, Lancashire OL10 1PX
T: (01706) 369606
F: (01706) 627914
E: mike@thealbanyhotel.co.uk
I: www.thealbanyhotel.co.uk

HIGHER BEBINGTON
Merseyside

The Bebington Hotel ◆◆◆
24 Town Lane, Higher
Bebington, Wirral, Merseyside
CH63 5JG
T: (0151) 645 0608 & 645 5478

HOLMES CHAPEL
Cheshire

Bridge Farm Bed and Breakfast
◆◆◆
Blackden, Jodrell Bank, Holmes
Chapel, Crewe, Cheshire
CW4 8BX
T: (01477) 571202
E: stay@bridgefarm.com

Padgate Guest House ◆◆◆◆
Twemlow Lane, Cranage,
Middlewich, Cheshire CW4 8EX
T: (01477) 534291
F: (01477) 544726
E: lynda@padgate.freeserve.
co.uk
♿

HOOLE
Cheshire

Glann Hotel ◆◆◆
2 Stone Place, Hoole, Chester
CH2 3NR
T: (01244) 344800
E: glannhot@supanet.com

Hamilton Court Hotel ◆◆◆◆
5-7 Hamilton Street, Hoole,
Chester CH2 3JG
T: (01244) 345387
F: (01244) 317404
E: hamiltoncourth@aol.com
I: www.smoothhound.co.uk

Holly House Guest House
◆◆◆
1 Stone Place, Hoole, Chester
CH2 3NR
T: (01244) 328967

Oaklea Guest House ◆◆
63 Oaklea Avenue, Hoole,
Chester CH2 3RG
T: (01244) 340516

HOYLAKE
Merseyside

Crestwood ◆◆◆
25 Drummond Road, Hoylake,
Wirral, Merseyside CH47 4AU
T: (0151) 632 2937

HUXLEY
Cheshire

Higher Huxley Hall ◆◆◆◆
Huxley, Chester CH3 9BZ
T: (01829) 781484
F: (01829) 781142
E: info@huxleyhall.co.uk
I: www.huxleyhall.co.uk

KIRKBY
Merseyside

Greenbank ◆◆
193 Rowan Drive, Westvale,
Kirkby, Liverpool L32 0SG
T: (0151) 546 9971
F: 1051 546 9971

KNUTSFORD
Cheshire

The Dog Inn
Rating Applied For
Well Bank Lane, Over Peover,
Knutsford, Cheshire WA16 8UP
T: (01625) 861421
F: (01625) 864800

**Laburnum Cottage Guest
House** ◆◆◆◆
Knutsford Road, Mobberley,
Knutsford, Cheshire WA16 7PU
T: (01565) 872464
F: (01565) 872464

Wash Lane Farm ◆◆◆
Allostock, Knutsford, Cheshire
WA16 9JP
T: (01565) 722215

LACH DENNIS
Cheshire

Melvin Holme Farm ◆◆◆
Pennys Lane, Lach Dennis,
Northwich, Cheshire CW9 7SJ
T: (01606) 330008

LANCASTER
Lancashire

Castle Hill Bed and Breakfast
◆◆◆
27 St Mary's Parade, Castle Hill,
Lancaster, LA1 1YX
T: (01524) 849137
F: (01524) 849137
E: gsutclif@aol.com.uk

Edenbreck House ♦♦♦♦
Sunnyside Lane, Lancaster,
LA1 5ED
T: (01524) 32464

Farmers Arms Hotel ♦♦
Penny Street, Lancaster, LA1 1XT
T: (01524) 36368

Farmhouse Tavern ♦♦♦
Morecambe Road, Lancaster,
LA1 5JB
T: (01524) 69255
F: (01524) 69255

Lancaster Town House ♦♦♦
11-12 Newton Terrace, Caton
Road, Lancaster, LA1 3PB
T: (01524) 65527
F: (01524) 65527
E: hedge-holmes@talk21.com
I: www.lancastertownhouse.
co.uk

Low House Farm ♦♦♦
Claughton, Lancaster, LA2 9LA
T: (01524) 221260
E: shirley@lunevalley.freeserve.
co.uk

Middle Holly Cottage ♦♦♦
Middle Holly Lane, Forton,
Preston PR3 1AH
T: (01524) 792399

The Old Station House ♦♦♦
25 Meeting House Lane,
Lancaster, LA1 1TX
T: (01524) 381060
F: (01524) 61845

**Priory Bed and Breakfast
♦♦♦♦**
15 St Mary's Parade, Castle Hill,
Lancaster, LA1 1YX
T: (01524) 845711

Railton Hotel ♦
2 Station Road, Lancaster,
LA1 5SJ
T: (01524) 388364
F: (01524) 388364

Shakespeare Hotel ♦♦♦♦
96 St Leonardgate, Lancaster,
LA1 1NN
T: (01524) 841041

Wagon and Horses ♦♦♦
27 St Georges Quay, Lancaster,
LA1 1RD
T: (01524) 34036 & 846094

LANGHO
Lancashire
**Petre Lodge Country Hotel
♦♦♦♦**
Northcote Road, Langho,
Blackburn BB6 8BG
T: (01254) 245506
F: (01254) 245506
E: aslambert@fsbdial.co.uk

LEYLAND
Lancashire
Oxen House Farm ♦♦♦
204 Longmeanygate, Leyland,
Preston PR5 3TB
T: (01772) 423749

LITHERLAND
Merseyside
**Litherland Park Bed and
Breakfast ♦♦♦**
34 Litherland Park, Litherland,
Bootle, Merseyside L21 9HP
T: (0151) 928 1085 & 0794 217
2357

LITTLEBOROUGH
Greater Manchester
**Hollingworth Lake Bed and
Breakfast ♦♦♦♦♦**
164 Smithy Bridge Road,
Hollingworth Lake,
Littleborough, Lancashire
OL15 0DB
T: (01706) 376583 &
07714 341078
E: karen@hollingworth.
masterflash.co.uk

Swing Cottage ♦♦♦♦
31 Lakebank, Hollingworth Lake
Country Park, Littleborough,
Lancashire OL15 0DQ
T: (01706) 379094
F: (01706) 379091
E: swingcottage@aol.com
I: www.hollingworthlake.com

LIVERPOOL
Merseyside
Aachen Hotel ♦♦♦
89-91 Mount Pleasant,
Liverpool, L3 5TB
T: (0151) 709 3477 & 709 3633
F: (0151) 709 1126
E: fpwaachen@netscapeonline.
co.uk
I: www.aachenhotel.co.uk

Antrim Hotel ♦♦
73 Mount Pleasant, Liverpool,
L3 5TB
T: (0151) 709 5239 & 709 9212
F: (0151) 709 7169
E: antrimhotel@ukbusiness.com

Blenheim Lodge ♦♦♦
37 Aigburth Drive, Liverpool,
L17 4JE
T: (0151) 727 7380
F: (0151) 727 5833
E: blenheimlodge@btinternet.
com

**Dolby Hotel Liverpool Ltd
♦♦♦**
36-42 Chaloner Street, Queen's
Dock, Liverpool, L3 4DE
T: (0151) 708 7272
F: (0151) 708 7266
E: liverpool@dolbyhotels.co.uk
I: www.dolbyhotels.co.uk

The Feathers Inn ♦♦
1 Paul Street, Vauxhall Road,
Liverpool, L3 6DX
T: 0870 236 1203
F: (0151) 236 0081

Holme Leigh Guest House ♦♦
93 Woodcroft Road, Wavertree,
Liverpool, L15 2HG
T: (0151) 734 2216 & 726 9980
F: (0151) 728 9521
E: bridges01@cableinet.co.uk

Lord Nelson ♦
Lord Nelson Street, Liverpool,
L3 5PD
T: (0151) 709 4362
F: (0151) 707 1321

Parkland ♦♦♦
38 Coachmans Drive, Croxteth
Park, Liverpool, L12 0HX
T: (0151) 259 1417

Redcroft ♦♦♦
12 Parkfield Road, Sefton Park,
Liverpool, L17 8UH
T: (0151) 727 3723

**Woolton Redbourne Hotel
♦♦♦♦**
Acrefield Road, Woolton,
Liverpool, L25 5JN
T: (0151) 421 1500
F: (0151) 421 1501
E: wooltonredbourne@cwcom.
net

LONGRIDGE
Lancashire
Oak Lea ♦♦♦♦
Clitheroe Road, Knowle Green,
Longridge, Preston PR3 2YS
T: (01254) 878486
F: (01254) 878486

LONGTON
Lancashire
Moorside Villa ♦♦♦♦
Drumacre Lane West, Longton,
Preston PR4 4SB
T: (01772) 616612

Willow Cottage ♦♦♦♦
Longton Bypass, Longton,
Preston PR4 4RA
T: (01772) 617570
E: info@
lancashirebedandbreakfast.co.uk
I: www.
lancashirebedandbreakfast.co.uk

LOWER WHITLEY
Cheshire
Tall Trees Lodge ♦♦♦
Tarporley Road, Lower Whitley,
Warrington WA4 4EZ
T: (01928) 790824 & 715117
F: (01928) 791330
E: booking@talltreeslodge.co.uk
I: www.talltreeslodge.co.uk

LYTHAM ST ANNES
Lancashire
Clifton Park Hotel ♦♦♦♦
299-301 Clifton Drive South,
Lytham St Annes, Lancashire
FY8 1HN
T: (01253) 725801
F: (01253) 721135
E: info@cliftonpark.co.uk
I: www.cliftonpark.co.uk

Fairmile Hotel ♦♦♦
9 St Annes Road East, Lytham St
Annes, Lancashire FY8 1TA
T: (01253) 728375
F: (01253) 728375
E: fairmilehotel@hotmail.com
I: www.hotellink.
co.uk/lytham/fairmile.html

Monarch Hotel ♦♦♦
29 St Annes Road East, Lytham
St Annes, Lancashire FY8 1TA
T: (01253) 720464 &
07778 422523
F: (01253) 720464
E: churchill@monarch91.
freeserve.co.uk
I: www.monarch-st-annes.co.uk

Strathmore Hotel ♦♦♦
305 Clifton Drive South, Lytham
St Annes, Lancashire FY8 1HN
T: (01253) 725478

MACCLESFIELD
Cheshire
Carr House Farm ♦♦♦
Mill Lane, Adlington,
Macclesfield, Cheshire SK10 4LG
T: (01625) 828337
F: (01625) 828337

Moorhayes House Hotel ♦♦♦
27 Manchester Road,
Tytherington, Macclesfield,
Cheshire SK10 2JJ
T: (01625) 433228
F: (01625) 429878
E: helen@moorhayes.co.uk
I: www.smoothhound.
co.uk/hotels/moorhaye

Oldhams Hollow Farm ♦♦♦
Manchester Road, Tytherington,
Macclesfield, Cheshire SK10 2JW
T: (01625) 424128 & 574280
F: (01625) 574280

Penrose Guest House ♦♦♦♦
56 Birtles Road, Whirley,
Macclesfield, Cheshire SK10 3JQ
T: (01625) 615323 &
07770 828795
F: (01625) 432284
E: info@penroseguesthouse.
co.uk
I: www.PenroseGuestHouse.
co.uk

Sandpit Farm ♦♦♦
Messuage Lane, Marton,
Macclesfield, Cheshire SK11 9HS
T: (01260) 224254

MAGHULL
Merseyside
Rosedene ♦♦♦
175 Liverpool Road South,
Maghull, Liverpool L31 8AA
T: (0151) 527 1897

MALPAS
Cheshire
**Hamilton House Bed and
Breakfast ♦♦♦**
Station Road, Hampton Heath,
Malpas, Cheshire SY14 8JF
T: (01948) 820421
E: katch&tted@hamiltonhouse.
com

MANCHESTER
Greater Manchester
Anbermar ♦♦♦
32 Gibwood Road, Northenden,
Manchester, M22 4BS
T: (0161) 998 2375

Bentley Guest House ♦♦♦
64 Hill Lane, Blackley,
Manchester M9 6PF
T: (0161) 795 1115

Commercial Hotel ♦♦
125 Liverpool Road, Castlefield,
Manchester, M3 4JN
T: (0161) 834 3504
F: (0161) 835 2725

**Dolby Hotel Manchester West
Ltd ♦♦♦**
55 Blackfriars Road, Manchester,
M3 7DB
T: (0161) 907 2277
F: (0161) 907 2266
E: manchester@dolbyhotels.
co.uk
I: www.dolbyhotels.co.uk

Luther King House ♦♦♦
Brighton Grove, Wilmslow Road,
Manchester, M14 5JP
T: (0161) 224 6404
F: (0161) 248 9201
E: reception@lkh.co.uk
I: www.lkh.co.uk

Monroe's ◆
38 London Road, Piccadilly,
Manchester, M1 1PE
T: (0161) 236 0564

The Ox Bar Restaurant Hotel
◆◆◆
71 Liverpool Road, Castleford,
Manchester, M3 4NQ
T: (0161) 839 7740
F: (0161) 839 7760
E: david@theox.uk

Palatine Hotel ◆◆◆
88 Palatine Road, West
Didsbury, Manchester, M20 3JW
T: (0161) 446 2222
F: (0161) 446 2233

Rembrandt Hotel ◆◆◆
33 Sackville Street, Manchester,
M1 3LZ
T: (0161) 236 1311 & 236 2435
F: (0161) 236 4257
E: rembrandthotel@aol.com
I: www.therembrandthotel.co.uk

MARTHALL
Cheshire

Moat Hall Motel ◆◆◆
Chelford Road, Marthall,
Knutsford, Cheshire WA16 8SU
T: (01625) 860367 & 861214
F: (01625) 861136
E: val@moathall.fsnet.co.uk
I: www.moathallmotel.co.uk

MICKLE TRAFFORD
Cheshire

Manor Guest House ◆◆◆
Mickle Trafford Manor,
Warrington Road, Mickle
Trafford, Chester CH2 4EA
T: (01244) 300555
F: (01244) 301909

MIDDLEWICH
Cheshire

Hopley House
Rating Applied For
Wimboldsley, Middlewich,
Cheshire CW10 0LN
T: (01270) 526292
F: (01270) 526292
E: margery@mreade.freeserve.
co.uk
I: www.mreade.freeserve.co.uk

MINSHULL VERNON
Cheshire

Higher Elms Farm ◆◆
Minshull Vernon, Crewe
CW1 4RG
T: (01270) 522252
F: (01270) 522252

MOBBERLEY
Cheshire

The Hinton ◆◆◆◆
Town Lane, Mobberley,
Knutsford, Cheshire WA16 7HH
T: (01565) 873484
F: (01565) 873484

MORECAMBE
Lancashire

Ashley Private Hotel ◆◆◆
371 Marine Road East,
Morecambe, Lancashire LA4 5AH
T: (01524) 412034
F: (01524) 421390
E: info@ashleyhotel.co.uk
I: www.ashleyhotel.co.uk

The Balmoral Hotel
Rating Applied For
34 Marine Road West,
Morecambe, Lancashire LA3 1BZ
T: (01524) 418526
F: (01524) 418526
I: www.
balmoralhotelmorecambe.co.uk

Belle Vue Hotel ◆◆
330 Marine Road, Morecambe,
Lancashire LA4 5AA
T: (01524) 411375
F: (01524) 411375

Berkeley Private Hotel ◆◆◆
39 Marine Road West,
Promenade West, Morecambe,
Lancashire LA3 1BZ
T: (01524) 418201

The Broadwater Private Hotel
◆◆
356 Marine Road, Morecambe,
Lancashire LA4 5AQ
T: (01524) 411333
F: (01524) 411 333

Caledonian Hotel ◆
60 Marine Road West,
Morecambe, Lancashire LA4 4ET
T: (01524) 418503
F: (01524) 401710

The Clifton Hotel ◆◆
43-46 Marine Road West,
Morecambe, Lancashire LA3 1BZ
T: (01524) 411573
F: (01524) 420839

Craigwell Hotel ◆◆◆
372 Marine Road East,
Morecambe, Lancashire LA4 5AH
T: (01524) 410095
F: (01524) 410095

The Durham Guest House
◆◆◆
73 Albert Road, Morecambe,
Lancashire LA4 4HY
T: (01524) 424790

Eidsforth Hotel ◆◆◆
317-318 Marine Road Central,
Promenade, Morecambe,
Lancashire LA4 5AA
T: (01524) 411691 & 420960
F: (01524) 832334

Glen Isla Guest House ◆◆
16 Clark Street, Morecambe,
Lancashire LA4 5HR
T: (01524) 418496

Glenthorn Private Hotel ◆◆
24-26 West End Road, Seaview
Parade, Morecambe, Lancashire
LA4 4DL
T: (01524) 411640
F: (01524) 411640
E: glenthorn@computerweekly.
com
I: www.glenthorn.co.uk

Jacaranda Guest House ◆◆
68 Clarendon Road, Morecambe,
Lancashire LA3 1QZ
T: (01524) 416915

Lakeland View Guest House
◆◆
130 Clarendon Road,
Morecambe, Lancashire LA3 1SD
T: (01524) 415873

The Marina Hotel ◆◆◆
324 Marine Road Central,
Morecambe, Lancashire LA4 5AA
T: (01524) 423979
F: (01524) 426699
E: marina@marina-hotel.
demon.co.uk
I: www.marina-hotel.demon.
co.uk

New Hazelmere Hotel ◆◆◆
391 Marine Road East,
Morecambe, Lancashire LA4 5AN
T: (01524) 417876
F: (01524) 414488

Roxbury Private Hotel ◆◆
78 Thornton Road, Morecambe,
Lancashire LA4 5PJ
T: (01524) 410561
F: (01524) 859734
E: ritall@bigfoot.com

St Winifred's Hotel ◆◆◆
Marine Road East, Morecambe,
Lancashire LA4 5AR
T: (01524) 412322 & 417903
F: (01524) 412322

Seacrest ◆◆◆
9-13 West End Road,
Morecambe, Lancashire LA4 4DJ
T: (01524) 411006

Seashelt Private Hotel ◆◆
85 Regent Road, Morecambe,
Lancashire LA3 1AD
T: (01524) 410265

Sunnyside Hotel ◆◆
8 Thornton Road, Morecambe,
Lancashire LA4 5PB
T: (01524) 418363

Tern Bay Hotel ◆◆◆
43 Heysham Road, Morecambe,
Lancashire LA3 1DA
T: (01524) 421209 &
07880 582544
F: (01524) 421209
E: info@ternbayhotel.co.uk
I: www.ternbayhotel.co.uk

Trevelyan Private Hotel ◆◆◆
27 West End Road, Morecambe,
Lancashire LA4 4DJ
T: (01524) 412013
E: thetrevelyan@supanet.com
I: www.thetrevelyan.freeserve.
co.uk

Westleigh Hotel ◆◆◆
9 Marine Road, Morecambe,
Lancashire LA3 1BS
T: (01524) 418352
F: (01524) 418352

The Wycollar Hotel ◆◆◆
28 Seaview Parade, West End
Road, Morecambe, Lancashire
LA4 4DL
T: (01524) 412335

Yacht Bay View Hotel ◆◆◆
359 Marine Road East,
Morecambe, Lancashire LA4 5AQ
T: (01524) 414481
E: yachtbayview@hotmail.com
I: www.yachtbay.co.uk

MOTTRAM ST ANDREW
Cheshire

Goose Green Farm ◆◆◆
Oak Road, Mottram St Andrew,
Macclesfield, Cheshire SK10 4RA
T: (01625) 828814
F: (01625) 828814
E: goosegreenfarm@talk21.com

MUCH HOOLE
Lancashire

The Barn Guest House ◆◆◆
204 Liverpool Old Road, Much
Hoole, Preston PR4 4QB
T: (01772) 612654 &
07932 735681

NANTWICH
Cheshire

Henhull Hall ◆◆◆◆
Welshmans Lane, Nantwich,
Cheshire CW5 6AD
T: (01270) 624158 &
07774 885305
F: (01270) 624158
E: philip.percival@virgin.net

Poole Bank Farm ◆◆◆
Wettenhall Road, Poole,
Nantwich, Cheshire CW5 6AL
T: (01270) 625169

NATEBY
Lancashire

Bowers Hotel and Brasserie
◆◆◆
Bowers Lane, Nateby, Preston
PR3 0JD
T: (01995) 601500
F: (01995) 603770

NELSON
Lancashire

Lovett House Guest House
◆◆◆
6 Howard Street, Off Carr Road,
Nelson, Lancashire BB9 7SZ
I: (01282) 697352 &
07719 599536
F: (01282) 700186
E: lovetthouse@cwcom.net
I: www.lovetthouse.co.uk

NETHER ALDERLEY
Cheshire

**Millbrook Cottage Guest
House** ◆◆◆◆
Congleton Road, Nether
Alderley, Macclesfield, Cheshire
SK10 4TW
T: (01625) 583567 &
07796 594229
F: (01625) 599556
E: millbrookcottage@hotmail.
com
I: www.millbrookcottage.co.uk

NEW BRIGHTON
Merseyside

Sea Level Hotel ◆◆◆
126 Victoria Road, New
Brighton, Wallasey, Merseyside
CH45 9LD
T: (0151) 639 3408
F: (0151) 639 3408

Sherwood Guest House ◆◆◆
55 Wellington Road, New
Brighton, Wirral, Merseyside
CH45 2ND
T: (0151) 639 5198
E: frankbreo@btinternet.com

Wellington House Hotel ◆◆◆
65 Wellington Road, New
Brighton, Wirral, Merseyside
CH45 2NE
T: (0151) 639 6594
F: (0151) 639 6594
I: www.wellington-house-hotel.
freeserve.co.uk

NORTHWICH
Cheshire

Ash House Farm ◆◆◆
Chapel Lane, Acton Bridge,
Northwich, Cheshire CW8 3QS
T: (01606) 852717
F: (01606) 852717
E: sue_schofield40@hotmail.com

Park Dale Guest House ◆◆◆
140 Middlewich Road,
Rudheath, Northwich, Cheshire
CW9 7DS
T: (01606) 45228
F: (01606) 331770

OLDHAM
Greater Manchester

Boothstead Farm ◆◆◆
Rochdale Road, Denshaw,
Oldham OL3 5UE
T: (01457) 878622
E: boothsteadfarm@
bushinternet.com

Globe Farm Guest House ◆◆◆
Huddersfield Road, Standedge,
Delph, Oldham OL3 5LU
T: (01457) 873040
F: (01457) 873040
E: globefarm@amserve.com
I: www.smoothhound.
co.uk/hotels/globef.html

Temple Bar Farm ◆◆◆◆
Wallhill Road, Dobcross, Oldham
OL3 5BH
T: (01457) 870099 & 872003
F: (01457) 872003
E: info@templebarfarm.co.uk
I: www.templebarfarm.co.uk

ORMSKIRK
Lancashire

The Meadows ◆◆◆◆
New Sutch Farm, Sutch Lane,
Ormskirk, Lancashire L40 4BU
T: (01704) 894048

OVER ALDERLEY
Cheshire

Lower Harebarrow Farm ◆◆
Over Alderley, Macclesfield,
Cheshire SK10 4SW
T: (01625) 829882

OVERTON
Lancashire

The Globe Hotel ◆◆◆
40 Main Street, Overton,
Morecambe, Lancashire LA3 3HG
T: (01524) 858228
F: (01524) 858 073
E: theglobe@talk21.com

PADIHAM
Lancashire

Windsor House ◆◆
71 Church Street, Padiham,
Burnley, Lancashire BB12 8JH
T: (01282) 773271

PICTON
Cheshire

The Fox Covert Guest House ◆◆◆◆
Fox Covert Lane, Picton, Chester
CH2 4HB
T: (01244) 300363 & 300963
F: (01244) 300963
E: george.derby@virgin.net
I: freespace.virgin.net/george.derby

PRESTON
Lancashire

County Hotel ◆◆
1 Fishergate Hill, Preston,
Lancashire PR1 8UL
T: (01772) 253188
F: (01772) 253188

Derby Court Hotel ◆◆
1 Pole Street, Preston, PR1 1DX
T: (01772) 202077
F: (01772) 252277

Olde Duncombe House ◆◆◆
Garstang Road, Bilsborrow,
Preston PR3 0RE
T: (01995) 640336
F: (01995) 640336
E: oldedunc@aol.com

Tulketh Hotel ◆◆◆◆
209 Tulketh Road, Ashton,
Preston, PR2 1ES
T: (01772) 728096 & 726250
F: (01772) 723743
I: www.smoothhound.
co.uk/hotels/tulketh.html

Ye Horns Inn ◆◆◆◆
Horns Lane, Goosnargh, Preston,
PR3 2FJ
T: (01772) 865230
F: (01772) 864299
E: enquiries@yehornsinn.co.uk
I: www.yehornsinn.co.uk

PRESTWICH
Greater Manchester

Church Inn ◆◆◆
Church Lane, Prestwich,
Manchester M25 1AJ
T: (0161) 798 6727
F: (0161) 773 6281
E: tom.gribben@virgin.net

RUSHTON
Cheshire

Hill House Farm Bed and Breakfast ◆◆◆
The Hall Lane, Rushton,
Tarporley, Cheshire CW6 9AU
T: (01829) 732238 &
07973 284863
F: (01829) 733929
E: rayner@hillhousefarm.fsnet.co.uk

SADDLEWORTH
Greater Manchester

Farrars Arms ◆◆
56 Oldham Road, Grasscroft,
Oldham OL4 4HL
T: (01457) 872124
F: (01457) 820351

ST ANNES
Lancashire

Elsinghurst Hotel ◆◆◆
34 Derbe Road, St Annes,
Lytham St Annes, Lancashire
FY8 1NJ
T: (01253) 724629
F: (01253) 7244629
E: elsinghursthotel@supanet.com

ST MICHAEL'S ON WYRE
Lancashire

Compton House ◆◆◆◆
Garstang Road, St Michael's on
Wyre, Preston PR3 0TE
T: (01995) 679378
F: (01995) 679378
E: dave@compton-hs.co.uk
I: www.compton-hs.co.uk

SALE
Greater Manchester

Cornerstones ◆◆◆◆
230 Washway Road, Sale,
Cheshire M33 4RA
T: (0161) 283 6909
F: (0161) 283 6909
E: cornerstones.hotel@aol.com
I: www.cornerstoneshotel.com

SALFORD
Greater Manchester

Hazeldean Hotel ◆◆◆
467 Bury New Road, Kersal Bar,
Salford, Lancashire M7 3NE
T: (0161) 792 6667 & 792 2079
F: (0161) 792 6668

White Lodge Private Hotel ◆
87-89 Great Cheetham Street
West, Salford, Lancashire
M7 2JA
T: (0161) 792 3047

SALTNEY
Cheshire

The Garden Gate Guest House ◆◆◆
8 Chester Street, Saltney,
Chester CH4 8BJ
T: (01244) 682306 &
07711 698361
F: 07769 723128

SANDBACH
Cheshire

Moss Cottage Farm ◆◆◆◆
Hassall Road, Winterley,
Sandbach, Cheshire CW11 4RU
T: (01270) 583018

SCORTON
Lancashire

Tuft Cottage ◆◆◆
Scorton, Preston PR3 1BT
T: (01524) 791955
E: tuftcottage@quista.net

SCOTFORTH
Lancashire

West View Farm ◆◆◆
Langthwaite Road, Scotforth,
Lancaster LA1 3JJ
T: (01524) 841336

SEALAND
Cheshire

The Elms Farmhouse Hotel ◆◆
Sealand Road, Sealand, Chester
CH1 6BS
T: (01244) 880747
F: (01244) 880920

SIDDINGTON
Cheshire

Golden Cross Farm ◆◆◆
Siddington, Macclesfield,
Cheshire SK11 9JP
T: (01260) 224358

SILVERDALE
Lancashire

Silverdale Hotel ◆◆◆
Shore Road, Silverdale,
Carnforth, Lancashire LA5 0TP
T: (01524) 701206

SLAIDBURN
Lancashire

Hark to Bounty Inn ◆◆◆
Slaidburn, Clitheroe, Lancashire
BB7 3EP
T: (01200) 446246
F: (01200) 446361
E: isobel@hark-to-bounty.co.uk
I: www.hark-to-bounty.co.uk

Pages Farm ◆◆◆
Woodhouse Lane, Slaidburn,
Clitheroe, Lancashire BB7 3AH
T: (01200) 446205

SLYNE
Lancashire

Slyne Lodge
Rating Applied For
92 Main Road, Slyne, Lancaster
LA2 6AZ
T: (01524) 825035
F: (01524) 823467
E: skilshaw@jenningsbrewery.co.uk
I: www.jenningsbrewery.co.uk

SOUTHPORT
Merseyside

Aaron Hotel ◆◆◆
18 Bath Street, Southport,
Merseyside PR9 0DA
T: (01704) 530283
F: (01704) 501055
E: info@aaronhotel.co.uk
I: www.aaronhotel.co.uk

Adelphi Hotel ◆◆
39 Bold Street, Southport,
Merseyside PR9 0ED
T: (01704) 544947
F: (01704) 538234
E: gromad@aol.com
I: www.merseyworld.
com/adelphi_hotel

Alhambra Hotel ◆◆◆
41 Bold Street, Southport,
Merseyside PR9 0ED
T: (01704) 534853
E: info@alhambrahotel.co.uk
I: www.alhambrahotel.co.uk

Ambassador Private Hotel ◆◆◆◆
13 Bath Street, Southport,
Merseyside PR9 0DP
T: (01704) 543998
F: (01704) 536269
E: ambassador.walton@virgin.net
I: www.ambassadorprivatehotel.co.uk

Brae Mar Private Hotel ◆◆◆
4 Bath Street, Southport,
Merseyside PR9 0DA
T: (01704) 535838
F: (01704) 535838

Carleton House Hotel ◆◆◆
17 Alexandra Road, Southport,
Merseyside PR9 0NB
T: (01704) 538035 & 530488
F: (01704) 538035
E: bookings@carleton-house.co.uk
I: www.carleton-house.co.uk

Carlton Lodge Hotel ◆◆◆◆
43 Bath Street, Southport,
Merseyside PR9 0DP
T: (01704) 542290 &
0500 400413
F: (01704) 542290
E: benvale@which.net
I: www.smoothhound.
co.uk/hotels/carlton

Club House Hotel ◆◆◆
15 Leicester Street, Southport,
Merseyside PR9 0ER
T: (01704) 533745
E: carolstan@clubhouse15.fsnet.co.uk

Cora Hotel ◆◆
29 Bath Street, Southport,
Merseyside PR9 0DP
T: (01704) 530204
F: (01704) 530204

Crescent House Hotel ◆◆◆
27 Bath Street, Southport,
Merseyside PR9 0DP
T: (01704) 530339
F: (01704) 530339
E: glynor@creshohotel.
freeserve.co.uk
I: www.smoothhound.
co.uk/hotels/crescnt.html

Fairfield Private Hotel ◆◆◆
83 Promenade, Southport,
Merseyside PR9 0JN
T: (01704) 530137

Le Maitre Hotel ◆◆◆◆
69 Bath Street, Southport,
Merseyside PR9 0DN
T: (01704) 530394 &
07889 399357
F: (01704) 548755
E: enquiries@hotel-lemaitre.
co.uk
I: www.hotel-lemaitre.co.uk

Leicester Hotel ◆◆◆
24 Leicester Street, Southport,
Merseyside PR9 0EZ
T: (01704) 530049
F: (01704) 530049
E: leicester.hotel@mail.cybase.
co.uk

Lynwood Private Hotel ◆◆◆◆
11a Leicester Street, Southport,
Merseyside PR9 0ER
T: (01704) 540794
F: (01704) 500724
I: www.smoothhound.
co.uk/lynwood.html.

Oakwood Private Hotel ◆◆◆◆
7 Portland Street, Southport,
Merseyside PR8 1LJ
T: (01704) 531858
E: oakwoodhotel@tinyworld.
co.uk
I: www.merseyworld.
com/oakwood

Penkelie Hotel ◆◆◆
34 Bold Street, Southport,
Merseyside PR9 0ED
T: (01704) 538510
F: (01704) 538510
E: info@penkelie.co.uk
I: www.penkelie.co.uk

Rosedale Hotel ◆◆◆◆
11 Talbot Street, Southport,
Merseyside PR8 1HP
T: (01704) 530604
F: (01704) 530604
E: info@
rosedalehotelsouthport.co.uk
I: www.rosedalehotelsouthport.
co.uk

Sandy Brook Farm ◆◆◆
52 Wyke Cop Road, Scarisbrick,
Southport, Merseyside PR8 5LR
T: (01704) 880337
F: (01704) 880337

Sidbrook Hotel ◆◆◆
14 Talbot Street, Southport,
Merseyside PR8 1HP
T: (01704) 530608
F: (01704) 530608
E: sidbrookhotel@tesco.net
I: www.sidbrookhotel.co.uk

Silverdale Hotel ◆◆◆◆
10 Victoria Street, Southport,
Merseyside PR9 0DU
T: (01704) 536479
F: (01704) 536479

Squires Hotel ◆◆◆
78/80 King Street, Southport,
Merseyside PR8 1LG
T: (01704) 544462 & 07957 747
4031
F: (01704) 544462
E: mail@squireshotel.co.uk
I: www.squireshotel.co.uk

Sunnyside Hotel ◆◆◆
47 Bath Street, Southport,
Merseyside PR9 0DP
T: (01704) 536521
F: (01704) 539237
E: sunnysidehotel@rapid.co.uk
I: www.sunny-lisa.co.uk

Waterford ◆◆◆◆
37 Leicester Street, Southport,
Merseyside PR9 0EX
T: (01704) 530559
F: (01704) 530559
E: waterfordhotel@rapidnet
I: www.waterford-hotel.co.uk

Whitworth Falls Hotel ◆◆◆
16 Lathom Road, Southport,
Merseyside PR9 0JH
T: (01704) 530074 & 534505
E: whitworthfalls@rapid.co.uk
I: www.whitworthfallshotel.
co.uk

Windsor Lodge Hotel ◆◆◆
37 Saunders Street, Southport,
Merseyside PR9 0HJ
T: (01704) 530070

Hallfield Guest House ◆◆◆
50 Hall Street, Offerton,
Stockport, Cheshire SK1 4DA
T: (0161) 429 8977 & 429 6153
F: (0161) 429 9017
E: hallfieldhouse@btconnect.
com
I: www.hallfieldguesthouse.
co.uk

Moss Deeping ◆◆◆
7 Robins Lane, Bramhall,
Stockport, Cheshire SK7 2PE
T: (0161) 439 1969
F: (0161) 439 9985
E: gbanks7872@aol.com

Needhams Farm
Uplands Road, Werneth Low,
Gee Cross, Hyde, Cheshire
SK14 3AG
T: (0161) 368 4610
F: (0161) 367 9106
E: charlotte@needhamsfarm.
demon.co.uk
I: www.needhamsfarm.co.uk

Alden Cottage ◆◆◆◆
Kemple End, Birdy Brow,
Stonyhurst, Clitheroe,
Lancashire BB7 9QY
T: (01254) 826468
E: carpenter@aldencottage.f9.
co.uk

Foresters Arms ◆◆◆
92 High Street, Tarporley,
Cheshire CW6 0AX
T: (01829) 733151
F: (01829) 730020

Roughlow Farm ◆◆◆◆
Willington, Tarporley, Cheshire
CW6 0PG
T: (01829) 751199
F: (01829) 751199
E: sutcliffe@roughlow.
freeserve.co.uk
I: www.roughlow.freeserve.co.uk

Broad Oak Farm ◆◆◆
Birds Lane, Tattenhall, Chester
CH3 9NL
T: (01829) 770325
F: (01829) 771546

Ford Farm ◆◆◆
Newton Lane, Tattenhall,
Chester CH3 9NE
T: (01829) 770307

Acorn of Oakmere ◆◆◆
Oakmere, 6 Wingate Drive,
Timperley, Altrincham, Cheshire
WA15 7PX
T: (0161) 980 8391
F: (0161) 980 8391
E: oakmere@cwctv.net

The Old House ◆◆◆
Woodhead Road, Torside,
Glossop, Derbyshire SK13 1HU
T: (01457) 857527

Dog and Partridge
Rating Applied For
Tosside, Skipton, North Yorkshire
BD23 4SQ
T: (01729) 840668

Peter Barn Country House
◆◆◆◆
Cross Lane, Waddington,
Clitheroe, Lancashire BB7 3JH
T: (01200) 428585 &
07797 826370
E: jean@peterbarn.fsnet.co.uk

Dean Lodge Guest House ◆
8 Dean Avenue, Wallasey,
Merseyside CH45 3HT
T: (0151) 630 2320
F: (0151) 630 2320

The Russell Hotel ◆◆◆
44 Church Road, Seacombe,
Wallasey, Merseyside CH44 7BA
T: (0151) 639 5723 & 637 2258
F: (0151) 639 5723

Cotestones Farm ◆◆◆
Sand Lane, Warton, Carnforth,
Lancashire LA5 9NH
T: (01524) 732418
F: (01524) 732418

Marlborough Hotel
Rating Applied For
21 Crosby Road outh, Waterloo,
Liverpool L22 1RG
T: (0151) 928 7709
F: (0151) 928 7709

Woodlands Guest House ◆◆◆
10 Haigh Road, Waterloo,
Liverpool L22 3XP
T: (0151) 920 5373

Blackmoor ◆◆◆
160 Blackmoor Drive, West
Derby, Liverpool L12 9EF
T: (0151) 291 1407 & 228 4886

Caldy Warren Cottage ◆◆◆◆
42 Caldy Road, West Kirby,
Wirral, Merseyside CH48 2HQ
T: (0151) 625 8740
F: (0151) 625 4115
E: graves@warrencott.demon.
co.uk
I: www.warrencott.demon.co.uk

Maconachie Guest House
◆◆◆
1 Victoria Road, West Kirby,
Wirral, Merseyside CH48 3HL
T: (0151) 625 1915

Daisy Hill Hotel ◆◆◆
3 Lower Leigh Road, Daisy Hill,
Westhoughton, Bolton BL5 2JP
T: (01942) 812096 & 797180
F: (01942) 797180
E: daisy.hill@cwcom.net
I: www.daisyhillhotel.co.uk

Snape Farm ◆◆◆
Snape Lane, Weston, Crewe
CW2 5NB
T: (01270) 820208
F: (01270) 820208

Bayley Arms Hotel ◆◆◆
Avenue Road, Hurst Green,
Whalley, Clitheroe, Lancashire
BB7 9QB
T: (01254) 826478
F: (01254) 826797

The Inn at Whitewell ◆◆◆◆
Whitewell, Clitheroe, Lancashire
BB7 3AT
T: (01200) 448222 & 448640
F: (01200) 448298

Chapel Fold Farm ◆◆◆◆
Chapel Lane, Whittle-le-Woods,
Chorley, Lancashire PR6 7DZ
T: (01257) 249518
I: www.lancashireoak.co.uk

WHITWORTH
Lancashire

Hindle Pastures
Rating Applied For
Highgate Lane, Whitworth,
Rochdale, Lancashire OL12 0TS
T: (01706) 643310
F: (01706) 653846
E: p-marshall@breathemail.net

WIGAN
Greater Manchester

Wilden ◆◆◆
11a Miles Lane, Shevington,
Wigan, Lancashire WN6 8EB
T: (01257) 251516 &
07798 935373
F: (01257) 255622
E: wildenads@aol.com

WILMSLOW
Cheshire

Dean Bank Hotel ◆◆◆
Adlington Road, Wilmslow,
Cheshire SK9 2BT
T: (01625) 524268
F: (01625) 549715
⅙

Finney Green Cottage ◆◆◆◆
134 Manchester Road,
Wilmslow, Cheshire SK9 2JW
T: (01625) 533343

**Hollow Bridge Guest House
◆◆◆◆**
90 Manchester Road, Wilmslow,
Cheshire SK9 2JY
T: (01625) 537303
F: (01625) 528718
E: lynandjack@hollowbridge.
com
I: www.hollowbridge.com

Marigold House ◆◆◆◆
132 Knutsford Road, Wilmslow,
Cheshire SK9 6JH
T: (01625) 584414 &
0793 9514609

**Rylands Farm Guest House
◆◆◆**
Altrincham Road, Wilmslow,
Cheshire SK9 4LT
T: (01625) 535646 & 548041
F: (01625) 535646

WINTERLEY
Cheshire

Field Mews ◆◆◆◆
The Fields, 36 Hassall Road,
Winterley, Sandbach, Cheshire
CW11 4RL
T: (01270) 761858 &
07973 867609

WISWELL
Lancashire

Pepper Hill ◆◆◆◆
Pendleton Road, Wiswell,
Clitheroe, Lancashire BB7 9BZ
T: (01254) 825098

WYCOLLER
Lancashire

Parson Lee Farm ◆◆◆
Wycoller, Colne, Lancashire
BB8 8SU
T: (01282) 864747
E: pathodgson@hotmail.com
I: www.parsonleefarm.co.uk

YORKSHIRE

ACKLAM
North Yorkshire

Trout Pond Barn ◆◆◆◆
Acklam, Malton, North Yorkshire
YO17 9RG
T: (01653) 658468 & 693088
F: (01653) 693088
E: margaret@troutpondbarn.
co.uk

ADDINGHAM
West Yorkshire

Ghyll House Farm ◆◆◆
Straight Lane, Addingham, Ilkley,
West Yorkshire LS29 9JX
T: (01943) 830370

**Lumb Beck Farmhouse Bed and
Breakfast◆◆◆◆**
Moorside Lane, Addingham,
Ilkley, West Yorkshire LS29 9JX
T: (01943) 830400

AINTHORPE
North Yorkshire

The Fox & Hounds Inn ◆◆◆◆
45 Brook Lane, Ainthorpe,
Whitby, North Yorkshire
YO21 2LD
T: (01287) 660218
F: (01287) 660370
E: ajbfox@globalnet.co.uk
I: www.foxandhounds.org

AIRTON
North Yorkshire

Lindon House ◆◆◆
Malhamdale, Airton, Skipton,
North Yorkshire BD23 4BE
T: (01729) 830418

AISLABY
North Yorkshire

**Blacksmiths Arms Restaurant
◆◆◆**
Aislaby, Pickering, North
Yorkshire YO18 8PE
T: (01751) 472182 &
07885 573808

ALDBROUGH
East Riding of Yorkshire

West Carlton ◆◆◆◆
Carlton Lane, Aldbrough, Hull,
East Yorkshire HU11 4RB
T: (01964) 527724 &
07767 830868
F: (01964) 527505
E: caroline_maltas@hotmail.
com
I: www.west-carlton.co.uk

ALDFIELD
North Yorkshire

Bay Tree Farm ◆◆◆◆
Aldfield, Ripon, North Yorkshire
HG4 3BE
T: (01765) 620394
F: (01765) 620394
E: baytree@wotz.freeserve.co.uk

ALLERTON
West Yorkshire

Victoria Hotel ◆◆◆
10 Cottingley Road, Sandy Lane,
Allerton, Bradford, West
Yorkshire BD15 9JP
T: (01274) 823820
F: (01274) 823820

AMOTHERBY
North Yorkshire

**Old Station Country Guest
House ◆◆◆◆**
High Street, Amotherby, Malton,
North Yorkshire YO17 6TL
T: (01653) 693683
F: (01653) 693683
E: info@oldstationfarm.co.uk
I: www.oldstationfarm.co.uk

AMPLEFORTH
North Yorkshire

Carr House Farm ◆◆◆
Shallowdale, Ampleforth, York
YO62 4ED
T: (01347) 868526 &
07977 113197
E: ampleforth@hotmail.com
I: www.guestaccom.co.uk

Daleside ◆◆◆◆
East End, Ampleforth, York
YO62 4DA
T: (01439) 788266

Shallowdale House ◆◆◆◆◆
West End, Ampleforth, York
YO62 4DY
T: (01439) 788325
F: (01439) 788885
E: stay@shallowdalehouse.
demon.co.uk
I: www.shallowdalehouse.
demon.co.uk

Spring Cottage ◆◆◆
Ampleforth, York YO62 4DA
T: (01439) 788579

The White Horse Inn ◆◆◆
West End, Ampleforth, York
YO62 4DX
T: (01439) 788378 & 788120

APPERSETT
North Yorkshire

Thorney Mire House ◆◆◆◆
Appersett, Hawes, North
Yorkshire DL8 3LU
T: (01969) 667159
E: sylvia@thorneymire.yorks.net
I: www.thorneymire.yorks.net

APPLETREEWICK
North Yorkshire

Knowles Lodge ◆◆◆◆
Appletreewick, Skipton, North
Yorkshire BD23 6DQ
T: (01756) 720228
F: (01756) 720381
E: chris.knowlesfitton@totalise.
co.uk
I: www.knowleslodge.com

ARKENGARTHDALE
North Yorkshire

Chapel Farmhouse ◆◆◆◆
Whaw, Arkengarthdale,
Richmond, North Yorkshire
DL11 6RT
T: (01748) 884062
F: (01748) 884062
E: chapelfarmbb@aol.com

**The Charles Bathurst Inn
◆◆◆◆**
Arkengarthdale, Richmond,
North Yorkshire DL11 6EN
T: (01748) 884567 & 884058
F: (01748) 884599
E: info@cbinn.co.uk
I: www.cbinn.co.uk

The Ghyll ◆◆◆
Arkle Town, Arkengarthdale,
Richmond, North Yorkshire
DL11 6EU
T: (01748) 884353
F: (01748) 884015
E: bookings@theghyll.co.uk
I: www.theghyll.co.uk

The White House ◆◆◆
Arkle Town, Arkengarthdale,
Richmond, North Yorkshire
DL11 6RB
T: (01748) 884203
F: (01748) 884088
I: www.yorkshirenet.
co.uk/stayat/thewhitehouse

ASKRIGG
North Yorkshire

**The Apothecary's House
◆◆◆◆**
Market Place, Askrigg, Leyburn,
North Yorkshire DL8 3HT
T: (01969) 650626

Helm ◆◆◆◆
Askrigg, Leyburn, North
Yorkshire DL8 3JF
T: (01969) 650443
F: (01969) 650443
E: holiday@helmyorkshire.com
I: www.helmyorkshire.com

Home Farm ◆◆◆
Stalling Busk, Askrigg, Leyburn,
North Yorkshire DL8 3DH
T: (01969) 650360

Milton House ◆◆◆◆
Askrigg, Leyburn, North
Yorkshire DL8 3HJ
T: (01969) 650217

YORKSHIRE

Stoney End ◆◆◆◆
Worton, Leyburn, North
Yorkshire DL8 3ET
T: (01969) 650652
F: (01969) 650077
E: stoneyendholidays@
btinternet.com
I: www.wensleydale.
org/links/stoneyendfrm.htm

Thornsgill Guest House ◆◆◆◆
Moor Road, Askrigg, Leyburn,
North Yorkshire DL8 3HH
T: (01969) 650617
E: gilyeatfamily@yahoo.co.uk

AUSTWICK
North Yorkshire
Dalesbridge House ◆◆◆◆
Austwick, Lancaster LA2 8AZ
T: (01524) 251021 & 0800 458
1021
F: (01524) 251051
E: info@dalesbridge.co.uk
I: www.dalesbridge.co.uk

Woodview Guest House
◆◆◆◆
The Green, Austwick, Lancaster
LA2 8BB
T: (01524) 251268

AYSGARTH
North Yorkshire
Cornlee ◆◆◆
Aysgarth, Leyburn, North
Yorkshire DL8 3AE
T: (01969) 663779 & 663053
F: (01969) 663779
E: cornlee@tesco.net
I: www.cornlee.co.uk

Field House ◆◆◆◆
East End, Aysgarth, Leyburn,
North Yorkshire DL8 3AB
T: (01969) 663556

Low Gill Farm ◆◆◆
Aysgarth, Leyburn, North
Yorkshire DL8 3AL
T: (01969) 663554

Stow House Hotel ◆◆◆◆
Aysgarth Falls, Aysgarth,
Leyburn, North Yorkshire
DL8 3SR
T: (01969) 663635
E: davidpeterburton@aol.com
I: www.wensleydale.org

Wheatsheaf Hotel ◆◆◆
Carperby, Leyburn, North
Yorkshire DL8 4DF
T: (01969) 663216
F: (01969) 663019
E: wheatsheaf@paulmit.
globalnet.co.uk
I: www.
wheatsheafinwensleydale.co.uk

BAILDON
West Yorkshire
**Ford House Farm Bed and
Breakfast** ◆◆◆◆
Buck Lane, Baildon, Shipley,
West Yorkshire BD177 7R
T: (01274) 584489 &
07747 002626
F: (01274) 584489
E: mick@mpadley.fsnet.co.uk

BAINBRIDGE
North Yorkshire
Hazel's Roost ◆◆◆
Bainbridge, Leyburn, North
Yorkshire DL8 3EH
T: (01969) 650400

High Force Farm ◆◆◆
Bainbridge, Leyburn, North
Yorkshire DL8 3DL
T: (01969) 650379
F: (01969) 650826
E: highforce@4free.net

BAINTON
East Riding of Yorkshire
Bainton Burrows Farm ◆◆◆
Bainton, Driffield, North
Humberside YO25 9BS
T: (01377) 217202

BALDERSBY
North Yorkshire
The Barn ◆◆◆
Nemur, Baldersby, Thirsk, North
Yorkshire YO7 4PE
T: (01765) 640561 &
07785 746015
F: (01765) 609399
E: sthain@zoom.co.uk

BARLOW
North Yorkshire
Berewick House ◆◆◆◆
Park Lane, Barlow, Selby, North
Yorkshire YO8 8EW
T: (01757) 617051 &
07961 919678
F: (01751) 617051
E: Wilson.Guesthouse@
Berewick.co.uk

BARNBY DUN
South Yorkshire
Gateway Inn & Restaurant
◆◆◆
Station Road, Barnby Dun,
Doncaster, South Yorkshire
DN3 1HA
T: (01302) 882849 & 880641
F: (01302) 891434
E: brnsmit@aol.com
I: www.gatewayinn.co.uk

BARNETBY
South Humberside
Reginald House ◆◆◆◆
27 Queens Road, Barnetby,
South Humberside DN38 6JH
T: (01652) 688566
F: (01652) 688510

BARNSLEY
South Yorkshire
Travellers Inn ◆◆◆
23 Green Road, Dodworth,
Barnsley, South Yorkshire
S75 3RR
T: (01226) 284173
F: (01226) 284173
E: jeremy@travellersinn.
freeserve.co.uk

BARROW UPON HUMBER
North Lincolnshire
Glebe Farm ◆◆◆
Cross Street, Barrow upon
Humber, South Humberside
DN19 7AL
T: (01469) 531548
F: (01469) 530034
E: glebe_farm@lineone.net

Haven Inn ◆◆◆
Ferry Road, Barrow Haven,
Barrow upon Humber, South
Humberside DN19 7EX
T: (01469) 530247
F: (01469) 530625
E: dmhav123@aol.com
I: www.haveninn.com

BARTON-LE-STREET
North Yorkshire
Laurel Barn Cottage ◆◆◆
Barton-le-Street, Malton, North
Yorkshire YO17 6QB
T: (01653) 628329

BARTON-UPON-HUMBER
North Lincolnshire
**The George Hotel
Rating Applied For**
George Street, Barton-upon-
Humber, South Humberside
DN18 5ES
T: (01652) 662001
F: (01652) 662002

BECK HOLE
North Yorkshire
Brookwood Farm ◆◆◆◆
Beck Hole, Whitby, North
Yorkshire YO22 5LE
T: (01947) 896402
I: www.brookwoodfarm.co.uk

BEDALE
North Yorkshire
The Castle Arms Inn ◆◆◆◆
Snape, Bedale, North Yorkshire
DL8 2TB
T: (01677) 470270
F: (01677) 470837
E: castlearms@aol.com

Elmfield Country House
◆◆◆◆◆
Arrathorne, Bedale, North
Yorkshire DL8 1NE
T: (01677) 450558
F: (01677) 450557
E: stay@elmfieldhouse.
freeserve.co.uk
I: www.countryhouse.co.uk

Georgian Bed and Breakfast
◆◆◆◆
16 North End, Stabann, Bedale,
North Yorkshire DL8 1AB
T: (01677) 424454

Milton House ◆◆◆◆◆
Londonderry, Northallerton,
North Yorkshire DL7 9NE
T: (01677) 423142
F: (01677) 423142
E: rachel@miltonhouse79.co.uk

BEESTON
West Yorkshire
Crescent Hotel ◆◆
274 Dewsbury Road, Beeston,
Leeds LS11 6JT
T: (113) 270 1819
F: (113) 270 1819

BELL BUSK
North Yorkshire
Tudor House ◆◆◆◆
Bell Busk, Skipton, North
Yorkshire BD23 4DT
T: (01729) 830301
F: (01729) 830037
E: bellbusk.hitch@virgin.net
I: www.tudorbellbusk.co.uk

BEN RHYDDING
West Yorkshire
Gracefield ◆◆◆
133 Bolling Road, Ben Rhydding,
Ilkley, West Yorkshire LS29 8PN
T: (01943) 600960
E: gracefield133@netscape.net
I: sites.netscape.
net/gracefield133/homepage

BEVERLEY
East Riding of Yorkshire
Beck View Guest House
◆◆◆
Beck View House, 1a Blucher
Lane, Beverley, North
Humberside HU17 0PT
T: (01482) 882332
E: BeckViewHouse@aol.com

Eastgate Guest House ◆◆◆
7 Eastgate, Beverley, North
Humberside HU17 0DR
T: (01482) 868464
F: (01482) 871899

Market Cross Hotel ◆◆◆
14 Lairgate, Beverley, North
Humberside HU17 8EE
T: (01482) 882573 & 679029

The Pipe and Glass Inn ◆◆◆
West End, South Dalton,
Beverley, North Humberside
HU17 7PN
T: (01430) 810246
F: (01430) 810246

Springdale Bed and Breakfast
◆◆◆
Springdale Stud, Long Lane,
Beverley, North Humberside
HU17 0RN
T: (01482) 888264

BILSDALE WEST
North Yorkshire
Hill End Farm ◆◆◆
Chop Gate, Middlesbrough,
Cleveland TS9 7JR
T: (01439) 798278

BINGLEY
West Yorkshire
Ashley End ◆◆◆
22 Ashley Road, Bingley, West
Yorkshire BD16 1DZ
T: (01274) 569679

Five Rise Locks Hotel ◆◆◆◆
Beck Lane, Bingley, West
Yorkshire BD16 4DD
T: (01274) 565296
F: (01274) 568828
E: 101731.2134@compuserve.
com
I: www.five-rise-locks.co.uk

March Cote Farm ◆◆◆◆
Off Woodside Avenue,
Cottingley, Bingley, West
Yorkshire BD16 1UB
T: (01274) 487433 &
07889 162257
F: (01274) 561074
E: jean.warin@nevisuk.net
I: www.wsshirenet.
co.uk/accqde/marchcote

BIRKBY
West Yorkshire
Cherry Tree Bed and Breakfast
◆◆◆◆
Stanwell Royd, Birkby Road,
Birkby, Huddersfield HD2 2BX
T: (01484) 546628
F: (01484) 546628
E: hyatt@royd2.fsnet.co.uk

BISHOP THORNTON
North Yorkshire
Bowes Green Farm ◆◆◆◆
Colber Lane, Bishop Thornton,
Harrogate, North Yorkshire
HG3 3JX
T: (01423) 770114
F: (01423) 770114

Dukes Place
Rating Applied For
Bishop Thornton, Harrogate,
North Yorkshire HG3 3JY
T: (01765) 620229
F: (01765) 620454
E: jakimoorhouse@onetel.net.uk

BISHOP WILTON
East Riding of Yorkshire

High Belthorpe ♦♦♦
High Belthorpe, Bishop Wilton,
York YO42 1SB
T: (01759) 368238 &
07881 812370
I: www.holidayswithdogs.com

BOLTBY
North Yorkshire

Willow Tree Cottage Bed and
Breakfast♦♦♦♦
Boltby, Thirsk, North Yorkshire
YO7 2DY
T: (01845) 537406
F: (01845) 537073
E: townsend.sce@virgin.net

BOLTON ABBEY
North Yorkshire

Holme House Farm ♦♦♦
Barden, Bolton Abbey, Skipton,
North Yorkshire BD23 6AT
T: (01756) 720661

BOLTON PERCY
North Yorkshire

Glebe Farm ♦♦♦♦
Bolton Percy, York YO23 7AL
T: (01904) 744228

BOROUGHBRIDGE
North Yorkshire

Primrose Cottage ♦♦♦♦
Lime Bar Lane, Grafton, York
YO51 9QJ
T: (01423) 322835 & 322711
F: (01423) 323985
E: primrosecottage@btinternet.
com

BOSTON SPA
West Yorkshire

Crown Hotel ♦♦♦
128 High Street, Boston Spa,
Wetherby, West Yorkshire
LS23 6BW
T: (01937) 842608
F: (01937) 541373

Four Gables ♦♦♦♦
Oaks Lane, Boston Spa,
Wetherby, West Yorkshire
LS23 6DS
T: (01937) 849031 &
07721 055497
F: (01937) 845592
E: info@fourgables.co.uk
I: www.fourgables.co.uk

Little Orchard ♦♦♦♦
Lime Tree Avenue, Boston Spa,
Wetherby, West Yorkshire
LS23 6DP
T: (01937) 843356
F: (01937) 841193
E: jolley@onetel.net.uk

BOUTHWAITE
North Yorkshire

Covill Barn ♦♦♦♦
Bouthwaite, Harrogate, North
Yorkshire HG3 5RW
T: (01423) 755306
F: (01423) 755322

BRADFORD
West Yorkshire

Brow Top Farm ♦♦♦♦
Baldwin Lane, Clayton, Bradford,
West Yorkshire BD14 6PS
T: (01274) 882178
F: (01274) 882178
E: ruthpriestley@
farmersweekly.co.uk
I: www.browtopfarm.co.uk

Carnoustie ♦♦♦
8 Park Grove, Frizinghall,
Bradford, West Yorkshire
BD9 4JY
T: (01274) 490561
F: (01274) 490561
E: carnoustie1@activemail.co.uk

Castle Hotel ♦♦♦
20 Grattan Road, Bradford, West
Yorkshire BD1 2LU
T: (01274) 393166
F: (01274) 393200
E: rooms@castle-bfd.freeserve.
co.uk
I: www.thecastlehotel.
britain-uk.con

Hillside House ♦♦♦
10 Hazelhurst Road, Daisy Hill,
Bradford, West Yorkshire
BD9 6BJ
T: (01274) 542621 & 830396

Ivy Guest House ♦♦
3 Melbourne Place, Bradford,
West Yorkshire BD5 0HZ
T: (01274) 727060
F: (01274) 306347
E: 101524.3725@compuserve.
com

New Beehive Inn ♦♦♦
171 Westgate, Bradford, West
Yorkshire BD1 3AA
T: (01274) 721784
F: (01274) 375092

Norland Guest House ♦♦♦
695 Great Horton Road,
Bradford, West Yorkshire
BD7 4DU
T: (01274) 571698
F: (01274) 503290
E: pipin@ic24.net
I: www.norlandguesthouse.co.uk

Shaw House ♦♦♦
35 bierley Lane, Bierley,
Bradford, West Yorkshire
BD4 6AD
T: (01274) 682929

Westleigh Hotel ♦♦♦
30 Easby Road, Bradford, West
Yorkshire BD7 1QX
T: (01274) 727089
F: (01274) 394658
E: westleigh@hotel27.freeserve.
co.uk
I: www.come.
to/the_westleigh_hotel

Woodlands Guest House
♦♦♦♦
2 The Grove, Shelf, Halifax, West
Yorkshire HX3 7PD
T: (01274) 677533 &
07710 760994

BRAMHOPE
West Yorkshire

The Cottages ♦♦♦♦
Moor Road, Bramhope, Leeds
LS16 9HH
T: (0113) 284 2754
F: (0113) 203 7496

BRAMLEY
South Yorkshire

The Ibis ♦♦♦♦
Moorhead Way, Bramley,
Rotherham, South Yorkshire
S66 1YY
T: (01709) 730333
F: (01709) 730444
E: h3163@accor-hotels.com

BREARLEY
West Yorkshire

Brearley Old Hall ♦♦♦
Brearley, Luddendenfoot,
Halifax, West Yorkshire HX2 6HS
T: (01422) 882301
F: (01422) 885747
E: arthur.c.welham@lineone.net

BRETTON
West Yorkshire

Birch Laithes Farm ♦♦
Bretton Lane, Bretton,
Wakefield, West Yorkshire
WF4 4LF
T: (01924) 252129
F: (01924) 252129

BRIDLINGTON
East Riding of Yorkshire

Bay Court Hotel ♦♦♦♦
35a Sands Lane, Bridlington,
East Riding of Yorkshire
YO15 2JG
T: (01262) 676288
E: bay.court@virgin.net
I: www.baycourt.co.uk

Bay Ridge Hotel ♦♦♦
11 Summerfield Road,
Bridlington, East Riding of
Yorkshire YO15 3LF
T: (01262) 673425
I: bridlington.
net/business/bayridge/index.
html

Belmont
Rating Applied For
27 Flamborough Road,
Bridlington, North Humberside
YO15 2HU
T: (01262) 673808

Blantyre House Hotel ♦♦♦
21 Pembroke Terrace,
Bridlington, East Yorkshire
YO15 3BX
T: (01262) 400660
E: baker.blantyre@cwcom.net

Bosville Arms Country Hotel
♦♦♦
High Street, Rudston, Driffield,
North Humberside YO25 4UB
T: (01262) 420259
F: (01262) 420259
E: hogan@bosville.freeserve.
co.uk
I: www.bosville.freeserve.co.uk

The Brockton Hotel ♦♦♦
4 Shaftesbury Road, Bridlington,
North Humberside YO15 3NP
T: (01262) 673967
F: (01262) 673967
E: grbrocktonhotel@aol.com

de Souza's Hotel and
Restaurant ♦♦♦
South Marine Drive, Bridlington,
East Riding of Yorkshire
YO15 3JJ
T: (01262) 674225
F: (01262) 678070
E: desouzasotel@onetel.net.uk

Dulverton Court Hotel ♦♦♦
17 Victoria Road, Bridlington,
East Riding of Yorkshire
YO15 2BW
T: (01262) 672600 & 609514

Glen Alan Hotel ♦♦♦
21 Flamborough Road,
Bridlington, East Yorkshire
YO15 2HU
T: (01262) 674650

The Grantlea Guest House
♦♦♦
2 South Street, Bridlington, East
Riding of Yorkshire YO15 3BY
T: (01262) 400190

Lansdowne Lodge ♦♦♦
14 Lansdowne Crescent,
Bridlington, North Humberside
YO15 2QR
T: (01262) 400760
F: (01262) 400760

London Hotel
Rating Applied For
1 Royal Crescent, York Road,
Bridlington, North Humberside
YO15 2PF
T: (01262) 675377

Longcroft Hotel ♦♦♦
100 Trinity Road, Bridlington,
East Riding of Yorkshire
YO15 2HF
T: (01262) 672180
F: (01262) 608240

The Mayville Guest House
♦♦♦
74 Marshall Avenue, Bridlington,
East Riding of Yorkshire
YO15 2DS
T: (01262) 674420
F: (01262) 674420

The Mount Hotel ♦♦♦
2 Roundhay Roud, Bridlington,
East Riding of Yorkshire
YO15 3JY
T: (01262) 672306
F: (01262) 672306

Newcliffe Hotel ♦♦♦
6 Belgrave Road, Bridlington,
East Riding Of Yorkshire
YO15 3JR
T: (01262) 674244

Northlands Hotel ♦♦♦
5 Flamborough Road,
Bridlington, East Riding of
Yorkshire YO15 2HU
T: (01262) 672207 &
07866 895723

Promenade Hotel ♦♦
121 Promenade, Bridlington,
East Riding of Yorkshire
YO15 2QN
T: (01262) 602949

Rags Restaurant & Dyl's Hotel
♦♦♦
South Pier, Southcliff Road,
Bridlington, East Riding of
Yorkshire YO15 3AN
T: (01262) 400355 & 674791

Rosebery House ♦♦♦
1 Belle Vue, Tennyson Ave,
Bridlington, East Riding of
Yorkshire YO15 2ET
T: (01262) 670336
F: (01262) 608381

St Aubyn's Hotel ◆◆◆
111-113 Cardigan Road,
Bridlington, East Riding of
Yorkshire YO15 3LP
T: (01262) 673002

Sandsend Hotel ◆◆
8 Sandslane, Bridlington, East
Riding of Yorkshire YO15 2JE
T: (01262) 673265

Shellbourne Hotel ◆◆◆
14-16 Summerfield Road,
Bridlington, East Riding of
Yorkshire YO15 3LF
T: (01262) 674697

Spinnaker House Hotel ◆◆◆
19 Pembroke Terrace,
Bridlington, East Riding of
Yorkshire YO15 3BX
T: (01262) 678440
F: (01262) 678440

Springfield Private Hotel ◆◆◆
12 Trinity Road, Bridlington, East
Riding of Yorkshire YO15 2EY
T: (01262) 672896 &
0500 131424

Sunflower Lodge ◆◆◆
24 Flamborough Road,
Bridlington, East Riding of
Yorkshire YO15 2HX
T: (01262) 400447

The Tennyson Hotel ◆◆◆
19 Tennyson Avenue,
Bridlington, East Riding of
Yorkshire YO15 2EU
T: (01262) 604382
I: www.bridlington.
net/accommodation/hotels/
tennyson

Three Gables Private Hotel
Rating Applied For
37 Windsor Crescent,
Bridlington, North Humberside
YO15 3HZ
T: (01262) 673826

Victoria Hotel ◆◆◆
25/27 Victoria Road, Bridlington,
East Riding of Yorkshire
YO15 2AT
T: (01262) 673871 &
07808 650600
F: (01262) 609431
E: victoria.hotel@virgin.net
I: www.victoriahotelbridlington.
co.uk

Waverley Hotel ◆◆◆
105 Cardigan Road, Bridlington,
East Riding of Yorkshire
YO15 3LP
T: (01262) 671040
E: waverley.hotel@bridlington.
worldonline.co.uk

The White Rose ◆◆◆
123 Cardigan Road, Bridlington,
East Riding of Yorkshire
YO15 3LP
T: (01262) 673245 &
07860 159208

Winston House Hotel ◆◆◆
5-6 South Street, Bridlington,
East Riding of Yorkshire
YO15 3BY
T: (01262) 670216
F: (01262) 670216
E: bob.liz@winstonhouse.fsnet.
co.uk
I: www.winston-house.co.uk

BRIGG
North Lincolnshire

Albert House ◆◆◆◆
23 Bigby Street, Brigg, South
Humberside DN20 8ED
T: (01652) 658081

Arties Mill ◆◆◆
Wressle Road, Castlethorpe,
Brigg, South Humberside
DN20 9LF
T: (01652) 652094 & 657107
F: (01652) 657107
E: www.artiesmill.co.uk

Holcombe Guest House ◆◆◆
34 Victoria Road, Barnetby,
South Humberside DN38 6JR
T: 07850 764002
F: (01652) 680841
E: holcombe.house@virgin.net
I: www.holcombeguesthouse.
co.uk

Lord Nelson Hotel & Hardy's
Cafe Bar ◆◆◆
Market Place, Brigg, South
Humberside DN20 8LD
T: (01652) 652127
F: (01652) 658952

The Woolpack Hotel ◆◆
4 Market Place, Brigg, South
Humberside DN20 8HA
T: (01652) 655649 &
07971 965826
F: (01652) 655649
E: harry@woolpack488.
freeserve.co.uk

BRIGHOUSE
West Yorkshire

The Black Bull ◆◆◆
46 Briggate, Thornton Square,
Brighouse, West Yorkshire
HD6 1EF
T: (01484) 714816
F: (01484) 721711
E: katrina@bilmember.net
I: www.westel.co.uk/blackbull.
htmlwww.dukeofyork.co.uk

BRIGSLEY
Lincolnshire

Prospect Farm ◆◆◆◆
Waltham Road, Brigsley,
Grimsby, South Humberside
DN37 0RQ
T: (01472) 826491
E: prospectfarm@btchick.com
I: www.nelincs.gov.uk

BROUGH
East Riding of Yorkshire

Woldway ◆◆◆
10 Elloughton Road, Brough,
North Humberside HU15 1AE
T: (01482) 667666
I: www.woldway.co.uk

BUCKDEN
North Yorkshire

East House Farm ◆◆◆
Beckermonds, Buckden, Skipton,
North Yorkshire BD23 5JL
T: (01756) 760816
F: (01756) 760816
I: www.thedalesway.
co.uk@easthousefarm

Low Raisgill ◆◆◆◆
Hubberholme, Skipton, North
Yorkshire BD23 5JQ
T: (01756) 760351

Redmire Farm ◆◆◆◆
Upper Wharfedale, Buckden,
Skipton, North Yorkshire
BD23 5JD
T: (01756) 760253

BULMER
North Yorkshire

Grange Farm ◆◆◆
Castle Howard, Bulmer, York
YO60 7BN
T: (01653) 618376
F: (01653) 618600
E: foster@grangefarm35.fsnet.
co.uk

Lower Barn ◆◆◆◆
Wandales Lane, Castle Howard,
Bulmer, York YO60 7ES
T: (01653) 618575 &
07930 756289
F: (01653) 618575
E: isabelhall@lowerbarn.fsnet.
co.uk
I: www.lowerbarn.fsnet.co.uk

BURLEY IN WHARFEDALE
West Yorkshire

Upstairs, Downstairs ◆◆◆
3 Elm Grove, Burley in
Wharfedale, Ilkley, West
Yorkshire LS29 7PL
T: (01943) 862567

BURNSALL
North Yorkshire

Valley View ◆◆◆◆
Burnsall, Skipton, North
Yorkshire BD23 6BN
T: (01756) 720314
F: (01756) 720314
E: fitton_valley_view@lineone.
net

BURNT YATES
North Yorkshire

High Winsley Farm ◆◆◆
Burnt Yates, Harrogate, North
Yorkshire HG3 3EP
T: (01423) 770376
E: highwinsley@got.com

The New Inn ◆◆◆◆
Burnt Yates, Harrogate, North
Yorkshire HG3 3EG
T: (01423) 771070 &
07710 513182
F: (01423) 771070
E: newinn@chrisgnaylor.force9.
co.uk
I: www.chrisgnaylor.force9.co.uk

CARLTON
North Yorkshire

Abbots Thorn ◆◆◆◆
Carlton, Leyburn, North
Yorkshire DL8 4AY
T: (01969) 640620
F: (01969) 640304
E: abbots.thorn@virgin.net
I: www.abbotsthorn.co.uk

Middleham House ◆◆◆
Carlton, Leyburn, North
Yorkshire DL8 4BB
T: (01969) 640645
E: trevorw.smith@virgin.net

CARLTON MINIOTT
North Yorkshire

Old Red House ◆◆
Station Road, Carlton Miniott,
Thirsk, North Yorkshire YO7 4LT
T: (01845) 524383
F: (01845) 525902
E: anthony@oldredhouse.
demon.co.uk
I: www.oldredhouse.demon.
co.uk

The Poplars ◆◆◆◆
Carlton Miniott, Thirsk, North
Yorkshire YO7 4LX
T: (01845) 522712
F: (01845) 522712
E: chrischilton.thepoplars@
virginnet
I: www.yorkshirebandb.co.uk

CARPERBY
North Yorkshire

Cross House ◆◆◆
Carperby, Leyburn, North
Yorkshire DL8 4DQ
T: (01969) 663457

CASTLETON
North Yorkshire

Crown End ◆◆◆◆
Castleton, Whitby, North
Yorkshire YO21 2HP
T: (01287) 660267

The Eskdale Inn ◆◆◆
Station Road, Castleton, Whitby,
North Yorkshire YO21 2EU
T: (01287) 660234

Greystones ◆◆◆
30 High Street, Castleton,
Whitby, North Yorkshire
YO21 2DA
T: (01287) 660744

CATTERICK
North Yorkshire

Rose Cottage Guest House
◆◆◆
26 High Street, Catterick,
Richmond, North Yorkshire
DL10 7LJ
T: (01748) 811164

CHAPEL ALLERTON
West Yorkshire

Green House ◆◆◆
5 Bank View, Chapel Allerton,
Leeds LS7 2EX
T: (0113) 268 1380
E: anniegreen11@hotmail.com

CHAPELTOWN
South Yorkshire

The Norfolk Arms
Rating Applied For
White Lane, Chapeltown,
Sheffield S35 2YG
T: (0114) 2402016
F: (0114) 2468414
E: norfharri@aol.com

CHOP GATE
North Yorkshire

Beacon Guest Farm ◆◆◆
Chop Gate, Middlesbrough,
Cleveland TS9 7JS
T: (01439) 798320
F: (01439) 798320

CLAPHAM
North Yorkshire

Brook House ◆◆◆
Station Road, Clapham,
Lancaster LA2 8ER
T: (01524) 251580

CLEASBY
North Yorkshire
Cleasby House ◆◆◆◆
Cleasby, Darlington, County
Durham DL2 2QY
T: (01325) 350160
E: junehirst@aol.com

CLEETHORPES
North East Lincolnshire
Hotel 77 ◆◆◆
77 Kingsway, Cleethorpes, South
Humberside DN35 0AB
T: (01472) 692035 &
0800 0354207
F: (01472) 692035
E: hotel77@knox24.fsbusiness.
comuk

Abbeydale Guest House ◆◆◆
39 Isaacs Hill, Cleethorpes,
South Humberside DN35 8JT
T: (01472) 692248 & 311088
F: (01472) 311088
E: info@abbeydaleguesthouse.
co.uk
I: www.abbeydaleguesthouse.
co.uk

Adelalde Hotel ◆◆◆◆
41 Isaacs Hill, Cleethorpes,
South Humberside DN35 8JT
T: (01472) 693594
F: (01472) 329717
E: robertcallison@ntlworld.com
I: www.adelaide-hotel.com

Alpine Guest House ◆◆◆
55 Clee Road, Cleethorpes,
South Humberside DN35 8AD
T: (01472) 690804

Ascot Lodge Guest House
◆◆◆
11 Princes Road, Cleethorpes,
South Humberside DN35 8AW
T: (01472) 290129
F: (01472) 290129
E: ascotclee@aol.com
I: www.ascotlodgeguesthouse.
co.uk

Brentwood Guest House ◆◆◆
9 Princes Road, Cleethorpes,
South Humberside DN35 8AW
T: (01472) 693982
E: brentwoodguesthouse@
hotmail.com
I: brentwoodguesthouse69@
hotmail.com

Brier Parks Guest House ◆◆
27 Clee Road, Cleethorpes,
South Humberside DN35 8AD
T: (01472) 605591 & 237456
E: a.brierley1@ntlworld.com
I: www.thebrierparks.co.uk

Carlton Lodge ◆◆◆
14 Isaacs Hill, Cleethorpes,
South Humberside DN35 8JS
T: (01472) 691844

Clee House ◆◆◆◆
31-33 Clee Road, Cleethorpes,
South Humberside DN35 8AD
T: (01472) 200850 & 200130
F: (01472) 200850
E: david@cleehouse.com
I: www.cleehouse.com

Comat Hotel ◆◆◆◆
26 Yarra Road, Cleethorpes,
South Humberside DN35 8LS
T: (01472) 694791 & 591861
F: (01472) 592823
E: comat-hotel@ntlworld.com
I: www.comat-hotel.co.uk

Ginnies ◆◆◆
27 Queens Parade, Cleethorpes,
South Humberside DN35 0DF
T: (01472) 694997
F: (01472) 316799
I: www.
ginniesguesthousecleethorpes.
co.uk

Gladson Guest House ◆◆◆
43 Isaacs Hill, Cleethorpes,
North East Lincolnshire
DN35 8JT
T: (01472) 694858 & 239642
F: (01472) 239642
E: gladson@tinyonline.co.uk
I: www.s-h-systems.
co.uk/hotels/gladson.html

London Guest House
Rating Applied For
49-51 Market Place,
Cleethorpes, South Humberside
DN35 8LY
T: (01472) 815242 & 692536

Sandside Guest House ◆◆◆
17 Kingsway, Cleethorpes, South
Humberside DN35 8QU
T: (01472) 694039

The Saxon House Hotel
Rating Applied For
70 St Peters Avenue,
Cleethorpes, South Humberside
DN35 8HP
T: (01472) 697427
F: (01472) 602696

Sherwood Guest House ◆◆◆
15 Kingsway, Cleethorpes, South
Humberside DN35 8QU
T: (01472) 692020
F: (01472) 239177
E: sherwood.guesthouse@
ntlworld.com
I: www.sherwoodguesthouse.
co.uk

Tudor Terrace Guest House
◆◆◆◆
11 Bradford Avenue,
Cleethorpes, North East
Lincolnshire DN35 0BB
T: (01472) 600800
F: (01472) 501395
E: enquiries.tudorterrace@
btinternet.com
I: www.tudorterrace.co.uk
🛉

White Rose Guest House ◆◆◆
13 Princes Road, Cleethorpes,
South Humberside DN35 8AW
T: (01472) 695060

CLIFTON
North Yorkshire
Avenue Guest House ◆◆◆
6 The Avenue, Clifton, York
YO30 6AS
T: (01904) 620575
E: allen@avenuegh.fsnet.co.uk
I: www.avenuegh.fsnet.co.uk

CLOUGHTON
North Yorkshire
Cober Hill ◆
Newlands Road, Cloughton,
Scarborough, North Yorkshire
YO13 0AR
T: (01723) 870310
F: (01723) 870271
E: enquireis@coberhill.co.uk
I: www.coberhill.co.uk

CONISTONE
North Yorkshire
Ebony House ◆◆◆◆
Conistone, Skipton, North
Yorkshire BD23 5HS
T: (01756) 753139
I: www.yorkshirenet.
co.uk/stayat/ebonyhouse

COTTINGHAM
East Riding of Yorkshire
Kenwood House ◆◆◆
7 Newgate Street, Cottingham,
North Humberside HU16 4DY
T: (01482) 847558

COUNTERSETT
North Yorkshire
Carr End House ◆◆◆◆
Countersett, Askrigg, Leyburn,
North Yorkshire DL8 3DE
T: (01969) 650346

COXWOLD
North Yorkshire
Oldstead Grange ◆◆◆◆◆
Oldstead, Coxwold, York
YO61 4BJ
T: (01347) 868634
F: (01347) 868634
E: oldsteadgrange@yorkshireuk.
com
I: www.yorkshireuk.com

CRACOE
North Yorkshire
Devonshire Arms ◆◆◆
Grassington Road, Cracoe,
Skipton, North Yorkshire
BD23 6LA
T: (01756) 730237
F: (01756) 730142
I: www.jennings

CRAGG VALE
West Yorkshire
Hinchliffe Arms ◆◆◆◆
Cragg Vale, Hebden Bridge, West
Yorkshire HX7 5TA
T: (01422) 883256
F: (01422) 886216
E: phil.chaplin@ukonline.co.uk
I: www.hinchliffearms.com

CRAYKE
North Yorkshire
The Hermitage ◆◆◆
Mill Lane, Crayke, York YO61 4TB
T: (01347) 821635

CROFTON
West Yorkshire
Redbeck Motel Ltd ◆◆
Doncaster Road, Crofton,
Wakefield, West Yorkshire
WF4 1RR
T: (01924) 862730 & 865269
F: (01924) 862937

CROPTON
North Yorkshire
High Farm ◆◆◆◆
Cropton, Pickering, North
Yorkshire YO18 8HL
T: (01751) 417461
F: (01751) 417807
E: highfarmcropton@aol.com

New Inn and Cropton Brewery
◆◆◆
Cropton, Pickering, North
Yorkshire YO18 8HH
T: (01751) 417330 & 417310
F: (01751) 417310
E: newinn@cropton.fsbusiness.
co.uk
I: www.croptonbrewery.co.uk

CROWLE
North Lincolnshire
Seven Lakes Motel ◆◆◆
Seven Lakes Leisure Park, Ealand,
Crowle, Scunthorpe, South
Humberside DN17 4JS
T: (01724) 710245
F: (01724) 711814

CROXTON
North Lincolnshire
Croxton House ◆◆◆
Croxton, Ulceby, South
Humberside DN39 6YD
T: (01652) 688306 &
07940 935343
F: (01652) 680577
E: k_gallimoreuk@yahoo.co.uk

CUNDALL
North Yorkshire
Cundall Lodge Farm ◆◆◆◆
Cundall, York YO61 2RN
T: (01423) 360203
F: (01423) 360805

DACRE BANKS
North Yorkshire
Dalriada ◆◆◆
Cabin Lane, Dacre Banks,
Harrogate, North Yorkshire
HG3 4EE
T: (01423) 780512 & 0771 280
5383

Gate Eel Farm ◆◆◆◆
Dacre Banks, Harrogate, North
Yorkshire HG3 4ED
T: (01423) 781707

The Royal Oak Inn ◆◆◆◆
Oak Lane, Dacre Banks,
Harrogate, North Yorkshire
HG3 4EN
T: (01423) 780200
T: (01423) 781748
E: royaloakdacre@aol.com
I: www.theroyaloak.uk.com

DALTON
North Yorkshire
Dalton Hall ◆◆◆◆
Dalton, Richmond, North
Yorkshire DL11 7HU
T: (01833) 621339

The Gables Guest House ◆◆
25-27 Broad Lane, Dalton,
Huddersfield HD5 9BX
T: (01484) 345500
F: (01484) 345500

Throstle Gill Farm ◆◆◆◆
Dalton, Richmond, North
Yorkshire DL11 7HZ
T: (01833) 621363
F: (01833) 621363

**Ye Jolly Farmers of Olden
Times** ◆◆◆
Dalton, Thirsk, North Yorkshire
YO7 3HY
T: (01845) 577359

DANBY
North Yorkshire
Botton Grove Farm ◆◆◆
Danby Head, Danby, Whitby,
North Yorkshire YO21 2NH
T: (01287) 660284
E: judytait@bottongrove.
freeserve.co.uk

Crag Farm ◆◆◆◆
Danby, Whitby, North Yorkshire
YO21 2LQ
T: (01287) 660279
F: (01287) 660279
E: sal.b.b.cragfarm.n.y.@
ukgateway.net

Crossley Gate Farm House
◆◆◆◆
Crossley Gate Farm, Little Fryup,
Danby, Whitby, North Yorkshire
YO21 2NR
T: (01287) 660165 &
07710 263149

Duke of Wellington Inn ◆◆◆
Danby, Whitby, North Yorkshire
YO21 2LY
T: (01287) 660351
E: landlord@dukeofwellington.
freeserve.co.uk
I: www.
danby-dukeofwellington.co.uk

Rowantree Farm ◆◆◆
Ainthorpe, Whitby, North
Yorkshire YO21 2LE
T: (01287) 660396
E: krbsatindall@aol.com

Stonebeck Gate Farm ◆◆◆
Little Fryup, Danby, Whitby,
North Yorkshire YO21 2NS
T: (01287) 660363
F: (01287) 660363
I: www.stonebeckgatefarm.co.uk

Sycamore House ◆◆◆
Danby Dale, Danby, Whitby,
North Yorkshire YO21 2NW
T: (01287) 660125 &
07703 714676
F: (01287) 669122
E: sycamore.danby@btinternet.
com
I: www.smoothhound.
co.uk/hotels/sycamore1.html

DARLEY
North Yorkshire

Brimham Guest house ◆◆◆◆
Brookfield, Silverdale Close,
Darley, Harrogate, North
Yorkshire HG3 2PQ
T: (01423) 780948

Elsinglea Guest House ◆◆◆◆
Sheepcote Lane, Darley,
Harrogate, North Yorkshire
HG3 2RW
T: (01423) 781069 & 0777 391
4642
I: www.elsingleaguesthouse.
homestead.com/homepage.html

Greenbanks ◆◆◆◆
Nidd Side, Station Road, Darley,
Harrogate, North Yorkshire
HG3 2PW
T: (01423) 780883
E: terryn'doris@nidd-side.fsnet.
co.uk

DEEPDALE
North Lincolnshire

West Wold Farmhouse
Rating Applied For
West Wold Farm, Deepdale,
Barton-upon-Humber, South
Humberside DN18 6ED
T: (01652) 633293
F: (01652) 633293

DEIGHTON
North Yorkshire

Grimston House ◆◆◆
Deighton, York YO19 6HB
T: (01904) 728328
F: (01904) 720093
E: grimstonhouse@talk21.com
I: www.grimstonhouse.com

Rush Farm ◆◆◆
Rush Farm, York Road, Deighton,
York YO19 6HQ
T: (01904) 728459
E: david@rushfarm.fsnet.co.uk
I: www.rushfarm.fsnet.co.uk

DENBY DALE
West Yorkshire

Eastfield Cottage ◆◆◆
248 Wakefield Road, Denby
Dale, Huddersfield HD8 8SU
T: (01484) 861562

DONCASTER
South Yorkshire

Ashlea Hotel ◆◆◆
81 Thorne Road, Doncaster,
South Yorkshire DN1 2ES
T: (01302) 363303 & 363374
F: (01302) 760215
E: brigby@ashlea25.freeserve.
co.u/k

The Balmoral Hotel ◆◆◆
129 Thorne Road, Doncaster,
South Yorkshire DN2 5BH
T: (01302) 364385
F; (01302) 364385
E: thebalmoralhotel@bt.
connect.com
I: www.thebalmoralhotel@bt.
connect.com

Low Farm ◆◆◆◆
The Green, Clayton, Doncaster,
South Yorkshire DN5 7DB
T: (01977) 648433 & 640472
F: (01977) 640472
E: bar@lowfarm.freeserve.co.uk
I: www.lowfarm.freeserve.co.uk

Lyntone Hotel ◆◆◆
24 Avenue Road, Wheatley,
Doncaster, South Yorkshire
DN2 4AQ
T: (01302) 361586
F: (01302) 361079

DOWNHOLME
North Yorkshire

Walburn Hall ◆◆◆◆
Downholme, Richmond, North
Yorkshire DL11 6AF
T: (01748) 822152
F: (01748) 822152

DRIFFIELD
East Riding of Yorkshire

Kelleythorpe Farm ◆◆◆
Driffield, North Humberside
YO25 9DW
T: (01377) 252297
E: jhopper@kelleythorpe.
fsbusiness.co.uk

The White Horse Inn ◆◆◆
Main Street, Hutton Cranswick,
Driffield, East Riding of
Yorkshire YO25 9QN
T: (01377) 270383 & 270136
F: (01377) 270383
E: c.tomlinson@amserve.net

EASINGWOLD
North Yorkshire

Allerton House
Rating Applied For
34 Uppleby, Easingwold, York,
North Yorkshire YO61 3BB
T: (01347) 821912

Dimple Wells ◆◆◆◆
Thormanby, York YO61 4NL
T: (01845) 501068
F: (01845) 501068

The Old Vicarage ◆◆◆◆
Market Place, Easingwold, York
YO61 3AL
T: (01347) 821015
F: (01347) 823465
E: kirman@oldvic-easingwold.
freeserve.co.uk

Yeoman's Course House ◆◆◆
Thornton Hill, Easingwold, York
YO61 3PY
T: (01347) 868126
F: (01347) 868129
E: chris@yeomanscourse.fsnet.
co.uk

EAST HESLERTON
North Yorkshire

Manor Farm ◆◆◆
East Heslerton, Malton, North
Yorkshire YO17 8RN
T: (01944) 728268 &
07977 934550
F: (01944) 728268
E: bandb@manorfarmholidays.
co.uk
I: members.netscapeonline.
co.uk/dclumley/

The Snooty Fox ◆◆
Scarborough Road, East
Heslerton, Malton, North
Yorkshire YO17 8EN
T: (01944) 710554
F: (01944) 711164
E: snootyfox@tinyworld.co.uk
I: www.thesnootyfox.co.uk

EAST MARTON
North Yorkshire

Drumlins ◆◆◆◆
Heber Drive, East Marton,
Skipton, North Yorkshire
BD23 3LS
T: (01282) 843521
I: www.yorkshiredales.
net/stayat/drumlins

EBBERSTON
North Yorkshire

Foxholm Hotel ◆◆◆
Ebberston, Scarborough, North
Yorkshire YO13 9NJ
T: (01723) 859550 &
07977 141656
F: (01723) 859550
E: kay@foxholm.freeserve.co.uk
I: www.foxholm.freeserve.co.uk

Givendale Head Farm ◆◆◆
Ebberston, Scarborough, North
Yorkshire YO13 9PU
T: (01723) 859383
F: (01723) 859383
E: sue.gwilliam@talk21.com
I: www.visityorkshire.com

Littlegarth ◆◆◆◆
High Street, Ebberston,
Scarborough, North Yorkshire
YO13 9PA
T: (01723) 850045 & 850151
F: (01723) 850151

EGTON
North Yorkshire

Flushing Meadow ◆◆◆
Egton, Whitby, North Yorkshire
YO21 1UA
T: (01947) 895395
F: (01947) 895395
E: flushing_meadow_egton@
yahoo.co.uk

EGTON BRIDGE
North Yorkshire

Broom House ◆◆◆◆
Broom House Lane, Egton
Bridge, Whitby, North Yorkshire
YO21 1XD
T: (01947) 895279
F: (01947) 895657
E: welcome@
broomhouseegtonbridge.
freeserve.co.uk
I: www.egton/bridge.co.uk

The Postgate ◆◆◆
Egton Bridge, Whitby, North
Yorkshire YO21 1UX
T: (01947) 895241 & 895111
F: (01947) 895111
I: www.touristnetuk.
com/ne/postgate

ELLERTON ABBEY
North Yorkshire

Ellerton Abbey ◆◆◆◆
Ellerton Abbey, Richmond, North
Yorkshire DL11 6AN
T: (01748) 884067
F: (01748) 884909
E: francis@ellertonabbey.co.uk
I: www.ellertonabbey.co.uk

ELLINGSTRING
North Yorkshire

Holybreen ◆◆◆
Ellingstring, Ripon, North
Yorkshire HG4 4PW
T: (01677) 460216
F: (01677) 460106
E: anne.wright@virgin.net

EMBSAY
North Yorkshire

Bondcroft Farm ◆◆◆◆
Embsay, Skipton, North
Yorkshire BD23 6SF
T: (01756) 793371
F: (01756) 793371
E: bondcroftfarm@
bondcroftfarm.yorks.net
I: www.bondcroft.yorks.net

EMLEY
West Yorkshire

Thorncliffe Farmhouse ◆◆◆
Thorncliffe Lane, Emley,
Huddersfield, West Yorkshire
HD8 9RS
T: (01924) 848277
F: (01924) 849041

FACEBY
North Yorkshire

Four Wynds Bed and Breakfast
◆◆◆
Whorl Hill, Faceby,
Middlesbrough, Cleveland
TS9 7BZ
T: (01642) 701315

FADMOOR
North Yorkshire
Mount Pleasant ◆◆◆
Rudland, Fadmoor, York, North
Yorkshire YO62 7JJ
T: (01751) 431579
E: info@
mountpleasantbedandbreakfast.
co.uk
I: www.
mountpleasantbedandbreakfast.
co.uk

FEATHERSTONE
West Yorkshire
Rolands Croft Guest House ◆◆
Waldenhowe Close, Ackton Lane,
Featherstone, Pontefract, West
Yorkshire WF7 6ED
T: (01977) 790802 &
07711 915330
F: (01977) 790802
E: peter@rolandscroft.co.uk
I: www.rolandscroft.co.uk

FILEY
North Yorkshire
Abbot's Leigh Hotel ◆◆◆
7 Rutland Street, Filey, North
Yorkshire YO14 9JA
T: (01723) 513334 &
07799 666544
E: barbara_abbots@yahoo.com

Athol Guest House ◆◆◆◆
67 West Avenue, Filey, North
Yorkshire YO14 9AX
T: (01723) 515189
E: baker@athol67.freeserve.
co.uk

Binton Guest House ◆◆◆
25 West Avenue, Filey, North
Yorkshire YO14 9AX
T: (01723) 513260 &
07712 657535
E: kdatbgh@aol.com

Cherries ◆◆◆◆
59 West Avenue, Filey, North
Yorkshire YO14 9AX
T: (01723) 513299
E: cherriesfiley@hotmail.com

Gables Guest House ◆◆◆◆
Rutland Street, Filey, North
Yorkshire YO14 9JB
T: (01723) 514750
E: kate_gables@talk21.com

Mayfield Guest House ◆◆◆
2 Brooklands, Filey, North
Yorkshire YO14 9BA
T: (01723) 514557

Pebbles Guest House ◆◆
5-6 Brooklands, Filey, North
Yorkshire YO14 9BA
T: (01723) 513366 &
07944 917238

Seafield Hotel ◆◆◆
9-11 Rutland Street, Filey, North
Yorkshire YO14 9JA
T: (01723) 513715

FREMINGTON
North Yorkshire
Broadlands Bed & Breakfast
◆◆◆
Fremington, Richmond, North
Yorkshire DL11 6AW
T: (01748) 884297
F: (01748) 884297

FRIDAYTHORPE
East Riding of Yorkshire
**Manor House Inn and
Restaurant** ◆◆◆
Fridaythorpe, Driffield, North
Humberside YO25 9RT
T: (01377) 288221
F: (01377) 288402

FRYUP
North Yorkshire
Crossley Side Farm ◆◆◆◆
Fryup, Danby, Whitby, North
Yorkshire YO21 2NR
T: (01287) 660313

Furnace Farm ◆◆◆
Fryup, Danby, Whitby, North
Yorkshire YO21 2AP
T: (01947) 897271

FYLINGTHORPE
North Yorkshire
Croft Farm ◆◆◆◆
Church Lane, Fylingthorpe,
Whitby, North Yorkshire
YO22 4PW
T: (01947) 880231
F: (01947) 880231

GANTON
North Yorkshire
Cherry Tree Cottage ◆◆◆
23 Main Street, Ganton,
Scarborough, North Yorkshire
YO12 4NR
T: (01944) 710507
E: iris@hallaways.freeserve.
co.uk

Key Cottage ◆◆◆◆
10 Main Street, Ganton,
Scarborough, North Yorkshire
YO12 4NR
T: (01944) 710807 & 710062

GARFORTH
West Yorkshire
Myrtle House ◆◆◆
31 Wakefield Road, Garforth,
Leeds LS25 1AN
T: (0113) 286 6445

GAYLE
North Yorkshire
Blackburn Farm/Trout Fishery
◆◆◆
Blackburn Farm, Gayle, Hawes,
North Yorkshire DL8 3NX
T: (01969) 667524
E: blackburnfarm@hotmail.com
I: www.dalesaccommodation.
com/blackburnfarm

Force Head Farm ◆◆◆
Gayle, Hawes, North Yorkshire
DL8 3RZ
T: (01969) 667518
F: (01969) 667518

Hunters Hill Bed and Breakfast
◆◆◆◆
Gayle, Hawes, North Yorkshire
DL8 3RZ
T: (01969) 667139
E: clive@firehunter.freeserve.
co.uk

**Rookhurst Country House
Hotel** ◆◆◆◆◆
West End, Gayle, Hawes, North
Yorkshire DL8 3RT
T: (01969) 667454
F: (01969) 667128
E: rookhurst@lineone.net
I: www.rookhurst.co.uk

Thimble Cottage ◆◆◆
Gayle Lane, Gayle, Hawes, North
Yorkshire DL8 3RP
T: (01969) 667828

GIGGLESWICK
North Yorkshire
Black Horse Hotel ◆◆◆
Church Street, Giggleswick,
Settle, North Yorkshire
BD24 0BE
T: (01729) 822506

The Old Station ◆◆◆
Brackenber Lane, Giggleswick,
Settle, North Yorkshire
BD24 0EA
T: (01729) 823623 & 823623
F: (01729) 825710
E: theoldstation@btinternet.
com

GILDERSOME
West Yorkshire
End Lea ◆◆◆◆
39 Town Street, Gildersome,
Morley, Leeds LS27 7AX
T: (0113) 252 1661 &
07702 223653

GILLAMOOR
North Yorkshire
Manor Farm ◆◆◆
Gillamoor, York, North Yorkshire
YO62 7HX
T: (01751) 432695
F: (01751) 432695

GILLING EAST
North Yorkshire
Hall Farm ◆◆◆
Gilling East, York YO62 4JW
T: (01439) 788314 & 0771 328
3492
E: virginia@collinson2.fsnet.
co.uk
I: www.collinson2.fsnet.co.uk

GLAISDALE
North Yorkshire
Egton Banks Farm ◆◆◆◆
Glaisdale, Whitby, North
Yorkshire YO21 2QP
T: (01947) 897289
E: egtonbanksfarm@agriplus.
net
I: www.egtonbanksfarm.
agriplus.net

Hollins Farm ◆◆◆
Glaisdale, Whitby, North
Yorkshire YO21 2PZ
T: (01947) 897516

London House Farm ◆◆◆
Dale Head, Glaisdale, Whitby,
North Yorkshire YO21 2PZ
T: (01530) 836122
F: (01947) 897166
E: marydanaher@hotmail.com

GOATHLAND
North Yorkshire
Barnet House Guest House
◆◆◆
Goathland, Whitby, North
Yorkshire YO22 5NG
T: (01947) 896201
F: (01947) 896201
E: barnethouse@gofornet.co.uk
I: www.smoothhound.
co.uk/hotels/barnethouse.html

The Beacon Guest House
◆◆◆◆
The Beacon, Goathland, Whitby,
North Yorkshire YO22 5AN
T: (01947) 896409
F: (01947) 896431
E: stewartkatz@compuserve.
com
I: www.touristnetuk.
com/ne/beacon.
&

Fairhaven Country Hotel ◆◆◆
The Common, Goathland,
Whitby, North Yorkshire
YO22 5AN
T: (01947) 896361
E: royellis@thefairhavenhotel.
co.uk
I: www.thefairhavenhotel.co.uk

Heatherdene Hotel ◆◆◆
The Common, Goathland,
Whitby, North Yorkshire
YO22 5AN
T: (01947) 896334
F: (01947) 896334
E: info@heatherdenehotel.co.uk
I: www.heatherdenehotel.co.uk

Heatherlands ◆◆◆
Darnholm, Goathland, Whitby,
North Yorkshire YO22 5LA
T: (01947) 896311
E: keiththompson@yorkcollege.
ac.uk

Prudom Guest House ◆◆◆◆
Goathland, Whitby, North
Yorkshire YO22 5AN
T: (01947) 896368
F: (01947) 896030
E: info@prudomhouse.co.uk
I: www.prudomhouse.co.uk

GOXHILL
North Lincolnshire
King's Well ◆◆
Howe Lane, Goxhill, Barrow
upon Humber, South
Humberside DN19 7HU
T: (01469) 532471
F: (01469) 532471

GRASSINGTON
North Yorkshire
Clarendon Hotel ◆◆◆
Hebden, Grassington, Skipton,
North Yorkshire BD23 5DE
T: (01756) 752446
E: clarhotel@aol.com
I: www.theclarendonhotel.co.uk

Craiglands Guest House ◆◆◆◆
1 Brooklyn, Threshfield,
Grassington, Skipton, North
Yorkshire BD23 5ER
T: (01756) 752093
E: craiglands@talk21.com
I: www.craiglands.yorks.net

The Devonshire Hotel ◆◆◆◆
Main Street, Grassington,
Skipton, North Yorkshire
BD23 3LA
T: (01756) 752525
E: suel@dev-pub.co.uk
I: www.
devonshirehotelgrassington.
co.uk

Foresters Arms Hotel ◆◆◆
20 Main Street, Grassington,
Skipton, North Yorkshire
BD23 5AA
T: (01756) 752349
F: (01756) 753633
E: theforesters@totalise.co.uk

Grange Cottage ◆◆◆◆
Linton, Skipton, North Yorkshire
BD23 5HH
T: (01756) 752527

Grassington Lodge ◆◆◆◆
8 Wood Lane, Grassington,
Skipton, North Yorkshire
BD23 5LU
T: (01756) 752518
F: (01756) 752518
E: grassington.lodge@totalise.
co.uk
I: grassingtonlodge.co.uk

Long Ashes Inn ◆◆◆◆
Long Ashes Park, Threshfield,
Skipton, North Yorkshire
BD23 5PN
T: (01756) 752434
F: (01756) 752937
E: info@longashesinn.co.uk
I: www.longashesinn.co.uk

New Laithe House ◆◆◆
Wood Lane, Grassington,
Skipton, North Yorkshire
BD23 5LU
T: (01756) 752764
E: enquiries@newlaithehouse.
co.uk
I: www.newlaithehouse.co.uk

Raines Close Guest House
◆◆◆◆
Station Road, Grassington,
Skipton, North Yorkshire
BD23 5LS
T: (01756) 752678
E: rainesclose@yorks.net
I: www.rainesclose.co.uk

Springroyd House ◆◆◆
8A Station Road, Grassington,
Skipton, North Yorkshire
BD23 5NQ
T: (01756) 752473 &
07703 203607
F: (01756) 752473
E: springroydhouse@hotmail.
com

Station House ◆◆◆
Station Road, Threshfield,
Skipton, North Yorkshire
BD23 5ES
T: (01756) 752667
E: peter@station-house.
freeserve.co.uk
I: www.yorkshirenet.
co.uk/stayat/stationhouse

Town Head Guest House
◆◆◆◆
1 Low Lane, Grassington,
Skipton, North Yorkshire
BD23 5AU
T: (01756) 752811

GREAT AYTON
North Yorkshire

Pinchinthorpe Hall ◆◆◆◆◆
Pinchinthorpe, Great Ayton,
Middlesbrough, Cleveland
TS14 8HG
T: (01287) 630200 & 632000
F: (01287) 630200

Royal Oak Hotel ◆◆◆
High Green, Great Ayton,
Middlesbrough, Cleveland
TS9 6BW
T: (01642) 722361
F: (01642) 724047

Susie D's B & B ◆◆◆◆
Crossways, 116 Newton Road,
Great Ayton, Middlesbrough,
Cleveland TS9 6DL
T: (01642) 724351
E: susieD's@crossways26.fsnet.
co.uk

The Wheelhouse ◆◆◆
Langbaurgh Grange, Great
Ayton, Middlesbrough,
Cleveland TS9 6QQ
T: (01642) 724523

GREAT BARUGH
North Yorkshire

Hill Brow ◆◆◆
Great Barugh, Malton, North
Yorkshire YO17 6UZ
T: (01653) 668426

White House Farm ◆◆◆◆
Great Barugh, Malton, North
Yorkshire YO17 6XB
T: (01653) 668317

GREAT BUSBY
North Yorkshire

Chestnut Farm ◆◆◆
Great Busby, Middlesbrough,
Cleveland TS9 5LB
T: (01642) 710676

Old Busby House ◆◆◆◆◆
Great Busby, Middlesbrough,
Cleveland TS9 7AX
T: (01642) 714550
F: (01642) 711713
E: cath@busbyguesthouse.
freeserve.co.uk

GREAT EDSTONE
North Yorkshire

Cowldyke Farm ◆◆◆
Great Edstone, York YO62 6PE
T: (01751) 431242
E: info@cowldyke-farm.co.uk

GREAT LANGTON
North Yorkshire

Wishing Well Inn ◆◆◆
Great Langton, Northallerton,
North Yorkshire DL7 0TE
T: (01609) 748233
E: liz.boynton@ukonline.co.uk

GREEN HAMMERTON
North Yorkshire

Bay Horse Inn ◆◆◆
York Road, Green Hammerton,
York YO26 8BN
T: (01423) 330338 & 331113
F: (01423) 331279
E: bayhorsepc@aol.com
I: www.thebayhorse.com

GRIMSBY
North East Lincolnshire

The Danish Lodge ◆◆◆◆
2-4 Cleethorpes Road, Grimsby,
South Humberside DN31 3LQ
T: (01472) 342257
F: (01472) 344156
E: danishlodge@aol.com
I: www.danishlodge.co.uk

Sunnyview Guesthouse
◆◆◆◆
Carr Lane, Healing, Grimsby,
South Humberside DN41 7QR
T: (01472) 885015
F: (01472) 885015
E: starian@btinternet.com

GROSMONT
North Yorkshire

Eskdale ◆◆◆
Grosmont, Whitby, North
Yorkshire YO22 5PT
T: (01947) 895385
E: counsell@supanet.com

GUISELEY
West Yorkshire

Bowood ◆◆◆
Carlton Lane, Guiseley, Leeds
LS20 9NL
T: (01943) 874556

GUNNERSIDE
North Yorkshire

Dalegarth House ◆◆◆
Gunnerside, Richmond, North
Yorkshire DL11 6LD
T: (01748) 886275
E: dalegarth@btinternet.com

HABROUGH
North East Lincolnshire

Church Farm ◆◆◆◆
Immingham Road, Habrough,
Immingham DN40 3BD
T: (01469) 576190

The Old Vicarage ◆◆◆◆
Killingholme Road, Habrough,
Immingham DN40 3BB
T: (01469) 575051
F: (01469) 577160
E: ken@theoldvicarge.freeserve.
co.uk

HACKFORTH
North Yorkshire

Ainderby Myers Farm ◆◆
Hackforth, Bedale, North
Yorkshire DL8 1PF
T: (01609) 748668 & 748424
F: (01609) 748424

HALIFAX
West Yorkshire

Beech Court ◆◆◆
40 Prescott Street, Halifax, West
Yorkshire HX1 2QW
T: (01422) 366004

Claytons ◆◆◆◆
146 Pye Nest Road, Halifax,
West Yorkshire HX2 7HS
T: (01422) 835053

The Elms ◆◆◆
Keighley Road, Illingworth,
Halifax, West Yorkshire HX2 8HT
T: (01422) 244430
E: sylvia@theelms.f9.co.uk

Field House ◆◆◆◆
Staups Lane, Stump Cross,
Halifax, West Yorkshire
HX3 6XW
T: (01422) 355457 &
0772 066580
E: stayatfieldhouse@yahoo.
co.uk
I: www.fieldhouse-bb.co.uk

Halifax Guest House ◆◆◆◆
130 Skircoat Road, Halifax, West
Yorkshire HX1 2RE
T: (01422) 355912
F: (01422) 344924

Heathleigh ◆◆◆◆
124 Skircoat Road, Halifax, West
Yorkshire HX1 2RE
T: (01422) 323957

Joan's Guest House ◆◆◆
13 Heath Park Avenue, Halifax,
West Yorkshire HX1 2PP
T: (01422) 369290

Mozart House ◆◆◆
34 Prescott Street, Halifax, West
Yorkshire HX1 2QW
T: (01422) 340319 & 256419
F: (01422) 340319

Victoria Hotel ◆◆
31-35 Horton Street, Halifax,
West Yorkshire HX1 1QE
T: (01422) 351209 & 358392
F: (01422) 351209

HAMPSTHWAITE
North Yorkshire

Graystone View Farm ◆◆◆◆
Grayston Plain Lane,
Hampsthwaite, Harrogate, North
Yorkshire HG3 2LY
T: (01423) 770324
F: (01423) 772536
E: graystoneviewfarm.
Btinternet.co.uk

Lonsdale House ◆◆◆
Hampsthwaite, Harrogate, North
Yorkshire HG3 2ET
T: (01423) 771311
F: (01423) 772810

HARDRAW
North Yorkshire

Bushby Garth ◆◆◆
Hardraw, Hawes, North
Yorkshire DL8 3LZ
T: (01969) 667644
E: andrea@focusonfelt.co.uk
I: www.focusonfelt.co.uk

HARMBY
North Yorkshire

Sunnyridge ◆◆◆
Argill Farm, Harmby, Leyburn,
North Yorkshire DL8 5HQ
T: (01969) 622478
E: richah@freenet.co.uk

HARPHAM
East Riding of Yorkshire

St Quintin Arms Inn ◆◆◆◆
Main Street, Harpham, Driffield,
North Humberside YO25 4QY
T: (01262) 490329
F: (01262) 490329

HARROGATE
North Yorkshire

Acomb Lodge ◆◆◆
6 Franklin Road, Harrogate,
North Yorkshire HG1 5EE
T: (01423) 563599

Acorn Lodge Hotel ◆◆◆
1 Studley Road, Harrogate,
North Yorkshire HG1 5JU
T: (01423) 525630
F: (01423) 564413

Alamah ◆◆◆◆
88 Kings Road, Harrogate, North
Yorkshire HG1 5JX
T: (01423) 502187
F: (01423) 566175

Alderside Guest House ◆◆◆
11 Belmont Road, Harrogate,
North Yorkshire HG2 0LR
T: (01423) 529400 &
10142 527531
F: (01423) 527531

The Alexander ◆◆◆◆
88 Franklin Road, Harrogate,
North Yorkshire HG1 5EN
T: (01423) 503348
F: (01423) 540230

Alexandra Court Hotel ◆◆◆◆
8 Alexandra Road, Harrogate,
North Yorkshire HG1 5JS
T: (01423) 502764
F: (01423) 523151
E: janette@alexandracourt.
co.uk
I: www.alexandracourt.co.uk

Alvera Court Hotel ◆◆◆◆
76 Kings Road, Harrogate, North
Yorkshire HG1 5JX
T: (01423) 505735
F: (01423) 507996

Amadeus Hotel ◆◆◆◆
115 Franklin Road, Harrogate,
North Yorkshire HG1 5EN
T: (01423) 505151
F: (01423) 505151
E: amadeushotel@btinternet.
com
I: www.acartha.
com/amadeushotel

Anro ◆◆◆
90 Kings Road, Harrogate, North
Yorkshire HG1 5JX
T: (01423) 503087
F: (01423) 561719
E: info@theanro.harrogate.net
I: www.theanro.harrogate.net

Arden House Hotel ◆◆◆◆
69-71 Franklin Road, Harrogate,
North Yorkshire HG1 5EH
T: (01423) 509224
F: (01423) 561170
I: www.ardenhousehotel.co.uk

Argyll House ◆◆◆
80 King's Road, Harrogate,
North Yorkshire HG1 5JX
T: (01423) 562408
F: (01423) 567166

Ashbrooke House Hotel
◆◆◆◆
140 Valley Drive, Harrogate,
North Yorkshire HG2 0JS
T: (01423) 564478
F: (01423) 564458
E: ashbrooke@harrogate.com
I: www.harrogate.
com/ashbrooke

Ashley House Hotel ◆◆◆◆
36-40 Franklin Road, Harrogate,
North Yorkshire HG1 5EE
T: (01423) 507474
F: (01423) 560858
E: ron@ashleyhousehotel.com
I: www.ashleyhousehotel.com

Ashwood House ◆◆◆◆
7 Spring Grove, Harrogate,
North Yorkshire HG1 2HS
T: (01423) 560081
F: (01423) 527928
E: ashwoodhouse@aol.com
I: www.ashwoodhouse.co.uk

Askern Guest House ◆◆◆
3 Dragon Parade, Harrogate,
North Yorkshire HG1 5BZ
T: (01423) 523057
F: (01423) 523057
E: john.coughtrey@virgin.net

Aston Hotel ◆◆◆
7-9 Franklin Mount, Harrogate,
North Yorkshire HG1 5EJ
T: (01423) 564262
F: (01423) 505542
E: astonhotel@btinternet.com

Azalea Court Hotel ◆◆◆
56-58 Kings Road, Harrogate,
North Yorkshire HG1 5JR
T: (01423) 560424
F: (01423) 505662
🚶

Barkers Guest House ◆◆◆
202-204 King's Road, Harrogate,
North Yorkshire HG1 5JG
T: (01423) 568494

Britannia Lodge ◆◆◆◆
16 Swan Road, Harrogate, North
Yorkshire HG1 2SA
T: (01423) 508482
F: (01423) 526840
E: britlodge3@aol.com
I: www.britannia-harrogate.net

Brookfield House ◆◆◆◆
5 Alexandra Road, Harrogate,
North Yorkshire HG1 5JS
T: (01423) 606646
F: (01423) 566470

Brooklands ◆◆◆◆
5 Valley Drive, Harrogate, North
Yorkshire HG2 0JJ
T: (01423) 564609

Camberley Hotel ◆◆◆◆
52-54 Kings Road, Harrogate,
North Yorkshire HG1 5JR
T: (01423) 561618
F: (01423) 536360
E: camberley.hotel@virgin.net
I: www.camberleyhotel.co.uk

Cavendish Hotel ◆◆◆◆
3 Valley Drive, Harrogate, North
Yorkshire HG2 0JJ
T: (01423) 509637
F: (01423) 504434

Claremont House ◆◆◆
8 Westcliffe Grove, Harrogate,
North Yorkshire HG2 0PL
T: (01423) 502738 & 07811 803
009

Conference View Guest House
◆◆◆◆
74 Kings Road, Harrogate, North
Yorkshire HG1 5JR
T: (01423) 563075 &
07778 143160
F: (01423) 563075
E: admin@conferenceview.f9.
co.uk
I: www.conferenceview.f9.co.uk

The Coppice ◆◆◆
9 Studley Road, Harrogate,
North Yorkshire HG1 5JU
T: (01423) 569626
F: (01423) 569005
E: coppice@harrogate.com
I: www.harrogate.com/coppice

Craigmoor Manor Hotel ◆◆◆
10 Harlow Moor Drive,
Harrogate, North Yorkshire
HG2 0JX
T: (01423) 523562
F: (01423) 523562

Crescent Lodge ◆◆◆◆
20 Swan Road, Harrogate, North
Yorkshire HG1 2SA
T: (01423) 503688
F: (01423) 503688
E: peter.humphris@dial.pipex.
com

Delaine Hotel ◆◆◆◆
17 Ripon Road, Harrogate,
North Yorkshire HG1 2JL
T: (01423) 567974
F: (01423) 561723

Dragon House ◆◆◆
6 Dragon Parade, Harrogate,
North Yorkshire HG1 5DA
T: (01423) 569888 &
07947 495584

Eton House ◆◆◆
3 Eton Terrace, Knaresborough
Road, Harrogate, North
Yorkshire HG2 7SU
T: (01423) 886850
F: (01423) 886850

Field House ◆◆◆
Clint Bank Lane, Clint,
Harrogate, North Yorkshire
HG3 3DS
T: (01423) 770638
E: annwoodclint@lineone.net

Franklin Hotel ◆◆◆
25 Franklin Road, Harrogate,
North Yorkshire HG1 5ED
T: (01423) 569028
E: flack@frantel74.freeserve.
co.uk
I: www.thefranklinhotel.com

Franklin View ◆◆◆◆
19 Grove Road, Harrogate,
North Yorkshire HG1 5EW
T: (01423) 541388
F: (01423) 547872
E: jennifer@franklinview.com
I: www.franklinview.com

The Gables Hotel ◆◆◆
2 West Grove Road, Harrogate,
North Yorkshire HG1 2AD
T: (01423) 505625
F: (01423) 561312
E: gablesshotel@auista.net
I: www.harrogategables.co.uk

Garden House Hotel ◆◆◆◆
14 Harlow Moor Drive,
Harrogate, North Yorkshire
HG2 0JX
T: (01423) 503059
F: (01423) 503059
E: gardenhouse@hotels.
harrogate.com
I: www.harrogate.
com/gardenhouse

Geminian Guest House ◆◆◆
11-13 Franklin Road, Harrogate,
North Yorkshire HG1 5ED
T: (01423) 523347 & 561768
F: (01423) 523347
E: geminian@talk21.com
I: www.geminian.org.uk

Gillmore Hotel ◆◆◆
98 Kings Road, Harrogate, North
Yorkshire HG1 5HH
T: (01423) 503699 & 507122
F: (01423) 563223
E: gillmoregh@aol.com

Glynhaven ◆◆◆
72 Kings Road, Harrogate, North
Yorkshire HG1 5JR
T: (01423) 569970
F: (01423) 569970

Grafton Hotel ◆◆◆◆
1-3 Franklin Mount, Harrogate,
North Yorkshire HG1 5EJ
T: (01423) 508491
F: (01423) 523168
E: enquiries@graftonhotel.co.uk
I: www.graftonhotel.co.uk

Half Moon Inn ◆◆
Main Street, Pool in Wharfedale,
Otley, West Yorkshire LS21 1LH
T: (0113) 284 2878
F: (0113) 203 7895

Hollins House ◆◆◆
17 Hollins Road, Harrogate,
North Yorkshire HG1 2JF
T: (01423) 503646
F: (01423) 503646
I: www.hollinshouse.co.uk

Kingsway Hotel ◆◆◆
36 Kings Road, Harrogate, North
Yorkshire HG1 5JW
T: (01423) 562179
F: (01423) 562179
E: baznoble@aol.com
I: www.kingswayhotel.com

Knabbs Ash ◆◆◆◆
Skipton Road, Felliscliffe,
Harrogate, North Yorkshire
HG3 2LT
T: (01423) 771040
F: (01423) 771515
E: colin&sheila@knabbsash.
freeserve.co.uk

Lamont House ◆◆◆◆
12 St Mary's Walk, Harrogate,
North Yorkshire HG2 0LW
T: (01423) 567143
F: (01423) 567143

Low Hall Hotel and Restaurant
◆◆◆
Ripon Road, Killinghall,
Harrogate, North Yorkshire
HG3 2AY
T: (01423) 508598
F: (01423) 560848
E: lowhall@fsbusiness.co.uk

Mrs Murray's Guest House
◆◆◆
67 Franklin Road, Harrogate,
North Yorkshire HG1 5EH
T: (01423) 505857
F: (01423) 530027
E: mrsmurrays@yahoo.co.uk

Oakbrae Guest House ◆◆◆◆
3 Springfield Avenue, Harrogate,
North Yorkshire HG1 2HR
T: (01423) 567682
F: (01423) 567682
E: oakbrae@nascr.net
I: www.nascr/-oakbrae

Parnas Hotel ◆◆◆◆
98 Franklin Road, Harrogate,
North Yorkshire HG1 5EN
T: (01423) 564493
F: (01423) 564493
E: robert@parho.freeserve.co.uk
I: www.scoot.
co.uk/parnas_hotel/

17 Peckfield Close ◆◆◆
Hampsthwaite, Harrogate, North
Yorkshire HG3 2ES
T: (01423) 770765

Quality Hotel Kimberley
◆◆◆◆
11-19 Kings Road, Harrogate,
North Yorkshire HG1 5JY
T: (01423) 505613
F: (01423) 530276
E: info@kimberley.scotnet.co.uk
I: www.choicehotels.europe.com

Royd Mount ◆◆◆◆
4 Grove Road, Harrogate, North
Yorkshire HG1 5EW
T: (01423) 529525
E: roydmount@btinternet.com

Ruskin Hotel ◆◆◆◆
1 Swan Road, Harrogate, North
Yorkshire HG1 2SS
T: (01423) 502045
F: (01423) 506131
E: ruskin.hotel@virgin.net
I: www.ruskinhotel.co.uk

Scotia House Hotel ◆◆◆
66-68 Kings Road, Harrogate,
North Yorkshire HG1 5JR
T: (01423) 504361
F: (01423) 526578
E: info@scotiahotel.harrogate.
net
I: www.scotiahotel.harrogate.net

Shannon Court Hotel ◆◆◆◆
65 Dragon Avenue, Harrogate,
North Yorkshire HG1 5DS
T: (01423) 509858
F: (01423) 530606
E: shannon@hotels.harrogate.
com
I. www.harrogate.com/shannon

Sherwood ◆◆◆
7 Studley Road, Harrogate,
North Yorkshire HG1 5JU
T: (01423) 503033
F: (01423) 564659
E: sherwood@hotels.harrogate.
com
I: www.sherwood-hotel.com

Spring Lodge Guest House
◆◆◆
22 Spring Mount, Harrogate,
North Yorkshire HG1 2HX
T: (01423) 506036
F: (01423) 506036

Staveleigh ◆◆◆◆
20 Ripon Road, Harrogate,
North Yorkshire HG1 2JJ
T: (01423) 524175
F: (01423) 524178
E: enquiries@staveleigh.co.uk
I: www.staveleigh.co.uk

Sunflower House ◆◆◆
61 Grantley Drive, Harrogate,
North Yorkshire HG3 2XU
T: (01423) 503261

Valley Hotel ◆◆◆◆
93-95 Valley Drive, Harrogate,
North Yorkshire HG2 0JP
T: (01423) 504868
F: (01423) 531940
E: valley@harrogate.com
I: www.valleyhotel.co.uk

The Welford ◆◆◆
27 Franklin Road, Harrogate,
North Yorkshire HG1 5ED
T: (01423) 566041 & 525344
F: (01423) 566041

Wharfedale House ◆◆◆
28 Harlow Moor Drive,
Harrogate, North Yorkshire
HG2 0JY
T: (01423) 522233

HARTWITH
North Yorkshire
Brimham Lodge ◆◆◆
Hartwith, Harrogate, North
Yorkshire HG3 3HE
T: (01423) 771770
F: (01423) 770370
E: neil.clarke@virgin.net

HARWOOD DALE
North Yorkshire
The Grainary ◆◆◆◆
Keasbeck Hill Farm, Harwood
Dale, Scarborough, North
Yorkshire YO13 0DT
T: (01723) 870026 &
07712 652633
F: (01723) 870026
E: thesimpsons@grainary.co.uk
I: www.grainary.co.uk

HAWES
North Yorkshire
Beech House ◆◆
Burtersett Road, Hawes, North
Yorkshire DL8 3NP
T: (01969) 667486

Bulls Head Hotel ◆◆◆◆
Market Place, Hawes, North
Yorkshire DL8 3RD
T: (01969) 667437
F: (01969) 667048
E: jeff@bullsheadhotel
I: www.bullsheadhotel.com

The Bungalow ◆◆◆
Spring Bank, Hawes, North
Yorkshire DL8 3NW
T: (01969) 667209

Cocketts Hotel and Restaurant
◆◆◆◆
Market Place, Hawes, North
Yorkshire DL8 3RD
T: (01969) 667312
F: (01969) 667162
E: enquiries@cocketts.co.uk
I: www.cocketts.co.uk

East House ◆◆◆◆
Gayle, Hawes, North Yorkshire
DL8 3RZ
T: (01969) 667405
E: lornaward@lineone.net
I: www.dalesaccommodation.
com/easthouse

Ebor Guest House ◆◆◆
Burtersett Road, Hawes, North
Yorkshire DL8 3NT
T: (01969) 667337
F: (01969) 667337
E: gwen@eborhouse.freeserve.
co.uk

Fairview House ◆◆◆◆
Burtersett Road, Hawes, North
Yorkshire DL8 3NP
T: (01969) 667348
F: (01969) 6677348
E: joan.bill.fairview@tinyonline.
co.uk
I: www.wensleydale.org

Herriots Hotel & Restaurant
◆◆◆◆
Main Street, Hawes, North
Yorkshire DL8 3QW
T: (01969) 667536
F: (01969) 667810
E: herriotshotel@aol.com
I: www.herriots.com

Laburnum House ◆◆◆
The Holme, Hawes, North
Yorkshire DL8 3QR
T: (01969) 667717
F: (01969) 667 041
E: janetbatty@hotmail.com

Old Station House ◆◆◆◆
Hardraw Road, Hawes, North
Yorkshire DL8 3NL
T: (01969) 667785
E: alan.watkinson@virgin.net
🏃

Pry House ◆◆◆
Hawes, North Yorkshire DL8 3LP
T: (01969) 667241

South View ◆◆◆
Gayle Lane, Hawes, North
Yorkshire DL8 3RW
T: (01969) 667447

Springbank House ◆◆◆
Springbank, Townfoot, Hawes,
North Yorkshire DL8 3NW
T: (01969) 667376
F: (01969) 667376

White Hart Inn ◆◆◆
Main Street, Hawes, North
Yorkshire DL8 3QL
T: (01969) 667259
F: (01969) 667259
E: whitehart@wensleydale.org
I: www.wensleydale.org

Widdale Foot ◆◆◆
Hawes, North Yorkshire DL8 3LX
T: (01969) 667383
F: (01969) 667471
E: widdalefoot@talk21.com
I: www.wensleydale.org

HAWNBY
North Yorkshire
Easterside Farm ◆◆◆
Hawnby, York YO62 5QT
T: (01439) 798277
F: (01439) 798277

HAWORTH
West Yorkshire
Aitches Guest House ◆◆◆◆
11 West Lane, Haworth,
Keighley, West Yorkshire
BD22 8OU
T: (01535) 642501
I: www.aitches.co.uk

The Apothecary Guest House
◆◆◆
86 Main Street, Haworth,
Keighley, West Yorkshire
BD22 8DA
T: (01535) 643642
F: (01535) 643642
E: apot@sisley86.freeserve.
co.uk
I: www.sisley86.freeserve.co.uk

Ashmount ◆◆◆◆
Mytholmes Lane, Haworth,
Keighley, West Yorkshire
BD22 8EZ
T: (01535) 645726
F: (01535) 645726
E: ashmounthaworth@aol.com
I: members.aol.
com/ashmounthaworth

Bronte Hotel ◆◆
Lees Lane, Haworth, Keighley,
West Yorkshire BD22 8RA
T: (01535) 644112
F: (01535) 646725
E: Brontehotel@btinternet.com
I: www.Binternet.
com/~brontehotel

Ebor House ◆◆◆
Lees Lane, Haworth, Keighley,
West Yorkshire BD22 8RA
T: (01535) 645869
E: derekbelle@aol.com

**Haworth Tea Rooms and Guest
House
Rating Applied For**
68 Main Street, Haworth,
Keighley, West Yorkshire
BD22 8DP
T: (01535) 644278 &
(01780) 751799

Heather Cottage Guest House
◆◆◆
25-27 Main Street, Haworth,
Keighley, West Yorkshire
BD22 8DA
T: (01535) 644511 &
07702 552076
E: heathercott@
haworthmsfreeserve.co.uk

Hole Farm ◆◆◆◆
Dimples Lane, Haworth,
Keighley, West Yorkshire
BD22 8QT
T: (01535) 644755
F: (01535) 644755
E: holefarm@bronteholidays.
co.uk
I: www.bronteholidays.co.uk

Jennrita Cottage ◆◆◆◆
3 Oldfield Gate, Haworth,
Keighley, West Yorkshire
BD22 0FW
T: (01535) 647121

Kershaw House ◆◆◆◆
90 West Lane, Haworth,
Keighley, West Yorkshire
BD22 8EN
T: (01535) 642074 &
07973 734758
F: (01535) 642074
E: kershawguesthouse@talk21.
com

Moorfield Guest House ◆◆◆
80 West Lane, Haworth,
Keighley, West Yorkshire
BD22 8EN
T: (01535) 643689
E: daveandann@moorfieldgh.
demon.co.uk
I: www.moorfieldgh.demon.
co.uk

The Old Registry ◆◆◆
2-4 Main Street, Haworth,
Keighley, West Yorkshire
BD22 8DA
T: (01535) 646503
F: (01535) 646503
E: oldregistry.haworth@virgin.
net
I: www.old-registry.co.uk

The Old Silent Inn ◆◆◆
Hob Lane, Stanbury, Keighley,
West Yorkshire BD22 0HW
T: (01535) 647437
F: (01535) 646449

Park Top House ◆◆◆◆
1 Rawdon Road, Haworth,
Keighley, West Yorkshire
BD22 8DX
T: (01535) 646102
E: gmilnes@parktophouse.fsnet.
co.uk

6 Penistone Mews ◆◆◆◆
Rawdon Road, Haworth,
Keighley, West Yorkshire
BD22 8DF
T: (01535) 647412
E: philip@haworth3.freeserve.
co.uk

**Woodlands Grange Private
Hotel** ◆◆◆
Woodlands Grange, Belle Isle,
Haworth, Keighley, West
Yorkshire BD22 8PB
T: (01535) 646814
F: (01535) 648282
E: woodlandsgrange@hotmail.
com

HAXEY
North Lincolnshire
Duke William ◆◆◆
Church Street, Haxey, Doncaster,
South Yorkshire DN9 2HY
T: (01427) 752210
F: (01427) 752210

HEADINGLEY
West Yorkshire
Boundary Hotel Express ◆◆
42 Cardigan Road, Headingley,
Leeds LS6 3AG
T: (0113) 275 7700
F: (0113) 275 7700
E: info@boundaryhotel.co.uk
I: www.boundaryhotel.co.uk

Oak Villa Hotel ◆◆◆
55/57 Cardigan Road,
Headingley, Leeds LS6 1DW
T: (0113) 275 8439
F: (0113) 275 8439

HEBDEN
North Yorkshire
Court Croft ◆◆◆
Church Lane, Hebden, Skipton,
North Yorkshire BD23 5DX
T: (01756) 753406

HEBDEN BRIDGE
West Yorkshire
Angeldale Guest House ◆◆◆
Hangingroyd Lane, Hebden
Bridge, West Yorkshire HX7 7DD
T: (01422) 847321
E: enq@angeldale.co.uk
I: www.angeldale.co.uk

Badger Fields Farm ◆◆◆◆
Badger Lane, Blackshaw Head,
Hebden Bridge, West Yorkshire
HX7 7JX
T: (01422) 845161
E: enquiries@badgerfields.com
I: www.badgerfields.com

8 Birchcliffe ◆◆◆
Off Sandy Gate, Hebden Bridge,
West Yorkshire HX7 8JA
T: (01422) 844777

The Grove Inn ◆◆◆
Burnley Road, Brearley,
Luddendenfoot, Halifax, West
Yorkshire HX2 6HS
T: (01422) 883235
F: (01422) 883905

Myrtle Grove ◆◆◆◆
Old Lees Road, Hebden Bridge,
West Yorkshire HX7 8HL
T: (01422) 846078 &
07905 174902

Nutclough House Hotel ◆◆◆
Keighley Road, Hebden Bridge,
West Yorkshire HX7 8EZ
T: (01422) 844361

1 Primrose Terrace ◆◆
Hebden Bridge, West Yorkshire
HX7 6HN
T: (01422) 844747

Prospect End ◆◆◆
8 Prospect Terrace, Savile Road,
Hebden Bridge, West Yorkshire
HX7 6NA
T: (01422) 843586

Robin Hood Inn ◆◆◆
Keighley Road, Pecket Well,
Hebden Bridge, West Yorkshire
HX7 8QR
T: (01422) 842593 &
07979 854338
F: (01422) 844938
E: info@robinhoodsinn.com
I: www.robinhoodsinn.com

1 St John's Close ◆◆◆
Hebden Bridge, West Yorkshire
HX7 8PD
T: (01422) 843321
E: angela.barrs@lineone.net

HELMSLEY
North Yorkshire
Argyle House ◆◆◆◆
Ashdale Road, Helmsley, York
YO62 5HD
T: (01439) 770590

Carlton Grange ◆◆◆
Helmsley, York YO62 5HH
T: (01439) 770259

Griff Farm Bed & Breakfast
◆◆◆◆
Griff Farm, Helmsley, York
YO62 5EN
T: (01439) 771600 &
07801 145049
F: (01439) 770462
E: j.fairburn@farmline.com

The Hawnby Hotel ◆◆◆
Hawnby, York YO62 5QS
T: (01439) 798202
F: (01439) 798344
E: info@hawnbyhotel.co.uk
I: www.hawnbyhotel.co.uk

High House Farm ◆◆◆
Sutton Bank, Thirsk, North
Yorkshire YO7 2HL
T: (01845) 597557

Laskill Farm ◆◆◆◆
Hawnby, York YO62 5NB
T: (01439) 798268
F: (01439) 798498
E: suesmith@laskillfarm.fsnet.
co.uk
I: www.laskillfarm.co.uk

Mount Grace Farm ◆◆◆◆
Cold Kirby, Thirsk, North
Yorkshire YO7 2HL
T: (01845) 597389 & 597389
F: (01845) 597872
E: joyce@mountgracefarm.com
I: www.mountgracefarm.com

Sproxton Hall ◆◆◆◆
Sproxton, York YO62 5EQ
T: (01439) 770225
F: (01439) 771373
E: info@sproxtonhall.demon.
co.uk
I: www.yorkshirenet.
co.uk/stayat/sproxtonhall

Stilworth House ◆◆◆◆
1 Church Street, Helmsley, York
YO62 5AD
T: (01439) 771072
E: carol@stilworth.co.uk
I: www.stilworth.co.uk

HEPTONSTALL
West Yorkshire
Poppyfields House ◆◆◆
29 Slack Top, Heptonstall,
Hebden Bridge, West Yorkshire
HX7 7HA
T: (01422) 843636
F: (01422) 845621

HEPWORTH
West Yorkshire
Uppergate Farm ◆◆◆◆
Hepworth, Holmfirth,
Huddersfield HD9 1TG
T: (01484) 681369
F: (01484) 687343
E: stevenal.booth@virgin.net
I: www.areas.co.uk/farm

HESSLE
East Riding of Yorkshire
Redcliffe House Luxury B&B
◆◆◆◆
Redcliffe Road, Hessle, North
Humberside HU13 0HA
T: (01482) 648655

Weir Lodge Guest House
◆◆◆◆
Tower Hill, Hessle, North
Humberside HU13 0SG
T: (01482) 648564
I: www.weirlodge.co.uk

HEWORTH
Yorkshire
The Nags Head ◆◆◆
56 Heworth Road, Heworth,
York YO3 0AD
T: (01904) 422989

HIBALDSTOW
North Lincolnshire
Thornfield Guest House ◆
23 Station Road, Hibaldstow,
Brigg, North Lincolnshire
DN20 9EA
T: (01652) 655555 &
07885 497149

HIGH BENTHAM
North Yorkshire
Fowgill Park ◆◆◆◆
High Bentham, Lancaster
LA2 7AH
T: (01524) 261630

Lane House Farm ◆◆◆◆
High Bentham, Lancaster
LA2 7DJ
T: (015242) 61479

HIGH STITTENHAM
North Yorkshire
Hall Farm ◆◆◆◆
High Stittenham, York
YO60 7TW
T: (01347) 878461
F: (01347) 878461
E: hallfarm@btinternet.com
I: www.hallfarm.btinternet.co.uk

HOLMBRIDGE
West Yorkshire
Corn Loft House ◆◆◆
146 Woodhead Road,
Holmbridge, Holmfirth,
Huddersfield HD7 1NL
T: (01484) 683147

HOLMFIRTH
West Yorkshire
Holme Valley Guest House
◆◆◆
97 Huddersfield Road,
Holmfirth, Huddersfield HD7 1JA
T: (01484) 681361
F: (01484) 681361
E: christine.assured@tinyworld.
co.uk
I: www.smoothhound.
co.uk/hotels/valley2.htmlwww.
s-hsystems.
co.uk/hotels/valley2-html

**Linden Grove Bed and
Breakfast** ◆◆
39 Huddersfield Road,
Holmfirth, Huddersfield
HD7 1JH
T: (01484) 683718

The Old Bridge Bakery ◆◆
15 Victoria Street, Holmfirth,
Huddersfield HD7 1DF
T: (01484) 685807

Red Lion Inn ◆◆◆
Sheffield Road, Jackson Bridge,
Holmfirth, Huddersfield
HD7 7HS
T: (01484) 683499

Springfield House ◆◆◆
95 Huddersfield Road,
Holmfirth, Huddersfield HD7 1JA
T: (01484) 683031
E: ann_brook@hotmail.com

HOLMPTON
East Riding of Yorkshire
**Elm Tree Farm
Rating Applied For**
Main Road, Holmpton,
Withernsea, North Humberside
HU19 2QR
T: (01964) 630957
E: cft-mcox@supanet.com

HOLTBY
Yorkshire
Sycamore House ◆◆◆◆
Holtby, York YO19 5UD
T: (01904) 488089
F: (01904) 488089

HOOTON PAGNELL
South Yorkshire
Rock Farm ◆◆◆
Hooton Pagnell, Doncaster,
South Yorkshire DN5 7BT
T: (01977) 642200 &
07785 916186

HORNSEA
East Riding of Yorkshire
Merlstead Private Hotel ◆◆◆
59 Eastgate, Hornsea, North
Humberside HU18 1NB
T: (01964) 533068
F: (01964) 536975

HORTON-IN-RIBBLESDALE
North Yorkshire
Crown Hotel ◆◆◆
Horton-in-Ribblesdale, Settle,
North Yorkshire BD24 0HF
T: (01729) 860209
F: (01729) 860444
E: minehost@crown-hotel.co.uk
I: www.crown-hotel.co.uk

Middle Studfold Farm ◆◆◆
Horton-in-Ribblesdale, Settle,
North Yorkshire BD24 0ER
T: (01729) 860236 &
07774 918908

The Rowe House ◆◆◆
Horton-in-Ribblesdale, Settle,
North Yorkshire BD24 0HT
T: (01729) 860212
E: therowehouse@lineone.net
I: www.therowehouse.co.uk

HUBBERHOLME
North Yorkshire
Church Farm ◆◆◆◆
Hubberholme, Skipton, North
Yorkshire BD23 5JE
T: (01756) 760240

HUDDERSFIELD
West Yorkshire
Ashfield Hotel ◆◆◆
93 New North Road,
Huddersfield, HD1 5ND
T: (01484) 425916
F: (01484) 537029
E: enquiries@theashfieldhotel.
co.uk
I: www.theashfieldhotel.co.uk

Cambridge Lodge ◆◆◆
4 Clare Hill, Huddersfield,
HD1 5BS
T: (01484) 519892
F: (01484) 534534

Croppers Arms ◆◆◆
136 Westbourne Road, Marsh,
Huddersfield, HD1 4LF
T: (01484) 421522
F: (01484) 301300

Ellasley Guest House ◆◆
86 New North Road,
Huddersfield, HD1 5NE
T: (01484) 423995
F: (01484) 432995

Holmcliffe Guest House ◆◆◆
16 Mountjoy Road, Edgerton,
Huddersfield, HD1 5PZ
T: (01484) 429598
F: (01484) 429598
E: jwilco@mwfree.net

Laurel Cottage Guest House
◆◆◆
34 Far Dene, Kirkburton,
Huddersfield, West Yorkshire
HD8 0QU
T: (01484) 607907

The Mallows Guest House
◆◆◆
55 Spring Street, Springwood,
Huddersfield, HD1 4AZ
T: (01484) 544684

Manor Mill Cottage ◆◆◆
21 Linfit Lane, Kirkburton,
Huddersfield HD8 0TY
T: (01484) 604109
E: manormill@paskham.
freeserve.co.uk

The White House ◆◆◆
Holthead, Slaithwaite,
Huddersfield HD7 5TY
T: (01484) 842245
F: (01484) 842245
E: whthouse@globalnet.co.uk
I: www.whitehouse-hotel.co.uk

Woods End Bed & Breakfast
◆◆◆◆
46 Inglewood Ave, Birkby,
Huddersfield HD2 2DS
T: (01484) 513580 &
07730 030993
F: (01484) 513580
E: smithmoorhouse@ntlworld.
com

HUGGATE
East Riding of Yorkshire
Greenwick Farm ◆◆◆
Huggate, York YO42 1YR
T: (01377) 288122
E: wf@talk21.com

HULL
East Riding of Yorkshire
Acorn Guest House ◆◆◆
719 Beverley High Road, Hull,
HU6 7JN
T: (01482) 853248 & 853148
F: (01482) 853148
E: janet@theacorns.karoo.net
I: www.theacorn.karoo.
net/theguesthouse

The Admiral Guest House ◆◆
234 The Boulevard, Hull,
HU3 3ED
T: (01482) 329664
F: (01482) 329664

Allandra Hotel ◆◆◆
5 Park Avenue, Hull, HU5 3EN
T: (01482) 493349 & 492680

The Arches ◆◆◆
38 Saner Street, Hull, HU3 2TR
T: (01482) 211558

Clyde House Hotel ◆◆◆
13 John Street, Hull, HU2 8DH
T: (01482) 214981 & 214981

Conway–Roseberry Hotel
◆◆◆◆
86 Marlborough Avenue, Hull,
HU5 3JT
T: (01482) 445256 &
07909 517328
F: (01482) 343215
I: www.smoothhound.
co.uk/hotels/conwayhtml

The Earlsmere Hotel ◆◆◆
76-78 Sunnybank, Off Spring
Bank West, Hull, HU3 1LQ
T: (01482) 341977
F: (01482) 473714
E: hotel7678.freeserve.co.uk
I: www.earlsmerehotel.karoo.net

West Park Hotel ◆◆◆
405-411 Anlaby Road, Hull,
HU3 6AB
T: (01482) 571888 & 505674
F: (01482) 351215
E: westparkhotel@mandp.
karoo.uk

HUNMANBY
North Yorkshire
Saxdale House Farm ◆◆◆◆
The Row, Hunmanby, Filey,
North Yorkshire YO14 0JD
T: (01723) 892346
F: (01723) 892400
E: saxdale.house@virgin.net
I: www.saxdale.co.uk

HUSTHWAITE
North Yorkshire
Flower of May ◆◆◆
Husthwaite, York, North
Yorkshire YO61 4PG
T: (01347) 868317

HUTTON-LE-HOLE
North Yorkshire
Barn Hotel and Tea Room
◆◆◆
Hutton-le-Hole, York YO62 6UA
T: (01751) 417311
E: fairhurst@lineone.net

Westfield Lodge ◆◆◆
Hutton-le-Hole, York YO62 6UG
T: (01751) 417261
F: (01751) 417876
E: sticklandrw@farmersweekly.
net

HUTTON SESSAY
North Yorkshire
Burtree Country House ◆◆◆◆
Burtree House, York Road,
Hutton Sessay, Thirsk, North
Yorkshire YO7 3AY
T: (01845) 501333 & 501562
F: (01845) 501596

HUTTONS AMBO
North Yorkshire
High Gaterley Farm ◆◆◆◆
Castle Howard Estate, Huttons
Ambo, York YO60 7HT
T: (01653) 694636 &
07703 188086
F: (01653) 694636
E: relax@highgaterley.com
I: www.highgaterley.com

ILKLEY
West Yorkshire
Archway Cottage ◆◆◆◆
24 Skipton Road, Ilkley, West
Yorkshire LS29 9EP
T: (01943) 603399
F: (01943) 603399

Cow & Calf ◆◆◆◆
Hangingstone Road, Ilkley, West
Yorkshire LS29 8BT
T: (01013) 607335
F: (01943) 604712
I: www.cowandcalf.co.uk

Grove Hotel ◆◆◆◆
66 The Grove, Ilkley, West
Yorkshire LS29 9PA
T: (01943) 600298
F: 0870 706 5587
E: info@grovehotel.org
I: www.grovehotel.org

One Tivoli Place ◆◆◆
Ilkley, West Yorkshire LS29 8SU
T: (01943) 600328 &
07860 293193
F: (01943) 600320
E: tivolipl@aol.com

**Roberts Family Bed and
Breakfast** ◆◆◆
63 Skipton Road, Ilkley, West
Yorkshire LS29 9HF
T: (01943) 817542
F: (01943) 817542
E: petraroberts1@activemail.
co.uk

Summerhill Guest House ◆◆◆
24 Crossbeck Road, Ilkley, West
Yorkshire LS29 9JN
T: (01943) 607067

Summerhouse ◆◆◆◆
Hangingstone Road, Ilkley, West
Yorkshire LS29 8RS
T: (01943) 601612 &
07957 986228
F: (01943) 601612
E: summerguesthouse@talk21.
com

Westwood Lodge, Ilkley Moor
◆◆◆◆
Wells Road, Ilkley, West
Yorkshire LS29 9JF
T: (01943) 433430
F: (01943) 433431
E: welcome@westwoodlodge.
co.uk
I: www.westwoodlodge.co.uk

ILLINGWORTH
West Yorkshire
Whitehill Lodge ◆◆◆
102 Keighley Road, Illingworth,
Halifax, West Yorkshire HX2 8HF
T: (01422) 240813 &
07931 765842
E: lodge102@Pgen.net

IMMINGHAM
North East Lincolnshire
The Poplars Guest House ◆◆◆
30 Church Lane, Immingham,
DN40 2EU
T: (01469) 573067

INGBIRCHWORTH
South Yorkshire
The Fountain Inn & Rooms
◆◆◆◆
Wellthorne Lane, Ingbirchworth,
Penistone, Sheffield S36 7GJ
T: (01226) 763125
F: (01226) 761336
E: reservations@fountain-inn.
co.uk
I: www.fountain-inn.co.uk

INGLEBY CROSS
North Yorkshire
Blue Bell Inn ◆
Ingleby Cross, Northallerton,
North Yorkshire DL6 3NF
T: (01609) 882272
E: david.kinsella@tesco.net

INGLEBY GREENHOW
North Yorkshire
Manor House Farm ◆◆◆◆
Ingleby Greenhow,
Middlesbrough, Cleveland
TS9 6RB
T: (01642) 722384
E: mbloom@globalnet.co.uk

INGLETON
North Yorkshire
The Dales Guest House ◆◆◆
Main Street, Ingleton, Carnforth,
North Yorkshire LA6 3HH
T: (015242) 41401
E: dalesgh@hotmail.com

**Ferncliffe Country Guest
House** ◆◆◆◆
55 Main Street, Ingleton,
Carnforth, North Yorkshire
LA6 3HJ
T: (01524) 242405
E: ferncliffe@hotmail.com

Gatehouse Farm ◆◆◆◆
Far Westhouse, Ingleton,
Carnforth, North Yorkshire
LA6 3NR
T: (01524) 241458 & 241307

**Ingleborough View Guest
House** ◆◆◆◆
Main Street, Ingleton, Carnforth,
North Yorkshire LA6 3HH
T: (01524) 241523
E: anne@ingleboroughview.
co.uk
I: www.ingleboroughview.co.uk

Inglenook Guest House ◆◆◆
20 Main Street, Ingleton,
Carnforth, North Yorkshire
LA6 3HJ
T: (01524) 241270
E: phillsmith@
inglenookguesthouse.fsbusiness.
co.uk
I: www.nebsweb.co.uk/inglenook

New Butts Farm ◆◆◆
High Bentham, Lancaster
LA2 7AN
T: (01524) 241238

Pines Country House ◆◆◆◆
Ingleton, Carnforth, North
Yorkshire LA6 3HN
T: (01524) 241252
F: (01524) 241252
E: pineshotel@aol.com
I: www.yorkshirenet.
co.uk/stayat/thepines

Riverside Lodge ◆◆◆
24 Main Street, Ingleton,
Carnforth, North Yorkshire
LA6 3HJ
T: (015242) 41359
E: andrewa@foleya.fsnet.co.uk
I: www.riversideingleton.co.uk
🅰

**Springfield Country House
Hotel** ◆◆◆
Main Street, Ingleton, Carnforth,
North Yorkshire LA6 3HJ
T: (01524) 241280
F: (01524) 241280
I: www.destination-england.
co.uk.springfield

Station Inn ◆◆◆
Ribblehead, Ingleton, Carnforth,
North Yorkshire LA6 3AS
T: (01524) 241274
I: www.smoothhound.
co.uk/hotelsstation2.html

Wheatsheaf Inn & Hotel
◆◆◆◆
22 High Street, Ingleton,
Carnforth, North Yorkshire
LA6 3AD
T: (01524) 241275
F: (01524) 241275
E: randall.d@ingleton01.
freeserve.co.uk
I: www.yorkshirenet.
co.uk/stayat/thewheatsheaf

KETTLESING
North Yorkshire

Green Acres ◆◆◆◆
Sleights Lane, Kettlesing,
Harrogate, North Yorkshire
HG3 2LE
T: (01423) 771524
E: christine@yorkshiredalesbb.
com

KETTLEWELL
North Yorkshire

**Blue Bell Inn
Rating Applied For**
Kettlewell, Skipton, North
Yorkshire BD23 5QX
T: (01756) 760230
F: (01756) 760230
E: info@bluebellinn.co.uk
I: www.bluebellinn.co.uk

Chestnut Cottage ◆◆◆
Kettlewell, Skipton, North
Yorkshire BD23 5RL
T: (01756) 760804

Lynburn ◆◆◆
Kettlewell, Skipton, North
Yorkshire BD23 5RF
T: (01756) 760803

KILBURN
North Yorkshire

The Forresters Arms Hotel
◆◆◆
Kilburn, York YO61 4AH
T: (01347) 868550 & 868386
F: (01347) 868386
E: forresters@
destination-england-co.uk
I: wwwdestination-england.
co.uk./forresters.html

KINGSTONE
South Yorkshire

Park View Guest House ◆◆
2 Beech Grove, Kingstone,
Barnsley, South Yorkshire
S70 6NG
T: (01226) 297268 & 779324

KIRBY HILL
North Yorkshire

Shoulder of Mutton Inn ◆◆◆
Kirby Hill, Richmond, North
Yorkshire DL11 7JH
T: (01748) 822772
E: john@homledale.com
I: www.holmedale.com

KIRKBURTON
West Yorkshire

The Woodman Inn ◆◆◆◆
Thunderbridge, Kirkburton,
Huddersfield HD8 0PX
T: (01484) 605778
F: (01484) 604110
E: thewoodman@connectfree.
co.uk

KIRKBY
North Yorkshire

Dromonby Hall Farm ◆◆◆
Busby Lane, Kirkby, Stokesley,
Middlesbrough, Cleveland
TS9 7AP
T: (01642) 712312
F: (01642) 712312
E: b-b@dromonby.co.uk
I: www.dromonby.co.uk

KIRKBY MALHAM
North Yorkshire

Yeoman's Barn ◆◆◆◆
Kirkby Malham, Skipton, North
Yorkshire BD23 4BL
T: (01729) 830639
E: c_d.turner@virgin.net
I: www.yeomansbarn.co.uk

KIRKBYMOORSIDE
North Yorkshire

Cartoft Lodge ◆◆◆◆
Keldholme, Kirkbymoorside,
York, North Yorkshire YO62 6NU
T: (01751) 431566

The Cornmill ◆◆◆◆
Kirby Mills, Kirkbymoorside,
York, North Yorkshire YO62 6NP
T: (01751) 432000
F: (01751) 432300
E: cornmill@kirbymills.demon.
co.uk
I: www.kirbymills.demon.co.uk
🅰

Dale End ◆◆◆
25 Dale End, Kirkbymoorside,
York YO62 6EE
T: (01751) 431689

High Blakey House ◆◆◆◆
Blakey Ridge, Kirkbymoorside,
York YO62 7LQ
T: (01751) 417186
E: highblakey.house@virginnet.
co.uk
I: freespace.virginnet.
co.uk/highblakey.house/

The Lion Inn ◆◆◆
Blakey Ridge, Kirkbymoorside,
York YO62 7LQ
T: (01751) 417320
F: (01751) 417717
I: www.lionblakey.co.uk

Red Lion House ◆◆◆◆
Crown Square, Kirkbymoorside,
York YO62 6AY
T: (01751) 431815
E: angela.thomson@
red-lion-house.freeserve.co.uk

Sinnington Common Farm
◆◆◆◆
Kirkbymoorside, York YO62 6NX
T: (01751) 431719
E: Felicity@scfarm.demon.co.uk
I: www.scfarmdemon.co.uk

White Horse Hotel ◆◆◆
5 Market Place, Kirkbymoorside,
York YO62 6AB
T: (01751) 431296

KIRKLINGTON
North Yorkshire

Upsland Farm ◆◆◆◆
Kirklington, Bedale, North
Yorkshire DL8 2PA
T: (01845) 567709
F: (01845) 567709
E: upsland@btinternet.com
I: www.btinternet.com/upsland

KIRKSTALL
West Yorkshire

Abbey Guest House ◆◆◆◆
44 Vesper Road, Kirkstall, Leeds
LS5 3NX
T: (0113) 278 5580
F: (0113) 2787780
E: abbeyleeds@aol.com

KNARESBOROUGH
North Yorkshire

Ebor Mount ◆◆◆
18 York Place, Knaresborough,
North Yorkshire HG5 0AA
T: (01423) 863315
F: (01423) 863315

**Hermitage Guest House & Tea
Garden** ◆◆◆
10 Waterside, Knaresborough,
North Yorkshire HG5 9AZ
T: (01423) 863349
I: www.smoothhound.
co.uk/hotels/hermitage1.html

Holly Corner ◆◆◆◆
3 Coverdale Drive, High Bond
End, Knaresborough, North
Yorkshire HG5 9BW
T: (01423) 864204 &
07713 135713
F: (01423) 864204
E: hollycorner@ukhotelguide.
net
I: www.knaresborough.
co.uk/guest-accom/

Kirkgate House ◆◆◆◆
17 Kirkgate, Knaresborough,
North Yorkshire HG5 8AD
T: (01423) 862704
F: (01423) 862704
I: www.knaresborough.
co.uk/guest-accom.

The Mitre Hotel ◆◆◆
4 Station Road, Knaresborough,
North Yorkshire HG5 9AA
T: (01423) 863589
F: (01423) 863589
E: the-mitre@bizhosting.com
I: www.
the-mitrehotelbizhosting.com

Newton House Hotel ◆◆◆◆
5-7 York Place, Knaresborough,
North Yorkshire HG5 0AD
T: (01423) 863539
F: (01423) 869748
E: newtonhouse@btinternet.
com
I: www.newtonhousehotel.com

Rosedale ◆◆◆
11 Aspin Way, Knaresborough,
North Yorkshire HG5 8HL
T: (01423) 867210
F: (01423) 860675
I: www.knaresborough.
co.uk/guest-accommodation

Watergate Lodge ◆◆◆
Watergate Haven, Ripley Road,
Knaresborough, North Yorkshire
HG5 9BU
T: (01423) 864627
F: (01423) 861087
E: watergate.haven@virgin.net
I: business.virgin.net/watergate.
haven

Windsor House ◆◆◆◆
16b Windsor Lane,
Knaresborough, North Yorkshire
HG5 8DX
T: (01423) 865398

Yorkshire Lass ◆◆◆
High Bridge, Harrogate Road,
Knaresborough, North Yorkshire
HG5 8DA
T: (01423) 862962
F: (01423) 869091
E: yorkshirelass@
knaresborough.co.uk
I: www.knaresborough.
co.uk/yorkshirelass

KNOTTINGLEY
West Yorkshire

Wentvale Bed and Breakfast
◆◆◆◆
Great North Road, Knottingley,
West Yorkshire WF11 8PF
T: (01977) 676714
F: (01977) 676714
E: wentvale@aol.com
I: www.wentvale.co.uk

LANGCLIFFE
North Yorkshire

**Langcliffe Lodge Bed and
Breakfast Accommodation**◆◆
Langcliffe Road, Langcliffe,
Settle, North Yorkshire BD24 9LT
T: (01729) 823362

LANGSETT
South Yorkshire

Waggon and Horses ◆◆◆
Langsett, Stocksbridge, Sheffield
S36 4GY
T: (01226) 763147
F: (01226) 763147
E: info@langsettinn.com
I: www.langsettinn.com

LANGTOFT
East Riding of Yorkshire

The Ship Inn ◆◆◆
Scarborough Road, Langtoft,
Driffield, North Humberside
YO25 3TH
T: (01377) 267243 &
07769 684647

LAYCOCK
West Yorkshire

Far Laithe Farm ◆◆◆◆
Laycock, Keighley, West
Yorkshire BD22 0PP
T: (01535) 661993

LEALHOLM
North Yorkshire
High Park Farm ♦♦♦
Lealholm, Whitby, North
Yorkshire YO21 2AQ
T: (01947) 897416

LEEDS
West Yorkshire
Adriatic Hotel ♦♦♦
87 Harehills Avenue, Leeds,
LS8 4ET
T: (0113) 262 0115 & 262 3606
F: (0113) 262 6071
E: adriatic87@hotmail.com
I: www.theadriatichotel.co.uk

Aintree Hotel ♦♦
38 Cardigan Road, Headingley,
Leeds LS6 3AG
T: (0113) 275 8290 & 275 7053
F: (0113) 275 8290

Avalon Guest House ♦♦♦
132 Woodsley Road, Leeds,
LS2 9LZ
T: (0113) 243 2545

Beechwood Hotel ♦♦♦
34 Street Lane, Roundhay, Leeds,
West Yorkshire LS8 2ET
T: (0113) 266 2578
F: (0113) 266 2578

Broomhurst Hotel ♦♦♦
12 Chapel Lane, Off Cardigan
Road, Headingley, Leeds
LS6 3BW
T: (0113) 278 6836 & 278 5764
F: (0113) 230 7099

Central Hotel ♦♦
35 - 47 New Briggate, Leeds,
LS2 8JD
T: (0113) 294 1456
F: (0113) 294 1551
E: reception@central-hotel.
freeserve.com.uk

City Centre Hotel ♦♦
51A New Briggate, Leeds,
LS2 8JD
T: (0113) 242 9019
F: (0113) 242 9019

17 Cottage Road ♦♦
Headingley, Leeds LS6 4DD
T: (0113) 275 5575

Fairbairn House ♦♦♦
71-75 Clarendon Road, Leeds,
LS2 9PL
T: (0113) 233 6633 & 233 6913
F: (0113) 233 6914
E: m.a.timm@leeds.ac.uk

Glengarth Hotel ♦♦♦
162 Woodsley Road, Leeds,
LS2 9LZ
T: (0113) 245 7940
F: (0113) 216 8033

Highbank Hotel & Restauarnt
♦♦
83 Harehills Lane, Leeds, West
Yorkshire LS7 4HA
T: 0870 741 9227 & 741 4230
F: 0870 741 4225
E: highbankhotel@hotmail.com
I: www.leedshotel.com

Hilldene Hotel ♦♦
99 Harehills Lane, Leeds,
LS8 4DN
T: (0113) 262 1292
F: (0113) 262 1292

Hinsley Hall ♦♦♦
62 Headingley Lane, Leeds,
LS6 2BX
T: (0113) 261 8000
F: (0113) 224 2406
E: info@hinsley-hall.co.uk
I: www.hinsley-hall.co.uk

**Kirkstall Hall, Trinity and All
Saints College**♦♦♦
Brownberrie Lane, Horsforth,
Leeds LS18 5HD
T: (0113) 283 7240 & 283 7100
F: (0113) 283 7239
E: commercial_services@tasc.
ac.uk
I: www.tasc.ac.uk

Manxdene Private Hotel ♦♦
154 Woodsley Road, Leeds,
LS2 9LZ
T: (0113) 243 2586

Number 23 ♦♦♦
23 St Chad's Rise, Far
Headingley, Leeds, LS6 3QE
T: (0113) 275 7825 & 226 9575

Pinewood Hotel ♦♦♦
78 Potternewton Lane, Leeds,
LS7 3LW
T: (0113) 262 2561 & 0800 096
7463

Premier Lodge ♦♦♦
City West Office Park, Gelderd
Road, Leeds, West Yorkshire
LS12 6SN
T: 0870 700 1414
F: 0870 700 1415

Rydal Bank Hotel ♦♦♦
20 Street Lane, Roundhay, Leeds
LS8 2ET
T: (0113) 266 1178 & 00113 266
8690
F: (0113) 266 1178

St Michael's Tower Hotel ♦♦♦
5 St Michael's Villas, Cardigan
Road, Headingley, Leeds LS6 3AF
T: (0113) 275 5557 & 275 6039
F: (0113) 230 7491

Sandylands ♦♦♦
44 Lidgett Lane, Leeds, LS8 1PQ
T: (0113) 266 1666
E: spackman@cwnet.com.net

Temple Manor ♦♦♦♦
2 Field End Garth, Temple
Newsam, Leeds, LS15 0QQ
T: (0113) 264 1384

Wheelgate Guest House ♦♦♦
7 Kirkgate, Sherburn-In-Elmet,
Leeds, LS25 6BH
T: (01977) 682231
F: (01977) 682231

LEEMING BAR
North Yorkshire
Little Holtby ♦♦♦♦
Leeming Bar, Northallerton,
North Yorkshire DL7 9LH
T: (01609) 748762
F: (01609) 748822
E: littleholtby@yahoo.co.uk
I: www.littleholtby.co.uk

LEVISHAM
North Yorkshire
Horseshoe Inn ♦♦♦
Levisham, Pickering, North
Yorkshire YO18 7NL
T: (01751) 460240
F: (01751) 460240

The Moorlands ♦♦♦♦♦
Levisham, Pickering, North
Yorkshire YO18 7NL
T: (01751) 460229
F: (01751) 460470
E: ronaldoleonardo@aol.com
I: www.smoothhound.
co.uk/hotels/moorlands.html

Rectory Farm House ♦♦♦♦
Levisham, Pickering, North
Yorkshire YO18 7NL
T: (01751) 460491 &
08707 059863
E: stay@levisham.com
I: www.levisham.com

LEYBURN
North Yorkshire
Clyde House ♦♦♦
5 Railway Street, Leyburn, North
Yorkshire DL8 5AY
T: (01969) 623941
F: (01969) 623941
E: info@clydehouseleyburn.
co.uk
I: www.clyehouseleyburn.co.uk

**Craken House Farm
Rating Applied For**
Middleham Road, Leyburn,
North Yorkshire DL8 5HF
T: (01969) 622204
F: (01969) 622204

Eastfield Lodge Private Hotel
♦♦♦
St Matthews Terrace, Leyburn,
North Yorkshire DL8 5EL
T: (01969) 623196
F: (01969) 624599

Greenhills ♦♦♦♦♦
5 Middleham Road, Leyburn,
North Yorkshire DL8 5EY
T: (01969) 623859
E: val.pringle@freenet.co.uk
I: www.yorkshirenet.co.uk

Grove Hotel ♦♦♦
8 Grove Square, Leyburn, North
Yorkshire DL8 5AE
T: (01969) 622569
E: grove@bensonk.freeserve.
co.uk
I: www.yorkshirenet.
co.uk/stayat/grovehotel

Hayloft Suite ♦♦♦
Foal Barn, Spennithorne,
Leyburn, North Yorkshire
DL8 5PR
T: (01969) 622580

Park Gate House ♦♦♦♦
Constable Burton, Leyburn,
North Yorkshire DL8 5RG
T: (01677) 450466 & 450466
E: parkgatehouse@freenet.co.uk

Secret Garden House ♦♦♦
Grove Square, Leyburn, North
Yorkshire DL8 5AE
T: (01969) 623589

LINTON
West Yorkshire
Glendales ♦♦♦
Muddy Lane, Linton, Wetherby,
West Yorkshire LS22 4HW
T: (01937) 585915

LITTLE RIBSTON
North Yorkshire
Beck House ♦♦♦♦
Wetherby Road, Little Ribston,
Wetherby, West Yorkshire
LS22 4EP
T: (01937) 583362

LOCKTON
North Yorkshire
Farfields Farmhouse ♦♦♦♦
Farfields Farm, Lockton,
Pickering, North Yorkshire
YO18 7NQ
T: (01751) 460239
E: farfieldsfarm@btinternet.
com

LOFTHOUSE
West Yorkshire
Hawthorne Villa Guest House
♦♦♦
Temple View, Lofthouse,
Wakefield, West Yorkshire
WF3 3LN
T: (01924) 822456 & 822437
F: 0870 1328032
E: hawthornevilla@topaddress.
com
I: www.hawthornevilla.
topaddress.com

Tall Trees ♦♦♦♦
188 Leeds Road, Lofthouse,
Wakefield, West Yorkshire
WF3 3LS
T: (01924) 827666 & (0113) 282
7874
F: (0113) 282 2095
E: gell@200553@aol.com

LONDESBOROUGH
East Riding of Yorkshire
Towthorpe Grange ♦♦
Towthorpe Lane,
Londesborough, York YO43 3LB
T: (01430) 873814

LONDONDERRY
North Yorkshire
Tatton Lodge ♦♦♦
Londonderry, Northallerton,
North Yorkshire DL7 9NF
T: (01677) 422222
F: (01677) 422222
E: enquiries@tattonlodge.co.uk
I: www.tattonlodge.co.uk

LOW ROW
North Yorkshire
Park End ♦♦♦
Kearton, Low Row, Richmond,
North Yorkshire DL11 6PL
T: (01748) 886287

Summer Lodge Farm ♦♦♦
Summer Lodge, Low Row,
Richmond, North Yorkshire
DL11 6NP
T: (01748) 886504

LUDDENDENFOOT
West Yorkshire
Bankfield Bed and Breakfast
♦♦♦♦
Danny Lane, Luddendenfoot,
Halifax, West Yorkshire
HX2 6AW
T: (01422) 883147
E: jenden@bankfieldbb.fsnet.
co.uk

2 Lane Ends ◆◆◆◆
Midgley, Luddendenfoot,
Halifax, West Yorkshire HX2 6TU
T: (01422) 883388 &
07775 904474
E: sandra@lane-ends-b-b.fsnet.
co.uk

Rockcliffe West ◆◆◆◆
Burnley Road, Luddendenfoot,
Halifax, West Yorkshire HX2 6HL
T: (01422) 882151
F: (01422) 882151
E: rockcliffe.b.b@virgin.net

LUND
East Riding of Yorkshire

**Clematis House, Farmhouse
Bed and Breakfast◆◆◆◆**
1 Eastgate, Lund, Driffield, East
Riding of Yorkshire YO25 9TQ
T: (01377) 217204
F: (01377) 217204
E: clematis@bblund.fsnet.co.uk
I: www.clematisfarm.co.uk

MALHAM
North Yorkshire

Beck Hall Guest House ◆◆◆
Malham, Skipton, North
Yorkshire BD23 4DJ
T: (01729) 830332

Miresfield Farm ◆◆◆
Malham, Skipton, North
Yorkshire BD23 4DA
T: (01729) 830414 & 830060
E: chris@miresfield.freeserve.
co.uk

River House Hotel ◆◆◆
Malham, Skipton, North
Yorkshire BD23 4DA
T: (01729) 830315
F: (01729) 830672
E: info@riverhousehotel.co.uk
I: www.riverhousehotel.co.uk
🏃

MALTBY
South Yorkshire

The Cottages Guest House ◆◆
1, 3 & 5 Blyth Road, Maltby,
Rotherham, South Yorkshire
S66 8HX
T: (01709) 813382

MALTON
North Yorkshire

The George Hotel ◆◆◆
19 Yorkersgate, Malton, North
Yorkshire YO17 7AA
T: (01653) 692884 &
07768 344337
F: (01653) 698674

Howe Cottage ◆◆◆◆
Malton, North Yorkshire
YO17 6RG
T: (01653) 699528 &
07971 566394
F: (01653) 696667

Leonard House ◆◆◆◆
45 Old Maltongate, Malton,
North Yorkshire YO17 7EH
T: (01653) 695711

The Old Rectory ◆◆◆◆
West Heslerton, Malton, North
Yorkshire YO17 8RE
T: (01944) 728285 &
07778 064580
F: (01944) 728436
E: bhillas@supanet.com
I: www.oldrectoryny.fsnet.co.uk/

MANKINHOLES
West Yorkshire

Cross Farm ◆◆◆◆
Mankinholes, Todmorden,
Lancashire OL14 6HB
T: (01706) 813481

MAPPLEWELL
South Yorkshire

The Grange ◆◆◆
29 Spark Lane, Mapplewell,
Barnsley, South Yorkshire
S75 6AA
T: (01226) 380078 &
07971 239974
E: the.grange@telinco.com

MARKET WEIGHTON
East Riding of Yorkshire

Arras Farmhouse ◆◆◆
Arras Farm, Market Weighton,
York YO43 4RN
T: (01430) 872404
F: (01430) 872404

MARSDEN
West Yorkshire

**Olive Branch Restaurant with
Rooms and Bar◆◆◆◆**
Manchester Road, Marsden,
Huddersfield HD7 6LU
T: (01484) 844487
E: reservations@olivebranch.uk.
com
I: www.olivebranch.uk.com

MARTON
North Yorkshire

Orchard House ◆◆◆◆
Main Street, Marton, Sinnington,
York YO61 6RD
T: (01751) 432904

Wildsmith House ◆◆◆◆
Marton, Sinnington, York
YO62 6RD
T: (01751) 432702
E: wildsmithhouse@talk21.com
I: www.swiftlink.pnc-uk.
net/bb/1102.htm

MASHAM
North Yorkshire

Garden House ◆◆◆◆
1 Park Street, Masham, Ripon,
North Yorkshire HG4 4HN
T: (01765) 689989
E: S.Furby@freenet.co.uk
I: www.ukfreenet.co.uk

Haregill Lodge ◆◆◆◆
Ellingstring, Masham, Ripon,
North Yorkshire HG4 4PW
T: (01677) 460272
F: (01677) 460272
E: haregilllodge@freenet.co.uk

Limetree Farm ◆◆◆◆
Hutts Lane, Grewelthorpe,
Ripon, North Yorkshire HG4 3DA
T: (01765) 658450

Pasture House ◆◆◆
Healey, Masham, Ripon, North
Yorkshire HG4 4LJ
T: (01765) 689149
F: (01765) 689990

Warren House Farm ◆◆◆
High Ellington, Masham, Ripon,
North Yorkshire HG4 4PP
T: (01677) 460244
F: (01677) 460244

MENSTON
West Yorkshire

Chevin End Guest House ◆◆◆
West Chevin Road, Menston,
Ilkley, West Yorkshire LS29 6DU
T: (01943) 876845
E: chevinend.guesthouse@
virgin.net
I: www.members.xoom.
com/chevinguest/

MIDDLEHAM
North Yorkshire

The Black Bull Inn ◆◆◆◆
Market Place, Middleham,
Leyburn, North Yorkshire
DL8 4NX
T: (01969) 623669
E: blackbull@tinyworld.co.uk

Chapelfields ◆◆◆
East Witton Road, Middleham,
Leyburn, North Yorkshire
DL8 4PY
T: (01969) 625075
F: (01765) 689991
E: tulip@tulipeve.demon.co.uk

Domus ◆◆◆◆
Market Place, Middleham, North
Yorkshire DL8 4NR
T: (01969) 623497
E: domus_2000@yahoo.co.uk

Jasmine House ◆◆◆◆◆
Market Place, Middleham,
Leyburn, North Yorkshire
DL8 4NU
T: (01969) 622858
E: enquiries@jasminehouse.net
I: jasminehouse.net

The Priory ◆◆◆
West End, Middleham, Leyburn,
North Yorkshire DL8 4QG
T: (01969) 623279

Richard III Hotel ◆◆◆
Market Place, Middleham,
Leyburn, North Yorkshire
DL8 4NP
T: (01969) 623240

**17th Century Castle Keep
◆◆◆◆**
Castle Hill, Middleham, Leyburn,
North Yorkshire DL8 4QR
T: (01969) 623665
E: tonymaddison@aol.co.uk

Yore View ◆◆◆◆
Leyburn Road, Middleham,
Leyburn, North Yorkshire
DL8 4PL
T: (01969) 622987
E: yore_view@hotmail.com

MIDGLEY
West Yorkshire

Midgley Lodge Motel ◆◆◆
Bar Lane, Midgley, Wakefield,
West Yorkshire WF4 4JJ
T: (01924) 830069
F: (01924) 830087
I: www.
co.uk/midgley-lodge-motel

MIDHOPESTONES
South Yorkshire

Ye Olde Mustard Pot ◆◆◆◆
Mortimer Road, Midhopestones,
Sheffield S36 4GW
T: (01226) 761 155

MILLINGTON
East Riding of Yorkshire

Laburnum Cottage ◆◆
Millington, York YO42 1TX
T: (01759) 303055

MUKER
North Yorkshire

Hylands ◆◆◆◆
Muker, Richmond, North
Yorkshire DL11 6QQ
T: (01748) 886003 &
07802 758198
E: jonesr3@btinternet.com

MYTHOLMROYD
West Yorkshire

Redacre Mill ◆◆◆◆
Redacre, Mytholmroyd, Hebden
Bridge, West Yorkshire HX7 5DQ
T: (01422) 885563 & 0771 340
3563
F: (01422) 885563
E: peters@redacremill.freeserve.
co.uk
I: www.redacremill.freeserve.
co.uk

NAWTON
North Yorkshire

Nawton Grange ◆◆◆
Gale Lane, Nawton, York
YO62 7SD
T: (01439) 771146
E. chrisbaxter@themall.co.uk

NEW WALTHAM
North East Lincolnshire

Peaks Top Farm ◆◆◆
Hewitts Avenue, New Waltham,
Grimsby, North East Lincolnshire
DN36 4RS
T: (01472) 812941
F: (01472) 812941
E: lmclayton@tinyworld.co.uk

NEWBY WISKE
North Yorkshire

Well House ◆◆◆◆
Newby Wiske, Northallerton,
North Yorkshire DL7 9EX
T: (01609) 772253
F: (01609) 772253

NEWMILLERDAM
West Yorkshire

On the Edge ◆◆◆
671 Barnsley Road,
Newmillerdam, Wakefield, West
Yorkshire WF2 6QG
T: (01924) 253310
E: ontheedge@lineone.net
I: www.
ontheedgenewmillerdam.co.uk

NEWTON-ON-OUSE
North Yorkshire

Village Farm Holidays ◆◆◆◆
Cherry Tree Avenue, Newton-
on-Ouse, York YO30 2BN
T: (01347) 848064
F: (01347) 848065
E: vfholidays@cs.com
I: www.yorkshirenet.
co.uk/stayat/villagefarm

NEWTON-ON-RAWCLIFFE
North Yorkshire

Elm House Farm ◆◆◆◆
Newton-on-Rawcliffe, Pickering,
North Yorkshire YO18 8QA
T: (01751) 473223

Swan Cottage ◆◆◆
Newton-on-Rawcliffe, Pickering,
North Yorkshire YO18 8QA
T: (01751) 472502

NORMANTON
West Yorkshire
The Village Motel ♦♦♦
Castleford Road, Normanton,
West Yorkshire WF6 1QY
T: (01924) 897171
F: (01924) 896009

NORTH CAVE
East Riding of Yorkshire
Albion House ♦♦
18 Westgate, North Cave,
Brough, North Humberside
HU15 2NJ
T: (01430) 422958
E: caroline@ccockin.freeserve.
co.uk

NORTH FERRIBY
East Riding of Yorkshire
B & B @103 ♦♦♦
103 Ferriby High Road, North
Ferriby, North Humberside
HU14 3LA
T: (01482) 633637 &
07808 387651
E: info@bnb103.co.uk
I: www.bnb103.co.uk

NORTH NEWBALD
North Yorkshire
The Gnu Inn ♦♦♦
The Green, North Newbald, York
YO43 4SA
T: (01430) 827799

NORTHALLERTON
North Yorkshire
Alverton Guest House ♦♦♦
26 South Parade, Northallerton,
North Yorkshire DL7 8SG
T: (01609) 776207
F: (01609) 776207

The Conifers ♦♦♦
18 Almond Grove, Northallerton,
North Yorkshire DL7 8RQ
T: (01609) 773361
E: ericpennypop@aol.com

Elmscott ♦♦♦♦
10 Hatfield Road, Northallerton,
North Yorkshire DL7 8QX
T: (01609) 760575
E: elmscott@freenet.co.uk
I: www.
elmscottbedandbreakfast.co.uk

Heyrose Farm ♦♦♦
Lovesome Hill, Northallerton,
North Yorkshire DL6 2PS
T: (01609) 881554
F: (01609) 881554
E: heyrosefarm@hotmail.com

Lovesome Hill Farm ♦♦♦♦
Lovesome Hill, Northallerton,
North Yorkshire DL6 2PB
T: (01609) 772311 & 774715
E: pearsonlhf@care4free.net
🏃

**Masham House Bed And
Breakfast ♦♦♦♦**
18 South Parade, Northallerton,
North Yorkshire DL7 8SG
T: (01609) 771541
E: jpbb@ukonline.co.uk

Porch House ♦♦♦♦
68 High Street, Northallerton,
North Yorkshire DL7 8EG
T: (01609) 779831
F: (01609) 778603

NORTON
North Yorkshire
Lynden ♦♦♦
165 Welham Road, Norton,
Malton, North Yorkshire
YO17 9DU
T: (01653) 694236

NORWOOD
North Yorkshire
The Old Primary ♦♦♦♦
Bland Hill, Norwood, Harrogate,
North Yorkshire HG3 1TB
T: (01943) 880472

NUNNINGTON
North Yorkshire
Sunley Court ♦♦♦
Nunnington, York YO62 5XQ
T: (01439) 748233
F: (01439) 748233

OAKWORTH
West Yorkshire
Railway Cottage ♦♦♦
59 Station Road, Oakworth,
Keighley, West Yorkshire
BD22 0DZ
T: (01535) 642693
E: railwaycottage@talk21.com

OLD MALTON
North Yorkshire
**The Wentworth Arms
Rating Applied For**
111 Town Street, Old Malton,
Malton, North Yorkshire
YO17 7HD
T: (01653) 692618
F: (01653) 600061
E: wentwortharms@btinternet.
com

OSMOTHERLEY
North Yorkshire
Oak Garth Farm ♦♦
North End, Osmotherley,
Northallerton, North Yorkshire
DL6 3BH
T: (01609) 883314

**Osmotherley Walking Shop
♦♦♦**
4 West End, Osmotherley,
Northallerton, North Yorkshire
DL6 3AA
T: (01609) 883818
E: walkingshop@osmotherley.
fsbusiness.co.uk
I: www.coast2coast.co.uk

Vane House ♦♦♦
11A North End, Osmotherley,
Northallerton, North Yorkshire
DL6 3BA
T: (01609) 883448 & 883406
F: (01609) 883448
I: www.coast2coast.
co.uk/vanehouse

OSSETT
West Yorkshire
Heath House ♦♦♦
Chancery Road, Ossett, West
Yorkshire WF5 9RZ
T: (01924) 260654 & 273098
F: (01924) 260654
E: jo.holland@amserve.net
I: www.heath-house.co.uk

Mews Hotel ♦♦♦♦
Dale Street, Ossett, West
Yorkshire WF5 9HN
T: (01924) 273982 &
07973 137547
F: (01924) 279389
E: enquiries@mews-hotel.co.uk
I: www.mews-hotel.co.uk

The Mill ♦♦
194-198 Dewsbury Road, Ossett,
West Yorkshire WF5 9QG
T: (01924) 277851 &
(01624) 267322
F: (01924) 277851

OTLEY
West Yorkshire
11 Newall Mount ♦♦♦
Otley, West Yorkshire LS21 2DY
T: (01943) 462898

Paddock Hill ♦♦♦
Norwood, Otley, West Yorkshire
LS21 2QU
T: (01943) 465977
E: chenbeaumont@connectfree.
co.uk

Scaife Hall Farm ♦♦♦♦
Blubberhouses, Otley, West
Yorkshire LS21 2PL
T: (01943) 880354
F: (01943) 880374
E: christine.a.ryder@btinternet.
com

**Wood Top Farm
Rating Applied For**
Off Norwood Edge, Lindley,
Otley, West Yorkshire LS21 2QS
T: (01943) 464010
F: (01943) 464010
E: mailwoodtop@aol.com

OUGHTERSHAW
North Yorkshire
Camm Farm ♦♦♦♦
Cam Houses, Oughtershaw,
Skipton, North Yorkshire
BD23 2JT
T: 07860 648045 & (0113) 271
1339
F: (0113) 277 9750

PATELEY BRIDGE
North Yorkshire
Bewerley Hall Farm ♦♦♦
Bewerley, Harrogate, North
Yorkshire HG3 5JA
T: (01423) 711636 & 0780 848
0417

Dale View ♦♦♦
Old Church Lane, Pateley Bridge,
Harrogate, North Yorkshire
HG3 5LY
T: (01423) 711506
F: (01423) 711506
E: bedandbreakfast@daleview.
com

Greengarth ♦♦♦
Greenwood Road, Pateley
Bridge, Harrogate, North
Yorkshire HG3 5LR
T: (01423) 711688
🏃

Knottside Farm ♦♦♦♦♦
The Knott, Pateley Bridge,
Harrogate, North Yorkshire
HG3 5DQ
T: (01423) 712927
F: (01423) 712927

Nidderdale Lodge Farm ♦♦♦
Fellbeck, Harrogate, North
Yorkshire HG3 5DR
T: (01423) 711677

North Pasture Farm ♦♦♦♦
Brimham Rocks, Summer Bridge,
Harrogate, North Yorkshire
HG3 4DW
T: (01423) 711470
F: (01423) 711470
I: www.yorkshirenet.
co.uk/stayat/northpasturefarm

Prospect House ♦♦♦
1 Millfield Street, Pateley Bridge,
Harrogate, North Yorkshire
HG3 5AX
T: (01423) 711167
F: (01423) 711591
E: writessc@supanet.com

PATRICK BROMPTON
North Yorkshire
Mill Close Farm ♦♦♦♦♦
Patrick Brompton, Bedale, North
Yorkshire DL8 1JY
T: (01677) 450257
F: (01677) 450585

PENISTONE
South Yorkshire
**Cubley Hall Freehouse Pub-
Restaurant-Hotel ♦♦♦♦**
Mortimer Road, Penistone,
Sheffield S36 9DF
T: (01226) 766086
F: (01226) 767335
E: cubley.hall@ukonline.co.uk

PICKERING
North Yorkshire
Barker Stakes Farm ♦♦♦
Lendales Lane, Pickering, North
Yorkshire YO18 8EE
T: (01751) 476759

Black Swan Hotel ♦♦♦
18 Birdgate, Pickering, North
Yorkshire YO18 7AL
T: (01751) 472286
F: (01751) 472928

**Bramwood Guest House
♦♦♦♦**
19 Hallgarth, Pickering, North
Yorkshire YO18 7AW
T: (01751) 474066

Bridge House ♦♦♦♦
8 Bridge Street, Pickering, North
Yorkshire YO18 8DT
T: (01751) 477234

**Burgate House Hotel &
Restaurant♦♦♦♦**
17 Burgate, Pickering, North
Yorkshire YO18 7AU
T: (01751) 473463
F: (01751) 473463
E: info@burgatehouse.co.uk
I: www.burgatehouse.co.uk

Burr Bank ♦♦♦♦♦
Cropton, Pickering, North
Yorkshire YO18 8HL
T: (01751) 417777 & 0776 884
2233
F: (01751) 417789
E: bandb@burrbank.com
I: www.burrbank.com

Cawthorne House ♦♦♦♦
42 Eastgate, Pickering, North
Yorkshire YO18 7DU
T: (01751) 477364 &
07818 273084

Clent House ◆◆◆
15 Burgate, Pickering, North
Yorkshire YO18 7AU
T: (01751) 477928 &
07960 243446
E: bb1315@swiftlink.pnc-uk.net
I: www.swiftlink.pnc-uk.
net/bb/1315.htm

Cottage Leas Country Hotel
◆◆◆◆
Nova Lane, Middleton, Pickering,
North Yorkshire YO18 8PN
T: (01751) 472129
F: (01751) 474930
E: cottageleas@aol.com

Eden House ◆◆◆◆
120 Eastgate, Pickering, North
Yorkshire YO18 7DW
T: (01751) 472289 & 476066
F: (01751) 476066
E: edenhouse@breathemail.net
I: www.edenhousebandb.co.uk

Fox and Hounds Country Inn
◆◆◆◆
Sinnington, York YO62 6SQ
T: (01751) 431577
F: (01751) 432791
E: foxhoundsinn@easynet.co.uk

Grindale House ◆◆◆◆
123 Eastgate, Pickering, North
Yorkshire YO18 7DW
T: (01751) 476636
F: (01751) 475727

Heathcote House ◆◆◆◆
100 Eastgate, Pickering, North
Yorkshire YO18 7DW
T: (01751) 476991
F: (01751) 476991
E: joanlovejoy@lineone.net

Munda Wanga ◆
14 Garden Way, Pickering, North
Yorkshire YO18 8BG
T: (01751) 473310

The Old Manse Guest House
◆◆◆◆
Middleton Road, Pickering,
North Yorkshire YO18 8AL
T: (01751) 476484
F: (01751) 477124
E: valerie-a-gardner@talk21.
com

Rains Farm ◆◆◆◆
Allerston, Pickering, North
Yorkshire YO18 7PQ
T: (01723) 859333
E: allan@rainsfarm.freeserve.
co.uk
I: www.rains-farm-holidays.
co.uk

Rose Folly ◆◆◆◆
112 Eastgate, Pickering, North
Yorkshire YO18 7DW
T: (01751) 475057
E: gail@rosefolly.freeserve.co.uk
I: www.rosefolly.freeserve.co.uk

Rosebank Bed & Breakfast
◆◆◆◆
61 Ruffa Lane, Pickering, North
Yorkshire YO18 7HN
T: (01751) 472531

Sunnyside ◆◆◆◆
Carr Lane, Middleton, Pickering,
North Yorkshire YO18 8PD
T: (01751) 476104
F: (01751) 476104

Vivers Mill ◆◆◆
Mill Lane, Pickering, North
Yorkshire YO18 8DJ
T: (01751) 473640
E: viversmill@talk21.com

POCKLEY
North Yorkshire
West View Cottage ◆◆◆◆
Pockley, York YO62 7TE
T: (01439) 770526

POCKLINGTON
East Riding of Yorkshire
Star Inn ◆◆◆
North Dalton, Driffield, East
Riding of Yorkshire YO25 9UX
T: (01377) 217688
F: (01377) 217791

POOL IN WHARFEDALE
West Yorkshire
Rawson Garth ◆◆◆
Pool Bank Farm, Pool in
Wharfedale, Otley, West
Yorkshire LS21 1EU
T: (0113) 284 3221
F: (0113) 284 3221

PRESTON
East Riding of Yorkshire
Little Weghill Farm ◆◆◆◆
Weghill Road, Preston, Hull
HU12 8SX
T: (01482) 897650 &
07941 368999
F: (01482) 897650

PUDSEY
West Yorkshire
Heatherlea House ◆◆◆
105 Littlemoor Road, Pudsey,
West Yorkshire LS28 8AP
T: (0113) 257 4397
E: heatherlea_pudsey.leeds@
excite.co.uk

Lynnwood House ◆◆◆
18 Alexandra Road, Uppermoor,
Pudsey, Leeds LS28 8BY
T: (0113) 257 1117

RASKELF
North Yorkshire
Old Black Bull Inn ◆◆◆
Raskelf, York, North Yorkshire
YO61 3LF
T: (01347) 821431
E: pjacksobbull@bizonline.co.uk

RASTRICK
West Yorkshire
Elder Lea House ◆◆◆◆◆
Clough Lane, Rastrick,
Brighouse, West Yorkshire
HD6 3QH
T: (01484) 717832 &
07721 046131
F: (01484) 717832
E: elderleahouse@amserve.net

RATHMELL
North Yorkshire
The Stables ◆◆◆◆
Field House, Rathmell, Settle,
North Yorkshire BD24 0LA
T: (01729) 840234
F: (01729) 840775
E: rosehyslop@easynet.co.uk

RAVENSCAR
North Yorkshire
Bide-a-While ◆◆◆
3 Loring Road, Ravenscar,
Scarborough, North Yorkshire
YO13 0LY
T: (01723) 870643
F: (01723) 871577

Cliff House ◆◆◆◆
Ravenscar, Scarborough, North
Yorkshire YO13 0LX
T: (01723) 870889
E: hodgson@cliffhouse.
fsbusiness.co.uk
I: www.clifftopstop.com

Smugglers Rock Country
House ◆◆◆
Staintondale Road, Ravenscar,
Scarborough, North Yorkshire
YO13 0ER
T: (01723) 870044
E: info@smugglersrock.co.uk
I: www.smugglersrock.co.uk

RAVENSWORTH
North Yorkshire
The Bay Horse Inn ◆◆◆
Ravensworth, Richmond, North
Yorkshire DL11 7ET
T: (01325) 718328

REETH
North Yorkshire
Arkle House ◆◆◆◆
Mill Lane, Reeth, Richmond,
North Yorkshire DL11 6SJ
T: (01748) 884815
E: info@arklehouse.com
I: www.arklehouse.com

Arkleside Hotel ◆◆◆◆
Reeth, Richmond, North
Yorkshire DL11 6SG
T: (01748) 884200
F: (01748) 884200
E: info@arklesidehotel.co.uk
I: www.arklesidehotel.co.uk

Black Bull Hotel ◆◆◆
High Row, Reeth, Richmond,
North Yorkshire DL11 6SZ
T: (01748) 884213
F: (01748) 884213
I: www.blackbull.co.uk

2 Bridge Terrace ◆◆◆
Reeth, Richmond, North
Yorkshire DL11 6TP
T: (01748) 884572
E: davidsizer@freenetname.
co.uk
I: coast2coast.
co.uk/2bridgeterrace

Buck Hotel ◆◆◆
Reeth, Richmond, North
Yorkshire DL11 6SW
T: (01748) 884210
F: (01748) 884802
E: enquiries@buckhotel.co.uk
I: www.buckhotel.co.uk

Elder Peak ◆◆◆
Arkengarthdale Road, Reeth,
Richmond, North Yorkshire
DL11 6QX
T: (01748) 884770

Hackney House ◆◆◆
Reeth, Richmond, North
Yorkshire DL11 6TW
T: (01748) 884302

Kernot Court ◆◆
Reeth, Richmond, North
Yorkshire DL11 6SF
T: (01748) 884662

Springfield House ◆◆◆◆
Quaker Close, Reeth, Richmond,
North Yorkshire DL11 6UY
T: (01748) 884634 &
(01794) 104 4048
E: springfield.house@
breathemail.net

REIGHTON
North Yorkshire
Reighton Hall
Rating Applied For
Church Hill, Reighton, Filey,
North Yorkshire YO14 9RX
T: (01723) 890601
F: (01723) 890260
E: dawn@reightonhall.com
I: www.reightonhall.com

RICCALL
North Yorkshire
South Newlands Farm ◆◆◆
Selby Road, Riccall, York
YO19 6QR
T: (01757) 248203
F: (01757) 249450
E: pswann3059@aol.com
I: www.yorkbandb.f9.co.uk

RICHMOND
North Yorkshire
The Buck Inn ◆◆
27-29 Newbiggin, Richmond,
North Yorkshire DL10 4DX
T: (01748) 822259 & 850141

Emmanuel Guest House ◆◆◆
41 Maison Dieu, Richmond,
North Yorkshire DL10 7AU
T: (01748) 823584 & 0585 272
2361
F: (01748) 821554

66 Frenchgate ◆◆◆
Richmond, North Yorkshire
DL10 7AG
T: (01748) 823421
E: Paul@66french.freeserve.
co.uk

Holmedale ◆◆◆
Dalton, Richmond, North
Yorkshire DL11 7HX
T: (01833) 621236
F: (01833) 621236
E: David@holmedale.
free-online.co.uk

27 Hurgill Road ◆◆
Richmond, North Yorkshire
DL10 4AR
T: (01748) 824092
F: (01748) 824092

Mount Pleasant Farm ◆◆◆◆
Whashton, Richmond, North
Yorkshire DL11 7JP
T: (01748) 822784
F: (01748) 822784
♿

Nunns Cottage ◆◆◆◆
5 Hurgill Road, Richmond, North
Yorkshire DL10 4AR
T: (01748) 822809
F: (01748) 822809
E: nunscottage@richmond.org.
uk
I: www.richmond.org.
uk/business/nunscottage

Pottergate Guest House ◆◆◆
4 Pottergate, Richmond, North
Yorkshire DL10 4AB
T: (01748) 823826

The Restaurant on the Green
◆◆◆
5-7 Bridge Street, Richmond,
North Yorkshire DL10 4RW
T: (01748) 826229
F: (01748) 826229
E: accom.bennett@talk21.com
I: www.coast2coast.
co.uk/restaurantonthegreen

Victoria House ◆◆◆
49 Maison Dieu, Richmond,
North Yorkshire DL10 7AU
T: (01748) 824830 &
07803 367276

West Cottage
Rating Applied For
Victoria Road, Richmond, North
Yorkshire DL10 4AS
T: (01748) 824046

West End Guest House ◆◆◆◆
45 Reeth Road, Richmond,
North Yorkshire DL10 4EX
T: (01748) 824783
E: westend@richmond.org
I: www.stayatwestend

Whashton Springs Farm
◆◆◆◆
(North Yorkshire), Richmond,
North Yorkshire DL11 7JS
T: (01748) 822884
F: (01748) 826285
E: whashton@turnbullg-f.
freeserve.co.uk
I: www.whashtonsprings.co.uk

Willance House Guesthouse
◆◆◆
24 Frenchgate, Richmond, North
Yorkshire DL10 7AG
T: (01748) 824467
F: (01748) 824467
E: willance@bun.com

Barn Close Farm ◆◆◆
Rievaulx, York YO62 5LH
T: (01439) 798321

Little Beck ◆◆◆◆
22 Low Moorgate, Rillington,
Malton, North Yorkshire
YO17 8JW
T: (01944) 758655 &
07761 237722
E: flinton@tinyworld.co.uk

Slate Rigg Farm ◆◆◆
Birthwaite Lane, Ripley,
Harrogate, North Yorkshire
HG3 3JQ
T: (01423) 770135

Bishopton Grove House ◆◆◆
Bishopton, Ripon, North
Yorkshire HG4 2QL
T: (01765) 600888
E: wimpress@bronco.co.uk

The Coopers ◆◆◆
36 College Road, Ripon, North
Yorkshire HG4 2HA
T: (01765) 603708
E: joe_cooper74@hotmail.com

Fremantle House ◆◆◆
35 North Road, Ripon, North
Yorkshire HG4 1JR
T: (01765) 605819
F: (01765) 601313
E: jcar105462@aol.com
I: www.riponforward.
homestead.com/freemantle.html

Mallard Grange ◆◆◆◆◆
Aldfield, Ripon, North Yorkshire
HG4 3BE
T: (01765) 620242 &
07720 295918
F: (01765) 620242
E: Mallard@Grange@
btinternet.com

Middle Ridge ◆◆◆◆
42 Mallorie Park Drive, Ripon,
North Yorkshire HG4 2QF
T: (01765) 690558
F: (01765) 690558
E: john@midrig.demon.co.uk

Moor End Farm ◆◆◆◆
Knaresborough Road,
Littlethorpe, Ripon, North
Yorkshire HG4 3LU
T: (01765) 677419
E: pspensley@ukonline.co.uk
I: www.yorkshirebandb.co.uk

River Side Guest House ◆◆◆
20-21 Iddesleigh Terrace,
Boroughbridge Road, Ripon,
North Yorkshire HG4 1QW
T: (01765) 603864 & 602707
F: (01765) 602707
E: christopher-pearson3@
virgin-net

St George's Court ◆◆◆◆
Old Home Farm, Grantley, Ripon,
North Yorkshire HG4 3EU
T: (01765) 620618
F: (01765) 620618
E: stgeorgescourt@bronco.co.uk

Sharow Cross House ◆◆◆◆
Dishforth Road, Sharow, Ripon,
North Yorkshire HG4 5BQ
T: (01765) 609866 & 0786 683
0741
E: sharowcrosshouse@
btinternet.com
I: www.sharowcrosshouse.com

Boathouse Bistro ◆◆◆
The Dock, Robin Hood's Bay,
Whitby, North Yorkshire
YO22 4SJ
T: (01947) 880099

Flask Inn ◆◆◆◆
Robin Hood's Bay, Whitby, North
Yorkshire YO22 4QH
T: (01947) 880305
F: (01947) 880592
E: flaskinn@aol.com
I: www.flaskinn.com

Flask Inn Travel Lodge ◆◆◆◆
Robin Hoods Bay, Fylingdales,
Whitby, North Yorkshire
YO22 4QH
T: (01947) 880692 & 880592
F: (01947) 880592
E: flaskinn@aol.com
I: www.flaskinn.com

Lee-Side ◆◆◆◆
Mount Pleasant South, Robin
Hood's Bay, Whitby, North
Yorkshire YO22 4RQ
T: (01947) 881143

Ravenswood Bed and Breakfast
◆◆◆
Ravenswood, Mount Pleasant
North, Robin Hood's Bay,
Whitby, North Yorkshire
YO22 4RE
T: (01947) 880690

Victoria Hotel ◆◆◆
Station Road, Robin Hood's Bay,
Whitby, North Yorkshire
YO22 4RL
T: (01947) 880205
F: (01947) 881170

The Crown at Roecliffe ◆◆◆
Roecliffe, York YO51 9LY
T: (01423) 322578
F: (01423) 324060
E: crownroecliffe@btinternet.
com

Bridge End ◆◆
159 Chantry Road, Romanby,
Northallerton, North Yorkshire
DL7 8JJ
T: (01609) 772655 & 07831 388
112
F: (01609) 772655

The Orange Tree ◆◆◆
Rosedale East, Pickering, North
Yorkshire YO18 8RH
T: (01751) 417219
F: (01751) 417219
E: relax@theorangetree.com
I: www.theorangetree.com

Sevenford House ◆◆◆◆
Rosedale Abbey, Pickering,
North Yorkshire YO18 8SE
T: (01751) 417283
F: (01751) 417505
E: sevenford@aol.com

Fernlea Hotel ◆◆◆
74 Gerard Road, Moorgate,
Rotherham, South Yorkshire
S60 2PW
T: (01709) 830884
F: (01709) 305951

Fitzwilliam Arms Hotel ◆◆◆
Taylors Lane, Parkgate,
Rotherham, South Yorkshire
S62 6EE
T: (01709) 522744
F: (01709) 710110

Phoenix Hotel ◆◆
1 College Road, Rotherham,
South Yorkshire S60 1EY
T: (01709) 364611 & 511121
F: (01709) 511121

Eastgate Farm Cottage ◆◆◆
Rudston, Driffield, East Riding of
Yorkshire YO25 0UX
T: (01262) 420150 &
07710 161897
F: (01262) 420150
E: ebrudston@aol.com
I: www.eastgatefarmcottage.
com

Cliffemount Hotel ◆◆◆◆
Runswick Bay, Saltburn-by-the-
Sea, Cleveland TS13 5HU
T: (01947) 840103
F: (01947) 841025
E: cliffemount@runswickbay.
fsnet.co.uk
I: www.cliffemounthotel.co.uk

Cockpit House ◆◆
The Old Village (Nr Whitby),
Runswick Bay, Saltburn-by-the-
Sea, Cleveland TS13 5HU
T: (01947) 840504 & 603047

Ellerby Hotel ◆◆◆◆
Ellerby, Saltburn-by-the-Sea,
Cleveland YO21 2DE
T: (01947) 840342
F: (01947) 841221
E: relax@ellerbyhotel.co.uk
I: www.ellerbyhotel.co.uk

The Firs ◆◆◆◆
26 Hinderwell Lane, Runswick
Bay, Nr Whitby TS13 5HR
T: (01947) 840433
F: (01947) 841616
E: mandy.shackleton@talk21.
com
I: www.the-firs.co.uk

Newgate Foot Farm ◆◆◆◆
Newgate Foot, Saltersgate,
Pickering, North Yorkshire
YO18 7NR
T: (01751) 460215
F: (01751) 460215

Church Farm ◆◆◆◆
Scackleton, York YO62 4NB
T: (01653) 628403
F: (01653) 628403
E: churchfarmhol@yahoo.com

Scagglethorpe Manor ◆◆◆◆
Main Street, Scagglethorpe,
Malton, North Yorkshire
YO17 8DT
T: (01944) 758909
F: (01944) 758909

Holly Croft ◆◆◆◆◆
28 Station Road, Scalby,
Scarborough, North Yorkshire
YO13 0QA
T: (01723) 375376
F: (01723) 360563

Aartswood Guest House ◆◆
27 - 29 Trafalgar Square,
Scarborough, North Yorkshire
YO12 7PZ
T: (01723) 360689
F: (01723) 381849

Abbey Court Hotel ◆◆◆
19 West Street, South Cliff,
Scarborough, North Yorkshire
YO11 2QR
T: (01723) 360659

Adene Hotel ◆◆◆
39 Esplanade Road,
Scarborough, North Yorkshire
YO11 2AT
T: (01723) 373658

Admiral
Rating Applied For
13 West Square, Scarborough,
North Yorkshire YO11 1TW
T: (01723) 375084 & 500321
F: (01723) 375084

Airedale Guest House ◆◆◆
23 Trafalgar Square,
Scarborough, North Yorkshire
YO12 7PZ
T: (01723) 366809
E: shaunatairedale@aol.com

Aldon Hotel ◆◆◆◆
120-122 Columbus Ravine,
Scarborough, North Yorkshire
YO12 7QZ
T: (01723) 372198

The Alexander Hotel ◆◆◆◆
33 Burniston Road,
Scarborough, North Yorkshire
YO11 6PG
T: (01723) 363178
F: (01723) 354821
E: alex@atesto.freeserve.co.uk
I: www.spiderweb.
co.uk/thealexanderhotel

Hotel Almar ◆◆◆
116 Columbus Ravine,
Scarborough, North Yorkshire
YO12 7QZ
T: (01723) 372887
F: (01723) 372887

**The Anchor Guest
Accommodation** ◆◆
61 Northstead Manor Drive,
Scarborough, North Yorkshire
YO12 6AF
T: (01723) 364518
F: (01723) 364518
E: theanchor@hotmail.com

Arlington Private Hotel ◆◆◆
42 West Street, South Cliff,
Scarborough, North Yorkshire
YO11 2QP
T: (01723) 503600
I: www.s-h.a.dipcon.co.uk./

Arran Licensed Hotel ◆◆◆
114 North Marine Road,
Scarborough, North Yorkshire
YO12 7JA
T: (01723) 364692

Atlanta Hotel ◆◆◆
62 Coloumbus Ravine,
Scarborough, North Yorkshire
YO12 7QU
T: (01723) 360996
F: (01723) 350322
E: atlanta62@aol.com
I: www.
atlantahotelscarborough.co.uk

Beaches Private Hotel ◆◆◆
167 Columbus Ravine,
Scarborough, North Yorkshire
YO12 7QZ
T: (01723) 374587

Boston Hotel ◆◆◆
1-2 Blenheim Terrace, North
Bay, Scarborough, North
Yorkshire YO12 7HF
T: (01723) 360296 & 362226
F: (01723) 353838
E: suzanne@whitton@
bostonhotel.freeserve.co.uk
I: www.200k.
com/ta/bostonhotel

Brincliffe Edge Hotel ◆◆◆
105 Queens Parade,
Scarborough, North Yorkshire
YO12 7HY
T: (01723) 364834
E: brincliffeedgehotel@hotmail.
com
I: www.brincliffeedgehotel.co.uk

Hotel Catania ◆◆
141 Queens Parade,
Scarborough, North Yorkshire
YO12 7HU
T: (01723) 364516
F: (01723) 372640
E: hotelcatania@aol.co.uk

Cavendish Private Hotel
◆◆◆◆
53 Esplanade Road, Southcliff,
Scarborough, North Yorkshire
YO11 2AT
T: (01723) 362108 &
07785 726236
E: cavendishhotel@hotmail.com
I: www.s-h.a.dircon.co.uk

Chessington Hotel ◆◆◆
The Crescent, Scarborough,
North Yorkshire YO11 2PP
T: (01723) 365207
F: (01723) 375206

Cliffside Hotel ◆◆◆
79-81 Queens Parade,
Scarborough, North Yorkshire
YO12 7HT
T: (01723) 361087
F: (01723) 366472
E: cliffside@fsmail.net
I: www.yorkshirecoast.
co.uk/cliffside

Cordelia Hotel ◆◆◆
51 Esplanade Road, South Cliff,
Scarborough, North Yorkshire
YO11 2AT
T: (01723) 363393
F: (01723) 363393

Earlsmere Hotel ◆◆◆◆
5 Belvedere Road, South Cliff,
Scarborough, North Yorkshire
YO11 2UU
T: (01723) 361340 &
07721 925188
F: (01723) 350924

Empire Hotel ◆◆
39 Albermarle Crescent,
Scarborough, North Yorkshire
YO11 1XX
T: (01723) 373564

Falcon Inn ◆◆◆
Whitby Road, Cloughton,
Scarborough, North Yorkshire
YO13 0DY
T: (01723) 870717

Gordon Hotel ◆◆◆◆
Ryndleside, Scarborough, North
Yorkshire YO12 6AD
T: (01723) 362177
E: sales@gordonhotel.co.uk
I: www.gordonhotel.co.uk

**The Grand Hotel
Rating Applied For**
St Nicholas Cliff, Scarborough,
North Yorkshire YO11 2ET
T: (01723) 375371 & 376205
F: (01723) 378518
E: sales@scarboro.
grandhotelgroup.co.uk
I: www.grandhotelgroup.co.uk

Granville Lodge Hotel ◆◆◆◆
Belmont Road, Scarborough,
North Yorkshire YO11 2AA
T: (01723) 367668
F: (01723) 363089
E: granville@scarborough.co.uk
I: www.granville.scarborough.
co.uk

Greno Seafront Hotel ◆◆
25 Blenheim Terrace, Queens
Parade, Scarborough, North
Yorkshire YO12 7HD
T: (01723) 375705
F: (01723) 355512

The Gresham Hotel ◆◆◆
18 Lowdale Avenue, Northstead,
Scarborough, North Yorkshire
YO12 6JW
T: (01723) 372117
F: (01723) 372117
E: karen.robinson3@tesco.net
I: www.thegreshamhotel.co.uk

Harcourt Hotel ◆◆◆
45 Esplanade, Scarborough,
North Yorkshire YO11 2AY
T: (01723) 373930
E: harcourthotel@
netscapeonline.co.uk

Harmony Country Lodge
◆◆◆◆
80 Limestone Road, Burniston,
Scarborough, North Yorkshire
YO13 0DG
T: (01723) 870276 &
07967 157689
F: (01723) 870276
E: harmonylodge@cwcom.net
I: www.spiderweb.
co.uk/Harmony

Harmony Guest House ◆◆◆
13 Princess Royal Terrace, South
Cliff, Scarborough, North
Yorkshire YO11 2RP
T: (01723) 373562
E: harmonyguesthouse@
hotmail.com

Headlands Hotel ◆◆◆
Weydale Avenue, Scarborough,
North Yorkshire YO12 6AX
T: (01723) 373717
F: (01723) 373717

Hotel Helaina ◆◆◆
14 Blenheim Terrace,
Scarborough, North Yorkshire
YO12 7HF
T: (01723) 375191

Hillcrest Private Hotel ◆◆◆◆
2 Peasholm Avenue,
Scarborough, North Yorkshire
YO12 7NE
T: (01723) 361981
E: peacock@hillcresthotel.fsnet.
co.uk
I: www.hillcresthotel.fsnet.co.uk

Howdale Hotel ◆◆◆
121 Queens Parade,
Scarborough, North Yorkshire
YO12 7HU
T: (01723) 372696 &
(01771) 8761864
F: (01723) 372696
E: maria_keith_howdalehotel@
yahoo.co.uk

Killerby Cottage Farm ◆◆◆◆
Killerby Lane, Cayton,
Scarborough, North Yorkshire
YO11 3TP
T: (01723) 581236
F: (01723) 585465
E: val@green-glass.demon.co.uk
I: www.yorkshire.co.uk/valgreen

La Baia Hotel ◆◆◆◆
24 Blenheim Terrace,
Scarborough, North Yorkshire
YO12 7HD
T: (01723) 370780

Langsett Hotel ◆◆◆
108 Columbus Ravine,
Scarborough, North Yorkshire
YO12 7QZ
T: (01723) 372094
F: (01723) 372094
I: www.s-h-a.dircon.co.uk

Lonsdale Villa Hotel ◆◆◆◆
Lonsdale Road, South Cliff,
Scarborough, North Yorkshire
YO11 2QY
T: (01723) 363383

Lyncris Manor Hotel ◆◆◆
45 Northstead Manor Drive,
Scarborough, North Yorkshire
YO12 6AF
T: (01723) 361052
E: lyncris@manorhotel.fsnet.
co.uk
I: www.manorhotel.fsnet.co.uk

Lysander Hotel ◆◆◆
22 Weydale Avenue,
Scarborough, North Yorkshire
YO12 6AX
T: (01723) 373369 &
07855 294517
E: joy-harry@lysanderhotel.
freeserve.co.uk
I: www.lysanderhotel.freeserve.
co.uk

Maynard Hotel ◆◆◆
16 Esplanade Gardens, South
Cliff, Scarborough, North
Yorkshire YO11 2AW
T: (01723) 372289

Moorings ◆◆◆◆
3 Burniston Road, Scarborough,
North Yorkshire YO12 6PG
T: (01723) 373786
F: (01723) 364276
I: www.s-h-a.dircon.
co.uk/moorings

Moseley Lodge Private Hotel
◆◆◆◆
26 Avenue Victoria, South Cliff,
Scarborough, North Yorkshire
YO11 2QT
T: (01723) 360564
F: (01723) 363088
I: www.yorkshirenet.
co.uk/moseleylodge

Mount House Hotel ◆◆◆◆
33 Trinity Road, South Cliff,
Scarborough, North Yorkshire
YO11 2TD
T: (01723) 362967
E: bookings@
mounthouse-hotel.co.uk
I: www.mounthouse-hotel.co.uk

**Mountview Private Hotel
(Non-Smoking)** ◆◆◆
32 West Street, South Cliff,
Scarborough, North Yorkshire
YO11 2QP
T: (01723) 500608
F: (01723) 501385
E: stay@mountview-hotel.co.uk
I: www.mountview-hotel.co.uk

Norbreck Hotel ◆◆◆
Castle Road, Scarborough, North
Yorkshire YO11 1HY
T: (01723) 366607
F: (01723) 500984

The Old Mill Hotel ♦♦♦
Mill Street, Scarborough, North Yorkshire YO11 1SZ
T: (01723) 372735
F: (01723) 377190
E: info@windmill-hotel.co.uk
I: www.windmill-hotel.co.uk

Parmelia Hotel ♦♦♦
17 West Street, Southcliff, Scarborough, North Yorkshire YO11 2QN
T: (01723) 361914
E: parmeliahotel@btinternet.com
I: parmeliahotel.co.uk

Peasholm Park Hotel ♦♦♦
21-23 Victoria Park, Columbus Ravine, Scarborough, North Yorkshire YO12 7TS
T: (01723) 375580 & 500954
E: peasholm.park.hote@amserve.net

Perry's Court ♦♦♦♦
1 & 2 Rutland Terrace, Queen's Parade, Scarborough, North Yorkshire YO12 7JB
T: (01723) 373768
F: (01723) 353274
E: john@perryscourthotel.fsnet.co.uk
I: www.perryscourthotel.co.uk

Philamon ♦♦♦
108 North Marine Road, Scarborough, North Yorkshire YO12 7JA
T: (01723) 373107 & 0771 320 6194

Philmore Hotel ♦♦♦♦
126 Columbus Ravine, Scarborough, North Yorkshire YO12 7QZ
T: (01723) 361516

The Phoenix ♦♦♦
157 Columbus Ravine, Scarborough, North Yorkshire YO12 7QZ
T: (01723) 368319
F: (01723) 368319

Powy's Lodge ♦♦♦♦
2 Westbourne Road, Scarborough, North Yorkshire YO11 2SP
T: (01723) 374019

Princess Court Guest House ♦♦♦
11 Princess Royal Terrace, Scarborough, North Yorkshire YO11 2RP
T: (01723) 501922
E: andy@princesscourt.co.uk
I: www.princesscourt.co.uk

Raincliffe Hotel ♦♦♦
21 Valley Road, Scarborough, North Yorkshire YO11 2LY
T: (01723) 373541
E: enquiries@raincliffehotel.co.uk
I: www.raincliffehotel.co.uk

Rex Hotel ♦♦
9 Crown Crescent, South Cliff, Scarborough, North Yorkshire YO11 2BJ
T: (01723) 373297 & 07771 697023
F: (01723) 373297
E: ibstewart@talk21.com

Rivelyn Hotel ♦♦
1-4 Crown Crescent, South Cliff, Scarborough, North Yorkshire YO11 2BJ
T: (01723) 361248
F: (01723) 361248

Riviera Hotel ♦♦♦
St Nicholas Cliff, Scarborough, North Yorkshire YO11 2ES
T: (01723) 372277

Rose Dene ♦♦♦
106 Columbus Ravine, Scarborough, North Yorkshire YO12 7QZ
T: (01723) 374252
F: (01723) 507356
I: www.rosedenehotel.co.uk

Russell Hotel
Rating Applied For
22 Ryndleside, Scarborough, North Yorkshire YO12 6AD
T: (01723) 365453
E: russellhotel.scarb@tinyworld.co.uk

St Michael's Hotel ♦♦♦
27 Blenheim Terrace, Scarborough, North Yorkshire YO12 7HD
T: (01723) 374631
E: v.rennie@stmichaels27.freeserve.co.uk

Selomar Hotel ♦♦♦♦
23 Blenheim Terrace, Scarborough, North Yorkshire YO12 7HD
T: (01723) 364964

Sylvern Hotel ♦♦♦
25 New Queen Street, Scarborough, North Yorkshire YO12 7HJ
T: (01723) 360952
E: sylvernhotel@aol.com
I: www.smoothhound.co.uk/hotels/sylvern.html

The Terrace Hotel ♦♦
69 Westborough, Scarborough, North Yorkshire YO11 1TS
T: (01723) 374937
E: theterracehotel@btinternet.com

Victoria Lodge
Rating Applied For
19 Avenue Victoria, South Cliff, Scarborough, North Yorkshire YO11 2QS
T: (01723) 370906

Victoria Seaview Hotel ♦♦♦♦
125 Queen's Parade, Scarborough, North Yorkshire YO12 7HY
T: (01723) 362164
E: victoria-seaview-hotel@tinyworld.co.uk

Villa Marina ♦♦♦♦
59 Northstead Manor Drive, Scarborough, North Yorkshire YO12 6AF
T: (01723) 361088

The Warren Hotel ♦♦♦
34 Princess Street, Scarborough, North Yorkshire YO11 1QR
T: (01723) 367790

Wharncliffe Hotel ♦♦♦♦
26 Blenheim Terrace, Scarborough, North Yorkshire YO12 7HD
T: (01723) 374635
F: (01723) 374635
E: wharncliffe.hotel@virgin.net
I: freespace.virgin.net/wharncliffe.hotel

The Whiteley Hotel ♦♦♦♦
99-101 Queens Parade, Scarborough, North Yorkshire YO12 7HY
T: (01723) 373514
F: (01723) 373007
E: Whiteley_Hotel@compuserve.com
I: www.s-h-a.dircon.co.uk/thewhiteleyhotel.htm

SCAWBY
North Lincolnshire

The Old School ♦♦♦♦
Church Street, Scawby, Brigg, North Lincolnshire DN20 9AH
T: (01652) 654239

Olivers ♦♦♦
Church Street, Scawby, Brigg, North Lincolnshire DN20 9AM
T: (01652) 650446
E: eileen_harrison@lineone.net

SCHOLES
West Yorkshire

24 The Avenue ♦♦♦
Arthursdale, Scholes, Leeds LS15 4AS
T: (0113) 273 0289
E: ian.mann@virgin.net

The Willows ♦♦♦
Scholes Moor Road, Scholes, Holmfirth, Huddersfield HD9 1SJ
T: (01484) 684231

The Willows ♦♦♦
Scholes Moor Road, Scholes, Holmfirth, Huddersfield HD9 1SJ
T: (01484) 684231

SCOTCH CORNER
North Yorkshire

Vintage Hotel ♦♦♦
Scotch Corner, Richmond, North Yorkshire DL10 6NP
T: (01748) 824424 & 822961
F: (01748) 826272

SCUNTHORPE
North Lincolnshire

Beverley Hotel ♦♦♦
55 Old Brumby Street, Scunthorpe, South Humberside DN16 2AJ
T: (01724) 282212
F: (01724) 270422

The Downs Guest House ♦♦♦
33 Deyne Avenue, Scunthorpe, South Humberside DN15 7PZ
T: (01724) 850710
F: (01724) 330928
I: www.thedownsguesthouse.co.uk

Dragonby Hotel
Rating Applied For
Winterton Road, Scunthorpe, South Humberside DN15 OBQ
T: (01724) 872101
F: (01724) 872101

Elm Field ♦♦
22 Deyne Avenue, Scunthorpe, South Humberside DN15 7PZ
T: (01724) 869306

Kirks Korner ♦♦
12 Scotter Road, Scunthorpe, South Humberside DN15 8DR
T: (01724) 855344 & 281637
E: paul.kirk1@ntlworld.com

Larchwood Hotel ♦♦
1-5 Shelford Street, off Mary Street, Scunthorpe, South Humberside DN15 6NU
T: (01724) 864712
F: (01724) 864712
I: www.thelarchwoodhotel.co.uk

Normanby Hotel ♦♦♦
9-11 Normanby Road, Scunthorpe, South Humberside DN15 6AR
T: (01724) 289982 & 341421

SELBY
North Yorkshire

Hazeldene Guest House ♦♦
34 Brook Street, Doncaster Road, Selby, North Yorkshire YO8 4AR
T: (01757) 704809
F: (01757) 709300
E: selbystay@breathe.com
I: www.hazeldene-selby.co.uk

SETTLE
North Yorkshire

Arbutus Guest House ♦♦♦♦
Riverside, Clapham, Lancaster LA2 8DS
T: (01524) 251240
F: (01524) 251197
E: info@arbutus.co.uk
I: www.arbutus.co.uk

Golden Lion Hotel ♦♦♦♦
Duke Street, Settle, North Yorkshire BD24 9DU
T: (01729) 822203
F: (01729) 824103
E: bookings@goldenlion.yorks.net
I: www.yorkshirenet.co.uk/stayat/goldenlion

Husbands Barn ♦♦♦♦
Stainforth, Settle, North Yorkshire BD24 9PB
T: (01729) 822240
F: (01729) 822240
I: www.husbands.force9.co.uk

Mainsfield ♦♦♦♦
Stackhouse Lane, Giggleswick, Settle, North Yorkshire BD24 ODL
T: (01729) 823549 & 07790 379247

Maypole Inn ♦♦♦
Maypole Green, Main Street, Long Preston, Skipton, North Yorkshire BD23 4PH
T: (01729) 840219
E: landlord@maypole.co.uk
I: www.maypole.co.uk

Oast Guest House ♦♦♦
5 Pen-Y-Ghent View, Settle, North Yorkshire BD24 9JJ
T: (01729) 822989
F: (01729) 822989
E: king@oast2000.freeserve.co.uk
I: www.yorkshirenet.co.uk/stayat/theoast

Ottawa ♦♦♦♦
Station Road, Giggleswick, Settle, North Yorkshire BD24 OAE
T: (01729) 822757

Penmar Court ◆◆◆◆
Duke Street, Settle, North
Yorkshire BD24 9AS
T: (01729) 823258
F: (01729) 823258
E: stay@penmarcourt.freeserve.
co.uk

Scar Close Farm ◆◆◆◆
Feizor, Austwick, Lancaster
LA2 8DF
T: (01729) 823496

Station House ◆◆◆
Settle, North Yorkshire
BD24 9AA
T: (01729) 822533
E: stationhouse@btinternet.
com
I: www.stationhouse.btinternet.
com

**Whitefriars Country Guest
House** ◆◆◆
Church Street, Settle, North
Yorkshire BD24 9JD
T: (01729) 823753
I: www.whitefriars-settle.co.uk

SEWERBY
East Riding of Yorkshire
The Poplars Motel ◆◆◆
45 Jewison Lane, Sewerby,
Bridlington, East Riding of
Yorkshire YO15 1DX
T: (01262) 677251
F: (01262) 677251

SHAROW
North Yorkshire
Half Moon Inn ◆◆◆
Sharow Lane, Sharow, Ripon,
North Yorkshire HG4 5BP
T: (01765) 600291
E: halfmoon@bronco.co.uk
I: www.ripon.
org/webads/halfmoon

SHEFFIELD
South Yorkshire
321 ◆◆◆
321 Psalter Lane, Brincliffe,
Sheffield, S11 8WA
T: (0114) 2555150
E: lynda321@hotmail.com

Abbey View House ◆◆◆
168 Prospect Road, Totley Rise,
Sheffield, S17 4HX
T: (0114) 235 1349

Anna's Bed and Breakfast ◆
981 Penistone Road,
Hillsborough, Sheffield, S6 2DH
T: (0114) 234 0108 &
0797 4660304
F: (0114) 234 0108

Ashford ◆◆◆
44 Westwick Crescent,
Beauchief, Sheffield, S8 7DH
T: (0114) 237 5900 & 0787 940
5335

Coniston Guest House ◆◆◆
90 Beechwood Road,
Hillsborough, Sheffield, S6 4LQ
T: (0114) 233 9680
F: (0114) 233 9680
E: conistonguest.freeuk.co.uk
I: www.conistonguest@freeuk.
co.uk

Etruria House Hotel ◆◆◆
91 Crookes Road, Broomhill,
Sheffield, S10 5BD
T: (0114) 266 2241 & 267 0853
F: (0114) 267 0853
E: etruria@waitrose.com

Gulliver's Bed And Breakfast
◆◆◆
167 Ecclesall Road South,
Sheffield, S11 9PN
T: (0114) 262 0729

Harvey House ◆◆◆◆
159 Dobcroft Road, Sheffield,
S7 2LT
T: (0114) 236 1018 &
07720 485946

Hillside ◆◆◆
28 Sunningdale Mount,
Ecclesall, Sheffield, S11 9HA
T: (0114) 2620833

Holme Lane Farm Private Hotel
◆◆◆◆
38 Halifax Road, Grenoside,
Sheffield S35 8PB
T: (0114) 246 8858
F: (0114) 246 8858

Ivory House Hotel ◆◆◆
34 Wostenholm Road, Sheffield,
S7 1LJ
T: (0114) 255 1853
F: (0114) 255 1578
E: ivoryhouse@fsmail.net

Lindrick Hotel ◆◆◆
226-230 Chippinghouse Road,
Sheffield, S7 1DR
T: (0114) 258 5041
F: (0114) 255 4758
E: reception@thelindrick.co.uk
I: www.thelindrick.co.uk

Lindum Hotel ◆◆◆
91 Montgomery Road, Nether
Edge, Sheffield, S7 1LP
T: (0114) 255 2356 &
0800 0352300
F: (0114) 249 4746
E: lindumhotel@freenetname.
co.uk

The Noose and Gibbet
Rating Applied For
97 Broughton Lane, Attercliffe,
Sheffield, South Yorkshire
S9 2DE
T: (0114) 261 7182

Parklands
Rating Applied For
113 Rustlings Road, Sheffield,
S11 7AB
T: (0114) 267 0692

Priory Lodge Hotel ◆◆
40 Wostenholm Road,
Netheredge, Sheffield, S7 1LJ
T: (0114) 258 4670 & 258 4030
F: (0114) 255 6672
I: www.priorylodgehotel.co.uk

Psalter House ◆◆◆◆
17 Clifford Road, Brincliffe,
Sheffield, S11 9AQ
T: (0114) 255 7758
F: (0114) 255 7758
E: psalterhouse@waitrose.com
I: www.smoothhound.
co.uk/hotels/psalter.html

Riverside Court Hotel ◆◆◆
4 Nursery Street, Sheffield,
S3 8GG
T: (0114) 273 1962 &
0800 0352228
F: (0114) 273 1962
E: enquiries@riversidecourt.
co.uk
I: www.riversidecourt.co.uk

The Rock Inn Hotel ◆◆◆◆
Cranemoor Road, Cranemoor,
Sheffield, South Yorkshire
S35 7AT
T: (0114) 288 3427 &
07778 386508
F: (0114) 288 3726
E: rmk@rockinn.co.uk
I: www.rockinn.co.uk

St Pellegrino ◆◆
2 Oak Park, Off Manchester
Road, Sheffield, S10 5DE
T: (0114) 268 1953 & 266 0151
F: (0114) 266 0151

Tyndale ◆◆◆
164 Millhouses Lane, Sheffield,
S7 2HE
T: (0114) 236 1660
F: (0114) 236 1660

SHELF
West Yorkshire
Duke of York Inn ◆◆◆
West Street, Shelf, Halifax, West
Yorkshire HL7 7LN
T: (01422) 202056
F: (01422) 206618
E: dukeofyork@england.com
I: www.dukeofyork.co.uk/

Rook Residence ◆◆◆
69 Shelf Hall Lane, Shelf, Halifax,
West Yorkshire HX3 7LT
T: (01274) 601586 &
0786 778602
F: (01274) 670179
E: rookbnb@btinternet.com

SHELLEY
West Yorkshire
Three Acres Inn and Restaurant
◆◆
Roydhouse, Shelley,
Huddersfield HD8 8LR
T: (01484) 602606
F: (01484) 608411
E: 3acres@globalnet.co.uk

SHERBURN
North Yorkshire
Cherry Tree Cottage ◆◆◆
37 St Hilda's Street, Sherburn,
Malton, North Yorkshire
YO17 8PG
T: (01944) 710851
E: Cherrybnb@aol.com
I: www.CherryBnB.co.uk

SHIBDEN
West Yorkshire
Ploughcroft Cottage ◆◆◆
53 Ploughcroft Lane, Shibden,
Halifax, West Yorkshire HX3 6TX
T: (01422) 341205
E: ploughcroft.cottage@
Care4free.net
I: www.ploughcroftcottage.co.uk

SHIPLEY
West Yorkshire
Beeties With Rooms ◆◆◆◆
7 Victoria Road, Saltaire Village,
Shipley, West Yorkshire
BD18 3LA
T: (01274) 581718 & 595988
F: (01274) 582118
E: maureen@beeties.co.uk
I: www.beeties.co.uk

Clifton Lodge ◆◆◆
75 Kirkgate, Shipley, West
Yorkshire BD18 3LU
T: (01274) 580509
F: (01274) 580343
E: j.e.foster@lineone.net

SILSDEN
West Yorkshire
Dalesbank Holiday Park ◆◆◆
Low Lane, Silsden, Keighley,
West Yorkshire BD20 9JH
T: (01535) 653321 & 656523

SINNINGTON
North Yorkshire
Green Lea ◆◆◆
Sinnington, York YO62 6SH
T: (01751) 432008

Sinnington Manor ◆◆◆◆
Sinnington, York YO62 6SN
T: (01751) 433296
F: (01751) 433296
E: charles.wilson@
sinningtonmanor.fsnet.co.uk

SKEEBY
North Yorkshire
The Old Chapel ◆◆◆◆
Richmond Road, Skeeby,
Richmond, North Yorkshire
DL10 5DR
T: (01748) 824170 & 0780 310
3871
E: hazel@theoldchapel.fsnet.
co.uk

SKIPSEA
East Riding of Yorkshire
The Grainary ◆◆◆
Skipsea Grange, Hornsea Road,
Skipsea, Driffield, North
Humberside YO25 8SY
T: (01262) 468745
F: (01262) 468840
E: francesdavies@btconnect.
com
I: www.the-grainary.co.uk

SKIPTON
North Yorkshire
Bourne House ◆◆◆
22 Upper Sackville Street,
Skipton, North Yorkshire
BD23 2EB
T: (01756) 792633
F: (01756) 701609
E: bournehouse@totalise.co.uk
I: www.
bournehouseguesthouse.co.uk

Craven Heifer Inn ◆◆◆
Grassington Road, Skipton,
North Yorkshire BD23 3LA
T: (01756) 792521 &
07767 476077
F: (01756) 794442
E: philandlynn@cravenheifer.
co.uk
I: www.cravenheifer.co.uk

Cravendale ◆◆◆
57 Keighley Road, Skipton,
North Yorkshire BD23 2LX
T: (01756) 795129 & 793866
F: (01756) 795129
E: cravendale@rapidial.co.uk
I: www.yorkshirenet.
co.uk/stayat/cravendale/
indexhtml

Dalesgate Lodge ◆◆◆◆
69 Gargrave Road, Skipton,
North Yorkshire BD23 1QN
T: (01756) 790672
E: dalesgatelodge@talk21.com

Napier's Restaurant ◆◆◆◆
Chapel Hill, Skipton, North
Yorkshire BD23 1NL
T: (01756) 799688
F: (01756) 798111
I: www.restaurant-skipton.co.uk

Skipton Park Guest'otel ◆◆◆
2 Salisbury Street, Skipton,
North Yorkshire BD23 1NQ
T: (01756) 700640
F: (01756) 700641
E: derekchurch@skiptonpark.
freeserve.co.uk
I: www.milford.
co.uk/go/skiptonpark.html

Spring Gardens Cottage
Rating Applicd For
20 Queens Street, Skipton, North
Yorkshire BD23 1HE
T: (01756) 790739

Tempest Arms ◆◆◆
Elslack, Skipton, North Yorkshire
BD23 3AY
T: (01282) 842450
F: (01282) 843331

SLAITHWAITE
West Yorkshire

Hey Leys Farm ◆◆◆◆
Marsden Lane, Cop Hill,
Slaithwaite, Huddersfield
HD7 5XA
T: (01484) 845404 &
07803 744499
F: (01484) 843188
I: www.yorkshireholidays.com

SLEDMERE
North Humberside

The Triton Inn ◆◆◆
Sledmere, Driffield, North
Humberside YO25 3XQ
I: (01377) 236644
E: thetritoninn@sledmere.
fsbusiness.co.uk

SLEIGHTS
North Yorkshire

The Lawns ◆◆◆◆◆
73 Carr Hill Lane, Sleights,
Whitby, North Yorkshire
YO21 1RS
T: (01947) 810310
F: (01947) 810310
E: lorton@onetel.net.uk

The Salmon Leap Hotel
Rating Applied For
6 Coach Road, Sleights, Whitby,
North Yorkshire YO22 5AA
T: (01947) 810233

SLINGSBY
North Yorkshire

Lowry's Restaurant and Guest House◆◆◆
Malton Road, Slingsby, York,
North Yorkshire YO62 4AF
T: (01653) 628417
F: (01653) 628417

SOUTH CAVE
East Riding of Yorkshire

Rudstone Walk Country Accommodation and Cottages ◆◆◆◆
South Cave, Brough, North
Humberside HU15 2AH
T: (01430) 422230
F: (01430) 424552
E: office@rudstone-walk.co.uk
I: www.rudstone-walk.co.uk

SOWERBY
North Yorkshire

Long Acre Bed and Breakfast ◆◆◆
Long Acre, 86A Topcliffe Road,
Sowerby, Thirsk, North Yorkshire
YO7 1RY
T: (01845) 522360

SOWERBY BRIDGE
West Yorkshire

Park Villa Guest House ◆◆◆
Bolton Brow, Sowerby Bridge,
West Yorkshire HX6 2BE
T: (01422) 832179

SPAUNTON
North Yorkshire

Holywell House ◆◆◆◆
Spaunton Bank Foot, Spaunton,
Appleton-le-Moors, York
YO62 6TR
T: (01751) 417624

STADDLEBRIDGE
North Yorkshire

Staddlebridge House ◆◆◆
Staddlebridge Farm,
Staddlebridge, Northallerton,
North Yorkshire DL6 3JF
T: (01609) 882264
E: staddlebridgehouse@
ntlworld.com

STAINFORTH
North Yorkshire

2 Bridge End Cottage ◆◆◆
Stainforth, Settle, North
Yorkshire BD24 9PG
T: (01729) 822149

STAINTONDALE
North Yorkshire

Island House ◆◆◆◆
Island Farm, Staintondale,
Scarborough, North Yorkshire
YO13 0ER
T: (01723) 870249
E: roryc@tinyworld.co.uk
I: www.islandhousefarm.co.uk

Wellington Lodge ◆◆◆◆
Staintondale, Scarborough,
North Yorkshire YO13 0EL
T: (01723) 871234
F: (01723) 871234
E: b&b@llamatreks.co.uk
I: www.llamatreks.co.uk

STAIRFOOT
South Yorkshire

The Old Coach House Guest House
Rating Applied For
255 Doncaster Road, Stairfoot,
Barnsley, South Yorkshire
S70 3RH
T: (01226) 290612

STAITHES
North Yorkshire

The Giardini Guest House ◆◆◆
Roxby Lane, Staithes, Saltburn-
by-the-Sea, Cleveland TS13 5DZ
T: (01947) 840572 & 841642
F: (01947) 841642

Springfields ◆◆◆
42 Staithes Lane, Staithes,
Saltburn-by-the-Sea, Cleveland
TS13 5AD
T: (01947) 841011

STAMFORD BRIDGE
East Riding of Yorkshire

High Catton Grange ◆◆◆
Stamford Bridge, York YO41 1EP
T: (01759) 371374
F: (01759) 371374

STANBURY
West Yorkshire

Ponden House ◆◆◆◆
Stanbury, Keighley, West
Yorkshire BD22 0HR
T: (01535) 644154
E: brenda.taylor@pondenhouse.
co.uk
I: www.pondenhouse.co.uk

STAPE
North Yorkshire

Grange Farm ◆◆◆◆
Stape, Pickering, North Yorkshire
YO18 8HZ
T: (01751) 473805
T: (01751) 477805
E: thelma_grange_farm@
yahoo.co.uk
I: www.smoothhound.
co.uk/hotels/grange.html

Rapers Farm ◆◆◆
Newtondale, Stape, Pickering,
North Yorkshire YO18 8HU
T: (01751) 476846
I: www.rapersfarm.co.uk

Rawcliffe House Farm ◆◆◆◆
Stape, Pickering, North Yorkshire
YO18 8JA
T: (01751) 473292
F: (01751) 473766
E: sheila@
yorkshireaccommodation.com
I: www.
yorkshireaccommodation.com

Seavy Slack ◆◆◆◆
Stape, Pickering, North Yorkshire
YO18 8HZ
T: (01751) 473131

STARBOTTON
North Yorkshire

Bushey Lodge Farm ◆◆◆◆
Starbotton, Skipton, North
Yorkshire BD23 5HY
T: (01756) 760424

STEARSBY
North Yorkshire

The Granary ◆◆◆◆
Stearsby, York YO61 4SA
T: (01347) 888652
F: (01347) 888652
E: robertturl@thegranary.org.uk

STOKESLEY
North Yorkshire

The Buck Inn Hotel ◆◆◆
Chopgate, Stokesley,
Middlesbrough, Cleveland
TS9 7JL
T: (01642) 778334 & 778205
T: (01642) 778205
E: buckinn@aol.com

Harker Hill Farm ◆◆◆
Harker Hill, Seamer, Stokesley,
Middlesbrough, Cleveland
TS9 5NF
T: (01642) 710431
T: (01642) 710431
E: harkerhill@freeuk.com
I: www.destination-england.
co.uk/harkerhill.html

STONEGRAVE
North Yorkshire

Manor Cottage Bed and Breakfast ◆◆◆◆
Manor Cottage, Stonegrave,
York YO62 4LJ
T: (01653) 628599
E: gideon.v@virgin.net
I: business.virgin.net/gideon.
v/index.html

STUDLEY ROGER
North Yorkshire

Downing House Farm ◆◆◆◆
Studley Roger, Ripon, North
Yorkshire HG4 3AY
T: (01765) 601014
F: (01765) 601014
E: dickhelen@supanet.com
I: www.downinghousefarm.
co.uk

SUTTON BANK
North Yorkshire

Greystones ◆◆◆
Sutton Bank, Thirsk, North
Yorkshire YO7 2HB
T: (01845) 597580 &
07980 138349

SUTTON-ON-THE-FOREST
North Yorkshire

Goose Farm ◆◆◆
Eastmoor, Sutton-on-the-
Forest, York YO61 1ET
T: (01347) 810577
T: (01347) 810577
E: stay@goosefarm.fsnet.co.uk
I: www.yorkshirenet.
co.uk/stayat/goosefarm

SWILLINGTON
West Yorkshire

Bridge Farm Hotel ◆◆◆
Wakefield Road, Swillington,
Leeds LS26 8PZ
T: (0113) 282 3718
F: (0113) 282 5135

TERRINGTON
North Yorkshire

Gate Farm ◆◆◆
Ganthorpe, Terrington, York
YO60 6QD
T: (01653) 648269
E: millgate001@aol.com

THIMBLEBY
North Yorkshire

Stonehaven ◆◆◆
Thimbleby, Northallerton, North
Yorkshire DL6 3PY
T: (01609) 883689

THIRSK
North Yorkshire

Fourways Guest House ◆◆
Town End, Thirsk, North
Yorkshire YO7 1PY
T: (01845) 522601
F: (01845) 522131
E: fourways@nyorks.fsbusiness.
co.uk

Kirkgate House Hotel ◆◆◆
35 Kirkgate, Thirsk, North
Yorkshire YO7 1PL
T: (01845) 525015 & 522181
F: (01845) 522181
E: kirkgate_hotel@hotmail.com
I: www.geocities.
com/kirkgate_hotel

Laburnum House ◆◆◆◆
31 Topcliffe Road, Thirsk, North
Yorkshire YO7 1RX
T: (01845) 524120

Lavender House ◆◆◆
27 Kirkgate, Thirsk, North
Yorkshire YO7 1PL
T: (01845) 522224
E: susie.dodds@btinternet.com
I: www.lavenderhouse.org

Lord Nelson Inn ♦♦♦
40/41 St James Green, Thirsk,
North Yorkshire YO7 1AQ
T: (01845) 522845 & 522845
F: (01845) 522845
E: cot@supanet.com

Plump Bank
Rating Applied For
Felixkirk Road, Thirsk, North
Yorkshire YO7 2EW
T: (01845) 522406

St James House ♦♦♦
36 St James Green, Thirsk, North
Yorkshire YO7 1AQ
T: (01845) 526565

Station House ♦♦
Station Road, Thirsk, North
Yorkshire YO7 4LS
T: (01845) 522063

Town Pasture Farm ♦♦♦
Boltby, Thirsk, North Yorkshire
YO7 2DY
T: (01845) 537298

THORALBY
North Yorkshire

Pen View ♦♦♦
Thoralby, Leyburn, North
Yorkshire DL8 3SU
T: (01969) 663319
F: (01969) 663319
E: audrey@penview.yorks.net
I: www.penview.yorks.net

THORNTON
West Yorkshire

Ann's Farmhouse ♦♦♦
New Farm, Thornton Road,
Thornton, Bradford, West
Yorkshire BD13 3QE
T: (01274) 833214 &
07974 119328

THORNTON DALE
North Yorkshire

Banavie ♦♦♦♦
Roxby Road, Thornton Dale,
Pickering, North Yorkshire
YO18 7SX
T: (01751) 474616 &
07803 098604
E: ella@banavie.fsbusiness.co.uk
I: www.smoothhound.co.uk/

Bridgefoot Guest House ♦♦♦
Thornton Dale, Pickering, North
Yorkshire YO18 7RR
T: (01751) 474749

The Buck Hotel ♦♦♦
Chestnut Avenue, Thornton
Dale, Pickering, North Yorkshire
YO18 7RW
T: (01751) 474212
F: (01751) 474212

Hall Farm ♦♦♦
Maltongate, Thornton Dale,
Pickering, North Yorkshire
YO18 7SA
T: (01751) 475526
E: hallfarmholidays@amserve.
net

Nabgate ♦♦♦♦
Wilton Road, Thornton Dale,
Pickering, North Yorkshire
YO18 7QP
T: (01751) 474279 &
07703 804859

New Inn ♦♦♦♦
Maltongate, Thornton Dale,
Pickering, North Yorkshire
YO18 7LF
T: (01751) 474226
F: (01751) 477715
E: newinntld@aol.com

The Old Granary Bed and
Breakfast ♦♦♦♦
Top Bridge Farm, Thornton Dale,
Pickering, North Yorkshire
YO18 7RA
T: (01751) 477217 &
07775 617107

Tangalwood ♦♦♦
Roxby Road, Thornton Dale,
Pickering, North Yorkshire
YO18 7SX
T: (01751) 474688

THORNTON RUST
North Yorkshire

Fellside ♦♦♦♦
Thornton Rust, Leyburn, North
Yorkshire DL8 3AP
T: (01969) 663504
F: (01969) 663965
E: harvey@plwmp.freeserve.
co.uk
I: www.wensleydale.
org/accommodation/fellside

THORPE
North Yorkshire

Langerton House Farm ♦♦♦
Cracoe, Thorpe Lane, Thorpe,
Skipton, North Yorkshire
BD23 5HN
T: (01756) 730260

THWAITE
North Yorkshire

Kearton Country Hotel ♦♦♦
Thwaite, Richmond, North
Yorkshire DL11 6DR
T: (01748) 886277
F: (01748) 886590
E: jdanton@aol.com
I: www.keartoncountryhotel.
co.uk

TODMORDEN
West Yorkshire

Cherry Tree Cottage ♦♦♦♦
Woodhouse Road, Todmorden,
Lancashire OL14 5RJ
T: (01706) 817492

Watty Farm ♦♦♦
Watty Lane, Todmorden,
Lancashire OL14 7JQ
T: (01706) 818531
F: (01706) 818531

Woodleigh Hall ♦♦♦♦
Ewood Lane, Todmorden,
Lancashire OL14 7DF
T: (01706) 814664 & 810788
F: (01706) 810673

TOLLERTON
North Yorkshire

Bungalow Farm ♦♦♦
Warehills Lane, Tollerton, York
YO61 1RG
T: (01347) 838732

TRIANGLE
West Yorkshire

The Dene ♦♦♦♦
Triangle, Sowerby Bridge, West
Yorkshire HX6 3EA
T: (01422) 823562
E: noble@thedene-triangle.
freeserve.co.uk

ULCEBY
North Lincolnshire

Gillingham Court ♦♦♦♦
Spruce Lane, Ulceby, South
Humberside DN39 6UL
T: (01469) 588427

UPPER GREETLAND
West Yorkshire

Crawstone Knowl Farm ♦♦♦
Rochdale Road, Upper
Greetland, Halifax, West
Yorkshire HX4 8PX
T: (01422) 370470

WADSWORTH
West Yorkshire

Hare & Hounds ♦♦♦
Billy Lane, Wadsworth, Hebden
Bridge, West Yorkshire HX7 8TN
T: (01422) 842671
I: www.hare.and.hounds.
connectfree.co.uk

WALSDEN
West Yorkshire

Birks Clough ♦♦♦
Hollingworth Lane, Walsden,
Todmorden, Lancashire
OL14 6QX
T: (01706) 814438
F: (01706) 819002
E: mstorah@mwfree.net

Highstones Guest House ♦♦♦
Lane Bottom, Walsden,
Todmorden, Lancashire
OL14 6TY
T: (01706) 816534

WEAVERTHORPE
North Yorkshire

The Blue Bell Inn ♦♦♦
Main Street, Weaverthorpe,
Malton, North Yorkshire
YO17 8EX
T: (01944) 738204
F: (01944) 738204

The Star Country Inn ♦♦♦
Weaverthorpe, Malton, North
Yorkshire YO17 8EY
T: (01944) 738273 &
07977 472221
E: info@starinn.net
I: www.starinn.net

WEETON
North Yorkshire

Arthington Lodge ♦♦♦♦
Jubilee Farm, Wescoe Hill Lane,
Weeton, Leeds LS17 0EZ
T: (01423) 734102

WENSLEYDALE
North Yorkshire

Ivy Dene Country Guesthouse
♦♦♦
West Witton, Leyburn, North
Yorkshire DL8 4LP
T: (01969) 622785
F: (01969) 622785

WEST BRETTON
West Yorkshire

The Old Manor House ♦♦♦
19 Sycamore Lane, West
Bretton, Wakefield, West
Yorkshire WF4 4JR
T: (01924) 830324
F: (01924) 830150

WEST BURTON
North Yorkshire

The Grange ♦♦♦♦♦
West Burton, Leyburn, North
Yorkshire DL8 4JR
T: (01969) 663348
I: www.
thegrange-yorkshiredales.co.uk

Grange House ♦♦♦♦
Walden Head, West Burton,
Leyburn, North Yorkshire
DL8 4LF
T: (01969) 663641
F: (01969) 663641

WEST WITTON
North Yorkshire

The Old Star ♦♦♦
West Witton, Leyburn, North
Yorkshire DL8 4LU
T: (01969) 622949
E: martins@the-old-star.
freeserve.co.uk

The Old Vicarage ♦♦♦
Main Street, West Witton,
Leyburn, North Yorkshire
DL8 4LX
T: (01969) 622108
E: info@dalesbreaks.co.uk
I: www.dalesbreaks.co.uk

WESTOW
North Yorkshire

Blacksmiths Arms Inn ♦♦♦
Westow, York, North Yorkshire
YO60 7NE
T: (01653) 618365 & 618343
E: blacksmithsinn@cwcom.net

Clifton Farm ♦♦♦
Parkhouse, Clifton Farm,
Westow, York YO60 7LS
T: (01653) 658557 &
07776 112530
F: (01653) 658 557
E: parkhouseclifton@aol.com

WETHERBY
West Yorkshire

Broadleys ♦♦♦
39 North Street, Wetherby, West
Yorkshire LS22 6NU
T: (01937) 585866

The Coach House Garden
Studio ♦♦♦♦
North Grove Approach,
Wetherby, West Yorkshire
LS22 7GA
T: (01937) 586100
F: (01937) 586100

Highfield ♦♦♦♦
6 Prospect Villas, Wetherby,
West Yorkshire LS22 6PL
T: (01937) 583351
F: (01937) 583351
E: robert@rolfe96.freeserve.
co.uk

Lindum Fields ♦♦♦♦
48a Spofforth Hill, Wetherby,
West Yorkshire LS22 6SE
T: (01937) 520389
F: (01937) 520389
E: peter@pstretton.freeserve.
co.uk

Linton Close ♦♦♦♦
2 Wharfe Grove, Wetherby, West
Yorkshire LS22 6HA
T: (01937) 582711
F: (01937) 588499

Prospect House ◆◆
8 Caxton Street, Wetherby, West
Yorkshire LS22 6RU
T: (01937) 582428

Swan Guest House ◆◆
38 North Street, Wetherby, West
Yorkshire LS22 6NN
T: (01937) 582381 & 0771 204
3931
F: (01937) 584908
E: info@swanguesthouse.co.uk
I: www.swanguesthouse.co.uk

14 Woodhill View ◆◆◆
Wetherby, West Yorkshire
LS22 6PP
T: (01937) 581200 &
07967 152091

WHITBY
North Yorkshire

Alexandra Hotel
Rating Applied For
12 Esplanade, Whitby, North
Yorkshire YO21 3HH
T: (01947) 820959
F: (01947) 602349

Anchorage Non Smoking Hotel
◆◆◆
3 Crescent Terrace, Whitby,
North Yorkshire YO21 3EL
T: (01947) 821888

Arches Guesthouse ◆◆◆
8 Havelock Place, Hudson Street,
Whitby, North Yorkshire
YO21 3ER
T: (01947) 601880
F: (01947) 601880
E: archeswhitby@freeola.com
I: www.whitbyguesthouses.co.uk

Argyle House ◆◆◆◆
18 Hudson Street, Whitby, North
Yorkshire YO21 3EP
T: (01947) 602733
E: pat.donegan@ntlworld.com
I: www.argyle-house.co.uk

Avalon Hotel
Rating Applied For
13-14 Royal Crescent, Whitby,
North Yorkshire YO21 3EJ
T: (01947) 820313
F: (01947) 602349
I: www.avalonhotel.at.freeserve.
co.uk

Boulmer ◆◆◆
23 Crescent Avenue, Whitby,
North Yorkshire YO21 3ED
T: (01947) 604284

Bramblewick Guest House
◆◆◆◆
3 Havelock Place, Whitby, North
Yorkshire YO21 3ER
T: (01947) 604504
E: bramblewick@nfieldhouse.
freeserve.co.uk
I: www.bramblewick.co.uk

Chiltern Guest House ◆◆◆◆
13 Normanby Terrace, West
Cliff, Whitby, North Yorkshire
YO21 3ES
T: (01947) 604981
F: (01947) 604981

Corner Guest House ◆◆◆◆
3-4 Crescent Place, Whitby,
North Yorkshire YO21 3HE
T: (01947) 602444

Crescent Lodge ◆◆◆◆
27 Crescent Avenue, Whitby,
North Yorkshire YO21 3EW
T: (01947) 820073

Esklet Guest House ◆◆◆
22 Crescent Avenue, West Cliff,
Whitby, North Yorkshire
YO21 3ED
T: (01947) 605663
E: les@llintott.freserve.co.uk
I: www.eskletguesthouse.co.uk

The Esplanade Hotel
Rating Applied For
2 Esplanade, Whitby, North
Yorkshire YO21 3HH
T: (01947) 605053
F: (01947) 605053

Glendale Guest House ◆◆◆◆
16 Crescent Avenue, Whitby,
North Yorkshire YO21 3ED
T: (01947) 604242

Grantley House ◆◆◆◆
26 Hudson Street, Whitby, North
Yorkshire YO21 3EP
T: (01947) 600895
F: (01947) 600895
E: kevin@thegrantley.freeserve.
co.uk
I: www.thegrantley.freeserve.
co.uk

Grove Hotel ◆◆◆
36 Bagdale, Whitby, North
Yorkshire YO21 1QL
T: (01947) 603551
I: www.smoothhound.
co.uk/hotels/grove2.html

Havelock Guest House ◆◆◆
30 Hudson Street, West Cliff,
Whitby, North Yorkshire
YO21 3EP
T: (01947) 602295
F: (01947) 602295

High Tor
Rating Applied For
7 Normanby Terrace, Whitby,
North Yorkshire YO21 3ES
T: (01947) 602507

Jaydee Guest House ◆◆◆
15 John Street, Whitby, North
Yorkshire YO21 3ET
T: (01947) 605422 &
07765 265718
F: (01947) 605422

Kom Binne Guest House ◆◆◆
5 Broomfield Terrace, Whitby,
North Yorkshire YO21 1QP
T: (01947) 602752

The Langley Hotel ◆◆◆◆
Royal Crescent, West Cliff,
Whitby, North Yorkshire
YO21 3EJ
T: (01947) 604250
F: (01947) 604250
E: langleyhotel@hotmail.co.uk
I: www.langleyhotel.com

Lansbury Guest House ◆◆◆
29 Hudson Street, Whitby, North
Yorkshire YO21 3EP
T: (01947) 604821
F: (01947) 604821
E: anne-tom.wheeler@
lansbury87.freeserve.co.uk
I: www.whitby-uk.
com/lansburyhse.html

Lavender House ◆◆◆◆
28 Love Lane, Whitby, North
Yorkshire YO21 3LJ
T: (01947) 602917 & 07748 201
049
F: (01947) 602917
E: dcrichmond@aol.com

Lavinia House ◆◆◆◆
3 East Crescent, Whitby, North
Yorkshire YO21 3HD
T: (01947) 602945 & 820656
F: (01947) 820656
E: tony@lavinia-whitby.
freeserve.co.uk

Leeway Guest House ◆◆◆◆
1 Havelock Place, Whitby, North
Yorkshire YO21 3ER
T: (01947) 602604
F: (01947) 601880
E: linda@leeway.co.uk
I: www.leeway.fsbusiness.co.uk

The Middleham ◆◆
3 Church Square, Whitby, North
Yorkshire YO21 3EG
T: (01947) 603423 & 0777 3199
2934
F: (01947) 603423

Morningside Hotel ◆◆◆◆
10 North Promenade, West Cliff,
Whitby, North Yorkshire
YO21 3JX
T: (01947) 602643 & 604030

Netherby House ◆◆◆◆
90 Coach Road, Sleights,
Whitby, North Yorkshire
YO22 5EQ
T: (01947) 810211
F: (01947) 810211
E: netherby-house@hotmail.
com

Number Five ◆◆◆
5 Havelock Place, Whitby, North
Yorkshire YO21 3ER
T: (01947) 606361
F: (01947) 606361

Number Seven Guest House
◆◆◆◆
7 East Cresent, Whitby, North
Yorkshire YO21 3HD
T: (01947) 606019
F: (01947) 606019
E: numberseven@whitbytown.
freeserve.co.uk
I: www.1up.co.uk/whitby

The Olde Ford ◆◆◆◆
1 Briggswath, Whitby, North
Yorkshire YO21 1RU
T: (01947) 810704 & 0798 989
8833
E: gray@theoldeford.fsnet.co.uk

Partridge Nest Farm ◆◆◆
Eskdaleside, Sleights, Whitby,
North Yorkshire YO22 5ES
T: (01947) 810450 & 811412
F: (01947) 811413
E: pnfarm@aol.com
I: www.tmis.uk.
com/partridge-nest/

Postgate Farm ◆◆◆◆
Glaisdale, Whitby, North
Yorkshire YO21 2PZ
T: (01947) 897353 &
07779 206347
F: (01947) 897353
E: j-m.thompson.bandb@talk21.
com
I: www.eskvalley.
com/postgate/postgate.html

Prospect Villa Hotel ◆◆◆
13 Prospect Hill, Whitby, North
Yorkshire YO21 1QE
T: (01947) 603118 &
07778 782638
F: (01947) 825445
E: chris@prospect.freeserve.
co.uk
I: www.prospectvilla.freederve.
co.uk

Riviera Hotel ◆◆◆
4 Crescent Terrace, Whitby,
North Yorkshire YO21 3EL
T: (01947) 602533
F: (01947) 606441
E: info@rivierawhitby.com
I: www.rivierawhitby.com

Rosewood Bed & Breakfast
◆◆◆◆
3 Ocean Road, Whitby, North
Yorkshire YO21 3HY
T: (01947) 820534
E: rose.wood@virgin.net

Rosslyn House ◆◆◆
11 Abbey Terrace, Whitby, North
Yorkshire YO21 3HQ
T: 0800 2985254 &
07768 963589
F: (01947) 604086
I: www.whitbyonline.co.uk

Rothbury ◆◆◆◆
2 Ocean Road, Whitby, North
Yorkshire YO21 3HY
T: (01947) 606282 &
07713 704574

Royal Hotel ◆◆◆
West Cliff, Whitby, North
Yorkshire YO21 3HA
T: (01947) 602234
F: (01947) 820355

Ryedale House ◆◆◆◆
156 Coach Road, Sleights,
Whitby, North Yorkshire
YO22 5EQ
T: (01947) 810534
F: (01947) 810534

Sandpiper Guest House
Rating Applied For
4 Belle Vue Terrace, Whitby,
North Yorkshire YO21 3EY
T: (01947) 600246
F: (01947) 600246

Seacliffe Hotel ◆◆◆◆
12 North Promenade, West Cliff,
Whitby, North Yorkshire
YO21 3JX
T: (01947) 603139 &
08000 191747
F: (01947) 603139
E: julie@seacliffe.fsnet.co.uk
I: www.seacliffe.co.uk

Seacrest Guest House ◆◆◆
10 Crescent Avenue, Whitby,
North Yorkshire YO21 3ED
T: (01947) 605541 &
07974 721147
F: (01947) 821400

Seaview ◆◆◆
5 East Crescent, Whitby, North
Yorkshire YO21 3HD
T: (01947) 604462

Storrbeck Guest House ◆◆◆
9 Crescent Avenue, Whitby,
North Yorkshire YO21 3ED
T: (01947) 605468
E: storrbeck@bigfoot.com
I: www.storrbeck.fsnet.co.uk

YORKSHIRE

Weardale Guest House ◆◆◆
12 Normanby Terrace, Whitby,
North Yorkshire YO21 3ES
T: (01947) 820389 &
07765 182843
F: (01947) 820389
I: www.weardaleguesthouse.
co.uk

Wheeldale Hotel ◆◆◆◆
11 North Promenade, Whitby,
North Yorkshire YO21 3JX
T: (01947) 602365 &
07710 994277
E: wheeldale_hotel@lineone.net
I: www.wheeldale-hotel.co.uk

The Willows ◆◆◆
35 Bagdale, Whitby, North
Yorkshire YO21 1QL
T: (01947) 600288

York House Hotel ◆◆◆◆
3 Back Lane, High Hawsker,
Whitby, North Yorkshire
YO22 4LW
T: (01947) 880314
F: (01947) 880314
E: yorkhtl@aol.com

WICKERSLEY
South Yorkshire

Millstone Farm ◆◆◆
Morthen Road, Wickersley,
Rotherham, South Yorkshire
S66 1EA
T: (01709) 542382

WIKE
West Yorkshire

Wike Ridge Farm ◆◆◆◆
Wike Ridge Lane, Wike, Leeds
LS17 9JF
T: (0113) 266 1190

WILBERFOSS
East Riding of Yorkshire

Cuckoo Nest Farm ◆◆◆
Wilberfoss, York YO41 5NL
T: (01759) 380365

The Steer Inn ◆◆◆
Hull Road, Wilberfoss, York
YO41 5PE
T: (01759) 380600
F: (01759) 388904
E: kevin@steerinn.co.uk
I: www.steerinn.co.uk

WILSDEN
West Yorkshire

Springhill Bed and Breakfast
◆◆
2 Spring Hill, Wilsden, Bradford,
West Yorkshire BD15 0AW
T: (01535) 275211 &
07974 959197

WILTON
North Yorkshire

The Old Forge ◆◆◆◆
Wilton, Pickering, North
Yorkshire YO18 7JY
T: (01751) 477399
F: (01751) 477464
E: theoldforge@themutual.net
I: www.forgecottages.
themutual.net/fc.html

WOLD NEWTON
East Riding of Yorkshire

The Wold Cottage ◆◆◆◆◆
Wold Newton, Driffield, North
Humberside YO25 3HL
T: (01262) 470696
F: (01262) 470696
E: woldcott@wold-newton.
freeserve.co.uk

WOMBLETON
North Yorkshire

Rockery Cottage ◆◆◆◆
Main Street, Wombleton, York
YO62 7RX
T: (01751) 432257 &
07771 657222

WORTLEY
South Yorkshire

Wortley Cottage Guest House
◆◆◆
Park Avenue, Wortley, Sheffield
S35 7DB
T: (01142) 881864 & 882179
F: (01142) 881095

Wortley Hall Ltd ◆◆
Wortley, Sheffield S35 7DB
T: (0114) 288 2100 & 288 5750
F: (0114) 283 0695
E: info@wortleyhall.org.uk
I: www.wortleyhall.org.uk

WRAWBY
North Lincolnshire

The Jolly Miller ◆◆◆
Brigg Road, Wrawby, Brigg,
South Humberside DN20 8RH
I: (01652) 655658
E: (01652) 652048
E: john@jollymiller.co.uk
I: www.jollymiller.co.uk

Wish 'u' Well Guest House
◆◆◆
Brigg Road, Wrawby, Brigg,
South Humberside DN20 8RH
T: (01652) 652301
F: (01652) 652301
E: wishuwell@talk21.com

WRELTON
North Yorkshire

Huntsman Restaurant ◆◆◆
Main Street, Wrelton, Pickering,
North Yorkshire YO18 8PG
T: (01751) 472530
F: (01751) 472530
E: howard@thehuntsman.
freeserve.co.uk
I: www.europage.
co.uk/huntsman

WROOT
North Lincolnshire

Green Garth Country Guest
House ◆◆◆◆
High Street, Wroot, Doncaster,
South Yorkshire DN9 2BU
T: (01302) 770416 &
07711 734128
F: (01302) 770416
E: greengarth@wroot.freeserve.
co.uk

YORK
North Yorkshire

Aaron Guest House ◆◆◆
42 Bootham Crescent, Bootham,
York, YO30 7AH
T: (01904) 625927

Abbey Guest House ◆◆◆
14 Earlsborough Terrace,
Marygate, York, YO30 7BQ
T: (01904) 627782
F: (01904) 671743
E: abbey@rsummers.cix.co.uk
I: www.cix.
co.uk/~munin/sworld/abbey.htm

Abbeyfields ◆◆◆◆
19 Bootham Terrace, York,
YO30 7DH
T: (01904) 636471 & 624197
F: (01904) 636471
E: info@abbeyfields.co.uk
I: www.abbeyfields.co.uk

The Abbingdon ◆◆
60 Bootham Crescent, Bootham,
York, YO30 7AH
T: (01904) 621761
F: (01904) 610002
E: paula@abbingdon.freeserve.
co.uk
I: www.abbingdon.co.uk

The Acer Hotel ◆◆◆◆
52 Scarcroft Hill, York, YO24 1DE
T: (01904) 653839 & 677017
F: (01904) 677017
E: info@acerhotel.co.uk
I: www.acerhotel.co.uk

Acorn Guest House ◆◆◆
1 Southlands Road, York, North
Yorkshire YO23 1NP
T: (01904) 620081 &
07710 507536
F: (01904) 613331
E: acorn.gh@btinternet.com

Acres Dene Guesthouse ◆◆◆
87 Fulford Road, York, YO10 4BD
T: (01904) 625280 & 623126
F: (01904) 637330
E: acresdene@bigwig.net

Airden House ◆◆◆
1 St Mary's, Bootham, York,
YO30 7DD
T: (01904) 638915

Alcuin Lodge ◆◆◆
15 Sycamore Place, Bootham,
York, YO30 7DW
T: (01904) 632222
F: (01904) 626630
E: alcuinlodg@aol.com

Aldwark Bridge House ◆◆◆
Ouseburn, Boat Lane, York,
YO26 9SJ
T: (01423) 331097
F: (01423) 331097
E: bbabh@netscapeonline.co.uk

Aldwark Guest House ◆◆
30 St Saviourgate, Aldwark,
York, YO1 8NN
T: (01904) 627781 &
07771 530160
E: aldwark@hotmail.com

Alexander House ◆◆◆◆◆
94 Bishopthorpe Road, York,
YO23 1JS
T: (01904) 625016 &
07799 490484
E: info@alexanderhouseyork.
co.uk
I: www.alexanderhouseyork.
co.uk

Alfreda Guest House ◆◆◆
61 Heslington Lane, Fulford,
York YO10 4HN
T: (01904) 631698
F: (01904) 411215

Ambleside Guest House ◆◆◆
62 Bootham Crescent, Bootham,
York, YO30 7AH
T: (01904) 637165
F: (01904) 637165
E: ambles@globalnet.co.uk
I: www.ambleside-gh.co.uk

Arndale Hotel ◆◆◆◆
290 Tadcaster Road, York,
YO24 1ET
T: (01904) 702424
F: (01904) 709800

Arnot House ◆◆◆◆
17 Grosvenor Terrace, Bootham,
York, YO30 7AG
T: (01904) 641966
F: (01904) 641966
E: kim.robbins@virgin.net
I: www.arnothouseyork.co.uk

Ascot House ◆◆◆◆
80 East Parade, York, YO31 7YH
T: (01904) 426826
F: (01904) 431077
E: j&k@ascot-house-york.
demon.co.uk
I: www.smoothhound.
co.uk/hotels/ascothou.html

Ashbourne House ◆◆◆◆
139 Fulford Road, York,
YO10 4HG
T: (01904) 639912
F: (01904) 631332
E: ashbourneh@aol.com

Ashbury Hotel ◆◆◆
103 The Mount, York, YO24 1AX
T: (01904) 647339
F: (01904) 647339
E: ashbury@talk21.com

Ashwood Guest House ◆◆◆
19 Nunthorpe Avenue, Scarcroft
Road, York, YO23 1PF
T: (01904) 623412
F: (01904) 623412

Astley House ◆◆◆
123 Clifton, York, YO30 6BL
T: (01904) 634745 & 621327
F: (01904) 621327
E: astley123@aol.com
I: www.astley123.co.uk

Avondale Guest House ◆◆◆
61 Bishopthorpe Road, York,
YO23 1NX
T: (01904) 633989
E: addyman@avondalehouse.
freeserve.co.uk
I: www.avondalehouse.co.uk

The Bar Convent Enterprises
Ltd ◆◆◆
17 Blossom Street, York,
YO24 1AQ
T: (01904) 643238 & 464902
F: (01904) 631792
E: info@bar-convent.org.uk
I: www.bar-convent.org.uk

Barbican House ◆◆◆◆
20 Barbican Road, York,
YO10 5AA
T: (01904) 627617
F: (01904) 647140
E: info@barbicanhouse.com
I: www.barbicanhouse.com

Barrington House ◆◆◆
15 Nunthorpe Avenue, Scarcroft
Road, York, YO23 1PF
T: (01904) 634539

Bay Tree Guest House ◆◆◆
92 Bishopthorpe Road, York,
YO23 1JS
T: (01904) 659462
F: (01904) 659462
E: d.ridley.baytree@ondigital.
co.uk

The Beckett ◆◆◆
58 Bootham Crescent, Bootham,
York, YO30 7AH
T: (01904) 644728
F: (01904) 639915
E: abrownyork@aol.com
I: www.mywebpage.
net/thebeckett

Bedford Hotel ◆◆◆
108-110 Bootham, York,
YO30 7DG
T: (01904) 624412
F: (01904) 632851
E: info@bedford-hotel.fsnet.
co.uk
I: www.bedford-hotel.fsnet.
co.uk

Beech House ◆◆◆
6-7 Longfield Terrace, Bootham,
York, YO30 7DJ
T: (01904) 634581 & 630951

Bentley Guest House ◆◆◆◆
25 Grosvenor Terrace, Bootham,
York, YO30 7AG
T: (01904) 644313 &
07860 199440
F: (01904) 644313
E: p.a.lefebve@tesco.net

Birchfield Guest House ◆◆◆
2 Nunthorpe Avenue, Scarcroft
Road, York, YO23 1PF
T: (01904) 636395

Bishopgarth Guest House
◆◆◆
3 Southlands Road,
Bishopthorpe Road, York,
YO23 1NP
T: (01904) 635220 &
07050 383711
F: (01904) 635220
I: web.ukonline.
co.uk/spreckley//index.html

Bishops Hotel ◆◆◆◆
135 Holgate Road, Holgate,
York, YO24 4DF
T: (01904) 628000
F: (01904) 628181
E: bishops@ukonline.co.uk
I: www.bishopshotel.co.uk

Blakeney Hotel ◆◆◆
180 Stockton Lane, York,
YO31 1ES
T: (01904) 422786
F: (01904) 422786
E: reception@
blakeneyhotel-york.co.uk
I: www.blakeneyhotel-york.co.uk

Blue Bridge Hotel ◆◆◆
Fishergate, York, YO10 4AP
T: (01904) 621193
F: (01904) 671571
E: info@bluebridgehotel.co.uk
I: www.bluebridgehotel.co.uk

Bootham Guest House ◆◆◆
56 Bootham Crescent, York,
YO30 7AH
T: (01904) 672123
F: (01904) 672123
E: boothamguesthouse@
btinternet.com

Bootham Park ◆◆◆◆
9 Grosvenor Terrace, Bootham,
York, YO30 7AG
T: (01904) 644262
F: (01904) 645647
I: boothampark@aol.com

Bowen House ◆◆◆
4 Gladstone Street, Huntington
Road, York, YO31 8RF
T: (01904) 636881
F: (01904) 338700
E: info@bowenhouse.co.uk
I: www.bowenhouse.co.uk

Brentwood Guest House ◆◆◆
54 Bootham Crescent, Bootham,
York, YO30 7AH
T: (01904) 636419
F: (01904) 636419
E: brentwood ps
I: www.visitus.co.uk

Briar Lea Guest House ◆◆◆
8 Longfield Terrace, Bootham,
York, YO30 7DJ
T: (01904) 635061 &
07703 344302
F: (01904) 330356
E: briargh8l@aol.com

Bridge House ◆◆
181 Haxby Road, York, YO31 8JL
T: (01904) 636161
F: (01904) 636161

Bronte Guesthouse ◆◆◆◆
22 Grosvenor Terrace, Bootham,
York, YO30 7AG
T: (01904) 621066
F: (01904) 653434
E: enquires@
bronte-guesthouse.com
I: www.bronte-guesthouse.com/

Bull Lodge Guest House ◆◆◆
37 Bull Lane, Lawrence Street,
York, YO10 3EN
T: (01904) 415522
F: (01904) 415522
E: stay@bulllodge.co.uk
I: www.bulllodge.co.uk

Burton Villa ◆◆◆
24 Haxby Road, York, YO31 8JX
T: (01904) 626364
E: burtonvilla@hotmail.com

Carlton House Hotel ◆◆◆
134 The Mount, York, YO24 1AS
T: (01904) 622265
F: (01904) 637157
E: etb@carltonhouse.co.uk
I: www.carltonhouse.co.uk

Carousel Guest House ◆◆◆
83 Eldon Street, off Stanley
Street, Haxby Road, York,
YO31 7NH
T: (01904) 646709

Cavalier Hotel ◆◆◆
39 Monkgate, York, YO31 7PB
T: (01904) 636615
F: (01904) 636615
E: julia@cavalierhotel.co.uk
I: www.cavalierhotel.co.uk

Chelmsford Place Guest House
◆◆◆
85 Fulford Road, York, YO10 4BD
T: (01904) 624491 &
07802 339681
F: (01904) 624491
E: chelmstordplace@btinternet.
com
I: www.chelmsfordplace.co.uk

Chilton Guest House ◆◆◆
1 Claremont Terrace, Gillygate,
York, YO31 7EJ
T: (01904) 612465
F: (01904) 612465

Chimneys ◆◆◆
18 Bootham Crescent, York,
YO30 7AH
T: (01904) 644334

City Guest House ◆◆◆◆
68 Monkgate, York, YO31 7PF
T: (01904) 622483
E: info@cityguesthouse.co.uk
I: www.cityguesthouse.co.uk

Clarence Gardens Hotel ◆◆◆
Haxby Road, York, YO31 8JS
T: (01904) 624252
F: (01904) 671293
E: clarencehotel@hotmail.com
I: www.clarencegardenhotel.
com

Claxton Hall Cottage ◆◆◆◆
Malton Road, York, YO60 7RE
T: (01904) 468697
E: claxcott@aol.com
I: www.claxtonhallcottage.com

Cook's Guest House ◆◆◆
120 Bishopthorpe Road, York,
YO23 1JX
T: (01904) 652519 &
07946 577247
F: (01904) 652519
E: cooks@talk21.com

**Cornmill Lodge Vegetarian
Guest House** ◆◆◆
120 Haxby Road, York, YO31 8JP
T: (01904) 620566
F: (01904) 620566
E: cornmillyork@aol.com
I: www.cornmillyork.co.uk

Cottage Hotel
Rating Applied For
1 Clifton Green, York, YO30 6LH
T: (01904) 643711
F: (01904) 611230

Crescent Guest House ◆◆
77 Bootham, York, YO30 7DQ
T: (01904) 623216
F: (01904) 623216
I: www.guesthousesyork.net

Crook Lodge ◆◆◆◆
26 St Mary's, Bootham, York,
YO30 7DD
T: (01904) 655614
F: (01904) 655614
E: crooklodge@hotmail.com
I: www.crooklodge.co.uk

Crossways Guest House ◆◆◆
23 Wigginton Road, York,
YO31 8HJ
T: (01904) 637250 &
0777 9873060
E: crossways@tinyonline.co.uk
I: www.crosswaysguesthouse.
freeserve.co.uk

Cumbria House ◆◆◆
2 Vyner Street, Haxby Road,
York, YO31 8HS
T: (01904) 636817
E: clark@cumbriahouse.
freeserve.co.uk
I: www.cumbriahouse.com

**Curzon Lodge and Stable
Cottages** ◆◆◆◆
23 Tadcaster Road, Dringhouses,
York YO24 1QG
T: (01904) 703157
F: (01904) 703157
I: www.smoothhound.
co.uk/hotels/curzon.html

Dairy Guest House ◆◆◆
3 Scarcroft Road, York,
YO23 1ND
T: (01904) 639367
E: filcis@globelnet.co.uk
I: www.dairyguesthouse.
freeserve.co.uk

Dalescroft Guest House ◆◆◆
10 Southlands Road,
Bishopthorpe Road, York,
YO23 1NP
T: (01904) 626801
E: dalescroftg.h.@aol.com

Eastons ◆◆◆◆
90 Bishopthorpe Road, York,
YO23 1JS
T: (01904) 626646
F: (01904) 626165
E: eastonsbbyork@aol.com
I: members.aol.
com/eastonsbbyork/home.htm

Elliotts ◆◆◆◆
Sycamore Place, Bootham
Terrace, York, YO30 7DW
T: (01904) 623333
F: (01904) 654908
E: elliottshotel@aol.com
I: www.elliottshotel.co.uk

Fairthorne ◆◆◆
356 Strensall Road, Earswick,
York YO32 9SW
T: (01904) 768609
F: (01904) 768609

Farthings Hotel ◆◆◆
5 Nunthorpe Avenue, York,
YO23 1PF
T: (01904) 653545
F: (01904) 628355
E: farthings@york181.
fsbusiness.co.uk

Ferns ◆◆
5 Claremont Terrace, off
Gillygate, York, North Yorkshire
YO31 7EJ
T: (01904) 636335
E: jferguson@supanet.com

**Feversham Lodge International
Guest House** ◆◆◆
No 1 Feversham Crescent, Off
Wigginton Road, York,
YO31 8HQ
T: (01904) 623882
F: (01904) 623882
E: feversham@lutyens.
freeserve.co.uk
I: www.s-h-systems.
co.uk/hotels/feversha.html

Foss Bank Guest House ◆◆◆
16 Huntington Road, York,
YO31 8RB
T: (01904) 635548

Four Seasons Hotel ◆◆◆◆
7 St Peter's Grove, Bootham,
York, YO30 6AQ
T: (01904) 622621
F: (01904) 620976
E: roe@fourseasons.netlineuk.
net
I: www.fourseasons-hotel.co.uk

Fourposter Lodge Hotel ◆◆◆
68-70 Heslington Road,
Barbican Road, York, YO10 5AU
T: (01904) 651170
F: (01904) 651170
E: fourposter.lodge@virgin.net
I: www.smoothhound.
co.uk/hotels/fourposter.html

Friars Rest Guest House ◆◆◆
81 Fulford Road, York, YO10 4BD
I: (01904) 629823 &
07802 798427
F: (01904) 629823
E: friarsrest@btinternet.com
I: www.smoothhound.
co.uk/hotels/friars.html

Gables Guest House ◆◆
50 Bootham Crescent, Bootham,
York, YO30 7AH
T: (01904) 624381 & 466377
F: (01904) 624381
I: www.thegablesofyork.co.uk

George Hotel ◆◆◆
6 St George's Place, Tadcaster
Road, York, YO24 1DR
T: (01904) 625056
F: (01904) 625009
E: sixstgeorg@aol.com
I: members.aol.com/sixstgeorg/

Grange Lodge ◆◆◆
52 Bootham Crescent, Bootham,
York, YO30 7AH
T: (01904) 621137
E: grangeldg@aol.com

Greenside ◆◆◆
124 Clifton, York, YO30 6BQ
T: (01904) 623631
F: (01904) 623631

The Hazelwood ◆◆◆◆
24-25 Portland Street, York,
YO31 7EH
T: (01904) 626548
F: (01904) 628032
E: Reservations@
thehazelwoodyork.com
I: www.thehazelwoodyork.com

Heworth Guest House ◆◆◆
126 East Parade, Heworth, York
YO31 7YG
T: (01904) 426384
F: (01904) 426384
E: chris.thompson1@virgin.net
I: www.yorkcity.co.uk

Hillcrest Guest House ◆◆◆
110 Bishopthorpe Road, York,
YO23 1JX
T: (01904) 653160
F: (01904) 656168
E: hillcrest@accommodation.
gbr.fm
I: www.accommodation.gbr.fm

Hobbits Hotel ◆◆◆◆
9 St Peter's Grove, York,
YO30 6AQ
T: (01904) 624538 & 642926
F: (01904) 651765
E: admin@ecsyork.co.uk
I: www.ecsyork.
co.uk/hobbitshotel/hobbits.html

Holgate Bridge Hotel ◆◆◆
106-108 Holgate Road, York,
YO24 4BB
T: (01904) 635971 & 647288
F: (01904) 670049
E: info@holgatebridge.co.uk

The Hollies Guest House ◆◆◆
141 Fulford Road, York,
YO10 4HG
T: (01904) 634279
F: (01904) 625435
E: enquiries@
hollies-guesthouse.co.uk
I: www.hollies-guesthouse.co.uk

Holly Lodge ◆◆◆◆
206 Fulford Road, York,
YO10 4DD
T: (01904) 646005
I: www.thehollylodge.co.uk

Holme Lea Manor Guest House ◆◆◆
18 St Peter's Grove, Bootham,
York, YO30 6AQ
T: (01904) 623529
F: (01904) 653584
E: holmeleamanor@themail.
co.uk

Holmlea Guest House ◆◆
6-7 Southlands Road,
Bishopthorpe Road, York,
YO23 1NP
T: (01904) 621010 &
07971 400991
F: (01904) 659566
E: steve@holmlea.co.uk
I: www.holmlea.co.uk

Holmwood House Hotel ◆◆◆◆
114 Holgate Road, York,
YO24 4BB
T: (01904) 626183
F: (01904) 670899
E: holmwood.house@dial.pipex.
com
I: www.holmwoodhousehotel.
co.uk

The Limes ◆◆◆◆
135 Fulford Road, York,
YO10 4HE
T: (01904) 624548
F: (01904) 624944
E: queries@limeshotel.co.uk
I: www.limeshotel.co.uk

Linden Lodge ◆◆◆
6 Nunthorpe Avenue, Scarcroft
Road, York, YO23 1PF
T: (01904) 620107
F: (01904) 620985
E: bookings@lindenlodge.yorks.
net
I: www.yorkshirenet.
co.uk/stayat/lindenlodge

The Lodge ◆◆◆
302 Strensall Road, Old
Earswick, York YO32 9SW
T: (01904) 761387
F: (01904) 761387
E: the.lodge@talk21.com

The Manor Country House ◆◆◆◆
Acaster Malbis, York YO23 2UL
T: (01904) 706723
F: (01904) 700737
E: manorhouse@selcom.co.uk
I: www.manorhse.co.uk

Martin's Guest House ◆◆
5 Longfield Terrace, York,
YO30 7DJ
T: (01904) 634551
F: (01904) 634551
E: martinsbandb@talk21.com
I: www.smoothhound.co.uk.
hotels/martins.html

Meadowcroft Hotel ◆◆◆
84 Bootham, York, YO30 7DF
T: (01904) 655194
F: (01904) 651384
E: mcroftyork@aol.com

Midway House Hotel ◆◆◆
145 Fulford Road, York,
YO10 4HG
T: (01904) 659272
E: midway.house@virgin.net
I: www.s-h-systems.
co.uk/hotels/midway.html

Millfield Lodge ◆◆
34 Millfield Road, Scarcroft
Road, York, YO23 1NQ
T: (01904) 653731
F: (01904) 643281

Minster Hotel
Rating Applied For
60 Bootham, York, YO30 7BZ
T: (01904) 621267
F: (01904) 654719
E: res@minsterhotel.co.uk
I: www.minsterhotel.co.uk

Minster View Guest House ◆◆◆
2 Grosvenor Terrace, Bootham,
York, YO30 7AG
T: (01904) 655034 & 643410

Monkgate Guest House ◆◆◆
65 Monkgate, York, YO31 7PA
T: (01904) 655947
E: jmb@monkgate.swinternet.
co.uk

Mont Clare Guest House ◆◆◆
32 Claremont Terrace, Gillygate,
York, YO31 7EJ
T: (01904) 627054 & 651011
F: (01904) 627054
E: montclarey@aol.com
I: www.mont-clare.co.uk

Moorgarth Guest House ◆◆◆
158 Fulford Road, York,
YO10 4DA
T: (01904) 636768
F: (01904) 636768
E: moorgarth@fsbdial.co.uk
I: www.avaweb.
co.uk/moorgarth.york.html

Moorland House ◆◆◆
1A Moorland Road, Fulford
Road, York, YO10 4HF
T: (01904) 629354
F: (01904) 629354

Moorlands of Hutton–Le–Hole
Rating Applied For
Huton-Le-Hole, North Yorkshire
Modes, York, YO62 6UA
T: (01751) 417548
F: (01751) 417760
E: moorlandshouse@yahoo.
co.uk
I: www.moorlandshouse.com

Mowbray House ◆◆◆
34 Haxby Road, York, YO31 8JX
T: (01904) 637710
E: carol@mowbrayhouse.co.uk
I: www.mowbrayhouse.co.uk

Northolme Guest House ◆◆◆
114 Shipton Road, Rawcliffe,
York YO30 5RN
T: (01904) 639132
E: g.liddle@tesco.net

Nunmill House ◆◆◆◆
85 Bishopthorpe Road, York,
YO23 1NX
T: (01904) 634047
F: (01904) 655879
E: info@nunmill.co.uk
I: www.nunmill.co.uk

Oaklands Guest House ◆◆◆
351 Strensall Road, Earswick,
York YO32 9SW
T: (01904) 768443
E: mavmo@oaklands5.fsnet.
co.uk
I: www.holidayguides.com

Olga's Licensed Guest House ◆◆
12 Wenlock Terrace, Fulford
Road, York, YO10 4DU
T: (01904) 641456 &
07850 225682
F: (01904) 641456
E: olgasguesthouseyork@
talk21.com
I: www.
olgas-guesthouse-york-
england-uk.com

Orillia House
Rating Applied For
89 The Village, Stockton-on-the-
Forest, York YO32 9UP
T: (01904) 400600
F: (01904) 400101
E: orillia@globalnet.co.uk
I: www.
s-h-systems/hotels/orillia

Palm Court Hotel ◆◆◆◆
17 Huntington Road, York,
YO31 8RB
T: (01904) 639387
F: (01904) 639387

Papillon Hotel ◆◆
43 Gillygate, York, YO31 7EA
T: (01904) 636505
F: (01904) 611968
E: papillonhotel@btinternet.
com
I: www.btinternet.
com/~papillonhotel

Park View Guest House ◆◆◆
34 Grosvenor Terrace, Bootham,
York, YO30 7AG
T: (01904) 620437
F: (01904) 620437
E: park_view@talk21.com

Primrose Lodge ◆◆◆
Hull Road, Dunnington, York
YO19 5LP
T: (01904) 489140

Priory Hotel & Garth
Restaurant ◆◆◆
126-128 Fulford Road, York,
YO10 4BE
T: (01904) 625280
F: (01904) 637330
E: reservations@
priory-hotelyork.co.uk
I: www.priory-hotelyork.co.uk

Queen Anne's Guest House ◆◆◆
24 Queen Anne's Road,
Bootham, York, YO30 7AA
T: (01904) 629389
F: (01904) 619529
E: info@queenannes.fsnet.co.uk
I: www.s-h-systems.
co.uk/hotels/queenann

Red Lion Motel and Country
Inn ◆◆◆
Boroughbridge Road, Upper
Poppleton, York, North Yorkshire
YO26 6PR
T: (01904) 781141
F: (01904) 785143
E: reservations@redlionhotel.
com
I: www.redlionhotel.com

Regency House ◆◆◆◆
7 South Parade, York, North
Yorkshire YO23 1BF
T: (01904) 633053 & 645053
F: (01904) 633053
E: enquiries@regency-house.
fsnet.co.uk
I: www.regencyhouseyork.co.uk

Riverside Walk Guest House
◆◆◆
9 Earlsborough Terrace,
Marygate, York, YO30 7BQ
T: (01904) 620769 & 646249
F: (01904) 671743
E: riverside@rsummers.cix.co.uk
I: www.riversidewalkbb.demon.
co.uk

Romley Guest House ◆◆◆
2 Millfield Road, Scarcroft Road,
York, YO23 1NQ
T: (01904) 652822
E: info@romleyhouse.co.uk
I: www.romleyhouse.co.uk

St Deny's Hotel ◆◆◆
51 St Denys Road, York,
YO1 9QD
T: (01904) 622207 & 646776
F: (01904) 624800
E: info@stdenyshotel.co.uk
I: www.stdenyshotel.co.uk

St Mary's Hotel ◆◆◆
17 Longfield Terrace, Bootham,
York, YO30 7DJ
T: (01904) 626972
F: (01904) 626972
E: stmaryshotel@talk21.com
I: www.stmaryshotel.co.uk

St Paul's Hotel ◆◆◆
120 Holgate Road, York,
YO24 4BB
T: (01904) 611514
F: (01904) 623188
E: normfran@supernet.com

St Raphael Guest House ◆◆
44 Queen Anne's Road,
Bootham, York, YO30 7AF
T: (01904) 645028 & 658788
F: (01904) 658788
E: straphael2000@yahoo.co.uk

Saxon House Hotel ◆◆◆
Fishergate, 71-73 Fulford Road,
York, YO10 4BD
T: (01904) 622106
F: (01904) 633764
E: saxon@househotel.freeserve.
co.uk
I: www.saxonhousehotel.co.uk

Skelton Grange Farmhouse
◆◆◆
Orchard View, Skelton, York
YO30 1XQ
T: (01904) 470780
F: (01904) 470229
E: info@skelton-farm.co.uk
I: www.skelton-farm.co.uk

Southlands Bed and Breakfast
◆◆◆◆
Huntington Road, Huntington,
York YO32 9PX
T: (01904) 766796
F: (01904) 764536
E: southlandsbandb.york@
btinternet.com
I: www.southlandsbandb.
freeserve.co.uk

Southland's Guest House
◆◆◆
69 Nunmill Street, South Bank,
York, YO23 1NT
T: (01904) 631203
E: jillhowcroft@hotmail.com
I: www.southlandsguesthouse.
co.uk/

23 St Marys ◆◆◆◆
Bootham, York, YO30 7DD
T: (01904) 622738
F: (01904) 621168

Stanley House ◆◆◆
Stanley Street, Haxby Road,
York, YO31 8NW
T: (01904) 637111
F: (01904) 659599
E: enquiry@stanleyhouse.uk.
com
I: www.stanleyhouse.uk.com

Staymor Guest House ◆◆◆
2 Southlands Road, York,
YO23 1NP
T: (01904) 626935
E: kathwilson@lineone.net
I: www.mywebpage.net/staymor

Sycamore Guest House ◆◆◆
19 Sycamore Place, Bootham,
York, YO30 7DW
T: (01904) 624712
F: (01904) 624712
E: thesycamore@talk21.com
I: www.guesthousesyork.co.uk

Tower Guest House ◆◆◆
2 Feversham Crescent,
Wigginton Road, York,
YO31 8HQ
T: (01904) 655571 & 635924
F: (01904) 655571
E: reservations@
towerguesthouse.fsnet.co.uk
I: www.towerguesthouse.fsnet.
co.uk

Tree Tops ◆◆◆
21 St Mary's, Bootham, York,
YO30 7DD
T: (01904) 658053 & 625749
F: (01904) 658053
E: treetops.guesthouse@virgin.
net
I: business.thisisyork.
co.uk/treetops

Turnberry House ◆◆◆
143 Fulford Road, York,
YO10 4HG
T: (01904) 658435
F: (01904) 658435

Tyburn House ◆◆◆
11 Albemarle Road, The Mount,
York, YO2 1EN
T: (01904) 655069
F: (01904) 655069
E: york@tyburnhotel.freeserve.
co.uk

Vegetarian Guest House ◆◆◆
21 Park Grove, York, North
Yorkshire YO31 7LG
T: (01904) 644790

The Victoria Hotel ◆◆◆
1 Heslington Road, York,
YO10 5AR
T: (01904) 622295
F: (01904) 677860

Victoria Villa ◆◆
72 Heslington Road, York,
YO10 5AU
T: (01904) 631647
F: (01904) 651170

Warrens Guest House ◆◆◆
30 Scarcroft Road, York,
YO23 1NF
T: (01904) 643139
F: (01904) 658297
I: www.warrens.ndo.co.uk

Waters Edge
Rating Applied For
5 Earlsborough Terrace,
Marygate, York, YO30 7BQ
T: (01904) 644625
F: (01904) 731516
E: julie@watersedgeyork.co.uk
I: www.watersedgeyork.co.uk

Wellgarth House ◆◆◆
Wetherby Road, Rufforth, York
YO23 3QB
T: (01904) 738592 & 738595
F: (01904) 738595

Westgate Hotel ◆◆◆
132 The Mount, York, YO24 1AS
T: (01904) 653303
F: (01904) 635717
E: westgateyork@gofornet.
co.uk
I: www.smoothhound.
co.uk/hotels/westgate.html

White Doves ◆◆◆
20 Claremont Terrace, Gillygate,
York, YO31 7EJ
T: (01904) 625957

York Lodge Guest House ◆◆◆
64 Bootham Crescent, Bootham,
York, YO30 7AH
T: (01904) 654289 &
07860 449460
F: (01904) 654289
E: moore.york@virgin.net
I: www.yorkshirenet.
co.uk/accgde/yorklodge

HEART OF ENGLAND

AB KETTLEBY
Leicestershire

White Lodge Farm ◆◆◆◆
Nottingham Road, Ab Kettleby,
Melton Mowbray, Leicestershire
LE14 3JB
T: (01664) 822286 & 823729
I: www.farm-holidays.co.uk

ABBEY DORE
Herefordshire

The Mynd ◆◆◆
Abbey Dore, Hereford HR2 0AE
T: (01981) 570440
F: (01981) 570440
E: roselloyd@themynd.co.uk
I: www.golden-valley.
co.uk/mynd

ABBOTS BROMLEY
Staffordshire

Crown Inn ◆◆
Market Place, Abbots Bromley,
Rugeley, Staffordshire
WS15 3BS
T: (01283) 840227
F: (01283) 840016
E: f.j.crown@aol.com
I: www.thecrowninn.net

ABBOTS MORTON
Worcestershire

The Cottage Apartment
◆◆◆◆
The Cottage, Gooms Hill, Abbots
Morton Manor, Abbots Morton,
Worcester WR7 4LT
T: (01386) 792783
F: (01386) 792783
E: cottage@bedbrek.fsnet.co.uk
I: www.bedbrek.co.uk

ABTHORPE
Northamptonshire

Rignall Farm Barns ◆◆◆◆
Handley Park, Abthorpe,
Towcester, Northamptonshire
NN12 8PA
T: (01327) 350766
F: (01327) 350766

ACTON BURNELL
Shropshire

Acton Pigot ◆◆◆◆
Acton Burnell, Shrewsbury
SY5 7PH
T: (01694) 731209 &
0797 1974643
E: acton@farmline.com
I: www.actonpigot.co.uk

ADSTONE
Northamptonshire

Manor Farm ◆◆◆
Adstone, Towcester,
Northamptonshire NN12 8DT
T: (01327) 860284
F: (01327) 860685

ALBRIGHTON
Shropshire

Parkside Farm ◆◆◆◆
Holyhead Road, Albrighton,
Wolverhampton WV7 3DA
T: (01902) 372310
F: (01902) 375013
E: jmshanks@farming.co.uk
I: www.patksidefarm.com

ALCESTER
Warwickshire

The Globe Hotel ◆◆◆◆
54 Birmingham Road, Alcester,
Warwickshire B49 5EG
T: (01789) 763287 &
07956 442767
F: (01789) 763287
E: info@theglobehotel.com
I: www.theglobehotel.com

Orchard Lawns ♦♦♦♦
Wixford, Alcester, Warwickshire
B49 6DA
T: (01789) 772668
E: margaret.orchardlawns@
farmersweekly.net

Sambourne Hall Farm ♦♦♦♦
Wike Lane, Sambourne, B96 6NZ
T: (01527) 852151

ALDERTON
Gloucestershire

Corner Cottage ♦♦♦
Stow Road, Alderton,
Tewkesbury, Gloucestershire
GL20 8NH
T: (01242) 620630 &
07770 225548
F: (01242) 620630
E: cornercottagebb@talk21.com

Moors Farm House ♦♦♦♦♦
32 Beckford Road, Alderton,
Tewkesbury, Gloucestershire
GL20 8NL
T: (01242) 620523
E: moorsfarmhouse@ukworld.
net
I: www.ukworld.
net/moorsfarmhouse

ALDSWORTH
Gloucestershire

The Old Chapel ♦♦♦♦
Aldsworth, Cheltenham,
Gloucestershire GL54 3QZ
T: (01451) 844547

ALDWARK
Derbyshire

Lydgate Farm ♦♦♦♦
Aldwark, DE4 4HW
T: (01629) 540250
F: (01629) 540250
E: lomas.lydgate@lineone.net
I: www.peakdistrictfarmhols.
co.uk

ALDWINCLE
Northamptonshire

Pear Tree Farm ♦♦♦♦
Aldwincle, Kettering,
Northamptonshire NN14 3EL
T: (01832) 720614
F: (01832) 720559
E: tim.hankins@zoom.co.uk

ALFRETON
Derbyshire

Crown Inn ♦♦
73 Sleetmoor Lane, Somercotes,
Alfreton, Derbyshire DE55 1RE
T: (01773) 602537

The Spinney Cottage ♦♦♦
Derby Road, Swanwick, Alfreton,
Derbyshire DE55 1BG
T: (01773) 609020

ALMELEY
Herefordshire

**Almeley House Bed and
Breakfast ♦♦♦♦**
Almeley House, Almeley,
Hereford HR3 6LB
T: (01544) 327269 &
07703 953066
F: (01544) 328406
E: gwenda@hamesg.freeserve.
co.uk

ALTON
Staffordshire

Admirals House ♦♦♦
Mill Road, Oakamoor, Stoke-on-
Trent ST10 3AG
T: (01538) 702187
F: (01538) 702957
E: admiralshouse@btinternet.
com
I: www.admiralshouse.co.uk

Alverton Motel ♦♦♦
Denstone Lane, Alton, Stoke-on-
Trent ST10 4AX
T: (01538) 702265
F: (01538) 703284
I: www.alvertonmotel.com

Bee Cottage ♦♦♦♦
Saltersford Lane, Alton, Stoke-
on-Trent, Staffordshire
ST10 4AU
T: (01538) 702802

Bradley Elms Farm ♦♦♦♦
Alton Road, Threapwood,
Cheadle, Cheshire ST10 4RB
T: (01538) 753135 & 750202
F: (01538) 750202

**Bramble Cottage
Rating Applied For**
Gallows Green, Alton, Stoke-on-
Trent ST10 4BN
T: (01538) 703805

Bulls Head Inn ♦♦♦
High Street, Alton, Stoke-on-
Trent ST10 4AQ
T: (01538) 702307
F: (01538) 702065
E: janet@alton.freeserve.co.uk
I: www.thebullsheadinn.
freeserve.co.uk

Church Grange ♦♦♦♦
Bradley in the Moors, Alton,
Stoke-on-Trent, Staffs ST10 4DF
T: (01889) 507525 &
0780 3530655
F: (01889) 507282
E: ddeb@lineone.net
I: www.staffordshire.gov.
uk/tourism/chgrange.htm
🅰

The Cross Inn ♦♦♦
Cauldon Low, Waterhouses,
Stoke-on-Trent, Staffs ST10 3EX
T: (01538) 308338 & 308767
F: (01538) 308767
E: adrian_weaver@hotmail.com
I: www.crossinn.co.uk

The Dale ♦♦♦♦
Off Battlesteads, Alton, Stoke-
on-Trent ST10 4BG
T: (01538) 702394 &
07711 891655
E: thedalealton@talk21.com

Fairview Guesthouse ♦♦♦
1 Vicarage Row, Alton, Stoke-
on-Trent ST10 4BL
T: (01538) 702086

Fernlea Guest House ♦♦♦
Cedar Hill, Alton, Stoke-on-Trent
ST10 4BH
T: (01538) 702327

Fields Farm ♦♦♦♦
Chapel Lane, Threapwood, Alton,
Stoke-on-Trent ST10 4QZ
T: (01538) 752721 &
07850 310381
F: (01538) 757404
E: pat.massey@ukonline.co.uk

Hansley Cross Cottage ♦♦♦
Cheadle Road, Alton, Stoke-on-
Trent ST10 4DH
T: (01538) 702189
F: (01538) 702189
E: jeanhcross@aol.com
I: www.hansleycrosscottage.
co.uk
🅰

The Hawthorns ♦♦♦
8 Tythe Barn, Alton, Stoke-on-
Trent ST10 4AZ
T: (01538) 702197
E: altonbb@aol.com
I: www.members.aol.
com/altonbb

Hillside Farm ♦♦♦
Alton Road, Denstone, Uttoxeter,
Staffordshire ST14 5HG
T: (01889) 590760
I: www.smoothhound.
co.uk/hotels/hillside.html

The Malthouse ♦♦♦♦
Malthouse Road, Alton, Stoke-
on-Trent ST10 4AG
T: (01538) 703273
I: www.themalthouse.gbr.fm

**The Old School House
♦♦♦♦♦**
Castle Hill Road, Alton, Stoke-
on-Trent ST10 4AI
T: (01538) 702151
F: (01538) 702151
E: old_school_house@talk21.
com
I: www.geocities.
com/dennisreardley

The Peakstones Inn ♦♦
Cheadle Road, Alton, Stoke-on-
Trent ST10 4DH
T: (01538) 755776

Rockhaven ♦♦♦
Smithy Bank, Alton, Stoke-on-
Trent ST10 4AA
T: (01538) 702066
F: (01538) 702066

Royal Oak ♦♦
Alton, Stoke-on-Trent ST10 4BH
T: (01538) 702625
E: enq@royaloak-alton.co.uk
I: www.royaloak-alton.co.uk

Trough Ivy House ♦♦♦♦
1 Hay Lane, Farley, Alton, Stoke-
on-Trent ST10 3BQ
T: (01538) 702683
F: (01538) 702683
E: bookings@trough-ivy-house.
demon.co.uk
I: www.trough-ivy-house.
demon.co.uk

Tythe Barn House ♦♦♦
Denstone Lane, Alton, Stoke-on-
Trent ST10 4AX
T: (01538) 702852

The Warren ♦♦♦
The Dale, Battlesteads, Alton,
Stoke-on-Trent ST10 4BG
T: (01538) 702493
F: (01538) 702493

Yoxall Cottage ♦♦♦
Malt House Road, Alton, Stoke-
on-Trent ST10 4AG
T: (01538) 702537

ALVASTON
Derbyshire

Grace Guesthouse ♦♦
1063 London Road, Alvaston,
Derby DE24 8PZ
T: (01332) 572522
F: (01332) 341916

ALVECHURCH
Worcestershire

Alcott Farm ♦♦♦
Weatheroak, Alvechurch,
Birmingham B48 7EH
T: (01564) 824051 &
07774 163253
F: (01564) 824051

ALVELEY
Shropshire

**Arnside Bed and Breakfast
Rating Applied For**
Arnside, Kidderminster Road,
Alveley, Bridgnorth, Shropshire
WV15 6LL
T: (01746) 780007

AMBERGATE
Derbyshire

Lord Nelson ♦♦♦
Bullbridge, Ambergate, Belper,
Derbyshire DE56 2EW
T: (01773) 852037

AMBERLEY
Gloucestershire

High Tumps ♦♦♦♦
St Chloe Green, Amberley,
Stroud, Gloucestershire GL5 5AR
T: (01453) 873584
F: (01453) 873587

APPLEBY MAGNA
Leicestershire

Elms Farm ♦♦♦♦
Appleby Magna, Swadlincote,
Derbyshire DE12 7AP
T: (01530) 270450
F: (01530) 272718

ARLEY
Worcestershire

Tudor Barn ♦♦♦♦
Nib Green, Arley, Bewdley,
Worcestershire DY12 3LY
T: (01299) 400129 &
0797 4817092
E: tudorbarn@aol.com
I: www.tudor-barn.co.uk

ARLINGHAM
Gloucestershire

Horseshoe View ♦♦
Overton Lane, Arlingham,
Gloucester GL2 7JJ
T: (01452) 740293

ARMSCOTE
Warwickshire

Willow Corner ♦♦♦♦
Armscote, Stratford-upon-Avon,
Warwickshire CV37 8DE
T: (01608) 682391 & 0780 371
0149
E: willowcorner@compuserve.
com
I: www.stratford-upon-avon.
co.uk/willowcorner.htm

ARNOLD
Nottinghamshire

Rufford Guesthouse ♦♦♦♦
117 Redhill Road, Arnold,
Nottingham NG5 8GZ
T: (0115) 926 1759
E: ruffordhouse@hotmail.com

ASFORDBY VALLEY
Leicestershire

Valley End ◆◆◆◆
17 North Street, Asfordby Valley,
Melton Mowbray, Leicestershire
LE14 3SQ
T: (01664) 812003

ASH MAGNA
Shropshire

Ash Hall ◆◆◆
Ash Magna, Whitchurch,
Shropshire SY13 4DL
T: (01948) 663151

ASHBOURNE
Derbyshire

The Black Horse Inn ◆◆◆
Main Road, Hulland Ward,
Ashbourne, Derbyshire DE6 3EE
T: (01335) 370206
F: (01335) 370206

Calton Moor House ◆◆◆◆
Calton Moor, Calton, Ashbourne,
Derbyshire DE6 2BU
T: (01538) 308328

Cross Farm ◆◆◆◆
Main Road, Ellastone,
Ashbourne, Derbyshire DE6 2GZ
T: (01335) 324668
F: (01335) 324039
E: janecliffe@hotmail.com

Cubley Common Farm ◆◆◆◆
Cubley, Ashbourne, Derbyshire
DE6 2EX
T: (01335) 330041 &
07710 591407

Dove House ◆◆◆◆
Bridge Hill, Mayfield, Ashbourne,
Derbyshire DE6 2HN
T: (01335) 343329

Foxgloves ◆◆◆◆
Calwich Rise, Ellastone,
Ashbourne, Derbyshire DE6 2HE
T: (01335) 324664

Green Gables ◆◆◆◆
107 The Green Road, Ashbourne,
Derbyshire DE6 1EE
T: (01335) 342431

Henmore Cottage ◆◆◆◆
Clifton, Ashbourne, Derbyshire
DE6 2GL
T: (01335) 344492 &
0786 7334835
F: (01335) 348094
E: mclarke@henmorecottagebb.
fsnet.co.uk
I: www.henmorecottagebb.fsnet.
co.uk

Hurtswood ◆◆◆
Buxton Road, Sandybrook,
Ashbourne, Derbyshire DE6 2AQ
T: (01335) 342031 & 347467
F: (01335) 347467
E: gl.hurtswood@virgin.net
I: www.hurtswood.co.uk

The Lilacs ◆◆◆◆
Mayfield Road, Ashbourne,
Derbyshire DE6 2BJ
T: (01335) 343749
F: (01335) 343749

Little Park Farm ◆◆◆
Mappleton, Ashbourne,
Derbyshire DE6 2BR
T: (01335) 350341

Mona Villas Bed and Breakfast
◆◆◆
1 Mona Villas, Church Lane,
Mayfield, Ashbourne, Derbyshire
DE6 2JS
T: (01335) 343773
F: (01335) 343773

Omnia Somnia ◆◆◆◆◆
The Coach House, The Firs,
Ashbourne, Derbyshire DE6 1HF
T: (01335) 300145
F: (01335) 300958
E: omnia.somnia@talk21.com

Overfield Farm ◆◆◆
Tissington, Ashbourne,
Derbyshire DE6 1RA
T: (01335) 390285

Shirley Hall Farm ◆◆◆◆
Shirley, Ashbourne, Derbyshire
DE6 3AS
T: (01335) 360346 & 360820
F: (01335) 360346
E: sylviafoster@shirleyhallfarm.
com
I: www.shirleyhallfarm.com

Stanshope Hall ◆◆◆◆
Stanshope, Ashbourne,
Derbyshire DE6 2AD
T: (01335) 310278
F: (01335) 310470
E: naomi@stanshope.demon.
co.uk
I: www.stanshope.demon.co.uk

Tan Mill Farm ◆◆◆◆
Mappleton Road, Ashbourne,
Derbyshire DE6 2AA
T: (01335) 342387
F: (01335) 342387

Thorpe Cottage ◆◆◆◆
Thorpe, Ashbourne, Derbyshire
DE6 2AW
T: (01335) 350466 &
07711 217475
F: (01335) 350217
I: www.peakdistrict-bandb.com

The Wheelhouse ◆◆◆◆
Belper Road, Hulland Ward,
Ashbourne, Derbyshire DE6 3EE
T: (01335) 370953
E: samax@supanet.com

White Cottage ◆◆◆◆
Wyaston, Ashbourne, Derbyshire
DE6 2DR
T: (01335) 345503

ASHBY-DE-LA-ZOUCH
Leicestershire

Church Lane Farm House
◆◆◆◆
Church Lane, Ravenstone,
Ravenstone, Leicester LE67 2AE
T: (01530) 810536 &
07973 772341
F: (01530) 810536
E: annthorne@
ravenstone-guesthouse.co.uk
I: www.ravenstone-guesthouse.co.uk

Holywell House Hotel ◆◆
58 Burton Road, Ashby-de-la-
Zouch, Leicestershire LE65 2LN
T: (01530) 412005

The Laurels Bed and Breakfast
◆◆◆
17 Ashby Road, Measham,
Ashby-de-la-Zouch,
Leicestershire DE12 7JR
T: (01530) 272567
F: (01530) 272567
E: evanslaurels@onetel.net.uk
I: www.thelaurelsguesthouse.
com

Measham House Farm ◆◆◆◆
Gallows Lane, Measham,
Swadlincote, Derbyshire
DE12 7HD
T: (01530) 270465 & 273128
F: (01530) 270465
E: jjlovett@meashamhouse.
freeserve.co.uk

ASHBY ST LEDGERS
Northamptonshire

The Olde Coach House Inn
Rating Applied For
Main Street, Ashby St Ledgers,
Rugby, Warwickshire CV23 8UN
T: (01788) 890349
F: (01788) 891922
E: info@theoldecoachhouse.
co.uk
I: theoldecoachhouse.co.uk

ASHFORD IN THE WATER
Derbyshire

Arncliffe House
Rating Applied For
Greaves Lane, Ashford in the
Water, Bakewell, Derbyshire
DE45 1QH
T: (01629) 813121

Chy-an-Dour ◆◆◆◆
Vicarage Lane, Ashford in the
Water, Bakewell, Derbyshire
DE45 1QN
T: (01629) 813162

Gritstone House ◆◆◆◆
Greaves Lane, Ashford in the
Water, Bakewell, Derbyshire
DE45 1QH
T: (01629) 813563
F: (01629) 813563

Marble Cottage ◆◆◆◆
The Dukes Drive, Ashford in the
Water, Bakewell, Derbyshire
DE45 1QP
T: (01629) 813624
F: (01629) 813832
E: marblecottage@aol.com
I: www.cressbrook.
co.uk/bakewell/marblecottage

Warlands ◆◆◆
Hill Cross, Ashford in the Water,
Bakewell, Derbyshire DE45 1QL
T: (01629) 813736

Woodland View ◆◆◆
John Bank Lane, Ashford in the
Water, Bakewell, Derbyshire
DE45 1PY
T: (01629) 813008
F: (01629) 813008
E: woodview@neilellis.
free-online.co.uk
I: www.woodlandviewbandb.
co.uk

ASHLEWORTH
Gloucestershire

Ashleworth Court ◆◆◆
Ashleworth, Gloucester
GL19 4JA
T: (01452) 700241
F: (01452) 700411
E: chamberlayne@farmline.com
I: members.farmline.
com/chamberlayne

ASHOVER
Derbyshire

Hardwick View ◆◆◆◆
Ashover Road, Littlemoor,
Ashover, Chesterfield,
Derbyshire S45 0BL
T: (01246) 590876
E: sueworsey@talk21.com

Old School Farm ◆◆◆◆
Uppertown, Ashover,
Chesterfield, Derbyshire S45 0JF
T: (01246) 590813

ASHPERTON
Herefordshire

Pridewood ◆◆◆
Ashperton, Ledbury,
Herefordshire HR8 2SF
T: (01531) 670416
F: (01531) 670416

ASTLEY
Worcestershire

Woodhampton House ◆◆◆
Weather Lane, Astley, Stourport-
on-Severn, Worcestershire
DY13 0SF
T: (01299) 826510
E: pete-a@sally-a.freeserve.
co.uk

ASTON MUNSLOW
Shropshire

Chadstone ◆◆◆◆
Aston Munslow, Craven Arms,
Shropshire SY7 9ER
T: (01584) 841675
E: chadstone.lee@btinternet.
com
I: www.chadstonebandb.co.uk

ATHERSTONE
Warwickshire

Hall Farm ◆◆◆◆
The Green, Orton-on-the-Hill,
Atherstone, Warwickshire
CV9 3NG
T: (01827) 880350 & 881041
F: (01827) 881041
E: hallfm101@aol.com

Manor Farm Bed and Breakfast
◆◆◆
Manor Farm, Ratcliffe Culey,
Atherstone, Warwickshire
CV9 3NY
T: (01827) 712269 & 716947
E: user880243@aol.com

Mythe Farm Bed & Breakfast
◆◆◆◆
Pinwall Lane, Sheepy Magna,
Atherstone, Warwickshire
CV9 3PF
T: (01827) 712367 &
07932 680254
F: (01827) 715738
E: bosworth/advertising@
connectfree.co.uk

AUDLEY
Staffordshire
The Domvilles Farm ◆◆◆◆
Barthomley Road, Audley,
Stoke-on-Trent ST7 8HT
T: (01782) 720378 &
07880 731436
F: (01782) 720883

AVON DASSETT
Warwickshire
Crandon House ◆◆◆◆◆
Avon Dassett, Leamington Spa,
Warwickshire CV47 2AA
T: (01295) 770652
F: (01295) 770632
E: crandonhouse@talk21.com

AWSWORTH
Nottinghamshire
Hog's Head Hotel ◆◆◆
Main Street, Awsworth,
Nottingham NG16 2RN
T: (0115) 938 4095
F: (0115) 945 9718

AYLBURTON
Gloucestershire
Bridge Cottage ◆◆
High Street, Aylburton,
Gloucester GL15 6BX
T: (01594) 843527

AYNHO
Northamptonshire
**Cartwright Arms Hotel and
Restaurant** ◆
Aynho, Banbury, Oxfordshire
OX17 3BE
T: (01869) 811111
F: (01869) 811110
E: eric@hotel25.freeserve.co.uk

BACTON
Herefordshire
Pentwyn Cottage Gardens
◆◆◆
Pentwyn Cottage, Bacton,
Hereford HR2 0AP
T: (01981) 240508
F: (01981) 240508
E: wendy@gunnsacre.co.uk
I: www.golden-valley.
co.uk/pentwyn

BADBY
Northamptonshire
Meadows Farm ◆◆◆◆◆
Newnham Lane, Badby,
Daventry, Northamptonshire
NN11 3AA
T: (01327) 703302
F: (01327) 703085

The Old House ◆◆◆◆
Church Hill, Badby, Daventry,
Northamptonshire NN11 3AR
T: (01327) 879053
F: (01327) 310967
E: rose.susan@talk21.com

BADSEY
Worcestershire
Orchard House ◆◆◆
99 Bretforton Road, Badsey,
Evesham, Worcestershire
WR11 5UQ
T: (01386) 831245

BAKEWELL
Derbyshire
Castle Cliffe ◆◆◆
Monsal Head, Bakewell,
Derbyshire DE45 1NL
T: (01629) 640258
F: (01629) 640258
E: relax@castle-cliffe.co.uk
I: www.castle-cliffe.com

Castle Inn ◆◆◆
Castle Street, Bakewell,
Derbyshire DE45 1DU
T: (01629) 812103
F: (01629) 814830

Easthorpe ◆◆◆◆
Buxton Road, Bakewell,
Derbyshire DE45 1DA
T: (01629) 814929
E: easthorpe@amserve.net

Ferndale Mews ◆◆◆◆
Buxton Road, Bakewell,
Derbyshire DE45 1DA
T: (01629) 814339

The Garden Room ◆◆◆◆
1 Park Road, Bakewell,
Derbyshire DE45 1AX
T: (01629) 814299
E: the.garden.room@talk21.com
I: www.smoothound.
co.uk/hotels/thegarden.html

Haddon House Farm ◆◆◆◆◆
Haddon Road, Bakewell,
Derbyshire DE45 1BN
T: (01629) 814024
F: (01629) 812759
E: bb@haddon-house.co.uk
I: www.haddon-house.co.uk

The Haven ◆◆◆◆
Haddon Road, Bakewell,
Derbyshire DE45 1AW
T: (01629) 812113 &
07790 790664
E: RoseArmstg@aol.com
I: members.aol.com/RoseArmstg

**Long Meadow House Bed and
Breakfast** ◆◆◆◆
Coombs Road, Bakewell,
Derbyshire DE45 1AQ
T: (01629) 812500
E: amshowarth@cs.com

Loughrigg ◆◆◆◆
Burton Close Drive, Bakewell,
Derbyshire DE45 1BG
T: (01629) 813173
E: john@bakewell55.freeserve.
co.uk
I: www.bakewell55.freeserve.
co.uk

2 Lumford Cottages ◆◆◆
Off Holme Lane, Bakewell,
Derbyshire DE45 1GG
T: (01629) 813273
F: (01629) 813273
I: www.cressbrook.
co.uk/bakewell/lumford

Mandale House ◆◆◆◆
Haddon Grove, Bakewell,
Derbyshire DE45 1JF
T: (01629) 812416
F: (01629) 812416

Melbourne House ◆◆◆
Buxton Road, Bakewell,
Derbyshire DE45 1DA
T: (01629) 815357 &
07812 714785
E: melbournehouse@amserve.
net

River Walk Bed and Breakfast
◆◆◆
River Walk, 3 New Lumford,
Bakewell, Derbyshire DE45 1GH
T: (01629) 812459

30 Riverside Crescent
◆◆◆◆◆
Bakewell, Derbyshire DE45 1HF
T: (01629) 815722
E: iain_mcbain@ibm.uk.com

Sheldon House ◆◆◆◆
Chapel Street, Monyash,
Bakewell, Derbyshire DE45 1JJ
T: (01629) 813067
F: (01629) 813067
E: sheldonhouse@lineone.net

Tannery House ◆◆◆◆◆
Matlock Street, Bakewell,
Derbyshire DE45 1EE
T: (01629) 815011 & 815327
F: (01629) 815327
I: www.tanneryhouse.co.uk
🏠

West Lawn Bed and Breakfast
◆◆◆◆
2 Aldern Way, Bakewell,
Derbyshire DE45 1AJ
T: (01629) 812243
I: www.westlawn.co.uk

BALSALL COMMON
West Midlands
Avonlea ◆◆
135 Kenilworth Road, Balsall
Common, Coventry CV7 7EU
T: (01676) 533003
F: (01676) 533003

Blythe Paddocks ◆◆◆
Barston Lane, Balsall Common,
Coventry CV7 7BT
T: (01676) 533050
F: (01676) 533050

Camp Farm ◆◆◆
Hob Lane, Balsall Common,
Coventry CV7 7GX
T: (01676) 533804
F: (01676) 533804

BALTERLEY
Staffordshire
Pear Tree Lake Farm ◆◆◆◆
Balterley, Crewe CW2 5QE
T: (01270) 820307 &
07970 158658
F: (01270) 820868

BAMFORD
Derbyshire
Pioneer House ◆◆◆◆
Station Road, Bamford, Hope
Valley S33 0BN
T: (01433) 650638
E: pioneerhouse@yahoo.co.uk
I: www.pioneerhouse.co.uk

BARBER BOOTH
Derbyshire
Brookfield Guesthouse ◆◆◆
Brookfield, Barber Booth, Edale,
Sheffield S33 7ZL
T: (01433) 670227

BARDNEY
Lincolnshire
The Black Horse ◆◆◆
16 Wragby Road, Bardney,
Lincoln LN3 5XL
T: (01526) 398900
F: (01526) 399281
E: black-horse@lineone.net

BARLASTON
Staffordshire
Hurden Hall Farm ◆◆◆
Barlaston, Stoke-on-Trent
ST12 9AZ
T: (01782) 372378

Wedgwood Memorial College
◆◆◆
Station Road, Barlaston, Stoke-
on-Trent ST12 9DG
T: (01782) 372105 & 373427
F: (01782) 372393
E: wedgwood.college@
staffordshire.gov.uk.
I: www.aredu.demon.
co.uk/wedgwoodcollege

BARLBOROUGH
Derbyshire °
Stone Croft Bed and Breakfast
◆◆◆
15 Church Street, Barlborough,
Chesterfield, Derbyshire S43 4ER
T: (01246) 810974 &
0771 8080904

BARLOW
Derbyshire
Millbrook ◆◆◆◆
Furnace Lane, Monkwood,
Barlow, Dronfield S18 7SY
T: (0114) 2890253 &
07831 398373
F: (0114) 2891365

Woodview Cottage ◆◆◆◆
Millcross Lane, Barlow, Dronfield
S18 7TA
T: (0114) 289 0724
F: (0114) 289 0724

BARNBY MOOR
Nottinghamshire
**White Horse Inn and
Restaurant** ◆◆◆
Great North Road, Barnby Moor,
Retford, Nottinghamshire
DN22 8QS
T: (01777) 707721
F: (01777) 869445

BARROW-ON-TRENT
Derbyshire
5 Nook Cottages ◆◆◆◆
The Nook, Barrow-on-Trent,
Derby DE73 1NA
T: (01332) 702050
F: (01332) 705927
E: nookcottage@nookcottage.
com
I: www.nookcottage.com

BARTON UNDER NEEDWOOD
Staffordshire
Fairfield Guest House ◆◆◆◆
55 Main Street, Barton under
Needwood, Burton upon Trent,
Staffordshire DE13 8AB
T: (01283) 716396
F: (01283) 716396
E: hotel@fairfield-uk.fsnet.co.uk

Three Way Cottage ◆◆◆
2 Wales Lane, Barton under
Needwood, Burton upon Trent,
Staffordshire DE13 8JF
T: (01283) 713572
E: marion@threewaycottage.
fsnet.co.uk
I: communities.msn.
co.uk/
threewayscottagebedbreakfast

BASLOW
Derbyshire
Bubnell Cliff Farm ◆◆◆
Wheatlands Lane, Baslow,
Bakewell, Derbyshire DE45 1RF
T: (01246) 582454
E: c.k.mills@ukgateway.net

Nether Croft ◆◆◆◆
Eaton Place, Baslow, Bakewell,
Derbyshire DE45 1RW
T: (01246) 583564
E: nethercroftB&B@aol.com

The Old School House ◆◆◆◆
School Lane, Baslow, Bakewell,
Derbyshire DE45 1RZ
T: (01246) 582488
F: (01246) 583323
E: yvonnewright@talk21.com

BASSINGTHORPE
Lincolnshire

Sycamore Farm ◆◆◆◆
Bassingthorpe, Grantham,
Lincolnshire NG33 4EB
T: (01476) 585274

BAUMBER
Lincolnshire

Baumber Park ◆◆◆◆
Baumber, Horncastle,
Lincolnshire LN9 5NE
T: (01507) 578235 &
07977 722776
F: (01507) 578417

BAYSTON HILL
Shropshire

**Lythwood Hall Bed and
Breakfast ◆◆◆**
2 Lythwood Hall, Lythwood,
Bayston Hill, Shrewsbury
SY3 0AD
T: (01743) 874747 &
07074 874747
F: (01743) 874747
E: lythwoodhall@amserve.net
I: www.smoothhound.co.uk

BEESTON
Nottinghamshire

Andrews Private Hotel ◆◆◆
310 Queens Road, Beeston,
Nottingham NG9 1JA
T: (0115) 925 4902
F: (0115) 917 8839

The Grove Guesthouse ◆◆
8 Grove Street, Beeston,
Nottingham NG9 1JL
T: (0115) 9259854

Hylands Hotel ◆◆◆
307 Queens Road, Beeston,
Nottingham NG9 1JB
T: (0115) 925 5472 & 9225678
F: (0115) 922 5574
E: hylands.hotel@telinco.co.uk
I: www.s-h-systems.
co.uk/hotels/hylands.html

BELPER
Derbyshire

Amber Hills ◆◆◆◆
Whitehouse Farm, Belper Lane,
Belper, Derbyshire DE56 2UJ
T: (01773) 824080 &
07808 393687
F: (01773) 824080
E: stew@scooke54.fsnet.co.uk

**Broadhurst Bed and Breakfast
◆◆◆◆**
West Lodge, Bridge Hill, Belper,
Derbyshire DE56 2BY
T: (01773) 823596
F: (01773) 880810
E: stel.broadhurst@talk21.com

The Cedars ◆◆◆◆
Field Lane, Belper, Derbyshire
DE56 1DD
T: (01773) 824157 &
07802 708389
F: (01773) 825573
E: enquiries@
derbyshire-holidays.com
I: www.derbyshire-holidays.com

Chevin Green Farm ◆◆◆◆
Chevin Road, Belper, Derbyshire
DE56 2UN
T: (01773) 822328
F: (01773) 822328
E: spostles@globalnet.co.uk
I: www.chevingreenfarm.co.uk

Hill Top Farm ◆◆◆◆
80 Ashbourne Road, Cowers
Lane, Belper, DE56 2LF
T: (01773) 550338

The Old Shop ◆◆◆
10 Bakers Hill, Heage, Belper,
Derbyshire DE56 2BL
T: (01773) 856796

32 Spencer Road ◆◆◆◆
Belper, Derbyshire DE56 1JY
T: (01773) 823877

BELTON IN RUTLAND
Rutland

The Old Rectory ◆◆
4 New Road, Belton in Rutland,
Oakham, Rutland LE15 9LE
T: (01572) 717279
F: (01572) 717343
E: bb@stablemate.demon.co.uk
I: www.rutnet.co.uk/orb

BENNIWORTH
Lincolnshire

Glebe Farm ◆◆◆◆
Benniworth, Market Rasen,
Lincolnshire LN8 6JP
T: (01507) 313231
F: (01507) 313231
I: www.glebe-farm.com

BENTHALL
Shropshire

Hilltop House ◆◆◆◆
Bridge Road, Benthall, Broseley,
Shropshire TF12 5RB
T: (01952) 884821
E: hilltophouse@ukonline.co.uk
I: www.smoothhound.
co.uk/hotels/hilltop.html

BEOLEY
Worcestershire

Windmill Hill ◆◆◆◆
Cherry Pit Lane, Beoley,
Redditch, Worcestershire
B98 9DH
T: (01527) 62284 & 64476
F: (01527) 64476
E: macotton@tinyworld.co.uk

BERKELEY
Gloucestershire

Pickwick Farm ◆◆◆
A38, Berkeley, Gloucestershire
GL13 9EU
T: (01453) 810241
E: piclwick@supanet.com

BESTHORPE
Nottinghamshire

Lord Nelson Inn ◆◆◆
Main Road, Besthorpe, Newark,
Nottinghamshire NG23 7HR
T: (01636) 892265

BETLEY
Staffordshire

Adderley Green Farm ◆◆◆◆
Heighley Lane, Betley, Crewe
CW3 9BA
T: (01270) 820203 & 820542
F: (01270) 820542
E: adderleygreenfarm@betley.
fsbusiness.co.uk

BEWDLEY
Worcestershire

Clay Farm ◆◆◆◆
Clows Top, Kidderminster,
Worcestershire DY14 9NN
T: (01299) 832421
F: (01299) 832421

Lightmarsh Farm ◆◆◆◆
Crundalls Lane, Bewdley,
Worcestershire DY12 1NE
T: (01299) 404027
I: www.farmstayworcs.co.uk

Sydney Place ◆◆◆
7 Kidderminster Road, Bewdley,
Worcestershire DY12 1AQ
T: (01299) 404832

Winbrook Cottage ◆◆◆
Cleobury Road, Bewdley,
Worcestershire DY12 2BA
T: (01299) 405686 &
07967 700758

BIBURY
Gloucestershire

Coln Cottage ◆◆◆◆
Coln Court, Bibury, Cirencester,
Gloucestershire GL7 5NL
T: (01285) 740314
F: (01285) 740314

Cotteswold House ◆◆◆◆
Arlington, Bibury, Cirencester,
Gloucestershire GL7 5ND
T: (01285) 740609
F: (01285) 740609
E: cotteswold.house@btclick.
com
I: www.home.btclick.
com/cotteswold.house

**The William Morris Bed &
Breakfast ◆◆◆◆**
11 The Street, Bibury,
Cirencester, Gloucestershire
GL7 5NP
T: (01285) 740555
F: (01285) 740049
E: info@thewilliammorris.com
I: www.thewilliammorris.com

BICKENHILL
West Midlands

**Church Farm Accommodation
◆◆**
Church Farm, Church Lane,
Bickenhill, Solihull, West
Midlands B92 0DN
T: (01675) 442641 &
07775 835799
F: (01675) 442905

BIDDULPH
Staffordshire

**Chapel Croft Bed and
Breakfast ◆◆◆**
Newtown Road, Biddulph Park,
Biddulph, Stoke-on-Trent
ST8 7SW
T: (01782) 511013 &
07970 022217
E: chapelcroft@biddulphpark.
freeserve.co.uk
I: www.chapelcroft.com

BIDFORD-ON-AVON
Warwickshire

Avonview House ◆◆◆◆
Stratford Road, Bidford-on-
Avon, Alcester, Warwickshire
B50 4LU
T: (01789) 778667
F: (01789) 778667
E: avonview@talk21.com

**Brook Leys Bed and Breakfast
◆◆◆◆**
Honeybourne Road, Bidford-on-
Avon, Alcester, Warwickshire
B50 4PD
T: (01789) 772785
E: brookleys@amserve.net
I: www.stratford-upon-avon.
co.uk/brookleys.htm

Broom Hall Inn ◆◆◆
Bidford Road, Broom, Alcester,
Warwickshire B50 4HE
T: (01789) 773757

Fosbroke House ◆◆◆◆
4 High Street, Bidford-on-Avon,
Alcester, Warwickshire B50 4BU
T: (01789) 772327
I: www.smoothhound.
co.uk/hotels/fosbroke.html

The Harbour ◆◆◆◆
Salford Road, Bidford-on-Avon,
Alcester, Warwickshire B50 4EN
T: (01789) 772975
E: pwarwick@theharbour-gh.
co.uk
I: www.theharbour-gh.co.uk

BIGGIN-BY-HARTINGTON
Derbyshire

The Kings at Ivy House ◆◆◆◆
Biggin-by-Hartington, Buxton,
Derbyshire SK17 0DT
T: (01298) 84709
F: (01298) 84710
E: kings.ivyhouse@lineone.net
I: www.SmoothHound.
co.uk/hotels/kingsivy.html

BILLINGHAY
Lincolnshire

Old Mill Crafts ◆◆◆
8 Mill Lane, Billinghay, Lincoln
LN4 4ES
T: (01526) 861996

BIRCH VALE
Derbyshire

Spinney Cottage ◆◆◆◆
Spinnerbottom, Birch Vale, High
Peak SK22 1BL
T: (01663) 743230

BIRCHOVER
Derbyshire

Uppertown Farmhouse ◆◆◆◆
Uppertown Lane, Birchover,
Matlock, Derbyshire DE4 2BH
T: (01629) 650112
F: (01629) 650112
E: jonliz@hudrow.
enterprise-plc.com
I: www.SmoothHound.
co.uk/hotels/uppertown.html

BIRDLIP
Gloucestershire

Beechmount ◆◆◆
Birdlip, Gloucester GL4 8JH
T: (01452) 862262
F: (01452) 862262
E: thebeechmount@
breathemail.net

BIRMINGHAM
West Midlands

Alden ◆◆◆
7 Elmdon Road, Marston Green,
Birmingham, B37 7BS
T: (0121) 779 2063
F: (0121) 788 0898

Ashley House ◆◆◆
18 Alcott Lane, Marston Green,
Birmingham, B37 7AT
T: (0121) 779 5368
F: (0121) 779 5368

Atholl Lodge ◆◆◆
16 Elmdon Road, Acocks Green,
Birmingham, B27 6LH
T: (0121) 707 4417
F: (0121) 707 4417

Central Guest House ◆◆◆
1637 Coventry Road, South
Yardley, Birmingham, B26 1DD
T: (0121) 706 7757
F: (0121) 706 7757
E: mmou826384@aol.com
I: www.centralguesthouse.com

Clay Towers ◆◆◆
51 Frankley Beeches Road,
Northfield, Birmingham,
B31 5AB
T: (0121) 6280053 &
07976 950784
F: (0121) 6280053

Cook House Hotel ◆◆
425 Hagley Road, Edgbaston,
Birmingham, B17 8BL
T: (0121) 429 1916

Elmdon Guest House ◆◆◆
2369 Coventry Road, Sheldon,
Birmingham, B26 3PN
T: (0121) 742 1626 & 688 1720
F: (0121) 7421626

Gables Nest ◆◆◆
1639 Coventry Road, South
Yardley, Birmingham, B26 1DD
T: (0121) 708 2712
F: (0121) 707 3396
E: malatgables@aol.com
I: www.guesthousebirmingham.
co.uk

The Glades Guest House ◆◆◆
2469 Coventry Road, Sheldon,
Birmingham, B26 3PP
T: (0121) 742 1871
F: (0121) 742 1871

Grants Guest House ◆◆◆
643 Walsall Road, Great Barr,
Birmingham, B42 1EH
T: (0121) 357 4826
F: (0121) 604 5910
E: wendygrant@
guesthouse643.fsnet.co.uk

Grasmere Guesthouse ◆◆
37 Serpentine Road, Harborne,
Birmingham, B17 9RD
T: (0121) 427 4546
F: (0121) 427 4546

Greenway House Hotel ◆◆
978 Warwick Road, Acocks
Green, Birmingham B27 6QG
T: (0121) 706 1361 & 624 8356
F: (0121) 706 1361

Homelea
2399 Coventry Road, Sheldon,
Birmingham B26 3PN
T: (0121) 742 0017
F: (0121) 688 1879

Kensington Guest House Hotel
◆◆◆
785 Pershore Road, Selly Park,
Birmingham, B29 7LR
T: (0121) 472 7086 & 414 1874
F: (0121) 472 5520

Knowle Lodge Hotel ◆◆
423 Hagley Road, Edgbaston,
Birmingham B17 8BL
T: (0121) 429 8366 & 429 3150

La Caverna Hotel & Restaurant
◆◆◆
2327 Coventry Road, Sheldon,
Birmingham B26 3PG
T: (0121) 743 7917
F: (0121) 722 3307

Lyndhurst Hotel ◆◆◆
135 Kingsbury Road, Erdington,
Birmingham B24 8QT
T: (0121) 373 5695
T: (0121) 373 5697
E: info@lyndhurst-hotel.co.uk
I: www.lyndhurst-hotel.co.uk

Rollason Wood Hotel ◆◆
130 Wood End Road, Erdington,
Birmingham B24 8BJ
T: (0121) 373 1230
F: (0121) 382 2578
E: rollwood@globalnet.co.uk

Royce Land ◆◆◆
33 Elmdon Road, Marston
Green, Birmingham, B37 7BU
T: (0121) 779 4343 &
07973 479122
F: (0121) 779 4343
I: www.roycelandguesthouse.
co.uk

Villanova Hotel ◆◆
2 Grove Hill Road, Handsworth
Wood, Birmingham, B21 9PA
T: (0121) 523 7787 & 551 1139
F: (0121) 523 7787

Wentworth Hotel ◆◆
103 Wentworth Road, Harborne,
Birmingham, B17 9SU
T: (0121) 427 2839 & 427 6818
F: (0121) 427 2839
E: wentworthhotel@freeuk.com
I: www.hotelbirminghamuk.com

Woodville House ◆
39 Portland Road, Edgbaston,
Birmingham B16 9HN
T: (0121) 454 0274
F: (0121) 454 5965

BISHAMPTON
Worcestershire

Bunns Leys
Rating Applied For
Bishampton, Pershore,
Worcestershire WR10 2LX
T: (01386) 462234
F: (01386) 555170
E: enquiries@bunnsleys.co.uk
I: www.bunnsleys.co.uk

BISHOP'S CASTLE
Shropshire

Broughton Farm ◆◆◆
Bishop's Castle, Shropshire
SY15 6SZ
T: (01588) 638393 &
07890 220859

The Castle Hotel ◆◆◆
The Square, Bishop's Castle,
Shropshire SY9 5BN
T: (01588) 638403
F: (01588) 638403
I: www.bishops-castle.
co.uk/castlehotel

Old Time ◆◆
29 High Street, Bishop's Castle,
Shropshire SY9 5BE
T: (01588) 638467 &
07890 875244
F: (01588) 638469
E: jane@oldtime.co.uk
I: www.oldtime.co.uk

The Sun at Norbury ◆◆◆◆
Norbury, Bishop's Castle,
Shropshire SY9 5DX
T: (01588) 650680
E: sun@norbury99.fsbusiness.
co.uk
I: www.thesunatnorbury.co.uk

BISHOP'S CLEEVE
Gloucestershire

Manor Cottage ◆◆
41 Station Road, Bishop's
Cleeve, Cheltenham,
Gloucestershire GL52 8HH
T: (01242) 673537

BLAKENEY
Gloucestershire

The Old Tump House ◆◆◆◆
New Road, Blakeney,
Gloucestershire GL15 4DG
T: (01594) 510608
F: (01594) 510608
E: oldtumphouse@fsbdial.co.uk

BLEDINGTON
Gloucestershire

Kings Head Inn and Restaurant
◆◆◆◆
The Green, Bledington, Oxford
OX7 6XQ
T: (01608) 658365
F: (01608) 658902
E: kingshead@orr-ewing.com
I: www.kingsheadinn.net

BLOCKLEY
Gloucestershire

Arreton House ◆◆◆◆
Station Road, Blockley,
Moreton-in-Marsh,
Gloucestershire GL56 9DT
T: (01386) 701077
F: (01386) 701077
E: bandb@arreton.demon.uk
I: www.arreton.demon.co.uk

Claremont Bed & Breakfast
Rating Applied For
The Greenway, Blockley,
Moreton-in-Marsh,
Gloucestershire GL56 9BQ
T: (01386) 700744
F: (01386) 700412
E: s.clarkson@care4free.net
I: www.claremontbandb.co.uk

The Malins ◆◆◆
21 Station Road, Blockley,
Moreton-in-Marsh,
Gloucestershire GL56 9ED
T: (01386) 700402
F: (01386) 700402
E: johnmalin@talk21.com
I: members.home.
com/panthers-3/TheMalinsBnB.
html

Mill Dene ◆◆◆
Mill Dene, Blockley, Moreton-in-
Marsh, Gloucestershire
GL56 9HU
T: (01386) 700457
F: (01386) 700526
E: wendy@milldene.co.uk
I: www.milldene.co.uk

The Old Bakery ◆◆◆◆◆
High Street, Blockley, Moreton-
in-Marsh, Gloucestershire
GL56 9EU
T: (01386) 700408
F: (01386) 700408

BLYTH
Nottinghamshire

Priory Farm Guesthouse ◆◆◆
Hodsock Priory Estate, Blyth,
Worksop, Nottinghamshire
S81 0TY
T: (01909) 591515
E: vera@guesthse.force9.co.uk.
I: www.guesthse.force9.co.uk.

BOBBINGTON
Staffordshire

Blakelands Country Guest
House and Restaurant ◆◆◆◆
Halfpenny Green, Bobbington,
Stourbridge, West Midlands
DY7 5DP
T: (01384) 221000 & 221000
F: (01384) 221585
E: enquiries@blakelands.com
I: www.blakelands.com

BODENHAM
Herefordshire

The Forge ◆◆◆◆
Bodenham, Hereford HR1 3JZ
T: (01568) 797144
E: bodenham.freeserve.co.uk
I: www.fsvo.
com/bodenhamforge

BOLEHILL
Derbyshire

Byways House Bed and
Breakfast ◆◆◆◆
Byways House, 61 Oakerthorpe
Road, Bolehill, Matlock,
Derbyshire DE4 4GP
T: (01629) 822602

BONSALL
Derbyshire

Townhead Farmhouse ◆◆◆◆
70 High Street, Bonsall, Matlock,
Derbyshire DE4 2AR
T: (01629) 823762
E: townhead70@hotmail.com

BOSTON
Lincolnshire

Bramley House ◆◆◆
267 Sleaford Road, Boston,
Lincolnshire PE21 7PQ
T: (01205) 354538
F: (01205) 354538
E: bramleyhouse@supanet.com

Fairfield Guesthouse
Rating Applied For
101 London Road, Boston,
Lincolnshire PE21 7EN
T: (01205) 362869

Park Lea Guesthouse
Rating Applied For
85 Norfolk Street, Boston,
Lincolnshire PE21 6PE
T: (01205) 356309

BOURNE
Lincolnshire

Angel Hotel ◆◆◆
Market Place, Bourne,
Lincolnshire PE10 9AE
T: (01778) 422346
F: (01778) 426113

Mill House ◆◆◆
64 North Road, Bourne,
Lincolnshire PE10 9BU
T: (01778) 422278
F: (01778) 422546
E: millhousebnb@fsbdial.co.uk

BOURTON-ON-THE-WATER
Gloucestershire

Alderley Guesthouse ◆◆◆◆
Rissington Road, Bourton-on-
the-Water, Cheltenham,
Gloucestershire GL54 2DX
T: (01451) 822788
F: (01451) 822788
E: boxpetlyn@aol.com

Berkeley Guesthouse ◆◆◆◆
Moore Road, Bourton-on-the-
Water, Cheltenham,
Gloucestershire GL54 2AZ
T: (01451) 810388
F: (01451) 821776

Broadlands Guest House
◆◆◆◆
Clapton Row, Bourton-on-the-
Water, Cheltenham,
Gloucestershire GL54 2DN
T: (01451) 822002
F: (01451) 821776

Coach and Horses ◆◆◆◆
Fosseway, A429, Bourton-on-
the-Water, Cheltenham,
Gloucestershire GL54 2HN
T: (01451) 821064
F: (01451) 810570
E: info@coach-horses.co.uk
I: www.coach-horses.co.uk

Coombe House ◆◆◆◆
Rissington Road, Bourton-on-
the-Water, Cheltenham,
Gloucestershire GL54 2DT
T: 1451 821966 & 822367
F: 1451 810477
E: coombe.house@virgin.net
I: www.coombehousecotswolds.
co.uk

**Cotswold Bed and Breakfast
'Rooftrees'** ◆◆◆◆
Rissington Road, Bourton-on-
the-Water, Cheltenham,
Gloucestershire GL54 2DX
T: (01451) 821943
F: (01451) 810614

Cotswold Carp Farm ◆◆◆◆
Bury Barn Lane, Bourton-on-
the-Water, Cheltenham,
Gloucestershire GL54 2HB
T: (01451) 821795

The Cotswold House ◆◆◆
Lansdowne, Bourton-on-the-
Water, Cheltenham,
Gloucestershire GL54 2AR
T: (01451) 822373

Elvington Bed and Breakfast
◆◆◆
Elvington, Rissington Road,
Bourton-on-the-Water,
Cheltenham, Gloucestershire
GL54 2DX
T: (01451) 822026

Fairlie ◆◆◆
Riverside, Bourton-on-the-
Water, Cheltenham,
Gloucestershire GL54 2DP
T: (01451) 821842

Farncombe ◆◆◆◆
Clapton, Bourton-on-the-Water,
Cheltenham, Gloucestershire
GL54 2LG
T: (01451) 820120 &
07714 703142
F: (01451) 820120
E: jwrightbb@aol.com
I: www.SmoothHound.
co.uk/hotels/farncomb.html
AND http://www.
farncombecotswolds.com

Fosseside House ◆◆◆◆
Lansdowne, Bourton-on-the-
Water, Cheltenham,
Gloucestershire GL54 2AT
T: (01451) 820574

Holly House ◆◆◆◆
Station Road, Bourton-on-the-
Water, Cheltenham,
Gloucestershire GL54 2ER
T: (01451) 821302
E: hollyhouse@amserve.net

The Kingsbridge Inn ◆◆◆◆
Riverside, Bourton-on-the-
Water, Cheltenham,
Gloucestershire GL54 2BS
T: (01451) 820371
F: (01451) 810179
E: book@lionheartinns.co.uk
I: www.lionheartinns.co.uk

Lamb Inn ◆◆◆
Great Rissington, Bourton-on-
the-Water, Cheltenham,
Gloucestershire GL54 2LP
T: (01451) 820388
F: (01451) 820724
I: www.thelamb-inn.com

Lansdowne House ◆◆◆◆
Lansdowne, Bourton-on-the-
Water, Cheltenham,
Gloucestershire GL54 2AT
T: (01451) 820812
F: (01451) 822484
E: heart@lansdownehouse.
co.uk
I: www.lansdownehouse.co.uk

Lansdowne Villa Guest House
◆◆◆◆
Lansdowne, Bourton-on-the-
Water, Cheltenham,
Gloucestershire GL54 2AR
T: (01451) 820673
F: (01451) 822099
E: lansdowne@star.co.uk
I: www.lansdownevilla.co.uk

Larch House ◆◆◆◆◆
Station Road, Bourton-on-the-
Water, Cheltenham,
Gloucestershire GL54 2AA
T: (01451) 821172
F: (01451) 821172
I: www.s-n-systems.
co.uk/hotels/larchhse

The Lawns ◆◆◆◆
Station Road, Bourton-on-the-
Water, Cheltenham,
Gloucestershire GL54 2ER
T: (01451) 821195
F: (01451) 821195

Manor Close ◆◆◆◆
High Street, Bourton-on-the-
Water, Cheltenham,
Gloucestershire GL54 2AP
T: (01451) 820339

Mousetrap Inn ◆◆◆
Lansdowne, Bourton-on-the-
Water, Cheltenham,
Gloucestershire GL54 2AR
T: (01451) 820579
F: (01451) 822393
E: mtinn@waverider.co.uk
I: www.mousetrap-inn.co.uk

Old New Inn ◆◆◆
Bourton-on-the-Water,
Cheltenham, Gloucestershire
GL54 2AF
T: (01451) 820467
F: (01451) 810236
E: old_new_inn@compuserve.
com
I: ourworld.compuserve.
com/homepages/old_new_inn

Polly Perkins ◆◆◆
1 The Chestnuts, Bourton-on-
the-Water, Cheltenham,
Gloucestershire GL54 2AN
T: (01451) 820244
F: (01451) 820558

**The Red House Bed and
Breakfast** ◆◆◆
Station Road, Bourton-on-the-
Water, Cheltenham,
Gloucestershire GL54 2EN
T: (01451) 810201
F: (01451) 810201
E: charlie@theredhouse@
bourton.co.uk

The Ridge ◆◆◆◆
Whiteshoots Hill, Bourton-on-
the-Water, Cheltenham,
Gloucestershire GL54 2LE
T: (01451) 820660
F: (01451) 822448

Station Villa
Rating Applied For
2 Station Villa, Station Road,
Bourton-on-the-Water,
Cheltenham, Gloucestershire
GL54 2ER
T: (01451) 810406
F: (01451) 821359
E: rooms@stationvilla.com
I: www.stationvilla.com

Strathspey
Rating Applied For
Lansdowne, Bourton-on-the-
Water, Cheltenham,
Gloucestershire GL54 2AR
T: (01451) 820694
F: (01451) 821466
E: mel@strathspey-bedfsnet.
co.uk

Sycamore House ◆◆◆
Lansdowne, Bourton-on-the-
Water, Cheltenham,
Gloucestershire GL54 2AR
T: (01451) 821647

Touchstone ◆◆◆◆
Little Rissington, Bourton-on-
the-Water, Cheltenham,
Gloucestershire GL54 2ND
T: (01451) 822481
F: (01451) 822481
E: touchstone.bb@lineone.net
I: website.lineone.
net/~touchstone.bb

Upper Farm ◆◆◆◆
Clapton on the Hill, Bourton-on-
the-Water, Cheltenham,
Gloucestershire GL54 2LG
T: (01451) 820453
F: (01451) 810185
I: www.tuckedup.
com/upperfarm.html

**Whiteshoots Cottage Bed and
Breakfast** ◆◆◆
Whiteshoots Hill, Fosseway,
Bourton-on-the-Water,
Cheltenham, Gloucestershire
GL54 2LE
T: (01451) 822698
E: whiteshootscottage@talk21.
com

Willow Crest ◆◆◆◆
Rissington Road, Bourton-on-
the-Water, Cheltenham,
Gloucestershire GL54 2DZ
T: (01451) 822073

BOYLESTONE
Derbyshire

Lees Hall Farm ◆◆◆
Boylestone, Ashbourne,
Derbyshire DE6 5AA
T: (01335) 330259
F: (01335) 330259

BRACKLEY
Northamptonshire

Astwell Mill ◆◆◆◆
Helmdon, Brackley,
Northamptonshire NN13 5QU
T: (01295) 760507
F: (01295) 768602
E: astwell01@aol.com

Brackley House Private Hotel
◆◆◆◆
Brackley House, 4 High Street,
Brackley, Northamptonshire
NN13 7DT
T: (01280) 701550
F: (01280) 704965
E: sales@brackleyhouse.com
I: www.brackleyhouse.com

The Thatches ◆◆◆
Whitfield, Brackley,
Northamptonshire NN13 5TQ
T: (01280) 850358

Walltree House Farm ◆◆◆◆
Steane, Brackley,
Northamptonshire NN13 5NS
T: (01295) 811235 &
07860 913399
F: (01295) 811147

Welbeck House ◆◆
Pebble Lane, Brackley,
Northamptonshire NN13 7DA
T: (01280) 702364
F: (01280) 702364
E: pebblelane06mac@aol.com

BRADLEY
Derbyshire

Yeldersley Old Hall Farm
◆◆◆◆
Yeldersley Lane, Bradley,
Ashbourne, Derbyshire DE6 1PH
T: (01335) 344504
F: (01335) 344504
E: janethindsfarm@yahoo.co.uk

BRADNOP
Staffordshire

Middle Farm Guest House
◆◆◆
Apesford, Bradnop, Leek,
Staffordshire ST13 7EX
T: (01538) 382839 & 399571
F: (01538) 382839

BRADWELL
Derbyshire

Stoney Ridge ♦♦♦♦
Granby Road, Bradwell, Hope
Valley S33 9HU
T: (01433) 620538
F: (01433) 623154
E: toneyridge@aol.com
I: www.cressbrook.
co.uk/hopev/stoneyridge

BRAILES
Warwickshire

Agdon Farm ♦♦♦
Brailes, Banbury, Oxfordshire
OX15 5JJ
T: (01608) 685226 &
07977 704240
F: (01608) 685226
E: maggie_cripps@hotmail.com

BRAMSHALL
Staffordshire

Bowmore House ♦♦♦
Stone Road, Bramshall,
Uttoxeter, Staffordshire
ST14 8SH
T: (01889) 564452
E: glovatt@furoris.com

BRASSINGTON
Derbyshire

Ivy Bank House
Rating Applied For
Church Street, Brassington,
Matlock, Derbyshire DE4 4HJ
T: (01629) 540818
E: june@ivybankhouse.co.uk
I: www.ivybankhouse.co.uk

BREAM
Gloucestershire

The Hedgehog Freehouse
♦♦♦
High Street, Bream, Lydney,
Gloucestershire GL15 6JS
T: (01594) 562358
F: (01594) 564273
E: thehedgehogfreehouse@
btinternet.com

**Lindum House Bed and
Breakfast** ♦♦♦
Oakwood Road, Bream, Lydney,
Gloucestershire GL15 6HS
T: (01594) 562051
I: www.indumhouse.fsworld.
co.uk

BREDENBURY
Herefordshire

Redhill Farm ♦♦
Bredenbury, Bromyard,
Herefordshire HR7 4SY
T: (01885) 483255 & 483535
F: (01885) 483535

BREDON
Worcestershire

Royal Oak Inn ♦♦♦♦
Main Road, Bredon, Tewkesbury,
Gloucestershire GL20 7LW
T: (01684) 772393

BREDON'S NORTON
Worcestershire

Round Bank House ♦♦♦♦
Lampitt Lane, Bredon's Norton,
Tewkesbury, Gloucestershire
GL20 7HB
T: (01684) 772983 & 772142
F: (01684) 773035

BREDWARDINE
Herefordshire

Old Court Farm ♦♦♦
Bredwardine, Hereford HR3 6BT
T: (01981) 500375
E: whittall@oldcourt74.co.uk

BRETFORTON
Worcestershire

**Bretforton House Farm Bed
and Breakfast**♦♦♦♦
Bretforton House Farm,
Bretforton, Evesham,
Worcestershire WR11 5JH
T: (01386) 830831
F: (01386) 830831
E: japplebya@aol.com

BREWOOD
Staffordshire

The Blackladies ♦♦♦♦♦
Kiddemore Green Road,
Brewood, Stafford ST19 9BH
T: (01902) 850210
F: (01902) 851782

BRIDGNORTH
Shropshire

The Albynes ♦♦♦♦
Nordley, Bridgnorth, Shropshire
WV16 4SX
T: (01746) 762261

Bassa Villa Bar and Grill ♦♦♦
48 Cartway, Bridgnorth,
Shropshire WV16 4BG
T: (01746) 763977 &
(01952) 691184
F: (01952) 691604
E: sugarloaf@globalnet.co.uk
I: www.bassavilla.com

Bear Inn ♦♦♦
Northgate, Bridgnorth,
Shropshire WV16 4ET
T: (01746) 763250

Bearwood Lodge Hotel
Rating Applied For
10 Kidderminster Road,
Bridgnorth, Shropshire
WV15 6BW
T: (01746) 762159
F: (01746) 762159
E: bearlodge@lineone.net

Bridgnorth Guest House ♦♦♦
45 Victoria Road, Bridgnorth,
Shropshire WV16 4LD
T: (01746) 766251 &
07958 561619
F: (01746) 762279
E: delbarters@netscapeonline.
co.uk

Bulls Head Inn ♦♦♦♦
Chelmarsh, Bridgnorth,
Shropshire WV16 6BA
T: (01746) 861469
F: (01746) 862074
E: dave@bullshead.fsnet.co.uk
I: www.virtual-shropshire.
co.uk/bulls-head-inn

Dinney Farm ♦♦
Chelmarsh, Bridgnorth,
Shropshire WV16 6AU
T: (01746) 861070
F: (01746) 861002
E: hedley.southport@virgin.net
I: www.smoothhound.
co.uk/hotels/dinney.html

Friar's Inn ♦♦♦
3 St. Mary's Street, Bridgnorth,
Shropshire WV16 4DW
T: (01746) 762396

The Golden Lion Inn ♦♦♦
83 High Street, Bridgnorth,
Shropshire WV16 4DS
T: (01746) 762016
F: (01746) 762016
I: www.midlandspubs.
co.uk/bridgnorth/goldenlion.htm

Haven Pasture ♦♦♦♦
Underton, Bridgnorth,
Shropshire WV16 6TY
T: (01746) 789632
F: (01746) 789333
E: havenpasture@underton.
co.uk
I: www.underton.co.uk

Highfields ♦♦♦♦
44 Ludlow Road, Bridgnorth,
Shropshire WV16 5AF
T: (01746) 763110 &
07974 501228
I: www.virtual-shropshire.
co.uk/highfields

Linley Crest ♦♦♦♦
Linley Brook, Bridgnorth,
Shropshire WV16 4SZ
T: (01746) 765527 &
07889 227875
F: (01746) 765527
E: linleycrest@easicom.com

Pen-y-Ghent ♦♦♦
7 Sabrina Road, Bridgnorth,
Shropshire WV15 6DQ
T: (01746) 762880
E: firman.margret@freeuk.com
I: pen-y-ghent.8m.com

Saint Leonards Gate ♦♦♦
6 Church Street, Bridgnorth,
Shropshire WV16 4EQ
T: (01746) 766647
E: Stewart.buchanan@
btinternet.com

Sandward Guesthouse ♦♦♦
47 Cartway, Bridgnorth,
Shropshire WV16 4BG
T: (01746) 765913

Severn Arms Hotel ♦♦♦
Underhill Street, Bridgnorth,
Shropshire WV16 4BB
T: (01746) 764616
F: (01746) 761750
E: severnarmshotel@
compuserve.com
I: www.virtual-shropshire.
co.uk/severn-arms-hotel

Severn Hall ♦♦♦♦
Stanley Lane, Bridgnorth,
Shropshire WV16 4SR
T: (01746) 763241

Severn House ♦♦♦♦
38 Underhill Street, Bridgnorth,
Shropshire WV16 4BB
T: (01746) 766976
F: (01746) 766976
E: severnhouse@faxvia.net
I: www/severnhouse.
bridgnorthshropshire.com

BRIMPSFIELD
Gloucestershire

Highcroft ♦♦♦♦♦
Brimpsfield, Gloucester GL4 8LF
T: (01452) 862405

BRINGHURST
Leicestershire

Castle View Farm
Rating Applied For
Bringhurst, Market Harborough,
Leicestershire LE16 8RJ
T: (01536) 770408
F: (01536) 771626
E: tommyandsal@hotmail.com

BRINKLOW
Warwickshire

White Lion ♦♦♦
32 Broad Street, Brinklow,
Rugby, Warwickshire CV23 0LN
T: (01788) 832579
T: (01788) 833844
E: brinklowlion@aol.com
I: www.thewhitelion-inn.co.uk

BRIXWORTH
Northamptonshire

The Rookery ♦♦♦♦
36 Church Street, Brixworth,
Northampton NN6 9BZ
T: (01604) 883699
F: (01604) 880886
E: cherryliell@
rookeryb- bfreeserve.co.uk
I: www.rookeryb-b.freeserve.
co.uk

BROAD CAMPDEN
Gloucestershire

Marnic House ♦♦♦♦
Broad Campden, Chipping
Campden, Gloucestershire
GL55 6UR
T: (01386) 840014 & 841473
F: (01386) 840441
E: marnichouse@zoom.co.uk

Primrose Cottage♦♦♦♦
3 The Bank, Broad Campden,
Chipping Campden,
Gloucestershire GL55 6US
T: (01386) 840921

BROADWAY
Worcestershire

Barn House ♦♦♦♦
152 High Street, Broadway,
Worcestershire WR12 7AJ
T: (01386) 858633
F: (01386) 858633
E: barnhouse@btinternet.com
I: btinternet.com/~barnhouse/

Bourne House ♦♦♦♦
Leamington Road, Broadway,
Worcestershire WR12 7DZ
T: (01386) 853486
F: (01386) 853793
E: maria@
bournehousebroadway.
freeserve.co.uk

Burhill Farm ♦♦♦♦♦
Buckland, Broadway,
Worcestershire WR12 7LY
T: (01386) 858171
F: (01386) 858171

Crown and Trumpet Inn ♦♦♦
Church Street, Broadway,
Worcestershire WR12 7AE
T: (01386) 853202
F: (01386) 834650
E: ascott@cotswoldholidays.
co.uk
I: www.cotswoldholidays.co.uk

Dove Cottage ♦♦♦
Colletts Fields, Broadway,
Worcestershire WR12 7AT
T: (01386) 859085
I: www.broadway-cotswolds.
co.uk

Highlands Country House Bed and Breakfast ◆◆◆◆
Highlands, Fish Hill, Broadway,
Worcestershire WR12 7LD
T: (01386) 858015 &
07774 700321
F: 0870 7348742
E: sue@adames.demon.co.uk

Knoll Bed and Breakfast ◆◆◆◆
The Knoll, Springfield Lane,
Broadway, Worcestershire
WR12 7BT
T: (01386) 858702

Leasow House ◆◆◆◆
Laverton Meadow, Broadway,
Worcestershire WR12 7NA
T: (01386) 584526
F: (01386) 584596
E: leasow@clara.net
I: www.leasow.co.uk

Lowerfield Farm ◆◆◆◆
Willersey, Broadway,
Worcestershire WR11 5HF
T: (01386) 858273 &
07703 343996
F: (01386) 854608
E: info@lowerfield-farm.co.uk
I: www.lowerfield-farm.co.uk

Milestone House ◆◆◆◆
Upper High Street, Broadway,
Worcestershire WR12 7AJ
T: (01386) 853432
F: milestone.house@talk21.com

Mount Pleasant Farm ◆◆◆◆
Childswickham, Broadway,
Worcestershire WR12 7HZ
T: (01386) 853424

Old Stationhouse Eastbank ◆◆◆◆
Station Drive, Broadway,
Worcestershire WR12 7DF
T: (01386) 852659
F: (01386) 852891
E: trueman@
eastbank-broadway.fsnet.co.uk
I: www.broadway-cotswolds.
co.uk/ebank.html

Olive Branch Guest House ◆◆◆◆
78 High Street, Broadway,
Worcestershire WR12 7AJ
T: (01386) 853440
F: (01386) 859070
E: broadway@theolive-branch.
co.uk
I: www.
theolivebranch-broadway.com

Pathlow House ◆◆◆
82 High Street, Broadway,
Worcestershire WR12 7AJ
T: (01386) 853444 &
(01527) 65861
F: (01386) 853444
E: pathlow@aol.com
I: www.pathlowguesthouse.
co.uk

Shenberrow Hill ◆◆◆◆
Stanton, Broadway,
Worcestershire WR12 7NE
T: (01386) 584468
F: (01386) 584468
E: michael.neilan@talk21.com
I: www.cotswold-way.co.uk

Small Talk Lodge ◆◆◆
32 High Street, Broadway,
Worcestershire WR12 7DP
T: (01386) 858953 & 854611
I: www.broadway-cotswolds.
co.uk

Southwold Guest House ◆◆◆◆
Station Road, Broadway,
Worcestershire WR12 7DE
T: (01386) 853681
F: (01386) 854610
E: sueandnick.southwold@
talk21.com

Whiteacres ◆◆◆◆
Station Road, Broadway,
Worcestershire WR12 7DE
T: (01386) 852320
E: whiteacres@btinternet.com
I: www.broadway-cotswolds.
co.uk/whiteacres.html

Windrush House ◆◆◆◆
Station Road, Broadway,
Worcestershire WR12 7DE
T: (01386) 853577 & 853790
F: (01386) 853790
E: richard@
broadway-windrush.co.uk
I: www.broadway-windrush.
co.uk

BROADWELL
Gloucestershire

The White House ◆◆◆
2 South Road, Broadwell,
Coleford, Gloucestershire
GL16 7BH
T: (01594) 837069 &
07074 837069
F: (01594) 833130
I: www.ukworld-int.co.uk

BROMSGROVE
Worcestershire

Bea's Lodge ◆◆
245 Pennine Road, Bromsgrove,
Worcestershire B61 0TN
T: (01527) 877613

Bromsgrove Country Hotel ◆◆◆◆
249 Worcester Road, Stoke
Heath, Bromsgrove,
Worcestershire B61 7JA
T: (01527) 835522
F: (01527) 871257
E: bchotel@talk21.com

The Durrance ◆◆◆◆
Berry Lane, Upton Warren,
Bromsgrove, Worcestershire
B61 9EL
T: (01562) 777533
F: (01562) 777533
E: helenhirons@thedurrance.
co.uk
I: www.thedurrance.co.uk

Fox Hollies
Rating Applied For
78 New Road, Bromsgrove,
Worcestershire B60 2LA
T: (01527) 574870

Honeypot ◆◆◆
305 Old Birmingham Road,
Lickey, Bromsgrove,
Worcestershire B60 1HQ
T: (0121) 445 2580 &
07803 473737

Merrivale ◆◆◆◆
309 Old Birmingham Road,
Lickey, Bromsgrove,
Worcestershire B60 1HQ
T: (0121) 445 1694 &
07721 641268
F: (0121) 445 1694
E: alincolnsmith@bushinternet.
com

12 Moorfield Drive ◆◆
Bromsgrove, Worcestershire
B61 8EJ
T: (01527) 835056 &
0796 8087966

Overwood Bed and Breakfast ◆◆◆◆
Woodcote Lane, Woodcote,
Bromsgrove, Worcestershire
B61 9EE
T: (01562) 777193
F: (01562) 777689
E: info@overwood.net
I: www.overwood.net

Sprite House ◆◆◆
58 Stratford Road, Bromsgrove,
Worcestershire B60 1AU
T: (01527) 874565 & 870935
F: (01527) 870935

BROMYARD
Herefordshire

The Granary Restaurant ◆◆◆
Church House Farm, Collington,
Bromyard, Herefordshire
HR7 4NA
T: (01885) 410345
F: (01885) 410555

Linton Brook Farm ◆◆◆
Malvern Road, Bringsty,
Worcester WR6 5TR
T: (01885) 488875
F: (01885) 488875

Littlebridge House ◆◆◆◆
Tedstone Wafre, Bromyard,
Herefordshire HR7 4PN
T: (01885) 482471
F: (01885) 482471

The Old Cowshed ◆◆◆◆
Avenbury Court Farm, Bromyard,
Herefordshire HR7 4LA
T: (01885) 482384
F: (01885) 482367
E: combes@cowshed.uk.com
I: www.cowshed.uk.com

Park House Hotel ◆◆◆
28 Sherford Street, Bromyard,
Herefordshire HR7 4DL
T: (01885) 482294
F: (01885) 482294
E: parkhouse@callnet.uk.com
I: www.bromyard.
co.uk/parkhouse

BROOM
Warwickshire

The Arrows ◆◆◆◆
Broom, Alcester, Warwickshire
B50 4HR
T: (01789) 772260 &
07788 140182
F: (01789) 772260
E: softly@compuserve.com
I: www.SmoothHound.
co.uk/hotels/arrows.html

BROSELEY
Shropshire

The Pheasant Inn ◆◆◆
56 Church Street, Broseley,
Telford, Shropshire TF12 5BX
T: (01952) 884499
F: (01952) 884499

Rock Dell ◆◆◆◆
30 Ironbridge Road, Broseley,
Shropshire TF12 5AJ
T: (01952) 883054
F: (01952) 883054
E: rockdell@ukgateway.net

BROUGHTON ASTLEY
Leicestershire

The Old Farm House ◆◆◆
Old Mill Road, Broughton Astley,
Leicester LE9 6PQ
T: (01455) 282254
E: annabelc@talk21.com

BROXWOOD
Herefordshire

Broxwood Court ◆◆◆◆◆
Broxwood, Leominster,
Herefordshire HR6 9JJ
T: (01544) 340245
F: (01544) 340573
E: mikeanne@broxwood.kc3.
co.uk

BUCKNELL
Shropshire

The Hall ◆◆◆
Bucknell, Shropshire SY7 0AA
T: (01547) 530249
F: (01547) 530249
E: hall@ukworld.net
I: www.ukworld.net/hall

The Willows ◆◆◆◆
Bucknell, Shropshire SG20 0AA
T: (01547) 530201

BUGBROOKE
Northamptonshire

The Byre ◆◆◆◆
2 Church Lane, Bugbrooke,
Northampton NN7 3PB
T: (01604) 830319

BULLO PILL
Gloucestershire

Grove Farm
Rating Applied For
Bullo Pill, Newnham-on-Severn,
Gloucestershire GL14 1DZ
T: (01594) 516304
F: (01594) 516304

BUNNY
Nottinghamshire

The Rancliffe Arms ◆◆◆◆
Loughborough Road, Bunny,
Nottingham NG11 6QT
T: (0115) 9844727

BURLTON
Shropshire

Petton Hall Farm ◆◆◆◆
Petton, Burlton, Shrewsbury
SY4 5TH
T: (01939) 270601
F: (01939) 270601
I: www.virtualshrops.co.
u/pettonhall

BURSTON
Staffordshire

Yew Tree House ◆◆◆
Burston, ST18 0DR
T: (01889) 508063
F: (01889) 508063
E: hazel@yewtreeburston.
freeserve.co.uk

BURTON DASSETT
Warwickshire

The White House Bed and Breakfast ◆◆◆◆
Burton Dassett, Southam, Warwickshire CV47 2AB
T: (01295) 770143 &
0476 458314
E: lisa@whitehouse10.freeserve. co.uk

BURTON LAZARS
Leicestershire

The Grange ◆◆◆◆
New Road, Burton Lazars, Melton Mowbray, Leicestershire LE14 2UU
T: (01664) 560775
F: (01664) 560775

BURTON UPON TRENT
Staffordshire

The Delter Hotel ◆◆◆
5 Derby Road, Burton upon Trent, Staffordshire DE14 1RU
T: (01283) 535115
F: (01283) 845261
E: delterhotel@hotmail.com
I: www.burtonontrenthotels. co.uk

Meadowview ◆◆◆
203 Newton Road, Winshill, Burton upon Trent, Staffordshire DE15 0TU
T: (01283) 564046

The New Inn ◆◆◆
Five Lanes End, Burton Road, Needwood, Burton upon Trent, Staffordshire DE13 9PB
T: (01283) 575392
F: (01283) 575708
E: barry@newinn.co.uk
I: www.newinn.co.uk

New Inn Farm ◆◆◆
Burton Road, Needwood, Burton upon Trent, Staffordshire DE13 9PB
T: (01283) 575435 &
07801 491482

Primrose Bank House ◆◆
194A Newton Road, Burton upon Trent, Staffordshire DE15 0TU
T: (01283) 532569

BUSHLEY
Worcestershire

Shiloh House ◆◆◆
Church End, Bushley, Tewkesbury, Gloucestershire GL20 6HT
T: (01684) 293435

BUTTERTON
Staffordshire

Black Lion Inn ◆◆◆
Butterton, Leek, Staffordshire ST13 7ST
T: (01538) 304232
E: theblacklion@clara.net
I: www.theblacklion.clara.net

Butterton House ◆◆◆
Park Road, Butterton, Newcastle-under-Lyme, Staffordshire ST5 4DZ
T: (01782) 619085
E: sjtoast@aol.com

Butterton Moor House ◆◆◆◆
Parsons Lane, Butterton, Leek, Staffordshire ST13 7PD
T: (01538) 304506
F: (01538) 304506

Coxon Green Farm ◆◆◆◆
Butterton, Leek, Staffordshire ST13 7TA
T: (01538) 304221

Greenhead Cottage ◆◆◆
Pot Hooks Lane, Butterton, Leek, Staffordshire ST13 7SY
T: (01538) 304541

Heathy Roods Farm ◆◆◆◆
Butterton, Leek, Staffordshire ST13 7SR
T: (01538) 304397

New Hayes Farm ◆◆◆◆
Trentham Road, Butterton, Newcastle-under-Lyme, Staffordshire ST5 4DX
T: (01782) 680889 &
07703 882593
E: newhayesfarm@ukworld.net
I: www.SmoothHound. co.uk/Hotels/newhayes.html

BUXTON
Derbyshire

Abbey Guesthouse ◆◆◆
43 South Avenue, Buxton, Derbyshire SK17 6NQ
T: (01298) 26419
E: aghbuxton@aol.com

All Seasons Guest House ◆◆◆◆
4 Wye Grove, Buxton, Derbyshire SK17 9AJ
T: (01298) 74628 &
07970 186715
E: chrisandruss@ allseasonsguesthouse.fsnet. co.uk
I: www.allseasonsguesthouse. fsnet.co.uk

Alpine Guesthouse ◆◆◆◆
1 Thornsett, Hardwick Mount, Buxton, Derbyshire SK17 6PS
T: (01298) 26155 &
07970 652238
E: exclusively.psandqs@talk21. com
I: www.exclusivelypsandqs.com

Barn House ◆◆◆◆
Litton Mill, Buxton, Derbyshire SK17 8SW
T: (01298) 872751
F: (01298) 872751

Braemar ◆◆◆◆
10 Compton Road, Buxton, Derbyshire SK17 9DN
T: (01298) 78050
E: buxtonbraemar@supanet. com
I: www.cressbrook. co.uk/buxton/braemar

Buxton View ◆◆◆◆
74 Corbar Road, Buxton, Derbyshire SK17 6RJ
T: (01298) 79222 &
07710 516846
F: (01298) 79222
E: rogerbuxtonview@aol.com

Buxton Wheelhouse Hotel ◆◆◆◆
19 College Road, Buxton, Derbyshire SK17 9DZ
T: (01298) 24869 & 26040
F: (01298) 24869
E: lyndsie@buxton-wheelhouse. com
I: www.buxton-wheelhouse.com

Buxton's Victorian Guesthouse ◆◆◆◆◆
3A Broad Walk, Buxton, Derbyshire SK17 6JE
T: (01298) 78759 &
07801 861227
F: (01296) 74732
E: buxvic@x-stream.co.uk
I: www.smoothhound.co.uk

Compton House Guesthouse ◆◆◆
4 Compton Road, Buxton, Derbyshire SK17 9DN
T: (01298) 26926
F: (01298) 26926
E: comptonbuxton@aol.com
I: www.cressbrook. co.uk/buxton/compton

Coningsby ◆◆◆◆◆
6 Macclesfield Road, Buxton, Derbyshire SK17 9AH
T: (01298) 26735
F: (01298) 26735
E: coningsby@btinternet.com

Cotesfield Farm ◆◆
Parsley Hay, Buxton, Derbyshire SK17 0BD
T: (01298) 83256 &
07850 051148
F: (01298) 83256

Devonshire Arms ◆◆◆
Peak Forest, Buxton, Derbyshire SK17 8EJ
T: (01298) 23875 &
07831 707325
I: www.devarms.com

Devonshire Lodge Guesthouse ◆◆◆◆
2 Manchester Road, Buxton, Derbyshire SK17 6SB
T: (01298) 71487

Fairhaven ◆◆
1 Dale Terrace, Buxton, Derbyshire SK17 6LU
T: (01298) 24481
F: (01298) 24481
E: paulandcatherine@ fairhavenguesthouse.freeserve. co.uk

Ford Side House ◆◆◆◆
125 Lightwood Road, Buxton, Derbyshire SK17 6RW
T: (01298) 72842
E: fordside.house@ukgateway. net

Grendon Guesthouse ◆◆◆◆
Bishops Lane, Buxton, Derbyshire SK17 6UN
T: (01298) 78831 &
07711 380143
F: (01298) 79257
E: parkerh1@talk21.com
I: www.cressbrook. co.uk/buxton/grendon/

Griff Guesthouse ◆◆
2 Compton Road, Buxton, Derbyshire SK17 9DN
T: (01298) 23628 & 71778

Grosvenor House ◆◆◆◆
1 Broad Walk, Buxton, Derbyshire SK17 6JE
T: (01298) 72439
F: (01298) 72439
I: www.SmoothHound. co.uk/hotels/grosvenr.html

Harefield ◆◆◆◆
15 Marlborough Road, Buxton, Derbyshire SK17 6RD
T: (01298) 24029
F: (01298) 24029
E: hardie@harefield1.freeserve. co.uk
I: www.harefield1.freeserve. co.uk

Hawthorn Farm Guesthouse ◆◆◆
Fairfield Road, Buxton, Derbyshire SK17 7ED
T: (01298) 23230
F: (01298) 71322

Kingscroft ◆◆◆◆
10 Green Lane, Buxton, Derbyshire SK17 9DP
T: (01298) 22757 &
07889 977971
F: (01298) 27858

Lakenham Guesthouse ◆◆◆◆
11 Burlington Road, Buxton, Derbyshire SK17 9AL
T: (01298) 79209
F: (01285) 711349
E: milton@farmersweekly.net
I: www.miltonfarm.co.uk

Lowther Guesthouse ◆◆◆◆
7 Hardwick Square West, Buxton, Derbyshire SK17 6PX
T: (01298) 71479 &
07803 693816

Nithen Cottage ◆◆◆◆
123 Park Road, Buxton, Derbyshire SK17 6SP
T: (01298) 24679 &
07703 717335
E: nithencott@netscape.co.uk

The Old Manse Private Hotel ◆◆◆
6 Clifton Road, Silverlands, Buxton, Derbyshire SK17 6QL
T: (01298) 25638
E: old_manse@yahoo.co.uk
I: www.oldmanse.co.uk

Oldfield House ◆◆◆◆
8 Macclesfield Road, Buxton, Derbyshire SK17 9AH
T: (01298) 24371
E: info@buxtonlet.com
I: www.buxtonlet.com

The Queens Head Hotel ◆◆◆
High Street, Buxton, Derbyshire SK17 6EU
T: (01298) 23841
F: (01298) 71238

Roseleigh Hotel ◆◆◆
19 Broad Walk, Buxton, Derbyshire SK17 6JR
T: (01298) 24904
F: (01298) 24904
E: enquiries@roseleighhotel. co.uk
I: www.roseleighhotel.co.uk

Staden Grange Country House ◆◆◆
Staden Lane, Staden, Buxton, Derbyshire SK17 9RZ
T: (01298) 24965
F: (01298) 72067
E: staden@grange100. fsbusiness.co.uk

Stoneridge ◆◆◆◆
9 Park Road, Buxton, Derbyshire SK17 6SG
T: (01298) 26120
E: hoskin@stoneridge.co.uk
I: www.stoneridge.co.uk

Templeton Guesthouse ◆◆
Compton Road, Buxton,
Derbyshire SK17 9DN
T: (01298) 25275 &
07831 606601
F: (01298) 25275
E: tembux@lineone.net

Westminster Hotel ◆◆◆
21 Broad Walk, Buxton,
Derbyshire SK17 6JR
T: (01298) 23929 &
07770 503629
F: (01298) 71121
E: cecelia@westminsterhotel.
demon.co.uk
I: www.westminsterhotel.
demon.co.uk

BYFIELD
Northamptonshire
Glebe Farm Bed and Breakfast
◆◆◆
Glebe Farm, 61 Church Street,
Byfield, Daventry,
Northamptonshire NN11 6XN
T: (01327) 260512 &
07773 398550
F: (01327) 260512
E: sagem12924@talk21.com

CALDECOTE
Warwickshire
**Hill House Country Guest
House**◆◆◆◆
Off Mancetter Road, Caldecote,
Nuneaton, Warwickshire
CV10 0RS
T: (024) 7639 6685
F: (024) 7639 6685

Leathermill Grange ◆◆◆◆◆
Leathermill Lane, Caldecote,
Nuneaton, Warwickshire
CV10 0RX
T: (01827) 714637
F: (01827) 716422
E: davidcodd@
leathermillgrange.co.uk
I: www.leathermillgrange.co.uk

CALLOW
Herefordshire
Knockerhill Farm ◆◆◆◆
Callow, Hereford HR2 8BP
T: (01432) 268460
F: (01432) 268460

CALLOW END
Worcestershire
Henwick House ◆◆◆◆
Jennett Tree Lane, Callow End,
Worcester WR2 4UB
T: (01905) 831736
F: (01905) 831886
E: henwick@lineone.net
I: www.henwickhouse.net

CALMSDEN
Gloucestershire
The Old House ◆◆◆◆
Calmsden, Cirencester,
Gloucestershire GL7 5ET
T: (01285) 831240 &
07720 779456
F: (01285) 831240
E: baxter@calmsden.freeserve.
co.uk

CALVER
Derbyshire
The Old Village Store ◆◆◆
High Street, Calver, Hope Valley
S32 3XP
T: (01433) 630523
I: www.oldvillagestore.com

Rose Cottage ◆◆◆◆
Main Street, Calver, Hope Valley
S32 3XR
T: (01433) 630769
E: cronksley@btclick.com

Valley View ◆◆◆◆
Smithy Knoll Road, Calver, Hope
Valley S32 3XW
T: (01433) 631407
F: (01433) 631407
E: sue@a-place-2-stay.co.uk
I: www.a-place-2-stay.co.uk

CANON PYON
Herefordshire
Nags Head ◆◆◆
Canon Pyon, Hereford HR4 8NY
T: (01432) 830252

CARDINGTON
Shropshire
Woodside Farm ◆◆◆◆
Cardington, Church Stretton,
Shropshire SY6 7LB
T: (01694) 771314

CARRINGTON
Nottinghamshire
**Paramount Hotel and Tandoori
Restaurant**◆◆
328 Mansfield Road, Carrington,
Nottingham NG5 2EF
T: (0115) 962 1621
F: (0115) 956 1561

CARSINGTON
Derbyshire
Breach Farm ◆◆◆◆
Carsington, Matlock, Derbyshire
DE4 4DD
T: (01629) 540265

CASTLE DONINGTON
Leicestershire
Castletown House ◆◆◆◆
4 High Street, Castle Donington,
Derby DE74 2PP
T: (01332) 812018 & 814550
F: (01332) 814550
E: enquiry@castletownhouse.
co.uk
I: www.castletownhouse.com

Little Chimneys Guesthouse
◆◆◆
19 The Green, Diseworth, Castle
Donington, Derby DE74 2QN
T: (01332) 812458 &
07889 338828
F: (01332) 853336
E: kay@little-chimneys.demon.
co.uk
I: www.little-chimneys.demon.
co.uk

**Scot's Corner Guesthouse Bed
and Breakfast**◆◆◆
82 Park Lane, Castle Donington,
Derby DE74 2JG
T: (01332) 811226 &
0771 2084119
E: scots-corner@amserve.net
I: www.scots-corner.com

CASTLEMORTON
Worcestershire
Hawthorne Cottage ◆◆◆
New Road, Castlemorton,
Malvern, Worcestershire
WR13 6BT
T: (01684) 833266 &
0780 8870722
F: (01684) 833857

CASTLETON
Derbyshire
Bargate Cottage ◆◆◆◆
Bargate, Market Place, Castleton,
Hope Valley S33 8WG
T: (01433) 620201
F: (01433) 621739
I: www.peakland.com/bargate

Causeway House ◆◆◆
Back Street, Castleton, Hope
Valley S33 8WE
T: (01433) 623291 & (0114) 236
8574
E: susanbridget@aol.com
I: www.causewayhouse.co.uk

Cryer House ◆◆◆
Castle Street, Castleton, Hope
Valley S33 8WG
T: (01433) 620244
F: (01433) 620244
E: FleeSkel@aol.com

Dunscar Farm Bed & Breakfast
◆◆◆◆
Dunscar Farm, Castleton, Hope
Valley S33 8WA
T: (01433) 620483
I: www.hopenet.
co.uk/dunscarfarm

Hillside House ◆◆◆◆
Pindale Road, Castleton, Hope
Valley S33 8WU
T: (01433) 620312
F: (01433) 620312

Ramblers Rest ◆◆◆
Mill Bridge, Castleton, Hope
Valley S33 8WR
T: (01433) 620125
F: (01433) 621677
E: peter.d.m.gillott@btinternet.
com
I: www.peakland.
com/ramblersrest

**Swiss House Hotel and Nero's
Italian Restaurant**◆◆◆
How Lane, Castleton, Hope
Valley S33 8WJ
T: (01433) 621098 & 623781
F: (01433) 623781
E: swisshousehotel@
castleton8WJ.fsnet.co.uk

Ye Olde Cheshire Cheese Inn
Rating Applied For
How Lane, Castleton, Hope
Valley S33 8WJ
T: (01433) 620330 &
07836 369636
F: (01433) 621847
I: www.peakland.com.
cheshirecheese

CAUNTON
Nottinghamshire
Knapthorpe Lodge ◆◆◆
Hockerton Road, Caunton,
Newark, Nottinghamshire
NG23 6AZ
T: (01636) 636262
F: (01636) 636415

CHADDESDEN
Derbyshire
Green Gables ◆◆◆
19 Highfield Lane, Chaddesden,
Derby DE21 6PG
T: (01332) 672298
E: us@sallyandtony.fsnet.co.uk
I: www.greengablesuk.com

CHALFORD
Gloucestershire
The Ragged Cot Inn ◆◆◆
Hyde, Chalford, Stroud,
Gloucestershire GL6 8PE
T: (01453) 884643 & 731333
F: (01453) 731166
E: david-savage@
oasis-holdings.com
I: home.btclick.com/ragged.cot

CHAPEL-EN-LE-FRITH
Derbyshire
The Potting Shed ◆◆◆◆
Bank Hall, Chapel-en-le-Frith,
High Peak SK23 9UB
T: (01298) 812656 & (0161) 338
8134

Ridge Hall ◆◆◆◆◆
Chapel-en-le-Frith, High Peak
SK23 9UD
T: (01298) 813130 & 815862
F: (01298) 815863
E: ridgehall@aol.com
I: www.ridge-hall.com

Slack Hall Farm ◆◆◆
Castleton Road, Chapel-en-le-
Frith, High Peak SK23 0QS
T: (01298) 812845

CHARLTON KINGS
Gloucestershire
Glenfall House ◆◆◆
Mill Lane, Charlton Kings,
Cheltenham, Gloucestershire
GL54 4EP
T: (01242) 583654
F: (01242) 251314
E: glenfall@surfaid.org
I: www.users.surfaid.
org/~glenfall

Orion House ◆◆◆
220 London Road, Charlton
Kings, Cheltenham,
Gloucestershire GL52 6HW
T: (01242) 233309
F: (01242) 233309
E: ena@orionhouse.fs.net.co.uk

CHEADLE
Staffordshire
Caverswall Castle ◆◆◆◆◆
Caverswall, Stoke-on-Trent
ST11 9EA
T: (01782) 393239
F: (01782) 394590
E: yarsargent@hotmail.com
I: www.caverswallcastle.com

The Church Farm ◆◆◆◆
Holt Lane, Kingsley, Stoke-on-
Trent ST10 2BA
T: (01538) 754759
F: (01538) 754759

Ley Fields Farm ◆◆◆◆
Leek Road, Cheadle, Cheshire
ST10 2EF
T: (01538) 752875
F: (01583) 752875
E: kathryn@leyfieldsfarm.
freeserve.co.uk

Park Lodge Guest House ◆◆◆
1 Tean Road, Cheadle, Cheshire
ST10 1LG
T: (01538) 753562
E: margaret.mower@amserver.
net

Park View Guest House ◆◆◆
15 Mill Road, Cheadle, Cheshire
ST10 1NG
T: (01538) 755412
I: www.theparkviewguesthouse.
com

**Woodhouse Farm Country
Guesthouse** ◆◆◆
Lockwood Road, Near Kingsley
Holt, Cheadle, Stoke-on-Trent,
Staffordshire ST10 4QU
T: (01538) 754250
F: (01538) 754470
E: ask@woodhousefarm.net
I: www.woodhousefarm.net

CHEDDLETON
Staffordshire

Brook House Farm ◆◆◆
Cheddleton, Leek, Staffordshire
ST13 7DF
T: (01538) 360296

Choir Cottage and Choir House
◆◆◆◆◆
Ostlers Lane, Cheddleton, Leek,
Staffordshire ST13 7HS
T: (01538) 360561 &
07703 622328
E: enquiries@choircottage.co.uk
I: www.choircottage.co.uk

Hillcrest ◆◆◆◆
74 Folly Lane, Cheddleton, Leek,
Staffordshire ST13 7DA
T: (01782) 550483

CHELMARSH
Shropshire

Hampton House ◆◆◆◆
Hampton Loade, Chelmarsh,
Bridgnorth, Shropshire
WV16 6BN
T: (01746) 861436

Unicorn Inn ◆◆
Hampton Loade, Chelmarsh,
Bridgnorth, Shropshire
WV16 6BN
T: (01746) 861515
F: (01746) 861515
E: unicorninn.bridgnorth@
virginnet.co.uk
I: freespace.virginnet.
co.uk/unicorninn.bridgnorth

CHELMORTON
Derbyshire

Ditch House ◆◆◆◆
Chelmorton, Buxton, Derbyshire
SK17 9SG
T: (01298) 85719
F: (01298) 85719

Shallow Grange ◆◆◆◆◆
Chelmorton, Buxton, Derbyshire
SK17 9SG
T: (01298) 23578
F: (01298) 78242
E: holland@shallowgrangefarm.
freeserve.co.uk

CHELTENHAM
Gloucestershire

The Abbey Hotel ◆◆◆◆
14-16 Bath Parade, Cheltenham,
Gloucestershire GL53 7HN
T: (01242) 516053
F: (01242) 513034
E: office@
abbeyhotel-cheltenham.com
I: www.abbeyhotel-cheltenham.
com

Barn End ◆◆◆◆
23 Cheltenham Road, Bishop's
Cleeve, Cheltenham,
Gloucestershire GL52 8LU
T: (01242) 672404
E: joymerrell@cs.com

The Battledown ◆◆◆
125 Hales Road, Cheltenham,
Gloucestershire GL52 6ST
T: (01242) 233881
F: (01242) 524198
E: smurth@fsbdial.co.uk

Beaumont House Hotel
◆◆◆◆
Shurdington Road, Cheltenham,
Gloucestershire GL53 0JE
T: (01242) 245986
F: (01242) 520044
E: rocking.horse@virgin.net
I: www.smoothhound.
co.uk/hotels/beauchel.html

Beechworth Lawn Hotel
◆◆◆◆
133 Hales Road, Cheltenham,
Gloucestershire GL52 6ST
T: (01242) 522583
F: (01242) 574800
E: beechworth.lawn@dial.pipcx.
com
I: www.beechworthlawnhotel.
co.uk

Bentleyville ◆◆◆
179 Gloucester Road,
Cheltenham, Gloucestershire
GL51 8NQ
T: (01242) 581476 &
07974 806229
F: (01242) 581476
E: bentleyville_179@hotmail.
com

Bentons ◆◆◆
71 Bath Road, Cheltenham,
Gloucestershire GL53 7LH
T: (01242) 517417 & 527772
F: (01242) 527772

Bibury House ◆◆◆
Priory Place, Cheltenham,
Gloucestershire GL52 6HG
T: (01242) 525014

Brennan Guest House ◆◆◆
21 St Lukes Road, Cheltenham,
Gloucestershire GL53 7JF
T: (01242) 525904 &
0771 2317494
F: (01242) 525904

Bridge House ◆◆◆◆
88 Lansdown Road, Cheltenham,
Gloucestershire GL51 6QR
T: (01242) 583559 &
07960 740816
F: (01242) 255920
E: bridgehouse@freeuk.com

Central Hotel ◆◆
7-9 Portland Street,
Cheltenham, Gloucestershire
GL52 2NZ
T: (01242) 582172 & 524789

Crossways Guest House ◆◆◆
Oriel Place, 57 Bath Road,
Cheltenham, Gloucestershire
GL53 7LH
T: (01242) 527683
F: (01242) 577226
E: cross.ways@btinternet.com
I: www.crossways.btinternet.
co.uk

Detmore House ◆◆◆
London Road, Charlton Kings,
Cheltenham, Gloucestershire
GL52 6UT
T: (01242) 582868
F: (01242) 582868

Elm Villa ◆◆
49 London Road, Cheltenham,
Gloucestershire GL52 6HE
T: (01242) 231909

Evington Hill Farm ◆◆◆◆
Tewkesbury Road, The Leigh,
Gloucester, GL19 4AQ
T: (01242) 680255

Glencree ◆◆◆◆
80 Lansdown Road, Cheltenham,
Gloucestershire GL51 6QW
T: (01242) 260242
F: (01242) 260242
E: jdn.hopkins@virgin.net

Ham Hill Farm ◆◆◆◆
Whittington, Cheltenham,
Gloucestershire GL54 4EZ
T: (01242) 584415 &
07711 832041
F: (01242) 222535

**Hannaford's
Rating Applied For**
20 Evesham Road, Cheltenham,
Gloucestershire GL52 2AB
T: (01242) 515181 & 524190
F: (01242) 257571
E: dc@hannafords-hotel.
demon.co.uk
I: www.hannafords-hotel.
demon.co.uk

Hollington House Hotel
◆◆◆◆
115 Hales Road, Cheltenham,
Gloucestershire GL52 6ST
T: (01242) 256652
F: (01242) 570280
E: hollingtonhscheltenham@
lineone.net

Home Cottage ◆◆◆
1 Priors Road, Cheltenham,
Gloucestershire GL52 5AB
T: (01242) 518144
F: (01242) 518144

Hope Orchard ◆◆◆
Gloucester Road, Staverton,
Cheltenham, Gloucestershire
GL51 0TF
T: (01452) 855556
F: (01452) 530037
E: info@hopeorchard.com
I: www.hopeorchard.com

Ivydene Guest House ◆◆◆
145 Hewlett Road, Cheltenham,
Gloucestershire GL52 6TS
T: (01242) 521726 & 525694
F: (01242) 525694
E: jvhopwood@ivydenehouse.
freeserve.co.uk
I: www.ivydenehouse.freeserve.
co.uk

Lawn Hotel ◆◆◆
5 Pittville Lawn, Cheltenham,
Gloucestershire GL52 2BE
T: (01242) 526638
F: (01242) 526638

Lawn House ◆◆◆◆
11 London Road, Cheltenham,
Gloucestershire GL52 6EX
T: (01242) 578486 &
07768 457403
F: (01242) 578486

Leeswood ◆◆
14 Montpellier Drive,
Cheltenham, Gloucestershire
GL50 1TX
T: (01242) 524813
F: (01242) 524813
E: leeswood@hotmail.com
I: www.leeswood.org.uk

Lonsdale House ◆◆◆
Montpellier Drive, Cheltenham,
Gloucestershire GL50 1TX
T: (01242) 232379
F: (01242) 232379
E: lonsdalehouse@hotmail.com

Milton House ◆◆◆◆◆
12 Bayshill Rod, Royal Parade,
Cheltenham, Gloucestershire
GL50 3AY
T: (01242) 582601
F: (01242) 222326
E: info@miltonhousehotel.co.uk
I: www.miltonhousehotel.co.uk

Montpellier Hotel ◆◆◆
33 Montpellier Terrace,
Cheltenham, Gloucestershire
GL50 1UX
T: (01242) 526009

Number 91 ◆◆◆◆
91 Montpellier Terrace,
Cheltenham, Gloucestershire
GL50 1XA
T: (01242) 579441
F: (01242) 579441

Old Rectory ◆◆◆◆
Woolstone, Cheltenham,
Gloucestershire GL52 4RG
T: (01242) 673766
E: fesey@aol.com
I: www.theoldrectory.com

Parkview ◆◆◆
4 Pittville Crescent, Cheltenham,
Gloucestershire GL52 2QZ
T: (01242) 575567
E: jospa@tr250.freeserve.co.uk

Pike House ◆◆◆◆
Fossebridge, Cheltenham,
Gloucestershire GL54 3JR
T: (01285) 720223 &
07765 482068
F: (01285) 720223

Pittville Gate Hotel ◆◆◆
12/14 Pittville Lawn,
Cheltenham, Gloucestershire
GL52 2BD
T: (01242) 221922
F: (01242) 244687

Saint Cloud ◆◆◆
97 Leckhampton Road,
Cheltenham, Gloucestershire
GL53 0BZ
T: (01242) 575245

St Michaels ◆◆◆◆
4 Montpellier Drive,
Cheltenham, Gloucestershire
GL50 1TX
T: (01242) 513587
F: (01242) 513587
E: st_michaels_guesthouse@
yahoo.com
I: st_michaels.future.easyspace.
com

Segrave ◆◆◆
7 Park Place, Cheltenham,
Gloucestershire GL50 2QS
T: (01242) 523606

Steyne Cross Bed and Breakfast ◆◆◆
Steyne Cross, Malvern Road,
Cheltenham, Gloucestershire
GL50 2NU
T: (01242) 255289
F: (01242) 255289
E: sumiko@susumago.f9.co.uk

Stray Leaves ◆◆◆
282 Gloucester Road,
Cheltenham, Gloucestershire
GL51 7AG
T: (01242) 572303
F: (01242) 708382

Stretton Lodge Hotel ◆◆◆◆
Western Road, Cheltenham,
Gloucestershire GL50 3RN
T: (01242) 570771
F: (01242) 528724
E: info@strettonlodge.demon.
co.uk
I: www.strettonlodge.demon.
co.uk

Westal Court ◆◆◆◆
2 Westal Court, 27 Hatherley
Road, Cheltenham,
Gloucestershire GL51 6EB
T: (01242) 696679
F: (01242) 696679
E: martinkw@onetel.net

Westcourt ◆◆◆
14 Old Bath Road, Cheltenham,
Gloucestershire GL53 7QD
T: (01242) 241777 & 228555
F: (01242) 228666
E: michael.seston@which.net

Whittington Lodge Farm
◆◆◆◆
Whittington, Cheltenham,
Gloucestershire GL54 4HB
T: (01242) 820603 &
07976 691589
F: (01242) 820603
E: i.boyd@farmline.com

Wishmoor Guest House
◆◆◆◆
147 Hales Road, Cheltenham,
Gloucestershire GL52 6TD
T: (01242) 238504
F: (01242) 226090
E: wishmoor@aol.com

The Wynyards ◆◆◆◆
Butts Lane, Woodmancote,
Cheltenham, Gloucestershire
GL52 4QH
T: (01242) 673876
E: graham@wynyards1.
freeserve.co.uk
I: www.SmoothHound.
co.uk/hotels/wynyards.html

CHESTERFIELD
Derbyshire

Abigails ◆◆◆
62 Brockwell Lane, Chesterfield,
Derbyshire S40 4EE
T: (01246) 279391 &
07970 777909
F: (01246) 854468
E: gail@abigails.fsnet.co.uk
I: www.abigailsguesthouse.co.uk

Anis Louise Guesthouse ◆◆◆
34 Clarence Road, Chesterfield,
Derbyshire S40 1LN
T: (01246) 235412
E: neil@anislouise.co.uk
I: www.anislouise.co.uk

Batemans Mill ◆◆◆◆
Mill Lane, Old Tupton,
Chesterfield, Derbyshire S42 6AE
T: (01246) 862296
F: (01246) 865672
E: tracey@batemansmillhotel.
co.uk
I: www.batemansmillhotel.co.uk

Brook House ◆◆◆◆
45 Westbrook Drive, Brookside,
Chesterfield, Derbyshire S40 3PQ
T: (01246) 568535

Clarendon Guesthouse ◆◆◆
32 Clarence Road, West Bars,
Chesterfield, Derbyshire S40 1LN
T: (01246) 235004

Fairfield House ◆◆◆
3 Fairfield Road, Chesterfield,
Derbyshire S40 4TR
T: (01246) 204905
F: (01246) 230155
E: 5p8@talk21.com.uk

Locksley ◆◆◆
21 Tennyson Avenue,
Chesterfield, Derbyshire S40 4SN
T: (01246) 273332

The Maylands ◆◆◆
56 Sheffield Road, Chesterfield,
Derbyshire S41 7LS
T: (01246) 233602

Shakespeare Villa ◆◆◆
3 Saint Margarets Drive,
Saltergate, Chesterfield,
Derbyshire S40 4SY
T: (01246) 200704

The Shoulder at Hardstoft
◆◆◆
Hardstoft, Chesterfield,
Derbyshire S45 8AF
T: (01246) 850276
F: (01246) 854760

Springbank Guesthouse ◆
35 Springbank Road,
Chesterfield, Derbyshire S40 1NL
T: (01246) 279232

CHETWYND ASTON
Shropshire

Woodcroft Bed and Breakfast
◆◆◆
Woodcroft, Pitchcroft Lane,
Chetwynd Aston, Newport,
Shropshire TF10 9AU
T: (01952) 812406
I: www.visit-shropshire.
co.uk/woodcroft

CHINLEY
Derbyshire

Mossley House Farm ◆◆◆
Maynestone Road, Chinley, High
Peak SK23 6AH
T: (01663) 750240
F: (01663) 750240

CHIPPING CAMPDEN
Gloucestershire

Badgers Hall Tearooms ◆◆◆◆
High Street, Chipping Campden,
Gloucestershire GL55 6HB
T: (01386) 840839
E: badgershall@talk21.com
I: www.stratford.upon.avon.
co.uk/badgershall.htm

Brymbo ◆◆◆◆
Honeybourne Lane, Mickleton,
Chipping Campden,
Gloucestershire GL55 6PU
T: (01386) 438890
F: (01386) 438113
E: enquiries@brymbo.com
I: www.brymbo.com

Dragon House ◆◆◆◆
High Street, Chipping Campden,
Gloucestershire GL55 6AG
T: (01386) 840734
F: (01386) 840734
E: valatdragonhouse@
btinternet.com
I: www.
dragonhouse-chipping-
campden.com

The Eight Bells ◆◆◆
Church Street, Chipping
Campden, Gloucestershire
GL55 6JG
T: (01386) 840371
F: (01386) 841669
I: www.eightbellsinn.co.uk

Home Farm House ◆◆◆◆
Ebrington, Chipping Campden,
Gloucestershire GL55 6NL
T: (01386) 593309
F: (01386) 593309
E: willstanley@farmersweekly.
net
I: www.stop.at/homefarm

The Kettle House ◆◆◆
Leysbourne, Chipping Campden,
Gloucestershire GL55 6HN
T: (01386) 840328
F: (01386) 841740
E: info@kettlehouse.co.uk
I: www.kettlehouse.co.uk

Manor Farm ◆◆◆◆
Weston Subedge, Chipping
Campden, Gloucestershire
GL55 6QH
T: (01386) 840390 &
07889 108812
F: 08701 640 638
E: lucy@manorfarmbnb.demon.
co.uk
I: www.manorfarmbnb.demon.
co.uk

M'Dina Courtyard ◆◆◆◆
Park Road, Chipping Campden,
Gloucestershire GL55 6EA
T: (01386) 841752
F: (01386) 840942
E: barbara@mdina-bandb.co.uk
I: www.mdina-bandb.co.uk

Nineveh Farm ◆◆◆◆
Campden Road, Mickleton,
Chipping Campden,
Gloucestershire GL55 6PS
T: (01386) 438923 &
07880 737649
E: stay@ninevehfarm.co.uk
I: www.ninevehfarm.co.uk

Orchard Rise
Rating Applied For
Sheep Street, Chipping
Campden, Gloucestershire
GL55 6DR
T: (01386) 840307

Sandalwood House ◆◆◆◆
Back-Ends, Chipping Campden,
Gloucestershire GL55 6AU
T: (01386) 840091
F: (01386) 840091

Weston Park Farm ◆◆◆
Dovers Hill, Chipping Campden,
Gloucestershire GL55 6UW
T: (01386) 840835
E: jane_whitehouse@hotmail.
com

Wyldlands ◆◆◆◆
Broad Campden, Chipping
Campden, Gloucestershire
GL55 6UR
T: (01386) 840478
F: (01386) 849031

CHURCH EATON
Staffordshire

Slab Bridge Cottage ◆◆◆◆
Little Onn, Church Eaton,
Stafford ST20 0AY
T: (01785) 840220
F: (01785) 840220.

CHURCH STRETTON
Shropshire

Acton Scott Farm ◆◆◆
Acton Scott, Church Stretton,
Shropshire SY6 6QN
T: (01694) 781260
E: edandm@clara.co.uk
I: welcome.to/acton-scott-h

Belvedere Guest House ◆◆◆◆
Burway Road, Church Stretton,
Shropshire SY6 6DP
T: (01694) 722232
F: (01694) 722232
E: belv@bigfoot.com
I: www.smoothhound.
co.uk/hotels/belvedere.html

Brereton's Farm ◆◆◆
Church Stretton, Shropshire
SY6 6QD
T: (01694) 781201
F: (01694) 781201

Brook House Farm ◆◆◆
Wall-under-Heywood, Church
Stretton, Shropshire SY6 7DS
T: (01694) 771308

Brookfields Guesthouse ◆◆◆
Watling St. North, Church
Stretton, Shropshire SY6 7AR
T: (01694) 722314

The Coates ◆◆
Rushbury, Church Stretton,
Shropshire SY6 7DZ
T: (01694) 771330 &
07779 854950
F: (01694) 771330
E: sarah-madeley@excite.co.uk

**Cwm Dale Farm Bed and
Breakfast** ◆◆◆
Cwm Dale Farm, Cwm Dale
Valley, Church Stretton,
Shropshire SY6 6JL
T: (01694) 722362 &
07860 108031
F: (01694) 724656
E: susan@cwmdale

Gilberries Cottage ◆◆◆◆
Wall-under-Heywood, Church
Stretton, Shropshire SY6 7HZ
T: (01694) 771400
F: (01694) 771663
E: griffiths@gilberries.freeserve.
co.uk

Grove Farm ◆◆
Cardington, Church Stretton,
Shropshire SY6 7JZ
T: (01694) 771451

Highcliffe ♦♦
Madeira Walk, Church Stretton,
Shropshire SY6 6JQ
T: (01694) 722908

Jinlye ♦♦♦♦♦
Castle Hill, All Stretton, Church
Stretton, Shropshire SY6 6JP
T: (01694) 723243
F: (01694) 723243
E: info@jinlye.co.uk
I: www.jinlye.co.uk

Juniper Cottage ♦♦♦♦
All Stretton, Church Stretton,
Shropshire SY6 6HG
T: (01694) 723427
F: (01694) 723427

Old Rectory Cottage ♦♦♦
Burway Road, Church Stretton,
Shropshire SY6 6DP
T: (01694) 722973

Old Rectory House ♦♦♦
Burway Road, Church Stretton,
Shropshire SY6 6DW
T: (01694) 724462
F: (01694) 724799
E: smamos@btinternet.com

Rheingold ♦♦♦♦
9 The Bridleways, Church
Stretton, Shropshire SY6 7AN
T: (01694) 723969

Sayang House ♦♦♦♦
Hope Bowdler, Church Stretton,
Shropshire SY6 7DD
T: (01694) 723981
E: madegan@aol.com
I: www.sayanghouse.com

Travellers Rest Inn ♦♦♦
Upper Affcot, Church Stretton,
Shropshire SY6 6RL
T: (01694) 781275
F: (01694) 781555
E: reception@travellersrestinn.
co.uk
I: www.travellersrestinn.co.uk

**Willowfield Country
Guesthouse** ♦♦♦♦♦
Lower Wood, All Stretton,
Church Stretton, Shropshire
SY6 6LF
T: (01694) 751471
F: (01694) 751471
I: www.willowfieldguesthouse.
co.uk

CHURCHAM
Gloucestershire

The Pinetum Lodge
Rating Applied For
Pinetum, Churcham, Gloucester
GL2 8AD
T: (01452) 750554
F: (01452) 750402

Woodgreen Farm ♦♦♦♦
Bulley, Churcham, Gloucester
GL2 8BJ
T: (01452) 790292

CIRENCESTER
Gloucestershire

Abbeymead ♦♦♦
39a Victoria Road, Cirencester,
Gloucestershire GL7 1ES
T: (01285) 653740
F: (01285) 720770
E: abbeymead@amserve.net
I: www.smoothhound.co.uk/shs.
htnl

Apsley Villa ♦♦♦
16 Victoria Road, Cirencester,
Gloucestershire GL7 1ES
T: (01285) 653489

The Black Horse ♦♦
17 Castle Street, Cirencester,
Gloucestershire GL7 1QD
T: (01285) 653187
F: (01285) 659772

Brooklands Farm ♦♦♦
Ewen, Cirencester,
Gloucestershire GL7 6BU
T: (01285) 770487
F: (01285) 770487
I: www.glosfarmhols.co.uk

The Bungalow ♦♦♦
93 Victoria Road, Cirencester,
Gloucestershire GL7 1ES
T: (01285) 654179 &
07778 985975
F: (01285) 656159
E: CBEARD7@compuserve.com

Catherine Wheel ♦♦♦
Arlington Bibury, Cirencester,
Gloucestershire GL7 5ND
T: (01285) 740250
F: (01285) 740779

Chesil Rocks ♦♦♦
Baunton Lane, Stratton,
Cirencester, Gloucestershire
GL7 2LL
T: (01285) 655031

**Claremont Villa Bed and
Breakfast** ♦♦♦
131 Cheltenham Road, Stratton,
Cirencester, Gloucestershire
GL7 2JF
T: (01285) 654759

Coleen Bed and Breakfast
♦♦♦♦
Ashton Road, Siddington,
Cirencester, Gloucestershire
GL7 6HR
T: (01285) 642203
E: bookings@coleen.co.uk
I: www.coleen.co.uk

Coltsmoor Farm ♦♦♦♦
Coln St Aldwyns, Cirencester,
Gloucestershire GL7 5AX
T: (01285) 750527
F: (01285) 750246

The Corner House ♦♦♦♦
101A Victoria Road, Cirencester,
Gloucestershire GL7 1EU
T: (01285) 641958
F: (01285) 640805
E: thecorner.house@virgin.net
I: www.freespace.virgin.
net/thecorner.house

Eliot Arms Hotel Free House
♦♦♦♦
Clarks Hay, South Cerney,
Cirencester, Gloucestershire
GL7 5UA
T: (01285) 860215
F: (01285) 861121
E: eliotarm@aol.uk

Horse and Groom ♦♦♦♦
Cricklade Road, South Cerney,
Cirencester, Gloucestershire
GL7 5QE
T: (01285) 860236

Hunters New House ♦♦♦♦♦
Cherry Tree Lane, Cirencester,
Gloucestershire GL7 5DT
T: (01285) 640790 &
07974 387385
F: (01285) 652275

The Ivy House ♦♦♦
2 Victoria Road, Cirencester,
Gloucestershire GL7 1EN
T: (01285) 656626
E: info@ivyhousecotswolds.com
I: www.ivyhousecotswolds.com

King's Head Hotel ♦♦♦♦
Market Place, Cirencester,
Gloucestershire GL7 2NR
T: (01285) 653322
F: (01285) 655103

Landage House ♦♦♦
Rendcomb, Cirencester,
Gloucestershire GL7 7HB
T: (01285) 831250

The Leauses ♦♦♦
101 Victoria Road, Cirencester,
Gloucestershire GL7 1EU
T: (01285) 653643
F: (01285) 640805
E: the.leauses@virgin.net

Manby's Farm ♦♦♦♦
Oaksey, Malmesbury, Wiltshire
SN16 9SA
T: (01666) 577399 & 577241
F: (01666) 577241
E: manbys@oaksey.junglelink.
co.uk
I: www.cotswoldbandb.com

The Masons Arms ♦♦♦
High Street, Meysey Hampton,
Cirencester, Gloucestershire
GL7 5JT
T: (01285) 850164
F: (01285) 850164
E: jane@themasonsarms.
freeserve.co.uk
I: www.SmoothHound.
co.uk/hotels/mason

Millstone ♦♦♦♦
Down Ampney, Cirencester,
Gloucestershire GL7 5QR
T: (01793) 750475

Oddfellows Arms ♦♦♦
12-14 Chester Street,
Cirencester, Gloucestershire
GL7 1HF
T: (01285) 641540
F: (01285) 640771
E: mike@oddfellowsfsnet.co.uk
I: www.oddfellowsarms.com

The Old Rectory ♦♦♦♦
Rodmarton, Cirencester,
Gloucestershire GL7 6PE
T: (01285) 841246 &
07970 434302
F: (01285) 841488
E: jfitz@globalnet.co.uk

Raydon House Hotel ♦♦♦
3 The Avenue, Cirencester,
Gloucestershire GL7 1EH
T: (01285) 653485
F: (01285) 653485

Smerrill Barns ♦♦♦♦
Kemble, Cirencester,
Gloucestershire GL7 6BW
T: (01285) 770907
F: (01285) 770706
E: gsopher@smerrillbarns.com
I: www.smerrillbarns.com

Sunset ♦♦♦
Baunton Lane, Cirencester,
Gloucestershire GL7 2NQ
T: (01285) 654822

The Talbot Inn
Rating Applied For
14 Victoria Road, Cirencester,
Gloucestershire GL7 1EN
T: (01285) 653760
F: (01285) 653760

The White Lion Inn ♦♦
8 Gloucester Street, Cirencester,
Gloucestershire GL7 2DG
T: (01285) 654053
F: (01285) 641316
E: roylion@aol.com.
I: www.
WHITE-LION-CIRENCESTER.co.uk

Willows ♦♦♦
2 Glebe Lane, Kemble,
Cirencester, Gloucestershire
GL7 6BD
T: (01285) 770667

Windrush ♦♦♦
Baunton, Cirencester,
Gloucestershire GL7 7BA
T: (01285) 655942
F: (01285) 655942

CLEEVE HILL
Gloucestershire

Malvern View ♦♦♦
Cleeve Hill, Cheltenham,
Gloucestershire GL52 3PR
T: (01242) 672017
F: (01242) 676207
E: vchoak@hotmail.com

CLEOBURY MORTIMER
Shropshire

Clod Hall ♦♦♦
Milson, Kidderminster,
Worcestershire DY14 0BJ
T: (01584) 781421
F: (01584) 781421
I: www.farmstayworcs.co.uk

Cox's Barn ♦♦♦♦
Bagginswood, Cleobury
Mortimer, Kidderminster,
Worcestershire DY14 8LS
T: (01746) 718415 & 718277

The Old Bake House ♦♦♦♦
46/47 High Street, Cleobury
Mortimer, Kidderminster,
Worcestershire DY14 8DQ
T: (01299) 270193
E: old-bake-house@amuserve.
net

The Old Cider House ♦♦♦♦
1 Lion Lane, Cleobury Mortimer,
Kidderminster, Worcestershire
DY14 8BT
T: (01299) 270304
F: (01299) 270304
E: lennox@old-cider-house.
fsnet.co.uk

Woodview ♦♦♦♦
Mawley Oak, Cleobury Mortimer,
Kidderminster, Worcestershire
DY14 9BA
T: (01299) 271422

CLEOBURY NORTH
Shropshire

Cleobury Court
Rating Applied For
Cleobury North, Bridgnorth,
Shropshire WV16 6RW
T: (01746) 787005
F: (01746) 787005

CLIFFORD
Herefordshire

Cottage Farm ♦♦♦
Middlewood, Clifford, Hereford
HR3 5SX
T: (01497) 831496
F: (01497) 831496
E: julie@hgjmjones.freeserve.
co.uk

CLIFTON
Derbyshire

Stone Cottage ♦♦♦
Green Lane, Clifton, Ashbourne,
Derbyshire DE6 2BL
T: (01335) 343377
F: (01335) 34117
E: info@stone-cottage.fsnet.
co.uk
I: www.stone-cottage.fsnet.
co.uk

CLUN
Shropshire

Cockford Hall ♦♦♦♦♦
Cockford Bank, Clun, Craven
Arms, Shropshire SY7 8LR
T: (01588) 640327
F: (01588) 640881
E: cockford.hall@virgin.net
I: www.go2.co.uk/cockfordhall

Crown House ♦♦♦♦
Church Street, Clun, Craven
Arms, Shropshire SY7 8JW
T: (01588) 640780
E: crownhouseclun@talk21.com

Hurst Mill Farm ♦♦♦
Clun, Craven Arms, Shropshire
SY7 0JA
T: (01588) 640224
F: (01588) 640224

Llanhedric Farm ♦♦♦
Clun, Craven Arms, Shropshire
SY7 8NG
T: (01588) 640203
F: (01588) 640203
E: llanhedric@21.com

New House Farm ♦♦♦♦♦
Clun, Craven Arms, Shropshire
SY7 8NJ
T: (01588) 638314

The Old Farmhouse ♦♦♦
Woodside, Clun, Craven Arms,
Shropshire SY7 0JB
T: (01588) 640695
F: (01588) 640501
E: helen@vuan1.freeserve.co.uk
I: www.tuckedup.
com/theoldfarmhouse.html

Springhill Farm ♦♦♦
Clun, Craven Arms, Shropshire
SY7 8PE
T: (01588) 640337
F: (01588) 640337

The Sun Inn ♦♦♦
High Street, Clun, Craven Arms,
Shropshire SY7 8JB
T: (01588) 640277 & 640559

CLUNGUNFORD
Shropshire

**Knock Hundred Cottage
♦♦♦♦**
Abcott, Clungunford, Craven
Arms, Shropshire SY7 0PX
T: (01588) 660594
F: (01588) 660594

COALBROOKDALE
Shropshire

The Grove Inn ♦♦♦
10 Wellington Road,
Coalbrookdale, Telford,
Shropshire TF8 7DX
T: (01952) 433269 & 432240
F: (01952) 433269
E: frog@fat-frog.co.uk
I: www.fat-frog.co.uk

The Lodge ♦♦♦
Sunniside, Coalbrookdale,
Telford, Shropshire TF8 7EX
T: (01952) 432423
E: thelodge.cbds.fsnet.co.uk

The Old Vicarage ♦♦♦♦
Church Road, Coalbrookdale,
Telford, Shropshire TF8 7NT
T: (01952) 432525 &
07831 348343
F: (01952) 433169
E: theoldvicarage@tf87nt.
freeserve.co.uk

COALEY
Gloucestershire

**Silver Street Farmhouse
♦♦♦♦**
Silver Street, Coaley, Dursley,
Gloucestershire GL11 5AX
T: (01453) 860514

COALPORT
Shropshire

Thorpe House ♦♦♦
High Street, Coalport, Telford,
Shropshire TF8 7HP
T: (01952) 586789
F: (01952) 586789

COALVILLE
Leicestershire

Broadlawns ♦♦♦
98 London Road, Coalville,
Leicester LE67 3JD
T: (01530) 836724 &
07702 056586

COATES
Gloucestershire

**Southfield House
Rating Applied For**
Coates, Cirencester,
Gloucestershire GL7 6NH
T: (01285) 770220
F: (01285) 770177
E: awberry@aol.com

COCKSHUTT
Shropshire

Highfields ♦♦♦♦
Stanwardine, Cockshutt,
Ellesmere, Shropshire SY12 0JL
T: (01939) 270659

COLD ASTON
Gloucestershire

Bangup Cottage ♦♦♦
Bangup Lane, Cold Aston,
Cheltenham, Gloucestershire
GL54 3BQ
T: (01451) 810127
E: chrisarmer@yahoo.com

**Grove Farm House
Rating Applied For**
Cold Aston, Cheltenham,
Gloucestershire GL54 3BJ
T: (01451) 821801
F: (01451) 821108
E: mstorey@btinternet.com
I: cotswoldbedandbreakfast.com

COLEFORD
Gloucestershire

Allary House ♦♦♦
14 Boxbush Road, Coleford,
Gloucestershire GL16 8DN
T: (01594) 835206
F: (01594) 835206

Forest House Hotel ♦♦
Cinder Hill, Coleford,
Gloucestershire GL16 8HQ
T: (01594) 832424

Graygill ♦♦♦
Duke of York Road, Staunton,
Coleford, Gloucestershire
GL16 8PD
T: (01600) 712536

Lower Perrygrove Farm ♦♦♦♦
Coleford, Gloucestershire
GL16 8QB
T: (01594) 833187

Meadow Cottage ♦♦♦
59 Coalway Road, Coleford,
Gloucestershire GL16 7HL
T: (01594) 833444
F: (01594) 833444

**Millend House and Garden
♦♦♦♦**
Newland, Coleford,
Gloucestershire GL16 8NF
T: (01594) 832128
F: (01594) 832128
E: apriljohnt@aol.com

Perouges ♦♦♦
31 Newland Street, Coleford,
Gloucestershire GL16 8AJ
T: (01594) 834287

Symonds Yat Rock Lodge ♦♦♦
Hillersland, Coleford,
Gloucestershire GL16 7NY
T: (01594) 836191
E: enquiries@rocklodge.co.uk
I: www.rocklodge.co.uk

COLEORTON
Leicestershire

Zion Cottage ♦♦♦♦
93 Zion Hill, Peggs Green,
Coleorton, Leicester,
Leicestershire LE67 8JP
T: (01530) 223914 &
07973 422668
F: (01530) 222488
E: zionbnb@aol.com
I: members.aol.com/zionbnb

COLESHILL
Warwickshire

The Old Rectory ♦♦♦♦
Church Lane, Maxstoke,
Coleshill, Birmingham B46 2QW
T: (01675) 462248
F: (01675) 481615
I: www.SmoothHound.
co.uk/hotels/oldrect.html

Packington Lane Farm ♦♦♦♦
Packington Lane, Coleshill,
Birmingham B46 3JJ
T: (01675) 462228
F: (01675) 462228

COLLINGHAM
Nottinghamshire

Lime Tree Farm ♦♦♦♦
Lunn Lane, Collingham,
Nottingham NG23 7LP
T: (01636) 892044 &
07976 902814

COLSTERWORTH
Lincolnshire

The Stables ♦♦♦♦
Stainby Road, Colsterworth,
Grantham, Lincolnshire
NG33 5JB
T: (01476) 861057
E: thestables@ondigital.com
I: www.stablesbandb.co.uk

COLWALL
Herefordshire

Brook House ♦♦♦♦♦
Walwyn Road, Colwall, Malvern,
Worcestershire WR13 6QX
T: (01684) 540604 &
07740 516605
F: (01684) 540604

**Old Library Lodge
Rating Applied For**
Stone Drive, Colwall, Malvern,
Worcestershire WR13 6QJ
T: (01684) 540077

CONINGSBY
Lincolnshire

The Lea Gate Inn ♦♦♦♦
Leagate Road, Coningsby,
Lincoln LN4 4RS
T: (01526) 342370
F: (01526) 345468
E: enquiries@theleagateinn.
co.uk
I: www.theleagateinn.co.uk

White Bull Inn ♦
55 High Street, Coningsby,
Lincoln LN4 4RB
T: (01526) 342439
F: (01526) 342818
E: thewhitebullconingsby@
tinyworld.co.uk
I: www.thewhitebull.Homestead.
com

CONISHOLME
Lincolnshire

Wickham House ♦♦♦♦♦
Church Lane, Conisholme, Louth,
Lincolnshire LN11 7LX
T: (01507) 358465
F: (01507) 358465
E: kenmor_wickham@hotmail.
com

CORBY GLEN
Lincolnshire

Stonepit Farmhouse ♦♦♦♦
Swinstead Road, Corby Glen,
Grantham, Lincolnshire
NG33 4NU
T: (01476) 550614
F: (01476) 550614
E: beds@stonepit.u-net.com

CORELEY
Shropshire

Brookfield House ♦♦♦♦
Coreley, Ludlow, Shropshire
SY8 3AS
T: (01584) 890059

CORRINGHAM
Lincolnshire

**The Old Hall
Rating Applied For**
Field Lane, Corringham,
Gainsborough, Lincolnshire
DN21 5QX
T: (01427) 838470
F: (01427) 839333
E: wayneturner@btinternet.com

639

COSBY
Leicestershire
The Vineries ◆◆◆◆
Countesthorpe Road, Cosby,
Leicester LE9 1UL
T: (0116) 2750817

COTGRAVE
Nottinghamshire
Heronbrook ◆◆◆◆
Peashill Lane, Cotgrave,
Nottingham NG12 3HD
T: (0115) 9899285

Jerico Farm ◆◆◆◆
Fosse Way, Cotgrave,
Nottingham NG12 3HG
T: (01949) 81733
F: (01949) 81733
E: herrick@jerico.swinternet.
co.uk
I: www.jericofarm.co.uk

COUGHTON
Herefordshire
Coughton House ◆◆◆◆
Coughton, Ross-on-Wye,
Herefordshire HR9 5SF
T: (01989) 562612 & 567322
F: (01989) 567322

COVENTRY
West Midlands
Abigail Guesthouse ◆◆◆
39 St. Patrick's Road, Coventry,
CV1 2LP
T: (024) 7622 1378
E: ag002a@netgates.co.uk
I: www.abigailuk.com

Aburley ◆◆◆◆
23 St Patricks Road,
Cheylesmore, Coventry, CV1 2LP
T: (024) 76251348 &
07957 925596
F: (024) 76223243

Acacia Guest House ◆◆◆◆
11 Park Road, Coventry, CV1 2LE
T: (02476) 633622 &
07970 966016
F: (02476) 633622
E: acaciaguesthouse@ukonline.
co.uk

Albany Guest House ◆◆◆
121 Holyhead Road, Coundon,
Coventry, CV1 3AD
T: (024) 7622 3601
F: (024) 7622 3601

Arlon Guest House ◆◆◆
25 St Patricks Road, Coventry,
CV1 2LP
T: (024) 7622 5942

Ashdowns Guest House ◆◆◆
12 Regent Street, Earlsdon,
Coventry, CV1 3EP
T: (024) 7622 9280

Ashleigh House ◆◆◆
17 Park Road, Coventry, CV1 2LH
T: (024) 7622 3804
F: (024) 76223804

Bourne Brook Lodge ◆◆◆◆
Mill Lane, Fillongley, Coventry
CV7 8EE
T: (01676) 541898
F: (01676) 541898

Brookfields ◆◆◆◆
134 Butt Lane, Allesley,
Coventry, CV5 9FE
T: (024) 7640 4866
F: (024) 7640 2022
E: brookfieldscoventry@
easicom.com

Chester House ◆◆◆
3 Chester Street, Coventry,
CV1 4DH
T: (024) 7622 3857

Crest Guest House ◆◆◆◆
39 Friars Road, Coventry,
CV1 2LJ
T: (024) 7622 7822
F: (024) 7622 7244
E: alanharve@aol.com
I: www.SmoothHound.
co.uk/hotels/crestgue.html

Fairlight Guest House ◆◆◆
14 Regent Street, Off Queen's
Road, Coventry, CV1 3EP
T: (024) 7622 4215
F: (024) 7622 4215
E: k.schofield@btinternet.com

Falcon Hotel ◆◆◆
13-19 Manor Road, Coventry,
CV1 2LH
T: (024) 7625 8615
F: (024) 7652 0680
E: falcon.hotel@talk21.co.uk

Highcroft Guest House ◆◆
65 Barras Lane, Coundon,
Coventry, CV1 4AQ
T: (024) 7622 8157
F: (024) 7663 1609

**Lodge Farm House Bed and
Breakfast** ◆◆◆
Westwood Heath Road,
Coventry, CV4 8AA
T: (024) 7646 6786
F: (024) 7646 6786
E: davidjohnhall@msn.com

Mount Guest House ◆◆◆
9 Coundon Road, Coventry,
CV1 4AR
T: (024) 7622 5998 &
07703 218238
F: (024) 7622 5998
E: enquiries@
guesthousecoventry.com
I: www.guesthousecoventry.com

Northanger House ◆◆◆
35 Westminster Road, Coventry,
CV1 3GB
T: (024) 7622 6780
F: (024) 7622 6780

St Mary's Cottage ◆◆◆
107 Kingsbury Road, Coventry,
CV6 1PT
T: (024) 7659 1557
F: (024) 7659 1557
E: afoster543@aol.com

Spire View Guest House ◆◆◆
36 Park Road(Near Railway
Station), Coventry, CV1 2LD
T: (024) 7625 1602
F: (024) 7622 2779
E: j-m@spireviewcov.freeserve.
co.uk

Vardre ◆◆
68 Spencer Avenue, Earlsdon,
Coventry, CV5 6NP
T: (024) 7671 5154
F: (024) 76715748
E: valvardre@aol.com
I: www.s-h.systems.co.uk

Westwood Cottage ◆◆◆
79 Westwood Heath Road,
Westwood Heath, Coventry,
CV4 8GN
T: (024) 7647 1084
F: (024) 7647 1084

COWLEY
Gloucestershire
Butlers Hill Farm ◆◆◆
Cockleford, Cowley, Cheltenham,
Gloucestershire GL53 9NW
T: (01242) 870455
F: (01242) 870455
E: butlershill@aol.com

CRADLEY
Herefordshire
Hollings Hill Farm ◆◆◆◆
Bosbury Road, Cradley, Malvern,
Worcestershire WR13 5LY
T: (01886) 880203 &
07966 184278
E: ajgkhollingshill@
farmersweekly.net

CRANWELL
Lincolnshire
Byards Leap Cottage ◆◆◆
Cranwell, Sleaford, Lincolnshire
NG34 8EY
T: (01400) 261537
F: (01400) 261537

CRAVEN ARMS
Shropshire
Blacksmith's Cottage ◆◆◆◆
9 Lower Corfton, Craven Arms,
Shropshire SY7 9LD
T: (01584) 861 241
F: (01584) 861 241
E: Beryl@corfton.freeserve.
co.uk

Castle View ◆◆◆◆
148 Stokesay, Craven Arms,
Shropshire SY7 9AL
T: (01588) 673712

Earnstrey Hill House ◆◆◆◆
Abdon, Craven Arms, Shropshire
SY7 9HU
T: (01746) 712579
F: (01746) 712631
E: hugh.scurfield@smwh.org.uk

The Firs ◆◆◆◆
Norton, Craven Arms, Shropshire
SY7 9LS
T: (01588) 672511 &
07977 697903
F: (01588) 672511
E: thefirs@go2.co.uk
I: www.go2.co.uk/firs

Glebelands ◆◆◆
25 Knighton Road, Clun, Craven
Arms, Shropshire SY7 8JH
T: (01588) 640442
F: (01588) 640442
E: Tourism@clun25.freeserve.
co.uk
I: www.clun25.freeserve.co.uk

Groveside ◆◆◆
Shrewsbury Road, Craven Arms,
Shropshire SY7 8BX
T: (01588) 672948

CRESSBROOK
Derbyshire
Cressbrook Hall ◆◆◆◆
Cressbrook, Buxton, Derbyshire
SK17 8SY
T: (01298) 871289 &
0800 3583003
F: (01298) 871845
E: stay@cressbrookhall.co.uk
I: www.cressbrookhall.co.uk

The Old Toll House ◆◆◆◆
Cressbrook, Buxton, Derbyshire
SK17 8SY
T: (01298) 872547
E: loy@oldtollhouse.freeserve.
co.uk
I: www.oldtollhouse.freeserve.
co.uk

CRICH
Derbyshire
Mount Tabor House ◆◆◆◆
Bowns Hill, Crich, Matlock,
Derbyshire DE4 5DG
T: (01773) 857008 &
07977 078266
E: mountabor@email.msn.com

**Penrose Avista Property
Partnership** ◆◆◆◆
Sandy Lane, Crich, Derbyshire
DE4 5DE
T: (01773) 852625 &
07889 297608
E: keith@avista.freeserve.co.uk
I: www.s-h-systems.
co.uk/hotels/avista.html

Upper Rosskeen Guesthouse
◆◆◆◆
Surgery Lane, Crich, Matlock,
Derbyshire DE4 5BP
T: (01773) 857186
E: elaine@stay-crich.co.uk
I: www.stay-crich.co.uk

CROPTHORNE
Worcestershire
The Cedars Guest House
◆◆◆◆
Evesham Road, Cropthorne,
Pershore, Worcestershire
WR10 3JU
T: (01386) 860219
E: cedarsguesthouse@ukonline.
co.uk

**Cropvale Farm Bed and
Breakfast**
Rating Applied For
Cropvale Farm, Smokey Lane,
Cropthorne, Pershore,
Worcestershire WR10 3NF
T: (01386) 860237
F: (01386) 860237
E: susan@hutchings22.
freeserve.co.uk
I: www.smoothhound.
co.uk/hotels/cropvale.html

CROWLAND
Lincolnshire
Abbey Hotel ◆◆◆
21 East Street, Crowland,
Peterborough PE6 0EN
T: (01733) 210200
F: (01733) 210938
E: AbbeyHotel@hotmail.com
I: www.
peterborough-net/abbeyhotel/

CROXDEN
Staffordshire
Farriers Cottage and Mews
◆◆◆◆
Woodhouse Farm, Nabb Lane,
Croxden, Uttoxeter,
Staffordshire ST14 5JB
T: (01889) 507507
F: (01889) 507282
E: ddeb@lineone.net
I: alton-towers.glo.uk

CUBBINGTON
Warwickshire
Bakers Cottage ◆◆◆◆
52/54 Queen Street, Cubbington,
Leamington Spa, Warwickshire
CV32 7NA
T: (01926) 772146

**Staddlestones Bed and
Breakfast** ◆◆◆
67 Rugby Road, Cubbington,
Leamington Spa, Warwickshire
CV32 7HY
T: (01926) 740253 &
07715 153756

CURBAR
Derbyshire
Bridgend ◆◆◆
Dukes Drive, Curbar, Calver,
Hope Valley S32 3YP
T: (01433) 630226
E: hunt@g3fwb.freeserve.co.uk

CUTTHORPE
Derbyshire
Cow Close Farm ◆◆◆
Overgreen, Cutthorpe,
Chesterfield, Derbyshire S42 7BA
T: (01246) 232055
E: cowclosefarm.cottages@
virginnet

DAGLINGWORTH
Gloucestershire
Windrush Cottage ◆◆◆
Itlay, Daglingworth, Cirencester,
Gloucestershire GL7 7H7
T: (01285) 652917

DARLEY ABBEY
Derbyshire
The Coach House ◆◆◆
185A Duffield Road, Darley
Abbey, Derby DE22 1JB
T: (01332) 551795 &
07971 772201

DARLEY BRIDGE
Derbyshire
Square and Compass ◆◆◆
Station Road, Darley Bridge,
Matlock, Derbyshire DE4 2EQ
T: (01629) 733255

DAVENTRY
Northamptonshire
Drayton Lodge ◆◆◆◆
Staverton Road, Daventry,
Northamptonshire NN11 4NL
T: (01327) 702449 & 876365
F: (01327) 872110
E: annspicer@farming.co.uk

Kingsthorpe Guesthouse ◆◆◆
18 Badby Road, Daventry,
Northamptonshire NN11 4AW
T: (01327) 702752
F: (01327) 301854

Threeways House ◆◆◆◆
Everdon, Daventry,
Northamptonshire NN11 6BL
T: (01327) 361631 &
07774 428242
F: (01327) 361359
E: elizabethbarwood@hotmail.
com
I: threewayshouse.com

DEFFORD
Worcestershire
**Brook Cottages Bed &
Breakfast** ◆◆◆
Upton Road, Defford, Pershore,
Worcestershire WR8 9BA
T: (01386) 750229 &
07768 384761
F: (01386) 750229
E: brook_cottages@tesco.net
I: www.homepages.tesco.
net~brook_cottages

DENSTONE
Staffordshire
Denstone Hall Farm ◆◆◆
Denstone, Uttoxeter,
Staffordshire ST14 5HF
T: (01889) 590253 &
07970 808151
F: (01889) 590930
E: denstonehallfarm@talk21.
com

Manor House Farm ◆◆◆◆
Prestwood, Denstone, Uttoxeter,
Staffordshire ST14 5DD
T: (01889) 590415 &
07976 767629
F: (01335) 342198
E: cm_ball@yahoo.co.uk
I: www.4posteraccom.com

Rowan Lodge ◆◆◆◆
Stubwood, Denstone, Uttoxeter,
Staffordshire ST14 5HU
T: (01889) 590913
E: rowanlodgecl@
netscapeonline.co.uk
I: www.smoothhound.
co.uk/hotels/rowanlodge.html

DERBY
Derbyshire
Alambie ◆◆◆
189 Main Road, Morley, Derby,
DE7 6DG
T: (01332) 780349 &
0780 3636130
F: (01332) 780349
E: alambie@beeb.net
I: www.alambieguesthouse.co.uk

Bonehill Farm ◆◆◆
Etwall Road, Mickleover, Derby
DE3 5DN
T: (01332) 513553
E: bonehillfarm@hotmail.com

Chuckles Guesthouse ◆◆◆
48 Crompton Street, Derby,
DE1 1NX
T: (01332) 367193 &
07711 379490
E: ianfraser@
chucklesguesthouse.freeserve.
co.uk

The Crompton Coach House
Rating Applied For
45 Crompton Street, Derby,
DE1 1NX
T: (01332) 365735
F: (01332) 365735
E: francescasmithw@aol.com

The Hill House Hotel ◆◆◆
294 Burton Road, Derby,
DE23 6AD
T: (01332) 361523
F: (01332) 361523
E: amandafearn@
hillhousehotel.co.uk
I: www.hillhousehotel-derby.
co.uk

Red Setters Guesthouse ◆◆◆
85 Curzon Street, Derby,
DE1 1LN
T: (01332) 362770
E: yvonne@derbycity.com
I: www.derbycity.
com/michael/redset.html

Rose & Thistle Guesthouse
◆◆◆
21 Charnwood Street, Derby,
DE1 2GU
T: (01332) 344103
F: (01332) 291006
E: rosethistle@gpanet.co.uk

Victoria Park Hotel ◆◆◆
312 Burton Road, Derby,
DE23 6AD
T: (01332) 341551

The Wayfarer Guesthouse
◆◆◆
27 Crompton Street, Derby,
DE1 1NY
T: (01332) 348350

DIGBETH
West Midlands
The Works Guesthouse ◆◆◆
29-30 Warner Street, Digbeth,
Birmingham B12 0JG
T: (0121) 7723326
F: (0121) 7723326

DIGBY
Lincolnshire
**Woodend Farm Bed and
Breakfast** ◆◆◆
Woodend Farm, Digby, Lincoln
LN4 3NG
T: (01526) 860347

DONNINGTON
Gloucestershire
Holmleigh ◆◆
Donnington, Moreton-in-Marsh,
Gloucestershire GL56 0XX
T: (01451) 830792

DORRINGTON
Shropshire
Meadowlands ◆◆◆
Lodge Lane, Frodesley,
Dorrington, Shrewsbury
SY5 7HD
T: (01694) 731350
F: (01694) 731350
E: Meadowlands@talk21.com

DORSTONE
Herefordshire
Haie Barn ◆◆◆◆
The Bage, Dorstone, Hereford
HR3 5SU
T: (01497) 831729
E: goodfood@haie-barn.co.uk
I: www.golden-valley.
co.uk/haiebarn

**Westbrook Manor Bed and
Breakfast** ◆◆◆
Westbrook Manor, Dorstone,
Hereford HR3 5SY
T: (01497) 831431
F: (01497) 831431
E: roddyandlibby@nextcall.net
I: www.golden-valley.
co.uk/wmamor

DROITWICH
Worcestershire
Foxbrook ◆◆◆
238A Worcester Road,
Droitwich, Worcestershire
WR9 8AY
T: (01905) 772414

Middleton Grange ◆◆◆◆
Ladywood Road, Salwarpe,
Droitwich, Worcestershire
WR9 0AH
T: (01905) 451678 & 453978
F: (01905) 453978
E: salli@middletongrange.com
I: www.middletongrange.com

The Old Farmhouse ◆◆◆◆◆
Hadley Heath, Droitwich,
Worcestershire WR9 0AR
T: (01905) 620837
F: (01905) 621722
E: judylambe@ombersley.
demon.co.uk
I: www.the-old-farmhouse.com

Richmond Guest House ◆◆◆
3 Ombersley St. West, Droitwich,
Worcestershire WR9 8HZ
T: (01905) 775722
F: (01905) 794642
I: www.infotel.
co.uk/hotels/36340.htm

Temple Broughton Farm
◆◆◆◆
Broughton Green, Droitwich,
Worcestershire WR9 7EF
T: (01905) 391456 &
07803 737501
F: (01905) 391515
E: suemaccoll@ukonline.co.uk

DRONFIELD
Derbyshire
Cassita ◆◆◆◆
Off Snape Hill Lane, Dronfield,
S18 2GL
T: (01246) 417303
F: (01246) 417303

DUNCHURCH
Warwickshire
Toft Hill ◆◆◆◆
Dunchurch, Rugby,
Warwickshire CV22 6NR
T: (01788) 810342

DUNTISBOURNE ABBOTS
Gloucestershire
Dixs Barn ◆◆◆
Duntisbourne Abbots,
Cirencester, Gloucestershire
GL7 7JN
T: (01285) 821249
E: wilcox@dixsbarn.freeserve.
co.uk

DURSLEY
Gloucestershire
Foresters ◆◆◆◆
Chapel Street, Upper Cam
Village, Dursley, Gloucestershire
GL11 5NX
T: (01453) 549996 &
07973 890477
F: (01453) 548200
E: foresters@freeuk.com
I: www.ibex.freeserve.
co.uk/foresters

DYMOCK
Gloucestershire
Granary ◆◆◆
Lower House Farm, Kempley,
Dymock, Gloucestershire
GL18 2BS
T: (01531) 890301
F: (01531) 890301

The White House ◆◆◆
Dymock, Gloucestershire
GL18 2AQ
T: (01531) 890516

HEART OF ENGLAND

EARDISLAND
Herefordshire

Eardisland Tea Room ♦♦
Church Lane, Eardisland,
Leominster, Herefordshire
HR6 9BP
T: (01544) 388226

The Manor House ♦♦♦♦
Eardisland, Leominster,
Herefordshire HR6 9BN
T: (01544) 388138

EARL STERNDALE
Derbyshire

Chrome Cottage ♦♦♦
Earl Sterndale, Buxton,
Derbyshire SK17 0BS
T: (01298) 83360
F: (01298) 83360
E: adgregg@bigwig.net

Fernydale Farm ♦♦♦♦
Earl Sterndale, Buxton,
Derbyshire SK17 0BS
T: (01298) 83236
F: (01298) 83605
E: jane@jmycock.fsnet.co.uk

EAST BARKWITH
Lincolnshire

Bodkin Lodge ♦♦♦♦♦
Grange Farm, Torrington Lane,
East Barkwith, Market Rasen,
Lincolnshire LN8 5RY
T: (01673) 858249
F: (01673) 858249

The Grange ♦♦♦♦
Torrington Lane, East Barkwith,
Market Rasen, Lincolnshire
LN8 5RY
T: (01673) 858670
E: sarahstamp@farmersweekly.
net
I: www.the-grange.f2s.com

EAST HADDON
Northamptonshire

East Haddon Lodge ♦♦♦
East Haddon, Northampton
NN6 8BU
T: (01604) 770240

EAST LANGTON
Leicestershire

The Bell Inn ♦♦♦♦
Main Street, East Langton,
Market Harborough,
Leicestershire LE16 7TW
T: (01858) 545278
F: (01858) 545748
E: achapman@thebellinn.co.uk
I: www.thebellinn.co.uk

EASTCOTE
Northamptonshire

West Farm ♦♦♦♦
Gayton Road, Eastcote,
Towcester, Northamptonshire
NN12 8NS
T: (01327) 830310
F: (01327) 830310
E: west.farm@eastcote97.fsnet.
co.uk

EASTNOR
Herefordshire

**Hill Farmhouse Bed and
Breakfast** ♦♦
Eastnor, Ledbury, Herefordshire
HR8 1EF
T: (01531) 632827

EASTWOOD
Nottinghamshire

Horseshoe Cottage ♦♦♦♦
25 Babbington Village,
Eastwood, Nottingham
NG16 2SS
T: (0115) 930 4769 &
0786 7507870
F: (0115) 930 4769
E: janet@jtserve.force9.co.uk

ECCLESHALL
Staffordshire

Cobblers Cottage ♦♦♦♦
Kerry Lane, Eccleshall, Stafford
ST21 6EJ
T: (01785) 850116
F: (01785) 850116
E: cobblerscottage@tinyonline.
co.uk

**Slindon House Farm
Rating Applied For**
Slindon, Eccleshall, Stafford
ST21 6LX
T: (01782) 791237

ECKINGTON
Worcestershire

The Anchor Inn and Restaurant
♦♦♦
Cotheridge Lane, Eckington,
Pershore, Worcestershire
WR10 3BA
T: (01386) 750356
F: (01386) 750356
E: anchoreck@aol.com
I: www.anchoreckington.co.uk

The Bell Inn ♦♦♦
Church Street, Eckington,
Pershore, Worcestershire
WR10 3AN
T: (01386) 750205
E: the_bell_uk@hotmail.com
I: www.jks.org/bell.html

Lantern House ♦♦♦
Boon Street, Eckington,
Pershore, Worcestershire
WR10 3BL
T: (01386) 750003 &
0771 3160402
E: ann@parker14.freeserve.
co.uk

Nafford House ♦♦♦♦
Eckington, Pershore,
Worcestershire WR10 3DJ
T: (01386) 750233

EDALE
Derbyshire

Mam Tor House ♦♦♦
Edale, Hope Valley S33 7ZA
T: (01433) 670253
E: mam.tor@ukgateway.net

Stonecroft ♦♦♦♦
Grindsbrook, Edale, Hope Valley
S33 7ZA
T: (01433) 670262 &
07879 427937
F: (01433) 670262
E: stonecroftedale@aol.com
I: www.edale-valley.
co.uk/stonecroft

EDGBASTON
West Midlands

The Kennedy ♦
38 York Road, Edgbaston,
Birmingham B16 9JB
T: (0121) 454 1284
F: (0121) 454 3040

Swiss Cottage Hotel ♦♦
475 Gillott Road, Edgbaston,
Birmingham B16 9LJ
T: (0121) 454 0371
F: (0121) 454 0371

EDGE
Gloucestershire

**Painswick View
Rating Applied For**
Back Edge Lane, Edge, Stroud,
Gloucestershire GL6 6PE
T: (01542) 813396
E: ascahill@hotmail.com

EDWINSTOWE
Nottinghamshire

Black Swan ♦♦♦
High Street, Edwinstowe,
Mansfield, Nottinghamshire
NG21 9QR
T: (01623) 822598
E: blackswan.fsbusiness.co.uk

ELLASTONE
Staffordshire

Chapel House ♦♦♦♦
Wootton, Ellastone, Ashbourne,
Derbyshire DE6 2GW
T: (01335) 324554
F: (01335) 324554
E: lizzy@weaverband.co.uk

ELLESMERE
Shropshire

The Ellesmere Hotel ♦♦♦
High Street, Ellesmere,
Shropshire SY12 0ES
T: (01691) 622055
F: (01691) 624110

The Grange ♦♦♦♦
Grange Road, Ellesmere,
Shropshire SY12 9DE
T: (01691) 623495
F: (01691) 623227
E: rosie@thegrange.uk.com
I: www.thegrange.uk.com

Hordley Hall ♦♦♦
Hordley, Ellesmere, Shropshire
SY12 9BB
T: (01691) 622772

Mereside Farm ♦♦♦♦
Ellesmere, Shropshire SY12 0PA
T: (01691) 622404
F: (01691) 622404
E: nicky@mereside.free-online.
co.uk
I: www.ellesmere.co.uk/mereside

Oakhill ♦♦♦♦
Dudleston, Ellesmere, Shropshire
SY12 9LL
T: (01691) 690548

ELMESTHORPE
Leicestershire

Badgers Mount ♦♦♦♦
6 Station Road, Elmesthorpe,
Leicester LE9 7SG
T: (01455) 848161
F: (01455) 848161
E: info@badgersmount.com
I: www.badgersmount.com

ELMLEY CASTLE
Worcestershire

The Old Mill Inn ♦♦♦♦
Mill Lane, Elmley Castle,
Pershore, Worcestershire
WR10 3HP
T: (01386) 710407 & 710066
F: (01386) 710066
E: oldmilin@dircon.co.uk
I: www.elmleymill.com

ELTON
Derbyshire

Elton Guesthouse ♦♦♦
Moor Lane, Elton, Matlock,
Derbyshire DE4 2DA
T: (01629) 650217 &
0771 2084699

Hawthorn Cottage ♦♦♦♦
Well Street, Elton, Matlock,
Derbyshire DE4 2BY
T: (01629) 650372

Homestead Farm ♦♦♦
Main Street, Elton, Matlock,
Derbyshire DE4 2BW
T: (01629) 650359

ENDON
Staffordshire

Hollinhurst Farm ♦♦♦
Park Lane, Endon, Stoke-on-
Trent ST9 9JB
T: (01782) 502633 &
07967 7784340
E: hjball@ukf.net

ENGLISH BICKNOR
Gloucestershire

Dryslade Farm ♦♦♦♦
English Bicknor, Coleford,
Gloucestershire GL16 7PA
T: (01594) 860259 &
0780 1732778
F: (01594) 860259
E: dryslade@agriplus.net
I: www.fweb.org.uk/dryslade

ETTINGTON
Warwickshire

White Horse Inn ♦♦♦
Banbury Road, Ettington,
Stratford-upon-Avon,
Warwickshire CV37 7SU
T: (01789) 740641
F: (01789) 740641

**Whitfield Farm
Rating Applied For**
Ettington, Stratford-upon-Avon,
Warwickshire CV37 7PN
T: (01789) 740260
F: (01789) 740260

EVESHAM
Worcestershire

Bredon View Guest House
♦♦♦♦
Village Street, Harvington,
Evesham, Worcestershire
WR11 5NQ
T: (01386) 871484
F: (01386) 871484
E: b.v.circa1898@bushinternet.
com
I: www.bredonview.heartuk.net

Park View Hotel ♦♦♦
Waterside, Evesham,
Worcestershire WR11 6BS
T: (01386) 442639
E: mike.spires@btinternet.com
I: www.superstay.co.uk

EWYAS HAROLD
Herefordshire

Kingstreet Farmhouse ♦♦♦
Ewyas Harold, Hereford,
Herefordshire HR2 0HB
T: (01981) 240208

The Old Rectory ♦♦♦♦
Ewyas Harold, Hereford HR2 0EY
T: (01981) 240498
F: (01981) 240498

EYAM
Derbyshire
The Old Rose and Crown ♦♦♦♦
Main Road, Eyam, Hope Valley
S32 5QW
T: (01433) 630858 &
07710 344688
E: drivermichael@hotmail.com
I: www.smoothhound.
co.uk/hotels/oldrose.html

EYDON
Northamptonshire
Crockwell Farm ♦♦♦♦
Eydon, Daventry,
Northamptonshire NN11 3QA
T: (01327) 361358 &
07850 050716
F: (01327) 361573
E: info@crockwellfarm.co.uk
I: www.crockwellfarm.co.uk

FAIRFIELD
Derbyshire
Barms Farm ♦♦♦♦
Fairfield, Buxton, Derbyshire
SK17 7HW
T: (01298) 77723 &
07957 863963
F: (01298) 78692
E: info@peakpracticegolf.co.uk

FAIRFORD
Gloucestershire
East End House ♦♦♦♦♦
Fairford, Gloucestershire
GL7 4AP
T: (01285) 713715
F: (01285) 713505
E: eastendho@cs.com
I: www.eastendhouse.co.uk

Kempsford Manor ♦♦♦
Fairford, Gloucestershire
GL7 4EQ
T: (01285) 810131
F: (01285) 810131
E: kempsford_manor@
acmemail.net
I: members.tripod.
co.uk/kempsford_manor

Milton Farm ♦♦♦
Fairford, Gloucestershire
GL7 4HZ
T: (01285) 712205
F: (01285) 711349
E: milton@farmersweekly.net
I: www.miltonfarm.co.uk

Waiten Hill Farm ♦♦
Fairford, Gloucestershire
GL7 4JG
T: (01285) 712652
F: (01285) 712652

FARNSFIELD
Nottinghamshire
Lockwell House ♦♦♦
Lockwell Hill, Old Rufford Road,
Farnsfield, Newark,
Nottinghamshire NG22 8JG
T: (01623) 883067

FARTHINGHOE
Northamptonshire
Grafton House ♦♦♦♦
Baker Street, Farthinghoe,
Brackley, Northamptonshire
NN13 5PH
T: (01295) 710741
F: (01295) 712249
E: jaymaddison@aol.com

Greenfield ♦♦♦
Baker Street, Farthinghoe,
Brackley, Northamptonshire
NN13 5PH
T: (01295) 712380
F: (01295) 712380
E: vivwebb@aol.com
I: www.webb52.freeserve.co.uk

FARTHINGSTONE
Northamptonshire
Glebe Farm ♦♦♦♦
Maidford Road, Farthingstone,
Towcester, Northamptonshire
NN12 8HE
T: (01327) 361558
F: (01327) 361558
E: gjbryce.glebefarm@virgin.net

FECKENHAM
Worcestershire
Orchard House ♦♦♦♦
Berrow Hill Lane, Feckenham,
Redditch, Worcestershire
B96 6QJ
T: (01527) 821497
F: (01527) 821497

The Steps ♦♦
6 High Street, Feckenham,
Redditch, Worcestershire
B96 6HS
T: (01527) 892678
E: jenny@thesteps.co.uk
I: www.thesteps.co.uk

FENNY BENTLEY
Derbyshire
Cairn Grove ♦♦♦♦
Ashes Lane, Fenny Bentley,
Ashbourne, Derbyshire DE6 1LD
T: (01335) 350538 &
07973 859992
E: keith.wheeldon@virgin.net

FENNY DRAYTON
Leicestershire
White Wings ♦♦♦♦♦
Quaker Close, Fenny Drayton,
Nuneaton, Warwickshire
CV13 6BS
T: (01827) 716100 &
07767 266215
F: (01827) 717191
E: lloyd@whitewings.freeserve.
co.uk

FERNHILL HEATH
Worcestershire
Dilmore House Hotel ♦♦♦
Droitwich Road, Fernhill Heath,
Worcester WR3 7UL
T: (01905) 451543
F: (01905) 452015
E: dilmorehouse@ukgateway.
net

Heathside ♦♦♦♦
Droitwich Road, Fernhill Heath,
Worcester WR3 7UA
T: (01905) 458245
F: (01905) 458245

FILLINGHAM
Lincolnshire
Church Farm ♦♦♦♦
Fillingham, Gainsborough,
Lincolnshire DN21 5BS
T: (01427) 668279
F: (01427) 668025
E: fillinghambandb@lineone.net

FILLONGLEY
Warwickshire
Manor House Farm ♦♦♦♦
Green End Road, Fillongley,
Coventry CV7 8DS
T: (01676) 540256

FINSTALL
Worcestershire
Stoke Cross Farm ♦♦♦
Dusthouse Lane, Finstall,
Bromsgrove, Worcestershire
B60 3AE
T: (01527) 876676
F: (01527) 874729

FOOLOW
Derbyshire
Housley Cottage ♦♦♦
Foolow, Hope Valley S32 5QB
T: (01433) 631505
E: kevin@housley-cottage.
freeserve.co.uk

FORTON
Shropshire
The Swan At Forton
Rating Applied For
Eccleshall Road, Forton,
Newport, Shropshire TF10 8BY
T: (01952) 812169
F: (01952) 812722

FOWNHOPE
Herefordshire
The Tan House ♦♦♦
Fownhope, Hereford HR1 4NJ
T: (01432) 860549
F: (01432) 860466
E: vera@ukbu.co.uk

FOXTON
Leicestershire
The Old Manse
Rating Applied For
Swingbridge Street, Foxton,
Market Harborough,
Leicestershire LE16 7RH
T: (01858) 545456
E: theoldmanse37@hotmail.
com

FRAMPTON MANSELL
Gloucestershire
The Crown Inn ♦♦♦♦
Frampton Mansell, Stroud,
Gloucestershire GL6 8JG
T: (01285) 760601
F: (01285) 760681
E: book@lionheartinns.co.uk
I: www.lionheartinns.co.uk

FRAMPTON-ON-SEVERN
Gloucestershire
Archway House ♦♦♦♦
The Green, Frampton-on-Severn,
Gloucester GL2 7DY
T: (01452) 740752
F: (01452) 741629
E: mike.brown@archwayhouse.
fsnet.co.uk

FRANKTON
Warwickshire
Frankton Grounds ♦♦♦
Frankton Grounds Farm,
Frankton, Rugby, Warwickshire
CV23 9PD
T: (01926) 632391
F: (01926) 632391
E: frankton.grounds@virgin.net

FULBECK
Lincolnshire
**The Hare and Hounds Country
Inn** ♦♦♦
The Green, Fulbeck, Grantham,
Lincolnshire NG32 3JJ
T: (01400) 272090
F: (01400) 273663

GAINSBOROUGH
Lincolnshire
The Beckett Arms ♦♦♦
25 High Street, Corringham,
Gainsborough, Lincolnshire
DN21 5QP
T: (01427) 838201

Swallow Barn ♦♦♦♦
Sturgate, Gainsborough,
Lincolnshire DN21 5PX
T: (01427) 839042 &
07905 246694
F: (01427) 839043
E: gwen.anselm@ntlworld.com

GARWAY
Herefordshire
The Old Rectory ♦♦♦♦
Garway, Hereford HR2 8RH
T: (01600) 750363 &
07860 366679
F: (01600) 750364

GAYTON
Northamptonshire
Queen Victoria Inn ♦♦♦
High Street, Gayton,
Northampton NN7 3HD
T: (01604) 858878

GAYTON LE MARSH
Lincolnshire
Westbrook House ♦♦♦♦
Gayton le Marsh, Alford,
Lincolnshire LN13 0NW
T: (01507) 450624

GEDNEY HILL
Lincolnshire
Sycamore Farmhouse ♦♦♦
6 Station Road, Gedney Hill,
Spalding, Lincolnshire PE12 0NP
T: (01406) 330445 &
07889 147001
F: (01406) 330445
E: sycamore.farm@virgin.net
I: www.
farmhousebedandbreakfast.
freeserve.co.uk

GLOOSTON
Leicestershire
**The Old Barn Inn and
Restaurant** ♦♦♦♦
Glooston, Market Harborough,
Leicestershire LE16 7ST
T: (01858) 545215
F: (01858) 545215

GLOSSOP
Derbyshire
Avondale ♦♦♦
28 Woodhead Road, Glossop,
Derbyshire SK13 7RH
T: (01457) 853132 &
07773 480684
F: (0161) 494 6078
E: avondale.glossop@talk21.
com

Peels Arms ♦♦♦
6-12 Temple Street, Padfield,
Hyde, Cheshire SK13 1EX
T: (01457) 852719
F: (01457) 860536
E: peels@talk21.com

White House Farm ♦♦♦
Padfield Main Road, Glossop,
Derbyshire SK13 1ET
T: (01457) 854695
F: (01457) 854695

GLOUCESTER
Gloucestershire

Albert Hotel ◆◆◆
56-58 Worcester Street,
Gloucester, GL1 3AG
T: (01452) 502081 & 300832
F: (01452) 311738
I: www.alberthotel.com

Alston Field Guest House ◆◆
88 Stroud Road, Gloucester,
GL1 5AJ
T: (01452) 529170

Brookthorpe Lodge ◆◆◆
Stroud Road, Brookthorpe,
Gloucester GL4 0UQ
T: (01452) 812645
F: (01452) 812645
E: enq@brookthorpelodge.
demon.co.uk
I: www.brookthorpelodge.
demon.co.uk

The Chestnuts ◆◆◆◆
9 Brunswick Square, Gloucester,
GL1 1UG
T: (01452) 330356 &
07887 650231
F: (01452) 330356
E: davidchampion1@
compurserve.com

The Coppins ◆◆◆◆
11c Kenilworth Avenue,
Gloucester, GL2 0QN
T: (01452) 302777

Cyder Press Farm ◆◆◆◆
The Leigh, Gloucester, GL19 4AG
T: (01242) 680661
F: (01242) 680023
E: archers@cyderpressfarm.
freeserve.co.uk

Georgian Guest House ◆
85 Bristol Road, Gloucester,
GL1 5SN
T: (01452) 413286
F: (01452) 413286

Gilbert's ◆◆◆◆
Brookthorpe, Gloucester,
GL4 0UH
T: (01452) 812364
F: (01452) 812364
E: jenny@gilbertsbb.demon.
co.uk
I: www.SmoothHound.
co.uk/hotels/gilberts.html

Kilmorie Small Holding ◆◆◆
Gloucester Road, Corse, Snigs
End, Staunton, Gloucester
GL19 3RQ
T: (01452) 840224
F: (01452) 840224
E: sheila-barnfield@supanet.
com
I: www.SmoothHound.
co.uk/hotels/kilmorie.html

Lulworth ◆◆◆
12 Midland Road, Gloucester,
GL1 4UF
T: (01452) 521881
F: (01452) 521881
E: themanager@lulworth.
swinternet.co.uk
I: www.lulworth.swinternet.
co.uk

Nicki's Hotel & Taverna ◆◆
105-107 Westgate Street,
Gloucester, GL1 2PG
T: (01452) 301359

Notley House and The Coach House ◆◆◆
93 Hucclecote Road, Hucclecote,
Gloucester GL3 3TR
T: (01452) 611584
F: (01452) 371229
E: notleyhouse@cs.com
I: ourworld.compuserve.
com/homepages/notleyhouse

Pembury Guest House ◆◆◆
9 Pembury Road, St. Barnabas,
Gloucester, GL4 6UE
T: (01452) 521856
F: (01452) 303418

Spalite Hotel ◆◆
121 Southgate Street,
Gloucester, GL1 1XQ
T: (01452) 380828

The Tailors House ◆◆◆
43-45 Westgate Street,
Gloucester, GL1 2NW
T: (01452) 521750
F: (01452) 521750

GNOSALL
Staffordshire

The Leys House ◆◆◆◆
Gnosall, Stafford, Staffordshire
ST20 0BZ
T: (01785) 822532
F: (01785) 822060

GOADBY
Leicestershire

The Hollies ◆◆◆◆
Goadby, Leicester LE7 9EE
T: (0116) 259 8301
F: (0116) 2598491
E: j.parr@btinternet.com

GOTHERINGTON
Gloucestershire

Pardon Hill Farm ◆◆◆
Prescott, Gotherington,
Cheltenham, Gloucestershire
GL52 9RD
T: (01242) 672468 &
07802 708814
F: (01242) 672468
E: janet@pardonhillfarm.
freeserve.co.uk
I: www.glosfarmhols.co.uk

GRANGEMILL
Derbyshire

Middle Hills Farm ◆◆◆◆
Grangemill, Derby DE4 4HY
T: (01629) 650368
F: (01629) 650368
E: l.lomas@btinternet.com
I: www.peakdistrictfarmhols.
co.uk

GRANTHAM
Lincolnshire

Beechleigh Town House Hotel ◆◆◆◆
55 North Parade, Grantham,
Lincolnshire NG31 8AT
T: (01476) 572213
F: (01476) 572213
E: info@beechleigh.com
I: www.beechleigh.com

The Red House ◆◆◆
74 North Parade, Grantham,
Lincolnshire NG31 8AN
T: (01476) 579869
F: (01476) 401597
E: redhousebb@aol.com
I: www.smoothhound.
co.uk/hotels/theredhouse1.html

GREAT COMBERTON
Worcestershire

Tibbitts Farm ◆◆◆◆
Russell Street, Great Comberton,
Pershore, Worcestershire
WR10 3DT
T: (01386) 710210
F: (01386) 710210
E: pixiefarr@aol.com

GREAT DALBY
Leicestershire

Dairy Farm ◆◆◆
8 Burrough End, Great Dalby,
Melton Mowbray, Leicestershire
LE14 2EW
T: (01664) 562783

GREAT HUCKLOW
Derbyshire

Holly House ◆◆◆◆
Windmill, Great Hucklow,
Buxton, Derbyshire SK17 8RE
T: (01298) 871568
E: holly.house@which.net

The Old Manse ◆◆◆◆
Great Hucklow, Buxton,
Derbyshire SK17 8RF
T: (01298) 871262
F: (01298) 872916
E: bedandbreakfast@angus.
co.uk
I: www.angus.
co.uk/bedandbreakfast/

GREAT LONGSTONE
Derbyshire

Fieldsview ◆◆◆◆
Station Road, Great Longstone,
Bakewell, Derbyshire DE45 1TS
T: (01629) 640593
E: mikes@ga-memik.demon.
co.uk
I: www.ga-memik.demon.co.uk

GREAT RISSINGTON
Gloucestershire

Lower Farmhouse ◆◆◆
Great Rissington, Cheltenham,
Gloucestershire GL54 2LH
T: (01451) 810163 & 810187
F: (01451) 810187
E: B&B@lowerfarmhouse.co.uk

Stepping Stone ◆◆◆
Rectory Lane, Great Rissington,
Cheltenham, Gloucestershire
GL54 2LL
T: (01451) 821385
E: stepping-stone-b-b@excite.
com

GREAT WITLEY
Worcestershire

Home Farm ◆◆◆◆
Great Witley, Worcester WR6 6JJ
T: (01299) 896825
F: (01299) 896176

GRETTON
Gloucestershire

Elms Farm ◆◆◆
Gretton, Cheltenham,
Gloucestershire GL54 5HQ
T: (01242) 620150 &
07774 461107
E: rose@elmfarm.demon.co.uk
I: www.elmfarm.demon.co.uk

Gretton Court ◆◆◆◆
Gretton, SY6 7HU
T: (01694) 771630

Welland House ◆◆◆◆
31 High Street, Gretton, Corby,
Northamptonshire NN17 3DE
T: (01536) 771102
F: (01536) 771102
E: ann@acraske.freeserve.co.uk
I: wellandhouse.co.uk

GRIMSTON
Leicestershire

Gorse House ◆◆◆◆
33 Main Street, Grimston,
Melton Mowbray, Leicestershire
LE14 3BZ
T: (01664) 813537 &
07768 341848
F: (01664) 813537
E: cowdell@gorsehouse.co.uk
I: www.gorsehouse.co.uk

GRINDLEFORD
Derbyshire

Woodlands ◆◆◆◆
Sir William Hill Road,
Grindleford, Hope Valley
S32 2HS
T: (01433) 631593

GRINDON
Staffordshire

Summerhill Farm ◆◆◆◆
Grindon, Leek, Staffordshire
ST13 7TT
T: (01538) 304264

GRINGLEY ON THE HILL
Nottinghamshire

Gringley Hall ◆◆◆◆
Gringley on the Hill, Doncaster
DN10 4QT
T: (01777) 817262
F: (01777) 816824
E: dulce@gringleyhall.fsnet.
co.uk

GUITING POWER
Gloucestershire

Castlett Bank ◆◆◆◆
Castlett Street, Guiting Power,
Cheltenham, Gloucestershire
GL54 5US
T: (01451) 850300
F: (01451) 850300
E: wilderspin.castlettbank@
btinternet.com
I: www.SmoothHound.
co.uk/hotels/castlett.html

Cobnutt Cottage ◆◆◆
Winchcombe Road, Guiting
Power, Cheltenham,
Gloucestershire GL54 5UX
T: (01451) 850658

Farmers Arms ◆◆◆
Guiting Power, Cheltenham,
Gloucestershire GL54 5TZ
T: (01451) 850358

Guiting Guesthouse ◆◆◆◆◆
Post Office Lane, Guiting Power,
Cheltenham, Gloucestershire
GL54 5TZ
T: (01451) 850470
F: (01451) 850034
E: guiting.guest_house@virgin.
net
I: freespace.virgin.net/guiting.
guest_house/

The Hollow Bottom ◆◆◆
Winchcombe Road, Guiting
Power, Cheltenham,
Gloucestershire GL54 5UX
T: (01451) 850392
F: (01451) 850945

Tally Ho Guesthouse ◆◆◆◆
1 Tally Ho Lane, Guiting Power,
Cheltenham, Gloucestershire
GL54 5TY
T: (01451) 850186
E: tallyhobb@aol.com

GUNBY
Lincolnshire

Brook House
Rating Applied For
Gunby, Grantham, Lincolnshire
NG33 5LF
T: (01476) 860010 &
0788 5454007
F: (01476) 860010

HACKTHORN
Lincolnshire

Honeyholes ◆◆◆◆
South Farm, Hackthorn, Lincoln
LN2 3PW
T: (01673) 861868
F: (01673) 861868

HADNALL
Shropshire

Hall Farm House ◆◆◆
Hadnall, Shrewsbury SY4 4AG
T: (01939) 210269 &
07989 235181

Saracens
Rating Applied For
Shrewsbury Road, Hadnall,
Shrewsbury SY4 4AG
T: (01939) 210877 &
07808 769272
F: (01939) 210877

HAGWORTHINGHAM
Lincolnshire

White Oak Grange ◆◆◆◆
Hagworthingham, Spilsby,
Lincolnshire PE23 4LX
T: (01507) 588376
F: (01507) 588377
I: whiteoakgrange.com

HALSE
Northamptonshire

Hill Farm ◆◆◆
Halse, Brackley,
Northamptonshire NN13 6DY
T: (01280) 703300 &
07860 865146
F: (01280) 704999
E: jg.robinson@farmline.com

HAMPTON IN ARDEN
West Midlands

The Cottage Guest House
◆◆◆
Kenilworth Road, On A452 to
Balsall Common, Hampton in
Arden, Solihull, West Midlands
B92 0LW
T: (01675) 442323
F: (01675) 443323

The Hollies ◆◆◆
Kenilworth Road, Hampton in
Arden, Solihull, West Midlands
B92 0LW
T: (01675) 442941 & 442681
F: (01675) 442941
E: thehollies@hotmail.com
I: www.theholliesguesthouse.
co.uk

White Lion ◆◆◆
High Street, Hampton in Arden,
Solihull, West Midlands B92 0AA
T: (01675) 442833
F: (01675) 443168

HANDSACRE
Staffordshire

The Olde Peculiar ◆◆◆
The Green, Handsacre, Rugeley,
Staffordshire WS15 4DP
T: (01543) 491891
F: (01543) 493733

HANLEY
Staffordshire

Northwood Hotel Limited
◆◆◆
146 Keelings Road, Northwood,
Hanley, Stoke-on-Trent ST1 6QA
T: (01782) 279729 &
07971 222130
F: (01782) 207507

HANLEY SWAN
Worcestershire

Meadowbank ◆◆◆◆
Picken End, Hanley Swan,
Worcester WR8 0DQ
T: (01684) 310917 &
07976 749866
E: dave@meadowbank.
freeserve.co.uk

**Pyndar Lodge Bed and
Breakfast** ◆◆◆◆◆
Roberts End, Hanley Swan,
Worcester WR8 0DN
T: (01684) 310716
F: (01684) 311402
E: info@pyndarlodge.co.uk
I: www.pyndarlodge.co.uk

**Yew Tree House Bed and
Breakfast** ◆◆◆◆◆
Yew Tree House, Hanley Swan,
Worcester WR8 0DN
T: (01684) 310736 &
07498 753543
F: (01684) 311709
E: yewtreehs@aol.com
I: www.yewtreehouse.co.uk

HARDWICK
Herefordshire

The Haven ◆◆◆◆
Hardwick, Hay on Wye, Hereford
HR3 5TA
T: (01497) 831254 & 831407
F: (01497) 831254
E: robinson@havenhay.demon.
co.uk
I: www.golden-valley.
co.uk/haven

HARESFIELD
Gloucestershire

Lower Green Farmhouse ◆◆◆
Haresfield, Stonehouse,
Gloucestershire GL10 3DS
T: (01452) 728264
E: lowergreen@lineone.net

HARLASTON
Staffordshire

The Old Rectory ◆◆◆◆
Churchside, Harlaston,
Tamworth, Staffordshire
B79 9HE
T: (01827) 383583 &
07973 756367
F: (01827) 383583

HARLEY
Shropshire

Rowley Farm Hospitality ◆◆◆
Harley, Shrewsbury SY5 6LX
T: (01952) 727348

HARMER HILL
Shropshire

Red Castle
Rating Applied For
Harmer Hill, Shrewsbury
SY4 3EB
T: (01939) 291071
F: (01939) 291071

HARRINGWORTH
Northamptonshire

White Swan ◆◆◆◆
Seaton Road, Harringworth,
Corby, Northamptonshire
NN17 3AF
T: (01572) 747543
F: (01572) 747323
E: white.swan1@virgin.net
I: www.thewhite-swan.com

HARTINGTON
Derbyshire

Bank Top Farm ◆◆◆
Pilsbury Road, Hartington,
Buxton, Derbyshire SK17 0AD
T: (01298) 84205 &
07885 021474

Manifold Inn ◆◆◆
Hulme End, Hartington, Buxton,
Derbyshire SK17 0EX
T: (01298) 84537

Wolfscote Grange ◆◆◆
Hartington, Buxton, Derbyshire
SK17 0AX
T: (01298) 84342
E: wolfscote@btinternet.com

HARTLEBURY
Worcestershire

Garden Cottages ◆◆◆◆
Crossway Green, Hartlebury,
Kidderminster, Worcestershire
DY13 9SJ
T: (01299) 250626
F: (01299) 250626
E: mamod@btinternet.com
I: gardencottages.co.uk

HASELOR
Warwickshire

Walcote Farm ◆◆◆◆
Walcote, Haselor, Alcester,
Warwickshire B49 6LY
T: (01789) 488264
F: (01789) 488264
E: john@walcotefarm.co.uk
I: www.walcotefarm.co.uk

HASSOP
Derbyshire

Flatts Farm ◆◆◆◆
Hassop, Bakewell, Derbyshire
DE45 1NU
T: (01629) 812983

HATHERSAGE
Derbyshire

Cannon Croft ◆◆◆◆
Cannonfields, Hathersage, Hope
Valley S32 1AG
T: (01433) 650005 &
0771 3352327
F: (01433) 650005
E: soates@cannoncroft.
fsbusiness.co.uk
I: www.cannoncroft.fsbusiness.
co.uk

The Plough Inn ◆◆◆◆
Leadmill Bridge, Hathersage,
Hope Valley S32 1BA
T: (01433) 650319 & 650180
F: (01433) 651049

Sladen ◆◆◆
Jaggers Lane, Hathersage, Hope
Valley S32 1AZ
T: (01433) 650706
F: (01433) 650315

Sladen Cottage
Rating Applied For
Castleton Road, Hathersage,
Hope Valley S32 1EH
T: (01433) 650104
E: colley@sladencottage.co.uk

HEATON
Staffordshire

Gun End Bed and Breakfast
◆◆◆
The Barn, Swythamley, SK11 0SJ
T: (01260) 227391

HENLEY-IN-ARDEN
Warwickshire

Holland Park Farm ◆◆◆
Buckley Green, Henley-in-Arden,
Solihull, West Midlands B95 5QF
T: (01564) 792625
F: (01564) 792625

HEREFORD
Herefordshire

Alberta ◆◆◆
7-13 Newtown Road, Hereford,
HR4 9LH
T: (01432) 270313
F: (01432) 270313

Ancroft ◆◆◆
10 Cheviot Close, Kings Acre,
Hereford, HR4 0TF
T: (01432) 274394 &
07803 430888

Aylestone Court Hotel ◆◆◆◆
Aylestone Hill, Hereford,
HR1 1HS
T: (01432) 341891 & 359342
F: (01432) 267691
E: ayleshotel@aol.com
I: aylestonecourthotel.
homestead.com

Bouvrie Guest House ◆
26 Victoria Street, Hereford,
HR4 0AA
T: (01432) 266265

The Bowens Country House
◆◆◆◆
Fownhope, Hereford HRI 4PS
T: (01432) 860430
F: (01432) 860430

Brandon Lodge ◆◆◆◆
Ross Road, Grafton, Hereford,
HR2 8BL
T: (01432) 355621
F: (01432) 355621
E: info@brandonlodge.co.uk
I: www.brandonlodge.co.uk

Cedar Guest House ◆◆◆
123 Whitecross Road,
Whitecross, Hereford, HR4 0LS
T: (01432) 267235
F: (01432) 267235
E: info@cedarguesthouse.com
I: www.cedarguesthouse.com

Charades ◆◆◆
34 Southbank Road, Hereford,
HR1 2TJ
T: (01432) 269444

Felton House ◆◆◆◆
Felton, Hereford HR1 3PH
T: (01432) 820366
F: (01432) 820366
E: bandb@ereal.net
I: www.bandbherefordshire.
co.uk

Grafton Villa Farm House
◆◆◆◆
Grafton, Hereford HR2 8ED
T: (01432) 268689
F: (01432) 268689
E: jennielayton@ereal.net
I: www.smoothhound.
co.uk/hotels/graftonv.html

Hedley Lodge ◆◆◆◆
Belmont Abbey, Abergavenny
Road, Hereford, HR2 9RZ
T: (01432) 277475
F: (01432) 277318
E: hedleylodge@aol.com
I: www.hedleylodge.com

Heron House Bed & Breakfast
◆◆◆
Heron House, Canon Pyon Road,
Portway, Burghill, Hereford
HR4 8NG
T: (01432) 761111
F: (01432) 760603
E: bb.hereford@tesco.net
I: www.homepages.tesco.
net/~bb.hereford/heron.html

Holly Tree Guest House ◆◆◆
21 Barton Road, Hereford,
IIR4 0AY
T: (01432) 357845

Hopbine Hotel ◆◆
The Hopbine, Roman Road,
Hereford, HR1 1LE
T: (01432) 268722
F: (01432) 268722

Montgomery House ◆◆◆◆
12 St Owen Street, Hereford,
HR1 2PL
T: (01432) 351454 &
07971 649787
F: (01432) 344463
E: lizforbes@lineone.net

Sink Green Farm ◆◆◆◆
Rotherwas, Hereford HR2 6LE
T: (01432) 870223
E: sinkgreenfarm@email.msn.
com

The Somerville ◆◆◆
12 Bodenham Road, Hereford,
HR1 2TS
T: (01432) 273991
F: (01432) 268719

HILCOTE
Derbyshire

Hilcote Hall ◆◆
Hilcote Lane, Hilcote, Alfreton,
Derbyshire DE55 5HR
T: (01773) 812608
F: (01773) 812608

HIMBLETON
Worcestershire

Phepson Farm ◆◆◆◆
Himbleton, Droitwich,
Worcestershire WR9 7JZ
T: (01905) 391205
F: (01905) 391338
E: havard@globalnet.co.uk
I: www.phepsonfarm.co.uk

HINTON IN THE HEDGES
Northamptonshire

The Old Rectory ◆◆◆
Hinton in the Hedges, Brackley,
Northamptonshire NN13 5NG
T: (01280) 706807
F: (01280) 706809
E: lavinia@lavinia.demon.co.uk

HOARWITHY
Herefordshire

Aspen House ◆◆◆◆
Hoarwithy, Hereford HR2 6QP
T: (01432) 840353 &
07796 671749
F: (01432) 840353
E: hoarwithy@aol.com

Old Mill ◆◆◆◆
Hoarwithy, Hereford HR2 6QH
T: (01432) 840602
F: (01432) 840602

HOCKLEY HEATH
West Midlands

Illshaw Heath Farm ◆◆◆◆
Kineton Lane, Hockley Heath,
Solihull, West Midlands B94 6RX
T: (01564) 782214

HOLBEACH
Lincolnshire

The Bull Inn ◆◆
Old Main Road, Fleet Hargate,
Holbeach, Spalding, Lincolnshire
PE12 8LH
T: (01406) 426866

Cackle Hill House ◆◆◆◆
Cackle Hill Lane, Holbeach,
Spalding, Lincolnshire PE12 8BS
T: (01406) 426721 &
07930 228755
F: (01406) 424659
E: cacklehill2@netscapeonline.
co.uk

Pipwell Manor ◆◆◆◆
Washway Road, Saracens Head,
Holbeach, Spalding, Lincolnshire
PE12 8AL
T: (01406) 423119
F: (01406) 423119

HOLBECK
Nottinghamshire

Browns ◆◆◆◆◆
The Old Orchard Cottage,
Holbeck, Worksop,
Nottinghamshire S80 3NF
T: (01909) 720659
F: (01909) 720659
E: Browns@holbeck.fsnet.co.uk
I: www.smoothhound.
co.uk/hotels/browns.html

HOLLINGTON
Staffordshire

The Raddle Inn
Rating Applied For
Quarry Bank, Hollington, Stoke-
on-Trent ST10 4HQ
T: 1889 507278 & 7779 264277
F: 1889 507520
E: peter@logcabin.co.uk
I: www.logcabin.co.uk

Reevsmoor ◆◆◆◆
Hoargate Lane, Hollington,
Ashbourne, Derbyshire DE6 3AG
T: (01335) 330318
F: (01335) 390798
E: hlivesey@aol.com

HOLMESFIELD
Derbyshire

Carpenter House ◆◆◆
Millthorpe, Holmesfield,
Dronfield S18 7WH
T: (0114) 289 0307

HOLYMOORSIDE
Derbyshire

Burnell ◆◆◆◆
Baslow Road, Holymoorside,
Chesterfield, Derbyshire S42 7HJ
T: 1246 567570
I: www.geocities.
com/burnellbnb

HOPE
Derbyshire

The Poachers Arms ◆◆◆
95 Castleton Road, Hope, Hope
Valley S33 6SB
T: (01433) 620380
F: (01433) 621915

Underleigh House ◆◆◆◆◆
Off Edale Road, Hope, Hope
Valley S33 6RF
T: (01433) 621372 & 621324
F: (01433) 621324
E: underleigh.house@
btinternet.com
I: www.underleighhouse.co.uk

Woodroffe Arms ◆◆◆
1 Castleton Road, Hope, Hope
Valley S33 6SB
T: (01433) 620351

HOPE BAGOT
Shropshire

Croft Cottage ◆◆◆◆
Cumberley Lane, Hope Bagot,
Ludlow, Shropshire SY8 3LJ
T: (01584) 890664
F: 0870 1299897
E: croft.cottage@virgin.net
I: freespace.virgin.
net/david-elizabeth.hatchell

HOPE MANSELL
Herefordshire

Sutton House ◆◆◆◆
Hope Mansell, Ross-on-Wye,
Herefordshire HR9 5TJ
T: (01989) 750351 &
0771 2230320
F: (01989) 750351
E: sutton.house@virgin.net

HOPTON CASTLE
Shropshire

Upper House Farm ◆◆◆◆
Hopton Castle, Craven Arms,
Shropshire SY7 0QF
T: (01547) 530319
I: www.go2.co.uk/upperhouse

HORSLEY
Derbyshire

Horsley Lodge ◆◆◆◆
Smalley Mill Road, Horsley,
Derby DE21 5BL
T: (01332) 780838
F: (01332) 781118
E: enquiries@horsleylodge.co.uk
I: www.horsleylodge.co.uk

HORTON
Staffordshire

Croft Meadows Farm ◆◆◆
Horton, Leek, Staffordshire
ST13 8QE
T: (01782) 513039
&

HULLAND
Derbyshire

Hulland Nurseries ◆◆◆
The Green, Hulland, DE6 3EP
T: (01335) 370052

HULME END
Staffordshire

Raikes Farm ◆◆◆
Raikes, Hulme End, Buxton,
Derbyshire SK17 0HJ
T: (01298) 84344
F: (01298) 84344

Riverside
Rating Applied For
Hulme End, Buxton, Derbyshire
SK17 0EZ
T: (01298) 84474
F: (01298) 84474
E: roger@riversidevilla.co.uk
I: www.riversidevilla.co.uk

HUMBERSTONE
Leicestershire

The Squirrels
Rating Applied For
9 Widford Close, Humberstone,
Leicester LE5 0AN
T: (0116) 2202894
F: (0116) 2768424

HUNTLEY
Gloucestershire

Birdwood Villa Farm ◆◆
Main Road, Birdwood, Huntley,
Gloucester GL19 3EQ
T: (01452) 750451

Forest Gate ◆◆◆
Huntley, Gloucester GL19 3EU
T: (01452) 831192 &
(01836) 632415
F: (01452) 831192
E: forest.gate@huntley-glos.
demon.co.uk
I: www.huntley-glos.demon.
co.uk

The Kings Head Inn ◆◆◆
Birdwood, Huntley, Gloucester
GL19 3EF
T: (01452) 750348
F: (01452) 750348

HUSBANDS BOSWORTH
Leicestershire

Mrs Armitage's ◆◆
31-33 High Street, Husbands
Bosworth, Lutterworth,
Leicestershire LE17 6LJ
T: (01858) 880066

IDRIDGEHAY
Derbyshire

**Millbank Cottage Bed and
Breakfast** ◆◆◆◆
Idridgehay, Belper, Derbyshire
DE56 2SH
T: (01629) 823 161 & 822 318

ILAM
Staffordshire

Beechenhill Farm ◆◆◆◆
Ilam, Ashbourne, Derbyshire
DE6 2BD
T: (01335) 310274
F: (01335) 310274
E: beechenhill@btinternet.com
I: www.beechenhill.co.uk

Throwley Hall ◆◆◆◆
Ilam, Ashbourne, Derbyshire
DE6 2BB
T: (01538) 308202 & 308243
F: (01538) 308243
E: throwleyhall@talk21.com
I: www.throwleyhallfarm.co.uk

INCHBROOK
Gloucestershire

The Crown Inn ◆◆◆
Bath Road, Inchbrook, Stroud,
Gloucestershire GL5 5HA
T: (01453) 832914 &
07977 096224
F: (01453) 832914
E: inchbrook@cwcom.net
I: www.inchbrook.cwc.net

INKBERROW
Worcestershire

Bulls Head Inn ◆◆◆
The Village Green, Inkberrow,
Worcester WR7 4DY
T: (01386) 792233
F: (01386) 793090

IRONBRIDGE
Shropshire

Bird in Hand Inn ◆◆◆
Waterloo Street, Ironbridge,
Telford, Shropshire TF8 7HG
T: (01952) 432226

Bridge House ◆◆◆◆◆
Buildwas, Telford, Shropshire
TF8 7BN
T: (01952) 432105
F: (01952) 432105
E: janethedges@talk21.com
I: www.smoothhound.co.uk

Bridge View ◆◆◆
10 Tontine Hill, Ironbridge,
Telford, Shropshire TF8 7AL
T: (01952) 432541 & 433914
F: (01952) 433405
I: www.ironbridgeview.co.uk

The Calcutts House ◆◆◆
Jackfield, Ironbridge, Telford,
Shropshire TF8 7LH
T: (01952) 882631
F: (01952) 882951
E: alan&linda@calcuttshouse.
co.uk
I: www.calcuttshouse.co.uk

Coalbrookdale Villa ◆◆◆◆
Paradise, Coalbrookdale,
Ironbridge, Telford, Shropshire
TF8 7NR
T: (01952) 433450
F: (01952) 433450
E: coalbrookdalevilla@
currantbun.com
I: www.coalbrookdale.f9.co.uk

The Firs Guest House
Rating Applied For
32 Buildwas Road, Ironbridge,
Telford, Shropshire TF8 7BJ
T: (01952) 432121 & 433688
F: (01952) 433010

The Golden Ball Inn
Rating Applied For
Newbridge Road, Ironbridge,
Telford, Shropshire TF8 7BA
T: (01952) 432179
F: (01952) 433123
E: matrowland@hotmail.com

Greenways Guest House ◆◆◆
57 High Street, Telford,
Shropshire TF7 5AT
T: (01952) 583118 & 408777
F: (01952) 408777
I: www.greenwaysguesthouse.
com

The Library House ◆◆◆◆
11 Severn Bank, Ironbridge,
Telford, Shropshire TF8 7AN
T: (01952) 432299
F: (01952) 433967
E: info@libraryhouse.com
I: www.libraryhouse.com

Lord Hill Guest House ◆◆
Duke Street, Broseley,
Shropshire TF12 5LU
T: (01952) 884270 & 580792

The Malthouse ◆◆◆◆
The Wharfage, Ironbridge,
Telford, Shropshire TF8 7NH
T: (01952) 433712
F: (01952) 433298
E: malthse@globalnet.co.uk
I: malthousepubs.co.uk

The Old Church Guest House
◆◆◆◆
Park Avenue, Madeley, Telford,
Shropshire TF7 5AB
T: (01952) 583745
F: (01952) 583745

Orchard House ◆◆◆
40 King Street, Broseley,
Shropshire TF12 5NA
T: (01952) 882684

Post Office House ◆◆◆
6 The Square, Ironbridge,
Telford, Shropshire TF8 7AQ
T: (01952) 433201
F: (01952) 433582
E: Hunter@pohouse-ironbridge.
fsnet.co.uk
I: www.pohouse-ironbridge.
fsnet.co.uk

Severn Lodge ◆◆◆◆
New Road, Ironbridge, Telford,
Shropshire TF8 7AS
T: (01952) 432148
F: (01952) 432062
E: bookings@severnlodge.com
I: www.severnlodge.com

Sunny Croft Guest House
Rating Applied For
Orchard Lane, Ironbridge,
Telford, Shropshire TF8 7PB
T: (01952) 432397
F: (01952) 432635

Tontine Hotel ◆◆◆
The Square, Ironbridge, Telford,
Shropshire TF8 7AL
T: (01952) 432127
F: (01952) 432094
E: tontinehotel@
netscapeonline.co.uk
I: www.tontine-ironbridge.co.uk

Wharfage Cottage ◆◆◆
17 The Wharfage, Ironbridge,
Telford, Shropshire TF8 7AW
T: (01952) 432721
F: (01952) 432639

Woodlands Farm ◆◆
Beech Road, Ironbridge, Telford,
Shropshire TF8 7PA
T: (01952) 432741

KEGWORTH
Leicestershire

Kegworth Lantern Hotel ◆◆
1 Market Place, Kegworth, Derby
DE74 2EE
T: (01509) 673989 & 672538
F: (01509) 670725

KEMERTON
Worcestershire

Wings Cottage ◆◆◆◆
Wing Lane, Kemerton,
Tewkesbury, Gloucestershire
GL20 7JG
T: (01386) 725273
F: (01386) 725273
E: jway@wingscottage.demon.
co.uk
I: www.wingscottage.demon.
co.uk/index.html

KEMPSEY
Worcestershire

Malbre House ◆◆
Baynhall, Kempsey, Worcester
WR5 3PA
T: (01905) 820412

KENILWORTH
Warwickshire

Abbey Guest House ◆◆◆◆
41 Station Road, Kenilworth,
Warwickshire CV8 1JD
T: (01926) 512707
F: (01926) 859148
E: the-abbey@virgin.net

Avondale B & B ◆◆◆
18 Moseley Road, Kenilworth,
Warwickshire CV8 2AQ
T: (01926) 859072 &
07811 688136

Bridgend ◆◆◆
15 Farmer Ward Road,
Kenilworth, Warwickshire
CV8 2DJ
T: (01926) 511995 &
07713 141396
E: bridgenddbb@hotmail.com

Castle Laurels Hotel ◆◆◆◆
22 Castle Road, Kenilworth,
Warwickshire CV8 1NG
T: (01926) 856179
F: (01926) 854954
E: moores22@aol
I: www.castlelaurelshotel.co.uk

The Cottage Inn ◆◆◆
36 Stoneleigh Road, Kenilworth,
Warwickshire CV8 2GD
T: (01926) 853900
F: (01926) 856032

Enderley Guest House ◆◆◆◆
20 Queens Road, Kenilworth,
Warwickshire CV8 1JQ
T: (01926) 855388
F: (01926) 850450
E: enderleyguesthouse@
supanet.com

Ferndale Guest House ◆◆◆◆
45 Priory Road, Kenilworth,
Warwickshire CV8 1LL
T: (01926) 853214
F: (01926) 858336
E: derekwilson1@canpuserve.
com

Howden House ◆◆
170 Warwick Road, Kenilworth,
Warwickshire CV8 1HS
T: (01926) 850310

Oldwych House Farm ◆◆◆◆
Oldwych Lane, Fen End,
Kenilworth, Warwickshire
CV8 1NR
T: (01676) 533552
F: (01676) 530177

The Priory Guesthouse ◆◆◆
58 Priory Road, Kenilworth,
Warwickshire CV8 1LQ
T: (01926) 856173
F: (01926) 856173

The Quince House ◆◆◆◆
29 Moseley Road, Kenilworth,
Warwickshire CV8 2AR
T: (01926) 858652
E: georgina.thomas@ntlworld.
com
I: www.balldesi.demon.
co.uk/b_b.html

Victoria Lodge Hotel ◆◆◆◆
180 Warwick Road, Kenilworth,
Warwickshire CV8 1HU
T: (01926) 512020
F: (01926) 858703
E: info@victorialodgehotel.
co.uk
I: www.victorialodgehotel.co.uk

KETTERING
Northamptonshire

Dairy Farm ◆◆◆◆
Cranford St Andrew, Kettering,
Northamptonshire NN14 4AQ
T: (01536) 330273

**Hawthorn House (Private)
Hotel** ◆◆◆
2 Hawthorn Road, Kettering,
Northamptonshire NN15 7HS
T: (01536) 482513
F: (01536) 513121

Pennels Guesthouse ◆◆◆
175 Beatrice Road, Kettering,
Northamptonshire NN16 9QR
T: (01536) 481940 &
07713 899508
F: (01536) 410798
E: pennelsgh@aol.com
I: www.members.aol.
com/pennelsgh

2 Wilkie Close ◆◆◆◆
Kettering, Northamptonshire
NN15 7RD
T: (01536) 310270 &
(01961) 541369
F: (01536) 310270
E: roxmere@aol.com

KEXBY
Lincolnshire

The Grange ◆◆◆
Kexby, Gainsborough,
Lincolnshire DN21 5PJ
T: (01427) 788265

KEYWORTH
Nottinghamshire

Flinders Farm Bed & Breakfast
◆◆◆◆
33 Main Street, Keyworth,
Nottingham NG12 5HA
T: (0115) 937 2352

KIDDERMINSTER
Worcestershire

Bewdley Hill House ◆◆◆◆
8 Bewdley Hill, Kidderminster,
Worcestershire DY11 6BS
T: (01562) 60473
F: (01562) 60473
E: judy-john@bewdleyhillhouse.
fsnet.co.uk

Collingdale Private Hotel ◆◆◆
197 Comberton Road,
Kidderminster, Worcestershire
DY10 1UE
T: (01562) 515460 & 862839
F: (01562) 863937

Hollies Farm Cottage ◆◆◆◆
Hollies Lane, Franche,
Kidderminster, Worcestershire
DY11 5RW
T: (01562) 745677 &
0777 5645183
F: (01562) 824580
E: pete@top-floor.fsbusiness.
co.uk

Victoria Hotel ◆◆◆
15 Comberton Road,
Kidderminster, Worcestershire
DY10 1UA
T: (01562) 67240
F: (01562) 67240

KILCOT
Gloucestershire

Withyland Heights Bed and Breakfast ◆◆◆
Withyland Heights, Beavans Hill,
Kilcot, Newent, Gloucestershire
GL18 1PG
T: (01989) 720582
F: (01989) 720238
E: withyland@farming.co.uk

KILSBY
Northamptonshire

The Hollies Farm ◆◆◆
Main Road, Kilsby, CV23 8XR
T: (01788) 822629

KINETON
Warwickshire

The Castle ◆◆◆
Edgehill, Kineton, Warwick
OX15 6DJ
T: (01295) 670255
F: (01295) 670521
E: castleedgehill@msn.com.
I: www.our-web-site.
com/the-castle-inn

KING'S CLIFFE
Northamptonshire

19 West Street ◆◆◆◆
King's Cliffe, Peterborough
PE8 6XB
T: (01780) 470365
F: (01780) 470623
E: bjdixon@compuserve.com

KINGS CAPLE
Herefordshire

Ruxton Farm ◆◆◆◆
Kings Caple, Hereford HR1 4TX
T: (01432) 840493
F: (01432) 840493

KINGSLAND
Herefordshire

The Buzzards ◆◆◆
Kingsland, Leominster,
Herefordshire HR6 9QE
T: (01568) 708941
E: booking@bakerpovey.co.uk
I: www.bakerpovey.co.uk

The Corners Inn ◆◆◆
Kingsland, Leominster,
Herefordshire HR6 9RY
T: (01568) 708385
T: (01568) 709033
E: enq@cornersinn.co.uk
I: www.cornersinn.co.uk

Holgate Farm ◆◆◆◆
Kingsland, Leominster,
Herefordshire HR6 9QS
T: (01568) 708275

KINGSTONE
Herefordshire

Mill Orchard ◆◆◆◆
Kingstone, Hereford HR2 9ES
T: (01981) 250326
F: (01981) 250520
E: cleveland@millorchard.co.uk
I: www.millorchard.co.uk

Webton Court Farmhouse ◆◆
Kingstone, Hereford HR2 9NF
T: (01981) 250220
F: (01981) 250220
E: juliet@pudgefsnet.co.uk

KINGTON
Herefordshire

Tumbledown ◆◆◆
Headbrook, Kington,
Herefordshire HR5 3DZ
T: (01544) 231380

KINLET
Worcestershire

Catsley Farm ◆◆
Kinlet, Bewdley, Worcestershire
DY12 3AP
T: (01299) 841323 & 841231

KINVER
Staffordshire

Anchor Hotel ◆◆◆
Dark Lane, Kinver, Stourbridge,
West Midlands DY7 6NR
T: (01384) 872085 & 873291
F: (01384) 878824
E: anchorhotel@kinver2000.
freeserve.co.uk
I: www.anchorhotel.com

KIRTON
Nottinghamshire

The Fox at Kirton ◆◆◆
Main Street, Kirton, Newark,
Nottinghamshire NG22 9LP
T: (01623) 860502 & 861909
F: (01623) 861909
E: foxkirton@aol.com

KISLINGBURY
Northamptonshire

The Elms ◆◆◆
Kislingbury, Northampton
NN7 4AH
T: (01604) 830326

KNOCKDOWN
Gloucestershire

Avenue Farm ◆◆◆
Knockdown, Tetbury,
Gloucestershire GL8 8QY
T: (01454) 238207
F: (01454) 238033
I: www.glosfarmhols.co.uk

KNOWLE
West Midlands

Ivy House Guest House ◆◆◆
Warwick Road, Heronfield,
Knowle, Solihull, West Midlands
B93 0EB
T: (01564) 770247
F: (01564) 778063
E: @ivy-guest-house.freeserve.
co.uk
I: www.smoothhound.
co.uk/hotels/ivyguest.html

LAMBLEY
Nottinghamshire

Magnolia Guest House ◆◆◆◆
22 Spring Lane, Lambley,
Nottingham NG4 4PH
T: (0115) 9314404
F: (0115) 9314582
E: magnoliahouse@lineone.net

LAXTON
Nottinghamshire

Lilac Farm ◆◆◆
Laxton, Newark,
Nottinghamshire NG22 0NX
T: (01777) 870376
F: (01777) 870376

Manor Farm ◆◆
Moorhouse Road, Laxton,
Newark, Nottinghamshire
NG22 0NU
T: (01777) 870417

Spanhoe Lodge ◆◆◆◆
Harringworth Road, Laxton,
Corby, Northamptonshire
NN17 3AT
T: (01780) 450328 &
07867 520917
F: (01780) 450328
E: jennie.spanhoe@virgin.net
I: www.spanhoelodge.co.uk

LEA MARSTON
West Midlands

Reindeer Park Lodge ◆◆◆◆
Kingsbury Road, Lea Marston,
Sutton Coldfield, West Midlands
B76 0DE
T: (01675) 470811 & 470710
F: (01675) 470710

LEADENHAM
Lincolnshire

George Hotel ◆◆◆
High Street, Leadenham, Lincoln
LN5 0PN
T: (01400) 272251
F: (01400) 272091

LEAMINGTON SPA
Warwickshire

Adelaide ◆◆◆
15 Adelaide Road, Leamington
Spa, Warwickshire CV31 3PN
T: (01926) 450633
F: (01926) 450633

Almond House ◆◆◆◆
8 Parklands Avenue, Lillington,
Leamington Spa, Warwickshire
CV32 7BA
T: (01926) 424052 &
07931 286945

**Avenue Lodge Guest House
◆◆◆**
61 Avenue Road, Leamington
Spa, Warwickshire CV31 3PF
T: (01926) 338555 &
07932 652521

Buckland Lodge Hotel ◆◆
35 Avenue Road, Leamington
Spa, Warwickshire CV31 3PG
T: (01926) 423843
F: (01926) 423843
E: buckland.lodge1@btinternet.
com
I: www.Buckland-Lodge.co.uk.

Bungalow Farm ◆◆◆◆
Windmill Hill, Cubbington,
Leamington Spa, Warwickshire
CV32 7LW
T: (01926) 423276 &
07970 818305

Charnwood Guest House ◆◆◆
47 Avenue Road, Leamington
Spa, Warwickshire CV31 3PF
T: (01926) 831074
F: (01926) 831074

8 Clarendon Crescent ◆◆◆◆
Leamington Spa, Warwickshire
CV32 5NR
T: (01926) 429840
F: (01926) 424641
E: lawson@lawson71.fsnet.
co.uk
I: www.shakespeare-country.
co.uk

The Coach House ◆◆◆◆
Snowford Hall Farm,
Hunningham, Leamington Spa,
Warwickshire CV33 9ES
T: (01926) 632297
F: (01926) 633599
E: the_coach_house@lineone.
net
I: lineone.
net/~the_coach_house

**Corkill Bed and Breakfast
◆◆◆**
27 Newbold Street, Leamington
Spa, Warwickshire CV32 4HN
T: (01926) 336303
F: (01926) 336303
E: mrscorkill@aol.com

The Dell Guesthouse ◆◆◆
8 Warwick Place, Leamington
Spa, Warwickshire CV32 5BJ
T: (01926) 422784
F: (01926) 422784
E: dellguesthouse@virgin.net
I: www.dellguesthouse.co.uk

**Flowerdale
Rating Applied For**
29A Coventry Road, Warwick,
CV34 5HN
T: (01926) 496393
F: (01926) 496393

Fountain House ◆◆◆
4 Willes Road, Leamington Spa,
Warwickshire CV32 4PY
T: (01926) 424822
E: fountain@apswabey.demon.
co.uk

5 The Grange ◆◆◆
Cubbington, Leamington Spa,
Warwickshire CV32 7LE
T: (01926) 744762

**Hedley Villa Guest House
◆◆◆**
31 Russell Terrace, Leamington
Spa, Warwickshire CV31 1EZ
T: (01926) 424504 &
07778 895124
F: (01926) 745801
E: pat.ashfield@ntlworld.com
I: www.hedleyvilla.freeserve.
co.uk

Hill Farm ◆◆◆◆
Lewis Road, Radford Semele,
Leamington Spa, Warwickshire
CV31 1UX
T: (01926) 337571

Lansdowne Hotel ◆◆◆◆
87 Clarendon Street,
Leamington Spa, Warwickshire
CV32 4PF
T: (01926) 450505
F: (01926) 421313
E: thelansdowne@cwcom.net
I: www.thelansdowne.cwc.net

4 Lillington Road ◆◆◆
Leamington Spa, Warwickshire
CV32 5YR
T: (01926) 429244
E: pauline.burton@btinternet.
com

Milverton House Hotel ◆◆◆◆
1 Milverton Terrace, Leamington
Spa, Warwickshire CV32 5BE
T: (01926) 428335
F: (01926) 428335

Trendway Guest House ◆◆◆
45 Avenue Road, Leamington
Spa, Warwickshire CV31 3PF
T: (01926) 316644
F: (01926) 337506

Victoria Park Hotel ◆◆◆◆
12 Adelaide Road, Leamington
Spa, Warwickshire CV31 3PW
T: (01926) 424195
F: (01926) 421521
I: www.
victoriaparkhotelleamingtonspa.
co.uk

The Willis ◆◆◆
11 Eastnor Grove, Leamington
Spa, Warwickshire CV31 1LD
T: (01926) 425820

Wymondley Lodge ◆◆◆◆
8 Adelaide Road, Leamington
Spa, Warwickshire CV31 3PW
T: (01926) 882669
F: (01926) 882669

York House Hotel ◆◆◆
9 York Road, Leamington Spa,
Warwickshire CV31 3PR
T: (01926) 424671
F: (01926) 832272
E: yorkhouse@leamington.
freeserve-co-uk

LEASINGHAM
Lincolnshire

Manor Farm ◆◆
Leasingham, Sleaford,
Lincolnshire NG34 8JN
T: (01529) 302671
F: (01529) 414946

LECHLADE
Gloucestershire

Apple Tree Guest House ◆◆◆
Buscot, Faringdon, Oxfordshire
SN7 8DA
T: (01367) 252592
E: emreay@aol.com

Cambrai Lodge ◆◆◆◆
Oak Street, Lechlade,
Gloucestershire GL7 3AY
T: (01367) 253173 &
07860 150467

New Inn Hotel ◆◆◆
Market Square, Lechlade-on-
Thames, Lechlade,
Gloucestershire GL7 3AB
T: (01367) 252296
F: (01367) 252315
E: info@newinnhotel.com
I: www.newinnhotel.co.uk

LEDBURY
Herefordshire

Brook House ◆◆◆◆
Birtsmorton, Malvern,
Worcestershire WR13 6AF
T: (01531) 650664
F: (01531) 650664
E: maryd@lineone.net

Church Farm ◆◆◆
Coddington, Ledbury,
Herefordshire HR8 1JJ
T: (01531) 640271

The Hopton Arms ◆◆◆
Ashperton, Ledbury,
Herefordshire HR8 2SE
T: (01531) 670520
E: peter@hoptonarms.co.uk
I: www.hoptonarms.co.uk

Kilmory ◆◆◆◆◆
Bradlow, Ledbury, Herefordshire
HR8 1JF
T: (01531) 631951
E: seymore@clara.co.uk

Little Marcle Court ◆◆◆◆
Little Marcle, Ledbury,
Herefordshire HR8 2LB
T: (01531) 670936

Mainstone House ◆◆◆
Trumpet, Ledbury, Herefordshire
HR8 2RA
T: (01531) 670230

**Wall Hills Country Guest
House** ◆◆◆◆
Hereford Road, Ledbury,
Herefordshire HR8 2PR
T: (01531) 632833
I: www.smoothhound.
co.uk/hotels/wallhill.html

LEEK
Staffordshire

Abbey Inn ◆◆◆
Abbey Green Road, Leek,
Staffordshire ST13 8SA
T: (01538) 382865
F: (01538) 398604
E: martin@abbeyinn.co.uk
I: www.abbeyinn.co.uk

Bank End Farm Motel ◆◆◆
Leek Old Road, Longsdon, Stoke-
on-Trent ST9 9QJ
T: (01538) 383638

Beechfields ◆◆◆◆
Park Road, Leek, Staffordshire
ST13 8JS
T: (01538) 372825
E: judith@beech-fields.fsnet.
co.uk
I: www.cressbrook.
co.uk/leek/beechfields

The Green Man ◆◆◆
38 Compton, Leek, Staffordshire
ST13 5NH
T: (01538) 388084

The Hatcheries ◆◆
Church Lane, Leek, Staffordshire
ST13 5EX
T: (01538) 399552 & 383544
F: (01538) 399552
E: the.hatcheries@faxvia.net
I: www.thehatcheries.co.uk

Little Brookhouse Farm
◆◆◆◆
Cheddleton, Leek, Staffordshire
ST13 7DF
T: (01538) 360350

New House Farm ◆◆◆
Bottomhouse, Leek,
Staffordshire ST13 7PA
T: (01538) 304350 &
07850 183208
F: (01538) 304338
E: newhousefarm@btinternet.
com

Peak Weavers Hotel ◆◆◆
21 King Street, Leek,
Staffordshire ST13 5NW
T: (01538) 383729 & 387475
F: (01538) 387475
E: peak.weavers@virgin.net
I: www.peakweavershotel.com

Prospect House ◆◆◆◆
334 Cheadle Road, Cheddleton,
Leek, Staffordshire ST13 7BW
T: (01782) 550639 &
07973 179478
E: prospect@talk21.com
I: www.touristnetuk.
com/wm/prospect/index.htm

LEICESTER
Leicestershire

Beaumaris Guesthouse ◆◆◆
18 Westcotes Drive, Leicester,
LE3 0QR
T: (0116) 254 0261 &
07957 763922
E: beaumarisgh@talk21.com

Burlington Hotel ◆◆◆
Elmfield Avenue, Stoneygate,
Leicester, LE2 1RB
T: (0116) 270 5112
F: (0116) 270 4207
E: welcome@burlingtonhotel.
co.uk
I: www.burlingtonhotel.co.uk

Glenfield Lodge Hotel
Rating Applied For
4 Glenfield Road, Leicester,
LE3 6AP
T: (0116) 262 7554

Scotia Hotel ◆◆
10 Westcotes Drive, Leicester,
LE3 0QR
T: (0116) 254 9200
F: (0116) 254 9200
E: scotiahotel@hotmail.com

South Fork Guesthouse ◆◆◆
464-466 Narborough Road,
Leicester, LE3 2FT
T: (0116) 2999960
F: (0116) 2994332
E: southfork@ntlworld.com

Spindle Lodge Hotel ◆◆◆
2 West Walk, Leicester, LE1 7NA
T: (0116) 233 8801
F: (0116) 233 8804
E: spindlelodgeleicester@
orange.net
I: www.smoothhound.
co.uk/hotels/spindle.html

LEIGH SINTON
Worcestershire

Chirkenhill ◆◆◆◆
Leigh Sinton, Malvern,
Worcestershire WR13 5DE
T: (01886) 832205
E: wenden@eidosnet.co.uk

LEINTWARDINE
Herefordshire

Lower House ◆◆◆◆
Adforton, Leintwardine, Craven
Arms, Shropshire SY7 0NF
T: (01568) 770223
F: (01568) 770592
E: cutler@sy7.com
I: www.sy7.com/lowerhouse

LEOMINSTER
Herefordshire

Bedford House ◆◆◆
Dilwyn, Hereford HR4 8JJ
T: (01544) 388260

Bramlea ◆◆◆
Barons Cross Road, Leominster,
Herefordshire HR6 8RW
T: (01568) 613406
F: (01568) 613406
E: lesbramlea@netlineUK.net

Chesfield ◆◆◆
112 South Street, Leominster,
Herefordshire HR6 8JF
T: (01568) 613204

Copper Hall ◆◆◆◆
South Street, Leominster,
Herefordshire HR6 8JN
T: (01568) 611622
E: sccrick@copperhall.freeserve.
co.uk

Heath House ◆◆◆◆
Stoke Prior, Leominster,
Herefordshire HR6 0NF
T: (01568) 760385
F: (01568) 760385
E: heathhouse@onetel.net.uk

Highfield ◆◆◆◆
Ivington Road, Newtown,
Leominster, Herefordshire
HR6 8QD
T: (01568) 613216
E: info@stay-at-highfield.co.uk
I: www.stay-at-highfield.co.uk

Highgate House ◆◆◆◆
29 Hereford Road, Leominster,
Herefordshire HR6 8JS
T: (01568) 614562
F: (01568) 614562
E: highgatehouse@easicom.
com

Home Farm ◆◆◆◆
Bircher, Leominster,
Herefordshire HR6 0AX
T: (01568) 780525

Little Bury Farm ◆◆◆
Luston, Leominster,
Herefordshire HR6 0EB
T: (01568) 611575

Lower Bache House ◆◆◆◆
Kimbolton, Leominster,
Herefordshire HR6 0ER
T: (01568) 750304
E: leslie.wiles@care4free.net

The Paddock ◆◆◆◆
Shobdon, Leominster,
Herefordshire HR6 9NQ
T: (01568) 708176
F: (01568) 708829
E: thepaddock@talk21.com

Rossendale Guesthouse ◆◆◆
46 Broad Street, Leominster,
Herefordshire HR6 8BS
T: (01568) 612464

Tyn-Y-Coed ◆◆◆
Shobdon, Leominster,
Herefordshire HR6 9NY
T: (01568) 708277
F: (01568) 708277
E: jandrews@shobdondesign.
kc3.co.uk

LICHFIELD
Staffordshire

Altair House ◆◆◆
21 Shakespeare Avenue,
Lichfield, Staffordshire
WS14 9BE
T: (01543) 252900 &
07968 265843

32 Beacon Street ◆◆◆◆
Lichfield, Staffordshire
WS13 7AJ
T: (01543) 262378

8 The Close ◆◆◆◆
Lichfield, Staffordshire
WS13 7LD
T: (01543) 418483
F: (01543) 418483
E: gilljones@talk21.com
I: www.ldb.
co.uk/accommodation.htm

Coppers End Guest House ◆◆◆
Walsall Road, Muckley Corner,
Lichfield, Staffordshire
WS14 0BG
T: (01543) 372910
F: (01543) 360423
I: www.coppersendguesthouse.
co.uk

Davolls Cottage ◆◆◆◆
156 Woodhouses Road,
Burntwood, Lichfield,
Staffordshire WS7 9EL
T: (01543) 671250

16 Dimbles Lane ◆◆◆
Lichfield, Staffordshire
WS13 7HW
T: (01543) 251107

The Farmhouse ◆◆◆◆
Lysway Lane, Longdon Green,
Rugeley, Staffordshire
WS15 4PZ
T: (0121) 378 4552 &
(01543) 490416
F: (0121) 311 2915
E: jaynetdrury@aol.com
I: www.chez.com/thefarmhouse

Freeford Farm ◆◆◆
Freeford, Lichfield, Staffordshire
WS14 9QL
T: (01543) 263330

Green View ◆◆◆◆
Knowle Lane, Lichfield,
Staffordshire WS14 9RB
T: (01543) 256224

4 Hayes View ◆◆◆
Lichfield, Staffordshire
WS13 7BT
T: (01543) 253725

Holly House Bed and Breakfast ◆◆◆
198 Upper St John Street,
Lichfield, Staffordshire
WS14 9EF
T: (01543) 263078

Netherstowe House North ◆◆
Netherstowe Lane, Lichfield,
Staffordshire WS13 6AY
T: (01543) 254631

Pauline Duvals Bed and Breakfast ◆◆◆
21-23 Dam Street, The Bogey
Hole, Lichfield, Staffordshire
WS13 6AE
T: (01543) 264303

Twenty Three The Close ◆◆◆◆
23 The Close, Lichfield,
Staffordshire WS13 7LD
T: (01543) 306140 &
0780 3689897
E: charles.taylor@
lichfield-cathedral.org

The White House ◆◆
Market Lane, Wall, Lichfield,
Staffordshire WS14 0AS
T: (01543) 480384

LINCOLN
Lincolnshire

AA and M Guesthouse ◆◆◆
79 Carholme Road, Lincoln,
LN1 1RT
T: (01522) 543736
F: (01522) 543736

Aaron Whisby Guest House ◆◆◆
262 West Parade, Lincoln,
LN1 1LY
T: (01522) 526930

Allwood Guesthouse ◆◆
258 West Parade, Lincoln,
LN1 1LY
T: (01522) 887868

Damon's Motel ◆◆◆◆
997 Doddington Road, Lincoln,
LN6 3ES
T: (01522) 887733
F: (01522) 887734
♿

D'isney Place Hotel ◆◆◆◆
Eastgate, Lincoln, LN2 4AA
T: (01522) 538881
F: (01522) 511321
E: info@disneyplacehotel.co.uk
I: www.disneyplacehotel.co.uk

Hamilton Hotel ◆◆
2 Hamilton Road, Lincoln,
LN5 8ED
T: (01522) 528243
F: (01522) 528243

Jaymar ◆◆
31 Newland St West, Lincoln,
LN1 1QQ
T: (01522) 532934 &
(01552) 820182
F: (01522) 820182
E: ward.jaymar4@ntlworld.com

Manor Farm Stables ◆◆◆◆
Broxholme, Lincoln, LN1 2NG
T: (01522) 704220 &
07890 812323
E: pfieldson@lineone.net

Manor House ◆◆◆◆
Bracebridge Heath, Lincoln
LN4 2HW
T: (01522) 520825
F: (01522) 542418
E: mikescoley@farming.co.uk

New Farm ◆◆◆
Burton, Lincoln LN1 2RD
T: (01522) 527326
F: (01522) 576572

Newport Cottage ◆◆◆◆
21 Newport, Lincoln, LN1 3DQ
T: (01522) 534470

Newport Guest House ◆◆◆
26-28 Newport, Lincoln,
LN1 3DF
T: (01522) 528590
F: (01522) 542868
E: info@newportguesthouse.
co.uk
I: www.newportguesthouse.
co.uk

The Old Bakery Guesthouse
Rating Applied For
26-28 Burton Road, Lincoln,
LN1 3LB
T: (01522) 576057
F: (01522) 576057

Ridgeways Guesthouse ◆◆◆
243 Burton Road, Lincoln,
LN1 3UB
T: (01522) 546878 &
07970 425130
F: (01522) 546878
E: ridgeways@talk21.com

Savill Guesthouse ◆◆◆◆
203 Yarborough Road, Lincoln,
LN1 3NQ
T: (01522) 523261
F: (01522) 568018
E: vvn@themail.co.uk

73 Station Road ◆◆◆
Branston, Lincoln, LN4 1LG
T: (01522) 828658 &
07932 162940

Tennyson Hotel ◆◆◆◆
7 South Park, Lincoln, LN5 8EN
T: (01522) 521624
F: (01522) 521355
E: tennyson.hotel@virgin.net
I: www.tennysonhotel.com

Truro House ◆◆◆◆
421 Newark Road, North
Hykeham, Lincoln, LN6 9SP
T: (01522) 882073 &
07798 791484

Welbeck Cottage ◆◆◆
Meadow Lane, South Hykeham,
Lincoln LN6 9PF
T: (01522) 692669 &
07799 741000
F: (01522) 692669
E: mad@wellbeck1.demon.co.uk

LINTON
Derbyshire

The Manor ◆◆◆◆
Hillside Road, Linton,
Swadlincote, Derbyshire
DE12 6RA
T: (01283) 761177
E: themanor@ukonline.co.uk

LITTLE BYTHAM
Lincolnshire

The Mallard Inn ◆◆◆◆
1 High Street, Little Bytham,
Grantham, Lincolnshire
NG33 4PP
T: (01780) 410470
F: (01780) 410245
E: john@mallard-inn.freeserve.
co.uk
I: www.mallard-inn.co.uk

The Willoughby Arms
Rating Applied For
Station Road, Little Bytham,
Grantham, Lincolnshire
NG33 4RA
T: (01780) 410276
F: (01780) 410190
E: willo@willoughbyarms.co.uk
I: www.willoughbyarms.co.uk

LITTLE COWARNE
Herefordshire

Three Horseshoes Inn ◆◆◆
Little Cowarne, Bromyard,
Herefordshire HR7 4RQ
T: (01885) 400276 & 40035
F: (01885) 400276

LITTLE HAYFIELD
Derbyshire

Lantern Pike Inn ◆◆◆
Glossop Road, Little Hayfield,
High Peak SK22 2NG
T: (01663) 747590
F: (01663) 749045

LITTLE INKBERROW
Worcestershire

Perrymill Farm ◆◆◆
Little Inkberrow, Worcester
WR7 4JX
T: (01386) 792177
F: (01386) 793449
E: alexander@estatesgazette.
net

LITTLE RISSINGTON
Gloucestershire

Weaveley Cottage ◆◆◆◆
Little Rissington, Cheltenham,
Gloucestershire GL54 2ND
T: (01451) 822482 & 821091
F: (01451) 822482
E: bourtonb@aol.com

LITTLE WENLOCK
Shropshire

Wenboro Cottage ◆◆◆
Church Lane, Little Wenlock,
Telford, Shropshire TF6 5BB
T: (01952) 505573
E: rcarter@wenboro.freeserve.
co.uk

LITTLEDEAN
Gloucestershire

Brayne Court ◆◆◆
High Street, Littledean,
Cinderford, Gloucestershire
GL14 3JY
T: (01594) 822163 &
07887 524991
F: (01594) 822163
E: jan@greenhalghj.fsnet.co.uk

The Cottage
Rating Applied For
Green Bottom, Cinderford,
Gloucestershire GL14 3LH
T: (01594) 823665 &
07909 717966
E: pmccoy45@aol.com

LITTON
Derbyshire

Beacon House ◆◆◆
Litton, Buxton, Derbyshire
SK17 8QP
T: (01298) 871752

Hall Farm House ◆◆◆◆
Litton, Buxton, Derbyshire
SK17 8QP
T: (01298) 872172

LLANGROVE
Herefordshire

Prospect Place ◆◆◆
Llangrove, Ross-on-Wye,
Herefordshire HR9 6ET
T: (01989) 770596 & 770159
E: prospectplacehr9bet@
btinternet.com

LONG BUCKBY
Northamptonshire

Murcott Mill ◆◆◆
Murcott, Long Buckby,
Northampton NN6 7QR
T: (01327) 842236
F: (01327) 844524
E: bhart6@compuserve.com

LONG CLAWSON
Leicestershire

Elms Farm ◆◆◆◆
East End, Long Clawson, Melton
Mowbray, Leicestershire
LE14 4NG
T: (01664) 822395
F: (01664) 823399
E: elmsfarm@whittard.net
I: www.whittard.net

LONG COMPTON
Warwickshire

Ashby House Bed and Breakfast ♦♦♦♦
Ashby House, Clarks Lane, Long Compton, Shipston-on-Stour, Warwickshire CV36 5LB
T: (01608) 684286 &
07976 700763
F: (01608) 684286
E: epfield@fieldashby.demon.co.uk
I: www.travel-uk.com/country/stratford.htm

Butlers Road Farm ♦♦♦
Long Compton, Shipston-on-Stour, Warwickshire CV36 5JZ
T: (01608) 684262
F: (01608) 684262
E: eileenwhittaker@easicom.com

Manor House Hotel & Restaurant ♦♦♦♦
Long Compton, Shipston-on-Stour, Warwickshire CV36 5JJ
T: (01608) 684218 &
07885 621177
F: (01608) 684218
E: themanor@gleneldon.fsbusiness.co.uk
I: www.accofind.com

LONGBOROUGH
Gloucestershire

Luckley Farm Bed and Breakfast ♦♦♦
Luckley Farm, Longborough, Moreton-in-Marsh, Gloucestershire GL56 0RD
T: (01451) 870885
F: (01451) 831481
E: luckleyholidays@talk21.com
I: www.luckley-holidays.co.uk

LONGDON
Staffordshire

Grand Lodge ♦♦♦♦
Horsey Lane, Longdon, Rugeley, Staffordshire WS15 4LW
T: (01543) 686103
F: (01543) 676266
E: grandlodge@edbroemt.demon.co.uk

LONGHOPE
Gloucestershire

New House Farm ♦♦♦
Barrel Lane, Aston Ingham, Longhope, Gloucestershire GL17 0LS
T: (01452) 830484
F: (01452) 830484
E: scaldbrain@aol.com
I: www.newhousefarm-accommodation.co.uk

The Old Farm ♦♦♦♦
Barrel Lane, Longhope, Gloucestershire GL17 0LR
T: (01452) 830252 &
0789 9831998
F: (01452) 830252
E: lucyr@avnet.co.uk
I: www.avnet.co.uk/theoldfarm

Royal Spring Farm ♦♦♦♦
(A4136), Longhope, Gloucestershire GL17 0PY
T: (01452) 830550

The Temple ♦♦♦♦♦
Old Monmouth Road, Longhope, Gloucestershire GL17 0NZ
T: (01452) 831011
F: (01452) 831776
E: tricia.ferguson@virgin.net

LONGLEVENS
Gloucestershire

Gemini Guest House ♦♦
83a Innsworth Lane, Longlevens, Gloucester GL2 0TT
T: (01452) 415849

LONGNOR
Staffordshire

Crewe and Harpur Arms Hotel ♦♦♦
Longnor, Buxton, Derbyshire SK17 0NS
T: (01298) 83205

LONGTOWN
Herefordshire

Olchon Cottage Farm ♦♦♦
Longtown, Hereford HR2 0NS
T: (01873) 860233
F: (01873) 860233
I: www.golden-valley.co.uk/Olchon

LOUGHBOROUGH
Leicestershire

The Beauchief Hotel ♦♦♦
29 Pinfold Gate, Loughborough, Leicestershire LE11 1BE
T: (01509) 268096
F: (01509) 268586
I: www.thebeauchiefhotel.co.uk

Charnwood Lodge ♦♦♦
136 Leicester Road, Loughborough, Leicestershire LE11 2AQ
T: (01509) 211120
F: (01509) 211121
E: charnwoodlodge@charwat.freeserve.co.uk
I: www.charnwoodlodge.com

Demontfort Hotel ♦♦♦
88 Leicester Road, Loughborough, Leicestershire LE11 2AQ
T: (01509) 216061
F: (01509) 233667

Forest Rise Hotel Ltd ♦♦♦
55-57 Forest Road, Loughborough, Leicestershire LE11 3NW
T: (01509) 215928
F: (01509) 210506

Garendon Park Hotel ♦♦♦
92 Leicester Road, Loughborough, Leicestershire LE11 2AQ
T: (01509) 236557
F: (01509) 265559
E: info@garendonparkhotel.co.uk
I: www.garendonparkhotel.co.uk

The Highbury Guesthouse ♦♦♦
146 Leicester Road, Loughborough, Leicestershire LE11 2AQ
T: (01509) 230545
F: (01509) 233086
E: emkhighbury@supanet.com
I: www.thehighburyguesthouse.co.uk

Holywell House ♦♦♦
40 Leicester Road, Loughborough, Leicestershire LE11 2AG
T: (01509) 267891 &
07899 755556
F: (01509) 214075
E: lezdes@holywellhouse.fsbusiness.co.uk
I: www.holywell.here.co.uk

Lane End Cottage ♦♦♦♦
45 School Lane, Old Woodhouse, Loughborough, Leicestershire LE12 8UJ
T: (01509) 890706
E: maryhudson@talk21.com

The Mountsorrel Hotel ♦♦♦
217 Loughborough Road, Mountsorrel, Loughborough, Leicestershire LE12 7AR
T: (01509) 412627 & 416105
F: (01509) 416105
E: mountsorrelhotel@route56.co.uk
I: www.uktourism.com/le-mountsorrel

New Life Guesthouse ♦♦♦
121 Ashby Road, Loughborough, Leicestershire LE11 3AB
T: (01509) 216699
F: (01509) 210020
E: jean_of_newlife@assureweb.com

Peachnook ♦♦
154 Ashby Road, Loughborough, Leicestershire LE11 3AG
T: (01509) 264390 & 217525
I: www.SmoothHound.co.uk/hotels/peachnohtml

LOUTH
Lincolnshire

Masons Arms ♦♦♦
Cornmarket, Louth, Lincolnshire LN11 9PY
T: (01507) 609525 & 609526
F: 0870 7066450
E: justin@themasons.co.uk
I: www.themasons.co.uk

LOWER BODDINGTON
Northamptonshire

Sears Cottage ♦♦♦♦
Owl End Lane, Lower Boddington, Daventry, Northamptonshire NN11 6XZ
T: (01327) 260271 & 262476
F: (01327) 262476
E: lynne.sydenham@mcmail.com
I: www.searscottage.cwc.net

LOWER CATESBY
Northamptonshire

The Old Coach House ♦♦♦♦
Lower Catesby, Daventry, Northamptonshire NN11 6LF
T: (01327) 310390 & 312220
F: (01327) 312220
E: coachhouse@lowercatesby.co.uk
I: www.lowercatesby.co.uk

LOWER SLAUGHTER
Gloucestershire

Greenfingers ♦♦♦♦
Wyck Rissington Lane, Lower Slaughter, Cheltenham, Gloucestershire GL54 2EX
T: (01451) 821217 &
07710 798385

LOXLEY
Warwickshire

Elm Cottage ♦♦♦♦
Stratford Road, Loxley, Warwick CV35 9JW
T: (01789) 840609

Oldborough Farmhouse ♦♦♦♦
Loxley Road, Loxley, Warwick CV35 9JW
T: (01789) 840938
F: (01789) 840938

LUBENHAM
Leicestershire

The Old Bakehouse ♦♦♦♦
9 The Green, Lubenham, Market Harborough, Leicestershire LE16 9TD
T: (01858) 463401

LUDLOW
Shropshire

Arran House ♦♦♦
42 Gravel Hill, Ludlow, Shropshire SY8 1QR
T: (01584) 873764

The Brakes ♦♦♦♦
Downton, Ludlow, Shropshire SY8 2LF
T: (01584) 856485
F: (01584) 856485
E: thebrakes@cwcom.net
I: www.ludlow.org.uk/brakes

Bull Hotel ♦♦♦
14 The Bull Ring, Ludlow, Shropshire SY8 1AD
T: (01584) 873611
F: (01584) 873666
E: bull.ludlow@btinternet.com
I: www.ludlow.org.uk/bullhotel

Castle View ♦♦♦
7 Castle View Terrace, Ludlow, Shropshire SY8 2NG
T: (01584) 875592
F: (01584) 875592

Cecil Guest House ♦♦♦
Sheet Road, Ludlow, Shropshire SY8 1LR
T: (01584) 872442
F: (01584) 872442

Crown Inn ♦♦♦♦
Hopton Wafers, Cleobury Mortimer, Kidderminster, Worcestershire DY14 0NB
T: (01299) 270372
F: (01299) 271127
E: desk@crownathopton.co.uk
I: www.go2.co.uk/crownathopton

Eight Dinham ♦♦♦♦
Dinham, Ludlow, Shropshire SY8 1EJ
T: (01584) 875661

Elsich Manor Cottage ♦♦♦
Seifton, Ludlow, Shropshire SY8 2DL
T: (01584) 861406 &
07989 623813
F: (01584) 861406

The Hen and Chickens Guesthouse ♦♦♦
103 Old Street, Ludlow, Shropshire SY8 1NU
T: (01584) 874318
E: sally@hen-and-chickens.co.uk
I: www.hen-and-chickens.co.uk

Henwick House ◆◆◆
Gravel Hill, Ludlow, Shropshire
SY8 1QU
T: (01584) 873338 &
07951 642159

Longlands ◆◆◆
Woodhouse Lane, Richards
Castle, Ludlow, Shropshire
SY8 4EU
T: (01584) 831636
E: iankemsley@aol.com
I: www.ludlow.org.uk/longlands

Lower House Farm ◆◆◆◆
Cleedownton, Ludlow,
Shropshire SY8 3EH
T: (01584) 823648
E: gsblack@talk21.com
I: www.ludlow.org.
uk/lowerhouse

Manna Oak ◆◆◆
Mill Street, Ludlow, Shropshire
SY8 1BE
T: (01584) 873204 &
07811 312800

Mill House ◆◆◆
Squirrel Lane, Lower Ledwyche,
Ludlow, Shropshire SY8 4JX
T: (01584) 872837
E: millhousebnb@aol.com

Mr Underhills ◆◆◆◆◆
Dinham Weir, Dinham, Ludlow,
Shropshire SY8 1EH
T: (01584) 874431
F: (01584) 874431
I: www.mr-underhills.co.uk

Nelson Cottage ◆◆◆
Rocks Green, Ludlow, Shropshire
SY8 2DS
T: (01584) 878108
F: (01584) 878108
E: nelsoncottage@hotmail.com
I: www.ludlow.uk.com

Number Twenty Eight
◆◆◆◆◆
28 Lower Broad Street, Ludlow,
Shropshire SY8 1PQ
T: (01584) 876996 &
0800 0815000
F: (01584) 876860
E: ross@no28.co.uk
I: www.no28.co.uk

Old Downton House ◆◆◆◆◆
Donnton on the Rock, Ludlow,
Shropshire SY8 2HU
T: (01568) 770389 &
07976 579006
F: (01568) 770776
E: barbara@old-downton.fsnet.
co.uk

Ravenscourt Manor ◆◆◆◆
Woofferton, Ludlow, Shropshire
SY8 4AL
T: (01584) 711905
F: (01584) 711905
I: www.virtual-shropshire.
co.uk/ravenscourt-manor

Spring Cottage ◆◆◆◆◆
Abdon, Craven Arms, Shropshire
SY9 9HU
T: (01746) 712551
F: (01746) 712001

The Wheatsheaf Inn ◆◆◆◆
Lower Broad Street, Ludlow,
Shropshire SY8 1PQ
T: (01584) 872980
F: (01584) 877990
E: karen.wheatsheaf@tinyworld.
co.uk

LUSTON
Herefordshire

Knapp House ◆◆◆
Luston, Leominster,
Herefordshire HR6 0EB
T: (01568) 615705

Ladymeadow Farm ◆◆◆◆
Luston, Leominster,
Herefordshire HR6 0AS
T: (01568) 780262

LUTTERWORTH
Leicestershire

The Greyhound Coaching Inn
◆◆◆
9 Market Street, Lutterworth,
Leicestershire LE17 4EJ
T: (01455) 553307
F: (01455) 554558
E: bookings@greyhoundinn.
fsnet.co.uk
I: www.greyhoundinn.co.uk

Orchard House ◆◆◆◆
Church Drive, Gilmorton,
Lutterworth, Leicestershire
LE17 5LR
T: (01455) 559487
F: (01455) 553047
E: diholman@hotmail.com

LYDBURY NORTH
Shropshire

Brunslow ◆
Lydbury North, Shropshire
SY7 8AD
T: (01588) 680244
F: (01588) 680244

The Powis Arms ◆◆◆
Lydbury North, Shropshire
SY7 8AU
T: (01588) 680254

Walcot Farm ◆◆◆◆
Lydbury North, Shropshire
SY7 8AA
T: (01588) 680243
F: (01588) 680243

LYDDINGTON
Rutland

Lydbrooke
Rating Applied For
2 Colley Rise, Lyddington,
Oakham, Leicestershire LE15 9LL
T: (01572) 821471
F: (01572) 821471

LYONSHALL
Herefordshire

Penrhos Farm ◆◆◆◆
Lyonshall, Kington,
Herefordshire HR5 3LH
T: (01544) 231467
F: (01544) 340273
E: sallyw@totalise.co.uk
I: www.penrhosfarm.ukfarmers.
com

Royal George Inn ◆◆◆◆
Lyonshall, Kington,
Herefordshire HR5 3JN
T: (01544) 340210
E: rtae.b@virgin.net

MACKWORTH
Derbyshire

Thames House ◆◆◆◆
6 Thames Close, Mackworth,
Derby DE22 4HT
T: (01332) 513526
F: (01332) 513526
E: jswarbrooke@aol.com

MADELEY
Staffordshire

Bar Hill House ◆◆◆◆
Bar Hill, Madeley, Crewe
CW3 9QE
T: (01782) 752199
F: (01782) 750981
E: barhillbb@hotmail.com
I: www.touristnet.com

MALTBY LE MARSH
Lincolnshire

Farmhouse Bed and Breakfast
◆◆◆
Grange Farm, Maltby le Marsh,
Alford, Lincolnshire LN13 0JP
T: (01507) 450267
F: (01507) 450180
E: graves_ann@hotmail.co.uk
I: www.grange-farmhouse.co.uk

MALVERN
Worcestershire

Berewe Court ◆◆◆◆
Whiting Lane, Berrow, Malvern,
Worcestershire WR13 6AY
T: (01531) 650250 &
07702 303810
E: susanmaryprice@hotmail.
com
I: www.ourworcester.
net/berewecourt

Clevelands ◆◆◆
41 Alexandra Road, Malvern,
Worcestershire WR14 1HE
T: (01684) 572164
F: (01684) 576691
E: jonmargstocks@aol.com

Como House ◆◆◆
Como Road, Malvern,
Worcestershire WR14 2TH
T: (01684) 561486
E: mary@como-house.
freeserve.co.uk

Cowleigh Park Farm ◆◆◆◆
Cowleigh Road, Malvern,
Worcestershire WR13 5HJ
T: (01684) 566750
F: (01684) 566750
E: cowleighparkfarm@talk21.
com

Danemoor Farm ◆◆◆
Welland, Malvern,
Worcestershire WR13 6NL
T: (01684) 310905
F: (01684) 310905

Edgeworth ◆◆◆
4 Carlton Road, Malvern,
Worcestershire WR14 1HH
T: (01684) 572565 & 0775 287
2460

The Firs ◆◆◆
243 West Malvern Road,
Malvern, Worcestershire
WR14 4BE
T: (01684) 564016 &
07885 789609
F: (01684) 564016
E: valshearerthefirs@hotmail.
com
I: www.smoothhound.co

Guarlford Grange ◆◆◆◆
11 Guarlford Road, Malvern,
Worcestershire WR14 3QW
T: (01684) 575996
F: (01684) 575996

Harcourt Cottage ◆◆◆
252 West Malvern Road, West
Malvern, Malvern,
Worcestershire WR14 4DQ
T: (01684) 574561
F: (01684) 574561
E: harcourtcottage@lineone.net

Homestead Lodge ◆◆◆
25 Somers Park Avenue,
Malvern, Worcestershire
WR14 1SE
T: (01684) 573094 &
07880 874537
F: (01684) 573094
E: trant@homesteadlodge.
freeserve.co.uk
I: www.homesteadlodge.
freeserve.co.uk

Mellor Heights ◆◆◆
46A West Malvern Road,
Malvern, Worcestershire
WR14 4NA
T: (01684) 565105
F: (01684) 565105
E: mellorheights@onetel.net.uk

Montrose Hotel ◆◆◆
23 Graham Road, Malvern,
Worcestershire WR14 2HU
T: (01684) 572335
F: (01684) 575 707
I: www.cotfordhotel.co.uk

Priory Holme ◆◆◆◆
18 Avenue Road, Malvern,
Worcestershire WR14 3AR
T: (01684) 568455

Rathlin ◆◆◆◆
1 Carlton Road, Malvern,
Worcestershire WR14 1HH
T: (01684) 572491
E: quiver@rathlin-malvern.
fsnet.co.uk

The Red Gate ◆◆◆◆
32 Avenue Road, Malvern,
Worcestershire WR14 3BJ
T: (01684) 565013
F: (01684) 565013
E: enquires@the-red-gate.co.uk
I: www.SmoothHound.co.uk/shs.
html

Robin's Orchard ◆◆◆
New Road, Castlemorton,
Malvern, Worcestershire
WR13 6BT
T: (01684) 833251

Rosendale The View
Rating Applied For
66 Worcester Road, Malvern,
Worcestershire WR14 1NU
T: (01684) 566159

Sunnydale ◆◆◆◆
69 Tanhouse Lane, Malvern,
Worcestershire WR14 1LQ
T: (01886) 832066

The White Cottage ◆◆◆◆
260 Wells Road, Malvern,
Worcestershire WR14 4HD
T: (01684) 576426 &
07751 878025
F: (01684) 561881
E: fiona@
fionacowleylanguageservices.
co.uk
I: www.thewhitecottagemalvern.
co.uk

Wyche Keep Country House
◆◆◆◆
22 Wyche Road, Malvern,
Worcestershire WR14 4EG
T: (01684) 567018
F: (01684) 892304
E: wychekeep@aol.com
I: www.jks.org/wychekeep

MANSFIELD
Nottinghamshire
Blue Barn Farm ◆◆◆
Nether Langwith, Mansfield,
Nottinghamshire NG20 9JD
T: (01623) 742248 &
07885 485346
F: (01623) 742248
E: ibbotsonbluebarn@
netscape-online.co.uk

Clifton Hotel ◆◆
Terrace Road, Mansfield,
Nottinghamshire NG18 2BP
T: (01623) 623876

MARCHINGTON
Staffordshire
Forest Hills ◆◆◆◆
Moisty Lane, Marchington,
Uttoxeter, Staffordshire
ST14 8JY
T: (01283) 820447

MARDEN
Herefordshire
Vauld House Farm ◆◆◆◆
Marden, Hereford HR1 3HA
T: (01568) 707347
F: (01568) 797366
E: wellthevauld@talk21.com

MARKET DRAYTON
Shropshire
Crofton ◆◆◆◆
80 Rowan Road, Market
Drayton, Shropshire TF9 1RR
T: (01630) 655484
F: (01630) 655484

Heath Farm Bed and Breakfast
◆◆
Heath Farm, Wellington Road,
Hodnet, Market Drayton,
Shropshire TF9 3JJ
T: (01630) 685570
F: (01630) 685570
E: adrysdale@telco4u.net

Marton ◆◆
7 Broom Hollow, Loggerheads,
Market Drayton, Shropshire
TF9 4NT
T: (01630) 673329

Milford ◆◆◆◆
Adderley Road, Market Drayton,
Shropshire TF9 3SW
T: (01630) 655249

Millstone ◆◆◆◆
Adderley Road, Market Drayton,
Shropshire TF9 3SW
T: (01630) 657584

Red House Cottage ◆◆◆
31 Shropshire Street, Market
Drayton, Shropshire TF9 3DA
T: (01630) 655206

The Tudor House Hotel and Restaurant◆◆◆
1 Cheshire Street, Market
Drayton, Shropshire TF9 1PD
T: (01630) 657523 &
(01952) 691184
F: (01630) 657806
E: sugarloaf@globalnet.co.uk

Willow House ◆◆◆◆
Shrewsbury Road, Tern Hill,
Market Drayton, Shropshire
TF9 3PX
T: (01630) 638326
F: (01630) 638326
E: moira@willowhouse.
free-online.co.uk

MARKET HARBOROUGH
Leicestershire
The Fox Inn ◆◆◆
Church Street, Wilbarston,
Market Harborough,
Leicestershire LE16 8QG
T: (01536) 771270
F: (01536) 518141

The George at Great Oxendon
◆◆◆◆
Great Oxendon, Market
Harborough, Leicestershire
LE16 8NA
T: (01858) 465205
F: (01858) 465205

The Old House ◆◆◆
Church Street, Wilbarston,
Market Harborough,
Leicestershire LE16 8QG
T: (01536) 771724
F: (01536) 771622
E: oldhousebb@aol.com.uk

MARKET RASEN
Lincolnshire
Beechwood Guesthouse
◆◆◆◆
54 Willingham Road, Market
Rasen, Lincolnshire LN8 3DX
T: (01673) 844043
F: (01673) 844043
E: beechwoodgh@aol.com

East Farmhouse ◆◆◆◆
Middle Rasen Road,
Buslingthorpe, Market Rasen,
Lincolnshire LN3 5AQ
T: (01673) 842283
E: gilliannannegrant@hotmail.
co.uk
I: www.oas.
co.uk/ukcottages/eastfarm

Waveney Cottage Guesthouse
◆◆◆◆
Willingham Road, Market Rasen,
Lincolnshire LN8 3DN
T: (01673) 843236
F: (01673) 843236
E: vacancies@waveneycottage.
co.uk
I: www.waveneycottage.co.uk

MARSTON
Lincolnshire
Gelston Grange Farm ◆◆◆◆
Marston, Grantham, Lincolnshire
NG32 2AQ
T: (01400) 250281
F: (01400) 250281

Thorold Arms ◆◆◆
Main Street, Marston,
Grantham, Lincolnshire
NG32 2HH
T: (01400) 250899 &
07796 545783
F: (01400) 251030

MARSTON MONTGOMERY
Derbyshire
The Old Barn ◆◆◆◆
Marston Montgomery,
Ashbourne, Derbyshire DE6 2FF
T: (01889) 590848
F: (01889) 590698

MARTIN HUSSINGTREE
Worcestershire
Knoll Farm Bed and Breakfast
◆◆◆
Knoll Farm, Ladywood Road,
Martin Hussingtree, Worcester
WR3 7SX
T: (01905) 455565
E: aligriggs@hotmail.com

MARTLEY
Worcestershire
The Chandlery ◆◆◆◆
Worcester Road, Martley,
Worcester, Worcestershire
WR6 6QA
T: (01886) 888318
F: (01886) 889047
E: john.nicklin@virgin.net
I: freespace.virgin.net/john.
nicklin

MATLOCK
Derbyshire
Bank House ◆◆◆◆◆
12 Snitterton Road, Matlock,
Derbyshire DE4 3LZ
T: (01629) 56101
F: (01629) 56101

The Beeches ◆◆◆
29 Snitterton Road, Matlock,
Derbyshire DE4 3LZ
T: (01629) 55775

Derwent House ◆◆◆
Knowleston Place, Matlock,
Derbyshire DE4 3BU
T: (01629) 584681

Dimple House ◆◆◆◆
Dimple Road, Matlock,
Derbyshire DE4 3JX
T: (01629) 583228

Edgemount ◆◆
16 Edge Road, Matlock,
Derbyshire DE4 3NH
T: (01629) 584787

Ellen House ◆◆◆◆
37 Snitterton Road, Matlock,
Derbyshire DE4 3LZ
T: (01629) 55584 & 07752 598
637

Henmore Grange ◆◆◆◆
Hopton, Wirksworth, Derby
DE4 4DF
T: (01629) 540420
F: (01629) 540720
E: marycollins@
henmoregrange.freeserve.co.uk
I: www.henmoregrange.
freeserve.co.uk

Home Farm ◆◆◆
Ible, Grange Mill, Matlock,
Derbyshire DE4 4HS
T: (01629) 650349

Jackson Tor House Hotel ◆◆◆
76 Jackson Road, Matlock,
Derbyshire DE4 3JQ
T: (01629) 582348
F: (01629) 582348

The Old English Hotel ◆◆
77 Dale Road, Matlock,
Derbyshire DE4 3LT
T: (01629) 55028
F: (01629) 55028

Riverbank House ◆◆◆◆
Derwent Avenue, (Off Old
English Road), Matlock,
Derbyshire DE4 3LX
T: (01629) 582593
E: bookings@riverbankhouse.
co.uk
I: www.riverbankhouse.co.uk

Robertswood Guesthouse
◆◆◆◆◆
Farley Hill, Matlock, Derbyshire
DE4 3LL
T: (01629) 55642
F: (01629) 55642
E: robertswood@supanet.com
I: www.robertswood.com

Sheriff Lodge
Rating Applied For
51 Dimple Road, Matlock,
Derbyshire DE4 3JX
T: (01629) 760760 &
07753 679563
F: (01629) 760860
E: sheriff.lodge@ntlworld.com
I: www.sherifflodge.co.uk

Warren Carr Barn ◆◆◆◆
Warren Carr, Matlock,
Derbyshire DE4 2LN
T: (01629) 733856
E: cherry@warrencarrbarn.
freeserve.co.uk
I: www.SmoothHound.
co.uk/hotels/warrenca.html

Wayside Farm ◆◆◆
Matlock Moor, Matlock,
Derbyshire DE4 5LZ
T: (01629) 582967 & 07890 536
747

The White Lion Inn ◆◆◆◆
195 Starkholmes Road, Matlock,
Derbyshire DE4 5JA
T: (01629) 582511
F: (01629) 582511
E: whitelion@ntlworld.com
I: www.rightfast.com/whitelion/

MATLOCK BATH
Derbyshire
Ashdale ◆◆
92 North Parade, Matlock Bath,
Matlock, Derbyshire DE4 3NS
T: (01629) 57826 &
07714 106402
E: ashdale@matlockbath.fsnet.
co.uk
I: www.ashdaleguesthouse.co.uk

The Firs ◆◆◆
180 Dale Road, Matlock Bath,
Matlock, Derbyshire DE4 3PS
T: (01629) 582426 & 581235
F: (01629) 582426
E: moira@thefirs180.demon.
co.uk

Fountain Villa ◆◆◆◆
86 North Parade, Matlock Bath,
Matlock, Derbyshire DE4 3NS
T: (01629) 56195
F: (01629) 581057
E: enquiries@fountainvilla.co.uk
I: www.fountainvilla.co.uk

Hodgkinsons Hotel ◆◆◆◆
150 South Parade, Matlock Bath,
Matlock, Derbyshire DE4 3NR
T: (01629) 582170
F: (01629) 584891
E: enquiries@
hodgkinsons-hotel.co.uk
I: www.hodgkinsons-hotel.co.uk

Old Museum Guesthouse
♦♦♦
170-172 South Parade, Matlock
Bath, Matlock, Derbyshire
DE4 3NR
T: (01629) 57783
E: lindsayandstewartbailey@
tinyworld.co.uk

Sunnybank Guesthouse
♦♦♦♦
37 Clifton Road, Matlock Bath,
Matlock, Derbyshire DE4 3PW
T: (01629) 584621
E: sunward@lineone.net
I: www.SmoothHound.
co.uk/hotels/sunbankgh.html

Temple Hotel ♦♦♦♦
Temple Walk, Matlock Bath,
Matlock, Derbyshire DE4 3PG
T: (01629) 583911
F: (01629) 580851
I: www.temple.co.uk

MAVESYN RIDWARE
Staffordshire
The Old Rectory ♦♦♦♦
Mavesyn Ridware, Rugeley,
Staffordshire WS15 3QE
T: (01543) 490792

MEDBOURNE
Leicestershire
Homestead House ♦♦♦♦
5 Ashley Road, Medbourne,
Market Harborough,
Leicestershire LE16 8DL
T: (01858) 565724
F: (01858) 565324

MELBOURNE
Derbyshire
Burdett House ♦♦
Derby Road, Melbourne, Derby
DE73 1DE
T: (01332) 862105
E: jjvglaze@btinternet.com

MELTON MOWBRAY
Leicestershire
Amberley Gardens B&B
♦♦♦♦
4 Church Lane, Asfordby, Melton
Mowbray, Leicestershire
LE14 3RU
T: (01664) 812314
F: (01664) 813740
E: doris@amberleygardens.net
I: www.amberleygardens.net

Hillside House ♦♦♦♦
27 Melton Road, Burton Lazars,
Melton Mowbray, Leicestershire
LE14 2UR
T: (01664) 566312
F: (01664) 501819
E: Hillhs27@aol.com
I: www.hillside-house.co.uk

Tole Cottage ♦♦♦♦
10 Main Street, Kirby Bellars,
Melton Mowbray, Leicestershire
LE14 2EA
T: (01664) 812932
E: michael@handjean.freeserve.
co.uk

MELVERLEY
Shropshire
Church House ♦♦♦♦
Melverley, Oswestry, Shropshire
SY10 8PJ
T: (01691) 682754 &
07752 323048
E: melverley@aol.com
I: members.aol.com/melverley

MEOLE BRACE
Shropshire
Meole Brace Hall ♦♦♦♦♦
Church Road, Meole Brace,
Shrewsbury SY3 9HF
T: (01743) 235566 &
07710 644696
F: (01743) 236886
E: meolebracehall@onetel.net.
uk
I: www.meolebracehall.co.uk

MERIDEN
West Midlands
Barnacle Farm ♦♦♦♦
Back Lane, Meriden, Coventry,
West Midlands CV7 7LD
T: (024) 7646 8875
F: (024) 7646 8875

Bonnifinglas Guest House ♦♦
3 Berkswell Road, Meriden,
Coventry CV7 7LB
T: (01676) 523193 &
07900 20116
F: (01676) 523193

Cooperage Farm Bed and
Breakfast ♦♦
Old Road, Meriden, Coventry
CV7 7JP
T: (01676) 523493
F: (01676) 523876
E: lucy@cooperagefarm.co.uk
I: www.cooperagefarm.co.uk

Innellan House ♦♦♦
Eaves Green Lane, Meriden,
Coventry CV7 7JL
T: (01676) 523005 & 522548
F: (01676) 523005
I: www.smoothhound.
co.uk/hotels/innellan.html

MICHAELCHURCH ESCLEY
Herefordshire
The Grove Farm ♦♦♦♦
Michaelchurch Escley, Hereford
HR2 0PT
T: (01981) 510229
F: (01981) 510229

MICKLETON
Gloucestershire
Bank House ♦♦♦
Mickleton, Chipping Campden,
Gloucestershire GL55 6RX
T: (01386) 438302

Myrtle House ♦♦♦♦
High Street, Mickleton, Chipping
Campden, Gloucestershire
GL55 6SA
T: (01386) 430032 &
07971 938085
E: kate@myrtlehouse.co.uk
I: www.myrtlehouse.co.uk

Old Barn House ♦♦♦
Mill Lane, Mickleton, Chipping
Campden, Gloucestershire
GL55 6SE
T: (01386) 438668
F: (01386) 438668

MIDDLE DUNTISBOURNE
Gloucestershire
Manor Farm ♦♦♦
Middle Duntisbourne,
Cirencester, Gloucestershire
GL7 7AR
T: (01285) 658145 &
07866 450417
F: (01285) 641504
E: tina.barton@farming.co.uk
I: www.smoothhound.
co.uk/hotels/manorfar.html

MIDDLETON
Derbyshire
Eastas Gate ♦♦♦♦
18 Main Street, Middleton,
Matlock, Derbyshire DE4 4LQ
T: (01629) 822790
E: eastasgate@hotmail.com

Middleton House Farm
Rating Applied For
Tamworth Road, Middleton,
Tamworth, Staffordshire
B78 2BD
T: (01827) 873474
F: (01827) 872246
E: rob.jane@tinyonline.co.uk
I: middletonhousefarm.co.uk

Valley View ♦♦♦
3 Camsdale Walk, Middleton,
Market Harborough,
Leicestershire LE16 8YR
T: (01536) 770874

MIDDLETON-BY-YOULGREAVE
Derbyshire
Castle Farm ♦♦♦
Middleton-by-Youlgreave,
Derby, Derbyshire DE45 1LS
T: (01629) 636746

Smerrill Grange ♦♦♦
Middleton-by-Youlgreave,
Derby, Derbyshire DE45 1LQ
T: (01629) 636232

MILLTHORPE
Derbyshire
Cordwell House ♦♦♦♦
Cordwell Lane, Millthorpe,
Holmesfield, Dronfield S18 7WH
T: (0114) 289 0271

MILTON
Nottinghamshire
The Stables ♦♦♦♦
Milton, Newark,
Nottinghamshire NG22 OPW
T: (01777) 871920
F: (01777) 871920
E: wellez@hotmail.com

MINCHINHAMPTON
Gloucestershire
Hyde Wood House ♦♦♦♦
Cirencester Road,
Minchinhampton, Stroud,
Gloucestershire GL6 8PE
T: (01453) 885504
F: (01453) 885504
E: bettyandjohn@
hydewoodhouse.co.uk
I: www.hydewoodhouse.co.uk

The Old Ram Bed and Breakfast
♦♦♦♦
Market Square,
Minchinhampton, Stroud,
Gloucestershire GL6 9BW
T: (01453) 882287
E: awheeler@btinternet.com
I: oldram.cjg.net/

Vale View ♦♦♦♦
Besbury, Minchinhampton,
Stroud, Gloucestershire GL6 9EP
T: (01453) 882610
F: (01453) 882610
E: reservations@vale-view.co.uk
I: www.vale-view.co.uk

MINSTERLEY
Shropshire
The Callow Inn ♦♦♦
Bromlow, Minsterley,
Shrewsbury SY5 0EA
T: (01743) 891933
F: (01743) 891933
E: del@callowinn.freeserve.
co.uk
I: www.callowinn.freeserve.co.uk

Cricklewood Cottage ♦♦♦♦
Plox Green, Minsterley,
Shrewsbury SY5 0HT
T: (01743) 791229
E: paul.crickcott@bushinternet.
com
I: www.smoothhound.
co.uk/hotels/crickle

Mandalay Bed and Breakfast
♦♦♦♦
The Grove, Minsterley,
Shrewsbury SY5 0AG
T: (01743) 791758 &
07980 135888

MITCHELDEAN
Gloucestershire
Gunn Mill House ♦♦♦♦
Lower Spout Lane, Mitcheldean,
Gloucestershire GL17 0EA
T: (01594) 827577
F: (01594) 827577
E: info@gunnmillhouse.co.uk
I: www.gunnmillhouse.co.uk

MONSAL DALE
Derbyshire
Upperdale House ♦♦♦
Monsal Dale, Buxton, Derbyshire
SK17 8SZ
T: (01629) 640536
F: (01629) 640536
E: bookings@upperdale.fsnet.
co.uk
I: www.monsaldale.com

MONSAL HEAD
Derbyshire
Cliffe House ♦♦♦
Monsal Head, Bakewell,
Derbyshire DE45 1NL
T: (01629) 640376
F: (01629) 640376
E: enquires@cliffehouse.co.uk
I: www.cliffehouse.co.uk

Monsal Head Hotel ♦♦♦
Monsal Head, Bakewell,
Derbyshire DE45 1NL
T: (01629) 640250
F: (01629) 640815
E: christine@monsalhead.com
I: www.monsalhead.com

MONYASH
Derbyshire
Chapel View Farm ♦♦♦♦
Chapel Street, Monyash,
Bakewell, Derbyshire DE45 1JJ
T: (01629) 814317

High Rakes Farm ♦♦♦♦
Rakes Road, Monyash, Bakewell,
Derbyshire DE45 1JL
T: (01298) 84692 &
07715 818336

MOORHOUSE
Nottinghamshire

Brecks Cottage Bed and Breakfast ◆◆◆◆
Green Lane, Moorhouse, Newark, Nottinghamshire NG23 6LZ
T: (01636) 822445 &
07968 327914
E: BandB@breckscottage.co.uk
I: www.breckscottage.co.uk

MORETON-IN-MARSH
Gloucestershire

Acacia ◆◆
2 New Road, Moreton-in-Marsh, Gloucestershire GL56 0AS
T: (01608) 650130

The Bell Inn ◆◆◆
High Street, Moreton-in-Marsh, Gloucestershire GL56 0AF
T: (01608) 651688
F: (01608) 652195
I: bellinncotswold.com

Blue Cedar House ◆◆◆
Stow Road, Moreton-in-Marsh, Gloucestershire GL56 0DW
T: (01608) 650299
E: gandsib@dialstart.net

Bran Mill Cottage ◆◆◆
Aston Magna, Moreton-in-Marsh, Gloucestershire GL56 9QP
T: (01386) 593517 &
07971 253544
F: (01386) 593 517
E: enquiries@branmillcottage.co.uk
I: www.branmillcottage.co.uk

Ditchford Farmhouse ◆◆◆
Stretton on Fosse, Moreton-in-Marsh, Gloucestershire GL56 9RD
T: (01608) 663307 &
07812 415357
E: randb@ditchford-farmhouse.co.uk
I: www.ditchford-farmhouse.co.uk

Fosseway Farm B&B ◆◆◆◆
Stow Road, Moreton-in-Marsh, Gloucestershire GL56 0DS
T: (01608) 650503

Fourshires Bed and Breakfast ◆◆◆◆
Fourshires House, Great Wolford Road, Moreton-in-Marsh, Gloucestershire GL56 0PE
T: (01608) 651412 & 652069
F: (01608) 651412
E: M1aff@aol.com
I: www.fourshires.com

Kymalton House ◆◆◆◆
Todenham Road, Moreton-in-Marsh, Gloucestershire GL56 9NJ
T: (01608) 650487

Neighbrook Manor
Rating Applied For
Near Aston Magna, Moreton-in-Marsh, Gloucestershire GL56 9QP
T: (01386) 593232
F: (01386) 593500
E: info@neighbrookmanor.com
I: www.neighbrookmanor.com

New Farm ◆◆◆
Dorn, Moreton-in-Marsh, Gloucestershire GL56 9NS
T: (01608) 650782
F: (01608) 652704
E: cath.righton@amserve.net
I: www.smoothhound.co.uk

The Old Chequer ◆◆◆◆
Draycott, Moreton-in-Marsh, Gloucestershire GL56 9LB
T: (01386) 700647
F: (01386) 700647
E: g.f.linley@tesco.net

Old Farm ◆◆◆
Dorn, Moreton-in-Marsh, Gloucestershire GL56 9NS
T: (01608) 650394
F: (01608) 650394
E: simon@righton.freeserve.co.uk

Roosters ◆◆◆◆
Todenham, Moreton-in-Marsh, Gloucestershire GL56 9PA
T: (01608) 650645
F: (01608) 650645
I: www.touristnet.uk.com/wm/roosters/indexhtm

Staddle Stones Guest House ◆◆◆
Rowborough, Stretton-on-Fosse, Moreton-in-Marsh, Gloucestershire GL56 9RE
T: (01608) 662774

Townend Cottage and Coach House ◆◆◆
High Street, Moreton-in-Marsh, Gloucestershire GL56 0AD
T: (01608) 650846
E: townend-cottage@moreton.junglelink.co.uk
I: www.townend-cottage.co.uk

Treetops ◆◆◆◆
London Road, Moreton-in-Marsh, Gloucestershire GL56 0HE
T: (01608) 651036
F: (01608) 651036
E: treetops1@talk21.com
♿

Warwick House ◆◆◆
London Road, Moreton-in-Marsh, Gloucestershire GL56 0HH
T: (01608) 650773
F: (01608) 650773
E: charlie@warwickhousebnb.demon.co.uk
I: www.snoozeandsizzle.com

MORETON PINKNEY
Northamptonshire

Englands Rose ◆◆◆
Upper Green, Moreton Pinkney, Daventry, Northamptonshire NN11 3SG
T: (01295) 760353
F: (01295) 760353
E: sheila@englandsrose.freeserve.co.uk

The Old Vicarage ◆◆◆◆
Moreton Pinkney, Daventry, Northamptonshire NN11 3SQ
T: (01295) 760057
F: (01295) 760057
E: tim@tandjeastwood.fsnet.co.uk
I: www.tandjeastwood.fsnet.co.uk

MORVILLE
Shropshire

Hannigans Farm ◆◆◆◆
Morville, Bridgnorth, Shropshire WV16 4RN
T: (01746) 714332
E: Hanningansfarm@btinternet.com

MUCH BIRCH
Herefordshire

The Old School ◆◆◆
Much Birch, Hereford HR2 8HJ
T: (01981) 541317

MUCH MARCLE
Herefordshire

Bodenham Farm ◆◆◆◆
Much Marcle, Ledbury, Herefordshire HR8 2NJ
T: (01531) 660222

New House Farm ◆◆◆
Much Marcle, Ledbury, Herefordshire HR8 2PH
T: (01531) 660674 & 660604

MUCH WENLOCK
Shropshire

Broadstone Mill ◆◆◆◆◆
Broadstone, Much Wenlock, Shropshire TF13 6LE
T: (01584) 841494
F: (01584) 841515
E: hargreaves@broadstones.fsnet.co.uk
I: www.broadstonemill.co.uk

Danywenollt ◆◆◆
Farley Road, Much Wenlock, Shropshire TF13 6NB
T: (01952) 727892

Gaskell Arms Hotel ◆◆◆
Much Wenlock, Shropshire TF13 6AQ
T: (01952) 727212
F: (01952) 728505
E: maxine@gaskellarms.co.uk
I: www.smoothhound.co.uk/gaskell/hotel

The Longville Arms ◆◆◆
Longville in the Dale, Much Wenlock, Shropshire TF13 6DT
T: (01694) 771206
F: (01694) 771742

Old Quarry Cottage ◆◆◆◆
Brockton, Much Wenlock, Shropshire TF13 6JR
T: (01746) 785596

Talbot Inn ◆◆◆
Much Wenlock, Shropshire TF13 6AA
T: (01952) 727077
F: (01952) 728436

MUNSLOW
Shropshire

The Old Laundry ◆◆◆◆◆
Beambridge, Munslow, Craven Arms, Shropshire SY7 9HA
T: (01584) 841520
E: diana@theoldlaundry.free-online.co.uk

MUNSTONE
Herefordshire

Munstone House
Rating Applied For
Munstone, Hereford HR1 3AH
T: (01432) 267122

MUXTON
Shropshire

Muxton House ◆◆◆◆◆
Muxton Lane, Muxton, Telford, Shropshire TF2 8PF
T: (01952) 603312
F: (01952) 603312
E: sarahcarlton@compuserve.com

MYDDLE
Shropshire

Oakfields ◆◆◆
Oakfields, Baschurch Road, Myddle, Shrewsbury SY4 3RX
T: (01939) 290823

NAILSWORTH
Gloucestershire

Aaron Farm ◆◆◆◆
Nympsfield Road, Nailsworth, Stroud, Gloucestershire GL6 0ET
T: (01453) 833598
F: (01453) 833626
E: aaronfarm@aol.com
I: www.aaronfarm-bedandbreakfast.co.uk

Heavens Above Bed and Breakfast ◆◆◆
3 Cossack Square, Above Mad Hatters Restaurant, Nailsworth, Stroud, Gloucestershire GL6 0DB
T: (01453) 832615
F: (01453) 832615

Highlands ◆◆◆◆
Shortwood, Nailsworth, Stroud, Gloucestershire GL6 0SJ
T: (01453) 832591
F: (01453) 833590

1 Orchard Mead ◆◆
Chestnut Hill, Nailsworth, Stroud, Gloucestershire GL6 0RE
T: (01453) 833581

The Upper House ◆◆◆◆
Spring Hill, Nailsworth, Stroud, Gloucestershire GL6 0LX
T: (01453) 836606
F: (01453) 836769

NANTMAWR
Shropshire

Four Gables ◆◆◆◆
Nantmawr, Oswestry, Shropshire SY10 9HH
T: (01691) 828708

NASSINGTON
Northamptonshire

Sunnyside ◆◆◆
62 Church Street, Nassington, Peterborough PE8 6QG
T: (01780) 782864

NAUNTON
Gloucestershire

Fox Hill ◆◆◆
Old Stow Road, Naunton, Cheltenham, Gloucestershire GL54 5RL
T: (01451) 850496 &
07798 822477
F: (01451) 850602

Naunton View Guesthouse ◆◆◆
Naunton, Cheltenham, Gloucestershire GL54 3AS
T: (01451) 850482
F: (01451) 850482

NAVENBY
Lincolnshire
The Barn ◆◆◆◆
North Lane, Navenby, Lincoln
LN5 0EH
T: (01522) 810318
F: (01522) 810318
E: peter.sheila@
thebarnnavenby.freeserve.co.uk.
co.uk

NETHER HEYFORD
Northamptonshire
Heyford Bed and Breakfast ◆◆
27 Church Street, Nether
Heyford, Northampton NN7 3LH
T: (01327) 340872

NETHER WESTCOTE
Gloucestershire
Cotswold View Guesthouse
◆◆◆
Nether Westcote, Oxford
OX7 6SD
T: (01993) 830699
F: (01993) 830699
E: info@
cotswoldview-guesthouse.co.uk
I: www.
cotswoldview-guesthouse.co.uk

NEW DUSTON
Northamptonshire
Rowena ◆◆◆◆
569 Harlestone Road, New
Duston, Northampton NN5 6NX
T: (01604) 755889
E: info@rowenaBB.co.uk
I: www.rowenaBB.co.uk

NEWARK
Nottinghamshire
The Boot and Shoe Inn ◆◆◆◆
Main Street, Flintham, Newark,
Nottinghamshire NG23 5LA
T: (01636) 525246

**Crosshill House Bed and
Breakfast** ◆◆◆◆
Crosshill House, Laxton, Newark,
Nottinghamshire NG22 ONT
T: (01777) 871953 &
07971 864446
E: roberta@crosshillhouse.
freeserve.co.uk
I: www.crosshillhouse.com

St Clares ◆◆◆◆
1 Elm Close, Elm Avenue,
Newark, Nottinghamshire
NG24 1SG
T: (01636) 685347
F: (01636) 685347
E: pat@gregg.ukf.net

Willow Tree Inn ◆◆◆
Front Street, Barnby-in-the-
Willows, Newark,
Nottinghamshire NG24 2SA
T: (01636) 626613
F: (01636) 626060
E: info@willowtreeinn.co.uk
I: www.info@willowtreeinn.
co.uk

NEWCASTLE-UNDER-LYME
Staffordshire
Graythwaite Guest House
◆◆◆
106 Lancaster Road, Newcastle-
under-Lyme, Staffordshire
ST5 1DS
T: (01782) 612875 &
07977 541422
E: cooke@graythwaite.fsnet.
co.uk
I: www.smoothhound.
co.uk/hotels/grayth

NEWENT
Gloucestershire
George Hotel ◆◆◆
Church Street, Newent,
Gloucestershire GL18 1PU
T: (01531) 820203
F: (01531) 822899
E: enquiries@georgehotel.uk.
com
I: www.georgehotel.uk.com

Newent Golf and Lodges ◆◆◆
Newent Golf Course,
Coldharbour Lane, Newent,
Gloucestershire GL18 1DJ
T: (01531) 820478
F: (01531) 820478
E: tomnewentgolf@aol.com
I: www.short-golf-break.com

The Old Winery ◆◆◆◆◆
Welsh House Lane, Dymock,
Newent, Gloucestershire
GL18 1LR
T: (01531) 890824

**Sandyway Nurseries
Countryside B & B** ◆◆◆◆
Redmarley Road, Newent,
Gloucestershire GL18 1DR
T: (01531) 820693

Three Ashes House ◆◆◆◆
Ledbury Road, Newent,
Gloucestershire GL18 1DE
T: (01531) 820226
F: (01531) 820226
E: jrichard.cockroft@tinyworld.
co.uk

Three Choirs Vineyards
◆◆◆◆◆
Newent, Gloucestershire
GL18 1LS
T: (01531) 890223
F: (01531) 890877
E: info@threechoirs.com
I: www.threechoirs.com

NEWLAND
Gloucestershire
Rookery Farm ◆◆◆
Newland, Coleford,
Gloucestershire GL16 8NJ
T: (01594) 832432

Scatterford Farm ◆◆◆◆
Newland, Coleford,
Gloucestershire GL16 8NG
T: (01594) 836562
F: (01594) 836323
E: benson@scatterford-farm.
demon.co.uk
I: www.scatterford-farm.demon.
co.uk

Tan House Farm ◆◆◆
Newland, Coleford,
Gloucestershire GL16 8NP
T: (01594) 832222
F: (01594) 833501

NEWNHAM-ON-SEVERN
Gloucestershire
Hayden Lea ◆◆◆
Dean Road, Newnham-on-
Severn, Gloucestershire
GL14 1AB
T: (01594) 516626

Swan House ◆◆◆◆
High Street, Newnham-on-
Severn, Gloucestershire
GL14 1BY
T: (01594) 516504
F: (01594) 516177
E: joanne@
swanhouse-newnham.freeserve.
co.uk
I: www.swanhouse-newnham.
freeserve.co.uk
🏃

The White House World ◆◆◆
Popes Hill, Newnham-on-
Severn, Gloucestershire
GL14 1LE
T: (01452) 760463
F: (01452) 760776
E: whitehouseworld@talk21.
com
I: www.fweb.org.uk/whitehouse

NEWPORT
Shropshire
Lane End Farm ◆◆◆◆
Chetwynd, Newport, Shropshire
TF10 8BN
T: (01952) 550337 &
0777 1632255
F: (01952) 550337
E: lane1.endfarm@ondigital.
com
I: www.virtual-shropshire.
co.uk/lef

**Norwood House Hotel and
Restaurant** ◆◆◆
Pave Lane, Newport, Shropshire
TF10 9LQ
T: (01952) 825896
F: (01952) 825896

Pear Tree Farmhouse ◆◆◆◆
Farm Grove, Newport,
Shropshire TF10 7PX
T: (01952) 811193
F: (01952) 812115
E: patgreen@peakfarmhouse.
co.uk
I: www.peartreefarmhouse.co.uk

Sambrook Manor ◆◆◆
Sambrook, Newport, Shropshire
TF10 8AL
T: (01952) 550256

NEWTON SOLNEY
Derbyshire
The Unicorn Inn ◆◆◆◆
Repton Road, Newton Solney,
Burton upon Trent, Staffordshire
DE15 0SG
T: (01283) 703324
F: (01283) 703324
E: unicorn.newtonsolney@
barbox.net

NEWTOWN LINFORD
Leicestershire
Wondai ◆◆◆
47-49 Main Street, Newtown
Linford, Leicester LE6 0AE
T: (01530) 242728 &
07980 950941
E: j_weazel@eggconnect.net

NORBURY
Shropshire
Oulton House Farm ◆◆◆◆
Norbury, Whitchurch,
Shropshire ST20 0PG
T: (01785) 284264
F: (01785) 284264
E: judy@oultonhousefarm.co.uk
I: www.oultonhousefarm.co.uk

Shuttocks Wood ◆◆◆◆
Norbury, Bishop's Castle,
Shropshire SY9 5EA
T: (01588) 650433
F: (01588) 650492
E: shuttockswood@barclays.net
I: www.go2.
co.uk/shuttockswood/

NORTH COTES
Lincolnshire
Fleece Inn ◆◆◆
Lock Road, North Cotes,
Grimsby, South Humberside
DN36 5UP
T: (01472) 388233
F: (01472) 388 233

NORTH HYKEHAM
Lincolnshire
Lakeview Guesthouse ◆◆◆◆
50 Station Road, North
Hykeham, Lincoln LN6 9AQ
T: (01522) 680455

NORTH KYME
Lincolnshire
Old Coach House Motel & Cafe
◆◆◆◆
Church Lane, North Kyme,
Lincolnshire LN4 4DJ
T: (01526) 861465
F: (01526) 861658
E: Barbara@motel-plus.co.uk
I: www.Motel-Plus.co.uk

NORTH SOMERCOTES
Lincolnshire
**Pigeon Cottage Bed &
Breakfast & LLA Summer
Camps** ◆◆
Conisholme Road, North
Somercotes, Louth, Lincolnshire
LN11 7PS
T: (01507) 359063
F: (01507) 359063

NORTH WINGFIELD
Derbyshire
South View ◆◆◆
95 Church Lane, North
Wingfield, Chesterfield,
Derbyshire S42 5HR
T: (01246) 850091

NORTHAMPTON
Northamptonshire
**Aarandale Regent Hotel and
Guesthouse** ◆◆
6-8 Royal Terrace, Barrack Road
(A508), Northampton,
Northamptonshire NN1 3RF
T: (01604) 631096
F: (01604) 621035
E: info@aarandale.co.uk
I: www.aarandale.co.uk

Abington Park Guesthouse
◆◆◆
407 Wellingborough Road,
Abington, Northampton
NN1 4EY
T: (01604) 635072

The Gables Guest House
♦♦♦♦
74 Fulford Drive, Links View,
Northampton, NN2 7NR
T: (01604) 713858 &
07713 062713

Paddock Cottage Bed and Breakfast ♦♦♦♦
Paddock Cottage, The Gated
Road, Watford, Northampton
NN6 7UE
T: (01788) 823615 &
07801 978326

Poplars Hotel ♦♦♦♦
Cross Street, Moulton,
Northampton NN3 7RZ
T: (01604) 643983
F: (01604) 790233
E: poplars@btclick.com

Upton Mill ♦♦♦
Northampton, NN5 4UY
T: (01604) 753277
F: (01604) 753277

NORTHLEACH
Gloucestershire
Cotteswold House ♦♦♦♦
Market Place, Northleach,
Cheltenham, Gloucestershire
GL54 3EG
T: (01451) 860493
F: (01451) 860493
E: cotteswoldhouse@talk21.
com

The Eastington Suite ♦♦♦♦♦
Japonica, Upper End Eastington,
Northleach, Cheltenham,
Gloucestershire GL54 3PJ
T: (01451) 861117 &
07774 680091
F: (01451) 861117
I: members.tripod.
co.uk/the2eastingtonsuite/

Long Barrow ♦♦♦♦
Farmington, Northleach,
Cheltenham, Gloucestershire
GL54 3NQ
T: (01451) 860428 &
07979 802600
F: (01451) 860166
E: ghowson@longbarrow.fsnet.
co.uk

The Mead House ♦♦♦
Sherborne, Cheltenham,
Gloucestershire GL54 3DR
T: (01451) 844239

Northfield Bed and Breakfast
♦♦♦♦
Cirencester Road (A429),
Northleach, Cheltenham,
Gloucestershire GL54 3JL
T: (01451) 860427
F: (01451) 860820
E: nrthfield0@aol.com

The Sherborne Arms ♦♦
Market Place, Northleach,
Cheltenham, Gloucestershire
GL54 3EE
T: (01451) 860241

Wheatsheaf Hotel ♦♦♦
Northleach, Cheltenham,
Gloucestershire GL54 3EZ
T: (01451) 860244
F: (01451) 861037
E: whtshfhtl@aol.com
I: www.glosbp.
co.uk/hotels/wheatsheaf.htm

NOTTINGHAM
Nottinghamshire
Acorn Hotel ♦♦♦
4 Radcliffe Road, West
Bridgford, Nottingham
NG2 5FW
T: (0115) 981 1297
F: (0115) 981 7654
E: reservations@acorn-hotel.
co.uk

Calerin House ♦♦♦♦
21 Redcliffe Road, Mapperley
Park, Nottingham, NG3 5BW
T: (0115) 960 5366
F: (0115) 985 8423

Cotswold Hotel ♦♦♦
330-332 Mansfield Road,
Nottingham, NG5 2EF
T: (0115) 955 1070
F: (0115) 955 1071
E: cotswoldhotel@btinternet.
com

Grantham Hotel ♦♦♦
24-26 Radcliffe Road, West
Bridgford, Nottingham
NG2 5FW
T: (0115) 981 1373
F: (0115) 981 8567
E: granthamhotel@netlineuk.
net

Greenwood Lodge City Guesthouse ♦♦♦♦♦
Third Avenue, Sherwood Rise,
Nottingham NG7 6JH
T: (0115) 962 1206
F: (0115) 962 1206
E: coolspratt@aol.com
I: www.SmoothHound.
co.uk/hotels/greenwo.html

Milford Hotel ♦♦
Pavilion Road, West Bridgford,
Nottingham NG2 5FG
T: (0115) 981 1464 & 9811044
F: (0115) 982 2204

Nelson and Railway Inn ♦♦
Station Road, Kimberley,
Nottingham, NG16 2NR
T: (0115) 938 2177

Orchard Cottage ♦♦♦♦
The Old Workhouse, Trowell,
Nottingham NG9 3PQ
T: (0115) 9280933 &
07790 817597
F: (0115) 9280933
E: orchardcottage.bandb@
virgin.net
I: www.orchardcottages.com

Park Hotel City Centre ♦♦
7 Waverley Street, Nottingham,
NG7 4HF
T: (0115) 978 6299 & 942 0010
F: (0115) 942 4358
E: enquiries@
parkhotelcitycentre.co.uk
I: www.parkhotelcitycentre.co.uk

Yew Tree Grange ♦♦♦♦
2 Nethergate, Clifton Village,
Nottingham, NG11 8NL
T: (0115) 984 7562 & 9142886
F: (0115) 984 7562
E: yewtreel@nascr.net
I: www.yewtreegrange.co.uk

NUNEATON
Warwickshire
Astley House ♦♦♦♦
1 Slade Close, Nuneaton,
Warwickshire CV11 6UW
T: (024) 76371144

La Tavola Calda ♦♦
70 Midland Road, Abbey Green,
Nuneaton, Warwickshire
CV11 5DY
T: (024) 7638 3195 &
07747 010702
F: (024) 7638 1816

Royal Arms ♦♦♦♦
Main Street, Sutton Cheney,
Nuneaton, Warwickshire
CV13 0AG
T: (01455) 290263
F: (01455) 290124
I: www.royalarms.co.uk

OAKAMOOR
Staffordshire
Bank House ♦♦♦♦♦
Farley Road, Oakamoor, Stoke-
on-Trent, Staffordshire
ST10 3BD
T: (01538) 702810
F: (01538) 702810
E: john.orme@dial.pipex.com
I: www.smoothhound.
co.uk/hotels/bank.html

Beehive Guest House ♦♦♦
Churnet View Road, Oakamoor,
Stoke-on-Trent ST10 3AE
T: (01538) 702420
E: thebeehiveoakamoor@
btinternet.com

Crowtrees Farm ♦♦♦♦
Oakamoor, Stoke-on-Trent
ST10 3DY
T: (01530) 702260
F: (01538) 702260
E: crowtrees@fenetre.co.uk
I: www.touristnetuk.
com/wm/crowtrees

The Laurels ♦♦♦♦
Star Bank, Oakamoor, Stoke-on-
Trent ST10 3BN
T: (01538) 702629 &
0771 2008802
F: 07884 368137
E: bbthelaurels@aol.com
I: www.thelaurels.co.uk

The Lord Nelson
Rating Applied For
Carr Bank, Oakamoor, Stoke-on-
Trent ST10 3DQ
T: (01538) 702242

Ribden Farm ♦♦♦♦
Oakamoor, Stoke-on-Trent
ST10 3BW
T: (01538) 702830
F: (01538) 702830
E: chris@ribden.fsnet.co.uk
I: www.ribdenfarm.com

Tenement Farm ♦♦♦♦
Three Lows, Ribden, Oakamoor,
Stoke-on-Trent ST10 3BW
T: (01538) 702333 & 703603
F: (01538) 703603
E: stanleese@aol.com
I: www.tenementfarm.co.uk

OAKENGATES
Shropshire
Chellow Dene ♦♦♦
Park Road, Malinslee, Dawley,
Telford, Shropshire TF3 2AY
T: (01952) 505917

OAKHAM
Leicestershire
Hall Farm ♦♦♦
Cottesmore Road, Exton,
Oakham, Leicestershire
LE15 8AN
T: (01572) 812271 &
07711 979628
F: (01572) 812271

The Tithe Barn ♦♦♦
Clatterpot Lane, Cottesmore,
Oakham, Leicestershire
LE15 7DW
T: (01572) 813591
F: (01572) 812719
E: jpryke@thetithebarn.co.uk
I: www.tithebarn-rutland.co.uk

Westgate Lodge ♦♦♦♦
9 Westgate, Oakham,
Leicestershire LE15 6BH
T: (01572) 757370
F: (01572) 757370
E: westgatelodge@gofornet.
co.uk
I: www.rutnet.co.uk

OAKRIDGE LYNCH
Gloucestershire
Lower Weir Farm ♦♦♦♦
Oakridge Lynch, Stroud,
Gloucestershire GL6 7NS
T: (01285) 760701
F: (01285) 760690

OASBY
Lincolnshire
The Pinfomar
Rating Applied For
Mill Lane, Oasby, Grantham,
Lincolnshire NG32 3ND
T: (01529) 455400
F: (01529) 455681

OLD
Northamptonshire
Wold Farm ♦♦♦♦
Old, Daventry,
Northamptonshire NN6 9RJ
T: (01604) 781258
F: (01604) 781258
E: www.woldfarm.co.uk
I: www.northantsfarmholidays.
co.uk

OLD TUPTON
Derbyshire
Rose Cottage Guest House
♦♦♦
Derby Road, Old Tupton,
Chesterfield, Derbyshire S42 6LA
T: (01246) 864949
F: (01246) 864949
E: bookings@
rosecottagetupton.freeserve.
co.uk
I: www.rosecottage.freeservers.
com

OMBERSLEY
Worcestershire
Eden Farm ♦♦♦♦
Ombersley, Droitwich,
Worcestershire WR9 0JX
T: (01905) 620244

Greenlands ♦♦♦♦
Uphampton, Ombersley,
Droitwich, Worcestershire
WR9 0JP
T: (01905) 620873
E: xlandgreenlands@onetel.net.
uk

ONECOTE
Staffordshire
The Old Vicarage ◆◆◆◆
Onecote, Leek, Staffordshire
ST13 7SD
T: (01538) 304125
F: (01538) 304479
E: dominic.tighe@care4free.net
I: onecotevicarage.co.uk

ORLETON
Worcestershire
**Hope Cottage Bed and
Breakfast ◆◆◆**
Hope Cottage, Orleton, Ludlow,
Shropshire SY8 4JB
T: (01584) 831674
F: (01584) 831124
E: hopecott@aol.com

Line Farm ◆◆◆◆◆
Tunnel Lane, Orleton, Ludlow,
Shropshire SY8 4HY
T: (01568) 780400

OSGATHORPE
Leicestershire
Royal Oak House ◆◆◆
20 Main Street, Osgathorpe,
Loughborough, Leicestershire
LE12 9TA
T: (01530) 222443 &
07885 377652

OSWESTRY
Shropshire
Ashfield Farmhouse ◆◆◆◆
Maesbury, Oswestry, Shropshire
SY10 8JH
T: (01691) 653589 &
07712 406413
F: (01691) 653589
E: marg@ashfieldfarmhouse.
co.uk
I: www.ashfieldfarmhouse.co.uk

Bridge House ◆◆◆◆
Llynclys, Oswestry, Shropshire
SY10 8AE
T: (01691) 830496
F: (01691) 830496
E: jenny@llynclys.freeserve.
co.uk

Foel Guesthouse ◆◆◆
18 Hampton Road, Oswestry,
Shropshire SY11 1SJ
T: (01691) 652184 &
07752 882129

Frankton House ◆◆◆◆
Welsh Frankton, Oswestry,
Shropshire SY11 4PA
T: (01691) 623422 &
07803 955823

Greyhound Inn ◆◆
Willow Street, Oswestry,
Shropshire SY11 1AJ
T: (01691) 653392

Llwyn Guesthouse ◆◆◆
5 Llwyn Terrace, Oswestry,
Shropshire SY11 1HR
T: (01691) 670746
E: llwyn@virtual-shropshire.
co.uk
I: www.virtual-shropshire.
co.uk/llwyn

Montrose ◆◆◆
Weston Lane, Oswestry,
Shropshire SY11 2BG
T: (01691) 652063
I: www.shropshiretourism.
com/placestostay

35 Oak Drive ◆◆◆
Oswestry, Shropshire SY11 2RX
T: (01691) 655286

The Old Rectory ◆◆◆
Selattyn, Oswestry, Shropshire
SY10 7DH
T: (01691) 659708

**Railway Cottage
Rating Applied For**
51 Gobowen Road, Oswestry,
Shropshire SY11 1HU
T: (01691) 654851
F: (01691) 654851
E: pmull36823@aol.com

Red Lion ◆◆◆◆
Bailey Head, Oswestry,
Shropshire SY11 1PZ
T: (01691) 655459 &
07976 225409
F: (01691) 655459

Top Farm House ◆◆◆◆
Knockin, Oswestry, Shropshire
SY10 8HN
T: (01691) 682582
F: (01691) 682070
E: p.a.m@knockin.freeserve.
co.uk
I: www.topfarmknockin.co.uk

Westbourne House ◆◆◆◆
11 Top Street, Whittington,
Oswestry, Shropshire SY11 4DR
T: (01691) 661824

OUNDLE
Northamptonshire
Ashworth House ◆◆◆◆
75 West Street, Oundle,
Peterborough PE8 4EJ
T: (01832) 275312
F: (01832) 275312
E: sue@ashworthhse.fsnet.co.uk

2 Benefield Road ◆◆◆◆
Oundle, Peterborough PE8 4ET
T: (01832) 273953
F: (01832) 273953

**Castle Farm Guesthouse
◆◆◆◆**
Castle Farm, Fotheringhay,
Peterborough PE8 5HZ
T: (01832) 226200
F: (01832) 226200

Lilford Lodge Farm ◆◆◆◆
Barnwell, Oundle, Peterborough
PE8 5SA
T: (01832) 272230
F: (01832) 272230
E: trudy@lilford-lodge.demon.
co.uk
I: www.lilford-lodge.demon.
co.uk

OVER HADDON
Derbyshire
Lathkill Cottage ◆◆◆◆
Over Haddon, Bakewell,
Derbyshire DE45 1JE
T: (01629) 814518
F: (01629) 814518
E: judithparker@talk21.com

OXLYNCH
Gloucestershire
Tiled House Farm ◆◆◆◆
Oxlynch, Stonehouse,
Gloucestershire GL10 3DF
T: (01453) 822363 &
07778 841853
F: (01453) 822363
E: nigel.jeffery@ukgateway.net

OXTON
Nottinghamshire
Far Baulker Farm ◆◆◆
Oxton, Southwell,
Nottinghamshire NG25 0RQ
T: (01623) 882375 &
0797 1087605
F: (01623) 882375
E: j.esam@virgin.net

PAINSWICK
Gloucestershire
Cardynham House ◆◆◆◆
The Cross, Painswick, Stroud,
Gloucestershire GL6 6XX
T: (01452) 814006
F: (01452) 812321
E: info@cardynham.co.uk
I: www.cardynham.co.uk

Hambutts Mynd ◆◆◆
Edge Road, Painswick, Stroud,
Gloucestershire GL6 6UP
T: (01452) 812352
F: (01452) 813862
E: ewarland@aol.com
I: www.accommodation.uk.
net/painswick.htm

Meadowcote ◆◆◆◆
Stroud Road, Painswick, Stroud,
Gloucestershire GL6 6UT
T: (01452) 813565

Skyrack ◆◆◆
The Highlands, Painswick,
Stroud, Gloucestershire GL6 6SL
T: (01452) 812029
F: (01452) 813846
E: wendyskyrack@hotmail.com

Thorne ◆◆◆
Friday Street, Painswick, Stroud,
Gloucestershire GL6 6QJ
T: (01452) 812476
I: www.painswick.co.uk.
forward/thorne.

Upper Doreys Mill ◆◆◆
Edge, Painswick, Stroud,
Gloucestershire GL6 6NF
T: (01452) 812459 &
07971 300563
F: (01452) 814756
E: sylvia@painswick.co.uk
I: www.painswick.co.uk/doreys

Wheatleys ◆◆◆◆◆
Cotswold Mead, Painswick,
Stroud, Gloucestershire GL6 6XB
T: (01452) 812167
F: (01452) 814270
E: wheatleys@dial.pipex.com
I: www.wheatleys-b-and-b.
freeserve.co.uk

Wickridge Farm ◆◆◆
Folly Lane, Stroud,
Gloucestershire GL6 7JT
T: (01453) 764357

PANT
Shropshire
The Palms ◆◆◆
Pant, Oswestry, Shropshire
SY10 8JZ
T: (01691) 830813
F: (01691) 830813

PAPPLEWICK
Nottinghamshire
Forest Farm ◆◆◆
Mansfield Road, Papplewick,
Nottingham NG15 8FL
T: (0115) 963 2310

PARKEND
Gloucestershire
Deanfield ◆◆◆
Royal Forest Of Dean, Parkend,
Lydney, Gloucestershire
GL15 4JF
T: (01594) 562256
F: (01594) 562524

Edale House ◆◆◆
Folly Road, Parkend, Lydney,
Gloucestershire GL15 4JF
T: (01594) 562835
F: (01594) 564488
E: edale@lineone.net
I: www.edalehouse.co.uk

**The Fountain Inn & Lodge
◆◆◆**
Fountain Way, Parkend, Lydney,
Gloucestershire GL15 4JD
T: (01594) 562189
F: (01594) 564448
E: thefountaininn@aol.com
I: smoothhound.
co.uk/hotels/fount.html

PARWICH
Derbyshire
Flaxdale House ◆◆◆◆
Parwich, Ashbourne, Derbyshire
DE6 1QA
T: (01335) 390252
F: (01335) 390644
E: mike@flaxdale.demon.co.uk
I: www.flaxdale.demon.co.uk

PEMBRIDGE
Herefordshire
**Lowe Farm Bed and Breakfast
◆◆◆◆**
Lowe Farm, Pembridge,
Leominster, Herefordshire
HR6 9JD
T: (01544) 388395 &
07855 904715
E: williams-family@lineone.net
I: www.lowe-farm.co.uk

PENTRICH
Derbyshire
Coney Grey Farm ◆◆
Chesterfield Road, Pentrich,
Ripley, Derbyshire DE5 3RF
T: (01773) 833179

PERRY BARR
West Midlands
Park Hotel ◆◆◆
131 Aldridge Road, Perry Barr,
Birmingham B24 2ET
T: (0121) 3560707
F: (0121) 3314450
E: parkhoteldavidsue@hotmail.
com
I: www.members.xoom.
com/thehussar/

PERSHORE
Worcestershire
Aldbury House ◆◆◆◆
George Lane, Wyre Piddle,
Pershore, Worcestershire
WR10 2HX
T: (01386) 553754
F: (01386) 553754
E: aldbury@onetel.net.uk

Arbour House ◆◆◆◆
Main Road, Wyre Piddle,
Pershore, Worcestershire
WR10 2HU
T: (01386) 555833
F: (01386) 555833
E: arbourhouse@faxvia.net

The Barn ◆◆◆◆◆
Pensham Hill House, Pensham,
Pershore, Worcestershire
WR10 3HA
T: (01386) 555270
F: (01386) 552894

Byeways ◆◆◆
Pershore Road, Little
Comberton, Pershore,
Worcestershire WR10 3EW
T: (01386) 710203
F: (01386) 710203
E: pwbyeways@aol.com

PILLERTON HERSEY
Warwickshire

The Old Vicarage ◆◆◆◆◆
Pillerton Hersey, Warwick
CV35 0QJ
T: (01789) 740185 &
07836 796674
E: oldvicarage98@hotmail.com

PITCHCOMBE
Gloucestershire

Gable End ◆◆◆
Pitchcombe, Stroud,
Gloucestershire GL6 6LN
T: (01452) 812166
F: (01452) 812719

PITSFORD
Northamptonshire

Ashley House ◆◆◆◆
19 Broadlands, Pitsford,
Northampton NN6 9AZ
T: (01604) 880691
F: (01604) 880691

PONTESBURY
Shropshire

Jasmine Cottage ◆◆◆◆
Pontesford, Pontesbury,
Shrewsbury SY5 0UA
T: (01743) 792771
E: joyce@jasmine-cottage.fsnet.
co.uk
I: www.jasminecottage.net

PONTRILAS
Herefordshire

Station House ◆◆
Pontrilas, Hereford HR2 0EH
T: (01981) 240564
F: (01981) 240564
E: john.pring@tesco.net
I: www.golden-valley.
co.uk/stationhouse

PONTSHILL
Herefordshire

Rowan Lea ◆◆
Pontshill, Ross-on-Wye,
Herefordshire HR9 5SY
T: (01989) 750693

POULTON
Gloucestershire

Sprucewood ◆◆◆◆
Elf Meadow, Poulton,
Cirencester, Gloucestershire
GL7 5HQ
T: (01285) 851351
F: (01285) 851351

PRIORS HARDWICK
Warwickshire

Hill Farm ◆◆◆
Priors Hardwick, Southam,
Warwickshire CV47 7SP
T: (01327) 260338 &
07740 853085
E: simon.darbishire@farming.
co.uk
I: www.farming_holidays.co.uk

PULVERBATCH
Shropshire

Lane Farm ◆◆◆
Wilderley, Pulverbatch,
Shrewsbury SY5 8DF
T: (01743) 718935
F: (01743) 728448
E: bgreig@enterprise.net
I: www.homepages.enterprise.
net/bgreig

QUENIBOROUGH
Leicestershire

Three Ways Farm ◆◆◆
Melton Road, Queniborough,
Leicester LE7 3FN
T: (0116) 260 0472

RAGNALL
Nottinghamshire

Ragnall House ◆◆◆
Main Street, Ragnall, Newark,
Nottinghamshire NG22 0UR
T: (01777) 228575 &
07774 455792
F: (01777) 228575
E: ragnallhouse@gofornet.co.uk

RAITHBY
Lincolnshire

The Red Lion Inn
Rating Applied For
Main Street, Raithby, Spilsby,
Lincolnshire PE23 4DS
T: (01790) 753727
E: alcaprawn@aol.com

REDDITCH
Worcestershire

Avonhill Lodge Guest House
◆◆◆
Alcester Road, Beoley, Redditch,
Worcestershire B98 9EP
T: (01564) 742413
F: (01564) 741873

REDMILE
Leicestershire

**Peacock Farm Guesthouse and
The Feathers Restaurant** ◆◆◆
Redmile, Nottingham NG13 0GQ
T: (01949) 842475
F: (01949) 843127
E: peacockfarm@primeuk.net
I: www.peacock-farm.co.uk

Peacock Inn
Rating Applied For
Church Corner, Main Street,
Redmile, Nottingham NG13 0GA
T: (01949) 842554
F: (01949) 843746
E: peacock@redmile.fsbusiness.
co.uk

RETFORD
Nottinghamshire

The Barns Country Guesthouse
◆◆◆◆
Morton Farm, Babworth,
Retford, Nottinghamshire
DN22 8HA
T: (01777) 706336
F: (01777) 709773
E: harry@thebarns.co.uk
I: www.thebarns.co.uk

Bolham Manor
Rating Applied For
Retford, Nottinghamshire
DN22 9SG
T: (01777) 703528
E: bolhammanor@hotmail.com

The Brick and Tile ◆◆◆
81 Moorgate, Retford,
Nottinghamshire DN22 6RR
T: (01777) 703681
E: foster.2000@virgin.net

RICHARDS CASTLE
Shropshire

The Barn
Rating Applied For
Ryecroft, Richards Castle,
Ludlow, Shropshire SY8 4EU
T: (01584) 831224
F: (01584) 831224
E: ryecroftbarn@hotmail.com
I: www.ludlow.org.uk/ryecroft

RIPLEY
Derbyshire

Spinney Lodge Guesthouse
◆◆◆
Coach Road, Butterley Park,
Ripley, Derbyshire DE5 3QU
T: (01773) 740168

RIPPLE
Worcestershire

Green Gables ◆◆◆
Ripple, Tewkesbury,
Gloucestershire GL20 6EX
T: (01684) 592740
F: (01684) 592740

RISLEY
Derbyshire

Braeside Guest House ◆◆◆◆
113 Derby Road, Risley,
Draycott, Derby DE72 3SS
T: (0115) 939 5885

ROADE
Northamptonshire

**Roade House Restaurant and
Hotel** ◆◆◆◆
16 High Street, Roade,
Northampton NN7 2NW
T: (01604) 863372
F: (01604) 862421
E: chris@roadehousehotel.
demon.co.uk

ROCK
Worcestershire

The Old Forge ◆◆◆
Gorst Hill, Rock, Kidderminster,
Worcestershire DY14 9YG
T: (01299) 266745

ROSS-ON-WYE
Herefordshire

The Arches ◆◆◆
Walford Road, Ross-on-Wye,
Herefordshire HR9 5PT
T: (01989) 563348
F: (01989) 563348
E: the.arches@which.net

Ashe Leigh ◆◆◆
Bridstow, Ross-on-Wye,
Herefordshire HR9 6QB
T: (01989) 565020

Brookfield House ◆◆◆
Over Ross, Ross-on-Wye,
Herefordshire HR9 7AT
T: (01989) 562188
F: (01989) 564053
E: reception@brookfieldhouse.
co.uk
I: www.brookfieldhouse.co.uk

The Falcon Guest House ◆◆◆
How Caple, Hereford HR1 4TF
T: (01989) 740223
F: (01989) 740223
E: falconguesthouse@
tinyworld.co.uk

Forest Edge ◆◆◆◆
4 Noden Drive, Lea, Ross-on-
Wye, Herefordshire HR9 7NB
T: (01989) 750682 &
07974 770358
E: don@wood11.freeserve.co.uk
I: www.wood11.freeserve.co.uk

Four Seasons ◆◆◆◆
Coughton, Walford, Ross-on-
Wye, Herefordshire HR9 5SE
T: (01989) 567884

Haslemere ◆◆◆◆
Ledbury Road, Ross-on-Wye,
Herefordshire HR9 7BE
T: (01989) 563046
F: (01989) 563046
E: bandb@rossonwye.fsnet.
co.uk

The Hill House ◆◆◆
Howle Hill, Ross-on-Wye,
Herefordshire HR9 5ST
T: (01989) 562033
E: welcome@thehillhouse.
dabsol.co.uk
I: www.thehillhouse.dabsol.
co.uk/index.html

Lavender Cottage ◆◆◆
Bridstow, Ross-on-Wye,
Herefordshire HR9 6QB
T: (01989) 562836 &
07790 729131
F: (01989) 762129
E: barbara_lavender@yahoo.
co.uk

Lea House Bed and Breakfast
◆◆◆◆
Lea House, The Lea, Ross-on-
Wye, Herefordshire HR9 7JZ
T: (01989) 750652 &
07889 521797
F: (01989) 750652
E: leahouse@wyenet.co.uk
I: www.leahouse.wyenet.co.uk/

Linden House ◆◆◆◆
14 Church Street, Ross-on-Wye,
Herefordshire HR9 5HN
T: (01989) 565373
F: (01989) 565575
I: www.lindenhouse.wyenet.co.
uk

Lumleys ◆◆◆◆
Kerne Bridge, Bishopswood,
Ross-on-Wye, Herefordshire
HR9 5QT
T: (01600) 890040
F: (01600) 891095
E: helen@lumleys.force9.co.uk
I: www.lumleys.force9.co.uk

Lyndor Bed and Breakfast
◆◆◆
Lyndor, Hole-in-the-Wall, Ross-
on-Wye, Herefordshire HR9 7JW
T: (01989) 563833

The Mill House ◆◆◆
Walford, Ross-on-Wye,
Herefordshire HR9 5QS
T: (01989) 764339 &
07780 812507
F: (01989) 763231

Norton House ◆◆◆◆
Whitchurch, Ross-on-Wye,
Herefordshire HR9 6DJ
T: (01600) 890046
F: (01600) 890045
E: jackson@osconwhi.source.
co.uk

The Old Rectory ◆◆◆◆
Hope Mansell, Ross-on-Wye,
Herefordshire HR9 5IL
T: (01989) 750382
F: (01989) 750382
E: rectory@mansell.wyenet.
co.uk

Radcliffe Guest House ◆◆◆
Wye Street, Ross-on-Wye,
Herefordshire HR9 7BS
T: (01989) 563895
E: Radcliffegh@btinternet.com

Rudhall Farm ◆◆◆◆
Ross-on-Wye, Herefordshire
HR9 7TL
T: (01989) 780240

Sunnymount Hotel ◆◆◆◆
Ryefield Road, Ross-on-Wye,
Herefordshire HR9 5LU
T: (01989) 563880
F: (01989) 566251

Thatch Close ◆◆◆
Llangrove, Ross-on-Wye,
Herefordshire HR9 6EL
T: (01989) 770300
E: thatch.close@virgin.net

Vaga House ◆◆◆
Wye Street, Ross-on-Wye,
Herefordshire HR9 7BS
T: (01989) 563024
E: vagahouse@hotmail.com

Walnut Tree Cottage Hotel
◆◆◆◆
Symonds Yat West, Ross-on-
Wye, Herefordshire HR9 6BN
T: (01600) 890828
F: (01600) 890828
E: enquiries@walnuttreehotel.
co.uk
I: www.walnuttreehotel.co.uk

Warren Farm ◆◆◆◆
Warren Lane, Lea, Ross-on-Wye,
Herefordshire HR9 7LT
T: (01989) 750272 &
07802 167395
F: (01989) 750272

Welland House ◆◆◆
Archenfield Road, Ross-on-Wye,
Herefordshire HR9 5BA
T: (01989) 566500
F: (01989) 566500
E: wellandhouse@hotmail.com

ROWSLEY
Derbyshire

The Old Station House ◆◆◆◆
4 Chatsworth Road, Rowsley,
Matlock, Derbyshire DE4 2EJ
T: (01629) 732987
F: (01629) 735169
E: patches@proach.fsnet.co.uk

Vernon House ◆◆◆◆
Bakewell Road, Rowsley,
Matlock, Derbyshire DE4 2EB
T: (01629) 734294

1 Vicarage Croft ◆◆◆
Church Lane, Rowsley, Matlock,
Derbyshire DE4 2EA
T: (01629) 735429

ROWTON
Shropshire

Church Farm ◆◆◆
Rowton, Telford, Shropshire
TF6 6QY
T: (01952) 770381
F: (01952) 770381
E: church.farm@bigfoot.com
I: www.
virtual-shropshire/churchfarm
(符)

RUARDEAN
Gloucestershire

The Malt Shovel Inn ◆◆◆
Ruardean, Gloucestershire
GL17 9TW
T: (01594) 543028
E: mark@maltshovel.u-net.com
I: www.maltshovel.u-net.com

Oakleigh Farm House ◆◆
Crooked End, Ruardean,
Gloucestershire GL17 9XF
T: (01594) 542284
F: (01594) 543610
E: christine@iconmodel2.
demon.co.uk

RUGBY
Warwickshire

The Croft Bed and Breakfast
Rating Applied For
69 Rugby road, Dunchurch,
Rugby, Warwickshire CV22 6PQ
T: (01788) 816763 &
07977 502734
E: tlong79@hotmail.com

Diamond House Hotel ◆◆◆
30 Hillmorton Road, Rugby,
Warwickshire CV22 5AA
T: (01788) 572701
F: (01788) 572701

The Golden Lion Inn of
Easenhall ◆◆◆◆
Easenhall, Rugby, Warwickshire
CV23 0JA
T: (01788) 832265
F: (01788) 832878
E: goldenlioninn@aol.com
I: www.goldenlion-easenhall.
co.uk

Lawford Hill Farm ◆◆◆◆
Lawford Heath Lane, Rugby,
Warwickshire CV23 9HG
T: (01788) 542001
F: (01788) 537880
E: lawford.hill@talk21.com
I: www.lawford.co.uk

Marston House ◆◆◆◆
Priors Marston, Rugby,
Southam, Warwickshire
CV47 7RP
T: (01327) 260297
F: (01327) 262846
E: john.mahon@coltel.co.uk
I: www.ivabestbandb.co.uk

The Old Rectory ◆◆◆◆
Main Street, Harborough
Magna, Rugby, Warwickshire
CV23 0HS
T: (01788) 833151 &
07803 054509
F: (01788) 833151
E: oldrectory@cwcom.net
I: www.
theoldrectorywarwickshire.co.uk

Village Green Hotel ◆◆◆◆
The Green, Dunchurch, Rugby,
Warwickshire CV22 6NX
T: (01788) 813434 &
07710 576867
F: (01788) 814714
E: villagegreenhotel.rugby@
btinternet.com
I: www.villagegreenhotelrugby.
com

White Lion Inn ◆◆◆
Coventry Road, Pailton, Rugby,
Warwickshire CV23 0QD
T: (01788) 832359
F: (01788) 832359

RUGELEY
Staffordshire

Park Farm ◆◆◆
Hawkesyard, Armitage Lane,
Rugeley, Staffordshire
WS15 1ED
T: (01889) 583477
F: (01889) 583477

RUSHWICK
Worcestershire

Laugherne Grange
Rating Applied For
Bransford Road, Rushwick,
Worcester WR2 5SJ
T: (01905) 428 047

RUSKINGTON
Lincolnshire

Sunnyside Farm ◆◆◆
Leasingham Lane, Ruskington,
Sleaford, Lincolnshire NG34 9AH
T: (01526) 833010
E: daphneluke@talk21.com

ST OWENS CROSS
Herefordshire

Amberley ◆◆◆◆
Aberhall Farm, St Owens Cross,
Hereford HR2 8LL
T: (01989) 730256
F: (01989) 730256
E: freda-davies@ereal.net
I: www.SmoothHound.
co.uk/hotels/amberley2.html

SANDHURST
Gloucestershire

Brawn Farm ◆◆◆◆
Sandhurst, Gloucester GL2 9NR
T: (01452) 731010 &
07989 779440
F: (01452) 731102
E: williams.sally@excite.com

SAXILBY
Lincolnshire

Orchard Cottage ◆◆◆◆
3 Orchard Lane, Saxilby, Lincoln
LN1 2HT
T: (01522) 703192
F: (01522) 703192
E: margaretallen@
orchardcottage.org.uk
I: www.smoothhound.
co.uk/hotels/orchardcot.html

SCALDWELL
Northamptonshire

The Old House ◆◆◆◆
East End, Scaldwell,
Northampton NN6 9LB
T: (01604) 880359 & 882287
F: (01604) 880359
E: mrsv@scaldwell43.fsnet.
co.uk
I: www.the-oldhouse.co.uk

SCOTTER
Lincolnshire

Ivy Lodge Hotel ◆◆◆◆
4 Messingham Road, Scotter,
Gainsborough, Lincolnshire
DN21 3UQ
T: (01724) 763723 & 761704
F: (01724) 763770
I: www.SmoothHound.
co.uk/hotels/ivylodge.html

SEATON
Rutland

Grange Farm Bed & Breakfast
◆◆◆◆
Grange Farm, Seaton, Oakham,
Leicestershire LE15 9HT
T: (01572) 747664
E: david.reading@farmline.com

SHAWBURY
Shropshire

Unity Lodge ◆◆◆
Moreton Mill, Shawbury,
Shrewsbury SY4 4ER
T: (01939) 250831

SHEEPSCOMBE
Gloucestershire

Sen Sook ◆◆◆
Far End Lane, Sheepscombe,
Stroud, Gloucestershire GL6 7RL
T: (01452) 812047

SHEPSHED
Leicestershire

Croft Guesthouse ◆◆◆
21 Hall Croft, Shepshed,
Loughborough, Leicestershire
LE12 9AN
T: (01509) 505657
F: 0870 0522266
E: ray@croftguesthouse.demon.
co.uk
I: www.croftguesthouse.demon.
co.uk

The Grange Courtyard ◆◆◆◆
The Grange, Forest Street,
Shepshed, Loughborough,
Leicestershire LE12 9DA
T: (01509) 600189
E: lindalawrence@
thegrangecourtyard.co.uk
I: www.thegrangecourtyard.
co.uk

SHIFNAL
Shropshire

Cross Keys Guest House ◆◆◆
62 Broadway, Shifnal,
Shropshire TF11 8AZ
T: (01952) 460173
E: ruth@xkeys.fsnet.co.uk
I: www.xkeys.fsnet.co.uk

Naughty Nell's Limited ◆◆◆
1 Park Street, Shifnal, Shropshire
TF11 9BA
T: (01952) 411412
F: (01952) 463336

Odfellows – The Wine Bar
◆◆◆
Market Place, Shifnal,
Shropshire TF11 9AU
T: (01952) 461517
F: (01952) 463855
E: matt@odley.co.uk

SHILTON
Warwickshire

Barnacle Hall ◆◆◆◆◆
Shilton Lane, Shilton, Coventry
CV7 9LH
T: (024) 76612629

SHIPSTON-ON-STOUR
Warwickshire

Tallet Barn Bed and Breakfast ♦♦♦♦
Yerdley Farm, Long Compton,
Shipston-on-Stour,
Warwickshire CV36 5LH
T: (01608) 684248
I: www.country-accom.co.uk

White Bear Hotel ♦♦♦
High Street, Shipston-on-Stour,
Warwickshire CV36 4AJ
T: (01608) 661558
F: (01608) 661558
E: inisfallen@aol.com

SHIRLEY
Derbyshire

The Old Byre Guesthouse ♦♦♦♦
Hollington Lane, Shirley,
Ashbourne, Derbyshire DE6 3AS
T: (01335) 360054
F: (01335) 360054
E: alan@theoldbyre.fsbusiness.
co.uk
I: www.theoldbyre.fsbusiness.
co.uk

SHOBDON
Herefordshire

Four Oaks ♦♦♦
Uphampton, Shobdon,
Leominster, Herefordshire
HR6 9PA
T: (01568) 708039
F: (01568) 708039
E: fouroaksbandb@hotmail.com

SHOBY
Leicestershire

Shoby Lodge Farm ♦♦♦♦
Shoby, Melton Mowbray,
Leicestershire LE14 3PF
T: (01664) 812156 &
07802 961300

SHREWSBURY
Shropshire

Abbey Court House ♦♦♦
134 Abbey Foregate,
Shrewsbury, SY2 6AU
T: (01743) 364416
F: (01743) 358559

Abbey Lodge Guest House ♦♦♦
68 Abbey Foregate, Shrewsbury,
SY2 6BG
T: (01743) 235832 &
07947 925134
F: (01743) 235832
E: lindsay.abbeylodge@virgin.
net
I: www.abbeylodgeshrewsbury.
co.uk

Anton Guest House ♦♦♦♦
1 Canon Street, Monkmoor,
Shrewsbury, SY2 5HG
T: (01743) 359275
E: antonhouse@supanet.com
I: www.antonhouse.supanet.
com

Ashton Lees ♦♦♦♦
Dorrington, Shrewsbury
SY5 7JW
T: (01743) 718378

Avonlea ♦♦
33 Coton Crescent, Coton Hill,
Shrewsbury, SY1 2NZ
T: (01743) 359398

Bancroft ♦♦♦
17 Coton Crescent, Shrewsbury,
SY1 2NY
T: (01743) 231746
F: (01743) 231746
E: bancroft01@aol.com

**164 Bed and Continental
Breakfast** ♦♦♦
164 Abbey Foregate,
Shrewsbury, SY2 6AL
T: (01743) 367750
F: (01743) 367750
E: chris@164bedandbreakfast.
co.uk
I: www.chrisyatesroberts.freeola.
com

The Boars Head ♦
18 Belle Vue Road, Shrewsbury,
SY3 7LL
T: (01743) 350590

Brambleberry ♦♦♦♦
Halfway House, Shrewsbury,
SY5 9DD
T: (01743) 884762

The Burlton Inn ♦♦♦♦
Burlton, Shrewsbury, SY4 5TB
T: (01939) 270284
F: (01939) 270204
E: bean@burltoninn.co.uk
I: www.burltoninn.co.uk

Cardeston Park Farm ♦♦♦
Ford, Shrewsbury SY5 9NH
T: (01743) 884265
F: (01743) 886265

Castlecote ♦♦♦
77 Monkmoor Road,
Shrewsbury, SY2 5AT
T: (01743) 245473
E: btench@castlecote.
fsbusiness.co.uk

Chatford House ♦♦♦
Bayston Hill, Shrewsbury,
SY3 0AY
T: (01743) 718301

College Hill Guest House ♦♦
11 College Hill, Shrewsbury,
SY1 1LZ
T: (01743) 365744
F: (01743) 365744

Cromwells Hotel & Wine Bar ♦♦
11 Dogpole, Shrewsbury,
SY1 1EN
T: (01743) 361440
F: (01743) 341121
E: theresa@cromwellsinn.co.uk
I: www.cromwellshotel.co.uk

Eye Manor ♦♦♦♦
Leighton, Shrewsbury, SY5 6SQ
T: (01952) 510066
F: (01952) 510967

Golden Cross Hotel ♦♦♦
14 Princess Street, Shrewsbury,
SY1 1LP
T: (01743) 362507

Jasmine House ♦♦♦
102 Copthorne Road,
Shrewsbury, SY3 8NA
T: (01743) 232208

Lyth Hill House ♦♦♦♦
28 Old Coppice, Lyth Hill,
Shrewsbury, SY3 0BP
T: (01743) 874660 &
07967 375702
E: bnb@lythhillhouse.com
I: www.lythhillhouse.com
🚶

Noneley Hall ♦♦♦♦
Noneley, Near Wem,
Shrewsbury, SY4 5SL
T: (01939) 233271
F: (01939) 233271
E: cpbirch@callnetuk.com

North Farm ♦♦♦♦
Eaton Mascot, Shrewsbury,
Shropshire SY5 6HF
T: (01743) 761031
F: (01743) 761854
E: northfarm@talk21.com
I: www.northfarm.co.uk

The Old Station ♦♦♦♦
Leaton, Bomere Heath,
Shrewsbury SY4 3AP
T: (01939) 290905 &
07885 526307

The Old Vicarage ♦♦♦♦
Leaton, Shrewsbury, SY4 3AP
T: (01939) 290989
F: (01939) 290989
E: m-j@oldvicleaton.com
I: www.oldvicleaton.com

Pinewood House ♦♦♦♦♦
Shelton Park, The Mount,
Shrewsbury, SY3 8BL
T: (01743) 364200

Prynce's Villa ♦♦
15 Monkmoor Road,
Shrewsbury, Shropshire SY2 5AG
T: (01743) 356217

Restawhile ♦♦♦
36 Coton Crescent, Coton Hill,
Shrewsbury, SY1 2NZ
T: (01743) 240969
F: (01743) 231841
E: restawhile@breathemail.net
I: www.virtual-shropshire.
co.uk/restawhile

Sandford House Hotel ♦♦♦
St Julian's Friars, Shrewsbury,
SY1 1XL
T: (01743) 343829
F: (01743) 343829
E: sandfordhouse@lineone.net
I: www.sandfordhouse.co.uk

Severn Cottage ♦♦♦♦
4 Coton Hill, Shrewsbury,
SY1 2DZ
T: (01743) 358467 &
07971 569339
F: (01743) 340254
E: david.tudor1@virgin.net
I: www.shrewsburynet.com

Shenandoah ♦♦♦
Sparrow Lane, Abbey Forgate,
Shrewsbury, SY2 5EP
T: (01743) 363015 &
07989 888172
F: (01743) 244918

Shorthill Lodge ♦♦♦♦
Shorthill, Lea Cross, Shrewsbury,
SY5 8JE
T: (01743) 860864
E: shorthilllodge@hotmail.com
I: www.go2.co.uk/shorthill

The Stiperstones Guest House ♦♦♦♦
18 Coton Crescent, Coton Hill,
Shrewsbury, SY1 2NZ
T: (01743) 246720 & 350303
F: (01743) 350303
E: stiperstones@aol.com
I: www.stiperstones.net

Sydney House Hotel ♦♦♦
Coton Crescent, Coton Hill,
Shrewsbury, SY1 2LJ
T: (01743) 354681 &
0800 2981243
F: (01743) 354681

Trevellion House ♦♦♦
1 Bradford Street, Monkmoor,
Shrewsbury, SY2 5DP
T: (01743) 249582 &
07713 394396
F: (01743) 232096
E: marktaplin@
bradfordstreetjunglelink.co.uk

Upper Brompton Farm ♦♦♦♦♦
Brompton, Cross Houses,
Shrewsbury SY5 6LE
T: (01743) 761629
F: (01743) 761679
E: upper-brompton.farm@dial.
pipex.com
I: www.smoothound.
co.uk/hotels/upperbro.html

Ye Olde Bucks Head Inn ♦♦♦
Frankwell, Shrewsbury, SY3 8JR
T: (01743) 369392
E: jennyhodges@onetel.net.uk

SHUSTOKE
Warwickshire

Ye Olde Station Guest House ♦♦♦
Church Road, Shustoke,
Coleshill, Birmingham B46 2AX
T: (01675) 481736
F: (01675) 481736
E: yeoldestationguestho@
talk21.com
I: www.yeoldstationguesthouse.
activehotels.com

SKEGNESS
Lincolnshire

Chatsworth Hotel ♦♦♦
North Parade, Skegness,
Lincolnshire PE25 2UB
T: (01754) 764177
F: (01754) 761173
E: Altipper@aol.com
I: www.chatsworthskegness.
co.uk
🚶

Clarence House Hotel ♦♦♦
32 South Parade, Skegness,
Lincolnshire PE25 3HW
T: (01754) 765588
E: barbarahartley@aol.com

Crawford Hotel ♦♦♦
104 South Parade, Skegness,
Lincolnshire PE25 3HR
T: (01754) 764215
F: (01754) 764215

Eastleigh ♦♦♦
60 Scarbrough Avenue,
Skegness, Lincolnshire PE25 2TB
T: (01754) 764605 &
07719 626232
F: (01754) 764605
I: www.eastleigh-skegness.co.uk

Fountaindale Hotel ♦♦♦
69 Sandbeck Avenue, Skegness,
Lincolnshire PE25 3JS
T: (01754) 762731 &
0500 515259
I: www.fountaindale.co.uk
♿

Merton Hotel ◆◆◆
14 Firbeck Avenue, Skegness,
Lincolnshire PE25 3JY
T: (01754) 764423
F: (01754) 766627

North Parade Hotel ◆◆◆
20 North Parade, Skegness,
Lincolnshire PE25 2UB
T: (01754) 762309 & 765235
F: (01754) 610949
E: northparadehotel@
btinternet.com

Palm Court Hotel ◆◆◆
74 South Parade, Skegness,
Lincolnshire PE25 3HP
T: (01754) 767711
F: (01754) 767711

Rufford Hotel ◆◆◆
5 Saxby Avenue, Skegness,
Lincolnshire PE25 3JZ
T: (01754) 763428

Savoy Hotel ◆◆◆
12 North Parade, Skegness,
Lincolnshire PE25 2UB
T: (01754) 763371
F: (01754) 761256
F: info@savoy-skegness.co.uk
I: www.savoy-skegness.co.uk

Saxby Hotel ◆◆◆
12 Saxby Avenue, Skegness,
Lincolnshire PE25 3LG
T: (01754) 763905
F: (01754) 763905
[symbol]

Stoneleigh Private Hotel ◆◆◆
67 Sandbeck Avenue, Skegness,
Lincolnshire PE25 3JS
T: (01754) 769138
E: enquiries@stoneleigh-hotel.
freeserve.co.uk
I: www.stoneleigh-hotel.
freeserve.co.uk

Sun Hotel ◆◆◆
19 North Parade, Skegness,
Lincolnshire PE25 2UB
T: (01754) 762364
F: (01754) 762364

Sunnybank Hotel ◆◆◆
29 Ida Road, Skegness,
Lincolnshire PE25 2AU
T: (01754) 762583 &
0794 6647485
E: sunnybank.hotel@amserve.
net

Woodthorpe Private Hotel ◆◆
64 South Parade, Skegness,
Lincolnshire PE25 3HP
T: (01754) 763452

SKILLINGTON
Lincolnshire

Jackson's House ◆◆◆◆
Middle Street, Skillington,
Grantham, Lincolnshire
NG33 5EU
T: (01476) 861634

Sproxton Lodge Farm ◆◆
Sproxton Lodge, Skillington,
Grantham, Lincolnshire
NG33 5HJ
T: (01476) 860307

SLEAFORD
Lincolnshire

The Tally Ho Inn ◆◆◆
Aswarby, Sleaford, Lincolnshire
NG34 8SA
T: (01529) 455205
F: (01529) 455773

SMISBY
Derbyshire

Hillside Lodge ◆◆◆◆
Derby Road, Smisby, Ashby-de-
la-Zouch, Leicestershire
LE65 2RG
T: (01530) 416411
E: david.ball99@virgin.net

SNELSTON
Derbyshire

Sidesmill Farm ◆◆◆◆
Snelston, Ashbourne, Derbyshire
DE6 2GQ
T: (01335) 342710

SOLIHULL
West Midlands

Acorn Guest House ◆◆◆◆
29 Links Drive, Solihull, West
Midlands B91 2DJ
T: (0121) 7055241
E: acorn.wood@btinternet.com

Boxtrees Farm ◆◆◆
Stratford Road, Hockley Heath,
Solihull, West Midlands B94 6EA
T: (01564) 782039 &
07970 736156
F: (01564) 784661
E: b&tb@boxtrees.co.uk
I: boxtrees.co.uk

Cedarwood House ◆◆◆
347 Lyndon Road, Solihull, West
Midlands B92 7QT
T: (0121) 743 5844
F: (0121) 743 5844
E: mail@cedarwooduk.co.uk
I: www.cedarwooduk.co.uk

Chale Guest House ◆◆◆
967 Stratford Road, Shirley,
Solihull, West Midlands B90 4BG
T: (0121) 744 2846 &
07974 323018
F: (0121) 6240044
E: chale.guesthouse@iname.
com
I: www.smoothhound.
co.uk/hotels/chalegue.htm

Chelsea Lodge ◆◆◆◆
48 Meriden Road, Hampton in
Arden, Solihull, West Midlands
B92 0BT
T: (01675) 442408
F: (01675) 442408
E: chelsealodgebnb@aol.com
I: www.chelsealodgebnb.co.uk
ALSO www.tempera.
co.uk/pchapman

Clovelly Guest House ◆◆◆
Coleshill Heath Road, Marston
Green, Solihull, West Midlands
B37 7HY
T: (0121) 779 2886 &
07885 412780

**The Edwardian Guest House
◆◆◆◆**
7 St Bernards Road, Olton,
Solihull, West Midlands B92 7AU
T: (0121) 706 2138

The Gate House ◆◆◆
Barston Lane, Barston, Solihull,
West Midlands B92 0JN
T: (01675) 443274
F: (01675) 443274
E: gatehouse@jjemmett.fsnet.
co.uk

Ravenhurst ◆◆◆
56 Lode Lane, Solihull, West
Midlands B91 2AW
T: (0121) 7055754 &
07973 954930
F: (0121) 704 0717

Triangle Guest House ◆◆
512-514 Stratford Road, Shirley,
Solihull, West Midlands B90 4AY
T: (0121) 744 4182 &
0797 7666489
F: (0121) 744 4182

SOUTH HYKEHAM
Lincolnshire

**The Hall Farm Farmhouse
◆◆◆**
Meadow Lane, South Hykeham,
Lincoln LN6 9PF
T: (01522) 686432
F: (01522) 686432
E: maps@oden.org.uk

SOUTH NORMANTON
Derbyshire

The Boundary Lodge ◆◆◆◆
Lea Vale, Broadmeadows, South
Normanton, Alfreton, Derbyshire
DE55 3NA
T: (01773) 819066
E: manager@boundarylodgefs.
net.co.uk
I: theboundary.co.uk

SOUTH WINGFIELD
Derbyshire

Platts Farm Guesthouse ◆◆◆
High Road, South Wingfield,
Alfreton, Derbyshire DE55 7LX
T: (01773) 832280

SOUTH WITHAM
Lincolnshire

Barn Owl House ◆◆◆◆
20 High Street, South Witham,
Grantham, Lincolnshire
NG33 5QB
T: (01572) 767688 &
07932 000870
F: (01572) 767688
E: margaret@mcclambert.fsnet.
co.uk
I: www.rutnet.co.uk/barnowl

**The Blue Cow Inn and Brewery
◆◆◆**
29 High Street, South Witham,
Grantham, Lincolnshire
NG33 5QB
T: (01572) 768432
F: (01572) 768432
E: richard@tithwell.fslife.co.uk
I: www.thebluecowinn.co.uk

Rose Cottage ◆◆◆◆
7 High Street, South Witham,
Grantham, Lincolnshire
NG33 5QB
T: (01572) 767757 &
07961 317011
F: (01572) 767199
E: bob@vankimmenade.
freeserve.co.uk

SOUTHAM
Warwickshire

Briarwood ◆◆◆
34 Warwick Road, Southam,
Warwickshire CV47 0HN
T: (01926) 814756

SOUTHWELL
Nottinghamshire

Barn Lodge ◆◆◆
Duckers Cottage, Brinkley,
Southwell, Nottinghamshire
NG25 0TP
T: (01636) 813435
E: barnlodge@hotmail.com

**Church Street Bed and
Breakfast
Rating Applied For**
56 Church Street, Southwell,
Nottinghamshire NG25 0HG
T: (01636) 812004 & 0798 995
1665
E: ian.wright5@btinternet.com

SPALDING
Lincolnshire

**Belvoir House
Rating Applied For**
13 London Road, Spalding,
Lincolnshire PE11 2TA
T: (01775) 723901
F: (01775) 711816
E: belvoir@fsbdial.co.uk

STAFFORD
Staffordshire

Cedarwood ◆◆◆◆
46 Weeping Cross, Stafford,
ST17 0DS
T: (01785) 662981

The Foxes ◆◆◆
2A Thorneyfields Lane, Stafford,
ST17 9YS
T: (01785) 602589 &
07946 324092
F: (01785) 602680
E: thefoxes.beech@ntlworld.
com

Littywood House ◆◆◆◆
Bradley, Stafford, ST18 9DW
T: (01785) 780234 & 780770
F: (01785) 780770

Park Farm ◆◆◆
Weston Road, Stafford,
ST18 0BD
T: (01785) 240257
F: (01785) 240257

Woodhouse Farm ◆◆◆◆
Woodhouse Lane, Haughton,
Stafford, ST18 9JJ
T: (01785) 822259

Wyndale Guest House ◆◆
199 Corporation Street,
Stafford, ST16 3LQ
T: (01785) 223069

STAMFORD
Lincolnshire

**Abbey House and Coach House
◆◆◆◆**
West End Road, Maxey,
Peterborough PE6 9EJ
T: (01778) 344642 & 347499
F: (01778) 342706
E: sales@abbeyhouse.co.uk
I: www.abbeyhouse.co.uk

Birch House ◆◆◆
4 Lonsdale Road, Stamford,
Lincolnshire PE9 2RW
T: (01780) 754876
F: (01780) 754876
E: Birch_House@faxvia.net

86 Casterton Road ◆◆◆
Stamford, Lincolnshire PE9 2UB
T: (01780) 754734

Chestnut View Bed & Breakfast ♦♦♦
Chestnut View, 94 Casterton Road, Stamford, Lincolnshire PE9 2UB
T: (01780) 763648
F: (01780) 480 663
E: jstimson@uk.packardbell.org
I: www.angelfire.com/ga3/chestnutview

Dolphin Guesthouse ♦♦
12 East Street, Stamford, Lincolnshire PE9 1QD
T: (01780) 757515 & 481567
F: (01780) 757515
E: mikdolphin@mikdolphin.demon.co.uk

4 Kings Road ♦♦
Stamford, Lincolnshire PE9 1HD
T: (01780) 752172 & 481883
F: (01780) 752172

Martins ♦♦♦♦
20 High Street, Saint Martin's, Stamford, Lincolnshire PE9 2LF
T: (01780) 752106
F: (01780) 482691
E: marie@martins-b-b.demon.co.uk

Midstone Farmhouse ♦♦♦♦
Southorpe, Stamford, Lincolnshire PE9 3BX
T: (01780) 740136
F: (01780) 749294
E: ahsmidstonehouse@amserve.net

The Oak Inn ♦♦♦
48 Stamford Road, Easton on the Hill, Stamford, Lincolnshire PE9 3PA
T: (01780) 752286
F: (01780) 752286
E: peter@klippon.demon.co.uk

Rock Lodge ♦♦♦♦♦
1 Empingham Road, Stamford, Lincolnshire PE9 2RH
T: (01780) 481758
F: (01780) 481757
E: rocklodge@innpro.co.uk

5 Rock Terrace ♦♦♦♦
Scotgate, Stamford, Lincolnshire PE9 2YJ
T: (01780) 755475
E: averdieckguest@talk21.com

STANDISH
Gloucestershire

Oaktree Farm ♦♦♦
Little Haresfield, Standish, Stonehouse, Gloucestershire GL10 3DS
T: (01452) 883323
E: Jackie@oaktreefarm.fsnet.co.uk

STANFORD BISHOP
Herefordshire

The Hawkins Farm ♦♦♦
Stanford Bishop, Worcester WR6 5TQ
T: (01886) 884250
F: (01886) 884250

STANTON–BY–BRIDGE
Derbyshire

Ivy House Farm ♦♦♦
Stanton-by-Bridge, Derby DE73 1HT
T: (01332) 863152 & 07780 991983
F: (01332) 863152
E: mary@guesthouse.fsbusiness.co.uk

St Brides Farmhouse ♦♦♦♦
Stanton-by-Bridge, Derby DE73 1JQ
T: (01332) 865255
E: stbrides.bb@talk21.com

STANTON IN PEAK
Derbyshire

Congreave Farm ♦♦♦♦
Congreave, Stanton in Peak, Matlock, Derbyshire DE4 2NF
T: (01629) 732063
E: deborahbettney@congreave.junglelink.co.uk
I: www.matsam16.freeserve.co.uk/congreave/

STANTON-ON-THE-WOLDS
Nottinghamshire

Laurel Farm ♦♦♦
Browns Lane, Stanton-on-the-Wolds, Keyworth, Nottingham NG12 5BL
T: (0115) 937 3488
F: (0115) 9376490
E: laurelfarm@yahoo.com
I: www.s-h-systems.co.uk/laurelfa.html

STAPLETON
Shropshire

Stapleton Cottage
Rating Applied For
Stapleton, Dorrington, Shrewsbury SY5 7EQ
T: (01743) 719132 & 718314
F: (01743) 718314
E: wilkinson@ichthusltd.fsnet.co.uk

STAPLOW
Worcestershire

Woodleigh ♦♦♦♦
Staplow, Ledbury, Herefordshire HR8 1NP
T: (01531) 640204
F: (01531) 640767

STAVELEY
Derbyshire

Foresters Arms ♦♦
Market Street, Staveley, Chesterfield, Derbyshire S43 3UT
T: (01246) 477455
E: info@theforesters.co.uk
I: www.theforesters.co.uk

STIPERSTONES
Shropshire

The Old Chapel ♦♦♦♦
Perkins Beach Dingle, Stiperstones, SY5 0PE
T: (01743) 791449
E: jean@a-lees.freeserve.co.uk
I: www.s-h-systems.co.uk/hotels/oldchapel.html

STOCKINGFORD
Warwickshire

Aberglynmarch Guest House ♦♦♦
198 Church Road, Stockingford, Nuneaton, Warwickshire CV10 8LH
T: (02476) 342793 & 07765 407541
F: (02476) 342793

STOCKTON ON TEME
Worcestershire

Wharf Farm ♦♦♦
Pensax Lane, Stockton on Teme, Worcester WR6 6XF
T: (01584) 881341
E: wharf.farm@cwcom.net

STOKE BRUERNE
Northamptonshire

Beam End ♦♦♦♦
Stoke Park, Stoke Bruerne, Towcester, Northamptonshire NN12 7RZ
T: (01604) 864802 & 864638
F: (01604) 864637
E: beamend@bun.com

3 Rookery Barns ♦♦♦♦
Rookery Lane, Stoke Bruerne, Towcester, Northamptonshire NN12 7SJ
T: (01604) 862274

STOKE DOYLE
Northamptonshire

Shuckburgh Arms ♦♦♦♦
Stoke Doyle, Peterborough PE8 5TG
T: (01832) 272339
F: (01832) 275230
E: paulkirkby@shuckburgharms.co.uk
I: www.shuckburgharms.co.uk

STOKE-ON-TRENT
Staffordshire

Cedar Tree Cottage ♦♦♦
41 Longton Road, Trentham, Stoke-on-Trent, ST4 8ND
T: (01782) 644751

Flower Pot Hotel ♦
44-46 Snow Hill, Shelton, Stoke-on-Trent, ST1 4LY
T: (01782) 207204

The Hollies ♦♦♦
Clay Lake, Endon, Stoke-on-Trent ST9 9DD
T: (01782) 503252 & 07790 762815
F: (01782) 503252
E: theholliesendon@faxvia.net

Holly Trees ♦♦♦♦
Crewe Road, Alsager, Stoke-on-Trent, ST7 2JL
T: (01270) 876847
F: (01270) 883301
E: hollytreeshotel@aol.com
I: www.hollytreeshotel.co.uk

The Limes ♦♦♦
Cheadle Road, Blythe Bridge, Stoke-on-Trent ST11 9PW
T: (01782) 393278

The Old Dairy House ♦♦♦♦♦
Trentham Park, Stoke-on-Trent, ST4 8AE
T: (01782) 641209
F: (01782) 712904
E: olddairyhouse@hotmail.com

Old Vicarage Guesthouse ♦♦♦♦
Birchenwood Road, Newchapel, Stoke-on-Trent ST7 4QT
T: (01782) 785270
E: peter.kent-baguley@birchenwood.freeserve.co.uk

Reynolds Hey ♦♦♦♦
Park Lane, Endon, Stoke-on-Trent ST9 9JB
T: (01782) 502717

Shaw Gate Farm ♦♦♦
Shay Lane, Foxt, Stoke-on-Trent, ST10 2HN
T: (01538) 266590
F: (01538) 266590
E: Ken_morris@lineone.net
I: www.shawgatefarm.co.uk

Star Hotel ♦♦♦
92 Marsh Street North, Hanley, Stoke-on-Trent ST1 5HH
T: (01782) 207507 & 289989
F: (01782) 289989

Verdon Guest House ♦♦♦
44 Charles Street, Hanley, Stoke-on-Trent ST1 3JY
T: (01782) 264244 & 07711 514682
F: (01782) 264244
E: debbie@howlett18.freeserve.co.uk
I: business.thisisstaffordshire.co.uk/verdon

STONE
Staffordshire

Lock House ♦♦♦♦
74 Newcastle Road, Stone, Staffordshire ST15 8LB
T: (01785) 811551 & 814822
F: (01785) 286587
E: mbd@fsbdial.co.uk

STONEHOUSE
Gloucestershire

Beacon Inn Hotel ♦♦♦
Haresfield, Stonehouse, Gloucestershire GL10 3DX
T: (01452) 728884
F: (01452) 728884
E: beaconinn@aol.com

The Grey Cottage ♦♦♦♦♦
Bath Road, Leonard Stanley, Stonehouse, Gloucestershire GL10 3LU
T: (01453) 822515
F: (01453) 822515

Merton Lodge ♦♦
8 Ebley Road, Stonehouse, Gloucestershire GL10 2LQ
T: (01453) 822208

STOTTESDON
Worcestershire

Hardwicke Farm ♦♦♦♦
Stottesdon, Kidderminster, Worcestershire DY14 8TN
T: (01746) 718220
E: Hardwickefarm@hotmail.com
I: www.farm-holidays.co.uk

STOULTON
Worcestershire

Caldewell ♦♦♦
Pershore Road, Stoulton, Worcester WR7 4RL
T: (01905) 840894
F: (01905) 840894
E: sheila@caldewell.demon.co.uk
I: www.caldewell.com

STOURBRIDGE
West Midlands

St. Elizabeth's Cottage ♦♦♦♦
Woodman Lane, Clent, Stourbridge, West Midlands DY9 9PX
T: (01562) 883883
F: (01562) 885034
E: st_elizabeth_cot@btconnect.com

STOURPORT-ON-SEVERN
Worcestershire

Baldwin House ♦♦♦
8 Lichfield Street, Stourport-on-Severn, Worcestershire DY13 9EU
T: (01299) 877221 & 824613
F: (01299) 877221
E: baldwinhousebb@aol.com

STOW-ON-THE-WOLD
Gloucestershire

Aston House ◆◆◆◆
Broadwell, Moreton-in-Marsh,
Gloucestershire GL56 0TJ
T: (01451) 830475 &
07773 452037
E: fja@netcomuk.co.uk
I: www.netcomuk.
co.uk/~nmfa/aston_house.html

The Beeches ◆◆◆
Fosse Lane, Stow-on-the-Wold,
Cheltenham, Gloucestershire
GL54 1EH
T: (01451) 870836

Corsham Field Farmhouse
◆◆◆
Bledington Road, Stow-on-the-
Wold, Cheltenham,
Gloucestershire GL54 1JH
T: (01451) 831750

**The Cotswold Garden Tea
Room & B&B.** ◆◆◆
Wells Cottage, Digbeth Street,
Stow-on-the-Wold,
Cheltenham, Gloucestershire
GL54 1BN
T: (01451) 870999

Crestow House ◆◆◆◆
Stow-on-the-Wold,
Gloucestershire GL54 1JX
T: (01451) 830969
F: (01451) 832129
E: fjsimon@compuserve.com
I: ourworld.compuserve.
com/homespaces/fjsimon

Cross Keys Cottage ◆◆◆
Park Street, Stow-on-the-Wold,
Cheltenham, Gloucestershire
GL54 1AQ
T: (01451) 831128
F: (01451) 831128

Fairview Farmhouse ◆◆◆◆
Bledington Road, Stow-on-the-
Wold, Gloucestershire GL54 1JH
T: (01451) 830279 &
07711 979944
F: (01451) 830279
E: sdavis0145@aol.com
I: www.SmoothHound.co.uk/shs

The Fox Inn ◆◆◆◆
Stow-on-the-Wold,
Cheltenham, Gloucestershire
GL56 0UR
T: (01451) 870555
F: (01451) 870669
E: info@foxinn.net
I: www.foxinn.net

The Gate Lodge ◆◆◆◆
Stow Hill, Stow-on-the-Wold,
Cheltenham, Gloucestershire
GL54 1JZ
T: (01451) 832103

Honeysuckle Cottage ◆◆◆◆
Kings Arms Lane, Stow-on-the-
Wold, Cheltenham,
Gloucestershire GL54 1AF
T: (01451) 830973 &
07733 126430
E: hsucklecottage@aol.com

Littlebroom ◆◆◆◆
Maugersbury, Stow-on-the-
Wold, Cheltenham,
Gloucestershire GL54 1HP
T: (01451) 830510
E: davidandbrenda@talk21.com
I: www.accofind.com/

Maugersbury Manor ◆◆◆
Stow-on-the-Wold,
Cheltenham, Gloucestershire
GL54 1HP
T: (01451) 830581
F: (01451) 870902
E: karen@manorholidays.co.uk
I: www.manorholidays.co.uk

Mount Pleasant Farm
Rating Applied For
Oddington Road, Stow-on-the-
Wold, Cheltenham,
Gloucestershire GL54 1JJ
T: (01451) 832078
F: (01451) 832078
E: sgaden72@aol.com

Number Nine ◆◆◆◆
9 Park Street, Stow-on-the-
Wold, Cheltenham,
Gloucestershire GL54 1AQ
T: (01451) 870333 &
07836 205431
F: (01451) 870445
E: numbernine@talk21.com

Old Farmhouse Hotel ◆◆◆◆
Lower Swell, Stow-on-the-Wold,
Cheltenham, Gloucestershire
GL54 1LF
T: (01451) 830232 &
0800 0561150
F: (01451) 870962
E: oldfarm@globalnet.co.uk
I: www.oldfarm.co.uk

Pear Tree Cottage ◆◆◆
High Street, Stow-on-the-Wold,
Cheltenham, Gloucestershire
GL54 1DL
T: (01451) 831210
E: peartreecottage@btinternet.
com

South Hill Farmhouse ◆◆◆
Fosseway, Stow-on-the-Wold,
Cheltenham, Gloucestershire
GL54 1JU
T: (01451) 831888
F: (01451) 832255
E: info@southhill.co.uk
I: www.southhill.co.uk

South Hill Lodge ◆◆◆◆
Fosseway, Stow-on-the-Wold,
Cheltenham, Gloucestershire
GL54 1JU
T: (01451) 831083 & 870694
F: (01451) 870694
E: digby@southilllodge.
freeserve.co.uk
I: www.SmoothHound.
co.uk/hotels/southhill

Tall Trees ◆◆◆
Oddington Road, Stow-on-the-
Wold, Cheltenham,
Gloucestershire GL54 1AL
T: (01451) 831296
F: (01451) 870049
E: talltreestow@aol.com

White Hart Inn ◆◆
The Square, Stow-on-the-Wold,
Cheltenham, Gloucestershire
GL54 1AF
T: (01451) 830674
F: (01451) 830090

Woodlands ◆◆◆◆
Upper Swell, Stow-on-the-Wold,
Cheltenham, Gloucestershire
GL54 1EW
T: (01451) 832346

Wyck Hill Lodge ◆◆◆◆◆
Burford Road, Stow-on-the-
Wold, Cheltenham,
Gloucestershire GL54 1HT
T: (01451) 830141
E: gkhwyck@compuserve.com

STOWE-BY-CHARTLEY
Staffordshire

The Plough Inn ◆◆◆
Amerton, Stowe-by-Chartley,
Stafford ST18 0LA
T: (01889) 270308
F: (01889) 271131

STRAGGLETHORPE
Lincolnshire

Stragglethorpe Hall ◆◆◆◆
Stragglethorpe, Lincoln LN5 0QZ
T: (01400) 272308
F: (01400) 273816
E: stragglethorpe@compuserve.
com
I: www.stragglethorpe.com

STRATFORD-UPON-AVON
Warwickshire

Aberfoyle Guest House ◆◆◆
3 Evesham Place, Stratford-
upon-Avon, Warwickshire
CV37 6HT
T: (01789) 295703
F: (01789) 295703

Aidan Guest House ◆◆◆◆
11 Evesham Place, Stratford-
upon-Avon, Warwickshire
CV37 6HT
T: (01789) 292824 &
0709 1000445
F: (01789) 269072
E: john2aidan@aol.com
I: www.aidanhouse.co.uk

Alderminster Farm ◆◆◆◆
Alderminster, Stratford-upon-
Avon, Warwickshire CV37 8BP
T: (01789) 450774
F: (01789) 450924
E: christopher_denley.wright@
virgin.net
I: www.tpointmc.demon.
co.uk/alderminster/.

All Seasons ◆◆
51 Grove Road, Stratford-upon-
Avon, Warwickshire CV37 6PB
T: (01789) 293404
F: (01789) 293404

Amelia Linhill Guesthouse
◆◆◆
35 Evesham Place, Stratford-
upon-Avon, Warwickshire
CV37 6HT
T: (01789) 292879
F: (01789) 299691
E: Linhill@bigwig.net
I: Linhillguesthouse.co.uk

The Applegarth ◆◆◆
Warwick Road, Stratford-upon-
Avon, Warwickshire CV37 6YW
T: (01789) 267388
F: (01789) 267388
E: applegarth@supanet.com

Arden Park Hotel ◆◆◆
6 Arden Street, Stratford-upon-
Avon, Warwickshire CV37 6PA
T: (01789) 296072 &
0798 0479025
F: (01789) 296072

Arrandale Guesthouse ◆◆◆
208 Evesham Road, Stratford-
upon-Avon, Warwickshire
CV37 9AS
T: (01789) 267112

Ashley Court Hotel ◆◆◆
55 Shipston Road, Stratford
upon-Avon, Warwickshire
CV37 7LN
T: (01789) 297278
F: (01789) 204453
E: info@ashleycourthotel.co.uk
I: www.ashleycourthotel.co.uk

Avon View Hotel ◆◆◆◆
121 Shipston Road, Stratford-
upon-Avon, Warwickshire
CV37 7LW
T: (01789) 297542
F: (01789) 292936
E: avon.view@lineone.net

Avonlea ◆◆◆◆
47 Shipston Road, Stratford-
upon-Avon, Warwickshire
CV37 7LN
T: (01789) 205940
F: (01789) 209115
E: avonlea-stratford@lineone.
net
I: www.avonlea-stratford.co.uk

34 Banbury Road ◆◆◆
Stratford-upon-Avon,
Warwickshire CV37 7HY
T: (01789) 269714
E: clodagh@lycosmail.com
I: www.smoothhound.
co.uk/hotels/34banbur.html

Barbette ◆◆◆
165 Evesham Road, Stratford-
upon-Avon, Warwickshire
CV37 9BP
T: (01789) 297822

The Blue Boar Inn ◆◆◆
Temple Grafton, Alcester,
Warwickshire B49 6NR
T: (01789) 750010
F: (01789) 750635
E: blueboar@covlink.co.uk
I: www.stratford.upon.avon.
co.uk/blueboar

Bradbourne House ◆◆◆◆
44 Shipston Road, Stratford-
upon-Avon, Warwickshire
CV37 7LP
T: (01789) 204178
F: (01789) 262335
I: www.bradbourne-house.co.uk

Brett House ◆◆◆
8 Broad Walk, Stratford-upon-
Avon, Warwickshire CV37 6HS
T: (01789) 266374
F: (01789) 414027
I: www.bretthouse.co.uk

Broadlands Guest House ◆◆◆
23 Evesham Place, Stratford-
upon-Avon, Warwickshire
CV37 6HT
T: (01789) 299181
F: (01789) 551382
E: broadlands.com@virgin.net

Brook Lodge Guest House
◆◆◆◆
192 Alcester Road, Stratford-
upon-Avon, Warwickshire
CV37 9DR
T: (01789) 295988
F: (01789) 295988
E: brooklodgeguesthouse@
btinternet.com
I: www.smoothhound.
co.uk/hotels/brooklod.html

Burton Farm ◆◆◆◆
Bishopton, Stratford-upon-
Avon, Warwickshire CV37 0RW
T: (01789) 293338
F: (01789) 262877
E: tony.crook@ukonline.co.uk

Carlton Guest House ◆◆◆
22 Evesham Place, Stratford-
upon-Avon, Warwickshire
CV37 6HT
T: (01789) 293548
F: (01789) 293548

Chadwyns Guest House
◆◆◆◆
6 Broad Walk, Stratford-upon-
Avon, Warwickshire CV37 6HS
T: (01789) 269077
F: (01789) 298855
E: reservations@chadwyns.
freeserve.co.uk
I: www.chadwyns.freeserve.
co.uk

Church Farm ◆◆◆
Dorsington, Stratford-upon-
Avon, Warwickshire CV37 8AX
T: (01789) 720471 &
07831 504194
F: (01789) 720830
E: chfarmdorsington@aol.com
I: www.churchfarmstratford.
co.uk
(symbol)

Church Farm ◆◆◆
Long Marston, Stratford-upon-
Avon, Warwickshire CV37 8RH
T: (01789) 720275
F: (01789) 720275
E: wiggychurchfarm@hotmail.
com
I: www.churchfarmhouse.co.uk

Clomendy Bed and Breakfast
◆◆◆
10 Broad Walk, Stratford-upon-
Avon, Warwickshire CV37 6HS
T: (01789) 266957

Courtland Hotel ◆◆
12 Guild Street, Stratford-upon-
Avon, Warwickshire CV37 6RE
T: (01789) 292401
F: (01789) 292401
E: bridget.johnson4@virgin.net
I: www.uk-vacation.
com/courtland

**Craig Cleeve House Hotel &
Restaurant**◆◆◆◆
67-69 Shipston Road, Stratford-
upon-Avon, Warwickshire
CV37 7LW
T: (01789) 296573
F: (01789) 299452
E: craigcleev@aol.com

Curtain Call ◆◆◆
142 Alcester Road, Stratford-
upon-Avon, Warwickshire
CV37 9DR
T: (01789) 267734
F: (01789) 267734
E: curtaincall@btinternet.com
I: www.curtaincallguesthouse.
co.uk

Cymbeline House ◆◆◆
24 Evesham Place, Stratford-
upon-Avon, Warwickshire
CV37 6HT
T: (01789) 292958
F: (01789) 292958

Dylan Guesthouse ◆◆◆
10 Evesham Place, Stratford-
upon-Avon, Warwickshire
CV37 6HT
T: (01789) 204819
E: dylanguesthouse@lineone.
net
I: www.thedylan.co.uk

East Bank House ◆◆◆◆
19 Warwick Road, Stratford-
upon-Avon, Warwickshire
CV37 6YW
T: (01789) 292758
F: (01789) 292758
E: eastbank.house@virgin.net
I: www.east-bank-house.co.uk
(symbol)

Eastnor House Hotel ◆◆◆◆
Shipston Road, Stratford-upon-
Avon, Warwickshire CV37 7LN
T: (01789) 268115
F: (01789) 266516
E: enquiries@eastnorhouse.com
I: www.eastnorhouse.com

The Emsley Guest House
◆◆◆◆
4 Arden Street, Stratford-upon-
Avon, Warwickshire CV37 6PA
T: (01789) 299557
F: (01789) 299023
E: emsleygh@bigfoot.com
I: www.theemsley.co.uk

**Ettington Chase Conference
Centre** ◆◆◆◆◆
Banbury Road, Ettington,
Stratford-upon-Avon,
Warwickshire CV37 7NZ
T: (01789) 740000
F: (01789) 740909
E: ettconf@hayleycc.co.uk
I: www.hayley-conf.co.uk

Eversley Bears' Guest House
◆◆◆◆
37 Grove Road, Stratford-upon-
Avon, Warwickshire CV37 6PB
T: (01789) 292334
F: (01789) 292334
E: eversleybears@btinternet.
com
I: www.stratford-upon-avon.
co.uk/eversleybears.htm

Faviere ◆◆◆◆
127 Shipston Road, Stratford-
upon-Avon, Warwickshire
CV37 7LW
T: (01789) 293764
F: (01789) 269365
E: guestsfaviere@cwcom.net
I: www.faviere.com

Folly Farm Cottage ◆◆◆◆
Back Street, Ilmington,
Shipston-on-Stour,
Warwickshire CV36 4LJ
T: (01608) 682425
F: (01608) 682425
E: slowe@follyfarm.co.uk
I: www.follyfarm.co.uk

Gravelside Barn ◆◆◆◆◆
Binton, Stratford-upon-Avon,
Warwickshire CV37 9TU
T: (01789) 750502
F: (01789) 750502
E: denise@gravelside.fsnet.
co.uk

Green Gables ◆◆◆
47 Banbury Road, Stratford-
upon-Avon, Warwickshire
CV37 7HW
T: (01789) 205557
E: jeankerr@talk21.com
I: www.stratford-upon-avon.
co.uk/greengables.htm

Green Haven ◆◆◆◆
217 Evesham Road, Stratford-
upon-Avon, Warwickshire
CV37 9AS
T: (01789) 297874
E: information@green-haven.
co.uk
I: www.green-haven.co.uk

Grosvenor Villa ◆◆◆
9 Evesham Place, Stratford-
upon-Avon, Warwickshire
CV37 6HT
T: (01789) 266192
F: (01789) 297353
E: grosvenorvilla.fsbusiness.
co.uk

Hampton Lodge Guest House
◆◆◆◆
38 Shipston Road, Stratford-
upon-Avon, Warwickshire
CV37 7LP
T: (01789) 299374 & 267742
F: (01789) 299374
E: hamptonlodge@aol.com
I: www.hamptonlodge.co.uk

Harvard Private Hotel ◆◆◆
89 Shipston Road, Stratford
upon-Avon, Warwickshire
CV37 7LW
T: (01789) 262623 & 261354
F: (01789) 261354

Heron Lodge ◆◆◆
260 Alcester Road, Stratford-
upon-Avon, Warwickshire
CV37 9JQ
T: (01789) 299169
E: chrisandbob@heronlodge.
com
I: www.heronlodge.com

Highcroft ◆◆◆
Banbury Road, Stratford-upon-
Avon, Warwickshire CV37 7NF
T: (01789) 296293
F: (01789) 415236
E: suedavies_highcroft@
hotmail.com
I: www.Smoothhound.co.uk

Houndshill House ◆◆◆
Banbury Road, Ettington,
Stratford-upon-Avon,
Warwickshire CV37 7NS
T: (01789) 740267
F: (01789) 740075

Howard Arms ◆◆◆◆◆
Lower Green, Ilmington,
Shipston-on-Stour,
Warwickshire CV36 4LT
T: (01608) 682226
F: (01608) 682226
E: howard.arms@virgin.net
I: www.howardarms.com

Ingon Bank Farm ◆◆◆
Warwick Road, Stratford-upon-
Avon, Warwickshire CV37 0NY
T: (01789) 292642
F: (01789) 292642

Kawartha House ◆◆◆
39 Grove Road, Stratford-upon-
Avon, Warwickshire CV37 6PB
T: (01789) 204469
F: (01789) 292837
E: mavis@kawarthahouse.
freeserve.co.uk
I: www.stratford-upon-avon.
co.uk/kawartha.htm

Marlyn Hotel ◆◆◆
3 Chestnut Walk, Stratford-
upon-Avon, Warwickshire
CV37 6HG
T: (01789) 293752 &
07973 492673
F: (01789) 293752
E: evansmarlynhotel@aol.com

Mary Arden Inn ◆◆◆◆
The Green, Wilmcote, Stratford-
upon-Avon, Warwickshire
CV37 9XJ
T: (01789) 267030
F: (01789) 204875

Melita Private Hotel ◆◆◆◆
37 Shipston Road, Stratford-
upon-Avon, Warwickshire
CV37 7LN
T: (01789) 292432
F: (01789) 204867
E: Melita37@email.msn.com
I: www.melitahotel.co.uk

Meridian Guest House ◆◆◆
3 St. Gregory's Road, Stratford-
upon-Avon, Warwickshire
CV37 6UH
T: (01789) 292356
E: meridian.guesthouse@virgin.
net
I: www.meridianguesthouse.
co.uk

Midway ◆◆◆◆
182 Evesham Road, Stratford-
upon-Avon, Warwickshire
CV37 9BS
T: (01789) 204154

Mil-Mar ◆◆◆◆
96 Alcester Road, Stratford-
upon-Avon, Warwickshire
CV37 9DP
T: (01789) 267095
F: (01789) 262205
E: milmar@btinternet.com

Minola Guest House ◆◆◆
25 Evesham Place, Stratford-
upon-Avon, Warwickshire
CV37 6HT
T: (01789) 293573
F: (01789) 551625

Moonlight Bed & Breakfast
◆◆◆
144 Alcester Road, Stratford-
upon-Avon, Warwickshire
CV37 9DR
T: (01789) 298213

Moss Cottage ◆◆◆◆
61 Evesham Road, Stratford-
upon-Avon, Warwickshire
CV37 9BA
T: (01789) 294770
F: (01789) 294770
E: pauline_rush@onetel.net.uk

The Myrtles Bed and Breakfast
◆◆◆◆
6 Rother Street, Stratford-upon-
Avon, Warwickshire CV37 6LU
T: (01789) 295511

Nando's ◆◆
18-19 Evesham Place, Stratford-upon-Avon, Warwickshire
CV37 6HT
T: (01789) 204907
F: (01789) 204907

Newlands ◆◆◆◆
7 Broad Walk, Stratford-upon-Avon, Warwickshire CV37 6HS
T: (01789) 298449
F: (01789) 267806
E: newlandslynwalter@hotmail.com
I: www.smoothhound.co.uk/hotels/newlands.html

Oxstalls Farm ◆◆◆
Warwick Road, Stratford-upon-Avon, Warwickshire CV37 0NS
T: (01789) 205277 & 730224
F: (01789) 205277

Park View ◆◆◆◆
57 Rother Street, Stratford-upon-Avon, Warwickshire
CV37 6LT
T: (01789) 266839
F: (01789) 266839

Parkfield ◆◆◆
3 Broad Walk, Stratford-upon-Avon, Warwickshire CV37 6HS
T: (01789) 293313
F: (01789) 293313
E: parkfield@btinternet.com
I: www.parkfieldbandb.co.uk

Payton Hotel ◆◆◆◆
6 John Street, Stratford-upon-Avon, Warwickshire CV37 6UB
T: (01789) 266442
F: (01789) 294410
E: info@payton.co.uk
I: www.payton.co.uk

Peartree Cottage ◆◆◆◆
7 Church Road, Wilmcote, Stratford-upon-Avon, Warwickshire CV37 9UX
T: (01789) 205889
F: (01789) 262862
E: manager@peartreecot.co.uk
I: www.peartreecot.co.uk

Penryn Guesthouse ◆◆◆◆
126 Alcester Road, Stratford-upon-Avon, Warwickshire
CV37 9DP
T: (01789) 293718 & 07889 486345
F: (01789) 266077
E: penrynhouse@btinternet.com
I: www.stratford-upon-avon.co.uk/penryn.htm

Penshurst Guesthouse ◆◆◆
34 Evesham Place, Stratford-upon-Avon, Warwickshire
CV37 6HT
T: (01789) 205259 & 295322
F: (01789) 295322
E: penshurst@cwcom.net
I: www.smoothhound.co.uk/hotels/penshurs/html

The Poplars ◆◆◆
Mansell Farm, Newbold-on-Stour, Stratford-upon-Avon, Warwickshire CV37 8BZ
T: (01789) 450540
F: (01789) 450540
E: rspencer@farming.co.uk
I: www.SmoothHound.co.uk/hotel/poplars2html

The Queens Head ◆◆◆◆
Ely Street, Stratford-upon-Avon, Warwickshire CV37 6LN
T: (01789) 204914
F: (01789) 772983
E: richard@distinctivepubs.freeserve.co.uk
I: www.distinctivepubs.co.uk

Quilt and Croissants ◆◆◆
33 Evesham Place, Stratford-upon-Avon, Warwickshire
CV37 6HT
T: (01789) 267629
F: (01789) 551651
E: rooms@quilt-croissants.demon.co.uk
I: www.smoothhound.co.uk/hotels/quilt.html

Ravenhurst ◆◆◆
2 Broad Walk, Stratford-upon-Avon, Warwickshire CV37 6HS
T: (01789) 292515
E: ravaccom@waverider.co.uk
I: www.ravenhurstguesthouse.co.uk

Salamander Guest House ◆◆◆
40 Grove Road, Stratford-upon-Avon, Warwickshire CV37 6PB
T: (01789) 205728 & 297843
F: (01789) 205728
E: sejget@nova88.freeserve.co.uk

Shakespeare's View ◆◆◆◆◆
Kings Lane, Snitterfield, Stratford-upon-Avon, Warwickshire CV37 0QB
T: (01789) 731824 & 07973 144151
F: (01789) 731824
E: shakespeares.view@btinternet.co.uk
I: www.shakespeares.view.btinternet.co.uk

Stratheden Hotel ◆◆◆
5 Chapel Street, Stratford-upon-Avon, Warwickshire CV37 6EP
T: (01789) 297119
F: (01789) 297119
E: richard@stratheden.fsnet.co.uk
I: www.stratheden.co.uk

Sunnydale Guest House ◆◆◆
64 Shipston Road, Stratford-upon-Avon, Warwickshire CV37 7LP
T: (01789) 295166

Victoria Spa Lodge ◆◆◆◆
Bishopton Lane, Bishopton, Stratford-upon-Avon, Warwickshire CV37 9QY
T: (01789) 267985
F: (01789) 204728
E: ptozer@victoriaspalodge.demon.co.uk
I: www.stratford-upon-avon.co.uk/victoriaspa.htm

Virginia Lodge Guest House ◆◆◆◆
12 Evesham Place, Stratford-upon-Avon, Warwickshire CV37 6HT
T: (01789) 292157 & 266605
F: (01789) 292157
E: pamela83@btinternet.com

Whitchurch Farm ◆◆◆
Wimpstone, CV37 8NS
T: (01789) 450275 & 07799 280 564
F: (01789) 450275

Woodstock Guest House ◆◆◆◆
30 Grove Road, Stratford-upon-Avon, Warwickshire CV37 6PB
T: (01789) 299881
F: (01789) 299881
E: woodstockhouse@compuserve.com

| STRETTON |
| Staffordshire |

Dovecliff Hall ◆◆◆◆◆
Dovecliff Road, Stretton, Burton upon Trent, Staffordshire
DE13 0DJ
T: (01283) 531818
F: (01283) 516546

| STRETTON ON FOSSE |
| Warwickshire |

Jasmine Cottage ◆◆◆
Stretton on Fosse, Moreton-in-Marsh, Gloucestershire
GL56 9SA
T: (01608) 661972 & 07701 002990

The Little House
Rating Applied For
4 Carsons Close, Stretton on Fosse, Moreton-in-Marsh, Gloucestershire GL56 9SJ
T: (01608) 664592

| STROUD |
| Gloucestershire |

Ashleigh House ◆◆◆◆
Bussage, Stroud, Gloucestershire GL6 8AZ
T: (01453) 883944
F: (01453) 886931

Beechcroft ◆◆◆
Brownshill, Stroud, Gloucestershire GL6 8AG
T: (01453) 883422 & 07976 657797

Burleigh Farm ◆◆◆◆
Minchinhampton, Stroud, Gloucestershire GL5 2PF
T: (01453) 883112
F: (01453) 883112

The Clothier's Arms ◆◆◆
1 Bath Road, Stroud, Gloucestershire GL5 3JJ
T: (01453) 763801
F: (01453) 757161
E: luciano@clothiersarms.demon.co.uk
I: www.clothiersarms.co.uk

Downfield Hotel ◆◆◆
134 Cainscross Road, Stroud, Gloucestershire GL5 4HN
T: (01453) 764496
F: (01453) 753150
E: messenger@downfieldotel.demon.co.uk
I: www.downfieldotel.demon.co.uk

Edendale Guesthouse ◆◆◆
92 Westward Road, Cainscross, Stroud, Gloucestershire GL5 4JA
T: (01453) 751490
F: (01453) 751490

The Firs Bed and Breakfast ◆◆◆◆
Selsley Road, North Woodchester, Stroud, Gloucestershire GL5 5NQ
T: (01453) 873088 & 07932 172553
F: (01453) 873053
E: cwalsh3088@aol.com

Grove Cottage ◆◆◆◆
Browns Hill, Stroud, Gloucestershire GL6 8AJ
T: (01453) 882561

Pretoria Villa ◆◆◆◆
Wells Road, Eastcombe, Stroud, Gloucestershire GL6 7EE
T: (01452) 770435
F: (01452) 770435
E: Glynis@G.salomon.freeserve.co.uk

Threeways ◆◆◆
Bisley Road, Lypiatt Hill, Stroud, Gloucestershire GL6 7LQ
T: (01453) 756001
E: threewaysbedandbreakfast@tinyworld.co.uk

The Yew Tree Bed and Breakfast ◆◆◆
Walls Quarry, Brimscombe, Stroud, Gloucestershire GL5 2PA
T: (01453) 887594
F: (01453) 883428
E: elizabeth.peters@tesco.net
I: www.uk-bedandbreakfasts.com/Gloucestershire/Stroud

| STURTON-BY-STOW |
| Lincolnshire |

Ivy Cottage ◆◆◆
Stow Road, Sturton-by-Stow, Lincoln LN1 2BZ
T: (01427) 788023

| SULGRAVE |
| Northamptonshire |

Rectory Farm ◆◆◆
Little Street, Sulgrave, Banbury, Oxfordshire OX17 2SG
T: (01295) 760261
F: (01295) 760089
E: rectoryfarm@talk21.com

Wemyss Farm
Rating Applied For
Sulgrave, Banbury, Oxfordshire OX17 2RX
T: (01295) 760323
F: (01295) 760323

| SUTTON CHENEY |
| Leicestershire |

The Almshouse ◆◆◆
Sutton Cheney, Nuneaton, Warwickshire CV13 0AH
T: (01455) 291050
F: (01455) 290601

| SUTTON-ON-SEA |
| Lincolnshire |

Athelstone Lodge Hotel ◆◆◆
25 Trusthorpe Road, Sutton-on-Sea, Mablethorpe, Lincolnshire LN12 2LR
T: (01507) 441521
I: www.athelstonelodge.co.uk

Bacchus Hotel ◆◆◆
High Street, Sutton-on-Sea, Mablethorpe, Lincolnshire LN12 2EY
T: (01507) 441204
F: (01507) 441204

| SUTTON-ON-TRENT |
| Nottinghamshire |

Fiveways ◆◆◆
Barrel Hill Road, Sutton-on-Trent, Newark, Nottinghamshire NG23 6PT
T: (01636) 822086

SWADLINCOTE
Derbyshire

Ferne Cottage ♦♦♦
5 Black Horse Hill, Appleby
Magna, Swadlincote, Derbyshire
DE12 7AQ
T: (01530) 271772
F: (01503) 270652

Hurst Farm Guesthouse
♦♦♦♦
Netherseal Road, Chilcote,
Swadlincote, Derbyshire
DE12 8DQ
T: (01827) 373853 &
07967 044162
E: suehfgh@aol.com

SWANNINGTON
Leicestershire

Hillfield House ♦♦♦♦
52 Station Hill, Swannington,
Leicester LE67 8RH
T: (01530) 837 414
F: (01530) 458 233

SWARKESTONE
Derbyshire

October House ♦♦♦♦
The Water Meadows,
Swarkestone, Derby DE73 1JA
T: (01332) 705849
E: longsons@hotmail.com

SWAYFIELD
Lincolnshire

The Royal Oak Inn ♦♦♦
High Street, Swayfield,
Grantham, Lincolnshire
NG33 4LL
T: (01476) 550247
F: (01476) 550996

SWINSCOE
Staffordshire

Common End Farm ♦♦♦♦
Swinscoe, Ashbourne,
Derbyshire DE6 2BW
T: (01335) 342342 & 342342
I: cartman/commonendfarm/
Index.html

SWYNNERTON
Staffordshire

Home Farm ♦♦
Swynnerton, Stone,
Staffordshire ST15 0RA
T: (01782) 796241

SYMONDS YAT EAST
Herefordshire

Garth Cottage ♦♦♦♦
Symonds Yat East, Ross-on-
Wye, Herefordshire HR9 6JL
T: (01600) 890364
F: (01600) 890364

Rose Cottage Tea Gardens
♦♦♦
Symonds Yat East, Ross-on-
Wye, Herefordshire HR9 6JL
T: (01600) 890514 &
07721 423890
F: (01600) 890498
I: www.SmoothHound.
co.uk/hotels/rose2.html

SYRESHAM
Northamptonshire

The Priory ♦♦
36 Wappenham Road,
Syresham, Brackley,
Northamptonshire NN13 5HH
T: (01280) 850218 & 850603
F: (01280) 850576
E: info@signpost.co.uk

TADDINGTON
Derbyshire

Ade House ♦♦♦♦
Taddington, Buxton, Derbyshire
SK17 9TY
T: (01298) 85203

The Old Bake and Brewhouse
♦♦♦
Blackwell Hall, Blackwell in the
Peak, Taddington, Buxton,
Derbyshire SK17 9TQ
T: (01298) 85271
F: (01298) 85271
E: christine.gregory@btinternet.
com
I: www.peakdistrictfarmhols.
co.uk

TAMWORTH
Staffordshire

Bonehill Farm House ♦♦♦
Bonehill Road, Tamworth,
Staffordshire B78 3HP
T: (01827) 310797
E: james@bonehill.junglelink.
co.uk

Oak Tree Farm ♦♦♦♦♦
Hints Road, Hopwas, Tamworth,
Staffordshire B78 3AA
T: (01827) 56807 &
07836 387887
F: (01827) 56807

The Peel Hotel ♦♦♦♦
14b Aldergate, Tamworth,
Staffordshire B79 7DL
T: (01827) 87070
F: (01827) 69812

TANSLEY
Derbyshire

Packhorse Farm ♦♦♦♦
Tansley, Matlock, Derbyshire
DE4 5LF
T: (01629) 580950
F: (01629) 580950

Packhorse Farm Bungalow
♦♦♦♦
Tansley, Matlock, Derbyshire
DE4 5LF
T: (01629) 582781

TEDDINGTON
Gloucestershire

Bengrove Farm ♦♦♦
Bengrove, Teddington,
Tewkesbury, Gloucestershire
GL20 8JB
T: (01242) 620332
F: (01242) 620851

TELFORD
Shropshire

Albion Inn ♦♦♦
West Street, St Georges, Telford,
Shropshire TF2 9AD
T: (01952) 614193

Allscott Inn ♦♦
Walcot, Wellington, Telford,
Shropshire TF6 5EQ
T: (01952) 248484
F: (01952) 222622
E: allscottinn@telfordlife.co.uk

Coppice Heights ♦♦♦
Spout Lane, Little Wenlock,
Telford, Shropshire TF6 5BL
T: (01952) 505655

Falcon Hotel ♦♦♦
Holyhead Road, Wellington,
Telford, Shropshire TF1 2DD
T: (01952) 255011
F: falconhotel@hotmail.com

The Golden Ball Inn
Rating applied for
Newbridge Road, Ironbridge,
Telford, Shropshire TF8 7BA
T: (01952) 432179
F: (01952) 433123
E: matrowland@hotmail.com

Grove House Guesthouse ♦♦♦
Stafford Street, St Georges,
Telford, Shropshire TF2 9JW
T: (01952) 616140
F: (01952) 616140

The Mill House ♦♦♦♦
Shrewsbury Road, High Ercall,
Telford, Shropshire TF6 6BE
T: (01952) 770394
F: (01952) 770394
E: mill-house@talk21.com
I: www.virtual-shropshire.
co.uk/millhouse

Old Rectory ♦♦♦♦
Stirchley Village, Telford,
Shropshire TF3 1DY
T: (01952) 596308 & 596518
F: (01952) 596308
E: hazelmiller@waitrose.co.uk

**The Old Vicarage Country
House** ♦♦♦♦
Church Street, St George's,
Telford, Shropshire TF2 9LZ
T: (01952) 616437
F: (01952) 616952
E: skristian@aol.com
I: www.oldvicarage.uk.com

Stone House ♦♦♦♦
Shifnal Road, Priorslee, Telford,
Shropshire TF2 9NN
T: (01952) 290119 &
07976 847278
F: (01952) 290119
E: dave@
stonehouseguesthouse.
freeserve.co.uk
I: www.smoothhound.
co.uk/hotels/stonehou.html

West Ridge Bed and Breakfast
♦♦♦♦
Kemberton, Shifnal, Shropshire
TF11 9LB
T: (01952) 580992
F: (01952) 580992
E: westridge.bb@ntlworld.com
I: www.westridgebb.com

Westbrook House ♦♦
78a Holy Head Road, Ketly,
Telford, Shropshire TF1 4DJ
T: (01952) 615535 &
07752 612192
F: (01952) 615535

Willow House ♦♦♦
137 Holyhead Road, Wellington,
Telford, Shropshire TF1 2DH
T: (01952) 223817
F: (01952) 223817

TENBURY WELLS
Worcestershire

Court Farm ♦♦♦♦
Hanley Childe, Tenbury Wells,
Worcestershire WR15 8QY
T: (01885) 410265

Elliott House Farm ♦♦♦♦
Vine Lane, Kyre, Tenbury Wells,
Worcestershire WR15 8RL
T: (01885) 410302 &
07836 533049
F: (01885) 410240

Peacock Inn ♦♦♦♦
Worcester Road, Boraston,
Tenbury Wells, Worcestershire
WR15 8LL
T: (01584) 810506 & 811236
F: (01584) 811236
E: juidler@fsbdial.co.uk
I: www.smoothhound.
co.uk/hotels/peacockinn.html

TETBURY
Gloucestershire

Folly Farm Cottages ♦♦
Long Newnton, Tetbury,
Gloucestershire GL8 8XA
T: (01666) 502475
F: (01666) 502358
E: info@gtb.co.uk
I: www.gtb.co.uk

The Old Rectory ♦♦♦♦
Didmarton, Badminton, Avon
GL9 1DS
T: (01454) 238233
F: (01454) 238909

TEWKESBURY
Gloucestershire

**Abbey Antiques Bed and
Breakfast** ♦♦♦
62 Church Street, Tewkesbury,
Gloucestershire GL20 5RZ
T: (01684) 298145
F: (01684) 292378

The Abbey Hotel ♦♦
67 Church Street, Tewkesbury,
Gloucestershire GL20 5RX
T: (01684) 294247
F: (01684) 297208
E: reservations@abbey-hotel.
totalserve.co.uk

Abbots Court Farm ♦♦♦
Church End, Twyning,
Tewkesbury, Gloucestershire
GL20 6DA
T: (01684) 292515
F: (01684) 292515
E: bernieabbotscourt.fsbusiness.
co.uk

Alstone Fields Farm ♦♦♦♦♦
Teddington Hands, Stow Road,
Tewkesbury, Gloucestershire
GL20 8NG
T: (01242) 620592 & 621527

Carrant Brook House ♦♦♦
3 Rope Walk, Tewkesbury,
Gloucestershire GL20 5DS
T: (01684) 290355 & 0771 808
5136
E: lorraine@carrantbrookhouse.
co.uk

The Fleet Inn ♦♦♦♦
Twyning, Tewkesbury,
Gloucestershire GL20 6DG
T: (01684) 274310
F: (01684) 291612
E: fleetinn@hotmail.com
I: www.fleetinn.com

Jessop House Hotel ♦♦♦♦
65 Church Street, Tewkesbury,
Gloucestershire GL20 5RZ
T: (01684) 292017
F: (01684) 273076
E: LesThurlow@aol.com
I: www.jessophousehotel.com

Malvern View Guest House ♦♦
1 St. Mary's Road, Tewkesbury,
Gloucestershire GL20 5SE
T: (01684) 292776

Town Street Farm
Rating Applied For
Tirley, Gloucester GL19 4HG
T: (01452) 780442
F: (01452) 780890
E: townstreetfarm@hotmail.com

Two Back of Avon ◆◆◆
2 Back of Avon, Riverside Walk,
Tewkesbury, Gloucestershire
GL20 5BA
T: (01684) 298935 &
07711 947016

THORPE
Derbyshire
Hillcrest House ◆◆◆
Dovedale, Thorpe, Ashbourne,
Derbyshire DE6 2AW
T: (01335) 350436
F: (01335) 350436
E: hillcresthouse@freenet.co.uk
I: www.ashbourne-towncom/accom/hillcrest

The Old Orchard ◆◆◆
Stoney Lane, Thorpe, Ashbourne,
Derbyshire DE6 2AW
T: (01335) 350410
F: (01335) 350410

THRAPSTON
Northamptonshire
The Poplars ◆◆◆◆
50 Oundle Road, Thrapston,
Kettering, Northamptonshire
NN14 4PD
T: (01832) 732499

THURLBY
Lincolnshire
6 The Pingles ◆◆◆◆
Thurlby, Bourne, Lincolnshire
PE10 0EX
T: (01778) 394517

TIBSHELF
Derbyshire
Rosvern House Bed and Breakfast ◆◆◆◆
High Street, Tibshelf, Alfreton,
Derbyshire DE55 5NY
T: (01773) 874800
F: (01773) 874800

TICKNALL
Derbyshire
Limeyards Stables ◆◆◆◆
136 Main Street, Ticknall, Derby
DE73 1JZ
T: (01332) 864802
E: info@limeyard.co.uk
I: www.limeyard.co.uk

The Staff of Life Public House and Restaurant
Rating Applied For
7 High Street, Ticknall, Derby
DE73 1JH
T: (01332) 862479
F: (01332) 862479
I: www.thestaffoflife.com

TINWELL
Rutland
The Old Village Hall
Rating Applied For
Main Road, Tinwell, Stamford,
Lincolnshire PE9 3UD
T: (01780) 763900

TISSINGTON
Derbyshire
Bassett Wood Farmhouse Bed and Breakfast ◆◆◆
Bassett Wood Farm, Tissington,
Ashbourne, Derbyshire DE6 1RD
T: (01335) 350254
E: janet@bassettwood.freeserve.co.uk
I: www.peakdistrictfarmhols.co.uk

TOTON
Nottinghamshire
Brookfield Cottage ◆◆◆
108 Carrfield Avenue, Toton,
Beeston, Nottingham NG9 6FB
T: (0115) 9178046 &
07949 592590
E: sheila.done@amserve.net

TOWCESTER
Northamptonshire
Green's Park ◆◆◆◆
Woodend, Towcester,
Northamptonshire NN12 8SD
T: (01327) 860386
F: (01327) 861003

The Leys ◆◆◆◆
Field Burcote, Towcester,
Northamptonshire NN12 8AL
T: (01327) 350431
F: (01327) 350431

Monk and Tipster ◆◆
36 Watling Street, Towcester,
Northamptonshire NN12 6AF
T: (01327) 350416

TRUSTHORPE
Lincolnshire
The Ramblers Hotel ◆◆◆
Sutton Road, Trusthorpe,
Mablethorpe, Lincolnshire
LN12 2PY
T: (01507) 441171

TUNSTALL
Staffordshire
Victoria Hotel ◆◆◆
4 Roundwell Street, Tunstall,
Stoke-on-Trent ST6 5JJ
T: (01782) 835964
F: (01782) 835964
E: victoria-hotel@tunstall51.fsnet.co.uk

TUTBURY
Staffordshire
Woodhouse Farm Bed and Breakfast ◆◆◆
Woodhouse Farm, Tutbury,
Burton upon Trent, Staffordshire
DE13 9HR
T: (01283) 812185 & 814046
F: (01283) 815743
E: enquiries@tutbury.co.uk
I: www.tutbury.co.uk/woodhouse

TWO DALES
Derbyshire
Hazel House ◆◆◆◆
Chesterfield Road, Two Dales,
Matlock, Derbyshire DE4 2EZ
T: (01629) 734443

Norden House ◆◆◆◆
Chesterfield Road, Two Dales,
Matlock, Derbyshire DE4 2EZ
T: (01629) 732074 &
07710 839985
F: (01629) 735805
E: david.a.pope@talk21.com
I: www.geocities.com/nordenhouse

UCKINGTON
Gloucestershire
3 Homecroft Drive
Rating Applied For
Uckington, Cheltenham,
Gloucestershire GL51 9SN
T: (01242) 680146

ULLINGSWICK
Herefordshire
The Steppes ◆◆◆◆◆
Ullingswick, Hereford HR1 3JG
T: (01432) 820424
F: (01432) 820042
E: info@steppeshotel.co.uk
I: www.steppeshotel.co.uk

UPPER COBERLEY
Gloucestershire
Upper Coberley Farm ◆◆◆◆
Upper Coberley, Cheltenham,
Gloucestershire GL53 9RB
T: (01242) 870306
E: allen@uppercoberley.freeserve.co.uk

UPPER HULME
Staffordshire
Paddock Farm Bed and Breakfast ◆◆◆◆
Paddock Farm, Upper Hulme,
Leek, Staffordshire ST13 8TY
T: (01538) 300345 & 300145

Roaches Hall ◆◆◆◆
Upper Hulme, Leek,
Staffordshire ST13 8UB
T: (01538) 300115

UPPER QUINTON
Warwickshire
Winton House ◆◆◆◆
The Green, Upper Quinton,
Stratford-upon-Avon,
Warwickshire CV37 8SX
T: (01789) 720500 &
07831 485483
E: gail@wintonhouse.com
I: www.wintonhouse.com

UPPINGHAM
Rutland
Boundary Farm ◆◆◆◆
Glaston Road, Uppingham,
Oakham, Leicestershire LE15 9PX
T: (01572) 822354

The Vaults ◆◆◆
Market Place, Uppingham,
Oakham, Leicestershire
LE15 9QH
T: (01572) 823259 & 820019

UPTON BISHOP
Herefordshire
Bishops Acre ◆◆◆
Upton Bishop, Ross-on-Wye,
Herefordshire HR9 7TT
T: (01989) 780318
F: (01989) 780318

UPTON SNODSBURY
Worcestershire
The French House Inn ◆◆◆
Worcester Road, Upton
Snodsbury, Worcester WR7 4NW
T: (01905) 381631
F: (01905) 381635
I: www.frenchhousepub.co.uk

UPTON ST LEONARDS
Gloucestershire
Bullens Manor Farm ◆◆◆◆
Portway, Upton St Leonards,
Gloucester GL4 8DL
T: (01452) 616463

UPTON-UPON-SEVERN
Worcestershire
Bridge House ◆◆◆◆
Welland Stone, Upton-upon-Severn, Worcester WR8 0RW
T: (01684) 593046
F: (01684) 593046
E: merrymichael@clara.net
I: www.malvern.net/commerce/bridge-house.htm

The Hill
Rating Applied For
Upton-upon-Severn, Worcester
WR8 0QL
T: (01684) 592120 &
07966 370340
F: (01684) 593353
E: info@thehillupton.co.uk
I: www.thehillupton.co.uk

Kimberlee ◆◆◆
The Beeches, Ryall, Upton-upon-Severn, Worcester WR8 0QQ
T: (01684) 591234 &
07702 307207
F: (01684) 591234

Ryall House Farm ◆◆◆◆
Ryall, Upton-upon-Severn,
Worcester WR8 0PL
T: (01684) 592013
F: (01684) 592013

Tiltridge Farm and Vineyard ◆◆◆◆
Upper Hook Road, Upton-upon-Severn, Worcester WR8 0SA
T: (01684) 592906
F: (01684) 594142
E: elgarwine@aol.com

Welland Court ◆◆◆◆
Upton-upon-Severn, Worcester
WR8 0ST
T: (01684) 594426
F: (01684) 594426
E: wellandcourt@onetel.net.uk
I: www.wellandcourt.co.uk

UTTOXETER
Staffordshire
Oldroyd Guest House & Motel ◆◆◆
18-22 Bridge Street, Uttoxeter,
Staffordshire ST14 8AP
T: (01889) 562763
F: (01889) 568916
E: oldroyd@netcom.co.uk
I: www.scoot.co.uk/oldroyd-guest-house

VOWCHURCH
Herefordshire
New Barns Farm ◆◆◆◆
Vowchurch, Hereford HR2 0QA
T: (01981) 250250 &
07765 654131
F: (01981) 250250
E: lloydnewbarns@tesco.net
I: www.golden-valley.co.uk

The Old Vicarage ◆◆◆◆
Vowchurch, Hereford HR2 0QD
T: (01981) 550357
F: (01981) 550357
I: www.golden-valley.co.uk/vicarage

Upper Gilvach Farm ◆◆◆◆
St. Margarets, Vowchurch,
Hereford HR2 0QY
T: (01981) 510618
F: (01981) 510618
E: ruth@uppergilvach.freeserve.
co.uk
I: www.golden-valley.
co.uk/gilvach

WADDINGTON
Lincolnshire

Horse and Jockey ◆◆◆◆
High Street, Waddington,
Lincoln LN5 9RF
T: (01522) 720224
F: (01527) 722551
E: ltott@globelnet.com
I: www.vanguardpubs.
com/horseandjockey

WADENHOE
Northamptonshire

The Kings Head ◆◆◆◆
Church Street, Wadenhoe,
Peterborough PE8 5ST
T: (01832) 720024
F: (01832) 720024

WADSHELF
Derbyshire

Hillcrest ◆◆◆◆
Baslow Road, Wadshelf,
Chesterfield, Derbyshire S42 7BZ
T: (01246) 567082

Temperance House Farm
◆◆◆◆
Bradshaw Lane, Wadshelf,
Chesterfield, Derbyshire S42 7BT
T: (01246) 566416

WALTERSTONE
Herefordshire

Coed Y Grafel ◆◆
Coed Y Grafel, Walterstone,
Hereford, Herefordshire HR2 0DJ
T: (01873) 890675
F: (01873) 890675

Lodge Farm Cottage ◆◆◆
Walterstone Common,
Walterstone, Hereford,
Herefordshire HR2 0DT
T: (01873) 890263

WARWICK
Warwickshire

Agincourt Lodge Hotel ◆◆◆◆
36 Coten End, Warwick,
CV34 4NP
T: (01926) 499399 & 497252
F: (01926) 499399

Apothecary's ◆◆◆◆
The Old Dispensary, Stratford
Road, Wellesbourne, Warwick
CV35 9RN
T: (01789) 470060
E: apothband@aol.com
I: www.apothbandb@aol.com

Ashburton Guest House ◆◆◆
74 Emscote Road, Warwick,
CV34 5QG
T: (01926) 401082 &
07977 973780
F: (01926) 419237
E: 100534.444@compuserve.
com
I: www.smoothhound.co.uk

Austin House ◆◆◆
96 Emscote Road, Warwick,
Warwickshire CV34 5QJ
T: (01926) 493583
F: (01926) 493679
E: mike@austinhouse96.
freeserve.co.uk

Avon Guest House ◆◆◆
7 Emscote Road, Warwick,
CV34 4PH
T: (01926) 491367
E: sue@comphouse.demon.uk
I: www.comphouse.demon.co.uk

Avonside Cottage ◆◆◆◆◆
1 High Street, Barford, Warwick
CV35 8BU
T: (01926) 624779

Brome House ◆◆◆◆
35 Bridge End, Warwick,
CV34 6PB
T: (01926) 491069
F: (01926) 491069
E: brome.house@virgin.net
I: www.smoothhound.
co.uk/hotel/brome.html

Cambridge Villa Hotel ◆◆
20A Emscote Road, Warwick,
CV34 4PP
T: (01926) 491169
F: (01926) 491169

Charter House ◆◆◆◆◆
87-91 West Street, Warwick,
CV34 6AH
T: (01926) 496965
F: (01926) 411910
E: penon@charterhouse8.
freeserve.co.uk
I: www.smoothhound.
co.uk/hotels/charter.html

**Cliffe Hill House Bed and
Breakfast** ◆◆◆◆
37 Coventry Road, Warwick,
CV34 5HW
T: (01926) 496431 &
07771 630006
E: quirke@cliffehillhouse.
freeserve.co.uk
I: www.cliffehillhouse.freeserve.
co.uk

The Coach House ◆◆◆◆
Old Budbrooke Road, Budbrooke,
Warwick, CV35 7DU
T: (01926) 410893
F: (01926) 490453
E: johnmannion@hotmail.com

The Croft Guesthouse ◆◆◆◆
Haseley Knob, Warwick
CV35 7NL
T: (01926) 484447
F: (01926) 484447
E: david@croftguesthouse.co.uk
I: www.croftguesthouse.co.uk

Crown and Castle Inn ◆◆◆
2-4 Coventry Road, Warwick,
CV34 4NT
T: (01926) 492087
F: (01926) 410638

Dinas ◆◆◆◆
30 Eastley Crescent, Warwick,
CV34 5RX
T: (01926) 496480
E: dinasbb@talk21.com

Forth House ◆◆◆◆
44 High Street, Warwick,
CV34 4AX
T: (01926) 401512
F: (01926) 490809
E: info@forthhouseuk.co.uk
I: www.forthhouseuk.co.uk

High House ◆◆◆◆
Old Warwick Road, Rowington,
Warwick CV35 7AA
T: (01926) 843270 &
0774 8592656
F: (01926) 843689

Hill House ◆◆◆◆
Hampton Lucy, Warwick,
CV35 8AU
T: (01789) 840329
E: eliz_hunter@hotmail.com
I: www.stratford-upon-avon.
co.uk/hillhouse.htm

Jersey Villa Guest House ◆◆◆
69 Emscote Road, Warwick,
CV34 5QR
T: (01926) 774607
F: (01926) 774607
E: jerseyvillaguesthouse@
emscote.freeserve.co.uk

**Longbridge Farm
Rating Applied For**
Stratford Road, Warwick,
CV34 6RB
T: (01926) 401857

Lower Rowley ◆◆◆◆
Wasperton, Warwick, CV35 8EB
T: (01926) 624937
F: (01926) 620053
E: cliffordveasey@lower-rowley.
freeserve.co.uk

Lower Watchbury Farm
◆◆◆◆
Wasperton Lane, Barford,
Warwick CV35 8DH
T: (01926) 624772 &
07880 557668
F: (01926) 624772
E: eykyn@barford.
spacomputers.com
I: www.farmaccommodation.
com

Merchant's House ◆◆◆◆◆
Hampton Lucy, Warwick,
CV35 8BE
T: (01789) 842280 &
07747 002770
E: hwaterworth@hotmail.com

Northleigh House ◆◆◆◆
Five Ways Road, Hatton,
Warwick CV35 7HZ
T: (01926) 484203 &
07774 101894
F: (01926) 484006
I: www.northleigh.co.uk

The Old Rectory Hotel ◆◆◆
Vicarage Lane, Sherbourne,
Warwick, CV35 8AB
T: (01926) 624562 &
077206 35317
F: (01926) 624995

Park Cottage ◆◆◆◆
113 West Street, Warwick,
CV34 6AH
T: (01926) 410319
F: (01926) 410319
E: parkcott@aol.com

Park House Guest House ◆◆◆
17 Emscote Road, Warwick,
CV34 4PH
T: (01926) 494359
F: (01926) 494359
E: park.house@ntlworld.com
I: parkhousewarwick.co.uk

Peacock Lodge ◆◆◆
97 West Street, Warwick,
CV34 6AH
T: (01926) 411892
F: (01926) 776268

The Seven Stars Public House
◆◆◆◆
Friars Street, Warwick,
CV34 6HD
T: (01926) 492658
F: (01926) 411747
E: sevenstars@gofornet.co.uk
I: www.smoothhound.co.uk

Shrewley Pools Farm ◆◆◆◆
Haseley, Warwick CV35 7HB
T: (01926) 484315
E: cathydodd@hotmail.com
I: www.s-h-systems.
co.uk/hotels/shrewley.html

The Tilted Wig ◆◆◆◆
11 Market Place, Warwick,
CV34 4SA
T: (01926) 410466 & 411740
F: (01926) 495740

Tudor House Inn ◆◆◆
90-92 West Street, Warwick,
CV34 6AW
T: (01926) 495447
F: (01926) 492948
I: www.oldenglish.co.uk

Warwick Lodge Guest House
◆◆◆
82 Emscote Road, Warwick,
CV34 5QJ
T: (01926) 492927

Westham Guest House ◆◆◆
76 Emscote Road, Warwick,
CV34 5QG
T: (01926) 491756
F: (01926) 491756
E: westhamhouse@aol.com
I: www.smoothhound.
co.uk/hotels/westham.html

Woodside ◆◆◆
Langley Road, Claverdon,
Warwick CV35 8PJ
T: (01926) 842446
F: (01926) 843697
E: ab021@dial.pipex.com
🏃

WATERHOUSES
Staffordshire

Broadhurst Farm ◆◆◆
Waterhouses, Stoke-on-Trent
ST10 3LQ
T: (01538) 308261

Lee House Farm ◆◆◆◆
Leek Road, Waterhouses, Stoke-
on-Trent ST10 3HW
T: (01538) 308439

WEEDON
Northamptonshire

Mullions ◆◆◆◆
9 Oak Street, Upper Weedon,
Weedon, Northampton
NN7 4RQ
T: (01327) 341439
F: (01327) 341439

WEEDON LOIS
Northamptonshire

Green Farm ◆◆◆
Green Farm, Weedon Lois,
NN12 8PL
T: (01327) 860249
F: (01327) 860249

WELDON
Northamptonshire
Thatches on the Green ◆◆◆◆
9 School Lane, Weldon, Corby,
Northamptonshire NN17 3JN
T: (01536) 266681
F: (01536) 266659
E: tom@
thatches-on-the-green.fsnet.
co.uk
I: www.thatches-on-the-green.
fsnet.co.uk

WELFORD
Northamptonshire
West End Farm ◆◆◆◆
5 West End, Welford,
Northampton NN6 6HJ
T: (01858) 575226
E: bevin@uklynx.net

WELFORD-ON-AVON
Warwickshire
Bridgend ◆◆◆
Binton Road, Welford-on-Avon,
Stratford-upon-Avon,
Warwickshire CV37 8PW
T: (01789) 750900
F: (01789) 750900
E: bridgend.g.house@amserve.
net

Mullions ◆◆◆◆
Greenhill, Binton Road, Welford-
on-Avon, Stratford-upon-Avon,
Warwickshire CV37 8PP
T: (01789) 750413
F: (01789) 750413
E: bandbpmw@aol.com

WELLAND
Worcestershire
The Lovells ◆◆◆◆
Welland, Malvern,
Worcestershire WR13 6NF
T: (01684) 310795

WELLESBOURNE
Warwickshire
Brook House ◆◆◆◆
9 Chestnut Square,
Wellesbourne, Warwick
CV35 9QS
T: (01789) 840922

WELLINGTON
Shropshire
Barnfield House ◆◆
5 Barnfield Court, Wellington,
Telford, Shropshire TF1 2ET
T: (01952) 223406

The Paddock ◆◆◆◆
Arleston Manor, Arleston Lane,
Wellington, Telford, Shropshire
TF1 2LT
T: (01952) 243311 &
07836 329568
F: (01952) 243311

WEM
Shropshire
Aston Lodge ◆◆◆
Souton Road, Wem, Shrewsbury
SY4 5BG
T: (01939) 232577
F: (01939) 232577

Chez Michael ◆◆◆
23 Roden Grove, Wem,
Shrewsbury SY4 5HJ
T: (01939) 232947
F: (01939) 232947

Forncet ◆◆
Soulton Road, Wem, Shrewsbury
SY4 5HR
T: (01939) 232996

Lowe Hall Farm ◆◆◆◆
Wem, Shrewsbury SY4 5UE
I: (01939) 232236
F: (01939) 232236
E: bandb@lowehallfarm.demon.
co.uk
I: www.lowehallfarm.demon.
co.uk

Polstead House ◆◆◆
Shawbury Road, Wem,
Shrewsbury SY4 5PF
T: (01939) 233530

WENLOCK EDGE
Shropshire
The Wenlock Edge Inn ◆◆◆◆
Hilltop, Wenlock Edge, Much
Wenlock, Shropshire TF13 6DJ
T: (01746) 785678
F: (01746) 785285
E: info@wenlockedgeinn.co.uk
I: www.wenlockedgeinn.co.uk

WENTNOR
Shropshire
Crown Inn ◆◆◆◆
Wentnor, Bishop's Castle,
Shropshire SY9 5EE
T: (01588) 650613
F: (01588) 650436
E: crowninn@wentnor.com
I: www.wentnor.com

Inn on the Green ◆◆
Wentnor, Bishop's Castle,
Shropshire SY9 5EF
T: (01588) 650105 &
07974 670691
E: thegreen@redhotant.com

WEOBLEY
Herefordshire
Garnstone House ◆◆◆
Weobley, Hereford HR4 8QP
T: (01544) 318943
F: (01544) 318197

The Marshpools Country Inn
◆◆◆
Ledgemoor, Weobley, Hereford
HR4 8RN
T: (01544) 318215 & 318847
F: (01544) 318847
E: burgoyne@marshpools.
freeserve.co.uk
I: www.country-inn.co.uk

WESSINGTON
Derbyshire
Crich Lane Farm ◆◆◆◆
Moorwood Moor Lane,
Wessington, Alfreton,
Derbyshire DE55 6DU
T: (01773) 835186 &
07775 881423

WEST BARKWITH
Lincolnshire
The Manor House ◆◆◆◆
Louth Road, West Barkwith,
Market Rasen, Lincolnshire
LN8 5LF
T: (01673) 858253
F: (01673) 858253

WEST BRIDGFORD
Nottinghamshire
The Croft Hotel ◆◆
6-8 North Road, West Bridgford,
Nottingham NG2 7NH
T: (0115) 981 2744
F: (0115) 9812744
E: croft.hotel.wb@talk21.com
I: www.smoothhound.co.uk

The Gallery Hotel ◆◆◆
8-10 Radcliffe Road, West
Bridgford, Nottingham
NG2 5FW
T: (0115) 981 3651 & 981 1346
F: (0115) 981 3732
I: www.yell.
co.uk/sites/galleryhotel/

Number 56 ◆◆
56 Melton Road, West Bridgford,
Nottingham NG2 7NF
T: (0115) 9821965

WEST HADDON
Northamptonshire
Pear Trees ◆◆◆◆
31 Station Road, West Haddon,
Northampton NN6 7AU
T: (01788) 510389
E: peartrees@lineone.net

WESTBURY-ON-SEVERN
Gloucestershire
Boxbush Barn ◆◆◆◆◆
Rodley, Westbury-on-Severn,
Gloucestershire GL14 1QZ
T: (01452) 760949
F: (01452) 760949
E: bed&breakfast@
boxbushbarn.fsnet.co.uk

WESTON
Staffordshire
Canalside Bed and Breakfast
◆◆◆
Bridge Cottage, Green Road,
Weston, Stafford ST18 0HZ
T: (01889) 271403
E: melgodridge@
canalsidebbweston.fsnet.co.uk

WESTON UNDER PENYARD
Herefordshire
The Hill ◆◆◆
Weston under Penyard, Ross-
on-Wye, Herefordshire HR9 7PZ
T: (01989) 750225
F: (01989) 750225
E: gill@gevans.fsnet.co.uk

**Wharton Farm Bed and
Breakfast** ◆◆◆◆
Wharton Farm, Weston under
Penyard, Ross-on-Wye,
Herefordshire HR9 5SX
T: (01989) 750255
F: (01989) 750255
E: jesavage@breathemail.com

WETTON
Staffordshire
Croft Cottage ◆◆◆◆
Wetton, Ashbourne, Derbyshire
DE6 2AF
T: (01335) 310402

The Old Chapel ◆◆◆◆
Wetton, Ashbourne, Derbyshire
DE6 2AF
T: (01335) 310450
F: (01335) 310089

WHALEY BRIDGE
Derbyshire
Cote Bank Farm ◆◆◆◆
Buxworth, Whaley Bridge, High
Peak SK23 7NP
T: (01663) 750566
F: (01663) 750566
E: cotebank@btinternet.com
I: www.peakdistrictfarmhols.
co.uk

WHAPLODE
Lincolnshire
Westgate House ◆◆◆◆
Little Lane, Whaplode, Spalding,
Lincolnshire PE12 6RU
T: (01406) 370546
E: bandb@westgatehouse.f9.
co.uk
I: www.westgatehouse.f9.co.uk

WHATSTANDWELL
Derbyshire
Meerbrook Farm ◆◆◆
Wirksworth Road,
Whatstandwell, Matlock,
Derbyshire DE4 5HU
T: (01629) 824180 &
07850 103927

Riverdale ◆◆◆◆
Middle Lane, Whatstandwell,
Matlock, Derbyshire DE4 5EG
T: (01773) 853905
F: (01773) 853905

WHATTON
Nottinghamshire
The Dell ◆◆◆◆
Church Street, Whatton,
Nottingham NG13 9EL
T: (01949) 850832
E: thedell@bushinternet.com

WHISTON
Staffordshire
Heath House Farm ◆◆◆
Ross Road, Whiston, Stoke-on-
Trent ST10 2JF
T: (01538) 266497
E: heathhousefarm@aol.com
I: www.heathhousefarm.com

WHITCHURCH
Shropshire
**Barmere House Bed and
Breakfast** ◆◆◆
Barmere House, Bickley,
Whitchurch, Shropshire
SY13 4HH
T: (01943) 663748

The Laurels ◆◆◆
Tushingham, Cum Grindley
Brook, Whitchurch, Shropshire
SY13 4QL
T: (01948) 664203
F: (01948) 664203

**The Old Pound Bed and
Breakfast** ◆◆◆
The Old Pound House,
Whitchurch, Ross-on-Wye,
Herefordshire HR9 6DW
T: (01600) 890637 &
07711 283328
F: (01600) 890508
E: tiffykabir@aol.com

Pheasant Walk ◆◆◆
Terrick Road, Whitchurch,
Shropshire SY13 4JZ
T: (01948) 667118

Roden View ◆◆◆◆
Dobsons Bridge, Whixall,
Whitchurch, Shropshire
SY13 2QL
T: (01948) 710320 &
07974 785318
F: (01948) 710320
E: rodenview@talk21.com

Wood Farm ◆◆◆◆
Old Woodhouses, Whitchurch,
Shropshire SY13 4EJ
T: (01948) 871224 &
07977 920429

WHITFIELD
Northamptonshire
Chestnut View ◆◆
Mill Lane, Whitfield, Brackley,
Northamptonshire NN13 5TQ
T: (01280) 850246
F: (01280) 850246

WHITTINGTON
Staffordshire
The Dog Inn and Restaurant
◆◆◆
Main Street, Whittington,
Lichfield, Staffordshire
WS14 9JU
T: (01543) 432252
F: (01543) 433748
E: thedoginn@leighnadi.
freeserve.co.uk

Hawthorns House ◆◆◆
44A Church Street, Whittington,
Lichfield, Staffordshire
WS14 9JX
T: (01543) 432613

WICKEN
Northamptonshire
The Pound House ◆◆◆
7 Pound Close, Wicken, Milton
Keynes MK19 6BN
T: (01908) 568729

WICKHAMFORD
Worcestershire
Avonwood ◆◆◆◆
30 Pitchers Hill, Wickhamford,
Evesham, Worcestershire
WR11 6RT
T: (01386) 834271 &
07790 672004
F: (01386) 834271

WIGMORE
Herefordshire
Compasses Hotel ◆◆
Ford Street, Wigmore,
Leominster, Herefordshire
HR6 9UN
T: (01568) 770203
F: (01568) 770705

Gotherment Farmhouse ◆◆◆
Wigmore, Leominster,
Herefordshire HR6 9UF
T: (01568) 770547
E: blair@gotherment.freeserve.
co.uk

Pear Tree Farm ◆◆◆◆
Wigmore, Leominster,
Herefordshire HR6 9UR
T: (01568) 770140 & 770141
F: (01568) 770140
E: steveandjill@peartreefarmco.
freeserve.co.uk
I: www.peartreefarmco.
freeserve.co.uk

WILLERSEY
Gloucestershire
Bowers Hill Farm ◆◆◆◆
Bowers Hill, Willersey,
Broadway, Worcestershire
WR11 5HG
T: (01386) 834585 &
07966 171861
F: (01386) 830234
E: sarah@bowershillfarm.com
I: www:bowershillfarm.com

Garnons Chase ◆◆◆◆
Collin Close, Willersey,
Broadway, Worcestershire
WR12 7PP
T: (01386) 853718
F: (01386) 853795
E: jgooding@clara.co.uk

WILTON
Herefordshire
Benhall Farm ◆◆◆
Wilton, Ross-on-Wye,
Herefordshire HR9 6AG
T: (01989) 563900 &
07900 264612
F: (01989) 563900
E: carol_m_brewer@hotmail.
com

**Benhall House Bed and
Breakfast** ◆◆◆
Wilton, Ross-on-Wye,
Herefordshire HR9 6AG
T: (01989) 567420
F: (01989) 567420

Copperfield House ◆◆◆◆
Wilton Lane, Wilton, Ross-on-
Wye, Herefordshire HR9 6AH
T: (01989) 764379 &
07710 282878
E: fran_brown@talk21.com
I: www.copperfieldhouse.co.uk

The White Lion Inn ◆◆
Wilton Lane, Wilton, Ross-on-
Wye, Herefordshire HR9 6AQ
T: (01989) 562785
E: lois@thewhitelion.fsbusiness.
co.uk

WINCHCOMBE
Gloucestershire
Blair House ◆◆◆
41 Gretton Road, Winchcombe,
Cheltenham, Gloucestershire
GL54 5EG
T: (01242) 603626
F: (01242) 604214

Cleveley ◆◆◆
Wadfield Farm, Corndean Lane,
Winchcombe, Cheltenham,
Gloucestershire GL54 5AL
T: (01242) 602059

Gower House ◆◆◆
16 North Street, Winchcombe,
Cheltenham, Gloucestershire
GL54 5LH
T: (01242) 602616

Greenhyde ◆◆◆◆
Langley Road, Winchcombe,
Cheltenham, Gloucestershire
GL54 5QP
T: (01242) 602569

The Homestead ◆◆◆
Footbridge, Broadway Road,
Winchcombe, Cheltenham,
Gloucestershire GL54 5JG
T: (01242) 602536 &
07787 542738
F: 08701 375598
E: homestead.bandb@virgin.net
I: www.homesteadbandb.
simplybedandbreakfast.com

Ireley Grounds ◆◆◆◆
Broadway Road, Winchcombe,
Cheltenham, Gloucestershire
GL54 5NY
T: (01242) 603736 &
07836 322230
F: (01242) 603736
E: mike@ireley.fsnet.co.uk
I: www.ireleygrounds.freeserve.
co.uk/

Isbourne Manor House
◆◆◆◆◆
Castle Street, Winchcombe,
Cheltenham, Gloucestershire
GL54 5JA
T: (01242) 602281
F: (01242) 602281
E: felicity@isbourne-manor.
co.uk
I: www.isbourne-manor.co.uk

Manor Farm ◆◆◆◆
Greet, Winchcombe,
Cheltenham, Gloucestershire
GL54 5BJ
T: (01242) 602423 &
07748 077717
F: (01242) 602423
E: janet@dickandjanet.fsnet.
co.uk

Mercia ◆◆◆◆
Hailes Street, Winchcombe,
Cheltenham, Gloucestershire
GL54 5HU
T: (01242) 602251
E: jonathanhupton@hotmail.
com

The Old Bakehouse ◆◆◆◆
Castle Street, Winchcombe,
Cheltenham, Gloucestershire
GL54 5JA
T: (01242) 602441
F: (01242) 602441
E: deniseparker@onetel.net.uk

Old Station House ◆◆◆
Greet Road, Winchcombe,
Cheltenham, Gloucestershire
GL54 5LB
T: (01242) 602283
F: (01242) 602283

Parks Farm ◆◆◆◆
Sudeley, Winchcombe,
Cheltenham, Gloucestershire
GL54 5JB
T: (01242) 603874
F: (01242) 603874
E: rosmaryawilson@hotmail.
com

The Plaisterers Arms
Rating Applied For
Abbey Terrace, Winchcombe,
Cheltenham, Gloucestershire
GL54 5LL
T: (01242) 602358
F: (01242) 602360
E: plaisterers.arms@btinternet.
com

Postlip Hall Farm ◆◆◆◆
Winchcombe, Cheltenham,
Gloucestershire GL54 5AQ
T: (01242) 603351
F: (01242) 603351
E: val@postliphallfarm.
free-online.co.uk
I: www.smoothhound.
co.uk/hotels/postlip

1 Stancombe View ◆◆◆
Winchcombe, Cheltenham,
Gloucestershire GL54 5LE
T: (01242) 603654

Sudeley Hill Farm ◆◆◆◆
Winchcombe, Cheltenham,
Gloucestershire GL54 5JB
T: (01242) 602344
F: (01242) 602344
E: scudamore4@aol.com

The White Hart Inn and
Restaurant ◆◆◆
High Street, Winchcombe,
Cheltenham, Gloucestershire
GL54 5LJ
T: (01242) 602359 & 609220
F: (01242) 602703
E: enquiries@
the-white-hart-inn.com
I: www.the-white-hart-inn.co.uk

WING
Rutland
Kings Arms Inn ◆◆◆◆
Top Street, Wing, Oakham,
Leicestershire LE15 8SE
T: (01572) 737634
F: (01572) 737255
E: neil@thekingsarms-wing.
co.uk
I: www.thekingsarms-wing.co.uk

WINKHILL
Staffordshire
Country Cottage ◆◆◆◆
Back Lane Farm, Winkhill, Leek,
Staffordshire ST13 7XZ
T: (01538) 308273
F: (01538) 308098
E: mjb6435@netscapeonline.
co.uk
I: www.biophysics.umn.
edu/~bent/

WINSLOW
Worcestershire
Munderfield Harold ◆◆
Winslow, Bromyard,
Herefordshire HR7 4SZ
T: (01885) 483231

WINSTER
Derbyshire
Brae Cottage ◆◆◆◆
East Bank, Winster, Matlock,
Derbyshire DE4 2DT
T: (01629) 650375

The Dower House ◆◆◆◆◆
Main Street, Winster, Matlock,
Derbyshire DE4 2DH
T: (01629) 650931
F: (01629) 650932
E: fosterbig@aol.com
I: www.SmoothHound.
co.uk/hotels/dowerho

Old Shoulder of Mutton
◆◆◆◆
West Bank, Winster, Matlock,
Derbyshire DE4 2DQ
T: (01629) 650778

WIRKSWORTH
Derbyshire
Avondale Farm ◆◆◆◆
Grangemill, Matlock, Derbyshire
DE4 4HT
T: (01629) 650820
F: (01629) 650233
E: avondale@tinyworld.co.uk

Old Lock Up ◆◆◆◆◆
North End, Wirksworth, Derby
DE4 4FG
T: (01629) 826272 & 826929
F: (01629) 826272
E: wheeler@theoldlockup.co.uk
I: www.theoldlockup.co.uk

WISHAW
Warwickshire

Ash House ◆◆◆
The Gravel, Wishaw, Sutton
Coldfield, West Midlands
B76 9QB
T: (01675) 475782 &
07850 414000
E: kate@rectory80.freeserve.
co.uk

WITCOMBE
Gloucestershire

Crickley Court
Rating Applied For
Dog Lane, Witcombe, Gloucester
GL3 4UF
T: (01452) 863634
F: (01452) 863634

Springfields Farm ◆◆
Little Witcombe, Gloucester,
GL3 4TU
T: (01452) 863532

WITHINGTON
Shropshire

Garden Cottage ◆◆◆
Withington, Shrewsbury
SY4 4QA
T: (01743) 709511 &
(01771) 3818743
F: (01743) 709511
E: silvia-hopper@
garden-cottage.fsnet.co.uk

Willowside Farm ◆◆◆
Withington, Cheltenham,
Gloucestershire GL54 4DA
T: (01242) 890362
F: (01242) 890556

WOLLASTON
Northamptonshire

Duckmire ◆◆◆◆
1 Duck End, Wollaston,
Northampton, NN29 7SH
T: (01933) 664249
F: (01933) 664249
E: kerry@foreverengland.
freeserve.co.uk

WOLSTANTON
Staffordshire

Whispering Pines ◆◆◆◆
11A Milehouse Lane,
Wolstanton, Newcastle-under-
Lyme, Staffordshire ST5 9JR
T: (01782) 639376
F: (01782) 639376
E: timpriestman@
whisperingpinesbb45.freeserve.
co.uk
I: whisperingpinesbb45.
freeserve.co.uk

WOLSTON
Warwickshire

The Byre ◆◆◆◆
Lords Hill Farm, Coalpit Lane,
Wolston, Coventry CV8 3GB
T: (024) 7654 2098

WOODCHESTER
Gloucestershire

Southfield Mill ◆◆◆◆
Southfield Road, Woodchester,
Stroud, Gloucestershire GL5 5PA
T: (01453) 872896
F: (01453) 872896
E: judysutch@hotmail.com

WOODHALL SPA
Lincolnshire

Claremont Guesthouse ◆◆
9-11 Witham Road, Woodhall
Spa, Lincolnshire LN10 6RW
T: (01526) 352000

The Dower House Hotel ◆◆◆
The Manor Estate, Woodhall Spa,
Lincolnshire LN10 6PY
T: (01526) 352588
F: (01526) 352588
E: cplumb_dowerhouse@yahoo.
co.uk
I: www.web-marketing.
co.uk/dowerhouse

Newlands ◆◆◆◆
56 Woodland Drive, Woodhall
Spa, Lincolnshire LN10 6YG
T: (01526) 352881

Pitchaway Guesthouse ◆◆◆
The Broadway, Woodhall Spa,
Lincolnshire LN10 6SQ
T: (01526) 352969
E: barry@pitchaway.fsnet.co.uk

WOONTON
Herefordshire

Rose Cottage ◆◆◆◆
Woonton, Hereford HR3 6QW
T: (01544) 340459
F: (01544) 340459

WORCESTER
Worcestershire

Barbourne ◆◆◆
42 Barbourne Road, Worcester,
WR1 1HU
T: (01905) 27507
F: (01905) 27507

The Boot Inn ◆◆◆◆
Radford Road, Flyford Flavell,
Worcester WR7 4BS
T: (01386) 462658 & 792931
F: (01386) 462547
E: thebootinn@yahoo.com

The Croft ◆◆◆
25 Station Road, Fernhill Heath,
Worcester, WR3 7UJ
T: (01905) 773174 & 453482

Foresters Guest House ◆◆◆
2 Chestnut Walk, Arboretum,
Worcester, WR1 1PP
T: (01905) 20348
F: (01905) 20348

Green Farm ◆◆◆◆
Crowle Green, Crowle,
Worcester WR7 4AB
T: (01905) 381807 &
07721 029023
F: (01905) 381807
E: lupa@beeb.net

Hidelow House ◆◆◆◆
Acton Green, Acton Beauchamp,
Malvern, Worcestershire
WR6 5AH
T: (01886) 884547
F: (01886) 884060
E: bta@hidelow.co.uk
I: www.hidelow.co.uk

Ivy Cottage ◆◆◆◆
Sinton Green, Hallow, Worcester
WR2 6NP
T: (01905) 641123
E: rendle@ukgateway.net

Little Lightwood Farm ◆◆◆◆
Lightwood Lane, Cotheridge,
Worcester WR6 5LT
T: (01905) 333236
F: (01905) 333236
E: lightwood.holidays@virgin.
net

**Manor Arms Country Inn and
Hotel** ◆◆◆
Abberley Village, Worcester,
WR6 6BN
T: (01299) 896507
F: (01299) 896723
E: themanorarms@btconnect.
com
I: themanorarms.co.uk

Oaklands ◆◆◆◆
Claines, Worcester WR3 7RR
T: (01905) 458871 &
07885 378771
F: (01905) 759362
E: barbaragadd@hotmail.com
I: www.ukbed.
com/heart-of-england/oaklands.
htm

The Old Smithy ◆◆◆◆
Pirton, Worcester WR8 9EJ
T: (01905) 820482
E: welcome@theoldsmithy.
co.uk
I: www.smoothound.
co.uk/hotels/oldsmith.html

**Oldbury Farm Bed and
Breakfast** ◆◆◆◆
Oldbury Farm, Lower
Broadheath, Worcester,
WR2 6RQ
T: (01905) 421357 &
07751 075126

Osborne House ◆◆◆
17 Chestnut Walk, Worcester,
Worcestershire WR1 1PR
T: (01905) 22296
F: (01905) 22296
E: enquiries@osborne-house.
freeserve.co.uk
I: www.a1tourism.
com/uk/hotels/osborneh.html

**Park House Guest
Accommodation** ◆◆◆
12 Droitwich Road, Worcester,
WR3 7LJ
T: (01905) 21816 & 612029

Retreat Farm ◆◆◆◆
Camp Lane, Grimley, Worcester,
WR2 6LX
T: (01905) 640266
F: (01905) 641397

Shrubbery Guest House ◆◆◆
38 Barbourne Road, Worcester,
WR1 1HU
T: (01905) 24871
F: (01905) 23620

Yew Tree House ◆◆◆◆
Norchard, Crossway Green,
Stourport-on-Severn,
Worcestershire DY13 9SN
T: (01299) 250921 &
07971 112621
F: (01299) 253472
E: paul@knightp.swinternet.
co.uk
I: www.yewtreeworcester.co.uk

WORKSOP
Nottinghamshire

Carlton Road Guesthouse
◆◆◆
67 Carlton Road, Worksop,
Nottinghamshire S80 1PP
T: (01909) 483084

The Old Blue Bell ◆◆◆
30 Park Street, Worksop,
Nottinghamshire S80 1HF
T: (01909) 500304
F: (01909) 500304

Sherwood Guesthouse ◆◆◆
57 Carlton Road, Worksop,
Nottinghamshire S80 1PP
T: (01909) 474209
F: (01909) 476470
E: CHERWOULD@aol.com

WORMELOW
Herefordshire

Lyston Villa ◆◆◆
Wormelow, Hereford HR2 8EL
T: (01981) 540130
F: (01981) 540130

WORMHILL
Derbyshire

Wellhead Farm ◆◆◆
Wormhill, Buxton, Derbyshire
SK17 8SL
T: (01298) 871023

WOTTON-UNDER-EDGE
Gloucestershire

Falcon Cottage ◆◆◆◆
15 Station Road, Charfield,
Wotton-under-Edge,
Gloucestershire GL12 8SY
T: (01453) 843528

Hillesley Mill ◆◆◆
Alderley, Wotton-under-Edge,
Gloucestershire GL12 7QT
T: (01453) 843258

Warren Farm ◆◆◆
Blackquarries Hill, Wotton-
under-Edge, Gloucestershire
GL12 7QE
T: (01453) 842212

WYMONDHAM
Leicestershire

The Old Rectory ◆◆◆
Sycamore Lane, Wymondham,
Melton Mowbray, Leicestershire
LE14 2AZ
T: (01572) 787583
F: (01572) 787347
I: www.theold-rectory.com

WYSALL
Nottinghamshire

Lorne House Bed & Breakfast
◆◆◆◆
Lorne House, Bradmore Road,
Wysall, Nottingham NG12 5QR
T: (01509) 881433 &
07974 710037
F: (0115) 942 3350
E: haymin@ukonline.co.uk

YARDLEY
West Midlands

Olton Cottage Guest House
◆◆◆◆
School Lane, Yardley,
Birmingham B33 8PD
T: (0121) 783 9249 &
07885 163291
F: (0121) 789 6545
E: olton.cottage@virgin.net
I: www.olton-cottage.com

Yardley Guesthouse ◆◆◆
330 Church Road, Yardley,
Birmingham B25 8XT
T: (0121) 783 6634
F: (0121) 7836634

YARKHILL
Herefordshire

Garford Farm ◆◆◆
Yarkhill, Hereford HR1 3ST
T: (01432) 890226
F: (01432) 890707
E: garfordfarm@lineone.net

YORTON HEATH
Shropshire
Country Bed & Breakfast
Rating Applied For
Mayfield, Yorton Heath,
Shrewsbury SY4 3EZ
T: (01939) 210860
F: (01939) 210860
E: macdonalds@
mayfieldyortonheath.freeserve.
co.uk
I: www.shropshiretourism.com

YOULGREAVE
Derbyshire
Bankside Cottage ♦♦♦
Bankside, Youlgreave, Bakewell,
Derbyshire DE45 1WD
T: (01629) 636689

Fairview ♦♦♦
Bradford Road, Youlgreave,
Bakewell, Derbyshire DE45 1WG
T: (01629) 636043
F: (01629) 636043

The Farmyard Inn ♦♦♦
Main Street, Youlgreave,
Bakewell, Derbyshire DE45 1UW
T: (01629) 636221

The Old Bakery ♦♦♦
Church Street, Youlgreave,
Bakewell, Derbyshire DE45 1UR
T: (01629) 636887
E: croasdell@
oldbakeryyoulgrave.freeserve.
co.uk
I: www.cressbrook.
co.uk/youlgve/oldbakery

YOXALL
Staffordshire
Thimble Hall ♦♦♦♦
School Green, Yoxall, Burton
upon Trent, Staffordshire
DE13 8NB
T: (01543) 472226
F: (01543) 472226
E: jo@thimble.fsbusiness.co.uk

EAST OF ENGLAND

ACTON
Suffolk
Barbie's ♦♦
25 Clayhall Place, Acton,
Sudbury, Suffolk CO10 0BT
T: (01787) 373702

Lime Tree House ♦♦♦♦
Lime Tree Green, Acton,
Sudbury, Suffolk CO10 0UU
T: (01787) 373551 & 312413

ALBURY
Hertfordshire
Tudor Cottage ♦♦♦♦
Upwick Green, Albury, Ware,
Hertfordshire SG11 2JX
T: (01279) 771440 &
07770 898424

ALDBOROUGH
Norfolk
Butterfly Cottage ♦♦♦
The Green, Aldborough, Norwich
NR11 7AA
T: (01263) 768198
F: (01263) 768198

ALDBURY
Hertfordshire
**Livingston's Bed & Breakfast
♦♦♦**
Chimanimani, Toms Hill Road,
Aldbury, Tring, Hertfordshire
HP23 5SA
T: (01442) 851527

ALDEBURGH
Suffolk
East Cottage ♦♦
55 King Street, Aldeburgh,
Suffolk IP15 5BZ
T: (01728) 453010
F: (01728) 453010
E: anglian55@hotmail.com

Faraway ♦♦♦
28 Linden Close, Aldeburgh,
Suffolk IP15 5JL
T: (01728) 452571

Lime Tree House B&B ♦♦♦
Benhall Green, Saxmundham,
Suffolk IP17 1HU
T: (01728) 602149

Margaret's ♦♦♦
50 Victoria Road, Aldeburgh,
Suffolk IP15 5EJ
T: (01728) 453239

Sanviv ♦♦♦
59 Fairfield Road, Aldeburgh,
Suffolk IP1 5JN
T: (01728) 453107

Wateringfield ♦♦♦♦
Golf Lane, Aldeburgh, Suffolk
IP15 5PY
T: (01728) 453163 &
07711 745962
E: wateringfield@tesco.net

ALDEBY
Norfolk
The Old Vicarage ♦♦♦
Rectory Road, Aldeby, Beccles,
Suffolk NR34 0BJ
T: (01502) 678229
E: butler@beccles33.freeserve.
co.uk

ALDHAM
Essex
Old House ♦♦♦
Ford Street, Aldham, Colchester
CO6 3PH
T: (01206) 240456
F: (01206) 240456

ALDRINGHAM
Suffolk
Fern House ♦♦♦
6 The Follies, Aldringham,
Leiston, Suffolk IP16 4LU
T: (01728) 830759
E: gallowaymd@aol.com

ALPHETON
Suffolk
Amicus ♦♦♦♦
Old Bury Road, Alpheton,
Sudbury CO10 9BT
T: (01284) 828579 &
07779 076519
F: (01284) 828579

ARDLEIGH
Essex
Malting Farm ♦♦♦♦
Malting Farm Lane, Ardleigh,
Colchester CO7 7QG
T: (01206) 230207

Old Shields Farm ♦♦♦♦
Waterhouse Lane, Ardleigh,
Colchester CO7 7NE
T: (01206) 230251
F: (01206) 231825

ARKESDEN
Essex
Parsonage Farm ♦♦♦♦
Arkesden, Saffron Walden, Essex
CB11 4HB
T: (01799) 550306

ASHDON
Essex
Cobblers ♦♦♦♦
Bartlow Road, Ashdon, Saffron
Walden, Essex CB10 2HR
T: (01799) 584666
E: cobblers@ashdon2000.
freeserve.co.uk

ASHILL
Norfolk
**Moat Farm G C Pickering and
Son**
Rating Applied For
Ashill, Thetford, Norfolk
IP25 7BX
T: (01760) 440357
F: (01760) 441447

ASPLEY GUISE
Bedfordshire
Chain Guest House ♦♦♦♦
Church Street, Aspley Guise,
Milton Keynes MK17 8HQ
T: (01908) 586511
F: (01908) 586511
E: chainhouse@ukgateway.net
I: www.chainhouse.ukgateway.
net

ATTLEBOROUGH
Norfolk
Scales Farm ♦♦♦♦
Old Buckenham, Attleborough,
Norfolk NR17 1PE
T: (01953) 860324

AYLMERTON
Norfolk
Felbrigg Lodge ♦♦♦♦♦
Aylmerton, Holt, Norfolk
NR11 8RA
T: (01263) 837588
F: (01263) 838012
E: info@felbrigglodge.co.uk
I: www.felbrigglodge.co.uk

AYLSHAM
Norfolk
The Old Pump House ♦♦♦♦
Holman Road, Aylsham, Norwich
NR11 6BY
T: (01263) 733789 & 733789
F: (01263) 733789

AYOT ST LAWRENCE
Hertfordshire
The Brocket Arms ♦♦
Ayot St Lawrence, Welwyn,
Hertfordshire AL6 9BT
T: (01438) 820250
F: (01438) 820068
I: www.brocketarms.com

BACTON-ON-SEA
Norfolk
Keswick Hotel ♦♦♦
Walcott Road, Bacton-on-Sea,
Norwich NR12 0LS
T: (01692) 650468
F: (01692) 650788

BADINGHAM
Suffolk
Colston Hall ♦♦♦♦
Badingham, Woodbridge,
Suffolk IP13 8LB
T: (01728) 638375 &
07773 359193
F: (01728) 638084
E: lizjohn@colstonhall.com
I: www.colstonhall.com

BARHAM
Suffolk
**The Sorrel Horse Inn Various
Ltd♦♦♦**
Old Norwich Road, Barham,
Ipswich IP6 0PG
T: (01473) 830327
F: (01473) 833149
E: matt@sorrelhorse.freeserve.
co.uk
I: www.sorrelhouse.freeserve.
co.uk

Tamarisk House ♦♦♦♦
Sandy Lane, Barham, Ipswich
IP6 0PB
T: (01473) 831825 &
07932 174821
I: www.hotelmaster.co.uk

BASILDON
Essex
38 Kelly Road ♦♦♦♦
Bowers Gifford, Basildon, Essex
SS13 2HL
T: (01268) 726701 & 246195
F: (01268) 246060
E: patricia.jenkinson@tesco.net
I: www.uk-visit.co.uk

BATTLESBRIDGE
Essex
The Cottages Guest House ♦♦
The Cottages, Beeches Road,
Battlesbridge, Wickford, Essex
SS11 8TJ
T: (01702) 232105 &
07753 634933
E: cottage2000@totalise.co.uk

BAWBURGH
Norfolk
The Old Lodge
Rating Applied For
New Road, Bawburgh, Norwich
NR9 3LZ
T: (01603) 742798
E: peggy@theoldlodge.
freeserve.co.uk

BECCLES
Suffolk
Catherine House ♦♦♦♦
2 Ringsfield Road, Beccles,
Suffolk NR34 9PQ
T: (01502) 716428
F: (01502) 716428

Colville Arms Motel ◆◆◆
Lowestoft Road, Worlingham,
Beccles, Suffolk NR34 7EF
T: (01502) 712571
F: (01502) 712571
E: pat@thecolvillearms.
freeserve.co.uk

The Kings Head ◆◆◆
New Market, Beccles, Suffolk
NR34 9HA
T: (01502) 712147
F: (01502) 715386
E: enquiries@
kingsheadhotel-uk.co.uk
I: www.kingsheadhotel-uk.co.uk

Plantation House ◆◆◆◆
Rectory Road, Haddiscoe,
Beccles, Suffolk NR14 6PG
T: (01502) 677778
F: (01502) 677778
E: plantationhouse@ukonline.
co.uk
I: www.broadland.
com/plantationhouse

BEDFORD
Bedfordshire

**Cornfields Restaurant and
Hotel
Rating Applied For**
Wilden Road, Colmworth,
Bedford, MK44 2NJ
T: (01234) 378990
F: (01234) 376370
E: reservations@
cornfieldsrestaurant.co.uk
I: www.cornfieldsrestaurant.
co.uk

1 Ravensden Grange ◆◆◆
Sunderland Hill, Ravensden,
Bedford MK44 2SH
T: (01234) 771771

BEESTON
Norfolk

Holmdene Farm ◆◆◆
Beeston, King's Lynn, Norfolk
PE32 2NJ
T: (01328) 701284
E: holmdenefarm@
farmersweekly.net
I: www.northnorfolk.
co.uk/holmdenefarm

BEESTON REGIS
Norfolk

**Sheringham View Cottage
Rating Applied For**
Cromer Road, Beeston Regis,
Cromer, Norfolk NR26 8RX
T: (01263) 820300 &
07961 921009

BEETLEY
Norfolk

Peacock House ◆◆◆◆
Peacock Lane, Beetley, East
Dereham, Norfolk NR20 4DG
T: (01362) 860371 &
0797 9013258
E: PeackH@aol.com
I: www.smoothhound.
co.uk/hotels/peacockh.html/

Shilling Stone ◆◆◆
Church Road, Beetley, East
Dereham, Norfolk NR20 4AB
T: (01362) 861099 &
07721 306190
F: (01362) 869153
E: jeannepartridge@ukgateway.
net
I: www.norfolkshillingstone.
co.uk

BEIGHTON
Norfolk

**Beech House Bed & Breakfast
◆◆◆**
Southwood Road, Beighton,
Norwich NR13 3AB
T: (01493) 750870 &
07790 976611

BELCHAMP ST PAUL
Essex

The Plough ◆◆◆◆
Gages Road, Belchamp St Paul,
Sudbury, Suffolk CO10 7BT
T: (01787) 278882
E: info@theplough-belchamp.
co.uk
I: www.theplough-belchamp.
co.uk

BENHALL GREEN
Suffolk

Honeypot Lodge ◆◆◆
Aldecar Lane, Benhall Green,
Saxmundham, Suffolk IP17 1HN
T: (01728) 602449

BERKHAMSTED
Hertfordshire

Broadway Farm ◆◆◆◆
Berkhamsted, Hertfordshire
HP4 2RR
T: (01442) 866541
F: (01442) 866541
E: a.knowles@broadway.
nildram.co.uk

BEYTON
Suffolk

Brook Farm ◆◆◆◆
Drinkstone Road, Beyton, Bury
St Edmunds, Suffolk IP30 9AQ
T: (01359) 270733

BIGGLESWADE
Bedfordshire

Old Warden Guesthouse ◆◆◆
Shop and Post Office, Old
Warden, Biggleswade,
Bedfordshire SG18 9HQ
T: (01767) 627201

BILDESTON
Suffolk

Christmas Hall ◆◆◆◆
Market Square, Bildeston,
Ipswich IP7 7EN
T: (01449) 741428
F: (01449) 744161

**The Crown Hotel
Rating Applied For**
104 High Street, Bildeston,
Ipswich IP7 7EB
T: (01449) 740510
F: (01449) 740510
I: www.crownhotel.uk.net

BILLERICAY
Essex

Badgers Rest ◆◆◆◆
2 Mount View, Billericay, Essex
CM11 1HB
T: (01277) 625384 &
07778 444169
F: (01277) 633912

BINHAM
Norfolk

Field House ◆◆◆◆
Field House, Walsingham Road,
Binham, Fakenham, Norfolk
NR21 0BU
T: (01328) 830639

BIRCHAM
Norfolk

Country Stores ◆◆◆
Lynn Road, Bircham, King's
Lynn, Norfolk PE31 6RJ
T: (01485) 578502

BISHOP'S STORTFORD
Hertfordshire

5 Ascot Close ◆◆◆
Bishop's Stortford, Hertfordshire
CM23 5BP
T: (01279) 652228 &
07889 662292

6 Ascot Close ◆◆◆
Bishop's Stortford, Hertfordshire
CM23 5BP
T: (01279) 651027 &
07787 562288
E: 113714.2346@compuserve.
com

Chippendales ◆◆◆
7 Stort Lodge, Off Hadham
Road, Bishop's Stortford,
Hertfordshire CM23 2QL
T: (01279) 656315 & 0780 801
4985

The Cottage ◆◆◆◆
71 Birchanger Lane, Birchanger,
Bishop's Stortford, Hertfordshire
CM23 5QA
T: (01279) 812349
F: (01279) 815045

Lancasters ◆◆◆◆
Castle House, Market Square,
Bishop's Stortford, Hertfordshire
CM23 3UU
T: (01279) 501307

The Lawns ◆
46 Windhill, Bishop's Stortford,
Hertfordshire CM23 2NH
T: (01279) 654114 &
(01585) 457014

Pleasant Cottage ◆◆◆◆
Woodend Green, Henham,
Bishop's Stortford, Hertfordshire
CM22 6AZ
T: (01279) 850792
F: (01279) 850792

Saint Vincent ◆◆◆
24 Elm Road, Bishop's Stortford,
Hertfordshire CM23 2SS
T: (01279) 658884 &
0787 0335887
E: hilarydave@lineone.net

47 Southmill Road ◆◆◆
Bishop's Stortford, Hertfordshire
CM23 3DH
T: (01279) 755536 &
07966 490748
E: stortfordbnb@aol.com
I: www.
stanstedairportaccomodation.
com

Tap Hall ◆◆◆
15 The Street, Takeley, Bishop's
Stortford, Hertfordshire
CM22 6QS
T: (01279) 871035

52 Thorley Hill ◆◆◆◆
Bishop's Stortford, Hertfordshire
CM23 3NA
T: (01279) 658311
F: (01279) 658311

17 Windhill ◆◆◆
Bishop's Stortford, Hertfordshire
CM23 2NE
T: (01279) 834797
F: (01279) 834797
E: admill@ntlworld.com

52 Windhill ◆◆◆
Bishop's Stortford, Hertfordshire
CM23 2NH
T: (01279) 651712
I: aspence@btinternet.com

Woodlands Lodge ◆◆◆
Dunmow Road, Bishop's
Stortford, CM23 5QX
T: (01279) 504784
F: (01279) 461474
E: lynn_kingsbury@yahoo.com
I: www.woodlandslodge.co.uk

BLAKENEY
Norfolk

**Navestock Bed & Breakfast
Rating Applied For**
Cley Road, Blakeney, Holt,
Norfolk NR25 7NL
T: (01263) 740998
F: (01263) 740998

Ryecroft ◆◆◆◆
Back Lane, Blakeney, Holt,
Norfolk NR25 7NP
T: (01263) 740701
F: (01263) 740701

BLAXHALL
Suffolk

The Ship Inn ◆◆
Blaxhall, Snape, Saxmundham,
Suffolk IP12 2DY
T: (01728) 688316
F: (01728) 688316

BLETSOE
Bedfordshire

North End Barns ◆◆◆◆
North End Farm, Risley Road,
Bletsoe, Bedford MK44 1QT
T: (01234) 781320
F: (01234) 781320

BLICKLING
Norfolk

**The Buckinghamshire Arms
◆◆◆**
Blickling, Norwich NR11 6NF
T: (01263) 732133

BOTESDALE
Suffolk

Virginia Cottage ◆◆◆◆
The Street, Botesdale, Diss,
Norfolk IP22 1BZ
T: (01379) 890128
E: mmwebbe@hotmail.com

BOXFORD
Suffolk

Hurrells Farmhouse ◆◆◆◆
Boxford Lane, Boxford, Sudbury,
Suffolk CO10 5JY
T: (01787) 210215 & 211806
F: (01787) 211806
E: hurrellsf@a.o.l.com
I: members.a.o.l.
com/hurrellsf/index.htm

BOXTED
Essex

Round Hill House ◆◆◆◆
Parsonage Hill, Boxted,
Colchester, Essex CO4 5ST
T: (01206) 272392
F: (01206) 272392
E: jermar@appleonline.net
I: www.information-britain.
co.uk

BRADFIELD
Essex
Emsworth House ◆◆◆
Ship Hill, Bradfield,
Manningtree, Essex CO11 2UP
T: (01255) 870860 &
07767 477771
E: emsworthhouse@hotmail.
com
I: www.emsworthhouse.co.uk

BRADFIELD COMBUST
Suffolk
Church Farm ◆◆◆◆
Bradfield Combust, Bury St
Edmunds, Suffolk IP30 0LW
T: (01284) 386333
F: (01284) 386155
E: paul@williamsonff.freeserve.
co.uk

BRADWELL
Essex
Park Farmhouse ◆◆◆
Church Road, Bradwell,
Braintree, Essex CM7 8EP
T: (01376) 563584

BRAINTREE
Essex
16 Acorn Avenue ◆◆
Braintree, Essex CM7 2LR
T: (01376) 320155

**Brook Farm c/o Mrs A Butler
◆◆◆**
Wethersfield, Braintree, Essex
CM7 4BX
T: (01371) 850284 &
07770 881966
F: (01371) 850284

**Greengages Bed & Breakfast
◆◆◆◆**
268 Broad Road, Braintree, Essex
CM7 5NJ
T: (01376) 345868 &
0787 9284195

70 High Garrett ◆◆
Braintree, Essex CM7 5NT
T: (01376) 345330

The Old House ◆◆◆
11 Bradford Street, Braintree,
Essex CM7 9AS
T: (01376) 550457
F: (01376) 343863
E: old_house@talk21.com
I: theoldhousebraintree.co.uk

BRANDON
Suffolk
The Laurels ◆◆◆
162 London Road, Brandon,
Suffolk IP27 0LP
T: (01842) 812005

BRENT ELEIGH
Suffolk
Wroughton Lodge ◆◆◆◆
Brent Eleigh, Sudbury, Suffolk
CO10 9PB
T: (01787) 247495
E: elizabethknight@
wroughtonlodge.fsnet.co.uk
I: www.wroughtonlodge.fsnet.
co.uk

BRENTWOOD
Essex
Brentwood Guesthouse ◆◆◆
75/77 Rose Valley, Brentwood,
Essex CM14 4HJ
T: (01277) 262713 &
07710 523757
F: (01277) 211146

Chestnut Tree Cottage ◆◆◆
Great Warley Street, Great
Warley Village Green,
Brentwood, Essex CM13 3JF
T: (01277) 221727 &
0780 3131731

BRESSINGHAM
Norfolk
Hazel Barn ◆◆◆
Lodge Lane, Bressingham, Diss,
Norfolk IP22 2BE
T: (01379) 644396
E: hazelbarn@net-traders.co.uk

BRICKET WOOD
Hertfordshire
Little Oaks ◆◆◆◆
Lye Lane, Bricket Wood, St
Albans, Hertfordshire AL2 3TE
T: (01923) 681299
F: (01923) 681299

BRIGHTLINGSEA
Essex
Paxton Dene ◆◆◆◆
Church Road, Brightlingsea,
Colchester CO7 0QT
T: (01206) 304560
F: (01206) 302877
E: nora@paxtondene.freeserve.
co.uk
I: www.brightlingsea-town.
co.uk/business

BRISLEY
Norfolk
**The Brisley Bell Inn and
Restaurant
Rating Applied For**
The Green, Brisley, East
Dereham, Norfolk NR20 5DW
T: (01362) 668686
F: (01362) 668686

BROCKDISH
Norfolk
Grove Thorpe ◆◆◆◆◆
Grove Road, Brockdish, Diss,
Norfolk IP21 4JE
T: (01379) 668305
F: (01379) 668305
E: b-b@grovethorpe.freeserve.
co.uk
I: www.grovethorpe.co.uk

BROOKE
Norfolk
Hillside Farm ◆◆◆◆
Welbeck Road, Brooke, Norwich
NR15 1AU
T: (01508) 550260
F: (01508) 550260
E: carrieholl@tinyworld.co.uk
I: www.hillside-farm.com

The Old Vicarage ◆◆◆◆
48 The Street, Brooke, Norwich
NR15 1JU
T: (01508) 558329

BROOME
Norfolk
Outlaws Cottage ◆◆◆◆
Lugs Lane, Broome, Bungay,
Suffolk NR35 2HT
T: (01508) 518559
F: (01508) 518559

BRUNDALL
Norfolk
Braydeston House ◆◆◆
9 The Street, Brundall, Norwich,
Norfolk NR13 5JY
T: (01603) 713123
E: ann@braydeston.freeserve.
co.uk

3 Oak Hill ◆◆◆
Brundall, Norwich NR13 5AQ
T: (01603) 717903

BULPHAN
Essex
Bonny Downs Farm ◆◆◆
Doesgate Lane, Bulphan,
Upminster, Essex RM14 3TB
T: (01268) 542129

BUNGAY
Suffolk
Castles ◆◆◆◆
35 Earsham Street, Bungay,
Suffolk NR35 1AF
T: (01986) 892283
E: castles@lineone.net

Cleveland House ◆◆◆◆
2 Broad Street, Bungay, Suffolk
NR35 1EE
T: (01986) 896589
F: (01986) 892311

Dove Restaurant ◆◆◆
Holbrook Hill, Alburgh,
Harleston, Norfolk IP20 0EP
T: (01986) 788315
E: thedovenorfolk@freeola.com

Earsham Park Farm ◆◆◆◆
Harleston Road, Earsham,
Bungay, Suffolk NR35 2AQ
T: (01986) 892180 &
07887 648139
E: (01986) 892180
E: watchorn_s@freenet.co.uk

Manor Farm House ◆◆◆◆
St Margarets Road, Bungay,
Suffolk NR35 1PQ
T: (01986) 896895 &
07976 693506
F: 10986 896840

BUNTINGFORD
Hertfordshire
Buckland Bury Farm ◆◆◆◆
Buckland Bury, Buntingford,
Hertfordshire SG9 0PY
T: (01763) 272958 &
07881 802441
F: (01763) 274722
E: buckbury@farming.co.uk

Southfields Farm ◆◆◆
Throcking, Buntingford,
Hertfordshire SG9 9RD
T: (01763) 281224 &
07730 966898
F: (01763) 281224
E: iamurchie@hotmail.com

BURES
Suffolk
Queen's House ◆◆◆
Church Square, Bures, Suffolk
CO8 5AB
T: (01787) 227760 &
07802 841448
F: (01787) 227082
E: rogerarnold1@cs.com
I: www.ourworld.compuserve.
com/homepage/rogerarnold1

BURGH ST PETER
Norfolk
Shrublands Farm ◆◆◆◆
Burgh St Peter, Beccles, Suffolk
NR34 0BB
T: (01502) 677241
F: (01502) 677241

BURNHAM MARKET
Norfolk
Wood Lodge ◆◆◆◆
Millwood, Burnham Market,
King's Lynn, Norfolk PE31 8DP
T: (01328) 730152
F: (01328) 730158

BURNHAM-ON-CROUCH
Essex
Holyrood House ◆◆◆
46 Green Lane, Ostend,
Burnham-on-Crouch, Essex
CM0 8PU
T: (01621) 784759 & 784759

Mill Lodge ◆◆◆◆
Mill Green, Burnham-on-
Crouch, Essex CM0 8HT
T: (01621) 785321
E: royandsharon@martinson.
fsnet.co.uk

BURNHAM OVERY STAITHE
Norfolk
Domville ◆◆◆
Glebe Lane, Burnham Overy
Staithe, King's Lynn, Norfolk
PE31 8JQ
T: (01328) 738298

BURNHAM THORPE
Norfolk
Whitehall Farm ◆◆◆◆
Burnham Thorpe, King's Lynn,
Norfolk PE31 8HN
T: (01328) 738416 &
07831 794029
F: (01328) 730937
E: barry.southerland@amserve.
net

BURY ST EDMUNDS
Suffolk
**Abbotts House Bed &
Breakfast ◆◆◆**
2 Grove Road, Bury St Edmunds,
Suffolk IP33 3BE
T: (01284) 749660
F: (01284) 749660
E: robert.everitt@talk21.com
I: www.abbottshouse.co.uk

Brighthouse Farm ◆◆◆◆
Melford Road, Lawshall, Bury St
Edmunds, Suffolk IP29 4PX
T: (01284) 830385 &
07711 829546
F: (01284) 830385
E: brighthousefarm@supanet.
com
I: www.brighthousefarm.fsnet.
co.uk

Craufurd House ◆◆◆
Howe Lane, Cockfield, Bury St
Edmunds, Suffolk IP30 0HA
T: (01284) 828216

**Dunston Guesthouse/Hotel
◆◆◆**
8 Springfield Road, Bury St
Edmunds, Suffolk IP33 3AN
T: (01284) 767981

Hilltop ◆◆
22 Bronyon Close, Bury St
Edmunds, Suffolk IP33 3XB
T: (01284) 767066
E: bandb@hilltop22br.freeserve.
co.uk
I: www.hilltop22br.freeserve.
co.uk

Kent House
Rating Applied For
20 St Andrews Street North,
Bury St Edmunds, Suffolk
IP33 1TH
T: (01284) 769661 &
07801 735234
E: lizkent@supanet.com
I: you.genie.co.uk/I.kent/Default.
htm

Manorhouse ◆◆◆◆◆
The Green, Beyton, Bury St
Edmunds, Suffolk IP30 9AF
T: (01359) 270960
E: manorhouse@beyton.com
I: www.beyton.com

Northgate House ◆◆◆◆
8 Northgate Street, Bury St
Edmunds, Suffolk IP33 1HQ
T: (01284) 760469
F: (01284) 724008
E: northgate_hse@hotmail.com

The Old Bakery ◆◆◆◆
Farley Green, Wickhambrook,
Newmarket, Suffolk CB8 8PX
T: (01440) 820852 &
07778 380538
F: (0144U) 820852
E: info@theoldbakery.freeserve.
co.uk

Park House ◆◆◆
22A Mustow Road, Bury St
Edmunds, Suffolk IP33 1XL
T: (01284) 703432
F: (01284) 703432

Regency House Hotel
Rating Applied For
3 Looms Lane, Bury St Edmunds,
Suffolk IP33 1HE
T: (01284) 764676
F: (01284) 752718

82 Risbygate Street Bed &
Breakfast ◆◆◆
Bury St Edmunds, Suffolk
IP33 3AQ
T: (01284) 760594
E: harold@par4.fsnet.co.uk

South Hill House ◆◆◆◆
43 Southgate Street, Bury St
Edmunds, Suffolk IP33 2AZ
T: (01284) 755650
F: (01284) 752718
E: southill@cwcom.net
I: www.southill.cwc.net

Sycamore House ◆◆◆
23 Northgate Street, Bury St
Edmunds, Suffolk IP33 1HP
T: (01284) 755828
E: m.chalkley@ntlworld.com
I: www.sycamorehouse.net

Toad Hall ◆◆◆◆
Gedding, Bury St Edmunds,
Suffolk IP30 0QA
T: (01449) 736488 &
07747 621096
F: (01449) 736706
E: selucy@compuserve.com

BUXTON
Norfolk

Belair ◆◆◆
Crown Road, Buxton, Norwich
NR10 5EN
T: (01603) 279637 &
0790 1655348
F: (01603) 279637
E: johnblake1234@aol.com

CAMBRIDGE
Cambridgeshire

Acer House ◆◆◆
3 Dean Drive, Holbrook Road,
Cambridge, CB1 7SW
T: (01223) 210404
E: carol.dennett@btinternet.
com
I: www.smoothhound.
co.uk/hotels/acerhous.html

Acorn Guesthouse ◆◆◆◆
154 Chesterton Road,
Cambridge, CB4 1DA
T: (01223) 353888
F: (01223) 350527
E: info@acornguesthouse.co.uk
I: www.acornguest.co.uk

Alpha Milton Guesthouse
◆◆◆
61-63 Milton Road, Cambridge,
CB4 1XA
T: (01223) 311625 & 565100
F: (01223) 565100

Arbury Lodge Guesthouse
◆◆◆
82 Arbury Road, Cambridge,
CB4 2JE
T: (01223) 364319 & 566988
F: (01223) 566988
E: arburylodge@ntlworld.com
I: www.guesthousecambridge.
com

Ashley Hotel ◆◆◆
74 Chesterton Road, Cambridge,
CB4 1ER
T: (01223) 350059
F: (01223) 350900
E: info@arundelhousehotels.
co.uk
I: www.arundelhousehotels.
co.uk

Ashtrees Guesthouse ◆◆◆
128 Perne Road, Cambridge,
CB1 3RR
T: (01223) 411233
F: (01223) 411233
E: mandy@mhill22.fsnet.co.uk
I: www.smoothhound.
co.uk/hotels/ashtrees.html

Assisi Guesthouse ◆◆◆
193 Cherry Hinton Road,
Cambridge, CB1 7BX
T: (01223) 246648 & 211466
F: (01223) 412900

Aylesbray Lodge Guesthouse
◆◆◆◆
5 Mowbray Road, Cambridge,
CB1 7SR
T: (01223) 240089
F: (01223) 528678
E: aylesbray.lodge@ntlworld.
com
I: www.smoothhound.
co.uk/hotels/aylesbray.html

Brooklands Guesthouse ◆◆◆
95 Cherry Hinton Road,
Cambridge, CB1 7BS
T: (01223) 242035
F: (01223) 242035

Cam Guesthouse ◆◆◆
17 Elizabeth Way, Cambridge,
CB4 1DD
T: (01223) 354512
F: (01223) 353164
E: camguesthouse@btinternet.
com
I: www.camguesthouse.co.uk

Cambridge Lodge Hotel
◆◆◆◆
139 Huntingdon Road,
Cambridge, CB3 0DQ
T: (01223) 352833
F: (01223) 355166

Carolina Bed & Breakfast ◆◆◆
148 Perne Road, Cambridge,
CB1 3NX
T: (01223) 247015 &
07716 83424
F: (01223) 247015
E: carolina.amabile@tesco.net
I: www.smoothhound.
co.uk/hotels/carol.html

Cristinas ◆◆◆
47 St Andrews Road, Cambridge,
CB4 1DH
T: (01223) 365855 & 327700
F: (01223) 365855
E: cristinas.guesthouse@
ntlworld.com
I: www.smoothhound.
co.uk/hotels/cristina.html

Dresden Villa Guesthouse
◆◆◆
34 Cherry Hinton Road,
Cambridge, CB1 7AA
T: (01223) 247539
F: (01223) 410640

Dykelands Guesthouse ◆◆◆
157 Mowbray Road, Cambridge,
CB1 7SP
T: (01223) 244300
F: (01223) 566746
E: dykelands@fsbdial.co.uk
I: www.dykelands.com

Finches ◆◆◆◆
144 Thornton Road, Girton,
Cambridge CB3 0ND
T: (01223) 276653 &
07710 179214
F: (01223) 276653
E: liz.green.b-b@talk21.com
I: www.smoothhound.
co.uk/hotels/finches

Gransden Lodge Farm ◆◆◆◆
Little Gransden, Longstowe,
Cambridge SG19 3EB
T: (01767) 677365
F: (01767) 677647

Hamilton Hotel ◆◆◆
156 Chesterton Road,
Cambridge, CB4 1DA
T: (01223) 365664
F: (01223) 314866

Hills Guesthouse ◆◆◆◆
157 Hills Road, Cambridge,
CB2 2RJ
T: (01223) 214216
F: (01223) 214216

King's Tithe ◆◆◆◆
13a Comberton Road, Barton,
Cambridge CB3 7BA
T: (01223) 263610
F: (01223) 263610
E: thornebarton@lineone.net

Lensfield Hotel ◆◆◆◆
53 Lensfield Road, Cambridge,
CB2 1EN
T: (01223) 355017
F: (01223) 312022
E: reservations@lensfield.co.uk
I: www.lensfieldhotel.co.uk

Lovell Lodge Hotel ◆◆◆
365 Milton Road, Cambridge,
CB4 1SR
T: (01223) 425478
F: (01223) 426581

Segovia Lodge ◆◆◆
2 Barton Road, Newnham,
Cambridge, CB3 9JZ
T: (01223) 354105
F: (01223) 323011

Southampton Guest House
◆◆◆
7 Elizabeth Way, Cambridge,
CB4 1DE
T: (01223) 357780
F: (01223) 314297
E: southamptonhouse@telco4u.
net
I: www.smoothhound.
co.uk/hotels/sout.htlm

The Suffolk House ◆◆◆◆
69 Milton Road, Cambridge,
CB4 1XA
T: (01223) 352016
F: (01223) 566816
E: suffolkhouse@btinternet.com

Sycamore House ◆◆◆◆
56 High Street, Great
Wilbraham, Cambridge CB1 5JD
T: (01223) 880751 &
07711 845300
F: (01223) 880751
E: barry@thesycamorehouse.
co.uk
I: www.thesycamorehouse.co.uk

Victoria ◆◆◆◆
57 Arbury Road, Cambridge,
CB4 2JB
T: (01223) 350086
F: (01223) 350086
E: vicmaria@globalnet.co.uk
I: www.victoriaguesthouse.co.uk

Woodfield House ◆◆◆◆
Madingley Road, Coton,
Cambridge CB3 7PH
T: (01954) 210265
F: (01954) 212650
E: wendy_
johnawsadlerfreeserve.co.uk

Worth House ◆◆◆◆
152 Chesterton Road,
Cambridge, CB4 1DA
T: (01223) 316074
F: (01223) 316074
E: enquiries@worth-house.
co.uk
I: www.worth-house.co.uk

CAMPSEA ASHE
Suffolk

The Old Rectory ◆◆◆◆◆
Campsea Ashe, Woodbridge,
Suffolk IP13 0PU
T: (01728) 746524
F: (01728) 746524

CARBROOKE
Norfolk

White Hall ◆◆◆◆
Carbrooke, Thetford, Norfolk
IP25 6SG
T: (01953) 885950
F: (01953) 884420
E: shirleycarr@whitehall.uk.net

CARLETON RODE
Norfolk

Upgate Farm ◆◆◆
Carleton Rode, Norwich
NR16 1NJ
T: (01953) 860300
F: (01953) 860300
E: upgatefarm@btinternet

CASTLE ACRE
Norfolk

Pilgrims Cottage ◆◆
3 Stocks Green, Castle Acre,
King's Lynn, Norfolk PE32 2AE
T: (01328) 820044 &
07889 902818
F: (01328) 821006
E: valguinness@hotmail.com

CASTLE HEDINGHAM
Essex

Fishers ◆◆◆◆
St James Street, Castle
Hedingham, Halstead, Essex
CO9 3EW
T: (01787) 460382
F: (01787) 460382
E: Fishers@hutchingsh.
freeserve.co.uk

The Old School House ◆◆◆
St James Street, Castle
Hedingham, Halstead, Essex
CO9 3EW
T: (01787) 461629
E: trish@pmsacc.demon.co.uk

CASTOR
Cambridgeshire

Cobnut Cottage ◆◆◆◆
45 Peterborough Road, Castor,
Peterborough PE5 7AX
T: (01733) 380745
F: (01733) 380745
E: huckle.cobnut@talk21.com

Old Smithy ◆◆◆◆
47 Peterborough Road, Castor,
Peterborough PE5 7AX
T: (01733) 380186
F: (01733) 380186
E: julie.e.m.taylor@lineone.net

CAVENDISH
Suffolk

**Embleton House Bed &
Breakfast ◆◆◆◆**
Melford Road, Cavendish,
Sudbury, Suffolk CO10 8AA
T: (01787) 280447
F: (01787) 282396
E: silverned@aol.com
I: www.smoothhound.
co.uk/hotels/embleton

**The Red House Bed and
Breakfast ◆◆◆◆**
Stour Street, Cavendish,
Sudbury, Suffolk CO10 8BH
T: (01787) 280611
F: (01787) 280611
E: theredhousebandb@lineone.
net
I: www.SmoothHound.
co.uk/hotels/theredh.html

CHELMSFORD
Essex

Aarandale ◆◆◆
9 Roxwell Road, Chelmsford,
CM1 2LY
T: (01245) 251713
F: (01245) 251713
E: aarandaleuk@aol.com

Almond Lodge ◆◆◆
The Bringey, Great Baddow,
Chelmsford CM2 7JW
T: (01245) 471564
E: resnorfolk@btinternet.com

Aquila ◆◆
11 Daffodil Way, Springfield,
Chelmsford, CM1 6XB
T: (01245) 465274

Beechcroft Private Hotel ◆◆◆
211 New London Road,
Chelmsford, CM2 0AJ
T: (01245) 352462 & 250861
F: (01245) 347833
E: beechcroft.hotel@btinternet.
com
I: www.beechcrofthotel.com

Boswell House Hotel ◆◆◆◆
118 Springfield Road,
Chelmsford, CM2 6LF
T: (01245) 287587
F: (01245) 287587

Brook House ◆◆◆◆
Chelmsford Road, Great
Waltham, Chelmsford, CM3 1AQ
T: (01245) 360776 &
07723 006154

The Chelmer Hotel ◆◆
2-4 Hamlet Road, Chelmsford,
CM2 0EU
T: (01245) 353360 & 609055
F: (01245) 609055
E: collingsnick@hotmail.com

Fitzjohns Farmhouse ◆◆◆
Mashbury Road, Great Waltham,
Chelmsford, CM3 1EJ
T: (01245) 360204 & 361224
F: (01245) 361724
E: rosrenwick@aol.com

Neptune Cafe Motel ◆◆
Burnham Road, Latchingdon,
Chelmsford CM3 6EX
T: (01621) 740770

Old Bakery ◆◆◆◆
Waltham Road, Terling,
Chelmsford, CM3 2QR
T: (01245) 233363

Pemajero ◆◆◆
Cedar Avenue West, Chelmsford,
CM1 2XA
T: (01245) 264679
F: (01245) 264679

Sherwood ◆◆◆
Cedar Avenue West, Chelmsford,
CM1 2XA
T: (01245) 257981
F: (01245) 257981
E: jeremy.salter@btclick.com

Silvertrees ◆◆
565 Galleywood Road,
Chelmsford, CM2 8AA
T: (01245) 268767

Springford ◆◆◆
8 Well Lane, Galleywood,
Chelmsford CM2 8QY
T: (01245) 257821

Stump Cross House ◆◆◆◆
Moulsham Street, Chelmsford,
CM2 9AQ
T: (01245) 353804

Tanunda Hotel ◆◆◆
217-219 New London Road,
Chelmsford, CM2 0AJ
T: (01245) 354295 & 258799
F: (01245) 345503

Wards Farm ◆◆
Loves Green, Highwood Road,
Highwood, Chelmsford CM1 3QJ
T: (01245) 248812
F: (01245) 248812
E: alsnbrtn@aol.com

CLACTON-ON-SEA
Essex

**Le'Vere House Hotel
Rating Applied For**
15 Agate Road, Clacton-on-Sea,
Essex CO15 1RA
T: (01255) 423044
F: (01255) 423044

Sandrock Hotel ◆◆◆
1 Penfold Road, Marine Parade
West, Clacton-on-Sea, Essex
CO15 1JN
T: (01255) 428215
F: (01255) 428215

Stonar Hotel ◆◆◆
19 Agate Road, Clacton-on-Sea,
Essex CO15 1RA
T: (01255) 221011 &
07802 387778
F: (01255) 422973

CLAPHAM
Bedfordshire

**Narly Oak Lodge Narly Oak
◆◆◆◆**
The Baulk, Green Lane, Clapham,
Bedford MK41 6AA
T: (01234) 350353
F: (01234) 350353
E: fostert@csd.bedfordshire.
gov.uk

CLARE
Suffolk

The Clare Hotel ◆◆◆
19 Nethergate Street, Clare,
Sudbury, Suffolk CO10 8NP
T: (01787) 277449
F: (01787) 277161
E: rhrng@netscapeonline.co.uk

Cobbles ◆◆◆
26 Nethergate Street, Clare,
Sudbury, Suffolk CO10 8NP
T: (01787) 277539
F: (01787) 278252
E: cobbles@tuffillverner.com

Ship Stores ◆◆◆
22 Callis Street, Clare, Sudbury,
Suffolk CO10 8PX
T: (01787) 277834
E: shipclare@aol.com
I: www.ship-stores.co.uk

CLEY NEXT THE SEA
Norfolk

**Cooke's of Cley
Rating Applied For**
High Street, Cley next the Sea,
Holt, Norfolk NR25 7RX
T: (01263) 740776
F: (01263) 740776
I: www.broadland./cookesofcley

The George Hotel ◆◆◆
High Street, Cley next the Sea,
Holt, Norfolk NR25 7RN
T: (01263) 740652
F: (01263) 741275
E: thegeorge@cleynextthesea.
com
I: www.thegeorgehotelcley.com

CLOPHILL
Bedfordshire

**Shallmarose Bed & Breakfast
◆◆◆**
32 Bedford Road, Clophill,
Bedford MK45 4AE
T: (01525) 861565

COLCHESTER
Essex

Apple Blossom House ◆◆◆
8 Guildford Road, Colchester,
CO1 2YL
T: (01206) 512303
F: (01206) 870260

Athelstan House ◆◆◆◆
201 Maldon Road, Colchester,
CO3 3BQ
T: (01206) 548652
E: mackman@mcmail.com

Four Sevens Guesthouse ◆◆◆
28 Inglis Road, Colchester,
CO3 3HU
T: (01206) 546093
F: (01206) 546093
E: calypsod@hotmail.com
I: www.cdemetri.freeserve.com.
uk

Fridaywood Farm ◆◆◆◆
Bounstead Road, Colchester,
CO2 0DF
T: (01206) 573595 &
07970 836285
F: (01206) 547011

Glinska House ◆◆◆◆
6 St Johns Green, Colchester,
CO2 7HA
T: (01206) 578961 &
07850 215598
F: (01206) 503406
E: rhawki@email.msn.com

Hampton House ◆◆◆
224 Maldon Road, Colchester,
CO3 3BD
T: (01206) 579291

11 Harvest End ◆◆◆
Stanway, Colchester, CO3 5YX
T: (01206) 543202

Lemoine ◆◆◆◆
2 Whitefriars Way, Colchester,
CO3 4EL
T: (01206) 574710

11a Lincoln Way ◆◆◆
Colchester, CO1 2RL
T: (01206) 867192 &
07710 208168
F: (01206) 799993
E: j.medwards@easicom.com

Nutcrackers ◆◆◆
6 Mayberry Walk, Colchester,
CO2 8PS
T: (01206) 543085
E: jean@aflex.net.

Old Courthouse Inn ◆◆◆◆
Harwich Road, Great Bromley,
Colchester, CO7 7JG
T: (01206) 250322 & 251906
F: (01206) 251346
E: oldcourthoseinn@21.com

Pescara House ◆◆◆
88 Manor Road, Colchester,
CO3 3LY
T: (01206) 520055
F: (01206) 512127
E: dave@pescarahouse.co.uk
I: www.pescarahouse.co.uk

Peveril Hotel ◆◆
51 North Hill, Colchester,
CO1 1PY
T: (01206) 574001
F: (01206) 574001

The Red House ◆◆◆◆
29 Wimpole Road, Colchester,
CO1 2DL
T: (01206) 509005
F: (01206) 500311
E: theredhousecolchester@
hotmail.com

76 Roman Road ◆◆◆
Colchester, CO1 1UP
T: (01206) 514949

Scheregate Hotel ◆◆
36 Osborne Street, via St John's
Street, Colchester, CO2 7DB
T: (01206) 573034
F: (01206) 541561

Seven Arches Farm ◆◆
Chitts Hill, Lexden, Colchester,
CO3 5SX
T: (01206) 574896
F: (01206) 574896

Tall Trees ◆◆◆◆
25 Irvine Road, Colchester,
CO3 3TP
T: (01206) 576650 & 0794 122
3688
E: whitehead.talltrees@lineone.
net

Telstar ◆◆◆
Layer Breton, Colchester,
CO2 0PS
T: (01206) 331642

4 Wavell Avenue ◆◆
Colchester, CO2 7HP
T: (01206) 571736

COLTISHALL
Norfolk
The Hedges Guesthouse
◆◆◆◆
Tunstead Road, Coltishall,
Norwich NR12 7AL
T: (01603) 738361
F: (01603) 738983
E: thehedges@msn.com
I: www.hedgesbandb.co.uk

Kings Head ◆◆◆
26 Wroxham Road, Coltishall,
Norwich NR12 7EA
T: (01603) 737426
F: (01603) 736542

The Old Railway Station ◆◆◆
The Old Railway Station, Station
Road, Coltishall, Norwich
NR12 7JG
T: (01603) 737069 &
07879 671865

Terra Nova Lodge ◆◆◆◆
14 Westbourne Road, Coltishall,
Norwich NR12 7HT
T: (01603) 736264

CORTON
Suffolk
Barn Owl Lodge ◆◆◆
Yarmouth Road, Corton,
Lowestoft, Suffolk NR32 5NH
T: (01502) 733105

Holly Cottage ◆◆◆◆
11 Mill Lane, Corton, Lowestoft,
Suffolk NR32 5HZ
T: (01502) 731224

COTTENHAM
Cambridgeshire
Denmark House
Rating Applied For
58 Denmark Road, Cottenham,
Cambridge CB4 8QS
T: (01954) 251060 & 250448
F: (01954) 251629
E: denmark.house@tesco.net

CRANFIELD
Bedfordshire
The Swan ◆◆
2 Court Road, Cranfield, Bedford
MK43 0DR
T: (01234) 750332
F: (01234) 750332

CREETING ST MARY
Suffolk
St Eia ◆◆◆◆
All Saints Road, Creeting St
Mary, Needham Market, Ipswich
IP6 8PP
T: (01449) 721977

CRETINGHAM
Suffolk
The Cretingham Bell ◆◆◆◆
The Street, Cretingham,
Woodbridge, Suffolk IP13 7BJ
T: (01728) 685419

Shrubbery Farmhouse ◆◆◆◆
Chapel Hill, Cretingham,
Woodbridge, Suffolk IP13 7DN
T: (01473) 737494 &
07860 352317
F: (01473) 737312
F: sm@marmar.co.uk
I: www.shrubberyfarmhouse.
co.uk

CROMER
Norfolk
Birch House ◆◆◆
34 Cabbell Road, Cromer,
Norfolk NR27 9HX
T: (01263) 512521

Cambridge House ◆◆◆
Sea Front, Cromer, Norfolk
NR29 9HD
T: (01263) 512085
I: www.broadland.
com/cambridgehouse

The Grove Guesthouse ◆◆◆
95 Overstrand Road, Cromer,
Norfolk NR27 0DJ
T: (01263) 512412
F: (01263) 513416
E: thegrove@barclays.net
I: www.thegrovecromer.co.uk

Knoll Guesthouse ◆◆◆
23 Alfred Road, Cromer, Norfolk
NR27 9AN
T: (01263) 512753
E: ian@knollguesthouse.co.uk
I: www.knollguesthouse.co.uk

Morden House ◆◆◆◆
20 Cliff Avenue, Cromer, Norfolk
NR27 0AN
T: (01263) 513396
E: rosemary@broadland.co.uk
I: www.broadland.
com/mordenhouse

Seaspray ◆◆◆◆
1 Cliff Drive, Cromer, Norfolk
NR27 0AW
T: (01263) 512116

Shrublands Farm ◆◆◆◆
Northrepps, Cromer, Norfolk
NR27 0AA
T: (01263) 579297
F: (01263) 579297
E: youngman@farming.co.uk
I: www.broadland.
com/shrublands

Stenson ◆◆◆◆
32 Overstrand Road, Cromer,
Norfolk NR27 0AJ
T: (01263) 511308

DALLINGHOO
Suffolk
Old Rectory ◆◆◆
Dallinghoo, Woodbridge, Suffolk
IP13 0LA
T: (01473) 737700

DANBURY
Essex
Southways ◆◆◆
Copt Hill, Danbury, Chelmsford
CM3 4NN
T: (01245) 223428

DARSHAM
Suffolk
Priory Farm ◆◆◆
Darsham, Saxmundham, Suffolk
IP17 3QD
T: (01728) 668459

White House Farm ◆◆◆
Main Road, Darsham,
Saxmundham, Suffolk IP17 3PP
T: (01728) 668632

DEBDEN
Essex
Redbrick House ◆◆◆
Deynes Road, Debden, Saffron
Walden, Essex CB11 3LG
T: (01799) 540221
F: 0870 1643639
E: bandb@redbrick-house.fsnet.
co.uk

DEDHAM
Essex
Good Hall ◆◆◆◆
Coggeshall Road, Dedham,
Colchester CO7 7LR
T: (01206) 322100
F: (01206) 323902
E: goodhall@ic24.net

The Marlborough ◆◆◆
Mill Lane, Dedham, Colchester
CO7 6DH
T: (01206) 323250
F: (01206) 322331
E: themarlborough@fsmail.net
I: www.oldenglish.co.uk

May's Barn Farm ◆◆◆◆
May's Lane, Off Long Road West,
Dedham, Colchester CO7 6EW
T: (01206) 323191
E: maysbarn@talk21.com
I: www.mays.barn.btinternet.
co.uk

DENNINGTON
Suffolk
Grange Farm Bed & Breakfast
◆◆◆
Grange Farm, Dennington,
Woodbridge, Suffolk IP13 8BT
T: (01986) 798388 &
07774 182835
I: www.framlingham.
com/grangefarm

DENVER
Norfolk
Westhall Cottage ◆◆◆
20-22 Sluice Road, Denver,
Downham Market, Norfolk
PE38 0DY
T: (01366) 382987
F: (01366) 385553

DEPDEN
Suffolk
Elms Farm Bed & Breakfast
◆◆◆◆
Elms Farm, Depden, Bury St
Edmunds, Suffolk IP29 4BS
T: (01284) 850289 &
07887 875943
F: (01284) 851085
E: elmsfarm@supanet.com

DEREHAM
Norfolk
Greenbanks Country Hotel
◆◆◆◆
Swaffham Road, Wendling,
Dereham, Norfolk NR19 2AR
T: (01362) 687742
F: (01362) 687742
E: greenbanks@skynow.net
I: www.greenbankshotel.co.uk
(🐾)

Park Farm ◆◆◆◆
Bylaugh, East Dereham, Norfolk
NR20 4QE
T: (01362) 688584
E: lakeparkfm@aol.com

DERSINGHAM
Norfolk
Ashdene House ◆◆◆
Dersingham, King's Lynn,
Norfolk PE31 6HQ
T: (01485) 540395
I: www.mistral.co.uk/ashdene

The Corner House ◆◆◆◆
2 Sandringham Road,
Dersingham, King's Lynn,
Norfolk PE31 6LL
T: (01485) 543532

Dove Lodge ◆◆◆◆
21 Woodside Avenue,
Dersingham, King's Lynn,
Norfolk PE31 6QB
T: (01485) 540053 &
07703 790789
F: (01485) 540053

Tall Trees ◆◆◆
7 Centre Vale, Dersingham,
King's Lynn, Norfolk PE31 6JR
T: (01485) 542638
F: (01485) 542638
E: frosty-trees@classicfm.net
I: www.talltrees-norfolk.co.uk

The White House ◆◆◆
44 Hunstanton Road,
Dersingham, King's Lynn,
Norfolk PE31 6HQ
T: (01485) 541895 & 544880
F: (01485) 544880
E: whitehouseguestaccom@
ukonline.co.uk

Woodroyal ◆◆◆◆
Manor Road, Dersingham, King's
Lynn, Norfolk PE31 6LD
T: (01485) 543156

DISS
Norfolk
Abbey Farm ◆◆◆
Great Green, Thrandeston, Diss,
Norfolk IP21 4BN
T: (01379) 783422
E: jean.carlisle@virgin.net
I: wwwdiss.co.uk

Dickleburgh Hall ◆◆◆◆◆
Semere Green Lane, Dickleburgh,
Diss, Norfolk IP21 4NT
T: (01379) 741259 &
07702 273497
I: www.dickhall.co.uk

Ducksfoot Farm ◆◆◆
Bush Green, Pulham Market,
Diss, Norfolk IP21 4YB
T: (01379) 608561
F: (01379) 608562
E: mvenables@duckfoot.fsnet.
co.uk
I: www.abreakwithtradition.
co.uk

Koliba ◆◆◆
8 Louie's Lane, Diss, Norfolk
IP22 4LR
T: (01379) 650046 &
07788 400040
F: (01379) 650046
E: olgakoliba@aol.com

Oxfootstone Granary ◆◆◆◆
Low Common, South Lopham,
Diss, Norfolk IP22 2JS
T: (01379) 687490
E: oxfoot@cwcom.net

Rose Cottage ◆◆◆
Diss Road, Burston, Diss, Norfolk
IP22 5TP
T: (01379) 740602 &
07770 410534
F: (01379) 740602
E: cyrilbrom@aol.com

South View ◆◆◆
High Road, Roydon, Diss,
Norfolk IP22 5RU
T: (01379) 651620

Strenneth ◆◆◆◆
Airfield Road, Fersfield, Diss,
Norfolk IP22 2BP
T: (01379) 688182
F: (01379) 688260
E: ken@strenneth.co.uk
I: www.strenneth.co.uk

DOCKING
Norfolk

Bakers Cottage ◆◆◆
Station Road, Docking, King's
Lynn, Norfolk PE31 8LR
T: (01485) 518510

Jubilee Lodge ◆◆◆
Station Road, Docking, King's
Lynn, Norfolk PE31 8LS
T: (01485) 518473
F: (01485) 518473
E: eqhoward62@hotmail.com
I: www.jubilee-lodge.co.uk

DOVERCOURT
Essex

Dudley Guesthouse ◆◆
34 Cliff Road, Dovercourt,
Harwich, Essex CO12 3PP
T: (01255) 504927

Homebay ◆◆◆
9 Bay Road, Dovercourt,
Harwich, Essex CO12 3JZ
T: (01255) 504428
E: sydie@dialstart.net

Sun View ◆◆
42 Cliff Road, Dovercourt,
Harwich, Essex CO12 3PP
T: (01255) 507816

Tudor Rose ◆◆◆
124 Fronks Road, Dovercourt,
Harwich, Essex CO12 4EQ
T: (01255) 552398
E: jane@morgan-co12.
freeserve.co.uk

DOWNHAM MARKET
Norfolk

Chestnut Villa ◆◆◆
44 Railway Road, Downham
Market, Norfolk PE38 9EB
T: (01366) 384099
E: chesnutvilla@talk21.com

**Lion House Licensed
Restaurant and Guest House**
◆◆◆
Lion House, 140 Lynn Road,
Downham Market, Norfolk
PE38 9QF
T: (01366) 382017
E: lionhouse@supanet.com
I: www.lionhouse.supanet.com

DUNSTABLE
Bedfordshire

Cherish End B & B ◆◆◆◆
21 Barton Avenue, Dunstable,
Bedfordshire LU5 4DF
T: (01582) 606266
F: (01582) 606266
E: dandg4bandb@tinyworld.
co.uk

EARITH
Cambridgeshire

Riverview Hotel ◆◆◆
37 High Street, Earith,
Huntingdon, Cambridgeshire
PE28 3PP
T: (01487) 841405
E: riverviewhotel@tinyworld.
co.uk
I: www.riverviewhotel.co.uk

EARL SOHAM
Suffolk

Bridge House ◆◆◆◆
Earl Soham, Woodbridge,
Suffolk IP13 7RT
T: (01728) 685473 & 685289
T: (01728) 685289
E: bridgehouse46@hotmail.com
I: www.jenniferbaker.co.uk

EARLS COLNE
Essex

Chalkney Wood Cottage
◆◆◆◆
Tey Road, Earls Colne, Colchester
CO6 2LD
T: (01787) 223522
F: (01787) 224267

Riverside Lodge ◆◆◆
40 Lower Holt Street, Earls
Colne, Colchester CO6 2PH
T: (01787) 223487
F: (01787) 223487

EAST BARSHAM
Norfolk

White Horse Inn ◆◆◆
Fakenham Road, East Barsham,
Fakenham, Norfolk NR21 0LH
T: (01328) 820645
F: (01328) 820645

EAST BERGHOLT
Suffolk

Rosemary ◆◆◆
Rectory Hill, East Bergholt,
Colchester CO7 6TH
T: (01206) 298241
E: s.finch@bcs.org.uk

EAST MERSEA
Essex

Bromans Farm ◆◆◆◆
Mersea Island, East Mersea,
Colchester CO5 8UE
T: (01206) 383235
F: (01206) 383235

Mersea Island Vineyard
◆◆◆◆
Rewsalls Lane, East Mersea,
Colchester CO5 8SX
T: (01206) 385900
F: (01206) 383600
E: jacqui.barber@merseawine.
com
I: www.merseawine.com

EASTON
Suffolk

Atlantis Stud Farm ◆◆◆◆
Framlingham Road, Easton,
Woodbridge, Suffolk IP13 0EW
T: (01728) 621553
F: (01728) 621553
E: atlantisbandb@yahoo.co.uk

ELMSWELL
Suffolk

Elmswell Hall Bed & Breakfast
◆◆◆◆
Elmswell Hall, Elmswell, Bury St
Edmunds, Suffolk IP30 9EN
T: (01359) 240215
F: (01359) 240215
E: kate@elmswellhall.freeserve.
co.uk
I: www.elmswellhall.co.uk

Kiln Farm ◆◆◆
Kiln Lane, Elmswell, Bury St
Edmunds, Suffolk IP30 9QR
T: (01359) 240442 & 242604
E: barry-sue@kilnfarm.fsnet.
co.uk

Mulberry Farm ◆◆◆◆
Ashfield Road, Elmswell, Bury St
Edmunds, Suffolk IP30 9HG
T: (01359) 244244 &
07885 934309
F: (01359) 244244

ELSENHAM
Hertfordshire

Aspens ◆◆◆
Park Road, Elsenham, Bishop's
Stortford, Hertfordshire
CM22 6DF
T: (01279) 816281 &
0788 4047273

ELY
Cambridgeshire

Cambridge House ◆◆◆
2 Ship Lane, Ely, Cambridgeshire
CB7 4BB
T: (01353) 662088
E: info@ukdomains.net
I: www.ukdomains.net

Cathedral House ◆◆◆◆
17 St Mary's Street, Ely,
Cambridgeshire CB7 4ER
T: (01353) 662124
F: (01353) 662124
E: farndale@cathedralhouse.
co.uk
I: www.cathedralhouse.co.uk

**The Flyer Restaurant, Public
House & Hotel** ◆◆◆
69 Newnham Street, Ely,
Cambridgeshire CB7 4PQ
T: (01353) 669200
F: (01353) 669100
E: graham@flyerhotel.co.uk
I: www.flyerhotel.co.uk

The Grove ◆◆◆◆
Bury Lane, Sutton Gault, Ely,
Cambridgeshire CB6 2BD
T: (01353) 777196
F: (01353) 777425

Hill House Farm ◆◆◆◆
9 Main Street, Coveney, Ely,
Cambridgeshire CB6 2DJ
T: (01353) 778369
F: (01353) 778369
E: hill_house@madasafish.com

Nyton Hotel ◆◆◆
7 Barton Road, Ely,
Cambridgeshire CB7 4HZ
T: (01353) 662459
F: (01353) 666217
E: nytonhotel@yahoo.co.uk

Rosendale Lodge ◆◆◆◆◆
223 Main Street, Witchford, Ely,
Cambridgeshire CB6 2HT
T: (01353) 667700
F: (01353) 667799
&

Spinney Abbey ◆◆◆◆
Stretham Road, Wicken, Ely,
Cambridgeshire CB7 5XQ
T: (01353) 720971
E: spinney.abbey@tesco.net
I: www.spinneyabbey.co.uk

Springfields
Rating Applied For
Ely Road, Little Thetford, Ely,
Cambridgeshire CB6 3HJ
T: (01353) 663637
F: (01353) 663130
E: springfields@talk21.com
I: www.smoothhound.
co.uk/hotels/springfields.html

Sycamore House ◆◆◆◆
91 Cambridge Road, Ely,
Cambridgeshire CB7 4HX
T: (01353) 662139
F: (01353) 662795
E: sycamore_house@hotmail.
com

Waterside Bed & Breakfast
◆◆◆◆
52 Waterside, Ely,
Cambridgeshire CB7 4AZ
T: (01353) 667570
E: jane.latimer@classicfm.net
I: www.waterside-ely.co.uk

EPPING
Essex

Brooklands ◆◆◆
1 Chapel Road, Epping, Essex
CM16 5DS
T: (01992) 575424
I: www.abrookland@aol.com

**Country House Bed &
Breakfast** ◆◆◆◆
16 Beulah Road, Epping, Essex
CM16 6RH
T: (01992) 576044
F: (01992) 570430
E: epping.accomm@btinternet.
com

ERPINGHAM
Norfolk

Saracens Head Inn ◆◆◆
Wolterton, Erpingham, Norwich
NR11 7LX
T: (01263) 768909
F: (01263) 768993
I: www.broadland.
com/saracenshead

EYE
Suffolk

The White Horse Inn ◆◆◆
Stoke Ash, Eye, Suffolk IP23 7ET
T: (01379) 678222
F: (01379) 678557
E: whitehorse@stokeash.
fsbusiness.co.uk

EYKE
Suffolk

The Old House ◆◆◆◆
Eyke, Woodbridge, Suffolk
IP12 2QW
T: (01394) 460213

FAKENHAM
Norfolk

Abbott Farm ◆◆◆
Walsingham Road, Binham,
Fakenham, Norfolk NR21 0AW
T: (01328) 830519 & 0780 884
7582
F: (01328) 830519
E: abbot.farm@btinternet.com

Erika's Bed and Breakfast
◆◆◆
3 Gladstone Road, Fakenham,
Norfolk NR21 9BZ
T: (01328) 863058

Hardlands ◆◆◆◆
East Raynham, Fakenham,
Norfolk NR21 7EQ
T: (01328) 862567 &
07710 232441
E: harlands@waitrose.com
I: harlands@waitrose.com

Highfield Farm ◆◆◆◆
Great Ryburgh, Fakenham,
Norfolk NR21 7AL
T: (01328) 829249
F: (01328) 829422
E: jegshighfield@onet.co.uk
I: www.broadland.com/highfield

Hillside Bed & Breakfast
◆◆◆◆
47 Wells Road, Fakenham,
Norfolk NR21 9HQ
T: (01328) 855128
E: mhillside@cs.com

Holly Lodge ◆◆◆◆◆
The Street, Thursford Green,
Fakenham, Norfolk NR21 0AS
T: (01328) 878465
F: (01328) 878465
E: hollyguestlodge@talk21.com
I: www.hollylodgeguesthouse.
co.uk

Mulberry Cottage ◆◆◆◆
Green Farm Lane, Thursford
Green, Fakenham, Norfolk
NR21 0RX
T: (01328) 878968

The Old Brick Kilns Guesthouse
◆◆◆◆
Little Barney Lane, Little Barney,
NR21 0NL
T: (01328) 878305
F: (01328) 878948
E: enquire@old-brick-kilns.
co.uk
I: www.old-brick-kilns.co.uk

Southview ◆◆◆◆
Lynn Road, Sculthorpe,
Fakenham, Norfolk NR21 9QE
T: (01328) 851300

FARCET
Cambridgeshire

Red House Farm ◆◆◆
Broadway, Farcet, Peterborough
PE7 3AZ
T: (01733) 243129 &
07968 011803
F: (01733) 243129
E: gill.emberson@totalise.co.uk

FEERING
Essex

The Old Anchor ◆◆◆◆
132 Feering Hill, Feering,
Colchester CO5 9PY
T: (01376) 572855
F: (01376) 572855

Old Wills Farm ◆◆◆
Feering, Colchester CO5 9RP
T: (01376) 570259
F: (01376) 570259
E: janecrayston@barclays.net

FELIXSTOWE
Suffolk

Dolphin Hotel ◆◆
41 Beach Station Road,
Felixstowe, Suffolk IP11 2EY
T: (01394) 282261
F: (01394) 278319

Dorincourt Guesthouse ◆◆◆
41 Undercliff Road West,
Felixstowe, Suffolk IP11 2AH
T: (01394) 270447 & 270577
F: (01394) 270447
🏃

The Grafton Guesthouse
◆◆◆◆
13 Sea Road, Felixstowe, Suffolk
IP11 2BB
T: (01394) 284881
E: geoff.harvey@btinternet.com

Mansard Cottage ◆◆◆◆
Golf Road, Felixstowe, Suffolk
IP11 7NB
T: (01394) 282817
E: bathomas47@lineone.com

Primrose Gate Bed & Breakfast
◆◆◆◆
263 Ferry Road, Felixstowe,
Suffolk IP11 9RX
T: (01394) 271699
F: (01394) 283614
E: lesley_berry@hotmail.com

FELMINGHAM
Norfolk

Larks Rise ◆◆
North Walsham Road,
Felmingham, North Walsham,
Norfolk NR28 0JU
T: (01692) 403173
I: www.broadland.com/larksrise

FELSTED
Essex

Potash Farm ◆◆◆◆
Cobblers Green, Causeway End
Road, Felsted, Dunmow, Essex
CM6 3LX
T: (01371) 820510
F: (01371) 820510
E: rgspotash@compuserve.com

FENSTANTON
Cambridgeshire

Orchard House ◆◆◆
6A Hilton Road, Fenstanton,
Huntingdon, Cambridgeshire
PE28 9LH
T: (01480) 469208
F: (01480) 497487
E: ascarrow@aol.com

FINCHAM
Norfolk

**Rose Cottage Bed and
Breakfast** ◆◆◆◆
Downham Road, Fincham, King's
Lynn, Norfolk PE33 9HF
T: (01366) 347426
F: (01366) 347426
E: vaughanarbuckle@aol.com

FINCHINGFIELD
Essex

The Red Lion Inn ◆◆◆
6 Church Hill, Finchingfield,
Braintree, Essex CM7 4NN
T: (01371) 810400
F: (01371) 851062
E: franktyler_new.uk@excite.
co.uk
I: www.red-lion-finchingfield.
com

FLATFORD MILL
Suffolk

The Granary
Rating Applied For
Granary Museum, Flatford Mill,
East Bergholt, Colchester
CO7 6UL
T: (01206) 298111 & 299100
E: flatfordmill@fsdial.co.uk

FOULDEN
Norfolk

The White Hart Inn ◆◆◆
White Hart Street, Foulden,
Thetford, Norfolk IP26 5AW
T: (01366) 328638
E: sylvia.chisholm@virgin.net

FRAMLINGHAM
Suffolk

Fieldway Bed & Breakfast
◆◆◆◆
Saxtead Road, Dennington,
Woodbridge, Suffolk IP13 8AP
T: (01728) 638456
F: (01728) 638456
E: dianaturan@hotmail.com

High House Farm ◆◆◆
Cransford, Framlingham,
Woodbridge, Suffolk IP13 9PD
T: (01728) 663461
F: (01728) 663409
E: bb@highhousefarm.co.uk
I: www.highhousefarm.co.uk

Shimmens Pightle ◆◆◆
Dennington Road, Framlingham,
Woodbridge, Suffolk IP13 9JT
T: (01728) 724036

FRESSINGFIELD
Suffolk

Chippenhall Hall ◆◆◆◆◆
Fressingfield, Eye, Suffolk
IP21 5TD
T: (01379) 588180 & 586733
F: (01379) 586272
E: info@chippenhall.co.uk
I: www.chippenhall.co.uk

Elm Lodge ◆◆◆◆
Chippenhall Green, Fressingfield,
Eye, Suffolk IP21 5SL
T: (01379) 586249
E: sheila-webster@elm-lodge.
fsnet.co.uk
I: www.elm-lodge.fsnet.co.uk

FRINTON-ON-SEA
Essex

Uplands Guesthouse ◆◆◆
41 Hadleigh Road, Frinton-on-
Sea, Essex CO13 9HQ
T: (01255) 674889 & 679232
E: info@uplandsguesthouse.
freeserve.co.uk

FRISTON
Suffolk

The Flint House ◆◆◆◆
Aldeburgh Road, Friston,
Saxmundham, Suffolk IP17 1PD
T: (01728) 689123
E: handsel@eidosnet.co.uk

The Old School ◆◆◆◆
Aldeburgh Road, Friston,
Saxmundham, Suffolk IP17 1NP
T: (01728) 688173
E: oldschool@fristonoldschool.
freeserve.co.uk

GARBOLDISHAM
Norfolk

Ingleneuk Lodge ◆◆◆◆
Hopton Road, Garboldisham,
Diss, Norfolk IP22 2RQ
T: (01953) 681541
F: (01953) 681138
E: info@ingleneuklodge.co.uk
🏃

GOOD EASTER
Essex

Treloyhan Bed & Breakfast
◆◆◆
Treloyhan, Chelmsford Road,
Good Easter, Chelmsford
CM1 4PU
T: (01245) 231425
E: tdellar@barclays.net

GREAT BADDOW
Essex

Homecroft ◆◆◆
Southend Road, Great Baddow,
Chelmsford CM2 7AD
T: (01245) 475070 & 0788 181
6560
F: (01245) 475070

Little Sir Hughes ◆◆◆◆◆
West Hanningfield Road, Great
Baddow, Chelmsford CM2 7SZ
T: (01245) 471701
F: (01245) 478023
E: accom@englishlive.co.uk
I: www.smoothhound.
co.uk/a51878

Orchard House ◆◆◆
The Bringey, Church Street,
Great Baddow, Chelmsford
CM2 7JW
T: (01245) 474333

Rothmans ◆◆◆
22 High Street, Great Baddow,
Chelmsford CM2 7HQ
T: (01245) 473837 & 477144
F: (01245) 476833
E: eliz_barron@excite.co.uk
I: www.city2000.
com/h/rothmans-b&b.
essex-html

GREAT BARTON
Suffolk

Cherry Trees ◆◆◆
Mount Road, Great Barton, Bury
St Edmunds, Suffolk IP31 2QU
T: (01284) 787501
E: marigoldsalmon@hotmail.
com

40 Conyers Way ◆◆◆
Great Barton, Bury St Edmunds,
Suffolk IP31 2SW
T: (01284) 787632

GREAT BRICETT
Suffolk

Riverside Cottage ◆◆◆◆
The Street, Great Bricett, Ipswich
IP7 7DH
T: (01473) 658266
E: chasmhorne@aol.com

GREAT CHESTERFORD
Essex

White Gates ◆◆◆◆
School Street, Great
Chesterford, Saffron Walden,
Essex CB10 1NN
T: (01799) 530249
E: margaret-mortimer@lineone.
net
I: www.welcometowhitegates.
co.uk

GREAT CORNARD
Suffolk

Richmond Lodge ◆◆◆
Kings Hill, Great Cornard,
Sudbury, Suffolk CO10 0EH
T: (01787) 373728 & 379232
F: (01787) 373728
E: jenny@digitalfinecut.co.uk
I: digitalfinecut.co.uk

GREAT CRESSINGHAM
Norfolk

The Vines ◆◆◆
The Street, Great Cressingham,
Swaffham, Norfolk IP25 6NL
T: (01760) 756303
E: the.vines@eidosnet.co.uk

GREAT DUNMOW
Essex

Harwood Guest House ◆◆◆◆
52 Stortford Road, Great
Dunmow, CM6 1DN
T: (01371) 874627
F: (01371) 874627

Homelye Farm ◆◆◆◆
Homelye Chase, Braintree Road,
Dunmow, Essex CM6 3AW
T: (01371) 872127 & 0771 825
9076
F: (01371) 876428
E: homelye@supanet.com
I: www.homelyefarm.co.uk

Mallards ◆◆◆◆
Star Lane, Great Dunmow,
CM6 1AY
T: (01371) 872641

Rose Cottage ◆◆◆◆
Pharisee Green, Great Dunmow,
CM6 1JN
T: (01371) 872254

GREAT ELLINGHAM
Norfolk

Home Cottage Farm
Rating Applied For
Pewhill Road, Great Ellingham,
Attleborough, Norfolk NR17 1LS
T: (01953) 483734
E: royandmaureen@mail.com

Manor Farm ◆◆◆◆
Hingham Road, Great Ellingham,
Attleborough, Norfolk NR17 1JE
T: (01953) 453388
F: (01953) 453388

GREAT EVERSDEN
Cambridgeshire

Red House Farm
Rating Applied For
44 High Street, Great Eversden,
Cambridge CB3 7 HW
T: (01223) 262154
F: (01223) 264875

GREAT FINBOROUGH
Suffolk

Dairy Farmhouse ◆◆◆◆
Valley Lane, Great Finborough,
Stowmarket, Suffolk IP14 3BE
T: (01449) 615730
F: (01449) 615730

GREAT HOCKHAM
Norfolk

Manor Farm Bed & Breakfast
◆◆◆
Manor Farm, Vicarage Road,
Great Hockham, Thetford,
Norfolk IP24 1PE
T: (01953) 498204
F: (01953) 498204
E: manorfarm@ukf.net

GREAT RYBURGH
Norfolk

The Boar Inn ◆◆◆
Great Ryburgh, Fakenham,
Norfolk NR21 0DX
T: (01328) 829212
E: boarinn@aol.com
I: ourworld.compuserve.
com/homepages/boar_inn

GREAT SAMPFORD
Essex

Stow Farmhouse ◆◆◆◆
High Street, Great Sampford,
Saffron Walden, Essex CB10 2RG
T: (01799) 586060
F: (01799) 586060
E: joanne.barratt@lineone.net

GREAT WALDINGFIELD
Suffolk

Jasmine Cottage ◆◆◆◆
The Heath, Lavenham Road,
Great Waldingfield, Sudbury,
Suffolk CO10 0RN
T; (01787) 374665
I: www.jasminecottage-b-and-b.
co.uk

GREAT YARMOUTH
Norfolk

Alexandra Hotel ◆◆◆
9 Kent Square, Great Yarmouth,
Norfolk NR30 2EX
T: (01493) 853115

Barnard House ◆◆◆◆
2 Barnard Crescent, Great
Yarmouth, Norfolk NR30 4DR
T: (01493) 855139
F: (01493) 843143
E: barnardhouse@btinternet.
com
I: www.btinternet.
com/~barnardhouse.com

The Bromley Hotel ◆◆
63 Apsley Road, Great
Yarmouth, Norfolk NR30 2HG
T: (01493) 842321
E: malcolm-barber@hotmail.
com
I: bromleyhotel.homstead.com

Carlton Hotel ◆◆◆
Marine Parade, Great Yarmouth,
Norfolk NR30 3JE
T: (01493) 855234
F: (01493) 852220

Cleasewood Private Hotel
◆◆◆
55 Wellesley Road, Great
Yarmouth, Norfolk NR30 1EX
T: (01493) 843960 &
07940 911424

Concorde Private Hotel ◆◆◆
84 North Denes Road, Great
Yarmouth, Norfolk NR30 4LW
T: (01493) 843709
F: (01493) 843709
E: concordeyarmouth@hotmail.
com

The Edwardian Hotel ◆◆
18-20 Crown Road, Great
Yarmouth, Norfolk NR30 2JN
T: (01493) 856482
E: sandy@eaglemont.freeserve.
co.uk
I: www.edwardianhotel.co.uk

Filby Hall
Rating Applied For
Filby, Great Yarmouth, Norfolk
NR29 3HN
T: (01493) 368259 &
07740 822002
E: filbyhall@filbyhall.com
I: www.filbyhall.com

Fjaerland Hotel ◆◆◆
24-25 Trafalgar Road, Great
Yarmouth, Norfolk NR30 2LD
T: (01493) 856339 &
0780 3859951
F: (01493) 856339

Hadleigh Gables Hotel ◆◆◆
6-7 North Drive, Great
Yarmouth, Norfolk NR30 1ED
T: (01493) 843078
F: (01493) 843078
E: mike@hadleigh-gables.co.uk
I: www.hadleigh-gables.co.uk

Midland Hotel ◆◆◆
7-9 Wellesley Road, Great
Yarmouth, Norfolk NR30 2AP
T: (01493) 330046 &
07850 047999
F: (01493) 330046

Oasis Hotel ◆◆◆
Tower Building, Marine Parade,
Great Yarmouth, Norfolk
NR30 2EW
T: (01493) 855281
F: (01493) 330697

Royston House ◆◆
11 Euston Road, Great
Yarmouth, Norfolk NR30 1DY
T: (01493) 844680
F: (01493) 844680

Ryecroft Licensed Guesthouse
◆◆◆
91 North Denes Road, Great
Yarmouth, Norfolk NR30 4LW
T: (01493) 844015 &
07713 815569
F: (01493) 856096
E: theryecroft@aol.com
I: www.ryecroft-guesthouse.
co.uk

Sandy Acres ◆◆
80-81 Salisbury Road, Great
Yarmouth, Norfolk NR30 4LB
T: (01493) 856553
E: sandyacres@talk21.com
I: www.sandyacres.co.uk

Shadingfield Lodge ◆◆◆◆
Marine Parade, Great Yarmouth,
Norfolk NR30 3JG
T: (01493) 843915 & 847200
F: (01493) 847206
E: shadlodge@aol.com
I: www.shadingfieldlodge.co.uk

Silverstone House ◆◆◆
29 Wellesley Road, Great
Yarmouth, Norfolk NR30 1EU
T: (01493) 844862

Southern Hotel ◆◆◆
46 Queens Road, Great
Yarmouth, Norfolk NR30 3JR
T: (01493) 843313
F: (01493) 853047
E: southern.hotel@tinyonline.
co.uk
I: www.southernhotel.co.uk

Sunnydene Hotel ◆◆◆
83 North Denes Road, Great
Yarmouth, Norfolk NR30 4LW
T: (01493) 843554 & 332391
F: (01493) 332391
E: greatyarmouthhotel@yahoo.
co.uk
I: www.sunnydenehotel.co.uk

Taunton House Hotel ◆◆◆
9 Nelson Road South, Great
Yarmouth, Norfolk NR30 3JL
T: (01493) 850043
E: taunton@wilkinsonb.
fsbusiness.co.uk

Trotwood Private Hotel ◆◆◆
2 North Drive, Great Yarmouth,
Norfolk NR30 1ED
T: (01493) 843971
E: richard@trotwood.fsbusiness.
co.uk
I: www.trotwood.fsbusiness.
co.uk

The Waverley Hotel ◆◆◆
32-37 Princes Road, Great
Yarmouth, Norfolk NR30 2DG
T: (01493) 842508
F: (01493) 842508
E: malcolm@waverley-hotel.
co.uk
I: www.waverley-hotel.co.uk

GRIMSTON
Norfolk

The Bell Inn ◆◆◆
1 Gayton Road, Grimston, King's
Lynn, Norfolk PE32 1BG
T: (01485) 601156 &
07961 304833

GRISTON
Norfolk

Hall Farm Bed & Breakfast ◆◆
Hall Farm, Griston, Thetford,
Norfolk IP25 6PR
T: (01953) 881626
F: (01953) 883131

Park Farm Bed & Breakfast
◆◆◆◆
Park Farm, Caston Road, Griston,
Thetford, Norfolk IP25 6QD
T: (01953) 483020 &
07974 772485
F: (01953) 483056
E: parkfarm@eidosnet.co.uk
I: www.parkfarmbreckland.co.uk

HADDISCOE
Norfolk

Brook House ◆◆◆◆
Aldeby Road, Haddiscoe,
Norwich NR14 6PQ
T: (01502) 677772

HADLEIGH
Suffolk

Edgehall Hotel ◆◆◆◆
2 High Street, Hadleigh, Ipswich
IP7 5AP
T: (01473) 822458
F: (01473) 827751

Odds and Ends House ◆◆◆◆
131 High Street, Hadleigh,
Ipswich IP7 5EJ
T: (01473) 822032 & 829825
F: (01473) 829816
E: gordonranson@aol.com

Weavers ◆◆◆◆
25 High Street, Hadleigh,
Ipswich IP7 5AG
T: (01473) 827247 & 823185
F: (01473) 822802
E: cyndymiles@aol.com
I: www.weaversrestaurant.co.uk

The White Hart ◆◆◆
46 Bridge Street, Hadleigh,
Ipswich IP7 6DB
T: (01473) 822206
F: (01473) 822206
E: enquiries@
whitehearthadleight.co.uk
I: www.whitehearthadleigh.co.uk

HALESWORTH
Suffolk

The Angel Hotel ◆◆◆
Thoroughfare, Halesworth,
Suffolk IP19 8AH
I: (01986) 873365
F: (01986) 874891
E: angel@halesworth.ws
I: www.halesworth.ws/angel/

The Croft ◆◆◆
Ubbeston Green, Halesworth,
Suffolk IP19 0HB
T: (01986) 798502 &
0771 2414274

Fen Way Guest House ◆◆◆
Fen Way, School Lane,
Halesworth, Suffolk IP19 8BW
T: (01986) 873574

The Huntsman and Hounds
◆◆◆
Stone Street, Spexhall,
Halesworth, Suffolk IP19 0RN
T: (01986) 781341
E: huntmanspexhall@aol.com

Stradbroke Town Farm ◆◆◆◆
Westhall, Halesworth, Suffolk
IP19 8NY
T: (01502) 575204

HALSTEAD
Essex

The Dog Inn ◆◆◆
37 Hedingham Road, Halstead,
Essex CO9 2DB
T: (01787) 477774

**Hedingham Antiques Bed &
Breakfast** ◆◆◆
100 Swan Street, Sible
Hedingham, Halstead, Essex
CO9 3HP
T: (01787) 460360
F: (01787) 469109
E: patriciapatterson@totalise.
co.uk
I: www.hedinghamantiques.
co.uk

Townsford Mill ◆◆◆◆
Mill House, The Causeway,
Halstead, Essex CO9 1ET
T: (01787) 474451
F: (01787) 473893
E: stuckey@townsford.
freeserve.co.uk
I: www.townsford.freeserve.
co.uk.

HALVERGATE
Norfolk

**School Lodge Country
Guesthouse** ◆◆◆
Marsh Road, Halvergate,
Norwich NR13 3QB
T: (01493) 700111 & 700808
F: (01493) 700808

HAPPISBURGH
Norfolk

**Cliff House Guesthouse
Teashop and Restaurant**◆◆◆
Beach Road, Happisburgh,
Norwich NR12 0PP
T: (01692) 650775

Manor Farmhouse ◆◆◆
Happisburgh, Norwich
NR12 0SA
T: (01692) 651262 & 650220
I: www.broadland.
com/manorfarmhouse

HARDWICK
Cambridgeshire

Wallis Farm ◆◆◆◆
98 Main Street, Hardwick,
Cambridge CB3 7QU
T: (01954) 210347
F: (01954) 210988
E: wallisfarm@mcmail.com

HARLESTON
Suffolk

Green Farmhouse ◆◆◆◆
Harleston, Stowmarket, Suffolk
IP14 3HW
T: (01449) 736841
F: (01449) 736894
E: grnfarm@globalnet.co.uk

Weston House Farm ◆◆◆
Mendham, Harleston, Norfolk
IP20 0PB
T: (01986) 782206 &
07803 099203
F: (01986) 782414
E: holden@farmline.com

HARPENDEN
Hertfordshire

Hall Barn ◆◆◆◆
20 Sun Lane, Harpenden,
Hertfordshire AL5 4EU
T: (01582) 769700

The Laurels Guest House
◆◆◆◆
22 Leyton Road, Harpenden,
Hertfordshire AL5 2HU
T: (01582) 712226
F: (01727) 712226

Milton Hotel ◆◆◆
25 Milton Road, Harpenden,
Hertfordshire AL5 5LA
T: (01582) 762914

HARSTON
Cambridgeshire

Hoffers Brook Farm ◆◆◆
Royston Road, Harston,
Cambridge CB2 5NJ
T: (01223) 870065

HARTEST
Suffolk

The Hatch ◆◆◆◆◆
Pilgrims Lane, Cross Green,
Hartest, Bury St Edmunds,
Suffolk IP29 4ED
T: (01284) 830226
F: (01284) 830226

HARWICH
Essex

New Farm House ◆◆◆
Spinnels Lane, Wix,
Manningtree, Essex CO11 2UJ
T: (01255) 870365
F: (01255) 870837
E: newfarmhouse@which.net
I: www.newfarmhouse.com

Oceanview ◆◆
86 Main Road, Dovercourt,
Harwich, Essex CO13 3LH
T: (01255) 554078 &
07801 689002
F: (01255) 554519
E: oceanview@dovercourt.org.
uk
I: www.oceanview.fsbusiness.
co.uk

Paston Lodge ◆◆◆
1 Una Road, Parkeston, Harwich,
Essex CO12 4PP
T: (01255) 551390 &
07867 888498
F: (01255) 551390
E: dwright@globalnet.co.uk

HATFIELD BROAD OAK
Essex

The Cottage ◆◆◆
Dunmow Road, Hatfield Broad
Oak, Bishop's Stortford,
Hertfordshire CM22 7JJ
T: (01279) 718230

HATFIELD HEATH
Essex

The Barn ◆◆◆
Great Heath Farm, Chelmsford
Road, Hatfield Heath, Bishop's
Stortford, Hertfordshire
CM22 7BQ
T: (01279) 739093

Friars Farm ◆◆◆
Hatfield Heath, Bishop's
Stortford, Hertfordshire
CM22 7AP
T: (01279) 730244
F: (01279) 730244

**Hunters' Meet Restaurant and
Hotel** ◆◆◆◆
Chelmsford Road, Hatfield
Heath, Bishop's Stortford,
Hertfordshire CM22 7BQ
T: (01279) 730549
F: (01279) 731587
E: info@huntersmeet.co.uk
I: www.huntersmeet.co.uk

Oaklands ◆◆◆◆
Hatfield Heath, Bishop's
Stortford, Hertfordshire
CM22 7AD
T: (01279) 730240 &
07774 904002

HATFIELD PEVEREL
Essex

The Swan Inn ◆◆
The Street, Hatfield Peverel,
Chelmsford CM3 2DW
T: (01245) 380238
F: (01245) 380238

HAUGHLEY
Suffolk

Red House Farm ◆◆◆◆
Station Road, Haughley,
Stowmarket, Suffolk IP14 3QP
T: (01449) 673323
F: (01449) 675413
E: mary@noy1.fsnet.co.uk
I: www.farmstayanglia.co.uk

HEACHAM
Norfolk

Allington Bed and Breakfast
◆◆◆◆
10 Neville Road, Heacham,
King's Lynn, Norfolk PE31 7HB
T: (01485) 571148

The Grove ◆◆◆◆
Collins Lane, Heacham, King's
Lynn, Norfolk PE31 4DZ
T: (01485) 570513
F: (01485) 570513
E: tm.shannon@virgin.net

Holly House ◆◆◆
3 Broadway, Heacham, King's
Lynn, Norfolk PE31 7DF
T: (01485) 572935

Saint Annes Guesthouse ◆◆◆
53 Neville Road, Heacham,
King's Lynn, Norfolk PE31 7HB
T: (01485) 570021
F: (01485) 570021
I: www.smoothhound.co.uk/

HELLESDON
Norfolk

**The Old Corner Shop
Guesthouse** ◆◆◆
26 Cromer Road, Hellesdon,
Norwich NR6 6LZ
T: (01603) 419000
F: (01603) 419000

HEMEL HEMPSTEAD
Hertfordshire

The Red House ◆◆◆
34 Alexandra Road, Hemel
Hempstead, Hertfordshire
HP2 5BS
T: (01442) 246665

HENGRAVE
Suffolk

Minstrels ◆◆◆
Bury Road, Hengrave, Bury St
Edmunds, Suffolk IP28 6LT
T: (01284) 703677 &
07788 148337
F: (01284) 703677

HETHEL
Norfolk

Old Thorn Barn ◆◆◆◆
Corporation Farm, Wymondham
Road, Hethel, Norwich
NR14 8EU
T: (01953) 607785
F: (01953) 607785
E: enquiries@oldthornbarn.
co.uk
I: www.oldthornbarn.co.uk

HETHERSETT
Norfolk

Magnolia House ◆◆◆
Cromwell Close, Hethersett,
Norwich NR9 3HD
T: (01603) 810749
F: (01603) 810749

HEVINGHAM
Norfolk

Marsham Arms Inn ◆◆◆◆
Holt Road, Hevingham, Norwich
NR10 5NP
T: (01603) 754268
F: (01603) 754839
E: nigelbradley@marshamarms.
co.uk
I: www.marshamarms.co.uk

HICKLING
Norfolk

**Hickling Broad Bed &
Breakfast ◆◆◆**
Paddock Cottage, Staithe Road,
Hickling, Norwich NR12 0YJ
T: (01692) 598259 &
07790 461776

HIGH KELLING
Norfolk

**Lynton Loft
Rating Applied For**
Vale Road, High Kelling, Holt,
Norfolk NR25 6RA
T: (01263) 712933
E: lynton@highkelling.fsnet.
co.uk
I: www.olivetreebreaks.co.uk

HILGAY
Norfolk

**Crosskeys Riverside Hotel
◆◆◆**
Bridge Street, Hilgay, Downham
Market, Norfolk PE38 0LD
T: (01366) 387777
F: (01366) 387777

HINDRINGHAM
Norfolk

Field House ◆◆◆◆◆
Moorgate Road, Hindringham,
Fakenham, Norfolk NR21 0PT
T: (01328) 878726
F: (01328) 878955
E: wendyfieldhouse@lineone.
net
I: www.northnorfolk.
co.uk/fieldhouse

HINTLESHAM
Suffolk

College Farm ◆◆◆◆
Hintlesham, Ipswich IP8 3NT
T: (01473) 652253
F: (01473) 652253
E: bryce1@agripro.co.uk

HITCHIN
Hertfordshire

The Greyhound ◆◆◆
London Road, St Ippolyts,
Hitchin, Hertfordshire SG4 7NL
T: (01462) 440989

The Lord Lister Hotel ◆◆◆
1 Park Street, Hitchin,
Hertfordshire SG4 9AH
T: (01462) 432712 & 459451
F: (01462) 438506

HOLBROOK
Suffolk

Highfield ◆◆◆◆
Harkstead Road, Holbrook,
Ipswich IP9 2RA
T: (01473) 328250
F: (01473) 328250

HOLKHAM
Norfolk

**Peterstone Cutting Bed &
Breakfast ◆◆◆◆**
Peterstone Cutting, Peterstone,
Holkham, Wells-next-the-Sea,
Norfolk NR23 1RR
T: (01328) 730171
F: (01328) 730171

HOLME NEXT THE SEA
Norfolk

Meadow Springs ◆◆◆
15 Eastgate Road, Holme next
the Sea, Hunstanton, Norfolk
PE36 6LL
T: (01485) 525279

HOLT
Norfolk

Hempstead Hall ◆◆◆◆
Holt, Norfolk NR25 6TN
T: (01263) 712224 &
07721 827246
F: (01263) 710137
I: www.broadland.
com/hempsteadhall

Lawns Hotel ◆◆◆◆
Station Road, Holt, Norfolk
NR25 6BS
T: (01263) 713390
F: (01263) 710642
E: info@lawnshotel.co.uk
I: www.lawnshotel.co.uk

Three Corners ◆◆◆
12 Kelling Close, Holt, Norfolk
NR25 6RU
T: (01263) 713389
E: «roncox@supanet.com»

The White Cottage ◆◆◆
Norwich Road, Holt, Norfolk
NR25 6SW
T: (01263) 713353 &
07833 324030

HOLTON
Suffolk

Blythwood House ◆◆◆
Beccles Road, Holton,
Halesworth, Suffolk IP19 8NQ
T: (01986) 873379 &
07960 535324
F: (01986) 873379

HOLTON ST MARY
Suffolk

Stratford House ◆◆◆◆
Holton St Mary, Colchester
CO7 6NT
T: (01206) 298246
F: (01206) 298246
E: fjs.stratho@quista.net

HONINGTON
Suffolk

North View Guesthouse ◆◆
North View, Malting Row,
Honington, Bury St Edmunds,
Suffolk IP31 1RE
T: (01359) 269423

HORRINGER
Suffolk

12 The Elms ◆◆◆
Horringer, Bury St Edmunds,
Suffolk IP29 5SE
T: (01284) 735400
E: neca56@onetel.net.uk

HORSEHEATH
Cambridgeshire

**Chequer Cottage
Rating Applied For**
Streetly End, Horseheath,
Cambridge CB1 6RR
T: (01223) 891522
F: (01223) 890266

HORSEY
Norfolk

The Old Chapel ◆◆◆◆
Horsey Corner, Horsey, Great
Yarmouth, Norfolk NR29 4EH
T: (01493) 393498
F: (01493) 393498
I: rectoryh@aol.com
I: www.hitelregister.
co.uk/hotel/oldirectory.asp
🖈

HORSFORD
Norfolk

Lower Farm B&B ◆◆◆◆
Lower Farm, Horsford, Norwich
NR10 3AW
T: (01603) 891291
E: lowerfarm@lowerfarm.f9.
co.uk
I: norfolkbroads.com/lowerfarm

HORSTEAD
Norfolk

Beverley Farm ◆◆◆
Norwich Road, Horstead,
Norwich NR12 7EH
T: (01603) 737279

HOVETON
Norfolk

The Willows ◆◆◆◆
Marsh Road, Hoveton, Norwich
NR12 8UH
T: (01603) 782844
F: (01603) 782 844

HUNSTANTON
Norfolk

Burleigh Hotel ◆◆◆◆
7 Cliff Terrace, Hunstanton,
Norfolk PE36 6DY
T: (01485) 533080

Cobblers Cottage ◆◆◆
3 Wodehouse Road, Old
Hunstanton, Hunstanton,
Norfolk PE36 6JD
T: (01485) 534036

Eccles Cottage ◆◆◆
Heacham Road, Sedgeford,
Hunstanton, Norfolk PE36 5LU
T: (01485) 572688
E: mike99.barker@virgin.net

Fieldsend House ◆◆◆◆
Homefields Road, Hunstanton,
Norfolk PE36 5HL
T: (01485) 532593
F: (01485) 532593

The Gables ◆◆◆◆
28 Austin Street, Hunstanton,
Norfolk PE36 6AW
T: (01485) 532514
E: bbatthegables@aol.com

Garganey House ◆◆◆
46 Northgate, Hunstanton,
Norfolk PE36 6DR
T: (01485) 533269
E: Garganey1.@f.s.net.co.uk

Gate Lodge ◆◆◆
2 Westgate, Hunstanton,
Norfolk PE36 5AL
T: (01485) 533549
F: (01485) 533549
E: sagemo2206@talk21.com

**Glenberis
Rating Applied For**
6 St Edmunds Avenue,
Hunstanton, Norfolk PE36 6AY
T: (01485) 533663

**Kiama Cottage Guesthouse
◆◆◆**
23 Austin Street, Hunstanton,
Norfolk PE36 6AN
T: (01485) 533615

Lakeside ◆◆◆
Waterworks Road, Old
Hunstanton, Hunstanton,
Norfolk PE36 6JE
T: (01485) 533763

**The Linksway Country House
Hotel ◆◆◆**
Golf Course Road, Old
Hunstanton, Hunstanton,
Norfolk PE36 6JE
T: (01485) 532209 & 532653
F: (01485) 532209
I: www.linkswayhotel.co.uk

Miramar Guesthouse ◆◆◆
7 Boston Square, Hunstanton,
Norfolk PE36 6DT
T: (01485) 532902 & 0771 202
3134
I: www.miramar.co.uk

Neptune Inn ◆◆
85 Old Hunstanton Road, Old
Hunstanton, Hunstanton,
Norfolk PE36 6HZ
T: (01485) 532122

Oriel Lodge ◆◆◆◆
24 Homefields Road,
Hunstanton, Norfolk PE36 5HJ
T: (01485) 532368
F: (01485) 535737
E: info@oriellodge.co.uk
I: www.oriellodge.co.uk

Peacock House ◆◆◆◆
28 Park Road, Hunstanton,
Norfolk PE36 5BY
T: (01485) 534551
E: peacockhouse@onetel.net.uk
I: www.web.onetel.net.
uk/~peacockhouse

Queensbury House ◆◆◆
18 Glebe Avenue, Hunstanton,
Norfolk PE36 6BS
T: (01485) 534320

Rosamaly Guesthouse ◆◆◆
14 Glebe Avenue, Hunstanton,
Norfolk PE36 6BS
T: (01485) 534187

The Shelbrooke Hotel ◆◆◆
9 Cliff Terrace, Hunstanton,
Norfolk PE36 6DY
T: (01485) 532289
F: (01485) 535385
E: mikrac@shelbrooke.f9.co.uk
I: www.shelbrooke.force9.co.uk

Sunningdale Hotel ◆◆◆
3-5 Avenue Road, Hunstanton,
Norfolk PE36 5BW
T: (01485) 532562
F: (01485) 534915
E: reception@sunningdalehotel.
com
I: www.sunningdalehotel.com

**Troon Cottage Bed and
Breakfast ◆◆**
4 Victoria Avenue, Hunstanton,
Norfolk PE36 6BX
T: (01485) 533290 &
0800 654321

HUNTINGDON
Cambridgeshire

Grange Hotel ◆◆◆
115 High Street, Brampton,
Huntingdon, Cambridgeshire
PE28 4RA
T: (01480) 459516
F: (01480) 459391
E: enquiries@
grangehotelbrampton.com
I: www.grangehotelbrampton.
com or .co.uk

Prince of Wales ◆◆◆◆
Potton Road, Hilton,
Huntingdon, Cambridgeshire
PE28 9NG
T: (01480) 830257
F: (01480) 830257
E: princeofwales.hilton@talk21.
com

HUNTINGFIELD
Suffolk

Huntingfield Arms ◆◆
The Street, Huntingfield,
Halesworth, Suffolk IP19 0PU
T: (01986) 798320

ICKLETON
Cambridgeshire

Hessett Grange ◆◆◆◆
60 Frogge Street, Ickleton,
Saffron Walden, Essex CB10 1SH
T: (01799) 530300

IPSWICH
Suffolk

Carlton Hotel ◆◆
41-43 Berners Street, Ipswich,
IP1 3LN
T: (01473) 254955
F: (01473) 211145
E: carltonhotel@hotmail.com

The Gatehouse Hotel Ltd
◆◆◆◆◆
799 Old Norwich Road, Ipswich,
IP1 6LH
T: (01473) 741897
F: (01473) 744236
E: info@gatehousehotel.co.uk
I: www.gatehousehotel.co.uk

231 Humber Doucy Lane ◆◆◆
Ipswich, IP4 3PE
T: (01473) 402664

Lattice Lodge Guest House
◆◆◆◆
499 Woodbridge Road, Ipswich,
IP4 4EP
T: (01473) 712474 &
07931 737663
F: (01473) 272239
E: lattice.lodge@btinternet.com
I: www.latticelodge.co.uk

Mockbeggars Hall ◆◆◆◆
Paper Mill Lane, Claydon,
Ipswich IP6 0AH
T: (01473) 830239 &
0770 2627770
F: (01473) 832989
E: pru@mockbeggars.co.uk
I: www.mockbeggars.co.uk

Redholme ◆◆◆◆
52 Ivry Street, Ipswich, IP1 3QP
T: (01473) 250018 & 233174
E: johnmcneil@
redholmeipswich.freeserve.co.uk
I: redholmeipswich.co.uk

Sidegate Guesthouse ◆◆◆◆
121 Sidegate Lane, Ipswich,
IP4 4JB
T: (01473) 728714
F: (01473) 728714

Stebbings ◆◆◆◆
Back Lane, Washbrook, Ipswich,
IP8 3JA
T: (01473) 730216 &
07989 061088
E: carolinefox@netscapeline.
co.uk

KEDINGTON
Suffolk

The White House ◆◆◆◆◆
Silver Street, Kedington,
Haverhill, Suffolk CB9 7QG
T: (01440) 707731 &
07778 986693
F: (01440) 707731

KELSALE
Suffolk

Mile Hill Barn ◆◆◆◆◆
Main Road, Kelsale,
Saxmundham, Suffolk IP17 2RG
T: (01728) 668519
E: richard@milehillbarn.
freeserve.co.uk
I: www.milehillbarn.freeserve.
co.uk

KELVEDON
Essex

Highfields Farm ◆◆◆◆
Kelvedon, Colchester CO5 9BJ
T: (01376) 570334
T: (01376) 570334
E: HighfieldsFarm@
farmersweekly.net

KERSEY
Suffolk

Red House Farm ◆◆◆
Wickerstreet Green, Kersey,
Ipswich IP7 6EY
T: (01787) 210245

KETTLEBASTON
Suffolk

Box Tree Farm ◆◆◆
Kettlebaston, Ipswich IP7 7PZ
T: (01449) 741318
F: (01449) 741318

KETTLEBURGH
Suffolk

Rookery Farm ◆◆◆
Framlingham Road, Kettleburgh,
Woodbridge, Suffolk IP13 7LL
T: (01728) 723248
I: bazin@btinternet.com

KING'S LYNN
Norfolk

The Beeches Guesthouse ◆◆
2 Guanock Terrace, King's Lynn,
Norfolk PE30 5QT
T: (01553) 766577
F: (01553) 766664

Fairlight Lodge ◆◆◆◆
79 Goodwins Road, King's Lynn,
Norfolk PE30 5PE
T: (01553) 762234
F: (01553) 770280
E: joella@nash42.freeserve.
co.uk
I: www.fairlightlodge.co.uk

Flint's Hotel ◆◆
73 Norfolk Street, King's Lynn,
Norfolk PE30 1AD
T: (01553) 769400

Hall Farm Bed & Breakfast ◆
Shouldham Thorpe, King's Lynn,
Norfolk PE33 0DP
T: (01366) 347940 &
07768 208673
F: (01366) 347946
E: hallfarm@freenetname.co.uk
I: www.
hall-farmbedandbreakfast.co.uk

Maranatha Guesthouse ◆◆◆
115-117 Gaywood Road, King's
Lynn, Norfolk PE30 2PU
T: (01553) 774596 & 772331
F: (01553) 763747

Marsh Farm ◆◆◆◆
Wolferton, King's Lynn, Norfolk
PE31 6HB
T: (01485) 540265
F: (01485) 543143
E: info@
marshfarmbedandbreakfast.
co.uk
I: www.
marshfarmbedandbreakfast.
co.uk

The Old Rectory ◆◆◆◆
33 Goodwins Road, King's Lynn,
Norfolk PE30 5QX
T: (01553) 768544
E: clive@
theoldrectory-kingslynn.com
I: www.theoldrectory-kingslynn.
com

KINGS LANGLEY
Hertfordshire

Woodcote House ◆◆◆◆
7 The Grove, Whippendell,
Chipperfield, Kings Langley,
Hertfordshire WD4 9JF
T: (01923) 262077
F: (01923) 266198
E: leverldge@btinternet.com

KIRBY CANE
Norfolk

Butterley House ◆◆◆
Leet Hill Farm, Kirby Cane,
Bungay, Suffolk NR35 2HJ
T: (01508) 518301
F: (01508) 518301

KNAPTON
Norfolk

Cornerstone House
Rating Applied For
The Street, Knapton, North
Walsham, Norfolk NR28 0AD
T: (01263) 722884

LANGHAM
Essex

Oak Apple Farm ◆◆◆◆
Greyhound Hill, Langham,
Colchester CO4 5QF
T: (01206) 272234
E: rosie@oakapplefarm.fsnet.
co.uk
I: www.smoothhound.
co.uk/hotels/oak.html

LAVENHAM
Suffolk

Anchor House ◆◆◆◆
27 Prentice Street, Lavenham,
Sudbury, Suffolk CO10 9RD
T: (01787) 249018 &
07974 212629
E: suewade@tinyworld.co.uk
I: www.anchorhouse.co.uk

Angel Gallery ◆◆◆◆
17 Market Place, Lavenham,
Sudbury, Suffolk CO10 9QZ
T: (01787) 248417
F: (01787) 248417
E: angel-gallery@gofornet.co.uk
I: www.angel-gallery@gofornet.
co.uk

Brett Farm ◆◆◆◆
The Common, Lavenham,
Sudbury, Suffolk CO10 9PG
T: (01787) 248533

Hill House Farm ◆◆◆◆
Preston St Mary, Lavenham,
Sudbury, Suffolk CO10 9LT
T: (01787) 247571
F: (01787) 247571

The Island House ◆◆◆◆
Lower Road, Lavenham,
Sudbury, Suffolk CO10 9QJ
T: (01787) 248181
E: islandhouse@dial.pipex.com
I: lavenham.co.uk/islandhouse/

Lavenham Great House Hotel
◆◆◆◆
Market Place, Lavenham,
Sudbury, Suffolk CO10 9QZ
T: (01787) 247431
F: (01787) 248007
E: info@greathouse.co.uk
I: www.greathouse.co.uk

Lavenham Priory ◆◆◆◆◆
Water Street, Lavenham,
Sudbury, Suffolk CO10 9RW
T: (01787) 247404
F: (01787) 248472
E: mail@lavenhampriory.co.uk
I: www.lavenhampriory.co.uk

Mortimer's Barn ◆◆◆◆
Preston St Mary, Lavenham,
Sudbury, Suffolk CO10 9ND
T: (01787) 248231 & 248075
F: (01787) 248075
E: mervyn@mortimers.
freeserve.co.uk
I: www.diggins.co.uk/mortimers/

The Old Convent ◆◆◆◆
The Street, Kettlebaston, Ipswich
IP7 7QA
T: (01449) 741557
E: holidays@kettlebaston.fsnet.
co.uk
I: www.kettlebaston.fsnet.co.uk

The Red House ◆◆◆◆
29 Bolton Street, Lavenham,
Sudbury, Suffolk CO10 9RG
T: (01787) 248074 &
07885 536148
I: www.lavenham.
co.uk/redhouse

Sunrise Cottage ◆◆◆
32 The Glebe, Sudbury Road,
Lavenham, Sudbury, Suffolk
CO10 9SN
T: (01787) 248439 &
07778 709964
E: deallen@talk21.com

LAXFIELD
Suffolk

The Villa Stables ◆◆◆◆
The Villa, High Street, Laxfield,
Woodbridge, Suffolk IP13 8DU
T: (01986) 798019
F: (01986) 798019
E: laxfieldleisure@talk21.com

LEIGH-ON-SEA
Essex

Undercliff B & B ◆◆◆
52 Undercliff Gardens, Leigh-
on-Sea, Essex SS9 1EA
T: (01702) 474984 &
07967 788873

LEISTON
Suffolk

Field End ◆◆◆◆
1 Kings Road, Leiston, Suffolk
IP16 4DA
T: (01728) 833527
F: (01728) 833527
E: pwright@field-end.freeserve.
co.uk
I: www.field-end.freeserve.co.uk

LEVINGTON
Suffolk

Lilac Cottage ◆◆◆◆
Levington Green, Levington,
Ipswich IP10 0LE
T: (01473) 659509

LINTON
Cambridgeshire

Springfield House ◆◆◆◆
16 Horn Lane, Linton, Cambridge
CB1 6HT
T: (01223) 891383
F: (01223) 890335
I: www.smoothhound.
co.uk/hotels/springf2.html

LITTLE BADDOW
Essex

Chestnuts ◆◆◆
Chestnut Walk, Little Baddow,
Chelmsford CM3 4SP
T: (01245) 223905

LITTLE BEALINGS
Suffolk

10 Michaels Mount ◆◆◆
Little Bealings, Woodbridge,
Suffolk IP13 6LS
T: (01473) 610466

Timbers ◆◆◆
Martlesham Road, Little
Bealings, Woodbridge, Suffolk
IP13 6LY
T: (01473) 622713

LITTLE CANFIELD
Essex

Canfield Moat ◆◆◆◆◆
High Cross Lane West, Little
Canfield, Dunmow, Essex
CM6 1TD
T: (01371) 872565 & 07881 165
049
F: (01371) 876264
E: falk@canfieldmoat.co.uk
I: www.canfieldmoat.co.uk

LITTLE GLEMHAM
Suffolk

The Lion Inn ◆◆◆
Main Road, Little Glemham,
Woodbridge, Suffolk IP13 0BA
T: (01728) 746505
F: (01728) 746505
E: pauline@theglemhamlion.
co.uk

LITTLE HALLINGBURY
Hertfordshire

Little Hallingbury Mill ◆◆◆
Old Mill Lane, Gaston Green,
Little Hallingbury, Bishop's
Stortford, Hertfordshire
CM22 7QT
T: (01279) 726554
F: (01279) 724162
I: www.littlehallingburymill.net

LITTLE LEIGHS
Essex

Little Leighs Hall
Rating Applied For
Little Leighs, Chelmsford
CM3 1PG
T: (01245) 361462 & 361221
F: (01245) 361221

LITTLE SAMPFORD
Essex

Bush Farm ◆◆◆
Little Sampford, Saffron Walden,
Essex CB10 2RY
T: (01799) 586636 &
07702 955290
E: aimreso@iname.com

Woodlands ◆◆◆◆
Hawkins Hill, Little Sampford,
Saffron Walden, Essex
CB10 2QW
T: (01371) 810862 &
07811 937381
E: lynne.jameson@amserve.net

LITTLE WALSINGHAM
Norfolk

The Old Bakehouse ◆◆◆◆
33 High Street, Little
Walsingham, Walsingham,
Norfolk NR22 6BZ
T: (01328) 820454
F: (01328) 820454
E: chris@cpadley.freeserve.co.uk

St David's House ◆◆
Friday Market, Little
Walsingham, Walsingham,
Norfolk NR22 6BY
T: (01328) 820633 &
07710 044452
E: stdavidshouse@amserve.net
I: www.stilwell.co.uk

LITTLE WALTHAM
Essex

Little Belsteads ◆◆◆◆
Back Lane, Little Waltham,
Chelmsford CM3 3PP
T: (01245) 360249
F: (01245) 360996

Windmill Motor Inn ◆◆
Chatham Green, Little Waltham,
Chelmsford CM3 3LE
T: (01245) 361188
F: (01245) 362992
E: a131windmill.essex@virgin.
net

LODDON
Norfolk

Poplar Farm ◆◆◆
Sisland, Loddon, Norwich
NR14 6EF
T: (01508) 520706
E: milly@hemmant.myhome.
org.uk
I: www.hemmant.myhome.org.
uk

LONDON COLNEY
Hertfordshire

The Conifers ◆◆◆
42 Thamesdale, London Colney,
St Albans, Hertfordshire AL2 1TL
T: (01727) 823622

LONG MELFORD
Suffolk

The Crown Hotel ◆◆◆
Hall Street, Long Melford,
Sudbury, Suffolk CO10 9JL
T: (01787) 377666
F: (01787) 379005

The George & Dragon ◆◆◆◆
Long Melford, Sudbury, Suffolk
CO10 9JB
T: (01787) 371285
F: (01787) 312428
E: geodrg.@ mail.globalnet.
co.uk

High Street Farmhouse ◆◆◆◆
Long Melford, Sudbury, Suffolk
CO10 9BD
T: (01787) 375765 &
07710 375765
F: (01787) 375765
E: anroy@lineone.net
I: www.longmelford.co.uk/index.
html

Perseverance Hotel ◆◆
Rodbridge Hill, Long Melford,
Sudbury, Suffolk CO10 9HN
T: (01787) 375 862
F: (01787) 375 862

LONG STRATTON
Norfolk

Greenacres Farm ◆◆◆◆
Woodgreen, Long Stratton,
Norwich NR15 2RR
T: (01508) 530261
F: (01508) 530261
E: greenacresfarm@hayworld.
co.uk

LOUGHTON
Essex

Forest Edge ◆◆◆
61 York Hill, Loughton, Essex
IG10 1HZ
T: (020) 8508 9834
F: (020) 8281 1894
E: arthur@catterallarthur.fsnet.
co.uk

9 Garden Way ◆◆◆
Loughton, Essex IG10 2SF
T: (020) 8508 6134

LOWER LAYHAM
Suffolk

Badgers ◆◆◆◆
Rands Road, Lower Layham,
Ipswich IP7 5RW
T: (01473) 823396 &
07774 184613
E: catbadgers@aol.com

LOWESTOFT
Suffolk

Albany Hotel ◆◆◆◆
400 London Road South,
Lowestoft, Suffolk NR33 0BQ
T: (01502) 574394
F: (01502) 581198
E: geoffrey.ward@btclick.com
I: www.albanyhotel-lowestoft.
co.uk

All Seasons Guest House ◆◆◆
17 Wellington Esplanade,
Lowestoft, Suffolk NR33 0QQ
T: (01502) 530870
E: allseasons@netscapeonline.
co.uk
I: www.allseasons.lowestoft.org.
uk

The Blinking Owl ◆◆◆
30 Marine Parade, Lowestoft,
Suffolk NR33 0QN
T: (01502) 563717
F: (01502) 563717

Church Farm ◆◆◆◆◆
Corton, Lowestoft, Suffolk
NR32 5HX
T: (01502) 730359
F: (01502) 733426
E: medw149227@aol.com

Hall Farm ◆◆◆◆
Jay Lane, Church Lane, Lound,
Lowestoft, Suffolk NR32 5LJ
T: (01502) 730415
E: josephashley@compuserve.
com

Homelea Guest House ◆◆
33 Marine Parade, Lowestoft,
Suffolk NR33 0QN
T: (01502) 511640

Longshore Guesthouse ◆◆◆◆
7 Wellington Esplanade,
Lowestoft, Suffolk NR33 0QQ
T: (01502) 565037
F: (01502) 582032
E: longshore@7wellington.
fsnet.co.uk

Oak Farm ◆◆◆
Market Lane, Blundeston,
Lowestoft, Suffolk NR32 5AP
T: (01502) 731622

St Catherines House ◆◆◆
186 Denmark Road, Lowestoft,
Suffolk NR32 2EN
T: (01502) 500951

The Sandcastle ◆◆◆
35 Marine Parade, Lowestoft,
Suffolk NR33 0QN
T: (01502) 511799
F: (01502) 511799
E: rocketfuel@lineone.net

LUTON
Bedfordshire

Adara Lodge ◆◆◆
539 Hitchin Road, Luton,
LU2 7UL
T: (01582) 731361

The Pines Hotel ◆◆◆
10 Marsh Road, Luton,
Bedfordshire LU3 3NH
T: (01582) 651130 & 651140
F: (01582) 615182
E: pineshotelluton@aol.com
I: www.pineshotel.com

44 Skelton Close ◆◆
Barton Hills, Luton, LU3 4HF
T: (01582) 495205

MALDON
Essex

Anchor Guesthouse ◆◆◆
7 Church Street, Maldon, Essex
CM9 5HW
T: (01621) 855706
F: (01621) 850405

Barges Galore ◆◆◆
28 The Hythe, Maldon, Essex
CM9 5HN
T: (01621) 853520

Home While Away ◆◆◆
25c Spital Road, Maldon, Essex
CM9 6DZ
T: (01621) 851470

Jolly Sailor ◆◆
Hythe Quay, Maldon, Essex
CM9 5HP
T: (01621) 853463
F: (01621) 840253

The Limes ◆◆◆
21 Market Hill, Maldon, Essex
CM9 4PZ
T: (01621) 850350 &
07761 282676
F: (01621) 850350
E: thelimes@ukonline.co.uk
I: www.smoothhound.co.uk

Little Owls ◆◆◆
Post Office Road, Woodham
Mortimer, Maldon, Essex
CM9 6ST
T: (01245) 224355 &
07889 964584
F: (01245) 224355
E: the.bushes@virgin.net

4 Lodge Road ◆◆◆
Maldon, Essex CM9 6HW
T: (01621) 858736

The Swan Hotel ◆◆◆
73 High Street, Maldon, Essex
CM9 5EP
T: (01621) 853170
F: (01621) 854490
E: john@swanhotel.freeserve.
co.uk
I: swanhotel_maldon.co.uk

Tatoi Bed & Breakfast ◆◆◆◆
31 Acacia Drive, Maldon, Essex
CM9 6AW
T: (01621) 853841 &
07860 162328
E: diana.rogers@tesco.net

**Wilsons Motel & Bed and
Breakfast ◆◆**
154 High Street, Maldon, Essex
CM9 5BX
T: (01621) 853667 & 851850
F: (01621) 851850

MARCH
Cambridgeshire
Woodpecker Cottage ◆◆◆
20 Kingswood Road, March,
Cambridgeshire PE15 9RT
T: (01354) 660188
E: johnliz.spencer@talk21.com
I: www.smoothhound.
co.uk/hotel/woodpecker.html

MARGARET RODING
Essex
Garnish Hall ◆◆◆◆
Margaret Roding, Dunmow,
Essex CM6 1QL
T: (01245) 231209 & 231224
F: (01245) 231224

Greys ◆◆◆
Ongar Road, Margaret Roding,
Dunmow, Essex CM6 1QR
T: (01245) 231509

MARKYATE
Hertfordshire
Beechwood Home Farm ◆◆◆
Markyate, St Albans,
Hertfordshire AL3 8AJ
T: (01582) 840209

MARSHAM
Norfolk
Plough Inn ◆◆◆
Old Norwich Road, Marsham,
Norwich NR10 5PS
T: (01263) 735000
T: (01263) 735407
E: enquiries@
ploughinnmarsham.co.uk
I: www.ploughinnmarsham.
co.uk

MARSTON MORETAINE
Bedfordshire
The White Cottage ◆◆◆◆
Marston Hill, Cranfield, Bedford
MK43 0QJ
T: (01234) 751766 &
0830 554778
F: (01234) 757823
E: stay@thewhitecottage.
fsbusiness.co.uk
I: www.smoothhound.
co.uk/hotels/whitecottage

MARTHAM
Norfolk
3 Nursery Close ◆◆◆
Bell Meadow, Martham, Great
Yarmouth, Norfolk NR29 4UB
T: (01493) 740307
E: davena@
vk-bedandbreakfasts.com

MELTON CONSTABLE
Norfolk
Lowes Farm ◆◆◆◆
Edgefield, Melton Constable,
Norfolk NR24 2EX
T: (01263) 712317

MESSING
Essex
Crispin's Restaurant ◆◆◆◆
The Street, Messing, Colchester
CO5 9TR
T: (01621) 815868
E: dine@crispinsrestaurant.
co.uk
I: www.crispinsrestaurant.co.uk

MILDENHALL
Suffolk
Oakland House ◆◆◆
9 Mill Street, Mildenhall, Bury St
Edmunds, Suffolk IP28 7DP
T: (01638) 717099
F: (01638) 714852
E: lardnerjk@eggconnect.net
I: www.oaklandhouse.co.uk

Pear Tree House ◆◆◆◆
Chapel Road, West Row,
Mildenhall, Bury St Edmunds,
Suffolk IP28 8PA
T: (01638) 711112
F: (01638) 711112
E: peartree@12stay.co.uk
I: www.peartree.12stay.co.uk

MILTON BRYAN
Bedfordshire
Town Farm ◆◆◆◆
Milton Bryan, Milton Keynes
MK17 9HS
T: (01525) 210001
F: (01525) 210001

MISTLEY
Essex
Thorn Hotel ◆◆◆
High Street, Mistley,
Manningtree, Essex CO11 1HE
T: (01206) 392821
F: (01206) 392133

MUCH HADHAM
Hertfordshire
Hall Cottage
Rating Applied For
High Street, Much Hadham,
Hertfordshire SG10 6BZ
T: (01279) 842640

MUNDESLEY
Norfolk
The Grange ◆◆◆◆
High Street, Mundesley, Norwich
NR11 8JL
T: (01263) 722977 &
07949 068750

Newlands ◆◆◆◆
31 Trunch Road, Mundesley,
Norwich NR11 8JU
T: (01263) 720205
F: (01263) 720205
E: newlands@mcmail.com
I: www.newlands.cwc.net

Overcliff Lodge ◆◆◆
46 Cromer Road, Mundesley,
Norwich NR11 8DB
T: (01263) 720016
E: overclifflodge@btinternet.
com
I: www.broadland.
com/overclifflodge/

MUNDFORD
Norfolk
Colveston Manor ◆◆◆◆
Mundford, Thetford, Norfolk
IP26 5HU
T: (01842) 878218
F: (01842) 879218
I: www.farmstayanglia.co.uk

NARBOROUGH
Norfolk
Park Cottage ◆◆◆
Narford Road, Narborough,
King's Lynn, Norfolk PE32 1HZ
T: (01760) 337220

NAYLAND
Suffolk
Gladwins Farm ◆◆◆◆
Harpers Hill, Nayland, Colchester
CO6 4NU
T: (01206) 262261
F: (01206) 263001
E: gladwinsfarm@compuserve.
com
I: www/gladwinsfarm.co.uk

The White Hart Inn ◆◆◆◆
High Street, Nayland, Colchester
CO6 4JF
T: (01206) 263382
F: (01206) 263638
E: nayhart@aol.com
I: www.whitehart-nayland.co.uk

NEATISHEAD
Norfolk
Allens Farmhouse ◆◆◆
Three Hammer Common,
Neatishead, Norwich NR12 8XW
T: (01692) 630080
E: allensfarmhouse@lineone.net

**The Barton Angler Country Inn
◆◆◆**
Irstead Road, Neatishead,
Norwich NR12 8XP
T: (01692) 630740
F: (01692) 631122

Ramblers ◆◆◆
School Lane, Neatishead,
Norwich NR12 8XW
T: (01692) 630864

Regency Guesthouse ◆◆◆◆
The Street, Neatishead, Norwich
NR12 8AD
T: (01692) 630233
F: (01692) 630233
E: wrigleyregency@talk21.com
I: www.norfolkbroads.
com/regency

NEWMARKET
Suffolk
2 Birdcage Walk ◆◆◆◆
Newmarket, Suffolk CB8 0NE
T: (01638) 669456
F: (01638) 669456

The Meadow House ◆◆◆◆
2A High Street, Burwell,
Cambridge CB5 0HB
T: (01638) 741926 & 741354
F: (01638) 743424
E: hilary@themeadowhouse.
co.uk
I: www.themeadowhouse.co.uk

NORTH FAMBRIDGE
Essex
Ferry Boat Inn ◆◆◆
North Fambridge, Chelmsford
CM3 6LR
T: (01621) 740208
F: (01621) 740208
E: sylviaferryboat@aol.com

NORTH LOPHAM
Norfolk
Church Farm House ◆◆◆◆◆
North Lopham, Diss, Norfolk
IP22 2LP
T: (01379) 687270
F: (01379) 687270
E: b&b@bassetts.demon.co.uk
I: www.churchfarmhouse.org

NORTH MYMMS
Hertfordshire
Wood View ◆◆
23 Dixon Hill Close, North
Mymms, Hatfield, Hertfordshire
AL9 7EF
T: (01707) 263802

NORTH WALSHAM
Norfolk
Dolphin Lodge
Rating Applied For
Trunch, North Walsham, Norfolk
NR18 0QE
T: (01263) 720961

Kings Arms Hotel ◆◆◆
Kings Arms Street, North
Walsham, Norfolk NR28 9JX
T: (01692) 403054
F: (01692) 500095
E: kahotel@fsbdial.co.uk

Pinetrees ◆◆◆◆
45 Happisburgh Road, North
Walsham, Norfolk NR28 9HB
T: (01692) 404213

NORTH WOOTTON
Norfolk
Red Cat Hotel ◆◆◆
Station Road, North Wootton,
King's Lynn, Norfolk PE30 3QH
T: (01553) 631244 & 631574
F: (01553) 631574
E: enquiries@redcathotel.com
I: www.redcathotel.com

NORWICH
Norfolk
The Abbey Hotel ◆◆◆
16 Stracey Road, Thorpe Road,
Norwich, NR1 1EZ
T: (01603) 612915
F: (01603) 612915

Arbor Linden Lodge ◆◆◆◆
Linden House, 557 Earlham
Road, Norwich, Norfolk
NR4 7HW
T: (01603) 451303
F: (01603) 250641
E: info@guesthousenorwich.
com
I: www.guesthousenorwich.com

Aylwyne House ◆◆◆
59 Aylsham Road, Norwich,
NR3 2HF
T: (01603) 665798

Becklands ◆◆◆
105 Holt Road, Horsford,
Norwich NR10 3AB
T: (01603) 898582
F: (01603) 754223

**Hotel Belmonte and Belmonte
Restaurant◆◆◆**
60-62 Prince of Wales Road,
Norwich, NR1 1LT
T: (01603) 622533
F: (01603) 760805
E: bar7seven@yahoo.com
I: www.geocities.
com/bar7seven/

The Blue Boar Inn ◆◆◆
259 Wroxham Road, Sprowston,
Norwich NR7 8RL
T: (01603) 426802
F: (01603) 487749
E: turnbull101@hotmail.com
I: www.norwich2nite.
co.uk/pubs/blue boar/blueboar.
htm

Blue Cedar Lodge Guesthouse
◆◆◆
391 Earlham Road, Norwich,
NR2 3RQ
T: (01603) 458331 &
07836 792659
F: (01603) 458331

Cavell House ◆◆◆
Swardeston, Norwich NR14 8DZ
T: (01508) 578195

Church Farm Guesthouse
◆◆◆
Church Street, Horsford,
Norwich NR10 3DB
T: (01603) 898020
F: (01603) 891649
E: churchfarm.guesthouse@
btinternet.com
I: www.btinternet.
com/~churchfarm.guesthouse

Conifers Hotel ◆◆◆
162 Dereham Road, Norwich,
NR2 3AH
T: (01603) 628737

Farlham Guesthouse ◆◆◆◆
147 Earlham Road, Norwich,
NR2 3RG
T: (01603) 454169
F: (01603) 454169
E: earlhamgh@hotmail.com

Eaton Bower ◆◆◆◆
20 Mile End Road, Norwich,
NR4 7QY
T: (01603) 462204
E: eaton_bower@hotmail.com
I: www.eatonbower.co.uk

Edmar Lodge ◆◆◆
64 Earlham Road, Norwich,
NR2 3DF
T: (01603) 615599
F: (01603) 495599
E: edmar@btconnect.com
I: www.edmarlodge.co.uk

Elm Farm Country House
◆◆◆◆
55 Norwich Road, St Faiths,
NR10 3HH
T: (01603) 898366
F: (01603) 897129
E: pmpbelmfarm@aol.com

309 Fakenham Road ◆◆◆
Taverham, Norwich, NR8 6LF
T: (01603) 860103 & 07719 409
709
E: jeanshepherd@lineone.net

The Gables Guesthouse ◆◆◆◆
527 Earlham Road, Norwich,
NR4 7HN
T: (01603) 456666
F: (01603) 250320

Garden House Hotel ◆◆◆
Salhouse Road, Rackheath,
Norwich NR13 6AA
T: (01603) 720007
F: (01603) 720019
E: gardenhousebandb@aol.com
I: www.gardenhouse.uk.com

Harvey House Guesthouse
◆◆◆
50 Harvey Lane, Norwich,
NR7 0AQ
T: (01603) 436575
F: (01603) 436575
E: harveyhouse@which.net

Kingsley Lodge ◆◆◆◆
3 Kingsley Road, Norwich,
NR1 3RB
T: (01603) 615819
F: (01603) 615819
E: kingsley@paston.co.uk

The Limes ◆◆◆
188 Unthank Road, Norwich,
NR2 2AH
T: (01603) 454282 &
0771 3026517

Manor Barn House ◆◆◆◆
Back Lane, Rackheath, Norwich
NR13 6NN
T: (01603) 783543

Marlborough House Hotel
◆◆◆
22 Stracey Road, Norwich,
NR1 1EZ
T: (01603) 628005
F: (01603) 628005

Mousehold Lodge Guesthouse
◆◆◆
53-55 Mousehold Lane,
Norwich, NR7 8HL
T: (01603) 426026
F: (01603) 413009
E: info@mouseholdlodge.co.uk
I: www.mousehold-lodge.co.uk

The Old Rectory ◆◆◆◆
Hall Road, Framingham Earl,
Norwich NR14 7SB
T: (01508) 493590
F: (01508) 495110
E: brucewellings@drivedevice.
freeserve.co.uk

Rosedale ◆◆
145 Earlham Road, Norwich,
NR2 3RG
T: (01603) 453743 &
07949 296542
F: (01603) 259887
E: drcbac@aol.com
I: www.members.aol.com/drcbac

Wedgewood House ◆◆◆
42 St Stephens Road, Norwich,
NR1 3RE
T: (01603) 625730
F: (01603) 615035
E: stay@wedgewoodhouse.
co.uk
I: www.wedgewoodhouse.co.uk

Witton Hall Farm ◆◆◆
Witton, North Walsham, Norfolk
NR13 5DN
T: (01603) 714580
E: wittonhall@cwcom.net

OCCOLD
Suffolk

The Cedars Guesthouse ◆◆◆◆
Church Street, Occold, Eye,
Suffolk IP23 7PS
T: (01379) 678439

OLD CATTON
Norfolk

Catton Old Hall ◆◆◆◆◆
Lodge Lane, Old Catton, Norwich
NR6 7HG
T: (01603) 419379
F: (01603) 400339
E: enquiries@catton-hall.co.uk
I: catton-hall.co.uk

ORSETT
Essex

The Larches ◆◆◆
Rectory Road, Orsett, Grays,
Essex RM16 3EH
T: (01375) 891217 &
07778 873612
F: (01375) 891747

ORTON LONGUEVILLE
Cambridgeshire

Orton Mere Guest House
◆◆◆◆
547 Oundle Road, Orton
Longueville, Peterborough
PE2 7DH
T: (01733) 708432
F: (01733) 708425

OULTON
Suffolk

Laurel Farm ◆◆◆◆
Hall Lane, Oulton, Lowestoft,
Suffolk NR32 5DL
T: (01502) 568724 &
(01788) 147758
F: (01502) 568724
E: laurelfarm@hodgkin.
screaming.net

OVERSTRAND
Norfolk

Danum House ◆◆◆
22 Pauls Lane, Overstrand,
Cromer, Norfolk NR27 0PE
T: (01263) 579327
F: (01263) 579327

PAKEFIELD
Suffolk

Pipers Lodge Hotel & Motel
◆◆◆
41 London Road, Pakefield,
NR33 7AA
T: (01502) 569805
F: (01502) 565383

PALGRAVE
Suffolk

The Paddocks B & B ◆◆◆
3 The Paddocks, Palgrave, Diss,
Norfolk IP22 1AG
T: (01379) 642098 & 640518
F: (01379) 652796
E: rod@rodjones.force9.co.uk
I: www.rodjones.force9.co.uk

PAMPISFORD
Cambridgeshire

**South Cambridgeshire
Guesthouse** ◆◆
2 and 4 London Road,
Pampisford, Cambridge, CB2 4EF
T: (01223) 834523 &
07971 073758
F: (01223) 570379
E: south.cambs@lineone.net
I: www.southcambs.
co.uk/guesthouse.htm

PEBMARSH
Essex

Timbers ◆◆◆
Cross End, Pebmarsh, Halstead,
Essex CO9 2NT
T: (01787) 269330

PENTLOW
Essex

Fiddlesticks ◆◆◆◆
Pentlow Ridge, Pentlow,
Sudbury, Suffolk CO10 7JW
T: (01787) 280154
F: (01787) 280154

PETERBOROUGH
Cambridgeshire

The Anchor Lodge ◆◆◆
28 Percival Street, Peterborough,
PE3 6AU
T: (01733) 312724 &
07767 611911

Aragon House ◆◆◆
75-77 London Road,
Peterborough, PE2 9BS
T: (01733) 563718
F: (01733) 563718
E: aragon@fsbdial.co.uk
I: www.
peterboroughaccommodation.
co.uk

Arman Lodge House ◆◆
3 Scotney Street, Newengland,
Peterborough, PE1 3NG
T: (01733) 554232
E: rajna@talk21.com
I: www.armanlodgehouse.com

Blue Wisteria House ◆◆◆
Church Lane, Helpston,
Peterborough PE6 7DT
T: (01733) 252272

The Brandon ◆◆◆
161 Lincoln Road, Peterborough,
PE1 2PW
T: (01733) 568631
F: (01733) 568631
I: www.
peterboroughaccommodation.
co.uk

Clarks ◆◆◆◆
21 Oundle Road, Peterborough,
PE2 9PB
T: (01733) 342482

Courtyard Cottage ◆◆◆◆
2 West End, Langtoft,
Peterborough, PE6 9LS
T: (01778) 348354
F: (01778) 348354
E: david_tinegate@ic24.net
I: www.courtyardcottage.8m.
com/

Da Rosalia Hotel ◆◆
25 Burghley Road,
Peterborough, PE1 2QA
T: (01733) 568020 & 553331
F: (01733) 897816
E: darosaliahotel.2@virginnet.
co.uk

The Graham Guesthouse ◆◆◆
296 Oundle Road, Peterborough,
PE2 9QA
T: (01733) 567824
F: (01733) 567824

Hawthorn House ◆◆◆◆
89 Thorpe Road, Peterborough,
PE3 6JQ
T: (01733) 340608 & 313470
F: (01733) 763800
E: peggy.warren@tesco.net
I: www.
peterboroughaccomodation.
co.uk

Longueville Guesthouse
◆◆◆◆
411 Oundle Road, Orton
Longueville, Peterborough,
PE2 7DA
T: (01733) 233442 &
07703 540059
F: (01733) 233442

Montana ◆◆◆
15 Fletton Avenue,
Peterborough, PE2 8AX
T: (01733) 567917
F: (01733) 567917
I: www.stilwell.co.uk / www.
peterboroughaccomodation.
co.uk

Newark Hotel ◆◆◆
239-241 Eastfield Road,
Peterborough, PE1 4BH
T: (01733) 569811
F: (01733) 312550

Park Road Guesthouse ◆◆◆
67 Park Road, Peterborough,
PE1 2TN
T: (01733) 562220
F: (01733) 344279

PETTISTREE
Suffolk

The Three Tuns Coaching Inn
◆◆◆
Main Road, Pettistree,
Woodbridge, Suffolk IP13 0HW
T: (01728) 747979 & 746244
F: (01728) 746244
E: jon@threetuns-coachinginn.
co.uk
I: www.threetuns-coachinginn.
co.uk

PLAYFORD
Suffolk

Glenham ◆◆◆
Hill Farm Road, Playford,
Ipswich IP6 9DU
T: (01473) 624939 & 410115
E: glenham@tesco.net
I: glenham.hypermart.net

PLESHEY
Essex

Acreland Green ◆◆◆◆
Pleshey, Chelmsford CM3 1HP
T: (01245) 231277 & 251263
F: (01245) 231277

POLSTEAD
Suffolk

Polstead Lodge ◆◆◆◆
Mill Street, Polstead, Colchester
CO6 5AD
T: (01206) 262196
E: polsteadlodge@bushinternet.
com

POTTER HEIGHAM
Norfolk

Falgate Inn ◆◆◆
Ludham Road, Potter Heigham,
Great Yarmouth, Norfolk
NR29 5HZ
T: (01692) 670003 &
07899 847262
E: malber@cypress72.freeserve.
co.uk

POTTERS BAR
Hertfordshire

Bruggen Lodge ◆◆◆◆
13 The Drive, Potters Bar,
Hertfordshire EN6 2AP
T: (01707) 655904 & 665070
F: (01707) 857287
E: andreaseggie@lineone.net

PULHAM MARKET
Norfolk

The Old Bakery ◆◆◆◆◆
Church Walk, Pulham Market,
Diss, Norfolk IP21 4SJ
T: (01379) 676492
F: (01379) 676492

RACKHEATH
Norfolk

Barn Court ◆◆◆
6 Back Lane, Rackheath,
Norwich NR13 6NN
T: (01603) 782536
F: (01603) 782536

RAMSEY
Essex

Woodview Cottage ◆◆◆◆
Wrabness Road, Ramsey,
Harwich, Essex CO12 5ND
T: (01255) 886413 &
07714 600134
E: pcohen@cix.co.uk
I: www.woodview-cottage.co.uk

RAMSHOLT
Suffolk

The Ramsholt Arms ◆◆◆
Dock Road, Ramsholt,
Woodbridge, Suffolk IP12 3AB
T: (01394) 411229
F: (01394) 411818

RAVENSDEN
Bedfordshire

Tree Garth ◆◆◆◆
Church End, Ravensden, Bedford
MK44 2RP
T: (01234) 771745
F: (01234) 771745
E: treegarth@ukonline.co.uk
I: treegarth.co.uk

REEDHAM
Norfolk

Briars ◆◆◆
10 Riverside, Reedham, Norwich
NR13 3TF
T: (01493) 700054
F: (01493) 700054

The Pyghtle ◆◆◆◆
26A The Hills, Reedham,
Norwich NR13 3AR
T: (01493) 701262
F: (01493) 701635
E: oporeedham@zoo.co.uk
I: www.reedham-oldpostoffice.
co.uk

RENDHAM
Suffolk

Rendham Hall ◆◆◆
Rendham, Saxmundham, Suffolk
IP17 2AW
T: (01728) 663440
F: (01728) 663245
E: dc.strachan@talk21.com

REPPS WITH BASTWICK
Norfolk

Grove Farm Bed & Breakfast
◆◆◆
Grove Farm, Repps With
Bastwick, Great Yarmouth,
Norfolk NR29 5JN
T: (01692) 670205
F: (01692) 670205
E: jenny@grovefarmholidays.
co.uk

RETTENDON
Essex

Crossways ◆◆◆
Main Road, Rettendon Common,
Chelmsford CM3 8DY
T: (01245) 400539
F: (01245) 400127
E: crossways@somnific.
freeserve.co.uk

REYDON
Suffolk

Broadlands ◆◆◆
68 Halesworth Road, Reydon,
Southwold, Suffolk IP18 6NS
T: (01502) 724384
F: (01502) 724384

Newlands Country House
◆◆◆◆
72 Halesworth Road, Reydon,
Southwold, Suffolk IP18 6NS
T: (01502) 722164
F: (01502) 724696
E: broadside@beeb.net
I: www.southwold.blythweb.
co.uk/newlands/
&

The Randolph Hotel ◆◆◆◆
41 Wangford Road, Reydon,
Southwold, Suffolk IP18 6PZ
T: (01502) 723603
F: (01502) 722194
E: randolph_hotel@demon.
co.uk

Ridge Bed & Breakfast ◆◆◆
The Ridge, 14 Halesworth Road,
Reydon, Southwold, Suffolk
IP18 6NH
T: (01502) 724855 &
07773 924105

RICKINGHALL
Suffolk

The Bell Inn ◆◆◆◆
The Street, Rickinghall, Diss,
Norfolk IP22 1BN
T: (01379) 898445

RIDLINGTON
Norfolk

Mill Common House ◆◆◆◆
Mill Common Road, Ridlington,
North Walsham, Norfolk
NR28 9TY
T: (01692) 650792
F: (01692) 651480
E: johnpugh@millcommon.
freeserve.co.uk
I: www.broadland.
com/millcommon

RIVENHALL
Essex

North Ford Farm ◆◆◆◆
Church Road, Rivenhall,
Witham, Essex CM8 3PG
T: (01376) 583321 &
07957 862112
F: (01376) 583321

**Rickstones Farmhouse Bed &
Breakfast** ◆◆◆◆
Rickstones Farmhouse,
Rickstones Road, Rivenhall,
Witham, Essex CM8 3HQ
T: (01376) 514351
F: (01376) 514351
E: rickstonesfarmhouse@
btinternet.com

ROXTON
Bedfordshire

Church Farm ◆◆◆◆
41 High Street, Roxton, Bedford
MK44 3EB
T: (01234) 870234
F: (01234) 870234
E: churchfarm@amserve.net

ROXWELL
Essex

Cross Keys ◆◆◆
Boyton Cross, Roxwell,
Chelmsford CM1 4LP
T: (01245) 248201

ROYDON
Essex

Roydon Motel ◆◆◆◆
Roydon Mill Leisure Park,
Roydon, Harlow, Essex CM19 5EJ
T: (01279) 792777 & 792695
E: motel@roydonpark.com
I: www.roydonpark.com

ROYSTON
Hertfordshire

Hall Farm ◆◆◆◆
Great Chishill, Royston,
Hertfordshire SG8 8SH
T: (01763) 838263
F: (01763) 838263
E: wisehall@farming.co.uk
I: www.hallfarmbb.co.uk

RUMBURGH
Suffolk

Rumburgh Farm ◆◆◆◆
Rumburgh, Halesworth, Suffolk
IP19 0RU
T: (01986) 781351
F: (01986) 781351
E: binder@rumburghfarm.
freeserve.co.uk
I: www.rumburghfarm.freeserve.
co.uk

SAFFRON WALDEN
Essex

Archway Guesthouse ◆◆◆◆
Archway House, Church Street,
Saffron Walden, Essex CB10 1JW
T: (01799) 501500 &
07779 397669
F: (01799) 506003

Ashleigh House ◆◆◆
7 Farmadine Grove, Saffron
Walden, Essex CB11 3DR
T: (01799) 513611 &
07752 417575
E: deborah@anngilder.fsnet.
co.uk

The Bell House ◆◆◆◆
53-55 Castle Street, Saffron
Walden, Essex CB10 1BD
T: (01799) 527857

The Cricketers ◆◆◆◆
Clavering, Saffron Walden, Essex
CB11 4QT
T: (01799) 550442
F: (01799) 550882
E: cricketers@lineone.net
I: www.thecricketers.co.uk

11 Dawson Close ◆◆◆
Saffron Walden, Essex CB10 2AR
T: (01799) 528491

Grimalkins B & B
Rating Applied For
49 Castle Street, Saffron
Walden, Essex CB10 1BD
T: (01799) 521557
E: gertrud@hill-castle.freeserve.
co.uk

1 Gunters Cottages ◆◆◆◆
Thaxted Road, Saffron Walden,
Essex CB10 2UT
T: (01799) 522091

30 Lambert Cross ◆◆
Saffron Walden, Essex CB10 2DP
T: (01799) 527287

Oak House ◆◆◆
40 Audley Road, Saffron
Walden, Essex CB11 3HD
T: (01799) 523290 &
07802 705555
E: oakhouse@appleonline.net

The Plough Inn at Radwinter
◆◆◆
Sampford Road, Radwinter,
Saffron Walden, Essex CB10 2TL
T: (01799) 599222 & 599161
F: (01799) 599161

Pudding House ◆◆◆
9a Museum Street, Saffron
Walden, Essex CB10 1JL
T: (01799) 522089

Redgates Farmhouse ◆◆◆◆
Redgate Lane, Sewards End,
Saffron Walden, Essex CB10 2LP
T: (01799) 516166

Rockells Farm ◆◆◆◆
Duddenhoe End, Saffron
Walden, Essex CB11 4UY
T: (01763) 838053

Rowley Hill Lodge ◆◆◆◆
Little Walden, Saffron Walden,
Essex CB10 1UZ
T: (01799) 525975
F: (01799) 516622
E: eh@clara.net

Saffron Lodge ◆◆◆◆
11 Mount Pleasant Road,
Saffron Walden, Essex CB11 3EA
T: (01799) 522179

10 Victoria Avenue ◆◆◆
Saffron Walden, Essex CB11 3AE
T: (01799) 525923

Yardley's ◆◆◆◆
Orchard Pightle, Hadstock,
Cambridge CB1 6PQ
T: (01223) 891822
F: (01223) 891822
E: yardleys@waitrose.com
I: www.users.waitrose.
com/~yardleys/

Cranford House ◆◆◆◆
Ovington Road, Saham Toney,
Thetford, Norfolk IP25 7HF
T: (01953) 885292
F: (01953) 885611
E: dsf@anstruthers.com
I: www.cranfordhouse.net

5 Approach Road ◆◆
St Albans, Hertfordshire AL1 1SP
T: (01727) 852471 & 858571
T: (01727) 847408
E: nigelcocks@compuserve.com

22 Ardens Way ◆◆◆
St Albans, Hertfordshire AL4 9UJ
T: (01727) 861986 &
07931 722493

Ardmore House ◆◆◆
54 Lemsford Road, St Albans,
Hertfordshire AL1 3PP
T: (01727) 859313
F: (01727) 859313
E: info@ardmorehousehotel.
altodigital.co.uk
I: www.ardmorehousehotel.com

Avona ◆◆◆
478 Hatfield Road, St Albans,
Hertfordshire AL4 0SX
T: (01727) 842216 &
07956 857353

Black Lion Inn ◆◆◆
198 Fishpool Street, St Albans,
Hertfordshire AL3 4SB
T: (01727) 851786
F: (01727) 859243
E: info@blacklioninn.abelgratis.
com

Braemar House ◆◆◆◆
89 Salisbury Avenue, St Albans,
Hertfordshire AL1 4TY
T: (01727) 839641
F: (01727) 839641

55 Charmouth Road ◆◆◆
St Albans, Hertfordshire AL1 4SE
T: (01727) 860002
E: terry@charmouthfsnet.co.uk

35 Chestnut Drive ◆◆◆
St Albans, Hertfordshire AL4 0ER
T: (01727) 833401

5 Cunningham Avenue ◆◆◆
St Albans, Hertfordshire AL1 1JJ
T: (01727) 857388

Fern Cottage ◆◆◆◆
116 Old London Road, St Albans,
Hertfordshire AL1 1PU
T: (01727) 834200 &
07957 484349
E: dorotheabristow@ntlworld.
com
I: www.ferncottage.uk.net

Fleuchary House ◆◆◆◆
3 Upper Lattimore Road, St
Albans, Hertfordshire AL1 3UD
T: (01727) 766761
E: linda@fleucharyhouse.
freeserve.co.uk

32 Gurney Court Road ◆◆◆
St Albans, AL1 4RL
T: (01727) 835819 & 760250
E: the-salisburys@cwcom.net

8 Hall Place Gardens ◆◆◆
St Albans, Hertfordshire AL1 3SP
T: (01727) 858939

2 The Limes ◆◆◆
Spencer Gate, St Albans,
Hertfordshire AL1 4AT
T: (01727) 831080
E: hunter.mitchell@virgin.net

178 London Road ◆◆◆◆
St Albans, Hertfordshire AL1 1PL
T: (01727) 846726 & 831267
F: (01727) 831267

7 Marlborough Gate ◆◆◆
St Albans, Hertfordshire AL1 3TX
T: (01727) 865498 &
07960 095940
F: (01727) 812965
E: michael.jameson@btinternet.
com

Park House ◆◆◆
30 The Park, St Albans,
Hertfordshire AL1 4RY
T: (01727) 832054

36 Potters Field ◆◆◆
St Albans, Hertfordshire AL3 6LJ
T: (01727) 766840 &
07790 452920
F: (01727) 766840
E: manners-smith@compuserve

Riverside ◆◆◆◆
24 Minister Court, St Albans,
Hertfordshire AL2 2NF
T: (01727) 758780 &
0771 5824936
F: (01727) 758760
E: Ellispatriciam@aol.com

56 Sandpit Lane ◆◆◆◆
St Albans, Hertfordshire
AL1 4BW
T: (01727) 856799
F: (01727) 856799

Tresco ◆◆◆◆
76 Clarence Road, St Albans,
Hertfordshire AL1 4NG
T: (01727) 864880
F: (01727) 864880
E: pat.leggatt@talk21.com
I: www.twistedsilicon.
co.uk/76/index.htm

The White House ◆◆
28 Salisbury Avenue, St Albans,
Hertfordshire AL1 4TU
T: (01727) 861017

Wren Lodge ◆◆◆◆
24 Beaconsfield Road, St Albans,
Hertfordshire AL1 3RB
T: (01727) 855540 &
07836 285196
F: (01727) 766674
E: wren.lodge@ntlworld.com
I: www.destination-england.
co.uk/wrenlodge.html

16 York Road ◆◆◆
St Albans, Hertfordshire AL1 4PL
T: (01727) 853647

The Nags Head Hotel ◆◆◆
2 Berkley Street, Eynesbury, St
Neots, Huntingdon,
Cambridgeshire PE19 2NA
T: (01480) 476812
F: (01480) 391881

The Lodge Inn
Rating Applied For
Vicarage Road, Salhouse,
Norwich NR13 6HD
T: (01603) 782828
E: thelodgeinn@salhouse.f.s.
business.co.uk

Oldfield ◆◆◆◆
Vicarage Road, Salhouse,
Norwich NR13 6HA
T: (01603) 781080
F: (01603) 781083

Highfield Farm ◆◆◆◆◆
Great North Road, Sandy,
Bedfordshire SG19 2AQ
T: (01767) 682332
F: (01767) 692503
E: stay@highfield-farm.co.uk

Village Farm ◆◆
Thorncote Green, Sandy,
Bedfordshire SG19 1PU
T: (01767) 627345

7 Church Walk ◆◆◆
Sawbridgeworth, Hertfordshire
CM21 9BJ
T: (01279) 723233
E: kent@sawbridgeworth.co.uk

A1 Bed & Breakfast ◆◆
5 High Street, Sawtry,
Huntingdon, Cambridgeshire
PE28 5SR
T: (01487) 830201
F: (01487) 830201

The Map House ◆◆◆◆
The Map House, Smokers Hole,
Saxlingham, Holt, Norfolk
NR25 7JU
T: (01263) 741304
F: (01263) 741439
E: enquiries@maphouse.net
I: www.maphouse.net

Foxhole Farm ◆◆◆◆
Windy Lane, Foxhole,
Saxlingham Thorpe, Norwich
NR15 1UG
T: (01508) 499226
F: (01508) 499226
E: foxholefarm@hotmail.com

Moat House Farm ◆◆◆◆
Rendham Road, Carlton,
Saxmundham, Suffolk IP17 2QN
T: (01728) 602228
F: (01728) 602228
E: sally@goodacres.com
I: www.goodacres.com

North Lodge Guest House
◆◆◆◆◆
6 North Entrance, Saxmundham,
Suffolk IP17 1AY
T: (01728) 603337
E: northlodgetoto@aol.com

Poppy Cottage ◆◆◆
7 Stour Close, Saxmundham,
Suffolk IP17 1XX
T: (01728) 602936
E: sonis.byard@ic24.net

Stratford Hall ◆◆◆◆
Stratford St Andrew,
Saxmundham, Suffolk IP17 1LH
T: (01728) 602025

Ivy Forge ◆◆◆◆
The Green, Saxtead, Woodbridge,
Suffolk IP13 9QG
T: (01728) 685054
F: (01728) 6865054
E: george@ivyforge.freeserve.
co.uk

Holmwood House ◆◆◆◆
Tunstead Road, Scottow,
Norwich NR10 5DA
T: (01692) 538386
F: (01692) 538386
E: holmwoodhouse@lineone.
net
I: www.norfolkbroads.
com/holmwood

Manor Farm Bed & Breakfast
◆◆◆◆
Manor Farm, Sculthorpe,
Fakenham, Norfolk NR21 9NJ
T: (01328) 862185
F: (01328) 862033
E: mddwo2@dial.pipex.com

Achimota ◆◆◆◆
31 North Street, Sheringham,
Norfolk NR26 8LW
T: (01263) 822379
I: www.broadland.com/achimota

Alverstone ◆◆
33 The Avenue, Sheringham,
Norfolk NR26 8DG
T: (01263) 825527

The Bay Leaf Guest House
◆◆◆
10 St Peters Road, Sheringham,
Norfolk NR26 8QY
T: (01263) 823779
F: (01263) 820041
E: thebayleaf@bushinternet.
com
I: www.broadland.com/bayleaf

The Burlington Lodge ◆◆◆
5 St Nicholas Place, Sheringham,
Norfolk NR26 8LF
T: (01263) 820931 & 822053
F: (01263) 820964
E: r.mcdermott@hemscott.net

Camberley Guesthouse ◆◆◆
62 Cliff Road, Sheringham,
Norfolk NR26 8BJ
T: (01263) 823101
F: (01263) 821433
E: graham@
camberleyguesthouse.co.uk
I: www.camberleyguesthouse.
co.uk

Holly Cottage ◆◆◆◆
14a The Rise, Sheringham,
Norfolk NR26 8QB
T: (01263) 822807
F: (01263) 824822
E: hollyperks@aol.com
I: sheringham-network.co.uk

The Melrose ◆◆◆
9 Holway Road, Sheringham,
Norfolk NR26 8HN
T: (01263) 823299
E: jparsonage@btconnect.com
I: www.themelrsosesheringham.
co.uk

Olivedale Guesthouse ◆◆◆◆
20 Augusta Street, Sheringham,
Norfolk NR26 8LA
T: (01263) 825871 &
0774 8850951
F: (01263) 821104
E: info@olivedale.co.uk
I: www.olivedale.co.uk

Pentland Lodge ◆◆
51 The Avenue, Sheringham,
Norfolk NR26 8DQ
T: (01263) 823533
F: (01263) 823533
E: janetnolson@btinternet.com

Pinecones ◆◆◆◆
70 Cromer Road, Sheringham,
Norfolk NR26 8RT
T: (01263) 824955
F: (01263) 824955
E: TonyandPat@pinecones.
fsnet.co.uk

Priestfields ◆◆◆◆
6B North Street, Sheringham,
Norfolk NR26 8LW
T: (01263) 820305
F: (01263) 820125
E: david.phillips10@which.net

Sheringham Lodge ◆◆◆
Cromer Road, Sheringham,
Norfolk NR26 8RS
T: (01263) 821954
E: mikewalker19@hotmail.com
I: www.sheringhamlodge.co.uk

The Two Lifeboats Hotel ◆◆◆
2 The High Street, Sheringham,
Norfolk NR26 8JR
T: (01263) 822401
F: (01263) 823130
E: info@twolifeboats.co.uk
I: www.twolifeboats.co.uk

Westwater B&B Guest House
◆◆◆
28 Norfolk Road, Sheringham,
Norfolk NR26 8HJ
T: (01263) 822321
F: (01263) 825932
E: westwater@x-stream.co.uk
I: smoothhound.co.uk

Willow Lodge ◆◆◆◆
6 Vicarage Road, Sheringham,
Norfolk NR26 8NH
T: (01263) 822204
F: (01263) 822204

SHIMPLING
Suffolk

Gannocks House ◆◆◆◆
Old Rectory Lane, Shimpling,
Bury St Edmunds, Suffolk
IP29 4HG
T: (01284) 830499 &
07702 833240
F: (01284) 830499
E: gannocks-house@lineone.net
I: www.countrybreak.co.uk

SHOTLEY
Suffolk

Hill House Farm
Rating Applied For
Wades Lane, Shotley, Ipswich
IP9 1EW
T: (01473) 787318 & 787111
F: (01473) 787111
E: richard@rjwrinch.fsnet.co.uk

SHUDY CAMPS
Cambridgeshire

Old Well Cottage ◆◆◆◆
Main Street, Shudy Camps,
Cambridge CB1 6RA
T: (01799) 584387 & 584486
F: (01799) 584486

SIBLE HEDINGHAM
Essex

Brickwall Farm ◆◆◆◆
Queen Street, Sible Hedingham,
Halstead, Essex CO9 3RH
T: (01787) 460329
F: (01787) 460329
E: brickwallfarm@btinternet.
com

Tocat House ◆◆◆◆
9 Potter Street, Sible
Hedingham, Halstead, Essex
CO9 3RG
T: (01787) 461942

SIBTON
Suffolk

Church Farm ◆◆◆◆◆
Yoxford Road, Sibton,
Saxmundham, Suffolk IP17 2LX
T: (01728) 660101
F: (01728) 660102
E: dixons@church-farmhouse.
demon.co.uk
I: www.church-farmhouse.
demon.co.uk

Park Farm ◆◆◆◆
Sibton, Saxmundham, Suffolk
IP17 2LZ
T: (01728) 668324
F: (01728) 668564
E: margaret.gray@btinternet.
com
I: www.farmstayanglia.
co.uk/parkfarm

SNAPE
Suffolk

Flemings Lodge ◆◆◆◆
Gromford Lane, Snape,
Saxmundham, Suffolk IP17 1RG
T: (01728) 688502
F: (01728) 688502

SNETTISHAM
Norfolk

The Hollies ◆◆◆◆
12 Lynn Road, Snettisham,
King's Lynn, Norfolk PE31 7LS
T: (01485) 541294 &
07798 827485
F: (01485) 541294

The Rose & Crown ◆◆◆◆
Old Church Road, Snettisham,
King's Lynn, Norfolk PE31 7LX
T: (01485) 541382
F: (01485) 543172
I: www.14th-century-inn.co.uk

The Round House ◆◆◆◆
131 Lynn Road, Snettisham,
King's Lynn, Norfolk PE31 7QG
T: (01485) 540580
E: zipha.christopher@virgin.net

Violet Cottage ◆◆◆◆
24 Common Road West,
Snettisham, King's Lynn, Norfolk
PE31 7PE
T: (01485) 544081 &
07930 332088
F: (01485) 544081
E: mwatts@749@aol.com

SOUTH LOPHAM
Norfolk

Malting Farm ◆◆◆
Blo' Norton Road, South
Lopham, Diss, Norfolk IP22 2HT
T: (01379) 687201
I: www.farmstayanglia.co.uk

SOUTH WALSHAM
Norfolk

Old Hall Farm ◆◆◆◆
Newport Road, South Walsham,
Norwich NR13 6DS
T: (01603) 270271 & 270017
F: (01603) 270017
E: rdewing@freenet.co.uk
I: www.oldhallfarm.co.uk

SOUTHEND-ON-SEA
Essex

Atlantis Guest House ◆◆◆◆
63 Alexandra Road, Southend-
on-Sea, SS1 1EY
T: (01702) 332538
F: (01702) 392736

The Bay Guesthouse ◆◆◆◆
187 Eastern Esplanade, Thorpe
Bay, Southend-on-Sea, Essex
SS1 3AA
T: (01702) 588415
E: thebayguesthouse@hotmail.
com

Beaches ◆◆◆◆
192 Eastern Esplanade, Thorpe
Bay, Southend-on-Sea, SS1 3AA
T: (01702) 586124
F: (01702) 588377
E: beaches@quista.net
I: www.smoothhound.
co.uk/hotels/beaches

Gladstone Guesthouse
Rating Applied For
40 Hartington Road, Southend-
on-Sea, SS1 2HS
T: (01702) 462776

Haven House Hotel ◆◆
47 Heygate Avenue, Southend-
on-Sea, SS1 2AN
T: (01702) 619246

Lee Villas Guesthouse ◆
1 & 2 Hartington Place,
Southend-on-Sea, SS1 2HP
T: (01702) 613768 & 317214
E: SMCK764100@aol.com

Pebbles Guesthouse ◆◆◆◆
190 Eastern Esplanade, Thorpe
Bay, Southend-on-Sea, SS1 3AA
T: (01702) 582329
F: (01702) 582329

Strand Guesthouse ◆◆
165 Eastern Esplanade, Thorpe
Bay, Southend-on-Sea, SS1 2YB
T: (01702) 586611

The Waverley Guesthouse ◆◆
191 Eastern Esplanade, Thorpe
Bay, Southend-on-Sea, SS1 3AA
T: (01702) 585212 &
07939 508806
E: waverleyguesthouse@
hotmail.com

SOUTHMINSTER
Essex

New Moor Farm ◆◆◆◆
Tillingham Road, Burnham-on-
Crouch, Southminster, Essex
CM0 7DS
T: (01621) 772840
F: (01621) 774087

Saxegate Guesthouse ◆◆◆
44 North Street, Southminster,
Essex CM0 7DG
T: (01621) 773180
F: (01621) 774116

SOUTHREPPS
Norfolk

Avalon ◆◆◆◆
Lower Southrepps, Southrepps,
Norwich NR11 8UJ
T: (01263) 834461 &
07833 563005
F: (01263) 834461
E: mokies@msn.com

SOUTHWOLD
Suffolk

Amber House ◆◆◆
24 North Road, Southwold,
Suffolk IP18 6LT
T: (01502) 723303
E: spring@amberhouse.fsnet.
co.uk
I: www.southwold.blythweb.
co.uk/amber_house/index.htm

The Angel Inn ◆◆◆
39 High Street, Wangford,
Southwold, Suffolk NR34 8RL
T: (01502) 578636
F: (01502) 578535
E: inn@wangford.freeserve.
co.uk
I: www.angel-wangford.co.uk

Avocet House ◆◆◆◆
1 Strickland Place, Southwold,
Suffolk IP18 6HN
T: (01502) 724 720
E: barnett@beeb.net
I: www.southwold.
ws/avocet-house

Brenda's ◆◆◆
Wellesley House, 3 Strickland
Place, Southwold, Suffolk
IP18 6HN
T: (01502) 722403

Dunburgh Guesthouse ◆◆◆◆
28 North Parade, Southwold,
Suffolk IP18 6LT
T: (01502) 723253
I: www.southwold.ws/dunburg

Links Cottage Private Hotel
◆◆◆
Godyll Road, Southwold, Suffolk
IP18 6AJ
T: (01502) 723521
F: (01502) 724364
E: annette@linkscottage.co.uk
I: www.linkscottage.co.uk/hotel

Northcliffe Guesthouse
◆◆◆◆
20 North Parade, Southwold,
Suffolk IP18 6LT
T: (01502) 724074 &
07702 588554
F: (01502) 724074
I: www.s-h-systems.
co.uk/hotels/northcli.html

Number Three ◆◆◆
3 Cautley Road, Southwold,
Suffolk IP18 6DD
T: (01502) 723611

The Old Vicarage ◆◆◆◆
Wenhaston, Halesworth, Suffolk
IP19 9EG
T: (01502) 478339
F: (01502) 478068
E: theycock@aol.com
I: www.world.blythweb.
co.uk/oldvicarage

Prospect Place ◆◆◆◆
33 Station Road, Southwold,
Suffolk IP18 6AX
T: (01502) 722757
E: sally@prospect-place.demon.
co.uk
I: www.prospect-place.demon.
co.uk

Saxon House ◆◆◆
86 Pier Avenue, Southwold,
Suffolk IP18 6BL
T: (01502) 723651

Shanklin House ◆◆◆◆
6 Chester Road, Southwold,
Suffolk IP18 6LN
T: (01502) 724748
E: ratcliffshanklin@aol.com

Ventnor Villas ◆◆◆
4 Hurn Crag Road, Reydon,
Southwold, Suffolk IP18 6RG
T: (01502) 723619 &
07979 727059
F: (01502) 723619
E: sue@ventnorvillas.co.uk
I: www.ventnorvillas.co.uk

Victoria House ◆◆◆◆
9 Dunwich Road, Southwold,
Suffolk IP18 6LJ
T: (01502) 722317
E: victoria@southwold.ws
I: www.southwold.
ws/victoria_house/

'No 21' North Parade ◆◆◆
Southwold, Suffolk IP18 6LT
T: (01502) 722573
F: (01502) 724326
E: richard.comrie@cwcom.net

SPORLE
Norfolk

Corfield House ◆◆◆◆
Sporle, Swaffham, Norfolk
PE32 2EA
T: (01760) 723636
E: corfield.house@virgin.net

SPROUGHTON
Suffolk

Finjaro ◆◆◆◆
Valley Farm Drive, Hadleigh
Road, Sproughton, Ipswich
IP8 3EL
T: 0705 0065465 &
(01473) 652581
F: (01473) 652139
E: jan@finjaro.freeserve.co.uk
I: www.s-h-systems.
co.uk/hotels/finjaro.html

SPROWSTON
Norfolk

Driftwood Lodge ◆◆◆◆
102 Wroxham Road, Sprowston,
Norwich NR7 8EX
T: (01603) 444908
E: johnniekate@driftwood16.
freeserve.co.uk
I: www.driftwoodlodge.co.uk

STALHAM
Norfolk

Bramble House ◆◆◆◆
Cat's Common, Norwich Road,
Smallburgh, Norwich NR12 9NS
T: (01692) 535069
F: (01692) 535069
E: bramblehouse@tesco.net
I: www.norfolkbroads.
com/bramblehouse

Chapelfield Cottage ◆◆◆◆
Chapelfield, Stalham, Norwich
NR12 9EN
T: (01692) 582173 &
07775 650656
F: (01692) 583009
E: gary@cinqueportsmarine.
freeserve.co.uk
I: www.whiteswan.u-net.com

STANDON
Hertfordshire

Fox and Hounds House ◆◆◆◆
Bromley, Standon, Ware,
Hertfordshire SG11 1NX
T: (01279) 842722 & 842277
E: timakerz@aol.com
I: www.smoothhound.
co.uk/hotels/foxandhounds.html

Leamington House ◆◆◆
1 Churchfields, Standon, Ware,
Hertfordshire SG11 1QR
T: (01920) 821926

16 Vicarage Close ◆◆◆
Standon, Ware, Hertfordshire
SG11 1QP
T: (01920) 821065 & 07880 628
813

STANSTEAD
Suffolk

The White Hart Inn ◆◆◆
Lower Street, Stanstead,
Sudbury, Suffolk CO10 9AH
T: (01787) 280902 & 280417

STANSTED
Essex

High Trees ◆◆◆
Parsonage Road, Takeley,
Bishop's Stortford, Hertfordshire
CM22 6QX
T: (01279) 871306 &
07767 431491

STANSTED MOUNTFITCHET
Essex

Chimneys
Rating Applied For
44 Lower Street, Stansted
Mountfitchet, Stansted, Essex
CM24 8LR
T: (01279) 813388
F: (01279) 813388
E: info@chimneysguesthouse.
co.uk
I: www.chimneysguesthouse.
co.uk

The Laurels Hotel ◆◆◆
84 St Johns Road, Stansted
Mountfitchet, Stansted, Essex
CM24 8JS
T: (01279) 813023
F: (01279) 813023

Norman House ◆◆◆
Alsa Street, Stansted
Mountfitchet, Stansted, Essex
CM24 8SX
T: (01279) 812343
F: (01279) 816876
E: david.shepherd@tesco.net

STEBBING
Essex

Motts Cottage ◆◆◆◆
High Street, Stebbing, Dunmow,
Essex CM6 3SE
T: (01371) 856633
E: dianekittow@hotmail.com

STEEPLE BUMPSTEAD
Essex

Yew Tree House ◆◆◆
15 Chapel Street, Steeple
Bumpstead, Haverhill, Suffolk
CB9 7DQ
T: (01440) 730364
F: (01440) 730364
E: yewtreehouse@talk21.com

STOKE-BY-NAYLAND
Suffolk

The Angel Inn ◆◆◆◆
Polstead Street, Stoke-by-
Nayland, Colchester CO6 4SA
T: (01206) 263245
F: (01206) 263373
I: www.angelhotel.com

Ryegate House ◆◆◆◆
Stoke-by-Nayland, Colchester,
Suffolk CO6 4RA
T: (01206) 263679
E: ryegate@lineone.net
I: www.w-h-systems.
co.uk/hotels/ryegate.html

Thorington House ◆◆◆
Stoke-by-Nayland, Colchester
CO6 4SS
T: (01206) 337329

STOKE HOLY CROSS
Norfolk

Salamanca Farm ◆◆◆
116-118 Norwich Road, Stoke
Holy Cross, Norwich NR14 8QJ
T: (01508) 492322
I: www.smoothhound.
co.uk/salamanc.html

STONHAM ASPAL
Suffolk

Morgans ◆◆◆
East End Lane, Stonham Aspal,
Stowmarket, Suffolk IP14 6AS
T: (01449) 711419
E: joanna.hase@btinternet.com
I: www.btinternet.com~joanna.
hase/morgans

STOWMARKET
Suffolk

Gipping Heights Hotel ◆◆◆◆
Creeting Road, Stowmarket,
Suffolk IP14 5BT
T: (01449) 675264

The Step House ◆◆◆◆
Hockey Hill, Wetheringsett,
Stowmarket, Suffolk IP14 5PL
T: (01449) 766476
F: (01449) 766476
E: stephouse@talk21.com

Stricklands
Rating Applied For
Stricklands Road, Stowmarket,
Suffolk IP14 1AP
T: (01449) 612450
F: (01449) 614944
E: poppy_robinson@hotmail.
com

The Three Bears House
Mulberrytree Farm ◆◆◆
Blacksmiths Lane, Middlewood
Green, Stowmarket, Suffolk
IP14 5EU
I: (01449) 711707 &
07711 112114
F: (01449) 711707

Verandah House ◆◆◆◆
29 Ipswich Road, Stowmarket,
Suffolk IP14 1BD
T: (01449) 676104
F: (01449) 616127
E: verandahhs@aol.com
I: www.verandah-house.co.uk

STRETHAM
Cambridgeshire

The Red Lion ◆◆◆
High Street, Stretham, Ely,
Cambridgeshire CB6 3JQ
T: (01353) 648132
F: (01353) 648327
E: frank.hayes@gateway.net
I: www.redlion.org

SUDBOURNE
Suffolk

Long Meadows ◆◆◆
Gorse Lane, Sudbourne,
Woodbridge, Suffolk IP12 2BD
T: (01394) 450269

SUDBURY
Suffolk

The Hall ◆◆◆◆
Milden, Lavenham, Sudbury,
Suffolk CO10 9NY
T: (01787) 247235
F: (01787) 247235
E: gjb53@dial.pipex.com
I: www.farmstayanglia.co.uk

Lychgate ◆◆◆
45 Clarence Road, Sudbury,
Suffolk CO10 1NJ
T: (01787) 466912
F: (01787) 880494

Old Bull Hotel and Restaurant ◆◆◆
Church Street, Ballingdon,
Sudbury, Suffolk CO10 2BL
T: (01787) 374120
F: (01787) 379044
E: old-bull.8sudbury@virgin.net
I: www.theoldbullhotel.co.uk

West House ◆◆◆
59 Ballingdon Street, Sudbury,
Suffolk CO10 2DA
T: (01787) 375033

SWAFFHAM
Norfolk

Glebe Bungalow ◆◆◆◆
8a Princes Street, Swaffham,
Norfolk PE37 7BP
T: (01760) 722764 &
07778 163706
🏃

Lodge Farm ◆◆◆◆
Castle Acre, King's Lynn, Norfolk
PE32 2BS
T: (01760) 755506
F: (01760) 755103
E: coghill@
lodgefarm-castleacre.co.uk

Strattons ◆◆◆◆◆
Strattons, 4 Ash Close,
Swaffham, Norfolk PE37 7NH
T: (01760) 723845
F: (01760) 720458
E: strattonshotel@btinternet.
com
I: www.stratton-hotel.co.uk

SWAFFHAM BULBECK
Cambridgeshire

**Black Horse Motel, Public
House and Restaurant ◆◆◆**
High Street, Swaffham Bulbeck,
Cambridge CB5 0HP
T: (01223) 811366

SWAFFHAM PRIOR
Cambridgeshire

Sterling Farm ◆◆◆
Heath Road, Swaffham Prior,
Cambridge CB5 0LA
T: (01638) 741431

SWEFFLING
Suffolk

**Wayside Bed and Breakfast
◆◆◆◆**
Glemham Road, Sweffling,
Saxmundham, Suffolk IP17 2BQ
T: (01728) 663256

TAKELEY
Essex

Crossroads B & B ◆◆
2 Hawthorn Close, Takeley,
Bishop's Stortford, Hertfordshire
CM22 6SD
T: (01279) 870619 &
07790 302813
E: ajcaiger@netscapeonline.
co.uk

Jan Smiths B&B ◆◆◆
The Cottage, Jacks Lane, Takeley,
Bishop's Stortford, Hertfordshire
CM22 6NT
T: (01279) 870603
F: (01279) 870603

Joseph's Drive ◆◆
2 Joseph's Drive, The Street,
Takeley, Bishop's Stortford,
Hertfordshire CM22 6QT
T: (01279) 870652 &
07990 671824
E: ethlyn_king@hotmail.com

Joyners ◆◆◆
The Street, Takeley, Bishop's
Stortford, Hertfordshire
CM22 6QU
T: (01279) 870944
F: (01279) 870944
E: andersonsi@joyners99.
freeserve.co.uk

**Little Bullocks Farm
Rating Applied For**
Hope End, Takeley, Bishop's
Stortford, Hertfordshire
CM22 6TA
T: (01279) 870464 &
07702 361591
F: (01279) 871430
E: julie@waterman-farm.fsnet.
co.uk

Pippins ◆◆◆
Smiths Green, Takeley, Bishop's
Stortford, Hertfordshire
CM22 6NR
T: (01279) 870369
F: (01279) 871216
E: kevinmatthews@
pippinsbandb.co.uk

San Michele ◆◆◆◆
Jacks Lane, Takeley, Bishop's
Stortford, Hertfordshire
CM22 6NT
T: (01279) 870946

TANNINGTON
Suffolk

Tannington Hall ◆◆◆
Tannington, Woodbridge,
Suffolk IP13 7NH
T: (01728) 628226
F: (01728) 628646
E: info@tannington-hall.co.uk
I: www.tannington-hall.co.uk

TERRINGTON ST JOHN
Norfolk

Somerville House ◆◆◆◆
Church Road, Terrington St
John, Wisbech, Cambridgeshire
PE14 7RY
T: (01945) 880952
F: (01945) 880952
E: somervillemc@hotmail.com
I: www.somervillehouse.co.uk

THAXTED
Essex

Crossways Guesthouse ◆◆◆◆
32 Town Street, Thaxted,
Dunmow, Essex CM6 2LA
T: (01371) 830348

The Farmhouse Inn ◆◆◆
Monk Street, Thaxted, Dunmow,
Essex CM6 2NR
T: (01371) 830864
F: (01371) 831196

THEBERTON
Suffolk

The Alders ◆◆◆
Potters Street, Theberton,
Leiston, Suffolk IP16 4RL
T: (01728) 831790
F: (01728) 831790

The Granary ◆◆◆◆
Theberton, Leiston, Suffolk
IP16 4RR
T: (01728) 831633 & 07811 808
085
F: (01728) 831633
E: GranaryTheberton@aol.com

THETFORD
Norfolk

East Farm ◆◆◆◆
Euston Road, Barnham,
Thetford, Norfolk IP24 2PB
T: (01842) 890231
F: (01842) 890457

THOMPSON
Norfolk

The Chequers Inn ◆◆◆◆
Griston Road, Thompson,
Thetford, Norfolk IP24 1PX
T: (01953) 483360
F: (01953) 488092
E: themcdowalls@barbox.net
I: www.thompsonchequers.com

THORNDON
Suffolk

Moat Farm ◆◆◆◆
Thorndon, Eye, Suffolk IP23 7LX
T: (01379) 678437 &
07775 761318
E: geralde@clara.co.uk
I: www.moatfarm.co.uk

THORNHAM
Norfolk

Rushmeadow ◆◆◆◆
Main Road, Thornham,
Hunstanton, Norfolk PE36 6LZ
T: (01485) 512372
F: (01485) 512372
E: rushmeadow@lineone.net
I: www.rushmeadow.com

THORPE MARKET
Norfolk

Manorwood ◆◆◆
Church Road, Thorpe Market,
Norwich NR11 8UA
T: (01263) 834938

THORPE MORIEUX
Suffolk

Mount Farm House ◆◆◆◆
Thorpe Morieux, Lavenham,
Sudbury, Suffolk IP30 0NQ
T: (01787) 248428
F: (01787) 248428
E: mntfarm@waitrose.com

TOFT
Cambridgeshire

Orchard Farmhouse ◆◆◆◆
56 Comberton Road, Toft,
Cambridge CB3 7RY
T: (01223) 262309
F: (01223) 263979
E: tebbit.bxb.toft@talk21.com
I: www.smoothhound.
co.uk/hotels/orchfarm.html

West View ◆◆◆
6 Hardwick Road, Toft,
Cambridge CB3 7RQ
T: (01223) 263287 & 264202

TOLLESBURY
Essex

Fernleigh ◆◆◆
16 Woodrolfe Farm Lane,
Tollesbury, Maldon, Essex
CM9 8SX
T: (01621) 868245
F: (01621) 868245
E: gill.willson@ntlworld.com

TOLLESHUNT MAJOR
Essex

Mill Lodge ◆◆◆
Mill Lane, Tolleshunt Major,
Maldon, Essex CM9 8YF
T: (01621) 860311

Wicks Manor Farm ◆◆◆◆
Witham Road, Tolleshunt Major,
Maldon, Essex CM9 8JU
T: (01621) 860629
F: (01621) 860629
E: rhowie@aspects.net

TOTTENHILL
Norfolk

**Andel Lodge Hotel &
Restaurant ◆◆◆◆**
48 Lynn Road, Tottenhill, King's
Lynn, Norfolk PE33 0RH
T: (01553) 810256
F: (01553) 811429

TRUNCH
Norfolk

**North Barn
Rating Applied For**
Mundesley Road, Trunch, North
Walsham, Norfolk NR28 0QB
T: (01263) 722256
F: (01263) 722256
E: uchardjelliff@hotmail.com

UFFORD
Suffolk

Strawberry Hill ◆◆◆◆
Loudham Lane, Ufford,
Woodbridge, Suffolk IP13 6ED
T: (01394) 460252
E: strawberryhilly@yahoo.co.uk
I: www.smoothhound.
co.uk/hotels/strawber.html

UPPER SHERINGHAM
Norfolk

**Lodge Cottage
Rating Applied For**
Lodge Hill, Upper Sheringham,
Sheringham, Norfolk NR26 8TJ
T: (01263) 821445

UPWELL
Cambridgeshire

The Olde Mill Hotel ◆◆◆◆
Town Street, Upwell, Wisbech,
Cambridgeshire PE14 9AF
T: (01945) 772614
F: (01945) 772614
E: oldmill@lineone

WAKES COLNE
Essex

**Rosebank Bed and Breakfast
◆◆◆◆**
Rosebank Station Road, Wakes
Colne, Colchester CO6 2DS
T: (01787) 223552 &
07970 046629
F: (01787) 220415

WALBERSWICK
Suffolk

Dickon ◆◆
Main Street, Walberswick,
Southwold, Suffolk IP18 6UX
T: (01502) 724046

WALSHAM-LE-WILLOWS
Suffolk

Wagner Cottage ◆◆
Walsham-le-Willows, Bury St
Edmunds, Suffolk IP31 3AA
T: (01359) 259380

WALTON-ON-THE-NAZE
Essex

The Regency Hotel ◆◆◆
45 The Parade, Walton-on-the-
Naze, Essex CO14 8AS
T: (01255) 676300
F: (01255) 676300

WANGFORD
Suffolk

Poplar Hall ♦♦♦♦
Frostenden Corner, Frostenden, Wangford, Beccles, Suffolk NR34 7JA
T: (01502) 578549
I: www.southwold.
co.uk/poplar-hall/

WANSFORD
Cambridgeshire

The Cross Keys ♦♦♦
21 Elton Road, Wansford, Peterborough PE8 6JD
T: (01780) 782266
F: (01780) 782266

WASHBROOK
Suffolk

High View ♦♦♦♦
Back Lane, Washbrook, Ipswich IP8 3JA
T: (01473) 730494
E: rosanna.steward@virgin.net

WATTON
Norfolk

The Willow House ♦♦♦♦
2 High Street, Watton, Thetford, Norfolk IP25 6AE
T: (01953) 881181 &
(01760) 440760
F: (01953) 885885
E: willowhousewatton@barbox.net
I: www.willowhouse.net

WELLINGHAM
Norfolk

Manor House Farm ♦♦♦♦
Wellingham, King's Lynn, Norfolk PE32 2TH
T: (01328) 838227
F: (01328) 838348
E: robinellis@farming.co.uk

WELLS–NEXT–THE–SEA
Norfolk

Blenheim House ♦♦♦♦
Theatre Road, Wells-next-the-Sea, Norfolk NR23 1DJ
T: (01328) 711368
F: (01328) 711368
E: marjorams@lineone.net
I: www.marjorams.co.uk

The Cobblers ♦♦♦
Standard Road, Wells-next-the-Sea, Norfolk NR23 1JU
T: (01328) 710155 & 710155
E: ina@cobblers.co.uk
I: www.cobblers.co.uk

Corner House ♦♦♦
Staithe Street, Wells-next-the-Sea, Norfolk NR23 1AF
T: (01328) 710701
E: lmoney@ukonline.co.uk

Crossways Bed & Breakfast ♦♦
2 Park Road, Wells-next-the-Sea, No NR23 1DQ
T: (01328) 711392 &
0778 7348631
E: annette@crossways-bb.co.uk

Glebe Barn ♦♦♦♦
7a Glebe Road, Wells-next-the-Sea, Norfolk NR23 1AZ
T: (01328) 711809
E: glebebarn@supanet.com

Hideaway ♦♦♦
Red Lion Yard, Wells-next-the-Sea, Norfolk NR23 1AX
T: (01328) 710524
F: (01328) 710524
E: hideaway.wells@btinternet.com

Ilex House ♦♦♦
Bases Lane, Wells-next-the-Sea, Norfolk NR23 1DH
T: (01328) 710556
F: (01328) 710556
E: tommcjay@aol.com
I: www.broadland.com/ilexhouse

Machrimore ♦♦♦♦
Burnt Street, Wells-next-the-Sea, Norfolk NR23 1HS
T: (01328) 711653 &
0771 3225990
E: dorothy.maccallum@ntlworld.com

Mill House Guesthouse ♦♦♦
Mill House, Northfield Lane, Wells-next-the-Sea, Norfolk NR23 1JZ
T: (01328) 710739
I: www.broadland.com/millhouse

The Normans ♦♦♦♦
Invaders Court, Standard Road, Wells-next-the-Sea, Norfolk NR23 1JW
T: (01328) 710657
F: (01328) 710468

The Old Custom House ♦♦♦
East Quay, Wells-next-the-Sea, Norfolk NR23 1LD
T: (01328) 711463
F: (01328) 710277
E: b&b@eastquay.co.uk

Old Police House ♦♦♦♦
Polka Road, Wells-next-the-Sea, Norfolk NR23 1ED
T: (01328) 710630 &
07767 660213
F: (01328) 710630
E: ophwells@yahoo.co.uk
I: www.northnorfolk.co.uk/oldpolicehouse

27 Staithe Street ♦♦
Wells-next-the-Sea, Norfolk NR23 1AG
T: (01328) 710480
F: (01328) 710480
E: jaspinks@freeuk.com

WEST BERGHOLT
Essex

The Old Post House ♦♦♦
10 Colchester Road, West Bergholt, Colchester CO6 3JG
T: (01206) 240379
F: (01206) 243301

WEST DEREHAM
Norfolk

Bell Barn ♦♦♦♦
Lime Kiln Road, West Dereham, King's Lynn, Norfolk PE33 9RT
T: (01366) 500762
F: (01366) 500762
E: chris@woodbarn.freeserve.co.uk

WEST LYNN
Norfolk

The Rectory ♦♦♦
St Peters Road, West Lynn, King's Lynn, Norfolk PE34 3JT
T: (01553) 775093 &
07773 658456
E: ruth.sansom@west-lynn.demon.co.uk

WEST MERSEA
Essex

Hazel Oak ♦♦♦
28 Seaview Avenue, West Mersea, Colchester CO5 8HE
T: (01206) 383030
E: ann.blackmore@btinternet.com
I: www.btinternet.com/~daveblackmore/

WEST RUNTON
Norfolk

The Old Barn ♦♦♦♦
Cromer Road, West Runton, Cromer, Norfolk NR27 9QT
T: (01263) 838285

Village Inn ♦♦♦
Water Lane, West Runton, Cromer, Norfolk NR27 9QP
T: (01263) 838000
F: (01263) 837877

WEST SOMERTON
Norfolk

The White House Farm ♦♦♦♦
The Street, West Somerton, Great Yarmouth, Norfolk NR29 4EA
T: (01493) 393991
E: prued@hotmail.com

WESTCLIFF–ON–SEA
Essex

Chilton House ♦♦♦
3 Trinity Avenue, Westcliff-on-Sea, Essex SS0 7PU
T: (01702) 342282
F: (01702) 342282

Mariner's Reach Guesthouse ♦♦♦
8 Clifton Drive, Westcliff-on-Sea, Essex SS0 7SW
T: (01702) 332031
E: mariners_reach@btinternet.com
I: www.marinersreach.btinternet.co.uk

Pavilion Hotel ♦♦
1 Trinity Avenue, Westcliff-on-Sea, Essex SS0 7PU
T: (01702) 332767
F: (01702) 332767

Retreat Guesthouse ♦♦♦
12 Canewdon Road, Westcliff-on-Sea, Essex SS0 7NE
T: (01702) 348217 & 337413
F: (01702) 391179
E: retreatguesthouse.co.uk@tinyworld.co.uk
I: www.retreatguesthouse.co.uk

Welbeck Hotel ♦♦♦♦
27 Palmerston Road, Westcliff-on-Sea, Essex SS0 7TA
T: (01702) 347736
F: (01702) 339140
E: welbeck@tinyworld.co.uk

WESTLETON
Suffolk

Pond House ♦♦♦♦
The Hill, Westleton, Saxmundham, Suffolk IP17 3AN
T: (01728) 648773

WHITE RODING
Essex

Marks Hall Farmhouse ♦♦♦♦
Marks Hall, White Roding, Dunmow, Essex CM6 1RT
T: (01279) 876438 & 876236
F: (01279) 876236
E: jane@markshall.fsnet.co.uk

WHITTLESEY
Cambridgeshire

Whitmore House ♦♦♦♦
31 Whitmore Street, Whittlesey, Peterborough PE7 1HE
T: (01733) 203088

WICKHAM BISHOPS
Essex

Meadow Bank ♦♦♦♦
Station Road, Wickham Bishops, Witham, Essex CM8 3JN
T: (01621) 892743
F: (01621) 892930
E: james.cravensmith@btinternet.com

WIGHTON
Norfolk

Shrublands ♦♦♦♦
Wells Road, Wighton, Wells-next-the-Sea, Norfolk NR23 1PR
T: (01328) 820743
F: (01328) 820088
E: shrublands@shrub-lands.freeserve.co.uk

WIMBISH
Essex

Blossom Cottage ♦♦♦
Rowney Corner, Thaxted road, Wimbish, Saffron Walden, Essex CB10 2UZ
T: (01799) 599430

Newdegate House ♦♦♦♦
Howlett End, Wimbish, Saffron Walden, Essex CB10 2XW
T: (01799) 599748
F: (01799) 599748

WINGFIELD
Suffolk

Gables Farm ♦♦♦♦
Earsham Street, Wingfield, Diss, Norfolk IP21 5RH
T: (01379) 586355 &
07808 448272
F: (01379) 586355
E: sue.harvey@lineone.net
I: www.gablesfarm.co.uk

WISBECH
Cambridgeshire

Marmion House Hotel ♦♦♦
11 Lynn Road, Wisbech, Cambridgeshire PE13 3DD
T: (01945) 582822
F: (01945) 475889

WITHAM
Essex

Abbotts ♦♦♦
45 Collingwood Road, Witham, Essex CM8 2DZ
T: (01376) 512586

Chestnuts ◆◆◆◆
8 Octavia Drive, Witham Lodge,
Witham, Essex CM8 1HQ
T: (01376) 515990 &
07885 456803
F: (01376) 515990
E: KBMONEY2@aol.com
I: www.chestcars@aol.com

WITNESHAM
Suffolk
Burnbank House ◆◆◆◆
Church Lane, Witnesham,
Ipswich IP6 9JD
T: (01473) 785854

WIX
Essex
Dairy House Farm ◆◆◆◆◆
Bradfield Road, Wix,
Manningtree, Essex CO11 2SR
T: (01255) 870322
F: (01255) 870186
E: bridgetwhitworth@hotmail.
com

WOOD DALLING
Norfolk
Westwood Barn ◆◆◆◆
Crabgate Lane South, Wood
Dalling, Norwich NR11 6SW
T: (01263) 584108 &
07990 760124

WOOD NORTON
Norfolk
Manor Farm Bed and Breakfast
◆◆◆◆
Manor Farm, Hall Lane, Wood
Norton, East Dereham, Norfolk
NR20 5BE
T: (01362) 683231
F: (01362) 683231

WOODBRIDGE
Suffolk
Deben Lodge ◆◆
Melton Road, Woodbridge,
Suffolk IP12 1NH
T: (01394) 382740
I: www.SmoothHound.co.uk/shs.
html

Grove House ◆◆◆
39 Grove Road, Woodbridge,
Suffolk IP12 4LG
T: (01394) 382202
F: (01394) 380652
E: reception@grovehousehotel.
com
I: www.grovehousehotel.com
&

Lark Cottage ◆◆◆◆
Shingle Street, Woodbridge,
Suffolk IP12 3BE
T: (01394) 411292

Moat Barn ◆◆◆
Bredfield, Woodbridge, Suffolk
IP13 6BD
T: (01473) 737520
F: (01473) 737520
I: www.moat-barn.co.uk

Moat Farmhouse ◆◆◆
Dallinghoo Road, Bredfield,
Woodbridge, Suffolk IP13 6BD
T: (01473) 737475

The Station Hotel ◆◆
Station Road, Woodbridge,
Suffolk IP12 4AU
T: (01394) 384831
F: (01394) 384831
E: enquiries@
woodbridge-station.co.uk
I: www.woodbridge-station.
co.uk

WOODHAM MORTIMER
Essex
Chase Farm Bed & Breakfast
◆◆◆
Chase Farm, Hyde Chase,
Woodham Mortimer, Maldon,
Essex CM9 6TN
T: (01245) 223268 &
07703 409444

WOODSTON
Cambridgeshire
White House Guesthouse
◆◆◆
White House, 318 Oundle Road,
Woodston, Peterborough
PE2 9QP
T: (01733) 566650

WOOLPIT
Suffolk
The Bull Inn & Restaurant
◆◆◆
The Street, Woolpit, Bury St
Edmunds, Suffolk IP30 9SA
T: (01359) 240393
E: trevor@howling.fsbusiness.
co.uk

Grange Farm ◆◆◆◆
Woolpit, Bury St Edmunds,
Suffolk IP30 9RG
T: (01359) 241143
F: (01359) 244296
E: grangefarm@btinternet.com
I: www.farmstayanglia.
co.uk/grangefarm/

Swan Inn ◆◆◆
The Street, Woolpit, Bury St
Edmunds, Suffolk IP30 9QN
T: (01359) 240482

WOOTTON
Bedfordshire
Maple Tree Cottage ◆◆◆◆
Wootton Green, Wootton,
Bedford MK43 9EE
T: (01234) 768631
F: (01234) 768631
E: francy.mtc@cwcom.net

WORLINGTON
Suffolk
**Worlington Hall Country
House Hotel** ◆◆◆◆
The Street, Worlington, Bury St
Edmunds, Suffolk IP28 8RX
T: (01638) 712237
F: (01638) 712631

WORSTEAD
Norfolk
Hall Farm Guesthouse ◆◆◆◆
Hall Farm, Sloley Road,
Worstead, North Walsham,
Norfolk NR28 9RS
T: (01692) 536124 &
07768 991894
E: d.lowe4@tinyworld.co.uk OR
j.lowe4@tinyworld.co.uk

The Ollands ◆◆◆◆
Swanns Loke, Worstead, North
Walsham, Norfolk NR28 9RP
T: (01692) 535150
F: (01692) 535150
E: ollands@worstead.freeserve.
uk

WOTHORPE
Cambridgeshire
Firwood ◆◆◆◆
First Drift, Wothorpe, Stamford,
Lincolnshire PE9 3JL
T: (01780) 765654
F: (01780) 765654

WRENTHAM
Suffolk
The Garden Flat ◆◆◆
68 Southwold Road, Wrentham,
Beccles, Suffolk NR34 7JF
T: (01502) 675692
F: (01502) 675692
E: r.ashton@ecosse.net

Southwold Lodge ◆◆◆◆
67 Southwold Road, Wrentham,
Beccles, Suffolk NR34 7JE
T: (01502) 676148 &
(01986) 784214
F: (01986) 784797
E: qhbfield@aol.com

WRESTLINGWORTH
Bedfordshire
Orchard Cottage ◆◆◆
1 High Street, Wrestlingworth,
Sandy, Bedfordshire SG19 2EW
T: (01767) 631355
F: (01767) 631355

WRITTLE
Essex
Moor Hall ◆◆◆◆
Newney Green, Writtle,
Chelmsford CM1 3SE
T: (01245) 420814 &
07946 584636
E: moorhall@talk21.com

WROXHAM
Norfolk
The Dragon Flies ◆◆◆◆
5 The Avenue, Wroxham,
Norwich NR12 8TN
T: (01603) 783822
F: (01603) 783822
E: geoff.g.kimberley@talk21.
com

Garden Cottage ◆◆◆◆
The Limes, 96 Norwich Road,
Wroxham, Norwich, Norfolk
NR12 8RY
T: (01603) 784376 & 0771 224
2388
F: (01603) 783734

Ridge House ◆◆◆◆
7 The Avenue, Wroxham,
Norwich NR12 8TN
T: (01603) 782130

Wroxham Park Lodge ◆◆◆◆
142 Norwich Road, Wroxham,
Norwich NR12 8SA
T: (01603) 782991
E: prklodge@nascr.net
I: www.smoothhound.
co.uk/hotels/wroxhamp.html

WYMONDHAM
Norfolk
Witch Hazel ◆◆◆◆
Church Lane, Wicklewood,
Wymondham, Norfolk
NR18 9QH
T: (01953) 602247 & 0771 391
1853
F: (01953) 602247

YOXFORD
Suffolk
The Griffin ◆◆◆
High Street, Yoxford,
Saxmundham, Suffolk IP17 3EP
T: (01728) 668229 & 668749
E: i.terry@thegriffin.co.uk
I: www.thegriffin.co.uk

The Old Methodist Chapel
◆◆◆◆
High Street, Yoxford,
Saxmundham, Suffolk IP17 3EU
T: (01728) 668333 &
07931 668681
F: (01728) 668333
E: browns@chapelsuffolk.co.uk
I: www.chapelsuffolk.co.uk

SOUTH WEST

ABBOTSBURY
Dorset
Corfe Gate House ◆◆◆◆
Coryates, Abbotsbury,
Weymouth, Dorset DT3 4HW
T: (01305) 871483 &
07498 904602
F: (01305) 264024
E: maureenadams@
corfegatehouse.co.uk
I: www.corfegatehouse.co.uk

Linton Cottage ◆◆◆◆
Abbotsbury, Weymouth, Dorset
DT3 4JL
T: (01305) 871339
F: (01305) 871339
E: queenbee@abbotsbury.co.uk
I: www.lintoncottage.co.uk

Swan Lodge ◆◆◆
Rodden Row, Abbotsbury,
Weymouth, Dorset DT3 4JL
T: (01305) 871249
F: (01305) 871249

ALDERBURY
Wiltshire
Wisteria Cottage ◆◆◆
Silver Street, Alderbury,
Salisbury, Wiltshire SP5 3AN
T: (01722) 710274

ALHAMPTON
Somerset
The Barn at Yew Tree Cottage
◆◆◆
No Through Road, Alhampton,
Shepton Mallet, Somerset
BA4 6PZ
T: (01749) 860615
F: (01749) 860512
E: hhassoc@lineone.net

ALLERFORD
Somerset

Exmoor Falconry & Animal Farm ◆◆◆
West Lynch Farm, Allerford, Minehead, Somerset TA24 8HJ
T: (01643) 862816
F: (01643) 862816
E: exmoorfalcon@freenet.co.uk
I: www.exmoorfalconry.co.uk

Fern Cottage ◆◆◆◆
Allerford, Minehead, Somerset TA24 8HN
T: (01643) 862215
F: (01643) 862215
E: ferncottage@bushinternet.com
I: www.smoothhound.co.uk/hotels/ferncott

AMESBURY
Wiltshire

Enford House ◆◆◆
Enford, Pewsey, Wiltshire SN9 6DJ
T: (01980) 670414

Fairlawn Hotel ◆◆
42 High Street, Amesbury, Salisbury SP4 7DL
T: (01980) 622103
F: (01980) 624888

Mandalay
Rating Applied For
15 Stonehenge Road, Amesbury, Salisbury SP4 7BA
T: (01980) 623733
F: (01980) 626642

The Old Bakery ◆◆◆
Netton, Salisbury SP4 6AW
T: (01722) 782351
E: valahen@aol.com
I: members.aol.com/valahen

Solstice Farmhouse ◆◆◆
39 Holders Road, Amesbury, Salisbury SP4 7PH
T: (01980) 625052 &
07944 709869
E: williams@btinternet.com

Vale House ◆◆◆
Figheldean, Salisbury SP4 8JJ
T: (01980) 670713

Westavon ◆◆◆
76 Countess Road, Amesbury, Salisbury, Wiltshire SP4 7AT
T: (01980) 623698

ASHBRITTLE
Somerset

Lower Westcott Farm ◆◆◆
Ashbrittle, Wellington, Somerset TA21 0HZ
T: (01398) 361296

ASHBURTON
Devon

Gages Mill ◆◆◆◆
Buckfastleigh Road, Ashburton, Newton Abbot, Devon TQ13 7JW
T: (01364) 652391
F: (01364) 652391
E: moore@gagesmill.co.uk
I: www.gagesmill.co.uk

The Rising Sun ◆◆◆◆
Woodland, Ashburton, Newton Abbot, Devon TQ13 7JT
T: (01364) 652544
F: (01364) 654202
E: mail@risingsunwoodland.co.uk
I: www.risingsunwoodland.co.uk

Sladesdown Farm ◆◆◆◆
Landscove, Ashburton, Newton Abbot, Devon TQ13 7ND
T: (01364) 653973
F: (01364) 653973
E: sue@sladesdownfarm.co.uk
I: www.sladesdownfarm.co.uk

ASHTON
Somerset

Ashton Road Farm ◆◆◆
Ashton, Wedmore, Somerset BS28 4QE
T: (01934) 713462 &
07970 289518
F: (01934) 713462

ASHTON KEYNES
Wiltshire

Corner Cottage ◆◆◆
Fore Street, Ashton Keynes, Swindon SN6 6NP
T: (01285) 861454

ASKERSWELL
Dorset

Hembury House ◆◆◆◆
Askerswell, Dorchester, Dorset DT2 9EN
T: (01308) 485297 & 485032
F: (01308) 485032
E: askers@askers.free-online.co.uk
I: www.freeyellow.com/members5/hembury/page1.html

ATWORTH
Wiltshire

Church Farm ◆◆◆
Atworth, Melksham, Wiltshire SN12 8JA
T: (01225) 702215 &
07974 786387
F: (01225) 702215
E: chrchfarm@tinyonline.co.uk
I: www.churchfarm-atworth.freeserve.co.uk

AVEBURY
Wiltshire

Manor Farm
Rating Applied For
Avebury, Marlborough, Wiltshire SN8 1RF
T: (01672) 539294
F: (01672) 539294

The New Inn ◆◆◆
Winterbourne Monkton, Swindon, Wiltshire SN4 9NW
T: (01672) 539240
F: (01672) 539150

AVEBURY TRUSLOE
Wiltshire

Manor Farm ◆◆◆
Avebury Trusloe, Marlborough, Wiltshire SN8 1QY
T: (01672) 539243
F: (01672) 539230

AVETON GIFFORD
Devon

Helliers Farm ◆◆◆◆
Ashford, Aveton Gifford, Kingsbridge, Devon TQ7 4ND
T: (01548) 550689
F: (01548) 550689
E: helliersfarm@ukonline.co.uk
I: www.helliersfarm.co.uk

AWLISCOMBE
Devon

Birds Farm ◆◆
Awliscombe, Honiton, Devon EX14 3PU
T: (01404) 841620

Godford Farm ◆◆◆◆
Awliscombe, Honiton, Devon EX14 3PW
T: (01404) 42825
F: (01404) 42825
E: lawrencesally@hotmail.com
I: www.devon-farm-holidays.co.uk

AXBRIDGE
Somerset

Waterside ◆◆◆
Cheddar Road, Axbridge, Somerset BS26 2DP
T: (01934) 743182

Ye Olde School
Rating Applied For
Back Lane, Axbridge, Somerset BS26 2PH
T: (01934) 713360

AXMINSTER
Devon

Chalfont House ◆◆◆◆
Crewkerne Road, Raymonds Hill, Axminster, Devon EX13 5SX
T: (01297) 33852

Coaxdon Farm ◆◆◆◆
Axminster, Devon EX13 7LP
T: (01297) 35540

Kerrington House Hotel
Rating Applied For
Musbury Road, Axminster, Devon EX13 5JR
T: (01297) 35333
E: ja.reaney@kerringtonhouse.com

BABBACOMBE
Devon

Birch Tor ◆◆◆
315 Babbacombe Road, Babbacombe, Torquay TQ1 3TB
T: (01803) 292707
E: terry@birchtor.worldonline.co.uk
I: freespace.virgin.net/birch.tor/index.html

Regency Hotel ◆◆◆◆
33,35 Babbacombe Downs Road, Babbacombe, Torquay, Devon TQ1 3LN
T: (01803) 323509

Seabury Hotel ◆◆◆◆
Manor Road, Babbacombe, Torquay TQ1 3JX
T: (01803) 327255
F: (01803) 315321

BACKWELL
North Somerset

Ambassadors Health Farm ◆◆◆
Backwell Hill House, Backwell, Bristol BS48 3DA
T: (01275) 464462
F: (01275) 462951

Moorlands ◆◆◆◆
Backwell Hill, Backwell, Bristol BS48 3EJ
T: (01275) 462755

BAMPTON
Devon

Bampton Gallery ◆◆◆◆
2-4 Brook Street, Bampton, Tiverton, Devon EX16 9LY
T: (01398) 331354
F: (01398) 331119
E: bampgall@aol.com
I: www.exmoortourism.org/bamptongallery.htm

Exeter Inn ◆◆
Tiverton Road, Bampton, Tiverton, Devon EX16 9DY
T: (01398) 331345
F: (01398) 331345
E: exeterinn@farmersweekly.net
I: www.exeterinn.co.uk

Lodfin Farm Bed & Breakfast ◆◆◆◆
Morebath, Bampton, Tiverton, Devon EX16 9DD
T: (01398) 331400
F: (01398) 331400
E: lodfin.farm@eclipse.co.uk
I: www.lodfinfarm.com

Manor Mill House ◆◆◆◆
Bampton, Tiverton, Devon EX16 9LP
T: (01398) 332211
F: (01398) 332009
E: stay@manormill.demon.co.uk
I: www.manormill.demon.co.uk

BANWELL
North Somerset

Banwell Castle ◆◆◆
Banwell, Somerset BS29 6NX
T: (01934) 822263
F: (01934) 823946
E: banwellcastle@supanet.com
I: www.banwellcastle.co.uk

BARBROOK
Devon

Manor Hotel and Beggars Roost Inn ◆◆◆
Barbrook, Lynton, Devon EX35 6LD
T: (01598) 752404
F: (01598) 753636
E: beggars.roost.inn@tinyworld.co.uk
I: www.smoothhound.co.uk/hotels/manorho1.html

BARFORD ST MARTIN
Wiltshire

Briden House ◆◆◆◆
West Street, Barford St Martin, Salisbury SP3 4AH
T: (01722) 743471 & 741292
F: (01722) 743471
E: bridenhouse@barford25.freeserve.co.uk
I: www.smoothhound.co.uk/hotels/bridenho.html

BARNSTAPLE
Devon

Bradiford Cottage ◆◆◆◆
Bradiford, Barnstaple, Devon EX31 4DP
T: (01271) 345039
F: (01271) 345039
E: tony@humesfarm.co.uk
I: www.humesfarm.co.uk

The Red House ◆◆◆◆
Brynsworthy, Roundswell, Barnstaple, Devon EX31 3NP
T: (01271) 345966
F: (01271) 379966

The Spinney ◆◆◆◆
Shirwell, Barnstaple, Devon EX31 4JR
T: (01271) 850282
E: thespinny@shirwell.fsnet.co.uk
I: www.northdevon.com

Waytown Farm ◆◆◆◆
Shirwell, Barnstaple, Devon
EX31 4JN.
T: (01271) 850396
F: (01271) 850396
E: hazel@waytown.
enterprise-plc.com
I: www.waytownholidays.co.uk

BASONBRIDGE
Somerset

Merry Farm ◆◆◆◆
Merry Lane, Basonbridge,
Highbridge, Somerset TA9 3PS
T: (01278) 783655
🏃

BATCOMBE
Somerset

Valley View Farm ◆◆◆
Batcombe, Shepton Mallet,
Somerset BA4 6AJ
T: (01749) 850302 &
07974 442284
F: (01749) 850302

BATH
Bath and North East Somerset

Abbey Rise ◆◆◆◆
97 Wells Road, Bath, BA2 3AN
T: (01225) 316177
F: (01225) 316177

Abbot House ◆◆◆
168 Newbridge Road, Bath,
BA1 3LE
T: (01225) 314151
F: (01225) 314151
E: sandra.ashley@btinternet.
com
I: www.abbothouseguesthouse.
co.uk

The Albany Guest House
◆◆◆◆
24 Crescent Gardens, Upper
Bristol Road, Bath, BA1 2NB
T: (01225) 313339
E: the_albany@lineone.net
I: www.bath.org/hotel/albany.
htm

Apartment 1 ◆◆◆
60 Great Pulteney Street, Bath,
BA2 4DN
T: (01225) 464134 & 483663
F: (01225) 483663
E: chanloosmith@aptone.fsnet.
co.uk

Ashgrove Guest House ◆◆◆
39 Bathwick Street, Bath,
BA2 6PA
T: (01225) 421911
F: (01225) 461287

Ashley House ◆◆◆
8 Pulteney Gardens, Bath,
BA2 4HG
T: (01225) 425027

Ashley Villa Hotel ◆◆◆◆
26 Newbridge Road, Bath,
BA1 3JZ
T: (01225) 421683 & 428887
F: (01225) 313604
E: ashleyvilla@clearface.co.uk
I: www.ashleyvilla.co.uk

Astor House ◆◆◆
14 Oldfield Road, Bath, BA2 3ND
T: (01225) 429134
F: (01225) 429134
E: astorhouse.visitus@virgin.net

Athelney Guest House ◆◆◆
5 Marlborough Lane, Bath,
BA1 2NQ
T: (01225) 312031
F: (01225) 312031
E: colin-davis@supanet,com

Athole Guest House ◆◆◆◆◆
33 Upper Oldfield Park, Bath,
BA2 3JX
T: (01225) 334307
F: (01225) 320000
E: info@atholehouse.co.uk
I: www.atholehouse.co.uk

Avoca ◆◆
16 Newbridge Road, Bath,
BA1 3JX
T: (01225) 333665

Avon Guest House ◆◆
1 Pulteney Gardens, Bath,
BA2 4HG
T: (01225) 313009
F: (01225) 313009

Ayrlington Hotel ◆◆◆◆◆
24/25 Pulteney Road, Bath,
BA2 4EZ
T: (01225) 425495
F: (01225) 469029
E: mail@ayrlington.com
I: www.ayrlington.com

Badminton Villa ◆◆◆◆
10 Upper Oldfield Park, Bath,
BA2 3JZ
T: (01225) 426347
F: (01225) 420393
E: badmintonvilla@cableinet.
co.uk
I: www.smoothhound.
co.uk/hotels/badmintn.html

Bailbrook Lodge Hotel ◆◆◆
35/37 London Road West, Bath,
BA1 7HZ
T: (01225) 859090
F: (01225) 852299
E: hotel@bailbrooklodge.
demon.co.uk
I: www.bailbrooklodge.demon.
co.uk

The Belmont
Rating Applied For
7 Belmont, Lansdown Road,
Bath, BA1 5DZ
T: (01225) 423082
E: archie_watson@hotmail.com

Bloomfield House ◆◆◆◆◆
146 Bloomfield Road, Bath,
BA2 2AS
T: (01225) 420105
F: (01225) 481958
E: bloomfieldhouse@
compuserve.com
I: www.bloomfield.house.co.uk

16 Bloomfield Road ◆◆◆
Bear Flat, Bath, BA2 2AB
T: (01225) 337804

Brinsley Sheridan Guest House
◆◆◆◆
95 Wellsway, Bear Flat, Bath,
BA2 4RU
T: (01225) 429562
F: (01225) 429616
E: post@sheridan-house.com
I: www.sheridan-house.com

Brompton House ◆◆◆◆
St John's Road, Bath, BA2 6PT
T: (01225) 420972
F: (01225) 420505
E: bromptonhouse@btinternet.
com
I: www.bromptonhouse.co.uk

Carfax Hotel ◆◆◆◆
Great Pulteney Street, Bath,
BA2 4BS
T: (01225) 462089
F: (01225) 443257
E: reservations@carfaxhotel.
co.uk
I: www.carfaxhotel.co.uk
♿

Cherry Tree Villa ◆◆◆
7 Newbridge Hill, Bath, BA1 3PW
T: (01225) 331671

Chesterfield House ◆◆◆
11 Great Pulteney Street, Bath,
BA2 4BR
T: (01225) 460953
F: (01225) 448770
E: info@chesterfieldhouse.com
I: www.chesterfieldhouse.com

Church Farm ◆◆◆
Monkton Farleigh, Bradford-on-
Avon, Wiltshire BA15 2QJ
T: (01225) 858583 &
07889 596929
F: (01225) 852474
E: rebecca@tuckerb.fsnet.co.uk
I: www.tuckerb.fsnet.co.uk

Corston Fields Farm ◆◆◆◆
Corston, Bath BA2 9EZ
T: (01225) 873305 &
07900 056586
E: corston.fields@btinternet.
com
I: www.corstonfields.com

County Hotel ◆◆◆◆◆
18-19 Pulteney Road, Bath,
BA2 4EZ
T: (01225) 425003
F: (01225) 466493
E: reservations@county-hotel.
co.uk
I: www.county-hotel.co.uk

Crescent Guest House ◆◆◆
21 Crescent Gardens, Bath,
BA1 2NA
T: (01225) 425945

Edgar Hotel ◆◆◆
64 Great Pulteney Street, Bath,
BA2 4DN
T: (01225) 420619
F: (01225) 466916

Elgin Villa ◆◆◆◆
6 Marlborough Lane, Bath,
BA1 2NQ
T: (01225) 424557
F: (01225) 424557
E: stay@elginvilla.co.uk
I: www.elginvilla.co.uk

The Firs
Rating Applied For
2 Newbridge Hill, Bath, BA1 3PU
T: (01225) 334575

Flaxley Villa ◆◆◆
9 Newbridge Hill, Bath, BA1 3PW
T: (01225) 313237 & 480574

Forres House ◆◆◆
172 Newbridge Road, Bath,
BA1 3LE
T: (01225) 427698
E: Jj.forres@btinternet.co.uk

The Gainsborough ◆◆◆◆
Weston Lane, Bath, BA1 4AB
T: (01225) 311380
F: (01225) 447411
E: gainsborough_hotel@
compuserve.com
I: www.gainsboroughhotel.co.uk

Georgian Guest House ◆◆◆
34 Henrietta Street, Bath,
BA2 6LR
T: (01225) 424103
F: (01225) 425279
E: georgian@georgian-house.
co.uk
I: www.georgian-house.co.uk

Glan Y Dwr ◆◆◆
14 Newbridge Hill, Bath,
BA1 3PU
T: (01225) 317521 &
07968 263343
F: (01225) 317521
E: glanydwr@hotmail.com

Glen View ◆◆◆◆
162 Newbridge Road, Bath,
BA1 3LE
T: (01225) 421376
F: (01225) 310271
E: info@glenviewbath.co.uk
I: www.glenviewbath.co.uk

Glentworth ◆◆◆◆
12 Marlborough Lane, Bath,
BA1 2NQ
T: (01225) 334554
F: (01225) 425239
E: stay@glentworth.co.uk
I: www.glentworthbath.co.uk

Grove Lodge Guest House
Rating Applied For
11 Lambridge, London Road,
Bath, BA1 6BJ
T: (01225) 310860
F: (01225) 429630
E: grovelodge@bath24.fsnet.
co.uk

Hatt Farm ◆◆◆◆
Old Jockey, Box, Corsham,
Wiltshire SN13 8DJ
T: (01225) 742989
F: (01225) 742779
E: hattfarm@netlineuk.net

Haute Combe Hotel ◆◆◆◆
174/176 Newbridge Road, Bath,
BA1 3LE
T: (01225) 420061 & 339064
F: (01225) 446077
E: enquiries@hautecombe.com
I: www.hautecombe.com

Haydon House ◆◆◆◆◆
9 Bloomfield Park, Bath,
BA2 2BY
T: (01225) 444919 & 427351
F: (01225) 444919
E: stay@haydonhouse.co.uk
I: www.haydonhouse.co.uk

Henrietta Hotel ◆◆◆
32 Henrietta Street, Bath,
BA2 6LR
T: (01225) 447779
F: (01225) 444150

Hermitage ◆◆◆
Bath Road, Box, Corsham,
Wiltshire SN13 8DT
T: (01225) 744187
F: (01225) 743447
E: hermitage@telecall.co.uk

Highways House ◆◆◆◆
143 Wells Road, Bath, BA2 3AL
T: (01225) 421238 &
0800 0749250
F: (01225) 481169
E: stay@highwayshouse.co.uk
I: www.highwayshouse.co.uk

The Hollies ◆◆◆◆
Hatfield Road, Wellsway, Bath,
BA2 2BD
T: (01225) 313366
F: (01255) 313366
I: www.visitus.co.uk/bath/hotel.
hollies.html

Holly Lodge ◆◆◆◆◆
8 Upper Oldfield Park, Bath,
BA2 3JZ
T: (01225) 424042 &
(01255) 339187
F: (01225) 481138
E: stay@hollylodge.co.uk
I: www.hollylodge.co.uk

Kennard Hotel ◆◆◆◆◆
11 Henrietta Street, Bath,
BA2 6LL
T: (01225) 310472
F: (01225) 460054
E: reception@kennard.co.uk
I: www.kennard.co.uk

**Kinlet Villa Guest House
◆◆◆◆**
99 Wellsway, Bath, BA2 4RX
T: (01225) 420268
F: (01225) 420268
E: kinlet@inbath.freeserve.co.uk
I: www.visitus.
co.uk/bath/hotel/kinlet.htm

Lamp Post Villa ◆◆◆
3 Crescent Gardens, Upper
Bristol Road, Bath, BA1 2NA
T: (01225) 331221
F: (01225) 426783

Laura Place Hotel ◆◆◆◆
3 Laura Place, Great Pulteney
Street, Bath, BA2 4BH
T: (01225) 463815
F: (01225) 310222

Lavender House ◆◆◆◆◆
17 Bloomfield Park, Bath,
BA2 2BY
T: (01225) 314500
F: (01225) 448564
E: lavenderhouse@btintenet.
com
I: www.lavenderhouse-bath.com

Leighton House ◆◆◆◆◆
139 Wells Road, Bath, BA2 3AL
T: (01225) 314769 & 420210
F: (01225) 443079
E: welcome@leighton-house.
co.uk
I: www.leighton-house.co.uk

**Lindisfarne Guest House
◆◆◆◆**
41a Warminster Road,
Bathampton, Bath BA2 6XJ
T: (01225) 466342 &
07740 741541
F: (01225) 444062
E: lindisfarne-bath@talk21.com
I: www.bath.
org/hotel/lindisfarne.htm

The Manor House ◆◆◆
Mill Lane, Monkton Combe, Bath
BA2 7HD
T: (01225) 723128
F: (01225) 722972
E: beth@manorhousebath.co.uk
I: www.manorhousebath.co.uk

Marisha's Guest House ◆◆◆
68 Newbridge Hill, Bath,
BA1 3QA
T: (01225) 446881
F: (01225) 446881
E: marishasinbath@amserve.net

Marlborough House ◆◆◆◆
1 Marlborough Lane, Bath,
BA1 2NQ
T: (01225) 318175
F: (01225) 466127
E: mars@manque.dircon.co.uk
I: www.marlborough-house.net

Meadowland ◆◆◆◆◆
36 Bloomfield Park, Bath,
BA2 2BX
T: (01225) 311079
F: (01225) 311079
E: meadowland@bath92.
freeserve.co.uk
I: www.bath.
org/hotel/meadowland.htm

Membland Guest House ◆
7 Pulteney Terrace, Pulteney
Road, Bath, BA2 4HJ
T: (01958) 599572 &
07958 599572
E: prmoore@wimpey.co.uk

Midway Cottage ◆◆◆◆
10 Farleigh Wick, Bradford-on-
Avon, Wiltshire BA15 2PU
T: (01225) 863932
F: (01225) 866836
E: midway_cottage@hotmail.
com

Milton Guest House ◆◆◆
75 Wellsway, Bear Flat, Bath,
BA2 4RU
T: (01225) 335632
E: sue@milton-house.fsnet.
co.uk
I: www.milton-house.fsnet.co.uk

Monkshill ◆◆◆◆◆
Shaft Road, Monkton Combe,
Bath BA2 7HL
T: (01225) 833028
F: (01225) 833028
E: monks.hill@virgin.net

**Number 30 Crescent Gardens
◆◆◆◆**
Bath, BA1 2NB
T: (01225) 337393
F: (01225) 337393
E: david.greenwood12@
btinternet.com
I: www.stay@numberthirty.
co.uk

Parkside ◆◆◆◆
11 Marlborough Lane, Bath,
BA1 2NQ
T: (01225) 429444
F: (01225) 429444
E: parkside@lynall.freeserve.
co.uk
I: www.visitus.
co.uk/bath/hotel/parkside.html

Poplar Farm ◆◆◆
Stanton Prior, Bath BA2 9HX
T: (01761) 470382
F: (01761) 470382
E: poplarfarm@talk21.com

Pulteney Hotel ◆◆◆
14 Pulteney Road, Bath,
BA2 4HA
T: (01225) 460991 & 421261
F: (01225) 460991
E: pulteney@tinyworld.co.uk
I: www.pulteneyhotel.co.uk

14 Raby Place ◆◆◆◆
Bathwick Hill, Bath, BA2 4EH
T: (01225) 465120

Radnor Guesthouse ◆◆◆◆
9 Pulteney Terrace, Pulteney
Road, Bath, BA2 4HJ
T: (01225) 316159
F: (01225) 319199

Rainbow Wood Farm ◆◆
Claverton Down Road, Bath,
BA2 7AR
T: (01225) 466366
F: (01225) 466366

Ravenscroft ◆◆◆◆
Sydney Road, Bath, BA2 6NT
T: (01225) 469267
F: (01225) 448722
E: chmbaker@gatewayuk.net

**Roman City Guest House
◆◆◆◆**
18 Raby Place, Bathwick Hill,
Bath, BA2 4EH
T: (01225) 463668 &
07899 777953
E: romancityguesthse@
amserve.net
I: www.romancityguesthouse.
co.uk

Rosemary House ◆◆◆
63 Wellsway, Bath, BA2 4RT
T: (01225) 425667
F: (01225) 425667
E: rosemary.house@which.net
I: www.visitus.co.uk

Royal Park Guest House ◆◆
16 Crescent Gardens, Upper
Bristol Road, Bath, BA1 2NA
T: (01225) 317651
E: royal@parkb-b.freeserve.
co.uk

Hotel Saint Clair ◆◆◆
1 Crescent Gardens, Upper
Bristol Road, Bath, BA1 2NA
T: (01225) 425543
F: (01225) 425543
E: hotel-st-clair@ukonline.co.uk
I: web.ukonline.
co.uk/hotel-st-clair

St Leonards ◆◆◆◆
Warminster Road, Bathampton,
Bath BA2 6SQ
T: (01225) 465838
F: (01225) 442800
E: stleon@dircon.co.uk
I: www.smoothhound.
co.uk/hotels/stleonar.html

Sampford ◆◆
11 Oldfield Road, Bath, BA2 3ND
T: (01225) 310053
E: robert.dolby@btinternet.com

Somerset House Hotel ◆◆◆◆
35 Bathwick Hill, Bath, BA2 6LD
T: (01225) 466451 & 463471
F: (01225) 317188
E: somersethouse@compuserve.
com
I: www.somersethouse.co.uk

Stoke Bottom Farm ◆◆
Stoke St Michael, Bath BA3 5HW
T: (01761) 232273

Sydney Gardens Hotel ◆◆◆◆
Sydney Road, Bath, BA2 6NT
T: (01225) 464818 & 445362
F: (01225) 484347
E: pete@sydneygardens.co.uk
I: www.sydneygardens.co.uk

Thirty Five ◆◆◆◆
35 Upper Oldfield Park, Bath,
Somerset BA2 3LB
T: (01225) 484034

3 Thomas Street ◆◆◆
Bath, BA1 5NW
T: (01225) 789540

Toghill House Farm ◆◆◆
Wick, Bristol BS30 5RT
T: (01225) 891261
F: (01225) 892128
I: www.toghillhousefarm.co.uk

The Town House ◆◆◆◆
7 Bennett Street, Bath, BA1 2QJ
T: (01225) 422505

Villa Magdala Hotel ◆◆◆◆
Henrietta Road, Bath, BA2 6LX
T: (01225) 466329
F: (01225) 483207
E: office@villamagdala.co.uk
I: www.villamagdala.co.uk

Walton Villa ◆◆◆◆
3 Newbridge Hill, Bath, BA1 3PW
T: (01225) 482792
F: (01225) 313093
E: walton.villa@virgin.net
I: www.walton.izest.com

Wellsway Guest House ◆◆
51 Wellsway, Bath, BA2 4RS
T: (01225) 423434

The Wheatsheaf Inn ◆◆◆◆
Combe Hay, Bath BA2 7EG
T: (01225) 833504
F: (01225) 833504
I: www.the-wheatsheaf.
freeserve.co.uk

Wheelwrights Arms ◆◆
Monkton Combe, Bath BA2 7HD
T: (01225) 722287
F: (01225) 723029
E: debbie@gillespie.fslife.co.uk
I: www.yell.
co.uk/sites/the-wheelwright-
arms/

BATHEASTON
Bath and North East Somerset

Brook Lodge ◆◆◆◆
199 London Road East,
Batheaston, Bath BA1 7NB
T: (01225) 851158 & 851100
F: (01225) 851158
E: bobmatthews@
netscapeonline.co.uk

BATHFORD
Bath and North East Somerset

Garston Cottage ◆◆◆
28 Ashley Road, Bathford, Bath
BA1 7TT
T: (01225) 852510 &
07771 998120
F: (01225) 852793
E: garstoncot@aol.com
I: www.garstoncottage.
freeservers.com

The Lodge Hotel ◆◆◆◆
Bathford Hill, Bathford, Bath
BA1 7SL
T: (01225) 858467 & 858575
F: (01225) 858172
E: lodgethe@aol.com
I: www.lodgehotelbath.co.uk

BATHWICK
Bath and North East Somerset

Ravenscroft ◆◆◆◆
North Road, Bathwick, Bath
BA2 6HZ
T: (01225) 461919
F: (01225) 461919
E: patrickbryanr@cs.com
I: www.ravenscroftbandb.co.uk

BAWDRIP
Somerset

Kings Farm ◆◆◆
10 Eastside Lane, Bawdrip,
Bridgwater, Somerset TA7 8QB
T: (01278) 683233 &
07801 079138

BEAMINSTER
Dorset

Beam Cottage ◆◆◆◆
16 North Street, Beaminster,
Dorset DT8 3DZ
T: (01308) 863639
E: magie@beam-cottage.fsnt.
co.uk

Jenny Wrens ◆◆◆
1 Hogshill Street, Beaminster,
Dorset DT8 3AE
T: (01308) 862814
F: (01308) 861191

Kitwhistle Farm ◆◆◆
Beaminster Down, Beaminster,
Dorset DT8 3SG
T: (01308) 862458
F: (01308) 862 458

North Buckham Farm ◆◆◆
Beaminster, Dorset DT8 3SH
T: (01308) 863054 &
07967 499720
F: (01308) 863054
E: andrew@northbuckham.
fsnet.co.uk

Slape Hill Barn ◆◆◆◆
Waytown, Bridport, Dorset
DT6 5LQ
T: (01308) 488429

The Walnuts ◆◆◆◆
2 Prout Bridge, Beaminster,
Dorset DT8 3AY
T: (01308) 862211

Water Meadow House ◆◆◆◆
Bridge Farm, Hooke, Beaminster,
Dorset DT8 3PD
T: (01308) 862619
F: (01308) 862619
E: enquiries@
watermeadowhouse.co.uk
I: www.watermeadowhouse.
co.uk

BEAWORTHY
Devon

Longcross House ◆◆◆
Black Torrington, Beaworthy,
Devon EX21 5QG
T: (01409) 231219

Three Oaks ◆◆◆
Henford Barton, Ashwater,
Beaworthy, Devon EX21 5DA
T: (01409) 211417

BECKINGTON
Somerset

Eden Vale Farm ◆◆◆
Mill Lane, Beckington, Bath
BA3 6SN
T: (01373) 830371

BEECHINGSTOKE
Wiltshire

Taw Cottage ◆◆◆
Broad Street, Beechingstoke,
Pewsey, Wiltshire SN9 6HW
T: (01672) 851609
F: (01672) 851130

BELSTONE
Devon

The Cleave House ◆◆◆◆
Belstone, Okehampton, Devon
EX20 1QY
T: (01837) 840055
E: manuel@cleavehouse99.
freeserve.co.uk
I: www.caterham.force9.
co.uk/cleavehouse.htm

BERROW
Somerset

Berrow Links House ◆◆◆◆
Coast Road, Berrow, Burnham-
on-Sea, Somerset TA8 2QS
T: (01278) 751422

Martins Hill Farmhouse ◆◆◆
Red Road, Berrow, Burnham-
on-Sea, Somerset TA8 2RW
T: (01278) 751726
F: (01278) 751230
I: www.marinshillfarm.co.uk

Yew Tree House ◆◆◆◆
Hurn Lane, Berrow, Burnham-
on-Sea, Somerset TA8 2QT
T: (01278) 751382
F: (01278) 751382
I: www.yewtree-house.co.uk
&

BERRY POMEROY
Devon

Berry Farm ◆◆◆
Berry Pomeroy, Totnes, Devon
TQ9 6LG
T: (01803) 863231

BERRYNARBOR
Devon

Langleigh House ◆◆◆
The Village, Berrynarbor,
Ilfracombe, Devon EX34 9SG
T: (01271) 883410
F: (01271) 882396
E: langleigh@hotmail.com

The Lodge ◆◆◆◆
Pitt Hill, Berrynarbor, Ilfracombe,
Devon EX34 9SG
T: (01271) 883246
F: (01271) 882984
E: teem.mabin@virgin.net
I: www.thelodgeberrynarbor.
co.uk

Mill Park House ◆◆◆◆
Mill Lane, Berrynarbor,
Ilfracombe, Devon EX34 9SH
T: (01271) 882990
F: (01271) 882682
E: ian_smith@millparkhouse.
freeserve.co.uk
I: www.millparkhouse.freeserve.
co.uk

BETTISCOMBE
Dorset

Marshwood Manor ◆◆◆◆
Bettiscombe, Bridport, Dorset
DT6 5NS
T: (01308) 868442 & 868825

BIDDESTONE
Wiltshire

The Granary ◆◆◆
Cuttle Lane, Biddestone,
Chippenham, Wiltshire
SN14 7DA
T: (01249) 715077
E: penny.lloyd@virgin.net
I: freespace.virgin.net/penny.
lloyd

Home Farm ◆◆◆◆
Harts Lane, Biddestone,
Chippenham, Wiltshire
SN14 7DQ
T: (01249) 714475 &
07966 549759
F: (01249) 701488
E: audrey.smith@
homefarmbandb.co.uk
I: www.homefarmbandb.co.uk

Home Place ◆◆
The Green, Biddestone,
Chippenham, Wiltshire
SN14 7DG
T: (01249) 712928

BIDEFORD
Devon

The Mount ◆◆◆◆
Northdown Road, Bideford,
Devon EX39 3LP
T: (01237) 473748
F: (01271) 342268
E: andrew@themountbideford.
fsnet.co.uk
I: www.themount1.cjb.net

Sunset Hotel ◆◆◆
Landcross, Bideford, Devon
EX39 5JA
T: (01237) 472962
F: (01237) 422520
E: hazellamb@hotmail.com

BILBROOK
Somerset

Steps Farmhouse ◆◆◆◆
Bilbrook, Minehead, Somerset
TA24 6HE
T: (01984) 640974
E: info@stepsfarmhouse.co.uk
I: www.stepsfarmhouse.co.uk

BINEGAR
Somerset

Mansefield House ◆◆◆◆
Binegar, Shepton Mallet,
Somerset BA3 4UG
T: (01749) 840568 &
07976 705157
F: (01749) 840572
E: mansfieldhouse@aolcomm

BISHOP SUTTON
Bath and North East Somerset

Centaur ◆◆◆
Ham Lane, Bishop Sutton, Bristol
BS39 5TZ
T: (01275) 332321

Withymede ◆◆◆
The Street, Bishop Sutton,
Bristol BS39 5UU
T: (01275) 332069

BISHOP'S LYDEARD
Somerset

The Kingfisher ◆◆◆
Taunton Road, Bishop's Lydeard,
Taunton, Somerset TA4 3LR
T: (01823) 432394
E: ivor@kingfisherinn.co.uk
I: www.kingfisherinn.co.uk

The Mount ◆◆◆◆
32 Mount Street, Bishop's
Lydeard, Taunton, Somerset
TA4 3AN
T: (01823) 432208
E: d.hinton@talk21.com

West View
West View ◆◆◆◆
Minehead Road, Bishop's
Lydeard, Taunton, Somerset
TA4 3BS
T: (01823) 432223
F: (01823) 432223
E: westview@pattemore.
freeserve.co.uk

BISHOPS HULL
Somerset

The Old Mill ◆◆◆◆◆
Roughmoor, Bishops Hull,
Taunton, Somerset TA1 5AB
T: (01823) 289732
F: (01823) 289732

BISHOPSTON
Bristol

Basca Guest House ◆◆◆
19 Broadway Road, Bishopston,
Bristol BS7 8ES
T: (0117) 9422182

BISHOPSWOOD
Somerset

Hawthorne House ◆◆◆
Bishopswood, Chard, Somerset
TA20 3RS
T: (01460) 234482 &
07710 255059
F: (01460) 234482
E: roger-sarah@supanet.com
I: www.roger-sarah.co.uk

BLACK DOG
Devon

Hele Barton Farm Guest House
◆◆◆
Black Dog, Crediton, Devon
EX17 4QJ
T: (01884) 860278
F: (01884) 860278
E: gillbard@eclipse.co.uk
I: www.eclipse.co.uk/helebarton

BLACKAWTON
Devon

The Normandy Arms ◆◆◆◆
Chapel Street, Blackawton,
Totnes, Devon TQ9 7BN
T: (01803) 712316
F: (01803) 712191
E: normandyarms@hotmail.com

BLUE ANCHOR
Somerset

Camelot ◆◆◆
Carhampton Road, Blue Anchor,
Minehead, Somerset TA24 6LB
T: (01643) 821348
E: d.thrush@btinternet.com

The Langbury ◆◆◆
Blue Anchor, Minehead,
Somerset TA24 6LB
T: (01643) 821375
F: (01643) 821375
E: post@langbury.co.uk
I: www.langbury.co.uk

BODMIN
Cornwall

Bedknobs ◆◆◆
Polgwyn, Castle Street, Bodmin,
Cornwall PL31 2DX
T: (01208) 77553
F: (01208) 77885
E: gill@bedknobs.co.uk
I: www.bedknobs.co.uk

Bokiddick Farm ◆◆◆◆◆
Lanivet, Bodmin, Cornwall
PL30 5HP
T: (01208) 831481
F: (01208) 831481
E: gillhugo@bokiddickfarm.
co.uk
I: www.bokiddickfarm.co.uk

Castle Canyke Farmhouse
◆◆◆◆
Priors Barn Road, Bodmin,
Cornwall PL31 1HG
T: (01208) 79109
F: (01208) 79216
E: castlecanykefarmhouse@aol.
com
I: www.castlecanykefarmhouse.
com

Colliford Tavern ◆◆◆◆
Colliford Lake, St Neot, Liskeard,
Cornwall PL14 6PZ
T: (01208) 821335
F: (01208) 821335
E: colliford@hotmail.com
I: www.cornwall-online.
co.uk/colliford-tavern

Higher Windsor Cottage
◆◆◆◆
18 Castle Street, Bodmin,
Cornwall PL31 2DU
T: (01208) 76474
E: johntrishpencheon@
tinyworld.co.uk
I: www.ji77.dial.pipex.com/

BOLVENTOR
Cornwall

Jamaica Inn ◆◆◆
Bolventor, Launceston, Cornwall
PL15 7TS
T: (01566) 86250
F: (01566) 86177
I: jamaicainn@eclipse.co.uk

BOSCASTLE
Cornwall

Bridge House
Rating Applied For
Boscastle, Cornwall PL35 0HE
T: (01840) 250554

The Old Coach House ◆◆◆◆
Tintagel Road, Boscastle,
Cornwall PL35 0AS
T: (01840) 250398
F: (01840) 250346
E: parsons@old-coach.co.uk
I: www.old-coach.co.uk
⚓

**Tolcarne House Hotel and
Restaurant** ◆◆◆◆
Tintagel Road, Boscastle,
Cornwall PL35 0AS
T: (01840) 250654
F: (01840) 250654
E: crowntolhouse@eclipse.co.uk
I: www.milford.
co.uk/go/tolcarne

Trerosewill Farmhouse
◆◆◆◆◆
Paradise, Boscastle, Cornwall
PL35 0BL
T: (01840) 250545
F: (01840) 250545
E: trerosewill@talk21
I: www.trerosewill.com

BOSSINGTON
Somerset

Buckley Lodge ◆◆◆◆
Bossington, Minehead, Somerset
TA24 8HQ
T: (01643) 862521
E: bucklodgeuk@yahoo.co.uk

BOVEY TRACEY
Devon

Brookfield House ◆◆◆◆
Challabrook Lane, Bovey Tracey,
Newton Abbot, Devon TQ13 9DF
T: (01626) 836181
F: (01626) 836182
E: brookfieldh@tinyworld.co.uk
I: www.hotellink.
co.uk/bovey/brookfield/index.
htm

The Cromwell Arms Hotel
◆◆◆
Fore Street, Bovey Tracey,
Newton Abbot, Devon TQ13 9AE
T: (01626) 833473
F: (01626) 836873

Frost Farmhouse ◆◆◆
Frost Farm, Hennock Road,
Bovey Tracey, Newton Abbot,
Devon TQ13 9PP
T: (01626) 833266
F: (01626) 833266
E: linda@frostfarm.co.uk
I: www.frostfarm.co.uk

BOWERHILL
Wiltshire

The Court ◆◆◆◆
9 Brampton Court, Bowerhill,
Melksham, Wiltshire SN12 6TH
T: (01225) 702390

32 Duxford Close ◆◆◆
Bowerhill, Melksham, Wiltshire
SN12 6XN
T: (01225) 704679

BOWLISH
Somerset

Kakadu ◆◆◆
2 Coombe Dell, Bowlish,
Shepton Mallet, Somerset
BA4 5JJ
T: (01749) 345403

BOX
Wiltshire

Cheney Cottage ◆◆◆◆
Ditteridge, Box, Corsham,
Wiltshire SN13 8QF
T: (01225) 742346
F: (01225) 742346
E: cheneycottage@btinternet.
com
I: www.visitus.
co.uk/bath/hotel/cheney.htm

Highfield House ◆◆◆
London Road, Box, Corsham,
Wiltshire SN13 8LU
T: (01225) 743030
F: (01225) 743030
E: liz.millward@talk21.com

Lorne House ◆◆◆◆
London Road, Box, Corsham,
Wiltshire SN13 8NA
T: (01225) 742597
E: lornehousebandb@aol.com

Norbin Farmhouse ◆◆◆◆
Box, Corsham, Wiltshire
SN13 8JJ
T: (01225) 866907 & 0797 485
4274
E: gillhillier@yahoo.co.uk

BRADFORD ABBAS
Dorset

Purbeck House ◆◆◆◆
North Street, Bradford Abbas,
Sherborne, Dorset DT9 6SA
T: (01935) 474817

BRADFORD-ON-AVON
Wiltshire

Applegates ◆◆◆◆
32 Winsley Village, Bradford-on-
Avon, Wiltshire BA15 2LU
T: (01225) 723803
F: (01225) 722174
E: stay@applegatesbandb.co.uk
I: www.applegatesbandb.co.uk

The Beeches Farmhouse
◆◆◆◆◆
Holt Road, Bradford-on-Avon,
Wiltshire BA15 1TS
T: (01225) 863475 &
07774 607417
F: (01225) 863996
E: beeches-farmhouse@
netgates.co.uk
I: www.beeches-farmhouse.
co.uk

Brookfield House ◆◆◆◆
Vaggs Hill, Southwick,
Trowbridge, Wiltshire BA14 9NA
T: (01373) 830615 & 0777 160
3842
F: (01373) 830615

Great Ashley Farm ◆◆◆◆
Ashley Lane, Bradford-on-Avon,
Wiltshire BA15 2PP
T: (01225) 864563 & 0790 997
1319
F: (01225) 309 117
E: greatashleyfarm@
farmersweekly.net
I: www.greatashleyfarm.co.uk

Hillside Lodge Bed & Breakfast
◆◆◆◆◆
Hillside Lodge, Jones Hill,
Bradford-on-Avon, Bath
BA15 2EE
T: (01225) 866312
F: (01225) 866312
E: barnes@hillsidelodge.fsnet.
co.uk

Springfields ◆◆◆
182a Great Ashley, Bradford-
on-Avon, Wiltshire BA15 2PP
T: (01225) 866125
E: christine.rawlings@
farmersweekly.net
I: www.bed-and-breakfast.org

Woodpeckers ◆◆◆◆
Holt Road, Bradford-on-Avon,
Wiltshire BA15 1TR
T: (01225) 865616
F: (01225) 865615
E: b+b@wood-peckers.co.uk
I: www.wood-peckers.co.uk

BRADPOLE
Dorset

Spray Copse Farm ◆◆◆◆
Lee Lane, Bradpole, Bridport,
Dorset DT6 4AP
T: (01308) 458510 &
07850 300044
F: (01308) 421015
E: spraycopse@lineone.net

BRADWORTHY
Devon

Lake House Cottages & B&B
◆◆◆
Lake Villa, Bradworthy,
Holsworthy, Devon EX22 7SQ
T: (01409) 241962
E: lesley@lakevilla.co.uk
I: www.lakevilla.co.uk

BRATTON FLEMING
Devon

Bracken House Country Hotel
◆◆◆◆◆
Bratton Fleming, Barnstaple,
Devon EX31 4TG
T: (01598) 710320
F: (01598) 710115
E: holidays@
brackenhousehotel.com
I: www.brackenhousehotel.com
⚓

Haxton Down Farm ◆◆◆
Bratton Fleming, Barnstaple,
Devon EX32 7JL
T: (01598) 710275
F: (01598) 710275

BRAUNTON
Devon

Moorsands ◆◆◆
34 Moor Lane, Croyde Bay,
Braunton, Devon EX33 1NP
T: (01271) 890781
I: www.croyde-bay.
com/moorsands.htm

Povers Hotel ◆◆◆
Wrafton, Braunton, North Devon
EX33 2DN
T: (01271) 812149
I: www.poyers.co.uk

BRAYFORD
Devon

Rockley Farmhouse ◆◆◆◆
Brayford, Barnstaple, Devon
EX32 7QR
T: (01598) 710429
F: (01598) 710429
E: rockley@hicon.co.uk
I: www.hicon.co.uk/rockley

BREAN
Somerset

Berrow Heath Guest House
◆◆◆
South Road, Brean, Burnham-
on-Sea, Somerset TA8 2RD
T: (01278) 751385
F: (01278) 751542
E: walter@robertprice.freeserve.
co.uk

Brean Farm ◆◆◆
Brean Down, Brean, Burnham-
on-Sea, Somerset TA8 2RR
T: (01278) 751055
F: (01278) 751055

The Old Rectory Motel ◆◆◆
Church Road, Brean, Burnham-
on-Sea, Somerset TA8 2SF
T: (01278) 751447
F: (01278) 751800
I: www.old-rectory.fsbusiness.
co.uk

BREMHILL
Wiltshire

Hilltop Farm ◆◆◆
Bremhill, Calne, Wiltshire
SN11 9HQ
T: (01249) 740620

BRENDON
Devon

Brendon House Hotel ◆◆◆
Brendon, Lynton, Devon
EX35 6PS
T: (01598) 741206
E: dave@brendonhouse.
freeserve.co.uk
I: www.brendonvalley.co.uk

Shilstone Farm ◆◆◆
Brendon, Lynton, Devon
EX35 6PU
T: (01598) 741262

Southernwood Farm ◆◆◆
Brendon, Lynton, Devon
EX35 6NU
T: (01598) 741277 &
07710 299504
E: 113726.65@compuserve.com
I: www.brendonvalley.co.uk

BRENT KNOLL
Somerset

The Hawthorns ◆◆◆◆
Crooked Lane, Brent Knoll,
Highbridge, Somerset TA9 4BQ
T: (01278) 760181

Yonder Hill Bed and Breakfast ◆◆◆
Yonder Hill, Crooked Lane, Brent
Knoll, Highbridge, Somerset
TA9 4BQ
T: (01278) 760181
F: (01278) 760181

BRIDESTOWE
Devon

The Knole Farm ◆◆◆◆
Bridestowe, Okehampton, Devon
EX20 4HA
T: (01837) 861241
F: (01837) 861241

Way Barton Barn ◆◆◆
Bridestowe, Okehampton, Devon
EX20 4QH
T: (01837) 861513

White Hart Inn ◆◆◆
Fore Street, Bridestowe,
Okehampton, Devon EX20 4EL
T: (01837) 861318
F: (01837) 861318
E: whihartinn@aol.com
I: members.aol.
com/whihartinn/bridestowe.
html

BRIDGWATER
Somerset

Admirals Rest ◆◆◆
5 Taunton Road, Bridgwater,
Somerset TA6 3LW
T: (01278) 458580
F: (01278) 458580
E: sueparker@admiralsrest.
freeserve.co.uk
I: www.admiralsrest.co.uk

Ash–Wembdon Farm ◆◆◆◆
Hollow Lane, Wembdon,
Bridgwater, Somerset TA5 2BD
T: (01278) 453097 &
07702 272755
F: (01278) 445856
E: mary.rowe@btinternet.com
I: www.farmaccommodation.
co.uk

Bower Green Pub Restaurant ◆◆◆
Bower Lane, Bridgwater,
Somerset TA6 4TY
T: (01278) 422926
F: (01278) 434426

Brookland Hotel ◆
56 North Street, Bridgwater,
Somerset TA6 3PN
I: (01278) 423263
F: (01278) 452988

Cokerhurst Farm ◆◆◆◆
87 Wembdon Hill, Bridgwater,
Somerset TA6 7QA
T: (01278) 422330 &
07850 692065
F: (01278) 422330
E: cokerhurst@clara.net
I: www.cokerhurst.clara.net

Manor Farm ◆◆◆
Waterpitts, Broomfield,
Bridgwater, Somerset TA5 1AT
T: (01823) 451266

Manor Farmhouse ◆◆◆
Wembdon, Bridgwater,
Somerset TA5 2BB
T: (01278) 427913

Model Farm ◆◆◆◆
Perry Green, Wembdon,
Bridgwater, Somerset TA5 2BA
T: (01278) 433999
E: rmodelfarm@aol.com
I: www.modelfarm.com

Quantock View Guest House ◆◆◆
Bridgwater Road, North
Petherton, Bridgwater, Somerset
TA6 6PR
T: (01278) 663309
E: irene@quantockview.
freeserve.co.uk

BRIDPORT
Dorset

Bridport Arms Hotel ◆◆◆
West Bay, Bridport, Dorset
DT6 4EN
T: (01308) 422994
F: (01308) 425141

Britmead House ◆◆◆◆
West Bay Road, Bridport, Dorset
DT6 4EG
T: (01308) 422941
F: (01308) 422516
E: britmead@talk21.com
I: www.britmeadhouse.co.uk

The Bull Hotel ◆◆
34 East Street, Bridport, Dorset
DT6 3LF
T: (01308) 422878
F: (01308) 422878

Candida House ◆◆◆◆
Whitchurch Canonicorum,
DT6 6RQ
T: (01297) 489629
F: (01297) 489629
E: candida@globalnet.co.uk
I: www.holidayaccom.
com/candida-house.htm

Durbeyfield Guest House ◆◆◆
10 West Bay, West Bay, Bridport,
Dorset DT6 4EL
T: (01308) 423307 &
0870 1166478
F: (01308) 423307
E: manager@durbeyfield.co.uk
I: www.durbeyfield.co.uk

**Eypeleaze
Rating Applied For**
117 West Bay Road, Bridport,
Dorset DT6 4EQ
T: (01308) 423363
F: (01308) 420228
E: cdan@walker42.freeserve.
co.uk

New House Farm ◆◆◆
Mangerton Lane, Bradpole,
Bridport, Dorset DT6 3SF
I: (01308) 422884
F: (01308) 422884
E: jane@mangertonlake.
freeserve.co.uk
I: www.mangertonlake.co.uk

Patchwork House ◆◆◆
47 Burton Road, Bridport, Dorset
DT6 4JE
T: (01308) 456515
E: loveridge1@netlineuk.net
I: loveridge1@netlineuk.net

Polly's ◆◆◆◆
22 West Allington, Bridport,
Dorset DT6 5BG
T: (01308) 458095 &
07957 856112
F: (01308) 421834
E: mail@hime.org.uk

Rudge Farm ◆◆◆◆◆
Chilcombe, Bridport, Dorset
DT6 4NF
T: (01308) 482630
F: (01308) 482635
E: sue@rudgefarm.co.uk
I: www.rudgefarm.co.uk

Southcroft ◆◆◆◆
Park Road, Bridport, Dorset
DT6 5DA
T: (01308) 423335
F: (01308) 423335
E: info@southcroftguesthouse.
com
I: www.southcroftguesthouse.
com

Southview ◆◆◆
Whitecross, Netherbury,
Bridport, Dorset DT6 5NH
T: (01308) 488471
E: southviewbb@lineone.net
I: website.lineone.
net/~southviewbb/index.htm

Urella ◆◆◆◆
65 Burton Road, Bridport, Dorset
DT6 4JE
T: (01308) 422450
E: urella_uk@yahoo.co.uk
I: geocities.com/urellauk

The Well ◆◆◆
St Andrews Well, Bridport,
Dorset DT6 3DL
T: (01308) 424156

BRISLINGTON
Bristol

The Beeches ◆◆◆◆
Broomhill Road, Brislington,
Bristol BS4 5RG
T: (0117) 972 8778
F: (0117) 971 1968

Kingston House ◆◆
101 Hardenhuish Road,
Brislington, Bristol BS4 3SR
T: (0117) 9712456

Woodstock ◆◆◆
534 Bath Road, Brislington,
Bristol BS4 3JZ
T: (0117) 987 1613
F: (0117) 987 1613
E: woodstock@blueyonder.co.uk
I: www.homestead.com/wstock/

BRISTOL

A4 Hotel ◆◆◆
511 Bath Road, Brislington,
Bristol BS4 3LA
T: (0117) 9715492
F: (0117) 9711791
E: a4hotel@lineone.net

Arches Hotel ◆◆◆
132 Cotham Brow, Cotham,
Bristol BS6 6AE
T: (0117) 9247398
F: (0117) 9247398
E: ml@arches-hotel.co.uk
I: www.arches-hotel.co.uk

Cumberland Guest House ◆◆◆
6 Clift House Road, Ashton,
Bristol BS3 1RY
T: (0117) 966 0810
F: (0117) 966 0810
E: cumberlandguesthouse@
talk21.com

The Hunters Rest ◆◆◆◆◆
King Lane, Clutton Hill, Bristol,
BS39 5QL
T: (01761) 452303
F: (01761) 453308
E: paul@huntersrest.co.uk
I: www.huntersrest.co.uk

Mayfair Hotel ◆◆◆
5 Henleaze Road, Westbury-on-
Trym, Bristol BS9 4EX
T: (0117) 9622008 & 9493924

Naseby House Hotel ◆◆◆
105 Pembroke Road, Clifton,
Bristol BS8 3EF
T: (0117) 9737859 & 9080011
F: (0117) 9737859
I: www.nasebyhousehotel.co.uk

Norfolk House ◆◆◆
577 Gloucester Road, Horfield,
Bristol, BS7 0BW
T: (0117) 9513191
F: (0117) 9513191

Oakfield Hotel ◆◆◆
52 Oakfield Road, Clifton, Bristol
BS8 2BG
T: (0117) 973 5556 & 973 3643
F: (0117) 974 4141

The Old Court ◆◆◆◆◆
Main Road, Temple Cloud,
Bristol BS39 5DA
T: (01761) 451101
F: (01761) 451224
E: oldcourt@gifford.co.uk
I: www.theoldcourt.com

The Paddock ◆◆◆
Hung Road, Shirehampton,
Bristol BS11 9XJ
T: (0117) 9235140 & 9829748

Rockleaze House ◆◆◆
91 Gloucester Road North,
Filton, Bristol BS34 7PT
T: (0117) 9692536

Rowan Lodge Hotel ◆◆◆
41 Gloucester Road North, Filton
Park, Bristol, BS7 0SN
T: (0117) 931 2170
F: (0117) 975 3601

Thornbury House ◆◆◆◆
80 Chesterfield Road, St
Andrews, Bristol BS6 5DR
T: (0117) 924 5654
F: (0117) 944 1620
E: kaysmith@thornburyhouse.
fsbusiness.co.uk

Treborough ◆◆◆
3 Grove Road, Coombe Dingle,
Bristol BS9 2RQ
T: (0117) 968 2712

Tricomo House B & B ◆◆◆
183 Cheltenham Road, Cotham,
Bristol BS6 5RH
T: (0117) 9248082
F: (0117) 9248082
E: tricomohouse1@activemail.
co.uk

Washington Hotel ◆◆◆
11-15 St Paul's Road, Clifton,
Bristol, BS8 1LX
T: (0117) 973 3980
F: (0117) 973 4740
E: washington@cliftonhotels.
com
I: www.cliftonhotels.com

BRIXHAM
Devon

Anchorage Guest House ◆◆◆
170 New Road, Brixham, Devon
TQ5 8DA
T: (01803) 852960
F: (01803) 852960

Black Cottage Guest House
◆◆◆
17 Milton Street, Brixham,
Devon TQ5 0BX
T: (01803) 853752

Brioc Hotel ◆◆◆
11 Prospect Road, Brixham,
Devon TQ5 8HS
T: (01803) 853540

Lamorna ◆◆◆
130 New Road, Brixham, Devon
TQ5 8DA
T: (01803) 853954
E: lamornabrixham@aol.com

Melville Hotel ◆◆◆
45 New Road, Brixham, Devon
TQ5 8NL
T: (01803) 852033
E: melvillehotel@brixham45.
fsnet.co.uk
I: www.smoothhound.
co.uk/hotels.melville2.html

Raddicombe Lodge ◆◆◆◆
Kingswear Road, Brixham,
Devon TQ5 0EX
T: (01803) 882125
F: (01803) 882125
E: val-trev@
raddicombe-fsbusiness.co.uk

Ranscombe House Hotel
◆◆◆◆
Ranscombe Road, Brixham,
Devon TQ5 9UP
T: (01803) 882337
F: (01803) 882337
E: ranscombe@lineone.net
I: www.RanscombeHouseHotel.
co.uk

Redlands Hotel ◆◆◆
136 New Road, Brixham, Devon
TQ5 8DA
T: (01803) 853813
F: (01803) 853813
E: redlandsbrixham@aol.com
I: www.members.aol.
com/redlandsbrixham/index.
html

Richmond House Hotel ◆◆◆
Higher Manor Road, Brixham,
Devon TQ5 8HA
T: (01803) 882391
F: (01803) 882391
E: juliegiblett@richmondhse.
hoteloneman.fsnet.co.uk

Sampford House ◆◆◆
57-59 King Street, Brixham,
Devon TQ5 9TH
T: (01803) 857761
F: (01803) 857761
E: carole.boulton@btinternet.
com

Sea Tang Guest House ◆◆◆
67 Berry Head Road, Brixham,
Devon TQ5 9AA
T: (01803) 854651
F: (01803) 854651
E: b&tb@seatang.freeserve.co.uk

The Shoalstone Hotel ◆◆◆
105 Berry Head Road, Brixham,
Devon TQ5 9AG
T: (01803) 857919 & 850550
F: (01803) 850540

Tor Haven Hotel ◆◆◆
97 King Street, Brixham, Devon
TQ5 9TH
T: (01803) 882281

Westbury Guest House ◆◆◆
51 New Road, Brixham, Devon
TQ5 8NL
T: (01803) 851684
F: ann.hurt@lineone.net

BRIXTON
Devon

Venn Farm ◆◆◆◆
Brixton, Plymouth, Devon
PL8 2AX
T: (01752) 880378
F: (01752) 880378

BROAD CHALKE
Wiltshire

The Queens Head Inn ◆◆◆◆
1 North Street, Broad Chalke,
Salisbury SP5 5EN
T: (01722) 780344
F: (01722) 780344

BROAD HINTON
Wiltshire

Huntersley ◆◆◆
Post Office Lane, Broad Hinton,
Swindon SN4 9PB
T: (01793) 731115
F: (01793) 731115

BROADHEMBURY
Devon

Lane End Farm ◆◆◆
Broadhembury, Honiton, Devon
EX14 3LU
T: (01404) 841563

Stafford Barton Farm
◆◆◆◆◆
Broadhembury, Honiton, Devon
EX14 3LU
T: (01404) 841403
E: djwalters@uk.packardbell.org

BROADOAK
Dorset

Dunster Farm ◆◆◆◆
Broadoak, Bridport, Dorset
DT6 5NR
T: (01308) 424626

BROADWOODWIDGER
Devon

Frankaborough Farm ◆◆◆
Broadwoodwidger, Lifton, Devon
PL16 0JS
T: (01409) 211308 &
07971 525550

BROMHAM
Wiltshire

The Cottage ◆◆◆
Westbrook, Bromham,
Chippenham, Wiltshire
SN15 2EE
T: (01380) 850255
E: rjsteed@cottage16.freeserve.
co.uk

Paddock House
Rating Applied For
104 Devizes Road, Bromham,
Chippenham, Wiltshire
SN15 2DZ
T: (01380) 850970

Sandycroft ◆◆◆◆
Chittoe Heath, Bromham,
Chippenham, Wiltshire
SN15 2EQ
T: (01380) 850030 &
07702 364324

BROUGHTON GIFFORD
Wiltshire

Frying Pan Farm ◆◆◆
Broughton Gifford, Melksham,
Wiltshire SN12 8LL
T: (01225) 702343
F: (01225) 793652
E: fr65@dial.pipex.com

Honeysuckle Cottage ◆◆◆◆
95 the Common, Broughton
Gifford, Melksham, Wiltshire
SN12 8ND
T: (01225) 782463 &
07747 754157
E: dmehta@globalnet.co.uk
I: www.users.globalnet.
co.uk/~dmehta/index.htm

BRUTON
Somerset

Gants Mill ◆◆◆◆
Gants Mill Lane, Bruton,
Somerset BA10 0DB
T: (01749) 812393
E: shingler@gantsmill.co.uk
I: www.gantsmill.co.uk

BRYHER
Cornwall

Bank Cottage Guest House
◆◆◆◆
Bryher, Isles of Scilly TR23 0PR
T: (01720) 422612
F: (01720) 422612
E: macmace@patrol.i-way.co.uk

Soleil D'or ◆◆◆◆
Bryher, Isles of Scilly TR23 0PR
T: (01720) 422003

BUCKFAST
Devon

Furzeleigh Mill Country Hotel
◆◆◆
Dartbridge, Buckfast, Devon
TQ11 0JP
T: (01364) 643476 & 642245
F: (01364) 643476

BUCKFASTLEIGH
Devon

Wellpark Farm ◆◆◆◆
Dean Prior, Buckfastleigh, Devon
TQ11 0LY
T: (01364) 643775
F: (01364) 643775
E: rosiepalmer@btinternet.com

BUCKLAND
Devon

The Drive Inn
Rating Applied For
Haytor Drive, Buckland, Newton
Abbot, Devon TQ12 4DU
T: (01626) 365597

BUCKLAND NEWTON
Dorset

Holyleas House ◆◆◆◆
Buckland Newton, Dorchester,
Dorset DT2 7DP
T: (01300) 345214 &
07968 341887
F: (01305) 264488
E: tiabunkall@holyleas.fsnet.
co.uk

Rew Cottage ◆◆◆◆
Buckland Newton, Dorchester,
Dorset DT2 7DN
T: (01300) 345467
F: (01300) 345467

**Whiteways Farmhouse
Accommodation** ◆◆◆◆
Bookham, Buckland Newton,
Dorchester, Dorset DT2 7RP
T: (01300) 345511
F: (01300) 345511
E: bookhamfarm@
netscapeonline.co.uk

BUDE
Cornwall

Atlantic Calm ◆◆◆◆
30 Downs View, Bude, Cornwall
EX23 8RG
T: (01288) 359165
E: atlanticcalm@btinternet.com
I: www.atlanticcalm.co.uk

Brendon Arms
Rating Applied For
Bude, Cornwall EX23 8SD
T: (01288) 354542 & 352713
F: (01288) 354542

Cliff Hotel ◆◆◆◆
Crooklets Beach, Bude, Cornwall
EX23 8NG
T: (01288) 353110
F: (01288) 353110
I: www.cliffhotel.co.uk

Clovelly House ◆◆◆
4 Burn View, Bude, Cornwall
EX23 8BY
T: (01288) 352761
F: (01288) 352761

Corisande Hotel ◆◆◆
24 Downs View, Bude, Cornwall
EX23 8RG
T: (01288) 353474
F: (01288) 353474
E: janerouse@compuserve.com
I: www.bude-cornwall.
co.uk/corisande

The Elms ◆◆◆
37 Lynstone Road, Bude,
Cornwall EX23 8LR
T: (01288) 353429

Hallagather Farmhouse ♦♦♦♦
Crackington Haven, Bude,
Cornwall EX23 0LA
T: (01840) 230276
F: (01840) 230276

Link's Side ♦♦♦♦
7 Burn View, Bude, Cornwall
EX23 8BY
T: (01288) 352410
E: linksidebude@
north-cornwall.co.uk
I: www.north-cornwall.
co.uk/bude/client/linkside

Lower Tresmorn ♦♦♦♦
Lower Tresmorn Farm,
Crackington Haven, Bude,
Cornwall EX23 0LQ
T: (01840) 230667
F: (01840) 230667

**Penleaze Farm Bed and
Breakfast ♦♦♦♦**
Penleaze, Marham Church, Bude,
Cornwall EX23 0ET
T: (01288) 381226
F: (01288) 381226

Seagulls Guest House ♦♦♦
11 Downs View, Bude, Cornwall
EX23 8RF
T: (01288) 352059 &
07855 088318
F: (01288) 359259
E: seagullsgh@ukonline.co.uk
I: web.ukonline.co.uk/seagullsgh

**Stratton Gardens Hotel
♦♦♦♦**
Cot Hill, Stratton, Bude,
Cornwall EX23 9DN
T: (01288) 352500
F: (01288) 352256
E: stratton.gardens@which.net
I: www.cornwall-online.
co.uk/stratton-gardens

Sunrise Guest House ♦♦♦♦
6 Burn View, Bude, Cornwall
EX23 8BY
T: (01288) 353214

Tee-Side Guest House ♦♦♦
2 Burn View, Bude, Cornwall
EX23 8BY
T: (01288) 352351
F: (01288) 352351
E: tee-side@hotmail.com

Wyvern House ♦♦♦♦
7 Downs View, Bude, Cornwall
EX23 8RF
T: (01288) 352205
F: (01288) 356802
E: eileen@wyvernhouse.co.uk
I: www.wyvernhouse.co.uk

BUDLEIGH SALTERTON
Devon

Lufflands ♦♦♦♦
Yettington, Budleigh Salterton,
Devon EX9 7BP
T: (01395) 568422
F: (01395) 568810
E: Lufflands@compuserve.com
I: www.lufflands.co.uk

BUDOCK WATER
Cornwall

Higher Kergilliack Farm ♦♦♦
Budock Water, Falmouth,
Cornwall TR11 5PB
T: (01326) 372271

**The Home Country House
Hotel ♦♦♦**
Penjerrick, Budock Water,
Falmouth, Cornwall TR11 5EE
T: (01326) 250427 & 250143
F: (01326) 250143

BURLAWN
Cornwall

Pengelly Farmhouse ♦♦♦
Burlawn, Wadebridge, Cornwall
PL27 7LA
T: (01208) 814217

BURNHAM-ON-SEA
Somerset

Alstone Court Farm ♦♦
Alstone Lane, Highbridge,
Somerset TA9 3DS
T: (01278) 789417
F: (01278) 784582

Ar Dhachaedh ♦♦♦
36 Abingdon Street, Burnham-
on-Sea, Somerset TA8 1PJ
T: (01278) 783652

Boundrys Edge ♦♦♦
40 Charlestone Road, Burnham-
on-Sea, Somerset TA8 2AP
T: (01278) 783128 &
0771 2737033
F: (01278) 783128

Cresta B&B ♦♦
230 Berrow Road, Burnham-on-
Sea, Somerset TA8 2JG
T: (01278) 795626

Dunstan House Inn ♦♦♦
Love Lane, Burnham-on-Sea,
Somerset TA8 1EU
T: (01278) 784343

Knights Rest ♦♦♦
9 Dunstan Road, Burnham-on-
Sea, Somerset TA8 1ER
T: (01278) 782318

Priors Mead ♦♦♦
23 Rectory Road, Burnham-on-
Sea, Somerset TA8 2BZ
T: (01278) 782116 &
07790 595585
F: (01278) 782116
E: priorsmead@aol.com
I: www.smoothhound.
co.uk/hotels/priors.html

**Prospect Farm Guest House
♦♦♦**
Strowlands, East Brent,
Highbridge, Somerset TA9 4JH
T: (01278) 760507

Sandhills Guest House ♦♦♦
3 Poplar Road, Burnham-on-
Sea, Somerset TA8 2HD
T: (01278) 781208

Shalimar Guest House ♦♦
174 Berrow Road, Burnham-on-
Sea, Somerset TA8 2JE
T: (01278) 785898

Somewhere House ♦♦♦
68 Berrow Road, Burnham-on-
Sea, Somerset TA8 2EZ
T: (01278) 795236
E: di@somewherehouse.com
I: www.somewherehouse.com

Thornbury ♦♦
4 Manor Road, Burnham-on-
Sea, Somerset TA8 2AS
T: (01278) 784882

Walton House ♦♦♦
Burnham-on-Sea, Somerset
TA8 2PN
T: (01278) 780034
E: auntflo@dialstart.net

The Warren Guest House ♦♦♦
29 Berrow Road, Burnham-on-
Sea, Somerset TA8 2EZ
T: (01278) 786726 & 788204
F: (01278) 786726
E: TheWarren@compuserve.com
I: www.warrenguesthouse.co.uk

BURTLE
Somerset

The Tom Mogg Inn ♦♦♦
Station Road, Burtle, Bridgwater,
Somerset TA7 8NU
T: (01278) 722399
F: (01278) 722724
E: tommogg@telinco.com

BURTON BRADSTOCK
Dorset

Bridge Cottage Stores ♦♦♦
87 High Street, Burton
Bradstock, Bridport, Dorset
DT6 4RA
T: (01308) 897222

Burton Cliff Hotel ♦♦♦
Cliff Road, Burton Bradstock,
Bridport, Dorset DT6 4RB
T: (01308) 897205
F: (01308) 898111
&

Pebble Beach Lodge ♦♦♦♦
Coast Road, Burton Bradstock,
Bridport, Dorset DT6 4RJ
T: (01308) 897428
F: (01308) 897428
E: pebblebeachlodge@supanet.
com
I: www.burtonbradstock.org.
uk/pebblebeachlodge

BUTCOMBE
North Somerset

Butcombe Farm ♦♦♦♦
Aldwick Lane, Butcombe, Bristol
BS40 7UW
T: (01761) 462380
F: (01761) 462300
E: info@butcombe-farm.
demon.co.uk
I: www.butcombe-farm.demon.
co.uk

CADLEY
Wiltshire

Kingstones Farm ♦♦♦♦
Cadley, Marlborough, Wiltshire
SN8 4NE
T: (01672) 512039
F: (01672) 515947

CALLINGTON
Cornwall

Dozmary ♦♦♦
Tors View Close, Tavistock Road,
Callington, Cornwall PL17 7DY
T: (01579) 383677
E: dozmarybb@aol.com

Green Pastures ♦♦♦
Longhill, Callington, Cornwall
PL17 8AU
T: (01579) 382566
E: greenpast@aol.com

Higher Manaton ♦♦♦
Callington, Cornwall PL17 8PX
T: (01579) 370460
F: (01579) 370460
E: dtrewin@manaton.fsnet.
co.uk

CALNE
Wiltshire

Chilvester Hill House ♦♦♦♦♦
Calne, Wiltshire SN11 0LP
T: (01249) 813981 & 815785
F: (01249) 814217
E: gill.dilley@talk21.com
I: www.wolsey-lodges.co.uk

**Manor Farm (Calstone)
♦♦♦♦**
Calstone Wellington, Calne,
Wiltshire SN11 8PY
T: (01249) 816804 &
07050 208886
F: (01249) 817966
E: calstonebandb@
farmersweekly.net
I: www.calstone.co.uk

Maundrell House ♦♦♦♦
Horsebrook, The Green, Calne,
Wiltshire SN11 8DL
T: (01249) 821267
F: (01249) 821267
E: liz@mundrell.bigwig.net
I: www.maundrell.bigwig.net

**Queenwood Golf Lodge
♦♦♦♦♦**
Bowood Golf & Country Club,
Calne, Wiltshire SN11 9PQ
T: (01249) 822228
F: (01249) 822218
I: www.bowood-estate.co.uk

White Hart Hotel ♦♦
2 London Road, Calne, Wiltshire
SN11 0AB
T: (01249) 812413 & 812467
F: (01249) 812467

CANNINGTON
Somerset

Blackmore Farm ♦♦♦♦♦
Cannington, Bridgwater,
Somerset TA5 2NE
T: (01278) 653442
F: (01278) 653427
E: dyerfarm@aol.com
I: www.dyerfarm.co.uk
&

The Friendly Spirit ♦♦♦
Brook Street, Cannington,
Bridgwater, Somerset TA5 2HP
T: (01278) 652215
F: (01278) 653636

Gurney Manor Mill ♦♦♦♦
Gurney Street, Cannington,
Bridgwater, Somerset TA5 2HW
T: (01278) 653582
F: (01278) 653993
E: gurneymill@yahoo.co.uk
I: www.gurneymill.freeserve.
co.uk

Kings Head Inn ♦♦♦
12-14 High Street, Cannington,
Bridgwater, Somerset TA5 2HE
T: (01278) 652293

CARBIS BAY
Cornwall

Howards Hotel ♦♦♦
St Ives Road, Carbis Bay, St Ives,
Cornwall TR26 2SB
T: (01736) 795651
F: (01736) 795535
E: dmgill@hhotel.fsbusiness.
co.uk
I: www.cornwall-online.
co.uk/howardshotel

Trelowena Guest House ♦♦♦
27 Richmond Way, Carbis Bay,
St Ives, Cornwall TR26 2JY
T: (01736) 798276

CARLYON BAY
Cornwall

Horizon House ◆◆◆◆
Sea Road, Carlyon Bay, St
Austell, Cornwall PL25 3SG
T: (01726) 817221
F: (01726) 817221

CASTLE CARY
Somerset

Bond's ◆◆◆◆
Ansford Hill, Castle Cary,
Somerset BA7 7JL
T: (01963) 350464
F: (01963) 350464
E: bonds-bistro@faxvia.net

Clanville Manor ◆◆◆◆
Castle Cary, Somerset BA7 7PJ
T: (01963) 350124 &
07966 512732
F: (01963) 350719
E: info@clanvillemanor.co.uk
I: www.clanvillemanor.co.uk

The Horse Pond Inn and Motel
◆◆◆
The Triangle, Castle Cary,
Somerset BA7 7BD
T: (01963) 350318 & 351762
F: (01963) 351764
E: horsepondinn@aol.com

Orchard Farm ◆◆◆
Cockhill, Castle Cary, Somerset
BA7 7NY
T: (01963) 350418
F: (01963) 350418
E: boyeroj@talk21.com

CASTLE COMBE
Wiltshire

Fosse Farmhouse ◆◆◆◆
Nettleton Shrub, Nettleton,
Chippenham, Wiltshire
SN14 7NJ
T: (01249) 782286 &
07780 694935
F: (01249) 783066
E: caroncooper@compuserve.
com
I: www.fossefarmhouse.8m.com

Goulters Mill Farm ◆◆◆
Goulters Mill, Nettleton,
Chippenham, Wiltshire SN14 7LL
T: (01249) 782555

Thorngrove Cottage ◆◆◆
Summer Lane, Castle Combe,
Chippenham, Wiltshire
SN14 7LG
T: (01249) 782607 &
0780 1304676
E: chrisdalene@compuserve.
com

CATTISTOCK
Dorset

Greystones ◆◆◆
Cattistock, Dorchester, Dorset
DT2 0JB
T: (01300) 320477
E: j_f.fletcher@virgin.net

Sandhills Cottage ◆◆◆◆
Sandhills, Cattistock, Dorchester,
Dorset DT2 0HQ
T: (01300) 321146
F: (01300) 321146
E: m.roca@lineone.net

CERNE ABBAS
Dorset

Badger Hill ◆◆◆◆
11 Springfield, Cerne Abbas,
Dorchester, Dorset DT2 7JZ
T: (01300) 341698
F: (01300) 341698

Cerne River Cottage ◆◆◆◆
8 The Folly, Cerne Abbas,
Dorchester, Dorset DT2 7JR
T: (01300) 341355
E: b&b@w-ellis.freeserve.co.uk
I: www.cernerivercottage.co.uk

CHAGFORD
Devon

Glendarah House ◆◆◆◆
Lower Street, Chagford, Newton
Abbot, Devon TQ13 8BZ
T: (01647) 433270
F: (01647) 433483
E: enquiries@glendarah-house.
co.uk
I: www.glendarah-house.co.uk

Throwleigh Manor ◆◆◆◆
Throwleigh, Okehampton, Devon
EX20 2JF
T: (01647) 231630
F: (01647) 231630

CHALLACOMBE
Devon

Twitchen Farm ◆◆◆
Challacombe, Barnstaple, Devon
EX31 4TT
T: (01598) 763500
F: (01598) 763310
E: holidays@twitchen.co.uk
I: www.twitchen.co.uk

CHARD
Somerset

Bellplot House Hotel ◆◆◆◆◆
High Street, Chard, Somerset
TA20 1QB
T: (01460) 62600
F: (01460) 62600
E: bellplothousehotel@talk21.
com

Home Farm ◆◆◆
Hornsbury Hill, Chard, Somerset
TA20 3DB
T: (01460) 63731

Hornsbury Mill ◆◆◆◆
Eleighwater, Chard, Somerset
TA20 3AQ
T: (01460) 63317
F: (01460) 63317
E: horsburymill@btclick.com
I: www.hornsburymill.co.uk

Wambrook Farm ◆◆◆
Wambrook, Chard, Somerset
TA20 3DF
T: (01460) 62371
F: (01460) 68827

CHARLESTOWN
Cornwall

Rashleigh Arms ◆◆◆
Charlestown Road, Charlestown,
St Austell, Cornwall PL25 3NJ
T: (01726) 73635
F: (01726) 73635

T'Gallants ◆◆◆
6 Charlestown Road,
Charlestown, St Austell,
Cornwall PL25 3NJ
T: (01726) 70203

CHARLTON HORETHORNE
Somerset

Ashclose Farm ◆◆◆
Blackford Road, Charlton
Horethorne, Sherborne, Dorset
DT9 4PG
T: (01963) 220360 &
07710 235494
F: 08704 034570
E: gooding@ashclosefarm.
freeserve.co.uk

Longbar ◆◆◆
Level Lane, Charlton Horethorne,
Sherborne, Dorset DT9 4NN
T: (01963) 220266
E: longbar@tinyworld.co.uk
I: www.longbarfarm.co.uk

CHARMINSTER
Dorset

The Inn For All Seasons ◆◆◆
16 North Street, Charminster,
Dorchester, Dorset DT2 9QZ
T: (01305) 264694
F: (01305) 257824

Slades Farm ◆◆◆◆
North Street, Charminster,
Dorchester, Dorset DT2 9QZ
T: (01305) 265614
F: (01305) 265614

Three Compasses Inn ◆◆◆
Charminster, Dorchester, Dorset
DT2 9QT
T: (01305) 263618

CHARMOUTH
Dorset

Cardsmill Farm ◆◆◆
Whitchurch Canonicorum,
DT6 6RP
T: (01297) 489375
F: (01297) 489375
E: cardsmill@aol.com
I: www.farmhousedorest.com

Fernhill Hotel
Rating Applied For
Charmouth, Bridport, Dorset
DT6 6BX
T: (01297) 560492
F: (01297) 560492

Queen's Armes Hotel
Rating Applied For
The Street, Charmouth, Bridport,
Dorset DT6 6QF
T: (01297) 560339
F: (01297) 560339
E: peterm@netcomuk.co.uk

CHEDDAR
Somerset

Chedwell Cottage ◆◆◆◆
59 Redcliffe Street, Cheddar,
Somerset BS27 3PF
T: (01934) 743268
I: www.westcountrynow.com

Constantine ◆◆◆
Lower New Road, Cheddar,
Somerset BS27 3DY
T: (01934) 741339 &
07710 966695

Gordons Hotel ◆◆◆
Cliff Street, Cheddar, Somerset
BS27 3PT
T: (01934) 742497
F: (01934) 744965
I: gordons.hotel@virgin.net

Market Cross Hotel ◆◆◆
The Cross, Church Street,
Cheddar, Somerset BS27 3RA
T: (01934) 742264
F: (01934) 741411
E: annfieldhouse@aol.com
I: www.marketcrosshotel.co.uk

Neuholme ◆◆◆◆
The Barrows, Cheddar, Somerset
BS27 3BG
T: (01934) 742841 &
07977 644712

South Barn B & B ◆◆
The Hayes, Cheddar, Somerset
BS27 3AN
T: (01934) 743146 &
0471 579593
F: (01934) 743146

Tor Farm ◆◆◆◆
Nyland, Cheddar, Somerset
BS27 3UD
T: (01934) 743710
F: (01934) 743710
E: bcjbkj@aol.com

Wassells House ◆◆◆◆
Upper New Road, Cheddar,
Somerset BS27 3DN
T: (01934) 744317 &
07977 580453
E: aflinders@wassells99.
freeserve.co.uk

CHEDZOY
Somerset

Apple View ◆◆◆◆
Temple Farm, Chedzoy,
Bridgwater, Somerset TA7 8QR
T: (01278) 423201 &
07710 594063
E: templefarm@netscapeonline.
co.uk
&

CHELSTON
Devon

Colindale Hotel ◆◆◆◆
20 Rathmore Road, Chelston,
Torquay, Devon TQ2 6NY
T: (01803) 293947

Elmdene Hotel ◆◆◆◆
Rathmore Road, Chelston,
Torquay TQ2 6NZ
T: (01803) 294940
F: (01803) 294940
E: elmdenehoteltorqy@
amserve.com
I: www.s-h-systems.
co.uk/hotels/elmdene.html

Millbrook House Hotel
◆◆◆◆◆
Old Mill Road, Chelston,
Torquay, Devon TQ2 6AP
T: (01803) 297394
F: (01803) 297394
E: millbrookhotel@virgin.net

Parks Hotel ◆◆◆◆
Rathmore Road, Chelston,
Torquay TQ2 6NZ
T: (01803) 292420 &
08000 191799
F: (01803) 405267

Strathnaver Hotel ◆◆◆
Rawlyn Road, Chelston, Torquay
TQ2 6PQ
T: (01803) 605523
F: (01803) 605529

Tower Hall Hotel ◆◆◆
Solsbro Road, Chelston, Torquay
TQ2 6PF
T: (01803) 605292
E: johnbutler@towerhallhotel.
co.uk

White Gables Hotel ◆◆◆
Rawlyn Road, Chelston, Torquay,
Devon TQ2 6PQ
T: (01803) 605233
F: (01803) 606634

Windsurfer Hotel ◆◆◆
St Agnes' Lane, Chelston,
Torquay TQ2 6QD
T: (01803) 606550

CHELYNCH
Somerset

The Old Stables ◆◆◆◆
Hurlingpot Farm, Chelynch,
Shepton Mallet, Somerset
BA4 4PY
T: (01749) 880098 &
07798 600752
E: maureen.keevil@amserve.net
I: www.the-oldstables.co.uk

CHERHILL
Wiltshire

Cricketers Rest ◆◆◆◆
Quemerford Gate, Cherhill,
Calne, Wiltshire SN11 8UL
T: (01249) 812388

CHEW MAGNA
Bath and North East Somerset

Valley Farm ◆◆◆◆
Sandy Lane, Stanton Drew,
Bristol BS39 4EL
T: (01275) 332723
F: (01275) 332723
E: valley.farm@faxvia.net

Woodbarn Farm ◆◆◆
Denny Lane, Chew Magna,
Bristol BS40 8SZ
T: (01275) 332599
F: (01275) 332599
E: woodbarnfarm@hotmail.com

CHEW STOKE
Bath and North East Somerset

Dewdown Cottage ◆◆◆
Nempnett Thrubwell, Chew
Stoke, Bristol BS40 8YF
T: (01761) 462917
E: dewdown@hotmail.com

Orchard House ◆◆◆
Bristol Road, Chew Stoke, Bristol
BS40 8UB
T: (01275) 333143
F: (01275) 333754
E: orchardhse@ukgateway.net
I: www.orchardhse.ukgateway.
net

CHEWTON MENDIP
Somerset

The Pantiles ◆◆◆◆
Bathway, Chewton Mendip,
Bath BA3 4NS
T: (01761) 241519

CHICKERELL
Dorset

Stonebank ◆◆◆◆◆
14 West Street, Chickerell,
Weymouth, Dorset DT3 4DY
T: (01305) 760120
F: (01305) 760871
E: BB@stonebank-chickerell.
co.uk
I: www.stonebank-chickerell.
co.uk

CHICKLADE
Wiltshire

The Old Rectory ◆◆◆◆
Chicklade, Hindon, Salisbury
SP3 5SU
T: (01747) 820226
F: (01747) 820783
E: vbronson@old-rectory.co.uk
I: www.old-rectory.co.uk

CHIDEOCK
Dorset

Betchworth House ◆◆◆◆
Chideock, Bridport, Dorset
DT6 6JW
T: (01297) 489478
F: (01297) 489932
E: jffldg@aol.com
I: www.lymeregis.co.uk

CHILSWORTHY
Devon

Ugworthy Barton ◆◆◆◆
Chilsworthy, Holsworthy, Devon
EX22 7JH
T: (01409) 254435
F: (01409) 254435

CHILTON CANTELO
Somerset

Higher Farm ◆◆◆◆
Chilton Cantelo, Yeovil,
Somerset BA22 8BE
T: (01935) 850213
E: susankerton@tinyonline.
co.uk

CHILTON TRINITY
Somerset

Chilton Farm ◆◆◆◆
Chilton Trinity, Bridgwater,
Somerset TA5 2BL
T: (01278) 421864
E: warmt@supanet.com

CHIPPENHAM
Wiltshire

Church Farm ◆◆◆◆
Hartham Park, Corsham,
Wiltshire SN13 0PU
T: (01249) 715180 &
07977 910775
F: (01249) 715572
E: kmjbandb@aol.com
I: www.churchfarm.cjb.net

Fairfield Farm ◆◆◆◆
Upper Wraxall, Chippenham,
Wiltshire SN14 7AG
T: (01225) 891750
F: (01225) 891050
E: mcdonoug@globalnet.co.uk

London Road Guest House ◆◆◆
122 London Road, Chippenham,
Wiltshire SN15 3BA
T: (01249) 660027 &
07976 740060
E: ron@read122a.fsnet.co.uk

New Road Guest House ◆◆◆
31 New Road, Chippenham,
Wiltshire SN15 1HP
T: (01249) 657259
F: (01249) 657259

Oakfield Farm ◆◆◆◆
Easton Piercy Lane, Yatton
Keynell, Chippenham, Wiltshire
SN14 6JU
T: (01249) 782355
F: (01249) 783458

75 Rowden Hill ◆◆
Chippenham, Wiltshire
SN15 2AL
T: (01249) 652981

**Teresa Lodge (Glen Avon)
◆◆◆**
43 Bristol Road, Chippenham,
Wiltshire SN15 1NT
T: (01249) 653350
F: (01249) 653 350

CHIPPING SODBURY
South Gloucestershire

**The Sodbury House Hotel
◆◆◆◆**
Badminton Road, Old Sodbury,
Bristol BS37 6LU
T: (01454) 312847
F: (01454) 273105
E: sodhousehotel@tesco.net

CHISELDON
Wiltshire

Norton House ◆◆◆◆
46 Draycott Road, Chiseldon,
Swindon, Wiltshire SN4 0LS
T: (01793) 741210 &
07976 750767
E: sharian@clara.co.uk
I: www.nortonhouse.uk.com

CHITTLEHAMPTON
Devon

Higher Blddacott Farm ◆◆◆
Chittlehampton, Umberleigh,
Devon EX37 9PY
T: (01769) 540222
F: (01769) 540222
E: waterers@sosi.net
I: www.heavyhorses.net

CHRISTIAN MALFORD
Wiltshire

Beanhill Farm ◆◆◆
Main Road, Christian Malford,
Chippenham, Wiltshire
SN15 4BS
T: (01249) 720672 &
07775 660000

The Ferns ◆◆◆
Church Road, Christian Malford,
Chippenham, Wiltshire
SN15 4BW
T: (01249) 720371
E: ault.ferns@amserve.net

CHRISTOW
Devon

Weir Park Farm ◆◆◆
Waterwell Lane, Christow, Exeter
EX6 7PB
T: (01647) 252549 &
0797 4752734
F: (01647) 252549
E: louise@baber.co.uk
I: www.devonfarms.co.uk

CHUDLEIGH
Devon

Farmborough House ◆◆◆◆
Old Exeter Road, Chudleigh,
Newton Abbot, Devon TQ13 0DR
T: (01626) 853258
F: (01626) 853258
E: holidays@
farmborough-house.com
I: www.farmborough-house.
com

CHUDLEIGH KNIGHTON
Devon

Church House ◆◆◆◆
Chudleigh Knighton, Newton
Abbot, Devon TQ13 0HE
T: (01626) 852123
F: (01626) 852123
E: brandon@churchhouse100.
freeserve.co.uk
I: www.smoothhound.
co.uk/hotels/churchho.html

CHURCHILL
North Somerset

Clumber Lodge ◆◆◆
New Road, Churchill,
Winscombe BS25 5NW
T: (01934) 852078 &
0771 5001441

Hillslee House ◆◆◆◆
New Road, Churchill,
Winscombe BS25 5NP
T: (01934) 853035
F: (01934) 852470

CHURCHINFORD
Somerset

The York Inn ◆◆◆◆
Honiton Road, Churchinford,
Taunton, Somerset TA3 7RF
T: (01823) 601333
F: (01823) 601026
E: wdatheyorkinn@aol.com
I: www.the-york-inn.freeserve.
co.uk

CHURCHSTANTON
Somerset

Pear Tree Cottage ◆◆
Stapley, Churchstanton,
Taunton, Somerset TA3 7QA
T: (01823) 601224
F: (01823) 601224
E: colvin.parry@virgin.net
I: www.smoothhound.
co.uk/hotels/thatch.html

CLAWTON
Devon

**The Old Vicarage
Rating Applied For**
Clawton, Holsworthy, Devon
EX22 6PS
T: (01409) 271100

CLENCH
Wiltshire

Clench Farmhouse ◆◆◆
Clench, Marlborough, Wiltshire
SN8 4NT
T: (01672) 810264 &
07774 784601
F: (01672) 811458
E: clarissaroe@btinternet.com
I: www.clenchfarmhouse.co.uk

CLEVEDON
North Somerset

Highcliffe Hotel ◆◆◆
Wellington Terrace, Clevedon,
Avon BS21 7PU
T: (01275) 873250
F: (01275) 873572

Maybank Guest House ◆◆
4 Jesmond Road, Clevedon,
Avon BS21 7SA
T: (01275) 876387

CLIFTON
Bristol

**Downs View Guest House
◆◆◆**
38 Upper Belgrave Road, Clifton,
Bristol BS8 2XN
T: (0117) 973 7046 &
07976 432430
F: (0117) 973 8169

Number 31 ◆◆◆◆
31 Royal York Crescent, Clifton,
Bristol BS8 4JU
T: (0117) 9735330

Rosebery House ♦♦♦
Clifton, Bristol BS8 4PU
T: (0117) 9149508 &
0777 1871251
F: (0117) 9149508
E: anne@amalindine.freeserve.
co.uk

Westbourne Hotel
Rating Applied For
40-44 St Paul's Road, Clifton,
Bristol BS8 1LR
T: (0117) 973 4214
F: (0117) 974 3552
E: westbourne@clemshaws.
freeserve.co.uk
I: www.westbournehotel-bristol.
co.uk

CLOVELLY
Devon
Dyke Green Farm ♦♦♦♦
Clovelly, Bideford, Devon
EX39 5RU
T: (01237) 431699 & 431279
E: edward@ecjohns.freeserve.
co.uk

Fuchsia Cottage ♦♦♦♦
Burscott, Clovelly, Bideford,
Devon EX39 5RR
T: (01237) 431398
E: tomsuecurtis.fuchsiacot@
currantbun.com
I: www.clovelly-holidays.co.uk

Holloford Farm ♦♦♦♦
Higher Clovelly, Bideford, Devon
EX39 5SD
T: (01237) 441275
I: www.wade@holloford.
freeserve.co.uk

CLUTTON
Bath and North East Somerset
Cholwell Hall ♦♦♦
Clutton, Bristol BS39 5TE
T: (01761) 452380
I: www.cholwellhall.co.uk

CODFORD ST MARY
Wiltshire
Glebe Cottage ♦♦♦♦
Church Lane, Codford St Mary,
Warminster, Wiltshire BA12 0PJ
T: (01985) 850565
F: (01985) 850666

COLEFORD
Somerset
Brook Cottage ♦♦
Highbury Street, Coleford, Bath
BA3 5NW
T: (01373) 812633
F: (01373) 812633

COLLINGBOURNE KINGSTON
Wiltshire
Cum-Bye ♦♦♦
Aughton, Collingbourne
Kingston, Marlborough,
Wiltshire SN8 3RZ
T: (01264) 850256

COLYTON
Devon
Smallicombe Farm ♦♦♦♦
Northleigh, Colyton, Devon
EX24 6BU
T: (01404) 831310
F: (01404) 831431
E: maggie_todd@yahoo.com
I: www.smallicombe.com

COMBE DOWN
Bath and North East Somerset
Beech Wood ♦♦♦♦
Beech Wood, Shaft Road, Combe
Down, Bath BA2 7HP
T: (01225) 832242 & 836060
F: (01225) 836060
E: info@beechwoodbath.co.uk
I: www.beechwoodbath.co.uk

The Glade ♦♦♦
Shaft Road, Combe Down, Bath
BA2 7HP
T: (01225) 833172

Grey Lodge ♦♦♦♦
Summer Lane, Combe Down,
Bath, BA2 7EU
T: (01225) 832069
F: (01225) 830161
E: greylodge@freenet.co.uk
I: www.visitus.
co.uk/bath/hotel/grey_lodge.
htm

COMBE FLOREY
Somerset
Redlands ♦♦♦♦
Trebles Holford, Combe Florey,
Taunton, Somerset TA4 3HA
T: (01823) 433159
E: redlandshouse@hotmail.com
I: www.escapetothecountry.
co.uk

COMBE MARTIN
Devon
Channel Vista ♦♦♦
Woodlands, Combe Martin,
Ilfracombe, Devon EX34 0AT
T: (01271) 883514
E: channelvista@freeuk.com
I: www.smoothhound.
co.uk/hotels/channelvista.html

The London Inn ♦♦
Lynton Road, Combe Martin,
Ilfracombe, Devon EX34 0NA
T: (01271) 883409
F: (01271) 883409

Saffron House Hotel ♦♦♦
King Street, Combe Martin,
Ilfracombe, Devon EX34 0BX
T: (01271) 883521

COMBPYNE
Devon
1 Granary Cottage ♦♦♦♦
Combpyne, Axminster, Devon
EX13 8SX
T: (01297) 442856

COMPTON BASSETT
Wiltshire
The White Horse ♦♦♦♦
Compton Bassett, Calne,
Wiltshire SN11 8RG
T: (01249) 813118
F: (01249) 811595

COMPTON DUNDON
Somerset
Rickham House ♦♦♦♦
Compton Dundon, Somerton,
Somerset TA11 6QA
T: (01458) 445056
F: (01458) 445056
E: rickham.house@talk21.com

COOMBE BISSETT
Wiltshire
Evening Hill ♦♦♦
Blandford Road, Coombe Bissett,
Salisbury SP5 4LH
T: (01722) 718561 &
07730 034039
E: henrys@tesco.net
I: www.smoothhound.
co.uk/hotels/eveninghillhtml

CORSHAM
Wiltshire
Boyds Farm ♦♦♦♦♦
Gastard, Corsham, Wiltshire
SN13 9PT
T: (01249) 713146
F: (01249) 713146
E: boydsfarmdorothy@aol.com
I: www.webscape.
co.uk/farmaccom/england/wilts/
index.nt

Fairfield House
Rating Applied For
44 High Street, Corsham,
Wiltshire SN13 0HF
T: (01249) 713121 & 713121

Heatherly Cottage ♦♦♦♦
Ladbrook Lane, Gastard,
Corsham, Wiltshire SN13 9PE
T: (01249) 701402
F: (01249) 701412
E: ladbrook1@aol.com
I: www.smoothhound.
co.uk/hotels/heather3.html

Pickwick Lodge Farm ♦♦♦♦
Guyers Lane, Corsham, Wiltshire
SN13 0PS
T: (01249) 712207 &
07710 287263
F: (01249) 701904
E: pickwickfarm.freeserve.co.uk
I: www.smoothand.
co.uk/hotels/pickworld.html

Saltbox Farm ♦♦♦
Drewetts Mill, Box, Corsham,
Wiltshire SN13 8PT
T: (01225) 742608
F: (01225) 742608

CORSLEY
Wiltshire
Sturford Mead ♦♦♦♦
Corsley, Warminster, Wiltshire
BA12 7QT
T: (01373) 832039
F: (01373) 832104
E: bradshaw@sturford.co.uk
I: www.sturford.co.uk

CORTON
Wiltshire
The Dove Inn ♦♦♦♦
Corton, Warminster, Wiltshire
BA12 0SZ
T: (01985) 850109
F: (01985) 851041
E: info@thedove.co.uk
I: www.thedove.co.uk

COSSINGTON
Somerset
Brookhayes Farm ♦♦♦♦
Bell Lane, Cossington,
Bridgwater, Somerset TA7 8LR
T: (01278) 722559
F: (01278) 722559

COTHAM
Bristol
Farle Villa ♦♦♦
45 Sydenham Hill, Cotham,
Bristol BS6 5SL
T: (0117) 9420809
F: (0117) 9420809
E: joysyd@farleyvilla.fsnet.co.uk

COVERACK
Cornwall
The Paris Hotel ♦♦♦
Coverack, Helston, Cornwall
TR12 6SX
T: (01326) 280258
F: (01326) 280774

Tregwenyn ♦♦♦
School Hill, Coverack, Helston,
Cornwall TR12 6SA
T: (01326) 280774
F: (01326) 280774

CRANMORE
Somerset
Lynfield ♦♦♦
Frome Road, Cranmore, Shepton
Mallet, Somerset BA4 4QQ
T: (01749) 880600
E: rsgildo@aol.com
I: www.shepton-mallet.co.uk

CRANTOCK
Cornwall
Highfield Lodge Hotel ♦♦♦
Halwyn Road, Crantock,
Newquay, Cornwall TR8 5TR
T: (01637) 830744
E: highfieldlodge@tinyworld.
co.uk

Tregenna House ♦♦♦♦
West Pentire Road, Crantock,
Newquay, Cornwall TR8 5RZ
T: (01637) 830222
F: (01637) 831267
E: dench@cix.compulink.co.uk

Treringey Farm
Rating Applied For
Crantock, Newquay, Cornwall
TR8 5EN
T: (01637) 830265

CREDITON
Devon
Great Park Farm ♦♦
Crediton, Devon EX17 3PR
T: (01363) 772050

CREECH ST MICHAEL
Somerset
Curvalion Villa ♦♦♦♦
Curvalion Road, Creech St
Michael, Taunton, Somerset
TA3 5QQ
T: (01823) 444630 &
07711 569589
F: (01823) 444629
E: curvalion_villa@btinternet.
com

CREWKERNE
Somerset
The George Hotel & Courtyard
Restaurant ♦♦♦
Market Square, Crewkerne,
Somerset TA18 7LP
T: (01460) 73650
F: (01460) 72974
E: eddie@thegeorgehotel.
saqehost.co.uk
I: www.thegeorgehotel.saganet.
co.uk

The Manor Arms ◆◆◆
North Perrott, Crewkerne,
Somerset TA18 7SG
T: (01460) 72901
F: (01460) 72901
E: info@manorarmshotel.co.uk
I: www.manorarmshotel.co.uk

CRICKLADE
Wiltshire

Waterhay Farm ◆◆◆
Leigh, Leigh, Swindon SN6 6QY
T: (01285) 861253

The White Lion ◆◆
50 High Street, Cricklade,
Swindon SN6 6DA
T: (01793) 750443
E: info@whitelion-inn.com
I: www.whitelion-inn.com

CROCKERTON
Wiltshire

Stoneyside ◆◆◆
Potters Hill, Crockerton,
Warminster, Wiltshire BA12 8AS
T: (01985) 218149

CROWCOMBE
Somerset

Hooks House ◆◆◆◆
Crowcombe, Taunton, Somerset
TA4 4AE
T: (01984) 618691

CROWCOMBE HEATHFIELD
Somerset

Meadowsweet ◆◆◆◆
3 Bakers Orchard, Crowcombe
Heathfield, Taunton, Somerset
TA4 4PA
T: (01984) 618305
E: ajcorwood@lineone.net

CROYDE
Devon

Combas Farm ◆◆◆
Putsborough, Croyde, Braunton,
Devon EX33 1PH
T: (01271) 890398

**Denham Farm and Country
House** ◆◆◆◆
North Buckland, Braunton,
Devon EX33 1HY
T: (01271) 890297
F: (01271) 890297

CROYDE BAY
Devon

West Winds ◆◆◆◆
Moor Lane, Croyde Bay,
Braunton, Devon EX33 1PA
T: (01271) 890489
F: (01271) 890489
E: chris@croydewestwinds.
freeserve.co.uk
I: www.westwindsguesthouse.
co.uk

CULLOMPTON
Devon

Upton House ◆◆◆◆◆
Cullompton, Devon EX15 1RA
T: (01884) 33097
F: (01884) 33097

Weir Mill Farm ◆◆◆◆
Jaycroft, Willand, Cullompton,
Devon EX15 2RE
T: (01884) 820803
F: (01884) 820973
E: parish@weirmillfarm.
freeserve.co.uk
I: www.smoothound.
co.uk/hotels/weirmill.html

Wishay ◆◆◆
Trinity, Cullompton, Devon
EX15 1PE
T: (01884) 33223
F: (01884) 33223
E: wishaytrinity@hotmail.com

CURRY RIVEL
Somerset

Orchard Cottage ◆◆◆◆
Townsend, Curry Rivel, Langport,
Somerset TA10 0HT
T: (01458) 251511
F: (01458) 251511

CURY
Cornwall

Cobblers Cottage ◆◆◆◆◆
Nantithet, Cury, Helston,
Cornwall TR12 7RB
T: (01326) 241342
F: (01326) 241342

DARTMOUTH
Devon

Barrington House ◆◆◆◆
Mount Boone, Dartmouth,
Devon TQ6 9HZ
T: (01803) 835545 &
07968 080410
F: (01803) 835545
E: enquiries@barrington-house.
com
I: www.barrington-house.com

Campbells ◆◆◆◆◆
5 Mount Boone, Dartmouth,
Devon TQ6 9PB
T: (01803) 833438
F: (01803) 833438
I: www.webmachine.
co.uk/campbells

Nonsuch House ◆◆◆◆◆
Church Hill, Kingswear,
Dartmouth, Devon TQ6 0BX
T: (01803) 752829 & 752297
F: (01803) 752357
E: enquiries@nonsuch-house.
co.uk
I: www.nonsuch-house.co.uk

Sunnybanks ◆◆◆
1 Vicarage Hill, Dartmouth,
Devon TQ6 9EW
T: (01803) 832766
F: (01803) 832766
E: sue@sunnybanks.com
I: www.sunnybanks.com

**Woodside Cottage Bed &
Breakfast** ◆◆◆◆
Blackawton, Totnes, Devon
TQ9 7BL
T: (01803) 712375
F: (01803) 712375
E: woodside-cottage@lineone.
net
I: www.
woodside-cottage-devon.co.uk

DAUNTSEY
Wiltshire

Olivemead Farm ◆◆◆
Olivemead Lane, Dauntsey,
Chippenham, Wiltshire
SN15 4JQ
T: (01666) 510205 &
07974 815305
F: (01666) 510205
E: olivemead@farming.co.uk

DAWLISH
Devon

Radfords Country Hotel
◆◆◆◆
Lower Dawlish Water, Dawlish,
Devon EX7 0QN
T: (01626) 863322
F: (01626) 888515
E: radfords@eclipse.co.uk
I: www.eclipse.co.uk/radfords

Smallacombe Farm ◆◆◆
Dawlish, Devon EX7 0PS
T: (01626) 862536

DENBURY
Devon

Tornewton ◆◆◆◆
Denbury, Newton Abbot, Devon
TQ12 6EF
T: (01803) 812257
F: (01803) 812257

DEVIZES
Wiltshire

Asta ◆◆
66 Downlands Road, Devizes,
Wiltshire SN10 5EF
T: (01380) 722546

Blounts Court Farm ◆◆◆◆◆
Coxhill Lane, Potterne, Devizes,
Wiltshire SN10 5PH
T: (01380) 727180
E: blountscourtfarm@tinyworld.
co.uk

The Chestnuts ◆◆◆◆
Potterne Road, Devizes,
Wiltshire SN10 5DD
T: (01380) 724532

Eastcott Manor ◆◆◆
Easterton, Devizes, Wiltshire
SN10 4PL
T: (01380) 813313

Eastleigh House ◆◆◆◆
3 Eastleigh Road, Devizes,
Wiltshire SN10 3EE
T: (01380) 726918
F: (01380) 726918

The Gate House ◆◆◆
Wick Lane, Devizes, Wiltshire
SN10 5DW
T: (01380) 725283 &
07889 637047
F: (01380) 722382

Heathcote House ◆◆◆
The Green, Devizes, Wiltshire
SN10 5AA
T: (01380) 725080 &
(01672) 515311
F: (01672) 515312

Littleton Lodge ◆◆◆◆
Littleton Panell (A360), West
Lavington, Devizes, Wiltshire
SN10 4ES
T: (01380) 813131
F: (01380) 816969
E: stay@littletonlodge.co.uk
I: www.littletonlodge.co.uk

Longwater ◆◆◆
Lower Road, Erlestoke, Devizes,
Wiltshire SN10 5UE
T: (01380) 830095
F: (01380) 830095
E: pam.hampton@talk21.com
⌖

Melbourne House
Rating Applied For
Melbourne Place, Devizes,
Wiltshire SN10 2AB
T: (01380) 720555
F: (01380) 720777
E: accom@melbhouse.co.uk
I: www.melbhouse.co.uk

The Old Manor ◆◆◆◆
Chirton, Devizes, Wiltshire
SN10 3QS
T: (01380) 840777
F: (01380) 840927

DINTON
Wiltshire

Morris' Farm House ◆◆◆
Baverstock, Dinton, Salisbury
SP3 5EL
T: (01722) 716874
F: (01722) 716874
E: marriott@dircon.co.uk
I: www.kgp-publishing.co.uk

The Penruddocke Arms ◆◆◆
Hindon Road, Dinton, Salisbury
SP3 5EL
T: (01722) 716253
F: (01722) 716253

DITTISHAM
Devon

The Red Lion Inn ◆◆◆
Dittisham, Dartmouth, Devon
TQ6 0ES
T: (01803) 722235

DODDISCOMBSLEIGH
Devon

Whitemoor Farm ◆
Doddiscombsleigh, Exeter
EX6 7PU
T: (01647) 252423
E: blaceystaffyrescue@easicom.
com

DORCHESTER
Dorset

The Beagles ◆◆◆
37 London Road, Dorchester,
Dorset DT1 1NF
T: (01305) 267338
E: joycegraham@talk21.com

The Casterbridge Hotel
◆◆◆◆◆
49 High East Street, Dorchester,
Dorset DT1 1HU
T: (01305) 264043
F: (01305) 260884
E: reception@casterbridgehotel.
co.uk
I: www.casterbridgehotel.co.uk

Churchview Guest House ◆◆◆
Winterbourne Abbas,
Dorchester, Dorset DT2 9LS
T: (01305) 889296
F: (01305) 889296
E: stay@churchview.co.uk
I: www.churchview.co.uk

Higher Came Farmhouse
◆◆◆◆
Higher Came, Dorchester, Dorset
DT2 8NR
T: (01305) 268908
F: (01305) 268908
E: highercame@eurolink.ltd.net
I: http://www.smoothound.
co.uk/hotels/highercame.html

Hillfort View ◆◆
10 Hillfort Close, Dorchester,
Dorset DT1 2QT
T: (01305) 268476

Joan's Bed and Breakfast ◆◆◆
119 Bridport Road, Dorchester,
Dorset DT1 2NH
T: (01305) 267145 &
0774 8947610
F: (01305) 267145
E: b_and_b@joancox.freeserve.
co.uk

Junction Hotel Dorchester
◆◆◆◆
42 Great Western Road,
Dorchester, Dorset DT1 1UF
T: (01305) 263094
F: (01305) 751949
I: www.stayhereuk.com

5 Little Britain Farmhouse
◆◆◆
Fordington, Dorchester, Dorset
DT1 1NN
T: (01305) 263431

Maiden Castle Farm ◆◆◆◆
Dorchester, Dorset DT2 9PR
T: (01305) 262356
F: (01305) 251085
E: maidencastlefarm@euphony.
net

The Old Manor ◆◆◆◆◆
Kingston Maurward, Dorchester,
Dorset DT2 8PX
T: (01305) 261110
F: (01305) 263734
E: thomson@
kingston-maurward.co.uk
I: www.kingston-maurward.
co.uk

The Old Rectory ◆◆◆◆
Winterbourne Steepleton,
Dorchester, Dorset DT2 9LG
T: (01305) 889468
F: (01305) 889737
E: trees@eurobell.co.uk
I: www.trees.eurobell.co.uk

Port Bredy ◆◆◆◆
107 Bridport Road, Dorchester,
Dorset DT1 2NH
T: (01305) 265778
F: (01305) 265778
E: B&Benquires@portbredy.
fsnet.co.uk

Sunrise Guest House ◆◆◆
34 London Road, Dorchester,
Dorset DT1 1NE
T: (01305) 262425

Tarkaville ◆◆◆◆
30 Shaston Crescent, Manor
Park, Dorchester, Dorset DT1 2EB
T: (01305) 266253 &
07769 923095
E: tarkaville@lineone.net

Westwood House Hotel
◆◆◆◆
29 High West Street, Dorchester,
Dorset DT1 1UP
T: (01305) 268018
F: (01305) 250282
E: reservations@
westwoodhouse.co.uk
I: www.westwoodhouse.co.uk

The White House ◆◆◆
9 Queens Avenue, Dorchester,
Dorset DT1 2EW
T: (01305) 266714
E: lees.twh@tinyonline.co.uk

Whitfield Farm Cottage
◆◆◆◆
Poundbury Whitfield,
Dorchester, Dorset DT2 9SL
T: (01305) 260233
F: (01305) 260233
E: dc.whitfield@clara.net
I: www.milford.co.uk & www.dc.
whitfield.clara.net

**Yalbury Cottage Hotel and
Restaurant**◆◆◆◆◆
Lower Bockhampton,
Dorchester, Dorset DT2 8PZ
T: (01305) 262382
F: (01305) 266412
E: yalburycottage@aol.com
I: www.smoothhound.
co.uk/hotels/yalbury.html

Yalbury Park ◆◆◆◆
Frome Whitfield Farm, Frome
Whitfield, Dorchester, Dorset
DT2 7SE
T: (01305) 250336
F: (01305) 260070
E: yalburypark@tesco.net

Yellowham Farm ◆◆◆◆
Yellowham Wood, Dorchester,
Dorset DT2 8RW
T: (01305) 262892
F: (01305) 257707
E: b&b@yellowham.freeserve.
co.uk
I: www.yellowham.freeserve.
co.uk

DOWNTON
Wiltshire

The Bull
Rating Applied For
The Headlands, Downton,
Salisbury SP5 3HL
T: (01725) 510374

Witherington Farm ◆◆◆◆◆
Downton, Salisbury SP5 3QT
T: (01722) 710222
F: (01722) 710405
E: fergiewoods@ntlworld.com
I: www.smoothhound.
co.uk/hotels/witherin.html

DREWSTEIGNTON
Devon

The Drewe Arms ◆◆◆◆
Drewsteignton, Exeter EX6 6QN
T: (01647) 281224

DULOE
Cornwall

Carglonnon Farm ◆◆◆◆
Duloe, Liskeard, Cornwall
PL14 4QA
T: (01579) 320210
F: (01579) 320210

DULVERTON
Somerset

Dassels Country House ◆◆◆◆
Dassels, Dulverton, Somerset
TA22 9RZ
T: (01398) 341203
F: (01398) 341561
E: margaret.spencer@dassels.
demon.co.uk

Exton House Hotel ◆◆◆◆
Exton, Dulverton, Somerset
TA22 9JT
T: (01643) 851365
F: (01643) 851213

Highercombe Farm ◆◆◆◆
Dulverton, Somerset TA22 9PT
T: (01398) 323616
F: (01398) 323616
E: abigail@highercombe.demon.
co.uk
I: www.highercombe.demon.
co.uk

Penlee ◆◆◆◆
31 Battleton, Dulverton,
Somerset TA22 9HU
T: (01398) 323798
F: (01398) 323780
E: info@penlee-bnb.co.uk
I: www.penlee-bnb.co.uk

Springfield Farm ◆◆◆◆
Ashwick Lane, Dulverton,
Somerset TA22 9QD
T: (01398) 323722
F: (01398) 323722
E: info@springfieldfarms.
freeserve.co.uk

Town Mills ◆◆◆◆
High Street, Dulverton, Somerset
TA22 9HB
T: (01398) 323124
E: townmills@onetel.net.uk

Winsbere House ◆◆◆
64 Battleton, Dulverton,
Somerset TA22 9HU
T: (01398) 323278

DUNBALL
Somerset

Admiral's Table
Rating Applied For
Bristol Road, Dunball,
Bridgwater, Somerset TA6 4TW
T: (01278) 685671
F: (01278) 685672

DUNSFORD
Devon

Oak Lodge ◆◆◆◆
The Court, Dunsford, Exeter
EX6 7DD
T: (01647) 252829 & 0771 404
0648
E: shirley.hodge@virgin.net
I: www.oaklodge-devon.co.uk

DUNSTER
Somerset

Cobbles Bed & Breakfast
◆◆◆◆
14-16 Church Street, Dunster,
Minehead, Somerset TA24 6SH
T: (01643) 821305
F: (01643) 821305

Conygar House ◆◆◆◆
2A The Ball, Dunster, Minehead,
Somerset TA24 6SD
T: (01643) 821872
F: (01643) 821872
E: bale.dunster@virgin.net
I: homepage.virgin.net/bale.
dunster

Exmoor House Hotel ◆◆◆◆
12 West Street, Dunster,
Minehead, Somerset TA24 6SN
T: (01643) 821268

Higher Orchard ◆◆◆◆
30 St Georges Street, Dunster,
Minehead, Somerset TA24 6RS
T: (01643) 821915

The Old Bakery
Rating Applied For
14 West Street, Dunster,
Minehead, Somerset TA24 6SN
T: (01643) 822123

Spears Cross Hotel ◆◆◆◆
1 West Street, Dunster,
Minehead, Somerset TA24 6SN
T: (01643) 821439
E: mjcapel@aol.com
I: www.smoothhound.
co.uk/hotels/spearsx.html

EAST ALLINGTON
Devon

Higher Torr Farm ◆◆◆
East Allington, Totnes, Devon
TQ9 7QH
T: (01548) 521248
E: helen@hrtorr.freeserve.co.uk

EAST COKER
Somerset

Chesells Guest House ◆◆◆◆
Yeovil Road, East Coker, Yeovil,
Somerset BA22 9HD
T: (01935) 428581

Granary House ◆◆◆◆
East Coker, Yeovil, Somerset
BA22 9LY
T: (01935) 862738
E: granary.house@virgin.net
I: www.granaryhouse.co.uk

EAST LAMBROOK
Somerset

Penryn ◆◆◆◆
Southay, East Lambrook, South
Petherton, Somerset TA13 5HQ
T: (01460) 241358
E: pjandea@tesco.net

EAST TYTHERTON
Wiltshire

Barnbridge ◆◆
East Tytherton, Chippenham,
Wiltshire SN15 4LT
T: (01249) 740280
F: (01249) 651 472
E: bgiffard@aol.com
I: www.smoothhound.
co.uk/hotels/barnbrdg.html

EASTLEIGH
Devon

The Pines at Eastleigh ◆◆◆◆
Old Barnstaple Road, Eastleigh,
Bideford, Devon EX39 4PA
T: (01271) 860561
F: (01271) 861248
E: barry@thepinesateastleigh.
co.uk
I: www.thepinesateastleigh.
co.uk

EASTON ROYAL
Wiltshire

Follets B & B ◆◆◆◆
Easton Royal, Pewsey, Wiltshire
SN9 5LZ
T: (01672) 810619 &
07768 560302
F: (01672) 810619
E: margaretlandless@talk21.
com
I: www.folletsbb.com

EGLOSHAYLE
Cornwall

Goosey Cottage ◆◆◆
Clapper, Egloshayle,
Wadebridge, Cornwall PL27 6HZ
T: (01208) 814997

EVERCREECH
Somerset

The Bell Inn ◆◆◆
Bruton Road, Evercreech,
Shepton Mallet, Somerset
BA4 6HY
T: (01749) 830287

Crossdale Cottage ◆◆◆
Pecking Mill, Evercreech,
Shepton Mallet, Somerset
BA4 6PQ
T: (01749) 830293
F: (01749) 830293

EVERLEIGH
Wiltshire

The Crown Hotel
Rating Applied For
Everleigh, Marlborough,
Wiltshire SN8 3EY
T: (01264) 850229

EVERSHOT
Dorset

The Acorn Inn ◆◆◆◆
Fore Street, Evershot,
Dorchester, Dorset DT2 0JW
T: (01935) 83228
F: (01935) 83707
E: stay@acorn-inn.co.uk
I: www.acorn-inn.co.uk

Westwood Farm B&B ◆◆◆◆
Evershot, Dorchester, Dorset
DT2 0PG
T: (01935) 83351 &
0797 0052785

EXETER
Devon

Bickham Farmhouse ◆◆◆◆
Kenn, Exeter EX6 7XL
T: (01392) 832206 &
07773 456194
F: (01392) 832206

The Grange ◆◆◆◆
Stoke Hill, Exeter, EX4 7JH
T: (01392) 259723
E: dudleythegrange@aol.com

Hayne Barton ◆◆◆◆
Whitestone, Exeter EX4 2JN
T: (01392) 811268

Hayne House ◆◆◆
Silverton, Exeter EX5 4HE
T: (01392) 860725
F: (01392) 860725
E: haynehouse@ukonline.co.uk

Lochinvar ◆◆◆
Shepherds Park Farm,
Woodbury, Exeter EX5 1LA
T: (01395) 232185 & 232284
F: (01395) 232284
E: jglanuil@devon-cc-gov.uk

Park View Hotel ◆◆◆◆
8 Howell Road, Exeter, EX4 4LG
T: (01392) 271772
F: (01392) 253047
E: philbatho@parkviewhotel.
freeserve.co.uk
I: www.parkviewhotel.freeserve.
co.uk

Raffles Hotel ◆◆◆◆
11 Blackall Road, Exeter,
EX4 4HD
T: (01392) 270200
F: (01392) 270200
E: rafflesthl@btinternet.com

Rydon Farm ◆◆◆◆
Woodbury, Exeter EX5 1LB
T: (01395) 232341
F: (01395) 232341
E: sallyglanvill@hotmail.com
I: www.devonbandb.co.uk

St Andrews Hotel ◆◆◆◆
28 Alphington Road, Exeter,
EX2 8HN
T: (01392) 276784
F: (01392) 250249
🏃

Silversprings ◆◆◆◆◆
12 Richmond Road, St Davids,
Exeter, DEVON EX4 4JA
T: (01392) 494040 &
07768 637103
F: 0870 0561615
E: juliet@silversprings.co.uk
I: www.silversprings.co.uk

EXFORD
Somerset

Edgcott House ◆◆◆
Exford, Minehead, Somerset
TA24 7QG
T: (01643) 831495
F: (01643) 831495
E: edgcott@whatsonexmoor.f9.
co.uk
I: www.whatsonexmoor.
co.uk/edgcott

Hunters Moon ◆◆◆
Church Hill, Exford, Minehead,
Somerset TA24 7PP
T: (01643) 831695
F: (01643) 831576

EXMOUTH
Devon

The Imperial ◆◆◆◆
The Esplanade, Exmouth, Devon
EX8 2SW
T: (01395) 274761
F: (01395) 265161
I: www.shearingsholidays.com

Noble House ◆◆◆◆
1 Stevenstone Road, Exmouth,
Devon EX8 2EP
T: (01395) 264803 & 272501

The Swallows ◆◆◆◆
11 Carlton Hill, Exmouth, Devon
EX8 2AJ
T: (01395) 263937
F: (01395) 271040
E: firus@globalnet.co.uk
I: www.smoothhound.
co.uk/hotels/swallows.html

FALMOUTH
Cornwall

Apple Tree Cottage ◆◆◆◆
Laity Moor, Ponsanooth, Truro,
Cornwall TR3 7HR
T: (01872) 865047
E: appletreecottage@talk21.
com
I: www.cornwall-online.co.uk

Chelsea House Hotel ◆◆◆
2 Emslie Road, Falmouth,
Cornwall TR11 4BG
T: (01326) 212230
F: (01326) 814308
E: enquiries@
chelseahousehotel.com
I: www.chelseahousehotel.com

Dolvean Hotel ◆◆◆◆◆
50 Melvill Road, Falmouth,
Cornwall TR11 4DQ
T: (01326) 313658
F: (01326) 313995
E: reservations@dolvean.
freeserve.co.uk
I: www.dolvean.co.uk

Headlands Hotel ◆◆◆
4 Avenue Road, Falmouth,
Cornwall TR11 4AZ
T: (01326) 311141
F: (01356) 311141
E: acoddington@headlands1.
freeserve.co.uk
I: www.cornwall-online.
co.uk/headlands-falmouth

Ivanhoe Guest House ◆◆◆◆
7 Melvill Road, Falmouth,
Cornwall TR11 4AS
T: (01326) 319083
F: (01326) 319083
E: ivanhoe@enterprise.net
I: www.smoothhound.
co.uk/hotels/ivanhoe

The Trevelyan ◆◆
6 Avenue Road, Falmouth,
Cornwall TR11 4AZ
T: (01326) 311545 &
07974 732366
F: (01326) 311545
E: gaunt@tre6.freeserve.co.uk

Wickham Guest House ◆◆◆
21 Gyllyngvase Terrace,
Falmouth, Cornwall TR11 4DL
T: (01326) 311140 &
07977 573575
E: enquiries@wickhamhotel.
freeserve.co.uk

FARMBOROUGH
Bath and North East Somerset

Barrow Vale Farm ◆◆◆◆
Farmborough, Bath BA2 0BL
T: (01761) 470300
F: (01761) 470300
E: cherilynlangley@hotmail.com

FARRINGTON GURNEY
Bath and North East Somerset

Home Farm ◆◆◆◆
Farrington Gurney, Bristol
BS39 6UB
T: (01761) 452287 & 0797 153
8971
F: (01761) 452287
E: tish_andy@tish-andy.
freeserve.co.uk
I: www.firstspace.
com/msn&r/smallpages/
homefarm.htm

FAULKLAND
Somerset

Lime Kiln Farm ◆◆◆◆
Faulkland, Bath BA3 5XE
T: (01373) 834305
E: limekiln@btinternet.com

FENNY BRIDGES
Devon

Skinners Ash Farm ◆◆◆
Fenny Bridges, Honiton, Devon
EX14 3BH
T: (01404) 850231
F: (01404) 850231
I: www. cottageguide.
co.uk/skinnersash

FLEET
Dorset

Highfield ◆◆◆◆
Fleet, Weymouth, Dorset
DT3 4EB
T: (01305) 776822
E: highfield.fleet@lineone.net

FONTHILL BISHOP
Wiltshire

Riverbarn ◆◆◆
Fonthill Bishop, Salisbury
SP3 5SF
T: (01747) 820232
F: (01747) 820232
E: rbarn@globalnet.co.uk

FOVANT
Wiltshire

The Pembroke Arms ◆◆◆
Fovant, Salisbury SP3 5JH
T: (01722) 714201
F: (01722) 714201
E: mwillo@aol.com

FOWEY
Cornwall

Carnethic House Hotel ◆◆◆◆
Lambs Barn, Fowey, Cornwall
PL23 1HQ
T: (01726) 833336
F: (01726) 833296
E: carnethic@btinternet.com
I: www.carnethic.co.uk

The Old Ferry Inn ◆◆◆
Bodinnick, Fowey, Cornwall
PL23 1LX
T: (01726) 870237
F: (01726) 870116

Seahorses Bed and Breakfast
◆◆◆◆
14 Fimbarrus Road, Fowey,
Cornwall PL23 1JJ
T: (01726) 833148
F: (01726) 833148
E: jandh@globalnet.co.uk
I: www.users.globalnet.
co.uk/~jandh/fowey.htm

FRAMPTON
Dorset

The Stables ◆◆◆
Hyde Crook, Frampton,
Dorchester, Dorset DT2 9NW
T: (01300) 320075

FREMINGTON
Devon

Lower Yelland Farm ◆◆◆◆
Fremington, Barnstaple, Devon
EX31 3EN
T: (01271) 860101 &
07803 933642
F: (01271) 860101
E: pday@loweryellandfarm.
co.uk
I: www.loweryellandfarm.co.uk

FRESHFORD
Bath and North East Somerset

Longacre ◆◆◆
17 Staples Hill, Freshford, Bath
BA3 6EL
T: (01225) 723254
F: (01225) 723254

FROME
Somerset

Abergele Guest House ◆◆◆◆
2 Fromefield, Frome, Somerset
BA11 2HA
T: (01373) 463998

Fourwinds Guest House
◆◆◆◆
19 Bath Road, Frome, Somerset
BA11 2HJ
T: (01373) 462618
F: (01373) 453029
🏃

The Full Moon at Rudge
◆◆◆◆
Rudge, Frome, Somerset
BA11 2QF
T: (01373) 830936
F: (01373) 831366
E: fullmoon@lineone.net
I: www.thefullmoon.co.uk

Kozy-Glen ◆◆◆◆
Rooks Lane, Berkley Marsh,
Frome, Somerset BA11 5JD
T: (01373) 464767

North Parade House ◆◆◆◆
7 North Parade, Frome,
Somerset BA11 1AT
T: (01373) 474249
F: (01373) 474024
E: annie@nphouse.fsnet.co.uk

Number Four Rating Applied For
Catherine Street, Frome,
Somerset BA11 1DA
T: (01373) 455690
F: (01373) 455992

Stonewall Manor ♦♦♦
Culver Hill, Frome, Somerset
BA11 4AS
T: (01373) 462131

The Sun Inn ♦♦♦
6 Catherine Street, Frome,
Somerset BA11 1DA
T: (01373) 471913

Wadbury House ♦♦♦
Mells, Frome, Somerset
BA11 3PA
T: (01373) 812359
E: sbrinkmann@btinternet.com

GALMPTON
Devon

Rose Cottage ♦♦♦♦
Galmpton, Hope Cove,
Kingsbridge, Devon TQ7 3EU
T: (01548) 561953
F: (01548) 561953
I: www.rosecottagesalcombe.
co.uk

GITTISHAM
Devon

Catshayes Farm ♦♦
Gittisham, Honiton, Devon
EX14 3AE
T: (01404) 850302 & 850267
F: (01404) 850302
E: christine@bapt.org.uk
I: www.devonfarms.co.uk

GLASTONBURY
Somerset

Abbey Garth ♦♦♦
5 Bere Lane, Glastonbury,
Somerset BA6 8BD
T: (01458) 832675
E: ann.matkins@freenet.co.uk
I: www.glastonbury.co.uk.
accommodation

Avalon Barn ♦♦♦♦
Lower Godney, Wells, Somerset
BA5 1RZ
T: (01458) 835005
F: (01458) 835636
E: william.n@virgin.net

The Barn ♦♦♦
84b Bove Town, Glastonbury,
Somerset BA6 8JG
T: (01458) 832991

The Bolthole ♦♦♦
32 Chilkwell Street, Glastonbury,
Somerset BA6 8DA
T: (01458) 832800

46 Bove Town ♦♦♦
Glastonbury, Somerset BA6 8JE
T: (01458) 833684

Coig Deug ♦♦
15 Helyar Close, Glastonbury,
Somerset BA6 9LQ
T: (01458) 835945 &
07773 145395
E: kath@coigdeug.freeserve.
co.uk
I: www.coigdeug.freeserve.co.uk

Divine Light Holiday Flat ♦♦♦
16a Magdalene Street,
Glastonbury, Somerset BA6 9EH
T: (01458) 035909
E: glastonburyrose@lineone.net

Hawthornes Hotel and Restaurant ♦♦
8-12 Northload Street,
Glastonbury, Somerset BA6 9JJ
T: (01458) 831255
F: (01458) 831255
E: walker@hawthorneshotel.
fsnet.co.uk

The Heart Centred Bed & Breakfast with Morning Meditation ♦♦♦
24 Bove Town, Glastonbury,
Somerset BA6 8JE
T: (01458) 833467
I: www.glastonbury.
co.uk/users/mitchell-a.html

46a High Street ♦♦
Glastonbury, Somerset BA6 9DX
T: (01458) 832214

Highlands Guest House ♦♦♦♦
21 Rowley Road, Glastonbury,
Somerset BA6 8HU
T: (01458) 834587
F: (01458) 834587
E: highlands@eclipse.co.uk
I: www.glastonbury.co.uk

The Lightship ♦♦♦
82 Bove Town, Glastonbury,
Somerset BA6 8JG
T: (01458) 833698
E: roselightship@
netscapeonline.co.uk

Little Orchard ♦♦♦
Ashwell Lane, Glastonbury,
Somerset BA6 8BG
T: (01458) 831620
E: the.littleorchard@lineone.net
I: www.smoothhound.
co.uk/hotels/orchard.html

Mafeking ♦♦♦♦
67 Wells Road, Glastonbury,
Somerset BA6 9BY
T: (01458) 833379
E: mafeking@wellsroad.
freeserve.co.uk

Meadow Barn ♦♦♦
Middlewick Farm, Wick Lane,
Glastonbury, Somerset BA6 8JW
T: (01458) 832351
F: (01458) 832351
I: www.smoothhound.
co.uk/hotels/middlewi.html

Meare Manor ♦♦♦♦
60 St Marys Road, Meare,
Glastonbury, Somerset BA6 9SR
T: (01458) 860449
F: (01458) 860449
E: info@mearemanor.co.uk
I: www.mearemanor.co.uk

Melrose ♦♦♦
Coursing Batch, Glastonbury,
Somerset BA6 8BH
T: (01458) 834706 &
07973 108646
I: www.
nick&sarahmelroseglastonbury.
uk

Merryall House ♦♦♦
50 Roman Way, Glastonbury,
Somerset BA6 8AD
T: (01458) 834511 & 830208
E: francidev@hotmail.com
I: www.merriyallhouse.com

Number Three ♦♦♦♦♦
3 Magdalene Street,
Glastonbury, Somerset BA6 9EW
T: (01458) 832129
F: (01458) 834227
E: info@numberthree.co.uk
I: www.numberthree.co.uk

The Old Bakery ♦♦♦
84A Bove Town, Glastonbury,
Somerset BA6 8JG
T: (01458) 833400
E: oldbakery@talk21.com

1 Park Terrace ♦♦♦
Street Road, Glastonbury,
Somerset BA6 9EA
T: (01458) 835845 & 833296
F: (01458) 833296
E: info@no1parkterrace.co.uk
I: www.no1parkterrace.co.uk

Perks Croft ♦♦♦
95 The Roman Way,
Glastonbury, Somerset BA6 8AD
T: (01458) 832326

Pilgrims ♦♦♦
12/13 Norbins Road,
Glastonbury, Somerset BA6 9JE
T: (01458) 834650 & 834606
E: pbrown0848@aol.com
I: www.glastonbury.
co.uk/users/brown-alison.html

Pippin ♦♦♦
4 Ridgeway Gardens,
Glastonbury, Somerset BA6 8ER
T: (01458) 834262
E: daphneslater@talk21.com
I: www.smoothhound.
co.uk/hotels/pippin.html

15 Saint Brides Close ♦♦
Glastonbury, Somerset BA6 9JU
T: (01458) 835909

Sheffern ♦♦♦
38 Hamlyn Road, Glastonbury,
Somerset BA6 8HT
T: (01458) 832587

Tordown Guest House ♦♦♦
5 Ashwell Lane, Glastonbury,
Somerset BA6 8BG
T: (01458) 832287
F: (01458) 831100
E: torangel@aol.com
I: www.tordown.com

Villa Khiron ♦♦♦♦
12 Hexton Road, Glastonbury,
Somerset BA6 8HL
T: (01458) 830321 & 830151
F: (01458) 830151
E: villakhiron@bigfoot.com
I: www.villakhiron.freeserve.
co.uk

Wearyall Hill House ♦♦♦♦♦
78 The Roman Way,
Glastonbury, Somerset BA6 8AD
T: (01458) 835510 &
07976 978060
E: enquiries@wearyallhillhouse.
co.uk
I: www.wearyallhillhouse.co.uk

The Who'd A Thought It Inn ♦♦♦
17 Northload Street,
Glastonbury, Somerset BA6 9JJ
T: (01458) 834460
F: (01458) 831039
E: reservations@
whodathoughtit.co.uk
I: www.reservations.
whodathoughtit.co.uk

GOATHURST
Somerset

Willowburn ♦♦♦
Goathurst, Bridgwater, Somerset
TA5 2DJ
T: (01278) 662398
F: (01278) 662398
E: scarborough@willowburn.
fsnet.co.uk

GODNEY
Somerset

Double-Gate Farm ♦♦♦♦
Godney, Wells, Somerset
BA5 1RX
T: (01458) 832217
F: (01458) 835612
E: hilary@doublegate.demon.
co.uk
I: www.doublegatefarm.com
&

GOLDSITHNEY
Cornwall

Penleen ♦♦♦
South Road, Goldsithney,
Penzance, Cornwall TR20 9LF
T: (01736) 710633
F: (01736) 710633
E: jimblain@penleen.fsbusiness.
co.uk

GOONHAVERN
Cornwall

September Lodge ♦♦♦
Wheal Hope, Goonhavern, Truro,
Cornwall TR4 9QJ
T: (01872) 571435
F: (01872) 571435
E: jc.septlodge@virgin.net

GRAMPOUND
Cornwall

Perran House ♦♦♦
Fore Street, Grampound, Truro,
Cornwall TR2 4RS
T: (01726) 882066
F: (01726) 882936

GREAT BEDWYN
Wiltshire

The Cross Keys Inn ♦♦♦
High Street, Great Bedwyn,
Marlborough, Wiltshire
SN8 3NU
T: (01672) 870678

GREAT DURNFORD
Wiltshire

Meadow Croft ♦♦♦♦
Great Durnford, Salisbury
SP4 6AY
T: (01722) 782643
F: 07714 158791

GREENHAM
Somerset

The Granary ♦♦♦♦
Bishops Barton, Greenham,
Wellington, Somerset TA21 0JJ
T: (01823) 672969
E: bishopsbarton@talk21.com

Greenham Hall ♦♦
Greenham, Wellington,
Somerset TA21 0JJ
T: (01823) 672603
F: (01823) 672307
E: peterjayre@cs.com

GREINTON
Somerset
The Greylake Inn
Rating Applied For
Greinton, Bridgwater, Somerset
TA7 9BP
T: (01458) 210383
F: (01458) 210383
E: scottstavely@freeuk.com

GRITTLETON
Wiltshire
Garden House ♦♦♦♦
Grittleton, Chippenham,
Wiltshire SN14 6AJ
T: (01249) 782507
F: (01249) 782507

The Neeld Arms Inn ♦♦♦
The Street, Grittleton,
Chippenham, Wiltshire
SN14 6AP
T: (01249) 782470
F: (01249) 782470
E: neeldarms@genie.co.uk
I: www.neeldarms.co.uk

GULWORTHY
Devon
Colcharton Farm ♦♦♦♦
Gulworthy, Tavistock, Devon
PL19 8HU
T: (01822) 616435 &
07970 863974
F: (01822) 616435

Hele Farm ♦♦♦
Gulworthy, Tavistock, Devon
PL19 8PA
T: (01822) 833084
F: (01822) 833084

GURNEY SLADE
Somerset
The Old Mendip Coaching Inn
♦♦♦
Gurney Slade, Bath BA3 4UU
T: (01749) 841234
E: floella@tinyonline.co.uk

HALSE
Somerset
New Inn ♦♦♦
Halse, Taunton, Somerset
TA4 3AF
T: (01823) 432352

HALSTOCK
Dorset
Quiet Woman House
Rating Applied For
Halstock, Yeovil, Somerset
BA22 9RX
T: (01935) 891218
E: quietwomanhouse@ukonline.
co.uk

HALWELL
Devon
Orchard House ♦♦♦♦♦
Horner, Halwell, Totnes, Devon
TQ9 7LB
T: (01548) 821448
I: www.orchard-house-halwell.
co.uk

HAM
Wiltshire
Crown & Anchor ♦♦♦
Ham, Marlborough, Wiltshire
SN8 3RB
T: (01488) 668242

HARLYN BAY
Cornwall
The Harlyn Inn ♦♦♦
Harlyn Bay, Padstow, Cornwall
PL28 8SB
T: (01841) 520207
F: (01841) 520722
E: harlyninn@aol.com

Polmark Hotel ♦♦♦
Harlyn Bay, Padstow, Cornwall
PL28 8SB
T: (01841) 520206
F: (01841) 520206
E: dplum9705@aol.com

HARTLAKE
Somerset
Hartlake Farm ♦♦♦♦
Hartlake, Glastonbury, Somerset
BA6 9AB
T: (01458) 835406
F: (01749) 670373
I: www.hartlakebandb.co.uk

HARTLAND
Devon
Elmscott Farm ♦♦♦♦
Hartland, Bideford, Devon
EX39 6ES
T: (01237) 441276
F: (01237) 441076

Golden Park ♦♦♦♦♦
Hartland, Bideford, Devon
EX39 6EP
T: (01237) 441254

Hartland Quay Hotel ♦♦♦
Hartland, Bideford, Devon
EX39 6DU
T: (01237) 441218
F: (01237) 441371

Trutrese ♦♦♦
Harton Cross, Hartland,
Bideford, Devon EX39 6AE
T: (01237) 441274

HATHERLEIGH
Devon
The George ♦♦♦
Market Street, Hatherleigh,
Okehampton, Devon EX20 3JN
T: (01837) 810454
F: (01837) 810901
E: jfpozzetto@yahoo.co.uk

Orchard House ♦♦♦♦
Hatherleigh, Okehampton,
Devon EX20 3LE
T: (01837) 810911
E: jden@euphony.net

Seldon Farm ♦♦
Monkokehampton, Winkleigh,
Devon EX19 8RY
T: (01837) 810312

HAYLE
Cornwall
Penellen Hotel ♦♦♦
Riviere Towans, Hayle, Cornwall
TR27 5AF
T: (01736) 753777 & 753819
F: (01736) 753777

HELSTON
Cornwall
Longstone Farm ♦♦♦
Coverack Bridges, Trenear,
Helston, Cornwall TR13 0HG
T: (01326) 572483
F: (01326) 572483
E: longstonehse@lineone.net
I: www.longstonehse.co.uk

Lyndale Guest House ♦♦♦
4 Greenbank, Meneage Road,
Helston, Cornwall TR13 8JA
T: (01326) 561082
F: (01326) 565813
E: enquiries@lyndale1.freeserve.
co.uk
I: www.lyndale1.freeserve.co.uk

Mandeley Guest House ♦♦♦
Clodgey Lane, Helston, Cornwall
TR13 8PJ
T: (01326) 572550

Strathallan ♦♦♦♦
6 Monument Road, Helston,
Cornwall TR13 8HF
T: (01326) 573683
F: (01326) 565777
E: strathallan@compuserve.com
I: www.connexions.
co.uk/strathallan

HENLADE
Somerset
Barn Close Nurseries ♦♦♦
Henlade, Taunton, Somerset
TA3 5DH
T: (01823) 443507

HENSTRIDGE
Somerset
Fountain Inn Motel ♦♦
High Street, Henstridge,
Templecombe, Somerset
BA8 0RA
T: (01963) 362722
F: (01963) 362722
I: www.fountaininn.fsnet.co.uk
🅰

Quiet Corner Farm ♦♦♦♦
Henstridge, Templecombe,
Somerset BA8 0RA
T: (01963) 363045
F: (01963) 363045
E: quietcorner.thompson@
virgin.net

HEXWORTHY
Devon
The Forest Inn ♦♦♦♦
Hexworthy, Yelverton, Devon
PL20 6SD
T: (01364) 631211
F: (01364) 631515
E: forestinn@hotmail.com

HEYTESBURY
Wiltshire
Red Lion Hotel ♦♦
42a High Street, Heytesbury,
Warminster, Wiltshire BA12 0EA
T: (01985) 840315

HIGHBRIDGE
Somerset
46 Church Street ♦♦
Highbridge, Somerset TA9 3AQ
T: (01278) 788365

Knoll Farm
Rating Applied For
Jarvis Lane, Highbridge,
Somerset TA9 4HS
T: (01278) 760227

Sandacre ♦♦
75 Old Burnham Road,
Highbridge, Somerset TA9 3JG
T: (01278) 781221
F: (01278) 781221

HIGHWORTH
Wiltshire
Roves Farm ♦♦♦
Sevenhampton, Highworth,
Swindon, Wiltshire SN6 7QG
T: (01793) 763939
F: (01793) 763939
E: jb@rovesfarm.freeserve.co.uk
I: www.rovesfarm.co.uk

HILMARTON
Wiltshire
Burfoots ♦♦♦♦
The Close, Hilmarton, Calne,
Wiltshire SN11 8TH
T: (01249) 760492
F: (01249) 760609
E: anncooke@burfoots.co.uk
I: www.burfoots.co.uk

HOLBETON
Devon
Bugle Rocks ♦♦♦♦
The Old School, Battisborough,
Holbeton, Plymouth PL8 1JX
T: (01752) 830422
F: (01752) 830558
E: buglerocks@hotmail.com

HOLNE
Devon
Mill Leat Farm ♦♦♦
Holne, Newton Abbot, Devon
TQ13 7RZ
T: (01364) 631283
F: (01364) 631283

HOLNEST
Dorset
Common Gate Farm ♦♦♦
Holnest, Sherborne, Dorset
DT9 6HY
T: (01963) 210411
F: (01963) 210411

HOLSWORTHY
Devon
Bason Farm ♦♦♦♦
Bradford, Holsworthy, Devon
EX22 7AW
T: (01409) 281277
E: info@basonfarmholidays.
co.uk
I: www.basonfarmholidays.co.uk

Highbre Crest
Rating Applied For
Whitstone, Holsworthy, Devon
EX22 6UF
T: (01288) 341002

**Leworthy Farmhouse Bed &
Breakfast** ♦♦♦♦
Leworthy Farmhouse, Lower
Leworthy, Pyworthy,
Holsworthy, Devon EX22 6SJ
T: (01409) 259469

HONITON
Devon
Barn Park Farm
Rating Applied For
Stockland Hill, Honiton, Devon
EX14 9JA
T: 0800 3282605
F: (01404) 861297
I: www.stockland.cx

The Bliss Centre ♦♦♦♦
Snodwell Farm, Stockland Hill,
Honiton, Devon EX14 9HZ
T: (01404) 861696
F: (01404) 861696
E: blisscentre@hotmail.com

Fairmile Inn ◆◆◆◆
Fairmile, Ottery St Mary, Devon
EX11 1LP
T: (01404) 812827
F: (01404) 815806

Lelamarie ◆◆◆
Awliscombe, Honiton, Devon
EX14 3PP
T: (01404) 44646 & 42308
F: (01404) 42131

The New Dolphin Hotel ◆◆◆
115 High Street, Honiton, Devon
EX14 8LS
T: (01404) 42377
F: (01404) 47662

The Old Vicarage ◆◆◆◆
Yarcombe, Honiton, Devon
EX14 9BD
T: (01404) 861594
F: (01404) 861594
E: jonannstockwell@aol.com
I: members.aol.
com/Jonannstockwell/

Wessington Farm ◆◆◆◆
Awliscombe, Honiton, Devon
EX14 3NU
T: (01404) 42280
F: (01404) 45271
E: b&b@eastdevon.com
I: www.eastdevon.
com/bedandbreakfast

HORNINGSHAM
Wiltshire

Mill Farm ◆◆◆◆
Horningsham, Warminster,
Wiltshire BA12 7LL
T: (01985) 844333
E: millfarm_horningsham@
yahoo.com

Woodlands ◆◆◆
White Street, Horningsham,
Warminster, Wiltshire BA12 7LH
T: (01985) 844335
F: (01985) 844335
E: wheelerfam@talk21.com

HORSINGTON
Somerset

Half Moon Inn ◆◆◆
Horsington, Templecombe,
Somerset BA8 0EF
T: (01963) 370140
F: (01963) 371450
E: halfmoon@horsington.co.uk
I: www.horsington.co.uk

HORTON
Somerset

Lympool House ◆◆◆
Forest Mill Lane, Horton,
Ilminster, Somerset TA19 9QU
T: (01460) 57924

Partacre ◆◆
Horton, Devizes, Wiltshire
SN10 3NB
T: (01380) 860261

HUISH EPISCOPI
Somerset

Spring View ◆◆◆
Wagg Drove, Huish Episcopi,
Langport, Somerset TA10 9ER
T: (01458) 251215

Wagg Bridge Cottage ◆◆◆◆
Ducks Hill, Huish Episcopi,
Langport, Somerset TA10 9EN
T: (01458) 251488 &
07939 374234
F: 0820 4055 2077
E: sandy@waggbridgecottage.
freeserve.co.uk
I: www.waggbridgecottage.co.uk

HULLAVINGTON
Wiltshire

Bradfield Manor
Rating Applied For
Hullavington, Chippenham,
Wiltshire SN14 6EU
T: (01666) 838000
F: (01666) 838200
E: enquiries@bradfieldmanor.
co.uk
I: www.bradfieldmanor.co.uk

IDDESLEIGH
Devon

Parsonage Farm ◆◆◆◆
Iddesleigh, Winkleigh, Devon
EX19 8SN
T: (01837) 810318

IFORD
Wiltshire

Dog Kennel Farm Cottage ◆◆
Iford, Bradford-on-Avon,
Wiltshire BA15 2BB
T: (01225) 723533

ILCHESTER
Somerset

Liongate House ◆◆◆
Northover, Ilchester, Yeovil,
Somerset BA22 8NG
T: (01935) 841193
F: (01935) 841037

ILFRACOMBE
Devon

Avalon Hotel ◆◆◆◆
6 Capstone Crescent, Ilfracombe,
Devon EX34 9BT
T: (01271) 863325
F: (01271) 866543
E: christine@avalon hotel.
force9.co.uk
I: www.avalon-hotel.co.uk

Capstone Hotel and Restaurant
◆◆◆
St James Place, Ilfracombe,
Devon EX34 9BJ
T: (01271) 863540
F: (01271) 862277
E: steve@capstone.freeserve.
co.uk
I: www.ilfracombe2000.
freeserve.co.uk

The Collingdale Hotel ◆◆◆
Larkstone Terrace, Ilfracombe,
Devon EX34 9NU
T: (01271) 863770
F: (01271) 863770
E: collingdale@onet.co.uk
I: www.ilfracombe-guide.
co.uk/collingdale.htm

Dedes Hotel ◆◆◆
1-4 The Promenade, Ilfracombe,
Devon EX34 9BD
T: (01271) 862545
F: (01271) 862234
E: jackie@dedes.fsbusiness.
co.uk
I: www.dedesshootingholidays.
co.uk

Dilkhusa Grand Hotel ◆◆◆
Wilder Road, Ilfracombe, Devon
EX34 9AH
T: (01271) 863505
F: (01271) 864739

Dorchester Hotel ◆◆
59 St Brannocks Road,
Ilfracombe, Devon EX34 8EQ
T: (01271) 865472

The Epchris Hotel ◆◆◆
Torrs Park, Ilfracombe, Devon
EX34 8AZ
T: (01271) 862751
F: (01271) 879077
E: epchris-hotel@ic24.net
I: www.epchrishotel.co.uk

Glen Tor Hotel ◆◆◆◆
Torrs Park, Ilfracombe, Devon
EX34 8AZ
T: (01271) 862403
F: (01271) 862403
E: info@glentorhotel.co.uk
I: www.glentorhotel.co.uk

Grosvenor Hotel ◆◆◆
Wilder Road, Ilfracombe, Devon
EX34 9AF
T: (01271) 863426
F: (01271) 863714

Laston House Hotel ◆◆◆
Hillsborough Road, Ilfracombe,
Devon EX34 9NT
T: (01271) 866557
F: (01271) 864440
E: robinlasto@hotmail.com
I: www.s-h-systems.
co.uk/hotels/laston.html

Lyncott House ◆◆◆◆
56 St Brannock's Road,
Ilfracombe, Devon EX34 8EQ
T: (01271) 862425
F: (01271) 862425
E: david@ukhotels.com
I: www.s-h-systems.
co.uk/hotels/lyncott.html and
www.lyncottdevon.com

Rivendell Guest House ◆◆◆
28 St Brannocks Road,
Ilfracombe, Devon EX34 8EQ
T: (01271) 866852

Strathmore Hotel ◆◆◆◆
57 St Brannocks Road,
Ilfracombe, Devon EX34 8EQ
T: (01271) 862248 & 862243
F: (01271) 862243
E: strathmore@ukhotels.com
I: www.strathmore.ukhotels.com

**Sunnymeade Country House
Hotel** ◆◆◆
Dean Cross, West Down,
Ilfracombe, Devon EX34 8NT
T: (01271) 863668
F: (01271) 863668
E: info@sunnymeade.co.uk
I: www.sunnymeade.co.uk

The Towers Hotel ◆◆◆
Chambercombe Park Road,
Ilfracombe, Devon EX34 9QN
T: (01271) 862809
F: (01271) 879442
E: info@thetowers.co.uk
I: www.thetowers.co.uk

Varley House ◆◆◆◆
Chambercombe Park,
Ilfracombe, Devon EX34 9QW
T: (01271) 863927
F: (01271) 879299
E: info@varleyhouse.co.uk
I: www.varleyhouse.co.uk

Westaway ◆◆◆
Torrs Park, Ilfracombe, Devon
EX34 8AY
T: (01271) 864459 &
07932 032017
F: (01271) 863486
E: westaway@onetel.net.uk
I: www.westaway.net

Wildersmouth Hotel ◆
Sommers Crescent, Ilfracombe,
Devon EX34 9DP
T: (01271) 862002 & 862015
F: (01271) 862803
E: booking@devoniahotel.co.uk
I: www.devoniahotels.co.uk

ILMINSTER
Somerset

Dillington House ◆◆◆◆
Ilminster, Somerset TA19 9DT
T: (01460) 52427
F: (01460) 52433
E: dillington@somerset.gov.uk
I: www.dillington.co.uk

Graden ◆◆◆
Peasmarsh, Ilminster, Somerset
TA19 0SG
T: (01460) 52371
F: (01460) 52371

Hermitage ◆◆◆
29 Station Road, Ilminster,
Somerset TA19 9BE
T: (01460) 53028
I: www.home.freeuk.
net/hermitage

Minster View ◆◆◆
8 Butts Road, Ilminster,
Somerset TA19 0AX
T: (01460) 54619 &
07833 391131
F: 07833 391131
E: trishlee@freenet.co.uk
I: www.minsterview.co.uk

IPPLEPEN
Devon

Fir Tree House ◆◆◆◆
North Street, Ipplepen, Newton
Abbot, Devon TQ12 5RT
T: (01803) 812280
F: (01803) 812280

June Cottage ◆◆◆◆
Dornafield Road, Ipplepen,
Newton Abbot, Devon TQ12 5SH
T: (01803) 813081

ISLES OF SCILLY

Hotel Beachcomber ◆◆◆
Thorofare, St Mary's, Isles of
Scilly TR21 0LN
T: (01720) 422682
F: (01720) 422532

Nundeeps ◆◆◆
Rams Valley, St Mary's, Isles of
Scilly TR21 0JX
T: (01720) 422517

Polreath Guest House ◆◆◆
Higher Town, St Martin's, Isles of
Scilly TR25 0QL
T: (01720) 422046
F: (01720) 422046
E: polreath.scilly@virginnet.
co.uk
I: www.polreath.
scilly@virginnet.co.uk

Seaview Moorings ◆◆◆◆◆
The Strand, St Mary's, Isles of
Scilly TR21 0PT
T: (01720) 422327
E: enquiries@
islesofscillyestateagents.com
I: www.islesofscillyestateagents.
com

IVYBRIDGE
Devon

Hillhead Farm ◆◆◆◆
Ugborough, Ivybridge, Devon
PL21 0HQ
T: (01752) 892674 &
07785 915612
F: (01752) 690111

Venn Farm ◆◆◆
Ugborough, Ivybridge, Devon
PL21 0PE
T: (01364) 73240
F: (01364) 73240

KEINTON MANDEVILLE
Somerset

Stangray House ◆◆◆◆
Church Street, Keinton
Mandeville, Somerton, Somerset
TA11 6ER
T: (01458) 223984
F: (01458) 224 295
E: david.moran@btinternet.com

KELSTON
Bath and North East Somerset

Old Crown ◆◆◆
Kelston, Bath BA1 9AQ
T: (01225) 423032
F: (01225) 480115

KENN
Devon

Lower Thornton Farm ◆◆◆◆
Kenn, Exeter EX6 7XH
T: (01392) 833434 &
07970 972012
F: (01392) 833434

KENTON
Devon

Devon Arms ◆◆◆
Fore Street, Kenton, Exeter
EX6 8LD
T: (01626) 890213
F: (01626) 891678
E: devon.arms@ukgateway.net

KEPNAL
Wiltshire

Eastfield House ◆◆◆
Kepnal, Pewsey, Wiltshire
SN9 5JL
T: (01672) 562489

KEYNSHAM
Bath and North East Somerset

Chewton Place ◆◆◆
Chewton Road, Keynsham,
Bristol BS31 2SX
T: (0117) 986 3105
F: (0117) 986 5948
E: conferenceoffice@
chewton-place.co.uk
I: www.hanover_international.
com

KILVE
Somerset

The Old Mill ◆◆◆◆
Kilve, Bridgwater, Somerset
TA5 1EB
T: (01278) 741571

KINGSAND
Cornwall

Halfway House Inn ◆◆◆
Fore Street, Kingsand, Torpoint,
Cornwall PL10 1NA
T: (01752) 822279
F: (01752) 823146
E: halfway@eggconnect.net
I: www.crappot.co.uk

KINGSBRIDGE
Devon

The Ashburton Arms ◆◆◆
West Charleton, Kingsbridge,
Devon TQ7 2AH
T: (01548) 531242

Ashleigh House ◆◆◆
Ashleigh Road, Kingsbridge,
Devon TQ7 1HB
T: (01548) 852893 &
07967 737875
E: reception@ashleigh-house.
co.uk
I: www.ashleigh-house.co.uk

Combe Farm B & B ◆◆◆◆
Loddiswell, Kingsbridge, Devon
TQ7 4DT
T: (01548) 550560
F: (01548) 550560
E: Combefarm@Hotmail.com

Coombe Farm ◆◆◆◆
Kingsbridge, Devon TQ7 4AB
T: (01548) 852038
F: (01548) 852038

Globe Inn ◆◆
Frogmore, Kingsbridge, Devon
TQ7 2NR
T: (01548) 531351
F: (01548) 531351
E: enquiries@theglobeinn.co.uk
I: www.theglobeinn.co.uk

Shute Farm ◆◆◆
South Milton, Kingsbridge,
Devon TQ7 3JL
T: (01548) 560680

Sloop Inn ◆◆◆
Bantham, Kingsbridge, Devon
TQ7 3AJ
T: (01548) 560489 & 560215
F: (01548) 561940

South Allington House ◆◆◆◆
Chivelstone, Kingsbridge, Devon
TQ7 2NB
T: (01548) 511272
F: (01548) 511421
E: barbara@sthallingtonbnb.
demon.co.uk
I: www.sthallingtonbnb.demon.
co.uk

KINGSBURY EPISCOPI
Somerset

The Retreat ◆◆◆◆
Kingsbury Episcopi, Martock,
Somerset TA12 6AZ
T: (01935) 823500

KINGSKERSWELL
Devon

Harewood Guest House ◆◆
17 Torquay Road, Kingskerswell,
Newton Abbot, Devon TQ12 5HH
T: (01803) 872228

KINGTON LANGLEY
Wiltshire

The Moors ◆◆◆
Malmesbury Road, Kington
Langley, Chippenham, Wiltshire
SN14 6HT
T: (01249) 750288
F: (01249) 7508814

KINGWESTON
Somerset

Lower Farm ◆◆◆◆
Kingweston, Somerton,
Somerset TA11 6BA
T: (01458) 223237 &
07860 350426
F: (01458) 223276
E: lowerfarm@kingweston.
demon.co.uk
I: www.lowerfarm.net

KNOWSTONE
Devon

West Bowden Farm ◆◆◆
Knowstone, South Molton,
Devon EX36 4RP
T: (01398) 341224

LACOCK
Wiltshire

King John's Hunting Lodge
◆◆◆◆
21 Church Street, Lacock,
Chippenham, Wiltshire
SN15 2LB
T: (01249) 730313
F: (01249) 730313

**Lacock Pottery Bed &
Breakfast** ◆◆◆◆
1 The Tanyard, Church Street,
Lacock, Chippenham, Wiltshire
SN15 2LB
T: (01249) 730266
F: (01249) 730946
E: simonemcdowell@
lacockbedandbreakfast.com
I: www.lacockbedandbreakfast.
com

Lower Lodge ◆◆◆
35 Bowden Hill, Lacock,
Chippenham, Wiltshire
SN15 2PP
T: (01249) 730711
F: (01249) 730955

The Old Rectory ◆◆◆◆
Cantax Hill, Lacock,
Chippenham, Wiltshire SN15 2JZ
T: (01249) 730335 &
07730 884003
F: (01249) 730166
E: sexton@oldrectorylacock.
co.uk
I: www.oldrectorylacock.co.uk

Pen-Y-Brook ◆◆◆
Notton, Lacock, Chippenham,
Wiltshire SN15 2NF
T: (01249) 730376 &
07711 111643

Videl ◆◆◆
6A Bewley Lane, Lacock,
Chippenham, Wiltshire
SN15 2PG
T: (01249) 730279

LADOCK
Cornwall

Swallows Court ◆◆◆◆
Treworyan, Ladock, Truro,
Cornwall TR2 4QD
T: (01726) 883488
F: (01726) 882689
E: sarah@swallowscourt.fsnet.
co.uk

LAMERTON
Devon

New Court Farm ◆◆◆
Lamerton, Tavistock, Devon
PL19 8RR
T: (01822) 614319

LANDFORD
Wiltshire

New Forest Lodge ◆◆◆◆
Southampton Road, Landford,
Salisbury SP5 2ED
T: (01794) 390999
F: (01794) 390066
E: reservations@
newforestlodge.co.uk
I: www.newforestlodge.co.uk

LANDSCOVE
Devon

Thornecroft ◆◆◆◆
Landscove, Ashburton, Newton
Abbot, Devon TQ13 7LX
T: (01803) 762500
E: tonymatthews@lineone.net
I: www.b&b@thornecroft.co.uk

LANEAST
Cornwall

Stitch Park ◆◆◆◆
Laneast, Launceston, Cornwall
PL15 8PN
T: (01566) 86687
E: stitchpark@hotmail.com

LANGFORD
North Somerset

Miltons ◆◆◆
Stock Lane, Lower Langford,
Langford, Bristol BS40 5EU
T: (01934) 852352
F: (01934) 852352
E: hotelmil@globalnet.co.uk

Newcourt Barton ◆◆◆
Langford, Cullompton, Devon
EX15 1SE
T: (01884) 277326
F: (01884) 277326
E: newcourtbarton@btinternet.
com
I: www.
newcourtbarton@btinternet.
com

LANGPORT
Somerset

Amberley ◆◆◆◆
Long Load, Langport, Somerset
TA10 9LD
T: (01458) 241542
E: jeanatamberley@talk21.com

Gothic House ◆◆◆◆
Muchelney, Langport, Somerset
TA10 0DW
T: (01458) 250626
E: joy_thorne@totalserve.co.uk

Muchelney Ham Farm ◆◆◆◆◆
Muchelney, Langport, Somerset
TA10 0DJ
T: (01458) 250737
F: (01458) 250737
I: www.muchelneyhamfarm.
co.uk

The Old Pound Inn ◆◆◆
Aller, Langport, Somerset
TA10 0RA
T: (01458) 250469
F: (01458) 250469

LANIVET
Cornwall

Tremeere Manor ◆◆◆
Lanivet, Bodmin, Cornwall
PL30 5BG
T: (01208) 831513
F: (01208) 832417
E: oliver.tremeere.manor@
farming.co.uk

Willowbrook ◆◆◆◆
Old Coach Road, Lamorick,
Lanivet, Bodmin, Cornwall
PL30 5HB
T: (01208) 831670 &
07799 762221
F: (01208) 831670
E: miles.willowbrook@
btinternet.com
I: www.cornwall-online.
co.uk/willowbrook

o LANSALLOS
Cornwall

Lesquite ◆◆◆◆
Lansallos, Looe, Cornwall
PL13 2QE
T: (01503) 220315
F: (01503) 220137
E: lesquite@farmersweekly.net
I: www.lesquite-polperro.fsnet.
co.uk

West Kellow Farmhouse ◆◆◆
Lansallos, Looe, Cornwall
PL13 2QU
T: (01503) 272089
F: (01503) 272089

LATTON
Wiltshire

Dolls House ◆◆◆
55 The Street, Latton, Swindon
SN6 6DJ
T: (01793) 750384
F: (01793) 750384
E: gemma-maraffi@
bbdollshouse.freeserve.co.uk

LAUNCESTON
Cornwall

Berrio Bridge House ◆◆◆◆
North Hill, Launceston, Cornwall
PL15 7NL
T: (01566) 782714
F: (01566) 782714

11 Castle Street ◆◆◆◆
Launceston, Cornwall PL15 8BA
T: (01566) 773873 &
07801 066031

Hurdon Farm ◆◆◆◆
Launceston, Cornwall PL15 9LS
T: (01566) 772955

Laneast Barton ◆◆◆
Laneast Barton, Launceston,
Cornwall PL15 8PN
T: (01566) 880104
F: (01566) 880104
E: affb@totalise.co.uk

Middle Tremollett Farm ◆◆◆
Coad's Green, Launceston,
Cornwall PL15 7NA
T: (01566) 782416 &
07974 682603
F: (01566) 782416

The Old Vicarage ◆◆◆◆
Treneglos, Launceston, Cornwall
PL15 8UQ
T: (01566) 781351
F: (01566) 781351
E: maggie@fancourt.freeserve.
co.uk
I: www.fancourt.freeserve.co.uk

Trethorne Leisure Farm ◆◆◆
Kennards House, Launceston,
Cornwall PL15 8QE
T: (01566) 86324 & 86992
F: (01566) 86981
E: trethorneleisure@eclipse.
co.uk
I: www.cornwall-online.
co.uk/trethorne

Trevadlock Farm ◆◆◆◆
Trevadlock, Congdon Shop,
Launceston, Cornwall PL15 7PW
T: (01566) 782239
F: (01566) 782239
E: trevadlockfarm@compuserve.
com
I: www.trevadlock.co.uk

Wheatley Farm ◆◆◆◆
Maxworthy, Launceston,
Cornwall PL15 8LY
T: (01566) 781232
F: (01566) 781232
E: wheatley@farming.co.uk
I: www.wheatleyfrm.com

White Hart Hotel ◆◆◆
15 Broad Street, Launceston,
Cornwall PL15 8AA
T: (01566) 772013 & 773567
F: (01566) 773668

LAVERSTOCK
Wiltshire

20 Potters Way ◆◆◆
Laverstock, Salisbury SP1 1PY
T: (01722) 335031
F: (01722) 335031

1 Riverside Close ◆◆◆◆
Laverstock, Salisbury SP1 1QW
T: (01722) 320287
F: (01722) 320287
E: marytucker2001@yahoo.com

The Twitterings ◆◆◆
73 Church Road, Laverstock,
Salisbury SP1 1QY
T: (01722) 321760

LAVERTON
Somerset

Hollytree Cottage ◆◆◆◆
Laverton, Bath BA2 7QZ
T: (01373) 830786 & 0790 186
7694
F: (01373) 830786

LEIGH
Wiltshire

Leighfield Lodge Farm ◆◆◆◆
Malmesbury Road, Leigh,
Swindon SN6 6RH
T: (01666) 860241
F: (01666) 860241

LEWDOWN
Devon

Old Cottage ◆◆◆◆
Dippertown, Lewdown,
Okehampton, Devon EX20 4PT
T: (01566) 783250

Stowford Grange Farm ◆◆
Lewdown, Okehampton, Devon
EX20 4BZ
T: (01566) 783298

LISKEARD
Cornwall

Elnor Guest House ◆◆◆
1 Russell Street, Station Road,
Liskeard, Cornwall PL14 4BP
T: (01579) 342472
F: (01579) 345673
E: Elnor@btclick.com

Hyvue House ◆◆◆
Barras Cross, Liskeard, Cornwall
PL14 6BN
T: (01579) 348175

Pencubbitt Hotel ◆◆◆◆
Station Road, Liskeard, Cornwall
PL14 4EB
T: (01579) 342694
I: www.penc.co.uk

Tregondale Farm ◆◆◆◆
Menheniot, Liskeard, Cornwall
PL14 3RG
T: (01579) 342407
F: (01579) 342407
E: tregondale@connectfree.
co.uk
I: www.tregondalefarm.co.uk

Trewint Farm ◆◆◆◆
Menheniot, Liskeard, Cornwall
PL14 3RE
T: (01579) 347155
F: (01579) 347155

LITTLE BEDWYN
Wiltshire

Bridge Cottage ◆◆◆
Little Bedwyn, Marlborough,
Wiltshire SN8 3JS
T: (01672) 870795
F: (01672) 870795
E: rwdaniel@bridgecott.fsnet.
co.uk
I: www.bridgecott.co.uk

LITTLE LANGFORD
Wiltshire

Little Langford Farmhouse ◆◆◆◆◆
Little Langford, Salisbury
SP3 4NR
T: (01722) 790205
F: (01722) 790086
E: bandb@littlelangford.co.uk
I: www.dmac.co.uk/llf

LITTLE PETHERICK
Cornwall

Molesworth Manor ◆◆◆
Little Petherick, Padstow,
Cornwall PL27 7QT
T: (01841) 540292

LITTLE TORRINGTON
Devon

Smytham Manor Leisure ◆◆◆
Smytham Manor, Little
Torrington, Torrington, Devon
EX38 8PU
T: (01805) 622110
F: (01805) 625451
E: info@smytham.fsnet.co.uk

LITTON CHENEY
Dorset

Charity Farm ◆◆◆
Litton Cheney, Dorchester,
Dorset DT2 9AP
T: (01308) 482574
E: charityfarm@eurolink.ltd.net

LODDISWELL
Devon

The Shippen ◆◆◆◆
Rake Farm, Loddiswell,
Kingsbridge, Devon TQ7 4DA
T: (01548) 550016
E: theshippen@barclays.net
I: james.dircon.co.uk /
theshippen.html

LONG BREDY
Dorset

Middle Farm ◆◆◆
Long Bredy, Dorchester, Dorset
DT2 9HW
T: (01308) 482215
F: (01308) 482215

LONG LOAD
Somerset

Fairlight ◆◆◆
Martock Road, Long Load,
Langport, Somerset TA10 9LG
T: (01458) 241323

LONGBRIDGE DEVERILL
Wiltshire

The George Inn ◆◆◆◆
Longbridge Deverill, Warminster,
Wiltshire BA12 7DG
T: (01985) 840396
F: (01985) 841333
W: www.
thegeorgeinnlongbridgedeveril.
co.uk

LONGLEAT
Wiltshire

Post Office Farm ◆◆◆
Corsley Heath, Longleat,
Warminster, Wiltshire BA12 7PR
T: (01373) 832734 &
07074 832734
F: (01373) 832734
E: kmyoudan@lineone.net

LOOE
Cornwall

Barclay House
Rating Applied For
St Martins Road, Looe, Cornwall
PL13 1LP
T: (01503) 262929
F: (01503) 262632
E: info@barclayhouse.co.uk
I: www.barclayhouse.co.uk

Bucklawren Farm ◆◆◆◆
St Martin-by-Looe, Looe,
Cornwall PL13 1NZ
T: (01503) 240738
F: (01503) 240481
E: bucklawren@compuserve.
com
I: www.cornwallexplore.
co.uk/bucklawren

Coombe Farm Country House Hotel ◆◆◆◆
Widegates, Looe, Cornwall
PL13 1QN
T: (01503) 240223 & 240329
F: (01503) 240895
E: coombe_farm@hotmail.com
I: www.coombefarmhotel.co.uk

Downend Country House
Rating Applied For
Widegates, Looe, Cornwall
PL13 1QN
T: (01503) 340213

Little Larnick Farm ◆◆◆◆
Pelynt, Looe, Cornwall PL13 2NB
T: (01503) 262837
F: (01503) 262837
E: littlelarnick@btclick.com

The Panorama Hotel ◆◆◆◆
Hannafore Road, Looe, Cornwall
PL13 2DE
T: (01503) 262123
F: (01503) 265654
E: stay@looe.co.uk
I: www.looe.co.uk

Stonerock Cottage ◆◆
Portuan Road, Hannafore, West
Looe, Cornwall PL13 2DN
T: (01503) 263651
F: (01503) 263414

Trehaven Manor ◆◆◆◆
Station Road, Looe, Cornwall
PL13 1HN
T: (01503) 262028
F: (01503) 262028
E: enquiries@trehavenhotel.
co.uk
I: www.trehavenhotel.co.uk

SOUTH WEST

Trevanion Hotel ◆◆◆
Hannafore, Looe, Cornwall
PL13 2DE
T: (01503) 262003 &
07802 447544
F: (01503) 265408
E: hotel@looecornwall.co.uk
I: www.looecornwall.co.uk

LOWER WOODFORD
Wiltshire

**Swallow Cottage Bed &
Breakfast ◆◆◆◆**
Swallow Cottage, Lower
Woodford, Salisbury SP4 6NQ
T: (01722) 782393 &
07973 265419
F: (01722) 782739
E: swallow.cottage@amserve.net

LYDIARD TREGOZE
Wiltshire

Park Farm ◆◆◆
Hook Street, Lydiard Tregoze,
Swindon SN5 3NY
T: (01793) 853608

LYME REGIS
Dorset

**Charnwood Guest House
◆◆◆◆**
21 Woodmead Road, Lyme
Regis, Dorset DT7 3AD
T: (01297) 445281
E: charnwood@lymeregis62.freeserve.co.uk
I: www.lymeregisaccommodation.com

Clappentail House ◆◆◆◆◆
Uplyme Road, Lyme Regis,
Dorset DT7 3LP
T: (01297) 445739
F: (01297) 444794
E: pountain@clappentail.freeserve.co.uk

Cliff Cottage ◆◆◆
Cobb Road, Lyme Regis, Dorset
DT7 3JE
T: (01297) 443334
E: merry.bolton@btinternet.com

Coombe House ◆◆◆
41 Coombe Street, Lyme Regis,
Dorset DT7 3PY
T: (01297) 443849
E: dunc@hughduncan.freeserve.co.uk

Devon Hotel ◆◆◆
Lyme Road, Uplyme, Lyme Regis,
Dorset DT7 3TQ
T: (01297) 443231
F: (01297) 445836
E: thedevonhotel@virgin.net
I: www.lymeregis.com/devon-hotel

Devonia Guest House ◆◆◆
2 Woodmead Road, Lyme Regis,
Dorset DT7 3AB
T: (01297) 442869
F: (01297) 442869
E: roysue@fsmail.net.co.uk

Dorset Hotel ◆◆◆
Silver Street, Lyme Regis, Dorset
DT7 3HX
T: (01297) 442482
F: (01297) 443970
E: dorsethotel@lymeregis.com
I: www.lymeregis.com/dorset-hotel

Higher Spence ◆◆◆
Wootton Fitzpaine, Bridport,
Dorset DT6 6DF
T: (01297) 560556
E: higherspence@eurolink.ltd.net

**The London Bed and Breakfast
◆◆◆**
40 Church Street, Lyme Regis,
Dorset DT7 3DA
T: (01297) 442083

Lucerne ◆◆◆
View Road, Lyme Regis, Dorset
DT7 3AA
T: (01297) 443752
E: lucerne@lineone.net

Lydwell House ◆◆◆
Lyme Road, Uplyme, Lyme Regis,
Dorset DT7 3TJ
T: (01297) 443522
E: brittain16@fsbusiness.co.uk
I: www.smoothhound.co.uk/hotels/lydwell.html

Manaton B & B ◆◆◆◆
Hill Road, Lyme Regis, Dorset
DT7 3PE
T: (01297) 445138

Mermaid House ◆◆◆◆
32 Coombe Street, Lyme Regis,
Dorset DT7 3PP
T: (01297) 445351
E: mermaidhouse@talk21.com
I: www.smoothhound.co.uk

Ocean View ◆◆◆◆
2 Hadleigh Villas, Silver Street,
Lyme Regis, Dorset DT7 3HR
T: (01297) 442567

Old Lyme Guest House ◆◆◆◆
29 Coombe Street, Lyme Regis,
Dorset DT7 3PP
T: (01297) 442929
F: (01297) 444652
E: oldlyme.guesthouse@virgin.net
I: www.oldlymeguesthouse.co.uk

Orchard Country Hotel ◆◆◆◆
Rousdon, Lyme Regis, Dorset
DT7 3XW
T: (01297) 442972
F: (01297) 443670
E: the.orchard@btinternet.com

The Red House ◆◆◆◆
Sidmouth Road, Lyme Regis,
Dorset DT7 3ES
T: (01297) 442055
F: (01297) 442055
E: red.house@virgin.net
I: www.smoothhound.co.uk/hotels/redhous2.html

Rotherfield ◆◆◆
View Road, Lyme Regis, Dorset
DT7 3AA
T: (01297) 445585
E: rotherfield@lymeregis.com
I: www.lymeregis.com/rotherfield/

Southernhaye ◆◆◆
Pound Road, Lyme Regis, Dorset
DT7 3HX
T: (01297) 443077
F: (01297) 443077

Springfield ◆◆◆
Woodmead Road, Lyme Regis,
Dorset DT7 3LJ
T: (01297) 443409
F: (01297) 443685
E: springfield@lymeregis.com
I: www.lymeregis.com/springfield

Thatch ◆◆◆◆
Uplyme Road, Lyme Regis,
Dorset DT7 3LP
T: (01297) 442212
F: (01297) 443485
E: thethatch@lineone.net
I: www.uk-bedandbreakfasts.com

**Thatch Lodge Hotel &
Restaurant ◆◆◆◆◆**
The Street, Charmouth, Bridport,
Dorset DT6 6PQ
T: (01297) 560407 _35333_
F: (01297) 560407
E: thatchlodgehotel@cs.com
I: www.thatchlodgehotel.com

Tudor House Hotel ◆◆◆
Church Street, Lyme Regis,
Dorset DT7 3BU
T: (01297) 442472
E: tudor@eclipse.co.uk
I: www.thetudorhouse.co.uk

Victoria Hotel ◆◆◆
Uplyme Road, Lyme Regis,
Dorset DT7 3LP
T: (01297) 444801
F: (01297) 442949
E: info@vichotel.co.uk
I: www.vichotel.co.uk

Westwood Guest House ◆◆◆
1 Woodmead Road, Lyme Regis,
Dorset DT7 3LJ
T: (01297) 442376

White House ◆◆◆◆
47 Silver Street, Lyme Regis,
Dorset DT7 3HR
T: (01297) 443420

Woodberry Down ◆◆
Colway Lane, Lyme Regis, Dorset
DT7 3HF
T: (01297) 444655
F: (01297) 444655

LYNMOUTH
Devon

**Bonnicott House Hotel
◆◆◆◆◆**
Watersmeet Road, Lynmouth,
Devon EX35 6EP
T: (01598) 753346

Coombe Farm ◆◆◆
Countisbury, Lynton, Devon
EX35 6NF
T: (01598) 741236 & 741227
F: (01598) 741236

Ferndale House ◆◆◆
Summerhouse Path,
Watersmeet Road, Lynmouth,
Devon EX35 6EP
T: (01598) 753431

Orchard House Hotel ◆◆◆◆
12 Watersmeet Road, Lynmouth,
Devon EX35 6EP
T: (01598) 753247
F: (01598) 753855
E: orchardhouse@lynmouth.fsnet.co.uk
I: www.welcome.to/orchardhouse

Seaview Villa ◆◆◆◆
6 Summerhouse Path,
Lynmouth, Devon EX35 6ES
T: (01598) 753460
F: (01598) 752399
E: seaviewvilla.lynmouth@virgin.net

**Tregonwell Riverside
Guesthouse ◆◆◆**
1 Tors Road, Lynmouth, Devon
EX35 6ET
T: (01598) 753369
I: www.smoothhound.co.uk/hotels/tregonwl.html

The Village Inn ◆◆◆
19 Lynmouth Street, Lynmouth,
Devon EX35 6EH
T: (01598) 752354

LYNTON
Devon

Alford House Hotel ◆◆◆
3 Alford Terrace, Lynton, Devon
EX35 6AT
T: (01598) 752359
F: (01598) 752359
E: alfordhouse@btinternet.com
I: www.smoothhound.co.uk/hotels/alford.html

Caffyns Heanton Farm ◆◆◆◆
Lynton, Devon EX35 6JW
T: (01598) 753770
F: (01598) 753770

Croft House Hotel ◆◆◆◆
Lydiate Lane, Lynton, Devon
EX35 6HE
T: (01598) 752391
F: (01598) 752391
E: jane.woolnough@lineone.net
I: www.smoothhound.co.uk/hotels/crofthou.html

The Denes Guest House ◆◆◆
15 Longmead, Lynton, Devon
EX35 6DQ
T: (01598) 753573
F: (01598) 753573
E: j.e.mcgowan@btinternet.com
I: www.thedenes.com

**The Exmoor Sandpiper Inn
Rating Applied For**
Countisbury, Lynton, Devon
EX35 6NE
T: (01598) 741263
F: (01598) 741358
E: clair@exmoorsandpiper.demon.co.uk
I: www.exmoor-hospitality-inns.co.uk

Fairholme Hotel ◆◆◆
North Walk, Lynton, Devon
EX35 6ED
T: (01598) 752263
F: (01598) 752263
I: www.fairholme-hotel.co.uk

Fernleigh Guest House ◆◆◆◆
Park Street, Lynton, Devon
EX35 6BY
T: (01598) 753575
F: (01598) 753575
E: hugh_mcdonnell@hotmail.com
I: www.s-h-systems.co.uk/hotels/fernleighexmoor.html

Ingleside Hotel ◆◆◆◆
Lee Road, Lynton, Devon
EX35 6HW
T: (01598) 752223
E: johnpauldevon@aol.com
I: www.inglesidehotel.co.uk

Kingford House ◆◆◆◆
Longmead, Lynton, Devon
EX35 6DQ
T: (01598) 752361
E: kingfordhousehotel@
compuserve.com
I: www.kingfordhouse.co.uk

Lauraleigh ◆◆◆◆
14 Park Street, Lynton, Devon
EX35 6BY
T: (01598) 752613

Lee House ◆◆◆
27 Lee Road, Lynton, Devon
EX35 6BP
T: (01598) 752364
F: (01598) 752364
E: leehouse@freeuk.com
I: www.smoothhound.
co.uk/hotels/lee.html

Longmead House Hotel
◆◆◆◆
9 Longmead, Lynton, Devon
EX35 6DQ
T: (01598) 752523
F: (01598) 752523
E: info@longmeadhouse.co.uk
I: www.longmeadhouse.co.uk

Meadhaven ◆◆
12 Crossmead, Lynton, Devon
EX35 6DG
T: (01598) 753288

Millslade Country House Hotel
◆◆◆
Brendon, Lynton, Devon
EX35 6PS
T: (01598) 741322
F: (01598) 741355
E: bobcramp@millslade.
freeserve.co.uk
I: www.brendonvalley.
co.uk/millslade.htm

North Walk House ◆◆◆◆
North Walk, Lynton, Devon
EX35 6HJ
T: (01598) 753372
E: murphynwh@tesco.net

Pine Lodge ◆◆◆◆
Lynway, Lynton, Devon
EX35 6AX
T: (01598) 753230
E: info@pinelodgehotel.com
I: www.pinelodgehotel.com

Rockvale Hotel ◆◆◆◆
Lee Road, Lynton, Devon
EX35 6HW
T: (01598) 752279 & 753343
E: JudithWoodland@rockvale.
fsbusiness.co.uk
I: www.rockvalehotel.co.uk

Rodwell House ◆◆◆
21 Lee Road, Lynton, Devon
EX35 6BP
T: (01598) 753324

Sinai House
Rating Applied For
Lynway, Lynton, Devon
EX35 6AY
T: (01598) 753227
F: (01598) 752633
E: enquiries@sinaihouse.co.uk
I: www.sinaihouse.co.uk

South View Guest House ◆◆◆
23 Lee Road, Lynton, Devon
EX35 6BP
T: (01598) 752289 & 752289

Southcliffe ◆◆◆◆
34 Lee Road, Lynton, Devon
EX35 6BS
T: (01598) 753328
F: (01598) 753328

The Turret ◆◆◆
33 Lee Road, Lynton, Devon
EX35 6BS
T: (01598) 753284
F: (01598) 753284
I: www.smoothhound.
co.uk/hotels/theturre.html

Valley House ◆◆◆
Lynbridge Road, Lynton, Devon
EX35 6BD
T: (01598) 752285
E: valleyhouse@westcountry.
net
I: www.westcountry.net

Valley of Rocks ◆◆
Lee Road, Lynton, Devon
EX35 6HS
T: (01598) 752349
F: (01598) 753720

Victoria Fernery ◆◆◆
Lydiate Lane, Lynton, Devon
EX35 6AJ
T: (01598) 752440
F: (01598) 752396
E: enquiries@theferney.co.uk
I: www.theferney.co.uk

MALBOROUGH
Devon

The Lodge ◆◆◆◆
Higher Town, Malborough,
Kingsbridge, Devon TQ7 3RN
T: (01548) 561405
F: (01548) 561111
E: accom@compuserve.com
I: ourworld.compuserve.
com/homepages/accom

MALMESBURY
Wiltshire

Bremilham House ◆◆◆
Bremilham Road, Malmesbury,
Wiltshire SW16 0DQ
T: (01666) 822680

Honeysuckle ◆◆◆
Foxley Road, Malmesbury,
Wiltshire SN16 0JQ
T: (01666) 825267

The Kings Arms Hotel ◆◆◆◆
High Street, Malmesbury,
Wiltshire SN16 9AA
T: (01666) 823383
F: (01666) 825327
E: kingsarmshotel@
malmesburywilts.freeserve.co.uk
I: www.malmesburywilts.
freeserve.co.uk

Lovett Farm ◆◆◆◆
Little Somerford, Chippenham,
Wiltshire SN15 5BP
T: (01666) 823268 &
07808 858612
F: (01666) 823268
E: lovetts_farm@hotmail.com

Manor Farm ◆◆◆◆
Corston, Malmesbury, Wiltshire
SN16 0HF
T: (01666) 822148
F: (01666) 826565
E: ross@manorfarmbandb.fsnet.
co.uk
I: www.manorfarmbandb.co.uk

Marsh Farmhouse ◆◆◆
Crudwell Road, Malmesbury,
Wiltshire SN16 9JL
T: (01666) 822208 &
07785 535944

Oakwood Farm ◆◆◆
Upper Minety, Malmesbury,
Wiltshire SN16 9PY
T: (01666) 860286 &
07785 916039
F: (01666) 860286

The Old Manor House ◆◆
6 Oxford Street, Malmesbury,
Wiltshire SN16 9AX
T: (01666) 823494

Rothay ◆◆◆◆
Milbourne Lane, Malmesbury,
Wiltshire SN16 9JQ
T: (01666) 823509 &
07870 892486

Stonehill Farm ◆◆◆◆
Charlton, Malmesbury, Wiltshire
SN16 9DY
T: (01666) 823310
F: (01666) 823310
E: johnedna@stonehillfarm.
fsnet.co.uk

Trucklebridge ◆◆◆
Foxley Road, Malmesbury,
Wiltshire SN16 0JE
T: (01666) 826027
F: (01666) 824805

Whychurch Farm ◆◆◆◆
Whychurch Hill, Malmesbury,
Wiltshire SN16 9JL
T: (01666) 822156
E: chriswhychurch@aol.com

Winkworth Farm ◆◆◆◆
Lea, Malmesbury, Wiltshire
SN16 9NH
T: (01666) 823267

MANNAMEAD
Devon

Devonshire Guest House ◆◆◆
22 Lockyer Road, Mannamead,
Plymouth, Devon PL3 4RL
T: (01752) 220726
F: (01752) 220766
E: phil@devshire.demon.co.uk
I: www.devshire.demon.co.uk

MANNINGFORD ABBOTS
Wiltshire

Huntlys ◆◆◆
Manningford Abbots, Pewsey,
Wiltshire SN9 6HZ
T: (01672) 563663
F: (01672) 851249

MANTON
Wiltshire

Sunrise ◆◆◆
Manton, Marlborough, Wiltshire
SN8 4HL
T: (01672) 512878
F: (01672) 512878

MARAZION
Cornwall

Chymorvah Private Hotel
◆◆◆
Marazion, Cornwall TR17 0DQ
T: (01736) 710497 & 710508
F: (01736) 710508
I: www.smoothhound.
co.uk/hotels/chymorvah.html

MARK
Somerset

Burnt House Farm ◆◆◆
Yarrow Road, Mark, Highbridge,
Somerset TA9 4LR
T: (01278) 641280 &
07909 888692
F: (01278) 641280
E: carmen@burnthousefarm.
fsnet.co.uk

Laurel Farm ◆◆◆
The Causeway, Mark,
Highbridge, Somerset TA9 4PZ
T: (01278) 641216
F: (01278) 641447

MARLBOROUGH
Wiltshire

Ash Lodge ◆◆◆
Choppingknife Lane,
Marlborough, Wiltshire SN8 2AT
T: (01672) 516745

Cartref ◆◆◆
63 George Lane, Marlborough,
Wiltshire SN8 4BY
T: (01672) 512771

Fishermans House ◆◆◆◆
Mildenhall, Marlborough,
Wiltshire SN8 2LZ
T: (01672) 515390 &
07785 225363
F: (01672) 519009

13 Hyde Lane ◆◆◆
Marlborough, Wiltshire SN8 1JL
T: (01672) 514415
F: (01672) 514415

The Lamb Inn ◆◆◆
The Parade, Marlborough,
Wiltshire SN8 1NE
T: (01672) 512668
F: (01672) 512668

Manton Weir ◆◆◆◆
Marlborough, Wiltshire SN8 4HR
T: (01672) 511398

Merlin Hotel ◆◆◆
36/39 High Street, Marlborough,
Wiltshire SN8 1LW
T: (01672) 512151
F: (01672) 514656

Wernham Farm ◆◆◆
Clench Common, Marlborough,
Wiltshire SN8 4DR
T: (01672) 512236 &
07880 728980
F: (01672) 515001
E: margglvsf@aol.com

West View ◆◆◆
Barnfield, Marlborough,
Wiltshire SN8 2AX
T: (01672) 515583 &
0771 2165258
F: (01672) 519014
E: maggiestewart@euphony.net
I: www.westviewb-b.co.uk

Westcourt Bottom ◆◆◆◆
165 Westcourt, Burbage,
Marlborough, Wiltshire
SN8 3BW
T: (01672) 810924 & 811723
F: (01672) 810924
E: westcourt.b-and-b@virgin.
net

MARSTON
Wiltshire

Home Farm ◆◆◆◆
Close Lane, Marston, Devizes,
Wiltshire SN10 5SN
T: (01380) 725484

MARTOCK
Somerset

Bartletts Farm ◆◆◆◆
Isle Brewers, Taunton, Somerset
TA3 6QN
T: (01460) 281423 &
07808 960668
F: (01460) 281423
E: sandjpeach@tesco.net
I: www.pcmanyeouil.co.uk/bnb.
html

Madey Mills
Rating Applied For
Martock, Somerset TA12 6NN
T: (01935) 823268

The Nags Head ◆◆◆
East Street, Martock, Somerset
TA12 6NF
T: (01935) 823432
E: Thenagschef@aol.com

The White Hart Hotel ◆◆◆◆
East Street, Martock, Somerset
TA12 6JQ
T: (01935) 822005
F: (01935) 822056

Wychwood ◆◆◆◆
7 Bearley Road, Wychwood,
Martock, Somerset TA12 6PG
T: (01935) 825601
F: (01935) 825601
E: wychwoodmartock@yahoo.
co.uk
I: www.theaa.
co.uk/region8/76883.html

MAWGAN PORTH
Cornwall

Bre-Pen Farm ◆◆◆◆
Mawgan Porth, Newquay,
Cornwall TR8 4AL
T: (01637) 860420
E: jill.brake@virgin.net

MEAVY
Devon

Callisham Farm ◆◆◆
Meavy, Yelverton, Devon
PL20 6PS
T: (01822) 853901
F: (01822) 853901
E: wills@callishamfarm.fsnet.
co.uk
I: www.callishamfarm.fsnet.
co.uk

MELKSHAM
Wiltshire

Longhope Guest House ◆◆◆
9 Beanacre Road, Melksham,
Wiltshire SN12 8AG
T: (01225) 706737
F: (01225) 706737

The Old Manor ◆◆◆
48 Spa Road, Melksham,
Wiltshire SN12 7NY
T: (01225) 793803
F: (01225) 793803
E: theoldmanor@yahoo.co.uk

The Regency Hotel ◆◆
10-12 Spa Road, Melksham,
Wiltshire SN12 7NS
T: (01225) 702971
F: (01225) 790745
E: regency.hotel@btinternet.
com
I: www.regencyhotel.co.uk

The Spa Bed & Breakfast ◆◆
402 The Spa, Melksham,
Wiltshire SN12 6QL
T: (01225) 707984
I: www.melksham.org.uk/thespa

18 Spa Road ◆◆◆
Melksham, Wiltshire SN12
T: (01225) 700125

Springfield B & B ◆◆◆◆
403 The Spa, Melksham,
Wiltshire SN12 6QL
T: (01225) 703694
F: (01225) 703694

MELPLASH
Dorset

Mount Meadow Farm ◆◆◆
The Mount, Melplash, Bridport,
Dorset DT6 3TV
T: (01308) 488524
E: rosie@mountmeadow
I: www.mountmeadow.co.uk

MEMBURY
Devon

Goodmans House ◆◆◆◆
Furley, Membury, Axminster,
Devon EX13 7TU
T: (01404) 881690
F: (01404) 881690

MERE
Wiltshire

The Beeches ◆◆◆
Chetcombe Road, Merc,
Warminster, Wiltshire BA12 6AU
T: (01747) 860687

Downleaze ◆◆◆
North Street, Mere, Warminster,
Wiltshire BA12 6HH
T: (01747) 860876

Talbot Hotel ◆◆◆◆
The Square, Mere, Warminster,
Wiltshire BA12 6DR
T: (01747) 860427

MERRYMEET
Cornwall

Higher Trevartha Farm ◆◆◆◆
Pengover, Merrymeet, Liskeard,
Cornwall PL14 3NJ
T: (01579) 343382

MEVAGISSEY
Cornwall

Kerry Anna Country House
◆◆◆◆
Treleaven Farm, Mevagissey, St
Austell, Cornwall PL26 6RZ
T: (01726) 843558
F: (01726) 843558
E: linda.hennah@talk21.com
I: www.kerryanna.co.uk

Seapoint House Hotel ◆◆◆
Battery Terrace, Mevagissey, St
Austell, Cornwall PL26 6QS
T: (01726) 842684 & 844627
F: (01726) 842266
E: mevatele@compuserve.com

MIDDLEMARSH
Dorset

White Horse Farm ◆◆◆
Middlemarsh, Sherborne, Dorset
DT9 5QN
T: (01963) 210222
E: enquiries@whitehorsefarm.
co.uk
I: www.whitehorsefarm.co.uk

MILLBROOK
Cornwall

Stone Farm Bed and Breakfast
◆◆◆◆
Whitsand Bay, Millbrook,
Torpoint, Cornwall PL10 1JJ
T: (01752) 822267
F: (01752) 822267

MILVERTON
Somerset

Cullendown ◆◆
Springrove, Milverton, Taunton,
Somerset TA4 1NL
T: (01823) 400731

MINEHEAD
Somerset

Alcombe Cote Guest House
◆◆◆
19 Manor Road, Alcombe,
Minehead, Somerset TA24 6EH
T: (01643) 703309
F: (01643) 709901
E: collopalcombecote@
bushinternet.com

Allington House ◆◆◆◆
30 Ponsford Road, Minehead,
Somerset TA24 5DY
T: (01643) 703898

Avill House ◆◆◆
Townsend Road, Minehead,
Somerset TA24 5RG
T: (01643) 704370

Avondale ◆◆◆◆
Martlet Road, Minehead,
Somerset TA24 5QD
T: (01643) 706931

Bactonleigh Hotel ◆◆◆
20 Tregonwell Road, Minehead,
Somerset TA24 5DU
T: (01643) 702147

Baytree
Rating Applied For
29 Blenheim Road, Minehead,
Somerset TA24 5PZ
T: (01643) 703374 &
07990 623383
E: derekcole@onetel.net.uk

Fernside ◆◆◆
The Holloway, Minehead,
Somerset TA24 5PB
T: (01643) 707594 & 708995
E: colin.cjs@btinternet.com

Field House ◆◆◆
The Parks, Minehead, Somerset
TA24 8BU
T: (01643) 706958
F: (01643) 704335

Finial ◆◆◆◆
24 Ponsford Road, Minehead,
Somerset TA24 5DY
T: (01643) 703945
E: greenfinial@lineone.net

Foxes Hotel ◆◆◆
The Esplanade, Minehead,
Somerset TA24 5PQ
T: (01643) 704450
F: (01643) 708249
E: foxeshotel@aol.com

Gascony Hotel ◆◆◆◆
The Avenue, Minehead,
Somerset TA24 5BB
T: (01643) 705939

Higher Rodhuish Farm ◆◆◆
Rodhuish, Minehead, Somerset
TA24 6QL
T: (01984) 640253
F: (01984) 640253

Hillside ◆◆◆◆
Higher Allerford, Allerford,
Minehead, Somerset TA24 8HS
T: (01643) 862831
F: (01643) 862279
E: michael.prideaux@virgin.net

Kingsway Hotel ◆◆◆◆
36 Ponsford Road, Minehead,
Somerset TA24 5DY
T: (01643) 702313
F: (01643) 702313

Lorna Doone ◆◆◆
26 Tregonwell Road, Minehead,
Somerset TA24 5DU
T: (01643) 702540
F: (01643) 709905
E: lornadoone@tregonwell.
freeserve

Lyn Valley Guest House ◆◆◆
3 Tregonwell Road, Minehead,
Somerset TA24 5DT
T: (01643) 703748
F: (01643) 703748

Marshfield Hotel ◆◆◆◆
18 Tregonwell Road, Minehead,
Somerset TA24 5DU
T: (01643) 702517 &
0500 600734
F: (01643) 702517
E: marshfield.hotel@
minehead18.freeserve.co.uk
I: www.marshfield-hotel.co.uk

Mayfair Hotel ◆◆◆◆
25 The Avenue, Minehead,
Somerset TA24 5AY
T: (01643) 702719
F: (01643) 702719
E: info@hotelmayfair.com
I: www.hotelmayfair.com

1 Moorlands ◆◆◆
Moor Road, Minehead, Somerset
TA24 5RT
T: (01643) 703453
E: moorlands@amserve.net

Old Ship Aground ◆◆◆
Quay Street, Minehead,
Somerset TA24 5UL
T: (01643) 702087 & 709065
F: (01643) 709066
E: enquiries@oldshipaground.
co.uk
I: www.oldshipaground.co.uk

Promenade Hotel ◆◆◆
The Esplanade, Minehead,
Somerset TA24 5QS
T: (01643) 702572
F: (01643) 702572
E: jgph@globalnet.co.uk
I: www.johngroons.org.uk
&

Sunfield Private Hotel ◆◆◆
83 Summerland Avenue,
Minehead, Somerset TA24 5BW
T: (01643) 703565
F: (01643) 705822
E: sunfield@primex.co.uk
I: www.hotelsminehead.com

Tranmere House ◆◆◆
24 Tregonwell Road, Minehead,
Somerset TA24 5DU
T: (01643) 702647

Tregonwell House ◆
1 Tregonwell Road, Minehead,
Somerset TA24 5DT
T: (01643) 703595

Wanneroo Farm ◆◆◆
Timberscombe, Minehead,
Somerset TA24 7TU
T: (01643) 841493
F: (01643) 841693
E: bandbwanneroo@cs.com
I: www.smoothhound.
co.uk/hotels/wanneroo.html

MINSTER
Cornwall

Branarth ◆◆◆◆
Minster, Boscastle, Cornwall
PL35 0BN
T: (01840) 250102
F: (01840) 250102
E: arthur.bradley1@which.net

Home Farm ◆◆◆
Minster, Boscastle, Cornwall
PL35 0BN
T: (01840) 250195
F: (01840) 250195
E: jackie.haddy@btclick.com

MODBURY
Devon

Goutsford ◆◆◆◆
Ermington, Modbury, Ivybridge,
Devon PL21 9NY
T: (01548) 831299 &
07977 200324
F: (01752) 601728
E: carolinefarrand@
compuserve.com

Weeke Farm ◆◆◆
Modbury, Ivybridge, Devon
PL21 0TT
T: (01548) 830219
F: (01548) 830219

MOLLAND
Devon

Great Woods Farm ◆
Molland, South Molton, Devon
EX36 3NL
T: (01769) 550203

MONKLEIGH
Devon

Annery Barton ◆◆◆
Monkleigh, Bideford, Devon
EX39 5JL
T: (01237) 473629
F: (01237) 424468

MONTACUTE
Somerset

Carents House ◆◆◆◆
7A Middle Street, Montacute,
Somerset TA15 6UZ
T: (01935) 824914 &
07779 776050
E: carentshouse@amserve.net

Mad Hatters Tearooms ◆◆◆
1 South Street, Montacute,
Somerset TA15 6XD
T: (01935) 823024
E: montacutemuseum@aol.com
I: www.montacutemuseum.com

The Phelips Arms
Rating Applied For
The Borough, Montacute,
Somerset TA15 6XB
T: (01935) 822557
E: thephelipsarms@aol.com

Slipper Cottage
Rating Applied For
41 Bishopston, Montacute,
Somerset TA15 6UX
T: (01935) 823073 &
07812 145402
E: sue.weir@ntlworld.com
I: www.slippercottage.co.uk

MORCOMBELAKE
Dorset

Wisteria Cottage ◆◆◆
Taylors Lane, Morcombelake,
Bridport, Dorset DT6 6ED
T: (01297) 489019

MORELEIGH
Devon

Higher Barton ◆◆◆◆
Moreleigh, Totnes, Devon
TQ9 7JN
T: (01548) 821475 &
07721 068181

Island Farm ◆◆◆◆
Moreleigh, Totnes, Devon
TQ9 7JH
T: (01548) 821441

MORETONHAMPSTEAD
Devon

Cookshayes Country Guest
House ◆◆◆
33 Court Street,
Moretonhampstead, Newton
Abbot, Devon TQ13 8LG
T: (01647) 440374
F: (01647) 440374
E: cookshayes@eurobell.co.uk
I: www.cookshayes.co.uk

Great Doccombe Farm ◆◆◆◆
Doccombe, Moretonhampstead,
Newton Abbot, Devon TQ13 8SS
T: (01647) 440694

Great Sloncombe Farm ◆◆◆◆
Moretonhampstead, Newton
Abbot, Devon TQ13 8QF
T: (01647) 440595
F: (01647) 440595
E: hmerchant@sloncombe.
freeserve.co.uk
I: www.greatsloncombefarm
co.uk

Great Wooston Farm Bed &
Breakfast ◆◆◆◆
Moretonhampstead, Newton
Abbot, Devon TQ13 8QA
T: (01647) 440367 &
07798 670590
F: (01647) 440367

Little Wooston Farm ◆◆◆
Moretonhampstead, Newton
Abbot, Devon TQ13 8QA
T: (01647) 440551 &
07850 098789
F: (01647) 440551

Midfields ◆◆◆◆
North Bovey Road,
Moretonhampstead, Newton
Abbot, Devon TQ13 8PB
T: (01647) 440462 &
07951 199505
F: (01647) 440039
E: sharon@ridgetor.freeserve.
co.uk
I: www.guestbeds.com

Moorcote Guest House ◆◆◆◆
Chagford Cross,
Moretonhampstead, Newton
Abbot, Devon TQ13 8LS
T: (01647) 440966
E: moorcote@smartone.co.uk

Yarningale ◆◆◆
Exeter Road,
Moretonhampstead, Newton
Abbot, Devon TQ13 8SW
T: (01647) 440560
F: (01647) 440560
E: sally-radcliffe@virgin.net

MORTEHOE
Devon

Baycliffe Hotel ◆◆◆◆
Chapel Hill, Mortehoe,
Woolacombe, Devon EX34 7DZ
T: (01271) 870393
F: (01271) 870393

The Cleeve House ◆◆◆◆
North Morte Road, Mortehoe,
Woolacombe, Devon EX34 7ED
T: (01271) 870719
F: (01271) 870719
E: info@cleevehouse.co.uk
I: www.cleevehouse.co.uk
🐾

Sunnycliffe Hotel ◆◆◆◆
Chapel Hill, Mortehoe,
Woolacombe, Devon EX34 7EB
T: (01271) 870597
F: (01271) 870597
E: jj@sunnycliffe.freeserve.co.uk

MORWENSTOW
Cornwall

Cornakey Farm ◆◆◆
Morwenstow, Bude, Cornwall
EX23 9SS
T: (01288) 331260

MOSTERTON
Dorset

Yeabridge Farm ◆◆◆◆
Whetley Cross, Mosterton,
Beaminster, Dorset DT8 3HE
T: (01308) 868944 &
07967 687994
F: (01308) 868944

MOUSEHOLE
Cornwall

Kerris Farmhouse ◆◆◆◆
Kerris, Paul, Penzance, Cornwall
TR19 6UY
T: (01736) 731309
E: susangiles@btconnect.com
I: www.cornwall-online.
co.uk/kerris-farm

MULLION
Cornwall

Meaver Farm ◆◆◆◆
Mullion, Helston, Cornwall
TR12 7DN
T: (01326) 240128
F: (01326) 240128
E: meaverfarm@eclipse.co.uk
I: www.meaverfarm.freeserve.
co.uk

Polhormon Farm ◆◆◆
Polhormon Lane, Mullion,
Helston, Cornwall TR12 7JE
T: (01326) 240304 &
0796 7810063
F: (01326) 240304
E: polhormonfarm@
farmersweekly.net

Tregaddra Farm ◆◆◆◆
Cury, Helston, Cornwall
TR12 7BB
T: (01326) 240235
F: (01326) 240235
E: holidays@tregaddra.
freeserve.co.uk
I: www.tregaddra.freeserve.co.uk

Trenance Farmhouse ◆◆◆◆
Mullion, Helston, Cornwall
TR12 7HB
T: (01326) 240639
F: (01326) 240639
E: trenancefarm@cwcom.net

MUSBURY
Devon

Kate's Farm Bed & Breakfast ◆
Lower Bruckland Farm, Musbury,
Axminster, Devon EX13 8ST
T: (01297) 552861

MUTLEY
Devon

The Dudley Hotel ◆◆◆◆
42 Sutherland Road, Mutley,
Plymouth PL4 6BN
T: (01752) 668322
F: (01752) 673763
E: butler@dudleyhotel.fsnet.
co.uk

NANCEGOLLAN
Cornwall

Little Pengwedna Farm ◆◆◆◆
Nancegollan, Helston, Cornwall
TR13 0AY
T: (01736) 850649
F: (01736) 850649
E: ray@good-holidays.demon.
co.uk
I: www.good-holidays.demon.
co.uk

NETHER STOWEY
Somerset

Castle of Comfort Country
House ◆◆◆◆
Dodington, Nether Stowey,
Bridgwater, Somerset TA5 1LE
T: (01278) 741264 &
07050 642002
F: (01278) 741144
E: reception@
castle-of-comfort.co.uk
I: www.castle-of-comfort.co.uk

Rose and Crown ◆◆
St Mary Street, Nether Stowey,
Somerset TA5 1LJ
T: (01278) 732265

NETHERAVON
Wiltshire

Paddock House Bed and
Breakfast ◆◆◆
Paddock House, High Street,
Netheravon, Salisbury SP4 9QP
T: (01980) 670401
F: (01980) 670401

NETHERBURY
Dorset

Jasmine Cottage ◆◆◆◆
St James Road, Netherbury,
Bridport, Dorset DT6 5LP
T: (01308) 488767

NEWBRIDGE
Cornwall

Wheal Buller ◆◆◆◆
North Road, Newbridge,
Penzance, Cornwall TR20 8PS
T: (01736) 787999
E: rwrgibson@supanet.com

NEWQUAY
Cornwall

Aloha ◆◆◆
122 Henver Road, Newquay,
Cornwall TR7 3EQ
T: (01637) 878366
E: Alohanewqu@aol.com
I: www.mjiggins.freeserve.
co.uk/mjaloha/index.html

Beresford Hotel ◆◆◆
Narrowcliff, Newquay, Cornwall
TR7 2PR
T: (01637) 873238
F: (01637) 851874

Chichester ◆◆◆
14 Bay View Terrace, Newquay,
Cornwall TR7 2LR
T: (01637) 874216
F: (01637) 874216
E: sheila.harper@virgin.net
I: www.freespace.virgin.
net/sheila.harper

Degembris Farmhouse ◆◆◆◆
St Newlyn East, Newquay,
Cornwall TR8 5HY
T: (01872) 510555
F: (01872) 510230
E: kathy@degembris.co.uk
I: www.degembris.co.uk

Edwardian Hotel Island Crescent ◆◆◆
3-7 Island Crescent, Newquay,
Cornwall TR7 1DZ
T: (01637) 874087

The Harbour Hotel ◆◆◆◆
North Quay Hill, Newquay,
Cornwall TR7 1HF
T: (01637) 873040
E: alan@harbourhotel.co.uk
I: www.harbourhotel.co.uk

Marina Hotel ◆◆◆◆
Narrowcliff, Newquay, Cornwall
TR7 2PL
T: (01637) 873012
F: (01637) 851273

Pendeen Hotel ◆◆◆◆
Alexandra Road, Porth,
Newquay, Cornwall TR7 3ND
T: (01637) 873521
F: (01637) 873521
E: pendeen@cornwall.net
I: www.cornwall.net/pendeen/

Rose Cottage ◆◆◆◆
Shepherds Farm, Fiddlers Green,
St Newlyn East, Newquay,
Cornwall TR8 5NW
T: (01872) 540502
F: (01872) 540340

Tir Chonaill Lodge Hotel ◆◆◆
106 Mount Wise, Newquay,
Cornwall TR7 1QP
T: (01637) 876492
E: gerardwatts@tinyworld.co.uk
I: www.conniexions.
co.uk/tirchon@naill

Trevilla ◆◆◆
18 Berry Road, Newquay,
Cornwall TR7 1AR
T: (01637) 871504

Wenden Guest House ◆◆◆
11 Berry Road, Newquay,
Cornwall TR7 1AU
T: (01637) 872604
F: (01637) 872604
E: wenden@newquay-holidays.
co.uk
I: www.newquay-holidays.co.uk

Windward Hotel ◆◆◆◆
Alexandra Road, Porth,
Newquay, Cornwall TR7 3NB
T: (01637) 873185 & 852436
F: (01637) 852436
E: caswind@aol.com
I: www.windwardhotel.com

NEWTON ABBOT
Devon

Keyberry Hotel ◆◆◆
17 Kingskerswell Road, Decoy,
Newton Abbot, Devon TQ12 1DQ
T: (01626) 352120

The Rowans ◆◆◆
85 Highweek Village, Highweek,
Newton Abbot, Devon TQ12 1QQ
T: (01626) 365584

NEWTON FERRERS
Devon

Broadmoor Farm ◆◆◆
Newton Ferrers, Plymouth
PL8 2NE
T: (01752) 880407
E: agfarms@hotmail.com

NEWTON ST LOE
Bath and North East Somerset

Pennsylvania Farm ◆◆◆◆
Newton St Loe, Bath BA2 9JD
T: (01225) 314912
F: (01225) 314912
E: info@pennsylvaniafarm.co.uk
I: ww.pennsylvaniafarm.co.uk

NORTH BRADLEY
Wiltshire

49a Church Lane ◆◆◆
North Bradley, Trowbridge,
Wiltshire BA14 0TA
T: (01225) 762558

NORTH CADBURY
Somerset

Ashlea House ◆◆◆◆
High Street, North Cadbury,
Yeovil, Somerset BA22 7DP
T: (01963) 440891
F: (01963) 440891
E: ashlea@btinternet.com
I: www.ashlea.btinternet.co.uk

The Catash Inn ◆◆
North Cadbury, Yeovil, Somerset
BA22 7DH
T: (01963) 440248
F: (01963) 440248
E: clive&sandra@catash.com
I: www.catash.com

NORTH TAWTON
Devon

Kayden House Hotel ◆◆◆
High Street, North Tawton,
Devon EX20 2HF
T: (01837) 82242

Lower Nichols Nymet Farm ◆◆◆◆
Lower Nichols Nymet, North
Tawton, Devon EX20 2BW
T: (01363) 82510
F: (01363) 82510

Oaklands Farm ◆◆◆
North Tawton, Devon EX20 2BQ
T: (01837) 82340

NORTH WOOTTON
Dorset

Stoneleigh Barn ◆◆◆◆
North Wootton, Sherborne,
Dorset DT9 5JW
T: (01935) 815964
E: stoneleigh@ic24.net

NORTH WRAXALL
Wiltshire

Court Close House ◆◆◆◆
North Wraxall, Chippenham,
Wiltshire SN14 7AD
T: (01225) 891930
E: vickyosborne@delomosne.
co.uk

NORTON ST PHILIP
Somerset

George Inn ◆◆◆◆
High Street, Norton St Philip,
Bath BA2 7LH
T: (01373) 834224
F: (01373) 834861

The Old Police House ◆◆◆
Town Barton, Norton St Philip,
Bath BA3 6LN
T: (01373) 834308
F: (01373) 834145
E: grahamjenkinson@
compuserve.com

NORTON SUB HAMDON
Somerset

Brook House ◆◆◆◆
Little Street, Norton Sub
Hamdon, Stoke sub Hamdon,
Somerset TA14 6SR
T: (01935) 881789
F: (01935) 881789

NOSS MAYO
Devon

Netton Farmhouse ◆◆◆◆◆
Noss Mayo, Plymouth, Devon
PL8 1HB
T: (01752) 873080 &
07899 923444
F: (01752) 873107
E: lesley@brunning-host.co.uk
I: www.brunning-host.co.uk

OAKFORD
Devon

Harton Farm ◆◆◆
Oakford, Tiverton, Devon
EX16 9HH
T: (01398) 351209
F: (01398) 351209
E: harton@eclipse.co.uk

OAKHILL
Somerset

Blakes Farm ◆◆◆
Radstock, Oakhill, Bath BA3 5HY
T: (01749) 840301

The Boltons ◆◆◆
Sumach House, Neighbourne,
Oakhill, Bath BA3 5BQ
T: (01749) 840366
F: (01749) 840366
E: sumachhouse@aol.com
I: www.members.aol.
com/sumachhouse

OBORNE
Dorset

The Grange Restaurant and Hotel ◆◆◆◆◆
Oborne, Sherborne, Dorset
DT9 4LA
T: (01935) 813463
F: (01935) 817464

OGBOURNE ST ANDREW
Wiltshire

The Wheatsheaf Inn with Rooms
Rating Applied For
Ogbourne St Andrew,
Marlborough, Wiltshire SN8 1RZ
T: (01672) 841229
F: (01672) 841114

OKEHAMPTON
Devon

Higher Cadham Farm ◆◆◆◆
Jacobstowe, Okehampton,
Devon EX20 3RB
T: (01837) 851647
F: (01837) 851410
I: www.highercadham.co.uk

The Tuit
Rating Applied For
Lewdown, Okehampton, Devon
EX20 4BS
T: (01566) 783301

Week Farm Country Holidays ◆◆◆◆
Bridestowe, Okehampton, Devon
EX20 4HZ
T: (01837) 861221
F: (01837) 861221
E: accom@weekfarmonline.com
I: www.weekfarmonline.com

OLD SODBURY
South Gloucestershire

Dornden Guest House ◆◆◆◆
Church Lane, Old Sodbury,
Bristol BS37 6NB
T: (01454) 313325
F: (01454) 312263
E: dorndenguesthouse@
tinyworld.co.uk
I: westcountrytouristboard

ORCHESTON
Wiltshire

The Crown Inn ◆◆◆
Stonehenge Park, Orcheston,
Salisbury, Wiltshire SP3 4SH
T: (01980) 620304
F: (01980) 621121
F: stp@orcheston.freeserve.
co.uk
I: www.orcheston.freeserve.
co.uk

OSMINGTON
Dorset

Halls Farm ◆◆◆
Church Lane, Osmington,
Weymouth, Dorset DT3 6EW
T: (01305) 837068 &
07747 803317
F: (01305) 837068
E: hallsfarm@lineone.net

Rosedale ◆◆◆
Lower Church Lane, Osmington,
Weymouth, Dorset DT3 6EW
T: (01305) 832056

OTTERY ST MARY
Devon

Normandy House Hotel and Bistro ◆◆◆◆
5 Cornhill, Ottery St Mary,
Devon EX11 1DW
T: (01404) 811088
F: (01404) 811023
E: petergfield@dial.pipex.com

Pitt Farm ◆◆◆◆
Fairmile, Ottery St Mary, Devon
EX11 1NL
T: (01404) 812439
F: (01404) 812439
I: www.smoothhound.co.uk.
/hotels/pittfarm.html

OWERMOIGNE
Dorset

Chilbury Lodge ◆◆◆◆
5 Wareham Road, Owermoigne,
Dorchester, Dorset DT2 8HL
T: (01305) 854773
E: susanl@euphony.net

PADSTOW
Cornwall

Althea Library Bed and Breakfast ◆◆◆◆
27 High Street, Padstow,
Cornwall PL28 8BB
T: (01841) 532717 & 532679
F: (01841) 532717

Beau Vista ◆◆◆◆
Sarah's Lane, Padstow, Cornwall
PL28 8EL
T: (01841) 533270 &
07767 405550
F: (01841) 533270
E: beauvista@padstow.uk.com
I: www.padstow.uk.
com/beauvista

Cally Croft ◆◆◆◆
26 Raleigh Close, Padstow,
Cornwall PL28 8BQ
T: (01841) 533726
E: john@cally26.freeserve.co.uk
I: www.padstow-callycroft.co.uk

The Dower House Hotel ◆◆◆◆◆
Fentonluna Lane, Padstow,
Cornwall PL28 8BA
T: (01841) 532317
F: (01841) 532667
E: dower@btinternet.com
I: www.padstow.uk.
com/dowerhouse/

The Old Mill House
Rating Applied For
Little Petherick, Wadebridge,
Cornwall PL27 7QT
T: (01841) 540388
F: 0870 056 9360
E: dwalker@oldmillbandb.
demon.co.uk

Petrocstowe ◆◆◆
30 Treverbyn Road, Padstow,
Cornwall PL28 8DW
T: (01841) 532429 &
07818 451485

Trealaw ◆◆◆
22 Duke Street, Padstow,
Cornwall PL28 8AB
T: (01841) 533161
F: (01841) 533161

Tregea Hotel ◆◆◆◆◆
16-18 High Street, Padstow,
Cornwall PL28 8BB
T: (01841) 532455
F: (01841) 533542
E: reservations@tregea.co.uk
I: www.tregea.co.uk

Treverbyn House ◆◆◆◆
Station Road, Padstow, Cornwall
PL28 8AD
T: (01841) 532855
F: (01841) 532855
I: www.treverbynmembers.
easyspace.com

Trevone Bay Hotel ◆◆◆◆
Trevone Bay, Padstow, Cornwall
PL28 8QS
T: (01841) 520243
F: (01841) 521195
E: hamilton@trevonebay.
demon.co.uk

Trevorrick Farm ◆◆◆
St Issey, Wadebridge, Cornwall
PL27 7QH
T: (01841) 540574
F: (01841) 540574
E: info@trevorrick.co.uk
I: www.trevorrick.co.uk

The White Hart ◆◆◆◆
1 New Street, Padstow, Cornwall
PL28 8EA
T: (01841) 532350
E: whthartpad@aol.com
I: www.padstow.uk.
com/whitehart

PAIGNTON
Devon

Arcadia Hotel
Rating Applied For
Marine Gardens, Preston,
Paignton, Devon TQ3 2NT
T: (01803) 551039
F: (01803) 551039
E: jwest@talk21.com

Arden House Hotel ◆◆◆
10 Youngs Park Road, Paignton,
Devon TQ4 6BU
T: (01803) 558443
F: (01803) 558443

Arrandale ◆◆◆
34 Garfield Road, Paignton,
Devon TQ4 6AX
T: (01803) 552211 &
0771 9452715
I: www.paigntondevon.
co.uk/arrandale.htm

Bay Sands Hotel ◆◆◆◆
14 Colin Road, Paignton, Devon
TQ3 2NR
T: (01803) 524877
F: (01803) 557827
E: enquiries@baysands.co.uk
I: www.baysands.co.uk

Beach House ◆◆◆
39 Garfield Road, Paignton,
Devon TQ4 6AX
T: (01803) 525742
F: 0870 403 2953
E: lesjt@altavista.co.uk
I: www.geocities.
com/beach_house_uk

Bella Vista Guest House ◆◆◆
5 Berry Square, Paignton, Devon
TQ4 6AZ
T: (01803) 558122

Beresford Hotel ◆◆◆◆
5 Adelphi Road, Paignton, Devon
TQ4 6AW
T: (01803) 551560
F: (01803) 551560
E: lek42@aol.com

Birchwood House Hotel ◆◆◆◆
33 St Andrews Road, Paignton,
Devon TQ4 6HA
T: (01803) 551323
F: (01803) 401301
E: yates3048@aol.com
I: www.birchwoodhouse.net

Birklands Guest House ◆◆◆
33 Garfield Road, Paignton,
Devon TQ4 6AX
T: (01803) 556970

Blue Waters Hotel ◆◆◆
4 Leighon Road, Paignton,
Devon TQ3 2BQ
T: (01803) 557749
E: bluewaterhtl@aol.com

The Briars Hotel ◆◆◆◆
26 Sands Road, Paignton, Devon
TQ4 6EJ
T: (01803) 557729
E: enquiries@thebriarshotel.
co.uk

Bronte Hotel ◆◆◆◆
7 Colin Road, Paignton, Devon
TQ3 2NR
T: (01803) 550254
F: (01803) 391489

Bruce Lodge Guest House ◆◆◆
2 Elmsleigh Road, Paignton,
Devon TQ4 5AU
T: (01803) 550972
F: (01803) 550972
E: roger_kingdon@lineone.net
I: www.paigntondevon.
co.uk/brucelodge/htm

Carrington Hotel ◆◆
10 Beach Road, Paignton, Devon
TQ4 6AY
T: (01803) 558785

Cherwood Hotel ◆◆◆◆
26 Garfield Road, Paignton,
Devon TQ4 6AX
T: (01803) 556515
F: (01803) 555126
E: james-pauline.
cherwood-hotel.co.uk
I: www.cherwood-hotel.co.uk

Cleve Court Hotel ◆◆◆◆
3 Cleveland Road, Paignton,
Devon TQ4 6EN
T: (01803) 551444
F: (01803) 664617

Cliveden ◆◆◆
27 Garfield Road, Paignton,
Devon TQ4 6AX
T: (01803) 557461
F: (01803) 557461
E: cliveden@lineone.net
I: www.clivedenguesthouse.
co.uk

Colin House ◆◆◆
2 Colin Road, Paignton, Devon
TQ3 2NR
T: (01803) 550609
F: (01803) 550609
E: colin-house@talk21.com
I: www.paigntondevon.
co.uk/colinhouse.htm

Craigmore Guest House ◆◆◆
54 Dartmouth Road, Paignton,
Devon TQ4 5AN
T: (01803) 557373

Dalmary Guest House ◆◆◆
21 Garfield Road, Paignton,
Devon TQ4 6AX
T: (01803) 528145

Danethorpe Hotel ◆◆◆◆
23 St Andrews Road,
Roundham, Paignton, Devon
TQ4 6HA
T: (01803) 551251
F: (01803) 557075

Devon House Hotel ◆◆◆
20 Garfield Road, Paignton,
Devon TQ4 6AX
T: (01803) 559371
F: (01803) 550054
E: devon.house.hotel@lineone.
net
I: www.lineone.net/~devon.
house.hotel/

Earlston House Hotel ◆◆◆◆
31 St Andrews Road, Paignton,
Devon TQ4 6HA
T: (01803) 558355
F: (01803) 556085
E: earlstonhouse@tinyworld.
co.uk

Esplanade Hotel ◆◆◆
Sands Road, Paignton, Devon
TQ4 6EG
T: (01803) 556333
F: (01803) 666786

Hotel Fiesta ◆◆◆
2 Kernou Road, Paignton, Devon
TQ4 6BA
T: (01803) 521862 &
07802 427401
F: (01803) 521862

Florida Hotel ◆◆◆◆
9 Colin Road, Paignton, Devon
TQ3 2NR
T: (01803) 551447
I: www.mlemm@floridahotel.
fsbusiness.co.uk

Greenford Lodge Private Hotel ◆◆◆
56 Dartmouth Road, Paignton,
Devon TQ4 5AN
T: (01803) 553635

Harbour Lodge ◆◆◆
4 Cleveland Road, Paignton,
Devon TQ4 6EN
T: (01803) 556932
E: harbourlodge@theseed.net

Kingswinford Hotel ◆◆◆◆
32 Garfield Road, Paignton,
Devon TQ4 6AX
T: (01803) 558358
E: kingswinford@garfieldroad.
freeserve.co.uk
I: www.kingswinfordhotel.co.uk

The Linton Hotel ◆◆◆◆
7 Elmsleigh Road, Paignton,
Devon TQ4 5AX
T: (01803) 558745
F: (01803) 527345

Lyncourt Hotel ◆◆◆
14 Elmsleigh Park, Paignton,
Devon TQ4 5AT
T: (01803) 557124

Mandalay Hotel
Rating Applied For
7 Cleveland Road, Paignton,
Devon TQ4 6EN
T: (01803) 525653
F: (01803) 525193
E: mandalayhotel@btconnect.
com
I: www.mandalay-hotel.co.uk

Mayfield Hotel ◆◆◆
8 Queens Road, Paignton, Devon
TQ4 6AT
T: (01803) 556802

Meadowfield Hotel ◆◆◆◆
36 Preston Down Road,
Paignton, Devon TQ3 2RW
T: (01803) 522987
F: (01803) 554605
E: rpitchell@aol.com
I: www.meadowfieldhotel.co.uk

Middlepark Hotel ◆◆◆
3 Marine Drive, Paignton, Devon
TQ3 2NJ
T: (01803) 559025
F: (01803) 559025

Norbreck ◆◆◆
35 New Street, Paignton, Devon
TQ3 3HL
T: (01803) 558033
F: (01803) 665755

Paignton Court Hotel ◆◆◆
17-19 Sands Road, Paignton,
Devon TQ4 6EG
T: (01803) 553111
E: paigntoncourt@aol.com
I: www.paignton-court-hotel.
co.uk

Richmond Guest House ◆◆◆
19 Norman Road, Paignton,
Devon TQ3 2BE
T: (01803) 558792 &
(017802) 398040
F: (01803) 558792

Rockview Guest House ◆◆◆
13 Queens Road, Paignton,
Devon TQ4 6AT
T: (01803) 556702

Roscrea Hotel ◆◆◆◆
2 Alta Vista Road, Paignton,
Devon TQ4 6BZ
T: (01803) 558706
F: (01803) 558706
E: roscrea@globalnet.co.uk
I: www.paigntonhotels.com

Rosemead Guest House ◆◆◆
22 Garfield Road, Paignton,
Devon TQ4 6AX
T: (01803) 557944
E: pauldgama@aol.com

Rougemont Hotel ◆◆◆
23 Roundham Road, Paignton,
Devon TQ4 6DN
T: (01803) 556570
F: (01803) 556570
E: beds@rougemonthotel.co.uk
I: www.rougemonthotel.co.uk

Roundham Lodge ◆◆◆◆◆
16 Roundham Road, Paignton,
Devon TQ4 6DN
T: (01803) 558485
F: (01803) 553090
E: alan@vega68.freeserve.co.uk
I: www.smoothhound.
co.uk/hotels/round1.html

Rowcroft Private Hotel ◆◆◆
14 Youngs Park Road, Paignton,
Devon TQ4 6BU
T: (01803) 559420

St Edmund's Hotel ◆◆◆
25 Sands Road, Paignton, Devon
TQ4 6EG
T: (01803) 558756
E: stedmunds@currantbun.com
I: www.stedmundshotel.com

St Weonards Private Hotel
◆◆◆
12 Kernou Road, Paignton,
Devon TQ4 6BA
T: (01803) 558842
F: (01803) 558842

The Sands Hotel ◆◆◆
32 Sands Road, Paignton, Devon
TQ4 6EJ
T: (01803) 551282
F: (01803) 407269
E: sands.hotel@virgin.net

Sea Spray Hotel
Rating Applied For
1 Beach Road, Paignton, Devon
TQ4 6AY
T: (01803) 553141
E: seasprayhotel.co.uk
I: www.seasprayhotel.co.uk

Seacroft Guest House ◆◆◆◆
41 Sands Road, Paignton, Devon
TQ4 6EG
T: (01803) 523791

Seaford Sands Hotel ◆◆◆
17 Roundham Road, Paignton,
Devon TQ4 6DN
T: (01803) 557722
F: (01803) 665026

Sealawn Hotel ◆◆◆
Sea Front, 20 Esplanade Road,
Paignton, Devon TQ4 6BE
T: (01803) 559031

Seaways Hotel ◆◆◆◆
30 Sands Road, Paignton, Devon
TQ4 6EJ
T: (01803) 551093
F: (01803) 551093

Sonachan House Hotel ◆◆◆
35 St Andrews Road, Paignton,
Devon TQ4 6HA
T: (01803) 558021

Sundale Hotel ◆◆◆
10 Queens Road, Paignton,
Devon TQ4 6AT
T: (01803) 557431

Two Beaches Hotel ◆◆◆
27 St Andrews Road, Paignton,
Devon TQ4 6HA
T: (01803) 522164

Wulfruna Hotel ◆◆◆◆
8 Esplanade, Paignton, Devon
TQ4 6EB
T: (01803) 555567
F: (01803) 555567
E: julieatwulf@aol.com

Wynncroft Hotel ◆◆◆◆
2 Elmsleigh Park, Paignton,
Devon TQ4 5AT
T: (01803) 525728
F: (01803) 526335
E: wynncroft@fsbdial.co.uk
I: www.wynncroft.co.uk

PANBOROUGH
Somerset

Garden End Farm ◆◆◆
Panborough, Wells, Somerset
BA5 1PN
T: (01934) 712414
E: sheila@gardenendfarm.
freeserve.co.uk
I: www.gardenendfarm.
freeserve.co.uk

PATCHWAY
South Gloucestershire

Willow Hotel ◆◆◆
209 Gloucester Road, Patchway,
Bristol BS34 6ND
T: (01454) 612276
F: (01454) 201107
E: colinm@gifford.co.uk.
I: www.gifford.co.uk.willowhotel

PATTERDOWN
Wiltshire

Bennetts ◆◆◆◆
Holywell House, Patterdown,
Chippenham, Wiltshire
SN15 2NP
T: (01249) 652922
E: holywell-house@btinternet.
com
I: www.smoothhound.
co.uk/hotels/bennetts.htm

PAYHEMBURY
Devon

Yellingham Farm ◆◆◆◆
Payhembury, Honiton, Devon
EX14 3HE
T: (01404) 850272
F: (01404) 850873
E: JanetEast@compuserve.com

PEASEDOWN ST JOHN
Bath and North East Somerset

Eastfield Farm Guest House
◆◆◆
Eastfield, Dunkerton Hill,
Peasedown St John, Bath
BA2 8PF
T: (01761) 432161

PEDWELL
Somerset

Barncroft ◆◆◆
20a Taunton Road, Pedwell,
Bridgwater, Somerset TA7 9BG
T: (01458) 211011

Sunnyside ◆◆◆◆
34 Taunton Road, Pedwell,
Bridgwater, Somerset TA7 9BG
T: (01458) 210097 &
07971 527771

PELYNT
Cornwall

Bake Farm ◆◆◆
Pelynt, Looe, Cornwall PL13 2QQ
T: (01503) 220244
F: (01503) 220244

Cardwen Farm
Rating Applied For
Pelynt, Looe, Cornwall PL13 2LU
T: (01503) 220213
F: (01503) 220213

Penkelly Farm ◆◆◆
Pelynt, Looe, Cornwall PL13 2QH
T: (01503) 220348
I: www.penkellyfarm.co.uk

Trenderway Farm ◆◆◆◆◆
Pelynt, Polperro, Looe, Cornwall
PL13 2LY
T: (01503) 272214
F: (01503) 272991
E: trenderwayfarm@hotmail.
com
I: www.trenderwayfarm.co.uk

PENDEEN
Cornwall

Field House ◆◆◆◆
8 Trewellard Road, Pendeen,
Penzance, Cornwall TR19 7ST
T: (01736) 788097
E: fieldhousetrewellard@talk21.
com
I: www.cornwall-online.
co.uk/field-house

Trewellard Manor Farm
◆◆◆◆
Pendeen, Penzance, Cornwall
TR19 7SU
T: (01736) 788526

PENSFORD
Bath and North East Somerset

Green Acres ◆◆◆
Stanton Wick, Pensford,
BS39 4BX
T: (01761) 490397
F: (01761) 490397

Leigh Farm ◆◆
Old Road, Pensford, BS39 4BA
T: (01761) 490281 &
07866 251409
F: (01761) 490281

The Model Farm ◆◆◆
Norton Hawkfield, Pensford,
BS39 4HA
T: (01275) 832144
F: (01275) 832144
E: margarethasell@hotmail.com

PENSILVA
Cornwall

**Penharget Farm Bed and
Breakfast**
Rating Applied For
Penharget Farm, Pensilva,
Liskeard, Cornwall PL14 5RJ
T: (01579) 362221
F: (01579) 363965
E: penhargetfarm@ukonline.
co.uk

PENZANCE
Cornwall

Carnson House Hotel ◆
2 East Terrace, Penzance,
Cornwall TR18 2TD
T: (01736) 365589
F: (01736) 365594
E: carnson@netcomuk.co.uk
I: www.chycor.
co.uk/carnson-house

Con Amore ◆◆◆
38 Morrab Road, Penzance,
Cornwall TR18 4EX
T: (01736) 363423
F: (01736) 363423

Cornerways Guest House
Rating Applied For
5 Leskinnick Street, Penzance,
Cornwall TR18 2HA
T: (01736) 364645
F: (01736) 364645
E: enquiries@
cornerways-penzance.co.uk
I: penzance.co.uk/cornerways

Glencree Private Hotel ◆◆◆
2 Mennaye Road, Penzance,
Cornwall TR18 4NG
T: (01736) 362026
F: (01736) 362026

Halcyon Guest House ◆◆◆
6 Chyandour Square, Penzance,
Cornwall TR18 3LW
T: (01736) 366302
F: (01736) 366302
E: pat+bob@halcyon/.co.uk

Lombard House ◆◆◆◆
16 Regent Terrace, Penzance,
Cornwall TR18 4DW
T: (01736) 364897
F: (01736) 364897
E: rita.kruge@talk21.com
I: www.cornwall-online.
co.uk/lombard-house

Lynwood Guest House ◆◆◆
41 Morrab Road, Penzance,
Cornwall TR18 4EX
T: (01736) 365871
F: (01736) 365871
E: lynwoodpz@aol.com
I: www.penzance.
co.uk/lynwood-guesthouse

Menwidden Farm ◆◆◆
Ludgvan, Penzance, Cornwall
TR20 8BN
T: (01736) 740415

Penmorvah Hotel ◆◆◆
Alexandra Road, Penzance,
Cornwall TR18 4LZ
T: (01736) 363711
F: (01736) 363711

Richmond Lodge ◆◆◆
61 Morrab Road, Penzance,
Cornwall TR18 4EP
T: (01736) 365560
E: ivor@richmondlodge.fsnet.
co.uk
I: www.geocities.
com/richmondlodge_uk

Rose Farm ◆◆◆
Chyanhal, Buryas Bridge,
Penzance, Cornwall TR19 6AN
T: (01736) 731808
F: (01736) 731808
E: lally@rosefarm.co.uk
I: www.rosefarmcornwall.co.uk

Roseudian ◆◆◆◆
Crippas Hill, Kelynack, St. Just,
Penzance, Cornwall TR19 7RE
T: (01736) 788556

The Summer House ◆◆◆◆◆
Cornwall Terrace, Penzance,
Cornwall TR18 4HL
T: (01736) 363744
F: (01736) 360959
E: summerhouse@dial.pipex.
com
I: www.summerhouse-cornwall.
com

Treventon Guest House ◆◆◆
Alexandra Place, Penzance,
Cornwall TR18 4NE
T: (01736) 363521
F: (01736) 361873
I: www.
ukholidayaccommodation.
com/treventonguesthouse

Warwick House Hotel ◆◆◆
17 Regent Terrace, Penzance,
Cornwall TR18 4DW
T: (01736) 363881
F: (01736) 331078

Woodstock House ◆◆◆
20 Morrab Road, Penzance,
Cornwall TR18 4AZ
T: (01736) 369049
F: (01736) 369049
E: woodstocp@aol.com
I: www.ivaccommodations.
com/woodstock.html

PERRANPORTH
Cornwall

Chy-an-Kerensa Guest House
◆◆◆
Cliff Road, Perranporth,
Cornwall TR6 0DR
T: (01872) 572470
F: (01872) 572470

Ponsmere Hotel ◆◆◆
Ponsmere Road, Perranporth,
Cornwall TR6 0BW
T: (01872) 572225 & 572519
F: (01872) 573075
E: info@ponsmere.co.uk
I: www.ponsmere.co.uk

Trevie Guest House ◆◆◆
Mill Road, Bolingey,
Perranporth, Cornwall TR6 0AP
T: (01872) 573475
F: (01872) 573475

PIDDLEHINTON
Dorset

Muston Manor ◆◆◆◆
Piddlehinton, Dorchester, Dorset
DT2 7SY
T: (01305) 848242
F: (01305) 848242

Whites Dairy House
Rating Applied For
High Street, Piddlehinton,
Dorchester, Dorset DT2 7TD
T: (01300) 348386
F: (01300) 348368
E: robin.adeney@care4free.web
I: www.whitesdairyhouse.co.uk

PIDDLETRENTHIDE
Dorset

Fern Cottage ◆◆
Piddletrenthide, Dorchester,
Dorset DT2 7QF
T: (01300) 348277
F: (01300) 348277
E: ferncottage@onetel.net.uk

The Poachers Inn ◆◆◆◆
Piddletrenthide, Dorchester,
Dorset DT2 7QX
T: (01300) 348358
F: (01300) 348153
E: thepoachersinn@
piddletrenthide.fsbusiness.co.uk
I: www.thepoachersinn.co.uk

PILLATON
Cornwall

The Weary Friar Inn ◆◆◆
Pillaton, Saltash, Cornwall
PL12 6QS
T: (01579) 350238
F: (01579) 350238

PINKNEY
Wiltshire

Home Farm House ◆◆◆
Pinkney, Malmesbury, Wiltshire
SN16 0NX
T: (01666) 840772

PLUSH
Dorset

The Old Barn House ◆◆◆
Plush, Dorchester, Dorset
DT2 7RQ
I: (01300) 348730

PLYMOUTH
Devon

Athenaeum Lodge ◆◆◆◆
4 Athenaeum Street, The Hoe,
Plymouth, PL1 2RQ
T: (01752) 665005
F: (01752) 665005

Berkeleys of St James ◆◆◆◆
4 St James Place East, The Hoe,
Plymouth, PL1 3AS
T: (01752) 221654
F: (01752) 221654
I: www.smoothhound.
co.uk/hotels/berkely2html.

Blackhall Lodge ◆◆◆◆
Old Staddiscombe Road,
Plymouth, Devon PL9 9NA
T: (01752) 482482
F: (01752) 482482
E: johnm@jboocock.freeserve.
co.uk
I: www.jboocock.freeserve.co.uk

Bowling Green Hotel ◆◆◆◆◆
9-10 Osborne Place, Lockyer
Street, Plymouth, PL1 2PU
T: (01752) 209090 & 667485
F: (01752) 209092
E: dave@bowlinggreenhotel.
freeserve.co.uk
I: www.smoothhound.
co.uk/hotels/bowling.html

Gabber Farm ◆◆◆
Down Thomas, Plymouth
PL9 0AW
T: (01752) 862269
F: (01752) 862269

The George Guest House ◆◆◆
161 Citadel Road, The Hoe,
Plymouth, PL1 2HU
T: (01752) 661517
F: (01752) 661517
E: georgeguesthouse@faxvia.
net
I: www.
accommodationplymouth.co.uk

Hotspur Guest House ◆◆
108 North Road East, Plymouth,
PL4 6AW
T: (01752) 663928
F: (01752) 261493
E: info@hotspur.co.uk
I: www.hotspur.co.uk

Lamplighter Hotel ◆◆◆
103 Citadel Road, The Hoe,
Plymouth, PL1 2RN
T: (01752) 663855
F: (01752) 228139
E: lampligherhotel@ukonline.
co.uk

Mayflower Guest House ◆◆◆
209 Citadel Road East, The Hoe,
Plymouth, PL1 2JF
T: (01752) 202727 & 667496
F: (01752) 202727
E: info@mayflowerguesthouse.
co.uk
I: www.mayflowerguesthouse.
co.uk

Mountbatten Hotel ◆◆◆
52 Exmouth Road, Stoke,
Plymouth PL1 4QH
T: (01752) 563843
F: (01752) 606014

The Old Pier Guest House
◆◆◆
20 Radford Road, West Hoe,
Plymouth, Devon PL1 3BY
T: (01752) 268468
E: enquiries@oldpier.freeserve.
co.uk
I: www.oldpier.freeserve.
co.uk/oldpier

Osmond Guest House ◆◆◆◆
42 Pier Street, Plymouth,
PL1 3BT
T: (01752) 229705
F: (01752) 269655
E: mike@osmondgh.freeserve.
co.uk
I: plymouth-explore.co.uk

Rosaland Hotel ◆◆◆◆
32 Houndiscombe Road,
Plymouth, PL4 6HQ
T: (01752) 664749
F: (01752) 256984
E: manager@rosalandhotel.com
I: www.rosalandhotel.com

The Roscoff Guest House ◆◆◆
32 Grand Parade, West Hoe,
Plymouth, PL1 3DJ
T: (01752) 257900

Smeatons Tower Hotel ◆◆◆◆
40-42 Grand Parade, The Hoe,
Plymouth, PL1 3DJ
T: (01752) 221007
F: (01752) 221664
E: info@smeatonstowerhotel.
co.uk
I: www.smeatonstowerhotel.
co.uk

Squires Guest House ◆◆◆◆
7 St James Place East, The Hoe,
Plymouth, PL1 3AS
T: (01752) 261459
F: (01752) 261459
E: pagea8@aol.com
I: www.squiresguesthouse.co.uk

The Teviot Guest House
◆◆◆◆
20 North Road East, Plymouth,
Devon PL4 6AS
T: (01752) 262656
F: (01752) 251660
E: teviotgh@btinternet.com
I: www.btinternet.
com/~teviotgh

Westwinds Hotel ◆◆◆
99 Citadel Road, The Hoe,
Plymouth, PL1 2RN
T: (01752) 601777 &
08007 315717
F: (01752) 662158
E: paul.colman@btinternet.com
I: business.thisisplymouth.
co.uk/westwindshotel

POLBATHIC
Cornwall

Hendra Farm ◆◆◆◆
Polbathic, Torpoint, Cornwall
PL11 3DT
T: (01503) 250225
F: (01503) 250225

POLPERRO
Cornwall

Brent House ◆◆
1 Brent House, Talland Hill,
Polperro, Looe, Cornwall
PL13 2RY
T: (01503) 272495

Penryn House ◆◆◆
The Coombes, Polperro, Looe,
Cornwall PL13 2RQ
T: (01503) 272157
F: (01503) 273055

POLZEATH
Cornwall

The White Heron ◆◆◆
Polzeath, Wadebridge, Cornwall
PL27 6TJ
T: (01208) 863623
E: info@whiteheronhotel.co.uk
I: www.whiteheronhotel.co.uk

PORLOCK
Somerset

Burley Cottage Guest House
◆◆◆◆
Parsons Street, Porlock,
Minehead, Somerset TA24 8QJ
T: (01643) 862563 &
07957 721568
F: (01643) 862563
E: burleycottage@aol.com
I: www.bandbsomerset.co.uk

Leys B & B ◆◆◆◆
The Ridge, Off Bossington Lane,
Porlock, Minehead, Somerset
TA24 8HA
T: (01643) 862477
F: (01643) 862477

The Lorna Doone Hotel ◆◆◆
High Street, Porlock, Minehead,
Somerset TA24 8PS
T: (01643) 862404
F: (01643) 863018
E: lorna@doone99.freeserve.
co.uk

Myrtle Cottage ◆◆◆
High Street, Porlock, Minehead,
Somerset TA24 8PU
T: (01643) 862978
F: (01243) 862978
E: bob.steer@talk21.com
I: www.smoothhound.co.uk

Seapoint ◆◆◆◆
Upway, Porlock, Minehead,
Somerset TA24 8QE
T: (01643) 862289
F: (01643) 862289

PORT ISAAC
Cornwall

**The Slipway Hotel &
Restaurant ◆◆◆**
Harbour Front, Port Isaac,
Cornwall PL29 3RH
T: (01208) 880264
F: (01208) 880408
E: slipwayhotel@portisaac.com
I: www.portisaac.com

PORTESHAM
Dorset

The Old Fountain ◆◆◆
36 Front Street, Portesham,
Weymouth, Dorset DT3 4ET
T: (01305) 871278
F: (01305) 871278

PORTH
Cornwall

Porth Cliff Hotel ◆◆◆
Watergate Road, Porth,
Newquay, Cornwall TR7 3LX
T: (01637) 872503
F: (01637) 872503
E: porthcliff@hotel163.
freeserve.co.uk
I: www.porthcliffhotel.co.uk

PORTHCURNO
Cornwall

The Porthcurno Hotel ◆◆◆◆
The Valley, Porthcurno, St Levan,
Penzance, Cornwall TR19 6JX
T: (01736) 810119
F: (01736) 810711
E: porthcurnohotel@
netscapeonline.co.uk
I: www.porthcurnohotel.co.uk

PORTHLEVEN
Cornwall

Seefar ◆◆◆
Peverell Terrace, Porthleven,
Helston, Cornwall TR13 9DZ
T: (01326) 573778
E: seefar@talk21.com
I: www.cornwall-online.co.uk

PORTLAND
Dorset

Alessandria Hotel ◆◆◆
71 Wakeham Easton, Portland,
Dorset DT5 1HW
T: (01305) 822270 & 820108
F: (01305) 820561
I: www.s-h-systems.
co.uk/hotels/alessand.html

PORTMELLON
Cornwall

Bodrugan Barton ◆◆◆◆
Portmellon, Mevagissey, St
Austell, Cornwall PL26 6PT
T: (01726) 842094
F: (01726) 844378
E: bodruganbarton@ukonline.
co.uk

POULSHOT
Wiltshire

Higher Green Farm ◆◆
Poulshot, Devizes, Wiltshire
SN10 1RW
T: (01380) 828355
F: (01380) 828355

Middle Green Farm ◆◆◆
The Green, Poulshot, Devizes,
Wiltshire SN10 1RT
T: (01380) 828413
F: (01380) 828826

Poulshot Lodge Farm ◆◆
Poulshot, Devizes, Wiltshire
SN10 1RQ
T: (01380) 828255

POYNTINGTON
Dorset

Welgoer ◆◆◆
Poyntington, Sherborne, Dorset
DT9 4LF
T: (01963) 220737

PRESTON
Devon

Innisfree Hotel ◆◆◆◆
12 Colin Road, Preston, Newton
Abbot, Devon TQ3 2NR
T: (01803) 550692
F: (01803) 550692

PUNCKNOWLE
Dorset

The Crown Inn ◆◆◆
Church Street, Puncknowle,
Dorchester, Dorset DT2 9BN
T: (01308) 897711
F: (01308) 898282
E: thecrowninn@
puncknowle48.fsnet.co.uk

PURITON
Somerset

Canns Farm ◆◆◆
Canns Lane, Puriton, Bridgwater,
Somerset TA7 8AY
T: (01278) 684773 & 0797 143
2483
F: (01278) 684773
E: cannsfarm@minim.com
I: www.minim.com/cannsfarm

QUEEN CAMEL
Somerset

Mildmay Arms ◆◆
High Street, Queen Camel,
Yeovil, Somerset BA22 7NJ
T: (01935) 850456
F: (01935) 851610
E: mike@mildmayarms.
greatxscape.net
I: www.mildmayarms.
greatxscape.net

QUETHIOCK
Cornwall

Trecorme Barton ◆◆◆◆
Quethiock, Liskeard, Cornwall
PL14 3SH
T: (01579) 342646

RADSTOCK
Bath and North East Somerset

The Rookery ◆◆◆◆
Wells Road, Radstock, Bath
BA3 3RS
T: (01761) 432626
F: (01761) 432626
E: rookery@iname.com
I: www.therookeryguesthouse.
co.uk

RAMSBURY
Wiltshire

Marridge Hill Cottage ◆◆◆
Marridge Hill, Ramsbury,
Marlborough, Wiltshire
SN8 2HG
T: (01672) 520486

Marridge Hill House ◆◆◆◆
Ramsbury, Marlborough,
Wiltshire SN8 2HG
T: (01672) 520237
F: (01672) 520053
E: judy.davies@lineone.net

RATTERY
Devon

Knowle Farm ◆◆◆◆
Rattery, Totnes, Devon TQ10 9JY
T: (01364) 73914
F: (01364) 73914
E: lynn@knowle-farm.co.uk
I: www.knowle-farm.co.uk/b&b

REDLYNCH
Wiltshire

**Orchards Country House Bed &
Breakfast ◆◆◆◆**
Kiln Road, Redlynch, Salisbury,
Wiltshire SP5 2HT
T: (01725) 510372
F: (01725) 510372
E: alanjj1@hotmail.com
I: www.hompepages.tesco.
net/~alanjj

**Templeman's Old Farmhouse
◆◆◆◆**
Redlynch, Salisbury SP5 2JS
T: (01725) 510331
F: (01752) 510331

ROADWATER
Somerset

Briar Cottage ◆◆◆◆
The Old Mineral Line, Roadwater,
Watchet, Somerset TA23 0RJ
T: (01984) 640020

Stamborough Farm ◆◆◆◆
Roadwater, Watchet, Somerset
TA23 0RW
T: (01984) 640258
F: (01984) 641051
E: rileystamco@compuserve.
com

ROCK
Cornwall

Silvermead ◆◆◆
Rock, Wadebridge, Cornwall
PL27 6LB
T: (01208) 862425
F: (01208) 862919
E: barbara@silvermead.
freeserve.co.uk
I: www.silvermeadguesthouse.
co.uk

ROCKBEARE
Devon

Lower Marsh Farm ◆◆◆
Marsh Green, Rockbeare, Exeter
EX5 2EX
T: (01404) 822432
F: (01404) 823330
E: lowermarfarm@talk21.com
I: www.smoothhound.
co.uk/hotels/lowermar.html

RODE
Somerset

Rode Farm ◆◆◆
Rode, Bath BA3 6QQ
T: (01373) 831479 &
07971 929398

ROOKSBRIDGE
Somerset

Rooksbridge House ◆◆◆◆
Rooksbridge, Axbridge, Somerset
BS26 2UL
T: (01934) 750630

ROWDE
Wiltshire

Lower Foxhangers Farm ◆◆◆
Rowde, Devizes, Wiltshire
SN10 1SS
T: (01380) 828254
F: (01380) 828254

RUSHALL
Wiltshire

Little Thatch ◆◆◆
Rushall, Pewsey, Wiltshire
SN9 6EN
T: (01980) 635282 &
07977 562533
F: (01980) 635282

ST AGNES
Cornwall

Covean Cottage ◆◆◆◆
St Agnes, Isles of Scilly TR22 0PL
T: (01720) 422620
F: (01720) 422620

Penkerris ◆◆
Penwinnick Road, Penkerris, St
Agnes, Cornwall TR5 0PA
T: (01872) 552262
F: (01872) 552262
E: info@penkerris.co.uk
I: www.penkerris.co.uk

ST ANNS CHAPEL
Cornwall

The Rifle Volunteer Inn ◆◆◆
St Anns Chapel, Gunnislake,
Cornwall PL18 9HL
T: (01822) 832508

ST AUSTELL
Cornwall

Polgreen Farm ◆◆◆◆
London Apprentice, St Austell,
Cornwall PL26 7AP
T: (01726) 75151
F: (01726) 75151
E: polgreen.farm@btclick.com

ST BREWARD
Cornwall

Tarny Guesthouse ◆◆◆◆
Row, St Breward, Bodmin,
Cornwall PL30 4LW
T: (01208) 850583
I: www.bodminmoor.co.uk/tarny

Treswallock Farm ◆◆◆
St Breward, Bodmin, Cornwall
PL30 4PL
T: (01208) 850255
E: treswallockfarm@cwcom.et

ST BURYAN
Cornwall

Boskenna Home Farm ◆◆◆◆
St Buryan, Penzance, Cornwall
TR19 6DQ
T: (01736) 810705
F: (01736) 810705
E: julia.hosking@btclick.com

Higher Leah Farm ◆◆
St Buryan, Penzance, Cornwall
TR19 6EJ
T: (01736) 810424

Tregurnow Farm ◆◆◆◆
St Buryan, Penzance, Cornwall
TR19 6BL
T: (01736) 810255
F: (01736) 810255
E: tregurno@eurobell.co.uk
I: homepage.eurobell.
co.uk/tregurnol

Trelew Farm ◆◆◆
St Buryan, Penzance, Cornwall
TR19 6ED
T: (01736) 810308
E: trelew@btclick.com
I: www.cornwall-online.
co.uk/trelew-farm

ST EWE
Cornwall

Higher Kestle Farm ◆◆◆◆
St Ewe, Mevagissey, St Austell,
Cornwall PL26 6EP
T: (01726) 842001
F: (01726) 842001
E: vicky@higherkestle.freeserve.
co.uk

Lower Barn
Rating Applied For
Bosue, St Ewe, St Austell,
Cornwall PL26 6EU
T: (01726) 844881
E: janie@www.bosue.co.uk
I: www.bosue.co.uk

ST ISSEY
Cornwall

Ring O'Bells ◆◆◆
Church Town, St Issey,
Wadebridge, Cornwall PL27 7QA
T: (01841) 540251
E: ringersstissey-freeserve.co.uk

ST IVES
Cornwall

The Anchorage Guest House
◆◆◆◆
5 Bunkers Hill, St Ives, Cornwall
TR26 1LJ
T: (01736) 797135
F: (01736) 797135
E: james@theanchoragebb.
fsnet.co.uk
I: www.theanchoragebb.fsnet.
co.uk

Blue Hayes Hotel ◆◆◆◆
Trelyon Avenue, St Ives,
Cornwall TR26 2AD
T: (01736) 797129
F: (01736) 797129
E: malcolm@bluehayes.
fsbusiness.co.uk
I: www.bluehayes.co.uk

Carlill
Rating Applied For
9 Porthminster Terrace, St Ives,
Cornwall TR26 2DQ
T: (01736) 796738

Chy-an-Creet Hotel ◆◆◆
Higher Stennack, St Ives,
Cornwall TR26 2HA
T: (01736) 796559
F: (01736) 796559
E: relax@chy.co.uk
I: www.chy.co.uk

Cornerways ◆◆◆
Bethesda Place, St Ives, Cornwall
TR26 1PA
T: (01736) 796706 &
07070 800577
E: bryan.pyecroft@lineone.net
I: www.tregenna.
com/cornerways

The Countryman at Trink
◆◆◆◆
Old Coach Road, St Ives,
Cornwall TR26 3JQ
T: (01736) 797571
F: (01736) 797571
I: countrymanstives@
bushinternet.com

Dean Court Hotel ◆◆◆◆
Trelyon Avenue, St Ives,
Cornwall TR26 2AD
T: (01736) 796023
F: (01736) 796233

The Grey Mullet Guest House
◆◆◆
2 Bunkers Hill, St Ives, Cornwall
TR26 1LJ
T: (01736) 796635
E: greymulletguesthouse@
lineone.net
I: www.touristnetuk.
com/sw/greymullet

Longships Hotel ◆◆◆◆
Talland Road, St Ives, Cornwall
TR26 2DF
T: (01736) 798180
F: (01736) 798180
E: enquiries@longships-hotel.
co.uk
I: www.longships-hotel.co.uk

Pierview Guesthouse ◆◆◆
32-34 Back Road East, St Ives,
Cornwall TR26 1PD
T: (01736) 794268
F: (01736) 794268
I: www.pierview.f2s.com

The Pondarosa ◆◆◆◆
10 Porthminster Terrace, St Ives,
Cornwall TR26 2DQ
T: (01736) 795875
F: (01736) 797811
E: pondarosa.hotel@talk21.com
I: www.cornwall-online.co.uk

Porthmeor Hotel ◆◆◆
Godrevy Terrace, St Ives,
Cornwall TR26 1JA
T: (01736) 796712
F: (01736) 796712
E: info@porthmeor.com
I: www.porthmeor.com

St Ives Bay Hotel ◆◆◆
The Terrace, St Ives, Cornwall
TR26 2BP
T: (01736) 795106
F: (01736) 793216

Tregony Guest House ◆◆◆◆
1 Clodgy View, St Ives, Cornwall
TR26 1JG
T: (01736) 795884
F: (01736) 798942
E: info@tregony.com
I: www.tregony.com

ST JULIOT
Cornwall

Higher Pennycrocker Farm
◆◆◆◆
St Juliot, Boscastle, Cornwall
PL35 0BY
T: (01840) 250488
F: (01840) 250488
E: Jackiefarm@aol.com

The Old Rectory ◆◆◆◆◆
St Juliot, Boscastle, Cornwall
PL35 0BT
T: (01840) 250225
F: (01840) 250225
E: sally@stjuliot.com
I: www.stjuliot.com

ST JUST-IN-PENWITH
Cornwall

Bosavern House ◆◆◆
St Just-in-Penwith, TR19 7RD
T: (01736) 788301
F: (01736) 788301
E: marcol@bosavern.u-net.com
I: www.bosavern.u-net.com

Boscean Country Hotel ◆◆◆◆
Boswedden Road, St Just-in-
Penwith, Cornwall TR19 7QP
T: (01736) 788748
F: (01736) 788748
E: boscean@aol.com
I: www.connexions.
co.uk/boscean/index.htm

Boswedden House ◆◆◆
Cape Cornwall, St Just-in-
Penwith, Cornwall TR19 7NJ
T: (01736) 788733
F: (01736) 788733
E: relax@boswedden.org.uk
I: www.smoothhound.
co.uk/hotels/boswedden.html

ST KEVERNE
Cornwall

Eden House ◆◆◆◆
Lemon Street, St Keverne,
Helston, Cornwall TR12 6NE
T: (01326) 280005
E: rf.hughes@talk21.com

Gallen-Treath Guest House
◆◆◆
Porthallow, St Keverne, Helston,
Cornwall TR12 6PL
T: (01326) 280400
E: gallentreath@btclick.com
I: www.gallen-treath.com

ST KEW
Cornwall

Tregellist Farm ◆◆◆◆
Tregellist, St Kew, Bodmin,
Cornwall PL30 3HG
T: (01208) 880537
F: (01208) 881017
E: jillcleave@tregellist.
fsbusiness.co.uk

ST MABYN
Cornwall

Treglown House ◆◆◆
Haywood Farm, St Mabyn,
Wadebridge, Cornwall PL30 3BU
T: (01208) 841896
F: (01208) 841896
E: treglownhouse@stmabyn.
fsnet.co.uk

ST MARY'S
Isles of Scilly

Anjeric Guest House ◆◆◆
The Strand, St Mary's, Isles of
Scilly TR21 0PS
T: (01720) 422700
F: (01720) 422700
I: www.scillyonline.
co.uk/accomm/anjeric.html

Annet ◆◆◆◆
Porthlow, St Mary's, Isles of
Scilly TR21 0NF
T: (01720) 422441 &
07771 663772

April Cottage ◆◆◆◆
Church Road, St Mary's, Isles of
Scilly TR21 0NA
T: (01720) 422279
F: (01720) 423247

Armeria ◆◆
1 Porthloo Terrace, St Mary's,
Isles of Scilly TR21 0NF
T: (01720) 422961
E: b.holt@talk21.com

Auriga Cottage
Rating Applied For
7 Porthcressa Road, St Mary's,
Isles of Scilly TR21 0JL
T: (01720) 422817
F: (01720) 422988

Beachfield House ◆◆◆◆
Porthloo, St Mary's, Isles of
Scilly TR21 0NE
T: (01720) 422463
F: (01720) 422463
E: whomersley@supanet.com

Belmont ◆◆◆◆
Church Road, St Mary's, Isles of
Scilly TR21 0NA
T: (01720) 423154
F: (01720) 423357
E: enquiries@the-belmont.
freeserve.co.uk
I: www.the-belmont.freeserve.
co.uk

Blue Carn Cottage ◆◆◆
Old Town, St Mary's, Isles of
Scilly TR21 0NH
T: (01720) 422309

The Boathouse ◆◆◆
Thorofare Hugh Town, St Mary's,
Isles of Scilly TR21 0LN
T: (01720) 422688

Broomfields ◆◆◆
Church Road, St Mary's, Isles of
Scilly TR21 0NA
T: (01720) 422309

Buckingham House ◆◆
The Bank, St Mary's, Isles of
Scilly TR21 0HY
T: (01720) 422543

The Bylet ◆◆◆
Church Road, St Mary's, Isles of
Scilly TR21 0NA
T: (01720) 422479
F: (01720) 422479

Carn Vean Guest House ◆◆◆
Pelistry, St Mary's, Isles of Scilly
TR21 0NX
T: (01720) 422462

Cornerways ◆◆◆◆
Jackson's Hill, St Mary's, Isles of
Scilly TR21 0JZ
T: (01720) 422757
F: (01720) 422797

Crebinick House ◆◆◆◆
Church Street, St Mary's, Isles of
Scilly TR21 0JT
T: (01720) 422968
F: (01720) 422968
E: enquiries@crebinick.co.uk
I: www.crebinick.co.uk

Evergreen Cottage Guest
House ◆◆◆◆
The Parade, Hugh Town, St
Mary's, Isles of Scilly TR21 0LP
T: (01720) 422711

Garrison House ◆◆◆◆
Garrison Hill, St Mary's, Isles of
Scilly TR21 0LS
T: (01720) 422972
F: (01720) 422972
E: garrisonhouse@aol.com
I: www.isles-of-scilly.
co.uk/guesthouses

Gunners Rock
Rating Applied For
Jackson's Hill, St Mary's, Isles of
Scilly TR21 0JZ
T: (01720) 422595

Guthers ◆◆
Church Road, St Mary's, Isles of
Scilly TR21 0NA
T: (01720) 422345

Hazeldene ◆◆◆◆
Church Street, St Mary's, Isles of
Scilly TR21 0JT
T: (01720) 422864

High Lanes Farm ◆◆◆
Atlantic View, St Mary's, Isles of
Scilly TR21 0NW
T: (01720) 422684

Higher Trenoweth ◆◆◆◆
St Mary's, Isles of Scilly
TR21 0NS
T: (01720) 422419

Innisidgen Guest House ◆◆◆
Church Street, St Mary's, Isles of
Scilly TR21 0JT
T: (01720) 422899 & 422736
F: (01720) 422899
E: innisidgcn@yahoo.co.uk
I: www.isles-of-scilly.co.uk

Kistvaen ◆◆◆◆
St Mary's, Isles of Scilly TR21 0JE
T: (01720) 422002
F: (01720) 422002
E: chivy002@aol.com

Lamorna ◆◆◆
Rams Valley, St Mary's, Isles of
Scilly TR21 0JX
T: (01720) 422333

Lynwood ◆◆◆◆
Church Street, St Mary's, Isles of
Scilly TR21 0JT
T: (01720) 423313
F: (01720) 423313

Lyonnesse Guest House ◆◆◆
The Strand, St Mary's, Isles of
Scilly TR21 0PS
T: (01720) 422458

Marine House ◆◆◆
Church Street, Hugh Town, St
Mary's, Isles of Scilly TR21 0JT
T: (01720) 422966
E: peggy@rowe55.freeserve.
co.uk

Men-a-Vaur ◆◆◆
Church Road, St Mary's, Isles of
Scilly TR21 0NA
T: (01720) 422245

Morgelyn ◆◆◆
McFarlands Down, St Mary's,
Isles of Scilly TR21 0NS
T: (01720) 422897
E: info@morgelyn.co.uk
I: www.morgelyn.co.uk

Pier House ◆◆◆
The Bank, St Mary's, Isles of
Scilly TR21 0HY
T: (01720) 423061

Rose Cottage ◆◆◆◆
The Strand, St Mary's, Isles of
Scilly TR21 0PT
T: (01720) 422078
F: (01720) 422078
E: rosecottage@infinnet.co.uk

St Hellena ◆◆◆◆
13 Garrison Lane, St Mary's, Isles
of Scilly TR21 0JD
T: (01720) 423231 & 422536

Santa Maria ◆◆◆◆
Sallyport, St Mary's, Isles of
Scilly TR21 0JE
T: (01720) 422687
F: (01720) 422687

Scillonia ◆◆
Bank, St Mary's, Isles of Scilly
TR21 0HY
T: (01720) 422101 & 422798

Shearwater Guest House ◆◆◆
The Parade, Hugh Town, St
Mary's, Isles of Scilly TR21 0LP
T: (01720) 422402
F: (01720) 422351
E: ianhopkin@aol.com
I: www.
shearwater-guest-house.co.uk

Strand House ◆◆◆
The Strand, St Mary's, Isles of
Scilly TR21 0PS
T: (01720) 422808
F: (01720) 423009

Sylina ◆◆◆
McFarlands Downs, St Mary's,
Isles of Scilly TR21 0NS
T: (01720) 422129
F: (01720) 422129

Trelawney Guest House ◆◆◆
Church Street, St Mary's, Isles of
Scilly TR21 0JT
T: (01720) 422377 &
07900 016113
F: (01720) 422377
E: dtownend@netcomuk.co.uk

Veronica Lodge ◆◆◆◆
The Garrison, St Mary's, Isles of
Scilly TR21 0LS
T: (01720) 422585

Westford House ◆◆◆
Church Street, St Mary's, Isles of
Scilly TR21 0JT
T: (01720) 422510
F: (01720) 422510

The Wheelhouse ◆◆◆◆
Porthcressa, St Mary's, Isles of
Scilly TR21 0JG
T: (01720) 422719 & 423043
F: (01720) 422719

Wingletang Guest House ◆◆◆
The Parade, St Mary's, Isles of
Scilly TR21 0LP
T: (01720) 422381

The Withies ◆◆◆◆
Trench Lane, Old Town, St
Mary's, Isles of Scilly TR21 0PA
T: (01720) 422986

ST MARYS
Devon

The Town House ◆◆◆◆
Little Porth, St Marys, Lifton,
Devon TR21 0JG
T: (01720) 422793
E: scillytownhouse@btclick.com

ST MAWES
Cornwall

The Ship and Castle ◆◆◆
The Waterfront, St Mawes,
Truro, Cornwall TR2 5DG
T: (01326) 270401
F: (01326) 270152

ST MAWGAN
Cornwall

The Falcon Inn ◆◆◆◆
St Mawgan, Newquay, Cornwall
TR8 4EP
T: (01637) 860225
F: (01637) 860884
E: abanks@cwcom.net
I: www.falcon-inn.net

ST MERRYN
Cornwall

Tregavone Farm
Rating Applied For
St Merryn, Padstow, Cornwall
PL28 8JZ
T: (01841) 520148

Trewithen Farm ◆◆◆◆
St Merryn, Padstow, Cornwall
PL28 8JZ
T: (01841) 520420

ST MINVER
Cornwall

Porteath Barn
Rating Applied For
St Minver, Wadebridge, Cornwall
PL27 6RA
T: (01208) 863605
F: (01208) 863954

ST NEOT
Cornwall

The London Inn ◆◆◆
St Neot, Liskeard, Cornwall
PL14 6NG
T: (01579) 320263 &
07710 419527
F: (01579) 320263

ST TUDY
Cornwall

Polrode Mill Cottage ◆◆◆◆◆
Allen Valley, St Tudy, Bodmin,
Cornwall PL30 3NS
T: (01208) 850203
E: polrode@tesco.net
I: www.cornwall-online.
co.uk/polrode-mill

ST WENN
Cornwall

Wenn Manor Hotel ◆◆◆◆
St Wenn, Bodmin, Cornwall
PL30 5PS
T: (01726) 890240
F: (01726) 890680

SALCOMBE
Devon

Burton Farm ◆◆◆◆
Galmpton, Kingsbridge, Devon
TQ7 3EY
T: (01548) 561210
F: (01548) 561210

Torre View Hotel ◆◆◆◆
Devon Road, Salcombe, Devon
TQ8 8HJ
T: (01548) 842633
F: (01548) 842633
E: bouttle@torreview.eurobell.
co.uk
I: www.smoothhound.
co.uk/hotels/torreview.html

SALISBURY
Wiltshire

11 Assisi Road
Rating Applied For
Salisbury, Wiltshire SP1 3QZ
T: (01722) 410789

Avila ◆◆◆
130 Exeter Street, Salisbury,
SP1 2SG
T: (01722) 421093

The Avon Brewery Inn
Rating Applied For
75 Castle Street, Salisbury,
SP1 3SP
T: (01722) 416184
F: (01722) 326219

The Barford Inn ◆◆◆◆
Barford St Martin, Salisbury
SP3 4AB
T: (01722) 742242
F: (01722) 743606
E: ido@barfordinn.co.uk
I: www.barfordinn.co.uk

Barlings ◆◆◆◆
41 Gravel Close, Downton,
Salisbury, Wiltshire SP5 3JQ
T: (01725) 510310

The Bell Inn ◆◆◆
Warminster Road, South
Newton, Salisbury SP2 0QD
T: (01722) 743336
F: (01722) 744202

40 Belle Vue Road ◆◆
Salisbury, Wiltshire SP1 3YD
T: (01722) 325773

78 Belle Vue Road ◆◆◆
Salisbury, SP1 3YD
T: (01722) 329477

Beulah ◆◆
144 Britford Lane, Salisbury,
SP2 8AL
T: (01722) 333517

Bridge Farm ◆◆◆◆
Lower Road, Britford, Salisbury
SP5 4DY
T: (01722) 332376
F: (01722) 332376
E: mail@bridgefarmbb.co.uk
I: www.bridgefarmbb.co.uk

Burcombe Manor
Rating Applied For
Burcombe, Salisbury, SP2 0E3
T: (01722) 744288

Byways House ◆◆◆
31 Fowlers Road, City Centre,
Salisbury, SP1 2QP
T: (01722) 328364
F: (01722) 322146
E: byways@
bed-breakfast-salisbury.co.uk
I: www.bed-breakfast-salisbury.
co.uk
🌳

Castlewood ◆◆◆
45 Castle Road, Salisbury,
SP1 3RH
T: (01722) 324809 &
07733 331599
F: (01722) 421494

132 Coombe Road ◆◆◆◆
Salisbury, Wiltshire SP2 8BL
T: (01722) 320275
E: jim.izzard@ukonline.co.uk

The Devizes Inn ◆◆
53 Devizes Road, Salisbury,
Wiltshire SP2 7LQ
T: (01722) 327842

The Edwardian Lodge ◆◆◆◆
59 Castle Road, Salisbury,
SP1 3RH
T: (01722) 413329 & 502147
F: (01722) 503105
E: richardwhite@edlodge.
freeserve.co.uk
I: www.edwardianlodge.co.uk

Farthings ◆◆◆
9 Swaynes Close, Salisbury,
SP1 3AE
T: (01722) 330749
F: (01722) 330749
E: farthings@shammer.
freeserve.co.uk
I: www.shammer.freeserve.co.uk

Gerrans House ◆◆◆◆
91 Castle Road, Salisbury,
SP1 3RW
T: (01722) 334394
F: (01722) 332508
E: gerranshouse@robinsg.fsnet.
co.uk

Glenshee ◆◆◆◆
3 Montague Road, West
Harnham, Salisbury, Wiltshire
SP2 8NJ
T: (01722) 322620 &
07971 827804
F: (01722) 322620
E: glenshee@breathemail.net
I: www.dmac.co.uk/glenshee

Griffin Cottage ◆◆◆◆
10 St Edmunds Church Street,
Salisbury, Wiltshire SP1 1EF
T: (01722) 328259 &
07767 395898
F: (01722) 416928
E: mark@brandonasoc.demon.
co.uk
I: www.smoothhound.
co.uk/hotels/griffinc.html

Highveld ◆◆◆
44 Hulse Road, Salisbury,
SP1 3LY
T: (01722) 338172
E: icedawn@amserve.net

Holly Tree House ◆◆
53 Wyndham Road, Salisbury,
SP1 3AH
T: (01722) 322955

Holmhurst Guest House ◆◆
Downton Road, Salisbury,
SP2 8AR
T: (01722) 410407
F: (01722) 323164
E: holmhurst@talk21.com

Leena's Guest House ◆◆◆
50 Castle Road, Salisbury,
SP1 3RL
T: (01722) 335419
F: (01722) 335419

The Limes
Rating Applied For
5 Marlborough Road, Salisbury,
SP1 3TH
T: (01722) 336040
F: (01722) 413269

The Little House ◆◆
38 Fairview Road, Salisbury,
Wiltshire SP1 1JX
T: (01722) 320381 &
07885 100918

Malvern ◆◆◆◆
31 Hulse Road, Salisbury,
SP1 3LU
T: (01722) 327995

Manor Farm ◆◆◆◆
Burcombe, Salisbury SP2 0EJ
T: (01722) 742177
F: (01722) 744600
E: SACombes@talk.com

94 Milford Hill ◆◆◆
Salisbury, SP1 2QL
T: (01722) 322454

Newton Farm House ◆◆◆◆◆
Southampton Road,
Whiteparish, Salisbury, SP5 2QL
T: (01794) 884416
F: (01794) 884416
E: enquiries@
newtonfarmhouse.co.uk
I: www.newtonfarmhouse.co.uk

Number Eighty Eight ◆◆◆◆
88 Exeter Street, Salisbury,
SP1 2SE
T: (01722) 330139 &
07971 561349
E: enquiries@no88.co.uk
I: www.no88.co.uk

The Old Bakery ◆◆
35 Bedwin Street, Salisbury,
SP1 3UT
T: (01722) 320100

Old Chequers Cottage ◆◆
17 Guilder Lane, Salisbury,
SP1 1HW
T: (01722) 325335
F: (01722) 325335
E: old_chequers@onetel.net.uk

**The Old Rectory Bed &
Breakfast** ◆◆◆◆
75 Belle Vue Road, Salisbury,
SP1 3YE
T: (01722) 502702
F: (01722) 501135
E: stay@theoldrectory-bb.co.uk
I: www.theoldrectory-bb.co.uk

Pathways ◆◆
41 Shady Bower, Salisbury,
Wiltshire SP1 2RG
T: (01722) 324252

The Priory
Rating Applied For
95 Brown Street, Salisbury,
SP1 2BA
T: (01722) 502337
E: scredland@ntlworld.com

Richburn Guest House ◆◆◆
25 Estcourt Road, Salisbury,
SP1 3AP
T: (01722) 325189 & 411551
F: (01722) 325189

The Rokeby Guest House
◆◆◆◆
3 Wain-a-Long Road, Salisbury,
SP1 1LJ
T: (01722) 329800
F: (01722) 329800
I: www.smoothhound.
co.uk/hotels/rokeby.html

Saddlers ◆◆◆◆
Princes Hill, Redlynch, Salisbury
SP5 2HF
T: (01725) 510571
F: (01725) 510571
E: sadd.lers@virgin.net
I: www.s-h-systems.
co.uk/hotels/saddlers.html

34 Salt Lane ◆◆
Salisbury, Wiltshire SP1 1EG
T: (01722) 326141

Spire House ◆◆◆◆
84 Exeter Street, Salisbury,
Wiltshire SP1 2SE
T: (01722) 339213
F: (01722) 339213
E: lois.faulkner@talk21.com
I: www.smoothhound.
co.uk/hotels/spire.html

Spire-View ◆◆◆◆
118 Harnham Road, Harnham,
Salisbury, SP2 8JY
T: (01722) 335525
E: spireview@lineone.net

Stratford Lodge ◆◆◆◆
4 Park Lane, Castle Road,
Salisbury, SP1 3NP
T: (01722) 325177
F: (01722) 325177
E: enquiries@stratfordlodge.
co.uk
I: www.stratfordlodge.co.uk

Swaynes Firs Farm ◆◆◆
Grimsdyke, Coombe Bissett,
Salisbury SP5 5RF
T: (01725) 519240
E: swaynes.firs@virgin.net
I: www.swaynesfirs.co.uk

Tamar House ◆◆◆
237 Castle Road, Salisbury,
Wiltshire SP1 3RY
T: (01722) 502254 &
07710 297053
E: w.rampton@ntlworld.com
I: www.smoothhound.
co.uk/hotels/tamar.html

Tiffany ◆◆◆
2 Bourne Villas, off College
Street, Salisbury, SP1 3AW
T: (01722) 332367

Torrisholme ◆◆◆
Stratford Sub Castle, Salisbury
SP1 3LQ
T: (01722) 320080
F: (01722) 321363
E: torrisholme@hotmail.com

Vale View Farm ◆◆◆
Slab Lane, Woodfalls, Salisbury,
SP5 2NE
T: (01725) 512116

Victoria Lodge Guest House
◆◆◆
61 Castle Road, Salisbury,
SP1 3RH
T: (01722) 320586
F: (01722) 414507
E: mail@viclodge.co.uk
I: www.viclodge.co.uk

Websters ◆◆◆◆
11 Hartington Road, Salisbury,
SP2 7LG
T: (01722) 339779
F: (01722) 339779
E: websters.salis@eclipse.co.uk
I: www.websters-bed-breakfast.
com
&

White Horse Inn ◆◆
38 Castle Street, Salisbury,
Wiltshire SP1 1BN
T: (01722) 327844
F: (01722) 336226

Wyndham Park Lodge ◆◆◆◆
51 Wyndham Road, Salisbury,
SP1 3AB
T: (01722) 416517
F: (01722) 328851
E: enquiries@
wyndhamparklodge.co.uk
I: www.wyndhamparklodge.
co.uk

48 Wyndham Road ◆◆◆◆
Salisbury, Wiltshire SP1 3AB
T: (01722) 327757

SALTASH
Cornwall

Haye Farm ◆◆◆◆
Landulph, Saltash, Cornwall
PL12 6QQ
T: (01752) 842786
F: (01752) 842786

SALTFORD
Bath and North East Somerset

Brunels Tunnel House Hotel
◆◆◆◆
High Street, Saltford, Bristol
BS31 3BQ
T: (01225) 873873
F: (01225) 874875
E: info@brunelstunnelhouse.
com
I: www.brunelstunnelhouse.com

SAMPFORD COURTENAY
Devon

Langdale ◆◆
Sampford Courtenay,
Okehampton, Devon EX20 2SY
T: (01837) 82433 &
07989 936425

SAND
Somerset

Townsend Farm ◆◆◆◆
Sand, Wedmore, Somerset
BS28 4XH
T: (01934) 712342
F: (01934) 712405
E: smewillcox0@farmersweekly.
net

SEATON
Devon

Beaumont ◆◆◆◆
Castle Hill, Seaton, Devon
EX12 2QW
T: (01297) 20832
F: 0870 0554708
E: tony@lymebay.demon.co.uk
I: www.smoothhound.
co.uk/hotels/beaumont.html

Blue Haven Hotel ◆◆◆
Looe Hill, Seaton, Torpoint,
Cornwall PL11 3JQ
T: (01503) 250310
F: (01503) 250310
E: bluehaven@btinternet.com
I: www.smoothhound.
co.uk/hotels/bluehave.html

Four Seasons ◆◆◆
3 Burrow Road, Seaton, Devon
EX12 2NF
T: (01297) 20761

Gatcombe Farm ◆◆◆◆
Seaton, Devon EX12 3AA
T: (01297) 21235 &
07971 941096
F: (01297) 23010
E: gatcombefarm@tinyworld.
co.uk

Hill House ◆◆◆◆
Highcliffe Crescent, Seaton,
Devon EX12 2PS
T: (01297) 20377
E: jphil.beard@lineone.net

Mariners Hotel ◆◆◆◆
The Esplanade, Seaton, Devon
EX12 2NP
T: (01297) 20560
F: (01297) 20560

SOUTH WEST

SEMINGTON
Wiltshire
Newhouse Farm ◆◆◆
Littleton, Semington,
Trowbridge, Wiltshire BA14 6LF
T: (01380) 870349

SHALDON
Devon
Glenside House ◆◆◆
Ringmore Road, Shaldon,
Teignmouth, Devon TQ14 0EP
T: (01626) 872448
F: 1626 872448
I: www.smoothhound.
co.uk/hotels/glensideho.html

Potters Mooring
Rating Applied For
30 The Green, Shaldon,
Teignmouth, Devon TQ14 0DN
T: (01626) 873225
F: (01626) 872909
E: mail@pottersmooring.co.uk
I: www.pottersmooring.co.uk

SHARCOTT
Wiltshire
The Old Dairy House ◆◆◆◆
Sharcott, Pewsey, Wiltshire
SN9 5PA
T: (01672) 562287
E: old.dairy@virgin.net
I: business.virgin.net/neville.
burrell/sharcott.htm

SHEPTON MALLET
Somerset
Belfield Guest House ◆◆◆
34 Charlton Road, Shepton
Mallet, Somerset BA4 5PA
T: (01749) 344353
F: (01749) 344353
E: andrea@belfield-house.co.uk
I: www.belfield-house.co.uk

Bowlish House ◆◆◆◆
Coombe Lane, Shepton Mallet,
Somerset BA4 5JD
T: (01749) 342022
F: (01749) 342022

Burnt House Farm ◆◆◆◆
Waterlip, West Cranmore,
Shepton Mallet, Somerset
BA4 4RN
T: (01749) 880280
F: (01749) 880004

Hillbury House ◆◆◆
65 Compton Road, Shepton
Mallet, Somerset BA4 5QT
T: (01749) 345473
E: patandjerry@ukonline.co.uk

Hurlingpot Farm ◆◆◆◆
Chelynch, Shepton Mallet,
Somerset BA4 4PY
T: (01749) 880256
I: www.smoothhound.
co.uk/hotels/hurling.html

Knapps Farm ◆◆◆◆◆
Doulting, Shepton Mallet,
Somerset BA4 4LA
T: (01749) 880471

Leamount ◆◆◆
60 Compton Road, Shepton
Mallet, Somerset BA4 5QT
T: (01749) 344278 &
07970 947068

Middleton House ◆◆◆
68 Compton Road, Shepton
Mallet, Somerset BA4 5QT
T: (01749) 343720 &
07833 123967

Pecking Mill Inn and Hotel ◆◆◆
A371 Evercreech, Evercreech,
Shepton Mallet, Somerset
BA4 6PG
T: (01749) 830336 & 830006
F: (01749) 831316

Temple House Farm ◆◆◆◆
Doulting, Shepton Mallet,
Somerset BA4 4RQ
T: (01749) 880294
F: (01749) 880688

SHEPTON MONTAGUE
Somerset
Lower Farm ◆◆◆◆
Shepton Montague, Wincanton,
Somerset BA9 8JG
T: (01749) 812253
E: susiedowding@
netscapeonline.co.uk
I: lowerfarm.org.uk

SHERBORNE
Dorset
The Alders ◆◆◆◆
Sandford Orcas, Sherborne,
Dorset DT9 4SB
T: (01963) 220666
F: (01963) 220106
E: jonsue@thealdersbb.com
I: www.thealdersbb.com

Bay Trees ◆◆
Bristol Road, Sherborne, Dorset
DT9 4HP
T: (01935) 816527

Bridleways ◆◆◆
Oborne Road, Sherborne, Dorset
DT9 3RX
T: (01935) 814716
F: (01935) 814716

The Britannia Inn ◆◆◆
Westbury, Sherborne, Dorset
DT9 3EH
T: (01935) 813300

Clatcombe Grange ◆◆◆◆
Bristol Road, Sherborne, Dorset
DT9 4RH
T: (01935) 814355

Cromwell House ◆◆◆◆
Long Street, Sherborne, Dorset
DT9 3BS
T: (01935) 813352
I: www.smoothhound.
co.uk/a53281.html

Crown Inn ◆◆◆
Green Hill, Sherborne, Dorset
DT9 4EP
T: (01935) 812930
F: (01935) 812930

Heartsease Cottage ◆◆◆◆◆
North Street, Bradford Abbas,
Sherborne, Dorset DT9 6SA
T: (01935) 475480 &
07929 717019
F: (01935) 475480
E: heartsease@talk21.com

Huntsbridge Farm ◆◆◆◆
Batcombe Road, Leigh,
Sherborne, Dorset DT9 6JA
T: (01935) 872150
F: (01935) 872150
E: huntsbridge@lineone.net

The Old Vicarage Hotel ◆◆◆◆◆
Sherborne Road, Milborne Port,
Sherborne, Dorset DT9 5AT
T: (01963) 251117
F: (01963) 251515
E: theoldvicarage@
milborneport.freeserve.co.uk
I: www.milborneport.freeserve.
co.uk

Village Vacations ◆◆◆
Brookmead, Rimpton, Yeovil,
Somerset BA22 8AQ
T: (01935) 850241
F: (01935) 850241
E: villagevac@aol.com
I: www.villagevacations.co.uk

SHERSTON
Wiltshire
Widleys Farm ◆◆◆
Sherston, Malmesbury, Wiltshire
SN16 0PY
T: (01666) 840213
F: (01666) 840156

SHIPHAM
Somerset
Herongates ◆◆◆
Horseleaze Lane, Shipham,
Winscombe BS25 1UQ
T: (01934) 843280
F: (01934) 843280

Penscot Farmhouse Hotel ◆◆◆
The Square, Shipham,
Winscombe BS25 1TW
T: (01934) 842659
F: (01934) 842576
I: www.minotel.com

SHIPTON GORGE
Dorset
Cairnhill ◆◆◆◆◆
Shipton Gorge, Bridport, Dorset
DT6 4LL
T: (01308) 898203
F: (01308) 898203
E: cairnhill@talk21.com

SHREWTON
Wiltshire
Maddington House ◆◆◆◆
Maddington Street, Shrewton,
Salisbury SP3 4JD
T: (01980) 620406
F: (01980) 620406
E: rsrobathan@freenet.co.uk

SIDBURY
Devon
Cotfordbridge Hotel and Restaurant ◆◆◆◆
Cotford Road, Sidbury,
Sidmouth, Devon EX10 0SQ
T: (01395) 597351

SIDFORD
Devon
The Salty Monk ◆◆◆◆◆
Church Street, Sidford,
Sidmouth, Devon EX10 9QP
T: (01395) 513174
F: (01395) 514722
E: andy@
saltymonkhotelsidmouth.co.uk
I: www.
saltymonkhotelsidmouth.co.uk

SIDMOUTH
Devon
Berwick Guest House ◆◆◆◆
Salcombe Road, Sidmouth,
Devon EX10 8PX
T: (01395) 513621

Canterbury Guest House ◆◆◆
Salcombe Road, Sidmouth,
Devon EX10 8PR
T: (01395) 513373 & 0800 328
1775
E: cgh@eclipse.co.uk

Coombe Bank Guest House ◆◆◆◆
86 Alexandria Road, Sidmouth,
Devon EX10 9HG
T: (01395) 514843 & 515181
F: (01395) 515181
E: info@coombebank.com
I: www.coombebank.com

Ferndale ◆◆◆◆
92 Winslade Road, Sidmouth,
Devon EX10 9EZ
T: (01395) 515495 &
07889 332492
F: (01395) 515495

Higher Coombe Farm ◆◆◆
Tipton St John, Sidmouth, Devon
EX10 0AX
T: (01404) 813385
F: (01404) 813385
E: KerstinFarmer@farming.co.uk
I: www.smoothhound.
co.uk/hotels/higherco.html

Lower Pinn Farm ◆◆◆◆
Pinn, Sidmouth, Devon
EX10 0NN
T: (01395) 513733
F: (01395) 513733
E: liz@lowerpinnfarm.co.uk
I: www.lowerpinnfarm.co.uk

Lynstead ◆◆◆◆
Vicarage Road, Sidmouth, Devon
EX10 8UQ
T: (01395) 514635
F: (01395) 578954
E: lynstead@aol.com
I: wwwsmoothhound.
co.uk/hotels/lynstead.html

Pinn Barton Farm ◆◆◆◆
Peak Hill, Pinn Lane, Sidmouth,
Devon EX10 0NN
T: (01395) 514004
F: (01395) 514004
I: www.smoothhound.
co.uk/hotels/pinn.html

Willow Bridge Private Hotel ◆◆◆◆
Millford Road, Sidmouth, Devon
EX10 8DR
T: (01395) 513599 &
07966 531132
F: (01395) 513599
E: willowframing@c.s.com

Wiscombe Linhaye Farm ◆◆◆◆
Southleigh, Colyton, Devon
EX24 6JF
T: (01404) 871342
F: (01404) 871342
E: rabjohns@btinternet.com

SILVERTON
Devon
Three Tuns Inn ◆◆◆
14 Exeter Road, Silverton, Exeter
EX5 4HX
T: (01392) 860352
F: (01392) 860636
I: www.threetuninn.co.uk

SIMONSBATH
Somerset

Emmett's Grange ◆◆◆
Simonsbath, Minehead,
Somerset TA24 7LD
T: (01643) 831138
F: (01643) 831093
E: emmetts.grange@virgin.net
I: www.whatsonexmoor.co.uk

SITHNEY
Cornwall

Parc-An-Ithan House Hotel ◆◆◆
Sithney, Helston, Cornwall
TR13 0RN
T: (01326) 572565
F: (01326) 572565
E: parchotel@btinternet.com
I: www.smoothhound.
co.uk/parcanit.html

SKILGATE
Somerset

Chapple Farm ◆
Skilgate, Taunton, Somerset
TA4 2DP
T: (01398) 331364

SLAPTON
Devon

Little Pittaford ◆◆◆◆◆
Slapton, Kingsbridge, Devon
TQ7 2QG
T: (01548) 580418
F: (01548) 580406
E: LittlePittaford@compuserve.
com
I: www.littlepitaford.co.uk

Start House ◆◆◆
Start, Slapton, Kingsbridge,
Devon TQ7 2QD
T: (01548) 580254

SOMERTON
Somerset

Littleton House ◆◆◆
New Street, Somerton, Somerset
TA11 7NU
T: (01458) 273072

Mill House ◆◆◆◆◆
Barton St. David, Somerton,
Somerset TA11 6DF
T: (01458) 851215
F: (01458) 851372
E: knightsmillhouse@aol.com
I: www.smoothhound.
co.uk/hotels/millhouse3.html

SOUTH MOLTON
Devon

Huxtable Farm ◆◆◆◆
West Buckland, Barnstaple,
Devon EX32 0SR
T: (01598) 760254
F: (01598) 760254
E: info@huxtablefarm.co.uk
I: www.huxtablefarm.co.uk

Kerscott Farm ◆◆◆◆◆
Ash Mill, South Molton, Devon
EX36 4QG
T: (01769) 550262
F: (01769) 550910
E: kerscott.farm@virgin.net
I: www.greencountry.
co.uk/kerscott

Old Coaching Inn ◆◆
Queen Street, South Molton,
Devon EX36 3BJ
T: (01769) 572526 & 572397

SOUTH NEWTON
Wiltshire

Salisbury Old Mill House ◆◆◆◆
Warminster Road, South
Newton, Salisbury, Wiltshire
SP2 0QD
T: (01722) 742458 &
07860 542475
F: (01722) 742458

SOUTH PERROTT
Dorset

Shepherds Farmhouse ◆◆◆
South Perrott, Beaminster,
Dorset DT8 3HU
T: (01935) 891599 &
07977 422916
F: (01935) 891977
E: shepherds@eclipse.co.uk
I: www.shepherds.eclipse.co.uk

SOUTH PETHERTON
Somerset

Kings Pleasure ◆◆◆◆
24 Silver Street, South
Petherton, Somerset TA13 5BZ
T: (01460) 241747
E: n.veit@kingspleasure.fsnet.
co.uk

SOUTH ZEAL
Devon

Poltimore ◆◆◆
Ramsley, South Zeal,
Okehampton, Devon EX20 2PD
T: (01837) 840209

SOUTHVILLE
Bristol

Walmer House ◆◆◆
94 Stackpool Road, Southville,
Bristol BS3 1NW
T: (0117) 966 8253
F: (0117) 966 8253

SPREYTON
Devon

The Tom Cobley Tavern ◆◆◆
Spreyton, Crediton, Devon
EX17 5AL
T: (01647) 231314
F: (01647) 231506
E: fjwfilor@tomcobley.fsnet.
co.uk

STANTON DREW
Bath and North East Somerset

Greenlands ◆◆◆◆
Stanton Drew, Bristol BS39 4ES
T: (01275) 333487
F: (01275) 331211

STANTON WICK
Bath and North East Somerset

The Carpenters Arms ◆◆◆◆
Stanton Wick, Pensford, Bristol
BS39 4BX
T: (01761) 490202
F: (01761) 490763
E: carpenters@dial.pipex.com

STAPLEFORD
Wiltshire

The Parsonage ◆◆◆◆
Stapleford, Salisbury SP3 4LJ
T: (01722) 790334

STARCROSS
Devon

The Croft Guest House ◆◆◆
Cockwood Harbour, Starcross,
Exeter EX6 8QY
T: (01626) 890282
F: (01626) 891768

The Old Vicarage ◆◆◆
Starcross, Exeter EX6 8PX
T: (01626) 890206
F: (01626) 890206
E: maggie@theoldvicarage.
clara.co.uk
I: www.theoldvicarage.clara.net

STATHE
Somerset

Black Smock Inn ◆◆◆
Stathe Road, Stathe, Bridgwater,
Somerset TA7 0JN
T: (01823) 698352
F: (01823) 698352
E: blacksmock@aol.com
I: www.blacksmock.co.uk

STAVERTON
Devon

Kingston House ◆◆◆◆◆
Staverton, Totnes, Devon
TQ9 6AR
T: (01803) 762235
F: (01803) 762444
E: info@kingston-estate.net
I: www.kingston-estate.net

STEEPLE ASHTON
Wiltshire

Church Farm ◆◆◆◆
Steeple Ashton, Trowbridge,
Wiltshire BA14 6EL
T: (01380) 870518
E: church.farm@farmline.com

Longs Arms Inn ◆◆◆
High Street, Steeple Ashton,
Trowbridge, Wiltshire BA14 6FU
T: (01380) 870245
F: (01380) 870245
E: chantal@stayatthepub.
freeserve.co.uk
I: www.stayatthepub.freeserve.
co.uk

STERT
Wiltshire

Hill House ◆◆◆
Stert, Devizes, Wiltshire
SN10 3JB
T: (01380) 722356
F: (01380) 722356

Orchard Cottage ◆◆
Stert, Devizes, Wiltshire
SN10 3JD
T: (01380) 723103

STICKLEPATH
Devon

Higher Coombe Head House ◆◆◆◆
Sticklepath, Okehampton, Devon
EX20 1QL
T: (01837) 840240
E: coombehead@btinternet.com

STOCKWOOD
Dorset

Church Farm ◆◆◆◆
Stockwood, Dorchester, Dorset
DT2 0NG
T: (01935) 83221
F: (01935) 83771
E: ruth@churchfarm.co.uk
I: www.churchfarm.co.uk

STOGUMBER
Somerset

Hall Farm ◆◆◆
Stogumber, Taunton, Somerset
TA4 3TQ
T: (01984) 656321

Northam Mill
Northam Mill ◆◆◆◆
Water Lane, Stogumber,
Taunton, Somerset TA4 3TT
T: (01984) 656916 & 656146
F: (01984) 656144
E: bmsspicer@aol.com
I: www.northam-mill.co.uk

STOGURSEY
Somerset

West End Cottage ◆◆◆◆
Stolford, Stogursey, Bridgwater,
Somerset TA5 1TN
T: (01278) 653149

STOKE-IN-TEIGNHEAD
Devon

Deane Thatch Accommodation ◆◆◆
Deane Road, Stoke-in-
Teignhead, Newton Abbot,
Devon TQ12 4QU
T: (01626) 873724 &
07971 939364
F: (01626) 873724
E: deanethatch@hotmail.com
I: www.deanethatch.co.uk

STOKE ST GREGORY
Somerset

Ashgrove ◆◆◆◆
Meare Green, Stoke St Gregory,
Taunton, Somerset TA3 6HZ
T: (01823) 490209
E: sueperowne@hotmail.com

Meare Green Farm ◆◆◆◆
Meare Green, Stoke St Gregory,
Taunton, Somerset TA3 6HT
T: (01823) 490759
F: (01823) 490759
E: jane.pine@kitesourcing.com

STOKE SUB HAMDON
Somerset

Castle Farm ◆◆◆◆
Stoke sub Hamdon, Somerset
TA14 6QS
T: (01935) 822231
F: (01935) 822057

The Cavern ◆◆◆◆
Stoke Cross, Stoke High Street,
Stoke sub Hamdon, Yeovil,
Somerset TA14 6PP
T: (01935) 826826
F: (01935) 826565
E: info@caverncafe.com
I: www.caverncafe.com

STOKENHAM
Devon

Brookfield ◆◆◆
Stokenham, Kingsbridge, Devon
TQ7 2SL
T: (01548) 580615

STONEY STRATTON
Somerset

Stratton Farm ◆◆◆◆
Stoney Stratton, Shepton Mallet,
Somerset BA4 6DY
T: (01749) 830830
F: (01749) 831080

STRATFORD SUB CASTLE
Wiltshire

Carp Cottage ◆◆◆◆
Stratford Sub Castle, Salisbury
SP1 3LH
T: (01722) 327219 &
07967 153298

STRATTON
Cornwall

Cann Orchard ◆◆◆◆
Howard Lane, Stratton, Bude,
Cornwall EX23 9TD
T: (01288) 352098
F: (01288) 352098

STRATTON-ON-THE-FOSSE
Somerset

Oval House ◆◆◆
Stratton-on-the-Fosse, Bath
BA3 4RB
T: (01761) 232183
F: (01761) 232183
E: mellotte@clara.co.uk
I: www.mellotte.clara.co.uk

STREET
Somerset

Leigh Nook ◆◆◆◆
Marshalls Elm, Somerton Road,
Street, Somerset BA16 0TZ
T: (01458) 443511 &
07971 430278

Marshalls Elm Farm ◆◆◆
Street, Somerset BA16 0TZ
T: (01458) 442878

Old Orchard House ◆◆◆◆
Middle Brooks, Street, Somerset
BA16 0TU
T: (01458) 442212
E: oldorchardhouse@amserve.
net

STRETE
Devon

Skerries Bed & Breakfast
◆◆◆◆
Skerrries, Strete, Dartmouth,
Devon TQ6 0PH
T: (01803) 770775
F: (01803) 770950
E: jam.skerries@rya-online.net

SUTTON POYNTZ
Dorset

Brookfield ◆◆◆
White Horse Lane, Sutton
Poyntz, Weymouth, Dorset
DT3 6LU
T: (01305) 833674

Selwyns ◆◆◆
Puddledock Lane, Sutton Poyntz,
Weymouth, Dorset DT3 6LZ
T: (01305) 832239
E: selwyns-b-and-b@hotmail.
com

SWINDON
Wiltshire

Courtleigh House ◆◆◆◆
40 Draycott Road, Chiseldon,
Swindon SN4 0LS
T: (01793) 740246

SYDLING ST NICHOLAS
Dorset

Magiston Farm ◆◆◆
Sydling St Nicholas, DT2 9NR
T: (01300) 320295

TAUNTON
Somerset

Acorn Lodge ◆
22 Wellington Road, Taunton,
Somerset TA1 4EQ
T: (01823) 337613

Fursdon House ◆◆◆
88-90 Greenway Road, Taunton,
Somerset TA2 6LE
T: (01823) 331955

Gatchells ◆◆◆◆
Angersleigh, Taunton, Somerset
TA3 7SY
T: (01823) 421580 &
07808 164276
E: gatchells@somerweb.co.uk
I: www.somerweb.
co.uk/gatchells

Heathercroft ◆◆◆
118 Wellington Road, Taunton,
Somerset TA1 5LA
T: (01823) 275516

**Higher Yarde Farm Country
Bed & Breakfast**◆◆◆◆
Higher Yarde Farm, Staplegrove,
Taunton, Somerset TA2 6SW
T: (01823) 451553 &
07770 866848
E: anita.hyf@rya-online.net

Lowdens House ◆◆◆
26 Wellington Road, Taunton,
Somerset TA1 4EQ
T: (01823) 334500

**North Down Farm Bed &
Breakfast** ◆◆◆
Pyncombe Lane, Wiveliscombe,
Taunton, Somerset TA4 2BL
T: (01984) 623730 & 077 9 0
858450
F: (01984) 623730

Orchard House ◆◆◆◆
Fons George, Middleway,
Taunton, Somerset TA1 3JS
T: (01823) 351783
F: (01823) 351785
E: orch-hse@dircon.co.uk
I: www.smoothhound.
co.uk/hotels/orchard2.html

Prockters Farm ◆◆◆
West Monkton, Taunton,
Somerset TA2 8QN
T: (01823) 412269
F: (01823) 412269

Southview ◆
2 St Andrew's Road, Taunton,
Somerset TA2 7BW
T: (01823) 284639
E: southstyle@easicom.com

The Spinney ◆◆◆◆
Curland, Taunton, Somerset
TA3 5SE
T: (01460) 234362 & 234193
F: (01460) 234362
E: bartlett.spinney@zetnet.co.uk
I: www.somerweb.
co.uk/spinney-bb

Staplegrove Lodge ◆◆◆◆
Staplegrove, Taunton, Somerset
TA2 6PX
T: (01823) 331153
I: www.staplegrovelodge.co.uk

Yallands Farmhouse ◆◆◆◆
Staplegrove, Taunton, Somerset
TA2 6PZ
T: (01823) 278979
F: 0870 2849194
E: mail@yallands.co.uk
I: www.yallands.co.uk

TAVISTOCK
Devon

April Cottage ◆◆◆◆
Mount Tavy Road, Tavistock,
Devon PL19 9JB
T: (01822) 613280

Beera Farmhouse ◆◆◆◆
Milton Abbot, Tavistock, Devon
PL19 8PL
T: (01822) 870216
F: (01822) 870216
E: robert.tucker@farming.co.uk
I: www.
beerafarmbedandbreakfast.com

Carmel Heights ◆◆◆◆
57 Whitchurch Road, Tavistock,
Devon PL19 9BD
T: (01822) 617340
E: m.aggiss@talk21.com

Eko Brae Guest House ◆◆◆◆
4 Bedford Villas, Spring Hill,
Tavistock, Devon PL19 8LA
T: (01822) 614028
F: (01822) 613693
E: ekobrae@aol.com.

**Harrabeer Country House
Rating applied for**
Harrowbeer Lane, Yelverton,
Devon PL20 6EA
T: (01822) 853302 & 855811
F: (01822) 853302
E: reception@harrabeer.co.uk
I: www.harrabeer.co.uk

Kingfisher Cottage ◆◆◆
Mount Tavy Road, Vigo Bridge,
Tavistock, Devon PL19 9JB
T: (01822) 613801 &
07721 772095

Mallards ◆◆◆◆
48 Plymouth Road, Tavistock,
Devon PL19 8BU
T: (01822) 615171

Old Rectory Farm ◆◆◆◆
Mary Tavy, Tavistock, Devon
PL19 9PP
T: (01822) 810102

Rubbytown Farm ◆◆◆◆
Gulworthy, Tavistock, Devon
PL19 8PA
T: (01822) 832493

Tor Cottage ◆◆◆◆◆
Chillaton, Tavistock, Devon
PL16 0JE
T: (01822) 860248
F: (01822) 860126
E: info@torcottage.co.uk
I: www.torcottage.co.uk

Westward ◆◆◆
15 Plymouth Road, Tavistock,
Devon PL19 8AU
T: (01822) 612094
F: (01822) 611206

TEIGNMOUTH
Devon

Belvedere Hotel ◆◆◆
Barn Park Road, Teignmouth,
Devon TQ14 8PJ
T: (01626) 774561

Hill Rise Hotel ◆◆◆
1 Winterbourne Road,
Teignmouth, Devon TQ14 8JT
T: (01626) 773108
F: (01626) 773108

Leicester House ◆◆◆
2 Winterbourne Road,
Teignmouth, Devon TQ14 8JT
T: (01626) 773043 &
07710 772097

Thomas Luny House ◆◆◆◆◆
Teign Street, Teignmouth, Devon
TQ14 8EG
T: (01626) 772976
E: alisonandjohn@
thomas-luny-house.co.uk
I: www.thomas-luny-house.
co.uk

THE LIZARD
Cornwall

Trethvas Farmhouse ◆◆◆◆
The Lizard, Helston, Cornwall
TR12 7AR
T: (01326) 290720
F: (01326) 290720

THORNBURY
Devon

Forda Farm ◆◆◆
Thornbury, Holsworthy, Devon
EX22 7BS
T: (01409) 261369

THORNE
Somerset

Thorne Cottage ◆◆◆◆
Thorne, Yeovil, Somerset
BA21 3PZ
T: (01935) 421735

THORNE ST MARGARET
Somerset

Thorne Manor ◆◆◆◆
Thorne St Margaret, Wellington,
Somerset TA21 0EQ
T: (01823) 672264
E: thorne.manor@euphony.net

TILSHEAD
Wiltshire °

Black Horse Inn ◆◆◆
High Street, Tilshead, Salisbury,
Wiltshire SP3 4RY
T: (01980) 620104
F: (01980) 620104

TIMBERSCOMBE
Somerset

The Dell ◆◆◆
Cowbridge, Timberscombe,
Minehead, Somerset TA24 7TD
T: (01643) 841564
E: hcrawford@zetnet.co.uk

**Knowle Manor and Riding
Centre** ◆◆◆
Timberscombe, Minehead,
Somerset TA24 6TZ
T: (01643) 841342
F: (01643) 841644
E: knowlemnr@aol.com
I: www.ridingholidaysuk.com

TINHAY
Devon

Tinhay Mill Restaurant ◆◆◆◆
Tinhay, Lifton, Devon PL16 0AJ
T: (01566) 784201
F: (01566) 784201

TINTAGEL
Cornwall

Bosayne Guest House ◆◆◆
Atlantic Road, Tintagel, Cornwall
PL34 0DE
T: (01840) 770514
E: clark@clarky100.freeserve.
co.uk
I: www.clarky100.freeserve.co.uk

Camelot Hotel ◆◆
Atlanta Road, Tintagel, Cornwall
PL34 0DQ
T: (01840) 770202
F: (01840) 770978

The Cornishman Inn ◆◆◆
Fore Street, Tintagel, Cornwall
PL34 0DB
T: (01840) 770238
F: (01840) 770078
E: info@cornishmaninn.com
I: www.cornishmaninn.com

Cottage Teashop ◆◆◆◆
Bossiney Road, Tintagel,
Cornwall PL34 0AH
T: (01840) 770639
E: cotteashop@talk21.com

Pendrin House ◆◆◆◆
Atlantic Road, Tintagel, Cornwall
PL34 0DE
T: (01840) 770560
F: (01840) 770560
E: pendrin@tesco.net

Polkerr Guest House ◆◆◆◆
Tintagel, Cornwall PL34 0BY
T: (01840) 770382 & 770132

Port William Inn ◆◆◆◆
Trebarwith Strand, Tintagel,
Cornwall PL34 0HB
T: (01840) 770230
F: (01840) 770936
E: william@eurobell.co.uk

**Trewarmett Lodge Hotel and
Restaurant**◆◆
Trewarmett, Tintagel, Cornwall
PL34 0ET
T: (01840) 770460

TIVERTON
Devon

Bridge Guest House ◆◆◆
23 Angel Hill, Tiverton, Devon
EX16 6PE
T: (01884) 252804
F: (01884) 252804
I: www.smoothhound.
co.uk/hotels/bridgegh.html

Great Bradley Farm ◆◆◆◆
Withleigh, Tiverton, Devon
EX16 8JL
T: (01884) 256946
F: (01884) 256946

Lodgehill Farm Hotel ◆◆◆
Tiverton, Devon EX16 5PA
T: (01884) 251200 & 252907
F: (01884) 242090
E: Lodgehill@dial.pipex.com
I: www.lodgehill.co.uk

Lower Collipriest Farm ◆◆◆◆
Tiverton, Devon EX16 4PT
T: (01884) 252321
F: (01884) 252321
E: linda@lowercollipriest.co.uk
I: www.lowercollipriest.co.uk

Quoit-at-Cross Farm ◆◆◆
Stoodleigh, Tiverton, Devon
EX16 9PJ
T: (01398) 351280
F: (01398) 351351
E: quiot-at-cross@talk21.com
I: www.quoit-at-cross.co.uk

TOLLER PORCORUM
Dorset

Barrowlands ◆◆◆
Toller Porcorum, Dorchester,
Dorset DT2 0DW
T: (01300) 320281
E: jrdovey@ukgateway.net

Colesmoor Farm ◆◆◆◆
Toller Porcorum, Dorchester,
Dorset DT2 0DU
T: (01300) 320812
F: (01300) 321402
E: geddes.colesmoor@eclipse.
co.uk

Grays Farmhouse ◆◆◆◆
Clift Lane, Toller Porcorum,
Dorchester, Dorset DT2 0EJ
T: (01308) 485574
E: rosie@farmhousebnb.co.uk
I: www.farmhousebnb.co.uk

The Kingcombe Centre ◆◆
Lower Kingcombe, Toller
Porcorum, Dorchester, Dorset
DT2 0EQ
T: (01300) 320684
F: (01300) 321409
E: nspring@kingcombe-centre.
demon.co.uk
I: www.kingcombe-centre.
demon.co.uk

The Manor ◆◆◆◆◆
5 Kingcombe Road, Toller
Porcorum, Dorchester, Dorset
DT2 0DG
T: (01300) 320010 &
0797 1956120

TOPSHAM
Devon

**The Galley Restaurant with
Cabins**
Rating Applied For
41 Fere Street, Topsham, Exeter
EX3 0HY
T: (01392) 876078
F: (01392) 876078
E: fish@galleyrestaurant.co.uk
I: www.galleyrestaurant.co.uk

TORCROSS
Devon

Cove Guest House ◆◆◆
Torcross, Kingsbridge, Devon
TQ7 2TH
T: (01548) 580350
F: (01548) 580350

TORQUAY
Devon

Abbeyfield Hotel ◆◆◆◆
Bridge Road, Torquay, TQ2 5AX
T: (01803) 294268
F: (01803) 296310

Acorn Lodge ◆◆◆
28 Bridge Road, Torquay, Devon
TQ2 5BA
T: (01803) 296939
F: (01803) 296939
E: acronlodgehotel@aol.com

Alstone Hotel ◆◆◆
22 Bridge Road, Torquay,
TQ2 5BA
T: (01803) 293243
E: alstonehotel@hotmail.com

Ascot House Hotel ◆◆
7 Tor Church Road, Torquay,
Devon TQ2 5UR
T: (01803) 295142
F: (01803) 295142
E: ascothousehotel@
holidaymail.co.uk

Ashfield Guest House ◆◆◆
9 Scarborough Road, Torquay,
TQ2 5UJ
T: (01803) 293537

Ashleigh House ◆◆◆
61 Meadfoot Lane, Torquay,
TQ1 2BP
T: (01803) 294660

Avenue Park Guest House
◆◆◆
3 Avenue Road, Torquay,
TQ2 5LA
T: (01803) 293902
F: (01803) 293902
E: avenuepark@bushinternet.
com
I: www.torbay.gov.
uk/tourism/t-hotels/avepark.htm

Avron Hotel ◆◆◆
70 Windsor Road, Torquay,
TQ1 1SZ
T: (01803) 294182
F: (01803) 403112
E: avronhotel@hotmail.com
I: www.avronhotel.com

Bahamas Hotel ◆◆◆
17 Avenue Road, Torquay,
TQ2 5LB
T: (01803) 296005 &
0500 526022

Barclay Court Hotel ◆◆◆
29 Castle Road, Torquay, Devon
TQ1 3BB
T: (01803) 292791
F: (01803) 215715
E: reservations@barclaycourt.
co.uk
I: www.barclaycourt.co.uk

Beverley House Hotel ◆◆◆
9 Clifton Grove, Old Torwood
Road, Torquay, TQ1 1PR
T: (01803) 294626

Blue Haze Hotel ◆◆◆◆
Seaway Lane, Torquay, Devon
TQ2 6PS
T: (01803) 607186 & 606205
F: (01803) 607186
E: mail@bluehazehotel.co.uk
I: www.bluehazehotel.co.uk

Braddon Hall Hotel ◆◆◆
70 Braddon Hill Road East,
Torquay, TQ1 1HF
T: (01803) 293908
F: (01803) 293908

Brampton Court Hotel ◆◆◆◆
St Luke's Road South, Torquay,
TQ2 5NZ
T: (01803) 294237
F: (01803) 294237
E: stay@bramptoncourt.co.uk
I: www.bramptoncourt.co.uk

Brandize Hotel ◆◆◆
19 Avenue Road, Torquay,
TQ2 5LB
T: (01803) 297798
F: (01803) 297798
E: ted@brandize20.freeserve.
co.uk
I: www.brandizehotel.com

Brantwood Hotel ◆◆◆◆
Rowdens Road, Torquay, Devon
TQ2 5AZ
T: (01803) 297241

Briarfields Hotel ◆◆◆
84/86 Avenue Road, Torquay,
TQ2 5LF
T: (01803) 297844
F: (01803) 297844
E: briarfieldshotel@aol.com
I: www.smoothhound.
co.uk/hotels/briar.html

Brocklehurst Hotel ◆◆◆
Rathmore Road, Torquay, Devon
TQ2 6NZ
T: (01803) 292735 &
0500 505450
F: (01803) 403204
E: enquiries@brocklehursthotel.
co.uk
I: www.brocklehursthotel.co.uk

Brooklands Guest House ◆◆◆
5 Scarborough Road, Torquay,
TQ2 5UJ
T: (01803) 296696

Burleigh House ◆◆◆
25 Newton Road, Torquay,
Devon TQ2 5DB
T: (01803) 291557

Capri Hotel ◆◆◆◆
12 Torbay Road, Livermead,
Torquay, TQ2 6RG
T: (01803) 293158
I: www.capri-hotel.co.uk

Carysfort Guest House ◆◆
13 Warren Road, Torquay,
TQ2 5TQ
T: (01803) 294160

Cedar Court Hotel ◆◆◆◆
3 St Matthew's Road, Chelston,
Torquay, TQ2 6JA
T: (01803) 607851

Charterhouse Hotel
Rating Applied For
Cockington Lane, Torquay,
Devon TQ2 6QT
T: (01803) 605804

The Chelston Manor Hotel
◆◆◆
Old Mill Road, Torquay, Devon
TQ2 6HW
T: (01803) 605142
F: (01803) 605267

Chester Court Hotel ◆◆◆
30 Cleveland Road, Torquay,
TQ2 5BE
T: (01803) 294565
F: (01803) 294565
E: kevin@kpmorris.freeserve.
co.uk
I: www.kpmorris.freeserve.
co.uk/cch.html

Chesterfield Hotel ◆◆◆◆
62 Belgrave Road, Torquay,
TQ2 5HY
T: (01803) 292318
F: (01803) 293676

Clovelly Guest House ◆◆◆
91 Avenue Road, Chelston,
Torquay, TQ2 5LH
T: (01803) 292286
F: (01803) 242286
E: clovellyguesthouse@
ntlworld.com
I: homepage.ntlworld.
com/clovelly.guesthouse

Collingwood Hotel ◆◆◆
38 Braddons Hill Road East,
Torquay, Devon TQ1 1HB
T: (01803) 293448

Coombe Court Hotel ◆◆◆◆
Babbacombe Downs Road,
Torquay, TQ1 3LP
T: (01803) 327086 & 344840
F: (01803) 327097
E: phil&jackie@
coombecourthotel
I: www.coombecourthotel.co.uk

Cranborne Hotel ◆◆◆◆◆
58 Belgrave Road, Torquay,
TQ2 5HY
T: (01803) 298046
F: (01803) 215477

The Cranmore ◆◆◆◆
89 Avenue Road, Torquay,
Devon TQ2 5LH
T: (01803) 298488
F: (01803) 298488
E: dave@thecranmore.fsnet.
co.uk

Crimdon Dene Hotel ◆◆◆
12 Falkland Road, Torquay,
TQ2 5JP
T: (01803) 294651
I: www.crimdondenehotel.
homestead.com/index.html

Crowndale Hotel ◆◆◆
18 Bridge Road, Torquay,
TQ2 5BA
T: (01803) 293068
F: (01803) 293068
I: www.torquayhotels.com

Daylesford Hotel ◆◆◆◆
60 Bampfylde Road, Torquay,
TQ2 5ΛY
T: (01803) 294435
I: www.daylesfordhotel.com

The Downs Hotel ◆◆◆
43 Babbacombe Downs Road,
Babbacombe, Torquay TQ1 3LN
T: (01803) 328543
F: (01803) 328543
E: manager@downshotel.co.uk
I: www.downshotel.co.uk

Ellington Court Hotel ◆◆◆
St Lukes Road South, Torquay,
TQ2 5NZ
T: (01803) 294957
F: (01803) 201383
E: ellington-court-hotel@
supanet.com

Everglades Hotel ◆◆◆
32 St Marychurch Road,
Torquay, Devon TQ1 3HY
T: (01803) 295389
F: (01803) 214357

Fairmount House Hotel
◆◆◆◆
Herbert Road, Chelston, Torquay
TQ2 6RW
T: (01803) 605446
F: (01803) 605446

Fairways ◆◆◆◆
72 Avenue Road, Torquay,
TQ2 5LF
T: (01803) 298471
F: (01803) 298471

Ferndale Hotel ◆◆◆◆
22 St Marychurch Road,
Torquay, TQ1 3HY
T: (01803) 295311

Hotel Fleurie ◆◆◆◆
50 Bampfylde Road, Torquay,
TQ2 5AY
T: (01803) 294869
F: (01803) 389589

Gainsboro Hotel ◆◆◆
22 Rathmore Road, Torquay,
Devon TQ2 6NY
T: (01803) 292032
F: (01803) 292032
E: gainsboro@freeuk.com

The Garlieston Hotel ◆◆◆
Bridge Road, Torquay, TQ2 5BA
T: (01803) 294050
E: garliestonhotel@jridewood.
fsnet.co.uk

Glendower Hotel ◆◆◆
Falkland Road, Torquay, TQ2 5JP
T: (01803) 299988
F: (01803) 299988
E: peter@hoteltorquay.co.uk
I: www.hoteltorquay.co.uk

Glenross Hotel ◆◆◆◆
25 Avenue Road, Torquay,
Devon TQ2 5LB
T: (01803) 297517
F: (01803) 299033
E: holiday@glenross-hotel.co.uk
I: www.glenross-hotel.co.uk

Glenroy Hotel ◆◆
10 Bampfylde Road, Torquay,
TQ2 5AR
T: (01803) 299255 &
07768 415045
F: (01803) 299255
E: glenroy@bun.com

The Green Park Hotel ◆◆◆
25 Morgan Avenue, Torquay,
TQ2 5RR
T: (01803) 293618
E: greenpark@eclipse.co.uk
I: www.greenpark.eclipse.co.uk

Grosvenor House Hotel ◆◆◆
Falkland Road, Torquay, TQ2 5JP
T: (01803) 294110
E: pearce@grosvenor-hse.fsnet.
co.uk

Haytor Hotel ◆◆◆
Meadfoot Road, Torquay,
TQ1 2JP
T: (01803) 294708
F: (01803) 292511
E: enquiries@haytorhotel.com
I: www.haytorhotel.com

Hillcroft Hotel ◆◆◆
9 St Luke's Road, Torquay,
TQ2 5NY
T: (01803) 297247
E: chris_hoyte@hotmail.com

The Hotel Newburgh ◆◆
14 Scarborough Road, Torquay,
TQ2 5UJ
T: (01803) 293270
E: the-newburgh-torquay@
hotels.activebooking.com

Howard Court Hotel
Rating Applied For
31 St Efrides Road, Torquay,
TQ2 5SG
T: (01803) 295494

Ingoldsby Hotel ◆◆◆◆
1 Chelston Road, Torquay,
TQ2 6PT
T: (01803) 607497
F: (01803) 607497
E: ingoldsby.hotel@virgin.net

Jesmond Dene Hotel ◆◆
85 Abbey Road, Torquay,
TQ2 5NN
T: (01803) 293062

Kings Hotel ◆◆◆◆
44 Bampfylde Road, Torquay,
TQ2 5AY
T: (01803) 293108
F: (01803) 292482
E: kingshotel@bigfoot.com
I: www.kingshoteltorquay.co.uk

Kingston House ◆◆◆◆
75 Avenue Road, Torquay,
TQ2 5LL
T: (01803) 212760
F: (01803) 201425
E: butto@kingstonhousehotel.
co.uk

Kingsway Lodge ◆◆◆
95 Avenue Road, Torquay,
TQ2 5LH
T: (01803) 295288
I: www.
smoothhoundco.uk/hotels/
kingsway.html

Lee Hotel ◆◆
Torbay Road, Livermead,
Torquay, TQ2 6RG
T: (01803) 293946
F: (01803) 293946
I: www.leehotel.co.uk

Lindum Hotel ◆◆◆
105 Abbey Road, Torquay, Devon
TQ2 5NP
T: (01803) 292795
F: (01803) 299358
E: lindum@eurobell.co.uk
I: www.lindum-hotel.co.uk

Maple Lodge ◆◆◆
36 Ash Hill Road, Torquay,
TQ1 3JD
T: (01803) 297391

Marstan Hotel ◆◆◆◆
Meadfoot Sea Road, Torquay,
TQ1 2LQ
T: (01803) 292837
F: (01803) 299202
E: enquiries@
marstan-hotel-torquay.co.uk
I: www.marstan-hotel-torquay.
co.uk

Melba House Hotel ◆◆◆
62 Bampfylde Road, Torquay,
TQ2 5AY
T: (01803) 213167
F: (01803) 211953

Melbourne Tower Hotel ◆◆◆
Solsbro Road, Chelston, Torquay
TQ2 6PF
T: (01803) 607252
F: (01803) 607252
E: wilson@
melbournetowerhotel.co.uk
I: www.melbournetowerhotel.
co.uk

Mount Edgcombe Hotel
◆◆◆◆
23 Avenue Road, Torquay,
TQ2 5LB
T: (01803) 292310
F: (01803) 292310

Mount Nessing Hotel ◆◆◆
St Luke's Road North, Torquay,
TQ2 5PD
T: (01803) 294259
F: (01803) 294259
E: mount_nessing@hotmail.
com
I: www.smoothhound.co.uk

Newlyn Hotel ◆◆◆◆
62 Braddons Hill Road East,
Torquay, TQ1 1HF
T: (01803) 295100
E: Barbara@newlyn-hotel.co.uk
I: www.newlyn-hotel.co.uk

Norwood Hotel ◆◆◆◆
60 Belgrave Road, Torquay,
TQ2 5HY
T: (01803) 294236
F: (01803) 294236
E: enquires@norwood-hotel.
co.uk
I: www.norwood-hotel.co.uk

The Pines ◆◆
19 Newton Road, Torre, Torquay,
Devon TQ2 5DB
T: (01803) 292882

Richwood Hotel ◆◆◆
20 Newton Road, Torquay,
Devon TQ2 5BZ
T: (01803) 293729
F: (01803) 213632
E: enq@
richwood-hotel-torquay.co.uk
I: www.richwood-hotel-torquay.
co.uk

Robin Hill International Hotel
◆◆◆◆
74 Braddons Hill Road East,
Torquay, TQ1 1HF
T: (01803) 214518
F: (01803) 291410
E: jo@robinhillhotel.co.uk
I: www.robinhillhotel.co.uk

Sandpiper Hotel ◆◆◆
Rowdens Road, Torquay,
TQ2 5AZ
T: (01803) 292779

Sandpiper Lodge Hotel ◆◆◆
96 Avenue Road, Torquay,
TQ2 5LF
T: (01803) 293293

Seapoint Hotel ◆◆◆
Old Torwood Road, Torquay,
TQ1 1PR
T: (01803) 211808
E: seapointhotel@hotmail.com

Shirley Hotel ◆◆◆◆
Braddons Hill Road East,
Torquay, TQ1 1HF
T: (01803) 293016
E: shirleyhotel@eurobell.co.uk

Silverlands ◆◆◆
27 Newton Road, Torquay,
TQ2 5DB
T: (01803) 292013

South View Hotel ◆◆◆◆
12 Scarborough Road, Torquay,
TQ2 5UJ
T: (01803) 296029
E: dianesouthview@aol.com

Southbank Hotel ◆◆◆◆
15/17 Belgrave Road, Torquay,
TQ2 5HU
T: (01803) 296701 &
07774 948850
F: (01803) 292026

Suite Dreams Hotel ◆◆◆◆
Steep Hill, Maidencombe,
Torquay TQ1 4TS
T: (01803) 313900
F: (01803) 313841
E: suitedreams@suitedreams.
co.uk
I: www.suitedreams.co.uk

Sunnymead ◆◆◆
501 Babbacombe Road, Torquay,
TQ1 1HL
T: (01803) 296938

Tor Dean Hotel ◆◆◆
27 Bampfylde Road, Torquay,
TQ2 5AY
T: (01803) 294669
F: (01803) 299547
E: jeffmillen@postmaster.co.uk

Tor Park Hotel ◆◆◆
24 Vansittart Road, Torquay,
TQ2 5BW
T: (01803) 295151
F: (01803) 200584
I: www.shearings-holidays.co.uk

Torbay Hotel ◆◆◆
Torbay Road, Torquay, TQ2 5EY
T: (01803) 295218
F: (01803) 291127

Torbay Rise Hotel ◆◆◆
Old Mill Road, Torquay, TQ2 6HL
T: (01803) 605541
E: vivienne.plewes@IC24.net
I: www.torbayrisehotel.
freeservers.com

Torbay Star Guest House ◆◆◆
73 Avenue Road, Torquay,
TQ2 5LL
T: (01803) 293998
F: (01803) 293998

Trafalgar House Hotel ◆◆◆
30 Bridge Road, Torquay,
TQ2 5BA
T: (01803) 292486
E: s.collett@ntlworld.com
I: www.torquayhotelsuk.com

Tree Tops Hotel ◆◆◆
St Albans Road, Torquay, Devon
TQ1 3NP
T: (01803) 325135

Trelawney Hotel ◆◆◆
48 Belgrave Road, Torquay,
TQ2 5HS
T: (01803) 296049
F: (01803) 296049
E: trelawneyj@aol.com
I: www.trelawneyhotel.co.uk

Trouville Hotel ◆◆◆
70 Belgave Road, Torquay,
TQ2 5HY
T: (01803) 294979

Villa Marina ◆◆◆
Tor Park Road, Torquay, Devon
TQ2 5BQ
T: (01803) 292187 &
07790 433897

The Wayland Hotel & Belgravia Self-Catering Holiday Suites ◆◆◆
31-47 Belgrave Road, Torquay,
TQ2 5HX
T: (01803) 293417
F: (01803) 293417

West Bank Hotel ◆◆◆
54 Bampfylde Road, Torquay,
TQ2 5AY
T: (01803) 295271

Westbourne Hotel ◆◆◆◆
106 Avenue Road, Torquay,
TQ2 5LQ
T: (01803) 292927
F: (01803) 292927

Whitburn Guest House ◆◆◆
St Lukes Road North, Torquay,
TQ2 5PD
T: (01803) 296719
E: joe@lazenby15.freeserve.
co.uk

Wilsbrook Guest House ◆◆◆
77 Avenue Road, Torquay,
TQ2 5LL
T: (01803) 298413
E: wilsbrook@amserve.net
I: www.wilsbrook.freeserve.co.uk

Woodgrange Hotel ◆◆◆
18 Newton Road, Torquay,
TQ2 5BZ
T: (01803) 212619
F: (01803) 212619

TORRINGTON
Devon

Beaford House Hotel ◆◆◆◆
Beaford, Winkleigh, Devon
EX19 8AB
T: (01805) 603305 & 603330
F: (01805) 603305

Locksbeam Farm ◆◆◆◆
Torrington, Devon EX38 7EZ
T: (01805) 623213
F: (01805) 623213
I: www.tarka-country.
co.uk/locksbeamfarm

West of England Inn ◆◆◆
18 South Street, Torrington,
Devon EX38 8AA
T: (01805) 624949

TOTNES
Devon

Buckyette Farm ◆◆◆
Buckyette, Totnes, Devon
TQ9 6ND
T: (01803) 762638
F: (01803) 762638

The Elbow Room ◆◆◆◆◆
North Street, Totnes, Devon
TQ9 5NZ
T: (01803) 863480 &
0797 1516824

Foales Leigh ◆◆◆◆
Harberton, Totnes, Devon
TQ9 7SS
T: (01803) 862365
F: (01803) 862365

Four Seasons Guest House ◆◆◆
13 Bridgetown, Totnes, Devon
TQ9 5AB
T: (01803) 862146
F: (01803) 867779
E: eecornford@netscapeonline.
co.uk

Great Court Farm ◆◆◆◆
Weston Lane, Totnes, Devon
TQ9 6LB
T: (01803) 862326
F: (01803) 862326

The Hungry Horse Restaurant ◆◆◆◆
Old Road, Harbertonford, Totnes,
Devon TQ9 7TA
T: (01803) 732441
F: (01803) 732780

Old Follaton ◆◆◆◆◆
Plymouth Road, Totnes, Devon
TQ9 5NA
T: (01803) 865441
F: (01803) 863597
E: bandb@oldfollaton.co.uk
I: www.oldfollaton.co.uk

The Old Forge at Totnes ◆◆◆◆
Seymour Place, Totnes, Devon
TQ9 5AY
T: (01803) 862174
F: (01803) 865385

The Watermans Arms ◆◆◆◆◆
Bow Bridge, Ashprington,
Totnes, Devon TQ9 7EG
T: (01803) 732214
F: (01803) 732314

TREATOR
Cornwall

Woodlands Close ◆◆◆
Treator, Padstow, Cornwall
PL28 8RU
T: (01841) 533109
E: john@stock65.freeserve.co.uk
I: www.cornwall-online.
co.uk/woodlands-close

TREGASWITH
Cornwall

Tregaswith Farmhouse ◆◆◆◆
Tregaswith, Newquay, Cornwall
TR8 4HY
T: (01637) 881181
F: (01637) 881181

TREGONY
Cornwall

Tregonan ◆◆◆◆
Tregony, Truro, Cornwall
TR2 5SN
T: (01872) 530249
F: (01872) 530249

TRELIGHTS
Cornwall

Long Cross Hotel and Victorian Garden ◆◆◆
Trelights, Port Isaac, Cornwall
PL29 3TF
T: (01208) 880243
F: (01208) 880 560

TRESILLIAN
Cornwall

Polsue Manor Farm ◆◆◆
Tresillian, Truro, Cornwall
TR2 4BP
T: (01872) 520234
F: (01872) 520616
E: geraldineholliday@hotmail.
com

TREVALGA
Cornwall

Trehane Farm ◆◆◆
Trevalga, Boscastle, Cornwall
PL35 0EB
T: (01840) 250510

TREVAUNANCE COVE
Cornwall

Driftwood Spars Hotel ◆◆◆
Trevaunance Cove, St Agnes,
Cornwall TR5 0RT
T: (01872) 552428 & 553323
F: (01872) 553701
E: driftwoodspars@hotmail.com
I: driftwoodspars.co.uk

TROWBRIDGE
Wiltshire

26 The Beeches ◆◆◆
Trowbridge, Wiltshire BA14 7HG
T: (01225) 760760

Herons Knoll ◆◆
18 Middle Lane, Trowbridge,
Wiltshire BA14 7LG
T: (01225) 752593
F: (01225) 752593

Lion and Fiddle ◆◆◆
Devizes Road, Hilperton,
Trowbridge, Wiltshire BA14 7QS
T: (01225) 776392
F: (01225) 774501

Old Manor Hotel ◆◆◆◆◆
Trowle, Trowbridge, Wiltshire
BA14 9BL
T: (01225) 777393
F: (01225) 765443
E: oldbeams@oldmanorhotel.
com
I: www.oldmanorhotel.com

62b Paxcroft Cottages ◆◆◆
Devizes Road, Hilperton,
Trowbridge, Wiltshire BA14 6JB
T: (01225) 765838
E: paxcroftcottages@hotmail.
com

Sue's B & B ◆◆◆
25 Blair Road, Trowbridge,
Wiltshire BA14 9JZ
T: (01225) 764559 &
07977 655017
E: sue_b_n_b@yahoo.com
I: www.visitbritain.com

Welam House ◆◆◆
Bratton Road, West Ashton,
Trowbridge, Wiltshire BA14 6AZ
T: (01225) 755908

TRULL
Somerset

The Winchester Arms
Rating Applied For
Church Road, Trull, Taunton,
Somerset TA3 7LG
T: (01823) 284723
F: (01823) 284723

TRURO
Cornwall

Bissick Old Mill ◆◆◆◆
Ladock, Truro, Cornwall TR2 4PG
T: (01726) 882557
F: (01726) 884057

Great Hewas Farm ◆◆◆
Grampound Road, Truro,
Cornwall TR2 4EP
T: (01726) 882218 &
07860 117572

Marcorrie Hotel ◆◆◆◆
20 Falmouth Road, Truro,
Cornwall TR1 2HX
T: (01872) 277374
F: (01872) 241666
E: marcorrie@aol.com
I: www.hotelstruro.com

Moonfleet House
Rating Applied For
20 St Georges Road, Truro,
Cornwall TR1 3JD
T: (01872) 263105

Rock Cottage ◆◆◆◆
Blackwater, Truro, Cornwall
TR4 8EU
T: (01872) 560252 &
07971 941399
F: (01872) 560252
E: rockcottage@yahoo.com

Trevispian-Vean Farm Guest House ◆◆◆◆
St Erme, Truro, Cornwall TR4 9AT
T: (01872) 279514
F: (01872) 263730
I: www.guesthousestruro.com

UFFCULME
Devon

Waterloo Cross Inn ◆◆
Waterloo Cross, Uffculme,
Cullompton, Devon EX15 3ES
T: (01884) 840328
F: (01884) 840908

UPLODERS
Dorset
Uploders Farm ◆◆◆
Dorchester Road, Uploders,
Bridport, Dorset DT6 4NZ
T: (01308) 423380

UPLYME
Devon
Elton ◆◆◆◆
Lyme Road, Uplyme, Lyme Regis,
Dorset DT7 3TH
T: (01297) 445986
E: mikecawte@aol.com

Hill Barn ◆◆◆◆
Gore Lane, Uplyme, Lyme Regis,
Dorset DT7 3RJ
T: (01297) 445185
F: (01297) 445185
E: jwb@
lymeregis-accomodation.com
I: lymeregis-accomodation.com

UPOTTERY
Devon
Robins Cottage ◆◆◆◆
Upottery, Honiton, Devon
EX14 9PL
T: (01404) 861281

UPTON
Cornwall
**The Chough Hotel &
Restaurant** ◆◆◆
Marine Drive, Upton, Bude,
Cornwall EX23 0LZ
T: (01288) 352386
F: (01288) 352386
E: bull-ji@choughhotel.
swinternet.co.uk
I: www.activebooking.com

Harefield Cottage
Rating Applied For
Upton, Bude, Cornwall EX23 0LY
T: (01288) 352350
F: (01288) 352712
E: sales@coast-countryside.
co.uk
I: www.coast-countryside.co.uk

UPTON LOVELL
Wiltshire
Prince Leopold ◆◆◆
Upton Lovell, Warminster,
Wiltshire BA12 0JP
T: (01985) 850460
F: (01985) 850737
E: princeleopold@lineone.net
I: www.princeleopoldinn.co.uk

UPTON NOBLE
Somerset
Kingston House ◆◆◆◆
Upton Noble, Shepton Mallet,
Somerset BA4 6BA
T: (01749) 850805
F: (01749) 850806
E: timstroud220@
netscapeonline.co.uk

UPWEY
Dorset
Bankside Cottage ◆◆◆
Church Street, Upwey,
Weymouth, Dorset DT3 5QE
T: (01305) 812320
E: edward.bird@care4free.net

URCHFONT
Wiltshire
The Nags Head ◆
High Street, Urchfont, Devizes,
Wiltshire SN10 4QH
T: (01380) 840346

VICTORIA
Cornwall
Auberge Asterisk ◆◆◆
Victoria, Roche, St Austell,
Cornwall PL26 8LH
T: (01726) 890863 & 890062
F: (01726) 890642
E: aubasterisk@hotmail.com

WADEBRIDGE
Cornwall
Kivells ◆◆◆◆
Chapel Amble, Wadebridge,
Cornwall PL27 6EP
T: (01208) 841755
E: kivells@cwcom.net
I: www.kivellsbandb.co.uk

Tregolls Farm ◆◆◆
St Wenn, Bodmin, Cornwall
PL30 5PG
T: (01208) 812154
F: (01208) 812154
E: tregollsfarm@btclick.com
I: www.tregollsfarm.co.uk

WAMBROOK
Somerset
Woodview
Rating Applied For
Wambrook, Chard, Somerset
TA20 3EH
T: (01460) 65368

WARMINSTER
Wiltshire
Angel Cottage B & B ◆◆◆
34B Upton Scudamore,
Warminster, Wiltshire BA12 0AQ
T: (01985) 218504
F: (01985) 218504

Bugley Barton ◆◆◆◆◆
Victoria Road, Warminster,
Wiltshire BA12 7RB
T: (01985) 213389
F: (01985) 300450
E: bugleybarton@aol.com

Lane End Cottage ◆◆◆
72 Lane End, Corsley,
Warminster, Wiltshire BA12 7PG
T: (01373) 832592
F: (01373) 832935
E: hugh-kay@moredent.fsnet.
co.uk

Old Bell Hotel ◆◆◆
42 Market Place, Warminster,
Wiltshire BA12 9AN
T: (01985) 216611
F: (01985) 217111

Sturford Mead Farm ◆◆◆◆
Corsley, Warminster, Wiltshire
BA12 7QU
T: (01373) 832213
F: (01373) 832213
E: lynn_sturford.bed@virgin.net

WARMLEY
Gloucestershire
Ferndale Guest House ◆◆◆
37 Deanery Road, Warmley,
Bristol BS15 9JB
T: (0117) 9858247
F: (0117) 9044855
E: alexandmikewake@yahoo.
co.uk

WASHBOURNE
Devon
Penny Rowden ◆◆◆◆
Washbourne, Totnes, Devon
TQ9 7DN
T: (01803) 712485
F: (01803) 712485
E: ap@pennyrowden.freeserve.
co.uk

WASHFORD
Somerset
Green Bay ◆◆◆
Washford, Watchet, Somerset
TA23 0NN
T: (01984) 640303
E: greenbay@tinyonline.co.uk

WATCHET
Somerset
Esplanade House ◆◆◆◆
The Esplanade, Watchet,
Somerset TA23 0AJ
T: (01984) 633444

Wyndham House ◆◆◆◆
4 Sea View Terrace, Watchet,
Somerset TA23 0DF
T: (01984) 631881
F: (01984) 631881
E: rhv@dialstart.net

WATERGATE BAY
Cornwall
The White House ◆◆◆◆
Watergate Bay, Newquay,
Cornwall TR8 4AD
T: (01637) 860119
F: (01637) 860449
E: jenny.vallance@virgin.net
I: www.cornwallwhitehouse.
co.uk

WATERROW
Somerset
Handley Farm Accommodation
◆◆◆◆
Waterrow, Taunton, Somerset
TA4 2BE
T: (01398) 361516
F: (01398) 361516
I: www.handleyfarm.co.uk

WELLS
Somerset
Beaconsfield Farm ◆◆◆◆◆
Easton, Wells, Somerset
BA5 1DU
T: (01749) 870308
E: carol@beaconsfieldfarm.
co.uk
I: www.beaconsfieldfarm.co.uk

Beryl ◆◆◆◆◆
Wells, Somerset BA5 3JP
T: (01749) 678738
F: (01749) 670508
E: stay@beryl.co.uk
I: www.smoothhound.co.uk

**Burcott Mill Historic
Watermill and Guesthouse**
◆◆◆
Wookey Road, Wookey, Wells,
Somerset BA5 1NJ
T: (01749) 673118
F: (01749) 677376
E: theburts@burcottmill.com
I: www.burcottmill.com

Cadgwith ◆◆◆◆
Hawkers Lane, Wells, Somerset
BA5 3JH
T: (01749) 677799
E: rplettscadgwith@aol.com

Canon Grange ◆◆◆◆
Cathedral Green, Wells,
Somerset BA5 2UB
T: (01749) 671800
E: canongrange@email.com
I: www.canongrange.co.uk

Carmen B & B ◆◆◆◆
Bath Road, Wells, Somerset
BA5 3LQ
T: (01749) 677331 &
07977 098607
E: carmenbandb@tesco.net

Franklyns Farm ◆◆◆
Chewton Mendip, Bath BA3 4NB
T: (01761) 241372

Glengarth ◆◆◆
7 Glastonbury Road, Wells,
Somerset BA5 1TW
T: (01749) 673087

Highfield ◆◆◆◆
93 Portway, Wells, Somerset
BA5 2BR
T: (01749) 675330

Highgate Cottage ◆◆◆
Worth, Wells, Somerset
BA5 1LW
T: (01749) 674201
F: (01749) 674201

Hillside Cottage ◆◆◆
5-6 Keward, Glastonbury Road,
Wells, Somerset BA5 1TR
T: (01749) 673770
E: hillsidecott@compuserve.
com

Hillview Cottage ◆◆◆◆
Paradise Lane, Croscombe, Wells,
Somerset BA5 3RL
T: (01749) 343526
E: cathyhay@yahoo.co.uk
I: www.smoothhound.co.uk

Littlewell Farm Guest House
◆◆◆◆
Coxley, Wells, Somerset BA5 1QP
T: (01749) 677914

30 Mary Road ◆◆◆
Wells, Somerset BA5 2NF
T: (01749) 674031
F: (01749) 674031
E: triciabailey30@hotmail.com

The Old Stores ◆◆◆
Westbury-sub-Mendip, Wells,
Somerset BA5 1HA
T: (01749) 870817 &
07721 514306
F: (01749) 870980
E: moglin980@aol.com

The Pound Inn ◆◆◆
Burcott Lane, Coxley, Wells,
Somerset BA5 1QZ
T: (01749) 672785
E: poundinnwells@aol.com

Southway Farm ◆◆◆◆
Polsham, Wells, Somerset
BA5 1RW
T: (01749) 673396 &
07971 694650
F: (01749) 670373
I: www.southwayfarm.co.uk

Wookey Hole Inn
Rating Applied For
Wookey Hole, Somerset, Wells,
Somerset BA5 1BP
T: (01749) 676677
F: (01749) 676677
E: toadhall@lineone.net
I: www.wookeyholeinn.com

Worth House Hotel ◆◆◆◆
Worth, Wookey, Wells, Somerset
BA5 1LW
T: (01749) 672041
F: (01749) 672041
E: mblomeley2001@yahoo.
co.uk

WEMBURY
Devon

Bay Cottage ◆◆◆
150 Church Road, Wembury,
Plymouth PL9 0HR
T: (01752) 862559
F: (01752) 862559
E: thefairies@aol.com
I: www.bay-cottage.com

WEST ANSTEY
Devon

Greenhills Farm ◆◆◆◆
Yeo Mill, West Anstey, South
Molton, Devon EX36 3NU
T: (01398) 341300

Jubilee House ◆◆◆◆
Highaton Farm, West Anstey,
South Molton, Devon EX36 3PJ
T: (01398) 341312
F: (01398) 341323
E: denton@exmoorholiday.co.uk
I: www.exmoorholiday.co.uk

WEST BAY
Dorset

Egdon ◆◆
Third Cliff Walk, West Bay,
Bridport, Dorset DT6 4HX
T: (01308) 422542

The George Hotel ◆◆◆
West Bay, Bridport, Dorset
DT6 4EY
T: (01308) 423191

Heatherbell Cottage ◆◆◆
Hill Close, West Bay, Bridport,
Dorset DT6 4HW
T: (01308) 422998 &
07967 859896
E: heatherbell4bnb@onetel.net.
uk

WEST BUCKLAND
Somerset

Causeway Cottage ◆◆◆◆
West Buckland, Wellington,
Somerset TA21 9JZ
T: (01823) 663458
F: (01823) 663458
E: orrs@westbuckland.freeserve.
co.uk
I: welcome.to/causeway-cottage

WEST CAMEL
Somerset

The Walnut Tree ◆◆◆◆
Fore Street, West Camel, Yeovil,
Somerset BA22 7QW
T: (01935) 851292
F: (01935) 851292
I: www.thewalnuttreehotel.com

WEST COKER
Somerset

Millbrook House ◆◆◆◆
92 High Street, West Coker,
Yeovil, Somerset BA22 9AU
T: (01935) 862840
F: (01935) 863846

WEST DOWN
Devon

The Long House ◆◆◆◆
The Square, West Down,
Ilfracombe, Devon EX34 8NF
T: (01271) 863242

WEST HARPTREE
Bath and North East Somerset

The Wellsway Inn ◆◆◆
Harptree Hill, West Harptree,
Bristol BS40 6EJ
T: (01761) 221382

WEST HUNTSPILL
Somerset

Greenwood Lodge ◆◆◆◆
76 Main Road, West Huntspill,
Highbridge, Somerset TA9 3QU
T: (01278) 795886
F: (01278) 795886

Ilex House ◆◆◆◆
102 Main Road, West Huntspill,
Highbridge, Somerset TA9 3QZ
T: (01278) 783801 &
07989 601705
F: (01278) 794254
E: rogwyn@onetel.net.uk

WEST KNIGHTON
Dorset

Church Cottage ◆◆◆◆
West Knighton, Dorchester,
Dorset DT2 8PF
T: (01305) 852243
E: info@church-cottage.com
I: www.church-cottage.com

WEST MONKTON
Somerset

Springfield House ◆◆◆◆
Walford Cross, West Monkton,
Taunton, Somerset TA2 8QW
T: (01823) 412116
F: (01823) 412116
E: tina@ridout13.freeserve.
co.uk
I: www.mycbsite.com/bestbandb

WEST OVERTON
Wiltshire

Cairncot ◆◆◆
West Overton, Marlborough,
Wiltshire SN8 4ER
T: (01672) 861617 &
07798 603455

WEST PENNARD
Somerset

Clover Cottage ◆◆◆
Glastonbury Road, West
Pennard, Glastonbury, Somerset
BA6 8NN
T: (01458) 831174
E: cloverpennard@aol.com
I: www.glastonbury.
co.uk/accommodation/
bb_around_glaston/
clovercottage

WEST PORLOCK
Somerset

West Porlock House ◆◆◆◆
West Porlock, Minehead,
Somerset TA24 8NX
T: (01643) 862880

WEST STAFFORD
Dorset

Barton Barn
Rating Applied For
Barton Close, West Stafford,
Dorchester, Dorset DT2 8AD
T: (01305) 269949
E: ruth@barnarts.com
I: www.barnarts.com

Keepers Cottage ◆◆◆◆
West Stafford, Dorchester,
Dorset DT2 8AA
T: (01305) 264389 &
07979 316046
F: (01305) 264389
E: keeperscottage@tinyworld.
co.uk
I: www.keeperscottage.net

WESTBURY
Wiltshire

Black Dog Farm ◆◆◆
Chapmanslade, Westbury,
Wiltshire BA13 4AE
T: (01373) 832858
E: im.mills@virgin.net

Sherbourne House ◆◆◆
47 Station Road, Westbury,
Wiltshire BA13 3JW
T: (01373) 864865

WESTHAY
Somerset

New House Farm ◆◆◆◆
Burtle Road, Westhay,
Glastonbury, Somerset BA6 9TT
T: (01458) 860238 &
07944 828819
F: (01458) 860568
E: newhousefarm@
farmersweekly.net

WESTON
Devon

Higher Weston Farm ◆◆◆◆
Weston, Honiton, Devon
EX10 0PH
T: (01395) 513741

WESTON-SUPER-MARE
North Somerset

Algarve Guest House ◆◆◆
24 Quantock Road, Weston-
super-Mare, Avon BS23 4DT
T: (01934) 626128

Ashcombe Court ◆◆◆◆
17 Milton Road, Weston-super-
Mare, Avon BS23 2SH
T: (01934) 625104
F: (01934) 625104
E: ashcombecourt@tinyonline.
co.uk

Braeside Hotel ◆◆◆◆
2 Victoria Park, Weston-super-
Mare, Avon BS23 2HZ
T: (01934) 626642
F: (01934) 626642
E: braeside@tesco.net
I: www.braesidehotel.co.uk

Cornerways ◆◆◆
14 Whitecross Road, Weston-
super-Mare, Avon BS23 1EW
T: (01934) 623708

The Grand Atlantic ◆◆◆
Beach Road, Weston-super-
Mare, BS23 1BA
T: (01934) 626543
F: (01934) 415048
I: www.skypages.com

The Milton Lodge Hotel
◆◆◆◆
15 Milton Road, Weston-super-
Mare, Avon BS23 2SH
T: (01934) 623161
F: (01934) 623210
E: vallen@miltonlodge.
freeserve.co.uk
I: www.miltonlodge.com

Moorlands Country
Guesthouse ◆◆◆
Hutton, Weston-super-Mare,
Avon BS24 9QH
T: (01934) 812283
F: (01934) 812283
E: margaret_holt@email.comm
I: www.guestaccom.co.uk/35.
htm

Orchard House ◆◆◆◆
Summer Lane, West Wick,
Weston-super-Mare, BS24 7TF
T: (01934) 520948
F: (01934) 520948

Saxonia ◆◆◆
95 Locking Road, Weston-super-
Mare, Avon BS23 3EW
T: (01934) 633856
F: (01934) 623141
E: saxonia@lineone.net
I: www.smoothhound.
co.uk/hotels/saxonia.html

Spreyton Guest House ◆◆◆
72 Locking Road, Weston-super-
Mare, Avon BS23 3EN
T: (01934) 416887

Welbeck Hotel ◆◆◆
Knightstone Road, Marine
Parade, Weston-super-Mare,
Avon BS23 2BB
T: (01934) 621258
F: (01934) 643585
E: info@weston-welbeck.co.uk
I: www.weston-welbeck.co.uk

WESTONZOYLAND
Somerset

Staddlestones Guest House
◆◆◆◆
3 Standards Road,
Westonzoyland, Bridgwater,
Somerset TA7 0EL
T: (01278) 691179
F: (01278) 691333
E: staddlestones@euphony.net
I: www.
staddlestonesguesthouse.co.uk

WESTROP
Wiltshire

Park Farm Barn ◆◆◆◆
Westrop, Corsham, Wiltshire
SN13 9QF
T: (01249) 715911
F: (01249) 715911

WESTWARD HO!
Devon

Brockenhurst ◆◆◆
11 Atlantic Way, Westward Ho!,
Bideford, Devon EX39 1HX
T: (01237) 423346
F: (01237) 423346
E: snowball@brockenhurst1.
freeserve.co.uk

Eversley ◆◆◆◆
1 Youngaton Road, Westward
Ho!, Bideford, Devon EX39 1HU
T: (01237) 471603
E: lsharrat@ndevon.co.uk

The Puffins Inn ◆◆◆
123 Bay View Road, Westward
Ho!, Bideford, Devon EX39 1BJ
T: (01237) 473970
F: (01237) 422815
E: thepuffins@breathemail.net

WEYMOUTH
Dorset

Albatross Hotel ◆◆◆
96 The Esplanade, Weymouth,
Dorset DT4 7AT
T: (01305) 785191
F: (01305) 785191

Bay Lodge ◆◆◆◆◆
27 Greenhill, Weymouth, Dorset
DT4 7SW
T: (01305) 782419
F: (01305) 782828
E: barbara@baylodge.co.uk
I: www.baylodge.co.uk

Bay View Hotel ◆◆◆◆
35 The Esplanade, Weymouth,
Dorset DT4 8DH
T: (01305) 782083
F: (01305) 782083

Brunswick Guest House ◆◆◆
9 Brunswick Terrace, Weymouth,
Dorset DT4 7RW
T: (01305) 785408 &
07776 485600

Chadwood House ◆◆◆◆
77 Preston Road, Weymouth,
Dorset DT3 6PY
T: (01305) 834887

The Channel Hotel ◆◆◆
93 The Esplanade, Weymouth,
Dorset DT4 7AY
T: (01305) 785405
F: (01305) 785405
E: lee@thechannel.freeserve.
co.uk
I: www.resort-guide.
co.uk/channel

The Chatsworth ◆◆◆◆
14 The Esplanade, Weymouth,
Dorset DT4 8EB
T: (01305) 785012
F: (01305) 766342
E: david@thechatsworth.co.uk

Crofton Guest House ◆◆◆
36 Lennox Street, Weymouth,
Dorset DT4 7HD
T: (01305) 785903 &
0777 5905149
F: (01305) 750165
E: stevemerrill1@excite.com

Cumberland Hotel ◆◆◆◆
95 Esplanade, Weymouth,
Dorset DT4 7BA
T: (01305) 785644
F: (01305) 785644
I: www.theaa.co.uk/hotels

Cunard Guest House ◆◆◆
45-46 Lennox Street,
Weymouth, Dorset DT4 7HB
T: (01305) 771546
F: (01305) 771546
E: cunardhotel@hotmail.com

Eastney ◆◆◆◆
15 Longfield Road, Weymouth,
Dorset DT4 8RQ
T: (01305) 771682
E: eastneyhotel@aol.com
I: www.resort-guide.
co.uk/eastney

Elwell Manor Guest House
◆◆◆
70 Rodwell Road, Weymouth,
Dorset DT3 8QU
T: (01305) 782434
F: (01305) 782434
E: elwell@burville.fsnet.co.uk
I: www.tawdryandvulgar.co.uk

Florian ◆◆◆
59 Abbotsbury Road,
Weymouth, Dorset DT4 0AQ
T: (01305) 773836 &
07808 934138
F: (01305) 750160

The Freshford Hotel
Rating Applied For
3 Grange Road, Weymouth,
Dorset DT4 7PQ
T: (01305) 775862
F: (01305) 775862
E: freshfondhotel@handbag.
com

Green Gables ◆◆◆◆
14 Carlton Road South,
Weymouth, Dorset DT4 7PJ
T: (01305) 774808 &
07761 106525
E: greengables@w-a-g.co.uk
I: www.w-a-g.co.uk/greengables

Harlequin House Guest House
◆◆◆
9 Carlton Road South,
Weymouth, Dorset DT4 7PL
T: (01305) 785598

Kenora Private Hotel ◆◆◆◆
5 Stavordale Road, Weymouth,
Dorset DT4 0AB
T: (01305) 771215 &
07976 826067
E: kenora.hotel@wdi.co.uk

**Kimberley Family Run Guest
House** ◆◆◆
16 Kirtleton Avenue, Weymouth,
Dorset DT4 7PT
T: (01305) 783333
F: (01305) 839603

Kings Acre Hotel ◆◆◆◆
140 The Esplanade, Weymouth,
Dorset DT4 7NH
T: (01305) 782534
F: (01305) 782534

The Kingsley Hotel ◆◆◆◆
10 Kirtleton Avenue, Weymouth,
Dorset DT4 7PT
T: (01305) 777715
E: thekingsleyhotel@fs.mail
I: www.thekingsleyhotel.com

Hotel Kinley ◆◆◆
98 The Esplanade, Weymouth,
Dorset DT4 7AT
T: (01305) 782264
F: (01305) 786676
E: hotelkinley@hotmail.com
I: hotelkinley.co.uk

Lichfield House Hotel ◆◆◆
8 Brunswick Terrace, Weymouth,
Dorset DT4 7RW
T: (01305) 784112

Morven House Hotel ◆◆◆
2 Westerhall Road, Weymouth,
Dorset DT4 7SZ
T: (01305) 785075

The Pebbles Guest House ◆◆◆
18 Kirtleton Avenue, Weymouth,
Dorset DT4 7PT
T: (01305) 784331
F: (01305) 784695
E: blackwoodg@aol.com

Royal Hotel ◆◆◆◆
90-91 The Esplanade,
Weymouth, Dorset DT4 4AX
T: (01305) 782777
F: (01305) 761088

The Seaham ◆◆◆◆
3 Waterloo Place, Weymouth,
Dorset DT4 7NU
T: (01305) 782010
E: stay@theseaham.co.uk
I: www.theseaham.co.uk

Southbrook ◆◆◆
13 Preston Road, Weymouth,
Dorset DT3 6PU
T: (01305) 832208

Southville Guest House ◆◆◆
5 Dorchester Road, Weymouth,
Dorset DT4 7JR
T: (01305) 770382
E: southvillehotel@aol.com

Hotel Sunnywey ◆◆◆
23 Kirtleton Avenue, Weymouth,
Dorset DT4 7PS
T: (01305) 786911
F: (01305) 767084

Weyside Guest House ◆◆◆
1a Abbotsbury Road,
Weymouth, Dorset DT4 0AD
T: (01305) 772685
E: weysideguesthouse@
btinternet.com
I: www.weysideguesthouse.
btinternet.com

WHEDDON CROSS
Somerset

Cutthorne Farm ◆◆◆◆
Luckwell Bridge, Wheddon
Cross, Minehead, Somerset
TA24 7EW
T: (01643) 831255
F: (01643) 831255
E: durbin@cutthorne.co.uk
I: www.cutthorne.co.uk

Exmoor House ◆◆◆◆
Wheddon Cross, Somerset
TA24 7DU
T: (01643) 841432
F: (01643) 841811
E: exmoorhouse@hotmail.com
I: www.exmoorhotel.co.uk

Little Brendon Hill Farm
◆◆◆◆◆
Wheddon Cross, Minehead,
Somerset TA24 7BG
T: (01643) 841556
F: (01643) 841556
E: info@exmoorheaven.co.uk
I: www.exmoorheaven.co.uk

Little Quarme Farm ◆◆◆◆◆
Wheddon Cross, Minehead,
Somerset TA24 7EA
T: (01643) 841249
F: (01643) 841249
E: 106425.743@compuserve.
com
I: www.littlequarme.co.uk

The Rest And Be Thankful Inn
◆◆◆◆
Wheddon Cross, Minehead,
Somerset TA24 7DR
T: (01643) 841222
F: (01643) 841222
E: enquiries@
restandbethankful.co.uk
I: www.restandbethankful.co.uk

Sundial House ◆◆◆◆
Wheddon Cross, Minehead,
Somerset TA24 7DP
T: (01643) 841188
F: (01643) 841870
E: admin@sundialguesthouse.
co.uk
I: www.sundialguesthouse.co.uk

Triscombe Farm ◆◆◆◆
Wheddon Cross, Minehead,
Somerset TA24 7HA
T: (01643) 851227
F: (01643) 851227

WHIDDON DOWN
Devon

Fairhaven Farm ◆◆◆
Gooseford, Whiddon Down,
Okehampton, Devon EX20 2QH
T: (01647) 231261

WHIMPLE
Devon

Higher Southbrook Farm
Rating Applied For
Southbrook Lane, Whimple,
Exeter EX5 2PG
T: (01404) 823000

WICK ST LAWRENCE
North Somerset

Icelton Farm ◆◆◆
Wick St Lawrence, Weston-
super-Mare, Avon BS22 7YJ
T: (01934) 515704
F: (01934) 515704
E: iceltonfarm@faxria.net

WIDECOMBE-IN-THE-MOOR
Devon

Higher Venton Farm ◆◆◆
Widecombe-in-the-Moor,
Newton Abbot, Devon TQ13 7TF
T: (01364) 621235
F: (01364) 621382

Sheena Tower ◆◆◆
Widecombe-in-the-Moor,
Newton Abbot, Devon TQ13 7TE
T: (01364) 621308
E: sheenatower@compuserve.
com

WIDEMOUTH BAY
Cornwall

Brocksmoor Hotel ◆◆◆
Widemouth Bay, Bude, Cornwall
EX23 0DF
T: (01288) 361207 & 361589

WILCOT
Wiltshire

Wilcot Lodge ◆◆◆◆
Wilcot, Pewsey, Wiltshire
SN9 5NS
T: (01672) 563465 &
07974 700735
F: (01672) 569040
E: gmikegswimdells@hotmail.
com
I: www.bed-breakfast-uk.
com/bb-uk-wilts.htm

WILTON
Wiltshire

The Pembroke Arms Hotel
◆◆◆◆
Minster Street, Wilton,
Marlborough, Wiltshire SP2 0BH
T: (01722) 743328
F: (01722) 744886
E: reservations@pembrokearms.
co.uk

Pit Folly ◆◆◆◆
The Avenue, Wilton, Salisbury
SP2 0BU
T: (01722) 742108
E: damer.colville@virgin.net
I: www.uk-bedandbreakfasts.
com/wiltshire/salisbury/
Pit_Folly/

WINKLEIGH
Devon
The Old Parsonage ♦♦♦
Court Walk, Winkleigh, Devon
EX19 8JA
T: (01837) 83772
F: (01837) 680074

WINSCOMBE
North Somerset
Home Farm ♦♦♦♦
Barton, Winscombe, Cheddar,
Somerset BS25 1DX
T: (01934) 842078
E: chris@homefarmcottages.
co.uk
I: www.homefarmcottages.co.uk

WINSFORD
Somerset
Karslake House Hotel ♦♦♦♦
Halse Lane, Winsford, Minehead,
Somerset TA24 7JE
T: (01643) 851242
F: (01643) 851242
E: karslakehouse@aol.com
I: www.karslakehouse.co.uk

Kemps Farm ♦♦♦
Winsford, Minehead, Somerset
TA24 7HT
T: (01643) 851312

Larcombe Foot ♦♦♦♦
Winsford, Minehead, Somerset
TA24 7HS
T: (01643) 851306

WINSLEY
Wiltshire
The Conifers ♦♦
4 King Alfred Way, Winsley,
Bradford-on-Avon, Wiltshire
BA15 2NG
T: (01225) 722482

Stillmeadow ♦♦♦♦
18 Bradford Road, Winsley,
Bradford-on-Avon, Wiltshire
BA15 2HW
T: (01225) 722119
F: (01225) 722633
E: sue.gilby@btinternet.com

WINTERBOURNE STOKE
Wiltshire
Scotland Lodge Farm ♦♦♦♦
Winterbourne Stoke, Salisbury
SP3 4TF
T: (01980) 621199
F: (01980) 621188
E: william.lockwood@bigwig.
net
I: www.smoothhound.
co.uk/hotels/scotlandl.html

WINTERSLOW
Wiltshire
Shiralee Bed & Breakfast ♦♦
Tytherley Road, Winterslow,
Salisbury SP5 1PY
T: (01980) 862004 &
07818 415354
F: (01980) 862004
E: anything@faisa.co.uk
I: www.faisa.co.uk

WITHAM FRIARY
Somerset
**Higher West Barn Farm
♦♦♦♦**
Witham Friary, Frome, Somerset
BA11 5HH
T: (01749) 850819 &
07976 162207
E: ea.harrison@tesco.net

WITHERIDGE
Devon
Thelbridge Cross Inn ♦♦♦
Thelbridge, Crediton, Devon
EX17 4SQ
T: (01884) 860316
F: (01884) 861318
E: thelbridgexinn@cwcom.net
I: www.westcountry-hotels.
co.uk/thelbridgexinn

WIVELISCOMBE
Somerset
Greenway Farm ♦♦♦
Wiveliscombe, Taunton,
Somerset TA4 2UA
T: (01984) 623359
F: (01984) 624051

Mill Barn ♦♦♦♦
Jews Farm, Maundown,
Wiveliscombe, Taunton,
Somerset TA4 2HL
T: (01984) 624739 &
07779 448720
F: (01984) 624408
E: Tony&Marilyn@mill-barn.
freeserve.co.uk
I: www.mill-barn.freeserve.co.uk

WOODBOROUGH
Wiltshire
Pantawick ♦♦♦♦
Woodborough, Pewsey,
Wiltshire SN9 5PG
T: (01672) 851662
F: (01672) 851662
E: pantawick@aol.com

Well Cottage ♦♦♦
Honey Street, Woodborough,
Pewsey, Wiltshire SN9 5PS
T: (01672) 851577 &
07966 298863
E: b_trowbridgewellcottage@
yahoo.com

WOODY BAY
Devon
Moorlands ♦♦♦
Woody Bay, Parracombe,
Barnstaple, Devon EX31 4RA
T: (01598) 763224
E: info@moorlandshotel.
freeserve.co.uk
I: www.moorlandshotel.co.uk

WOOKEY HOLE
Somerset
Broadleys ♦♦♦♦
21 Wells Road, Wookey Hole,
Wells, Somerset BA5 1DN
T: (01749) 674746
F: (01749) 674746
E: broadleys@bobmilton.
totalserve.co.uk

Glencot House ♦♦♦♦♦
Glencot Lane, Wookey Hole,
Wells, Somerset BA5 1BH
T: (01749) 677160
F: (01749) 670210
E: glencot@ukonline.co.uk
I: web.ukonline.co.uk/glencot

Whitegate Cottage ♦♦♦
Milton Lane, Wookey Hole,
Wells, Somerset BA5 1DG
T: (01749) 675326
E: sueandnic@whitegate.
freeserve.co.uk

WOOLACOMBE
Devon
Camberley ♦♦♦
Beach Road, Woolacombe,
Devon EX34 7AA
T: (01271) 870231
E: camberley@tesco.net

Castle Hotel ♦♦♦♦
The Esplanade, Woolacombe,
Devon EX34 7DJ
T: (01271) 870788
F: (01271) 870788

Gull Rock Hotel ♦♦♦♦
Mortehoe, Woolacombe, Devon
EX34 7EA
T: (01271) 870534
F: (01271) 870534
E: info@thegullrockhotel.co.uk
I: www.thegullrockhotel.co.uk

Ossaborough House ♦♦♦♦
Ossaborough Lane,
Woolacombe, Devon EX34 7HJ
T: (01271) 870297
E: info@ossaboroughhouse.
co.uk
I: www.ossaboroughhouse.co.uk

Sunnyside House ♦♦♦
Sunnyside Road, Woolacombe,
Devon EX34 7DG
T: (01271) 870267

WOOLAVINGTON
Somerset
Chestnut House ♦♦♦♦♦
Hectors Stone, Lower Road,
Woolavington, Bridgwater,
Somerset TA7 8EF
T: (01278) 683658
F: (01278) 684333
I: www.chestnuthouse.freeserve.
co.uk

WOOLLEY
Cornwall
East Woolley Farm ♦♦♦♦
Woolley, Bude, Cornwall
EX23 9PP
T: (01288) 331525
F: (01288) 331525

WOOLVERTON
Somerset
The Old School House ♦♦♦
Woolverton, Bath BA3 6RH
T: (01373) 830200
F: (01373) 830200

WOOTTON BASSETT
Wiltshire
1 Highgate Cottages ♦♦♦
Brinkworth Road, Wootton
Bassett, Swindon SN4 8DU
T: (01793) 848054

The Hollies ♦♦♦
Greenhill, Hook, Wootton
Bassett, Swindon SN4 8EH
T: (01793) 770795
F: (01793) 770795

**Tockenham Court Farm
♦♦♦♦**
Tockenham, Swindon SN4 7PH
T: (01793) 852315 &
07836 241686
F: (01793) 852315

WRAXALL
Somerset
Rose's Farm ♦♦♦♦
Wraxall, Shepton Mallet,
Somerset BA4 6RQ
T: (01749) 860261
F: (01749) 860261

WRINGTON
North Somerset
Bracken Hill ♦♦♦♦
Wrington Hill, Wrington, Bristol
BS40 5PN
T: (01934) 862261
F: (01934) 862875
E: brackenhill@btinternet.com

YARCOMBE
Devon
Crawley Farm ♦♦♦
Yarcombe, Honiton, Devon
EX14 9AX
T: (01460) 64760
F: (01460) 64760
E: info@crawleyfarm.com
I: www.crawleyfarm.com

YELVERTON
Devon
Eggworthy Farm ♦♦♦
Sampford Spiney, Yelverton,
Devon PL20 6LJ
T: (01822) 852142
F: (01822) 852142

**Knightstone Tearooms and
Restaurant ♦♦**
Crapstone Road, Yelverton,
Devon PL20 6BT
T: (01822) 853679
F: (01822) 856479
E: knightstonetea@yahoo.co.uk

The Old Orchard ♦♦♦♦
Harrowbeer Lane, Yelverton,
Devon PL20 6DZ
T: (01822) 854310
T: (01822) 854310
E: babs@baross.demon.co.uk
I: www.baross.demon.
co.uk/theoldorchard

Peek Hill Farm ♦♦♦
Dousland, Yelverton, Devon
PL20 6PD
T: (01822) 854808 & 852908
F: (01822) 854808
E: colton@peekhill.freeserve.
co.uk

**The Rosemont Guest House
♦♦♦♦**
Greenbank Terrace, Yelverton,
Devon PL20 6DR
T: (01822) 852175
E: office@rosemontgh.fsnet.
co.uk

Torrfields ♦♦♦♦
Sheepstor, Yelverton, Devon
PL20 6PF
T: (01822) 852161
E: torrfields@beeb.net

YEOVIL
Somerset
Cartref ♦♦♦
10 Home Drive, Yeovil, Somerset
BA21 3AP
T: (01935) 421607
E: tere@lattanzio.freeserve.
co.uk

Greystones Court ♦♦♦♦
152 Hendford Hill, Yeovil,
Somerset BA20 2RG
T: (01935) 426124 &
07970 897580
F: (01935) 426124
E: rich&isobel@greystones.
freeserve.co.uk
I: www.greystones.freeserve.
co.uk

Jessops ◆◆◆◆
Vagg Lane, Chilthorne Domer,
Yeovil, Somerset BA22 8RY
T: (01935) 841097
F: (01935) 841097

The Sparkford Inn ◆◆◆
Sparkford, Yeovil, Somerset
BA22 7JN
T: (01963) 440218
F: (01963) 440358

Sunnymede ◆◆◆◆
26 Lower Wraxhill Road, Yeovil,
Somerset BA20 2JU
T: (01935) 425786

White Horse Inn ◆◆
10 St Michaels Avenue, Yeovil,
Somerset BA21 4LB
T: (01935) 476471

YEOVILTON
Somerset

Cary Fitzpaine ◆◆◆◆
Yeovilton, Yeovil, Somerset
BA22 8JB
T: (01458) 223250 &
07932 657140
F: (01458) 223372
E: acrang@aol.com
I: www.caryfitzpaine.com

Courtry Farm ◆◆◆
Bridgehampton, Yeovil,
Somerset BA22 8HF
T: (01935) 840327
F: (01935) 840964
I: www.courtryfarm@hotmail.
com

YETMINSTER
Dorset

Bingers Farm ◆◆◆◆
Ryme Road, Yetminster,
Sherborne, Dorset DT9 6JY
T: (01935) 872555
F: (01935) 872555
E: bingersfarm@talk21.com

Old Mill House ◆◆◆◆
Mill Lane, Yetminster, Sherborne,
Dorset DT9 6ND
T: (01935) 873672
F: (01935) 873672
E: theparks@inyetminster.
freeserve.co.uk

ZEALS
Wiltshire

Cornerways Cottage ◆◆◆◆
Longcross, Zeals, Warminster,
Wiltshire BA12 6LL
T: (01747) 840477
F: (01747) 840477
E: cornerways.cottage@
btinternet.com
I: www.smoothhound.
co.uk/hotels/cornerwa.html

SOUTH OF ENGLAND

ABBOTTS ANN
Hampshire

Carinya Farm ◆◆◆
Cattle Lane, Abbotts Ann,
Andover, Hampshire SP11 7DR
T: (01264) 710269
E: carinyafarm@virgin.net
I: www.carinyafarm.co.uk

East Manor House ◆◆◆◆◆
Abbotts Ann, Andover,
Hampshire SP11 7BH
T: (01264) 710031

Virginia Lodge ◆◆◆
Salisbury Road, Abbotts Ann,
Andover, Hampshire SP11 7NX
T: (01264) 710713
E: b_stuart@talk21.com

ABINGDON
Oxfordshire

Dinckley Court ◆◆◆◆
Burcot, Abingdon, Oxfordshire
OX14 3DP
T: (01865) 407763 &
07976 883925
F: (01865) 407010
E: annette@dinckleycourt.co.uk
I: www.dinckleycourt.co.uk

ADDERBURY
Oxfordshire

The Bell Inn ◆◆◆
High Street, Adderbury, Banbury,
Oxfordshire OX17 3LS
T: (01295) 810338
F: (01295) 812221
E: tim@thebell-adderbury.com
I: www.thebell@adderbury.com

**Le Restaurant Francais at
Morgans Orchard** ◆◆◆
9 Twyford Gardens, Adderbury,
Banbury, Oxfordshire OX17 3JA
T: (01295) 812047
F: (01295) 81241
E: morgarest@aol.co.uk
I: www.banbury-cross.
co.uk/morgans

ADSTOCK
Buckinghamshire

The Folly Inn ◆◆
Buckingham Road, Adstock,
Buckingham MK18 2HS
T: (01296) 712671
F: (01296) 712671

AKELEY
Buckinghamshire

Badgers Rest ◆◆◆
46 Manor Road, Akeley,
Buckingham, Buckinghamshire
MK18 5HQ
T: (01280) 860009
F: (01280) 860331

ALDERHOLT
Dorset

Blackwater House ◆◆◆◆
Blackwater Grove, Alderholt,
Fordingbridge, Hampshire
SP6 3AD
T: (01425) 653443
E: bandb@blackwater47.fsnet.
co.uk

Merrimead ◆◆◆◆
12 Station Road, Alderholt,
Fordingbridge, Hampshire
SP6 3RB
T: (01425) 657544
F: (01425) 650400
E: merrimead@ic24.net
I: www.newforest.demon.
co.uk/merrimead.htm

ALDWORTH
West Berkshire

Fieldview Cottage ◆◆◆◆
Bell Lane, Aldworth, Reading
RG8 9SB
T: (01635) 578964
E: chunt@fieldview.freeserve.
co.uk

ALTON
Hampshire

Boundary House B & B ◆◆◆◆
Gosport Road, Lower
Farringdon, Alton, Hampshire
GU34 3DH
T: (01420) 587076
F: (01420) 587047
E: BoundaryS@messages.co.uk

The Vicarage ◆◆◆
East Worldham, Alton,
Hampshire GU34 3AS
T: (01420) 82392 &
07778 800804
F: (01420) 82367
E: wenrose@bigfoot.com
I: www.altonbedandbreakfast.
co.uk

AMERSHAM
Buckinghamshire

Coldmoreham House ◆◆◆◆
172 High Street, Amersham,
Buckinghamshire HP7 0EG
T: (01494) 725245

The Dacha ◆◆◆
118 Chestnut Lane, Amersham,
Buckinghamshire HP6 6DZ
T: (01494) 433063
F: (01895) 843307

127 High Street ◆◆◆◆
Amersham, Buckinghamshire
HP7 0DY
T: (01494) 725352

63 Hundred Acres Lane ◆◆◆
Amersham, Buckinghamshire
HP7 9BX
T: (01494) 433095

La Fosse
Rating Applied For
Fagnall Lane, Winchmore Hill,
Amersham, Buckinghamshire
HP7 0PG
T: (01494) 433458
F: (01494) 433458

39 Quarrendon Road ◆◆◆◆
Amersham, Buckinghamshire
HP7 9EF
T: (01494) 727959

St Catherins ◆◆◆
9 Parkfield Avenue, Amersham,
Buckinghamshire HP6 6BE
T: (01494) 728125
E: jelliott@callnetuk.com

The White House ◆◆◆◆
20 Church Street, Amersham,
Buckinghamshire HP7 0DB
T: (01494) 433015
F: (01494) 433015

AMPFIELD
Hampshire

The Taj ◆◆◆◆
2 Hook Crescent, Ampfield,
Romsey, Hampshire SO51 9DE
T: (023) 8027 0810 &
07702 227366
E: christine@jeaves.freeserve.
co.uk

AMPORT
Hampshire

Broadwater ◆◆◆◆
Amport, Andover, Hampshire
SP11 8AY
T: (01264) 772240
F: (01264) 772240
E: carolyn@dmac.co.uk
I: www.dmac.co.uk/carolyn

Tilehurst ◆◆◆◆
Furzedown Lane, Amport,
Andover, Hampshire SP11 8BW
T: (01264) 771437
F: (01264) 773651
E: tilehurst@compuserve.com

ANDOVER
Hampshire

18 Altona Gardens ◆◆◆◆
Andover, Hampshire SP10 4LG
T: (01264) 351932

Amberley Hotel ◆◆◆
70 Weyhill Road, Andover,
Hampshire SP10 3NP
T: (01264) 352224 & 364676
F: (01264) 392555
E: amberleyand@fsbdial.co.uk.

Amport Inn
Rating Applied For
Amport, Andover, Hampshire
SP11 8AE
T: (01264) 710371
F: (01264) 710112

Fernihurst ◆◆◆◆
1 Strathfield Road, Andover,
Hampshire SP10 2HH
T: (01264) 361936

Holmdene Guest House ◆◆
1 Winchester Road, Andover,
Hampshire SP10 2EG
T: (01264) 365414

Malt Cottage ◆◆◆◆
Upper Clatford, Andover,
Hampshire SP11 7QL
T: (01264) 323469
F: (01264) 334100
E: info@maltcottage.co.uk
I: www.maltcottage.co.uk

Old Grange ◆◆◆◆
86 Winchester Road, Andover,
Hampshire SP10 2ER
T: (01264) 352784

**Salisbury Road Bed &
Breakfast** ◆◆◆
99 Salisbury Road, Andover,
Hampshire SP10 2LN
T: (01264) 362638
F: (01264) 396597
E: jenny@mosaicevents.co.uk
I: www.exploretestvalley.
com/salisr

Shangri-La Guest House ◆◆◆
Walworth Road, Andover,
Hampshire SP11 6LU
T: (01264) 354399

78 Springfield Close ◆◆
Andover, Hampshire SP10 2QT
T: (01264) 350489

Sutherland Guest House
◆◆◆◆
Micheldever Road, Andover,
Hampshire SP10 2BH
T: (01264) 365307
E: mikejkelly@talk21.com

ARDLEY
Oxfordshire
The Old Post Office ◆◆◆
Church Road, Ardley, Bicester,
Oxfordshire OX27 7NP
T: (01869) 345958
F: (01869) 345958

ASCOT
Berkshire
Ascot Corner ◆◆◆◆
Wells Lane, Ascot, Berkshire
SL5 7DY
T: (01344) 627722
F: (01344) 873965
E: susan.powell@easynet.co.uk

**Ennis Lodge Private Guest
House** ◆◆◆
Winkfield Road, Ascot, Berkshire
SL5 7EX
T: (01344) 621009
F: (01344) 621009

Tanglewood ◆◆◆
Birch Lane, off Longhill Road,
Chavey Down, Ascot, Berkshire
SL5 8RF
T: (01344) 882528

ASCOTT-UNDER-WYCHWOOD
Oxfordshire
College Farm ◆◆◆◆
Ascott-under-Wychwood,
Oxford OX7 6AL
T: (01993) 831900
F: (01993) 831900
E: walkers@collegefarmbandb.
fsnet.co.uk

Crown Farm Bed & Breakfast
◆◆◆◆
Crown Farm, 13 The Green,
Ascott-under-Wychwood,
Oxford OX7 6AB
T: (01993) 832083 & 830045
F: (01993) 832083
E: chris&janet@farming.co.uk
I: www.uk-world-int.co.uk

The Mill ◆◆◆
Ascott-under-Wychwood,
Oxford OX7 6AP
T: (01993) 831282
F: (01993) 831282
E: Mill@auwoxon32.freeserve.
co.uk

ASHENDON
Buckinghamshire
The Gatehangers ◆◆◆
Lower End, Ashendon, Aylesbury,
Buckinghamshire HP18 0HE
T: (01296) 651296
F: (01296) 651340

ASHEY
Isle of Wight
Little Upton Farmhouse
◆◆◆◆◆
Little Upton Farm, Gatehouse
Road, Ashey, Ryde, Isle of Wight
PO33 4BS
T: (01983) 563236
F: (01983) 563236
E: alison@littleuptonfarm.co.uk
I: www.littleuptonfarm.co.uk

ASHLEY HEATH
Dorset
Fir Tree Cottage ◆◆◆
4 Forest Edge Drive, Ashley
Heath, Ringwood, Hampshire
BH24 2ER
T: (01425) 477977

Lions Hill Farm ◆◆
Horton Road, Ashley Heath,
Ringwood, Hampshire BH24 2EX
T: (01425) 472115
F: (01425) 472115
I: www.internetonline.
co.uk/holidays/493752u6html

Yorkland ◆◆◆◆
12 Ashley Drive West, Ashley
Heath, Ringwood, Hampshire
BH24 2JW
T: (01425) 472869
E: beaumontgarethsm@
netscapeonline.co.uk

ASHMORE
Dorset
Glebe Cottage Farm ◆◆◆◆
Ashmore, Shaftesbury, Dorset
DT5 5AE
T: (01747) 811974
T: (01747) 811104
E: all@glebe.force9.co.uk

ASHURST
Hampshire
Forest Gate Lodge ◆◆◆
161 Lyndhurst Road, Ashurst,
Southampton SO40 7AW
T: (023) 8029 3026

Kingswood Cottage ◆◆◆◆
10 Woodlands Road, Ashurst,
Southampton SO40 7AD
T: (023) 8029 2582
F: (023) 8029 3435

ASTON ABBOTTS
Buckinghamshire
The Royal Oak Inn ◆◆
Wingrave Road, Aston Abbotts,
Aylesbury, Buckinghamshire
HP22 4LT
T: (01296) 681262
E: moulty.towers@btinternet.
com

Windmill Hill Barns ◆◆◆◆
Moat Lane, Aston Abbotts,
Aylesbury, Buckinghamshire
HP22 4NF
T: (01296) 681714

ASTON CLINTON
Buckinghamshire
Baywood Guest House ◆◆
98 Weston Road, Aston Clinton,
Aylesbury, Buckinghamshire
HP22 5EJ
T: (01296) 630612

ASTON UPTHORPE
Oxfordshire
Middle Fell ◆◆◆◆
Moreton Road, Aston Upthorpe,
Didcot, Oxfordshire OX11 9ER
T: (01235) 850207 &
07889 489870
F: (01235) 850207
E: middlefell@ic24.net

AWBRIDGE
Hampshire
**Crofton Country
Accommodation** ◆◆◆◆
Kents Oak, Awbridge, Romsey,
Hampshire SO51 0HH
T: (01794) 340333
F: (01794) 340333

AYLESBURY
Buckinghamshire
Amber Court ◆
116 Bierton Road, Aylesbury,
Buckinghamshire HP20 1EN
T: (01296) 432184 &
07801 958116

Dovedale Court Guest House
Rating Applied For
46 Wendover Road, Aylesbury,
Buckinghamshire HP21 9LB
T: (01296) 339400 & 07808 628
307

The Old Forge Barn ◆◆◆
Ridings Way, Cublington,
Leighton Buzzard, Bedfordshire
LU7 0LW
T: (01296) 681194
F: (01296) 681194
E: waples@ukonline.co.uk

The Town House ◆
35 Tring Road, Aylesbury,
Buckinghamshire HP20 1LD
T: (01296) 395295

331 Tring Road ◆◆◆◆
331 Tring Road, Aylesbury,
Buckinghamshire HP20 1PJ
T: (01296) 424012 &
07790 737583

Wallace Farm ◆◆◆
Dinton, Aylesbury,
Buckinghamshire HP17 8UF
T: (01296) 748660
F: (01296) 748851
E: jackiecook@wallacefarm.
freeserve.co.uk
I: www.wallacefarm.co.uk

BAMPTON
Oxfordshire
Chimney Farm House ◆◆◆◆
Chimney, Bampton OX18 2EH
T: (01367) 870279
F: (01367) 870279
I: www.country-accom.
co.uk/chimneyfarmhouse

The Granary ◆◆◆
Main Street, Clanfield, Bampton
OX18 2SH
T: (01367) 810266

BANBURY
Oxfordshire
Amberley Guest House ◆◆
151 Middleton Road, Banbury,
Oxfordshire OX16 8QS
T: (01295) 255797
F: (01295) 255797

Ark Guest House
Rating Applied For
120 Warwick Road, Banbury,
Oxfordshire OX16 2AN
T: (01295) 254498
F: (01295) 254498

Ashlea Guest House ◆
58 Oxford Road, Banbury,
Oxfordshire OX16 9AN
T: (01295) 250539
F: (01295) 250539
E: johnatashlea1@tinyworld.
co.uk

Avonlea Guest House ◆◆
41 Southam Road, Banbury,
Oxfordshire OX16 7EP
T: (01295) 267837
F: (01295) 271 946

Banbury Cross Bed & Breakfast
◆◆◆◆
1 Broughton Road, Banbury,
Oxfordshire OX16 9QB
T: (01295) 266048
F: (01295) 266698

College Farmhouse ◆◆◆◆
Kings Sutton, Banbury,
Oxfordshire OX17 3PS
T: (01295) 811473
F: (01295) 812505
E: sallday@compuserve.com
I: www.banburytown.
co.uk/accom/collegefarmhouse

Cotefields Bed & Breakfast ◆◆
Opposite Bodicote Park,
Banbury, Oxfordshire OX15 4AQ
T: (01295) 264977 &
07899 901743
F: (01295) 264977
E: tony.stockford@ic24.net

Fernleigh Guest House ◆◆◆
67 Oxford Road, Banbury,
Oxfordshire OX16 9AJ
T: (01295) 250853
T: (01295) 269349
E: mark-gill@bidwell.fsbusiness.
co.uk

George & Dragon ◆◆◆
Silver Street, Chacombe,
Banbury, Oxfordshire OX17 2JR
T: (01295) 711500

The Glebe House ◆◆◆◆
Village Road, Warmington,
Banbury, Oxfordshire OX17 1BT
T: (01295) 690642

Grafton Lodge ◆◆◆
63 Oxford Road, Banbury,
Oxfordshire OX16 9AJ
T: (01295) 257000
F: (01295) 258545

The Lodge ◆◆◆◆
Main Road, Middleton Cheney,
Banbury, Oxfordshire OX17 2PP
T: (01295) 710355

119 Middleton Road ◆◆◆
Banbury, Oxfordshire OX16 3QS
T: (01295) 253236

Prospect House Guest House ◆◆◆
70 Oxford Road, Banbury,
Oxfordshire OX16 9AN
T: (01295) 268749 &
07798 772578
F: (01295) 268749

St Martins House ◆◆◆
Warkworth, Banbury,
Oxfordshire OX17 2AG
T: (01295) 712684
F: (01295) 712838

Treetops Guest House ◆◆
28 Dashwood Road, Banbury,
Oxfordshire OX16 8HD
T: (01295) 254444

Winstons ◆◆◆
65 Oxford Road, Banbury,
Oxfordshire OX16 9AJ
T: (01295) 270790

BARTLEY
Hampshire
Bartley Farmhouse ◆◆◆◆
Ringwood Road, Bartley,
Southampton, Hampshire
SO40 7LD
T: (023) 8081 4194
F: (023) 8081 4117

BARTON ON SEA
Hampshire
Cleeve House ◆◆◆◆
58 Barton Court Avenue, Barton
on Sea, New Milton, Hamphire
BH25 7HG
T: (01425) 615211
F: (01425) 615211
I: cleeve.house@btinternet.com

Eureka Guest House ◆◆◆
Christchurch Road, Barton on
Sea, New Milton, Hamphire
BH25 6QQ
T: (01425) 610289
E: eureka@eurolink.ltd.net

Everglades ◆◆◆◆
81 Sea Road, Barton on Sea,
New Milton, Hamphire
BH25 7ND
T: (01425) 617350 & 0773 017
7625

Hotel Gainsborough ◆◆◆◆
Marine Drive East, Barton on
Sea, New Milton, Hamphire
BH25 7DX
T: (01425) 610541

Laurel Lodge ◆◆◆
48 Western Avenue, Barton on
Sea, New Milton, Hampshire
BH25 7PZ
T: (01425) 618309

The Old Coastguard Hotel
◆◆◆
53 Marine Drive East, Barton on
Sea, New Milton, Hampshire
BH25 7DX
T: (01425) 612987
F: (01425) 612987
E: dp@theoldcoastguardfsnet.
co.uk
I: www.theoldcoastguardfsnet.
co.uk

Westbury House ◆◆◆
12 Greenacre, Barton on Sea,
New Milton, Hampshire
BH25 7BS
T: (01425) 620935 &
07976 871756
E: les@westbury-house.
freeserve.co.uk
I: www.westbury-house.
freeserve.co.uk

The Wight House ◆◆◆◆
41 Marine Drive East, Barton on
Sea, New Milton, Hampshire
BH25 7DX
T: (01425) 614008

BARTON STACEY
Hampshire
Swan Inn ◆◆◆
Barton Stacey, Winchester,
Hampshire SO21 3RL
T: (01962) 760470

BASINGSTOKE
Hampshire
Cedar Court ◆◆◆
Reading Road, Hook, Hampshire
RG27 9DB
T: (01256) 762178
F: (01256) 762178

Fernbank Hotel ◆◆◆◆
4 Fairfields Road, Basingstoke,
Hampshire RG21 3DR
T: (01256) 321191
F: (01256) 321191
E: availability@fernbankhotel.
co.uk
I: www.fernbankhotel.co.uk

Street Farm House ◆◆◆◆
The Street, South Warnborough,
Hook, Hampshire RG29 1RS
T: (01256) 862225
F: (01256) 862225
E: streetfarmhouse@btinternet.
com

96 Worting Road ◆◆◆
Basingstoke, Hampshire
RG21 8TT
T: (01256) 320136

BEACONSFIELD
Buckinghamshire
Beacon House ◆◆◆
113 Maxwell Road, Beaconsfield,
Buckinghamshire HP9 1RF
T: (01494) 672923 & 681769
F: (01494) 672923
E: Ben.Dickinson@Tesco.net

Highclere Farm ◆◆◆◆
Newbarn Lane, Seer Green,
Beaconsfield, Buckinghamshire
HP9 2QZ
T: (01494) 875665 & 874505
F: (01494) 875238

BEAULIEU
Hampshire
2-3 Northern Cottages ◆◆◆◆
Lyndhurst Road, Beaulieu,
Brockenhurst, Hampshire
SO42 7YE
T: (01590) 612127
F: (01590) 612127
E: christine.hills@btinternet

Dale Farm House ◆◆◆
Manor Road, Applemore Hill,
Dibden, Southampton SO45 5TJ
T: (023) 8084 9632
F: (023) 8084 0285
E: chris@dalefarmhouse.fsnet.
co.uk

Leygreen Farm House ◆◆◆
Lyndhurst Road, Beaulieu,
Brockenhurst, Hampshire
SO42 7YP
T: (01590) 612355
F: (01590) 612355
I: www.newforest.demon.
co.uk/leygreen.htm

Old School House ◆◆◆◆
High Street, Beaulieu,
Brockenhurst, Hampshire
SO42 7YD
T: (01590) 612062
F: (01590) 612062
E: jeanie@eurolink.ltd.net

The Rectory ◆◆◆◆
Palace Lane, Beaulieu,
Hampshire SO42 7YG
T: (01590) 612242
F: (01590) 612242

BEMBRIDGE
Isle of Wight
The Crab and Lobster ◆◆◆◆
32 Forelands Field Road,
Bembridge, Isle of Wight
PO35 5TR
T: (01983) 872244

Harbour Farm ◆◆◆◆
Embankment Road, Bembridge,
Isle of Wight PO35 5NS
T: (01983) 872610 & 874080
F: (01983) 874080

Sea Change ◆◆◆◆
22 Beachfield Road, Bembridge,
Isle of Wight PO35 5TN
T: (01983) 875558 & 875557
F: (01983) 875667
E: curzon@compuserve.com

BENSON
Oxfordshire
Brookside ◆◆◆
Brook Street, Benson,
Wallingford, Oxfordshire
OX10 6LJ
T: (01491) 838289
F: (01491) 838289

The Crown Inn ◆◆◆
52 High Street, Benson,
Wallingford, Oxfordshire
OX10 6RP
T: (01491) 838247

Fyfield Manor ◆◆◆◆
Benson, Wallingford,
Oxfordshire OX10 6HA
T: (01491) 835184
F: (01491) 825635
E: ffbrown@fifield-software.
demon.co.uk

Rainbow Cottage
Rating Applied For
19 Littleworth Road, Benson,
Wallingford, Oxfordshire
OX10 6LY
T: (01491) 837488

BENTLEY
Hampshire
Pittersfield
Rating Applied For
Bentley, Farnham, Surrey
GU10 5LT
T: (01420) 22414
F: (01420) 22414

BERE REGIS
Dorset
The Dorsetshire Golf Lodge
◆◆◆◆
East Dorset Golf Club, Bere
Regis, Wareham, Dorset
BH20 7NT
T: (01929) 472244
F: (01929) 471294
E: eastdorsetgc@aol.com

The Royal Oak ◆◆◆◆
West Street, Bere Regis,
Wareham, Dorset BH20 7HQ
T: (01929) 471203
F: (01929) 472636
E: info@theroyaloakhotel.co.uk
I: www.theroyaloakhotel.co.uk

BICESTER
Oxfordshire
Manor Farm Bed & Breakfast
◆◆◆
Poundon, Bicester, Oxfordshire
OX27 9BB
T: (01869) 277212 & 277166
F: (01869) 277166
E: jeanettecollett@aol.com
I: www.smoothhound.
co.uk/hotels/manor3.html

Priory House ◆◆◆
86 Chapel Street, Bicester,
Oxfordshire OX26 6BD
T: (01869) 325687
E: anderson@prioryhouse.fsnet.
co.uk

BINSTEAD
Isle of Wight
Elm Close Cottage ◆◆◆◆
Elm Close, Ladies Walk, Binstead,
Ryde, Isle of Wight PO33 3SY
T: (01983) 567161 &
0771 3540134
E: elm_cottage@hotmail.com

**Newnham Farm Bed &
Breakfast** ◆◆◆◆
Newnham Lane, Binstead, Ryde,
Isle of Wight PO33 4ED
T: (01983) 882423
F: (01983) 882423
E: newnhamfarm@talk21.com
I: www.newnhamfarm.co.uk

BIX
Oxfordshire
The Barn ◆◆◆◆
Bix, Henley-on-Thames,
Oxfordshire RG9 4RS
T: (01491) 414062
E: tgb@btinternet.com
I: www.thebarnbix.btinternet.
co.uk

BLACKTHORN
Oxfordshire
Limetrees Farm ◆◆◆◆
Lower Road, Blackthorn,
Bicester, Oxfordshire OX25 1TG
T: (01869) 248435
F: (01869) 325843
E: limetreesfarm@hotmail.com
I: www.limetreesfarm.freeserve.
co.uk

BLANDFORD FORUM
Dorset
Farnham Farm House ◆◆◆◆
Farnham, Blandford Forum,
Dorset DT11 8DG
T: (01725) 516254
F: (01725) 516306
E: patricia.bed.and.breakfast@
farmersweekly.net

Meadow House ◆◆◆◆
Tarrant Hinton, Blandford
Forum, Dorset DT11 8JG
T: (01258) 830498
F: (01258) 830498

BLEDLOW
Buckinghamshire

Cross Lanes Guest House
◆◆◆◆
Cross Lanes Cottage, Bledlow,
Aylesbury, Buckinghamshire
HP27 9PF
T: (01844) 345339
F: (01844) 274165

BLEDLOW RIDGE
Buckinghamshire

Old Callow Down Farm
Rating Applied For
Wigans Lane, Bledlow Ridge,
High Wycombe,
Buckinghamshire HP14 4BH
T: (01844) 344416
F: (01844) 344703

BLEWBURY
Oxfordshire

The Barley Mow ◆◆◆
London Road, Blewbury, Didcot,
Oxfordshire OX11 9NU
T: (01235) 850296
F: (01235) 850296

BLOXHAM
Oxfordshire

Brook Cottage ◆◆
Little Bridge Road, Bloxham,
Banbury, Oxfordshire OX15 4PU
T: (01295) 721089

BOLDRE
Hampshire

Fernbrake ◆◆◆
Coxhill, Boldre, Lymington,
Hampshire SO41 8PS
T: (01590) 622257
F: (01590) 624256

Kingston Cottage ◆◆◆
Lower Sandy Down, Boldre,
Lymington, Hampshire
SO41 8PP
T: (01590) 623051

Passford Farm ◆◆◆
Southampton Road, Boldre,
Lymington, Hampshire
SO41 8ND
T: (01590) 674103

Pinecroft ◆◆
Coxhill, Boldre, Lymington,
Hampshire SO41 8PS
T: (01590) 624260 &
07980 309384
F: (01590) 624025
E: enquiries@pinecroftbandb.
co.uk
I: www.pinecroftbandb.co.uk

The Well House ◆◆◆◆
Southampton Road, Boldre,
Lymington, Hampshire SO41 8PT
T: (01590) 689055
F: (01590) 688993
E: darver@msn.com
I: www.thewellhouse.bnb.com

BOLTER END
Buckinghamshire

Summerhill House ◆◆◆
Fingest Lane, Bolter End, High
Wycombe, Buckinghamshire
HP14 3LS
T: (01494) 882113
F: (01494) 882028

BONCHURCH
Isle of Wight

The Lake Hotel ◆◆◆◆
Shore Road, Bonchurch,
Ventnor, Isle of Wight PO38 1RF
T: (01983) 852613
F: (01983) 852613
E: enquiries@lakehotel.co.uk
I: www.lakehotel.co.uk

Under Rock Country House Bed
& Breakfast ◆◆◆
Shore Road, Bonchurch,
Ventnor, Isle of Wight PO38 1RF
T: (01983) 855274
E: enquiries@under-rock.co.uk
I: www.under-rock.co.uk

BOSCOMBE
Dorset

Aloha Wyvern Hotel
Rating Applied For
24 Glen Road, Boscombe,
Bournemouth BH5 1HR
T: 1202 397543
F: 1202 256175

Au-Levant Hotel ◆◆◆
15 Westby Road, Boscombe,
Bournemouth BH5 1HA
T: (01202) 394884

Audmore Hotel ◆◆◆
3 Cecil Road, Boscombe,
Bournemouth BH5 1DU
T: (01202) 395166
I: www.audmorehotel.co.uk

Dramcote Hall Hotel ◆◆◆
1 Glen Road, Boscombe,
Bournemouth BH5 1HR
T: (01202) 395555 & 398623
F: (01202) 398623
E: bramcotehall@lineone.net

Denewood Hotel ◆◆◆
1 Percy Road, Boscombe,
Bournemouth, Dorset BH5 1JE
T: (01202) 394493
F: (01202) 391155
E: peteer@denewood.co.uk
I: www.denewood.co.uk

Knightlow Hotel ◆◆◆
5 Percy Road, Boscombe,
Bournemouth, Dorset BH5 1JE
T: (01202) 396415 & 255973
F: (01202) 387871
E: ros@knightlow-hotel.co.uk
I: www.knightlow-hotel.co.uk

The Marven Hotel ◆◆◆
5 Watkin Road, Boscombe,
Bournemouth BH5 1HP
T: (01202) 397099

Rosemount Hotel
Rating Applied For
11 Argyll Road, Boscombe,
Bournemouth BH5 1EB
T: (01202) 395460
F: (01202) 385461

Siena Private Hotel ◆◆◆◆
17 Cecil Road, Boscombe,
Bournemouth BH5 1DU
T: (01202) 394159
F: (01202) 309798
E: barbara_hall16@yahoo.com

Hotel Sorrento ◆◆◆◆
16 Owls Road, Boscombe,
Bournemouth, Dorset BH5 1AG
T: (01202) 394019
F: (01202) 394019
E: mail@hotelsorrento.co.uk
I: www.hotelsorrento.co.uk

Southlands Private Hotel
◆◆◆◆
11 Crabton Close Road,
Boscombe, Bournemouth,
Dorset BH5 1HN
T: (01202) 394887
F: (01202) 397882
E: southlandshotel@ukonline.
co.uk
I: www.southlandshotel.com

BOTLEY
Hampshire

Steeple Court Farm ◆◆◆
Church Lane, Botley,
Southampton, Hampshire
SO30 2EQ
T: (01489) 798824
E: theblue.room@btinternet.
com

BOTOLPH CLAYDON
Buckinghamshire

Hickwell House ◆◆◆◆
40 Botyl Road, Botolph Claydon,
Buckingham MK18 2LR
T: (01296) 712217 &
07703 115972
F: (01296) 712217

BOURNE END
Buckinghamshire

Hollands Farm ◆◆◆◆
Hedsor Road, Bourne End,
Buckinghamshire SL8 5EE
T: (01628) 520423
F: (01628) 531602

BOURNEMOUTH
Dorset

Alexander Lodge Hotel ◆◆◆◆
21 Southern Road, Southbourne,
Bournemouth BH6 3SR
T: (01202) 421662
F: (01202) 421662
E: alexanderlodge@yahoo.com
I: www.smoothhound.
co.uk/a28852.html

Ardene Hotel ◆
12 Glen Road, Boscombe,
Bournemouth, Dorset BH5 1HR
T: (01202) 394928 & 393856
F: (01202) 394928

Avonwood Hotel ◆◆◆
20 Owls Road, Boscombe,
Bournemouth BH5 1AF
T: (01202) 394704
E: avonwood.hotel@tinyworld.
co.uk

Balincourt Hotel ◆◆◆◆
58 Christchurch Road,
Bournemouth, BH1 3PF
T: (01202) 552962
F: (01202) 552962
E: rooms@balincourt.co.uk
I: www.balincourt.co.uk

Bay View Hotel ◆◆◆
Southbourne Overcliff Drive,
Bournemouth, BH6 3SS
T: (01202) 427924 & 429315
F: (01202) 429315
E: bayview@btinternet.com

Bonnington Hotel ◆◆◆
44 Tregonwell Road,
Bournemouth, Dorset BH2 5NT
T: (01202) 553621
F: (01202) 317797
E: bonnington.bournemouth@
btinternet.com
I: www.bonnington-hotel.com

Cairnsmore Hotel ◆◆◆
37 Beaulieu Road, Alum Chine,
Bournemouth, Dorset BH4 8HY
T: (01202) 763705
E: ritacoombs@hotmail.com

Carisbrooke Hotel ◆◆◆
42 Tregonwell Road,
Bournemouth, BH2 5NT
T: (01202) 290432
F: (01202) 310499
E: all@carisbrooke58.freeserve.
co.uk
I: www.carisbrooke.co.uk

Chase Lodge ◆◆◆
4 Herbert Road, Alum Chine,
Bournemouth, BH4 8HD
T: (01202) 768515
F: (01202) 757847
E: chaselodge@hotmail.com
I: www.tuckedup.
com/chaselodge.html

Chine Cote Hotel ◆◆◆
25 Studland Road, Alum Chine,
Bournemouth, Dorset BH4 8HZ
T: (01202) 761208
E: t.f.sanford@skynow.net
I: www.bournemouth-hotels.
co.uk/chinecote

Coniston Hotel ◆◆◆
27 Studland Road, Alum Chine,
Bournemouth, BH4 8HZ
T: (01202) 765386
E: coniston.hotel

Cransley Hotel ◆◆◆◆
11 Knyveton Road, East Cliff,
Bournemouth, Dorset BH1 3QG
T: (01202) 290067
F: (01202) 294368
E: info@cransley.com
I: www.cransley.com

Crosbie Hall Hotel ◆◆◆
21 Florence Road, Boscombe,
Bournemouth BH5 1HJ
T: (01202) 394714
F: (01202) 394714
E: david@crosbiehall.fsnet.co.uk
I: www.crosbiehall.fsnet.co.uk

Earlham Lodge ◆◆◆◆
91 Alumhurst Road, Alum Chine,
Bournemouth, BH4 8HR
T: (01202) 761943
F: (01202) 768223
E: info@earlhamlodge.com
I: www.earlhamlodge.com

East Cliff Cottage Hotel ◆◆◆
57 Grove Road, Bournemouth,
BH1 3AT
T: (01202) 552788
F: (01202) 556400
E: len@l.wallen.freeserve.co.uk
I: www.smoothhound.
co.uk/hotels/eastcliff.html

Fairmount Hotel ◆◆◆◆
15 Priory Road, West Cliff,
Bournemouth, BH2 5DF
T: (01202) 551105
F: (01202) 551105
E: reservations@
fairmount-hotel.co.uk
I: www.fairmount-hotels.co.uk

Gervis Court Hotel ◆◆◆
38 Gervis Road, Bournemouth,
BH1 3DH
T: (01202) 556871
F: (01202) 467066
E: enquiries@gerviscourthotel.
co.uk
I: http:www.gerviscourthotel.
co.uk

Glenbourne Hotel ♦♦♦
81 Alumhurst Road, Alum Chine,
Bournemouth, Dorset BH4 8HR
T: (01202) 761607

Hawthorns Hotel ♦♦♦
40 Alumhurst Road,
Westbourne, Bournemouth,
Dorset BH4 8EY
T: (01202) 760220
E: liz_mcdonald@yahoo.co.uk

The Inverness Hotel ♦♦♦♦
26 Tregonwell Road,
Bournemouth, BH2 5NS
T: (01202) 554968
F: (01202) 294197
E: inverness.hotel@tesco.net
I: www.hotelsbournemouth.uk.
com

Kings Langley Hotel ♦♦♦
1 West Cliff Road,
Bournemouth, BH2 5ES
T: (01202) 557349 & 553736
F: (01202) 789739
E: john@kingslangley.fsnet.
co.uk
I: www.kingslangleyhotel.co.uk
🕅

Langdale Hotel ♦♦♦♦
6 Earle Road, Alum Chine,
Bournemouth, BH4 8JQ
T: (01202) 761174
F: (01202) 761174
E: mikepark@freenetname.co.uk
I: www.langdalehotel.com

Lawnswood Hotel ♦♦♦
22A Studland Road, Alum Chine,
Bournemouth, BH4 8JA
T: (01202) 761170
F: 44012 02761170
E: lawnswood_hotel_uk@
yahoo.com
I: www.lawnswoodhotel.co.uk

Majestic Hotel ♦♦♦♦
34 Derby Road, East Cliff,
Bournemouth, BH1 3QE
T: (01202) 294771
F: (01202) 310962

Mayfield Guest House ♦♦♦♦
46 Frances Road, Knyveton
Gardens, Bournemouth,
BH1 3SA
T: (01202) 551839
F: (01202) 551839
E: accom@may-field.co.uk
I: www.may-field.co.uk

Mount Lodge Hotel ♦♦♦
19 Beaulieu Road, Alum Chine,
Bournemouth, BH4 8HY
T: (01202) 761173
F: (01202) 540502

Oxford Hall Hotel ♦♦♦♦
6 Sandbourne Road,
Bournemouth, BH4 8JH
T: (01202) 761016
F: (01202) 540465
E: oxfordhall@eurolinkltd.net

Parklands Hotel ♦♦♦♦
4 Rushton Crescent,
Bournemouth, Dorset BH3 7AF
T: (01202) 552529 &
07768 716217
F: (01202) 249013
E: parklandshotel@redhotant.
com
I: www.parklandshotel.
redhotant.com

Redlands Hotel
Rating Applied For
79 St Michaels Road, West Cliff,
Bournemouth, BH2 5DR
T: (01202) 553714
E: enquiries@redlandshotel.
co.uk
I: www.redlandshotel.co.uk

Rosedene Cottage Hotel ♦♦♦
St Peter's Road, Bournemouth,
BH1 2LA
T: (01202) 554102
F: (01202) 246995
E: enquiries@
rosedenecottagehotel.co.uk
I: www.rosedenecottagehotel.
co.uk

St Winifrides Hotel ♦♦♦♦
1 Studland Road, Alum Chine,
Bournemouth, BH4 8HZ
T: (01202) 761829

Shoreline Hotel ♦♦♦♦
7 Pinecliffe Avenue,
Southbourne, Bournemouth
BH6 3PY
T: (01202) 429654
F: (01202) 429654
E: timjonshorelinebb@amserve.
net

Silver How Hotel ♦♦♦
5 West Cliff Gardens,
Bournemouth, BH2 5HL
T: (01202) 551537
F: (01202) 551456
E: reservations@silverhowhotel.
co.uk
I: www.silverhowhotel.co.uk

Southern Comfort Hotel
♦♦♦♦
10 Earle Road, Alum Chine,
Bournemouth, BH4 8JQ
T: (01202) 767349
F: (01202) 752504
E: sales@southerncomforthotel.
co.uk
I: www.southerncomforthotel.
co.uk

Southernhay Hotel ♦♦♦
42 Alum Chine Road,
Westbourne, Bournemouth,
Dorset BH4 8DX
T: (01202) 761251
F: (01202) 761251

Tiffanys ♦♦♦♦
31 Chine Crescent, West Cliff,
Bournemouth, Dorset BH2 5LB
T: (01202) 551424
F: (01202) 318559

Trelawny Guest House
Rating Applied For
34 Wellington Road,
Bournemouth, BH8 8JW
T: (01202) 554015
F: (01202) 554015

The Twin Tops ♦♦♦♦
33 Wheelers Lane,
Bournemouth, BH11 9QQ
T: (01202) 570080 &
07890 332742
F: (01202) 570080
E: twintops@btinternet.com
I: www.thetwintops.com

The Ventura Hotel ♦♦♦♦
1 Herbert Road, Bournemouth,
BH4 8HD
T: (01202) 761265
F: (01202) 757673
E: enquiries@venturahotel.com
I: www.venturahotel.co.uk

The Vine Hotel ♦♦♦
22 Southern Road, Southbourne,
Bournemouth BH6 3SR
T: (01202) 428309
F: (01202) 428309
E: thevinehotel@faxvia.net

45 Wheelers Lane ♦♦♦
Bearwood, Bournemouth, Dorset
BH11 9QQ
T: (01202) 572760

Whitley Court Hotel ♦♦♦
West Cliff Gardens,
Bournemouth, BH2 5HL
T: (01202) 551302
F: (01202) 551302

Willowdene Hotel ♦♦♦♦
43 Grand Avenue, Southbourne,
Bournemouth BH6 3SY
T: (01202) 425370
F: (01202) 425 370
E: willowdenehotel@aol.com
I: www.willowdenehotel.co.uk

Winter Dene Hotel ♦♦♦♦
11 Durley Road South, West
Cliff, Bournemouth, BH2 5JH
T: (01202) 554150
F: (01202) 555426
E: winterdene@
bournemouth-hotels.co.uk
I: www.bournemouth-hotels.
co.uk/winterdene

Wood Lodge Hotel ♦♦♦♦
10 Manor Road, East Cliff,
Bournemouth, Dorset BH1 3EY
T: (01202) 290891
F: (01202) 290892
🕅

Woodside Private Hotel
♦♦♦♦
29 Southern Road, Southbourne,
Bournemouth BH6 3SR
T: (01202) 427213
F: (01202) 417609
E: ann.jeff@btinternet.com
I: www.smoothhound.
co.uk/hotels/woodsid3.html

Wrenwood Hotel ♦♦♦
11 Florence Road, Boscombe,
Bournemouth BH5 1HH
T: (01202) 395086 & 250793
F: (01202) 396511
E: bookings@wrenwood.co.uk
I: www.wrenwood.co.uk

Wychcote Hotel ♦♦♦♦
2 Somerville Road, West Cliff,
Bournemouth, BH2 5LH
T: (01202) 557898
E: info@wychcote.co.uk
I: www.wychcote.co.uk

BRACKNELL
Berkshire

Elizabeth House ♦♦♦
Wokingham Road, Bracknell,
Berkshire RG42 1PB
T: (01344) 868480 &
07050 176674
F: (01344) 648453
E: rooms@elizabeth-house.
freeserve.co.uk
I: www.elizabeth-house.
freeserve.co.uk

22 Evedon ♦♦
Birch Hill, Bracknell, Berkshire
RG12 7NF
T: (01344) 450637 &
07967 300676

BRAISHFIELD
Hampshire

Tregoyd House ♦♦♦
Crook Hill, Braishfield, Romsey,
Hampshire SO51 0QB
T: (01794) 368307
F: (01794) 368307
E: tregoyd@yahoo.co.uk
I: www.geocities.
com/eureka/park/2485

BRAMSHAW
Hampshire

Forge Cottage ♦♦♦
Stocks Cross, Bramshaw,
Lyndhurst, Hampshire SO43 7JB
T: (023) 8081 3873 &
07850 305606
F: (023) 8081 1241
E: idavies1@cs.com
I: www.newforest-uk.
com/forgecottage.htm

BRANKSOME PARK
Dorset

Grovefield Manor Hotel
♦♦♦♦
18 Pinewood Road, Branksome
Park, Poole, Dorset BH13 6JS
T: (01202) 766798

BRANSGORE
Hampshire

The Corner House ♦♦♦♦
Betsy Lane, Bransgore,
Christchurch, Dorset BH23 8AQ
T: (01425) 673201

Wiltshire House ♦♦♦♦
West Road, Bransgore,
Christchurch, Dorset BH23 8BD
T: (01425) 672450
F: (01425) 672450
E: hooper@wiltshirehouse.
freeserve.co.uk
I: www.smoothhound.
co.uk/hotels/wiltshirehouse.html

BRIGHSTONE
Isle of Wight

Buddlebrook Guest House
♦♦♦
Moortown Lane, Brighstone,
Newport, Isle of Wight
PO30 4AN
T: (01983) 740381
F: (01983) 740381
E: buddle.brook.bb@
bushinternet.com

Chilton Farm ♦♦♦
Chilton Lane, Brighstone,
Newport, Isle of Wight
PO30 4DS
T: (01983) 740338
F: (01983) 741370
E: info@chiltonfarm.co.uk
I: www.chiltonfarm.co.uk

Moortown Cottage ♦♦♦
Moortown Lane, Brighstone,
Newport, Isle of Wight
PO30 4AN
T: (01983) 741428 & 740575
E: denise_moortown@beeb.net

BRILL
Buckinghamshire

Laplands Farm ♦♦♦♦
Ludgershall Road, Brill,
Aylesbury, Buckinghamshire
HP18 9TZ
T: (01844) 237888
F: (01844) 238870
E: enquiries@intents-marquees.
co.uk
I: www.intents-marquees.co.uk

Poletrees Farm ◆◆◆
Ludgershall Road, Brill,
Aylesbury, Buckinghamshire
HP18 9TZ
T: (01844) 238276
F: (01844) 238276

BRIZE NORTON
Oxfordshire

Anvil Croft ◆◆◆
64 Station Road, Brize Norton,
Oxford OX18 3QA
T: (01993) 843655
F: (01993) 843655
E: judyleckyt@aol.com

Carpenters ◆◆◆
96 Station Road, Brize Norton,
Carterton, Oxford OX18 3QA
T: (01993) 844222 &
07889 246500
E: bonniehigh@aol.com

Foxbury Farmhouse ◆◆◆
Burford Road, Brize Norton,
Oxford OX18 3NX
T: (01993) 844141
F: (01993) 844141
E: foxburyfarm@cs.com
I: foxburyfarm.co.uk

The Long Barn ◆◆◆◆
26 Carterton Road, Brize Norton,
Oxford OX18 3LY
T: (01993) 843309
F: (01993) 843309
E: kgillians@the-long-barn.
co.uk
I: www.the-long-barn.co.uk

The Priory Manor Farm
Rating Applied For
Manor Road, Brize Norton,
Carterton, Oxfordshire
OX18 3NA
T: (01993) 843062 & 0771 838
6264

The Willows ◆◆◆◆
Quarry Dene, Burford Road,
Brize Norton, Oxford OX18 3NN
T: (01993) 842437 &
07950 868930
E: willowsbbbrize@aol.com

BROADSTONE
Dorset

Avon House ◆◆◆
54A York Road, Broadstone,
Dorset BH18 8ET
T: (01202) 696938 & 257160
F: (01202) 604543

Honey Lodge ◆◆◆◆
41 Dunyeats Road, Broadstone,
Dorset BH18 8AB
T: (01202) 694247

Tarven ◆◆◆
Corfe Lodge Road, Broadstone,
Dorset BH18 9NF
T: (01202) 694338

Weston Cottage ◆◆◆◆
6 Macaulay Road, Broadstone,
Dorset BH18 8AR
T: (01202) 699638
F: (01202) 699638
E: westoncot@aol.com

BROCKENHURST
Hampshire

Briardale ◆◆◆
11 Noel Close, Brockenhurst,
Hampshire SO42 7RP
T: (01590) 623946
F: (01590) 623946
E: briardale@brockenhurst.
fsbusiness.co.uk
I: www.brockenhurst.fsbusiness.
co.uk

Broad Oak ◆◆◆◆
Broadlands, Brockenhurst,
Hampshire SO42 7SX
T: (01590) 622208 & (023) 8032
1198
F: (01590) 622208

Brookside Cottage ◆◆◆
Collyers Road, Brockenhurst,
Hampshire SO42 7SE
T: (01590) 623973

Caters Cottage ◆◆◆
Latchmoor, Brockenhurst,
Hampshire SO42 7UP
T: (01590) 623225

Evergreen ◆◆◆◆
Sway Road, Brockenhurst,
Hampshire SO42 7RX
T: (01590) 623411

The Filly Inn ◆◆◆
Lymington Road, Setley,
Brockenhurst, Hampshire
SO42 7UF
T: (01590) 623449
F: (01590) 622915
E: pub@fillyinn.co.uk
I: www.fillyinn.co.uk

Garlands Cottage ◆◆◆◆
2 Garlands Cottage, Lyndhurst
Road, Brockenhurst, Hampshire
SO42 7RH
T: (01590) 623250
F: (01590) 623250
E: rkdalley@tcp.co.uk

Goldenhayes ◆◆
9 Chestnut Road, Brockenhurst,
Hampshire SO42 7RF
T: (01590) 623743

Hilden Bed & Breakfast ◆◆◆
Southampton Road, Boldre,
Lymington, Hampshire SO41 8PT
T: (01590) 623682 &
07802 668658
F: (01590) 624444
I: www.newforestbandb-hilden.
co.uk

Jacmar Cottage ◆◆◆
Mill Lane, Brockenhurst,
Hampshire SO42 7UA
T: (01590) 622019

Little Heathers ◆◆◆◆
Whitemoor Road, Brockenhurst,
Hampshire SO42 7QG
T: (01590) 623512 &
07889 141523
F: (01590) 624255
E: little_heathers@hotmail.com
I: www.newforest.demon.
co.uk/littleheathers.htm

Mansfield ◆◆◆
Partridge Road, Brockenhurst,
Hampshire SO42 7RZ
T: (01590) 623877
E: chippie.lorri@virgin.net

Old Oak ◆◆◆
Meerut Road, Brockenhurst,
Hampshire SO42 7TD
T: (01590) 623735
F: (01590) 623735

BUCKINGHAM
Buckinghamshire

5 Bristle Hill ◆◆◆
Buckingham, MK18 1EZ
T: (01280) 814426 &
0780 1258455
F: (01280) 814426

Churchwell ◆◆
23 Church Street, Buckingham,
MK18 1BY
T: (01280) 815415 & 822223
F: (01280) 815415

Folly Farm ◆◆◆
Padbury, Buckingham
MK18 2HS
T: (01296) 712413
F: (01296) 714923

Huntsmill House Bed &
Breakfast
Rating Applied For
Huntsmill Farm, Shalstone,
Buckingham, Buckinghamshire
MK18 5ND
T: (01280) 704852
F: (01280) 704852

Radclive Dairy Farm ◆◆◆◆
Radclive Road, Gawcott,
Buckingham MK18 4AA
T: (01280) 813433
F: (01280) 813433

The Whale Hotel
Rating Applied For
14 Market Hill, Buckingham,
Buckinghamshire MK18 1JX
T: (01280) 815537
F: (01280) 815537

The White Hart Hotel ◆◆◆
Market Square, Buckingham,
Buckinghamshire MK18 1NL
T: (01280) 815151
F: (01280) 823165

BURFORD
Oxfordshire

The Bird in Hand ◆◆◆◆
Whiteoak Green, Hailey, Witney,
Oxfordshire OX29 9XP
T: (01993) 868321 & 868811
F: (01993) 868702
E: birdinhand@heavitreeinns.
co.uk
I: www.oxfordpages.
co.uk/birdinhand

Burford House Hotel ◆◆◆◆◆
99 High Street, Burford, Oxford
OX18 4QA
T: (01993) 823151
F: (01993) 823240
E: stay@burfordhouse.co.uk
I: www.burford-house.co.uk.

The Fox Inn
Rating Applied For
Great Barrington, Burford,
Oxfordshire OX18 4TB
T: (01451) 844385

The Highway ◆◆◆
117 High Street, Burford, Oxford
OX18 4RG
T: (01993) 822136
F: (01993) 824740
E: rbx20@dial.pipex.com
I: www.oxlink.co.uk/burford

Jonathan's at The Angel
◆◆◆◆◆
14 Witney Street, Burford,
Oxford OX18 4SN
T: (01993) 822714
F: (01993) 822069
E: jo@theangel-uk.com

Manor Lodge ◆◆◆◆
Shilton, Burford, Oxfordshire
OX18 4AS
T: (01993) 841444
F: (01993) 841446
E: enquiries@manorlodgebnb.
co.uk
I: www.manorlodgebnb.co.uk

Merryfield ◆◆◆
High Street, Fifield, Oxford,
Oxfordshire OX7 6HL
T: (01993) 830517
E: jpmgtd@freeuk.com
I: www.merryfieldbandb.co.uk

The Old Bell Foundry ◆◆◆◆
45 Witney Street, Burford,
Oxford OX18 4RX
T: (01993) 822234 &
07989 818970
F: (01993) 822234
E: barguss@ukgateway.net

Potters Hill Farm ◆◆◆
Leafield, Burford, Oxford,
Oxfordshire OX8 5QB
T: (01993) 878018 &
07711 045207
F: (01993) 878018
E: k.stanley@virgin.net
I: www.country-accom.
co.uk/potters-hill-farm

St Winnow ◆◆◆
160 The Hill, Burford, Oxford
OX18 4QY
T: (01993) 823843
I: www.stwinnow.com

Tudor Cottage ◆◆◆
40 Witney Street, Burford,
Oxford OX18 4SN
T: (01993) 823251
F: (01993) 823251

Willow Cottage ◆◆◆◆
Shilton, Burford, Oxford
OX18 4AB
T: (01993) 842456
F: (01993) 842456
I: www.smoothhound.
co.uk/hotels/willowcot.html

BURLEY
Hampshire

Bay Tree House ◆◆◆
1 Clough Lane, Burley,
Ringwood, Hampshire BH24 4AE
T: (01425) 403215
F: (01425) 403215
E: Baytreehousebandb@
burleyhants.freeserve.co.uk

Burbush Farm ◆◆◆◆◆
Pound Lane, Burley, Ringwood,
Hampshire BH24 4EF
T: (01425) 403238 &
07711 381924
F: (01425) 403238
E: burbush-farmexcite.com
I: www.burbush-farm.com

Great Wells House ◆◆◆◆◆
Beechwood Lane, Burley,
Ringwood, Hampshire BH24 4AS
T: (01425) 402302
F: (01425) 402302
E: chrisstewart@compuserve.
com

Holmans ◆◆◆◆
Bisterne Close, Burley,
Ringwood, Hampshire BH24 4AZ
T: (01425) 402307
F: (01425) 402307

Little Deeracres ◆◆◆
Bisterne Close, Burley,
Ringwood, Hampshire BH24 4BA
T: (01425) 402477

BUSCOT WICK
Oxfordshire

Weston Farm ◆◆◆◆
Buscot Wick, Faringdon,
Oxfordshire SN7 8DJ
T: (01367) 252222
F: (01367) 252222
I: www.farm-holiday.co.uk

CADMORE END
Buckinghamshire

South Fields ◆◆◆
Cadmore End, High Wycombe,
Buckinghamshire HP14 3PJ
T: (01494) 881976 &
07968 214389
F: (01494) 883765
E: crichtons@crichtonville.
freeserve.co.uk
I: www.crichtonville.freeserve.
co.uk

CADNAM
Hampshire

**The Old Well Hotel &
Restaurant** ◆◆◆
Romsey Road, Copythorne,
Southampton SO40 2PE
T: (023) 8081 2321 & 8081 2700
F: (023) 8081 2158
I: www.yell.
co.uk/sites/old-well-restaurant/

The Willows ◆◆◆
Holly Farm, Pound Lane,
Copythorne, Cadnam,
Southampton SO40 2PD
T: (023) 8081 3168

CARISBROOKE
Isle of Wight

Alvington Manor Farm ◆◆◆
Carisbrooke, Newport, Isle of
Wight PO30 5SP
T: (01983) 523463
F: (01983) 523463

CASHMOOR
Dorset

Cashmoor House ◆◆◆
Cashmoor, Blandford Forum,
Dorset DT11 8DN
T: (01725) 552339
E: spencer.jones@ukonline.
co.uk
I: www.cashmoorhouse.cjb.net

CASSINGTON
Oxfordshire

St Margaret's Lodge ◆◆◆
The Green, Cassington, Oxford
OX8 1DN
T: (01865) 880361
F: (01865) 731314

CASTLETHORPE
Buckinghamshire

Balney Grounds ◆◆◆◆
Home Farm, Hanslope Road,
Castlethorpe, Milton Keynes,
Buckinghamshire MK19 7HD
T: (01908) 510208
F: (01908) 510208
E: mary.stacey@tesco.net
I: www.lets-stay-mk.co.uk

Lincoln Lodge Farm ◆◆◆
Castlethorpe, Milton Keynes,
Buckinghamshire MK19 7HJ
T: (01908) 510152
F: (01908) 511022

CHADLINGTON
Oxfordshire

Stone Croft ◆◆◆
East End, Chadlington, Oxford
OX7 3LX
T: (01608) 676551 &
07860 472605

CHALE
Isle of Wight

Cortina ◆◆◆
Gotten Lane, Chale, Ventnor, Isle
of Wight PO38 2HQ
T: (01983) 551292

Gotten Manor ◆◆◆
Gotten Lane, Chale, Ventnor, Isle
of Wight PO38 2HQ
T: (01983) 551368
F: (01983) 551368
E: caroline.smith6@virgin.net

Little Atherfield Farm ◆◆◆
Chale, Ventnor, Isle of Wight
PO38 2LQ
T: (01983) 551363
F: (01983) 551033
E: david's.farm@virgin.net

CHALFONT ST GILES
Buckinghamshire

Gorelands Corner ◆◆◆
Gorelands Lane, Chalfont St
Giles, Buckinghamshire
HP8 4HQ
T: (01494) 872689
F: (01494) 872689
E: bickfordcsg@compuserve.
com

Holmdale ◆◆◆◆
Cokes Lane, Little Chalfont,
Amersham, Buckinghamshire
HP8 4TX
T: (01494) 762527
F: (01494) 764701
E: judy@holmdalebb.freeserve.
co.uk
I: www.smoothhand.
co.uk/hotels/holmdale.html

Pickwicks ◆◆◆
Nightingales Lane, Chalfont St
Giles, Buckinghamshire HP8 4SH
T: (01494) 874123
F: (01494) 870442

The White Hart Inn ◆◆◆◆
Three Households, Chalfont St
Giles, Buckinghamshire HP8 4LP
T: (01494) 872441

CHALFONT ST PETER
Buckinghamshire

Whitewebbs ◆◆◆
Grange Road, Off Lower Road,
Chalfont St Peter, Gerrards
Cross, Buckinghamshire SL9 9AQ
T: (01753) 884105
F: (01753) 884105

CHALGROVE
Oxfordshire

Cornerstones ◆◆◆
1 Cromwell Close, Chalgrove,
Oxford OX44 7SE
T: (01865) 890298
F: (01865) 890298

CHANDLERS FORD
Hampshire

Blackbird Hill ◆◆◆
24 Ashbridge Rise, Chandlers
Ford, Eastleigh, Hampshire
SO53 1SA
T: (023) 8026 0398
E: dotsid@onetel.net.uk

Landfall ◆◆◆
133 Bournemouth Road,
Chandlers Ford, Eastleigh,
Hampshire SO53 3HA
T: (023) 8025 4801
F: (023) 8025 4801

Little Oak ◆◆◆
176 Hiltingbury Road, Chandlers
Ford, Eastleigh, Hampshire
SO53 5NS
T: (023) 8090 3063

Monks House ◆◆◆◆◆
111 Hocombe Road, Chandlers
Ford, Eastleigh, Hampshire
SO53 5QD
T: (023) 8027 5986
F: (023) 8027 1505
E: info@monkshouse.com
I: www.monkshouse.com

Thornbury ◆◆◆◆
243 Winchester Road, Chandlers
Ford, Eastleigh, Hampshire
SO53 2DX
T: (023) 8026 0703 &
07775 862133
F: (023) 8061 3100

CHARLBURY
Oxfordshire

Banbury Hill Farm ◆◆◆◆
Enstone Road, Charlbury,
Oxford, Oxfordshire OX7 3JH
T: (01608) 810314
F: (01608) 811891
E: angelawiddows@gfwiddows.
f9.co.uk
I: www.charlburyoxfordaccom.
co.uk

Tanyer's House ◆◆◆◆
Hundley Way, Charlbury, Oxford
OX7 3QX
T: (01608) 811711 &
0780 3867424
E: jrose@charlburybb.co.uk
I: www.charlburybb.co.uk

CHARLTON MARSHALL
Dorset

Keston House ◆◆◆◆
314 Bournemouth Road,
Charlton Marshall, Blandford
Forum, Dorset DT11 9NQ
T: (01258) 451973
F: (01258) 451973
E: bandb@kestonhouse.co.uk

CHARLTON-ON-OTMOOR
Oxfordshire

Home Farm ◆◆
Mansmoor Lane, Charlton-on-
Otmoor, Kidlington, Oxfordshire
OX5 2US
T: (01865) 331267 &
07774 710305
F: (01865) 331267

CHECKENDON
Oxfordshire

Larchdown Farm ◆◆◆◆
Whitehall Lane, Checkendon,
Reading, Berkshire RG8 0TT
T: (01491) 682282
F: (01491) 682282
E: larchdown@onetel.net.uk
I: www.larchdown.com

CHESHAM
Buckinghamshire

49 Lowndes Avenue ◆◆
Chesham, Buckinghamshire
HP5 2HH
T: (01494) 792647

**May Tree House Bed &
Breakfast
Rating Applied For**
32 Hampden Avenue, Chesham,
Buckinghamshire HP5 2HL
T: (01494) 784019
F: (01494) 776896

Wychelm Farm ◆◆
Pednor Vale, Chesham,
Buckinghamshire HP5 2ST
T: (01494) 782309

CHESTERTON
Oxfordshire

Larchmont ◆◆◆
Alchester Road, Chesterton,
Bicester, Oxfordshire OX6 8UN
T: (01869) 245033
F: (01869) 245033

CHIEVELEY
Berkshire

19 Heathfields ◆◆◆
Chieveley, Newbury, Berkshire
RG20 8TW
T: (01635) 248179
F: (01635) 248799
E: ingandco@aol.com

CHILBOLTON
Hampshire

Sycamores ◆◆◆
Meadow View, Chilbolton,
Stockbridge, Hampshire
SO20 6AZ
T: (01264) 860380 &
07796 164664
E: maureen@sycamoresbb.
freeserve.co.uk
I: www.sycamoresbb.freeserve.
co.uk/sycamores2

Uplands ◆◆◆
Drove Road, Chilbolton,
Stockbridge, Hampshire
SO20 6AD
T: (01264) 860650
F: (01264) 860650
E: june@haymanjoyce.freeserve.
co.uk
I: www.haymanjoyce.freeserve.
co.uk

CHILDREY
Oxfordshire

Ridgeway House ◆◆◆◆
West Street, Childrey, Wantage,
Oxfordshire OX12 9UL
T: (01235) 751538 &
07774 182154
E: robertsfamily@compuserve.
com

CHIPPING NORTON

Kings Arms Hotel ◆◆◆
18 West Street, Chipping
Norton, Oxfordshire OX7 5AA
T: (01608) 642668
F: (01608) 646673

Lower Park Farm ◆◆◆◆
Great Tew, Oxford OX7 4DE
T: (01608) 683170
F: (01608) 683859
E: lowerparkfarm@talk21.com
I: members.tripod.
co.uk/lowerparkfarm

The Old Vicarage ◆◆◆
5 Church Street, Chipping
Norton, Oxfordshire OX7 5NT
T: (01608) 641562
E: anthony.ross@virgin.net

**Southcombe Lodge Guest
House ◆◆◆**
Southcombe, Chipping Norton,
Oxfordshire OX7 5QH
T: (01608) 643068
F: (01608) 642948
E:
georgefinlysouthcombelodge@
tinyworld.co.uk

Parkhouse Motel ◆◆◆◆
Cholderton, Salisbury SP4 0EG
T: (01980) 629256
F: (01980) 629256

The Well Cottage ◆◆◆
Caps Lane, Cholsey, Wallingford,
Oxfordshire OX10 9HQ
T: (01491) 651959 &
07887 958920
F: (01491) 651675
E: thewellcottage@talk21.com
I: www.thewellcottage.co.uk

The Beech Tree ◆◆◆◆
2 Stuart Road, Highcliffe,
BH23 5JS
T: (01425) 272038

Belvedere Guest House ◆◆
3 Twynham Avenue,
Christchurch, Dorset BH23 1QU
T: (01202) 485978
F: (01202) 485978
E: belvedere@eurolink.ltd.net

**Beverly Glen Guest House
◆◆◆◆**
1 Stuart Road, Highcliffe,
BH23 5JS
T: (01425) 273811

Bure Farm House ◆◆◆
107 Bure Lane, Friars Cliff,
Christchurch, Dorset BH23 4DN
T: (01425) 275498
I: www.burefarmhouse.co.uk

**Cafe 39 – The Pines Hotel
◆◆◆**
39 Mudeford, Christchurch,
Dorset BH23 3NQ
T: (01202) 475121 & 475121
F: (01202) 476646
E: pineshotelcafe39@ic24.net
I: www.mudeford.com

Druid House ◆◆◆◆◆
26 Sopers Lane, Christchurch,
Dorset BH23 1JE
T: (01202) 485615
F: (01202) 473484
E: druid_house@yahoo.com
I: www.druidhouse.co.uk

Grosvenor Lodge ◆◆◆◆
53 Stour Road, Christchurch,
Dorset BH23 1LN
T: (01202) 499008 &
07970 979881
F: (01202) 486041
E: grosvenorlodge@bigfoot.com
I: www.grosvenorlodge.co.uk

**Salmons Reach Guest House
◆◆**
28 Stanpit, Christchurch, Dorset
BH23 3LZ
T: (01202) 477315
F: (01202) 477315

Seapoint ◆◆◆
121 Mudeford, Christchurch,
Dorset BH23 4AF
T: (01425) 279541
F: (01425) 279541
I: www.seapointb-b.com

**Stour Lodge Guest House
◆◆◆**
54 Stour Road, Christchurch,
Dorset BH23 1LW
T: (01202) 486902
E: kcat@stourbridge.fsnet.co.uk

Three Gables ◆◆◆
11 Wickfield Avenue,
Christchurch, Dorset BH23 1JB
T: (01202) 481166 & 486171
F: (01202) 486171
E: rfgill@3gables.fsnet.co.uk

The White House ◆◆◆◆
428 Lymington Road, Highcliffe,
BH23 5HF
T: (01425) 271279
F: (01425) 276900
E: thewhitehouse@themail.
co.uk
I: www.thewhite-house.co.uk

The Forge ◆◆◆◆
Churchill, Oxford OX7 6NJ
T: (01608) 658173
F: (01608) 659262
E: jon@theforge.co.uk
I: www.theforge.co.uk

Long Barrow House ◆◆◆◆
Cole Henley, Whitchurch,
Hampshire RG28 7QJ
T: (01256) 895980
E: info@longbarrowhouse.co.uk
I: www.longbarrowhouse.co.uk

Long Lane Farmhouse ◆◆◆◆
Long Lane, Colehill, Wimborne
Minster, Dorset BH21 7AQ
T: (01202) 887829
E: paddysmyth@aol.com
I: www.eastdorsetdc.gov.
uk/tourism

Chine Cottage ◆◆◆
Colwell Chine Road, Colwell Bay,
PO40 9RU
T: (01983) 752808
E: enq1999@hotmail.com

Rockstone Cottage ◆◆◆◆
Colwell Chine Road, Colwell Bay,
PO40 9NR
T: (01983) 753723
F: (01983) 753721
E: enquiries@rockstonecottage.
co.uk
I: www.rockstonecottage.co.uk

Shorefield House ◆◆◆◆
Madeira Lane, Colwell Bay,
PO40 9SP
T: (01983) 752232
E: shorefield.house@btinternet.
com

Manor House ◆◆
Place Lane, Compton,
Winchester, Hampshire
SO21 2BA
T: (01962) 712162

The Old Forge ◆◆◆◆
Fanners Yard, Compton Abbas,
Shaftesbury, Dorset SP7 0NQ
T: (01747) 811881
F: (01747) 811881
E: theoldforge@hotmail.com
I: www.smoothhound.co.uk/

Wylie Cottage ◆◆◆
School Lane, Cookham,
Maidenhead, Berkshire SL6 9QJ
T: (01628) 520106
F: (01628) 520106
E: crowegc@ntlworld.com

Highfield ◆◆◆
Coombe Keynes, Wareham,
Dorset BH20 5PS
T: (01929) 463208
F: (01929) 463208
E: jmitchell@coombekeynes.
freeserve.co.uk
I: www.highfield-bb.co.uk

**West Coombe Farmhouse
◆◆◆◆**
Coombe Keynes, Wareham,
Dorset BH20 5PS
T: (01929) 462889
F: (01929) 405863
E: west.coombe.farmhouse@
barclays.net
I: www.westcoombefarmhouse.
co.uk

Bankes Hotel ◆◆◆
East Street, Corfe Castle,
Wareham, Dorset BH20 5ED
T: (01929) 480206 & 481288
F: (01929) 480186
E: bankeshotel.corfecastle@
telinco.co.uk
I: www.dorset-info.
co.uk/bankes_arms_hotel

Bradle Farmhouse ◆◆◆◆
Bradle Farm, Church Knowle,
Wareham, Dorset BH20 5NU
T: (01929) 480712
F: (01929) 481144
E: hole.bradle@farmersweekly.
net
I: www.smoothhound.
co.uk/hotels/bradle.html

Furzyhurst Farmhouse ◆◆◆
69 Oxford Street, Northwood,
Cowes, Isle of Wight PO31 8PT
T: (01983) 292513
F: (01983) 292513
E: mary.mcbride@pmail.net
I: www.geocities.
com/furzyhurst/

Halcyone Villa ◆◆◆
Grove Road, Cowes, Isle of
Wight PO31 7JP
T: (01983) 291334
E: sandra@halcyone.freeserve.
co.uk
I: www.halcyonevilla.freeuk.com

Noss Mayo ◆◆◆◆
66a Baring Road, Cowes, Isle of
Wight PO31 8DW
T: (01983) 200266
E: nossmayo.one@freeuk.com

Skye Villa Guest House ◆◆
11 Newport Road, Cowes, Isle of
Wight PO31 7PA
T: (01983) 292803 &
07768 960732
F: (01983) 292803
E: sharonounsworth@hotmail.
com

Acorns ◆◆◆◆
55a The Green, Woodlands,
Wimborne Minster, Dorset
BH21 8LN
T: (01202) 823991
E: wgac@tesco.net
I: www.dorsetbandb.com

The Fleur de Lys ◆◆◆
5 Wimborne Street, Cranborne,
Wimborne Minster, Dorset
BH21 5PP
T: (01725) 517282 & 517765
F: (01726) 517631
E: fleurdelys@btinternet.com
I: www.btinternet.
com/fleurdelys/

La Fosse at Cranborne ◆◆◆◆
London House, The Square,
Cranborne, Wimborne Minster,
Dorset BH21 5PR
T: (01725) 517604
F: (01725) 517778
E: mac@la-fosse.com
I: www.la-fosse.com

Poplars Farm ◆◆◆◆
Claydon Road, Cropredy,
Banbury, Oxfordshire OX17 1JP
T: (01295) 750561
E: colkathpoplars@supanet.com

Homeground Farm ◆◆◆
Ridings Way, Cublington,
Leighton Buzzard, Bedfordshire
LU7 0LW
T: (01296) 681107 &
07968 264769
F: (01296) 681107

The Compasses Inn ◆◆◆
Damerham, Fordingbridge,
Hampshire SP6 3HQ
T: (01725) 518231
F: (01725) 518880

Hill Barn ◆◆
Milton Gated Road, Deddington,
Banbury, Oxfordshire OX15 0TS
T: (01869) 338631
F: (01869) 338631
E: hillbarn-bb@supanet.com

The Little House ◆◆◆◆
Clifton Road, Deddington,
Banbury, Oxfordshire OX15 0TP
T: (01869) 337319
F: (01869) 337355
E: clarkejs@msn.com

Stonecrop Guest House ◆◆
Hempton Road, Deddington,
Banbury, Oxfordshire OX15 0QH
T: (01869) 338335 & 338496
F: (01869) 338505

The Unicorn Inn
Rating Applied For
Market Place, Deddington,
Banbury, Oxfordshire OX15 0SE
T: (01869) 338838
F: (01869) 338592

DENMEAD
Hampshire

Bellchamber House
Rating Applied For
80 Anmore Road, Denmead,
Waterlooville, Hampshire
PO7 6NT
T: (023) 9236 0978

DINTON
Buckinghamshire

Dinton Cottage ◆◆◆
Dinton, Aylesbury,
Buckinghamshire HP17 8UH
T: (01296) 748270
F: (01296) 748370
E: scribe@blankpage.freeserve.
co.uk
I: www.amicitiam.com

Perryfield ◆◆◆◆
New Road, Dinton, Aylesbury,
Buckinghamshire HP17 8UT
T: (01296) 748265 &
07885 273574
F: (01296) 747765
E: bandb@perryfield.co.uk

DORCHESTER ON THAMES
Oxfordshire

Harley's Lodge ◆
14 Bridge End, Dorchester on
Thames, Wallingford,
Oxfordshire OX10 7JP
T: (01865) 340830 &
07850 394090
F: (01865) 340248
E: tsawtell@harleys-lodge.
freeserve.co.uk
I: www.scoot.
co.uk/harleys_lodge/

DOWNLEY
Buckinghamshire

Avon Guest House ◆◆
2 Grays Lane, Downley, High
Wycombe, Buckinghamshire
HP13 5TZ
T: (01494) 523014

DRAYTON PARSLOW
Buckinghamshire

Crossroads Farm B & B ◆◆◆◆
Crossroads Farm, Newton Road,
Drayton Parslow, Milton Keynes,
Buckinghamshire MK17 0LB
T: (01908) 372440
F: (01908) 372388

The Three Horseshoes ◆◆◆
10 Main Road, Drayton Parslow,
Milton Keynes, Buckinghamshire
MK17 0JS
T: (01296) 720296
F: (01296) 720841
E: 3shoes@threehorseshoes.
idps.co.uk
I: www.threehorseshoes.
free-online.uk

DUMMER
Hampshire

Oakdown Farm Bungalow
◆◆◆
Oakdown Farm, Dummer,
Basingstoke, Hampshire
RG23 7LR
T: (01256) 397218

DUNBRIDGE
Hampshire

The Mill Arms ◆◆◆◆
Barley Hill, Dunbridge, Romsey,
Hampshire SO51 0LF
T: (01794) 340401
F: (01794) 340401
E: the-mill-arms@river-dun.
demon.co.uk
I: www.river-dun.demon.co.uk/

EARLEY
Berkshire

Elmhurst Hotel ◆◆
51 Church Road, Earley, Reading
RG6 1EY
T: (01189) 661588 & 265273
F: (01189) 352180
E: elmhurst_hotel@hotmail.
com

EAST COWES
Hampshire

Crossways House ◆◆◆
Crossways Road, East Cowes,
Isle of Wight PO32 6LJ
T: (01983) 298282 &
07771 623129
F: (01983) 298282

The Doghouse ◆◆◆◆
Crossways Road, East Cowes,
Isle of Wight PO32 6LJ
T: (01983) 293677
E: timindoghouse@beeb.net

EAST END
Oxfordshire

**The Leather Bottel Guest
House** ◆◆◆
East End, North Leigh, Witney,
Oxfordshire OX8 6PX
T: (01993) 882174 &
07711 782302

EAST MEON
Hampshire

Coombe Cross House & Stables
◆◆◆
Coombe Road, East Meon,
Petersfield, Hampshire
GU32 1HQ
T: (01730) 823298
F: (01730) 823515

Drayton Cottage ◆◆◆◆
East Meon, Petersfield,
Hampshire GU32 1PW
T: (01730) 823472 &
07703 642085
E: draytoncottage@btinternet.
com

Dunvegan Cottage ◆◆◆◆
Frogmore Lane, East Meon,
Petersfield, Hampshire
GU32 1QJ
T: (01730) 823213
F: (01730) 823858
E: dunvegan@btinternet.com
🏛

EAST STOUR
Dorset

Aysgarth ◆◆◆◆
Back Street, East Stour,
Gillingham, Dorset SP8 5JY
T: (01747) 838351
E: aysgarth@lineone.net

EAST WELLOW
Hampshire

Country Views B & B ◆◆◆◆
Willowbend, Dunwood Hill, East
Wellow, Romsey, Hampshire
SO51 6FD
T: (01794) 514735 & 521867
F: (01794) 521867
E: elsoncvee@madasafish.com

EASTLEIGH
Hampshire

Carinya B & B ◆◆◆
38 Sovereign Way, Boyatt Wood,
Eastleigh, Hampshire SO50 4SA
T: (023) 8061 3128
F: (023) 8061 3128

EDGCOTT
Buckinghamshire

Perry Manor Farm ◆◆
Buckingham Road, Edgcott,
Aylesbury, Buckinghamshire
HP18 0TR
T: (01296) 770257

EMBERTON
Buckinghamshire

Ekeney House ◆◆◆
Wood Farm, Emberton, Olney,
Buckinghamshire MK46 5JH
T: (01234) 711133
F: (01234) 711133

EMSWORTH
Hampshire

Apple Blossom ◆◆◆
19A Bosmere Gardens,
Emsworth, Hampshire PO10 7NP
T: (01243) 372201

Bunbury Lodge ◆◆◆
10 West Road, Emsworth,
Hampshire PO10 4JT
T: (01243) 432030
F: (01243) 432030
E: Bunbury.Lodge@breathemail.
net
I: www.guestaccom.co.uk

The Merry Hall Hotel ◆◆◆
73 Horndean Road, Emsworth,
Hampshire PO10 7PU
T: (01243) 431377
F: (01243) 431411

EPWELL
Oxfordshire

Yarnhill Farm ◆◆◆
Epwell, Banbury, Oxfordshire
OX15 6JA
T: (01295) 780250
F: (01295) 780250

EWELME
Oxfordshire

Mays Farm ◆◆◆◆
Ewelme, Oxford OX10 6QF
T: (01491) 641294 & 642056
F: (01491) 641697

EYNSHAM
Oxfordshire

Grange House ◆◆◆
Station Road, Eynsham, Oxford
OX8 1HX
T: (01865) 880326 &
07803 012805
F: (01865) 880326
E: bookings@grangehouse.co.uk
I: www.grangehouse.co.uk

The White Hart Inn ◆◆◆◆
31 Newland Street, Eynsham,
Oxford OX8 1LB
T: (01865) 880711
F: (01865) 880169

FAREHAM
Hampshire

Bridge House ◆◆◆
1 Waterside Gardens,
Wallington, Fareham, Hampshire
PO16 8SD
T: (01329) 287775 &
07751 674400
F: (01329) 287775
E: maryhb@fish.co.uk

Catisfield Cottage Guest House
◆◆
1 Catisfield Lane, Catisfield,
Fareham, Hampshire PO15 5NW
T: (01329) 843301
F: (01329) 841652

Seven Sevens Guest House
◆◆◆
56 Hill Head Road, Hill Head,
PO14 3JL
T: (01329) 662408

Springfield Hotel ◆◆◆◆
67 The Avenue, Fareham,
Hampshire PO14 1PE
T: (01329) 828325

Travelrest Avenue House Hotel
◆◆◆
22 The Avenue, Fareham,
Hampshire PO14 1NS
T: (01329) 232175
F: (01329) 232196
🏛

FARINGDON
Oxfordshire

Ashen Copse Farm ◆◆◆
Coleshill, Faringdon, Oxfordshire
SN6 7PU
T: (01367) 240175
F: (01367) 241418
E: pat@hodd.demon.co.uk
I: www.hodd.demon.co.uk

Bowling Green Farm ◆◆◆
Stanford Road, Faringdon,
Oxfordshire SN7 8EZ
T: (01367) 240229
F: (01367) 242568
E: della@bowling-green-farm.
co.uk
I: www.leading.co.uk/bgfarm

Portwell House Hotel ◆◆◆
Market Place, Faringdon,
Oxfordshire SN7 7HU
T: (01367) 240197 & 242413
F: (01367) 244330
E: portwellh@aol.com

FARNBOROUGH
Hampshire

Colebrook Guest House ◆◆
56 Netley Street, Farnborough,
Hampshire GU14 6AT
T: (01252) 542269
F: (01252) 542269
E: derek.clark@ukonline.co.uk

The Oak Tree Guest House
Rating Applied For
112 Farnborough Road,
Farnborough, Hampshire
GU14 6TN
T: (01252) 545491
F: (01252) 545491

The White Residence Town House Hotel ◆◆◆◆
Farnborough Park, 76 Avenue
Road, Farnborough, Hampshire
GU14 7BG
T: (01252) 375510 & 371817
F: (01252) 655567
E: info@countyapartments.com
I: www.countyapartments.co.uk

FAWLEY
Hampshire

Walcot House ◆◆◆
Blackfield Road, Fawley,
Southampton SO45 1ED
T: (023) 8089 1344

FERNDOWN
Dorset

Woodridings ◆◆◆◆
73 Beaufoys Avenue, Ferndown,
Wimborne Minster, Dorset
BH22 9RN
T: (01202) 876729

FIFEHEAD ST QUINTON
Dorset

Lower Fifehead Farm ◆◆◆◆
Fifehead St Quinton,
Sturminster Newton, Dorset
DT10 2AP
T: (01258) 817335
F: (01258) 817335

FORDINGBRIDGE
Hampshire

A Green Patch ◆◆◆◆
Furze Hill, Fordingbridge,
Hampshire SP6 2PS
T: (01425) 652387
F: (01425) 656594

Appletree ◆◆◆◆
159 Station Road, Alderholt,
Fordingbridge, Hampshire
SP6 3AZ
T: (01425) 652154
E: blanham@appletree159.
fsnet.co.uk
I: www.appletree159.co.uk

The Augustus John ◆◆◆◆
116 Station Road,
Fordingbridge, Hampshire
SP6 1DG
T: (01425) 652098
E: peter@augustusjohn.com
I: www.augustusjohn.com

Broomy ◆◆◆◆
Ogdens, Fordingbridge,
Hampshire SP6 2PY
T: (01425) 653264

The Crown Inn ◆◆◆
62 High Street, Fordingbridge,
Hampshire SP6 1AX
T: (01425) 652552
F: (01425) 655752
E: CandM.Bell@ukgateway.net

Drummond House ◆◆◆◆
Bowerwood Road,
Fordingbridge, Hampshire
SP6 1BL
T: (01425) 653165
E: drumbb@btinternet.com

Hillbury ◆◆◆
2 Fir Tree Hill, Camel Green
Road, Alderholt, Fordingbridge,
Hampshire SP6 3AY
T: (01425) 652582
F: (01425) 657587
I: www.newforest.demon.
co.uk/hillbury.htm

Noarlunga ◆◆◆◆
16 Broomfield Drive, Alderholt,
Fordingbridge, Hampshire
SP6 3HY
T: (01425) 650491

Primrose Cottage ◆◆◆◆
Newgrounds, Godshill,
Fordingbridge, Hampshire
SP6 2LJ
T: (01425) 650447 &
07712 469394
F: (01425) 650447
E: ann@blake98.freeserve.co.uk

The Ship Inn
Rating Applied For
68 High Street, Fordingbridge,
Hampshire SP6 1AX
T: (01425) 651820
F: (01425) 651825

The Three Lions ◆◆◆◆◆
Stuckton, Fordingbridge,
Hampshire SP6 2HF
T: (01425) 652489
F: (01425) 656144
E: the3lions@btinternet.com

FREELAND
Oxfordshire

Wintersbrook ◆◆◆◆
15 Broadmarsh Lane, Freeland,
Oxford OX29 8QP
T: (01993) 883602

FRESHWATER
Isle of Wight

Brookside Forge Hotel ◆◆◆
Brookside Road, Freshwater, Isle
of Wight PO40 9ER
T: (01983) 754644

Cherry Trees ◆◆◆◆
29 School Green Road,
Freshwater, Isle of Wight
PO40 9AW
T: (01983) 756000
F: (01983) 752681
E: cherrytrees@cuemedianet.
com

Field House ◆◆◆◆
Pound Green, Freshwater, Isle of
Wight PO40 9HG
T: (01983) 754190

Royal Standard Hotel ◆◆◆
School Green Road, Freshwater,
Isle of Wight PO40 9AJ
T: (01983) 753227
E: sue.stephenson84@freeserve.
co.uk

Seahorses ◆◆◆◆
Victoria Road, Freshwater, Isle of
Wight PO40 9PP
T: (01983) 752574
F: (01983) 752574
E: lanterncom@aol.com

Traidcraft ◆◆
119 School Green Road,
Freshwater, Isle of Wight
PO40 9AZ
T: (01983) 752451

FRESHWATER BAY
Isle of Wight

Wighthaven ◆◆◆◆
Afton Road, Freshwater Bay, Isle
of Wight PO40 9TT
T: (01983) 753184 & 755957
E: wighthaven@btinternet.com

FRITHAM
Hampshire

Amberwood Cottage ◆◆◆
Fritham, Lyndhurst, Hampshire
SO43 7HL
T: (023) 8081 2359

Fritham Farm ◆◆◆◆
Fritham, Lyndhurst, Hampshire
SO43 7HH
T: (023) 8081 2333
F: (023) 8081 2333
E: frithamfarm@supanet.com

FROYLE
Hampshire

West End Farm
Rating Applied For
Froyle, Alton, Hampshire
GU34 4JG
T: (01420) 22130
F: (01420) 22930

GARSINGTON
Oxfordshire

Hill Copse Cottage ◆◆◆
Wheatley Road, Garsington,
Oxford OX44 9DT
T: (01865) 361478 &
07778 776209
F: (01865) 361478

GATCOMBE
Isle of Wight

Freewaters ◆◆◆◆
New Barn Lane, Gatcombe,
Newport, Isle of Wight
PO30 3EQ
T: (01983) 721439 & 294 173
F: (01983) 294173
E: john@pitstopmodels.demon.
co.uk

Little Gatcombe Farm ◆◆◆◆
New Barn Lane, Gatcombe,
Newport, Isle of Wight
PO30 3EQ
T: (01983) 721580 &
07968 462513
E: littlegatcombefarm@
gatcombelow.fsnet.co.ukl
I: www.littlegatcombefarm.co.uk

GERRARDS CROSS
Buckinghamshire

15 Howards Wood Drive ◆◆◆
Gerrards Cross,
Buckinghamshire SL9 7HR
T: (01753) 884911
F: (01753) 884911
E: james.crosby@tesco.net

GIFFARD PARK
Buckinghamshire

Cheslyn B & B
Rating Applied For
12 Cheslyn Gardens, Giffard
Park, Milton Keynes,
Buckinghamshire MK14 5JU
T: (01908) 611429

Giffard House ◆◆◆
10 Broadway Avenue, Giffard
Park, Milton Keynes MK14 5QF
T: (01908) 618868
F: (01908) 618868
E: phil.mason@lineone.net

GODSHILL
Hampshire

Croft Cottage ◆◆◆
Southampton Road, Godshill,
Fordingbridge, Hampshire
SP6 2LE
T: (01425) 657955 &
07977 142745

Vennards Cottage ◆◆◆
Newgrounds, Godshill,
Fordingbridge, Hampshire
SP6 2LJ
T: (01425) 652644
F: (01425) 656646
E: gillian.bridgeman@virgin.net

GORING
Oxfordshire

The John Barleycorn ◆
Manor Road, Goring, Reading,
Berkshire RG8 9DP
T: (01491) 872509

Miller of Mansfield ◆◆◆
High Street, Goring, Reading
RG8 9AW
T: (01491) 872829
F: (01491) 874200
I: www.millerofmansfield.co.uk

GOSPORT
Hampshire

Spring Garden Guest House ◆
Spring Garden Lane, Gosport,
Hampshire PO12 1LP
T: (023) 9251 0336
F: (023) 9251 0336

West Wind Guest House
◆◆◆◆
197 Portsmouth Road, Lee on
the Solent, Gosport, Hampshire
PO13 9AA
T: (023) 9255 2550
F: (023) 9255 4657
E: maggie@west-wind.co.uk
I: www.west-wind.co.uk
⌘

GRATELEY
Hampshire

Gunville House ◆◆◆◆
Grateley, Andover, Hampshire
SP11 8JQ
T: (01264) 889206
F: (01264) 889060
E: pct@onetel.net.uk

GREAT KINGSHILL
Buckinghamshire

Hatches Farm ◆◆
Hatches Lane, Great Kingshill,
High Wycombe,
Buckinghamshire HP15 6DS
T: (01494) 713125
F: (01494) 714666

GREAT TEW
Oxfordshire

The Falkland Arms ◆◆◆◆
Great Tew, Oxford OX7 4DB
T: (01608) 683653
F: (01608) 683656
E: sjcourage@btconnect.com
I: www.banbury-cross.
co.uk/falklandarms

GURNARD
Isle of Wight

Hillbrow Private Hotel ◆◆◆◆
Tuttons Hill, Gurnard, Cowes,
Isle of Wight PO31 8JA
T: (01983) 297240
F: (01983) 297240

The Woodvale Hotel ◆◆◆
1 Princes Esplanade, Gurnard,
Cowes, Isle of Wight PO31 8LE
T: (01983) 292037
F: (01983) 292037
E: woodvaleparkin@aol.com

HADDENHAM
Buckinghamshire

The Majors ◆◆◆◆
19-21 Townside, Haddenham,
Aylesbury, Buckinghamshire
HP17 8BQ
T: (01844) 292654
F: (01844) 299050

HAMBLE
Hampshire

Farthings Bed & Breakfast
◆◆◆◆
Farthings, School Lane, Hamble,
Southampton, Hampshire
SO31 4JD
T: (023) 8045 2009 &
07979 746717
F: (023) 8045 2613
E: strakers@hamble2.fsnet.
co.uk
I: www.hamble.net

Honeysuckle ◆◆◆
Flowers Close, Hamble,
Southampton, Hampshire
SO31 4LU
T: (023) 8045 3209
F: (023) 8045 3209

HAMBLEDON
Hampshire

Cams ◆◆◆
Hambledon, Waterlooville,
Hampshire PO7 4SP
T: (023) 9263 2865
F: (023) 9263 2691

Mornington House ◆◆◆
Speltham Hill, Hambledon,
Waterlooville, Hampshire
PO7 4RU
T: (023) 9263 2704
F: (023) 9263 2704

HAMWORTHY
Dorset

Harbourside Guest House
◆◆◆
195 Blandford Road,
Hamworthy, Poole, Dorset
BH15 4AX
T: (01202) 673053
F: (01202) 673053

Holes Bay B & B ◆◆◆
365 Blandford Road,
Hamworthy, Poole, Dorset
BH15 4JL
T: (01202) 672069

ITP Lodge ◆◆◆◆
53 Branksea Avenue,
Hamworthy, Poole, Dorset
BH15 4DP
T: (01202) 673419 &
07710 725301
F: (01202) 667260
E: johnrenate@lineone.net

San-Michele Guest House
◆◆◆
237 Blandford Road,
Hamworthy, Poole, Dorset
BH15 4AZ
T: (01202) 675442

Seashells ◆◆◆
4 Lake Road, Hamworthy, Poole,
Dorset BH15 4LH
T: (01202) 671921
F: (01202) 671921

HANSLOPE
Buckinghamshire

Cuckoo Hill Farm ◆◆
Hanslope, Milton Keynes
MK19 7HQ
T: (01908) 510748
F: (01908) 511669

Woad Farm ◆◆◆
Tathall End, Hanslope, Milton
Keynes MK19 7NE
T: (01908) 510985 & 07940 506
439
F: (01908) 510985
E: mail@sarahstacey.freeserve.
co.uk

HAVANT
Hampshire

High Towers ◆◆◆
14 Portsdown Hill Road,
Bedhampton, Havant,
Hampshire PO9 3JY
T: (023) 9247 1748

HAYLING ISLAND
Hampshire

Ann's Cottage ◆◆
45 St Andrews Road, Hayling
Island, Hampshire PO11 9JN
T: (023) 9246 7048

16 Charleston Close ◆◆◆
Hayling Island, Hayling Island,
Hampshire PO11 0JY
T: (023) 9246 2527

Maidlings ◆◆◆
55 Staunton Avenue, Hayling
Island, Hampshire PO11 0EW
T: (023) 9246 6357

The Nook
Rating Applied For
11 Fishery Lane, Hayling Island,
Hampshire PO11 9NP
T: (02392) 787366

The Rook Hollow Hotel ◆◆◆
84 Church Road, Hayling Island,
Hampshire PO11 0NX
T: (023) 9246 7080
F: (023) 9246 1078

The Shallows
Rating Applied For
Woodgaston Lane, Hayling
Island, Hampshire PO11 0RL
T: (023) 9246 3713

Tide Reach ◆◆◆
214 Southwood Road, Hayling
Island, Hampshire PO11 9QQ
T: 0800 970 1670 &
(023) 924607828
F: (023) 9246 7828

White House ◆◆◆
250 Havant Road, Hayling
Island, Hampshire PO11 0LN
T: (023) 9246 3464

HEADINGTON
Oxfordshire

Conifers Guest House ◆◆◆
116 The Slade, Headington,
Oxford, Oxfordshire OX3 7DX
T: (01865) 763055
F: (01865) 742232

Red Mullions ◆◆◆
23 London Road, Headington,
Oxford, Oxfordshire OX3 7RE
T: (01865) 742741
F: (01865) 769944
E: redmullion@aol.com
I: http://www.oxfordcity.
co.uk/accom/redmullions

HEADLEY
Hampshire

Knightsbridge Farm ◆◆
Newbury Road, Headley,
Thatcham, Berkshire RG19 8JY
T: (01635) 268210

HEDGE END
Hampshire

Montana Guest House ◆◆◆
90 Lower Northam Road, Hedge
End, Southampton SO30 4FT
T: (01489) 782797
F: (01489) 782797

HEELANDS
Buckinghamshire

Butter's Guest House ◆◆
51 Langcliffe Drive, Heelands,
Milton Keynes MK13 7LA
T: (01908) 312166

Fallty Towers ◆◆◆
110 Langcliffe Drive, Heelands,
Milton Keynes MK13 7LD
T: (01908) 315867 &
07941 258915
F: (01908) 315867
E: ryandorothy@aol.com

Rovers Return ◆◆
49 Langcliffe Drive, Heelands,
Milton Keynes MK13 7LA
T: (01908) 310465

HENLEY-ON-THAMES
Oxfordshire

Abbottsleigh
Rating Applied For
107 St Marks Road, Henley-on-
Thames, Oxfordshire RG9 1LP
T: (01491) 572982 & 07958 424
337
F: (01491) 572982

Alftrudis ◆◆◆◆
8 Norman Avenue, Henley-on-
Thames, Oxfordshire RG9 1SG
T: (01491) 573099 &
07802 408643
F: (01491) 411747
E: b&b@alftrudis.fsnet.co.uk
I: www.alftrudis.co.uk

Avalon ◆◆◆
36 Queen Street, Henley-on-
Thames, Oxfordshire RG9 1AP
T: (01491) 577829
E: avalon@henleybb.fsnet.co.uk
I: www.henleybb.fsnet.co.uk

Azalea House ◆◆◆
55 Deanfield Road, Henley-on-
Thames, Oxfordshire RG9 1UU
T: (01491) 576407 &
07712 446076
F: (01491) 576407
I: masseyp@globalnet.co.uk

Bank Farm ◆◆
The Old Road, Pishill, Henley-on-
Thames, Oxfordshire RG9 6HS
T: (01491) 638601 & 07799 752
933
F: (01491) 638601
E: bankfarm@btinternet.com

16 Baronsmead
Rating Applied For
Henley-on-Thames, Oxfordshire
RG9 2DL
T: (01491) 578044

4 Coldharbour Close ◆◆◆
Henley-on-Thames, Oxfordshire
RG9 1QF
T: (01491) 575297
F: (01491) 575297
E: jenny_bower@email.com
I: www.henley-bb.freeserve.
co.uk

Coldharbour House ◆◆◆◆
3 Coldharbour Close, Henley-
on-Thames, Oxfordshire
RG9 1QF
T: (01491) 575229
F: (01491) 575229
E: coldharbourhouse@cs.com

Denmark House
Rating Applied For
Northfield Road, Henley-on-
Thames, Oxfordshire RG9 2HN
T: (01491) 572028
F: (01491) 572458

Five New Street ◆◆◆
Henley-on-Thames, Oxfordshire
RG9 2BP
T: (01491) 411711
E: fivenewstreet@aol.com

Gablehurst ◆◆◆
34 Cromwell Road, Henley-on-
Thames, Oxfordshire RG9 1JH
T: (01491) 575876
F: (01491) 575876
E: gablehurst@rg91jh.
free-online.co.uk

Henley House ◆◆◆
School Lane, Medmenham,
Marlow, Buckinghamshire
SL7 2HJ
T: (01491) 576100
F: (01491) 571764
E: dres@crownandanchor.co.uk
I: www.crownandanchor.co.uk

Holmwood ◆◆◆◆
Shiplake Row, Binfield Heath,
Henley-on-Thames, Oxfordshire
RG9 4DP
T: (0118) 947 8747
F: (0118) 947 8637

The Knoll ◆◆◆◆
Crowsley Road, Shiplake,
Henley-on-Thames, Oxfordshire
RG9 3JT
T: (01189) 402705 & 406538
F: (01189) 402705
E: theknollhenley@aol.com
I: www.theknollhenley.com

Lenwade ◆◆◆◆◆
3 Western Road, Henley-on-
Thames, Oxfordshire RG9 1JL
T: (01491) 573468 &
07774 941629
F: (01491) 573468
E: lenwadeuk@compuserve.com
I: www.w3b-ink.com/lenwade

Little Parmoor Farm ◆◆◆◆
Frieth, Henley-on-Thames,
Oxfordshire RG9 6NL
T: (01494) 881600
F: (01494) 883634
E: francesemmett@
netscapeonline.co.uk

New Lodge ◆◆◆
Henley Park, Henley-on-Thames,
Oxfordshire RG9 6HU
T: (01491) 576340
F: (01491) 576340
E: newlodge@mail.com

Park View Farm ◆◆
Lower Assendon, Henley-on-Thames, Oxfordshire RG9 6AN
T: (01491) 414232 & 0786 766 0814
F: (01491) 577515
E: thomasmartin@globalnet.co.uk
I: www.thomasmartin.co.uk

Pennyford House ◆◆◆
Peppard Common, Henley-on-Thames, Oxfordshire RG9 5JE
T: (01491) 628272
F: (01491) 628779

The Rise ◆◆◆◆
Rotherfield Road, Henley-on-Thames, Oxfordshire RG9 1NR
T: (01491) 579360
F: (01491) 579360

12 Rupert Place ◆◆◆◆
Rupert Lane, Henley-on-Thames, Oxfordshire RG9 2JE
T: (01491) 573810 &
07932 312889
E: jo.bausor@virgin.net
I: www.12rupertplace.com

Slaters Farm ◆◆◆
Peppard Common, Henley-on-Thames, Oxfordshire RG9 5JL
T: (01491) 628675
F: (01491) 628675

Somewhere to Stay ◆◆◆◆
c/o Loddon Acres, Bath Road, Twyford, Reading RG10 9RU
T: (0118) 934 5880 &
07798 801088
F: (0118) 934 5880

Stag Hall
Peppard, Henley-on-Thames, Oxfordshire RG9 5NX
T: (01491) 680338
F: (01491) 680338

Thamesmead House Hotel ◆◆◆◆◆
Remenham Lane, Remenham, Henley-on-Thames, Oxfordshire RG9 2LR
T: (01491) 574745
F: (01491) 579944
E: thamesmead@supanet.com
I: www.thamesmeadhousehotel.co.uk

Windy Brow ◆◆◆◆
204 Victoria Road, Wargrave, Reading RG10 8AJ
T: (0118) 940 3336
F: (0118) 940 1260
E: heathcar@aol.com

HETHE
Oxfordshire

Manor Farm ◆◆◆◆
Hethe, Bicester, Oxfordshire OX27 8ES
T: (01869) 277602
F: (01869) 278376
E: chrmanor@aol.com

HIGH WYCOMBE
Buckinghamshire

Ayam Manor ◆◆◆
Hammersley Lane, High Wycombe, Buckinghamshire HP10 8HS
T: (01494) 816932
F: (01494) 816932
E: jeansenior@ayammanor.freeserve.co.uk
I: www.ayammanorguesthouse.co.uk

The Birches ◆◆
30 Lucas Road, High Wycombe, Buckinghamshire HP13 6QG
T: (01494) 533547

Bird in Hand ◆◆◆
81 West Wycombe Road, High Wycombe, Buckinghamshire HP11 2LR
T: (01494) 523502
F: (01494) 459449

P A Smails Guest Accommodation ◆◆◆
106 Green Hill, High Wycombe, Buckinghamshire HP13 5QE
T: (01494) 524310 &
07940 544776
E: pauline.smails@talk21.com

Sunnydale ◆◆◆
425 Amersham Road, Hazlemere, High Wycombe, Buckinghamshire HP15 7JG
T: (01494) 711439

HIGHCLIFFE
Dorset

10 Brook Way ◆◆◆
Friars Cliff, Highcliffe, BH23 4HA
T: (01425) 276738
E: midgefinn@hotmail.com

Castle Lodge ◆◆◆◆
173 Lymington Road, Highcliffe, BH23 4JS
T: (01425) 275170
F: (01425) 275170

The Close ◆◆◆
12 Shelley Close, Highcliffe, BH23 4HW
T: (01425) 273559

Rothesay Hotel ◆◆◆◆
175 Lymington Road, Christchurch, Dorset BH23 4JS
T: (01425) 274172
F: (01425) 270780
E: rothesay.hotel@virgin.net

HILLESDEN
Buckinghamshire

Field Cottage ◆◆◆
Hillesden Hamlet, Hillesden, Buckingham MK18 4BX
T: (01280) 815360
F: (01280) 815360
E: martin.tessa@virgin.net

HINTON ST MARY
Dorset

The Old Post Office Guest House ◆◆◆◆
Hinton St Mary, Sturminster Newton, Dorset DT10 1NG
T: (01258) 472366
F: (01258) 472173
E: sofields@aol.com

HOLT
Dorset

Bumble Bee Cottage ◆◆◆
Gods Blessing Lane, Holt, Wimborne Minster, Dorset BH21 7DE
T: (01202) 849747 & 0771 256 8778
F: (01202) 849747

HOLTON
Oxfordshire

Home Farm House ◆◆◆◆
Holton, Oxford OX33 1QA
T: (01865) 872334
F: (01865) 876220
E: sonjab@btinternet.com

HOOK
Hampshire

Cherry Lodge Guest House ◆◆◆
Reading Road, Hook, Hampshire RG27 9DB
T: (01256) 762532
F: (01256) 762532

Oaklea Guest House ◆◆◆
London Road, Hook, Hampshire RG27 9LA
T: (01256) 762673
F: (01256) 762150

HOOK NORTON
Oxfordshire

Manor Farm ◆◆◆
Hook Norton, Banbury, Oxfordshire OX15 5LU
T: (01608) 737204
E: jdyhughes@aol.com

Symnel ◆◆
High Street, Hook Norton, Oxfordshire OX15 5NH
T: (01608) 737547
E: cornelius@hooky13.freeserve.co.uk

HORDLE
Hampshire

Long Acre Farm ◆◆◆
Vaggs Lane, Hordle, Lymington, Hampshire SO41 0FP
T: (01425) 610443 &
07946 577530
F: (01425) 613026
E: long.acre@amserve.net

Miranda ◆◆◆◆
Vaggs Lane, Hordle, Lymington, Hampshire SO41 0FP
T: (01425) 621561

Spinney Cottage ◆◆◆◆
219 Everton Road, Hordle, Lymington, Hampshire SO41 0HE
T: (01590) 644555 &
07711 138555
F: (01590) 644555
E: spinneycottage@aol.com
I: www.spinneycottage.co.uk

HORLEY
Oxfordshire

Sor Brook House Farm ◆◆◆◆
Horley, Banbury, Oxfordshire OX15 6BL
T: (01295) 738121

HORNDEAN
Hampshire

Rosedene ◆◆◆◆
63 Rosemary Way, Horndean, Waterlooville, Hampshire PO8 9DQ
T: (023) 9261 5804
T: (023) 9242 3948
E: pbbatt@aol.com

The Ship & Bell Hotel ◆◆◆
6 London Road, Horndean, Waterlooville, Hampshire PO8 0BZ
T: (023) 9259 2107
F: (023) 9257 1644

HORTON
Dorset

The Horton Inn ◆◆◆◆
Cranborne Road, Horton, Wimborne Minster, Dorset BH21 5AD
T: (01258) 840252
F: (01258) 841400
E: thehorton@btinternet.com
I: www.welcome.to/thehortoninn

HOUGHTON
Hampshire

Rowans ◆◆◆◆
Houghton, Stockbridge, Hampshire SO20 6LT
T: (01794) 388551

HUNGERFORD
Berkshire

Alderborne House ◆◆◆◆
33 Bourne Vale, Hungerford, Berkshire RG17 0LL
T: (01488) 683228
E: honeybones@hungerford.co.uk
I: www.smoothhound.co.uk/hotels/alderborne.html

Anne's B & B ◆◆◆
59 Priory Avenue, Hungerford, Berkshire RG17 0AS
T: (01488) 682290
F: (01488) 686993

Fishers Farm ◆◆◆◆
Ermin Street, Shefford Woodlands, Hungerford, Berkshire RG17 7AB
T: (01488) 648466 &
07973 691901
F: (01488) 648706
E: mail@fishersfarm.co.uk
I: www.fishersfarm.co.uk

Marshgate Cottage Hotel ◆◆◆◆
Marsh Lane, Hungerford, Berkshire RG17 0QX
T: (01488) 682307
F: (01488) 685475
E: reservations@marshgate.co.uk
I: www.marshgate.co.uk

Wilton House ◆◆◆◆
33 High Street, Hungerford, Berkshire RG17 0NF
T: (01488) 684228
F: (01488) 685037
E: welfares@hotmail.com
I: www.wiltonhouse.freeserve.co.uk

HUNTINGFORD
Dorset

Huntingford Oak ◆◆◆◆
Huntingford, Gillingham, Dorset SP8 5QH
T: (01747) 860574

HURN
Dorset

Avon Causeway Inn ◆◆◆
Hurn, Christchurch, Dorset BH23 6AS
T: (01202) 482714
F: (01202) 477416
E: avoncauseway@wadworth.co.uk
I: www.avoncausewayhotel.co.uk

SOUTH OF ENGLAND

HURSTBOURNE PRIORS
Hampshire
The Hurstbourne ◆◆◆
Hurstbourne Priors, Whitchurch,
Hampshire RG28 7SE
T: (01256) 892000
F: (01256) 895351
E: jwessen@hotmail.com

HYTHE
Hampshire
Changri-La ◆◆◆◆
12 Ashleigh Close, Hythe,
Southampton SO45 3QP
T: (023) 8084 6664

IBTHORPE
Hampshire
Staggs Cottage ◆◆
Windmill Hill, Ibthorpe, Andover,
Hampshire SP11 0BP
T: (01264) 736235
F: (01264) 736597
E: staggscottage@aol.com

IFFLEY
Oxfordshire
Bramley House ◆◆◆
76 Iffley Turn, Iffley, Oxford
OX4 4HN
T: (01865) 770824
E: joyce.stephen@talk21
I: www.bramleyhouse.20m.com/

INKPEN
Berkshire
The Crown & Garter ◆◆◆◆
Great Common, Inkpen,
Hungerford, Berkshire
RG17 9QR
T: (01488) 668325
F: (01488) 669072
I: www.crownandgarter.com

The Swan Inn ◆◆◆◆
Inkpen, Hungerford, Berkshire
RG17 9DX
T: (01488) 668326
F: (01488) 668306
E: enquiries@
theswaninn-organics.co.uk
I: www.theswaninn-organics.
co.uk

IVINGHOE
Buckinghamshire
The Old Forge ◆◆◆◆
5 High Street, Ivinghoe, Leighton
Buzzard, Bedfordshire LU7 9EP
T: (01296) 668122
F: (01296) 668122
E: hotelsainfotel.co.uk.h25076

IWERNE MINSTER
Dorset
Cleff House ◆◆◆◆◆
Brookmans Valley, Iwerne
Minster, Blandford Forum,
Dorset DT11 8NG
T: (01747) 811129 & 811112
F: (01747) 811112

JORDANS
Buckinghamshire
**Old Jordans Guest House &
Conference Centre** ◆◆◆
Jordans Lane, Jordans,
Beaconsfield, Buckinghamshire
HP9 2SW
T: (01494) 879700
F: (01494) 875657
E: info@oldjordans.org.uk
I: www.oldjordans.org.uk

KELMSCOTT
Oxfordshire
Bradshaws Farmhouse
Rating Applied For
Kelmscott, Lechlade,
Gloucestershire GL7 3HD
T: (01367) 252519
F: (01367) 244800

KENNINGTON
Oxfordshire
The Lawns ◆◆◆
10 Jackson Drive, Kennington,
Oxford OX1 5LL
T: (01865) 739595
F: (01865) 437520

The Poplars ◆◆
204 Poplar Grove, Kennington,
Oxford, Oxfordshire OX1 5QT
T: (01865) 326443
F: (01865) 739133

KIDLINGTON
Oxfordshire
Breffni House ◆◆
9 Lovelace Drive, Kidlington,
Oxfordshire OX5 2LY
T: (01865) 372569

55 Nethercote Road ◆◆◆
Tackley, Kidlington, Oxford,
OX5 3AT
T: (01869) 331255 &
07790 338225
F: (01869) 331670

Warsborough House
Rating Applied For
52 Mill Street, Kidlington,
Oxfordshire OX5 2EF
T: (01865) 370316
F: (01865) 370316

Wise Alderman Inn ◆◆◆
249 Banbury Road, Kidlington,
Oxford, Oxfordshire OX5 1BF
T: (01865) 372281
F: (01865) 370153

KIMMERIDGE
Dorset
Kimmeridge Farmhouse
◆◆◆◆
Kimmeridge, Wareham, Dorset
BH20 5PE
T: (01929) 480990
F: (01929) 481503
E: kimmeridgefarmhouse@
hotmail.com

KINGHAM
Oxfordshire
The Plough Inn ◆◆◆
17 The Green, Kingham, Oxford,
Oxfordshire OX7 6YD
T: (01608) 658327

KINGSTON
Hampshire
Greenacres Farmhouse ◆◆◆◆
Christchurch Road, Kingston,
Ringwood, Hampshire BH24 3BJ
T: (01425) 480945
F: (01425) 480945
E: paddy@strongarm.freeserve.
co.uk

Kingston Country Courtyard
◆◆◆◆
Greystone Court, Kingston,
Corfe Castle, Wareham, Dorset
BH20 5LR
T: (01929) 481066
F: (01929) 481256
E: kingstoncountrycourt@
talk21.com
I: www.
kingstoncountrycourtyard.co.uk
♿

KINGTON MAGNA
Dorset
Kington Manor Farm ◆◆◆◆
Church Hill, Kington Magna,
Gillingham, Dorset SP8 5EG
T: (01747) 838371
F: (01747) 838371

KINTBURY
Berkshire
Holt Lodge ◆◆◆◆
Kintbury, Hungerford, Berkshire
RG17 9SX
T: (01488) 668244
F: (01488) 668244
E: johnfreeland@holtlodge.
freeserve.co.uk

KIRTLINGTON
Oxfordshire
Vicarage Farm ◆◆◆◆
Kirtlington, Oxford OX5 3JY
T: (01869) 350254
F: (01869) 350254
E: jahunter@freenet.co.uk
I: www.country-accom.
co.uk/vicaragefarm

LAKE
Isle of Wight
Ashleigh House Hotel ◆◆◆◆
81 Sandown Road, Lake,
Sandown, Isle of Wight
PO36 9LE
T: (01983) 402340 & 403835

Cliff Lodge ◆◆◆
13 Cliff Path, Lake, Sandown,
Isle of Wight PO36 8PL
T: (01983) 402963

Haytor Lodge ◆◆◆◆
16 Cliff Path, Lake, Sandown,
Isle of Wight PO36 8PL
T: (01983) 402969

Osterley Lodge ◆◆◆
62 Sandown Road, Lake,
Sandown, Isle of Wight
PO36 9JX
T: (01983) 402017
F: (01983) 402017
E: osterleylodge@netguides.
co.uk
I: www.netguides.
co.uk/wight/basic/osterley.html

Pebblecombe Guest House ◆◆
48 Sandown Road, Lake,
Sandown, Isle of Wight
PO36 9JT
T: (01983) 402609
F: (01983) 402609

Piers View Guest House ◆◆◆
20 Cliff Path, Lake, Sandown,
Isle of Wight PO36 8PL
T: (01983) 404646
E: piers-view@zoom.co.uk

LANGFORD
Oxfordshire
Dovecote House ◆◆◆◆
Filkins Road, Langford, GL7 3LW
T: (01367) 860289 & 860711
F: (01367) 860711
E: dovecote@hotmail.com

LANGTON LONG
Dorset
The Old Brew House ◆◆◆◆◆
Langton Long, Blandford Forum,
Dorset DT11 9HR
T: (01258) 452861
F: (01258) 450718

LEAFIELD
Oxfordshire
Greenside Cottage ◆◆◆
The Ridings, Leafield, Oxford
OX29 9NN
T: (01993) 878368
F: (01993) 878368

Langley Farm ◆◆◆
Langley, Oxford OX29 9QD
T: (01993) 878686 &
0797 0955924

Pond View ◆◆◆
Fairspear Road, Leafield, Oxford
OX8 9NT
T: (01993) 878133

LECKHAMPSTEAD
Buckinghamshire
Weatherhead Farm
Rating Applied For
Leckhampstead, Buckingham
MK18 5NP
T: (01280) 860502 &
07779 264074
F: (01280) 860535

LEE ON THE SOLENT
Hampshire
Apple Tree Cottage ◆◆◆
159 Portsmouth Road, Lee on
the Solent, Hampshire
PO13 9AD
T: (023) 9255 1176
F: (023) 9235 2492
E: lmgell@aol.com

Avon Manor Guest House
◆◆◆
12 South Place, Lee on the
Solent, Hampshire PO13 9AS
T: (023) 9255 2773
E: karen@avonmanor.fsnet.
co.uk
I: www.avonmanor.co.uk

Chester Lodge ◆◆◆
20 Chester Crescent, Lee on the
Solent, Hampshire PO13 9BH
T: (023) 9255 0894 & 9255 0894
F: (023) 9255 6291

Kings Lodge Guest House
◆◆◆
16 Kings Road, Lee on the
Solent, Hampshire PO13 9NU
T: (023) 9255 2118
E: john@kings-lodge.fsbusiness.
co.uk
I: www.kingslodgeguesthouse.
co.uk

LEWKNOR
Oxfordshire
Moorcourt Cottage
Rating Applied For
Weston Road, Lewknor, Oxford
OX49 5RU
T: (01844) 351419
F: (01844) 351419
E: p.hodgson@freeuk.com

LIPHOOK
Hampshire

The Bailiff's Cottage ◆◆◆
Hollycombe, Liphook, Hampshire
GU30 7LR
T: (01428) 722171
F: (01428) 729394
E: jenner@bailiffs.fsnet.co.uk

LISS
Hampshire

Greywalls House ◆◆◆
London Road, Hillbrow, Liss,
Hampshire GU33 7QR
T: (01730) 894246 & 895596
F: (01730) 894865
E: hillbrow.la@lineone.net
I: www.bidbury.co.uk

LITTLE CHESTERTON
Oxfordshire

Cover Point ◆◆◆◆
Little Chesterton, Bicester,
Oxfordshire OX6 8PD
T: (01869) 252500
F: (01869) 252500
E: lamb@coverpoint100.
freeserve.co.uk

LOCKERLEY
Hampshire

Dunmeads ◆◆◆◆
Butts Green, Lockerley, Romsey,
Hampshire SO51 0JG
T: (01794) 340568
E: alecraymond@thew99.co.uk

St Brelade ◆◆
Top Green, Lockerley, Romsey,
Hampshire SO51 0JP
T: (01794) 340603
E: goodrg@waitrose.com

LONG HANBOROUGH
Oxfordshire

The Close Guest House ◆◆◆
Witney Road, Long Hanborough,
Oxford OX8 8HF
T: (01993) 882485 & 883819
F: (01993) 883819

Old Farmhouse ◆◆◆◆
Station Hill, Long Hanborough,
Oxford, Oxfordshire OX8 8JZ
T: (01993) 882097
E: old.farm@virgin.net

LONGPARISH
Hampshire

Yew Cottage Bed & Breakfast
◆◆◆
Yew Cottage, Longparish,
Andover, Hampshire SP11 6QE
T: (01264) 720325 &
0777 1675341
E: yewcottage@ukgateway.net

LOUDWATER
Buckinghamshire

Trevona
Rating Applied For
7 Derehams Lane, Loudwater,
High Wycombe,
Buckinghamshire HP10 9RH
T: (01494) 526715

LYMINGTON
Hampshire

Angel Inn ◆◆◆
108 High Street, Lymington,
Hampshire SO41 9AP
T: (01590) 672050
F: (01590) 671661
I: www.stayhere.uk.com

Birchcroft ◆◆◆
Westfield Road, Lymington,
Hampshire SO41 3QB
T: (01590) 688844
F: (01590) 688766

Britannia House ◆◆◆◆◆
Mill Lane, Lymington, Hampshire
SO41 9AY
T: (01590) 672091
F: (01590) 672091
E: enquiries@britannia-house.
com
I: www.britannia-house.com

Cedars ◆◆◆
2 Linden Way, Highfield,
Lymington, Hampshire SO41 9JU
T: (01590) 676468

Dolphins ◆◆◆◆
6 Emsworth Road, Lymington,
Hampshire SO41 9BL
T: (01590) 676108 &
07958 727536
F: (01590) 688275
E: dolphins@easynet.co.uk

Durlston Guest House ◆◆◆◆
Durlston House, Gosport Street,
Lymington, Hampshire
SO41 9EG
T: (01590) 676908 & 677364

Efford Cottage ◆◆◆◆◆
Everton, Lymington, Hampshire
SO41 0JD
T: (01590) 642315
F: (01590) 641030
E: effcottage@aol.com
I: www.SmoothHound.
co.uk/hotels/effordco.html

Gleneagles ◆◆◆◆
34 Belmore Road, Lymington,
Hampshire SO41 3NT
T: (01590) 675958
F: (01590) 675958
E: gleneagles34@hotmail.com

Gorse Meadow Guest House
◆◆◆
Gorse Meadow, Sway Road,
Lymington, Hampshire SO41 8LR
T: (01590) 673354
F: (01590) 673336
E: gorsemeadow.guesthouse@
wildmushrooms.co.uk
I: www.@wildmushrooms.co.uk

Hideaway ◆◆◆
Middle Common Road,
Pennington, Lymington,
Hampshire SO41 8LE
T: (01590) 676974 &
07956 520802
F: (01590) 676974
I: www.newforest.demon.
co.uk/hideaway.htm

The Hillsman House ◆◆◆◆◆
74 Milford Road, Lymington,
Hampshire SO41 8DP
T: (01590) 674737
E: caroline@hillsman-house.
co.uk
I: www.newforest.demon.
co.uk/hillsman.htm

The Mayflower Inn ◆◆◆◆
Kings Saltern Road, Lymington,
Hampshire SO41 3QD
T: (01590) 672160
E: mayflower@lymington.
fsbusiness.co.uk

Monks Pool ◆◆◆◆
Waterford Lane, Lymington,
Hampshire SO41 3PS
T: (01590) 678850
F: (01590) 678850
E: cam@monkspool.swinternet.
co.uk
I: www.camandjohn.com

Moonraker Cottage ◆◆◆◆
62 Milford Road, Lymington,
Hampshire SO41 8DU
T: (01590) 678677 &
07790 057727
F: (01590) 678677

Our Bench ◆◆◆◆
9 Lodge Road, Pennington,
Lymington, Hampshire
SO41 8HH
T: (01590) 673141
F: (01590) 673141
E: enquiries@ourbench.co.uk
I: www.ourbench.co.uk
♿

Pennavon House ◆◆◆◆
Lower Pennington Lane,
Lymington, Hampshire SO41 8AL
T: (01590) 673984

Rosefield House ◆◆◆◆◆
Sway Road, Lymington,
Hampshire SO41 8LR
T: (01590) 671526
F: (01590) 689007

The Rowans ◆◆◆◆
76 Southampton Road,
Lymington, Hampshire
SO41 9GZ
T: (01590) 672276 &
07860 630361
F: (01590) 688610
E: the.rowans@totalise.co.uk

40 Southampton Road ◆◆◆◆
Lymington, Hampshire
SO41 9GG
T: (01590) 672237
F: (01590) 673592

Tranmere House ◆◆◆◆
Tranmere Close, Lymington,
Hampshire SO41 3QQ
T: (01590) 671983 &
07967 845334
E: tranmere.house@tesco.net
I: www.tranmere_house.co.uk

The Vicarage ◆◆◆
Grove Road, Lymington,
Hampshire SO41 3RF
T: (01590) 673847
F: (01590) 673847
E: junovicarage@hotmail.com

Woodslee ◆◆◆◆
Sway Road, Lymington,
Hampshire SO41 8LR
T: (01590) 676572
F: (01590) 676572

LYNDHURST
Hampshire

Beechen House ◆◆◆
Clay Hill, Lyndhurst, Hampshire
SO43 7DN
T: (023) 8028 3584

Beechwood House
Rating Applied For
Allum Green, Lyndhurst,
Hampshire SO43 7GR
T: (023) 8028 4746

Burwood Lodge ◆◆◆◆
27 Romsey Road, Lyndhurst,
Hampshire SO43 7AA
T: (023) 8028 2445
F: (023) 8028 4104

Clayhill House ◆◆◆◆
Clayhill, Lyndhurst, Hampshire
SO43 7DE
T: (023) 8028 2304 &
07989 536837
F: (023) 8028 2093
E: clayhillhouse@tinyworld.
co.uk
I: www.newforest.demon.
co.uk/clayhill.htm

Englefield ◆◆◆◆
Chapel Lane, Lyndhurst,
Hampshire SO43 7FG
T: (023) 8028 2685

Forest Cottage ◆◆◆◆
High Street, Lyndhurst,
Hampshire SO43 7BH
T: (023) 8028 3461
I: www.forestcottage.i12.com

Little Hayes ◆◆◆◆
43 Romsey Road, Lyndhurst,
Hampshire SO43 7AR
T: (023) 8028 3816

Lyndhurst House ◆◆◆◆
35 Romsey Road, Lyndhurst,
Hampshire SO43 7AR
T: (023) 8028 2230
F: (023) 8028 2230
E: bcjwood@lyndhouse.
freeserve.co.uk
I: www.newforest.demon.
co.uk/lynho.html

Pen Cottage ◆◆◆
Bournemouth Road, Swan
Green, Lyndhurst, Hampshire
SO43 7DP
T: (023) 8028 2075

The Penny Farthing Hotel
◆◆◆◆
Romsey Road, Lyndhurst,
Hampshire SO43 7AA
T: (023) 8028 4422
F: (023) 8028 4488
E: stay@pennyfarthinghotel.
co.uk
I: www.pennyfarthinghotel.
co.uk

Reepham House ◆◆◆◆
12 Romsey Road, Lyndhurst,
Hampshire SO43 7AA
T: (023) 8028 3091
F: (023) 8028 3091

Rose Cottage ◆◆◆◆
Chapel Lane, Lyndhurst,
Hampshire SO43 7FG
T: (023) 8028 3413
F: (023) 8028 3413
E: cindy@rosecottageb-b.
freeserve.co.uk
I: www.rosecottageb-b.
freeserve.co.uk/

Rosedale Bed & Breakfast
◆◆◆
24 Shaggs Meadow, Lyndhurst,
Hampshire SO43 7BN
T: (023) 8028 3793
E: jenny@theangels.freeserve.
co.uk

Rufus House Hotel ◆◆◆◆
Southampton Road, Lyndhurst,
Hampshire SO43 7BQ
T: (023) 8028 2930 & 8028 2200
F: (023) 8028 2930
E: rufushotel@dcintra.fsnet.
co.uk

Southview ◆◆◆
Gosport Lane, Lyndhurst,
Hampshire SO43 7BL
T: (023) 8028 2224
E: gburbidge@virgin.net

Temple Lodge Guest House
◆◆◆◆
Queens Road, Lyndhurst,
Hampshire SO43 7BR
T: (023) 8028 2392
F: (023) 8028 4590
E: templelodge@lineone.net

MAIDENHEAD
Berkshire

Cartlands Cottage ◆
Kings Lane, Cookham Dean,
Cookham, Maidenhead,
Berkshire SL6 9AY
T: (01628) 482196

Clifton Guest House ◆◆◆
21 Crauford Rise, Maidenhead,
Berkshire SL6 7LR
T: (01628) 623572 & 620086
F: (01628) 623572
E: clifton@aroram.freeserve.
co.uk
I: www.cliftonguesthouse.co.uk

Moor Farm ◆◆◆◆
Ascot Road, Holyport,
Maidenhead, Berkshire SL6 2HY
T: (01628) 633761
F: (01628) 636167
E: moorfm@aol.com

Sheephouse Manor ◆◆◆
Sheephouse Road, Maidenhead,
Berkshire SL6 8HJ
T: (01628) 776902
F: (01628) 625138
E: info@sheephousemanor.
co.uk
I: www.sheephousemanor.co.uk

MARLOW
Buckinghamshire

Acha Pani ◆◆
Bovingdon Green, Marlow,
Buckinghamshire SL7 2JL
T: (01628) 483435
F: (01628) 483435
E: mary@achapani.freeserve.
co.uk

Acorn Lodge ◆◆◆
79 Marlow Bottom Road,
Marlow Bottom, Marlow,
Buckinghamshire SL7 3NA
T: (01628) 472197 &
0771 8757601
F: (01628) 472197

The Boundary ◆◆◆◆
Seymour Plain, Marlow,
Buckinghamshire SL7 3DA
T: (01628) 476674 &
07768 351459

16 Claremont Road ◆◆
Marlow, Buckinghamshire
SL7 1BW
T: (01628) 471334 &
07774 107445
E: sue@gladeend.com
I: www.gladeend.com

The Country House ◆◆◆◆
Bisham, Marlow,
Buckinghamshire SL7 1RP
T: (01628) 890606
F: (01628) 890983

Four Winds ◆◆◆
18 Bovingdon Heights, Marlow,
Buckinghamshire SL7 2JS
T: (01628) 476567 & 481710
F: (01628) 481711
E: gooding@globalnet.co.uk

Granny Anne's
Rating Applied For
54 Seymour Park Road, Marlow,
Buckinghamshire SL7 3EP
T: (01628) 473086
F: (01628) 472721

Holly Tree House ◆◆◆◆
Burford Close, Marlow Bottom,
Marlow, Buckinghamshire
SL7 3NE
T: (01628) 891110
F: (01628) 481278

The Inn on the Green Limited
◆◆◆◆
The Old Cricket Common,
Cookham Dean, Cookham,
Maidenhead, Berkshire SL6 9NZ
T: (01628) 482638
F: (01628) 487474
E: enquiries@theinnonthegreen.
com
I: www.theinnonthegreen.com

31 Institute Road ◆◆
Marlow, Buckinghamshire
SL7 1BJ
T: (01628) 485662

10 Lock Road ◆◆◆
Marlow, Buckinghamshire
SL7 1QP
T: (01628) 473875 &
07899 913805

Merrie Hollow ◆◆◆
Seymour Court Hill, Marlow
Road, Marlow, Buckinghamshire
SL7 3DE
T: (01628) 485663
F: (01628) 485663

Nia Roo ◆◆◆
4 Pound Crescent, Marlow,
Buckinghamshire SL7 2BG
T: (01628) 486679
F: (01628) 486679

Oak Lodge ◆◆◆
29 Oaktree Road, Marlow,
Buckinghamshire SL7 3ED
T: (01628) 472145 &
07973 842616

Red Barn Farm ◆◆◆
Marlow Road, Marlow,
Buckinghamshire SL7 3DQ
T: (01494) 882820
F: (01494) 883545

Riverdale ◆◆◆
Marlow Bridge Lane, Marlow,
Buckinghamshire SL7 1RH
T: (01628) 485206
E: chrisrawlings@onetel.net.uk

18 Rookery Court ◆◆◆
Marlow, Buckinghamshire
SL7 3HR
T: (01628) 486451 &
07970 555814
F: (01628) 486451
E: gillbullen@compuserve.com

**Rosemary Cottage Bed &
Breakfast** ◆◆◆◆
99 Heath End Road, Flackwell
Heath, High Wycombe,
Buckinghamshire HP10 9ES
T: (01628) 520635
F: (01628) 520635
E: mike.1@virgin.net
I: www.reservation.co.uk

Sneppen House ◆◆◆◆
Henley Road, Marlow,
Buckinghamshire SL7 2DF
T: (01628) 485227

Sunnyside ◆◆
Munday Dean Lane, Marlow,
Buckinghamshire SL7 3BU
T: (01628) 485701
E: ruthandtom@tinyworld.co.uk

The White House ◆◆◆
194 Little Marlow Road, Marlow,
Buckinghamshire SL7 1HX
T: (01628) 485765
F: (01628) 485765

MARLOW BOTTOM
Buckinghamshire

61 Hill Farm Road ◆◆
Marlow Bottom, Marlow,
Buckinghamshire SL7 3LX
T: (01628) 475145 &
07768 923331
F: (01628) 475775
E: p.simmons@ukonline.co.uk

63 Hill Farm Road ◆◆
Marlow Bottom, Marlow,
Buckinghamshire SL7 3LX
T: (01628) 472970 &
07958 524438

50A New Road ◆◆◆
Marlow Bottom, Marlow,
Buckinghamshire SL7 3NW
T: (01628) 472666

Number One B & B ◆◆◆
1 Meadow View, Marlow
Bottom, Buckinghamshire
SL7 3PA
T: (01628) 483426
E: number.one.bed.and.
breakfast@dial.pipex.com

T J O'Reillys ◆◆◆
61 Marlow Bottom Road,
Marlow Bottom, Marlow,
Buckinghamshire SL7 3NA
T: (01628) 891187
F: (01628) 484926

MARNHULL
Dorset

The Old Bank ◆◆◆
Burton Street, Marnhull,
Sturminster Newton, Dorset
DT10 1PH
T: (01258) 821019
F: (01258) 821019

Yew House Farm ◆◆◆◆
Husseys, Marnhull, Sturminster
Newton, Dorset DT10 1PD
T: (01258) 820412
F: (01258) 821044

MARSH GIBBON
Buckinghamshire

Judges Close ◆◆◆
West Edge, Marsh Gibbon,
Bicester, Oxfordshire OX27 0HA
T: (01869) 278508 & 277528
F: (01869) 277189
E: royllambourne1@
farmersweekly.net

MENTMORE
Buckinghamshire

The Orchard ◆◆◆
Mentmore, Leighton Buzzard,
Bedfordshire LU7 0QF
T: (01296) 662189 & 668976
F: (01296) 662189
E: jan.hc@virgin.net

MERSTONE
Isle of Wight

Redway Farm ◆◆◆◆
Merstone, Newport, Isle of
Wight PO30 3DJ
T: (01983) 865228
F: (01983) 865228
E: redway@wrightfarmholidays.
co.uk
I: www.wrightfarmholidays.
co.uk OR www.redway-farm.
co.uk

MIDDLE ASTON
Oxfordshire

Home Farm House ◆◆◆
Middle Aston, Oxford OX25 5PX
T: (01869) 340666
F: (01869) 347789
E: cparsons@telinco.co.uk
I: www.country-accom.
co.uk/home-farm-house

MIDDLE WALLOP
Hampshire

**The George Inn – Middle
Wallop** ◆◆◆◆
The Crossroads, Middle Wallop,
Stockbridge, Hampshire
SO20 8EG
T: (01264) 781224
E: joanne.george@virgin.net

MIDGHAM
Berkshire

The Paddock ◆◆◆
Midgham Green, Midgham,
Reading RG7 5TT
T: (0118) 971 3098
F: (0118) 971 2925
E: david.cantwell@virgin.net

MILFORD-ON-SEA
Hampshire

Alma Mater ◆◆◆◆
4 Knowland Drive, Milford-on-
Sea, Lymington, Hampshire
SO41 0RH
T: (01590) 642811
F: (01590) 642811
E: bandbalmamater@aol.com
I: www.almamater.org.uk

The Bay Trees ◆◆◆◆◆
8 High Street, Milford-on-Sea,
Lymington, Hampshire
SO41 0QD
T: (01590) 642186
F: (01590) 645461
E: thebaytrees@netscapeonline.
co.uk
I: www.newforestbandb.com

Briantcroft
Rating Applied For
George Road, Milford-on-Sea,
Lymington, Hampshire
SO41 0RS
T: (01590) 644355
F: (01590) 644355

Compton Hotel ◆◆◆
59 Keyhaven Road, Milford-on-
Sea, Lymington, Hampshire
SO41 0QX
T: (01590) 643117
F: (01590) 643117
E: dbembo@talk21.com

Ha'Penny House ◆◆◆◆
16 Whitby Road, Milford-on-
Sea, Lymington, Hampshire
SO41 0ND
T: (01590) 641210
F: (01590) 641227
E: info@hapennyhouse.co.uk

Laburnum Cottage ◆◆◆
19 Carrington Lane, Milford-on-
Sea, Lymington, Hampshire
SO41 0RA
T: (01590) 644225

Sun Cottage ◆◆◆◆
Barnes Lane, Milford-on-Sea,
Lymington, Hampshire
SO41 0RR
T: (01590) 644840
F: (01590) 642064

MILTON ABBAS
Dorset

Dunbury Heights ◆◆◆◆
Milton Abbas, Blandford Forum,
Dorset DT11 0DH
T: (01258) 880445

MILTON COMMON
Oxfordshire

Byways ◆◆◆◆
Old London Road, Milton
Common, Oxford OX9 2JR
T: (01844) 279386
F: (01844) 279386

MILTON KEYNES
Buckinghamshire

Chantry Farm ◆◆◆
Pindon End, Hanslope, Milton
Keynes MK19 7HL
T: (01908) 510269 &
07850 166122
F: (01908) 510269

Conifers Bed & Breakfast ◆◆
29 William Smith Close,
Woolstone, Milton Keynes
MK15 0AN
T: (01908) 674506
F: (01908) 550628

The Croft ◆◆◆
Little Crawley, Newport Pagnell,
Buckinghamshire MK16 9LT
T: (01234) 391296

Furtho Manor Farm ◆◆◆
Old Stratford, Milton Keynes,
MK19 6NR
T: (01908) 542139
F: (01908) 542139
E: dsansome@farming.co.uk

The Grange Stables ◆◆◆
Winslow Road, Great Horwood,
Milton Keynes MK17 0QN
T: (01296) 712051
F: (01296) 714991
E: grangestables@suncheck.
demon.co.uk

Haversham Grange ◆◆◆◆
Haversham, Milton Keynes
MK19 7DX
T: (01908) 312389
F: (01908) 312389
E: smithers@
haversham-grange.co.uk

Kingfishers ◆◆◆
9 Rylstone Close, Heelands,
Milton Keynes MK13 7QT
T: (01908) 310231 & 318601
F: (01908) 318601
E: sheila-derek@m-keynes.
freeserve.co.uk
I: www.smoothhound.
co.uk/hotels/kingfishers.html

Manor Farm House ◆◆◆
South Street, Castlethorpe,
Milton Keynes MK19 7EL
T: (01908) 510216
F: (01908) 510216
E: manorfarmhouse@aol.com

Milford Leys Farm ◆◆
Castlethorpe, Milton Keynes
MK19 7HH
T: (01908) 510153

Mill Farm ◆◆◆
Gayhurst, Newport Pagnell,
Buckinghamshire MK16 8LT
T: (01908) 611489 &
07714 719640
F: (01908) 611489
E: adamsmillfarm@aol.com

The Old Bakery Hotel ◆◆◆◆
Main Street, Cosgrove, Milton
Keynes MK19 7JL
T: (01908) 263103 & 262255
F: (01908) 263620

The Old Rectory ◆◆◆
Drayton Road, Newton Longville,
Milton Keynes, Buckinghamshire
MK17 0BH
T: (01908) 375794

Oldhams Field House
Rating Applied For
Nash Road, Beachampton,
Milton Keynes, Buckinghamshire
MK19 6EA
T: (01908) 568094

Rose Cottage Guest
Accommodation ◆◆◆◆
Broughton Road, Salford, Milton
Keynes, Buckinghamshire
MK17 8BQ
T: (01908) 582239 &
07702 587648
F: (01908) 282029
E: info@rosecottagemk.co.uk
I: www.rosecottagemk.co.uk

Spinney Lodge Farm ◆◆◆
Forest Road, Hanslope, Milton
Keynes MK19 7DE
T: (01908) 510267

Vignoble ◆◆◆
2 Medland, Woughton Park,
Milton Keynes MK6 3BH
T: (01908) 666804
F: (01908) 666626
E: vignoblegh@aol.com

MINSTEAD
Hampshire

Grove House ◆◆
Newtown, Minstead, Lyndhurst,
Hampshire SO43 7GG
T: (023) 8081 3211

The Trusty Servant ◆◆◆
Minstead, Lyndhurst, Hampshire
SO43 7FY
T: (023) 8081 2137

MINSTER LOVELL
Oxfordshire

Hill Grove Farm ◆◆◆◆
Crawley Road, Minster Lovell,
Oxford OX29 0NA
T: (01993) 703120
F: (01993) 700528
E: kbrown@eggconnect.net

MORETON
Oxfordshire

Elm Tree Farmhouse ◆◆◆◆
Moreton, Thame, Oxfordshire
OX9 2HR
T: (01844) 213692
F: (01844) 215369
E: wendy@elmtreefarmhouse.
co.uk
I: www.elmtreefarmhouse.co.uk

MOTCOMBE
Dorset

The Coppleridge Inn ◆◆◆◆
Elm Hill, Motcombe,
Shaftesbury, Dorset SP7 9HW
T: (01747) 851980
F: (01747) 851858
E: thecoppleridgeinn@
btinternet.com
I: www.coppleridge.com
🏠

Manor Farm ◆◆◆◆
Motcombe, Shaftesbury, Dorset
SP7 9PL
T: (01747) 853811
F: (01747) 853811
E: manor.motcombe@talk21

Shorts Green Farm ◆◆◆◆
Motcombe, Shaftesbury, Dorset
SP7 9PA
T: (01747) 852260
F: (01747) 852260

MOTTISTONE
Isle of Wight

Mottistone Manor Farm
◆◆◆◆
Mottistone, Newport, Isle of
Wight PO30 4ED
T: (01983) 740232

MOULSFORD ON THAMES
Oxfordshire

White House ◆◆◆◆
Moulsford on Thames,
Wallingford, Oxfordshire
OX10 9JD
T: (01491) 651397 &
07831 372243
F: (01491) 652560

MUDEFORD
Dorset

Seahaze ◆◆◆◆
4 Rook Hill Road, Friars Cliff,
Mudeford, Christchurch, Dorset
BH23 4DZ
T: (01425) 270866
F: (01425) 278285
E: seahaze@eggconnect.net

MURSLEY
Buckinghamshire

Fourpenny Cottage ◆◆◆◆
Main Street, Mursley, Milton
Keynes, Buckinghamshire
MK17 0RT
T: (01296) 720544
F: (01296) 720906

Richmond Hill Farm ◆◆◆
Stewkley Lane, Mursley, Milton
Keynes MK17 0JD
T: (01296) 720385
F: (01296) 730385

NAPHILL
Buckinghamshire

Woodpeckers ◆◆◆
244 Main Road, Naphill, High
Wycombe, Buckinghamshire
HP14 4RX
T: (01494) 563728 &
07775 694015
E: angela.brand@virgin.net

NETHER WALLOP
Hampshire

Halcyon ◆◆◆
Church Hill, Nether Wallop,
Stockbridge, Hampshire
SO20 8EY
T: (01264) 781348

York Lodge ◆◆◆◆
Nether Wallop, Stockbridge,
Hampshire SO20 8HE
T: (01264) 781313 &
07776 126508
F: (01264) 781313
E: bradley@yorklodge.fslife.com

NETLEY ABBEY
Hampshire

The Prince Consort ◆◆◆
71 Victoria Road, Netley Abbey,
Southampton, Hampshire
SO31 5DQ
T: (023) 8045 2676
F: (023) 8045 6334

NEW MILTON
Hampshire

Canada Cottage ◆◆◆◆
New Lane, Bashley, New Milton,
Hamphire BH25 5TE
T: (01425) 627446 & 07790 850
562

Jobz-A-Gudn ◆◆◆◆
169 Stem Lane, New Milton,
Hamphire BH25 5ND
T: (01425) 615435 &
07866 881426
F: (01425) 615435

St Ursula ◆◆◆
30 Hobart Road, New Milton,
Hamphire BH25 6EG
T: (01425) 613515
🏠

Taverners Cottage ◆◆◆◆
Bashley Cross Road, Bashley,
New Milton, Hampshire
BH25 5SZ
T: (01425) 615403 &
07966 463466
F: (01425) 615403
E: jbaines@supanet.com
I: www.taverners.cottage.bandb.
baines.com

Willy's Well ◆◆◆
Bashley Common Road,
Wootton, New Milton, Hamphire
BH25 5SF
T: (01425) 616834
E: myoramac@hotmail.com

NEWBRIDGE
Isle of Wight

Homestead Farmhouse ◆◆◆
Newbridge, Yarmouth, Isle of
Wight PO41 0TZ
T: (01983) 531270 &
07836 583982
F: (01983) 531270

NEWBURY
Berkshire

The Bacon Arms ◆◆◆
10 Oxford Street, Newbury,
Berkshire RG14 1JB
T: (01635) 31822
F: (01635) 552496

10 Cheviot Close ◆◆◆
Wash Common, Newbury,
Berkshire RG14 6SQ
T: (01635) 48887
E: taciliaok@aol.com

Little Paddocks ◆◆◆
Woolhampton Hill,
Woolhampton, Reading
RG7 5SY
T: (0118) 971 3451
F: (0118) 971 3451
E: annie_pat@gardner38.
freeserve.co.uk

Livingstone House ◆◆◆
48 Queens Road, Newbury,
Berkshire RG14 7PA
T: (01635) 45444
F: (01635) 45444

The Old Farmhouse ◆◆◆◆
Downend Lane, Chieveley,
Newbury, Berkshire RG20 8TN
T: (01635) 248361 &
07970 583373
F: (01635) 528195
E: palletts@aol.com
I: www.smoothhound.
co.uk/hotels/oldfarmhouse

Rookwood Farmhouse ◆◆◆◆
Stockcross, Newbury, Berkshire
RG20 8JX
T: (01488) 608676
F: (01488) 657961

White Cottage ◆◆◆
Newtown, Hungerford, Berkshire
RG20 9AP
T: (01635) 43097 &
07721 613224
F: (01635) 43097
E: ellie@p-p-i.fsnet.co.uk

The White Hart Inn ◆◆◆◆
Kintbury Road, Hamstead
Marshall, Newbury, Berkshire
RG20 0HW
T: (01488) 658201
F: (01488) 657192

NEWINGTON
Oxfordshire

Ewe Farm ◆◆
Newington, Wallingford,
Oxfordshire OX10 7AF
T: (01865) 891236

Hill Farm
Rating Applied For
Newington, Wallingford,
Oxfordshire OX10 7AL
T: (01865) 891173

NEWPORT
Isle of Wight

L'Abri ◆◆◆
8 Ulster Crescent, Newport, Isle
of Wight PO30 5RU
T: (01983) 520596

Litten Park Guest House ◆◆◆
48 Medina Avenue, Newport,
Isle of Wight PO30 1EL
T: (01983) 526836

Magnolia House ◆◆◆◆
6 Cypress Road, Newport, Isle of
Wight PO30 1EY
T: (01983) 529489
E: magnoliaiw@aol.com

Newclose House East ◆◆◆◆
134 Watergate Road, Newport,
Isle of Wight PO30 1YP
T: (01983) 826290

Newport Quay Hotel ◆◆◆
41 Quay Street, Newport, Isle of
Wight PO30 5BA
T: (01983) 528544
F: (01983) 527143
I: keith@newportquayhotel.
freeserve.co.uk

Wheatsheaf Hotel ◆◆◆
St Thomas Square, Newport, Isle
of Wight PO30 1SG
T: (01983) 523865
F: (01983) 528255
E: information@
wheatsheaf-iow.co.uk
I: www.wheatsheaf-iow.co.uk

NEWPORT PAGNELL
Buckinghamshire

The Limes ◆◆◆◆◆
North Square, Newport Pagnell,
Buckinghamshire MK16 8EP
T: (01908) 617041 &
07860 908925
F: (01908) 217292
E: royandruth@8thelimes.
freeserve.co.uk

Rectory Farm ◆◆◆
North Crawley, Newport Pagnell,
Buckinghamshire MK16 9HH
T: (01234) 391213

Rosemary House ◆◆◆
7 Hill View, Wolverton Road,
Newport Pagnell,
Buckinghamshire MK16 8BE
T: (01908) 612198
F: (01908) 612198

5 Walnut Close ◆◆
Newport Pagnell,
Buckinghamshire MK16 8JH
T: (01908) 611643
F: (01908) 611643
E: shirleyderek.clitheroe@
btinternet.com

NORTH GORLEY
Hampshire

The Gorley Tea Rooms ◆◆◆◆
Ringwood Road, North Gorley,
Fordingbridge, Hampshire
SP6 2PB
T: (01425) 653427
F: (01425) 653720

NORTH LEIGH
Oxfordshire

Elbie House ◆◆◆◆
East End, North Leigh, Witney,
Oxfordshire OX8 6PZ
T: (01993) 880166 &
07712 462405
E: buck@elbiehouse.freeserve.
co.uk
I: www.smoothhound.
co.uk/hotels/elbiehouse.htm/

Forge Cottage ◆◆
East End, North Leigh,
Woodstock, Oxford OX8 6PZ
T: (01993) 881120
E: jill.french@talk21.com
I: www.country-accom.co.uk
(Forge Cottage)

The Woodman Inn ◆◆◆
New Yatt Road, North Leigh,
Witney, Oxfordshire OX8 6TT
T: (01993) 881790
F: (01993) 881790

NORTH NEWINGTON
Oxfordshire

The Blinking Owl Country Inn
◆◆◆
Main Street, North Newington,
Banbury, Oxfordshire OX15 6AE
T: (01295) 730650

**La Madonette Country Guest
House** ◆◆◆◆
North Newington, Banbury,
Oxfordshire OX15 6AA
T: (01295) 730212
F: (01295) 730363
E: lamadonett@aol.com
I: www.lamadonette.co.uk

NORTHMOOR
Oxfordshire

Rectory Farm ◆◆◆◆
Northmoor, Oxford, Oxfordshire
OX8 1SX
T: (01865) 300207 &
07974 102198
F: (01865) 300559
E: pj.florey@farmline.com

NURSLING
Hampshire

Conifers ◆◆
6 Nursling Street Cottages,
Nursling, Southampton
SO16 0XH
T: (023) 8034 9491 &
07775 830539
F: (023) 8034 9491
E: barbara.hinton@lineone.net

OAKDALE
Dorset

Heathwood Guest House
◆◆◆◆
266 Wimborne Road, Oakdale,
Poole, Dorset BH15 3EF
T: (01202) 679176 & 679746
F: (01202) 679176

OAKLEY
Buckinghamshire

New Farm ◆◆◆
Oxford Road, Oakley, Aylesbury,
Buckinghamshire HP18 9UR
T: (01844) 237360

OLNEY
Buckinghamshire

Colchester House ◆◆◆◆
26 High Street, Olney,
Buckinghamshire MK46 4BB
T: (01234) 712602
F: (01234) 240564
I: www.olneybucks.co.uk

The Lindens ◆◆◆
30A High Street, Olney,
Buckinghamshire MK46 4BB
T: (01234) 712891

OVER NORTON
Oxfordshire

Cleeves Farm ◆◆◆
Over Norton, Chipping Norton,
Oxfordshire OX7 5RB
T: (01608) 645019
F: (01608) 645021
E: tillylamb@hotmail.com

Woodhaven Cottage
Rating Applied For
The Green, Over Norton,
Chipping Norton, Oxfordshire
OX7 5PT
T: (01608) 646265

OWER
Hampshire

Octagon Lodge
Rating Applied For
Romsey Road, Ower, Romsey,
Hampshire SO51 6AH
T: (02380) 814233

OXFORD
Oxfordshire

Acorn Guest House ◆◆
260-262 Iffley Road, Oxford,
OX4 1SE
T: (01865) 247998
F: (01865) 247998
🚶

Adams Guest House ◆◆
302 Banbury Road, Oxford,
OX2 7ED
T: (01865) 556118
F: (01865) 514066

All Seasons Guest House ◆◆◆
63 Windmill Road, Headington,
Oxford, Oxfordshire OX3 7BP
T: (01865) 742215
F: (01865) 432691
E: admin@
allseasonsguesthouse.com
I: www.allseasonsguesthouse.
com

Arden Lodge ◆◆◆
34 Sunderland Avenue, off
Banbury Road, Oxford, OX2 8DX
T: (01865) 552076 & 512265

Beaumont Guest House ◆◆
234 Abingdon Road, Oxford,
Oxfordshire OX1 4SP
T: (01865) 241767
F: (01865) 241767
E: info@beaumont.sagehost.
co.uk
I: www.beaumont.sagehost.
co.uk

Becket House ◆◆
5 Becket Street, Oxford, OX1 7PP
T: (01865) 724675 & 513045
F: (01865) 724675

Bravalla Guest House ◆◆◆
242 Iffley Road, Oxford,
Oxfordshire OX4 1SE
T: (01865) 241326 & 250511
F: (01865) 250511
E: bravalla.guesthouse@virgin.
net
I: oxfordcity.
co.uk/accom/bravalla

Bronte Guest House
Rating Applied For
282 Iffley Road, Oxford,
OX4 4AA
T: (01865) 244594

Brown's Guest House ◆◆◆
281 Iffley Road, Oxford,
OX4 4AQ
T: (01865) 246822
F: (01865) 246822
I: brownsgh@hotmail.com

The Bungalow ◆◆◆
Cherwell Farm, Mill Lane, Old
Marston, Oxford OX3 0QF
T: (01865) 557171 &
07703 162125

Casa Villa Guest House ◆◆
388 Banbury Road,
Summertown, Oxford, OX2 7PW
T: (01865) 512642
F: (01865) 512642
E: stoya@casavilla.fsnet.co.uk
I: www.casavilla.fsnet.co.uk

Chestnuts ◆◆◆
72 Cumnor Hill, Oxford,
OX2 9HU
T: (01865) 863602 & 865070

Chestnuts Guest House ♦♦♦♦♦
45 Davenant Road, Off
Woodstock Road, Oxford,
OX2 8BU
T: (01865) 553375
F: (01865) 553375
E: stay@chestnutsguesthouse.
co.uk

The Coach & Horses Inn ♦♦♦
Watlington Road,
Chiselhampton, Oxford
OX44 7UX
T: (01865) 890255
F: (01865) 891995
E: david-mcphillips@lineone.
net
I: www.coachhorsesinn.co.uk

Cock and Camel ♦♦♦♦
24-26 George Street, Oxford,
OX1 2AE
T: (01865) 203705
F: (01865) 792130
E: cockandcamel@youngs.co.uk
I: www.youngs.co.uk

College Guest House ♦♦
103-105 Woodstock Road,
Oxford, OX2 6HL
T: (01865) 552579
F: (01865) 311244
E: r.pal@ukonline.co.uk

Conifer Lodge ♦♦♦
159 Eynsham Road, Botley,
Oxford, Oxfordshire OX2 9NE
T: (01865) 862280

Cornerways Guest House ♦♦♦
282 Abingdon Road, Oxford,
OX1 4TA
T: (01865) 240135
F: (01865) 247652
E: jeakings@btinternet.com

Cotswold House ♦♦♦♦♦
363 Banbury Road, Oxford,
OX2 7PL
T: (01865) 310558
F: (01865) 310558
E: d.r.walker@talk21.com
I: www.house363.freeserve.co.uk

Dial House ♦♦♦
25 London Road, Headington,
Oxford OX3 7RE
T: (01865) 769944
F: (01865) 769944
E: dialhouse@aol.com
I: www.oxfordcity.
co.uk/accom/dialhouse

Earlmont Guest House ♦♦♦
322-324 Cowley Road, Oxford,
Oxfordshire OX4 2AF
T: (01865) 240236
F: (01865) 434903
E: beds@earlmont.prestel.co.uk
I: www.oxfordcity.
co.uk/accom/earlmont.html

Euro Bar & Hotel Oxford ♦♦♦
48 George Street, Oxford,
OX1 2AQ
T: (01865) 725087 & 242998
F: (01865) 243367
E: eurobarox@aol.com
I: www.oxfordcity.
co.uk/accom/eurobar/

Falcon Private Hotel ♦♦♦
88-90 Abingdon Road, Oxford,
OX1 4PX
T: (01865) 511122
F: (01865) 246642
E: reservations@thefalconhotel.
freeserve.co.uk
I: www.oxfordcity.
co.uk/hotels/falcon

Five Mile View Guest House
♦♦♦
528 Banbury Road, Oxford,
OX2 8EG
T: (01865) 558747 &
07802 758366
F: (01865) 558747
E: fivemileview@aol.com
I: www.oxfordpages.
co.uk/fivemileview

Gables ♦♦♦♦
6 Cumnor Hill, Oxford,
Oxfordshire OX2 9HA
T: (01865) 862153
F: (01865) 864054
E: stay@gables-oxford.co.uk
I: www.oxfordcity.
co.uk/accom/gables/

Green Gables ♦♦♦
326 Abingdon Road, Oxford,
Oxfordshire OX1 4TE
T: (01865) 725870
F: (01865) 723115
E: green.gables@virgin.net

Head of the River ♦♦♦♦
Folly Bridge, St Aldates, Oxford,
OX1 4LB
T: (01865) 721600
F: (01865) 726158

Heather House B & B ♦♦
192 Iffley Road, Oxford,
Oxfordshire OX4 1SD
T: (01865) 249757
F: (01865) 249757

High Hedges ♦♦♦♦
8 Cumnor Hill, Oxford, OX2 9HA
T: (01865) 863395
F: (01865) 437351
E: tompkins@btinternet.com
I: www.smoothhound.
co.uk/hotels/highhedges

Highfield West ♦♦♦
188 Cumnor Hill, Oxford,
Oxfordshire OX2 9PJ
T: (01865) 863007
E: highfieldwest@email.msn.
com

Hollybush Guest House ♦♦♦
530 Banbury Road, Oxford,
Oxfordshire OX2 8EG
T: (01865) 554886
F: (01865) 554886
E: heather@hollybush.
fsbusiness.co.uk
I: www.angelfire.co.
/on/hollybush

Homelea Guest House ♦♦♦♦
356 Abingdon Road, Oxford,
OX1 4TQ
T: (01865) 245150
F: (01865) 245150
E: homelea@talk21.com
I: www.guesthouseoxford.com

Isis Guest House ♦♦
45-53 Iffley Road, Oxford,
OX4 1ED
T: (01865) 248894 & 242466
F: (01865) 243492
E: isis@herald.ox.ac.uk

Lakeside Guest House ♦♦♦
118 Abingdon Road, Oxford,
OX1 4PZ
T: (01865) 244725
F: (01865) 244725

21 Lincoln Road ♦♦♦♦
Oxford, Oxfordshire OX1 4TB
T: (01865) 246944
E: lbaleham@cwcom.net

Lonsdale Guest House ♦♦♦
312 Banbury Road, Oxford,
OX2 7ED
T: (01865) 554872
F: (01865) 554872

Marlborough House Hotel
♦♦♦♦
321 Woodstock Road, Oxford,
OX2 7NY
T: (01865) 311321
F: (01865) 515329
E: enquiries@marlbhouse.
win-uk.net
I: www.oxfordcity.
co.uk/hotels/marlborough

Milka's Guest House ♦♦♦
379 Iffley Road, Oxford,
Oxfordshire OX4 4DP
T: (01865) 778458
F: (01865) 776477
E: reservations@milkas.co.uk
I: www.milkas.co.uk

Mulberry Guest House ♦♦♦
265 London Road, Headington,
Oxford, Oxfordshire OX3 9EH
T: (01865) 767114
F: (01865) 767114
E: mulberryguesthouse@
hotmail.com

Newton House ♦♦♦
82-84 Abingdon Road, Oxford,
OX1 4PL
T: (01865) 240561
F: (01865) 244647
E: newton.house@btinternet.
com
I: www.oxfordcity.
co.uk/accom/newton

The Old Black Horse Hotel
♦♦♦
102 St Clements, Oxford,
OX4 1AR
T: (01865) 244691
F: (01865) 242771

Oxford Guest House ♦♦♦
107 Botley Road, Oxford,
OX2 0HB
T: (01865) 243620

Parklands Hotel ♦♦♦
100 Banbury Road, Oxford,
Oxfordshire OX2 6JU
T: (01865) 554374
F: (01865) 559860
E: theparklands@freenet.co.uk
I: www.oxfordcity.
co.uk/hotels/parklands

Pembroke House ♦♦♦♦♦
379 Woodstock Road, Oxford,
OX2 8AA
T: (01865) 310782
F: (01865) 310649
E: gaynordean@aol.co.uk

Pickwicks Guest House ♦♦♦♦
15-17 London Road,
Headington, Oxford OX3 7SP
T: (01865) 750487
F: (01865) 742208
E: pickwicks@x-stream.co.uk
I: www.oxfordcity.
co.uk/accom/pickwicks/

Pine Castle Hotel ♦♦♦♦
290 Iffley Road, Oxford, OX4 4AE
T: (01865) 241497 & 728887
F: (01865) 727230
E: stay@pinecastle.co.uk
I: www.oxfordcity.
co.uk/hotels/pinecastle

The Ridings ♦♦♦
280 Abingdon Road, Oxford,
OX1 4TA
T: (01865) 248364
F: (01865) 251348
E: ringsoxi@aol.com
I: www.members@aol.
com/ridingsoxi

River Hotel ♦♦♦
17 Botley Road, Oxford,
OX2 0AA
T: (01865) 243475
F: (01865) 724306
E: info@southerntb.co.uk
I: www.riverhotel.co.uk

Ryan's Guest House ♦♦♦
164 Banbury Road,
Summertown, Oxford,
Oxfordshire OX2 7BU
T: (01865) 558876
F: (01865) 558876

St Michael's Guest House
Rating Applied For
26 St Michael's Street, Oxford,
OX1 2EB
T: (01865) 242101

Sandfield House ♦♦♦♦
19 London Road, Headington,
Oxford, Oxfordshire OX3 7RE
T: (01865) 762406
F: (01865) 762406
E: stay@sandfieldguesthouse.
co.uk
I: www.sandfieldguesthouse.
co.uk

Sportsview Guest House ♦♦♦
106-110 Abingdon Road,
Oxford, OX1 4PX
T: (01865) 244268 &
07798 818190
F: (01865) 249270
E: stay@sportsview.
guest-house.freeserve.co.uk
I: www.smoothhound.
co.uk/hotels/sportsvi.html

The Tower House ♦♦♦♦
15 Ship Street, Oxford, OX1 3DA
T: (01865) 246828
F: (01865) 246828

West Farm ♦♦♦
Eaton, Appleton, Abingdon,
Oxfordshire OX13 5PR
T: (01865) 862908
F: (01865) 865512

The Westgate Hotel ♦♦
1 Botley Road, Oxford, OX2 0AA
T: (01865) 726721
F: (01865) 722078

Whitehouse View ♦♦
9 Whitehouse Road, Oxford,
OX1 4PA
T: (01865) 721626 &
07702 816050

PADWORTH COMMON
Berkshire

Lanteglos House ♦♦
Rectory Road, Padworth
Common, Reading RG7 4JD
T: (01189) 700333

PANGBOURNE
Berkshire

Weir View House ◆◆◆
9 Shooters Hill, Pangbourne,
Reading RG8 7DZ
T: (01189) 842120
F: (01189) 842120

PARK GATE
Hampshire

Four Winds Guest House ◆◆◆
17 Station Road, Park Gate,
Southampton SO31 7GJ
T: (01489) 584433 & 570965
F: (01489) 570965

Little Park Lodge
Rating Applied For
5 Bridge Road, Park Gate,
Fareham, Hampshire SO31 7GD
T: (01489) 600500
F: (01489) 605231
E: julie@manicmike.com
I: www.manicmike.com

60 Southampton Road ◆◆◆
Park Gate, Southampton
SO31 6AF
T: (01489) 573994

PARKSTONE
Dorset

Casa Ana Guest House ◆◆◆
93 North Road, Parkstone, Poole,
Dorset BH14 0LT
T: (01202) 741367

Danecourt Lodge ◆◆◆◆
58 Danecourt Road, Parkstone,
Poole, Dorset BH14 0PQ
T: (01202) 730957

Toad Hall ◆◆◆◆
30 Church Road, Parkstone,
Poole, Dorset BH14 0NS
T: (01202) 733900 &
07748 488103
F: (01202) 746814
E: toadhallguesthouse@
btinternet.com
I: www.smoothhound.
co.uk/hotels/toadhall.html

Viewpoint Guest House
◆◆◆◆
11 Constitution Hill Road,
Parkstone, Poole, Dorset
BH14 0QB
T: (01202) 733586 &
07850 164934
F: (01202) 733586
E: viewpointgh@viewpoint-gh
I: www.viewpoint-gh.co.uk

PENN
Buckinghamshire

Little Penn Farmhouse ◆◆◆◆
Penn Bottom, Penn, High
Wycombe, Buckinghamshire
HP10 8PJ
T: (01494) 813439
F: (01494) 817740
E: sally@saundersharris.co.uk

Little Twyford ◆◆◆
Hammersley Lane, Penn, High
Wycombe, Buckinghamshire
HP10 8HG
T: (01494) 816934
F: (01494) 816934
E: tandt@twyfoed.freeserve.
co.uk

PENNINGTON
Hampshire

Restormel Bed & Breakfast
◆◆◆◆
Restormel, Sway Road,
Pennington, Lymington,
Hampshire SO41 8LJ
T: (01590) 673875 &
07703 918188
F: (01590) 673875
E: judy@restormel-newforest.
co.uk
I: smoothhound.
co.uk/hotels/restorme.html

PETERSFIELD
Hampshire

Beaumont ◆◆◆
22 Stafford Road, Petersfield,
Hampshire GU32 2JG
T: (01730) 264744
F: (01730) 264744
E: jenny.bewes@btinternet.com

Heath Farmhouse ◆◆◆
Heath Road East, Petersfield,
Hampshire GU31 4HU
T: (01730) 264709
E: info@heathfarmhouse.co.uk
I: www.heathfarmhouse.co.uk

Heathside ◆◆◆
36 Heath Road East, Petersfield,
Hampshire GU31 4HR
T: (01730) 262337
F: (01730) 262337

The Holt ◆◆◆
60 Heath Road, Petersfield,
Hampshire GU31 4EJ
T: (01730) 262836

Pipers ◆◆◆
1 Oaklands Road, Petersfield,
Hampshire GU32 2EY
T: (01730) 262131

Ridgefield ◆◆
Station Road, Petersfield,
Hampshire GU32 3DE
T: (01730) 261402
E: ymcokw@hants.gov.uk

Rose Cottage ◆◆◆
1 The Mead, Liss, Hampshire
GU33 7DU
T: (01730) 892378

South Gardens Cottage ◆◆◆
South Harting, Petersfield,
Hampshire GU31 5QJ
T: (01730) 825040
F: (01730) 825040
E: rogerandjulia@beeb.net

1 The Spain ◆◆◆
Sheep Street, Petersfield,
Hampshire GU32 3JZ
T: (01730) 263261 & 261678
F: (01730) 261084
E: allantarver@cwcom.net

Ye Olde George ◆◆◆
Church Street, East Meon,
Petersfield, Hampshire
GU32 1NH
T: (01730) 823481
F: (01730) 823759

PICKET PIECE
Hampshire

Cherry Trees ◆◆◆
Picket Piece, Andover,
Hampshire SP11 6LY
T: (01264) 334891 & 357 150
F: (01264) 334 891

PILLEY
Hampshire

Mistletoe Cottage ◆◆◆◆
3 Jordans Lane, Pilley Bailey,
Pilley, Lymington, Hampshire
SO41 5QW
T: (01590) 676361

PISHILL
Oxfordshire

Orchard House ◆◆◆
Pishill, Henley-on-Thames,
Oxfordshire RG9 6HJ
T: (01491) 638351
F: (01491) 638351

POOLE
Dorset

Annelise ◆◆◆
41 Danecourt Road, Lower
Parkstone, Poole, Dorset
BH14 0PG
T: (01202) 744833 &
07702 025442
F: (01202) 744833
E: vincent41.fsnet.co.uk

Ashdell ◆◆
85 Dunyeats Road, Broadstone,
Dorset BH18 8AF
T: (01202) 692032
E: ian@ashdell.fsnet.co.uk
I: www.ashdell.co.uk

B & B on the Quay ◆◆◆
23 Barbers Wharf, Poole, Dorset
BH15 1ZB
T: (01202) 669214 &
07802 410520
F: (01202) 669214

Corkers ◆◆◆◆
1 High Street, The Quay, Poole,
Dorset BH15 1AB
T: (01202) 681393
F: (01202) 667393
E: corkers@corkers.co.uk
I: www.corkers.co.uk/corkers

Fernway ◆◆◆
56 Fernside Road, Poole, Dorset
BH15 2JJ
T: (01202) 252044 &
07802 351033
F: (01202) 666587
E: dave.way@sequencecontrols.
co.uk
I: www.fernway.co.uk

Fleetwater Guest House ◆◆◆
161 Longfleet Road, Poole,
Dorset BH15 2HS
T: (01202) 682509

The Golden Sovereign Hotel
◆◆◆◆
97 Alumhurst Road, Alum Chine,
Bournemouth, BH4 8HR
T: (01202) 762088 &
07788 977132
F: (01202) 762088
E: goldensov@aol.com

The Grange Guest House
Rating Applied For
1 Linthorpe Road, Poole, Dorset
BH15 2JS
T: (01202) 671336

Harbour Lea ◆◆◆
1 Whitecliff Road, Poole, Dorset
BH14 8DU
T: (01202) 744346
F: (01202) 268930
E: harbourlea@easicom.com

Harlequins B & B ◆◆◆◆
134 Ringwood Road, Poole,
Dorset BH14 0RP
T: (01202) 677624 &
07887 888074
E: harlequins@tinyworld.co
I: www.harlequins.freeuk.com

Highways ◆◆◆
29 Fernside Road, Poole, Dorset
BH15 2QU
T: (01202) 677060

Laurel Cottages ◆◆◆◆
41 Foxholes Road, Poole, Dorset
BH15 3NA
T: (01202) 730894 &
07748 713681
F: (01202) 730894
E: anne.howarth@cwcom.net
I: www.laurel-cottages.cwc.net

Lytchett Mere ◆◆◆◆
191 Sandy Lane, Upton, Poole,
Dorset BH16 5LU
T: (01202) 622854

The Mariners Guest House
◆◆◆
26 Sandbanks Road, Poole,
Dorset BH14 8AQ
T: (01202) 247218

Minster Bed & Breakfast
Rating Applied For
826 Ringwood Road,
Bournemouth, BH11 8NF
T: (01202) 249977

26 Porter Road ◆◆◆
Creekmoor, Poole, Dorset
BH17 7AW
T: (01202) 678835

Quay House ◆◆◆
3A Thames Street, Poole, Dorset
BH15 1JN
T: (01202) 686335

The Saltings ◆◆◆◆
5 Salterns Way, Lilliput, Poole,
Dorset BH14 8JR
T: (01202) 707349
E: saltings_poole@yahoo.co.uk
I: www.thesaltingsfsnet.co.uk

Sarnia Cherie ◆◆◆◆
375 Blandford Road,
Hamworthy, Poole, Dorset
BH15 4JL
T: (01202) 679470 &
07885 319931
F: (01202) 679470
E: criscollier@aol.com

The Shah of Persia ◆◆◆◆
173 Longfleet Road, Poole,
Dorset BH15 2HS
T: (01202) 676587 & 685346
F: (01202) 679327

Tatnam Farm ◆◆◆◆
82 Tatnam Road, Poole, Dorset
BH15 2DS
T: (01202) 672969
F: (01202) 682732
E: helenbishop@jrb.netkonect.
co.uk

Vernon ◆◆
96 Blandford Road North,
Beacon Hill, Poole, Dorset
BH16 6AD
T: (01202) 625185

PORCHFIELD
Isle of Wight

Youngwoods Farm ◆◆◆
Whitehouse Road, Porchfield,
Newport, Isle of Wight PO30 4LJ
T: (01983) 522170
F: (01983) 522170
E: judith@youngwoods.com
I: www.youngwoods.com

PORTCHESTER
Hampshire

Harbour View ◆◆
85 Windmill Grove, Portchester,
Fareham, Hampshire PO16 9HH
T: (023) 9237 6740

PORTMORE
Hampshire

A Thatched House ◆◆◆
Hundred Lane, Portmore,
Lymington, Hampshire
SO41 5RG
T: (01590) 679977
F: (01590) 679977

Cherry Tree ◆◆◆◆
Hundred Lane, Portmore,
Lymington, Hampshire
SO41 5RG
T: (01590) 672990
E: cherry.tree@lineone.net

PORTSMOUTH & SOUTHSEA
Hampshire

Abbey Lodge ◆◆◆
30 Waverley Road, Southsea,
Hampshire PO5 2PW
T: (023) 9282 8285
F: (023) 9287 2943
E: linda@abbeylodge.co.uk
I: www.abbeylodge.co.uk

The Albatross Guest House
◆◆◆◆
51 Waverley Road, Southsea,
Hampshire PO5 2PJ
T: (023) 9282 8325

Amberley Court ◆◆◆
97 Waverley Road, Southsea,
Portsmouth, Hampshire PO5 2PL
T: (023) 9273 7473 &
07801 379514
F: (023) 9235 6911
E: nigelward@compuserve.com
I: www.amberley-court.co.uk

Aquarius Court Hotel ◆◆◆
34 St Ronans Road, Southsea,
Hampshire PO4 0PT
T: (023) 9282 2872 & 9282 0148
F: (023) 9261 9065
E: enquiries@aquariuscourt.
freeserve.co.uk
I: www.aquariuscourt.com

Arden Guest House ◆◆◆
14 Herbert Road, Southsea,
Hampshire PO4 0QA
T: (023) 9282 6409
F: (023) 9282 6409

Avarest Guest House ◆◆
10 Waverley Grove, Southsea,
Hampshire PO4 0PZ
T: (023) 9282 9444

Bembell Court Hotel ◆◆◆
69 Festing Road, Southsea,
Hampshire PO4 0NQ
T: (023) 9273 5915 & 9275 0497
F: (023) 9275 6497
E: keith@bembell.freeserve.
co.uk
I: www.bembell.com

Birchwood Guest House ◆◆◆
44 Waverley Road, Southsea,
Hampshire PO5 2PP
T: (023) 9281 1337 &
07711 897789
F: (023) 9236 1161
E: ged@birchwoodguesthouse.
freeserve.co.uk
I: www.smoothound.
co.uk/hotels/birchwod/hmtl

Britannia Guest House ◆◆◆
8 Outram Road, Southsea,
Hampshire PO5 1QU
T: (023) 9281 4234
F: (023) 9281 4234

Corran Guest House ◆◆◆
25 Herbert Road, Southsea,
Hampshire PO4 0QA
T: (023) 9273 3006

The Dorcliffe ◆◆◆
42 Waverley Road, Southsea,
Hampshire PO5 2PP
T: (023) 9282 8283
E: dorcliffe@supanet.com

The Elms Guest House ◆◆◆
48 Victoria Road South,
Southsea, Hampshire PO5 2BT
T: (023) 9282 3924
F: (023) 9282 3924
E: theelmsgh@aol.com
I: www.
resort-guide/portsmouth/elms

Esk Vale Guest House ◆◆◆
39 Granada Road, Southsea,
Hampshire PO4 0RD
T: (023) 9286 2639
F: (023) 9235 5589
I: www.interalpha.
net/eskvale-guesthouse

Everley Guest House ◆◆◆
33 Festing Road, Southsea,
Hampshire PO4 0NG
T: (023) 9273 1001
F: (023) 9278 0995

Fairlea ◆◆
19 Beach Road, Southsea,
Hampshire PO5 2JH
T: (023) 9273 3090
F: (023) 9273 3090

The Festing Grove Guest House
◆◆◆
8 Festing Grove, Southsea,
Hampshire PO4 9QA
T: (023) 9273 5239
E: festinggrove@lineone.co.uk

Fortitude Cottage ◆◆◆
51 Broad Street, Spice Island,
Portsmouth, PO1 2JD
T: (023) 9282 3748
F: (023) 9282 3748
E: fortcott@aol.com
I: www.fortitudecottage.co.uk

Gainsborough House ◆◆
9 Malvern Road, Southsea,
Hampshire PO5 2LZ
T: (023) 9282 2604

Glenroy Guest House ◆◆
28 Waverley Road, Southsea,
Hampshire PO5 2PW
T: (023) 9281 4922
F: (023) 9275 4196
E: glenroygh@btinternet.com

Granada House Hotel ◆◆◆
29 Granada Road, Southsea,
Hampshire PO4 0RD
T: (023) 9286 1575
F: (023) 9271 8343

Greenacres Guest House ◆◆◆
12 Marion Road, Southsea,
Hampshire PO4 0QX
T: (023) 9235 3137 & 9275 1312
E: katad@greenacres80.
freeserve.co.uk

Hamilton House ◆◆◆◆
95 Victoria Road North,
Southsea, Hampshire PO5 1PS
T: (023) 9282 3502
F: (023) 9282 3502
E: sandra@hamiltonhouse.co.uk
I: www.resort-guide.
co.uk/portsmouth/hamilton

Hillside Lodge ◆
1 Blake Road, Farlington,
Portsmouth PO6 1ET
T: (023) 9237 2687

Homestead Guest House ◆◆◆
11 Bembridge Crescent,
Southsea, Hampshire PO4 0QT
T: (023) 9273 2362

Kilbenny Guest House ◆◆◆
2 Malvern Road, Southsea,
Hampshire PO5 2NA
T: (023) 9286 1347

Kingsley Guest House ◆◆◆
16 Craneswater Avenue,
Southsea, Hampshire PO4 0PB
T: (023) 9273 9113 & 07979 594
915
F: (023) 9273 9113

Lamorna Guest House ◆◆
23 Victoria Road South,
Southsea, Hampshire PO5 2BX
T: (023) 9281 1157
F: (023) 9281 1157

Langdale Guest House ◆◆◆
13 St Edwards Road, Southsea,
Hampshire PO5 3DH
T: (023) 9282 2146
F: (023) 9235 3303
E: langdalegh@btinternet.com
I: www.smoothhound.
co.uk/hotels/langdal.html

Mandalay ◆◆◆
31 St Andrews Road, Southsea,
Hampshire PO5 1EP
T: (023) 9282 9600
F: (023) 9282 9600

Marmion Lodge Guest House
◆◆◆◆
71 Marmion Road, Southsea,
Hampshire PO5 2AX
T: (023) 9282 2150
F: (023) 9282 2150
E: marmionlodge@btinternet.
com
I: www.marmionlodge.co.uk

Oakdale ◆◆◆◆
71 St Ronans Road, Southsea,
Hampshire PO4 0PP
T: (023) 9273 7358
F: (023) 9273 7358
E: oakdale@btinternet.com

Oakleigh Guest House ◆◆◆
48 Festing Grove, Southsea,
Hampshire PO4 9QD
T: (023) 9281 2276
E: dwillett@cwtv.net
I: www.oakleighguesthouse.
co.uk

The Pembroke Park Hotel
◆◆◆
1 Bellevue Terrace, Southsea,
Portsmouth, Hampshire PO5 3AT
T: (023) 9229 6817
F: (023) 9229 6817
E: pph@bandb.uk.net
I: www.bandb.uk.net/pph.htm

**Rees Hall University of
Portsmouth** ◆◆◆
Southsea Terrace, Southsea,
Hampshire PO5 3AP
T: (023) 9284 3884
F: (023) 9284 3888
E: reservation@port.ac.uk
I: www.port.ac.uk

The Rowans ◆◆◆◆
43 Festing Grove, Southsea,
Hampshire PO4 9QB
T: (023) 9273 6614
F: (023) 9282 3711

Sailmaker's Loft ◆◆
5 Bath Square, Spice Island,
Portsmouth, PO1 2JL
T: (023) 9282 3045 & 9229 5961
F: (023) 9229 5961
E: sailmakersloft@aol.com
I: www.smoothhound.co.uk

Sally Port Inn ◆◆
57-58 High Street, Portsmouth,
PO1 2LU
T: (023) 9282 1860
F: (023) 9282 1293

Stacey Court Hotel ◆◆
42 Clarence Parade, Southsea,
Hampshire PO5 2EU
T: (023) 92826827
F: (023) 92361365

Uplands Hotel ◆◆◆
34 Granada Road, Southsea,
Hampshire PO4 0RH
T: (023) 9282 1508
F: (023) 9283 2211
I: www.canterburyhotelgroup.
com

Victoria Court ◆◆◆
29 Victoria Road North,
Southsea, Hampshire PO5 1PL
T: (023) 9282 0305
F: (023) 9283 8277
E: stay@victoriacourt.co.uk
I: www.victoriacourt.co.uk

Walsingham Guest House
◆◆◆
18 Festing Road, Southsea,
Hampshire PO4 0NG
T: (023) 9283 2818
F: (023) 9283 2818

**Waverley Park Lodge Guest
House** ◆◆◆
99 Waverley Road, Southsea,
Hampshire PO5 2PL
T: (023) 9273 0402 & 9278 1094
I: www.waverleyparklodge.co.uk

The White House Hotel ◆◆◆
26 South Parade, Southsea,
Hampshire PO5 2JF
T: (023) 9282 3709 & 9273 2759
F: (023) 9273 2759
E: keastlkline@aol.com

Wolverton Guest House ◆◆◆
22 Granada Road, Southsea,
Hampshire PO4 0RH
T: (023) 9273 2819 & 9234 5474
F: (023) 814234

Woodville Hotel ◆◆◆
6 Florence Road, Southsea,
Hampshire PO5 2NE
T: (023) 9282 3409
F: (023) 9234 6089
I: woodvillehotel@cwcom.net

POULNER
Hampshire

A Secret Garden ◆◆◆
132 Kingfisher Way, Poulner,
Ringwood, Hampshire
BH24 3LW
T: (01425) 477563 &
07957 7356748
F: (01425) 477563
E: jennybandb@aol.com
I: www.secretgardenbandb.co.uk

PRINCES RISBOROUGH
Buckinghamshire

Grahurst ◆◆◆
6 Abbotswood, Speen, Princes
Risborough, Aylesbury,
Buckinghamshire HP27 0SR
T: (01494) 488544

Solis Ortu ◆◆◆
Aylesbury Road, Askett, Princes
Risborough, Aylesbury,
Buckinghamshire HP27 9LY
T: (01844) 344175
F: (01844) 343509

PRIVETT
Hampshire

Thatched Cottage Farm
◆◆◆◆
Filmore Hill, Privett, Alton,
Hampshire GU34 3NX
T: (01730) 828278

QUAINTON
Buckinghamshire

The White Hart ◆◆◆
4 The Strand, Quainton,
Aylesbury, Buckinghamshire
HP22 4AS
T: (01296) 655234

Woodlands Farmhouse ◆◆◆
Doddershall, Quainton,
Aylesbury, Buckinghamshire
HP22 4DE
T: (01296) 770225

QUARLEY
Hampshire

Lains Cottage ◆◆◆◆
Quarley, Andover, Hampshire
SP11 8PX
T: (01264) 889697
F: (01264) 889227
E: lains-cott-hols@dial.pipex.
com
I: dspace.dial.pipex.
com/lains-cott-hols/

RADNAGE
Buckinghamshire

Highlands ◆◆◆◆
26 Green Lane, Radnage, High
Wycombe, Buckinghamshire
HP14 4DN
T: (01494) 484835
F: (01494) 482633
E: janekhighlands@aol.com
I: www.country-accom.co.uk

RAMSDEN
Oxfordshire

Akeman Cottage ◆◆◆◆◆
Ramsden, Oxford OX7 3AU
T: (01993) 868383
F: (01993) 868075
E: akeman.cottage.bb@anserve.
net
I: www.oxlink.
co.uk/burford/akeman-cottage/

Ann's Cottage ◆◆◆
Lower End, Ramsden, Oxford
OX7 3AZ
T: (01993) 868592
E: foxwoodfamily@lineone.net

READING
Berkshire

Abadair House ◆◆
46 Redlands Road, Reading,
Berkshire RG1 5HE
T: (0118) 986 3792
F: (0118) 986 3792
E: abadair@globalnet.co.uk
I: www.smoothhound.
co.uk/hotels/abadair/.html

Bath Hotel ◆◆◆
54 Bath Road, Reading,
RG1 6PG
T: (0118) 957 2019
F: (0118) 950 3203

Caversham Lodge ◆◆
133a Caversham Road, Reading,
Berkshire RG1 8AS
T: (01189) 573529 & 612110

Crescent Hotel ◆◆◆
35 Coley Avenue, Reading,
RG1 6LL
T: (01189) 507980
F: (01189) 574299

Dittisham Guest House ◆◆◆
63 Tilehurst Road, Reading,
RG30 2JL
T: (0118) 956 9483 &
07889 605193
E: dittishamgh@aol.com

The Elms ◆◆
Gallowstree Road, Rotherfield
Peppard, Henley-on-Thames,
Oxfordshire RG9 5HT
T: (0118) 972 3164
F: (0118) 972 4594

10 Greystoke Road ◆◆◆◆
Caversham, Reading RG4 5EL
T: (01189) 475784 &
07891 30237
E: greystoke.guesthouse@
freedomland.co.uk

The Old Forge ◆◆◆
109 Grovelands Road, Reading,
RG30 2PB
T: (0118) 958 2928
F: (0118) 958 2408
E: rees.family@virgin.net

The Six Bells ◆◆◆
Beenham Village, Beenham,
Reading RG7 5NX
T: (0118) 971 3368

Warren Dene Hotel ◆◆◆
1017 Oxford Road, Tilehurst,
Reading, Berkshire RG31 6TL
T: (0118) 942 2556
F: (0118) 945 1096
E: wdh@globalnet.co.uk

RINGWOOD
Hampshire

Amberwood ◆◆◆◆
3-5 Top Lane, Mansfield,
Ringwood, Hampshire BH24 1LF
T: (01425) 476615
F: (01425) 476615
E: maynsing@aol.com
I: www.amberwoodbandb.co.uk

The Auld Kennels ◆◆◆
215 Christchurch Road,
Moortown, Ringwood,
Hampshire BH24 3AN
T: (01425) 475170
F: (01425) 461577

Beau Cottage ◆◆◆
1 Hiltom Road, Ringwood,
Hampshire BH24 1PW
T: (01425) 461274
F: (01425) 461274
E: sagemo5734@talk21.com

Fraser House ◆◆◆
Salisbury Road, Blashford,
Ringwood, Hampshire BH24 3PB
T: (01425) 473958
F: (01425) 473958
E: fraserhouse@btinternet.com

Old Stacks ◆◆◆◆
154 Hightown Road, Ringwood,
Hampshire BH24 1NP
T: (01425) 473840
F: (01425) 473840
E: oldstacksbandb@aol.com

Original White Hart ◆◆◆
Market Place, Ringwood,
Hampshire BH24 1AW
T: (01425) 472702
F: (01425) 471993

Picket Hill House ◆◆◆◆
Picket Hill, Ringwood,
Hampshire BH24 3HH
T: (01425) 476173
F: (01425) 470022
E: b&b@pickethill.freeserve.
co.uk

Torre Avon ◆◆◆◆
21 Salisbury Road, Ringwood,
Hampshire BH24 1AS
T: (01425) 472769
F: (01425) 472769
E: b&b@torreavon.freeserve.
co.uk
I: www.torreavon.freeserve.co.uk

ROMSEY
Hampshire

Abbey Hotel ◆◆◆
11 Church Street, Romsey,
Hampshire SO51 8BT
T: (01794) 513360
F: (01794) 524318
E: di@abbeyhotelromsey.co.uk
I: www.abbeyhotelromsey.co.uk

**Aylwards Bottom
Rating Applied For**
Top Green, Lockerley, Romsey,
Hampshire SO51 0JP
T: (01794) 340864

The Chalet Guest House ◆◆◆
Botley Road, Whitenap, Romsey,
Hampshire SO51 5RQ
T: (01794) 517299 &
07703 638550
E: b-and-b@the-chalet.
freeserve.co.uk

3 Cherville Mews ◆◆◆◆
Romsey, Hampshire SO51 8FY
T: (01794) 830518
F: (01794) 830518
E: pat.townson@lineone.net

79 Mercer Way ◆◆
Romsey, Hampshire SO51 7PH
T: (01794) 502009
F: (01794) 503009

Pauncefoot House ◆◆◆
Pauncefoot Hill, Romsey,
Hampshire SO51 6AA
T: (01794) 513139
F: (01794) 513139
E: lendupont@netscapeonline.
co.uk

Pillar Box Cottage ◆◆◆
Toothill, Romsey, Hampshire
SO51 9LN
T: (023) 8073 2390 &
07719 738603

Pyesmead Farm ◆◆◆
Plaitford, Romsey, Hampshire
SO51 6EE
T: (01794) 323386
F: (01794) 323386
E: pyesmead@talk21.com

Ranvilles Farm House ◆◆◆
Ower, Romsey, Hampshire
SO51 6AA
T: (023) 8081 4481
F: (023) 8081 4481

Roselea ◆◆◆◆
Hamdown Crescent, East
Wellow, Romsey, Hampshire
SO51 6BJ
T: (01794) 323262
F: (01794) 323262
E: pennyc@tcp.co.uk

Southernwood ◆◆
Plaitford Common, Salisbury
Road, Plaitford, Romsey,
Hampshire SO51 6EE
T: (01794) 323255

Stoneymarsh Cottage ◆◆◆
Stoneymarsh, Romsey,
Hampshire SO51 0LB
T: (01794) 368867
F: (01794) 368867
E: m.m.moran@btinternet.com

RYDE
Isle of Wight

Bridge House ◆◆◆◆
Kite Hill, Wootton Bridge, Ryde,
Isle of Wight PO33 4LA
T: (01983) 884163

Claverton ◆◆◆◆
12 The Strand, Ryde, Isle of
Wight PO33 1JE
T: (01983) 613015
F: (01983) 613015

The Dorset Hotel ◆◆◆
31 Dover Street, Ryde, Isle of
Wight PO33 2BW
T: (01983) 564327 & 563892
F: (01983) 614635
E: hoteldorset@aol.com
I: www.thedorsethotel.co.uk

Elmfield Lodge ◆◆◆◆
35 Marlborough Road, Elmfield,
Ryde, Isle of Wight PO33 1AB
T: (01983) 614131

Fern Cottage ◆◆◆
8 West Street, Ryde, Isle of
Wight PO33 2NW
T: (01983) 565856
F: (01983) 565856
E: sandra@psd-ferguson.
freeserve.co.uk

Kemphill Farm ◆◆◆◆
Stroudwood Road, Upton, Ryde,
Isle of Wight PO33 4BZ
T: (01983) 563880
F: (01983) 563880
E: ron.holland@farming.co.uk
I: www.kemphill.com

Royal Esplanade Hotel ◆◆◆
16 The Esplanade, Ryde, Isle of
Wight PO33 2ED
T: (01983) 562549
F: (01983) 563918

Sea View ◆◆◆
8 Dover Street, Ryde, Isle of
Wight PO33 2AQ
T: (01983) 810976

Seahaven Hotel ◆◆◆
36 St Thomas Street, Ryde, Isle
of Wight PO33 2DL
T: (01983) 563069
F: (01983) 563570
E: seahaven@netguides.co.uk

Seaward Guest House ◆◆◆
14-16 George Street, Ryde, Isle
of Wight PO33 2EW
T: (01983) 563168 & 0800 915
2966
F: (01983) 563168
E: seaward@fsbdial.co.uk

Sillwood Acre ◆◆◆◆
Church Road, Binstead, Ryde,
Isle of Wight PO33 3TB
T: (01983) 563553
E: sillwood.acre@virgin.net

Stonelands ◆◆◆◆
Binstead Road, Binstead, Ryde,
Isle of Wight PO33 3NJ
T: (01983) 616947
F: (01983) 812857

The Vine Guest House ◆◆◆
16 Castle Street, Ryde, Isle of
Wight PO33 2EG
T: (01983) 566633
F: (01983) 566633
E: vine@guesthouse49.
freeserve.co.uk

ST LAWRENCE
Isle of Wight
Little Orchard ◆◆◆◆
Undercliff Drive, St Lawrence,
Ventnor, Isle of Wight PO38 1YA
T: (01983) 731106

SANDFORD
Isle of Wight
The Barn ◆◆◆◆
Pound Farm, Shanklin Road,
Sandford, Ventnor, Isle of Wight
PO38 3AW
T: (01983) 840047
F: (01983) 840047
E: barnpoundfarm@
barnpoundfarm.free-online.
co.uk

SANDLEHEATH
Hampshire
**Sandleheath Post Office &
Stores** ◆◆◆
Sandleheath, Fordingbridge,
Hampshire SP6 1PP
T: (01425) 652230
F: (01425) 652230
E: david@cordelle.co.uk
I: www.cordelle.
co.uk/sandleheath

SANDOWN
Isle of Wight
Alendel Hotel ◆◆
1 Leed Street, Sandown, Isle of
Wight PO36 9DA
T: (01983) 402967

The Belgrave Hotel
Rating Applied For
14-16 Beachfield Road,
Sandown, Isle of Wight
PO36 8NA
T: (01983) 404550
F: (01983) 404550

Belmore Private Hotel ◆◆◆
101 Station Avenue, Sandown,
Isle of Wight PO36 8HD
T: (01983) 404189 & 404169
F: (01983) 405942
E: lowbelmore@talk21.com
I: www.
islandbreaksco.uk/belmore

Bernay Hotel ◆◆◆
24 Victoria Road, Sandown, Isle
of Wight PO36 8AL
T: (01983) 402205
F: (01983) 402205
E: bernayhotel@btconnect.com

Carisbrooke House Hotel ◆◆◆
11 Beachfield Road, Sandown,
Isle of Wight PO36 8NA
T: (01983) 402257
E: carisbrookehotel@aol.com

Cavalier Guest House ◆◆◆
9 Carter Street, Sandown, Isle of
Wight PO36 8BL
T: (01983) 403269

The Danebury ◆◆◆
26 Victoria Road, Sandown, Isle
of Wight PO36 8AL
T: (01983) 403795
E: danebury@madasafish.com

Denecroft ◆◆◆
53 Grove Road, Sandown, Isle of
Wight PO36 8HH
T: (01983) 404412
F: (01983) 404412

Denewood Hotel ◆◆◆◆
7 Victoria Road, Sandown, Isle of
Wight PO36 8AL
T: (01983) 402980 & 403517
F: (01983) 402980

Heathfield House Hotel ◆◆◆
52 Melville Street, Sandown, Isle
of Wight PO36 8LF
T: (01983) 400002
F: (01983) 400002
E: mike.sollis@ic24.net
I: www.netguides.
co.uk/wight/heathfieldhouse.
html

Homeland Private Hotel ◆◆◆
38 Grove Road, Sandown, Isle of
Wight PO36 8HH
T: (01983) 404305

Inglewood Guest House ◆◆◆
15 Avenue Road, Sandown, Isle
of Wight PO36 8BN
T: (01983) 403485

Iona Guest House ◆◆◆
44 Sandown Road, Lake,
Sandown, Isle of Wight
PO36 9JT
T: (01983) 402741
F: (01983) 402741
E: ionahotel@supanet.com

Kingswood Hotel ◆◆
15 Melville Street, Sandown, Isle
of Wight PO36 9DP
T: (01983) 402685
F: (01983) 402685

Lanowlee ◆◆◆
99 Station Avenue, Sandown,
Isle of Wight PO36 8HD
T: (01983) 403577

The Lawns Hotel ◆◆◆
72 The Broadway, Sandown, Isle
of Wight PO36 9AA
T: (01983) 402549
F: (01983) 402549
E: kdlawns@ukgateway.net
I: www.netguides.
co.uk/wight/lawns.html

Lyndhurst Hotel ◆◆◆
8 Royal Crescent, Sandown, Isle
of Wight PO36 8LZ
T: (01983) 403663

Montpelier Hotel ◆◆◆
Pier Street, Sandown, Isle of
Wight PO36 8JR
T: (01983) 403964
F: (01983) 403074
E: enquiries@montpelier-hotel.
co.uk
I: www.montpelier-hotel.co.uk

Oakfields ◆
26 Melville Street, Sandown, Isle
of Wight PO36 8HX
T: (01983) 405410

The Regent ◆◆
Esplanade, Sandown, Isle of
Wight PO36 8AE
T: (01983) 403219
F: (01983) 400067
E: theregent@sarahsandown.
freeserve.co.uk

Rooftree Hotel ◆◆◆◆
26 Broadway, Sandown, Isle of
Wight PO36 9BY
T: (01983) 403175
F: (01983) 407354
E: rooftree@netguides.co.uk

St Catherines Hotel ◆◆◆◆
1 Winchester Park Road,
Sandown, Isle of Wight
PO36 8HJ
T: (01983) 402392
F: (01983) 402392
E: stcathhotel@hotmail.com
I: www.isleofwight-holidays.
co.uk

St Michaels Hotel ◆◆◆◆
33 Leed Street, Sandown, Isle of
Wight PO36 8JE
T: (01983) 403636

St Ninians Guest House ◆◆◆
19 Avenue Road, Sandown, Isle
of Wight PO36 8BN
T: (01983) 402755
F: (01983) 400112

Sandhill Hotel ◆◆◆
6 Hill Street, Sandown, Isle of
Wight PO36 9DB
T: (01983) 403635 & 403695
F: (01983) 403695
E: sandhill.hotel@ukgateway.
net
I: www.sandhill-hotel.com

Shachri ◆◆◆
31 Avenue Road, Sandown, Isle
of Wight PO36 8BN
T: (01983) 405718

Shangri-La Hotel ◆◆
30 Broadway, Sandown, Isle of
Wight PO36 9BY
T: (01983) 403672 & 403415
F: (01983) 403672
E: shangrilahotel0@aol.com

Victoria Lodge ◆◆◆
4-6 Victoria Road, Sandown, Isle
of Wight PO36 8AP
T: (01983) 403209

Westfield Hotel ◆◆◆◆
17 Broadway, Sandown, Isle of
Wight PO36 9BY
T: (01983) 403802 & 408225
F: (01983) 408225

SAUNDERTON
Buckinghamshire
Hunters Gate ◆◆◆
Deanfield, Saunderton,
Aylesbury, Buckinghamshire
HP14 4JR
T: (01494) 481718
E: dadykes@attglobal.net

SEAVIEW
Isle of Wight
1 Cluniac Cottages ◆◆◆◆
Priory Road, Seaview, Isle of
Wight PO34 5BU
T: (01983) 812119
E: bill.elfenjay@virgin.net
I: www.cluniaccottages.fsnet.
co.uk/

Maple Villa ◆◆◆
Oakhill Road, Seaview, Isle of
Wight PO34 5AP
T: (01983) 614826
E: dveccles@free4all.co.uk
I: www.maplevilla.co.uk

SELBORNE
Hampshire
8 Goslings Croft ◆◆◆◆
Selborne, Alton, Hampshire
GU34 3HZ
T: (01420) 511285
F: (01420) 587451

Ivanhoe ◆◆◆◆
Oakhanger, Selborne, Alton,
Hampshire GU35 9JG
T: (01420) 473464

The Queen's & The Limes ◆◆◆
High Street, Selborne, Alton,
Hampshire GU34 3JJ
T: (01420) 511454
F: (01420) 511272
E: enquiries@queens-selborne.
co.uk
I: www.queens-selborne.co.uk

Seale Cottage ◆◆◆
Gracious Street, Selborne, Alton,
Hampshire GU34 3JE
T: (01420) 511396 & 07799 474
471
E: cw.gibson@virgin.net

Thatched Barn House ◆◆◆◆
Grange Farm, Gracious Street,
Selborne, Alton, Hampshire
GU34 3JG
T: (01420) 511007
F: (01420) 511008
E: bandb@bobt.dircon.co.uk
I: www.bobt.dircon.co.uk

SHAFTESBURY
Dorset

Cliff House ◆◆◆◆◆
Breach Lane, Shaftesbury,
Dorset SP7 8LF
T: (01747) 852548 &
07990 574849
F: (01747) 852548
E: dianaepow@aol.com
I: www.cliff-house.co.uk

The Grove Arms Inn ◆◆◆◆
Ludwell, Shaftesbury, Dorset
SP7 9ND
T: (01747) 828328
F: (01747) 828960
I: www.wiltshireaccommodation.
com

The Kings Arms Inn ◆◆◆◆
East Stour Common, East Stour,
Gillingham, Dorset SP8 5NB
T: (01747) 838325
E: jenny@kings-arms.fsnet.
co.uk

The Knoll ◆◆◆◆
Bleke Street, Shaftesbury, Dorset
SP7 8AH
T: (01747) 855243
E: pickshaftesbury@
compuserve.com
I: www.pick-art.org.uk

Paynes Place Barn ◆◆◆◆
New Road, Shaftesbury, Dorset
SP7 8QL
T: (01747) 855016
F: (01747) 855016
E: xstal@globalnet.co.uk
I: www.accomodata.
co.uk/140498.htm

The Retreat ◆◆◆◆
47 Bell Street, Shaftesbury,
Dorset SP7 8AE
T: (01747) 850372
F: (01747) 850372
E: at.retreat@virgin.net
I: www.the-retreat.org.uk

SHALFLEET
Isle of Wight

HEBBERDENS
Rating Applied For
Yarmouth Road, Shalfleet,
Newport, Isle of Wight
PO30 4NB
T: (01983) 531364

The Old Malthouse ◆◆
1 Mill Road, Shalfleet, Newport,
Isle of Wight PO30 4NE
T: (01983) 531329
E: b&b@oldmalthouse.demon.
co.uk

SHALSTONE
Buckinghamshire

Barnita ◆◆◆
Wood Green, Shalstone,
Buckingham MK18 5DZ
T: (01280) 850639 &
07778 304163
I: www.aylesburyvale.
net/buckingham/barnita.htm

SHANKLIN
Isle of Wight

Atholl Court Guest House
◆◆◆
1 Atherley Road, Shanklin, Isle of
Wight PO37 7AT
T: (01983) 862414 & 07721 924
182
F: (01983) 868985
E: info@atholl-court.co.uk
I: www.atholl-court.co.uk

Bedford Lodge Hotel ◆◆◆
4 Chine Avenue, Old Village,
Shanklin, Isle of Wight
PO37 6AQ
T: (01983) 862416
F: (01983) 868704
E: bta@bedfordlodge.co.uk
I: www.bedfordlodge.co.uk

Birkdale Hotel ◆◆◆◆
Grange Road, Shanklin, Isle of
Wight PO37 6NN
T: (01983) 862949
F: (01983) 862949
E: enq@birkdalehoteliowfsnet.
co.uk
I: enq@birkdalehoteliowfsnet.
co.uk

Brooke House Hotel ◆◆◆
2 St Pauls Avenue, Shanklin, Isle
of Wight PO37 7AL
T: (01983) 863162
E: brookhousehotel@hotmail.
com
I: www.islandbreaks.co.uk

The Burlington Hotel ◆◆◆
6 Chine Avenue, Shanklin, Isle of
Wight PO37 6AG
T: (01983) 862090
F: (01983) 862191
E: mtulett@zoom.uk
I: www.isleofwighthotels.org.uk

Cedar Lodge Hotel ◆◆◆
28 Arthurs Hill, Shanklin, Isle of
Wight PO37 6EX
T: (01983) 863268
F: (01983) 863268

Celebration Hotel ◆◆◆◆
6 Avenue Road, Shanklin, Isle of
Wight PO37 7BG
T: (01983) 862746
F: (01983) 867704

Chestnuts Hotel ◆◆◆
Hope Road, Shanklin, Isle of
Wight PO37 6EA
T: (01983) 862162

Claremont Guest House ◆◆◆
4 Eastmount Road, Shanklin, Isle
of Wight PO37 6DN
T: (01983) 862083

Clifton Hotel
Rating Applied For
Keats Green, 1 Queens Road,
Shanklin, Isle of Wight
PO37 6AN
T: (01983) 863015
F: (01983) 865911

Cliftonville Hotel ◆◆◆
6 Hope Road, Shanklin, Isle of
Wight PO37 6EA
T: (01983) 862197
F: (01983) 862197
E: cliftonvillehotel@talk21.com

Courtlands Hotel ◆◆◆
Paddock Road, Shanklin, Isle of
Wight PO37 6PA
T: (01983) 862167
F: (01983) 863308
E: simon@courtlandshotel.co.uk
I: www.courtlandshotel.co.uk

Culham Lodge Hotel ◆◆◆◆
31 Landguard Manor Road,
Shanklin, Isle of Wight
PO37 7HZ
T: (01983) 862880
F: (01983) 862880
E: metcalf@culham99.freeserve.
co.uk
I: www.isleofwight-hotel.co.uk

Duncroft Hotel ◆◆◆
2 Wilton Park Road, Shanklin,
Isle of Wight PO37 7BT
T: (01983) 862427
F: (01983) 862963
E: angela@duncrofthotel.
freeserve.co.uk
I: www.duncrofthotel.freeserve.
co.uk

The Edgecliffe Hotel ◆◆◆◆
7 Clarence Gardens, Shanklin,
Isle of Wight PO37 6HA
T: (01983) 866199
F: (01983) 868841
E: edgecliffehtl@aol.com
I: www.wightonline.
co.uk/edgecliffehotel

The Empress of the Sea Hotel
◆◆◆◆
Luccombe Road, Shanklin, Isle of
Wight PO37 6RQ
T: (01983) 862178
F: (01983) 868636
E: empress.sea@virgin.net
I: www.empressofthesea.com

Esplanade Hotel
Rating Applied For
33 The Esplanade, Shanklin, Isle
of Wight PO37 6BG
T: (01983) 863001

Farringford Hotel ◆◆◆◆
19 Hope Road, Shanklin, Isle of
Wight PO37 6EA
T: (01983) 862176
E: crrome@excite.com
I: www.farringfordhotel.com

Fawley Guest House ◆◆◆
12 Hope Road, Shanklin, Isle of
Wight PO37 6EA
T: (01983) 868898 & 868828

Foxhills ◆◆◆◆◆
30 Victoria Avenue, Shanklin,
Isle of Wight PO37 6LS
T: (01983) 862329
F: (01983) 866666
E: info@foxhillshotel.co.uk
I: www.foxhillshotel.co.uk

The Glen Hotel ◆◆◆
4 Avenue Road, Shanklin, Isle of
Wight PO37 7BG
T: (01983) 862154

Grange Bank Hotel ◆◆◆◆
Grange Road, Shanklin, Isle of
Wight PO37 6NN
T: (01983) 862337
F: (01983) 862787
E: Grangebankhotel@aol.com
I: www.grangebank.co.uk

The Havelock Hotel ◆◆◆◆
2 Queens Road, Shanklin, Isle of
Wight PO37 6AN
T: (01983) 862747

Hazelwood Hotel ◆◆◆
14 Clarence Road, Shanklin, Isle
of Wight PO37 7BH
T: (01983) 862824
F: (01983) 862824
E: barbara.tubbs@
thehazelwood.free-online.co.uk
I: www.thehazelwood.
free-online.co.uk

Holly Lodge B & B ◆◆◆
29 Queens Road, Shanklin, Isle
of Wight PO37 6DQ
T: (01983) 863604

Hope Lodge Hotel ◆◆◆◆
21 Hope Road, Shanklin, Isle of
Wight PO37 6EA
T: (01983) 863140
F: (01983) 863140
E: janetwf@aol.com
I: placestostay.com

Jasmine Lodge ◆◆
156 Sandown Road, Shanklin,
Isle of Wight PO37 6HF
T: (01983) 863296
F: (01983) 863296

Kenbury Hotel ◆◆◆
Clarence Road, Shanklin, Isle of
Wight PO37 7BH
T: (01983) 862085
E: kenbury@isleofwighthotel.
co.uk
I: www.isleofwighthotel.co.uk

The Lincoln Hotel
Rating Applied For
30 Littlestairs Road, Shanklin,
Isle of Wight PO37 6HS
T: (01983) 861171
F: (01983) 862147

Meyrick Cliffs Hotel ◆◆
Esplanade, Shanklin, Isle of
Wight PO37 6BH
T: (01983) 862691
F: (01983) 862648

Miclaran Hotel ◆◆◆
37 Littlestairs Road, Shanklin,
Isle of Wight PO37 6HS
T: (01983) 862726
F: (01983) 862726

Mount House Hotel ◆◆◆
20 Arthurs Hill, Shanklin, Isle of
Wight PO37 6EE
T: (01983) 862556
F: (01983) 867551
E: mounthouse@netguides.
co.uk
I: www.netguides.co.uk

The Norfolk House Hotel
◆◆◆◆
The Esplanade, Shanklin, Isle of
Wight PO37 6BN
T: (01983) 863023
E: thenorfolkhousehotel@
tinywould.co.uk
I: www.nebsweb.
co.uk/thenorfolkhousehotel

Overstrand Hotel ◆◆◆
5 Howard Road, Shanklin, Isle of
Wight PO37 6HD
T: (01983) 862100
F: (01983) 862100

Palmerston Hotel ◆◆◆
Palmerston Road, Shanklin, Isle
of Wight PO37 6AS
T: (01983) 865547
F: (01983) 868008
E: info@palmerston-hotel.co.uk
I: www.palmerston-hotel.co.uk

Pink Beach Hotel ◆◆◆
20 The Esplanade, Shanklin, Isle
of Wight PO37 6BN
T: (01983) 862501

The Richmond Hotel ◆◆◆
23 Palmerston Road, Shanklin,
Isle of Wight PO37 6AS
T: (01983) 862874
F: (01983) 862874
E: richmondhotel.shanklin@
virgin.net

The Roseglen Hotel ◆◆◆
12 Palmerston Road, Shanklin,
Isle of Wight PO37 6AS
T: (01983) 863164
F: (01983) 862271
E: david@roseglen.co.uk

Rowborough Private Hotel
◆◆◆
32 Arthurs Hill, Shanklin, Isle of
Wight PO37 6EX
T: (01983) 866072
F: (01983) 867703

The Royson ◆◆◆◆
26 Littlestairs Road, Shanklin,
Isle of Wight PO37 6HS
T: (01983) 862163
F: (01983) 865403
I: www.theroyson.co.uk

Rozelle Hotel ◆◆◆
Atherley Road, Shanklin, Isle of
Wight PO37 7AT
T: (01983) 862745
F: (01983) 862745

Ryedale Private Hotel ◆◆◆
3 Atherley Road, Shanklin, Isle of
Wight PO37 7AT
T: (01983) 862375 &
07831 413233
F: (01983) 862375
E: ryedale@dottydots.co.uk
I: www.smoothhound.
co.uk/hotels/ryedalep.html

St Brelades Hotel ◆◆◆
15 Hope Road, Shanklin, Isle of
Wight PO37 6EA
T: (01983) 862967
E: julie@st-brelades-hotel.co.uk
I: www.st-brelades-hotel.co.uk

St Leonards Hotel ◆◆◆◆
22 Queens Road, Shanklin, Isle
of Wight PO37 6AW
T: (01983) 862121
F: (01983) 868895
E: les@stleonardsiw.freeserve.
co.uk
I: www.wight-breaks.co.uk

Seamer House ◆◆◆◆
30 Atherley Road, Shanklin, Isle
of Wight PO37 7AT
T: (01983) 864926
F: (01983) 864926
E: seamerhouse@tinyworld.
co.uk

Somerville Hotel ◆◆◆
14 St Georges Road, Shanklin,
Isle of Wight PO37 6BA
T: (01983) 862821

The Steamer Inn ◆◆◆◆
18 The Esplanade, Shanklin, Isle
of Wight PO37 6BS
T: (01983) 862641
F: (01983) 862741

Suncliffe Private Hotel ◆◆◆
8 Hope Road, Shanklin, Isle of
Wight PO37 6EA
T: (01983) 863009
F: (01983) 864868
E: suncliffe@pmorter.tcp.co.uk
I: www.homepages.tcp.
co.uk/~pmorter

Swiss Cottage Hotel ◆◆◆
10 St Georges Road, Shanklin,
Isle of Wight PO37 6BA
T: (01983) 862333
F: (01983) 862333
E: mail@swiss-cottage.co.uk
I: www.swiss-cottage.co.uk

The Triton Hotel ◆◆
23 Atherley Road, Shanklin, Isle
of Wight PO37 7AU
T: (01983) 862494

Westbourne Guest House
◆◆◆
23 Queens Road, Shanklin, Isle
of Wight PO37 6AW
T: (01983) 862360

Whitegates Guest House ◆◆◆
18 Wilton Park Road, Shanklin,
Isle of Wight PO37 7BT
T: (01983) 866126

Willow Bank Hotel ◆◆◆◆
36 Atherley Road, Shanklin, Isle
of Wight PO37 7AU
T: (01983) 862482 & 862486
F: (01983) 862486
E: willowbank.hotel@virgin.net
I: www.willowbankhotel.com

SHENINGTON
Oxfordshire

Sugarswell Farm ◆◆◆◆
Shenington, Banbury,
Oxfordshire OX15 6HW
T: (01295) 680512
F: (01295) 688149

Top Farm House ◆◆◆
Shenington, Banbury,
Oxfordshire OX15 6LZ
T: (01295) 670226
F: (01295) 678170
E: cc.services@virgin.net

SHENLEY CHURCH END
Buckinghamshire

3 Selby Grove ◆◆◆◆
Shenley Church End, Milton
Keynes, Buckinghamshire
MK5 6BN
T: (01908) 504663
E: ceyesmk@aol.com

SHILLINGFORD
Oxfordshire

The Kingfisher Inn
Rating Applied For
27 Henley Road, Shillingford,
Wallingford, Oxfordshire
OX10 7EL
T: (01865) 858595
F: (01865) 858286
E: enquiries@kingfisher-inn.
co.uk
I: www.kingfisher-inn.co.uk

Marsh House ◆◆◆
7 Court Drive, Shillingford,
Wallingford, Oxfordshire
OX10 7ER
T: (01865) 858496
F: (01865) 858496
E: marsh.house@talk21.com

SHIPTON BELLINGER
Hampshire

Parsonage Farm ◆◆◆◆
Shipton Bellinger, Tidworth,
Hampshire SP9 7UF
T: (01980) 842404
F: (01980) 842404

SHIPTON-UNDER-WYCHWOOD
Oxfordshire

Court Farm ◆◆◆◆
Mawles Lane, Shipton-under-
Wychwood, Oxford OX7 6DA
T: (01993) 831515
F: (01993) 831813
E: belinda@courtfarmbb.fsnet.
co.uk

Courtlands ◆◆◆◆
6 Courtlands Road, Shipton-
under-Wychwood, Oxford,
Oxfordshire OX7 6DF
T: (01993) 830551
E: j-jfletcher@which.net
I: www.homepages.which.
net/~j-jfletcher/j-jfletcher/index.
html

Garden Cottage ◆◆◆
Fiddlers Hill, Shipton-under-
Wychwood, Chipping Norton,
Oxfordshire OX7 6DR
T: (01993) 830640 &
07803 399697
E: charmian@ukgateway.net

Lodge Cottage ◆◆◆
Shipton-under-Wychwood,
Oxford OX7 6DG
T: (01993) 830811

SHIRRELL HEATH
Hampshire

Highdown
Rating Applied For
Twynhams Hill, Shirrell Heath,
Southampton SO32 2SL
T: (01329) 835876
F: (01329) 835876

SHOOTASH
Hampshire

Lower Frenchwood Farm ◆◆◆
The Frenches, Shootash,
Romsey, Hampshire SO51 6FE
T: (01794) 322939

SHORWELL
Isle of Wight

Bucks Farm ◆◆◆◆
Shorwell, Newport, Isle of Wight
PO30 3LP
T: (01983) 551206
F: (01983) 551206

Northcourt ◆◆◆◆
Main Road, Shorwell, Newport,
Isle of Wight PO30 3JG
T: (01983) 740415
F: (01983) 740409
E: john@north-court.demon.
co.uk

Westcourt Farm ◆◆◆◆
Limerstone Road, Shorwell,
Newport, Isle of Wight PO30 3LA
T: (01983) 740233

SHOTTESWELL
Oxfordshire

Slated Barn Guest House
Rating Applied For
Slated Barn, Warwick Road,
Shotteswell, Banbury,
Oxfordshire OX17 1GA
T: (01295) 738999
F: (01295) 738807

SONNING COMMON
Oxfordshire

21 Red House Drive
Rating Applied For
Sonning Common, Reading
RG4 9NT
T: (0118) 972 2312
F: (0118) 972 2312

The Spinney ◆◆◆
40 Woodlands Road, Sonning
Common, Reading RG4 9TE
T: (0118) 9723248
E: john.terry@bushinternet.com

SOULDERN
Oxfordshire

The Fox Inn ◆◆
Fox Lane, Souldern, Bicester,
Oxfordshire OX27 7JW
T: (01869) 345284
F: (01869) 345667

Tower Fields ◆◆◆
Tusmore Road, Souldern,
Bicester, Oxfordshire OX27 7HY
T: (01869) 346554
F: (01869) 345157
E: hgould@strayduck.com

SOUTH GORLEY
Hampshire

Hucklesbrook Farm ◆◆◆◆
South Gorley, Fordingbridge,
Hampshire SP6 2PN
T: (01425) 653180
E: dh.sampson@btinternet.com

SOUTH LEIGH
Oxfordshire

Stow Cottage ◆◆◆
Station Road, South Leigh,
Witney, Oxfordshire OX29 6XN
T: (01993) 704005 &
07703 681920
F: (01993) 704005

SOUTHAMPTON
Hampshire

Acorn Lodge Guest House
◆◆◆
75 Morris Road, Polygon,
Southampton, SO15 2QB
T: (023) 8022 4837

Addenro House Hotel ◆◆
40-42 Howard Road, Shirley,
Southampton, SO15 5BL
T: (023) 8022 7144

Alcantara Guest House ◆◆◆
20 Howard Road, Shirley,
Southampton, SO15 5BN
T: (023) 8033 2966 & 8049 6163
F: (023) 8049 6163
E: alcantara@supanet.com
I: www.alcantaraguesthouse.
co.uk

Argyle Lodge ◆◆◆
13 Landguard Road, Shirley,
Southampton, SO15 5DL
T: (023) 8022 4063
F: (023) 8033 3688

Ashelee Lodge ◆◆◆
36 Atherley Road, Shirley,
Southampton, SO15 5DQ
T: (023) 8022 2095
F: (023) 8022 2095

Banister House Hotel ◆◆
Banister Road, Southampton,
SO15 2JJ
T: (023) 8022 1279 & 8022 5753
F: (023) 8022 6551
E: banisterhouse@lineone.net

The Bosun's Locker
Rating Applied For
Castle Square, Upper Bugle
Street, Southampton, SO14 2EE
T: (02380) 333364
F: (02380) 333364

Carmel Guest House ◆◆◆
306 Winchester Road, Shirley,
Southampton, SO16 6TU
T: (023) 8077 3579

Cliffden Guest House ◆◆◆
43 The Polygon, Southampton,
SO15 2BP
T: (023) 8022 4003

Eaton Court Hotel ◆◆◆
32 Hill Lane, Southampton,
SO15 5AY
T: (023) 8022 3081
F: (023) 8032 2006
E: ecourthot@aol.com
I: www.eatoncourtsouthampton.
co.uk

Ellenborough House ◆◆◆
172 Hill Lane, Shirley,
Southampton, SO15 5DB
T: (023) 8022 1716
F: (023) 8034 8486

Fenland Guest House ◆◆◆
79 Hill Lane, Southampton,
SO15 5AD
T: (023) 8022 0360
F: (023) 8022 6574
E: sde5999756@aol.com

Hunters Lodge Hotel ◆◆◆◆
25 Landguard Road, Shirley,
Southampton, SO15 5DL
T: (023) 8022 7919
F: (023) 8023 0913
E: hunterslodge.hotel@virgin.
net

Linden Guest House ◆◆◆
51-53 The Polygon,
Southampton, SO15 2BP
T: (023) 8022 5653
F: (023) 8063 0808

The Lodge ◆◆◆
No 1 Winn Road, The Avenue,
Southampton, SO17 1EH
T: (023) 8055 7537
F: (023) 8055 3586
E: lodgehotel@faxvia.net
I: www.yell.co.uk/siteslodgeso17

Madeleine Guest House
Rating Applied For
55 The Polygon, Southampton,
SO15 2BP
T: (023) 8033 3331
F: (023) 8033 3331

Madison House
Rating Applied For
137 Hill Lane, Southampton,
Hampshire SO15 5AF
T: (023) 8033 3374
F: (023) 8033 1209
E: foley@madisonhouse.co.uk
I: www.madisonhouse.co.uk

The Mayfair Guest House
◆◆◆◆
11 Landguard Road, Shirley,
Southampton, SO15 5DL
T: (023) 8022 9861
F: (023) 8021 1552

Mayview Guest House ◆◆◆
30 The Polygon, Southampton,
SO15 2BN
T: (023) 8022 0907
E: j_cole_new.uk@excite.co.uk

Nirvana Hotel ◆◆
386 Winchester Road, Bassett,
Southampton, Hampshire
SO16 7DH
T: (023) 8079 0087 & 8079 0993
F: (023) 8079 0575

Rivendell ◆◆◆
19 Landguard Road, Shirley,
Southampton, SO15 5DL
T: (023) 80 223240
E: rivendellbb@amserve.net

The Royal Standard ◆◆◆
Western Esplanade,
Southampton, Hampshire
SO14 2AZ
T: (023) 8063 3344
F: (023) 8063 3344

The Spinnaker ◆◆◆
Bridge Road, Lower Swanwick,
Southampton, Hampshire
SO31 7EB
T: (01489) 572123
F: (01489) 577394

Villa Capri Guest House ◆◆◆
50-52 Archers Road,
Southampton, SO15 2LU
T: (023) 8063 2800
F: (023) 8063 0100

Acorns Hotel ◆◆◆◆
14 Southwood Avenue,
Southbourne, Bournemouth
BH6 3QA
T: (01202) 422438
F: (01202) 418384
E: acornshotel@hotmail.com

Hawkesmore Hotel ◆◆◆
3 Beech Avenue, Southbourne,
Bournemouth BH6 3ST
T: (01202) 426787 & 416959

Newpoint Hotel
Rating Applied For
25 Pinecliffe Avenue,
Southbourne, Bournemouth,
Dorset BH6 3PY
T: (01202) 425047

Pennington Hotel ◆◆◆◆
26 Southern Road, Southbourne,
Bournemouth BH6 3SS
T: (01202) 428653 & 420912
F: (01202) 428653
E: vranderton@btinternet.co.uk

Shearwater Hotel ◆◆◆
61 Grand Avenue, Southbourne,
Bournemouth, Dorset BH6 3TA
T: (01202) 423396
F: (01202) 423396
E: shearwaterbb@hotmail.com
I: www.theshearwater.freeserve.
co.uk

Sherbourne House Hotel
◆◆◆◆
14 Southern Road, Southbourne,
Bournemouth BH6 3SR
T: (01202) 425680
F: (01202) 257423
E: ian@sherbournehousehotel.
co.uk
I: www.sherbournehousehotel.
co.uk

Pinkhill Cottage ◆◆◆◆
45 Rack End, Standlake, Witney,
Oxfordshire OX29 7SA
T: (01865) 300544
E: pinkhill@madasafish.com

Stanford Park House ◆◆◆
Park Lane, Stanford in the Vale,
Faringdon, Oxfordshire SN7 8PF
T: (01367) 710702 &
07831 242694
F: (01367) 710329
E: gjd34@dial.pipex.com
I: www.stanfordpark.co.uk

The Talkhouse
Rating Applied For
Wheatley Road, Stanton St John,
Oxford, Oxfordshire OX33 1EX
T: (01865) 351648
F: (01865) 351085
E: talkhouse@stantonstjohn.
fsnet.co.uk

Westfield Farm Motel ◆◆◆◆
Fenway, Steeple Aston, Oxford
OX25 4SS
T: (01869) 340591
F: (01869) 347594
E: info@westfieldmotel.u-net.
com
I: www.oxlink.
co.uk/accom/westfield-farm/

Carbery Guest House ◆◆◆
Salisbury Hill, Stockbridge,
Hampshire SO20 6EZ
T: (01264) 810771
F: (01264) 811022

Hallbottom Farm
Rating Applied For
Park Lane, Stokenchurch, High
Wycombe, Buckinghamshire
HP14 3TQ
T: (01494) 482520 &
07878 216024

Vicarage Farmhouse ◆◆◆◆
Churchway, Stone, Aylesbury,
Buckinghamshire HP17 8RG
T: (01296) 748182 &
07885 181435

The Old School ◆◆◆
Mill Road, Stratton Audley,
Bicester, Oxfordshire OX6 9BJ
T: (01869) 277371
E: sawertheimer@euphony.net
I: www.old-school.co.uk

West Farm ◆◆◆◆
Launton Road, Stratton Audley,
Bicester, Oxfordshire OX27 9AS
T: (01869) 278344
F: (01869) 278344
E: sara.westfarmbb@virgin.net
I: www.westfarm.supaweb.co.uk

The Bull ◆◆◆
Reading Road, Streatley,
Reading, Berkshire RG8 9JT
T: (01491) 872392
F: (01491) 875231

Pennyfield ◆◆◆◆
The Coombe, Streatley, Reading
RG8 9QI
T: (01491) 872048 &
07774 946182
F: (01491) 872048
E: mandrvanstone@hotmail.
com
I: web.onetel.net.
uk/~mandrvanstone

The Bankes Arms Hotel ◆◆◆
Manor Road, Studland,
Swanage, Dorset BH19 3AU
T: (01929) 450225 & 450310
F: (01929) 450307

Fairfields Hotel ◆◆◆◆
Swanage Road, Studland,
Swanage, Dorset BH19 3AE
T: (01929) 450224
F: (01929) 450571

Melrose ◆◆◆
16 Charborough Way,
Sturminster Marshall, Wimborne
Minster, Dorset BH21 4DH
T: (01258) 858359
E: hjewitt@btinternet.com
I: www.four-runner.
com/melrose

The Homestead ◆◆◆
Hole House Lane, Sturminster
Newton, Dorset DT10 2AA
T: (01258) 471390
F: (01258) 471090
E: townsend@dircon.co.uk
I: www.townsend.dircon.co.uk/

The Old Manor ◆◆◆◆◆
Whitehouse Green,
Sulhamstead, Reading RG7 4EA
T: (0118) 983 2423
F: (0118) 983 6262
E: rags-r@theoldmanor.
fsbusiness.co.uk

Partway House ◆◆◆◆◆
Swalcliffe, Banbury, Oxfordshire
OX15 5HA
T: (01295) 780246
F: (01295) 780988

Amberlea Hotel ◆◆◆◆
36 Victoria Avenue, Swanage,
Dorset BH19 1AP
T: (01929) 426213
E: amberlea-guesthouse@
excite.co.uk

Bella Vista Hotel ◆◆◆◆
Burlington Road, Swanage,
Dorset BH19 1LS
T: (01929) 422873
F: (01929) 426220
E: mail@bellavista-hotel.com
I: www.bellavista-hotel.com

The Castleton Hotel ◆◆◆◆
1 Highcliffe Road, Swanage,
Dorset BH19 1LW
T: (01929) 423972
F: (01929) 422901

Easter Cottage ◆◆◆◆
9 Eldon Terrace, Swanage,
Dorset BH19 1HA
T: (01929) 427782

Firswood Hotel ◆◆◆
29 Kings Road West, Swanage,
Dorset BH19 1HF
T: (01929) 422306 &
07957 181652
E: firswood@aol.com
I: www.firswoodguesthouse.
co.uk

Glenlee Hotel ◆◆◆◆
6 Cauldon Avenue, Swanage,
Dorset BH19 1PQ
T: (01929) 425794
F: (01929) 421530
E: martin@glenleehotel.
freeserve.co.uk

Goodwyns ◆◆◆◆
2 Walrond Road, Swanage,
Dorset BH19 1PB
T: (01929) 421088

The Limes Hotel ◆◆◆
48 Park Road, Swanage, Dorset
BH19 2AE
T: (01929) 422664 & 0870 054
8794
F: 0870 054 8794
E: info@limeshotel.demon.co.uk
I: www.limeshotel.demon.co.uk

Millbrook Guest House ◆◆◆
56 Kings Road West, Swanage,
Dorset BH19 1HA
T: (01929) 423443
F: (01929) 423443
E: bob.millbrook@virgin.net
I: freespace.virgin.net/bob.
millbrook

St Michael ◆◆◆◆
31 Kings Road, Swanage, Dorset
BH19 1HF
T: (01929) 422064

Sandringham Hotel ◆◆◆
20 Durlston Road, Swanage,
Dorset BH19 2HX
T: (01929) 423076
F: (01929) 423076
E: silk@sandhot.fsnet.co.uk

White Lodge Hotel ◆◆◆◆
Grosvenor Road, Swanage,
Dorset BH19 2DD
T: (01929) 422696
F: (01929) 425510
E: whitelodge.hotel@virgin.net
I: www.whitelodgehotel.co.uk

SWANMORE
Hampshire

Hill Top ◆◆◆◆
Upper Swanmore, Swanmore,
Southampton, Hampshire
SO32 2QQ
T: (01489) 892653
F: (01489) 892653

SWAY
Hampshire

Forest Heath Hotel ◆◆◆
Station Road, Sway, Lymington,
Hampshire SO41 6BA
T: (01590) 682287
F: (01590) 682626

Little Arnewood Cottage ◆◆◆
Linnies Lane, Sway, Lymington,
Hampshire SO41 6ES
T: (01590) 682920 &
07866 852679
E: littlearnewoodcottage@
eurolink.ltd.net

Little Purley Farm ◆◆◆
Chapel Lane, Sway, Lymington,
Hampshire SO41 6BS
T: (01590) 682707
F: (01590) 682707

Manor Farm ◆◆◆
Coombe Lane, Sway, Lymington,
Hampshire SO41 6BP
T: (01590) 683542

The Nurse's Cottage ◆◆◆◆◆
Station Road, Sway, Lymington,
Hampshire SO41 6BA
T: (01590) 683402
F: (01590) 683402
E: nurses.cottage@lineone.net
I: www.hants.gov.
uk/tourist/hotels
🏃

The Old Chapel ◆◆◆◆
Chapel House, Coombe Lane,
Sway, Lymington, Hampshire
SO41 6BP
T: (01590) 683382
F: (01590) 682979

Squirrels ◆◆◆
Broadmead, (off Silver Street),
Sway, Lymington, Hampshire
SO41 6DH
T: (01590) 683163
I: www.newforest.demon.
co.uk/squirrels.htm

Tiverton ◆◆◆
9 Cruse Close, Sway, Lymington,
Hampshire SO41 6AY
T: (01590) 683092
F: (01590) 683092
E: ronrowe@talk21.com

TAPLOW
Buckinghamshire

Bridge Cottage Guest House
◆◆◆
Bath Road, Taplow, Maidenhead,
Berkshire SL6 0AR
T: (01628) 626805
F: (01628) 788785

TARRANT LAUNCESTON
Dorset

Ramblers Cottage ◆◆◆◆
Tarrant Launceston, Blandford
Forum, Dorset DT11 8BY
T: (01258) 830528
E: sworrall@ramblerscottage.
fsnet.co.uk
I: www.ramblerscottage.fsnet.
co.uk

THAME
Oxfordshire

The Dairy ◆◆◆◆◆
Moreton, Thame, Oxfordshire
OX9 2HX
T: (01844) 214075
F: (01844) 214075
E: thedairy@freeuk.com
I: www.thedairy.freeuk.com

Field Farm ◆◆◆
Rycote Lane, North Weston,
Thame, Oxfordshire OX9 2HQ
T: (01844) 215428

Langsmeade House ◆◆◆◆
Milton Common, Thame,
Oxfordshire OX9 2JY
T: (01844) 278727
F: (01844) 279256

Oakfield ◆◆◆◆
Thame Park Road, Thame,
Oxfordshire OX9 3PL
T: (01844) 213709 &
07785 764447

THATCHAM
Berkshire

The Swan ◆◆◆
Station Road, Thatcham,
Berkshire RG13 4QL
T: (01635) 862084
F: (01635) 871851

THREE LEGGED CROSS
Dorset

Thatch Cottage ◆◆◆◆
Ringwood Road, Three Legged
Cross, Wimborne Minster,
Dorset BH21 6QY
T: (01202) 822042
F: (01202) 821888
E: dthatchcottage@aol.com
I: www.thatch-cottage.co.uk

THRUXTON
Hampshire

May Cottage ◆◆◆◆
Thruxton, Andover, Hampshire
SP11 8LZ
T: (01264) 771241 &
07768 242166
F: (01264) 771770

TILEHURST
Berkshire

Beethovens Hotel ◆◆
De Hillier Taverns plc, Oxford
Road, Tilehurst, Reading,
Berkshire RG31 6TG
T: (0118) 942 7517
F: (0118) 941 7629

2 Cotswold Way ◆◆
Tilehurst, Reading RG31 6SH
T: (0118) 9413286

TITCHFIELD
Hampshire

Westcote Bed & Breakfast
◆◆◆◆
325 Southampton Road,
Titchfield, Fareham, Hampshire
PO14 4AY
T: (01329) 846297 &
07711 293421
F: (01329) 846297

TOTLAND BAY
Isle of Wight

Chart House ◆◆◆◆
Madeira Road, Totland Bay, Isle
of Wight PO39 0BJ
T: (01983) 755091

**Frenchman's Cove Country
Hotel** ◆◆◆
Alum Bay Old Road, Totland Bay,
Isle of Wight PO39 0HZ
T: (01983) 752227
F: (01983) 755125
E: boatfield@frenchmanscove.
co.uk
I: www.frenchmanscove.co.uk

The Highdown Inn ◆◆◆
Highdown Lane, Totland Bay,
Isle of Wight PO39 0HY
T: (01983) 752450
F: (01983) 752450

Latton House ◆◆◆
Madeira Road, Totland Bay, Isle
of Wight PO39 0BJ
T: (01983) 754868
F: (01983) 754868

Littledene Lodge ◆◆◆
Granville Road, Totland Bay, Isle
of Wight PO39 0AX
T: (01983) 752411
F: (01983) 752411

Lomarick ◆◆◆
Church Hill, Totland Bay, Isle of
Wight PO39 0EU
T: (01983) 753364
E: lomarick.isleofwight@virgin.
net
I: www.wightonline.
co.uk/lomarick

The Nodes Country Hotel
◆◆◆
Alum Bay Old Road, Totland Bay,
Isle of Wight PO39 0HZ
T: (01983) 752859 & 752859
E: (023) 9220 1226

Norton Lodge ◆◆◆
Granville Road, Totland Bay, Isle
of Wight PO39 0AZ
T: (01983) 752772 &
07971 815460
E: jacquie.simmons@talk21.com

Sandford Lodge ◆◆◆◆
61 The Avenue, Totland Bay, Isle
of Wight PO39 0DN
T: (01983) 753478
F: (01983) 753478
E: sandfordlodge@cwcom.net

Sandy Lane Guest House ◆◆◆
Colwell Common Road, Totland
Bay, Isle of Wight PO39 0DD
T: (01983) 752240
F: (01983) 752240
E: jane@sandylaneguesthouse.
fsnet.co.uk

TOTTON
Hampshire

Colbury Manor ◆◆◆◆
Jacobs Gutter Lane, Eling,
Totton, Southampton SO40 9FY
T: (023) 8086 2283
F: (023) 8086 5545

Ivy Lawn ◆◆◆◆
Eling Hill, Totton, Southampton
SO40 9HE
T: (023) 8066 0925 &
07803 246202
I: www.ivylawn.co.uk

TWYFORD
Berkshire

Chesham House ◆◆◆
79 Wargrave Road, Twyford,
Reading RG40 9PE
T: (0118) 932 0428
E: maria.ferguson@virgin.net

UPPER BUCKLEBURY
Berkshire

Brockley ◆◆◆
Little Lane, Upper Bucklebury,
Reading RG7 6QX
T: (01635) 869742 &
07887 870226

UPTON
Oxfordshire

The White House ◆◆◆
Reading Road, Upton, Didcot,
Oxfordshire OX11 9HP
T: (01235) 850289

VENTNOR
Isle of Wight

Bellevue House ◆◆◆◆
Bellevue Road, Ventnor, Isle of
Wight PO38 1DB
T: (01983) 855047

Bermuda Guest House ◆◆◆
3 Alexandra Gardens, Ventnor,
Isle of Wight PO38 1EE
T: (01983) 852349

Brunswick House ◆◆◆
Victoria Street, Ventnor, Isle of
Wight PO38 1ET
T: (01983) 852656
E: graemebarker@aol.com

Cornerways ◆◆◆
39 Madeira Road, Ventnor, Isle
of Wight PO38 1QS
T: (01983) 852323
I: www.cornerwaysventnor.co.uk

Delamere Guest House ◆◆◆◆
Bellevue Road, Ventnor, Isle of
Wight PO38 1DB
T: (01983) 852322
F: (01983) 852322

Sterlings ◆◆◆◆
11 Altofts Gardens, Ventnor, Isle
of Wight PO38 1DT
T: (01983) 853479
F: (01983) 853479

VERNEY JUNCTION
Buckinghamshire
The White Cottage ◆◆◆
Verney Junction, Buckingham
MK18 2JZ
T: (01296) 714416 &
07836 642191

VERNHAM DEAN
Hampshire
Upton Cottage ◆◆◆
Vernham Dean, Andover,
Hampshire SP11 0JY
T: (01264) 737640
F: (01264) 737640

VERWOOD
Dorset
Verwood Farmhouse ◆◆◆◆
Margards Lane, Verwood,
Wimborne Minster, Dorset
BH31 6JQ
T: (01202) 822083
E: sue@verwoodfarmhouse.net
I: www.verwoodfarmhouse.net

Woodside Cottage ◆◆◆
Sutton Holmes, Verwood,
Wimborne Minster, Dorset
BH21 6NQ
T: (01202) 829763
F: (01202) 829840

WADDESDON
Buckinghamshire
The Georgian Doll's Cottage
◆◆◆◆
High Street, Waddesdon,
Aylesbury, Buckinghamshire
HP18 0NE
T: (01296) 655553 &
07956 941820

The Old Dairy
Rating Applied For
4 High Street, Waddesdon,
Aylesbury, Buckinghamshire
HP18 0JA
T: (01296) 658627

WALKFORD
Dorset
Acorns ◆◆◆
37 Walkford Road, Walkford,
Christchurch, Dorset BH23 5QD
T: (01425) 270903 & 270476
F: (01425) 270476
E: kevin.prouten@virgin.net

WALLINGFORD
Oxfordshire
Fords Farm ◆◆◆◆
Ewelme, Wallingford,
Oxfordshire OX10 6HU
T: (01491) 839272
E: fordsfarm@callnetuk.com

Little Gables ◆◆◆
166 Crowmarsh Hill, Crowmarsh
Gifford, Wallingford,
Oxfordshire OX10 8BG
T: (01491) 837834 &
07860 148882
F: (01491) 834426
E: jill@stayingaway.com
I: www.stayingaway.com

North Farm ◆◆◆◆
Shillingford Hill, Wallingford,
Oxfordshire OX10 8NB
T: (01865) 858406
F: (01865) 858519
E: northfarm@compuserve.com
I: www.country-accom.
co.uk/north-farm/

WAREHAM
Dorset
The Old Granary
Rating Applied For
The Quay, Wareham, Dorset
BH20 4LP
T: (01929) 552010
F: (01929) 552482

The Old Granary ◆◆◆◆
West Holme Farm, Wareham,
Dorset BH20 6AQ
T: (01929) 552972
F: (01929) 551616
E: venngoldsack@lineone.net

WARGRAVE
Berkshire
Appletree Cottage ◆◆◆◆
Backsideans, Wargrave, Reading
RG10 8JS
T: (0118) 940 4306
E: trishlangham@
appletreecottage.co.uk
I: www.appletreecottage.co.uk

WARRINGTON
Buckinghamshire
Home Farm ◆◆◆◆◆
Warrington, Olney,
Buckinghamshire MK46 4HN
T: (01234) 711655
F: (01234) 711855
E: ruth@oldstonebarn.co.uk
I: www.oldstonebarn.co.uk

WARSASH
Hampshire
Dormy House Hotel ◆◆◆◆
21 Barnes Lane, Sarisbury Green,
Southampton SO31 7DA
T: (01489) 572626
F: (01489) 573370
E: dormyhousehotel@warsash.
globalnet.co.uk
I: www.silverblue.co.uk/dormy

Solent View Hotel ◆◆◆◆
33 Newtown Road, Warsash,
Southampton SO31 9FY
T: (01489) 572300
F: (01489) 572300

WATER STRATFORD
Buckinghamshire
The Rolling Acres ◆◆◆◆
Water Stratford, Buckingham
MK18 5DX
T: (01280) 847302 &
07770 608366
F: 07929 336694
E: david.abbotts@talk21.com

WATERLOOVILLE
Hampshire
Clibdens
Rating Applied For
Chalton, Waterlooville,
Hampshire PO8 0BG
T: (02392) 592172
F: (02392) 596320

Holly Dale ◆◆◆
11 Lovedean Lane, Waterlooville,
Hampshire PO8 8HH
T: (023) 9259 2047

WATLINGTON
Oxfordshire
Huttons ◆◆◆
Britwell Salome, Watlington,
Oxford OX49 5LH
T: (01491) 614389
F: (01491) 614993
E: efonwell@mail.com

WENDOVER
Buckinghamshire
Belton House ◆
26 Chiltern Road, Wendover,
Aylesbury, Buckinghamshire
HP22 6DB
T: (01296) 622351

Dunsmore Edge ◆◆◆
London Road, Wendover,
Aylesbury, Buckinghamshire
HP22 6PN
T: (01296) 623080
E: uron@lineone.net.uk

Field Cottage ◆◆◆◆
St Leonards, Tring, Hertfordshire
HP23 6NS
T: (01494) 837602 &
07803 295337

17 Icknield Close ◆◆◆
Wendover, Aylesbury,
Buckinghamshire HP22 6HG
T: (01296) 583312
E: grbr@cwcom.net
I: www.visitbritain.com

46 Lionel Avenue ◆◆◆
Wendover, Aylesbury,
Buckinghamshire HP22 6LP
T: (01296) 623426

WEST LULWORTH
Dorset
Gatton House ◆◆◆◆
West Lulworth, Wareham,
Dorset BH20 5RU
T: (01929) 400252
F: (01929) 400252
E: mikedale@gattonhouse.co.uk
I: gattonhouse.co.uk

Graybank ◆◆◆
Main Road, West Lulworth,
Wareham, Dorset BH20 5RL
T: (01929) 400256

Lulworth Cove Hotel ◆◆◆
Main Road, West Lulworth,
Wareham, Dorset BH20 5RQ
T: (01929) 400333
F: (01929) 400534
E: hotel@lulworth-cove.com
I: www.lulworth-cove.com

The Old Barn ◆◆◆
Lulworth Cove, West Lulworth,
Wareham, Dorset BH20 5RL
T: (01929) 400305
F: (01929) 400516

WEST MEON
Hampshire
Brocklands Farm ◆◆◆
West Meon, Petersfield,
Hampshire GU32 1JN
T: (01730) 829228
F: (01730) 829325
E: hf.morris@virgin.net

WEST WELLOW
Hampshire
Lukes Barn ◆◆◆
Maury's Lane, West Wellow,
Romsey, Hampshire SO51 6DA
T: (01794) 324431
F: (01794) 324431

WESTBURY
Buckinghamshire
Mill Farm House ◆◆◆
Westbury, Brackley,
Northamptonshire NN13 5JS
T: (01280) 704843
F: (01280) 704843

WESTON-ON-THE-GREEN
Oxfordshire
Weston Grounds Farm ◆◆◆
Weston-on-the-Green, Bicester,
Oxfordshire OX25 3QX
T: (01869) 351168
F: (01869) 350887

WESTON TURVILLE
Buckinghamshire
Brickwall Farm Cottage
Rating Applied For
Mill Lane, Weston Turville,
Aylesbury, Buckinghamshire
HP22 5RG
T: (01296) 612656
F: (01296) 614017
E: davidwleech@totalise.co.uk

The Hideaway ◆◆◆
Main Street, Weston Turville,
Aylesbury, Buckinghamshire
HP22 5RR
T: (01296) 612604
F: (01296) 615705

Loosley House ◆◆◆◆
87 New Road, Weston Turville,
Aylesbury, Buckinghamshire
HP22 5QT
T: (01296) 428285 & 484157
F: (01296) 428285

WEYHILL
Hampshire
Juglans ◆◆◆◆
Red Post Lane, Weyhill, Andover,
Hampshire SP11 0PY
T: (01264) 772651 &
07802 664540

WHERWELL
Hampshire
New House Bed & Breakfast
◆◆◆
New House, Fullerton Road,
Wherwell, Andover, Hampshire
SP11 7JS
T: (01264) 860817
E: DiWoodWherwell@aol.com

WHIPPINGHAM
Isle of Wight

1 Truckles Cottage ◆◆◆
Beatrice Avenue, Whippingham,
East Cowes, Isle of Wight
PO32 6LW
T: (01983) 292606
E: wrighttruckles@freeserve.
co.uk

WHITCHURCH
Hampshire

Peak House Farm ◆◆◆
Cole Henley, Whitchurch,
Hampshire RG28 7QJ
T: (01256) 892052
E: peakhousefarm@tesco.net

White Hart Hotel ◆◆
Newbury Street, Whitchurch,
Hampshire RG28 7DN
T: (01256) 892900
F: (01256) 896628

WHITWELL
Isle of Wight

The Old Rectory ◆◆◆
Ashknowle Lane, Whitwell,
Ventnor, Isle of Wight PO38 2PP
T: (01983) 731242
F: (01983) 731288
E: rectory@ukonline.co.uk
I: www.wightonline.
co.uk/oldrectory

WICKHAM
Hampshire

Chiphall Acre ◆◆◆
Droxford Road (A32), Wickham,
Fareham, Hampshire PO17 5AY
T: (01329) 833188
F: (01329) 833188
E: mavis.stevens@zoom.co.uk
I: www.smoothhound.
co.uk/hotels/chiphall.html

Montrose ◆◆◆◆
Solomons Lane, Shirrell Heath,
Southampton, Hampshire
SO32 2HU
T: (01329) 833345
F: (01329) 833345
E: bb@montrose78.fsnet.co.uk

WIDMER END
Buckinghamshire

The White House ◆◆◆
North Road, Widmer End, High
Wycombe, Buckinghamshire
HP15 6ND
T: (01494) 712221
F: (01494) 712221

WIMBORNE MINSTER
Dorset

Ashton Lodge ◆◆◆◆
10 Oakley Hill, Wimborne
Minster, Dorset BH21 1QH
T: (01202) 883423
F: (01202) 886180
E: ashtonlodge@ukgateway.net
I: www.ashtonlodge.ukgateway.
net

Crab Apple Corner ◆◆◆
40 Lacy Drive, Wimborne
Minster, Dorset BH21 1DG
T: (01202) 840993
E: andrew.curry@virgin.net

**Hemsworth Manor Farm
◆◆◆◆**
Witchampton, Wimborne
Minster, Dorset BH21 5BN
T: (01258) 840216
F: (01258) 841278

Henbury Farm ◆◆◆◆
Dorchester Road, Sturminster
Marshall, Wimborne Minster,
Dorset BH21 3RN
T: (01258) 857306
F: (01258) 857928

Homestay ◆◆◆
22 West Borough, Wimborne
Minster, Dorset BH21 1NF
T: (01202) 849015
F: (01202) 849015

Hopewell ◆◆◆◆
Little Lonnen, Colehill,
Wimborne Minster, Dorset
BH21 7BB
T: (01202) 880311
E: hopewell@cwcom.net

Lantern Lodge ◆◆◆◆
47 Gravel Hill, Merley,
Wimborne Minster, Dorset
BH21 1RW
T: (01202) 884183

Meadbank ◆◆◆
5 Greenclose Lane, Wimborne
Minster, Dorset BH21 2AL
T: (01202) 849941

No 2 Stoneleaze ◆◆◆◆
Stone Lane, Wimborne Minster,
Dorset BH21 1HD
T: (01202) 842739

The Old George ◆◆◆◆
2 Corn Market, Wimborne
Minster, Dorset BH21 1JL
T: (01202) 888510
F: (01202) 888513

Old Merchant's House ◆◆◆◆
44 West Borough, Wimborne
Minster, Dorset BH21 1NQ
T: (01202) 841955

Peacehaven B & B ◆◆
282 Sopwith Crescent, Merley,
Wimborne Minster, Dorset
BH21 1XL
T: (01202) 880281

Pear Tree Cottage ◆◆
248 Wimborne Road West,
Stapehill, Wimborne Minster,
Dorset BH21 2DZ
T: (01202) 890174
E: ca.whiteman@ntlworld.com

Silvertrees ◆◆◆
Merley House Lane, Wimborne
Minster, Dorset BH21 3AA
T: (01202) 880418
F: (01202) 881415
E: philfihammick@hotmail.com

Twynham ◆◆◆
67 Poole Road, Wimborne
Minster, Dorset BH21 1QB
T: (01202) 887310

96 West Borough ◆◆◆
Wimborne Minster, Dorset
BH21 1NH
T: (01202) 884039

**38 Wimborne Road West
◆◆◆**
Wimborne Minster, Dorset
BH21 2DP
T: (01202) 889357

Woodlands ◆◆◆◆
29 Merley Ways, Wimborne
Minster, Dorset BH21 1QN
T: (01202) 887625

WINCHESTER
Hampshire

Acacia ◆◆◆◆
44 Kilham Lane, Winchester,
Hampshire SO22 5PT
T: (01962) 852259 &
04801 537703
F: (01962) 852259
E: eric.buchanan@mcmail.com
I: www.btinternet.com/~eric.
buchanan

12 Christchurch Road ◆◆
Winchester, Hampshire
SO23 9SR
T: (01962) 854272

85 Christchurch Road ◆◆◆◆
Winchester, Hampshire
SO23 9QY
T: (01962) 868661
F: (01962) 868661
E: fetherstondilke@x-stream.
co.uk

Dawn Cottage ◆◆◆◆
Romsey Road, Winchester,
Hampshire SO22 5PQ
T: (01962) 869956
F: (01962) 869956

Dellbrook ◆◆
Hubert Road, St Cross,
Winchester, Hampshire
SO23 9RG
T: (01962) 865093
F: (01962) 865093
E: dellbrook2@aol.com

East View ◆◆◆◆
16 Clifton Hill, Winchester,
Hampshire SO22 5BL
T: (01962) 862986

The Farrells ◆◆◆
5 Ranelagh Road, St Cross,
Winchester, Hampshire
SO23 9TA
T: (01962) 869555
F: (01962) 869555
E: thefarrells@easicom.com

Portland House ◆◆◆◆
63 Tower Street, Winchester,
Hampshire SO23 8TA
T: (01962) 865195 &
07710 425577
F: (01962) 865195
E: tony@knightworld.com

St Margaret's ◆◆◆
3 St Michael's Road, Winchester,
Hampshire SO23 9JE
T: (01962) 861450 &
07802 478926
E: brigid.brett@amserve.net
I: www.winchesterbandb.com

Shawlands ◆◆◆◆
46 Kilham Lane, Winchester,
Hampshire SO22 5QD
T: (01962) 861166
F: (01962) 861166
E: kathy@pollshaw.u-net.com

54 St Cross Road ◆◆◆◆
Winchester, Hampshire
SO23 9PS
T: (01962) 852073
F: (01962) 852073

Stanmore Hotel ◆◆◆
Stanmore Lane, Stanmore,
Winchester, Hampshire
SO22 4BL
T: (01962) 852720
F: (01962) 850467

Sullivan's ◆◆
29 Stockbridge Road,
Winchester, Hampshire
SO22 6RW
T: (01962) 862027
E: sullivans_bandb@amserve.
net

Sycamores ◆◆◆◆
4 Bereweeke Close, Winchester,
Hampshire SO22 6AR
T: (01962) 867242
F: (01962) 620300
E: sycamores.b-and-b@virgin.
net

WINDRUSH
Oxfordshire

Dellwood ◆◆◆
Quarry Lane, Windrush, Oxford
OX18 4TR
T: (01451) 844268

WINDSOR
Berkshire

Alma House ◆◆◆
56 Alma Road, Windsor,
Berkshire SL4 3HA
T: (01753) 862983
F: (01753) 862983
E: info@almahouse.co.uk
I: www.almahouse.co.uk

Beaumont Lodge ◆◆◆◆
1 Beaumont Road, Windsor,
Berkshire SL4 1HY
T: (01753) 863436 &
07774 841273
F: (01753) 863436
E: bhamshere@beaumontlodge.
demon.co.uk
I: www.smoothhound.co.uk.
/hotels/beaulos.html

Clarence Hotel ◆◆
9 Clarence Road, Windsor,
Berkshire SL4 5AE
T: (01753) 864436
F: (01753) 857060

Halcyon House ◆◆◆
131 Clarence Road, Windsor,
Berkshire SL4 5AR
T: (01753) 863262 &
07768 034128
F: (01753) 863262
E: halcyonhouse@hotmail.com

Honeysuckle Cottage ◆◆◆◆
61 Fairfield Approach,
Wraysbury, Windsor, Berkshire
TW19 5DR
T: (01784) 482519
F: (01784) 482305
E: B&B@berks.force9.co.uk
I: www.berks.force9.co.uk

Jeans ◆◆
1 Stovell Road, Windsor,
Berkshire SL4 5JB
T: (01753) 852055
F: (01753) 842932

Melrose House ◆◆◆
53 Frances Road, Windsor,
Berkshire SL4 3AQ
T: (01753) 865328
F: (01753) 865328

Oscar Hotel ◆◆◆
65 Vansittart Road, Windsor,
Berkshire SL4 5DB
T: (01753) 830613
F: (01753) 833744
E: info@oscarhotel.com
I: www.oscarhotel.com

22 York Avenue ◆◆◆
Windsor, Berkshire SL4 3PD
T: (01753) 865775

WINFRITH NEWBURGH
Dorset
Wynards Farm
Rating Applied For
Winfrith Newburgh, Dorchester,
Dorset DT2 8DQ
T: (01305) 852660
F: (01305) 854094

WINSLOW
Buckinghamshire
The Congregational Church ◆◆◆
15 Horn Street, Winslow,
Buckingham MK18 3AP
T: (01296) 715717
F: (01296) 715717

The Old Manse ◆◆
9 Horn Street, Winslow,
Aylesbury, Buckinghamshire
MK18 3AP
T: (01296) 712048 &
0859 313339

Puzzletree ◆◆◆◆
3 Buckingham Road, Winslow,
Buckingham MK18 3DT
T: (01296) 712437
F: (01296) 712437
E: puzzletree@hotmail.com

'Witsend' ◆◆
9 Buckingham Road, Winslow,
Buckingham, Buckinghamshire
MK18 3DT
T: (01296) 712503 & 715499
E: sheila.spatcher@tesco.net

WINSOR
Hampshire
Trees ◆◆◆
Tatchbury Lane, Winsor,
Southampton SO40 2HA
T: (023) 8081 3128 &
07773 263305
F: (023) 8081 3128

WINTERBORNE STICKLAND
Dorset
Stickland Farmhouse ◆◆◆◆
Stickland Farmhouse,
Winterborne Stickland,
Blandford Forum, Dorset
DT11 0NT
T: (01258) 880119 &
07932 897774
F: (01258) 880119
E: sticklandfarmhouse@
sticklanddorset.fsnet.co.uk

WINTERBORNE ZELSTON
Dorset
Brook Farm ◆◆◆
Winterborne Zelston, Blandford
Forum, Dorset DT11 9EU
T: (01929) 459267 & 459284
F: (01929) 459267

Rainbow View Farm ◆◆◆
Winterborne Zelston, Blandford
Forum, Dorset DT11 9EU
T: (01929) 459529 &
0797 0032278
F: (01929) 145216

WITNEY
Oxfordshire
The Court Inn ◆◆◆
43 Bridge Street, Witney,
Oxfordshire OX8 6DA
T: (01993) 703228
F: (01993) 700980
E: info@thecourt.co.uk

Crofters Guest House ◆◆◆◆
29 Oxford Hill, Witney,
Oxfordshire OX28 3JU
T: (01993) 778165
F: (01993) 778165
E: crofers.ghouse@virgin.net

Ducklington Farm ◆◆◆
Coursehill Lane, Ducklington,
Witney, Oxfordshire OX8 7YG
T: (01993) 772175
I: www.country-accom.co.uk

Field View ◆◆◆◆
Wood Green, Witney,
Oxfordshire OX8 1DE
T: (01993) 705485 &
07768 614347
E: jsimpson@netcomuk.co.uk
I: www.netcomuk.
co.uk/~kearse/index.html

Hawthorn House ◆◆◆
79 Burford Road, Witney,
Oxfordshire OX8 5DR
T: (01993) 772768
E: roland@hawthorn79.
freeserve.co.uk
I: www.hawthornguesthouse.
co.uk

North Leigh Guest House ◆◆◆◆
28 Common Road, North Leigh,
Witney, Oxfordshire OX8 6RA
T: (01993) 881622

Quarrydene ◆◆
17 Dene Rise, Witney,
Oxfordshire OX8 5LU
T: (01993) 772152
F: (01993) 772152

**Springhill Farm Bed &
Breakfast** ◆◆◆
Cogges, Witney, Oxfordshire
OX8 6UL
T: (01993) 704919 &
07808 229569

The Witney Hotel ◆◆
7 Church Green, Witney,
Oxfordshire OX28 4AZ
T: (01993) 702137
F: (01993) 705337
E: bookings@thewitneyhotel.
co.uk

WOBURN SANDS
Buckinghamshire
The Old Stables ◆◆◆◆
Woodleys Farm, Bow Brickhill
Road, Woburn Sands, Milton
Keynes MK17 8DE
T: (01908) 281340 &
07778 313906
F: (01908) 584812

WOKINGHAM
Berkshire
South Lodge ◆◆◆◆
1A South Drive, Wokingham,
Berkshire RG40 2DH
T: (0118) 9789413
F: (0118) 9789413

WOODCOTE
Oxfordshire
Hedges ◆◆◆
South Stoke Road, Woodcote,
Reading RG8 0PL
T: (01491) 680461

**The Highwayman Inn, Country
Restaurant & Freehouse**
Rating Applied For
Exlade Street, Woodcote,
Reading, Berkshire RG8 0UA
T: (01491) 682020
F: (01491) 682229

WOODFALLS
Hampshire
The Woodfalls Inn ◆◆◆◆
The Ridge, Woodfalls, Salisbury
SP5 2LN
T: (01725) 513222
F: (01725) 513220
E: woodfallsi@aol.com
I: www.woodfallsinn.co.uk

WOODLEY
Berkshire
72 Butts Hill Road ◆◆◆
Woodley, Reading, Berkshire
RG5 4NP
T: (01189) 693295

WOODSTOCK
Oxfordshire
**Blenheim Guest House & Tea
Rooms** ◆◆◆◆
17 Park Street, Woodstock,
Oxford OX20 1SJ
T: (01993) 813814
F: (01993) 813810
E: Theblenheim@aol.com
I: www.theblenheim.com

Burleigh Farm ◆◆◆
Bladon Road, Cassington, Oxford
OX29 4EA
T: (01865) 881352
E: j.cook@farmline.com

Gorselands Hall ◆◆◆◆
Boddington Lane, North Leigh,
Witney, Oxfordshire OX29 6PU
T: (01993) 882292 & 881895
F: (01993) 883629
E: hamilton@gorselandshall.
com
I: www.gorselandshall.com

The Kings Head Inn ◆◆◆◆
Chapel Hill, Wootton,
Woodstock, Oxford, Oxfordshire
OX20 1DX
T: (01993) 811340
F: (01993) 811340
E: t.fay@kings-head.co.uk
I: www.kings-head.co.uk

The Laurels ◆◆◆◆
Hensington Road, Woodstock,
Oxford OX20 1JL
T: (01993) 812583
F: (01993) 812583
I: www.smoothhound.
co.uk/hotels/thelaur.html

The Lawns ◆◆
2 Flemings Road, Woodstock,
Oxford OX20 1NA
T: (01993) 812599
F: (01993) 812599
E: thelawns@amserve.net
I: www.smoothhound.
co.uk/hotels/thelawns2

Pine Trees Bed & Breakfast ◆◆◆◆
44 Green Lane, Woodstock,
Oxford, Oxfordshire OX20 1JZ
T: (01993) 813300
F: (01608) 646658

Plane Tree House ◆◆◆◆
48 Oxford Street, Woodstock,
Oxford OX20 1TT
T: (01993) 813075

The Punchbowl Inn ◆◆◆
12 Oxford Street, Woodstock,
Oxford OX20 1TR
T: (01993) 811218
F: (01993) 811393
E: info@punchbowl-woodstock.
co.uk
I: www.punchbowl-woodstock.
co.uk

Shepherds Hall Inn ◆◆◆
Witney Road, Freeland, Oxford
OX29 8HQ
T: (01993) 881256
F: (01993) 883455

Shipton Glebe ◆◆◆◆◆
Woodstock, Oxford OX20 1QQ
T: (01993) 812688
F: (01993) 813142
E: stay@shipton-glebe.com
I: www.shipton-glebe.com

The Townhouse ◆◆◆◆
15 High Street, Woodstock,
Oxford, Oxfordshire OX20 1TE
T: (01993) 810843 & 0780 359
9001
F: (01993) 810843
E: info@woodstock-townhouse.
com
I: www.woodstock-townhouse.
com

WOOLHAMPTON
Berkshire
River View House ◆◆◆◆
Station Road, Woolhampton,
Reading RG7 5SF
T: (0118) 971 3449
F: (0118) 971 3475

WOOLSTONE
Buckinghamshire
Ediths Cottage
Rating Applied For
21 Newport Road, Woolstone,
Milton Keynes MK15 0AB
T: (01908) 604916

WOOTTON
Hampshire
Cottage Bed & Breakfast ◆◆◆◆
Appledore, Holmsley Road,
Wootton, New Milton, Hamphire
BH25 5TR
T: (01425) 629506 &
07773 527626
E: cottagebb@eurolink.ltd.net

WOOTTON BRIDGE
Isle of Wight
Grange Farm ◆◆◆◆
Staplers Road, Wootton Bridge,
Ryde, Isle of Wight PO33 4RW
T: (01983) 882147
F: (01983) 882147

Island Charters Sea Urchin ◆◆
26 Barge Lane, Wootton Creek,
Wootton Bridge, Ryde, Isle of
Wight PO33 4LB
T: (01983) 882315 &
07889 038877
F: (01983) 882315

WORMINGHALL
Buckinghamshire
Crabtree Barn ◆◆◆◆
Field Farm, Worminghall,
Aylesbury, Buckinghamshire
HP18 9JY
T: (01844) 339719
F: (01844) 339719
E: issymcguinness@
crabtreebarn.co.uk

Oaktree Copse ◆◆◆
Wood Farm, Menmarsh Road,
Worminghall, Aylesbury,
Buckinghamshire HP18 9UP
T: (01865) 351695 &
07715 926850

WOUGHTON ON THE GREEN
Buckinghamshire

Apple Tree House ◆◆◆◆
16 Verley Close, Woughton on
the Green, Milton Keynes
MK6 3ER
T: (01908) 669681
F: (01908) 669681
E: apples@mrobinson5.fsnet.
co.uk
I: www.smoothhound.
co.uk/hotels/appletree2.html

WRAYSBURY
Berkshire

The Oast Barn ◆◆◆
Staines Road, Wraysbury,
Staines, Berkshire TW19 5BS
T: (01784) 481598 &
07867 504424
F: (01784) 483022
E: theoastbarn@netscapeonline.
co.uk

WROXALL
Isle of Wight

The Grange
Rating Applied For
Wroxall, Ventnor, Isle of Wight
PO38 3DA
T: (01983) 857424

Little Span Farm ◆◆◆
Rew Lane, Wroxall, Ventnor, Isle
of Wight PO38 3AU
T: (01983) 852419
E: info@spanfarm.co.uk
I: www.spanfarm.co.uk

YARMOUTH
Isle of Wight

Marlborough Cottage ◆◆◆
High Street, Yarmouth, Isle of
Wight PO41 0PN
T: (01983) 760338

Medlars ◆◆◆
Halletts Shute, Yarmouth, Isle of
Wight PO41 0RH
T: (01983) 761541 &
07941 196977
F: (01983) 761541
E: grey@lineone.net
I: www.milford.
co.uk/go/medlars.html

Rosemead ◆◆
Tennyson Road, Yarmouth, Isle
of Wight PO41 0PX
T: (01983) 761078
E: barbara_boon@hotmail.com

YARNTON
Oxfordshire

Eltham Villa Guest House
◆◆◆◆
148 Woodstock Road, Yarnton,
Kidlington, Oxfordshire
OX5 1PW
T: (01865) 376037 &
07802 722595
F: (01865) 376037

King's Bridge Guest House
◆◆◆
Woodstock Road, Yarnton,
Kidlington, Oxfordshire OX5 1PH
T: (01865) 841748
F: (01865) 370215
E: kingsbridgegh@aol.com

YATELEY
Hampshire

Carisbrooke Cottage ◆◆◆
Millmere, Mill Lane, Yateley,
Hampshire GU46 7TQ
T: (01252) 409526 &
07811 462581

Holly Lodge ◆◆◆
24 Sandhurst Road, Yateley,
Hampshire GU46 7UU
T: (01252) 870716
F: (01252) 668471
E: eshanks@aol.com

SOUTH EAST ENGLAND

ABINGER COMMON
Surrey

Leylands Farm ◆◆◆◆
Leylands Lane, Abinger
Common, Dorking, Surrey
RH5 6JU
T: (01306) 730115 &
0781 8422881
F: (01306) 731675

Park House Farm ◆◆◆◆
Hollow Lane, Abinger Common,
Dorking, Surrey RH5 6LW
T: (01306) 730101
F: (01306) 730643
E: peterwallis@msn.com
I: www.smoothhound.
co.uk/hotels/parthous.html

ACRISE
Kent

Ladwood Farm ◆◆◆
Acrise, Folkestone, Kent
CT18 8LL
T: (01303) 891328 &
07778 498455
F: (01303) 891427
E: mail@ladwood.com
I: www.ladwood.com

ALBURY
Surrey

Barn Cottage ◆◆◆◆
Brook Hill, Farley Green, Albury,
Guildford, Surrey GU5 9DN
T: (01483) 202571

ALDINGBOURNE
West Sussex

Limmer Pond House ◆◆◆
Church Road, Aldingbourne,
Chichester, West Sussex
PO20 6TU
T: (01243) 543210

ALDINGTON
Kent

Hogben Farm ◆◆◆◆
Church Lane, Aldington,
Ashford, Kent TN25 7EH
T: (01233) 720219
F: (01233) 720285
E: ros.martin@talk21.com

ALFRISTON
East Sussex

Meadowbank ◆◆◆◆
Sloe Lane, Alfriston, Polegate,
East Sussex BN26 5UR
T: (01323) 870742

Riverdale House ◆◆◆◆
Seaford Road, Alfriston,
Polegate, East Sussex BN26 5TR
T: (01323) 871038
I: www.cuckmere-valley.
co.uk/riverdale/

Russets ◆◆◆◆
14 Deans Road, Alfriston,
Polegate, East Sussex BN26 5XJ
T: (01323) 870626
F: (01323) 870626
E: russets@yahoo.co.uk

AMBERLEY
West Sussex

The Sportsman
Rating Applied For
Rackham Road, Amberley,
Arundel, West Sussex B18 9NR
T: (01798) 831787
F: (01798) 831787
E: mob.club@virgin.net

ANSTY
West Sussex

Netherby ◆◆◆◆
Bolney Road, Ansty, Haywards
Heath, West Sussex RH17 5AW
T: (01444) 455888
F: (01444) 455888

APPLEDORE
Kent

Horne's Place ◆◆◆
Appledore, Ashford, Kent
TN26 2BS
T: (01233) 758305

Park Farm Barn ◆◆◆
School Lane, Appledore, Ashford,
Kent TN26 2AR
T: (01233) 758159
F: (01233) 758159

ARDINGLY
West Sussex

Stonelands West Lodge ◆◆◆
Ardingly Road, West Hoathly,
East Grinstead, West Sussex
RH19 4RA
T: (01342) 715372

ARPINGE
Kent

Pigeonwood House ◆◆◆◆
Grove Farm, Arpinge, Folkestone,
Kent CT18 8AQ
T: (01303) 891111
F: (01303) 891019
E: samandmary@aol.com
I: www.pigeonwood.com

ARUNDEL
West Sussex

Arundel House ◆◆◆
11 High Street, Arundel, West
Sussex BN18 9AD
T: (01903) 882136
F: (01909) 882136
E: arundelhouse@btinternet.
com
I: btinternet.
com/~arundelhouse/

Dukes of Arundel ◆◆◆
65 High Street, Arundel, West
Sussex BN18 9AJ
T: (01903) 883847
F: (01903) 889601
E: info@dukesofarundel.co.uk
I: www.dukesofarundel.co.uk

Houghton Farm ◆◆◆◆
Amberley, Arundel, West Sussex
BN18 9LW
T: (01798) 831327 & 831100
F: (01798) 831183
E: rosemarylock@ukonline.co.uk

Medlar Cottage ◆◆◆
Poling Street, Poling, Arundel,
West Sussex BN18 9PT
T: (01903) 883106
F: (01903) 883106

Mill Lane House ◆◆◆
Slindon, Arundel, West Sussex
BN18 0RP
T: (01243) 814440
F: (01243) 814436
&

Pindars ◆◆◆◆
Lyminster, Littlehampton, West
Sussex BN17 7QF
T: (01903) 882628
F: (01903) 882628

Woodpeckers ◆◆◆◆
15 Dalloway Road, Arundel,
West Sussex BN18 9HJ
T: (01903) 883948 &
07879 212489

ASH
Kent

Great Weddington ◆◆◆◆
Ash, Canterbury, Kent CT3 2AR
T: (01304) 813407 & 812531
F: (01304) 812531
E: traveltale@aol.com
I: www.greatweddington.co.uk

ASHFORD
Kent

Ashford Guest House ◆◆◆◆
15 Canterbury Road, Ashford,
Kent TN24 8LE
T: (01233) 640460
F: (01233) 626504
E: srcnoel@netcomuk.co.uk
I: www.mounteverest.uk.com

Croft Hotel ◆◆◆
Canterbury Road, Kennington,
Ashford, Kent TN25 4DU
T: (01233) 622140
F: (01233) 635271
E: crofthotel@btconnect.com

Dalmeny House
Rating Applied For
18 Magazine Road, Ashford,
Kent TN24 8NN
T: (01233) 627596

Dean Court Farm ◆◆◆
Challock Lane, Westwell,
Ashford, Kent TN25 4NH
T: (01233) 712924

Glenmoor ◆◆◆
Maidstone Road, Ashford, Kent
TN25 4NP
T: (01233) 634767

Goldwell Manor ◆◆◆
Great Chart, Ashford, Kent
TN23 3BY
T: (01233) 631495
F: (01233) 631495

Mayflower House ◆◆◆
61 Magazine Road, Ashford,
Kent TN24 8NR
T: (01233) 621959
F: (01233) 621959

New Flying Horse Inn ◆◆◆
Upper Bridge Street, Wye,
Ashford, Kent TN25 5AN
T: (01233) 812297
F: (01233) 813487
E: newflyhorse@
shepherd-neame.co.uk
I: www.shepherd-neame.co.uk

Quantock House ◆◆◆
Quantock Drive, Ashford, Kent
TN24 8QH
T: (01233) 638921
E: tucker100@madasafish.com

20 Spelthorne Lane ◆◆◆
Ashford, Sunbury, Middlesex
TW15 1UJ
T: (01784) 420256

Warren Cottage Hotel and
Restaurant ◆◆◆
136 The Street, Willesborough,
Ashford, Kent TN24 0NB
T: (01233) 621905 & 632929
F: (01233) 623400
E: general@warrencottage.
co.uk
I: www.warrencottage.co.uk

AYLESFORD
Kent

Wickham Lodge ◆◆◆◆
The Quay, High Street, Aylesford,
Kent ME20 7AY
T: (01622) 717267
F: (01622) 792855
E: wickhamlodge@aol.com

BALCOMBE
West Sussex

Rocks Lane Cottage ◆◆◆
Rocks Lane, Balcombe,
Haywards Heath, West Sussex
RH17 6JG
T: (01444) 811245 &
07989 197348
E: kpa@fsbdial.co.uk

BALLS CROSS
West Sussex

The Stag Inn ◆◆◆
Balls Cross, Petworth, West
Sussex GU28 9JP
T: (01403) 820241

BARHAM
Kent

Heaseland House ◆◆◆◆
South Barham Road, Barham,
Canterbury, Kent CT4 6LA
T: (01227) 831643

BARNHAM
West Sussex

Downhills ◆◆◆
87 Barnham Road, Barnham,
Bognor Regis, West Sussex
PO22 0EQ
T: (01243) 553104 & 07951 457
909

Todhurst Farm ◆◆◆
Lake Lane, Barnham, Bognor
Regis, West Sussex PO22 0AL
T: (01243) 551959
E: nigelsedg@aol.uk

BATTLE
East Sussex

Abbey View Bed & Breakfast
◆◆◆◆
Caldbec Hill, Battle, East Sussex
TN33 0JS
T: (01424) 775513
F: (01424) 775513

April Cottage ◆◆◆
46 North Trade Road, Battle,
East Sussex TN33 0HU
T: (01424) 775108

Clematis Cottage ◆◆◆
The Green, 3 The High Street,
Battle, East Sussex TN33 0TD
T: (01424) 774261

Farthings Farm ◆◆◆◆
Farthings Lane, Catsfield, Battle,
East Sussex TN33 9BA
T: (01424) 773107
I: www.farthingsfarm.co.uk

The Gateway Restaurant ◆◆◆
78 High Street, Battle, East
Sussex TN33 0AG
T: (01424) 772856

High Hedges ◆◆◆◆
28 North Trade Road, Battle,
East Sussex TN33 0HB
T: (01424) 774140 &
0780 8551064

Kelklands ◆◆◆
Off Chain Lane, Battle, East
Sussex TN33 0HG
T: (01424) 773013

Little Hemingfold Hotel ◆◆◆
Telham, Battle, East Sussex
TN33 0TT
T: (01424) 774338
F: (01424) 775351

Moons Hill Farm ◆◆◆
The Green, Ninfield, Battle, East
Sussex TN33 9LH
T: (01424) 892645
F: (01424) 892645

BEAN
Kent

Black Horse Cottage ◆◆◆
High Street, Bean, Dartford
DA2 8AS
T: (01474) 704962

BEARSTED
Kent

88 Ashford Road ◆◆◆
Bearsted, Maidstone, Kent
ME14 4LT
T: (01622) 738278
F: (01622) 738346

Hurstfield House ◆◆◆
24 Nursery Avenue, Bearsted,
Maidstone, Kent ME14 4JS
T: (01622) 737584
E: jacquiSV@globalnet.co.uk
I: www.hurstfield.com

Tollgate House ◆◆◆
Ashford Road, Bearsted,
Maidstone, Kent ME14 4NS
T: (01622) 738428

BELLS YEW GREEN
East Sussex

Rushlye Barn ◆◆◆
Bells Yew Green, Royal
Tunbridge Wells, Kent TN3 9AP
T: (01892) 750398

BENENDEN
Kent

The Bull At Benenden
Rating Applied For
The Street, Benenden,
Cranbrook, Kent TN17 4DE
T: (01580) 240054
E: thebullatbenenden@
btinternet.com

BEPTON
West Sussex

Park House Hotel ◆◆◆◆◆
Bepton, Midhurst, West Sussex
GU29 0JB
T: (01730) 812880
F: (01730) 815643
I: www.Freepages.
co.uk/parkhouse_hotel/

BERWICK
East Sussex

Lower Claverham Farm ◆◆◆
Berwick, Polegate, East Sussex
BN26 6TJ
T: (01323) 811267
F: (01323) 811267
E: paul.rossi@talk21.com

BETHERSDEN
Kent

Cloverlea ◆◆◆
Hothfield Road, Bethersden,
Ashford, Kent TN26 3DU
T: (01233) 820353 &
07711 739690
F: (01233) 820353

The Coach House ◆◆◆
Oakmead Farm, Bethersden,
Ashford, Kent TN26 3DU
T: (01233) 820583
F: (01233) 820583

Little Hodgeham ◆◆◆◆
Smarden Road, Bethersden,
Ashford, Kent TN26
T: (01233) 850323
E: little.hodgeham@virgin.net

The Old Stables ◆◆◆◆
Wissenden, Bethersden, Ashford,
Kent TN26 3EL
T: (01233) 820597 &
07770 388501
F: (01233) 820199
E: pennygillespie@
theoldstables.co.uk
I: www.theoldstables.co.uk

Potters Farm ◆◆◆
Bethersden, Ashford, Kent
TN26 3JX
T: (01233) 820341
F: (01233) 820469
E: ianmcanderson@cs.com
I: www.smoothhound.
co.uk/hotels/potters.html

BEXHILL
East Sussex

Albany House ◆◆◆
30 Magdalen Road, Bexhill, East
Sussex TN40 1SB
T: (01424) 223012

Annamaria's at Southolme
◆◆◆◆
129 Cooden Drive, Cooden,
Bexhill, East Sussex TN39 3AJ
T: (01424) 843811 &
07889 912628
E: southolme@aol.com

The Arosa Hotel ◆◆◆◆
6 Albert Road, Bexhill, East
Sussex TN40 1DG
T: (01424) 212574 &
08000 748041
F: (01424) 212574

Barnoak ◆◆◆◆
22 Barnhorn Road, Little
Common, Bexhill, East Sussex
TN39 4QA
T: (01424) 843269

Barrington B & B ◆◆◆◆
14 Wilton Road, Bexhill, East
Sussex TN40 1HY
T: (01424) 210250
F: (01424) 211433
E: mick@barrington14.
freeserve.co.uk
I: www.barrington14.freeserve.
co.uk

Buenos Aires Guest House
◆◆◆
24 Albany Road, Bexhill, East
Sussex TN40 1BZ
T: (01424) 212269
F: (01424) 212269

Collington Lodge Guest House
◆◆◆
41 Collington Avenue, Bexhill,
East Sussex TN39 3PX
T: (01424) 210024
F: (01424) 210024
E: info@collington.co.uk
I: www.collington.co.uk

Dunselma ◆◆◆
25 Marina, Bexhill, East Sussex
TN40 1BP
T: (01424) 734144

Hartfield House ◆◆◆◆
27 Hartfield Road, Cooden,
Bexhill, East Sussex TN39 3EA
T: (01424) 845715
F: (01424) 845715
E: mansi@hartfieldhouse.
free-online.co.uk
I: www.aplacetostayuk.
com/sussex/hartfield-house.htm

Henry House ◆◆◆
16 Linden Road, Bexhill-on-Sea,
Bexhill, East Sussex TN40 1DN
T: (01424) 225528
E: sylvia.laidlaw@henry.dialnet.
com

Linden Lodge ◆◆◆
31 Linden Road, Bexhill, East
Sussex TN40 1DN
T: (01424) 225005
F: (01424) 222895
E: lindenlodge@hotmail.com

Little Shelter ◆◆◆
5 Ashdown Road, Bexhill-on-
Sea, Bexhill, East Sussex
TN40 1SE
T: (01424) 225386

16 Magdalen Road ◆◆◆
Bexhill, East Sussex TN40 1SB
T: (01424) 218969

Manor Barn ◆◆◆
Lunsford Cross, Bexhill, East
Sussex TN39 5JJ
T: (01424) 893018
F: (01424) 893018

Marabou Mansions ◆◆
60 Devonshire Road, Bexhill,
East Sussex TN40 1AX
T: (01424) 212189
F: (01424) 212189

Messens Farmhouse ◆◆◆◆
Potmans Lane, Lunsford Cross,
Bexhill, East Sussex TN39 5JL
T: (01424) 893456 &
07976 644652
F: (01424) 893456

Mulberry ◆◆◆
31 Warwick Road, Bexhill, East
Sussex TN39 4HG
T: (01424) 219204

Park Lodge Hotel ◆◆◆
16 Egerton Road, Bexhill, East
Sussex TN39 3HH
T: (01424) 216547 & 215041
F: (01424) 217460

Sackville Hotel ◆◆◆◆
De La Warr Parade, Bexhill-on-
Sea, Bexhill, East Sussex
TN40 1LS
T: (01424) 224694
F: (01424) 734132

Sunshine Guest House ◆◆◆
Sandhurst Lane, Little Common,
Bexhill, East Sussex TN39 4RH
T: (01424) 842009

Treforfan Guest House ◆◆◆
33 Woodville Road, Bexhill, East
Sussex TN39 3ET
T: (01424) 223767

Westwood Farm ◆◆◆
Stonestile Lane, Hastings, East
Sussex TN35 4PG
T: (01424) 751038
F: (01424) 751038
E: york@westwood-farm.fsnet.
co.uk

BEXLEYHILL
West Sussex

Elidge Farm ◆◆◆
Bexleyhill, Petworth, West
Sussex GU28 9EA
T: (01798) 861617
F: (01798) 861617

BIDDENDEN
Kent

Birchley House West ◆◆◆◆
Fosten Green, Biddenden,
Ashford, Kent TN27 8DZ
T: (01580) 291124
F: (01580) 291416
E: birchley@globalnet.co.uk
I: www.birchleywest.co.uk

Bishopsdale Oast ◆◆◆◆
Biddenden, Ashford, Kent
TN27 8DR
T: (01580) 291027 & 292065
F: (01580) 292321
E: bishopsdale@pavilion.co.uk
I: www.bishopsdaleoast.co.uk

Heron Cottage ◆◆◆◆
Biddenden, Ashford, Kent
TN27 8HH
T: (01580) 291358

Tudor Cottage ◆◆◆◆
25 High Street, Biddenden,
Ashford, Kent TN27 8AL
T: (01580) 291913
E: suemorris.biddenden@virgin.
net
I: freespace.virgin.net/suemorris.
biddenden

BILLINGSHURST
West Sussex

Groom Cottage ◆◆◆
Station Road, Billingshurst, West
Sussex RH14 9RF
T: (01403) 782285

BILSINGTON
Kent

Willow Farm ◆◆◆
Stone Cross, Bilsington, Ashford,
Kent TN25 7JJ
T: (01233) 720484 & 721700
F: (01233) 720484
E: renee@willow-farm.
freeserve.co.uk

BIRDHAM
West Sussex

The Red House ◆◆◆◆
Lock Lane, Birdham Pool,
Birdham, Chichester, West
Sussex PO20 7BB
T: (01243) 512488
F: (01243) 514563
E: susie.redhouse@ukonline.
co.uk
I: www.redhousehideaway.co.uk

BIRLING
Kent

The Stable Block
Rating Applied For
25 Ryarsh Road, Birling, West
Malling, Kent ME19 5JW
T: (01732) 873437
F: (01732) 849320
E: carolinemoorhead@hotmail.
com

BLACKHAM
East Sussex

Salehurst Farm ◆◆◆
Blackham, Royal Tunbridge
Wells, Kent TN3 9UB
T: (01892) 740357
F: (01892) 740158

BLADBEAN
Kent

Molehills ◆◆◆◆
Bladbean, Canterbury, Kent
CT4 6LU
T: (01303) 840051 &
07808 639942
E: molehills84@hotmail.com

BOARS HEAD
East Sussex

Wareham Lodge ◆◆◆◆
Boars Head, Crowborough, East
Sussex TN6 3HE
T: (01892) 653444

BODIAM
East Sussex

Northlands House ◆◆◆◆
Bodiam, Robertsbridge, East
Sussex TN32 5UX
T: (01580) 831849
F: (01580) 831949

BOGNOR REGIS
West Sussex

Alancourt Hotel ◆◆◆
Marine Drive West, Bognor
Regis, West Sussex PO21 2QA
T: (01243) 864844
F: (01243) 864844

Homestead Guest House ◆◆◆
90 Aldwick Road, Bognor Regis,
West Sussex PO21 2PD
T: (01243) 823443
F: (01243) 823443

Jubilee Guest House ◆◆◆
5 Gloucester Road, Bognor
Regis, West Sussex PO21 1NU
T: (01243) 863016 &
07702 275967
F: (01243) 868017
E: jubileeguesthouse@
breathemail.net
I: www.jubileeguesthouse.com

Regis Lodge ◆◆◆
3 Gloucester Road, Bognor
Regis, West Sussex PO21 1NU
T: (01243) 827110 &
07768 117770
F: (01243) 827110
E: frank@regislodge.fsbusiness.
co.uk
I: www.regislodge.tripod.com

St Albans ◆◆◆◆
The Esplanade, Bognor Regis,
West Sussex PO21 1NY
T: (01243) 860516

Sea Crest Private Hotel ◆◆◆
19 Nyewood Lane, Bognor Regis,
West Sussex PO21 2QB
T: (01243) 821438

Swan Guest House ◆◆◆◆
17 Nyewood Lane, Bognor Regis,
West Sussex PO21 2QB
T. (01243) 020000
F: (01243) 826880
E: swanhse@globalnet.co.uk
I: www.users.globalnet.
co.uk/~swanhse

Tudor Cottage Guest House
◆◆◆◆
194 Chichester Road, Bognor
Regis, West Sussex PO21 5BJ
T: (01243) 821826
F: (01243) 862189
E: tudorcottage@supernet.com

BOLNEY
West Sussex

Broxmead Paddock ◆◆◆◆
Broxmead Lane, Bolney,
Haywards Heath, West Sussex
RH17 5RG
T: (01444) 881458
F: (01444) 881491
E: bishop4goats@bishop4goats.
screaming.net

Butchers Bed & Breakfast
◆◆◆◆
Butchers, Ryecroft Road, Bolney,
Haywards Heath, West Sussex
RH17 5PS
T: (01444) 881503
E: karen.darby@
butchers-sussex.co.uk
I: www.butchers-sussex.co.uk

Colwood Manor West ◆◆◆◆
Spronketts Lane, Bolney,
Haywards Heath, West Sussex
RH17 5SA
T: (01444) 461331
E: dmartin@ricsonline.org

New Farm House ◆◆◆◆
Nyes Hill, Wineham Lane,
Bolney, Haywards Heath, West
Sussex RH17 5SD
T: (01444) 881617 &
(01410) 710555
F: (01444) 881850
E: newfarmhouse@btinternet.
com
I: www.newfarmhouse.co.uk

BOROUGH GREEN
Kent

Yew Tree Barn ◆◆◆◆
Long Mill Lane, Crouch, Borough
Green, Sevenoaks, Kent
TN15 8QB
T: (01732) 883107
F: (01732) 883107
E: yewtreebarnbb@hotmail.com

BOSHAM
West Sussex

Crede Farmhouse ◆◆◆◆
Crede Lane, Bosham, Chichester,
West Sussex PO18 8NX
T: (01243) 574929
E: lesley@credefarmhouse.
fsnet.co.uk

Good Hope ◆◆◆◆
Delling Lane, Bosham,
Chichester, West Sussex
PO18 8NR
T: (01243) 572487
F: (01243) 530760

Govers ◆◆◆
Crede Lane, Bosham, Chichester,
West Sussex PO18 8NX
T: (01243) 573163

Hatpins ◆◆◆◆◆
Bosham Lane, Old Bosham,
Chichester, West Sussex
PO18 8HG
T: (01243) 572644
F: (01243) 572644
E: mary@hatpins.co.uk
I: www.hatpins.co.uk

Kenwood ◆◆◆◆
Bosham, Chichester, West
Sussex PO18 8PH
T: (01243) 572727
F: (01243) 572738

BOUGH BEECH
Kent

Bank View ◆◆◆
Chequers Hill, Bough Beech,
Edenbridge, Kent TN8 7PD
T: (01732) 700315
F: (01732) 700315
E: t.dalladay@ukgateway.net

BOUGHTON
Kent

Brenley Farm House ◆◆◆
Brenley Lane, Boughton,
Faversham, Kent ME13 9LY
T: (01227) 751203
F: (01227) 751203
E: maggie@brenley.freeserve.
co.uk

10 Horselees Road ◆◆◆
Boughton under Blean,
Boughton, Faversham, Kent
ME13 9TG
T: (01227) 751332
F: (01227) 751332
E: keyway@bigfoot.com

Wellbrook Farmhouse ♦♦♦♦
South Street, Boughton,
Faversham, Kent ME13 9NA
T: (01227) 750941
F: (01227) 750807
E: reservations@
wellbrookfarmhouse.co.uk
I: www.wellbrookfarmhouse.
co.uk

BOUGHTON MONCHELSEA
Kent

Hideaway ♦♦♦
Heath Road, Boughton
Monchelsea, Maidstone, Kent
ME17 4JD
T: (01622) 747453
F: (01622) 747453

Wierton Hall Farm ♦♦♦
East Hall Hill, Boughton
Monchelsea, Maidstone, Kent
ME17 4JU
T: (01622) 743535
F: (01622) 743535

BOXGROVE
West Sussex

The Brufords ♦♦♦♦
66 The Street, Boxgrove,
Chichester, West Sussex
PO18 0EE
T: (01243) 774085
F: (01243) 781235
E: brendan@bjcoffey.freeserve.
co.uk

BOXLEY
Kent

Barn Cottage ♦♦♦
Harbourland, Boxley, Maidstone,
Kent ME14 3DN
T: (01622) 675891
F: (01622) 675891

BRABOURNE LEES
Kent

Meadowsweet ♦♦♦
Manor Pound Lane, Brabourne
Lees, Ashford, Kent TN25 5LG
T: (01303) 814050
F: (01303) 814050
E: meadowsweet@onet.co.uk

BRAMLEY
Surrey

The Granary ♦♦♦♦
Chinthurst Farmhouse,
Chinthurst Lane, Bramley,
Guildford, Surrey GU5 0DR
T: (01483) 898623
F: (01483) 898623

Highpoint ♦♦♦♦
Munstead View Road, Bramley,
Guildford, Surrey GU5 0DA
T: (01483) 893566
F: (01483) 894205
E: chriscard@compuserve.com
I: www.come.to/highpoint

BRASTED
Kent

Lodge House ♦♦
High Street, Brasted,
Westerham, Kent TN16 1HS
T: (01959) 562195
F: (01959) 562195
E: lodgehouse@brastedbb.
freeserve.co.uk

The Mount House ♦♦♦
Brasted, Westerham, Kent
TN16 1JB
T: (01959) 563617
F: (01959) 561296
E: jpaulco@webspeed.net

The Orchard House ♦♦♦
Brasted Chart, Westerham, Kent
TN16 1LR
T: (01959) 563702
E: david.godsal@tesco.net

BREDE
East Sussex

**Brede Court Country House
♦♦♦♦**
Brede Hill, Brede, Rye, East
Sussex TN31 6EJ
T: (01424) 883105
F: (01424) 883104
E: bredecrt@globalnet.co.uk
I: www.english-training.com

2 Stonelink Cottages ♦♦♦
Stubb Lane, Brede, Rye, East
Sussex TN31 6BL
T: (01424) 882943 &
07802 573612
F: (01424) 883052
E: stonelinkc@aol.com

BRENCHLEY
Kent

The Bull of Brenchley ♦♦♦♦
High Street, Brenchley,
Tonbridge, Kent TN12 7NQ
T: (01892) 722701
F: (01892) 722760
I: www.users.globalnet.
co.uk/~bullinn/.

Chillmill Manor ♦♦♦♦
Fairmans Road, Brenchley,
Tonbridge, Kent TN12 7AL
T: (01892) 722518 &
07721 586632
F: (01892) 722003

Woodlands Cottage ♦♦♦♦
Fairmans Road, Brenchley,
Tonbridge, Kent TN12 7BB
T: (01892) 722707
F: (01892) 724946
E: chris.omalley@virgin.net

BRIDGE
Kent

**East Bridge Country Hotel
♦♦♦♦**
Bridge Hill, Bridge, Canterbury,
Kent CT4 5AS
T: (01227) 830808
F: (01227) 832181

Harrow Cottage ♦♦♦
2 Brewery Lane, Bridge,
Canterbury, Kent CT4 5LD
T: (01227) 830218
F: (01227) 830218
E: pamela@phooker.fsbusiness.
co.uk

BRIGHTLING
East Sussex

Orchard Barn ♦♦♦
3 Twelve Oaks Cottages,
Brightling, Robertsbridge, East
Sussex TN32 5HS
T: (01424) 838263

Swallowfield Farm ♦♦♦♦
Brightling, Robertsbridge, East
Sussex TN32 5HB
T: (01424) 838225
F: (01424) 838225
E: jssp@swallowfieldfarm.
freeserve.co.uk
I: www.swallowfieldfarm.co.uk

BRIGHTON & HOVE
East Sussex

The Acropolis Hotel ♦♦
14-15 Burlington Street, Marine
Parade, Brighton, BN2 1AU
T: (01273) 698195
F: (01273) 698991

Adelaide Hotel ♦♦♦♦
51 Regency Square, Brighton,
BN1 2FF
T: (01273) 205286
F: (01273) 220904
E: adelaide@pavilion.co.uk

Aegean Hotel ♦♦♦
5 New Steine, Brighton, East
Sussex BN2 1PB
T: (01273) 686547
F: (01273) 625613

Ainsley House Hotel ♦♦♦♦
28 New Steine, Brighton,
BN2 1PD
T: (01273) 605310
F: (01273) 688604
E: ahhotel@fastnet.co.uk
I: www.ainsleyhotel.com

Allendale Hotel ♦♦♦
3 New Steine, Brighton, East
Sussex BN2 1PB
T: (01273) 675436
F: (01273) 602603

Amalfi Hotel ♦♦
44 Marine Parade, Brighton, East
Sussex BN2 1PE
T: (01273) 607956

Ambassador Hotel ♦♦♦♦
22 New Steine, Marine Parade,
Brighton, BN2 1PD
T: (01273) 676869
F: (01273) 689988
E: ambassadorhoteluk@
hotmail.com
I: www.
ambassadorhotelbrighton.com

Andorra Hotel ♦♦♦
15-16 Oriental Place, Brighton,
BN1 2LJ
T: (01273) 321787 & 725485
F: (01273) 721418

Aquarium Guest House ♦♦♦
13 Madeira Place, Brighton, East
Sussex BN2 1TN
T: (01273) 605761

Arlanda Hotel ♦♦♦♦
20 New Steine, Brighton,
BN2 1PD
T: (01273) 699300
F: (01273) 600930
E: arlanda@brighton.co.uk
I: www.arlandahotel.co.uk

Atlantic Hotel ♦♦♦
16 Marine Parade, Brighton, East
Sussex BN2 1TL
T: (01273) 695944
F: (01273) 695944

Aymer ♦♦♦♦
13 Aymer Road, Hove, Brighton
BN3 4GB
T: (01273) 271165 &
07770 488764
F: (01273) 321653
I: www.sussexlive.com

The Beach Hotel ♦♦♦
2-4 Regency Square, Brighton,
East Sussex BN1 2GP
T: (01273) 323776
F: (01273) 747028
I: www.beachotel.co.uk

Beynon House ♦♦♦
24 St George's Terrace, Brighton,
East Sussex BN2 1JJ
T: (01273) 681014
E: beynonhouse@hotmail.com
I: www.brightonpages.
co.uk/beynonhouse

Brighton House Hotel ♦♦♦♦
52 Regency Square, Brighton,
East Sussex BN1 2FF
T: (01273) 323282

**Brighton Marina House Hotel
♦♦♦**
8 Charlotte Street, Marine
Parade, Brighton, BN2 1AG
T: (01273) 605349 & 819806
F: (01273) 679484
E: rooms@jungs.co.uk
I: www.s-h-systems.
co.uk/hotels/brightma

Brighton Pavilions ♦♦♦
7 Charlotte Street, Brighton,
BN2 1AG
T: (01273) 621750 & 621725
E: sanchez-crespo@lineone.net
I: www.brightonpavilions.com

**Brighton Twenty One Hotel
♦♦♦♦**
21 Charlotte Street, Marine
Parade, Brighton, BN2 1AG
T: (01273) 686450 & 681617
F: (01273) 695560
E: rooms@the21.co.uk
I: www.s-h-systems.
co.uk/hotels/21

Brunswick Square Hotel ♦♦
11 Brunswick Square, Hove,
Brighton, East Sussex BN3 1EH
T: (01273) 205047
F: (01273) 205047
E: brunswick@brighton.co.uk
I: www.brighton.
co.uk/hotels/brunswick

Cavalaire Hotel ♦♦♦
34 Upper Rock Gardens,
Brighton, BN2 1QF
T: (01273) 696899
F: (01273) 600504
E: welcome@cavalaire.co.uk
I: www.cavalaire.co.uk

Chatsworth Hotel ♦♦♦
9 Salisbury Road, Hove, Brighton
BN3 3AB
T: (01273) 737360
F: (01273) 737360

Churchill Guest House ♦♦♦
44 Russell Square, Brighton, East
Sussex BN1 2EF
T: (01273) 700777
F: (01273) 700887
E: enquiries@
churchillguesthouse.com
I: www.churchillguesthouse.com

Cinderella Hotel ♦♦♦
48 St Aubyns, Hove, Brighton,
East Sussex BN3 2TE
T: (01273) 727827
F: (01273) 746272

Cosmopolitan Hotel ♦♦♦
31 New Steine, Marine Parade,
Brighton, BN2 1PD
T: (01273) 682461
F: (01273) 622311
E: enquiries@
cosmopolitanhotel.co.uk
I: www.cosmopolitanhotel.co.uk

Diana House ◆◆
25 St Georges Terrace, Brighton,
East Sussex BN2 1JJ
T: (01273) 605797
F: (01273) 600533
E: diana@enterprise.net
I: www.dianahouse.co.uk

Dove Hotel ◆◆◆
18 Regency Square, Brighton,
East Sussex BN1 2FG
T: (01273) 779222
F: (01273) 746912
E: dovehotel@
dovehotelfree-online.co.uk

Dudley House ◆◆◆
10 Madeira Place, Brighton, East
Sussex BN2 1TN
T: (01273) 676794
E: dudleyhousebrighton@
btinternet.com

Funchal Guest House ◆◆◆
17 Madeira Place, Brighton,
BN2 1TN
T: (01273) 603975
F: (01273) 603975

Fyfield House ◆◆◆◆
26 New Steine, Brighton,
BN2 1PD
T: (01273) 602770
F: (01273) 602770
E: fyfield@aol.com
I: www.brighton.
co.uk/hotels/fyfield

Georjan Guest House ◆◆◆
27 Upper Rock Gardens,
Brighton, BN2 1QE
T: (01273) 694951
F: (01273) 694951
E: georjan.gh@virgin.net

Granada House Hotel ◆◆◆
35 Walsingham Road, Hove,
Brighton, East Sussex BN3 4FE
T: (01273) 723855
F: (01273) 723855

Harveys ◆◆◆
1 Broad Street, Brighton, East
Sussex BN2 1TJ
T: (01273) 699227
F: (01273) 699227

Hudsons Guest House ◆◆◆
22 Devonshire Place, Brighton,
East Sussex BN2 1QA
T: (01273) 683642
F: (01273) 696088
E: hudsons@brighton.co.uk
I: brighton.co.uk/hotels/hudsons

The Kelvin Guest House ◆◆◆
9 Madeira Place, Brighton,
BN2 1TN
T: (01273) 603735 & 687992
F: (01273) 603735

Kingsway Hotel ◆◆◆◆
2 St Aubyns, Hove, East Sussex
BN3 2TB
T: (01273) 722068
F: 0870 0554661
E: admin@kingswayent.demon.
co.uk

Leona House ◆◆
74 Middle Street, Brighton,
BN1 1AL
T: (01273) 327309

Lichfield House ◆◆◆
30 Waterloo Street, Hove,
Brighton, East Sussex BN3 1AN
T: (01273) 777740 &
07970 945464
E: feelgood@lichfieldhouse.
freeserve.co.uk
I: www.lichfieldhouse.freeserve.
co.uk

Madeira Guest House ◆◆◆
14 Madeira Place, Brighton,
BN2 1TN
T: (01273) 681115
F: (01273) 681115

Miami Hotel ◆◆◆
22 Bedford Square, Brighton,
East Sussex BN1 2PL
T: (01273) 730169 &
07889 582797
F: (01273) 730169
E: themiami@pavilion.co.uk
I: www.brighton.
co.uk/hotels/miami

New Madeira Hotel ◆◆◆
19-23 Marine Parade, Brighton,
BN2 1TL
T: (01273) 698331
F: (01273) 606193
E: info@newmadeirahotel.com
I: www.newmadeirahotel.com

Oriental Hotel ◆◆◆
9 Oriental Place, Brighton,
BN1 2LJ
T: (01273) 205050 &
07974 976839
F: (01273) 821096
E: info@orientalhotel.co.uk
I: www.orientalhotel.co.uk

The Palace Hotel ◆◆◆
10-12 Grand Junction Road,
Brighton, BN1 1PN
T: (01273) 202035
F: (01273) 202034
E: palacehotel@connectfree.
co.uk

Pavilion Guest House ◆◆◆
12 Madeira Place, Brighton,
BN2 1TN
T: (01273) 683195

Penny Lanes ◆◆◆
11 Charlotte Street, Brighton,
BN2 1AG
T: (01273) 603197 & 684041
F: (01273) 689408
E: welcome@pennylanes.co.uk
I: www.pennylanes.co.uk

Russell Guest House ◆◆◆
19 Russell Square, Brighton,
BN1 2EE
T: (01273) 327969
F: (01273) 821535
E: russell.brighton@btinternet.
com

Sandpiper Guest House ◆◆
11 Russell Square, Brighton,
BN1 2EE
T: (01273) 328202
F: (01273) 329974
E: sandpiper@brighton.co.uk

Sea Spray ◆◆◆
25 New Steine, Marine Parade,
Brighton, East Sussex BN2 1PD
T: (01273) 680332
E: seaspray@brighton.co.uk
I: www.brighton.
co.uk/hotels/seaspray

Hotel Seafield ◆◆◆
23 Seafield Road, Hove, Brighton
BN3 2TP
T: (01273) 735912
F: (01273) 323525
I: www.brighton.
co.uk/hotels/seafield/

Strawberry Fields Hotel ◆◆◆
6-7 New Steine, Brighton, East
Sussex BN2 1PB
T: (01273) 681576 & 693397
F: (01273) 693397
E: strawberryfields@pavilion.
co.uk
I: www.brighton.
co.uk/hotels/strawberryfields

BROAD OAK
East Sussex

Layces Bed & Breakfast
◆◆◆◆
Chitcombe Road, Broad Oak,
Rye, East Sussex TN31 6EU
T: (01424) 882836
F: (01424) 882281
E: stephens@layces.fsnet.co.uk
I: www.layces.fsnet.co.uk

BROADSTAIRS
Kent

Admiral Dundonald Hotel
◆◆◆
43 Belvedere Road, Broadstairs,
Kent CT10 1PF
T: (01843) 862236

Bay Tree Hotel ◆◆◆
12 Eastern Esplanade,
Broadstairs, Kent CT10 1DR
T: (01843) 862502
F: (01843) 860589

Cintra Hotel ◆◆◆
24 Victoria Parade, Broadstairs,
Kent CT10 1QL
T: (01843) 862253

Devonhurst Hotel ◆◆◆◆
Eastern Esplanade, Broadstairs,
Kent CT10 1DR
T: (01843) 863010
F: (01843) 868940
E: info@devonhurst.co.uk
I: www.devonhurst.co.uk

East Horndon Hotel
Rating Applied For
4 Eastern Esplanade,
Broadstairs, Kent CT10 1DP
T: (01843) 868306

Gull Cottage Hotel ◆◆◆◆
5 Eastern Esplanade,
Broadstairs, Kent CT10 1DP
T: (01843) 861936

Hanson Hotel ◆◆◆
41 Belvedere Road, Broadstairs,
Kent CT10 1PF
T: (01843) 868936

Merriland Hotel ◆◆◆◆
The Vale, Broadstairs, Kent
CT10 1RB
T: (01843) 861064
F: (01843) 861064

Oakfield Private Hotel ◆◆◆◆
11 The Vale, Broadstairs, Kent
CT10 1RB
T: (01843) 862506 & 864021
F: (01843) 600659
E: oakfield.hotel@lineone.net
I: www.travelcheck.co.uk

The Queens Hotel ◆◆◆
31 Queens Road, Broadstairs,
Kent CT10 1PG
T: (01843) 861727
F: (01843) 600993
E: enquiries@queenshotel.org
I: www.queenshotel.org

Seaview Cottage
Rating Applied For
1 Seaview Cottages, Broadstairs,
Kent CT10 3RY
T: (01843) 604784

Sunnydene Hotel ◆◆◆◆
10 Chandos Road, Broadstairs,
Kent CT10 1QP
T: (01843) 863347
F: (01843) 863347
E: eileendocherty@sunnydene.
co
I: www.sunnydene.co.uk

Velindre Hotel ◆◆◆
10 Western Esplanade,
Broadstairs, Kent CT10 1TG
T: (01843) 601081

The Victoria ◆◆◆◆
23 Victoria Parade, Broadstairs,
Kent CT10 1QL
T: (01843) 871010
F: (01843) 860888
E: mullin@
thevictoriabroadstairs.co.uk
I: www.thevictoriabroadstairs.
co.uk

BURGESS HILL
West Sussex

Daisy Lodge ◆◆◆
26 Royal George Road, Burgess
Hill, West Sussex RH15 9SE
T: (01444) 870570
F: (01444) 870571

49 Ferndale Road ◆◆◆
Burgess Hill, West Sussex
RH15 0EZ
T: (01444) 241778
E: marlenwatsonbnb@hotmail.
com

8 Hammonds Gardens
◆◆◆◆◆
Burgess Hill, West Sussex
RH15 9QN
T: (01444) 250160

The Homestead ◆◆◆◆
Homestead Lane, Valebridge
Road, Burgess Hill, West Sussex
RH15 0RQ
T: (01444) 246899
F: (01444) 246899
E: homestead@burgess-hill.
co.uk
I: www.burgess-hill.co.uk

87 Meadow Lane ◆◆◆
Burgess Hill, West Sussex
RH15 9JD
T: (01444) 248421
F: (01444) 248421

Roselands ◆◆◆
3 Upper St Johns Road, Burgess
Hill, West Sussex RH15 8HB
T: (01444) 870491

St Owens ◆◆◆
11 Silverdale Road, Burgess Hill,
West Sussex RH15 0ED
T: (01444) 236435
E: n.j.bakers@amserve.net

Wellhouse ♦♦♦♦
Wellhouse Lane, Burgess Hill,
West Sussex RH15 0BN
T: (01444) 233231
F: (01444) 233231

BURMARSH
Kent

Dolly Plum Cottage ♦♦♦♦
Burmarsh Road, Burmarsh,
Romney Marsh, Kent TN29 0JT
T: (01303) 874558

BURPHAM
West Sussex

Anderton House
Rating Applied For
51 Marlyns Drive, off Burpham
Lane, Burpham, Guildford,
Surrey GU4 7LU
T: (01483) 826951

BURWASH
East Sussex

Glydwish Place ♦♦♦♦♦
Fontridge Lane, Burwash,
Etchingham, East Sussex
TN19 7DG
T: (01435) 882869 &
07860 624197
F: (01435) 882740
E: collins@collinsdolores.
screaming.net
I: www.glydwish.co.uk

BURWASH WEALD
East Sussex

Church House ♦♦♦
Heathfield Road, Burwash
Weald, Etchingham, East Sussex
TN19 7LA
T: (01435) 882688

CAMBERLEY
Surrey

Abacus ♦♦♦
7 Woodside, Blackwater,
Camberley, Surrey GU17 9JJ
T: (01276) 38339

CANTERBURY
Kent

Abberley House ♦♦♦
115 Whitstable Road,
Canterbury, Kent CT2 8EF
T: (01227) 450265
F: (01227) 478626

Acacia Lodge ♦♦♦♦
39 London Road, Canterbury,
Kent CT2 8LF
T: (01227) 769955 &
0975 433486
F: (01227) 769955
E: michael.cain1@virgin.net

Alexandra House ♦♦♦♦
1 Roper Road, Canterbury, Kent
CT2 7EH
T: (01227) 767011
F: (01227) 786617

Alicante Guest House ♦♦♦
4 Roper Road, Canterbury, Kent
CT2 7EH
T: (01227) 766277
F: (01227) 766277

**Anchor House Restaurant &
Guest House** ♦♦♦
25 North Lane, Canterbury, Kent
CT2 7EE
T: (01227) 768105
F: (01227) 768105

Anns House ♦♦♦
63 London Road, Canterbury,
Kent CT2 8JZ
T: (01227) 768767
F: (01227) 768172
E: annshotel.canterbury@
btinternet.com

Ashley Guest House ♦♦
9 London Road, Canterbury,
Kent CT2 8LR
T: (01227) 455863

Bower Farm House ♦♦♦♦
Stelling Minnis, Canterbury,
Kent CT4 6BB
T: (01227) 709430
E: anne@bowerbb.freeserve.
co.uk
I: www.kentac.co.uk/bowerfm

Castle Court Guest House ♦♦
8 Castle Street, Canterbury, Kent
CT1 2QF
T: (01227) 463441
F: (01227) 463441
E: guesthouse@castlecourt.
fsnet.co.uk
I: www.SmoothHound.
co.uk/hotels/castlecourt.html

Cathedral Gate Hotel ♦♦♦
36 Burgate, Canterbury, Kent
CT1 2HA
T: (01227) 464381
F: (01227) 462800
E: cgate@cgate.demon.co.uk
I: www.smoothhound.
co.uk/cathedra.html

Chaucer Lodge ♦♦♦♦
62 New Dover Road, Canterbury,
Kent CT1 3DT
T: (01227) 459141
F: (01227) 459141
E: wchaucerldg@aol.com
I: www.thechaucerlodge.co.uk

Clare-Ellen Guest House
♦♦♦♦
9 Victoria Road, Wincheap,
Canterbury, Kent CT1 3SG
T: (01227) 760205
F: (01227) 784482
E: loraine.williams@
clareellenguesthouse.co.uk
I: www.clareellenguesthouse.
co.uk

The Coach House ♦
34 Watling Street, Canterbury,
Kent CT1 2UD
T: (01227) 784324

**The Dickens Inn at House of
Agnes Hotel** ♦♦♦
71 St Dunstan's Street,
Canterbury, Kent CT2 8BN
T: (01227) 472185
F: (01227) 464527
E: enq@dickens-inn.co.uk
I: www.dickens-inn.co.uk

Four Seasons ♦♦♦
77 Sturry Road, Canterbury,
Kent CT1 1BU
T: (01227) 787078
F: (01227) 787078
E: fourseasonsbnb@aol.com
I: members.aol.
com/fourseasonsbnb

The Green House ♦♦♦
86 Wincheap, Canterbury, Kent
CT1 3RS
T: (01227) 453338
F: (01227) 452185
E: chrismac@greenhouse48.
fsnet.co.uk
I: www.bednbreakfastkent.co.uk

Greyfriars House ♦♦♦
6 Stour Street, Canterbury, Kent
CT1 2NR
T: (01227) 456255 & 830931
F: (01227) 455233
E: christine@greyfriars-house.
co.uk
I: www.greyfriars-house.co.uk

Harriet House ♦♦♦♦
3 Broad Oak Road, Canterbury,
Kent CT2 7PL
T: (01227) 457363
F: (01227) 788214

Homewood Farm ♦♦♦♦
Agester Lane, Denton,
Canterbury, Kent CT4 6NR
T: (01227) 832611
F: (01227) 832611

Iffin Farmhouse ♦♦♦♦
Iffin Lane, Canterbury, Kent
CT4 7BE
T: (01227) 462776
F: (01227) 462776
E: iffinfarmhouse@btinternet.
com

The Kings Head ♦♦♦
204 Wincheap, Canterbury, Kent
CT1 3RY
T: (01227) 462885
F: (01227) 459627

Kingsbridge Villas ♦♦♦
15 Best Lane, Canterbury, Kent
CT1 2JB
T: (01227) 766415

Kingsmead House ♦♦♦
68 St Stephen's Road,
Canterbury, Kent CT2 7JF
T: (01227) 760132
E: kingsmead@cwcom.net

Lindens Guest House ♦♦♦
38b St Dunstans Street,
Canterbury, Kent CT2 8BY
T: (01227) 462339
E: ellencommon@ukgateway.
net
I: www.canterbury.
co.uk/pages/linden.htm

London Guest House ♦♦♦
14 London Road, Canterbury,
Kent CT2 8LR
T: (01227) 765860
F: (01227) 456721
E: londonguesthousecabnkz@
supanet.com

Magnolia House ♦♦♦♦♦
36 St Dunstans Terrace,
Canterbury, Kent CT2 8AX
T: (01227) 765121 &
07885 595970
F: (01227) 765121
E: magnolia_house_
canterbury@yahoo.com
I: freespace.virgin.net/magnolia.
canterbury

The Millers ♦♦♦
2 Mill Lane, Canterbury, Kent
CT1 2AW
T: (01227) 456057
F: (01227) 452421

Oriel Lodge ♦♦♦♦
3 Queens Avenue, Canterbury,
Kent CT2 8AY
T: (01227) 462845
F: (01227) 462845
E: info@oriel-lodge.co.uk
I: www.oriel-lodge.co.uk

Peregrine House ♦♦♦
18 Hawks Lane, Canterbury,
Kent CT1 2NU
T: (01227) 472153 & 830931
F: (01227) 455233
E: christine@greyfriars-house.
co.uk
I: www.cantweb.co.uk/peregrine

Pilgrims Hotel ♦♦♦
18 The Friars, Canterbury, Kent
CT1 2AS
T: (01227) 464531
F: (01227) 762514
E: pilhot@easynet.co.uk
I: www.pilgrimshotel.com

The Plantation ♦♦♦♦
Iffin Lane, Canterbury, Kent
CT4 7BD
T: (01227) 472104
E: plantation@excite.co.uk
I: www.media-p.
co.uk/plantation/

Raemore House ♦♦♦
33 New Dover Road, Canterbury,
Kent CT1 3AS
T: (01227) 769740 &
07836 786020
F: (01227) 769432
E: tom@raemore.demon.co.uk

Renville Oast ♦♦♦
Bridge, Canterbury, Kent
CT4 5AD
T: (01227) 830215
F: (01227) 830215
E: renville.oast@virgin.net
I: freespace.virgin.net/joan.
hill/index.html

St Lawrence Guest House
♦♦♦
183 Old Dover Road, Canterbury,
Kent CT1 3EP
T: (01227) 451336
F: (01227) 451148
E: stlawrence@ic24.net

St Stephens Guest House
♦♦♦
100 St Stephens Road,
Canterbury, Kent CT2 7JL
T: (01227) 767644
F: (01227) 767644
E: info@st-stephens.fsnet.co.uk
I: www.come.to/st-stephens

Tanglewood Cottage ♦♦♦♦
40 London Road, Canterbury,
Kent CT2 8LF
T: (01227) 786806
F: (01227) 478960

Thanington Hotel ♦♦♦♦♦
140 Wincheap, Canterbury, Kent
CT1 3RY
T: (01227) 453227
F: (01227) 453225
E: thanington@lineone.net
I: www.thanington-hotel.co.uk

Tudor House ♦♦♦
6 Best Lane, Canterbury, Kent
CT1 2JB
T: (01227) 765650

Twin Mays ◆◆◆◆
Plumpudding Lane, Dargate,
Faversham, Kent ME13 9EX
T: (01227) 751346
E: janetm@harper128.freeserve.
co.uk

Waltham Court Hotel ◆◆◆◆
Kake Street, Petham, Canterbury,
Kent CT4 5SB
T: (01227) 700413
F: (01227) 700127
E: enquiries@
walthamcourthotel.co.uk
I: www.walthamcourthotel.co.uk

White Horse Inn ◆◆◆◆
Boughton, Faversham, Kent
ME13 9AX
T: (01227) 751700 & 751343
F: (01227) 751090
E: whitehorse@
shepherd-neame.co.uk
I: www.shepherd-neame.co.uk

The White House ◆◆◆◆
6 St Peters Lane, Canterbury,
Kent CT1 2BP
T: (01227) 761836
E: whwelcome@aol.com

Wincheap Guest House ◆◆◆
94 Wincheap, Canterbury, Kent
CT1 3RS
T: (01227) 762309
F: (01227) 762309

Woodlands Farm ◆◆◆
The Street, Adisham, Canterbury,
Kent CT3 3LA
T: (01304) 840401 &
07720 861765
F: (01304) 841985
E: woodlands.farm@btinternet.
com

The Woolpack Inn ◆◆◆
High Street, Chilham,
Canterbury, Kent CT4 8DL
T: (01227) 730208 & 730351
F: (01227) 731053
E: woolpack@shepherd-neame.
co.uk
I: www.shepherd-neame.co.uk

Yorke Lodge ◆◆◆◆
50 London Road, Canterbury,
Kent CT2 8LF
T: (01227) 451243
T: (01227) 462006
E: yorke-lg@dircon.co.uk
I: www.users.dircon.
co.uk/~yorke-lg

Zan Stel Lodge ◆◆◆◆
140 Old Dover Road, Canterbury,
Kent CT1 3NX
T: (01227) 453654

Barnfield ◆◆◆
Charing, Ashford, Kent
TN27 0BN
T: (01233) 712421 &
07798 686168
F: (01233) 712421

Royal Oak Inn ◆◆◆
5 High Street, Charing, Ashford,
Kent TN27 0HU
T: (01233) 712612
F: (01233) 713355
E: theroyal-oak.charingtn27@
barbox.net

Timber Lodge ◆◆◆◆
Charing Hill, Charing, Ashford,
Kent TN27 0NG
T: (01233) 712822
F: (01233) 712822

White House Farm ◆◆◆
Green Lane, Chart Sutton,
Maidstone, Kent ME17 3ES
T: (01622) 842490
F: (01622) 842490

Stour Farm ◆◆◆◆
Riverside, Chartham,
Canterbury, Kent CT4 7NX
T: (01227) 731977
F: (01227) 731977
E: info@stourfarm.co.uk
I: www.stourfarm.co.uk

Normandy House ◆◆◆
143 Maidstone Road, Chatham,
Kent ME4 6JE
T: (01634) 843047

Officers Hill ◆◆◆◆
7 College Road, Historic
Dockyard, Chatham, Kent
ME4 4QW
T: (01634) 828436
F: (01634) 828735
F: carol.chambers@ukgateway.
net

10 Officers Terrace ◆◆◆◆
Historic Dockyard, Chatham,
Kent ME4 4LJ
T: (01634) 847512
E: sandrawsparks@aol.com

35 Sandling Way ◆◆◆◆
St Marys Island, Chatham, Kent
ME4 3AZ
T: (01634) 890982
E: marcellomori@learndirect.
com

Holly House ◆◆◆◆
Beaconsfield Road, Chelwood
Gate, Haywards Heath, West
Sussex RH17 7LF
T: (01825) 740484
F: (01825) 740172
E: deebirchell@hollyhousebnb.
demon.co.uk
I: hollyhousebnb.demon.co.uk

Crossways House ◆◆◆◆
Chevening, Sevenoaks, Kent
TN14 6HF
T: (01732) 456334
F: (01732) 452312
E: info@cheveningconferences.
co.uk
I: www.cheveningconferences.
co.uk

Abelands Barn ◆◆◆◆
Bognor Road, Merston,
Chichester, West Sussex
PO20 6DY
T: (01243) 533826 & 551234
F: (01243) 555533
I: www.accomodata.
co.uk/170998.htm

Annas ◆◆◆
27 Westhampnett Road,
Chichester, West Sussex
PO19 4HW
T: (01243) 788522 &
07885 446077
F: (01243) 788522
E: nick@annas.freeserve.co.uk
I: www.annasofchichester.co.uk

**Apuldram Manor Farm Bed &
Breakfast** ◆◆◆◆
Dell Quay, Apuldram Lane,
Chichester, West Sussex
PO20 7EF
T: (01243) 782522
F: (01243) 782052
E: ma.sawday@farmersweekly.
net

Barford ◆◆◆
Bosham Lane, Bosham,
Chichester, West Sussex
PO18 8HL
T: (01243) 573393
F: (01243) 573393
E: tony@aflanagan.freeserve.
co.uk

Bayleaf ◆◆◆
16 Whyke Road, Chichester,
West Sussex PO19 2HN
T: (01243) 774330

21 Brandy Hole Lane ◆◆◆
Chichester, West Sussex
PO19 4RL
T: (01243) 528201
F: (01243) 528201
E: anneparry@anneparry.
screaming.net

The Chichester Inn ◆◆◆
38 West Street, Chichester, West
Sussex PO19 1RP
T: (01243) 783185

The Coach House ◆◆◆◆
Binderton, Chichester, West
Sussex PO18 0JS
T: (01243) 539624 &
07710 536085
F: (01243) 539624
E: spightling@aol.com

The Cottage ◆◆◆
22B Westhampnett Road,
Chichester, West Sussex
PO19 4HW
T: (01243) 774979
E: mbc_techincal@madasfish.
com

Draymans ◆◆◆
112 St Pancras, Chichester, West
Sussex PO19 4LH
T: (01243) 789872
F: (01243) 785474
E: liz@jaegerl.freeserve.co.uk
I: www.jaegerl.freeserve.co.uk

Encore ◆◆◆◆
11 Clydesdale Avenue,
Chichester, West Sussex
PO19 2LW
T: (01243) 528271

Englewood ◆◆◆◆
East Ashling, Chichester, West
Sussex PO18 9AS
T: (01243) 575407 &
07712 545570
F: (01243) 575407
E: sjenglewood@tinyworld.
co.uk

Finisterre ◆◆◆◆
9 Albert Road, Chichester, West
Sussex PO19 3JE
T: (01243) 532680 &
07889 285407
F: (01243) 532680

Forge Hotel ◆◆◆◆◆
High Street, Chilgrove,
Chichester, West Sussex
PO18 9HX
T: (01243) 535333
F: (01243) 535363
E: reservations@forgehotel.com
I: www.forgehotel.com

Friary Close ◆◆◆◆
Friary Lane, Chichester, West
Sussex PO19 1UF
T: (01243) 527294
F: (01243) 533876
E: friaryclose@argonet.co.uk

George and Dragon ◆◆
51 North Street, Chichester,
West Sussex PO19 1NQ
T: (01243) 775525 & 785660

Hedgehogs ◆◆◆
45 Whyke Lane, Chichester,
West Sussex PO19 2JT
T: (01243) 780022

Herons ◆◆◆
6 Orchard Gardens, Chichester,
West Sussex PO19 1DG
T: (01243) 531424

Home Farm House ◆◆◆◆
Elms Lane, West Wittering,
Chichester, West Sussex
PO20 8LW
T: (01243) 514252

Kia-ora Nursery ◆◆◆
Main Road, Nutbourne,
Chichester, West Sussex
PO18 8RT
T: (01243) 572858
F: (01243) 572858
E: ruthiefp@aol.com

4 The Lane ◆◆◆◆
Summersdale, Chichester, West
Sussex PO19 4PY
T: (01243) 527293 &
07711 499685
E: ynyo5@dial.pipex.com

Leef Daal ◆◆◆
Warren Farm Lane, Chichester,
West Sussex PO19 4RU
T: (01243) 790692
F: (01243) 790535
E: leefdaal@elmac.demon.co.uk
I: www.elmac.co.uk/leefdaal

Litten House ◆◆◆◆
148 St Pancras, Chichester, West
Sussex PO19 1SH
T: (01243) 774503
F: (01243) 539187
E: victoria@littenho.demon.
co.uk
I: www.littenho.demon.co.uk

5A Little London ◆◆◆
Chichester, West Sussex
PO19 1PH
T: (01243) 788405

Longmeadow Guest House
◆◆◆
Pine Grove, Chichester, West
Sussex PO19 3PN
T: (01243) 782063
E: bbeeching@lineone.net

1 Maplehurst Road ◆◆◆◆
Chichester, West Sussex
PO19 4QL
T: (01243) 528467 & 07879 963
8244
F: (01243) 528467
E: philandsuespooner@talk21.
com

Millstone Cottage ◆◆◆
Church Lane, Pagham, Bognor
Regis, West Sussex PO21 4NU
T: (01243) 262495
F: (01243) 262668
E: reception@theinglenook.com
I: www.the-inglenook.com

The Old Store Guest House
◆◆◆◆
Stane Street, Halnaker,
Chichester, West Sussex
PO18 0QL
T: (01243) 531977
F: (01243) 531977
E: alandavis@theoldstore.fsnet.
co.uk
I: www.smoothhound.
co.uk/hotels/store.html

Palm Tree Cottage ◆◆◆◆
110 Fishbourne West,
Fishbourne, Chichester, West
Sussex PO19 3JR
T: (01243) 782110 & 785285
F: (01243) 785285

Primrose Cottage ◆◆◆
Old Broyle Road, West Broyle,
Chichester, West Sussex
PO19 3PR
T: (01243) 788873

Riverside Lodge ◆◆◆
7 Market Avenue, Chichester,
West Sussex PO19 1JU
T: (01243) 783164
E: tregeardavid@hotmail.com
I: www.riverside-lodge.
chichester.co.uk

Sycamores ◆◆◆◆
16 Hunters Way, Chichester,
West Sussex PO19 4RB
T: (01243) 528294
F: (01243) 839747
E: sally.bassett@sycamores16.
freeserve.co.uk

1 Tower Street ◆◆◆
Chichester, West Sussex
PO19 1QH
T: (01243) 782526

University College Chichester
◆◆◆
Bishop Otter Campus, College
Lane, Chichester, West Sussex
PO19 4PE
T: (01243) 816070 & 816068
F: (01243) 816068
E: conference@ucc.ac.uk
I: www.ucc.ac.uk

Whyke Cottage ◆◆◆◆
17 Whyke Lane, Chichester,
West Sussex PO19 2JR
T: (01243) 788767

5 Willowbed Avenue ◆◆◆
Chichester, West Sussex
PO19 2JD
T: (01243) 786366

Xavier House ◆◆◆◆
Old Broyle Road, Chichester,
West Sussex PO19 3PR
T: (01243) 784930

CHIDDINGSTONE
Kent

Hoath House ◆◆◆
Chiddingstone Hoath,
Edenbridge, Kent TN8 7DB
T: (01342) 850362
E: jstreatfield@hoath-house.
freeserve.co.uk
I: www.hoath_house.freeserve.
co.uk

CHILHAM
Kent

Folly House ◆◆◆◆
Chilham, Canterbury, Kent
CT4 8DD
T: (01227) 738669 & 730425
F: (01227) 730425

The Old Alma ◆◆◆
Canterbury Road, Chilham,
Canterbury, Kent CT4 8DX
T: (01227) 731913
F: (01227) 731078
E: oldalma@aol.com

Woodchip House ◆◆◆
Maidstone Road, Chilham,
Canterbury, Kent CT4 8DD
T. (01227) 730386 &
07889 321978
E: woodchip@talk21.com

CHIPSTEAD
Kent

Chevers ◆◆◆◆
Moat Close, Homedean Road,
Chipstead, Sevenoaks, Kent
TN13 2HZ
T: (01732) 779144 &
07887 717429
E: japarish@supanet.com

Windmill Farm ◆◆◆◆
Chevening Road, Chipstead,
Sevenoaks, Kent TN13 2SA
T: (01732) 452054

CHURT
Surrey

Anne's Cottage ◆◆◆◆
Green Cross Lane, Churt,
Farnham, Surrey GU10 2ND
T: (01428) 714181

CLIFTONVILLE
Kent

Carnforth Hotel ◆◆◆
103 Norfolk Road, Cliftonville,
Margate, Kent CT9 2HX
T: (01843) 292127

Debenham Lodge Hotel ◆◆◆
25 Norfolk Road, Cliftonville,
Margate, Kent CT9 2HU
T: (01843) 292568

Ferndale Hotel ◆◆
26-30 Athelstan Road,
Cliftonville, Margate, Kent
CT9 2BA
T: (01843) 229192
🕎

Lynton House Hotel ◆◆
24-26 Sweyn Road, Cliftonville,
Margate, Kent CT9 2DH
T: (01843) 292046

Hotel Marina ◆◆◆
8 Dalby Square, Cliftonville,
Margate, Kent CT9 2ER
T: (01843) 230120
F: (01843) 230120
E: hotelmarina_margate@
hotmail.com
I: www.hotel_marina.co.uk

Marsdon Hotel ◆◆◆
7 Ethelbert Crescent, Cliftonville,
Margate, Kent CT9 2AY
T: (01843) 220175
F: (01843) 280920
E: enquiries@marsdon.
freeserve.co.uk
I: www.marsdon.freeserve.co.uk

Mentone Lodge ◆◆◆
5 Norfolk Road, Cliftonville,
Margate, Kent CT9 2HU
T: (01843) 292152 &
07775 515741
E: mentone@libertysurf.co.uk

Ocean View Hotel
Rating Applied For
8-10 Ethelbert Terrace,
Cliftonville, Margate, Kent
CT9 1RX
T: (01843) 220641
F: (01843) 571045
E: hoteloceanview@cs.com
I: www.oceanviewhotel.co.uk

St Malo Hotel ◆
54 Surrey Road, Cliftonville,
Margate, Kent CT9 2LA
T: (01843) 224931

CLIMPING
West Sussex

Amberley Court ◆◆◆◆
Crookthorn Lane, Climping,
Littlehampton, West Sussex
BN17 5SN
T: (01903) 725131
F: (01903) 732264

COBHAM
Kent

Burleigh Farmhouse ◆◆◆◆
Sole Street Road, Cobham,
Gravesend, Kent DA12 3AR
T: (01474) 814321
F: (01474) 813843

Roxena ◆◆◆
34 Manor Road, Sole Street,
Cobham, Gravesend, Kent
DA13 9BN
T: (01474) 814174

COLEMANS HATCH
East Sussex

Gospel Oak ◆◆◆
Sandy Lane, Colemans Hatch,
Hartfield, East Sussex TN7 4ER
T: (01342) 823840

COMPTON
West Sussex

Apiary Cottage ◆◆◆
Compton, Chichester, West
Sussex PO18 9EX
T: (023) 9263 1306

Compton Farmhouse ◆◆
Church Lane, Compton,
Chichester, West Sussex
PO18 9HB
T: (023) 9263 1597

COOKSBRIDGE
East Sussex

Lower Tulleys Wells Farm
◆◆◆
Beechwood Lane, East
Chiltington Road, Cooksbridge,
Lewes, East Sussex BN7 3QG
T: (01273) 472622

COOLHAM
West Sussex

Selsey Arms ◆◆◆
Coolham, Horsham, West Sussex
RH13 8QJ
T: (01403) 741536

COWBEECH
East Sussex

Batchelors ◆◆◆
Cowbeech Hill, Cowbeech,
Hailsham, East Sussex BN27 4JB
T: (01323) 832215

The Mill ◆◆◆◆
Trolliloes Lane, Cowbeech,
Hailsham, East Sussex BN27 4JG
T: (01323) 833952

COWDEN
Kent

Becketts Bed & Breakfast
◆◆◆◆
Pylegate Farm, Hartfield Road,
Cowden, Edenbridge, Kent
TN8 7HE
T: (01342) 850514 &
07884 427550
F: (01342) 851281
E: bed-breakfast.becketts@
tinyworld.co.uk
I: www.becketts-bandb.co.uk

Saxbys ◆◆◆◆
Cowden, Royal Tunbridge Wells,
Kent TN8 7DU
I: (01342) 850581
F: (01342) 850830
I: www.saxbys@cowden.fsnet.
com.uk

Southernwood House ◆◆◆◆
(The Old Rectory), Church Street,
Cowden, Edenbridge, Kent
TN8 7JE
T: (01342) 850880

COWFOLD
West Sussex

Coach House ◆◆◆
Horsham Road, Cowfold,
Horsham, West Sussex
RH13 8BT
T: (01403) 864247
F: (01403) 865329
E: coachhousecowfold@talk21.
com

CRANBROOK
Kent

Bargate House ◆◆◆◆
Angley Road, Cranbrook, Kent
TN17 2PQ
T: (01580) 714254

Folly Hill Cottage ◆◆◆◆
Friezley Lane, Hocker Edge,
Cranbrook, Kent TN17 2LL
T: (01580) 714299
F: (01580) 714299
E: decarlej@aol.com
I: members.aol.com:/decarlej

Guernsey Cottage ◆◆◆
Wilsley Green, Cranbrook, Kent
TN17 2LG
T: (01580) 712542

Hallwood Farm House ◆◆◆
Hallwood Farm, Cranbrook, Kent
TN17 2SP
T: (01580) 713204
F: (01580) 713204

Millfields House ◆◆◆◆
The Hill, Cranbrook, Kent
TN17 3AJ
T: (01580) 714344 & 720045
F: (01580) 720045
E: janepugh@millfieldshouse.
freeserve.co.uk
I: www.millfieldshouse.
freeserve.co.uk

Old Rectory ◆◆◆◆
The Old Rectory, Frittenden,
Cranbrook, Kent TN17 2DG
T: (01580) 852313
F: (01580) 852313

Sissinghurst Castle Farm
◆◆◆◆
Sissinghurst, Cranbrook, Kent
TN17 2AB
T: (01580) 712885
F: (01580) 712601

Swattenden Ridge ◆◆◆
Swattenden Lane, Cranbrook,
Kent TN17 3PR
T: (01580) 712327

Tolehurst Barn ◆◆◆◆
Cranbrook Road, Frittenden,
Cranbrook, Kent TN17 2BP
T: (01580) 714385
F: (01580) 714385

White Horse Inn ◆◆
High Street, Cranbrook, Kent
TN17 3EX
T: (01580) 712615

CRANLEIGH
Surrey

Pathstruie
Rating Applied For
Stouolds Hill, Cranleigh, Surrey
GU6 8LE
T: (01483) 273551

CRAWLEY
West Sussex

Little Foxes Hotel ◆◆◆◆
Charlwood Road, Ifield Wood,
Crawley, West Sussex RH11 0JY
T: (01293) 529206
F: (01293) 551434
E: info@littlefoxeshotel.co.uk
I: www.littlefoxeshotel.co.uk

The Manor House ◆◆◆
Bonnetts Lane, Ifield, Crawley,
West Sussex RH11 0NY
T: (01293) 510000 & 512298
F: (01293) 518046
E: info@manorhouse-gatwick.
co.uk
I: www.manorhouse-gatwick.
co.uk

Three Bridges Lodge ◆◆◆
190 Three Bridges Road,
Crawley, West Sussex RH10 1LN
T: (01293) 612190
F: (01293) 553078
E: nisangah@yahoo.com

Waterhall Country House
◆◆◆
Prestwood Lane, Ifield Wood,
Crawley, West Sussex RH11 0LA
T: (01293) 520002
F: (01293) 539905
E: info@waterhall.co.uk
I: www.
smoothhound/hotels/waterhall

CROWBOROUGH
East Sussex

Alpina ◆◆◆◆
27 Beacon Close, Crowborough,
East Sussex TN6 1DX
T: (01892) 655743
F: (01892) 652545

Bathurst ◆◆◆◆
Fielden Road, Crowborough,
East Sussex TN6 1TR
T: (01892) 665476 & 654189
F: (01892) 654189

Braemore ◆◆◆◆
Eridge Road, Steel Cross,
Crowborough, East Sussex
TN6 2SS
T: (01892) 665700

Bryher Patch ◆◆◆
18 Hydehurst Close,
Crowborough, East Sussex
TN6 1EN
T: (01892) 663038

Hope Court ◆◆◆◆
Rannoch Road, Crowborough,
East Sussex TN6 1RA
T: (01892) 654017 &
07710 289138

CUCKFIELD
West Sussex

The Wheatsheaf Inn ◆◆◆
Broad Street, Cuckfield,
Haywards Heath, West Sussex
RH17 5DW
T: (01444) 454078
F: (01444) 417265

CUXTON
Kent

27 James Road ◆◆◆
Cuxton, Rochester, Kent
ME2 1DH
T: (01634) 715154

DANEHILL
East Sussex

New Glenmore ◆◆◆◆
Sliders Lane, Furners Green,
Uckfield, East Sussex TN22 3RU
T: (01825) 790783
E: alan.robinson@bigfoot.com

DARTFORD
Kent

Chashir ◆◆
3 Tynedale Close, Fleet Estate,
Dartford, DA2 6LL
T: (01322) 227886

DEAL
Kent

Cannongate Guest House ◆◆
26 Gilford Road, Deal, Kent
CT14 7DJ
T: 1304 375238

Hardicot Guest House ◆◆◆◆
Kingsdown Road, Walmer, Deal,
Kent CT14 8AW
T: (01304) 373867 & 389234
F: (01304) 389234
E: guestboss@talk21.com
I: www.smoothhound.
co.uk/hotels/hardicot.html

The Hole in the Roof Hotel
◆◆◆
42-44 Queen Street, Deal, Kent
CT14 6EY
T: (01304) 374839 & 373768
F: (01304) 373768

Ilex Cottage ◆◆◆◆
Temple Way, Worth, Deal, Kent
CT14 0DA
T: (01304) 617026
F: (01304) 620890
E: info@ilexcottage.com
I: www.ilexcottage.com

Keep House ◆◆◆
1 Deal Castle Road, Deal, Kent
CT14 7BB
T: (01304) 368162
F: (01304) 368162
E: keephouse@talk21.com
I: www.keephouse.co.uk

Kings Head Public House ◆◆◆
9 Beach Street, Deal, Kent
CT14 7AH
T: (01304) 368194
F: (01304) 364182

The Malvern ◆◆◆
5-7 Ranelagh Road, Deal, Kent
CT14 7BG
T: (01304) 372944
F: (01304) 372944

Richmond Villa Guest House
◆◆◆◆
1 Ranelagh Road, Deal, Kent
CT14 7BG
T: (01304) 366211
E: richmondvilla@supanet.com
I: www.richmondvilla.co.uk

The Roast House Lodge ◆◆◆
224 London Road, Deal, Kent
CT14 9PW
T: (01304) 380824
F: (01304) 380824

Sondes Lodge B & B ◆◆◆◆
14 Sondes Road, Deal, Kent
CT14 7BW
T: (01304) 368741
F: (01304) 368741

DENSOLE
Kent

Garden Lodge ◆◆◆◆
324 Canterbury Road, Densole,
Folkestone, Kent CT18 7BB
T: (01303) 893147 &
07885 933683
F: (01303) 894581
E: gardenlodge@tritontek.com
I: www.garden-lodge.com

DETLING
Kent

East Lodge ◆◆◆◆
Harple Lane, Detling, Maidstone,
Kent ME14 3ET
T: (01622) 734205
F: (01622) 735500

DODDINGTON
Kent

Palace Farmhouse ◆◆◆
Chequers Hill, Doddington,
Sittingbourne, Kent ME9 0AU
T: (01795) 886820

DORKING
Surrey

Bulmer Farm ◆◆◆◆
Holmbury St Mary, Dorking,
Surrey RH5 6LG
T: (01306) 730210

Fairdene Guest House ◆◆◆
Moores Road, Dorking, Surrey
RH4 2BG
T: (01306) 888337
E: zoe@fairdene5.freeserve.
co.uk

Kerne Hus ◆◆◆◆
Walliswood, Dorking, Surrey
RH5 5RD
T: (01306) 627548 &
07719 595107
E: kerne_hus@lineone.net

Sturtwood Farm ◆◆◆
Partridge Lane, Newdigate,
Dorking, Surrey RH5 5EE
T: (01306) 631308
F: (01306) 631908

Torridon Guest House ◆◆◆
Longfield Road, Dorking, Surrey
RH4 3DF
T: (01306) 883724
F: (01306) 880759

DOVER
Kent

Amanda Guest House ◆◆
4 Harold Street, Dover, Kent
CT16 1SF
T: (01304) 201711
E: pageant@port-of-dover.com
I: www.amandaguesthouse.
co.uk

Beulah House ◆◆◆◆
94 Crabble Hill, Dover, Kent
CT17 0SA
T: (01304) 824615

Blakes of Dover ◆◆◆
52 Castle Street, Dover, Kent
CT16 1PJ
T: (01304) 202194 & 211263
F: (01304) 202194
E: blakes-of-dover@hotels.
activebooking.com

Castle Guest House ◆◆◆
10 Castle Hill Road, Dover, Kent
CT16 1QW
T: (01304) 201656
F: (01304) 210197
E: dimechr@aol.com
I: www.castle-guesthouse.co.uk

Clare Guest House ◆◆◆
167 Folkestone Road, Dover,
Kent CT17 9SJ
T: (01304) 204553

Cleveland Guest House ◆◆◆
2 Laureston Place, off Castle Hill
Road, Dover, Kent CT16 1QX
T: (01304) 204622
F: (01304) 211598
E: albetcleve@aol.com
I: www.albetcleve.homestead.
com

Colret House ◆◆◆◆
The Green, Coldred, Dover, Kent
CT15 5AP
T: (01304) 830388
F: (01304) 830388
E: jackie.colret@evnet.co.uk

The Dell Guest House ◆◆◆
233 Folkestone Road, Dover,
Kent CT17 9SL
T: (01304) 202422
F: (01304) 204816
E: mail@dell-guesthouse.co.uk
I: www.dell-guesthouse.co.uk

Esther House ◆◆◆
55 Barton Road, Dover, Kent
CT16 2NF
T: (01304) 241332
F: (01304) 241332

Frith Lodge ◆◆◆
14 Frith Road, Dover, Kent
CT16 2PY
T: (01304) 208139

Gladstone Guest House ◆◆◆
3 Laureston Place, Dover, Kent
CT16 1QX
T: (01304) 208457
F: (01304) 208457
E: kkd3gladstone@aol.com
I: www.doveraccommodation.
co.uk/gladstone.htm

Le Clermont
Rating Applied For
15 Park Avenue, Dover, Kent
CT16 1ES
T: 1304 202302
F: 1304 202302

Linden Guest House ◆◆◆◆
231 Folkestone Road, Dover,
Kent CT17 9SL
T: (01304) 205449
F: (01304) 212499
E: Lindenrog@aol.com
I: www.smoothhound.
co.uk/hotels/linden.html

Loddington House Hotel
◆◆◆◆
14 East Cliff, (Seafront - Marine
Parade), Dover, Kent CT16 1LX
T: (01304) 201947
F: (01304) 201947

Longfield Guest House ◆◆◆
203 Folkestone Road, Dover,
Kent CT17 9SL
T: (01304) 204716

Maison Dieu Guest House ◆◆
89 Maison Dieu Road, Dover,
Kent CT16 1RU
T: (01304) 204033
F: (01304) 242816
E: lawrie@brguest.co.uk
I: www.brguest.co.uk

The Norman Guest House
◆◆◆
75 Folkestone Road, Dover, Kent
CT17 9RZ
T: (01304) 207803

Owler Lodge ◆◆◆◆
Alkham Valley Road, Alkham,
Dover, Kent CT15 7DF
T: (01304) 826375
F: (01304) 826375
E: owlerlodge@aol.com
I: www.smoothhound.
co.uk/hotels/owlerlodge.html

The Park Inn ◆◆◆◆
1-2 Park Place, Ladywell, Dover,
Kent CT16 1DQ
T: (01304) 203300
F: (01304) 203324
E: theparkinn@cs.com
I: www.theparkinnatdover.co.uk

St Brelades Guest House
◆◆◆◆
80-82 Buckland Avenue, Dover,
Kent CT16 2NW
T: (01304) 206126
F: (01304) 211486
E: stbrelades@compuserve.com
I: www.stbrelades-dover.co.uk

**St Margaret's Holiday Park
Hotel** ◆◆◆◆
Reach Road, St-Margarets-at-
Cliffe, Dover, Kent CT15 6AE
T: (01304) 853262 & 852 255
F: (01304) 853434

Swingate Inn and Hotel ◆◆◆
Deal Road, Dover, Kent
CT15 5DP
T: (01304) 204043
F: (01304) 204043
E: terry@swingate.com
I: www.swingate.com

Talavera House ◆◆◆◆
275 Folkestone Road, Dover,
Kent CT17 9LL
T: (01304) 206794
F: (01304) 207067
E: john-jan@talavera-house.
freeserve.co.uk
I: www.smoothhound.
co.uk/hotels

Victoria Guest House ◆◆◆◆
1 Laureston Place, Dover, Kent
CT16 1QX
T: (01304) 205140 &
07967 692872
F: (01304) 205140
E: WHam101496@aol.com

Westbank Guest House ◆◆◆◆
239-241 Folkestone Road,
Dover, Kent CT17 9LL
T: (01304) 201061 & 205609
F: (01304) 214718
E: WSEbnk111@netscapeonline.
co.uk
I: www.westbankguesthouse.
co.uk

Whitmore Guest House ◆◆◆
261 Folkestone Road, Dover,
Kent CT17 9LL
T: (01304) 203080 &
07812 711887
F: (01304) 240110
E: whitmoredover@aol.com
I: www.smoothhound.
co.uk/hotels/whitmore.html.

DUDDLESWELL
East Sussex
Duddleswell Manor ◆◆◆◆
Duddleswell, Uckfield, East
Sussex TN22 3JL
T: (01825) 712701
F: (01825) 712701
E: davidsmith@crosscastle.
fsnet.co.uk

DUNCTUN
West Sussex
Duncton Mill House ◆◆◆◆◆
Dye House Lane, Dunctun,
Petworth, West Sussex
GU28 0LF
T: (01798) 342294
F: (01798) 344122
E: sheila@duntonmill.com
I: www.dunctonmill.com

Wild Cherries ◆◆◆
Dyehouse Lane, Dunctun,
Petworth, West Sussex
GU28 0LF
T: (01798) 342313 &
07971 828020

DUNTON GREEN
Kent
Lilac Cottage ◆◆◆
15 Pounsley Road, Dunton
Green, Sevenoaks, Kent
TN13 2XP
T: (01732) 469898

DYMCHURCH
Kent
The Ship Inn ◆◆
118 High Street, Dymchurch,
Romney Marsh, Kent TN29 0LD
T: (01303) 872122
F: (01303) 872311
E: bookings@theshipinn.co.uk
I: www.theshipinn.co.uk

Waterside Guest House
◆◆◆◆
15 Hythe Road, Dymchurch,
Romney Marsh, Kent TN29 0LN
T: (01303) 872253
F: (01303) 872253
E: info@watersideguesthouse.
co.uk
I: www.watersideguesthouse.
co.uk

EARNLEY
West Sussex
Millstone ◆◆◆◆
Clappers Lane, Earnley,
Chichester, West Sussex
PO20 7JJ
T: (01243) 670116 &
07768 958223
F: (01243) 672280
E: michaelharrington@
btinternet.com

EAST ASHLING
West Sussex
Horse & Groom ◆◆◆
East Ashling, Chichester, West
Sussex PO18 9AX
T: (01243) 575339
F: (01243) 575339

EAST GRINSTEAD
West Sussex
Cranston House ◆◆◆
Cranston Road, East Grinstead,
West Sussex RH19 3HW
T: (01342) 323609
F: (01342) 323609
E: accommodation@
cranstonhouse.screaming.net
I: www.cranstonhouse.co.uk

The Star Inn ◆◆◆
Church Road, Lingfield, Surrey
RH7 6AH
T: (01342) 832364
F: (01342) 832364
E: thestarinn@breathemail.net
I: www.starinnlingfield.com

Town House ◆◆
6 De La Warr Road, East
Grinstead, West Sussex
RH19 3BN
T: (01342) 300310
F: (01342) 315122

EAST LAVANT
West Sussex
The Flint House ◆◆◆◆◆
Pook Lane, East Lavant,
Chichester, West Sussex
PO18 0AS
T: (01243) 773482
E: theflinthouse@ukonline.co.uk

EAST PECKHAM
Kent
Roydon Hall ◆◆◆
Seven Mile Lane, East Peckham,
Tonbridge, Kent TN12 5NH
T: (01622) 812121
F: (01622) 813959
E: roydonhall@btinternet.com
I: www.tourismsoutheast.
com/member/webpages/A5224.
htm

EAST PRESTON
West Sussex
Roselea Cottage ◆◆◆
2 Elm Avenue, East Preston,
Littlehampton, West Sussex
BN16 1HJ
T: (01903) 786787
F: (01903) 770220
E: roselea.cottage@tesco.net

EAST WITTERING
West Sussex
Apples & Pears ◆◆◆◆
65 Stocks Lane, East Wittering,
Chichester, West Sussex
PO20 8NH
T: (01243) 670551
F: (01243) 672069

Stubcroft Farm ◆◆◆
Stubcroft Lane, East Wittering,
Chichester, West Sussex
PO20 8PJ
T: (01243) 671469
E: sigreen@cix.co.uk

EASTBOURNE
East Sussex
The Alfriston Hotel ◆◆◆
16 Lushington Road,
Eastbourne, East Sussex
BN21 4LL
T: (01323) 725640
E: alfristonhotel@fsbdial.co.uk

Bay Lodge Hotel ◆◆◆
61-62 Royal Parade, Eastbourne,
East Sussex BN22 7AQ
T: (01323) 732515
F: (01323) 735009
E: Beryl@mnewson.freeserve.
co.uk

Bella Vista ◆◆◆◆
30 Redoubt Road, Eastbourne,
East Sussex BN22 7DH
T: (01323) 724222

Birling Gap Hotel ◆◆◆
Birling Gap, Seven Sisters Cliffs,
East Dean, Eastbourne, East
Sussex BN20 0AB
T: (01323) 423197
F: (01323) 423030
E: info@birlinggaphotel.co.uk
I: www.birlinggaphotel.co.uk

Boyne House ◆◆◆
12 St Aubyns Road, Eastbourne,
East Sussex BN22 7AS
T: (01323) 430245
E: derek@derekandjoan.fsnet.
co.uk

Brayscroft Hotel ◆◆◆◆
13 South Cliff Avenue,
Eastbourne, East Sussex
BN20 7AH
T: (01323) 647005
F: (01323) 720705
E: brayscroft@hotmail.com
I: www.brayscrofthotel.co.uk

Cambridge House ◆◆◆
6 Cambridge Road, Eastbourne,
East Sussex BN22 7BS
T: (01323) 721100

Cherry Tree Hotel ◆◆◆◆
15 Silverdale Road, Eastbourne,
East Sussex BN20 7AJ
T: (01323) 722406
F: (01323) 648838
E: anncherrytree@aol.com
I: www.eastbourne.
org/cherrytree-hotel

Cornerways Hotel ◆◆◆
60 Royal Parade, Eastbourne,
East Sussex BN21 7AQ
T: (01323) 721899
F: (01323) 724422

Cromwell Private Hotel ♦♦♦♦
23 Cavendish Place, Eastbourne,
East Sussex BN21 3EJ
T: (01323) 725288
F: (01323) 725288
E: cromwell-hotel@lineone.net
I: www.SmoothHound.
co.uk/hotels/cromwell

Edelweiss Private Hotel ♦♦♦
10-12 Elms Avenue, Eastbourne,
East Sussex BN21 3DN
T: (01323) 732071
F: (01323) 732071
E: peterbutler@fsbdial.co.uk

Gladwyn Hotel
Rating Applied For
16 Blackwater Road, Eastbourne,
East Sussex BN21 4JD
T: (01323) 733142

Hanburies Hotel ♦♦♦
4 Hardwick Road, Eastbourne,
East Sussex BN21 4NY
T: (01323) 730698
F: (01323) 730698

Jenric Guest House ♦
36 Ceylon Place, Eastbourne,
East Sussex BN21 3JF
T: (01323) 728857
E: jenric@lineone.net

Little Foxes ♦♦♦♦
24 Wannock Road, Eastbourne,
East Sussex BN22 7JU
I: (01323) 640670
F: (01323) 640670
E: chris@foxholes55.freeserve.
co.uk

Loriston Guest House ♦♦♦
17 St Aubyns Road, Eastbourne,
East Sussex BN22 7AS
T: (01323) 726193

The Lynwood Hotel ♦♦♦
31-33 Jevington Gardens,
Eastbourne, East Sussex
BN21 4HP
T: (01323) 638716
F: (01323) 412846
E: gm.lyn@barbox.net
I: www.shearingholidays.co.uk

Majestic Hotel ♦♦♦
26-34 Royal Parade, Eastbourne,
East Sussex BN21 7AN
T: (01323) 730311

Nirvana Private Hotel ♦♦♦
32 Redoubt Road, Eastbourne,
East Sussex BN22 7DL
T: (01323) 722603

Pinnacle Point ♦♦♦♦♦
Foyle Way, Eastbourne, East
Sussex BN20 7XL
T: (01323) 726666 &
0796 7209958
F: (01323) 643946
I: www.pinnaclepoint.co.uk

St Omer Hotel ♦♦♦
13 Royal Parade, Eastbourne,
East Sussex BN22 7AR
T: (01323) 722152
F: (01323) 723400
E: st.omer@lineone.net
I: www.st-omer.co.uk

Sea Beach House Hotel ♦♦♦♦
39-40 Marine Parade,
Eastbourne, East Sussex
BN22 7AY
T: (01323) 410458 & 410459
E: enquiries@
seabeachhousehotel.com
I: www.seabeachhousehotel.com

Sherwood Hotel ♦♦♦
7 Lascelles Terrace, Eastbourne,
East Sussex BN21 4BJ
T: (01323) 724002
F: (01323) 439989
E: sherwood-hotel@supanet.
co.uk
I: www.
sherwood-hotel-eastbourne.
co.uk

Southcroft Hotel ♦♦♦♦
15 South Cliff Avenue,
Eastbourne, East Sussex
BN20 7AH
T: (01323) 729071
E: southcroft@eastbourne34.
freeserve.co.uk
I: www.southcrofthotel.co.uk

Stratford Hotel & Restaurant ♦♦
59 Cavendish Place, Eastbourne,
East Sussex BN21 3RL
T: (01323) 724051 & 726391
F: (01323) 726391

Trevinhurst Lodge ♦♦♦♦
10 Baslow Road, Meads,
Eastbourne, East Sussex
BN20 7UJ
T: (01323) 410023
F: (01323) 643238
E: enquiries@trevinhurstlodge.
com
I: www.trevinhurstlodge.com

EASTCHURCH
Kent

Dunmow House ♦♦♦
9 Church Road, Eastchurch,
Sheerness, Kent ME12 4DG
T: (01795) 880576
F: (01795) 880 230
E: mepordage@msn.com

EASTERGATE
West Sussex

Highfield ♦♦♦
Cherry Tree Drive, Eastergate,
Chichester, West Sussex
PO20 6RR
T: (01243) 545194
F: (01243) 545194
E: jenny.price@talk21.com

EASTLING
Kent

Carpenters Arms ♦♦♦
The Street, Eastling, Faversham,
Kent ME13 0AZ
T: (01795) 890234
F: (01795) 890654
E: www.carpenters-arms@
lineone.net
I: www.carpenters-arms.com

EDENBRIDGE
Kent

Black Robins Farm ♦♦♦♦
Grants Lane, Edenbridge, Kent
TN8 6QP
T: (01732) 863212

Mowshurst Farm House ♦♦♦♦
Swan Lane, Edenbridge, Kent
TN8 6AH
T: (01732) 862064

Shoscombe ♦♦♦♦
Mill Hill, Edenbridge, Kent
TN8 5DA
T: (01732) 866781
F: (01732) 867807

Ye Old Crown Inn ♦♦♦♦
74-76 The High Street,
Edenbridge, Kent TN8 5AR
T: (01732) 867896
F: (01732) 868316
I: www.lionheartinns.co.uk

ELHAM
Kent

Abbot's Fireside Hotel ♦♦♦♦
High Street, Elham, Canterbury,
Kent CT4 6TD
T: (01303) 840265
F: (01303) 840852
E: info@abbotsfireside.com
I: www.abbotsfireside.com

The Rose and Crown ♦♦♦
High Street, Elham, Canterbury,
Kent CT4 6TD
T: (01303) 840226
F: (01303) 840141
E: info@roseandcrown.co.uk
I: www.roseandcrown.co.uk

ELMSTED
Kent

Oak Cottage ♦♦♦♦
Elmsted, Ashford, Kent TN25 5JT
T: (01233) 750272 & 750543
T: (01233) 750543
E: nichols@oakcottage.
invictanet.co.uk

ELSTED
West Sussex

Three Elsted ♦♦♦
Elsted, Midhurst, West Sussex
GU29 0JY
T: (01730) 825065
E: rh@rhill.ftech.co.uk

EPSOM
Surrey

White House Hotel ♦♦♦♦
Downs Hill Road, Epsom, Surrey
KT18 5HW
T: (01372) 722472
F: (01372) 744447
E: hopkins.epsom@virgin.net

ERIDGE GREEN
East Sussex

The Goodwood Lodge ♦♦♦
Eridge Green, Royal Tunbridge
Wells, Kent TN3 9JB
T: (01892) 750470
F: (01892) 750470

ESHER
Surrey

The Bear Inn ♦♦♦♦
71 High Street, Esher, Surrey
KT10 9LQ
T: (01372) 469786
F: (01372) 468378

EWHURST
Surrey

Sixpenny Buckle ♦♦♦♦
Gransden Close, Ewhurst,
Cranleigh, Surrey GU6 7RL
T: (01483) 273988
E: patriciamortimore@legenie.
co.uk
I: my.genie.
co.uk/patriciamortimore01

Yard Farm ♦♦♦
Ewhurst, Cranleigh, Surrey
GU6 7SN
T: (01483) 276649
F: (01483) 276649

FAIRLIGHT
East Sussex

Fairlight Cottage ♦♦♦♦
Warren Road, (Via Coastguard
Lane), Fairlight, Hastings, East
Sussex TN35 4AG
T: (01424) 812545
F: (01424) 812545
E: fairlightcottage@supanet.
com

FAIRWARP
East Sussex

Broom Cottage ♦♦♦♦
Browns Brook, Fairwarp,
Uckfield, East Sussex TN22 3BY
T: (01825) 712942

FARNHAM
Surrey

A to B&B ♦♦♦
The Wrens, 16 Aveley Lane,
Farnham, Surrey GU9 8PR
T: (01252) 715046
F: (01252) 715046
E: colin-barbara-wrens@talk21.
com

High Wray ♦♦♦
73 Lodge Hill Road, Farnham,
Surrey GU10 3RB
T: (01252) 715589
F: (01252) 715746
E: crawford@highwray73.co.uk
&

Mala Strana ♦♦♦♦
66 Roundstone Road, Farnham,
Surrey GU10 4TR
T: (01252) 793262

14 Nutshell Lane ♦♦
Farnham, Surrey GU9 0HG
T: (01252) 710147
F: (01252) 710147

South Lodge ♦♦♦♦♦
Gravel Hill Road, Holt Pound,
Farnham, Surrey GU10 4LG
T: (01420) 520960
F: (01420) 520961
E: southlodge1@aol.com
I: www.southlodge.org.uk

FAVERSHAM
Kent

Barnsfield ♦♦♦
Fostall, Hernhill, Faversham,
Kent ME13 9JH
T: (01227) 750973 &
07889 836259
F: (01227) 273098
E: barnsfield@yahoo.com
I: www.barnsfield.co.uk

The Granary ♦♦♦♦
Plumford Lane, Off Brogdale
Road, Ospringe, Faversham, Kent
ME13 0DS
T: (01795) 538416 &
07710 199177
F: (01795) 538416
E: annette@the-granary.co.uk
I: www.the-granary.co.uk

Heronsmere, 19 Nobel Court ♦♦♦
Faversham, Kent ME13 7SD
T: (01795) 536767
E: keith@griff16.freeserve.co.uk

Leaveland Court ♦♦♦♦
Leaveland, Faversham, Kent
ME13 0NP
T: (01233) 740596
F: (01233) 740015

March Cottage ◆◆◆
5 Preston Avenue, Faversham,
Kent ME13 8NH
T: (01795) 536514

Owens Court Farm ◆◆◆
Selling, Faversham, Kent
ME13 9QN
T: (01227) 752247
F: (01227) 752247

Preston Lea ◆◆◆◆
Canterbury Road, Faversham,
Kent ME13 8XA
T: (01795) 535266
F: (01795) 533388
E: preston.lea@which.net
I: homepages.which.net/~alan.
turner10

FAYGATE
West Sussex

The Willows ◆◆◆◆
Wimlands Lane, Faygate,
Horsham, West Sussex
RH12 4SP
T: (01293) 851030
F: (01293) 852466

FINDON
West Sussex

Findon Tower ◆◆◆◆
Cross Lane, Findon, Worthing,
West Sussex BN14 0UG
T: (01903) 873870

FIRLE
East Sussex

New House Farm ◆◆◆
Firle, Lewes, East Sussex
BN8 6ND
T: (01273) 858242
F: (01273) 858242
E: hecks@farming.co.uk

FISHBOURNE
West Sussex

Maycroft ◆◆◆◆
Clay Lane, Fishbourne,
Chichester, West Sussex
PO19 3PX
T: (01243) 778338
F: (01243) 536596
E: jbumfrey@aol.co

FITTLEWORTH
West Sussex

Fleet Bungalow ◆◆◆
The Fleet, Fittleworth,
Pulborough, West Sussex
RH20 1HS
T: (01798) 865634 & 0772 0085
010
F: (01798) 865 634
E: linda.wagstaff@ntlworld.com
I: www.the-fleet.co.uk

The Old Post Office ◆◆◆◆
Lower Street, Fittleworth,
Pulborough, West Sussex
RH20 1JE
T: (01798) 865315
F: (01798) 865315
E: sue.moseley@ukgateway.net

Street Farm B & B ◆◆◆◆
Street Farm, Lower Street,
Fittleworth, Pulborough, West
Sussex RH20 1EN
T: (01798) 865885
F: (01798) 865870

Swan Inn ◆◆◆◆
Lower Street, Fittleworth,
Pulborough, West Sussex
RH20 1EN
T: (01798) 865429
F: (01798) 865721
E: hotel@swaninn.com
I: www.swaninn.com

FIVE OAK GREEN
Kent

Ivy House ◆◆◆
Five Oak Green, Tonbridge, Kent
TN12 6RB
T: (01892) 832041
F: (01892) 832041

FLETCHING
East Sussex

The Griffin Inn ◆◆◆◆
High Street, Fletching, Uckfield,
East Sussex TN22 3SS
T: (01825) 722890
F: (01825) 722810
E: nigelpullan@thegriffininn.
co.uk
I: www.thegriffininn.co.uk

FLIMWELL
Kent

St Annes ◆◆◆◆
5 Chaplefield, High Street,
Flimwell, Wadhurst, East Sussex
TN5 7PF
T: (01580) 879880
E: gemwilsonmoir@supanet.
com

FOLKESTONE
Kent

Banque Hotel ◆◆◆
4 Castle Hill Avenue, Folkestone,
Kent CT20 2QT
T: (01303) 253797
F: (01303) 253797
E: banquehotel4@hotmail.com
I: www.banquehotel.com

Beachborough Park ◆◆◆
Newington, Folkestone, Kent
CT18 8BW
T: (01303) 275432
F: (01843) 845131
I: www.kentaccess.org.uk

Chandos Guest House ◆◆◆
77 Cheriton Road, Folkestone,
Kent CT20 1DG
T: (01303) 851202
F: (01303) 272073
E: don@chandosguesthouse.
co.uk
I: www.chandosguesthouse.com

Chilton House Hotel ◆◆◆
14-15 Marine Parade,
Folkestone, Kent CT20 1PX
T: (01303) 249786
F: (01303) 247525
E: chiltonhousehotel@
btinternet.com
I: www.chiltonhousehotel.co.uk

Cliffside
Rating Applied For
Radnor Cliff Crescent,
Folkestone, Kent CT20 2JH
T: (01303) 248328
F: (01303) 240115

Granada Guest House ◆◆◆
51 Cheriton Road, Folkestone,
Kent CT20 1DF
T: (01303) 254913

Harbourside Hotel ◆◆◆◆◆
12-14 Wear Bay Road,
Folkestone, Kent CT19 6AT
T: (01303) 256528 &
07768 123884
F: (01303) 241299
E: joy@harboursidehotel.com
I: www.harboursidehotel.com

Kentmere Guest House
Rating Applied For
76 Cheriton Road, Folkestone,
Kent CT20 1DG
T: (01303) 259661
F: (01303) 259661
E: kentmere.guesthouse@
ntlworld.com
I: www.smoothhound.
co.uk/hotels/kentmere

The Rob Roy Guest House ◆
227 Dover Road, Folkestone,
Kent CT19 6NH
T: (01303) 253341
F: (01303) 770060
E: therobroy@cwcom.net
I: www.therobroy.freeserve.
co.uk

Windsor Hotel ◆◆
5-6 Langhorne Gardens,
Folkestone, Kent CT20 2EA
T: (01303) 251348
E: williams.windsor@virginnet.
co.uk

FONTWELL
West Sussex

Woodacre ◆◆◆◆
Arundel Road, Fontwell, Arundel,
West Sussex BN18 0SD
T: (01243) 814301
F: (01243) 814344
E: wacrebb@aol.com
I: www.woodacre.co.uk

FOUR ELMS
Kent

Oak House Barn ◆◆◆◆◆
Mapleton Road, Four Elms,
Edenbridge, Kent TN8 6PL
T: (01732) 700725

FRAMFIELD
East Sussex

Beggars Barn ◆◆◆◆
Barn Lane, Framfield, Uckfield,
East Sussex TN22 5RX
T: (01825) 890869 &
07770 687686
F: (01825) 890868
E: caroline@beggarsbarn.co.uk
I: www.beggarsbarn.co.uk

Gatehouse Green Farm ◆◆◆◆
Gatehouse Lane, Framfield,
Uckfield, East Sussex TN22 5RS
T: (01825) 890212
F: (01825) 890212

The Old Farmhouse ◆◆◆◆
Honey's Green, Framfield,
Uckfield, East Sussex TN22 5RE
T: (01825) 841054
F: 0870 122 9055
E: stay@honeysgreen.com
I: www.honeysgreen.com

FRENSHAM
Surrey

The Mariners Hotel ◆◆◆
Millbridge, Frensham, Farnham,
Surrey GU10 3DJ
T: (01252) 792050 & 794745
F: (01252) 792649

GATWICK
West Sussex

Brooklyn Manor Hotel ◆◆◆
Bonnetts Lane, Ifield, Gatwick,
West Sussex RH11 0NY
T: (01293) 546024
F: (01293) 510366

Collendean Barn ◆◆◆
Collendean Lane, Norwood Hill,
Horley, Surrey RH6 0HP
T: (01293) 862433
F: (01293) 863102
E: collendean.barn@amserve.
net

Gainsborough Lodge ◆◆◆
39 Massetts Road, Horley,
Surrey RH6 7DT
T: (01293) 783982 & 430830
F: (01293) 785365
E: gainsbor@eurobell.co.uk
I: www.gainsboroughlodge.co.uk

GILLINGHAM
Kent

Mayfield Guest House ◆◆
34 Kingswood Road, Gillingham,
Kent ME7 1DZ
T: (01634) 852606

Primrose House ◆◆◆◆
4 Primrose Avenue, Wigmore,
Gillingham, Kent ME8 0TD
T: (01634) 365668
F: (01634) 263600
E: primrosebb@aol.com
I: www.smoothhound.
co.uk/hotels/primrosehouse.
html

Ramsey House ◆◆◆
228A Barnsole Road, Gillingham,
Kent ME7 4JB
T: (01634) 854193

GODALMING
Surrey

Heath Hall Farm ◆◆◆
Bowlhead Green, Godalming,
Surrey GU8 6NW
T: (01428) 682808
F: (01428) 684025
E: heathhallfarm@btinternet.
com

GODDARDS GREEN
West Sussex

Orchard House ◆◆◆
Gatehouse Lane, Goddards
Green, Hassocks, West Sussex
BN6 9LE
T: (01444) 233511

GODMERSHAM
Kent

Waggoners Lodge ◆◆◆
Eggarton Lane, Godmersham,
Canterbury, Kent CT4 7DY
T: (01227) 731118 & 731221
F: (01227) 730292
E: maud@waggoners.freeserve.
co.uk
I: waggoners.de5.de

GOODWOOD
West Sussex

1 Pilleygreen Lodge ◆◆◆◆
Goodwood, Chichester, West
Sussex PO18 0QE
T: (01243) 811467 &
07779 417709
F: (01243) 811408
E: j.robinson@worthing.ac.uk
I: www.sussexlive@enta.net

GORING-BY-SEA
West Sussex
The Court House Guest House ◆◆◆
Sea Lane, Goring-by-Sea,
Worthing, West Sussex
BN12 4NY
T: (01903) 248473

GOUDHURST
Kent
Lidwell Lodge Nursery ◆◆
Lidwell Lane, Goudhurst,
Cranbrook, Kent TN17 1EJ
T: (01580) 211188

Mill House ◆◆◆◆
Church Road, Goudhurst,
Cranbrook, Kent TN17 1BN
T: (01580) 211703 &
07702 714195
E: therussellsuk@yahoo.com
I: www.goudhurst-online.
freeserve.co.uk

Mount House ◆◆◆◆
Ranters Lane, Goudhurst,
Cranbrook, Kent TN17 1HN
T: (01580) 211230 &
07808 170944
E: DavidMargaretSargent@
compuserve.com

GRAFFHAM
West Sussex
Brook Barn ◆◆◆◆◆
Selham Road, Graffham,
Petworth, West Sussex
GU28 0PU
T: (01798) 867356
E: jollands@lineone.net

GRAFTY GREEN
Kent
Who'd A Thought It ◆◆◆
Headcorn Road, Grafty Green,
Maidstone, Kent ME17 2AR
T: (01622) 858951
F: (01622) 858078

GRAVESEND
Kent
48 Clipper Crescent ◆◆◆
Riverview Park, Gravesend, Kent
DA12 4NN
T: (01474) 365360

Eastcourt Oast ◆◆◆◆
14 Church Lane, Chalk,
Gravesend, Kent DA12 2NL
T: (01474) 823937
F: (01474) 823937
E: mary.james@lineone.net
I: www.eastcourtoast.co.uk

South Hill Bank B & B ◆
1 Parrock Road, Gravesend, Kent
DA12 1PY
T: (01474) 352929

23 St James' Road ◆◆◆
Gravesend, Kent DA11 0HF
T: (01474) 321193
E: dot@agassiz.worldonline.
co.uk

GREATSTONE
Kent
Holm–Lea ◆◆◆
66 Coast Drive, Greatstone, New
Romney, Kent TN28 8NR
T: (01797) 364677

White Horses Cottage ◆◆◆◆
180 The Parade, Greatstone,
New Romney, Kent TN28 8RS
T: (01797) 366626

GROOMBRIDGE
East Sussex
Hunters Hall ◆◆◆
Tophill Farm, Groombridge Hill,
Groombridge, Royal Tunbridge
Wells, Kent TN3 9LY
T: (01892) 864021

GUESTLING
East Sussex
Mount Pleasant Farm ◆◆◆◆
White Hart Hill, Guestling,
Hastings, East Sussex TN35 4LR
T: (01424) 813108 &
07711 717695
F: (01424) 813818
E: angelajohn@
mountpleasantfarm.fsbusiness.
co.uk

GUILDFORD
Surrey
Acorn Croft ◆◆◆
15 Wykeham Road, Merrow,
Guildford, Surrey GU1 2SE
T: (01483) 570286
F: (01483) 563515

Beevers Farm ◆◆◆
Chinthurst Lane, Bramley,
Guildford, Surrey GU5 0DR
T: (01483) 898764
F: (01483) 898764
E: beevers@onetel.net.uk

Bluebells ◆◆◆
21 Coltsfoot Drive, Burpham,
Guildford, Surrey GU1 1YH
T: (01483) 826124
E: hughes.a@ntlworld.co.uk

9 Boxgrove Lane
Rating Applied For
9 Boxgrove Lane, Guildford,
Surrey GU1 2TE
T: (01483) 565524

Chalklands ◆◆◆
Beech Avenue, Effingham,
Leatherhead, Surrey KT24 5PJ
T: (01372) 454936
F: (01372) 459569
E: rreilly@onetel.net.uk

Crawford House Hotel
Rating Applied For
73 Farnham Road, Guildford,
Surrey GU2 5PF
T: (01483) 579299
F: (01483) 579299

Hampton ◆◆◆◆
38 Poltimore Road, Guildford,
Surrey GU2 7PN
T: (01483) 572012 &
07973 343495
F: (01483) 572012
E: vgmorris@aol.com

High Edser ◆◆◆
Shere Road, Ewhurst, Cranleigh,
Surrey GU6 7PQ
T: (01483) 278214 &
0777 5865125
F: (01483) 278200
E: franklinadams@highedser.
demon.co.uk

29 Liddington Hall Drive
Rating Applied For
Guildford, Surrey GU3 3AE
T: (01483) 232347 &
07799 626198
E: bill.white@amserve.net

Littlefield Manor ◆◆◆
Littlefield Common, Guildford,
Surrey GU3 3HJ
T: (01483) 233068 &
07860 947439
F: (01483) 233686

Matchams ◆◆◆
35 Boxgrove Avenue, Guildford,
Surrey GU1 1XQ
T: (01483) 567643
F: (01483) 567643

The Old Malt House ◆◆◆
Bagshot Road, Worplesdon,
Guildford, Surrey GU3 3PT
T: (01483) 232152

Patcham
Rating Applied For
44 Farnham Road, Guildford,
Surrey GU2 4LS
T: (01483) 570789

Plaegan House ◆◆◆◆
96 Wodeland Avenue, Guildford,
Surrey GU2 4LD
T: (01483) 822181 &
07961 919430
E: roxanne@plaegan.fsnet.co.uk

Westbury Cottage
Rating Applied For
1 Waterden Road, Guildford,
Surrey GU1 2AN
T: (01483) 822602
F: (01483) 822602

HADLOW
Kent
Leavers Oast ◆◆◆◆
Stanford Lane, Hadlow,
Tonbridge, Kent TN11 0JN
T: (01732) 850924
F: (01732) 850924
E: denis@leavers-oast.freeserve.
co.uk

HAILSHAM
East Sussex
Longleys Farm Cottage ◆◆◆
Harebeating Lane, Hailsham,
East Sussex BN27 1ER
T: (01323) 841227
F: (01323) 841227

Windesworth ◆◆◆◆
Carters Corner, Hailsham, East
Sussex BN27 4HT
T: (01323) 847178 & 440696
F: (01323) 440696
E:
windesworthbedandbreakfast@
virgin.net

HALLAND
East Sussex
Shortgate Manor Farm ◆◆◆◆
Halland, Lewes, East Sussex
BN8 6PJ
T: (01825) 840320
F: (01825) 840320
E: ewalt@shortgate.co.uk
I: www.shortgate.co.uk

Tamberry Hall ◆◆◆◆
Eastbourne Road, Halland,
Lewes, East Sussex BN8 6PS
T: (01825) 880090
F: (01825) 880090
E: bedandbreakfast@
tamberryhall.fsbusiness.co.uk

HALNAKER
West Sussex
Veronica Cottage ◆◆◆◆
Halnaker, Chichester, West
Sussex PO18 0NG
T: (01243) 774929
F: (01243) 774929

HAMBROOK
West Sussex
Ridge Farm ◆◆◆◆
Scant Road (East), Hambrook,
Chichester, West Sussex
PO18 8UB
T: (01243) 575567
F: (01243) 576797

Willowbrook Riding Centre
◆◆◆
Hambrook Hill South, Hambrook,
Chichester, West Sussex
PO18 8UJ
T: (01243) 572683

HARRIETSHAM
Kent
Homestay ◆◆◆
14 Chippendayle Drive,
Harrietsham, Maidstone, Kent
ME17 1AD
T: (01622) 858698
F: (01622) 858698
E: johnbtaylor@homestay14.
freeserve.co.uk
I: www.skybusiness.com/jonba

HARTFIELD
East Sussex
Bolebroke Castle Ltd ◆◆◆
Edenbridge Road, Hartfield, East
Sussex TN7 4JJ
T: (01892) 770061
F: (01892) 771041
E: bolebroke@btclick.com
I: www.bolebrokecastle.co.uk

HARTLEY
Kent
Squirrels Haunt ◆◆◆
Gorsewood Road, Hartley,
Longfield, Kent DA3 7DE
T: (01474) 702352
F: (01474) 702352
E: rosebrainirene@btinternet

HASLEMERE
Surrey
Chawton ◆◆◆
17 Marley Combe Road,
Haslemere, Surrey GU27 3SN
T: (01428) 658023
E: hannah@hlnewman.
freeserve.co.uk

Little Hoewyck ◆◆◆◆
Lickfold Road, Fernhurst,
Haslemere, Surrey GU27 3JH
T: (01428) 653059
E: suehodge@hoewyck.
freeserve.co.uk

Sheps Hollow ◆◆◆
Henley Common, Haslemere,
Surrey GU27 3HB
T: (01428) 653120

Strathire ◆◆◆◆
Grayswood Road, Haslemere,
Surrey GU27 2BW
T: (01428) 642466
F: (01428) 656708

Town House ◆◆◆◆
High Street, Haslemere, Surrey
GU27 2JY
T: (01428) 643310
F: (01428) 641080

HASSOCKS
West Sussex

New Close Farm ◆◆◆
London Road, Hassocks, West
Sussex BN6 9ND
T: (01273) 843144
E: sharon.ballard@
newclosefarm.co.uk
I: www.newclosefarm.co.uk

HASTINGLEIGH
Kent

Crabtree Farm ◆◆◆
Tamley Lane, Hastingleigh,
Ashford, Kent TN25 5HW
T: (01233) 750327 & 750507

HASTINGS
East Sussex

Amberlene Guest House ◆◆◆
12 Cambridge Gardens,
Hastings, East Sussex TN34 1EH
T: (01424) 439447

Apollo Guest House ◆◆◆
25 Cambridge Gardens,
Hastings, East Sussex TN34 1EH
T: (01424) 444394
F: (01424) 444394
E: jim@apollogh.freeserve.co.uk
I: www.apolloguesthouse.co.uk

Ashleigh Guest House ◆
4 Millward Crescent, Hastings,
East Sussex TN34 3RU
T: (01424) 439066

Badgers Run Guest House
◆◆◆
167 Old London Road, Hastings,
East Sussex TN35 5LU
T: (01424) 712082 &
07703 975755
E: badgers.run@talk21.com
I: www.badgersrun.thenetzone.
co.uk

Beechwood Hotel ◆◆◆
59 Baldslow Road, Hastings,
East Sussex TN34 2EY
T: (01424) 420078
F: (01424) 435655
E: beechwoodhastings@talk21.
com

Bell Cottage ◆◆◆◆
Vinehall Road, Robertsbridge,
Hastings, East Sussex TN32 5JN
T: (01580) 881164
F: (01580) 880519
E: patricia.lowe@tesco.net
I: homepages.tesco.net/timothy.
lowe/bellcottage.html

Bryn-Y-Mor ◆◆◆◆◆
12 Godwin Road, Hastings, East
Sussex TN35 5JR
T: (01424) 722744
F: (01424) 445933

Churchills Hotel ◆◆◆◆
3 St Helens Crescent, Hastings,
East Sussex TN34 2EN
T: (01424) 439359
F: (01424) 439359
E: churchills.hotel@btinternet.
com

Croft Place ◆◆◆◆
2 The Croft, Hastings, East
Sussex TN34 3HH
T: (01424) 433004

Eagle House Hotel ◆◆◆◆
12 Pevensey Road, St Leonards-
on-Sea, Hastings, East Sussex
TN38 0JZ
T: (01424) 430535 & 441273
F: (01424) 437771
E: info@eaglehousehotel.com
I: www.eaglehousehotel.com

Ecclesbourne Lodge ◆◆◆
Barley Lane, Hastings, East
Sussex TN35 5NT
T: (01424) 443172
F: (01424) 443172
E: ecclesbournelodge@supanet.
com
I: www.business-uk.com

The Elms ◆◆◆
9 St Helens Park Road, Hastings,
East Sussex TN34 2ER
T: (01424) 429979

Emerydale ◆◆◆◆
6 King Edward Avenue, Hastings,
East Sussex TN34 2NQ
T: (01424) 437915
F: (01424) 444124

Europa Hotel ◆◆◆
2 Carlisle Parade, Hastings, East
Sussex TN34 1JG
T: (01424) 717329

Fantail Cottage ◆◆◆◆
Rosemary Lane, Fairlight,
Hastings, East Sussex TN35 4EB
T: (01424) 813637

The Gallery ◆◆◆◆
19 Fearon Road, Hastings, East
Sussex TN34 2DL
T: (01424) 718110 &
07974 804752
E: info@thegallerybnb.
freeserve.co.uk
I: www.thegallerybnb.freeserve.
co.uk

Glastonbury Guest House ◆◆
45 Eversfield Place, St Leonards
On Sea, Hastings, East Sussex
TN37 6DB
T: (01424) 422280 & 444711
E: glastonburybandb@
btinternet.com
I: www.hastings.gov.uk

Grand Hotel ◆◆◆
Grand Parade, St Leonards,
Hastings, East Sussex TN38 0DD
T: (01424) 428510
F: (01424) 428510
(symbol)

Harbour View Guest House
◆◆◆
21 Priory Road, Hastings, East
Sussex TN34 3JL
T: (01424) 721435 &
07957 909521

64 High Street ◆◆◆
Old Town, Hastings, East Sussex
TN34 3EW
T: (01424) 712584

Highlands Inn ◆◆
Boscobel Road, St Leonards-on-
Sea, Hastings, East Sussex
TN38 0LU
T: (01424) 420299
F: (01424) 465065

Holyers ◆◆◆
1 Hill Street, Old Town, Hastings,
East Sussex TN34 3HU
T: (01424) 430014
E: max@holyers.co.uk
I: www.holyers.co.uk

Lavender & Lace Guest House
◆◆◆◆
106 All Saints Street, Old Town,
Hastings, East Sussex TN34 3BE
T: (01424) 716290
F: (01424) 716290

Lionsdown House ◆◆◆◆
116 High Street, Old Town,
Hastings, East Sussex TN34 3ET
T: (01424) 420802
F: (01424) 420802
E: sharonlionsdown@aol.com
I: www.lionsdownhouse.co.uk

Mayfair Hotel ◆◆
9 Eversfield Place, St Leonards-
on-Sea, Hastings, East Sussex
TN37 6BY
T: (01424) 434061 & 422821
F: (01424) 434125
E: simmonds@jacqui60.fsnet.
co.uk

Millifont Guest House ◆◆◆
8-9 Cambridge Gardens,
Hastings, East Sussex TN34 1EH
T: (01424) 425645
F: (01424) 425645

The Pines ◆◆◆
50 Baldslow Road, Hastings,
East Sussex TN34 2EY
T: (01424) 435838
F: (01424) 435838
E: robert-jean@beeb.net

The Priory Guest House
◆◆◆◆
13-15 Priory Avenue, Hastings,
East Sussex TN34 1UH
T: (01424) 443306
F: (01424) 439078

Sea Spray Guest House ◆◆◆
54 Eversfield Place, St Leonards,
Hastings, East Sussex TN37 6DB
T: (01424) 436583
F: (01424) 436583
E: seaspraybb@faxvia.net
I: www.seaspraybb.co.uk

South Riding Guest House
◆◆◆
96 Milward Road, Hastings, East
Sussex TN34 3RT
T: (01424) 420805

Summerfields House ◆◆◆◆
Bohemia Road, Hastings, East
Sussex TN34 1EX
T: (01424) 718142
F: (01424) 420135

Tower House ◆◆◆◆
26-28 Tower Road West, St
Leonards, Hastings, East Sussex
TN38 0RG
T: (01424) 427217
F: (01424) 427217
E: towerhot@dial.pipex.com

West Hill Cottage ◆◆◆
Exmouth Place, Old Town,
Hastings, East Sussex TN34 3JA
T: (01424) 716021

Woodhurst Lodge ◆◆◆
Ivyhouse Lane, Hastings, East
Sussex TN35 4NN
T: (01424) 754147
F: (01424) 754147

Hotel '66 ◆◆◆
9 White Rock Road, Hastings,
East Sussex TN34 1LE
T: (01424) 460510
F: (01424) 447334
E: htl66@aol.com
I: www.hotel66.com

HAWKHURST
Kent

Conghurst Farm ◆◆◆◆◆
Conghurst Lane, Hawkhurst,
Cranbrook, Kent TN18 4RW
T: (01580) 753331
F: (01580) 754579
E: rosa@conghurst.co.uk

Patricks ◆◆◆◆
Horns Hill, Hawkhurst,
Cranbrook, Kent TN18 4XH
T: (01580) 752143
F: (01580) 754649
I: elliotpat@aol.com.

The Wren's Nest ◆◆◆◆◆
Hastings Road, Hawkhurst,
Cranbrook, Kent TN18 4RT
T: (01580) 754919
F: (01580) 754919

HAWKINGE
Kent

Braeheid Bed & Breakfast
◆◆◆◆
2 Westland Way, Hawkinge,
Folkestone, Kent CT18 7PW
T: (01303) 893928
E: bill@forrest68.fsnet.co.uk

Terlingham Manor Farm
◆◆◆◆
Gibraltar Lane, Hawkinge,
Folkestone, Kent CT18 7AE
T: (01303) 894141
F: (01303) 894144
E: diana@terlinghammanor.
co.uk

HAYWARDS HEATH
West Sussex

**Copyhold Hollow Bed &
Breakfast** ◆◆◆◆
Copyhold Lane, Borde Hill,
Haywards Heath, West Sussex
RH16 1XU
T: (01444) 413265
E: 2@copyholdhollow.freeserve.
co.uk
I: www.copyholdhollow.
freeserve.co.uk

HEADCORN
Kent

Bon Anse ◆◆◆
2 Station Road, Headcorn,
Ashford, Kent TN27 9SA
T: (01622) 890627 &
07885 968076

Four Oaks ◆◆◆
Four Oaks Road, Headcorn,
Ashford, Kent TN27 9PB
T: (01622) 891224 &
07931 603104
F: (01622) 890630
E: info@fouroaks.uk.com
I: www.fouroaks.uk.com

Waterkant Guest House ◆◆◆
Moat Road, Headcorn, Ashford,
Kent TN27 9NT
T: (01622) 890154

HEATHFIELD
East Sussex

Iwood B & B ◆◆◆◆
Mutton Hall Lane, Heathfield,
East Sussex TN21 8NR
T: (01435) 863918 &
07768 917816
F: (01435) 468575
E: iwoodbb@aol.com
I: www.iwoodbb.co.uk
(symbol)

Establishments printed in blue have a detailed entry in this guide

Spicers Bed & Breakfast
◆◆◆◆
21 Spicers Cottages, Cade Street,
Heathfield, East Sussex
TN21 9BS
T: (01435) 866363 &
07973 188138
F: (01435) 866363
E: beds@spicersbb.co.uk
I: www.spicersbb.co.uk

HEMPSTEAD
Kent

Applewood Lodge ◆◆◆
320 Hempstead Road,
Hempstead, Gillingham, Kent
ME7 3QH
T: (01634) 261364

4 The Rise ◆◆◆
Hempstead, Gillingham, Kent
ME7 3SF
T: (01634) 388156
F: (01634) 388156

HENFIELD
West Sussex

1 The Laurels ◆◆◆◆
Martyns Close, Henfield, West
Sussex BN5 9RQ
T: (01273) 493518 &
07788 713864
E: malc.harrington@lineone.net
I: www.no1thelaurels.co.uk

HERONS GHYLL
East Sussex

Tanglewood ◆◆◆◆
Oldlands Hall, Herons Ghyll,
Uckfield, East Sussex TN22 3DA
T: (01825) 712757

HERSHAM
Surrey

Bricklayers Arms ◆◆◆◆
6 Queens Road, Hersham,
Walton-on-Thames, Surrey
KT12 5LS
T: (01932) 220936
F: (01932) 230400

HERSTMONCEUX
East Sussex

Conquerors ◆◆◆◆
Stunts Green, Herstmonceux,
Hailsham, East Sussex BN27 4PR
T: (01323) 832446
E: Conquerors@ukgateway.net

Sandhurst ◆◆◆◆
Church Road, Herstmonceux,
Hailsham, East Sussex
BN27 1RG
T: (01323) 833088
F: (01323) 833088
E: junerussell@compuserve.com

The Stud Farm ◆◆◆
Bodle Street Green,
Herstmonceux, Hailsham, East
Sussex BN27 4RJ
T: (01323) 833201
F: (01323) 833201
E: philippa@miroted.freeserve.
co.uk

Waldernheath Country House
Rating Applied For
Amberstone, Herstmonceux,
Hailsham, East Sussex BN27 1PJ
T: (01323) 442259 &
09973 191610
F: (01323) 442259
E: waldernheath@lineone.net

HEYSHOTT
West Sussex

Amberfold ◆◆◆◆
Heyshott, Midhurst, West Sussex
GU29 0DA
T: (01730) 812385

Little Hoyle ◆◆◆◆
Hoyle Lane, Heyshott, Midhurst,
West Sussex GU29 0DX
T: (01798) 867359 & 871943
F: (01798) 867359

HIGH HALDEN
Kent

Badgers ◆◆◆◆
Ashford Road, High Halden,
Ashford, Kent TN26 3LY
T: (01233) 850158
E: wendy@badgers-bb.co.uk
I: www.badgers-bb.co.uk

Draylands ◆◆◆
Woodchurch Road, High Halden,
Ashford, Kent TN26 3JG
T: (01233) 850048 & 850830
F: (01233) 850048

11 The Martins ◆◆◆◆
High Halden, Ashford, Kent
TN26 3LD
T: (01233) 850013

HIGH HURSTWOOD
East Sussex

Chillies Granary ◆◆◆◆
Chillies Lane, High Hurstwood,
Uckfield, East Sussex TN6 3TB
T: (01892) 655560
F: (01892) 655560

Huckleberry ◆◆◆◆
Perrymans Lane, High
Hurstwood, Uckfield, East Sussex
TN22 4AG
T: (01825) 733170

The Orchard ◆◆◆◆
Rocks Lane, High Hurstwood,
Uckfield, East Sussex TN22 4BN
T: (01825) 732946 &
07710 205554
F: (01825) 732946
E: TurtonOrchard@aol.com
I: www.networkclub.
co.uk/theorchard

HIGHAM
Kent

Kinsale ◆◆◆
1A School Lane, Mid Higham,
Higham, Rochester, Kent
ME3 7AT
T: (01474) 822106

HILDENBOROUGH
Kent

Froxfield ◆◆◆
98 Tonbridge Road,
Hildenborough, Tonbridge, Kent
TN11 9BT
T: (01732) 833759
F: (01732) 833759
E: dobson@tinyonine.co.uk

150 Tonbridge Road ◆◆
Hildenborough, Tonbridge, Kent
TN11 9HW
T: (01732) 838894

HOLLINGBOURNE
Kent

Eyhorne Manor ◆◆◆
Eyhorne Green, Hollingbourne,
Maidstone, Kent ME17 1UU
T: (01622) 880263
E: eyhorne.manor@virginnet.
co.uk

The Limes ◆◆◆◆
53 Eyhorne Street,
Hollingbourne, Maidstone, Kent
ME17 1TS
T: (01622) 880554
F: (01622) 880063
E: thelimes@btinternet.com

Woodhouses ◆◆◆◆
49 Eyhorne Street,
Hollingbourne, Maidstone, Kent
ME17 1TR
T: (01622) 880594
F: (01622) 880594

HORAM
East Sussex

Oak Mead Bed & Breakfast
◆◆◆
Oak Mead Nursery, Cowden Hall
Lane, Horam, Heathfield, East
Sussex TN21 9HD
T: (01435) 812962

Wimbles Farm ◆◆◆
Vines Cross, Horam, Heathfield,
East Sussex TN21 9HA
T: (01435) 812342
F: (01435) 813603
E: susan_ramsay@madasafish.
com
I: www.sussexcountry.com

HORLEY
Surrey

The Beeches ◆◆◆◆
60 Massetts Road, Horley,
Surrey RH6 7DS
T: (01293) 023457
F: (01293) 415595

Berrens Guest House ◆◆
62 Massetts Road, Horley,
Surrey RH6 7DS
T: (01293) 786125 & 430800
F: (01293) 786125

Copperwood Guest House
◆◆◆◆
Massetts Road, Horley, Gatwick,
West Sussex RH6 7DJ
T: (01293) 783388
F: (01293) 420156
E: copperwood@blueyonder.
co.uk
I: www.copperwood.co.uk

The Corner House ◆◆◆◆
72 Massetts Road, Horley,
Surrey RH6 7ED
T: (01293) 784574
F: (01293) 784620
E: info@thecornerhouse.co.uk
I: www.thecornerhouse.co.uk

Gables Guest House ◆
50 Bonehurst Road, Horley,
Surrey RH6 8QJ
T: (01293) 774553
F: (01293) 430006
I: www.thegables.com.ok

Gatwick Belmont ◆◆◆
46 Massetts Road, Horley,
Surrey RH6 7DS
T: (01293) 820500
F: (01293) 783812
E: stay@gatwickbelmont.com
I: www.gatwickbelmont.com

The Lawn Guest House ◆◆◆◆
30 Massetts Road, Gatwick,
West Sussex RH6 7DE
T: (01293) 775751 & 784370
F: (01293) 821803
E: info@lawnguesthouse.co.uk
I: www.lawnguesthouse.co.uk

Lenton Lodge ◆◆◆
36 Massetts Road, Horley,
Surrey RH6 7DS
T: (01293) 772571
F: (01293) 432391

Masslink House ◆◆◆
70 Massetts Road, Horley,
Surrey RH6 7ED
T: (01293) 785798
F: (01293) 783279

Melville Lodge Guest House
◆◆
15 Brighton Road, Horley,
Gatwick, West Sussex RH6 7HH
T: (01293) 784951
F: (01293) 785669
E: melvillelodge.guesthouse@
tesco.net

Prinsted Guest House ◆◆◆
Oldfield Road, Horley, Surrey
RH6 7EP
T: (01293) 785233
F: (01293) 820624
E: prinsted@tinyworld.co.uk
I: www.networkclub.
co.uk/prinsted

Rosemead Guest House
◆◆◆◆
19 Church Road, Horley, Surrey
RH6 7EY
T: (01293) 784965
F: (01293) 430547
E: rosemead@globalnet.co.uk
I: www.rosemeadguesthouse.
co.uk

Springwood Guest House
◆◆◆
58 Massetts Road, Horley,
Surrey RH6 7DS
T: (01293) 775998
F: (01293) 823103
E: ernest@springwood58.u-net.
com
I: www.networkclub.
co.uk/springwood

Trumbles Guest House ◆◆◆◆
Stanhill, Charlwood, Horley,
Surrey RH6 0EP
T: (01293) 862925 & 863418
F: (01293) 862925
E: info@trumbles.co.uk
I: www.trumbles.co.uk

The Turret Guest House ◆◆◆
48 Massetts Road, Horley,
Surrey RH6 7DS
T: (01293) 782490 & 431491
F: (01293) 431492
E: info@theturret.com
I: www.theturret.com

Yew Tree ◆
31 Massetts Road, Horley,
Surrey RH6 7DQ
T: (01293) 785855
F: (01293) 785855
I: www.smoothound.
co.uk/hotels/yewtree.html.

HORSHAM
West Sussex

49 Broadwood Close ◆◆◆
Horsham, West Sussex RH12 4JY
T: (01403) 263651

The Deans ◆◆◆
8 Wimblehurst Road, Horsham,
West Sussex RH12 2ED
T: (01403) 268166 &
07802 843866
F: (01403) 268166
E: contact@thedeans.co.uk
I: www.thedeans.co.uk

163 Heathway ◆◆
Horsham, West Sussex
RH12 5XX
T: (01403) 257066
F: (01403) 257066

The Larches ◆◆◆
28 Rusper Road, Horsham, West
Sussex RH12 4BD
T: (01403) 263392
F: (01403) 249980

Orchard Cottage ◆◆◆
Tower Hill, Horsham, West
Sussex RH13 7JT
T: (01403) 253034 &
07747 013293
F: (01403) 253034

The Studio
Rating Applied For
The Hermitage, Tower Hill,
Horsham, West Sussex RH13 7JS
T: (01403) 270808

The Wirrals ◆◆◆
1 Downsview Road, Horsham,
West Sussex RH12 4PF
T: (01403) 269400 &
07774 745262
F: (01403) 269400
E: p.archibald@lineone.net
I: website.lineone.net/~p.
archibald/webba.htm

HOUGHAM
Kent

Old Vicarage ◆◆◆◆◆
Chilverton Elms, Hougham,
Dover, Kent CT15 7AS
T: (01304) 210668
F: (01304) 225118
E: vicarage@csi.com

HUNSTON
West Sussex

2 Meadow Close ◆◆◆◆
Hunston, Chichester, West
Sussex PO20 6PB
T: (01243) 788504

HUNTON
Kent

Barn Hill Oast ◆◆◆◆
Barn Hill, Hunton, Maidstone,
Kent ME15 0QT
T: (01622) 820206 &
07778 266515
F: (01622) 820886
E: jean.searle@btclick.com

HURSTPIERPOINT
West Sussex

The Vinyard Lodge ◆◆◆◆
42 The High Street,
Hurstpierpoint, Hassocks, West
Sussex BN6 9RG
T: (01273) 835000
F: (01273) 835041
E: vinyards@btconnect.com
I: www.smoothhound.
co.uk/hotels/vinyard.html

Wickham Place ◆◆◆◆
Wickham Drive, Hurstpierpoint,
Hassocks, West Sussex BN6 9AP
T: (01273) 832172
F: (01273) 832172
E: stay@wickham-place.co.uk

HYTHE
Kent

Seabrook House ◆◆◆◆
81 Seabrook Road, Hythe, Kent
CT21 5QW
T: (01303) 269282
F: (01303) 237822
E: seabhouse@globalnet.co.uk
I: www.smoothhound.
co.uk/hotels/seabrook.html

ICKHAM
Kent

Baye Oast ◆◆◆◆
1 Baye Oast, Baye Lane, Ickham,
Canterbury, Kent CT3 1RB
T: (01227) 720813
E: enquiries@bayeoast.co.uk
I: www.bayeoast.co.uk

ICKLESHAM
East Sussex

The Old Farmhouse ◆◆◆
Snaylham Farm, Icklesham,
Winchelsea, East Sussex
TN36 4AT
T: (01424) 814711 &
07966 282569
F: (01424) 814007
E: oldfrmhse@aol.com
I: www.members.aol.
com/oldfrmhse

ISFIELD
East Sussex

Farm Place ◆◆◆◆
Lewes Road, Isfield, Uckfield,
East Sussex TN22 5TY
T: (01825) 750485
F: (01825) 750411

The Faulkners ◆◆◆◆
Isfield, Uckfield, East Sussex
TN22 5XG
T: (01825) 750344
F: (01825) 750577

ITCHENOR
West Sussex

Itchenor Park House ◆◆◆◆
Itchenor, Chichester, West
Sussex PO20 7DN
T: (01243) 512221
E: susie.green@lineone.net

The Ship Inn ◆
The Street, Itchenor, Chichester,
West Sussex PO20 7AH
T: (01243) 512284
F: (01243) 513817

KENNINGTON
Kent

Heather House ◆◆◆
40 Burton Road, Kennington,
Ashford, Kent TN24 9DS
T: (01233) 661826 & 0793 11
50489
F: (01233) 661821

Stone House ◆◆◆
Faversham Road, Kennington,
Ashford, Kent TN25 4PQ
T: (01233) 623776

KINGSDOWN
Kent

**Blencathra Country Guest
House** ◆◆◆
Kingsdown Hill, Kingsdown,
Deal, Kent CT14 8EA
T: (01304) 373725

Sparrow Court ◆◆◆
Chalk Hill Road, Kingsdown,
Deal, Kent CT14 8DP
T: (01304) 389253
F: (01304) 389016

KIRDFORD
West Sussex

Half Moon Inn ◆◆◆
Kirdford, Billingshurst, West
Sussex RH14 0LT
T: (01403) 820223
F: (01403) 820224
I: www.the-halfmoon-inn.com

LADDINGFORD
Kent

The Chequers
Rating Applied For
The Street, Laddingford,
Maidstone, Kent ME18 6BP
T: (01622) 871266
F: (01622) 873115

LAMBERHURST
Kent

Chequers Oast ◆◆◆
The Broadway, Lamberhurst,
Royal Tunbridge Wells, Kent
TN3 8DB
T: (01892) 890579
F: (01892) 890579
E: avrilandterry@yahoo.co.uk

LANCING
West Sussex

Edelweiss Guest House ◆◆◆
17 Kings Road, Lancing, West
Sussex BN15 8EB
T: (01903) 753412
F: (01903) 527424

LANGLEY
Kent

Orchard House ◆◆◆◆
Sutton Road, Langley,
Maidstone, Kent ME17 3LZ
T: (01622) 862694
F: (01622) 862694

LARKFIELD
Kent

Mead Cottage ◆◆◆
433 Lunsford Lane, Larkfield,
Aylesford, Kent ME20 6JA
T: (01634) 241133

LAUGHTON
East Sussex

Holly Cottage ◆◆◆◆
Lewes Road, Laughton, Lewes,
East Sussex BN8 6BL
T: (01323) 811309 &
07771 956350
F: (01323) 811106
E: hollycottage@tinyworld.
co.uk

Spences Farm ◆◆◆
Laughton, Lewes, East Sussex
BN8 6BX
T: (01825) 840489
F: (01825) 840489

LAVANT
West Sussex

47 Mid Lavant ◆◆◆◆
Lavant, Chichester, West Sussex
PO18 0AA
T: (01243) 785883

LEEDS
Kent

West Forge ◆◆◆
Back Street, Leeds, Maidstone,
Kent ME17 1TF
T: (01622) 861428

LEIGH
Kent

Charcott B & B ◆◆◆◆
Charcott, Leigh, Tonbridge, Kent
TN11 8LG
T: (01892) 870024
F: (01892) 870158
E: nicholasmorris@charcott.
freeserve.co.uk
I: www.smoothhound.
co.uk/hotels/charcott.html

Herons Head Farm ◆◆◆◆
Mynthurst, Leigh, Reigate,
Gatwick, West Sussex RH2 8QD
T: (01293) 862475
F: (01293) 863350
E: heronshead@clara.net
I: seetb.org.uk/heronshead

LENHAM
Kent

Bramley Knowle Farm ◆◆◆
Eastwood Road, Ulcombe,
Maidstone, Kent ME17 1ET
T: (01622) 858698
F: (01622) 851121

The Dog & Bear Hotel ◆◆◆
The Square, Lenham, Maidstone,
Kent ME17 2PG
T: (01622) 858219
F: (01622) 859415
E: dogbear@shepherd-neame.
co.uk
I: www.shepherd-neame.co.uk
🏃

East Lenham Farm ◆◆◆◆
Lenham, Maidstone, Kent
ME17 2DP
T: (01622) 858686
F: (01622) 859474
E: eastlenham@farmline.com
I: www.members.farmline.
com/abarr

LEWES
East Sussex

Barn House ◆◆◆
Rodmell, Lewes, East Sussex
BN7 3HE
T: (01273) 477865
F: (01273) 476317
E: sharifindgn.apc.org
I: www.knowledge.
co.uk/barnhouse/

The Crown Inn ◆◆
High Street, Lewes, East Sussex
BN7 2NA
T: (01273) 480670
F: (01273) 480679
E: sales@crowninn-lewes.co.uk
I: www.crowninn-lewes.co.uk

Downsview ◆◆◆
15 Montacute Road, Lewes, East
Sussex BN7 1EW
T: (01273) 472719

Eckington House ◆◆◆◆
Ripe Lane, Ripe, Lewes, East
Sussex BN8 6AR
T: (01323) 811274
F: (01323) 811140
E: sue@eckingtonhouse.co.uk
I: www.eckingtonhouse.co.uk

Foxwood House ◆◆◆◆
14 Southdown Avenue, Lewes,
East Sussex BN7 1EL
T: (01273) 471768
E: chris@foxwoodhouselewes.
co.uk
I: www.foxwoodhouselewes.
co.uk

6 Gundreda Road ◆◆◆◆
Lewes, East Sussex BN7 1PX
T: (01273) 472106
E: jacquelinelucas@yahoo.co.uk

Hale Farm House ◆◆◆
Chiddingly, Lewes, East Sussex
BN8 6HQ
T: (01825) 872619 &
07702 340631
F: (01825) 872619
E: s.burrough@virgin.net
I: www.cuckmere-valley.
co.uk/hale

13 Hill Road ◆◆◆
Lewes, East Sussex BN7 1DB
T: (01273) 477723 &
07881 911929
F: (01273) 486032
E: kmyles@btclick.com

Number Seven ◆◆◆◆
7 Prince Edwards Road, Lewes,
East Sussex BN7 1BJ
T: (01273) 487038
E: numberseven@
lewesbedandbreakfast.com
I: www.lewesbedandbreakfast.
com

Racecourse House ◆◆◆◆
Old Lewes Racecourse, Lewes,
East Sussex BN7 1UR
T: (01273) 480804
F: (01273) 486478
E: a.heyes@btinternet.com

Settlands ◆◆◆◆
Wellgreen Lane, Kingston,
Lewes, East Sussex BN7 3NP
T: (01273) 472295
F: (01273) 472295
E: diana-a@solutions-inc.co.uk

Studfarm House ◆◆◆
Telscombe Village, Lewes, East
Sussex BN7 3HZ
T: (01273) 302486
F: (01273) 302486

**Sussex Countryside
Accommodation** ◆◆◆◆
Crink House, Barcombe Mills,
Lewes, East Sussex BN8 5BJ
T: (01273) 400625
E: crinkhouse@hgaydon.fsnet.
co.uk

Whitesmith Barn ◆◆◆◆
Whitesmith, Lewes, East Sussex
BN8 6HA
T: (01825) 872867

LEYSDOWN ON SEA
Kent

Muswell Manor ◆◆
Shellness Road, Leysdown on
Sea, Sheerness, Kent ME12 4RJ
T: (01795) 510245

LIGHTWATER
Surrey

Carlton Guest House ◆◆◆◆
63-65 Macdonald Road,
Lightwater, Camberley, Surrey
GU18 5XY
T: (01276) 473580 &
07703 868994
F: (01276) 453595
E: carltongh@aol.com
I: www.carltonguesthouse.co.uk

LINDFIELD
West Sussex

Little Lywood ◆◆◆
Ardingly Road, Lindfield,
Haywards Heath, West Sussex
RH16 2QX
T: (01444) 892571
E: nick@littlelywood.freeserve.
co.uk

LITTLEBOURNE
Kent

King William IV
Rating Applied For
4 High Street, Littlebourne,
Canterbury, Kent CT3 1UN
T: (01227) 721244
F: (01227) 721244

LITTLEHAMPTON
West Sussex

Arun Sands ◆◆◆
84 South Terrace, Seafront,
Littlehampton, West Sussex
BN17 5LJ
T: (01903) 732489
F: (01903) 732489
E: info@arun-sands.co.uk
I: www.arun-sands.co.uk

Arun View Inn ◆◆
Wharf Road, Littlehampton,
West Sussex BN17 5DD
T: (01903) 722335
F: (01903) 722335

Quayside Guest House ◆◆◆
36 Pier Road, Littlehampton,
West Sussex BN17 5LW
T: (01903) 721958
F: (01903) 721958

Racing Greens ◆◆◆
70 South Terrace, Littlehampton,
West Sussex BN17 5LQ
T: (01903) 732972 & 719389
F: (01903) 732932
E: urban.surfer@easynet.co.uk

Sharoleen Guest House ◆◆◆
85 Bayford Road, Littlehampton,
West Sussex BN17 5HW
T: (01903) 713464
F: (01903) 713464

Tudor Lodge Guest House
◆◆◆
2 Horsham Road, Littlehampton,
West Sussex BN17 6BU
T: (01903) 716203 &
07803 821440
F: (01903) 716203

LONGFIELD
Kent

Kaye Cottage ◆◆◆◆
Old Downs, Hartley, Longfield,
Kent DA3 7AA
T: (01474) 702384 &
07778 250650
F: (01474) 702384
E: b-b@kayecottage.freeserve.
co.uk

The Rising Sun Inn ◆◆◆
Fawkham Green, Longfield, Kent
DA3 8NL
T: (01474) 872291
F: (01474) 872291

LOOSE
Kent

Vale House ◆◆◆
Old Loose Hill, Loose, Maidstone,
Kent ME15 0BH
T: (01622) 743339 & 743400
F: (01622) 743103
E: vansegethin@hotmail.com

LOWER BEEDING
West Sussex

The Village Pantry ◆◆◆
Handcross Road, Plummers
Plain, Lower Beeding, Horsham,
West Sussex RH13 6NU
T: (01403) 891319
F: (01403) 891319
E: village-pantry@faxvia.net

LOWER STOKE
Kent

Larkspur ◆◆◆
Cuckolds Green Road, Lower
Stoke, Rochester, Kent ME3 9QU
T: (01634) 272261 &
0773 0032288
E: larkspurgood@cs.com

LYMINSTER
West Sussex

Sandfield House ◆◆◆◆
Lyminster, Littlehampton, West
Sussex BN17 7PG
T: (01903) 724129
F: (01903) 715041
E: thefbs@aol.com

MAIDSTONE
Kent

Aylesbury Hotel ◆◆◆
56-58 London Road, Maidstone,
Kent ME16 8QL
T: (01622) 762100 & 664673
F: (01622) 762100
E: aylesbury@onetel.net.uk

The Bower House
Rating Applied For
64 Tonbridge Road, Maidstone,
Kent ME16 8SE
T: (01622) 763448

51 Bower Mount Road ◆◆◆
Maidstone, Kent ME16 8AX
T: (01622) 762948
F: (01622) 202753
E: sylviabnb@compuserve.com

Conway House ◆◆◆◆
12 Conway Road, Maidstone,
Kent ME16 0HD
T: (01622) 688287
F: (01622) 662589
E: conwayhouse@ukgateway.
net
I: www.conwayhouse.
ukgateway.net

The Flower Pot ◆◆
96 Sandling Road, Maidstone,
Kent ME14 2RJ
T: (01622) 757705
F: (01622) 833051
I: www.homleighgroup.co.uk

The Hazels ◆◆◆◆
13 Yeoman Way, Bearsted,
Maidstone, Kent ME15 8PQ
T: (01622) 737943
F: (01622) 737943
E: dbuse@totalise.co.uk
I: www.redrival.com/thehazels

The Howard Hotel ◆◆
22-24 London Road, Maidstone,
Kent ME16 8QL
T: (01622) 758778
F: (01622) 609984

King Street Hotel ◆◆◆
74 King Street, Maidstone, Kent
ME14 1BH
T: (01622) 663266
F: (01622) 663123
E: reservations@
kingstreethotelmaidstone.co.uk
I: www.
kingstreethotelmaidstone.co.uk

The Limes ◆◆◆◆
118 Boxley Road, Maidstone,
Kent ME14 2BD
T: (01622) 750629
F: (01622) 691266

514 Loose Road ◆◆◆
Maidstone, Kent ME15 9UF
T: (01622) 741001

39 Marston Drive
Rating Applied For
Vinters Park, Maidstone, Kent
ME14 5NE
T: (01622) 202196
E: steveandlesley@steleybrown.
freeserve.co.uk

54 Mote Avenue ◆◆
Maidstone, Kent ME15 7ST
T: (01622) 754016

Raigersfeld House ◆◆
Mote Park, Ashford Road,
Maidstone, Kent ME14 4AE
T: (01622) 685211 & 687377
F: (01622) 691013
E: chipdbs@aol.com

**The Ringlestone Inn &
Farmhouse Hotel** ◆◆◆◆◆
Ringlestone Hamlet,
Harrietsham, Maidstone, Kent
ME17 1NX
T: (01622) 859900 &
07973 612261
F: (01622) 859966
E: bookings@ringlestone.com
I: www.ringlestone.com

Rock House Hotel ◆◆◆
102 Tonbridge Road, Maidstone,
Kent ME16 8SL
T: (01622) 751616
F: (01622) 756119

Rose Cottage ◆◆◆
10 Fant Lane, Maidstone, Kent
ME16 8NL
T: (01622) 729883 &
07885 162566

Roslin Villa ◆◆◆
11 St Michael's Road,
Maidstone, Kent ME16 8BS
T: (01622) 758301
F: (01622) 695646

Wealden Hall House ◆◆◆◆
East Street, Hunton, Maidstone,
Kent ME15 0RB
T: (01622) 820246
F: (01622) 820246
I: www.smoothhound.
co.uk/hotels/wealden.html

West Belringham ◆◆◆
Chart Road, Sutton Valence,
Maidstone, Kent ME17 3AW
T: (01622) 843995
F: (01622) 843995
E: west.belringham@tesco.net
I: www.travelengland.org.uk

4 White Rock Court ◆◆◆
White Rock Place, Maidstone,
Kent ME16 8HX
T: (01622) 753566 &
0771 2239936
F: (01622) 753566
E: catnap.farnham@amserve.
net

Willington Court ◆◆◆◆
Willington Street, Maidstone,
Kent ME15 8JW
T: (01622) 738885
F: (01622) 631790
E: Willingtoncourt@AOL.com
I: www.bbchannel.
com/bbc/p604332.aspwww.
hotelkent.com

Wits End Guest House ◆◆◆
78 Bower Mount Road,
Maidstone, Kent ME16 8AT
T: (01622) 752684 & 762696
F: (01622) 688943

63 Woolley Road ◆◆◆
Senacre Wood, Maidstone, Kent
ME15 8PZ
T: (01622) 761052

MARDEN
Kent

Tanner House ◆◆◆◆
Tanner Farm, Goudhurst Road,
Marden, Tonbridge, Kent
TN12 9ND
T: (01622) 831214
F: (01622) 832472
E: tannerhouse@cs.com
I: www.tannerfarmpark.co.uk

MARGATE
Kent

Burlington Hotel ◆◆
8 Buenos Ayres, Margate, Kent
CT9 5AE
T: (01843) 292817

Luxor Hotel
Rating Applied For
23 Fort Crescent, Margate, Kent
CT9 1HX
T: (01843) 290889
F: (01843) 290889

MARK CROSS
East Sussex

Houndsell Cottage ◆◆◆
Mark Cross, Crowborough, East
Sussex TN6 3PF
T: (01892) 782292

Rose Cottage ◆◆◆◆
Mill Lane, Mark Cross,
Crowborough, East Sussex
TN6 3PJ
T: (01892) 852592
F: (01892) 853268

MARSHBOROUGH
Kent

Honey Pot Cottage ◆◆◆◆
Marshborough Road,
Marshborough, Sandwich, Kent
CT13 0PQ
T: (01304) 813374 &
07798 804920
F: (01304) 813374
E: honeypotcottage@lycos.com
I: www.honeypotcottage.co.uk

MATFIELD
Kent

Maycotts ◆◆◆◆◆
Matfield, Tonbridge, Kent
TN12 7JU
T: (01892) 723983
F: (01892) 722203
E: debbie.jolley@dial.pipex.com
I: www.bbgl.co.uk

MEOPHAM
Kent

Lamplights ◆◆◆
Wrotham Road, Meopham,
Gravesend, Kent DA13 0QW
T: (01474) 813869
F: (0208) 306 1189

Nurstead Court ◆◆
Meopham, Gravesend, Kent
DA13 9AD
T: (01474) 812121
F: (01474) 815133

MERSTON
West Sussex

The White House ◆◆◆
Merston, Chichester, West
Sussex PO20 6EF
T: (01243) 783669

MIDHURST
West Sussex

10 Ashfield Close ◆◆◆◆
Midhurst, West Sussex
GU29 9RP
T: (01730) 814858

Carron Dune ◆◆◆
Carron Lane, Midhurst, West
Sussex GU29 9LD
T: (01730) 813558

The Elsted Inn ◆◆◆
Elsted Marsh, Midhurst, West
Sussex GU29 0JT
T: (01730) 813662
F: (01730) 813662

20 Guillards Oak ◆◆◆◆
Midhurst, West Sussex
GU29 9JZ
T: (01730) 812550
F: (01730) 816765
E: coljen@tinyworld.co.uk

Moonlight Cottage ◆◆◆
Chichester Road, Cocking,
Midhurst, West Sussex
GU29 0HN
T: (01730) 813336
F: (01730) 813362
E: enquiries@moonlightcottage.
net
I: www.moonlightcottage.net

Oakhurst Cottage ◆◆◆
Carron Lane, Midhurst, West
Sussex GU29 9LF
T: (01730) 813523

Pear Tree Cottage ◆◆◆
Lamberts Lane, Midhurst, West
Sussex GU29 9EF
T: (01730) 817216

18 Pretoria Avenue
Rating Applied For
Midhurst, West Sussex
GU29 9PP
T: (01730) 814868

Rumbolds House ◆◆◆
Rumbolds Hill, Midhurst, West
Sussex GU29 9BY
T: (01730) 816175 &
07970 015214
F: (01730) 816175
E: anngr@atd.net

Ye Olde Tea Shoppe
Rating Applied For
North Street, Midhurst, West
Sussex GU29 9DY
T: (01730) 817081
F: (01730) 810228

MILFORD
Surrey

Chesil Cottage ◆◆◆
Moushill Lane, Milford,
Godalming, Surrey GU8 5BH
T: (01483) 422831
F: (01483) 422831
E: abanmcandrew@aol.com
I: www.athomeinengland.co.uk

MILSTEAD
Kent

The Cottage ◆◆◆◆
Frinsted Road, Milstead,
Sittingbourne, Kent ME9 0SA
T: (01795) 830367

MINSTER-IN-SHEPPEY
Kent

Abbots Gate ◆◆◆◆
Falcon Gardens, Minster-in-
Sheppey, Sheerness, Kent
ME12 3QE
T: (01795) 872882
E: b&b@abbotsgate.demon.
co.uk

Glen Haven Farm ◆◆◆
Lower Road, Minster-in-
Sheppey, Sheerness, Kent
ME12 3ST
T: (01795) 877064
F: (01795) 871746
E: johnstanford@btinternet.
com

Mia Crieff ◆◆◆◆
Mill Hill, Chequers Road,
Minster-in-Sheppey, Sheerness,
Kent ME12 3QL
T: (01795) 870620

Sheppey Guest House
Rating Applied For
214 Queenborough Road,
Halfway, Minster-in-Sheppey,
Sheerness, Kent ME12 3DF
T: (01795) 665950
F: (01795) 661200
E: sophie.allen@btinternet.com

NETHERFIELD
East Sussex

Upper Homestead Farm
◆◆◆◆
Darwell Hill, Netherfield, Battle,
East Sussex TN33 9QH
T: (01424) 838457

NETTLESTEAD
Kent

The Granary Bed & Breakfast
◆◆◆◆
Rock Farm, Gibbs Hill,
Nettlestead, Maidstone, Kent
ME18 5HT
T: (01622) 814547
F: (01622) 813905
E: robcorfe@thegranary-bnb.
co.uk
I: www.thegranary-bnb.co.uk

Rock Farm House ◆◆◆◆
Gibbs Hill, Nettlestead,
Maidstone, Kent ME18 5HT
T: (01622) 812244
F: (01622) 812244

NEW ROMNEY
Kent

Martinfield Manor ◆◆◆◆
Lydd Road, New Romney, Kent
TN28 8HB
T: (01797) 363802

Warren Lodge Motel ◆◆◆
Dymchurch Road, New Romney,
Kent TN28 8UE
T: (01797) 362138
F: (01797) 367377
E: admin@warrenlodge.co.uk
I: www.warrenlodge.co.uk

NEWHAVEN
East Sussex

Brighton Motel
Rating Applied For
1 Southcoast Road, Peacehaven,
East Sussex BN10 8SY
T: (01273) 583736
F: (01273) 586599
🅰

Newhaven Lodge Guest House
◆
12 Brighton Road, Newhaven,
East Sussex BN9 9NB
T: (01273) 513736 &
07776 293398
F: (01273) 734619
E: newhavenlodge@aol.com

NEWICK
East Sussex

Firle Cottage ◆◆◆
High Street, Newick, Lewes, East
Sussex BN8 4LG
T: (01825) 722392

Holly Lodge ◆◆◆
Oxbottom Lane, Newick, Lewes,
East Sussex BN8 4RA
T: (01825) 722738
F: (01825) 722624

NINFIELD
East Sussex

Hollybank House ◆◆◆
Lower Street, Ninfield, Battle,
East Sussex TN33 9EA
T: (01424) 892052
F: (01424) 892052

London House ◆◆◆◆
Manchester Road, Ninfield,
Battle, East Sussex TN33 9JX
T: (01424) 893532
F: (01424) 893595

NORTH BERSTED
West Sussex

Lorna Doone Bed & Breakfast
◆◆◆◆
58 Sandymount Avenue, North
Bersted, Bognor Regis, West
Sussex PO22 9EP
T: (01243) 822203 & 0780 149
3678
F: (01243) 822203
E: joan@lornadoone.freeserve.
co.uk
I: www.lornadoone.freeserve.
co.uk

Willow Rise ◆◆◆
131 North Bersted Street, North
Bersted, Bognor Regis, West
Sussex PO22 9AG
T: (01243) 829544
F: (01243) 829544

NORTH MUNDHAM
West Sussex

The Cottage ◆◆◆◆
Church Road, North Mundham,
Chichester, West Sussex
PO20 6JU
T: (01243) 784586
E: lambrinudi-bandb@supanet.
com

NORTHFLEET
Kent

The Nook ◆◆◆
3 Falcon Mews, Vale Road,
Northfleet, Gravesend, Kent
DA11 8BW
T: (01474) 350748

NUTFIELD
Surrey
Hillside Cottage ♦♦♦
Coopers Hill Road, Nutfield,
Redhill RH1 4HX
T: (01737) 822916
F: (01737) 822916

NUTLEY
East Sussex
The Court House ♦♦♦♦
School Lane, Nutley, Uckfield,
East Sussex TN22 3PG
T: (01825) 713129
F: (01825) 712650
E: execrelocation@compuserve.com

OARE
Kent
Mount House ♦♦♦
Mount Pleasant, Oare,
Faversham, Kent ME13 0PZ
T: (01795) 534735

OCKLEY
Surrey
The Kings Arms Inn ♦♦♦♦
Stane Street, Ockley, Dorking,
Surrey RH5 5TP
T: (01306) 711224
F: (01306) 711224

OLD ROMNEY
Kent
Rose & Crown Inn ♦♦♦
Old Romney, Romney Marsh,
Kent TN29 9SQ
T: (01797) 367500
F: (01797) 361262

OTFORD
Kent
Darenth Dene ♦♦♦♦
Shoreham Road, Otford,
Sevenoaks, Kent TN14 5RP
T: (01959) 522293

The Garden Room
Rating Applied For
3 Darnetsfield, Otford,
Sevenoaks, Kent TN15 5LB
T: (01959) 522521
E: gardenroom@otford.org
I: www.otford.org/garden-room

The Hop Barn ♦♦♦
Park Farm, High Street, Otford,
Sevenoaks, Kent TN14 5PQ
T: (01959) 523509
F: (01959) 525326

9 Warham Road ♦♦
Otford, Sevenoaks, Kent
TN14 5PF
T: (01959) 523596

OTHAM
Kent
Valley View ♦♦♦
Greenhill, Otham, Maidstone,
Kent ME15 8RR
T: (01622) 862279
F: (01622) 862279

OUTWOOD
Surrey
The Coach House ♦♦♦♦
Millers Lane, Outwood, Redhill
RH1 5PZ
T: (01342) 843193
F: (01342) 842544
E: coachselgw@aol.com

OVING
West Sussex
The Willows ♦♦♦♦
High Street, Oving, Chichester,
West Sussex PO20 6DD
T: (01243) 789493 &
07977 593347
F: (01243) 789493
E: mbstocker@aol.com

OXTED
Surrey
Arawa ♦♦♦
58 Granville Road, Limpsfield,
Oxted, Surrey RH8 0BZ
T: (01883) 714104 & 0800 298 5732
F: (01883) 714104
E: david@davidgibbs.co.uk

Meads ♦♦♦♦
23 Granville Road, Oxted, Surrey
RH8 0BX
T: (01883) 730115
E: Holgate@meads9.fsnet.co.uk

The New Bungalow ♦♦♦
Old Hall Farm, Tandridge Lane,
Oxted, Surrey RH8 9NS
T: (01342) 892508
F: (01342) 892508
E: donnunn@compuserve.com

PADDOCK WOOD
Kent
Little Fowle Hall Oast ♦♦
Lucks Lane, Paddock Wood,
Tonbridge, Kent TN12 6PA
T: (01892) 832602

PARTRIDGE GREEN
West Sussex
**Pound Cottage Bed &
Breakfast** ♦♦♦
Mill Lane, Littleworth, Partridge
Green, Horsham, West Sussex
RH13 8JU
T: (01403) 710218 & 711285
F: (01403) 711337
E: poundcottagebb@amserve.net
I: www.horsham.co.uk/poundcottage.html

PEASMARSH
East Sussex
Busti ♦♦♦
Barnetts Hill, Peasmarsh, Rye,
East Sussex TN31 6YJ
T: (01797) 230408

PEMBURY
Kent
Gates House ♦♦♦
5 Lower Green Road, Pembury,
Royal Tunbridge Wells, Kent
TN2 4DZ
T: (01892) 822866
F: (01892) 824626
E: simon@s.galway.freeserve.co.uk

**Horse Pastures Bed &
Breakfast** ♦♦♦♦
2 Horse Pasture Cottages, Little
Hawkwell Farm, Pembury, Royal
Tunbridge Wells, Kent TN2 4AQ
T: (01892) 824754
F: (01892) 824754
E: sommervillescr@aol.com

PETHAM
Kent
South Wootton House ♦♦♦
Capel Lane, Petham, Canterbury,
Kent CT4 5RG
T: (01227) 700643
F: (01227) 700613
E: mountfrances@farming.co.uk

PETT
East Sussex
Pendragon Lodge ♦♦♦♦♦
Watermill Lane, Pett, Hastings,
East Sussex TN35 4HY
T: (01424) 814051

PETT LEVEL
East Sussex
Cliff End ♦♦♦♦
Pett Level Road, Pett Level,
Hastings, East Sussex TN35 4EE
T: (01424) 813135
F: (01424) 813135
E: roastbeef@zoom.co.uk
I: www.rye.org.uk

PETWORTH
West Sussex
Badgers Tavern
Rating Applied For
Coultershaw Bridge, Petworth,
West Sussex GU28 0JF
T: (01798) 342651
F: (01798) 343649

Burton Park Farm ♦♦♦
Petworth, West Sussex GU28 0JT
T: (01798) 342431

Eedes Cottage ♦♦♦♦
Bignor Park Road, Bury Gate,
Pulborough, West Sussex
RH20 1EZ
T: (01798) 831438
F: (01798) 831942

The Horse Guards Inn ♦♦♦♦
Tillington, Petworth, West
Sussex GU28 9AF
T: (01798) 342332
F: (01798) 344351
E: mail@horseguardsinn.co.uk
I: www.horseguardsinn.co.uk

The Old Railway Station ♦♦♦♦♦
Coultershaw Bridge, Petworth,
West Sussex GU28 0JF
T: (01798) 342346 &
07860 435370
F: (01798) 342346
E: mlr@old-station.co.uk
I: www.old-station.co.uk

Rectory Cottage ♦♦♦
Rectory Lane, Petworth, West
Sussex GU28 0DB
T: (01798) 342380
E: dcradd@aol.com

Stonemasons Inn ♦♦♦
North Street, Petworth, West
Sussex GU28 9NL
T: (01798) 342510
F: (01798) 344111

White Horse Inn ♦♦♦
The Street, Sutton, Pulborough,
West Sussex RH20 1PS
T: (01798) 869221
F: (01798) 869291

PILTDOWN
East Sussex
Deerview Farm ♦♦♦
Down Street, Piltdown, Uckfield,
East Sussex TN22 3XX
T: (01825) 713139
F: (01825) 713139
E: b&b@deerviewfarm.freeserve.co.uk

The Piltdown Man Free House ♦♦♦
Piltdown, Uckfield, East Sussex
TN22 5XL
T: (01825) 723563
F: (01825) 721087
E: enquiries@thepiltdownman.com
I: www.thepiltdownman.com

PLAYDEN
East Sussex
The Corner House ♦♦♦
Playden, Rye, East Sussex
TN31 7UL
T: (01797) 280439
E: richard.turner5@virgin.net
I: http://www.smoothhound.co.uk/hotels/corner2.html

Houghton Farm ♦♦♦♦
Houghton Green Lane, Playden,
Rye, East Sussex TN31 7PJ
T: (01797) 280175

The Playden Oast Hotel ♦♦♦
Peasmarsh Road, Playden, Rye,
East Sussex TN31 7UL
T: (01707) 223502
F: (01797) 223502

PLUCKLEY
Kent
Elvey Farm Country Hotel ♦♦♦
Elvey Farm, Pluckley, Ashford,
Kent TN27 0SU
T: (01233) 840442
F: (01233) 840726

PLUMMERS PLAIN
West Sussex
Cinnamon Cottage ♦♦♦
Handcross Road, Plummers
Plain, Horsham, West Sussex
RH13 6NZ
T: (01444) 400539 &
07885 424579

POLEGATE
East Sussex
The Cottage ♦♦♦
Dittons Road, Polegate, East
Sussex BN26 6HS
T: (01323) 482011
F: (01323) 482011

POYNINGS
West Sussex
Poynings Manor Farm ♦♦♦
Poynings, Brighton BN45 7AG
T: (01273) 857371
F: (01273) 857371
E: manor-farm@faxvia.com
I: www.smoothhound.co.uk/hotels/poynings.html

PRESTON
Kent
The Windmill Inn ♦♦
Canterbury Road, Preston,
Faversham, Kent ME13 8LT
T: (01795) 536505
E: terry@thewindmillinn.free-online.co.uk

PULBOROUGH
West Sussex

Barn House Lodge ♦♦♦♦
Barn House Lane, Pulborough,
West Sussex RH20 2BS
T: (01798) 872682
F: (01798) 872682

Hurston Warren ♦♦♦
Golf Club Lane, Wiggonholt,
Pulborough, West Sussex
RH20 2EN
T: (01798) 875831
F: (01798) 874989
E: kglazier@btinternet.com
I: www.sussexlive.com

Moseleys Barn ♦♦♦♦
Hardham, Pulborough, West
Sussex RH20 1LB
T: (01798) 872912
F: (01798) 872912

PUNNETTS TOWN
East Sussex

Ringwood ♦♦♦♦
Forest Lane, Punnetts Town,
Heathfield, East Sussex
TN21 9JA
T: (01435) 830630

QUEENBOROUGH
Kent

**The Trafalgar Hotel &
Restaurant ♦♦**
10-13 Rushenden Road,
Queenborough, Kent ME11 5HB
T: (01795) 662342 & 663365
F: (01795) 580885
E: trafalgarhotel@bardays.net

RAINHAM
Kent

Abigails ♦♦♦
17 The Maltings, Rainham,
Gillingham, Kent ME8 8JL
T: (01634) 365427

Sans Souci ♦♦♦
43 Wakeley Road, Rainham,
Gillingham, Kent ME8 8HD
T: (01634) 370847 &
0771 8551663

RAMSGATE
Kent

Abbeygail Guest House ♦♦♦
17 Penshurst Road, Ramsgate,
Kent CT11 8EG
T: (01843) 594154
F: (01843) 594154
E: lindi.groom@ukf.net

The Crescent ♦♦♦
19 Wellington Crescent,
Ramsgate, Kent CT11 8JD
T: (01843) 591419
F: (01843) 591419

Glendevon Guest House ♦♦♦
8 Truro Road, Ramsgate, Kent
CT1 8DB
T: (01843) 570909 &
0800 0352110
F: (01843) 570909
E: glendevon@currantbun.com
I: www.glendevon-guesthouse.
co.uk

Glenholme ♦♦
6 Crescent Road, Ramsgate,
Kent CT11 9QU
T: (01843) 595149

The Jalna Hotel ♦♦♦
49 Vale Square, Ramsgate, Kent
CT11 9DΛ
T: (01843) 593848
F: (01843) 593848
E: rosemary@jalna8.freeserve.
co.uk
I: www.placestostay.
com/ramsgate-jalnahotel

The Royal Harbour Hotel ♦
8 Nelson Crescent, Ramsgate,
Kent CT11 9JF
T: (01843) 584198
F: (01843) 586759

The Royale Guest House ♦♦♦
7 Royal Road, Ramsgate, Kent
CT11 9LE
T: (01843) 594712
F: (01843) 594712
E: theroyaleguesthouse@talk21.
com

Sion Hill Hotel ♦♦
2 Sion Hill, Ramsgate, Kent
CT11 9HZ
T: (01843) 591908
F: (01843) 850283

Spencer Court Hotel ♦♦♦
37 Spencer Square, Ramsgate,
Kent CT11 9LD
T: (01843) 594582
F: (01843) 594582

Sunnymede Hotel ♦♦♦
10 Truro Road, Ramsgate, Kent
CT11 8DP
T: (01843) 593974
F: (01843) 594327

Westcliff Hotel ♦♦
9 Grange Road, Ramsgate, Kent
CT11 9NG
T: (01843) 581222
F: (01843) 581222
E: westrams@call21.com

REDFORD
West Sussex

Redford Cottage ♦♦♦♦
Redford, Midhurst, West Sussex
GU29 0QF
T: (01428) 741242
F: (01428) 741242

REDHILL
Surrey

Ashleigh House Hotel ♦♦♦♦
39 Redstone Hill, Redhill,
RH1 4BG
T: (01737) 764763
F: (01737) 780308

REIGATE
Surrey

Highview ♦♦♦
78 Woodcrest Walk, Reigate,
Surrey RH2 0JL
T: (01737) 768294
F: (01737) 760433
E: highview@creative-eye.
demon.co.uk

RHODES MINNIS
Kent

Monsoon Lodge ♦♦♦
Rhodes Minnis, Canterbury, Kent
CT4 6XX
T: (01303) 863272 &
07712 580441
F: (01303) 863272
E: jm@farmersweekly.net

RINGMER
East Sussex

Bethany ♦♦♦
25 Ballard Drive, Ringmer,
Lewes, East Sussex BN8 5NU
T: (01273) 812025
F: (01273) 812025
E: dybethany@aol.com

Bryn-Clai ♦♦♦
Uckfield Road (A26), Ringmer,
Lewes, East Sussex BN8 5RU
T: (01273) 814042

Drove Park ♦♦♦♦
Half Mile Drove, Ringmer, Lewes,
East Sussex BN8 5NL
T: (01273) 814470
F: (01273) 814470
E: pru@drovepark.com
I: www.drovepark.com

Gote Farm ♦♦♦♦
Gote Lane, Ringmer, Lewes, East
Sussex BN8 5HX
T: (01273) 812303
F: (01273) 812303
E: janecraig@ukgateway.net

RIVER
Kent

Woodlands ♦♦♦
29 London Road, River, Dover,
Kent CT17 0SF
T: (01304) 823635

RIVERHEAD
Kent

Bramber ♦♦♦
45 Shoreham Lane, Riverhead,
Sevenoaks, Kent TN13 3DX
T: (01732) 457466
F: (01732) 457466

ROBERTSBRIDGE
East Sussex

Glenferness ♦♦♦♦
Brightling Road, Robertsbridge,
East Sussex TN32 5DP
T: (01580) 881841
E: ktwright@ukonline.co.uk

ROCHESTER
Kent

10 Abbotts Close ♦♦♦♦
Priestfields, Rochester, Kent
ME1 3AZ
T: (01634) 811126

Ambleside Lodge ♦♦♦
12 Abbotts Close, Priestfields,
Rochester, Kent ME1 3AZ
T: (01634) 815926

The Cottage ♦♦♦
66 Borstal Road, Rochester, Kent
ME1 3BD
T: (01634) 403888

Glaisdale ♦♦♦
29 Langdon Road, Bishop
Square, Rochester, Kent
ME1 1UN
T: (01634) 409559 &
07947 390515
E: hlsinclair29@supanet.com
I: www.medway.gov.uk

Holly House ♦♦♦
144 Maidstone Road, Rochester,
Kent ME1 3ED
T: (01634) 815998

King Charles Hotel ♦♦♦
Brompton Road, Gillingham,
Kent ME7 5QT
T: (01634) 830303
F: (01634) 829430
E: enquiries@kingcharleshotel.
co.uk
I: www.kingcharleshotel.co.uk

2 King Edward Road ♦♦♦
Rochester, Kent ME1 1UA
T: (01634) 844148

Kings Head Hotel ♦♦
58 High Street, Rochester, Kent
ME1 1LD
T: (01634) 831103
F: (01634) 831103

Linden House ♦♦♦
10 Nag's Head Lane, Rochester,
Kent ME1 1BB
T: (01634) 819438
E: carolyn@cpidgeon.freeserve.
co.uk

Longley House ♦♦♦
Boley Hill, Rochester, Kent
ME1 1TE
T: (01634) 819108
F: (01634) 819108
E: marguerita@jtq.globalnet.
co.uk
I: www.users.globalnet.
co.uk/~jtq

North Downs Barn ♦♦♦♦
Bush Road, Rochester, Kent
ME2 1HF
T: (01634) 296829
F: (01634) 296829

The Old Priory ♦♦
4 Mill Road, Frindsbury,
Rochester, Kent ME2 3BT
T: (01634) 714053
F: (01634) 717716

Riverview Lodge ♦
88 Borstal Road, Rochester, Kent
ME1 3BD
T: (01634) 842241 &
07956 279628
F: (01634) 843404

St Martin ♦♦♦
104 Borstal Road, Rochester,
Kent ME1 3BD
T: (01634) 848192
E: icolvin@stmartin.freeserve.
co.uk

St Ouen ♦♦♦
98 Borstal Road, Rochester, Kent
ME1 3BD
T: (01634) 843528
E: m.s.beggs@98borstal.
freeserve.co.uk

Sunshine House ♦♦
14 Beech Road, Rochester, Kent
ME2 2LP
T: (01634) 724291
E: melzo@strood1950.freeserve.
co.uk

ROGATE
West Sussex

Trotton Farm ♦♦♦
Trotton, Petersfield, Hampshire
GU31 5EN
T: (01730) 813618
F: (01730) 816093
E: baigentfarms@
farmersweekly.net

ROLVENDEN
Kent

Duck & Drake Cottage ♦♦♦
Sandhurst Lane, Rolvenden,
Cranbrook, Kent TN17 4PQ
T: (01580) 241533

ROTTINGDEAN
East Sussex

Braemar Guest House ♦♦♦
Steyning Road, Rottingdean,
Brighton BN2 7GA
T: (01273) 304263

ROWLEDGE
Surrey

Borderfield Farm ♦♦♦
Boundary Road, Rowledge,
Farnham, Surrey GU10 4EP
T: (01252) 793985 &
07885 581443

ROYAL TUNBRIDGE WELLS
Kent

Ash Tree Cottage ♦♦♦♦
7 Eden Road, Royal Tunbridge
Wells, Kent TN1 1TS
T: (01892) 541317 &
07050 160322
F: (01892) 541317
E: rogersashtree@excite.co.uk

Badgers End ♦♦
47 Thirlmere Road, Royal
Tunbridge Wells, Kent TN4 9SS
T: (01892) 533176 &
07929 553938

Bankside ♦♦♦
6 Scotts Way, Royal Tunbridge
Wells, Kent TN2 5RG
T: (01892) 531776

4 Bedford Terrace ♦♦♦
Royal Tunbridge Wells, Kent
TN1 1YJ
T: (01892) 532084

Blinkbonnie ♦♦
4 Beltring Road, Royal Tunbridge
Wells, Kent TN4 9UA
T: (01892) 527908

Blundeston ♦♦♦♦
Eden Road, Royal Tunbridge
Wells, Kent TN1 1TS
T: (01892) 513030
F: (01892) 540255
E: daysblundeston@excite.co.uk

Braeside ♦♦♦
7 Rusthall Road, Royal
Tunbridge Wells, Kent TN4 8RA
T: (01892) 521786
F: (01892) 521786
E: itucker@eggconnect.net

Chequers ♦♦♦♦
Camden Park, Royal Tunbridge
Wells, Kent TN2 5AD
T: (01892) 532299
F: (01892) 526448
E: stubbsmcd@btinternet.com

Cheviots ♦♦♦
Cousley Wood, Wadhurst, East
Sussex TN5 6HD
T: (01892) 782952
F: (01892) 782952
E: b&b@cheviots99.freeserve.
co.uk
I: www.cheviots99.freeserve.
co.uk

Clarken Guest House ♦♦♦
61 Frant Road, Royal Tunbridge
Wells, Kent TN2 5LH
T: (01892) 533397
F: (01892) 617121
E: barrykench@virgin.net

The Coach House ♦♦♦
51A Frant Road, Royal Tunbridge
Wells, Kent TN2 5LE
T: (01892) 530615
F: (01892) 530615

69 Culverden Park ♦♦♦
Royal Tunbridge Wells, Kent
TN4 9QS
T: (01892) 533314
E: peterbell8@aol.com

Danehurst ♦♦♦♦♦
41 Lower Green Road, Rusthall,
Royal Tunbridge Wells, Kent
TN4 8TW
T: (01892) 527739
F: (01892) 514804

Ephraim Lodge ♦♦♦♦♦
The Common, Royal Tunbridge
Wells, Kent TN4 8BX
T: (01892) 523053
F: (01892) 523053

Ford Cottage ♦♦♦♦
Linden Park Road, Royal
Tunbridge Wells, Kent TN2 5QL
T: (01892) 531419
E: fordcottage@tinyworld.co.uk

Hadleigh ♦♦♦
69 Sandown Park, Royal
Tunbridge Wells, Kent TN2 4RT
T: (01892) 822760
F: (01892) 823170

Hamsell Wood Farm ♦♦♦
The Forstal, Eridge, Royal
Tunbridge Wells, Kent TN3 9JY
T: (01892) 864326

Hawkenbury Farm ♦♦♦♦
Hawkenbury Road, Royal
Tunbridge Wells, Kent TN3 9AD
T: (01892) 536977
F: (01892) 536200

Hazelwood House ♦♦♦
Bishop's Down Park Road, Royal
Tunbridge Wells, Kent TN4 8XS
T: (01892) 545924
E: judith02@globalnet.co.uk

Manor Court Farm ♦♦♦
Ashurst, Royal Tunbridge Wells,
Kent TN3 9TB
T: (01892) 740279
F: (01892) 740919
E: jsoyke@jsoyke.freeserve.co.uk
I: www.manorcourtfarm.co.uk

Nightingales ♦♦♦
London Road, Southborough,
Royal Tunbridge Wells, Kent
TN4 0UJ
T: (01892) 528443
F: (01892) 511376
E: the_nightingales@bigfoot.
com
I: www.bcity.
com/the_nightingales

Number Ten ♦♦♦
Modest Corner, Southborough,
Royal Tunbridge Wells, Kent
TN4 0LS
T: (01892) 522450
F: (01892) 522450
E: modestanneke@lineone.net

Orchard House ♦♦♦♦
Kingswood Road, Royal
Tunbridge Wells, Kent TN2 4UJ
T: (01892) 521549
F: (01892) 618637
E: bennettryanassociates@
btinternet.com

19 Ravenswood Avenue ♦
Royal Tunbridge Wells, Kent
TN2 3SG
T: (01892) 530167

80 Ravenswood Avenue ♦♦
Royal Tunbridge Wells, Kent
TN2 3SJ
T: (01892) 523069

Rosnaree ♦♦
189 Upper Grosvenor Road,
Royal Tunbridge Wells, Kent
TN1 2EF
T: (01892) 524017
E: david@rosnaree.freeserve.
co.uk

Southview House ♦♦♦
21 Rusthall Road, Royal
Tunbridge Wells, Kent TN4 8RD
T: (01892) 518832

Studley Cottage ♦♦♦♦
Bishops Down Park Road, Royal
Tunbridge Wells, Kent TN4 8XX
T: (01892) 539854 &
0771 848333

Triton ♦♦♦
46 Broadwater Down, Royal
Tunbridge Wells, Kent TN2 5PE
T: (01892) 530547

191 Upper Grosvenor Road
♦♦♦
Royal Tunbridge Wells, Kent
TN1 2EF
T: (01892) 537305

Vale Royal Hotel ♦♦♦
54-57 London Road, Royal
Tunbridge Wells, Kent TN1 1DS
T: (01892) 525580 & 525968
F: (01892) 526022
E: reservations@valeroyalhotel.
co.uk
I: www.valeroyalhotel.co.uk

40 York Road ♦♦♦
Royal Tunbridge Wells, Kent
TN1 1JY
T: (01892) 531342
F: (01892) 531342
I: www.wolsey-lodge.co.uk

RUDGWICK
West Sussex

The Mucky Duck Inn ♦♦♦
Loxwood Road, Tismans
Common, Rudgwick, Horsham,
West Sussex RH12 3BW
T: (01403) 822300
F: (01403) 822300
E: mucky_duck_pub@msn.com
I: www.mucky-duck-inn.co.uk

RUNCTON
West Sussex

Springdale Cottage ♦♦♦
Runcton Lane, Runcton,
Chichester, West Sussex
PO20 6PS
T: (01243) 783912

RUSTINGTON
West Sussex

Kenmore ♦♦♦♦
Claigmar Road, Rustington,
Littlehampton, West Sussex
BN16 2NL
T: (01903) 784634
F: (01903) 784634
E: kenmoreguesthouse@
amserve.net
I: www.kenmoreguesthouse.
co.uk

RYE
East Sussex

Arndale Cottage ♦♦♦♦
Northiam Road, Broad Oak
Brede, Rye, East Sussex
TN31 6EP
T: (01424) 882813 & 882852
F: (01424) 882813

Aviemore Guest House ♦♦♦
28-30 Fishmarket Road, Rye,
East Sussex TN31 7LP
T: (01797) 223052
F: (01797) 223052
E: aviemore@lineone.net
I: www.SmoothHound.
co.uk/hotels/aviemore.html

Benson Hotel ♦♦♦♦♦
15 East Street, Rye, East Sussex
TN31 7JY
T: (01797) 225131
F: (01797) 225512

Cinque Ports Hotel ♦♦♦
Cinque Ports Street, Rye, East
Sussex TN31 7AN
T: (01797) 222319
F: (01797) 224184
E: jane@fiveports.freeserve.
co.uk
I: www.rye.org.uk

The Clocks ♦♦♦
8 Rock Channel Quay, Rye, East
Sussex TN31 7DL
T: (01797) 226466

Culpeppers ♦♦♦♦
15 Love Lane, Rye, East Sussex
TN31 7NE
T: (01797) 224411
F: (01797) 224411
E: peppersrye@aol.com
I: www.rye-tourism.
co.uk/culpeppers

Durrant House Hotel ♦♦♦♦
2 Market Street, Rye, East Sussex
TN31 7LA
T: (01797) 223182
F: (01797) 226940
E: kingslands@compuserve.com
I: www.durranthouse.com

Four Seasons ♦♦♦♦
96 Udimore Road, Rye, East
Sussex TN31 7DX
T: (01797) 224305
F: (01797) 229450
E: coxsam@btinternet.com

Furnace Lane Oast ♦♦♦♦
Broad Oak Brede, Rye, East
Sussex TN31 6ET
T: (01424) 882407
E: furnacelane@pavilion.co.uk
I: www.seetb.org.
uk/furnace-lane-oast/

Glencoe Farm ♦♦♦♦
West Undercliff, Rye, East
Sussex TN31 7DX
T: (01797) 224347 &
07971 692012

11 High Street ♦♦♦
Rye, East Sussex TN31 7JF
T: (01797) 223952

The Hope Anchor Hotel ♦♦♦
Watchbell Street, Rye, East
Sussex TN31 7HA
T: (01797) 222216
F: (01897) 223796

Jeake's House ◆◆◆◆◆
Mermaid Street, Rye, East Sussex
TN31 7ET
T: (01797) 222828
F: (01797) 222623
E: jeakeshouse@btinternet.com
I: www.jeakeshouse.com

Kimbley Cottage ◆◆◆
Main Street, Peasmarsh, Rye,
East Sussex TN31 6UL
T: (01797) 230514
F: (01797) 230850
E: kimbley@clara.co.uk

Little Orchard House ◆◆◆◆◆
West Street, Rye, East Sussex
TN31 7ES
T: (01797) 223831
F: (01797) 223831
I: www.littleorchardhouse.com

Llamedos ◆◆
11 Cadborough Cliff, Rye, East
Sussex TN31 7EB
T: (01797) 227220 & 225273
E: patsr_rye@virgin.net

Manor Farm Oast ◆◆◆◆◆
Workhouse Lane, Icklesham,
Winchelsea, East Sussex
TN36 4AJ
T: (01424) 813787
F: (01424) 813787
E: manor.farm.oast@lineone.net

The Mint B & B ◆◆◆
Rye Fine Art, 39 The Mint, Rye,
East Sussex TN31 7EN
T: (01797) 224968

Mint Court Cottage ◆◆◆
The Mint, High Street, Rye, East
Sussex TN31 7EN
T: (01797) 227780
F: (01797) 223432

Mint Lodge ◆◆◆
38 The Mint, Rye, East Sussex
TN31 7EN
T: (01797) 223268

Mountsfield ◆◆◆◆◆
Rye Hill, Rye, East Sussex
TN31 7NH
T: (01797) 227105
F: (01797) 227106

The Old Vicarage ◆◆◆
Rye Harbour, Rye, East Sussex
TN31 7TT
T: (01797) 222088
F: (01797) 229620
E: jonathan@
oldvicarageryeharbour.fsnet.
co.uk

Owlet ◆◆◆
37 New Road, Rye, East Sussex
TN31 7LS
T: (01797) 222544
E: owlet-rye@amserve.net

Playden Cottage Guesthouse
◆◆◆◆◆
Military Road, Rye, East Sussex
TN31 7NY
T: (01797) 222234
I: www.rye.org.uk.
playdencottage

The Queens Head Hotel ◆◆◆
19 Landgate, Rye, East Sussex
TN31 7LH
T: (01797) 222181
F: (01797) 229180

The Rise ◆◆◆◆
82 Udimore Road, Rye, East
Sussex TN31 7DY
T: (01797) 222285
E: therise@bb-rye.freeserve.
co.uk

St Margarets ◆◆◆
Dumbwomans Lane, Udimore,
Rye, East Sussex TN31 6AD
T: (01797) 222586

Ship Inn ◆◆◆
The Strand, Rye, East Sussex
TN31 7DB
T: (01797) 222233
F: (01797) 222715
E: shipinn@zoom.co.uk

The Strand House ◆◆◆◆
Tanyard's Lane, Winchelsea, Rye,
East Sussex TN36 4JT
T: (01797) 226276
F: (01797) 224806
E: strandhouse@winchelsea98.
fsnet.co.uk
I: www.s-h-systems.
co.uk/hotels/strand.html

Thacker House ◆◆◆
Old Brickyard, Rye, East Sussex
TN31 7EE
T: (01797) 226850
F: (01797) 226850
E: abb25@supanet.com

Tidings ◆◆◆◆
26A Military Road, Rye, East
Sussex TN31 7NY
T: (01797) 223760

Tillingham House ◆◆◆◆
75 Ferry Road, Rye, East Sussex
TN31 7DJ
T: (01797) 222225 & 223268

Top o'The Hill at Rye ◆◆◆
Rye Hill, Rye, East Sussex
TN31 7NH
T: (01797) 223284
F: (01797) 227030

Tower House ◆◆◆◆◆
(The Old Dormy), Hilders Cliff,
Rye, East Sussex TN31 7LD
T: (01797) 226865
F: (01797) 226865

Vine Cottage ◆◆◆
25a Udimore Road, Rye, East
Sussex TN31 7DS
T: (01797) 222822 &
0780 3431406
F: (01797) 222822

White Vine House ◆◆◆◆◆
24 High Street, Rye, East Sussex
TN31 7JF
T: (01797) 224748 & 227768
F: (01797) 223599
E: irene@whitevinehouse.
freeserve.co.uk

The Windmill Guest House
◆◆◆
Mill Lane, (off Ferry Road), Rye,
East Sussex TN31 7DW
T: (01797) 224027
F: (01797) 227211
I: www.rye-tourism.
co.uk/windmill

Wish House ◆◆◆
Wish Ward, Rye, East Sussex
TN31 7DH
T: (01797) 223672

**Wisteria Corner Bed &
Breakfast
Rating Applied For**
47 Ferry Road, Rye, East Sussex
TN31 7DJ
T: (01797) 225011

Woodpeckers ◆◆◆
West Undercliff, Rye, East
Sussex TN31 7DX
T: (01797) 223013 & 222264
F: (01797) 222264 ?

RYE FOREIGN
East Sussex

The Hare & Hounds ◆◆◆
Main Road, Rye Foreign, Rye,
East Sussex TN31 7ST
T: (01797) 230483

ST LEONARDS
East Sussex

Ashton House ◆◆◆
381 Battle Road, St Leonards on
Sea, St Leonards, Hastings, East
Sussex TN37 7BE
T: (01424) 853624

Hollington Croft ◆◆◆
272 Battle Road, St Leonards-
on-Sea, St Leonards, Hastings,
East Sussex TN37 7BA
T: (01424) 851795 &
07733 426062

Marina Lodge ◆◆◆
123 Marina, St Leonards-on-
Sea, St Leonards, Hastings, East
Sussex TN38 0BN
T: (01424) 715067
E: marinalodge@lineone.net
I: www.marinalodge.co.uk

May Tree House ◆◆◆
41 Albany Road, St Leonards,
Hastings, East Sussex TN38 0LJ
T: (01424) 421760 &
07973 283117
F: (01424) 421760
E: maytreehouse@hotmail.com

Melrose Guest House ◆◆◆
18 De Cham Road, St Leonards,
Hastings, East Sussex TN37 6JP
T: (01424) 715163 & 422578
F: (01424) 715163
E: melrose18@fsmail.net

Rutland Guest House ◆◆◆
17 Grosvenor Cres, St Leonards,
Hastings, East Sussex TN38 0AA
T: (01424) 714720
F: (01424) 714720

Sherwood Guest House ◆◆◆
15 Grosvenor Crescent, St
Leonards-on-Sea, St Leonards,
East Sussex TN38 0AA
T: (01424) 433331
F: (01424) 433331

The Windsor Hotel ◆◆◆
9 Warrior Square, St Leonards-
on-Sea, St Leonards, Hastings,
East Sussex TN37 6BA
T: (01424) 422709
F: (01424) 422709

ST MICHAELS
Kent

Forge House ◆◆◆
Biddenden Road, St Michaels,
Tenterden, Kent TN30 6SX
T: (01233) 850779
E: forgehouse@email.com
I: pages.eidosnet.
co.uk/~forgehouse

Whitelands Farm ◆◆◆
Grange Road, St Michaels,
Tenterden, Kent IN30 6TJ
T: (01580) 765971 &
07770 796288
E: whitelandsfarm@tinyonline.
co.uk

SALTDEAN
East Sussex

Grand Ocean Hotel ◆◆◆
Longridge Avenue, Saltdean,
Brighton BN2 8RP
T: (01273) 302291 &
0870 7780333
F: (01273) 304255
I: www.grandhotelgroup.co.uk

SANDGATE
Kent

Royal Norfolk Hotel ◆◆
7 Sandgate High Street,
Sandgate, Folkestone, Kent
CT20 3BD
T: (01303) 248262
F: (01303) 238433
E: coasthosts@cwctv.net

SANDHURST
Kent

Heronden Barn ◆◆◆◆
Rye Road, Sandhurst, Cranbrook,
Kent TN18 5PH
T: (01580) 850809
F: (01580) 850809
E: hdj@hdjohns.idps.co.uk
I: www.heronden.co.uk

Hoads Farm ◆◆◆
Crouch Lane, Sandhurst,
Cranbrook, Kent TN18 5PA
T: (01580) 850296
F: (01580) 850296

Hope Barn ◆◆◆◆
Crouch Lane, Sandhurst,
Cranbrook, Kent TN18 5PD
T: (01580) 850689
F: (01580) 850689
I: www.hopebarn.co.uk

Lamberden House ◆◆◆◆
Rye Road, Sandhurst, Cranbrook,
Kent TN18 5PH
T: (01580) 850968
F: (01580) 850121
E: croysdill@lamberden.
freeserve.co.uk
I: www.lamberden.freeserve.
co.uk

SANDWICH
Kent

Durlock Lodge ◆◆◆
Durlock, Minster-in-Thanet,
Ramsgate, Kent CT12 4HD
T: (01843) 821219 &
07880 725150
E: david@durlocklodge.co.uk
I: www.durlocklodge.co.uk

**Fleur De Lis Hotel Inn &
Restaurant** ◆◆◆
6-8 Delf Street, Sandwich, Kent
CT13 9BZ
T: (01304) 611131
F: (01304) 611199
E: thefleur@verinitaverns.co.uk
I: www.verinitaverns.co.uk

57 St Georges Road ◆◆◆
Sandwich, Kent CT13 9LE
T: (01304) 612772

SARRE
Kent

Crown Inn (The Famous Cherry Brandy House) ◆◆◆◆
Ramsgate Road, Sarre,
Birchington, Kent CT7 0LF
T: (01843) 847808
F: (01843) 847914
E: crown@shepherd-neame.
co.uk
I: www.shepherd-neame.co.uk
♿

SEAFORD
East Sussex

Copperfields ◆◆◆◆
12 Connaught Road, Seaford,
East Sussex BN25 2PU
T: (01323) 492152 &
07775 700625
F: (01323) 872311
E: sally.green@btinternet.com

Cornerways ◆◆◆
10 The Covers, Seaford, East
Sussex BN25 1DF
T: (01323) 492400

Holmes Lodge ◆◆◆
72 Claremont Road, Seaford,
East Sussex BN25 2BJ
T: (01323) 898331
F: (01323) 491346
E: holmes.lodge@freemail.co.uk
I: www.seaford.
co.uk/holmes/holmes.htm

Malvern House ◆◆◆
Alfriston Road, Seaford, East
Sussex BN25 3QG
T: (01323) 492058 &
07860 262271
F: (01323) 492000
E: MalvernBandB@cs.com
I: www.seaford.co.uk/malvern/

Oasis Clearview Hotel ◆◆
36-38 Claremont Road, Seaford,
East Sussex BN25 2BD
T: (01323) 890138
F: (01323) 896534

The Silverdale ◆◆◆◆
21 Sutton Park Road, Seaford,
East Sussex BN25 1RH
T: (01323) 491849
F: (01323) 891131
E: silverdale@mistral.co.uk
I: www.mistral.
co.uk/silverdale/silver.htm

Tudor Manor Hotel ◆◆◆◆
Eastbourne Road, Seaford, East
Sussex BN25 4DB
T: (01323) 896006
F: (01323) 896006

SEDLESCOMBE
East Sussex

Lower Marley Farm ◆◆◆
New Road, Sedlescombe, Battle,
East Sussex TN33 0RG
T: (01424) 871416 & 870728

SELSEY
West Sussex

Greenacre ◆◆◆◆
5 Manor Farm Court, Selsey,
Chichester, West Sussex
PO20 0LY
T: (01243) 602912 &
07973 392629
E: greenacre@zoom.co.uk
I: www.greenacre@zoom.co.uk

42 Kingsway ◆◆◆
Selsey, Chichester, West Sussex
PO20 0SY
T: (01243) 604711 &
07860 109819
F: (01243) 604711
E: stephen.lucas2@virgin.net

Norton Lea ◆◆◆
Upper Norton, Selsey,
Chichester, West Sussex
PO20 9EA
T: (01243) 605454
F: (01243) 605456
E: 100013.3142@compuserve.
com

St Andrews Lodge ◆◆◆◆
Chichester Road, Selsey,
Chichester, West Sussex
PO20 0LX
T: (01243) 606899
F: (01243) 607826
E: info@standrewslodge.co.uk
I: www.standrewslodge.co.uk
♿

SEVENOAKS
Kent

Beechcombe ◆◆◆◆
4 Vine Lodge Court, Holly Bush
Lane, Sevenoaks, Kent TN13 3XY
T: (01732) 741643
F: (01732) 741643
E: anthonytait@hotmail.com

The Bull Inn Hotel ◆◆◆
Wrotham, Sevenoaks, Kent
TN15 7RF
T: (01732) 789800 & 789819
F: (01732) 886288
E: bookings@bullhotel.
freeserve.co.uk
I: www.bullinnhotel.co.uk

Burley Lodge ◆◆◆
Rockdale Road, Sevenoaks, Kent
TN13 1JT
T: (01732) 455761
F: (01732) 458178
E: dilatter@aol.com

75 Clarendon Road ◆◆◆
Sevenoaks, Kent TN13 1ET
T: (01732) 456000
F: (01732) 456000
E: info@chocolateshop.uk.com

Crofters ◆◆◆◆
67 Oakhill Road, Sevenoaks,
Kent TN13 1NU
T: (01732) 460189
F: (01732) 460189
E: ritamarfry@talk21.com

56 The Drive ◆◆◆
Sevenoaks, Kent TN13 3AF
T: (01732) 453236
E: jwlloydsks@aol.com

Garden House ◆◆◆◆
Solefields Road, Sevenoaks, Kent
TN13 1PJ
T: (01732) 457225

Hornshaw House ◆◆◆◆
47 Mount Harry Road,
Sevenoaks, Kent TN13 3JN
T: (01732) 465262
E: embates@hornshaw47.
freeserve.co.uk
I: www.hornshaw-house.co.uk

Legh House ◆◆◆◆
Woodland Rise, Sevenoaks, Kent
TN15 0HZ
T: (01732) 761587

The Moorings Hotel ◆◆◆
97 Hitchen Hatch Lane,
Sevenoaks, Kent TN13 3BE
T: (01732) 452589 & 742323
F: (01732) 456462
E: theryans@mooringshotel.
co.uk
I: www.mooringshotel.co.uk

The Old Police House ◆◆◆◆
18 Shenden Way, Sevenoaks,
Kent TN13 1SE
T: (01732) 457150
F: (01732) 457150

The Pightle ◆◆◆◆
21 White Hart Wood, Sevenoaks,
Kent TN13 1RS
T: (01732) 451678
F: (01732) 464905
E: miketessa@pightle21.fsnet.
co.uk
I: www.pightle21.fsnet.co.uk

Robann ◆◆◆
5 Vestry Cottages, Old Otford
Road, Sevenoaks, Kent TN14 5EH
T: (01732) 456272

40 Robyns Way ◆◆◆
Sevenoaks, Kent TN13 3EB
T: (01732) 452401
E: valerie.ingram@centrenet.
co.uk

Rosewood ◆◆◆◆
Ismays Road, Ivy Hatch,
Sevenoaks, Kent TN15 0PA
T: (01732) 810496
F: (01732) 810400
E: rosewood@
covenantblessings.co.uk

Star House ◆◆◆
Star Hill, Sevenoaks, Kent
TN14 6HA
T: (01959) 533109 &
07774 281558

Welford ◆◆◆
6 Crownfields, Sevenoaks, Kent
TN13 1EE
T: (01732) 452689
F: (01732) 455422
E: rcjollye@compuserve.com

Wendy Wood ◆◆◆◆
86 Childsbridge Lane, Seal,
Sevenoaks, Kent TN15 0BW
T: (01732) 763755
E: wendywood@freeuk.com
I: www.wendywood.co.uk

SHADOXHURST
Kent

Park Farmhouse ◆◆◆◆
Woodchurch Road, Shadoxhurst,
Ashford, Kent TN26 1LE
T: (01233) 733264 & 733265
F: (01233) 733264

SHALFORD
Surrey

2 Northfield
Rating Applied For
Summersbury Drive, Shalford,
Guildford, Surrey GU4 8JN
T: (01483) 570431

SHARPTHORNE
West Sussex

Coach House ◆◆◆
Courtlands, Chilling Street,
Sharpthorne, East Grinstead,
West Sussex RH19 4JF
T: (01342) 810512 &
07930 977076
F: (01342) 810512
E: sussexlive@enta.net
I: www.sussexlive.com

SHEERNESS
Kent

Kingsferry House Bed and Breakfast ◆◆
247 Queenborough Road,
Halfway, Sheerness, Kent
ME12 3EW
T: (01795) 663606

SHEPPERTON
Surrey

Splash Cottage ◆◆◆
91 Watersplash Road,
Shepperton, Middlesex
TW17 0EE
T: (01932) 229987
F: (01932) 229987
E: info@lazy-river.co.uk
I: www.lazy-river.co.uk

SHIPLEY
West Sussex

Goffsland Farm ◆◆◆◆
Shipley, Horsham, West Sussex
RH13 7BQ
T: (01403) 730434
F: (01403) 730434

SHOLDEN
Kent

The Sportsman ◆◆◆◆
23 The Street, Sholden, Deal,
Kent CT14 0AL
T: (01304) 374973
F: (01304) 374973
E: rgri445880@aol.com

SHOREHAM
Kent

Church House ◆◆◆◆
Church Street, Shoreham,
Sevenoaks, Kent TN14 7SB
T: (01959) 522241
F: (01959) 522241
E: katehowie@compuserve.com
I: www.intacom.
co.uk/shore/churchouse.htm

Preston Farmhouse ◆◆◆◆
Preston Farm, Shoreham,
Sevenoaks, Kent TN14 7UD
T: (01959) 522029

SISSINGHURST
Kent

1 Hillview Cottage ◆◆◆
Starvenden Lane, Sissinghurst,
Cranbrook, Kent TN17 2AN
T: (01580) 712823 &
07850 909838

The Oast House ◆◆◆◆
Buckhurst Farm, Sissinghurst,
Cranbrook, Kent TN17 2AA
T: (01580) 720044
F: (01580) 720022

SITTINGBOURNE
Kent

Hempstead House ◆◆◆◆◆
London Road, Bapchild,
Sittingbourne, Kent ME9 9PP
T: (01795) 428020
F: (01795) 436362
E: info@hempsteadhouse.co.uk
I: www.hempsteadhouse.co.uk

Scuttington Manor Guest House ♦♦♦♦
Dully Road, Dully, Sittingbourne, Kent ME9 9PA
T: (01795) 521316
F: (01795) 521316

Woodstock Guest House
Rating Applied For
25 Woodstock Road, Sittingbourne, Kent ME10 4HJ
T: (01795) 421516
F: (01795) 421516

SLINFOLD
West Sussex

Oakwood House ♦♦♦
Five Oaks Road, Slinfold, Horsham, West Sussex RH13 7QW
T: (01403) 790402

Wendy's Cottage ♦♦♦
Five Oaks Road, Slinfold, Horsham, West Sussex RH13 7RQ
T: (01403) 782326
F: (01403) 782326

SMARDEN
Kent

Bardleden Manor ♦♦♦♦
Biddenden Road, Smarden, Ashford, Kent TN27 8QG
T: (01233) 770141
F: (01233) 770171
E: cathyallport@bardleden.co.uk

Chequers Inn ♦♦♦♦
The Street, Smarden, Ashford, Kent TN27 8QA
T: (01233) 770217
F: (01233) 770623

Dering Barn ♦♦♦♦
Pluckley Road, Smarden, Ashford, Kent TN27 8ND
T: (01233) 770836

Hereford Oast ♦♦♦♦
Smarden, Ashford, Kent TN27 8PA
T: (01233) 770541
F: (01233) 770045
E: peter@hill5050.fsnet.co.uk

SOUTHBOROUGH
Kent

The Croft ♦♦
Argyle Road, Southborough, Royal Tunbridge Wells, Kent TN4 0SU
T: (01892) 522671

SOUTHWATER
West Sussex

Meadow House ♦♦♦
Church Lane, Bonfire Hill, Southwater, Horsham, West Sussex RH13 7BT
T: (01403) 730324

ST-MARGARETS-AT-CLIFFE
Kent

Holm Oaks ♦♦♦♦
Dover Road, St-Margarets-at-Cliffe, Dover, Kent CT15 6EP
T: (01304) 852990 & 853473
F: (01304) 853433
E: holmoaks852@icqmail.com

Merzenich Guest House ♦♦♦
Station Road, St-Margarets-at-Cliffe, Dover, Kent CT15 6AY
T: (01304) 852260
F: (01304) 852167
E: robclaringbould@lineone.net
I: www.smoothhound.co.uk/hotels/merzen.html

STANSTED
Kent

The Black Horse ♦♦♦♦
Tumblefield Road, Stansted, Sevenoaks, Kent TN15 7PR
T: (01732) 822355
F: (01732) 824415

STAPLE
Kent

The Three Tuns Inn ♦♦♦
Staple, Canterbury, Kent CT3 1LN
T: (01304) 812317
F: (01304) 812317
E: johngunner@totalise.co.uk
I: www.three-tuns-staple.freeserve.co.uk

STAPLEHURST
Kent

Overbridge Barn ♦♦♦♦
Marden Road, Staplehurst, Tonbridge, Kent TN12 0JH
T: (01580) 890189
F: (01580) 893164
E: paula@overbridge.co.uk
I: www.overbridge.co.uk

Tudorhurst ♦♦♦♦
Pagehurst Road, Staplehurst, Tonbridge, Kent TN12 0JA
T: (01580) 891564 & 07711 760677
F: (01580) 890505
E: laurie@bluey39.freeserve.co.uk

The White Cottage ♦♦♦♦
Hawkenbury Road, Hawkenbury, Staplehurst, Tonbridge, Kent TN12 0DU
T: (01580) 892554 & 753573
F: (01580) 891553
E: batten.j.@talk21.com

STEDHAM
West Sussex

Meadowhills ♦
Stedham, Midhurst, West Sussex GU29 0PT
T: (01730) 812609

STELLING MINNIS
Kent

Great Field Farm ♦♦♦♦
Misling Lane, Stelling Minnis, Canterbury, Kent CT4 6DE
T: (01227) 709223
F: (01227) 709223
E: Greatfieldfarm@aol.com

STEYNING
West Sussex

Chequer Inn ♦♦♦
41 High Street, Steyning, West Sussex BN44 3RE
T: (01903) 814437
F: (01903) 879707
E: chequerinn@btinternet.com

Wappingthorn Farmhouse ♦♦♦♦
Horsham Road, Steyning, West Sussex BN44 3AA
T: (01903) 813236
F: (01903) 813236
E: arianne@wappingthorn.demon.co.uk
I: www.wappingthorn.demon.co.uk

STONE-IN-OXNEY
Kent

Tighe Farmhouse ♦♦♦♦
Stone-in-Oxney, Tenterden, Kent TN30 7JU
T: (01233) 758251
F: (01233) 758054

STORRINGTON
West Sussex

Chardonnay ♦♦♦♦
Hampers Lane, Storrington, Pulborough, West Sussex RH20 3HZ
T: (01903) 746688
E: annsearancke@bigfoot.com
I: www.sussexlive.co.uk

No 1 Lime Chase ♦♦♦♦♦
(off Fryern Road), Storrington, Pulborough, West Sussex RH20 4LX
T: (01903) 740437 & 07721 042826
F: (01903) 740437
E: fionawarton@limechase.co.uk
I: www.limechase.co.uk

STROOD
Kent

Cedars Hotel ♦♦♦
38 London Road, Strood, Rochester, Kent ME3 3HU
T: (01634) 290277
F: (01634) 290277

Squires Corner ♦♦♦
38 Sharfleet Drive, Strood, Rochester, Kent ME2 2TY
T: (01634) 296898
E: barry@blazell.freeserve.co.uk

The White Cottage ♦♦♦
41 Rede Court Road, Strood, Rochester, Kent ME2 3SP
T: (01634) 719988

SUTTON AT HONE
Kent

Hamilton ♦♦♦
Arnolds Lane, Sutton at Hone, Dartford DA4 9HE
T: (01322) 272535
F: (01322) 284856

SUTTON VALENCE
Kent

Sparks Oast Farm ♦♦♦
Forsham lane, Sutton Valence, Maidstone, Kent ME17 3EW
T: (01622) 842213
E: sparks-oast@supanet.com
I: www.s-h-systems.co.uk/hotels/sparksoa.html

SWANLEY
Kent

The Dees ♦♦♦
56 Old Chapel Road, Crockenhill, Swanley, Kent BR8 8LJ
T: (01322) 667645

TENTERDEN
Kent

Collina House Hotel ♦♦♦♦
East Hill, Tenterden, Kent TN30 6RL
T: (01580) 764852 & 764004
F: (01580) 762224
E: collina.house@dial.pipex.com
I: dspace.dial.pipex.com/collina.house

11 East Hill ♦♦♦
Tenterden, Kent TN30 6RL
T: (01580) 766805
F: (01580) 766805

Eight Bells Public House ♦♦♦
43 High Street, Tenterden, Kent TN30 6BJ
T: (01580) 762788
F: (01580) 766070

The Lemon Tree Restaurant with Rooms ♦♦♦♦
52-56 High Street, Tenterden, Kent TN30 6AU
T: (01580) 762060
F: (01580) 765146
E: nick.lemontree@talk21.com

Old Burren ♦♦♦
25 Ashford Road, Tenterden, Kent TN30 6LL
T: (01580) 764442 & 764254
F: (01580) 764157
E: poo@burren.fsbusiness.co.uk
I: www.oldburren.co.uk

Two Willows ♦♦♦♦
10 The Martins, High Halden, Ashford, Kent TN26 3LD
T: (01233) 850859
F: (01233) 850859

White Cottage ♦♦♦
London Beach, St Michaels, Tenterden, Kent TN30 6SR
T: (01233) 850583
I: www.smoothhound.co.uk/shs.html

White Lion Hotel ♦♦♦♦
High Street, Tenterden, Kent TN30 6BD
T: (01580) 765077
F: (01580) 764157

The Woolpack Hotel ♦♦
26 High Street, Tenterden, Kent TN30 6AP
T: (01580) 762934

THURNHAM
Kent

Court Farm Farmhouse ♦♦♦♦
Thurnham Lane, Thurnham, Maidstone, Kent ME14 3LH
T: (01622) 737305
F: (01622) 737305
E: monleggo1@hotmail.com
I: www.courtfarmfarmhouse.co.uk

TICEHURST
East Sussex

The Bull Inn ♦♦♦
Three Leg Cross, Ticehurst, Wadhurst, East Sussex TN5 7HH
T: (01580) 200586
F: (01580) 201289
E: michael@thebullinn.co.uk
I: www.thebullinn.co.uk

Cherry Tree Inn ♦♦♦
Dale Hill, Ticehurst, Wadhurst, East Sussex TN5 7DG
T: (01580) 201229
F: (01580) 201325
E: leondiane@aol.com

Pashley Farm ♦♦♦♦
Pashley Road, Ticehurst, Wadhurst, East Sussex TN5 7HE
T: (01580) 200362
F: (01580) 200832
E: pashleyfarm@btconnect.com

TILMANSTONE
Kent

Plough and Harrow ♦♦
Dover Road, Tilmanstone, Deal, Kent CT14 0HX
T: (01304) 617582

TONBRIDGE
Kent

Brown Bear's Den ♦♦♦
95 Barden Road, Tonbridge, Kent
TN9 1UR
T: (01732) 351195

9 The Crescent
Rating Applied For
Tonbridge, Kent TNG 1JH
T: (01732) 366919

86 Hadlow Road ♦♦
Tonbridge, Kent TN9 1PA
T: (01732) 357332

Lodge Oast ♦♦♦♦
Horns Lodge Lane, Shipbourne
Road, Tonbridge, Kent TN11 9NJ
T: (01732) 833976
F: (01732) 838394
E: maryann@lodgeoast.
freeserve.co.uk
I: www.lodgeoast.electricfence.
co.uk

Marigolds ♦♦♦
19 Old Hadlow Road, Tonbridge,
Kent TN10 4EY
T: (01732) 356539 & 07720 770
5155
E: jmtn10@aol.com
I: www.tonbridge-kent.com

Masters ♦♦♦
Matfield Green, Tonbridge, Kent
TN12 7LA
T: (01892) 722126
F: (01892) 722126

70 The Ridgeway ♦♦♦
Tonbridge, Kent TN10 4NN
T: (01732) 366459
F: (01732) 366459

30 Stacey Road ♦♦♦
Tonbridge, Kent TN10 3AR
T: (01732) 358027

UCKFIELD
East Sussex

Hooke Hall ♦♦♦♦♦
250 High Street, Uckfield, East
Sussex TN22 1EN
T: (01825) 761578
F: (01825) 768025
E: a.percy@virgin.net

Old Mill Farm ♦♦♦♦
High Hurstwood, Uckfield, East
Sussex TN22 4AD
T: (01825) 732279
F: (01825) 732279

The Old Oast
Rating Applied For
Underhill, Maresfield, Uckfield,
East Sussex TN22 3AY
T: (01825) 768886

Robins Wood ♦♦♦♦
Fairhazel, Piltdown, Uckfield,
East Sussex TN22 3XB
T: (01825) 763555
E: louise-edelston@excite.co.uk
I: www.smoothhound.co.uk

South Paddock ♦♦♦♦
Maresfield Park, Uckfield, East
Sussex TN22 2HA
T: (01825) 762335

UPCHURCH
Kent

Suffield House ♦♦♦♦
The Street, Upchurch,
Sittingbourne, Kent ME9 7EU
T: (01634) 230409 &
07715 691683

VINES CROSS
East Sussex

The Coach House ♦♦♦♦
Wellbrook Place, Hammer Lane,
Vines Cross, Heathfield, East
Sussex TN21 9HF
T: (01435) 812529
F: (01435) 812529
E: farrow@wellbrookplace.
freeserve.co.uk

WADHURST
East Sussex

Best Beech Inn ♦♦♦
Best Beech, Mayfield Lane,
Wadhurst, East Sussex TN5 6JH
T: (01892) 782046
F: (01892) 782052
I: www.bestbeechinn.com

Four Keys ♦♦
Station Road, Wadhurst, East
Sussex TN5 6RZ
T: (01892) 782252 & 784113

Little Tidebrook Farm ♦♦♦
Riseden Road, Wadhurst, East
Sussex TN5 6NY
T: (01892) 782688 &
07970 159988
E: sally-mike@marleyward.
freeserve.co.uk

Spring Cottage ♦♦♦
Best Beech Hill, Wadhurst, East
Sussex TN5 6JH
T: (01892) 783896
F: (01892) 784866
E: enquiries@
southerncrosstravel.co.uk

WALBERTON
West Sussex

Felsted Cottage ♦♦♦
Arundel Road, Walberton,
Arundel, West Sussex BN18 0QP
T: (01243) 814237 &
0788 7507122

Oaks Lodge ♦♦♦♦
Yapton Lane, Walberton,
Arundel, West Sussex BN18 0LS
T: (01243) 552865
F: (01243) 553862

WALDRON
East Sussex

Barns Oak ♦♦♦♦
Firgrove Road, Waldron,
Heathfield, East Sussex
TN21 0RE
T: (01435) 864574
E: davenporthomasbtinternet.
com

WALTHAM
Kent

Beech Bank ♦♦♦♦
Duckpit Lane, Waltham,
Canterbury, Kent CT4 5QA
T: (01227) 700302
F: (01227) 700302

WALTON-ON-THAMES
Surrey

Beech Tree Lodge ♦♦♦
7 Rydens Avenue, Walton-on-
Thames, Surrey KT12 3JB
T: (01932) 242738 & 886667
E: joanspiteri@aol.com

WARLINGHAM
Surrey

Glenmore ♦♦♦
Southview Road, Warlingham,
Oxted, Surrey CR6 9JE
T: (01883) 624530
F: (01883) 624199
E: croydon@southeastsurveys.
co.uk

WARNHAM
West Sussex

Nowhere House
Rating Applied For
Dorking Road, Warnham,
Horsham, West Sussex
RH12 3RZ
T: (01306) 627272
F: (01306) 627190

WATERSFIELD
West Sussex

Beacon Lodge B & B ♦♦♦♦
London Road, Watersfield,
Arundel, West Sussex RH20 1NH
T: (01798) 831026
F: (01798) 831026
E: beaconlodge@freeuk.com
I: www.beaconlodge.co.uk

WEALD
Kent

Church Cottage ♦♦
Glebe Road, Weald, Sevenoaks,
Kent TN14 6PB
T: (01732) 463583
F: (01732) 463583

WEST BRABOURNE
Kent

**Bulltown Farmhouse Bed &
Breakfast ♦♦♦**
Bulltown Lane, West Brabourne,
Ashford, Kent TN25 5NB
T: (01233) 813505
T: (01227) 709544
E: wiltons@bulltown.fsnet.co.uk

WEST CHILTINGTON
West Sussex

New Barn Cottage ♦♦♦♦
New Barn Lane, off Harborough
Hill, West Chiltington,
Pulborough, West Sussex
RH20 2PP
T: (01798) 813231
F: (01798) 813231

New House Farm ♦♦♦
Broadford Bridge Road, West
Chiltington, Pulborough, West
Sussex RH20 2LA
T: (01798) 812215
F: (01798) 813209
E: alma.steele@virgin.net

WEST CLANDON
Surrey

Ways Cottage ♦♦♦♦
Lime Grove, West Clandon,
Guildford, Surrey GU4 7UT
T: (01483) 222454

WEST DEAN
West Sussex

Lodge Hill Farm ♦♦♦
West Dean, Chichester, West
Sussex PO18 0RT
T: (01243) 535245

WEST FARLEIGH
Kent

Wynngarth Farmhouse ♦♦♦
Lower Road, West Farleigh,
Maidstone, Kent ME15 0PF
T: (01622) 812616
F: (01622) 812616

WEST HARTING
West Sussex

Three Quebec ♦♦♦♦
West Harting, Petersfield,
Hampshire GU31 5PG
T: (01730) 825386
F: (01730) 826652
E: stevens@threequebec.co.uk
I: www.threequebec.co.uk

WEST HORSLEY
Surrey

Brinford
Rating Applied For
off Shere Road, West Horsley,
Leatherhead, Surrey KT24 6EJ
T: (01483) 283636

Silkmore ♦♦♦♦
Silkmore Lane, West Horsley,
Leatherhead, Surrey KT24 6JQ
T: (01483) 282042 & 284109
F: (01483) 284109
E: kimpton@leporello.
free-online.co.uk

WEST MALLING
Kent

Appledene ♦♦♦♦
164 Norman Road, West
Malling, Kent ME19 6RW
T: (01732) 842071
F: (01732) 842071
E: appledene@westmalling.
freeserve.co.uk

The Barn ♦♦♦♦
16 West Street, West Malling,
Kent ME19 6UX
T: (01732) 846512
F: (01732) 846512

Westfields Farm ♦♦♦
St Vincents Lane, Addington,
West Malling, Kent ME19 5BW
T: (01732) 843209

WEST WITTERING
West Sussex

The Beach House ♦♦♦
Rookwood Road, West
Wittering, Chichester, West
Sussex PO20 8LT
T: (01243) 514800
F: (01243) 514798
E: info@beachhse.co.uk
I: www.beachhse.co.uk

Thornton Cottage ♦♦♦♦
Chichester Road, West
Wittering, Chichester, West
Sussex PO20 8QA
T: (01243) 512470
F: (01243) 512470
E: thornton@b-and-b.
fsbusiness.co.uk

WESTERHAM
Kent

Worples Field ♦♦♦♦
Farley Common, Westerham,
Kent TN16 1UB
T: (01959) 562869
E: marr@worplesfield.com
I: www.worplesfield.com

WESTGATE ON SEA
Kent

Seacroft ♦♦♦
108 St Mildreds Road, Westgate
on Sea, Margate, Kent CT8 8RL
T: (01843) 833334

White Lodge Guest House ◆◆
12 Domneva Road, Westgate on
Sea, Margate, Kent CT8 8PE
T: (01843) 831828
E: whitelodge.thanet@
btinternet.com
I: www.whitelodge.thanet.
btinternet.co.uk

WHITSTABLE
Kent

Alliston House ◆◆◆
1 Joy Lane, Whitstable, Kent
CT5 4LS
T: (01227) 779066 &
07702 203188
F: (01227) 779066

The Cherry Garden ◆◆◆
62 Joy Lane, Whitstable, Kent
CT5 4LT
T: (01227) 266497

Hotel Continental ◆◆◆
29 Beach Walk, Whitstable, Kent
CT5 2BP
T: (01227) 280280
F: (01227) 280257
I: www.oysterfishery.co.uk

Copeland House ◆◆◆
4 Island Wall, Whitstable, Kent
CT15 1EP
T: (01227) 266207
F: (01227) 266207

Horizons Bed & Breakfast
◆◆◆
7 St Swithins Road, Tankerton,
Whitstable, Kent CT5 2HT
T: (01227) 772468 &
07947 047482
E: horizonsbandb@hotmail.com

Marine ◆◆◆
Marine Parade, Tankerton,
Whitstable, Kent CT5 2BE
T: (01227) 272672
F: (01227) 264721
E: marine@shepherd-neame.
co.uk
I: www.shepherd-neame.co.uk

Marine Lodge ◆◆◆
82 Marine Parade, Tankerton,
Whitstable, Kent CT5 2BA
T: (01227) 273707
E: christine.tilley@tesco.net

Victoria Villa ◆◆◆◆
Victoria Street, Whitstable, Kent
CT5 1JB
T: (01227) 779191
F: (01227) 779191

Windyridge Guest House
◆◆◆◆
Wraik Hill, Whitstable, Kent
CT5 3BY
T: (01227) 263506
F: (01227) 771191

WILLESBOROUGH
Kent

Rosemary House ◆◆◆
94 Church Road, Willesborough,
Ashford, Kent TN24 0JG
T: (01233) 625215

WILMINGTON
Kent

66 Tredegar Road ◆◆◆
Wilmington, Dartford DA2 7AZ
T: (01322) 270659

WINCHELSEA
East Sussex

The New Inn ◆◆◆
German Street, Winchelsea, East
Sussex TN36 4EN
T: (01797) 226252
E: newinnwsea@aol.com

St Anthonys ◆◆◆◆
Castle Street, Winchelsea, East
Sussex TN36 4EL
T: (01797) 226255

Wickham Manor ◆◆◆
Pannel Lane, Winchelsea, East
Sussex TN36 4AG
T: (01797) 226216
F: (01797) 226216

**Winchelsea Lodge Motel &
Restaurant** ◆◆◆◆
Hastings Road (A259),
Winchelsea, East Sussex
TN36 4AD
T: (01797) 226211
F: (01797) 226312
E: orlandoatwinchelsealodge@
tinyworld.co.uk
I: winchelsea-lodge-motel.co.uk

WINGHAM
Kent

Dambridge Oast ◆◆◆◆
Staple Road, Wingham,
Canterbury, Kent CT3 1LU
T: (01227) 720082 &
07889 707828
F: (01227) 720082
E: pagoast@primex.co.uk
I: homepages.primex.
co.uk/~pagoast

WISBOROUGH GREEN
West Sussex

Lower Sparr Farm ◆◆◆◆
Skiff Lane, Wisborough Green,
Billingshurst, West Sussex
RH14 0AA
T: (01403) 820465
F: (01403) 820678
E: sclater@lowersparrbb.f9.
co.uk
I: www.lowersparrbb.f9.co.uk

Meadowbank House ◆◆◆
Petworth Road, Wisborough
Green, Billingshurst, West
Sussex RH14 0BJ
T: (01403) 700482

WISTON
West Sussex

**Buncton Manor Farm Bed &
Breakfast** ◆◆◆◆
Buncton Manor Farm, Wiston,
Steyning, West Sussex
BN44 3DD
T: (01903) 812736
F: (01903) 814838
E: bunctonmanor@email.com
I: www.bunctonmanor.supanet.
com

WITTERSHAM
Kent

Oxney Farm ◆◆◆◆◆
Moons Green, Wittersham,
Tenterden, Kent TN30 7PS
T: (01797) 270558 &
07850 219830
F: (01797) 270958
E: oxneyf@globalnet.co.uk
I: www.users.globalnet.
co.uk/~oxneyf

WOKING
Surrey

Amberhurst ◆◆◆
Hollybank Road, Hook Heath,
Woking, Surrey GU22 0JN
T: (01483) 762748
F: (01483) 762748

Grantchester ◆◆◆
Boughton Hall Avenue, Send,
Woking, Surrey GU23 7DF
T: (01483) 225383
F: (01483) 596490
E: gary@hotpotmail.com

Swallow Barn ◆◆◆
Milford Green, Chobham,
Woking, Surrey GU24 8AU
T: (01276) 856030 &
07768 972904
F: (01276) 856030
E: swallowbarn@compuserve.
com
I: www.bestbandb.co.uk

WOODCHURCH
Kent

Little Tiffenden Farm ◆◆◆◆
Redbrook Street, Woodchurch,
Ashford, Kent TN26 3QU
T: (01233) 860238
F: (01233) 860238
E: accommodation@
Lt-tiffendenfarm.ndirect.co.uk
I: www.Lt-tiffendenfarm.ndirect.
co.uk

Shirkoak Farm ◆◆◆◆
Bethersden Road, Woodchurch,
Ashford, Kent TN26 3PZ
T: (01233) 860056
F: (01233) 861402
E: shirkoakfarm@aol.com
I: www.shirkoakfarm.com

WORPLESDON
Surrey

Maytime
Rating Applied For
43 Envis Way, Worplesdon,
Guildford, Surrey GU3 3NJ
T: (01483) 235025

WORTH
Kent

The Blue Pigeons Inn ◆◆◆
The Street, Worth, Deal, Kent
CT14 0DE
T: (01304) 613245
F: (01304) 613245

WORTHING
West Sussex

Acacia Guest House ◆◆
5-7 Warwick Gardens, Worthing,
West Sussex BN11 1PE
T: (01903) 232995

Angel Lodge ◆◆◆◆
19 Malvern Close, Worthing,
West Sussex BN11 2HE
T: (01903) 233002 & 0777 921
7734
F: (01903) 233002
E: angellodge19@aol.com
I: www.angellodge.co.uk

The Beacons Hotel ◆◆◆◆
18 Shelley Road, Worthing, West
Sussex BN11 1TU
T: (01903) 230948
F: (01903) 230948
I: www.smoothhound.
com/worthing

Beechwood Hall Hotel ◆◆◆
Wykeham Road, Worthing, West
Sussex BN11 4JD
T: (01903) 205049

Blair House Hotel ◆◆◆◆
11 St Georges Road, Worthing,
West Sussex BN11 2DS
T: (01903) 234071
F: (01903) 234071
E: stay@blairhousehotel.
freeserve.co.uk
I: www.blairhousehotel.co.uk

Bonchurch House ◆◆◆◆
1 Winchester Road, Worthing,
West Sussex BN11 4DJ
T: (01903) 202492
F: (01903) 202492
E: bonchurch@enta.net
I: www.smoothhound.
co.uk/hotels/bonchurc.html

Brooke House ◆◆◆◆
6 Westbrooke, Worthing, West
Sussex BN11 1RE
T: (01903) 600291
F: (01903) 600291

The Brunswick ◆◆
Thorn Road, Worthing, West
Sussex BN11 3ND
T: (01903) 202141
E: b&b@brunswick.freeserve.
co.uk
I: www.brunswick.fsnet.co.uk

Bute House ◆◆◆◆
325 Brighton Road, Worthing,
West Sussex BN11 2HP
T: (01903) 210247
F: (01903) 208109

Camelot House ◆◆
20 Gannon Road, Worthing,
West Sussex BN11 2DT
T: (01903) 204334

Delmar Hotel ◆◆◆
1-2 New Parade, Worthing,
West Sussex BN11 2BQ
T: (01903) 211834 &
07889 890393
F: (01903) 219052
I: www.SmoothHound.
co.uk/hotels/delmar.html

Haytor Guest House ◆◆◆
5 Salisbury Road, Worthing,
West Sussex BN11 1RB
T: (01903) 235287

Heenefields Guest House ◆◆◆
98 Heene Road, Worthing, West
Sussex BN11 3RE
T: (01903) 538780
E: heenefields.guesthouse@
virgin.net
I: www.heenefields.com

High Beach ◆◆◆
201 Brighton Road, Worthing,
West Sussex BN11 2EX
T: (01903) 236389

High Trees Guest House
◆◆◆◆
2 Warwick Gardens, Worthing,
West Sussex BN11 1PE
T: (01903) 236668
F: (01903) 601688
E: bill@hightreesguesthouse.
co.uk
I: www.hightreesguesthouse.
co.uk

The Lantern Hotel ♦♦♦
54 Shelley Road, Worthing, West
Sussex BN11 4BX
T: (01903) 238476
F: (01903) 602429
&

Manor Guest House ♦♦♦
100 Broadwater Road,
Worthing, West Sussex
BN14 8AN
T: (01903) 236028 &
07880 557615
F: (01903) 230404
E: stay@manorworthing.com
I: www.manorworthing.com

Marcroft ♦♦♦♦
17 St Georges Road, Worthing,
West Sussex BN11 2DS
T: (01903) 233626
E: marcroftguesthouse@talk21.
com

Marine View Hotel ♦♦♦
111 Marine Parade, Worthing,
West Sussex BN11 3QG
T: (01903) 238413
F: (01903) 238630

Merton House ♦♦♦
96 Broadwater Road, Worthing,
West Sussex BN14 8AW
T: (01903) 238222
F: (01903) 238222
E: stay@mertonhouse.freeserve.
co.uk

The Moorings Hotel ♦♦♦♦
4 Selden Road, Worthing, West
Sussex BN11 2LL
T: (01903) 208882
F: (01903) 236878

Oakville Guest House ♦♦♦♦
13 Wyke Avenue, Worthing,
West Sussex BN11 1PB
T: (01903) 205026
F: (01903) 205026
E: oakville@denyert.fsbusiness.
co.uk
I: www.worthingnet.
com/oakville

Olinda Guest House ♦♦♦♦
199 Brighton Road, Worthing,
West Sussex BN11 2EX
T: (01903) 206114

Pebble Beach ♦♦♦
281 Brighton Road, Worthing,
West Sussex BN11 2HG
T: (01903) 210766
F: (01903) 210766
E: pebblebeach281@aol.com
I: www.worthingnet.
com/pebblebeach

Queens Lodge ♦♦♦♦
2 Queens Road, Worthing, West
Sussex BN11 3LX
T: (01903) 205519
E: enquiries.queenslodge@
virgin.net

Rosedale House ♦♦♦♦
12 Bath Road, Worthing, West
Sussex BN11 3NU
T: (01903) 233181
E: rosedale@amserve.net

St Albans Guest House ♦♦♦♦
143 Brighton Road, Worthing,
West Sussex BN11 2EU
T: (01903) 206623
F: (01903) 525597
E: suemurray@aol.com

School House ♦♦♦♦
11 Ambrose Place, Worthing,
West Sussex BN11 1PZ
T: (01903) 206823
F: (01903) 821902

Sea Lodge ♦♦♦
183 Brighton Road, Worthing,
West Sussex BN11 2EX
T: (01903) 201214
F: (01903) 201214

Southdene Guest House ♦♦
41 Warwick Gardens, Worthing,
West Sussex BN11 1PF
T: (01903) 232909

Tamara Guest House ♦♦♦
19 Alexandra Road, Worthing,
West Sussex BN11 2DX
T: (01903) 520332

Tudor Guest House ♦♦♦
5 Windsor Road, Worthing, West
Sussex BN11 2LU
T: (01903) 210265 & 202042
F: (01903) 210265
E: tudorguesthouse@fsbdial.
co.uk

Woodlands Guest House ♦♦♦
20-22 Warwick Gardens,
Worthing, West Sussex
BN11 1PF
T: (01903) 233557 & 231957
F: (01903) 536925
E: woodlandsghse@cwcom.net
I: www.woodlands20-22.
freeserve.co.uk

WROTHAM
Kent

Hillside House ♦♦♦
Gravesend Road, Wrotham,
Sevenoaks, Kent TN15 7JH
T: (01732) 822564
E: clive@broteham.freeserve.
co.uk

WYE
Kent

Farriers ♦♦♦
Little Olantigh Road, Wye,
Ashford, Kent TN25 5DQ
T: (01233) 813105
F: (01233) 813432
E: pam@hannibals.co.uk

Mistral ♦♦♦
3 Oxenturn Road, Wye, Ashford,
Kent TN25 5BH
T: (01233) 813011
F: (01233) 813011
E: geoff@chapman.invictanet.
co.uk
I: www.wye.org

YAPTON
West Sussex

Hawthorn Lodge ♦♦♦♦
North End Road, Yapton,
Arundel, West Sussex BN18 0DU
T: (01243) 551526

USE YOUR *i*s

There are more than 550 Tourist
Information Centres throughout
England offering friendly help with
accommodation and holiday ideas
as well as suggestions of places to
visit and things to do. There may well
be a centre in your home town which
can help you before you set out.
You'll find addresses in the
local Phone Book.

Finding
accommodation
is as easy as 1 2 3

Where to Stay makes it quick and easy to find a place to stay.
There are several ways to use this guide.

1

Town Index

The town index, starting on page 812, lists all the places with
accommodation featured in the regional sections. The index gives a page
number where you can find full accommodation and contact details.

2

Colour Maps

All the place names in black on the colour maps at the front have an
entry in the regional sections. Refer to the town index for the page
number where you will find one or more establishments offering
accommodation in your chosen town or village.

3

Accommodation listing

Contact details for **all** English Tourism Council assessed accommodation
throughout England, together with their national Star rating are given in
the listing section of this guide. Establishments with a full entry in the
regional sections are shown in blue. Look in the town index for the page
number on which their full entry appears.

Information

The National
Quality Assurance
Standards

English Tourism Council

GUEST
ACCOMMODATION

A rating you can trust

When you're looking for a place to stay, you need a rating system you can trust. The English Tourism Council's ratings are your clear guide to what to expect, in an easy-to-understand form. Properties are visited annually by our trained impartial assessors, so you can have confidence that your accommodation has been thoroughly checked and rated for quality before you make a booking.

Using a simple One to Five Diamond rating, the system puts a much greater emphasis on quality and is based on research which shows exactly what consumers are looking for when choosing accommodation.

'Guest Accommodation' covers a wide variety of serviced accommodation for which England is renowned, including guesthouses, bed and breakfasts, inns and farmhouses. Establishments are rated from one to five Diamonds. The same minimum requirement for facilities and services applies to all Guest Accommodation from One to Five Diamonds. Progressively higher levels of quality and customer care must be provided for each of the One to Five Diamond ratings. The rating reflects the unique character of Guest Accommodation, and covers areas such as cleanliness, service and hospitality, bedrooms, bathrooms and food quality.

Look out, too, for the English Tourism Council's Gold and Silver Awards, which are awarded to those establishments which not only achieve the overall quality required for their Diamond rating, but also reach the highest levels of quality in those specific areas which guests identify as being really important for them. They will reflect the quality of comfort and cleanliness you'll find in the bedrooms and bathrooms and the quality of service you'll enjoy throughout your stay.

Diamond ratings are your sign of quality assurance, giving you the confidence to book the accommodation that meets your expectations.

What to expect at each rating level

The Diamond ratings for Guest Accommodation reflect visitor expectations of this sector. The quality of what is provided is more important to visitors than a wide range of facilities and services. Therefore, the same minimum requirement for facilities and services applies to all Guest Accommodation from One to Five Diamonds, while progressively higher levels of quality and customer care must be provided for each of the One to Five Diamond ratings.

- **At One Diamond Guest Accommodation, you will find:**

An acceptable overall level of quality and helpful service. Accommodation offering, as a minimum, a full cooked or continental breakfast. Other meals, where provided, will be freshly prepared. You will have a comfortable bed, with clean bed linen and towels and fresh soap. Adequate heating and hot water available at reasonable times for baths or showers at no extra charge.

- **At Two Diamond Guest Accommodation, you will find** (in addition to what is provided at One Diamond):

A good overall level of quality and comfort, with a greater emphasis on guest care in all areas.

- **At Three Diamond Guest Accommodation, you will find** (in addition to what is provided at Two Diamond):

A very good overall level of quality. For example, good quality, comfortable bedrooms; well maintained, practical décor; a good choice of quality items available for breakfast; other meals, where provided, will be freshly cooked from good quality ingredients.
A greater degree of comfort provided for you, with good levels of customer care.

- **At Four Diamond Guest Accommodation, you will find** (in addition to what is provided at Three Diamond):

An excellent overall level of quality in all areas and customer care showing very good levels of attention to your needs.

- **At Five Diamond Guest Accommodation, you will find** (in addition to what is provided at Four Diamond):

An exceptional overall level of quality. For example, ample space with a degree of luxury, an excellent quality bed, high quality furniture, excellent interior design. Breakfast offering a wide choice of high quality fresh ingredients; other meals, where provided, featuring fresh, seasonal, and often local ingredients.

Excellent levels of customer care, anticipating your needs.

NB. En suite and private bathrooms contribute to the quality score at all Diamond levels. Please check when booking or see entry details.

Awaiting confirmation of rating

At the time of going to press some establishments featured in this guide had not yet been assessed for their rating for the year 2002 and so their new rating could not be included.

For your information, the most up-to-date information regarding these establishments' ratings is in the listings pages at the back of this guide.

General Advice & Information

MAKING A BOOKING

When enquiring about accommodation, make sure you check prices and other important details. You will also need to state your requirements, clearly and precisely - for example:

- **Arrival and departure dates,** with acceptable alternatives if appropriate.
- **The type of accommodation you need;** for example, room with twin beds, private bathroom.
- **The terms you want;** for example, room only, bed and breakfast, half board, full board.
- **If you have children with you;** their ages, whether you want them to share your room or be next door, any other special requirements, such as a cot.
- **Particular requirements you may have,** such as a special diet.

Booking by letter

Misunderstandings can easily happen over the telephone, so we strongly advise you to confirm your booking in writing if there is time.

Please note that the English Tourism Council does not make reservations - you should write direct to the accommodation.

DEPOSITS

If you make your reservation weeks or months in advance, you will probably be asked for a deposit. The amount will vary according to the time of year, the number of people in your party and how long you plan to stay. The deposit will then be deducted from the final bill when you leave.

PAYMENT ON ARRIVAL

Some establishments may ask you to pay for your room on arrival if you have not booked it in advance. This is especially likely to happen if you arrive late and have little or no luggage.

If you are asked to pay on arrival, it is a good idea to see your room first, to make sure it meets your requirements.

CANCELLATIONS

Legal contract

When you accept accommodation that is offered to you, by telephone or in writing, you enter a legally binding contract with the proprietor.

This means that if you cancel your booking, fail to take up the accommodation or leave early, the proprietor may be entitled to compensation if he cannot re-let for all or a good part of the booked period. You will probably forfeit any deposit you have paid, and may well be asked for an additional payment.

The proprietor cannot make a claim until after the booked period, however, and during that time every effort should be made by the proprietor to re-let the accommodation.

If there is a dispute it is sensible for both sides to seek legal advice on the matter.

If you do have to change your travel plans, it is in your own interests to let the proprietors know in writing as soon as possible, to give them a chance to re-let your accommodation.

And remember, if you book by telephone and are asked for your credit card number, you should check whether the proprietor intends charging your credit card account should you later cancel your reservation.

A proprietor should not be able to charge your credit card account with a cancellation unless he or she has made this clear at the time of your booking and you have agreed. However, to avoid later disputes, we suggest you check with the proprietor whether he or she intends to charge your credit card account if you cancel.

INSURANCE

A travel or holiday insurance policy will safeguard you if you have to cancel or change your holiday plans. You can arrange a policy quite cheaply through your insurance company or travel agent. Some hotels also offer their own insurance schemes.

ARRIVING LATE

If you know you will be arriving late in the evening, it is a good idea to say so when you book. If you are delayed on your way, a telephone call to say that you will be late will help prevent any problems when you arrive.

SERVICE CHARGES AND TIPPING

These days many places levy service charges automatically. If they do, they must clearly say so in their offer of accommodation, at the time of booking. Then the service charge becomes part of the legal contract when you accept the offer of accommodation.

If a service charge is levied automatically, there is no need to tip the staff, unless they provide some exceptional service. The usual tip for meals is ten per cent of the total bill.

TELEPHONE CHARGES

Guest Accommodation establishments can set their own charges for telephone calls made through their switchboard or from direct-dial telephones in bedrooms. These charges are often much higher than telephone companies' standard charges (to defray the cost of providing the service).

Comparing costs

It is a condition of the quality assurance standard, that unit charges for using the telephone are on display, by the phones or with the room information. But in practice it is not always easy to compare these charges with standard telephone rates. Before using the telephone for long-distance calls, you may decide to ask how the charges compare.

SECURITY OF VALUABLES

You can deposit your valuables with the proprietor or manager during your stay, and we recommend you do this as a sensible precaution. Make sure you obtain a receipt for them.

Some places do not accept articles for safe custody, and in that case it is wisest to keep your valuables with you.

Disclaimer

Some proprietors put up a notice which disclaims liability for property brought on to their premises by a guest. In fact, they can only restrict their liability to a minimum laid down by law (The Hotel Proprietors Act 1956).

Under that Act, a proprietor is liable for the value of the loss or damage to any property (except a motor car or its contents) of a guest who has engaged overnight accommodation, but if the proprietor has the notice on display as prescribed under that Act, liability is limited to £50 for one article and a total of £100 for any one guest. The notice must be prominently displayed in the reception area or main entrance. These limits do not apply to valuables you have deposited with the proprietor for safe-keeping, or to property lost through the default, neglect of wilful act of the proprietor or his staff.

BRINGING PETS TO ENGLAND

The quarantine laws have recently changed in England and a Pet Travel Scheme (PETS) is currently in operation. Under this scheme pet dogs are able to come into Britain from over 35 countries via certain sea, air and rail routes into England.

Dogs that have been resident in these countries for more than 6 months may enter the UK under the Scheme providing they are accompanied by the appropriate documentation.

For dogs to be able to enter the UK without quarantine under the PETS Scheme they will have to meet certain conditions and travel with the following documents: the Official PETS Certificate, a certificate of treatment against tapeworm and ticks and a declaration of residence.

For details of participating countries, routes, operators and further information about the PETS Scheme please contact the PETS Helpline, DEFRA (Department for

Environment, Food and Rural Affairs), 1a Page Street, London SW1P 4PQ

Tel: +44 (0) 870 241 1710 Fax: +44 (0) 20 7904 6834
Email: pets.helpline@defra.gsi.gov.uk, or visit their web site at www.defra.gov.uk/animalh/quarantine

CODE OF CONDUCT

All the places featured in this guide have agreed to observe the following Codes of Conduct:

1   To ensure high standards of courtesy and cleanliness, catering and service appropriate to the type of establishment.

2   To describe fairly to all visitors and prospective visitors the amenities, facilities and services provided by the establishment, whether by advertisement, brochure, word of mouth or any other means. To allow visitors to see accommodation, if requested, before booking.

3   To make clear to visitors exactly what is included in all prices quoted for accommodation, meals and refreshments, including service charges, taxes and other surcharges. Details of charges, if any, for heating or additional service or facilities should also be made clear.

4   To adhere to, and not to exceed, prices current at time of occupation for accommodation or other services.

5   To advise visitors at the time of booking, and subsequently of any change, if the accommodation offered is in an unconnected annexe, or similar, or by boarding out; and to indicate the location of such accommodation and any difference in comfort or amenities from accommodation in the main establishment.

6   To give each visitor, on request, details of payments due and a receipt if required.

7   To deal promptly and courteously with all enquiries, requests, reservations, correspondence and complaints from visitors.

8   To allow an English Tourism Council representative reasonable access to the establishment, on request, to confirm that the Code of Conduct is being observed.

COMMENTS AND COMPLAINTS

Guest accommodation and the law

Places that offer accommodation have legal and statutory responsibilities to their customers, such as providing information about prices, providing adequate fire precautions and safeguarding valuables. Like other businesses, they must also abide by the Trades Description Acts 1968 and 1972 when they describe their accommodation and facilities.

All the places featured in this guide have declared that they do fulfil all applicable statutory obligations.

Information

The proprietors themselves supply the descriptions of their establishments and other information for the entries, and they pay to be included in the regional sections of the guide. All the accommodation featured in this guide has also been assessed or has applied for assessment under the new quality assurance scheme.

The English Tourism Council cannot guarantee accuracy of information in this guide, and accepts no responsibility for any error or misrepresentation. All liability for loss, disappointment, negligence or other damage caused by reliance on the information contained in this guide, or in the event of bankruptcy or liquidation or cessation of trade of any company, individual or firm mentioned, is hereby excluded.

We strongly recommend that you carefully check prices and other details when you book your accommodation.

Problems

Of course, we hope you will not have cause for complaint, but problems do occur from time to time.

If you are dissatisfied with anything, make your complaint to the management immediately. Then the management can take action at once to investigate the matter and put things right. The longer you leave a complaint, the harder it is to deal with it effectively.

In certain circumstances, the English Tourism Council may look into complaints. However, the Council has no statutory control over establishments or their methods of operating. The Council cannot become involved in legal or contractual matters.

If you do have problems that have not been resolved by the proprietor and which you would like to bring to our attention, please write to: Quality Standards Department, English Tourism Council, Thames Tower, Black's Road, Hammersmith, London W6 9EL.

About the Guide Entries

LOCATIONS

Places to stay are listed under the town, city or village where they are located. If a place is out in the countryside, you will find it listed under the nearest village or town.

Town names are listed alphabetically within each regional section of the guide, along with the name of the county or unitary authority they are in (see note on page 15), and their map reference.

MAP REFERENCES

These refer to the colour location maps at the front of the guide. The first figure shown is the map number, the following letter and figure indicate the grid reference on the map.

Some entries were included just before the guide went to press, so they do not appear on the maps.

ADDRESSES

County names, which appear in the town headings, are not repeated in the entries. When you are writing, you should of course make sure you use the full address and postcode.

TELEPHONE NUMBERS

Telephone numbers are listed below the accommodation address for each entry. Area codes are shown in brackets.

PRICES

The prices shown in Where to Stay 2002 are only a general guide; they were supplied to us by proprietors in summer 2001. Remember, changes may occur after the guide goes to press, so we strongly advise you to check prices when you book your accommodation.

Prices are shown in pounds sterling and include VAT where applicable. Some places also include a service charge in their standard tariff so check this when you book.

Standardised method

There are many different ways of quoting prices for accommodation. We use a standardised method in the guide to allow you to compare prices.

For example when we show:

Bed and breakfast, the prices shown are for overnight accommodation with breakfast, for single and double rooms.
The double-room price is for two people. If a double room is occupied by one person there is sometimes a reduction in price.
Halfboard, the prices shown are for room, breakfast and evening meal, per person per day, and are usually based on two people sharing a room.

Some places provide only a continental breakfast in the set price, and you may have to pay extra if you want a full English breakfast.

Checking prices

According to the law, hotels and guest accommodation with at least four bedrooms or eight beds must display their overnight accommodation charges in the reception area or entrance. In your own interests, do make sure you check prices and what they include.

Children's rates

You will find that many places charge a reduced rate for children especially if they share a room with their parents.

Some places charge the full rate, however, when a child occupies a room which might otherwise have been let to an adult.

The upper age limit for reductions for children varies from one hotel to another, so check this when you book.

Seasonal packages and special promotions

Prices often vary through the year, and may be significantly lower outside peak holiday weeks. Many places offer special package rates - fully inclusive weekend breaks, for example - in the autumn, winter and spring. A number of establishments have included in their enhanced entry information about any special offers, themed breaks, etc. that are available.

You can get details of other bargain packages that may be available from the establishment themselves, the Regional Tourist Boards or your local Tourist Information Centre (TIC).

Your local travel agent may also have information, and can help you make bookings.

BATHROOMS

Each accommodation entry shows you the number of en suite and private bathrooms available, the number of private showers and the number of public bathrooms.

'En suite bathroom' means the bath or shower and WC are contained behind the main door of the bedroom. 'Private bathroom' means a bath or shower and WC solely for the occupants of one bedroom, on the same floor, reasonably close and with a key provided. 'Private shower' means a shower en suite with the bedroom but no WC.

Public bathrooms normally have a bath, sometimes with a shower attachment. If the availability of a bath is important to you, remember to check when you book.

MEALS

If an establishment serves evening meals, you will find the starting time and the last order times shown in the entry; some smaller places may ask you at breakfast or at midday whether you want an evening meal.

The prices shown in each entry are for bed and breakfast or half board, but many places also offer lunch, as you will see indicated in the entry.

OPENING PERIOD

All places are open for the months indicated in their entry. If opening period is not shown, please check with the establishment.

SYMBOLS

The at-a-glance symbols included at the end of each entry show many of the services and facilities available at each place. You will find the key to these symbols on the back cover flap. Open out the flap and you can check the meanings of the symbols as you go.

ALCOHOLIC DRINKS

Many places listed in the guide are licensed to serve alcohol. The licence may be restricted - to diners only, for example - so you may want to check this when you book. If they have a bar this is shown by the ♀ symbol.

SMOKING

Many places provide non-smoking areas - from no-smoking bedrooms and lounges to no-smoking sections of the restaurant. Some places prefer not to accommodate smokers, and in such cases the descriptions and symbols in each entry makes this clear.

PETS

Many places accept guests with dogs, but we do advise that you check this when you book, and ask if there are any extra charges or rules about exactly where your pet is allowed. The acceptance of dogs is not always extended to cats and it is strongly advised that cat owners contact the establishment well in advance. Some establishments do not accept pets at all. Pets are welcome where you see this symbol 🐕.

The quarantine laws have recently changed in England and pet dogs are able to come into Britain from selected European countries. For details of the Pet Travel Scheme (PETS) please turn to page 796.

CREDIT AND CHARGE CARDS

The credit and charge cards accepted by a place are listed in the entry following the letters CC.

If you do plan to pay by card, check that the establishment will take your card before you book.

Some proprietors will charge you a higher rate if you pay by credit card rather than cash or cheque. The difference is to cover the percentage paid by the proprietor to the credit card company.

If you are planning to pay by credit card, you may want to ask whether it would, in fact, be cheaper to pay by cheque or cash. When you book by telephone, you may be asked for your credit card number as 'confirmation'. But remember, the proprietor may then charge your credit card account if you cancel your booking. See under Cancellations on page 795.

CONFERENCES AND GROUPS

Places which cater for conferences and meetings are marked with the symbol ♣. Rates are often negotiable, depending on the time of year, numbers of people involved and any special requirements you may have.

Distance Chart

The distances between towns on the chart below are given to the nearest mile, and are measured along routes based on the quickest travelling time, making maximum use of motorways or dual-carriageway roads. The chart is based upon information supplied by the Automobile Association.

To calculate the distance in kilometres multiply the mileage by 1.6

For example: Brighton to Dover
82 miles x 1.6
=131.2 kilometres

Distances are read from the triangular chart. Each row is labelled (reading down the diagonal) by a town, and the columns (reading along the diagonal) are, in order: Aberdeen, Aberystwyth, Barnstaple, Birmingham, Brighton, Bristol, Cambridge, Cardiff, Carlisle, Carmarthen, Colchester, Dorchester, Dover, Edinburgh, Exeter, Fort William, Glasgow, Gloucester, Guildford, Holyhead, Hull, Inverness, Kendal, Leeds, Lincoln, Liverpool, Maidstone, Manchester, Middlesbrough, Newcastle, Norwich, Nottingham, Oxford, Penzance, Perth, Plymouth, Sheffield, Southampton, Stranraer, Taunton, York, London.

```
Aberystwyth   468
Barnstaple    603 214
Birmingham    431 124 180
Brighton      605 288 208 171
Bristol       513 128  99  90 169
Cambridge     462 215 267  97 120 170
Cardiff       531 110 127 109 201  44 203
Carlisle      231 236 372 199 375 282 257 300
Carmarthen    513  48 190 171 264 106 266  67 282
Colchester    516 289 292 171 112 195  48 227 310 290
Dorchester    595 206  94 172 119  62 179 119 363 182 206
Dover         587 325 273 207  82 206 124 238 400 301 116 200
Edinburgh     125 335 470 298 473 380 333 398  98 381 385 462 458
Exeter        585 196  53 162 175  82 249 109 353 172 274  55 245 453
Fort William  156 446 581 409 584 491 466 509 209 491 518 573 590 133 563
Glasgow       147 333 468 296 472 379 353 397  96 379 405 461 478  49 451 102
Gloucester    479 111 125  56 155  35 150  61 247 124 171 117 192 347 107 456 343
Guildford     563 224 175 128  44 106  91 138 332 201 103  97  97 432 147 541 428  99
Holyhead      459 101 339 167 343 250 259 201 227 149 333 332 369 327 322 436 323 215 300
Hull          375 228 321 140 258 231 138 249 170 312 191 313 262 247 303 379 266 196 239 219
Inverness     106 494 630 457 633 540 514 558 257 540 566 622 639 158 612  66 174 505 591 485 428
Kendal        279 190 325 153 329 236 245 254  47 236 319 318 355 147 308 256 181 201 286 181 164 305
Leeds         331 174 302 121 263 212 146 230 126 220 200 294 271 202 284 335 222 177 220 165  60 383  71
Lincoln       387 199 276  89 216 186  95 204 182 267 147 245 220 258 258 391 278 151 173 204  46 439 176  72
Liverpool     357 110 274 102 277 184 193 202 126 163 268 266 304 225 256 335 222 150 235 101 128 383  79  74 140
Maidstone     548 286 234 168  50 167  85 199 361 262  77 161  41 419 206 570 458 153  58 329 223 619 315 233 181 263
Manchester    356 134 261  89 264 171 160 189 123 180 212 253 291 223 243 332 219 137 222 125  97 381  77  44  85  35 251
Middlesbrough 276 245 357 177 318 268 198 286  95 291 251 350 322 147 340 280 191 233 276 236  89 308  84  63 123 145 283 115
Newcastle     234 276 388 208 349 299 229 317  60 322 282 381 353 106 371 239 154 264 307 267 142 266 102  94 154 176 314 146  38
Norwich       488 277 329 159 171 233  63 264 282 327  61 241 175 359 311 491 379 212 162 320 150 540 276 173 104 241 135 186 223 254
Nottingham    393 162 234  54 195 144  86 163 188 226 139 226 218 265 216 397 284 110 153 178  92 446 164  74  38 112 179  71 129 160 119
Oxford        503 159 170  68 109  73  81 105 271 168 124 115 146 371 152 480 367  48  67 239 189 529 225 171 130 173 106 161 226 257 144 103
Penzance      697 308 108 274 287 194 361 221 465 284 386 167 357 565 111 674 562 219 259 433 414 723 419 396 369 367 317 355 451 482 423 328 264
Perth          87 382 518 345 521 428 402 446 145 428 454 510 527  42 500 102  62 393 478 373 315 114 193 268 327 271 487 266 192 151 428 334 418 611
Plymouth      628 239  67 205 218 125 292 152 396 215 316  98 288 496  45 605 492 150 190 364 345 654 350 326 300 298 248 286 382 413 354 259 195  77 542
Sheffield     365 167 272  76 233 182 122 201 159 254 204 236 254 368 255 148 191 158  66 417 125  36  47  79 207  39 100 131 147  44 141 366 281 297  ...
Southampton   570 225 142 135  66 106 131 138 339 201 159  53 152 439 109 548 435 100  49 307 257 596 292 238 197 241 112 228 293 324 193 171  67 221 484 152 208
Stranraer     232 342 478 305 481 388 363 406 106 388 415 470 487 133 460 188  86 354 439 333 276 258 153 228 288 231 448 226 201 163 388 294 378 572 146 503 265 446
Taunton       554 165  50 112 233 160  51 218  79 323 142 243  45 224 423  32 532 419   7 272 581 225 225 211 286 212 308 339 280 186 121 144 469  75 223  94 429
York          322 202 315 134 276 225 155 243 117 248 209 307 280 193 297 326 213 191 233 193  38 374  91  24  80 103 240  72  50  89 180  86 184 409 238 340  58 251 223 266
London        544 238 216 120  59 120  60 152 313 215  61 128  79 413 198 522 409 102  30 281 186 571 266 198 143 215  39 202 253 284 115 131  56 310 458 241 168  80 419 167 211
```

National Rail network

- ▬▬ Principal routes
- ── Other selected routes
- ✈ Airport interchange
- ✈ Railair coach link with Heathrow Airport
- ⛴ Ferry interchange

LONDON TERMINALS

C	Charing Cross
E	Euston
F	Fenchurch Street
K	Kings Cross
L	Liverpool Street
M	Marylebone
P	Paddington
S	St Pancras
V	Victoria
W	Waterloo

Channel Tunnel services
LILLE, BRUSSELS, PARIS

National Rail Enquiries
08457 48 49 50
www.nationalrail.co.uk © ATOC 2000. All rights reserved. MCD/BAJS-2S 11/00

≋ National Rail

01/NRE/1169

A selection of **events** for **2002**

This is a selection of the many cultural, sporting and other events that will be taking place throughout England during 2001. Please note, as changes often occur after press date, it is advisable to confirm the date and location before travelling.

* Provisional at time of going to press.

January 2002

1 January
The New Year's Day Parade - London
Parliament Square,
SW1 to Berkeley Square, London W1
Tel: (020) 8566 8586
Email: markp@londonparade.co.uk
www.londonparade.co.uk

3-13 January
London International Boat Show
Earls Court Exhibition Centre, Warwick Road,
London SW5 9TA
Tel: (01784) 472222 (Boatline)
www.bigblue.org.uk

13 January
Antique and Collectors' Fair
Alexandra Palace,
Alexandra Palace Way, London N22 7AY
Tel: (020) 8883 7061
Email: info@pigandwhistlepromotions.com
www.allypally-uk.com

27 January
Charles I Commemoration
Banqueting House,
Whitehall, London SW1A 2ER
Tel: (01430) 430695

31 January-3 February
Wakefield Rhubarb Trail and Festival of Rhubarb
Various venues, Wakefield
Tel: (01924) 305841
Email: pventom@wakefield.gov.uk
www.wakefield.gov.uk

February 2002

1 February*
Cheltenham Folk Festival
Town Hall, Imperial Square, Cheltenham
Tel: (01242) 226033
Email: Antoniac@cheltenham.gov.uk
www.visitcheltenham.gov.uk

9-16 February
Jorvik Viking Festival - Jolablot 2002
Various venues - Jorvik, Coppergate, York
Tel: (01904) 643211
Email: marketing.jorvik@lineone.net
www.jorvik-viking.centre.co.uk

17 February
Chinese New Year Celebrations
Centered on Gerrard Street and Leicester Square,
London WC2
Tel: (020) 7287 1118

17 February-24 March
Lambing Sunday and Spring Bulb Days
Kentwell Hall, Long Melford, Sudbury

26 February-3 March
Fine Art and Antiques Fair
Olympia, Hammersmith Road, London W14
Tel: (020) 7370 8212
Email: olympia.antiques@eco.co.uk
www.olympia-antiques.co.uk

March 2002

6 March-1 April
Ideal Home Show
Earls Court Exhibition Centre,
Warwick Road, London SW5 9TA
Tel: (0870) 606 6080

7 March-10 March*
Crufts 2002
National Exhibition Centre, Birmingham

12 March-14 March
Cheltenham Gold Cup National Hunt Racing Festival
Cheltenham Racecourse, Prestbury Park, Cheltenham
Tel: (01242) 513014
www.cheltenham.co.uk

16 March-17 March
Ambleside Daffodil and Spring Flower Show
The Kelsick Centre, St Mary's Lane, Ambleside
Tel: (015394) 32252
www.ambleside-show.org.uk

17 March
Antique and Collectors' Fair
Alexandra Palace, Alexandra Palace Way,
London N22 7AY
Tel: (020) 8883 7061
Email: info@pigandwhistlepromotions.com
www.allypally-uk.com

23 March
Head of the River Race
River Thames, London
Tel: (01932) 220401
Email: secretary@horr.co.uk
www.horr.co.uk

23 March-24 March*
Thriplow Daffodil Weekend
Various Venues, Thriplow, Royston
Tel: (01763) 208132
Email: jmurray@thriplow.fsnet.co.uk
www.thriplow.org.uk

29 March
British and World Marbles Championship
Greyhound Public House,
Radford Road, Tinsley Green, Crawley
Tel: (01403) 730602

29 March-5 April*
Harrogate International Youth Music Festival
Various venues, Harrogate
Tel: (01306) 744360
Email: peurope@kuoni.co.uk
www.performeurope.co.uk

29 March-6 April
Ulverston Walking Festival
Various Venues, Ulverston
Tel: (01229) 585588

30 March
Oxford and Cambridge Boat Race
River Thames, London
Tel: (020) 7611 3500

April 2002

1 April
Old Custom: World Coal Carrying Championship
Start: Royal Oak Public House,
Owl Lane, Ossett
Tel: (01924) 218990
Email: bwilding@gawthorpe.ndo.co.uk
www.gawthorpe.ndo.co.uk

1 April
London Harness Horse Parade
Battersea Park, London SW11
Tel: (01733) 371156
Email: t-g@ic24.net
www.eastofengland.org.uk

1 April-30 April*
Old Custom: Pace Egg Plays
Upper Calder Valley, Various venues, Todmorden,
Heptonstall, Hebden Bridge
Tel: (01422) 843831
Email: calderdale_tourism@lineone.net

1 April-30 April*
Trigg Morris Men's Easter Monday Tour
Various Venues Starting in the
Market Square, Launceston
Tel: (01637) 880394
www.triggmorris.freeserve.co.uk

4 April-6 April*
Horse-racing: Martell Grand National Festival
Aintree Racecourse,
Ormskirk Road, Aintree, Liverpool
Tel: (0151) 523 2600
Email: aintree@rht.net
www.aintree.co.uk

14 April
London Marathon
Greenwich Park, London SE10
Tel: (020) 8948 7935

18 April-20 April
Maltings Beer Festival
Tuckers Maltings, Teign Road, Newton Abbot
Tel: (01626) 334734

20 April-6 May
World Snooker Championships
Crucible Theatre, Norfolk Street, Sheffield
Tel: (0114) 249 6006
www.embassysnooker.com

24 April-27 April
Bury St Edmunds Beer Festival
Corn Exchange, Cornhill, Bury St Edmunds
Tel: (01842) 860063

25 April-28 April
Harrogate Spring Flower Show
Great Yorkshire Showground, Harrogate
Tel: (01423) 561049
Email: info@flowershow.org.uk
www.flowershow.org.uk

May 2002

1 May-6 May*
Cheltenham International Jazz Festival
Various venues throughout Cheltenham

1 May-31 May*
Bexhill 100 Festival of Motoring
Seafront, De La Warr Parade, Bexhill
Tel: (01424) 730564
Email: brian@bexhill100.co.uk
www.bexhill100.co.uk

1 May-31 May*
Hay on Wye Literature Festival
Various Venues in Hay-on-Wye,
Hay-on-Wye, Hereford
Tel: (01497) 821299

1 May-31 May*
Jennings Keswick Jazz Festival
Keswick
Tel: (01900) 602122
Email: carnegie@allerdale.gov.uk

1 May-31 Aug
Glyndebourne Festival Opera
Glyndebourne Opera House,
Glyndebourne, Glynde, Lewes

3 May-6 May
**Hastings Traditional Jack in the
Green Morris Dance and Folk Festival**
Various venues, Hastings
Tel: (01424) 781122
Email: greenman@britishlibrary.net
www.jack-in-the-park.co.uk

4 May*
Downton Cuckoo Fair
Village Centre, Downton, Salisbury
Tel: (01725) 510646

4 May-27 May*
Rhododendron and Azalea Time
Leonardslee Gardens,
Lower Beeding, Horsham
Tel: (01403) 891212
Email: leonardslee.gardens@virgin.net
www.leonardslee.com

5 May-6 May*
2002 Dover Pageant
Dover College Grounds, Dover
Tel: (01304) 242990
Email: pageant@port-of-dover.com
www.port-of-dover.com/pageant

6-May
Dunstable Carnival
Bennett Memorial Recreation Ground,
Bull Pond Lane, Dunstable
Tel: (01582) 607895
Email: promotions.dunstable@towns.bedfordshie.gov.uk

11 May-19 May*
Tiverton Spring Festival
Various venues, Tiverton
Tel: (01884) 258952

12 May
Antique and Collectors' Fair
Alexandra Palace, Alexandra Palace Way,
London N22 7AY
Tel: (020) 8883 7061
Email: info@pigandwhistlepromotions.com
www.allypally-uk.com

12-May
South Suffolk Show
Point-to-Point Course, Ampton Park,
Ingham, Bury St Edmunds
Tel: (01638) 750879
Email: geoff@southsuffolkshow.co.uk
www.southsuffolkshow.co.uk

15 May-19 May
Royal Windsor Horse Show
Windsor Home Park, Datchet Road, Windsor
Tel: (01753) 860633
Email: mail@hpower.co.uk
www.royal-windsor-horse-show.co.uk

18 May-19 May
London Tattoo
Wembley Arena, Empire Way, Wembley
Tel: (01189) 303239
Email: normanrogerson@telinco.co.uk
www.telinco.co.uk/maestromusic

21 May-24 May
Chelsea Flower Show
Royal Hospital Chelsea,
Royal Hospital Road,
Chelsea, London SW3 4SR

24 May-27 May*
Old Custom: The Hunting of the Earl of Rone
Various venues, Combe Martin, Ilfracombe
Tel: (01271) 882 366
Email: tom.brown1@virgin.net

25 May-26 May*
Air Fete
RAF Mildenhall,
100ARW/CV USAF, Mildenhall,
Bury St Edmunds
Tel: (01638) 543341
www.mildenhall.af.mil/airfete

25 May-26 May
Hertfordshire County Show
Hertfordshire Agricultural Society, Dunstable Road,
Redbourn, St Albans
Tel: (01582) 792626

26 May-27 May
Battle Medieval Fair
Abbey Green, High Street, Battle
Tel: (01424) 774447
Email: chpsmith@lineone.net

27 May-7 Jun
Isle of Man T.T. Motorcycle Festival
Various venues Isle of Man
Tel: (01624) 686801

29 May-30 May
Corpus Christi Carpet of Flowers and Floral Festival
Cathedral of Our Lady and St Philip Howard,
Cathedral House, Arundel
Tel: (01903) 882297
Email: aruncathl@aol.com

31 May-2 Jun
Holker Garden Festival
Holker Hall and Gardens, Cark in Cartmel,
Grange-over-Sands
Tel: (015395) 58328
Email: publicopening@holker.co.uk
www.holker-hall.co.uk

June 2002

1 June-3 June*
Orange WOW
North Shields Fishquay and Town Centre, North Shields
Tel: (0191) 200 5164
Email: carol.alevroyianni@northtyneside.gov.uk
www.orangewow.co.uk

1 June-4 June*
Chatham Navy Days
The Historic Dockyard, Chatham
Tel: (01634) 823800
www.worldnavalbase.org.uk

1 June-31 July*
Exeter Festival
Various Venues, Exeter
Tel: (01392) 265118
www.exeter.gov.uk

6 June-12 June
Appleby Horse Fair
Fair Hill, Roman Road,
Appleby-in-Westmorland
Tel: (017683) 51177
Email: tic@applebytowncouncil.fsnet.co.uk
www.applebytowncouncil.fsnet.co.uk

6 June-16 June
Fine Art and Antiques Fair
Olympia, Hammersmith Road, London W14
Tel: (020) 7370 8212
Email: olympia.antiques@eco.co.uk
www.olympia-antiques.com

7 June*
Robert Dover's Cotswold Olimpick Games
Dovers Hill, Weston Subedge, Chipping Campden
Tel: (01384) 274041
Email: a.greenwood@cix.co.uk

7 June-8 June*
Vodafone Derby Horse Race Meeting
Epsom Racecourse, Epsom
Tel: (01372) 470047
Email: epsom@rht.net
www.epsomderby.co.uk

11 June-13 June*
Three Counties Show
Three Counties Showground, Malvern
Tel: (01684) 584900
Email: info@threecounties.co.uk
www.threecounties.co.uk

12 June-18 June
Grosvenor House Art and Antiques Fair
Le Meridien Grosvenor House, Park Lane,
London W1A 3AA
Tel: (020) 7399 8100
Email: olivia@grosvenor-antiquesfair.co.uk
www.grosvenor-antiquesfair.co.uk

15 June
Trooping the Colour - The Queen's Birthday Parade
Horse Guards Parade, London SW1
Tel: (020) 7414 2479

15 June-23 June
Broadstairs Dickens Festival
Various Venues, Broadstairs
Tel: (01843) 865265
www.broadstairs.gov.uk/dickensfestival.html

18 June-19 June*
Cheshire County Show
The Showground, Tabley, Knutsford
Tel: (01829) 760020

18 June-21 June
Royal Ascot
Ascot Racecourse, Ascot
Tel: (01344) 876876
www.ascot.co.uk

19 June-23 June
Covent Garden Flower Festival
Covent Garden Piazza, London WC2
Tel: 09064 701 777 (60p per minute)
Email: info@cgff.co.uk
www.cgff.co.uk

21 June-30 June
Newcastle Hoppings
Town Moor, Grandstand Road, Newcastle upon Tyne
Tel: (07831) 458774

22 June
HOYA Round the Island Race
Isle of Wight Coast, c/o Island Sailing Club,
70 High Street, Cowes
Tel: (01983) 296621
Email: islandsc.org.uk
www.island.org.uk

24 June-7 July
Wimbledon Lawn Tennis Championships
All England Lawn Tennis and Croquet Club,
Church Road, London SW19 5AE
Tel: (020) 8946 2244

28 June-30 June*
The Ordnance Survey Balloon and Flower Festival
Southampton Common, The Avenue, Southampton
Tel: (023) 8083 2525
Email: southampton.gov.uk

29 June-17 July*
Chester Mystery Plays
Cathedral Green, Chester
Tel: (01244) 682617

July 2002

5 July-14 July
Lichfield International Arts Festival
Throughout City of Lichfield
Tel: (01543) 306270
Email: Lichfield.fest@Lichfield-arts.org.uk
www.lichfieldfestival.org

5 July-14 July
York Early Music Festival
Various venues, York
Tel: (01904) 645738
Email: enquiry@yorkearlymusic.org
www.yorkearlymusic.org

6 July-7 July
Sunderland International Kite Festival
Northern Area Playing Fields, District 12, Washington
Tel: (0191) 514 1235
Email: jackie.smithr@edcom.sunderland.gov.uk
www.sunderland.gov.uk/kitefestival

6 July-18 August
Cookson Country Festival
Various Venues in South Shields
Tel: (0191) 424 7985
Email: andy.buyers@s-tyneside-mbc.gov.uk
www.s-tyneside-mbc.gov.uk

10 July-14 July*
Henley Festival
Royal Regatta, Henley-on-Thames
Tel: (01491) 843400
Email: info@henley-festival.co.uk
www.henley-festival.co.uk

13 July
Tendring Hundred Show
Lawford House Park, Lawford,
Manningtree
Tel: (01206) 571517
Email:
anne@tendringshow.demon.co.uk
www.tendringshow.demon.com

13 July-14 July
Tewkesbury Medieval Festival
The Gastons, Gloucester Road, Tewkesbury
Tel: (01386) 871908

19 July-21 July*
Netley Marsh Steam and Craft Show
Meadow Farm, Ringwood Road, Netley Marsh,
Southampton
Tel: (023) 8086 7882

19 July-14 September
BBC Henry Wood Promenade Concerts
Royal Albert Hall, Kensington Gore, London SW7 2AP
Tel: (020) 7765 5575
Email: proms@bbc.co.uk
www.bbc.co.uk/proms

23 July-28 July*
Chulmleigh Old Fair
Various Venues, Chulmleigh
Tel: (01769) 580276

25 July-4 August*
Manchester 2002
- The 17th Commonwealth Games
Various venues, Manchester
Tel: (0161) 228 2002

26 July-28 July
Gateshead Summer Flower Show
Gateshead Central Nurseries, Whickham Highway, Lobley Hill, Gateshead
Tel: (0191) 433 3838
Email: g.scott@leisure.gatesheadmbc.gov

27 July-28 July*
Sunderland International Air Show
Promenade, Sea Front, Seaburn, Sunderland
Tel: (0191) 553 2000

31 July
Nantwich and South Cheshire Show
Dorfold Hall, Nantwich
Tel: (01270) 780306

August 2002

1 August-30 August
Last Night of the Proms Outdoor Concert
Castle Howard, York
Tel: (01653) 648444
Email: mec@castlehoward.co.uk
www.castlehoward.co.uk

1 August-31 August*
Lowther Horse Driving Trials and Country Fair
Lowther Castle , Lowther Estate, Lowther, Penrith
Tel: (01931) 712378

1 August-31 August*
Maryport Songs of the Sea Festival
The Harbour, Maryport
Tel: (01900) 813738

3 August*
Stoke Gabriel Grand Carnival Procession
Village Centre, Stoke Gabriel, Totnes
Tel: (01803) 782483

3 August-4 August
Woodvale International Rally
R A F Woodvale, 43 Kenilworth Road, Southport
Tel: (01704) 578816

4 August-11 August
Alnwick International Music Festival
Market-place, Alnwick
Tel: (01665) 510417
Email: jim@alnwick0.demon.co.uk

10 August-17 August
Billingham International Folklore Festival
Town Centre, Queensway, Billingham
Tel: (01642) 651060
www.billinghamfestival.co.uk

16 August-26 August*
Ross on Wye International Festival
Various venues around Ross on Wye, mainly by the riverside, Rope Walk, Ross-on-Wye
Tel: (01594) 544446
Email: info@festival.org.uk
www.festival.org.uk

22 August-27 August
International Beatles Festival
Various venues, Liverpool
Tel: (0151) 236 9091
Email: cavern@fsb.dial.co.uk
www.cavern-liverpool.co.uk

25 August-26 August
Western Union Notting Hill Carnival
Streets around Ladbroke Grove , London W11
Tel: (020) 8964 0544

28 August-1 September
Great Dorset Steam Fair
South Down Farm, Tarrant Hinton, Blandford Forum
Tel: (01258) 860361
Email: enquiries@steam-fair.co.uk
www.steam-fair.co.uk

30 August-3 November
Blackpool Illuminations
Promenade, Blackpool
Tel: (01253) 478222
Email: tourism@blackpool.gov.uk
www.blackpooltourism.gov.uk

31 August-1 September*
Lancashire Vintage and Country Show
Hamilton House Farm, St Michael's on Wyre, Preston
Tel: (01772) 687259

September 2002

1 September*
Egremont Crab Fair and Sports
Baybarrow, Orgill, Egremont
Tel: (01946) 821554
Email: crabfair.homestead.com/mainpage.html

1 September*
Kendal Torchlight Procession
Kendal
Tel: (015395) 63018
Email: ronc@torchlight.net1.co.uk
www.lakesnet.co.uk/kendaltorchlight

1 September-30 September*
Southampton International Boat Show
Western Esplanade, Southampton
Tel: (01784) 223600
Email: boatshow@boatshows.co.uk
www.bigblue.org.uk

5 September-8 September
The Blenheim Petplan International Three Day Event
Blenheim Palace, Woodstock
Tel: (01993) 813335
Email: blenheimht@btconnect.com

7 September-8 September
Berwick Military Tattoo
Berwick Barracks, Berwick-upon-Tweed
Tel: (01289) 307426

7 September-8 September*
Kirkby Lonsdale Victorian Fair
Kirkby Lonsdale
Tel: (015242) 71570

13 September-15 September
Thames Festival
River Thames, London
Tel: (020) 7928 0960
Email: festival@coin-street.org
www.ThamesFestival.org

18 September-21 September*
Barnstaple Ancient Chartered Fair
Seven Brethren Bank, Barnstaple
Tel: (01271) 373311
Email: barnstaple_com_council@northdevon.gov.uk

21 September-22 September*
Newbury and Royal County of Berkshire Show
Newbury Showground, Priors Court, Hermitage,
Thatcham

22 September
Antique and Collectors' Fair
Alexandra Palace, Alexandra Palace Way,
London N22 7AY
Tel: (020) 8883 7061
Email: info@pigandwhistlepromotions.com
www.allypally-uk.com

October 2002

1 October-6 October
Horse of the Year Show
Wembley Arena, Empire Way, Wembley
Tel: (020) 8900 9282
Email: info@hoys.co.uk
www.hoys.co.uk

11 October-19 October
Hull Fair
Walton Street Fairground, Walton Street, Hull
Tel: (01482) 615625
Email: city.entertainments@hull.gov.uk

20 October
Trafalgar Day Parade - The Sea Cadet Corps
Trafalgar Square, London WC2
Tel: (020) 7928 8978
Email: rbusby@sea-cadets.org

November 2002

1 November-30 November*
International Guitar Festival of Great Britain
Various venues, Wirral
Tel: (0151) 666 5060
Email: rob@bestguitarfest.com
www.bestguitarfest.com

1 November-31 December*
Marwell's Winter Wonderland
Marwell Zoological Park, Colden Common, Winchester
Tel: (01962) 777407
Email: events@marwell.org.uk

3 November
London to Brighton Veteran Car Run
Hyde Park, London W2
Tel: (01753) 765035

9 November
Lord Mayor's Show
City of London, London
Tel: (020) 7606 3030

10 November
Remembrance Day Service and Parade
Cenotaph, Whitehall, London SW1
Tel: (020) 7273 3498
Email: frances.bright@homeoffice.gsi.gov.uk

11 November*
Highbridge and Burnham-on-Sea
Guy Fawkes Carnival
Town Centre, Burnham-on-Sea
Tel: (01278) 794557

16 November-23 December
Thursford Christmas Spectacular
Thursford Collection, Thursford Green,
Thursford, Fakenham
Tel: (01328) 878477

17 November
Antique and Collectors' Fair
Alexandra Palace, Alexandra Palace Way,
London N22 7AY
Tel: (020) 8883 7061
Email: info@pigandwhistlepromotions.com
www.allypally-uk.com

December 2002

18 December-22 December
Showjumping: Olympia International
Championships
Olympia, Hammersmith Road, London W14
Tel: (020) 7370 8206
Email: olympia-show-jumping@eco.co.uk
www.olympia-show-jumping.co.uk

Calendar 2002

JANUARY

M	T	W	T	F	S	S
	1	2	3	4	5	6
7	8	9	10	11	12	13
14	15	16	17	18	19	20
21	22	23	24	25	26	27
28	29	30	31			

FEBRUARY

M	T	W	T	F	S	S
				1	2	3
4	5	6	7	8	9	10
11	12	13	14	15	16	17
18	19	20	21	22	23	24
25	26	27	28			

MARCH

M	T	W	T	F	S	S
				1	2	3
4	5	6	7	8	9	10
11	12	13	14	15	16	17
18	19	20	21	22	23	24
25	26	27	28	**29**	30	31

APRIL

M	T	W	T	F	S	S
1	2	3	4	5	6	7
8	9	10	11	12	13	14
15	16	17	18	19	20	21
22	23	24	25	26	27	28
29	30					

MAY

M	T	W	T	F	S	S
		1	2	3	4	5
6	7	8	9	10	11	12
13	14	15	16	17	18	19
20	21	22	23	24	25	26
27	28	29	30	31		

JUNE

M	T	W	T	F	S	S
					1	2
3	**4**	5	6	7	8	9
10	11	12	13	14	15	16
17	18	19	20	21	22	23
24	25	26	27	28	29	30

JULY

M	T	W	T	F	S	S
1	2	3	4	5	6	7
8	9	10	11	12	13	14
15	16	17	18	19	20	21
22	23	24	25	26	27	28
29	30	31				

AUGUST

M	T	W	T	F	S	S
			1	2	3	4
5	6	7	8	9	10	11
12	13	14	15	16	17	18
19	20	21	22	23	24	25
26	27	28	29	30	31	

SEPTEMBER

M	T	W	T	F	S	S
30						1
2	3	4	5	6	7	8
9	10	11	12	13	14	15
16	17	18	19	20	21	22
23	24	25	26	27	28	29

OCTOBER

M	T	W	T	F	S	S
	1	2	3	4	5	6
7	8	9	10	11	12	13
14	15	16	17	18	19	20
21	22	23	24	25	26	27
28	29	30	31			

NOVEMBER

M	T	W	T	F	S	S
				1	2	3
4	5	6	7	8	9	10
11	12	13	14	15	16	17
18	19	20	21	22	23	24
25	26	27	28	29	30	

DECEMBER

M	T	W	T	F	S	S
30	31					1
2	3	4	5	6	7	8
9	10	11	12	13	14	15
16	17	18	19	20	21	22
23	24	**25**	**26**	27	28	29

Calendar 2003

JANUARY

M	T	W	T	F	S	S
	1	2	3	4	5	
6	7	8	9	10	11	12
13	14	15	16	17	18	19
20	21	22	23	24	25	26
27	28	29	30	31		

FEBRUARY

M	T	W	T	F	S	S
					1	2
3	4	5	6	7	8	9
10	11	12	13	14	15	16
17	18	19	20	21	22	23
24	25	26	27	28		

MARCH

M	T	W	T	F	S	S
					1	2
3	4	5	6	7	8	9
10	11	12	13	14	15	16
17	18	19	20	21	22	23
24	25	26	27	28	29	30
31						

APRIL

M	T	W	T	F	S	S
	1	2	3	4	5	6
7	8	9	10	11	12	13
14	15	16	17	**18**	19	20
21	22	23	24	25	26	27
28	29	30				

MAY

M	T	W	T	F	S	S
			1	2	3	4
5	6	7	8	9	10	11
12	13	14	15	16	17	18
19	20	21	22	23	24	25
26	27	28	29	30	31	

JUNE

M	T	W	T	F	S	S
						1
2	3	4	5	6	7	8
9	10	11	12	13	14	15
16	17	18	19	20	21	22
23	24	25	26	27	28	29
30						

JULY

M	T	W	T	F	S	S
	1	2	3	4	5	6
7	8	9	10	11	12	13
14	15	16	17	18	19	20
21	22	23	24	25	26	27
28	29	30	31			

AUGUST

M	T	W	T	F	S	S
				1	2	3
4	5	6	7	8	9	10
11	12	13	14	15	16	17
18	19	20	21	22	23	24
25	26	27	28	29	30	31

SEPTEMBER

M	T	W	T	F	S	S
1	2	3	4	5	6	7
8	9	10	11	12	13	14
15	16	17	18	19	20	21
22	23	24	25	26	27	28
29	30					

OCTOBER

M	T	W	T	F	S	S
		1	2	3	4	5
6	7	8	9	10	11	12
13	14	15	16	17	18	19
20	21	22	23	24	25	26
27	28	29	30	31		

NOVEMBER

M	T	W	T	F	S	S
					1	2
3	4	5	6	7	8	9
10	11	12	13	14	15	16
17	18	19	20	21	22	23
24	25	26	27	28	29	30

DECEMBER

M	T	W	T	F	S	S
1	2	3	4	5	6	7
8	9	10	11	12	13	14
15	16	17	18	19	20	21
22	23	24	**25**	**26**	27	28
29	30	31				

Notes

USE YOUR *i*'s

There are more than 550 Tourist Information Centres throughout England offering friendly help with accommodation and holiday ideas as well as suggestions of places to visit and things to do.

You'll find TIC addresses in the local Phone Book.

www.travelengland.org.uk

Log on to travelengland.org.uk and discover something different around every corner. Meander through pages for ideas of places to visit and things to do. Spend time in each region and discover the diversity - from busy vibrant cities to rural village greens; rugged peaks to gentle rolling hills; dramatic coastline to idyllic sandy beaches. England might be a small country but it is brimming with choice and opportunity. Visit www.travelengland.org.uk and see for yourself.

England